ISBN 978-0-483-48540-2
PIBN 10783494

THE

Saturday Review

OF

Politics, Literature, Science and Art

VOLUME CVIII

LONDON:
PUBLISHED AT THE OFFICE, 10 KING STREET, COVENT GARDEN

INDEX TO VOL. CVIII.

LEADERS.

MIDDLES.

MIDDLES—(*continued*).

VERSE.

CORRESPONDENCE.

REVIEWS.

REVIEWS—(*continued*).

Spottiswoode & Co. Ltd., Printers, New-street Square, London.

THE

SATURDAY REVIEW

OF

POLITICS, LITERATURE, SCIENCE, AND ART.

No. 2,801 Vol. 108. 3 July 1909. [REGISTERED AS A NEWSPAPER.] 6*d*.

CONTENTS.

NOTES OF THE WEEK.

Peculiarly revolting are the circumstances of Sir Curzon Wyllie's assassination at the Imperial Institute. The victim was either the guest or the host of the assassin and his fellows. He had gone out of his way to meet them and lend his official and personal support to the promotion of social intercourse between the two races. No doubt the creature that took this useful, honourable, harmless life will pose as a patriot martyr—an Indian Charlotte Corday—or his friends will so represent him. The murder of his own political aide-de-camp may help Lord Morley to feel the danger of weakening executive authority by the infusion of a prominent Indian element.

Which was to go, Lord Kitchener or Lord Curzon? This may be brutal, but it is a true way of putting the position. The Government in 1905 had to make up their minds whether they would lose Lord Kitchener or Lord Curzon. And they elected to keep Lord Kitchener. Before the Lords debate this week on the Indian Army delicacy might have forbidden this rough speaking; but Lord Morley, Lord Midleton, and Lord Curzon did not scruple to tell the world everything about this miserable business: so it is no good for us to be diplomatic. Henceforward the Commander-in-Chief was to be supreme in military matters, and no one supposed the wraith of the Military Member, to be called the Military Supply Member, would have any terror for the triumphant Commander-in-Chief. The comments at the time, both of those for and those against the change, assumed this. So it seems rather unreal for Lord Lansdowne and Lord Curzon now to be arguing as if the supremacy of the Commander-in-Chief sprang from the disappearance of the Military Supply Member. His passing does not make a new situation; and as Lord Morley is now converted to Lord Midleton's policy, there can hardly be a reversion to the old system, no matter which side is in office.

Lord Curzon fortified his case by an appeal to army organisation here. This was clever, for it almost compelled Lord Lansdowne to support him, seeing that Lord Lansdowne as War Minister had abolished the British Commandership-in-Chief, so fearful was he and his colleagues of a "one-man show". How they got out of this poser in 1905 when they set up Lord Kitchener we do not know. But while it was a very effective reply to Ministers that made the Commander-in-Chief supreme in India, it has no merits. We should take the story of army administration here since the abolition of the Commander-in-Chief as just so much evidence in favour of keeping a Commander-in-Chief and trusting him. Lord Wolseley's scheme, referred to by Lord Curzon as condemned by a commission, would have done better than an Army Council of mediocrities has done. We know now that had Lord Wolseley been listened to more, much of our South African war trouble might have been saved.

Mr. Haldane and the Army Council are fortunate in being able to obtain at desire the approbation of Sir John French, the Inspector-General. When doubts were cast by every known artillery expert on the wisdom of relying on a mass of sham Territorial artillery for the defence of the country Sir John French's opinion was produced in favour of the proposal. Now that many people, including Lord Roberts, have serious doubts as to the adequacy of our defence arrangements, Sir John French once again fills the breach. As to the regular army most of us will agree with him that, both as to knowledge and training, it is in a high state of efficiency, and well prepared to take the field at short notice. Indeed, so far as it goes, it is probable that the regular army has never been more efficient than it is to-day. Accompanying Sir John French's report is a memorandum by the Army Council sketching the history of the organisation of the army since the Cromwell period, and claiming that the new plans are only the logical outcome of that system. The favourite

Haldanean device of counting things twice over is, of course, resorted to. It is stated that we now have 265,515 men to send abroad, as against 185,828 before the days of the Millennium. This, of course, simply means the militiamen are now liable for foreign service —when they are old enough to go—and that they are now called Special Reservists.

Whatever may be the view of the Government, the City takes Lord Charles Beresford seriously, and the opinion of the City still counts even in these Georgian days. And it was more as expert than as hero that Lord Charles was heard with rapt attention for an hour and a half by the overcrowded meeting in the hall of the Merchant Taylors' Company. The speaker's obvious curb upon himself, his desire to offend none but the merely party man, his depreciation of criticism of other nations' naval action, strengthened his case. He was terribly in earnest. Lord Charles is not an orator, but he has the sailor's knack of getting home.

We must commend for its good taste and judgment, in a speech not the most conclusive in thought, the passage bearing on our relations with Germany. As Lord Charles says, Germany has her own interests to consult. If she wants to build a big fleet, if she thinks it to her own advantage to do it, what right have we or any other country to complain? It was interfering insolence asking Germany at all to stop building. There is no grievance against Germany, but there is every reason for being on our guard against so powerful a rival. We cannot be content to be less than twice as strong on the sea as Germany, which is more than twice as strong as we on land. We see nothing "wild" in this standard.

A very interesting point was raised by questions in the House of Lords about the visit of the fleet to the Thames. It was pointed out by Lord Ellenborough and Lord Cawdor that, according to the Admiralty plans published in the newspapers, a great part of the fleet would be "bottled up" in the narrow waters of the Thames and be placed in an extremely risky position. Lord Crewe would not deny positively that this plan had been authorised by the Admiralty. It seems then to have been worth while to raise the question, and according to the now authorised plan the large ships are to be placed at Southend in a channel so broad that "bottling up" need not be feared. Lord Crewe may argue against the possibility of a coup de main on the ground that it would be a brigand attack not to be contemplated from any civilised Power, but it is better to be on the safe side.

There is a "Chancellor crisis" in Germany, and the question agitating all the parties is whether Prince Bülow will resign. It seems to be settled in the meantime as the result of the meeting of the Chancellor with the Kaiser at Kiel that Prince Bülow will go on at least until an arrangement is made as to the new taxation. There is still some scepticism as to the seriousness of the threat of retirement. It is represented as a move to bring pressure on the Conservatives and the Centre who defeated the inheritance taxation proposals. This may be considered the prominent feeling, though the "North German Gazette" has announced with official gravity that the intention of Prince Bülow to retire is irrevocable.

Already the Conservative and Centre newspapers are beginning to intimate that they are willing to come to terms which would make the retirement unnecessary. The "Kreuz Zeitung", the Conservative paper, states that no occasion for retirement can be recognised, and the "Germania", the Centre organ, states that the majority are ready for an agreement between themselves and the Government. Insistence on their victory would, as the Conservatives see, leave Prince Bülow no alternative but retirement; and this would involve an offence against all their principles. They would dislike above all that a Minister should resign as a consequence of the action of a parliamentary majority. They would be setting a precedent in the new constitutionalism which they intensely hate. An arrangement may yet conceivably be made with the Chancellor on the hypothesis that the Kaiser has expressed his personal will in the matter. Prince Bülow will have no objection to the theory if he gets what he wants; and so the retirement may yet not be absolutely irrevocable.

Our own Chancellor of the Exchequer's methods in the Budget debate recall Santerre's at the Place de la Révolution. When the most distinguished victims of the Terror raised their voices Santerre drowned them with the drums lest the people should be shaken. Mr. Lloyd George drowns them with the ringing of electric bells. In the intervals between the guillotining of one batch of speakers and amendments and the guillotining of the next, he occasionally offers a few words of defence or defiance. Argument and admission, perhaps, hardly count in this business—the thing that really counts to-day is the action of the guillotine, and the thing that will really count to-morrow will be the action of the House of Lords. Yet we must welcome Mr. Lloyd George's admission as to the moral rights of landowners. On Wednesday, interrupting Mr. Austen Chamberlain, he declared strongly and clearly that the owners of land had an absolute moral right to the increment!

These are far and away the most valuable words spoken by any member of the Government during the Budget debate. If owners of land have an absolute moral right to the increment, it follows they have an absolute moral right to the land itself. That they have a legal right we suppose not even Tower Hill orators would dispute. What, then, are we to think of those "reformers" who have it in their hearts, even in their mouths, to take away from the landowner that which he holds by moral as well as by legal right? After all, is the word "robber" too hard a word to use of land reformers with a letch for getting hold of other people's property?

This handsome admission by the Government—which Mr. Hughes, we hope, will have printed as a leaflet at the Central Office and distributed throughout the country—was made during the only interesting debate on the Budget this week. The debates on Monday and Tuesday for the most part were legal technicality. They did, however, draw from Mr. Lloyd George a strong condemnation of the whole leasehold system. For building purposes this system is, he thinks, thoroughly immoral. We suppose the only moral houses ever built on leased land are the houses of the artificial smallholders whom the Government are trying to establish. It is odd to reflect that a session or two ago leasing land for smallholders to build on was so much better than selling land for smallholders to build on! In what way exactly the leasehold house is an immoral or "thoroughly vicious" place, Mr. Lloyd George, though Mr. Balfour pressed him, refused to say.

As to this increment duty which has been discussed this week, peer after peer has written to the press announcing that he intends, if the Budget pass, to sell some of his land or to turn away some of the hands he now employs. This is a sort of sport from a Radical view. Sneers and guffaws greet every addition to the list of "splendid paupers" whom this first real democratic Budget is smiting well. Yet the jest will appear wretched enough when the estate workmen lose their work and lose their homes. We might mention several cases where arrangements are now being made to reduce the staffs. The worst of it is that those who will lose their jobs are not the younger and more active, but the older hands—men who are too old to be sure of getting fresh work and not old enough for the Government's five shillings a week.

And as to an owner being forced to sell his land, is this not, too, a wretched theme for a jest? Surely any man who can think somewhat higher than his stomach or his pocket will find merit in the landowner who cares for his estate and greatly wishes to live on it because it has long been in his family. This is care for property that has nothing gross or carnal about it. There are thousands of landowners still who have this kind of entirely honourable pride. By a hard struggle against thirty years of farming depression they have just managed to keep their estates, large or small, in the family. The disappearance of this class can be nothing but an ill.

At the meeting of the Unionist Free Trade Clubs it was decided that the executive should carefully consider the desirability of attacking certain Tariff Reform seats unless some proposals were made for the cessation of the Tariff Reform attacks on Free Trade Unionists. This will probably be about as effective as the alternative Budgets on Free Trade lines Lord Cromer and Lord Avebury are exercising their wits upon. It is very natural that they should want to hit out, but Lord Hugh Cecil's view is that he would rather let the matter alone. Lord Cromer wants the Government to be defeated by the Tariff Reformers for two reasons. It would put an end to the socialist attack on property and show that Tariff Reform itself is impossible. Why, then, should Unionist Free Traders want to win a few seats from Tariff Reformers?

From a letter of Lord Bessborough it appears that the East Marylebone branch of the Tariff Reform League are bent on making mischief. A Unionist Association, independent of the Marylebone Constitutional Union, is to be formed for East Marylebone. This, of course, means an association to oppose Lord Robert Cecil. Lord Bessborough and his followers evidently think it better not to have a Unionist as member at all than a Unionist who is not a Tariff Reformer. They will not get in a Tariff Reformer against Lord Robert Cecil. Either Lord Robert will be elected again in their despite, or a Liberal will get in. Neither event would be without prejudice to the Conservative cause. The best thing, of course, would be for Lord Robert to become a Tariff Reformer; the next best that he should be returned by grace of Conservatives who do not agree with his tariff views. This Unionist tomfoolery, to use Mr. Gladstone's phrase, should be squashed.

The promotion of Mr. Herbert Samuel to Cabinet rank is neither unexpected nor undeserved. His abilities are of a kind peculiarly fitted to holders of office. Clear-headed and clever-tongued, alert, precise and self-possessed, he brings to the advocacy of a measure, or in aid of its defence, a brain full of facts, each in its place and ready for instant service. The details of his subject are at the ends of his fingers, and he loses no time looking for them elsewhere. He stands for a type that results from the twin virtues of earnestness and application, and his success is eminently the reward of merit. It is quite possible that he may climb very high, as he has a tenacious grasp and is the reverse of giddy; but a drain of hot blood is not to be despised in politics, and the man who seldom smiles and never makes mistakes may find admirers but draws no enthusiastic followers. It is the chief of Mr. Samuel's faults that he is so faultless.

The Under-Secretary to the Home Office has fortune as well as himself to thank, however, for his present advancement. His conduct of several Bills through the Grand Committees—notably the Eight Hours Coal Miners Bill—has been admirable from the party point of view. This demands that a Bill shall come downstairs in much the same shape as it went up; if it returns to the floor of the House in a tumbled, unrecognisable condition, it is evident that those in charge have bungled and been bested by the Opposition. Amendments proposed in Committee should be either answered or accepted, but Mr. Samuel has frequently accomplished the difficult task of scotching a proposal against which his chief, the Home Secretary, could find no adequate reply. The seal was set on his reputation during the debates on the Licensing Bill of last session, when it became apparent, after experiments had been made by almost every member of the Government bench, that he alone understood the measure and could explain its provisions. If Mr. Samuel has seized his opportunities, Mr. Herbert Gladstone has provided them; spectacular rescues can be effected only through the flounderings of a victim, and from them who seek rewards thanks are in measure due to those who cannot swim. We hope the recognition is mutual.

Mr. Seymour Keay's name dropped out of politics long ago. But a good many people must remember him as a very quaint House of Commons figure. There was a Mr. Pickwick in the House not many years ago, but Mr. Seymour Keay represented a much more difficult Dickens figure, Simon Tappertit. The likeness was quite extraordinary; and, like Simon, Mr. Keay was for waging heroic combats with giants. He came out fearlessly on the subject of finance. He loved to hold forth on Budgets, and Mr. Gladstone would listen to him quite seriously on this subject. We have heard a Chancellor of the Exchequer say in the Lobby that there was something in what Seymour Keay argued, though the House of Commons and the Press took him for a bore.

The split between the Government and the cow-hunters in the House of Commons has developed through revolt to conflict, deep, definite, and likely to last until such time as the bishops order " the boys " to change their opinions " in the interests of Ireland ". The talk of " the boys " is about " betrayal ", but they must keep it strictly private. Had they been independent of the Government, how could the Government have betrayed them? Their independence of the Government has been their boast in Ireland, but if Ireland got to know about the " betrayal " she might ask awkward questions about the " independence ". On the other hand, the members of the Government, at least among themselves and their closer friends, are very free about their contempt for " the boys ". For the present, feeling is very hot, but the honourable member for Cardinal Logue and the honourable member for Archbishop Healy will no doubt be able to bring " the boys " to order when the proper time comes and the bishops give the word.

The motives and methods of Irish Nationalism betray themselves once again in the treatment of Sir Horace Plunkett's interview on the Land Bill published in the " Morning Post " for Thursday. His statements are clearly set out and marked off, but other statements, which he never made, are deliberately attributed to him and scattered broadcast through Ireland, with the evident purpose of hindering his industrial propaganda. In one of these statements falsely attributed to him leaders of the League are described by the interviewer himself as " political hooligans ", but by this time the peasants are reading that description of themselves as coming from Sir Horace, who has never used such language regarding any of his fellow-countrymen. It is pitiful that men in charge of publicism can descend to such thoughtful falsehood, but, on the other hand, does it not look like the desperation of failure?

The Miners' Eight Hours Act has begun very badly. It has almost led to the greatest strike that has ever been known. When it was in the House of Commons one argument against it was that it would give rise to new labour troubles. It has already done this, and though the threatened strike has been averted the fear of it has sent up prices immensely and caused great loss to the South Wales ports. The dispute is only put off, and whether the miners shall work the sixty extra hours allowed by the Act may come up again. The miners may refuse to work the extra hours in any particular instance proposed to them. And, besides, this point may arise elsewhere than in Wales. At present there is a great strike of miners threatened in Scotland. There has been great want of consideration for Mr. Churchill. The Welsh coalowners and colliers actually settled the dispute without waiting for him.

M. Homyakoff, the President of the Douma, who is now in England with representatives of its various parties, has given himself the trouble of explaining to the Labour party that it is as ignorant of Russia as it is of ordinary decency in its attacks on the Tsar. He and his colleagues are insulted by the distinction made between the Tsar and the Russian nation. We should translate M. Homyakoff's polite phrases into the advice that the cobblers of the Labour party should stick to their last and not interfere with matters they have neither the education nor the experience to understand. When the troubles in Russia broke out, there were too many Englishmen who imagined that they might insult the Tsar in the name of Russia. They have learned better, and now leave it to the Labour party to stand for the fool Englishman.

"Deeds, not words", said Mrs. Pankhurst in "an emotional speech" as she took the women "forth to battle" at Westminster. Then she slapped a policeman for the offence of attending to his duties, including the duty of protecting her; and in return he behaved like a gentleman. She might knock off his cap, but he would not have his dignity farther disturbed, and he continued to protect her until she was quietly locked up. The "battle" really ended with the cap and the breaking of the official windows. The rest was for the unemotional machinery of the police court. Happily our police-magistrates are too sensible to allow any consideration of sex to affect them in court.

The Anti-socialist League held a successful meeting in the Whitehall Room of the Hôtel Métropole on Tuesday. Mr. Walter Long is a pleasant speaker. His voice and manner are good, and he makes his points with an ease and perspicuity which are exactly suited to a well-dressed, comfortable audience. But the ladies and gentlemen who applauded Mr. Long at the Hôtel Métropole are not the horny-handed sons of toil who make up the bulk of the electors. We do not quite know why the managers of the meeting put up Sir Charles Euan-Smith to talk finance to the West End. Like Lord Avebury, Sir Charles Euan-Smith has not been wholly successful in his handling of the finance of other people in the City. To give him precedence of Sir John Rolleston, who has fought Leicester several times and sat for it in one Parliament, and who is, besides, a really capable man of business, does not show much discrimination.

A well-known novelist once told Lord Grey that he considered the chief function of a Governor-General was to flap his wings and crow. At the Dominion Day dinner on Thursday, if Lord Grey resisted the temptation to flap his wings he found it impossible not to crow. Where every other member of a happy brood is so engaged it would be too much to expect Chanticleer in chief not to take the lead. Canadians have indeed better reason than a good many to demonstrate on occasions, and in Mr. R. L. Borden's opinion Lord Grey is perhaps the best Canadian of them all. His enthusiasm is natural. During the years of his Viceroyalty, Canada has rushed ahead; it may astonish some people to learn that the Dominion to-day has a population of 7,000,000. And we have Lord Grey's assurance that the American invaders, 80,000 apparently last year with more to come, will not leaven but be absorbed.

The censorship discussion is becoming a bore. The thing, we mean the censorship—we are not so sanguine about the discussion—cannot go on much longer, and the sooner the end comes the better. Right or wrong on paper, it has failed practically. A censorship that has nothing to say to immoral suggestion but is shocked at truth is a fraud. It seems to us that a dishonest playwright would find it easy enough to get round Mr. Pigott or Mr. Redford; while the unusually honest ones are the victims. Mr. Alexander's apology for the censor is frankly immoral. He thinks it grand for the theatre manager that once a play has got past the censor nobody can touch it. The manager is to leave his responsibility and conscience with the censor, who, you know, never says anything so long as you observe the conventions. But Mr. Bernard Shaw would do well to leave the matter alone for a time. A daily letter even from him palls.

PRINCE BÜLOW'S LEGACY.

As is his way, Prince Bülow is making the best of a bad job. He will get as much money as he can and then he will go, leaving the new problems just emerging in German politics to be dealt with by a new man. But he is not to go just yet. First he is to act as mediator between the Reichstag and the Federal Council, and thus once more to show his adroitness in combining elements apparently irreconcileable—a fitting curtain to the career of one who these eight years has picked so delicate a way and avoided so deftly the political crevasses that threatened to engulf him. His qualities have proved his ruin. No one but Prince Bülow could have dreamt of a working majority composed of Conservatives and Liberals—who, after all, disagree about most things under the sun. And now nemesis has overtaken this most skilful juggler with political combinations. Less than three years ago he appealed to the country against the Catholic Centre and the Socialist Left. The clericals returned with undiminished strength and formed the chief element of the combination by which the Chancellor has been defeated. The Socialist representation was diminished by nearly fifty per cent., and in the critical division on the succession duty, when the Government was beaten by only eight votes, the Socialists voted with the minority. The whole episode should prove instructive to Prince Bülow's successor.

In every political crisis there is a tendency to take too personal a view of the situation. The Chancellorship of the German Empire is, of course, too great an office for a change in its tenure to be immaterial; and the retirement of one of the ablest diplomatists in Europe is an important event. At the same time the German Empire stands where it did; its policy and its ambitions remain, despite all changes of persons. What really concerns England and Europe is whether Germany will manage to pay her way, and what is really material in the present situation is not that Prince Bülow is about to resign but that the revenues of the Empire are to be increased by a sum little short of £20,000,000 annually. There are some who still cling to the view that Germany is a poverty-stricken country whose inhabitants live on black bread and questionable sausages. Such notions are absurd; there is plenty of money in Germany, but the Government finds it very difficult to reach. Two great obstacles block the way to every financial reform. The first is the monetary relations between the Empire and the Federated States; the second is the quarrel between the agrarians and the industrialists. Neither of these obstacles has been overcome, though the reforms of last November proposed to deal with both. The constitutional question has been shelved; the party conflict has become more bitter than ever—and in spite of this double failure Germany is able to look forward to an increase of revenue which will yield a very satisfactory number of Dreadnoughts. Nothing could be more profoundly significant of the vast financial capacity of the modern German Empire than that this result should have been attained without the most obvious new sources of revenue being so much as tapped.

Nevertheless it is certain that £20,000,000 will not carry Germany through. It is probably not quite enough to cover the expenditure of the moment, and the future will bring heavy obligations both as regards armaments and in matters of social policy. Moreover the financial problem, deliberately shelved for some years past by the device of annual loans, has now been definitely raised. The fight must go forward to a finish, and its direction will occupy much of the attention of Prince Bülow's successor. First stands the problem of matricular contributions, at present scarcely ripe for settlement because the States do not know what they want. On the one hand they are repudiating further burdens, and they have been so far successful in their efforts that sums for which they are constitutionally liable have been transferred to the imperial debt. On the other hand they are extremely jealous of their authority, and for this reason they have refused to sanction an imperial income tax, which, if once accepted, would provide all the money necessary for many years to come. Their position is thus hopelessly illogical; they cannot both eat their cake and have it. If the Empire is to raise the revenue it must be provided with the necessary powers; if the States are to retain their powers unimpaired they must raise the revenue. It is the dilemma which confronts every federation. It accounts for the absence of an income tax in the U.S.A. and is responsible for the financial deadlock in the Australian Commonwealth. In Germany it has been the cause of more than one political crisis, and on paper the position of the States is so overwhelmingly strong that they may not shirk other crises in future. But the present position of European affairs tends to augment the power of the Empire, which is entrusted with the business of defence, and it appears likely that the Empire will prevail in the long run because time is on its side.

The issue of the struggle between the agrarians and the industrialists is at once more doubtful and more pressing. The present phase opened in 1894 when Count Caprivi concluded a series of commercial treaties which involved a reduction of the duty on imported foodstuffs. At the same time an exceptionally good harvest brought about a further decline in price, and the agrarians raised the cry "We are betrayed". Then was formed the famous Agricultural League (Bund der Landwirte), which speedily made itself the strongest force in German politics. It commands a solid block of fifty to sixty votes in the Reichstag; it dominates the whole of rural Germany; and it is mainly responsible for the collapse of Prince Bülow's financial scheme. Fifteen years were to elapse before the industrialists retorted on this move. Early in June, however, when it became apparent that the Government was resolved on compromise if not on surrender, a huge meeting was held in Berlin at which it was decided to form a new Hanseatic League. The new body has lost no time in getting to work. Its manifesto has been issued broadcast over the country and is backed by some of the greatest names in industrial Germany. The league is to be representative of every form of trade, commerce, or industry, and aspires to a membership running into hundreds of thousands. Membership is open to heads of firms on payment of a minimum contribution of 3s. annually; from employees the payment of a single shilling will suffice. The league is avowedly a counterblast to the agricultural Bund. Like it, it will run candidates for election and bring pressure to bear on the Government, and it contemplates the holding of meetings and the distribution of literature among the whole industrial population, thereby intruding on the preserves of the social democracy.

There is already no doubt that the new organisation will achieve a fair measure of success. It has been indiscriminately abused by the agrarian press, and it is even rumoured that the Conservatives, by refusing to withdraw the taxes on dividends, flour mills, and coal, to which the Government objects as injurious to industry, will force a dissolution and thus precipitate a crisis before worse things befall. The present fears are doubtless exaggerated, but it is likely enough that the new body will exercise an enormous influence on German politics. It is, indeed, on large bodies of this kind that the German Government is forced to depend. Outside the centre there are no real parties in Germany; there are only groups of interests, and even in the case of the centre the bond of union is not political but religious. The Government very properly refuses to identify itself with any one interest, and relies on a scratch majority formed of a number of groups. But impromptu combinations of this character are necessarily without that widespread external organisation such as is at the use of English parties. Accordingly, when embarking on some new and important policy, the Government favours the creation of some special organisation for the influence of public opinion. Hence the importance of the Navy League, without whose propaganda the German Navy would never have been built. Hence, too, it is that the Agricultural League has been able to tie the Government to an agrarian policy which it once showed some disposition to abandon. Hitherto, however, industrialism has remained unorganised, and though its interests have assuredly not been neglected, it has received no favours at the hands of the State and has not been able to demand support. Those days of passive acceptance are over, and Junkertum suddenly finds itself confronted with a foe whom it may be unable to resist. No wonder that Prince Bülow, already weary of his perpetual task of combination and bargaining, determined to resign on the emergence of the powerful engine which his own policy has called into being.

"WHY NOT LEAVE IT ALONE?"

AN adviser like Lord Melbourne was sadly wanted during the Lords' debate on Indian military administration. The discussion brought up a melancholy category of things that had better have been left alone. First, we find Lord Morley of his own initiative forcing on the Government of India the abolition of the "Supply Member". Everyone concerned knew very well that the post was useless. It was invented as a rather clumsy compromise by a Government that had to choose between Lord Curzon and Lord Kitchener. Like many another compromise, it finally failed. The measure of its mischief however is the £10,000 a year it is computed to have cost the Exchequer. The Indian Government thought the avoidance of a very unpleasant and undignified public controversy to be worth the money. Why not leave it alone? But in matters of greater moment Lord Morley has not hesitated to initiate the policy and reject the advice of the best authorities in India. He has saddled the revenues with immense charges for Councils not wanted, and fraught with great potential dangers. But a lakh and a half for a sinecure just to cover up the blunder of political adversaries is quite another thing. So economy won the day. Incidentally Lord Morley found an opportunity to praise his own "reforms" on the singular ground that they conciliate the population from which the Native Army is recruited. The people who ought to be—but apparently are not—conciliated by the "reforms" are the middle-class Bengalis. But the whole population of Bengal does not contribute, and never has contributed, a single soldier to the Native Army. Was it to placate the Sikhs and Pathans that Lord Morley appointed a Bengali lawyer to rule over them? Or did he intend thereby to recognise and strengthen the loyal adherence of the ruling chiefs to British rule? He must know that the new representatives of the people will be drawn chiefly from the classes and races that the Army holds in contempt. This unhappy obiter dictum is another thing that might very well have been left alone.

Lord Midleton naturally regrets the premature and violent death of an arrangement which was his own child. Nothing in life is more pathetic than the affection always shown by a parent for his deformed or sickly offspring. But there is no place in politics for a parade of this natural feeling. And why contest the title of a "compromise"? The only justification for it is that it really was what Lord Morley justly describes as a provisional and tentative proposal, made in the forlorn hope of averting an unedifying strife between two great public servants which must otherwise result in the loss of one or other to an Administration that had great need of both. Had the present change been made promptly on Lord Curzon's resignation all this would have been avoided and the resuscitation of a very disagreeable incident have been avoided. Lord Midleton almost seems to claim for his "reform" that it has enabled Lord Kitchener to increase the number of officers in the Indian Army, and so avert a peril to which the Home Army is exposed to-day. He might have left this out. The Indian Government was able to strengthen its staff because it could, and did, provide funds to pay them. That £10,000 would have supplied another half-score or so.

If, as we must hold, Lord Curzon's resignation

was the episode in his memorable Viceroyalty least becoming his office and himself, what is to be said of his action in reviving this infructuous controversy? The unpleasant personal element that must come in ought to have deterred him, even if he were incontestably in the right and able to prove it. He has failed to do this. Most people will share Lord Morley's difficulty in discovering any practical object in the discussion. Answering this challenge, Lord Curzon has explained that his object was to call attention to a system of military administration that the present Government had condemned when in opposition, that would not be tolerated in England, and has no parallel anywhere. The general principles of Lord Kitchener's scheme were formulated, discussed, and decided four years ago. That scheme extends far beyond a mere reconstruction of the dispositions at headquarters, which are an integral and necessary part of the organisation, but nothing more. It has so far stood the test of time and experience. By general admission the efficiency of the Indian armies has been immensely increased. The little campaigns that have afforded any test, however inadequate, of its practical working have been in every case a signal success. None of Lord Curzon's lurid prophecies of red ruin and the breaking-up of laws, of the establishment of a military autocracy and the dethronement of civil power, none of these serious prognostications shows any signs of fulfilment. The only forecast of the late Viceroy that has come true is the one where he followed the wise principle of "never prophesy unless you know". Like the rest of the world, he certainly did foretell the disestablishment of the Supply Member. Even then it was common knowledge. And this is all that has happened to justify Lord Curzon in disinterring an unhappy controversy out of which he emerged with some loss of dignity, if not of reputation. Lord Curzon, in short, has been badly advised. And to those who with us admire his great qualities and recognise both the high importance of his achievements in the past and the equally high prospect of his future services to the State, the worst is that he seems in this matter to have been his own adviser. Why could he not have left it alone?

As to the merits of the question it is unnecessary again to go over old ground. The constitutional reasons have receded, and the main attack is now directed against the Atlantean load piled on the Commander-in-Chief by the removal of the Supply Member. Even Lord Roberts can now find no other reason for keeping him. On the hypothesis, the post is abolished because experience has shown that there is not enough work in quantity or quality to justify its retention. The money it has cost has been well spent if it has done nothing more than prove that the Army Administration can get on very well without it. As for the rest, one would think, to read some parts of this debate, that there was only one efficient soldier at a time in all India, and he the Commander-in-Chief. There are scores of them as good to-day as India has ever produced, though they may not have filled the public eye, ready and able to take the place of those above or below them who may be called elsewhere. And, further, though no one in the House of Lords thought fit to repel the charge, there will be no lack of qualified advisers ready to give their opinion frankly and freely, when it is wanted, even if it is unpalatable. The officers of the Indian Army are not a body of time-servers.

Among the speakers who seemed to find relief in irrelevancy was Lord Wolverhampton. India has not often had so good a Secretary of State. But even pride in an office he so worthily filled can hardly justify his suggestion that the supreme authority in India should be other than the Governor-General in Council, or that salvation may be sought in the personal initiative of the Secretary of State. These matters he might have let alone. But assuredly in the immediate question under debate he struck the right note when he declared that the best course which can now be taken is to "let the thing work on" and deal with improvements in detail as events suggest them.

LORD CHARLES BERESFORD.

If Sir John Fisher is really about to retire from the post of First Sea Lord, then rather than endanger the great constructive work of building up our preparations for 1913 and 1914 we would urge on contending parties a truce to all the bitter feeling which he has created in a service he but imperfectly understood. We have ourselves from time to time urged that the Board of Admiralty has a collective responsibility, but, unfortunately, it was impossible to ignore the letter in which Lord Esher revealed Sir John Fisher as the sole author of the evils from which the Navy suffers. That Lord Esher regards the changes which have caused the notorious dissensions afloat as blessings is of little interest beside the importance of his testimony that he was shown the whole of these changes in outline by Sir John Fisher before he had joined the Board, and at a time when he could not have consulted his future colleagues or studied the evidence on which his predecessors had pursued a more orderly policy. Rushed upon a great service governed by traditions which have ever been a source of immense strength to it in war, these changes were made without the slightest regard for evidence or tradition. They were supported by methods such as the notorious Bacon-Mann letters and the Admiralty pamphlet "The Truth about the Navy", all of which were circulated at the public expense. It is easy to understand the intense bitterness excited, and to see how demoralisation on the one side produced demoralisation on the other until a state of affairs was evolved in which both sides could be accused of intriguing with politicians and journalists. So ardently did one camp desire the removal of Sir John Fisher for the salvation of the Navy that their opponents alleged they could always be used by the less reputable and scrupulous Cabinet Ministers for the purpose of terrorising the Admiralty into curtailing naval expenditure. "We have admirals ready to hand who will place at our disposal the advice suited to reduced Navy estimates" is a potent argument in the hands of a Government. We are opposed to the Board of Admiralty and most of its works during recent years, and if we have said hard things about any officer on it this has been because he ceased to act up to the noble traditions of the Navy and chose to be a politician. It was an example which was bound to spread both among friends and opponents until the Navy stood in danger of forgetting that its chief business was "to keep the foreigners from fooling us".

While we find much to approve of in Lord Charles Beresford's demands in regard to cruisers and other small craft and the absolute necessity of providing for the defence of our commerce, we deplore the line he took about battleships as heartily as his detractors will welcome it. It is so far removed from what was looked for, and not in vain, from Lord Charles Beresford in his prime that one cannot resist the suspicion that the Government have succeeded only too well in their ill-omened project of creating political sailors by playing off one camp against another, while Germany goes steadily ahead with the nation and navy at one. When Lord Charles Beresford characterises a demand that we should lay down two Dreadnoughts for every one Germany lays down as the insane demand of wild men, and as "ludicrously absurd", does he not prompt a suspicion that the demand is anathema because it happens to be inspired by Sir John Fisher and backed by the latter's supporters, Mr. Stead, Lord Esher, and Mr. Garvin? When he says that twenty-six Dreadnoughts to Germany's twenty-one and sixty-six large armoured ships to forty-one for Germany are enough, is he not pandering to the very self-deception in which the Cabinet have indulged of casting out the United States from the two-Power standard? In days when the outlook was far less threatening Lord Charles Beresford was not satisfied with a Government which was laying down two ships for each one laid down by France, and by his impetuous advocacy rendered great service to his country by causing the Government to introduce the Naval Defence Act. It is true that he says the eight

Dreadnoughts demanded for this year must be laid down at once, and so brings himself into apparent agreement with Imperialists, the Navy Committee of the House of Commons, and the Guildhall Meeting. After this year, however, his programme stipulates for laying down only six Dreadnoughts up to 31 March 1912, so that the six should be completed by 31 March 1914. This provides for three a year as compared with four a year in the programme of Germany. How is it possible to justify eight this year to be laid down at once if only three are required next year, and wild words can be quoted from the distinguished admiral that prior to the Dreadnought we were on a four-Power basis? What will happen as the result of Lord Charles Beresford's intervention? His plea in regard to Dreadnoughts will be quoted for all it is worth by the Little Navy party, while the advocates of a strong Navy will hesitate to use his authority, which in their view he has thus damaged, by quoting his powerful advocacy of cruisers and other small craft as well as a proper reserve of stores. It is right that Lord Charles Beresford should draw the attention of the great commercial men at the City meeting to the dangers threatening our trade routes and to the absolute need of cruisers for hunting down the enemy's commerce destroyers, but the historical lesson is that the defence of commerce ultimately rests on the successful operations of the fleets, and it would be an ill service to England if in a future war we were to find all our operations hampered by the fact that our margin of superiority in battleships is too narrow to provide for the requirements of fulfilling our traditional policy of keeping the sea in a position to bring the enemy's fleets to action the moment they leave their harbours. The supremacy of the battleship fleets is the first consideration, for without it no provision of cruisers, destroyers, stores, or coaling stations will avail. On the battleships depends the command of the sea. Then come the other considerations. The cruisers are the eyes of a fleet. Large ships cannot be wasted or dispersed to hunt for small commerce destroyers; therefore more cruisers are wanted for this purpose. The fleets are liable to torpedo attack at night when the crews need rest. Therefore picquets of destroyers must be kept at sea to hunt down torpedo craft. In each case they must be in sufficient strength so as not to be driven off, and as ships which keep the seas must coal, they have to be very numerous. We do not think that Lord Charles Beresford exaggerates our requirements when he demands thirty-six cruisers and seventy-six destroyers (twenty-four of our enlarged type) to be completed by March 1913. Of these we have only provided six cruisers and twenty destroyers under this year's programme, leaving us in two programmes to average fifteen cruisers and twenty-eight destroyers per annum with the colonial assistance which he commends to the empire for this purpose. The demand is tremendous, but it has been brought about by the wicked policy of deferring our liabilities. It is one based on a consideration of the naval strength of Germany alone. Lord Charles Beresford, in respect of the two-Power standard, might contend that his business as a sailor is to leave the standard to the Government, and to indicate only what is required to keep to it. If so, it is our emphatic opinion that he should have made his position clearer before he indicated a programme which provides in 1910 and 1911 for only three Dreadnoughts per annum as compared with four per annum for Germany. We believe that to act on such advice would stimulate the naval pretensions of Germany, whereas the policy of two keels to one would render the race so hopeless as to lead to its abandonment.

THE GENESIS OF A CRIME.

THERE is no longer any mystery about the mechanism by which the London and South Western Bank was fooled and robbed by the two young men King and Robert. After months of painstaking labour the detectives and the bank agents worked it out. King, a young man aged twenty-nine, took advantage of his knowledge of the bank's business procedure to devise a scheme which was as simple as it was ingenious, as the most effective schemes always are. Robert, a youth we might almost say of twenty-three, took on himself the part of the gentlemanly impersonator of the fictitious person whose account had been transferred from one branch to another. Seven or eight branch bank managers fell into the trap; King and Robert had nearly £3,000 to share between them; and the bank had the problem before them of discovering which out of their numerous clerks was the possible and probable culprit. The demonstration was complete that King had sent the transfer notes to the branch banks. Part of the proof, indeed, consisted of similarity of handwriting; and this of recent years has become very much suspect. But there remained no doubt when the father of King gave evidence that his son had confessed to having "engineered that D. S. Windell business". This fictitious name introduces us to the most curious feature of this daring raid. The concoction of it is the first thing that suggests that this crime has a more than usually interesting psychological history. An ordinary common-sense man would not imagine that a person of determined criminal mind could start a coolly nefarious crime by playing a practical joke. It was almost a danger signal in itself to the bank manager to suspect something. King devised the name, and he was described as a young man with a genius for friendship to whom everybody was devoted. This does not seem to be the sort of temperament which plots cautiously and takes cold-blooded precautions. The people who are liked are the impulsive, rattle-brained fellows, the practical jokers, who, with more vitality than brains, get themselves and others into trouble by doing something without realising its consequences. Robert has given as extraordinary an account of himself as was ever written. He is a visionary, fantastic, with an imagination which more even than is usual in the adolescent confounds all the boundaries of the real and the possible. We should not think of taking his account of himself literally. Probably half of it is pure fantasy; but this would only show that he lives on the borderland where genius and insanity meet. One worthy witness told how Robert wanted him to believe that a stone had life in it, and witness could not convince him that it had not.

Now fancy this 'inspired idiot'" being brought into contact with King, "the commonplace type with a stick and a pipe and a half-bred black-and-tan". A coarse-natured, insensitive fellow, who could remark airily to his distressed father, who spoke to him of his crime, "Nonsense, that's only my arrears of salary". We do not know how the two met, but we think we see how they stood to each other. King prided himself on his knowledge of the world and common-sense, and was amused with Robert as a poor fool who only appeared the more foolish for the accomplishments which King lacked. Robert was a vain fool. He had sense enough at first not to take the suggestion of the enterprise seriously. But King knew the man he was getting his amusement out of. "I listened to the details", says Robert, "like a novelist may consider the details of a plot which ultimately he will employ in some shape or form in his projected novel. Until it came to filling up the forms the scheme in my mind was wholly disconnected with myself. Then what I can only describe as a curious psychological process took place. Till that time it had been the hero of the romance who was going round to the banks. All of a sudden I substituted myself in his place. Instead of the plot remaining imaginary I became very excited with the prospect of making it a reality, with myself the hero of one of the most daring and ingenious schemes of modern times."

Up to this point we can believe that King had no other intention than to see how far he could fool Robert. He had gulled and "spoofed" Robert into posing as a hero of romance. Then came Robert's turn to react on King. From this moment Robert became the leader by the force of his superior character over King. Robert the visionary had had a life of adventures and made a way successfully for himself where King would have starved. King was not adventurous; he had been for years an ordinary plodding bank clerk "with the best of characters", and living on £150 a year and the prospect of a pension. Robert had engaged in half a dozen different intellectual occupations with equal facility. We imagine that when Robert began to consider himself a hero of romance he carried King off his feet by his energy and eloquence, and excited him to dare the risks of the adventure. King was not really the master mind. Robert was his intellectual superior. There remained only a shred of King's original joke in the contribution of "D. S. Windell". It is possible that Robert, being a foreigner, did not appreciate the play on the letters and word or there would have been no such joke for the delight of the evening papers.

It may be objected that the way we have "reconstructed" the crime was not the way in which it was presented in court. There King was put forward as the master criminal, deliberately perverting the mind of Robert and entrapping him through designing villainy into being his subordinate accomplice. But the procedure of the courts is very mechanical, and its methods do not allow much for investigation into unusual psychological histories. It was sufficient for the court that King was the one who was a servant of the bank, and had access to the necessary documents, for him to be treated as the principal offender, and to be punished more severely than Robert. One of the detectives said King was a man of iron nerves. But if possession of nerve is to be taken as a test, in what respect did he show himself superior to Robert, who, when he found his visits to the branches were being suspected by the cabman, ordered him to drive to the head offices of the bank which he had just robbed of over two thousand pounds? Nor did Robert make any weak attempt to throw blame on King for having corrupted and persuaded him into crime. It is quite possible that Robert's quick imagination played on the position of King in the bank, and set King to explain how by a particular method a fraud could be committed. This inquisitive, restless, vain spirit of Robert, an impracticable, visionary, foolish fellow as King conceived him to be, may have been the start of what we have called King's practical joke on Robert. The probabilities are all against King being the tempter and Robert the tempted. The danger for Robert was not so great as it was for King. When the criminals were sought for Robert could disappear more easily and with better chances of escape. This is what happened. King's disappearance would be equivalent to confession. He had to stay and bear the whole ordeal of investigation. Robert went on his travels and was found in Spain. The clever confession in which he made himself out to be not so much a criminal as having made a slip through romanticism of character is a masterpiece of plausibility. It was an invention which saved him from penal servitude. King had not, it is true, equally good material out of which to frame a similar defence unless indeed he had adopted the line which we have suggested. That he did not, we hold, proves that he was not capable of it, and that he was quite inferior intellectually to the clever youth who was supposed to be his dupe.

THE CITY.

THE settlement of the coal strike and the simultaneous appearance of the sun had perhaps something to do with the return of cheerfulness to the stock markets towards the end of the week. Liquidation, like all other mortal things, must have an end: and after "the dreary drip" of the last three weeks in the Kaffir Circus, one would think that the last and most incorrigible West-end dabbler must have been driven out. They are difficult to please, these South African magnates. When the lords and ladies with whom the magnates dine and bridge at the other end of the town are not in the market, we hear complaints of public apathy: and when the lords and ladies are in the market, then we are told that they must be "shaken out". As we have pointed out before, the danger of the South African market lies in the ease with which Tom, Dick and Harry can buy a hundred shares here, and a hundred shares there. Really the brokers are as much to blame as anybody for these slumplets in Kaffirs: they give credit to the first comer far too easily. Whether there will be a revival in the South African market this side of the holidays, or during, or after the holidays, it is impossible to say. The people who have bought shares during the last fortnight, being "in the kitchen", will probably not hold them too long. We can only indicate a few shares which in our judgment are good and cheap investments at present prices, namely Knights, Simmer and Jack, City Deep, Durban Deeps, Nourse, and among the low-priced shares Boksburgs. In the Rhodesian market, Lomagundas and Rhodesian Coppers are our favourites. The improvement in South Africa is shown in the Report of the General Mining and Finance Corporation for 1908: there is a working profit for the year of £148,347, and after paying a dividend of 5 per cent. the balance carried forward amounts to £62,661.

In the foreign railway market a mild sensation was caused by the rise of Mexican Southern Ordinary from 55 to 62; and by the fall of Buenos Ayres and Pacifics to 102½, from which price they, however, quickly recovered to 104. Buenos Ayres Great Southerns and Buenos Ayres Western also fell, and these two latter lines have much more reason for falling than Pacifics; for when the Government of Buenos Ayres builds its own line, for which it recently issued a loan, undoubtedly the Southern and the Western will be hard hit. That astonishing little company, the National Minerals Corporation (to which we have often drawn the attention of our readers), has just issued its report and balance-sheet. With an issued capital of £15,000 (in 300,000 shares of 1s.) it has made a profit for the first year of £9781, which is not bad. Against property which it bought for £15,000 in shares the company holds 102,000 shares in the St. Ives Consolidated Mines, valued in the market at £204,000, which is no mean profit: it has in addition £29,869 in cash at the bank, and investments at cost £27,000, besides debtors £7690, making roughly £240,000. Besides its capital of £15,000, however, the company has issued £46,820 of participating bonds, which are repayable in 1918 at a premium of £1 per bond, provision for which amortisation is made every year. But with the bonds, the capital of the National Minerals Corporation is only £61,820, against which it holds £240,000 in shares and cash. The Corporation has sold its "pitchblende rights" to the St. Ives Consolidated Mines for 122,000 shares in that concern, and the St. Ives Consolidated has passed on these rights to the British Radium Corporation, which is going to erect a factory capable of producing 1000 milligrammes of radium and a proportionate quantity of uranium compounds per month. The Minerals Corporation has "various other properties", which are going to be consolidated with several adjoining mines. On the top of all these things, the Minerals Corporation has secured what the directors call "an epoch-making process for the treatment of complex ores". All patents are a gamble, but if this process should do what is claimed for it, it will not only make an epoch, but, what is more important, it will make a market for the shares of the National Minerals Corporation at prices beside which the present price of 11*s.* will seem ridiculous.

Among the new issues of the week are the Canadian Government £6,500,000 Three-and-a-Half per Cent. Stock at £98½ per cent., and the Rembia Rubber Estates, Limited,, with a capital of £60,000.

INSURANCE: THE NORWICH UNION.

IN times gone by there were quite a number of life offices which worked with fire companies in the same offices, frequently with the same directors and the same branch officials, while yet remaining distinct associations. Several of these have, in one way or another, disappeared, and the only remaining arrangements of the kind are those of the Norwich Union Fire and Life Offices and the Sun Fire and Life. Whether they will maintain their separate existence to an indefinite future, or will respectively amalgamate, may not be of great moment to the insured. The plan seems to work well, since the connexions of one are available for the other, some economy apparently results from this co-operation, while the chief officials of the life office are left free to devote their whole attention to the life business and those of the fire company to the fire and other forms of insurance undertaken. There is reason to think that even greater benefits to both fire and life offices would result from amalgamation.

The Norwich Union Life Office, although it observed its centenary last year, keeping at the same time the bi-centenary of the Amicable Society, which the Norwich took over, did not rise to any great prominence until the present general manager was appointed something like twenty years ago. Since then its progress has been most remarkable. It has not merely grown to be one of the biggest of British life offices, but it has steadily improved its financial strength, while at the same time increasing its rate of bonus, and, as the necessary consequence of greater financial strength, has even better bonus prospects for the future. The report for 1908 tells of the issue of over 9000 policies, assuring nearly £5,000,000 and carrying a new premium income of £229,000. In spite of the efforts made to secure exceptional results for the centenary year, the new business now reported is still larger. We always regard a large new business as a good feature in a life assurance report, provided it is obtained at a moderate rate of expenditure. It is unfortunately a common practice for companies which aim at very rapid extension to pay a great deal too much for their new business. The Norwich Union, while as energetic as any, is more economical than the majority even of humdrum companies who do little more than maintain the amount of their premium income year by year. The average expenditure of British companies is 80 per cent. of the first year's premium and 8 per cent. of renewals; these ratios do not include as an expense the dividends paid to shareholders of proprietary companies, which are, in effect, an expenditure borne by the participating policyholders. The Norwich works at a cost of only 57 per cent. of new premiums and 5.7 per cent. of renewals.

Another good feature of the Norwich Union Life Office is that it systematically earns a high rate of interest upon its funds. Last year the return was £4 4s. 6d. per cent. after deducting income tax, which shows a very large margin for surplus or profit when compared with the £2 10s. per cent. employed in the valuation. The finance of the society is more enterprising than that of some life offices, with the result that while earning a high rate of interest it has managed to escape that depreciation in the value of securities which has been experienced by many companies who have managed their investments on more old-fashioned and conventional lines. The record of the society constitutes a strong argument against regulations by the State as to the securities in which life offices may invest.

The Norwich Union Fire Office also has a good account to render of its operations last year. The fire premium income was £1,101,505, of which 60 per cent. was absorbed in the payment of claims and 35 per cent. for commission and expenses of management. The proportionate amount paid for claims was heavier than usual, but the significant thing about the account is that although the shareholders received a dividend at the rate of 37½ per cent. of the paid-up capital, which absorbed £55,000, more than £50,000 of this amount was derived from interest on funds, and less than one-tenth of the trading profit was applied for dividend purposes, the balance of the profits being used to strengthen the financial resources of the society.

The Norwich Union Fire stands very high in the fire insurance world: it deals liberally with its policyholders and its security is strong in the extreme. An explanation of this is afforded by the systematic way in which the bulk of the profit earned each year is allowed to accumulate, instead of being distributed to the proprietors. It is the adoption of sound methods of this kind which has made British insurance at its best famous throughout the world.

"SCHOOL" AND "THE GROTESQUES".

By Max Beerbohm.

It must be ten years since Tom Robertson's plays were last revived in London. "School" is now being played at the Coronet Theatre, and is to be followed by "Ours" and "Caste". Ten years ago it filled me with scorn, which I expressed with all possible vehemence in this Review. In those days one was still fighting. Mr. Clement Scott was alive, decrying as a sign of decadence whatever in drama was non-Robertsonian; and there were many other critics hardly less hostile than he to the new movement which a few of us were trying to speed forward. The majority of popular playwrights were still working in the Robertsonian vein: their plays were simply Robertson up-to-date; and, so long as they were there to impede progress, one could not be fair to Robertson: he was the enemy. Well, there is no fighting nowadays. One by one, the old critics have disappeared, and their successors are, one and all, friends of—I was going to say the new movement; but the movement is no longer new: the battle is won, the formula established; realism sits crowned. Presently there will be a revolt, of course. The best among the youngest brains will find that realism, as a method of presenting life in drama, has been exhausted. New banners will appear, with some strange device on them. And we elders will fume and fret and fight, shoulder to shoulder, against these silly striplings who were in swaddling-clothes when we were founding the national drama on a rock which never, never will be shaken! And that rock will crumble, and our grey hairs be brought down in sorrow to the grave, and our posts be filled by persons whose ideas Time has not ossified. Our old age will be as stormy as our youth was. We shall be as fierce in defence as erst we were in attack. For the present we sit successful, unchallenged; amenable, a trifle smug. We can enjoy such plays as "School". We can give Tom Robertson due credit for the much that there was of charm and talent in him.

Not even in our hot youth did we ever deny his instinct for dramatic form, and for all that appertains to the theatre. The theatre was his very home, and he never looked out of the window; but he was, unlike the playwrights who preceded him, a student: he had actually read the works of Mr. Thackeray and Mr. Dickens. To the former he owed his notions of the upper class; to the latter his notions of the middle and lower classes. Not one of his characters has the strength that belongs to a faithful copy from life, or to a fantasy founded on fact: all his characters are founded on fiction—the fiction of Mr. Dickens and Mr. Thackeray respectively. But they have a charm of their own. Robertson had, besides a keen sense of humour, a pretty fancy. His touch was a trifle common, but it was tender. His presentment of the young ladies in Dr. Sutcliffe's academy is idyllic in its way. It is in no relation to actual fact, but it is a skilful realisation of a charming man's ideal. I do not wonder that it still enchants the public. And the enchantment would be greater if the play had been produced with the costumes proper to the period. It is disturbing to see these figments of the 'sixties tricked out in the fashion of 1909. David Garrick playing Hamlet in a periwig was all very well; for archæology was not expected in the theatre; and its absence did not hurt illusion. Nowadays, Hamlet in a top hat would be very deleterious; but no more so than is Robertson's Beau Farintosh as presented in the clothes of a dandy of to-day. This Beau, of course, was already somewhat out of date when the play was written: Robertson had faked him up from Major Pendennis. He might, however, pass muster in peg-top trousers. As it is, the anomaly is too grotesque. "His language is like Tom Moore's", says Jack Poyntz, when the Beau has been complimenting the young ladies. Such a remark as this would have a sentimental interest for us, helping us into the heart of the period, if Poyntz and the rest were properly attired. Otherwise, it merely makes us jump. And the matter is even worse when Poyntz tries to match his costume by speaking of the time when he was in Ladysmith—he, the Crimean "heavy swell"! The most ludicrous moment of all is when Lord Beaufoy, having in a long soliloquy declared Bella to be "as fresh as nature, and as artless as moss" and "very different from the young persons that one sees in Paris, and the great tame tiger-lilies that one meets in town", proceeds to cry out "Oh simplicity, sweet simplicity, how you are neglected in this twentieth century". Of course this change of date is the logical accompaniment to the change of costumes. The absurdity of it is the measure of the costumes' absurdity. I suppose Mr. Robert Arthur does not think it worth while to go to the expense and trouble of procuring appropriate costumes for three plays that are timed to run only a month or so in all, if the public will come and fill his theatre without such inducement. From his own point of view, he is wise. But the shade of poor Tom Robertson will not be appeased, nor I. Nor, I think, will the players at the Coronet. It is impossible for them, in modern clothes, to comport themselves in a manner befitting their utterances. They cannot, being outwardly tethered to their own time, retroject themselves into the Robertsonian spirit. They can only make uncomfortable efforts. These they loyally make.

I saw "The Grotesques" one day this week at the Queen's Hall. Mr. Vere Smith, like Mr. Pélissier, is a composer and writer of songs, as well as a singer of them; and he has gathered around him a small troupe of comedians, male and female, who unite in a very gay and clever little entertainment, somewhat in the manner of "The Follies". The troupe is a good one all round; but the outstanding figures are Mr. Vere Smith himself, who is a light, genial, and resourceful droll, and Miss Dorothy Doria, an actress to her finger-tips, and evident possessor of a keen intelligence and sense of humour. In the second part of the programme, which consists of a burlesque of a village concert, Miss Doria impersonated a very well-brought-up young lady singing a musical-comedy song entitled "I'm a ripping sort of gal". The singer's perfect composure and complacency in her well-meant effort to reproduce the right effect, and the completeness of her unconscious failure, were beautifully rendered by Miss Doria, with a sense not less of pathos than of fun. "The Grotesques" are likely to have a vogue. I hope they will not confine themselves to ridicule of comic and sentimental songs and their singers. Let them ridicule things in general.

THE PRINCESS.

SHE was a little German maiden, six years old, who was stopping at an English seaside hotel with her father and mother. As an addition to her pleasure, her escort was of the greatest service to her. As to her material wants, she seemed quite capable of attending to them without superintendence. It happened two or three times that she arrived at the breakfast table first of her family. Saluting by the way those of the guests who were honoured by her acquaintance, she gravely took her seat and held up a small forefinger. Instantly there was an avalanche of waiters. Even the head waiter forgot his high estate, and hurried to take her order, invariably one for porridge. Little Princess Juliana could not have been more enthusiastically waited on.

Nor was it only her compatriots the waiters who succumbed. The guests in the hotel, except, perhaps, some who had English children of their own, showed themselves quite as eager. They, one and all, crabbéd old bachelors and invalid old ladies, voted her "a dear".

How she came by her unquestioned supremacy seemed a puzzle. She was not a particularly pretty child—a nice straight little thing and that was all. Nor did she in any way lay herself out for conquest. She accepted homage when it came, but did not try to attract it. She was never shy, and, therefore, never bold.

Two reasons there seem to have been for her rule. First, as already foreshadowed, her perfect manners. The little formal curtsey with which she greeted her father and mother, the curtsey that seems so natural and pretty in German children, was of a piece with her whole demeanour. To strangers she curtsied not. They were neither der Herr Papa nor die Frau Mutter. Why should she? But if talked to she answered quite simply and unaffectedly, evidently liking to talk, but able, if unaddressed, to "keep herself to herself".

That same formal respect to parents we once had in England. Some of us are able to remember the last dying echoes of it. But somewhere about the beginning of the last century all the fools in London got up and said "It is not our duty to make our children respect us, but love us". The aforesaid collective wisdom decided that it was quite impossible to love a man whom you called "Sir". What syllogism led it to this conclusion remains a mystery. Perhaps there was no syllogism. Collective wisdom is quite as capable as an individual of rushing to a conclusion. Anyhow they reached it. Ergo, since love is more than courtesy, and the two are incompatible, away with courtesy. And they awayed with it. There must have been something wrong with their logic. To call a man "Sir" does not, in fact, prevent affection for him. One has heard of servants who loved their masters, boys who loved their tutors, and even of a few courtiers who loved their king. Formal courtesy means, perhaps, very little. But it adds to the amenities of life and it costs very little, for it soon becomes instinctive. To one bred to the manner it is no trouble to take off his hat to a funeral, to a parson on his own ground, or to Goody Bounce when he meets her on the road. He caps the Duchess of Omnium, not as duchess but as woman—for nobody caps the Duke. And Goody is a woman too, and thinks a lot of such small attentions, much more than does the Duchess. It must be owned that taking it off is rather bad for a hat. "Kneeling", said George Herbert (untruly), "ne'er spoilt silk stocking." Perpetual capping does spoil silk hats. But kind hearts are more than coronets, and politeness better than beavers.

Since England, under the guidance of collective wisdom, adopted as its watchwords the simple words "Push", "Hustle", "Get on or get out", courtesy is not to the fore. Manners, however, like morals, ebb and flow. They may return, and meanwhile we must do without them.

The second reason for our little maid's empire was the English she talked. It was quite fluent, evidently came as naturally to her as her mother tongue. But it had been taught her by those who had learned it as a foreign speech, and it was simple, real English, the prettiest book-English conceivable. As an instance: She was working a present for mother, a great secret, which she announced one afternoon she meant to finish that day. Asked next morning whether she had done so she said, "No, I did intend it; but the flowers were many and I became weary." An ordinary English child would have said she "got tired". If, indeed, she belonged to Father Vaughan's criminal classes she might have said that she "was fed up with the rotten thing". But "got tired" is bad enough. We all, in our laziness, say it—but it isn't English, and is not worthy of adoption into the language.

In "Harper's Magazine" there is an article by Professor Lounsbury, in which he falls foul of the language which romance writers make their characters speak. He says, quite truly, that one and all, Scott, Thackeray, Reade, Stevenson give to them a piebald jargon which never was talked and never will be—"Wardour Street English". The poets, too, offend, especially Spenser and Thomson. In fact, no writer ever made his characters talk as real people do. Every lover of Trollope will admit that his men and women are, almost all, deadly natural. Yet we would make a small bet that no sentence of two lines is placed in the mouth of any of them which would not seem unnatural, spoken by a real live archdeacon or Civil Service clerk. Therein lies the art. Conversation, quasi-photographically reproduced, is as uninteresting as the snapshots in the "Daily Mirror". While it is moving it sounds all right; fixed on paper it becomes impossible. The novelist's, as the painter's, art lies in so altering it as to make it seem natural.

This sort of corrected English we very seldom hear from anyone—least of all from children. Pedants, old and young, we have in plenty. They pride themselves on speaking grammatically. Very few talk in such a way that their words could be printed without offence. Our little German friend talked so, and the prettiness of the effect cannot be described. Might it not be worth while to attempt to imitate her? The elders must begin and the children would soon follow—if nobody laughed. And why should anyone laugh at an effort to prevent a noble language from being loaded out of existence with uninventive parrot slang, corrupted and bedevilled by sheer laziness? Some Greek and Latin dictionaries contain Indices Vitandorum. When the student of the future studies English as a dead language we fear this index will swell to half his book. The first most pressing need is to preserve England. But an England that talks and writes a bastard American is hardly worth preserving. One hears great outcry that the Germans are outstripping us in the race for many things. Are they, haply, doing so by being able to talk English?

DOCTORS, DEMOCRATS AND DRYDEN.

THE century that had begun with Elizabeth and the splendid despotism of the Tudors ended, placid and uninspiring, with the constitutionalism of the Restoration. Everywhere there was confirmed the triumph of the practical over the sentimental, of the useful over the beautiful, of the democratic in particular over the oligarchical, and literature had not stood apart from the tendencies of the time. Indeed, the prose written under William and Mary seems to become the new limited monarchy as Raleigh and Sir Thomas Urquhart became the days of Elizabeth. When the seventeenth century opened, when Burton and Hobbes and Bacon wrote, prose literature was the servant of an oligarchy. Doctors and dilettanti held it in vile durance, and the nation as yet had made no claim to it. Prose-writing belonged to the learned, and literary English was redolent at every point of far-sought knowledge and ancient idiom. In early times it had been adapted from the native speech to convey and hold the learning of old Rome, and still it bore upon it the marks of its double origin. It had been bruised at Hastings by heavy Norman hands and touched more lovingly by a later French when Romance came over and dwelt with Malory; Lyly's Euphuism had hung it with ornaments stolen out of Spain and Sidney had lent it to his shepherdesses from beyond the Alps; but through all these things the influence of its first master had remained supreme, and, when the great days of the Elizabethans came, the English of the prose-writers was still a learned tongue, steeped in the Latin whence all learning came. Even the simple things with which the Doctors had no part—

"The tendre Croppes and the yonge Sonne
And smale Fowles maken melodie"—

were dragged sometimes into prose and decked out there with ornaments that ill suited them. The birds were constrained to sing "diapasons", and the sun, distinguished with the name of "Titan", had to "pierce the crepuscle line matutine" when he rose. Indeed, the faults of the Latin manner were not few, though Milton was to prove it capable of splendid things; the syntactic sentences became easily too intricate, the heavy phrases cumbersome, the big words pompous and obese, and in the hands of such a man as Urquhart (of the "Logopandecteision" and other "gnathoclastic" works) the most active argument is often lost in a wilderness of wandering clauses and dazed syllables. But in the narrow brotherhood of the erudite such failings were not of great account, for the practised brain could unravel any intricacy, and the mind nourished on folios found few things too ponderous for it. Not until the writers of English prose looked to a wider audience than the doctors formed did simplicity and clarity seem even greatly to be desired. And so the mass of English prose remained both intricate and ponderous. Even the giant intellects such as Hobbes, even torrential orators like Donne, were not free from the prevailing vices. The "Anatomie of Melancholie" itself, the only book that ever drew Dr. Johnson from his bed before custom and conscience had made it untenable—though Burton could on occasion be both brief and clear—seems sometimes almost to caricature the failings of the "Latinesque". Breathless sentences labour down the pages bowed beneath a load of classic learning and goaded on at every pause by the importunities of an endless argument; long Latin words abound in native or in English dress, dicta from Cicero, jests from Erasmus; and though a wealth of mellow wisdom and a not always melancholy humour give the whole work a certain affinity with common, human things, yet there are many among the wise soliloquies and exalted jests that an education were needed to make accessible. Milton carried all this, save the humour, to its highest power. Nothing has been found to replace the gentle aloofness of the learned aristocrat, the scholar's consciousness of a scholar's worth, that unites such different men as Jeremy Taylor and Sir Thomas Browne, and there can never again appear that quality of richness and rarity which the princely profusion of Browne's learning gives to that wonderful prose of his, making it strange and beautiful like Eastern jewellery.

Long before these three masters of the old tradition brought it to its highest perfection the spirit of the new had been born. In the sudden youthfulness of Elizabethan England a new curiosity was questioning all things with the wide-eyed wonder of a child, and to the questioners of those days (save only hyperborean lands and red gold stored at the world's edge) nothing under the heavens seemed able in interest to compare with Man. So the thought of the age had turned to Man, and the anatomy of human sentiment formed a fitting subject for the epigrams of that brilliant Court. In the "Essays" of Bacon the Court epigram is made literature. In those brief, brilliant studies of humanity and human things is collected a host of pungent sayings and wise reflections happily expressed, coined or gathered in the course of a long life and grouped about various subjects almost carelessly, and a literature so composed came to the ordinary man with an absolutely new appeal. Here were things treated that were of interest to every man, and treated in a way that every man could understand; here were brilliant sayings, like the best of tavern wit, seven times refined, and observations upon men and things that confirmed, corrected or crystallised those that thinking people had been making vaguely all their lives. The language too in which these things were dressed was clear and brief and pointed, like the essence of spoken wit, and yet most manifestly it was literature. In fact a real extension of the literary franchise had been made, and it was never in history to be repealed. Overbury and Earle and a host of witty moralists followed in the new tradition, and the great name of Montaigne added a reflected dignity to the young democracy of letters. Bacon's condescension had been perhaps not even in part intended, and Overbury, who for a time had kept the Elizabethan spirit alive in the Court of James, was not more consciously a democrat, but Earle came designedly a step further from the high places of the oligarchy, and sometimes the "Microcosmographie" comes quite down to the level of good popular wit. What could be better in its way and what less aristocratic than this of "A Child": "The older he grows he is a stair lower from God; and like his first father much worse in his breeches"? And there is a startling modernity in the account of the "Mere Young Gentleman of the University" who "of all things endures not to be mistaken for a scholar". On a higher plane Bunyan, the tinker's son and best of English narrators, with Izaak Walton and Cowley among the artists, carried on the work that the first essayist had begun, and last of all to complete the changes of the century came the prefaces and prologues of John Dryden.

The favour of rich patrons as a means of sustenance could now be supplanted by a lucrative popularity, which meant the favour of booksellers and actor-managers, and to both these sources of income, to the dukes and to the nation, Dryden applied himself assiduously. The nation he found become newly serious. That it should enter at all into the question was indeed new enough, but just when Dryden presented himself before it a change in its attitude had appeared. The great war had shown men at close view the fierce reality of the ultimate things—of love and hate and death—and there had resulted a certain impatience of all that was not deep and genuine, of all affectations and assumed superiorities. The demand was everywhere for sound sense in literature rather than for passion, wit or learning, and that demand Dryden did his best to satisfy. He is the first writer of serious English prose who bent deliberately to the popular level, and the result is a style that is always simple and sometimes elaborately colloquial. Clause is added to clause without any too scrupulous regard for grammar, and though the loss of power is obvious and immense yet there is great gain in agility and suppleness. Sometimes indeed there is a glimpse of real strength, a phrase direct and forceful almost to nobility. Of Ben Jonson's borrowings he finely says: "He has done his robberies so openly that one may see he fears not to be taxed by any law. He invades authors like a monarch, and what would be theft in others is only victory in him." And his judgment of Collier is very happy: "He is too much given to horseplay in his raillery, and comes to battle like a dictator from the plough." But generally Dryden's prose level is an even one; he is lucid and pleasing, but not often great.

"'Tis with a poet as with a man who designs to build, and is very exact, as he supposes, in casting up the cost beforehand; but, generally speaking, is mistaken in his account, and reckons short of the expense he first intended: he alters his mind as the work proceeds, and will have this or that convenience more of which he had not thought when he began. So has it happened to me. I have built a house where I intended but a lodge; yet with better success than a certain nobleman, who, beginning with a dog-kennel, never lived to finish the palace he had contrived."

Here is a prose by worlds removed from Bacon. Very nearly it is Montaigne, but with something more of balance and a simplicity more carefully prepared. For Dryden's ease is the ease of art. He is natural because he labours to be so, and his rhythms are so well ordered that they can only be the result of patient anvil work. This he was always willing to give, for though he yields to the need of saying plain things to plain men, he takes some pride in the grace with which he says them, and, except when prostrate before a duke, he is very careful of his self-respect. But he dared not seem to make beauty itself an end, for the practical sense of the "bourgeois" class, his master, would not permit. The solid and worthy middle classes had successfully claimed the deciding word in literature, and indeed it was a time when solidity and worthiness were prevailing virtues. The thin shadow of a splendid monarchy, a people's spirit flameless and spent, and a slumbrous peace born of the knowledge of war, these things did not make the blood move fast in the nation's veins, and if in these years the "bourgeois" stability was first achieved it was at the cost of all the Elizabethan fire and the brilliancy of the Cavaliers. Splendour and spirit were lost beyond recovery; and yet there was still possible greatness of another kind, refinement, delicacy, grace, an inspiration more ordered than the Elizabethan, a gentler wit and a milder wisdom, and something of all this Dryden himself had added with his solid sanity to our tongue. But the greater part lay waiting across the border of the century. In 1700 Dryden died, and in the next year Joseph Addison published his first work in prose.

THE GARDENS OF ALCINOUS.

If any critical observer of changing modes should be inclined to doubt the permanence of the present taste for gardening, he would find some colour for his unbelief in a certain one-sidedness of the vogue. The prominence of the lady-gardener and the care lavished upon the flower garden—related as cause and effect though they may be—tend to a disproportionate mixture of the utile and the dulce which (though it may carry every vote in the present constitution of things) is not altogether of good omen for the prospects of the art as a whole. The large and increasing garden literature with a feminine authorship shows, by its excellent photographs or ravishingly pretty colour-prints, how successfully woman can deal with the soil in its lighter and more ornamental uses. If there is sometimes an almost provocative air about a paragraph or a photograph—a sense of "There! what do you think of that for a Lilium giganteum, or a Munstead polyanthus?" it would be peculiarly graceless not to approve the admirable specimens of the growers' skill all the more for the occasional touch of Nature in their presentation. Yet when all is said and done, admitted the charm of the rhododendron wood, and the border that changes from scarlet through yellows and mauves to delphinium blue like a shaded ribbon, and Lady So-and-so's pergola photographed in four positions, the feeling will sometimes come that the products of all this tasteful enthusiasm and accomplishment lack a certain actuality and force, a sort of consistency which may after all be the prerogative of the masculine mind exercised to more direct purpose than in wheeling heavy barrows and digging stiff clay under command. One divines possible effects of divorcing the poetry of the parterre from the solid science of the kitchen garden, of the absence of the presiding genius of an older day, the elderly man, taciturn, laborious, weather-beaten, with "a life experience in all branches, indoor and out", as the consecrated phrase has it, whose Cattleyas were but the apex of a skill which, taking unsurpassable peaches and melons on the way, was rooted in the deep foundations of celery and Brussels sprouts. The modern tendency to glorify the flower garden at the expense of the kitchen quarters, to devote oneself to roses and rockeries, and to leave the peas and cabbages to a hireling, or worse, to the greengrocer, should be resisted by all who care for the true character of English horticulture. Market vegetables, on the supply of which the townsman is apt of all things to plume himself, are only endurable by people who have no palate for the nicer degrees of freshness and staleness, or who, for want of opportunity, have never learned the meaning of better things. Anyone of an inquiring turn of mind who has observed fruit pickers at work in the fields, or has seen a train-load of Penzance broccoli on its way to the north wilting in a siding under a broiling sun, or a stack of watercress baskets receive a cloud of dust and dirt on a windy platform, will begin to have his doubts about the efficiency of Covent Garden. No one who has known what asparagus is like when it comes to table within an hour of being cut, or spring cabbages that reach the cook's hands with the dew still on their leaves, will accept shop wares save as one of those helpless makeshifts with which man has to piece out the splendours of his destiny. More and more in the future, it is to be hoped, the man of palate will grasp the necessity of having a kitchen garden of his own. At present too many are content to get their greenstuff in a way which is analogous to sending out to the nearest public-house for one's wine.

There are hopeful signs of progress in the right way. Appreciation of the value of ever so small a patch of ground as a source of wholesome provender —of actual "wealth" in the Ruskin sense—is much more general than it was twenty years ago. We seldom hear now the ignorant nonsense about the amateur's lettuces which cost a guinea apiece. There is constant evidence of the easiness of the apprenticeship required for the pursuit, and of its enduring attraction, in the frequent conversions of even elderly and hitherto quite urban-minded persons to the production of their own green peas and early potatoes. The output of books on vegetable growing, though not comparable with the more ornamental literature of the flower garden, is sufficient to show the existence of a multitude of inquiring amateurs of every degree, from the beginner who is not quite sure of his mustard and cress to the ambitious soul who dreams of a tomato house and mushroom beds in the potting shed. For every sort of novice there are instructors ready to teach the art which no man ever learned from print unless he had the root of the matter within himself; instructors who have a sound knowledge of their subjects, but are by no means always gifted with the power of expounding it lucidly to the lay mind. Here is one of the most recent guide-books to the kitchen garden,* where the "experts" who—as the title-page rather sweepingly informs us—are responsible for the text give their information in a rather general and indefinite way, stopping short of really intimate and circumstantial direction in details which, though second nature to the skilled hand, are often the crux of the tiro and the cause of most depressing failures. By far the best part of the book is the section on vegetable cookery, whose counsels, if cooks could be prevailed on to carry them out, would marvellously improve our national way of feeding. Such chapters are an excellent appendix to a book on the olitory art; the connexion between the cook's domain and the gardener's ought to be close and friendly. In France, perhaps, there is a better understanding of the natural harmony between the two provinces: with us the relation between them is apt to be a little difficult, if not strained. There is often a conviction on one side that the gardener out of pure perversity keeps back the peas till they are only fit for soup, and on the other an injured sense of rapacious demands for impossibly early asparagus or limitless salading in a drought. A little education in the rudiments of each other's science would work wonders in improving the results of the complementary and inseparable crafts.

But a kitchen garden—one, at least, of the traditional English type—has other uses besides that of growing things for the pot. The vegetable ground, if tended as it ought to be, is a very pleasant place to walk in. If it has not the gay charm of the flower borders, it affords a sober yet cheerful solace for a meditative stroll when work is over. The trimness and order, the wealth of present store, and the signs of careful provision for the future, the sense of man's control of Nature—for once wholly profitable—in the successions and relays of harvest, please the mind while the senses are refreshed by the monotony of green, the deep healthy colour which tells of thriving roots and generous sap, and by the fine mixed aroma of all the plots and lines, smells of bean flower, of strawberries beginning to turn colour, of the herb beds, the lavender bushes, the onion rows. The best type of English vegetable garden is one in a mean somewhere between the great walled ranges of a country seat or show place and the cottage patch—say a compact piece between one and two acres, including the small-fruit quarters and the frame-ground. A door in the middle of an old wall at the end of the flower garden should open into a square like Alcinous' home-piece—

"Beds of all various herbs for ever green
In beauteous order"—

a still-busy world, silently springing and maturing at once, where supreme method controls the rampant growth among the straight-drawn drills of seedlings, the broad hedges of peas, the bean trellises, the balanced espaliers. Yet with all the good order there is room here and there for stray graces of a less rigid fashion; an ancient fig tree rambles unchecked, a noble ne'er-do-well, with gnarled bole and smooth lusty rods, against the lichened wall; a hollyhock or a patch of lily-of-the-valley trespasses in a corner; the gourds riot over their hillocks with almost tropical vigour. Everywhere the quantities are above the reckoning of actual needs; there are large margins, a wide-minded liberality going together with the neatest order; signs of age and of other men's plannings harmonise the whole. Here, howsoever the world outside may conspire, is peace, and leisure to think a little, and room for traces of beauty. If ever we come to getting all our vegetables from market fields and railway trucks, from acres where every foot of space carries its calculated allowance of forced cropping, we shall have lost, in exchange for the drooping asparagus, the just-fermenting strawberry and the well-handled "shelled peas", the truth that really fresh garden stuff is connected, curiously but irrevocably, with the possession of leisure and ease of mind.

* "The English Vegetable Garden." Written by Experts. London: The Offices of "Country Life". 8s. 6d. net.

THE GREAT BORDEAUX WINES.

(In three articles.)

I.—CHÂTEAU HAUTBRION.

MUCH has been written and said in all languages of the four great Bordeaux wines, Château Hautbrion, Château Margaux, Château Latour, and Château Lafite; but although its name is by no means so well known in England as those of its great rivals in the Médoc, the greatest of all these wines is Château Hautbrion. The excellence of its wines has been undisputed since the fifteenth century, when the vintage is mentioned for the first time. Of late years its price has ruled higher than that of any other claret, and it has been able to hold its own notwithstanding the ravages of phylloxera and the adulteration which at one time was damaging claret in the British market. The proprietors of the château knew well they had a good thing, and they preferred not to sell at all rather than lower its price.

In some ways Château Hautbrion holds an exceptional position. Few Englishmen outside the trade know that it is the most expensive of clarets and it is not, as all the other high-priced clarets, a product of the Médoc. Bordeaux is but twenty hours from Charing Cross, and Hautbrion is but three miles from Bordeaux. Indeed, the electric tramway from Bordeaux to Péssac passes by the gates of the château, which is itself on the borders of the Graves district, far better known for its white than for its red wines. The grounds lie on the borders of the three Communes of Péssac, Talence, and Mérignac.

The domain is an old one, for a deed of 1360 speaks of the Manor of Hautbrion. In 1509 the estate belonged to Jean de Ségur. In the following century it was the property of Jean Duhalde, who sold it to the President de Pontac. By 1700 it had fallen into the hands of the Fumels, who owned many other vineyards. The Latresnes, Valences, and Talleyrands then succeeded in their turn to the estate. Later on M. Michel bought the vineyard, but sold it in his turn to M. Beyermann in 1824. In fact the property passed through a succession of families in no way connected with one another, until it eventually reached the hands of M. Eugène Larrieu, whose son Monsieur Amédée Larrieu was for so many years Député and Préfet of the Gironde. In July 1896 it became the property of his father's heirs and cousins Madame P. de Laistre and M. Norbert Milleret, who zealously follow the traditions of their illustrious relative and have entrusted the management of the vineyard to M. Albert Sanchon, the present "Maître de Chaix".

The château stands in the midst of a fine well-wooded park in a part of the Gironde which is decidedly prettier than the Médoc. Péssac is, it is true, fast becoming a mere suburb of Bordeaux, and its restaurants attract crowds of customers every Sunday. The road leads us into the Landes, that strange forest of pines broken by a few cultivated fields whose monotony is relieved by red-roofed wooden houses and the occasional shepherd who watches his flocks from the height of his stilts.

The château has been again and again transformed in the course of centuries; but its high pointed roofs and two wings jutting out on either side retain many characteristics of style prevalent in the sixteenth century when it was rebuilt, though there are bits here and there which remain from an earlier date.

The plantations are all made in the same way. The earth is dug up to a depth of from twenty-two to twenty-four inches, the soil which was on the surface being placed at the bottom, and vice versa. The whole is then levelled with the greatest care, but a sufficient incline is left to allow all the rain to run off. The stocks are then planted and manured with the best mould, whilst earth is heaped round the root of each tree. A month before the vintage, companies of from eighty to a hundred women are occupied in removing any defective grapes. The vintage itself takes place between 20 and 25 September. The vendangeurs, who come from all parts of the Gironde and indeed of the South of France, are divided into gangs, each one of which is under the control of a "commandant de manœuvre", whose duty it is to hasten the task of the cutters, to see that they leave no bunches on the stocks, that they take only ripe and sound fruit, pick up the fallen fruits, and collect nothing else but fruit into their baskets. Care must then be taken that all unsound fruit is rejected, and with that object the grapes are carefully examined before pressing.

What gives Château Hautbrion and the three great "crus" of the Médoc that wonderful bouquet and aroma which distinguish them from all other kinds of claret? In the first place they do not allow the grapes to be crushed by that rough-and-ready machinery which, if it possesses the merit of carrying out the work rapidly, does not distinguish green from ripe grapes, and crushes the stones, whose empyreumatical oil gives a harsh taste to the wine. In all these cases the more flexible human foot is used, for whilst the weight of the body does the work efficiently, it neither crushes the green grapes nor the stones. Then again, at all these great "crus" the yeast is cultivated. At the latter end of June a grey down forms itself upon the grape during vegetation. The best grapes are collected and allowed to ferment in a small vat, whose contents are poured into a larger one which contains half a tun. Generation is so rapid that two cells of yeast mixed with the must of the grape produce eight cells in two hours. As each one of these new cells is equally active, some sixteen million cells are generated in the course of twenty-four hours. The yeast also accelerates fermentation, which, however, at Hautbrion lasts from five to six days. The wine thus made is not affected by mildew or exposure to bad weather, is far healthier, its quality is more equable, whilst its body and bouquet are substantially improved. It is a great pity that this process, which more than repays the trouble, is not adopted more generally. Even where the grapes were inferior this practice would certainly improve the quality of the wine.

The wine is drawn off when there is no more sugar in the must. The vats are then mixed and the barrels filled and immediately placed upon their stands. The first racking takes place in December or January, and is followed by further rackings at each equinox, or even sooner should this be found essential.

At least ten years must pass before one can say certainly what will be the quality of a vintage. They are all different, for a wine which may be good in one "cru" may be inferior in another. Temperature is a most important factor, and has a great deal to do with the quality. Thus where the vintage weather has been warm with little or no rain the wine is sure to be better than where it has rained incessantly. In the latter case the wines will be flat and not have much body.

CONSOLATION.

(Catullus xcvi.)

FRIEND, if the mute and shrouded dead
  Are touched at all by tears,
By love long fled and friendship sped
  And the unreturning years:

O then, to her that early died,
  Know surely, bridegroom, to thy bride
Thy love is sweet and sweeteneth
  The very bitterness of death.

H. W. Garrod.

CORRESPONDENCE.

MODERN LITERARY CRITICISM.

To the Editor of the Saturday Review.

Sir,—Is it quite true that modern literary criticism, the modern literary taste of the buying public and the absorption of publishers in money-getting are in such a parlous state as some of your correspondents suggest?

We must not kick against the pricks: we must consider the merits or demerits of any man or any class in relation to the existing state of society. And, as things are, no publisher could remain a publisher unless he carried on his business at a profit; he must offer wares to the public which will sell. But the true question as to publishers is this, Have works of genius or even of exceptional merit as good a chance of being published now as in past days? I submit the chance is as good now as it ever was, and I know personally that publishers may now, at their own risk, introduce literature to the public because, though they think it will not pay, they think the few should have a chance of reading it.

Again, is it true that the taste of readers is illiterate, crude, and depraved? Bear in mind that now there are perhaps one thousand readers for every single one in past days. I think there are many more readers of sound literature in the present day than formerly, while, though many of the mass want—and get—illiterate excitement and immoral titillation, there are many others who want—and get—what is the best. Ask any assistant at any bookstall what sells. He will tell you the sixpenny editions of classic writers in literature—even in art and science—sell by hundreds of thousands. If it be admitted that the middle and upper middle classes read trash, there are still innumerable individuals of the educated working classes who choose the better part.

Society is thick with writers, the profession is overcrowded, and most write in competition for money or social position. They must take their chance of success or failure with tradesmen and politicians. And so Brown, who has failed, must not be hurt or surprised if his inferiors Jones and Robinson, who have succeeded, have beaten him by better use of the tricks of the trade. The man, however, who writes from sheer love of art or under the stress of genius stands on a different footing. He—a human being—may be moved by desire of public appreciation, but the less he is so moved the more freely and truly will he manifest his power in output of work. What is the reward of such a man? Delight in his labour; consciousness of justifying himself.

We often forget that barely one of us ever recognises genius when first manifested; as a body we confine appreciation to genius which is successful. Many of genius—probably the most—fall by the way, unknown. A Meredith in romance, a Turner in painting, a Carlyle in philosophy, or a Keats or even a Tennyson in poetry must have the pluck, in love of his art, to work through a slough of despond in public contempt or boycott before he can hope for full recognition of his genius. He alone is assured of the palm of victory in his own days who is just a leetle superior to us; the giants are fearsome to us till they have grown smaller in the distance of time.

And literary criticism?

Now literary critics are men, not demigods. Wherein do they fail? I say that if they fail it is in giving too much praise, not too little. I think it is ridiculous to suggest that men of genius should be viewed as the infants of critics, to be cradled and fed with the sop of enervating adulation. The man of genius must live on his own work and take the chance of sop from public recognition. Even with such men the law of the survival of the fittest applies; their output is purified by conflict with public contempt or boycott; coddle them with appreciation from the first and they become mere playthings of society.

As sane men and women let us try to get rid of humbug. I have failed; you, the reader, have failed to get public recognition. It is our own fault or misfortune, not that of the public taste, critics, or publishers. But still the delight of production remains our own and unaffected; that supreme success we have not failed to attain. And men of genius? They have their reward—a reward which has nothing to do with publishers or the reading public—the reward of personal satisfaction in the delight of work and self-manifestation. Only one critic do they bow to—the one immaculate critic, Time.

Your obedient servant,

F. C. Constable.

HOW TO KEEP OUR PICTURES.

To the Editor of the Saturday Review.

19 June 1909.

Sir,—A short time ago (I am purposely a little vague) an official connected with one of our public galleries informed me that his gallery had just arranged to hang a certain number of old masters belonging to a noble owner. He added that the mere fact of thus bringing them to the public notice would add something like £10,000 to their value. Surely it should not be beyond the wit of man to devise an equitable scheme whereby a goodly share of this unearned increment should revert to the gallery should the pictures in question be subsequently sold. It might indeed be possible further to arrange that in event of such a sale being contemplated the gallery should have the right of pre-emption. Had some such scheme been in existence before the notorious Holbein came on the market, the public would not have had to pay so dearly through the nose for it, but the National Gallery authorities would have been able, in return for the cachet of authenticity and distinction that exhibition in the gallery had conferred, to buy the picture at a cost of, say, 25 per cent. below what the first purchaser in the field had offered.

Yours faithfully,

Cloudesley Brereton.

A TAX ON PARIS GOWNS.

To the Editor of the Saturday Review.

Perros-Guirec, C. du N., France.

Sir,—The taxation of imported luxuries is certainly excellent in principle. I should suggest to the Chancellor of the Exchequer and to the Prime Minister a very heavy duty on dresses imported from Paris. The tax would not be unpopular, as there are so many people who value dresses more the more they pay for them (I speak of ladies, and not of their husbands or fathers). The dresses might all be sent to Downing Street to be estimated.

The gentler sex would then be enabled to contribute more than they do to the cost of those engines of murder which are daily becoming more indispensable for civilised nations.

Your obedient servant,

W. B. Paton.

A SNAKE-COLLECTOR'S ESCAPE.

To the Editor of the Saturday Review.

Sir,—Mr. Edward H. Cooper's article on South America, and his reference to its poisonous snakes, reminds me of an interesting adventure of a friend of mine in Northern Brazil.

My friend was making a collection of the poisonous snakes of the neighbourhood; and, as everyone round us was aware of the fact, many gifts of the kind were offered to him. One evening he was writing at a table in our hut when a local person brought him a small living specimen of one of the most deadly poisonous snakes of the neighbourhood. My friend, who was very busy, asked him to put it in a glass jar on the table, which was accordingly done.

Unfortunately the hot night and other soporific influences proved too much for my friend's waking powers. He went to sleep, with his head on the table, and slept peacefully till awakened by a fearful crash. He had knocked the table over, with the lamp on it; the lamp had naturally been put out; and, as his senses slowly returned, the awakened sleeper remembered that the glass jar also had fallen on to the floor, and the snake must now be loose.

Obviously the best thing to do was to jump on the bed and shout for help and light. But the hut was empty, and no help came. One could not spend the night standing on a bed roaring for help, so, as there was only a space of about eight feet between him and the door, the snake-collector jumped down from the bed, resolved to make a rush for it. He had taken his boots off at an early part of the evening; and, as he jumped, he felt a sharp vicious nip in the heel of his right foot.

My friend was a person with plenty of cool presence of mind. A servant entered the hut at the moment; he summoned him, told him curtly that he had not five minutes to live, and proceeded to dictate a will and various directions to his travelling companion and one or two other persons. But death tarried an unaccountably long time, and presently the reason of this became apparent. The snake was curled up in a far corner of the room, swaying and hissing angrily; and my friend had jumped off the bed on to a piece of the broken glass with which the floor of his room was liberally strewn.

I am, Sir, etc.,

Traveller.

GREEN'S "SHORT HISTORY".

To the Editor of the Saturday Review.

Buckhurst Hill, 30 June 1909.

Sir,—The Rev. Douglas Macleane's letter, following up your note on the subject of the previous week, induces wonder how Green's "Short History" ever secured such a hold not only on the public but on those responsible for the education of our boys and girls. Mr. Macleane makes a sufficiently serious indictment from the point of view of Churchmen. I am not at all sure that Green's History would stand the test of critical examination any better on the Imperial side. Recently in looking up all that I could find as to the life of General James Wolfe, I turned over the pages of ordinary histories, Green's among them, on the chance that some point of importance might have escaped me. Green devotes one page to the conquest of Quebec, and I freely confess that if you read that page in ignorance of the facts you will feel that in the course of fifty lines or so he presents you with a picture which it seems could hardly be made more clear in fifty pages.

But let us examine it carefully. He says "Wolfe fought at Fontenoy". Wolfe was never at Fontenoy. He says "For six weeks Wolfe saw his men wasting away in inactivity, while he himself lay prostrate with sickness and despair". That implies that Wolfe was prostrate during six weeks, whereas he was not prostrate for six days, and ignores the unsuccessful effort Wolfe made to get at Montcalm less than five weeks after he reached the Quebec basin and some six weeks before the battle was fought on the Heights of Abraham. Of course, Green tells the story of Wolfe's reciting Gray's "Elegy" as he floated down the S. Lawrence, without any suggestion that it was highly improbable he ever did anything so insane at such a time. Green says "Wolfe was the first to leap on shore and to scale the narrow path where no two men could go abreast". Wolfe was not the first to scale the path, for the reason that the path was blocked by abattis and the heights had been secured before Wolfe pulled himself up the cliff. Wolfe was not thirty-three, as Green says, when Pitt selected him for the Quebec command, but some weeks short of thirty-two, and his army was not drawn up on the battle-ground "at daybreak on the 12th of September", but the 13th.

These may be small points, but they at least serve to show that if facts are the raw material of history, Green's work is not history.

Yours very truly,

Edward Salmon.

REVIEWS.

A FLAMBOYANT NEW-YORKER.

"Egoists." A Book of Supermen. By James Huneker. London: Laurie. 1909. 6s. net.

MR. JAMES HUNEKER is a literary ostrich for discrimination and a ravening wolf for appetite. Ostriches and wolves do not publish lists of the victims and objects they have swallowed; Mr. Huneker does, and amazing reading they are. This, his latest volume —called "Egoists" on the title-page and "*The* Egoists" on Mr. Werner Laurie's pretty cover—contains many formidable strings of names, and the owner of each would stare to find himself in such strange company. Blake and Walter Pater are thrown together as "mystics", Stendhal, Flaubert and Huysmans as mere "egoists"; Ibsen stands in solitary grandeur; and Max Stirner is described as the very fount of all the great, good and new in the philosophy and art of the nineteenth century, though Mr. Huneker declares that few people have heard of him. Such a jumble of authors, books and notions has rarely been hurled at a reviewer's head. We cannot say, we can only guess, what Mr. Huneker would be at. Like an ostrich in catholicity of taste, Mr. Huneker's power of digestion is hardly that of an ostrich. He gorges himself with good and bad literature, but assimilates nothing, reduces nothing to order. In one respect he certainly resembles the broad-minded bird of the desert that hides its head in the sand and reposes in blissful unconsciousness of what is going on around it. Mr. Huneker shoved his head into the dreary sands of Romanticism long ago and there he remains, oblivious of the great world-changes that have taken place. The heroes of his boyhood are his heroes still. This fidelity is touching, but does not always make for good literary criticism.

Though he may occasionally lift up his head to deal with living authors, he cannot rub the sands of Romanticism out of his eyes; he views everything through Romantic spectacles in the perpetual glow of a Romantic sunset. His own language is ultra-Romantic—flamboyant only weakly describes it. Extremely fond of fine words for their own sake, as deeply stirred by them as the old woman was by "Mesopotamia", he incessantly talks of "jewelled prose" and seems to have ransacked the dictionary in search of jewels for his own prose. Also, the choicest diction of Wall Street—for Mr. Huneker is a New Yorker—delights his soul. The talent for talking a very great deal and saying singularly little, and for warping words away from their true or best sense, is peculiarly American; and Mr. Huneker stands in the first rank. Only grim and resolute analysis of this collection of essays reveals the purpose—or rather, purposes—with which it is written. After making an effort we think the fact is that all the prolixity and wealth of confusion are due to an attempt, so to speak, to assume several different attitudes in one and the same moment.

First of all, a title had to be found: no good American can hope ever to go to Paris if he calls his essays simply essays. Mr. Huneker sought a common denominator for his varied demigods; and when we turn to his last chapter we see where he unearthed it. Max Stirner was born in Bayreuth in 1806 and died fifty years later, a broken man, in Berlin. He made the astonishing discovery that in each of us the Ego is the all-important factor, because we—whoever "we" may be—can only know of the existence of the universe through the Ego. This, it will be conceded, was a charming metaphysical novelty to bring forth to the light of the nineteenth century; and many a philosopher would have retired on it, as having achieved what he came into the world to do. Not so Stirner. The times were fast growing ripe for Board-schools, and this thinker, with an inexorable logic prescient of the coming dispensation of sham-learning, proceeded thus: Since all I know and am sure of is in my Ego, my Ego *is* the All. I need not take account of anything but my Ego, am answerable only to my Ego for my deeds; everything is illusion save my Ego; other people's Egos are nothing to me, lions and tigers are nothing to me. Satisfied with this irrefragable reasoning, Stirner wrote the book which (according to Mr. Huneker) has exerted such influence, though no one read it till the other day; then he went out to try conclusions with other people, other Egos—which of course were not real. However, the other Egos illogically insisted on acting as though they were real. Twice they put Stirner in gaol, Ego and all, and they left him to die miserably; and only at the last, when his Ego seemed well out of the way, some friends of former days came to save the Ego's empty tenement from a parish burial.

Here, then, Mr. Huneker found his common denominator—Egoism; and it may be granted that a reliance on one's Ego, personality, individuality, rather than on authority, marks the literature and art of the nineteenth century. But it must also be said that only the small, barren, undistinguished Egos, personalities, show jealousy for their independence; the great men carelessly let their Egos draw nourishment "from art, from nature and the schools"—wherever there is food to enrich and strengthen them we find them eagerly absorbing it, dreadless of being absorbed. It was not the mighty Wagner or Beethoven who fretfully consoled himself, "God has my individuality in His keeping": it was the little Bülow: Wagner and Beethoven never gave the matter a thought. However, Mr. Huneker traces Egoism through all his authors, from Flaubert, bent only on perfect art, to noisy, prattling Maurice Barrès, bent only on advertising his soul. Next to Stirner Mr. Huneker admires Nietzsche, whom he nevertheless calls "the expiring voice of the old-fashioned romanticism in philosophy". And we too bow before Nietzsche with his bad science, his lying historical facts, his imbecile conceit; and we say, Hail Prophet of the one-tenth educated, of the Higher-grade schools and the Polytechnics! Nietzsche, by the way, claimed to be an intellectual Aristocrat: the daughters of retired buttermen sometimes call themselves aristocrats. One token of an aristocrat is his silence about his aristocracy: Nietzsche was a parvenu, without the money, the "coinage of the brain", to pay his way into the society of the elect.

Egoism provides Mr. Huneker with attitude number one; number two is Romanticism. The Romantics are the paladins of Mr. Huneker's boyhood, with their drug-taking, carefully disordered hair, blue-black beards, melancholy yet fiery eyes, secret gnawing sorrows, sallow complexions and defiance of the Almighty, Whom nevertheless they fear. "Evil be thou my good", they cried, with heroic voice and gesture; and then slid swiftly into a church to pray (see the paper on Baudelaire). They all wrote "jewelled prose", not to mention endless guide-book accounts of pictures, statuary, cathedrals, and scenery; and one would be astonished to find a critic who has read Georg Brandes (and dedicates his book to him) gushing over such tiresome stuff were not that critic Mr. Huneker. Tender memories of boyhood's hours are all-potent with him, and he apotheosises the small and less small Romantics alike—if we may so classify a group that had no great ones. The surging sea of indiscriminate praise makes one yawn. Understand some of the Romantics better—this we are willing to do: worship the best of them, no; and when we are asked to adore their latter-day descendants, chiefly young Paris journalists "on the make", we suspect that Mr. Huneker is pulling the reader's leg.

Egoism in a man's literature or journalism sets it high in Mr. Huneker's view; so does Romanticism; but more than by his love of egoism, more than by his boyish delight in Romanticism, Mr. Huneker is induced to take an attitude to literature which is frightfully complicated—indeed grotesque—by the modern journalist's passion to be the first to "discover" or rediscover a genius. Under the sway of this master-passion—praiseworthy of course in a commercial journalist: not so praiseworthy in a would-be serious man of letters—Mr. Huneker's sense of proportion finally disappears. Lest some other adventurer should be there before him, he dashes on Barrès, Huysmans, and Anatole France, and drags them into his book as his prey. In his haste he honours them all alike; they would all seem to write nothing but that eternal, and very wearisome, "jewelled prose". In fact Mr. Huneker's familiar set of epithets is becoming as fatiguing as the prose and verse he descants on. Will he not give us something serious? Can he not, instead of dashing through important provinces of French, English, German, and Scandinavian literature, reeling off scores of names of big and little men, trying to sum up whole schools in an epigram—can he not, instead of thus bewildering us, devote a little patient study to one or two subjects which we believe he really knows, and give us a few real estimates, from a modern point of view, of men worth estimating? This book is a jungle, but not a jungle with a tropical profusion of green growths. Rather the profusion is that of a marine-store where rarities may be seen heaped with things that men have apparently forever done with and—in the appropriate American phrase—"have no use for". Mr. Huneker, as has been said, sees the heap transfigured in the glow of a Romantic sunset, but the magic tints are visible to him alone.

LESSONS FROM ADVERSITY.

"The Russian Army and the Japanese War." By General Kouropatkin. London: Murray. 1909. 2 vols. 28s. net.

"The Russo-Japanese War: a Sketch." First Period —The Concentration. By Captain F. R. Sedgwick. London: Swan Sonnenschein. 1909. 5s. net.

MANY, perhaps, will seize upon this book with a view of enjoying the personal recriminations and the tittle-tattle about strained relations between Russian commanders such as the gossips delight in. They will find something of the kind, revelations of methods of business and conduct of affairs such as we may be said to be unaccustomed to in this country, even when recognition of our hideous blunders in connexion with the war in South Africa is duly made. But many more will be attracted less by the food for gossip and scandal than the information as to Russian ideas of political strategy which the pages supply. The veil that is raised by Kouropatkin the statesman will in other words reveal more of interest that what is found behind that which shrouded Kouropatkin the General. With the General during the course of the war we more than once expressed our sincere sympathy. We shall have something more to say on that side of his activity presently, but meanwhile we wish to draw attention to the system of administration of the Russian Government, of which we are given a glimpse, and to those preparations for hostilities which that portion of statesmanship known as peace strategy deals with.

Not everyone on whose lips the name of Kouropatkin was often a few years ago realised that immediately before he commanded in Manchuria he had been the Russian War Minister for some six years. Thus it was he to whom it would have fallen, had he been uninterfered with, to organise and train the forces of the Tsar for the wars which were before them, and that any failure under these headings may therefore with some show of justice be laid at his door.

Kouropatkin's views on Russian policy are of the highest interest, and he is clearly justified in the endeavour to vindicate them now. They will be read with more attention than the pages which deal with the tactical errors that may be culled from the narrative of fighting subsequently supplied. War, we learn—not for the first time—must in these days be carried on by a whole nation. When a Russian general thinks it necessary to reiterate the lesson of 1870 it is time for us surely to wake up to its significance? The size and cost of an efficient modern army have light thrown upon them too, and we are given a most valuable sketch of Russian history and development. The discussion of the frontiers of Russia will also be of assistance to those who study the strategical geography of the Continent, and the problems that have to be faced by the general staffs of the great European Powers. The ex-Minister of War goes on to give us his views on German policy, some most instructive remarks on the Austrian situation and questions connected with it, and proceeds in due course to discuss Persia, India, and the Far East. To read what is said as to the real needs of Russia will be illuminating to many, and they will be surprised at the moderation and good sense displayed by a Russian chiefly known in his fighting capacity. Most interesting of all is the account of Russian designs on India. Here we find an officer formerly Chief of the Staff to Skobeleff, who might reasonably be supposed to be a "thruster" of pronounced type, roaring as gently as any sucking dove, and explaining to his countrymen the doctrine of give and take and the blessings of a policy of peace and goodwill to us. In short, these pages proclaim Kouropatkin as a broad-minded and far-seeing statesman, who holds most sagacious opinions as to the future prosperity of his country, and who did his best to prevent her from rushing into war with Japan. It was the Finance Minister, against whose powers the writer of these pages again and again protests, who stood between efficiency and the military advisers of the Tsar. If war were to come, Kouropatkin saw that certain steps must be taken and certain preparations made. Russia must be ready to endure a prolonged strain, and must sharpen her sword before she threw it into the scales. The Russian War Minister had, however, to fight the Finance Minister before he fought the Japanese, as many a British general has had to struggle with the Treasury before he meets his opponents. Then the real causes of the war are revealed, the party currents and intrigues, the selfish interests, greed and ambition that wrecked Russia in the face of unheeded warnings. Thus far Kouropatkin's book cannot be termed an apologia; it is more a page or two of the secret history of our times given broadcast to the world. In the interests of his country, says our author—we need not analyse motives—it should benefit other countries if his own decline to listen to it.

But subsequently the story sags down in places to a recrimination of his colleagues in the field and to criticisms of the personal conduct of his officers and men, which are no doubt justified, but are none the less regrettable. The causes of the Russian defeat are writ so large already that it is unnecessary for a Russian general to dwell upon them in public. Kouropatkin had done so much in an all but impossible task, displayed so much magnanimity of soul in serving on in a subordinate position where he had been supreme, that everyone with knowledge of military history has recognised some of the highest qualities of a leader in him. It would have been more worthy of the man who was almost the last corps commander to leave Manchuria if he had kept silence as to the deficiencies of those he led. He and certain heroes nearer home might with advantage have imitated Wellington, who took care to avoid washing dirty linen in public. Moreover, what he has to say in this respect is already discounted. Russia rushed into war inadequately prepared against the advice of her experts owing to the malign influence of a certain set of politicians of whom Alexieff was the head. Kouropatkin was in supreme command for only four and a half months, and even when he had no official superior in Manchuria was controlled by wires from S. Petersburg. How much the strategy of the war was his or that of the wire-pullers we do not yet know, and perhaps shall never do so; but it is at least certain that a general with so short a lease of power, only entered upon after the great strategical plans had been set on foot, cannot be severely blamed if things went wrong. And when one examines the tactical deficiencies of the Russian one meets a state of things which nothing short of the highest military genius working absolutely uncontrolled could have balanced. The Russian officers were in many cases ignorant, self-indulgent, and without a sense of duty to those they commanded or to their country. That was the outcome of a vicious state of society, of lack of moral responsibility. No one man could supply the officers of an army, selected as they had been, with new ideals and aspirations in a few months or a few years. The Russian soldier was physically magnificent, brave and patient in the highest degree. But he went in many cases to the war without knowing how to handle the weapon with which he was armed. He had not been taught to shoot, he had been brought up indeed to use his rifle with a heavy bayonet always fixed upon it after a fashion which rendered accuracy of aim impossible. The system thus indicated exhibited in certain cases results even more deplorable. Men were sent to fight with units of arms other than those with which they had been trained and for which they had enlisted. Thus a gunner might find himself with a battalion and an infantry soldier with a battery. An army of which such things can be said was pitted against the most perfect military machine in the world, against an army which had not only been trained for war in general but for the particular war we are discussing. It needs no secret revelations to tell to which side victory fell and the reason why. We are sorry Kouropatkin condescended to take up the subject, though we do not regret that he has drawn attention to deficiencies in connexion with preparation for war and peace strategy which are in the highest degree instructive. The Japanese were victorious not so much because they were better trained as because their organisation for war and their foresight during peace time rendered them fit to take the field in full strength at once. This book is valuable, in fact, because a great deal of it constitutes an excellent treatise on the art of war, on the value of good communications, of the necessity for politics and strategy being in harmony with one another, on the need for resolution and foresight on the part of the governing powers of a country as well as for efficiency in tactical respects on the part of the troops. It shows how even a man of Kouropatkin's knowledge and experience could do nothing in the face of Russian systems, and it goes a long way to prove his main contention that Russia, had his counsels been followed, need never have owned herself beaten at all.

Captain Sedgwick in a modest preface asks the indulgence of his readers because he is only a beginner. He has written quite a clear and intelligible sketch, and deserves credit for the diligence and care he has displayed. He has been almost over-scrupulous in acknowledging assistance, because occasionally it has been of so slight a nature that he might have done equally well without it, and he is too fond of quoting other writers verbatim in place of assimilating their ideas and putting forth his own after the process in his own way. Such faults are, however, those of a beginner, and no doubt Captain Sedgwick will get over them. It must nevertheless remain a question whether a beginner is best employed in writing a work which is intended for the serious study of officers, and whether it is fair that he should educate himself at the expense of his readers. There is an old-fashioned prejudice in favour of men filling themselves with ideas and knowledge before they venture to instruct others, and it is certainly more helpful to students when they are given criticism and opinions the outcome of matured experience or wide study. Possibly there is so pressing a demand for a book such as this that it was desirable to bring it out at once and there was no time for much search or choice as regards authors. Perhaps no abler pen could be found, but the fact remains that we are here given but bald comments when with due economy of space there was room for close though brief discussion. The book is in fact clearly got up for purposes of examination. It is a primer to enable unhappy and ill-prepared candidates to meet the papers set them; in other words, it is intended for cramming purposes, and is a hasty compilation to meet the demands of the moment. The Russo-Japanese War has so lately come to an end that, as our author tells us, the data for writing a detailed account are not yet available. Would it not then have been better to wait until they were available before writing?—for certainly some of the questions discussed and disposed of very briefly here will in all probability be viewed a few years hence in quite a different light. The comments with reference to the battle of the Yalu on page 57, for example, state that the strategical situation required that the Japanese advance should be stayed. The reasons why the Russians offered battle were by no means based on sound strategy, however, and it is even now practically certain that political wire-pulling had far more to do with their action than generalship. Neither is our author happy in his illustration from military history, as when he quotes the action of Ziethen on the Sambre as similar to that of the Russians on the Yalu. Again, in a sketch such as this dealing mainly with a strategical concentration it seems hardly worth while to criticise such tactical details as the posting of the Russian howitzers at the Yalu, or to mention such minutiæ as that the air-line telephones in the Russian position were destroyed early in the action. The half-page or so devoted to a few bald tactical comments had been better utilised in amplification of the discussion of more important points. On page 127 we find the authority of Sir Ian Hamilton invoked to make comments such as that the Russian officers exposed themselves too much, that the Russians fired section volleys, that the men were at close interval without reference to cover. Our author seems to have forgotten his preface and his statement that it was yet too early to write a detailed account of the great war. Why fill up a little sketch with such petty trivialities as these, and skimp the discussion of the bigger questions about which already there is no doubt? A sense of proportion is, in fact, lacking throughout these pages. After touching on minor tactical points very briefly, really large strategical, political, and financial questions are taken up, but these are sketched in so crudely that we doubt any student gaining any benefit from them except as an aide-mémoire. Some excellent but disjointed extracts are quoted from the utterances of various authors and officers, and then we are led away from the subject into a dissertation on intelligence duties. Finally, after only some half-dozen pages have been devoted to strategy and intelligence, our author turns once more to tactics. Again we are given quotations (with the exception of Sir Ian Hamilton) not from officers who have been in Manchuria, and whose evidence was therefore the best, but from secondary testimony, with but small attempt on the part of the author towards discrimination or comment of his own.

We doubt if any but a victim to a system of examination will read the book, and he will wish he had a better one to guide him.

SAINTE-BEUVE THE MAN.

"Sainte-Beuve." By George McLean Harper. London: Lippincott. 1909. 6s. net.

IN French there already exists a considerable "literature" of Sainte-Beuve. In English there is nothing beyond a few scattered articles and reviews. It was, in fact, only a few months ago that anyone thought it worth while systematically to translate him. It was then that Mr. Trechmann began upon the "Causeries du Lundi"; and we are still waiting to see whether Mr. Trechmann's publisher will find a public anxious to read Sainte-Beuve in English—at a shilling a volume. Criticism in France falls more swiftly, and in this case it has not neglected to fall upon the critic. Brunetière has passed judgment in his inevitable and final manner; M. Michaut has discovered that Sainte-Beuve had a system, and has at least convinced himself; M. Léon Séché has been busy among the documents. It must be confessed that comparatively the English have neglected him. Professor Harper explains this neglect by suggesting that "it has perhaps been taken for granted that to criticise a critic would be to carry the thing too far ". It is interesting to speculate as to what Professor Harper will think about the criticisms upon his book. It is a case of " Juges jugés " twice over.

It is a really great adventure to seek among the critics of Sainte-Beuve either for a true picture of the man or a trustworthy estimate of his achievements. For those who want a portrait of him in black, there is no lack of pitch; and for those who wish to deny him genius there is no lack of authority. Let us frame an indictment upon collected testimony. He was a renegade, seven-and-seventy times forsworn. On the word of a noble lady his private life was " beastly ", and his relations with the Hugos formed one of the nastiest series of events in the history of literature. He was utterly lacking in courage, as is proved by the fact that he published opinions in a provincial journal which he would not have dreamed of signing in Paris. He went about sighing because he was not a handsome young dragoon, and seeking a religion that would condone a breach of the seventh commandment. His poetry was trivial, and his ambition to figure as a poet was absurd. His " Port Royal " was the work of a journalist who changed his allegiance while his work was in progress. Many of his portraits were malignant caricatures. He was a good critic, because he had failed at everything else.

What kind of answer can be made to all this? A flat denial seems best, and the hoisting of the accuser upon the horns of a dilemma. He was not a renegade, but a many-sided man who sympathised and understood many of the movements in progress during his generation. He was not a " beast ", for his life was one long struggle of the spiritual and sensual element in human nature, a struggle already exemplified in David and S. Anthony. He was not a coward, for he hurried back to his post in 1830, and bearded the Senate in his declining years. Also did he not fight a duel with an umbrella in his left hand, saying that he did not mind being killed, but that he did mind getting wet? Moreover, it is no sin even in a serious man of letters to want to be good-looking; and his search for a religion was a long and earnest endeavour after truth. His poetry was, on the word of Béranger, of a kind absolutely new in France. " Port Royal " was a noble, historical monument, and the splendid effort of a divided mind to find itself. His portraits are true in outline, just a little coloured with a natural feeling that is by no means insidious, and consequently not at all harmful. Finally, he was a good critic, not because he had failed in everything, but because he had, to a certain extent, succeeded in everything.

Needless to say, Professor Harper has little sympathy with a dilemma of this kind. The spirit and purpose of his book is one which Sainte-Beuve would have commended. He approaches the works entirely through the man. His book is a sympathetic and just endeavour to get at the real Sainte-Beuve. If the real Sainte-Beuve has eluded him, there is only one thing to be said about it—that the real Sainte-Beuve will elude posterity just as he eluded his contemporaries. His mind was too delicately balanced to permit of the weighing of that hair which always turned the scale. There was scarcely a thought or a tendency of his age that he did not reflect. He touched every movement, and was caught by none. He served a novitiate in every creed, and believed in none. He turned into every path along the journey of his life, and remained in none. He essayed every branch of literature, and gave himself entirely to none. If he eluded his contemporaries, it is equally true that he eluded himself. Sainte-Beuve was perhaps the one phenomenon that Sainte-Beuve failed utterly to probe and value. The accounts which he gives of himself are as contradictory as the accounts of his critics. Those who raise the cry of insincerity may profitably be referred, by way of Professor Harper, to a closer reading of their subject. Professor Harper is, indeed, to be congratulated. If there are occasional inconsistencies and some vagueness of outline, it is difficult to see how they could have been avoided. No hardness of outline is possible when a character so elusive as that of Sainte-Beuve has to be brought upon the canvas. Concerning the style of the book it is only necessary to hint that American readers will perhaps enjoy it more than English. To speak of " bursting foolish bubbles by endeavouring to clasp them to one's heart " is to mix metaphor a little too boldly for this side the Atlantic.

CORPUS DOMINI APUD ANGLOS.

"A History of the Holy Eucharist in Great Britain." By T. E. Bridgett C.Ss.R. London: Fisher Unwin and Burns and Oates. 1908. 21s. net.

"A History of the Doctrine of the Holy Eucharist." By Darwell Stone. London: Longmans. 1909. 2 vols. 30s. net.

A TALL folio, nobly printed, is so seldom now produced that the critic is disposed to enquire rather jealously whether the contents are worthy of the honour. Father Thurston, who has edited the present reissue, in a considerably pruned and rearranged form, of Bridgett's very discursive treatise, which first appeared in 1881, tells us that the idea was to commemorate the recent Eucharistic Congress by reprinting the most important historical work on the Blessed Sacrament which has as yet appeared on English soil. The occasion and subject were worthy of a fine and scholarly volume.

Father Bridgett's, however, opens badly with three popular fallacies in the first paragraph. Why is he still allowed to confuse the King's Accession Declaration with the Coronation Oath, which is a poor modern Whig thing, but is not vulgar and blasphemous? Why is he allowed to paraphrase the sacrificia missarum condemned in Article XXXI. as a late mediæval abuse by the phrase " the doctrine of Masses ", meaning, as the context shows, the authoritative doctrine of the Mass? And it is a cheap misstatement, which ought not to have been suffered to stand, that " the worship of our Lord beneath the sacramental veils " is stigmatised by the reformed Church of England as idolatry, when the Black Rubrick distinctly says that it is the worship of the sacramental veils in themselves which is idolatrous, and only condemns, with some of the best Roman doctors, adoration of " a corporal presence of Christ's natural Flesh and Blood ", the older phrase " real and essential " having been deliberately altered in 1661. Similarly, the transubstantiation which, as Article XXVIII. cautiously avers, cannot be proved by Holy Writ, was in the original draft of that Article described as " transubstantiatio in Corpus et Sanguinem Christi ", but the phrase was not allowed to remain, " the change of the substance of bread and wine " being substituted. Such a change is declared to overthrow the nature of a sacrament, which is essentially the union of two realities, a heavenly and an earthly. It is a ghostly mystery rather than a mere miracle.

The English Reformation, like most human things, was a sadly mixed business, and the Eucharistic teaching of the earlier Reformers was confused and self-contradictory. But certain main motives underlay the appeal to a more primitive doctrine of the Holy Eucharist. One was insistence on the actuality of the outward part or sign in the Cœna Domini, which for Aquinas is mere sense-illusion—" Visus, tactus, gustus in Te fallitur ". And a further element of unreality and uncertainty was introduced into a subject where all should be real and certain by the school doctrine that when the Sacrament is physically digested it ceases to be Christ's Body and once more becomes the substance of bread. The second motive of reform was the restoration of Communion in both kinds. An excessively dialectical use of the doctrine of Concomitance had argued that, since entire Christ is given in either species, it is unnecessary for anyone but the celebrant to receive the Cup of the Lord. But the practice had only dated at earliest from the twelfth century, and seemed a perilous tampering with the evangelical institution. We think, by the bye, that Bridgett is right in holding that the English and French Kings received an unconsecrated chalice—like the newly ordained. But, if so, it seems to have been because they waived their privilege.

A third straining of logic had come to be the regular employment of the Host, with all the attributes deducible from the words "Hoc est Corpus meum", for extra-Eucharistic purposes, processional, benedictional, and as an Object of perpetual adoration. The Presence is thus sundered from the Mass—that is to say, from the pleading of the atoning Sacrifice of Calvary. Here again the English Articles content themselves with temperately pointing out that the Sacraments were not ordained of Christ to be gazed upon or to be carried about, but that we should duly use them. Attractive as is the idea of resort in secret prayer to the "Prisoner of the Tabernacle", Father Bridgett's rhetoric about the banishing of the Redeemer from His ancient homes, so that the Son of Man hath not now where to lay His head, should have been restrained by the remembrance that reservation for such a purpose, whether in sacrament-house, pyx or tabernacle, came in at a comparatively late date. Father Thurston, with the candour which we should expect from so good a scholar, remarks: "The strange thing is that in all the Christian literature of the first thousand years no one has apparently yet found a single clear and definite statement that any person visited a church in order to pray before the Body of Christ, kept upon the altar. Almost equally remarkable is the fact that no one seems to have been yet able to quote a prayer addressed to the Blessed Sacrament, apart from prayers intended for the time of Communion". He adds that in the Oriental Church to this day no extra-liturgical cultus of the Sacrament is practised. Bridgett himself points out that side-chapels for reservation were in former times unknown.

On the other hand, if our author is usually rather unnecessarily polemical, it must be confessed that the writers whom he calls "Protestant" have been accustomed seriously to misrepresent history. They have not been satisfied with urging such considerations as those which we have touched on, with discussing (as the Bishop of Durham has done so well) the history of Elevation, with testing modern practices and theories by the ancient liturgies or by the old Ordo Romanus, or with castigating the abuses and corruptions which gathered round the Sacrament of the Altar, some of which Father Bridgett himself describes. But the fashion has been to draw a wholly imaginary and fictitious picture of a pure, non-papal, unsacerdotal, unsuperstitious Anglo-Saxon Church, in which the dignitaries of Barchester Close would find themselves at home and an eleven-o'clock congregation of colonels and farmers could worship comfortably. The slightest acquaintance with the facts gives a rude shock to this vision of ecclesiastical continuity. The essentials may be there, but the atmosphere of belief and practice is completely different. Both sides in this controversy have much to learn and unlearn. Nor is it merely a question how far mediæval Christianity, with its tender idealism and exquisite love of beauty, its frightful scandals, its magnificent creativeness and its tendency to dissolution, is to be admired. For Roman Catholicism is no longer mediæval. Its tawdry modern altars contrasted with the dignified simplicity of those at which our forefathers were houseled are a symptom of much else. There then is the difficulty. Christians have all drifted.

We have left ourselves but little space in which to refer to the massive and impartial history of Eucharistic doctrine which comes fittingly from the Pusey House; but Mr. Darwell Stone's book is an expansion of articles, and of a volume in the "Oxford Library of Practical Theology", which have been for some years before the world. It is as severe and student-like—almost grittily so—as Bridgett's work is picturesque and popular. There is room for both presentations of a subject austerely high and difficult but throbbing with poetic light and colour. Mr. Stone's plan is to let the authorities speak for themselves. But a history, as he says, must be something more than a collection of facts or a catena of quotations. Such collections and catenæ are seldom really fair. As regards the Eucharist, the difficulty is that in the early non-controversial days writers expressed themselves too freely and incautiously, while after controversy had begun they were so afraid of giving opponents an advantage that they narrowed their own language and jealously circumscribed their own standpoint. Thus Mr. Stone shows that the Western mediæval teaching was by no means mainly mechanical and materialist. Yet the necessity of opposing the Berengarians, Lollards and other heretics led, on the whole, to a one-sided presentation of Catholic truth. Similarly our own post-Reformation divines—even the Non-jurors—are so haunted by the Roman spectre that they often seem to talk mere virtualism or receptionism, or to say on one page what they unsay on another. Thus they speak of a "transmutation" or "transelementation" effected by consecration, of a "true and substantial" presence of the Body and Blood, of bodily veneration towards the altar, as being "the greatest place of God's residence upon earth, the throne where His Body is usually present". And almost in the same breath the change which has passed upon the elements is spoken of as one of use rather than of nature. Transubstantiation is "a monster", yet on the altar "God is here prepared and drest", and the priest "at Communion times is in a great confusion as being not only to receive God but to break and administer Him". So again what is made is only a commemoration. Yet "the thing offered is the Body of Christ, which is an eternal and propitiatory sacrifice", and the Eucharist is "profitable to very many not only of the living but also of the dead". It is really not till our own time that a calm and balanced effort to co-ordinate in one view the various aspects of this central Ordinance of Christianity becomes possible. The materials for it now lie ready to hand in Mr. Stone's great book.

SOME GREAT SEAMEN.

"Nelson, and other Naval Studies." By James R. Thursfield. London: Murray. 1909. 12s. net.

OF the ten naval studies which Mr. Thursfield has bound up together, only one, the sketch of Paul Jones' career, has not appeared before. The remainder consists of articles drawn from the "Times", "United Service Magazine", "National Review", "Quarterly Review", and "Naval Annual", the dates of publication ranging between 1898 and 1906. The second essay of the series recalls the brilliant part taken by Mr. Thursfield in the dispute whether the battle of Trafalgar was or was not fought in accordance with the famous memo. and his clever summing-up against the theory of a "mad perpendicular attack". The conclusions he arrived at in the centenary year on the evidence then available have since received striking confirmation in the findings of the independent inquiry undertaken by Colonel Desbrière, Chief of the Historical Section of the General Staff of the French Army, who has had the advantage of examining documents preserved in the French and Spanish archives.

Nelson the tactician vindicated, and Mahan taken to task for allowing the shadow of fair Emma to blur his vision of the hero, Mr. Thursfield rounds off his inspection of the admiral with an appreciation of Nelson the man.

The ground cleared of Nelson, one of the "suppressed characters of naval history" gets sea-room. The distinguished officer to whom Mr. Thursfield has happily applied the nickname of "Single-Action Duncan" has been rather shabbily treated by penmen; although Nelson owns to borrowing a tip from Duncan for the Nile, and the ruse of Collingwood of Cadiz bears a strong family likeness to the game of make-believe played off the "Texel", the victor of Camperdown had to wait for a descendant in the third generation to take his biography in hand.

Corbett, referring to the manœuvres at Camperdown and their place in the evolution of tactics, is of opinion that their result "was an action almost exactly like that of Nelson at Trafalgar ". Mr. Thursfield professes also to see a close resemblance between "the mode of attack adopted by Duncan at Camperdown and that adopted by Nelson at Trafalgar", but he holds the curious view that the breaking through to attack the Dutchmen from to leeward was a novel operation "sanctioned by no recent precedent save that of Rodney at the Saints". The precedent appears to us unfortunate, as it ignores the fundamental difference between breaking the line and leading through, and Mr. Thursfield must have forgotten Howe as well as his signal-book when he called the breaking manœuvre "novel".

Duncan's report runs: "I made the signal to bear up, break the enemy's line, and engage them to leeward". The effect produced was excellent, but whether he really admired his tactics or grasped their significance must remain doubtful, since he explained afterwards in a letter to a relative, "We were obliged from being so near to the land to be rather rash in our attack, by which we suffered more".

A good eye for country, sea instinct and fine seamanship won Camperdown, and this is probably what St. Vincent meant when he wrote "Lord Duncan's action was fought pell-mell (without plan or system)". The accusation of "littleness" brought against Jervis for thus expressing himself is not supported by the quotation taken from Duncan's own letter, which contains nothing to justify the belief held by Mr. Thursfield that "inattention to form and order was the calculated means to a clearly perceived end".

Kempenfelt, another suppressed character of history, in pointing out the necessity for a regular system of tactics eighteen years before Camperdown was fought, had written to Middleton, "Our enemies have theory, we were superior in practice"; and superiority in practice was still the principal British asset at Camperdown. St. Vincent probably knew his man; the sailors of the eighteenth century were quick to recognise a conscious tactician, and Kempenfelt is a case in point, his abilities extracting a grudging tribute even from Paul Jones, the worthy for whom Mr. Thursfield next asks a hearing. The Father of the American Navy has certainly no reason to complain of his advocate for letting slip any point that might tell in his favour, for the plea for a new trial is partly grounded on an ingenious suggestion to credit him with something he might have done had fortune favoured him with greater opportunities. This reminds us of the hunt hen and the eggs she might have laid. The Last Post has rung out over many mute inglorious Nelsons, but, whatever else he may have been, Jones was not mute, he cannot be called inglorious, he was not Nelson. His correspondence proves him to have been a painstaking student of tactics with a keen ear and eye for everything that touched the art of warfare at sea, and no contemptible exponent of what has been well called the higher strategy. Whether he was also the great sea-captain cast in heroic mould, whose "extraordinary gifts and astonishing achievements" have induced Mr. Thursfield and the American Eagle to rolic in hyperbole, or only the bold bad pirate of distinguished talent, originality, and tenacious courage, of whom Sir John Laughton's imagination has drawn a picture for the "Dictionary of National Biography", must always be largely a matter of opinion.

In presenting a case for the sailor of fortune Mr. Thursfield acknowledges his debt to Mr. Buell and also to the "Memoirs" published anonymously in 1825, the authorship of which Mr. John Murray assigns to Benjamin Disraeli. Buell has described friend Paul as "the dark, slender distingué, chevalier sans titre de la mer"; the "Memoirs" speak of him as being a "short, thick little fellow, about five feet eight in height, of a dark, swarthy complexion". No two persons see a man or woman in quite the same light, and Mr. Thursfield has a perfect right to take Jones at his own estimate, but when he places John Paul alongside the one and only Horatio for the purpose of comparison, we cannot help feeling that another client has been sacrificed to too keen a sense of humour in counsel.

The last four studies give hero-worship no chance: they carry us forward to our own times, and prove that over-indulgence in the superlative is best and quickest cured by putting the patient through a short course of responsibility.

NOVELS.

"Sixpenny Pieces." By A. Neil Lyons. London: Lane. 1909. 6s.

Books dealing with the London poor, either on their humorous or their pathetic side, have been of late years things to be shunned, being mostly written not because the author knew or cared anything about them but because they made good copy. Mr. Lyons' description of them makes good copy, but his interest and his knowledge absolves him from the imputation of that being his first care. He is an artist, yet his human concern for his material is always discernible under his occasionally relentless handling. Both qualities are to be felt in such sketches as "An April Barge", which tells of the drowning of a bargeman in the Regent's Canal viewed from the top of an omnibus. It is quite pitiless in its simplicity, in its unsentimental rendering of the fatuity of the man's death, yet it is steeped in a true tragic sense of the thing, and gives half a dozen philosophies of life in the mere attitude of the observers—the flower-girl, the cornet-player, the wife, the baby and the fat man—upon the 'bus. Their insistence on the unessential is what seems most to impress Mr. Lyons in the poor, but he often contrives in relating it to make the essence come out. He has a happy gift, moreover, of making them explain themselves, as in "The Case of Mrs. Roper", who, comparing herself with a rival when bemoaning her husband's indifference, says "*I* am on'y 'is wife. *I* don't flatter 'im. *I* don't make a fuss of 'im. *I* don't make meself agreeable. *I'm* on'y 'is wife." For the few false notes in the book the poor in it are not responsible. The author has sufficient detachment from them to describe them almost as another species. He may not always see them as they are; not, at any rate, as they see themselves, but he can always see them—as part of a picture: they rest quietly within the frame. His own species he cannot render with so sure a touch. Dr. Brink is all right, but of him there is very little direct drawing; but James and Mr. Baffin and the other supernumeraries have always a distracting effect when they appear. The humorous and descriptive vigour with which they are rendered might not sound so much forced in other company.

"Sir Guy and Lady Rannard." By H. N. Dickinson. London: Heinemann. 1909. 6s.

If it is impossible to feel liking for Sir Guy and his wife, it is also impossible not to be interested in them, and, if the tedium of the earlier part of their history is endured, not to be absorbed in and impressed by the description of the sinister development of Guy's nature. The growth of his abnormalities, his suspiciousness and secretiveness, his oblique moral vision in political matters, his violent pugnacity, his inability to adapt himself to his political fellow-workers' methods, all his eccentricities finally culminate in the insanity of a fixed idea. There is something of medical accuracy in the account of the confused workings of his brain; it is in fact a pathological study of merit. His wife, a woman of considerable strength of will and intellectual power, who from indifference has passed to passionate devotion to her husband, is confronted with the horrible realisation that she is in love with a madman, "that she had lavished her worship on the symptoms of imbecility, hung upon his neck, and caressed the framework of a morbid process, adoring a disease and cherishing its ordered characteristics as they arose; that his boyish waywardness and charm had been the phases of a malady, and his tenderness a mental decay; that his affection for her had been a pathological incident; that the force of his manhood had been a by-product of demented energy".

"Attainment." By Mrs. Havelock Ellis. London: Alston Rivers. 1909. 6s.

We cannot quite understand Mrs. Ellis' aim in writing this story. The note on the cover says it is "founded on experiments in Socialism and philanthropy, it points to the value of a natural life in every respect." She certainly does not altogether sympathise with the absurd Socialistic Brotherhood which she describes, and which, impossible as it may seem, is quite a conventional household in comparison with an actually existing colony she may have had in mind. Though she is quite earnest and sincere in her exposition of their ridiculous and crude wind-bag philosophy, she, perhaps reluctantly, makes the experiment end in failure. Yet, on the other hand, the story is not a satire; it is quite unpardonably dull, and there is no humour in the description of these tiresome people, some of whom we recognise as well-known cranks. The plot is so incoherent that when a lover comes to claim, in most conventional fashion, the heroine with the Socialist ideals, we have not the faintest idea who he is, and only by diligent search can we find a previous brief mention of him, though apparently in that short appearance he succeeded in winning her heart. It is altogether an indigestible, crude, and tiresome piece of work, and as far as we can discover quite pointless.

"Set in Silver." By C. M. and A. M. Williamson. London: Methuen. 1909. 6s.

Mr. and Mrs. Williamson appear to have travelled in a motor car round the English and Welsh coast from Chichester to Liverpool and then struck across into Northumberland. So if anyone wishes to read impressions of cathedrals from Winchester to Chester, of castles from Tintagel to Bamborough, and of the intervening scenery, he will now know where they can be found. But the thread of story on which these rather conventional pearls are strung is amusing. A retired Anglo-Indian comes to pick up a girl-ward in Paris, but as the young lady was engaged in eloping with a Frenchman she persuaded her dearest friend to impersonate her during the critical period. The story is told in letters, and the friend in question (believed by the Anglo-Indian and by Mr. and Mrs. Williamson to be altogether charming) suggests reflections on the odd blend of minx and sentimentalist in the modern girl which we have not time to formulate.

"The Shuttles of the Loom." By K. M. Edge. London: Murray. 1909. 6s.

This discursive tale, which begins in Southern India and brings us via Trieste and Lucerne to London, contains enough topographical information to show that the writer is well acquainted with all these places; but it is difficult, even in these days of elderly young men, to be much interested in an ex-Deputy-Conservator of Forests, aged fifty, whose fancy turns to thoughts of love on the voyage home—though all right-minded ladies will be sorry for him.

SHORTER NOTICES.

"The British Empire, Past, Present and Future. Edited by A. F. Pollard. London: The League of the Empire. 1909. 5s. net.

"The Colonies and Imperial Defence." By P. A. Silburn. London: Longmans. 1909. 6s.

Two books which may usefully be read together—one giving a concise account of the Empire in its beginnings, its development, and its present position; the other concerned with the best means of preserving against any enemy, European or other, who might challenge it, what Ralegh and Wolfe and Clive and John Macdonald and Cecil Rhodes secured to the British flag. Mr. Pollard's book is mainly history, though he devotes a good many pages to the needs of the future; Mr. Silburn's only glances at history sufficiently to illustrate his points. "The British Empire" will make an admirable guide for schools and popular purposes; "The Colonies and Imperial Defence" should be studied by all who may have a voice in deciding what part the colonies should play in imperial defence. It is a disquieting reflection that in an Empire of 430 millions of people barely one in 450 is available for its defence. The problems to be considered are manifold: of some the solution rests with the Home Government, of others with the colonies, of others, again, with both the home and the colonial Governments. True imperial defence demands the co-ordination of imperial resources, so that the whole shall be available for the defence of the whole without exposing any part to unnecessarily grave risks. Mr. Silburn enters in detail into the nature of the risks which have to be met in the various parts of the Empire, and makes a variety of suggestions for meeting them. In his opinion great good to the solidity of the Empire would be derived from the creation of a colonial nobility, which would put new life into imperialism and crush out the self-sufficient tendency, sometimes manifest in Australia and Canada. "The staying power of all monarchical government is an aristocracy", he says, and the colonies have no aristocracy. It is, he urges, one of the weaknesses of Australia, with the menace of Japan ever before her, that she should be engrossed in legislating for the immediate present along extreme Socialistic lines—a weakness to which the Australians are not wholly blind if we may judge from recent events. On the eve of the Imperial Defence Conference, Mr. Silburn's book should be of real service, on the practical not less than the speculative side. It will show the colonies that there is as much need for them as for the mother country to think imperially, and that the idea of little navies for colonial defence must be abandoned if the resources of the outer Empire are to be used to the full.

"The English Bible, 1611." Edited by William Aldis Wright. Cambridge: At the University Press. 1909. 5 vols. 20s. net.

The inclusion of the Authorised Version of the English Bible in the series of Cambridge English Classics will seem to many to need explanation. Most people are quite unaware that the text they read to-day differs very much from that first issued in 1611. Spelling and punctuation, even words and phrases, have been altered; while barely a seventh part of the marginal references is due to the original translators. Mr. Aldis Wright's name is sufficient guarantee of the scholarly accuracy of this reissue of the Authorised Version exactly as it was first given to the English people. There were two issues in 1611, commonly known as the He Bible and the She Bible, from the fact that the phrase in Ruth iii. 15, "he went into the citie", was

(Continued on page 24.)

changed in the second issue into "she went into the city". Modern Bibles are variations of the She Bible. In this edition we are brought back with literal accuracy to the He Bible. The reprint is not only accurate, but has wide margins, large spaces, and clear print. If it has not the dignity of the original edition—a handsome black-letter folio, with two columns on a page—a link with the old form has been preserved by rigidly keeping the folio column to a page of the octavo reprint. The edition has a real interest, not only for the student, but for all English-speaking people, who rightly regard the Authorised Version of the Bible as "the noblest example of the English tongue".

"A Holiday in Connemara." By Stephen Gwynn M.P. London: Methuen. 10s. 6d.

This book looks as if specially written to illustrate the difference between journalism and literature, a mixture of both, by a writer capable of either according as required. The price is 10*s.* 6*d.*, but about 9*s.* 6*d.* worth is journalism, that is, a product of necessities other than literary. The other shilling's worth arises from the author's own mind and feeling. The distinction is as obvious as the causes controlling it. The question is suggested on almost every page, How far can a clever man write what he thinks about Galway and hold a seat for Galway in the House of Commons? Outside Ireland Mr. Gwynn can write gracefully about human things, mental and moral interests included. Inside Ireland he writes about fish. The subject of fish is one that need not raise any serious questions of mental and moral interest; and so long as a man avoids these, he may hold a seat for Galway. Hence the 9*s.* 6*d.* worth of fish-writing and the odd shilling's worth of human interest. There is "writing" about women, all of the kind to secure "the man for Galway"; but when he comes to clothes the mind is free, and the man of letters, taking the place of the journalist, is worth reading: "Modern dress (for women) conveys as a rule the notion of a creature with an upper and lower half, more or less neatly put together at the waist". If he were as free to write about men and women, we might have had 9*s.* 6*d.* worth of literature. It appears that a man may have opinions of his own on clothes and keep his seat for Galway. He observes of others who write about Ireland: "Any man writing from the standpoint of a professed Catholic, or of a professed Nationalist, who will undertake to show the seamy side either of Irish Catholicism or Irish Nationalism, finds his books bought up with avidity by the enemies of Ireland". Mr. Gwynn seems to be thinking of his famous contemporary Mr. M. J. McCarthy, with whom he is substantially in agreement, but cannot say so and remain the man for Galway.

"The Foundations of the Origin of Species." By Charles Darwin. Edited by Francis Darwin. Cambridge: At the University Press. 1909. 7s. 6d. net.

The Syndics of the University Press printed in a separate volume the first sketch made by Darwin in 1842, entitled "The Foundations of the Origin of Species". It was intended for presentation on the occasion of the celebration at Cambridge of the centenary of Darwin's birth and of the fiftieth anniversary of the publication of "The Origin of Species". The essay is edited by Mr. Francis Darwin, with an introduction discussing the growth of Darwin's ideas and the origin of the essay.

Besides this essay the Syndics have published the book mentioned above, which contains, in addition to the essay of 1842, another and longer one of 1844. The earlier sketch is too inchoate, except for adepts in science who are capable of quickly seizing hints and suggestions, and its interest is chiefly historical. Of the 1844 essay, however, Mr. Dalton remarks that its freshness and the fuller discussion of some subjects make it good reading even for those who are familiar with the "Origin". The reader may also put to himself the question, What effect would have been produced if this, instead of the "Origin", had been published? and speculate on the answer.

"The Life Story of the Otter." By J. C. Tregarthen. London: Murray. 1909. 6s. net.

The true sportsman is instinctively in sympathy with his quarry; he is anxious to know him and shake hands with him, as it were, before putting the gloves on. Whether Mr. Tregarthen is a sportsman or merely a keen observer of wild life we do not know. He manages to put into his books just those touches which will appeal to every follower of the hounds, whether fox or otter be the quest. Mr. Tregarthen has made himself familiar with the otter's most intimate doings: his study must have meant midnight as well as daylight vigils, winter and summer, over wide stretches of country. He throws his chapters into the form of a biography—a form which enables him vividly to illustrate the animal's moods and fears and emotions. It is a pity Mr. Tregarthen did not confine his book to the otter: when he writes of human beings he seems to lose his insight and his grip. It is no mean compliment to say that the general reader and the old otter-hunter will alike find this "life story" extremely entertaining.

"Notes by the Way, with Memoirs of Joseph Knight and Joseph Woodfall Ebsworth." By John Collins Francis. London: Fisher Unwin. 1909. 10s. 6d. net.

Mr. Francis' "Notes by the Way" consist mainly of reprints of notes and articles from "Notes and Queries" with records of its history, its editors, and many notable contributors. The intention of the book is to commemorate the sixtieth year of the founding of "Notes and Queries". Mr. Francis has written for this volume the two above-mentioned memoirs. As to the memoir of Joseph Knight, while there is much in it which all admirers of that remarkable man will read with interest, it is not such a biography as we are entitled to expect, and it ought not to be considered as a satisfactory substitute. Such a rare character and career as Knight's call for a record more regular and substantial.

The Industrial Law Committee, York Mansion, York Street, Westminster, has issued the Report of its work for 1908, and of that of the Industrial Law Indemnity Fund for 1907 and 1908. It is pleasant to see that the operations of this very useful committee have been extended during the last year, so much so that the whole instead of the half time of the secretary has been employed. Increased work naturally means more expense, both in spreading information and procuring the redress of the many injustices which are committed on factory workers due to wilful or ignorant breaches of the laws passed for their protection. This work is so important that there ought to be no question of the inadequacy of funds.

We have received from Mr. John Murray No. 20 of the "**Journal of the Society of Comparative Legislation**" (5s. net). The articles in this number show how invaluable the journal of the society is as the record of the ideas of British jurists on International Law and Comparative Jurisprudence. It is no longer open to the criticism which we ourselves once made, that some of its articles were too much of the ordinary monthly or quarterly magazine type. The Aristotelian motto of the title-page is lived up to in the two-hundred-pages review of foreign and British and Colonial legislation.

For this Week's Books see page 26.

IN GASTRIC DISORDERS.

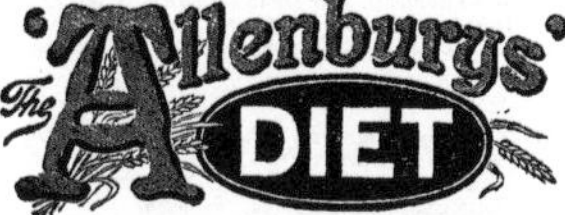

A Pancreatised Milk and Wheaten Food.

From its being so bland and readily digestible, the "Allenburys" DIET has been found a particularly valuable food in all gastric disorders. It can be retained and assimilated when other forms of nourishment fail to agree, improving the capacity for general assimilation. It is readily made by the addition of boiling water only. In tins, 1/6 and 3/-, of Chemists.

A large sample for three penny stamps to cover postage.

Allen & Hanburys Ltd., Lombard St., London.

CONNOISSEURS OF COFFEE

DRINK THE

RED WHITE & BLUE

DELICIOUS FOR BREAKFAST & AFTER DINNER.

In making, use less quantity, it being much stronger than ordinary COFFEE.

BRAGG'S CHARCOAL BISCUITS

Cure Indigestion

SPEEDILY CURE ACIDITY, FLATULENCE, HEARTBURN, IMPURE BREATH, INDIGESTION, DIARRHŒA, &c.

PREVENT MANY AN ILLNESS. Highly recommended by the Medical Profession. Sold by all Chemists and Stores. Biscuits, 1s., 2s. and 4s. per tin; Powder, 2s. and 4s. per bottle; Lozenges, 1s. 1½d. tin.

SAMPLES FREE to anyone in the United Kingdom sending this Coupon to J. L. BRAGG, Ltd., 14 Wigmore Street, London, W. (19)

POOLE & LORD

INDIAN AND GENERAL OUTFITTERS,

322 OXFORD STREET, LONDON, W.

(NEARLY OPPOSITE BOND STREET.)

INVENTORS OF THE

"Sans-Plis" SHIRT.

Prices from 7s. 6d.

The "SANS-PLIS" Shirt is superior to any other for Indian and Colonial wear. Being entirely free from gathers, it is cooler, much stronger, and will bear the Indian mode of washing better than any shirt in use.

A single shirt, or other article, made to *measure*, and accurate patterns preserved to ensure correctness in the execution of future orders.

Makers of Drawers with Flexible Hip Belt Bands.

"BREECHES CUT."

GUY'S HOSPITAL.—PRELIMINARY SCIENTIFIC (M.B. LONDON).—The next Course of Lectures and Practical Classes for this Examination will begin on October 1.

Full particulars may be obtained on application to

The DEAN, Guy's Hospital, London Bridge, S.E.

HAMPSTEAD.—FROGNAL PARK, LONDON, N.W. St. Basil's Roman Catholic PREPARATORY SCHOOL for BOYS. Beautiful grounds on the top of Hampstead Hill, close to Hampstead Heath.

ELY CATHEDRAL.

Visitors will find First Class Hotel Accommodation at the "LAMB" Family Hotel, which is situated close to the Cathedral. **MODERATE TERMS.** Omnibus meets all trains.

Proprietor, S. AIREY.

WHAT SHALL I GIVE?

is a question often put in connection with Birthdays, Weddings, Christmas, New Year, and many other occasions when the giving of presents is customary. And the question is not always easy to answer satisfactorily.

WHY NOT A PICTURE?

Everybody likes pictures of some kind or other, and nothing can be more generally acceptable or appropriate than a framed PERMANENT AUTOTYPE *reproduction of the work of some favourite painter.*

AT THE AUTOTYPE FINE ART GALLERY

will be found a selection of framed Autotypes sufficiently large and varied to suit the greatest diversities of taste. Ancient and Modern Art in all its phases is fully represented.

PERMANENT AUTOTYPE REPRODUCTIONS

are decorative in character and appeal to all lovers of art. Their reasonable price brings them within reach of the most modest picture buyer.

A Visit of Inspection is Invited.

THE AUTOTYPE COMPANY,

74 New Oxford Street, London, W.C.

(*A few doors west of Mudie's Library.*)

REAL HAMBURG GROUND

KROPP RAZOR

NEVER REQUIRES GRINDING.

DO NOT BE PUT OFF WITH SUBSTITUTES.

Black Handle ... ... 5s. 6d.	A pair Ivory Handles in
Ivory Handle ... ... 7s. 6d.	Russia Leather Case 21s.
Kropp DUPLEX STROP 7s. 6d.	Kropp Strop Paste ... 6d.

Wholesale: OSBORNE, GARRETT, & Co., LONDON, W.

R. ANDERSON & CO.,

BRITISH, INDIAN, AND COLONIAL ADVERTISEMENT CONTRACTORS,

14 KING WILLIAM STREET, STRAND, W.C.,

GIVE THE BEST TERMS for Company and General Advertising. Advice, Estimates, and all information free of charge. Replies received.

P. & O. AUTUMN PASSENGER SAILINGS (1909)

(Carrying Mails under Contract with H.M. Government.)

EGYPT, INDIA, STRAITS, CHINA, JAPAN, AUSTRALASIA.

STRAITS, CHINA and JAPAN DIRECT.

Steamer.	Tons.	From London.	
NAMUR ...	7,000	Sept. 11	Carrying First and Second Saloon Passengers at Reduced Fares without transhipment.
NORE ...	7,000	Sept. 25	
PALAWAN ...	5,000	Oct. 9	
SICILIA ...	7,000	Oct. 23	
SYRIA ...	7,000	Nov. 6	
SUMATRA ...	5,000	Nov. 20	

P. & O. Return Tickets, available for 2 years, at a Fare and a Half. For Passage and all information apply at the Company's Offices, 122 Leadenhall St., E.C., or Northumberland Ave., W.C., London.

AUSTRALIA by ORIENT LINE,

UNDER CONTRACT TO CARRY HIS MAJESTY'S MAILS.

FROM LONDON EVERY ALTERNATE FRIDAY, calling at PLYMOUTH, GIBRALTAR, MARSEILLES, NAPLES, PORT SAID, and COLOMBO.

Managers—F. GREEN & CO.: ANDERSON, ANDERSON & CO.

Head Offices—FENCHURCH AVENUE, LONDON.

For Passage apply to the latter firm at 5 Fenchurch Avenue, E.C., or to the Branch Office, 28 Cockspur Street, Charing Cross, S.W.

UNION-CASTLE LINE.

ROYAL MAIL SERVICE.—To SOUTH and EAST AFRICA.—Via Madeira, Canaries, Ascension, St. Helena, and Lobito Bay.

Steamers	Service	London	Southampton
* SAXON	Royal Mail	—	July 3
§ GUELPH	Intermediate	July 2	July 3
* KILDONAN CASTLE ..	Royal Mail		July 10
† GALICIAN	Intermediate	July 9	July 10

* Via Madeira. § Via Teneriffe. † Via Las Palmas.

Special Trains from Waterloo to Southampton every Saturday.

Donald Currie and Co., Managers, 3 and 4 Fenchurch Street, E.C. West End Agencies—Sleeping Car Co., 20 Cockspur Street, S.W., and Thos. Cook and Son, 13 Cockspur Street, S.W.

THIS WEEK'S BOOKS.

BIOGRAPHY

General Wolfe (Edward Salmon). Sir Isaac Pitman. 3s. 6d. net.
The Real Francis-Joseph (Henri De Weindel). Long. 15s. net.
Recollections of a Long Life (Lord Broughton, 2 vols.). Murray. 24s. net.

FICTION

Marriage as a Trade (Cicely Hamilton). Chapman and Hall. 6s.
A Tramp's Schooling (A. N. Cooper). Fisher Unwin. 3s. 6d. net.
The Ramblings of an Old Mummer (Russell Crauford); The Human Mole (Colin Collins). Greening. 6s. each.
The Invincible Amelia; or, The Polite Adventuress (E. Maria Albanesi). Methuen. 6s.
Oliver (Henry C. ff. Castleman); A White Lie (G. Russell Beardmore). Long. 6s. each.
Multitude and Solitude (John Masefield). Grant Richards. 6s.
Dragon's Blood (Henry Milner Rideout); Low Society (Robert Halifax). Constable. 6s. each.

HISTORY

The Secret History of the Court of Spain during the Last Century (Rachel Challice). Long. 15s. net.
The Last Days of Papal Rome, 1850-1870 (R. De Cesare). Constable. 12s. 6d. net.
Napoleon III. and Italy (Robert Holmes Edleston). Darlington: Bailey.

LAW

The Small Holdings and Allotments Act, 1908 (Aubrey John Spencer). Stevens and Sons, Ltd. 7s. 6d.
Accidental Injuries to Workmen (H. Norman Barnett). Rebman. 7s. 6d. net.

REPRINTS AND TRANSLATIONS

Dante's Convivio (William Walrond Jackson). Oxford: At the Clarendon Press. 3s. 6d. net.
Self-Government in Canada and How it was Achieved (F. Bradshaw). King. 3s. 6d. net.

SCIENCE AND PHILOSOPHY

Scientific Idealism (William Kingsland). Rebman. 7s. 6d. net.
The Campaign against Microbes (Etienne Burnet). Bale, Sons and Danielson. 5s. net.
The Berlin Discussion of the Problem of Evolution (Erich Wasmann). Kegan Paul. 6s. net.
The Foundations of the Origin of Species: Two Essays, written in 1842 and 1844 (Charles Darwin). Cambridge: At the University Press. 7s. 6d. net.

THEOLOGY

The Gospel of Rightness (C. E. Woods). Williams and Norgate. 5s. net.
Ecclesiasticus: The Greek Text of Codex (J. H. A. Hart). Cambridge: At the University Press. 10s. net.

TRAVEL

Letters from Malabar and on the Way (Henry Bruce). Routledge. 6s. net.
Portugal, its Land and People (W. H. Koebel). Constable. 16s. net.
Round the World in a Motor Car (Antonio Scarfoglio), 15s. net; Spain: a Study of her Life and Arts (Royall Tyler), 12s. 6d. net. Grant Richards.

MISCELLANEOUS

Charles Darwin as Geologist (Sir Archibald Geikie). Cambridge: At the University Press. 2s. net.
Conscience and Criticism (Rev. Geoffrey Hughes). Duckworth. 5s. net.
Empire in Pawn, An (A. J. Wilson). Fisher Unwin. 10s. 6d. net.
New English Dictionary, The (Edited by Sir James A. H. Murray). Vol. IX. Frowde. 5s.
Register of the Members of St. Mary Magdalen College, Oxford, A (William Dunn Macray). Frowde. 7s. 6d. net.
Shuttlecock for Critics, A (James J. Eaton). Stockwell. 2s. net.
Sovranty of Society The (Hugh E. M. Stutfield). Fisher Unwin. 5s. net.
Woman Suffrage: A National Danger (Heber Hart). Murby 1s. net.

REVIEWS AND MAGAZINES FOR JULY.—The East and the West, 1s.; The Antiquary, 6d.; The Nineteenth Century and After, 2s. 6d.; The Connoisseur, 1s.; The Financial Review of Reviews, 1s.; National Defence, 1s.; The Englishwoman, 1s.; Harper's Monthly, 1s.; The Musical Times, 4d.; Hibbert's Journal, 2s. 6d. net; The Fortnightly Review, 2s. 6d.; Blackwood's Magazine, 2s. 6d.; The Cornhill Magazine, 1s.; The Century, 1s. 4d.; The Treasury, 6d.; The Contemporary, 2s. 6d.; Scribner's, 1s.

TWO NEW BOOKS PUBLISHED LAST WEEK.

THE MANIAC. 6s.

A REALISTIC STUDY OF MADNESS FROM THE MANIAC'S POINT OF VIEW.

The Publishers are perfectly satisfied that this book is a genuine record of a case of madness from the patient's point of view, and therefore have no hesitation in recommending it as a most valuable psychological study. To the general reader it is offered as being more weirdly sensational than any novel.

The Times says :—"Certainly a curious record and bears the impress of truth."

OLD AS THE WORLD. 6s.

A ROMANCE OF THE WESTERN ISLANDS.

By J. W. BRODIE INNES, Author of "Morag the Seal."

"The story is well imagined, interesting, and told with a fine artistic haziness of suggestion proper to its subject . . . should be read with enjoyment."—*Scotsman.*

SECOND IMPRESSION NOW READY. 6s.

THE ROMANCE OF A NUN.

By ALIX KING, Author of "The Little Novice."

"An extraordinary book . . . the narrative style is quick and interesting."

FRANK HARRIS, in *Vanity Fair.*

JUST ISSUED. In 2 demy 8vo. vols. Over 1,000 pp. **21s. net.**

Descriptive Circular Free.

PROGRESSIVE CREATION.

A RECONCILIATION OF RELIGION WITH SCIENCE.

By Rev. HOLDEN E. SAMPSON.

"His (the author's) two vast volumes . . . are the outcome of thought at first hand : I will say on my part that the thought is often arresting . . . There are serious and important views on the Eucharist and on the other Sacraments, especially that of marriage, and references that seem sympathetic and enlightening to many holy offices and observances which are too lightly set aside in these days. . . . It is of the quality of revelation. . . ."

Mr. A. E. WAITE, in the *Occult Review.*

"The author's symbolical interpretation of the Fall in terms of Eugenics is startling . . . It is a work of the greatest value, both as an endeavour to turn the human mind from an utterly mischievous literal interpretation of the Bible to its true aspect as a Book of Poetry and Symbols, and as an endeavour to bring about a loftier spiritual perception of the future of the world, and to supply humanity with a new and poetic impulse and a new religious aspiration."

HUNTLEY CARTER, in *New Age.*

PUBLISHED LAST WEEK. Demy 8vo. 452 pp. Cloth, **7s. 6d. net.**

Descriptive Circular Free.

SCIENTIFIC IDEALISM;

Or, MATTER AND FORCE, AND THEIR RELATION TO LIFE AND CONSCIOUSNESS.

By WILLIAM KINGSLAND, Author of "The Mystic Quest," "The Esoteric Basis of Christianity," &c.

Extract from the first review received to date:—"Freshly thought out, if not actually original, it will prove suggestive reading to speculative students keen to reach some understanding, even if a mystical one, of the philosophic problems of personality and the inner life." —*Scotsman.*

London: REBMAN, Ltd. 129 Shaftesbury Avenue, W.C.

Sir ISAAC PITMAN & SONS, Ltd.,
No. 1 Amen Corner, LONDON, E.C.

Now Ready.

THE LATEST ADDITION TO PITMAN'S MAKERS OF NATIONAL HISTORY SERIES.

Edited by W. H. HUTTON, B.D.

GENERAL WOLFE.

By EDWARD SALMON.

In crown 8vo. cloth gilt, with Frontispiece and Map, **3s. 6d.** net.

In the ensuing September Canada will be celebrating the 150th anniversary of the capture of Quebec and the death of General Wolfe. Previous accounts of this famous soldier and accomplished man have been written without reference to facts and documents that are now accessible. The writer of this Life has gathered from authentic sources many new materials for compiling a thoroughly trustworthy biography, and for clearing up certain points that were previously obscure. Moreover, he has been at pains to correct the positive errors which only too abundantly have crept into the accounts of the conqueror of Quebec. The time for a new Life of Wolfe would seem to be opportune.

"A new and notable series of comprehensive and scholarly historical manuals." *Glasgow Herald.*

"The three volumes which have already appeared in this new library of historical manuals fully demonstrate the value of such a series, the immediate object of which is 'to commemorate important men whose share in the making of national history seems to need a more complete record than it has yet received.' Each volume is obviously the work of a practised historian." *Daily Graphic.*

Previous Volumes in the Series.

CARDINAL BEAUFORT. By L. B. RADFORD, D.D.

VISCOUNT CASTLEREAGH. By ARTHUR HASSALL, M.A.

ARCHBISHOP PARKER. By W. M. KENNEDY, B.A.

READY SHORTLY.

FRANCIS ATTERBURY. By H. C. BEECHING, D.Litt.

"No scheme could be more admirable than that of the series of volumes entitled, 'Makers of National History.'" *Sphere.*

"The new series ought to make a place for itself in school and public libraries." *Saturday Review.*

A NEW 16 pp. PROSPECTUS IS IN PREPARATION, and will be sent to anyone gratis on application.

NOW READY.

With Portraits. 2 vols. demy 8vo. 24s. net.

RECOLLECTIONS OF A LONG LIFE

By LORD BROUGHTON

(John Cam Hobhouse).

With additional Extracts from his private Diaries.

Edited by his Daughter, LADY DORCHESTER.

With a Preface by the EARL OF ROSEBERY, K.G.

Mr. (afterwards Sir) John Cam Hobhouse, who in later life was raised to the peerage as Lord Broughton, is too well known to require a detailed description. As the intimate friend of Lord Byron both at Trinity College, Cambridge, and afterwards, he was brought into close touch with the poet in all the affairs of his life. They travelled together in the Mediterranean when "Childe Harold" was written, and when Byron's domestic troubles were passing Hobhouse was his confidant and daily adviser. These volumes throw much new and most important light on Byron's affairs. In 1813 Hobhouse made a lengthy tour in Central Europe, Austria, Hungary, &c., and saw many of the leading personages of the day. He succeeded in reaching Paris during the Hundred Days, and was there while Waterloo was fought and when Napoleon returned. In 1816 he joined the exiled Byron in Switzerland and Italy. Besides all this the volumes contain many new and interesting reminiscences of *le beau monde* in London and the principal European capitals, and Mr. Hobhouse's full and careful record of the circumstances attending the Byron separation.

JOHN MURRAY, ALBEMARLE STREET, W.

THE

NINETEENTH CENTURY & AFTER.

JULY.

THE UNITY AND DEFENCE OF THE EMPIRE. By the Right Hon. Sir CHARLES TUPPER, Bart., G.C.M.G. (ex-Prime Minister of Canada and late High Commissioner in London).
ARE THE DEATH DUTIES AN ECONOMICALLY SOUND FORM OF TAXATION? By Sir FELIX SCHUSTER, Bart.
A BENGAL CIVILIAN'S VIEW OF THE INDIAN DEPORTATIONS. By H. C. STREATFEILD (late District Magistrate of Backergunge).
THE CREED OF IMPERIALISM. By WALTER FREWEN LORD.
"CABLE" REFORM. By Sir EDWARD SASSOON, Bart., M.P.
HENRY THE EIGHTH AND THE MONASTERIES: A REPLY TO THE REV. G. MONROE ROYCE. By Dr. JAMES GAIRDNER, C.B.
THE CULT OF "TEDDY BEAR." By AUSTIN HARRISON.
PERSONAL RECOLLECTIONS OF ABDUL HAMID II. AND HIS COURT (concluded). By Professor A. VAMBERY, C.V.O.
BRITISH ART AT VENICE. By MARCUS B. HUISH.
THE EXTINCTION OF THE UPPER CLASSES. By W. C. D. WHETHAM, F.R.S., and Mrs. WHETHAM.
FRERE JACQUES. By ROSE M. BRADLEY.
THE REVISION OF THE PRAYER BOOK PSALTER. By the Rev. Canon VAUGHAN.
"TRUE TEMPERANCE" AND THE PUBLIC HOUSE: A REPLY TO MR. EDWYN BARCLAY. By GEORGE B. WILSON (Secretary of the United Kingdom Alliance).
DECENTRALISATION OF GOVERNMENT IN INDIA.—II. By Sir ARUNDEL ARUNDEL, K.C.S.I. (late Member of the Viceroy's Council).
THE BUDGET AND SOCIAL REVOLUTION. By S. ROSENBAUM (Statistician to the Tariff Commission).
IMPERIALIST AUSTRIA: AN IMPRESSION FROM VIENNA. By ÆNEAS O'NEILL.

LONDON: SPOTTISWOODE & CO. LTD., 5 NEW-STREET SQUARE.

THE BRITISH EMPIRE:

ITS PAST, ITS PRESENT, AND ITS FUTURE.

Edited by **A. F. POLLARD, M.A.** Pp. 896, 5s. net.

Fifteen special Contributors and over a Hundred Authorities in all parts of the Empire have collaborated in its production.

LEAGUE OF THE EMPIRE, Caxton Hall, Westminster;
AND ALL BOOKSELLERS.

WHO WAS SWEDENBORG?

A Lecture on **EMANUEL SWEDENBORG: HIS LIFE AND CHARACTER,** will be sent **free and post free** to all applicants on their sending their names and addresses to the SECRETARY OF THE SWEDENBORG SOCIETY, 1 BLOOMSBURY STREET, LONDON, W.C.

SALES BY AUCTION.

THE HAZLITT COLLECTION OF COINS.

MESSRS. SOTHEBY, WILKINSON & HODGE will SELL by AUCTION, at their House, No. 13 Wellington Street, Strand, W.C., on MONDAY, JULY 5, and Four Following Days, and on MONDAY, JULY 12, and Three Following Days, at One o'clock precisely, the valuable Collection of GREEK, ROMAN, ORIENTAL, CONTINENTAL and FOREIGN and BRITISH and COLONIAL COINS, in Gold, Electrum, Silver, Bronze, &c., consisting chiefly of Choice Specimens in Preservation and Artistic Merit, formed during the last thirty years by W. C. Hazlitt, Esq., of Barnes Common (Surrey).

May be viewed. Catalogues may be had. Illustrated copies, price 2s. 6d. each.

THE LIBRARY OF THE LATE DR. FRANCIS ELGAR.

MESSRS. SOTHEBY, WILKINSON & HODGE will SELL by AUCTION, at their House, No. 13 Wellington Street, Strand, W.C., on THURSDAY, JULY 8, and Following Day, at One o'clock precisely, the LIBRARY of the late Dr. Francis Elgar, comprising a Collection of Rare Works connected with Shipping, Navigation, and the Navy: First and Collected Editions of Modern Authors, and Standard Works in the Various Branches of Literature; also ORIENTAL BOOKS and MANUSCRIPTS, the property of the late A. C. Kay, Esq., M.R.A.S., and other Oriental Scholars.

May be viewed two days prior. Catalogues may be had.

ENGRAVINGS, ETCHINGS AND WOODCUTS PRINCIPALLY BY THE OLD MASTERS.

MESSRS. SOTHEBY, WILKINSON & HODGE will SELL by AUCTION, at their House, No. 13 Wellington Street, Strand, W.C., on MONDAY, JULY 12, at One o'clock precisely, ENGRAVINGS, ETCHINGS and WOODCUTS principally by the Old Masters, comprising Engravings and Etchings by A. DURER, M. SCHONGAUER, SIR A. VANDYCK, H. S. BEHAM, REMBRANDT, and other celebrated Old Masters; Engravings by MARC ANTONIO RAIMONDI and his Pupils, Engravings by W. HOGARTH, mostly in the First State; Modern Etchings, and a few miscellaneous prints of the English and French Schools. A fine impression of the Rare Etching of "Ephraim Bonus," by Rembrandt. Engravings and Woodcuts by A. Dürer, including a fine Impression of the "Melancolia," and other Engravings by Old Masters.

May be viewed two days prior. Catalogues may be had.

ILLUMINATED AND OTHER MANUSCRIPTS AND VALUABLE OLD PRINTED BOOKS.

MESSRS. SOTHEBY, WILKINSON & HODGE will SELL by AUCTION, at their House, No. 13 Wellington Street, Strand, W.C., on TUESDAY, JULY 13, and following day, at One o'clock precisely, Illuminated and other Manuscripts and Rare and Valuable Old Printed Books, Collections of Early Engravings and Woodcuts, First Editions of Modern Authors, Works on America, Extra-Illustrated Books, Volumes of Rare Old Plays, including some First Editions by Shakespeare and his Contemporaries; many fine Illuminated Manuscript Service Books of the XIIIth, XIVth and XVth Centuries, English, Italian, Flemish and French. A Series of Separate Miniatures from Ancient Manuscripts, Speculum Christiani, printed by Machlinia; First Edition of Queen Elizabeth's Prayer Book; First Mozarabic Missal and Breviary; Contrat du Mariage de Louis de Lorraine et Francoise de Valois; A Full-length Statuette of Shakespeare, originally in the possession of the Hart Family; First Editions of Milton; Mary Farrar's (Collet) of Little Gidding Manuscripts and Bindings; Dickens's Original Letters on a Proposed Shakespeare Memorial, and many other Interesting and Valuable Items.

May be viewed two days prior. Catalogues may be had.

ENGRAVINGS.

MESSRS. SOTHEBY, WILKINSON & HODGE will SELL by AUCTION, at their House, No. 13 Wellington Street, Strand, W.C., on THURSDAY, JULY 15, and following day, at One o'clock precisely, COLLECTION of ENGRAVINGS, the Property of a Gentleman recently deceased, who lived in the West of England, comprising Portraits in Mezzotint and Stipple after Sir J. Reynolds, including an impression of "Mrs. Hardinge," by T. Watson; others by J. McArdell, J. Jones, C. H. Hodges, C. Watson, and others; Mezzotint Portraits, by J. Beckett, A. Blooteling, A. Browne, J. Faber, J. Smith, J. McArdell, R. Tompson, T. Watson, and other Early Engravers; Engravings, Etchings, &c., by Old Masters, including H. S. Beham, C. le Lorraine, A. Durer, A. Van Ostade, Rembrandt van Rhyn, C. Visscher, A. Waterloo, &c.; English and Foreign Line Portraits, by P. Drevet, R. Nanteuil, G. Edelinck, W. J. Delft, W. Faithorne, W. Hollar, A. Masson, J. Morin, and others; Modern Italian and other Line Engravings, by A. B. Desnoyers, J. T. Richomme, R. Morghen, and others; Fancy Subjects of the French School, after A. Watteau, F. Boucher, N. Lancret, J. M. Nattier, C. Vanloo, &c.; Miscellaneous Engravings, comprising Modern Etchings by C. Meryon, J. M. Whistler, and Seymour Haden; Line Engravings by W. Woollett, W. Sharp, R. Strange, and J. G. Wille; Mezzotints after Rembrandt by different engravers, some fine proofs before letters; Engravings after J. M. W. Turner; London, and other Views; Engravings after W. Hogarth, some in the first state; A collection of Reference Books on Engravings of different Schools, &c., including British Mezzotint Portraits, by J. Chaloner Smith, illustrated with 125 reproductions from original engravings; Catalogue Raisonne of the Engraved Works of Sir J. Reynolds, illustrated by the insertion of 40 portraits and other illustrations; Bryan's Dictionary of Painters and Engravers, extra-illustrated; Granger's Biographical History of England, 6 vols. in 2, extra-illustrated; and others.

May be viewed two days prior. Catalogues may be had.

THE LIBRARY OF MAJOR-GENERAL SIR M. W. E. GOSSET, K.C.B., DECEASED, WESTGATE HOUSE, DEDHAM.

MESSRS. SOTHEBY, WILKINSON & HODGE will SELL by AUCTION, at their House, No. 13 Wellington Street, Strand, W.C., on MONDAY, JULY 19, at One o'clock precisely, the LIBRARY OF MAJOR-GENERAL SIR M. W. E. GOSSET, K.C.B., deceased, Westgate House, Dedham, comprising First Editions of the Writings of Barrie, Bridges, George Eliot, Henley, Hewlett, Kipling, Meredith, Morris, Shaw, Stevenson, Swinburne, Symonds, Wilde, &c.; works on Sport and Travel Biography, History, and other properties, including a Magnificent Set of the Sporting Magazine, complete in 156 vols., in crimson calf, uncut; Annals of Sporting, 13 vols; Valuable Botanical and Ornithological Works, including Reichenbach, Icones Florae Germanicae et Helveticae; Parkinson's Paradisi in Sole, Second Edition; Fuchsius, De Historia Stirpium; Lord Lilford's Birds, Original Subscribers' copies; Dresser's Birds of Europe; Gould's Birds of Great Britain; &c.

May be viewed two days prior. Catalogues may be had.

THE CONDUIT STREET AUCTION GALLERIES.

The attention of Executors, Trustees, Solicitors, and Owners, who may be desirous of selling Works of Art, Family Jewels, Old Silver, Furniture, Pictures, Prints, Miniatures, China, Coins, Books, Old Lace, Furs, Musical Instruments, Guns, and other Valuables, is drawn to Messrs.

KNIGHT, FRANK & RUTLEY'S

AUCTION GALLERIES, 9 CONDUIT STREET, AND 23A MADDOX STREET, W., which are Open Daily to receive goods intended for early sales.

VALUATIONS are prepared for Fire Insurance, Estate Duty, and all other purposes. As to Insurance, owners are reminded that, for security, Messrs. KNIGHT, FRANK & RUTLEY'S detailed inventory and valuation of the contents of a Town or Country Mansion is an important adjunct to their Fire Insurance Policies.

THE BUDGET.

A MASS MEETING
of the
WHOLESALE and RETAIL LICENSED TRADE
To Protest Against the
Increase in Licence Duties
As proposed in the Budget,
Will be held in the
QUEEN'S HALL, LANGHAM PLACE, London
(Sole Lessees, Chappell & Co., Ltd.),
On TUESDAY, July 6, at 3 p.m.
Chairman—Alderman E. JOHNSON.

Licensed Victuallers' Central Protection Society of London (Ltd.).
Offices, 27 Russell Square, W.C ALBERT B. DEANE, Secretary.

DO YOU WRITE PLAYS?

THE INTERNATIONAL COPYRIGHT BUREAU, LTD.,
CAN BE OF SERVICE TO YOU.

We act as Agents for placing Plays, Operettas, Operas, Sketches, &c., in England and abroad on the best possible terms.
We have placed Plays with almost all leading Managers.
We copyright dramatic property and collect Author's fees.
We arrange Invitation Performances.
We review, advise upon, and remodel Plays and Musical Compositions.
We undertake Translations and Adaptations from and into all European languages.
All English Plays submitted to the Bureau are read by Mr. A. L. Ellis, so well known as a dramatic critic, and now joint director of the International Copyright Bureau. Mr. Ellis' advice and assistance are placed at our Clients' disposal.

THE INTERNATIONAL COPYRIGHT BUREAU, LTD.

ERNEST MAYER, ANTHONY L. ELLIS, } *Directors.*
DEWAR HOUSE, HAYMARKET, S.W.

The full Prospectus has been filed with the Registrar of Joint Stock Companies.

No Underwriting Commission has been or will be paid.

The Subscription List will open this day, Saturday, the 3rd July, 1909, and will close on or before Tuesday, 6th July, 1909, for Town and Country.

THE REMBIA RUBBER ESTATES, LIMITED

(Incorporated under the Companies (Consolidation) Act, 1908).

CAPITAL - - £60,000,
divided into
45,000 Six per cent. Cumulative Participating Preference Shares of £1 each,
and
15,000 Ordinary Shares of £1 each.

The Six per cent. Cumulative Participating Preference Shares are preferential both as to capital and dividend.

The profits available for distribution are to be applied:—First, in payment of a Cumulative Preferential Dividend at the rate of 6 per cent. per annum on the amounts paid up on the Preference Shares; secondly, in payment of a dividend of 6 per cent. on the Ordinary Shares, subject to which the remaining profits will be divisible amongst the holders of both the Preference and Ordinary Shares in proportion to the amount paid up on each share.

The 15,000 Ordinary Shares will be issued to the Vendors as fully paid in part satisfaction of the purchase price of the property.

Issue of 35,000 Six per cent. Cumulative Participating Preference Shares of £1 each.

Offered for Subscription at Par, payable as follows:—

2s. 6d. per share on Application,
7s. 6d. „ „ on Allotment,
2s. 6d. „ „ Two months after Allotment;

And the balance as and when required at intervals of not less than One month.

Of the total Capital 31,500 Preference Shares are available for working capital and the general purposes of the Company.

DIRECTORS.

THEODORE CHARLES OWEN, 4, Lloyd's Avenue, London, E.C., Chairman, The General Ceylon Rubber and Tea Estates, Limited (Chairman).
JOHN CORNELIUS SANDERSON, 36/37, Mincing Lane, London, E.C., Director, The East India Tea and Produce Company, Limited.
COSBY FRANCIS DEANE-DRAKE, 4, Clydesdale Mansions, London W., Director, The Cicely Rubber Estates Company, Limited.

BANKERS.

THE CAPITAL & COUNTIES BANK, LIMITED, Finsbury Circus Branch, 3, Broad Street Place, London, E.C., Head Office and Branches.
THE CHARTERED BANK OF INDIA, AUSTRALIA, AND CHINA, 32, Bishopsgate Street Within, London, E.C.

SOLICITORS.

PARKER & RICHARDSON, Friars House, New Broad Street, London, E.C.

PRODUCE BROKERS.

SANDERSON & CO., 36/37, Mincing Lane, London, E.C.

BROKERS.

BROWNING, TODD & CO., 18, Old Broad Street, London, E.C., and Stock Exchange.

AUDITOR.

FRANK DAVIES, Chartered Accountant, Moorgate Station Chambers, London, E.C.

SECRETARIES, COMMERCIAL AGENTS AND REGISTERED OFFICE.
ROWE, WHITE & CO., LIMITED, 4, Lloyd's Avenue, London, E.C.

This Company has been formed to acquire as a going concern the Rembia, Cheng, Paya Rumput, &c., Group of Estates, and to further cultivate and develop the same. They are situated in the territory of Malacca, in the Malay Peninsula.

Applications for Shares should be made on the Form accompanying the Full Prospectus, and sent to the Company's Bankers with the amount payable on application. If no allotment is made, the application money will be returned in full, and if the number of Shares allotted is less than that applied for, the surplus will be credited in reduction of the amount payable on allotment, and any balance will be returned.

Prospectuses and Forms of Application may be obtained from the Bankers, Brokers, and Solicitors, and at the Offices of the Company.

GENERAL MINING AND FINANCE CORPORATION, LIMITED.

(INCORPORATED IN THE TRANSVAAL.)

CAPITAL - - - - £1,875,000

AUTHORISED AND ISSUED.

In Shares of £1 each, of which Nos. 1 to 1000 are Founders' Shares.

DIRECTORS.

GEORGE ALBU, Chairman and Managing Director in South Africa.
LEOPOLD ALBU, Managing Director in London.
EUGEN GUTMANN.
MARTIN LUEDECK.
JACOB FREUDENTHAL.
DR. ARTHUR SALOMONSOHN.
ALBERT BLASCHKE.
REGIERUNGSRATH S. SAMUEL.

LONDON SECRETARY.
F. W. CHAMBERS.

OFFICES.

HEAD OFFICE: JOHANNESBURG, General Mining Buildings, Marshall Square, P.O. Box 1242.
BRANCHES: LONDON, Winchester House, Old Broad Street, E.C.
BERLIN, 51 Markgrafenstrasse, W., 56; PARIS, 29 Rue Taitbout.

Abridged Report of the Directors for the year ended 31st December, 1908.

ACCOUNTS.

The Working Profit for the year ended 31st December, 1908, after deducting administration expenses and depreciation of office furniture, &c., amounted to £148,347 2s. 9d., which, added to the balance of unappropriated profit brought forward from 1907 of £8,064 9s. 6d., makes a total credit to Appropriation Account of £156,411 12s. 3d. Out of this will be paid Dividend No. 4 of 5 per cent., declared April 1909, on the issued capital, and absorbing £93,750, leaving a balance of unappropriated profit (subject to sundry commissions due to certain members of the staff) carried forward to 1909 of £62,661 12s. 3d.

The usual practice has been followed of taking the Share and Stock holdings into the Balance Sheet either at cost or at the Stock Exchange making-up prices current at the date the accounts were made up, whichever is the lower. The book cost of the share investments is considerably less than the market prices at the date of the accounts, but of this unrealised profit no account has been taken, and in no case has an asset been written up. There is also a considerable appreciation in the value of mining claims above the cost at which they stand in the books.

DIVIDEND.

Out of the realised profits for the past year your Directors, on the 6th April, 1909, declared a dividend of 5 per cent. (equal to 1s. per share) on the issued capital payable to shareholders registered on the 23rd April, 1909, and absorbing £93,750.

GOLD MINING COMPANIES MANAGED BY THE CORPORATION.

The major portion of the share investments are in the nine mines under the management and control of the Corporation. These are Meyer & Charlton Gold Mining Company, Limited; Roodepoort United Main Reef Gold Mining Company, Limited; New Goch Gold Mines, Limited; Van Ryn Gold Mines Estate, Limited; Aurora West United Gold Mining Company, Limited; West Rand Consolidated Mines, Limited; New Steyn Estate Gold Mines, Limited; Rand Collieries, Limited; and Cinderella Deep, Limited.

The total issued share capitals at 31st December, 1908, of these nine Companies amounted to £4,754,424. They own properties on the Main Reef Series comprising 5,760 claims, and also freehold land 18,243 acres in extent, and coal rights over about 5,910 acres.

In reviewing the collective results obtained by the producing mines under the control of the Corporation, your Directors have pleasure in recording the entry into the list during the past twelve months of three new contributors—the Aurora West United, the Cinderella Deep, and the West Rand Consolidated Mines. As, however, these three mines only commenced crushing operations during the latter part of the year, only a partial effect of their output capacity is reflected in the results attained when taken over the whole period. In the aggregate, the seven mines (the Meyer and Charlton, New Goch, Roodepoort United, Van Ryn, Aurora West, Cinderella Deep, and West Rand Consolidated) treated 1,081,178 tons of ore, yielding gold and other revenue to the amount of £1,662,566, for a gross profit of £679,586. During the previous year the tonnage crushed was 839,107 tons, producing a total revenue of £1,427,559 and giving a gross profit of £528,744. The operations for the year under review therefore show an additional tonnage of 242,071 tons, with an increase in revenue of £235,007 and augmented profits to the extent of £150,842. At the end of the past year the total number of stamps running was 655, as compared with 460 in December 1907. The working expenditure of the Group for the year 1908 amounted to £982,980, equivalent to 18s. 2.2d. per ton crushed, as compared with £1 1s. 5d. per ton for 1907, £1 3s. 1d. for 1906, and £1 2s. 5d. for 1905. It will be seen therefore, that the steady diminution in the average working costs which has been effected in recent years has been more than maintained during the year under report, and this decrease is emphasised in a striking manner by a comparison of the comparatively low average figure of 18s. 2.2d. per ton attained for the past year with the average working cost of £1 8s. per ton for the year 1903. The payable ore reserves at 31st December, 1908, of these producing mines amounted to 3,351,000 tons of an average assay value of 7.1 dwts. over stoping width. The Meyer and Charlton declared dividends for the year equal to 60 per cent. (and a further 40 per cent. as bonuses), amounting in all to £100,000; the Van Ryn distributions aggregated 42½ per cent. for the year, absorbing £212,500, and the Roodepoort United declared 25 per cent. for the period, amounting to £73,750. The total dividends paid by these three mines since their inception amount in the aggregate to £1,985,808.

MISCELLANEOUS PROPERTIES.

Shares held by your Company in other mining, estate, financial, and miscellaneous companies are valued in the books at £74,821 3s. 2d.

MINING PROPERTIES, CLAIM HOLDINGS AND REAL ESTATE, &c.

The Corporation holds various mining properties, claims, real estate and house property, &c., standing in the Balance Sheet at £264,117 11s. 10d. They include 654½ Main Reef claims on various sections of the Witwatersrand, which on the basis of current valuations show a considerable appreciation over the price at which they stand in the books of your Corporation. The real estate and house properties are all situate in Johannesburg, and produce fair rentals.

GENERAL.

It is a source of gratification to your Directors that they are able not only to record a continued and marked improvement during the past year in the returns from the producing mines under the control of the Corporation, but also to point to the fact that the unreasonable scepticism of twelve months ago has ceased to exist and is replaced by a growing confidence in the values and potentialities of mining properties on these fields. The practical result of this more rational view is happily illustrated in the absence from the accompanying accounts of the Corporation of any depreciation of assets, and its consequent re-entry into the dividend-paying list. The incessant care which your Directors have devoted to the management of the subsidiary companies has resulted in the material reduction of working expenditure on the producing and developing mines to a highly satisfactory extent, but there is no intention of allowing that watchfulness to lessen, but rather that the success so far achieved shall act as a spur to further efforts in the direction of legitimate but economical improvements.

Johannesburg, 15th May, 1909. GEORGE ALBU, Chairman.

ABRIDGED BALANCE SHEET AT 31ST DECEMBER, 1908.

Dr.

		£ s. d.
To capital (Authorised and Issued)— As per Balance Sheet at 31st December, 1907—		
1,874,000 Shares of £1 each	£1,874,000 0 0	
1,000 Founders' Shares of £1 each ...	1,000 0 0	
		1,875,000 0 0
,, Deposits		460,228 8 3
,, Bills Payable, Creditors for Stock Bought, but not yet taken up, Sundry Creditors, and Unclaimed Dividends ...		308,567 9 6
,, House Property Redemption and Depreciation Reserve Account— As at 31st December, 1907		20,000 0 0
,, Appropriation Account— Balance from 31st December, 1907... ...	£8,064 9 6	
Profit for the year ended 31st December, 1908, as per Profit and Loss Account ...	148,347 2 9	
		156,411 12 3
,, Contingent Liability in respect of Uncalled Capital on Shares and Investments	£920 0 0	
		£2,821,207 10 0

Cr.

		£ s. d.
By Stocks and Shares (at or under Cost)—In companies under the Management of the Corporation	£1,032,180 17 8	
In other Companies	74,821 3 2	
		1,107,002 0 10
,, Debentures of Public Companies, &c.		116,428 10 8
,, Mining Properties, Claim Holdings, Real Estate and House Property in Johannesburg, and other Assets and Office Furniture		266,893 1 2
,, Advanced against Securities (including Stocks and Shares taken in), Sundry Debtors (including advances to Mining and other Companies) and Debtors for Stock Sold, but not yet delivered		1,083,397 16 8
,, Cash at Banks and in hand		247,486 1 4
		£2,821,207 10 0

PROFIT AND LOSS ACCOUNT FOR THE YEAR ENDED 31ST DECEMBER, 1908.

Dr.

	£ s. d.
To Administration Expenses in Johannesburg, London, Berlin, and Paris, including Managing Directors' Fees, Salaries of Staff and Engineering Department, Rents, Stationery, Printing, Advertising, Travelling Expenses, Cable and General Expenses, less Amounts received from other Companies	34,559 15 7
,, Directors' Fees	2,000 0 0
,, Depreciation—Office Furniture, Fixtures, Fittings, &c. ...	1,410 16 2
,, Balance, being Profit for Year, taken to Appropriation Account	148,347 2 9
	£186,317 14 6

Cr.

	£ s. d.
By Profits on Stocks and Shares Realised	121,673 4 5
By Sundry Revenue in respect of Dividends, Interest, Transfer Fees, Commissions, Rent of House Property, &c.	64,644 10 1
	£186,317 14 6

ABRIDGED PROSPECTUS.

The Lists will close for Cash Applications on or before Monday, 5th July, and for Conversion Applications on Monday, 12th July.

GOVERNMENT OF THE DOMINION OF CANADA

Issue of £6,500,000 3½% Stock,

Redeemable at par in London, 1st July, 1950, with option to the Government to redeem at par on or after 1st July, 1930, on giving six months' notice.

Interest payable 1st January and 1st July. Six months' Interest payable 1st January, 1910.

PRICE OF ISSUE, £98½ PER CENT.

Holders of the £4,295,776 outstanding 4 per cent. Reduced Bonds and Stock, maturing 1st January, 1910, can exchange for an equivalent amount of this Stock on the terms stated in the full Prospectus, and applications from such holders will receive preferential allotment.

The Government of the Dominion of Canada having complied with the requirements of the Colonial Stock Act 1900, Trustees are empowered, subject to the restrictions set forth in the Trustee Act 1893, to invest in this Stock.

The BANK OF MONTREAL, the Financial Agents of the Government of the Dominion of Canada, is authorised by the Minister of Finance to offer the above Stock for subscription at 98½ per cent. payable in respect of cash applications as follows:—

£5	per cent. on Application.	
£18 10s.	„	„ 19th July, 1909.
£35	„	„ 24th August, 1909.
£40	„	„ 23rd September, 1909.
£98 10s.		

Payment in full may be made on or after 19th July under discount at the rate of 2½ per cent. per annum.

The Loan is issued under the authority of Chapter 23 of the Statutes of Canada, 1909, to provide for the outstanding balance (£4,295,776) of the Loan maturing 1st January, 1910, and Chapter 19 of the Statutes of Canada, 1909, to provide for the advance of $10,000,000 (say, £2,054,794 10s. 5d.) to the Grand Trunk Pacific Railway Company to assist in the construction of the National Transcontinental Railway.

By an Order in Council, dated 23rd June, 1909, the Government of the Dominion of Canada has created a Cumu'ative Sinking Fund of ½ per cent. per annum in respect of this Stock, including the £8,000,000 previously issued.

Cash applications for £10 and multiples thereof should be lodged, with a deposit of £5 per cent. on the amount applied for, at the Bank of Montreal, 47 Threadneedle Street, London, E.C.

Scrip Certificates to bearer in respect of cash applications will be issued against Allotment Letters, and, when fully paid, will be exchangeable for Definitive Stock Certificates.

The Stock will be registered and transferable in any amount by deed, free of Stamp duty, at the Bank of Montreal, London, at which Bank the principal will be payable.

The Revenues of the Dominion of Canada alone are liable in respect of this Stock and the Dividends thereon, and the Consolidated Fund of the United Kingdom and the Commissioners of His Majesty's Treasury are not directly or indirectly liable or responsible for the payment of the Stock or of the Dividends thereon or for any matter relating thereto.—(*Colonial Stock Acts*, 1877 *to* 1900.)

Stock Certificates to Bearer, with coupons for the half-yearly dividends attached, will be obtainable in exchange for Registered Stock at the Bank of Montreal on payment of the prescribed fees, and such Certificates can be reregistered as Stock at the will of the holder.

Full Prospectuses and Forms of Application may be obtained from the Bank of Montreal, 47 Threadneedle Street, London, E.C., or of Messrs. R. Nivison & Co. Bank Buildings, Princes Street, London, E.C.

London: 1st July, 1909.

This Form may be used.

GOVERNMENT OF THE DOMINION OF CANADA

Issue of £6,500,000 3½ per Cent. Stock.

Price £98½ per cent.

CASH APPLICATION FORM.

To BANK OF MONTREAL,
47 Threadneedle Street, London, E.C.

GENTLEMEN,

Having paid to you the sum of £ being a deposit £5 per cent. on £ of the above Stock I/we hereby request that you will allot me/us that amount of Stock, and I/we hereby agree to accept the same or any less amount that may be allotted to me/us and to pay the further sums due on such allotment, according to the terms of your Prospectus dated 1st July 1909.

Name (in full)...
(Mr., Mrs., or Miss)

Address (in full)..

....

Date..............................July, 1909.

Cheques should be drawn to BEARER, and crossed BANK OF MONTREAL.
Applications must be for multiples of £10 Stock.

MEXICAN LIGHT AND POWER COMPANY, LIMITED.

(INCORPORATED UNDER THE LAWS OF CANADA.)

THREADNEEDLE HOUSE,
31 BISHOPSGATE STREET WITHIN, E.C.
1st July, 1909.

To the Shareholders of the
MEXICAN LIGHT AND POWER COMPANY, LIMITED.

GENTLEMEN,

In view of the exaggerated and inconsistent reports which have been circulated with reference to the extent of the accident which occurred at Necaxa in May last, the Board have deemed it desirable that I should make a short report to the Shareholders of the result of the investigation which I made on my recent visit to Mexico.

As soon as the accident occurred I proceeded to Necaxa in conjunction with Mr. James D. Schuyler, the Consulting Engineer of the Company in charge of the construction of the Company's dams.

As it is evident from the rumours which have been circulated that an entire misconception exists regarding the accident, as well as the extent to which the dam at Necaxa is essential to the operation of the Company's business, it will not be out of place to shortly outline the hydraulic development of the Company.

The capacity of the Power Station is at present 48,000 H.P., but the enlargement of the station is now under construction, and by the 1st January next it will have a capacity of 64,000 H.P., and by July 1st, 1910, the present works will be completed, when the Company will have a Power Station with a capacity of 96,000 H.P.

The reservoir system, when completed, will consist of six large reservoirs, with a capacity of about 192,000,000 cubic metres of water, which will be sufficient to store the flood waters during the rainy season, and provide more than the supply of water necessary during the dry season for the operation of the Company's Power Station to its full and enlarged capacity above mentioned.

The business of the Company has increased so rapidly that it has not been possible during construction to keep pace with the demands for power, and, in consequence, the Company has been obliged to operate partly by steam plant during each dry season to make up for the water deficiency, and this was done during the last dry season which has just ended. I am of opinion, however, that there will be no necessity to operate the steam plant in the future, as two large reservoirs have now been completed and can be used to store water to their full capacity during the present rainy season. The capacity of the two reservoirs referred to is approximately 68,000,000 cubic metres, which alone will be sufficient t provide all the water necessary for the Company's operation during the next dry season. Before the dry season of 1911 all the reservoirs now under construction should be completed, and ther will then be sufficient water stored to operate the power station to its full capacity under any condition of load in the driest season

The dam at Necaxa by which the third reservoir is formed and which is under construction, is the one to which the acciden happened in May last. This accident consisted of a slide, into th reservoir on the up-stream side of the dam, of earth and rock which had recently been sluiced into the dam and had not solidified As the slide occurred at the top of the dam it did not affect th lower portions, which are intact; nor did it affect the down-strea side of the dam, which remains in first-class condition, and whic is proved by the accident to be capable of resisting all the wate pressure to which it can be subject when the reservoir is full. T repair the damage it will only be necessary to replace the materi which has slid out. All the pumps, flumes, and other apparatus used in the construction of the dam, were uninjured by the slid and, consequently, the only expense in connection with the replacement is the actual cost of labour in handling the material, an this can be accurately estimated from the cost of doing thi character of work during the past two years. On this basis th cost of the replacement should amount to approximately £40,00 making the total cost of the dam about £368,000 instead o £328,000 as originally estimated. The accident will only dela the completion of the dam by about six months. At the presen time, in spite of the accident, the reservoir formed by the da can store 15,000,000 cubic metres of water, which is as much, in a probability, as would have been stored during this rainy seaso in any event. The accident has not affected the actual operatio of the power house, except for a short time when the slide occurred nor has it affected the supply of power to any of the customers o the Company. The earth filling, which has been in place for som time at the dams which are already completed, has solidified satisfactorily, and no anxiety need be felt as to permanency of thes dams or the dams under construction.

As a result of my recent visit to Mexico, I can assure all Shareholders that the Company's business is in a sound and flourishin condition, and that the accident will not adversely affect the presen or future earnings of the Company. I am also glad to be abl to state that the relations existing between the Company's official and its customers and the Government are most satisfactory an harmonious.

Yours faithfully,

For MEXICAN LIGHT & POWER COMPANY, LIMITED

F. S. PEARSON,
President.

MARCONI WIRELESS TELEGRAPH.

The Twelfth Ordinary General Meeting of Marconi's Wireless Telegraph Company, Ltd., was held on Monday at River Plate House, Mr. G. Marconi (Chairman and Managing Director) presiding. The Chairman, in proposing the adoption of the report and balance-sheet, said that he was occupying the position of Chairman in consequence of the resignation, through ill-health, of Sir Charles Euan-Smith, whose valuable services to the Company were warmly appreciated. In regard to the report he had not much to add except that since it was issued the position of the Company continued rapidly to improve. Important orders for stations and plant had been received from the Portuguese and Greek Governments, and he was glad to be able to say that the value of orders in hand amounted to over £100,000, with every prospect of a very substantial increase in the immediate future. The Transatlantic station at Clifden in Ireland had been completed, and though there had been delay through the failure of certain manufacturers to deliver, the plant had in every way come up to his expectations in regard to efficiency. In regard to the corresponding station at Glace Bay the machinery was now on the way to Canada, and he did not expect that more than a month would be required for its efficient erection. The limited service across the Atlantic which had now been established for over 18 months had continued to give satisfaction to its principal users, but the service, although exceedingly useful to the Company, had been very difficult to maintain efficiently, while additions and alterations were being constantly carried out at the terminal stations. No doubt a very great extension of the Transatlantic service might be anticipated as soon as the complete duplication of the station in Canada had taken place, which would enable the Company to accept from 15,000 to 20,000 words per day for transmission across the Atlantic between Clifden and Glace Bay. The board expected about the end of August to be in a position to invite the Post Office to give effect to their agreement with the Postmaster-General relative to the acceptance and delivery of the Company's Transatlantic messages at all the Government telegraph offices throughout the United Kingdom. A considerable addition had been made to the number of ships carrying the Marconi system. He thought this was an eloquent proof that even under what certain foreign Governments or their representatives called conditions of open competition, the system controlled by the Company had been able more than to hold its own against other systems, even although the latter were powerfully assisted by Governments which considered their development a question of national and political importance. The assistance rendered by the Company's organisation of wireless telegraphy to the steamship "Slavonia" was still fresh in the memories of all. The two assisting ships, the "Princess Irene," of the North-German Lloyd, and the "Batavia," of the Hamburg-American line, were among the vessels fitted with the Marconi system shortly after the accident to the White Star liner "Republic" in the North Atlantic on January 23 last, on which occasion also the efficiency of wireless telegraphy, as worked by the Company's employée, was fully demonstrated. It should be gratifying to the shareholders to know that wireless telegraphy was beginning to be considered every day more and more by the Press and the general public as likely to afford the most efficient and economical method for satisfactory telegraphic communication between the distant parts of the British Empire. After quoting from the leading article in the "Times" of the 26th ult. and referring to the resolution which was passed at the meeting of the Imperial Press Conference last Friday (urging upon the Governments concerned "the desirability of establishing a chain of wireless telegraph stations between all British countries"), he said that the stations of his systems erected by the Italian Government on the Somaliland coast in East Africa had now been completed and were working satisfactorily. Since the last meeting arrangements had been made on satisfactory terms with the Meteorological Offices in London and Hamburg for the supply of weather reports from vessels crossing the Atlantic. The Company's relations with his Majesty's Government were now on a most satisfactory basis. While the complete financial success of the Company was dependent on the full and efficient working of the Transatlantic stations, a very large measure of success could now be obtained by the execution of orders in hand, which were coming in from all parts of the world. In regard to the balance-sheet, the board had every reason to be satisfied with the position of the Company and with the amount of work which had been carried out during the time under review. The Directors, after careful consideration and with the approval of the Auditors, agreed that it would be unnecessary and inadvisable, if not misleading, to present a profit and loss account with the balance-sheet for the period ended December 31, 1908, for the reason stated by the Chairman at the last annual general meeting —namely, that, pending the completion of the long-distance stations, it would be a matter of considerable difficulty to prepare a reliable profit and loss account, on which point there would be a considerable difference of opinion as to the proper amount to be capitalised. In conclusion, he had pleasure in announcing that Mr. Hammersley Heenan (of Messrs. Heenan and Froude, engineers, Manchester and Worcester), Mr. Frederick Whowell (Managing Director of the Bleachers' Association, Manchester), and Captain Henry R. Sankey (late of Messrs. Willans and Robinson) had joined the board. After warmly recognising the services of the staff, he concluded by moving the adoption of the report. Colonel Sir C. Euan-Smith seconded the motion, after which Mr. Heenan and Mr. Whowell addressed the meeting.

A vote of thanks to the Chairman concluded the proceedings.

BOOTS CASH CHEMISTS (EASTERN).

The Seventeenth Ordinary General Meeting of shareholders of Boots Cash Chemists (Eastern), Limited, was held on Wednesday at the St. Pancras Hotel, under the presidency of Mr. Jesse Boot (the Chairman and Managing Director of the Company).

The Chairman said: Gentlemen,—Our annual meeting is held rather later than usual this year. The fact is, I could not very well get back earlier from a prolonged trip I have been making abroad, and after being at every meeting since the formation of the Company I felt that I must, if possible, be present—hence the delay. I am pleased to say there is no remarkable feature about our accounts. You will see from the figures we have earned slightly more than last year. Taking into account the depression in trade that has prevailed in most of the districts where our eastern depots are situated, I think we may congratulate ourselves upon being able to pay our usual dividend. That we are able to do so is, in part, owing to the fact that many of the businesses belonging to the Company are old-established, and so well in favour with the public that any little competition we get seems to benefit the business rather than otherwise. A number of our premises are held on long leaseholds at reasonable rents, and a good proportion of the most important are our own freeholds, therefore free from any exorbitant rises in rent. The splendid up-to-date character of our premises has been a prominent feature in the business. We wish to continue this policy, as its success has fully justified the expenditure, and in the present balance-sheet you will notice that we have taken £1,000 from the profits for renewals and displacements. One event—which, however, does not affect our Company alone, though we played a leading part in it—and an event which might be considered historical in the history of the retail drug trade, was the passing of the Poisons and Pharmacy Act at the close of the last Session of Parliament. I am not going to inflict upon you a history of our twenty years' contest for the right to trade as chemists and druggists, but merely say that we are now on a friendly footing with the pharmaceutical authorities, who are the regulating body in everything that respects the technical part of the business—that we retain our signs, our house-flag, so to speak, under which we compete for our business, the well-known name of Boots Cash Chemists, not a mere Boots drug stores; and last, but not least, we have established a better status for qualified chemists, of whom we have over 500 in our associated companies, and whom I regard as the finest staff of educated and diplomaed men connected with the chemist's business in the country. With these few remarks I commend the adoption of the report to you with confidence, and now formally propose: "That the accounts be received, and that the distribution of the profits as recommended in the Directors' report be and is hereby adopted."

Sir James Duckworth, M.P., seconded the resolution, which was unanimously adopted.

A vote of thanks to the Chairman, Mr. Boot, and the staff was proposed by Sir James Duckworth, M.P., seconded by Mr. Batty Langley, and unanimously agreed to.

The Chairman having acknowledged the compliment, the proceedings terminated.

NOTICE.

The Terms of Subscription to the SATURDAY REVIEW are:—

	United Kingdom.	Abroad.
	£ s. d.	£ s. d.
One Year ...	1 8 2	1 10 4
Half Year ...	0 14 1	0 15 2
Quarter Year	0 7 1	0 7 7

Cheques and Money Orders should be crossed and made payable to the Manager, SATURDAY REVIEW Offices, 10 King Street, Covent Garden, London, W.C.

In the event of any difficulty being experienced in obtaining the SATURDAY REVIEW, the Publisher would be glad to be informed immediately.

Printed for the Proprietors by SPOTTISWOODE & Co. LTD., 5 New-street Square, E.C., and Published by REGINALD WEBSTER PAGE, at the Office, 10 King Street, Covent Garden, in the Parish of St. Paul, in the County of London.—*Saturday*, 3 *July*, 1909.

THE

SATURDAY REVIEW

OF

POLITICS, LITERATURE, SCIENCE, AND ART.

CONTENTS.

NOTES OF THE WEEK.

To the horror of Mr. Byles and others the Government has made one or two concessions to the Opposition this week. Mr. Lloyd George has promised to consider the question of appeals against the valuations of the Inland Revenue Commissioners. This is a most important point, and we note the alarm of Mr. Wedgwood lest the landowners should go to the judges of the High Court and get protection there from his ideal Treasury. There are some folks who talk at least as if they would like to deprive the landowners even of habeas corpus. For the old idea that a man should be tried by his peers, we suppose Mr. Wedgwood would try him by the Treasury officials. But, happily, there are Liberals who see the thing in a very different light. Mr. Buckmaster's speech on Tuesday must be valued by all who care for the liberty of the subject. It is significant that the real despots should be discovered in a little group below the Ministerial gangway.

Is the increment tax a tax on the increment or a tax on the holder of the land? This conundrum was put to the House on Monday by Mr. Warner. There seems no end to the debating ability on the Government side, and it is to be hoped Mr. Warner of Lichfield will enrich many of these Budget discussions. Lichfield has had its famous man of letters and its famous swan: it may now boast a famous political economist. According to Mr. Warner, the buyer or owner of land likely to grow in value through the growth of towns and population is "very much the same sort" of speculator as the backer of a horse or as he who deals in "gambling counters". It follows—if we have disentangled Mr. Warner's logic rightly—that the increment tax is not a tax on the person at all but on the commodity; though Heaven knows why it follows.

If the man who puts five hundred pounds into a plot of suburban land on the chance of its rising in value is a gambler, so obviously is the man who puts five hundred into a grocery or undertaker's business in a promising suburb on the chance of its rising in value. We always thought Suburbia a very dull place, but most respectable and virtuous. Radical reasoners have thrown an entirely new light on the borderlands of cities. If we are to take Mr. Warner seriously, these places are as wicked as any racecourse, very hotbeds indeed for gamblers. There was an old theory—to which Lord Robert Cecil referred the other day—that all property is simple theft. Property in the suburbs has, it seems, the added vice of gambling.

Mr. Warner was not the only signal addition to Budget debaters this week. Mr. Masterman's speech on an amendment by Mr. Pretyman on Wednesday was quite arresting. True, he did not try to give the answer to his riddle "What is the community?" but we may find this interesting and curious point in his speech: If the land of a small owner benefits through the exertions and improvements of a neighbouring large owner, the increment should go—not to the small owner, not to the large owner, it should go to the community. The community has not earned it; but never mind—this is a clear case of unearned increment so far as the small owner goes: therefore let us take the lot in the name of the community!

Observe—the energetic and enterprising man who has "earned" the whole of his neighbour's increment by building the esplanade, or whatever the improvement be, is not to have a farthing of the loot. The community is to get its bit, and we suppose the local authority—if the dividing-up ever takes place—will get its bit. These are delightful ethics.

Not everybody who talks like General Harbottle is really a Harbottle. Mealy mouths sometimes go with hard hearts—could one but read them—or the reverse. We must know our man before we judge him by his words. Mr. Harold Cox's friends were a little staggered when they found him described in the "Times" of Wednesday as "robust". Were we asked to name a tree which Mr. Cox resembled, we would as soon name a willow as an oak. Leader writers who want the right epithet to hit off a man they know not should consult the descriptive writers at Westminster.

In the old days a Prime Minister was early and late on the scene when a great Government Bill was being hotly debated in Parliament. Peel, Gladstone, Disraeli kept this law. Palmerston kept it; and we remember a Father of the House telling us years ago how that great Minister would sit hour after hour on the front bench, following every word of the debate. Mr. Asquith is severely amending this rule—which, we are bound to say, has been somewhat amended by one or two other Prime Ministers of late years. On Tuesday Mr. Asquith strolled in towards midnight by way of change: he had not been in the House at all on Monday night. He explained his rule of conduct to the House: After long experience he has decided that it is a waste of time, is inconvenient and leads to general misunderstanding, for a Minister to intervene spasmodically "in technical and complex discussions".

So when anything technical and complex crops up in the chief Bill of the session, in the chief Bill of the Parliament, the leader of the House should get out of the House as fast as he can. (By the way, was Glasgow distress technical?) It saves time and temper. It is convenient. By hurrying away and keeping away he will spare the House general misunderstandings. It sounds quite plausible and pleasant, but where is the line to be drawn? Who will stay on the front bench—till four in the morning—when staying and "spasmodically intervening" leads to waste of time, general inconvenience? In the end it may come to this: only an Attorney- or Solicitor-General will stay, and he will confound the confusion of the Committee. Prime Ministers will enjoy longer life and better health, and there will be more elbow-room on Government benches. But may not the public vote the thing a bigger farce than ever?

Mr. Asquith's speech at Southport has brought an old, not-much-heard word into currency. "Windfall" will take the place of "efficiency", now obsolete; and it will be used till everybody gets tired of it. Since then we have heard nothing but "windfall", and the "Daily Chronicle" has promptly started a column of "Windfalls". Mr. Asquith constructs elaborate sentences, but not happily expressive words or phrases. His style is Gladstone's, not Beaconsfield's. He has not invented "windfall", he has only popularised it. Professor Pigou is the inventor of it. In a letter he told the "Times" that the Budget does not tax land but "windfalls". Mr. Asquith pounced on the word like a capitalist on a poor inventor and brings it into popular use.

Has it occurred to Professor Pigou that professors and other professional men get "windfalls" too? If there were a tax in addition to the income tax, when a professor exchanges a poor chair for one better paid, this would not be taxing professorships, would it? No; only "windfalls". Or if a clergyman is appointed to a better living, that, too, would be a tax on a "windfall", and not on livings. Professor Pigou has thought of a new word, but not a new argument, for the Budget. It does not lessen any such dangers as he himself points out. An estate, he says, owing to differences of nominal money prices, might have to pay on £20,000 when it was only worth £10,000. He even states that the portentous system of index numbers, which nobody, unless it is a political economy professor, understands, would have to be adopted.

The Irish Land Bill is now in Committee. Some of its curiosities are worth mentioning. For instance, at this moment "the boys" and their newspapers keep Ireland in complete ignorance that the £1,000,000 promised for congestion is to be taken from the cash available for ordinary land purchase, leaving that source a fifth less, though it is already exactly a third too little for the recent rate of buying and selling. Another curiosity is the provision for compulsory sale, without any compulsion on the buyer to buy—and without any hope that the League will allow the Congests to come on to the land when it is compulsorily sold for them!

Mr. John Redmond has attributed "infamous falsehood" to Sir Horace Plunkett. It is going all over Ireland now, and the political "hooligans" will be expected to denounce the economic movement, which becomes an increasing danger to "the Cause". Mr. Redmond's charge against Sir Horace is based on a statement attributed to him which he never made. The statement appeared in the "Morning Post" interview, but by the interviewer, and clearly marked off as such from all the statements by Sir Horace.

A quartette of bye-elections. Four Liberal seats strongly held are being strenuously attacked, and the Government would be the happier no doubt if victory could be "forecasted"—the word belongs to Mr. Lloyd George and the "Times" Literary Supplement—with confidence. Unionist readiness and energy in Yorkshire, in Derbyshire, and in Dumfries have been a little disconcerting to the Radicals. Of course the Budget is much in evidence. Tariff Reform is well to the front as the Unionist alternative, and Mr. Samuel thought it necessary to bribe the miners of the Cleveland division with promises of amendment to the Eight Hours Act, which has given rise to numerous grievances. In Dumfries the American tariff has been severely felt, so that the Unionist candidate will find support among the woollen workers, and in Mid-Derby Mr. Creswell has scored a point at the very outset by his attitude on the question of religious teaching.

Lord Portsmouth's interrogation on Wednesday of the Under-Secretary for War as to the value of the Territorial Army was amusing. Until Mr. Asquith's accession to the Premiership Lord Portsmouth was the representative of the War Office in the Lords. But now that he is free from Haldane influences he has apparently been converted by Lord Roberts and his adherents. He asks two very pertinent questions. Is the Territorial Force intended to be able to meet an invasion in the absence of the striking force; and how is it anticipated they will shape, if opposed man to man by continental regular troops? He also pointed out that according to the best expert opinion a serious invasion was not only possible but was within the region of probability.

Lord Lucas, his successor in the Under-Secretaryship, very truly stated that it was difficult to answer his questions. Indeed it would have taxed even Mr. Haldane's ingenuity to frame a convincing reply. We, like many other critics of the Territorial scheme, have pointed out over and over again that the inherent weakness of the whole affair was the supposition that an enemy would kindly allow us a six months' period of grace wherein to organise the Territorial Army for its primary function of taking the field against a highly trained invader. Lord Lucas frankly admitted so much. Consequently the whole scheme is a sham. Next Monday, when Lord Roberts' Bill for compulsory national service comes up for discussion, the matter will be threshed out.

The naval manœuvres have served to show how wrong Lord Charles Beresford was as to battleships and how right as to small craft. Lord Charles Beresford belongs to the school which contends that the larger vessels are far too valuable both as regards fighting capacity, size of crews and coal expenditure to detach from a fleet for the work of scouting, for thus they are not only liable to be absent on the day of battle, but may be captured altogether. The loss of a small cruiser of 4500 tons is relatively trifling. As to the manœuvres, it is perfectly evident that owing to scarcity of cruisers there was a great waste of armoured fighting force, so that when battle was joined last Saturday both fleets were in a depleted condition, though the manœuvres had lasted only three days. The manœuvres illustrate the immense importance of Togo tactics in keeping the armoured force intact and using unimportant small craft for scouting.

As we anticipated, the Little Navy party have quite ignored this side of Lord Charles Beresford's case, on which of course he is an authority as a tactician, and have, like Mr. Robert Harcourt M.P., concentrated on the strategical-political side, where Lord Charles Beresford is content in a war with Germany alone with sixty-six battleships to forty-one, or twenty-six Dreadnoughts to twenty-one, in March 1914. As the figures become sixty-six to seventy-five and twenty-six Dreadnoughts to thirty-three if we take in the United States as well, it is clear, both from political and strategical standpoints, without allowing for German acceleration, the Beresford programme is inadequate. The two-keels-to-one policy will give us thirty-six Dreadnoughts in March 1914 and seventy-six battleships and Invincibles, which is a far more satisfactory result.

Nothing of any particular importance came out at the inquests on Sir W. H. Curzon Wyllie and Dr. Lalcaca. What had happened was all too plain from the evidence of eye-witnesses, and the jury quickly returned verdicts of wilful murder. Several interesting details were given. One was why Dhingra failed to shoot himself. Dhingra in the hurry and the awkward position of pointing a revolver at his own head could not bring the necessary pressure to bear, though he was a practised revolver shot. The same thing happened with one of the Tottenham murderers, as it has also in many other cases. Another suggestion, that Dhingra had previously taken bhang, appears not unlikely to those who know India. For the murderer's purpose of blunting his sensibilities without depriving him of coolness it is a more subtle drug than alcohol.

There is something like panic in the eagerness with which the community of Indians resident here hasten to join in public expression of horror and indignation at the crime of their fellow-countryman. They need not fear that the innocent individually will suffer for the guilty. Men like H.H. Agha Khan, Sir M. Bhownaggree, and many another do not need to protest. Neither can they expect that a body which contains persons of different degrees of loyalty or disloyalty can be accepted by the standard of the highest or acquitted collectively because it includes some who are innocent of all offence. If the resident Indian community wishes to dissociate itself collectively from all connexion with such deeds, it must begin by open repudiation of those of its own members whose acts, speeches or writings have been directly or indirectly an encouragement to violence or sedition.

The Persian revolutionaries, or nationalists, or whatever they are, have overreached themselves. Russia has had to intervene again to save both Shah and Europeans in Teheran and other cities, and, as Sir Edward Grey says, the situation is one of confusion and suspense. Not satisfied with the withdrawal of Russia from Tabriz in loyal conformity with her undertaking, the malcontents insisted that every foreign element in the Shah's service should be abolished. In other words, they wished to be free to deal with him on their own terms, and to hold every foreign interest at their mercy. The result is that Russian forces are returning in hot haste, and the Nationalists realise that the game is up. Russia is acting with British approval; and if she stays this time longer than the Persians like, the responsibility must be shared by the Shah who cannot maintain order, and the Nationalists who demand the impossible.

The man Burzeff, who got M. Loupoukhin into trouble in the Azeff affair, has denounced to the French Government M. Harting, who has been the head of the Russian secret police in Paris, as an anarchist. He declares that M. Harting is one Landesen, who was the ringleader of the conspiracy to murder Alexander III. on his visit to Paris in 1890. Landesen was not arrested, and under the name of Harting he entered the Russian secret police. The story is not believed in Paris, and it is supposed that Burzeff has concocted it now to discredit the Russian police when the Tsar visits the President at Cherbourg, as he is afraid of being expelled. M. Harting is a general in the Russian army and is an officer of the Legion of Honour. M. Clemenceau has ordered an official inquiry into an incredible story which, if it were true, would be the most extraordinary case on record of poacher turned gamekeeper.

From the accounts of the interviews and speeches in French papers of the members of the Douma, who have just left us, we fear they have not been so discreet in France as they were over here. M. Homiakoff and M. Guchkoff have both shown that a good deal of the pleasure of their visit depends on the belief that warmth towards the Russian delegates means coolness towards Germany. The intended visit to France will be used with the same idea. They dwell on the popular resentment in Russia at Germany's action in the Bosnia question. We doubt whether in such circumstances inter-parliamentary visits make for peace.

It is announced that the Labour Party have got leave to demonstrate against the Tsar in Trafalgar Square on Sunday, 25 July. This seems contemptibly feeble in the Government. Sir Edward Grey suppressed the objecting Labour members with little ceremony in the House, and now the Government allow them to insult the Tsar publicly in Trafalgar Square just before his arrival in England. It is hardly decent. The Government are much more to be blamed than the Labour Party, most of whom do not know any better. They know nothing about the Tsar or about Russia. We can hardly believe that Mr. Bernard Shaw, though announced, is going to be one of the performers in this company. No man knows better than he that British indignation at Russian policy, especially in social questions, is either ignorance or hypocrisy.

Government servants have always had the privilege of snubbing the general public. Post Office clerks, especially the ladies, at one time seemed inclined to abuse the privilege. We believe there has been an improvement, and there is less of the aggravating indifference and condescension, youthful and more often feminine, which the Postmaster-General still mildly reproves in his little lecture on "Civility at the Public Counter". Maybe the girl behind the post-office counter might have something to say on the manners of the public she serves. The woman customer and the woman clerk intensely dislike each other, and complaints come more from women than from men. Shopgirls dare not show their annoyance as freely as women postal clerks dare, though they have much worse provocation.

We feel pretty sure the Government is not to be blamed for the meanness of granting £25 a year to the grandchildren of Charles Dickens. Many harsh words must be spoken in party spirit; it must always be the custom in a country where government by party exists; but we believe that the leading men in the Government would be generous, not mean, in dealing with a case like this. The whole Civil List is paltry enough—a scrap or a pittance to authors who spend their health and heart in writing books that are to the public good; or a scrap of a still minuter pittance perhaps here and there to the widows and children of these workers in the barren fields of literature! The Civil List in its meagreness is a disgrace to this great and wealthy country.

Fancy the contempt that Civil servants must have for it! They, at any rate, do get respectable pensions for their work. They, at any rate, do get such pay as enables them to carry on their public work. But there are hundreds of writers of good, unremunerative books who serve the public well if anybody in the world serves it so. Surely the State should recognise their work and worth, and help them, seriously help them to live—and die—in moderate comfort. The Civil List might be large enough for some country like Switzerland or Finland. It is grotesque when applied to literature and learning in this country.

Lord Curzon's speech on the opening of the new science buildings of S. Paul's School on Wednesday was most happy. It is no small thing for a speaker to be felicitous under rain; but rain could not damp the zest with which Lord Curzon was listened to. He seemed himself to be in good spirits, which perhaps stimulated his ridicule of modern English pessimism. He may be quite right in suggesting that this self-depreciation, which is now writ large in our newspapers, has a good deal of cant in it. Certainly to be dejected because we lose a cricket match or two or a boatrace is childish, but there is very little harm in a chastened mood. We are more likely to suffer by over-rating ourselves than by self-belittlement. That is not at all the Anglo-Saxon way.

Especially in education are we now questioning ourselves and our ways. Yet, Lord Curzon pointed out, foreign countries are sending over here to find out our ways. What is the secret, they want to know, of our public school and University life? Whence its influence on character? Certainly they will hardly find outside of this country any parallel to S. Paul's School. A day-school that with perhaps greater intellectuality combines the dominant characteristics of the social life of the great public boarding-school is a wonderful growth. The outcome of the New Learning, on the whole the noblest reform movement in history, S. Paul's School has not fallen below its birth. Lord Curzon rightly, indeed, put in the forefront of his speech a graceful allusion to Mr. F. W. Walker, the famous High Master, perhaps the greatest schoolmaster of the day. If S. Paul's School can keep up to the standard of its recent past it will do well enough. We could wish it nothing better on its quatercentenary.

Lake Champlain and Ticonderoga are names of picturesque significance in the story of American discovery and the hundred and fifty years' struggle for empire between France and England. The lake was the first link unconsciously forged in the great chain by which France ultimately hoped to hem in the English settlements between the Alleghanies and the sea; it was the initial step in exploration, after the occupation of Quebec, which led the French under men like La Salle from Canada to Louisiana. At Ticonderoga Montcalm routed Abercromby, and, but for Amherst and Wolfe and British sea power, might have overrun New England. The tercentenary celebrations this week have been the excuse for an outburst of rhetoric. Mr. Root surpassed himself, exclaiming that only Britons and French had the audacious courage needed for expansion across the Atlantic. The Spaniards never got to America, did they?

Miss Lind-af-Hageby's anti-vivisection procession to Hyde Park is a striking demonstration. It discovers her movement in the true light. This vulgar sensationalism, these methods of electioneering claptrap, would not be needed if there were any reality in these people's humanitarian claims. Apparently in desperation they are now turning to ignorant prejudice for sympathy. It is well the police have stopped the exhibition of some of their offensive banners. Kindness to animals does not need this sort of advocacy. Sane anti-vivisectionists should hasten to repudiate Miss Lind-af-Hageby's methods. Really the public has to put up with too much from hysterical women and their street nuisances in these days.

THE TRAP TO CATCH THE LORDS.

THE broad lines of the Finance Act, its unjust and unworkable land taxes, its crushing death duties, and its ruinous proposals to extinguish the liquor trade, are now familiar to the public. Its details are being laboriously threshed out, in the teeth of overwhelming odds and under the pitiless application of the closure, by the Unionist party in the House of Commons. The technical points raised in Committee are too difficult for the man in the street to follow: but everyone who has anything to lose is deeply indebted to every member of the present Opposition and to Mr. Harold Cox—and Mr. Buckmaster—for their conduct in Parliament. While, however, the financial proposals of the Government are being one by one stripped of justification, the hidden and deeper side of the Budget is still concealed from the attention of the country. The Budget is in reality a political conspiracy, a premeditated and carefully prepared design to destroy the power of the second chamber to amend or reject the Bills of the first chamber. Indeed, it has been admitted to be so by the Prime Minister, and we are astonished that Mr. Asquith's speech about the use of finance as a weapon to solve constitutional problems has not been made greater use of by the leaders of the Opposition. Every member of the House of Commons is now perfectly aware that the question has resolved itself into one of political manœuvring—how to manœuvre the House of Lords into a false or dangerous position, and then to appeal to the masses against the Constitution. This is an exciting game for the players we only wish the stakes were not other people's money The Government and their supporters believe that i they can only get the House of Lords to amend th Finance Act by deleting the clauses relating to th taxation of land, or to reject it on the ground that thes clauses ought to be embodied in a separate Bill, th Lords will be caught in a trap, as then the Radical can say to the electors, You see, the peers only car about their own dirty acres!

The trap is cunningly laid, and can only be avoide by courage on the part of the House of Lords, courag based on confidence in the justice and common-sens of the nation. The Lords should in the first plac clearly and unequivocally state that though they hav waived they have never renounced their constitution right to amend as well as to reject every Bill sent u to them by the House of Commons. "Autres temp autres mœurs"; and the statements made by Lo Salisbury and Mr. Balfour about the interference of th Lords with Finance Bills ought not to be binding in fa of a revolutionary conspiracy to mine the Constitutic and to redistribute property upon socialistic principle Having explicitly and boldly asserted their constit tional position, whether the Lords should amend reject the Finance Bill must be a matter of strateg and Lord Lansdowne must show that he can manœuv as well as Mr. Lloyd George. But of one thing we a quite sure, that whether amendment or rejection decided on, the grounds for the action of the House Lords should not be the clauses relating to the taxati of land alone. The small class which pays income t has, unwisely and indeed cruelly in our judgment, co to be regarded as fair game for every tax-huntin Chancellor of the Exchequer, and nothing will, suppose, be done for the reputed rich. But the Unioni party is bound, by expediency and justice, to protect t brewers and their shareholders and their tenants, well as the consuming public, from the bankrupt which would follow the imposition of anything like t proposed licence duties. Nor ought the death duti (really the most serious tax of all) to be excluded fro the purview of the revising chamber. To sum up, t opposition of the House of Lords should be to the la taxes, the licence duties, and the death duties, not the land taxes alone. We do not underrate the pra tical inconvenience of amending or rejecting the Budg in the late autumn: it will be very great. But t inconvenience will be the fault of the Government, n of the House of Lords. You cannot defeat a revol tion without inconvenience, any more than you can make an omelette without breaking eggs.

Here is a sketch of what may take place in the next few months, according to some who are not ill informed. The House of Lords will refuse to read the Finance Act a second time for reasons which will be elaborately set forth. A conference of the two Houses of Parliament will be held at which the points of difference will be discussed. The Finance Act amended to meet in some respects the Lords' objections will be sent up to the second chamber, and presumably passed by them. The Government will then remain in for the session of 1910 and go to the country at the beginning of 1911. This forecast squares with the often-declared Radical intention not to allow the Lords to dictate a dissolution. The concessions of the Government would be based on the great practical inconvenience of not carrying the Budget, and as a set-off to the triumph of the Lords the Government would obtain a fresh lease of life and a new grievance against the peers. According to another theory, Mr. Lloyd George may wish to risk a dissolution in order to get rid of his pledge about Welsh disestablishment. The Chancellor of the Exchequer has been forced by the Welsh members, much against his will, to promise that the next session shall be devoted to the Bill for disestablishing the Church in Wales, and the Prime Minister has endorsed the pledge. No one knows better than Mr. Lloyd George that the fifth session devoted to Welsh disestablishment would be very bad electioneering business. There is no enthusiasm for disestablishment, even amongst the Radicals, and the Lords would throw out the Bill. It would therefore be a session wasted on an unpopular subject merely to please the Welsh members, between whom and the Chancellor of the Exchequer there is little love lost. Mr. Lloyd George and Mr. Winston Churchill, who dominate the Cabinet, may think the time has come to disembarrass themselves of Mr. Asquith, Sir Edward Grey, and Mr. Haldane, and for that object a few years in Opposition would be the very thing. These conjectures as to the future course of politics during the next few weeks may be moonshine, but the people who make them are better informed than the leader-writers of the "Times". Nothing is more absurd than the airy omniscience with which the "Times" lectures and dogmatises and dismisses everything but its own opinion as "nonsense". The directors and leader-writers of the "Times" know just as little and just as much what is going to happen as any other interested and ordinarily well-informed person. Nobody knows what course Lord Lansdowne is going to take, for the excellent reason that Lord Lansdowne cannot know either. Nobody knows what line the peers as a body may take, for the same reason. The House of Lords is composed of independent English gentlemen who see, or believe that they see, in the Finance Act not only their own destruction but the sacrifice to the socialists of all that makes England a great country—its social, political and commercial interests. Possessed by this conviction—the sound instinct of a class trained by centuries of government—who shall say what view of their duty may be taken by the peers? We know that there is a growing feeling among a not inconsiderable number of peers that if they pass this Budget, it would be far better to abolish the House of Lords and replace it by an elective Senate on the model of the United States. Democracy would certainly not gain by that change, as American politicians who have been "up against" their Senate could tell us. But for the scribes of Fleet Street to lecture the Lords on their duty is a piece of fatuity of which the silliness is only surpassed by the presumption. Undoubtedly the event will be greatly influenced by such bye-elections as may take place between now and October.

TROUBLE IN EGYPT.

WE fear that there is trouble brewing in Egypt, and trouble due not to outside intrigue or interference but to the mistakes of our own administrators. A good deal of apprehension was excited at one time by the idea that the Young Turks might encourage the so-called Nationalist party, but, to do them justice, they took a very different line when they were asked to support Egyptian aspirations. The Nationalists were told that they had an excellent government and should be thankful. Neither have the agitations in Morocco or the missionaries of Pan-Islamism anything to answer for in the development of difficulties which threaten to become serious. Whatever may come out of the existing muddle, we shall have no one but our own officials to thank for it. The home Government, which may be at the present moment insufficiently informed, will do well to take steps betimes to avert worse trouble than that which already exists and to remedy the evils that have grown up in the last two years.

It is quite true that these evils have not altogether originated since Lord Cromer's departure. In fact he himself indicated some of them in his valedictory report. He pointed out that respect for the law was dwindling, though the contrary result might have been expected from the definite establishment of a strong and just government. Unfortunately this evil has grown and strengthened under the present régime, and if the latest statistics as to undiscovered criminals and unpunished crime (often murder) were published they would shock and disturb the public mind. The reasons advanced by Lord Cromer for this unfortunate condition of things in his report were that witnesses dared not or would not speak the truth. The less the protection of British force is apparent the less frequently will the native dare to offend others by coming forward. Under the present régime the tendency is more and more to eliminate the European judicial element and substitute natives. This is true of all the posts in the administration, but its effects are becoming most disastrously evident in the department known as the Parquet. This institution, which roughly corresponds to the office of our Public Prosecutor, has a much greater analogy with the functions of the Procureur-Général in France and his subordinates. The elimination of British supervision in these departments is having disastrous consequences in the increase of crime and the immunity of its perpetrators. In these matters slackness and lack of vigilance are unfortunately too evident in every direction, though the reimportation of a British official has been found in a month or two to restore the tone of a district. The fact is that the police will not act for lack of encouragement. Like all Oriental officials, they will move readily enough if supported and encouraged, but their natural tendency is to let things slide, and, unless very sure of protection, they will not be in a hurry to stir up trouble. On the other hand, if they are pressed to show results they will not be scrupulous as to the methods by which they secure convictions before a native judge. The belief in the justice of British authority and its determination to punish crime justified the attempt to institute civilised methods of administering justice in Egypt. The result of the present policy has already undermined that belief. The wholesale manner in which high native officials are being allowed to pack the Parquet with other natives and the reckless methods by which native judges are being placed everywhere in responsible situations are rapidly obscuring the idea of British supervision in the mind of the mass of the people.

It is very difficult for the impartial observer not to infer that the native judge is falling into the common Oriental habit of taking bribes. This is easy to infer, but difficult to prove. In any case there is no doubt as to the delight of the Fellaheen when an Englishman is on the bench. Not long ago when an Englishman on a tour of inspection was sitting beside a native judge he was embarrassed by a native shouting to the crowd outside, "God be thanked!—an Englishman is sitting to-day", the statement being welcomed by shouts of joy. Even if neither corrupt nor unfair, the native judge is almost certain to treat the majority of suitors or prisoners with contempt and discourtesy. This tendency is checked and discouraged where European supervision is strict and constant as in India; where it is the deliberate policy to leave the native to act for himself, and British control is palpably weakening, the tendency will and does develop and flourish.

The evil in this matter at present is not even that British officials are too scarce to do the work that is required, but that many of them are not employed upon the work of supervision which is so urgently required, and sit in their offices in enforced idleness. The idea apparently is to allow the natives to work out their own salvation or damnation unimpeded. To teach the native to govern himself is a worthy ideal, and it has been the aim of all the best English statesmen who have controlled the destinies of Egypt; but, as in all enterprises, there is a right and a wrong way of conducting the experiment. The right way is being tried in the Soudan. The present system in Egypt is to obtain the approval of the upper classes and the Khedive and ignore the mass of the population. This is a scheme that has advantages. The official and educated classes are vocal, very vocal, while the masses are dumb. The former can get at the Foreign Office and Parliament, the poor cannot. Therefore so long as the so-called Nationalists are pleased, Englishmen will hear little of the complaints of the Fellaheen. But after all it is by the well- or ill-being of the mass of the people that British rule in Egypt will be judged by history. The Nationalists care nothing for the lower classes. It is British control of the country that stands between the plutocrats and officials and the people, whom they oppressed before we arrived on the scene, and they have never forgiven us. Into the hands of this class, from the Khedive downwards, Sir Eldon Gorst has played deliberately ever since he was put into Lord Cromer's place. It is quite true that he went out to Egypt with instructions to give the natives progressively as large a share in the administration as possible, but he has been exaggerating the scope of his mandate in a fashion that we are sure Sir Edward Grey could never have intended. But unhappily if the Nationalists and the British representative are working together, there can be little chance either for the mass of the Egyptian people or the less important British officials to make their voices heard. No official would dare to compromise himself with a chief whose diplomatic tact is great but in whom magnanimity has never been a distinguishing trait. Unfortunate, like his distinguished father, he inspires anything rather than confidence among his subordinates. Men cannot do their best when experience tells them they cannot trust their chief.

The approval of the Egyptian beys, pachas, and plutocrats makes things easy for a high official, and the Khedive, who is a born intriguer, will not intrigue against him personally, which also makes things pleasant for the Government at home. But it may be well to remember that this Nationalist class is bitterly hated by the masses. When they go home to their country houses, they shut themselves up after dark for fear of being shot. These men will hardly hesitate to free themselves of their enemies if they can use their official positions for the purpose. It would appear to be the policy of the Consul-General to give them that opportunity at once and on a large scale. A measure is being prepared, and we believe is now before the Legislative Council in Egypt, authorising the Government to deport without trial thousands of persons stigmatised as dangerous characters. The lists have been drawn up, almost entirely, by leading natives, who have very naturally put upon them their personal enemies. The total number of names is said to be as many as twenty thousand. This of course must be greatly reduced before any sanction could be hoped for from the Foreign Office or the Cabinet, but the mere contemplation or possibility of such a move is enough to condemn the present régime. The policy pursued by Sir Eldon Gorst of exalting the native official class on every occasion and minimising British control, of flattering the Khedive and the plutocrats, stands convicted by the action of the Egyptian Government itself of glaring and egregious failure. Deportation without trial may be defended in a few specific and well-guarded instances, as in India, but only in analogous and limited cases. The measure now maturing in Egypt is indeed a brilliant object-lesson in the policy of "Egypt for the Egyptians" as understood by Sir Eldon Gorst. Two years of its application have led the Egyptian Ministry to recognise that it has engendered such discontent and disloyalty that nothing but the most stringent act of irresponsible despotism can save the situation. But it would be unfair to blame the native Ministry or the home Government for what is happening. Sir Eldon Gorst is alone really responsible, and it is incredible that the Foreign Secretary can be properly informed as to the strange developments Sir Eldon has thought fit to give to his instructions.

One thing is quite clear. If a healthy state of things is to be restored in Egypt, Sir Eldon Gorst must be relegated without delay to another sphere of usefulness. It is true he was no great success as Permanent Under-Secretary at the Foreign Office, but there is more than one great capital where his undoubted gifts for diplomacy might be well and safely employed. Unfortunately Cairo is not one of them.

POLITICAL ASSASSINATION.

WHEN a murder such as that of Sir Curzon Wyllie is committed, we shed tears or hold up our hands or curse, according to the way we are made; and with some such emotional vent we are content. It is indispensable, no doubt, this outburst; it is right; but is it ever enough? Is it enough now? Here is a young man born and bred in a land under English rule, educated according to English methods, a student finally in the capital of the Empire. English thought must necessarily have exercised a tremendous influence upon his mental and moral development; and as a result he kills a distinguished servant of the State to whom he had never spoken and of whose work he knew but little. Whereupon we, who can by no means be free from responsibility, are horrified that such things should be.

Is there anything wrong with English thought as to political assassination? On principle the average Englishman will maintain that murder is always murder, and therefore abominable. Unhappily however principle is seldom allowed to appear. The English have a dislike for generalisations; they prefer to consider every case on its merits. And when a political assassination is considered on its merits, extenuating circumstances emerge which gradually come to dominate the situation. It was an evil deed, but —and the "but" is emphasised—it was done in a good cause. A blow has been struck for liberty, as the phrase goes. Let us forget the means in the end; let us even glorify the deed in the light of the result. Or, maybe, apart from all question of political beliefs, the victim himself was some infamous wretch, crime-stained, vice-stained, loathsome and deservedly loathed. We thank God that the world is rid of a monster and write the name of his murderer on the roll of the heroes of history. Condonation of this sort is common enough. With a vague idea of the facts, most chime in with the praise of Harmodius and Aristogeiton and Brutus and Cassius. All the casuistry of sentiment has been brought into play in favour of Charlotte Corday, and a political murderess is held up as one of the noblest types of womankind. To come to our own day, our way of thinking is admirably illustrated by the tolerance bordering on approval which has been extended to the perpetrators of anarchist outrages in Russia. The victim was assumed either to have been justly punished for his own crimes or to have paid the penalty for the oppressive system of government of which he was the representative. The murderer, should he succeed in making good his escape, could be sure of a comfortable home in London. Such condemnation as was expressed was equally casuistical. It was said that the Russian bureaucracy had obtained too firm a hold to be shaken by sporadic outrages; that the method was clumsy and calculated to defeat its own ends. It was never boldly said, This is murder and an accursed thing. In fact, as a people we are practically prepared to tolerate political assassination in the concrete. We make exceptions to the rule so numerous that they can be classified, and so important that in effect they outweigh the rule itself altogether. The result is seen in the writings of Mr. Krishnavarma. In defending assassination as a political weapon that person is able to urge with some justice that he is only generalising from the verdicts of some of our historians or carrying to their logical conclusion the doctrines of our philosophers.

It is curious, this English tolerance of murder, curious not because it is immoral but because it is unnatural. For it runs contrary to the whole trend of European thought. Western philosophy has always been characterised by the stress which it has laid upon the sanctity of human life. Guided by this principle Europe has worked out its political evolution, and we ourselves, who in this matter have been the most Western of the Westerns, have banished efficient autocracy in favour of a free life in a free state. The Oriental, on the other hand, being more tolerant of that power of life and death which marks all despotisms, lives under them to this day. And yet in our attitude towards political assassination we are approximating to the Oriental point of view and denying the very principle which more than anything else has brought the British Constitution into existence. The inconsistency is too great to be explained by the fact that we were always an illogical people. The real cause lies deeper. Our tolerant attitude towards the murder of tyrants and villains is symptomatic of the general tone of nineteenth-century thought. Tom Paine, Bentham, Mill, Spencer, and indeed all the representatives of the thought of their day, have glorified the value of the individual judgment. Great were the achievements and unbounded the capacities of the untrammelled mind. The bold free intellect of the investigator could formulate the laws of Nature, could pry into all things on the earth or in the waters beneath it, could comprehend the mysteries of the universe and criticise God Himself. There was a crusade against authority whether in Church or State. The traditions of centuries were broken and cast aside. Nothing was to be allowed to impose shackles on man's freedom of thought or of action. Hence it was that principles were banished. Every case was to be considered on its merits, and one man's view was as good as another's. In practice this worked very well at first. Traditions continue to exercise their influence, though nominally disregarded, and tradition saw to it that the private judgments of individual Englishmen coincided on all important matters. But observe the effect of bringing an alien into this intellectual atmosphere. He is in very truth a free being, uncontrolled by the influence of a past in which he has had no share. He strikes out a line for himself, and when called upon to defend his conduct claims that it is justified at the tribunal of his own conscience. What reply can the individualist make to such a plea as this? He is answered out of his own mouth.

There is indeed but one reply possible. It takes the form of an assertion of authority, an enunciation of a principle. We say that murder is wrong under every form, wrong because it is utterly subversive of the social instinct which cannot find scope where there is no security and a man's hand may at any moment be raised against his fellow. It is of course possible to deny the existence of this social instinct. It is equally possible to deny the existence of the law of gravitation; but the man who does so will assuredly get hurt. And in just the same way the man who commits an outrage against the law of social fellowship will get hurt. He will find society crumbling to pieces about him. All history endorses this view. It is not an accident that Aristotle, living amongst those who worshipped the memory of tyrannicides, found himself compelled to devote a whole book to the study of revolutions; nor that Augustus, given a free hand to save the world from the anarchy into which the murder of Cæsar had plunged it, erected a system which turned out to be far more autocratic than anything which his uncle had planned; nor that Napoleon, called upon to put an end to a state of things in which murder had become the rule, established a cast-iron administrative despotism which no subsequent revolutionary has had either the power or the courage to overthrow. Such penalties must be paid. A sin against society recoils, if not on the sinner, at any rate on the people who have tolerated his sin. That lesson is one we ourselves have need to take to heart. We have trifled with the law. Our casuists have elaborated exceptions and qualifications; our philosophers have subordinated principles to the individual judgments; our poets have exalted murder as the handmaid of freedom. And now our self-satisfaction has received this tremendous shock. In the very building which Empire has called into existence a deed has been perpetrated which deals defiance not merely at British imperial rule but at any form of rule whatever. And the most terrifying reflection of all is that the blame for what has been done lies largely on our own heads.

MR. BIRRELL'S FINANCE.

MR. BIRRELL'S Irish comedy is to be revived this week at Westminster, in three acts, "Money", "Purchase", and "Congestion"; but money will take all the time they can give to this Bill for many a long day.

The excessive success of the Wyndham scheme was the cause of its failure, with land sold at the rate of about ten millions a year beyond the Treasury provision for it, and with a "bonus" of 12 per cent. to encourage sales at the expense of the taxpayer over and above the sale price. The person legally empowered to sell got the whole of the bonus, though he might not be the real owner, which naturally brought many insolvent and vicarious estates into the gamble, farther extending the success that made the failure, until we got a total of £53,000,000 worth of land sold and no money to pay for it. All this land was sold for cash, and now it is to be paid for in paper, on conditions that make it quite impossible for the seller to know what he can realise in cash when he finally parts with his land and puts his paper on the market. The absence of effective government has an influence on the value of property, and if we take the 12 per cent. bonus as the measure of the difference, then the price of Irish crime to the taxpayer under this head alone is a total of £12,000,000, apart from the selling price of the land and apart from any additional concessions to crime in the future. It was felt at the time that if the Government could not stop crime the taxpayer ought to provide the difference which it made in the price of land, and so the bonus of 12 per cent. was enacted, probably not enough to meet the minus value in property, though it stimulated sales so far beyond the £5,000,000 a year which was the statutory obligation of the Treasury.

As sale went up, the value of Land Stock went down, until we find it now at a discount of more than 14 per cent.; but the bonus of 12 per cent. must be added to realise the proper magnitude of the agrarian slump, since the taxpayer would have to make good the whole 26 per cent. in respect of any estate now sold under the Wyndham Act. This is 26 per cent. on the purchase money, and in addition to it. The man selling under the Wyndham Act is entitled to cash, not paper; so that if he sold £100 worth of land to-day, with the paper at 85-6, he would have to get £126 worth of Land Stock, registering that liability against the taxpayer, who in return can get back from the purchasing peasant only the £100. The £12 worth of bonus and the £14 worth of slump remain to be met by the taxpayer as an absolutely unsecured charge, apart from the selling price of the land, which, in addition, has its own uncertainties. Of course the policy of organised crime encouraged by "government in accordance with Irish ideas" had its effect on the Land Stock as well as on the price of the land; and the Irish county councils have flatly refused to meet their statutory share of the slump, while triumphantly organising the crime contributing to it. Is it not time that the taxpayer opened his eyes to his increasing liabilities in this statutory combination of crime and land purchase? We do not question that purchase must proceed, at least until a majority of the new owners find themselves strong enough and wise enough to insist on peace in the interest of their new possessions; but is it fair to the taxpayer to extend the confusion just now, under a Government that makes the process unnecessarily expensive at every point? An addition to the Wyndham provision of more than £80,000,000 is demanded, and demanded by the very men who, laughing at crime, have so obviously contributed to the unnecessary increase.

To get out of that puzzle, Mr. Birrell proposes this: The peasant is to pay for the crime organised by his leaders an increase of 5s. per cent. in the purchase annuity; and the same 5s. increase is to be handed on by the Irish Land Commission to the Treasury for the use of the purchase money, as an increased margin to meet slumps. That is the tenant's share towards making ends meet; and now let us see the landlord's. Cash purchase stops at the discretion of the Treasury. The landlord is to get paper for his land, guaranteed against slumping down to 92, a difference of £8 per cent. plus, to be borne by the taxpayer, apart from the price of the land; but the guarantee against slumping does not go below 92, and the landlord has to meet the unknowable remainder out of his purchase money. Will he? The landlord's bonus also is to be transformed. Instead of the level 12 per cent. on all sales, there is to be a "sliding scale", falling as the sale price of the land rises in terms of "years' purchase". The two extremes within which the bonus "slides" are fixed in figures, from 17 up to 24. At 25 there is no bonus, but it rises from 3 per cent. at 24 years' purchase to 16 per cent. at 18 years' purchase. The man who sells £100 worth of land for 24 times the rent gets £103, and it "slides" in proportion until the man who sells £100 worth of land for 18 times the rent gets £116. Mr. Redmond got 24½ for his own, plus 12 per cent. bonus. We will leave the landlord to think it out for himself, adding merely the terse opinion of Judge Ross, who presides over the Land Court in Dublin: "The sliding scale is a joke".

Now comes a sliding scale of a vastly more important kind, not provided by Mr. Birrell, but arising directly on his paper proposals. The market value of the paper is not to be secured against slumping below 92; but the present stock, on Mr. Wyndham's cash basis, is down within a fraction of 85. Can the new paper fare better at Throgmorton Street, with Mr. Birrell's government by "Irish ideas" encouraging crime in Connaught? Assuming the new stock at the same price, the selling landlord stands to lose every penny of the difference between 92 and 85. His loss on the £100 worth of land sold graduates from £1 when the paper sells at 91, to about £8 10s. when it sells at 84, which is only about 1½ below the present ruling of the present stock. On the average quotations for several months, the landlord stands to lose £6 to £7 on every £100 of his purchase money. Before selling he may, of course, try to meet this by exacting an increase in the "years' purchase" from the tenant; but, on the other hand, assuming sales much extended, the increase of the paper on the market must tend to depress its selling price in proportion, until a point is reached at which the landlord can sell no more, and the whole business is automatically stopped. The ingenious idea behind this part of the scheme seems to be an automatic brake on the purchase machine, so that the landlord may stop selling to restore the market price of the paper when he finds himself putting enough of it on the market to increase the slump beyond the loss that he can bear. The trick is quite clever, and the working of it would give a new interest to the dreary routine of financial method—if it worked at all. At the same time it is more like the calculation of a bookmaker than the insight of a statesman, allowing for the fullest responsiveness of the Irish character to speculative appeal and sporting uncertainty.

There are several hard facts against the chances of the landlord getting an increased price from the tenant to meet a slump in the paper below 92. The Estates Commissioners are empowered to decline a sale if they think the land is not security for the price agreed by the landlord and the tenant, a reservation which has often been exercised already, and for which the need would be increased by any increase in the prices stipulated. Then we have Mr. Birrell's Irish allies and their League organised and pledged to prevent the landlord getting a penny more on his sales than he gets now.

This statutory experiment in paper purchase applies to future sales, and the landlord has at least the use of his faculties still left him for self-defence; but the real hardship is in the attempt to apply it also to the £53,000,000 worth of land already sold without money to pay for it. Every sod of this was sold for cash, so that the seller knew exactly what he expected for his land when he closed the bargain; but now that bargain is to be virtually broken, and instead of cash the seller is asked to accept paper, the value of which no man can estimate beyond the fact that agrarian paper at least as good is now at a discount that means a net sacrifice of £6 10s. to £8 on every £100 of the £53,000,000. This paper panacea is offered as an "option" to the landlord who has sold, which looks fair until we examine the alternative: to wait his chance for cash liquidation, which might give him his money some time about the year 1921—it would take at least twelve years to work off the arrears at the recent rates of purchase and payment. The choice is between impossible paper and impossible patience. Can Mr. Birrell be in earnest? There is talk of amendments in Committee, and we must await these for final judgment. It is hard enough to anticipate the practical value of an Irish Land Act even at that.

THE GAMBLER WITHIN THE GATE.

THE news that M. Marquet, the proprietor of the Ostend Casino, has won his appeal in the Belgian superior Courts, and may now resume gambling at Ostend in peace and comfort, will cause a little mild amusement to the majority of people in this country, coupled with some wonder as to how much in bribes the judgment cost the appellant and under what heading such disbursements appear in the Casino balance sheet. The undertaking in question is still, we presume, a company, with M. Marquet and his distinguished friend and ally, the King of the Belgians, as its chief shareholders. It is not a matter for pride to reflect that a famous English statesman and a well-known English financier were among the founders and first shareholders of the business; but that unfortunate incident is, we are glad to remember, past history.

We are certainly not among those who regard the reopening of this pestilent gambling hell with equanimity. Fortunately the respectability of our own country, coupled with its unrecognised depths of common-sense, and with a good deal of luck thrown in, have combined so far to keep us singularly free from temptations to mere gambling. The sporting, open-air business of English racing is a totally different matter. The gaming-tables of German baths have been shut up; those at French pleasure resorts have been reduced to childish games such as petits-chevaux, except at Aix-les-Bains, where baccarat is still allowed; and the two great gambling clubs of Paris, the Jockey Club and the Cercle de la Rue Royale, are, of course, private establishments. So far as this country is concerned—and in dealing with temptations to vice it is a case of every man for himself and every country for its own inhabitants—fate could not have been kinder. Scotland Yard in London and the detective forces of all our large provincial towns hear of gaming establishments before the decorators have finished painting the ceilings, and "raid" them and shut them up exactly when it suits official convenience. So a man goes to play there with the uncomfortable certainty—or at any rate a good "10 to 1 on" chance—that his friends will see his name sooner or later in a police-court narrative. A journey to Aix-les-Bains or Monte Carlo costs a sum of money and takes an amount of time which put both places out of the range of ordinary common temptations. At any rate, a man who goes to either of these places for the purpose of gambling can hardly complain that temptation has been thrust in his way. Other nations have kindly carried out for our benefit the advice of the famous French Chef de la Sureté: "Keep gambling at the greatest possible distance; make access to it as difficult and costly as possible; then regulate it with the most iron law and the sternest police force, when you have got the thing, so to speak, with its back against the wall at the farthest possible extremity of the earth".

But Ostend is another matter. Here you have a place within five or six hours' journey and a few shillings fare of London; a public, ill-managed, vice-pervaded gambling hell of the most infamous description, with all the scandals and shames of Monte Carlo about it, and without any of the rigid financial honesty and strict outward decency which are maintained there. Moreover, we understand that the chief hotel in the place is opening a second baccarat establishment in its building, access to which will be equally free under the same childish farce of "election". We do not know whether the hotel has "squared" M. Marquet and the King of the Belgians; if not, we shall recall hopefully the proverb which tells us that honest men gain "when thieves fall out". But the hotel in question is a very wealthy establishment; and neither of the two gentlemen mentioned is likely to have overlooked such an obvious source of blackmail.

The English authorities are, of course, perfectly helpless in the matter. No Government could condescend to offer remonstrances of the usual diplomatic kind to King Leopold, and threats would be unavailing. There is nothing to be done except what can be and, we are convinced, will be done by all decent-minded Englishmen, give Ostend as wide a berth as they would give to a fever hospital. There is nothing except the gambling which could take anybody there. As a route into Northern and Central Europe the Dover-Ostend journey, with its slow, rickety boats and miserable, exposed landing-stage and platforms at Ostend, is beneath notice. The Ostend hotels are among the dearest and most uncomfortable in the world; its bathing machines "de luxe", with their sofas, lace-covered dressing-tables, silver looking-glasses and hair brushes, and charge of ten francs for the morning, tell you without further words the class of lady who uses them; and the drain odours of the town, humorously described by the inhabitants as ozone, are—well, they are easily distinguishable from the ozone of other health resorts. It is inconceivable that any decent-minded Englishman should continue to regard such a town as a fit place for the summer holidays of himself and his family. But we wish to make a further suggestion to such a man. When he goes there for a bachelor week-end, he is contributing largely to the maintenance of gambling rooms for young and less wealthy Englishmen of the middle class, whose unsupported patronage could not possibly maintain such an establishment. Does he wish to do that? Would the extra hours and railway fare of a journey to Aix-les-Bains or Monte Carlo seriously trouble him? And, to introduce a lower and more commercial consideration, do not all of us know business and private friends who, if they take to gambling, will nvolve ourselves in some very troublesome negotiations?

There is one more point connected with the kingdom f Belgium which is accentuated by the present impuent proceedings of M. Marquet, but has been forcing :self into prominence for some years past. How much onger will English parents regard Brussels and its eighbourhood as a proper place to which they may end their children for educational purposes? Fight ıs it may against such fate, a country cannot help aking its tone from its rulers; and, in spite of gallant efforts, which everyone cordially recognises and sympathises with, on the part of the Chamber of Deputies and the present Ministry, there is only one uler in Belgium to-day. King Leopold is a person ıbout whom the world writes and talks quite frankly nowadays. He is in no way peculiar to Belgium; men like him litter New York, whose papers have lately been discussing whether it is allowable to shoot such folk at sight; and in England—chiefly in and round Portland, Dartmoor, and Parkhurst—there are plenty of them. But their influence here is limited, and their fights for supremacy take place either with the police or with prison warders. When they become paramount in a town or country, as King Leopold and his friends are paramount in Brussels and Ostend, such places become plague spots, each of which can corrupt the whole neighbourhood for fifty miles round. Education in Belgium is cheap and passable. You learn French of a sort; music and drawing lessons are not much worse than you can get for the same money in Dresden or Leipsic; above all, Brussels and its neighbourhood are the nearest and most convenient point to which you can send a child in search of that adventure so dear to child life, a foreign school. But when M. Marquet meets you at Ostend and King Leopold in Brussels, the extra expense and trouble of a journey to Dresden seem eminently worthy of consideration.

THE CITY.

BUSINESS on the Stock Exchange has been at a standstill for the last week. This is now the third bad settlement for the bulls, and it is hoped that it may be the last. Anything like a boom is of course out of the question, as there is nothing on which to base a boom. But prices may improve slowly, if there is any buying at all, and stockbrokers are almost unanimous in predicting a return of the public to the market. We are not so sure. We have ascertained by inquiry that the shaking-out process is not directed against the West-end speculators, but against the members of the Stock Exchange itself. There are a lot of small jobbers and brokers who, having no clients or not enough, plunge wildly at the expense of their colleagues. These small fry, with little or no means to back them, think nothing of having four or five thousand Kaffir shares open, and this is a real danger, which, for their own protection, the big people are obliged to stop. The trouble is that in pulling up these domestic punters the outside public are hurt, and get disgusted with the market. The prices in the South African market were almost exactly the same on Friday as they were a fortnight ago.

The flatness of the Argentine railway market is partially explained by the issue of £1,000,000 debentures by the Buenos Ayres and Pacific Railway Four-and-a-Half per Cents. at 103. The outstanding debentures were put down 2 from 106 to 104. These debentures are, of course, a first-rate investment, and they ought to be easily subscribed, particularly with cheap money. With a Bank rate at 2½, and every prospect of its being reduced to 2, a 4½-per-cent. debenture on a system like the Buenos Ayres and Pacific ought to be largely over-subscribed. Pacific shares have had a heavy fall to 102, partly on the bond issue, but more, perhaps, on one or two decreases of traffic, and the widely entertained idea that the dividend will be reduced to 6, if not to 5 per cent. This is a matter on which the directors are at present probably as ignorant as the public.

The creation of new capital during the first six months of 1909 has been unprecedentedly large. In the first two quarters of the year the new capital issued amounted to £121,073,600, against £109,673,500 created in the first half of 1908. It is indeed more than the whole of the new capital created in 1906, which was £120,173,200, and almost as much as the whole of the capital created in 1907, which was £123,630,000. Last year the new capital created was £192,203,700; but if the capital applications go on at the present rate for the next six months it will amount to £240,000,000, which is enormous, seeing that the Government and the municipal authorities have been unusually moderate in their demands. This rapid conversion of circulating into fixed capital invariably results in stringency later on, sometimes in panic, as happened in the United States in 1907. Indeed, nothing but the increasing output of gold by the Transvaal mines saves us from a financial catastrophe. It has been calculated that in the seventeen years between 1890 and 1907 the production of gold is equivalent to half the production of the preceding four centuries—a prodigious fact if we take into consideration that for two years the mines were shut down owing to the war. It is also remarkable that during the war wages in England were never higher or trade brisker. Trade is gradually recovering, as the imports show; but the prices of cotton, wheat and meat are inconveniently high, and now there seems every prospect of coal being dearer. The stupid, mischievous and unnecessary Eight Hours Act for Miners has produced the results which everyone acquainted with the trade predicted. The miners, of course, thought that they would get the same wages for shorter hours; but the masters do not see that, and trouble is brewing in Scotland, Staffordshire and Derbyshire. A big coal strike would make industrial shares weak, though it is lucky it is not winter. People are beginning to ask what will happen if the Lords reject the Finance Bill? Will the Chancellor of the Exchequer issue Treasury bills for £100,000,000? And if so, where will the money come from? The period of cheap money might come to a speedy end if the national expenditure had to be financed by a short loan.

MIDDLE-CLASS LIFE FROM WITHOUT.

By Max Beerbohm.

I have often urged our dramatists to give the aristocracy a rest, and write plays about the class to which they themselves belong. An intimate and complete study of Mrs. Brown is of more account than a presentment of the Duchess of Hampshire as she is vaguely and respectfully supposed to be. In real life, doubtless, and as woman to woman, Mrs. Brown is at a disadvantage. Where is her tiara? Where are her electric and other cars? Her house has no courtyard, and on the inner walls hang no portraits of her husband's forbears by master hands. And, as against a battalion of powdered footmen, what is a houseparlourmaid? Mr. Robinson, Mr. Jones, and the other callers at Mrs. Brown's—how far less obviously exciting they are than the statesmen, the sportsmen, the diplomats, and the few carefully-selected millionaires, who surround Her Grace! I don't pretend not to be dazzled, even in this outer darkness, by the thought of them; and, if I were a dramatist, I daresay my plays would be exclusively about that exclusive world. Dazzled, blinded, I should trust inspiration to guide my reverent pen aright. The chances are that my confidence would be misplaced. Certainly, the average play about the aristocracy leaves me unconvinced of its truth. It *may* be all right, but I feel that it somehow isn't. That is why I have often wished that some aristocrat, or somebody whose life has been spent mainly among the aristocracy, would find time to write a play. For aught it might lack of technical merit, "connaissance de cause" would amply compensate us. My heart began to beat quickly, therefore, and my pulse throbbed, and my temperature rose, when I heard that Mrs. George Cornwallis-West had written a play. We know that for many years she has been in the midst of the beau monde. She was the wife of one distinguished politician, and is the mother of a second. Also, her foreign birth must have tended to prevent her from taking her environment as a matter of course—must have kept her keenly alert and watchful, sensitive to impressions. Here, then, thought I, will be the play I have long looked for. Alas, I reckoned without the law of human discontent. The Olympian gods, whom struggling mortals envied their luminous repose, looked down and contemplated and were amused. But the Olympian mortals, whom we of the middle class envy, are envious of us. There is a magnificence about all things unknown. It is ever sweet to escape from one's own familiar knowledge, and let fancy go flying where it listeth. Strawberry-leaves and stars-and-garters, whispered secrets of high policy, all the paraphernalia that are so dear to the brooding heart of you and me, are as dust and sand to Mrs. Cornwallis-West. She swishes them aside and makes a bee-line for our abject selves.

Well, it is a proud moment for us. But we do wish, in the interest of dramatic art, and for general enlightenment, that "His Borrowed Plumes" had been a play about the sort of people the author really knows, and not about the sort of people she fondly imagines. At the very outset her ignorance betrays her. It was convenient to her purpose that she should get all her characters staying together under one roof. But here she was confronted by a grave difficulty. She remembered having heard or read somewhere that middle-class people don't have big country-houses in which to entertain their friends. "What," she wondered, "does a lady of the middle class do when she wishes to have a big house-party?" After prolonged thought, and after fruitless search under "M" and "C" in the Encyclopædia Britannica, it occurred to her that middle-class house-parties are probably given in river-side hotels hired for the purpose. To make sure, she telephoned to some of her friends, who one and all assured her that it sounded likely enough. To us, however, the notion is more than a mild surprise, and strikes a key-note of fantasy that prepares us for other surprises in store. The middle-class hostess, Mrs. Sumner by name, is a distinguished novelist. It is always rather difficult to believe that any one of the characters in a play is really a great writer or painter, or excels in any other kind of art—except, possibly, in the art of acting. In reading a book, if the author has (as Mr. Henry James so pre-eminently has) an insight into the minds of creative artists, we can believe in the artistic achievements of this or that character: we can believe in the masterpieces that are hinted at. But when we see a well-known actor dabbing at a canvas on an easel, or complacently fingering a sheaf of MS., we do but smile. The dramatist may have a keen insight into the soul of a painter or writer; but we cannot be illuded by the actual presentment on the stage. I am afraid that not even in reading the script of "His Borrowed Plumes" should I be able to believe in Mrs. Sumner as a distinguished novelist. As a woman she is brave, affectionate, pure, self-sacrificing, what you will: a perfect "heroine", of a mould far more nobly heroinic, indeed, than is ever found in a member of the middle class; but at no point can a trace of the literary artist be detected in her. True, she does show something of the artist's pride and aloofness when Mr. Delaine K.C. asks her to tell him the plot of her forthcoming book. She says she prefers to keep such things to herself. But she instantly relents when he asks her to show him the MS. "as a mark of confidence". This somewhat sinister phrase had prepared me, as a man of the world, to see Delaine instantly decamp with the lady's property. I wronged him. He merely adjusted a pince-nez, and, fifteen seconds later, having turned the pages with lightning rapidity, pronounced Mrs. Sumner's latest work to be her strongest, and predicted that it would be her greatest success. Whether his literary judgment was as sure as his rapidity in mastering a brief, is a point which will never be cleared up. Fate, in her wisdom or her folly, ordained that the MS. should never be given to the world. One of the members of Mrs. Sumner's house-party was an adventuress, Mrs. Cranfield by name, a very wicked woman, but one to whom much might be forgiven because she was such an arrant fool. Mrs. Cornwallis-West may have met an adventuress or two in her time; and I daresay that adventuresses, when they come among the aristocracy, lose their heads and carry on in the strangest fashion. But Mrs. Cornwallis-West may take it from me that any adventuress who behaved among the middle class as Mrs. Cranfield behaves would presently find herself in a lunatic asylum. What other place would be fit to receive a lady who, sitting with a gentleman in the hall of a river-side hotel just after the other guests had gone to bed, and hearing this gentleman's wife approach, insisted on being shut into his bedroom, with a view to preserving her good name? Yet this is not the full measure of poor Mrs. Cranfield's madness. Major Sumner, whom she adores, is, like his wife, a writer. Only, his work does not amount to much. Mrs. Cranfield is struck by what seems to her a happy thought. Why not steal the type-written scenario of Mrs. Sumner's book, read it carefully to herself, and then suggest it to the Major as the scenario for a play? Of course she will be presently found out, and her beloved will spurn her from him, and there will be the deuce to pay all round. But what of that? The adventuress nabs the scenario, and the Major writes the play. You would not expect that a cape-and-sword romance, written at second hand by a very mediocre writer who had never essayed a play before, would be accepted for production at the National Theatre. Mrs. Cornwallis-West, peering into the future, is convinced that such a thing might be. As she is an active supporter of the scheme for a National Theatre, this conviction of hers is the more surprising. It is only fair to the Major to say that he himself is very much surprised. That he does not, however, describe the play to his wife until it has been accepted, is a lamentable proof of the distance he has drifted away from her. As soon as he does begin to tell her all about it, she sees what has happened. Rather than humiliate him, she holds her counsel and burns her MS. But she is not above a good strong scene with Mrs. Cranfield in private. Trust Mrs. Cranfield to have been fool enough to write blackmailing letters to a Frenchman, on the strength of which documents a confession is wrung from her by the K.C. And trust the Major to tell the enraptured first-night audience, in a soldierly and a gentlemanly fashion, that the author of the play is none other than his wife.

Now, from the standpoint of the average simple playgoer, "His Borrowed Plumes" is a very good entertainment. From the standpoint of the purely technical critic, it is a very good piece of work: a story conceived and set forth clearly, without halting, with a thorough grasp of dramatic form. From the standpoint of a critic who desires an illusion of real life, it does not pass muster. The characters have been sacrificed to the story. Now and again, as in the scene between the two jealous women, the characters emerge and are natural, real, and moving. There is much that rings true in the relations of Mrs. Cranfield and the Major. But, for the rest, Mrs. Cornwallis-West has let herself be led into the temptation that awaits every one who essays dramaturgy for the first time—the temptation to write not as a seer of life, but as a playgoer who knows all about the theatre. I conjure her not to bother, henceforth, about what she thinks is needed to make a good play, but rather to let her characters do just as they would in real life. Having, as she evidently has, an instinct for dramatic form, she need not fear for the result of this process. But of course she must select her characters from the milieu that she knows. They must be the kind of people on whose behaviour she can regard herself as an authority. I daresay she thought that the strange things which happen in "His Borrowed Plumes" were really not less usual in the middle class than in the theatre. That is a notion which she must banish for ever from her mind.

MADOX BROWN.

By Laurence Binyon.

DELACROIX, who wrote of painting with such insight, and who was fond of illustrating the faults of the French school by the virtues of the English (a compliment repaid by many of our own critics), has a passage in one of his letters on the change which had come over our art since his youth and since the days of Lawrence. He notes the "prodigieuse conscience" that Englishmen can put even into works of imagination; and he finds our painters more in their element when they adopt the extreme detail of the Pre-Raphaelites than when, as in the Reynolds period, they imitated the colourists of Italy and Flanders. And yet, he remarks, under this change of manner, how English these painters remain at heart! Visitors to the Leicester Galleries may be reminded of this criticism as they survey the choice and, within its limits, representative exhibition of works by Madox Brown. Here is indeed a transformation, from early works like the "Manfred" and "Parisina" to "The Last of England" and "The Pretty Baa-Lambs". And it is true that in the later, detailed manner Madox Brown is, as Delacroix says, far more at home than in that youthful black, Byronic vein; the style he learned on the Continent gave so little scope to that "prodigious conscientiousness" which this artist possessed in an acute degree. A thorough Northerner in his instincts, with no bent to suppleness and suavity, Madox Brown was particularly and redoubtably English in his art. Stubborn independence and obstinacy of conviction were alike his strength and his weakness. A certain grim intensity was his finest imaginative gift, and he is at his best in subjects which call this out, such as the splendid "Prisoner of Chillon" design, engraved on wood for an edition of Byron. This design is not in the exhibition; but the quality is seen in the various images of King Lear, a figure that haunted him—Lear crouching in impotent fury in his chair before Goneril, or asleep and watched by Cordelia. This gift of passion and concentration finds completest expression in "The Last of England", a picture truly historic, so entirely does it belong to the painter's time and race, and, one may add, to his own essential, uncompromising nature. The manner of its execution is significant of the main stream of tendency in the art of the time; "it was painted in the open air on dull days, and, when the flesh was being painted, on cold days"! I quote from the artist's own note which, with other commentary of his on his work, is printed in the admirably compiled catalogue of the exhibition. The passion for reality, which took hold on most of the strongest and sincerest minds of that generation, finds, as I have said, in this picture full and fortunate expression. The material is fused with the design, as it certainly is not in pictures like the "Cromwell", which needs a commentary to explain it. "Work", again, represented here, like "The Last of England", by a replica of smaller size, is an amazing effort, but it does not succeed in its main object; for the figures of the workers make no predominant impression, while the accessories and details provoke curiosity without satisfying it. By thinking about it you can work out all the intended contrasts between the toilers and the idle; but the contrast is not a pictorial contrast, it is not impressed immediately on our senses. In parts of this picture, and still more in "The Three Stages of Cruelty", the artist's intensity becomes something incongruous, between painful and comic. The latter picture is a Hogarth subject, and Madox Brown's mind had a good deal of affinity with Hogarth's. The nineteenth-century artist was less of the born painter, and cannot be said to have a light touch. And yet in this collection is a little canvas, "The Pretty Baa-Lambs", which is quite charming, and a wonderful rendering of sunshine on a warm blue April day.

It is curious to note in the notes on "Work" and "The Last of England" how anxious Madox Brown was to dissociate himself from any particular movement or party-cry in art. He is at pains to declare that the minute detail in the latter picture was necessary "to bring the pathos of the subject more home to the beholder", and that the hot July sunshine in the former was introduced "because it seems peculiarly fitted to display *work* in all its severity, and not from any predilection for this kind of light over any other". He will not be set down as a Pre-Raphaelite, nor as a painter of sunlight. I admire this determined liberty, abhorring the fetishes so dear to inferior talents; and yet it may be we should be more impressed by a less defiant attitude. Probably Madox Brown would have been still stronger if he had been more flexible, more ready to ally himself frankly with the forces congenial to his own aims which were stirring in his generation.

An exhibition like this prompts to a comparison with the imaginative effort in English art of to-day. Well, we have reason to despond; far from it. It is portraiture and landscape that bulk largest in our exhibitions and secure the popular praise. But a school of painting can have no powerful pulse of life which has not the imaginative sense; has not, that is, whatever be the ostensible material and surface subject, a grasp of, and affinity with, the universal and enduring. Realism is intolerable or merely null without imagination; yet, conversely, reality is the essential condition of imaginative success; we must be persuaded of life, even though it be a life our senses have never known. In the exhibition of "Chosen Pictures" at the Grafton Gallery, to which I have already referred once or twice in these columns, may be seen something of what our English school of to-day is doing. Gathered together in a few days, on a sudden opportunity, this collection might, of course, be greatly enriched; but it suffices to prove, and has already proved to intelligent visitors from abroad, that there is in English painting, not only the cleverness abundant almost everywhere, but an inner glow of independent life. Subject-painters who show imagination are never, or very rarely, appreciated in their own day save by a few; unless, at least, they live long enough to create their own public. How bitterly reviled were the Pre-Raphaelites; and now just those people who would have abused them in that generation demand of imaginative work to-day the methods and the vision of those now canonised masters. Yet the Pre-Raphaelites received more encouragement and support than their successors. It is significant that Mr. Shannon, Mr. Strang, and Mr. Ricketts (not to mention others) have all had to develop their imaginative gift in lithography, etching, and wood-engraving before being able to exercise it on an ampler scale; each of them has perforce come late to painting. So, too, Mr. John, denied a favourable outlet for his power of monumental painting, has had to spend his gift in studies and drawings. These conditions have reacted on these artists' painting, and are then made a reproach to them. But it is the public which ought to reproach itself. How many of the best pictures in the Grafton Gallery exhibition might have been bought, I wonder, for the sum given by the Chantrey Trustees for the one insignificant example of Sir Lawrence Alma-Tadema in this year's Academy?

DECADENCE IN CRICKET.

THERE is nothing to be said of the University match of 1909 which has not already been said in daily papers. The match, which Oxford seemed likely to win, was ruined by rain, and the little chance there was of a finish was destroyed by over-cautious batting by Oxford on Wednesday morning and a late declaration in the afternoon. The spectator of modern cricket expects to be disappointed, but it is no ordinary vexation when one out of the over-few matches in the year which promise complete satisfaction is thus frustrated. The game for the most part was played under one of those end-of-the-world skies to be seen in such perfection in the neighbourhood of Lord's and the Zoo. Truly, as the Roman historian said nearly two thousand years ago, we live in a climate "foul with clouds and rain".

Few men of feeling or sense can go to the University or Eton and Harrow matches without uttering the hard words about first-class cricket which the contrast of these two games suggests. The atmosphere compels such utterance. As you walk through the pavilion the young athlete will, of course, be found complaining—that is his privilege—and you will see the senators of the game exulting in the ecstasies of torture, for that is their solace. In the reading-room, should you fly there for quiet, an even sterner indictment in the pages of the "Times" will confront you; but still the grievances, and they are true grievances, persevere. Hayward, Hirst, Harry, Huddleston, and Hitch, the names are taken at random in the interests of an obvious euphony, pursue the ancient paths. The target, for all the arrows, remains immune. It is a matter of some debate whether Hayward reads the "Times".

Let us return to an historian, still a Roman historian, but modern, very modern—Signor Ferrero. Talking of standards of living he maintains that what we ca[ll] progress the Romans called corruption. And is n[ot] this true of cricket? Is not its development—that is [a] non-committal word—in truth its degeneration? Th[e] highest form of cricket, or cricket exhibited at it[s] highest, should be the cricket, if development be pro[gress], of a Test match. That is the apex of cricket. But everybody knows about the Test matches of 1909. Three have been already played, and they have all bee[n] as joyless as the spectacle of two fat wrestlers on a mat. In all three a definite result has been attained, bu[t] nothing has happened. It is the old contrast of pastim[e] and trade. What would Francis Thompson, ou[r] greatest cricket poet, have said of such an exhibition and what John Nyren? The heroic cricket of Joh[n] Nyren's day produced an heroic prose. What doe[s] the cricket of to-day produce? Turn to the cricket pag[e] of the "Tatler". In the whole of current literatur[e] there are few more degenerate pages than that.

The development of cricket is ruining cricket. Ther[e] are many features in this development, but, to take one look at the long fixture lists and you will see why it i[s] that the men who should be playing first-class crick[et] to-day no longer play it. Under the old dispensatio[n] Mr. R. E. Foster, Mr. B. T. J. Bosanquet, Mr. R. H. Spooner would probably still be in the field; and thi[s] defection of amateurs will go on increasing. Crick[et] will fall more and more into the hands of the profes[sional]; that is to say, into the hands of the class whic[h] plays for safety—the gamekeeper shots of cricke[t]. And there is another danger of the same kind workin[g] at the roots of cricket. There is over-developmen[t] at the roots as well as at the summits of cricke[t]. Cricket is being organised at private schools and publi[c] schools in a way quite out of proportion to its impor[t]ance and in a way which does not really tend to it[s] improvement. Monotony of type is the general resul[t] and more often still a premature distaste for the gam[e] which is the result of so laborious a training. For thi[s] reason many boys come up to the University as wear[y] of cricket as of Greek, and turn to the fresh and un[disciplined] delights of lawn-tennis and golf.

All this is bad. The outlook for cricket is dar[k]. Every lamentation is justified. But from anoth[er] point of view, emphatically not the point of vie[w] of cricket, there is a brighter side. Cricket is [a] long game, and wastes time, and there is a gener[al] feeling among the strenuous—an increasing class—th[at] there are quicker and far surer methods of enjoyme[nt] and recreation. But this is a large question. It i[n]volves the whole question of the place of this game [as] a recreation for the ordinary man of moderate ambiti[on] and means, and anyone who considers things will se[e] wherever he looks, which way the struggle goes. Mea[n]while, under present conditions, the spectator [of] modern first-class matches must be content if he se[es] one or two of those contests in the course of a seas[on] which even the players themselves regard as fortuna[te] exceptions, as bright oases in a barren desert, and t[he] players in their turn must be content with a simil[ar] destiny.

The judicious, if they have not already crept off [to] golf, will prefer in increasing numbers to take risks [on] country pitches far from the click of the turnstile, [and] leave the mob of the cities for the "agri Venafrani" [of] cricket.

THE COUNTRYSIDE.

THE views of the countryman about weather [do] not always agree with those of the mere tow[n] dweller, still less with those of the holiday-maker, b[ut] all can fervently unite in detesting the present seaso[n]. "June, June that we desire so," put up a variety [of] records for unseasonableness in the south and ea[st] of England, and though a dripping June is said [to] put all things in tune it must have been a farmer w[ho] had got his roots sown and was in no hurry for his h[ay] who gave the start to such a heresy. As it was, m[ost] men were muddling about all the month trying to g[et] their land ready for swedes, and when the time ca[me] for the great annual holiday to the Royal Agricultu[ral]

Show that pleasant reunion was almost completely spoilt, and must prove a financial failure, owing to the recurrent downpours which visited Gloucester. Although the remarkable recovery which the society has made from the disaster it nearly incurred through attempting to retain its show in London has enabled it to put aside a considerable reserve for a rainy week such as occurred this year, the necessity of trenching upon this reserve has come at a very awkward time. The society fell into a bad habit of regarding the show as the be-all and end-all of its existence; its other activities like its journal, its experimental farm, its expert assistance for its members—all great advances when they were started—have either lost their quality or have become of less account because so many other agencies have grown up to provide the same privileges for all farmers. Without doubt the society lost the initiative that had distinguished it for many years after its foundation, and ceased to be a leader and inspirer in the agricultural community. It is well known that several of the men who now have the guidance of the society wish to see this policy rectified, to show some enterprise, and to devise new methods of bringing help and guidance to the general run of farmers. Such a policy, however, demands expenditure, and it is to be feared that the movement may be checked by the loss resulting from the Gloucester show. But some change must take place; at present the farmer who has no very vital interest in the show gets little or no return for his subscription, except the feeling that he is doing the proper thing and backing up an ancient and honourable institution. Even the show, like every other agricultural show, wants reconsidering by some active minds who are not too much oppressed by tradition and can attain a detached point of view. The exhibition of live-stock at the great shows is becoming every year more and more a fancier's business, a pleasant social contest in which rich men alone can engage and the longest purse goes far towards winning; the whole thing is uneconomical, and it may be doubted whether it is reacting favourably on farming at large. We have too many breeds, both of cattle and sheep, in the British Isles, and the show system perpetuates and even resurrects many small local races which would be better merged in something of more general utility. British farming is too individual and looks at its business in too retail a fashion to be able to make the best of the great world's markets with which it is now thrown into competition. Our farmers sell their beasts singly and aim at fattening off each as a separate artistic result; the beef producer of the Argentine or the middle West or Canada tries to turn out reasonably marketable stuff in uniform hundreds. And, as far as shows go, the time has come for someone to turn round and ask himself how they can be made to bear upon the workaday business of the ordinary farmer.

But to return to the season, its prospects as regards crops may be summed up as—wheat good, barley good, oats bad: the latter were sown late, and all over the south country at least they are very ragged and patchy, having been affected by various root parasites. Roots are generally good, though some of the early-sown mangels suffered during May and are rather a poor plant; for once in a way the early man is the victim of his energies. The hay is very late, thanks to the backward spring and the cool and sunless weather of June; so far also there has been little chance of getting it up in good condition, and the comparatively high prices which ruled in the spring are likely to be maintained. But the ever-extending use of motor-cars is beginning to tell upon the hay and straw market, just as it has already raised the price of the stable manure coming out of London and the other large towns. As regards the more special crops, the fruit-growers are complaining of continual and heavy attacks of all kinds of insect pests; earlier in the year there was a plague of caterpillars which almost defoliated the trees where spraying was not carried out, and aphis of sorts are now very troublesome. Although England is full of birds, gloriously so as compared with the fruit-growing districts in the north of France and Belgium, we seem to get every year more and more destructive insects. The raisers of soft fruit are greatly in need of sunshine and warmth, and the strawberry-growers are making but a poor season of it. Hops seem generally to be growing well, but in most parts are being punished by a very severe attack of aphis; this is probably a blessing in disguise, for another large crop would complete the demoralisation of an already broken market; all the same, the grower whose capital has almost disappeared through the losses of the last three seasons is hard put to it to find the extra materials and labour necessitated by the continuous washing. Although grass was scarce and late, and has also been rather thin and innutritious since it began to grow, the beef trade has been good, and graziers who have been pushing on their fattening stock have found the markets in their favour. But the sheep trade has gone to pieces, notwithstanding the drop of nearly ten shillings a head which sheep experienced last summer; men who bought lambs in the early autumn and have wintered and fatted them can get no more for their fat sheep than they gave for the lambs.

It is difficult to account for this great drop in value; importations from abroad have certainly been large, but the real cause seems to be that the world's stock of sheep has at last righted itself after the enormous decline that was due to the succession of Australian droughts. Moreover, any rise or fall in price has always some tendency to be cumulative; the butchers maintain that they are no longer able to purchase so many sheep, because their poorer customers make it a point of honour to buy beef now that mutton is cheap. Curiously enough, wool maintains a fair price, and has even been rising a little.

These fluctuations, however, seem an inevitable part of the stock market; they are always defeating the plans and foresight of the grazier, and make it a question whether much of the poorer grass land of the country ought not to be put under the plough again, since wheat promises to remain above 40s. per quarter for some time to come. Despite these difficulties the general prospects of farming seem to be reasonably bright; nobody is likely to make money, but it appears to be possible once more to earn a living by actual farming rather than by dealing. The best sign of this reasonable quiet prosperity is the fact that sound farms cannot be hired; there are plenty of local and private applications for any good bit of land long before it is publicly known that the old tenancy is falling in. A more hopeful and energetic spirit pervades the farmers; they are organising and working together in a manner full of promise for the future of the industry; and whatever may be our opinions on the Budget as a whole, the new "development grant" does repair a serious defect in the dealings of the State with agriculture, and comes at a very useful time when farmers are beginning to have more courage to take advantage of whatever opportunities may be open to them.

THE GREAT BORDEAUX WINES.

II.—CHÂTEAU MARGAUX.

MANY a French poet has sung of the merits of "Château Margaux", which with Château Latour and Château Lafite form the three "grands crus" of the Médoc. Biarnez, the Girondist poet, has recognised its proud pre-eminence over the other two when he sang:

"Inclinez votre front, fléchissez le genou,
Amis, Château Margaux se lève devant nous;
Voilà l'un des trois rois, l'un des trois dieux du monde.

. . . .

Idole des gourmets c'est le plus grand des trois,
Il est seul sur son trône, il est le roi des rois".

The surrounding country, which is entirely devoted to vineyards, may not be the most beautiful part of the Gironde or even of the Médoc, but it is extremely rich. Château-Durfort, Vivens, Rausan-Ségla, Rausan-Gassies, Lascombes, second-classed growths; Châteaux Malescot-Saint-Exupery, Ferrière, and Desmirail, third-classed growths, are all at Margaux; whilst, as we go towards S. Julien on the one side or back to

Bordeaux on the other, we pass through many a vineyard whose wines enjoy a world-wide reputation. A fine view can be had of the Gironde, which is particularly lovely in a red autumn sunset, from Port Margaux, a mile off, though the river is much finer at Port Macau, a few miles lower down. Château Margaux itself is a mile from Margaux station and twenty-two miles from Bordeaux on the Paris-Orleans railway. Charing Cross can be left at ten o'clock in the morning, and Margaux reached at nine o'clock the following morning by the little line which runs from the Gare du Médoc to Lesparre and Soulac-les-Bains.

As a vintage the château is of far more modern growth than some of its rivals. In the fifteenth century Château Lamothe, which stood where the modern château now stands, was a fortified castle, and belonged to the Seigneurs de Montferrand, who were succeeded by the Seigneurs de Durfort. In 1760 M. de Fumel, the owner at the time, made some important plantations of the very best vines, and it is their quality combined with the soil and situation of Château Margaux which has placed it in the very forefront of the growths of the Médoc. Forty years afterwards the estate was purchased by the Marquis de Lacolonilla, who pulled down the old feudal castle and erected in its place the present château. It stands at the end of a short straight avenue, which leads down to a fine flight of stone steps at the top of which an impressive portico resting upon Doric columns gives the whole what the French call a "grand air" of its own. In 1862 the Lacolonillas gave way to the Vicomte d'Aguado, who in 1870 sold the whole domain to Count Pillett-Will, the representative of an old Savoyard family ennobled by the King of Sardinia, who is now at the head of one of the wealthiest banking houses in Paris. His family portraits hang in the billiard-room, and in the dining and drawing rooms are some fine pictures and good Empire furniture. The estate itself is small, consisting of some four hundred acres, of which one hundred and sixty are planted with the choicest vines, 20,000 plants to the acre, and are cultivated with the very greatest care. There are some fertile fen lands to the east, but most of the soil rests upon siliceous earth, which is mixed with pebbles and forms a stratum of unequal depth. To the north the subsoil is clay, to the north-east marl, whilst it is alluvial to the east and gravel to the south and west. The whole is ploughed four times a year during cultivation, and manured once every nine years. The vines used are in the first place Cabernet-Sauvignon, the best growth in the Médoc, Cabernet-Gris, Merlot, Malbec, Petit Verdot, and Carmenère. The original plants are still used, and there has been no grafting of that strong American vine whose produce is by no means delicate but whose strength has overcome the phylloxera. On the other hand the most careful precautions against disease have been taken by spraying the soil round every plant with carbonate of soda.

There is not any very striking difference between the vintage practice at Château Margaux and the common practice elsewhere in the Médoc except that the greater value of the crop involves the adoption of special precautions. Thus the "commandants de manœuvre" do not come from a distance, but are men who belong to the estate, and, working as they do from year's end to year's end, know all its peculiarities. Again, each of these inspectors looks after five workers, and gives them a personal superintendence that would scarcely pay elsewhere. These men watch the cutters and see that they do their work rapidly and efficiently. No bunches must be left uncut, every good grape must be gathered in, all that is collected must be thoroughly ripe and sound, and nothing is to be put into the basket besides the grape itself. The women and children who collect the grapes are placed one in each row with the wooden basket to receive the fruit. Each cutter then hands his basket to the "vide panier", who empties his basket into a baste containing six gallons. These bastes are carried by porters to the vats, which are taken by horses or oxen to the presshouse. Every precaution is taken to preserve that yeast which gives the first "crus" of the Gironde their peculiar bouquet; whilst the human foot is used to crush the grape, as, indeed, at all the other great crus, instead of machinery. A week after fermentation, when there is no more sugar in the must, the wine is poured out, the contents of the vats are then mixed together and are poured into barrels, whose contents are under constant supervision. They are filled up twice a week as the wood absorbs the wine, for a tenth of the wine evaporates annually. Many purchasers who have bought the wine keep it in barrel on the spot for two or three years before having it bottled. This is in fact the only way by which the growth can be guaranteed, for each cork bears the special mark of Château Margaux, including Count Pillett-Will's arms, stating whether the wine is a first or second growth. Some time ago a wine merchant on a large scale complained that his corks and labels had suffered by time, and asked to have twenty thousand corks and labels to take their place. He was told he could easily have them, but that a representative of the firm must superintend the bottling. Nothing further was heard of this request, which may have been made with the object of securing the corks and labels for other purposes.

Vintages differ in many respects from one another. Thus 1882, 1883, and 1884 turned out badly; whilst 1896, 1899, 1900, 1904, 1906, and 1908 have given very good wines. Prices have varied in the same way. In 1899 the tun cost the trade 2000 francs, in 1900 the price was 1150, in 1901 1100, in 1902 1400, in 1903 2000, and in 1904 4000. The year 1905 was a very speculative one. Its prospects were doubtful, and the wine was sold to the trade for 1500 francs, but it turned out far superior to what was expected, and very soon doubled in value. The average output used to be two hundred tuns, but the wine has suffered in quantity of late through rain, blight, and spring frosts. Only 112 tuns were produced in 1906, in 1907 160 tuns of light pleasant wine, whilst spring frosts and blight have reduced the output in 1908, which was of the very best quality, to 99 tuns. Of late years an understanding has been come to with different wine merchants, and little or no wine can be secured on the spot, all having been sold for a period of years to the trade.

CORRESPONDENCE.

THE LAND CLAUSES OF THE BUDGET.

To the Editor of the SATURDAY REVIEW.

National Liberal Club, Whitehall Place S.W.

SIR,—As a humble member of the rank and file of Liberals I naturally look to our party leaders for light and guidance, and it was in these proper dispositions that I listened yesterday at the National Liberal Club to the lucid address of the Lord Advocate (Mr. Ure) in defence of the land clauses of the Budget. It was the unearned increment, so he told us, in the value of the land—an increment to which the landowner had contributed nothing of his own money or industry, but which was provided wholly and solely by the industry and expenditure of the community—which the Government now proposed specially to tax. On the sale of land by its owner and upon its devolution on his death this unearned increment was to be ascertained and 20 per cent. of it to be appropriated by the State. Again, on the falling-in of the reversion on long leases this increment was to be taxed at 10 per cent. While, with regard to undeveloped lands, so much of their estimated capital value as may be due to their vicinity to a town was to be rated at an annual tax of ½d. in the £. There were naturally certain equitable exceptions to the general application of these imposts. The proposal was clear enough. It only remained to justify the measure. This was Mr. Ure's justification. As it was the community, and the community only, which bestowed the unearned increment on the landowner, so it was only just that he should contribute to the burdens of the community by a special tax levied on the increment which the community had gratuitously bestowed upon him. But Mr. Ure never met the difficulty that land constitutes no exception, and that the same form of unearned increment occurs in the case of almost every kind of property besides land. Take Consols. The State may borrow £100 from me, and issue to me £100 2½ per cent. stock at par. Ten years hence, by wise economies and sound administration of the State, that same £100 stock may rise to be worth £200 cash. I then sell at £200, say: why should not the Government regard the £100 profit realised on the sale as unearned increment, seeing that it was solely the industry and thrift of the community or State, not my own efforts, which created the increment? And if a needy Government requires 20 per cent. of it, why should not a still more necessitous Government require 80 per cent. or, in fact, the whole of it? As the community gave the whole increment gratuitously, why should it not, to meet its necessities, take the whole increment away from me? Does not all increment, and indeed does not the maintenance of any value at all in any marketable commodity, be it land, Consols or merchandise, depend solely on the industry, energy and wealth of the community at large where such commodities are situate or circulate and are marketable? The diamond mines of Kimberley would be practically valueless to their owners but for the wealth and cultured tastes of the civilised communities that purchase diamonds. And cannot the community collectively take away for its own purposes and needs the very value which it has collectively bestowed? In answering these questions in the affirmative I would unwittingly and as a reductio ad absurdum find myself landed in socialism: but it is thitherto, I fear, that the Lord Advocate's justification leads me logically.

Mr. Asquith, while admitting that land has no special monopoly in unearned increment, insists that no Government is ever likely to seize any of the unearned increment won in commercial enterprises, because such increment in the shape of increased revenue of the business already pays sufficient toll in income tax. But surely not all unearned increment in commerce is carried to revenue account, any more than any realised increment in the value of land escapes the income-tax assessor. Land round a growing town legitimately required for the town's proper expansion and development should be acquired—though I speak of course as a fool—rather under some wise extension of the "Towns Improvements" and "Lands Clauses" Acts, by which the landowner receives the fair market value of his land, than under penal confiscatory measures such as the Government now proposes.

Sir, I would, as a good Liberal, willingly lay these fiscal burdens on the broad shoulders of ducal and other landowners of notorious wealth, but for the life of me I cannot see why, on the like principles, I should not also be made to disgorge to the Government the profits of my small investments, or, logically, even the whole of my inherited wealth and other my property of every shape and kind possibly besides.

I am your obedient servant,
Francis O. Clutton.

CIVIL LIST PENSIONS AND COPYRIGHT.

To the Editor of the Saturday Review.

Sir,—The new Civil List pensions should be seized upon by all who consider that our present copyright laws are wrong. "Miss Mary Angela Dickens, Miss Dorothy Gertrude Dickens, Miss Cecil Mary Dickens, and Miss Evelyn Bessie Dickens, in recognition of the literary eminence of their grandfather, the late Mr. Charles Dickens, and in consideration of their straitened circumstances, £25 each." Could you put what I venture to think is an iniquity into more concrete form? Dickens created a vast amount of valuable property; if he had made a business or built houses or produced anything else that might continue to be commercially valuable for generations after his death, the rights would have gone to his family. But because he created books only his rights were sharply limited, and anybody to-day may produce a new edition of Dickens to his own profit, without obligation to contribute a penny to Dickens' descendants.

If there is one form of property the proceeds from which should specially belong to a man and his family it is surely that created by his brain. It is the one form in which his rights beyond a certain time are not recognised. But let us assume that his rights should be restricted. To whom should the benefit go? To the State, it would seem. Under our present system the benefit goes to individuals who rush out new editions of popular works directly the copyright limit is reached. There are innumerable editions of Dickens on the market to-day, and huge profits have been, and are being, made by publishers who have never paid one halfpenny in royalty. Yet the taxpayer is asked to provide £100 a year for the granddaughters of Dickens because of their straitened circumstances. Could anything be more preposterous?

What should happen, in my opinion, is this: Absolute copyright might be given for a period of years as now; at the end of that time anyone might have the right to produce new editions subject to a royalty to be paid either to the author's heirs or to the State which is called upon to meet their necessities out of the Civil List. Probably ten per cent. on the profits from the sale of Dickens' works to-day would give much more than the £100 now to be allowed to his granddaughters. Mr. Lloyd George is looking out for new sources of taxation: here surely is one to which he might give attention.

I am yours &c. Bookman.

BACK TO THE LAND.

To the Editor of the Saturday Review.

21 Harcourt Road, Sheffield,
3 July 1909.

Sir,—In connexion with the Children's Country Holiday movement may I point out a hopeful development? Some of the boys who are taken into the country by means of the various funds have been placed in situations upon farms, largely in Devonshire.

Those who prove unsuited for farm work often go into the Navy, following, in this respect, the example of so many native-born Devonians.

Local correspondents of the central organisation (the Secretary of which is Miss Iles, 18 Buckingham Street, Strand) report that last June twenty-eight of these town-bred lads were doing well on various farms.

I remain, yours faithfully,
Frank J. Adkins.

"CORPUS DOMINI APUD ANGLOS."

To the Editor of the Saturday Review.

31 Farm Street W., 4 July 1909.

Sir,—While gratefully acknowledging the courteous tone of your notice of Father Bridgett's "Holy Eucharist" which I have recently edited, may I call attention to one criticism which does not seem warranted by the text? Father Bridgett, speaking of the changes at the Reformation, remarks: "Altars of sacrifice were broken in pieces or condemned to the vilest uses. The doctrine of Masses was called 'a blasphemous fable and dangerous deceit', the worship of our Lord beneath the sacramental veils 'idolatry'. The offering of Mass by Catholic priests was punished with cruel death", &c. Upon this your reviewer observes: "It is a cheap misstatement, which ought not to have been suffered to stand, that 'the worship of our Lord beneath the sacramental veils' is stigmatised by the Reformed Church of England as idolatry". But Father Bridgett does not in any way mention "the Reformed Church of England". So far as I can see he is only speaking of what his next paragraph calls "the Protestant view". May I respectfully submit that, quite apart from the Black Rubric, "the Protestant view" did and does treat the adoration of the Blessed Sacrament as idolatry? At any rate I do not see how otherwise to understand the terms of the King's declaration on transubstantiation, or the language of the "Sermon concerning the Sacrament" in the Book of Homilies. "What hath been the cause of this gross idolatry?" asks the latter, speaking of the Holy Eucharist.

I am, Sir, your obedient servant,
HERBERT THURSTON S.J.

To the Editor of the SATURDAY REVIEW.

Holland House, Great Malvern,
3 July 1909.

SIR,—May I venture to express a doubt as to whether your reviewer, when he speaks of "the outward part or sign in the Cœna Domini" as being for S. Thomas Aquinas "mere sense-illusion", quite correctly represents the great schoolman?

The language quoted, "Visus, tactus, gustus in Te fallitur", is rather devotional than dogmatic; in the domain of pure theology it would imply that the Res Sacramenti is an object, not of sight, but of faith. And, consistently with this, the Sacramentum is, in S. Thomas's view, an object of sense-perception; that it is "mere sense-illusion" is by no means a valid conclusion from his teaching.

I am, Sir, yours obediently,
WATKIN W. WILLIAMS.

SCHOOLS AND THE HOLIDAY RUSH.

To the Editor of the SATURDAY REVIEW.

30 June 1909.

SIR,—As the holiday season approaches every year a problem confronts the father of a family which becomes more and more anxious. It is a problem from which bachelors and spinsters are comparatively free. All schools break up about the same time, and there is a period of some five or six weeks during which parents are in eager competition for rooms and houses at the seaside. Everybody wants to go to the sea nowadays; a fortnight or so in the country does not suffice, as it did even a generation ago. Children must be given the opportunity of digging in the sands, of bathing and paddling to their hearts' content for a month. The money for seaside holidays must be found if paterfamilias is to have any autumn peace. The consequence is obvious. The rush for quarters in August is so keen that tiny houses, jerry built to the last degree, or uncomfortable rooms with a minimum of so-called furniture—including generally a tuneless piano—realise prices which are ruinous because paterfamilias dare not say they are prohibitive. He is called upon to spend money he cannot afford to secure accommodation in a crowded resort under conditions which bring him no compensation in rest to much-tired nerves; the time so spent is not a pleasant memory, and the return of the holiday season is looked to with not unnatural dread by men whose families and incomes are possibly in inverse ratio. And all because schools must break up at one time.

In July as in September apartments and houses let for two-thirds, sometimes one-half, what is asked for them in August. It would be a boon and a blessing to parents, if there could be some rearrangement among the schools which would enable a more equable distribution of the holiday pressure. If one-third of the schools broke up at the end of June, another third at the end of July, and the other third at the end of August, the pressure would be relieved, and the father might take his family of five or six away for a sum not exceeding, say, that spent by half-a-dozen bachelors who escape the August rush. Money apart, the relief in other directions would be welcome. At present the anxiety to get rooms during the period of the children's holiday is really serious, involving several visits—costly in themselves—to likely places in the hope of finding tolerable vacation quarters. I do not know quite what regulates the school holidays; what I do know is the worry and the cost of the present system, and I ask the SATURDAY REVIEW to let me ventilate a domestic grievance in the hope that some more resourceful mind may suggest a way to the remedy.

Yours truly,
A HOLIDAY VICTIM.

REVIEWS.

THE FAERIE QUEENE.

"The Faerie Queene." By Edmund Spenser. Cambridge: At the University Press. 1909. 2 vols. 73s. 6d. net.

NO writer has a securer place in the affections of real lovers of poetry than the author of the most serenely beautiful of all great poems, and their devotion to him can only be increased by the possession of this very handsome reprint of the edition of 1596, plus the introductory verses and epistle from that of 1590 and the fragments from that of 1609. The size is sumptuous and the type a model of clearness. The paper is, perhaps, not quite on the same high level, and bears the watermark "Van Gelder Zonen". We are told that a few obvious misprints have been corrected, but we could provide the publishers with a list of a score of others which have escaped notice. But the production as a whole does the Cambridge Press great credit, and if it were in the hands of all readers of Spenser the company would be neither very few nor very weary which was "in at the death" of the Blatant Beast, that lusty animal as to whose subsequent career the poet, as though with prophetic anticipation of Macaulay, took so much pains to inform us. It is an ancient superstition that the "Faerie Queene" is a wearisome composition, particularly among those who have not taken the pains to read it. Allegories are by nature wearisome, it is thought, whether portrayed in print by Spenser or in paint by Watts. They certainly would be, if we were only permitted to enjoy the work of art after we had dosed ourselves with pages of flamboyant explanation. If that were necessary we should never have landed safely even in the House of Pride, let alone the Gulf of Greediness. But, mercifully, in Spenser's case there is no necessity for us to trouble whether Timias was Sir Walter Ralegh or Arthegill Lord Grey of Wilton, or whether Una's ass was the same as Tertullian's, or how Britain can be Fairyland and Britain at the same moment, or whether the Dragon, like other more respectable creatures, was killed by being compelled to swallow the Sword of Righteousness or some less radical weapon. We bathe ourselves in the sensuous splendour of the verse and it suffices us. Spenser was doubtless inferior to Boiardo or Ariosto as a teller of stories, but he invented for himself that flawless means of expression, the stanza which bears his name, the legitimate successor of Chaucer's rime royal and Sackville's seven-line compound, a stanza which makes Boiardo's and Ariosto's eight-line metre, with its six alternating rhymes and concluding couplet, seem almost nerveless in comparison. His mastery of his metre seems to have been complete from the very first, a striking testimony to his genius if we contrast it, for instance, with Dante's comparative technical imperfection in the earlier part of the "Commedia". Only once has a simile been suggested to him metri gratia, so far as we have discovered, as against numerous instances in the "Inferno". Indeed the luxuriant ease of rhythmic diction, which is Spenser's chief characteristic, is more noteworthy in the former than in the latter half of the poem. In Books IV. to VI. there is greater restraint and less spontaneity, but the technical accomplishment seems to be no greater. Again, in the Mutability cantos, which are usually attributed to the seventh book, but which appear to us to date from a much later period, and to postulate the intervention of rimed composition between them and the end of Book VI., we find another somewhat indefinable change in the character of the verse. It is at once clearer cut and more facile than the verse of the latter half of the main poem, and stands at the very highest point of Spenser's achievement. No one surely, with this sublime fragment before him, could fail to lament the loss of so much of the great work and to execrate Tyrone and his patriotic brigands.

What is the most perfect single stanza in the poem?

We have hesitated long in our choice, but are inclined to give our vote for this one:

"The lily, Lady of the flowering field,
The Floure de luce, her lovely Paramoure,
Bid thee to them thy fruitlesse labours yield,
And soon leave off this toilsome wearie stoure;
Loe, loe, how brave she decks her bounteous boure
With silken curtains and gold coverlets,
Therein to shrowd her sumptuous Belamoure,
Yet neither spinnes nor cardes, ne cares nor frets,
But to her mother Nature all her cares she lets."

More beautiful in some ways, or at any rate of a more elaborate beauty, is the stanza which follows, but it is marred by the echo rhyme in the fourth and fifth lines. In French this would be an additional grace, but in English it gives a sense of weakness at the very point where strength is most required:

"The joyous brides shrouded in chearefull shade
Their notes unto the voyce attempered sweet;
Th' Angelicall soft trembling voyces made
To th' instruments divine respondence meet;
The silver sounding instruments did meet
With the base murmurs of the waters' fall;
The waters' fall with difference discreet,
Now soft, now loud, unto the winds did call;
The gentle warbling wind low answered to all."

If any other stanzas are to be put into competition with these we should select the angel stanza (II. 8, 2) or the wonderful simile describing the bore on the Shannon (IV. 3, 2). There are single lines, too, or pairs of lines which, for mere beauty, can scarcely find their parallel in English literature—some lines in Arthur's address to Belphebe, Ulysses "that for his love refused deitie", "the fields, the floods, the heavens with one consent Did seeme to laugh at me and favour mine intent", "I feared love; but they that love do live, But they that die doe neither love nor hate"—and there are lines of scarcely surpassable vigour, "ne mortall steele empearce his miscreated mould", "with blasphemous bannes high God in peeces tare", or this, which may with justice be placed above its Vergilian original:

"His sinfull soule with desperate disdaine,
Out of her fleshly ferme fled to the place of paine".

But it is in more continuous passages, especially of description, that the genius of Spenser is even more fully displayed. Most of these are so celebrated that it is unnecessary to refer to them. The first three books abound with them, and it will depend upon our individual taste whether we admire more the pictures of the horrible or of the ecstatically lovely, of the virtues or of the vices. Occasionally Spenser shows himself to be as great in reflection as in description, for example, in the Lucretian exaltation of the dialogue between the Red Cross Knight and Despair or in the second of the Mutability cantos; and indeed his tendency in later years seems to have been more reflective and less descriptive, to pass, so to speak, from "Armide" to "Iphigénie en Tauride", a change causing or corresponding with the change in technique to which we have already referred.

We have pointed out that the allegorical basis of the "Faerie Queene" need prove no obstacle to its enjoyment. Another obstacle which has been much exaggerated is Spenser's alleged archaism. It would be remarkable if a poet of his enormous power and facility of expression had been deliberately archaistic to the extent to which the vice of sham archaism has been attributed to him. Such introduction of antique expressions as we find is probably due to the fact that his chief model was his only great predecessor, Chaucer; but we venture to suggest that the charge of archaism has been largely fostered by the fact that, for some reason or other, it has always been the custom to print his works in their original spelling, while those of his contemporaries have almost invariably been modernised. Modernise the spelling of any portion of the "Faerie Queene" and the impression of antiquity vanishes almost entirely. Take, for instance, the two stanzas which we have quoted above. In the former there is nothing at all which could not be found in the most ordinary Elizabethan English, except, perhaps, the word "stoure"; and in the latter there is nothing whatever which might not occur even in Dryden, or later still. Yet some critics speak of Spenser's style almost as if it were that of "Piers Plowman", and we have met persons who seem to be almost as much afraid of him as they would be of Beowulf. It is not Spenser's unsullied diction, but Milton's latinised vocabulary, we had almost said jargon, which should alarm true lovers of the English tongue.

SIR JOHN ARDAGH.

"The Life of Major-General Sir John Ardagh." By his Wife, Susan Countess of Malmesbury. London: Murray. 1909. 15s. net.

SIR JOHN ARDAGH would have distinguished himself in almost any profession; and, even in the comparatively narrow one he chose to adopt, he achieved success in spheres of activity which strictly speaking are outside the soldier's usual curriculum. He sat on innumerable commissions and committees; he was a leading authority on international law; he was private secretary to a Viceroy of India; he was Chief of the Military School of Engineering at Chatham; and he accompanied Lord Beaconsfield to the Berlin Congress as one of his military advisers, to say nothing of the numerous appointments of a purely military character he held in peace and war time during various phases of his career. In all of these sometimes diverse posts he did well, and earned the unstinted praise of his superiors. But perhaps the most important crisis in his career was his appointment as Director of Military Intelligence in the momentous years which immediately preceded the South African war. The Intelligence Department of the War Office is now rightly given a very prominent place. But at the time Sir John Ardagh took over its direction its importance had by no means been properly appreciated. Now it is manned by a very large staff, and housed in close proximity to the War Secretary and the Chief of the General Staff. But in 1896 it was hidden away in Queen Anne's Gate, and manned by a mere handful of officers. The funds at its use were exiguous, and had the information which it provided as to the coming struggle been on a similar scale, it would not have been altogether fair to blame either Sir John Ardagh or his small band of zealous assistants. The reverse, however, was the fact; and both the evidence given before the War Commission and its report amply proved this, even before Lady Malmesbury wrote this admirably clear and sensible Life of Sir John. Not only were the strength of the Boer forces and armaments most accurately gauged, but the authorities were expressly warned of the advisability of taking into consideration the practical certainty of the Orange Free State throwing in its lot with the Transvaal if war should break out. It was then no fault of the Intelligence branch that its warnings and estimates were disregarded by the Government of the day, in fact, hardly read. But the cruel injustice of the whole business is that even to-day, and in spite of the strongly worded report of the War Commission, the average well-informed man will tell you that the War Office grossly underestimated the strength of the Boer forces and the nature of their armaments. "Remarkably accurate", indeed, to quote the verdict of the War Commission on Sir John Ardagh's forecast of events.

Considering his abilities and the admirable though quiet work he had done for his country over a long space of years, he should certainly have reaped greater rewards and higher rank in the Army. As it was he was only a major-general when he retired. A propos we must tell a story which is not alluded to in Lady Malmesbury's book. Towards the close of the South African war Sir John Ardagh was sent to South Africa, where he arrived in January 1902. His duty was to represent the Government with respect to certain claims then before the Central Board, sitting at that time in South Africa. During his sojourn there he was granted the local rank of lieutenant-general. Now a regulation exists that an officer who has held a higher rank on active service than the one under which he retires may be granted that rank as an honorary one. There are consequently cases of colonels who are honorary major-generals, and major-generals who are honorary lieutenant-generals, in their retirement. It is true that Sir John held no command, and saw no service in the field at that time. Still he held the local rank in South Africa whilst the war was still going on; and most fair-minded men would surely say that this placed him within the terms of the regulation. After his retirement the point was raised that he should be granted the honorary rank. It was a modest request. When one considers the great services he had rendered the nation and how inadequately they had been rewarded, and when, moreover, one realises that this carries no increase of pension, a point might surely have been stretched in his favour, if indeed it was necessary to stretch anything. The question came before the then military chief at the War Office and his advisers in such matters, and the request was unceremoniously refused; and, as it was a purely military matter, the War Secretary acquiesced. One may be sure that had Sir John Ardagh belonged to the military party which was then in the ascendant no difficulty would have been made. As no question of pay was involved, there was no reason to fear that the Treasury, the supreme arbiter in most military matters, would intervene. He might be made an honorary Field-Marshal for all the Treasury cared, so long as no extra pay was asked. Of course it would have been a barren honour, but still it should have been granted. We imagine that the real reason why Ardagh did not reach a higher position in the Army was because his composition did not include "push", and because the science of self-advertisement, as now practised by some of our modern generals, was not amongst the many subjects he had studied.

THE WORSHIPFUL COMPANY OF MUSICIANS.

"An Illustrated Catalogue of the Music Loan Exhibition, held . . . by the Worshipful Company of Musicians at Fishmongers' Hall, June and July 1904." London: Novello. 1909. 21s. to Subscribers.

PROBABLY few people have heard of the existence of the Company of Musicians, and this is scarce surprising in view of the very little the company ever does for music. As, however, good King James the First of England granted its Charter on 8 July 1604, the company determined to show that it was still alive and doing well on its three-hundredth birthday; and to this end it arranged a public exhibition of printed and manuscript music, musical instruments, and portraits of celebrated and uncelebrated musicians. The exhibition was open in Fishmongers' Hall for three days in June and fourteen days of July 1904, and it was, we believe, fairly attended by the curious. In the list of names of the committee who arranged this festive matter we note those of a few musicians, an organ-builder, a clergyman, a military gentleman, a bank clerk, a music-publisher, a pianoforte-maker, and several amateurs, so that all classes may be said to have been represented. The committee seems to have expended all its spare energy over the festival itself; for it has taken it nearly five years to get out this catalogue. Messrs. Novello, in an apologetic Note, "regret the delay . . . due to the great difficulties which have been encountered in preparing the work". Our experience in such enterprises is that the principal difficulty lies, after the first glorious thrills of excitement have passed, in persuading the buoyant gentlemen to do what they promised. However, at last the catalogue is here, and a very handsome volume it is, beautifully printed on good paper, and the illustrations—particularly the reproductions of the portraits of Handel, Monteverde, and Haydn—beyond all praise. The edition, we may say, is limited to five hundred copies at a guinea apiece to subscribers before a certain date; after that date the price was raised to two guineas. When we examine the contents with some care there appears no great reason to be joyful. The committee of the Company of Musicians had apparently no definite aim beyond that of heaping together a lot of quaint musical curiosities. The earliest specimens of printing have of course an interest; the early viols and fiddles have an interest; the great musicians' autographs have an interest. But these things can always be seen, if not under one roof, by those who really wish to see them; and when all has been said, what good was done by getting them together without the purpose of illustrating some intelligible artistic scheme? This exhibition—a musical exhibition—might at least have been so arranged as to show us what has been lost or gained during the last three centuries or more in the engraving of music and the making of instruments. Most folk connected with music stand urgently in need of such a lesson to-day. The best engraved music issued at present cannot match the best of the eighteenth century for beauty and clearness; though it is undoubtedly cheaper—and more trying to the eyes. In the case of organs and pianos, of flutes, clarinets, oboes, horns and trumpets, the quality of tone has grown worse during even the last fifty years. But from the shop-window, commercial point of view our modern instruments are vastly superior to the old—see how they shine, highly polished, neat and new-looking, full of or covered with complicated mechanical contrivances! We have no doubt that many an honest musical amateur left Fishmongers' Hall with contentment in his heart, perfectly satisfied that music was holding its own in that extraordinary race, the "progress" of the arts. Neither the little introductions to the sections of this catalogue nor the lectures delivered at the exhibition (and since published under the editorship of that very wonderful busybody, Mr. P. L. Southgate) are calculated to disillusion him. The quite untenable, though orthodox, view is taken: music, musical instruments and all things connected with music have improved and are improving. And the sad truth is that while a real and marvellous advance has been made on the mechanical side of the instruments the tone is steadily growing poorer. Most of the writers here, and also the exhibition lecturers, seem without sense of beauty. Any ordinary man will instantly feel the rare loveliness of the tone of an old spinet or viol if you play it for him; but these gentlemen calmly assure their readers that things are unmistakeably getting better and will soon be as right as can be. Neither have they any historical sense: doubtless they would hold a modern schoolboy's exercise to be finer than Chaucer's poems, on the ground that Chaucer did not spell correctly. However, the exhibition is over and forgotten; this catalogue will be useful to some folk; and the fine portraits are worth tearing out to frame. They are cheap at a guinea, though we would not willingly give two guineas for them. We beg leave to ask a question. We do not deny that an exhibition once in three centuries is a proof of striking vitality; but we think that the £866 given by the Worshipful Company to the hospitals out of the profits on a musician's work was deplorably misapplied; and we inquire, with all respect, what else, during the three centuries, the Company of Musicians has done to justify its charter and existence?

THEISM AND CHRISTIANITY.

"The Christian Doctrine of God." By W. N. Clarke. Edinburgh: Clark. 1909. 10s. 6d.

THE author of this book has arranged his subject on a system quite his own. The great theme is treated in three main divisions: first, God as He is in Himself; secondly, God in relation to man; and, finally, God in relation to the universe. Under the first division is considered, among other attributes, Personality and Love. But these attributes are regarded without reference to the doctrine of the Trinity. Thus the discussion so far is theistic without being Christian. Under the second division God is considered as Creator, as

Father, as Saviour, as Trinity, and as God in human life—that is to say, as incarnate.

The disadvantages of this treatment of the subject are obvious. In the first place, Divine Personality is considered without reference to the Trinity. This is essentially non-Christian; for the Christian doctrine is not theism plus trinitarianism as a sort of appendix; it is inherently and essentially trinitarian. And the consequence of this treatment is that Divine Personality is discussed twice over, once under the aspect of God as He is in Himself and again under His relation to mankind. The effect of this is that God is made to appear essentially unitarian, and only trinitarian relatively to mankind. This may not be what the author intends to teach: but it is nevertheless what his system suggests. No other effect can result when a philosophic discussion of Divine personality is conducted without the light which the doctrine of inner distinctions within God, and this alone, can give. A second disadvantage of this division is that the doctrine that God is Love is discussed apart from reference either to the Trinity or to mankind. The necessary result of this treatment is that the Divine Love is deprived of all object; even one merely finite and created. But surely it is quite impossible to do justice to this loftiest of all Divine attributes, apart from those inner differentiations within Deity which give it an eternal significance. A third disadvantage of this division is that the Fatherhood of God is considered exclusively in relation to mankind: to Jesus indeed as He is human, and then to all other men. But this is not the Christian doctrine: God is, in Christianity, "the Father, of Whom all fatherhood in heaven and on earth is named". "According to this notable utterance of S. Paul", says the present Dean of Westminster, "God is not only the universal Father, but the archetypal Father, the Father of Whom all other fathers are derivatives and types. So far from regarding the Divine fatherhood as a mode of speech in reference to the Godhead, derived by analogy from our conception of human fatherhood, the Apostle maintains that the very idea of fatherhood exists primarily in the Divine nature, and only by derivation in every other form of fatherhood, whether earthly or heavenly. The All-Father is the source of fatherhood wherever it is found." If this is the apostolic conception, then it follows that the assignment of God's Fatherhood to the department of relative attributes, contingent on the existence of mankind, is wholly inadequate, and indeed gravely misleading. A fourth disadvantage of the system before us is that the Doctrine of the Trinity is discussed exclusively on its experimental side; in relation, that is, to mankind.

And this leads us to say that there are clearly two distinct methods in which the Christian doctrine of God can be treated: there is the historic method and there is the dogmatic method. The historic method is to trace the process by which God revealed Himself to man, and man gradually came to realise the Divine characteristics. This is the experimental, the religious, way. The dogmatic method is that which begins with the sum total of the conception of God as presented in its most matured and completed form. This is the theological, the systematic, way. Each of these methods has its own distinct advantages. They may well be employed independently and successively. But they are wholly different, and they are more valuable when not confused. If we adopt the historic method, then we survey the field of religious experience from the crude, rudimentary, vague, unformed ideas of early mankind up to their perfected and profound conceptions of Deity. We trace the gradual evolution through the various stages of Polytheism, Pantheism, Dualism, Monotheism up to the Christian, the Trinitarian conception. In the process of this study of religions it is easy to show how all the great terms, Person, Love, Fatherhood, become filled with profounder contents as the religious, experimental and intellectual development of mankind matures. It is easily shown in this method how the knowledge of God as Trinity came to men in an experimental way, through their recognition of Jesus as Redeemer and the Spirit as Sanctifier. They had to co-ordinate their conceptions of Divine Unity with their acknowledgment of Jesus as, in the highest sense, God's Son. Thus Fatherhood became filled with profounder meaning. It denoted an essential Divine characteristic and Divine distinction. It is also clear that the full revelation of God as Love waited for the correlative revelation of the Father and the Son. The author has stated part of this. "The early Christian experience contained the elements out of which was formed the doctrine of the Trinity." "It was indebted for this fresh manifestation of God to Jesus." But we cannot feel that adequate emphasis is laid on the distinctive sense in which Christ revealed the Fatherhood of God. We miss the recognition of the fact, which Harnack sees but cannot account for, that Jesus puts into the words *My* God and *My* Father something which belongs to no one but Himself.

But, in addition to the historic treatment of the Doctrine of God, there is the dogmatic exposition of the perfected Christian conception. Here the position is reversed. We begin with no crude and partial statement of the Christian truth. We start with no mere Unitarian view, but with the distinctively Christian features of the doctrine in their fulness and completion. We do not regard the Trinitarian conception as an extra to be tacked on to a theory of Deity otherwise complete. On the contrary, we begin with the Christian doctrine as essentially and inherently Trinitarian. The metaphysics of personality may be here introduced for the elucidation and confirmation of a doctrine traditionally known and proclaimed by the Christian Society. The sublime assertion that God is Love will, in this aspect, run no risk of being watered down into a theory of universal benevolence. It will be shown as another form of affirming the Trinity. The doctrine of Fatherhood will, in this method, be recognised as by no means primarily a "tenderer equivalent for creatorship", but as archetypal and correlative to the existence of the Eternal Son. And in this dogmatic exposition it will be from the essential characteristics of God that thought will proceed to develop His relation to mankind.

These are the contrasted ways. They are here briefly indicated in outline as a reminder of their difference. Either way may be advantageously pursued. But they ought not to be confused. The advantages of placing the dogmatic or theoretic method after the historical are numerous. This order is congenial to the historic spirit of the age. It does ample justice to the experimental side of religion. It forms a natural basis for abstract and theological exposition. What men have thought may conduce to indicate what men should think.

But the method pursued in this volume sets a crude dogmatic exposition of a doctrine which is Theism, but not Christianity, in the forefront of an exposition of the teaching of Jesus about God; with the grave disadvantages already noted.

Apart from these serious disadvantages of method, there is much clear and readable exposition of these great themes. There is no attempt to demonstrate that the Christian God exists. The attempt is considered "quite contrary to the Christian idea". There is a decided belief that "finality has never been reached", and that, in conceptions of God, it is unattainable. On the whole the author's earlier book, "Outlines of Christian Theology", is an abler volume than the present.

MARSHALS OF FRANCE.

"Napoleon's Marshals." By R. P. Dunn-Pattison. London: Methuen. 1909. 12s. 6d. net.

ALL who have studied the Napoleonic wars and the far greater number of readers of general history of that period must have been puzzled at times by the meteoric appearance of some of Napoleon's Marshals on some particular theatre of war. Whence did they come and whither did they go and for what reasons? The problems thus presented were not made less complex by the kaleidoscopic changes in rank and titles which Napoleon made it a part of his system to bestow upon those whom he elected to honour, at any rate outwardly. What his private opinions were of them and their capabilities can best be gathered from his brutal remarks on them made at S. Helena and elsewhere. The General of yesterday became the Count of to-day and the Duke, Prince, or Marshal of the morrow, and in Napoleon's bulletins were referred to by their latest titles with bewildering promptitude. We have known keen students of military history who have found it necessary to tabulate the Generals and Marshals of the Empire under their various titles for ready reference. Mr. Dunn-Pattison has evidently experienced the same difficulties and has wisely begun his book with a synopsis of the twenty-six soldiers of various nationalities who attained the rank of Marshal of France under Napoleon's rule. This records their names, dates of birth, and various titles, and gives a column showing " how disposed of ", and their ages when they died. It is a curious commentary upon the risks of warfare of this period, at any rate among the higher ranks, that among these twenty-six warriors who had taken part in almost countless engagements from 1804 onwards two, and two only, Lannes and Bessières, actually met their deaths on the battlefield. With the exception of the gallant Poniatowski, who was drowned in the Elster whilst nobly covering Napoleon's retreat from Leipzig, Ney, Murat, and Brune, who were shot or murdered in 1815 after the cessation of hostilities, and Mortier, who was slain by Fieschi's bomb in 1842, all the other Marshals died natural deaths at an average age of over seventy-one, six exceeding eighty years of age. Apparently the employment of a Marshal of France during the incessant fighting between 1804 and 1815 would hardly be classified as a dangerous trade nowadays.

It was a common and accepted saying of our forefathers that Napoleon's armies were composed of brigands. The lapse of time may have softened our views, but it is notorious that Napoleon's system of making war support war led to an enormous amount of plundering and rapine, both official and unofficial. Readers of this book will see how just was the old verdict and how those Marshals were, with but few exceptions, simply brigand chiefs, adorned with brilliant uniforms and mushroom titles and enriched by their brigand leader with the plunder of the nations he successively crushed, as well as by their own private efforts in imitation of his methods. The conditions were, of course, altogether exceptional, for owing to the Revolution many of the Marshals had sprung from the lower classes, and it is instructive to note how often when they rose to the occasion and acted in other respects as honourable and high-class soldiers, they could not avoid the besetting sin of the adventurer—avarice. Thus Masséna, certainly one of the very ablest of the Marshals, repeatedly showed the greed and cruelty of the low-class Italian he undoubtedly was. Napoleon's drastic step in calmly appropriating the three million francs which Masséna had wrung from the luckless Neapolitans and placed to his own account in the bank at Leghorn is a delightful example of a thief catching a thief.

For the well-read in Napoleonic literature there is little new in this book, yet we imagine that many readers will find some of the details both interesting and instructive. But in setting forth the brilliant services of these Marshals the whole pitiful tale of their jealousies and foibles has of necessity been repeated. We read of Murat's insane vanity which led him to masquerade in ridiculous costumes and caused his stern master to say : " Go and put on your uniform, you look like a clown " ; of Soult's audacious schemes, of Ney's and Victor's rebellious conduct, of the mutual hatreds and jealousies of one and all. Even in Mortier, who was conspicuously free from jealousy, the mean avarice of the peasant was painfully apparent. Soult was equally avaricious and jealous to boot. It is interesting to note how many of the men whom Napoleon selected to promote had, in the chaos due to the Revolution, risen from the ranks to high command in a few months. Thus Victor was only nine months from private soldier to battalion commander, and several others were not much longer. Often the command of a brigade was followed only a few weeks later by that of a division; colonels were twenty-one years of age and generals twenty-four. Such early promotion, combined with defective education due to their obscure origin, was not seldom detrimental to the subsequent development of these fortunate young soldiers. Much can be learned in the field, but the absence of a good military education was one of the causes why so many of the Marshals were poor tacticians and utterly ignorant of strategy. On the other hand, it is fair to note that some of them who had served for long periods in subordinate positions seemed incapable of exercising independent command. Serurier had thirty-four years' regimental service, and was a case in point. Even the gifted Berthier, the famous Chief of the Staff to the Emperor, although his twenty-three years' prior service had made him admirable at staff duties, was declared by his master to be unfit to command independently, nor did he wish to, but was content to serve with " dog-like fidelity ". Again, some of the Marshals lacked the moral courage to act decisively and to expend troops at critical moments in order to secure or to confirm a victory. Ney pointed out to Napoleon that the battle of Smolensk was no victory, since the Russians had been " dislodged, not beaten ".

How Napoleon was led to select his Marshals is a study in itself. His primary object was to strengthen his position by linking their destinies with his own, but he had also to provide for men such as Brune and Lefèbvre, whose dangerous Republican principles were prejudicial to his schemes. Others, such as Serurier, Kellermann, and Pérignon, had to be selected as connecting the victories of the Revolutionary wars with those of the Empire. As strategists, Masséna and Soult stand first; Davout was a great tactician, and Napoleon showed his appreciation of this by giving him the command of 140,000 men in Prussia in 1811. It was his far-reaching victory of Aüerstadt which made his reputation as a tactician for all time. The author refers to this as a masterpiece of minor tactics ! Davout commanded 23,000 men, and by his brilliant manœuvres beat 45,000 Prussians on this day. There are a few slips and misprints—Crawford for Craufurd, Ulces for Ucles, El Bodin for El Bodon. The book is decidedly good, and would be even better had the author refrained from repeating sundry French accounts of the prodigies of valour of the one man against a hundred type ascribed to some of the Marshals, which are painfully suggestive of some of Baron Marbot's performances.

NOVELS.

" Studies in Wives." By Mrs. Belloc Lowndes. London: Heinemann. 1909. 6s.

If you come to think of it, most modern novels are studies in wives, but the title chosen by Mrs. Lowndes fits well enough this collection of six short stories. They are obviously the work of a clever journalist with a keen eye for character and an uncertainty about style. The themes demand a more crisp kind of writing, a greater determination to reject the superfluous word, than their writer has given them. The wives range from a lady who spends an illicit honeymoon in London with a stranger met by chance in the train, and then poisons her elderly husband, to the blameless and rather stupid wife of a brilliant politician. We are reminded, rather too frequently for our old-fashioned taste, that many modern young women refuse to bear children. Mrs. Lowndes is very uncertain about those little touches—rather unnecessary in any case—which show the reader that the author knows some trifling fact which will perhaps be new to the public. For example, she describes excellently in the main the effect which a brilliant young Irish singer and her old Irish nurse produce as residents in a dull English provincial town. But it is not, as she thinks, " an Irish idiosyncrasy " for a servant to call her master " Mr. So-and-so ". This is exactly what the inferior English domestic invariably does, but no Irish servant would use any style but " Sir " unless meaning deliberately to be impertinent. We rather like the notion of a singer so oppressed by her husband's bourgeois Anglo-Saxon surroundings that she sent him an entirely imaginary confession of unfaithfulness in order to escape back to the concert-room. Another story is an apt study of a young wife living in a London set which is far too rich for her means by drawing subsidies from a male friend while remaining strictly virtuous. When honour goes out of date virtue is doubtless regarded as a merely physical fact. There is a brilliant description of a ten-year leasehold liaison masquerading as marriage, with its unexpected results upon the man and the woman. In fact every story is clever and readable—though we in our innocence cannot quite see why, if a Cabinet Minister falls dead in the afternoon in a respectable drawing-room where he is known to take tea constantly, the fact should be regarded as so fatal to his middle-aged hostess' reputation that his wife must be summoned on the telephone to get the corpse away in a cab. Can it be that for all the cleverness and up-to-dateness and all the rest of it the writer of these stories is slightly lacking in humour?

"Frank Burnet." By Dorothy V. Horace Smith. London: Murray. 1909. 6s.

Marchington Manor belonged to Miss Phillis, and Frank belonged to Marchington Vicarage, which was the family living. After philandering with art to near the end of the book he followed at last his hereditary bent; though he would hardly develop into the more robust type of parson, unless Miss Phillis greatly altered him. The real artist was Wattie, the blacksmith's boy, whose study of horses got mixed up in a rather unconvincing way with Frank's work, and was accepted by the Academy. There is here some good if sketchy character-drawing, a pleasant picture of country life, and apparently a touching faith in the cachet of Burlington House.

"The First Law." By Lady Troubridge. London: Mills and Boon. 1909. 6s.

A valued waiter of our acquaintance used every morning to ask us to return the halfpenny paper after breakfast because his wife was "absorbed in" its serial story. He was so anxious about it that presently we began to glance at the story ourselves. This novel reminds us of it. The suburban sentiment, wholesome if sticky, the adroit piling-up of sensational incident, and the implicit insistence on the great gulf fixed between "the quality" and the lower orders (beginning with the family solicitor) are excellently devised to render the book absorbing to a certain class of reader.

"The Road of No Return." By A. C. Inchbold. London: Chatto and Windus. 1909. 6s.

This is a serious novel from which the reader will glean information about the Russian revolutionary party, the Orthodox Greek Church, and the shrines and scenery of the Holy Land. There is a story as well, serving as a vehicle for all this, but not otherwise of great interest or originality.

"The Runaways." By R. Andom. London: Greening. 1909. 3s. 6d.

"Being", says the sub-title, "some early adventures of Troddles and us"—four schoolboys, whose nautical and other experiences are as incredible as the drawing of the lads themselves is conventional; but as a sort of slangy juvenile extravaganza the story is ingenious, and at least it is all en plein air.

SHORTER NOTICES.

"On the Oxford Circuit, and Other Verses." By Mr. Justice Darling. London: Smith, Elder. 1909. 5s. net.

Mr. Justice Darling is our only poet who wears the ermine as well as the bays. We may say of his poetry what may be said of his judicial humour, that it is not so striking by its merit as by its unexpectedness in coming from such a professionally incongruous source. There is the curiosity of seeing the trick performed at all, as has been remarked about canine dancing. In his little collection of verse Mr. Justice Darling gives us both the grave and the gay, and we find that both as poet and judge it is his lighter and not his more solemn note that pleases us most. The grave is represented by some three hundred lines of hexameters and by thirteen sonnets. Both forms are admittedly the most difficult of verse to handle, and unless the poetic fire is very strongly glowing it is more apt to be extinguished than to shine through. Mr. Justice Darling in his sonnets celebrates Rodin, Coquelin, General Picquart, Viscount Milner, J. McNeill Whistler and some others. One appreciates the difficulty of writing on these admirable subjects so as to avoid the appearance of the epitaph and to give the effect of the Shakespearean or Miltonian or Wordsworthian sonnet, and Mr. Justice Darling more evidently achieves the epitaph. Besides he cultivates the sonnet's measured plot of ground with so many awkward ditches of parenthetical dashes that it is only to be crossed in a risky steeplechase. Mr. Justice Darling is as dashing a sonneteer as he is a judge. We turn with pleasure to the "Occasional Verses" and admire their ease and cleverness and brightness. Meditans nugarum Mr. Justice Darling can write even a sonnet, as that to E.H.P. K.C., which is not heavy. It is easy enough, bar the dashes, to go with the "Occasional Verses". "On the Oxford Circuit" describes a judge's progress on circuit, and the burlesque hexameters are not inappropriate to the subject so far. But Mr. Justice Darling had in mind a particular judge, Sir Thomas Noon Talfourd, who in 1854 died on the Bench at Stafford while charging the Grand Jury. The end comes as an unexpected and startling climax to the reader. The piece is successful and Mr. Justice Darling is justified of his mock hexameters. They were instinctively well chosen to produce the ghastly bizarre effect of death in such surroundings. The legal epigrams, "Marginal Memoranda" prompted by certain well-known legal maxims, will be better appreciated for their twists and quirks by the lawyer than by the layman. To show the characteristic Darlingesque manner we quote one, the only one non-legal, which is in French—"Le Pécheur Dévot":

"Au diable tenir une chandelle
L'Eglise condamne, comme grave péché.
Pour que l'offense ne soit mortelle,
J'en offre de mauvaise qualité."

"The School of Madrid." By A. de Beruete y Moret. Translated by Mrs. Steuart Erskine. London: Duckworth. 1909. 7s. 6d. net.

In his study of a group of painters, imitators, and successors of Velasquez, of whom little has hitherto been known, Señor de Beruete y Moret continues and supplements the work of his father, whose book on Velasquez, published some three years ago, has already become a classic. Velasquez himself Señor Beruete declines for obvious reasons to discuss in any detail. His task is the exploration of that unknown country from which the figure of the great Spanish master emerges so unexpectedly. The period to be studied covers some seventy-five years from the arrival of Velasquez at the Court of Madrid in 1623 to the death of Claudio Coello at the end of the century. Of these successors of Velasquez who go to form the school of Madrid, that artist's pupil and son-in-law Del Mazo is the protagonist and the hero of the story. To this Amico di Velasquez, who so successfully "concealed his want of originality under an undeniable talent", working always before the master's eye, using the same materials in the same surroundings, are now ascribed with all confidence many canvases which bear a close resemblance to the work of Velasquez himself, and yet just lack something of his distinction and brio. While perhaps some few may not grudge Del Mazo the superb Admiral of the National Gallery, there will surely be many dissentient voices with regard to the curiously fascinating "Lady with a Mantilla" belonging to the Duke of Devonshire, a picture which, when shown for the first time in 1901 at the Guildhall, riveted all attention, and though disclaimed by the elder Beruete was unhesitatingly recognised by most English critics as from the hand of Velasquez himself. Several of the reproductions have been photographed for the first time especially for this book, which to students of the Spanish school should prove invaluable.

"Recent Progress in the Study of Variation, Heredity and Evolution." By Robert Heath Lock. London: Murray. 1909. 5s. net.

One very important feature in Mr. Lock's book is its insistence on the practical results which flow from the researches and experiments of recent years into the laws of variation and heredity. Apart from the theoretical student of biology there are two classes of readers who will find in the book the history of discoveries and experiments bearing directly on problems which interest them. They are the cultivators and breeders of plants and animals and the students of sociology, whose science is futile unless it is based upon the laws of man's physical life. The experiments on the Cambridge experimental farm show how the art of producing strains with desired qualities may be founded on definitely ascertained laws so that the product is of greatly increased commercial value. The sociologist may also see in these results a promise of a time when the eugenics of human beings may have still more important consequences on our politics and social conditions. It must be understood also that the book, which is now in its second edition, is addressed mainly to scientific students to whom the views of the Mendelians and Mutationists are phases of the Darwinian controversy which need to be mastered. But the Mendelian laws as expounded by Mr. Lock remain, after all his efforts to make them familiar to the general reader, hard reading. For those possessing a fair groundwork of biological science, however, this book may be recommended, as Dr. Wallace recommends it, for the thorough comprehension of one side in a great dispute.

"Sir Redvers Buller." By Lewis Butler. London: Smith, Elder. 1909. 6s.

This work does not pretend to be in any way an exhaustive account of Sir Redvers Buller's career. That will appear in due time by an experienced pen; and then perhaps at last we shall know the real truth about a man who was undoubtedly treated with great injustice by his contemporaries, military and political, and whose later actions have purposely been enshrouded in considerable mystery. Mr. Butler gives us a very clear picture, drawn by a sympathetic hand, of one who was a conspicuous leader of men, a strong personality, and a great organiser and administrator. Even from the standpoint of his severest detractors, he was largely the victim of circumstances, and the worst possible construction was placed on what he did. His failure in South Africa is by no means yet proven. And as to his previous career, there cannot be two opinions. With Sir Evelyn Wood he was the life and soul of the Zulu campaign. After his work in Egypt and the Soudan came his long, perhaps too long, sojourn at the War Office, during the course of which he filled the post of Adjutant-General more successfully, it is universally admitted, than almost any other holder of that office in modern times. He might have been Commander-in-Chief in India, and he was very nearly being the Chief at home. He might at least have been given his bâton. His services clearly entitled him to this honour.

"Rambles in Sussex." By F. G. Brabant M.A. London: Methuen. 1909. 6s. net.

The reference which Mr. Brabant in his preface makes to his earlier handbook to Sussex in the "Little Guides" series invites a comparison which is rather hard on the present volume. The Little Guide was distinguished by a gift of compendious accuracy almost amounting to genius; the "Rambles", though they are both exact and full, and as a book for the study make an excellent complement to the pocket gazetteer, yet suffer (as the author in his preface seems to fear they may) from an inevitable likeness to other books of that increasing class which presents the history, archæology, natural beauties, and local humours of a county in a readable form. Mr. Brabant adopts the peripatetic method in showing us the country, making excursions from successive centres. His strongest point is the summary descriptions of the architectural features of the village churches. The number of cases in which we are told that "the church has unfortunately been quite spoilt by restoration", or has been "modernised", or "contains little of interest" is a decidedly depressing list.

"Revue des Deux Mondes." 1 Juillet.

This is a strong number. It contains an article of great political interest by M. Tardieu on the relations between France and Germany. His conclusions are preceded by a sketch of events during the last three years, and this is more useful than the programme he lays down for the future, which is in truth neither particularly illuminating nor original. He laughs at the idea of the financial arrangements dreamed of by some hot-headed partisans of an entente. But very excellent reasons against France quarrelling with anyone are supplied by M. Blanchon in his "Balance-sheet of the French Navy", in which he elaborates in a most damaging catalogue the grave defects we already knew in brief. France, in fact, has not a Navy sufficient either to defend her own shores or her colonies; the efficient ships she does possess form a catalogue of samples rather than a coherent fighting force. There is anarchy in all the sections of controlling authorities, and also in the lower ranks. At least forty millions sterling are wanted to put things on a moderately sound footing. This is the result of forty years of the Republic, and a naval department conducted solely with an eye to party politics and pots de vin.

THE JULY REVIEWS.

Imperial defence and the Budget are the outstanding topics in the Reviews. In the "Fortnightly" Mr. Archibald Hurd makes a suggestion towards an imperial fleet and Mr. Geoffrey Drage cries "Back to the Sea". Mr. Hurd's scheme is to maintain the two-Power standard without subvention or other assistance from the oversea dominions, the self-governing colonies agreeing to a "dual scheme of defence" which would aim at their own protection if they were in jeopardy and at the wider duties involved in command of the sea; all should contribute a definite sum to the maintenance of an imperial flying squadron which would be the nucleus of the imperial navy. The Empire should decide upon "a fitting measure of naval defence" to-day so that it might be prepared to fight, if necessary, in 1913. Mr. Drage would not only send our boys to sea, but he would have an imperial organisation for sea service. Every elementary and secondary school would have a sub-target, and he says "the time is very near at hand when the golf links will have to be exchanged for the rifle range". In the "Nineteenth Century" Sir Charles Tupper is energetically patriotic, but a little vague on the question of the precise part the colonies should play in imperial defence, whilst Mr. Frewen Lord is precise as he is emphatic. He would not allow a Cabinet to hold office in any part of the Empire which was not sound on five points—a supreme Navy, universal military service, the preservation of our "Anglo-Saxon" stock throughout the world, a preferential tariff, and the teaching of imperial rights and duties in every school and university throughout the Empire. To Mr. Lord these five points are like the fingers of one's hand, "they cannot be separated". Dreadnought in the "National", who meets the possible charge that he is giving valuable information to foreign Powers with the crushing remark that he is merely telling Englishmen what every foreigner knows, demands the entire reorganisation of the Board of Admiralty, and the raising of a loan of £100,000,000. Dreadnought seems to be a Beresford man on all points except the amount of money to be spent; on that he demands £40,000,000 more than Lord Charles would spend. "Blackwood" calls the naval policy of the Government the great betrayal. "To leave the Empire defenceless, while they are destroying the institutions on which it has hitherto reposed, is now the policy of a Cabinet supported by a majority of three hundred in the House of Commons." "Blackwood" looks to the Lords to provide means, "however sharp or unfamiliar", which shall deliver the country from "this Government of treachery and tyranny". In the "Empire Review" Colonel St. John Fancourt, with more restraint than "Blackwood", says that the Government have made changes vitally affecting imperial interests. He discusses imperial defence under geographical limitations. Recent strategical changes in the distribution of the fleet, he says, have not secured the country against invasion, though they have seriously weakened the military strength of our imperial frontiers, and he demands a fleet which will enable the Empire in time of war to act on interior lines so that the parts can come to each other's assistance as emergencies may render necessary.

Baron d'Estournelles de Constant in the "Fortnightly" enters a plea for a Franco-German rapprochement: a reconciliation would, he says, be a deliverance for the whole world, by which apparently he means a deliverance from the crushing burden of an "armed peace". It would of course be a relief chiefly to France and Germany; it would not break the tension in other directions, and would probably convince the editor of the "National" that Germany had seized the opportunity of composing all differences with France in order to be free to deal with Great Britain. This month he finds that Germany is "the grand international agent provocateur" and derives comfort only from the fact that Prince Bülow has not Prince Bismarck's genius for controlling "the machinery of mischief-making". As to the Bismarckian rôle Mr. Charles Lowe has an extremely interesting article in the "Contemporary", in which he sets forth "the true causes" of the Franco-German war. He traces them to French fears and desire to frustrate the unification of Germany, and warns Great Britain that her suspicions of Germany to-day are on all fours with French suspicions forty years ago. In the same Review Dr. Dillon

(Continued on page 56.)

suggests that the next great war in Europe will not be waged between Germany and Great Britain, Germany and Russia, or Germany and France, but by one group of States against another. Germany and Austria, he says, will henceforth present a united front. Mr. Brailsford in the "English Review" denounces groups, and urges that we should end their latent antagonism by a real concert of Europe. Mr. Æneas O'Neill in the "Nineteenth Century" declares it to be a mistake to regard the Dual Monarchy as the prisoner of Germany. He finds that a basis for a good understanding between Austria, Russia, and England exists, which, while leaving the Triple Alliance free to maintain the balance of power, would prevent its being made an instrument in the hands of "Prussia-Germany".

The Budget has a confident defender in Mr. J. A. Hobson in the "English Review"; he is of course delighted with the land, liquor, and income taxes; they express and enforce the new Liberal finance which he regards as "a defence and a justification of Free Trade, by showing that a large increase of revenue can be obtained without recourse to protective duties". To Mr. Hobson the significance of the Budget is that it paves the way to an "economic survey, indispensable to the provident conduct of public finance". The article is a fine sample of perverted principle, due to the necessity of bolstering up an exploded fiscal ideal. We get into closer touch with fact when we turn to Mr. Pretyman in the "National", and Sir Felix Schuster and Mr. W. S. Rosenbaum in the "Nineteenth Century". What Mr. Hobson regards as provident is seen to be the providence of the spendthrift, under the sanction of an inquisition. Mr. Pretyman, as a landowner who has given the question attention from both the personal and the public point of view, says that if the forced valuation is enacted the landowner's security is gone, and with it his responsibility. Incidentally Mr. Pretyman points out that to escape a tariff which would provide all we want in the way of fresh revenue the Government are imposing new taxes on tobacco, spirits and licences that will cost the consumer some £22,000,000. Sir Felix Schuster in his denunciation of the "unsound and demoralising" death duties, appeals to Adam Smith, but Adam Smith is only listened to by Radical financiers when the principles he laid down can be made to apply to circumstances totally different from those of which he had cognisance. Mr. Rosenbaum is naturally statistical; he shows up anomalies and actual errors in the estimates, explains the intolerable burden which the Government is putting upon capital, and can find only one principle in the Budget—an attempt to justify the confiscation of wealth, a principle "too hazardous and revolutionary to be tamely submitted to by the nation".

Lord Selborne contributes a very judicial article on the native problem in South Africa to "The East and the West". No problem, either on the political or on the social side, is more anxious and in its development more charged with pathos. Lord Selborne says plainly that the white man must make himself responsible for the education of the black and must see that justice is done. With notable exceptions, the black man after a hundred years of contact with civilisation cannot hope to place himself on an equality with the white man, who has two thousand years of civilisation behind him. That is a natural barrier from the racial point of view, but what of the exceptions? Perhaps the best answer is to be found in a powerful study of the social relations of an educated and gifted negro with the white man given by Mr. Cunninghame Graham in the "English Review". If Mirahuano could not be taken to the homes of his white friends, what chance has the black man ever of being regarded as little else than a pariah? And the bitterness of it to the sensitive man! "Think of my life: my very God is white, made in your image, imposed upon my race by yours." Mirahuano's end, told with a few graphic and dramatic touches, was inevitable. Native problems of a different order are those of India, on which Mr. H. C. Streatfeild writes in the "Nineteenth Century", and of Morocco under Mulai Hafid—or any other Sultan for that matter—of which Mr. Ashmead-Bartlett gives a picturesque account in the "National". Affairs in Morocco have become a tragi-farce. Officers who know no Arabic drill, troops who know no English, and a disorganised rabble march to the strains of "The British Grenadiers" and the "Marseillaise". Mulai Hafid is unhappy on the throne, whilst Abd el Aziz plays polo, enjoys life in Tangier, and looks back upon his reign as a nightmare.

Among the miscellaneous items in the Reviews is an article by Mr. and Mrs. Whetham in the "Nineteenth Century" on the extinction of the upper classes which is worth serious study. The upper classes include professional men and the best artisans as well as the aristocracy. The diminution in the number of children born to parents whose attributes of mind and body or professional and business attainments make it desirable that the stock should be handed down is shown to be rapid and continuous; there is no falling-off in the families begotten by the improvident and the feeble-minded; and hence the nation is no longer being recruited from above, but from below. The warning as to the certain consequences should not go unheeded. Of George Meredith Mr. Edward Clodd gives some intimate recollections in the "Fortnightly"; and Mr. G. K. Chesterton discusses his philosophy in paradoxical and wholly Chestertonian vein in the "Contemporary". Mr. Chesterton also writes in the "Oxford and Cambridge Review" on Milton and his age; the most important article in the "Oxford and Cambridge" is, however, not Mr. Chesterton's, but Major Silburn's on the possible secession of South Africa as the result of allowing the Boers to supersede Lord Milner's great work. Major Silburn has the courage to say what many feel but try to disguise in a rush of false sentiment.

For this Week's Books see page 58.

THIS WEEK'S BOOKS.

BIOGRAPHY

The Life and Times of Laurence Sterne (Wilbur L. Cross). Macmillan. 10s. 6d. net.

FICTION

The Lady of the Strand (Bram Stoker); A Reaping (E. F. Benson). Heinemann. 6s. each.
Deep Sea Warriors (Basil Lubbock). Methuen. 6s.
The Veil (E. S. Stevens); Cardillac (Robert Barr); Mary up at Gaffries and Letitia her Friend (S. C. Nethersole); Harm's Way (Lloyd Osbourne). Mills and Boon. 6s. each.
The Vulture's Prey (Tyler De Saix). Fisher Unwin. 6s.
The Coming of Aurora (Mrs. P. C. De Crespigny); The Romance of Beauty (Roy Horniman). Nash. 6s. each.
The House of the Soul (J. B. Harris-Burland). Chapman and Hall. 6s.
The Cliffs (Charles M. Doughty). Duckworth. 6s.
The Bride of the Mistletoe (James Lane Allen). Macmillan. 2s. 6d. net.
With the Warden of the Marches (Howard Pease). Constable. 6s.

HISTORY

Eton Memories (An Old Etonian). Long. 10s. 6d. net.
The Romance of Fra Filippo Lippi (A. J. Anderson). Paul. 10s. 6d. net.
Survey of the Lands of William, First Earl of Pembroke (with an Introduction by the Transcriber. 2 vols.). Oxford: The Roxburghe Club.

SCIENCE

A Study of the Principles of Nature (Frederick Hovenden). Chapman and Hall. 6s.

TRAVEL

The Voice of the Orient (Mrs. Walter Tibbits). Long. 3s. 6d. net.
The Journal of an Expedition across Venezuela and Colombia, 1906-1907 (Hiram Bingham). Fisher Unwin. 10s. net.
The Isle of Man (Agnes Herbert). Lane. 10s. 6d. net.

VERSE

Verses of Various Moods (John Clark). Simpkin. 3s. 6d. net.
Peter of Cortona (Eleanor Gray), 2s. 6d. net; Thoughts and Pastimes (M. E. R.), 3s. 6d. net; The Sh'ahnama of Firdausi (Arthur George Warner and Edmond Warner. Vol. IV.), 10s. 6d. Kegan Paul.
Wind and Hill (Geoffrey Winthrop Young). Smith, Elder. 3s. 6d. net.

MISCELLANEOUS

British Terriers (J. Maxtee). Gill. 3s. net.
Safety of British Railways, The (H. Raynar Wilson), 3s. 6d. net; By What Authority? (John H. Muirhead), 2s. net. King.
Town Planning: Past, Present, and Possible (H. Inigo Triggs). Methuen. 15s.

REVIEWS AND MAGAZINES FOR JULY.—The National Review, 2s. 6d.; The Empire Review, 1s.; The Open Courts, 10c.; Current Literature, 25c.; The Book Monthly, 6d.; Mercure de France, 1f. 25c.; Revue des Deux Mondes, 3f.; The Scottish Historical Review, 2s. 6d.

SALES BY AUCTION.

THE HAZLITT COLLECTION OF COINS.

MESSRS. SOTHEBY, WILKINSON & HODGE will SELL by AUCTION, at their House, No. 13 Wellington Street, Strand, W.C., on MONDAY, JULY 12, and Three Following Days, at One o'clock precisely, the valuable Collection of GREEK, ROMAN, ORIENTAL, CONTINENTAL and FOREIGN and BRITISH and COLONIAL COINS, in Gold, Electrum, Silver, Bronze, &c., consisting chiefly of Choice Specimens in Preservation and Artistic Merit, formed during the last thirty years by W. C. Hazlitt, Esq., of Barnes Common (Surrey).

May be viewed. Catalogues may be had. Illustrated copies, price 2s. 6d. each.

ENGRAVINGS.

MESSRS. SOTHEBY, WILKINSON & HODGE will SELL by AUCTION, at their House, No. 13 Wellington Street, Strand, W.C., on THURSDAY, JULY 15, and following day, at One o'clock precisely, COLLECTION of ENGRAVINGS, the Property of a Gentleman recently deceased, who lived in the West of England, comprising Portraits in Mezzotint and Stipple after Sir J. Reynolds, including an impression of "Mrs. Hardinge," by T. Watson; others by J. McArdell, J. Jones, C. H. Hodges, C. Watson, and others; Mezzotint Portraits, by J. Beckett, A. Blooteling, A. Browne, J. Faber, J. Smith, J. McArdell, R. Tompson, T. Watson, and other Early Engravers; Engravings, Etchings, &c., by Old Masters, including H. S. Beham, C. le Lorraine, A. Dürer, A. Van Ostade, Rembrandt van Rhyn, C. Visscher, A. Waterloo, &c.; English and Foreign Line Portraits, by P. Drevet, R. Nanteuil, G. Edelinck, W. J. Delft, W. Faithorne, W. Hollar, A. Masson, J. Morin, and others; Modern Italian and other Line Engravings; Fancy Subjects of the French School, after A. Watteau, F. Boucher, N. Lancret, J. M. Nattier, C. Vanloo, &c.; Modern Etchings by C. Méryon, J. M. Whistler, and Seymour Haden; Books on Engravings, including British Mezzotint Portraits, by J. Chaloner Smith; Catalogue Raisonné of the Engraved Works of Sir J. Reynolds, illustrated by the insertion of 40 portraits and other illustrations; Bryan's Dictionary of Painters and Engravers, extra-illustrated; Granger's Biographical History of England, 6 vols. in 2, extra-illustrated; and others.

May be viewed two days prior. Catalogues may be had.

THE LIBRARY OF MAJOR-GENERAL SIR M. W. E. GOSSET, K.C.B., DECEASED, WESTGATE HOUSE, DEDHAM.

MESSRS. SOTHEBY, WILKINSON & HODGE will SELL by AUCTION, at their House, No. 13 Wellington Street, Strand, W.C., on MONDAY, JULY 19, at One o'clock precisely, the LIBRARY OF MAJOR-GENERAL SIR M. W. E. GOSSET, K.C.B., deceased, Westgate House, Dedham, comprising First Editions of the Writings of Barrie, Bridges, George Eliot, Henley, Hewlett, Kipling, Meredith, Morris, Shaw, Stevenson, Swinburne, Symonds, Wilde, &c.; works on Sport and Travel, Biography, History, and other properties, including a Magnificent Set of the Sporting Magazine, complete in 156 vols., in crimson calf, uncut; Annals of Sporting, 13 vols.; Valuable Botanical and Ornithological Works, including Reichenbach, Icones Florae Germanicae et Helveticae; Parkinson's Paradisi in Sole, Second Edition; Fuchsius, De Historia Stirpium; Lord Lilford's Birds, Original Subscribers' copies; Dresser's Birds of Europe; Gould's Birds of Great Britain; &c.

May be viewed two days prior. Catalogues may be had.

ENGRAVINGS AND DRAWINGS.

MESSRS. SOTHEBY, WILKINSON & HODGE will SELL by AUCTION, at their House, No. 13 Wellington Street, Strand, W.C., on TUESDAY, JULY 20, at One o'clock precisely, ENGRAVINGS and DRAWINGS, including the COLLECTION of LIEUT.-COL. PAUL THOMAS GOODWIN, V.D. (deceased), comprising English and Foreign Portraits by different Engravers, Engravings, Etchings, and Woodcuts by Old Masters, and Portraits by R. Nanteuil. Other properties comprising Fancy Subjects, some printed in Colours, Portraits in Mezzotint and Stipple by different Engravers, Views, Naval Engagements, etc. Modern Engravings by G. H. Every, M. Cormack, W. Henderson, H. T. Greenhead, E. Stamp, J. Jacquet, and others after Sir T. Lawrence, J. Hoppner, Sir J. Reynolds, J. L. E. Meissonier, Sir F. Leighton, etc., and a few Drawings in Water Colours, etc.

May be viewed two days prior. Catalogues may be had.

BOOKS AND MANUSCRIPTS.

MESSRS. SOTHEBY, WILKINSON & HODGE will SELL by AUCTION, at their House, No. 13 Wellington Street, Strand, W.C., on WEDNESDAY, JULY 21, at One o'clock precisely, BOOKS and MANUSCRIPTS, including the Alpine Library of Thomas Blandford Esq. (an original Member of the Alpine Club); the Library of Books on Freemasonry of the late T. B. Whytehead, Esq., J.P. (of Acomb, Yorkshire); the Library of the late Mrs. Aubert (of Stoke Newington); and other properties, comprising Standard Works in the various branches of Literature; a Series of First Editions of Swinburne, Dickens, and other Modern Writers; Books on Sport, Science, Archæology, Topography; Old and Rare Books and Pamphlets; Fine Art Publications, etc.

May be viewed two days prior. Catalogues may be had.

AUTOGRAPH LETTERS.

MESSRS. SOTHEBY, WILKINSON & HODGE will SELL by AUCTION, at their House, No. 13 Wellington Street, Strand, W.C., on THURSDAY, JULY 22, at One o'clock precisely, AUTOGRAPH LETTERS and HISTORICAL DOCUMENTS written by Carlyle, Dickens, Thackeray, "George Eliot," Shelley, Lamb, Robert Burns, Cowper; Important Unpublished Letters of Lord Byron; Signatures of British and Foreign Sovereigns; Interesting Series of Letters by D. G. Rossetti, and of Ruskin to Mr. H. Stacy Marks; Manuscript Music and Letters of Celebrated Composers, etc.

May be viewed two days prior. Catalogues may be had.

THE CONDUIT STREET AUCTION GALLERIES.

The attention of Executors, Trustees, Solicitors, and Owners, who may be desirous of selling Works of Art, Family Jewels, Old Silver, Furniture, Pictures, Prints, Miniatures, China, Coins, Books, Old Lace, Furs, Musical Instruments, Guns, and other Valuables, is drawn to Messrs.

KNIGHT, FRANK & RUTLEY'S

AUCTION GALLERIES, 9 CONDUIT STREET, AND 23A MADDOX STREET, W., which are Open Daily to receive goods intended for early sales.

VALUATIONS are prepared for Fire Insurance, Estate Duty, and all other purposes. As to Insurance, owners are reminded that, for security, Messrs. KNIGHT, FRANK & RUTLEY'S detailed inventory and valuation of the contents of a Town or Country Mansion is an important adjunct to their Fire Insurance Policies.

NOTICE.

In the event of any difficulty being experienced in obtaining the SATURDAY REVIEW, the Publisher would be glad to be informed immediately.

SALES BY AUCTION.

THE CALGARTH PARK LIBRARY.

MESSRS. HODGSON & CO. will SELL by AUCTION, at their Rooms, 115 Chancery Lane, W.C., on THURSDAY, JULY 15, at One o'clock, the above interesting LIBRARY collected by Dr. Richard Watson, Bishop of Llandaff, during the later years of the Eighteenth Century, and now removed from Calgarth Park, Westmorland, comprising a Collection of Curious and Early Works on Alchemy, Metallurgy, Chemistry, Mathematics, &c. —Watson's History of Halifax, with a fore-edge painting, and other Topographical and Antiquarian Books; a fine copy of the rare Complutensian Polyglott Bible, 6 vols., 1514-17; the first Greek Bible, Venice, 1518; Folio Editions of the Fathers; a Presentation Copy of the "Proposed" Prayer Book, Philadelphia, 1786; an extensive Collection of Historical, Political, and Economic Pamphlets; Combe's First Tour of Dr. Syntax, First Edition, and Life of Napoleon, coloured plates, 2 vols.; Old Novels and Poetry, &c., all in good condition, and mostly in the original Calf Bindings.

To be viewed and Catalogues had.

THE LIBRARY OF THE LATE DR. THOMAS GOUGH (REMOVED FROM WESTMORLAND, AND OTHER PROPERTIES).

MESSRS. HODGSON & CO. will SELL by AUCTION, at their Rooms, 115 Chancery Lane, W.C., on FRIDAY, JULY 16, at One o'clock, the above LIBRARY, comprising early Herbals; Natural History Books; White's Selborne, first edition; Old Books on Physics and Mathematics, &c., to which are added OTHER PROPERTIES comprising a rare copy of Boydell's Shakespeare Gallery, with the plates in duplicate; remarkably fine copies of Apperley's Life of a Sportsman, 1842, Life of John Mytton, 1851, and Surtees' Analysis of the Hunting Field, 1846, coloured plates, original cloth; Burchell's Travels in South Africa, 2 vols., half-russia; Wallis's New South Wales; a few Books relating to America; Hakluyt Society's Publications, 49 vols.; Dibdin's Bibliotheca Spenceriana, 4 vols.; Books in Sixteenth and Seventeenth Century Literature, &c.

To be viewed and Catalogues had.

VALUABLE MISCELLANEOUS BOOKS, INCLUDING THE MODERN LIBRARY OF A GENTLEMAN (REMOVED FROM IRELAND).

MESSRS. HODGSON & CO. will SELL by AUCTION, at their Rooms, 115 Chancery Lane, W.C., on WEDNESDAY, JULY 21, and Two following days, the VALUABLE MISCELLANEOUS BOOKS, including the above LIBRARY, comprising Modern Historical Works; Editions and Translations of the Classics, both English and Foreign; a Collection of Books on Dante; the Writings of the Victorian Poets and Essayists; Books on Art; Recent Works in General Literature, etc.

Catalogues on application

THE LIBRARY OF THE LATE AUGUSTUS A. VANSITTART, BY DIRECTION OF THE EXECUTORS OF THE HONBLE. MRS. R. F. A. VANSITTART, DECEASED (REMOVED FROM BROMLEY PARK, KENT).

MESSRS. HODGSON & CO. will SELL by AUCTION, at their Rooms, 115 Chancery Lane, W.C., at the END OF JULY, the above LIBRARY, comprising the Coronation of Louis XV., in a Morocco Binding by Padeloup; Folio Morocco Albums of Engravings and Original Drawings; Topographical Books, and Books of Travel; Standard Works in General Literature, many in Calf and Morocco Bindings.

Catalogues are preparing.

GUY'S HOSPITAL.—ENTRANCE SCHOLARSHIPS to be competed for in September 1909. Two Open Scholarships in Arts, one of the value of £100, open to candidates under twenty years of age, and one of £50, open to candidates under twenty-five years of age. Two Open Scholarships in Science, one of the value of £150, and another of £60, open to candidates under twenty-five years of age. One Open Scholarship for University Students who have completed their study of anatomy and physiology, of the value of £50.—Full particulars may be obtained on application to the DEAN, Guy's Hospital, London Bridge, S.E.

GUY'S HOSPITAL MEDICAL SCHOOL

(University of London).

THE WINTER SESSION commences on Friday, October 1st. Entrance Scholarships of the combined value of £410 are offered for competition annually in September.

For particulars as to Entrance Scholarships, Special Classes for Preliminary Scientific M.B. (Lond.), prospectuses of Medical and Dental Schools, regulations for residence in the College, new scheme for payment of composition fees, &c., apply personally or by letter to the DEAN, Guy's Hospital, London Bridge, S.E.

SECRETARIAL WORK WANTED, Daily or Resident; Temporary or Permanent; Notes worked up from and for MSS. (Literary, Military, or Political); typist, no shorthand. Good testimonials; organising experience; Conservative; not a Suffragist.

Miss X, c/o of "Saturday Review", 10 King Street, Covent Garden, W.C.

BOARD AND TUITION for 1st B.Sc. or Science Scholarship Examination offered in return for help given in Chemical and Physics Laboratories. Post suitable for a gentleman's son just leaving a good school.

Apply Headmaster, Trent College, Derbyshire.

ELY CATHEDRAL.

Visitors will find First Class Hotel Accommodation at the "LAMB" Family Hotel, which is situated close to the Cathedral. **MODERATE TERMS.** Omnibus meets all trains.

Proprietor, S. AIREY.

R. ANDERSON & CO.,

BRITISH, INDIAN, AND COLONIAL ADVERTISEMENT CONTRACTORS,

14 KING WILLIAM STREET, STRAND, W.C.,

GIVE THE BEST TERMS for Company and General Advertising. Advice, Estimates, and all information free of charge. Replies received.

RAPHAEL TUCK AND SONS.

THE Eighth Annual Ordinary General Meeting of Raphael Tuck & Sons, Limited, was held on Thursday at Salisbury House, Finsbury Circus, E.C., Mr. Adolph Tuck (Chairman of the Company) presiding.

The Chairman, in moving the adoption of the report, pointed out that the many millions decrease officially recorded in both the import and export trade of the country during the past year included among them some of the more modest thousands lost to the turnover of this Company, with the natural sequence that the dividend showed a decrease, namely, 5 per cent. against the 6 per cent. declared last year. Another reassuring feature was that it was practically the home trade alone which was responsible for their set-back. With the single exception of South Africa, which, despite its gold mine boom, made but slow recovery from the trade stagnation since the war, their over-seas trade had actually showed an advance during the past year, while their trade in European countries also showed an increase, the one exception being France, the set-back there, however, being more than made up by the advance in their German trade. While both France and Germany were countries where high protective tariffs existed, there was this distinction in the policy of these two great Continental nations, that whereas all art productions in their particular sphere were heavily taxed in France, Germany, rightly viewing art culture as an important adjunct to education generally, admitted both printed and painted works of art of every kind practically free. At no time in the history of the firm had Tuck's Christmas and New Year's cards occupied a higher plane than they did at the present moment, and this in every part of the world. If the opinion of the trade and the entire trade Press counted for anything, the magnificent collection of upwards of 4,000 designs they had placed on the market this year exhibited a far greater than the ordinary year's advance over every one of its predecessors. Their Royal collection of cards this year contained an entirely new series after the originals, which they again had the honour of painting for the various Royal houses, who granted them their gracious permission to reproduce their Royal Christmas cards last year, this unique honour being again accorded them this year, and also for the first time by their Imperial Majesties the Emperor and Empress of Russia, and their Majesties the King and Queen of Italy. With regard to the other departments, the engraving and photogravure occupied a firmer position each year, and the picture postcards promised to prove a considerable advantage to the Company. The net profits of the year total £29,973 9s. 3d., and adding thereto the balance brought forward from last year—£3,288 14s.—there is a grand total of £33,262 3s. 3d. From this deduct directors' remuneration £3,500, preference dividends paid to shareholders to January 1, 1909, £9,166 13s. 4d., further preference dividends paid from January 1, 1909, to April 30, 1909—£4,583 6s. 8d.—and the interim dividend paid on the ordinary shares at the rate of 5 per cent. per annum to the half-year ended October 31, 1908, £6,250. These totals already paid out of profits during the past year amount to exactly £20,000, thus leaving the sum of £9,762 3s. 3d. for disposal. Out of this the directors recommend a dividend on the ordinary shares at the rate of 5 per cent. per annum for the half-year ended April 30, 1909, making, with the interim dividend already paid on the ordinary shares, 5 per cent. for the year. This leaves the sum of £3,512 3s. 3d. to be carried forward to next year. The directors have closely followed last year's precedent—that is, they are dividing practically the whole of the profits made during the year, placing nothing to the reserve account, for the second time in the history of the Company, but withdrawing nothing therefrom, so that the financial position remains unimpaired, the capital reserve account standing, as last year, at £8,845 5s. 2d.; the general reserve account the same as last year, at £32,500; the special dividend reserve of £33,690 2s. 7d., against £32,822 10s. 9d., a grand reserve total of £75,035 7s. 9d., this giving an increase of £867 11s. 10d. over last year. He trusted that the recommendations made by the directors would commend themselves as sound finance, and that the principle followed by them to maintain the strong financial position of the Company would have the shareholders' unanimous support. The net liquid assets of nearly £100,000, after providing for every liability, a total of over £80,000 in outstanding accounts, stocks, taken below cost, at over £60,000, valuable long leasehold buildings absolutely unencumbered—all these would give the best possible proof that at no period in its history had the Company been in a sounder financial position than at this present moment. The slightest upward movement in trade, which would be easily met by present expenditure, must, perforce, react to the advantage of the Company, and produce an immediate appreciable increase in its profits.

Sir Arthur Conan Doyle seconded the motion, which was carried unanimously.

NATIONAL MINERALS CORPORATION.

THE Ordinary General Meeting of the National Minerals Corporation, Limited, was held on Tuesday, at Salisbury House, London Wall, E.C., Mr. Horace Barrett (Chairman of the Company) presiding.

The Secretary (Mr. F. A. Donne, F.C.I.S.) having read the notice convening the meeting and the report of the auditors,

The Chairman said: We consider we are in a very satisfactory condition, and I think that you will agree that there is good ground for that when you refer to the balance-sheet and see the profit that we have made. We might have declared a dividend, but we are a young company, and we prefer to conserve our strength, especially as we intend, if fortune continues to favour us, to declare substantial dividends in the future. I hope, speaking for myself, that ere long an interim dividend may be declared. You are aware that this Company was formed essentially with a view to acquiring mining properties, and you also know that we have made the county of Cornwall the active scene of our operations. There are undoubtedly in Cornwall most valuable minerals, and we have no doubt that we have the pick and hold some of the very best properties. Your company is a parent and finance company. It has floated—and successfully floated—the St. Ives Consolidated Mines, Limited, which took over the St. Ives group of your Company's properties, including the Trenwith Mine, to which I shall refer presently, and which latter, by reason of its value and the absolute necessity for independent attention, could not well be worked in conjunction with the other properties of the group. The British Radium Corporation was therefore formed to take it over and work it. That company has a capital of £40,000, and the whole of its issued shares are held by the St. Ives Consolidated Mines, Limited, in which, as you will have gathered from the report and accounts, your Company has the predominating holding. Formerly all the mining setts were worked as separate units, which often proved costly and disadvantageous. We have altered that, and have proceeded to consolidate the setts and to work out a policy of centralisation. We thus achieve economy by generating power at a central station, which will enable us to work all the setts from one head under the most economical conditions. There will be pumps, mills, hauling-gear, rock-drills, and air-compressor plants—everything, in fact, necessary for driving from the central power station at a minimum cost. At the Giew Mine the electrical power plant is actually finished and ready for operation. In this connection I may refer you to the latest progress report of our consulting mining engineer, Mr. Dietzsch, a print of which was sent to you with the notice convening this meeting. The entire plant is of the most modern type, selected with great care under the superintendence of the consulting civil engineers (Sir Douglas Fox and Partners) and the consulting mining engineer (Mr. Ferdinand Dietzsch). We consider that we are very fortunate in acquiring in the St. Ives properties mines which in the past—though worked under the most crude and antiquated methods, and in comparatively shallow depths only—have produced very large sums. Now that we are able to tackle them with up-to-date and modern methods, we have no doubt that their yield will reach the highest possible expectations. There is the Trenwith Mine, which was formerly worked for copper only. The preliminary development has been proceeded with to our entire satisfaction, and we have no doubt that before we meet again results more than satisfactory will be available to the shareholders. Sir Wm. Ramsay (the chief consulting chemist to the British Radium Corporation, Limited) has justified the original prognosis. He has produced radium—and he has produced it by his new and secret process. The stage of the laboratory is past, and he has been able to produce this precious article on a commercial scale. Samples of the radium are in the Company's office. We are, as to the recovery of radium, in a unique position; we have the control of a new and successful process (to which I shall refer presently) for the treatment of pitchblende and other ores, and we have also the benefit of Sir William Ramsay's new process for the extraction of radium, which process is cheaper, quicker, and more effective than any process hitherto known. So satisfied are the directors of the British Radium Corporation, Limited, that steps have been taken to acquire a site on which to erect a suitable factory with the necessary plant for the production of radium, and as the St. Ives Consolidated Mines, Limited, hold the issued shares of the British Radium Corporation, and have a call at par on the unissued shares, and as your Company has the very large holding to which I have referred in the St. Ives Consolidated Mines, Limited, there can be no doubt as to the value of your Company's interest in that direction. The plans and specifications for the factory are now in possession of the Company, so that we may expect to hear something very satisfactory with regard to the erection of a factory and the production of further radium at a very early date. There is no anxiety whatever on the part of the directors as to their being able to dispose of the radium upon highly remunerative terms. Indeed, some of your directors have already been approached by influential persons, one of whom, I understand, is a shareholder of this Company, who are prepared to offer a good and substantial price for the radium produced. I should mention, also, that there is a large demand for crude pitchblende and pitchblende concentrates. Many applications have been made to your Board to supply pitchblende and pitchblende concentrates, but we have made no contract in that connection; we much prefer to sell radium. Apart from the radium, the uranium oxide (many pounds in weight of which have been extracted and furnished by Sir William Ramsay) is of itself a valuable commodity, and will alone produce handsome profits. And now, let me pass to another matter—a very important matter. In the properties to which I have referred we have no doubt that we have very valuable holdings; but there is something else, the value of which it is impossible at this moment to estimate. After much thought, much consideration, and mainly through the indefatigable exertions of some of your directors, we have acquired a process for the treatment of complex and refractory ores, which we believe will be of inestimable value to the mining industries of the world. This process has been tried. Practical trials of supreme importance and of all sorts of complex and refractory ores have taken place, with results which more than justify the anticipated possible expectations. The process will revolutionise tin and copper mining in the county of Cornwall. It will make possible an absolute recovery of the various mineral constituents of most of the refractory or complex ores subjected to it. In support of what I have stated—and it has been stated with the concurrence, and at the request, of my co-directors—sulphide ores containing zinc and lead intimately mixed with copper, gold, silver, and other metals have been treated by the process with most gratifying success, and I am also authorised by the technical directors of your board to say with results to the fullest possible satisfaction of our experts. I may add that pitchblende from the Trenwith Mine has been subjected to this process with great success, which will no doubt tend to increase the value of our financial interest in that mine. Apart from the interest in the Trenwith, the pitchblende, uranium oxides, and bromide of radium, there will be the valuable interests arising from the process of which I have told you. What this will mean to your Company time alone—not far distant—will show. Later on, those of you who hold 1s. shares of the Company—not to mention the valuable bonds of which you are holders—will no doubt shake hands with yourselves when you reflect that you have been fortunate enough to acquire the 1s. shares of this Company at less than 20s. per share. I beg to move: "That the report of the directors, together with the annexed statement of the accounts duly audited, be received, approved, and adopted."

Mr. Sigismund Moritz seconded the resolution, and it was carried unanimously.

A vote of thanks to the Chairman terminated the proceedings.

This Prospectus has been filed with the Registrar of Joint Stock Companies.

The List Opened on **FRIDAY**, the 9th July, 1909, and will Close on or before **TUESDAY**, the 13th July, 1909.

THE BUENOS AYRES AND PACIFIC RAILWAY COMPANY, LIMITED.

Incorporated under the Companies (Consolidation) Act, 1908.

SHARE CAPITAL.

5 per Cent. First Preference Stock, issued	£1,200,000
5 per Cent. Second Preference Stock, issued ...	1,000,000
300,000 Ordinary (1911) Shares of £10 each, issued and fully paid	3,000,000
Ordinary Stock, issued	7,000,000
	£12,200,000

DEBENTURE CAPITAL.

4 per Cent. First Debenture Stock, issued	£2,925,000
4½ per Cent. Second Debenture Stock, issued	2,075,000
5 per Cent. Debenture Stock, issued	1,250,000
4½ per Cent. Consolidated Debenture Stock, issued ...	4,000,000
	£10,250,000

ISSUE OF £1,000,000 FOUR-AND-A-HALF PER CENT. CONSOLIDATED DEBENTURE STOCK.

Secured by a Trust Deed reserving to the Company the right to create further Debenture Stock for £1,000,000 (the present issue), carrying interest at 4½ per cent. per annum and ranking *pari passu* with the £4,000,000 Consolidated Debenture Stock already issued, and a further amount at the rate of £4,000 per mile of additional line hereafter acquired by the Company or of new line for the time being constructed or in course of construction, or about to be constructed (including the extra track taken at £4,000 a mile where existing lines are doubled) in excess of the mileage belonging to the Company in operation on May 28, 1907, and also for such a further amount as shall be sufficient to redeem prior issues at not exceeding the par value of the Stock for the time being redeemed, and any premium payable on redemption under the terms of the issue thereof.

At £103 per cent. payable as follows:—

£5	0	0	on Application.
15	0	0	,, Allotment.
25	0	0	,, August 24, 1909.
25	0	0	,, October 1, 1909.
33	0	0	,, on November 24, 1909.
Total £103	0	0	per £100 Stock.

Bearer Scrip will be issued to be exchanged for Debenture Stock Certificates on completion of all the payments, the Stock being transferable in amounts not involving a fraction of £1. The interest is payable by warrant to the Registered Holders of the Stock on January 1 and July 1 in each year. The first payment of interest will be made on January 1, 1910, and will be calculated on the instalments as due. Payment in full on allotment and on August 24 and October 1 can be made under discount at the rate of 3 per cent. per annum.

The Directors of the Buenos Ayres and Pacific Railway Company, Limited, have authorised the London Joint Stock Bank, Limited, and Martin's Bank, Limited, as bankers of the Company, to receive applications for £1,000,000 4½ per cent. Consolidated Debenture Stock of the Company, ranking *pari passu* with the existing issue of £4,000,000.

The whole or any part of the 4½ per Cent. Consolidated Debenture Stock is redeemable at any time at the Company's option after 30th June, 1920, at 110 per cent., on six calendar months' notice to the Stockholders. This Stock is secured by a charge upon the undertaking of the Company (subject to the First, Second, and Five per Cent. Debenture Stock), under Trust Deeds, dated 28th May, 1907, 11th October, 1907, 1st April, 1908, 26th May, 1908, and 1st July, 1909, made between the Company and the Trustees.

The Company owns and has in operation 1,204 miles of broad gauge (5 ft. 6 in.) railway in the Argentine Republic, extending westward from the City of Buenos Ayres to Villa Mercedes, the main line forming part of the system which is to connect the Atlantic and Pacific seaboards of the South American Continent. Beyond the branch lines already opened to public traffic the Company has under construction, or is about to construct, additional branches of a length of about 165 miles.

The Company also works the Bahia Blanca and North-Western Railway (665 miles now open) and the Villa Maria and Rufino Railway (141 miles). On the 1st July, 1907, the working of the Argentine Great Western and Argentine Transandine Railways (644 miles now open) was also taken over, and, by this means, the control of the whole transcontinental line from Buenos Ayres to Valparaiso, in so far as it is situated in Argentine territory, has been secured by this Company; and with the Bahia Blanca and North-Western Railway and its recently constructed extensions, this Company has placed its system in direct communication with the rapidly developing Port of Bahia Blanca. The total length of the entire system now in operation is 2,654 miles. The results of past expenditure of Capital on the system now controlled and worked by the Company is shown by the following table:—

	1904–1905	1905–1906	1906–1907	1907–1908
	£	£	£	£
Gross Receipts .	1,913,760	2,392,943	3,063,547	3,655,772
Working Expenses .	1,138,370	1,408,206	1,892,542	2,300,732
Net Receipts . .	£775,390	£984,737	£1,171,005	£1,354,990

Since the 1st July, 1908, the estimated gross receipts of the whole Pacific system to the 30th June last are £4,129,986, as against £3,655,772, an increase of £474,214.

The General Manager recently estimated that the maize crop in the zone served by the Company would be more or less double that of last year. He reports by cable under date of the 2nd instant as follows: "Ploughing has been delayed in some parts due to drought, but it will continue for wheat crop till end July and for linseed till end August. Up to the present we have every reason to look for an increase in the area under cultivation, as we have not suffered so much from drought as other regions, and if rain falls soon the increase will be considerable. General prospects good."

The expansion of all classes of traffic and the development of new districts have rendered it necessary to provide additional traffic facilities, and to increase the carrying capacity of the Railway generally. Dividends at the rate of 7 per cent. per annum have been paid on the Ordinary Stock of the Company since the year 1902-1903. The annual interest on the Company's Debenture Capital is £452,875, which will now be increased by £45,000. The proceeds of the present issue will be applied towards meeting the expenditure on branch lines, and the equipment of lines recently opened to public service, providing additional traffic facilities, and to the general requirements of the Railway. A preference in the allotment as regards 50 per cent. of this issue will be given to applications received before the actual closing of the list from existing Preference Stockholders and Ordinary Stock and Shareholders of the Company.

Applications on the form accompanying this prospectus, together with the deposit of £5 per cent., should be forwarded to the London Joint Stock Bank, Limited, 5 Princes Street, London, E.C., or to Martin's Bank, Limited, 68 Lombard Street, London, E.C.

If no allotment is made the deposit will be returned without deduction. Should a smaller amount be allotted than applied for the surplus paid on application will be appropriated towards the balance due on allotment. Non-payment of any instalment upon the due date will render the amount previously paid liable to forfeiture. Application will in due course be made to obtain a Stock Exchange quotation for this issue.

Apart from the contracts made by the Company in the ordinary course of business, the following have been entered into within the two years immediately preceding the date hereof: Contract dated July 16, 1907, and made between the Company, the Argentine Great Western Railway Company, Limited, and the Argentine Transandine Railway Company, Limited. Contracts made between the Company and Messrs. Sheppards, Pelly, Price and Pott, and dated respectively October 11, 1907, November 28, 1907, April 1, 1908, May 26, 1908, and July 7, 1909, for the underwriting of this and previous issues. Under the last-mentioned contract the Company agrees to pay a commission of 3 per cent. in respect of the present issue. Contracts dated March 18, 1908, and June 19, 1908, and made between the Company and the Argentine Government. Contracts dated November 9, 1908, and May 19, 1909, and made between the Company and the Argentine Great Western Railway Company, Limited. Contract dated November 17, 1908, and made between the Company and the Bahia Blanca and North-Western Railway Company, Limited. The above Contracts may be inspected at the Offices of the Solicitors on any day while the List remains open, between the hours of 11 and 4. During the last two years the Company has paid underwriting commissions amounting to £132,500. The Preferred Stocks carry equal rights of attending meetings and voting with the Ordinary Stock and Shares, every £20 in Stock or Shares carrying one vote on a poll.

A Brokerage at the rate of quarter per cent. will be paid by the Company on allotments made to the public in respect of applications bearing a Broker's stamp.

Prospectuses and Forms of Application may be obtained at the Offices of the Company, Dashwood House, 9, New Broad Street, London, E.C.; of the Bankers; and of Messrs. Sheppards, Pelly, Price, and Pott, the Brokers of the Company.

Registered Offices:
Dashwood House,
9 New Broad Street,
London, E.C.

8th July, 1909.

TRUSTEES FOR THE FOUR-AND-A-HALF PER CENT. CONSOLIDATED DEBENTURE STOCK.

The Rt. Hon. the EARL OF COVENTRY.
JOHN SOANE AUSTEN.

DIRECTORS.

The Rt. Hon. LORD ST. DAVIDS (Chairman).
T. PENN GASKELL, M.Inst.C.E.
C. E. GUNTHER.
EDWARD NORMAN.
Hon. ARTHUR STANLEY, M.P.
F. O. SMITHERS (Managing Director).

BANKERS.

THE LONDON JOINT STOCK BANK, LIMITED, 5 Princes Street, London, E.C.
MARTIN'S BANK, LIMITED, 68, Lombard Street, London, E.C.

BANKERS IN ARGENTINA.

THE ANGLO SOUTH AMERICAN BANK, LIMITED.

SOLICITORS.

ASHURST, MORRIS, CRISP & CO., 17 Throgmorton Avenue, London, E.C.

BROKERS.

SHEPPARDS, PELLY, PRICE & POTT, 57, Old Broad Street, London, E.C.

AUDITORS.

TURQUAND, YOUNGS & CO., 41, Coleman Street, London, E.C.

SECRETARY.

W. R. CRONAN.

This form of application may be used.

THE BUENOS AYRES AND PACIFIC RAILWAY COMPANY, LIMITED.

ISSUE OF £1,000,000 4½ PER CENT. CONSOLIDATED DEBENTURE STOCK.

To the Directors of

THE BUENOS AYRES AND PACIFIC RAILWAY COMPANY, LIMITED.

Gentlemen,—Having paid to your Bankers the sum of £.................... as a deposit of Five per cent. on application for £.................... 4½ per cent. Consolidated Debenture Stock of the Buenos Ayres and Pacific Railway Company, Limited, I request that this amount may be allotted to me, and I agree to accept the same, or any smaller amount that may be allotted to me, upon the terms of the Prospectus dated 8th July, 1909.

Ordinary Signature ....
Name (in full)* ....
Address ....

Date ...., 1909.

* Please say whether "Mrs.," "Miss," "Reverend," or give other distinctive description.

This Form is to be filled up and forwarded to the London Joint Stock Bank, Limited, 5 Princes Street, London, E.C., or Martin's Bank, Limited, 68, Lombard Street, London, E.C.

Printed for the Proprietors by SPOTTISWOODE & CO. LTD., 5 New-street Square, E.C., and Published by REGINALD WEBSTER PAGE, at the Office, 10 King Street, Covent Garden, in the Parish of St. Paul the County of London.—*Saturday, 10 July, 1909.*

THE

SATURDAY REVIEW

OF

POLITICS, LITERATURE, SCIENCE, AND ART.

No. 2,803 Vol. 108. 17 July 1909. [REGISTERED AS A NEWSPAPER.] 6d.

CONTENTS.

NOTES OF THE WEEK.

The work of cropping the ears of the landowning dogs began again in Parliament on Monday, and has gone on through most of this week. The Government, fearful they should hurt some of their own small hounds, made a concession on Monday. The very little dogs are to go scot-free; after all, it is the big ones that good Radicals want to serve out—and it is the big ones that can be made to pay something substantial. We must always bear in mind that, in the main taxes of this Budget, the Government have two distinct ends in view—the Budget no doubt is designed to punish, but the Budget is designed to pay; Lord Hugh Cecil sees chiefly malice, but money is an equal motive. Now there is no wish to punish the very small owners. Some may be Radicals; moreover, they are hardly worth a Treasury official's attention. So the Government let them off.

The Ministerial cave may be not a grave matter for Liberalism, but what of the Ministerial cave-in? After Cleveland and before High Peak the Government appear in full retreat. Captain Pretyman likened them to mariners fearful of shipwreck and jettisoning the cargo. Perhaps it will be truer, before these debates are done, to describe them as land-wrecked. The Government have suddenly found out that a large number of very small owners—one- or two-acre without even a cow owners—would be hurt by their Bill. So on Tuesday Mr. Lloyd George announces that no one need pay increment whose property is not worth more than five hundred pounds. Yet a few hours earlier Mr. Wedgwood blessed the Budget as the work of Henry—not Lloyd—George, and vowed the land proposals meant business!

However, having collapsed on Monday through dread of the bye-elections, the Government stiffened somewhat on Wednesday. Mr. Dickinson was put up by the Government to move an amendment in effect compelling every landowner, large and small, to report himself at Somerset House. The cursed landowner may be able to escape the increment tax if he can show his holding is worth under £500—but he is to be chased and fleeced none the less in the showing of it. It is like a cat playing with a mouse; the Government lets the wretched victim crawl away a little one minute, only to claw him again the next.

As to Mr. Wedgwood's description of the Budget as Henry George's Budget and as good business, Liberals should really make up their minds whether the principles of it are Liberal, democratic, socialist, or what. The "Daily News" vows that the last thing in the world the Budget is is socialist. Mr. Lloyd George scouts the very word, and flouts Mr. Philip Snowden's and Henry George's claims alike. Whereas Mr. Keir Hardie, always honest and uncompromising, has just said: "We have in this Budget for the first time a systematic attempt to socialise a portion of the national income." If there is not some hard lying among these various contradicting witnesses, there must be a slight confusion of thought.

People who are forced to discuss what Mr. Asquith styles a "highly complex and technical measure" from 1 P.M. till nine next day are likely to take an inflamed view of each other. There was a good deal of this inflammation in the House on Wednesday night and Thursday morning. Things were seen out of their right proportions by several people. Mr. Pointer M.P. could see in a speech by Captain Clive only a "silly farce"; and he suggested to the Chairman the use of the gag. Mr. Pointer should read the Duke of Rutland's plan of campaign against the labour leaders. The Duke of Rutland is, at any rate, for doing the thing thoroughly. He would gag Gargantua.

These all-night sittings are bad for the House in every way. Nobody's temper can stand the strain; and the Labour members no more than other people. These gentlemen's conduct during the whole debate was so offensively provocative that it is remarkable it ended in only one member being suspended and he, as the House decided yesterday, wrongfully. It is only fair to point out that Liberals cannot hear the Labour members' running comments on speeches, or rather on speakers. If they could, they would no doubt restrain their indignation at offensive comments on their opponents; but let the same sort of thing be said of themselves, and Lord Winterton would be distanced by their repartee altogether.

Mr. Ramsay Macdonald got in a little bit of advertisement business by way of winding up the sitting. The Chancellor of the Exchequer had just accepted a motion to report progress; so Mr. Macdonald, seeing release and rest assured, intervenes, standing up nobly for hard work and the traditions of the House. Knowing that every member present was only too thankful Mr. Lloyd George had accepted the motion, Mr. Macdonald deemed it safe to divide against it. So the Labour party could pose as the strenuous men, the men who would sit for ever while both Tories and Liberals were for stopping work. But that they should also pose as the champions of House of Commons traditions—well, at least that is superfluous, for their electors would care nothing for that. Labour electors care as little for the House as they do as a rule for their members.

Mr. Winston Churchill's article in "The World" on procedure is written for members of Parliament, for, as the writer says, the subject is "not understood by and consequently uninteresting to the public". We agree with Mr. Churchill that the chief interest of the Opposition is to choose the topics, while Government controls the time. Again and again we have urged in this Review the desirability of selecting, by previous arrangement, the clauses against which the attack should be directed, instead of practising, as at present, indiscriminate obstruction. What generally happens now is that the first six or twelve sections of a Bill are fiercely fought, line by line, simply because they come first, and the fighting men are fresh. As a consequence, the most important clauses, which come later, are closured wholesale. Mr. Churchill suggests that every Bill should be introduced with its time-table printed upon it, which time-table—the number of days for second reading, committee, and report—should be fixed by a committee of business, "overwhelmingly unofficial in its character", but with a party majority.

Unless some scheme for the devolution of business to local bodies can be devised, we suppose that the system of Grand Committees must be widely employed. We are not enamoured of this method of legislation, which gives ample scope to the assiduous amateur, sometimes to the danger of the public: but we see no help for it. The enforcement of a ten-minutes limit to speeches in Committee would be a great nuisance: we think it might be extended to a quarter of an hour, which presumably would not be applied to the Committee of Ways and Means which passes the Budget resolutions.

Mr. Churchill is, moreover, right in regretting that "the old right of moving the adjournment of the House, with all its lively and sensational characteristics, is now practically extinct", and that "the process of moving the Speaker out of the chair upon Supply is at an end". In former days, we mean in Victorian, not Georgian, times, some of the greatest historical debates have arisen on the Speaker's saying "The question is that I do now leave the chair". If the House of Commons wishes to retain its hold upon the attention of the nation, it should recover "its old freedom over the subjects of debate"; for undoubtedly what the House does best is to express the mind of the public upon great subjects. At present it is drowned in a sea of details: eloquence is becoming a lost art, and everybody is bored to death—so much so that the newspaper reports are getting shorter and shorter.

Mr. Runciman has vetoed his latest educational reform almost before he promulgated it. Certainly it does not seem unreasonable that teachers who are to give Cowper-Temple teaching should be instructed in Cowper-Templeism at the training colleges. Mr. Runciman regulated accordingly. But the nonconformists were up in arms at once. They would have none of this. Religious instruction, albeit undenominational, a part of the training-college curriculum, not to be thought of! And Mr. Runciman has submissively taken his instructions from his nonconformist friends, and religious instruction is not to be required in undenominational training colleges. This is a telling test of the sincerity of undenominational concern for religious teaching. Cowper-Templeism is a dishonest unreality; and it is now clearer than ever that it is only denominational schools and colleges that save religious teaching from dropping out of the elementary schools altogether. We are glad to find Mr. Runciman admitting that absolute religious equality is the only way out of the religious difficulty—precisely the opposite of Mr. Birrell's view, who tried to establish Cowper-Templeism as a State religion in elementary schools.

The Government may take what comfort they can from the result of the elections in Cleveland and Mid-Derby. Their candidates score a win in both cases, but by majorities which tell the same story that the bye-elections have told ever since January 1907. Mr. Samuel's majority was reduced from over two thousand to under one thousand, notwithstanding that the poll in his favour was larger than at the last contested election. Mr. Hancock's majority is reduced by over twelve hundred and his poll is less. The gratifying thing is the increase in the Unionist poll in both cases. Where the Radicals do not actually lose votes, they fail to put on more than half the Unionist increase. If a Samuel in Cleveland and a Hancock in Mid-Derby can do no better than this, Radical prospects are indeed gloomy.

The Marquess of Ripon was the son of that "transient and embarrassed phantom" who, under the name of Lord Goderich, flitted across the stage of politics on Canning's death. Old Cobbett nicknamed this statesman "Prosperity Robinson", because in the distress that followed Waterloo he was always assuring the public that the country was flourishing. It cannot be said that his son, the last lord, was a great statesman, though he filled the highest posts in the State. He will be remembered as the Viceroy of India who pushed partiality for the natives to danger-point, and who, if he had not been recalled, would probably have provoked something like a mutiny among the British Civil Servants. He was First Lord of the Admiralty, Secretary of State for War, for India, and for the Colonies, as well as Lord President of the Council, in various Liberal Governments. He succeeded Lord Kimberley as leader of the Liberal party in the Lords, and during the last few years had become inarticulate and inaudible.

Nothing but party pressure and political fear prevented Lord Roberts' Compulsory Service Bill getting a large majority on second reading. Even a glance at the list of speakers on each side shows the weight of opinion behind the Bill. Not a single independent peer, whose voice counts, spoke against the Bill; not a single soldier of any note. All the most distinguished Unionist peers who were not fettered by official memories or fears spoke for the Bill. What had the opponents of compulsion to put against Lord Curzon's and Lord Milner's speeches? Or against Lord Newton and Lord Ampthill? And practical soldiers like the Earl of Erroll were all for compulsion. Lord Lansdowne, looking to future office and fearing to commit himself, whipped his faithful followers to vote for a sort of compromise; but even so the Bill was only rejected by twenty. Is not this a record? Has any Bill before been officially opposed by both parties and yet only been beaten by twenty votes?

The debate justified the one or two peers who, in Lord Lansdowne's words, when asked where wisdom was to be found, said they did not know exactly, but on no account must we look for it on either front bench. We doubt if anybody did look for it there. There is not much wisdom in putting political and party considerations above the safety of the Empire. We are the only people in Europe who play at soldiers after we are grown up. A Navy we have, and want it to be strong; an Army we only pretend to have. Is this bubble of pretence to be pricked by thought before disaster or repentance after? This is the great practical question for the country at this moment. It is a pity front-bench politicians cannot face it honestly. Instead of thinking whether conscription is right, they are all thinking, is it popular?

Lord Portsmouth has clearly had the latest laugh, whether it prove the best or not. He was made Under-Secretary for War when this Government came in. Then he was asked to resign. He resigned. Next Mr. Asquith offered him an Ecclesiastical Commissionership. He took it. And now came Lord Portsmouth's turn. He moved a motion condemning the military policy of the Government. It is well to throw a sop to Cerberus; but how if Cerberus take the sop and yet turn upon the thrower?

The sinking of the submarine C11 with nearly all hands is a sinister stroke of reality before the pageant in the Thames next week. She has been lost, it may be, through one of those blunders in peace that are simply incident to ships of war, and for which often no man can be blamed. The highways of the sea are narrow even for these lesser battle and steam ships.

The Navy League has now set its house in order—not to soon. At an extraordinary meeting held at the United Service Institute yesterday it reorganised itself on a broad and businesslike basis. One especially sound reform is the reduction of the number of the Executive Committee to fourteen. As to the need of a new start, the facts of the League as it is are argument enough. Its membership is insignificant, its influence slight in the extreme: in a country which is accustomed to regard its supremacy at sea as vital to its existence. We are sanguine, however, that it has now turned the corner and will soon multiply exceedingly and be fruitful in influence.

If Lord Kitchener's ready acceptance of an invitation to visit Australia has no other effect, it will probably strengthen Mr. Deakin's hand in the matter of universal training. Mr. Cook, the Minister for Defence, believes in an Imperial General Staff and hopes to assist in developing the principle of the interchangeability of imperial and local forces. Mr. Cook is not among the advocates of local self-sufficiency in defence, and is prepared to make the offer of £2,000,000 to the Imperial Government unconditionally. If the money is spent on swift cruisers for commerce protection rather than on Dreadnoughts he would perhaps be pleased, and of course he is anxious to create a local naval force, but always on condition that it becomes the Australian section of the Imperial Navy.

The Persian Nationalists have stolen a march on the Government; for the moment they have the upper hand in the capital, and the Shah is outside, either bombarding or preparing to bombard the city. Beyond this there is nothing very definite. The Shah's fate depends mainly upon what Russia may do. He is now a refugee at the Russian Legation. The topsy-turvy situation which Russia's intervention originally brought about continues. The Nationalists and the Shah's forces sank their differences for a while in order to oppose Russia, and when the Shah refused to part with the Russian commander of the Persian Cossacks the Nationalists turned upon him again. Russia advanced once more because foreigners were in danger, but Teheran was then threatened not by the Nationalists but by the Shah, who now seeks Russian protection.

Prince Bülow has retired after being Imperial Chancellor for nine years, and he is succeeded by Herr von Bethmann-Hollweg, who has been Prince Bülow's lieutenant since 1907, when he became Imperial Secretary of State in succession to Count Posadowsky. It was Herr von Bethmann-Hollweg who is supposed, in 1906, to have encouraged Prince Bülow to dissolve the Reichstag in opposition to the advice of Count Posadowsky. The move was successful, and the Prince in the elections had his revenge on the Centre and Socialist parties which had opposed his foreign and colonial policy in the Reichstag. In two years the Centre has turned the tables on the Prince. The bloc of Conservatives and Liberals, so adroitly formed and maintained in spite of nature, goes to pieces under the Budget.

What the effects of the change may be on international and German domestic policies no one can yet tell; but it seems as though the most conspicuous ministerial political position in Europe had suddenly lost its brilliancy. The new Chancellor did his work at the Interior—our Home Office—admirably, but his personality is strangely dim when we think of the eager interest with which the public appearances of Prince Bülow were looked for by his own countrymen and all foreigners. It would be hard to say whether the Kaiser's or his Chancellor's speeches were anticipated, and discussed, and criticised with more zest. If it is true that the departure of the Prince is not wholly unconnected with certain speeches made by the Kaiser himself, one of the interesting speculations as to the future is how the Kaiser and his new Chancellor will settle their speeches between them. A great figure undoubtedly goes with Prince Bülow, even when by comparison with the gigantic figure of Bismarck it is attempted to disparage him.

How is it that French humour never seems to reach French oratory? The orators of France are now eloquent on two profound convictions—that Free Trade is good for England, on the ground that she is an old country; and that the opposite is better for France, on the ground that she is an older country. The French faculty for prime distinctions has been noted by international criticism; but if it still exists it does not appear much in politics, unless in the odd case of a frank statesman like M. Pichon, who honestly begs his compatriots to save France from the Free Trade fate of England. The final shape of the new tariff is not yet on paper, but the fact that M. Pichon and his followers have exercised a powerful influence on it does not suggest much of the entente cordiale in the scheme. On Tuesday the Chamber definitely approved the new commercial treaty with Canada, "the mother country" having no voice in it; but even in this M. Klotz points out that "France is left absolutely free to compose the tariffs as she wishes, so that, consequently, there is no danger". The "danger" is the same thing which is so good for England, but so bad for France.

When President Taft announced his fiscal project to "revise downward", there was uneasiness among the manufacturers; but these are strong in the Legislature, and now the "uneasiness" has definitely shifted to those who expected the President to keep his word. In the Western States particularly, where the high prices on the consumer are not compensated equally by his share in the high profits of production, the press has begun to denounce the Tariff Bill as a "betrayal" of the President's pledges, and we may trust these people to know the inwardness of it more accurately than we can here in London. In their judgment, a definite revision upward has been achieved, and, they explain, "in the interests of the manufacturers"—which shows again how it is easier for capital to employ labour when the process is not at the mercy of the world's industrial accidents.

In September next will fall the three-hundredth anniversary of Henry Hudson's discovery of the eponymous river. It was suggested that Holland should send over an exact replica of the "Half Moon", the Dutch ship in which he made the voyage. When the project was put in hand it was found that there was not sufficient material on which to reconstruct the vessel. Weight, size and shape had alike to be determined. The records disappeared years ago when the Dutch Government sold for mere waste-paper tons of documents believed to be worthless which had belonged to the old East India Company. Inquiries were made in museums, in libraries, of every curiosity dealer, by scholars, the Dutch naval authorities and others interested. Scraps of evidence slowly and laboriously collected and collated enabled the designers to set to work, and the vessel, an eighty-ton three-masted yacht built throughout of oak, is now complete.

The yachting season in the Thames is evidently going to be a dull affair this year. Several of the County Council vessels were put up this week again and hardly anybody would bid. Fancy Dick Whittington and rare Ben Jonson offered at five hundred pounds apiece! There is an old fort off Bembridge in the Isle of Wight which is now for sale. Perhaps if this fort were put up with one or two of the London County Council steamers the curious offer might draw an imaginative customer.

Escape from the disaster of a general colliers' strike, with all the attendant dislocation of trade, was only just secured by the settlement of the Welsh dispute. But it was clear that similar disputes might arise in connexion with the Eight Hours Act in other parts of the country. This has happened. Now 80,000 Scottish miners having decided to stop work in a fortnight, the Miners' Federation of Great Britain at a meeting in London on Friday decided that the question of a national strike should be referred to a ballot of its members. Then, without reckoning minor strikes, there are 30,000 men in Staffordshire who have stopped work, and the iron and pottery trades are almost at a standstill for want of coal. Even if an arrangement that has been made is confirmed, the pits will not be at work for a fortnight. No prediction was ever more literally fulfilled than that the Eight Hours Act would raise new disputes and cause immediate loss to trade, even if the present disputes should be settled without further trouble.

If Lord Gorell's proposal to extend jurisdiction to the County Courts in divorce cases goes to a Committee of Inquiry its chances of becoming law are very remote. The Lord Chancellor and Lord Gorell both admitted that a matter of such importance could not be dealt with offhand without inquiry, and the resolution was withdrawn. We do not believe the Government will start an inquiry into the general subject of marriage and divorce laws; and a limited one as to the County Courts would not touch the subject of most importance. If divorce is not yet cheap enough, the County Courts will not make it so for many people, unless the expenses are paid by the rate or tax payers. Perhaps we shall have this proposed next. We were glad to find the Archbishop of Canterbury taking courage to oppose the Bill. Divorce should be neither cheap nor easy. The talk about giving relief to innocent parties is bosh. Nine times out of ten one party is as bad as the other.

A vast deserted building at the top of Marylebone Road, formerly known as "The Yorkshire Stingo" Brewery, is soon to disappear, and on its site will stand the new buildings of the Church Army. Where the vats stood will be the chapel for the inmates of the two homes. The work depots are for discharged convicts of the "star" class who had previously good characters and for unemployed married men. Wood-chopping is an art at which skilled men can earn four shillings a day. The management charges six shillings a week for residence, and the men are kept four months until they find regular situations. In winter Embankment men will receive food and bed in return for work. We wish every success to this useful enterprise. The sum of £16,000 is wanted, and we hope the advertisement of this want, which was begun with the ceremony of lunch at the "Yorkshire Stingo" on Monday, will be answered by ample subscriptions.

THE GERMAN CHANCELLOR'S SHADE.

HISTORY is repeating itself in Germany. When Count Posadowsky was dismissed from the Ministry of the Interior through the Conservative objection to his Liberal tendencies, it was Herr von Bethmann-Hollweg who took his place; and now again Herr von Bethmann-Hollweg is chosen to succeed a Chancellor for whose retirement the Conservatives are primarily responsible. The German Constitution expressly denies the responsibility of Ministers to Parliament. A Chancellor remains in office so long as he retains the confidence of the Emperor. It was because of the withdrawal of the imperial confidence that Prince Bismarck laid down his office, and the same official explanation was given of the resignations of Count Caprivi and Prince Hohenlohe. But in the case of Prince Bülow there is not the least pretence of imperial dissatisfaction. On the contrary, it is common knowledge that the Emperor was extremely loth to part with him, and that the present change has been brought about by the majority in the Reichstag. The new Chancellor is a man whose past is sure evidence of his willingness to serve a party. He is in fact a constitutional Minister, and the whole course of his future conduct will be profoundly affected by the circumstances of his appointment. Never has Germany known so paradoxical a political situation. The Conservative Junkers are notoriously of absolutist views. They are true to the traditions of Frederick the Great; they detest the new-fangled notions of parliamentarianism and democracy which the French Revolution brought into Germany; they grumbled at the constitutional position which Prince Bülow took up in the critical days of last November; and now they find themselves hailed by the less myopic organs of German Liberalism as the pioneers of constitutional progress! Times have indeed changed since Bismarck was dismissed not twenty years ago.

Rapid as this development has been, it is in no way surprising. The German Constitution is not yet forty years old, but for the first half of its short life it was worked by its author and meant exactly what he chose it to mean. During these important years Germany was acquiring a political self-consciousness which was bound to assert itself when once the controlling hand was removed. Moreover, the new arrangement contained from the first elements of instability which are now becoming apparent. In making his Constitution Bismarck left out two of the political forces of the time. One was the Liberal party. The omission was deliberate. Bismarck had fought it at the crisis of his career. He had beaten it, and by beating it had made the Empire possible. He regarded it as a sham, broken for the moment and useless for the future. Nor was he mistaken. Eugen Richter's party was a sham; it consisted of a number of middle-class gentlemen who pretended to be democrats. Bismarck saw that the middle classes were too feeble to count, and overlooked the masses altogether. Modern Germany has both a middle class and a working class. The former has come into being with the industry which it has created. Numerically small, it is the richest party in Germany, and gold weighs heavily in the political scales. Politically that working class was created by the suffrage which Bismarck granted, but it was denied adequate expression. Deprived of any form of Ministerial control, the Reichstag found itself a fifth wheel to the political coach, and the democrats were driven to a policy of passive resistance. The tactics pursued by the Socialist Left have brought about the extraordinary situation that a party which is now supported by more than three million voters has never exercised the slightest influence on the course of legislation. A policy of pure negation stands self-condemned, but in justice to Herr Bebel and his colleagues it must be admitted that their position was largely forced upon them by circumstances.

The financial scheme propounded by Prince Bülow was, in one aspect, a concession to the claims of the industrialists and the multitude. It was on the left wing—on the Liberals and on the Socialists—that he had to rely, and in the critical division he was beaten by it. He had attempted to give the Left that position in politics which it had a certain right to hold. He had aimed at a change in the balance of the Constitution, and he was defeated. And here the question arises: Why did Prince Bülow resign? Why not dissolve, and if necessary dissolve again and again until he had at last convinced the reactionaries that he had behind him a combination of money and votes which was stronger than any Constitution and for which any workable Constitution must find room? It is at this point that we come upon the second of Bismarck's omissions. He forgot the Chancellor. He forgot, that is, to provide for an office which was something in itself apart from the dominant personality of its first occupant. Even as it was, Bismarck had to clothe himself with powers belonging properly to the Emperor as head of the Executive, and it was by depriving him of these powers that William II. eventually forced his resignation. But not until the crisis of last November did the full weakness of the Chancellor's position become apparent. At first sight, indeed, there never was a moment when the Chancellor was more powerful. For the first time since Bismarck's dismissal he found himself in direct opposition to the Emperor, and it was the Emperor who surrendered. But the victory was won not by the Chancellor but by the forces behind him. He spoke as the representative of the Federal Council, he had at his back all the influence of the Federated Governments, thoroughly scared at the difficult position in which the Empire had been placed by an irresponsible manager of foreign politics. Prince Bülow was far too astute a man to mistake his position. By himself he knew he was helpless. Behind him must stand either the Emperor or the Federal Council. Circumstances forced him to rely on the Council, and it was with their support that he formulated his scheme of financial reform.

At the critical moment that support was withdrawn. He had prepared plans so generous to the States in the matter of their financial contributions to the Empire that the Liberals were up in arms from the first. Somewhat to the surprise of the Federated Governments the majority in the Reichstag proved to be even more particularist than themselves. Prince Bülow was supported by the entire Left, by the very parties which regard the States Governments as the pillars of reaction and which are pledged to diminish their authority. Only by a dissolution which would result in the return of these parties in greater strength could the reforms be carried. Is it to be wondered that the Council refused to render a service to their bitterest enemies? The Prince found himself helpless. The Emperor could not support him. He had promised to efface himself seven months before, and an Emperor does not break his word. The Federal Council would not support him; the Reichstag, apparently the dominant factor, was in reality only able to force its will through the tacit concurrence of the Council, and was itself constitutionally inadequate to carry through a constructive policy. The Chancellorship suddenly emerged in all its weakness as the mouthpiece of the strongest political force in the State.

There is then no need to trouble about Herr von Bethmann-Hollweg's programme, which will probably not be disclosed until the new session is opened in the autumn. But, whatever it be, it will not be his own programme, but that of the victorious particularists. He is indeed in an even weaker position than was his predecessor during the last fortnight of his term of office. Prince Bülow held a deserved reputation as an expert in foreign politics. He had been a most successful ambassador, and as a diplomatist was probably unsurpassed in Europe. His successor knows nothing of diplomatic work. The Emperor has chosen an expert in home affairs to deal with the domestic crisis which now confronts Germany. There is no need to question the absolute disinterestedness of his motives, but he cannot be blind to the increase in his own influence which the new appointment involves. He has pledged his word to be a constitutional Sovereign, but the Constitution expressly states that he is to represent the Empire in foreign affairs. His Chancellor is to accept responsibility for foreign policy as far as the people at home are concerned, but that in no way permits a Chancellor to dictate a policy to his master. Prince Bülow, indeed, could possibly venture to do so, but that was because of the experience of the man and not on account of the importance of his office. Herr von Bethmann-Hollweg is a cipher in foreign affairs, and in the constitutional conflict he is not the protagonist but the prize of victory. There are three forces contending for supremacy in Germany to-day—there is the Emperor with his military and naval authority and his position as representative of the Empire as regards foreign States; there are the States, whose organ is the Federal Council; and there is the people as represented, or misrepresented, by the Reichstag. The Chancellor does not count, and History, who is a divinity with a sense of humour, smiles ironically over Bismarck's work.

THE COMING OF COMPULSION.

WHO would have thought even five years ago that an amendment hostile to compulsory service would be carried in the House of Lords only by a majority of twenty votes, in spite of the official condemnation of compulsion by the leaders on either side? We regret that Lord Lansdowne advised his followers to reject the Bill; and that the official Unionist whips should have acted as tellers. Nor can we believe that the Unionist party as a whole will welcome his action. A second reading of the Bill in the House of Lords would have brought the matter prominently before the nation without committing the party to any definite policy on the issue, and it is the work of the Lords to give a lead to public opinion. That is the great use of a second chamber, removed from the hysterical turmoil of a general election, and possessing men eminently qualified to speak with authority on any great national issue. We are glad that at any rate one party politician, who has held one of the greatest posts under the British Crown, should have spoken in no uncertain terms of the absolute necessity for introducing compulsion. Lord Curzon was not afraid of his convictions. None now can treat compulsion as the irresponsible idea of a few enthusiasts. In one respect Lord Midleton was not quite fair to Lord Roberts. Lord Roberts, he said, had already all the facts on the subject when he held his high post at the War Office; and the present state of affairs in no way justified his forming any new opinion. The European situation, however, has appreciably changed in the interim; and we think we are right in saying that Lord Roberts, when Commander-in-Chief, only agreed with Mr. Brodrick on the adequacy of our existing military preparations on the understanding that we should, in a European war, have the support of Germany.

When we come to consider in detail the arguments adduced by the opponents of Lord Roberts' Bill, they appear trivial and ill-informed. Lord Crewe ridicules as a platitude the historic idea that a citizen's first duty is to be qualified to defend his fatherland; and other speakers tell us that the influence of the barrack-room must be contaminating, whilst Lord Lansdowne, after telling us that public opinion is not yet ripe for such a change, has no more effective remedy to offer us than the formation of cadet corps and military training in schools. These remedies, as no doubt the speakers realised, are totally inadequate; and what can be said of the forethought of the politician who is ready to allow the very life of the Empire to depend upon so uncertain a factor as the outcome of perhaps even one naval battle? The issue of a great battle or a great campaign on land is uncertain, as all history shows. But it can rarely happen that either can lead to the annihilation of an army. But a navy can be wiped out in a single action; indeed we have not to carry our memories very far back to see that this is a possible result. Moreover, as Lord Milner truly pointed out, the primary duty of the Navy in time of war is not to be tied to our shores to ensure their integrity, but to protect our commerce and keep open our lines of communication. Some speakers again relied mainly on the argument that the cost would be prohibitive; and although the War Office officials have discarded the absurd figures which were issued on the subject under Mr. Arnold-Forster's régime, they still claim that the estimates of the National Service League are very much under the mark. We concede the point; for we have never yet known any new military scheme which has not far outrun the original estimates of its cost. Mr. Haldane's scheme is a case in point. But even granting that Lord Roberts' scheme may cost twice as much as is estimated, the amount is insignificant when the great issue of the security of the country is at stake. It was said that it would be unwise to tamper with Mr. Haldane's Territorial Army, which has already received the sanction of the Upper Chamber; and some speakers denied Lord Roberts' contention that a scheme of compulsion could easily be engrafted on Mr. Haldane's measures. As a fact, the one really good thing about the Territorial plan is that it does provide the plant for compulsion. We have now all the materials at hand. The country has been apportioned out into districts which should produce their requisite quota of men. The agricultural districts have to produce yeomanry and the densely populated areas their due supply of infantry. The force also has been provided with an adequate staff. We have already divisional and brigadier-generals and their staffs. Nothing but compulsion is wanted to make Mr. Haldane's scheme live. Ex-War Secretaries who, when in power, were not remarkable for the attention they paid to the advice of their military experts, now take refuge in the argument that as the present military advisers of the War Secretary are content with things as they are, it would be unwise to embark on any change. It is a remarkable fact, however, that whilst almost every soldier outside the War Office whose opinion counts is in favour of compulsion and distrusts Mr. Haldane's schemes, those inside that institution admire them. The entire brain of the Army, however, cannot be concentrated in the War Office. There must be some left without. So surely the opinion of the very large remainder, though not official, is worth considering. As Lord Newton wittily says, it is amusing to note how Lord Roberts' views are regarded in official circles. When they are in favour of some Government proposal they are treated as being as infallible as those of a Supreme Pontiff; but when they disagree with the proposals of those in power they are merely relegated to the background as being those of an obsolete Victorian soldier.

But whilst we support Lord Roberts' Bill, and regret its rejection, we are not departing from our original standpoint. We still maintain, as some of the adverse critics did in the debate, that it does not go far enough, and that its provisions as to training and service are inadequate. An initial training of four months, with an annual one of a fortnight afterwards, is not enough, though it is good as far as it goes. But what can we think of a country which will not accept such a modicum of compulsion? We do not admit, however, that popular opinion is so adverse as is generally supposed. The present conditions are extremely unsatisfactory. The man who is patriotic enough to serve in the Territorial Army is likely to be absolutely handicapped in time of stress. Two men are working side by side. The "terrier" is taken, whilst his fellow-workman actually scores by his patriotic endeavour, because as workmen become scarce wages rise. Compulsion would rectify this. The burden would fall equally on all. Moreover, it is quite clear now that compulsion must come. Let us pray that it may not come only as the outcome of some terrible national disaster, when all efforts at redress will be unavailing. We agree with Lord Lansdowne that it would be lamentable if the introduction of compulsion had the effect of starving the Regular forces and the Navy; but we do not agree with him in thinking that recruiting for the Regular Army would be prejudiced. Indeed, the weight of probability is all the other way. Military training and military life, as it is nowadays, are incentives to recruiting; and in any case the class from which we draw recruits for the Regular Army—mainly those who, possibly through no fault of their own, have not done well in the labour market—would not be affected. One point remains which we wish once more to emphasise. There is still the idea that most men in the prime of life would be called upon to serve. But were compulsion introduced to-morrow, not one single voter would be taken. No man can exercise the franchise until he is twenty-one. But the military age in all conscribed countries is twenty. It is not putting patriotism very high to call attention to this. But it is true; and when once our patriotic electors realise that conscription will not mean *their* being conscribed, not a man of them will hesitate to support conscription.

THE SHAH AND HIS ENEMIES.

IT was the late Musaffer-ed-Din Shah, as everyone knows, who granted a Constitution to Persia. He had suffered for some years from Bright's disease, and when he last journeyed to Europe, with all the disastrous expenditure that the moving of a Persian Court demands, it was not to be photographed with the Prince of Wales or Kaiser, but to be given new prescriptions by the doctors of Berlin and Paris. Always he had this idea of dying slowly, and so he was easily "brought to reason" by some ten thousand "agitators", who used the time-honoured method of "Bast"; that is to say, he was frightened into submission when his enemies retired to the grounds of a sympathetic Legation, though it would seem they were thereby only suggesting that he was no sportsman. Musaffer rests now in a corner of the Takieh, or theatre, which stands among the Royal buildings in Teheran. This town palace of the Shahs has been deserted and emptied by Mahommed Ali, and certainly as one goes through its deserted gardens, courts and council chambers it seems very certain that the old régime is at an end. Luxurious of body during his lifetime, Musaffer-ed-Din looked for a luxury of soul after death, and he gave instructions that he should be removed early to some chosen and holier shrine. But who now cares for his dying wishes?

Freedom, then, had no very glorious beginnings in Persia, and perhaps that is why Mahommed Ali has never learned to respect the word. He does not, however, admit that he has been animated by any hostility to representative institutions; and as he is a keen-sighted, vigorous-minded observer, his attitude is well worth attention. In his view certain mischief-makers took advantage of the unfortunate circumstances in which he came into his inheritance. Obviously his father bequeathed a very unpleasant situation—the State was pretty well bankrupt, the dignity of the Kajars gone, the traditions of their policy broken, the Bab heresy abroad in the Church. Still he was determined to make the best of things, and had no intention of falling out even with so foolish and unnecessary a body as the Medjliss. As a matter of fact he did fall out, quite in the approved fashion of kings, with his Parliament; but that was all the doing of those evilly disposed persons in the background.

The mischief-makers have been of his own household. One of his brothers started a revolt in the province of Hamadan immediately after the coronation. He imagined himself a Napoleon, and so dreamt among other things of the conquest of India. This prince was suppressed. If he still lives, even his most credulous friends must have ceased to be interested in his imaginings now that they have noted Persian military capacities as displayed during the present civil war. Among the members of the royal family to-day there does, however, stand out one considerable personage, the Zill-es-Sultan, a brother of the late Shah. A consideration of his position and claims leads at once into the complicated domain of royal relationships. The Zill only failed to secure the throne on Nasr-ed-Din's death because his mother was not of royal blood. But he made his name as Governor of Ispahan. While there he was more than once in trouble with his brother, but he outlived Musaffer-ed-Din, and was ruling practically over the whole of Southern Persia when his nephew came to the throne; he had become exceedingly wealthy, and was not yet past middle age. Now Mahommed Ali had scarcely a better claim to the throne than the Zill had had, for his mother was of royal blood on one side only; moreover, she was a divorced wife. It is easy to understand how the new Shah became suspicious of his kinsman, and how his suspicions deepened into certainties when he found himself threatened and thwarted by the Anjumans and the Medjliss, and later again when he heard of those well-fed, well-armed European mercenaries who were pouring into Northern Persia on evil intent all last spring. Meanwhile the Zill had hurried to Europe; he had left his country before the Royalist triumph in June last year, and was not home again when the Shah in May of this year seemed to be giving up the fruits of that triumph. About a week ago at a significant moment there came the news that he had landed at Enzeli.

On the whole it seems very likely that court rivalries have in the past been largely responsible for the Shah's difficulties. Certainly he would seem to have been swayed very often by personal animosities and prejudices, and thus only can the worse features of his conduct be explained. At the present moment, however, the ambitions of the Zill will probably have a limited scope. The vague hopes of the Persian people run in other directions. So capable a tax-collector could have no place in the Utopia. Curiously enough, the duel between Zill and Shah has a bearing on the more or less international aspect of the situation. The Zill, it should be known, has always been a self-constituted protégé of England—hence last year when his activities caused anxiety the Shah telegraphed to King Edward on the subject. The Shah on the other hand regards himself as a protégé of Russia—hence the number of Caucasians and other disaffected subjects of the Tsar who have entered Teheran in the name of Liberty and the Constitution. The fact is that neither the Royalists nor the Nationalists have accepted the Anglo-Russian agreement as an accomplished fact, signifying an entire change in the British and Russian policies in Persia. Like the Zill the Nationalists fancy that they are England's protégés; they argue that the Shah has been encouraged in his resistance by Russian support and promises, and that, therefore, England ought to stand by them in the arena. The complaints hich they make of a British betrayal do not however em very serious, for, after all, the constitutional movement cannot on their own showing be of value unless t represents a desire on the part of the people to learn he habit of self-reliance and to prove their capacity for he independent conduct of their own affairs. Still, rom Great Britain's point of view, a closer association n her part with these would-be allies of hers might ave been good policy. The Nationalist picture of ussian intrigue is no doubt grossly exaggerated. It s not proved that Russia has tried to take advantage f Persia's distracted state. At the same time events ave shaped themselves to give her the opportunity and o damage England's prestige rather badly. This ountry has so obviously played second fiddle.

But that is Great Britain's affair, not Persia's. And t would be well if patriotic Persians were in the future o refrain from over-estimating the importance of their ountry's fate, as it concerns Great Britain or Russia r any other Power. If Persia—Royalist or Nationalist wishes to be taken seriously, she must renew her nergy and courage, and cease to depend upon the hance and changing circumstances of British and ussian necessities. Neither England nor England's spiritual child", the Medjliss, can of itself make ersian life worth living. For the moment we wait or the smoke to clear from Teheran, and then we ought o know if there is really any hope for an unfortunate ountry.

ELECTIONEERING FINANCE.

ON Tuesday night, under excellent stage management, and after evident rehearsal with "the play boys of the western world", Mr. Lloyd George exempted small holdings from the increment tax, so that a millionaire may go free, while a penniless man must pay merely because it is his misfortune to hold a few perches more. It was done under an Irish disguise, all "in response to an invitation from Mr. Redmond and his colleagues", whose care for the comfort of agricultural land is so well known.

It has been discovered lately that many people have small holdings, that many more would like to have them, that they all could influence bye-elections, and even general elections. Before that discovery, there was little thought of exempting the small holder, and no need of the "invitation from Mr. Redmond" to disguise the Radical fear of British public opinion. Such is the tactical prudence with which heroic ideals can be trimmed to party convenience; but things that are inherently wrong have a way of exposing themselves in practice, and though the raw Radical of the villages may be slow to see it, this exemption of the small holdings starts a play of motives that must reveal the absurdity in the end. Can Mr. Lloyd George have fully considered the effects of his concession?

The usual place for a small holding is near a town, on the border of the building margin, where the holder may live while earning wages in the town, and where the market gardener may be near his customers; and the main idea is to exempt the land so long as it is not used for building, no matter how much its building value may grow in the meantime. So far, there is an inducement to convert idle building sites into market gardens, and that is to the good; but as the purpose is only temporary, there is an equal inducement to do the thing hideously. There will not be much concern with architecture about the building of new houses that may have to come down before five years; and, on a tenure so precarious, there will not be much reason to maintain a reserve of fertility in the soil. The outlook is to assure poverty in production and ugliness in aspect; yet in proportion to the extent of the tax evaded, there must be an economic need for this temporary tinkering while the site "matures" for the jerry builder. The exemption does not extend to a small holding worth more than £500, the Welsh conscience having reduced British justice to a question of arithmetic.

Take the man who has a holding in the same situation worth £10,000. He bears the new tax, but, in proportion to its extent, it will pay him to divide it up into twenty small holdings, each below the taxable limit. Even apart from the tax, he might sell it for more in twenty lots than in one; but, the tax in force, he can certainly secure by the division an increase in some proportion to the impost evaded. It is claimed that the tax will not lessen the selling value of the land bearing it; but it must certainly increase the value of the land exempted; so that, on the basis of the claim, the owner of the big plot may at once pocket a handsome profit out of Mr. Lloyd George's methods. Then comes the question of economy in building, which affects rent and housing. The smaller the plot, the harder to build on it at a profit, and the greater the inducement to build badly. A builder may have a handsome and economic scheme on the £10,000 basis; but with this divided into twenty, he may be able to secure only three of the twenty plots together, making a little scheme on the basis of £1,500 only. Buying on the smaller scale, the builder pays more for his material. His mortar-mill is enough for a scheme ten times as large, and in every other way his fixed charges are high in proportion to the scope and profit of his undertaking. The law of diminishing return is against him, and, to build at a profit, he must try to produce the worst possible buildings at the highest possible rents. With the economics of the affair thus subdivided on small margins, the architecture must be mean to match, and only the more disreputable class of builders can be attracted. With one little building scheme completed, there is every inducement for the small holders round it to hold out for still higher prices, and so long as they make a fair pretence that the land is in small holdings worth no more than £500, the tax cannot touch them. Care will be taken to hold on to the fee simple and work the small holdings on the tenancy principle, so that the owner may draw the equivalent of a double rent, constantly increasing, first from the agricultural tenant, and secondly from the increasing value of the fee simple. Is it not obvious that the whole thing makes for the comparative increase of house-rent and the comparative degradation of the building standard? Yet the boast at the beginning of the Budget was that it would "force building land into the market", and so reduce rent. That, however, was before the bye-elections had revealed the influence of the small holders at the ballot-box. Whatever the action of the Lords on the Finance Bill, the Budget ought to be kept before the House of Commons as long as possible, so that the largest possible number of bye-elections may take place before the Upper House make their decision. In so far as can be seen from their methods, the Government are prepared to drop any part of the Budget that may be found inconvenient to their party purposes.

Take the man who has a £10,000 plot and wishes to evade the tax while keeping the land in his own possession. He can lockspit the twenty patches himself and sell them to twenty of his family and friends, with properly legal conveyances; and then they can sell them all back again to him, so that he remains the owner all the time, but in shape to evade the tax-gatherer. So long as the transfers are duly registered, Mr. Lloyd George cannot interfere without a farther and still more obvious betrayal of his methods; and the whole shuffle can be achieved even without calling on the bank for a temporary overdraft to finance it. If necessary, the owner of the twenty plots can put up wooden shanties and collect twenty tramps to do a little digging; or, if he be a strong man in the County Council, he may contrive a combination of labour colonies and market gardening until such time as his estate has "matured". Then he can throw the whole twenty plots back again into one if it pays him; and the Treasury is defeated from beginning to end, though the land is all the time really a building estate held for higher prices. In short, there is no end to the trickeries necessitated in the lower places when trickery has become the standard in the Chancellorship of the Exchequer.

Is it that the significance of the bye-elections was revealed too suddenly for Mr. Lloyd George to mature his exemptions before announcing them? It is hard to think that a man of his cleverness could have made such a muddle if he had had time to reflect. One of his own reasons for the exemptions is that taxes on small holdings are expensive to collect; but is not this a further reason for every victim to convert his land into some form of small holdings as soon as he can? The trickery can but hurt Radicalism itself in the end, multiplying small holders, and creating for each a business necessity to oppose the methods of Radical finance. The active extent of the causes and motives which we have indicated will depend on the pressure and effect of the exactions. If great enough to produce revenue, the exactions must certainly make it worth while to apply those methods of evasion in self-defence; and if the evasions be not worth the trouble, the new scheme can produce no revenue worth considering.

THE WORK OF THE CANCER RESEARCH FUND.

THE distinguished pathologists who are engaged in investigating cancer must ardently wish for a public educated in the history of scientific research. They themselves lose neither heart nor hope, and they are assured that in the end their labours will benefit the world. To the ordinary man seven years spent by experts in the study of one scientific problem without any decisive result that can be communicated in popular language appear wasted. He asks, in the case of cancer investigation, Have you found out what causes cancer, and have you found a cure for it or a means of prevention? If he finds that no definite answer can be given to him as a plain man, one knows that his interest will cool and his subscriptions fall off. This is unfortunately the state of mind of the general public when the seventh annual report of the Imperial Cancer Research Fund appears and its annual meeting is held. Subscriptions will fall off and the faith of many wax cold, but we cannot believe that wealth and intelligence are so divorced that the investigations will be crippled for lack of funds. If the investigators were themselves losing heart we might despair, or if they were too eager to publish conclusions which excited our hopes we might distrust them. But they have a "scientific conscience", and those who know the history of scientific discovery are aware that the great discoverers do not make premature and immature disclosures. Usually they work for years in silence, and only an inner circle knows what is going on. Then a Newton or Darwin, a Pasteur or a Lister comes into the mouth of a public that is informed of a result without having an idea of the long process that has preceded. The investigations of the Cancer Fund started in circumstances known to the public. A yearly scientific balance sheet had to be presented which few understood. The process was as mysterious as making diamonds, but diamonds were expected and large dividends immediately.

This impatience is quite natural and quite unreasonable. Cancer has been investigated and treated by the medical profession for centuries. The Cancer Fund organised investigation more completely than it had been before; but it was never imagined by those who understood the nature of the disease that organisation would make a short cut to its origin and cure. Let us take an illustration from a different subject. We organise our polar expeditions now with far more completeness and with much better knowledge of the conditions than the early explorers had, but after so many years the poles are not yet reached. The explorers know much better than we others why they are so often baffled. If our lives and health, our happiness and misery were dependent on their success, how ignorantly impatient we should be at their failures! As it is we are free to be reasonable. We can allow for what we do not understand. We have confidence in the character and accomplishments of the explorers; and if they believe they will ultimately plant the flag at the poles, we catch their enthusiasm and are willing to subscribe for an indefinite number of expeditions. We ought to think of the Cancer Fund's investigations in a similar way. It is a fact of great importance to have proved that the course of cancer as it can be observed in the laboratory agrees with it as it occurs in man, and forms a sound foundation for studying the disease in the human species. The study of cancer is thus put on the same experimental basis as all other studies in physical science. It is evidently a great advantage if the phenomena of cancer in animals are established as being essentially the same as those of cancer in man. One interesting fact is mentioned by Sir William Church bearing on the question of heredity of cancer: "The breeding experiments from mice derived from cancerous stocks are as yet insufficient for determining the frequency of cancer in mice with a cancerous ancestry." Anti-vivisectionists leap at an admission of this kind, and assert that it shows experiments on animals prove nothing as to man. But this is a fallacy. All the experiments that can be made on man so far have left the question of heredity in obscurity. The experiments in breeding animals as yet cannot be taken one way or the other; but in this case there is far more control over the experiments; and it is this control that makes experiment more trustworthy than mere observation or intuition—than guesswork in short. And so with other results which cannot be stated in a positive form.

Certain negative results are already of great importance to the public. Many hypotheses that put research on wrong tracks have been shown to be untenable. With them go mistaken methods of treatment and pretended "cures" founded on erroneous theories or on imposture facilitated by imperfect knowledge. Beyond these claims the investigators will not go, though their reticence conceals the fact of many important pathological discoveries which would be unintelligible to the untrained. But they enable those by whose authority we should be guided to declare confidently that the ultimate objects of the Fund will be attained. To them the progress has been quite as decided and rapid as they expected it to be at the outset; and the public which has no interest but in a proclaimed cure must know that without patient scientific investigation, no matter how many years it may occupy, there will be no "cure". There is strong temptation to exaggerate the effect of what has been done. Mr. Gerard Fiennes pointed out that even negative results if they could be announced would be of enormous value to the health of the community and they would certainly bring in subscriptions. For instance, Mr. Fiennes said, "if as soon as the fact was scientifically established, a declaration could go forth that cancer was not hereditary and not communicable, it would have a vast therapeutic effect on the army of the well. It was only the other day that an acquaintance of his told him that he was living in dread of the onset of the disease of which one relative after another had died. That condition of mind, he had reason to know, was not uncommon". Many of us know that it is quite common. Surely, however impatient the public may be, it must see in the work of the Cancer Research Fund the one chance of learning some day that this burden of evil has no longer to be borne. Hardly less insidious is the temptation to exaggerate results owing to the attitude of the opponents of experiments on animals. The absence of announced discoveries by the Fund enables the Anti-Vivisection Societies to disparage its work and to persuade the public that it loses nothing by withdrawing its support. This we are convinced is altogether a mistake; and there is a real danger that the Fund may suffer. Quite evidently it is at a critical moment in its history. It needs an endowment to make it independent of ignorant popular feeling, which is far too precarious a basis on which to found scientific research.

THE CITY.

THE Stock markets have been very dull and uninteresting all through the week, and the Mining market has been actually weak. Notwithstanding the active liquidation that has been proceeding in the South African market for the last three accounts, and the sensibly diminished volume of the commitments for the rise, it appears that all the weak bulls have not yet been eliminated. Or, to put it more accurately, those who bought stock to help the lame ducks during the slump have been disappointed in their hope of unloading at a profit; so that they are still pressing shares upon the market. The big houses will do nothing for the present, and the public naturally holds aloof from a stagnant market. How long this state of things will continue it is impossible to predict. The holidays do not make so much difference as formerly, as the telephone and telegraph are more handy than they used to be at seaside resorts and in country houses. The Jungle always sympathises with the Kaffir circus, and things are sluggish there too, though the backers of West African shares are more earnest and enthusiastic than the Kaffir dealers. Undoubtedly such shares as Fanti Mines and Gold Coast Agency are cheap at present prices. The only mining share that has dared to lift its head is the Alaska Treadwell, which has risen to 6¼ on very favourable developments at the mine. Amongst industrials, Pekin shares and Shansis have been strong, the former being bid for at 11; and it is whispered—though tell it not in Gath—that certain people are buying for control with a view to changing the chairman.

The Argentine railway market is steady at lower prices. The issue of Buenos Ayres and Pacific debentures has not been taken quite so well as it deserved to be, considering its security and the prevalent cheapness of money. Mexican Southerns remain about 70, despite the rupture of negotiations with the Mexican railway. Leopoldina ordinary are slowly rising, and Yankee rails continue to defy bears and the crop reports that are always used at this time of year to disturb values. Steel Commons have risen to 72, and are talked of as likely to go to 90. An addition to the Cobalt properties dealt in on the London market is shortly to be made by La Rose Consolidated Mines Company, which has a capital of seven and a half million dollars.

The price of rubber has risen to 7s. a pound, and some people predict that it will rise to 10s. This has caused the shares of a great many rubber companies to advance to very high premiums, such as Malacca Preference, Linggi, Bukit Raja, Consolidated Malay, Anglo-Ceylon, Vallambrosa, Kapar Paras and many others. Nearly all these companies have very small capitals, on which they are able to pay very high dividends, in many cases 60 or 70 per cent. This gives the public rather an inaccurate notion of the rubber-producing industry. The capital is raised to cover the jungle value of the estate, usually from £2 to £3 an acre, plus the amount that must be spent on clearing, planting, weeding and tapping. This comes to between £30 and £40 an acre. The cost of producing a pound of rubber in Ceylon and Malaya is pretty uniformly 1s. 4d., and the freight, insurance, dock charges and brokerage in London another 3d., bringing the cost of a pound of rubber up to 1s. 7d. In the present market the best rubber can be sold at 6s. 7d. or more, leaving the producer the enormous profit of 5s. a pound. This of course cannot last for ever, though it may easily last for another year. The Brazilian rubber, compared with which the output of plantation rubber is a mere fleabite, is in the hands of three or four firms, all acting for the United States Rubber Trust; and it is said that these men, foreseeing the great increase in plantation rubber that is coming fast, are determined to make hay while the sun shines; in other words, to keep up the price of rubber while they can. We are of opinion therefore that the market for rubber shares is not likely to collapse for some time to come. We hear that there is a new process brought from France for treating the latex, or raw gum, which will save the elaborate rolling and drying that is now done in the estate factories in Ceylon and the Malay Peninsula. There is also a new process for treating and remaking old rubber.

INSURANCE: CONFEDERATION LIFE.

COLONIAL life offices earn with safety a rate of interest that is appreciably higher than that yielded by the funds of English and Scottish life offices. We have recently been examining the valuation returns made to the British Board of Trade by the Confederation Life Association of Canada, the first returns of this kind which have been published. One significant fact is that the total life funds invested and uninvested yielded interest at rates which increased from £4 12s. per cent. in 1903 to £5 per cent. in 1906 and to more than £5 3s. per cent. in 1907. These are high rates of interest which can be obtained in Canada with entire safety. The measure of the surplus derived from interest is not, however, the actual rate earned, but the difference between the rate assumed in valuing the liabilities and the actual return upon the funds. Very fairly, as it seems to us, life offices in the colonies and the United States do not value all their liabilities on the same basis. The Confederation Life, for instance, values all policies issued since 1899 on a 3 per cent. basis, and policies issued at previous dates are valued at higher rates of interest. The effect of this plan is to avoid diminishing bonuses on old policies by using the surplus to strengthen the reserves instead of distributing it among the assured. Since the Confederation Life commenced business in the United

Kingdom all its policies here have reserves held for them on a 3 per cent. basis, and, the rate of interest earned being over 5 per cent., there is the very large margin of more than 2 per cent. per annum of the funds accumulating for bonus purposes.

For various reasons, which we have explained from time to time, a very high rate of interest is normally accompanied by a high rate of expenditure, and the Confederation Life is no exception to this general rule. The expenses absorb 29 per cent. of the total premium income, which is a high rate of expenditure. To judge fairly of the economy or otherwise of management we ought to know the amount of the premium income on the new policies issued each year. We have reason to believe that it is large, in which case even 29 per cent. of the premium income might not prove an excessive expenditure. The association was founded in 1871, and is developing vigorously: this is of necessity an expensive process, but it may well prove a wise expenditure, and in any case a large influx of lives that have been medically examined recently tends to produce favourable mortality. For these and other reasons the tests which are applicable to very old offices doing a moderate new business and earning a comparatively low rate of interest on their funds break down when applied to a vigorous colonial society exhibiting rapid expansion and earning with safety a very high rate of interest.

Sooner or later—probably next year—a new insurance law will be passed by the Canadian Parliament which, though by no means in accordance with English notions, is calculated to make certain of financial security without unduly interfering with the free development of the companies. Canada, like most countries outside the United Kingdom, is committed to State supervision and control of insurance companies, and at the International Congress of Actuaries, where the subject has been discussed, the English and the Scottish representatives for the most part stood alone in deprecating that State supervision which prevails in most countries and which is wisely avoided in the Bill at present before the House of Lords.

Colonial offices such as the Confederation Life are in a position to offer great advantages to policyholders and annuitants under contracts where a large surplus from interest plays the most important part: this happens in the more expensive kind of policies, such as endowment assurances, particularly those for short terms, and annuities. The wise man wanting to invest his money in assurance naturally takes advantage of the peculiarities of different companies, and the good colonial life offices afford him the opportunity of benefiting in certain circumstances by the enterprise and prosperity of our British colonies.

The Confederation Life has recently changed its management in the United Kingdom, and has appointed as its representative in this country Mr. L. H. Senior, who has a long and successful record with important offices in England. This should mean the prosperous development of the company here by the combination of English methods of management backed up by colonial enterprise and the financial advantages which Canada has to offer.

NEVILLE CHAMBERLAIN.*

By Field-Marshal Sir Evelyn Wood V.C.

THE character of Neville Bowles Chamberlain would be perhaps most aptly described by the opening lines in the Prologue to Chaucer's "Canterbury Tales":

> "A Knight ther was, and that a worthy man,
> That from the time that he first began
> To riden out, he loved chevalrie,
> Trouthe and honour".

I have been told by old officers who knew both Neville and Crawford that the younger brother, who was comparatively unknown, was equally grand in character, and some considered that he was a greater man than his elder brother. It is impossible indeed to imagine anything finer than the determination, prompt decision and tact shown by Crawford Chamberlain in June 1857 in disarming two Bengal infantry battalions at Multan without the aid of any Europeans, except a few Garrison Artillerymen.

On the other hand, I cannot recall the name of any soldier in all the stories of the glorious hand-to-hand fighting warriors in our frontier expeditions and Indian Mutiny in whom was united to so remarkable a degree the burning desire to fight individually any number of our foes, coupled with such sincere pity and compassion for the vanquished, as we find in all records and opinions of Neville Chamberlain's character. It is probable indeed that many British officers would have shown the same solicitude as he did for the safety of the native women and children captured at Istaliffe on 29 September 1842; but there can scarcely have been other fighting men who were as sensitive and compassionate as this hero, who had himself been three times wounded before he attained his twenty-third birthday.

On 29 October 1842, during the retirement of the force under General Pollock from Jelalabad to Peshawur, Neville Chamberlain was in command of the rearguard. The morning having been very wet, the march was delayed, and Neville Chamberlain rode alone in front of his command before it had marched off into a ravine, where he came suddenly on three of the enemy; drawing his sword, the young man charged at them. The matches of their firelocks were not lighted, and, being frightened by Chamberlain's bold attack, one Afghan threw himself over a crag, a second hid himself behind rocks, while the third awaited the young Englishman's attack, who, having killed him, wrote thus to Mrs. Chamberlain: "I would now give back any honour or reputation I have gained not to have committed that one act". Sir Charles Napier, whose personal courage was remarkable, named Chamberlain "Cœur de Lion", and Sir James Outram wrote of him as "the most noble and bravest soldier who ever trod in Afghanistan".

Our hero was born at Rio de Janeiro in 1820, and joined the Woolwich Academy in 1833, where his tastes tended more to muscular than to intellectual exercises. When his mother and sister went to see him he was in the infirmary with "erysipelas in the head, the result of a fight, and we heard that he had spent a great deal of his probationary year in fighting".

At fifteen years of age the lad was sent home, it being considered he was unlikely to pass the final examination; but he received an appointment in the Bengal Army in the East India Service, and, sailing for India in February 1837, reached Calcutta early in June. He landed in stirring times, for in spite of the fact that the Burmese, Mahratas and Nepaulese were in an excitable state, the Governor-General, Lord Auckland, had just been instructed by the home Government "that the time had arrived when it would be right to interfere decidedly in the affairs of Afghanistan".

The Governor-General determined to replace the then ruler of Afghanistan, Dost Muhammad Khan, a Barukzye, by Shah Sooja, a Saddukzye, who had been ousted by his brother five years previously. Lord Auckland made a tripartite treaty with Runjit Singh, the ruler of the Punjab, and Shah Sooja. The Governor-General had been assured by our officers who had visited Afghanistan that the Amir Dost Muhammad was detested by the people, and that Shah Sooja would be welcomed by a powerful party in Kabul.

This was an entire misapprehension, for which Lord Auckland can scarcely be held responsible, but it is impossible to accept Mr. Forrest's apology for Lord Auckland's memory that "he had no means of knowing Shah Sooja was the most incapable and feeble of men".

The Afghan was sixty years of age, known to be feeble and worn out in constitution; he was carried about in a chair, and was obviously no match for the active and energetic ruler whom it was proposed to dethrone. As Shah Sooja had lived for five years ou[r] pensioner in British territory at Ludiana there can be no excuse for ignorance as to his capacity.

* "Life of Field-Marshal Sir Neville Chamberlain G.C.B., G.C.S.I." By G. W. Forrest. Edinburgh and London: Blackwood. 1909. 18s. net.

Before the force designed for the invasion of Afghanistan crossed the Indus the Persians had raised the siege of Herat, and, one of the objectives being no longer in question, the so-called army of the Indus was reduced, but the two Chamberlains belonged to the troops which went forward.

It required seven days to pass through the Bolan Pass, a distance of sixty miles (over which there now runs a railway), for the track ascended over five thousand feet on the road to Quetta, then a small village of mud huts.

The Bengal column reached Kandahar, after suffering severe privations, on 23 April 1839. It had marched over a thousand miles, mainly across deserts and mountains, and was joined a fortnight later by the column from Bombay.

When the troops quitted Kandahar for Kabul at the end of June it was confidently stated that it would not fire a shot on the march, but Sir Alexander Burnes was misinformed, for on approaching Ghazni to reconnoitre it the General, Sir John Keane, was fired on.

It stood on a plain with parapets sixty feet high; and besides the difficulty of escalading, from the height of the walls, which could not be breached, as the heavy guns had been left at Kandahar, the place was surrounded by a wet ditch. There was a large wooden door closing the entrance on the Kabul side; and Sir John Keane, having only three days' food, determined to move round to the northern or Kabul side, blow in the gateway, and assault the fortress.

Mr. Forrest's account, as does also that of Neville Chamberlain, omits the most interesting and dramatic episode, the historian writing "The bugler had been shot through the head". This is an error, though a bugler was doubtless shot, for *the* Ghazni bugler was alive as a retired paymaster and honorary major just before the South African War.

Lieut.-Colonel Butler (now General Sir William K.C.B.), in "Far Out Rovings Retold", tells the story of "The Ghazni Bugler".

"As the powder exploded the massive gate disappeared and the walls fell inwards." One of the sappers, running back to where the main body of the assaulting column, 13th (now Somerset) Light Infantry, was halted, reported "The passage is choked with fallen masonry; the forlorn hope cannot force it". On this an officer ordered Bugler Luke White, 13th Light Infantry, to sound the "Retire". He replied "The 13th don't know it", and sounded the "Advance". Thus the strongest fortress in Afghanistan was carried, and Dost Muhammad, mistrusting his followers, crossed the Oxus River, and Shah Sooja re-entered Kabul on 7 August.

Sir Alexander Burnes, capable as he was, remained as ignorant of Afghan character as was one of our greatest Britons, John Lawrence, of Hindustani plots fifteen years later. Burnes reported in September "The noses of the Durranee chiefs have been brought to the grindstone", "Afghanistan is as quiet as an Indian district", and arranged to send back to India a part of the small garrison. On 2 November he was informed by a friendly Afghan that he was to be attacked, but he refused to believe him. Then Shah Sooja's Prime Minister warned him to go to the cantonment, but all such advice was disregarded, and shortly afterwards he, with his brother, was murdered.

In a few days all the Kabul district rose against the puppet Amir and his British protectors. Chamberlain was then at Kandahar, disabled by a severe wound received when leading a pursuit after a successful fight on the Argandab River. He was riding up a very stony narrow passage when he was attacked simultaneously by two Afghans. One of them, jumping from a rock, lit on Chamberlain's horse and drove a dagger into the young Briton's thigh; they rolled to the ground and, while the Afghan tried to force his dagger into Chamberlain's stomach, he, flinging his arms around him, bit the man's biceps so severely that he dropped the dagger and was killed by one of the native troopers.

When Chamberlain returned from Afghanistan with a great reputation he was appointed to the native Bodyguard then being formed, but suffered too much from exfoliating bones from his leg to enable him to join at once. After having a finger amputated he was carried in a doli up to the battlefield of Maharajpur, and took part in the action. He was obliged to go to hospital again after the action, and after his wound had been treated vainly by injections of nitric acid, the diseased bone was removed by a painful operation which he underwent without an anæsthetic. He went to England to recover his health, but was back at duty in time to fight at Chilianwala in January 1849.

After acting as Military Secretary to the Punjab Board he suffered so much from fever that he took two years' leave to South Africa, and on his return was appointed to command the Punjab Frontier Force. He instituted for it what is now termed "field training", though, as he wrote in 1862, he was never able "to rise to the Horse Guards standard, despising slow time and toe-pointing parades".

Successive wounds had no effect on his nerves, for when at Delhi he saw on 14 July 1857 some infantry hesitate to advance, "he leaped his horse clean over the wall into the midst of the enemy and dared the men to follow him, which they did, but Chamberlain got a ball in his shoulder" (Lord Roberts' "Forty-one Years in India").

Again, in the Umbeyla campaign on 20 November 1863, when in command of the whole force, he actually led a column to retake for the third time the Crag Picquet, and was severely wounded.

In February 1876 Chamberlain got command of the Madras Army, returning to England in 1880. He was appointed a Field-Marshal in 1902, two years before his death.

The opening lines of this appreciation indicate the reason for his great influence over races which esteem courage as the first of virtues. He wrote well and with a keen enjoyment of the beauties of Nature, but he did not write willingly, and it was this probably which induced the author's treatment of the Life. It contains the most readable account of the British disasters in Afghanistan, but we learn in that part comparatively little of the hero, whose name for instance does not once appear in sixteen consecutive pages of Chapter IV.

"TESS" IN GRAND OPERA.

By Filson Young.

I feel sure that if Mr. Max Beerbohm had attended the first performance in England of Baron F. d'Erlanger's opera "Tess", which took place at Covent Garden on Wednesday evening, he would have had something more interesting to say about it than I have. Quite apart from what he would have said about the music, which would certainly have been interesting, he would have had most important things to say about the drama itself and the way in which M. Luigi Illica has constructed an Italian libretto out of the very English story which is Mr. Thomas Hardy's masterpiece. Dramatically the opera is interesting not because it is good, but because it is so very odd and strange, and this quality of oddity and strangeness is exactly what I should have liked Mr. Max Beerbohm to analyse and expound.

Mr. Hardy's story reeks of the soil; the smells of earth, the colour of the sky, the voices of birds and animals, and the drip and gurgle of the milk-pails are leading motives which are hardly ever absent from that complex composition. All this has been most wonderfully eliminated from the opera, and it is all done by the librettist; for the music is nearer the spirit of the "Tess" we know than Italian words can ever be. Indeed, one is tempted to wish that the opera could be sung to the admirable English prose translation of Claud Aveling, which is a model of what such things should be, and would help a little to produce some sense of the English soil to assist our illusion. As it is, I dare say it seemed very English in Naples; but at Covent Garden it was very modern Italian, very remote indeed from the land of Wessex.

The story of course has been altered—quite rightly;

but as it stands it is a drama without movement. The first act merely explains the poverty of the Durbeyfields, the rumour of their kinship with the family of d'Urbeville, and Tess's decision to go and seek for help from them. The second merely reveals a quarrel among the servants at D'Urbeville House, and the subsequent catastrophe to Tess. Instead of the splendid psychology of Mr. Hardy accounting for this catastrophe, however, the dramatic reason as shown on the stage is that a spiteful servant has locked the doors, so that Tess cannot get in in the evening, not even through the very practicable Tudor windows; and that consequently she yields to her seducer in the garden. Somehow the motive seems a little insufficient; one is under the impression that things do not happen quite so simply in real life. It is like those novels of Mr. Robert Hichens in which the whole courses of people's lives and characters are changed by their drinking a glass of liqueur or witnessing the performance of a country dance. The third act shows us that Tess has partly recovered from her mishap and put behind her the dark memory of her child, and is looking forward to a possible happy future with Angel Clare. And the last act shows us the bridal chamber, and Angel's paralysing discovery of poor Tess's history, and her acceptance of destiny in the shape of suicide. You see how little movement there is in all this, how little actually happens on the stage; and this makes the acts sometimes seem long where a little movement and incident would have sustained our interest.

The really weak point is the manner of Tess's downfall. A seduction is always an immensely popular theme with a theatre audience; it has made "Faust" immortal on the stage; people are so interested and thrilled, now sharing the wicked anticipation of the villain, now the maiden flutterings of the victim, and in the end having the privilege of sitting, quite unharmed, and shaking their heads over the consequences of sin. But the interest, like the interest of so many things in life, is almost all in anticipation. When it comes to the chase round the garden or room we are dangerously near the grotesque. The dramatically weak point of this opera is that the seduction does not take long enough, is too easily accomplished—the sole mechanism of the thing being, as I have said, two closed doors and a run round the garden.

It will be seen that I cling to the Wagnerian tradition that the drama itself is at least of as much importance as the music, although it is the fashion to say, "After all, the music is the thing". If you have to sit for three hours in a theatre, it is only half the thing. In the case of M. d'Erlanger's opera it is far and away the best half; from the beginning of the first act the music pleased me and won my sympathy, partly because it was very melodious without being banal, and so old-fashioned as to be almost Wagnerian. In fact one would describe M. d'Erlanger's style as a modern Italian version of Wagner. Often the orchestral accompaniment reminded me of the flowing score of "Meistersinger"; that kind of busy and happy animation of the orchestra that makes a background for one's thoughts while one is observing the drama is admirably achieved throughout the score. Often M. d'Erlanger has carried the flattery of his imitation a little too far; there are whole groups of bars at a time that have been lifted bodily from Wagner, both in sequence and in scoring and even in key—as, for example, certain passages, strangely reminiscent of "Walküre", which accompany the love duet in the third act. But the saving merit of this kind of thing is that it is unconscious imitation. M. d'Erlanger is so steeped in the music of his master that it comes straight out of his head in preference to something of his own. I cannot help contrasting this music with that of "The Wreckers", which we have lately been hearing—that angular and arid composition, so much deeper and cleverer than the music of "Tess", yet so much less human and beautiful. It is precisely those more obvious human qualities which one missed in Miss Ethel Smyth's work which are present in the score of "Tess". Sometimes there is almost a superfluity; the long-drawn Italianised Wagnerian melodies become sometimes a little sugary, and one feels as though the conductor's fingers were getting sticky. But it is not for long; there are always relief and correction sooner or later. The thing flows on in a sequence of admirable vocal music accompanied by those deeper and more significant orchestral utterances which serve to represent the great talking voice of Destiny muttering its majestic monologue throughout the drama.

I know nothing about the conditions under which this work was produced at Covent Garden, nor to what extent, if any, Baron F. d'Erlanger's position as director of the syndicate may have given him advantage over other composers. All I know is that his opera was deserving of production on its own merits, and that it was very admirably produced. The scenery reflects the greatest credit on Mr. Harry Brooke, and both the colouring and lighting of the scene in the second act were singularly beautiful. As for the performance, it is very seldom that a new work receives such thorough justice at the hands of its interpreters. Mlle. Destinn was at her best and happiest in the high, bird-like music of Tess; Signor Zenatello as Angel Clare and Signor Sammarco as Alec both supported her admirably; M. Gilibert as Jack Durbeyfield, Mme. Lejeune as his wife, and Mlle. de Lys as Aby happily represented the atmosphere of Tess's old home; and I am inclined to think the first act and the early morning music that accompanies it the freshest and best piece of work in the opera. Of course a work that derives itself so directly from another composer cannot be put in the highest rank of art, but one can say truthfully of M. d'Erlanger's opera that it stands high in the second rank.

ROSES AND ROSE SHOWS.

"How vainly men themselves amaze
To win the palm, the oak, the bays."

So sang the poet, and surely to strive for the palm by exhibiting roses seems the idlest of all reasons for submitting oneself to the indignities of competition. The most ardent hunter of medals and cups must feel a qualm sometimes when he cuts a glorious bloom in all its unfolding freshness, wires it rigidly to a stick, and sets it up, stolid and expressionless, on a board in a mathematical pattern. Really to appreciate the fullness of beauty of a rose you must go out after breakfast when the sun is beginning to attain some power and the last dewdrops are evaporating: then the roses have just loosened their outer robes sufficiently to reveal the full glow of the petals and the tender changing shades which lie deep within. No hint of laxity has yet touched the form, and the colour has to its full that intoxicating quality which is shared by no other flower. By the afternoon a subtle change has come over the blooms, the breath of age has opened out the point, the red roses have taken on an indefinable purple shade, the pink roses are growing ashen, gone is the consecration and the poet's dream. Even the white roses which stand the best are now dead white, no longer maize-coloured or that faintest primrose which seems purer than white itself.

Of course there are those to whom all of the exhibitor's roses, the great built-up blooms of fold upon fold of petals, are anathema wholly. Like Perdita they hate the art which shares with great creating nature. The briar, whether exotic or from our own hedgerows, with its five unconfused petals curving into the perfect wine cup, brimmed up with colour and faint pervasive scent, crowned with the golden anthers, is for them the ideal flower which man civilises but to spoil.

But why be so intolerant? Why deny oneself any form of beauty in order to worship a principle? The symphony on the full orchestra is none the less glorious because there are times when the simple flute music of the solitary shepherd winds more subtly into the heart.

Let us grow and admire every kind of briar and rambler and the many loose decorative roses with their easy grace and wealth of colour, but none the less we will keep one section of the garden where the general effect is subordinated to a system of regular planting and close pruning that shall give us the finest possible individual blooms. There will always be two classes of gardeners, those who grow flowers to make glad their gardens and those who maintain gardens in order to grow flowers. But the mind of man is sufficiently divers et ondoyant to be able to harbour both ideals. And even the exhibitor of late years has come to recognise "garden" roses as worthy of a place in his shows, though in judging the competition he has had to abandon his insistence upon form as the prime criterion of excellence.

The first of the National Rose Society's shows held this year in the Botanic Gardens was by no means up to the usual standard. After so cold and sunless a June even the southern growers found the date very early, and the wonder only was how so many fine blooms had been got together. It is true that the finest blooms of all are those which develop slowly in cool weather, but the cool weather should follow heat, and the heat has been denied us. Still, here and there in the show were magnificent specimens which would satisfy the fancier in any year. But they were the exceptions, and the majority bore traces of the persistent rainy weather in their stained and spotted outer petals, which no amount of protection can obviate. Fortunately the London district practically had a second show this year, for Luton, where one of the provincial shows of the National Society was held last Wednesday, is not an hour out of town, and the date suited the majority of professional growers, especially the Colchester firms, to a nicety. Of course the great firms, the Dicksons and the Cants and their rivals, showed their boxes of forty-eight and thirty-six distinct varieties as wonderfully as ever; as wonderfully and, it must be said, as unattractively. There is no getting away from the necessity of showing flowers isolated on stands, when they are going to be judged absolutely and solely from a florist's point of view. The classes which have been created for exhibition roses in vases will continue to play only a secondary part in the exhibition, and the stand, however unadorned, must remain the dock in which the rose awaits its trial. There is, however, one defect in the ideal adopted by the judges which makes the show table so unattractive; shape, fullness, size, texture of petal are the items of excellence; colour and freshness are not regarded at all until the judge is driven to split straws in order to discriminate between two exhibits. Consequently the stands are over-full of blooms of a pale and undecided colour, enormous, rotund, with a technical point but otherwise distinctly ungraceful. These roses also by reason of their solidity and stoutness of petal have often been kept in a cut state for many days and have acquired a dull and livid complexion. The Dicksons of Newtownards have done so much for the modern rose that it is unkind to reproach them for any of their productions, but Marchioness of Londonderry, Alice Linsdell, Florence Pemberton, Bessie Brown, and others of that type are apt to be terribly dull and even unpleasing roses, though their size and formal regularity are such that the judges always award them high marks. Colour and freshness ought to count, and though the judge will tell you that such qualities are matters of opinion and cannot be marked on definite lines like form, we doubt the validity of the argument. At its best it would only mean that the roses must be submitted to judges and not to marking machines. We miss, too, nowadays the full scarlets and deep velvety crimsons of the old hybrid perpetuals. Neither in shape nor in size can such glowing fragrant favourites as Victor Hugo, Prince Camille de Rohan, Charles Lefebvre, La Havre stand up against the modern hybrid tea, but the colours of this latter class range almost exclusively among the pinks and creams. Certainly some deeper reds have been introduced of late, but none of them possesses that velvety dark shaded petal which is the glory of the older hybrid perpetuals. It is a common complaint, too, that the newer roses are scentless; but though there are some striking instances, for example that otherwise perfect white rose, Frau Karl Druschki, the reproach was equally true thirty years ago, when such widely grown flowers as Baroness Rothschild and Her Majesty were also wholly without scent. However, the predominance of the hybrid tea nowadays does mean that the majority of roses possess only a faint odour of the "tea-scented" kind instead of the rich and almost fruity smell associated only with the deep-red hybrid perpetuals.

On first thoughts it may seem a pity that the judges should give so many points to size, but putting aside the instinctive and often irrational bent of human nature towards size which is seen in all the arts, every grower knows how difficult it is to attain the perfect shape in a big rose, although little ones that satisfy the eye can be picked by the half-dozen. In big blooms the faults leap to the eye, and the extra vigour which confers greatness is apt to bring errors and distortion in its train, a fact which is not without its bearing on our judgments of men.

Just as the "National" rose show is not exactly the place in which to enjoy roses, so it is very far from the best place for their choice when the stocking of your own garden is in question. Many of the varieties which yield "medal" blooms exhaust all their energies in the production of one or two flowers in the first year only of their life, so that the exhibitor has to rebud them every year, and the amateur who buys them as "cut-backs" only sees their lingering decline. No; selection is best made on a visit to the grounds of a nurseryman or even to the garden of a rose-growing friend when the season is at its height. The big shows are for the experts, the little local shows do the most to spread the true worship of the rose. There the blooms may be inferior, and the judge may often be put to it to decide between degrees of badness, but it is wonderful how an annual opportunity of displaying one's flowers to one's neighbours tunes up the care and attention given to the garden, and brings about the replacement of poor "anyhow" varieties by others which are equally easy to grow and take up no more room, but which will yield roses and not scrubs. Above all a little local show stimulates one's gardener and gives him a soul above cabbages. The love of the rose is latent everywhere, and it takes but a little training and opportunity to make it active. Not for nothing is the rose called the queen of flowers. It is more, for in all ages it has stood to men as the symbol of the passion and the purity hid in the heart of the woman.

SPORT, THE PRESS, AND HENLEY.

By Reginald P. P. Rowe.

THERE was surely never a time when sport was so much advertised as at present. Every newspaper devotes many columns to it daily, and the doings of our prominent sportsmen are exhaustively chronicled and criticised. Yet never surely had England so little claim to pre-eminence in sport. The question naturally arises: "Is this because our opponents from oversea have improved or because we have deteriorated?" It would perhaps be some consolation to know that the colonies and other countries had learnt to better their teachers. It would at any rate be a net gain to sport as a science. But is there any ground for such a supposition? The Australians have beaten us twice at cricket at least as much through our bad play as through any super-excellence of theirs. The American polo players are undoubtedly a fine team, but the performance of our men was by everyone regarded as disappointing. The Belgians came to Henley with an eight a little less good than usual, but once again they carried off the chief prize of the rowing world.

One is unwillingly driven to the conclusion that in England sport has inclined to deterioration rather than improvement, and one cannot help wondering if there is any connexion between this tendency and the excessive newspaper advertisement with which it is coincident.

It is hard to trace any direct connexion between the two, but indirectly it can be seen that this newspaper talk adversely affects the true interests of sport. In the first place it has created a small but increasing minority who bitterly resent the hold of sport upon the country. "Flannelled fools at the wicket" was not a phrase which increased the popularity of its author, but many people felt that, though extravagantly expressed, there was some ground for the view adopted. That was years ago, and there is more excuse for it to-day. It may be that to the man of sober judgment the extreme militarist exceeds wisdom by no less than the worshipper of sport falls short of it, but this does not justify the ideals of the latter. Resentment to these ideals increases probably in proportion to their glorification in the sporting pages of the newspapers. But there is another much more serious indictment to be brought against the press in its attitude towards sport. Recent plays have suggested to our minds the problem "Does the press merely reflect or does it largely create public opinion?" Probably it does both—that is to say it increases any tendency which it discovers. The tendency it has discovered in sport is one which makes for the falsification of its very name. Sport is being turned into a business. The Americans began it, and we follow their example. To be any use as a sportsman nowadays one must specialise to the verge of professionalism. Otherwise one is relegated to the ever-increasing ranks of the lookers-on, for whom the sporting pages of the newspapers chiefly exist and who are content to play nothing themselves.

It might have been thought that specialisation in sport would have tended to increase skill. Unhappily experience has not taught us this. In cricket, for instance, though everyone writes to the papers to inform the Selection Committee what the England eleven should be, the very variety of the teams suggested makes it evident that there is less prominent talent among players of the game than formerly. A worse feature than this is that the men chosen have hitherto shown themselves notably lacking in nerve and self-reliance; and if sport fails to produce qualities such as these there must be something very wrong with it and little justification for its existence. In these circumstances can it be a matter of surprise that many good sportsmen of the cricket world should long for the day when the publication of averages (with its paralysing effect on the game as *sport*) shall be done away with, or that many true sportsmen of all kinds should condemn the rage for international matches and sigh for a future when sport will again be sport and not a specialised, much-advertised business?

Of all sports rowing is probably as yet the least professionalised. It is also perhaps the least advertised. The strictness of the amateur rule in rowing is little short of daring in these democratic days, but its existence is amply justified by results. For there is no doubt that rowing in England is still purely a sport, and as such productive of the best qualities of sportsmanship. Yet the Belgians have again carried off the Grand Challenge Cup at Henley Regatta. At first sight it would seem that rowing was suffering from the same disease as other sports, but its position, I think, is somewhat different and the trouble from which it has been suffering is peculiarly its own. It is true that it has suffered from "internationalism". Foreign crews, representing combined clubs, have come over to compete against our clubs and colleges represented separately. But this would not have mattered if the standard of our own oarsmanship had not fallen for quite other reasons. These reasons have to do with style, a matter of more importance to rowing than to any other sport because oarsmanship is essentially a science. On the whole orthodox opinion on style has been completely vindicated by the experience of the last few years, and never more emphatically than at last week's Henley Regatta. At the time when the Belgians were first victorious at Henley the English rowing world showed some inclination to lose faith in established principles, and powerful crews were winning races with a heavy dragging stroke in which "beginning" was conspicuous by its absence. The Belgians came with a stroke which was little else than "beginning" and proved invincible. A small band of extremists immediately flew to the conclusion that the way to attain pace was virtually to eliminate all other elements of the stroke. The representatives of this new extreme of heterodoxy made so poor a showing at Henley that one cannot help believing that they themselves must see the error of their ways. At any rate, if the ardour of their faith is undiminished it is not likely to find fresh adherents. But the most hopeful sign at Henley was the marked improvement in the quality of many crews which frankly accepted the older ideals of good oarsmanship. Magdalen College, Oxford, rowing a long well-marked stroke, raced the Belgians to half a length from the inferior station on one of the worst "station" days seen of late years at the regatta. It is annoying, of course, to have results influenced by the luck of the draw, but it was a satisfaction to see at least one college crew well up to the level of the Belgians. So much it is necessary to say, even if it sounds ungracious to our visitors, in defence of English style. Mr. Kirby, the chief Magdalen heavyweight, was rowing under a serious disadvantage, being partially crippled, and Mr. Stanhope at stroke, though he raced pluckily, was obviously too light for the post. If the crew had possessed a stroke of the class of Mr. Bourne and if Mr. Kirby had been sound, most English rowing men would with some confidence have entrusted them with the defence of the cup against any Belgian eight which has yet come over. The Belgians were perhaps slightly less good than on some previous occasions, but they showed considerable pace and raced as pluckily as ever. Though many would with good reason wish Henley reserved exclusively for English club crews and would relegate international matches to rare and special occasions, it may be hoped that the Belgians will come once again next year, if only to learn that we have profited by what they had to teach, and not been content with merely imitating their shortcomings. We may even at last have something to teach them.

With regard to Henley there is little to add save that with few exceptions the rowing of club and college crews showed all-round improvement, and that the Eton and Radley eights were well above the average. Both schools were unlucky in the draw, and their representatives had little opportunity of showing their quality. Oxford crews were remarkably successful, no less than four out of the eight finals falling to Oxford colleges. In rowing at least England cannot fairly be said to be on the down grade. If this, as has been contended, is the fruit of amateurism, it is some excuse for the bias which has perhaps been shown against the tendency towards professionalism in other fields of sport.

THE GREAT BORDEAUX WINES.

III.—CHÂTEAU LATOUR.

THE banks of the Gironde were defended in the Middle Ages against the fleets of pirates that then infested the western seaboard of Gascony and Guyenne by a series of forts built by the noblemen of the country for the defence of themselves and their peasantry. No doubt a castle once stood to the south of the tower which is still to be seen in the middle of the vineyard of Château Latour. The Sire de Larzan, who held it, was one of the last to stand by the Plantagenets in their endeavour to keep the hereditary lands of the house of Aquitaine. When England was finally driven from Guyenne he had to seek refuge across the seas, whilst his castle was sacked and razed to the ground. It is upon the ruins of this castle that the present press-house was built, and its castellated portico of cut stone still preserves the illusion that it is fortified. In 1477 the lordship was owned by Gaston de la Touche; in 1606 it became the property of Denis de Mullet, whose family was replaced by the Clausels in 1677. They held it until Marie Thérèse de Clausel married Alexandre de Ségur. When the Marquis de Ségur died one of his daughters, the Comtesse de

Miroménil, succeeded to Château Latour, which was divided at her death between her two daughters, Madame de la Pallu and Countess de Beaumont, whose heirs are the present owners. Such incalculable mischief has, however, been done to land properties and vineyards by the compulsory subdivision which was established by the Code Napoléon that its owners determined to preserve the estate intact by turning it into a limited liability company through a series of deeds made by the de Flers, de Beaumonts, and de Courtiesons between 1842 and 1866. They even went to the extent of repurchasing what had been confiscated during the Emigration. The estate therefore is now some 185 acres, of which there are 40 acres of pasture, 40 acres of wood, and 100 acres of vineyard. The whole is beautifully situated on the banks of the fine river formed by the junction of the Garonne and the Dordogne near Bordeaux.

It would be hard to hit off the chief characteristics of Château Latour, one of the three great "crus" of the Médoc, than is furnished in the words of the Girondist poet Biarnez:

"Latour n'a pas besoin d'un éclat emprunté,
Pas de lambris dorés, pas de pompe illusoire;
A ses seules vertus, il veut devoir la gloire.
C'est le vin le plus riche et le plus coloré,
Et pourtant il est fin, vif, délicat, ambré,
Quand il est dépouillé de son tannin par l'âge
D'Œnantine et d'alcool c'est un noble assemblage".

These qualities of richness and colour are due in the first place to the nature of its soil; as are its bouquet—a mixture of rose and violet—as well as its peculiarly delicate body, which grows in bottle and lasts for many years. The vineyard consists of a gravel soil whose pebbles are mixed with an earth which becomes so hard when dry weather has followed upon rain that two powerful oxen find it all they can do to plough it up. The owners have therefore to use particularly heavy ploughs, first for raising the earth round the roots of the plants and secondly for baring them, the former plough being called the "courbe" and the latter the "cabat". Seven-tenths of the vineyard is planted with Cabernet-Sauvignon, the rest with the Malbec, the Merlot and White Cabernet. Cabernet-Sauvignon gives the greater body, and the wine lasts longer. Though the three latter vines give a wine which tastes better at the start, it loses both colour and body after it has been a year in the wood, and loses somewhat more when bottled. The phylloxera attacked Château Latour with great energy, and the owners had to take strong measures to avert the scourge. M. Jouet the manager sprayed the plants with carbonate of sulphur generally with marked success. Where, however, the position of the vines made this difficult, fresh vines were grafted on to the old plants; but this process has only been carried out gradually during the last eighteen years on little more than a seventh of the vineyard, so that the average age of the plants has not been much modified and the general quality of the wine has not suffered. The average annual output of Château Latour has been 116 tuns of first-class wine, 10 tuns of second-class wine, and 19 tuns of "vin de presse".

As in the other "grands crus", the greatest care is taken at the vintage that nothing but ripe grapes in good condition shall be used, and that no unripe or defective grapes are mixed with them. Many of the old-fashioned practices remain. Thus the berries are taken from the grapes by rubbing them on wooden hurdles, and the grapes are crushed by the men's feet. Until very lately a fiddler played whilst this process was going on. If by any chance he was not to be found, or fell asleep at his work, he was put astride upon a ladder and carried under the pump by two men. All were then given some glasses of good wine. The must is cultivated in the same way as in the other "grands crus", but it is not drawn off until it has not only cooled but become thoroughly clear, which takes from eighteen to twenty days. The "vin de presse" at Château Latour used at one time to be drunk by the men; but since M. Jouet became manager it is kept for three years, treated with the greatest care, and, though not quite up to the standard of the wine itself, is good tipple. The great vintages of Château Latour used to be 1858, 1862, 1864, 1865, 1868 and 1870. From 1871 to 1875 they were good, but then fell off. Of late years the vintages of 1893, 1896, 1899, 1904 and 1906 all promise well. 1900 was a very good year, whilst there is every reason to believe that 1905 will take the same position as the five vintages from 1871 to 1875.

THE BASTILLE: 14 JULY 1789.

It is Tuesday, the fourteenth day of July 1789—the last day of the Bastille. On the morning of the day the old castle which has frowned over the eastern gate of Paris since the days of Charles the Wise makes an impressive picture of the dying monarchy of S. Louis. Its eight grim towers mounted with artillery, its double moat, its raised drawbridges, its arched gateways, its bastions, and its mazes of barracks and courts and gardens wear as terrible a look as they wore in the days of the Fronde, when la grande Mademoiselle turned its cannons on Turenne and his advancing host, and its fame is known in all lands. And not only is it in the eyes of France and Europe the impregnable fortress of despotism against which a people's discontent may beat in vain, it is also a terrible palace of vengeance, a place of mystery and horror where innocent captives pine away their lives in abodes always of misery, often of torture. But the hard truth is that whether we contemplate it as a fortress or as a State prison the Bastille of 14 July 1789 is a mere historic phantom. The fifteen guns on the towers that strike terror into the rue S. Antoine are useless except to fire salvos, and are mounted on naval carriages and cannot be lowered. And for the garrison. There are some eighty-two pensioners, aged men and much resembling the old Beefeaters of the Tower, and thirty-two petits Suisses who joined the pensioners just a week ago, under the command of Lieutenant De Flue, the one soldier among the many officers in the castle. And if the Bastille is in no sense a strong fortress it is no longer a terrible prison. There are to-day just seven prisoners within its walls. Of these captives four are common-place forgers. Two more are madmen, one of whom was put there for an attempt on the life of Louis quinze, and the other, said to be an Englishman, was mad when he arrived. The remaining one is a noble-man of dissipated habits, who has been locked up there at his family's request. It may be said that for at least two centuries the régime of this establishment has been milder in most cases than that of any other prison in France or England. The State prisoners have a pretty garden and permission to walk round the battlements under escort. There is further at their use a library of some hundred volumes, and their dinner includes dessert and wine. When the Breton aristocrats were here the other day a billiard-table was placed for their accommodation in the major's room.

The governor of the doomed castle, the Marquis de Launey, makes this morning the saddest sight of all as, nervous, worried and hatless, he moves about court and bastion in his grey frock-coat, a gold-nobbed sword-cane in his hand and the poppy-coloured ribbon of S. Louis on his breast. He is a true child of the place, for he was born within its walls when his father, Jourdan de Launey, was governor in the days of Louis quinze. He has been an officer in the Gardes Françaises and a cavalry captain, and thirteen years have passed since he became governor of the Bastille. And he has guarded here in his time some notable captives—the bitter-tongued Linguet and the women of the diamond necklace, and elixir-making Cagliostro and the patriots of Brittany. But he is no soldier, and ever since he saw the flames of Reveillon's factory he has been ill at ease. When he goes into the street he hears bitter words, and at night time, as he gazes on the trees in that garden where so many captive feet have trod, he mistakes the shadows of the foliage for enemies and calls his staff to arms. He has found comfort the last week in talking to De Flue of the preparations that he has made for the day when the rabble comes. He shows him the loopholes that he has opened and the loopholes that he has stopped in the walls. He points out the heap of stones that weary men have dragged to the top of the towers to hurl on the besiegers. It has never occurred to him to get guns that will go off, or to lay in provisions. And as the days pass his terrors increase. Paris, he hears, is in the hands of the mob or of the revolutionary Committee of the Electors at the Hôtel de Ville. Worse still, the Gardes Françaises, the garrison of Paris, whose uniform he has once worn, have gone over to the enemy. And, worst of all, the Baron de Bensenval has led such troops as remain loyal across the Seine, after bidding the forsaken Bastille hold out to the last. On this morning perverse folly has pushed forward the useless old cannons, so that they seem to threaten S. Antoine, and timid burghers hurry to the Committee at the Hôtel de Ville to implore its aid. The Committee nominates a deputation of three soldiers to interview the governor, but this deputation takes its time on the way, and only reaches the castle gates at 10 A.M. Meanwhile, cannons or no cannons, a great mob has gathered around the outworks, and is furiously shouting for arms.

And it is a strange and savage crowd. There is in it, indeed, a sprinkling of the quality, gentlemen in ruffles and with swords and even abbés in their cassocks. Young Chateaubriand, who has lately come from Brittany, is there, an interested if indignant spectator. But the rough element of the Faubourg S. Antoine, male and female, preponderates, an element all the rougher and fiercer seeing that it has had naught to eat. And worse than these S. Antoine fellows are the groups of cut-throats and ruffians in the background, the offscouring of all France, which, in these days of stress and storm and famine, has drifted into the capital, and which the sack of the barracks of Paris has armed with muskets and daggers. This uncanny assembly watches the gates for the deputation to come forth, and as it comes not and as the cannons on the towers are being pushed back to load them (so some think), wild cries arise. The local revolutionary committee accordingly sends an envoy, Elector Thuriot. He passes through the castle gates some time after noon to find the governor and the first deputation drinking their last glass of wine after a déjeûner over which they have wasted a precious hour. The governor has promised the deputation to push back his cannons, and this is all that has been done, only the mob has misunderstood. But this will not content Elector Thuriot, who advises a surrender and asks to see the castle, a request to which the governor meekly assents. Thuriot walks into the inner castle and climbs with the governor to the battlements. The guns have been pulled back; but their position is unchanged. Some of the pensioners in their blue or red uniforms are on the towers, others are in the court behind the inner drawbridge, with De Flue and his Swiss, whose regimentals are covered by their holland jackets. But what are they against the swarms below on which he and De Launey are gazing? The poor governor loses his head and talks as he comes down of surrender, but his officers cheer him up, and he only promises that he will not fire unless attacked. Partly satisfied, Thuriot makes his adieux. But still the mob grows and grows and still the shouts continue: "Nous voulons la Bastille; à bas la troupe." Then suddenly from the front rank comes an ugly rush on the outworks. Here victory is easy, for there is only an unarmed pensioner to face. The chains of the drawbridge are cut, the gate is forced, and the crowd rushes on past the governor's house to the second drawbridge, presenting their guns and firing casual shots at the soldiers. From the towers comes first a cry of warning. It is unheeded or misunderstood, and then the order is given, and from above pours the deadly volley on the mob. At once a wild cry of "Treason!" is raised. Still the mob does not disperse. Only it puts stone walls between itself and the fire, and in comparative safety keeps up desultory and ineffective shots. In time this excitement palls, and the idea is started that the governor shall be burnt out. Conveniently at the moment the horses and waggons of Santerre's brewery, which many know so well, appear; but the popular young brewer, thinking discretion the better part of valour, keeps away from the fray. The waggons are filled with straw and pushed near the inner drawbridge, and fire is set to the government buildings, and this fire ignites the straw. It is a roundabout method, but necessary, for these heroes will not face the bullets for a minute. And then once and once only, when the rascals are threatening to burn a girl who is flying from the governor's house unless the fortress is yielded, a cannon from the towers speaks. And so the hurly-burly goes on until the beating of a drum announces another deputation from the Hôtel de Ville to urge the governor to surrender or to admit "civic troops". But the deputation may not enter the castle. Possibly the governor suspects treachery. So the muskets sputter lead until three o'clock, and so far the honours are with the besieged.

But towards three o'clock the weary, starving garrison must face different foes. Companies of the Gardes Françaises, fusiliers and gunners, are drawing nigh with five pieces of artillery, and the cry "La Bastille ou la mort". The new host has two half-pay officers, Hulin and Jacob Job Elié, who wears the uniform of the Queen's regiment, to lead them. The newcomers are advancing from the garden of the Arsenal to the inner drawbridge; but it is a dangerous way to tread, when they shall pass from the shelter of the barracks into la cour de l'Orme. For here they will be raked by the fire from the tour de la Basinière and exposed to the shot and balls that De Flue and his Swiss will pour on them from the court behind. For the Swiss have with them a small gun that can be fired, and through the hole that they have made in the raised drawbridge comes the hail of death.

It is two hours' hard work ere Hulin and Elié can get their cannons face to face with that drawbridge. It is necessary first to make feint with some of their pieces in various directions, so as to distract the fire from the tower. They must then, and this is no easy task, force back the burning waggons that block the approach. It is, lastly, imperative to hustle away the unarmed rabble who are left free to sack the governor's house, and then three cannons are pushed through la cour de l'Orme, through la cour de Gouvernement, right up to the inner drawbridge. De Launey sees from the tower the enemies' guns before his gate; he looks at his hungry and dispirited men, and bids the drummer beat the rappel. In place of the red-and-white flag a white handkerchief is raised on the Basinière. And from below comes the savage shout, "Bas les ponts, point de capitulation". The miserable governor descends into the council chamber and writes that he has twenty thousand pounds of powder and will blow up the castle and district if terms are refused. De Flue, who has gone there for instructions, then pleads with him. Let him still hold out. The castle is not damaged. The gates are uninjured and he has only lost one man. It is useless, the governor cannot understand. So De Flue sadly takes the note, and next essays to pass it through one of the holes that he has made in the drawbridge. A man steps on a plank that is laid over the moat and catches it and hands it to Elié. "Foi d'officier nous acceptons", cries the man of the Queen's regiment; but there are still ugly shouts "Point de capitulation". De Flue joins his Swiss, and the brave men wait expecting the dread explosion. But it comes not. The pensioners accept the foi d'officier, De Launey has indeed rushed with a lighted torch to the tower where the powder lies; but a hand, that the mob will soon hack off, holds him back. The drawbridge is lowered and the gate thrown open. The cut-throats are now in the castle, while the Gardes Françaises remain outside. The place is looted, and the garrison is disarmed and dragged forth. De Launey stands by his blazing house almost a martyr. His wig has been torn off, his cane snatched from him, and he is pushed forward a poor dishevelled wretch, while Hulin and another rebel officer in their resplendent uniforms walk by his side and try to shield him in vain from stabs and thrusts and stones. After him on the via dolorosa to the Hôtel de Ville comes the brave De Flue, walking on mid curses and blows, and expecting every moment death. Two of his soldiers are stabbed almost by his side, and as he reaches the Hôtel de Ville he sees the head of De Launey on a pike and the major of the Bastille lying on the ground bathed in blood. Another officer, he notes, is being hanged on a lamp-post. So does the Revolution observe the "foi d'officier". But his guardians bear him safely into the hall, and here there is safety and even a cry "Bravo, bravo, brave Suisse". Meanwhile others of the assassins are drinking the red beer at Santerre's brewery, and exhibiting a poor maniac whom they have dragged from his Bastille cell.

TOOTH FOR A TOOTH.

By George A. B. Dewar.

GRUBBIT'S daughter has long had a piano, but Grubbit could never bring himself to the expense of replacing his missing eye tooth. Knowing the Squire and Grubbit so well, the story of how that tooth went fascinates me, and I cannot go to the manor without begging the squire's wife to tell it me once more. It happened years ago, when landlord and tenant were near their wits' end to make both ends meet, for most of the land was plough and corn was at about twenty shillings a quarter. Driving home one evening the Squire drew rein at West End and halloed to Grubbit, Would he please come out and have a few words as to some estate matter? The faithful Grubbit came and stood by the dogcart, and the two went deep into the matter. Now the squire had an absent-minded way of twirling something round and round. It would revolve first this way, then that way, like one of the little wheels set in a kitchen garden to scare the birds. Nothing could break him of the trick. There was a little cane in the cart, and getting hold of this the squire twirled it as he talked to his man of all advice.

The squire's wife was in a reverie, her eyes fixed on the landscape of little fields and copses and thatched roofs all in the dreamy haze of sundown in idyll England. How I know those midsummer sundown scenes at the very quiet hamlet of West End! scenes steeped in a peace past understanding, scenes of God.

She started out of this reverie at a smothered cry of pain, looked round and saw Grubbit's hand clapt to his mouth.. It rushed on her in an instant what had been done. The prophecy had come true: the squire had twirled his stick once too often. Grubbit had lost an eye tooth. Now Grubbit was the last man the squire would have wished to offend. I remember when Grubbit peppered me slightly rabbit shooting, the squire asked me as a favour not to mention it. Yet so wrapped up was the squire in his estate detail that he did not become conscious of the enormity of his deed. An "Eh? What did you say? What's that, Grubbit?" was all the squire said; and in two moments he had plunged again into the estate detail. The squire's wife, overwhelmed with shame, saw Grubbit take out a handkerchief and mop an agonised mouth. But the wretched man was swept back into the discussion as to heifers or the gravel pit, and he went through, or spluttered through, with the matter.

It was like some wounded creature going through with the business it began; a willow wren singing out its faery song though in the midst a boy has catapulted off one of its lovely little legs, or a wasp that cut in two by a knife still sucks at the jam pot—and was not all land business song and jam to Grubbit?

Then the squire, having settled the estate detail, gathered the reins and drove off, and it was not till some fifteen years later that he realised what he had done that evening. After I had got the squire's wife to tell me the story twice in his presence, he jumped to it. Vaguely he seemed to recall that something had stopped his twirling cane that evening at West End farm, and that there had been a cry and a splutter. The squire smiled a grim smile and said, "Ah, did I? Well, never mind. Many's the tooth Grubbit has drawn of mine".

Eye for an eye, tooth for a tooth. Seeing what Grubbit has done for himself and his family in life, and knowing that he started on the best capital for a man—if the worst for a mouse—the capital of nothing, I can well believe what the squire said. He has drawn many teeth from many men in his forty year of hard practice. I should like to open the drawer and look at his collection. Some of them so white and sharp and strong!—the teeth of men nearly but not quite his match in the market. Others growing black—teeth of men in decay, teeth of weaklings, teeth of soakers, teeth of wasters, teeth of bad bargainers, all bested by Grubbit in the dentistry of life.

And, mind, all bested straight enough as business in the market goes. Briton, Scot, Irishman, church-goer, chapel-goer, whig, radical, tory, all who go into the market of life with their million varied wares, wares of hand and head, think of number one. This is the law. The selfish man must act through number one; so must the unselfish. Beware of the man who affects to overlook number one. He is a sly one. Pass by his stall. Grubbit made no pretences of this kind.

Grubbit was an intensive farmer. A friend took me over his farm one day, and showed me his intensive turnips, intensive hay, intensive beans, everything twice the usual size, everything well before its time. Grubbit's intensity was not of that kind. It ran not so much to the latest in science or the latest in seeds as, first, to sheer hard work or grind, and, second, striking a bargain. I have watched him swinking in the hay-dust in the blaze of July. Then there was a field on the brow of the hill that grew nothing but bracken and furze. It grows nothing but grass now, and thirty head of cattle fatten on it. Grubbit got that field for a song. He cut and tugged up, root and all, the furze and the fern, and he burnt them and spread the ash over the ground, and when some of them appeared again drew up anew and burnt anew. Grubbit grubbed them. In the end he had the better of Nature with her furze and fern. To-day, looking at the field, you would hardly guess it had been a waste won over by a single brave arm.

Then he went to market, and the tooth-drawing business, as we have seen, followed the furze-drawing business. He drew teeth so well that to-day he is his own owner and has put by, I have heard, several thousand pounds. His children are now all out in the world; and after a life of ungrudging labour, labour with the hand and labour with the head—for, starting on nothing, a man wants a head to do very well in the markets—Grubbit may think about retiring from the dentist profession. Many people like him and all respect him. Grubbit, they tell me, is all right. Lately they have made him a churchwarden.

CORRESPONDENCE.

SPENSER ON THE FINANCE BILL.

To the Editor of the Saturday Review.

Sir,—In the Fifth Book of the "Faërie Queene" Sir Artegall, the embodiment of Justice, accompanied by his squire Talus, comes across an anonymous giant standing on a rock, probably somewhere in Wales, and wielding a large pair of scales, for the purpose, as he alleges, of weighing up everything and arriving at an equal division:

"Then would he ballaunce heaven and hell together,
And all that did within them all containe;
Of all whose weight he would not misse a fether,
And looke what *surplus* did of each remaine."

I have italicised the word "surplus". His proceedings are said to have made him momentarily popular with some classes of the populace:

"Therefore the vulgar did about him flocke,
And cluster thicke unto his leasings vaine,
Like foolish flies about an honycrocke,
In hope by him great benefite to gaine".

Artegall points out to him that, before he decides to reduce everything to an equality, he must first make sure that equality was originally intended by nature; otherwise there may be a general upset. The giant is amazed at the interruption:

"'Thou foolishe Elfe' (said then the Gyant wroth),
'Seest not how badly all things present bee,
And each estate quite out of order goth?

. . . .

Were it not good that wrong were then surceast,
And from the most that some were given to the least?

. . . .

Tyrants, that make men subject to their law,
I will suppresse, that they no more may raine;
And Lordings curbe that commons overaw,
And all the wealth of rich men to the poore will draw'".

Artegall retorts that his estimate for the future is likely to be wrong since his knowledge of the present obviously is:

"'Of things unseene how canst thou deeme aright,'
Then answered the righteous Artegall,
'Sith thou misdeem'st so much of things in sight?'"

The giant, "much abashed", asserts that he cares nothing for details, but is quite capable of weighing the wrong and the right against one another in his scales. The knight therefore invites him to make the experiment, which he does, with unfortunate results:

"So first the right he put into one scale;
And then the Gyant strove with puissance strong
To fill the other scale with so much wrong.
But all the wrongs that he therein could lay
Might not it peise; yet did he labour long,
And swat, and chauf'd, and proved every way:
Yet all the wrongs could not a litle right downe way".

The giant is so much amazed with this that he wants to smash his scales, and disdains Artegall's suggestion that he should turn his attention wholly to the right. It then becomes obvious to the knight that what the giant wants is not really equality but inequality of the opposite kind to that which exists already:

"For it was not the right which he did seeke,
But rather strove extremities to way,
Th' one to diminish, th' other for to eeke.
For of the meane he greatly did misleeke".

Talus therefore pushes him off the rock and drowns him in the sea.

Yours obediently,

G. S. R.

LORD CREWE ON NATIONAL MILITARY SERVICE.

To the Editor of the Saturday Review.

15 July.

Sir,—Some points in the speech made by Lord Crewe on Tuesday night will earn the sympathy of all generous opponents. It is, for instance, a pathetic testimony to the impressions made upon him by his term of office as Lord Lieutenant of Ireland that he should regard Lord Roberts' Bill as more likely to endanger the Empire by arming the constituents of Irish Nationalist members than to aid it by arming the somewhat larger population of Great Britain. Again, probably no one but a member of the present Cabinet could have spoken with such evident conviction of the unpleasantness arising from the fusion of classes, and of the tragedy of sitting upon the same benches with persons of humble origin. The bearer of a peerage nearly fifty years old is horrified at a vision of enforced camaraderie with the lower orders which the Duke of Norfolk contemplates without dismay.

But what are we to think of the historical knowledge of the Minister responsible for the affairs of the Dominion of Canada, if the "Times" of the 14th instant correctly represents Lord Crewe as saying that, during the Napoleonic wars, the British Army was rescued from disgrace by Abercromby and Wolfe? As the "Times" reporter is unable to spell the name Wolfe correctly, he may be equally in error in his version of the speech made by the Secretary of State for the Colonies. If this is so, Lord Crewe should surely hasten to put himself right with the patriotic public, which is beginning to know that Wolfe died thirty years before the French Revolution, and beginning to expect Colonial Secretaries to have a rudimentary acquaintance with the history of the British Empire.

I am, Sir, your obedient servant,

"Damn Everything Low."

THE DEMONSTRATION AGAINST THE TSAR.

To the Editor of the Saturday Review.

10 Adelphi Terrace, London W.C.
15 July 1909.

Sir,—In your issue of the 10th, commenting on the announced Trafalgar Square demonstration of the 25th July, you say that you can hardly believe that I am going to be one of the performers, adding that no man knows better that British indignation against Russian policy, especially on social questions, is either ignorance or hypocrisy.

I have to observe on this that there is no such thing as British indignation, one and indivisible. Certain Britishers loathe the Russian policy, just as certain other Britishers loathe Mr. Lloyd George's fiscal policy. The only way in which these sections can make their sentiments known, and thereby get counted in that estimate of public opinion which statesmen must have continually before them, is to demonstrate. There is to be a tremendous demonstration in the Solent in favour of the Tsar. If there were to be no counter-demonstration the Government would be justified in concluding that the nation was unanimously in favour of the Solent demonstration. The object of the Trafalgar Square demonstration is to make such a disastrous and dishonourable inference impossible.

Nothing is more natural and proper than that I should take part in such a demonstration, as I happen to believe that all England's advantages over Russia depend on the fact that when kings behave in England as the Tsar behaves in Russia we either cut their heads off or replace them by their nearest well-behaved relative.

You are, I think, a little unjust to your own country in implying that it is as bad as Russia. It is quite true that England behaves in Ireland, Egypt, and India as the Tsar behaves in Russia; but Ireland, Egypt and India are conquered countries, held in that position by simple force, exactly as England would have to be held if conquered by Ireland, Egypt or India. That would be no excuse for the tyranny of an English king over his own country; and it gives no countenance to the abominable tyranny of which the Tsar is the representative. The Englishman who neglects this opportunity of throwing a brick at him (metaphorically, of course) is utterly unworthy of his country and its traditions. I hope the Saturday Review will charter a canal barge, paint its name in bold white letters on both sides of it, hang it with Union Jacks surmounted by caps of liberty and black flags of mourning for the Tsar's victims, and place it well in evidence in the Solent on the day of our national disgrace.

Yours truly,
G. Bernard Shaw.

THE RIFLE BRIGADE.

To the Editor of the Saturday Review.

Hartford Bridge, Winchester, 15 July 1909.

Sir,—Field-Marshal H.R.H. the Duke of Connaught, Colonel-in-Chief of the Rifle Brigade, has approved of the history of the regiment being written by me.

I write to ask any of your readers who may happen to possess any documents, pictures, medals, badges or other things of interest connected with the early history of the regiment to be good enough to communicate with me. I may mention that the regiment when first raised in 1800 was known as "The Rifle Corps"; in 1803 it was numbered the 95th, and it was known as "The 95th" or "The Rifles" throughout the Peninsular War and at Waterloo. In 1816 it was taken out of the numbered regiments of the line and styled the Rifle Brigade.

I am, Sir, your obedient servant,
Willoughby Verner, Colonel, late Rifle Brigade.

PRESIDENT TAFT'S MODESTY.

To the Editor of the Saturday Review.

12 Charlotte Street, Bath.

Sir,—The mental calibre of American presidents is always a subject for wonderment. A sentence or two from Mr. Taft's latest speech, at Vermont, on Canada and international friendship, is worth quoting: "We Americans have been going ahead so rapidly in our own country that our heads have been somewhat swollen with the idea that we were carrying on our shoulders all the progress there was in the world. But that is not true, as you will realise when you think for a moment."

The "when you think for a moment" is especially good. When American Presidents talk in such a strain, it is not surprising that the "nation of villagers" (to quote Mr. Bernard Shaw) appropriates all knowledge, learning and progress to itself.

Mr. Taft then points out, in splendid disdain of Europe, that America has not been sufficiently conscious of that other young nation, Canada, for whom also there is a great deal to be said. He might have added that—as far as true progress, law, and order are concerned—Canada is a hundred years ahead of the United States.

I suppose this ignorance and cocksureness is the natural result of a purely material civilisation, which has given us the first great instance of how reactionary a democracy may become under certain conditions. As for "carrying on its shoulders all the progress of the world", it is well to remember that, except in the matter of technology, there is not a single American university which can be said to rank with those of Europe. The newspapers and reviews which an educated man can read are easily counted on the fingers of one hand. With a few brilliant exceptions, the painters and sculptors cut a very poor figure. In poetry the sterility is even more marked. A dramatist they have never had, while in the realm of empirical science their achievements are trivial.

President Taft evidently shares the belief that others invariably take you at your own valuation.

Yours faithfully,
Hugh Blaker.

SCHOOLS AND THE SUMMER HOLIDAYS.

To the Editor of the Saturday Review.

12 July 1909.

Sir,—The complaint of "A Holiday Victim" is not unreasonable, but it is doubtful whether his suggestion is practicable. The public school year, like the Gaul of Cæsar's time, in tres partes divisa est, and the preparatory schools obviously have to follow the lead as regards both terms and holidays. Moreover, supposing that the time of the summer vacations were varied as suggested, there would ensue quite a chaotic disproportion in the length of the previous and the subsequent terms, highly embarrassing where brothers were at different places of education, not to mention that parents as a rule like to be with their boys (and girls), and that the majority of them cannot take their own holiday before August.

Yours faithfully,
Preparatory.

HOLIDAYS FOR THE SICK AND THE POOR.

To the Editor of the Saturday Review.

S. Giles' Christian Mission, 4 Ampton Street, Regent Square, W.C., 12 July 1909.

Sir,—I shall be very grateful if you will kindly permit me, through the columns of your valuable paper, to make an appeal to your readers to aid us in sending away to our seaside country homes numbers of poor, deserving children, women and men, as we have hitherto done for many years past. The Mission is now in its jubilee year, and its work amongst the poor, the sick and the fallen is universally known. Cheques and postal orders (crossed "Messrs. Barclay and Co.") will be thankfully received and acknowledged by

Yours faithfully,
Wm. Wheatley, Superintendent.

"CORPUS DOMINI APUD ANGLOS."

To the Editor of the Saturday Review.

Ely, Cambs, 10 July 1909.

Sir,—Let me suggest that (to borrow the schoolmen's terminology of exactitude) it is the Res Sacramenti and not the Sacramentum upon which the incidence of adoration has ever been intended and directed throughout Catholic Christendom; in fact, just that "Lord beneath the sacramental veil" of Father Bridgett, rather than that which is connoted by "the Blessed Sacrament" outside and apart from its Res.

I humbly submit that herein, awaiting discovery by pilgrims with better charts than I have, lies common ground for many.

I am, Sir, your obedient servant,
J. Vicars Foote
(Late Vicar of East Clevedon).

THE ANTI-VIVISECTION AGITATION.

To the Editor of the Saturday Review.

32 Queen's Road, Bayswater, 11 July 1909.

Sir,—Referring to a paragraph in your issue of the 10th inst. implying that Miss Lind-af-Hageby's anti-vivisectionist procession to Hyde Park was got up by and consisted of "hysterical women", I wish to state as an eye-witness that the procession contained quite as many men as women, if not more. It is true that anti-vivisectionists are now appealing to "ignorant prejudice", but they are doing so with the object of making that prejudice no longer ignorant but enlightened. I maintain that this is precisely the sort of advocacy that kindness to animals does need. As to the offensive banners which were stopped, their number is one, and that banner the reproduction of an illustration in a medical journal ("Journal of Pathology"). That an illustration of vivisection should be of such a revolting character that it cannot be carried through the streets without fear of creating a disturbance is sufficient justification for the striking demonstration of Saturday last.

Yours sincerely,
Edward Cahen.

REVIEWS.

"MY BOY HOBBIE O!"

"Recollections of a Long Life." By Lord Broughton. Edited by his Daughter, Lady Dorchester. London: Murray. 1909. 2 vols. 24s. net.

JOHN CAM HOBHOUSE began his political career in Newgate and ended it as a Minister on the benches of the House of Lords, thus resembling the rise of a living statesman from the tub in Hyde Park to the Cabinet. Not that Hobhouse did anything very dreadful or really suffered durance vile. He merely wrote a pamphlet in which he said that were it not for the military the members of the House of Commons would be drawn from their places by the ears, which seems to modern readers a very harmless remark, but which in the days of Lord Liverpool was voted a breach of privilege, and consigned its author to a comfortable room in the Governor of Newgate's house. It was exactly the advertisement that Hobhouse wanted. He had just contested Westminster unsuccessfully: he now became a martyr in the cause of the Westminster Reformers (the best known of whom were Burdett, Bentham, Cobbett, Place, and James Mill), and on his release he was almost immediately returned for Westminster, which he represented continuously until his elevation to the peerage. Byron, incorrigible poseur as he was, disliked the poses of others, especially of his friends. He was annoyed at Hobhouse, a gentleman by birth and culture, posing as the People's Friend. It was all very well for Lord Byron to denounce Castlereagh and praise regicide in verse: but Hobhouse putting these principles, or some of them, into practice or speeches was intolerable. Byron, though he was really very fond of Hobhouse—had Hobhouse not been his groomsman at that weird wedding in Sir Ralph Milbanke's drawing-room?—could not help writing the ode which made Hobhouse so angry, though, like the good fellow he was, he quickly got over it. We have only space for two stanzas:

" Who are now the people's men,
My boy Hobbie O?
There's I and Burdett—gentlemen,
And blackguard Hunt and Cobby O.

But when we at Cambridge were,
My boy Hobbie O,
If my memory doesn't err,
You founded a Whig Clubbie O."

Hobhouse soon recurred to the Whiggism of his Cambridge days, and subsided into office and a coronet. There are some good stories. Here is one which has been told in many variant versions since: " A.: May I ask what your father was? B.: My father was a cobbler. A.: Hum! I wonder he didn't bring you up to the same profession. B.: May I ask what your father was? A.: My father was a gentleman. B.: Hum! I wonder he didn't bring you up to the same profession." There is a good deal about Sheridan in his decline, including his opinion of Burke, which, as it was given long after the latter's death, is probably sincere and well considered. " Sheridan then spoke with the highest admiration of Burke, put him next to Bacon, and said he would always be reckoned amongst the three or four great men that our country had produced. 'I am sure', continued he, 'that Charles Fox, and much more my humble self, will be known to future ages as having stood by the side of Burke. He was a wonderful speaker in early life, and also in his latter parliamentary days; but intermediately he wearied the House, speaking on every subject and not speaking well.' This was Sheridan's panegyric, and he then came to the other portion of his portrait. 'But he was a bad man, an interested man; in company vulgar, either haughty and overbearing or mean and cringing; he loved flattery. . . . Burke spoke with a brogue, and sometimes with much violence of voice and gesture. Burke was a very indolent man, and once, talking of the North American Indians, said "They enjoy the highest boon of Heaven, supreme and perpetual indolence" '." Considering Burke's enormous intellectual output, it is interesting to learn from one who knew him as well as Sheridan that he was naturally lazy. The two central figures of these volumes are, of course, Napoleon and Byron, the author's heroes: and there is much about them both that has not been previously published, and is consequently of surpassing interest. But we cannot imagine why Lady Dorchester has thought it worth while to reopen the Byron separation. Hobhouse played an important part in that wretched business, trying hard to induce Lady Byron either to return to her husband or to state explicitly her reason for leaving him, in both of which he failed. But Lady Dorchester, in publishing Hobhouse's papers on this subject, tells us nothing new, nothing that has not already been published. Neither the literary nor the social world is interested any more in the quarrel, having heard all the evidence and judged the parties long ago. As these volumes only bring us up to 1822, we suppose that they are a first instalment, and we look forward to their continuance. Apart from what we consider the Byron blunder, Lady Dorchester has done her work in editing and arranging these papers very well.

SPREADING THE EAGLE.

"Alaska, the Great Country." By Ella Higginson. London: Bell. 1909. 7s. 6d.

UP to the moment when the vessel which proudly conveys Miss (or Mrs.) Higginson sets her prow westward from Sitka, this book has scarcely anything to recommend it, except its pictures. It is marked alternately by a naïve lack and excess of information which merely moves us to smile. Take her account of the Treadwell Mine, including her own daring ascent of a ladder and her amazement at the harmless and elementary word " winze ", or her description of the Greek church at the former capital of the country, or her explanation how the waves break apart at the bows of a steamer and reunite at the stern. One would think she was trying to convince us that she had never been down a mine, inside an Orthodox church or on the deck of a steamer before. Or take her powers of mensuration. The Devil's Thumb, perhaps the most prominent feature of the mountains of South-Eastern Alaska, is marked by her as rising " more than 2000 feet "; it rises in fact more than 9000. Mount Edgecumbe, she says, is " only 8000 feet in height "; in reality it is about 3467. Yet she undoubtedly saw both of these, however uncertain we may feel, as to some parts of her narrative, whether she is describing things from her own experience or from the books which she cites so copiously in the appendix. Lucidity of description, indeed, is not her strong point. At Ketchikan the captain led her forth at 7 A.M. to see " one of the beautiful things of Alaska ". She tells us all about it for two pages, but at the end we have no idea whether this marvel of nature was a river, or a waterfall, or a wood, or a ravine, or all or any of them. She is perpetually gibing at Vancouver's and Whidbey's descriptions, but in fact they give us a clearer picture in five lines than she can produce in five pages, and her criticisms of their style merely show that she is ignorant of eighteenth-century English. But her monotonous abuse of Vancouver is only one feature of her Anglophobia. This spreadeagleism is of a sporadic and peculiar type, and we notice that it becomes a little subdued after she has had an opportunity of contrasting American and Canadian methods of government on each side of the boundary line. There is still one monarch, she tells us, to be " retired " from " our continent ", and perhaps she hopes to assist his retirement by telling a preposterous tale about the British Royal Family, which we are rather surprised to find in a book published by an English firm of repute. The egregious Lieutenant Zarembo becomes an " intrepid young officer ", though all he did was to bully an unarmed British trader out of the Stikine

River with a fourteen-gun brig. But we must not go to Miss Higginson for history. She would have us believe that there was real foundation in fact for her countrymen's claim to the Pacific coast up to 54° 40′, and speaks of the Oregon Treaty as "infamous"; she obviously knows nothing of the truth as to the suggested cession of Pyramid Harbour in 1898; she has read the Alaska Boundary Proceedings to so little advantage that she speaks of Pearse and Wales Islands as having "belonged to us"; she is apparently not familiar with the way in which the White Pass and Yukon Railway was promoted, and her narrative would lead us to believe that Mr. Heney, one of the prime movers in the matter, was a native of the United States. It is only in the latter part of her book that she admits that even at the present day there is no practicable justice in Alaska, that the United States Government has done next to nothing for the aborigines, and that (perhaps for political reasons) the coast has never been properly lighted or buoyed. She relates without a blush of shame the state of civil war which prevailed recently at Katalla, but she tells us nothing of the exploits of "Soapy Smith" and his brigands at Skaguay unchecked by the "Deputy United States Marshal" who was supposed to be keeping order; and the evasion of the laws as to the drink traffic at S. Michael's evidently strikes her as rather smart than blameworthy. No wonder the squaws at Sitka laughed at her.

But, as we have said, as soon as she gets west of Sitka her book becomes meritorious. It is true that she produces no valid reason, so far as we can see, why anyone should visit the Aleutian Islands, but there are some capital descriptions of her doings in the country behind Valdez. The atmosphere enlivened her so much that she even believes that the Alaskan Central Railroad will be completed some day. Her anti-British obsession gradually disappears, and she goes so far as to confess that she was rescued by two Englishmen in Unga Bay. Here was a case of between the devil and the deep sea, if you will! Her accounts of some of the inhabitants of land and water are as picturesque as those of some of the little mining towns and their "society" are inflated and absurd. This latter portion of her book, however, does make us feel what a magnificent country Alaska would be if it were well developed and governed, and makes us regret more than ever that it was purchased by the nation which purchased it.

REMNANTS OF CHURCH PLATE.

"Church Plate of Hants." By P. R. P. Braithwaite. London: Simpkin. 1909. 31s. 6d. net.

WHEN, at the nod of England's crowned cracksman and champion churchbreaker, shrines were spoiled and religious houses ruthlessly wrecked, the Guild of Barabbas may well have felt no world was left for thieves to conquer. "Sacrilegus omnium praedonum cupiditatem et scelera superat." From Canterbury alone twenty-six cartloads of chalices, ciboria, crucifixes, candlesticks, censers, cruets, pyxes, patens, and other treasure are said to have gone to replenish the royal hoard and reward royal favourites. The thought of those twenty-six wagons jolting along the Kentish roads is enough to make our present Chancellor of the Exchequer green with envy, for £1155 has been given at Christie's for a censer of the reign of Edward III., £900 for an incense-boat of early Tudor work, and only last year a ciborium of the thirteenth century, of copper-gilt, with champ-levé enamel of English work, reported to have been at one time the property of Malmesbury Abbey, sold for £6000. Of course S. Thomas was an exceptional swell, and the splendid pillage of Christ Church stands out a unique event in the annals of burglary; but it is wonderful those pious pilferers Somerset and Cranmer, on looking round for more spoil, paused to filch from humble chantries, since the parish churches were found to provide fair opportunities for profitable peculation when in the last year of King Edward's reign Protestant zeal again proved stronger than respect for the eighth commandment. Cripps speaks of S. Olave, Southwark, possessing no less than 1062 ounces of silver plate so late as 1552, and the same authority refers to a church in Norwich returning to the Commissioners a list of 857 ounces. From this it may be gathered that parish churches held goods of a commercial value quite sufficient to attract the greedy advisers of the boy King, and anything that slipped through their fingers stood little chance of being missed by the sanctimonious counsellors of Elizabeth, who were always ready to put commissions afoot with instructions to inquire "to what purpose is this waste". The restless seventeenth century was naturally a bad time for such church plate as escaped Tudor clutches, and appropriation of particular pieces by private persons has proceeded merrily ever since King Henry first found a more "fruteful" use for vessels dedicated to the service of religion. If anything more were needed to explain the modernity of so many of the marks on existing plate, there are plenty of tell-tale entries in churchwardens' accounts placing on record the barter of old lamps for new by foolish custodians anxious to be in the latest fashion.

Hampshire has had her share of knaves and simpletons, and unfortunately Canon Braithwaite, in cataloguing the plate of that county, has been obliged to mention several cases of larceny which have occurred there in comparatively recent times, but his repeated use of the word "remade" suggests that in Hampshire as elsewhere ignorance has been a more frequent cause of loss than dishonesty.

In 1867, on a presentation of new plate to the parish church of Bredhurst in Kent, the old Communion cup was sold for the trifling sum of £1 13s. 6d., and the ancient paten being laid aside was soon forgotten. Forty years afterwards the despised paten, which had been temporarily lost sight of, was returned to its proper home, and on examination by Mr. St. John Hope it was pronounced to be a fine copper-gilt specimen of the thirteenth century. Canon Braithwaite has nothing quite so romantic as this to report from Hampshire, but his catalogue raises a suspicion that here and there churches may still hold valuables waiting for a duster. At an inspection of plate undertaken at Southampton eight years ago, All Saints, Fawley, was found to possess a paten with six-foil depression and the Vernicle for device, and on the same occasion S. Michael, Southampton, produced an Edwardian chalice of an interesting and uncommon pattern. Even more surprising was the discovery that S. Michael was the lucky owner of an early Elizabethan tazza which turned out to be one of the best examples of its class and period left in England.

It is disappointing to find no pre-Reformation chalice has been preserved in Hampshire, but, by way of compensation, two rare Edwardian cups survive within her borders. "Alteracon of the Massing Chalosse" seems to have been earlier in this county than further west, as assay marks for 1562 and 1568 constantly catch the eye. Cripps points out that a great number of the Elizabethan cups in the Archdiocese of Canterbury belong to the year 1562. It is curious to see two cups of Irish make figuring amongst the ecclesiastical valuables of Hampshire: the charming Beaulieu chalice made in 1734, of which the history is unknown, was evidently designed for a "Massing chalice"; perhaps it came from Cowdray in the next county, where Mass had been said without break until the Lord Montague who succeeded to the title as a boy in 1717 put off allegiance to Rome.

Even if funeral stuff be included, the number of pre-Reformation pieces Hampshire can show is small compared with the sixteen of her neighbour Wiltshire, but she has an advantage over her richer sister in being able to claim the oldest bit of church plate still remaining in actual use in England, namely the paten at S. Mary's, Wyke, which Cripps assigns to a date about 1200. Canon Braithwaite has accepted the amended figure of 1280 suggested by Mr. Hope, and a photograph of this paten makes a handsome frontispiece for his book. Two other patens, one at Fawley, the other at Bishop's Sutton, complete the list of Hampshire plate in existence before the Dissolution.

We wish Canon Braithwaite had supplied a schedule with dates, and we should have liked something more than a record of height on which to reconstruct a lost chalice, but he has our entire sympathy when he expresses a hope that his book may help to prevent alienation of ecclesiastical plate. The church goods in most parishes are of small pecuniary value, but all sacred vessels are worthy of the most jealous care of their guardians. Canon Braithwaite has done a good work, and we trust that he will find many imitators to make similar inventories in other parts of the country.

NOVELS.

"Margery Pigeon: a Novel." By Jane Wardle. London: Arnold. 1909. 6s.

We can forgive many coincidences and improbabilities in a story which introduces us to characters as amusing as most of the actors in this little comedy. The barmaid heroine, adopted as a niece by a rich old woman for an amazing reason, is a girl with several attractive qualities, but the most rare study in the book is a young cockney solicitor's clerk with a passion for bar-loafing and music-halls. Miss Wardle evidently forgets the close parallel between his ultimate phase and that of Mr. Mantalini, which is a pity. For her Richard Fendick is very much more than a modern copy from a type suggested by Dickens. The hero is a pleasant boy—one of those likeable products of our public schools who find life very perplexing when forced to earn a living with no capital in the background—and his efforts at journalism seem to be studied from life. Then there is an amusing sketch of a minor poet, who fifteen years ago would have cultivated æstheticism, but to-day dresses in oilskins and writes ballads about sailors. Altogether, as the hero says in the first review he writes for a great newspaper which gives him an opening because the editor had been at the same public school, "This book is of very great excellence, very interesting, and well worth reading". At least it is great fun.

"The Cage." By Harold Begbie. London: Hodder and Stoughton. 1909. 6s.

The most remarkable thing about the hero of this book is that, standing in Edinburgh on what Mr. Begbie is pleased to call the "Carlton" Hill, and looking northward, he "rested his troubled gaze on the mist-wreathed peak of Ben Lomond, swimming like a cloud above the haze of the sea". Ben Lomond would have to swim far in order to get north of, or within sight of, Edinburgh, and a writer who does not know the difference between the low Lomond hills in Fife and the western mountain would be well advised to lay his scene nearer the Carlton Hotel than the Carlton Hill. The heroine is married to a rake, and the story consists mainly of long discussions as to the propriety of her refusing to return to him. Mr. Begbie is a sound moralist, but he has not much that is new to say about this particular problem.

"Much Ado about Something." By C. E. Laurence. London: Murray. 1909. 6s.

If anyone were so brutal as to call this book slightly silly, our answer would probably depend upon the amount, and the quality, of the wine we had drunk at dinner. There are pretty fancies in it such as appeal to the man who has dined well. But it is all very obvious, now that it has become a mark of intelligence to associate fairies with Kensington Gardens. The fairy June, accompanied by the gnome Bim, comes to London on a sort of revivalist mission. She turns hard City men—even a Jewish moneylender—into active philanthropists, creates a sense of beauty in architecture and sculpture amongst Londoners, makes an Archdeacon unworldly, a Duchess tolerant, and the Smart Set decent. The author has some shrewd observations to make, and can write gracefully, and he has really borrowed nothing from either "Iolanthe" or "Peter Pan", though Lord Geoffrey Season's maiden speech sends our minds back to Strephon's exploits in Parliament. But a writer who claims to be an expert on fairies and nightingales really ought to know that the latter are not to be heard in Irish woods.

"In a Good Cause: Stories and Verses on behalf of the Hospital for Sick Children." By F. Anstey, Sir Gilbert Parker M.P., Owen Seaman, W. Pett Ridge, Marjorie Bowen, Richard Pryce, Henry Newbolt, W. Graham Robertson, and Tom Gallon. London: Murray. 1909. 3s. 6d.

The title of "Omnium Gatherum" which we saw the other day affixed to a book of this kind says little about quality, and if this volume also has the miscellaneousness of a variety-show it should be added that it resembles one with an all-star cast, as befits a charity performance. And besides, miscellaneous though they are, the contributions are most of them so appropriate to the occasion that it is impossible for anyone whilst enjoying the fare provided to forget all about the bénéficiaire, as we know sometimes happens. First in this regard, as in place, comes Mr. Anstey's pretty story of "Winnie", the account of whose sojourn in the Hospital for Sick Children in Great Ormonde Street and in the Convalescent Home at Highgate has been specially written as a curtain-raiser—in more than one sense. Then appears that squalling small person whom Phil May drew so often, and whose distress is here attributed by the management to an unsatisfied yearning for Great Ormonde Street—without really making the picture a bit less funny. Two poems by Sir Gilbert Parker are followed by a humorous story about a hospital patient by Mr. Pett Ridge, and then we have some serio-comic verses by Mr. Henry Newbolt, and Mr. Richard Pryce gives an engaging sketch of an enfant terrible. The Editor of "Punch", whose turn comes next, appears in that kindly, serious vein of his; and after him begins a weird scene through which stalk figures à la Beardsley coloured by Miss Marjorie Bowen—creatures with no need of hospitals because apparently they are invulnerable. And after a bit of bright verse by Mr. Graham Robertson the curtain falls on Mr. Tom Gallon's idyll, "The Love Train from Loughborough", in which the child-note is again cunningly introduced. Walk up, ladies and gentlemen, please!

"An Honest Man." By Ralph Harold Bretherton. London: Methuen. 1909. 6s.

The honest man was a well-to-do manufacturer who came a financial cropper through the defalcations of a partner, and whose proud determination to pay his creditors twenty shillings in the pound (which they did not demand or expect), developed into a mania for small meannesses at home and deliberate cruelty to his wife and children. The book is smoothly written and shows a keen eye for detail; as a character-study, however, it either goes too far or not far enough. For though Mr. Bretherton contrives a happy ending through the supposed curative effects of an attack of brain fever, his honest man on the evidence presented was as mad as a hatter. Insolvent manufacturers who are sane as well as honest do not include their children's toys in a list of assets.

"Someone Pays." By Noel Barwell. London: Lane 1909. 6s.

The telling of a story by means of letters is an old convention, which had a considerable vogue in the eighteenth century and had some notable successes. Within recent years it has been revived in some much-talked-about books, which is not quite the same thing. Mr. Barwell's venture in this method is not without cleverness, but it lacks any compelling qualities. In the course of a hundred and thirty-three letters it develops a simple story of the love affair of a Cambridge undergraduate and the "fall" of a housemaid in the estab-

(*Continued on page* 88.)

lishment of the clergyman who badly plays the part of holiday tutor to that same undergraduate. The letters are by all sorts and conditions of men and women—from the Home Secretary, who happens to be the father of the undergraduate, to the betrayed "skivvy"—and the author has managed to indicate the varying characters of his correspondents with some ability, but he never really interests us. The book can be laid down at any point without the reader feeling any curiosity as to what happens later; it might be taken up, we fancy, and be begun anywhere without the reader feeling any particular desire to hark back and find what all the pother was about. There are not wanting signs that Mr. Barwell can tell a story and that he has an eye for character.

"Agnès: a Romance of the Siege of Paris." Translated from the French of Jules Claretie by Ada Solly-Flood. London: Stock. 1909. 3s. 6d.

This is a theatrically effective little story of the Siege of Paris, interesting chiefly for the description of scenes at the Conservatoire and at the Comédie Française. The foyer of this most august theatre was turned into a hospital, where Madeleine Brohan, Marie Favart, and other actresses became admirable devoted nurses. In the original the writing was probably vivid and, to a certain extent, distinguished; the translation is crude and bald, on the level of a school exercise.

"A Fair Refugee." By Morice Gerard. London: Hodder and Stoughton. 1909. 6s.

This story is so entirely inoffensive that we must not be misunderstood when we express surprise that it should occur to anyone either to write or to print or to read it. French Revolution. Orphaned Vicomtesse escapes to an English ship and is wrecked on the Cornish coast. Saved from the sea by a brave and handsome young gentleman, given a home at the vicarage by a kindly parson, she behaves exactly as might be expected, and the things that happen to her will be guessed by anyone who has ever read a conventional English novel.

For this Week's Books see page 90.

A Delightful Book for Summer and Holiday Reading.

ALL WHO LOVE GARDENS,
WATERWAYS, SPORT, AND
OLD-TIME TRAVEL

should secure a copy of

MEMORIES OF GARDENS.

By ALEXANDER INNES SHAND,

With a Special Memoir by
SIR ROWLAND BLENNERHASSETT, Bart.

CONTENTS:

10s. 6d. Net.

THE WEST STRAND PUBLISHING CO. LTD.
10 King Street, Covent Garden, W.C.

THE CONDUIT STREET AUCTION GALLERIES.

The attention of Executors, Trustees, Solicitors, and Owners, who may be desirous of selling Works of Art, Family Jewels, Old Silver, Furniture, Pictures, Prints, Miniatures, China, Coins, Books, Old Lace, Furs, Musical Instruments, Guns, and other Valuables, is drawn to Messrs.

KNIGHT, FRANK & RUTLEY'S

AUCTION GALLERIES, 9 CONDUIT STREET, AND 23A MADDOX STREET, W., which are Open Daily to receive goods intended for early sales.

VALUATIONS are prepared for Fire Insurance, Estate Duty, and all other purposes. As to Insurance, owners are reminded that, for security, Messrs. KNIGHT, FRANK & RUTLEY'S detailed inventory and valuation of the contents of a Town or Country Mansion is an important adjunct to their Fire Insurance Policies.

NOTICE.

In the event of any difficulty being experienced in obtaining the SATURDAY REVIEW, the Publisher would be glad to be informed immediately.

Readers of "The Saturday Review" should order a copy of

FRY'S MAGAZINE.

The AUGUST Number contains:

The Sporting Estates of England.
An Article describing Highclere Castle, the country seat of the Earl of Carnarvon.
By "EAST SUSSEX."

The Thirteenth Australian Team.
Illustrated by Chas. Ambrose. By E. H. D. SEWELL.

Freak Golf Matches.
By "DREADNOUGHT."

A Single-handed Cruise.
By CHAS. PEARS.

The Genesis of the Motor Car.
By DOUGLAS LEECHMAN.

A Night with the Bustard.
A Trout-Fishing Article. By W. CARTER PLATTS.

Racehorse and Trainer at Home
(Mr. Andrew Joyner at Ballaton Lodge, Newmarket).
By A. SIDNEY GALTREY.

Wood-Pigeon Practice.
By OWEN JONES ("Gamekeeper").

Still-Hunting Moose in New Brunswick.
By DOUGLAS W. CLINCH.

"Needs Must When—"
A Cricket Story. By G. L. JESSOP.

A Shameless Minx.
A Golf Story. By BERNARD DARWIN.

A Camp on the Beach.
By F. INNES.

And many other items, including Articles and Stories upon Tennis, Golf, Travel, Racing, Game Breeding, Cycling, Rifle Shooting, Motor Cycling, Fishing, etc.

NOW ON SALE. SIXPENCE NET.

THIS WEEK'S BOOKS.

FICTION

The Adventures of Captain Jack (Max Pemberton). Mills and Boon. 6s.
A Dog's Life in Burma (Told by the Dog). Drane. 3s. 6d.
The Fun of the Fair (Eden Phillpotts), 2s. 6d. net; The Score (Lucas Malet), 6s. Murray.
A Lighted Candle (Priscilla Craven). Rivers. 6s.
The Enterprise of Ella (Jay Jelf); Cackling Geese (Brenda Girvin). Long. 6s. each.
Dark House (Wynoth Dale). Nutt. 6s.
The Waking Hour (Harold Wintle). Fisher Unwin. 6s.
The Marquis Catilini (Rowland Strong). Greening. 6s.

HISTORY

The Central Period of the Middle Age, 918-1273 (Beatrice A. Lees). Methuen. 2s. 6d.
La Jeanne d'Arc de M. Anatole France (Andrew Lang). Paris: Perrin. 2fr.
Mysore and Coorg from the Inscriptions (B. Lewis Rice). Constable. 12s. 6d. net.

LAW

The Law and Custom of the Constitution (Sir William R. Anson). Oxford: At the Clarendon Press. 12s. 6d. net.
The Law of Compensation for Industrial Diseases (Edward Thornton Hill Lawes). Stevens and Sons, Ltd. 7s. 6d.

NATURAL HISTORY

Fertilisers and Manures (A. D. Hall). Murray. 5s. net.

TRAVEL

Pre-Historic Rhodesia (R. N. Hall). Fisher Unwin. 12s. 6d. net.

VERSE

Seven Short Plays (Lady Gregory). Dublin: Maunsel. 2s. 6d. net.

MISCELLANEOUS

Agriculture in the Tropics (J. C. Willis). Cambridge: At the University Press. 7s. 6d. net.
Dictionary of National Biography (Edited by Sidney Lee. Vol. XVII.). Smith, Elder. 15s. net.
Essays in Politics (Andrew Macphail). Longmans, Green. 6s. net.
Introduction to Military Geography, An (Brigadier-General E. S. May C.B., C.M.G.), 8s. 6d. net; Lectures on the Strategy of the Franco-German War 1870 up to the Battle of Sedan (Brevet-Major W. D. Bird), 6s. Hugh Rees.
Practical Arithmetic for Schools (W. G. Borchardt). Rivington. 4s. 6d.
Supplementary Catalogue of Hindustani Books acquired during the years 1889-1908, A (J. F. Blumhardt). Printed by order of the Trustees. British Museum. £2.
Taxation of Land. Wyman. 2s. 7d.
Works of James Buchanan, The (Edited by John Bassett Moore. Vol. VIII.). Lippincott. £12 12s. for 12 vols.

REVIEWS AND MAGAZINES.—The Dublin Review, 5s. 6d.; Revue des Deux Mondes, 3fr.

LA ROSE CONSOLIDATED MINES COMPANY.

Big Cobalt Consolidation for the London Market.

Few mining fields have had a more brilliant history of rapid and successful achievement than Cobalt, which has turned out more "big things" in a shorter time than any centre of mining effort discovered for many years past. One of the biggest dividend-paying combinations, the La Rose Consolidated Mines Company (incorporated under the laws of the State of Maine), will shortly be dealt in on the London market, and some particulars of the concern, which has a capital of $7,500,000, divided into 1,500,000 shares of a par value of $5, practically all of which are issued, will doubtless be interesting to readers.

Many of the most influential men of the Cobalt camp are concerned in its management. Mr. John McMartin is president, Mr. L. H. Timmins vice-president, and Mr. D. A. Dunlop secretary and treasurer.

The board of directors, which is an influential one, is composed of the following gentlemen: Mr. David Fasken, Toronto; Mr. Duncan McMartin, Montreal; Mr. Noah A. Timmins, Haileybury, Ont.; Mr. Ellis P. Earle, New York; Mr. Frank W. Holmes, New York; and Mr. Richard T. Greene, New York.

Cobalt in less than six years has achieved the position of being the largest silver-producing camp in the world. The steady increase in production is shown by the following: 1904, $136,217; 1905, $1,485,570; 1906, $3,573,908; 1907, $6,476,555; and 1908, over $10,000,000. So rapid has this increase been that to-day, after but four years of mining upon a serious scale, this fabulously rich district is producing at the rate of 30,000,000 oz. per annum, or approximately one-seventh of the world's silver output.

The holdings of the La Rose Consolidated Mines Company are among, if not the best, mines in the district. They differ from most of the other properties in having a relatively large quantity of ore blocked out ready for mining. As they are located in the heart of this wealthy district, and as only a small portion of their properties is prospected, the discovery of additional bonanza ore bodies may be expected.

The La Rose Consolidated Mines Company owns stock in the following operating companies, all of which are incorporated under the laws of the Province of Ontario, Canada:—

La Rose Mines, Limited. All of the capital stock. Properties include La Rose, La Rose Extension, Princess, Fisher, Eplett, and Silver Hill.

Lawson Mine, Limited. All of the capital stock.

University Mines, Limited. 98 per cent. of the capital stock.

Violet Mining Company, Limited. All of the capital stock.

The holdings aggregate 359.5 acres, all held under Crown patents. Certificates of title have been granted under the Land Titles Act.

The consolidation is already dividend-paying, the following distributions having been made: No. 1, October 20, 1908, 3 per cent., $171,505.20; No. 2, January 20, 1909, 3 per cent. and 1 per cent. bonus, $228,840.60; No. 3, April 20, 1909, 3 per cent. and 1 per cent. bonus, $228,886.20. A fourth dividend of 3 per cent. and 1 per cent. bonus ($229,600) has just been declared, payable July 20, to shareholders registered on July 1, 1909.

La Rose Mines, Limited.

To June 1, 1908, at which time the Consolidated Company acquired its interest and the properties started with a clean sheet, 2,675,161 oz. of silver had been produced by the La Rose Mine, mostly from development work alone, netting the owners $1,204,862. A preliminary estimate for the year ending May 31, 1909, shows an output of 6,164 tons of a gross value of $1,573,979, and net earnings of $1,093,572.

During the past year development has shown the ore at greater depth; the old veins have been extended, and new ones, showing good silver values, discovered. Messrs. R. B. and Wm. Watson, in their report of June 15, 1908, stated that at that time the La Rose mine alone had practically developed and indicated ore reserves containing 4,894,065 oz., with an estimated net profit of $2,017,878, figuring silver at 55c. per ounce. Since the examination of Messrs. R. B. and Wm. Watson approximately $1,093,572 of net values have been extracted from the La Rose. This, however, was not entirely from ore embraced in their estimates of net values, for the reason that, as before stated, after their reports were made, the known ore bodies have been extended and new ones opened up.

Professor Willet G. Miller, the eminent Provincial Geologist of Canada, in his report dated August 9, 1907, stated that at that time there were 8,020,870 oz. of silver. He further estimates, including the above, a possible yield from the La Rose mine alone, 12,871,750 oz., and states: "To this is to be added the possible production of veins on the unprospected part of the three properties." Since Professor Miller's examination, approximately $2,300,000 has been extracted from the La Rose. His report did not include several claims since acquired by the La Rose Mines, Limited, and the properties of the other companies now in the consolidation.

Lawson Mine, Limited.

This property is considered one of the most valuable of the La Rose holdings. There are now exposed several very rich veins, assaying from 3,000 to 14,000 oz. of silver to the ton. Due to the fact that it has been tied up by litigation (now settled) since its discovery, only a small percentage of the total area has been prospected by trenching, and there are only a few shallow shafts upon the property. After it had lain practically idle for four years, the La Rose Consolidated Mines Company acquired all interest, and entered into possession in April, 1909. Work was immediately started, and the development of the property will be pushed with all possible despatch. The property on the north side of the Lawson has developed high grade ore to a depth of 200 feet, and the property adjoining on the west has still high grade ore at a depth of 400 feet.

Mr. R. B. Watson, consulting engineer of the Consolidated Company, in his report dated June 1, 1909, states that the Lawson mine has "partly developed" and "indicated" 556.9 tons of ore assaying 3,462 oz. to the ton, containing 2,274,077 oz. of silver, which will yield an estimated net profit of $1,084,621, figuring silver at 53 c. per ounce. Concluding his report, Mr. Watson says: "Some of the best mines in the district surround the Lawson, and have developed high grade ore at much greater depths than the 50 feet to which the ore is calculated. Considering, therefore, the present surface showings and the known richness of the immediate district, the Lawson, no doubt, has a wonderful future ahead."

Other Holdings.

The small amount of exploration work done on the property known as University Mines, Limited, last year has disclosed additional high grade ore. Aggressive work will be started soon, from which results are expected.

No work has been done on the Violet Mining Company, Limited, during the past year, development being more advantageously concentrated on other sections.

La Rose, the man after whom this great consolidation is named, is, of course, the original discoverer of Cobalt. In laying the foundations of a new railway, he accidentally struck off a glittering specimen, which led to the establishment of the famous camp. The very spot where the discovery was made is still preserved, and visitors to the camp are shown the glittering side of the rock—within a stone's throw of La Rose Mine—where the first modest contribution to Cobalt's total mineral production was made. The name is consequently of happy augury.

Printed for the Proprietors by SPOTTISWOODE & Co. LTD., 5 New-street Square, E.C., and Published by REGINALD WEBSTER PAGE, at the Office, 10 King Street, Covent Garden, in the Parish of St. Paul, in the County of London.—*Saturday, 17 July, 1909.*

SUPPLEMENT TO THE

SATURDAY REVIEW

OF

POLITICS, LITERATURE, SCIENCE, AND ART.

No. 2,803 Vol. 108. 17 July 1909. GRATIS.

AND BACK,

Visiting the finest Fjords,

BY FAMOUS YACHTING STEAMER

"OPHIR"

AND

s.s. "OTRANTO," 12,000 tons.

From GRIMSBY 17th, 31st JULY; & 14th, 28th AUG.

LUXURIOUS ACCOMMODATION.

13 DAYS FOR 12 GUINEAS AND UPWARDS.

Write for Free Illustrated Booklet to ORIENT STEAM NAVIGATION COMPANY, 5 Fenchurch Avenue, London, E.C., and 28 Cockspur Street, S.W.
Managers—F. GREEN & CO. and ANDERSON, ANDERSON & CO.

GOOD SERVICE. CHEAP FARES. RESTAURANT CARS.

TO THE

BRACING BREEZES

— OF —

SCARBORO'
BRIDLINGTON
WHITBY
CLEETHORPES
N.E. COAST

SOUTHPORT
LYTHAM
BLACKPOOL
ISLE OF MAN
N.W. COAST

CHILTERN HILLS and SHAKESPEARE'S COUNTRY

— BY —

GREAT CENTRAL R[LY].

From LONDON (Marylebone).

A.B.C. PROGRAMME of Tourist and Excursion Facilities to over 600 Seaside and Inland Health Resorts for Week-End and longer periods can be obtained free at Marylebone Station, and Company's Town Offices, or by post from Publicity Dept., 216 Marylebone Road, N.W.

SAM FAY, General Manager.

SUMMER TOURS

FOR HEALTH AND PLEASURE.

Before arranging your Holidays write for particulars of the

CHEAPEST SEA TRIP IN THE WORLD

12 Guineas

for FIRST-CLASS Return Ticket to the

Canary Islands and Madeira.

Including One Week's Hotel Accommodation at the Métropole, Las Palmas, Hôtel Victoria, Monte, or (if open) at the Hôtel Pino de Oro, Teneriffe.

OR FOR PARTICULARS OF TRIPS TO

Jamaica (the New Riviera).

22 Guineas

covers FIRST-CLASS Return, with about Six Days' Accommodation at the Palatial Constant Spring Hotel. The whole Trip occupying one Month.

ELDER DEMPSTER & CO.,

Head Office: **Colonial House, LIVERPOOL.**

4 St. Mary Axe, London: 30 Mosley St., Manchester; Bristol, Cardiff, Birmingham, &c., &c.

TRAVEL BOOK SUPPLEMENT

LONDON: 17 *JULY,* 1909.

SOME BOOKS ON EGYPT PAST AND PRESENT.

"An Egyptian Oasis." By H. J. Llewellyn Beadnell London: Murray. 1909. 10s. 6d.

"Au Temps des Pharaons." By A. Moret. Paris Armand Colin. 1908.

"The Story of the Pharaohs." By James Baikie. London: Black. 1908. 7s. 6d.

"Egypt in Asia." By George Cormack. London: Black. 1908. 7s. 6d.

"Egypt and the English." By Douglas Sladen. London: Hurst and Blackett. 1908. 21s.

TO those who belittle the work of the English in Egypt "An Egyptian Oasis" will give a good idea of the work done by an individual Englishman in Government service. Told in a simple style without any embellishments, it is a record of solid and painstaking work conducted under many difficulties and real hardships. Mr. Beadnell gives a very fair account of the historical monuments of Khargeh, but he is at his best when describing things of a more modern and practical nature, such as artesian wells, desert routes, and the work of the Geological Survey. In "Au Temps des Pharaons" Monsieur Moret has compressed into a small compass some of the results of modern archæological investigations. The most interesting chapter is that entitled "La Restauration des Temples Egyptiens", in which he treats of the subject of restoration from the earliest known instances down to the present day. Restoration, according to the methods of the ancient rulers of Egypt, consisted largely of pulling down and breaking in pieces the works of their predecessors, and rebuilding as their own fancy and will dictated. The temples of Egypt have always needed careful and regular inspection, and to-day no less than in ancient times judicious restoration and strengthening are required. This demands good taste no less than architectural knowledge. A too lavish use of cement is disastrous from the artist's point of view, and although much valuable work has been done at Karnac and elsewhere, one cannot but regret the patchy and almost new appearance of many of the temples nowadays. But despite restored temples, modernised Cairo and Egyptians who ape the European and think that with their Frankish clothes they don Western culture, to the scholar and traveller Egypt must still retain her glamour of romance. As one nears the long, flat coast one remembers that off this self-same shore, crouching low on a mudbank, Odysseus shivered from cold and fright. And as the train takes us to Cairo through the seemingly limitless fields of the delta there comes to one's mind the same hero's tale to Eumæus of the raid by sea rovers on the crops and cattle of the Egyptians.

As the authors of "The Story of the Pharaohs" and "Egypt in Asia" show us, the Levant and Eastern Mediterranean traded with Egypt for centuries before Christ. As early as the third millennium B.C. Seneferu, last king of the third dynasty, fetched cedar logs from Lebanon, and in the tombs of the early dynastic kings at Abydos Petrie has found pottery that he identifies with the wares of Crete and the Ægean Islands. In the eighteenth dynasty, when the Cretan Empire—perhaps the Lost Atlantis of the Classics—was at the height of its glory artistically and as a naval power, the Egyptian ports and the Nile were thronged with the shipping, and the merchant vessels of every known nationality sailed right up to Thebes the hundred-gated, at that period the capital and emporium of the civilised world. Thither flowed the rich merchandise of Asia, South Europe, and Africa. Syria sent her woollen fabrics dyed purple, enriched with embroidery, and Nubia and the Sudan ivory, ebony, spices and the curious wares of Central Africa: in the storehouses of gods and kings the gold lay piled up in heaps. At this period, perhaps the most interesting to ourselves, Egypt after the expulsion of her alien rulers, the Hyksos of Josephus, awakened into a new and vigorous life and her past weakness forgotten, had, like her own Nile in flood, overflowed all her borders and, sweeping her foes before her, poured into Palestine. Then the princes of Syria became her vassals, the lands beyond the Euphrates paid her tribute, the peoples of the Tigris region and in the islands of the Mediterranean brought gifts. While Egypt spread north-east, she also extended her Empire southward, and brought civilisation and ordered government into the Sudan, which was ruled by an Egyptian viceroy and subordinate officials.

For about three hundred years this Empire lasted, except for a short interval at the end of the eighteenth dynasty. The break-up commenced at the death of the third Rameses, second king of the twentieth dynasty, in the year 1167 B.C. After his death Egypt plays no important part in world-politics till the twenty-sixth dynasty, the age of Psammetichus and the archaic revival, except for a brief period under Shishak of the twenty-second dynasty, when Egypt once more obtained a foothold in Palestine and enjoyed a short-lived predominance in Asiatic affairs. But the inevitable collapse soon followed, and Egypt once more became a collection of petty principalities, each one struggling for the mastery over the others, as in the more recent age of the Mamelukes. Under the twenty-sixth dynasty rulers, for instance Psammetichus and Amasis, Egypt for the first time comes in contact with modern Europe. This period sees the advent of the Greeks, who rapidly became, as they are to this day, the traders and money-lenders of the country. The characteristic of this dynasty is archaism in art and religion and modernism in politics. While seaport towns are founded especially for trade with the foreigners, and the monarch makes alliance with Greek potentates and encourages intercourse with other nations, the priest and artist, instead of seizing their inspirations from the present, with all its possibilities, look far into the dim and distant past, beyond the days of the great emperors, beyond the days of Sesostris and the Middle Kingdom, back to the times of the Pyramid-builders, when Mykerinus reigned at Memphis and the fifth-dynasty religious texts were engraved on the walls of the royal tombs at Saqqarah. So the State religion and art became more and more something apart from daily life, and priest, scholar and artist looked askance at the modern world and held themselves aloof. No longer, as in the days of Egypt's real greatness, did they express the national spirit and ideals. The religious hymns of the Empire, written in the popular language, were succeeded by a dry and archaic formalism and a jumble of ancient texts hardly understood and utterly out of touch with the spirit of the times. The newly arisen might of Persia soon shattered this outworn Empire, and Persia gave place to Alexander and his successors, only to be followed by Rome, the Arabs and the Turks, and finally the English. This severance of art and State religion from the life of the present, so prominent under the twenty-sixth dynasty rulers, increased more and more under the Greek Ptolemies, and everything was done to make them unintelligible to the masses; so the inscriptions became hieroglyphic indeed, a priestly writing. The condition of Egypt in this later period is not altogether unlike that of to-day. The foreign element is getting more and more pronounced, and as the upper classes become imbued with Western culture so they become the more out of touch with the feelings of the masses. As in the past, so to-day, the priest looks askance at the trend of events, as the old order changes. The best element in Egypt loves the old paths and sighs over the lapses of the semi-Europeanised Effendi. Mr. Sladen unfortunately appears to know but little Arabic, and seems ignorant of the habits and condition of the country people, the backbone of Egypt. His opinions are culled from officials and from what he has seen of the town-bred clerk in his ill-assorted Frankish garb and the natives who have been contaminated by tourists. Lady Duff-Gordon draws a very different picture of the fellah and country landowner. If the Egyptian has deteriorated in the last twenty years it is largely owing to the misconduct of the tourists with a moral tone far lower than that of the well-conducted fellahin. Despite what Mr. Sladen may say, there are Egyptians who are capable of loyalty, pluck, endurance and gratitude—even of telling the truth. No man has a right to judge the Egyptian nation as a whole unless he has some knowledge of Arabic and knows at any rate a little of the country people. The fellahin believe in the English, and look upon them as their protectors against the greed and corruption of the native official. This belief has so far withstood all attacks in the scurrilous native press and the seditious utterances of Nationalist agitators and disloyal English members of Parliament. But unless there is some change in present methods it is likely to be imperilled.

GIRDLING THE EARTH ANEW.

"Round the World in a Motor Car." By Antonio Scarfoglio. Translated by J. Parker Heyes. London: Richards. 1909. 15s. net.

THE Italian seems to have developed something in the nature of a passion for motoring through half-explored continents. Eighteen months ago we noticed Signor Barzini's account of Prince Borghese's remarkable trip from "Peking to Paris". Now we have a sort of companion volume in which Signor Scarfoglio describes in amusing detail the incidents, the adventures, the thoughts, the emotions which accompanied his motor race from Paris round the world.

The experiences of the little party in this rush across America, Asia, and Europe were not of a kind to induce any save a few speed-maniacs to embark on a similar enterprise. Nothing is to be proved by driving a motor car over mountains and across deserts which can be traversed with much less cost and trouble otherwise. The ordeal is not faced in the interest of health, of science, of anything that really matters. The object is not exploration or inquiry into the customs and ways of life of little-known peoples, but to arrive somewhere in record time and be gone as soon as mechanical contrivance will allow. With none of the joyousness of the ancient mariner but all the pent-up feverishness of the age the motorist on his world-tour makes speed his ideal. There is novelty, perhaps notoriety, but the novelty and the notoriety are rarely worth seeking. The thing brings no special pleasure whilst it lasts; it involves many hardships, on occasion tragedy even; and when it is all over, the plaudits which greet the adventurers' return are drowned in nightmare as the dangers they have passed crowd upon the memory.

The spirit in which Signor Scarfoglio and his companions started on this wild eight-months-long adventure is clear from what he says of his disappointment when a telegram received at Seattle ordered him to abandon the idea of crossing Alaska. A too late start from New York or a too early break-up of the ice and snow made the attempt hopeless. "Thus ends the daring dream of our adventure!" cries Signor Scarfoglio. Whatever else happened, it was not possible now to try their fortune on the virgin tracks of the Behring Sea. Signor Scarfoglio was not a bit concerned at the information that they would never have returned to their applauding friends in Paris if the attempt had been made. "That would matter little. We had set out to perpetrate an act of splendid folly, not to open up a new way for men. We wished to be madmen, not pioneers. And we are disappointed of our madness. Our dream is dispelled."

As showing how man and the machine can overcome difficulties which might appear insuperable, the race is perhaps worth running once or twice. But how futile and incongruous seems all this ploughing of desert sands, this plunging into Manchurian morasses, this taking of desperate chances, as when they groped their way in the dark through Japanese ravines and along the edge of precipices in order to catch a boat from Tsuruga to Vladivostock! We follow the well-told story with almost as little breath as the motorists had left after some of their nerve-racking trials, and then we wonder, What purpose is served? The risks taken are not less from the jealousy of unscrupulous rivalry or the superstitions of ignorance than from purely mechanical or natural causes. A hundred miles from anywhere it is unpleasant to find that something has gone wrong with the differential. On investigation it is worse than unpleasant to discover that the cause is a nail which could not have got in the machinery by accident. "It must have been placed there by some patriotic Yankee who thus wished to ensure the victory of his own country." It was not the only occasion on which the "patriotic Yankee" paid the car attention. "We could not help reflecting", says Signor Scarfoglio, "on the predatory instincts which still find a home in the depths of the American soul, and are ready at any moment to explode violently." The sporting instinct of some Americans is apparently little to be distinguished from the business instinct of the Siberian hotel-keeper who carried brigandage to the point of a fine art. In Siberia the innkeeper is not only "a pirate by his articles of faith" but "something more. He is a man of genius", who robs you with the most charming assurance and provides you with what you do not want at a charge which would be extortion if you were well served.

PERSIAN HOME LIFE.

"Behind the Veil in Persia and Turkish Arabia." By Mrs. Hume-Griffith. London: Seeley. 1909. 16s. net.

THIS book is not altogether free from the faults generally to be found in missionary writings; but it is easily written, and Mrs. Hume-Griffith has been careful to keep strictly within the limits of her experience and sympathy. The chapters in which she deals with the life of the Persian anderun, or women's apartments, are not only interesting but have a special value. Other writers upon Persian life have generally been men and have made little or no attempt to deal with the inner life of Persian women. Not less valuable are the chapters in which Dr. Hume-Griffith deals with his medical experiences both in Kerman and in Mosul.

But we are disappointed with the scanty attention paid to religion both in Persia and Turkish Arabia, the mission work apart. It would have been particularly interesting if Mrs. Hume-Griffith had dwelt on the attitude of the women in both countries towards the twin sects of Islam, and above all towards that widely spread but most mysterious religion, Babism. She briefly sketches the story of the Bab, but she makes no attempt whatever at an analysis or to give the baldest of accounts of the practice or theory of this little-understood faith. Yet there is no greater influence at work to-day in or near the frontiers of Persia than that of Babism, and it is not impossible that the whole National movement owes to it its origin. Too little credit, moreover, is given to whatever of good there is—and it is beyond question that there is much—in the Mohammedan creed. The suggestion is inevitable that in other matters also the book may not be entirely impartial. A writer's inability to recognise the good qualities of those from whom he differs may, of course, be confined to his religious antagonisms, but it makes his work open to suspicion.

Subject to these general criticisms Mrs. Hume-Griffith's book is a true and pleasant description of Persian life at the present day. Sometimes she seems not to have used the latest knowledge which she must possess, as, for example, in her statement that Persian women in the great centres still wear European ballet costume. To judge from her description this would seem to be the rule instead of the rarest of exceptions. Nor is she quite fair in some cases to the customs of the country. It is less than just to all concerned to suggest that the girls who weave carpets in the towns of Persia and the mountain villages suffer in health or spirits from what may be a monotonous but is certainly not an injurious occupation. But these faults of detail are few, and Mrs. Hume-Griffith's book is the best of the numerous volumes which have appeared lately dealing with the vie intime of the Persian people. Of the present political crisis she says nothing, nor is there more than a passing reference to the interesting archæological remains of Persia; but political troubles pass while home life remains, and there are not a few antiquaries who would willingly give Persepolis and Susa for just such a knowledge of the inner life of their builders as that which is so pleasantly given by Mrs. Hume-Griffith of the present inhabitants of Persia.

SHORTER NOTICES.

"Five Months in the Himalaya." By A. L. Mumm. London: Arnold. 1909. 21s. net.

In the record of mountain travel this account of five months spent amid the lonely peaks of Garhwal and Kashmir will take a prominent place. Mr. Mumm says in his Preface: "The mountainous portion of Garhwal and Kumaon, which forms a section of the great parallel ranges of the Himalayan chain, contains not only the highest summit but the largest and finest field for combined climbing and exploration in British territory; and in Nanda Devi, the summit referred to, and the mountains surrounding it possesses a group which, for individuality and striking and characteristic features of configuration and structure, may challenge comparison with any in the world. Its natural attractions gain an additional interest from the fact that the whole country is of immemorial sanctity, and was the scene of the marriage of Siva and many other capital events of the theogony of Brahminism." It was originally intended by Major Bruce and his friends to attack Mount Everest, but the powers that be forbad the expedition, and the party had to fall back on Garhwal. Mr. Mumm is a mountaineering enthusiast, and eagerly seized Major Bruce's invitation to join him in an expedition which was full of incident, hardship, and discovery of the kind that delights the true mountaineer's heart. There is much that is novel in these graphic and picturesque pages; for instance, the snow bridges, which are among the most remarkable features of a remarkable region. "Nothing impresses upon one so much the stupendous dimensions of the Himalayan snowfall as the spectacle of largish rivers covered over at midsummer by solid masses of hard snow, many feet in thickness, which completely fill their channels sometimes for miles together. They often facilitate travel and make ordinary routes shorter and easier; sometimes they themselves constitute the sole available route. There is a pass into Tibet a little north-west of Mava which is described in the G. T. S. map in these terms: 'Gumrang, or winter pass, closed between May and September, the snow bridges all being swept away.'" The book affords a very full idea of the character of the peaks and valleys, the passes and people in the Himalaya; an idea which is assisted by the many admirable illustrations.

"Tyrol and its People." By Clive Holland. London: Methuen. 1909. 10s. 6d. net.

In "Tyrol and Its People" Mr. Clive Holland has an ideal subject for a book which forms one of Messrs. Methuen's "Books for Travellers" series. The Tyrol is already in some parts a favourite playground for travellers, while in others there are still little-known regions inviting the tourist who seeks less travelled ways. Mr. Clive Holland must deprecate in the usual form the spoiling of these sequestered regions of the "Land within the Mountains" as yet unspoiled by crowds of tourists and general sophistication and the deterioration which arises therefrom. But still the purpose of his book is to make them known. If he does violence to his feelings by revealing these secrets he may plead the example of Tyrolese authors and associations whose excellent publications have been of so much assistance to him in writing his book. They are quite anxious that tourists should come to their beautiful land, and are willing to run any risk of desecration. And as tourists cannot be kept out of any country worth visiting, nothing could be better for them than reading such a book as this. Tourists are not irreverent who associate with the scenes they visit their historic story, connecting the past with the present, and are acquainted with the legends and folklore and customs of the people they are amongst. And the Tyrol is rich in all these things. It has been the battle ground of Romans and of Teutons, of Italians, French, Austrians and Prussians. Its mediæval towns are as romantic for their past as they are a delight to the eye that has grown weary of the monotony of modern buildings. Mr. Holland's descriptions of such towns as Innsbruck, Salzburg, Bregenz, Botzen, Meran, and Trent are an incitement to go to see them instead of to avoid them, as so many guide-book descriptions are. And though by a curious slip he makes the Tyrolese maidens' superstition against marriage in May different from our own, his accounts of the customs of the people enhance the pleasure we take in their country. This slip is the more curious because the common superstition is of Roman origin, and Mr. Holland emphasises the Roman and Italian influences on the Tyrol. Mr. Holland's book is as pleasant to read before or after visiting the Tyrol as it will be useful to the visitor who is fortunate enough to find himself there.

"The Buried City of Kenfig." By Thomas Gray. London: Fisher Unwin. 1909. 10s. 6d. net.

This is a book of extraordinary antiquarian research devoted to the restoration of the past history of a town that has for ages lain buried on the coast of Glamorgan. Mr. Walter De Gray Birch, librarian to the Marquis of Bute at Cardiff Castle, writes an introduction, in which he says "The sand-girt town of Kenfig, like many another town in similar plight set on the Wirral of Cheshire, has had its day of fame and glory, its long array of noble owners, its active populace, its trade and its commerce, but those have fled, and it has been left to the author to recover from the veiled past a multitude of interesting records of facts which throw light on the history of Glamorgan." It is the history of this town that Mr. Gray has reconstructed from ancient manuscripts with a skill as evident as his learning. If his book is not of wide general interest it must be attractive to all Welshmen, for whom he has made the dry bones of antiquity stir with the past life of their country.

"The Isle of Man." Described by Agnes Herbert. Illustrated by Donald Maxwell. London: Lane. 1909. 10s. 6d. net.

In a "Foreword" Mr. A. W. Moore, the Speaker of the House of Keys, commends Miss Herbert's book as "bright, breezy, and bracing", like Mona's Isle itself, as described in the advertisements. That is precisely the sort of literary effect to be expected of Miss Herbert when we recall her books on Somaliland and Alaska. She is here on her own ground, and her style is not less racy when dealing with the native and the tripper, the history, the customs, and the scenery of Manxland, than when she was engaged in explaining how she shot lions in Africa or bears in America, and incidentally turned the mere male person into her willing servitor. Unfortunately for herself Miss Herbert starts out with the confession that she has been invited to write the text for a colour book, and she asks what is a colour book? It would be a pity if the want of spontaneous origin were allowed to prejudice the reader against a book which is really admirable. Mona's Isle is never likely to find a more vivacious chronicler. But it would have added somewhat to its character if she had discussed the colour pictures which she was commissioned to write up to. Mr. Donald Maxwell is not by any means the conventional three-colour process man. There is in some of his pictures a touch of Mr. Rackham's imagination. Several of them are quite good. But we should like Miss Herbert's frank answer whether she ever saw in Manxland some of the effects Mr. Maxwell produces. There might have been a certain piquancy at any rate in the writer's opinion of the pictures which formed the excuse for her book.

"The Norfolk and Suffolk Coast." By W. A. Dutt. London: Fisher Unwin. 1909. 6s. net.

To Mr. Dutt the interest, human and topographical, of his beloved East Anglia is inexhaustible. This volume belongs to the County Coast series, and in a measure supplements his "Highways and Byways in East Anglia". He takes us from the south-eastern corner of Suffolk up through places familiar or unfamiliar on or near the shore and round Norfolk to the Wash and King's Lynn. There is hardly a mile in this long stretch of coast-line—all the longer because the Norfolk coast faces east, north, and west—which has not something worth special note either in its history or its present condition. Mr. Dutt, who has traversed parts of the coast which are so little known that the map-maker fails as a guide, was familiar with what are now popular holiday resorts in the days when they were visited only by the fortunate few who knew their charms and proclaimed them too widely for the taste of nature-lovers like Mr. Dutt. The note of regret in this book is unavailing. For some of the popularity which the East Coast now enjoys Mr. Dutt may perhaps himself be held responsible; he looks back wistfully to the more primitive days of Cromer and other places now grown almost out of recognition, but he must blame, not the railways and the builders, but writers like himself, who have made others eager to share the delights of sea and land which they describe so well. Mr. Dutt's account of the Norfolk and Suffolk coast is sufficient to send many pioneers to the likely spots for future holiday resorts. If the sea has made inroads which have changed the coast-line, so that towns have disappeared, the holiday-maker has provided an excuse for the building of other towns which the engineer does his best to protect by groin and sea-wall. The waves, thwarted at one spot, wreak their fury upon others adjacent, and some of the coast towns of East Anglia will probably in time become tiny islands. At places like Mundesley, as Mr. Dutt says, "new houses are being built rather more quickly than the sea can demolish the old ones"; but when we think of the fate of Dunwich we can only wonder what will be the issue of the challenge to Nature which man seems to be throwing down at intervals along the Norfolk and Suffolk coast. A dozen years hence much of the coast we know now may be non-existent.

"The Short Cut to India." By David Fraser. London: Blackwood. 1909. 12s. 6d. net.

Events have moved so fast in the Near East recently that Mr. Fraser's record of his journey along the route of the Baghdad Railway, so far as his chapters touch on politics, is already out of date. His book, however, does not depend for its value on political considerations. It gives an excellent account of the state of the Baghdad Railway, of the reasons why construction has not been continued, and of the international significance of the line. Somebody, if his figures are correct, has already made a fat profit out of the section of the line which has been laid, and if part of that profit is not to be disgorged more millions will have to be found. Are the New Turks any more likely to be able to provide the necessary guarantees than were the old, especially as present conditions make it quite impossible, according to Mr. Fraser, that the railway can pay its way? Politically, commercially, and strategically he shows what the line would mean to the British Empire, and how essential it is that it should remain in Turkish control. Of the country through which the railway would pass Mr. Fraser affords a very graphic idea, and he is able to give official documents relating to the enterprise which have not hitherto been published. The book is a most useful contribution to our knowledge of the Euphrates Valley.

"Worcestershire." Painted by Thomas Tyndale. Described by A. G. Bradley. London: Black. 1909. 7s. 6d. net.

Mr. Bradley is at home on the borders of Wales. The past and present of Worcestershire need no enthusiast to make them attractive. Simon de Montfort and King John, Charles II. and Cromwell, contributed most to its history, whilst the Severn, the Malverns, and the Vale of Evesham are among its natural features. Bishop Creighton and Professor Freeman were agreed that Worcestershire in many vital particulars was "the most illuminating county in England to the historical student". King John, "who had a passion for the remoter provinces, whether due to a more than common turn for sport which by modern ethics would be a saving clause in his long list of delinquencies, or because it was cheaper to live in the country at the expense of his unwilling friends there", showed his preference for Worcestershire by insisting on being buried beside the saints in the Cathedral. The county was, says Mr. Bradley, "the cockpit of the Civil War", and at Worcester was fought the last great battle upon English soil. "With it Worcester and its fertile shire pass into the humdrum life of an inland English county, to pursue with even more success and in more varied paths than most other ones the arts of peace." To most people Worcester is famous chiefly for its sauce and its china. Mr. Bradley's book will show that it has other and larger claims to notice. The coloured pictures are inoffensive, but the value of the book so far as it has value is literary. Mr. Bradley is picturesque without the aid of the three-colour process.

"Round the Lake Country." By the Rev. H. D. Rawnsley. Glasgow: Maclehose. 1909. 5s. net.

Canon Rawnsley's new collection of sketches dealing with the fringe of the Lake Country is little more than ornamental reporting. Such various subjects as the Gosforth and Bewcastle crosses, the gulls' breeding-ground at Ravenglass, the purchase of Gowbarrow Fell by the National Trust, and Brough Hill fair are treated with close local knowledge and capable use of authorities; but all is spoiled by an apparently irrepressible gift for seeing "copy" everywhere. The book is put together with so little care that not only do repetitions of matter scarcely varied in form occur (e.g. Agricola's hypocaust at Walls Castle and the miraculous snowstorm at S. Bees, with a scientific explanation by means of straying ice-floes), but paragraphs are copied, and even a whole chapter ("The Arnside Lilies") bodily lifted from an earlier work of the author's, which is advertised in this volume. A reasonable recension of the papers as a whole would have prevented such blemishes as these; it might also have suggested that the general reader may find the references to the Vikings more than enough, and that dangers lurk in the use of the modest but precarious "one" in place of the personal pronoun. "As a Balliol man", says the author, "one cannot look upon that ruin to-day without the thought", etc. We all know the ubiquity of Balliol men to-day, but this vision of the college as co-extensive with humanity is a very pleasing touch.

ABOUT GUIDE BOOKS.

Travel has always appealed to the literary and philosophical mind. It appealed to Bacon and Montaigne, as it appeals to-day to Mr. W. A. Dutt, Mr. A. G. Bradley, and Mr. Arthur Norway. Not everybody can enjoy the opportunity which Bacon regarded as essential—"to see the secretaries and employed men with ambassadors", so that in travelling in one country he may "suck the experience of many"—but at least to-day he may carry with him "some book where he travelleth which will be a key to his inquiry".

Whether the guide book or the travel book is always to be depended on is another matter. Montaigne deemed travel to be a profitable exercise, not merely because it enabled him to "mark things unknown", but because it showed that things are not always quite as described. "I know no better school to fashion a man's life than incessantly to propose unto him the diversity of so many other men's lives, customs, humours, and fantasies." At the same time Montaigne could not resist his little dig at the traveller's pretence. To be able to mention "the number of paces the Church of Santa Rotunda is in length or breadth", or "to dispute how much longer or broader the face of Nero is as seen in some old ruins of Italy than that which is made for him in monuments elsewhere", was among the incidental advantages of travel which Montaigne indicated.

Of all the developments which popular book-making has undergone in recent years none is perhaps more noteworthy than the increase in books by or for travellers. Every globe-trotter elects to be a minor Hakluyt, and every country, every county, every town even, seems now to have a dozen or more eager historians. Great changes have occurred since Murray's "Handbooks" were first put upon the market; there is no end to the number of so-called series, from Black's Colour Books, which would generally be better without the colour, to Methuen's Little Guides, which are among the handiest available. Methuen's Little Guides and Macmillan's Highways and Byways series together cover the ground pretty thoroughly on all sides, from the picturesque to the practical.

As though these books were not sufficient to meet the demands of the public, many of the railway and steamship lines themselves issue brochures on the places of interest which they serve. Thus the Belgian State Railways, the Great Western, the London and Brighton, the Great Central, the Elder Dempster, the Orient, and others are all prepared to supply the holiday maker with "literature" of a kind which makes the ordinary book, from the practical point of view, unnecessary. The average tourist wants to know little more about Scandinavia than he can learn from the Orient Line's booklet on Cruises in Norway. And where, as in the case of the Great Central, the country tapped is at once Shakespeare's and Miss Marie Corelli's—the two extremes surely—the literary interest is not confined to the brochure which may be had for the asking. It is in the country itself, which railway enterprise has placed within easiest accessibility. A day in "Shakespeare's country" is now one of the most popular of outings.

Guide books share one advantage in common with the classics: they go on for ever, though not always with the original publisher. Murray's Handbooks have for the last few years been issued by Mr. Stanford; Baedeker's are now controlled in England by Mr. Fisher Unwin. There is as keen a competition between the German and the English guide book as between the German and the English Navy; where Murray originally swept the field, Baedeker elected to follow, until he invaded the British Isles themselves with translations that speedily found their way to the hands of the tourist. Baedeker to-day covers Europe, America, the British Empire, and some parts of Africa and Asia.

There are, of course, many others, such as Grieben's Guide Books, to which Switzerland has just been added—they are published in England by Williams and Norgate—and Darlington's, which generally have a more literary touch than most. In the new edition of Darlington's London, for instance, Mr. E. T. Cook writes on the British Museum, the National Portrait and other galleries. Guide-book rivalry is in the public interest. It means that editors and publishers seize every opportunity to keep the volumes up to date.

Printed for the Proprietors by SPOTTISWOODE & CO. LTD., 5 New-street Square, E.C., and Published by REGINALD WEBSTER PAGE, at the Office, 10 King Street, Covent Garden, in the Parish of St. Paul, in the County of London.—*Saturday, 17 July, 1909.*

THE

SATURDAY REVIEW

OF

POLITICS, LITERATURE, SCIENCE, AND ART.

No. 2,804 Vol. 108. 24 July 1909. [REGISTERED AS A NEWSPAPER.] 6*d*.

CONTENTS.

NOTES OF THE WEEK.

The housebreaker working in guilty haste and confusion has been shown again this week in the Budget debates. After increment, reversion; and here once more, in the name of the community, the Government grabs the property of the man on the same plea—that he has not built it up by "his own brain or muscle". On this line no one who inherits property, whether five pounds or five million, is entitled to hold it. He has not made it by "his own brain or muscle". The community will seize it, and there will be reversion with a vengeance—reversion to simple chaos. Why, the naked barbarian of the paleolithic age with his flints and arrow-heads had as civilised a code of property as this.

But scared by noises in the house, the Government dare not after all act up to this principle of take all you can get hold of. They let a certain amount of their booty slip from their hands. First, they let off from the new duty reversions where the lease ends within thirty years of the date of purchase; and an hour or two later—one of their own band siding against them—they change thirty years into forty. We imagine that had a dozen Ministerialists threatened mutiny the Government would have run the period up to fifty years. If the duty is just, these exemptions, said Mr. Balfour, cannot be just. Logically of course they can't. But it is not logic the Government are after, it is loot.

Then land valuation has been to the fore all the week. There are two schools of opinion in the Liberal party on this. One school is for a policy of Thorough. Mr. Churchill appears to be its headmaster, Mr. Philip Morrell and Mr. Wedgwood—the inevitable Mr. Wedgwood—among its most promising pupils. It is for valuing every rod of land owned by a private individual, now whilst there is a good—or evil—excuse to value it. True, the Government propose to let the owner of agricultural land off lightly under the Budget—so far as the increment, development, and revenue clauses go. Never mind, say the Thorough school, let us none the less take this opportunity to find out what he is worth. We may want to fleece and flay him later. Remember, he is mostly a Tory and has always voted against us.

The other school is either more charitable or more cautious—we incline to think more cautious. It argues that the Government had better not tack a new Domesday Book on to the Budget lest the whole prove too cumbrous. The House of Lords must not be given a decent excuse for tampering with the Budget on the plea that it is a great deal more than a Budget. We note that Mr. C. J. O'Donnell M.P. is dead against adding a Domesday to the seventy-odd clauses of the Budget. But to him Mr. Morrell M.P. tartly retorts that for purposes hereafter it is absolutely necessary to value all the land, every marsh, we suppose, and every mountain-top. If the landowners object to the cost of valuation, why, let the Government do it for them. But we wonder how the British taxpayer would like this arrangement. Mr. Morrell's constituents are even more patient asses than the ordinary taxpayer if they are ready to pay for a State valuation of marshes and mountain-tops that yield them nought in return.

Yesterday there was a City of London meeting in favour of the Budget. Lord Rothschild is not to have it all his own way any longer. The full list of gentlemen who were present in support of the Prime Minister and the Chancellor of the Exchequer is worth reading. We noticed, among the names, these: Sir Henry Norman, Mr. Raymond Asquith, Mr. Hemmerde. So the Liberal party has got some of the City magnates after all.

Mr. Churchill has blundered badly twice this week, both times about the House of Lords. There was his great rhetorical speech about Lord Lansdowne "mincing" the Budget. But all the gas went out of it when it turned out that Lord Lansdowne never mentioned mincing. By the mouth of Mr. Asquith Mr. Churchill shrivelled his Edinburgh speech into a stupid platitude in the House of Commons on Wednesday. The audience at Edinburgh believed that Mr. Churchill was committing one of his audaciously planned "indiscretions" when he told them that if the Lords amended the Budget there would be an appeal to the country. They thought he was "betraying" a Cabinet secret. Now he explains that the speech did not mean there would be an immediate dissolution. But this is as stale as ditch-water.

Who is responsible in the House of Commons for the conduct of the Budget? Mr. Asquith, as we know, is not responsible—it is improper for him to "intervene spasmodically in a highly technical and complex measure" which he has not studied closely. Mr. Lloyd George, as Mr. Balfour says, obviously cannot be always present to conduct his Bill. And now the great law officers of the Crown are declaring they are not paid to do this job at all! "It is not my business", said Sir William Robson warmly on Tuesday night or Wednesday morning, "I am paid to do legal work only, though I am glad to oblige my friends". It comes to this—the only person whose business it is to be present is the Chairman—and he is roundly abused for his pains by the "Daily News".

But this talk about the Attorney- or Solicitor-General only helping the Government with their bills through good nature is nonsense. An Attorney- or Solicitor-General, Liberal or Conservative, helps his Government with their bills because the Prime Minister gave him office. Does Sir William Robson imagine that Mr. Asquith would have allowed him to fill the splendid post of Attorney-General at £7,000 a year and the chance of a still greater post by and bye, on any other understanding? Sir William Robson *is* paid to help with the Government Bills; it is too absurd to pretend otherwise. No Prime Minister who is not a perfect fool will ever offer these highly paid posts to anyone who is not ready to work hard at the ordinary front-bench work. The thing is simply past all dispute.

By the way, talking of great Law Officers, is the Lord Advocate an "exceptional monarch" in the Government? He has been preaching the doctrine that the land apart from the buildings belongs to the People. Therefore, he says, the People have a right to appropriate a part of the value of the land. Lord Crewe was shy and adroit when asked in the House of Lords whether this was the view of the Government. He could not tell what was the Government's view on this abstract question—Governments have no time for abstractions. We suspect that the Lord Advocate has been doing a little electioneering in the wilds of Scotland "on his own".

The affair of honour in the House of Commons last week ended this week in apologies all round. Everything has been expunged. It is a good ending to what for a little while looked quite a thorny affair. But Liberals cannot crow after all, for at the last moment of the incident a fearful Liberal offender was dragged in and he too had to apologise! Mr. Wilson, M.P. for South S. Pancras, worn down, poor man, by an eighteen-hour sitting, did a "sketch" for the "Daily News" accusing the Chairman of Ways and Means of at least discourtesy to Mr. Lloyd George. It is monstrous for the Government to keep irritated sketch-writers up till five and six in the morning. Has not the Chancellor of the Exchequer himself journalised in the "Manchester Guardian" in past times? He must know what nerve-racking work it is.

If wit is, as Selden said, "upon the sudden turn", Mr. Harcourt's little speech on the House of Commons bar can scarcely be called witty, seeing he had time to prepare it. Yet one knows not by what other word it can be described. A catchy saying has it that small things amuse small minds. As a fact they please large minds quite as much; and doubtless big men in the House were quite as much tickled as small men by the question of the removal of the bar—that sacred bit of constitutional wood. We like to think of Mr. Harcourt, sweet and cool as George Herbert's day, in these scenes of turmoil. He can make us laugh and be happy, whilst his colleagues make us curse. May he float serene to leadership one day!

The Liberals have held their seats in Dumfries and at High Peak, but with their 1906 majority reduced in both places. Save in 1906, High Peak has for many elections past been a near thing, and though disappointed we cannot say we are much surprised at the result. But this is one of the seats that will have to be won at the general election if we are to get a good working majority over Liberals, Labour and Irish. The personal interest no doubt was important at High Peak; Mr. Partington being a bright and clever candidate.

When is a peer interfering in an election not a peer interfering in an election? The Duke of Norfolk writing to say he hoped Mr. Profumo would win High Peak was, according to Mr. Dillon and Mr. Asquith, a peer who interfered; and his letter, the House decided on Tuesday, is to go before the Committee of Privilege. But when Lord Rosebery made a strong party speech at Leith when an election was being fought at Edinburgh—"not very far off", as Mr. Asquith slily admitted—Lord Rosebery was not interfering. Besides, he engaged himself months before to speak—and one must not interfere with contracts! The whole thing, however, is a storm in a teacup. A Conservative said to a friend in the Cabinet the other day, "I see you are in trouble again. There seems to be a storm in a teacup over your business". "Yes", replied the Minister, "but I'm not sure whether I'm the storm or the teacup." This is very much the position of peers accused of this terrible offence.

A statue to Sir Wilfrid Lawson on the Embankment was unveiled by Mr. Asquith on Tuesday. The Embankment is a chosen spot for raising statues to unlikely men. They are all ugly: John Stuart Mill, in his well-known attitude of sitting on a pin, Brunel, Forster, Raikes; and there is a medallion of Fawcett on a fountain, which would be an appropriate enough memorial for Sir Wilfrid Lawson, but does not seem so apposite for Fawcett. The statue is intended to commemorate Sir Wilfrid's apostolate on behalf of Local Option. But the effective martyr to that cause was Sir William Harcourt, as both Mr. Asquith and Mr. Lewis Harcourt may have recalled to each other. Mr. Asquith, thinking probably of the Licensing Bill, denied that Sir Wilfrid was the advocate of lost causes. His causes were all making headway, he said; but the Government has done singularly little to propitiate his manes in the matter of Local Option. There was little Local Option and much bureaucracy in this Government's Licensing Bill.

The 29th of this month was to be given to a discussion in the House of Commons of how Mr. Birrell earns his salary, an attractive subject for debate; but Mr. Birrell's friends got this thing done suddenly and unexpectedly last Wednesday, as if it were a cattle drive or a visit from Dublin Castle to Cardinal Logue for directions in the "government" of Ireland. The Nationalists had been taken into confidence in the tactics, but the Irish Unionists had been left in ignorance, most of them away, so that the record of Mr. Birrell's moonlit year went through without any criticism beyond a sham challenge by a few of "the boys" to show their village publicans that they were looking after "the cause". The urbanity of Mr. Long's protest left him helpless against the manœuvre, and there was not one to point out the fact that the taxpayer would gain greatly by giving Mr. Birrell his salary for avoiding Ireland in her "government".

Of course there is a recent fall in the criminal statistics of Ireland, as admitted by Mr. Long in the House on Wednesday; but it is most distinctly not due to the Government. It coincides exactly with the recent discovery of the bishops that crime was contrary to the Ten Commandments. Even after they "gave Birrell a chance and got the money for the new Universities", cattle driving was not stopped until several of the hierarchy announced that it was "immoral", and the Irish legislators were left to find some other kind of crime to cultivate as a "national policy". They have not yet hit on any other kind of crime to cultivate, but they have threatened to do so unless Mr. Birrell puts enough of the League into the new Land Bill.

Sir Edward Grey's speech on the Foreign Office Vote was statesmanship of a high order—the pity is such speeches are thrown away when addressed to canaille that would bespatter a foreign sovereign coming here as the guest of the King. Sir Edward even reasoned with these people, and his reasoning will tell with the country generally. "It is not our business even to know what passes in the internal affairs of other countries where we have no treaty rights." "To criticise the internal administration of a foreign country or to justify it is almost equally offensive to the country concerned." Obviously (to any person with any knowledge of affairs). Also, if interference is justifiable ever, it can only be when we are prepared to back our advice with force; the last thing any of these Tsar-baiters desire. If their meddling landed us in a war, how they would run behind a bushel or any other hiding-place!

On Wednesday Lord Curzon made a speech to the Turkish Parliamentary delegates who are now touring the country. They are getting a good reception and being handsomely entertained, as the representatives of every responsible foreign body should be. Perhaps, however, that is not a very happy word for the Turkish Parliament, for in fact it is not responsible, since it has not power. The power is with the military authorities in Turkey and with them only. They are governing the country, and the show of a Parliament makes it easier for them to do it. There was real humour in Lord Curzon's warning that they had to "retain the loyalty of their valiant army". The delegates must have smiled grimly at this, knowing that the question is whether the valiant army will retain them.

The Shah has had to go. Wanting a Shah they could control to their own ends, the revolutionaries have put his small son on the throne. The Nationalists have shown some energy and initiative since they entered Teheran, and it may be that if the Persians will only cease from troubling there need be little fear of foreign intervention. Persia now has popular government, whatever that may be; the Persian Cossacks and the rest have for the moment all fallen into line with the triumphant revolutionists. It is really a pity Persia could not be left alone to muddle along until the welter threw up a big man who could take the country over and compel respect. That is the only government for Persia and its likes. But no European politician has the courage to advise it.

M. Clemenceau, who has survived so many assaults that ought to have driven him from office, has succumbed at last to the attack of M. Delcassé. When M. Delcassé carried his motion for the appointment of a Commission to inquire into the state of the French Navy, and was appointed its President, it might have been foreseen that danger to the Ministry was imminent. Yet the crisis came suddenly and unexpectedly, and, brilliantly though M. Delcassé conducted his operations, it was really because M. Clemenceau lost his head that M. Delcassé accomplished his long-deferred revenge for his sacrifice to the Kaiser.

It was a bêtise of the worst kind for M. Clemenceau to reply as he did to M. Delcassé's accusations that he was personally responsible for the present state of the Navy. M. Delcassé simply overwhelmed him by a review of the foreign policy of France while M. Delcassé was Foreign Minister. M. Clemenceau might have got through the debate safely if his hatred of M. Delcassé had not got the better of him. But he was drawn; and when he foolishly made it the issue whether France had been humiliated at Algeciras or when M. Delcassé was dismissed at the dictation of Germany, what else could the Chamber do than back up M. Delcassé and give the vote which put M. Clemenceau out of office?

The Bill for registering the decisions of the South African Union Convention, which will come up for second reading in the Lords on Monday, should not escape critical examination. If it cannot be amended, at least it should not be rushed through on a torrent of rhetoric which there is nothing in the history of South Africa to justify. The South Africans only agree to do now what they might have done with profit to themselves and the Empire when Lord Carnarvon attempted to give them a lead and was roundly abused for his pains. On one point the Imperial Government, in the preliminary negotiations with the delegates, have secured a not unimportant change. The interests of Asiatics are not to be left to the tender mercies of the provincial councils, but are to be in the control of the Governor-General. With the native question the Imperial authorities are not likely to interfere: the future of the black, provided he be treated humanely, must be left in South African hands.

It appears that the Americans cannot get all the taxes they want and at the same time keep the President's promise to "revise downward". This makes the President in a way responsible for the balance, and he is fighting for an income tax; but the lawyers hold that it cannot be imposed in the ordinary way, and so the President is trying to impose it through the business concerns. The objections are naturally strong, based on the dollar and also on the national disgrace of possibly finding the tax uncollectible. They had an income tax before, but found that the national sense of truth made it nearly unproductive. That was long ago, when the new eagle was doubly inflated with the spirit of George Washington; and there is fear that the substituted spirit of Wall Street may not be more flattering to the national honour. Is it not curious that the people who produced George Washington should be so free from truth as to make an income tax uncollectible among them?

The Lord Chancellor's troubles are greater than he can bear in the matter of appointing Justices of the Peace. One can tell from his passionate utterance what he has had to put up with from the efforts of the Liberal wirepullers to get their own men appointed. Lord Loreburn has done what no other Liberal Chancellor has dared to do before; he has spoken the truth about his own side. Liberals are just as bad as Conservatives, he says, and they want their own men appointed, whether they are fit or not. He wants to be saved from his friends; and a Royal Commission is to be appointed to find out a way to do it. The greatest trouble is in the boroughs. Lord Loreburn and the Lords-Lieutenants would get on well enough together. He admits they are fair about politics. When Lord Halsbury speaks of "political partisans" he means Liberals—the Mayors of boroughs in this case. And, strange to say, Lord Loreburn means exactly the same thing.

Lawyers expect a slump in divorce under the new judge, on the ground that he will attach less weight to women's pleas of cruelty, narrowing the basis of actionable activity under his jurisdiction. No doubt there are limits within which the judge may influence the volume of "business", but any prospect of a fall in briefs is likely to be exaggerated by those who take the fees, and there appears to be no sign of a slump in the activities that lead to the Divorce Court. A narrowing of the pleas might stimulate the activities, still securing equilibrium for the lawyers. On the whole we do not expect an unemployment problem.

From the account given by the Home Secretary of the doings of the suffragist women in Holloway they are turning their prison into a lunatic asylum. Their latest plan for getting the vote is to kick and bite the female warders and to throw their food out of the cell windows. It is quite a common symptom of confirmed lunacy for patients to refuse food and try to starve themselves to death. Hysterical women in prison often break out and smash things; more often, indeed, than men do. But we never heard that they were discharged because they were giving the warders too much trouble. The doctors and the governor manage the matter amongst them. Why should they not do it with the suffragist women? They would, but the Home Secretary interferes and the women are discharged without serving their sentences. The magistrates might as well dismiss the cases against them, if they can get out of prison by making themselves as great a nuisance inside as they are outside.

The appointment of Mr. Kenyon, Assistant Keeper of the Manuscripts, to succeed to Sir E. Maunde Thompson as Director of the British Museum is the best that could have been made. There may from time to time be justification for taking a man from without the Museum, for a good second in command is not always fit to command in chief. But when a fit man can be found on the staff he ought to be preferred to a stranger. This time a fit man could be found and has been appointed. Mr. Kenyon has a searching task before him—it is not a joke to draw Sir E. Maunde Thompson's bow—but we fancy he will be equal to it. Honesty compels one to admit that satisfaction at Mr. Kenyon's appointment is partly relief from fear of terrible things that might have happened.

Father Tyrrell was without a doubt one of the true intellectuals of the Roman Church in this country, and though one cannot place him on a level with Newman he was a bold theological thinker and an impressive writer. With the Jesuits he always got on well; but his relations with his Hierarchy were never altogether friendly. With many of the views that he put forward in his later writings Anglicans must necessarily be in sympathy. This position was practically indistinguishable from Febronianism. It was anti-curia. It was scandalous that he was denied Christian burial: perhaps, as in the case of Mivart, the omission will be rectified in years to come.

Mr. Latham, the first flyer to attempt the Channel, failed; Captain Webb, the first swimmer, succeeded. But the future story may be different. The interest has almost died out about Channel swimming, and it has only just begun about flying. Either Mr. Latham or M. Bleriot may cross long before either Holbein or Woolf succeeds. All sorts of reasons might be given why the swimmers may fail; but there is no particular reason why a flyer should not get over the Channel. The distance is not greater than has already been done; and the weather may be as good for flying the Channel as on the land. It is quite likely there may be many Channel fliers when the swimmers have given up in despair. Mr. Latham's experience shows it is not so dangerous to flutter into the sea as on to the land; and the sensationalism will not be so stimulating in any future attempt as it was in Mr. Latham's first adventure.

Even the man that had no soul for ships could hardly help expanding to the magnificent effect off Southend. Him that has the soul this sight must have carried straight away into the Navy, making him a sailor if a boy, regretful that he is not a sailor if a man. Really, one need not regret the wooden walls. This arc of ironclads is so tremendous a sight that its awe makes up easily for loss of grace. More beautiful of course would be a crescent of Nelson's ships, but they would not hit the imagination so hard. There is charm in power. A modern battleship may be an unlovely thing—we do not feel it so ourselves—but multiply it in orderly arrangement and any unloveliness is lost in the magnificence of might.

THE FALL OF M. CLEMENCEAU.

M. CLEMENCEAU will not, after all, have the opportunity of engineering another election. This perhaps will be his bitterest reflection on the results of his huge blunder on Tuesday night. He might by the methods so well known to French officials have secured for himself another lease of office—it would be hardly correct to call it power. That he is not still Prime Minister is due entirely to his own inflammable temper. It would probably not be inaccurate to say that had the debate followed instead of preceded his visit to Carlsbad, he would never have given rein in so ill-advised a manner to his hatred of M. Delcassé. The vote of the Chamber was clearly intended as a rebuke to the Premier rather than as a condemnation of his Cabinet. Unfortunately for M. Clemenceau, the Cabinet decided recently to do away with the scandalous misuse of the proxy system which had become too common among deputies, and, owing to this unfortunate homage paid to the first principles of parliamentary government, M. Clemenceau ceases to be Premier, for scores of his supporters were absent in their constituencies.

A more dramatic illustration of Time's revenges has been rarely known in history. M. Clemenceau was the engineer of M. Delcassé's fall, and caused his second offer of resignation to be accepted. This of course was the real humiliation inflicted on France at that time, and since then everyone has learned how little French support is worth in a European crisis. Therefore even the not over-sensitive patriotism of the Chamber resented the extreme ill-taste of the taunts he directed against the ex-Foreign Minister. It is also, though this is a minor point, rather amusing to find M. Clemenceau describing Algeciras as a humiliation for France. Some of us might perhaps be minded to agree with him, but it is quite contrary to what we have been told by our would-be instructors in this country among pressmen and politicians of both parties. The Chamber took a perfectly correct view of the quarrel, and thus vindicated the reputation of M. Delcassé, who may now, if he be so disposed, rest on his laurels. If he be still desirous of taking a leading part in administration, there is plenty for him to do. Parliamentary government was never more thoroughly exposed as a hollow sham in France than by the course of events during the Clemenceau Ministry, and the rottenness of the administrative system stands confessed. It may well be that the condition of the navy was not the proximate cause of M. Clemenceau's fall, but it may be safely predicted that if an efficient substitute were at hand, or even if scrutin de liste took the place of the existing system, the parliamentary Republic would cease to exist.

The feeling of unrest and dissatisfaction throughout France has been growing during the Clemenceau régime. The advance of the Revolutionary party in every direction is exciting the apprehensions of the bourgeoisie and the peasantry who own land. And these classes have formed the bodyguard of the Republic throughout its existence. They believed it gave them peace and quiet enjoyment of what they possessed. They care little, it is true, about the prestige of their country or the scandals in which the Republic has been plunged time after time. Corruption has been accepted as the inevitable accompaniment of parliamentary government, and forgiven because that system of conducting affairs seemed to disturb least the ordinary current of French middle-class life. But now the existing régime is losing even that excuse for its continuance. It cannot even ensure the ordinary necessities of civilised life to its supporters, and now it has just been brought home to the French people that they have no navy worthy of the name, and that government by deputies means not only humiliation abroad but insecurity at home.

Under M. Clemenceau the Radical-Socialist group have had a fair opportunity of showing how they can conduct the business of the country. The result is not encouraging for the ordinary Frenchman who has no ambitions and only asks to be let alone to enjoy life. Strikes and riots have followed one another with alarming frequency, and anything in the nature of courageous repression has been always followed by some unnecessary surrender on the part of the Ministry which has sterilised any good effect their momentary firmness might have had.

A brief recapitulation will show the state of France during the last four years. The General Election, engineered by M. Clemenceau while Minister of the Interior with incomparable skill, took place amid scenes of riot and industrial disturbances. Paris was filled with troops, and a Monarchist conspiracy had to be invented to help Republican candidates. In October 1906 M. Clemenceau became Prime Minister, and the ejection of bishops and curés throughout the country led to religious riots. In 1907 took place the strike of naval reservists, the dockers' strike at Nantes, and the far more serious revolt of the wine-growers of the Midi. In 1908 occurred the deplorable labour riots at Villeneuve, when three persons were killed and twenty wounded. It may also be remembered that in spite of Government prohibition the public teachers continued to maintain their unions in defiance of authority. There were also riots of medical students in Paris which made a pandemonium on the left bank of the Seine. It is hardly necessary to recall postal strikes, telegraphists' strikes and others which, though failures from the point of view of the promoters, have caused serious dislocation of business and annoyance to society in general.

But beyond these overt acts on the part of revolutionary organisations, there have been grave symptoms of a general decay in the sense of public duty. The budget has been habitually hurried through the Chamber without adequate discussion. The tendency has been to abandon the proper functions of a popular Chamber, and to leave the matter entirely in the hands of the Budget Committee. There is consequently now no proper supervision of public expenditure. This general slackness is further shown by the disposition to pass the most dubious legislation in the Chamber in the hope that it may be rectified when it gets to the Senate. But the Senate has also shown that its members are adepts at shirking their duties. On several occasions Government Bills have been saved by the interposition of M. Clemenceau, who made the matter one of confidence. This was so with the Bill for buying the Chemin de fer de l'Ouest, when the Senate clearly voted against its convictions. The tendency of all popularly elected bodies to pander to the lowest strata of voters has been emphasised by the reduction of the reservists' terms of service, which was passed by the Senate (though under protest), and by the discharge of the recruits before their due time. Amnesty Bills have undone any good wrought by momentary firmness. The gross election scandals and the worse corruption shown in the disposal of the Church property have all helped to weaken confidence in the Republic as a reputable form of government.

The navy scandals have given the coup de grâce to public confidence. True it is not easy to interest the mass of French people in the navy. It only occupies a secondary place in the popular favour; hence neglect and corruption in this case have been more readily condoned when exposed than perhaps they might have been in some other branches of the public service. For many years French naval estimates have been deliberately cut down in order that the money might be devoted to other objects more likely to attract votes. The system is greatly to blame, but M. Pelletan, more than any other individual, is the author of the present feeble condition of the French navy. His policy was deliberately to foster opposition to authority in ships and dockyards and to sacrifice the officers to the men, encouraging mutiny and revolt. The construction of ships has been taken advantage of for purposes of corruption, or at best marked by ineptitude and the lack of any coherent policy. Large ships are approaching completion which will find no docks ready for them. The units of the fleet are distributed not with a view to common action or the defence of the country but in order to please the constituencies. Every port must have a ship or two, so there is no real fleet in being ready and accustomed to work together. One catastrophe after another reveals either treachery and mutiny among the crews or gross faults in construction and management. The following catastrophes have marked the last four years: Explosions of boilers on the "Jules Ferry", the "Chamois", the "Jeanne d'Arc", and the "Descartes"; guns bursting on the "Victor Hugo", the "Couronne", the "Latouche-Tréville"; the loss of the "Sully", "Chanzy", "Jean Bart", "Nive", "Latin", "Farfadet"; the sinking of the "Gymnote", the "Fresnel"; fires on the "Algeciras", "Latouche-Tréville", "Brennus" and "Charles Martel"; the burning of the arsenal at Toulon, and, finally, the explosion on the "Jena"—an appalling catalogue indeed.

This is the administrative record of the Clemenceau Ministry and its immediate predecessor in administration. It is characteristic that the Chambers have given the ex-Premier votes of confidence again and again for his conduct of affairs. They have dismissed him at last, but on a personal matter. The Chambers have indeed sunk low, and the Republic is hopelessly discredited. Henceforth it will exist on sufferance, only because a man cannot be found to take its place.

LORD LANSDOWNE AND MR. CHURCHILL.

LORD LANSDOWNE is a serious and responsible statesman: is Mr. Winston Churchill? Lord Lansdowne speaks for the majority in the House of Lords: does Mr. Churchill speak for the majority in the House of Commons? These are the questions which men have been asking themselves during the last week. If Mr. Churchill spoke at Edinburgh for the Cabinet of which he is a member, then there must be a General Election within the next few months. Nothing can be clearer than the issue raised by the speeches of Lord Lansdowne and the President of the Board of Trade. Mr. Churchill declared that the Finance Act "must leave the House of Commons in its final form"; in other words, that the House of Lords must not amend it, but must accept it "tel quel", or reject it. It does not matter whether Lord Lansdowne said "mincing" or "wincing", or neither, for his meaning was clear as crystal. The House of Lords is not to be ousted from its place in the Constitution by an aristocratic renegado like Mr. Churchill, nor elbowed into the gutter by an exhausted agitator like Mr. Lloyd George. In calm, even good-humoured, language Lord Lansdowne exposed the revolutionary character of the claim put forward by a chance majority in the House of Commons to lay any kind of imposition it chooses upon a class, or to single out for spoliation any kind of property it dislikes, and at the same time to exclude the second chamber from any interference with its decrees. Anyone who swallows Mr. Churchill's doctrine must be a one-chamber man. If it be possible to exclude the House of Lords from discussing and amending a licensing Bill and a land valuation Bill by merely incorporating them in the Finance Act, then it is plain that the second chamber has ceased to exist in all but name. There is hardly any first-class political measure that does not involve the raising and spending of money. The hatred of the Radicals is to-day centred on landowners and publicans. Who knows when the professional classes will come in for their turn? Suppose it should be decided to subject to special taxation Stock Exchange profits, or barristers' fees? According to the fashionable doctrine, these taxes would go into the Finance Act, and once there would be immune from any action on the part of the House of Lords. In all seriousness, what class and what kind of property is safe under such a régime? And why talk any more about the two branches of the Legislature?

The Prime Minister, when questioned in the House of Commons on Wednesday as to whether the President of the Board of Trade spoke on behalf of the Government, replied: "My right hon. friend informs me that he did not use the language attributed to him in some of these questions. He said nothing of any immediate dissolution. All he intended to convey was that the constitutional conflict between the two Houses must be ultimately settled by the people ". We do not wonder that this answer was received by the Opposition with laughter, for a more impudent prevarication was never resorted to by a public man. What did Mr. Churchill say, according to the report in the "Times"?: "When the Finance Bill leaves the House of Commons, I think you will agree with me that it ought to leave the House of Commons in its final form. No amendments, no excision, no modifying or mutilating will be agreed to by us. We will stand no mincing, and unless Lord Lansdowne and his landlordly friends choose to eat their own mince again, Parliament will be dissolved, and we shall come to you in a moment of high consequence for every cause for which Liberalism has ever fought. See that you do not fail us in that hour ". The utterer of these words has within seventy-two hours the incredible effrontery to inform the House of Commons, by the lips of the Prime Minister, that "he said nothing of any immediate dissolution. All he intended to convey was that the constitutional conflict between the two Houses must be ultimately settled by the people ". After this, who can treat Mr. Winston Churchill seriously, or as other than the pitiful braggart that he is? What demagogue's bluff is this? The really painful part about the business is that Mr. Asquith lends himself, with apparent complacency, to the disgusting farce of Mr. Churchill eating his own mince, hot, not cold, in the very sight of the House of Commons. Can the gossip that one hears about the Prime Minister's apolaustic indifference to aught save the pleasures of society be true? Or are the other rumours true, that he is afraid of Mr. Churchill and Mr. Lloyd George? It is but too obvious that the Prime Minister is not master in his own Cabinet; else he would tell the President of the Board of Trade to eat his own mince or leave the Ministry. It is almost incredible that so clever a man as Mr. Asquith should not see that vulgar boasting and cheap threats followed by mendacious denial merely strengthen the hands of Lord Lansdowne and cover the Government with ridicule. The President of the Board of Trade chalks up "Dissolution" on the wall, and when the Prime Minister appears runs away protesting he didn't do it. We doubt whether any Administration of modern times has ever been placed in a more ludicrous and undignified position. We leave Mr. Churchill to the digestion of his own meal of mince; but we earnestly appeal to the Prime Minister to exert his authority over his younger colleagues, in the interests of public decency, and for the sake of that Cabinet responsibility which is still a political tradition. If Mr. Asquith does not assert himself, he will discover, when it is too late, that power has slipped from him into the hands of a brace of the most unscrupulous demagogues that ever disturbed the destiny of this or any other country.

This is strong language, but already it is acknowledged by men of all parties that government by Messrs. Churchill and Lloyd George is fast drifting to the rapids of confusion and scandal. While the President of the Board of Trade is neglecting his duties at Whitehall and Westminster, in order to trapese about the country delivering inflammatory harangues, the Chancellor of the Exchequer is a tragical exhibition of failure in the House of Commons. He does not understand, and cannot therefore explain, still less manage his own Finance Bill. The relief of Ministerialists is intense when Mr. Haldane takes Mr. Lloyd George's place opposite the box, for if the problem is insoluble, at least "the plain blunt soldier" of the Chancery Bar brings to its handling a cool and trained mind. It is now the common talk of the lobbies and clubs that only urban land is to be valued, and that at the expense of the State; that the duties on undeveloped land and ungotten minerals are to be dropped; and that the licensing duties are to be charged not on annual value but on sales of liquor. This will involve a recasting of the Budget and a new resolution in Committee of Ways and Means. Was there ever a more disgraceful muddle? All this comes of entrusting the finances of the richest country in the world to the management of a triumvirate composed of a provincial attorney, a S. James' Street house-agent, and a lower-division clerk, drunk with socialist theories.

THE THAMES PAGEANT.

LONDON has turned out in great style to show its enthusiasm for "Jack". "Jack" indeed has been as constantly on the lips of the crowd and as large in the halfpenny papers as "Tommy" was in the early days of the South African War. Fortunately neither our Poet Laureate nor anyone else has composed a beggar's song for the sailor. Much, however, of the moral of that famous ditty applies to the patriotism of this week as to the patriotism of 1898. Enthusiastic affection for "Jack", ruling the waves, wooden walls (or iron), hearts of oak, and so forth is all very good and amiable and jolly no doubt. But we want a little business too. Not that sentiment is to be ruled out. It would be a bad sign if the people could take this great assemblage of ships without feeling. He that is not moved at all by such a sight must be very dull, probably very stupid. He had better be moved even to antipathy or indignation than not moved at all. There is always hope for the man who feels wrongly: there is no hope for the man who does not feel anything. Defect on this side there has been none in London. One may dismiss all fear as to interest in naval things declining or of the Navy losing popularity—at least as a show. Some of our peace-at-any-price friends, our anti-armament apostles, must be a little sick to find the people on whose especial behalf they demur to our bloated expenditure on ships utterly wanting in indignation at the sight of so many of these wasteful monsters. The people cannot even be decently indifferent to them. Why did not Mr. Mackarness and his kind go on to the Embankment or the Southend Pier and harangue the crowd on the iniquity of these ships of war they were all gaping at? Surely it was a splendid opportunity lost. Here were all these object-lessons in the waste and wickedness of expenditure on armaments ready to hand, and no use made of them; not a moral pointed. We suppose Mr. Mackarness and the rest did not care to take the risk of a ducking. Very certainly a ducking would have been the fate of anyone who attempted to address the gazing crowds on the enormity of spending money on Dreadnoughts. On these things the instinct of the people is sound enough. They have no use for anti-armament drivel. During the reign of the old Liberal saints they may have been hypnotised and narcotised and generally drugged by the policy of peace and plenty, the gospel of creature comfort which meant all for self and nothing for country, to which all self-sacrifice was unintelligible. But the drug lost its strength and the people regained theirs. The average Englishman is an imperialist—certainly at heart if not always in head. He may not always have a good reason for his faith; he may not know what he means by imperialism when he is enthusiastically proclaiming it; he may be doing very little for it when he is talking very much about it. But the idea is there all the same. It needs to be educated, refined, guided; but it has not to be put in the Englishman from without. Preachers of kosmopolitanism, to whom patriotism is a fallacy, have to start with the difficult operation of extracting from the Englishman the imperialist instinct. This is so difficult that they generally prefer an opiate to the knife, but they know it is no cure. Imperialism is still there, and will recrudesce—as they would say—some time.

As imperialists we have no fear for the Englishman's heart; but we often have for his head. He does not require much stimulus, but he does want much teaching. We want him to learn, perhaps we should rather say to realise, that he will help the empire much more by perceiving its weak points than by insisting on its bigness; that he will not keep up the fleet by shouting patriotic songs; that he should have an intelligent idea of the part the Navy has to play for the empire. He should also have some knowledge of the money side of the matter; what he gets for the large sums spent on ships; what assurance of safety in war and insurance against war. He should know something of the progress of other countries in naval matters, and how we stand to them in naval power and how we ought to stand. Instructed on these heads the man in the street here can be trusted to keep the Government up to the mark in matters of armament. Put before the country a single clear issue as to armaments and make it understood, and we have no doubt that the country will always decide in favour of the larger policy. We believe it would cheerfully vote many millions more for the Navy than any Government has yet asked. If the public had any means of voting on a naval issue by itself, it would be seen that the little-navy men were a negligible handful. But naval expenditure for the ordinary voter is mixed up with all the other items. He sees that the total amount of expenditure is large and taxes high; so he grumbles, though he has been calling loudly for an increased Navy. But all who this week have been swelling with pride at the magnificence of our warships—and the magnificence of their spectacle could hardly be exceeded—must be willing to pay for them, and willing always to be paying more. If a man believes in great armaments, he should be chary of grumbling about high taxation. Warships cannot be made cheaply and well. No care in administration, no finesse of economy, can prevent the bill for a big fleet being a very stiff one. We ought to pay it when presented not with resignation but with zest, knowing that for once we are getting full value for our money. We believe the great majority of Englishmen of all classes alike would pay cheerfully enough if they realised what ships cost and that it was ships they were paying for.

TSAR-TEASING.

WHERE are the people's steamboats? We do not know; and Sir J. W. Benn's little band of hardy demonstrators, with the assistance of one banner at least per man, in Trafalgar Square last Sunday afternoon seemed to be unable to find them. Neither has the "Morning Leader's" pathetic poster so far led to their discovery. It is unfortunate that they should have disappeared at this particular moment, as Mr. Bernard Shaw might have found them very useful for a naval demonstration against the potentate who is to visit our shores. Displays in Trafalgar Square have become a little stale, but the spectacle of Mr. Shaw mounted upon the conning-tower of the "King Alfred" or the "William Caxton", with the indignant Commons of England manning the cabin hatchway, and leading the attack upon the port quarter of the "Standart", would be an interesting, and possibly an amusing, novelty. When kings behave in England as the Tsar behaves in Russia we either cut their heads off, according to Mr. Shaw, or replace them by their nearest well-behaved relative. The Government have apparently found the problem of the disposal of Mr. Shaw a more difficult one. Mr. Shaw minus his head is inconceivable and plus his head he is unreplaceable. Perhaps they hope to kill him with ridicule by allowing him to demonstrate to his heart's content on dry land in the absence of the "Richard Whittington", "or other suitable vessel", as the shipping advertisements say. Continental papers please note. We know the value of our members of Parliament, especially of those who are likely to take part in Mr. Shaw's demonstration, but our knowledge has not permeated abroad so far as could be wished, except among certain Continental hotel-keepers, for value not received, and among the more astute of the Bengali leaders. Foreigners may not always bear in mind that these parliamentary heroes find their chief pleasure in demonstrating against anything and everything, from the Black Eagle of Russia to the Brown Dog of Battersea. They may not know any more about the internal politics of Russia than about vivisection, but that is a matter of indifference to them. Neither do they care whether the grievance under discussion is one which can be settled by talking or one which can only be remedied by force of arms. Such a consideration must necessarily be immaterial to persons for whom speech is delirium and war is anathema. In the midst of their "raptures of platonic lashings" they do not pause to consider what their feelings would be if some of the less respectable members of the Duma, accompanied by a motley collection of mouzhiks and presided over by a Slavonic avatar of Mr. Shaw, met in the Mariinskii Square in S. Petersburg to pass fulminatory resolutions on some of the misdoings of the Labour Party. Probably they would say that such proceedings were beneath contempt, and the retort of the Russians would be obvious. But at least the Russian meeting would be exempt from the reproach of scandalous bad manners. Neither, we fancy, would those who participated in the Russian demonstration cast abuse upon English administration in Ireland, Egypt, and India, as Mr. Shaw does so unctuously. We do not wish to draw any "disastrous and dishonourable inference" (the words are Mr. Shaw's) from this—such wild talk has become so common among a certain class of Englishmen that it scarcely calls for comment and attracts no one's attention, either here or abroad—but when such reckless statements are applied to the internal affairs of a friendly nation the matter becomes more serious. Perhaps some day, under stress of misfortune it may be, this nation may discover that foreign politics are not suitable for discussion by transfigured provincial labourers. Meanwhile it would be as well if Mr. Shaw and his friends would counter-demonstrate, if they must do so, by showing that a democracy goaded by socialists is superior to an autocracy tempered by chinovniks at least in good manners and in common-sense.

Anyone who knows the Tsar or even anything about him can hardly help being tickled, in the midst of his disgust, at this making of him a bogey-man. It is so delightfully childish; so naïvely of the nursery. Mr. Shaw and his company must have an ogre, a giant that goes about devouring little children. Why don't they make a terrific guy and set it up in the Square? It would be a great draw; too much for their liking, perhaps, for none would trouble to listen to them when he had a guy to look at. All this lifting-up of hands in horror at the Tsar is nothing but the nursery alarm at Fee-Fo-Fum, with Mr. Shaw as the nursemaid telling the awful story. Were there no bogey-man, no Tsar, to put up for cockshy, these fiery avengers would not come near Trafalgar Square, though things were done in Russia ten times as bad as the horrors they invent to deck their speeches. One word of advice. By making themselves a nuisance in this way Mr. Shaw and his company merely force one to appreciate the advantage of a Government that would be able to suppress them summarily, and would certainly do it, over a Government like ours that would like to but is afraid! Is that the lesson they want to teach?

THE COUNTY COURTS JOKE.

WE have become accustomed to queer performances on the part of the present Government, and the introduction of the County Courts Bill, 1909, is one of the queerest. A committee, under the presidency of Lord Gorell, sat for a long period to consider the question of county court jurisdiction and the relation of the county courts to the High Court. It duly made its report to the effect that the true solution of the problem with regard to the disposal of High Court business in the provinces, the chief problem at issue, was the remodelling of the circuit system so as to concentrate the civil work in centres, and the allowance of more time and the making of more convenient arrangements for dealing with such business. The promoters of the present Bill have merely ignored this recommendation, presumably because it did not suit the views which they had evolved for themselves, just as they brushed aside Mr. Justice Hamilton's findings in the Swansea School case. The Government, moreover, does not seem to have much respect for committees. The other day, it will be remembered, certain noble lords were appointed to sit upon the Censor, and the next morning we were told that the same noble lords had been transferred to a committee to inquire into the state of business in the King's Bench Division. Obviously persons who are fitted to examine Mr. Redford's vagaries are equally fitted to scrutinise the Middlesex Special Jury List. The proposals embodied in the County Courts Bill are those which are described by the majority of Lord Gorell's committee as "dangerous" unless they are preceded by the other reforms which the committee recommends. They involve the giving of unlimited jurisdiction in common-law actions to the county courts, subject to an absolute power of removal on the application of the defendant, except in actions of ejectment or where the title to hereditaments, tolls, fair or markets is in question, or for libel, slander, seduction or breach of promise of marriage. The only reason given by the Lord Chancellor for these exceptions is that they form "a class of cases which has always been considered unsuitable for trial in county courts". This lucid description applies equally to all the other actions which it is now proposed to fling into the county court. The reason given by Lord Gorell's committee for these exceptions, in which they concurred, is no better. Libel, slander, seduction and breach of promise, they declare, "form a class by themselves", and the county courts, if they had to try them, "might find themselves inundated by petty squabbles between quarrelsome neighbours". It would puzzle the most acute logician to find any connecting link between libel and breach of promise of marriage, and we have not hitherto regarded an action for seduction as a "petty squabble between quarrelsome neighbours". We imagined it generally arose from an excess of neighbourly affection. The committee was no more fortunate in its reason for excluding actions relating to tolls, markets or franchises. They are "as a rule of so much importance and generally take so much time". In Heaven's name, are they of more importance and do they take more time than a heavy commercial cause in which thousands of pounds are involved? Yet the pundits on the county court bench are thought good enough to try that.

A still more disagreeable feature of the Bill is the effect it may have on the status of the judiciary in this country. The chief pride of the English judicial system has generally been considered to be the dispensing of justice by a trained body of lawyers of high standing, who are practically irremovable and therefore independent of the favours or frowns of those in power. It is an extraordinary thing that the party which has owed most to the independence of the judicial bench in past times should be so anxious to reduce its dignity and influence. Our legal proceedings are, it seems, to be submitted to a hierarchy ranging from the High Court judge to the county court registrar, who may or may not have sufficient judicial capacity to try cases involving less than five pounds. Later on, perhaps, room will be found for the usher (limited to two pounds) and the charwoman, entrusted with litigation up to the amount of her weekly wage, say ten shillings. And this glorious company is not even to be entirely permanent and irremovable (though irremovability might add political lustre even to a charwoman). There are to be not more than five assistant judges, appointed for such time as the Lord Chancellor may authorise, at such remuneration as the Treasury may allow. They are to step up from the Bar to enjoy their brief judicial reign, and then step down again and address the bench on which they have just been sitting. We ought to be thankful that except in the Westminster County Court of Middlesex they are not to practise as barristers in the district in which they are sitting as judges. But there is nothing to prevent their practising next door. Even the universally reprobated system of appointing temporary deputies is encouraged. They are to be remunerated, on the recommendation of the Lord Chancellor, out of moneys provided by Parliament, instead of looking to the judge, whose place they take, for their hard-earned guinea. It is evident, therefore, that a large stock of judicial and non-judicial talent is placed at the service of litigants by the Bill. We may fairly compare its promoters to the enterprising salesman not many miles from the Law Courts and the House of Lords who "begs respectfully to inform his customers that in future they can have their fish or potatoes fried either in oil or in dripping".

THE CITY.

THE dullness of ditch-water would be sparkling compared with the utter stagnation on the Stock Exchange during the past week, particularly in the African mining markets, the Kaffir Circus and the Jungle. Americans have been firm, but not sensational, Union Pacifics at last passing the 200 limit, and Steel Commons remaining at 72. Canadian Pacifics have touched 192, their record price. The Canadians imitate the Americans in many things, particularly in finance. But the large importation of Scotsmen has dashed the national character with caution; so that the Canadians are not such wild speculators as Yankees. Accordingly Canada did not suffer so much last year as the United States, and the return of good business has been quicker. Cobalt is to the production of silver what the Witwatersrand is to the production of gold. The approximate output of silver by the Cobalt camp is 2,000,000 oz. per month, and it is estimated that the total output for the year will be between 25,000,000 and 30,000,000 oz., which is rather less gold than the Rand produces. The value of the ore ranges from 100 oz. to 8000 oz. of silver per ton, and the charges of treatment and transportation from £3 to £5 per ton. The La Rose Consolidated Mines Company (incorporated under the laws of Maine, U.S.A.) has a capital of £1,500,000, in shares of $5 or £1. It is a combination of La Rose Mines, Lawson Mine, University Mines, and Violet Mining Company, all mining companies in the Cobalt district, and is already earning dividends. In the last quarter of 1908 a dividend of 3 per cent. was distributed, and this year 6 per cent. in dividends and 2 per cent. bonus have been distributed, making 8 per cent. in six months. La Rose Consolidated are about to be dealt in on the London Stock Exchange, and would seem to be a respectable mining speculation in its infancy. Now is, of course, the time to buy good Kaffir shares, when markets are quiet; but those who want to make money in September must buy with discrimination. City Deeps at 4¼ are undoubtedly cheap, as are Knight's Witwatersrand at the same price, and Nourse, Crown Mines, and Durban Deeps at present figures. All these shares should be bought now and held for a few months for a rise in capital value. In the Rhodesian market the share to buy is Rhodesian Copper at 9s.; they are pretty sure to go to £1 before the end of the year, when the Tanganyika railway reaches them. But for the moment the mining market for the speculator is the Mexican and Alaskan. Kaffirs and West Africans are suffering from over-speculation, but nobody has as yet touched these out-of-the-way markets. For the past year we have been advising our readers to buy Alaska Treadwell, and now they have suddenly risen from 4⅞ to 6. But an even better share to buy is Alaska Mexican at 3½. This mine is earning 75 per cent. profit on its capital, so that at 3 it would yield 27 per cent. It is, however, not dividing up to the hilt at present, but paying about 14 per cent. at its present price. The share of a mine which divides 75 per cent. is certainly worth 5, at which figure it yields 15 per cent., whereas most good mines return between 8 and 10 per cent. The Alaska Mexican has a life of at least thirty years, and therefore a yield of 15 per cent. is good. We should say these shares will touch £4 within the next three months, and £5 by Christmas. Of course these fine calculations and this talk of sinking fund are thrown away on the average patron of the mining markets, for he is not an investor, but a speculator. But whether as investment or gamble, Alaska Mexicans are the thing, at anything under 3½. National Minerals Corporation shares were 13s. the last time we heard of them. A great deal depends on the value of their patent for the treatment of refractory ore; it may beat the Murex Magnetic out of the field; but then it may not.

The sensation in foreign rails has been the rise of Mexican Southerns to 88.

The Commonwealth Oil Corporation, Ltd., formed in 1905 for the purpose of developing deposits of oil shale in the Wolgan and Capertee Valleys in New South Wales, invites subscriptions for £300,000 6 per cent. Convertible Debentures. The Cincinnati Gas Transportation Company offers for sale, through the London and County Banking Co., Ltd., $3,000,000 First Mortgage 25-year 5 per cent. Gold Bonds at 97½ per cent.

INSURANCE: CLERGY MUTUAL.

THE eightieth annual report of the Clergy Mutual Assurance Society was presented to the assured members on Tuesday. As usual it is a very good one and helps to explain how it is that the policies of the Clergy Mutual are among the very best that can be obtained. The society is one of those which employ no agents and pay no commission for the introduction of business. The adoption of this plan has two consequences: first that the expenses of management are at a low rate, and second that the amount of new business transacted each year is very small. The Clergy Mutual, however, issues a larger amount of new assurances than any of the other non-commission-paying offices, and this in spite of the fact that to be eligible for with-profit policies it is necessary to be a clergyman of the Church of England or Ireland or of the Established Church of Scotland, or in some way related to one. The small new business is immaterial to the existing policyholders of the Society, and is sufficient to maintain a small but steady increase in the premium income, as well as regular additions to the funds. The expenditure is only 7 per cent. of the premium income, and as the average premiums of the Clergy Mutual are at an extremely low rate, the economy of management is even better than it appears to be. The main reason for regretting the small amount of new business done each year is that people who could, to their own advantage, assure in the Clergy Mutual must be taking policies elsewhere. The premium income of the Society is only £264,000, and it is absurd to suppose that the clergy and their relations are not paying between them a vastly larger sum than this. It is an indubitable fact that a great many of the policies issued by this society are the best that can be obtained; the premiums are low, the bonuses are large; and it is foolish for people who are qualified for membership to effect their assurance elsewhere.

When the sources of surplus are analysed they are seen to be large. The provision for future expenses exceeds the actual expenditure by 8 per cent. of the premium income, and the rate of interest earned exceeds by £1 6s. per cent. per annum of the funds the rate necessary to meet the liabilities, which are valued on a 2½ per cent. basis. There is a further source of surplus due to favourable mortality: the claims by death last year amounted to £259,000, which is £71,000 less than the amount which would have had to be paid had the mortality occurred in accordance with the British Offices Table of Mortality. This means that money which in other circumstances must have been paid away remains in the possession of the society, earning interest; it means also that a larger number of premiums was received than would otherwise have been the case.

Especially in a mutual society like this, the policyholders reap the full benefit of these large contributions to surplus or bonuses. A life office is merely the machinery which enables people to co-operate for their common good. This co-operation enables two things to be done which people cannot accomplish individually. They obtain compound interest upon their savings, and they pay the average cost of premature death in such cases as their own. Clearly it would be foolish for a lot of healthy people to combine with a lot of unhealthy people on equal terms when payment out of a common fund at death is a feature of the transaction. The unhealthy ones would gain and the healthy ones would lose. It is better for the healthy ones to associate among themselves. Statistics show that the longevity of the clergy is greater than among people in general; manifestly, therefore, the most sensible thing for the clergy to do is to combine among themselves, take advantage of the average long life which prevails among them, and thus secure their life assurance on the best possible terms. The Clergy Mutual Society is the mechanism by means of which this advantageous result can be accomplished. Financially it is among the strongest life offices in existence. For profitableness of results to the policyholders it has few, if any, equals; and the conditions of its policies in regard to surrender values of various kinds are of an exceptionally liberal character. The clergy as a class have great need of life assurance and are the least able to afford the serious loss of money which results from taking a bad or indifferent policy when in their own society they could obtain a good one. Every clergyman must know of the existence of the Clergy Mutual Society, and when approached by the agent of any other office he should at least make a point of ascertaining what the Clergy Mutual can do for him, since it is probable in the extreme that he will gain if he assures with this society, and will lose if he yields to the persuasion of an agent.

THE GREAT BORDEAUX WINES.

(Concluding article.)

IV.—CHÂTEAU LAFITE.

IT is not perhaps an easy matter to determine which is intrinsically the best or finest of the three great "crus" of the Médoc. Of late years Château Margaux has frequently commanded the highest price; but they vary from time to time, and very many an old vintage of Château Lafite will be better appreciated than its rivals; for the quality of the wine depends upon how it has been treated after it has left home. It may, however, be said that Château Lafite is better known in England, at least to the general public; for the estate has belonged for over forty years to members of the great house of Rothschild, who are perhaps more in touch with England and things English than are French country gentlemen or even great Savoyard bankers. It may be argued that "good wine needs no bush", but still the fact remains that the reputation of a vintage is made by collateral circumstances.

Château Lafite was before the Revolution the property of a family who emigrated and was sold as national property in 1793 for £48,000. In 1818 its then owners resold it for £40,000. By 1868, when the property was purchased by Baron James de Rothschild, its value had risen to £180,000. It now belongs to his heirs, Barons Gustave, Edmond and Edouard de Rothschild. Since 1906 "Rothschild" has been added to the name on the labels, the corks, and the cases, whilst the date of the year was put on for the first time in 1875. The château cannot boast of any special kind of architecture. It is a fine house built in the style which prevailed in the middle of the eighteenth century. It lies not far from the main road which leads to Vertheuil and Lesparre, and thence on to Montalivet-les-Bains, Soulac-les-Bains, and Amélie-les-Bains, on the Atlantic sea-coast. The gates of the domain are a couple of miles from Pauillac, and are reached after Château-Mouton-d'Armailhaig and Château-Mouton-Rothschild, two "deuxièmes-crus" of no mean order, have been passed. It is very easily reached either by the Chemin-de-fer du Médoc or by the steamer which connects Pauillac with Bordeaux and thence with Charing Cross in twenty-four hours. It is well worth while making the river journey with anyone who is interested in the wine trade and who is able to point out the different vineyards as he passes them. It is true that Château Beychevelle is not a "premier cru"; still it is amongst the best wines of the Médoc, and the castle may be seen as we approach Pauillac. Its name is derived from its robber-owner who used in the fifteenth century to compel every vessel that passed by to lower sail (baisser-voile) and then to levy toll. Perhaps in memory of this a well-known English wine merchant used to take off his hat as he passed by each noted "cru". Château Lafite lies rather lower down, not far from the riverside, and may be seen, but only after Pauillac has been passed. The vineyard is split up into three parts. Most of it surrounds the château. There is a fine portion of Château Lahte in S. Estephe, whilst a third portion is situated on the tableland of Carruades, whose crop is almost as valuable as that of the château itself. It sells for 25 per cent. less than the "grand vin". There is not much difference between the methods adopted here and at Château Latour. The plants used are the same, Cabernet Sauvignon predominating over the others. There are some five thousand separate vines to the acre planted three feet one from another and not rising more than three feet from the ground. The branches are trained to rise about a foot from the soil, and are kept in their place by either strips of wood attached horizontally to the stand or by the wire which is gradually taking their place. As the leaves are also trained, the vineyard looks severely regular when seen from a distance. The phylloxera gave the same amount of trouble here as it did elsewhere in the Médoc, and it has been necessary to adopt the same precautions. There has not been much grafting at Château Lahte, and what has been done in this direction has been so gradual that its effect is scarcely perceptible. Spraying has, however, been largely used, so that it has been possible in most cases to preserve the old plants which gave Château Lafite its world-wide reputation in the past. The soil is carefully prepared and renewed every year, the plants are carefully examined one by one, and the greatest trouble is taken to secure that the grapes are each one of them up to the mark. It may well be said that each separate bunch is scrutinised so that no grape may be taken to the Chaix that is in any way defective. In the same way the bouquet is perfectly natural and proceeds from the adoption of the same precautions to preserve the yeast which are adopted at the leading vineyards in the Médoc. No strange substance is added; there may be differences between one year and another, but they arise from such natural causes as the weather during the spring and summer months, but especially when the vintage approaches and whilst it is going on.

There can be no good in repeating what has already been said with regard to the vintage itself. The same "vendangeurs" who work during the vintage are chosen, but with the greatest care, and it is a picturesque sight to see the workmen treading the grapes with their feet in the Chaix which stands to the right of the château, so that the visitor can easily assure himself that none of that rough-and-ready modern machinery is used which mars the quality of the finest wine. Prices vary also, but as a general rule they preserve an average of from 2000 to 3000 francs the tun, though in some exceptional cases when the vintage has been particularly good or prices have ruled high as much as 6000 or even 6500 francs have been paid. These prices necessarily rise gradually, as the wine ripens on the spot, where it remains until it is bottled, three years after it has been put into the wood. In 1907 the crop was sold to two great local houses, part for five years to Messrs. Lébégue et Compagnie of Cantenac, whilst Messrs. Le Rosenheim and Sons, of Bordeaux, have bought their portion of the crop down to 1916.

It must be mentioned that no bad year is ever allowed to get into the market as Château Lafite. It is sold, but simply as claret and on the express condition that the purchaser shall not say where it has been grown. On one occasion we visited the Château with an eminent wine merchant who knew the year had been particularly bad and hoped to make a deal in consequence. There was no difficulty about buying the wine. It was not bad, but was certainly not up to the mark, and the steward was ready to sell it at the rate of a franc a bottle. There, however, he stopped. No corks with the trade mark or labels were to be used; in fact the wine was disowned as coming from the vineyard. As the wine merchant did not see what he could do with this nameless claret he broke off the bargain. The reputation of the brand can only gain by such care. None who has bought Château Lafite as such can complain that he has been put off with an inferior article. It may of course happen that in course of time the wine may have found its way into bad cellars or been roughly handled after it has been put into bottle; but this may happen to the very best article.

Much more might be written not only about the great wines of Bordeaux, but on the second, third and fourth growths, which in many cases are almost as good as the four wines already quoted; for the classification was made many years ago, and much has happened to enhance or depreciate the qualities of these various brands since then. Suffice it to say that a "Congrès Vinicole" will be held in September at Bordeaux, when merchants and amateurs will assemble from all parts of the world. Samples will in all probability be accessible to everyone who attends or cares to visit the vineyards at the time. An expert taster is bound to profit, and may secure for himself and for his friends bargains which can only be obtained on the spot.

PLEASURE IN HARNESS.

NO one needs to be told that pleasure cannot be had by taking thought. The caprice of pleasure is a moral commonplace we must not call trite, for it wears too well, but ancient indeed. Hardly a child of ten but has discovered that he is not enjoying the long-planned treat as he expected. Another day—quite a sober occasion—somehow he is enjoying himself hugely—he hardly knows why. When one has reached a subtler age—self-studying, analysing its own feelings—we are often clearly conscious that everything about us is pleasant, no drawbacks, all radiant, and yet we are not touched—there is no zest of enjoyment. Another moment and we know we are enjoying ourselves, and the moment after we are back in the shade. All for no reason in the world. Shade is the most nicely fitting figure. It is exactly as sunshine breaking over a gay garden that wanted only to be lit, and then going again. Butterfly is another good (and old) figure; meant in opprobrium, it is a compliment; and, unlike most compliments, true. The butterfly spoilt in the catching—you cannot beat it for an illustration of the strenuous pursuit of pleasure. Fancy harnessing a butterfly, trying to make him fly in a regular course, on regular days, in cloud as well as in sunshine! And that is just what in London we are always doing in these days, and seem condemned to do. If we don't take pleasure seriously we can't take it at all, and pleasure can't be taken seriously. Happy impasse! You feel in the mood to hear some music; you stroll into the Queen's Hall, and you find you can't get a seat. You have done some hard work in the day; you would like a modest frivol. A second-rate Italian opera will do very well. You go to Covent Garden, sure the article will be supplied there; so it is, but you cannot get a seat. Suddenly it occurs to you to make up a little party of intimates to dine quietly, and then go out somewhere or not, as you may feel inclined. The impromptu touch is part of the charm. You try your friends one after another. Every one of them—you know it well enough, both of you—would much rather dine with you than do what he is going to do; but he has been engaged at least three weeks. He cannot get off. There are three people whom you think should meet one another. You choose a day a week off. One can come but the others cannot. A week later two can come on the day named, but the first man cannot. So you go on exhausting the combinations and permutations of days and friends until you have at last all three fixed up six weeks hence. Who knows what may happen six weeks hence? They may all be dead then. At least one out of any four is likely to be ill six weeks hence. And the hope of no compelling circumstance arising to keep somebody away is small enough.

And this is what we are reduced to. The sensible man who will not make these things a business, knowing they are pleasant only when spontaneous, finds himself knocked out. The fools who organise their recreation with as much care as they do their work have forced everybody else to come into line with them. The first man who insisted on booking a theatre or concert seat more than a week beforehand should have been shut up in an asylum. A week's invitation should be the longest ever given. The idea that this would lead to confusion or congestion is sheer fallacy. There would be just as much time for everything as now, and if nobody gave long invitations, the chance of getting the guests you want would be quite as good as now. But naturally when a man finds he can go to no place of amusement, and get no one to dine with him, unless he does give a long notice, he changes his habits and gives it. Knowing the better, he has to follow the worse. And he does it with perhaps a little vindictiveness in heart. If he must take his pleasures like a solemn game of chess, working out moves any number ahead, he will beat the fools who made him do it at their own game. So next time he books in advance to the utmost limit allowed; and wants to know why he cannot be allowed to book still earlier. And the manager begins to think he will have to allow still earlier bookings, and those who have always booked and invited absurdly early book and invite earlier still. So things get worse and worse until, at any rate from April to August, we find ourselves nothing but items in a programme. And so life becomes simply a thing to be got through; a process; a magic-lantern show, in which every slide is spoilt by the next one coming in upon it too early, till the whole merges into one long blurr. Being but an item in a series, every one is doing several things at the same time: for he is living partly in to-day, partly next week, partly next month, and so does not live on any day at all. Everything is under the curse of the shopman's odious "What next, please?"

And the unhappy man who has had to forsake reason for the programme view of pleasure knows that he is not only kept out of a number of things when he would enjoy them, but it is ten to one he is imposing them on himself when he won't enjoy them. He has got his opera stall, booking in a musical mood long ahead. When the night comes round, six weeks after, he has no desire for opera whatever. He would rather do twenty other things; amongst them, perhaps, stay at home. Let him stay at home then. If he is going alone, he can stay at home, no doubt; but having paid for his seat, he likes to get something for his money. He will hardly be philosophic enough to see, though true, that he will be getting more for his money by staying at home, where he would be, than by going to the opera, where he would not be. Most of us in his position would, like him, go to the opera and grumble. Or he had fixed up a dinner party a long time back. The night comes round. His thoughts are preoccupied; he is feeling extremely unsociable. And the poor chap has to spend his evening labouring to be pleasant to friends he is only wishing he had not been such a fool as to ask for that night.

When they have gone, he thinks what a failure he is; what an ass. He has been a miserable host; he is sure his friends are all saying there must be something wrong with him; they cannot have enjoyed themselves any more than he did. And to think of the enormous trouble he took to get them there! As much thought in planning and selecting, as much care, as about the most serious piece of business he ever did. He took seriously what was not serious; and gets nothing whatever for his pains. He can't even say he has done his duty.

A PAINTER ON PAINTING.

By Laurence Binyon.

Ruskin in England, Baudelaire in France, are conspicuous examples of men of letters who by bold championship and sympathetic interpretation of genius thwarted and decried have done great service to the art of their day. Let it not be forgotten that the opposition against which they contended came not least from professional artists. The many painters who are inclined to argue that none but a man of their own profession has a right to judge works of art might remember this more often. Those who practise an art are particularly liable to wrong judgments about their comrades and contemporaries. None the less, the fact remains that on the essential principles and inner life of an art it is those who are masters of it who speak with most insight and authority; poets on poetry, painters on painting. Of the latter, indeed, few have had the gift of articulate and luminous expression, or the necessary gift of analysis, or the leisure and inclination to write. Among these few Reynolds is eminent. A well-known scholar, M. Louis Dimier, has just published a French edition of the "Discourses"; and in his preface he does not hesitate to affirm that these discourses constitute the completest and most profound treatise on painting ever published. Again, "l'esthétique n'a rien produit de plus élevé ni de plus solide chez aucun peuple et sous la plume d'aucun auteur". The carefully chosen terms are just. But what a contrast is this high deliberate praise with the current opinion of the "Discourses" in Reynolds' own country! The reception of Mr. Roger Fry's recent edition of the book showed what our popular journalists thought of Sir Joshua's doctrine; one read of obsolete conventionalisms and hypocritical admirations. This was only to follow Ruskin's lead. Yet in such a matter critical French opinion has authority. The sanity, the solidity, the reasonableness of Reynolds are just what appeal to the clear intellect of France; we in England crave rather for eloquence, enthusiasm, rhapsody. It is quite true that for the general public Reynolds is not a very stimulating writer; his business was not that of the man of letters who, when he writes on art, aims at interpreting this or that work, at refining and enhancing the sense of sight and the sense for art in his readers; his business was to expound principles and methods to professional students, for whom alone he wrote. But in this province he stands beyond all other English critics.

I have been often reminded of the famous "Discourses" in reading the volume which the Slade Professor at Oxford has devoted to the same subject. The modest title, "Notes on the Science of Picture-Making" (Chatto and Windus), is inadequate to a book which covers the ground so thoroughly. Writing in a clear, plain, practical manner, Mr. Holmes is particularly to be praised for the sanity and logical coherence of his exposition; and his writing has always this vital source of interest, that it is not painting in the abstract which occupies his thought, but painting now and here in England. Very few working painters have so wide and full a knowledge of the art of the world as Mr. Holmes has; and this knowledge supplies apt illustration to each problem the contemporary artist has to face. Appeal to practical experience, the conditions of the material employed—this is the keynote of these discourses. I think Mr. Holmes exaggerates in affirming that the criticism of art is in a state of fundamental chaos, while the criticism of literature and of music proceeds from a secure basis of common agreement. Certain it is that in each case criticism has relied too much on abstract theory; if it is to be healthy and alive, criticism of any art must reckon first of all with the material of that art, and the laws implicit in that material. The moderns rail at the old talk of Ideal Form and the Grand Style; but Mr. Holmes shrewdly points out that Truth to Nature and Sincerity have proved just as perilous catchwords. In fact, the later attitude of mind has encouraged painters to be casual and purposeless, and to leave the main things to chance, while they are far less in touch with the inherent conditions of their art than the older masters, who still retained the craftsman's sense, however vainly they pursued the sublime and beautiful. A flagrant instance of this loss of a right instinct—there is no theory needed here—is in the matter of proportion of canvas to design. "In the present day for one picture that might well have been painted on a large canvas, a hundred, nay a thousand, are produced which would look infinitely better if they were a quarter of their present size." Another point which more vitally affects a painting is inconsistency of presentation. Mr. Holmes has some acute remarks on this subject. He points out how the artificiality of the school of Watteau is accentuated by the contrast between the carefully painted figures and the conventional landscape. This, however, was a frank and probably intentional device. Nowadays convention creeps in more subtly, without the artist's knowing it; and the result is a pseudo-realism without sap or savour. This poor-spirited compromise is especially apparent in what attempts to be imaginative work. As Mr. Holmes says, "Not the least difficulty of imaginative art is to secure this identity of symbolism where there is great diversity of generic character; to render for instance a cloud, a rivulet or a tree in precisely the same abstract terms that may be required for the human figure". I cannot help thinking that Reynolds' precept of "generalised form" might have been stated with much more felicity and persuasion if he had laid his stress on the need for consistency of style and unity of atmosphere, instead of making it appear as if a kind of vagueness and non-individual character of form were indispensable features of imaginative painting. It was against the Reynolds tradition that the Pre-Raphaelites revolted: but the success of their early masterpieces was due, not to any formula of method, but to the pitch of intensity to which their minds were strung, the emotion of discovery, the charged and stimulated atmosphere in which they were working. Rembrandt, from whom Reynolds had learned so much, might have taught them that the utmost character and the utmost spiritual intensity could be expressed in summary terms with a strictly limited palette and with the boldest artifice of illumination. The first need of an imaginative artist is to create a style, an efficient instrument of expression corresponding to the personal matter he desires to express. There is no style without emphasis and sacrifice; and Mr. Holmes very justly devotes the best part of his book to consideration of the various kinds of emphasis, of symbol, of plan, of spacing, etc., which every born artist employs by instinct. One is sometimes tempted to think that painters were best left to follow instinct alone. But it is easy to form corrupting habits; and an instinctive gift is worth little if it cannot be strengthened and enriched by mental training. The great value of the Slade Professor's book, that which ought to make it eminently serviceable to students of to-day, is the fact that, like Reynolds before him, he continually insists on the need of mental effort and alertness. There can, I think, be no question that the depressing dull accomplishment of most contemporary painting is due to a stupid literalness of obedience to the commandment uttered in one form or another by all the great masters, "Go to Nature". Yet all the great creative artists, as Mr. Holmes reminds us, painted their pictures, "not from Nature herself, but from memory assisted by studies made in the presence of Nature". Current fashion has abandoned this excellent habit; excellent, because it tests the artist's powers from the beginning to the end of his work, exacts their utmost from them, compels him to be synthetic and to render just that which has most vividly engaged his interest; in short, builds up for him unconsciously his own natural style. The opposite habit insensibly seduces him to dissipate his interest and encourages the lazy mind. Here I think Mr. Holmes might with advantage have said more on the general principle involved; I mean the truth that a picture is mind speaking to mind, emotion responding to emotion. This is a truth which both the public and the painter of our time seem continually to forget. They are always referring to external nature for countenance or disapproval, instead of to the enduring interests of men. It is not for Nature that art is made: she is totally unmoved by the sublimest masterpiece, which yet may rejoice and deepen life for a hundred generations of the master's kind.

On the more technical portions of Mr. Holmes' book I have no authority to speak. His terminology is not, I think, always quite happy; but in a practical treatise what is important is that the meaning should be clear, and no reader of this sane and stimulating volume can be in doubt as to that. More thought, more brain-work, deeper feeling; this is the marrow of Mr. Holmes' teaching; and what lesson could be apter or more needful for a time which, rich in talent as it is, produces so vast an amount of work from wholly inadequate motives, with immense skill and with laborious apathy?

THE HEART OF EARTH.

By Lord Dunsany.

As the poet walked through the moist, grey town thinking of Faëry and imperious Death, he saw the unthought-of pavement, monotonous, wet, clad with dirt, desolate. And, thinking of the long time that they had lain there under unheeding feet, unprotected by soil or grass against the will of the rain, he, being at peace because it was now evening, pitied the old grey stones. And the pavement felt his pity. Every stone felt it; stone told it unto stone for quite a mile. It had been trodden on for two hundred years by dogs as well as men, it had been spat upon and covered with filth, but had not before been pitied.

Deep in its core it felt the poet's pity; it had felt an earthquake less.

The pavement said nought in answer, but the echoes of the poet's footsteps felt its anger as they fled, and from stone to stone these thoughts whirled up and down through the pavement's fiery soul that was welded of old in the volcanic Prime or ever the hills were dumb. (The poet knew not what the pavement thought, for his dreams were now in Arcady.)

"What is this that dares to pity the heart of Earth? A thing of a few years and the toy of Time!

Is not Earth's heart of the lineage of the stars? What should it do with a man's pity when Earth has none for man?

Is not Earth true unto her old love Seismos? Or hath man lured her from him?

Man dallies awhile with Earth, but soon Seismos sees him. Man could not protect Earth against her old fierce lover even if she had willed it.

Am I not the heart of wandering Earth, child of the sun?

Who? Who has pitied me?

Brethren of mine stand watch by companies over trivial human dead. And the dead moulder, but not my brethren.

Twin am I to the granite who used to frolic with me when the old earthquake rocked our native hills.

The wind greets me and passes by, and then comes back again. He brings me foundered armies as a cloak and old uprooted cities. Still goeth about with the wind Tyre; and still he carrieth Sidon. Hannibal hath rested awhile with me and rested lightly; no heavier are all his elephants. All rest for a while with me. Then to drifting cities and armies the wind saith 'Come'. Unto me cometh also the soft far-travelled rain, the child of Heaven and Sea, coming from hovering uncertain over forests and fields. And in the name of the stars, whose herald she is, the soft rain giveth me greeting. For the stars come to me whenever the rain is here. They glide down between her chariots and shine with me; thou shalt find them even here, whosoever passeth at night when the rain has come and her chariots rolled away.

One has dared to pity the intimate of the stars, the wind's confidant and whom the rain loveth. And this pity hath come from his detested heart.

Dear to me indeed are the boots of men, but their hearts I hate. What love should Earth's heart have for the hearts of men, who have chosen cities as their foster-mothers, rejecting Earth? But their boots I love, for I have an enemy that lurks and waits, mine enemy the moss, and against him they guard me. If the boots came not forth, the rumour would spread at once through all the wild things; the moss would know it first and then the grass, the dandelion would launch his airy armies on the first townward breeze, and the great brambles would come creeping in, and they would all hide me away where the great stars could not find me or the soft rain come.

Vile indeed was this man's despised heart. Earth taught it not pity, but it learnt it from some unearthly evil thing.

Behold now coming down to me the lamps and stars because the rain is here.

I love the red lamps that watch, because they flame like the heads of the olden hills or ever they were dumb.

Am I not beautiful among my lamps and stars? See now the mud upon me: here rests Persepolis and here

Troy: the East wind brought them and the rain eased their wandering.

I am older than gods.

Here comes a man forgetful of me, scorning me; here comes one spitting at me, cursing me when he slips. They do not pity me.

That is well, very well. Even so Earth feels towards them, who is one with her old love Seismos whose child the avalanche is."

Thus thought the pavement, and awaited with hopeful joy the coming again of the old grey earthquake, Seismos.

The poet had long since passed into the distance; the echoes of his footsteps had fled away through the air from the pavement's sudden anger like bats disturbed in some terrific temple: and anger still burned like the primeval fires in the core of that heart of Earth.

THE PASSING OF "MIKE".

FOR two or three years it had begun to be assumed and the probability even mentioned aloud that "Mike" would some day die. Not that there was any evidence that would bear sifting by one who was intimate with him. He was strong and hearty, and never had any wretchedness except when I threw a stick at him in anger. Looking back, we could say that his life's thread was spun "round and full out of their softest and their whitest wool" by the Fates. He could still walk as far as ever. If I travelled twenty or thirty miles over the Downs he would walk and run two or three times as far. For he was nearly always hunting at full speed, visible or audible half a mile away, or he was examining every inch of the path, seeking an excuse to be off; and if that was not to be found he would look up to see whether I was thinking or otherwise inattentive to him, and then, his thievish thighs endued suddenly with all the wolf, he was off at his best speed which no shout could stop. In the rapture of the hunt his bark became a song, but as a rule it was hard and explosive.

Seven years before, when he became mine for five shillings—he was a stray—I used in my ignorance to beat him for hunting. Never having thought about it, I took it for granted that the habit was bad because dangerous and forbidden, and also a piece of wantonness and defiant self-indulgence. I did not cure him; I did not even make him dislike me; and therefore I began to laugh at the folly of lashing myself into a fury at the vice of disobedience under the pretext of improving the morals of an excellent dog. He forgave me so readily that it took some time for me to forgive myself. And so for seven years not a day passed but he hunted, and many were his whole nights spent in the woods. He was a magically fortunate dog, and it was fore-ordained that, however boldly he might be leaping through a wood, he was always to alight with his four feet clear of traps. Wire nooses he often ran into, and many a hare and rabbit he must have saved by first entering a snare intended for them and then freeing himself by force or subtlety, returning sometimes with the wire and its peg still fastened on his leg as an inconvenient decoration. As he hunted in his first year so he did when the judicial minds, who knew nothing of him except what they believe to be common to all dogs, began to aver that he was getting old, with a kind of smile that one so mighty and so much vaunted should be giving way before them. They pointed out that he was silvering everywhere, that his head was almost pure white, that he lay dozing long after the house was astir; but I could see no real reason for believing that this change might not go on, as the phrase is, "for ever", and then when he was all silver he might have another life as a silver dog. So with his teeth. It was evident that the fangs which held on to a stick while humourists swung him giddily round and round were now very much shorter (I concede this), but still they held on; he ate as well as ever; he drew blood from the enemy as before. If a stump was as useful as the polished and pointed fang, why should not the bare gum of the hero be equal to the stump?

Gradually I got into the fame of mind which was no longer violently hostile to the proposition that one day "Mike" would die. But this did not affect my faith; it was an intellectual position with no influence on life.

He was no ordinary dog. That, the sceptics tell me, goes without saying: they argue that because all people regard their favourite dogs as extraordinary, therefore all, including "Mike", are ordinary and will turn white, lose their teeth and die. In the main he was an Irish terrier. But his hair was longer than it "should have been", and paler and softer. His face was more pointed than was right; his ears, darker than the rest of him and silky (so that a child once fell asleep sucking one), usually hung down. His hindquarters approached those of a collie. Also his tail when he trotted along curled over his back and made children laugh aloud; but when he was thinking about the chase it hung in a horizontal bow; when stealing away or in full cry it was held slightly lower and no longer bent, and it flowed finely into the curves of his great speed. He was eloquent; his yawn alone, or the twitching of his eyebrows as he lay with head between extended paws, expressed a score of shades of emotion. He was very excitable, very tender-hearted, very pugnacious. He was a rough, swift dog, yellowish-brown above and almost white beneath, who was here, there and everywhere at once, importunate yet usually welcome and always forgiven. He would attack any dog of equal or greater size, and test the magnanimity of the mastiff and the churlishness of curs running behind carriers' carts. But if a little dog attacked him, he lifted up his head, fixed his eyes on me, and looked neither to left nor right, but muttered: "You are neither dog nor cat; go away". As for a mouse, he thought it a kind of beetle, and was curious but kind. He would, however, kill wasps, baring his teeth to avoid the sting and snapping many times before the dividing blow.

I should like to be able to say that he had no tricks. The most splendid array of tricks only gives colour to the vulgar notion that a dog is, as it were, a human being manqué, a kind of pitiable amusing creature unfortunately denied the gifts of Smith and Brown. But this loud-voiced dog of violent ways, who leaped through a window unscathed, this fighter, this hunter, had been taught one trick before I had him: he would beg when commanded, but unwillingly and badly. The postman, cobbler and parish clerk, a little wizened philosopher, would never let him beg for the lump of sugar which he carried as a daily gift: "I would never beg myself," he said, "and I don't like to see a noble animal beg neither". As for faults, I think he had them all, the faults, that is, which human beings call such in dogs—abruptness, invariable vivacity, the appetites . . .; they merged charmingly into his other qualities; isolated, they looked like faults, but good and bad together swelled the energy, courage and affection of his character.

So long as he was out of doors he was inexhaustible, and he took every opportunity of trying his strength by hunting, racing to and fro, and asking even strangers (with head on one side, eyes expectant, forelegs stamping as he alternately retreated slowly and leapt forward) to throw him a stick or stone. Perhaps it was in this expectant attitude that he looked his best, every limb braced, his steps firm and delicate as he tripped backward obliquely, his ears erect, his mouth open, and white teeth, flame-like tongue and brown eyes gleaming together as he repeated his commanding bark. And as profound as his energy was his repose. After a fight or a night in the wood he showed no fatigue until he was indoors. Then he fell flat on his side and slept with quiverings and snuffling yaps; and even then anyone's movement of preparation for going out discovered a new fount of activity, and he was up and had burst out of the door before the latch was released.

When he was at least ten years old and looked very white slipping through the beeches and troubling the loves of the foxes under a full moon, I confess that even I used sometimes to say that I hoped he would die in full career with a charge of shot in his brain. He never began to grow stout, and was never pampered; it could not be thought of that he should come down to lying in the sun and taking quiet walks of a mile or so, and living on pity, memory and medicine. Better far that if he had to make an end one or other of the keepers (a good shot) should help him to it in the middle of his hunting. That would have been a fortunate death, as deaths go.

But he did not die. He forced himself through a dense blackthorn hedge and came out combed and fine, stood hesitating among the first celandines, and was off after a hare. He never came back. If he could not bolt out of this world into a better, where there is hunting and fighting for ever, yet with his head on one side, ears cocked, eyes bright, he would not be refused admittance by any quadruped janitor of Paradise. But then we do not know what stage the belief in a future life has reached among dogs, and whatever the dogmas, heresies, scientific doctrines (that the fleshly dog manifestly does not survive, etc.), they doubtless have no power to influence the law unknown to those whom it most concerns. I only hope he is—or, rather, I wish he were—somehow, hunting still. There seemed no reason why he should not go on for ever.

CORRESPONDENCE.

PRESIDENT TAFT'S MODESTY.

To the Editor of the SATURDAY REVIEW.

Weston-super-Mare, 21 July 1909.

SIR,—Your correspondent Mr. Hugh Blaker seems to assume a very superior attitude in scouting President Taft's recent remarks on the progress of the United States. As an Englishman who has lived and taught eight years in the States, I should like humbly to controvert some of his sweeping and ill-founded assertions.

No one can deny that the United States—for a nation, practically speaking, not more than a century old—has made astounding progress in all branches, and the making and development of the U.S.A. is one of the wonders of the world—especially material, for material development always precedes intellectual and spiritual, and to the former no doubt President Taft especially referred. A century ago the United States had a population of about five millions; now it has a population of about ninety millions, rapidly increasing. The general well-being of the masses in America far exceeds that of any other country in the world. Wages are double and treble what they are in England, and actual cost of living no higher; and the working population in the U.S.A. live as well as, if not better than, the English middle class. There is no country in the world where the general level of prosperity, well-being and education is higher; and Prince Henry of Prussia when he visited America made a similar remark. The masses of America, taken collectively, are better instructed and better educated than the masses of Europe, and have more opportunities: all schools are free to rich and poor alike up to twenty-one years, and each State maintains a university, where instruction is free to all.

Apart from New York and one or two Eastern immigrant cities, there are no slums, no such degraded poverty as is to be found in Europe. To turn to the less material side of the matter, that there are few newspapers or magazines an educated man can read in America is as untrue as it is grotesque: a large proportion of the American press is sensational, if you like, but the average New York and Eastern papers provide quite as good literary pabulum (and more varied) for their readers as the average London and provincial papers. As to magazines, America is generally reputed to be a pioneer in that form of literature—as, for example, "Harper's", "Munsey", "Maclure's", etc.; of more serious literature the "Outlook", "Atlantic", "Arena", "North American", "Forum", etc., are in no way inferior to the same type of English journalism. There are a large number of rising novelists and writers in the U.S.A., besides Marion Crawford, Winston Churchill, Mark Twain, Bliss Carman, etc.

As to art, the country is almost too new to have developed a school of art, and a large number of American artists live in Europe; and there are a goodly number of Sargents and Whistlers members of European academies little heard of in England. There is a rising very creditable school of architecture in America. In technical education America leads, and in pure science she holds her own—and has two Nobel prizemen on her list.

With regard to universities, I humbly think that for a new country she can give a good account of herself. Is there a university in the United Kingdom founded during the last hundred and fifty years that is of a higher standard or superior to Yale, Harvard or Colombia or Princeton, either in the list of professors, the status of scholarship and achievement or in equipment and endowment? I venture to think not.

I know that the ordinary B.A. degree of the aforesaid universities is of a higher standard than that of the ordinary or pass degree of Oxford (I took the latter degree myself, so I do not speak without knowledge). A large number of distinguished German and Continental professors, attracted by the far larger stipends and pension fund, are to be found in American universities. Every State in America maintains a university, where tuition is free to all, and there are a hundred who have had a university education in America to one in England.

As to the lawlessness and lack of order in America of which your correspondent complains, life and property are as safe in Eastern America as in Europe; and it is a wonder any order is kept at all considering the low class of immigration that streams into the country. I should advise your correspondent to read Bryce's "American Commonwealth", which is considered the best and most authoritative account of modern America.

I am, Sir, yours truly,
E. GOUGH.

[We have read Mr. Bryce's book, perhaps with as much care as our correspondent. Its unreasoned optimism and uncritical pro-American bias seem to have found an imitator.—ED. S. R.]

THE BUDGET AND CHANNEL ISLANDERS.

To the Editor of the SATURDAY REVIEW.

Chiswick, 20 July 1909.

SIR,—Hitherto the inhabitant of the Channel Islands has been placed upon precisely the same footing as to abatement of income tax as an inhabitant of Great Britain. Under the Finance Bill he is to be deprived of abatement. He is to be treated as though he were a foreigner and relegated to the same position with respect to fiscal liabilities as the Frenchman or German.

The Channel Islands are all that remain to us of the Duchy of Normandy that conquered us. Are we getting back some of our own? Or are the remnants of feudal laws and tenures a reason to a Radical Government for swinging beyond the mean of no preference to that of disability?

There is no more loyal portion of the King's dominions than these islands. They pay their own way without the seeking for doles which has become a portion of our system of political cadging. They set us an example in maintaining a compulsory militia for the defence of their own shores.

A great portion of their men go afield for their work in life. They enter the imperial services both as officers and men, and upon the completion of their term of service with rare exceptions retire to their islands, for which they have an ineradicable affection.

In the past their modest incomes have been granted the tax abatements we grant our own people. In future the necessities of Radical finance are to deprive them of it. The result to the Treasury will be so infinitesimal as to be negligible. As there are but 100,000 of them all told, the hurt to their feelings as loyal members of the Empire may appear to a Radical Chancellor equally negligible. But it none the less seems contemptibly mean.

I am, Sir, yours obediently,
C. J. ANDERSON.

THE PEERS AND THE BUDGET MINCE.

To the Editor of the SATURDAY REVIEW.

SIR,—Mr. Winston Churchill, owing to a misapprehension of what Lord Lansdowne really said, has given the Peers notice that if they dare to "mince" the Budget they will be forced to eat the mince they have made. Does this mean that the Government intend to keep the Budget discussion going till Christmas-time? "Mince" will hardly be sufficiently seasonable before then to induce the Lords to swallow it, even though it be of their own making. About that time it will become so popular that the country itself will certainly welcome it. As Mr. Churchill was misled as to the word Lord Lansdowne used, so he may possibly be deceiving himself as to the Peers' autumnal powers of digestion.

Yours truly, EPICURE.

ACTORS' ELOCUTION.

To the Editor of the SATURDAY REVIEW.

Callendar House, Falkirk, Scotland, 18 July 1909.

SIR,—Players seem to imagine that the British public measures their greatness by the inordinate number of minutes they take over one speech or sentence. From long training and practice in this dreary and most exasperating art of spinning out their lines to their utmost extent the actors of the present generation are probably past correction. But are there no authorities on these matters who will bestir themselves and convince the actors now preparing for the stage that the human tongue is as yet subject to no law of speed limit? Yours faithfully, D. L. FORBES.

THE ANTI-VIVISECTION AGITATION.

To the Editor of the SATURDAY REVIEW.

Research Defence Society, 70 Harley Street, W.
22 July 1909.

SIR,—One of your correspondents last week said that the police stopped only one of the anti-vivisection banners prepared for the procession on Saturday the 10th inst. This statement directly contradicts facts published at the time in more than one newspaper. Still, as your correspondent alludes to one and no more of these prohibited banners, let me describe it. The inscription was "Is it nothing to you all ye that pass by?" The picture, which is in constant use among anti-vivisection societies, was that of the "Khartum Dog". This dog was inoculated for the study of an infective disease of animals, which is closely allied to sleeping sickness in man. This disease is a very heavy scourge to horses, mules, and cattle in the Gambia Territory, the Uganda Protectorate, and the Soudan. In parts of the Gambia Territory its ravages have been so extensive as almost to prevent the employment of horses. The dog was inoculated at the Wellcome Laboratories, Khartum, from one of three mules brought from the Southern Sudan. The object of the experiment was to study the germs of the disease. Without such experiments it is impossible for the men of science to understand fully either the properties of the germs of the disease or the influence on these germs of this or that drug. The dog died of the disease, just as thousands of animals, on whose lives human life is more or less dependent, are dying of the disease all across Africa. These animals have a right to protection against disease; and that is why the dog was inoculated.

It is part of the work of the Research Defence Society to answer all inquiries relating to experiments on animals, and to send to all applicants the Society's pamphlets. I shall be happy to send to any of your readers a series of pamphlets, stating clearly the facts as to experiments on animals in this country and the regulations under which they are conducted; the immense importance of such experiments to the welfare of mankind; and the great saving of human life and health which is already due to them.

I remain your obedient servant,
STEPHEN PAGET, Hon. Secretary.

REVIEWS.

POOR YORICK.

"The Life and Times of Laurence Sterne." By Wilbur L. Cross. London: Macmillan. 1909. 10s. 6d. net.

ADMIRERS of an author, if they be wise in their generation, fight rather shy of biographies of their favourite. Especially where the little they know of him is unfavourable. They fear one of two evils: either that a knowledge of the man's life may spoil their enjoyment of his work—

"Oh! that in darkness I had died,
Before my soul had ever sighed
To see you off the stage"—

or that the biography may be the work of a whitewasher. Of "rehabilitations" they have had enough. Everyone, from Catiline and Nero to Henry VIII. and Judge Jeffreys, who seemed to need it has been whitewashed, which is (though the rehabilitators do not think so) a very different thing from being washed white.

Lovers, therefore, of my Uncle Toby have, we should imagine, steered clear of knowing much about Laurence Sterne. They had read Thackeray's reluctant praise and cordial reprobation: they had heard (who has not?) the gentle sarcasm about "whining over a dead ass and neglecting a living mother", and decided that the less they knew of Sterne the better.

Professor Cross has, however, written a book about Sterne which they may read in safety. He shows the humourist in a light which is probably as near the true as anyone will ever get, his life as that which might be expected of a man who lived, on principle, "as the fly stung him". Whitewash him he assuredly does not. But one or two ugly stains he washes off. The "dead ass" epigram for instance, which was, it appears, the joint work of Walpole and Byron—Horace laid the egg and my lord hatched it—is untrue, a minor fault common to many epigrams. Sterne did "relieve a living mother". Handsomely, according to his means at the time, which were, by the way, the means of his wife. The mother was one of those who say, "Out of two hundred a year a man can easily spare eighty, and not miss it; even then he'll have more than I shall". She seems to have been one whom to relieve could not be unmixed pleasure. If Sterne had preferred "whining", no man could have blamed him. But, as a fact, he did his duty though he hated it, high praise for any man, but especially for the volatile Laurence. Nor can Professor Cross admit, with Thackeray, that Sterne was mean and cowardly. Thackeray, great as he was, was steeped in the prudery of his generation. Did he not reject a story of Trollope's (of all men!) as unfit virginibus puerisque? Nor need one be a prude to bar much of Sterne's writing. But of Sterne's life Professor Cross has had more opportunity of collecting particulars than Thackeray had, and he finds the meanness and cowardice not proven.

The book has excellent portraits of Sterne—two, taken in youth, by Gainsborough and Ramsay; a reproduction, direct from the painting, of the well-known Reynolds; and a quaint print of Yorick in his fashionable Paris days from a water-colour by Carmontelle, taken for the Duke of Orleans. There is, too, a portrait of Hall Stevenson, the Eugenius of "Shandy" and author of "Crazy Tales", and a print of his house, where the merry "Demoniacs" held revels like minor monks of Medmenham. And here Professor Cross has stopped, for which, in these days of over-illustration, we are duly grateful.

Sterne is so unapproachably great in his own line that a biography of him was bound to come, and we are glad to find it so well done. But poor Laurence, even in Professor Cross' hands, remains unsatisfactory, almost fitted to dispute with Villon for that sad place on the roll of fame which Stevenson assigned to the latter. Kissable, kickable, a most incorrigible, irritating, irresistible, irreplaceable dog.

With criticism of Sterne's work Professor Cross troubles himself little. What remains to be said? Uncle Toby walks the Elysian fields with as firm a tread as Falstaff himself. Praise is superfluous. Blame has rained thick as hail. His sentimentality is nauseous. It is "muckibus" which Horace Walpole said was "Irish for 'sentimental'". Knowing his genius, one is tempted to believe that the rogue is laughing at sentiment. But Mr. H. D. Traill was probably right in thinking that Sterne honestly admired "sentimentality". His weakest vice he thought his strongest virtue. He even fell—once—with Uncle Toby. The celebrated fly is sentimentality. "Paillasse has tumbled", and, that time, "missed his tip".

And to the graver charge of "indecorum" no defence is possible. We have before now been puzzled to know why men whom Rabelais did not frighten shrank from Sterne. One reason perhaps is the manner, the "perpetual appeal", as Thackeray called it. "He is always looking in my face, watching his effect", etc. When Voltaire hailed Sterne as "the second Rabelais of England" the Patriarch of Wit spoke as a fool. Sterne like Rabelais! Sterne was like Panurge, and Rabelais (if he must resemble any of his creatures) like Pantagruel, a calm, benevolent superman. Rabelais never buttonholes you, except in his prefaces. Another reason is pointed to by Coleridge when he compares Sterne's indecency to the "trembling daring with which a child touches a hot tea-urn because it has been forbidden". Mr. Traill speaks of "the dirty age" in boyhood. Sterne never emerged. The husband and father of forty-six years old, whose genius, if not quite expanded, was in full bud, thought, with any average bad boy of fourteen, that it was witty to be dirty!

"No less virginally lies
The lily on the mere,
Because at whiles her fixéd root
Has felt the fingers of the newt."

Superior beings, to use Pope's phrase, may view both flower and reptile with equal eye. The newt's wedding waistcoat and frills are, in fact, flowers. Convention adores the flower and ignores the newt. The average man is well aware of the newt, knows him much too well to be in the least afraid of him, but admires the lily more. Nor would he think a bunch of newts' heads as suitable for presentation to a lady as a bouquet of lilies. Little boys and decadents make a secret cult of the newt and value the lily only as a cockshy. But Sterne was an exception to all men. He admired, most honestly, beauty and goodness, and he revelled in dirt. His two great faults are that he will paint the lily, and that he thinks it awfully clever of himself to know a few common facts about the newt.

THE SCAPEGOAT.

"The Life of Major-General Sir Charles William Wilson K.C.B., F.R.S., D.C.L., LL.D." By Colonel Sir Charles M. Watson. London: Murray. 1909. 15s. net.

IT is surely one of the most cruel ironies of fate that a man like Sir Charles Wilson, who had done splendid services to the nation in many parts of the world for over forty years, should be best known by his conduct during less than forty hours of his strenuous career. The suspense of Gordon's defence of Khartum and the unchivalrous attempt made to hold Sir Charles responsible for the final catastrophe have so obscured the story of his varied and useful life that few people nowadays seem to be aware of what he achieved, nine out of ten connecting his name only with the failure to save Gordon. This story of Wilson's life, written by a brother officer of both him and Gordon—for all three were Royal Engineers and old and intimate friends—must surely once and for all make an end of the accusations made by Gladstone's Government when in search of a scapegoat to bear the blame of their abandonment of Gordon. When the troubles arose in the Sudan Lord Dufferin advised the Government to send Wilson to Khartum. Gordon was, however, sent early in 1884, and in April his position had become so serious that Lord Wolseley urged that a British force should be placed at Berber not later than 20 October, reckoning that Gordon might hold out until 14 November and no longer. But the Government refused to act, for had they not Gladstone's assurance that Gordon was not besieged: he was only "hemmed in"?

On 26 May Berber fell, and the Mahdist revolt surged northward. In August the Government decided upon sending an expedition up the Nile under Lord Wolseley, who asked Wilson to come out as his Chief of Intelligence, telling him he was "the only man" who could fill that important office, and that by taking it he would do a good service to the State. Wilson joined Wolseley in Cairo in September, and on 16 December they arrived at Korti. Wolseley has been blamed for advocating the river route, but it must be remembered that he asked for the boats to be built in April, and that the Government delayed four months before they ordered them, and that it took three months more to place the first of them on the Nile above the Second Cataract. In his diary of 16 December Wilson writes: "It is not Lord Wolseley's fault that there has been so much delay. How much labour would have been saved if the boats had only been ready a month or six weeks beforehand! We are just six weeks too late in everything". Meanwhile, Gordon had named 14 December as the latest date up to which he could hold out.

The situation had changed when Wolseley arrived at Korti, and he now decided to send a small force across the Bayuda Desert—not for the relief of Gordon, but to get into touch with him and assure him of the advance of the British. The bulk of the expedition was still to follow the river route, and was calculated to arrive at Metemmeh some time in March, and, most important of all, the desert column was not to move to the relief of Khartum until it had joined hands with the river column. Up to now all the delays had been directly caused by the procrastination and the vacillations of the Government, for the "boat scheme", if adopted when recommended by Wolseley in April, or even two months later in June, would have been in good time. But now came a delay which Lord Wolseley's critics lay at his door. Insufficient camels had been bought to enable a flying column to cross the desert in one movement. The precise share of blame for this to be divided between a Government at home seeking to evade responsibilities or minimise expenses and a harassed commander in the field will ever be a matter of opinion. Anyway, the results were simply to wreck the desert column, for advancing on 30 December, upon reaching Gakdul, ninety-six miles out, on 2 January, it had to return to Korti for more supplies, with the result that when the final advance was made from Gakdul on 14 January not only had the Mahdi had time to despatch a strong force to oppose it, but the camels were already worn out by overmarching and lack of time to feed.

Lord Wolseley had specified minutely the precise part and duties of every member of this curiously composed force. Herbert Stewart was to take and to garrison Metemmeh and return with a convoy to Gakdul. Beresford was "at once to take over and man any steamers and put one or more into an effective state". Wilson was "as soon as Lord C. Beresford reports that he is ready" to proceed with him to Khartum, where he was "to confer with General Gordon", and tell him that "he might be relieved in six weeks' time". There was no question of immediate relief. For Wilson was, after the conference, "to return to Metemmeh". Burnaby was to be left in command at that town. Then came the heavy fighting in the desert, and the assembly of the column on the banks of the Nile on the afternoon of 20 January, with its gallant chief mortally wounded, Burnaby slain, over fifteen per cent. of its numbers killed or wounded, Beresford in ill-health, and, last, but not least, with the camel transport completely broken down. The column had met, fought, and defeated in two exceptionally severe fights the two contingents sent down by the Mahdi; a third was known to be within a day's march, and a fourth was reported moving up from Berber. Wilson, the political officer ordered "to confer with Gordon", found himself suddenly the military officer in command of this sorely stricken force.

Gordon's steamers, sent from Khartum four months before, came on the scene on 21 January, and about 4 P.M. met the desert column on the river bank at Gubat. On the 22nd Wilson determined to ensure the safety of his shattered force by ascertaining whether the Mahdists were, according to report, in his vicinity, as he was strenuously urged by Beresford to do, though he never mentioned this. Obviously he could not foretell that the advancing Mahdists, alarmed by the recent victories of the British, would halt. The next day, the 23rd, every effort was made to get the steamers ready to start, but it was late—very late—in the afternoon of 23 January before Beresford, who had vigorously protested against the steamers starting until they had been overhauled, reported that they were ready. Wilson at once went on board, but owing to darkness the actual start was not made until dawn on the 24th, and he did not reach Khartum until the 28th. But Gordon had been slain at dawn on the 26th and some thousands of his garrison put to the sword. It was too late!

The basis of the whole attack on Wilson rested on the alleged delay at Gubat, and amid the fire of abuse and condemnation, adroitly fed by a most unscrupulous press attack, it was accepted as an axiom that it was these three days which were the cause of Gordon's death, and therefore Wilson, the senior officer, was to blame for the catastrophe. The controlling fact was ignored that had the steamers started off for Khartum at the first possible moment—namely, at daylight on the 22nd—travelling at the same rate as they did, they would not have reached Khartum till midday on the 26th, some hours after the catastrophe. Also it was reiterated that for this delay in starting Wilson, and Wilson alone, was to blame. Indeed, it was not until Sir William Butler wrote his fine memoir of Gordon for the "Men of Action" series that anybody ventured to point out that, if unnecessary delay did occur, the responsibility for it must at least be shared by the officer, Lord Charles Beresford, who was particularly charged by Lord Wolseley "at once to take over and man any steamers" and "report when they were ready". That Lord Charles did not complete his share of the task till late on the 23rd, too late for the steamers to start until dawn on the 24th, will strike all impartial critics as an important factor in the question of delay.

However, it is plain that whatever delay did occur between 4 P.M. on the 21st and dawn on the 24th was due to the extraordinary emergencies which had arisen owing to the precarious position of the British column and the reasonable wish of the commander to safeguard its shattered remnants. Field-Marshal Sir Lintorn Simmons, no mean judge of war, wrote to Wilson strongly approving of his conduct in this matter, and saying "it was your bounden duty to see to the safety of your force before leaving it". Everybody should read this letter, which is given in the book.

We, in common with all Lord Wolseley's true friends and admirers, must very deeply regret that he did not use his influence to crush these calumnies against Wilson. Lord Wolseley, above all others, knew the true causes of the loss of Khartum. But a scapegoat was wanted, and Wilson was taken. The very few who happened to know the whole truth were ignored. Everything that could elucidate the story was skilfully eliminated. Wilson's circumstantial account of the loss of Khartum and death of Gordon was not accepted, and a pitiful pretence was kept up that Gordon might yet be alive. What happened to Kitchener's report? For, retreating from Gubat, Buller called upon Major Kitchener, who had accompanied him across the desert, to write a report on the fall of Khartum. This Kitchener did, stating emphatically that, from the information he had received, after the loss of Omdurman early in January the Mahdi could have entered Khartum any day he liked, and that had Wilson's steamers arrived many days earlier the results would have been exactly the same. The Mahdi, in fact, like all Orientals, did not see any reason to accelerate his plans until necessity was obvious. The advance of Wilson's steamers on Khartum was the death-warrant of Gordon. This report was kept back, as was another giving details of the death of Gordon—the decapitation and exhibition of the head upon a spear at Omdurman—and the public were beguiled by hopes of Gordon having somehow escaped! As to the effect which Wilson's appearance on the 25th (had it been possible, which it was not) would have produced, anyone who knows the Sudan and its warriors, even in their degenerate days in 1898, will admit the absurdity of supposing that the Mahdi's hosts, over fifty thousand strong, would have abandoned their guns and other belongings, and fled at the sight of a rickety penny steamer containing four British officers and twenty-five infantry soldiers!

The public was not allowed to realise that (1) nothing would have induced Gordon to save his life by embarking on the steamers and abandoning the garrison which, by his brilliant example, he had induced to hold out for ten long months, and whose massacre upon surrender was inevitable; (2) that had Sir Charles Wilson, in direct defiance of Lord Wolseley's orders, landed his small party and joined the garrison of Khartum he and they would merely have perished along with Gordon, for no help could have reached them for weeks. The desert column was wrecked, without transport and incapable of advancing. The conclusion of the whole matter is that it was impossible *from the beginning* for the expedition to succeed. It started too late. Lord Wolseley probably realised this, but, knowing the uncertainties of war, he prefered to take the off-chance as every hard-fighting man would. The blame for failure lies with Gladstone and his Cabinet, and with them only.

His K.C.B. and subsequent promotion to major-general was sorry compensation to Wilson for the misrepresentation of his conduct. He was one of those men who, while outwardly impassive, feel none the less acutely, and they who knew him best believe that this persistent calumny shortened his life. Once when asked why he did not come forward and refute the story of the various "delays", he looked hard at his questioner and replied quietly: "Because I have ever thought that the man who seeks to justify his own conduct by casting blame upon his subordinates is a very poor sort of creature".

DARWIN AND MODERN THOUGHT.

"Darwin and Modern Science." Essays edited by A. C. Seward. Cambridge: At the University Press. 1909. 18s.

"The Making of Species." By Douglas Dewar and Frank Finn. London: Lane. 1909. 7s. 6d.

THE first and the more important of these books is by many authors—no less than thirty when its almost too self-effacing editor is reckoned—and is part of the Cambridge celebration of Darwin's centenary and of the jubilee of the publication of the "Origin of Species". Despite its eminent list of contributors, it is not at all of the nature of the "Festschrift" usual in Germany on such commemorative occasions—a collection of fresh individual investigations of special points of detail applying the principles and methods of the master: this is frankly a collection of essays, and avowedly addressed to the educated layman rather than the expert. Yet the latter will not be justified in thinking this a mere collection of popular lectures or in passing it over as of the nature of after-dinner speeches, though both these notes are occasionally struck, and this time rightly enough. For though in his own special field such a reader may not learn much or anything from its essayist but what he might previously have read in more technical form, its condensed restatement may have its interest, while he can hardly fail to profit from so varied a series of discussions, each dealing with some, or it may be many, of the almost innumerable questions which Darwin's work has advanced or aroused, or for which his doctrines have proved to be significant, and his influence and example fruitful. These handlings, as is natural with such heterogeneous and independent authorship, are of very various treatment as well as value, sometimes historical, sometimes contemporary or speculative. Most commonly their plan is that of a more or less comprehensive review of some section or aspect of the evolutionary field, like those of the presidents of sections of the British Association and corresponding gatherings. Some, too, are more or less critical in their tone—at times, as we shall see, even controversial—not as regards Darwin's main theses, but vigorously so as regards contemporaries and one another.

While then the progress of evolutionism in general and of the Darwinian theory of natural selection in particular is the main theme of the book, and the various summaries of advances in this and that department since Darwin's day are its most informative contents, it would be no true commemoration of Darwin's fertile and candid mind if it did not at the same time frankly express some of the differences in view and tendency of the contrasts in detailed interpretation and in larger theory which at present divide and subdivide the many inquirers into the evolution process—that vast and complex poly-logy of dramas to which Darwin has aroused us to become the awakening spectators. For the days of utilitarian cocksureness, when Darwin was proclaimed to have settled everything, are now, for speculative purposes at least, falling behind us almost as those in which Paley was given that bad eminence; and although, so marked is the isolation factor in University life, something both of Paleyan and of Darwinian formalism of teaching may linger side by side, the various streams of evolutionary thought and inquiry, despite their magnificent confluence in Darwin's life-work, are still traceable, indeed are running vigorously on, and this not without varying currents and contrasted eddies, unexpected turns and clashing waves. These essays then are to be welcomed as giving a frequent glimpse of that "onward rush of science" which was Darwin's fitting image and of which his own mind has been so vivid and copious a source.

Before he is plunged into this, however, the reader is somewhat oriented by means of an introductory essay, Professor Arthur Thomson's studiously uncoloured but well-composed and firmly outlined historic survey, of which the first page—that summarising Darwin's essential work—outlines his essential themes, of which the subsequent essays are necessarily the partial developments and mingled variations. First of these is, of course, the general Doctrine of Descent, which, though both ancient and recent, Darwin made current intellectual coin; and this, while necessarily assumed by all our essayists, is vividly recalled by Professor Haeckel as now well-nigh the oldest and for long one of the most active of its expositors. The paleontological record in its bearing on the descent of animals is sketched, lightly and popularly enough, by Professor W. B. Scott, of Princeton; but that for plants is much more fully and strongly summarised by Dr. D. H. Scott, now President of the Linnean Society. For he successively brings out the bearings of his fossils, first upon the doctrine of descent in general, then upon the actual course of plant evolution from ancient cryptogams to modern flowers, and finally upon the theory of natural selection, for all of which the materials have notably increased since Darwin's day, in as many chapters, which will each and increasingly demand some study, but will be found to reward it. With these essays, too, may be taken those of Thiselton-Dyer and Gadow on Plant and on Animal Distribution, and also the largely biographical and hence most easily readable essay of Professor Judd on "Darwin and Geology".

Darwin's second theme, his comprehensive application of the evolution idea to particular problems, is also exemplified by not a few of the other essays, such as Professor Schwalbe's on the Descent of Man. But, as is natural and right, pre-eminence is given to Darwin's third great service, at once the most individual and the most convincing for the success of the evolutionary doctrine, his labours toward elucidating the factors of the evolutionary process, especially by his all-embracing theory of natural selection; and this is naturally the theme of Professor Weismann's contribution. This is the largest and most continuously elaborated of the whole group, and one which, whether it be felt convincing or no, would alone give it wide general interest and value as its author's latest and most mature deliverance, his compactest and most emphatic plea against the Lamarckian principle of modification by use or disuse, and in favour of that "all-sufficiency of natural selection" which he has so long and so stoutly maintained. His "theory of the germ-plasm", with its subtle sub-hypotheses of germ-cell structure, and the application of all these to build up a theory of the origin of variations, are here briefly and clearly restated. So, too, are his contributions to the solution of various difficulties of natural selection, such as those presented by the sterile worker bee and ant, by cases of mimicry and so on. His controversy with Spencer is naturally but briefly mentioned, but a new and not less pretty fight is promised by his short but sweeping onslaught upon Professor Hugo de Vries, whose "Theory of Mutations"—great and sudden saltatory variations arising from internal causes—have given him such eminence in recent discussion, and his place in this volume also. Here at length the fat is fairly in the fire, and the reader may begin to feel enlivened accordingly; for de Vries goes back to Darwin's doctrine of Pangenesis, and has correspondingly little use for Weismann's germ-plasm.

Professor Bateson is frankly controversial, as is his wont; and not only abates the omnipotence of natural selection, but quotes Lamarck, and even that arch-scoffer and sceptic Samuel Butler, so long ignored by biologists, let alone Darwinians, in a way for which we may leave him to the next essay by Weismann or by his old and fierce adversary Professor Poulton.

Good botanical essays are contributed by Dr. Francis Darwin and Professor Goebel; but among the most readable and most instructive of all these papers is that of Professor Loeb, whose extraordinary wizardry in "The Experimental Study of the Influence of Environment on Animals" must be read in detail to be believed, and whose speculative boldness and suggestiveness are no less remarkable. With this new alchemy of life, in its way no less marvellous than that of radium, we must leave this varied and interesting volume—for the present at least.

Yet it contains another series of essays, what might have been a second volume in fact, bound up with these biological ones, and those of yet more varied scope and application, psychological and social, historical and religious; and to these again, somewhat incongruously perhaps, a couple of studies in physical evolution are appended. The various and far-reaching issues of evolution and of Darwinism are at any rate thus clearly enough displayed, if not as yet greatly advanced.

While the official representatives, the convinced and complacent exponents of the Darwinian and Neo-Darwinian schools have been of late so much in the public eye, in centenary celebrations, in "Darwin and Modern Science", and in the many books of which such a series of collected essays gives the substance or at least the clues, there are signs of coming trouble outside the gates, and mutterings of criticism more thorough-going than either Cambridge or the surrounding world has yet commonly realised: witness Messrs. Douglas Dewar and Finn's view of current evolution doctrines as a very "blight of dogma". There are not a few signs in fact that the predominant views of the evolution process are not continuing to satisfy the younger and rising generation, and that a new period of fresh observation and interpretation, of proportionately active controversy also, is at hand. Of this tendency "The Making of Species" is the latest example, though far from likely to be the last one. The authors are both Indian zoologists—ornithologists especially—and as such bring up not a few fresh observations and arguments. Like most writers of heretical tendency, they base their dissent from the predominant schools, and especially from the Neo-Darwinians ("Wallaceians" as they prefer to call them), upon the writings of the master himself, and notably recall his strenuous insistence that "I am convinced that natural selection has been the main, but not the exclusive, means of modification ".

Not that they are Neo-Lamarckians, at any rate in the ordinary sense of use-inheritance, but they sharply remind us that "the double assumption that variations are for all practical purposes haphazard in origin and indefinite in direction is necessary if natural selection is to be the main factor in evolution ". Without claiming to have solved the mystery of variation they allege many instances of mutation, yet without fully accepting the doctrines of de Vries. Among their discussions of hybridism, Mendelian heredity and other departments of concrete evolutionary research, perhaps the most interesting is that which assaults Professor Poulton's treatment of mimicry, and this in considerable detail, to which we hope to see before long Professor Poulton's reply. A similar onslaught is made on the accepted doctrines of the colouring of flowers and fruits and of the relation of flowers to insects. The universally popularised teaching that the visits of insects are responsible not only for flower colouring and marking, and that the dots and stripes are " honey-guides ", is thrown over, and Mr. Kay Robinson's recent interpretation is preferred—that " flower colouring is not so much to attract insects as to deter grazing and browsing animals " ! Other popular theories go the same way, in fact fare no better than so many tales of Uncle Remus.

Constructively the authors rediscuss, as the various factors of evolution, variation and correlation, heredity, natural selection, sexual selection and isolation, but without greatly advancing the solution of the mystery how species not only survive but originate. They predict its solution rather on the lines of experiment, especially in breeding, than from the speculative interpretations so common during the past generation and the present time. We shall look forward then to their own contributions towards this, but retain the feeling that we need some more thorough and searching analysis of the mystery of life and evolution than any of our teachers have yet given us, partially illuminating, or at least suggestive, though each may be.

A FALSE STEP.

"The Cliffs." By Charles M. Doughty. London: Duckworth. 1909. 6s.

" THE Battle of Dorking " in blank verse, with occasional inspiration from Mr. Thomas Hardy's " Dynasts ", was not an enterprise one expected from the author of " Travels in Arabia ". The dramatis personæ, which include Sirion, a " divine shining one from heaven ", other " strong heavenly spirits ", the " Souls of Britain's Sleepers ", " Ghosts of England's Hero-Dead ", and " Foreign Ghosts (Buonaparte and the Maid of Orleans) ", speak to his ambition, and the inclusion with them of coastguards, aeronauts, yachtsmen, newsboys, and intelligence officers, to his modernity and courage. At his achievement one can only marvel. The book has no doubt been hurriedly written, since it contains all the latest political cries, but no hurry could quite explain its bombastic badness. That one is entirely in agreement with its argument cannot reconcile one to the doggrel verse and the unconscionable English, much of which reads almost like a parody of the Baboo. " The stomach all day ached of Buonaparte " is really a typical specimen of the author's manner, as is his Vicar's " I go put off My scholar's gown, to do my khaki on " representative of his common forms of speech; and of his rhythm " They in church-yard mould lie graved now, under yewen bough, Arow " is not an unfavourable specimen. The " foreign militaires " who descend on the cliffs from an airship speak an even quainter jargon than the country folk, littered with needless morsels of German, Latin, and French, and one is not surprised to be confronted, when the " Elves of the Sack " arrive, with lines such as " Certain man-great we saw soul-quelling moths ", which not even a knowledge that it is descriptive of the House of Commons helps one to construe. Such things are, however, for those who like them, but a protest is demanded against the spelling. Mr. Doughty may have the best of reasons for writing " prowd ", " catterpillar ", and so forth; but while such spelling is held sufficient to debar men from the practice of a profession, it is the kindly duty of books to avoid giving it an apparent currency.

WESTMINSTER ABBEY DOCUMENTS.

1. "The Manuscripts of Westminster Abbey." By J. A. Robinson and M. R. James. 2. "Flete's History of Westminster Abbey." By J. A. Robinson. Cambridge: At the University Press. 5s. net each.

SINCE Dean Stanley published his " Memorials of Westminster Abbey ", more than thirty years ago, little or nothing has been added to our knowledge of its history. There have been one or two valuable treatises on the architecture, notably Mr. W. R. Lethaby's " Westminster Abbey and the King's Craftsmen ", and there has been a great deal of competitive letterpress issued by this or that publisher to accompany process-pictures of various sorts, but nothing has appeared based on original research. The reason is not far to seek. The materials of history repose in the muniment-room of the Dean and Chapter, and it is not every dignitary of the collegiate body who possesses the necessary leisure or skill to handle original documents. The present Dean of Westminster, however, has both; he has won his spurs in the field of theological palæography; and the Chapter have very wisely decided to publish under his editorship, from time to time, such documents in their archives as are of importance for the history of the great Benedictine house.

The first volume issued in pursuance of this scheme must be pronounced curious rather than important. It is a collection of catalogues, made by the Provost of King's, of the various libraries of manuscripts that have existed in times past, or still exist, at Westminster. There seem to have been three such libraries: first, that of the monastery; secondly, one given by the Lord Keeper Williams in 1623 and destroyed by fire seventy years later; and, thirdly, the present library consisting of chance accumulations. The catalogue of this last library has its obvious use; and the first has an obvious historical interest; but Dr. James' main care has been devoted to the second library, three several catalogues of which he collates. We have no doubt that all this labour serves some useful purpose, but what that purpose may be when the manuscripts are no longer in existence we cannot conjecture. Perhaps it is merely a monument of piety.

> " His saltem accumulem donis, et fungar inani
> Munere."

At any rate it is a monument to the patience of the Provost. We have no means of testing the accuracy of the third and practicable catalogue, but a document which has passed the scrutiny of the Dean of Westminster and the Provost of King's should be beyond suspicion. It cannot, however, be complete. In the time of the late librarian we were shown manuscripts in the Chapter Library of which there is here no mention; for example, an heraldic manuscript in the hand of Camden and a poetical miscellany that had once belonged to George Morley, afterwards Bishop of Winchester. A manuscript book of donations to Dean Williams' Library here inventoried contains many items of interest. Williams seems to have laid all his distinguished friends under contribution for books and manuscripts; and the books still survive. The Cursitors of Chancery give £12, the Serjeants of Law £100. Later Dean Dolben gave back to the library its own great Missal, made by Abbot Litlington, and the Hon. Robert Drummond, a prebendary, gave back the no less famous Islip Roll, which, after staying quietly in the library for a decade or two, paid a visit of more than a century's duration to the Society of Antiquaries, and has now once more been brought back to its friends.

The Dean of Westminster contributes to this first volume a collection of notes on the history of the library, with many interesting details drawn from unpublished documents; and also a description of the Westminster Chartularies; but the task by which he has laid under obligation every student of the history of the Abbey is the edition of Flete's history, which forms the second volume before us. Flete was a monk of Westminster in the fifteenth century. The Dean traces him through various offices up to that of Prior. He seems to have been responsible as Treasurer for a rebuilding of the monks' dormitory. But posterity remembers him as the first historian of his house. Widmore used his manuscript, and so did Stanley in a more fumbling manner, but it has never until now been printed. "It is probable", says the Dean, "that the excellence of Widmore's history has been the cause why Flete's own work has lain so long in obscurity. The present edition is an attempt to do tardy justice to a writer who, though he displays no graces of style and not the most rudimentary sense of humour, has devoted vast pains to his task, has copied actual documents in attestation of his statements, and refrains from guessing where he can find no evidence". In a short introduction the Dean discusses Flete's story of the consecration of the Abbey by S. Peter, and makes a careful examination of the Royal Charters and Papal Bulls on which he relies. He makes also some tentative notes on the dates of the Abbots. In this work upon Flete, and the papers on Simon Langham, Osbert de Clare, and "an unknown chronicler" read before the British Academy and other learned bodies, we have substantial contributions towards that history of the Abbey in its monastic period which we hope the Dean of Westminster will some day write.

STAR-GAZING.

"The Judgment of Paris and some other Legends Astronomically Considered." By the Hon. Emmeline M. Plunket. London: Murray. 1908. 7s. 6d. net.

THERE are few more fascinating intellectual pastimes than speculation on the meaning of legends and fairy tales. Do they represent actual events distorted and amplified by the unconscious exaggeration of continual repetition or by the consicous imagination of poets and dramatists of literary ages? Are they mere products of fancy? Are they in some sense allegorical or symbolic? To the uneducated Greek of the historic ages the story of the Trojan war, at any rate in its broad outlines, represented actual fact, much as the traditions of the creation, of Alfred and the cakes, and of Richard Coeur de Lion are all alike history to the uncritical Englishman of to-day. To the philosopher, however, Greek myths were already suspect as early as in Plato's time. Though some were still regarded as historical, others were rejected as meaningless and untrue, and others again were interpreted as moral or religious allegories.

A generation or two ago a new impulse was given to the study of mythology by the suggestion and systematic application of the theory that Greek and other myths were to be explained as imaginative descriptions of the more obvious astronomical and allied natural phenomena. In the hands of a body of enthusiastic scholars the solar myth became in effect the "key to all mythologies". Common-sense, however, suggests, and modern scholars confirm the suggestion, that the Greek legends, not to mention those of other countries, should not be subjected to a uniform method of interpretation. We may obviously believe in an historical siege of Troy, while rejecting in toto the war between the gods and the Titans. We may interpret the Golden Fleece, which Jason and his Argonauts sought in the East, as the dawn or the rising sun, while explaining the genesis of the stories about Herakles in some quite different way. In particular an important modern school of mythologists finds a key to the peculiarities of many stories in the annual changes of vegetation or the processes of agriculture, and associates them with seed-time, harvest and the like. In a subject which is so complex and so speculative we can have no confidence that these explanations will permanently hold their ground, but it may at least be said that the harvest myth is now in fashion, and that the solar myth has lost a good deal of its former lustre.

Miss Plunket's book would have had a better chance of attracting attention and of commanding assent thirty years ago. It is in effect an attempt to explain the chief divinities and heroes associated with the Trojan war as personifications not so much of the sun and its more obvious phenomena but of more recondite astronomical events, and in particular to connect them with certain peculiarities of the system of time measurement employed in the early civilisations of Western Asia. Her speculations presuppose a particular theory of the Accadian calendar, which she has developed in earlier writings. According to one interpretation there is some resemblance between the names of the Accadian months, as given in cuneiform inscriptions, and those of the familiar constellations of the Zodiac, and Miss Plunket finds reasons to suppose that the calendar originated about 6000 B.C., when the sun at midwinter would have been in the position indicated by the name of the first month. The argument is partly linguistic, partly chronological, and partly astronomic. It would be unreasonable to expect really satisfactory evidence on so obscure a subject. When, however, the language is so uncertain that a critical word is translated "twins" by one scholar and "bricks" by another, when a fundamental date is uncertain to the extent of a thousand years, and when there is some astronomic evidence, which the author does not seem to know, that the constellations were formed and named some three thousand years too late for her theory, it must be admitted that she has laid a very insecure foundation for her elaborate superstructure.

Even if we grant the fundamental theory we still find the subsequent speculations wholly unconvincing. If a legend has an astronomical meaning at all, it must clearly correspond to something that is familiar or very striking. The rising run, the phases of the moon, the evening star, or an eclipse may reasonably be invoked in explanation of a divinity or a myth; but the probability of an astronomical explanation obviously diminishes very rapidly as the complexity or unfamiliarity of the phenomenon in question increases. Can we conceive so familiar and important a goddess as Aphrodite invented, as Miss Plunket would have us believe, to symbolise "the moon at or near its full at the season of midsummer in the waters of Pisces and Aquarius", or Achilles to typify the appearance at a particular time of Fomalhaut, a fixed star which is not even of the first magnitude? Cannot we understand Hera's jealousy of her husband's numerous loves without explaining it in terms of the quarrels between the adherents of rival calendars? Before accepting such inherently improbable identifications we may reasonably ask for a good deal of evidence of a fairly convincing nature, certainly far more than is afforded by the slight and trivial resemblances which make up the greater part of the author's case.

NOVELS.

"Treasure-Trove." By C. A. Dawson-Scott. London: Heinemann. 1909. 6s.

The author of "The Burden" is to be congratulated on a novel which shows humour as well as insight, and centres in a virtuous widow, not a disloyal wife. Mrs. Richard Smart, it is true, has a very rudimentary sense of honesty, just because she is lacking in the finer sensibilities, but it is impossible to read her story without sympathising with her devotion to son and daughter. The opening episode is excellent. A burglar, disturbed in his attempt upon Mrs. Smart's plate, bolts in a panic, leaving behind a packet of valuable jewels just stolen from another house. To Mrs. Smart "finding is keeping", and the jewels are turned into the capital necessary to launch her children in life. But everything goes wrong with the ill-gotten wealth, and poor Mrs. Smart sees in the misfortunes of her family the punishment for what, too late, she discerns to have been her sin. The author proclaims stridently that this view is absurd, but—well, things do happen very oddly in real life on these lines. All the characters are well drawn, and the matron's two interviews with the burglar are delightful.

"Indian Dust." By Otto Rothfeld. Oxford: Alden. London: Simpkin, Marshall. 1909. 3s. 6d. net.

We hope that these picturesque and sympathetic sketches of life in Western India, where Rajputs and Bhils are still almost unspoiled by European influence, will not pass unnoticed amidst the more pretentious books of the season. Mr. Rothfeld can see how things look from the Oriental point of view, and though he does not set himself to preach a political creed, his book might give some very salutary information to members of Parliament. It is not always evident to our legislators that the transference of administrative powers from Englishmen to Hindus of the lawyer or shopkeeper class may entail much misery and wrong for the cultivator—who of course ought to prefer a corrupt and oppressive native official to a capable and honest white man. Else what becomes of the sacred doctrine of India for the Indians? The author of these stories can enter into the romantic charm of Rajputana and also enjoy the simple company of primitive forest tribesmen. He can feel for the bewildered product of Islam tempered by Oxford. And he can write a good short story. But his essay on the poetry of "Laurence Hope" is more eulogistic than critical.

"Sarah Tuldon's Lovers." By Orme Agnus. London: Ward, Lock. 1909. 6s

Amongst the numerous admirers of Mrs. Mockell, née Sarah Tuldon, must evidently be reckoned Mr. Orme Agnus, who has written a second book about the lady. This seems to have demanded she should be a widow when the curtain rises on this sequel, and though Mr.

(*Continued on page* 114.)

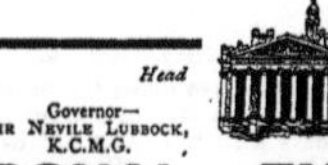

Agnus insists that she had not lost her "virginal bloom" and that no one looking at her would have thought it possible she could have been the mother of two children, his ingenuity did not entirely prevent our surprise when her best lover addressed so masterful and experienced a woman as "Princess of the Morning"! Unfortunately this poetical young man was shot dead in her presence by a less worthy suitor, who then committed suicide; and the old ogre Squire Deverill, another aspirant to her hand, had already been gathered to his fathers. There is really not a lover left, except Mr. Agnus; yet in the closing sentences of the book she is described as still young and of undiminished beauty and "athirst for full-orbed life". So there arises a fearful doubt whether she may not be given another long morning. For though Sarah is a "character" and her soft Dorset dialect is prettily rendered, we felt a good while before we reached the end of this lengthy novel how possible it is to have enough even of a good thing.

SHORTER NOTICES.

"A Tramp's Schooling." By A. N. Cooper. London: Fisher Unwin. 1909. 3s. 6d. net.

Mr. Cooper's "speciality" is walking, and he has achieved the distinction of being better known as "The Walking Parson" than by his own name. This book is a record of a good deal of walking he has done in England, Sweden and Denmark and Italy, and it is very amusing and even instructive reading. Mr. Cooper's method of seeing the world is not one which suits every taste, or everyone's circumstances, but when it does there is none better. Mr. Cooper is not like the countryman who sometimes sat and thought, and at other times just sat; when he walks he thinks, and in an informal, easy, chatty way, he gives his readers the benefit of what he thinks of the many different social and religious observances he has compared and contrasted in the countries through which he has passed. One of his claims for the educational advantages of walking is that it broadens the mind and produces toleration where the non-walker would have prejudices. This is what Mr. Cooper means by a "tramp's schooling". At the same time it is a useful preparation for learning the lessons to have been at Christ Church. This Mr. Cooper may perhaps intend to suggest by his description of himself on the title-page as of that college. There is nothing pregnant with wit or uncommon wisdom; and if Mr. Cooper's curiosity on some things is rather puerile, and his good opinion of himself a little prominent, this all adds to the amusement of a sort of book which is of the genre of Borrow on a small scale without the master's magic of genius.

"History of the Bank of England." By A. Andreades, Professor of Political Science in the University of Athens. Translated by Christabel Meredith. London: King. 1909. 10s. 6d. net.

From "tallies" to Treasury Bills is a long journey, lasting from the seventeenth to the nineteenth century. The Bank of England was founded in the reign of William III. by one Paterson—the Scots and the Swiss are the bankers of the world—and its first patron was Charles Montagu, Chancellor of the Exchequer and afterwards Lord Halifax. Its history is intimately bound up with the political and social history of England. The Old Lady of Threadneedle Street is as much a national institution as the House of Lords; and those who wish to trace its development and to master the intricacies of Sir Robert Peel's Bank Charter Act (which is more often referred to than understood) should read this accurate and scholarly work, written, we are a little ashamed to say, not by an English but a Greek professor.

"History of the German People at the Close of the Middle Ages." By Johannes Janssen. Vols. XIII. and XIV. Translated by A. M. Christie. London: Kegan Paul. 1909. 25s.

This is a celebrated work which has passed through fifteen or sixteen editions in Germany. We might hesitate to undertake the reading of the whole magnum corpus of such a German history. The greater part of it, however, consists of the political history, and there are certain volumes of very much more general interest to English readers. Amongst them is Vol. VII., which is now published as Vols. XIII. and XIV. of the English edition. These volumes treat of the German schools and universities, science, learning and culture down to the beginning of the Thirty Years War. The period is that of the religious reformation or revolution, and the standpoint both of the author and Dr. Ludwig Pastor, who after Janssen's death in 1888 edited and wrote some of the important sections in the present volumes, is the Roman Catholic. But this is an advantage for English readers, to whom this point of view is not so familiar as the Protestant. It is sufficient to know that scholarship and candour have presided over the composition of the work, not polemics. Dr. Janssen said of it: "Of stirring up sectarian feeling I have had no thought. This I can say with a good conscience". But the era is par excellence the era of passionate religious conflicts which disordered every department of life. We can only ask for honesty of intention and the erudition to bring together all the relevant facts. This history fulfils both conditions, and Janssen is to be placed amongst the great historians.

"Famous Women of Florence." By Edgcumbe Staley. London: Constable. 1909.

Mr. Staley has considerable knowledge of the history of Italy in mediæval and renaissance times, and has read widely in Italian literature. He is, therefore, quite qualified by reading to produce such a book as this. Unfortunately he has chosen to adopt a style of writing which would be offensive to the least fastidious. Besides he relates in this fashion hundreds of trivial incidents which may indeed have occurred, but are wholly immaterial. The following passage is a fair example of his method: "Each mounted messenger, descried afar, galloping over hill and dale, with the dust and sweat of battle at the heels of his charger, was halted by the fair watchers as he passed with his news from the front to the council chamber of the Signoria. Beatrice eagerly interrogated him. 'What news of Simone? Is he wounded? Is he well?' Then her concern passed on to her other warrior. 'And how does Dante bear himself? Is he, too, well and safe?' Happily Beatrice's fears of wounds and death upon the stricken field for her two braves were groundless; neither bit the ground, but both returned unscathed with honours fresh upon them." This kind of thing might please schoolgirls of the "establishment for young ladies" type, but it is difficult to characterise as it deserves such treatment of the immortal story of the Vita Nuova.

"The Dictionary of National Biography." Vol. XVII. London: Smith, Elder. 1909. 15s. net.

The new volume opens with fifty-seven pages of Robinsons, but they are beaten by sixty-three pages of Russells, who in turn have to give place to the Scotts with over one hundred pages. In the account of John Robison, the scientific writer and lecturer on chemistry in Glasgow University, Mr. George Stronach says that as a midshipman he saw much active service at the siege of Quebec and was with Wolfe the night before his death when he visited the posts on the river. As it was from Robinson that the story of Wolfe's reciting Gray's "Elegy" came originally, that fact is of some importance. Robison was apparently not with Wolfe in the boat when he drifted down the river to his last attack. The Elegy incident therefore occurred not at that peculiarly inopportune moment, but, as has been recently said, much earlier in the night. Mr. Stronach seems to confirm that view. The feature of the volume is of course Mr. Sidney Lee's "Shakespeare" to whom nearly fifty pages are allotted. The essay is not only exceptional in length, but in the method of setting. It was a happy idea to relieve the columns with paragraph titles.

"The South African Natives." London: Murray. 1909. 6s.

Just now, when the status of the native under the South African Union scheme is the cause of a certain amount of solicitude, this book ought to have a special value. It has been prepared by the South African Native Races Committee and is a supplement to the volume on the economic and social condition of the natives published by the same body a few years ago. Though, of course, much remains to be done, particularly in combating mere prejudice, it is satisfactory to know that the changes in the condition and position of the native since the war have been in the right direction, and that he is doing something to assist his own improvement. Experience shows that he is not as hopelessly indolent as he is generally supposed to be. Two things have saved the South African native from the fate of natives in contact with civilisation elsewhere—"the influence and teachings of the missionaries, and the almost insatiable demand of the white colonists for unskilled labour". The various aspects of the labour question, land administration and taxation, the legal status and the education of the native, and the Ethiopian movement in the various colonies are reviewed, so that those who would assist the transition from the old order to the new may easily understand the character of the problem involved. It is one of the gravest which will confront United South Africa from the very outset.

"Revue des Deux Mondes." 15 Juillet.

Madame "Marcelle Tinayre" begins in this number some very interesting notes de voyage on a visit to Constantinople in the spring of this year. She arrived there in the interval between the short-lived triumph of the counter-revolution and the entry of the Macedonian troops. The whole of the foreign colony was at the time in a state of great alarm, and expecting an attempt to massacre the Christians. The Kurds were expected every moment, and it is quite evident that M. Constans, the French Ambassador, was in a state of considerable anxiety. Madame Tinayre had some rather agitating experiences herself, but nevertheless she was not interfered with during her explorations of Stamboul. General de Négrier writes on the Japanese forces in 1909. He thinks that the spirit of old Japan is very much alive under Western trappings, and believes Japan intends to regenerate the East.

For this Week's Books see page 116.

THIS WEEK'S BOOKS.

BIOGRAPHY

Sir Randall Cremer (Howard Evans). Fisher Unwin. 5s. net.

FICTION

The Shadow of the Cathedral (Vincent Blaxo Ibañez). Constable. 6s.
The Third Circle (Frank Norris). Lane. 6s.
A Royal Indiscretion (Richard Marsh); Watchers by the Shore (J. E. Patterson). Methuen. 6s. each.
The House of Whispers (William Le Queux). Nash. 2s.
Arsène Lupin (Maurice Leblanc). Grant Richards. 6s.
Above all Things (W. Teignmouth Shore); The Lust of Power (Beatrice Selwyn and Russell Vaun). Long. 6s. each.
The Marriage of Hilary Garden (Stanley Portal Hyatt). Laurie. 6s.
Testimony (Alice and Claude Askew). Chapman and Hall. 6s.
Mary (Winifred Graham). Mills and Boon. 6s.
John Goodchild (R. W. Wright-Henderson); Fiona (Lady Napier of Magdala). Murray. 6s.
The Manuscript of Lettice Longnor (Edited by Elizabeth Longnor). Drane. 3s. 6d. net.

HISTORY

The History of the Universities' Mission to Central Africa, 1859-1909 (A. E. M. Anderson-Morshead). Mission to Central Africa. 2s. 6d.
History of the City of New York in the Seventeenth Century (Mrs. Schuyler Van Rensselaer. 2 vols.). New York: Macmillan.
A Century of French Poets (Francis Yvon Eccles). Constable. 10s. 6d. net.
The Gilded Beauties of the Second Empire (Frédéric Loliée). Long. 15s. net.
The Disappearance of the Small-Landowner (Arthur H. Johnson). Oxford: At the Clarendon Press. 5s. net.
Sailing Ships (E. Keble Chatterton). Sidgwick and Jackson. 16s. net.

THEOLOGY

Studies in Resurrection of Christ (Charles H. Robinson). Longmans, Green. 3s. 6d. net.

TRAVEL

Leaves from a Madeira Garden (Charles Thomas-Stanford). Lane. 5s. net.

VERSE

Poems at Home and Abroad (Rev. H. D. Rawnsley). Glasgow: Maclehose. 2s. 6d. net.
Heinrich Heine (Robert Levy). Melrose. 5s. net.

MISCELLANEOUS

Diversions in Sicily (Henry Festing Jones). Rivers. 6s.
Mines of the Transvaal (R. R. Mabson). "Statist." 15s. net.
REVIEWS AND MAGAZINES FOR JULY.—The North American Review, 1s.; Mercure de France, 1f. 50c.; The English Historical Review, 5s.; Science Progress, 5s.; The Law Quarterly Review, 5s.; The Church Quarterly Review, 3s.; The Atlantic Monthly, 1s.
FOR AUGUST.—Fry's Magazine, 6d.; The Pall Mall, 6d.; The Quarterly Review, 6s.

MESSRS. METHUEN'S NEW BOOKS

Messrs. METHUEN have ready a New Book of the highest interest, by H. INIGO TRIGGS, A.R.I.B.A., entitled **TOWN PLANNING: Past, Present, and Possible.** With 170 Illustrations. Wide royal 8vo. 15s. net.

Messrs. METHUEN will publish on July 29

ANNI DOMINI: A Gospel Study, by Lady MABEL LINDSAY. In two volumes. Super royal 8vo. 10s. net.

A splendid and marvellously cheap book.

THE YOUNG NATURALIST. By W. PERCIVAL WESTELL. With Coloured Plates and other Illustrations. Crown 8vo. 6s.; and

A CONSTITUTIONAL HISTORY OF ENGLAND. By A. M. CHAMBERS. Crown 8vo. 6s.

THE TERROR IN RUSSIA: an Appeal to the British Nation, by PRINCE KROPOTKIN, is now ready. Crown 8vo. 2d. net.

A NEW NOVEL BY HILAIRE BELLOC, M.P.

A CHANGE IN THE CABINET is Mr. BELLOC's New Novel. It is one of high politics. Please order it at once. Crown 8vo. 6s.

THE CASTLE BY THE SEA, by H. B. MARRIOTT WATSON, will be published on July 29. Crown 8vo. 6s.

Messrs. METHUEN have just published a New Edition of **OVER BEMERTON'S: an Easy-Going Story,** by E. V. LUCAS. Fcap. 8vo. 5s. It is uniform with Mr. Lucas's "Open Road."

GENERAL LITERATURE

THE CONDITION OF ENGLAND. By C. F. G. MASTERMAN, M.P. Second Edition. Crown 8vo. 6s. A book of enthralling interest and indispensable to the student of the new social and industrial conditions. *Daily Chronicle.*

"Mr. Masterman has essayed a great task, and has succeeded well."

"It is a brilliant, glowing work, the interest of which is unfailing throughout." *Daily News.*

THE PYRENEES. By HILAIRE BELLOC, M.P. With Maps and Plans by the Author. Demy 8vo. 7s. 6d. net.

Historical, descriptive, reminiscent, anecdotal, practical, geographical, political, and literary.

"The charm of a fine style is added to the practical man's grasp of commonplace detail."—*Morning Leader.*

"Mr. Belloc lays himself out to tell the traveller just those things which the guide books fail to tell him: the small essential things and the large interesting things."—*Daily News.*

TYROL AND ITS PEOPLE. By CLIVE HOLLAND. With 16 Illustrations in Colour by ADRIAN STOKES and many others. Demy 8vo. 10s. 6d. net.

This is a full and intimate account of that delightful province.

"A comprehensive volume, which does full justice to actual and legendary charms of the Tyrol."—*Evening Standard.*

"The illustrations are numerous and excellent, and those in colour are exquisite in themselves and beautifully reproduced."—*Daily Mail.*

THE SPIRIT OF THE DOWNS: Impressions and Reminiscences of the Sussex Downs, and Downland People and Places. By ARTHUR BECKETT. With 20 Illustrations in Colour by STANLEY INCHBOLD. Demy 8vo. 10s. 6d. net.

"A varied and delightful volume, with an individual touch and an individual enthusiasm."—*Daily Chronicle.*

"Of the people and their land Mr. Beckett writes delightfully; his knowledge is wide and his treatment sympathetic."—*Globe.*

THE CONFLICT OF RELIGIONS IN THE EARLY ROMAN EMPIRE. By T. R. GLOVER, M.A., Fellow of St. John's College, Cambridge. Second Edition. Demy 8vo 7s. 6d. net.

"The book has great literary distinction, and underlying it a foundation of firm and laborious scholarship. . . . The present reviewer may say that not a few passages in Mr. Glover's book have moved him with a feeling of which praise is a less fit expression than gratitude."—*Times.*

ENCHANTERS OF MEN. By ETHEL COLBURN MAYNE. With 24 Illustrations. Demy 8vo. 10s. 6d. net.

Contains vivid studies of twenty-three beautiful, witty, and fascinating women.

"The book is written with vivacity and succeeds in giving us living portraits." *Standard.*

"Miss Mayne's writing is in the best meaning of the word 'racy,' and is full of fragrance and a quivering eagerness to win sympathy for women as women." *Pall Mall Gazette.*

THE TURKISH PEOPLE. By LUCY M. GARNETT. With many Illustrations, demy 8vo. 10s. 6d. net.

A description of the life and customs of modern Turks.

"The curious home life of the East is described with unusual insight." *Daily Mail.*

"Miss Garnett writes with sympathy and knowledge."—*Observer.*

IN UNKNOWN TUSCANY. By EDWARD HUTTON. With 20 Illustrations, demy 8vo. 7s. 6d. net.

An account of a summer spent among the peasants of Southern Tuscany. It is full of delightful descriptions of the countryside.

HENRY VI. Parts I. and II. By WILLIAM SHAKESPEARE. Edited by H. C. HART and C. K. POOLER. Demy 8vo. 2 6d. net each. [*The Arden Shakespeare.*

THE BRETONS AT HOME. By FRANCES M. GOSLING. With 12 Illustrations in Colour by GASTON FANTY LESCURE and 32 from Photographs, demy 8vo. 10s. 6d. net.

A charming book, descriptive of Breton peasant life, with its rich harvest of legend and history. It is profusely illustrated.

"A keenly sympathetic picture of the Breton peasant folk."—*Daily Mail.*

"There has, perhaps, never been a more delightful account of the Bretons and their land from an English pen."—*Manchester Courier.*

A SUMMER IN TOURAINE. By FREDERIC LEES. With 12 Illustrations in Colour by MAXWELL ARMFIELD, and 87 from Photographs. Also a Map. Demy 8vo. 10s. 6d. net.

This magnificently illustrated book is a complete and absorbing description of France's most delightful province.

"At once accurate in topography, informing in history, appreciative in art, and complete in design."—*Liverpool Post.*

WALKS IN PARIS. By GEORGES CAIN. Translated by A. R. ALLINSON. With 118 Illustrations. Demy 8vo. 7s. 6d. net.

This is a delightful medley of gossip and antiquarian lore.

"A delightful book, vivaciously translated."—*Morning Leader.*

"An absolutely bewitching book, as full of fact as it is of fun." *Westminster Gazette.*

ENGLISH COSTUME. By G. CLINCH. With many Illustrations. Demy 8vo. 7s. 6d. net. [*Antiquary's Books.*

This important subject is traced from prehistoric times to the eighteenth century.

"A book of uncommon excellence and absorbing interest; a deep and safe well of illustration and erudition."—*Globe.*

"A veritable literary pageant of the dress of English men and women from the earliest age."—*World.*

DANTE IN ENGLISH LITERATURE. By PAGET TOYNBEE, M.A., D.Litt. Two vols. Demy 8vo. 21s. net.

An account of the connection of Dante with English literature, quoting all the references to the great poet from Chaucer to the death of Cary in 1844.

"Dr. Tonybee has fulfilled his task to admiration. His book is a treasure-house of English 'Dantism.'"—*Spectator.*

"This is a wonderful anthology of Dante criticism and eulogy."—*Sphere.*

EUROPE IN RENAISSANCE AND REFORMATION. By M. A. HOLLINGS. With many Maps. Crown 8vo. 2s. 6d. [*Six Ages of European History.*

THE CENTRAL PERIOD OF THE MIDDLE AGE, 918-1273. By BEATRICE A. LEES, Resident History Tutor, Somerville College, Oxford. With many Maps. Crown 8vo. 2s. 6d. [*Six Ages of European History.*

A SHORT HISTORY OF THE ROYAL NAVY. By DAVID HANNAY. Vol. II. 1689-1815. Demy 8vo. 7s. 6d. net.

This is the second and completing volume of Mr. Hannay's well-known history of the Royal Navy. It commences with the year 1689, and carries the history down to the year 1815.

"A book to captivate as well as to instruct."—*Daily Mail.*

THE NATURAL HISTORY OF IGNEOUS ROCKS. By ALFRED HARKER, M.A., F.R.S., Fellow of St. John's College. With 112 Diagrams and 2 Plates. Demy 8vo. 12s. 6d. net.

"A work of large erudition, freshly thought out, expounded on a well-considered system, and furnished with many serviceable illustrations."—*Scotsman.*

RAMBLES IN SUSSEX. By F. G. BRABANT. With many Illustrations. Crown 8vo. 6s.

"Mr. Brabant's qualities as a rambler contribute generally to our enjoyment. . . One of his best qualifications is his knowledge of architecture. . . He is a wide-awake and well-informed guide; he is also very companionable. He appreciates the literature, prose and poetry, ancient and modern, that bears on the county." *Athenæum.*

MONMOUTHSHIRE. By G. W. WADE, D.D., and J. H. WADE, M.A., Authors of "Somerset." With 32 Illustrations and 2 Maps. Small pott 8vo. gilt top, 2s. 6d. net; leather, 3s. 6d. net. [*Little Guides.*

FICTION

SET IN SILVER. By C. N. and A. M. WILLIAMSON, Authors of "The Lightning Conductor." With 4 Illustrations in Colour. Crown 8vo. 6s.

"The delightful authors are here found at their best as brilliant writers of romantic fiction."—*Scotsman.*

"It is a thoroughgoing Williamson book. It wakens and quickens love for the happy out-of-doors."—*Daily Chronicle.*

THE LIGHTNING CONDUCTOR. By C. N. and A. M. WILLIAMSON. Cheap Edition. Crown 8vo. 1s. net. [*Nineteeenth Edition.*

BARBARY SHEEP. By ROBERT HICHENS, Author of "The Garden of Allah." Crown 8vo. 3s. 6d. [*Second Edition.*

"The three chief characters are drawn with the finest strength and naturalness; they fit perfectly into the astonishing background. Mr. Hichens has done nothing better."—*Morning Leader.*

"Here is a clear little story, beautifully told, which is instinct with drama from the first page to the last."—*Daily Mail.*

THE CASTLE BY THE SEA. By H. B. MARRIOTT WATSON. Crown 8vo. 6s. [*Ready July 29.*

A ROYAL INDISCRETION. By RICHARD MARSH. Crown 8vo. 6s.

WATCHERS BY THE SHORE. By J. E. PATTERSON, Author of "Fishers of the Sea." Crown 8vo. 6s.

DEEP SEA WARRIORS. By BASIL LUBBOCK. With 4 Illustrations. Crown 8vo. 6s.

THE INVINCIBLE AMELIA: the Polite Adventuress. By E. MARIA ALBANESI, Author of "Susannah and One Other." Crown 8vo. 3s. 6d. *Second Edition.*

GALATEA OF THE WHEATFIELD. By M. E. FRANCIS (Mrs. Blundell), Author of "Hardy-on-the-Hill." Crown 8vo. 6s.

"All the characters have life and interest, and the writing is as delightful as all this author's writing."—*Observer.*

"An excellent story, told well and skilfully."—*Evening Standard.*

SISTER K. By MABEL HART. Crown 8vo. 6s.

AN HONEST MAN. By R. H. BRETHERTON, Author of "The Mill." Crown 8vo. 6s.

THE BISHOP AND THE LADY. By MARTIN LUTRELL SWAYNE. Crown 8vo. 6s.

THEIR OXFORD YEAR. By OONA H. BALL, Author of "Barbara Goes to Oxford." With 16 Illustrations. Crown 8vo. 6s.

"Descriptive, topical, and romantic interests are blended."—*Glasgow Herald.*

"Mrs. Ball's vignettes of Oxford scenes are full of charm, quiet, restrained, sympathetic."—*Guardian.*

METHUEN & CO., 36 Essex Street, London, W.C.

JOHN LONG'S NEW BOOKS

THE GILDED BEAUTIES OF THE SECOND EMPIRE.

By **FRÉDÉRIC LOLIÉE.** English Version by **BRYAN O'DONNELL, M.A.** With 34 Portraits of the Beauties of that period. Demy 8vo. **15s.** net. [*Just out.*

The Court, Society, Semi-Society, and the smaller fractions thereof are reviewed in the charming anecdotal style of Frédéric Loliée, the eminent historian and chronicler of the Second Empire. Dramatic and comic episodes abound, some of which concern contemporaneous personages of exalted rank. Paris, the centre of wit and pleasure, the home of mad revelry and wild gambling, the Paris of yesterday, is compared with the Paris of to-day.

THE REAL FRANCIS JOSEPH: the Private Life of the Emperor of Austria.

By **HENRI DE WEINDEL.** English Version by **PHILIP W. SERGEANT.** With Photogravure and 44 other Portraits. Demy 8vo. **15s.** net.

The *Daily Telegraph* says: "An entertaining—and in many respects saddening, if piquant—work. M. de Weindel tells many stories of various members of the Hapsburgs which will provide lively reading, and presents a tragic history of the *doyen* of European Monarchs in a distinctly readable fashion."

THE SECRET HISTORY OF THE COURT OF SPAIN, 1802-1906.

By **RACHEL CHALLICE,** Author of "Spanish Protestants in the Sixteenth Century," and Collaborator in "The Historians' History of the World." Illustrations by **JUAN COMBA,** Artist by appointment to the Court of Spain. Demy 8vo. **15s.** net.

The *Tatler* says: "The information is gained entirely from Spanish sources, and gives a new insight to many subjects which have hitherto to English people appeared mysterious and unaccountable. A very interesting book, and one as instructive as it is entertaining."

"In every way worthy of comparison with 'Tom Brown's Schooldays.'"—*The Times.*

ETON MEMORIES.

By an **OLD ETONIAN.** With numerous Illustrations. Demy 8vo. **10s. 6d.** net.

The *Times* says: "The author's memory goes back to the days of Keate, more than eighty years ago, and he gives a vigorous picture of life at Eton, which is in every way worthy of comparison with 'Tom Brown's Schooldays.' A word of high praise must be said for the admirable drawings which accompany the book, from sketches by an Old Etonian."

THE VOICE OF THE ORIENT.

By **Mrs. WALTER TIBBITS.** With Coloured Frontispiece and 20 Illustrations. Demy 8vo. **3s. 6d.** net. 2nd Edition.

The *Tatler* says: "We have nothing but praise for Mrs. Tibbits's volume, which is full of interest and the poetical glamour of the East."

"JOHN LONG'S Novels are read by everybody who is anybody."—*Madame.*

John Long's Popular Novels.

Mr. JOHN LONG has just published the following important New Novels:

"ABOVE ALL THINGS," by W. TEIGNMOUTH SHORE, Author of "A Soul's Awakening" **(6s.).** **"THE LUST OF POWER,"** a powerful and realistic Novel by BEATRICE SELWYN and RUSSELL VAUN **(6s.).** **"THE NATIVE WIFE,"** a Tale of Indian Love and Anarchism, by HENRY BRUCE, Author of "Letters from Malabar" **(6s.).**

SIX SHILLINGS EACH.

THE HAZARD OF THE DIE (see below) . . By a Peer
MOLLIE DEVERILL (Coloured Frontispiece) . . Curtis Yorke
THE RED HOT CROWN . . Dorothea Gerard
SYLVIA AND THE SECRETARY . . Olivia Ramsey
ASHES OF PASSION . . Mrs. Coulson Kernahan
BURNT WINGS . . Mrs. Stanley Wrench
OLIVER . . Henry C. ff. Castleman
A WHITE LIE . . G. Russell Beardmore
SHEILA OF DUNSLANE . . James Shannon
THE ENTERPRISE OF ELLA . . Jay Jelf
CACKLING GEESE . . Brenda Girvin

AN OUTSTANDING SUCCESS!

FOURTH EDITION PRINTING.

THE HAZARD OF THE DIE

THE NOVEL EVERYONE IS READING.

It is written by a Peer of the Realm, who last year jumped into fame with that powerful and realistic novel "THE HARD WAY."

The *Pall Mall Gazette* says:—"Never have the Smart—the Super-Smart—Set been exposed to more scathing and relentless attack. From black sin to mere foible there is hardly a trait of their characters or an act of their lives which is not here revealed. The book, with its smart dialogue, its shrewd observation, and its vraisemblance, must be written down a production of remarkable cleverness."

The *Globe* says:—"The Author's brilliant, if appalling, picture of a certain aspect of 'Smart' life is a bitter attack on the corruption of that class. 'The Hazard of the Die' is exceptionally powerful and dramatic, while the moral of the story is unimpeachable. It should make a real and forcible appeal to all thinking men and women."

Price 6s. at all Libraries and Booksellers.

NOTE.—A **1s.** Edition has just been published of "THE HARD WAY."

IMPORTANT ANNOUNCEMENT.

Nat Gould's New Novels at 1s.

Commencing July, 1909, all Mr. NAT GOULD'S **New** Novels will be published at the outset at **1s. net** picture cover and **2s.** cloth gilt, crown 8vo. The novels will be of the same length as heretofore, and **THE STOLEN RACER** is the first in the new series. Mr. Nat Gould is the Author with the largest public. The Sales of his stories to date exceed the stupendous number of **6,000,000** (six million) copies!

JOHN LONG, Ltd., are the Sole Publishers of all Mr. Nat Gould's **New** Novels. *Kindly write for List.*

John Long's Famous 1s. Series.

N.B.—In this Series none but Books of exceptional calibre are included. Price 1s. net each, or post free 1s. 3d. From all Booksellers, who hold large stocks.

MR. and MRS. VILLIERS . . Hubert Wales
CYNTHIA IN THE WILDERNESS . . Hubert Wales
LOVE'S FOOL . . Mrs. Stanley Wrench
THE HARD WAY . . By a Peer
KEEPERS OF THE HOUSE . . Cosmo Hamilton
ANNA LOMBARD . . Victoria Cross
CONFESSIONS OF A PRINCESS . . Anonymous
AMAZEMENT . . James Blyth
RUBINA . . James Blyth
CONFESSIONS OF CLEODORA . . Carlton Dawe
SECRET HISTORY OF THE COURT OF BERLIN . . H. W. Fischer

London: JOHN LONG, Ltd., Publishers, 12, 13, 14 Norris Street, Haymarket.

Printed for the Proprietors by SPOTTISWOODE & Co. LTD., 5 New-street Square, E.C., and Published by REGINALD WEBSTER PAGE, at the Office, 10 King Street, Covent Garden, in the Parish of St. Paul, in the County of London.—*Saturday*, 24 *July* 1909.

THE

SATURDAY REVIEW

OF

POLITICS, LITERATURE, SCIENCE, AND ART.

No. 2,805 Vol. 108. 31 July 1909. [Registered as a Newspaper.] 6d.

CONTENTS.

We beg leave to state that we decline to return or to enter into correspondence as to rejected communications; and to this rule we can make no exception. Manuscripts not acknowledged within four weeks are rejected.

NOTES OF THE WEEK.

The Spanish Government has serious work before it. The fighting at Melilla has grown into a war, and not a little one. The Moorish tribesmen are becoming more audacious daily, and are pressing the attack almost up to the gates of the city. So far the Spanish forces have succeeded in holding them in check. This may be said with truth, but it is the utmost that can be said. It has strained the Spanish forces on the spot to the utmost to do this; and their losses have been heavy. General Pintos has been killed, and according to Reuter about a thousand men, with from fifteen hundred to two thousand wounded. This is a list of casualties far exceeding that of most of the engagements in the South African war. Information as to the campaign is yet scanty, but it is evident that the Spanish general has his work cut out.

As ever, the revolutionaries in the population are taking advantage of the country's difficulties to help themselves. It seems likely that the outbreaks at Barcelona and elsewhere are part of a concerted plan, the work of a regular organisation. Apparently the war is unpopular in parts, as every war is, and the revolutionaries are playing on the discontent of the populace. In Barcelona there has been almost regular fighting, barricades and the usual revolutionary plant with artillery opposed. Fortunately the Government has acted with more or less readiness and firmness. The country has been placed under martial law, and there seems to be no disposition to take things easily. The revolutionaries should be put down with unsparing firmness. There is no room here for gentleness. Attacked within and without, Spain may very well be fighting for her life.

M. Clemenceau is succeeded by M. Briand, and the new Prime Minister has delivered a long phrase-mongering harangue to explain that he is going to carry on M. Clemenceau's policy. Until the elections M. Briand's Ministry can only be a makeshift. The question for M. Briand is, Will they give him such a majority that he will be more independent than he is at present and choose colleagues with more freedom than he has been able to do so far? In his new position he will be able to control things to this end. His Budget, which he inherits, is a handicap for him. The electors may be pleased with the very French sentiment of M. Briand's address to the Chamber; but when it comes to the hard facts of the Budget, their representatives will find it a hard task to please them and support M. Briand at the same time. Income tax and succession duties and "progressive" dog taxes and levies for old-age pensions will terribly dull the shine of M. Briand's beaux yeux.

How will M. Briand get on with his Tariff Bill or with the American Tariff Bill, which the French Ambassador to Washington says is so sorely trying France? Will he fare better than Mr. Taft in America? Mr. Taft is engaged in a struggle, apparently good-humoured, with both Houses of Congress. He has sent in an ultimatum demanding the lowest scale of tariffs on lumber, leather, gloves and hosiery, and free hides. The Conference are inclined to give in; in fact have given in. But neither the Senate nor the House is by any means so complacent. There is a deadlock. The President no doubt has popular support behind him. As is usual, the President represents the nation; Congress—well, rings and sections and trades; and on the whole it is more likely than not that the "interests" will beat the President.

The South Africa Union Bill was read a second time in the Lords on Tuesday. It received the blessing not only of Lord Crewe, but of the Archbishop of Canterbury and of Lord Lansdowne. The essential question now is, Will the Bill draw the sponge across the past? If we could shut our eyes to the history of a century—even to the history of a decade—we might share the optimism with which South Africa's union is hailed. But we cannot ignore patent facts. Has the Dutch ideal been abandoned? Have they gone back on their solemn oaths that the British flag must be superseded by the South African, in other words, the Dutch? If they have, then with Lord Milner and Mr. Chamberlain, who taught them respect for British power, not with Lord Elgin and Sir Henry Campbell-Bannerman, who gave them all they asked, rests the credit. The Boer became enthusiastic for Union when he became top dog. It is just because he is top dog that British enthusiasm should be sane.

We agree with Lord Curzon that Lord Crewe is leaving the truth about South Africa in dangerous hands if posterity is to rely on Macaulays and Froudes. Lord Crewe might have given posterity a more scientific historian, say a Gardiner or a Gairdner. It is not a clear prospect —only a mirage—if there is to be for the future only a repetition of Macaulay and Froude-like heroes and malefactors: picturesque but counterfeit presentments, in the modern sense of false. The newspaper would serve just as well if the newspaper man would, or could, only write English. The reference to Froude was the more unfortunate because Froude was Lord Carnarvon's misguided envoy in the seventies and the prophet of Dutch disloyalty. However, we are distinctly pleased to find Lord Crewe suggesting a name other than Green. He has at any rate read something beside the "Short History".

By the way, we may admire the little sermon in the "Westminster Gazette" on General Botha and Dr. Jameson sitting side by side on the steps of the Throne and yet doubt the text: for at the time Dr. Jameson was ill, and far away from the Throne.

The Foreign Secretary's phrasing is never the work of a wordsmith, it is the work of thought. His short speech on the unveiling of Lord Salisbury's statue at the Foreign Office had several very good points. He spoke of Lord Salisbury's simplicity and dignity combined—"the expression of an ease so often characteristic of the working of great minds". Lord Salisbury had "that detachment which comes not from indifference but from entire freedom from all small ambitions and petty personal anxieties". This is finely put. One may find the same freedom—the true independence—in the character and life of at least one of Lord Salisbury's successors at the Foreign Office.

The discussion on the Colonial Office vote ranged from the language question in South Africa to the opium traffic, from the case of Dinizulu to the grave misconduct of certain British officials in East Africa. Mr. Seely resented the reopening of the East Africa scandal, naturally. The case was a bad one, and the Government hardly seem to have realised their full responsibility in the matter. Both Mr. Lyttelton and Mr. Balfour condemned their action as inexcusably weak. High-placed officials who use their judicial position to gratify their own lust should be punished even more rigorously than men in inferior places. The Government regarded the matter apparently as in the nature of a first offence, punished the offenders accordingly, and sent out a circular to officials in other colonies warning them that any similar offence would be more drastically dealt with. This is just the sort of "justice" children and natives are quick to see through.

The Duke of Connaught's resignation of the Mediterranean command has not come altogether as a surprise. It was the almost inevitable end of what had become a rather ridiculous situation. Civil and military affairs in Gibraltar, Malta, and Egypt had long been "run" in well-established grooves. The responsibilities of the Governors of Malta and Gibraltar were well defined; and time had settled the exceptional nature of our position in Egypt. Two years ago, however, a High Commissioner and Commander-in-Chief of the Mediterranean was appointed. It will be monstrous if the Government appoints another holder of so anomalous and costly a post.

The so-called mobilisation of the First Division at Aldershot is said not to have been intended as a test in mobilisation, but merely as a tactical exercise. Possibly some useful experience may have been gained by one of the new divisions being seen and handled in the field. But in these lean days the money spent on the experiment might have been used better. One point has been made quite clear which can hardly be what the Government intended. The First Division could not be mobilised without denuding the Second and the Cavalry Brigade of its horses, wagons, and equipment. In fact, the whole affair was one of those elaborate shams which delight Mr. Haldane's heart. The regiments were made up to strength by borrowing officers and men from the Second Division, and the Cavalry Brigade horses were also taken away from their legitimate work and caretakers. What a spectacle for foreign nations!

Booms, as hitherto made, are apparently a vain defence. The destroyer cut through the boom at Portsmouth on Wednesday without much difficulty. It was not a matter of a knife going through butter or other such picturesque journalistic figure. At a certain point there was a tough struggle; for a moment the destroyer was held up. But it shore through all right, and was not damaged. The attack succeeded completely; they could have let off all the torpedoes they wished. The experiment showed that a new boom will have to be invented; at any rate, the old one is futile as an obstacle to attack.

Mr. Asquith on Thursday, as in the debate on the shipbuilding vote on Monday, agreed that the navy must be maintained at a point which assured command of the sea against any reasonably possible combination. That the Government have not worked up to that standard is admitted by their decision to lay down the further four ships the necessity for which has hitherto been denied. But even now they approach the question half-heartedly. The extra Dreadnoughts, or whatever they are to be, will not be put in hand immediately. There is no need, said Mr. McKenna, to lay down the keels of these vessels in the present financial year: they can be laid down next April. In other words, the Government admit the necessity but will not face the expense. Mr. George's Budget is of more urgency than the fleet. The Little Navy men could hardly adopt a more suicidal line of policy.

It is amusing to compare the different styles of Mr. Lloyd George and Mr. Asquith as surgeons. Both intend precisely the same operation, but how far apart their professional manner! Mr. George shows the patient his instruments, and openly proclaims that he must lop off the limb. Mr. Asquith's manner is so reassuring that the patient is almost lulled into the belief that there is not going to be an amputation after all. Mr. George hacks and hews like a doctor of old days. Mr. Asquith always employs anæsthetics. His speech in the City last week was a good example of this. We really believe that there are grown-up people so weak and gullible that after listening to Mr. Asquith they go away and imagine that Mr. Asquith's Budget is another than Mr. George's. They are tickled and soothed whilst they listen to Mr. Asquith; alarmed and enraged whilst they listen to Mr. George!

But is it really worth Mr. Asquith's while to go into the City for political purposes? A Liberal Minister with a socialist Budget is as much at home in the City of London as a Tory in Merthyr Tydvil or the wilds of Clare. Mr. Balfour, on the other hand, is very much at home nowadays in the City—though we recall that when he was elected there were wiseacres who thought he was not cut out for the work. His speech at the Cannon Street Hotel is one of the best he has made on the Budget. He touched on a feature of the Budget over which we hope there will be a fight quite as keen as any we have had on increment or reversion. The increased death duties are the most vengeful and crushing of all these new taxes; and they are, too, by common admission, a tax on capital. Mr. Balfour gives the party a good lead in this matter.

Valuation seems a more fissiparous thing than even increment or reversion. The Liberal party looks like splitting into two sections over it. One part is naked; the other ashamed. Mr. Wedgwood, Mr. Churchill, Mr. Morrell, and Mr. Dundas White belong to the former. Mr. White clearly goes on the principle that if a man is to be naked, he may as well be stark. He cries out for a great State valuation because agricultural land may by and by rise in worth. He wants the Government to look beyond " immediate finance ". How can there be any drastic land reform without a general valuation? " The scheme of valuation must be preserved in its entirety if the foundations of land reform are to be well and truly laid." In short, to cripple valuation is to crab the campaign against the Tory landowners—that is the line of Messrs. White, Wedgwood and Co.

So much for the naked section of the Liberal party. We must say it is courageous. It does not care a figleaf for respectability. The respectable section would clothe and disguise Budget designs against the traditional foes of Liberalism. It affects to be purist, quite pedantic, on the fine-spun constitutional questions of what should and what shouldn't be dealt with in the Budget, and of what the House of Lords can and what it can't touch. It quotes Erskine May and House of Lords clerks who write for the " Quarterly ". We find it uneasy lest the House of Lords may have a strong case for flinging out the Budget and smashing up the Liberal party at the General Election, if there is too much valuation.

There is not a shadow of doubt that if a great State valuation of all the land is tacked on to the Budget, the House of Lords will strike it out. Even the grammarians of the Constitution seem agreed that the Lords have the right to deal with tacking. And, indeed, if the Lords did not deal with this particular case, they would be too contemptibly weak. This scheme is quite irrelevant to the proposals of " immediate finance ", and, according to an ex-First Lord of the Treasury, would cost the taxpayers anything from ten to thirty millions of money. It is simply and solely a scheme to down the Tory landowners. From a party point of view we hope that Messrs. White, Wedgwood and Co. will prevail over the respectables. This will simplify the task of the House of Lords; and when the taxpayers come to see that the Budget proposes to put a huge expenditure of from ten to thirty millions on them, and only get a matter of thousands from land in return, they will back the Lords.

Once more the House is tinkering at its own machinery; rather the Prime Minister is tinkering at the machinery of the House. It seems reasonable, no doubt, that the Deputy Chairman of Committee should have the powers of the Chairman. None the less the general effect is to increase the power of the Government and render the House less its own master than ever. There can be no possible doubt that Lord Robert Cecil is right when he says that the House of Commons is rapidly falling in the public estimate. It is not that the calibre of its personnel has sunk (whether in fact it has sunk or not), nor that the debating is inferior, which we believe it is not. It is simply that people do not take the interest they used to take in House of Commons business, because they know it does not matter. They know the Government really control everything. The private member merely asks his whips, " Which side are we voting on? "

Mr. Dillon is concerned for the Roman Catholics in England. He sees " danger of the Catholics of England falling into the paths of those of France ". However, he promises them salvation on the footing that they allow themselves to be directed by himself and the rest of " the boys "; but their direction has been discovered by the Irish Bishops to be " immoral ". Mr. Dillon has not admitted these exact words; but if " the boys " are to lead any section of Englishmen, it is fair to assume that it must be in the way they lead Irishmen, that is, in opposition to the Ten Commandments. To be in the least consistent Mr. Dillon ought to start ten or eleven new Commandments of his own; because, in their leading of Englishmen, " the boys " will require some direct acquaintance with moral method which they seem at present unable to acquire on either side of the Channel.

Very short shrift has been given to the County Courts Bill. The Lords rejected Clause 1, giving unlimited jurisdiction to County Courts. This is the backbone of the Bill from the Government point of view. But it is a wrong view. In pique they may withdraw the Bill, though it has some good points. It is as well to notice when the Lords are represented as throwing out a useful measure of law reform that this clause was contrary to the recommendations of the majority of the Committee of inquiry. Lord Halsbury, who moved its rejection, expressed their views. The County Courts are not able to deal with the business that would have been thrust on them. The small litigants would be crowded out. The judges could not do the work, and in place of them there was to be a crowd of transient phantom judges. The Government will not appoint the necessary judges to the High Court and they devise a Bill which is an insidious attempt to undermine the rights of advocacy of the Bar.

The Duke of Richmond has won his case against the Crown's claim for about £55,000 estate duty. He and the present Earl of March had interests under a Scottish settlement, and their father, the preceding Duke, turned the entailed estates into freehold and gave bonds or mortgages for between seven and eight thousand pounds to secure these interests. This was admittedly done to save estate duty; and the Crown said that as the benefit was for the successors and not for the Duke himself, the amount of the bond could not be deducted. The House of Lords, Lord Collins and Lord Shaw dissenting, has decided that the deduction can be made; just as it might have been if money had been paid instead of the bonds being given. There is talk of an Act to stop such transactions. The Crown wants an Act to the effect that any arrangement whatever which benefits the successor is against the principle of the Finance Act. This would leave no sporting chance for the owner at all. But if the proposal is made, Lord Macnaghten in his judgment supplied arguments against it which will come in useful.

After many hours' sitting in London on Thursday the Board of Trade Conference on the troubles with the Scottish miners did not reach any conclusion and was adjourned again until Friday. All this seems very ominous after the failure of Mr. Askwith K.C., in the earlier conference at Glasgow on Tuesday, to persuade the employers and men to come to a peaceful settlement.

Friday too has passed, and yet after eight hours' sitting the Conference has again adjourned without the question of war or peace being settled. While the conferences have been going on the result of the ballot of all the miners included in the Miners' Federation of Great Britain has been announced, and an immense majority has voted for a national strike if the conference in London breaks up without composing the quarrel. If this should happen, a very serious position would be reached; and the Miners' Federation, acting on the ballot, will instruct the branches that their men shall send in their notices to stop work on the last day of August. All that can be said in such a case is that here, as in the similar Welsh trouble, a national strike, whatever the end of it might be or however quickly it might end, would be such a terrible disaster that its very seriousness seems the best ground for believing it will not be allowed to come to a head.

Mr. Asquith, unbending to humour in Latin, may trifle with less difficulty in that solemn tongue than in English. He is like that other rotund orator, "quem vivum tu socius atque amicus adjuvisti," referred to by the Prefect of Hall at Winchester on Tuesday. Latin might have been the mother-tongue both of Mr. Gladstone and Mr. Asquith, with its elaborate and balanced sentences and intercalated interwoven parentheses. It is a fine language for the gaiety of a serious man; the humour looks so like a statement of fact. The joke about "the furies to whom reference has been made", meaning the suffragettes, is a good example.

Crossing the Channel in twenty-five minutes, M. Blériot has done easily the greatest of feats so far with an aeroplane. Zeppelin and the Wrights were before him in their different aerial vessels; and each might claim, of his own craft, "in ætherias auras ego previus ibo"; but there is a sensation and a success about the Frenchman's adventure that far out-distances those of the German and the American. Mr. Wilbur Wright is, perhaps, the closest and cleverest student of artificial flight among them all; but the tour de force belongs to M. Blériot. He chose the right moment and he had the right vessel—a happy union of fortune and merit.

M. Latham in a much larger machine than M. Blériot has failed twice, and at the second try his monoplane seems to have been wrecked. This wreck is significant of much in the immediate future of aeroplaning. In squalls and storms these machines will often break up, and those who steer them will be killed. The whole thing is in its absolute babyhood, and those who have made any long or exact study of natural flight doubt very much whether the present generation or the coming generation will see anything in the nature of a real mastery of the air reached by aeroplane or airship. They are heavier than air, they are rapid, they can be steered—but the second and third of these conditions only apply when the air is in a state kindly to the "aviator". No sooner is the air really hostile than down comes the vessel. It is a matter of life and death to the "aviator" that he should pick and choose his hour with nicety. Even when he has chosen it he had better have a little fleet of boats preventing any following him if he dare to set sail over the water.

The feat is curious and beautiful; one is not inclined to regard it at present as a great deal more than this. A little gas about aerial adventures is natural and excusable, but it is childish to write and talk as some are writing of the aeroplane. Those who talk about the conquest of the air are like people who talk about the canals in Mars or the nursery gardens of Venus. Men are experimenting in a new and very interesting field—that is the more reasonable way of looking at it. We do feel, however, that the backwardness of this country in airship and aeroplane is almost shameful. Are the Army authorities making any progress? Their successes till now have not been dazzling.

THE SOUTH AFRICAN EPILOGUE.

It is, of course, always unwise not to shout with the multitude, to jump with the cat, to prophesy smooth things. The prophet of old knew that it would be much more to his advantage to tell the king to go and prosper in the war that was to be his undoing than to tell him the truth. And so he found; for he was put in prison for his honesty and nobody thanked him afterwards when his words came true. At least it is not recorded that anybody did; and there was no need to say so, for nobody ever does. The odd thing is that the man who does not fall in with the general rejoicing is thought not mistaken but actually wicked. It is no doubt very wicked of us to venture to think and to say anything of the South African Union except that it is a blessed, glorious, and magnificent thing. We ought to join in the chorus or hold our peace. To doubt the wisdom of the Union is wicked; to express the doubt monstrous. But, with all respect to the jubilation of the moment, we venture to say that there may be occasions when an honest man ought not to say nothing, even though he cannot say anything pleasant. That a thing has been done does not prove that it has been rightly done; nor is it making the best of a bad job to pretend that it is a good one. This unification of the South African colonies is now in effect an accomplished fact. Certainly we must accept it as a fact and make the best of it. The way to make the best of it is to look at it all round and be extremely well aware of its weak points.

This, however, is exactly what no speaker on the subject has dared to do. We are not surprised: it would be a very unpopular thing to do just now. The mot d'ordre is not to criticise the Union policy, but to praise it, which is easy. What more beautiful spectacle than Boer and Briton, pro-Boer and Jingo, Liberal and Tory, Bond and Free (or Progressive), Government and Opposition lying down together in unity? What sweeter music could there be than to hear Lord Curzon saying "The real issue is no longer one between British and Dutch. That is an issue that has gone by and been submerged; and we hope it is never again to be revived"? This is a perfectly pious hope in which we can all safely join. But it shows that Lord Curzon does not think the Dutch and British issue drowned; it is merely under water, out of sight. Ought not a great imperial policy to be founded on something more solid than hopes? Lord Curzon disposes of the racial issue exactly as people like to banish an unpleasant subject. N'en parlons plus. It is bad form to talk of it: it is taboo. And there is no doubt many people, by refusing steadily to think and speak of a thing, can convince themselves that the thing does not exist. Did Lord Curzon ever hear of a people who, having been burnt several times, found the thought of danger from fire irksome and so solemnly resolved that fire was not dangerous and never spoke of it from that day? Unfortunately they were burnt up. In the debate in the Lords, as in nearly all that has been said or written about South African union, there has been this note of make-believe: a determination to assume things are as we want them to be. We admit that the Government, certainly its pro-Boer members, are perfectly consistent in their present optimism: for this policy is carrying to its result the view they have always maintained. They believed in the Dutch and held that they ought to be predominant in South Africa. But Unionists thought otherwise, and it is idle for them to pretend that their enthusiastic acceptance of this Union policy is not a complete change of front. Neither shortly before nor during the war nor after it would any responsible Unionist leader have listened to a proposal to create a South African Parliament in which the British population was to be in a permanent minority. This does not, of course, prove that they are wrong in taking the opposite view now. But it does lay on them the burden of proving their present case very strictly. This present policy is a reversal of Lord Milner's plan.

It is mere playing with words to say that Lord Milner was in favour of a South African Union, and that his policy led up to this. Everybody is in favour of the ultimate union of South Africa; but Lord Milner acted on the single assumption that British supremacy was to be established in South Africa. British or Dutch supremacy was the issue of the war, and Lord Milner held himself bound to make the building-up of British supremacy the key to his whole policy. He believed, of course, that this supremacy was best for South Africa, and in the long run best for the Dutch themselves. Naturally everyone believes his own supremacy to be best for everybody else as well as himself. Lord Milner with true statesmanship would divert both Dutch and British thought from politics to business and agriculture. Crown Colony government equally avoided setting up a Parliament with a Dutch majority and a Parliament from which Dutch were excluded or reduced artificially to a minority. As the country developed the English population would grow, for the Boer is by nature and by tradition non-progressive. In time the British would be stronger in voting power than the Dutch in the Transvaal. Then self-government would be granted. The same process would have gone on in South Africa as a whole, and the Union would have been carried out safely.

This was a statesmanlike British policy. Now we set up a South African Parliament first, trusting to future development to reverse the balance now heavily in favour of the Dutch. Against the admitted great advantage of the Dutch in the meantime we are to put belief in Dutch reasonableness and love for their British brethren. Sentiment is to be our compensation for hard fact. Henceforth, we are told, there will be neither Dutch nor Englishmen, only South Africans. We are not sure every Englishman in South Africa will be so ready to give up his title to the name. The thickness of Dutch blood is proverbial. It was the standing excuse for the Cape rebels that they could not help regarding the Dutch throughout South Africa as of one family with themselves. It is no charge against General Botha and his followers to suggest that they will know how to take advantage of their majority in the Union Parliament. Why should they not? They have every right to do so. They will be much less sagacious than they have hitherto appeared if they do not. Politically the Dutch have beaten the English in South Africa everywhere and at every turn. The English population is fissiparous: it cannot hold together; it quarrels with itself in the face of the opponent: it breaks up into small parties, of which some invariably side with the Dutch. The Dutch, on the other hand, stick together to a man. They may hate each other in private, be jealous, envious, and uncharitable in every other way, but before the enemy they stand together and make a common front. Which of the two peoples, then, is likely to gain more by the setting up of this South African Parliament? Every responsible English statesman sees the danger, but shirks it. He puts us off by telling us that "progress" is going to save the situation. Its limitless wealth is going to draw ever more and more Englishmen to South Africa. In the process of development the Dutch must be beaten, for they are not so fond of money as the British, and have not enough energy to compete with them. Therefore in time the English will be in South Africa in numbers large enough to redress the political balance, now in favour of the Dutch. This may be a true forecast. But are the Dutch fools? Are they not at least as likely to foresee this as we? At best we are to trust to "progress" as a doubtful defence against an actual danger instead of using it, as we could have done, to prevent this danger ever coming into being.

Even those who bid us have confidence in the new régime have not confidence in it themselves: they dare not hand over to the South African Parliament the native protectorates without reservations and conditions. Most rightly; though it is doubtful whether the natives will see much gain in jumping from a colonial Parliament to a colonial Government. No wonder the natives fear the change. On the whole they have done well under British imperial administration, and they very certainly will not gain by the change proposed. Not a single British statesman has anything to say for it on merits. They find it hard enough decently to excuse it.

There are, indeed, splendid imperial paradoxes in this business. The Cape rebels find themselves in a few years, not only voters in their own colony, but masters of the destinies of all British South Africa equally with the rest of the electors. A Cape rebel may yet be Prime Minister of South Africa. How will this strike the Indian British subject, who is not allowed even to come into these African colonies or some of them? Maybe he is a descendant of certain other rebels who, instead of receiving a share in the government of India, with the chance of being Prime Minister, were blown from guns. We need not question the loyalty of the Dutch to the Union Jack and King Edward. Cogent reason is given for not doing so. The presence of the Germans in South Africa, we are told, is a guarantee of Dutch loyalty. They may not like us; but they like the Germans less. Is not this a dignified basis for the loyalty of South Africa to the British flag? The fear of the German? So we have something at any rate to thank the Germans for.

THE LITTLE NAVY PARTY.

I APPEAL to him whether I did not tell him, when I had urged many reasons for strengthening our fleet, which he only answered with 'You will be strong enough for the French', 'My Lord, I know my business, and will do my best with what I have; but pray remember it is not my fault that the fleet is no stronger. I own I am afraid now, in winter, whilst the danger may be remedied; and you will be afraid in summer, when it is past remedy!". The forecast was fully verified. This answer of the famous Admiral Lord Torrington to the Earl of Nottingham will serve perfectly well in reply to Mr. J. E. Ellis, who moved the reduction of the naval estimates to show his disdain for those who would warn the country against defective naval preparation. It is always the same with the economists. It was so with Sir Robert Walpole, for when that statesman found himself involved in a war he wrangled with the Admiralty as to whether it should be allowed to send a single line-of-battle ship, the "Salisbury", to the West Indies, and divested himself of responsibility for the conduct of the war and his inadequate peace preparations by saying in 1741, "As to the conduct of the war, as I am neither admiral nor general, as I have nothing to do with our Army or Navy, I am sure I am not answerable for the prosecution of it". The fact is that the real measure of the courage of the present Government in dealing with the Empire's safety is found in the miserable minority which opposed them in the division lobby on Monday on the Navy Estimates. It is this handful of votes which for three years has constrained them into starving the Navy, and, when appearances could no longer be kept up, abandoning the two-Power standard. As Mr. Balfour pointed out in his City speech on Tuesday, the naval controversy now is really whether we are building to a one-Power standard. Yet now we see, when it comes to voting as distinguished from shouting, the economist cave consists of a remnant of twenty-seven Liberals backed up by seventy-one Labour Socialists and Irish Nationalists. Even more significant of the educational value of the work of the Navy Committee in the House and of the agitation in the Press and on the platform is the fact that the number of Labour M.P.s voting in favour of the proposal to build eight Dreadnoughts instead of four outnumbered those who supported M. Barnes in his plea for reduction. More striking still is the result of any examination of the careers of the twenty-seven Liberals who were in the minority. The Society of Friends nor the Stay at Homes "who only England know" do not provide men of the governing stamp fitted to deal with imperial problems. The speech Mr. Ellis addressed to the Committee of the House in favour of reducing naval expenditure was of itself enough to show how incapable of argument are those who urge this course at a time when, as Mr. Balfour pointed out, we are actually submitting proposals to spend on new construction and armaments this year over half a million sterling less than Germany. Mr. Ellis did not submit one single argument dealing with the matter under discussion. Indeed, he protested vigorously against even attempting to base our naval strength on what a prospective enemy might do, saying, "As to Germany, I am bound to say I think it most unfortunate that we have drifted into a comparison of the naval powers and capacities and internal affairs of a friendly foreign Power". He declared that the spectacle of two leaders trying to make one another understand the particular number of ships that Germany was building was "what he had never seen in the House of Commons before", and was "most lamentable". It is lamentable only that it should become necessary because a British Government cannot be trusted to do its duty except in response to public indignation. It is unfortunately no rare event in our history. If Mr. Ellis will search the files of Hansard, he will find that it occurred on several occasions, notably in 1859, 1884, 1888 and 1893. It is regrettable because the publicity given to an agitation for the purpose of forcing the Government to act up to the necessities of our existence necessarily produces a reflex action on the Continent, and forces on us the extravagance of meeting extra armaments which are more or less indirectly of our own creation. 'Twas ever so under Liberal Governments. The limelight is turned on to our Navy and we have to pay doubly and dearly for our so-called economies. The expenditure is incurred in the most ostentatious manner after numerous official exaggerations of our real strength have been faithfully repeated in the Continental press. This is not all, since for years the harm goes on as the large number of ships built simultaneously become due for repair and ultimately fall obsolete together, producing mischief in the industrial ranks through the large variations of Government orders between one year and another.

It was as a cure to these evils that the Cawdor minimum programme was fixed at four large ships per annum. This document was so carefully considered that it has been stated it was revised three times in book form before its final issue at the end of November 1905. As the Liberal Government retained the same naval advisers as Lord Cawdor, it might have been supposed that with this policy publicly outlined we should have some continuity, especially as every vote in the estimates had been expressly fixed at the minimum of requirements. Not at all. In spite of speeches from Sir Edward Grey finding fault with the Unionists for reducing naval expenditure, in spite of Mr. Haldane being sent into the City of London during the General Election to give the assurances of the Prime Minister and the Cabinet that if necessary the expenditure would be increased, as a dog returns to its vomit the Liberal leaders were true to their worst traditions. They threw over the Cawdor programme at the behest of the party wastrels who have no other motive but mischief and no other task but talk. The excuses of setting an example in disarmament, the imaginary superiority in rapidity of building, the incubation of some wonderful design which is to be as superior to the "Neptune" laid down last February as that vessel outclassed the "Dreadnought", all these have served their turn, with but one object of staving off expenditure. Already Mr. Winston Churchill has begun to appropriate the four extra Dreadnoughts to next year's programme, for he speaks of this year's as embracing four ships, and "next year we should have to build at least four great capital ships". When next year comes the Government will be able to plead that there will be such a congestion of building that it will be physically impossible to lay down such a programme as will then be necessary. In the meantime the Government themselves have completely exploded the idea that we have any margin in pre-Dreadnought battleships by publishing figures showing we shall have of such vessels less than twelve years old on 1 April 1912, or fourteen years old on 1 April 1914, only fourteen, as compared with twelve for Germany and thirteen for the United States. Even if we allow a longer life and include pre-Dreadnoughts less than fifteen years old on 1 April 1912, or seventeen years old on 1 April 1914, we shall have only twenty-six, to eighteen for Germany and sixteen for the United States. The four extra Dreadnoughts are not to be ready at the earliest before 1 April 1912, and then only if no single important part of the numerous contracts is delayed by strikes. In the months prior to that date Germany will have ten Dreadnoughts and three Invincibles, while Great Britain will have twelve Dreadnoughts and four Invincibles. The distinction has to be made in view of Mr. McKenna's recent announcement that the Invincibles may be detached for the defence of commerce. As was pointed out in the debate, with an Admiralty interfering by wireless telegraphy and with such fundamentally unsound ideas of strategy as to believe two-million-pound Invincibles will be used for the attack on commerce, there can be no certainty that our Invincibles will not be detached, whether on true or false information, and the Germans may find themselves on the day of battle with ten Dreadnoughts and three Invincibles against our twelve Dreadnoughts. We use popular but erroneous language; for another of the grave dangers of the situation is that the German battleships are superior to the Dreadnoughts in the possession of powerful secondary batteries of six-inch guns. We understand that our future Dreadnoughts will again possess these batteries. If so, it is a clear confession that a grave error of policy was made, and it is a matter of the highest importance to ascertain by how much our position has been imperilled. It is equally desirable to estimate what margin is required in battleships by a nation whose policy must be to keep the sea, in order to keep open her trade routes, so as to allow for coaling, refits, and probable casualties from mines and torpedo attacks; and, finally, the antennæ of the fleets, in the shape of cruisers and destroyers, require the most detailed consideration. The manning of all these vessels and their proper supply and refit are matters which cannot be neglected if the situation is to be considered as a whole. Beside this great question of imperial safety all others pale into insignificance; and once it is clearly understood that the defence of the Empire is in dangerous hands, the country will not quibble about constitutional courtesies in putting better men in their place.

M. BRIAND'S DÉBUT.

M. BRIAND is a lucky man. A fortnight ago nothing would have seemed less likely than that he would have to "make" the next elections, except that he would within the same period become Prime Minister. Even in France there is still some distinction in holding that office. It is true that there are probably more ex-Prime Ministers in that country than there are in the City Aldermen who have passed the Chair. But it is also possible to be Prime Minister more than once, and M. Briand seems to possess many of the qualities which go to make in France a successful statesman. He started political life with the flourish and the réclame which attend the enunciation of Socialistic doctrines, and by easy gradations he has slid into that position which comes easily to the clever man who has known how to temper his Socialism below proof till it has been wholly absorbed into the easy and opportunist creed of the Radical-Socialist. This is a class of conviction which is now common among the young Republican lawyers "on the make". If we were to credit to their full extent all the dithyrambs which have been poured forth by the press of this country upon his head we should readily assume that M. Briand is worthy in every respect of the name Aristide which he bears in accordance with the grandiloquent taste of the lower French middle class, an assumption perhaps hardly justified. But we are called upon to consider the prospects of his future rather than the record of his distant past, and the outlook is entertaining rather than reassuring.

In any other country than France, where the system of government is conducted on a constitutional and parliamentary basis, the man who would be called upon to take the place of the defeated Premier would be the man who has been instrumental in turning him out of office, in this case M. Delcassé. But this is not so in French politics. Gambetta overturned several Ministries before he took office, M. Clemenceau even more, and M. Declassé might defeat the late Premier though he could not replace him. As things are now, he could neither form a Ministry nor command a majority. He would never be allowed to conduct an election even if he wished to do so, which may be doubted. M. Briand is a lucky rather than the inevitable man. M. Bourgeois, pursued by telegrams to the north of Europe, declined the invitation, but even before that M. Briand had reaped the advantage of being the man on the spot. This ere now has been the determining cause of success in politics no less than in love.

The world, which has before it already not only M. Briand's Cabinet, but also his programme and inaugural address, is in truth not much the wiser. The new Premier is an adroit and polished phrasemonger; he has also the art of saying nothing while allaying apprehension. It is exceedingly amusing to the foreign critic to contemplate him posing as the moderate man who abhors persecution and "dislikes useless cruelties". We might be deceived when we read this declaration into believing that he was really what he claims to be could we forget that he was the ruthless executor of M. Combes' designs. It is true that M. Combes may have appeared more harsh in his methods, but that was only because he was cruder and probably more honest in his persecution. M. Briand dealt with the Church like an astute politician who uses a certain situation as a stepping-stone for his own ambition. M. Combes was a real fanatic, and regarded his policy as beneficial to the State and only in the second place or in an equal degree to himself. The milder action of M. Briand may be safely attributed to a wise calculation as to how much injustice the ordinary Frenchman would allow to be committed in his name. M. Briand is an opportunist per sang, and he means to stay where he is as long as he can. As for his "Socialism", it may safely be assumed that it will not be allowed to lead him into any dangerous experiments on his own account. But he inherits a policy which he has already declared that he intends to carry out, and if this is to be effected before the elections are upon the country, then he will be a chief of more driving power than we give him credit for at present. If we may form an opinion from his declaration, then we are forced to the conclusion that his aim is to survive the elections, sailing to his goal on the inflated bladders of high-sounding phrases. If he can succeed in this, then he hopes that his ingenuity may be rewarded with a majority of his own kidney secured by the ingenious methods approved and practised by French politicians of all creeds.

But there are many difficulties in the way. He has to induce the Senate to pass the Income Tax Bill. If he succeeds he will have made that eminent body act contrary to its own convictions in the interest of what is supposed to be "Republican solidarity". The scheme itself is an ingenious concoction by the late M. Caillaux of German and English methods, and is of a nature foreign to French ideas, but pleasing, no doubt, to the large class who look with dislike on all people who have anything. This is the class largely cultivated at the present time by deputies who have voted themselves an extra £300 a year and want to be restored to the enjoyment of their incomes after the election. Then the long-promised old-age pension scheme has to become law; this again will raise much opposition. Also the Budget has to be passed, and that contains a large number of irritating taxes which will bring in no large amount but are highly disliked by many classes of the community. There is the "progressive" tax on dogs, the augmentation of the tax on petrol, the imposition of a halfpenny stamp on receipts for amounts between two and ten francs—a highly vexatious and troublesome way of raising revenue which will annoy everyone. There is also to be a tax on capital in the form of succession duty. Such a Budget in a country like France will require a good deal of energy to force through, unless the deputies really believe that it will be popular with the electors. If M. Cochery accepts in full M. Caillaux' legacy, which we understand he does, then he certainly has his work cut out. We must remember that MM. Ribot and Rouvier—both of them ex-Finance Ministers as well as ex-Premiers—have already attacked this Budget with energy, and that it has had to undergo the still more damaging onslaught of M. Poincaré. Though it may appear good electioneering to appeal to the "Have nots", it must not be forgotten that the people who have something to lose in France are very numerous, and they will be gravely affected by the new methods of taxation, whether they have much or little. In fact, we do not envy either the Ministry or the deputies, who have to make good their promises without knowing very precisely how these proposals may be viewed by their constituents. M. Briand will be safe through the vacation, and may think well to modify some of his predecessor's engagements before he actually tries to redeem them, but as a Minister of M. Clemenceau's Cabinet he can hardly repudiate a policy which he helped to engineer, and which he has been declaring for the past three years to be vital to the well-being of the country. But finance is only one of his difficulties. The regulation of the status of State officials is a graver one, and most urgent, which must be dealt with, for it involves the well-being not only of the business world but of society itself. No country can stand a succession of postal strikes and similar disorganisations of the ordinary course of civilised life. M. Briand has been lucky in obtaining M. Millerand to occupy the vital post of Minister of Posts. There he will have the opportunity of carrying out the policy somewhat vaguely described by the Premier as "reconciling the interests of national discipline and Government authority with those of justice". Unfortunately the word "justice" is one on the meaning of which all parties are never agreed in any country, and least of all in France. Unfortunately, also, the mass of public servants in France have not been taught by the Republican politician that they owe a duty to the public who employ them. There is a tendency in all democratic States to teach the worker that he has only rights and no duties. The approach of the elections does not lead us to hope that a politician like M. Briand will prove himself able to deal honestly and bravely as between the State and its employees. We confess that we shall be agreeably surprised if his eloquent exposition of his programme turns out to be anything better than mere phrase-making. There seems, however, some indication that he has grasped the fact that large masses of Frenchmen like a strong Government and are sick of social experiments made at the expense of the orderly classes. If M. Briand can secure a majority for the support of these views he may establish himself in power for a time at all events. He will not do it, however, by "sticking roses", as the "Temps" says, "on every thorn-bush". He will have to face the situation with something better than eloquence and sonorous platitudes. He claims to be "un homme de réalisation", but this is a claim which deeds alone can justify.

THE MEDITERRANEAN SINECURE.

ANOTHER costly unreality has been tested by experience and proved to be unnecessary. It has been announced that the Duke of Connaught has resigned the High Commissionership and Commandership-in-Chief of the Mediterranean. It is not, we are told, on account of any friction between the Duke and the Army Council. It is simply because he has found the office to be a sinecure, which fulfils no useful purpose and imposes an unnecessary charge on Army funds. This was of course obvious from the first; and one only wonders that it has taken two years to come out. The expense involved has nevertheless been considerable. Apart from the salaries of the Chief and his staff—no inconsiderable item—the travelling expenses must have been very heavy. Malta is practically a thousand miles from Gibraltar and Egypt, where the other component parts of the command are mainly situated. So the amount of travelling requisite to carry out the duties has been enormous. It was a strange experiment for a Government pledged to reduction in all possible ways to have sanctioned. To economise, the Regular Army was cut down and battalions disbanded. At the same time this perfectly unnecessary post was created. The whole business is really so absurd that we do not wonder that the Government should try to hush up comment. No doubt in time the Duke's letter of resignation will become public property, and will once more show up the extravagant inconsistencies to which the Government has committed itself. The Duke is a conscientious, hard-working soldier, and we are glad that he has shown his unwillingness any longer to be a party to useless waste and make-believe. It is an open secret that he has not found the position a bed of roses. He was practically a nonentity, and had not even the satisfaction of being a "post office", since, in order to save time, many important papers did not pass through his hands.

We do not follow the meaning of the "Times" in the assumption that the Duke's resignation of a sinecure office marks the close of his military career. As a Field-Marshal he is still on the active list, and indeed remains so till the day of his death; and he is certainly eligible for another military post. Moreover, he is under sixty, and really in the prime of life. So it would be regrettable if from henceforth his services should altogether be lost to the Army. It is true that there are few posts which an officer of his seniority could fitly hold. But it will occur to many that as the Army Council, after a five years' trial, is gradually losing the confidence both of the country and the Army, a return to the former system of a Commander-in-Chief might be desirable. In spite of the fact that for the first time since its creation a man of real ability is the principal military member of the Army Council, it does not appear that military advice is treated with much more respect than it was before Sir William Nicholson's appointment as Chief of the General Staff. The system of a Secretary of State and a Commander-in-Chief is by no means an ideal one. Under modern parliamentary conditions a Commander-in-Chief can never be Commander-in-Chief. But it is questionable whether the change has worked for the benefit of the Army. One authoritative soldier, with the prestige of a great office to back him up, is in a much stronger position than four ordinary General Officers, whose individual responsibility cannot be so well defined. One point at least is incontrovertible. The Army puts much more confidence in a Commander-in-Chief than in an Army Council. The post was once before abolished, but ten years later it was found necessary to restore it. So if it were again restored it would only once more be a case of history repeating itself. Should this happen in the course of the next few years, the Duke would certainly be the most suitable man available. Although, since its restoration in 1793, many very distinguished soldiers have held the post, it cannot be said that any of these have proved to be a remarkable success. Supreme commander as the Duke of Wellington was, he was not a successful Commander-in-Chief; nor can it be said that either Lord Wolseley or Lord Roberts was, though from different causes. On the other hand, although not distinguished commanders in the field, the two Royal chiefs, the Duke of York and the Duke of Cambridge, were successes and inspired confidence. This was of course largely due to the accident that they were Royal Princes, which placed them above political and social influence and above cliques. This may explain the strange rumours that, in spite of the announcement of a new Commander-in-Chief in India, a change of plan may take place at the last minute.

The post of Commander-in-Chief in the Mediterranean should in any case at once be abolished. It would be scandalous if the Government, in order to bolster up a grave bêtise which it has perpetrated, were to appoint another man. Again we cannot agree with the "Times" in thinking that such a post would be congenial to Lord Kitchener after his Indian command has ended. We should imagine, on the contrary, that the last post he would wish to fill would be a gilded sinecure which its first holder was resigning because he could do no useful work there. If we are wrong, then the nation's estimate of Lord Kitchener must be altogether wrong also. Whilst some economy might be effected by abolishing the Mediterranean command, we commend to Mr. Haldane's attention also possible reductions which might be effected at home, and especially in the War Office itself. The staff, civil as well as military, has grown enormously of late years. It is true that in the case of the "Intelligence" branch this was absolutely necessary. In the pre-South African War days Sir John Ardagh, in spite of excellent work done, had not nearly enough staff. But in almost every other branch the staff has increased enormously, and additional links of responsibility have been forged. Yet there is no indication that the work is better done. Indeed, it is said that over-many officials impede the course of business. For instance, in the days before the Esher millennium the War Office contained, including the Commander-in-Chief, sixteen general officers. Now, including the Inspector-General and his staff, the number has reached the generous proportions of twenty-four. Yet what have we gained for this expenditure?

THE INDIAN CONSPIRACY.

THE murderer of Sir Curzon Wyllie and Dr. Lalcaca faced his judges with the sullen courage of the fanatic and fatalist. Indian magistrates know this sort of criminal well, but people in this country are not familiar with the type. This temperament or mental state must not be confounded with insanity. Indian crime furnishes abundant disproof of any such assumption. Lenience to Dhingra in any shape would be misunderstood. The possible consequences are too serious. Mr. Stead, who is attempting to excite public opinion in favour of commutation of the sentence, does not seem to know that what he assumes as a reductio ad absurdum of Dhingra's sanity, the murder of every European in India, man, woman, and child, is actually advocated by anarchists like Mr. Krishnavarma, of whom Dhingra is only one disciple out of many. The principle was put into action in India before it had its victims in London.

But there is a more serious question than to determine the proper punishment of a convicted assassin. Behind Dhingra and his fellows is a secret conspiracy of violence and crime. Perhaps its only open advocate is the notorious Krishnavarma, whose vanity prevents him from being reticent as are the Western anarchists from whom he gets his ideas. It is curious how largely vanity enters into the composition of these patriots. It is conspicuous in Dhingra and no doubt was found useful by the astute conspirators who made him their instrument. For it is impossible to doubt that his act was the outcome of a conspiracy, with agents both here and in India, of which there is reason to fear much more will be heard. It was not the act of an isolated fanatic with motives peculiar and personal to himself. The whole circumstances contradict such a theory. His own words and acts, besides facts that have not yet been made public, discredit it. The meeting at the Caxton Hall included among those called to denounce and repudiate the murder both active and passive sympathisers with the murderer. It was left for an East Indian gentleman of European descent to answer the call from the platform to eject the Indian student who opposed the resolution reprobating the crime. In India the existence of the conspiracy is not denied, and a number of actual assassinations besides many more attempts are proofs of its activity.

Outside the inner ring of extremists and anarchists working in secret is a large organisation which professes to work by constitutional means for constitutional ends. The ultimate object of all is the same—to get rid of the British administration nd fill the vacancy themselves. This agitation conducted openly by methods which the imitave Bengali has fashioned on foreign models. hese methods are the boycott, the press, the platform, assive resistance, and incitement to race hatred; ısidious devices to create imaginary wrongs and rievances, to misrepresent motives and measures, and ɔ stir up hostility against those in authority. It is he story of the Land League over again under infinitely ıore dangerous conditions. Above the surface, teachıgs and preachings to inflammable and ignorant eople who can take hints. In India the hints were ery broad. Below the surface, organisations that plan and commit crimes when they can find and arm the fanatic hand. Then come denunciations of the crime—abhorrence, sympathy with the victim and his friends, the pose of horror to deceive the credulous Englishman at home—and the nauseous round begins again. Their orators talk to the ignorant Indian audiences, and still more ignorant English, as if the Indian population were enslaved. In their own persons and by their own words they prove that they enjoy a degree not merely of freedom but of licence which few European Governments allow their subjects.

In themselves these people present not a little that is pathetically ridiculous when they pose as liberators—bent on the overthrow of the only real liberty their country has ever known. Imagine William Tell or Garibaldi, in a speech of several days' duration, presenting to the oppressors of his fatherland a series of highly elaborate and technical arguments to prove that his words did not mean an appeal to his countrymen to rise and throw off the yoke of tyranny, but merely amounted to a constitutional claim to a large number of well-paid appointments under the hated foreigner!

The so-called "constitutionalists" know well that the agitation serves, and is designed, to create and keep alive a spirit of unrest, and they further must know that the doctrines they preach and the ends they propose cannot be effective without violence, and must and do lead up to outrage. The very reasons put forward by Dhingra in his vindication are evidence of this. The imaginary two millions of lives destroyed and the £100,000,000 filched from India every year by the British Government of which he spoke are merely an adaptation of the famine mortality and the "drain" or "tribute" brought up against our administration in the pages of such writers as Mr. Naoroji and Mr. Dutt. The agitators of this school confine themselves at best to repudiation in general terms of outrages after they have been committed. While posing as leaders they never appear to have given any active assistance to the authorities either in the prevention or detection of crime or in breaking up the conspiracies by which crime is organised. A recent correspondence in the "Times" between two former Lieutenant-Governors of Bengal and Mr. Banerjee and others throws some light on this aspect of the case. Mr. Banerjee had the effrontery to declare that unless the Partition of Bengal were reversed and the deported détenus released he could not assist the Administration. Apparently this is the price he puts on his loyal services.

This organisation, which professes to work in an open and legal manner, is really a greater and more permanent source of danger to public peace and order and to the stability of government than the secret conspiracies. It unsettles and it misleads ignorant people by appeal to imaginary wrongs; it creates a spirit of unrest and antagonism to authority by which the more forward and fanatical are emboldened to conceive and commit crime. It becomes thus ultimately responsible for disturbances which have to be repressed, and then it finds and preaches a new grievance in the repression. Unless the Government, both at home and in India, find nerve to put a stop to this mischievous agitation, both here and there, it will in the end have to face the anarchy and chaos of which Lord Morley has spoken. The people are well known and the means are ready to hand. Better a hundred or a thousand deportations than a cataclysm in which the worst sufferers will be the ignorant masses towards whom the Government will have neglected its first duty. The frontier Ghâzi is the creation of the Mullah. Equally these fanatics and assassins from the Indian provinces are the offspring of the political agitator.

THE CITY.

THE account open for the rise does at last seem to have been materially reduced, and after the carry-over the markets settled into a hard, quiet condition, as of a man who is determined to have a month's holiday undisturbed by ups or downs. Such appearances are, however, very deceptive on the Stock Exchange, as the jobbers are rather fond of laying in stock in quiet times, which, if the market is bare, sometimes produces a sharp rise. Americans are very firm, Union Pacifics having risen to 105 and Steel Commons to 73. The quarterly dividend on these latter has at length been raised to the rate of 3, which of course explains their recent rise, although their present yield, a little over 4 per cent., is not high enough for an ordinary industrial share. The price can only be justified by a further increase of dividend, and their backers say they will pay 6 per cent. and go to par.

In the Kaffir market the only share which has shown any real firmness is City Deep, which has recovered from 4¼ to 4½. Nourse seems to be a neglected and therefore a cheap share at 3¼; its life is put at twenty-five years. Alaska Mexicans are rising, and are now 3⅛. We told our readers to buy Alaska Treadwells when they were 5; they are now 6⅛. We recommend them to buy Alaska Mexicans, which will soon be at 4. It is an axiom of political economy that large profits in any industry attract so much capital that the dividends are speedily reduced to normal level. The rubber industry is a striking illustration of this truth. One or two companies with very small capitals, like Vallombrosa, Bukit Rajahs, and Linggi Plantations, pay dividends of 60 and 70 per cent. These companies planted their rubber trees ten years ago, when the commercial world was thinking of something else—gold or diamonds or oil or tea—and now these prudent planters are reaping their harvest. Their success, however, has attracted company promoters and other financiers who do not know a rubber tree from a tobacco plant or a sago palm, and a new rubber company comes out every day. Of course these promoting gentry have been assisted by the extraordinary rise in the price of rubber, to 8s. a pound, produced partly by increased demand, partly by "short" sales on behalf of speculators and partly by the disorganisation of the Brazilian industry that followed on the American crash of 1907, for the Yankees financed the Manaos industry. So much money has been invested by the public in rubber companies that we do not like to contemplate what will happen when these enthusiastic investors realise that they will not get any dividends for four or five years. There will be a slump in rubber shares, as there has often been a slump in Kaffir shares, as soon as buyers realise that they have been discounting the future rather freely, and as soon as they discover that no one will relieve them of their shares.

The Duke of Fife some time ago presented Duff House and 140 acres of grounds to the municipalities of Banff and Macduff. Duff House, to judge by the pictures on the prospectus, is not the ordinary hideous Scotch mansion, but a beautiful Palladian structure. The canny Councillors of Banff and Macduff have promptly leased it for ninety-nine years at £350 a year to the Banff Syndicate, a select company with £100 capital, held by six gentlemen, Messrs. Van Praagh, Dewynter, Randall, Harvey, Preston and Bryant. The Banff Syndicate has passed the lease on to the company, Duff House Limited, for the consideration of £25,000, and Duff House Limited is now asking the public for a capital of £60,000, out of which to pay Messrs. Van Praagh and Co. £25,000 and to convert the ducal residence into an hotel. There is said to be "excellent shooting on the lands adjoining Duff House", and salmon and trout fishing in the Deveron, "subject to the duke's fishing rights", and an 18-hole golf-course. We should say that the success of the hotel will depend entirely on the golf-links, for we do not much believe in hotel shooting-parties. Men who can shoot always get more invitations than they can accept; and men who cannot shoot would so quickly shoot one another that the hotel would become a mausoleum of duffers. No; the golf-links and the cooking are the things to make or mar the company.

The General Motor Cab Company has grown to be a big concern, and will shortly have 3,467 motor-cabs on the London streets, as well as an interest in the Provincial Motor Cab Company. Its issue of £400,000 debentures (5 per cent.) at 98 seems too good to pay an underwriting commission of 10 per cent.

MUSIC AT MEALS.

By G. S. Robertson.

FROM the boar's-head procession at Queen's College, Oxford, down to the parade of waiters bearing "illuminated ice creams" on a German liner music is used to whet the appetite and to lay stress upon the beauty of the viands which form its text. It is there employed as legitimately as in Messrs. Trench and Holbrooke's "Illuminated Symphony", and does not bore the audience half so much. The expectation of gastric pleasure titillates the auditory nerves. Purely culinary music, however, is rare and mostly obsolete. "The Roast Beef of Old England" is rather patriotic than gastronomic. In other cases the music is not specifically connected with the food, but is inseparable from it by some association of ideas. Thus at the dinner after the inter-University sports it has always been the custom to play Bishop's "The Chough and the Crow". No one has ever explained the reason of this, nor do I feel certain which bird is supposed to represent which University. But such a custom is unusual. Its only effect is to make the lusty athlete, who at that period of the evening is at his lustiest, shout louder than ever to drown the band. That, unfortunately, is the only practicable method in which the band can be drowned. Water is not available at a 'Varsity sports dinner. A far more insidious and detestable custom is that of providing meal-time melody which is purely irrelevant. In the humbler places of resort it is purveyed by two or three underfed and underpaid damsels sitting on the stairs outside the feeding chamber. As we mount the scale of luxury we find gentlemen in red coats, led by a more or less furious fiddler, playing so much of the music as they can manage on the usual combination of stringed instruments minus a viola, and filling up all the other parts on the piano. In higher regions still we have to endure the endeavours of the inferior soprano, and, worse still, the inferior baritone vocalist. Now the banqueter stands in a position of great inferiority to the concert-goer. The concert-goer can get up and go out, or he can imitate the deaf adder. The banqueter can do neither. If he stops his ears he has to lay down his knife and fork, and his plate is whisked away from him by the waiter; if he goes out he loses his dinner altogether. An alternative which might be suggested is that adopted by Ulysses in the case of the Sirens, but I have always been brought up to believe that making bread pills is bad manners. The person who dines at a modern restaurant is, indeed, in no better case than the guest at a German festive meal, where they make speeches between the courses. Once at a solemn lunch at Bayreuth a succulent dish was placed before me, but I had had no time to attack it when one of the Wagner family rose and delivered a speech on "Wissen durch Empfindung", which lasted for half an hour. I cannot even say that it benefited my "Wissen", though it certainly put a stop to my "Empfindung" as far as my lunch was concerned.

Conductors of restaurant bands should be careful to make their selections as abstract as possible. Sea music should be rigidly excluded—there are so many persons who cannot eat a comfortable meal on board ship. Military music does not help the digestion, I think. "Sacred music" may be safely tried, because the listener is in the same position as the church-goer—he cannot decently escape or protest. Vocal music has the disadvantage of being too specific. It is embarrassing to be treated to Tosti's "Good-bye" when you are only just commencing your hors d'œuvre. And, besides, vocal music labours under the disadvantage, for dining purposes, that the ordinary person, for some inscrutable reason, feels bound to stop talking and listen to it. Instrumental music, on the other hand, invariably encourages conversation, and loud conversation too, because you have to overcome the resistance of the orchestra; and active talk, they tell us, is especially good for the digestion. It will be found impossible to sit mum when a restaurant band is in full work, particularly when it is playing the overture to "Raymond". That piece is a favourite with theatre orchestras too, no doubt for the same reason—you are obliged to discuss the play, otherwise you would have to listen to the music. Suppé's "Leichte Cavallerie" overture, the intermezzo from "Cavalleria Rusticana", the "Lost Chord" on the cornet, and several other pieces, which it would be tedious to mention, inevitably produce a similar effect.

The proper position of a restaurant band presents a problem of some difficulty. If it is put too far away it is inaudible; if it is too near you cannot hear yourself speak. The relative disadvantage of these alternatives can only be determined if one has complete information as to the badness of the orchestra and the excellence of the conversation. If it is put too near the pantry the rattle of plates and cups provides a constant xylophone accompaniment, and if this is to be appropriate the répertoire will have to be confined practically to one piece by Saint-Saëns and one by Liszt, with short fragments from one or two more modern composers. If the pantry is at some distance from the instrumentalists, the constant competition of the pseudo-xylophones and the other instruments is annoying to the unmusical and maddening to the musical diner. If the band is too visible it distracts one's attention from one's food, which may or may not be an advantage according to the nature of the restaurant; if it is too invisible the leader becomes dispirited, and does not display his accustomed vigour. I am here speaking, of course, only of male orchestras. To a female orchestra invisibility is fatal. If the room is large, perhaps it will be best for us to place our orchestra in the very middle of it, like M. de Pachmann at the Albert Hall, and bury ourselves in the uttermost corner. If it is placed outside, its performance is apt to resemble too closely the "confused music without" of the Elizabethan dramatists.

My criticism has so far been mainly negative in its nature, and now, if space permitted, I should be happy to make suggestions for programmes to be performed by orchestras in restaurants, but it would be only possible to deal with restaurants where liquor is sold or imported from a public-house in the neighbourhood. There is a good deal of alcohol in music; take, for instance, the deplorable sentiments expressed in "Il segreto per esser felice" or "Fin ch'han dal vino calda la testa". No composer, so far as I know, has been inspired by ginger-pop, and the temperance and vegetarian eating-houses still wait for their musician. But there is great encouragement in the fact that the third act of "Tess" contains a large quantity of dairy music, and that the milky compound is quite in keeping with the remainder of the opera. So there is still hope that the A.B.C. and Lockhart's may be supplied with appropriate strains. Inappropriateness is the bane of music in restaurants. The other night I consumed my chop to the accompaniment of an air sung by Nebuchadnezzar in one of Verdi's earliest operas. Now if only I had been eating grass——

GOMBEEN GRABBIT.

By "Pat".

SOME said that was not his name in baptism, but it was his best, and we knew him as Tom Grabbit.

Grabbit first saw his wife spreading turf, in her bare feet, the only skirt tucked nearly to the knees, the arms bare to the shoulders, a mass of yellow hair sheltering an ample neck, the limbs tapering sensuously in pink and white among the mud; and, in addition, she would have a hundred pounds, which Grabbit knew before he went to see her spreading the turf. The description was his own, in somewhat different language, and she would listen smiling expansively behind the counter, but the sons and daughters must not hear this.

Before he met her, and for some years after, Grabbit was what they called a "spalpeen", that is, a migratory labourer, who went from Mayo every year to reap the harvest in Yorkshire, walking to Drogheda, a hundred and forty miles, in two days, walking again from Liverpool to the Holderness, carrying his food from home on his back, a bundle of oat-cake and a lump of salted butter, washed down from the wells on the way, with such odd glasses of beer as might be got from the five shillings he took to meet the expenses of the journey outside the price of his ticket on the cattle-boat. He slept in sheds and barns. He came back the same way, and counted himself lucky for ten pounds after six months. Knowing the value of money as Grabbit knew it, who will denounce him for permitting that hundred pounds to temper his appreciation of the pink-and-white, the tapering limbs and the yellow hair? Our refinements in these matters depend on our destiny as well as on our nature.

We did not know Grabbit personally in those days, but we knew him later, when he was sixty and looked forty; a man over six feet, on short legs, his head set forward over a mighty trunk, with a long, heavy face, an excess of jaw, a loose underlip, a flat strong nose, deep grey eyes, and the deliberate movements of a profound thinker, with all his outward appearance of a mere animal. Grabbit was always dirty, and seemed to glory in it, for it was the dirt of prosperity, and he knew how to travel five hundred miles on foot with five shillings as a necessity of his existence.

Not a penny was taken from his hundred pounds. He continued to bring the ten pounds a year from Yorkshire, and not a penny was taken from that. The wife and babies lived in the cottage shop in the little town of Kilcuddy, mainly by means of their five acres near, leaving something saved every year to put with the rest. Meantime Grabbit was not exactly a miser, but rather a man of enterprise, full of plans, deep and far-reaching; the brain of a Rockefeller in a Connaught village on a semi-savage training. He meant to make money. Was it not the only thing that he had ever known much worth considering?

Let us see the kind of place where this man set out to become rich. The population of Kilcuddy was two hundred and fifty, all very poor, with the sole exception of the parish priest and the pawnbroker. The peasants around were still poorer, on an average of ten acres to the holding, at five shillings an acre, and considered rack-rented at that. They, too, "went to the harvest", but they got no more than thirty pounds with their wives, and this was commonly paid away with the wives of others, a matrimonial system which keeps capital out of use where it is so badly wanted, always impeding production to save "the fortune". Within a radius of ten miles from Kilcuddy the whole taxable valuation was under fifteen shillings per head of the people. Not a region to attract a Rockefeller, but what if he should be there, seeing no way to a better? He must work out his motives on the scale of his means, in the conditions of his environment, and that was what Grabbit did.

When he found himself with two hundred pounds to spare, he lent a hundred to the peasants at forty per cent., taking care to "let it out" in the smallest possible sums, so as to annex the energies of the largest possible number, after which he got the farm work of the five acres done for nothing, in addition to the forty per cent. on his loans. With the remaining hundred he stocked the little shop with the stuff the peasants must buy, and sold it to his debtors at thirty per cent. above current prices, in addition to the trade profit. If they refused to buy at his shop, he could call in his "gombeen" when they were not ready, and charge them with ingratitude in view of his generosity in finding them money when they were in straits. He made it a point never to threaten them until Mrs. Grabbit had failed to coax them; but then he stopped at nothing; so that between the flatteries of the woman and the terrors of the man, not many peasants escaped. Grabbit soon found himself making at least fifty per cent. on his two hundred pounds, and on the additional hundred which he could put in every year, with the little farm increasingly productive, from labour free of wages, among a people who put little value on a day's work. If not working for Grabbit, they might be idle at home, and it was dangerous to displease the man in a position to crush them. With all the wretchedness of the region, the obvious way to wealth was simply to extend the process.

At first Grabbit paid "prompt cash" to his own creditors, which soon expanded his credit, and then he made the great discovery of his life—that he could get people into his debt without any money at all, by buying on credit, selling on credit, and charging "gombeen" on the goods as if they were money: nothing very original in other and greater places, but certainly a revolution at Kilcuddy, where no man had hitherto seen the possibilities of high finance in a maximum of poverty and a minimum of conscience. Grabbit saw the whole scheme in a flash. He examined it. Everything in it fitted logically with everything else. It was perfect, and it meant thousands instead of hundreds. "Thousands", he said to himself, and his great head leaned farther over his mighty trunk. His movements became still more deliberate. He was thinking, originating a complete Stock Exchange of his own, in the wilds of Mayo, though if anyone asked him what a Stock Exchange meant he could not answer. He had arrived at the great problem of multiplying his operations and his income from the credit of others, and he set about solving it with an enthusiasm impossible to a practised financier. He was at the point of determining the scope of his future life, the status of his family, and he knew it. The one drawback was the possibility of his own creditors coming down on him some day together when he could not grub up the money from the peasants; but he thought he saw a way even out of that.

Grabbit plunged, but he was all shrewdness, even in his plunging. In six months he ordered more goods than he could have paid for in the past seven years; more than he could ever hope to pay for except by forcing the creditors in Manchester and London to wait on his "gombeen" contracts with the peasants round Kilcuddy. "Now", he said to his wife, "let them come from London and Manchester as soon as they like. I can show them twinty shillin's in the pound an' a bit more; an' if they don't like to wait, I can aisily spare them a shillin' in the pound for the money while I'm gettin' seven shillin's for meself". He had seven thousand pounds scattered through the country, the capital of London and Manchester, used to put a whole community of Connaught peasants into pawn to one man; and seven thousand pounds is still regarded in this part of Ireland as the amount which a shopkeeper must find for the enslavement of the public to make money in a large way. He had at least thirty-five per cent. on the seven thousand, even after meeting accidents, so that he began to make over two thousand a year, still living on the scale of his cottage and the five acres, with bacon and cabbage for dinner six times a week. It would take him less than three years to pay off his creditors and have seven thousand pounds left, not to mention that he might "close" on a handsome balance in case they stopped him before the time. He kept no books but one, and neither himself nor his wife could write much more than his name; yet he was never known to lose sight of a debt due to him, though the County Court judge had often found him claiming more than his bond. Indeed, Tom Grabbit became "a character " in the County Court, and set an example that is followed still.

The day came when he had to meet his creditors, but he met them. They waited, and he was as good as his word, paying them 5 per cent. and the last of the principal at the end of three years, after which they renewed his credit most liberally, and he extended his plans in proportion. He built a great shop, with the drink counter across at the far end, so that when the people had well drunk, his wife caught them, and found it easier to sell them what they did not want along the counters on the way out. He got the post-office for the region, and it became a kind of disgrace to cash an order without leaving some of the money behind, so that even the Postmaster-General helped Tom Grabbit to make his fortune. He sent his sons to college, his daughters to boarding-school, and they returned " perfect ladies " and " perfect gintlemin ", though painfully ashamed of their parents. He bought landed estate, and he boasted that he had made seventy thousand pounds, which anyone could see was true.

I knew Tom well in his latter days, and saw him in his dirty clothes, his heavy head bent further than ever, and a dirty silk hat stuck on the back of it. It was the family that had started him with the silk hat; but they could never quite succeed in getting him to wash himself. He still stood behind the drink counter, beaming in an atmosphere of mixed smells, whisky and paraffin, tobacco and the china clay in the Manchester cottons, frizzling bacon and the endless dejectures in the awful yard, which ran uphill behind the shop, washed down against the back door on wet days without a farther thought of sanitation. Tom loved dirt so long as it was the sign of money-making, and when he got a new hat he did not feel at home with it until it had fallen against a flour-bag or into a bacon-box. Yet at times he was wistful in these latter days, and we all knew that when the family " had company " he dared not enter the drawing-room which his enterprise had provided for them. He died only ten years ago. The sons and daughters are already poor, having spent the money in trying to disguise their parentage. He had provided them with the money, but he never thought of providing them with a character. He died in the love of his victims, and had a great funeral of them—the Irish peasant's love for his enemies might make a poem but for it is always equalled by his hatred for his friends. Mrs. Grabbit had died a few years before him. Kilcuddy is here yet, as wretched as ever, and likely so to remain, with seven Grabbits now instead of one, and keen competition in the enterprise of enslavement. Any day I can point out the great shop, now nearly empty, where the " spalpeen " made the seventy thousand pounds, and was forbidden by his highly educated daughters from entering his own drawing-room.

HAY-TIME.

AGAIN the utmost of the year has been. Man's time has come, the time of the eager human onslaught. Already the banks by the roadside are garnered—shaven flat days ago—scorched now, brown and yellow, their rich grasses given their wealth of hemlock and meadowsweet, of fern and dock and campion to be piled away—a sweet withered bedding in stable and outhouse. Clinging and creeping close to earth, the wild strawberry has escaped, and here and there lords and ladies have held their own, rearing sturdy stems from the close-cropped slope, crowned with berries, shining emerald green.

The clipping of the hedges, properly the first victims, is in this leisurely neighbourhood mercifully sporadic. There are long reaches where the honeysuckle is still at its widest glory; the dog-rose lingers, and again we must wonder at eglantine beginning pallidly to utter its tardy challenge.

But the doom of the meadows has fallen.

You may fly; you may go far and deep into the humming stillness of the pinewood at the end of the lane, and in the scattered sunlight, as life streams up from the mossy floor and as the clean boles of the near trees stand intimate in a sudden fellowship, you may forget. You may dream, as the enchantment comes full circle in the branches above you, that the midmost splendour is not yet gone by, that beyond the woods lie the rich June meadows undisturbed—buttercup meadows and meadows where the lush grass has sprung to full measure unchallenged save for small weedy undergrowth; you may see meadows washed at sunset with the menacing flush of sheep-sorrel, and foremost and deepest in the vision a gently sloping fieldpiece where moon-daisies stand stark in the morning light, or bow and nod and ripple—foamy waves under the breeze—or glimmer, an unforgettable blanching, in the moonlight.

And you may still go down enchanted alleys, and, your footsteps marshalled by the ripening corn and all the music of the sunbaked field in your ears, may catch amongst the serried grey-gold stalks the flare of poppies. But the hour has struck; the fulness of the midsummer picture is touched.

Come into the hot open sunshine, come through the gap into the turnipfield—where the good haying days are taking toll of well-nigh the whole nursery—on up the rising ground to the head of the ridge running southward along the centre of the farmland and see away below across the level the hayfields, bathed in light.

There is no holding back. No escape from getting to handgrips with this clustered growth arresting and claiming us, borne up, as it were, on the south-west wind coming softly over the wide scene from the sea lying along the horizon a shimmering line, yielding free range and heightening all the picture. The three broad fields are defined from the afternoon countryside by wayward hedges rich and dark, opening here and there, for alluring access to and fro amongst the pale gold. The rattling mower eats in the near field into the last remaining strip of green, the clanking horse-rake piles the hay in shallow ridges, and away in the furthermost enclosure are the rows of gracious coned heapings, the gathered workers—redoubtable moving forms—and the clean flat stretch whence the enormous wain, slowly advancing along the head-land, has massed its scented burden.

All the arms in the countryside are toiling now throughout the hours of daylight. Women, cottage-bound for the rest of the year, escape their homes and tramp to join their husbands and give the help so precious now, until the last hops shall have been pressed. No one is out of work. Winter is still far off.

The village world is gathered together in its great effort. Early or late it must come, the broad open time, in the most capricious of summers, bringing the saving grace of the struggle, escape from the rural bondage, the goading isolation. Out they come into the fair wide days—for faint alleviation—to the place of welcome for all work-old and ever so little able. To all good strength there is an arena, and warm mead of witness.

Special talents shine. What a wholesome incense fills the afternoon air for the old thatcher pottering about in the stackyard away yonder beside the oasthouse. There is no one for miles round who can finish a rick as he can. It is his proud time. From farm to farm he tramps when haying comes, leaving his cottage and his trug-making, sleeping in outhouses and working from morning twilight until the short night falls. It is the good time.

SIMON'S FATHER.

TRANSLATED FROM GUY DE MAUPASSANT

By Alec Clark.

THE last stroke of noon had sounded, the school door was flung open, and the children poured out, jostling one another in their eagerness to escape as quickly as possible. But instead of dispersing rapidly and going home to dinner, as was their custom, they kept pausing, gathering into groups and holding whispered conversations.

La Blanchotte's son, Simon, had that morning come to school for the first time.

They had all heard talk of la Blanchotte at home; and although she was well enough received in public, the mothers were in the habit of mentioning her name with a kind of contemptuous pity, which made its impression on the children without their understanding its reason.

As for Simon, they did not know him, for he never came out to join their play in the village streets or by the riverside. Thus they had no particular liking for him, and it was with a measure of joy, mingled with considerable surprise, that they had heard certain words which they kept repeating from one to the other. The words had been said by a boy of fourteen or fifteen, whose sly winks indicated that he had known all about it for a long time; he had said: "Oh, Simon!—well—you know, he hasn't got a father ".

Simon in turn appeared at the school door. He was a child of seven or eight years, very pale, very neat, of appearance so timid as almost to seem awkward.

He was turning towards his mother's house, when the groups of his schoolmates gathered about him little by little, till in the end he was completely surrounded. They had never ceased to whisper, and they looked on him with the cruel and pitiless eyes of children who meditate an evil stroke. There Simon stood, planted in the middle of them, surprised and embarrassed, not understanding what they wanted with him. But the boy who had brought the news, puffed up by the success he had already obtained, demanded: "Hallo, youngster, what's your name?"

"Simon", came the reply.

"Simon what?" rejoined the other.

"Simon", repeated the child in confusion.

"Simon", cried the other, "Simon—that's no name—it must be Simon something."

And the child, on the verge of tears, replied for the third time, "My name is Simon".

The urchins around him began to laugh. The triumphant questioner raised his voice: "There, you see, he hasn't got a father".

There was a momentary silence. The children were stupefied by this extraordinary thing—a boy without a father—monstrous! impossible! They looked askance at him as an unnatural being; and they felt arising within them that hitherto unexplained despite which their mothers displayed towards la Blanchotte.

Simon was resting against a tree to keep himself from falling. He was motionless, as though overwhelmed by a disaster beyond repair. He wished to clear his position; but he knew not what to reply, or how to disprove the horrible charge that he had no father. Finally, beside himself he cried out impulsively, "Yes, I have one".

"Where is he?" asked the tormentor.

Simon could not answer: he did not know. The others, wild with glee, burst out laughing. They were children of the fields, with much of the wild beast in their nature; they were possessed by that same spirit which makes the fowls in a poultry-yard hasten to peck to death one of their number which has met with an injury. All at once Simon's eyes fell on a little neighbour, a widow's son, whom he had always seen alone with his mother, just like himself. "You haven't got a father", he said, "any more than I have."

"Oh, yes, I have," replied the other.

"Where is he?" retorted Simon.

"He is dead," declared the other with magnificent pride, "he is in the cemetery; that's where my father is."

A murmur of approbation ran through the scapegrace crew, as though the fact of having a father dead and in the cemetery had conferred a special honour on their comrade, so as to abase yet more this other, who had no father at all. And the little wretches—whose fathers were for the most part evildoers, drunkards, thieves, wifebeaters—jostled into one another and pressed closer and closer, as though they, the legitimate, wished to crush the life out of this being who had no lawful place in the world.

Suddenly the one who was nearest Simon thrust out his tongue with a leer, and cried: "Hasn't got a father, hasn't got a father!"

Simon threw himself on the boy, gripped his hair with both hands, and madly kicked his shins, at the same time trying to bite him. Then came a terrific commotion. The two combatants were separated, and Simon felt himself cuffed, torn, battered, rolled underfoot in the midst of the shrieking circle of ragamuffins. When he regained his feet he began mechanically to brush his little blouse, all filthy with dust. Someone shouted at him, "Go and tell your father".

Then he felt a great sinking of the heart. They were stronger than he, they had beaten him, and he could not answer them, for he knew that in truth he had no father. Pride alone buoyed him up, and for some seconds he sought to struggle against the tears which were trying to burst forth. He felt a choking, then he began to weep silently, and great sobs shook his frame.

At this his enemies burst into ferocious glee, and by natural instinct, like savages in their terrible merry-making, they joined hands and began to dance in a circle around him, repeating as a refrain, "Hasn't got a father! Hasn't got a father!" . . .

But all at once Simon ended his sobbing: an access of fury had seized upon him. Beneath his feet were some loose stones; he picked them up, and with all his force hurled them at his tormentors. Two or three were struck and ran away crying, and so formidable was Simon's appearance that the others were infected with panic. A crowd is always cowardly in the presence of an angry man, and they scattered in flight.

The fatherless child was left alone. He started running towards the fields, for something had come back to his memory and had quickened a great resolution in his spirit. He would drown himself in the river.

What he had remembered was that, a week before, a miserable beggar had thrown himself into the water because he had come to the end of his money. Simon had seen him dragged out. The poor creature had ordinarily seemed wretched, filthy, and repulsive; but what had struck Simon about the dead man was his tranquil appearance as he lay there with pale cheeks, long and dripping beard, and calm, wide-open eyes. "He is dead", someone had remarked; and another had added "Well, he is happy now". And Simon also was determined to drown himself because he had no father, like the poor wretch who had no money.

He had arrived at the brink and stood watching the flow of the water. Fishes were playing about, swiftly darting through the clear stream, and now and then one would make a little leap to catch the flies dancing above the surface. Simon was deeply interested; he watched and forgot his tears. But, like the gusts of wind which suddenly break the lull of a tempest and sweep over the horizon leaving a trail of shivered trees, from time to time the thought returned with a bitter pang, "I am going to drown myself because I have no father".

It was a warm and beautiful day. The grass was heated beneath the genial rays of the sun, and the water shone like a mirror. Simon had some moments of pure happiness, of that languor which is the sequence of tears, and the desire came over him to lay himself to sleep there in the warm meadow.

A little green frog jumped at his feet. He tried to catch it. It escaped. He ran after it and made three vain attempts to seize it, one after the other. At last he just caught hold of one of the hind feet, and it made him laugh to see the animal's attempts to get away. It doubled up its long legs, then suddenly shot straight out, its hind legs rigid like two metal bars, while it beat the air with its forepaws, which waved about like a pair of hands, and all the time its eyes stood out, glazed within their yellow rims. It reminded him of a plaything of his, tin soldiers at the end of a sort of zigzag latticework of wooden bars, which could be made to shoot out and back again like the frog's legs, and so to put the soldiers through their drill. That made him think of home, then of his mother, and then the bitterness came over him again, and the tears began anew. Shudders passed all through him; he knelt down and said his prayers as before going to sleep. But he could not finish, for the sobs came quickly and tempestuously, and at last quite overpowered him. He no longer thought or saw anything around him, but abandoned himself to his tears.

Suddenly a heavy hand was laid on his shoulder, and a deep voice demanded: "What is all the trouble about, my little man?"

Simon turned round. A big man in working clothes, with curly black hair and beard, was looking at him with a kindly expression. He replied in a choking voice, with his eyes still full of tears, "They have beaten me—be-cause—I—I have no father".

"Why," said the man, "everybody has a father."

Between his sobs the child forced out the words, "I—I—haven't—one".

The workman became grave. He had recognised la Blanchotte's son, and, though he was a newcomer to the district, he had learned something of her story. "Come," he said, "dry your tears, my lad, and let me take you home to your mother. Perhaps we'll find a father for you."

They set off together, Simon's little hand resting in the man's great fist. The man was smiling again. He was not sorry of a chance to see la Blanchotte, who was said to be one of the handsomest women of the district. They came to a little white cottage, beautifully kept. "Here we are", said the child, and he cried "Mama!"

A woman appeared, and the smile died suddenly from the workman's lips, for he understood in a flash that this woman was never again to be trifled with. Tall, pale, and dignified, she stood in the doorway as though to prohibit any man from entering that house where one man had already betrayed her. The workman was abashed; cap in hand, he stammered out: "Pardon, madam, I am bringing back your little boy, who had lost himself by the riverside".

But Simon flung both arms about his mother's neck and, bursting into fresh tears, said to her: "No, mother, I was going to drown myself, because the other boys have beaten me—beaten me—for not having a father".

A crimson flame blazed on the woman's face. With a movement of anguish she snatched up the child and kissed him passionately, while a swift burst of tears ran down her cheeks. The man stood still, affected by her emotion and not knowing how to leave. But Simon suddenly ran towards him and cried, "Will you be my father?"

There was a moment's silence. La Blanchotte, mute and overcome by shame, was leaning against the wall, pressing both hands to her heart. Seeing that none replied, the child began again: "If you won't be my father, I shall go back to drown myself".

The workman passed it off as a joke and replied with a laugh, "All right, I'll be your father".

"What do they call you?" was the child's next question, "so that I can tell the others when they ask me your name."

"Philip", replied the man.

Simon kept quiet a moment, to be certain that the name sank into his mind. Then, happy once more, he stretched out both hands, saying, "Very well, Philip, you are my father".

The workman lifted him from the ground and pressed a hasty kiss on each cheek, then fled as quickly as he could.

When the child arrived at school next morning he was greeted with derisive laughter, and after school his tormentor of the previous day was about to renew the attack. Simon, as though hurling a stone at his head, threw these words at him: "My father's name is Philip".

Shouts of laughter broke out on all sides. "Philip?—Philip who?—Philip what?—what's the good of a name like that?—where did you pick him up, this Philip of yours?"

Simon made no answer. His faith was unshaken, and he looked defiantly at them, ready to suffer anything rather than flee before them. The schoolmaster rescued him, and he returned to his mother's house.

During the next three months Philip, the big workman, often found himself near la Blanchotte's cottage. Sometimes when he saw her sewing at the window he summoned up courage to talk to her. She answered politely, yet always gravely, never laughing with him, and never letting him cross her threshold. But, like most men, Philip was a little conceited, and he fancied that when she spoke to him there was often more colour than usual on her cheeks.

But a shattered reputation is difficult to build up again, and is ever afterwards but fragile, and despite la Blanchotte's unyielding reserve, the gossips were already busy about her name.

Simon was immensely fond of his new father, and went out with him nearly every evening after work was over. He went regularly to school, and held his head very high among his fellows, never paying attention to their taunts. But one day the boy who had opened the attack on him began again: "You are a liar. You haven't got a father called Philip".

"How do you make that out?" asked Simon in agitation.

The boy leered and chuckled. "Because if you had one", he replied, "he would be married to your mother."

The argument was sound, and Simon was troubled. Nevertheless he answered "He is my father, all the same".

"Maybe," said the other with a grin, "but he is not a proper sort of father."

La Blanchotte's child went away with his head bowed, deep in thought. He went towards old Loizon's forge, where Philip worked.

The forge was buried among the trees. It was very dark, and only the red blaze of the furnace with its flickering glare illumined five bare-armed smiths, who filled the shed with the resounding clang of their hammers on the anvil. In the lurid glare of the forge they looked like five demons. They were standing upright, their eyes fixed on the white-hot iron which they were forging, and their heavy thoughts followed the rise and fall of their hammers.

Simon entered unnoticed. He went up and pulled his friend by the sleeve. Philip turned; suddenly the work ceased and all the men watched with great attention. In the midst of this unwonted silence, up rose the childish voice: "Tell me, Philip, what that boy meant who told me just now that you were not a proper sort of father":

"How did he make that out?" said Philip.

With childish innocence Simon replied "Because you are not married to my mother".

No one laughed. Philip stood lost in dreams, resting his brow on one great hand, while his elbow rested on the shaft of his hammer which stood on the anvil. His four companions stood watching him, and Simon, a tiny figure among the giants, waited anxiously. Suddenly one of the smiths, answering the thought which was in all their minds, spoke to Philip: "Well, they can say what they like, la Blanchotte is a fine girl and a good one, and she has plenty of grit and steadiness despite her misfortune. She would make as good a wife as anyone could wish, if she had the right man".

"That's true, every word of it", said the three others.

"Is it her fault, poor girl," continued the workman, "that she went wrong? The man had promised to marry her, and I know more than one woman who did just the same as this one and whom everybody respects now."

"True, every word," replied the three men in chorus.

He went on: "What suffering it has cost her, poor girl, to bring up this boy by herself, and what she has gone through during these years she has never left the house except to go to church, God only knows."

"True, every bit of it," said the others.

For a space nothing was heard but the whistle of the furnace-blast. Then Philip, with a brusque movement, bent towards Simon. "Go and tell your mother that I am coming to speak to her to-night."

Then he took the child by the shoulders and pushed him outside.

He returned to his work, and with a single sound the

five hammers fell together on the anvils. Powerful, vigorous, joyful in the mastery of their work, the five men continued to swing their hammers until nightfall. But just as the deep boom of a cathedral peal dominates over the tinkling carillons in the parish churches, so Philip's hammer smote the anvil, second after second, with a mighty clang that drowned the others. And there was a light in his eye as he turned passionately to his work amid the flying smithy sparks.

The sky was full of stars when he knocked at la Blanchotte's door. He was wearing his Sunday blouse and a new shirt, and his beard was carefully trimmed. The young woman appeared at the door. She had a pained expression, and she said to him "You ought not to come like this, after dark, Mr. Philip".

He would have liked to reply, but he could only stand before her, confused and stammering.

She continued: "And all the time you know perfectly well that I cannot have any more talk about my name".

Then he suddenly found his tongue: "But what does all that matter, if you will only be my wife?"

No answer came to this, but he thought he heard from the darkness of the room a noise as of a body sinking down. He entered quickly, and Simon, lying on his bed, heard the sound of a kiss and of some words murmured by his mother in a low voice. Then all at once he felt himself lifted in the hands of his friend, who, like the Hercules he was, held him out at arm's length and shouted, "You can tell your schoolmates that your father is Philip Remy the blacksmith, and that he will box anyone's ears who hurts you".

Next day, when the schoolroom was full and lessons were about to commence, little Simon rose, pale and with trembling lips, and said in a clear voice, "My father is Philip Remy the blacksmith, and he has promised to box anyone's ears who hurts me".

This time there was no longer any laughter, for everybody knew Philip Remy the blacksmith, and he was a man whom anyone might well be proud to have for father.

CORRESPONDENCE.

BLASTING THE HEATH.

To the Editor of the SATURDAY REVIEW.

27 July 1909.

SIR,—Slowness of speech in the actor, of which Mr. Forbes justly complains, may be due to a deficiency in dramatic instinct. More often than not the actor himself fails to realise that his method is false and unnatural. As with all the other arts, so it is with good acting, its excellence lies in restraint and in knowing what to surrender. If elocution is to imitate nature, a dozen or more words must be sacrificed, so that one word may predominate and thus give the keynote to the tune of the whole sentence. In this way, only, can the sound be made to echo the sense. But the last thing the actor cares to do is to give up making every word *tell*. Redundancy of emphasis is his besetting sin, especially in the speaking of verse. Thus, Shakespeare, without elaborate scenic accessories, is unattractive on our stage, because our actors rarely bring intelligence to bear upon what they are saying. Since the words are Shakespeare's it is imagined they should be spoken in some way that no human being ever did or could express his own thoughts. Only recently at a West End theatre, a leading actor of repute spoke the following words of "Macbeth" thus:

"or *why*
Upon this BLASTED *heath you* stop *our way*
With *such* prophetic *greeting*?"

All these words in italics were inflected, besides a double emphasis on the word "blasted"; but what the unfortunate heath had done to be thus "blasted" I cannot understand! The speech as spoken conveyed no sense to the listener. Now what did Shakespeare intend the sentence to mean? The Witches are standing in the middle of the path, barring Macbeth's return to the King's camp, and the chieftain says:

"or *why*
Upon this blasted heath you STOP our way
With such *prophetic* greeting?"

There are three words only that need inflecting in the sentence, with the emphasis either on "stop" or "prophetic". If these three words are rapped out and heard distinctly the listener knows what the rest of the sentence means, and the whole can be said very quickly. Of course to speak rapidly on the stage and clearly at the same time requires not only a flexible voice but severe training in exercises. But if elocutionists told their pupils that success on the stage depended upon voice and exercises, teachers would get no employment, so they uphold personality as the one essential, which all stage aspirants are privileged to possess. I certainly admit that of late our acting has wonderfully improved, but only in modern plays. It must be remembered besides that, compared to the French or the Germans, the English are bad listeners when they get inside a theatre. Our audiences, indeed, are taught to believe in the advantage of sight over hearing and forget to listen. Mr. Martyn Harvey is the slowest speaker on the stage I have ever heard, but I must add that neither he nor his audience seem to be in the least conscious of this slowness. An actress of considerable talent recently told me that she had given up playing in Shakespeare, because she found that the audience disliked her natural method. But the blame for this state of things lies with the actor. The appetite of an unæsthetic, unimaginative public grows by what it feeds on.

Yours faithfully,

WILLIAM POEL.

THE DUKE OF CONNAUGHT AND THE ARMY.

To the Editor of the SATURDAY REVIEW.

26 July 1909.

SIR,—As the Duke of Connaught has now relinquished his post as Field-Marshal Commanding-in-Chief the Mediterranean Forces, this would seem to be an opportune moment to make a radical change in the Army by creating His Royal Highness Field-Marshal Commander-in-Chief of His Majesty's Forces, with Lord Kitchener as the Chief of the Staff and Sir John French Adjutant-General. These officers have, at any rate, the confidence and respect of the Army. The present Board of Selection is an anomaly, which has long ago forfeited respect by its scandalous proceedings, and should be abolished forthwith as it has proved a dismal failure. Confidence would then be restored to the nation, whose position of defence still causes the gravest concern.

I am, Sir, your obedient servant,

PATRIOT.

PRESIDENT TAFT'S MODESTY.

To the Editor of the SATURDAY REVIEW.

12 Charlotte Street, Bath, 25 July 1909.

SIR,—Mr. E. Gough appears to be sufficiently Americanised to appreciate President Taft's spread-eagleism. In illustration of the progress of the United States he cites such things as the average newspaper, the illustrated magazine, the "rising novelist", the artist trained in Europe, and distinguished German and Continental professors holding posts in America. He further states that life and property are as safe as in Europe.

He finds his journalistic ideal in the average American newspaper. I have never been able to find anything in it but good printing. When he puts forward "Harper's", "Munsey's", and "Maclure's" as overwhelming proofs of American progress I am afraid I cannot follow him. It would be extraordinary if there were not good writers and novelists in a country which boasts a population of ninety millions, but the amazing part of it is that there are so few of them. The typical American novel, one remembers, was annihilated by Mr. Edmund Gosse some years ago.

I know something of picture galleries. The dexterity with which your correspondent's "goodly number of Whistlers and Sargents" manage to evade the hanging committee of English and Continental exhibitions is positively amazing. Native art criticism, too, supplies food for thought. Mr. Frederick Church, a well-known American painter, recently created a furore of patriotism among American editors by declaring, after a visit to Europe, that any Yankee dauber could give points to such a painter as Rubens. I quote from the "Herald": "To hell with Europe. I thought the Louvre a terror. The walls are plastered with pictures that are wholly mediocre. In all Europe I did not see a landscape painting, whether by Turner or any other artist, that touched Martin's sand dunes in the Metropolitan Museum." As we never see these priceless works it is only reasonable to suppose the existence of a trust which is creating a "corner" for the purpose of letting them loose on posterity.

How the employment of European brains can contribute to purely American greatness and enable it to "carry on its shoulders all the progress there is in the world" passes my comprehension. Your correspondent carefully omits to mention that hundreds of Englishmen hold important appointments in every branch of knowledge and industry. To take one instance, the Director, the Curator of Pictures, the Curator of Metal Work, and the Librarian of the Metropolitan Museum of New York are all Englishmen.

The universities which he mentions with such pride as belonging to the nation, "practically speaking, not more than a century old", were all established many years before the civil war between England and the colonists, Harvard being founded as far back as 1638. His statement as to the superiority of American graduates is without foundation. Mr. Risk, in his book on American colleges, compiled with the express purpose of comparing them with his own Glasgow University, declares that "they have not yet begun to produce scholars". Sir Joseph Thomson, head of the Cavendish Laboratory, recently stated that he had had helpers who had been educated in America, and that there was no comparison possible between the English and the American graduate. There are five hundred Britishers holding important positions in America to one American holding a similar position in England. Everyone knows that the majority of American industries were originally established by the wholesale importation of English draughtsmen and foreman mechanics—to say nothing of English capital.

Your correspondent says that every State in America maintains a university. Considering that nearly all the States are several times larger than Great Britain, this does not seem an over-generous proportion.

He says that life and property are as safe as in England. Our definitions of the word "safe" seem to differ. Since 1880 the number of white persons lynched in America is 1400, as against 2600 blacks—a grand average of three a week during the last twenty-eight years. Contrary to the general impression, rape is not the usual cause, only about one-third of the lynchings being for this crime. During the last generation eighty women, including twenty-five white women, have been lynched. The statistics of other forms of murder are even more appalling, the number of victims running into tens of thousands. Your correspondent's eight years' residence in the United States was hardly productive of accuracy.

He declares that the average working man is more prosperous than the English middle class. Only a few months ago there were 500,000 unemployed in New York State alone, while the percentage of unemployed in the trades unions is always far greater than in this country. One in every twenty-eight of the inhabitants of the United States is a registered pauper. How many unregistered ones there are I do not know. In New York City alone there are 300,000 inhabited windowless rooms. Considering the marvellous prosperity which these figures show, Mr. Gough's further ideas on the material condition of the English middle class would be interesting.

He imagines that the United States is a veritable literary, artistic, scientific and material Utopia. I think Mr. Kipling is as near the truth as anyone when he says "Most of their good luck lies in their woods and mines, and not in their brains".

Yours faithfully,

HUGH BLAKER.

THE ANTI-VIVISECTION AGITATION.

To the Editor of the SATURDAY REVIEW.

32 Charing Cross, Whitehall, London S.W.
27 July 1909.

SIR,—Mr. Stephen Paget's argument that a dog should be inoculated with a certain disease because other animals are suffering from it and "have a right to protection" is not very convincing. It would be an exactly analogous proposition that certain men should be inoculated with cancer because many other men are suffering from it, and require "protection" also. That does not alter the injustice towards the selected scapegoat.

But it is surely a wonderful thing that scientists can only study a disease by increasing the number of its victims. Is there not plenty of available material in the unhappy creatures that already have the disease, and whose sufferings might be relieved by experimental treatment undertaken with a genuine desire to benefit them? The fact is, the vivisector is far more interested in the "germ" than in the sufferer. When he begins to turn his attention to the latter, medical science will begin to make some real progress.

I remain your obedient servant,

BEATRICE E. KIDD,

Sec. British Union for Abolition of Vivisection.

MERCY FOR BEASTS.

To the Editor of the SATURDAY REVIEW.

30 July 1909.

SIR,—I do not often find myself in agreement with the Humanitarian League nor indeed with any professional humanitarian. He is generally much more concerned to spoil somebody's sport than to do a good turn to any animal. But for once I can congratulate the Humanitarian League wholeheartedly. They are doing real good work in pressing on the authorities (see memorial in to-day's papers signed by Sir James Crichton-Browne and others) the fulfilment of the recommendation of the Royal Commission that all private slaughter-houses be abolished and public abattoirs established in their place. This is not a pleasant subject, but to be excited about a few "Brown Dogs" and winged pheasants and turn a blind eye to all that may happen in the slaughter-house is hypocritical cowardice. Everyone who is not a vegetarian must bear personal responsibility in this matter. I notice with pleasure that both Houses of Parliament were yesterday considering the case of old and decrepit horses. Lord Carrington and Mr. Herbert Gladstone both promised attention. Surely they will do as much for the thousands of beasts whose lives have to be sacrificed for human food.

Yours etc., H.

May I in a postscript put in a word for cats at this season? They run a risk of being overlooked from their smallness; as do so many other beautiful things that are not big; butterflies, for instance.

REVIEWS.

THE UNPRODUCTIVE FALLACY.

"The Industrial System." By J. A. Hobson. London: Longmans. 7s. 6d.

THIS is the most important Free Trade document that we have seen for some time: "An Inquiry into Earned and Unearned Increment" by way of a scientific treatise which attempts in some essentials to start a new system of political economy, with the additional responsibility of the author's already considerable position as an economist. The method is severely scientific, and there is even a dictionary to fix original connotations. The whole expression is pruned to the niceties of a trained thinker and a practised writer. The field of data is elaborately examined, and there is no lack of mental subtlety to make order out of it in accordance with the new conception. Free Traders will naturally welcome the work as an achievement of value, but it is not of less interest to Tariff Reformers, because it states the case against Tariff Reform as well as it can possibly be stated, not merely exploiting the old claims, but also adding fresh ones, with carefully conducted arguments from premisses that had no point for Cobden.

The most distinctively new feature is an attempt at economic redistribution, conceived to react for the greater economy in production, with increased justice in the incidence of wealth and poverty. Mr. Hobson undertakes to show that our present distribution of wealth does not give back support to the productive factors in any proportion to assure their highest efficiency; and he propounds an alternative theory to correct this. He claims that land, labour, capital, and ability, as postulated by the preceding economists, are not in the proper proportion rewarded by rent, wages, interest and profit; but he goes farther and affirms that, in addition to the four receivers mentioned, there is a fifth, which he calls "unproductive surplus"; that is, an accumulating balance left after land, labour, capital and ability have got their shares. Of course, his "unproductive surplus" is the new name for "unearned increment".

He derives his fifth receiver first in gross, a total surplus after rewarding the familiar four; but then he subdivides it, deducting such proportion as sometimes returns to the productive process when this is extended, as in a progressive community, where additional units of productive power are induced beyond the upkeep of the existing scale. This, he admits, becomes indirectly a productive part of the fifth receiver or gross surplus; but after the deduction the remainder is purely "unproductive surplus", and, in his mind, the main "economic malady"; the source of "discord" in the economic system, holding the factors of production to scarcity prices when there is not scarcity, but monopoly.

This fifth division, the "unproductive surplus", alias "unearned increment", may be grabbed by any or all of the other four; but labour does not seem to be able to hold anything like its share, and so the bulk goes to the other three—the landlord, the capitalist, and the "entrepreneur", in addition to the proper rewards for their land, capital, and ability. Thus "unproductive surplus" includes "the whole of economic rent", and economic rent means all above the point at which there is no rent. Mr. Hobson will permit the landlord to take all he can get below that.

"Unproductive surplus" includes also "excessive" interest and "excessive" wages of management; but there is no scientifically workable definition of "excessive" in the context, though the concept is essential to the conclusion, which is scientifically strange. For the required distinction between interest and "excessive" interest, between profit and "excessive" profit, we turn with confidence to the opening dictionary of axioms, and find none there either, which is scientifically stranger. In short, with all our admiration of the author, we feel that he is driving us into suspicion of his new categories.

On reflection, "excessive" is an adjective, an adjective of quantity, and it is the very foundation of our science in the matter; but, to be decently scientific, we must at least know the quantity of the adjective, and this we do not know. When does an interest or a profit reach the point at which it ceases to be economically right, properly reacting for the factors in production; the point at which it begins to distort production and accumulate an "unproductive surplus"? We do not know. We expected Mr. Hobson to tell us, at least after he had founded a new theory of distribution on the distinction; but he does not, which surprises us. He is clear enough about "economic rent", and the whole of that goes at once; but "excessive" interest for the capitalist and "excessive" profit for the man of ability are no less sinners in the new decalogue, and our expert law-giver fails to tell us what he means by his newly discovered sins. We feel vaguely that he intends to mean something; but vague feeling does not satisfy our sense of science, though we by no means pretend to be severely scientific. It is the first time that we have been invited by such a severely scientific teacher to found a scientific system on something which we do not know, which he does not know, and which neither he nor we could pretend to measure with any scientific significance even if we knew. On the other hand, Mr. Hobson's distinction adds proportionate importance to his failure. His thoroughness makes us feel that if the thing could be done he was the man to do it, and so he increases our confidence in the failure of Free Trade.

Assuming the vague adjectivity scientific, which it obviously is not, and the fifth division safely founded in abstract reason, it could only make a still worse muddle in concrete practice. Let us assume for a moment that there is an accumulating balance beyond the four-headed division of orthodoxy, these questions arise: How is the fifth distinguishable from the other four? How can capital and ability be deprived of it without discouraging them, and in that measure reacting to the disadvantage of labour and production? Do not the capitalist and the man of ability enter the field now, induced by the expectation of the whole that they get? Could part of this be taken from them without in the same measure inducing them to take their capital and their brains elsewhere? Could they do this without in the same measure starving labour and impeding production here? Since the mobility of unemployed capital and ability is so much greater than that of labour, would not the labourer be the greatest sufferer by the displacement? Has any capitalist or man of ability ever entered the economic process content to give up what he may make beyond his cost of living? All these questions are essential, but the author does not attempt to answer one of them. Yet he founds on his new assumption the following propositions: "As 'unearned income' this unproductive surplus is seen to be the only properly taxable body. . . . The doctrine of a surplus affords a new interpretation to 'ability to bear' as a canon of taxation. Surplus alone has such ability"—though the "surplus" is an essential and indistinguishable part of the inducement for the capitalist and the man of ability to go into the productive process, without which inducement they remain out, distorting the productive process as a result of the new plan to improve it. In this way Mr. Hobson goes the circuit of his syllogisms until he arrives at defeating the purpose with which he set out.

Restrict the remuneration of capital and ability, and they can go to America by post, while the working man remains to carry a death's head in unemployed processions. They have begun to go already, as if anticipating Mr. Hobson and Mr. Lloyd George. Capital and ability accept anywhere the equivalent of what is offered elsewhere; and whether this be "excessive" or not depends on a score of considerations that are quite obviously beyond the reckoning of Mr. Hobson's syllogisms. His confusion about land is not less striking. He would bag the whole of the "differential rents", which means practically all rent whatever, but he does not stop to consider how far the rent of land is really interest on industrial capital sunk in it by the owners with the result of multiplying its productive contribution, and often only at rates of reward far below the average. We have in this country large estates highly and productively provided with fixed capital in this way at less than 2 per cent.; that is, below the rate at which the land could be capitalised for State credit. Does Mr. Hobson think 2 per cent. "excessive", and, if so, how is he to get the soil capitalised at less after he has taken the 2 per cent. in taxing the "differential rents" out of existence? There is an estate at the present moment changing hands for actually less than it cost to provide the farming fixed capital upon it; but when it is "heads" Mr. Hobson wins, and when it is "tails" he tries to put the loss on somebody else. Before taxing an increment value, the Germans allow for a decrement value; but Mr. Hobson's economic subtlety ignores all such equities, as if equity had nothing to do with economics. That is the result of perfecting syllogisms as if they had nothing to do with human nature.

The fatal defect in the treatise is its disregard of the national and international factors in determining the economic region. He admits himself that "political areas are not economic areas", but he evades the readiness of capital and ability to disregard political frontiers and to pass from one nation to another for the fittest region when they find themselves penalised in another. His vision of the difference between economic and political areas looks as if his evasion of the international factors in the problem were deliberate, in which case the book has not even the merit of sincerity. It is written as if one country could determine her remuneration to the factors in production without regard to the competitive inducements in other countries for these factors; and yet what we call an economic region comes every day to be more and more a place where the nation can determine nothing except as the outcome of international relationships in economic influence—a fact more applicable to a Free Trade country than to any other. As a Tariff Reformer, Mr. Hobson might have some sane chance of hedging round his economic frontiers to make his limitations workable and to give his "unproductive surplus" a thinkable significance; but he is a Free Trader, thereby advocating opposites, a new theory of wealth distribution and an old theory of taxation to make it more obviously impossible. Even his headlines are in obvious conflict. Here, for instance, are two of his fundamental propositions in succeeding chapters: (1) "All taxes are borne by producers"; (2) "The proportion of a wheat tax borne by the producer will be very small". These confusions belong to the brief, not to the advocate. The greater his ability, the more valuable his failure, and we welcome his work warmly as an implicit plea for Tariff Reform. It ought to be studied by every Tariff Reformer as the ablest effort yet to illustrate the intellectual and economic impossibility of defending Free Trade. We do not remember having seen such an acute mind, so highly fitted for the task, in such hopeless confusion.

CÆSAR AS GENERAL.

"Studies in Roman History." Second Series. By E. G. Hardy. London: Swan Sonnenschein. 1909. 6s.

THE title of this important but unpretentious little volume would fitly have been "Studies in Roman Military History", for it specially deals with that branch of historical research, and will be particularly valuable to those interested in it. It is much to be regretted that the pen of no soldier has yet given us a critical account of campaigns such as are dealt with here, notably those of Cæsar, probably the greatest or amongst the very greatest of the world's great captains. In the absence of professional insight we must, however, feel very grateful to Mr. Hardy for his most intelligent and able essays, which we trust will meet with the attention of officers as well as civilians. Military geography is a subject which has been sadly neglected amongst us until the last few years, and Mr. Hardy has done well to publish these essays on the German armies and frontier, even though, as he tells us, they were written fifteen years ago. Geography affects strategy now as it has affected it since wars were waged at all. The same physical features produce the same results. The line of rail coincides with the path of the legions; the modern invader treads in the footsteps of the barbarian. The second essay, that on "The Four Emperors Year", discusses events recently dealt with by Mr. Henderson in his "Civil War and Rebellion in the Roman Empire" and, as we showed when we reviewed Mr. Henderson's book, well exhibit the oft-reiterated truth that the principles of strategy are eternal. The strategical points that held the keys of success in the struggle for the purple are still those round which the struggle for supremacy in Italy will centre in the present and the future.

We cannot better illustrate our view as to the value modern students may derive from old-world records such as these than by a reference to the third of the essays which this volume contains, entitled "A Military Game of Chess." It is the shortest, and our author fears it may be looked on as superfluous since Cæsar's "Bellum Civile" is in future to be removed from the list of historical texts taken up at Oxford. We regard that decision as a great mistake. So great and comparatively modern an authority as Napoleon himself has enjoined students of war to study the writings of Cæsar. He expressly desired that the son he left behind him should be brought up to read and read again the works of the great captains. No student of history, whether officer or civilian, should neglect the great struggle between Cæsar and Pompey, for a study of this war will show us why Napoleon venerated Cæsar and why it is no exaggeration to extol his generalship as we have done. That the enemy's army and not a geographical point should be the objective of a general is a first principle of strategy which no commander can contravene without paying for it, witness the prolongation of the South African War. That truth Cæsar grasped. When he crossed the Rubicon, Rome, as Mr. Hardy well points out, was not his objective. His aim was Pompey's army in Italy, and its retention in Italy so that he might destroy it and end the war at once. Again, it is peace strategy or organisation which places victories within the general's grasp, as the Germans have shown twice within fifty years and the Japanese showed us the other day. It was Pompey and not his successful rival who was caught unprepared at the outbreak of hostilities in the year 49 B.C. Next to strategical instinct and powers of organisation the most prominent characteristic of great leaders has been resourcefulness on the battlefield. What better illustrations of that quality can be found in the annals of war than the manner in which Cæsar extricated himself from his difficulties during his Spanish campaign against Afranius, and snatched victory from the fire by sheer energy and readiness in combat? Further, it was by mobility that Cæsar's successes were usually attained. The sudden and unexpected were his, as they were Napoleon's and Wellington's hundreds of years later. The magic of his personality led his soldiers to demand to risk the passage of a dangerous ford just as the presence of the great Emperor, his disciple, elevated men to a kind of furious ecstasy when they met their foes. Cæsar's account of the siege of Massilia is as fresh as if written by a war correspondent of to-day, and vastly better literature. It is almost as instructive too, though the "agger" and the battering ram take the place of the emplacement and the howitzer. Even when we come to so modern a problem as the influence and limitations of sea power we can find examples from this very Civil War which must command our attention, and have indeed commanded it. Pompey was in command of the sea when Cæsar crossed the Hadriatic to attack him on his own ground. For Cæsar to embark his army and accept the hazardous risk it involved might well seem to his opponent impossible. But Cæsar not only accepted that risk but a still greater one, for he entered on his enterprise with only a portion of his army and left the remainder to follow. The story of the subsequent fighting round Dyrrhacium is full of living interest. Again we see the great qualities of Cæsar conspicuous, his swiftness and precision of stroke, his clear judgment, his resolution. He won the rubber just as he would win it to-day were he opposed to a general less highly gifted in these respects than himself, and an analysis and study of his methods are as valuable to the modern soldier as are those of the most-talked-of leader of our own time. Where all has been praise we regret to be obliged in conclusion to point out a serious deficiency. When questions of strategy and tactics are under discussion maps are an absolute necessity. These essays would be infinitely more instructive and interesting had maps been supplied in adequate number, and we trust that in any subsequent edition of this book almost the only flaw we have discovered in it may be removed.

THE FRANCISCANS IN SCOTLAND.

"The Scottish Grey Friars." By William Moir Bryce. Edinburgh: Green. 1909. 2 vols. 42s. net.

THESE two handsome volumes, recording the history of the Franciscans in Scotland, exhibit considerable care and research. The author shows such sympathy and large-minded tolerance for the work and character of the mendicant servants of Christ, that we doubted, until convinced by a few interlocutory remarks, if he could belong to a sect pledged to their extermination. His introductory notice of S. Francis of Assisi, and clear perception of the two different schools, Conventual and Observant, indicate emancipation from prejudice and diligent study of a difficult subject. The beautiful scheme of a body of evangelists, detached from all worldly encumbrance, living on alms, and bringing the sacraments and teaching of the Gospel to the humblest cottagers, is contrasted with the state of the secular clergy, while the impossibility of conducting any organised work without the aid of property is well stated. Mr. Bryce has collected evidence from national, municipal, and private records, has studied the printed histories of the friars, and has achieved his purpose of narrating the foundation, history and ruin of eight Conventual and nine Observantine friaries established in Scotland, from the first appearance of the order in Roxburgh to their violent suppression instigated by John Knox. It has been attempted of late by some Scottish writers to prove that the author of the destruction of the great monasteries of Scotland was not John Knox; but no one reading the pitiful story of the "Beggar's Warning" and subsequent destruction of the friaries can remain in serious doubt of his guilt. The attacks on the monasteries might be partly accounted for by English wars and the cupidity of inflamed mobs; the destruction of the friaries and persecution of the poorest ministers of religion in Christendom can be attributed only to the malignant hate which John Knox and his colleagues conceived for the Church and its faith.

But Mr. Bryce explains a deeper subject. Why was it that Rome hesitated and the Hierarchy disliked the disciples of S. Francis? The answer is that the decadence of practical Christianity and the corruption of the clergy, owing to their immoderate possessions, were exposed, when a body of ministers appeared living in accordance with the strictest view of Scriptural poverty. The new professors speedily attracted the love of the people. Nobles and peasants sought them as confessors and as trustees, desired their ministrations when living and their cemeteries after death, while their rule forbad the exchange of spiritual comfort for temporal wealth.

Then the secular clergy perceived how useful they could be in providing ministrations too long neglected and perhaps too often sold. The mendicant orders produced two results of great historical importance; they proved the State recognition and endowment of religion to be less imperative than the schoolmen taught, and they brought the Supreme Pontiff into personal relation with every Christian to a degree which the Hierarchy viewed with alarm. These are the general conclusions to which our study of this work leads us, and no reader can fail to admire the manipulation of his facts by the author. The narrative, however, though occasionally given in eloquent language, is on the whole so burdened with detail that perusal requires considerable patience.

If we approach Mr. Bryce's work critically, there are undoubtedly some faults. It is obvious that the work has occupied many years. We suspect, indeed, that it has been written wholly or partially long ago, for here and there we detect references to authorities in manuscript which have in recent years been printed. The Protocol books of Gavin Ros are an example. We also find some inaccuracy when accuracy did not appear to the author of much importance. He refers to an early grant by Sir William Lindsay, one of the most ancient of his proofs, describing the grantor as of Luffness, and giving as his evidence a page in a family history. He should have verified his reference. There was no such person as Sir William Lindsay of Luffness at the time, and he would have found him accurately described both in the family history and in better authorities there quoted. The author speaks of an Earl of Seton in 1409 when there was no such earldom, and translates Dominus sometimes as Sir and sometimes as Lord. These are small matters, but a more serious error—unless we ourselves are greatly mistaken—is the constant assertion, without reference to authority, that pensions were only paid to such expelled friars as conformed to the new religion. These pensions were, we apprehend, granted in mere justice by the King and Parliament without any such condition, but no doubt the "Ministers of the Gospel" did not approve such toleration. Very few friars apostatised, and all but two or three are impugned only on the author's assumption that those who received pensions must have denied their faith.

In England the "Reformation" was "rushed" by a masterful King. In Scotland a far more drastic change was violently imposed on the Sovereign and older nobles by the preachers and the mob. Consequently the Catholic clergy received greater consideration from the Scottish Court than they obtained in England, and were allowed to retain the greater part of their endowments for life. Those who have studied the history of Tiends are aware of the irritation caused by the refusal of Sovereigns to grant these reserved portions to the ministers even when vacated by death. Certainly the bishops who retained emoluments were not compelled to conform, and we know of no evidence that monks and friars were differently treated. If Mr. Bryce is wrong in his assertions part of his argument is undermined.

The capacity of the friars to take legacies is well discussed in Chapter XII. No friar could hold property for his own use or even for that of his house. Real property (rejected entirely by the Observants) was held by the Provincial Warden, and the ultimate owner was the Pope as trustee for the order. The sixth chapter concludes with a valuable table showing the property held by the friars when dispersed. The Dominicans held a few substantial rents—the Conventual Franciscans none of importance, the Observants none whatever.

There are a number of excellent illustrations in the work taken from office books and objects of art which must have been executed specially for the author. The work might perhaps have been condensed, and now that books based on original research are happily numerous, it is desirable that no unreasonable spacc on bookshelves should be claimed. The more bulky an antiquarian work the less it fetches at sales. We have ourselves seen nearly a score of publications of a Scottish Club, costing subscribers a guinea each, sold for little more than the amount of one subscription. We hope Mr. Bryce's work will escape such a fate, for the industry displayed in a chivalrous cause is magnificent, and in respect of paper, accurate printing, and illustration his volumes will be universally approved. A great part of the evidence collected in the second volume no one but a legal expert could have found or explained. We refer especially to the skilful use of the feudal law by two wardens, as expounded by Mr. Bryce.

NEW MEDITATIONS AMONGST THE TOMBS.

"The Philosophy of Long Life." By Jean Finot. London: Lane. 1909. 7s. 6d.

MODERN science no longer attempts to frown down speculations as to what happens after death, by taking an uncompromising materialistic view as to the belief in personal immortality. It lends itself readily either to supply analogies strengthening the belief, or facts which are considered as consistent or at least as not inconsistent with the belief. M. Finot, whose amiable object is to release our minds from abnormal fears of death, which are as a nightmare on life, does not attack that belief in immortality and individuality which is at present our best consolation against the horror of death. M. Finot professes optimism; and a too insistent optimism as to many facts of life and the supreme fact of death tends to become ludicrous in some aspects of it. Much of M. Finot's book makes one smile rather mournfully or bitterly, as though we were listening to the illusive mockeries of Christian Science and faith healing. Many are its seeming paradoxes; but it would be the vainest of paradoxes to attempt to destroy in the name of optimism the consolation of the hope of immortality.

M. Finot maintains that we need a new physical point of view, both as to life and death. The most convincing of his proofs that science has a consolation against death in store for us is found in what he says as to longevity. He works the theory, which may be taken as accepted by physiologists, that old age as we know it is a specific disease. The Law Courts would not define it as an "accident" in compensation cases, but, nevertheless, mostly it is an accident in the sense that it is not an inevitable condition of the organism implying death at the particular moment. The only "natural" death, according to Professor Metchnikoff, whom M. Finot follows, would be when the "instinct" of death has come to a man. Few are the "natural" deaths even amongst centenarians. Theoretically, there is a probability that even they succumb to "accidental" and not natural death. We need not here go into the details of investigations and experiments which have been made to discover a therapie that is to counteract the micro-organisms which are the particular enemies of vital organs whose destruction give rise to the symptoms of senility. These may be read in Professor Metchnikoff's well-known "Prolongation of Life" and in this book. In the meantime, as the therapie has not been discovered, it is sufficient to point out that we have to take the "instinct of death" on trust. Even if death were put off from time to time one might, for all that appears, still be in terror when serums lost their power at last. And there are the cases, too, that must fail; where serums would not give a new lease of life; nor would they be panacea for other ills than old age to which flesh is heir. We begin to recognise the humanity which will not substitute problematical longevity for the ancient aspirations and consolations.

On the scientific side, M. Finot's book has not the merits of Professor Metchnikoff's. It has few technicalities; it is popular; and the treatment is essentially literary. M. Metchnikoff is a great expert. M. Finot is not; we doubt if he is more than a clever Frenchman exercising a literary gift on a promising topic. On the literary side he much excels Professor Metchnikoff, and so he has made fuller and more interesting excerpts from a wider field of ancient and modern literature on the subjects of life and death, both from the view of optimism and pessimism. As we have implied, M. Finot's own contributions to the subject are not convincing. It may be that we ought to regard the processes of putrefaction as a series of new phenomena of life, and to rejoice in them as an exuberant manifestation of life processes. The time may come when we can find in the "entomology of the grave" a subject for pleasant and joyful contemplation. But at our present point of culture few of us can delight in that "immortality of the body" which takes the shape of putrefaction. Worse than the fact itself is an attempt like M. Finot's to make sentimental phrases about it, a somewhat ghastly kind of optimism reminding us of remonstrances sometimes addressed to those who cannot help shivering at fluttering, crawling, creeping things, though they may admit it is irrational. M. Finot is so enamoured, or professes to be, of the "entomology of the grave" that he devotes a chapter to an argument against cremation as being not only useless but an unnecessary interference with the coleoptera and lepidoptera about which he is so enthusiastic. There may be an unreasonable horror of the grave, but M. Finot is so lyrical about it that we suspect he hardly knows how near the ridiculous he gets. We have heard of many strange forms which the desire to perpetuate one's existence after death may take. But when M. Finot thinks to move us by our desire of leaving progeny, he will have to appeal to us by something else than that when we die, after being the fathers of some few human beings upon the earth, "we shall become the fathers of myriads of beings within its depths". These grotesque forms, not of science, but of sentimentalities about science, are suggestive of a special form of mental aberration, a sort of necrologic morbidity. They are more unnatural than excessive terror of death. George Eliot became lyrical over a conception of immortality too tenuous for most of us. But it seems we may understand better her rhapsody on "The Choir Invisible" than M. Finot's "And the dying man, whilst commending his soul to heaven, will salute with one of his last smiles the mysterious properties, the unknown joys, and the travelling company of his numerous descendants which await him in the tomb". This new conception of the resurrection of the body, we believe, will leave most people very unsympathetic.

FROM THE CITY TO THE MOUNTAIN.

"In Unknown Tuscany." By Edward Hutton. With Notes by William Heywood. London: Methuen. 1909. 7s. 6d. net.

"AMIATA mons est in agro Senensi." Thus opens the ninth book of the "Commentaries" of Æneas Sylvius, and there are few pages in the literature of the Renaissance more quick with the modern feeling for nature than those in which that most genial of pontiffs, "silvarum amator et varia videndi cupidus", describes his life on Monte Amiata in the summer of 1462. In the abbey of San Salvatore, on the eastern side of the mountain, Pius made his headquarters, leaving his more energetic courtiers to join the ambassador of Venice in the ascent, while he gave audience and signed his bulls under the shade of the oaks and chestnuts, or sat at evening in front of the convent, gazing over the valley of the Paglia outstretched beneath his feet.

The whole district is rich in historical associations and religious memories. Here lay the dominion of the Aldobrandeschi, the Counts of Santa Fiora, who boasted that they possessed more fortified places than there are days in the year, and whose "ancient blood and gallant deeds" are recorded by Dante himself in the "Purgatorio". At Radicofani still stands the castle of Boccaccio's magnanimous highwayman, Ghino di Tacco, where he cured the Abbot of his "male dello stomaco" with toasted bread and vernaccia wine. It was between Campiglia d'Orcia and San Quirico that S. Francis met the three mystical ladies of his vows, and heard with unspeakable joy their new salutation: "Bene veniat Domina Paupertas". We may see the scene of the vision in Sassetta's masterpiece at Chantilly, with Monte Amiata in the background. A century and a half later, with his rags replaced by the gray-and-white habit of a new religious order, Giovanni Colombini came to San Salvatore to die;

that strangely fascinating fourteenth-century repetition of the founder of the Waldenses, whom the Popes of that epoch, wiser in this than their predecessors, found means to retain within the Church.

It is curious to notice how figures, in external respects strongly resembling the ascetic saints of the Middle Ages, still reappear at intervals in Italy. Cosma, "il santo dei monti", in D'Annunzio's "Figlia di Iorio", and Benedetto in Fogazzaro's "Il Santo", have their prototypes in real life. We have seen a flagellant on the hills above Subiaco, performing his dreadful penance in the true mediæval fashion, and pilgrims, clad in sackcloth and bearing crosses, their faces all aglow with unearthly light, coming down from the mountains of the Abruzzi to worship at the distant shrines. Mr. Hutton gives us an extraordinarily interesting account of David Lazzaretti, "the Messiah of Monte Amiata", a latter-day mystic and visionary, who heard voices, underwent strange psychical experiences, and attempted to found the republic of the Holy Spirit foretold by the Abbot Joachim of old. In August 1878 he was shot by the carabinieri in a tumult, while his followers frantically acclaimed the new republic; and Mr. Hutton assures us that the peasants still point to the ruins of the tower that he built on Monte Labbro as all that is left of "David's Eternal City".

A complete and scientific monograph on the history of this region of the Sienese contado would be well worth writing. Mr. Hutton has, probably wisely, preferred to give a picturesque volume of impressions, stiffened in parts by a solid addition of facts and references from the pen of Mr. Heywood. The book is the record of a summer passed on Monte Amiata, apparently in the very abbey where Pius II. lodged, from which the various castelli, even in the August heat, can readily be reached, and where even "a German company mining for quicksilver" has not been able entirely to destroy the primitive life of rural Tuscany. Incidentally it supplies some new and vivid details concerning the part played by feudalism in the history of the republic of Siena, based upon the researches of Zdekauer, Lisini, Fumi, Calisse, and other distinguished local scholars whose work is still comparatively little known in this country. Nowhere in Tuscany can the relations of the feudal nobles of the contado with the great communes be so well studied as in the Casentino and in the Monte Amiata district. In the one, we have the various branches of the clan of the Conti Guidi struggling to maintain themselves against the power of Florence; in the other, these Aldobrandeschi of Santa Fiora and the Visconti of Campiglia, now at war, now in compulsory alliance with the Sienese, who ultimately drew their teeth and left their descendants to rule in peace as powerless subjects of the democracy.

From their stronghold of Castiglione d'Orcia, the Salimbeni make a fitful appearance in these pages. This famous Sienese family, which touched the life of S. Catherine much in the same way as the Conti Guidi had done that of Dante, has never received its due share of attention from historians. For more than two hundred years its nobles played a great part, for good and for evil, in the annals of Siena. Their men and women alike seem to have been gifted with strongly marked personalities. In the thirteenth century their commercial relations extended to England, and in the fourteenth they were able to withstand the whole military force of the commune in arms; but, by the latter part of the sixteenth century, we find Bargagli writing that "excepting their escutcheon and their palaces nought else now remains of the Salimbeni save their name". No comprehensive history of the Salimbeni has ever been written, though it would afford a splendid opportunity for an ardent student of mediæval documents to reconstruct the past "and bid the short-lived things, long dead, live long". The materials, in part at least, still exist in the Sienese Archivio di Stato.

The personal element always predominates in Mr. Hutton's descriptive passages. At times he lets sentiment run riot with his imagery and strikes an altogether false note, as where he finds the beauty of Siena "a little hysterical", or tells us that "the heat lay on the world like a woman thirsty for kisses". Other times he obtains effects that are undeniably beautiful. At his best Mr. Hutton has a peculiar power of interpreting the spirit of an Italian district. He feels it poetically, even passionately, and suggests its atmosphere with a fidelity that will be recognised by all who have followed the way from Siena to the mountain. He is finely touched, too, by that sense of the not far distant presence of Rome, which at times strangely overawes every imaginative traveller in southern Tuscany, and which Swinburne put to such dramatic use in "Songs before Sunrise".

We would suggest that Benvenuto da Imola is too important a writer to be quoted from an inaccurate Italian version. Dante's Emperor, in 1313, could hardly have been marching southwards to meet "his enemy", Clement V., as the latter was at Avignon. A passage, purporting to be an extract from Pius II.'s description of San Salvatore, is quaintly mistranslated, and bears only a somewhat remote resemblance to the original Latin of the "Commentaries". These, however, are but slight blemishes in a very charming and welcome book.

NOVELS.

"The Fun of the Fair." By Eden Phillpotts. London: Murray. 1909. 2s. 6d.

Mr. Phillpotts has more than one of the qualities we have a right to require of the writer of short stories. He can recognise, to begin with, the kind of material which should go to their making, and very seldom leaves us with the sense of having read a summary of what should have been a novel; which is the more surprising since he is rather given to diffuseness in the development of a romance. He has the gift also, and it is by no means a common one, of introducing his scene with the least possible preamble, and of bringing his persons upon it with something better than a mere attached tag of character. We are thus favourably adjusted at the outset to an interest in their adventures, and, when these prove insufficient to retain it, the character remains, and with it a pervasive and explanatory humour, distilled, as it should be, in most cases out of the character, which often provides a vivid quaintness in the point of view. He attains this by using as his narrator one of the persons of the story, and, as these are all country folk of Devon, he has the curious advantage that almost any form of dialect confers. He uses dialect with commendable restraint, never anxious to show his command of it or to force the note of a local colour. In consequence all his pictures of the country lie restfully within their frames, and obtrude none of the art with which they are drawn. Likewise the humour, to which reference has been made, has never the uncomfortable air of having been reproduced from a note-book, a certain allowance of it being allotted to every tale. It always seems to belong to the scene, and to be the natural comment of character upon it. One's appreciation of Mr. Phillpotts' qualities might fittingly conclude with gratitude for his avoidance of the sensational, since through that very virtue one of his weaknesses appears. Work in such determined monotone, that will not rely on incident for its relief, must obtain distinction from spiritual intensity. One requires to be made to feel the pressure of events on the souls instead of on the circumstances of the people in the story; and to conclude it with a sense of pity or of joy in something altered in their spiritual outlook, which has perhaps no visible influence on their days, and which even they might search in vain to specify. Maupassant, even when most carnally minded, owed the extraordinary grip of his short stories on the reader's consciousness to this very power of suggesting a spiritual influence. Mr. Thomas Hardy drives the sense of it like a stake through the trenchant compression of his shorter tales. But to obtain an exact comparison with Mr. Phillpotts' art one must put beside it some of the earlier stories of Miss Mary Wilkins, since she wrought with a material differing not at all from his, with the same disdain of incidental climax, with no greater command of humour, and with little finer sense of style. Yet where Mr. Phillpotts achieves only the atmosphere of an English country, Miss Wilkins commanded the tender and tragic territories of the soul, and always leaves us, as Mr. Phillpotts cannot, with a quickened sense of having breathed for a marvellous moment the essential air of being.

"Davina." By Frances G. Burmester. London: Smith, Elder. 1909. 6s.

The vital fault in this book is that Mrs. Burmester never discovers what a thorough cad her principal male character really is. Joe Lawson, a country gentleman with few merits except dislike for his blackguard brother, injures a girl's ear at hockey, and, when she suffers intense pain and partial loss of hearing, feels it his duty to marry her. But there was deafness in her family—as he discovers later—and before the accident her hearing was not very good. These facts apparently cancel his obligations towards her. She is rather stupid, and is capable of malice and treachery, but she is as much in love with him as her nature allows. And, after all, he had inflicted—by accident—so much physical pain upon her that he might have done his best to make her married life happy. It is due to no merit on his own part that he does not also wreck the life of Davina, a precocious schoolgirl who had loved him from her nursery days. Mrs. Burmester constructs her story neatly, and in the character of Davina shows considerable power of portraying a vivid unconventional nature.

"Their Oxford Year." By Oona H. Ball. London: Methuen. 1909. 6s.

This book is little more than a repetition of the same writer's "Barbara Goes to Oxford", and shows evidence of fatigue. But the public apparently likes encores. The writer of the letters which compose it is the Canadian wife of an Oxford man who is a professor at Harvard. She not only sees Oxford thoroughly, and enjoys a full store of its proverbial hospitality, but reads up diligently, and makes extracts from, various books—some rather out-of-the-way—about the past of the University. An element of originality is introduced by her preference for books and pamphlets on the early nineteenth century. That was not an interesting or stirring period of academic history, and Miss Ball is to be congratulated on finding in it so much that is entertaining. The vein of the story is even weaker than that in "Barbara", and if this sort of thing is to continue indefinitely, Miss Ball might try Cambridge next time.

"The Affair on the Bridge." By J. Morgan-de-Groot. Edinburgh and London: Blackwood. 1909. 6s.

This story is of Dutch life, and there is something un-English in the telling of it. The style is abrupt, crude, occasionally common and in bad taste, always a little uneasy, though fluently colloquial and even slangy. There are moments of vividness in the narration, and though often puzzling in the naïveté of their behaviour, the characters are something more than puppets. Evidently the author has information about Dutch colonial life: the horrors of the Atchinese outbreak are apparently authentically described in all their gruesome details. He accuses the home Government of increasing the difficulties and dangers of the colonials by their policy of a sentimental clemency towards the natives, a fault characteristic of many home governments, arising from obstinate ignorance of the real conditions of colonial existence, combined with distrust of the "man on the spot".

"The Red-hot Crown." By Dorothea Gerard. London: Long. 1909. 6s.

When the King and Queen of Moesia were assassinated, Prince Bazyl Kornelowicz, at the invitation of the regicides, ascended the throne. He wasn't altogether a success, and when Moesia got into trouble with Danubia he was mercifully killed in the first battle. But his son Marzian, to whom we are introduced in London wearing a faultless Eton jacket, was really the hero; and he escaped from the field—having first escaped a dreadful political union with the Princess Romualda of Therpissia—to find consolation for the loss of a crown in the charms of a nice girl called Yella, with whom he had of course fallen in love at first sight through a window one spring morning.

SHORTER NOTICES.

"We Two in West Africa." By Decima Moore and Major F. G. Guggisberg. London: Heinemann. 1909. 12s. 6d. net.
"Petticoat Pilgrims on Trek." By Mrs. Fred Maturin. London: Nash. 1909. 7s. 6d. net.

Among the departures which woman in the twentieth century is making from her conventional rôle, African travel is taking a distinct place. If she cannot become a pioneer of the jungle, she may at least indulge her propensity by trekking over the veldt. In these two books we have the narratives of women who went in search of novelty and adventure in different parts of Africa. Major Guggisberg is an old hand at travel in barbarous lands; he knows the hazards that must be run, and we admire his pluck almost more than his wife's in plunging with her into the very heart of a country whose physical character may easily be as treacherous as the natives themselves. Happily they came through unharmed. Mrs. Guggisberg's account of what she saw and did on the coast, in Kumasi, and in parts of Ashanti where no white woman, hardly a white man, had ever been seen before, is most entertaining and fresh. No doubt we owe it to her husband that so much of the information in the book as to the present position and future possibilities of various industrial enterprises is of a kind that we should not expect from a lady, however keen an explorer she might be. The Miss Decima Moore of other days appears when a native row, with its colour, its animation, and the spirited intervention of blue-uniformed black policemen, reminds her of a scene out of a Drury Lane drama. Major Guggisberg amusingly says "the book is most irritating to read"—apparently because he wanted to be the author of it himself. He will secure no sympathy: Mrs. Guggisberg has had the advantage of drawing on his experience, and writes—or "talks", as he puts it—with a vivacity which makes her account of West Africa, on both the native and the official side, extremely interesting. Mrs. Fred Maturin's book is of a very different character: it describes lightly and humorously her experiences with her maid in and about Johannesburg and other places in South Africa after the war. There is an occasional touch of the pathetic aftermath of war, and now and again we get a bright thought. Mrs. Maturin's idea is that "to analyse life is to spoil it". The Simple Life on trek is her way to happiness. Her adventures were chiefly domestic, and she describes them in the spirit of one to whom everything that happens, however trivial, is of some moment. The book is a novelty.

"The Place of Animals in Human Thought." By the Countess Evelyn Martinengo Cesaresco. London: Fisher Unwin. 1909 12s. 6d.

It would give a wrong impression of this very interesting book to say that it is an argument against experiments on animals or a plea for vegetarianism. This might repel many people who rightly believe that the discussion of such topics belongs to science and ought not to be meddled with by amateurs in the name of humanitarianism, philosophy, or religion. We have no objection, however, to a book about animals written as the author writes, though probably she makes one rather uneasier than one would be about vivisection or butchers' bills or killing animals for sport. The reason for this is that animals appear so very important in the history of human opinion, and speculation, and customs. Man has had to take animals into account when he has speculated about his own soul and the probabilities of his living or not living after his death. In some of his religions he has placed animals only a little lower than man in nature. Sometimes, as in Christian theology he has tended to do, he has put them very much lower. In all cases his perplexity about his own ignorance and doubt about himself and his future, or his most positive beliefs, have been reflected in his views about animals. The recital of this history by so well-informed and skilful a writer as the author is makes pleasant reading. It is very inconclusive about animals, just as a similar history about man would be. She may exaggerate the divinity in animals, as some philosophers have exaggerated the beast in man. On the whole she maintains the juster argument. We had better exalt animals, so it be "on this side idolatry", than not feel the

(*Continued on page* 144.)

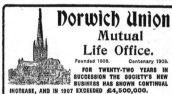

mystery of them. The best men everywhere have always regarded animals courteously and, shall we say? given them the benefit of the doubt.

"The Bird-Life of London." By Charles Dixon. London: Heinemann. 1909. 6s. net.

Mr. Dixon has made a very generous estimate as to area in his description of the birds of London. He deals with all the species found within the fifteen-miles radius, whether as residents, summer or winter migrants, or as casual wanderers occurring at irregular intervals. With Harrow, Hampstead, Epping, Richmond, and the Hounslow districts included, Mr. Dixon is able to write what may serve as a very fair general introduction to the study of British birds. But even in London strictly so-called there are many birds noted by Mr. Dixon which most people would think had not been seen there since the days when snipe were shot in Piccadilly. One would hardly expect, for instance, to see the kestrel, even in the wider area; but "it is by no means an uncommon sight about such spots as Hyde Park, Kensington Gardens, Regent's Park, Greenwich Park, Clapham Common, and Battersea Park." Mr. Dixon has written, he says, to encourage the observation of bird-life in London, and he points out how in many special ways London affects many of the problems of bird-life. He is severe on the nature instruction that is given in London schools, and we hope his book will find its way into the hands of many teachers who hitherto have used very imperfect text-books about birds.

"The Collected Works of Ambrose Beirce." Vol. I. "Ashes of the Beacon." New York: Neale Publishing Company.

The binding and printing of this book are perfect, recalling the best productions of Colburn and Rivingtons at the beginning of the last century. We wish that we could say as much for the interior as for the exterior of the volume. We do not know whether "Ambrose Beirce" is a real or assumed name; but we are quite sure that the author is not a twentieth-century Swift. The book is supposed to be written in 4930, and a great deal of it is thrown into the form of "Gulliver's Travels", the subjects of satire being American politics, society, and trusts. But Swift is a very difficult person to imitate well, though no one, of course, is easier to copy badly. The politicians and trust-mongers of the United States have been pretty frequently under the harrow of the satirist; and though we do not say Mr. Beirce says nothing true about his compatriots, he says nothing new. In the latter part of the volume the author drops allegory and appears as an old officer who fought in the Civil War. This is more interesting, though Ambrose Beirce is no more a descriptive historian than he is a political satirist.

"Psyche's Task." By J. G. Frazer. London: Macmillan. 1909. 2s. 6d. net.

This new book of Professor Frazer's has for explanatory title "A Discourse concerning the Influence of Superstition on the Growth of Institutions". It suggests a fascinating subject treated with the learning and charm that distinguish Professor Frazer's contributions to anthropology. The title "Psyche's Task" does not carry with it its own explanation, but the quotation from Milton throws light on it. "Good and evil we know in the field of this world grow up together; the knowledge of good is so involved and interwoven with the knowledge of evil, and in so many cunning resemblances hardly to be discerned, that these confused seeds, which were imposed on Psyche as an incessant labour to cull out and sort asunder, were not more intermixt." The object of the book is therefore to show that, though superstition is usually regarded as an unmitigated evil, yet it has been in many cases the basis of social institutions which are now defended as beneficial to society. The institutions considered and illustrated by much curious lore are government, private property, marriage, and respect for human life. Man, says Professor Frazer, may be the most rational of the beasts, but certainly he is the most absurd. The illustrations in this book of his absurdities are many and amusing; but its moral is consoling, that folly mysteriously deviates into wisdom, and good comes out of evil.

"A History of Ottoman Poetry." By the late E. J. W. Gibb. Vol. VI. Edited by E. G. Browne. London: Luzac. 1909. 21s. net.

The sixth volume of Mr. Gibb's "History of Ottoman Poetry", containing the Turkish texts of all the poems translated by him, is now published, and the editor, Professor Browne, has thus brought his laborious task to an end. It is needless to say that the publication reflects Professor Browne's usual care and scrupulous exactitude; the type is clear and the paper good. One volume yet remains to be published as a supplement. In this Riza Tewfik Bey will complete the work left unfinished by Mr. Gibb. When the fifth volume was published political reasons prevented Professor Browne from saying more than that the supplement would be written by "a very able Turkish man of letters", but the triumph of the "Young Turks" has now removed the necessity for suppressing his name. The chapter on Kemal Bey, the chief founder of the Young Turkish party, is, we are told by the editor, already in his hands.

"Brittany to Whitehall." By Mrs. Colquhoun Grant. London: Long. 1909. 12s. 6d. net.

"Brittany to Whitehall" is a biography of Louise Renée de Kéroualle, who sprang from a noble family in Brittany, came to Whitehall as mistress of Charles II., and was the ancestress of the Dukes of Richmond. How she came to Whitehall is the most curious and perhaps least known of all the scandalous stories told in this book. Her competition with the "English harlots", as Nell Gwynne described herself and the Duchess of Castelmane to distinguish them from the hated Duchess of Portsmouth, has been oftener told. Those who care to spend their time reading such malodorous hash and re-cooking of old stories of a licentious Court will find this book suit their tastes. As to others who have serious interests in reading they will think it is exactly the sort of book which is no book in any worthy sense.

For this Week's Books see page 146.

NOTICE.

The Terms of Subscription to the SATURDAY REVIEW are:—

	United Kingdom. £ s. d.	Abroad. £ s. d.
One Year	1 8 2	1 10 4
Half Year	0 14 1	0 15 2
Quarter Year	0 7 1	0 7 7

Cheques and Money Orders should be crossed and made payable to the Manager, SATURDAY REVIEW Offices, 10 King Street, Covent Garden, London, W.C.

In the event of any difficulty being experienced in obtaining the SATURDAY REVIEW, the Publisher would be glad to be informed immediately.

THIS WEEK'S BOOKS.

FICTION

The Castle by the Sea (H. B. Marriott-Watson). Methuen. 6s.
The Native Wife; or Indian Love and Anarchism (Henry Bruce). Long. 6s.
The Bill-Toppers (André Castaigne). Mills and Boon. 6s.
The Way Things Happen (Hugh De Sélincourt). Lane. 6s.
The Four Candles (Harry Tighe); Rolf the Imprudent (Coragh Travers). Long. 6s. each.

HISTORY

A Constitutional History of England (A. M. Chambers). Methuen. 6s.
A Short History of the Royal Navy, 1689-1815 (David Hannay). Methuen. 7s. 6d. net.
The Church of the Apostles (Lonsdale Ragg). Rivington. 4s. 6d. net.

LAW

Forms of Originating Summons and Proceedings connected therewith (George Nichols Marcy and Oswald R. A. Simpkin). Cox. 6s.

NATURAL HISTORY

Flowering Plants and Ferns (F. Hamilton Davey). Penryn: Chegwidden. 21s. net.

REPRINTS AND TRANSLATIONS

The Story of Roland (James Baldwin); Stories from Thucydides (H. L. Havell). Harrap. 2s. 6d. net each.

THEOLOGY

Anni Domini: A Gospel Study (Mabel M. Lindsay. 2 vols.). Methuen. 10s. net.

MISCELLANEOUS

Army Annual, The (Edited by Major B. F. S. Baden-Powell). Army Press. 7s. 6d. net.
Successful Jam Making and Fruit Bottling (Lucy H. Yates); Successful Dairy Work (A. T. Matthews); Small Estate Management (Albert C. Freeman). Rebman. 2s. 6d. net each.
Thom's Directory, 1909-10 (John E. Leggatt). Dublin: Thom. 10s.
Welsh Religious Revival, The (Rev. J. Vyrnwy Morgan). Chapman and Hall. 3s. 6d. net.
Wind and Wild, In (Eric Parker). Pitman. 5s. net.

REVIEWS AND MAGAZINES FOR JULY.—The Hindustan Review, 8 annas; The State, 6d.

FOR AUGUST.—The National Defence, 1s.; Scribner's, 1s.; Cornhill Magazine, 1s.; The Treasury, 6d.; The Connoisseur, 1s.; The Englishwoman, 1s.; The Fortnightly Review, 2s. 6d.; Harper's, 1s.; The Century, 1s. 4d.; Blackwood, 2s. 6d.; The Art Journal, 1s. 6d.; The Nineteenth Century, 2s. 6d.

Macmillan & Co.'s List.

The French Revolution.
A Short History. By R. M. JOHNSTON, M.A. Cantab. Crown 8vo. 5s. net.

JAMES LANE ALLEN'S NEW STORY.

The Bride of the Mistletoe.
By the Author of "The Choir Invisible," &c. Crown 8vo. 2s. 6d. net.

How to Identify the Stars.
By Professor WILLIS I. MILHAM, Ph.D. Illustrated. Crown 8vo. 3s. net.

THE CENTURY MAGAZINE.

Illustrated. Price 1s. 4d. Annual Subscription, 16s.

NOTRE DAME OF ROUEN. By ELIZABETH ROBINS PENNELL. Pictures by JOSEPH PENNELL.

THE FOURTEENTH GUEST: A Story of Thirteen at Table. The last of three stories with the same motive, by one of the following writers: MARGARET DELAND, S. WEIR MITCHELL, OWEN WISTER.

And numerous other Stories and Articles of General Interest.

MACMILLAN & CO., LTD., London.

THE

NINETEENTH CENTURY & AFTER.

AUGUST.

THE FOUNDATIONS OF INDIAN LOYALTY. By Sir BAMPFYLDE FULLER, K.C.S.I., C.I.E. (First Lieutenant-Governor of Eastern Bengal).
THE HOUSE OF LORDS AND THE BUDGET. By J. A. R. MARRIOTT.
GREAT BRITAIN AND RUSSIA: AN ALLIANCE OR AN ILLUSION? By Dr. E. J. DILLON.
THE TENNYSON CENTENARY. By FREDERIC HARRISON.
THE "NATIVE" PROBLEM AND SANE IMPERIALISM. By Sir HARRY H. JOHNSTON, G.C.M.G., K.C.B.
SOUTH AFRICAN UNION AND THE COLOUR QUESTION. By RODERICK JONES (Reuter's Agent in Charge in South Africa).
MARRIAGE LAW IN THE CHURCH OF ENGLAND. By the Rev. CHARLES J. SHEBBEARE.
FRANCIS BACON AS A POET. By Sir EDWARD SULLIVAN, Bart.
A LAST WORD TO MR. GEORGE GREENWOOD. By the Rev. Canon BEECHING.
THE HOUSE OF LORDS AND UNIVERSAL SERVICE. By Colonel the Earl of ERROLL, K.T.
FAULTS OF THE LONDONER. By W. PETT RIDGE.
RODDAM SPENCER-STANHOPE, PRE-RAPHAELITE. By Mrs. STIRLING.
THE "SLUMP" IN MODERN ART. By the Hon. JOHN COLLIER.
THE MISSING ESSENTIALS IN ECONOMIC SCIENCE. III. By W. H. MALLOCK.
HINDU STUDENTS IN ENGLAND. By EDWARD DICEY, C.B. (Resident Bencher of Gray's Inn).

LONDON: SPOTTISWOODE & CO. LTD., 5 NEW-STREET SQUARE.

THE

FORTNIGHTLY REVIEW.

CONTENTS—AUGUST 1909.

IMPERIAL AND FOREIGN AFFAIRS: A REVIEW OF EVENTS.
THE CULT OF THE UNFIT. By E. B. IWAN-MULLER.
TENNYSON: A RE-CONSIDERATION AND APPRECIATION. By the Rev. HENRY W. CLARK.
AN HOUR WITH THE POPE. By RENE LARA.
LORD CHARLES BERESFORD AS NAVAL EXPERT. By EXCUBITOR.
POLITICAL ASSASSINATION IN LONDON. By J. D. REES, C.V.O., C.I.E., M.P.
GEORGE MEREDITH AS PUBLISHER'S READER. By B. W. MATZ.
CHATEAUBRIAND'S THIRD AND FOURTH LOVES. By FRANCIS GRIBBLE.
PORSON AND JEBB. By Prof. W. RHYS ROBERTS.
THE INFLUENCE OF ITALY ON THE POETRY OF THE BROWNINGS. By Mrs. ARTHUR HARTER.
THE MADNESS OF LAUNCELOT. By KAUFMANN SPIERS.
LETTERS TO SANCHIA. II. By MAURICE HEWLETT.
CORRESPONDENCE: "MEREDITH'S POETRY." By LAURIE MAGNUS.

LONDON: CHAPMAN AND HALL, LIMITED.

THE BRITISH EMPIRE:

ITS PAST, ITS PRESENT, AND ITS FUTURE.

Edited by **A. F. POLLARD, M.A.** Pp. 896, **5s.** net.

Fifteen special Contributors and over a Hundred Authorities in all parts of the Empire have collaborated in its production.

LEAGUE OF THE EMPIRE, Caxton Hall, Westminster; AND ALL BOOKSELLERS.

STANLEY PAUL'S LIST

"The Novel of 1909."

SHOES OF GOLD

By HAMILTON DRUMMOND. 6s.

First Edition Exhausted. Second Edition Now Ready.

THE PRESS UNANIMOUS.

FIRST SIX OPINIONS.

Daily Telegraph: "A most excellent romance, thoroughly interesting, extremely well written and worked out, and should win high favour with all lovers of spirited historical fiction. He will find it hard to put down the volume when he has once got well into the story. Very ingeniously has the author worked out his plot. A really fine tale. We heartily recommend it to all readers in confidence that they will not be disappointed."

Times: "Mr. Drummond writes the historical novel with much talent. A racy, spirited story."

Truth: "A stirring picture of Eighteenth Century Court life at St. Petersburg and Versailles."

Guardian: "A spirited historical romance—wonderfully well rendered."

Morning Leader: "It might be imagined that no one could write a fresh, original, historical novel about France, but Mr. Drummond has done so. A striking, vigorous, and charming romance."

Observer: "The picture of the precarious Court life is vivid in the extreme, and makes the book one to read and remember."

Other New 6s. NOVELS IN DEMAND.

THE SECRET TERROR ... ... "Brenda."
THE GAY PARADINES ... Mrs. Stephen Batson.
THE CHIPPENDALES ... ... Robert Grant.
STOLEN HONEY ... Ada and Dudley James.
HEARTBREAK HILL ... Herman K. Viélé.
IN CALVERT'S VALLEY M. Prescott Montague.

THE ROMANCE OF FRA FILIPPO LIPPI

By A. J. ANDERSON.

Fully Illustrated. **10s. 6d.** net.

First large Edition sold out on day of publication. Second Edition Ready.

EARLY REVIEWS.

Sunday Chronicle, in devoting three columns to noticing the book, says:—"A great, fascinating, and picturesque romance."

Scotsman says: "The narrative is pervaded by human sentiment, the atmosphere of the Florence of the day is happily reproduced, and his 'reconstruction' of the scene in the convent, in which the 'Glad Friar,' as he was called, falls a victim to the charms of his model, has an air of verisimilitude which some of the older accounts do not possess."

Globe says: "The ways and manners of Florence and Prato during the middle of the fifteenth century are portrayed with carefulness, and the central figures of the story are well and clearly defined. The book should recommend itself to all interested in romance and in the life of the friar-artist. Its illustrations are excellently reproduced."

New Novels Ready Next Week.

LOVE, THE THIEF. 6s. ... Helen Mathers.
CO-HEIRESSES. 6s. ... E. Everett-Green.
BROTHER ROGUE AND BROTHER SAINT. 1s. net. Tom Gallon.
THE SINS OF SOCIETY. 1s. net. Cecil Raleigh.

London: STANLEY PAUL & CO., Clifford's Inn.

7th and Revised Impression.

"SATURDAY" BRIDGE,

By W. DALTON,

Is the Best Book on the Best Game.

That the popularity of Bridge is as great as ever is proved by the continuous steady demand for the work.

"'SATURDAY' BRIDGE"

is admitted to be the Standard book on the Game. It is the leading Bridge Authority, and takes its name from the "SATURDAY REVIEW," in which its chapters appeared.

Of all Booksellers 5s. net, or post free 5s. 3d., direct from the Office.

THE WEST STRAND PUBLISHING CO., Ltd., 10 King Street, Covent Garden, W.C.

RAIN—AND BOOKS!

The rain it raineth all the summer driving people to read the new books. If you want guidance as to them get the August ***BOOK MONTHLY,*** which is rich in literary information, articles and illustrations. It costs 6d. and is published by SIMPKIN, MARSHALL & CO., Stationers' Hall Court, London.

LA REVUE POLITIQUE ET LITTÉRAIRE

REVUE BLEUE

FONDÉE EN 1863. — DIRECTEUR : FÉLIX DUMOULIN.

Est à la tête des Revues françaises — *depuis près d'un demi-siècle* — par l'honorabilité, la variété et l'éclat de sa rédaction.

Chaque semaine elle publie de brillants articles *diplomatiques* et *politiques;* une *nouvelle* ou un *roman;* de spirituelles critiques *littéraire, dramatique* et *artistique;* des études d'*histoire*, de *philosophie;* une *poésie;* une *chronique* sur la vie parisienne ; etc.

Ses collaborateurs sont des Membres de l'Académie française, de l'Institut, du Parlement, de l'Université, etc.

Elle est indispensable aux Anglais, qui désirent se tenir au courant de la littérature, de l'art et de la politique de la France.

Abonnement : six mois, **20** fr.; un an, **35** fr.

PARIS — 41 *bis*, rue de Châteaudun — PARIS

Sir ISAAC PITMAN & SONS, Ltd.,
No. 1 Amen Corner, LONDON, E.C.

Now Ready.

THE LATEST ADDITION TO PITMAN'S MAKERS OF NATIONAL HISTORY SERIES.

Edited by W. H. HUTTON, B.D.

GENERAL WOLFE.

By EDWARD SALMON.

In crown 8vo. cloth gilt, with Frontispiece and Map, **3s. 6d.** net.

On September 13 will be celebrated the 150th anniversary of the capture of Quebec and the death of General Wolfe.

"Mr. Salmon's exhaustive account of the whole campaign should be read by every impartial student of military annals." *Outlook.*

"A careful and attractive study . . . Wolfe's life story, as a notable chapter in our national history, is here admirably told."—*Daily Telegraph.*

Previous Volumes in the Series.

CARDINAL BEAUFORT. By L. B. RADFORD, D.D.

VISCOUNT CASTLEREAGH. By ARTHUR HASSALL, M.A.

ARCHBISHOP PARKER. By W. M. KENNEDY, B.A.

READY SHORTLY.

FRANCIS ATTERBURY. By H. C. BEECHING, D.Litt.

"A new and notable series of comprehensive and scholarly historical manuals." *Glasgow Herald.*

"No scheme could be more admirable than that of the series of volumes entitled, 'Makers of National History.'" *Sphere.*

"The three volumes which have already appeared in this new library of historical manuals fully demonstrate the value of such a series, the immediate object of which is 'to commemorate important men whose share in the making of national history seems to need a more complete record than it has yet received.' Each volume is obviously the work of a practised historian." *Daily Graphic.*

"The new series ought to make a place for itself in school and public libraries." *Saturday Review.*

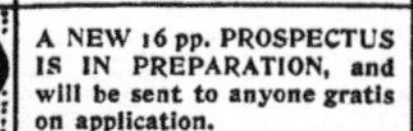

A NEW 16 pp. PROSPECTUS IS IN PREPARATION, and will be sent to anyone gratis on application.

KING'S COLLEGE (University of London).

THE THEOLOGICAL DEPARTMENT.

Complete instruction is given for all theological degrees in the University of London, and students are prepared for Holy Orders in the Church of England.

KING'S COLLEGE (University of London).

This includes the FACULTY OF ARTS (including ARCHITECTURE), the FACULTY OF LAWS. The classes in Laws are arranged by an inter-collegiate scheme with University College and the London School of Economics. The FACULTY OF SCIENCE with (*a*) DIVISION OF NATURAL SCIENCE. Preparation for Science degrees and also for the Institution of Chemistry examinations. (*b*) DIVISION OF MEDICAL SCIENCE. Preparation for preliminary and intermediate medical examinations, for which the college is a University centre. FACULTY OF ENGINEERING. Systematic courses in civil, mechanical, and electrical engineering and metallurgy. EVENING CLASS DEPARTMENT. Full courses for University degrees in arts and science, and various special classes.

KING'S COLLEGE FOR WOMEN

(University of London).

The College is in Kensington Square. The faculties represented are ARTS AND SCIENCE. There are also two other departments—viz. HOME SCIENCE AND ECONOMICS and FINE ART. The more advanced students in science attend classes at King's College.

For information and prospectus apply to the **Secretary**, King's College, Strand, W.C.

ELTHAM COLLEGE, KENT.

(THE ROYAL NAVAL SCHOOL.)

PUBLIC SCHOOL LIFE AND EDUCATION, with Special Classes for all Naval and Military Examinations. Special Fees for Officers in the Navy and Army. Recognised by the Army Council. Large Playing-fields. Gymnasium, Swimming Bath; Chemical and Physical Laboratories; Cadet Corps, &c. Recent Honours: Open Scholarship, Balliol College; 1st, Open Scholarships, Hertford and Merton Colleges; 1st place Naval Clerkships; Admissions to Sandhurst, Osborne, &c. NEXT TERM BEGINS SEPTEMBER 15th.

Apply Headmaster, Rev. A. E. RUBIE, D.D.

THE CONDUIT STREET AUCTION GALLERIES.

The attention of Executors, Trustees, Solicitors, and Owners, who may be desirous of selling Works of Art, Family Jewels, Old Silver, Furniture, Pictures, Prints, Miniatures, China, Coins, Books, Old Lace, Furs, Musical Instruments, Guns, and other Valuables, is drawn to Messrs.

KNIGHT, FRANK & RUTLEY'S

AUCTION GALLERIES, 9 CONDUIT STREET, AND 23A MADDOX STREET, W., which are Open Daily to receive goods intended for early sales.

VALUATIONS are prepared for Fire Insurance, Estate Duty, and all other purposes. As to Insurance, owners are reminded that, for security, Messrs. KNIGHT, FRANK & RUTLEY's detailed inventory and valuation of the contents of a Town or Country Mansion is an important adjunct to their Fire Insurance Policies.

THE

AFRICAN & EUROPEAN INVESTMENT COMPANY, LIMITED.

(Incorporated in the Transvaal.)

REPORT OF THE DIRECTORS.

To be submitted at the fifth ordinary general meeting of the company, to be held at the Company's Offices, Lewis and Marks Building, Johannesburg, on Friday, the 20th day of August, 1909, at twelve o'clock noon.

To the Shareholders.—Your directors beg to submit their fourth annual report and the audited statements of account for the twelve months ending the 31st December, 1908.

CAPITAL.

The capital of the company remains unchanged: 1,538,592 shares of £1 each being issued out of an authorised capital of £1,700,000.

LANDED PROPERTY.

The land holding of the company as at the 31st December, 1908, stands at 476,087 morgen, equal to 1,007,638 English acres. The difference in area—an increase of 629 morgen—between this figure and that given in the last annual report is due to the fact that one farm has been surveyed and its exact area defined, and several other farms in which your company hold undivided interests have been divided. Only one farm now remains.

In addition to the freehold land mentioned above, you are the virtual owners of 119,133 morgen 413 square roods of land, equivalent to 252,146 English acres, in the Vryburg and Mafeking districts of British Bechuanaland, registered as the Bechuanaland Farms, Limited, so that the total area of your land holding is 1,259,784 English acres.

Satisfactory progress continues to be made in the settlement of the land of your company. Nearly all the farms suitable for white occupation are now let to satisfactory tenants, and the revenues derived from rentals are increasing yearly and will continue to increase.

Energetic measures have been and continue to be taken by the Government of the Transvaal Colony to exterminate stock diseases; and encouragement is given to the export of agricultural products. The mealie growing and stock raising industries are now on a stable basis, and, with the extension of the railway system of the Transvaal, the outlook for the farming community is much brighter.

The settlement of farmers on so large an area of the company's estate has not only the direct effect of increasing the amount of income derived from rentals, but has a more important and far-reaching result. The tilling of the soil naturally leads to a closer acquaintance with the geological formation of a farm, and this has in many cases resulted in the discovery of mineral-bearing lodes, which, in the absence of agricultural operations, would have remained undiscovered. The land owned by your company is very widely distributed, and, as the greater part of it has been selected for its mineral possibilities, there is every reason to anticipate that important discoveries will be made on some of them which will justify development as mining propositions.

The prospecting and mining work carried out by the company during the year on the farms Snymansdrift, Palmietfontein, and Zandrivier, has disclosed no fresh feature of interest. Your directors considered that the ore bodies developed on these properties were not sufficiently large to justify the undertaking of more extensive work, and the mines have now been let on tribute, the lessees paying the company a royalty on the gold produced.

SHARE INTERESTS AND INVESTMENTS.

The severe market depression in South African shares which existed at the date of the last report was succeeded, towards the end of the financial year, by a revival of public confidence and a considerable appreciation in quotations, which has had the effect of reducing the depreciation on your company's securities from £300,828 10s. 9d., as shown in the balance sheet at 31st December, 1907, to £233,684 3s. 11d., as shown in the balance sheet now issued. Since the 31st December last the company has entered into several important transactions, and, as a result of these transactions and of the further general improvement which has taken place since the beginning of the year, your directors are pleased to report that a valuation of your shares and interests at the market quotations of to-day would show that the depreciation referred to in the balance sheet has been very largely reduced.

East Rand Mining Estates, Limited.—The past year has been marked by a strong revival of public confidence in the far east Rand as a result of the satisfactory developments obtained by companies working in this neighbourhood. Your company has a substantial holding in the East Rand Mining Estates, Limited, whose properties—Grootvlei and Palmeitkuil—adjoin the Welgedacht and Geduld farms, and as the existence of the main reef has already been proved by boreholes over the larger portion of the company's area, there is every reason to anticipate successful development results on these properties.

With the object of assisting the East Rand Mining Estates to finance its subsidiary undertakings, your directors have recently guaranteed an issue of 50,000 East Rand Mining Estates shares at 30s. per share, receiving as consideration for such guarantee a commission of 1s. per share and the option over a further 50,000 shares at 35s. for a period of twelve months. Your directors consider this transaction is likely to be a very profitable one for the company in view of the predominating interest held by the East Rand Mining Estates in the far eastern Rand, there being every indication that during the next few years the most active and important mining developments in the Transvaal will be centred in this neighbourhood.

The East Rand Mining Estates being now provided with funds will be in a position, if required, to render financial assistance to its subsidiaries. When the option over the reserve shares is exercised, the East Rand Mining Estates will have in hand a sum of over £200,000 for working capital.

Vereeniging Estates, Limited.—The prospects of this company, in which your company holds a substantial share interest, have greatly improved during the past year. A supplement agreement has been entered into with the Victoria Falls and Transvaal Power Company whereby the establishment of a 30,000 h.p. station on the property is provided for, the Vereeniging Estates having arranged a satisfactory contract for the supply of coal to them. The company will, moreover, largely benefit by the establishment of other industries on the property, the combination of cheap power and ample supplies of coal and water rendering the estate the most economically attractive position in the Transvaal for the purpose.

Roberts Victor Diamonds, Limited.—The returns of diamonds from this mine have maintained a high standard, 230,052 loads of ground having been washed during 1908, yielding 89,779½ carats of diamonds, equal to 39 carats per 100 loads. Since the commencement of washing operations in July 1906 until December 31, 1908, a total of 511,982 loads of ground have yielded 242,994¾ carats of diamonds, an average of 47.4 carats per 100 loads. For the six months ending June 30 last the washings have given a return of 67,837 carats from 144,419 loads washed, an average of 46.9 carats per 100 loads. The financial position of the Roberts Victor Diamonds, Limited, is a strong one, satisfactory profits having been earned during the latter part of 1908 under the new management, and a further dividend of 25 per cent. has recently been paid.

Giant Mines of Rhodesia, Limited.—The confidence your board have had in the company's investment in this undertaking has been well placed. These shares have steadily appreciated in value during the year, and now stand at a considerably higher price than that at which your company purchased.

East Rand Extension Gold Mining Company, Limited.—Your company has recently acquired an important share interest in the East Rand Extension Gold Mining Company, Limited, which possesses valuable mining interests on the farms Leeuwkuil and Finaalspan on the eastern section of the Rand. On one of the blocks of claims owned by this company—which adjoins the properties of the East Rand Proprietary Mines and the Apex Mines—a large amount of development work has been carried out, two shafts having been sunk to depths of 1,606 ft. and 1,239 ft. respectively. Prior to the closing down of the mine in 1906, three drives were put in from the No. 1 shaft, the last 260 ft. in the western drive giving assay results averaging 19.2 dwt. over a thickness of 12 to 15 in. The mine remained closed down for some time for want of funds, but arrangements for the supply of working capital on a large scale having now been made, the shafts have been dewatered and development work is being actively proceeded with. The engineering management of this property has been placed in the hands of the Consolidated Goldfields of South Africa, Limited.

In addition to its 229 claims the East Rand Extension Company has a large shareholding in the Hercules Deep and in the Eastern Gold Mines, two companies owning valuable mining areas in the same neighbourhood.

Crown Diamond Mining Co.—Your company also holds 50 per cent of the share capital of the Crown Diamond Mining and Exploration Co., Ltd., a company recently registered in the Orange River Colony with an issued capital of £100,000. The mine has been equipped with a thoroughly up-to-date direct-treatment plant and a new system of haulage has been installed, the modernised plant having a treatment capacity of 5,000 loads per day. All water requirements have been amply provided for and washing has recently been started. On a yield of 11 cts. per 100 loads (the average of the returns obtained by the previous owners) and taking the selling price of the diamonds at 22s. 6d. per carat (a contract for their sale at this price having been entered into), the manager estimates that a profit of £4,500 per month should be obtained. The company is exempt from payment of the 40 per cent. diamond tax, its only liability in this direction being the payment of claim licences at the rate of 5s. per claim per month.

Rhodesian Interests.—Your directors consider that the improved position of affairs in Rhodesia make it a good field for the investment of capital, and interests have already been secured in promising ventures there to which the directors attach considerable importance.

EXECUTIVE COMMITTEE.

In order to deal with the increasing business of the company Messrs. C. F. Rowsell and H. W. Smart have been appointed an executive committee of the board.

ISAAC LEWIS, Chairman.
CHAS. FRED. ROWSELL, } Directors.
H. W. SMART, }

London, July 23, 1909.

Copies of the Report and Accounts can be obtained at the London Office, Threadneedle House, 28-31 Bishopsgate Street Within, E.C.

THRELFALL'S BREWERY.

The twenty-second annual general meeting of Threlfall's Brewery Co., Limited, was held on Thursday at Cannon Street Hotel, Mr. Charles Threlfall, J.P., presiding.

The Chairman having read the auditors' report, said he had much pleasure in submitting it, together with the accounts for the year ended June 30 last. He continued: "I think you will agree with me that, taking into consideration the difficulties with which we have had to contend during the year, coupled with the depression in trade generally, we have very good ground for congratulation on the results attained. You have no doubt all studied the balance-sheet, and I need only draw attention to some of the more important figures. The profit from trading account for the year is £171,595, against £179,421 in 1908. This shows a decrease of £7,826, but we are passing through an anxious time, and we think that under the circumstances we have well held our own. We have written off £25,239 for depreciation, as compared with £20,875 last year, and we have carried forward £38,255, against £25,459 in 1908. I am sure that you will agree that your board is pursuing a sound policy in thus husbanding your resources. As you are aware, since our last meeting the Licensing Bill has been rejected, but the Chancellor of the Exchequer is now making an effort to impose additional heavy licence duties on the trade, notwithstanding the fact that we are already overburdened with taxation. And this is without taking into consideration the increased duty on spirits, which I may say has seriously interfered with our trade in that department. The sales have considerably declined through the consumer having had to pay the additional duty, but I am pleased to say that, on the other hand, there has been an increase in the sales of beer. The question of raising the price of beer is receiving the careful consideration of all the associations in the north of England, where we are most anxious to act unitedly, but up to the present no decision has been arrived at, pending the result of the Finance Bill. Before formally moving the adoption of the accounts there is another important matter I should like to mention. The time is not far distant when it will be to the benefit of the Company to make a further issue of our authorised but unissued capital, and when that time arrives the shareholders will have the first offer to subscribe to the issue. With a revival of trade—and there are strong signs of an improvement—your board believes that this Company will see a revival in their houses of that good business which for so many years they have been accustomed to enjoy, as the majority of their licensed houses are very valuable ones, suitable to the neighbourhood in which they are placed. I now beg to move the adoption of the report and accounts, and that dividends be paid at the rate of 6 per cent. per annum on the preference shares and at the rate of 10 per cent. per annum on the ordinary shares for the half-year ended June 30, which, with the interim dividend at the rate of 8 per cent. per annum, makes 9 per cent. for the year."

Mr. George Barker seconded the motion.

Mr. J. Hedges expressed a hope that the issue of fresh capital to which the Chairman had referred would not be made while the present Government was in office.

The Chairman having put the motion and declared it carried unanimously, stated, in reply to Mr. Hedges, that the issue of fresh capital was one which had been in the minds of the board for six months or more, and one in regard to which the shareholders must trust the board. The shareholders might be quite sure that nothing would be done by the directors to injure the business, which had been successfully carried on for 22 years. He could make no definite promise, but he thought that no fresh issue of capital would be made until the Finance Bill had passed.

The motion was unanimously adopted.

Mr. Buszard, K.C., proposed a hearty vote of thanks to the chairman, the directors, and the staff for the successful manner in which the business had been carried on in the past year.

Mr. Isaac Turner seconded the motion, which was carried unanimously.

NEW YORK TAXICAB.

The Annual General Meeting of the New York Taxicab Company, Limited, was held on Thursday at the offices, 32 Old Jewry, E.C., Mr. Charles Mascart (Chairman of the Company) presiding.

The Secretary (Mr. R. Gordon) having read the notice convening the meeting and the report of the auditors,

The Chairman said: At the last general meeting, held on April 6 this year, the chairman gave full particulars concerning the actual state of your Company's affairs. Since that time your directors have used the powers which were given to them at that meeting, in order to strengthen definitely the financial position of the Company. You will remember that a scheme to increase the number of cabs from 300 to 700, without the issue of further share capital, was unanimously carried at an extraordinary meeting held on May 20 last year. This scheme provided for a short loan to cover the extra expenditure incurred in the purchase of the additional cabs and the provision of the necessary garage accommodation, and, in favour of the charge given in connection with that loan, 25 per cent. of the cab takings was to be specifically set aside. This arrangement was duly carried out, but owing to the strike of last year the Company suffered heavy losses, and, unfortunately, in the middle of the troubles and anxieties which arose, consequent upon the strike, our bankers (Messrs. Tracy and Co., of New York) were obliged to inform us that, owing to their financial position, they were unable to allow us to deal with the money deposited with them; or that, at any rate, it would be necessary to spread the payments over a considerable period. The matter was at once put into the hands of our lawyers in New York, and they, after looking closely into the position, advised us that in order to avoid a complete loss of our deposits it would be wiser in the interests of the Company to enter into an agreement by which the money would be paid back in instalments over a specified period. At the same time Mr. W. W. Tracy resigned, both as a director and chairman of this Company. Messrs. Tracy and Co. fulfilled their undertaking in this respect until the payments were necessarily abruptly terminated by the failure of the firm, which occurred last May. The whole matter is now in the hands of our lawyers, and I need hardly say that the Company's rights will be carefully protected. The balance due on this account is, roughly speaking, £17,000. These various circumstances, as you will easily understand, were most embarrassing to the Company. We were short of money to pay the expenses of the strike, and we were no longer in a position to satisfy the conditions of the redemption of the loan which had been contracted under your authority for the extra number of cabs we have put out. We must say, in all fairness, that the gentlemen who advanced the money gave to the directors of the Company, all through this most trying period, their most generous support. They certainly were in a position to call in their loan; but, instead of taking such drastic steps, they readily fell in with a new suggestion, and agreed to the following arrangement: (1) They immediately readvanced to the Company the whole amount which had already been repaid them out of the daily takings prior to the strike. (2) They agreed to wait a considerable period for the payment of accrued interest. (3) They agreed to convert their short loan into debentures, which debentures have recently been issued under the powers given to the directors at your extraordinary meeting held on April 6 this year. It is certainly due to this generous attitude on the part of these gentlemen that the Company has had time to reorganise its affairs, to rebuild the cabs damaged during the strike, and practically to reconstruct the whole of its business. The accounts have been carefully examined in New York, up to the end of October last, by your auditors (Messrs. W. B. Peat and Co.), and from that time by Messrs. Price, Waterhouse and Co., of New York. There has been considerable work, not only in auditing the accounts for the past financial year, but also in establishing a close correlation between the books in New York and London. This work has been responsible for the delay in convening the present meeting, the directors having thought that no good purpose would be served by calling the shareholders together without being in a position to place before them the duly audited accounts. At your meeting in April last the Chairman told you that the business was now running smoothly and showed a decided improvement. Arriving recently from New York myself, I am in a position to give you more recent news. The new garage is a substantial building, well adapted to our requirements, and has cost us about £80,000. We believe that so well-designed and so suitable a building for the purpose of a taxicab business does not exist in the United States of America. The numbers of cabs operating daily is steadily increasing, although the summer season will always be a dull time. The local management is thoroughly efficient, and it appears from the accounts, audited each month by a first-class firm in New York, that the operating expenses are steadily and systematically decreasing. You will have seen from the accounts that up to the end of last year, notwithstanding all the difficulties with which the Company has had to contend, a gross operating profit was shown of £42,000. We hope to do much better in the future, as the number of our cabs in service is gradually increased and the item of general charges correspondingly reduced. The business is a good one, but, as in the case of every business, time is required to consolidate and organise it, and, although it may seem to some of you, not knowing all the circumstances, that the progress has been somewhat slow, still, if comparison be made with the results obtained by other similar companies in the early days of their existence, it will be seen that we have not done at all badly. I do not propose to go through the accounts in detail, but, of course, if any item appears to call for elucidation I shall be happy to give any further explanation in my power. According to all probability, we think you can now be safely assured that the business will soon be in a position to meet all its liabilities, including the annual instalments of the redemption fund and the interest on the debentures, and have a satisfactory balance of profit left in hand. Both my co-directors and I anticipate that a good future is open to your Company, and, in moving the adoption of the report and accounts, I would ask you to join me in a vote of thanks to the people who have supported your Company with their money, and who have shown such unbounded confidence in the stability of your enterprise. By the death of Mr. Winthrop Sands and of Admiral Sir Charles Fane, and by the resignations of Messrs. Tracy and H. N. Allen, of New York, we lost four of our directors. In their places the board nominated Messrs. François Ducasse, of New York, Léon Boulloche, of Paris, and J. S. Smith-Winby, of London, whose election we are asking you to confirm to-day. Within the last fortnight we have also had to deplore the loss of another of our directors in the person of Mr. George Dalziel, and we take this opportunity of expressing our deep sense of regret at losing so capable and amiable a colleague. I now move the resolution: "That the report of the directors and the balance-sheet and accounts to December 31, 1908, be, and are hereby, received and adopted."

Mr. J. S. Smith-Winby seconded the resolution, which, after some discussion, was put to the meeting and carried, with four dissentients.

The Chairman next moved: "That Mr. Lazare Weiller, a director retiring by rotation, and Mr. François Ducasse, Mr. Léon Boulloche, and Mr. J. S. Smith-Winby, retiring in accordance with the articles, be, and are hereby, re-elected directors of the Company."

The resolution was seconded and carried unanimously.

RAND MINES, LIMITED.

ABRIDGED TABULATED SUMMARY.

—	Glen Deep, Limited.	Rose Deep, Limited.	Geldenhuis Deep, Limited.	Jumpers Deep, Limited.	Nourse Mines, Limited.	Ferreira Deep, Limited.	Crown Deep, Ltd., now Crown Mines, Ltd.	Langlaagte Deep, Limited (*in Liquidation*).	Durban Roodepoort Deep, Ltd.
Financial Quarter ending	30th April,'09	30th June,'09	30th June,'09	30th June,'09	30th April,'09	30th June,'09	30th June,'09	Two months to 30th June,'09	30th June,'09
Mine.									
Development Work—									
No. of feet driven, sunk and risen, exclusive of Stopes ..	2,325·5	3,400	3,228	3,600	4,500	2,525	2,371·5	2,699	3,174
Estimated Tonnage of Ore exposed by drives, &c. ..	105,962	196,327	98,400	§ 159,829	‖ 174,621	161,285	221,123	116,225	114,650
Stoping—									
Tonnage Stoped, including Ore from development faces	64,172	138,253	106,200	80,727	126,943	114,281	130,766	91,760	74,097
Milling.									
No. of Stamps in operation	100	200	200	100	180	160	200	200	100
Ore milled (tons)	58,120	120,700	90,900	64,800	109,088	102,782	121,650	82,700	58,720
Duty per Stamp per 24 hours (tons)	8·063	7·273	5·619	7·674	7·509	7·756	7·488	7·683	7·129
Cyaniding.									
Total Tons treated	59,029	119,980	99,039	64,654	115,588	102,497	121,210	82,428	58,328
Gold Production.									
Milling (fine oz.)	12,537	23,879	17,546	15,238	29,137	38,547	30,975	19,875	15,010
Cyaniding (current milling) (fine oz.)	8,158	12,701	8,533	6,037	10,745	16,996	14,723	7,781	6,137
Do. (accumulations of Slimes) (fine oz.)	—	—	801	—	1,306	—	—	—	—
Total (fine oz.)	20,695	36,580	26,880	21,275	41,188	55,543	45,698	27,656	21,147
Total Yield per Ton Milled (fine dwt.)	7·121	6·061	† 5·737	6·566	† 7·311	10·807	7·513	6·688	7·202
Total Working Expenses.									
Cost	£59,763 5 8	£93,067 19 6	£99,006 3 8	£73,835 4 6	£112,724 11 9	£84,295 17 6	£89,808 12 4	£66,287 3 9	£63,295 19 10
Cost per Ton Milled ..	£1 0 6·785	£0 15 5·056	£1 1 9·402	£1 2 9·463	£1 0 8·000	£0 16 4·834	£0 14 9·180	£0 16 0·369	£1 1 6·702
Revenue.									
Value of Gold produced ..	£86,769 18 1	£153,411 11 6	£109,425 12 0	£89,207 14 6	£167,184 15 2	£233,164 0 0	£191,635 13 3	£116,067 0 3	£88,605 9 7
Value per Ton Milled ..	£1 9 10·305	£1 5 5·043	£1 4 0·912	£1 7 6·398	£1 10 7·816	£2 5 4·447	£1 11 6·072	£1 8 0·832	£1 10 2·147
Working Profit.									
Amount	£27,006 12 5	£60,343 12 0	£10,419 8 4	£15,372 10 0	£54,460 3 5	£148,868 2 6	£101,827 0 11	£49,779 16 6	£25,309 9 9
Per Ton Milled	£0 9 3·520	£0 9 11·987	£0 2 3·510	£0 4 8·935	£0 9 11·815	£1 8 11·612	£0 16 8·891	£0 12 0·463	£0 8 7·444
Interest.									
Credit	£434 16 11	£1,127 10 1	£447 11 4	*£789 18 2	*£1,020 14 5	*£1,758 2 11	£2,980 14 7	£686 5 6	£41 2 3
Net Profit	£27,441 9 4	£61,471 2 1	‡£12,835 9 9	£16,162 8 2	¶£59,700 9 8	£150,626 5 5	**113,907 15 6	£50,466 2 0	£25,350 12 0
Estimated Amount of 10% Tax on Profits	£1,620 0 0	£5,614 0 0	£782 0 0	£947 0 0	£3,789 0 0	£14,030 0 0	£9,069 0 0	£2,641 0 0	£1,812 0 0
Reserve Gold (fine oz.) ..	3,356	5,786	*Nil*	5,456	2,136	2,740	*Nil*	*Nil*	208
Capital Expenditure ..	£1,417 2 8	*Nil*	£301 6 10	£5,780 5 1	£8,136 4 11	£8 15 9	*Nil*	*Nil*	£1,556 11 2
Interim Dividends Declared.									
Payable to Shareholders registered on books as at	—	30th June,'09	30th June,'09	—	—	—	30th June,'09	30th June,'09	30th June,'09
Rate per cent.	—	25%	17½%	—	—	—	70%	8⅓%	10%
Total amount of distribution	—	£106,250 0 0	£52,500 0 0	—	—	—	£210,000 0 0	£66,666 13 4	£44,000 0 0

* Including Freehold Revenue.
† Not including yield from accumulations of Slimes.
‡ Including £1,968 10s. 1d., profit from treatment of accumulations of Slimes.
¶ Including £4,219 11s. 10d., profit from treatment of accumulations of Slimes.
§ Exclusive of 1,705 feet of development work done during the quarter, and charged to Capital Account.
‖ Exclusive of 1,418 feet of development work done during the quarter, and charged to Capital Account.
** Including £9,100 transferred from Suspense Account.

Printed for the Proprietors by SPOTTISWOODE & Co. LTD., 5 New-street Square, E.C., and Published by REGINALD WEBSTER PAGE, at the Office, 10 King Street, Covent Garden, in the Parish of St. Paul, in the County of London.—*Saturday*, 31 *July*, 1909.

THE

SATURDAY REVIEW

OF

POLITICS, LITERATURE, SCIENCE, AND ART.

No. 2,806 Vol. 108. 7 August 1909. [Registered as a Newspaper.] 6*d*.

CONTENTS.

NOTES OF THE WEEK.

The Tsar and the King have met; and the Ides of March are gone. Everything went off so happily that no one realised there could be anything in the world to guard against. The Tsar has received the freedom of the City, seen a great British fleet, and conversed with the King of England. The programme has been carried out without a hitch; and everybody is delighted—everybody save only Mr. Shaw, Mr. Hardie and a few others, who scowl in their corner, chiefly concerned that in the general rejoicing nobody marked them. They had done their best to spoil an act of courtesy, and had failed. We are glad to see that the Secretary of the knot of busybodies calling themselves by the big name of the Parliamentary Russian Committee has thought better of his ways and resigned. Mr. MacCallum Scott has the sense to see that, whatever defect there may be in Russian methods, it is not for the British Foreign Office to lecture the Tsar. He is shocked, too, by the discovery, familiar to everybody else, that the Parliamentary Russian Committee was hobnobbing with revolutionaries and advocates of assassination.

Why can no function of this kind be got through without some exhibition of gross bad taste by the British public? These gaucheries—to use the mildest word possible—are always apologised away as natural, after all, or explained as harmless fun. There is no malice in them, we are told. Of course there is no malice in bad taste; if there is, we call it by a harder name. It means nothing but total disregard for other people's comfort; counting it nothing compared with your own amusement. The English multitude may be slow-witted, but it is certainly not dull enough not to perceive that children—no matter how Royal and Imperial, Princesses, Archduchesses, or anything else—will not enjoy themselves the more for being followed about by a crowd. It is really humiliating to think that so few had delicacy enough to see that the very grace of these highnesses mixing freely with the crowd demanded from that crowd a similar courtesy. Recognise them, make a show of them, and the spirit of the whole thing is spoilt.

There was some irony in Mr. McKenna's explanation to the House that most of the money spent on these naval displays went in entertaining the press etc. The reporters do not seem to think they were entertained. On the Naval Review day they left home at eight in the morning, the guests of the Admiralty, and got no food until 10.30 at night, unless they bought it or begged it from the marines. They were all put on board one ship, and it looked as if somebody had carefully cleared that ship out of all food before their arrival. They appear to have explored the ship minutely. Some found bread, and it is reported that some found butter, but these were very few. Even at 10.30 the Admiralty had given them nothing to eat. The Government does not propose to charge them for his Majesty's bread and butter taken from the ship without an order from Mr. McKenna. He is "very sorry".

Spain seems to have got through her domestic trouble pretty well; strangely well, indeed, if one remembers she is under a parliamentary régime, and what parliamentary administration has meant in Spain. The present Prime Minister seems to be a better man than the usual run of Spanish politicians. Vigorous measures were taken at once, with the effect that the émeute soon collapsed. Evidently there was little sympathy with the revolutionaries. Had there been any truth in newspaper reports of general disaffection, the outbreak would not have been put down as quickly as this by any means, no matter how vigorous the Government might be. Most important of all, the army appears to have been perfectly sound; the troops doing their duty readily and well. The war in Morocco remains to finish. There, too, the Spaniards have every reason to be hopeful. They have greatly strengthened their forces; and their position seems to be daily improving. It was never nearly as serious as certain newsagents made out.

The South Africa Union Bill has passed through the House of Lords unamended. Proceedings in Committee can hardly be taken as serious, the amendments being few and not one of them pressed to a division. It is evident that the submission to the Imperial Parliament of any measure agreed on by a self-governing colony is now a mere form, or farce. Only one point even came up for discussion—the natives. Amendments were moved to give native electors of the Cape Colony the vote for the Union Parliament and to prevent the Union Parliament from passing a measure within ten years depriving the Cape natives of their present franchise. The answer was always that white South African opinion was against it. Certainly imperial policy, were there such a thing, would find it hard to explain why more civilised and more intelligent Indian peoples should not have a share in the government of India if Zulus and Hottentots were allowed the vote in South Africa.

The American Tariff Bill has passed. The President has had his way with the reductions or exemptions on the few outstanding products in dispute—gloves, hides, and lumber. The President's demand as to cotton, or most of it, had already been conceded, which will please Lancashire; and the free list is really large, though including little that can go from Great Britain, unless indirectly. As more expert merchants, better fitted to hunt for the odd products of the earth, the Germans ought to come out best under the free list. The main fact brought out by the whole controversy seems to be a distinct change in American opinion as to the relative importance of production and consumption; a recognition of the consumer's plea for checking increase in prices as against the producers' contention for increased protection as necessary to increased production. Is it not a splendid irony that the first effect of this lower tariff is to send up prices?

The naval debates this week showed the Government wedged tight—and most uncomfortable—between their friends who attacked them for spending too much and the Opposition who attacked them for spending too little. Mr. Lough and Mr. Byles were almost tearful over the Government's degeneracy and subservience to Opposition pressure. Sixteen millions for shipbuilding oppressed them as a nightmare. But all expenditure on armaments is relative; and Germany, Mr. Bellairs pointed out, was spending on new construction and armaments more than we. If Germany with her unequalled army can afford to spend so much on her navy, how can we think to spend any less? It is evident we want to spend much more, for at present we are keeping up neither a two-Power standard nor that of two keels to the next strongest navy's one. Mr. McKenna, in this debate, took his stand on Mr. Asquith's latest definition of Two Powers—not the next strongest two powers, but two within a certain distance of this country. This reduces the two-power standard to an illusion, and Mr. McKenna says it is final.

The Little Navy soul is not quite easy to fathom. Mr. Byles, for instance, says he greatly enjoyed the scene, which was the naval review at Cowes, on Saturday, yet it induced in him a feeling of sadness. "The great grey ugly monsters of destruction" were to him "a display of methods of barbarism". Might not this unhappy phrase be allowed to lie? Mr. Byles digs it up and worries it: he outdoes its author, who used it only of measures of severity regretted by those who most firmly urged their necessity. He did not apply it to British armies or British ships. An Englishman who can see nothing in a British battleship but "a grey ugly monster" should belong to some other country. But who would take him?

It is clear the Government is determined to keep the Mediterranean sinecure in being; and has even appointed a temporary occupant until a permanent appointment is made. Mr. Haldane was very reticent and uneasy about the affair. He says the post is necessary as a factor in the new defence organisation, and that there will be no extra expense. Still a cruiser is kept at the Commander-in-Chief's use. It is not easy to say why such a fifth wheel in the coach as a Mediterranean Commander-in-Chief is needed. The real reason for continuing the post is, perhaps, to be found in the statement that it had only been created by the Government after "careful consideration". An economising Government won't admit that it has created a sinecure.

Mr. Balfour's unfortunate speech about our immunity from invasion is always being used as an excuse for taking things easy. The Prime Minister, of course, used it in his speech on the Defence Committee. It is, however, now admitted that our position is not so secure as it was when Mr. Balfour made his original statement; and therefore home defence forces should be ready to cope with a foreign invasion of 70,000 men. Mr. Haldane's Territorial Army is obviously not equal to the demand. But now we have another scheme to strengthen the Territorials—a new reserve of three classes, styled respectively "The Territorial Force Reserve", "The Technical Reserve", and "The Veteran Reserve". Of course it is to the good to organise all the fighting power we possibly can. But all these forces will require officers; and the sketchy provisions for a reserve of officers will not produce them.

There was much gas about in the discussion of the airship vote. Seven columns in the "Times" is not bad for the first debate—parent of how many others in the future? We are far behind other nations in air navigation and flight. If it could have been proved that Mr. Haldane was wrong in saying that airships are of doubtful utility for war, we might have had a vote of censure. But nobody knew enough to disprove Mr. Haldane's optimism, and we have to hope that our backwardness is no danger. We must take it on trust too that we shall soon be on a level with other nations, though the three dirigibles we are to have "before a very long time is over" are only just beginning to be built. As to aeroplanes, they are not of great use in war according to Mr. Haldane, though he admits we should be foolish to neglect them, and we must push ahead. We shall soon, probably, have two. Nothing beyond this is to be got from the debate; except that as a pledge of "pushing ahead" £78,000 is to be spent this year on aeronautics for defence purposes.

There has been a great deal of factitious excitement in political circles over the supposed weakening of the Unionists on the Budget. Radical news-bills have bristled with wonderful legends, "Collapse of the Opposition: Great Triumph of Lloyd George". Behind most outbursts of this kind there is a spring of truth; and there is just something in this one. High Peak has caused some of the feebler Unionists, including a famous newspaper owner, to lose their heads. The "Daily Mail" has had a fright about the Budget; and fright is infectious among predisposed subjects. It is true there is a fall in buoyancy amongst a certain set of Unionists. Possibly, too, the licensing interest is afraid it may be overlooked if the opposition to the land clauses is insisted on à outrance. But "cause" for faintness of heart in the Opposition there is absolutely none. The party in the House remains where it did, determined to fight the Budget on every side to the last. There is no doubt the Government will be compelled to indulge in wholesale guillotining, or to extend the debate in the Commons till long past the 17th September.

The Duke of Westminster has shown the right way for gentlemen to deal with a politician of Mr. Lloyd

George's type. He has a very good legal case against Mr. George on the false statements in his Limehouse speech, but to bring an action for libel against a man implies some regard for his personality. Disraeli's famous "whom I do not respect but much regard" will not do for a politician who talks such vulgar clap-trap as the Limehouse speech. To abuse landlords was, of course, a safe draw; and Mr. George calculated, rightly enough, that none of those to whose prejudices he was pandering would ever see any of the exposures which would follow his speech. One instance will sufficiently show Mr. George's honesty. To the East-ender—whom he was addressing—a landlord usually means a speculative Jew house-farmer who makes ends meet by getting the most out of the tenant and spending the least on the house. From one learn all, says Mr. George.

Mr. Churchill at Wimborne was not to be out-vulgarised by Mr. Lloyd George at Limehouse. The talk of dignity in public affairs in his mouth is nothing but insolence and impertinence. Even the "Westminster Gazette" is tired of his diatribes about the House of Lords. He talks of it being a crime "against the British democracy if the Government acquiesce in the slightest mutilation of the Budget in the House of Lords". The "Westminster" tells him "it does not seem necessary to keep talking" about it. We should think his manner must repel even more than the matter. Mr. Long at Christchurch asked what Mr. Asquith thinks of the "more turbulent members of the party". Well, when he hears this—"The Government are not going to retreat. They are going on, and all who are with them will share the honour and glory of the victory"—we should think he feels very sick.

Liberal politicians and newspapers are furbishing up a very old weapon to defend the Budget. Mr. Lloyd George's example, we presume, of nosing into private matters accounts for it. Paul Pry is going to be very busy getting up particulars about family histories as arguments for the Budget. There should be a great demand for "Our Old Nobility" by Budget League speakers. The Duke of Portland makes some serious criticism of the Budget, and the "Daily Chronicle" responds with a column of "Ducal Family History". This is the sort of thing the Secularist Halls of Science used to do in Bradlaugh's and Holyoake's time. It is coming in again to back up Mr. Lloyd George's land taxation. Why restrict it? It is quite as valid for the 80 per cent. balance of increment that Mr. T. F. Richards M.P. still wants, as he said at Mr. Keir Hardie's meeting a few days ago.

Mr. Henderson did not take much by his attempt to pillory Lord Claud Hamilton for abusing the privileges of the House. The poor man was bowled out immediately on a highly technical point. The injurious remark was reported in the "Times" on Saturday. Mr. Henderson did not call the attention of the House to it until Tuesday. He could have done this on Monday; therefore he came within the rule requiring a motion of this kind to be made with the least possible delay. The Speaker suppressed him accordingly. On merits Mr. Henderson seems to have had something of a case. There certainly was a suggestion of partiality in the objection to the committee of sixteen members. But the Chairman of the Great Eastern had a very substantial point when he dwelt on the difficulties Labour members and others were putting in the way of railways. At any rate it is bringing railway development to a standstill. Railways should certainly be under the strictest public supervision as employers and otherwise, but not the sport of every crank's whim.

For the rather loose luxury of sitting Tory and voting Socialist Mr. Alexander Cross is dropped from the whip list, and he complains: "Such has always been the story of political life", neglect after consistent service! He has "crossed the floor", and it is a pity that people like him cannot find out on which side of it is their political conscience before they are forced. Because a man votes against one vague notion supposed to be entertained by some alleged number of Irishmen it does not follow that he must be free to vote against everything of value wanted in this country; and it is more than time that Ireland ceased to confuse the British conscience with her own. It has not been a matter of one question or two with Mr. Cross. Out of forty votes on the Budget he voted twenty-six times against the party with which he sat, and he complains! He ought to be an Irish "mimber".

The honourable "mimber" for Cardinal Logue has this week renewed his distrust of the Land Bill, wondering how land purchase can be "stimulated" by provisions that make it impossible at any point. The first clause, adding 5s. on £3 5s. to the tenants' annuities, charges them with £14,000,000 worth of organised crime, a total necessitated by the patriotic policy of "making government impossible". Then those who have sold £52,000,000 worth of land are to be paid by paper, at a minimum discount of six to seven per cent. on their bargains, with every prospect of farther slumps. The third great feature, which stood part of the Bill at the end of last week, graduates the bonus in such a way that the peaceful tenant may get nothing, and the law-breaker, who has reduced the "years' purchase" by crime, may get up to sixteen per cent.—or four per cent. more than under the Wyndham provision—at the expense of the taxpayer and in addition to the price of the land.

The "Irish Catholic", controlled by the clergy, denounces Mr. John Dillon, classing him with Cromwell, Satan, and other characters of doubtful reputation in Ireland. Mr. Dillon's mortal sin is in quoting the Pope to the priests. He used to talk of "going to Constantinople for his politics", but now he confesses that he went to Rome instead, and got the Pope's leave to obey his own conscience in his capacity as a British statesman, even on the education question. Very kind of His Holiness, but the "Irish Catholic" will have none of the story, denies that the Pope ever said it, and infers that Mr. Dillon must be lying. We had better leave the polemics between the "Irish Catholic", the Pope and Mr. Dillon; but the political split between "faith and country" must be deep and wide when Mr. Dillon is denounced as an anti-clerical, after his long devotion to "the cause". Most irritating of all, he is backed by Mr. Joe Devlin and his Molly Maguires, who defy the priests and boast of having "killed a bishop". The priests will find it very hard to make the people believe that Mr. Dillon is not a patriot.

Minor matters still remain after the coal dispute, but masters and men have agreed to settle them by arbitration. If the English federation had not interfered, the trouble would probably have been settled in the early days of the dispute, and more than once a rupture of the negotiations was only narrowly avoided. Success was due to the tact, knowledge, and courtesy of the Board of Trade officials. Both masters and men have publicly and privately expressed their satisfaction with the conduct of the proceedings throughout. The Board of Trade has again increased a reputation which was already very high. It succeeded, but it was touch and go.

The judgment of the King's Bench Divisional Court has exposed the injustice and illegality done to the Church school in Oxford Street, Swansea, by the local education authorities in league with the Board of Education. For several years the teachers of the Church school, against the protests of the managers, have been paid lower salaries than those of the Borough schools. This was for nothing else than that they were in the

Church school. It was "to larn them to be tooads". Under Mr. Birrell the Board admitted the illegality, but he took no action, and of course Mr. McKenna was not likely to do anything. Mr. Runciman sent Mr. Hamilton K.C. to report, and when he reported absolutely against the Swansea Council, Mr. Runciman threw over his report and refused to act on it. The managers of the school have now won a complete victory.

With Parliament sitting late into the autumn the Long Vacation will be rather a sorry time this year; especially for the Opposition lawyers. But the Bar may be thankful for a better prospect than it would have had if the County Courts Bill had passed. It asked for more judges so that there might be more cases in the High Court, and the Government proposed to send them to the County Courts where solicitors would flourish and the Bar wither. The question of barristers and solicitors lies at the root of every change in legal procedure that may be proposed. The Government have delayed appointing new judges, and they brought in their County Courts Bill because they have an idea of local courts replacing the High Court. This means either removing the distinction between barrister and solicitor, or the rise of the solicitors and ruin of the Bar.

Objectors to the censorship of plays have been giving their views before the Committee of Inquiry. They have made it clear that what they want is not an improved censorship but the abolition of the office. The evidence of Mr. Redford certainly suggests that there is nothing "intellectual" about the system as carried on in his office. If it were more intellectual, Mr. Shaw believes that many of the plays that now pass would be banned. This is probably true and to be desired. As to the plays which he calls "conscientiously immoral", such as he writes, those that satirise generally received opinions, an "intellectual" censorship would be more likely to be broader minded than the local authorities. But how are you to get your intellectual censorship? There is nothing for it, as we have said before, but to make Mr. Shaw examiner of plays.

We have supped so full of centenaries this year, and last, that one could almost wish that great men had never been born; certainly that they had never died. This Tennyson centenary is one of the silliest of these celebrations. He was with us far too recently, he was writing far too lately, for time yet to have enabled a better judgment, one nearer to finality, of his place as poet. Already the point of view from which he is regarded may have changed—has changed—but it will change again; and then will likely change back to the old standpoint. There is no advance in all this; nothing worth chronicling, nothing to survey. A hundred years from now a Tennyson celebration will have its use. One would like very much to know what people will think of Tennyson then. Will they be reading him? Will he then especially attract the particular type of society his average work, not his best, most appealed to in his lifetime? Or will he be but the cult of a coterie? These things lie in the lap of the gods. We shall get no nearer to them by taking thought now. Better say nothing and let Tennyson rest in peace.

Will the Philistines never cease from troubling? Now the Charles I. statue in Trafalgar Square, the one really satisfactory statue we have in London, is to be uprooted; just for the fun, we suppose, of seeing whether it will bear transplanting. Why cannot these meddlers leave well, indeed extremely well, alone? If they must be meddling, let them meddle with some of our bad statues: there are plenty for them to practise on. If they shifted Mill, now, from his seat, no one would mind though he never sat up again. But they must always worry the good things—James II. in Whitehall, for instance. Mr. Harcourt has not been bad in these things. Can he not let Charles I. be?

RUSSIA AND ENGLAND.

THE visit of the Tsar has been a complete success socially, but it is a success that may easily be exaggerated on the political side. It is hardly necessary for the SATURDAY REVIEW to emphasise its friendly attitude to Russia. Nothing can be more agreeable to us than the establishment of good relations with that great nation and its rulers. Any change from the suspicion and resentment with which it was once the habit in this country to speak and write of Russia would be welcome; but to no situation is the old maxim μηδὲν ἄγαν more applicable than to the relations between Great Powers. During the last few years we have seen strange and violent oscillations in the international barometer. At present so far as Russia is concerned the needle points "Set fair", but this is no assurance that it will never sink again to "Change", or even lower.

The present undoubted popularity of Russia in this country is due to two causes. In the first place it is believed that she is powerless for some time to come to do us any injury. We feel that to a very large extent this is due to ourselves. We brought her down by means of Japan, and the sporting instinct bids us have a good word for the man that is down. In the second place we are inclined to like the Russians because we believe that they dislike the Germans, and will prove useful in opposing German policy. This is a generalisation which may lead to some disappointment, but is undoubtedly founded on something. It is not a very worthy motive, but in the present condition of British feeling it is without doubt a strong one.

We cannot say that during the last year we have received any striking evidence of the value of Russian attachment in our international relations. This may be partly our own fault. Our Foreign Office might have known the binding nature of the engagements Russia had entered into with Austria. Sir Edward Grey could hardly have ignored the past as he did, had M. Isvolsky made it quite clear to his mind that Russia's policy could not go beyond platonic protests. We cannot believe that had a clear understanding been reached, the Foreign Secretary would have committed this country to a policy of conferences which were doomed from the first to come to nothing. The only result of the Anglo-Russian entente in Europe therefore has been to saddle us with Austrian hostility and to leave Germany with an easy triumph while our position in the Near East has been distinctly impaired.

We do not charge Russian policy with Machiavelism or with any wish to place England in an invidious position. On the contrary, we believe that at the present time Russian wishes coincide with ours. They desire to work with us as far as possible, and they believe that their potential adversaries are the same as ours at the moment; but we delude ourselves if we imagine that they are in the long run going to play for any hand but their own. There is no altruism in foreign policy, and if we desire to know how far any State may be credited with permanent friendship to ourselves, we have only to consider in what direction its permanent interests lie. Such a friendship has existed between us and Austria for many years, until it was rudely disturbed by our recent ill-calculated attitude on the Bosnian question. There is a similar congruity of interest between Italy and England which the keenest insight could find nothing to disturb. Is this so with Russia? We regret that we cannot find any valid reason for believing it. At the present time all hostility between us is banned, but causes, not to trouble about occasions, for a revival of rivalry are plentiful if latent. That this should be so is not the wish of either Power; it is the inevitable result of permanent forces over which neither of us can exercise control, unless one State or the other abandons her ambitions, which is inconceivable if we are both to maintain our position among nations.

It is not our own will, but the force of circumstances, which has brought us face to face in Persia. Here by the working of the Agreement the beau rôle has fallen to Russia. If that be hardly the correct expression in the circumstances, it may be more correct to say that Russia appears as the predominant partner. We have made it quite clear to the Persians that Russia and not England is the Power to be appeased, and that the future of Northern Persia at all events lies in her hands and not ours, and that we are henceforth estopped from any interference. Whether this is for the benefit or not of the "constitutional" régime we cannot say. It is hardly necessary at this time of day to demonstrate the absurdity of such an expression when applied to the Persians, but it will be the will of Russia and not ours which will henceforth make "la pluie et le beau temps" in Teheran. This is a fact the full significance of which can hardly be appreciated at present, but the deliberate execution of a religious leader for political reasons which took place the other day is so startling a development that the best authorities on Persian affairs will hesitate longest to predict its full import.

Another result of the Agreement may prove more injurious to us, and to this attention was called at the time by critics favourable to the policy of friendship with Russia. The right conceded to Russia of sending a commercial representative to the Amir was a most dangerous reversal of former policy. We have deliberately placed in the hands of the Tsar's Government a most powerful engine to manœuvre against us whenever we fall out in any quarter of the globe. If nothing worse comes of it, we shall almost certainly find this arousing suspicion (very likely groundless) directly our relations with Afghanistan become strained. This, unfortunately, is a possibility much nearer than is commonly supposed. Owing to the strange and heedless policy of the Indian Government the frontier tribes have been recently arming themselves with modern rifles at a low price. This is done with the connivance of the Amir, and the factories of Cabul supply the ammunition. The rifles are shipped from Muscat in dhows, and are met at the coast by strongly armed bodies of Afghans, who convey them to their destination. By what disastrous oversight or deliberate insanity the Indian Government allows the Sultan of Muscat, who is supposed to be under our protection, to carry on this trade it is impossible to imagine, but there the matter stands, and it is not difficult to see how gravely it may affect the relations between Afghanistan and ourselves, and ultimately between ourselves and Russia.

On the other side of India the policy of untempered enthusiasm for Russia may have dangerous results. Excessive regard for Russian susceptibilities has not tended to smooth our course in Tibet. It will always remain one of the mysteries of our diplomacy why, having obtained a predominant position in that country, we deliberately threw it over. After great labour and expense we had drawn all the cards into our own hands and then we handed them over to our rivals. Russia now enjoys greater consideration at Lhassa than we do. It was far worse policy to invade the country and then entirely abandon the field than never to have entered it at all. Having excited all the suspicion we could by allying ourselves with an Asiatic Power and having thereby sown the seeds of what may prove extremely dangerous developments in our own dominions, we failed to reap to the full the very considerable advantages that our diplomacy might have won. If we must incur the undoubted odium that attends an astute calculation and a daring manœuvre, it is only commonsense to reap from it the full advantage it is capable of yielding.

In many directions, therefore, it is wise to recognise that Russian policy and our own may not always coincide. We have only to look with an impartial eye on the geographical position of our possessions and the fact that we are both great and expanding Powers. To know this is in no way to take from our pleasure in the improved relations between the two countries and the exchange of civility and consideration for nagging and suspicion. The conduct of the Labour and Socialist parties is not only offensive but silly. If they knew anything of Russian legislation they would be aware that its tendencies are more in the direction of the socialist ideal than they are in most other countries, perhaps in any other. From every point of view let us cultivate nearer relations with Russia and stimulate intercourse between the nations, but not on that account ignore every permanent interest of our own policy. This could only make us before long again savagely anti-Russian.

SPAIN'S BLACK WEEK.

SPAIN has strong men. On the morrow of the hooligan outbreak at Barcelona a hundred leader-writers in a dozen capitals assured King Alfonso that his hour was come. King Alfonso remains. Señor Maura remains also. Throughout three dreadful days these strong and wise men were willing to be dubbed blundering weaklings. They knew the danger of commanding Catalan to fire on Catalan. But as soon as the Captain-General of Barcelona, telegraphing by way of the Balearic Isles, had made known the city's need, Castilian troops were hurled against the hooligans' barricades and the cosmopolitan gaol-birds' riot was ended before it could foment the hoped-for insurrection on behalf of Catalan autonomy. Hopeless and effete Spain, as untravelled journalists love to call her, has taught the world the quickest and kindest way of extinguishing a conflagration which may some day rekindle itself in New York, in London, or in any other wealthy city infested by criminal aliens.

Unhappily it cannot be said that our English press has been helpful, during this fiery crisis, to the proud nation with whom we have recently been seeking to improve our economic and diplomatic relations. Editors who angrily resented foreign strictures on our own Boer War have made haste to print exactly the same censures upon the operations in Morocco, and to affirm that Spanish and Moorish blood are being spilled solely to swell the gains of alien mine-owners. As for the disturbances in Catalonia, although everybody knows that Barcelona is the hottest of all Europe's hotbeds of anarchism, many of our leader-writers hurried to meet it as the heroic uprising of a people rightly struggling to be free from clerical and oligarchical oppression. As for "Our Own Correspondent", he has lived down to his reputation. Take, for example, the "Daily Telegraph's" news-finder in Madrid. Last Saturday this intrepid inquirer after truth dauntlessly "dined, in search of exact information, in a restaurant which is frequented by persons moving in Ministerial circles". After he had "prayed them by all the saints in heaven and by ancient friendship for complete details", the persons moving in Ministerial circles politely assured him that he himself was "the best-informed person in Madrid". Accordingly the readers of a great London daily which stands stoutly for religion and for monarchism have been treated to partisan attacks upon Spain's Conservative Government and to dark hints about an impending disaster to the reigning dynasty. They have been told that the strong Minister of the Interior is a danger to the public peace; that, without his presence at the head of affairs, the public peace would not have been disturbed; and that the same Minister "is simply furious at seeing that, through the 'Daily Telegraph', the whole of Europe has learned the truth about Barcelona". When, however, Our Own Correspondent was replaced by a Special Commissioner, the whole of Europe was informed that "the interruption of Barcelona's normal life has been slight and the revolution superficial". All this is bad; but unfortunately the "Telegraph" has not been the chief of sinners in this matter.

Like the disaster outside Melilla, the unpopularity of the war in the Riff, which furnished a pretext for the Barcelona outrages, has been enormously overstated. It is true that the best Spaniards, like the best men of every Christian nation, do not want to fight anybody. But it is false that the Spanish peasantry are abhorring the Riff as they abhorred Cuba. Spanish blood runs in Cuban veins, and the Cubans speak Spanish speech. But the wild hill-men of the Riff are Moors; and the hated name of a Moor still rings like a trumpet in Spanish ears. The least lettered muleteer knows that the Moor is an infidel, a denier of the Holy Trinity, a contemner of the Blessed Virgin. He knows that the Moor once lorded it arrogantly in Spain, and that Spain's greatness was built upon the Moor's defeat. Every good Spaniard has his bulla, with its privilege of meat-eating on Fridays in reward for Spain's prowess against the unbeliever; and, much as he is loth to leave Spanish soil and Spanish kindred, a Spaniard's blood runs quicker at the thought of striking down his Moor for faith and fatherland. As for the educated classes, they may bewail this untimely derangement of the national life and this unwelcome drain upon a half-plenished treasury; but they know that the Government has no alternative. We ourselves do not relish the news that a punitive expedition must needs brave the defiles of some mountain frontier; but we make our grimace and bear it. It is so with Spain. Noblesse oblige governments as well as individuals; and Spain is still a noble nation. The Riff is opposite Gibraltar; and Gibraltar, despite any number of Anglo-Spanish understandings, must always be a thorn in the side of proud Spain. During this week Fleet Street has lectured Madrid very solemnly upon her folly in retaining an African coastline of trivial economic importance. But the victory of economic over high-political considerations is not complete anywhere; and least of all is it complete in Spain. As the tribesmen have flouted Spain's flag and murdered her subjects, Spain must needs vindicate her sovereignty, as England would do in similar circumstances; and it is therefore entirely misleading to describe the present operations as a war of adventure.

Catalonia's opposition to the war is on all fours with the Irish Nationalists' opposition to our own South African campaign. The predominant partner's extremity is the malcontents' opportunity; and although the killings and burnings and lootings in Barcelona were the work of apaches, it is certain that the apaches were too cowardly to risk their necks if they had not confidently counted upon a successful Autonomist revolution to cover their own crimes. Catalonia, however, is no more wholly Separatist than England was wholly Radical at the last general election. The Republics which sprang into existence last week at Mataro and other places were proclaimed under a complete misunderstanding as to the course of events in Barcelona. The men of Mataro thought that the Catalan cat had jumped out of the historic Spanish unity, and they made headlong haste to show themselves on the winning side. But, as soon as it was found that the scum of the gaols and not the cream of the Autonomist party had temporarily risen to the top in the provincial capital, the new-born Republics made equal haste to commit suicide. After all, the industrial populations of Catalonia know on which side their bread is buttered. While they complain loudly that Catalonia pays an excessive share of Spain's taxes, they are silently conscious that Catalonia's access to Spain's protected markets brings into the province vastly more profit than the tax-collector carries out of it; and, if it came to a final choice, many a voluble Catalonian patriot would obey his Unionist head rather than his Home Rule heart.

No doubt Spain's black week has been black enough. As we have so often done ourselves, she began her campaign against an uncivilised enemy by underestimating his strength, and she has had to suffer. But, like ourselves, she will muddle through. As for Barcelona, it is sufficiently horrible that priests and religious and innocent lay-folk should have been done to death and that churches and orphanages and libraries should have been burnt to the ground. But it cannot be too plainly repeated that the Barcelona riot, bad as it was, had no revolutionary importance. It was merely an immense affair for the police. It was not a civil war. The soldiers who restored order were merely so many additional and more efficient policemen; and those who set them to their grim work just at the right moment and just in the right way have enhanced the prestige of their country in the eyes of all fair observers.

INDIAN FINANCE.

THE Commons debate on the Indian Budget was above the usual level this year. The Master of Elibank made a really good speech. The Rutherfords and Cottons did not occupy the entire stage this time. Still they manage the matter better in India—or have done so hitherto. Their Budget is an instance. On Monday it is presented to the Legislature with an explanatory speech by the Finance Minister. The honourable members have a week to scrutinise it and forge their thunder. Next Monday it comes up, is debated there and then, and that day becomes law. The heavy hand of reform has fallen on this simple and effective procedure. Next year will see a mimic Parliament with all the paraphernalia of resolutions, interpellations, and divisions—and what then?

Certainly the fiscal and financial questions coming this year to the front have been of a peculiarly complicated and technical character—in some ways disquieting. For the first time in twelve years the revised accounts disclose a deficit instead of a surplus, and it is a substantial one—£3,720,000. The causes of this sudden and startling lapse may be briefly stated. Bad rains, short harvests, high prices, slack trade, and epidemics of malaria and plague resulted in an increase of expenditure and a decrease of income under every important head except opium. Most notable is the fall in net railway revenue, which corresponds closely with the entire deficit. This is all the worse that in spite of a heavy decline in traffic the working expenses have increased by about one and a half million—which points to some defect in the administration. Opium has come to the rescue with a timely but unexpected increase of over a million sterling. This should give pause to a policy which would abandon this valuable revenue in subservience to the intrigues of America, who, for political reasons, has taken up a question with which she has no practical concern. At least we may insist that our Government shall not permit American interference to extend to our domestic arrangements in India. Any attempt to enforce a prohibition which the Commission of 1894 proved to be unnecessary and mischievous would furnish the enemies of British rule with just the sort of weapon they most want. The only thing that can really stir the masses is some such unjustifiable and gratuitous interference with their daily lives or their domestic industries.

It was foreseen by the experts that the present currency system would only work automatically in the matter of exchange as long as the balance of trade was in favour of India to the full extent of the annual remittances. Should that balance turn the other way, a very serious position would be at once created. But experience gave little reason to fear that such contingency would actually happen. The unforeseen as usual proved to be the certainty. A great and sustained rise in prices, to which the artificial inflation of the currency largely contributed, operated with other causes to diminish exports and stimulate imports, till in 1907-8 the favourable balance had been reduced to about £3,000,000, and in the following year it turned to an actual deficit. The causes which led to this difficult position are complex. The immediate consequence is simple enough. The Secretary of State was no longer able to obtain funds by sale of his Council bills on India. He had to rely on the usual annual loans, and when these were exhausted to draw on the gold reserves. Even these measures did not suffice to sustain exchange at specie point, and in March 1908 the Indian Government had to take the extreme step of selling sterling bills on London, which the Secretary of State was compelled to meet from his reserves in gold and gold securities. By the end of 1908 these funds were so depleted that the Secretary of State, as a precautionary measure, had to obtain borrowing powers. The tide, however, had turned, and it was not necessary to use them. The balance of trade began to resume a favourable condition, a portion of the outlay was replaced, and the close of the financial year found the two reserves still in possession of over nine millions in gold and gold securities available for a further campaign against falling exchange, should the necessity arise.

At present the conditions are favourable. Council bills have been freely sold at and around par; the flood of imports is decreasing, the introduction of foreign capital is checked, and the agricultural prospects, which so far leave little to be desired, promise a large export trade. Another factor has also come into operation. The immense withdrawals of rupee currency to counterbalance the gold disbursements have redressed the excessive coinage and note issue of preceding years, and may help to reduce the great rise in prices which coincided with that inflation. If this happens, a corresponding decline of imports may be expected and a favourable balance of trade will become firmly established.

The finance and particularly the currency system has come successfully through an extreme test in a manner which, on the whole, has justified the wisdom and skill of those concerned. It is possible nevertheless to learn a lesson from the danger that is past and may recur. In its hour of abounding prosperity the Indian Government was led to tamper with the gold reserves on which the stability of its system rested. In 1906-7 £4,000,000 was converted into silver and thus rendered useless for its only real and essential purpose. Later on it was decided to divert one half of the mintage profits to railway construction, and over a million sterling was so diverted. Had the exchange crisis lasted a little longer the gold thus lost might have saved the situation. This seems to be realised by the present Finance Minister in his welcome declaration that "it is our clear duty to develop and strengthen our gold resources by every means in our power". He would do well further to consider the question of excessive mintage of rupees. It is calculated that since 1900 the currency has been increased by a thousand million rupees. It is impossible to doubt that this has contributed largely to the great rise in prices which has directly and indirectly added to the difficulties of the position. The Government is finding itself gravely embarrassed by the additions it is compelled to make to the pay and allowances of its servants in the lower grades, both civil and military. Last year the extra compensation for dearness of food to civil employees alone came to nearly £600,000. The huge profits on mintage of silver afford a constant temptation to excessive coinage which must be firmly resisted. This resistance will be strengthened by the rigid application of all such profits to the currency gold reserve. It is still very far below safety point. Another danger which our own action threatens is the creation of new public wants which cannot be satisfied without more revenue and fresh taxation. The enlarged councils, with their greater facilities for pressure on the Government for funds, will increase this danger, and it is further enhanced by the recent tendency to abandon indirect taxation. No greater peril confronts the administration than that which may attend the imposition of some fresh and direct tax. In the light of present experience it is impossible to view all the recent remission with unmixed satisfaction.

After all, the financial position of India is such as any country in the world might envy. With a population of 232 millions, its public debts all told are only 277 millions sterling and are entirely covered by investments, loans, and deposits. The revenue from this source not only defrays the entire debt service but leaves a considerable annual profit besides. Even if met from taxation it would have an incidence only of 8d. per head—one-sixth that of any other important country. Even in a year like the last, of peculiar stress and trouble, a deficit of three and three-quarter millions has been met without seeking any fresh source of revenue or reimposing any of that recently remitted. The recuperative power of its resources is once again displayed by the rapidity with which improvement has declared itself in many directions. The fomenters of political and social unrest form at present the worst danger which the country has to face.

THE SWANSEA BOOMERANG.

THE Divisional Court judgment in the Swansea schools case must be decidedly unpleasant reading for the Government. Though an immediate appeal has been entered and the case started on its way for eventual consideration by the House of Lords, present comment is not without value.

The judges have found it necessary to remind a State department in no uncertain terms that the law must be administered as it is, and not as the Executive may find convenient to interpret it. The full disclosure of this amazing business reveals a contemptible trick on the part of the Government to gratify the spleen of its Welsh nonconformist supporters. The Board of Education has been made a catspaw to condone the illegal action of the Swansea Education Authority in their attempt to crush Church schools out of existence. The facts are so clear that only spite can cloud the issue. The Swansea Authority deliberately set up two scales of salaries for its teachers—the higher applicable to provided schools, and the lower to non-provided or voluntary schools. The avowed object of this discrimination was, by underpaying the teachers, to force the voluntary schools into such a condition of inefficiency that eventually their doors must be closed. The school managers at once appealed to the Board of Education, then under Mr. Birrell, and the Board did their best to make the Swansea Authority see reason. But they found the Welsh nonconformist very dour; to his mind, where the Church was concerned, the end justified the means, and he remained truculent and obstinate. Later Mr. Runciman, who in the meantime had succeeded Mr. Birrell, in reply to complaints of further and greater unfairness of treatment, appointed Mr. J. A. Hamilton K.C. (now a judge) to hold an inquiry. The result was a strong criticism of the Local Authority and a finding against it on every issue. The Welsh parliamentary party were at that time making themselves very awkward to the Government; a sop to Cerberus was needed, so the Cabinet deliberately passed over the Commissioner's report and directed the Board of Education to square the facts with local feeling. The managers took to their last resource, the courts—where, happily, there is no room for the importation of prejudice into points of law—and the courts, as Mr. Justice Hamilton was, are with them. The judges find, in effect, that the Board of Education never actually decided whether the Local Authority had the power to discriminate between the two classes of teachers, that they wriggled out of the difficulty by changing the form of the question put to them and deciding that so long as teachers could be procured at the lower rate the efficiency of the schools did not necessarily suffer. The real question at issue, say the judges, was whether the Local Authority had any right to discriminate between one class of school and another. That question the Board of Education is now ordered to consider, and to determine against the Local Authority. Discrimination is illegal; all schools must be treated alike and complete efficiency maintained. The Swansea Authority have throughout boldly maintained a theory which cuts right down to the roots of the Education Act. In effect they claimed the power to allocate money to the schools in their area in any proportion and in whatsoever manner seemed best to them, and that from their decision there was no appeal to anywhere; their only responsibility being to their own ratepayers. To pretensions so obviously impossible there could be only one answer, and to-day the Welsh political nonconformist is forcibly reminded that although his own party is in office an authority exists even beyond their manipulation. In the rest of England Swansea has found only one ally—Halifax—but in all probability many other nonconformist consciences have been itching while waiting the issue of the fight. The Swansea judgment will douche them.

This decision, whatever may be its ultimate fate on appeal, comes at an opportune moment, just as the Government, professedly loving freedom to excess, is making a determined attempt to set up in some of its new legislation a form of administrative law. In place of the open courts which to-day all may seek for the interpretation of a statute, we are being offered the closed doors of a Government department whose officials will be unfettered by any rules of law. The Swansea case conveniently reminds us that the Executive is able very effectively to influence a Government Department, and if that department should happen to be the final judge of its own proceedings, its decisions, whenever necessary, will subserve party expediency. The latest attempt to limit the right of appeal is contained in the land-valuation clauses of the Finance Bill now before Parliament, but, thanks to strong non-party opposition, landowners will probably still be able to rely on the protection of the courts against official juggling. How necessary such protection is recent death-duty cases all too clearly show. The knowledge that the courts have the power to review departmental actions is in itself a strong check on the illegality of decisions coloured by political expediency. Just by so much as that power of review is taken away will the independence and strength of the permanent Civil Service be undermined.

HOSPITAL ENTERTAINMENTS.

KING EDWARD'S Hospital Fund for London was in some doubt last year as to what it should do in the matter of charity entertainments for the hospitals. There was no particular scandal, but only an uneasy feeling that entertainments, bazaars, fancy fairs, balls, and all the paraphernalia of amusement in the name of charity were very doubtful resources and ought to be examined. A committee was appointed to inquire and advise the Fund what should be done on the question of expenses of these charity entertainments. If the Fund saw its way to bar these entertainments altogether it would be glad to be rid of the dubious element introduced by them into the constant and frantic efforts of the hospitals to raise funds. But doubtless it knew this would be a counsel of perfection, and was prepared for the finding of the committee that, dubious though charity entertainments may be, they have to be accepted as things are with the hospitals. The committee take the position that it is desirable not to look a gift-horse in the mouth, at least not too closely, if you cannot do without a steed of some kind, however broken-down a hack it may be. They say the practice of charity entertainments for hospitals has established itself as one of the recognised methods of raising funds, and is a means of securing income which could not be obtained in any other way. This is not quite an absolutely accurate way of putting the case. There are other possible ways. The hospitals might be a charge, for instance, on State funds, and this would at once put an end to the assumed necessity for amusements disguised as charity. What the committee really mean is that to a great number of the public the hospitals are not sufficiently serious institutions to be in the regular order of civic life. They rank them no higher than the local football or cricket club, and if you want their subscriptions they must be cajoled and entertained into giving them. It is a strange view to take of hospitals for the relief of all the most dreadful forms of suffering that our fellow-creatures endure. A stranger thing still is that those who will not contribute directly, but insist on getting some amusement for their subscriptions, plume themselves on their charity. We hardly know, however, whether they are really worse than that other class of persons who appear to be unaware of the existence of hospitals until a dance or bazaar, a concert or a play for the funds of a hospital calls their attention to the fact. Until the hospitals are put on a legal footing, and are able to draw on public funds, the patronage of these frivolous and ignorant people must be obtained by devices which exhaust the time and energies of officials who ought to be freed from such a humiliating necessity. They pay a great price for the money they get; but as money must be got, the committee was practically driven to sanction these entertainments and regard them as justifiable "if they are kept within reasonable limits and not associated with extravagance or abuse".

The committee submit to taking things as they are if there is a balance, and if the entertainments are some source of income. We do not find in the report any statement of what the balance is, and whether it is sufficient remuneration for the trouble and risk of preparing the entertainments. Admittedly the system is liable to the danger of waste and abuse, and the hospitals are cautioned to take measures to safeguard themselves. They say "We are glad to report that the evidence before us points to the conclusion that neither extravagance nor abuse prevails to any large or general extent. We have, however, come upon isolated instances which indicate the existence of certain dangers in this direction". The precautions that ought to be taken seem to us to prove that the system of hospitals getting up entertainments to raise funds is vicious in itself. The possible evils are so many that to guard against them the officials are advised to make inquiries and take precautions against being cheated. It is a ludicrous position that before accepting charitable assistance they have to take care that the benevolent donor does not pick their pockets. Charity is usually abused by the unworthiness of the receiver; here the receiver is unexceptionable, and it is the motives of the giver that are open to suspicion. If the hospitals are to follow the directions of the committee to protect themselves from fraud, it is clear much time will have to be spent by the officials which might more properly be spent on other matters. They may even have to increase their clerical staffs. The officials of a hospital ought to be employed in administering funds, not in raising them. Their functions are reversed in an expensive and laborious manner when they have to appeal as they do for charity in the ordinary way. But when they have to embark in the speculative and risky business of an entertainment entrepreneur, their functions become still more abnormal. What are our hospitals reduced to when to raise their funds, which are always inadequate, they have to go into enterprises so risky that we find such directions as the following given them in the report? "What we would here emphasise is the necessity of forming detailed estimates beforehand and of deciding, upon these estimates, whether or not the prospect of profit from the possible receipts is worth the risk involved in the inevitable expenditure. In making this calculation the chances of unexpected misfortunes must not be overlooked. Instances have been brought to our notice of disappointment through bad weather, through the clashing of other functions, and even through the incidence of national calamity. The degree of importance to be attached to such considerations depends on the amount at stake, and where thought desirable the danger might be to some extent covered by insurance." The hospitals are in desperate straits when the committee cannot advise them to drop such troublesome, and anxious, and harassing means of raising money. That the committee would do so if it could is evident. It dislikes the raising of money by entertainments undertaken by officials whose proper duties are strangely incongruous with the provision of popular amusements. But the hospitals, like importunate beggars, are always trying to attract the public either by wheedling or whining, and they must do so as long as their very existence depends on so-called charity. This report, though it is not sensational, is the latest piece of evidence that our hospital system rests on an unsound moral and inadequate pecuniary basis.

THE CITY.

THE week which includes the August Bank Holiday is, as a rule, the quietest in the year on the Stock Exchange. The last account was a sort of wiping up the remains of a bull account, which had run for nearly six months. The professional operators, the Kaffir "shops", and those who had the courage to be bulls of Yankees, had all made a lot of money since the settlement of the Eastern scare in the early spring. In the South African market there are always a lot of foolish dabblers who go in late and remain in late and have to be pushed out somehow. The pushing-out process began about the middle of June and lasted till the end of July. People will never remember or act upon the advice of Abraham, the father of speculators, who says "Go in early, go in big, and get out soon". Immediately after the Monday Bank Holiday the markets all round assumed a stolidly cheerful appearance, not active or booming of course, but a "noli-me-tangere" front towards the bears, which has succeeded in keeping those gentry off, at least for the time being. Indeed, with money a drug, and every prospect of its remaining so, with the mining industry in South Africa rapidly progressing, by means of amalgamations and cheapening of processes of production, with the strong manipulation of the American market by the magnates, he must take a very long view and have a very long purse who takes the "short" side in the market to-day. Mexico seems to be for the moment the centre of interest. Mexican Southern Railway ordinary shares are at 89, and seem to be pushing their way up to par. And Mexican mines, which have been doing remarkably well lately, are at last attracting the notice of operators. Alaska Treadwells, which we kept pushing on the notice of our readers at 5, are now at 6½, and will no doubt go to 7. It is perhaps a little late to buy them now, but Alaska Mexicans at 3½ are well worth buying, for the mine is earning 75 per cent.; and though it does not distribute all its profit, or anything like it, it soon will do so, and the shares ought certainly to reach 4 very soon, and ultimately go to 5. The price has risen ½ without the dividend during the last week. In the Kaffir section our favourites are Nourse, City Deep and Durban Deep. Consolidated Goldfields, which have now a large interest in West Africans, will undoubtedly rise very quickly—as soon as people begin to come back to town, or, bored in the country or at the seaside, take to telephoning their brokers. Goldfields are a very old favourite with the public, and it is high time that the company did something to encourage its backers by distributing a really handsome interim dividend. South African Gold Trust is not a good share to speculate in; but, from what we hear on the best authority, the shares are intrinsically worth £5, as they are sure to make a big division at the end of the year.

The American market is really astonishing. Steel Commons at 77, Union Pacifics at 207, Southern Pacifics at 139, all the dreams of the wise men have come true. Canadian Pacifics stick at 192; but there is a decided movement upward in all the securities of the Grand Trunk Railway, though we do not know the reason. Leopoldinas are slowly creeping up, and have risen from 69 to 72. For people in a hurry Leopoldinas are not to be recommended; but they are likely to rise to 80 between now and the spring. We do not know why Buenos Ayres Great Southern and Western of Buenos Ayres Railways keep so firm; as the provincial government has raised the money to build competing lines, it might be thought that they were too high, but "sufficient for the day" etc. is a maxim on the Stock Exchange. The shares of the Pekin Syndicate are certainly strong, the ordinary having risen to over 12, and Shansis to 25s. "To Meyer or not to Meyer?—that is the question", for this company. Mr. Carl Meyer may be a deep financier; but hitherto he has not been very successful as a director of companies.

It is curious how the commercial possibilities of Turkey for exploitation have been overlooked. Money has been poured into China and Japan; but Turkey is an excellent market for all English goods, and her tariff is very low, only an average of 9 per cent. One thing is quite certain, that if British traders and financiers let slip their opportunity Germany will step in and secure the Turkish market, and then a heavy protective tariff will be established, with a preference in favour of the subjects of Emperor William.

INSURANCE: POLICIES AT LOW PREMIUMS.

A FREQUENT requirement of people when effecting life assurance is to pay the lowest possible premium for the assurance of a given sum, or, to put the same thing in another way, to obtain a policy which for a given premium provides the largest amount of assurance. There are many ways of arriving at this result, and it depends upon circumstances which is the best in each case. The first thing to settle is whether or not it is likely to be feasible to pay an increased rate of premium later in life; when this is possible, there is much that is attractive about convertible term policies. An ordinary term policy is a contract which lasts for a fixed period only, such as one, five, or seven years, and guarantees the payment of the sum assured in the event of death within the term. Should the policyholder survive the agreed number of years no part of what he has paid in premiums is returned to him, and the contract is at an end. Convertible term policies provide this same kind of insurance protection, but, in consideration of a slightly increased premium, the policyholder has the right at any time within the term to exchange his policy for ordinary whole-life or endowment assurance, with or without profits, and without any further medical examination. On converting the original policy into a new one the premium for the new policy is at the prospectus rate for that kind of assurance for the age at which the change is made. A man of thirty paying £13 8s. 4d. a year for a term policy secures £1,000 for his estate in the event of his death within twenty years. The cheapest non-profit whole-life policy for age thirty at entry costs about £19 a year; that is to say, a premium which gives assurance for £1,000 under the former plan would assure only about £700 under the whole-life policy. If the holder of a convertible term policy came to the end of the twenty years without being able to convert this assurance into a policy of a permanent character, and if he still needed assurance, he would be in a bad way. For one thing he might find it impossible to pass a medical examination, or his health might be so far indifferent that he would have to pay an extra premium; in any case life assurance effected at age fifty is expensive.

He can, if he chooses, take a convertible policy for a term of thirty years at a cost of £15 a year (assuming the age at entry to be thirty), or for a term of thirty-five years at an annual cost of £16 2s. 6d. It may be that if a man survives for thirty or thirty-five years the imperative necessity for life assurance may have passed away; his children have grown up and may be able to look after themselves.

It is seldom advisable, however, to reckon that merely temporary life assurance protection will provide all that is required, and convertible term policies are generally advantageous only in cases where an increase of income is probable. In such instances this form of assurance has many attractions. Effected at age thirty a man may be able, by age thirty-five or forty, to afford a substantial premium. Instead of paying £13 8s. 4d. a year for the assurance of £1,000, he can possibly at age forty afford £31 15s. for ordinary whole-life assurance with profits, or about £41 a year, payable for twenty years at the most, to secure £1,000, with profits in addition, payable at his death whenever it happens. He may even be able to afford £51 a year to secure £1,000 and profits at age sixty, or at death if previous. Thus convertible term policies may not only provide a large amount of insurance protection during the years when it is especially necessary, but may be the means of enabling a man to take later in life a highly attractive form of policy, such as endowment assurance, which perhaps he would not be able to afford if he were already committed to paying a moderately high rate of premium.

In this case, as in all others, some disadvantage results from effecting assurance late in life. Thus, if at age thirty a man took an endowment assurance payable at age sixty, or death if previous, it would cost him £33 17s. 6d.; and should he live to sixty his total cash outlay would be £1,016, in return for which he would receive £1,000, and thirty years' bonuses in addition. If, starting at age thirty, he took a convertible term policy at a cost of £3 8s. 4d. a year, and at age forty changed it for endowment assurance with profits, payable at age sixty, costing him £51 7s. 6d. a year, his total cash outlay would be £1,162, in return for which he would obtain £1,000 and bonuses for only twenty years, as against a cash outlay of £1,016, which would yield him £1,000 and bonuses for thirty years.

Thus these convertible term policies are exceedingly useful in certain cases, but are not as a rule so advantageous for policyholders as taking permanent forms of assurance at the outset.

THE GUARDIA CIVIL OF SPAIN.

By Colonel Willoughby Verner.

On a winter's evening some few years ago I was sitting alone with my retriever in my castle in Spain in the wilds, many hours' ride from the nearest civilisation. Between me and that civilised spot lay a mountain pass liable to be barred at several points by the torrents when in flood. Outside the wind was howling and the rain cascading off the roof into the cobble-stoned patio below. My retriever suddenly stopped in his long-drawn-out effort to lick himself dry after a wet evening's flighting duck in the laguna hard by and gave a premonitory growl. Next moment I heard footsteps, soon followed by an imperious rap at the door obviously dealt by some hard and heavy substance. " Quien es? " " La pareja " was the sharp reply—" The pair ". For such is the universal term bestowed on the famous Guardia Civil of Spain owing to their invariably working in couples. I hastily rose and unbarred my door and saw before me two stalwart figures in black oilskin-covered cocked hats, worn " athwartship ", and long dark blue cloaks, and carrying rifles, the butt of one having just done service as a knocker. Polite inquiries followed as to my health and that of my family. Would they come in? " With pleasure." The long wet coats and cocked hats were removed, and the rifles, German Mausers, " modelo español ", balanced carefully between their knees as they took the seats I offered to them, for it is one of the maxims of the famous corps that no Guardia shall ever be parted from his arms.

All travellers in the Peninsula know well the smart uniform and immaculate turn-out of these " Civiles ". One expects as much from a corps d'élite at public places where they are on duty before the whole world, but here were these two men who had just performed an eight-mile march through a most desolate region on a dark night in heavy rain as immaculate, save for their shoe-leather, as any of their brethren at the railway stations or other places of public resort. Their buttons were burnished like silver, their yellow belts bright and clean, their red collars and cuffs unstained, and, marvel of all, their white linen collars unsoiled. Truly the huge turn-up collars of their capes must be well designed to afford complete protection in such desperate weather. Would they have a cigar? " With much pleasure." These were gravely accepted and safely stowed away with the greatest nonchalance for some more suitable occasion. Hastily I produced cigarettes, which were lighted at once. " May I ask the reason of my being thus honoured? " " O nothing particular; only the captain of our district sent word to our sergeant that the English coronel had passed through Algeciras last week and that we were to call and tell him that we were at his disposition." The small detachment of Civiles commanded by the sergeant in question is quartered in a remote hillside village some eight miles as the crow flies (or rather as flies the vulture, for there are no crows in these parts but many vultures) from my castle, which lies within the district for which he is responsible. Hence the visit. The Guardia Civil are all picked men chosen from among soldiers, generally non-commissioned officers who have served their time in the army. They are all men of good education, and are trained and expected to take all responsibility in an emergency, even to that of life or death. It is a sufficient voucher for their integrity and trustworthiness that complaints against them are almost unknown, whilst to the great mass of the Spanish nation they represent the only " law " which is universally respected and which appeals to the most untutored natures by reason of the swiftness and thoroughness of its application. No matter where one travels or how, by rail, by coach, by horse or pack animal, at regular intervals of the journey one encounters the inevitable " pareja ", always spick and span, always courteous and anxious to be of any assistance. To a wanderer like myself in the less trodden parts of Spain they are indeed a boon, for they not only act as a guard and rallying-point in case of emergency, but every couple is a complete " Intelligence Department " of its own, and ever willing and anxious to give information as to the condition of any district and the conduct of its inhabitants. It almost sounds like our Great General Staff when perfected by Mr. Haldane!

But to return to my visitors. Would they have some wine? " No." " What! Nothing? " " Well," with many shrugs and apologies, " possibly. a ' ponche inglés ' ". This request recalled the fact to me that about a year since I had met the same pareja and had seduced them into drinking hot Irish toddy.

The dose is now repeated and furtively taken with many remarks on its sweetness—it is mostly sugar and lemon-peel—and terrific strength. And now for the intelligence budget. Is the country quiet? Can I go into the Sierra? and suchlike conundrums, to which I get ready and voluble answers. There have been bad times in Andalucia, much severe famine and drought, and countless cattle and horses have perished. What about the road? I learn that there have been an unusual number of " mala gente "—bad people—drifting between Cadiz and La Linea outside of Gibraltar, but the road is well patrolled by the Civiles and there is no fear. Can I go through the passes? Certainly, but not alone. That is exactly what I usually do unfortunately. Explanations follow. The folk are not so very bad, but would it be fair for a solitary Englishman to go about in the Sierra just now when he might meet with some of the " mala gente ", who would be thus unfairly led into temptation, especially if there were no witness? " No! mi coronel, take a man with you: he will be useful." The point at issue between us was, however, amicably settled by an assurance that I could go wherever I liked and that they would take steps to see that I did not get into any danger or trouble. And what about the big Sierra, where José and his partida used to be? This evoked a duet of self-congratulation from the pareja. " The partida is gone. José was shot." Who shot him? " I did ", says the senior Guardia with becoming modesty. Why? " He had a desire to shoot me." The Spanish-speaker will appreciate the idiom. Further details are obviously unnecessary. The list of " persons wanted " is now produced, a heavy one, some thirty in all, and my attention is particularly called to the entry in the column of " How disposed of " affecting the unfortunate José.

" How many people have you shot since we met last? " I asked. " Two only ", says Guardia No. 1, upon which No. 2 gently reminds him sotto voce of a third case, but which is voted to be unimportant for some reason I cannot precisely grasp; possibly the third was a " pick-up ", some other man's " various ". Were they killed? " O dear no! But one has to fire when a man tries to escape." This brought us to a discussion as to the best methods of securing prisoners on the march. No. 1 opened one of his ammunition pouches and produced a chain of twisted brass wire interspersed with rings and fitted with a padlock, by means of which he asseverated that a man could be handcuffed and if necessary completely tamed by having a leg " thrown in " by using the manacles to connect his wrists with one of his knees. No. 2, not to be outdone, thereupon produced a neat pair of thumbscrews opened by a small key which he wore like a whistle. These he assured me, if used to secure the thumbs behind the back, were matchless! Much vivacious conversation ensued as to the merits of the rival implements, No. 1 asserting that the twisted chain can be tautened so as to bring the most bellicose prisoner to his senses, whereas No. 2 declared that the thumb-screws were *the* thing and insisted on trying them on me. I can vouch that after a couple of turns they hurt most horribly, and I hastily pleaded the instant necessity of preparing another ponche inglés, a suggestion that was considered very ready and appropriate, and I was forthwith unscrewed. Before they left I was asked to inspect their Mausers, which had the magazines fully charged, doubtless ready for another José. The big wet cloaks were donned, the collars turned up, and the pareja bade me a polite farewell, with many wishes for my good health and that of "la familia" before they disappeared into the darkness. They explained to me that on the morrow they were to meet another pareja and take over some prisoners from them who were being passed down the line, probably for Ceuta.

Two days after I was accosted at daylight by a smart-looking peasant, who informed me that he had been sent to accompany me on my expeditions "by order of the pareja". Doubtless as a "witness". Evidently the Guardia Civil consider that in my case prevention is better than cure. There is at any rate a good deal of common-sense in their methods.

The position of these fine fellows among their fellow-countrymen in the Peninsula is one of the curiosities of Spain. Some few years ago an ill-advised attempt was made to use them to aid in suppressing the ubiquitous contrabandistas. The Carabineros, the corps officially charged with the prevention of smuggling—especially that of tobacco—in Spain, are cordially hated, distrusted, and despised by every Spaniard, and the bare idea of the famous Guardia Civil being employed to aid and abet them aroused bitter anger and hostility among their erstwhile good friends. In a very few months the corps began to show unmistakable signs of breaking up, and the experiment was happily abandoned. Since then they have to a very great extent, if not completely, recovered their old prestige.

ROMANCE AND M. BLÉRIOT.

M. BLÉRIOT'S feat is a more disturbing intrusion into the realm of the spiritual than it is into the realm of the physical. He has not trespassed on our insularity but on our romance; and we are now in need not of a new type of field gun but a new type of poet.

M. Blériot has depoetised the "Ode to the West Wind", and the loss is ineffable. The physical metaphor which dominates the poem was till this moment one of the choicest recreation grounds to which the soul had access. The idea of being storm-driven round the world like a dead leaf was one of those glorious impossibilities which make glad the heart of man. As long as it was practically impossible it was poetically in our power. We possessed it. We could lie awake at night and listen to the wind, till our dour Teutonic souls had visions of the matchless strength and speed of the storm goddesses. But suddenly the Gallic voice of M. Blériot has answered us out of the whirlwind. It is all a question of the angle. We may no longer sigh for "the wings of a dove", for a monoplane arranged in wing fashion is to be the highest type of flight for the future. This is very serious. We cannot afford to have the stock of impossibilities in the world diminished, until we have a poet who can make new ones. Science is like paper money: its value depends on a backing of poetic gold; and the more paper money we issue without gold to back it, the more we depreciate its value. We were already in the unsound position of having far more current science than we could back with poetry; and now M. Blériot is simply giving us inconvertible paper when we have to take his monoplane in exchange for Shelley's metaphors.

The situation has never been quite so critical before, though it is not entirely new. Elizabethan literature, for instance, is full of an interest in mechanics which we are apt to think childish. An Elizabethan gentleman and a modern child have at least this in common, that a mechanical device is to them quite as wonderful as a living creature. To a child a living robin and a toy robin are both beautiful and unexplained, they are equally symbols of the Infinite. If one is superior to the other it is probably the toy, because it is possible to find in it the place of the squeak. The Elizabethan gentleman would also be more interested in the toy, because he would believe that art helps to explain nature, that, indeed, "The art is nature". He would feel that one cannot study the real robin before one has studied the imitation. This is the mental attitude whether in childhood or in Elizabethan England, where mechanics are in their infancy, and the Elizabethans could get romantic excitement from mechanical invention. Nashe, in his "Unfortunate Traveller", describes with gusto a bower composed of artificial trees, with artificial birds singing in the branches, and little pypes shedding artificial dew. We are not so moved. We know that Whiteley's could do the thing for us at a moderate cost. It was "the brightest Heaven of invention" when it was written.

Spenser, with no less enthusiasm, dreamed of the motor-boat:

> "Eftsoones the shallow ship began to slide
> More swift than swallow sheres the liquid sky,
> Withouten oar or pilot it to guide
> Or snowy sails before the wind to fly;
> Only she turned a pin, and by and by
> It cut away upon the yielding wave", etc.

The "pin" is probably suggested by Chaucer's "Squire's Tale", and it was full of romance for Spenser. But by Shelley's time the steamboat was carrying passengers, and when Shelley gives the "Witch of Atlas" her marvellous boat he describes her

> "Breathing the soul of swiftness into it"

until it lies on the pool

> "As on great Homer's heart a winged thought".

And this romance still holds good, for the mesmerism of inanimate objects is fortunately still impossible.

Thus science pricks the bubble of poetry, and clips the wings of imagination. It tends to make the whole world provincial. The Atlantic has shrunk since the days of Columbus; the chariot of the sun collapsed when the planetary revolution was calculated; and the west wind will never be so buoyant again now that it has carried M. Blériot. The only compensation possible is a poet greater than Spenser and Shelley. He must make the practicable thing impossible, the natural thing romantic. He must turn on science and show that it is itself as inexplicable as the things which it explains. Milton made an experiment which was rather ludicrously unsuccessful when he introduced field artillery in heaven.

We are not without romanticists who have attempted flight in the poetry of the future. Mr. Rudyard Kipling has seen visions in the engine-room of a ship or a locomotive shed, and there is poetic feeling in his strident treatment of those subjects. Some others have also felt that there might be new inspiration for the imagination in science. But most of our modern romanticists still invent impossibilities out of their own heads instead of revealing to us the impossibilities of the ordinary facts of life. If only Wordsworth had not objected to the Kendal and Windermere Railway, modern literature might have had a more robust imagination. It must always be regretted that his vision of the romance of common things should have failed at mechanics. If only he had realised, as he was bound to do by his philosophy, that a railway train is quite as natural as an old leech gatherer, poetry would have entered on a new world. We still lack the great poet who shall tell us all about what Turner suggested in "Rain, Steam, and Speed"; a poet who shall become as a little child (or an Elizabethan gentleman) to initiate us into the mysteries of mechanical contrivance. If such a poet is not soon forthcoming, M. Blériot, though he may appear just at present very wonderful, will have robbed us of all the poetry there has hitherto been in flight and will have reduced the very swallows to mechanic dullness.

GRABBIT'S SON.

By Pat.

WHEN Grabbit's eldest son got to know that he would go to college he raised his young nose in the air, and the altitude began the miseries of his happiness, the penalties of his pride to correct its distorted sense of proportion in the self-estimates of youth, in his case the more excessive through the isolation of circumstance, with no lad of his acquaintance so situated to qualify for the bitterness that belongs to the disregarded obligations of questionable privilege.

The child of different parents, he might have learnt to take the obligations with the privileges, but that was out of the question for him, and he excited hostility, an instinctive effort of social nature to repel individual distinction for the common security, in a region where individuals were not known to rise unless as a menace to the multitude. There can hardly be another country where men's advantages are so much at the expense of one another, a fact strongly enough personified in old Grabbit; and though the process is seldom understood, the effect is always felt among a people so much more tempered to feel than to understand, and so likely to express themselves in conduct that cannot be understood by others. An Englishman advances himself as a rule, advancing others along with him, but English rules are too often Irish exceptions.

In fairness to old Grabbit, he had not deliberately encouraged these painful tendencies in the son, but they were pressed on him as essential virtues by his mother, and especially by his sisters, already calculating the advantage of having a brother so much "better" than other girls' brothers; so that, prepared for the poison as he was, it permeated him rapidly, and he met the consequences in accordance with his preparation, a kind of campaign in which his money could only enlarge the triumph of his enemies against him, giving an early lesson from which he might gain much if he had anyone to explain it. It takes a Jew to enter with dignity on distinctions derived from the profits of pain; and an Irishman is as if specially designed by Providence for the opposite destiny, the more so in a very Irish place like Kilcuddy, where Fortune remains still a pagan deity, keeping character the creature of accident. Short of the capacity to control accident, life is a rather poor thing anywhere; but capacity was always controlled by accident at Kilcuddy, with the single and almost abnormal exception of old Grabbit, who, in working out the motives which controlled himself, directed the accidents which controlled his neighbours.

Young Grabbit put himself at a superior point of view, based on nothing better than material greed, satisfied at the expense of the public, with his degree above the crowd, in all things but money, as yet dangerously small, and contested at that. It is easier to be a long way above mediocrity than just a little, and his superior point of view was resented by his associates, who took care to make it painful for him in proportion to the superiority. Seventeen years of age, and still attending the Kilcuddy National School, among the children of his father's victims, he began to sit by himself away from the other lads; and in class, if he could not find himself in the top place, which was seldom, he made a point of going down to the bottom, determined to assert his distinction in this way if not in the other.

One day he made the further discovery that he was going to college to be "a counsellor", and that day he ceased to speak to all in the school except the master, even when they spoke to him; but at three o'clock, when they got out, the whole school, girls as well as boys, mobbed "the counsellor", pelted him down the hill to his door with mud, shouting in a wild chorus, "Gombeen Grabbit, Gombeen Grabbit, Gombeen Grabbit!"

The kitchen was still the Grabbit dining-room, and there he rushed, blackened with dirt his superior clothes, and even his lately elevated nose. In a weeping rage our future ornament of the Bar flung himself on the wooden bench, refused to speak, and repelled even the sympathies of his mother, as if in some remote way conscious how she and the sisters had so affectionately prepared his humiliation for him, without in any way preparing him to meet it. He did not go again to the school, and preparations were immediately started for the college.

In due course he left Kilcuddy, but without the least idea of the advantage, in itself, of either a college education or a place at the Bar. He only knew that it was a very great thing to be a "counsellor", perhaps the greatest of all things in Ireland short of being parish priest of Kilcuddy, which was not in his way as the heir to a country seat, expected to found a county family; a place with traditions, too, having once belonged to the De Veres before they took to writing hymns and exchanging the sword for the cloister. Tradition, however, appealed to young Grabbit no more than his opportunity to become an educated man. What appealed to him was that his neighbours could not be educated, that not one of them could become a "counsellor", that he was not as other people, and he did not even thank God for it. The maker of many victims may find one in his own house, and so far the Grabbit fortune from the gombeen shop had only made young Grabbit much more vicious than his destitute neighbours and very much more miserable.

With all this drifting between the women and the lad, old Grabbit knew his purpose precisely, and made for it definitely, as he always did. His younger son, Francis Xavier, was already articled to a Dublin solicitor, and he expected both to come out about the same time, the solicitor to prepare the briefs, the barrister to gather up what remained. Though nearly illiterate, the old man himself was an expert lawyer, and he grudged the great sum which he paid every year to lawyers in connexion with his enormously growing business and its necessities for litigation. Up to this he had depended on getting over his bad bookkeeping by his good swearing before the judge; but in spite of his amazing memory for details, the mass of his usury was getting too much for him, and more than a score of times he had looked like a perjurer before the court. With his two lawyers, supported by his own experienced capacity as a witness, he meant to conduct any case within the family, from the petty sessions to the House of Lords; but what he relied on most was that, himself fortified so completely, his customers and borrowers would be afraid to contest anything with him, so that he might extend the peculiarities of his bookkeeping even more profitably than before. What was the use of two lawyers in the family unless a return could be got for the money that made them lawyers? It never occurred to him that the "counsellor", a "perfect gentleman", with a fine sense of professional honour, might find himself in a compromising position with a bundle of usury briefs trying to defend the vagaries of his father's conscience in a way satisfactory to the future owner of the De Vere inheritance and to the social status properly attaching to that position.

People brought up one way to live another way have double need for thought, especially about themselves, and young Grabbit began his college career with several innovations that showed he had been thinking. His Christian name was simply Dominick, but he added De Vere and he put O' before his surname. He knew that numerous social classes would be represented at the college, and he adopted his sisters' advice to avoid all but those at the top, who might avoid him if he touched any lower down. Intelligent young ladies, these sisters, and they had not been to boarding-school without result; but this still left the brother to begin his career as a gentleman really on the footing of the father's level, with no idea that more than money was wanted for anything.

The " college " was really a public school for Catholic boys, conducted solely by priests, all good men, so good that education interested them merely as an accessory to religion; history because it could prove that the Church was the only true one, mathematics because it might give intellectual shape to the proof, literature because it was the vehicle of history, and so on. Nine-tenths of the students were young Grabbits from the gombeen public-houses all over Ireland, with a few of the Catholic aristocracy, sent there by their good parents on special request to give the " college " a social atmosphere, and relying on Oxford and Cambridge afterwards to counteract the intellectual damage done. These were the boys that Grabbit would make his friends; and from the first, as directed by his sisters, he would draw a severe line at all the other Grabbits, no matter how they might strain and strive for the privilege of his acquaintance.

His first shock at the " college " was the discovery that the other Grabbits would have nothing to do with him. Why should they? Had not they, too, sisters who had been to boarding-school? Kilcuddy was not the only place where " perfect ladies " had studied how to make headway in society; and, besides, the reputation of old Grabbit had already spread among all the other Grabbits, old and young. The freshman's next shock, still more unexpected, was to find the young aristocrats willing to speak to him, even civil; but he was again beyond his bearings when he found that they confined the friendship strictly to school, passing him coldly outside or merely nodding, even after he had confided to them all about the Bar, De Vere Manor, and how royally he would entertain them there when the right time came. They continued their civilities inside school, but increased their coldness outside in proportion to his advances, so that with the opposition of his own kind of people, now growing into active hostility, he was practically isolated, at the very time in a fellow's life when, without very high qualities in himself, he cannot bear isolation.

The greatest shock of all was poor Grabbit's discovery of young Mulligan in the " college ", the son of another gombeen family of Mayo who nursed a hundred hatreds against the Grabbits. Then post-cards began to reach the college from Mayo addressed " Dominick de Vere O'Grabbit, Esq. K.C. ", and on the back messages like this: " The Gombeen and your turnover at the Bar are going strong; but your father nearly got himself committed for perjury at the last sessions ". Sometimes as many as twenty such postcards would come in a day, and Mulligan managed in some way to get some of them and to show them round. The aristocrats, and they alone, refused to read them, and Grabbit's heart was full of gratitude to them for it; yet he could not understand why their friendship could never be extended beyond the door of the school, and he felt, as he really was, alone in a mob that mocked him to torture.

That was how young Grabbit got himself prepared to uphold the dignities of the Bar and to hand down the delicacies of the De Vere tradition. He might have gone elsewhere and read for a degree, but somebody had told his father that there was " no money in degrees ", and the son was sent on to read law as soon as he could pass the entrance examination. In short, his education was stopped at the point where other barristers began, if not behind it, his father relying on himself to make a real lawyer of his young advocate once B.L. had been secured from the Benchers.

The two brothers were qualified within three months, Dominick de Vere first, and he waited in Dublin for the other, so that they could come together and assume control of half Connaught; but, as if realising the true situation, Francis Xavier took a permanent post in Dublin, and refused to come altogether, the first great blow to the old man, who, for his gombeen litigation, had relied more on the solicitor than on the barrister. On the day Dominick was called, old Grabbit had handed him the deeds of De Vere Manor, so that he could marry into the aristocracy at once, and nothing was reserved but the income during the old man's life.

It was late on Saturday night at Kilcuddy, the night of the market day, just before Christmas, when the markets were big, the peasants plenty, and the takings heavy. The Misses Grabbit were upstairs in the drawing room, all in evening dress to honour the arrival of the brothers and to show their fitness for a greater destiny. The mixed smells from the yard, the kitchen, the china clay, the whisky, and the paraffin were as strong as ever; but they meant money, and old Grabbit was counting the receipts for the day's drinking behind the bar counter, when a young man, alone, stumbled from the mail car, jostled against the side of the door, and fell headlong on his face along the filthy floor of the shop, swearing in a way worthy of the floor, and as distinctly as his almost helpless drunkenness would allow. A crowd of the corner boys, sons of the gombeen borrowers, gathered round the door shouting " Gombeen Grabbit, Gombeen Grabbit, Gombeen Grabbit! "

Notwithstanding the doctor's diagnosis of " fatigue ", it proved to be delirium tremens. The day after his " call ", " Dominick de Vere O'Grabbit, Esquire, Barrister-at-law ", had pawned the De Vere inheritance for the last penny he could raise on it; and in these three months, between drink, Tyrone Street, the Stock Exchange and the bookmakers, he had made away with that last penny, borrowing his fare to Kilcuddy from the Jew who acted as his father's usury agent in Dublin. In trying to disguise himself as a gentleman he had ceased to be a man; and hopeless of surviving his father's reputation, at the Bar or elsewhere, he had sunk below the level of the beast, worthless even as a carcass.

As soon as he was able to move, old Grabbit showed him the door, and told him never to return. Then he " took chambers " at the nearest town, ten miles away, and there, a year later, drunk, as dirty as his father, wearing no shirt, in the commercial room of the O'Connell Arms, boasting, he passed round among the mocking commercial travellers a series of telegrams as they arrived from Mrs. O'Doolin, of Ballymuck, offering him her daughter, Maud Eugenie, who was also her barmaid, with £2,000, £2,500, £2,750, and then, finally, never to be repeated, going! gone!—£3,000! A good girl, too, Maud Eugenie, and her three thousand pounds bought back a patch of De Vere Manor, where she weeps nightly, and he grows cabbages daily, now wearing a shirt and all his father's manners, except the virile sincerities removed by his " college " education, if they ever existed. Francis Xavier prospered, far enough from his father to survive. The " young ladies " were distributed to young publicans of their class, and made bad wives. Both the father and mother died soon after the home-coming, and the " counsellor " remains unnoticed except when he gets drunk, and the boys shout " Gombeen Grabbit, Gombeen Grabbit, Gombeen Grabbit! "

A VILLAGE COMPETITION.

THE great day in the village year has come. Coronations and jubilees sweep comet-like across the firmament, uncharted and disconcerting. They bear no charm of familiar and confident activity. They are inconsiderable beside this day of days.

The annual herald, the printed syllabus and entry-form, was distributed weeks ago over all the area touched. It is an attractive document, with its comprehensive classes and the ingeniously careful discrimination of its divisions, sounding its keynote in a preliminary definition of a cottager as " a bona-fide labouring man ". Through page after page the challenge marches forward, rounding off at last with a list of the open competitions and of the several " events " in the athletic sports. In the whole straggling village there is hardly a soul that has not read it, scarcely a family standing uninvolved, excepting perhaps the nuclear members of the congregation of the tiny gospel hall in the brewery fields, living in active deprecation of revels and junketings.

For many days past women and girls have borne anxious or complacent witness to their sense of the momentous occasion. Much more fearful to them is this day of judgment than to any father or brother exhibiting merely the results of his garden-craft. Thought and care he has bestowed since the earliest budding days of the year, perhaps since last summer. He has watched day by day, selecting and rejecting, has at last chosen and committed himself, and there, for him, the matter ends. His trial under high focus will last but a moment, when the judges make their unwitnessed round. Long before evening his suspense will cease; satisfaction or disappointment will be his ascertained lot.

To some few of the women, however, the personal strain is mitigated by the relief of a practical stake. Prizes are to be had in the open list for the best loaf of home-baked bread, the best bunch of wild flowers, and the best table decoration; and the fact of holding office as an exhibitor, even as an unsuccessful exhibitor, sets one off to some extent for the whole day—while the winner of a prize stands propped on that dignity and makes a double challenge.

The dew still lies thick upon the squire's largest field when the conflict opens, and the family breakfasting within sight on the terrace may see their village, may be heartened and perplexed by the sight of their village at its best. They may watch effort, sustained and inspired, coming in its workaday clothes to stream along the headland of the ripe bracken meadow and through the wide gap into the great open space where the marquees stand ready. Proudly and affectionately the "stuff" is brought in carts and hand-trolleys, in cases and boxes, on tea-trays and dinner-plates, and in unsupplemented human hands. The splendours of hot-houses and lavishly nourished gardens, to arrive later on in smart gigs and dogcarts, will seem by contrast but cold achievements.

The little procession streams on and concentrates irregularly near the entrance of the largest tent, where the more zealous members of the committee are at work mapping out their space and allotting the fateful backgrounds. Many of the contributors execute on the grass outside the tent a preliminary grouping of their lots, braving the alternating stimulus and tension of conflicting suggestions. The more independent carry their things sternly through the gangway in the rough, setting them up in thoughtful solitude under the creamy shade of the canvas and leaving their adherents outside to the torment of tantalised impulse or the happiness of blind confidence.

To enter the tent towards the end of the hour set apart for exhibitors is instantly to be instructed in the private conscience of the crowding necessities of the situation, the controls and adjustments, the compelling presence of public opinion. The air is full of escapes and burgeonings, of illuminating recognitions of identity, of all the happy consequences of spontaneous human intercourse. For some there is obviously the great surprise, the first tasting of the essence of social satisfaction, the gladly tolerated going and coming amongst one's fellows, the delicious sense of common will towards a common end. On all hands there is rich circulation, the refreshment of contacts that are out of the ordinary, and are yet so much a part of the justified picture as to be welcomed and acclaimed. Many an unnecessary journey is made, many a halt and random comment in a sheer revel of human graciousness. There are during the morning moments when the personal stake fades and becomes a very little thing. The symbol of this stands out in the one garden-can which must serve for final dippings and freshenings, for the filling of the ranged jars destined to hold the competing bouquets and of the vases for the table decorations. These last are an innovation of this year's show and occupy a large share of the long centre table in the principal marquee between "pot plants" and plates of fruit from cottagers' gardens. And so it happens that upon the unprotesting ears of the old thatcher setting out his dozen of rosy Stibbards fall scraps of an anxious discussion between his neighbour the squire's daughter and her assistant as to a "broader scheme", "an accentuated note". The postmaster away beyond the last of these decorations is begged to manœuvre his scarlet begonias from the neighbourhood of pink sweet-peas shining faintly through a mist of gypsophila. At the head of the tent the squire's son is polishing and arranging prizes on a small platform, while the principal publican stands near him announcing in the intervals of their chat that none but exhibitors may be allowed in the tent.

This fresh morning of activity amidst a general busyness remains for most of the partakers the meaning of the day, leaves a freshness of spirit, a renewed capacity and hopefulness which nothing the afternoon has to offer is capable of sustaining. Indeed, so drifting are the later centres of interest that the accumulated stimulus of the morning tends to become an exasperation. None but the most resourceful of idlers could find means adequately to transmute it. The show, with its floating accompaniment of "visitors", is an immediate solvent of the familiar, and the combination does not in itself present to the overshadowed villagers any aspect from which more than a chance and momentary entertainment may be gleaned. The sports, it is true, provide a spectacle, intelligible and exciting, but they are in comparison and in the end but poor fun. The refreshment-marquee, too, is there, but the time spent under its shade almost certainly makes it necessary to provide entertainment in one's own person, to exhibit some measure of a quality which reaches in Sussex surely its extremest degree of attenuation. The morning was short, compact, and joyous. The afternoon is long, and brings at last a relaxed weariness.

Relief comes finally with the ending of the prescribed ritual, with the prize-giving and the squire's speech. The day comes gladly to its own once more, and for the remaining hours, under the pretext of games and dancing, may drive free.

The sultry heat has waned. Visitors have left. Fresh gossip is available and makes many a bridge for interchange. Everywhere is the watchful gaiety of an expectant interval. Then, fitfully, as children and old folk and the busier housewives are subtracted from the crowd, there comes a tension, a surging up of momentous things, a measuring of chances, a half-conscious summoning of the swift courage needed to encompass a presented opportunity. To many who stay on now, to many of the young and groping, to the bankrupt and stranded, will come a well-known helplessness, still there, in spite of all their hopefulness. And in this central human conflict there is no support. It is impossible to prepare, nothing can avail now, nothing but native wealth seen under the inspiration of the moment. That group of laughing girls reaps but a temporary "face" from its banded fronting of the arena in which each must in the end play her part alone.

CORRESPONDENCE.

"UNIFIKASIE"—AND AFTER.

To the Editor of the Saturday Review.

Nylstroom, Transvaal, 7 July 1909.

Sir,—"Unifikasie" is well nigh an accomplished fact: the Draft Act, that fine flower of South African statesmanship, has gone to London to be sub-edited by the young lions of the Colonial Office. With it goes a picked band of Colonial statesmen, jealous to see that sub-editing shall mean no more than investiture of the crude compromise with due imperial dignity of phrase; jealous—if all were known—each to see that his brother statesmen steal no march upon him with surreptitious amendment.

Writ large throughout this precious document are the results of the jealous suspicion which refused the chairmanship of the Congress to the one trained statesman in South Africa, whose urbanity and tact are yet unable to condone the fact that he was the deliberate choice of a Conservative Cabinet as Lord Milner's successor to prevent so far as might be the utter undoing of his inchoate work.

Root amendment of the draft is doubtless now impossible; yet a careful touch here and there might make it less unworkable, less manifestly a surrender of imperial interests.

Even the hasty stock-jobber on his way to his daily gamble might remark the chosen title of the new Dominion, and remarking it might infer from it the undercurrent of hope with which the Draft Act has been drawn up. Though at least two large provinces of South Africa are confessedly foreign, and not yet inclusive in the Union, the Act refers throughout to "South Africa", the "Executive Government of South Africa", the "Supreme Court of South Africa", and so on, with a consistent omission of the qualifying adjective "British". In the joyous picnic of Durban, with debate conducted in the sentimental hysteria bred of overnight junketing, such an omission might pardonably enough escape the notice of the British delegates, and the sober statesmanship of the Dutch delegates, while doubtless noticing it, was in no way bound to draw attention to it. Since then, however, the draft has been subjected to keen and businesslike criticism in every colony and parliament; yet in only one colony out of four was a mild suggestion put forward to insert here and there the little word "British", and even there, in Natal, the amendment was defeated.

Let it pass as a trifle if need be, though on the Continent of Europe, of which South Africa recks so little, it is taken as yet one more proof of British arrogance. It is hundreds of years since a foreign ambassador complained to his Government that English statesmen looked on England as a separate planet, and cries of "British arrogance" now as then may be looked on as envy's due tribute to British greatness.

A more serious and more wanton blunder stands in the Draft Act, even after clear-headed revision of the picnic's work. It is provided that the two languages, English and Dutch, shall enjoy complete equality; all records to be kept in both languages, all laws to be passed in both, and both to be equally authoritative.

Though not so specified, it may be taken that "Dutch" means High Dutch; the "taal" as understanded of the people not having scope for official records or legislation. And the simplest may ask "To what purpose is this waste?" Why duplicate all records at great expense in a language no more familiar to ninety per cent. of the Dutch than the alternative English? Still, if it pleases South Africa to have all records duplicated in Chinese or Greek it matters little, so long as South Africa does not apply for a further loan to pay the expense; it will at least provide employment and maintenance for a few needy nephews and brothers-in-law; though the critic may point out that the money were better spent on a version in a Bantu dialect.

But the glaring anomaly remains in the fact that the languages are to be equally authoritative: there is no provision for either version to be taken as definitive if they differ in translation.

No translator is truly bi-lingual, even in countries where education stands at a far higher level than in South Africa; one of the languages must always be his medium of thought, the other a tongue more or less foreign, the nuance of whose idiom is apt to elude him.

The translation into Dutch of the Orange River Colony Letters Patent taxed to the utmost the ingenuity of two of the ablest bi-lingual men in South Africa. Here and there an exact rendering was impossible, and an idiomatic passage had to be boldly recast. In legislative enactment such recasting is impossible; and with the utmost care, in the haste to promulgate an urgent law, delicate shades of meaning will be missed, idioms erroneously rendered.

It needs but little judicial experience to realise the possibilities thus opened up. In matters of civil law a landshark's harvest of litigation; in criminal statutes, every chance that the conviction or exculpation of an offender might depend on the choice by the prosecution of the language of the indictment; that the missing of some point by the translator might make conviction impossible under an indictment drawn in the language foreign to the translator. For the vista of possible consequences in a country inured to Krugerism let the reader unacquainted with South Africa study the immortal romance of "Prinsloo of Prinsloosdorp".

Such a blunder would hardly escape censure in a Draft Act drawn up in a mock parliament or a school debating society. Yet this draft is the matured product of the best business and political brains in British South Africa; and though the explanation is intelligble enough it is not one to reassure us of the wisdom of entrusting the business of half a continent and a great portion of an empire to men responsible for such a fatal flaw in the foundations. Readers of the SATURDAY REVIEW cannot have failed to notice the attitude of "gush and give way" which characterised at the conference the proceedings of certain of the British delegates, notably Dr. Jamieson, who seemed bent on diagnosing as nascent imperialism all symptoms in the Boer delegates of ordinary courtesy or native "slimness"; to these gentlemen, probably the section as it stands seemed a "chivalrous" concession to Boer feelings. Certain of the others, business men, doubtless care nothing for such matters so long as unification can be brought about to produce the desired boom; while, for the Boer delegates, the difficulty, if not actually an advantage, would seem merely academic, so certain is it that with a Parliament preponderatingly Boer the proceedings and statutes will primarily be drawn up in Dutch, with a perfunctory translation into English as a superfluous sop to a muzzled Cerberus.

One cannot blame the Boer delegates; yet British "statesmen" and business men might have been expected to see the fatuity of the section. In the name of sanity and commonsense, if the two languages must be placed on such a footing that neither can claim a technical precedence, let us have it on the lines of an international treaty, and provide for a third version in French, to be definitive in case of doubt.

Maybe the young lions who are to sub-edit it will have the moral courage to propound that in case of doubt the English version is to be final. Such a suggestion might serve as a good touchstone to determine the depth of Boer lip-loyalty: more probably it would prove the rock on which the somewhat ill-found ship "Unifikasie" would split. One is inclined to wonder and fear whether they will not be tempted to the further and semi-final "chivalrous concession" and provide that the Dutch version shall be final. The safest course, perhaps; from the Boer politicians it would meet with the customary meed of lip-gratitude and unspoken contempt; to the whilom English to whom South Africa is now perforce home, it would be little more than a last heart-breaking official recognition of the accomplished fact of Boer domination of British South Africa.

A hasty business, this "Unifikasie", calling to mind a certain rusty old saw anent hasty marriage. To the man in reach of the daily paper, whether in England or South Africa, the daily trumpetings of the press must have given the very false impression that all Africa is agog over the matter. In truth it is not so; the whole business has been engineered by a group of politicians, magnates, and business men, with the local press in pay to stimulate public interest. The passage of the Draft Act has been cleverly worked, with a slim avoidance, except in Natal, of any reference to the people. In the case of the Transvaal it is safe to say that the unbiassed verdict of the electorate—if such were by any miracle obtainable—would have been against the union. Knowing this, the Boer leaders arranged that the present Parliament should have authority to pass it without an election or a referendum: and the needful majority in the Parliament was secured by such provision of numbers of members of the Union Parliament and Provincial Council that each member of the Het Volk majority should feel secure of a seat and salary under the new arrangement. It may well have been with a far-sighted view to this eventuality that twelve months ago two members of the Upper House were jobbed out to secure a safe Het Volk majority there as well as in the Assembly.

There has been a show of consultation of the people in the holding of hurried meetings by Ministers touring the country: only a show, because only seldom has notice enough been given to allow of attendance of more than a handful; because, too, however he may grumble and doubt in conversation on his stoep, the country Boer is wont to sit dumb in the presence of a chairman and committee, and look furtively to his neighbour to raise those objections he so eloquently voiced last week at home; a mere circus, ruled by the crack of the ring-master's whip. But at home, on the stoep over the wayfarer's coffee, he has been eloquent enough in doubt and criticism; and the depth of the desire for union on the part of the back-veld Boer is shown clearly by his invariable question "If we have union, shall we be able to put a duty on mealies from Cape Colony?" an invariable question, the inevitable negative being followed by the comment "Then we don't want union, but I suppose it will come".

Yours faithfully,
C. R. Prance.

[Mr. Prance will resume this subject next week.—Ed. S.R.]

THE TSAR'S VISIT.

To the Editor of the Saturday Review.

31 Dorset Road, Bexhill, 5 August 1909.

Sir,—There are some aspects of the visit of the Tsar to England which have been too much neglected; I mean specially the importance of friendly relations existing between Russia and England in the present condition of European politics. The international relations of European Powers are at present dominated by two combinations, the Triple Alliance between Germany, Austria, and Italy, and the Triple Understanding between France, Russia, and England. For some years past Germany has felt herself in a position of isolation, and has regarded with suspicion the growing friendship between England and Russia, in addition to that already existing between England and France. When I was last at Marienbad, in 1906, I was urged by prominent German publicists to impress upon the English Prime Minister the importance of giving an assurance to the German Foreign Office that these friendly approachments were not meant as a slight upon Germany. Sir Henry very properly stated that his sole object was to remove causes of possible misunderstanding where such existed, but as there were no pending differences between England and Germany there was no reason for any formal agreement between the two countries. The relations between England and Germany have improved since that time, but there can be no doubt that Germany would be very glad, if possible, to weaken the ties of the Triple Understanding, and to restore the old Alliance between the three Emperors, which has played such an important part in the history of modern Europe.

If this were accomplished, England and France would find themselves alone. Many specious arguments can be used to effect this. Russia might be reminded of the unfriendly part played by England at the Congress of Berlin, and be assured that England and France can be of no use to her in her Balkan policy, to which recent events in Turkey have given new importance, and that the Triple Alliance can alone give her what she requires. It is important that Russia should not be seduced by these allurements, but, in order to effect this, demonstrations of English friendship are most valuable, and every sound-minded English statesman should support them to the utmost of his power. The good will of Russia towards us has been shown by the readiness with which she entered into the Anglo-Russian agreement, and by other proofs. Let us take care that there is no lukewarmness on our part, and that, if we can welcome the somewhat insubstantial phenomenon of a nascent liberal Turkey, we may sympathise, in stronger confidence, with the advent of constitutional government in Russia, under the guidance of a wise and far-seeing sovereign.

I am your obedient servant,
Oscar Browning.

ARMY COUNCIL OR COMMANDER-IN-CHIEF?

To the Editor of the Saturday Review.

4 August 1909.

Sir,—Whatever may be the opinion of civilians, by those most concerned, by the Army at large, the return of a Commander-in-Chief to their head would be acclaimed; and if, as suggested in your leading article, and as endorsed by the letter of "Patriot", the restored choice fell (as how should it not?) upon the Duke of Connaught, there can be no doubt as to its wisdom, its propriety, and its popularity.

As you correctly observe, the most successful soldier is not necessarily the best qualified for so delicate a post; and, in instancing the Dukes of York and of Cambridge—the "ready-made", so to speak, as against the "made" chiefs—you strike a note which cannot be too strongly insisted upon. They were "successes"; and why? Because they were "above political and social influence and above cliques". As such they inspired a confidence among their subordinates which is not to be paralleled elsewhere; and least of all in an agglomeration of mediocrities, call them Board or Council, even under the ablest of living civilians.

The idea may sound Utopian; but it is in the minds of many men, seeing a Secretary of State for War can thus de facto be a Commander-in-Chief, that, à fortiori, a Commander-in-Chief might make a Secretary of State for War—a distinction with a very great difference, be it said; for, the combined appointment being made irrespective of party as in the case supposed, its permanent occupant, with or without a seat in the Cabinet, would at least enjoy the ever-denied chance of seeing his schemes through.

Are we not all tired of incessant change without fruition? Of light-hearted amateurs who learn their raison d'être and its significance only to abdicate with the knowledge? "Quot homines tot sententiæ" is no motto wherewith to regulate an army.

Yours etc., Et Militavi.

MUSIC AT MEALS.

To the Editor of the Saturday Review.

Clacton-on-Sea, 4 August.

Sir,—Mr. G. S. Robertson suggests various reasons why "meal-time melody" is popular. He seems to me to have missed the real reason. Let me put it in the form of a question: Has he ever known music at meals welcome to people who have anything worth talking about to discuss? When people who are not devoid of ideas and conversational gifts are dining together, the one way to make the dinner wholly distracting is to secure an orchestra which "cuts in" with hopelessly inapposite strains at the very moment that the discussion of some point is most interesting.

Music at meals is useful, often a boon, where the company has no more absorbing topic to debate than the weather, or the excess charged by the taxicab, or the relationship of Mrs. Jones to Mr. Robinson's first wife. In such cases music covers up the awful pauses that even inanity cannot always bridge; it deflects conversation into channels which the diners would not open up for themselves, and a more or less familiar air provides one of the company with an excuse for reminiscences of opera or the theatre which fill in the gaps when the band is at rest. "Instrumental music invariably encourages conversation—and loud conversation too, because you have to overcome the resistance of the orchestra", says Mr. Robertson. Not "invariably" I think. Instrumental music, I have often noticed, silences conversation. The people who want to talk find the effort too great; the people who do not want to talk adopt the pensive air, and it would be difficult to say whether they are more absorbed in the meal or the music.

My view is that an orchestra at banqueting time is an irritant or a pleasure in precise proportion as one's immediate companion is or is not a congenial spirit.

Yours truly, Diner Out.

REVIEWS.

RELIGIOUS ART AND THE CRITICS.

"Francia's Masterpiece." By Montgomery Carmichael. London: Kegan Paul. 1909. 5s. net.

THIS is a book about a single picture, but Mr. Carmichael wants to drive into the minds of art critics a very general principle, namely, that an old religious picture can only be appreciated and understood in connexion with the purpose and surroundings for which it was originally painted. Such a picture is not simply an exhibition of technique, a piece of wall decoration, to be studied in meaningless isolation on an easel, in an art gallery, or even in any church or any part of a church. At least our great galleries ought to have a subjects index. But Mr. Carmichael's prime rule is, Connect the picture once more with its altar, and interrogate that; for, as Gaume observes, " L'autel est le plus éloquent de tous les livres ". Does it belong to a cathedral, a collegiate, a conventual, or a parochial church, and what was its original dedication? If, moreover, the art critic keeps up the absurd pretence of ignoring theologians, he is sure to flounder, for comprehension of a religious picture involves knowledge of the painter's theology. " By belief alone can he be judged; only if he were faithful to belief could he be great in his subject." We are not so confident as Mr. Carmichael is that the museum or pinacotheca view of religious pictures is " happily dying fast ", for Ruskinite enthusiasms have a decaying hold on the art-student world, and State-aided archæology is more than ever at work, in Rome especially, transferring everything from its locality to catalogued collections. But at any rate this monograph is a help towards the recovery of true principles of criticism.

For the subject of the noble picture in San Frediano's at Lucca, which Mr. Carmichael calls Francia's masterpiece, is one which the critics—including at one time Mr. Carmichael himself—have invariably misdescribed, for want of a little divinity and a little study of provenienza. They have called it a Coronation, or an Assumption, or a Reception of the Virgin into heaven. Mrs. Jameson comes nearest to truth in describing the subject as " the election or predestination of Mary as the immaculate vehicle or tabernacle of human redemption ". Mr. Carmichael now establishes beyond doubt that the picture is the altar-piece of the chapel on the north wall of which it hangs, that this chapel is a chapel of the Immaculate Conception, and that we have here almost the earliest representation of that mystery in art. Mr. Carmichael complains that the iconography of the Immaculate Conception has been neglected by modern writers. Partly this arises from the idea, expressed by Mrs. Jameson, that this subject does not appear in art until the seventeenth century, when all religious portrayal had become vulgarised—nude Adams and Eves being dragged in to parade the painter's skill, and the whole attitude to the mystery become sentimental, cheap, and shallow. Mr. Carmichael shows, however, that the subject was pictorially represented over altars from about 1400 onwards, while religious art still retained the note of dignity and devotion. There is such a picture in the Lucca gallery, painted in or about that year for the Confraternity of the Conception founded in the church of San Francesco, where it formerly hung. Francia's altar-piece in San Frediano bears a remarkable likeness to it—no doubt he was commissioned to paint another on the same lines —and Trenta is not the only writer who asserts the San Francesco picture to be a copy of Francia's. The shape of the episcopal mitre tells even a tiro in ecclesiology that it is the other way round. But art critics know little of ecclesiology. Mr. Carmichael's researches among the town archives have proved that Francia painted his Conception, under the will of Donna Maddalena Stiatta, not earlier than 1511, in the plenitude of his powers. This exquisite artist died in 1517.

Devotion to the mystery of the Conception of Mary the blessed Maid without spot of original sin had reached its height at the end of the fifteenth century, and had a special connexion with the " elect and for ever delectable city of Lucca ". It was still a pious and not uncontroverted opinion, rejected by S. Bernard in the twelfth century as a corruption of latter-day fraudulence, and traditionally obnoxious to the Dominicans. In 1477, however, Sixtus IV. sanctioned an Office and a Mass for it. Conservative Rome had been very slow to allow the festival official recognition, and Mr. Carmichael admits that " the grain of the Immaculate Conception was the tiniest of all seeds in the original deposit of the Faith " and practically undiscoverable in Holy Writ. As simply the Conception of our Lady, on the other hand, it had been observed for centuries on 8 December or 9 December, where it still stands in the kalendar of the Church of England. It was obviously not a subject lending itself to art, or only to the most mystical and delicately allusive treatment. Mr. Carmichael's analysis of the details of Francia's picture, however, demonstrates beyond the possibility of doubt that this is its theme, though we are not convinced that the kneeling friar is Duns Scotus rather than S. Anthony of Padua. That standard writers should have given the picture so many misnomers seems astonishing when we have once examined it with Mr. Carmichael's help. He has spared no pains to hunt down every scrap of evidence. The authorities gave him every possible assistance. On the other hand, the masterpiece itself hangs shrouded by a mercenary curtain, and actually so hung at a novena of the Conception which Mr. Carmichael happened to attend, while over the chapel altar was the usual conventional candle-lit Madonna. It is right to say that his remonstrances, poured into the patient ear of the Priore of San Frediano, produced the desired effect. The pious donor's sepulchre is gone beyond recall.

" O noble and pious Dame Magdalen Trenta," says our author in his quaint way, " true and faithful relict of that upright patrician merchant, Bartholomew Stiatta, thy tomb eclipsed, his tomb despoiled, thy Chapel of the Conception lost to sight and memory, thy Altar of the Conception gone the vulgar way to the haggling dealer, the Masses for this thy Altar all left unsaid, thy most honourable picture of the Conception ignobly treated as a show-piece and taken by the leading historians of art to be something else—all this were enough to make thee turn in thy tomb, but that they have robbed thee of this also. Yet the name of the woman who gave to God, without any thought of the world and its art galleries, Francesco Francia's incomparable masterpiece shall assuredly live, a dear and sweet memory, in the ages to come ".

CONCLUSION OF THE " TIMES " HISTORY OF THE SOUTH AFRICAN WAR.

"The 'Times' History of the War in South Africa, 1899-1902." Edited by L. S. Amery. Vol. VI. London: Sampson Low. 1909. 21s. net.

THE delay in producing the last volume in this history, as explained by the editor in a well-written preface, is due to a series of mishaps, the outcome of what can only be termed bad luck. The volume is in reality two, for its two parts are quite distinct. The first of these deals with the work of reconstructing South Africa both during and after the war, and with the subsequent political history of that country down to the early portion of the present year. Part II., on the other hand, is really a kind of special appendix to Volumes II.-V., and deals with the work of military services of a purely technical nature, or problems entirely of an administrative character. It was considered that to interrupt the flow of the narrative of military operations by entering into such matters in their proper place would have interfered seriously with the interest of the reader, and accordingly the arrangement which we have just described was adopted. In our opinion the judgment of the editor was sound. A narrative going so largely into detail as this one does and dealing with so many operations by such small forces over so wide a field is necessarily split up and disjointed to a regrettable extent. To discuss the special questions referred to in the sequence in which they first claimed attention would have added enormously to the embarrassment. We should add that another volume, VII., containing appendices and an index to the whole work, has now also been issued with this volume. The real end to the war is therefore only described in the nine chapters which form Part I. of Volume VI. But these adequately round off a narrative which from the first has been intended to deal with the war not as a military incident alone, but as a series of great historical and political events, forming one of the greatest crises in the development of the British Empire and certainly the greatest in the history of South Africa. No doubt it is too early, in the opinion of many, to attempt as yet to sum up the results of the war, or to come to any final conclusion on the subject. But we think Mr. Amery has nevertheless done well to make an effort towards a provisional estimate of its results, and he has certainly collected together for us data and information up to the very latest moment such as will enable us to form such a provisional judgment. In dealing with the work of Mr. Chamberlain and Lord Milner no doubt he will be accused of partiality and political partisanship. The politicians who were responsible for the placards and pictures dealing with Chinese labour during the last General Election will not be turned from their opinions or methods of controversy by any amount of judicial investigation. On the other hand, every man of honest and impartial mind, no matter to what party he may belong, will admit the level-headedness Mr. Amery displays, and will recognise his effort to be accurate and fair in all he has set down. In our view he has succeeded admirably, and if the vastness of Lord Milner's task and the courage and patience with which it was faced appear greater with every page we read, it is not because the writer exaggerates but because the facts are overpowering.

Part II. opens with an account of the mobilisation and improvisation of the South African Field Force. There is a satiric touch in the term adopted to express the latter process. It is mobilisation and organisation, not improvisation, that should go together, and we hope may do so in the future. But ten years ago we had no adequate organisation of our forces. After our accustomed manner we had to go into the byways and hedges to look for men. We did better than a hundred years ago, or during the Crimean period, when foreign mercenaries swelled our muster rolls, because it was not Poles and Germans but colonists of our flesh and blood who came to our assistance. In many respects Chapter I. of Part II. is the most interesting in the book, although it deals only with hard dry facts and has scarcely a tinge of sentiment in it. But it places on record how the vast numbers that we sent to South Africa were raised, and now, after ten years, when the methods adopted are half forgotten, it will strike many as marvellous that we accomplished what we did. The record of what was done by our naval transport department comes next, and the personality and industry of Captain Sir Edward Chichester are deservedly extolled. The railway work and the engineer work are discussed very fully and completely in the two following chapters. These are admittedly written by the officers themselves concerned, and interesting as they are they therefore lack the critical quality that would otherwise enhance the record of what was accomplished. Transport and supply in their turn are more absorbing. And the criticism directed against the manner in which the system of transport in South Africa was suddenly and chaotically jumbled up by Lord Roberts and Lord Kitchener seems to us just. Neither of these men, however able, had any knowledge or experience of the War Office system, and they would have done better to leave it alone rather than disorganise a system to which everyone was accustomed at a highly dangerous crisis in the campaign. That they were wrong was proved by subsequent events during the war, and the change which had brought about so much difficulty and confusion was allowed to die a natural death before peace was declared. The story of the local requisitioning, of the military farms, of the Field Force canteen, and of the surplus war stores is told temperately and accurately in a manner which will be of use towards educating us for future campaigns. Necessarily, however, the tale is somewhat dull and colourless and not very illuminating or convincing. Remounts and finance receive their due share of recognition, and the pages which discuss them embody valuable hints for future guidance. In conclusion we must not forget to notice the very able review of artillery progress in our army and the excellent account of the armament and employment of our batteries during the war.

ROME VERSUS FLORENCE.

"The Monuments of Christian Rome." By A. L. Frothingham. New York: The Macmillan Co. 1909. 10s. 6d.

WHEN we read on the first page "Handbooks of Archæology and Antiquities: The Monuments of Christian Rome", we thought of a single word, a proper name in the Old Testament with the curious meaning of "yet another", yet another of the handbooks that are already legion, yet another repetition of a tale that has been told ubique et ab omnibus ab urbe condita. Our only curiosity was to see whether this new production was a text-book after the manner of former generations or a sentimental journey after the fashion of to-day. In our attempt to classify it we found we had altogether misjudged it. Mr. Frothingham's book is not a handbook as are other handbooks. It is a really interesting study of Roman mediæval art, written by a man who has lived in Rome and worked in Rome, and written of Rome not because he wishes to say something but because he has something to say.

Handbooks are apt to be stodgy reading; a stream of facts can easily become turbid and confused. Its source must be kept clear; it cannot be allowed to meander aimlessly without a definite destination; if it has neither beginning nor end it ceases to fertilise, and collects into what the Campagnoli would call a "stagno". Mr. Frothingham does not allow his facts to stagnate. He cannot content himself with a catalogue raisonné, for he is out to prove something. In the Prologue he frankly states that he is a partisan—it is this parti pris that makes the book so thoroughly readable—"this handbook cannot, as such books usually do, give a summary of recognised facts, but must be itself often a pioneer and admit a large element of discussion and hypothesis". The facts are, to quote an epithet of Emile Faguet's, "talkative" facts; they talk like Dr. Johnson "for victory", and the conclusion of their talk is this, that Rome was the source of all art in Europe in the Middle Ages. The body of Vasari will turn in its grave; and those whose love of Florence takes the form of contempt of Rome will hold up their hands in horror. The very thought that Giotto should have taken his inspiration from Rome, and that Cavallini is a greater figure in the history of painting than Cimabue, verges on profanity. But even the fanatics of Florence will admit that Mr. Frothingham states his case with great force. He has been at some trouble to obtain his evidence. For various reasons it is not easily available. The Romans themselves are chiefly to blame; in the words of one of them: "Quod non fecerunt Barbari, fecerunt Barberini". A clause in the Code of Justinian shows that the evil was ingrained in the Roman character: "We the rulers of the State, with a view to restoring the beauty of our venerable city, desire to put an end to the abuses which have already long excited our indignation. It is well known that in several instances public buildings in which all the ornament of the city consisted have been destroyed with the criminal permission of the authorities, on the pretext that the materials were necessary for public works". It was a counsel of perfection remembered not for its observance but its breach. If the disiecta membra of Rome's mediæval splendour need searching out and piecing together, the fault is with the later generations of Romans, who could not keep their hands off anything mediæval. Not that we do not admire the magnificence of this later work. But when we say that they "make us regret the Vandals", it is because in building the new S. Peter's they destroyed the old, in decorating with the first gold of America the roof of Santa Maria Maggiore they mutilated the basilica of Liberius, in impressing the uniformity of the Council of Trent on their churches or the mannerisms of the classical revival on their villas, they laid their hands upon treasures of mediæval art such as no other city in Europe possessed. If we wish to gauge Rome's influence as a centre of art, we must first scrape away the whitewash of barocco Popes. Fortunately, however, some treasures have escaped them. The frescoes and mosaics, the campanili, the cloisters, the cosmatesque pavements and ambones, the tombs of thirteenth-century Popes, the remnants of mediæval domestic architecture, who can forget them in San Clemente, in San Giovanni in Laterano, in Santa Maria in Cosmedin, in the crypt of S. Peter's or the palace of the Crescentii?

Even if all the evidence had been destroyed in the city itself, there is enough left in the Roman Province to testify to the magnificence and originality of the Roman artists. Their work is writ large at Viterbo, at Subiaco, at the little-known Toscanella, or even in the holy of holies of the Florentines, Assisi. It is to be found further afield than the patrimony of S. Peter, or Tuscany, or even Lombardy and Venetia. Germany and France possess notable examples of it; and, what may come as a surprise to us, in England itself, it is represented in the very sanctuary of English national life, Westminster Abbey. Who could fail to be reminded of the Papal tombs at Viterbo when he sees the tomb of Henry III.? The cosmatesque pavement in the Choir may be seen in a hundred churches in and about Rome. The fluted column on Edward the Confessor's shrine is the work of the hands that fashioned the Paschal candles in the Roman basilicas. This is no idle conjecture, for on its east end the words may yet be traced, "duxit in actum Romanus civis." It is all that is left of the Roman artists' inscription:

"Anno milleno Domini cum sexageno
Et bis centeno cum completo quasi deno
Hoc opus est factum quod Petrus duxit in actum
Romanus civis. Homo causam noscere si vis,
Rex fuit Henricus Sancti presentis amicus".

If Peter the Roman's name is forgotten in England, and the Roman origin of some of the finest work in the Abbey is unrecognised, it is typical of the fate of Roman mediæval art generally.

Mr. Frothingham has done his best to restore it to its proper position. Even those who think that in his enthusiasm he has been led to exaggerate its influence will acknowledge that he has written a very interesting book. For Roman explorers there is much information for him who walks to read. If they stay at home they can find in it new ideas to give them to think. We will only suggest one. What might not have been the development of the Roman school if it had not been brought to an untimely end by the exile of the Popes and the Avignon captivity?

THE SCHOOL OF JAPAN.

"Japanese Education." Lectures delivered in the University of London by Baron Dairoku Kikuchi, President of the Imperial University of Kyoto. London: Murray. 1909. 5s. net.

WHEN the bishop who had just lost a train said to Father Healy that he put great faith in his watch, Father Healy replied that he would be inclined to suggest putting in good works instead. The story rises to the mind on reading Baron Kikuchi's interesting volume on "Japanese Education" and contrasting the Japanese system with our own. The Japanese system is pre-eminently a system of good works, while ours is a system of great faith. We have built up an educational structure in England which is ultimately based on an ideal of intellectual culture. The result of our system is to encourage and stimulate, within certain limits, a certain mental and moral independence; but it is contended on the other hand that the practical interests of the majority are sacrificed to the intellectual interests of the minority, and that such efficiency as we develop is incidental rather than deliberate.

The precise opposite holds in Japan. There everything is subordinate to morals and the efficient training of character. The Educational Code, which was from the first of the simplest and most practical kind, has been amended at short intervals, and always with a view to simplification and practical efficiency. The history of the whole movement is extremely interesting and instructive. The era of what is called "enlightened government" in Japan dates from the year 1868, and in 1872 the first Code of Education was promulgated. It was here clearly laid down that the habit of regarding education as a sort of polish, appropriate only to the governing classes, was a vicious one. "The cultivation of morals, the improvement of the intellect and proficiency in arts cannot be attained except through learning", the preamble states, adding "it is intended that henceforth universally, without any distinction of class or sex, in a village there shall be no house without education, and in a house no individual without education." The Code was more than once modified and reformed, but always on the same lines and with the same aim in view, namely to increase efficiency and to promote sound morals.

It is in this respect that the contrast between our own educational system and the Japanese system is so marked. Our ideal here has been originally humanistic and intellectual, and it has been hoped rather than intended that morality will be thereby incidentally promoted. In fact the chief defect of our own system has been that we have not begun by defining our aim. We laid down our system first, basing our elementary education in a general way upon the traditions of our secondary education. We are only now beginning to inquire what our aim is or ought to be; and it has been left until the last year or two to suggest that the aim of education is, primarily, the development of character and, secondarily, the increase of practical efficiency. But in Japan the aim has been clearly defined throughout, and whenever it has been suspected that the system was not producing the intended results, the system has been promptly modified.

The chief interest of the book lies in the description of Japanese elementary education, and the methods used in moral education. The child begins by simple lessons on ordinary virtues, such as order and punctuality; then follows instruction in home relations and loyalty, and then he passes on to more detailed lessons of daily conduct, such as friendship, honesty, kindness, generosity, modesty, courage, and manners. All these virtues are illustrated by tales and examples. Later on the children have lessons on the higher social virtues, such as patriotism, co-operation, honour, tenacity of purpose, public duty. It is enjoined on the teachers that, in addition to the formal lessons, every opportunity should be taken of instilling these and similar precepts into the minds of the children.

The subjects taught in the ordinary elementary course, besides morals, are the Japanese language, arithmetic, and gymnastics, to which drawing, singing, manual work, including sewing for girls, may be added according to local circumstances. In the higher elementary schools history and geography are added, with agriculture, commerce and the English language as additional subjects; the point being, as the Imperial Ordinance states, that elementary schools are designed to give children the rudiments of moral and civic education, together with such general knowledge and skill as are necessary for life, while due attention is paid to their bodily development.

It is interesting, in passing, to note how strictly these subjects are all subordinated to the central aim of conduct. Thus the Code states that the object of teaching history is to make boys attain to clear notions concerning the evolution of and changes in society, the rise, decline and fall of States; and therefore discussion or teaching of details must be avoided. Similarly the object of teaching science is declared to be that children should understand the relations of common natural objects and phenomena one to another and to mankind, and at the same time to train accurate observation and foster a love of nature; while the object of teaching drawing is to teach children to perceive clearly and represent correctly, and to foster the sense of the beautiful.

This is the striking part of the whole system, that a definite object is kept so clearly in view. Detailed knowledge is regarded as of no importance at all except in so far as the apprehension and retention of it develops and strengthens character and efficiency.

We have here been able only to touch one of the many problems which are aroused by this extremely interesting book; but all the problems with which it deals are subordinate to the main idea; we see a national aspiration embodying itself in a national ideal. That is the true motive of the book—the apparently sudden adolescence of a great nation; but the causes which make it possible for a nation suddenly to break—at least outwardly—with its past, to originate and realise a great national ideal—and this not only as a vague enthusiasm but as an intensely practical need—these are beyond the reach of speculation. What is clear is that the Japanese are hard at work, not feverishly but with a strenuous and calm diligence, at developing a certain type of character, not, as we Western nations do, valuing national prosperity for the sake of individual welfare, but subordinating all personal interests to public good. What the effects of this remarkable protest against individualism are, is visible to all; what its dangers may be it is easy enough to forecast; but the book stands as a record of a national movement absorbing into itself all the best energies of a virile and energetic people, and thus, though it is of peculiar interest to educational specialists, it has a wider and higher interest for historians and philosophers alike, and cannot be too highly commended.

A STUDY OF JERUSALEM.

"The City of Jerusalem." By C. R. Conder. London: Murray. 1909. 12s. net.

COLONEL CONDER has given us an interesting volume on Jerusalem and its history. It is well written, rising at times into passages of real eloquence, and brings the story of the city down to the close of the Crusades. The author is in sympathy with his subject, which indeed has been a lifelong study with him. The great survey made by the Palestine Exploration Fund will always be associated with his name, and where distances and levels are concerned no one should be able to speak with greater authority. His judgment, however, is not always equal to his information. Jerusalem is unfortunately a city of disputed sites, and Colonel Conder's conclusions in regard to them are apt to be formed hastily and upon insufficient grounds. His "cocksuredness" as to the site of Calvary and the Holy Sepulchre offers an unfavourable contrast to the cautious learning of Sir Charles Wilson's posthumous work upon the same subject. There is no question in his mind that the traditional site must be abandoned and that the real Calvary is to be found in a knoll north of the Damascus Gate. Bishop Macarius is not allowed the benefit of a doubt, and his identification of the tomb of Christ in the fourth century is dismissed as a "mistake". Sir Charles Wilson's careful inquiry, however, shows that such offhand treatment of the evidence is inadmissible, and that the contemporaries of Constantine were at least as well able as ourselves to determine whether or not the site of the Holy Sepulchre could be fixed by tradition. It is important to remember that Dr. Schick, the highest authority in our time on the topography of Jerusalem, returned before his death to a belief in the traditional site.

The non-archæological world might naturally suppose that the matter could be settled by excavation. Perhaps it could be if excavations could be made in the right places. But this is not always possible in Jerusalem. Houses and mosques come in the way, not to speak of cemeteries. The walls disinterred by Dr. Bliss for the Palestine Exploration Fund were either wholly or for the most part of a late age, and raised more problems than they solved. But though Colonel Conder adheres to his Calvary north of the Damascus Gate, he cannot away with the holy place of the modern Protestant, discovered by General Gordon. As he rightly says, General Gordon was not aware that the tomb associated with his name was already known and "attributed to a much later age than that of our Lord". Gordon's tomb is not a Jewish tomb, and Colonel Conder is probably correct in supposing that it is not older than the twelfth century. The Church of the Martyrion referred to in inscriptions found near the spot was built by Constantine.

The book contains a good account of the conquest of Jerusalem by the Arabs and of its fortunes in the time of the Crusades. It thus supplements the history of the city given by Professor G. A. Smith in his recently published work. The chapter on "The Roman City" should be read along with Sir Charles Wilson's "Golgotha", which will serve to supplement and also to correct or modify some of Colonel Conder's statements, which are not always as guarded as they should be. But the account of Hadrian's city is excellent, and, dealing as it does with a little-known period of Jewish history, will be very acceptable to most readers. Even better is the story of Jerusalem under the Arabs and Latins. The Jerusalem of the Crusades is described in detail, and the fact pointed out that after all the Christian Churches of the East preferred Mohammedan rule to that of the intolerant and ignorant Christians of the West. To the Crusader the native Christian was a schismatic and a heretic, and the want of education and culture of the European invader contrasted painfully with the Mohammedan civilisation of the time. It was not until the Turks appeared upon the scene that the Oriental Christian discovered that a Mohammedan conqueror could be as great a barbarian as a Christian. Colonel Conder, however, fails to notice what an important influence Saladin and his Kurds had not only on the fortunes of the Latin kingdom of Jerusalem but also upon those of Christianity in general in the East. Had it not been for the Kurds Amaury would have succeeded in his invasion of Egypt, with the result that Mohammedanism would have been expelled from its chief stronghold in the Near East, while it was the Kurds also, under Saladin, who eventually drove the Crusaders out of Palestine. They, in fact, saved the Mohammedan world. Without their help Egypt and Palestine must have become European, at all events politically and religiously, and the Byzantine Empire would have had a chance of maintaining itself in Asia Minor against the Turks. In the mediæval phase of what Professor Freeman used to call "the eternal struggle between East and West", it was the East that won.

The illustrations and maps in Colonel Conder's book have been well chosen and will be found useful. The one representing specimens of masonry from the age of Hyrcanus to that of the Crusades may be specially commended. But Colonel Conder's acquaintance with modern archæology is slight. A writer who believes that there was no neolithic age in Palestine "because (as in Egypt and Babylonia) instruments of stone and of flint are found at all levels in the excavations, and are contemporary with others of bronze and of iron" has indeed much to learn. The equanimity of the archæologist therefore need not be disturbed when he reads that "the frescoes and tablets of the palace of Knossos in Crete are probably not older than about 500 (not 1500) B.C."! Nor are Colonel Conder's quotations always accurate. It is odd, to say the least, to find Brugsch's "History of Egypt" quoted as the authority for the Aramaic papyri recently found in the island of Elephantinê.

LESSONS IN MILITARY GEOGRAPHY.

"An Introduction to Military Geography." By Brigadier-General E. S. May. With Maps and Sketches. London: Rees. 1909. 8s. 6d. net.

IT would be no small gain if some of the principles of military geography as well as its political aspects were understood not only by Staff officers but by every responsible citizen. We should at any rate be saved from such painful exhibitions of national ignorance as trusting in our fleet to stop a Russian advance in Asia Minor. All serious students of modern warfare are aware that in this country military geography is a branch of military art which has never received anything like the amount of attention it deserved, more especially in view of our world-wide geographical position. In fact, Brigadier-General May's book may be considered as the first of its sort written by a trained and capable officer of the Staff. For it is a systematised attempt to direct the attention of our officers to those portions of the world where, owing to political and strategical reasons, we have vast interests at stake or where we may expect in the near future to find ourselves face to face with most serious and complex problems. It would, of course, be impossible within the scope of a book of some two hundred and fifty pages to do more than outline briefly the broad conditions affecting every successive problem, and this the author has done most ably, leaving it to the serious student of war to elaborate and work out the details involved in the particular case.

What a blessing it would be if some of our "statesmen" in the House of Commons who attempt to pose as experts on all questions of national defence were to read this book and try to grasp a few of the general principles of what they talk about so glibly. But, whether they derived benefit or not, they would certainly stumble upon rather unpleasant facts, unpleasant because they are facts which cannot be refuted and which by no means tally with the imaginations of the uneducated M.P.

They would, for example, realise that a Switzerland relying upon her inaccessible mountains and her quasi-militia as a sure safeguard against invasion and conquest is a myth. It was Wordsworth's luckless lines anent the Voice of Freedom dwelling amid Swiss mountains and in the seas surrounding England that probably fostered the vulgar belief that there was something exceptionally sacred in the soil of both Switzerland and England. Since then Switzerland has been overrun by the foreigner, and only owes her existence to the jealousies and hatreds of her powerful neighbours and their unstable allies, tempered to a certain extent no doubt by the fact that she has no foreign possessions to cede as spoil to the victor. Could anything be more unlike the position of Great Britain to-day—with our world-wide and temptingly unfortified and inadequately garrisoned possessions to whet the cupidity of our jealous rivals, more especially those who are sorely in need of fresh territories for their ever-expanding peoples? The influences which a steadily growing population must exert in shaping the future of a nation are well described. Take, for example, Russia, whose population of one hundred and fifty millions is at present increasing annually by no less than two and a half millions. At this rate it will be about two hundred and fifty millions by the middle of the present century. In Asia lie vast territories which, despite adverse climatic conditions, are capable of enormous development. With this development of natural resources, aided by colonisation and the extension and improvement of the railways, the time will most surely come when nothing can prevent Russia overwhelming China, save indeed, as the author most truly remarks, China herself. Japan clearly foresees this, and hence her recent anxiety with reference to the projected railways in Manchuria.

Everybody should read General May's account of the probable effect of the proposed Georgian Bay Canal upon the development of Canada, as also the far-reaching strategical and political consequences of the opening of the Panama Canal. In fact, his is altogether a most instructive book and full of valuable information, with good maps to illustrate the various problems. But although the serious nature of the subject does not lend itself to light handling, we could wish at times that the author would remember that it is possible to be in deadly earnest without affording the unregenerate an excuse for saying that he is now and again deadly dull.

NOVELS.

"The Coming of Aurora." By Mrs. Philip Champion de Crespigny. London: Nash. 1909. 6s.

Aurora came to a French mountainside monastery. She came in a motor-car during a violent storm in which the car was snowbound. When the porter's lodge was opened to admit her servant and half-frozen chauffeur, she slipped through into the refectory where the monks were celebrating a feast, and refused to be banished to the guest-house, saying, "J'y suis, j'y reste". For about three weeks she remained at S. Olave's Priory, and then the weather permitted of her departure. An English novice, nearing the time for taking the vows, was in the priory, and coming thus into his life Aurora seduces him back to the world, though she has refused his offer of love made when they are imprisoned in the crypt by "the mad monk". Having behaved rudely, childishly, irresponsibly, Aurora leaves the place, where she has been an unwelcome guest. After a long interval she meets a man whom she could love but for the memory of S. Olave's novice—a memory so keen that she does not recognise that which she would have done at once had she been a reader of novels! It is all very unreal.

"The Romance of a Plain Man." By Ellen Glasgow. London: Murray. 1909. 6s.

The atmosphere of the life of the old landed gentry in Virginia remains mysterious to the self-made man of business whose autobiography is given in this story. Had the book been merely the presentment of his career from errand-boy to millionaire, it would have possessed little interest. But Ben Starr, son of a working mason, is deeply impressed in childhood by a pretty little girl who, when they first met, would not play with "a common boy", and from the first makes up his mind not to stay common. (O democracy!) He so far succeeds in his aim that the girl of good family marries him in spite of the horror of her relatives. Then follows a mode of life not unfamiliar to students of America—the husband absorbed in business in order that his wife may live in luxury. But since Mrs. Starr was not a society leader of New York, but a gentlewoman of the South with certain ideals, she found life unsatisfactory, for all its pleasures, when her husband allowed finance to absorb his soul. This is a fine novel, written with delicacy, and it is a good thing to be reminded that though the South was conquered, Richmond has not yet been annexed by Washington.

"Peter Homunculus." By Gilbert Cannan. London: Heinemann. 1909. 6s.

Mr. Cannan has taken a theme very like that discussed by Mr. Barrie in "Sentimental Tommy", the making of a man of letters. But there is nothing imitative in his treatment, and his Peter Davies has little in common with the dreamy Scots villager. Peter drifts from Leicestershire to London, and is engaged as shop-boy by a second-hand bookseller (decayed scholar and gentleman), who christens the queer imp "Homunculus", teaches him what books mean, and makes the boy his heir. We lose interest to some extent in our hero when the book-shop is closed and its old master buried, but the story is carefully told and the author can think. Peter becomes educated, is taken up by his social superiors, drifts into a boy-and-girl engagement with the precocious daughter of a kindly clergyman, but worships a brilliant actress whose fancy, for a moment, he seems to impress. Thus gradually he finds himself, and, if the discovery is not of great value, we must remember that worse men than Peter make reputations and earn hysterical eulogies when they die. Mr. Cannan has generally a sure touch, and, while his beautiful actress is very hard to comprehend, he has filled his story with odd people who arrest the reader's attention.

"My Lady of Shadows." By John Oxenham. London: Methuen. 1909. 6s.

Mary Dustan shot a man coming through her bedroom window on her bridal night. Then she fainted. When she recovered from the faint she had "lost her memory", and knew absolutely nothing in her life before the moment of her waking. She did not know that she was married. She did not know that she had shot the man. Her husband had no wife, and the question arose "Could they be married again?" Dr. Coffin advised this; but the vicar quoted the bishop's objections, and Dr. Coffin said "Hang the bishop". They were—but we must not write "My Lady of Shadows" over again. That is the footing of Mr. John Oxenham's latest novel; and yet, happily for authors, it will be found readable, the critical instinct being so rare in readers. Though Mary did not know that she was married, she knew that she was still in love with the bridegroom. How is it she did not forget that? Simply because the convenience of the story requires it so. Curious how people who fail in the probable can succeed in the impossible. In a "popular" way the telling is so satisfactory that the impossibility of the tale makes no difference to the thoughtless, who are always more numerous than the other people.

"The Adoption of Rhodope." By Thomas Pinkerton. London: Swan Sonnenschein. 1909. 6s.

Rhodope and Orion are two kidnapped children immured in an inn of ill repute in a Scotch glen. They run away, and after a hair's-breadth escape from recapture are picked up by a retired actress and her artist son, who is painting thereabouts. These amiable people, smitten by the children's beauty but with no more right to possession of them than the wicked pursuers, hurry them off to the banks of the Thames, where their neighbours are Mrs. Trefusis, the famous novelist, who adopts the girl as her daughter, and Sir Elphin Costorphine, to whose baronetcy Orion turns out to be the heir. If one can admit the rather unconvincing premises, what follows is good strong work, and amusing withal. Mr. Pinkerton's audacious word-coining will make most readers gasp, but they will probably smile immediately after.

"The Measure of our Youth." By Alice Herbert. London: Lane. 1909. 6s.

Miss Herbert has used a great variety of subject-matter in her book, too much indeed for singleness and clearness of purpose. We imagine that her intention is to show the vacillation between fleshliness and spirituality of a nature of mixed Oriental and British origin. Francis is a very pleasant, well-meaning young man, with strong natural passions. The temptations by various feminine allurements to which he time after time succumbs are very frankly narrated by Miss Herbert, with something of that insistence on sexual inclinations which is characteristic of feminine writers. What the author calls Francis' High Church tendencies are also described with an emotion and the sentimental enthusiasm for religious asceticism more likely to be found in a woman than in a man. But the story is a thoughtful piece of work, sometimes a little naïvely ignorant and crude in its philosophy of life, but written with sincerity and earnestness.

SHORTER NOTICES.

"The National Gallery." 100 Plates in Colour. General Editor: T. Leman Hare. Joint Authors: Paul G. Konody, Maurice W. Brockwell and F. W. Lippmann. London: Jack. 1909. Vol. I. 10s. 6d. net.

The latest variation on the numerous centuries of painting which have recently been given to the world in more or less sumptuous form is the series of one hundred coloured reproductions of pictures in the National Gallery. Whether or no the addition of colouring, which often bears only a remote resemblance to the original, is desirable must remain a moot point. It is also questionable whether such a collection is of real value to any section of the public. The initiated can feel but pity before these travesties and ghosts of paintings known and cared for by them. The Philistine will only get a wrong impression and become confirmed in his distaste for the colouring of the old masters, while the price of the publication puts it out of the reach of the humblest class of readers, who frankly prefer twopennyworth of colour. Taken altogether the illustrations are disappointing, and some, as, for example, Botticelli's "Nativity", Perugino's "Madonna and Child", and the Arnolfini portrait, reveal no trace of the beauty of the originals. On the other hand, such different works as the two single portraits of Jan Van Eyck and Piero della Francesca's "Nativity" are more successfully reproduced, and the little portrait of a girl with corn-coloured hair, officially ascribed to Ghirlandaio, though more probably by his assistant Mainardi, brings before one with quite pleasant reality the somewhat hard and clear brightness of the original. This first volume contains reproductions of Italian, Flemish, and German pictures, chosen presumably less for their importance than with regard to their possibilities for satisfactory reproduction. Neither of the Michaelangelos is given, and Veronese is represented by the doubtful "S. Helena", and not by the superb "Family of Darius". The accompanying text gives a clear and concise historical survey of the schools represented, with some passing mention of the more important painters whose works at present find no place in the Gallery.

"Chats on English Earthenware." By Arthur Hayden. London: Fisher Unwin. 1909. 5s. net.

This, the companion volume to the author's "Chats on English China", forms one of the series of so-called books for collectors. To the advanced collector they can scarcely appeal. The fact that the same author is responsible for the volumes on subjects so far removed as furniture and old prints is evidence of the very general character of the series. But for the large and ever-growing class which collects earthenware and stoneware because of its variety and decorative character, and because unimportant specimens can still be obtained at small cost, Mr. Hayden's "Chats" will be of considerable use. He begins well by pointing out the various provincial museums—Leeds, Bath, Swansea, Farnham, Chester, Bury S. Edmunds, Hanley, Burslem, Etruria, and many others little known even to the educated Englishman, in which the art of the British potter may be studied to advantage. The rest of the chapter for beginners is devoted to a short sketch of the methods and materials employed in the making of earthenware and to a table for use in identifying specimens dating from the fifteenth to the end of the first half of the nineteenth century. The different kinds of ware are then dealt with briefly and on the broadest possible lines, too broad indeed in some cases, we fear, to enable the novice to distinguish with any certainty those innumerable imitations and copies which, unless he be fortunate beyond his deserts, will inevitably form a considerable portion of his early acquisitions. Many of the less important yet not uninteresting wares, like those of Mortlake and Sussex, are not even mentioned, nor would the possessor of a piece signed by Absolon find by turning to the pages on Yarmouth ware any reference to the arrow which so often accompanies the signature, giving rise at one time to the belief that he was the manufacturer as well as the decorator of the dish or plate.

"Sea Kings of Britain: Albemarle to Hawke." By G. A. R. Callender. London: Longmans. 1909. 3s. 6d.

"A Short History of the Royal Navy, 1689-1815." By David Hannay. London: Methuen. 1909. 7s. 6d.

Mr. Callender and Mr. Hannay in these two volumes are both following up previous work on similar lines. They cover here a good deal of the same ground, but there is nothing in common in their methods. Mr. Callender's "Sea Kings of Britain" is a racy account of the outstanding achievements of individuals, whilst Mr. Hannay's is a serious connected narrative of policy and events. Both writers have been at pains to make their work authoritative so far as it goes, and for the student who does not want an exhaustive review of naval history, but is anxious to fix leading personalities and features in his mind, the reading of the two volumes together should be useful. He will learn more about individuals like Vernon and Anson and Hawke from Mr. Callender, but will get a more comprehensive idea of what the Navy did as a whole from Mr. Hannay. That some of England's victories on the sea were due to fortune, that others were due to the bad in our opponents rather than the good in ourselves, is the conclusion to which Mr. Hannay points. "The same national instinct, the healthy

(Continued on page 176.)

social order, the innate love of good work which have shaped our Navy are just subjects for pride. But they are also a lesson and a warning. Great navies are forming now which have thoroughly learned all we have taught." Mr. Hannay's caution as to his dates has not saved him from a quite remarkable slip with regard to the taking of Quebec. He gives the date as 17 August 1759, instead of 13 September.

"Explorers in the New World Before and After Columbus." By Mrs. Mulhall. London: Longmans. 1909. 6s. 6d. net.

Mrs. Mulhall's researches in the Vatican library and elsewhere have provided her with a certain amount of new material, especially concerning the rise and fall of the Jesuit Missions of Paraguay. But her book is rather a strange compound. It contains a portrait of her husband, the well-known statistician, which does not seem to have much bearing on the subject-matter of her pages. What she calls the Explorers' Preface, in which she makes them say that they have entrusted the recital of their adventures to the author, is also a quaint and rather meaningless conceit. She talks of Sebastian Cabot's voyage to South America, but omits all reference—perhaps because he only touched but did not explore America—to John Cabot, his father, with whom he first crossed the Atlantic in 1497. Or is it that she regards the New World as confined to South America and the Pacific? In none of her chapters does she deal with the North. So that the title will mislead many. For the rest, her pages are packed with facts about adventurers some of whose records are not easily available, and the compilation shows much industrious reading.

"Revue des Deux Mondes." 1 Aout.

Madame Marcelle Tinayre continues her diary of the events at Constantinople attending the entrance of the Macedonian army and the deposition of Abdul Hamid. She adds nothing to our political knowledge, but gives a brilliant account of the scenes which passed before her eyes. She attempts, it is true, to give an estimate of the reign and character of Abdul Hamid. For the most part this consists of legends we already have by heart. Some of them are founded on fact; the majority are romance pure and simple. But this matters not. Madame Tinayre writes delightfully, and gives us by far the best account we have seen of those momentous days. There are some interesting notes in this number made by the late Prince Napoleon of his mission to Verona on behalf of Napoleon III. in July 1859, in order to arrange the basis of a peace with the Emperor of Austria.

THE QUARTERLY REVIEWS.

The new quarterlies are more than usually full of good strong papers. On the lighter side we have an admirable essay in the "Edinburgh" on Richard Jefferies, who is treated as "a mystic, but a Western mystic, a mystic of the order of the Incarnation"; and an equally admirable concluding paper in the "Quarterly" on its own centenary, in which we are told something of the authorship of many of the articles that went to make the Review a power. The "Edinburgh" has articles on the naturalist transition in French fiction, on fallacies and superstitions, and on modern Dutch painting; the "Quarterly" deals with Darwin and his critics, with Firdausi and Homer, Tolstoy and Turgeneff, Sidney's Arcadia, and Early Flemish painters. Both Reviews have articles on the mystical element in religion—a subject on which Mr. J. Ellis McTaggart writes at some length in the "New Quarterly". South African Union is discussed by the "Edinburgh" and the "Church Quarterly". The "Edinburgh" sees manifold advantages in the union. South Africans, the writer says, "have shown their determination to break away for ever from the bad traditions of the Kruger régime", and in no direction will the advantages be greater than "in the gravest of all issues confronting South Africa—the administration of the natives". When the native question can be viewed as a whole, with the pick of South African officials for its service, an enlightened policy will, it is hoped, supersede panic and repression. The "Church Quarterly" devotes the larger part of its article to explaining what the native problem is, what the missionaries as well as the politicians have done, and what the status of the native should be. The writer is impressed with the novelty of the conditions: "Plato and Simple Simon, Hercules and Hop-o'-my Thumb do not present stranger contrasts than the white and black man, the senior and junior partners of South Africa". Lord Selborne's generous, cautious, and statesmanlike view of native claims is endorsed; the native must be treated with justice, he must be given adequate opportunity for ventilating his opinions through the pitsos, and his interests must be safeguarded in the South African Parliament. But there must be no hasty conferment of the franchise, and his qualifications must be those of genuine civilisation—"the average level of civilisation of the white man".

On the purely political side the "Quarterly" and the "Edinburgh" will be refreshing, perhaps informing, reading to the Government and their followers. It is true the "Edinburgh" is satisfied that "by virtue both of its foreign policy and of its naval and military preparation" the present Administration has "placed the nation in a singularly strong position to face, if need be, any threatened dangers from across the seas", but it cannot stand Radical finance at any price. Mr. George's Budget shocks the "Edinburgh" at least as badly as tariff reform—so badly that its criticisms are marked by italicised words as though the writer were afraid his perfectly simple points might be missed. The truth is the quarterlies are in the cleft stick of economics. They hate the Budget the more because it has made clear to so many Radicals that tariff reform is the only alternative. In a very able article in the "Quarterly" Sir Robert Giffen shows the utter impracticability from the standpoint of sane finance of many of Mr. George's proposals. The deficit, according to Sir Robert, can be made good by an overhauling of our present financial methods, by withdrawing old-age pensions on their present lines at least, and by the imposition of import duties—but not, let it be understood, for the purposes the wicked tariff reformer has in view. This is really pitiful. Sir Robert Giffen advocates less direct and more indirect taxation, but refuses to associate the very thing which the tariff reformer himself proposes with tariff reform. Sir Robert Giffen as a destructive economist is worthy of his reputation; on the constructive side he advocates the course dictated by every consideration of patriotism and common sense, and then waves the tattered Free Trade flag vigorously, as if scared at his own temerity. He would put us on the right road, but on no account must we call it by its proper name. The most valuable article in the "Quarterly" perhaps just now is that on the privileges of the Commons, by Mr. H. C. Malkin, who was for thirty years Clerk of Public Bills in the House of Lords. He goes fully into precedent, and from a mass of more or less technical detail shows that the Peers may reject but not amend a Money Bill. The "Quarterly" itself hopes they will not exercise their rights lest worse things than the Budget befall. It would rather see injustice done to a class than risk a fatal blow to the Upper Chamber on appeal to the country. We looked for more courage in the "Quarterly".

The "Church Quarterly Review" contains three articles of high merit; it is difficult to say which is the most interesting. Mr. Goodrick writes on Calvin. In a year of centenaries and commemorations, with their torrents of indiscriminate praise, it is refreshing to have a coldly critical account of the great reformer; and we can only say of Calvin, as of many a reformer, that the more we see of him the less we like him. Poor-law Reform is a well-worn and not very attractive subject, but the Warden of New College writes on it with such ripe wisdom and sympathy that he makes it attractive to us; his article is the best that we have read on the subject for a long time. Dr. Ball treats the problem of reunion with the Presbyterians from the Scottish Episcopal point of view, and we hope that his words will be carefully weighed. It seems clear that even if the Presbyterian Church has preserved an apostolical succession through presbyters this was without, or rather against, the intention of her reformers; what John Knox and his colleagues did was to organise a Church on fundamentally different lines and to substitute a hierarchy of courts for the traditional hierarchy of orders. The reputation of the "Church Quarterly" for more solid learning and thought is maintained by an article on the Greek contribution to spiritual progress by Miss Oakley; and the Dean of Westminster spends some time and ingenuity over the history of his abbey in the twelfth century.

The "Law Quarterly" maintains its usual studied aloofness from current legal affairs, though during the quarter there have been matters of more than usual importance in Parliament and the courts. Its learned historical and antiquarian articles on such subjects as "The Constitution of the Isle of Man", "Pleading Rules at Common Law", "Interest on Debts during War", are of the usual type, and only an exceptional one by the editor, entitled "The Dog and the Potman; or, 'Go it, Bob'," has the unusual combination of learning and style and even humour in the Pollock manner. The Notes and Reviews are, as always, excellent.

For this Week's Books see page 178.

Silky Silence.
Velvety Smoothness.

ARGYLLS negotiate the roughest roads with comfort, and fulfil all the requirements of modern conditions, whether for Business or Pleasure, at a minimum cost. The car for the thinking motorist.

ARGYLLS, LIMITED,
Works: Alexandria by Glasgow. London—6, Great Marlborough St., W.

ARGYLL CARS

POOLE & LORD

INDIAN AND GENERAL OUTFITTERS,

322 OXFORD STREET, LONDON, W.
(NEARLY OPPOSITE BOND STREET.)

INVENTORS OF THE
"Sans-Plis" SHIRT.
Prices from 7s. 6d.

The "SANS-PLIS" Shirt is superior to any other for Indian and Colonial wear. Being entirely free from gathers, it is cooler, much stronger, and will bear the Indian mode of washing better than any shirt in use.

A single shirt, or other article, made to *measure*, and accurate patterns preserved to ensure correctness in the execution of future orders.

Makers of Drawers with Flexible Hip Belt Bands.
"BREECHES CUT."

REAL HAMBURG GROUND

KROPP RAZOR

NEVER REQUIRES GRINDING.
DO NOT BE PUT OFF WITH SUBSTITUTES.

Black Handle	5s. 6d.	A pair Ivory Handles in Russia Leather Case	21s.
Ivory Handle	7s. 6d.		
Kropp DUPLEX STROP	7s. 6d.	Kropp Strop Paste ...	6d.

Wholesale: OSBORNE, GARRETT, & Co., LONDON, W.

AUSTRALIA by ORIENT LINE,

UNDER CONTRACT TO CARRY HIS MAJESTY'S MAILS.

FROM LONDON EVERY ALTERNATE FRIDAY, calling at PLYMOUTH, GIBRALTAR, MARSEILLES, NAPLES, PORT SAID, and COLOMBO.

Managers—F. GREEN & CO.: ANDERSON, ANDERSON & CO.

Head Offices—FENCHURCH AVENUE, LONDON.

For Passage apply to the latter firm at 5 Fenchurch Avenue, E.C., or to the Branch Office, 28 Cockspur Street, Charing Cross, S.W.

BELGIAN STATE RAILWAY AND MAIL PACKET SERVICE.

Cheapest Railway Tickets in the World.

RUNDREISE TICKETS AT OFFICIAL PRICES
MADE UP AT A FEW HOURS' NOTICE.

Apply, 53 GRACECHURCH STREET, or 72 REGENT STREET. And at Dover. Also, for information only, to P. DEFRANCE, 47 CANNON STREET, E.C.

PRUDENTIAL ASSURANCE COMPANY
(LIMITED)

HOLBORN BARS, LONDON, E.C.

INVESTED FUNDS - - £70,000,000.

BENGER'S

FOOD

is primarily a nutritive food for those suffering from digestive debility, or during severe illness, and convalescence. But a course of Benger's Food is also of the greatest advantage to those enjoying the best of health. Benger's Food is different from any other food obtainable—it can be served prepared to suit the exact physical condition of the person for whom it is intended.

Benger's Food is sold in tins by Chemists, &c., everywhere.

Bell's

THREE NUNS

Tobacco

The true Englishman likes the best and he will have it. If the true Englishman smokes, he likes "Three Nuns" and he will have it,

Or "King's Head," which is, however, stronger.

Rare mixtures of the choicest quality.

Obtainable everywhere.

1 oz. packets, 7*d.*; 2 oz. tins, 1*s.* 2*d.*; 4 oz. tins, 2*s.* 3*d.*

"THREE NUNS" CIGARETTES
4½*d.* per packet of 10.

468

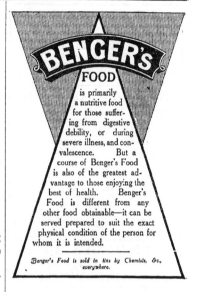

THIS WEEK'S BOOKS.

BIOGRAPHY

Semmelweis: His Life and His Doctrine (Sir William J. Sinclair). Manchester: At the University Press. 7s. 6d. net.

FICTION

The Last Lord Avanley (Gerald Maxwell). Mills and Boon. 6s.
Midsummer Madness (Morley Roberts). Nash. 6s.
Avenging Children (Mary E. Mann). Methuen. 6s.
Inexorable Nature. Drane. 6s.
Retribution (C. Ranger Gull); The Unseen Thing (Anthony Dyllington). Laurie. 6s. each.
The White Prophet (Hall Caine. 2 vols.). Heinemann. 4s. net.

HISTORY

Les Mavroyéni (Théodore Blanchard. 2 vols.). Paris: Leroux. 7fr. 50c.

SCIENCE AND PHILOSOPHY

Mesmerism and Christian Science (Frank Podmore). Methuen. 10s. 6d. net.

TRANSLATION

Modern Problems in Psychiatry (Ernesto Lugaro). Manchester: At the University Press. 7s. 6d. net.

TRAVEL

A Wanderer in Paris (E. V. Lucas). Methuen. 6s.

VERSE

Caradoc; or, The Church in the Sands (Sampson Waters). Letchworth: The Garden City Press. 10s. net.

MISCELLANEOUS

Adventures of Lally Helsmark (Marshall Kelly. 3 vols.). Drane. 18s.
Basis of Ascendancy, The (Edgar Gardner Murphy). Longmans, Green. 6s. net.
Nature (I. H. Crawford). Swan Sonnenschein. 5s.
REVIEWS AND MAGAZINES FOR AUGUST.—The Westminster Review, 2s. 6d.; Revue des Deux Mondes, 3fr.

NOTICE.

The Terms of Subscription to the SATURDAY REVIEW are:—

	United Kingdom. £ s. d.	Abroad. £ s. d.
One Year	1 8 2	1 10 4
Half Year	0 14 1	0 15 2
Quarter Year	0 7 1	0 7 7

Cheques and Money Orders should be crossed and made payable to the Manager, SATURDAY REVIEW Offices, 10 King Street, Covent Garden, London, W.C.

In the event of any difficulty being experienced in obtaining the SATURDAY REVIEW, the Publisher would be glad to be informed immediately.

Just weight is a delight

A very large edition of Mr. HALL CAINE'S new novel, "THE WHITE PROPHET," is now in the press, but intending purchasers are requested to place their orders without delay, so that Mr. HEINEMANN may be in a position to supply all immediate demands when this important book is published on Thursday, August 12, in two volumes, at 4s. net.

THE ENGLISH REVIEW.

CONTENTS OF AUGUST NUMBER.

1. Modern Poetry - - - - W. W. GIBSON, GERALD CUMBERLAND.
2. Norman Douglas - - - - - - TIBERIUS.
3. Henry James - - - - - MORA MONTRAVERS.
4. Walter de la Mare - - - THE ALMOND TREE.
5. P. Wyndham Lewis - - - LES SALTIMBANQUES.
6. E. Martindale - - - - THE ART OF DINING.
7. Ford Madox Hueffer - - - - - - A CALL.
8. The Month: Editorial - THE CRITICAL ATTITUDE: MILITANTS HERE ON EARTH.
9. C. E. Montague - - - THE WHOLESOME PLAY.
10. J. W. Williams - - SOME VICTORIAN CHANCELLORS.
11. Prof. Ed. S. Browne - - THE PERSIAN CRISIS: RE-BIRTH OR DEATH.
12. F.R. - - - REVIEW: THE CONDITION OF ENGLAND. By C. F. G. Masterman.

A special feature of this number will be the first instalment of a new serial story of modern life by FORD MADOX HUEFFER, entitled "A Call, the Tale of a Passion." The number will also contain a new short story by HENRY JAMES.

Subs. from Aug. till Dec. 12/6. For one year 30/-.
Half-a-Crown Monthly.

DUCKWORTH & CO., HENRIETTA STREET, W.C.

7th and Revised Impression.

"SATURDAY" BRIDGE,

By W. DALTON,

Is the Best Book on the Best Game.

That the popularity of Bridge is as great as ever is proved by the continuous steady demand for the work.

"'SATURDAY' BRIDGE"

is admitted to be the Standard book on the Game. It is the leading Bridge Authority, and takes its name from the "SATURDAY REVIEW," in which its chapters appeared.

Of all Booksellers 5s. net, or post free 5s. 3d., direct from the Office.

THE WEST STRAND PUBLISHING CO., Ltd.,
10 King Street, Covent Garden, W.C.

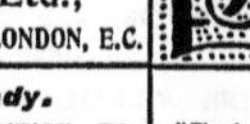

Sir ISAAC PITMAN & SONS, Ltd.,
No. 1 Amen Corner, LONDON, E.C.

Now Ready.

THE LATEST ADDITION TO PITMAN'S MAKERS OF NATIONAL HISTORY SERIES.

Edited by W. H. HUTTON, B.D.

GENERAL WOLFE.

By EDWARD SALMON.

In crown 8vo. cloth gilt, with Frontispiece and Map, **3s. 6d.** net.

On September 13 will be celebrated the 150th anniversary of the capture of Quebec and the death of General Wolfe.

"Mr. Salmon's exhaustive account of the whole campaign should be read by every impartial student of military annals." *Outlook.*

"A careful and attractive study . . . Wolfe's life story, as a notable chapter in our national history, is here admirably told."—*Daily Telegraph.*

Previous Volumes in the Series.

CARDINAL BEAUFORT.
By L. B. RADFORD, D.D.

VISCOUNT CASTLEREAGH.
By ARTHUR HASSALL, M.A.

ARCHBISHOP PARKER.
By W. M. KENNEDY, B.A.

READY SHORTLY.
FRANCIS ATTERBURY.
By H. C. BEECHING, D.Litt.

"A new and notable series of comprehensive and scholarly historical manuals." *Glasgow Herald.*

"No scheme could be more admirable than that of the series of volumes entitled, 'Makers of National History.'" *Sphere.*

"The three volumes which have already appeared in this new library of historical manuals fully demonstrate the value of such a series, the immediate object of which is 'to commemorate important men whose share in the making of national history seems to need a more complete record than it has yet received.' Each volume is obviously the work of a practised historian." *Daily Graphic.*

"The new series ought to make a place for itself in school and public libraries." *Saturday Review.*

A NEW 16 pp. PROSPECTUS IS IN PREPARATION, and will be sent to anyone gratis on application.

THE

"ARMY & NAVY CHRONICLE"

(*Established January* 1900. *Reconstituted January* 1905).

The only Illustrated Record of

Monthly Events in the Army and Navy, the Territorial Forces, and the Naval Reserves, in existence.

PRICE SIXPENCE.

SUBSCRIPTIONS, which can commence with any number, 8/6 per annum, post free.

A Specimen Copy, Scale of Charges for Advertisements, &c., will be sent on receipt of Eightpence-halfpenny, addressed to THE MANAGER, Offices of the ARMY & NAVY CHRONICLE (Department R.S.), 111 Jermyn Street, St. James's, London, S.W.

THE EVERSLEY SERIES.

Globe 8vo. cloth, 4s. net per Volume.

Matthew Arnold's Works. 8 vols.
Poems. 3 vols.
Essays in Criticism. First Series.
Essays in Criticism. Second Series.
American Discourses.
Letters, 1848–1888. Collected and Arranged by G. W. E. RUSSELL. 2 vols.

A Memoir of Jane Austen. By her Nephew, J. E. AUSTEN LEIGH. To which is added "Lady Susan," and Fragments of two other Unfinished Tales by Miss AUSTEN.

The Eversley Bible. Arranged in paragraphs, with an Introduction by J. W. MACKAIL, M.A.
Vol. II. **Deuteronomy—2 Samuel.**
Vol. III. **1 Kings—Esther.** Vol. IV. **Job—Song of Solomon.**
Vol. V. **Isaiah—Lamentations.** Vol. VI. **Ezekiel—Malachi.**
Vol. VII. **Matthew—John.** Vol. VIII. **Acts—Revelation.**
*** The Text is that of the Authorised Version.

Essays by George Brimley. Third Edition.

Calderon. Eight Dramas of Calderon freely translated. By EDWARD FITZGERALD.

Chaucer's Canterbury Tales. Edited by A. W. POLLARD. 2 vols.

Dean Church's Miscellaneous Writings. Collected Edition. 9 vols.
Miscellaneous Essays. | **Dante,** and other Essays.
St. Anselm. | **Bacon.** | **Spenser.**
The Oxford Movement. Twelve Years, 1833–1845.
The Beginning of the Middle Ages. (Included in this series by permission of Messrs. Longmans and Co.)
Occasional Papers. Selected from *The Guardian*, *The Times*, and *The Saturday Review*, 1846–1890. 2 vols.

Life and Letters of Dean Church. Edited by his Daughter, MARY C. CHURCH.

Lectures and Essays by the late W. K. Clifford, F.R.S. Edited by the late Sir LESLIE STEPHEN and Sir FREDERICK POLLOCK. Third Edition. In 2 vols.

Emerson's Collected Works. 6 vols. With Introduction by JOHN MORLEY, M.P.
Miscellanies. | **Essays.** | **Poems.**
English Traits and Representative Men.
The Conduct of Life, and Society and Solitude.
Letters and Social Aims.

Letters of Edward FitzGerald. Edited by W. ALDIS WRIGHT. 2 vols. New Edition.

Letters of Edward FitzGerald to Fanny Kemble, 1871–1883. Edited by W. A. WRIGHT.

More Letters of Edward FitzGerald. Edited by W. ALDIS WRIGHT.

Pausanias and other Greek Sketches. By J. G. FRAZER, D.C.L.

Goethe's Maxims and Reflections. Translated, with Introductions, by T. BAILEY SAUNDERS.
*** The Scientific and Artistic Maxims were Selected by Professor Huxley and Lord Leighton respectively.

Thomas Gray's Collected Works in Prose and Verse. Edited by EDMUND GOSSE. 4 vols.
Poems, Journals, and Essays.
Letters. 2 vols.
Notes on Aristophanes and Plato.

J. R. Green's Works. 16 vols.
History of the English People. 8 vols.
The Making of England. 2 vols.
The Conquest of England. 2 vols.
Stray Studies from England and Italy.
Oxford Studies.
Historical Studies.
Stray Studies. Second Series.

Guesses at Truth. By TWO BROTHERS.

Earthwork Out of Tuscany. Being Impressions and Translations of MAURICE HEWLETT, Author of "The Forest Lovers." Third Edition, revised.

R. H. Hutton's Collected Essays. 7 vols.
Literary Essays.
Theological Essays.
Essays on Some of the Modern Guides of English Thought in Matters of Faith.
Criticisms on Contemporary Thought and Thinkers. 2 vols.
Aspects of Religious and Scientific Thought. Edited by his Niece, ELIZABETH M. ROSCOE.
Brief Literary Criticism. Edited by his Niece, ELIZABETH M. ROSCOE.

The Choice of Books, and other Literary Pieces. By FREDERIC HARRISON.

The Meaning of History, and other Historical Pieces. By FREDERIC HARRISON.

Poems of Thomas Hood. Edited, with Prefatory Memoir, by the late Canon AINGER. In 2 vols.
Vol. I. **Serious Poems.**
Vol. II. **Poems of Wit and Humour.** With Vignettes and Portraits.

Thomas Henry Huxley's Collected Works. 12 vols.
Method and Results. | **Darwiniana.**
Science and Education.
Science and Hebrew Tradition.
Science and Christian Tradition.
Hume. With Helps to the Study of Berkeley.
Man's Place in Nature, and other Anthropological Essays.
Discourses: Biological and Geological.
Evolution and Ethics, and other Essays.
Life and Letters. 3 vols.

French Poets and Novelists. By HENRY JAMES.

Partial Portraits. By HENRY JAMES.

Modern Greece. Two Lectures delivered before the Philosophical Institution of Edinburgh, with Papers on "The Progress of Greece" and "Byron in Greece." By Sir RICHARD C. JEBB, Litt.D., D.C.L., LL.D. Second Edition.

Letters of John Keats to his Family and Friends. Edited by SIDNEY COLVIN.

Epic and Romance. By Prof. W. P. KER.

Charles Kingsley's Novels and Poems. 13 vols.
Westward Ho! 2 vols. | **Yeast.** 1 vol.
Alton Locke. 2 vols. | **Hypatia.** 2 vols.
Two Years Ago. 2 vols. | **Poems.** 2 vols.
Hereward the Wake. 2 vols.

Charles Lamb's Collected Works. Edited, with Introduction and Notes, by the late Rev. Canon AINGER, M.A. 6 vols.
The Essays of Elia.
Poems, Plays, and Miscellaneous Essays.
Mrs. Leicester's School, and other Writings.
Tales from Shakespeare. By CHARLES and MARY LAMB.
The Letters of Charles Lamb. Newly arranged, with additions, 1904. 2 vols.

Life of Charles Lamb. By the late Canon AINGER, M.A.

Historical Essays. By the late J. B. LIGHTFOOT, D.D., D.C.L., LL.D.

The Poetical Works of John Milton. Edited, with Memoir, Introduction, and Notes, by DAVID MASSON, M.A., LL.D. 3 vols.

John Morley's Collected Works. 14 vols.
Voltaire. 1 vol. | **Rousseau.** 2 vols.
Diderot and the Encyclopædists. 2 vols.
On Compromise. 1 vol. | **Miscellanies.** 3 vols.
Burke. 1 vol. | **Studies in Literature.** 1 vol.
Oliver Cromwell. 1 vol.
The Life of Richard Cobden. 2 vols.

Science and a Future Life, and other Essays. By F. W. H. MYERS, M.A.

Classical Essays. By F. W. H. MYERS.

Modern Essays. By F. W. H. MYERS.

Records of Tennyson, Ruskin, and Browning. By ANNE THACKERAY RITCHIE.

Works by Sir John R. Seeley, Litt.D. 5 vols.
The Expansion of England. Two Courses of Lectures.
Lectures and Essays.
Ecce Homo. | **Natural Religion.**
Introduction to Political Science. Two Series of Lectures.

Shakespeare. By WALTER RALEIGH.

The Works of Shakespeare. With short Introduction and Footnotes by Professor C. H. HERFORD. In 10 vols.
*** The Plays may also be had in separate volumes, cloth, 1s. each; roan, gilt tops, 2s. each.

Works by James Smetham. 2 vols.
Letters. With an Introductory Memoir. Edited by SARAH SMETHAM and WILLIAM DAVIES. With a Portrait.
Literary Works. Edited by WILLIAM DAVIES.

The Works of Alfred, Lord Tennyson. Annotated by the Author. Edited by HALLAM, LORD TENNYSON. 9 vols.
Vol. I. **Poems.** | Vol. II. **Poems.**
Vol. III. **Enoch Arden: In Memoriam.**
Vol. IV. **The Princess: Maud.**
Vol. V. **Idylls of the King.**
Vol. VI. **Ballads and other Poems.**
Vol. VII. **Demeter and other Poems.**
Vol. VIII. **Queen Mary and Harold.**
Vol. IX. **Becket and other Plays.**

Selections from the Writings of Thoreau.

Essays in the History of Religious Thought in the West. By BROOKE FOSS WESTCOTT, D.D., D.C.L., Lord Bishop of Durham.

The Works of Wordsworth. Edited by Professor KNIGHT. In 10 vols. Each volume contains a Portrait and Vignette etched by H. MANESSE.
Poetical Works. 8 vols.
Journals of Dorothy Wordsworth. 2 vols.

MACMILLAN & CO., LTD., LONDON.

Printed for the Proprietors by SPOTTISWOODE & Co. LTD., 5 New-street Square, E.C., and Published by REGINALD WEBSTER PAGE, at the Office, 10 King Street, Covent Garden, in the Parish of St. Paul, in the County of London.—*Saturday, 7 August*, 1909.

TURGENEFF'S GERMAN LETTERS.

TO LUDWIG PIETSCH.

1876—1878.

71.

50 Rue de Douai, Paris,

Friday, 28 January '76.

Dear Pietsch,—I have had a fine big letter from you, and a fine big photograph as well. I ought to have answered it at once, but I am just a lazy dog. Now here is my letter. It was not Mme. Viardot, who has not left Paris, but her daughter, Mme. Louise Nérisse Viardot, travelling from Brussels to Paris, who was a sufferer from this terrible railway affair. She was nearly crushed to death by one of the coaches, but a tree saved her. Her face was very much swollen and discoloured when she arrived here a fortnight ago, and one of her arms was badly crushed—almost broken. She has now recovered, and in a week's time, we hope, will bear no trace of what she has been through. She is still at this address. The whole family are well. I have had an attack of gout, fortunately not a severe one, and now it has almost gone.

I have written a tiny little thing which will appear in a few days in the "Deutsche Rundschau." Be lenient when you read it. Perhaps what I am writing now will be longer, if not greater. It is giving me some pleasure. I shall certainly come to Berlin in April or May.

Barlamoff has painted a wonderful portrait of myself. It has been in the gallery downstairs since yesterday. I am heartily delighted that you are enjoying life so much and always going ahead. My kind regards to your family and our friends.

I remain, as ever, yours,

Iw. TURGENJEW.

P.S.—I have just had a letter in lapidary style from Menzel, who tells me of an historical cartoon of his, which I should perhaps like to buy, not for myself but as a present for a drawing school at Moscow. Could you, perhaps, with that crafty, subtle diplomacy with which nature has endowed you, get some sort of an estimate of the price?

72.

50 Rue de Douai, Paris,

Saturday, 25 November '76.

My dear Pietsch,—It is quite scandalous that I did not answer your kind letter of good wishes at once, but I will not try to justify my conduct. You may feel sure it was due neither to forgetfulness nor to indifference. No, you are as much to me as ever, and your letter gave me intense pleasure; but I am old and lazy and slow, and, besides, I had to put the finishing touches to my manuscript, which only went off to S. Petersburg yesterday, and time seems to melt away before me like butter—et voilà! But now I set to work on your letter solemnly and without delay.

1. If war breaks out (I still have my doubts about it) I can send you two letters, one to the Minister of War (Dr. Milatin), the other to Prince Cherkasky, who will be given the control of all the hospital and sanitary services. I know them both, and perhaps they will pay some attention to my introduction. 2. I shall pass through Berlin on my way to S. Petersburg in the middle of January, and possibly we can travel together. My novel will not come out till January, and the translation of it probably not before February. 3. Herr M. Lebhardt has arrived and Storm has sent me his story "Aquis submersus." Herr M. seems to be a good sort of North German, and the story is delicate and poetical, though a little painful here and there. 4. All the Viardots are very well. Paul made his first appearance at the Cirque National in Mendelssohn's concerto with the greatest éclat. Mme. V. is well and vigorous. 5. My gout is silent, my kidneys have something to say occasionally. My mood is greyish, with a dash of yellow. A thousand remembrances to your family, and my heartiest greetings to yourself.

Yours,

I. TURGENJEW.

73.

Paris, Thursday, 28-12-'76.

A Happy New Year, dear Pietsch!

Many thanks for your letter. I fear it will be a gloomy year for Russia. I shall certainly go to S. Petersburg at the beginning of February, and, if you can and will, we will travel together from Berlin. I send you the book you asked for under cover. It was not easy to find. Your enclosed cartoon (I mean the photograph) was not enclosed. But now I am counting on getting it. Everything is well and cheerful here. Kathi* has sent your charming and kindly notice of Paul to Mme. Viardot. You are the same true old friend as ever.

À propos of photographs, tell Julian Schmidt when you see him "que je ne me tiens pas quitte" of the photographs of Zola and Flaubert which I promised him. He shall certainly have them in any case.

I have written to Storm and thanked him most courteously for the very elegant copy of "Aquis submersus" which he sent me. The story is delicately and tenderly told, but, in Heaven's name, how could he possibly, amongst other things, make the boy sing about Paradise and the angels just before he was drowned? Any sort of ordinary child's ditty would produce ten times as great an effect. The Germans *always* make two mistakes in their stories—they love painful themes and they persist in their damnable habit of idealising the truth. Grasp the truth simply and poetically, and the ideal element follows of itself. No, the Germans can conquer the whole world, but they have forgotten how to tell a story, or, rather, they have never known how. When a German author is relating something pathetic to me he cannot help pointing with one hand to his own weeping eye and giving me, his reader, a discreet signal with the other, for fear I should not notice the object of his emotions.

In S. Petersburg they have 40 degrees of frost; here we have a thaw. What is it like in Berlin? Kindest regards to your family and all our friends. My best remembrances to yourself.

I am, as ever, yours,

Iw. TURGENJEW.

74.

Paris, Sunday, 4 February '77.

My dear Pietsch,—I have to begin all my letters with an apology, this one included. I ought to have thanked you long ago for the photograph of Menzel's cartoon, which has arrived safely at last. But it is only the expression of my gratitude which has been delayed; the feeling has been there for a long time past. I like the thing extremely. It is serious and true and the work of a master. I am glad my little half-fanciful, half-physio-

* Eckert the conductor's wife.—L. P.

logical story was to your taste. I am afraid my long novel* will strike you as wearisome on account of its never-ending division into feuilletons, but I say, like Galileo, " E pur si muove ". If the boy in Storm's story was capable of singing such a song, all the same he ought not to have done it. The author will have it so, and that old saying of Goethe's is as true as ever : " Man merkt die Absicht," etc. My good German writers, give up your trick of pointing, however beautiful your finger may be and however delicate may be its movements. All the V. family is well. We had a dance here yesterday which lasted till 6 A.M. Didie and Marianne were, of course, " les reines du bal," and we had some very pretty Russians here as well. I am very sorry to hear that you are not very well, and have had to take to bismuth. This enemy must be rooted out at once, or it will be end of all of us. Remember me to Julian Schmidt. I am sending him Zola's " L'Assommoir ". It is a disreputable book, the word " merde " occurs a dozen times " en toutes lettres ", but it is a work of great talent. It will be too much for the Germans. I read it with a mixture of disgust and admiration, but disgust prevailed in the end. However, it is " un signe des temps," as the French say, and is an enormous success. Remember me to your family and all our friends. My heartiest greetings to yourself.

Yours, I. TURGENJEW.

P.S.—I shall arrive in Berlin on the 15th March, si vivo. Mme. Viardot sends her kindest regards.

75.

50 Rue de Douai, Paris,

Monday, 12 March '77.

Good heavens! is it possible? What, have you, with your eternal youth, and your invulnerable, undamageable, indiarubber corpus managed to go and break your arm? And in your own room, too, by a mere casual stumble, and not by being hurled from a swaying silken ladder tied to a Spanish lady's balcony or from the back of a fiery untamed steed! Joking apart, my poor friend, I am heartily sorry for you. I am " non ignotus mali " myself—my own arm has been broken three times. It is very disagreeable, but in six weeks' time everything is all right again, and so I hope it will not be long before you are again enjoying all the privileges and powers of that divine Greek form of yours. The whole family here uttered a groan of dismay when I told them the melancholy news, and they send you their best " compliments de condolence ". Everyone here is very well, " sin novedad ", as they say in Spain.

I am sorry that you have to swallow my novel drop by drop : in the first place, that is a bad way of publication ; and in the second place, between ourselves, the translation is very middling indeed. The translator knows dead Russian that can be found in the dictionaries, but he has a very feeble notion of the living language, and when he comes to something which he cannot understand he skips it. The French translation, which appeared in the " Temps ", is excellent ; you, and Julian Schmidt as well, shall have a copy as soon as the book appears. You had better not read the thing till then.

In spite of everything, I am coming to Berlin after all in April (à propos, Mme. Viardot's first journey to Russia was in 1843). Frl. Gerster has been engaged at the Grand Opera here, so we shall have a chance of hearing the marvel. I have not yet forgotten Frl. Busse's splendid voice—one does not forget such a thing as that. Give her my kind regards, if she still remembers me, and tell her that her high A (was it an A? but never mind) in Fesca's song is still ringing in my ears. My best remembrances to our other friends and your family. Get well cito, citius, citis[illegible]. I shake your injured hand cautiously but none t[illegible] less heartily, and remain

o[illegible] old friend,

IW. TURGENJEW.

Les Frêne[illegible],

[illegible], 17 September '77.

My dear Friend,—F[illegible] for not having answered you at once. I [illegible] utterly miserable—you know why. That w[illegible] reason why I slipped through Berlin so secretl[illegible] already saw everything on ahead, should have h[illegible] give explanations, etc., and wanted to escape, ve[illegible] that time, from the presence of mankind. The beginning of your letter is very melancholy ; let us hope that your asthma is not so bad as all that, and that you will soon burst from your wrappings and be once again the embodiment of imperishable youth. Everything is well here. Marianne sends her very best thanks for your congratulations ; she and he are both at the cooing turtle-dove stage. The wedding is to be at the end of October, and the whole family will return to Paris about that time. The letter etc. at the Hôtel [illegible] Louvre have been entirely lost. Who knows whose hands they have fallen into? But don't worry about the 100 fr.

My kind regards to your family and our friends. When things are better [illegible] will write again.

Yours, I. TURGENJEW.

P.S.—Send me your bo[illegible]. I shall certainly read it, as I have read all your th[illegible] books. My " Recollections " do not exist in a separate form. I put a few short notes together under the title " My Recollections of Life and Literature ", by way of preface to the Russian edition of my selected works. I speak there of my relations with Bienski (our great critic), Pushkin, Gogol, etc., and, naturally, as little as possible of myself. Julius Eckhart made a few extracts in his last book. The portion that he did not take would be of little use to you. I shall be glad to give you *something small* to translate but as I shall certainly never write anything more, either great or small, I cannot make any promise.

77.

Les Frênes, Bougival,

8 October 1878.

My dear Friend,—I have been here for some weeks, as you suppose, and was unfortunately only able to stay a few hours in Berlin, as I wanted to be present at the third Russian concert. I found all the family well when I arrived here. I am sincerely sorry that you and yours are not so well. I have certainly had very remarkable experiences in Russia, which we can talk over comfortably when you come to Paris. (It occurs to me that this is hopelessly ungrammatical German, but it doesn't matter in the least.)

You have reproduced my " Dream " correctly ; but I am a little surprised that you thought it worth while to communicate a thing like that to the worthy public. But, my alarming friend, you overwhelm me with a deluge of compliments Now I shan't be able to open my mouth without thinking : " Look out, now you are going to work your spells." I never imagined my magic art was so powerful.

I should be delighted to authorise you to translate " Le Partage " into German, but the little thing has already been translated, and will appear shortly in the illustrated Westermann series. Till our next meeting in the near future, with hearty good wishes from yours,

I. TURGENJEW.

*** *Further instalments of the second part of Turgeneff's German letters will appear during August and September.*

* " Virgin Soil."

THE

SATURDAY REVIEW

OF

POLITICS, LITERATURE, SCIENCE, AND ART.

No. 2,8.. Vol. 108. 14 August 1909. [Registered as a Newspaper.] 6d.

CONTENTS.

We beg leave to sta.. that we decline to return or to enter into correspon..ten.. as to rejected communications; and to this rule .e c.. make no exception. Manuscripts not acknowledged wi..'n four weeks are rejected.

NOTES OF THE WEEK.

Where are the g..es of the Government now? Last week the oppositio.. to the Budget had collapsed; the Government were t.. sail triumphantly into port, bringing with them the precious Budget, whole and unamended. Conces..on? the very idea was scouted. Mr. Churchill at S..tburn could not contain himself. "The party manag..rs of the Conservative party are shaking their heads ..nd shaking in their shoes." What a different tale W..enesday told. Then we had Mr. Asquith standing u.. meekly and giving up position after position which ..Ir. Lloyd George and the party had fought for so valia..ly. The great land valuation is to be charged on ..ie State; the tax on ungotten minerals is to be ab..ndoned altogether. Think of all the wealth of argum..nt wasted on these precious proposals. And how ..nany weary hours! Really this irresponsible way of ..reating the business of the country is a bit too much. ..hat an efficient Ministry!

The Opposition h..e never lost heart in their attack on the Budget; no.. wavered. But their spirits will be higher than ..er now. Their most serious criticisms are more th..n justified. They have compelled the Government—wi.. their two hundred majority—to adopt the suggestio..s of the Opposition on two vital points. It is a ver.. great feat. Mr. Asquith is hurt at the slight recog..ition of the Government's generosity. They should ..ave made their concessions earlier in the day; not gr..dgingly and of necessity. The Government gave w..y because they could not help it; it was very evident t..at they had no intention of yielding an inch until th.. found that the Opposition was too strong for them. It is well that even in these days brute force of voting cannot wholly suppress superior argument.

Certainly the changes make the Budget less objectionable than it was. A duty on royalties is full of pitfalls, but it is not grotesquely ludicrous as was the proposed ungotten minerals tax—a tax which might have cost mineowners more than their entire revenue from their mines. And the waste of public money on the general valuation is not quite so bad as the flagrant injustice of throwing the burden of the cost on the private landowner. Whether the mass of taxpayers will enjoy paying a million and a half on this valuation and some half a million a year hereafter we doubt. The socialists want it as a basis for future operations. But those who are not socialists, but taxpayers, will, if we mistake not, repent of the whole business long before it is carried through. They will be sick when they realise that all this turmoil of land taxation results in nothing but a deficit. They will take but small consolation from the large revenue these taxes are to bring in—according to Mr. Asquith—one day.

Mr. Balfour put the net balance as to the undeveloped land tax very neatly. The tax would yield just about double what the Government had spent on entertainments—some £40,000 in all. This is what Sir Edward Grey calls providing for the defence of the Empire. This tax is even worse than the increment tax; for increment is, at any rate, in a sense realised gain, while the undeveloped land gain is problematic. A man might be required to pay the tax on land which could not be built on. Undoubtedly owners very often will have to pay on land which they cannot sell or develop if they would. Mr. Haldane should find some better argument than that land can have no building value until it can find a purchaser. Had the L.C.C. land by Aldwych and Kingsway, which was in the market unlet and unsold for years, no building value? It is surprising how badly Mr. Haldane has done as expositor of the Budget.

logical story was to your taste. I am afraid my long novel* will strike you as wearisome on account of its never-ending division into feuilletons, but I say, like Galileo, "E pur si muove". If the boy in Storm's story was capable of singing such a song, all the same he ought not to have done it. The author will have it so, and that old saying of Goethe's is as true as ever: "Man merkt die Absicht," etc. My good German writers, give up your trick of pointing, however beautiful your finger may be and however delicate may be its movements. All the V. family is well. We had a dance here yesterday which lasted till 6 A.M. Didie and Marianne were, of course, "les reines du bal," and we had some very pretty Russians here as well. I am very sorry to hear that you are not very well, and have had to take to bismuth. This enemy must be rooted out at once, or it will be end of all of us. Remember me to Julian Schmidt. I am sending him Zola's "L'Assommoir". It is a disreputable book, the word "merde" occurs a dozen times "en toutes lettres", but it is a work of great talent. It will be too much for the Germans. I read it with a mixture of disgust and admiration, but disgust prevailed in the end. However, it is "un signe des temps," as the French say, and is an enormous success. Remember me to your family and all our friends. My heartiest greetings to yourself.

Yours, I. TURGENJEW.

P.S.—I shall arrive in Berlin on the 15th March, si vivo. Mme. Viardot sends her kindest regards.

75.

50 Rue de Douai, Paris,

Monday, 12 March '77.

Good heavens! is it possible? What, have you, with your eternal youth, and your invulnerable, undamageable, indiarubber corpus managed to go and break your arm? And in your own room, too, by a mere casual stumble, and not by being hurled from a swaying silken ladder tied to a Spanish lady's balcony or from the back of a fiery untamed steed! Joking apart, my poor friend, I am heartily sorry for you. I am "non ignotus mali" myself—my own arm has been broken three times. It is very disagreeable, but in six weeks' time everything is all right again, and so I hope it will not be long before you are again enjoying all the privileges and powers of that divine Greek form of yours. The whole family here uttered a groan of dismay when I told them the melancholy news, and they send you their best "compliments de condolence". Everyone here is very well, "sin novedad", as they say in Spain.

I am sorry that you have to swallow my novel drop by drop: in the first place, that is a bad way of publication; and in the second place, between ourselves, the translation is very middling indeed. The translator knows dead Russian that can be found in the dictionaries, but he has a very feeble notion of the living language, and when he comes to something which he cannot understand he skips it. The French translation, which appeared in the "Temps", is excellent; you, and Julian Schmidt as well, shall have a copy as soon as the book appears. You had better not read the thing till then.

In spite of everything, I am coming to Berlin after all in April (à propos, Mme. Viardot's first journey to Russia was in 1843). Frl. Gerster has been engaged at the Grand Opera here, so we shall have a chance of hearing the marvel. I have not yet forgotten Frl. Busse's splendid voice—one does not forget such a thing as that. Give her my kind regards, if she still remembers me, and tell her that her high A (was it an A? but never mind) in Fesca's song is still ringing in my ears. My best remembrances to our other friends and your family. Get well cito, citius, citissime. I shake your injured hand cautiously but none the less heartily, and remain

Your old friend,

IW. TURGENJEW.

76.

Les Frênes, Bougival,

Monday, 17 September '77.

My dear Friend,—Forgive me for not having answered you at once. I am feeling utterly miserable—you know why. That was the reason why I slipped through Berlin so secretly. I already saw everything on ahead, should have had to give explanations, etc., and wanted to escape, even at that time, from the presence of mankind. The beginning of your letter is very melancholy; let us hope that your asthma is not so bad as all that, and that you will soon burst from your wrappings and be once again the embodiment of imperishable youth. Everything is well here. Marianne sends her very best thanks for your congratulations; she and he are both at the cooing turtle-dove stage. The wedding is to be at the end of October, and the whole family will return to Paris about that time. The letter etc. at the Hôtel du Louvre have been entirely lost. Who knows whose hands they have fallen into? But don't worry about the 100 fr.

My kind regards to your family and our friends. When things are better I will write again.

Yours, I. TURGENJEW.

P.S.—Send me your book. I shall certainly read it, as I have read all your other books. My "Recollections" do not exist in a separate form. I put a few short notes together under the title "My Recollections of Life and Literature", by way of preface to the Russian edition of my collected works. I speak there of my relations with Bielinski (our great critic), Pushkin, Gogol, etc., and, naturally, as little as possible of myself. Julius Eckhardt made a few extracts in his last book. The portions that he did not take would be of little use to you. I shall be glad to give you *something small* to translate, but as I shall certainly never write anything more, either great or small, I cannot make any promise.

77.

Les Frênes, Bougival,

8 October 1878.

My dear Friend,—I have been here for some weeks, as you suppose, and was unfortunately only able to stay a few hours in Berlin, as I wanted to be present at the third Russian concert. I found all the family well when I arrived here. I am sincerely sorry that you and yours are not so well. I have certainly had very remarkable experiences in Russia, which we can talk over comfortably when you come to Paris. (It occurs to me that this is hopelessly ungrammatical German, but it doesn't matter in the least.)

You have reproduced my "Dream" correctly; but I am a little surprised that you thought it worth while to communicate a thing like that to the worthy public. But, my alarming friend, you overwhelm me with a deluge of compliments. Now I shan't be able to open my mouth without thinking: "Look out, now you are going to work your spells." I never imagined my magic art was so powerful.

I should be delighted to authorise you to translate "Le Partage" into German, but the little thing has already been translated, and will appear shortly in the illustrated Westermann series. Till our next meeting in the near future, with hearty good wishes from yours,

I. TURGENJEW.

. *Further instalments of the second part of Turgeneff's German letters will appear during August and September.*

* "Virgin Soil."

THE

SATURDAY REVIEW

OF

POLITICS, LITERATURE, SCIENCE, AND ART.

No. 2,807 Vol. 108. 14 August 1909. [Registered as a Newspaper.] 6d.

CONTENTS.

NOTES OF THE WEEK.

Where are the gibes of the Government now? Last week the opposition to the Budget had collapsed; the Government were to sail triumphantly into port, bringing with them their precious Budget, whole and unamended. Concession? the very idea was scouted. Mr. Churchill at Saltburn could not contain himself. "The party managers of the Conservative party are shaking their heads and shaking in their shoes." What a different tale Wednesday told. Then we had Mr. Asquith standing up meekly and giving up position after position which Mr. Lloyd George and the party had fought for so valiantly. The great land valuation is to be charged on the State; the tax on ungotten minerals is to be abandoned altogether. Think of all the wealth of argument wasted on these precious proposals. And how many weary hours! Really this irresponsible way of treating the business of the country is a bit too much. What an efficient Ministry!

The Opposition have never lost heart in their attack on the Budget; nor wavered. But their spirits will be higher than ever now. Their most serious criticisms are more than justified. They have compelled the Government—with their two hundred majority—to adopt the suggestions of the Opposition on two vital points. It is a very great feat. Mr. Asquith is hurt at the slight recognition of the Government's generosity. They should have made their concessions earlier in the day; not grudgingly and of necessity. The Government gave way because they could not help it; it was very evident that they had no intention of yielding an inch until they found that the Opposition was too strong for them. It is well that even in these days brute force of voting cannot wholly suppress superior argument.

Certainly the changes make the Budget less objectionable than it was. A duty on royalties is full of pitfalls, but it is not grotesquely ludicrous as was the proposed ungotten minerals tax—a tax which might have cost mineowners more than their entire revenue from their mines. And the waste of public money on the general valuation is not quite so bad as the flagrant injustice of throwing the burden of the cost on the private landowner. Whether the mass of taxpayers will enjoy paying a million and a half on this valuation and some half a million a year hereafter we doubt. The socialists want it as a basis for future operations. But those who are not socialists, but taxpayers, will, if we mistake not, repent of the whole business long before it is carried through. They will be sick when they realise that all this turmoil of land taxation results in nothing but a deficit. They will take but small consolation from the large revenue these taxes are to bring in—according to Mr. Asquith—one day.

Mr. Balfour put the net balance as to the undeveloped land tax very neatly. The tax would yield just about double what the Government had spent on entertainments—some £40,000 in all. This is what Sir Edward Grey calls providing for the defence of the Empire. This tax is even worse than the increment tax; for increment is, at any rate, in a sense realised gain, while the undeveloped land gain is problematic. A man might be required to pay the tax on land which could not be built on. Undoubtedly owners very often will have to pay on land which they cannot sell or develop if they would. Mr. Haldane should find some better argument than that land can have no building value until it can find a purchaser. Had the L.C.C. land by Aldwych and Kingsway, which was in the market unlet and unsold for years, no building value? It is surprising how badly Mr. Haldane has done as expositor of the Budget.

Later on the Government got into a quite awful tangle over this tax. Mr. Asquith has solemnly proclaimed that existing contracts were to be sacrosanct. But the Bill says that the undeveloped-land tax is to be payable by the owner any contract notwithstanding. Bang goes the Prime Minister's sanctity of existing contract. But Mr. Lloyd George makes things much worse by airily advising the landlord, if his tenant will not develop the land according to the lease, to call on the tenant to send him a cheque for the undeveloped-land tax or go. The Chancellor of the Exchequer advises the landlord to go behind the Act and the Attorney-General says it is all right. So we have the Government throwing over existing contracts in the face of the Prime Minister's solemn disclaimer and advising the landlord to make the tenant pay a tax which their own Bill says only the landlord is to pay, no matter what contract may stand in the way.

Mr. Hobhouse was caught out very neatly indeed by Lord Helmsley. Mr. Hobhouse had explained that the custom of the Woods and Forests Commissioners on renewing a lease was not to renew on the old basis, but to charge the tenant the rent the land would bear at the time of renewal. The rent of the United Service Club, for instance, was raised from £600 a year to £2560, with a premium of £10,000. This is precisely the kind of arrangement the Duke of Westminster made in the Gorringe renewal; but unfortunately the Chancellor of the Exchequer had called this blackmail. Was that which, done by a private person, was blackmail not blackmail when done by a public department? Mr. Hobhouse had no answer. To mutter that the gain went to the community is irrelevant, unless public advantage is to be held to condone robbery.

Sir Edward Grey had something to say about the Gorringe matter, too. He would find no fault with the Duke, who did only what he could not help doing. This was giving away Mr. Lloyd George with a vengeance. We wonder will the Liberal Publication Department circulate this speech along with Mr. Lloyd George's at Limehouse. We could not honestly advise them to; for it is a very uninspiring speech. Sir Edward cannot have it both ways. He has a great reputation as the safe sober man, the man whom the solid middle-class householder can trust in. But he cannot at the same time be the fiery partisan. When he has to make a party speech Sir Edward Grey does not come off. His sallies are slow and the general effect unhappy. They should not put him to such work, for his strength lies in his acceptance as something rather above party. If he loses that cachet, he will drop seriously in party value.

Indeed, we are really rather sorry for Sir Edward Grey. When a man has acquired the reputation of intense respectability, and of careful accuracy and moderation in the use of words, it is hard that his even platitudes should turn out to be quite as nonsensical as the wild, whirling words of Messrs. Churchill and Lloyd George. The Times gives Sir Edward Grey four columns and a half in his character as the safe man, and yet this speech at Leeds is as foolish a performance as any. Take, for instance, this sentence, "I ask, if money is really wanted, as it is wanted for the purposes I have described" (the Navy and old-age pensions), "if any man in this room was the Chancellor of the Exchequer looking round for what was a fair and reasonable source from which to draw money required for the national needs, could he find a fairer and more reasonable source than this unearned increment which I have described?" Here we have great affectation of fairness in expression—about a tax which was originally estimated to yield £50,000, and which it is now certain will cost more than it brings in. Really we prefer the robustious passion of Messrs. George and Churchill to the "smooth comforts false" of Sir Edward Grey.

Lord Lansdowne spoke at Bowood on Saturday. He is not exactly the man to answer Mr. Lloyd George. It is rather like putting a dignified constable to catch a gamin with a catapult. Of course, if the truncheon should fall on the hooligan's head, he is knocked down; but he is more likely to dodge and get in a shot with his catapult. Naturally Lord Lansdowne was not going to say anything about the intention of the Lords as to the Budget. Time enough for that when the Bill reaches his Chamber. The "swooping robber bird" was the one touch of colour relieving both Lord Lansdowne's speech and Sir Edward Grey's.

Really the country will soon have to come to the rescue of the House. "The debauch of late sittings" is telling seriously. Mr. Asquith says he can do nothing to help. The House once, he said, sat at eight in the morning; but this was not, apparently, by way of suggested reform. Can we not get someone to march a company of soldiers—perhaps Mr. Haldane's Territorials even would do—into the House every night at eleven and clear the room? If there were an absolutely fixed period the night end, things would soon accommodate themselves at the other.

Under a Radical Ministry the departments do strange things. We all know of the antics of the Board of Education since 1906—antics that seem doomed to bring the board up sharp against the courts, though it will still kick against the pricks. Now the Board of Agriculture is making itself ridiculous—unfortunately more than ridiculous, very mischievous. Everyone who has any feeling for architecture and historic association knows of Bramshill house and park, and grieved with Sir Anthony Cope over the ruin done by fire not long since to his glorious place. Thus the story Mr. C. T. O'Donnell told in yesterday's Times has quite a public interest. Sir Anthony, it appears, faced the situation pluckily, and decided to turn his ruined woodland—some two thousand acres—to agricultural use, tillage and then pasturage. This, of course, required some capital outlay, and the General Land Drainage and Improvement Company were quite ready to make an advance of £2,000. But the Board of Agriculture, unluckily having a locus standi under certain Acts, here came in, and vetoed the loan. Really one would have thought the turning of park-land into tillage was quite a democratic ideal and would have appealed to that popular champion, Lord Carrington. Why should a good landowner—in view of the character of his place, almost a trustee for the nation—be thus hampered and injured by the sheer cussedness of a Government Department?

A tenant of Mr. Pierce Mahoney's, in Kerry, has been six years without paying rent, and all the time in a position to pay. There was a dispute as to the terms of tenancy, submitted to the arbitration of the local priests, and the tenant repudiated the arbitration after having accepted it. Mr. Mahoney proceeded to evict. The County Council proceeded to object. At the eviction the police had to attend against breaches of the peace, and for this they were assaulted. The crime was proved, and the criminals identified, but the two local magistrates found them not guilty. Such magistrates, put on the Bench by the League and the clergy, are now all over Ireland.

From the report of the proceedings of the Committee of Privileges sitting on the alleged interference of the Duke of Norfolk in the High Peak election, this "offence" is about the obscurest to be found in the books. Indeed, it hardly is to be found there. Peers have frequently interfered with elections, but there is no record of proceedings against them. The Duke says he did not authorise the publication of the letter. Then the subtle point arises whether the mere writing is a breach of privilege. The Attorney-General thinks an action at common law would not lie against the Duke. It is a comical idea—an action by the House of Commons for damages. Would the damages go to the Government? The Government may be thinking of this as a new source of revenue from the peerage. Or perhaps they would go to the Kitchen Committee. Unless the Government has some such object as this in view, what purpose is to be gained by spending time and money and the energy and abilities of the Prime Minister, not to mention Mr. Swift MacNeill, on such solemn frivolities as this?

By issuing a communiqué to the Press, and by announcing that Lord Kitchener is to be made a Field-Marshal, the Government has attempted to invest the Mediterranean sinecure with increased importance, and by this means to draw a trail across the adverse comments which have been made on the extravagant folly. It is also said that in time Lord Kitchener is to be made Inspector of all our oversea forces. This, at any rate, solves the difficulty of finding employment for the retiring Indian Commander-in-Chief. He is also to have a seat on the Imperial Defence Committee. Thus, whilst appointing him to a very dignified position, the Government have the satisfaction of knowing that he must spend much of his time in the Mediterranean. So they will not be worried by having him too near: a soldier of his independent turn of mind is not persona grata within the purlieus of Downing Street and Whitehall.

It turns out now that exporters of goods to the United States will have the benefit of a reduction in tariffs that are prohibitive—provided that the reduction leaves them still prohibitive. To make up for concessions of this kind, over £160,000,000 worth of the goods now imported into the States will have the tariff raised on them. Thus the revision upward is on the goods that are imported, and the revision downward is on the goods that are not imported. Neither the manufacturer nor the Treasury can lose by conceding a fraction of nothing, and it will please the foreign exporters to know that such extensive concessions have been made in their favour. The whole of nothing has been made as large as possible, so that its fraction conceded should be large in proportion.

China and Japan have settled their dispute about the Antung line. Japan is to make the railway, so that the risk of a collision between the Chinese and Japanese soldiers, which just possibly might have led to war, is now removed. If there was anything more than the usual Chinese perversity in their resistance to the making of the line under the agreement of 1905, it may be accounted for by Japan having laid the original narrow-gauge line during the war without buying the land. As it is now agreed that the broad gauge is to be laid down, probably Japan has made arrangements for paying the owners both for the land originally taken and for the additional land required. If this has been the real difficulty, China was justified in holding out until it was settled.

Turkey managed her protest to Greece about the Cretan unrest very unskilfully. But the Young Turk Government is very nervous about losing the Cretan suzerainty as it lost the Bulgarian. Greece is as intriguing and malicious as Turkey assumes her to be; and the Turks got a fright when the Cretans planted the Greek flag where it had not flown before the troops of the four Powers were withdrawn. No doubt, too, the Turkish Government did a popular thing by having it out directly with the Greek Government. This was extremely risky, as the defiance by the Greek Government of the Turk would have been equally popular with the Cretans and their friends; and war might have been started before the Powers could stop it.

Fortunately the Greek Government, instead of doing the wrong thing, as Turkey did, and going on with the wrangle, appealed to the four Powers to manage the matter between it and Turkey. These Powers have declared that they intend to maintain the previous and present status of Turkey and Crete; and their first step has been successful. The Cretan Executive Committee were told that the Greek flag must be taken down from its unaccustomed position. This has been done, though there is a good deal of excitement about it in the island. Action of this kind, equally prompt if it again becomes necessary, will help the two Governments to resist being dragged into war either by Turks or by Cretans who want to be Greeks.

Now that the Spanish Government has completely put down the disorders, all the anti-Government parties are pretending that they had nothing to do with them. Everything from beginning to end was done by anarchists and socialists, and the Republicans were as much taken by surprise as anybody. This is not the general opinion in Spain. It is believed that there was a Republican conspiracy, badly planned, that broke down, whereupon the anarchists got their chance and used it mercilessly; but the way had been prepared for them by the gentry who are now talking of the constitutional movement. As the parties who have factiously opposed the war will keep quiet for some time there is a prospect of more decisive measures against the Riffs. The Spaniards have so far only been able to repel the attacks on their towns and fortresses and to keep open their supplies; but it is reported that the Government has ordered General Marina to begin an advance movement which it is now in a position to support.

After nearly a fortnight of effort to bring a general strike to a head, the Swedish Federation of Trade Unions seems to be beaten. The Swedish attempt has come as near if not nearer than any of the many previous efforts that have been made to paralyse general industry for the purpose of gaining the victory in some particular labour dispute. We have lately been on the edge of such a strike in the miners' troubles; but in future cases it is probable the threat of general strikes may not loom so terribly as it has hitherto done. The French attempt failed, the Spanish attempt also, and now the Swedish. What is proved is that it is easy to threaten, but almost impossible to get all the trades to carry out orders. In Sweden the strike began with a dispute over wages in the cotton, woollen, and paper industries. The most important classes that struck in sympathy with the men against the lock-out were the printing trades. The most important that refrained were the railway men. It was shown that society can get on moderately well without newspapers; though in Sweden the strain was mercifully lessened by the Socialist papers being allowed.

But the lukewarmness of the railway men prevented the maximum inconvenience being inflicted, and to do this is the essential principle of the general strike. This is not the greatest inconvenience that might be inflicted; but even general strikers cannot use what would be the most powerful instrument. The Swedish unions had to exempt the men engaged on waterworks, in the hospitals, and in the burial of the dead. In the Middle Ages, when the Interdict was the most analogous case to the general strike, the Church did not shrink from suspending some of these functions such as the burial of the dead. Even it, however, might have hesitated at the cutting off of all water supplies. And so also a limit to the terrors of a general strike remains in human nature, and they will probably never be successful.

It is a good idea to make better provision for the social wants of Indian students in this country. The new Indian Bureau of the India Office ought to be useful socially, educationally, and politically. Mr. Edward Dicey, in the "Nineteenth Century" this month, shows how very unfortunate the position of young Indians is in this country. The conditions throw them into the hands of agitators, and they are more likely to return with stronger anti-English feelings than they had when they came. One thing he does not mention. This is that by a change of examination at the Inns of Court a knowledge of English is required, which few Indian students possess. The Indian Bureau purposes to find lodgings in English families for students. This is exactly what many of them wish, but cannot manage for themselves. Young and inexperienced as they are, and in a strange country, they get into scrapes social and political. Both from sympathy and on public grounds we hope the Bureau may be successful. The murder of another official in India is announced; the motives are doubtful.

There is another class of law students who come from South Africa. Ample provision for teaching Roman-Dutch law, the law of South Africa, is made at the Inns of Court. To practise at the Cape Bar a law degree of the Cape University or being called as an English barrister is the present qualification. It makes one rather suspect the much-talked-of union of hearts to find that it is proposed to make a law degree at Leyden a sufficient qualification for the Cape Bar. The Transvaal Legislative Council also have a Bill to make a European law degree a qualification for the Transvaal Bar. This hankering after Dutch and German degrees, and ignoring the Universities in England and Ireland which make provision for teaching Roman-Dutch law, does not show any very ardent desire to cultivate the British connexion. The reason probably is that the Dutch dislike the influence English law has had on the Roman-Dutch law, and want to keep it for the future as free from this influence as they possibly can; and so they do not wish students to come to England.

Following closely on the report of the Imperial Cancer Research Fund deploring the falling-off in subscriptions from the public is an announcement of a great endowment for the treatment of cancer. This is the sum of £250,000, which the trustees of Mr. Harry Barnato have decided under the powers of his will to give to the Middlesex Hospital. At first sight there is some feeling of disappointment that these magnificent new resources for investigating cancer should not have been placed at the disposal of the Cancer Research Fund. Whatever treatment is at the command of present practice, whatever care cancer patients require, can be provided with our present means. What we lack is a sound theory and a scientific therapeutic founded on such a theory. Unfortunately we have neither, and our hope for it depends greatly on the researches of the Fund's savants. However, it appears provision is to be made under the Barnato bequest for research laboratories in connexion with the hospital work. The investigators will have the advantage, as all investigators now have, of working guided by the Fund's researches, and the connexion will be specially close as Sir Henry Morris, the secretary of the Fund, is consulting surgeon at the Middlesex Hospital.

In effect, the Whiskey Commission declares that there is no essential difference between the various kinds of whiskey, pot-still and patent-still, made from British barley and made from Indian corn. Now we understand Professor Hartley to declare that there is an essential difference, chemically, determinable, between pot-still and patent-still whiskeys. If that be so, the Commissioners have simply made a hash of the business. Professor Hartley lives in Dublin, has investigated in the chemistry of alcohol, and is one of Ireland's few men of science whose reputation extends farther than the Liffey. Has his assistance been asked?

Day after day Hyde Park is strewn with repellent bodies, the more objectionable because not dead. They are so thick on the grass that one is forced to go near them, and the sight leaves the mind sick for several hours. They infest the most beautiful spots, as if for the enjoyment of the pain they inflict. They are not the poor. Their most evident marks are liquid gluttony and vicious exhaustion. Was this the intention of Hyde Park, to make it unfit for decent people? If nothing better can be done, why not let them have a corner to themselves? It is an outrage on our children of all classes to let them see the kind of women that lie on the grass all day.

"It was a really magnificent spectacle", says the Times. What was this magnificent spectacle? The fleet at Southend or Spithead? Mr. Shackleton's fight with the elements? No; the "magnificent spectacle" was Mr. Ransford fielding in the test match.

THE VANISHING TAXES.

If the management of the national finance were not a very serious thing, involving the credit of Great Britain on the bourses of the world, one would shout with laughter at the position of the Government. Carlyle gives us a picture of a knight who, slashed and galloonєd and padded out in all the bravery of Elizabethan costume, caught his hose and doublet on a nail, and from out the rent there dribbled rapidly the sawdust, leaving a shrivelled, meagre mannikin. Those doughty knights, Messrs. Churchill and Lloyd George, have been prancing around on platforms telling an admiring proletariat how they were going at last to humble the pride of dukes, how the rapacious landlords were to be made to disgorge their spoils, and how with those spoils cupboards were to be filled, hearths brightened, and the country's pensioners conducted through waving cornfields (ravished from the dukes) to happy graves. The Prime Minister, who still retains his sanity, has found himself obliged to thrust quite a long nail into the puffing and stuffing of these swaggering Pistols, who are thereby suddenly reduced to very shrunken mannikins. For where are the spoils of the landlords? Where are the coppers for the poor old men of Limehouse? So far from the landlords being made to bleed, it appears that the general body of taxpayers are to bleed by paying £6 to get 10s. Taking the Prime Minister's figures, as given to the House of Commons on Wednesday, the estimated yield from the land taxes for the current year (or rather for the six months that remain of it) is £325,000, and the estimated cost of valuation, to be paid by the public, is £300,000. Of this yield one moiety is to be distributed amongst the local authorities; and we cannot agree with Mr. Asquith that this deduction should not be made on the ground that the taxpayer has nothing to do with the destination of a tax after it has once reached the Exchequer. The taxpayers have everything to do with the application of their taxes. It may or may not be necessary or expedient to give fresh grants in aid of local rates; we have not been told so: we have been told that a deficit of £16,000,000 has arisen by reason of old-age pensions and Dreadnoughts, and we (the opponents of the Budget) have been taunted with our unwillingness to pay for these national objects. The relief of local rates is perfectly irrelevant to the discussion, and we are entitled to deduct from the estimated yield of £325,000 from land taxes one-half, or £162,000. But in this £325,000 was included the duty on ungotten minerals, which is now dropped, and which Mr. Haldane told us stood for half the total, so that the net proceeds coming to the Treasury will be £81,000. We refuse to add the yield from the new 5 per cent. tax on mining royalties, for that is merely another form of income tax levied not on land but rent, and has nothing to do with the valuation. But only a fourth or a third of the above net estimated proceeds can reach the Exchequer this year, because all the land taxes are levied on site value, and the site values cannot be completely arrived at, again quoting the Prime Minister, for "three or four years". Until the site value on a property has been agreed by the owner and the Government valuer, or by the referee, or by a court of law, the owner, still quoting Mr. Asquith, will not be called upon to pay the duty—obviously he cannot be. Therefore the estimated net yield for the current year must be divided by three or four, if by three it comes to £27,000, if by four it comes to £20,000. So that the taxpayers are to be called on to pay £300,000 to get £27,000 or £20,000, leaving an actual deficit of £273,000 or £280,000. It must, we think, be allowed by the most ardent Radical that half a sovereign is dear at six sovereigns.

The above we believe to be an actual, accurate statement of the cost and yield of the increment duty, the undeveloped land duty, and the reversion duty, basing the calculation on the Prime Minister's figures and confining our purview to the current year. We decline altogether to be led into the realms of financial speculation, which are well enough on the Stock Exchange, but are grievously out of place in the Budget. The Finance Bill is an instrument for providing for the needs of the year that is passing over us. It may be that four or five years hence these land taxes may yield a net revenue of

£80,000, though at a cost of collection estimated between £300,000 and £400,000 there will still be a balance of £200,000 or so on the wrong side. But how absolutely justified has the conduct of the Opposition in the House of Commons and of the Unionists out of doors and in the press been by the amendments which were laid on the table by the head of the Government! We opposed these land taxes because they were unworkable, unjust and unremunerative. We denounced as oppressive the proposal to make the owners pay for the valuation on which they were to be taxed. Well, now it is admitted that the taxes will bring in next to nothing, and that the public must pay for the valuation. We have described these land taxes as vindictive taxation levied on a class politically opposed to the Government. What are the marks of punitive class taxation? That a class of the community should be vexed and alarmed, and that no money should be gained thereby. That is exactly what happens in this case. The owners of land are to be hunted for the sport of the public, or that section of the public which believes in Mr. Lloyd George. Thanks to the Unionist party, the public is to be made to pay for its sport.

Does the Prime Minister not now regret that he handed over the Exchequer to a provincial attorney, nursed in the crude socialism of the "Keltic fringe"? It was so obvious, and it would have been so easy, to make Mr. Haldane Chancellor of the Exchequer! As it is, Mr. Haldane is requisitioned whenever the metaphysical niceties of site value surpass the capacity of Mr. Lloyd George. And the question of the site value of undeveloped lands bristles with metaphysical subtleties, in which the Secretary for War, steeped in German philosophy, seems to revel. We confess that these distinctions and definitions, in which Mr. Haldane lovingly envelops his pure abstraction, fairly puzzles us. What is the site value of undeveloped land? Mr. Haldane has told us repeatedly, with some irritation at the stupidity of the ordinary man, that it means present, not potential, value, though not realised value, a price, that is, which is in the land, though it has not been obtained for the land. And what is undeveloped land? Agricultural land is said to be excluded, and land which is worth less than £50 an acre, and building land on which the owner has expended £100 an acre during the last ten years. These are large exceptions, and must materially reduce the estimated yield from the tax which we gave above. But how is agricultural land to be excluded? Land which is waiting for the builder is usually let out for grazing; when does such land cease to be agricultural and become building land? Mr. Haldane says "When it is wanted for building". But how is that want expressed except by an offer from a builder? Few landlords refuse such offers nowadays; so that it looks as if the undeveloped land duty would fall, not on the original owner, but on the building owner, in the interval between his buying and building on the land. The squire is not to be taxed until his land is "wanted", until an offer has been made for it. He accepts the offer, and, hey presto! the undeveloped land duty is straightway transferred to the builder who buys. It certainly would be a strange issue of Radical-Socialist finance if the murderous blow aimed at the old county families were to fall on the head of that dapper middle-class Prudhomme, the speculative builder. Yet such, we maintain, will be the undoubted effect of the duty on undeveloped land. When this is realised the Budget will become still less popular in those provincial circles which are at present so devoted to the chapel and Mr. Lloyd George. Let Lord Lansdowne consider the point, and he may arrive at the same conclusion as we have done—namely that, so far as the undeveloped land tax goes, it is not the squirearchy but the building trade that requires protection at the hands of the House of Lords.

CHINA AND JAPAN.

TOO much fuss has been made about China and Japan. It was assumed that, because certain matters were in dispute upon which one refused to yield and the other to arbitrate, there was risk of the quarrel being pushed to the verge if not the actuality of war. There might have been such risk in the case of European Powers. There was grave risk when British and Russian sentries were drawn up facing—almost touching—each other along a disputed frontage during the Boxer troubles, at Tientsin. There was perhaps the risk that a gun might go off, if it had come to Japanese guards pushing Chinese guards away from the Antung-Mukden railway this week; the Japanese are an excitable people, and might have jumped then to the conclusion that the national honour required vindication on an unnecessary scale, though it is almost inconceivable that even "Young China" should think itself able to resist by force of arms any action the Japanese might take. But the attitude of both was, as a matter of fact, normal. Japan observes agreements, though she may, upon occasion, strain somewhat severely the interpretation of a doubt: whereas of China it is true to-day, as a well-known writer said ten years ago: "We think when we have induced the Chinese Government to sign an agreement, that it is all over; but as a matter of fact it is only beginning: instead of irritating us by refusing a request abruptly, they have granted it in form without any intention of doing so in substance—farther than they are obliged. We stand aghast by-and-by at the discovery, and insist; and the mandarins put us off, and put us off again—as long as they dare". There is a very general feeling that the Japanese have pushed their interpretation of the 1905 treaty quite far enough in the case of Fakumen; while it will appear probably, to most people, that the construction of tunnels and adaptation of gauge are essential to the "improvement" of the Antung railway for which the same agreement provides. And so the mandarins have apparently recognised—assuming, that is, that there was ever any conviction in their resistance. Having resisted, characteristically, as long as they dared, they give way, veiling retreat behind reservations having no meaning other than "to save face". The Wai-wu-pu is, we know, ignorant enough; but if it did not know that in stipulating for identity of gauge with the Imperial Chinese railway, and for a survey of route by a joint commission, it was forcing an open door, one must be prepared to assume—well, that the mandarin mind is built upside down; for a joint commission has surveyed and reported, and the gauge of the two railways is the same. It would be easier to believe, even, that the solution was prearranged. It is no revelation to men who know China to read that the power of the Central Government over the provinces is weak: the article (in the "Fortnightly") from which we have already quoted satirised the futility with which we set ourselves, at the beginning of our treaty intercourse, to reform that condition of affairs. "We had chosen to assume the existence of an Imperial Authority supreme and centralised in all respects; whereas we were in presence, really, of a congeries of satrapies bound, each, to contribute its quota to the imperial exchequer and to obey imperial decrees, but possessing, each, a large degree of financial and administrative independence. We ignored these relations, and set ourselves to strengthen the Central Power: we were going to centralise the finances as well as the forces, and to use a Government which it was presumed would be grateful and docile, to impose reform on the Provinces from above. China being in case, things turned out, of course, exactly the reverse. . . ." So there is nothing new in the self-assertion of the Provinces; though it may perhaps be true that, in proportion as we have been urging the Central Government to impose more novel conditions, resistance has become more manifest. Neither is there anything new in the prevarication and procrastination of officials. It is a consequence of the peculiar conditions of balance under which the Chinese administration is carried on that the occupants of high office dread responsibility: the Peking correspondent of the "Times" has recently told us how abnormally weak is the personnel of the Wai-wu-pu. Where action is certain to be attacked, men less than strong—men, especially, bred in the atmosphere of Chinese officialdom—seek refuge in inaction; and the Japanese are not alone in complaining that, since Yuan Shih-kai left, there is no one at Peking to negotiate with. It is just conceivable, then, that such men as are left chose to have their hands forced, having provided a (Chinese) way of retreat.

But the Antung-Mukden railway is not the only question in dispute between the two Powers, nor are the others perhaps so easy of solution; though solution would be facilitated if both could be brought to see that the fault is not always on one side. If it be true, for instance, that the Japanese began the trouble by annexing instead of purchasing the land required for the Antung line, it is to be hoped that they will now rectify the wrong as an incident in present rearrangements. And so with respect to Chientao, and the difficulties about Yalu timber, and the questions of railway guards, and Fakumen. It would be matter for congratulation if the negotiations that are understood to have been reopened should result in a general settlement on the basis of give and take. Character and temperament will remain factors in any controversy between nations so different in temperament and character as the Chinese and Japanese; but attitude may be modified, facts taken into account; and above all the principle might be recognised that it is in the interests of both to pull together along the road of progress instead of wasting time and energy in disputes which give opportunity for intrigue and hinder the drastic reforms which alone can enable China to assume the position she desires. The sovereign rights about which she is so fond of talking must be based on the power to uphold them; and that power can only be attained by administrative and financial reforms of which there is no sign. Instead of projecting representative institutions for which her people are neither fit by nature nor prepared, or a navy for which she neither can nor is likely for many decades to be able to pay, let her make a beginning at reforming her finances and placing at the head of affairs a vigorous and clean-handed statesman, if such can be found. It is characteristic that she who has undertaken to abolish lekin should exact it to the detriment of the Shanghai-Nanking railway and find it a grievance that Japan refuses to collect it on the South Manchurian line, just as there is something characteristically puerile in the argument that Japan derives an unfair competitive advantage from action which she has only to imitate. It is characteristic that Japan should seek to make the most of the position she has gained at the cost of a war but for which China would have no word to say in respect of railways or gauge or lekin or any other matter in Manchuria at all. Still, it is not impossible that, if China were less ingrate, Japan might be more complaisant. But so long as exaction on one side is opposed by stolidity on the other, there can seemingly be no other solution than an assertion by might that it is right. It would be infinitely regrettable that this state of things should continue.

It is an old trick of China to play off one Power against another, but it is a game that, as her own annals show, may be played too often. The national vanity is of a quality that no rebuff, disaster, defeat, nor any other form of demonstration can, seemingly, shake. The misfortune is that corruption and inefficiency seem equally ingrained. Our postulate was questioned in some quarters when we characterised Yuan's dismissal as indicative of Manchu reaction, though it was admitted that his withdrawal was a loss; but it will hardly be questioned to-day that things have gone since from bad to worse. Progress of a kind there is; and people see in it more or less hope for the future, according to their temperaments and estimates of need. But it is still true, as Dr. Morrison remarked eight months ago, that "China has no budget, no rational financial system, no uniform currency", that the administration of justice is still unreformed and corruption as prevalent as ever. It may be added that debased coins have been multiplied, and that an unsecured paper currency has been issued with a freedom that has called forth earnest remonstrance at Peking. These defects are recorded against China with impatience it may be, but with a wish on the part of her critics that she would try to set her house in order for her own sake as well as ours. For a balance of power is desirable in the East as well as in the West. Opposite conditions make for unrest, as weakness makes for intrigue; and they are no true friends of China who flatter her with assurances of equality where there is no equality and of sympathy which is undeserved. The Regent was well spoken of, and people were willing to believe well of him when he assumed power. They are willing to believe that if the promise has not been fulfilled it is because his position is difficult, and that he lacks personality or prestige to direct the course of events. He would inspire better hope for the future if he would begin by placing at the head of affairs a statesman typical of the vaunted modern school in place of the elderly prince who typifies all that is worst of the traditions of the Tsung-li-Yamen and the vanity and incapacity of the old régime.

A BILL TO MAKE CRIMINALS.

THE Irish Land Bill began by charging the Irish peasants for £14,000,000 worth of organised crime, dear at the money. The capitalised estimate is by Mr. Hobhouse, an able member of the Government, and it is the difference made by raising the tenants' annual payments for interest and principal from £3 5s. to £3 10s. per cent. on the purchase-money. The £3 5s. was enough at the time of the Wyndham Act, when there was a Government to deal with crime; but since then we have had "government in accordance with Irish ideas", crime going up, security going down, and now the unfortunate peasant has to pay for his leaders' policy of "making government impossible". Crime does not attract investors, and the peasant can no longer buy his farm short of £3 10s. per cent.

Instead of charging the peasants, who are innocent of the "national policy", the £14,000,000 ought to be charged to the Irish parliamentary party, who alone profited by the crime; but then the bailiff would return "No effects", and Mr. Birrell would not like to place his valued allies in such an awkward position. Did they not "give Birrell a chance" and consent to stop crime for a time to make him look like a successful statesman? Men of expert ability cannot without a consideration be expected to suspend the practice of their profession and endanger their emoluments.

Irish "public opinion" being a private machine, worked by the professional criminals for their own profits, the peasants are kept in complete ignorance about the £14,000,000. There is no telling how it would endanger "the cause" if it came out that the people were paying for the crime organised by their leaders in the name of statesmanship, and penalised by their friend Mr. Birrell by £14,000,000 on the peasants' annuities. The Irish are the only people with a "national cause" that exists only on their own ignorance of it.

The increase of the terms against the tenant is not in the direction of "stimulating" land purchase, and the next provision approved by Committee is still more discouraging. There is £52,000,000 worth of land sold without money to pay for it, and the sellers are asked to accept £93 or £94 for every £100 that the tenants have agreed to pay with the approval of the judicial authority in Dublin. Even at £93-4 these victims of Mr. Birrell and his criminal allies must accept paper, without a cash basis, so that any increase in it on the market due to "stimulated" sales must go to make a further loss below £93 for the man who holds the paper. On the other hand, should the market price of the paper by any chance rise above par the Exchequer is held free to work in cash instead, and to save the premium against the investing public. It is paper as long as the public may lose by buying it, and it ceases to be paper as soon as the Treasury may lose by selling it. Even now £8 worth of "excess stock" must be issued at the expense of the taxpayer with every £100 worth of this paper to make it worth £100; but it is still not worth that, as it leaves a loss of £6 to £7 per cent. on the landlord, since the market price of the present stock, on a cash basis, is under £86. The Bill assumes it to be worth £92 when it is selling for 85½, and then, out of taxation, adds the £8, the difference between £92 and £100. Can the landlords afford to lose 6 to 7 per cent. on their settled bargains? If not, let them "wait for cash", that is, remain as they are, with their land sold and no payment for perhaps twelve years. Besides, a later provision in the Bill actually reduces the total cash available for purchase by one-fifth, since the million a year for congestion must come out of the present five millions a year for ordinary purchase. There is not an additional cent in cash at any point. It is hard to think that Mr. Birrell can be in earnest, but he appears to have got some hold on the Irish members. Few of them are capable of understanding the matter, and the fewer they are the easier to get them "squared". The ordinary Irish member trots from lobby to lobby under orders without the smallest notion how or why he is to vote. The few at the top know how and why, but the Government appear to be in touch with those.

The "sliding scale" for bonus now stands part of the Bill, graduated to rise as the years' purchase falls. A man selling his estate for twenty-five times the rent or more gets nothing. Selling at twenty-four times the rent he gets 3 per cent., and then up it slides until he gets 16 per cent. at seventeen years' purchase. The Bill assumes that no land can be sold either over twenty-four years' purchase or under seventeen years' purchase; yet the success claimed for the Congested Districts Board is based on thirteen years' purchase, that being the price paid for the great Dillon property in Mayo. It is known now that there has been no success, even with thirteen years' purchase, a price so low that Mr. Birrell excludes it from the calculation on which his Bill is based. With all the experienced ability of the people's leaders, neither the quantity nor the quality of their organised crime has been enough to prevent a rise in the landlord's price, which, in spite of everything, has risen in recent years at least at the rate of one year's purchase every year. Yet the £14,000,000 worth of organised crime was to drive down the landlord's price, and so the national policy of "making government impossible" is a failure even on its own ground, with its cost completely uncompensated to those who must now bear it. It is a pity that these Irish facts cannot be made known to the Irish people; but the organisation of crime is a profitable pursuit for the organisers, and they keep the unfortunate peasants in complete ignorance of the game that goes on between themselves and the Government. The local papers dare print nothing but what "the mimbers" like, and "the mimbers" do not like the people to know that they are paying for crime which fails to prevent the landlord's price from rising. If the people got to know this, they might stop the crime, "the cause" might burst, and the brilliant statesmen might have to go ploughing—if they could.

The Government admit, through Mr. Hobhouse, that they are going to save three millions by the "sliding" arrangement, as compared with Mr. Wyndham's level twelve all round; but this saving means so much less inducement for the landlord to sell, unless at prices increased to get the three millions out of the tenants, who are kept ignorant of this also. That is not the worst. The highest bonus is to go where the organised crime has been most successful. Where crime keeps the years' purchase at the lowest point, Mr. Birrell increases his bonus to 16 per cent., that is, 4 per cent. more than Mr. Wyndham's, and here the tenant may become the owner of his farm; but where peace permits the highest years' purchase there is no bonus at all, and the tenant remains as he is, though he is the tenant who really deserves to be helped. In short, Mr. Birrell fines the tenant who keeps the law, and with the fine rewards the tenant who breaks it. The man who is not enough of a criminal to make Mr. Birrell's Bill a "popular success" remains out in the cold, doing penance for his peaceful character; but the criminal is encouraged by a statutory premium at the expense of the taxpayers of the United Kingdom, since the whole of the bonus, sliding or fixed, comes out of taxation apart from the price of the land.

All that is bad enough, but Part III. of the Bill, still to go through Committee, is much worse, especially the clause which proposes compulsion, with nine county council hooligans to work it in the name of "Democracy", where "public opinion" is a private machine and nothing really democratic is possible. There is no provision to capitalise and work a test colony of the congests in a prairie, which ought to have been done from the start, instead of distributing money among parish favourites; yet the Congested Districts Board, of which Mr. Birrell is the head, have a colony scheme approved but in hiding, and the Government dare not produce it. Sir Horace Plunkett also has a colony scheme, and the Government have never asked him to produce it for the benefit of the Bill. Is this because of Mr. Dillon's recent confession that the League would not permit the congests to leave congestion? Then, if the statutory reward for crime be so obvious outside the compulsory areas, it must be still more obvious inside, with the very hooligans who organise the crime holding seats on the Board to work the compulsory provisions. The Bill cannot advance land purchase. What it can advance is crime, the thing most ruinous to Ireland but most necessary to those whom she sends to Parliament, and who have really no footing in public life unless on a basis of law-breaking.

WHISKEY.

WHISKEY remains the same as it was before, "a spirit obtained by distillation from a mash of cereal grains", with the difference that "Scotch whiskey is whiskey, as above defined, distilled in Scotland", and that "Irish whiskey is whiskey, as above defined, distilled in Ireland". Thus whiskey is a thing which is two different things in two different places at the same time, but remains one and the same thing all the time in both places. What was held to be a chemical difference becomes a geographical one, but is at the same time not a difference at all. We have thought deeply on this. Perhaps we shall think about it again, meantime keeping such an open mind as the effort requires. The definitions are the work of the best men on the subject, not done after dinner, and, as in our fifth-form days, we abstain from expressing ourselves rashly, on the possible ground that the thing is too profound for us.

At the same time, we may take leave to illustrate the limits of our own understanding. Any intelligent inquiry into the question "What is whiskey?" falls naturally into three divisions—the historical, the chemical and the psychological, which latter is obviously the primary one, the other two being merely subsidiary. The Commission itself admits most of this, dealing freely in the history and the chemistry. The history has to do with the evolution of processes. The chemistry has to do with the derivation through substances. The psychology is concerned with the effect in application, the primary purpose of the whole business. That is what makes the conduct of the Commission so strange, ignoring the most important matter of all.

Perhaps they had difficulty in attracting witnesses as to the effect, and there is complaint that they did not call sufficiently on Ireland for evidence. They might also have tried the Salvation Army. Neither history nor chemistry is a strong point with the Irishmen in the House of Commons, but they are irrepressible psychologists, and they ought to have been called. Their division of the subject, though belonging technically to the abstract region, was the one in which the most definite evidence as to distinctions could be produced. Even the learned differ in history and in chemistry; but, without learning, experience in the psychology of alcohol enables a man to know exactly the condition of his head next morning, Scotch or Irish, barley or treacle. Given time and means, as enjoyed in Parliament, an experienced man can know the exact distinctions by the delicate nervous promptings from the base of his skull. The

Irish members ought to have been called. We are always ready to acknowledge their legitimate grievances.

This conflict between science and experience is not confined to drink. A few years ago a gentleman in Dublin evolved a food for calves. It was a perfect food. The chemists sat on it and declared it so. The historians confirmed the chemists. The analysis showed something for calves which was better than cows' milk, and the historians dug up the alchemy of the subject to correspond. Learned men pondered in laboratories over the discovery, and could discover nothing wrong in it. Shares were bought and sold. Factories were set smoking. All was done that science and capital could do, but the cows were not consulted, and there was still one little defect in the new food—it killed the calves. More evidence, and on a broader basis, ought to have been taken from Irishmen on the great question, What is whiskey?

The report is vague even in its history and chemistry. For instance, it recognises no difference between barley malt and Indian corn for the basis of the preparatory "mash"; oats and rye may come among the barley in Ireland without making any official difference, and on the same footing barley may be imported if found inconveniently dear at home, so that the official definition of whiskey admits even an economic factor. Now, the average Irish member, without either chemistry or history, could have demonstrated most fundamental distinctions as regards these substances, based on better evidence than anything we can find in the report from beginning to end. The official effect, however hard to understand, makes a distinct disadvantage for the Irish distilleries, which stuck to the "pot-still" in preference to the more rapid process, claiming for the result a distinctive quality beyond the ken of the analyst and determinable solely through the nerves. On the analogy of the dead calves the Irishman would appear to be right; but, like the inventor of the food that killed the calves, the Commissioners appear to deny anything that cannot be chemically expressed and historically described. There is no chemical formula for the qualities of the sensations that radiate from the back of a man's head next morning, and nothing is more certain than the reality of these; but the Commissioners ignore any such experience as might guide them in this most interesting part of their business. Irish manufacturers of various products have been kept honest by their technical incapacity for novel adoptions. For instance, they do not yet know how to mix "shoddy" in their cloth, which keeps their tweeds as healthy as their whiskey. Some of what they lost in money-making they gained in reputation; but now, in the matter of whiskey, they stand to be deprived of both the reputation and the money.

THE CITY.

WE were not far wrong in our supposition last week that the little spurt on the Stock Exchange after the settlement was due to jobbers laying in stock against the autumn. The professionals always buy a certain amount of stock at quiet times and during the holidays, so as to be prepared for the public demand, which it is assumed will revive when people return to town. If the public do not buy Kaffirs in September or October there will be something like a slump, caused by the professionals throwing out the shares they bought last week. This forecast of course excludes the unexpected or abnormal, whether in the shape of good or bad news. There is, for instance, a rumour of a shortage of black labour on the Witwatersrand, to which the big people do not seem to pay any attention. On the other hand, there is the report of the discovery of another Rand in the Abercorn district of Rhodesia, which has served to put up Chartered and all Rhodesian shares. We long ago recommended the purchase of Rhodesian Coppers at 9s.; they are now at 11s., and as the railway will reach the mine in a few months the shares are confidently talked to £1. Mines outside the Transvaal are quite unaffected by ordinary market fluctuations. Alaska Treadwells, which our readers ought to have bought at 5, are now at 7; and Alaska Mexicans, after paying an interim dividend at the rate of 40 per cent., have risen from 3 to 3¼. For a pure gamble we should advise Chartereds, but it is too hot even to think of gambling, though Throgmorton Street is always in the shade.

Despite of the heat wave in New York, Wall Street is more active than ever, Union Pacifics having touched 210 and Steel Commons 80. Seeing that these latter shares have been at 42 during the last six months, the rise is sensational. We hope that it will be justified by the dividend. The United States Steel Corporation is to spend another £10,000,000 on the Gary plants. Another period of heavy steel and iron construction is said to be under way in the United States.

The traffics of the leading Argentine railways show declines, and Pacific ordinary stock has fallen to 102. But Buenos Ayres Western at 130 and Great Southerns at 124 are too high, and will have to come down in the next two years. The best foreign railway to buy for a slow rise is Leopoldina Ordinary, which have crept up from 69 to 72.

A new rubber company in some part of the Far East is introduced to the market every day. The Dutch stockbrokers in Amsterdam are beginning to incline their ear favourably to rubber flotations, partly because the shares in sugar companies have got too high for safety and partly because the tobacco companies in the Dutch East Indies have had two bad years. Java is of course a splendid country for growing rubber or any other tropical plant, and so is Dutch East Borneo. English investors would, however, do well to be careful how they put their money into Dutch companies. There are all sorts of Government taxes to be paid by Dutch companies, and Dutchmen are not particularly pleasant to do business with. But of all rubber speculations the most dangerous are those which are started in Brazil. The plantation rubber of Ceylon and the Malay States must in time knock out the Brazilian Para. It is said that some manufacturers of rubber goods find the plantation rubber not so tough as the Brazilian Para. It is possible, indeed probable, that the Ceylon and Malay planters "over-treat" their rubber, that is, roll, wash and bake it too much; it is also the fact that there is a good deal of premature tapping of young trees. The gum from young trees undoubtedly does not make such tough rubber as the gum from the wild forest trees in Brazil. But the Ceylon planters will learn their lesson, and, when they have learned it, wild rubber will not be able to stand against plantation. At the present extraordinarily high prices a great many companies have sold their output ahead for the next year: some even for the next two years.

INSURANCE: POLICIES AT LOW PREMIUMS.

ONE form of life assurance at low rates of premium was described last week. This was convertible term assurance, under which the policyholder pays for two chances: one is the chance that he may die within the term, and the second is the chance that his health may deteriorate before he converts this policy into one of another kind. It thus provides protection, and protection only, but does not carry with it the certainty that a claim will arise under the policy at some time or other. The assured may survive the term, may not exercise his right to take some other kind of policy at a higher rate of premium; and in these circumstances the transaction terminates when the end of the period is reached, and no part of the premiums that have been paid is returned to the policyholder. Although excellent for people who have small incomes at present and the prospect of considerably larger incomes later on, there is not much attraction in these policies under other conditions.

The next lowest rate of premium for life assurance is charged for whole-life policies, under which the sum assured is paid at death whenever it happens, premiums having to be paid throughout the whole lifetime of the assured.

Policies of this kind can be taken either without participation in the profits or on the discounted-bonus plan. Non-profit policies for £1000 involve a premium of £20 or a trifle less if the assurance is effected at age thirty and of about £26 a year if the policy commences at age forty. The Old Equitable Society have recently offered non-profit whole-life policies for sums not less than £1000, and taken out for the purposes of providing death duties, on still lower terms. The annual premium is £17 17s. at age thirty and £24 12s. at age forty for £1000.

The discounted-bonus system provides that policy-holders share in the profits of the life office, but instead of paying a high rate of premium, which is returned later on in one form or another by means of bonuses, the future profits or part of them are discounted and allowed from the outset as a reduction of the premium. The lowest annual cost for policies of this kind is £18 a year at age thirty and £25 a year at age forty. Under most of these policies it is provided that if the bonuses actually declared in the future prove to be larger than the bonuses discounted the difference is paid to the policyholder. Thus the Scottish Amicable Society, which introduced this system a great many years ago, discounts a bonus of 30s. per cent. per annum calculated upon sums assured and previous bonuses. The society gives a bonus at the higher rate of 35s., with the result that policies at extremely low rates of premium receive a reversionary bonus which increases the sum assured under a policy of £1000 by £2 10s. a year.

If, on the other hand, the bonuses declared fall short of the bonuses discounted, the policyholder has to make good the difference, either by paying up the premium or by incurring a small debt upon the policy. In view of the reductions which have been made in the premiums for non-profit policies in recent years, the discounted-bonus system is perhaps less attractive than it was when non-profit rates were higher. It is very unsatisfactory for policyholders to be called upon to pay more than the normal rate of premium, and on the whole a well-selected non-profit policy is now preferable to the discounted-bonus system.

Some offices issue policies under which the ordinary rate of premium is reduced to one-half for the first five years. At the end of this time the policyholder has to pay the full premium. If he dies meanwhile the sum assured is paid to the estate, but during the period that the lower rate of premium is being paid these policies carry no surrender value. They are in effect convertible term policies for a period of five years only, and are much less satisfactory than the convertible term policies which give people the right to change to more expensive kinds of assurance at any time within twenty or even thirty-five years. Premium rates for policies of this kind used to appear in many prospectuses in years gone by, but they are not attractive contracts, since the objects accomplished by means of them can be attained more effectively in other ways.

THE BUDGET AGITATION.

By Arthur A. Baumann.

A LETTER appeared in the "Times" at the beginning of the week complaining that the opposition to the Budget out of doors was weakening, and blaming the Central Office of the Conservative party for its failure to grasp the situation. This is not quite fair. The Central Office cannot suddenly create materials which at present it does not possess. The debates on the Budget in the House of Commons are too technical and difficult for the public to follow, while Ministers and their friends are only too eager to shift discussion from Parliament and the press to the platform. In the agitation of the market-place the Unionist party is always at a comparative disadvantage, but more particularly at the present time. Platform speakers may be divided into three classes: (1) Ministers and ex-Ministers; (2) members of Parliament (unofficial); (3) speakers, paid and unpaid, educated and uneducated, ranging from professors and barristers, through the "lecturer", down to the agitator and tub-thumper. In Class 1 it might be thought that the Opposition must have the advantage over the Government; and so it had in former days, when it was understood that Ministers were paid to look after the business of their departments, and afterwards to attend the House of Commons. But Messrs. Churchill and Lloyd George have changed all that. Mr. Churchill is the head of one of the largest and busiest of the public offices, the one which exercises a supervisory and auxiliary control over the commerce of the richest nation in the world. He makes on an average three platform speeches a week, generally in remote places such as Bournemouth, Edinburgh, and Norwich. Deducting the time necessary for the preparation of those speeches, the time consumed in travelling, and the hours between 4 and 6 P.M. when he must be in his place in the House of Commons, the residue of hours left over for attendance at the Board of Trade must be small. Likewise the Chancellor of the Exchequer, in charge of the most voluminous and complicated Budget ever submitted to Parliament, has apparently no difficulty in finding time constantly to occupy the platform. To this brace of demagogues, the most unscrupulous that ever disturbed the destiny of a nation, must be added the very effective second line of Ministerial speakers, such as Messrs. Samuel, Masterman, and Runciman. Against this band of propagandists, speaking with all the authority of high office, whom have the Unionists put up? Of the members of the late Government the only one who has grasped the importance of fighting the Budget outside Parliament is Mr. Walter Long. His labours, both in speaking and in organisation, have been unwearied; and deserve, as indeed they have excited, the liveliest gratitude from his party. But one swallow does not make a summer. It has to be admitted that in the first, or Ministerial, class of speakers the Unionists are out-numbered and out-talked by the Radicals. (2) In the second class of speakers, the unofficial members of Parliament, the Unionists are at a hopeless and irreparable disadvantage, through no fault of theirs or of the Central Office. The Government majority is so large that any number of Radical members can be spared for meetings. The number of Unionist members, making allowance for the sick and those abroad, is not much over a hundred, and they *must* be in their places in the House of Commons, pairing (except at the rate of one Unionist against two Radicals) being, I understand, discontinued. To be sure, there are the Unionist peers, and they, I think, ought to bestir themselves and take the platform far more frequently than they do. If every Conservative peer would take the chair or speak at a meeting in his own neighbourhood, a great deal of good could be done. The trouble with the peers is that "they will not sally forth and see their adversary". (3) But by far the most difficult problem is how to cope with the flood of socialist speeches which is poured forth by the nameless hirelings of the Radical party and of the various socialist agencies that are spread like a network over the country. There is much money and some real enthusiasm in the business. How are we to meet it? The mental temperament and the physical condition of the average Conservative does not equip him, disables him much rather, for the duty of haranguing a handful of costermongers on Margate sands or addressing a serious argument on unearned increment to the apple-woman and the butcher-boy at the street corner. Nevertheless, the thing having to be done, somebody must be found to do it, or, as Lord Charles Beresford said, "Good-night!" The view has been expressed that the Unionist candidates ought to do more in the way of propaganda. Alas! the Unionist candidates have been chosen for the most part on cheque-book considerations, and are no more fitted than the Conservative associations which pocket their subscriptions to educate our masters. Still, it is a question worth considering whether the Budget Protest League would not do well to use the existing Unionist organisations for the holding of meetings. The idea has been hitherto that meetings to protest against the Budget should not be party affairs, but open meetings of citizens, with a view to securing the adhesion of moderate Liberals. In so far as the anti-Budget meetings have, I believe, all been open, and sometimes numerously attended by Liberals, the idea has been well worked. But no Liberal, however he might secretly disapprove of the

Budget, would openly assist in his own neighbourhood in getting up a meeting to oppose it. The most we can expect of a sympathetic Liberal is that he should sit in the body of the hall and hold up his hand in favour of the condemnatory resolution. It will not matter to such a Liberal whether the meeting has been organised by the Budget Protest League or by the local Unionist association: the dissentient Liberal knows in either case that he is being cherished by his political opponents. And the local party organisation must have means of arranging a meeting superior to those possessed by the London people, however hard they may work. I think therefore that time would be saved and efficiency promoted by dropping the pretence of no-party politics. Messrs. Churchill and George certainly do not trouble themselves or their meetings with any make-believe on the subject. Our young barristers do fairly well, though it is to be feared their legal studies suffer. One or two professors, projected by the London School of Economics into politics, strive hard to forget their curves and polygons and to acquire the methods of the demagogue. They do better than the barristers, especially in the North, where they like statistics. Then there are the "lecturers", sometimes clever working men, who would do better if they were not suspected of being paid by capitalists. But lecturers, professors and barristers are a mere handful as compared with the army of mercenaries and enthusiasts fighting for the other side. We too must train and pay agitators, men who will speak anywhere and at all times, in parks, streets, workshops, mills, from tubs, waggons, pulpits. A new profession, like that of the chauffeur, has arisen, that, namely, of the political speaker. Let us see to it that the calling is respectable and adequately paid, for its practitioners will be more powerful than Board School teachers. Do not, however, let us blame the Central Office of the Conservative party because it cannot by a wave of the pen call these new apostles into being.

TEST-MATCH CRICKET.

If one cannot rejoice at the manner of the last test match's ending, we can rejoice fervently that it has ended and that it is the last. Naturally a draw is always unsatisfactory, but it never seemed probable that England would be victorious against the strong Australian batting on such a wicket within three days, and sure enough, in great heat, the game, which in Australia would have lasted a full five days, was forced to a spiritless conclusion, and Australia, content with a draw by virtue of her two wins at Lord's and at Leeds to the one victory of England at Birmingham, came out triumphant.

It is easy and true to say that England should have gone into the field on Monday with a fast bowler. Indeed, counting Mr. Carr as experimental, there was no bowler on the English side of the highest class save Barnes, and even he was bowling on a wicket unsuited to him. Other things, too, might be said, and again with truth, but they have been already said elsewhere and everywhere; for cricket like no other game unties the tongues and thoughts of the malignant. Nobody who shared in the discomforts of the vast crowd at the Oval during the last test match—and on no ground is less done to mitigate the hardships of the ordinary spectator than at the Oval—can have failed to be impressed by the hold of cricket on a long-suffering public. No other country could show so tolerant and good-natured a gathering at any contest of equal importance. There was no sign of impatience or ill-will; it sufficed apparently to be admitted, at the price of a shilling, into the same precinct with the twenty-two picked heroes. But the intelligence of such a crowd is inferior to its amiability. The wrong and irrelevant things are applauded—the individual record, the top score, the completion of a thousand runs; you will seek in vain for the synoptic view, and why wonder? It is so often wanting in the players themselves, who forget that the individual is as nothing, the side everything. This is a truism, and because it happens to be true the Australian eleven, a combination of players, will always in England, even if inferior in skill, have the pull over an English eleven which, with the best wish in the world, can only be an aggregate of players. The difference was very clear to anyone with eyes to see at the Oval this week. It is inevitable. The difficulties are, of course, increased when there are petty quarrels and jealousies between those who are playing and those who ought to be playing or who think they ought to be playing. There have been too many of these quarrels during the last few years, usually among the amateurs, who ought to know better than to cherish on the clean cricket-field sensibilities which would do credit to the members of an Italian orchestra.

It was said, when the Australians first came this year to England, that they fell considerably below the standard of former Australian elevens. This was true at the time of saying, and continues to be true. The mistake of critics lay in forgetting, or rather not truly foreseeing, that English batting and English fast bowling had receded even further from their former level. In other words, Australia has been lucky in finding, when herself weak, English cricket still weaker, and there is no immediate prospect of her recovery. No doubt nervousness in batting played its part—the nervousness, be it remembered, peculiar to the aggregate as opposed to the combination. But the nervousness which leads to bad cricket is almost bad cricket itself. In the near future we are threatened with triangular cricket, when test matches will be so common as to inspire no awe; but even so, at the present rate of actual degeneration, it will be no surprise if England succumbs not only to Australia but to South Africa also. To us all this multiplying and intensifying of serious cricket, already too serious, seems to be a perversion and not a development. There is a charm in cricket; but when cricket assumes a national aspect, that charm evaporates, and once more the true lover of the game is apt to sigh for the village green, for the cricket which is parochial.

A SPRAY OF SOUTHERNWOOD.

By W. H. Hudson.

It was hot and fatiguing on the Wiltshire Downs, and when I had got to the highest point of a big hill where a row of noble Scotch firs stood at the roadside I was glad to get off and rest in the shade. Fifty or sixty yards from the spot where I sat on the bank on a soft carpet of dry grass and pine-needles there was a small, old, thatched cottage, the only human habitation in sight except the little village at the foot of the hill, just visible among the trees a mile ahead—an old woman in the cottage had doubtless seen me going by, for she now came out into the road, and, shading her eyes with her hand, peered curiously at me. A bent and lean old woman in a dingy black dress, her face brown and wrinkled, her hair white. With her, watching me too, was a little mite of a boy; and after they had stood there a while he left her and went into the cottage garden, but presently came out into the road again and walked slowly towards me. It was strange to see that child in such a place! He had on a scarlet shirt or blouse, wide lace collar, and black knickerbockers and stockings; but it was his face rather than his clothes that caused me to wonder. Rarely had I seen a more beautiful child, such a delicate rose-coloured skin, and fine features, eyes of such pure intense blue, and such shining golden hair. How came this angelic little being in that poor remote cottage with that bent and wrinkled old woman for a guardian?

He walked past me very slowly, a sprig of southernwood in his hand; then after going by he stopped and turned, and approaching me in a shy manner and without saying a word offered me the little pale green feathery spray. I took it and thanked him and we entered into conversation, when I discovered that his little mind was as bright and beautiful as his little person. He loved the flowers, both garden and wild, but above everything he loved the birds: he watched them to find their nests; there was nothing he liked better than to look at the little spotted eggs in the nest.

He could show me a nest if I wanted to see one, only the little bird was sitting on her eggs. He was six years old, and that cottage was his home—he knew no other; and the old bent woman standing there in the road was his mother. They didn't keep a pig, but they kept a yellow cat, only he was lost now: he had gone away and they didn't know where he was. He went to school now—he walked all the way there by himself and all the way back every day. It was very hard at first, because the other boys laughed at and plagued him. Then they hit him, but he hit them back as hard as he could. After that they hurt him, but they couldn't make him cry. He never cried and always hit them back, and now they were beginning to leave him alone. His father was named Mr. Job, and he worked at the farm, but he couldn't do so much work now because he was such an old man. Sometimes when he came home in the evening he sat in his chair and groaned as if it hurt him. And he had two sisters: one was Susan; she was married and had three big girls; and Jane was married too, but had no children. They lived a great way off. So did his brother. His name was Jim, and he was a great fat man and sometimes came from London, where he lived, to see them. He didn't know much about Jim: he was very silent, but not with mother. Those two would shut themselves up together and talk and talk and talk, but no one knew what they were talking about. He would write to mother too; but she would always hide the letters and say to father, "It's only from Jim; he says he's well—that's all". But they were very long letters, so he must have said more than that.

Thus he prattled, while I, to pay him for the southernwood, drew figures of the birds he knew best on the leaves I tore from my note-book and gave them to him. He thanked me very prettily and put them in his pocket.

"And what is your name?" I asked.

He drew himself up before me and in a clear voice, pronouncing the words in a slow measured manner, as if repeating a lesson, he answered: "Edmund Donisthorpe Jasper Stanhope Overington".

"But why", said I, "do you call yourself Overington when your father's name is Job?"

"Oh, that is because I have two fathers—Mr. Job, my very old father, and Mr. Overington, who lives away from here. He comes to see me sometimes, and he is my father too; but I have only one mother—there she is looking at us."

I questioned him no further, and so we parted; but I never see a plant or sprig of southernwood, nor inhale its cedarwood smell, which one does not know whether to like or dislike, without recalling the memory of that bright cottage child with a queer history and numerous names.

THE DIVINE MOMENT.

IN the dew-fresh fields of Dawn I wander,
Immemorial Immortal Dawn!
Far-off goal of man's most High Adventure
Whence our Dream, and whence our Hope, is drawn.

This the Garden of Celestial Blossom!
They who call me by my mortal name
Seem to me my captors and my gaolers,
In the strongholds of the House of Shame.

They who harshly call and bring me Earthward,
Draw my lips from Springs of Paradise!
Hope and Fear shall bind our lives together,
Love and Hate shall dim our mortal eyes!

In the fragrant far-off fields I wander,
O keep silence! Let the soul be free!
Let the soaring bird unscathed win Heaven!
Aim no arrow of mortality.

ALTHEA GYLES.

THE GODWIT IN NEW ZEALAND.

By James Drummond.

THERE is nothing more interesting than the arrival of the southern godwit in New Zealand, and its departure from that country, year in and year out. This little brown-coated, slender-billed, long-legged, modest bird, impelled by a mysterious instinct and guided by an invisible hand, flies over great stretches of sea and land on its way to New Zealand and back again to its other home in a distant region of the Northern Hemisphere. After passing over a thousand miles of ocean without finding a resting-place for their pinions, godwits arrive in New Zealand in October, November, and December, where they spend most of their time on estuaries, the mouths of rivers, mud-banks, and spacious sand beaches, seeking for molluscs, marine insects, and other food supplies. They reach the northern parts first, and go down the coast line until they have spread out as far as Stewart Island and the Chatham Group. They remain in New Zealand throughout the Antipodean summer, flying about in flocks, clamouring in the search for food, wading in the wavelets, and leading a busy life, which, although it has no apparent object to human beings, is earnest enough to them. As the winter months approach they prepare to go. At the end of April or the beginning of May they start on their migration to the northern lands from which they came.

It seems to be almost past belief that the northern homes of these little migrants should be in Eastern Siberia, in the North Polar Regions in fact, ten thousand miles from their summer residence in the Antipodes. There are many eminent ornithologists, however, who, after careful investigation, have accepted the statement that the southern godwit migrates from Siberia to New Zealand and back again every year. It is believed that the birds breed in Eastern Siberia and other northern lands in June and July, and pass down over country after country until they reach New Zealand. They have not been known to breed in New Zealand, and their eggs have never been found there. Hundreds of them are shot by New Zealand sportsmen every year, but there is no record of a female bird having been found in New Zealand with eggs in her.

In their northern home, godwits have been seen by Dr. von Middendorf in seventy-four degrees north latitude. They appeared there in June and left at the beginning of August. Later in the year he found them further south, on the southern coast of the Sea of Okotsk. They have been seen in Formosa in September, and a few weeks later in the islands of the Malay Archipelago, the Polynesian Islands, Australia, and New Zealand. Dr. R. Bowdler Sharpe, of the British Museum, who examined nearly fifty specimens when he compiled his "Catalogue of Birds", obtained them from the two hemispheres, and described their habitat as extending from Alaska, Kamtscatka, and Eastern Siberia through Japan and China to the Malay Archipelago, and thence to Oceania, Australia, and New Zealand.

The late Captain F. W. Hutton, of New Zealand, and other investigators have pointed out that additional evidence of the extraordinary migration is supplied by the godwit's change of plumage. The godwit is one of those birds that have different plumage in summer and winter. In the Siberian summer, when the breeding-time comes, godwits are in their summer plumage. When they reach New Zealand, although they are there also in the summer, most of them are in their winter plumage. Godwits are sometimes seen in New Zealand in their summer plumage, but it is thought that these individuals have remained behind when the migration from New Zealand took place, or they may have moulted early. I have made inquiries for many years, but I have not been able to find any record of the godwits having bred regularly in any countries between Siberia and New Zealand, and it seems to be reasonable to accept the statement of observant men, trained to weigh evidence, that the birds which visit New Zealand go to Siberia to breed.

One of the godwit's favourite places of departure

from New Zealand is Spirits' Bay, near the North Cape. It is a bleak and lonely spot, from which, according to the ancient traditions of the Maoris, the spirits of the dead departed from this world to the World of Darkness in the regions below.

The migratory instinct is not absolutely constant. Large numbers of godwits remain in New Zealand all the year round, especially in the southern parts of the country. It is presumed that, for some hidden reason, they miss the ordinary time of departure and that, as the instinct does not prompt them to migrate at any other season, they wait until the proper time comes again.

Mr. S. Percy Smith, once Surveyor-General of New Zealand, who spent many years of his life in close touch with Nature before civilisation began to change the face of the country, states that in Kaipara Harbour, on the western coast of the Auckland province, he has seen godwits in countless numbers. The tidal waters in the harbour cover an enormous area. There is a coast line inside the harbour of over 400 miles. At low water many thousand acres of mud-banks and sand-banks are exposed, and in the season godwits assemble there in tens of thousands. In other New Zealand harbours and estuaries, where civilisation is not well represented, they are also seen. They crowd together so closely that sportsmen slaughter them with ease. Mr. Smith has told me that he has killed forty-three birds at one shot, and ninety-seven deaths with two barrels have been recorded. The New Zealand Government gives the godwit partial protection under the Animals Protection Act, which provides for unrestricted shooting in February, March, and April, but protects the bird at all other times of the year. My correspondents, however, state that the law is often ignored, and that godwit shooting takes place whenever a few of these birds are gathered together.

The arrival and departure of the godwits excited curiosity in the old days in New Zealand, and the ancient Maoris brought the birds into their interesting traditions and folk-lore. Mr. B. Keys, who is attached to the Native Land Court in New Zealand, and knows well the Maoris, has sent me a translation of a paper written by a Maori clergyman, the Rev. Wiki te Paa, a member of the Rarawa Tribe, which lives in the northernmost district, where the godwits first arrive on their annual visit, and from which many of them depart on their return journey to the Northern Hemisphere. Wiki te Paa's paper sets forth the theory that it was the godwits that guided the Maori navigators when the great migration to New Zealand from the Polynesian Islands took place, 500 or 600 years ago. The Maoris call their old home "Hawaiki", a place which is without definite location, but which is believed to be Tahiti Island, in the Society Group. The tradition recorded by Wiki te Paa states that when the Maoris lived in "Hawaiki" they inferred from the godwits' regular flight that there was land in the south. Knowing that godwits do not settle on the water like a sea-bird, and that they fly from shore to shore, and seeing them leave the islands and return again, the islanders concluded that in the distant south, far beyond the horizon, there was a country in which the birds spent the summer months. The Maoris therefore started out for a country which, although it may have been unknown, was not a myth, and the adventurers were convinced that if they steered for the south they would reach the land which gave haven to the godwits, and which would also give a haven to them.

Wiki te Paa carries his theory further. He believes that the Maoris used the birds as guides, the canoes following their tracks over the ocean. The Maoris also associated the godwit with the superstition that surrounds Spirits' Bay. They believed that at times the spirits might be heard in the night conversing together as they passed northward, sometimes sighing in grief at having to leave their relatives, and sometimes displaying a more cheerful mood. Educated Maoris suggest that this poetical superstition arose from the godwits' mysterious flights and from their cries and the sound of their wings, heard in the night.

To many people the most interesting feature of the godwits' flight over a large portion of the globe is the faculty that guides them and the irresistible charm that attracts them to New Zealand. The journey is arduous and perilous. Many of the birds arrive in New Zealand exhausted, and probably many perish on the way. What is the cause of this eagerness? New Zealand offers no special food supplies in the summer; the food they seek is available at all times. It is as good and as abundant in northern latitudes as it is in southern latitudes. Apparently, the best explanation is that the birds inherit a strong instinct, which impels them to follow old land lines, along which their ancestors often travelled. In past ages, probably in the Eocene Period, a ridge of land ran northwards from New Zealand to New Caledonia and New Guinea. In later times it sank into the ocean, and New Zealand was cut off from the mainland. It is believed that the godwits' migrations began when the lands were connected by the sunken ridge, or were separated by only narrow straits of water, no island being quite out of sight. As the ages passed this migratory habit became an instinct. It has been handed down from generation to generation, and the birds of the present time follow the old course, although they must fly over vast stretches of ocean from which no land can be seen.

IN ZACCARATH.

By Lord Dunsany.

"COME," said the King in sacred Zaccarath, "and let our prophets prophesy before us."

A far-seen jewel of light was the holy palace, a wonder to the nomads on the plains.

There was the King with all his under-lords, and the lesser kings that did him vassalage, and there were all his queens with all their jewels upon them.

Who shall tell of the splendour in which they sat; of the thousand lights and the answering emeralds; of the dangerous beauty of that hoard of queens or the flash of their laden necks?

There was a necklace there of rose-pink pearls beyond the art of dreamer to imagine. Who shall tell of the amethyst chandeliers where torches, soaked in rare Bhyrinian oils, burned and gave off a scent of blethany? *

Enough to say that when the dawn came up it appeared by contrast pallid and unlovely and stripped all bare of its glory, so that God covered it with rolling clouds.

"Come," said the King, "let our prophets prophesy."

Then the heralds stepped through the ranks of the King's silk-clad warriors who lay oiled and scented upon velvet cloaks, with a pleasant breeze among them caused by the fans of slaves; even their casting-spears were set with jewels; through their ranks the heralds went with mincing steps, and came to the prophets, clad in brown and black, and one of them they brought and set him before the King. And the King looked at him and said "Prophesy unto us".

And the prophet lifted his head, so that his beard came clear from his brown cloak, and the fans of the slaves that fanned the warriors wafted the tip of it a little awry. And he spake to the King and spake thus:

"Woe unto thee, King, and woe unto Zaccarath. Woe unto thee and woe unto thy women; for your fall shall be sore and soon. Already in Heaven the gods shun thy god: They know his doom and what is written of him: he sees oblivion before him like a mist. Thou hast aroused the hate of the mountaineers. They hate thee all along the crags of Droom. The evilness of thy days shall bring down the Zeedians on thee as the

* The herb marvellous, which growing near the summit of Mount Zaumnos scents all the Zaumnian range and is smelt far out on the Kepuscran plains, and even, when the wind is from the mountains, in the streets of the city of Ognoth. At night it closes its petals and is heard to breathe, and its breath is a swift poison. This it does even by day if the snows are disturbed abou it. No plant of this has ever been captured alive by a hunter.

suns of springtide bring the avalanche down. They shall do unto Zaccarath as the avalanche doth unto the hamlets of the valley." When the queens chattered or tittered among themselves, he merely raised his voice and still spake on: "Woe to these walls and the carven things upon them. The hunter shall know the camping-places of the nomads by the marks of the camp-fires on the plain, but he shall not know the place of Zaccarath."

A few of the recumbent warriors turned their heads to glance at the prophet when he ceased. Far overhead the echoes of his voice hummed on awhile among the cedarn rafters.

"Is he not splendid?" said the King. And many of that assembly beat with their palms upon the polished floor in token of applause. Then the prophet was conducted back to his place at the far end of that mighty hall; and for a while musicians played on marvellous curved horns, while drums throbbed behind them hidden in a recess. The musicians were seated cross-legged on the floor all blowing their huge horns in the brilliant torchlight, but as the drums throbbed louder in the dark they arose and moved slowly nearer to the King. Louder and louder drummed the drums in the dark, and nearer and nearer moved the men with the horns, so that their music should not be drowned by the drums before it reached the King.

A marvellous scene it was when the tempestuous horns were halted before the King, and the drums in the dark were like the thunder of God, and the queens were nodding their heads in time to the music, with their diadems flashing like heavens of falling stars, and the warriors lifted their heads and shook, as they lifted them, the plumes of those golden birds which hunters wait for by the Liddian lakes, in a whole lifetime killing scarcely six, to make the crests that the warriors wore when they feasted in Zaccarath. Then the King shouted and the warriors sang—almost they remembered then old battle-chaunts. And, as they sang, the sound of the drums dwindled and the musicians walked away backwards, and the drumming became fainter and fainter as they walked, and altogether ceased, and they blew no more on their fantastic horns. Then the assemblage beat on the floor with their palms. And afterwards the queens besought the King to send for another prophet. And the heralds brought a singer and placed him before the King; and the singer was a young man with a harp. And he swept the strings of it, and when there was silence he sang of the iniquity of the King. And he foretold the onrush of the Zeedians and the fall and the forgetting of Zaccarath and the coming again of the desert to its own and the playing about of little lion cubs where the courts of the palace had stood.

"Of what is he singing?" said a queen to a queen.

"He is singing of everlasting Zaccarath."

As the singer ceased the assemblage beat listlessly on the floor, and the King nodded to him and he departed.

When all the prophets had prophesied to them and all the singers sung, that royal company arose and went to other chambers, leaving the hall of festival to the pale and lonely dawn. And alone were left the lion-headed gods that were carven out of the walls; silent they stood and their rocky arms were folded. And shadows over their faces moved like curious thoughts as the torches flickered and the dull dawn crossed the fields. And the colours began to change in the chandeliers.

Never was greater splendour or a more famous hall. When the queens went away through the curtained door with all their diadems it was as though the stars should arise in their stations and troop together to the West at sunrise.

And only the other day I found a stone that had undoubtedly been a part of Zaccarath; it was three inches long and an inch broad; I saw the edge of it uncovered by the sand. I believe that only three other pieces have been found like it.

CORRESPONDENCE.

"UNIFIKASIE"—AND AFTER.

II.

To the Editor of the SATURDAY REVIEW.

Nylstroom, Transvaal, 7 July 1909.

SIR,—It is safe to say that this union is regarded by the farmers of British blood and of British birth with general distrust and fear; something of the feeling with which a man consents to a necessary operation which will perhaps cost him his life. Having done their best in a war which cost them the fruits of past labour, they were for the most part too manly really to grudge the Boer the strange new doctrine of "The spoils to the vanquished" which crippled their future: they know the Boer too well to cherish any Liberal illusions as to the dreams of his leaders; but having no means to start life yet once again elsewhere, Dutch or double-Dutch, this country is all they have; and if England chooses to abandon it to gratify the sentimental self-esteem or further the party moves of a group of half-informed Liberal politicians, they must swim with the tide and make the best of the pass to which misplaced and unrecognised loyalty has brought them.

As to the ultimate dreams of the Boer leaders and would-be leaders, the generals and the young hot-bloods for whom the generals are all too discreet and cautious, and above all the Predikants, who in the last resort pull the hidden strings of policy, he may cherish illusions who will, while others remember that "a fool is wise in his own conceit". Liberal politicians who have met the select Boer over a banquet, and Yeomanry officers who feasted them as fellow-soldiers at mess, may cling to their twopence-coloured ideal of a chivalrous simple-minded farmer-soldier, proud to be entrusted with a share in the destinies of a great Empire. Those who have lived amongst them in the veld realise that contempt and distrust of all things British have been bred into these people for three generations and more, in the home, at school, and in church; and that these feelings, intensified by the war, have not been eradicated by a policy of "gush and give way" which they are none the more prone to admire for being too simple-manly to be able to fathom it.

Mr. Kipling presents somewhere an Indian as saying that "Allah created the English mad, the maddest of all mankind"; and, indeed, this South African business will read to future ages like the dream of a frenzied pantomime-writer.

Ten years ago the conspiracy was just ripe, conspiracy between the leaders of the petty Boer States and traitors in Cape Colony for the overthrow of British power in South Africa and the establishment of a great Boer republic. Throughout the Boer States the mass of the people were red-hot for war; in Cape Colony active treason was so general that mere disaffection counted almost for righteousness: even the Cabinet, technically the advisers of her Majesty's deputy, gave more than passive assistance to the leaders of the conspiracy in the completion of their preparations.

Seven years ago, having raised and trained the needful army on the field itself, England and her colonies broke the last of the confederate forces and established undisputed supremacy, annexing the petty States where the conspiracy had been bred.

Seven years ago British power was a solid reality throughout South Africa, the development of the country along the normal lines of British colonisation fairly begun. He would have been accounted a fool indeed who had then prophesied a return of Boer supremacy and Boer traditions within seven years. All that was wanted to settle the country for ever on the lines of Canada, Australia, New Zealand, was ten years of careful and resolute government, with suppression of all show of disaffection. The Boer is accustomed to do what he is told: as Paul Kruger knew, the crack of the whip is what he respects; magnanimity, conciliation and apology he does not understand or admire.

But the rot set quickly in. Rebels taken in arms were not shot, merely disfranchised for just so long as there should be no election. A Boer general who had flogged and shot a peace envoy in cold blood was the hero of the hour in England: such of the conspirators as had not died in the war were allowed to return and form a nucleus for disaffection to rally on: the "Terms of Surrender" bloomed into the "Treaty of Vereeniging": an apology for martial law was printed in the Statute Book of one of the annexed States: an attempted rising was hushed up as a disturbance of the peace: an organised plan to thwart the educational system was bought off by compromise: the local press was allowed to preach treason and stir up dissension, unpunished by the Statute provided for the purpose: hardly anywhere in the two new colonies could the British flag fly or the National Anthem be sung safe from insult. In which circumstances, whether from honest conviction of crazy and ignorant ideologues or to suit the party ends of political gamblers, it was announced that his Majesty's Government felt the time ripe to hand over the government of the two new colonies to the men who five years before had been trying their utmost once more to raise rebellion in Cape Colony for the extermination of British influence in South Africa.

Two years later, struck by the success of the new Governments in their determination to uproot all the British influence and ideals so carefully implanted by Lord Milner, his Majesty's advisers consider the time ripe for extending over the hitherto British colonies of Natal, the Cape and Rhodesia the sway of these suborners of rebellion, killers of peace envoys, intriguers only ten years back for the substitution of Boer for British power throughout the sub-continent.

Ten years; not time enough for the African leopard to change his spots, had he, indeed, given any real earnest of his desire to do so; not time enough to have eradicated from the Boer the contempt, envy, and dislike of the English and all their ways and ideals bred into his very bone for fifty years past. One must suppose that no one will believe till he has bought his experience by residence among them that by Boer standards, to swindle—under the less crude guise of "verneuk"—is no disgrace, but a laudable accomplishment; to be "slim", or in plain English dishonest, is a virtue; to call a man a liar, rather a compliment which only a fool of an Englishman would resent as an insult.

Ten years since their incapacity for decent government was England's opportunity to put the country in order: and now with proof of their insidious intent added to their incapacity, the whole sub-continent is given them to mould as they will into the Boer Republic for which they played and lost ten years ago.

From London it may look like a triumph of magnanimous statesmanship: to the whilom Englishman in the veld, heart-sick at the steady change for the worse which has crept over all matters of public polity since Milner went, it seems like an abnegation on the part of England of all capacity for Empire.

How long it will be before Boer South Africa's independence of Britain becomes nominal as well as actual remains to be seen; it depends mainly on the native question. All things tend to a consolidation of the tribes into an overwhelming whole; from the prohibition of liquor on the mines and the consequent cessation of the inter-tribal faction fights to which the liquor led, to this very matter of unification, which has brought about for its consideration the first undreamed-of council of delegates from all the hitherto jealous and divided native races.

Who can doubt, with a seven years' record of "gush and give way", that if complete control of the natives is demanded by United South Africa, our "Government" will "gush and give way" once again?

Who can doubt that if it is granted, the time draws near for a general rising of allied tribes against Boer misrule? And should it come before Boer South Africa's Fourth of July, who doubts that once again, provided India keeps quiet and he has no European Power on his back, John Bull will pacify South Africa if it costs his last penny? Who doubts, finally, that his reward will be once again sneering criticism of his officers and men, and thankless permission to go home and leave the settlement to his betters?

Should the Fourth of July come before the natives are ready, perhaps after Africa is swept clean to Simonstown, John Bull may be wise at last in his generation and prefer to stand back and let his Continental neighbour try his prentice hand on the resettlement.

Yours faithfully,

C. R. Prance.

BY GRACE OF THE AMERICAN COUSIN.

To the Editor of the Saturday Review.

Plombières (Vosges), 2 August 1909.

Sir,—We are so accustomed to errors on the part of the British press (unfortunately both countries are equally culpable in this respect) that generally little attention ought to be given to these faults. But I am tempted to say a word in reply to an article upon the proposed income-tax law, now before the Congress of the United States, which appeared in the number of 24 July, in which you say, in speaking of my country: "They had an income tax before, but found that the national sense of truth made it nearly unproductive. . . . Is it not curious that the people who produced George Washington should be so free from truth as to make an income tax uncollectable among them?" Yes, we had an income tax. It was passed during the struggle of the North to maintain the integrity of the Union. This tax yielded sums large enough to enable the Government to put down the rebellion—a war which would have exhausted most countries. This income-tax law was afterwards repealed. During the administration of President Cleveland Congress imposed a new income-tax law which was declared unconstitutional by the Supreme Court on the ground that the tax was direct and should have been apportioned among the various States. On account of this decision, in the present Bill there is a clause submitting to the States an amendment to the Constitution to legalise the income tax. As the Government has present need of revenue, the Bill also contains a provision for a tax of one per cent. upon the income of corporations.

The newspapers of the two countries should use every endeavour to maintain cordiality between its citizens. If the time should ever arrive when the enemies of Great Britain shall feel themselves strong enough to attack her, you may be certain that the American people will have a hand in that fight. We have no great love for the mother country. We have not forgotten that during our War of Secession our flag was driven almost entirely from the seas by the "Alabama", fitted out in Liverpool and paid for by two hundred and ninety merchants of that city. But we shall take a hand against the enemies of England not from any sentimental ideas but for the commonplace and material reason that we shall not permit our commerce with Great Britain to be hurt, and because such a war will be against the peace and dignity of the commonweal made up of all civilised nations.

Albert Lapsley Wilson.

[Our correspondent appears never to have heard of the American "Revenue Collection Bill", enabling the tax-gatherer "to use force if necessary". When the American income tax was first levied, in 1862-3, instructions were issued that the returns should not be open to inspection, but owing to "various evasions" the order had to be reversed almost immediately. Two years later, in 1865, after several revisions, the tax was put on its final basis, with incomes up to 600 dollars free, five per cent. up to 5000 dollars, and ten per cent. on all incomes over that. In 1866 the scheme was in full working order, or at least as near it as American veracity could reach—it was already some time since the disappearance of Washington. In 1866 the American income tax produced 72,982,159 dollars; not a bad start, and with the young nation then growing rapidly, especially in dollars, the statesmen would naturally look forward to a fine and increasing purse. In the next seven years America grew enormously, always in dollars; but at the end of that period, in 1873, the revenue from the income tax had "gradually fallen" from nearly 73,000,000 dollars to a trifle over 5,000,000, a fall to about one-fourteenth in the seven years. For every £1 that they could collect in 1866 they could collect only about 1s. 5d. in 1873. Such a rapid fall in revenue from incomes rising so rapidly could hardly be due to Washingtonian ways, and so we get the New York correspondents of the London papers telling about "the difficulties of collection when America had an income tax"; but, apart from the newspapers, our American correspondent will find the details of the above facts at page 602 of "The New Encyclopædia of Social Reform". At page 121 of Woodburn's "American Political History" he will find this too: "The Constitution plainly gave Congress the power to levy and collect taxes; but it was certain that the power would be difficult and dangerous". This had not to do with any tax in particular, but it is all the more illuminating of American ways in tax-gathering.—Ed. S. R.]

To the Editor of the Saturday Review.

Duquesne Club, Pittsburg, 4 August 1909.

Sir,—In your editorial of 24 July you say: "Speaking of an income tax . . . the Americans cannot get all the taxes they want. . . . They had an income tax before, but found that the national sense of truth made it nearly unproductive. . . . Is it not curious that the people who produced George Washington should be so free from truth as to make an income tax uncollectible among them?"

As you well know, or ought to know, "the income tax before" was declared by the Supreme Court of the United States to be unconstitutional. Hence its failure. It was not a question whether productive or not. You therefore state as a fact what is not a fact. This you do wittingly or ignorantly. In any case, you evidently lie, under a mistake if we view your words charitably. Be good enough to boil the bile out of your brains, and tell of facts not fictions.

Yours truly,
William Seymour Edwards.

[We commend this specimen of American good taste to British admirers.—Ed. S.R.]

SMALL GUNS FOR SHIPS.

To the Editor of the Saturday Review.

Sir,—Like that of the scorpion, the tail of your leading article on the Navy is the "business end". You very truly say that the introduction of six-inch guns into our future Dreadnoughts is a clear confession that a grave error of policy was made in the original "Dreadnought", "and it is a matter of the highest importance to ascertain by how much our position has been imperilled".

But even your article, admirable as it is throughout, does not convey to the general reader the true significance of the "grave error". For years past in communications to the Government departments concerned, the press and otherwise, I have urged the important point that nothing bigger than a six-inch gun is necessary for the sinking or disablement of war vessels of all kinds. Dreadnoughts and super-Dreadnoughts are included. The authors of those vessels are not likely to take kindly to such a statement, as they would thereby stultify themselves; but the amour propre of individuals and "vested interests" should not be allowed to continue to block the road in matters of national defence.

On the advent to power of the present Government I specifically directed the attention of a highly placed member of the Government to the "grave error", and I have continued the warnings to members of the Cabinet. I have shown that the experiences of the battle of Tsushima proved that the penetration of armour is quite unnecessary for ship-sinking and ship-disabling purposes; that consequently monster guns, with their necessarily complicated, heavy and easily disabled machinery, are obsolete—seeing that a high-explosive projectile as used by the Japanese, fired from a man-handled six-inch gun, by acting against the submerged unprotected parts of armoured ships, can effect the required damage.

The logical conclusion from this is that if the six-inch gun can pump what Admiral Rozhdestvensky called "a kind of aerial torpedo, which led to the sinking of the Russian fleet", into an enemy, why should ships carry automobile torpedoes and their attendant complicated gear? Extending this reasoning, why the submarine? which has proved its dangerous proclivities to its users under peace conditions and seems scarcely likely to justify its existence in those of war.

The legitimate weapon of a warship, the small gun, sustained its reputation at close quarters in the Russo-Japanese War, wherein long-range firing was ineffective. The automobile torpedo made a poor show. These are indisputable facts upon which our legislators and others might advantageously ponder, as they directly affect this (to use your own words) "great question of imperial safety, beside which all others pale into insignificance".

Your obedient servant,
C. E. Kelway.

FRANCIA'S MASTERPIECE.

To the Editor of the Saturday Review.

Springbank, Hamilton N.B. 8 August 1909.

Sir,—For many years the Saturday Review has aided me in the study of art, if I may use so serious an expression for any little attention I have given to that subject. The "first aid" I remember having received many years ago was through my attention being drawn to the supreme excellence of the reproduction of Botticelli's famous picture "Primavera" by the Arundel Society. Since then, from week to week, I have never failed to read what was said in your columns on the subject of art. Yesterday I turned at once to the article headed "Religious Art and the Critics", but I read it with a feeling of disappointment. There is much said in it about a certain development of Catholic doctrine, which Francia's work is said to deal with; but it seems to me that the suggestion of such doctrines in a special degree is beyond the province of art. Even Raibolini's treatment of it so praised by Mr. Carmichael has left the subject of his painting so much in doubt that it has been described as a Coronation, an Assumption, or a Reception of the Virgin into heaven. Surely the indication of the Immaculate Conception in a picture, even a religious one, is to confound art with theology. M. Wyczewa, the art critic of the "Revue des deux Mondes", deals, I think, with religious art more wisely when he describes Botticelli's "Nativity", which we have the great good fortune to possess in the National Gallery, as not only a masterpiece, but as the most religious picture in all Italian art. There could never be any doubt as to the subject of that picture, and besides it suggests a beautiful religious lesson.

I have not seen even a reproduction of Francia's picture, but I humbly venture to ask Mr. Carmichael if he places it higher than that artist's beautiful "Adoration of the Infant Jesus" at Bologna, a fine group of saints with the Virgin, surrounding in simple devotion the Holy Child. This is another religious picture which needs no explanation.

Yours faithfully,
James Bell.

[Would it not be well to see the picture before criticising Mr. Carmichael and to read the book before criticising our review?—Ed. S. R.]

REVIEWS.

THE HOUSEHOLD CAVALRY.

"The Story of the Household Cavalry." By Captain Sir George Arthur Bart., late 2nd Life Guards. In 2 vols. London: Constable. 1909. 73s. 6d.

AS a record of soldierly service in peace and war extending over two centuries and a half the story of the Household Cavalry was well worth telling. Himself an old Lifeguardsman, Sir George Arthur is in many respects well equipped for the task. He has made judicious use of varied sources of information, some of it hitherto hidden amongst private papers. He has received valuable assistance from brother officers in recounting the campaigns in which he has himself taken part. His descriptions of battles have had the benefit of expert military criticism.

The outcome should have been a very good book, and up to a certain point Sir George Arthur has achieved a success. That he is master of his subject is evident, but this merit cannot avail to excuse faults of style which are equally patent. Sir George Arthur has made the mistake of affecting a literary brilliancy which is not at his command. His constant attempts at epigrammatic and graphic writing completely break down in the result. He has not the smallest gift either for epigram or for vivid description, and he would have been better advised had he avoided a laboured jocularity of tone and a recourse to the feeblest tricks of alliteration.

Wherever, eschewing these vagaries of style, Sir George Arthur is content to adopt a quiet straightforward manner of narration, his performance is far more satisfactory. The material which he has accumulated possesses an interest that is political and social as well as military, and in these pages many sidelights are thrown on the general history of the country.

The Household Cavalry was formed on a French model. The Life Guards whom Charles II. brought to England at the Restoration were soon disbanded, to be at once reconstituted on 26 January 1661. Of English Life Guards there were three troops, while a Scots troop had its headquarters at Edinburgh, the average strength being two hundred "private gentlemen" per troop. The officers enjoyed a rank in the Army much above their nominal rank in the corps, and many who held commissions in other regiments were glad to join the King's Life Guards as "private gentlemen".

To each troop there was shortly afterwards attached a number of Horse Grenadiers, whose tactics were those of mounted infantry and whose distinctive weapon was the hand-grenade—curiously enough reintroduced by the Japanese in the late war. William of Orange collected the Horse Grenadiers together into a single unit.

A fourth troop of Life Guards, intended to consist exclusively of Roman Catholics, was established by James II. Disbanded by William, it was replaced by a Dutch fourth troop until an Act of Parliament prohibited the presence of alien soldiery in England. Anne brought the Scots Life Guards south to form a new fourth troop, the Scots Horse Grenadiers also joining the English. George II. suppressed the third and fourth troops, and in 1788 the two surviving ones absorbed the Horse Grenadiers and were reconstituted as the First and Second Regiments of Life Guards.

The Royal Regiment of Horse Guards (Blue), originally the Earl of Oxford's Royal Regiment of Horse, was within living memory still familiarly known as the Oxford Blues. Its precursor, Unton Crook's Regiment of Horse, was taken into Charles II.'s service under Royalist officers. Like the Life Guards it was disbanded but quickly re-established. The Blues still cherish the memory of their first colonel, Aubrey de Vere, twentieth and last Earl of Oxford, who devoted forty years of his life to perfecting the efficiency of his regiment.

The Blues were not formally included in the Household Cavalry until after Waterloo. They stood in much the same relation to the Life Guards as the Gendarmerie de France did to the Maison du Roi, sharing many of their duties, particularly as mounted police. The Blues were temporarily brigaded with the Life Guards in the Peninsula in 1809. In 1814 the Prince Regent ordered their permanent inclusion in the Household Cavalry Brigade. Not till 1820 did their colonel acquire the right to take his share of the duty of Gold Stick with the colonels of the Life Guards.

The Household Cavalry, though restricted during long periods to home service, has gathered laurels on many foreign fields. The earliest successes of the Life Guards were won under Monmouth at Maastricht and under Marlborough at Walcourt. During the seven years' campaign in Flanders against France, from 1691 to 1697, they gained a reputation as "the finest body of horse in Europe", particularly by their rearguard actions at Leuse and Steenkirk, and still more by their victorious charge at Landen, where, headed by their King, they tackled and defeated the Maison du Roi itself.

The turn of "the Blew Guards" came in the middle of the next century. In company with the Life Guards they fought at Dettingen in 1743 and at Fontenoy in '45. Sir George Arthur devotes a whole chapter, one of the best in the book, to a detailed refutation of the slanderous charge brought against the Blues of misconduct at Dettingen. During the Seven Years' War from '56 to '63 the Blues took a creditable part in a series of arduous operations in Germany. Baulked by Sackville's treachery of their rightful share in the victory of Minden, they did themselves full justice under the immortal Granby at Warburg, besides putting in some good work at Wilhelmstahl. The end of the century saw the Blues winning fresh fame by their brilliant services at Villers-en-Cauchies, Bethencourt (otherwise Cateau) and Willems.

From this time onward Life Guards and Blues never fought apart. Denied by the mountainous character of the country any very prominent share in Wellington's Peninsula victories, they showed their great leader at Waterloo—somewhat to his astonishment—the stuff of which they were made, and his greeting, "Thank you, Life Guards", set his seal on the merit of their exploit.

Sixty-seven years were to elapse before the Household Cavalry again saw active service. That they saw it even then was in no small degree due to the raising, in the early 'seventies—conspicuously by the SATURDAY REVIEW—of the question whether it were worth while to maintain these costly regiments for ornament, not for use. The sequel of the controversy was that, at their own earnest entreaty, the Household Cavalry were in 1882 represented in the army that fought at Kassassin and Tel-el-Kebir. The experiment was successful enough to be repeated when the Nile expedition was sent to Khartum, and this twofold precedent was followed in South Africa.

The author's description of these three campaigns, though carefully done, exhibits occasionally a tendency to exaggerate. Thus on page 677 he writes: "The Household Cavalry had to pay another heavy toll in casualties". The first "heavy toll" had been one man killed and three wounded severely, besides eight others slightly. The second "heavy toll" was three killed and eight wounded. We are sure that no German soldier, and it is difficult to understand that an English soldier, could allow himself to write so.

We have another complaint to make. Surely no book descriptive of warlike operations was ever so starved in respect of maps and plans. At least if it were impossible to give good battle-plans, there was no need to offer such utterly bad ones as are several of those to be found here—Landen, for instance, which is incorrect as to the line occupied by the Allies, and Fontenoy, which, apart from its smudginess, is barely recognisable and wholly useless.

With whatever blemishes of execution, Sir George Arthur in compiling these stirring annals of a famous corps has rendered an important service. General Broadwood, as a part of whose command they served in South Africa, excused himself for "giving the Household Cavalry rather more than their fair share of work" on the ground that "they always did well anything he asked them to do, and never raised any difficulties". Sir George Arthur exhibits this uncomplaining devotion to duty as, in fact, their inherited tradition, and thereby provides his old comrades in arms with an additional incentive to maintain in the future the reputation they have so well upheld in the past.

THE DECORATION OF HOUSES.

"The Decoration and Furniture of English Mansions during the Seventeenth and Eighteenth Centuries." By Francis Lenygon. London: Laurie. 1909. 31s. 6d.

PEOPLE accustomed to rush and hurry, bitten by the craze for perpetual motion, which leaves no leisure for the contemplation of anything except motors and flying machines, are not so likely to find enjoyment in decorating their homes as those who dream away their lives in peaceful surroundings, and, if a knowledge of the art of decoration and correct use of ornament is becoming every day more general, it is chiefly because the camera has annihilated distance and brought the work of great artists within sight of everybody.

Mr. Lenygon has made free use of photographs to illustrate the growth of decorative art during the seventeenth and eighteenth centuries, and though it may be permissible to withhold admiration from a few of the objects chosen for representation, the plates must be highly commended for the accuracy with which they portray the detail of the examples selected. After some preliminary remarks on the Early English Renaissance, Mr. Lenygon introduces Inigo Jones, then passes on rapidly to Wren and Grinling Gibbons, and on leaving those worthies turns to William Kent, painter, sculptor, and architect, a man by whom he appears to be particularly attracted. The names of Kent and Burlington are very closely associated, otherwise this attention to the landscape gardener might suggest an attempt to start a cult for the doughty champion of Nature who utilised his talents to ruin the old-fashioned pleasaunce; however, the apology for Kent gives decided character to the book, and it is refreshing to find anyone taking up the cudgels on behalf of one whose laurels have withered so entirely. No doubt Mr. Lenygon is right in considering Kent did immense service to his patrons in helping them to adapt "Palladian architecture to the requirements of the mansions they were erecting and transforming in England", but we cannot account it to him for righteousness that he made himself useful in turning "stately-buildid housen" into magnificent and elegantly decorated edifices—so useful indeed that it is impossible to think of him apart from splendid structures, suitably embellished, designed to convey to strangers a high opinion of the riches of our nobility. Mr. Lenygon tries to refute the charge of clumsiness often brought against furniture designed by Kent, and excuses the heaviness of it on the ground that he did not work for people of small means: "His furniture and decoration were invariably intended for stately classic mansions." There is truth in this, and it is fortunate Mr. Lenygon has caught something of the stilted style of dialect affected by the superior person of the early eighteenth century, for it helps to explain his favourite. We do not blame Kent for not being ahead of his time; he was a pedant catering for pedants in an age when beauty had become confounded with grandeur.

Ruskin, defining "proud admiration" as "the delight most worldly people take in showy, large, or complete buildings for the sake of the importance which such buildings confer on themselves as their possessors or admirers", condemns the architect who courts that kind of applause, experience having led him to believe that the "love of largeness, and especially of symmetry (is) invariably associated with vulgarity and narrowness of mind".

In varying degrees we all worship with Ruskin, and maybe this is why the men of the early eighteenth century are no longer greatly venerated. Nevertheless, dislike of symmetry can be carried too far, decoration is a science to be studied with discretion, and we can learn much from the early Georgian architects who understood the importance of the fireplace, gave dignity to the chimneypiece, and remembered that in decorating a room nothing should clash with the design of the most prominent feature in it. Nowadays furnishing is apt to be a haphazard business, and the ornamentation of the interiors of our houses seldom shows any well-thought-out scheme; but there are signs that the architect is coming to his own again, and when he does perhaps he will kindly avoid some of the extravagance of his predecessors and bear in mind that art was made for man, not man for art.

There are over two hundred pictures in Mr. Lenygon's book, and they include examples of wood-panelling and plaster ornament, of velvets and damasks, of tapestries and floor carpets, besides specimens of articles of furniture of many different sorts. Decorative paintings have been allotted a proper share in the illustrations, and we are glad to find lacquer and English gessowork have not been forgotten.

The architect will agree with Mr. Lenygon that for artistic effect there is no covering for walls to compare with panelling; the plasterer will sympathise with the opinion that the possibilities of the plastic substance on which he endeavours to thrive are insufficiently appreciated; the upholsterer will be grateful for being reminded there was once a stuff describable as a strong, woollen, "watered" rep, which made an excellent covering for chairs and settees; the carpet manufacturer with yearnings towards perfection will doubtless own himself in debt for having his attention directed to the composition and colouring of the classic designs of the mid-eighteenth century. The collector and dealer must in like manner admit their obligation to Mr. Lenygon for drawing their notice to the merits of gessowork; and those about to marry owe him thanks for gently pointing out that Amorini will fly out of the window if objects displaying a trace of the "Grecian" taste are forced to keep company with anything belonging to an earlier period than their own.

Surely the benefactor of so large a number of people may be forgiven a pronounced preference for the split infinitive?

A CROAKER'S CHAGRIN.

"An Empire in Pawn." By A. J. Wilson. London: Fisher Unwin. 1909. 10s. 6d. net.

NEARLY twenty years ago Mr. A. J. Wilson made a prophecy. The prophecy was that the Empire, especially the colonies, must soon bankrupt, as a result of borrowing. The prophecy has not come true. Instead of bankrupting, they have borrowed more, whereupon the prophet has become cross and published a book, which would be a better book were he not cross. He wants to explain now that they upset his prophecy by their additional borrowing; in other words, that they defeated the disease by increasing the cause; but he confesses that he did not foresee how they might do it. Such oversight in a prophet makes us unsatisfied now with his renewal of the prophecy, even if he is wise enough on this occasion to extend the time. Why should they not again do something which he does not foresee, as they did before? He writes about the statesmen of the Empire as if they were specially occupied to injure his character as a prophet. He is very hard on Australia, and attributes "aberrations" to Mr. Deakin, merely because Mr. Deakin doubted the prophecy that was not true. No man ever wrote a good book on such a subject in such a temper. It is not a subject for prophecy. When a man comes to a subject like this in the character of a prophet, his need to make it appear that he is right makes impartial investigation psychologically impossible. Accordingly, he has done the colonies and their statesmen an undeserved injury, without any compensating service that can be seen.

Insolvency from borrowing depends on the use made of what is borrowed, and trustworthy investigation of this might be really instructive, but the author cannot be said to have attempted it. From the facts in our own knowledge we are satisfied that the borrowers can show assets for their liabilities.

ROME IN ITS LITERATURE.

"A Literary History of Rome." By J. Wight Duff. London and Leipsic: Fisher Unwin. 1909. 12s. 6d. net.

THOSE of us who remember Mr. Wight Duff's version of Catullus XXIV. ("Dianæ sumus in fide") in the "Classical Review" (November 1908) will be prepared for a display of poetic sympathy and insight in his appreciations of Roman poetry, and all through this volume we find versions of the Latin extracts executed with a good deal of grace by the author himself. It is an open question whether, in criticising Greek or Latin authors, one should do one's own translating or trust to well-known versions; but in this book a good deal of the translation, whether in prose or verse, is quite excellent, and an author who can render so many diverse writers adequately appeals to us at once as an understanding critic at any rate. "Catullus makes mouths at our speech", and not Catullus alone. Most translations are unsatisfactory, one way or another, but nevertheless, when translation and criticism are by the same hand the effect is greatly enhanced. Either reacts upon the other. In passing we may note that Vergil's plaintive

"Si qua fata aspera rumpas"

is rather misrepresented by the staccato abruptness of "couldst thou but cleave grim doom", and the well-nigh unapproachable pathos of

"Sunt lacrimæ rerum et mentem mortalia tangunt"

finds fitter expression in Arnold's

"The sense of tears in human things",

or in Myers' expansion of the line and a half,

"Tears answer tears and honour honour brings,
And mortal hearts are moved by mortal things",

than in our author's

"Tears haunt the world; man's fortunes touch man's heart".

But in this large and comprehensive volume there is infinitely more than a selection of well-rendered extracts. There is labour and erudition and a keen sense of literary values, which go far to justify the retracing of so much old familiar ground.

The work extends from the "origins" in the rude folk-songs and the hymns of the Arval Brethren to the close of the Golden Age in the "lepor" of Catullus, the "urbanitas" of Horace and the sonorous prose of Livy. The title is well chosen. "A Literary History of Rome" is not the same thing as "A History of Roman Literature". The standpoint is different and implies a scheme which shall trace the inevitable development of the literature from the nature, history and environment of the people who produce the literature, and this is perhaps the most valuable part of the book; herein it is an admirable counterpart to that remarkable "Latin Literature" of Professor Mackail, which came out so modestly and so effectively in the guise of a "University Extension Manual".

With the development of the town into the Empire came a corresponding extension of the literary frontiers; while in the early days Andronicus was a Greek and Terence an African, the Empire gives us Spaniards in Seneca, Lucan and Martial, and Africa in Apuleius and S. Augustine. For we must here note that though Mr. Duff does not pursue his investigations beyond the Golden Age, he closes his volume with these words: "So one is to realise that Latin prose runs on from Cicero to Lactantius, Jerome and Augustine, to Thomas Aquinas, Erasmus, Bacon, and Grotius; and that Latin poetry runs on from Virgil to Ausonius and Claudian, and from Catullus to Prudentius and Boethius, and so on to the Neo-Latin poets. Herein there is nothing derogatory to the dignity of the best work of the best period." Elsewhere also he reminds us, most usefully at the present moment, when classical studies are attacked on many sides, that Latin never really became a dead language, though it survived mainly as a literary medium. Church and State, lawyers, priests and diplomats, philosophers and scientists, all expressed themselves in Latin till comparatively a late date, and even now Latin is in active use as a vehicle of communication and of controversy between scholars of various aims and nationalities. Latin was the common tongue of the civilised world, and the world is a fool for not keeping it. At least it would have saved us from Esperanto or other invented jargon. Organisation, disciplined unity, this is the keynote of the Roman character, and this is reflected in the literature of the people. Gravitas, virtus, pietas, sobriety of outlook, manliness, duty to Heaven and one's kin, these moral qualities are valued as holding together family and State. Mr. Duff says well: "The practical largely determines the course and themes of Roman literature. The businesslike Roman character explains why Latin literary works have a more intimate bearing on contemporary circumstances than Greek literary works have. . . . Some of the best Greek literature rose divinely from individual inspiration. . . . Most Roman writers answered some definite demand of their day. They seem less instinct with subtly incalculable forces. Before their experiments comes not merely the suggestion of a want to be met, but also, as a stimulating model, the successful achievement of the Greeks. This is apt to make Roman literature appear by comparison unoriginal". The whole passage is too long for full citation, but will repay study.

This same practicality is well shown and even rhetorically exaggerated to the unnecessary disparagement of Roman oratory in Vergil's well-known lines:

"Excudent alii spirantia mollius æra,
Credo equidem, vivos ducent de marmore vultus;
Orabunt causas melius, cælique meatus
Describent radio, et surgentia sidera dicent.
Tu regere imperio populos, Romane, memento;
Hæ tibi erunt artes; pacisque imponere morem,
Parcere subjectis et debellare superbos."

We all remember how Mummius, when removing the priceless masterpieces of Greek art from captured Corinth, bade his workmen handle them carefully, as if they were damaged, they would have to be replaced. Yet the Roman mind was remarkably receptive. He borrowed freely and willingly from alien literatures and religions.

"Grecia capta ferum victorem cepit"

is a tag with some truth in it. But "the Roman borrowed in a Roman way. He left his impress on the Greek material. . . . Throughout the Roman mark abides, modified, but never obliterated". Between Homer and Vergil, Horace and the Greek lyrists there are fundamental differences of thought and of expression underlying surface resemblances, and the contrast produces new forms of art. The chapter on "The Invasion of Hellenism" in particular will be found informing, following closely as it does on an elaborate analysis of the primitive Latin writings, such as the Saturnian verse and the "Satura". The influence of the former on later poetry and the conflict of its qualitative scansion with the quantitative system adopted subsequently is well brought out in a little book "Stress Accent in Latin Poetry", which we reviewed some years since. It is a remarkable fact that the trochee, which in this form was so freely used by the early writers, was finally revived in the "Pervigilium Veneris", which is, at the same time, in its still rigorous quantitative scansion, one of the last efforts of expiring classicism, and yet, in its general coincidence of prose and verse stresses, brings us near to the accentual Latin poetry of the Middle Ages.

The Satura again is deeply interesting as the only absolutely native product which persisted in individuality and won a place in Roman literature. The term (full dish, lanx satura) implies an offering of first fruits to Ceres and Bacchus. From the varied contents thereof it comes to mean a medley, a farrago of rustic music and dialogue, originally half dramatic. This in time lost its grip of the stage, being displaced by the Greek type of play with a connected plot, but through Lucilius it developed into the "Satire" of Juvenal and Horace, Dryden and Pope; and Juvenal's phrase "farrago libelli" is clearly traceable to its origin.

The chapters on Ennius and Nævius, Plautus and Terence, are full of interest, though not strikingly novel; the short-lived Roman epic, the fragments of tragedy, which appears again in the hands of Seneca, are all carefully treated. But most readers will be more at home with the Golden Age, which Mr. Duff divides into two periods—the Ciceronian and the Augustan. In the former Lucretius is admirably handled, and it is interesting to compare our author's views with those of Sellar, Dr. Masson, and Professor Mackail. We have also chapters on Catullus, whom he interprets finely, Varro, Cicero, Sallust, and Cæsar. He deals with Cicero at great length, and his views, like all those expressed on that remarkable man of words, are open to controversy. If we have nothing altogether fresh on some of these authors, at any rate the old is restated clearly and vigorously. In the Augustan period we find Vergil, Horace, Tibullus, Propertius, and Ovid, and, passing over others of minor interest, he concludes with Livy. Here there is a statement concerning the style of Livy and Tacitus that one feels inclined to challenge. He says: "Like the 'Annals' of Tacitus, the preface opens with a metrical movement (Facturusne operæ pretium sim) sounding as it were a note in unison with that poetic ring in the earliest legends", etc. Also he quotes as "a piece of hexameter verse", conveying "poeticus color", the words (xxii. 50. 10): "Hæc ubi dicta dedit stringit gladium cuneoque facto per medios." But surely this "dropping into poetry", like the Tacitean opening he mentions, "Urbem Romam a principio reges habuere", is an accident and a blemish in prose, as rhymes are in blank verse. Moreover, the lines he quotes make very indifferent and prosaic verse. Tacitus does use Vergilian phrases in a prose rhythm, which is quite another matter.

So much has been written on Latin authors, especially those of the Golden Age, that it might appear a difficult and thankless task to take up the tale anew, but Mr. Duff's success is great enough to justify the experiment.

THE MENTAL MACHINERY.

"Psychology and Crime." By Hugo Münsterberg. London: Unwin. 5s. net.

THE mind, so far as we can perceive it, acts only through the physical medium, which is at all times liable to go wrong and to become abnormal or diseased. The old and arbitrary ideas according to which a person must be either perfectly sane or incoherently mad are no longer credited. A knowledge of the multiplication table is not now looked upon as a test of absolute compos-mentisness, although the alienist is looked on with some suspicion, as tending to upset the simplicity of assumptions, though they be often anachronical and false.

Professor Münsterberg has something to say about border-land cases, upon suggestion and hysteria as causes of crimes, and upon hypnotism as a means of cure; in this he is following on the path of Schrenck-Notzing, Milne Bramwell and many others, and it is well, for the unhappy victims of strange passions will receive rather treatment than punishment when the truth is realised. The present work, however, deals mainly with testimony, and we are reminded by means of experiments, and to an extent which would make a prospective juryman feel very uncomfortable, how great may be the difference between truth-intending and truth-telling by a person giving evidence. People constantly "see" what they expect to behold, easily picture anything suggested to them, and often, as Dr. Tylor tells us is the case with savages, confuse imaginings with actual facts: thus George IV. fancied he had fought at Waterloo, and frequently talked about it, to the embarrassment of his entourage. But in spite of the shortcomings of witnesses, it is very doubtful if the psychological precautions suggested by the author against mistaken and misleading evidence could be adopted in practice.

On the other hand the experiments carried out by Dr. Jung at Zurich, by the author from Harvard, and by Dr. Peterson in New York, do seem to point to ways of extracting confessions more subtle than the cross-examination of counsel and more humane and reliable than the bullying and cruelty of what in America seem to be called the "third degree" police. By means of such instruments as the psychometer and the chronoscope, both the nerve force expended and the time taken in replying to questions can be measured and noted. In using the latter, the normal time taken to answer by the person examined is ascertained. He is then given a number of words to which he must call, as quickly as possible, the associated ideas—as, for instance, black-white, cat-dog, rat-trap, and so on.

Amongst the words chosen are dangerous ones relating to the movements of the accused and to some details of the crime committed. If he is guilty, he will very likely make incriminating replies to them; or he will have to pause to select his words—and the hiatus is noted, down to fractions of a second, upon a dial. Again, if he thinks that he has committed himself there will be a shock, and a gap will come immediately after the telling word and may inhibit a perfectly harmless one, which would be ominous. Such a system of thought-analysis, worked out with all the refinements of which it is capable, would prove a deadly instrument of investigation in the hands of an acute and patient Juge d'Instruction with plenty of time, and might explain many a mystery which would otherwise rest unsolved.

THE LOT OF THE TAILORESS.

"Makers of our Clothes." By Mrs. Carl Meyer and Clementina Black. London: Duckworth. 1909. 5s.

IF it is the intention of the authors by writing this book to help the campaign against sweated industries, they are a little late in the field. Perhaps their idea is to keep the Government up to the mark, hence texts from Ecclesiasticus and a dedication to the President of the Board of Trade. The authors and their friends record the information gleaned from a series of visits (spread over a year) to workers employed in the wholesale tailoring trades, and although this work is spoken of as investigation, there appears to have been no systematic attempt to verify the stories told. In any event little is added to the long tale of newspaper articles, Parliament speeches, and drawing-room meetings which have been since the sweated-industries exhibition. It is difficult to gather whether Mrs. Meyer and Miss Black appeal to sentiment or to economics. Perhaps both; and the mixture may account for the evident confusion of thought which results in such expressions as "tolls levied by the landlords", "exorbitant rents", and "the duty of not underselling less fortunate competitors". Miss Black can do better than this; we regret she has not drawn on her long experience of labour questions to give us something more practical than cheap Radical denunciation. These "investigations" disclose good and bad employers, some well-paid and many ill-paid workers, a large proportion of the latter struggling along on wages much below any reasonable subsistence level. It is these underpaid workers whom the Trade Boards Bill now before Parliament is designed to help. The Bill is certain to become law; and to carry out its provisions trade boards, representing employers and employed, under the guiding influence of the Board of Trade, will be empowered to establish a minimum-wage standard.

The difficulty of fixing a minimum piece-work wage for home workers is fully recognised by Miss Black, as also is the not improbable transference of most of their work to factories and workshops. These workers, mainly women, are usually either lonely fighters in the industrial world, widows, or the wives of men in underpaid casual labour only. Some are efficient; the majority weak, sick, and inefficient. The standard of work must inevitably be set by the efficient, who will certainly benefit by the fixing of a minimum limit; while those whose inefficiency, from whatever cause resulting, prevents them reaching the standard, must as certainly be driven to seek public assistance. Probably the ultimate effect on the race will be all to the good, but in the meantime there must be for some years an increasing burden on the poor rate. In any event it will no longer be possible to exploit charity and occasional out-relief for bridging over the chasm between the sweated and the living wage. Social reformers will to that extent be nearer to the radical treatment of one form of unemployment. It is disappointing that Miss Black gives no indication of the manner in which it is proposed to organise the women workers in the tailoring trade. The difficulty is very real: there is no cohesion or unity of purpose among them, and often the lines between employer, middleman, and worker are very faintly defined. Yet if the scheme is to be successful the workers themselves must be directly represented; social reformers of another class, however devoted and experienced, cannot replace them for all purposes.

The possibility of competition from imported goods made under sweated conditions is very lightly regarded by Mrs. Meyer and Miss Black. In support of their belief nothing is advanced beyond a few of those well-worn economic platitudes which do duty in so many modern books on social reform. "In all Europe", they say, "the movement for the establishment of a minimum wage is now strong and growing." Possibly; but the standard of the rest of Europe is not so high as in England, and there are many people who think the preservation of their own standard would be best assured by a reasonable tariff. Evidently in this book tariff is taboo; but for the benefit of those who think there is some connexion between tariffs and social reform we may quote "it was interesting to find that piece-work rates for certain processes are practically the same in Breslau as in London", and again, one young married couple "investigated" in Tottenham Court Road had lived for some time in New York, "and the wife thinks that food and housing were no dearer there in proportion to wages and were much more comfortable". By way of appendix the facts concerning a number of cases investigated in Germany and in England are offered for examination. The social conditions disclosed are certainly interesting, but nothing very definite can be deduced.

NOVELS.

"The Pools of Silence." By H. de Vere Stacpoole. London: Fisher Unwin. 1909. 6s.

The Congo atrocities are the subject of Mr. Stacpoole's latest novel. He deals with them in characteristically vigorous fashion, and his lurid descriptions bring home even to the least imaginative an idea of the monstrous and unspeakable things that are committed by what the author calls "the greatest murder syndicate the world has ever seen". We do not know that Mr. Stacpoole is justified in calling King Leopold a "murderer". Such references to a reigning monarch are much better omitted, especially in the pages of a novel, where the writer can manipulate fact or fiction to suit his purpose. We are not in a position to test the truth of the author's general picture, but we observe that in the prefatory note he refers the reader to the report of H.M. Consul in the Congo in proof of his assertion that the condition of the country has remained practically unaltered since its transference from the hands of the King to the hands of the Belgian Government. Apart from its avowed purpose the novel, although it errs rather on the side of sensationalism, may be recommended. Its hero is a young American doctor who accompanies Captain Berselius on an expedition to Central Africa in search of big game and money. His horror at the treatment of the natives meets with no sympathy from Berselius, who is an interesting type of the primitive man with his ferocity and blood-lust. There are some thrilling descriptions of elephant hunting, and the scenic effects are vivid.

"Everybody's Secret." By Dion Clayton Calthrop. London: Alston Rivers. 1909. 6s.

This is an example of the successful treatment of a sexual problem from the healthy and common-sense standpoint. Mr. Calthrop handles a very delicate theme in his novel, and handles it tactfully and well. His book is quite devoid of offence, and is evidence once again of the intense importance of manner in treating of certain matters. For the story that the author tells turns upon the discovery by the hero that the woman whom he has married has had a child by another man. Toby Quarrenden is a delightful creation. He is one of those healthy, simple-minded, lovable people who believe in the goodness of everybody, and who consequently bring out as a rule the best in everybody. There is a general conspiracy on the part of his friends to keep up his belief in human nature. There is real tense drama in the author's description of Toby's discovery of his wife's past, and the situation is treated sympathetically and convincingly. The book is full of good things, and can be cordially recommended.

"Dromina." By John Ayscough. Bristol: Arrowsmith. London: Simpkin, Marshall. 1909. 6s.

Mr. Ayscough reminds us in this novel that there is no end and no beginning to any story, and this may be true if one thinks of a story as just a tiny section of an eternal thread extending both ways beyond it. But as applied to the novelist's art it is surely a theory making for formlessness. And there is a kinematograph-like lack of "composition" about the many figures crowded into this recital of the romantic fortunes of the house of M'Morogh, whose seat was Dromina Castle. Many people like the kinematograph; and they do not often see so many uncrowned kings jostling one another as here—the Cardinal Duke of York, the Dauphin Charles Louis Bourbon, and M'Morogh himself, who believes that he is de jure King of Ireland, not to mention his descendant who snatches an imperial throne by a coup d'état. It is magnificent, but it is not enough concentrated in interest to move us much.

"Diana Dethroned." By W. M. Letts. London: Lane. 1909. 6s.

The "note" of this novel is that mistakes in life are inevitable, and do not very much matter, so long as people behave nicely in the unfortunate circumstances that ensue. Perhaps this is true, but wise people are in favour of a little looking before leaping, even if thereby they—not to mention the others occasionally involved—escape much wholesome tribulation. But, be that as it may, this story, well written though it is, makes anything but exhilarating reading. Not on that account, of course, can we say it is untrue to life. Indeed, we feel sure that the emotional young ass of twenty-three, who sheds tears over a dead dog and desires when elated to slide down banisters, would be likely enough to marry twice—each time an unsuitable girl—and die early leaving offspring by both of them; and we gather that the author thinks the youth behaved as nicely as was possible in the circumstances. Perhaps this is true, also: and herein (and in like happenings) lies such force as the story has. As to the heroine, who is likened to Diana, she leaves us cold even when "dethroned"—that is to say, when developed through suffering into something like a normal human being.

"Moon of Valleys." By David Whitelaw. London: Greening. 1909. 6s.

This is a sensational story, written round a mysterious Oriental jewel. The characters themselves take a hand in the telling; and there is a hieroglyphic picture pointing to the whereabouts of the hidden treasure. If the book cannot claim much originality of theme or method, it is bright, and skilfully contrived to keep the attention of those readers who want excitement of a harmless kind, and do not pay too nice a regard to probabilities.

"The Waking Hour." By Harold Wintle. London: Unwin. 1909. 6s.

The three principal figures in this novel are a hard and unnatural woman, a vicious clerk in Holy Orders, and a duke who says "You ain't". They can hardly have been meant to be charming, and they fail to startle because, as presented, they are so palpably unreal.

SHORTER NOTICES.

"The Law and Custom of the Constitution." By Sir William R. Anson. Vol. I. 4th Edition. Oxford: At the Clarendon Press. 1909. 12s. 6d. net.

This volume is that one of the three forming the work which deals with Parliament, and has passed through four editions, while that on the Crown has passed through three, since the first publication in 1886. Sir William Anson revises his book when there are controversies pending which will have important results for the history and functions of Parliament. At present it is more than ever the case that while the British Constitution is being described it is changing its character. No one, says the author, "who tries to describe the Constitution of to-day can fail to be impressed with a sense of the passing and ephemeral character of nearly everything that is to be said and written on the subject, and with the instability of things as they are". In broad outline, our institutions are what they were when the first edition appeared, but "a change has come over their working which sooner or later may call for some change in their structure". So that though Sir William has no important changes to note in the relation of the House of Commons and the House of Lords, the present controversies give a new colour to what he says on this point. He has to handle as a lawyer questions on which as a Conservative politician he is at issue with a Liberal Government. On the dispute as to finance Bills he holds the view that the constitutional practice is against the power of rejection by the Lords; but it must be noted that it is only an opinion on the results of very recent precedents which have nothing like the force of those which prevent the Lords from imposing a tax. Moreover, it leaves open the question of "tacking" which arises on the present financial proposals; and as to this the right of the Lords is indisputable. On other matters, such as the strong claim which the defects of the representative system give the Lords to interpret the feeling of the country as to measures involving fundamental changes, or the Liberal plan to turn Parliament virtually into one Chamber, this book is a sound gospel. "If we are to contemplate", says the author, "the transfer of legislative sovereignty to a single Chamber, wherein the time of one Parliament would probably be engaged in undoing the work of its predecessor under conditions of discussion limited, as at present, by the guillotine, we should have departed a long way from the constitutional ideas of the nineteenth century".

"A History of Modern Banks of Issue." By Charles A. Conant. New York and London: Putnam. 1909.

This is a voluminous and erudite treatise on the banking systems of the world, too technical and elaborate for the general reader, but valuable for the students and practitioners of finance. There is an interesting account of the American panic in 1907 in the final chapter. Mr. Conant shows how events had for ten years (1897-1907) been making for a financial catastrophe. A financial crisis invariably occurs when the circulating capital of the world is converted too rapidly and disproportionately into fixed capital. In the decade in question there had been three wars—the South African war, the Russo-Japanese war, and the war between Spain and the United States. These wars had absorbed about £560,000,000 of the circulating capital of the world. After the conclusion of peace there was, as there always is, a great expansion of trade to replace the waste of material. There were innumerable issues by Governments, municipalities, railways, and combinations of commercial undertakings called trusts. This process of creating new securities converted circulating into fixed capital at too rapid a rate, and suddenly the world awoke to the fact that there was not enough money to go round. This produced the panic of 1907, which was one of the most violent and quite the shortest which the world has ever seen. The rapid recovery was due to the fact that the fixed capital, the instrument of industry, was there all the time. Amongst other interesting facts, Mr. Conant tells us that the gold produced between 1890 and 1907 was equal to half the production of gold in the preceding four centuries—an astounding thing.

"Through Uganda to Mount Elgon." By the Rev. J. B. Purvis. London: Unwin. 1909. 6s.

There have been published lately a good many books dealing incidentally or wholly with missionary enterprise in East Africa. Mr. Purvis however went beyond the now almost beaten track, and his book should be read by all interested in mission work. He has many notes of what he saw on the way up to Mount Elgon from the coast, but the chief novelty of the book is the description of the Masaba people and country. In Masaba the conditions are totally different from those in Uganda. The natives are friendly and trustful and "there is no king or feudal chief to influence his followers one way or the other. Every man, woman and child claims to be independent, and we often see the effect of this independence on our school children". The chief difficulty of the missionary is the unsettling of the native mind which follows his first efforts, and it is necessary to remember the Luganda proverb that "he who goes slowly reaches far".

"The Voice of the Orient." By Mrs. Walter Tibbits. London: Long. 1909. 3s. 6d. net.

Mrs. Tibbits has in her something of the spirit which secured her ancestor who settled in Ireland in Elizabeth's day the title of Adventurer. She adventures much: she has explored many of the hidden corners of India from Bombay to the Wangat Valley, and she reads more into what she sees than most people. "All sensitive natures feel to a greater or less degree the working within themselves of the ferment of the East" when they "pass down the Red Sea", she says. She appears to have passed down the Red Sea in a ferment the consequences of which have been to her momentous. The East has not called to her in vain, either on the spiritual or the material side. Everything in the peninsula appeals to her until she becomes almost more Eastern than the Indians themselves. For her India is everything that is romantic, picturesque, poetic and fateful. Of what she has seen she writes for the most part admirably, and there is more true colour in her chapters than in most colour-books. But she is a woman. That alone can explain the inclusion among the illustrations of two pictures of herself. It is a weakness which may lead many to regard "the Voice" not as that of the Orient, but of a fashionable woman of the Occident. To take such a view would be unfair to a book that is by no means ordinary.

THEOLOGY.

"The Pauline Epistles: a Critical Study." By R. Scott. Edinburgh: Clark. 1909. 6s. net.

The Epistles ascribed to S. Paul have been a critical problem for so long that it may seem impossible to say anything fresh about them. If we accept the traditional authorship and date they fall into four groups: (*a*) Thessalonians, (*b*) Galatians—Corinthians—Romans, (*c*) Ephesians—Philippians—Colossians—Philemon, and (*d*) Pastorals; and these groups are separated so widely from each other both in subject-matter and style that it is not an easy matter to answer a critic who urges that if S. Paul wrote the first he could not have written the last; the third and fourth groups have often been ruled out on these grounds. Dr. Scott has now carried the argument from internal evidence considerably further; he pleads that if we are to judge authorship by subject-matter, treatment, and style, we must be prepared not only to divide by groups but to cut up single epistles; for almost every epistle contains some features characteristic of others. He therefore boldly gives us four groups arranged on a new and original plan. The first, purely Pauline, consists of I. Corinthians (except xv. 20-34), II. Corinthians (except vi. 14-vii. 1, xiii. 11-14), Romans i.-xi., Galatians, Philippians, Romans xvi. 1-16, 21-24. The second comprises a series of documents mainly attributed to S. Paul, but in reality composed by Silas; these are: Ephesians, Hebrews, I. Peter, I. Thessalonians iv.-v., II. Thessalonians i.-ii., Romans xii., xiii., xv., I. Corinthians xv. 20-34, II. Corinthians vi. 14-vii. 1, the Gospel of S. Matthew in its present form, and perhaps slight elements in the Acts. The third consists of I. Thessalonians i.-iii., II. Thessalonians iii., Colossians, Philemon, Romans xiv., and the final editorship of S. Mark's Gospel; of these Timothy is the author. The fourth consists of the Pastoral Epistles which are assigned to

S. Luke. The documents are throughout divided according to authorship rather than date; thus Dr. Scott, though denying the direct Pauline authorship of the Pastorals, would separate II. Timothy from Philippians by only a few months, and regard it as a dying message of the Apostle, dictated by him to S. Luke, or written by the latter from memory soon after the Apostle's martyrdom.

The author has worked out his theory with care and ingenuity; but it is too complicated and elaborate, and only proves to us how subjective the "internal-evidence" argument can become, and consequently how weak. He has formed his own rigid conception of what S. Paul must have been, and everything which does not agree with it is rejected. It is a very narrow, limited S. Paul that is given us; one who writes on few subjects and always in the same way, who never uses a Greek word in more than one sense or in reference to more than one object. Diversities of thought or expression between an acknowledged or disputed epistle, or chapter, are always held to establish difference of authorship; and difference of authorship once assumed, similarities are put down to servile copying; instances are only allowed to count one way. The conservative student may reasonably protest that such a theory falls by its own weight; it is at least as likely that S. Paul's style was not absolutely uniform, or his mental attitude immoveable, as that every one of his epistles should be a mosaic. Dr. Scott himself is far more convincing when he is pointing out resemblances than when he is detecting discrepancies; he cannot for a moment make us doubt that Thessalonians or Philemon were written by S. Paul; but he has certainly succeeded in pointing out a series of surprising resemblances throughout the Pauline Epistles, Hebrews, I. Peter, the Synoptic Gospels, the Acts, and even I. John; and these can be best explained by supposing them to belong to much the same time, place, and atmosphere; to have proceeded from a very small circle of writers, intimately connected with each other, thinking the same thoughts, using the same terms; that is, from the Apostolic leaders of the primitive Church. This book is more conservative than the author imagines.

"The Old Testament in the Light of the Religion of Babylonia and Assyria." By J. Evans Thomas. London: Black. 1909.

Mr. Thomas has made a handy summary of the recent discoveries in Babylonia and Assyria, and of the traditions to which they bear witness; and he has carefully compared these with the corresponding records in the Old Testament, not always to the advantage of the latter. The reader who wishes, without going deeply into the subject, to know something about the Babylonian legends as to the Creation, the Fall of Man, the Flood, or such a legal code as the Laws of Hammurabi, will find them conveniently presented here; only he may feel inclined to protest that it is not a simple presentation that is placed before him, but a presentation with a purpose—that of showing that not only in its history and accounts of the origin of the world or of mankind, but even in its definitely religious teaching, the Old Testament occupies no unique position and gives evidence of no special revelation, but has simply assimilated the current beliefs of the greater nations of the East. Greater authorities, such as Dr. Driver, are somewhat more cautious not only in what they state but in what they suggest, and Mr. Thomas' compilation would have been valuable if his bias had not been so obvious.

"The Gospel of Human Needs." Being the Hulsean Lectures delivered before the University of Cambridge, 1908-9, with additions. By J. N. Figgis. London: Longmans. 1909. 4s. 6d. net.

The title of this book is a more accurate definition of its contents than the preface. There, Dr. Figgis describes his lectures as an attempt to show that miracles are a help rather than a stumbling-block to faith. After such a declaration we naturally look for a systematic defence or explanation of the miraculous element in Christianity. But we get something different—a protest, at times rising to eloquence, at times sinking to smartness, against the tyranny of intellectualism in the religious sphere; and a plea on behalf of the romantic element, of mystery and poetry, as being equally real things, and as answering equally deep needs of the human soul. The lecturer describes, and describes well, the religious unrest of the present day and its impatience, not only with the traditional creeds of the Church, but also with the triumphant secularism of the mid-Victorian epoch, and all its naïve faith in the saving virtues of education and physical science. He is at his best when criticising the critics; his constructive work is not very convincing, and it does not come to much more than saying "Life is real and grim for the masses; they do not want clever theories, and they will not chop logic; nothing but the presence of God Himself in their midst will give romance to their drudgery and victory to their moral struggles; let them grasp this great miracle—the perpetual presence of Christ in Church and Sacrament—and the other miracles will fall into their right place". We believe this is true; but it is not proved by simply saying so; it can only be proved by that same logic which we rate so highly when we can silence an opponent with it, and so cheaply when the opponent silences us. Dr. Figgis himself uses it deftly in attacking Modernism and showing that we cannot deny all the facts in the Gospel story and yet claim to believe in the Gospel religion; we wish there had been more argument and less rhetoric in the earlier lectures.

"God with us: a Study in Religious Idealism." By W. R. Boyce Gibson, Lecturer in Philosophy at the University of London. London: Black. 1909. 3s. 6d. net.

Mr. Boyce Gibson's book consists of a series of reviews of Professor Eucken, Professor Stanley Hall, Professor James, and others. The volume is dedicated to Rudolf Eucken, and very appropriately; for no man has done more than the writer to popularise Eucken among us, and Eucken's influence is in these pages apparent everywhere. There are good things in these essays, but they are not written in English. What language is this?—"The natural unself-conscious egoism of the prepubertal period", or "the phyletic inspiration of childhood is palæo-atavistic, that of adolescence neo-atavistic". We are told that the main credential for our religious vocation lies not so much in our being human as in our having been young. In adolescence "with the expansion of the love-life comes the urgent call for its control". "Nature and spirit battle for the empery of love. Nature, the passionate will to live, counsels abandonment; spirit urges restraint. . . . The premature passage from adolescence to maturity is above all things to be avoided. The inspirations of later life have their main source in this springtime of the soul". This is probably true. The whole chapter gains in significance from the author's eagerness to found the moral upon the religious.

"The Jew and Human Sacrifice [Human Blood and Jewish Ritual]. an Historical and Sociological Inquiry." By H. L. Strack. Translated from the Eighth Edition, with Corrections, New Preface, and Additions by the Author. London: Cope and Fenwick. 1909.

From time to time we still hear of anti-Semitic riots consequent on child murders, in distant parts of Europe. A child mysteriously disappears, or its body is found horribly mutilated; and, with a persistence that suggests either deep-rooted tradition or deliberate malice, the rumour spreads that the murder was committed by Jews, in order to secure the victim's blood for ritual purposes. Professor Strack, of Berlin, who is one of the foremost authorities on Jewish history in Europe, has produced an exhaustive treatise on the use of human blood in primitive medicine, magic and superstition; and his researches show not only that its use would be absolutely repugnant to the whole spirit of Jewish religion and tradition, but that sometimes Jews themselves have been murdered by Christians for blood-ritual purposes. To us in England his book will have mainly an academic interest; it will take its place among learned contributions to the science of comparative religion; the ordinary reader need not concern himself with the unpleasant beliefs and practices of half-civilised man, or with the dark stories of tortures inflicted upon unhappy Jews to make them confess crimes they had never committed. But the prefaces to Dr. Strack's numerous German editions make it clear that on the Continent the calumny is still sedulously circulated and widely believed; and in thus publicly refuting it he has stood up boldly for the cause of truth and righteousness.

"Life after Death." By S. C. Gayford. London: Masters. 1909. 2s. 6d. net.

Mr. Gayford knows how to give sober and reverent treatment to a very solemn subject. He sets forth what reason, the Bible, and the Church teach us as to the condition of the departed, the intermediate state, the Last Judgment, and the final condition of the saved and of the impenitent; and he sets it forth simply, but with adequate learning and a due sense of responsibility; if our junior clergy would study this little book before preaching on the last things it would be good both for themselves and for their congregations. On the question of eternal punishment we notice a slight wavering in the writer's position; he rejects the doctrines of conditional immortality and of universalism as being against Scripture, but is willing to believe that the Divine warnings as to hell-fire may prove in the end to have served their purpose so well that at the Last

(*Continued on page* 206.)

Day no human being will be found condemned to the extremest penalty; which looks like rejecting universalism theoretically, and practically accepting it. After all, almost everything that can be said by uninspired lips on this question was said many years ago by Dean Church in his sermon "Sin and Judgment", and we are glad that Mr. Gayford has drawn attention to that wonderful sermon, and to the fact that it has been published separately by the S.P.C.K.

THE AUGUST REVIEWS.

South Africa, India, and the Budget are the principal political topics discussed in the magazines this month. Only the "National Review" and the "Fortnightly" have articles dealing with the Navy, the one being "The Surrender of the Sea Lords", the other "Lord Charles Beresford as Naval Expert". In the "Nineteenth Century" Mr. Roderick Jones, Reuter's Agent in charge in South Africa, treats very fully the colour question, his point being that any material interference from the imperial side as to native and coloured political rights would put an end to the union. His answer to the question "What do we reap from the war except the right to send out a Governor-General and to police the Union sea-board?" seems to us naïve and unduly optimistic. He assumes that South Africa will become nothing less than are Canada, Australia, and New Zealand, and "Her people, Dutch and English, will be British in the broadest sense".

"Blackwood" puts the question from another point of view. It discusses the relative claims of the present Government and the Opposition to the credit "for an event which all welcome". After pointing out that there were good grounds for fear at the prospect of subjection to a Dutch Government, and the attitude of hostility to Union at the earlier stages from the Boer leaders, the writer proceeds: "The grant of self-government was, no doubt, a causa sine qua non of the Union of South Africa. Without it there would have been no means of repressing the natural desire. But it was not the causa causans. To those who say that it was, we would put this question: The Cape, the Transvaal, the Free State, and Natal, were all self-governing before the war—why did they not unify then? The true cause, in our opinion, was the war of 1899-1902, and, as such, we observe, it is now recognised by both races in South Africa. Rather, perhaps, we should say the war and the labours of Lord Milner after the war". He recalls what was done and he ends thus: "When self-government came South Africa could begin nearly where Canada and Australia left off, and the further step of unification followed almost of necessity. The edifice was completed by the co-operation of both races in South Africa, with the help of another High Commissioner appointed by the Conservatives; but the foundations were laid by Mr. Balfour's Government and their great Viceroy".

Both Mr. J. D. Rees M.P. in his article in the "Fortnightly Review" and Sir Bampfylde Fuller in his article in the "Nineteenth Century" on "The Foundations of Loyalty" lay stress on the fomenting of agitation and sedition in India by the encouragement it receives from Radical teaching in England. They show with what hypocrisy the so-called constitutional agitation is being conducted in India, and they both point their remarks by reference to Mr. Banerjee. Sir Bampfylde Fuller says: "In popular idea he is inseparably connected with the denunciation of British rule and of British morality, the initiation of the boycott, and the foundation of the school political associations which have demoralised thousands of youths". The effect of arresting certain ringleaders of sedition has been marred by "the distinction with which Mr. Banerjee has been received by us as one of the representatives of the Empire's press. . . . It may seem politic to win over so eloquent, so bitter an adversary. But the favours we have shown him must have caused some curious thoughts to his Bengali followers and his Mohammedan opponents, and cannot have strengthened the respect with which either regard us." Mr. Rees states that "on the day after the murder of Sir William Curzon Wyllie" his newspaper published a speech from the well-known agitator Arabindo Ghose, of which one sentence was: "There are three words which have the power of remoulding Governments—Liberty, Equality, and Fraternity. The fiat of God has gone out to the Indian nation to unite—unite, be free, be great". Mr. Rees comments: "Now, this means—Away with British rule, of which Arabindo Ghose has been a determined enemy, though he escaped conviction at a recent trial".

We may mention in this connexion a very apposite article by Mr. Edward Dicey in the "Nineteenth Century" on "Hindu Students in England", in which he explains the position of law students at the Inns of Court and the difficulties which have arisen owing to the great increase of students and the disaffection amongst them. He appears to think that the recent great increase dates from the defeat of Russia by Japan; and that it is a consequence of the demand of "India for the Indians". We suppose what he means is that these students come here to qualify themselves by study in England to be more efficient agitators when they return to their own country.

Also as to India, but leaving this class of topics, attention should be called to an article in "Blackwood", specially interesting just now when Lord Kitchener is about leaving India, on Lord Kitchener's work in the Indian Army. The article is critical, and not wholly eulogistic, but the writer believes that the scheme of Army reorganisation will be an abiding monument to Lord Kitchener's work in India.

Turning to the Budget, we find, as we should expect, that the "Nineteenth Century" and the "Contemporary" take precisely opposite views on the constitutional claim of the House of Lords to amend or reject the financial proposals of the House of Commons. The other magazines do not treat the subject in formal articles. Mr. J. A. R. Marriott's article in the "Nineteenth Century" argues that the precedents show the Lords' right of concurrence in taxation; hence the right to refuse to concur in its imposition and to reject it. This is distinct from the right to impose a tax, which the Lords do not possess, and it follows that neither can they alter or amend a proposed tax. Referring to the distinction which Lord Salisbury made in 1894 on the Finance Bill, Mr. Marriott points out the consequences if Lord Salisbury meant that the legal right could not expediently be exercised. He says this "means that the House of Lords must virtually surrender all its concurrent corporate rights in regard to taxation, that individual peers must accept a position inferior to that of the meanest voter in the Kingdom, and must shoulder burdens imposed upon them by the fiat of an assembly in which they have neither part nor lot. It means more than this. It means the constitutional omnipotence of a single-chamber legislature the like of which no great State has ever seen".

Mr. Harold Spender, in the "Contemporary", contends that this merely legal right is swallowed up in the constitutional question. He gives as illustration the Crown's right of veto; yet "None the less the King cannot exercise this right, and precisely by the same rule the Lords, as Lord Salisbury perceived, are debarred from rejecting or amending a Finance Bill". To this Mr. Marriott, judging from his treatment of the subject, would answer that even if this were so the Budget is revolutionary, and the House of Lords, as the bulwark against revolution, would be justified in meeting revolution by revolution. A propos of the Budget, we may also mention an article in the "National" on "The Burdened Landowner of England", in which Mr. Frank Fox, as an Australian, shows how much less are the burdens borne by land in Australia, where it is yet difficult to keep the people from flowing to the cities from the country. He asks: "How can England, pursuing a policy, as it seems to me, of casting large burdens on the landowning class, whilst denying them all protection, hope to keep a fair proportion of rural population?"

Lord Erroll, in the "Nineteenth", has a most sensible article on the compulsory service debate. Very good, too, are the notes in the "National" on the same subject.

Among the literary articles in the magazines the most interesting is Mr. B. W. Matz' in the "Fortnightly", on "George Meredith as Publisher's Reader", composed by Mr. Matz from the records of Messrs. Chapman and Hall, to whom Meredith was literary adviser for many years. Another article in the same magazine, for those to whom Greek scholarship appeals, is Professor N. Rhys Roberts' Plutarchian comparison of "Porson and Jebb". The "Fortnightly" and the "Nineteenth Century" celebrate the centenary of Tennyson: the one with an article by the Rev. Henry W. Clark, the other with a characteristically pontifical utterance by Mr. Frederic Harrison. Each taking the test of the prophetic gift and the gift of literary charm, the result of their appraisement of Tennyson's position as a poet amounts to the same thing, and may be guessed. In the "Contemporary" an article by the Count S. C. de Soissons on "Brunetière" is one which all who care for French literature will like to read.

The "English Review", which is in its ninth number, is almost entirely literary. There is the beginning of a novel by Mr. Henry James, called "Mora Montravers", and the rest of the contents perhaps one may compendiously describe as good for readers on holiday who are sufficiently fastidious to pass the usual holiday miscellanies.

For this Week's Books see page 208.

During the last half-century everyone travelling in hot climes has made a point of carrying some

DR. J. COLLIS BROWNE'S

CHLORODYNE

so as to stop immediately an attack of

DIARRHŒA, DYSENTERY, or CHOLERA.

Hot weather in the British Isles strikes suddenly, and everyone should take a little precaution. Don't wait until you actually need the Chlorodyne; but always keep it by you. Avoid disappointment, and insist on having DR. J. COLLIS BROWNE'S CHLORODYNE, it

ACTS LIKE A CHARM.

Of all Chemists, 1/1½, 2/9 & 4/6.

CONNOISSEURS OF COFFEE

DRINK THE

RED WHITE & BLUE

DELICIOUS FOR BREAKFAST & AFTER DINNER.

In making, use less quantity, it being much stronger than ordinary COFFEE.

POOLE & LORD

INDIAN AND GENERAL OUTFITTERS,

322 OXFORD STREET, LONDON, W.

(NEARLY OPPOSITE BOND STREET.)

INVENTORS OF THE

"Sans-Plis" SHIRT.

Prices from 7s. 6d.

The "SANS-PLIS" Shirt is superior to any other for Indian and Colonial wear. Being entirely free from gathers, it is cooler, much stronger, and will bear the Indian mode of washing better than any shirt in use.

A single shirt, or other article, made to *measure*, and accurate patterns preserved to ensure correctness in the execution of future orders.

Makers of Drawers with Flexible Hip Belt Bands.

"BREECHES CUT."

BRAGG'S CHARCOAL BISCUITS

Cure Indigestion

SPEEDILY CURE ACIDITY, FLATULENCE, HEARTBURN, IMPURE BREATH, INDIGESTION, DIARRHŒA, &c.

PREVENT MANY AN ILLNESS. Highly recommended by the Medical Profession. Sold by all Chemists and Stores. Biscuits, 1s., 2s. and 4s. per tin; Powder, 2s. and 4s. per bottle; Lozenges, 1s. 1½d. tin.

CHARCOAL CHOCOLATES. Highly nutritious and digestible. Sold in tins, 1/- each.

J. L. BRAGG, Ltd., 14 Wigmore Street, London, W.

THE CONDUIT STREET AUCTION GALLERIES.

The attention of Executors, Trustees, Solicitors, and Owners, who may be desirous of selling Works of Art, Family Jewels, Old Silver, Furniture, Pictures, Prints, Miniatures, China, Coins, Books, Old Lace, Furs, Musical Instruments, Guns, and other Valuables, is drawn to Messrs.

KNIGHT, FRANK & RUTLEY'S

AUCTION GALLERIES, 9 CONDUIT STREET, AND 23A MADDOX STREET, W., which are Open Daily to receive goods intended for early sales.

VALUATIONS are prepared for Fire Insurance, Estate Duty, and all other purposes. As to Insurance, owners are reminded that, for security, Messrs. KNIGHT, FRANK & RUTLEY'S detailed inventory and valuation of the contents of a Town or Country Mansion is an important adjunct to their Fire Insurance Policies.

P. & O. AUTUMN PASSENGER SAILINGS (1909)

(Carrying Mails under Contract with H.M. Government.)

EGYPT, INDIA, STRAITS, CHINA, JAPAN, AUSTRALASIA.

AUSTRALIA, CHINA & JAPAN; also BOMBAY via ADEN.

Steamer.	Tons.	From London.	From Marseilles.
MACEDONIA	10,500	Sept. 10	Sept. 17
MOLDAVIA	10,000	Sept. 24	Oct. 1
MONGOLIA	10,000	Oct. 8	Oct. 15
MARMORA	10,500	Oct. 22	Oct. 29
MOREA	11,000	Nov. 5	Nov. 12
MOOLTAN	10,000	Nov. 19	Nov. 26
MANTUA	11,000	Dec. 3	Dec. 10

P. & O. Return Tickets, available for 2 years, at a Fare and a Half. For Passage and all information apply at the Company's Offices, 122 Leadenhall St., E.C., or Northumberland Ave., W.C., London.

AUSTRALIA by ORIENT LINE,

UNDER CONTRACT TO CARRY HIS MAJESTY'S MAILS.

FROM LONDON EVERY ALTERNATE FRIDAY, calling at PLYMOUTH, GIBRALTAR, MARSEILLES, NAPLES, PORT SAID, and COLOMBO.

Managers—F. GREEN & CO.: ANDERSON, ANDERSON & CO.

Head Offices—FENCHURCH AVENUE, LONDON.

For Passage apply to the latter firm at 5 Fenchurch Avenue, E.C., or to the Branch Office, 28 Cockspur Street, Charing Cross, S.W.

BELGIAN STATE RAILWAY AND MAIL PACKET SERVICE.

Cheapest Railway Tickets in the World.

RUNDREISE TICKETS AT OFFICIAL PRICES.

MADE UP AT A FEW HOURS' NOTICE.

Apply, 53 GRACECHURCH STREET, or 72 REGENT STREET. And at Dover. Also, for information only, to P. DEFRANCE, 47 CANNON STREET, E.C.

UNION-CASTLE LINE.

ROYAL MAIL SERVICE.—To SOUTH and EAST AFRICA.—Via Madeira, Canaries, Ascension, St. Helena, and Lobito Bay.

Steamers	Service	London	Southampton
* NORMAN	Royal Mail	—	Aug. 14
§ DOVER CASTLE	Intermediate	Aug. 13	Aug. 14
* WALMER CASTLE	Royal Mail	—	Aug. 21
† GALEKA	Intermediate	Aug. 20	Aug. 21

* Via Madeira. § Via Teneriffe.
† Via Las Palmas, Ascension, and St. Helena.

Special Trains from Waterloo to Southampton every Saturday.

Donald Currie and Co., Managers, 3 and 4 Fenchurch Street, E.C. West End Agencies—Sleeping Car Co., 20 Cockspur Street, S.W., and Thos. Cook and Son, 13 Cockspur Street, S.W.

ELY CATHEDRAL.

Visitors will find First Class Hotel Accommodation at the "LAMB" Family Hotel, which is situated close to the Cathedral. **MODERATE TERMS.** Omnibus meets all trains.

Proprietor, S. AIREY.

R. ANDERSON & CO.,

BRITISH, INDIAN, AND COLONIAL ADVERTISEMENT CONTRACTORS,

14 KING WILLIAM STREET, STRAND, W.C.,

GIVE THE BEST TERMS for Company and General Advertising. Advice, Estimates, and all information free of charge. Replies received.

GUY'S HOSPITAL.—ENTRANCE SCHOLARSHIPS to be competed for in September 1909. Two Open Scholarships in Arts, one of the value of £100, open to candidates under twenty years of age, and one of £50, open to candidates under twenty-five years of age. Two Open Scholarships in Science, one of the value of £150, and another of £60, open to candidates under twenty-five years of age. One Open Scholarship for University Students who have completed their study of anatomy and physiology, of the value of £50.—Full particulars may be obtained on application to the DEAN, Guy's Hospital, London Bridge, S.E.

ELTHAM COLLEGE, KENT.

(THE ROYAL NAVAL SCHOOL.)

PUBLIC SCHOOL LIFE AND EDUCATION, with Special Classes for all Naval and Military Examinations. Special Fees for Officers in the Navy and Army. Recognised by the Army Council. Large Playing-fields. Gymnasium, Swimming Bath; Chemical and Physical Laboratories; Cadet Corps, &c. Recent Honours: Open Scholarship, Balliol College; 1st, Open Scholarships, Hertford and Merton Colleges; 1st place Naval Clerkships; Admissions to Sandhurst, Osborne, &c. NEXT TERM BEGINS SEPTEMBER 15th.

Apply Headmaster, Rev. A. E. RUBIE, D.D.

THIS WEEK'S BOOKS.

ART

Rubens (Edward Dillon). Methuen. 25s. net.

FICTION

The Kingdom of the Earth (Anthony Partridge). Mills and Boon. 6s.

The Master Schemer (Mrs. Vere Campbell); Sealed Orders (A. E. Carey). Greening. 6s. each.

The Book of the Golden Key (Edited by Hugo Ames and Flora Hayter). Kegan Paul. 6s.

Lords of the Sea (Edward Noble). Methuen. 6s.

HISTORY

The Court of Louis XIII. (K. A. Patmore), 10s. 6d. net; A Rose of Savoy (H. Noel Williams), 15s. net. Methuen.

Despatches from Paris 1784-1790 (Oscar Browning). St. Catherine Press.

TRAVEL

Among the Danes (F. M. Bullin). Methuen. 7s. 6d. net.

MISCELLANEOUS

Dictionary of National Biography (Edited by Sidney Lee. Vol. XVIII). Smith, Elder. 15s. net.

Paton's List of Schools, 1909. Paton. 2s.

Making of Gardens, On the (Sir George Sitwell). 5s. net.

World's Madonna, The (J. Shaw Mulholland). Burns and Oates.

Some Pages from the Life of Turkish Women (Demetra Vaka). Constable. 5s. net.

Your Week End Is Not Complete

WITHOUT

THE SATURDAY WESTMINSTER

The Weekly Issue of "The Westminster Gazette."

IT IS THE ONLY WEEKLY MAGAZINE REVIEW OF THE KIND.

"F. C. G.'s Cartoons of the Week.

An Unique Page of "Problems and Prizes."

Book Reviews and Special Literary Articles by the best known writers.

ONE PENNY.

Post, 6/6 per annum (home); 8/8 (abroad).

OFFICES: SALISBURY SQUARE, LONDON, E.C.

Sir ISAAC PITMAN & SONS, Ltd.,

No. 1 Amen Corner, LONDON, E.C.

Now Ready.

THE LATEST ADDITION TO PITMAN'S MAKERS OF NATIONAL HISTORY SERIES.

Edited by W. H. HUTTON, B.D.

GENERAL WOLFE.

By EDWARD SALMON.

In crown 8vo. cloth gilt, with Frontispiece and Map, **3s. 6d.** net.

On September 13 will be celebrated the 150th anniversary of the capture of Quebec and the death of General Wolfe.

"Mr. Salmon's exhaustive account of the whole campaign should be read by every impartial student of military annals." *Outlook.*

"A careful and attractive study . . . Wolfe's life story, as a notable chapter in our national history, is here admirably told."—*Daily Telegraph.*

"A new and notable series of comprehensive and scholarly historical manuals." *Glasgow Herald.*

"No scheme could be more admirable than that of the series of volumes entitled, 'Makers of National History.'" *Sphere.*

"The three volumes which have already appeared in this new library of historical manuals fully demonstrate the value of such a series, the immediate object of which is 'to commemorate important men whose share in the making of national history seems to need a more complete record than it has yet received.' Each volume is obviously the work of a practised historian." *Daily Graphic.*

"The new series ought to make a place for itself in school and public libraries." *Saturday Review.*

Previous Volumes in the Series.

CARDINAL BEAUFORT. By L. B. RADFORD, D.D.

VISCOUNT CASTLEREAGH. By ARTHUR HASSALL, M.A.

ARCHBISHOP PARKER. By W. M. KENNEDY, B.A.

READY SHORTLY.

FRANCIS ATTERBURY. By H. C. BEECHING, D.Litt.

A NEW 16 pp. PROSPECTUS IS IN PREPARATION, and will be sent to anyone gratis on application.

NOW READY.

THE RAMBLINGS OF AN OLD MUMMER

By RUSSELL CRAUFURD.

An interesting volume of bright, breezy anecdotes of well-known theatrical favourites—past and present.

PRICE SIX SHILLINGS.

Ask for the following Four Novels at your Library. They are all worth your attention.

SIX SHILLINGS EACH.

A *really* thrilling story. H. G. Wells outdone.

THE HUMAN MOLE

By COLIN COLLINS

is a startling story by a new writer, and is referred to by the *Morning Leader* as "that rare thing—a novel which may be legitimately described as both *sensational and original.*"

"The author has a knack of weaving plot and counterplot and piling peril upon peril that is somewhat reminiscent of Dumas."

That is what *BLACK AND WHITE* says of

MOON OF VALLEYS

A New Romance by **DAVID WHITELAW** (Author of "The Gang," &c.)

TRUTH says:—"Altogether a novel of absorbing interest."

DAILY CHRONICLE says:—"Considerably above the average."

"Seldom have we come across a brighter or more entertaining story than this."—Daily Mirror.

THE SPITFIRE

By EDWARD PEPLE, Author of "Semiramis."

"God made the lovers and the devil married them."

SEE

FRANCES FORBES-ROBERTSON'S

BRILLIANT ROMANCE

THE WANTON

MADAME says:—"There is the clash and the glamour of battle in these pages, and a fine heroic spirit breathes through the book."

Other Fiction from Messrs. Greening's List includes:

THE OLD MAN IN THE CORNER. (*3rd Edition.*) Baroness Orczy.

HENRY OF NAVARRE. (*6th Edition.*) May Wynne.

PENELOPE ANN. J. Henry Harris.

THE TRAGEDY OF A FLIRTATION. H. B. Vogel.

ONLY APRIL. Gurner Gillman.

DELUSION. Joseph Prague.

BEAUTY RETIRE. Dora Mellor.

A SON OF DESOLATION. M. Y. Halldom.

A STUDY IN SEPIA. Robert Castleton.

THE BREATH of SCANDAL. Ella Sawtell.

ALL AT SIX SHILLINGS EACH.

Also the following New Fiction Now Ready:

THE MARQUIS CATILINI. . . . Rowland Strong.

PETROVICH'S REVENGE . . . . C. de Lone.

JUSTIFIED . . . . C. E. Poulton.

A BLACK INHERITANCE. . . . John M'Enery.

ALL AT SIX SHILLINGS EACH.

Messrs. GREENING have the pleasure to announce that in the September Number of **"THE IMP"** *will appear the first instalment of a New Romance from the pen of* **THE BARONESS ORCZY,** *entitled* **"THE NEST OF THE SPARROWHAWK."** *Order* **"THE IMP"** *at once of your Newsagent, or subscribe direct for* **2s.** *for a year.*

GREENING & CO., Ltd., 91 St. Martin's Lane, W.C.

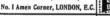

A Delightful Book for Summer and Holiday Reading.

ALL WHO LOVE GARDENS,
WATERWAYS, SPORT, AND
OLD-TIME TRAVEL

should secure a copy of

MEMORIES OF GARDENS.

By ALEXANDER INNES SHAND

With a Special Memoir by
SIR ROWLAND BLENNERHASSETT, Bart.

CONTENTS:

10s. 6d. Net.

THE WEST STRAND PUBLISHING CO. LTD.
10 King Street, Covent Garden, W.C.

THE
BYSTANDER
SIXPENCE. Every Tuesday.

Politics
Literature
Fiction

THE BEST OF THE LIGHT ILLUSTRATED WEEKLIES.
A PICTORIAL RECORD OF THE WEEK'S DOINGS.

TERSE AND TRUTHFUL CRITICISM.
"WORLDLY" SHORT STORIES.
SPORT: a Speciality. GOLF, HUNTING, LAWN TENNIS.

*** You do not only glance at "THE BYSTANDER," you READ it. It is Unique, Sparkling, Daring, Original.

Published by the Proprietors of the "GRAPHIC," Tallis House, Tallis Street, E.C.

7th and Revised Impression.

"SATURDAY" BRIDGE,

By W. DALTON,

Is the Best Book on the Best Game.

That the popularity of Bridge is as great as ever is proved by the continuous steady demand for the work.

"'SATURDAY' BRIDGE"

is admitted to be the Standard book on the Game. It is the leading Bridge Authority, and takes its name from the "SATURDAY REVIEW," in which its chapters appeared.

Of all Booksellers 5s. net, or post free 5s. 3d., direct from the Office.

THE WEST STRAND PUBLISHING CO., Ltd.,
10 King Street, Covent Garden, W.C.

LA REVUE POLITIQUE ET LITTÉRAIRE

REVUE BLEUE

FONDÉE EN 1863. — DIRECTEUR : FÉLIX DUMOULIN.

Est à la tête des Revues françaises — *depuis près d'un demi-siècle* — par l'honorabilité, la variété et l'éclat de sa rédaction.

Chaque semaine elle publie de brillants articles *diplomatiques* et *politiques*; une *nouvelle* ou un *roman*; de spirituelles critiques *littéraire, dramatique* et *artistique*; des études d'*histoire*, de *philosophie*; une *poésie*; une *chronique* sur la vie parisienne; etc.

Ses collaborateurs sont des Membres de l'Académie française, de l'Institut, du Parlement, de l'Université, etc.

Elle est indispensable aux Anglais, qui désirent se tenir au courant de la littérature, de l'art et de la politique de la France.

Abonnement : six mois, **20** fr.; un an, **35** fr.

PARIS — 41 *bis*, rue de Châteaudun — PARIS

NOTICE.

The Terms of Subscription to the SATURDAY REVIEW are:—

	United Kingdom.			Abroad.		
	£	s.	d.	£	s.	d.
One Year ...	1	8	2	1	10	4
Half Year ...	0	14	1	0	15	2
Quarter Year	0	7	1	0	7	7

Cheques and Money Orders should be crossed and made payable to the Manager, SATURDAY REVIEW Offices, 10 King Street, Covent Garden, London, W.C.

In the event of any difficulty being experienced in obtaining the SATURDAY REVIEW, the Publisher would be glad to be informed immediately.

Messrs. MILLS & BOON'S FIRST AUTUMN LIST

FICTION.

A few notes on the undermentioned Novels may be of assistance when making up Library lists. The published price of each volume. is **6s.**

The Veil. *(6th Edition of 1,500 Copies.)*
By E. S. STEVENS. A wonderful story of Tunis, its mysteries and passions.

Cardillac. *(4th Edition in the press.)*
By ROBERT BARR. A gallant and joyous tale of old Touraine, when swords and love went hand in hand.

Harm's Way.
By LLOYD OSBOURNE. A novel of stage life, in which a girl with an infinite capacity for loving becomes infatuated with and reforms an actor altogether unworthy of her.

Mary Up at Gaffries. *(2nd Edition.)*
By S. C. NETHERSOLE. An exquisite tale of life in a Kentish village.

The Bill-Toppers.
By ANDRÉ CASTAIGNE. A vivid narrative of Music Hall life from the inside.

The Last Lord Avanley.
By GERALD MAXWELL. A story of the fortunes of a noble house, in which the supernatural is amazingly blended with the matter-of-fact.

Mary.
By WINIFRED GRAHAM. The *chef d'œuvre* of this talented writer.

Miss Pilsbury's Fortune.
By CHRISTINE R. SHAND. A charmingly early Victorian account of the rise to affluence of Mr. Pilsbury and his family, and what wealth brought to them, in the days of crinolines and curtseys.

Mr. Burnside's Responsibility.
By THOMAS COBB. "Is (says the *P.M.G.*) a very agreeable and clever story, in which Mr. Cobb's ingenuity is at its best in devising compromising situations for the hero—an M.P. who is beginning to make a name for himself."

Mills & Boon's Thrilling Adventure Library

Comprises only Books of the highest excellence, of which the first three volumes are:—

The Lady Calphurnia Royal.
ALBERT DORRINGTON and A. G. STEPHENS.

The Adventures of Captain Jack.
(3rd Edition.) MAX PEMBERTON.

The Kingdom of Earth.
ANTHONY PARTRIDGE.

IN PREPARATION.

ARSÈNE LUPIN.
By EDGAR JEPSON and MAURICE LEBLANC.
The authentic Novel of the Play "ARSÈNE LUPIN," which will shortly be produced at the Duke of York's Theatre.

Ready next week.

Orpheus in Mayfair.
By MAURICE BARING. A volume of Stories and Sketches.

Ready the week after.

The Prodigal Father.
By J. STORER CLOUSTON, Author of "The Lunatic at Large." A fit successor to that universal favourite.

To be followed by

Draw in Your Stool. By OLIVER ONIONS.
Royal Lovers. By HÉLÈNE VACARESCO.
Tess of Ithaca. By GRACE MILLER WHITE.
My Lady Wentworth. By ALLAN FEA.

Mills & Boon's Laughter Library. 1s. net.

Wee Macgreegor. J. J. BELL.
Proofs Before Pulping. BARRY PAIN.
Thomas Henry. W. PETT RIDGE.

GENERAL LITERATURE.

Aviation.
Written from materials supplied by HENRI FARMAN (with a Special Chapter by him). By his Brother, D. FARMAN. Profusely Illustrated. Demy 8vo. 10s. 6d. net.

An Art Student's Reminiscences of Paris in the Eighties.
By SHIRLEY FOX, R.B.A. Illustrated by JOHN CAMERON and SHIRLEY FOX. Demy 8vo. 10s. 6d. net.

Sporting Stories.
By THORMANBY. Fully Illustrated. Demy 8vo. 10s. 6d. net.

Home Life in Ireland.
By ROBERT LYND. Fully Illustrated. Demy 8vo. 7s. 6d. net.

British Mountain Climbs.
By GEORGE D. ABRAHAM, Author of "The Complete Mountaineer," Member of the Climbers' Club, &c., &c. Fcap. 8vo. waterproof cloth, 7s. 6d. net.

Auction Bridge.
By ARCHIBALD DUNN. Containing the Revised Rules of the Game. Handsomely bound in cloth, and forming a Companion Volume to "Club Bridge," 5s. net.

Club Bridge.
By ARCHIBALD DUNN, Author of "Bridge and How to Play it." 5s. net.

The Children's Story of Westminster Abbey.
By Miss G. E. TROUTBECK, Author of "Westminster Abbey" (Little Guides). With 4 Photogravure Plates and 23 Illustrations from Photographs. Crown 8vo. 5s. net.

The Children's Story of the Bee.
By S. L. BENSUSAN, Author of "Wild Life Stories," "Heart of the Wild." Illustrated by C. MOORE PARK. Crown 8vo. 5s. net.

Deportmental Ditties.
By Captain HARRY GRAHAM, Author of "Ruthless Rhymes for Heartless Homes," "Misrepresentative Men," &c. Illustrated by LEWIS BAUMER. Royal 4to. 3s. 6d. net.

Through the Loopholes of Retreat.
A Cowper Day Book. By HANSARD WATT. Crown 8vo. 3s. 6d. net.

MILLS & BOON'S COMPANION SERIES.

The Chauffeur's Companion.
By "A FOUR-INCH DRIVER." With 4 Plates and 5 Diagrams, waterproof cloth. Crown 8vo. 2s. net

The Six-Handicap Golfer.
By "TWO OF HIS KIND." With Chapters by H. S. COLT and H. HILTON. Fully Illustrated. Crown 8vo. 2s. 6d. net.

The Gardener's Companion.
By SELINA RANDOLPH. With an Introduction by Lady ALWYNE COMPTON. Crown 8vo. 2s. net.

The Mother's Companion.
By Mrs. M. A. CLOUDESLEY-BRERETON (Officier d'Académie). 2s. 6d. net.

THE CHRISTMAS PRESENT FOR 1909.

Fully Illustrated, 2s. 6d. net.

A Book by those Wonderful Laughter-Makers:

THE FOLLIES.

Pure Folly. [*Ready in October.*

MILLS & BOON, LTD., 49 Whitcomb Street, Leicester Square, W.C.

Printed for the Proprietors by SPOTTISWOODE & Co. LTD., 5 New-street Square, E.C., and Published by REGINALD WEBSTER PAGE, at the Office, 10 King Street, Covent Garden, in the Parish of St. Paul in the County of London.—*Saturday, 14 August, 1909.*

TURGENEFF'S GERMAN LETTERS.

TO LUDWIG PIETSCH.

1879—1881.

78.

50 Rue de Douai, Paris,
Thursday, 9 January '79.

Dear Pietsch,—Now everything is at a standstill, and I must speak seriously. News has come from Weimar that if Louise's opera does not arrive in the next few days it will be impossible to produce it on the Grand Duchess' name-day, 8 March. The MS. with the translated text must come to Paris before it is sent to Weimar. Louise must fit the German version to her music, and perhaps alter and re-copy a good deal, and there is so far no sign of the MS.* Dohm has not even announced its receipt or sent a single line in answer to three urgent letters from Mme. Viardot. That is the utmost limit of (what shall I say?) unceremonious behaviour. That means that poor Louise, who truly does not need this blow to put a final touch to her bad luck, will lose her only chance of being performed. I beseech you by our ancient friendship to show this letter to Dohm and make him read it, and if nothing comes of it I shall know what to think of German punctuality, German friendship, etc., etc.

Further words are unnecessary. Best wishes.

Yours ever, I. TURGEN.

79.

50 Rue de Douai, Paris,
Tuesday, 14 January '79.

My dear Pietsch,—You quite misunderstood my letter. None of the severe expressions in it was intended for you. You have been as innocent as a lamb throughout the whole business. They were meant for Dohm, to whom you were to show the letter. If you look at the matter impartially, I hope you will admit that he has acted in a quite unaccountable manner. It would have been so easy for him to send a refusal and return the MS. As it is, in spite of all the goodwill of the Grand Duke, of Lassen, and of the management of the theatre, probably the whole affair will fall through, and Louise, in Bismarck's choice German (vide Busch), will take a knock, from which the poor thing will never recover. That's enough! Sapienti sat. You cannot doubt my friendship any more than I can doubt yours.

Yours, TURGENJEW.

80.

50 Rue de Douai, Paris,
Sunday, 8 October '79.

Here, my good friend, is the detailed explanation:

1. Yelitski is a S. Petersburg official, who understands nothing about rustic life and modes of expression, etc., and yet persists in trying to manage the property.

2. All the arable land, by very ancient custom extending down to the present day, is divided into three parts: the first is sown with rye, and the second with wheat and oats, while the third is left to lie fallow. There is a rotation every year. This is a primitive form of agriculture, but it is still employed, and is known as the three-field method. To this land must be added woodland and hayfields,* and finally the so-called unserviceable land, that is to say pleasure-grounds, bad or good, and, in particular, the site of the farm buildings. Each of the three parts above mentioned is called in Russian "clin", and when one wants to know how many desyatinas (a desyatina is rather more than an acre) a farm contains, one asks how many there are in the clin. If the reply is, for instance, that there are a hundred, one knows that the whole property contains some 400, some 300 in the three clins and about 100 (the usual proportion) divided among woodland, hayfields, and unserviceable land. Moreover till lately estates were divided into many separate portions, and only the high-class properties were compact and in a ring fence, translated in the French, "d'une seule semence". Yelitski naturally does not understand that they have translated "clin" by "sole". So when Kyov answers "275 desyatinas sur chaque sole", he means a total of more than 800. Yelitski does not understand that either, and is later on surprised at the large acreage. So when he afterwards speaks of the fallow land, Kyov thinks he wants to know how much unserviceable land there is and gives an approximate answer, because according to the old patriarchal custom it was not measured, but regarded as merely appendant to so much arable land.†

I think my exposition of the matter is quite as detailed as the famous discussion about the water at Cologne (do you remember?), so Heaven be with you.

Yours, IW. TURG.

81.

Les Frênes Chalet, Bougival, Seine-et-Oise,
Wednesday, 12 November '79.

Many thanks, my very dear Pietsch, for your warm letter of congratulation. Mme. Viardot rightly calls you "le vieux fidèle". I am glad you are well "en gros". I have also nothing much to complain of. Unfortunately all the Viardots are either ill or convalescent. Old Viardot himself alone stands erect, firm and unshaken like a granite peak, in spite of his eighty years. When we go out walking together people think I am his father.

I have been bombarded for some time past with letters from some journalistic individuals, who want something new out of me. I have nothing either new or old. Heaven be thanked and praised, I shall write nothing more. I have written to the editor of the "Berliner Tageblatt" that he can apply to you for the translation of "The Bread of Others", but (1) I feel very doubtful whether you have finished the translation, (2) I am still more doubtful whether a dramatic thing like that is suitable for a feuilleton. Of course I give you the fullest authority to do whatever you like with it. If the person in question wants to print it in book form as well, so much the better for you.

I am sorry for poor Kathi.‡ Give her my kind regards, if you see her, and remember me also to our other friends.

I shall go to Russia in December, via Berlin of course, and shall see you there. Meanwhile my best wishes of every sort.

Yours as ever, I. T.

P.S.—Great Heavens! I had nearly forgotten the political matter. You want my opinion upon the relations between Germany and Russia? Well, I think that before five years are over we shall have a war of annihilation between the two nations, and Germany will begin. But as I know with absolute certainty that I shall die in 1881 (probably in October), it is all a matter of pomade or caviar ad libitum as far as I am concerned.

---

* The text must be corrupt here. This appears to be the sense.—TRANSLATOR.

* Read Heu for neu in the text, "Wiesen wo neu gemacht wird".—TRANSLATOR.

† This is an explanation of a passage in the play "The Bread of Others".—L. P.

‡ Her husband, Eckert, the conductor, had just died suddenly.—L. P.

82.

Les Frênes, Bougival,
Thursday, 11 November '80.

My dear Friend,—Many thanks for your letter. Of all my friends outside France only you and a Russian girl, a sturdy little Nihilist, have sent me congratulations. Thank you again. All the Viardots have been in Paris since last Monday. I am all alone here. I will see if solitude can force me to do some work; probably not.

I am satisfied with my health. I have actually been able to take riding exercise, a thing I have not done for twenty years. Didie and her husband (such a pretty pair!) were in front all the time, of course; I followed behind on a big, solid horse. Didie asserts that I look like a retired general from Wurtemberg. All the family are well; Didie's children are perfect little cherubs. Mme. Viardot has been composing many fine things. Paul is on a concert tour in Spain, and most successful. Marianne is more fascinating than ever, but has not taken a husband yet.

I am grieved about poor Richter* and his wife. Give my kind regards to all our old friends, beginning with Kathi—I feel the greatest sympathy for the admirable creature, although she has perhaps good reason to doubt it.

Life is just what it is—sweet for the young and those who remain young, bitter for the old and for those who were born old. It is caviar to me, since, as you perhaps know, I shall die without fail at the beginning of October 1881—that is an absolute certainty.

Kindest regards to your family and yourself.

Are you shaking off your rheumatism? Just think of Pietschius grandiflorus, the Apollo on the Spree, with rheumatism. All good wishes.

Your old friend,
I. TURGENJEW.

83.

50 Rue de Douai,
Sunday, 21 November '80.

My dear Friend,—When I sent you an answer by telegram, to save time, authorising you to translate my essay on Pushkin I was silently wondering whether Pietsch had now added Russian to his accomplishments. There is no French essay of mine on Pushkin. Last May, in Moscow, at the unveiling of his statue, I delivered a fairly long address in Russian, but I never heard of a French translation of it. It was published in the following July in the S. Petersburg "European Courier". What? Can my old friend and patron imagine that I ever wrote a line in any other language than Russian? Can you inflict such an insult as that on me? A fellow who calls himself a writer and writes in any other language than his own mother tongue is, in my opinion, a scamp and a wretched brainless hog. Besides, this speech is only interesting to Russians; to foreigners it is mere caviar.

So let us leave this essay in peace and obscurity.

I am now in Paris again, and shall go to S. Petersburg at the end of this year. Of course I shall see you in Berlin. Meanwhile, my very best wishes.

Yours, I. T.

84.

50 Rue de Douai, Paris,
23 January '81.

My dear Pietsch,—I want you to do this for me: Go to Frau Eckert, and first of all give her my kindest regards. Then ask her if the scenario of a grand opera in five acts, called "Mirowitsch", has been found among her husband's papers. This fully completed scenario, written in German, is my composition, and Eckert translated it (I don't know whether scenario is masculine or neuter) in my presence, from the French. At that time he was still thinking of the possibility of composing an opera. Unfortunately his plan never came to fulfilment, and now the thing has no value for Frau Eckert. Perhaps she would be so kind as to hand the bit of paper to you, and you could then send it here to me. I would be very grateful to you, for perhaps something can still be made of it. A friend of mine, a young French composer, is looking for a text, and perhaps he might find "Mirowitsch" suitable. In any case, please inquire about it. I am only just recovering from a violent attack of gout. I have been in bed for three weeks, and still feel weak in the legs. This illness has delayed my journey to S. Petersburg, but I hope to pass through Berlin in six weeks' time and see you, Frau Eckert, and all my other friends.

Everyone here is well. They send their kindest regards, and I remain, with hearty good wishes,

Your old (very old) friend,
IW. TURGENJEW.

85.

Villa Les Frênes, Bougival,
Monday, 31 October '81.

My dear Pietsch,—I am sending to-day to Dernburg of the "National Zeitung" the corrected French proofs of my fantastic story,* and am asking him to hand the German proofs over to you for correction. It would be much better still if you would undertake the translation. The thing is very short, and of course the "National Zeitung" would have to pay you. There is no need to trouble about my own fee. Herr Dernburg will give me something or nothing, according to the amount which he has paid you. I shall stay here for a few weeks more and then go to Paris. The Viardots will move there earlier. I will see if I can do any work in my solitude.

Remember me to your family and our friends. Heartiest good wishes,

Yours, IW. TURGENJEW.

86.

Bougival,
Thursday, 10 November '81.

My dear Friend,—I have just received your letter, and want to thank you for all your hearty good wishes. I am now all alone here, as the Viardots have returned to Paris, and I will see whether I can still do some work. I am sorry that it is not you who are translating that Italian legend, though the thing is insignificant enough. But I promise you, if I ever finish the larger thing, no one but you shall translate it.

I sent Tolstoi's novel† to Julian Schmidt a month ago, but do not know whether he has received it or read it. Perhaps he didn't care about it? At any rate ask him about it, and, if possible, read it yourself. My own opinion of it is unchanged: it is the noblest epic of modern times. The translation is unfortunately rather weak and dull, a very feminine, amateurish piece of work.

I have received a telegram of congratulation from German and Russian artists, and I think I recognise your hand in it. But, to turn from your hand to your handwriting, its illegibility is something quite superb. What, for instance, in Heaven's name, does the following scrawl portend? I have copied it with meticulous accuracy. Apparently it is the name of the street in Brussels where your daughter is living. Send me the solution of the hieroglyphic, for it is quite possible that I shall go to Holland for a week this year, and of course I shall go to Brussels and see your charming Marie.

Kind regards to your family and our friends. With all good wishes,

Yours, I. TURGENJEW.

* The celebrated Berlin painter.

* "Le chant de l'amour triomphant."—L. P.
† "War and Peace."—L. P.

THE

SATURDAY REVIEW

OF

POLITICS, LITERATURE, SCIENCE, AND ART.

No. 2,808 Vol. 108. 21 August 1909. [REGISTERED AS A NEWSPAPER.] 6d.

CONTENTS.

NOTES OF THE WEEK.

The only innocent of any account to go this year is the Welsh Disestablishment Bill, but as that was hardly so much as even born but only shown to the light its massacre cannot move anybody very much. The day devoted to its discussion was sheer waste of time. That is what this Government does—wastes time on measures intended for nothing but party and electioneering purposes, with the result that it has to harry and goad the House into late sitting in order to get any business done at all. Mr. Asquith expects to pass a Finance Bill, the Irish Land Bill, and the London Elections Bill—all most contentious. If he does this it must mean keeping the House with its nose to the grindstone at least to the end of September, with all-night sittings if not the rule hardly an exception.

"It is the principle we want to establish", said one of Mr. Asquith's hearers at Bletchley. Well, it is very evident the Government will get very little out of their land taxes but principle. Mr. Asquith had to admit on Tuesday that these taxes might cost more to collect in their first year than their entire yield. Mr. Bonar Law showed that the Government would be spending two shillings in collecting every one shilling. Very possibly it will come out worse than that; for two millions is a low estimate of the cost of the valuation. And the grounds for the Government's expectation of a very large and very rapid rise in the yield of these taxes are not at all solid. Land does not steadily go up all over the country; it does not uniformly go up even in London. The taxes themselves will tend to keep the rise down. And the discount of ten per cent. allowed on the increment tax will keep out a vast amount of property altogether. Site values seldom increase by so much as ten per cent.; and every site value that does not will yield not a penny of increment tax.

The Chancellor of the Exchequer will never be clear of the entanglements of his Limehouse speech. "Blackmail" pursues him as nemesis. He struggled hard with it in trying to defend the clause letting local authorities off the payment of the new land taxes. Why is not holding up land and enjoying the unearned increment of land blackmail in a corporation if it is blackmail in a private owner? Mr. Lloyd George of course had absolutely no answer to give Mr. Balfour. It is not even a case of the country as a whole sharing in the immunity. One local area will gain at another's cost. Mr. Lloyd George could only talk irrelevancies about the object of the tax and corporations paying too much for land compulsorily bought. What nonsense this is! Corporations buy under the ordinary compensation law and pay the amount fixed after fair and open trial by jury. If the procedure is bad, let the Government amend it. It is no plea in excuse of letting these corporations off the tax.

The Prime Minister's "short and sharp" procedure with respect to the licensing clauses of the Finance Bill has been taken to foreshadow a drastic application of the guillotine. The true origin is probably far more in the direction of reasonable amendment. No defence has been attempted of the ridiculous and inequitable provisions which base increased duties on half the annual value of licensed premises irrespective of the nature of their trade. Hotels, restaurants, and dram-shops were all on the same footing. It has been strongly pressed on the Government that the only equitable basis of taxation is a percentage levy on the amount of liquor sold, and there is good ground for believing that new clauses are now being drafted to give effect to this view. We hope there will be no difference in this respect between the ordinary licensed houses and those unlicensed places termed Radical clubs. Such a basis of taxation will have the added advantage of being a useful guide to licensing justices in fixing compensation and monopoly values. To a large extent, also, the penal nature of the original proposals disappears.

Perhaps the most interesting item in the Budget programme for this week has been the epistolary duel between the Duke of Northumberland and Sir Edward

Grey. Sir Edward in his speech at Leeds had said, in an airy way most unwonted for him, that landowners hit by the Budget could easily find means of making up the difference without causing hardship to others. Any who might dismiss a workman he had hitherto employed was described by the way as vindictive. The Duke very naturally would like Sir Edward Grey to come to facts and tell him what he could dispense with without hurting others. Sir Edward in reply did not get to grips, but vaguely suggested giving up sporting rights or a London house, and then more vaguely that properties could be converted into small holdings and used for "scientific forestry". Scientific forestry! How easy to talk in these general terms. It was easy for Sir Edward to say landowners could do things, but he could not say what. The Duke of Northumberland was left where he was.

Sir Edward had not one practical proposal to make; so he ran off on abstract lines. One of his points was remarkable. He could not, he said, admit that any man need make any retrenchments that would bear hardly on others unless he was already spending the whole of his income. So, according to this economist and social reformer, a man ought to spend up to his last penny of income before he attempts provision by retrenchment to meet new and unavoidable claims on his income. This is how bankruptcy comes. A landowner must keep up his whole staff though to do so leaves him not a penny of margin to meet an unexpected demand. Then it comes and he breaks, and the whole staff, instead of a few of them, have to go. What sound economy! What thoughtful humanity!

The speech of a Liberal leader at Limehouse has been too much for a Liberal Leader at Sheffield. The Leaders there, who owned the "Sheffield Independent" for more than half a century, have been the incarnation of South Yorkshire and Sheffield Liberalism all that time. Until a few days ago Mr. Robert Leader had been ten years the treasurer of the Hallamshire Liberal Association. The Limehouse speech has driven him to desperation and resignation. There is no longer any room, he says, for moderate men and moderate counsels in a party that does not condemn the violence of that speech. He is a very unexpected coadjutor of the Duke of Norfolk, who has so many interests in Sheffield. The secession will have an effect, though Sheffield people now read the Conservative "Telegraph" more than the Liberal "Independent".

Lord Charles Beresford, not unreasonably, claims that the report of the Committee to inquire into his allegations as to the Navy justifies the charges that he made. It admits the facts he put forward are true. The changes in the arrangements of the fleets were in fact made as he said and there was danger while they were being so made. The defence is that the arrangement was provisional. Lord Charles' contention that while this provisional state continued there was danger is denied; but that is an opinion which might be expected from a Committee of the Government, not altogether an impartial judge of the Admiralty. Lord Charles is still entitled to maintain his own; though he cannot argue the Committee were prejudiced. He gave it too good a character at the beginning.

The South African Bill was passed by the House of Commons on Thursday. As the Government had made known that the Bill must pass exactly as presented and the Opposition had accepted this primary fact of the situation, it was evident what sort of a discussion would take place in Committee when the colour question came up. Naturally there would be a flood of irresponsible eloquence in assertion of the claim of Kaffirs to have the franchise and the right of sitting in the African Parliament. When a theory is not to be put into practice it is easy to rise to great moral heights in asserting it. As the Union Bill has been passed with the franchise question left to the new Parliament, if these eloquent speakers imagine their glowing periods will have any effect on that Parliament, they are more sanguine than sagacious.

President Taft seems bent on rivalling, even if he cannot eclipse, Mr. Roosevelt's reputation for spirited foreign policy. Naturally enough, President Taft has selected the East as his special field of operations. Unlike most American statesmen, he does know something about the Far East. The game of playing patron and champion to China is not a bad one, at least it is not bad for political purposes on paper. If we are to take the New York press, the line is that China cannot trust England being the ally of Japan, and America is to step in and protect the oppressed Empire against the bullying and machinations of the Japs. How far there is any political substance behind this kite one cannot say for certain. If the idea catches on with the public, it may develop into something of a real policy. President Taft, however, is reckoned a reasonable man, and would know that he cannot play this game for nothing or on a small scale. If he means to play the hand seriously he must be prepared for every issue, not stopping short of war. But we do not believe he has taken the matter so seriously at all.

The German press is much exercised by the King's not going to Ischl. But why doubt the official Austrian statement that the Emperor-King wants to make the most of his holiday? Last year it was carefully explained that the King's visit bore no deep political character, but was an act of friendly congratulation to the Emperor on the occasion of his jubilee. This year there is no jubilee, and therefore no need for any elaborate parade of courtesies. The Emperor has had an anxious time during the past winter, and the prolongation of the Hungarian Cabinet crisis compelled him to postpone his departure for Ischl. Moreover, at the beginning of next month he is to entertain his German ally at the manœuvres, a programme which might tax the strength of a younger man.

Germany is agog with excitement over Count Zeppelin and his flight to Berlin which has been fixed for next week. He is to be welcomed in state by the Emperor, and all Berlin will troop out to the Tempelhofer Feld to see the show. No one breathes a possibility of failure, although the voyage from Friedrichshafen to the capital will beat all records if accomplished. But the Count is a popular hero and so cannot fail. His portrait adorns all manner of metal, leather, and paper goods, and a huge variety of articles have been manufactured in the shape of his balloon. So great is the enthusiasm at something being done by a man who is not an official.

In France "on marche". The number of young men who refuse to come forward for their military training has almost trebled in the last three years. This is in the main the result of M. Hervé's propaganda, but is partly due to the contempt with which the average Frenchman views the present parliamentary régime. Why should he inconvenience himself for the sake of a few hundred "sous-vétérinaires" in Paris? If France possessed a single statesman with a real grip over his country's needs he would stop this national dry-rot. It could be done. The penalty for recalcitrance is mild enough—a year's imprisonment at most; but instead of making the best of so moderate a law, successive Cabinets have amnestied the culprits from fear of unpopularity. Very different is the practice across the Vosges, where disobedience of the military law is punished with lifelong expulsion from German soil.

Spain has rallied round the monarchy and is now determined to see the Moorish trouble through. It would be no light task for any Power. The Riff tribesmen are numerous and well-armed; they inhabit a mountainous country which has not been surveyed; their independence has never yet been seriously challenged; and, like all Mohammedans, they fight like demons when their religious fanaticism is stirred. Their subjection will cost both men and money, but in days gone by Spain spent both lavishly against the same Moorish foe, and in spending them found herself. It is for tradition's sake that so many young men of spirit are to-day volunteering for active service against the hereditary enemy. All Spain feels that in the fight against the Moors she is the champion of the civilisation and the religion of the West. That is why she is determined not to fail, and as reinforcements are now being hurried forward it will not be long before she strikes her blow.

It is really something of an international scandal that the Italian Government should allow the "Asino" of 15 August to be circulated. The whole issue is in effect an incentive to violence and riot in Spain. Criticism of a foreign Government is of course always legitimate—even what is popularly called "nasty" criticism—but there is a great difference between even violent criticism and the blackguardly abuse of the Spanish King and his Government which is bespattered over nearly every page of this outrageous sheet. It is nothing of course that all the mischief is put down to clerical influence, and King Alfonso lampooned as writing at the dictation of a priest. That goes without saying in this class of paper. But the open justification of violence and every other outrage committed by the revolutionaries ought not to be tolerated. Indeed all decent people have long wondered why the Italian Government has put up with the nauseous profanity of this rag so long.

There is a report of another engagement between the Moorish Pretender and Mulai Hafid's forces. The story is that the Pretender has been beaten and taken prisoner. Probably the truth is merely that in one of these eternal ups and down in Moorish campaigns the Pretender has this time got the worst of it. It is not at all likely he has been taken prisoner. Naturally the Sultan (for the time being) would make the most of his success. The "Times" gives exact and harrowing details of tortured prisoners. Even if absolute facts were known, horrors should not be placarded in this way; but it passes understanding how any serious paper can expose details of horrors admittedly speculative.

The Cretans have now been scolded, and the cane even brought out, but with ceremony. Each of the four protecting Powers has had to despatch a couple of warships to Suda Bay and each Power has solemnly landed a bluejacket. This little party formally lowered the offending flag and cut down the flagstaff which offered such irresistible temptation. Meanwhile the Cretan Parliament has promised to behave itself, and no doubt will keep its promise as long as the warships are in harbour. It certainly talked very firmly to the mutinous militiamen who re-hoisted the flag. "You Greeks are always children", an Egyptian philosopher told an Athenian visitor a good many centuries ago, and apparently they have not grown up yet. We dare say the Powers would be glad if Crete could only be united with Greece, and they be rid of their troublesome ward.

Unfortunately union is out of the question. Turkey has taken a firm stand on her new-found constitutional dignity, and refuses to let Crete go the way of Bulgaria. The Porte has addressed Notes to Athens carefully framed on the model of the Notes which the Powers once addressed to the Porte. Greece, with an exposed frontier and the memories of '97, has whimpered very plaintively and asked her strong friends to see she is not hurt. As yet there is no need to take the situation very seriously. Athens and Constantinople have long intrigued against one another. In the old days the sympathies of the Western Powers were rather with Greece, but of late their statesmen have done lip-service to the curious variety of constitutionalism which now lords it in Constantinople, and Turkey is anxious to show off her new respectability.

At last Denmark has a new Ministry. Six harmless members of the late Cabinet retain office, but there is a new Premier and two ex-Premiers have accepted important portfolios. The Government intends to deal with the question of national defence. Denmark has had to choose between three lines of policy. The Socialists are in favour of complete disarmament, since no efforts could avail against a great Power. This is not illogical, but is so unpatriotic that the country will have none of it. More sympathy has been won for the view that Denmark should concentrate her energies on ensuring the neutrality of the Sound. But there is a third party which insists that land defence also must not be neglected, and it is this policy which has received Royal support and which the new Cabinet hopes to carry out. Unhappily M. Christensen, the new Minister of Defence, was associated during his Premiership with some unsavoury political scandals. His appointment has therefore failed to satisfy the military party, and the Danish Commander-in-Chief has resigned by way of protest. Apparently the crisis is not yet over.

The general strike in Sweden shows signs of collapse. The railway men have refused to come out, and the mass of rural labourers are returning to work. There have been many skirmishes between Capital and Labour in Sweden these ten years, and the two forces have found themselves fairly evenly balanced. Public sympathy alone could turn the scale, and the appeal for it has led to what must be the most curious strike the world has seen. By way of preventing rioting in the capital the Government absolutely prohibited the sale of intoxicants and was able to enforce its prohibition without difficulty. Cut off from the public-houses, the workmen promenaded the streets in their best clothes and quietly waited. With all the shops closed and most of the traffic suspended, the whole thing resembled nothing so much as an English Sunday.

A decline in pauperism used to be quoted in answer to doubts about the condition of the working classes. This argument will have to be given up. It no longer holds after the recent Local Government Board Report. The rise of pauperism has been continuous since 1901, and there are now a hundred and eighteen thousand more paupers than there were in that year, twenty-one thousand being the increase for London alone. Depression of trade generally, in building, engineering and shipbuilding especially, and in London the transfer of some trades to other parts of the country, account for some of the increased pauperism. In London some of the Guardians, as those of Poplar, have manufactured paupers, according to the inspector. The decrease of adult labour owing to machinery is another cause. The youths employed instead of men are not wanted when they grow up, and they turn into unskilled labourers. This, apart from bad trade generally, is the most chronic cause of pauperism. Only old paupers over seventy are decreasing. They are being kept from the Poor Law to qualify for pensions.

Other reports, curious in detail, but difficult, as in many other cases, to follow in their real drift are that on the number of empty houses in London and other large towns, and that on the birth and death rate. Houses stand empty in towns, but building goes on in the suburbs; and if the birth rate declines, the death rate declines too, and on balance there is a steady gain. The empty houses are just the ordinary sort; not the town house that may have to be given up on account of the Budget. They are not empty because the population is declining, so that their tenants either overcrowd somewhere else in the town or go further out; and the probabilities are in favour of emigration in these quick-transit days. The decrement of the town will become increment in the suburb, to use the new financial phrase. As for the birth rate, that would require much analysis before we could be sure that the decline would satisfy the Eugenics Society.

The Government have granted Mr. Shackleton twenty thousand pounds towards the expenses of his antarctic expedition. We really do not believe a taxpayer could be found in the whole country to object to this. Even the most rigid of economic puritans would think that he had saved his face if he pretended to be shocked at the extravagance, but patronisingly excused it as allowable for once. It is quite delightful to find the State spending money on something that can add only to the sum of knowledge, not to the sum of money. Of what use? The question is an impertinence; knowledge is an end in itself.

There is still talk about amalgamating the Botanical and Zoological Societies. No doubt there is a good deal at first sight to be said for the idea. The Botanical evidently cannot stand on its own legs, and a marriage between the two sounds a very happy arrangement. Happy no doubt for the Botanical, but those who are advising such an alliance—alliance is the word ill-consecrated to arrangements of this kind—should remember that it is asking one very much going concern to embrace another that is not going at all. The Botanical has no funds, but has instead a very large debenture debt. They do no scientific work, their place scientifically being entirely taken by Kew and the Horticultural Society. In short, the Botanical has long given up work for play and has met with the idler's proper end.

Lord Rosebery's foreword to the Cramond Flower Show makes us wish he had been a gardener. Not that we would have him show much learning in floricultural lore—technical talk is always odious, and as expert he could hardly have been immune to the poison of competition. But we would have had him a gardener for the multitude of delightful discourses he would have given us on gardening. The Cramond speech makes one think what might have been. There be many that write well on gardening—to forget the very many that write badly—but few that speak well on it. Many public speakers are also gardeners, but somehow they cannot speak on gardening. Mr. Chamberlain has never made a gardening speech with any charm in it; nor could Mr. Harcourt. Lord Rosebery turns rather wistfully to gardening now as the ideal solace of old age; he knows that will not be taken up when you are old which you neglected when young.

Sir Theodore Martin, according to one account, began his literary career seventy years ago by editing Sir Thomas Urquhart's translation of Rabelais. If he did, it was a very venturesome thing for a young man of twenty-two. For though Sir Thomas was a fellow-countryman, the Presbyterian circles in which Martin was born would have considered the editing of this great translation, as Spencer said of the too clever billiard player, evidence of misspent time and misemployed talents. Besides, Martin could not have been equipped for such work at the age. There seems to be a mistake, and perhaps we are on the track of it when we note that the "Times" speaks of the ballads and parodies published by Aytoun and Martin in 1845 "under the Rabelaisian name of 'Bon Gaultier'" which went through sixteen editions between that year and 1902. So if he had not turned to more decorous pursuits, such as parliamentary agency and the "Life of the Prince Consort", he might have made a good editor of Rabelais after all.

The period of Sir Theodore's youth was much more Rabelaisian than ours, though he imagined as he grew older that the most boisterous and rollicking of literary periods had all the dignity. It was a curious delusion for the biographer of the Prince Consort and the friend of the Queen. Modern improvement in manners is usually dated from the Queen's reign. Motor omnibuses, it is true, came in before Sir Theodore's death, but many more undignified things that he knew of had passed away. Princes had ceased to ride in carriages with bruisers; young noblemen no longer went into the streets for rows under the protection of prize-fighters; there were no longer hideous crowds of all classes at prize-fights, dog-fights, cock-pits, and rat-pits; the night houses and gambling hells had been closed; and Baron Nicholson and the "Judge and Jury" had disappeared. It was not all Macready and Helen Faucit when the railway mania was on, and Theodore Martin was making a fortune or writing the life of the Prince Consort as the confidant of the Queen.

A SPLENDID OPPOSITION.

We regret to see in certain Unionist quarters an attempt to belittle and discountenance the opposition to the land taxes, both in and out of Parliament. The "Times", whose bad faith in matters of party is proverbial, is of course the leader of the sneaks, who are frightened by the bluff of Messrs. Churchill and George, and who are imploring the Unionist leaders to throw the landed interest to the wolves, in order, apparently, that the liquor interest may escape. According to this unworthy plan, a letter is inserted in what is supposed to be the leading organ of the Unionist party in the daily press from Sir Henry Norman, being an anthology of all the fictions invented by the "Daily News" and provincial Radical rags, to the effect that the meetings of the Budget Protest League have been failures. Another letter is printed in the same journal from a Tory Democratic candidate in Manchester, commanding the Unionist party to abandon its "futile" (sic) opposition to the land taxes, as if the landed interest was the only one worth preserving, and threatening our leaders with the wrath of the Tory Democratic working men of Lancashire if they do not at once hurry on to the increased duties on spirits and tobacco. We have never heard of Mr. Hiram Howell, whose democracy is more apparent than his Toryism; but we are quite sure that he libels the working men of Lancashire when he asserts that the only points in the Budget which interest them are the increased duties on tobacco and spirits. Lancashire artisans are very intelligent, and the majority of them take broad Imperial views. We are certain that they would resent the imputation that their only interest in national finance is the amount of the duties on drink and tobacco. Still more amazing and repellent is Mr. Howell's assertion that the Unionists have "no case" on the land taxes, and that their strongest case is the increase of the duties on drink and tobacco. As a matter of fact, we have little or no case on the increased duties on tobacco and drink, unless, indeed, our case is that the working men are to contribute nothing to the deficit of £16,000,000. Our experience, gathered from attendance at several meetings of the Budget Protest League (which were very successful), is that the working men, to whatever party they belong, are quite willing to pay the increased duties on tobacco and drink; and our belief, based on this experience, is that they would resent, instead of being grateful for, any attempt by the Unionist party to oppose these duties. We recommend the Unionist leaders to be very careful of the grounds on which they endeavour to reject these clauses of the Budget. We also found that the working men of both parties were interested in the land taxes, because they thought that a new, a rich, and a not unfair source of taxation was being tapped. When they realise, as they will only do slowly—for they think, not altogether without foundation, that half they hear at public meetings is false—that the land taxes will not only bring in nothing, but add to the burthen of the State, there may be a sharp reaction against the Budget.

The landed interest is not the only one worth preserving, but it is well worth preserving, and it is the interest which is most threatened by the Budget, by the death duties even more than by the land taxes. The discussion of the death duties is still some way off, coming after the new licensing duties. Let us just see, in the interval of waiting, what the Opposition, at which the "Times" and Mr. Hiram Howell sneer as futile, has actually done to help the landed interest and to hurt the Government. In the first place, it has forced the Government to throw the cost of valuation upon the public, a concession which is not only a great relief to the owners of land but exposes the gross injustice which the Government would have perpetrated if they had been strong enough. Mr. Lloyd George intended to throw an expense, which he and the Prime Minister put at £2,000,000 but which will be a great deal more, upon the owners of every acre of ground in the three kingdoms, in order that they might tell Mr. Lloyd George's officials how much taxation to levy upon them. Why not throw the salaries of the surveyors of income tax upon the payers of income tax? It would be just as fair, or just as unfair, as the Government has been forced to admit. Whilst we are writing of concessions, we should like to point out in passing that the business of the nation is not a game or a match, so that all the talk about gratitude is pure nonsense. When Mr. Lloyd George makes a concession, he does not give anybody anything that belongs to himself, as his language might lead an intelligent schoolboy to imagine. He merely modifies in the interest of the public a term or condition in a public transaction, and he only does so because he is forced by public opinion. Besides relieving the owners of land of the cost of the valuation, another very valuable concession is the exemption from undeveloped-land duty of those owners who have spent £100 an acre within the last ten years on developing their land. Here again we can best measure the value of the thing gained by considering what the Government originally intended. No matter what an owner might have spent on drains and roads to prepare his estate for the builder, he was still to have been taxed ½d. in the £ on the supposed capital value of the land, which he would have had to pay in addition to his loss of interest on the money so expended. That was a glaring injustice. But of course the greatest triumph of the Opposition has been the restoration of the right of appeal to a court of law upon the valuation, or indeed on any question connected with the taxation of the land. It is a little difficult to bring home to one's bosom that a modern Minister, a leader of a democratic party, in a modern Parliament, did really contemplate depriving Englishmen of the right of appealing to the law to protect his property. That the clause in the Finance Bill which took away the right of appeal to the court, and said that the Commissioners' decision must be final, was contrary to the one written instrument in our Constitution, the Bill or Act of Rights, is we think indisputable, and it could never really have stood. But that does not matter; the clause was there, drafted by the officials of Mr. Lloyd George, and printed after his approval and corrections. To deprive the owners of land of the protection of the law which is extended to every other the meanest subject of the King was therefore the original design of the Radical Chancellor of the Exchequer. There is still another very important change in the Budget, which is due to the line-by-line resistance of the Unionists in the House of Commons—namely, the dropping of the ludicrous tax on ungotten minerals and the substitution of the duty on mining royalties and dead rents. Unjust as this last duty is, for it is a mere duplication of an existing income tax, it will be at least clear in its amount, and certain in its operation—it will at least tax a man on what he has got, not on what he has not got. To recapitulate, the opposition to the land taxes, at which the "Times" and Mr. Hiram Howell sneer as futile, has obtained from the Government the following changes and modifications in the Budget: (1) Valuation at the public cost; (2) exemption from undeveloped-land duty of owners who have spent £100 an acre; (3) right of appeal to the courts of law; (4) dropping of the tax on ungotten minerals. When one reflects that these concessions have been wrung from an unwilling Government, which commands a majority of 350, by an Opposition which is rarely able to muster more than 100 followers, it is impossible to deny that a more splendid victory of sheer intellectual force is not recorded in the annals of Parliament.

In conclusion we must allude to some exceptions from the operation of the land taxes which have been made, not by the Opposition, but by the Government. Rating and local authorities are excepted from the payment of these taxes, as are charitable corporations and registered societies. The last exception is meant to cover the case of the great benefit and friendly and building societies, which have over £100,000,000 invested in land by the working men of this country. It is a grossly unfair exception, for it leaves corporations composed of working men free to exercise acts of ownership which, if done by individuals, are denounced as robbery and blackmail. The same remark applies to local and rating authorities, like the London County Council and the Corporation of Glasgow, who are to be allowed to hold up land for a good market and to pocket the increment accruing on reversions of leases. Indeed, these corporations are applauded for their wisdom in doing what, when done by a Duke of Westminster, is denounced as spoliation. Does not all this point to the conclusion, which the Lord Advocate for Scotland is the only member of the Government honest enough to admit, that the real and sole justification for these taxes is the political immorality of private ownership of land? That is the real basis of the Budget, and the sooner the country knows it the better. "Establishing the principle" means the assertion of the proposition that land ought not to be owned by individuals but by the municipalities and the State. If this be not pure socialism, we do not know the meaning of the term.

THE ADMIRALTY CIRCUIT.

HAPPY indeed is the report of the Cabinet Committee on the differences between Lord Charles Beresford and the Admiralty. It seems to have pleased everybody. We may be sure the Committee are pleased with their own report. It is true there is not a word of praise of the Admiralty, and there is much conditional fault-finding with them, while the most that is said for arrangements for which Cabinet and Admiralty are jointly responsible is that they did not imperil the country. Still the Admiralty are thoroughly satisfied with the report. Lord Charles Beresford is very nearly censured, while his own censures on the Admiralty, or some of them, are practically endorsed. He too writes to the papers to say he is satisfied with the report. Well, the chief naval adviser to the Admiralty, being now in his sixty-ninth year, has practically ended his career, and Lord Charles Beresford has been retired from his last active command: so their relative merits have no longer any living interest for the Navy. Each is delighted with the report, so each may contentedly chant his Nunc dimittis and leave us free to consider defence policy, unembarrassed by naval cliques and schools.

For the adequacy of the arrangements made by the Government for the defence, not of this country, to which the Cabinet Committee limits itself, but of the whole Empire and its trade, the Cabinet is directly responsible. Thus the Cabinet set itself to consider its own war plans, the sufficiency of its own programmes of cruisers and destroyers, and its own distribution of the fleet in home waters. It is remarkable that the Committee have so far condemned rather than condoned their own past. We need only point out that the Committee may be perfectly impartial and yet err grossly in judgment if its standpoint is wrong. Just before the appointment of the Cabinet Committee to inquire into Lord Charles Beresford's charges, the Prime Minister propounded the new doctrine that our naval strength was adequate if it could repel the force that the Government deemed likely to be used for aggressive purposes against *this island*. Hence the standpoint from which the verdict was to be delivered was fundamentally altered for the worse, and what would have been considered criminal neglect under the last Government became efficient preparation under their successors.

But while the Cabinet could dictate on the sufficiency of armament, it could not control the eternal principles of strategy. Of these principles, three bore directly on the questions the Cabinet Committee were investigating. The first is that one directing brain is indispensable to successful war, and that a divided command is fatal; the second is contained in the single word "comradeship", which involves the habit of working together; and the third is that untrained ships such as partially manned or nucleus-crew vessels must not be regarded as vessels ready for war. On all three the Admiralty set themselves right before the investigation, and excused their action throughout 1907 and 1908 on the absurd plea that the two years formed a transitional period. To argue in a circle may on a similar principle be called a transitional argument, but it does not carry us much further. The facts that strike the observer are that in 1903 we had a Home Fleet, a Mediterranean Fleet, and an Atlantic Squadron, then known as the Channel Squadron, free to reinforce in either direction. In 1904 one redistribution, in 1907 another, and in 1909, in fear of an inquiry, a third was carried through, bringing us exactly to the point from which we set out in 1903 of a Home Fleet, a Mediterranean Fleet and an Atlantic Squadron. Every one of these changes disorganised and demoralised the fleets during the real transitional period in which they were endeavouring to settle down and build up fresh active fleets even as ants have to work if the nest is destroyed. As Moltke has pointed out, a method of action not intrinsically the best may well succeed, whereas vacillation between better plans must fail. The whole case is governed according to an admirable principle laid down by Sir John Fisher that "Confidence is a plant of slow growth. Long and constant association of ships of a fleet is essential to success. A newcomer is often more dangerous than the enemy". That is one principle, and it was infringed at every point by redistributions carried out so ruthlessly, relentlessly and remorselessly as to destroy the entire organisations of fleets. There is another principle that just as an army with due proportions of infantry, artillery and cavalry must exercise together, so a fleet with due proportions of battleships, cruisers and destroyers must be trained as one homogeneous whole. In 1907 the only large fully commissioned and therefore ready fleet was deprived of the bulk of its small cruisers and of all its destroyers. In spite of entreaties and altercations in the House of Commons, which but for the tact of the Speaker might have become scenes, the Board of Admiralty refused for many months to alter the arrangement. The case was admirably stated by the second in command of the Channel Fleet, Admiral Sir Reginald Custance, in a speech reported in the "Liverpool Courier", 8 August 1907, as follows:

"He was treading on very dangerous ground, for he was an officer on full pay, and he could not tell them exactly what he thought, but he would give them a little illustration. He dared say that many of the gentlemen there had played football. They might think there was little relation between the Navy and football, but there really was. A Rugby football team was divided into heavy forwards, half-backs who passed the ball to the three-quarters, and the three-quarters were the fast ones who ran away with it. How did a football team try to win? They selected their team and always kept the same team, who always played in the same place and were constantly practised together. That was the secret of their success. If a team took up their forwards at one time and played one game with them, and in another place took up another set of forwards, they could not expect to win."

Sir Reginald Custance then explained that it was the same with a fleet. They must be trained and worked together, the backs knowing exactly what the forwards are going to do. The Channel Fleet without small cruisers and destroyers "had no forwards". The Liverpool people could see the battleships in the Mersey, but the forwards were not there. Read between the lines the speech was a pungent satire on the redistribution scheme of 1907. This was the scheme which the Admiralty treated as unimpeachable and ideal, and which they were yet forced to abandon in favour of the old arrangement. The truth is that the circular course which the Admiralty have taken in getting back to the point from which they started was deliberate; the Government's zeal for economy had to be humoured. It was necessary to put ships out of full commission in order to cut down expenses and yet mask the proceedings by an elaborate pretence of an increase of fighting force. Since 1906 the present Government, by carrying us back to the exact arrangement of fleets which existed in 1903, have reduced the number of ships in full commission by five battleships and ten cruisers, and so saved, say, 4000 men, besides many incidental expenses. The nucleus-crew ship as a reserve in the second line was the creation of the last Government and an idea borrowed from France. So long as it was regarded as a reserve there was no ground for complaint; but when the dangerous fallacy was put forward that it was capable of "immediate action" and of acting "without an hour's delay", and that it was therefore a substitute for fully manned ships constantly exercised in their proper places, the whole reasoning confirms us in the belief that while this country has no great reason to fear Germany and her allies, it has every reason to fear the present administration of the Navy. Take the following extract from the report: "He [Lord Charles Beresford] pointed out that a considerable proportion of the Home Fleet was manned with nucleus crews, and was therefore in his opinion ineffective as an instantly ready striking force. The evidence before the Committee showed, in their opinion, that the nucleus-crew ships were capable of very rapid mobilisation, and had attained a satisfactory standard of efficiency". Here the acceptance of these ships scattered between three ports, partially manned and only mobilised after weeks of preparation, as a substitute for fully manned ships in real fleets is implicitly assumed. We can only say that when such doctrines sway the minds of men, they sound the death-knell of nations.

BOERS AND KAFFIRS.

At this stage in the affairs of South Africa there seems nothing to do but to accept the accomplished fact and hope for the best. Everybody, Government and Opposition alike, is determined to sing a pæan, though it is done with shut eyes and a good deal of unexpressed misgiving. There is the union of South Africa, long prayed for, long worked for, unexpectedly taking shape and actually presenting itself in the form of a Bill for the assent of the British Parliament. It is all so wonderful that everybody speaks of it with bated breath; indeed is almost afraid to breathe lest the slightest wind of criticism should make the whole structure dissolve like Kubla Khan's fantastic palace. The reason is that we know the foundations it has are Boer foundations. The union of South Africa has been possible because all that the Boers demanded has been conceded and the future government of South Africa is to be in the hands of the Boers. We have made a bargain on the lines of the compromise between husband and wife as to the sheets of their bed. "I cannot bear linen", said the husband, "and my wife dislikes cotton, so we have arranged that they shall be linen". And so we in England have consented to a South African Union bed furnished in the Dutch fashion, and we have decided to hold our tongues. It is such a fine thing to have a bed in which British and Dutch can lie at all that we pretend to shut our eyes to the discomfort the British will have in Dutch wrappers.

This is the condition on which the game is to be played at present, and we must play according to the rules. We are practically shut up to accepting the Bill just as it is. We must believe with Mr. Balfour that there is now only one race question in South Africa, and that it is not the question of Boer and British but that of the white and the black races. We cannot help feeling a good deal of sympathy with the black races. They get nothing out of the deal and they run a risk of losing something they already have. Our rapidly developed fraternal affection for the Boers is not yet shared by them, and government by Boer Parliaments is not so fine a prospect for them as we have persuaded ourselves it is for us. Perhaps that is because they are simple savages; and as they look at things more directly they cannot cheat themselves so easily as we can into believing what we want to believe. Mr. Seely proves by arithmetical demonstration that the Kaffirs cannot be deprived of their franchise in Cape Colony by the South African Parliament. But very probably the Kaffirs, being merely savages, cannot go very far in arithmetical calculations and so will not be impressed by figures. They know quite well however, as the Scotch say, how many beans make five, and as the Dutch have often enough "given them beans" in the past, they are very much afraid their portion will be beans in the future. At any rate they know this much about politics, that they prefer Downing Street direct and unadulterated; and they know that Downing Street would be little protection to them against a Cape Parliament that had resolved to abolish the black man's franchise.

The same line of reasoning applies equally to the black man's position in the Protectorates whenever it shall please the South African Parliament to take any of them under its government. The black man's affection for Downing Street may pass for a mild joke with Mr. Seely and the politicians; but there is sound sense in the black man's view. He understands direct autocratic Crown Colony government. It fits in with his own customary way of thinking and his own notion of government. It is frank, open, honest, simple and above-board, and he can trust the Governor, who is not under the influence of secret and selfish and sinister motives, who has no covetous desire for other men's lands, and will not gerrymander him for taxation or other schemes in anybody else's interests than his own. Parliamentary government in which he has no share, especially when it is controlled by Dutch hands, must appear to him an ocean of treacherous cross-currents to which he has no chart, and in which he is always in danger of being caught. All those elaborate schedules which, according to Mr. Seely, are to make the black man even more secure than he is at present if he should fall into the grasp of the South African Parliament, are nothing to him but the meshes of a parliamentary net which he wants to keep out of. This sort of thing, which is useful for soothing the conscience of the British legislator, who is really very uneasy about the black man but must let the Boer take him if he wants to, is a hocus-pocus which the black man himself fears and wants to have nothing to do with. The black man knows very well that what the self-governing colony wants the British Parliament cannot hinder it from obtaining. Self-government is a word of art, a mystery, a formula, whereby is signified that a colony cannot be refused anything it wants. It is a self-governed child whose parents dare not refuse it anything for fear it should become hysterical and make itself ill and its parents miserable. All these references and things in the schedules are nought but the parents', the Imperial Government's, concealment of weakness in a flood of words. They do not deceive a British Member of Parliament, much less a Kaffir who is on the spot and has had his wits sharpened to expect possibilities just because he is a Kaffir and looks out for experiments on his corpus vile. We do not know if he reads the papers much; but if he does, and has followed the process by which it has been decided that he is to have no vote for and no seat in the South African Parliament, he will find out what will happen when the Parliament wants to annex his Protectorates.

There are plenty of arguments, we admit, against the black man voting or sitting in the South African Parliament. We do not want him either to vote or to sit there on account of his intellectual unfitness; just as for the same reason we do not want, though we have to submit to them, many of our own voters for the British Parliament. This is a minor reason, however, and the greater one is that it is the white and not the black race that must be dominant in South Africa. And it is better that the dominance of the white race should be asserted openly than that there should be a pretence of equality as there is in America, where the negroes are circumvented either by force or fraud. It would be the same in South Africa; and though the black man may not have much to hope for from the response of the South African Parliament to the eloquent appeals here made to it to be generous and magnanimous to the blacks, the blacks will not be the worse off for not having the franchise. Nor perhaps do they want it so badly as the friends of all natives but their own in the House of Commons want it for them. What they are really concerned with, and must be anxious about, is that the House of Commons agrees that they ought not to have the franchise mainly because the colonies are opposed to it. It is not a question of merits, as it would be if the proposal were to give a new class votes for the British Parliament. The really crucial proposition is that it would be absurd to admit the right to self-government sans phrase, and then to attempt to lay the colonies under any pledge as to enfranchisement or indeed anything else domestic. In this respect the Kaffirs are in the same position as women. Logically, when we admit the theory of the self-government of the colonies—and this is the very essence of the new South African Constitution—the British Parliament has no more locus standi to set terms for enfranchising Kaffirs than to set terms for enfranchising women. Anyone who is not within a certain highly eccentric circle of British politicians can see how ridiculous this would be. There is no getting away from the formula either for the black man or the British Parliament. And we sympathise with the unfortunate fellow. He will run against this cast-iron formula whenever he asks the British Parliament to protect him from his South African friends.

GOODWILL TO SPAIN.

SPAIN'S preparations for a decisive stroke against the truculent hill-men of the Riff are costing her more than she can easily afford. Her money, however, is being well invested. It is true that from the point of view of a short-sighted mercantile accountant the affair is bad business, and that it may take the whole hinterland of Melilla twenty years to repay the Spanish Exchequer this week's bill for cartridges. But proud and ancient nations are not exactly the same as hucksters' shops; and many things besides an immediate cash profit or loss must be brought into the balance-sheet of the Riff campaign.

First and foremost, Spain is recovering her prestige as a European Power—surely an inestimable asset. The Moors have already been taught that she is as unwilling as France to be injured and insulted. What is much more to the point, the greater Powers have been reminded that the disasters of Manila Bay and of Santiago de Cuba were not, after all, the oft-predicted "finis Hispaniæ". To many open-eyed and open-minded observers the events of the past three weeks have been a revelation. They have seen an effective remnant of the Spanish navy (popularly supposed to be non-existent) bombarding hill-fortresses, seizing contraband of war, and co-operating with land forces according to the modern rules of the game. They have seen military balloons mounting up through the fiery African airs in order that highly-trained aeronauts might direct by telephone the men behind the brand-new field-guns. They have seen an army of 30,000 men debarqued on an unfriendly coast without a hitch. The horses of the cavalry have moved every beholder to admiration. As for the officers, who were fondly reputed to have no heart or mind for anybody or anything save Lola and Carmen and espadas and bulls, they are proving themselves to be every inch of them soldiers and worthy leaders of the stout fighting men who form the rank and file. In short, Spain is showing in Morocco, as she showed in Barcelona, that she is not a mere geographical expression, or an outworn dynastic survival, but that she is a well-manned, self-respecting State, able both to enforce order at home and to wage war abroad.

For us in England all this has a significance which too many people are overlooking. It goes to prove that our lightly-regarded Anglo-Spanish understanding is distinctly worth having and worth fostering. Happily, Sir Edward Grey was on the right side in this matter long before Spain had shown her present mettle, but among Britons at large an entente with Spain has not been taken seriously. For years people felt drawn to the frank and generous boy-king. They were glad that Alfonso XIII. married an English princess and that his yacht won a cup at Cowes. They were still more pleased when the reconstruction of the Spanish navy was confided to English brains; but they found in this arrangement only a naval and financial compliment, and shut their eyes to its political importance. With the French, against whom we have fought fifty times more than we have fought against the Spanish, an entente has come to be treated as a matter of course, in spite of the worthlessness of France's navy and the studied selfishness of her fiscal attitude to her best customers. But an entente with the Spaniards, although it might prove distinctly more useful both on the low levels of commerce and on the mountain-tops of the highest high politics, is generally regarded as a sentimental chimera pursued by a meagre dozen or score of unpractical hobby-riders.

The chief reason for this English irresponsiveness towards an Anglo-Spanish understanding is not hard to find. Our schoolbooks and popular histories have kept alive in generation after generation of English boys and girls a religious hatred of the Spaniard almost comparable with the Spaniard's own hatred of the Moor. It is much more than three hundred years since the Spanish Armada was battered and scattered; and since that astounding day Englishmen and Spaniards have fought side by side against a dictator whose menace to England was at least as dire as the second Philip's. Modern historians have disproved slander after slander against the Church in the Peninsula; yet Englishmen, for all they have the Elizabethan penal laws upon their consciences, still feel that Tennyson exactly hit the mark when he burst out with his "Inquisition dogs and the devildoms of Spain". In the past France has behaved quite as badly as Spain to her English captives, and far worse to her own people; but because there is no such odium theologicum in the one case as in the other, the poor Spaniard must be hanged for stealing a lamb while the Frenchman is indulged in lifting a fat sheep. No doubt some slow good is being done by the thousands of English visitors to Spain who return home and contradict the more grotesque libels on the Spanish people; but probably many and many a year must pass before the exceeding high mountain of anti-Spanish prejudice is removed and cast into the sea of oblivion.

In this business, however, we have not many and many a year to spare. A certain subterranean influence has long been traceable under all the confused turmoil of Moorish affairs; and if we do not make reasonable haste in clinching a friendship with Spain, another Power may supplant us. We have Gibraltar, and we mean to keep it; but Gibraltar is not everything. As the mistress of strong points on both sides of the Strait, Spain can be either our very important enemy or our very important friend. There is no time to lose. Of course it would be pleasanter and easier if we could truthfully point to a great mass of pro-Spanish sentiment backing up our diplomacy; but, fortunately, the ravages of democracy have hardly reached the Foreign Office, and England can still make treaties and alliances in the light of a wisdom and a knowledge not necessarily shared by the man in the street. As the sanction of Parliament was not sought as a preliminary to our alliance with Japan, there would be nothing outrageous in sealing and signing and delivering a prudent document to the Spaniard, who is, after all, a white man, a European, and a Christian. Best of all, the Spaniard is well disposed to us just now. He is holding out his hand.

One historic obstacle to formal Anglo-Spanish friendship has quite lately begun to fade away. So long as responsible Spaniards dreamed of absorbing Portugal into a united Peninsular kingdom, England was forced to hold Spain at arm's length. Our bond with Portugal is more than an understanding. It is an alliance which, despite a tiff or two, has endured for more than five hundred years. Portuguese statesmen openly speak of the alliance with England as the keystone of their foreign policy and as the only effective guarantee of their nation's independence. We on our part enjoy the advantages of Lisbon and of the Açores, the vital importance of which is known to every naval strategist; and, in order to maintain friendship with Portugal, we have hitherto had to face the possibility of trouble with Spain. So long as the two countries were solidly monarchical, the danger was real. But it hardly exists to-day. Even if Spain had the men and the money and the temper for an old-fashioned war of aggression, she could not take the risk of placing herself between the two fires of Catalonian Separatism and Portuguese Nationalism. Besides, as the Republicans of Madrid have long been trying to worry the flank of monarchical Spain by fomenting Republican outbursts in Lisbon and Oporto, it is in every way the interest of Spain's present rulers to strengthen the hands of authority in the neighbouring kingdom and to maintain the existing status. There must still be a Spain and a Portugal, just as there must still be a Norway and a Sweden; and now that Spain is learning this truth, one of the greatest hindrances to her active and all-round friendship with England is nearly gone.

So much for the more portentous issues of the Anglo-Spanish understanding. They cannot, of course, mature in an hour or a day. Meanwhile, however, all men of good will towards Spain may accomplish something in the right direction. Mr. Arthur Keyser, our Consul at Seville, has written to the "Morning Post" making the timely suggestion that Englishmen who cherish "happy recollections of days spent in Spain may be glad of an opportunity for privately showing their sympathy with a people whose kindness to strangers is so well known". Any sums which reach the Consul will be sent to the Captain-General of Andalusia, for the needs of those whose fathers or sons have been killed in the war. The first aim of every Englishman who responds to this appeal will be to place a steaming puchero on many a table which would else stand bare; but, without rubbing the bloom off an act of disinterested benevolence, perhaps it is permissible to add that such an alms-deed will also be both an act of reparation for past malice and uncharitableness towards the Spaniards and an act of faith in a better future.

THE MISCHIEF-MAKER AT OXFORD.

As keen tariff reformers we can regard the interference in the Oxford representation by a few professors and lesser academics only as a piece of sheer gratuitous mischief-making. There are no such egregious busybodies as learned or professedly learned men who think they have a turn for affairs. Truly we are not surprised at this move. As soon as it was arranged, with the general approval of the best Unionist opinion throughout the country, that Lord Hugh Cecil should stand as Conservative candidate for the University, we were very sure that some academic statesman would find the opportunity to put himself forward too good to be missed. So Professor Bourne and his friends promptly began running about to find someone they could use as figurehead. To be known as the engineers of a domestic opposition to Lord Hugh Cecil would give them an importance and a publicity they could hardly even aspire to in ordinary circumstances. They would be talked of far beyond academic circles. So whatever might be the result of their intervention and the election, something would be gained. And Dr. Evans has apparently lent himself to their little plan with alacrity. His letter of acceptance is a very humorous document—unintentionally we are afraid. In the time-honoured style he first deprecates the honour that is thrust upon him—he would put it from him, but he hears the nation calling him; he must not fail the nation in the hour of need, and so he accepts the honour. Unlike a certain other man, Dr. Evans can dig, but he is not ashamed to beg—to beg for votes and favour; truly he takes himself sufficiently seriously in setting forth his claims. He evidently thinks in all sincerity that he alone can save Oxford from a great disaster; that he is a better man in every way than Lord Hugh Cecil; and that he deserves credit for really very considerable self-sacrifice in allowing himself to be put forward. He has the scientific mind which Lord Hugh Cecil lacks; he has intelligence for University reform which Lord Hugh has not; he has a soul above the self-sufficiency, the strange limitations, the inability to appreciate the need of scientific methods characteristic of the type of mind (Lord Hugh's type) produced by existing conditions. He is not, as poor Lord Hugh Cecil, a political refugee, the last resource of a worn-out Anglicanism. In fine, if Dr. Evans is not elected, the University will be virtually disfranchised.

This is truly and exactly the spirit of Dr. Evans' letter of acceptance, and not very far from its words. Its good taste may be left uncanvassed; its pompous self-importance smiled at. But its claims must be considered for a moment.

This letter put the matter plainly on a personal basis. That Dr. Evans should think that he is, and Lord Hugh is not, the man for Oxford University is natural enough. Others, in a better position to take a detached view, may not accept Dr. Evans' opinion of himself as conclusive. We have to choose between two men. Oxford, as any other University, ought not to choose its representative in Parliament just on the ordinary party lines: it ought to look for a distinguished personality, one that stands for an ideal as well as for a party; who will be able to contribute to public life something more than the mere politician, and yet be able to take his stand in the arena like the rest and to meet them on their own ground. Well we have Dr. Evans—academic, archæologist, unknown to public life—put forward as the orthodox Unionist candidate; we have Lord Hugh Cecil, the bearer of a great name, son of a Chancellor of Oxford University, a public man of experience and of real influence in the House of Commons, due, perhaps, mainly to regard for his character, an orator, and in some ways a genius. Which of the two is likely to represent Oxford University with more distinction in Parliament? The question has only to be put to show Dr. Evans' candidature in a farcical light. What disabling counts, then, are there against Lord Hugh? Dr. Evans is not above the cheap appeal to prejudice which suggests that his opponent is run by an extreme ecclesiastical party. It is true Lord Hugh Cecil has religious convictions, and Dr. Evans may think this a mistake in a public man, just as from the point of view of success it has been a mistake in Lord Hugh to have political convictions. Lord Hugh Cecil is a High Churchman; he is not a Ritualist. Churchmen will decide for themselves whether it is more against a candidate for Oxford University to be a High Churchman than, as Dr. Evans, not to be a Churchman at all. Lord Hugh is not an academic; Dr. Evans is. Is this indeed in Dr. Evans' favour? What University don or professor has ever been a really effective member of Parliament? Neither Lecky nor Jebb, each of them a much greater man than Dr. Evans, was a Parliamentary success. Moreover Oxford is already represented by one member of the Oxford inner, academic circle; so there is the more reason why the other should be chosen from without. Then, we are told, Lord Hugh would not assist University reform. Dr. Evans' claque are taking dangerous ground in urging this. If Convocation were really persuaded that Lord Hugh was against reform, or revolution, of the University, we have no doubt at all he would be elected. In fact, however, we suspect he would assist reasonable reform in the government of the University, the reform we all desire; but we dare say he is strongly opposed to flooding Oxford with Board-school boys, to making Oxford a training-ground for the organisation of strikes, to cutting her connexion with the Church of England, to putting a business course, bookkeeping, etc., in the place of classics. If these are Dr. Evans' ideals, no doubt Lord Hugh is a bad candidate for reform purposes. But he will not be alone in his iniquity.

But all this talk of unsympathy with Oxford reform is mere pretext. There is only one reason why Lord Hugh is opposed by a Unionist—because he is not a tariff reformer. Let him square his convictions for once and stand as a tariff reformer, and where would Dr. Evans be? Laughed out of his candidature. Not a word about Oxford reform would be listened to or indeed uttered. If Lord Hugh were a tariff reformer, not a Unionist would even criticise his candidature. And from the tariff reform point of view, which is ours, how does the case stand? In the first place, we are certain it will be hurtful to the good name of the tariff reform cause if it is associated with the hounding out of public life of such men as Lord Hugh Cecil and his brother. The Confederate game is making mischief and nothing else. But even on the result in votes in the House the effect of Dr. Evans' interference can only be hurtful. Lord Hugh Cecil will be elected—everyone knows there are forces behind him too strong to be beaten. So the real question is the effect of Dr. Evans' candidature on the other seat. There will be at any rate two candidates in the field for it—Sir William Anson and Dr. Evans. Why should anyone wish Dr. Evans to supplant Sir William Anson? And if Sir William is elected again, what will have been the use of Dr. Evans' intervention at all? But there is another far from impossible result. The Oxford Liberals will be foolish indeed if, seeing three Unionist candidates in the field for two seats, they do not put forward a man of their own. They would then vote for their own candidate, and not improbably for Lord Hugh as a free trader. It is not at all impossible that the Liberal candidate would come second on the poll. Then Dr. Evans' tariff reform friends will have the satisfaction of knowing they have caused Oxford University to be represented by two free-traders, one of them a Radical. This would be a fitting conclusion to the Evans movement, which is a deliberate attempt, with a good deal of petty spite in it, to breed bad blood among Unionists. These domestic feuds are always very bitter, and we cannot say that academic atmosphere seems at all likely to assuage the bitterness of this one. None who really cared for the interests of the Unionist party, still less for the health of public life, would have forced this domestic strife on the Unionists of Oxford University.

THE CITY.

WHAT is the motive of the extraordinary gyrations of the Harriman stocks we have not the least idea, nor do we believe that anybody in London knows, and even in New York the number of the initiated must be very small. On Wednesday Union Pacifics rose from 220 to 224, and then fell in the street market to 216. Steel Commons likewise fell from 81 to 78. The danger of outsiders dealing in these stocks may best be gauged by looking at the prices of options. The put or call of Unions for the end of September is 7 to 8 dollars, the put and call being 16 dollars. Till the end of November a single option costs 10 dollars. The put or call of Steel Commons for the end of September is 3½ dollars. Dabblers who sup with Mr. Harriman have need of a long spoon. As we are not equipped with such an article we confess to being afraid of this gentleman's stocks, and shall continue to be so until he takes us into his confidence. "Put" options in Unions and Steels are a fair gamble, like backing the red or the black, but the double option is too expensive, for after giving $20 for the put and call of Unions for the end of November they might hang about their present price for the next six months.

The Kaffir market is really dull, with the exception of Goldfields and Chartereds, where a certain amount of gambling is going on round the reputed Abercorn find. We can hardly believe in the shortage of black labour. It is the usual holiday talky-talky, for the financial editors must write about something in the dog days. If it were true, the slump might be pronounced, as the jobbers have been helping themselves pretty freely. Alaska Treadwells are over 7, and Alaska Mexicans have risen to $3\frac{5}{16}$-$3\frac{7}{16}$. The latter is the best mining share to buy at the moment.

Membakut Rubber Limited differs from the ordinary run of these companies in that it is the guaranteed offspring of the British North Borneo Company, which is a chartered company exercising sovereign rights in the Protectorate of North Borneo. It is, of course, a little pompous to speak of it in the prospectus as "the Government". It is a chartered company with a net or profit revenue of £54,020 (after defraying cost of administration) and a sum standing to the credit of the profit and loss account of £140,223. The Membakut Rubber Company has a capital of £150,000, divided into 100,000 guaranteed shares (5 per cent.) and 50,000 non-guaranteed shares (all of £1) reserved for future issue. Membakut is formed to acquire from the Government, i.e. the British North Borneo Company, a concession of 5000 acres of jungle, of which 500 acres have been cleared but not planted, for

£25,000 in cash. The estate is practically a freehold, and the British North Borneo Company guarantees 5 per cent. on 100,000 shares for six years, and in 1915 undertakes to buy all shares offered at par, provided that all moneys advanced by the B. N. B. Company for dividends shall be repaid by Membakut "without interest out of profits exceeding 6 per cent. in any year on the whole of the capital for the time being paid up, and that no debentures or other shares shall be issued until such repayment without the consent in writing of the Government". The British North Borneo Company, or the Government, has, moreover, underwritten 80,000 shares, the minimum subscription on which allotment may be made, for a commission of 6 per cent. in cash. It will thus be seen that with a cash consideration of £25,000, preliminary expenses put at £3000, underwriting commission £4800, and with, say, £500 for brokerage, a sum amounting to £33,300 has to be deducted from the £100,000 issued, leaving £66,700 for working capital, supposing 100,000 shares applied for; if only 80,000 shares are applied for, the working capital will be £44,700. Taking the larger sum, £66,000 is a wholly inadequate working capital to bring 5000 acres of jungle into the rubber-tapping stage. From the experience of Ceylon and the Federated Malay States, the minimum expenditure necessary is £30 per acre, in addition to the cost of the land. Membakut Rubber therefore ought to have a working capital of £150,000. It is true that it has 50,000 shares in reserve, and that, if the first clearing and planting are successful, it will have no difficulty in raising fresh capital. It is obvious that the shareholders are quite certain to get their 5 per cent. for six years, and if 200 acres are planted with 100 trees to the acre by the beginning of October, in six years' time the revenue might be nearly £5000. There is not any risk about Membakut, and if shareholders will be content with 5 per cent. for the next eight years they may be recommended to subscribe.

The smash-up of the Piccadilly Hotel and the report of the Official Receiver reveal a great defect in our company law. We do not mean the fact that the shareholders have lost £1,502,676—that is "an accident of hourly proof", and, besides, most of the shares were probably "boodle", or promoters' profit. We mean that the unsecured creditors—in other words, the tradesmen—have been let in for £854,641, and that a great part of these debts were incurred by the directors just before the debenture-holders foreclosed. It is true that the directors say that when they ordered the goods they were negotiating a loan of £500,000 with the trustees of the prior lien debentures, which fell through. But instances are constantly occurring of tradesmen supplying goods to companies, and then being cut out of payment by the debenture-holders. Of course, as the smash is a big one, great "sympathy" is expressed for the directors. Had the failure been for a tenth part of the sum, instead of sympathy they would probably have received writs.

INSURANCE: POLICIES AT LOW PREMIUMS.

III.

LIFE assurance policies under which the sum assured is paid at death whenever it happens, for which premiums have to be paid throughout life, and which do not share in the profits of the company, are frequently regarded with disfavour because, if a policyholder lives a reasonably long time, the total amount which he pays in premiums may exceed the sum payable to his estate at death. If a man commencing at age thirty pays a premium of £100 a year for a non-profit whole-life policy the sum assured is £5130. If he dies at age eighty-one, his estate gets back all the premiums he has paid, but without any interest. If he dies at age sixty-one, the premiums paid accumulated at 3 per cent. compound interest are returned to his estate. If he dies between sixty-one and eighty-one, the interest is less than 3 per cent.; and if he survives eighty-one, the sum assured is less than the total paid in premiums.

This, of course, is a wrong way of looking at the matter, because, as we have frequently explained, part of each premium is applied to pay for the chance of receiving a great deal more than the savings accumulated out of premiums, and only part of each premium is available for investment purposes. A prominent characteristic of non-profit whole-life assurance is the large amount of insurance protection which is provided. Death may occur before the second premium of £100 is paid, in which event more than £5100 would be paid to the heirs of the policyholder. The commercial value of this protection is approximately £40; that is to say, a man can go to a life office and pay about £8 for a term policy which guarantees the payment of £1000 to his estate in the event of his death within one year, but of nothing at all if he survives for twelve months.

Bearing this insurance protection in mind, let us see what a man of thirty could do with £100 a year paid for whole-life assurance with participation in profits. The sum assured in the first year would be about £3865, or £1265 less than under a non-profit policy. This protection for an additional £1265 is commercially worth about £10 a year. Thus under the non-profit policy about £40 out of the first annual premium is used for protection, and under the with-profit policy only about £30 is employed for this purpose. Ignoring any question of expenses, £60 is available for savings or investment under the non-profit policy, and £70 under the with-profit policy. It is clearly inappropriate to compare the results of saving £60 a year with those of saving £70 a year; the annual premium of £100 is employed differently in the two cases, there being more protection and less saving under one policy than under the other. Even if a man does take a non-profit policy at thirty, and lives to eighty, he is receiving a vast deal more than merely the return of all the premiums paid, although this is the apparent result, because all the time he has had a varying amount of insurance protection, the value of which ought not to be ignored because he happens to live long, any more than the value of fire-insurance protection should be disregarded because no fire occurs.

Under a good life policy sharing in the profits, the sum assured, if increased by the addition of bonuses, would equal the amount of the non-profit policy at the end of seventeen years, and thereafter the with-profit policy would be considerably and increasingly larger than the non-profit. The latter would remain constant at £5130 if taken at age thirty at an annual cost of £100, while the former policy would assure £5400 at the end of twenty years, £6400 at the end of thirty years, £7600 at the end of forty years, and £9000 when, after being assured for fifty years, the policyholder reached the age of eighty. The probable lifetime of a man effecting a policy at age thirty is a further thirty-seven years, by which time the with-profit policy would greatly exceed the non-participating assurance. Out of 1,000 people effecting their assurance at age thirty it is to be expected that the heirs of 155 would gain by taking non-profit policies, while those of 845 would benefit by taking really first-class with-profit assurance; but the dependants of the 845, no less than those of the minority, would have had the valuable benefit of the greater amount of insurance protection if without-profit assurance had been chosen. Thus the question between with-profit and without-profit policies is a matter for each individual according to his circumstances; if the largest amount of provision for dependants in the event of premature death is the greatest need, then a non-profit policy should be chosen. If less protection and a larger return in the event of living long is more desirable, then a with-profit policy should be taken.

THE FUTURE OF THE ZOOLOGICAL SOCIETY.

By Dr. P. Chalmers Mitchell F.R.S.

I.

THE Zoological Society of London has pursued an almost unbending course since its institution. It received a Royal Charter in 1829 for "the advancement of Zoology and Animal Physiology, and for the introduction of new and curious subjects of the Animal Kingdom". From the first it has been a scientific body, holding meetings for the discussion of scientific topics, entering into correspondence with learned societies and individuals throughout the world, publishing the memoirs presented at its meetings, exchanging these with the corresponding publications of similar bodies, and from this main source accumulating a library of high scientific importance. With a few notable exceptions the zoologists most active in the Society have been devoted to the systematic side of their subject, and the staff of the British Museum of Natural History has continued to supply a great proportion of those whose steady influence has moulded the character of the scientific work, scientific publications and library of the Society. The Council, the governing body, has always been drawn largely from systematic zoologists, the other and more fluctuating elements having consisted chiefly of noblemen and country gentlemen with a taste for natural history, wealthy amateur collectors, and an occasional professor of eminence.

An oligarchy of such a nature acting through presidents and secretaries of distinction and resource kept a firm grip on the fortunes of the Society, and treated the general body of Fellows, who subscribed chiefly because they were fond of animals and wished to see them on Sundays, with a benevolent tolerance. The offices, museum and library were in Central London, and there the Council met, keeping closely in touch with the scientific work of the Society and directing the Gardens from a distance.

By the provisions of the charter the secretary is the chief executive officer of the Society, and the post was held for a number of years by a series of learned gentlemen who were unpaid, and who were precisely of the type of the honorary officers who conduct the affairs of most of the learned societies. The Society met and discussed species, the experts of the Museum contributing largely; the "Scientific Proceedings" were published with a fair regularity, and the collection of skins and skulls and the library grew. A decent interest was taken in the Gardens at Regent's Park; good landscape gardening was carried out, and the animals, especially when they were of zoological interest, were sedulously chronicled and tolerably housed. The immediate management of the menagerie, however, was in the hands of servants. In such circumstances the Society slowly withered, and its annual income, which had been nearly £14,000 in 1829, sunk to £7,765 in 1847.

In 1847 the Council perceived the pass to which the Society had come, and changes of an important nature were brought about. The initial step was to appoint a secretary who should be a paid officer and give his whole time to the affairs of the Society. The new secretary, D. W. Mitchell, a man of high talent and great energy, was devoted to living animals, and redirected the attention of the Society to their living collection. The Council resolved that the menagerie was the "primary and almost sole object" of interest to Fellows and to the general public. It was agreed to abandon the museum, the collections being dispersed to provincial museums after the national Museum had selected what it required. The housing of the animals and the convenience of the public at the Gardens were greatly improved. Special efforts were made to secure the importation of animals by appointing as corresponding members of the Society persons in official positions in different parts of the world. Popular lectures on zoology at the Gardens were arranged for and a Guide to the Gardens, on the model which survived until 1903, was prepared. In the twelve years during which Mitchell was secretary the income of the Society doubled, the extent and interest of the collection at the Gardens increased greatly, and the foundation of their repute as a place of popular resort was firmly laid. This renewed prosperity, however, also affected the scientific side. The library was enriched by a beautiful series of studies from the living animals made by Wolf, one of the finest painters of animals that has ever lived. The scientific meetings flourished; the published "Scientific Proceedings" took their modern form, almost approached their modern size, and were illustrated by coloured plates. There remained, however, a steady bent in the direction of systematic zoology, and the isolation of the Gardens from the central offices and management crystallised the division of the Society into a scientific and menagerie side.

In 1859 D. W. Mitchell resigned, to undertake the direction of the new Jardin d'Acclimatation at Paris, and was succeeded by Dr. P. L. Sclater, who continued in office until 1903. Dr. Sclater proved to be a secretary of strong character and high capacity, widely interested in zoological science, but with a marked bent towards the systematic and museum side, his own great contributions to knowledge being chiefly in the sphere of naming new species and in studying the relation of species to geographical distribution. None the less he took a deep interest in other forms of zoological work, and was unwearied in his encouragement of young zoologists. Under his régime the library grew and prospered; the scientific meetings became a recognised arena for the discussion of zoological problems and for the exhibition of rarities, and the scientific publications increased in size and importance. His dominating interest, however, was systematic zoology, and as this was agreeable to the most persistent element on the Council, the character of the scientific work of the Society was inclined in that direction. In 1865 the office of prosector was created, with the object of making a proper use of the rich material provided by animals that died in the collection. The first prosector was a stubborn anatomist, with an abstract passion for descriptive anatomy as apart from any purpose to which it could be applied, but his successors, although of ability at the least equal, were more pliable, and their work was almost limited to anatomy as a guide to classification. The popular lectures at the Gardens slowly flickered out, and the funds devoted to them were applied towards the preparation of an annual "Record of Zoology", a publication of high technical importance, but useful primarily to systematists.

The divorce between the Gardens and the general work of the Society persisted, the gap, indeed, becoming wider. The Council gave the Gardens an intermittent and somewhat condescending attention, most of them being aroused to interest only by the arrival of hitherto undescribed forms or of additions "new to the collection". The active superintendence was in the hands of A. D. Bartlett, a man of humble origin and little education, certainly with a bent for the management of living things, but with an innate conservatism that silently acquiesced in a policy of drift. Scientific observation of living animals, not as museum specimens but as living things, was almost wholly confined to those who had no official connexion with the Society, and the management of the Gardens slowly fell behind that of similar institutions. With the growth of London, however, the Society grew slowly, and its income, which had doubled in the twelve years from 1847 to 1859, again doubled in the forty-three years from 1859 to 1903. Indications of the demand for a change became more and more plain, and in 1903, when Dr. Sclater retired, the Society showed its keen desire for new ideas, a desire equally plainly shown on the Council and amongst Fellows generally, and quite independent of any personal considerations.

THE SPORTSMAN OF 1909.

By Edward H. Cooper.

"THE new club-house at the S—— links", said an enthusiastic member, "is a marvellous place. The walls are papered with that new-fashioned stamped paper looking like tapestry. The sofas and arm-chairs are thick blue velvet, and the carpets are like old turf. The chef comes from the Savoy, and every dressing-room has got a bathroom attached to it. And there's a golf links too."

The man who was talking in this fashion meant to be sarcastic; except for this good intention he was a typical modern sportsman. Can you wonder at the contemptible condition of sport to-day when you study a golf house of this description, or the pavilion and luncheon arrangements at Lord's, or the arrangements for your comfort at Sandown Park, Kempton Park, Goodwood and such-like places?

Dealing with the racing world (because I chance to know it best) one is first and above all things anxious to know why half the people are here at all. The lawns at Brighton or the Botanical Gardens are quite as picturesque and healthy, and the visitors to them are not bothered by the sudden departure of their male escorts to Tattersall's Ring or to Stands whence they can look at some tiresome race. The casinos at Dinard or Dieppe are not very much farther off, and the petits-chevaux tables there are much more these people's "form". What on earth are they doing on an English racecourse? These are the folk, men and women, who go to bull-fights in Spain and almost weep with boredom if no man is killed or animal tortured to death at regular intervals; and who (the men at any rate) eighteen hundred years ago lay in hot baths in Rome or Pompeii while someone read witty poetry to them. Their programme of an agreeable afternoon's sport is a special train running into the middle of a club lawn, a five-course lunch with much whiskey-and-Perrier and black coffee and Grand Marnier to follow, three hours in an arm-chair varied by afternoon tea and a little comfortable successful gambling, and a return to London in the above-mentioned train. If you can imagine a pig in a sty making an occasional bet with another pig as to which of three cocks in the neighbouring yard will crow the oftenest, and spending the rest of his time lying on straw or eating at his trough, you have a model of the modern race-going Englishman.

I am moved to these reflections by the discovery during a recent visit to Newmarket that even this metropolis of the racing world is beginning to surrender itself to the modern craze for luxury. Here was a place which was the world's model for racing life of every description. "Our trainers are smarter than yours", said an American to me two or three years ago, "our jockeys are brainier, and our horses can leave yours standing still; but I always feel that we are there to play poker while you're out for sport." British mankind was walking or riding up the Bury Hills at 6 A.M. watching training gallops before the west wind had blown the October mists away across the hundred miles of level space which separate this high wide heath-land from The Wash. Horses with names almost world-famous strode past you in a swinging gallop; trainers, jockeys, newspaper correspondents and a bevy of friends stood in little groups, or sat on their hacks, to watch the horses, a score of newspaper folk being ready to flash the news through Great Britain if the Cambridgeshire favourite is seen to falter or heard to cough. Here comes the King trotting up the hill on a neat-looking hack; and, cantering behind him, a well-known trainer's son, with hands and heels well down, and his cap at that subtle inclination of the head which betokens that the wearer knows something to beat the favourite.

At nine you go in to an immense breakfast, and at 1.30 up to the racecourse—by no means to an armchair and overfed leisure. One race finishes at the Ditch Mile Post half a mile away, and you must walk down to the little Stand to see it; another at the Criterion Stands half a mile in the other direction, and you must go there too; while between every other race you must go to the Birdcage and listen to the sapient counsels of jockeys, trainers and owners. A man who has passed an afternoon of that description has won something besides money, and has certainly earned his dinner; just as the small stable-lad, who has arrived at the stable at 4.30 A.M., has "done" his horse, ridden him at exercise on Long Hill in the morning and in a race this afternoon, and stabled, groomed and fed him afterwards, has finished a healthy day's work.

But the languid sportsman of 1909 has decided that he cannot manage the walk up to the Criterion Stands, which have accordingly been abolished, and there is already some talk of the Ditch Mile Stand following them into oblivion. And some of the American trainers who have come over this year to afflict the English racing world with American methods of training, riding and managing horses, have decided that it is a mistake for a boy to ride the horse which he "does", and propose accordingly to introduce two sets of youths for these various purposes. I find no difficulty in believing that an American jockey requires an amount of knowledge for American racing purposes which it will take him all his time to acquire and utilise. The old-fashioned English method, it must be remembered, is only possible in the case of small boys who are required merely to win a race by honest, hard riding. I doubt very strongly whether the elder American jockeys, brilliant and straightforward riders such as Maher, learnt their business in such a miserable school.

Luxury of this sort, I fancy, came to us from Paris, whose racecourses are large and well-managed gardens, with comfortable garden-seats everywhere, big open fires standing about in cold weather, luncheon and tea rooms whose cooking you compare, sometimes favourably and sometimes unfavourably, with Durand's and Paillard's, and gorgeous flower-beds worthy of Hyde Park in June. The Parisian takes his wife—or the other lady—there to display her new hat, and incidentally (baccarat being unfortunately not available) to make a little money on the races, if Providence is kind, with which to pay for the aforesaid hat. He knows the horse merely as "No. 7" or "No. 10"; cries out, "Sacré! il gagne au pas!" about a stable companion who is making the running for it; and generally regards the racecourse as a large and rather ill-managed petits-chevaux table. Of course there are many French and very many Italian sportsmen to whom none of this applies in the least; but I fancy it represents the racing attitude of two-thirds of an ordinary assembly at Longchamps, Auteuil, Nice and Rome.

There are several reasons why armchair garden-party racing of this description is as undesirable as it is contemptible. In the first place, it is a good deal less healthy than an old-fashioned racing day at Newmarket, Epsom, Liverpool or Doncaster. An English trainer who dislikes being run in a special train up to an arm-chair on a lawn, and deposited there for the afternoon, told me the other day that he was going to clamour for Turkish baths at these "Park" racecourses, that being the only cure for the indigestion which they gave him. I suggested a return to the above-mentioned Roman baths; one might lie about the lawns and enclosures in gently running hot water, the baths being in rising tiers so that one need only just lift one's head to see an occasional race go by. The idea would certainly have appealed to the youth of Rome, though the climate might complicate matters at Sandown Park.

Chiefly, however, garden-party racing is much more expensive than the other kind, and allows far too much leisure for the proceedings by which one proposes to—but mostly does not—pay the extra cost. A man who gets up out of a cushioned garden-chair to make a bet, and then subsides into his seat again, is a gambler and not a sportsman. One wonders what the Marquis of Hastings or Admiral Rous would have said to a person who backed a horse which he saw for the first time as it cantered down to the starting-post; or would have replied to him if he had offered him afternoon tea between the races!

GARDENS WITHOUT FLOWERS.

By Sir William Eden Bart.

I HAVE come to the conclusion that it is flowers that ruin a garden, at any rate many gardens. Flowers in a cottage garden, yes. Hollyhocks against a grey wall; orange lilies against a white one; white lilies against a mass of green; aubretia and arabis and thrift to edge your walks. Delphiniums against a yew hedge and lavender anywhere. But the delight in colour, as people say, in large gardens is the offensive thing: flowers combined with shrubs and trees! The gardens of the Riviera, for instance; Cannes and the much praised vulgar Monte Carlo—beds of begonias, cinerarias at the foot of a palm, the terrible crimson rambler trailing around its trunk. I have never seen a garden of taste in France. Go to Italy, go to Tivoli, and then you will see what I mean by the beauty of a garden without flowers—yews, cypress, statues, steps, fountains—sombre, dignified, restful. And as every picture should have a bit of distance to let the eye out of it, here and there you get a peep at the hills. Distant beauty in a glimpse—given in a setting—a bit at a time. And you may add if you like a moving figure; "an Eve in this Eden of ruling grace". Above this as you look up, you recollect, is the Villa d'Este; classic—the garden and the architecture suited the one to the other. How I remember the noble stone pines in the Borghese at Rome. The sad and reticent cypress in the Boboli Gardens at Florence round about the fountains—what depth and dignity of background; a place to wander in and be free. After all, the suitability of things is what is admirable. Are they "in value", as artists say? The relation of tones correct? They do not swear? A woman suitably dressed, a man properly mounted, a picture well framed. People talk of colour; "I like a bit of colour in this cold and gloomy climate" they say. Agreed; but what is colour and where? Titian was a colourist, but always low in tone. Put a yellow viola beside the brightest tints of Titian and you will see. Keep your effects subdued. Never mix reds or pinks and yellow; put yellow and orange and green and white together; put blues and mauves and greys together; and let your backgrounds be broad, neutral, plain. If you have an herbaceous border against a wall, let the creepers on that wall be without flowers or nearly so. Let the wall be the background to frame it. You would not hang a Tintoretto on a Gobelin tapestried wall.

Have you ever been to Penshurst? There again is the beauty of a garden without flowers. It may have been accident; it may have been the time of year that made me like it so. There is an orchard and yew hedges and Irish yews and grass paths. And there is a tank with lovely pink brick edges and sides and water lilies and fish, and it is surrounded by a yew hedge and grass paths, and its four corners have steps down to the wall, and a ball on each pedestal at its base. And the apple blossom peeps over the hedge; and the raw sienna of the lichen everywhere on the stone gives the richness of gold; and that's all there is in the colour scheme. The only flowers I noticed were patches, unrestrained and unplanned, of auriculas, evidently from seed—all colours: many fringed with margins of gold like the eyes of "la fille aux yeux d'or" in Balzac's novel. All else was richness, depth, and calm, abstract but clearly felt.

Against this of course there is the garden of the Manor House, the wealth and luxuriance that is the result of the soil that suits and the flowers that dwell so happily against the grey old walls. There you can scarce go wrong—campanulas, foxgloves, endless lists of things. Flagged courtyards, flagged paths, sundials—you know it all. And if you can find a place with a moat, a clump of yews and a kingfisher, stay there if you can.

Never have flowers against a balustrade, only grass or gravel. Begonias, geraniums, calceolarias are hard to manage anywhere. Annuals are delightful, but their reign is short. Try nemophila called discoidalis—dull rather in colour as they say and like auriculas more or less. Linaria too you know—a very useful purple—it goes well with gypsophila.

You must have noticed that many flowers most beautiful cut are impossible grown in beds. Carnations, for instance, roses, and sweet peas. You take your lady down to dinner. She is fond of flowers. She knows what she likes, and she admires the decorations. They are certain to be either sweet peas and gypsophila or smilax and malmaisons. You try to make way amongst the smilax for her knick-knacks—her fan, her gloves, her scent, her powder puff, her matches and cigarettes. Eventually she puts half of them on her lap, and you have to get them from the floor after dinner—which you hate—and she is more amused at your annoyance than grateful for your trouble. Such is her sense of humour and her manners.

Fruit is the proper decoration for a dinner-table, not flowers. I am sure the Greeks only had fruit. Orchardson in that picture of "The Young Duke", I think it is, has fruit only in the wonderfully painted accessories of the dinner-table. The Dukes are all alike, but the fruit and plate are not. But all fruit is not beautiful. Oranges and bananas for instance are not. Grapes, apples, pears and pineapples are. What is more beautiful than black grapes with the bloom on them in a silver or gold dish?

AT PORCHESTER.

By W. H. Hudson.

To the historically and archæologically minded the castle and walls at Porchester are of great importance. Romans, Britons, Saxons, Normans—they all made use of this well-defended place for long centuries, and it still stands, much of it well preserved, to be explored and admired by many thousands of visitors every year. What most interested me was the sight of two small boys playing in the churchyard. The village church, as at Silchester, is inside the old Roman walls, in a corner, the village itself being some distance away. After strolling round the churchyard I sat down on a stone under the walls and began watching the two boys—little fellows of the cottage class from the village who had come, each with a pair of scissors, to trim the turf on two adjoining mounds. The bigger of the two, who was about ten years old, was very diligent and did his work neatly, trimming the grass evenly and giving the mound a nice smooth appearance. The other boy was not so much absorbed in his work; he kept looking up and making jeering remarks and faces at the other, and at intervals his busy companion put down his shears and went for him with tremendous spirit. Then a chase among and over the graves would begin; finally they would close, struggle, tumble over a mound and pommel one another with all their might. The struggle over, they would get up, shake off the dust and straws, and go back to their work. After a few minutes the youngest boy recovered from his punishment, and, getting tired of the monotony, would begin teasing again, and a fresh flight and battle would ensue.

By-and-by, after witnessing several of these fights, I went and sat down on a mound next to theirs and entered into conversation with them.

"Whose grave are you trimming?" I asked the elder boy.

It was his sister's, he said, and when I asked him how long she had been dead, he answered "Twenty years". She had died more than ten years before he was born. He said there had been eight of them born, and he was the youngest of the lot; his eldest brother was married and had children five or six years old. Only one of the eight had died—this sister, when she was a little girl. Her name was Mary, and one day every week his mother sent him to trim the mound. He did not remember when it began—he must have been very small. He had to trim the grass, and in summer to water it so as to keep it always smooth and fresh and green.

Before he had finished his story the other little fellow, who was not interested in it and was getting tired again, began in a low voice to mock at his companion, repeating his words after him. Then my little fellow, with a very serious, resolute air, put the scissors down, and in a moment they were both up and away, doubling this way and that, bounding over the mounds, like two young dogs at play, until, rolling over together, they fought again in the grass. There I left them and strolled away, thinking of the mother busy and cheerful in her cottage over there in the village, but always with that image of the little girl, dead these twenty years, in her heart.

CORRESPONDENCE.

UNDEVELOPED LAND.

To the Editor of the SATURDAY REVIEW.

16 August 1909.

SIR,—In your notes on the land tax you say that "undoubtedly owners very often will be required to pay the tax on land which they cannot sell or develop if they would". I had just read these words when I happened to be passing through a village—or perhaps it would call itself a town—the outskirts of which are decorated by two huge boards containing an announcement that is at once significant and amusing. The village is Thorpe-le-Soken, a charming old-world Essex village within half-a-dozen miles or so of places like Walton, Frinton and Clacton, and an excellent centre from which to make excursions. Land on the fringe of Thorpe has been valuable in times past for agricultural purposes, and might be again if agriculture were not regarded by a certain school of economists as negligible. Here is the announcement which arrested my attention:

"THORPE TOWN FREEHOLD BUILDING ESTATE.

"This land will be sold by auction in plots, in a marquee on the estate, during the seasons of 1902 and 1903, commencing in June next, by Messrs. Protheroe and Morris, on the following easy terms: ten per cent. deposit, balance by nine quarterly instalments, five per cent. discount for cash within a month of date of sale; no charge for roads; the land will be sold free of tithe and land tax; no law costs, free conveyances", etc.

New Thorpe Avenue was laid out long ago, but there are no houses in it, and a notice-board on the ground contains the words "Hotel Site".

Surely here we have a case in point. The land was sold six or seven years ago, and the opportunities for development along the lines intended by the men who put their money into it have been such that the very boards announcing the sale have remained standing all this time. The plots are simply derelict. One or two have been rented as allotments, one or two feed cattle. The capital put into the purchase, probably by speculative builders, has simply been sunk. No one wants the houses it was proposed to erect, and the only person who has done reasonably well is the original vendor. Presumably he found farming under existing conditions less profitable than the offers of the plot-purchasers, who thought they saw the possibility of enterprise which circumstances have defeated.

Here then is undeveloped land which the owners would be only too glad to develop—are they to be taxed? Are the plots on which horses, or a cow or two, now graze to be treated as agricultural land? This is the opposite side of the question of increment. Ought the Government not to compensate the men who have put good money into a bad bargain with a view to meeting social necessities, and to relieve them of the tax levied on others who have made profit from social necessities without expending a penny?

I am yours truly, S. G. E.

BENGALI LOYALTY.

To the Editor of the SATURDAY REVIEW.

Bengal, 10 July 1909.

SIR,—The recent anarchist outrage has been followed, as all the others have been followed, by an outburst of expressions of loyalty from public meetings and the Indian press. This matter of the loyalty of the educated classes in India, and particularly in Bengal, is one which, we are assured by members of Parliament and others at home, admits of no question. But is this really so? Lord Morley, of course, is bound to uphold this doctrine to the utmost of his power, for on any other supposition his scheme of reform would stand self-revealed as a most dangerous experiment. Sir Henry Cotton, apparently, would support any proposition, true or otherwise, provided it gave him an opportunity of vilifying his countrymen in India, while the other noisy questioners in the House of Commons know nothing about India. One could not, of course, expect Babu Surendranath Bannerjee to say anything but what he does say. If, however, we look carefully into the evidence as displayed in India itself, the question does not seem to be so entirely beyond the pale of discussion.

In the first place we are entitled to ask "What do you mean by loyalty?" If it means merely periodical outbursts of oratory, then doubtless the Bengalis are the loyalest of the loyal. But if it means anything more we must ask for proofs; and surely if it means anything it means support of the Government, tempered, no doubt, by reasonable criticism on points that admit of debate, but whole-hearted support in every genuine endeavour to put down crime or improve the condition of the people. Let us look at the facts. It is reasonable to suppose that unless the views expressed in the native press, both vernacular and English, found sympathetic audiences these papers would not be subscribed to, and the educated classes cannot blame us if we draw the inference that these views correspond with their own. But the most cursory examination of these publications will show that, with one or two exceptions, so far from extending any support to Government in any of its actions whatsoever, they systematically and bitterly oppose it. Nothing that it can do is right in their eyes. They denounce anarchism on one page, and on the next denounce Government for taking steps to frustrate the anarchists; they call out against the scandal of prolonged trials, and when Government devises more summary measures they cry out about Russian methods; they admit there is a conspiracy of anarchists, and when the police manage to lay hands on some of them they at once assume that the persons arrested are innocent and proceed to vilify the police. Throughout, their one motive idea is blind, unreasoning opposition to everything that Government does. This in itself would be bad enough, but the real mischief lies in their imputing the most malicious and sinister motives to Government, and crediting them with the one desire of suppressing all liberty and all signs of nascent nationality.

It is said that at least in the reception given to the Reform Scheme there was a unanimity of praise. It would not, indeed, be wonderful if persons who had received more than they ever expected or had any right to expect should find grace enough to bestow a word of thanks on the giver; but the fact is the unanimity was very short-lived. No sooner had Lord Morley indicated that he regarded not unfavourably the claims of the Mohammedans to separate representation than the Hindu papers began their campaign of calumny again. Babu Surendranath Bannerjee has been waxing eloquent at the Press Conference and elsewhere on the loyalty of the Bengalis. A certain editorial in "The Bengali", the paper of which he is editor, affords a curious comment on this. Formerly the paper had been the most strenuous supporter of the assertion that the interests of Hindus and Mohammedans were absolutely identical, but as soon as there was a talk of separate electorates "The Bengali" roundly asserted that the Mohammedan representatives would invariably vote with the Government and against the Hindus. (The underlying assumption that no Hindu will ever vote with the Government is worthy of note.) But the writer went on to assert that the whole device of separate representation was an elaborate plot on the part of the Government to nullify the concession of an unofficial majority in the Legislative Councils by securing the return of Mohammedans who would vote as directed by Government—note the gratuitous supposition that Government would order the representatives how to vote—and thus defeat the patriotic Hindu in his efforts to benefit his country. If this is loyalty as understood by Babu Surendranath Bannerjee, our definitions need revising.

In another respect also this loyalty is more than doubtful. Can it be supposed for a moment that the would-be assassin of the magistrate of Dacca could have eluded discovery for now nearly two years, had he not been screened by active sympathisers assisted by the dead weight of indifference on the part of the whole community? Again, it has transpired that the murder of the sub-inspector of police, Nanda Lal Bannerjee, in the streets of Calcutta took place when many persons were present and when all the shops in the neighbourhood were open. Yet when the police came to make investigations they found the street deserted and every one of the shops closed, and the shopkeepers swore they were closed at the time of the murder. Probably dozens of people saw the murderers, yet no one has come forward to assist the police in their search. If this is loyalty, open opposition would be preferable; but it seems to me the Bengalis have yet to do something to vindicate their much-vaunted loyalty.

I am etc., LOYALIST.

A HEAVY TOLL.

To the Editor of the SATURDAY REVIEW.

Carlton Club, Pall Mall S.W.
18 August 1909.

SIR,—Allow me to explain, with reference to one of the SATURDAY REVIEW'S criticisms of "The Story of the Household Cavalry", that the phrase "a heavy toll" was not intended—as you appear to suggest—for an expression of hysterical regret. It was employed from a purely military point of view in connexion with the regiment's reduced strength in the field.

The total strength of the Household Cavalry Regiment in Egypt in August 1882 was under 470. Its casualties on 24, 25 and 28 August amounted to twenty-three.

While a ratio of 5 per cent. would be considered insignificant in the case of a pitched battle, a similar wastage incurred in desultory skirmishing would be considered a "heavy toll" by any practical soldier.

I am your obedient servant,
GEORGE ARTHUR.

FRANCIA'S MASTERPIECE.

To the Editor of the SATURDAY REVIEW.

Cheltenham, 15 August 1909.

SIR,—I see the SATURDAY REVIEW has reviewed Montgomery Carmichael's monogram of Francia's capolavoro in the Church of San Frediano at Lucca, exciting some difference of opinion in certain quarters. My own interest in the city of Lucca culminated in a lament on the recent violation of its walls, expressed in a letter to the "Bath Chronicle" of 5th inst., and referred to in the "Athenæum" of 7th inst. My friend Signor P. Campetti, Director of the Pinacotheca of Lucca, sends me his criticism of this lately published book by Mr. Carmichael, and as his comments may be new to your readers I translate them below. He says:

"Francia worked in the old Basilica two altarpieces, one for the Chapel of the Buonvisi and the other for that of the Stiatta. The valuable picture of the Buonvisi, forming part of the Duke Carlo Ludovico's collection, was sold, and since 1841 has adorned the National Gallery. The masterpiece was removed from the Stiatta Chapel to that of the Guinigi" (I wrote in the Westminster Gazette of 12 July concerning Ilaria del Carretto, wife of Paolo Guinigi, whose tomb Ruskin so much admired in Lucca Cathedral), "where it may now be seen. Francia combined the qualities of Fra Angelico and Raffaello, the fervour and simplicity of the primitives with the knowledge of advanced technique, and in this picture it seems that in order to render all the purity of the Mystery represented he may have adopted the contours and colours of lilies and roses. At the top of the picture is the figure of the Almighty surrounded by angels, in the attitude of touching with His sceptre the humbly kneeling Virgin; below are represented S. Anselm, S. Augustine, David, Solomon, and a Franciscan saint who is thought to be Duns Scotus. On the lower step four lesser histories in chiaroscuro are depicted. Only a thorough connoisseur of our Renaissance like Mr. Carmichael could retrace in a painting so much matter for study and comparison. He is the first, except Michele Ridolfi, to cast aside the idea that this picture represents 'A Coronation of the Virgin', and, relying on the literal and symbolical meaning of the words written on the labels held by the Saints, demonstrates that the subject is 'The Conception'. Apropos of 'The Conception' in art, he writes many original pages of interest, coupled with acute inductions such as his recognition of the venerable Duns Scotus, a discovery both new and important. Examining the documentary evidence, he fixes with great probability the date of the picture, and, assisted by good fortune and his powers of research, has found in a chamber alongside the sacristy the lunette which was meant to complete the painting. Finally, by industry he exhausts everything that concerns the picture, its author, its vicissitudes and its previous historians. The book is enriched by clear copies of photographs executed by the writer. We hope that the illustrious author will continue to exercise his skill among our Lucchesi monuments and still further bind fast the intellectual bond which unites the country of Ruskin with that of Matteo Civitali."

I trust this end may be attained; but no countryman of Ruskin will ever consent patiently to suffer the Walls of the city of Lucca to be destroyed and desecrated without remonstrance by an act of vandalism such as is now threatening to break the continuity of the circlet which girds the city like a ring of emerald.

WILLIAM MERCER.

MUSIC AT MEALS.

To the Editor of the SATURDAY REVIEW.

74 Grosvenor Road, Highbury, London N.
9 August 1909.

SIR,—It would be easy to write a psychological essay on the subject of music at meals, but it would require a Frenchman to write it with the combined seriousness and lightness of touch which would make it at once interesting, lively and true.

To a vieux routier with enough accumulated experience upon which to found a generalisation, the opinion of "Diner Out", in your last issue, as to the reason of the popularity of music at meals sounds absolutely right. The fanciful picture of a number of highly respectable and, presumably, more or less educated English citizens of both sexes being goaded into loud conversation by the strains of an orchestra acting as an irritant is very amusing, and one is almost tempted to suspect Mr. Robertson of laughing in his sleeve as he sketched it.

Be that as it may, however, the fact remains that music at meals, for persons who have anything to say to each other, is out of place and a nuisance, and its popularity conclusively proves that among the pleasures of English dinner tables, at restaurants at any rate, conversation is not included. There are still one or two havens of refuge in London for those who believe that "Rien ne doit déranger l'honnête homme qui dîne", but should they too, following a bad and therefore highly popular example, go in for eating-concerts, then the fate of Berchoux' "honnête homme" would be forlorn indeed.

An allied subject is that of table d'hôte dinners. Why have they been universally instituted wherever English people do congregate? By parity of reasoning, Mr. Robertson might jocularly suggest that they are a kind of derivation from "à la carte" dining, which, in some mysterious way, acts as a derivative.

In this, as in the case of eating-house music, the simplest and most obvious would appear to be the correct explanation. Table d'hôte dinners are a great comfort and relief to those who do not know how to order a dinner. A man at sea among the (to him) terrible mysteries of a varied menu is in as little enviable a position as one who throws a square dance into confusion through his ignorance of its figures and their evolutions. Who would not take pity on such a man?

I am, Sir, your obedient servant,
D. N. SAMSON.

ANOTHER VILLAGE COMPETITION.

To the Editor of the SATURDAY REVIEW.

Brenchley, Kent, 9 August 1909.

SIR,—The committee of our village flower show, as doubtless others do, give prizes to the school-children—in needlework for the girls, in writing, drawing and "composition" for the boys. This year, a promised judge having failed them, they roped in me, multum reluctantem, to adjudicate the last. I have thus become possessed of answers given to the question "What I mean to be when I leave school, and why", by presumably the pick of our village boys. "Presumably" because entrance was voluntary, the work was done at home, and your truly bad boy is not a gentleman who enters for prizes.

Be it admitted that some of the competitors seem to feel, with Fielding and myself, that they are "fittest for a sinecure". A would-be policeman gives as the reason of his choice "because I could stroll about in the open air", another because "they have a holiday every year and get off on odd days for sports" (query: keeping order at football matches?). An engine-driver looks forward to the day when, on "a rather fast train but not so fast as an express but a little slower", "in the winter I can warm myself against the fire, and in summer I can take off my jacket and waistcoat and stand in the shade of the thing over my head". Tityrus sub tegmine. But these are exceptions.

The dozen boys who were "in the running" include one gardener, one butcher, one higgler (which, hereabouts, means the man who collects and fattens fowls for market), one engine-driver, one fireman, two postmen and four policemen. The twelfth means to be successively house-boy to a gentleman (because "you do not have to be out in a heavy rain"); clerk "for somebody because it is brainwork"; cotton manufacturer ("because I have took a fancy for machinery all my life"); "if I am spared another ten years" cattle-drover in Australia; after "a little while" going northwards to the sugar plantations. An ambitious programme "'I wish it may answer', said my Uncle Toby".

He is, however, the only one whose wishes are beyond what he may, quite possibly, compass. As a great believer in "Souhaits médiocres en matière de cognée", I look on this moderation as a hopeful sign. The boys seem to know what they want. The butcher for instance thinks he will make a good slaughterman, "as I have already (at thirteen) killed six sheep". A friend of mine thinks this boy "should be well on the way to the gallows", but I do not see it so. As long as sheep are killed and practice makes perfect, the more he kills the better. Vegetarianism may be a better diet, but, to parody Johnson, "Alas! sir, he that cannot get to Heaven on mutton-chops will hardly get there on cabbage".

As far as I can see, the chief dread of these boys is lest they be out of work. Hence the preference for post-office and police. As a postman sums it up, "When you are under Government, and honest, upright and steady, you are nearly always sure of work and sure of your money". The pension, too, counts. Next, they dread the weather. Nearly all mention it. It is natural that these two bugbears should loom large, for the two chief enemies of Rusticus are an empty cupboard and the rheumatics.

No boy wants farm work. Nor to have anything to do with horses—e.g. as waggoner or coachman—nor with cows. The last is a hard job, but I a little wonder that the second has no friend. It is not, as the daily press vainly talks, that these boys burn for town employ. They don't: the postman or policeman they envy is the country not the town man.

No boy intends to be a soldier, nor—except the fireman, who regards the sea as a preparatory school for the brigade—a sailor. This is from no lack of loyalty: one chooses the police "because I should like to do good and help guard our King". But soldiering is evidently unattractive. I am yours truly,

CECIL S. KENT.

REVIEWS.

"DRESSED ALL IN WHITE."

"The White Prophet." By Hall Caine. London: Heinemann. 1909. 2 vols. 2s. each.

IT is long since the earlier Mr. Caine gave up all pretence of a connexion with literature; and Mr. Hall Caine has since devoted himself exclusively to the production of novels which are popular in the worst meaning of the word. Therefore we fearlessly class this new achievement as fiction, though the statement that it "deals with various matters of importance from the National Political point of view" might mis-lead one to think it an essay on imperial affairs. Fiction it certainly is in the sense that not a word of it is truth. Though it may deal "with various matters of importance", that is not to say that Mr. Caine's treatment of them is of any importance whatever. It is not; it is not even interesting. Bold as the design of the novel is, we have rarely read anything more utterly wearisome. That anyone in cold or hot blood can sit down to read it for pleasure seems absolutely incredible; yet it is a book written by a gentleman for the uneducated, and, presumably, it will find its way into appreciative quarters.

As a purveyor of fiction for the uneducated and unthinking Mr. Caine has only one serious rival—Miss Corelli; and we trust that lady's finer feelings will not be outraged by a frank expression of our opinion that Mr. Caine is head of the trade. He neither spells society with a capital S nor sets the word in ironical quotation-marks; but he has honestly won his proud position largely by an unprecedented daring in "dealing" not only "with various matters of importance", but with quite recent events and living personages. Over the latter he throws the thinnest of veils. No disguise would be necessary if the occupation or position of the people was not described, for Mr. Caine's characters are completely unlike any human beings that ever lived. He had visited a good many places and made books of the material he found, and "The White Prophet" appears to be the fruit of his last trip to Egypt. His stay must have been rather a prolonged one. Judging from the acquaintance he displays with the topography and language—and allowing for a liberal use of guide-books—he cannot have stopped less than a quarter of an hour in Alexandria and twenty minutes in Cairo. A residence of thirty-five minutes in so strange a land as Egypt was, however, enough for Mr. Caine. That, and a brief study of old newspapers and certain hazy recollections of incidents that have occurred since the English occupation of the country, set the fiery imagination of Mr. Caine to work, and the result is a novel of Egyptian life and English life in Egypt which in many respects may be called unmatched.

A king of Spain once expressed the opinion that if he had made the world it would have been a much better one. Mr. Caine is of opinion that if he had had the management of Egyptian affairs he would have managed them much better. But Mr. Caine is bolder and has more resource than his royal forerunner, for in "The White Prophet" he endeavours to re-create the course of the events of the last quarter of a century as they ought to have happened. Many deluded good folk will doubtless believe they are reading genuine history, and the chronology is so artfully confused that the author may claim either that his tale is a forecast or that it is a retrospect—just as he thinks fit. According to Mr. Caine's story, Lord Nuneham had been Consul-General since the occupation; he had rescued the country from bankruptcy and made it a paying concern. But he grew ambitious, became a tyrant, lost his head, and by performing feats of imbecility brought about the disasters which form the subject-matter of the narrative. The Sirdar is Sir Reginald Mannering, called "Reg" (however that may be pronounced) for short. Lord Nuneham has a son named Colonel Gordon Lord, and he is persistently spoken of as "Gordon". For that reason, and because of many things he is made to say and do, we cannot but suppose him to be meant, partly at any rate, as a sketch of the real Gordon. General Graves is in

TURGENEFF'S GERMAN LETTERS.

TO LUDWIG PIETSCH.

1881—1883.

87.

50 Rue de Douai, Paris,
19 November '81.

My dear Pietsch,—I want you to do this for me: As you know, at the request of the editor of the "National Zeitung" I have sent him a proof of the French translation of my Italian story, and the German version was to appear on 15 November. He has never sent me any word whether he has received the thing. Probably he finds that he cannot use the story. It doesn't matter in the least to me whether it is translated or not, but now here comes another individual and asks for permission. I have told him that I have already given permission to someone else (as a matter of fact a translator needs no such permission, and anyone can turn the thing out of German into French without any qualms), but since nothing has appeared, he may do what he likes, and Heaven bless him. Will you be so kind as to tell the whole story to the editor of the "National Zeitung", that is, if you think "que le jeu vaut la chandelle".

I have been in Paris for the last few days. The Viardots are all tolerably well, and so am I. Heartiest good wishes from

Yours, I. TURGENJEW.

88.

Paris, 15 February '82.

Carissimo Pietsch,—Something entertaining has happened to me, which I must tell you about. A short time ago I received the January number of the "Magazine of Foreign Literature", containing an essay by G. H. Byr on my humble self (I enclose it herewith). The whole of this bright and thoroughgoing critic's argument (he thinks that he has expounded the whole nature of my literary activity, *which I do not understand myself*) is based on something which I never wrote at all; I mean the reflective appendix to my story "First Love", which was added by my French translator (Viardot, between ourselves) on moral grounds. There is not a trace of it in the original Russian edition. I did not make any protest against this. Perhaps I ought to have; but you know how little I bother about my things when once they have been published. Unfortunately, on this occasion the thing was transported, contrary to my express wishes, into the German version. You know very well how little anything of that kind appeals to me. This reflective method of digging up again and re-digesting what has gone before is as utterly useless as the cackle of a hen after she has laid her egg, and merely serves to confuse people's minds. What a prize example of *wry and high and dry* criticism! We don't find anything like that every day. Do you think it worth while to tell the magazine about it all, if only in order to beg my German readers to ignore the caudal appendage and its moralising?

We are all pretty well, and daily expecting Marianne's confinement. At the end of April I shall leave Paris for Berlin, where I shall certainly see you. Meanwhile remember me to your family and our friends. With hearty greetings,

Yours, I. TURGENJEW.

89.

50 Rue de Douai,
Saturday, 6 May '82.

My dear Pietsch,—It is true that I am ill, not in London, but merely in Paris, which I have never left. My ailment is an incurable one (angina pectoralis and gout combined). I am in the best hands here, but I know very well that my hopes must be limited to not being obliged to remain for ever on my back; in the best event, it may be possible for me to sit up. Of walking or standing (still less of mounting a staircase) there can never be any question. They have already burnt the whole of one of my shoulders with points de feu. To-morrow the roasting will begin again, but they only do it as a matter of principle. There is little hope that I shall ever recover. It is all up with my body; my mind may go crawling along a little longer. Of course there is no question of my taking another journey. I shall be delighted to see you and your daughter here. I wrote you a long letter six weeks ago, with a cutting from a paper. Probably you never received it, as you are usually such a punctual correspondent. With kind regards to your family and our friends, I remain,

Yours most sincerely,
I. TURGENJEW.

90.

50 Rue de Douai,
Monday, 22 May '82.

Pitschio Carissimo,—Mme. Viardot has just told me that Herr v. Voigtländer brought no dress clothes with him. In Paris it is impossible for one to go even to some of the theatres (such as the Grand Opera or the Théâtre Français), not to speak of a soirée, without dress clothes, particularly if one is a German. Don't deceive yourself: they still feel the greatest dislike for Germans here. But one can hire the finest dress coat (and trousers) here very easily and cheaply. Paul will tell you *where*. I thought I had better warn you beforehand. Au revoir before long.

Yours, I. TURGENJEW.

91.

Bougival, 30 July '82.

My dear Pietsch,—Here is my answer to your kind and affectionate letter. My ailment has now declared itself to be chronic, and how long it will sit enthroned in me no doctor can tell me. Unfortunately while it sits I must sit too. I can only walk or stand for a very short time, about five minutes, and that only with the aid of a little machine which presses on my left scapula (what is shoulder-blade in German?). Otherwise the pain is very disagreeable. I have also a constant shooting pain like toothache in my *right* shoulder-blade, which is usually very severe at night and forces me to have recourse to opium. But my appetite is good, and I have no trace of fever. I can only endure the movement of a carriage, or even of writing, for a short time. Result: Work and travelling are not to be thought of, and this may be my lot for years. Whether life seems very desirable under such conditions, I leave it to your sagacity to determine.

To-morrow Marianne with her husband and child are leaving us, and in a few days' time Claudie with her family. They will all come back in about six weeks' time. Till then the parents will be alone at Bougival. The weather is still horrible. Kind regards to your family and my other friends. With cordial feelings,

Yours, I. TURGENJEW.

92.

Bougival,
Sunday, 17 September '82.

Dear Pietsch,—I received your letters from Stockholm, and at once communicated the contents to the Viardots. The family is beginning to assemble again. Yesterday Marianne and her husband returned, and Claudie with her family will be here soon. All of them are very well, and I myself am a little better. I drink twelve glasses of milk a day, and that unfortunately gives me an even higher moral tone than I possess by nature. Of course I cannot dream of any active movement. I am still just a motionless something—"le patriarche des mollusques". I shall go to Paris at the end of October, and Heaven alone knows what will happen to me after that. After doing nothing for a long time, I have written a short story, which is pretty crazy. I have not yet translated it for Mme. Viardot, and so I do not know how the thing has turned out. I hope you and all your family are well. Haven't you yet become a grandfather?

Kindest regards to all our friends, and hearty greetings to yourself,

Yours, IW. TURGENJEW.

93.

Bougival,
Sunday, 8 October '82.

My dear Friend,—My new story is to appear at S. Petersburg in the "European Courier" on 13 January 1883, and about the same time a French translation will appear in Paris in the "Nouvelle Revue"—a week earlier. So you will receive the French proof sheets on 5 January, and you can also set to work on the German translation at once. The whole thing is about 50 (printed) pages in length. It rests chiefly with you to say what you will do with it. I do not require any fee at all. The whole of the Viardot family is now assembled here, and they are all well and happy. I am also well, except that I can neither walk nor stand nor take a drive, and have consequently been converted into a sort of stationary oyster. But as I feel no pain (so long as I remain motionless) and sleep pretty quietly of a night, I am content. "Cheerful inconsolability" is more my motto than ever. What more can an old fellow like me want?

I shall stay here till the end of November and take no thought for anything after that.

Kindest regards to your family and our friends, and hearty greetings to yourself.

Yours, I. TURGENJEW.

94.

Bougival,
Thursday, 19 October '82.

My dear Friend,—This is the answer to your question: My story called "After Death"* (the title must be kept a secret till its publicaion in Russia) would cover 48 pages of the "Revue des Deux Mondes" (45 lines to a page, 50 letters to a line). Make your arrangements accordingly. I hope you will receive the French proofs on 20 December. The German translation must not appear before 15 January. These are all conditiones sine qua non which my Russian publisher has imposed on me and on the strict observance of them the payment of my fee depends. So cave canem! I congratulate you on your "exceedingly lucky" summer, and hope the good luck will continue. All the family are well and send their kindest regards. With heartfelt good wishes, Yours very sincerely,

I. TURGENJEW.

95.

50 Rue de Douai, Paris,
8 December '82.

My dear Pietsch,—Here are the very carefully corrected proofs of my story. It will appear in S. Petersburg and Paris on 15 January. So you have plenty of time for the translation. The two conditions sine qua non are (1) the German translation is not to appear before 15 January, (2) you must not make known the title, the contents, etc., of your translation; otherwise it is entirely at your disposal. The "Berliner Tageblatt" has asked me about it, and I have referred the inquirer to you. Here everything is going on well. Duvernoy's † oratorio "Sardanapalus" was very successful. I can still neither walk nor stand, but otherwise I am well. Kindest regards to your family and our friends. Hearty greetings to yourself.

Yours, I. TURGENJEW.

P.S.—Send me a word to say that you have received the proofs.

96.

Rue de Douai, Paris,
28 December '82

Mr dear Pietsch,—You are right—that was a thorough oversight about the stereoscope.‡ Unfortunately it cannot now be corrected in the original, but you can easily set it right in the translation. Aratoff, instead of preparing the thing himself, can buy it at a photographic shop (Clara, being an actress, has had herself taken in Moscow in the same position as in the photograph), or her sister may give Aratoff a stereoscopic picture instead of a photograph. I give you carte blanche, as they say, in the matter.

As to the pages from the diary, it is a long story. For the last seven years, in which I have written nothing very large or very long, I have thrown off on loose leaves a series of little poems in prose (since, unfortunately, I am no poet). I never thought of publishing them, but my Russian publisher has come across some statement about them and has persuaded me to let him have some fifty of these "Senilia" (that was what they were called) for his "Review", of course with the careful omission of everything that is autobiographical and personal. Some thirty of them were translated into French with Mme. Viardot's help, and appeared here in the "Revue Poétique et Littéraire". I see, too, that the "Petersburger Zeitung" is publishing a translation of them. I have never set any special store by them, and have spoken very little about them. These little sketches only suit the few; to the general public, especially in Russia, they are caviar. If you like, I can send you the French translation, which at any rate is very accurate. But in fact these things are nothing but the last pious ejaculations (to speak politely) of an old man. It is still the old story with me—a little worse during the last few days. I feel grieved that you too, with your radiant youthfulness, must bite the sour apple of old age. But I rejoice with my whole heart at your domestic happiness. All of my dear ones here are very well, and that is the principal thing.

Kindest regards and good wishes for the new year, and Adieu.

Yours, Iw. TURGENJEW.

* Also called "Clara Militch".—L. P.
† Marianne Viardot's husband.
‡ Turgeneff had made the mistake of narrating how the hero of his story, after Clara Militch's death, had a stereoscopic portrait of his beloved made from existing photographs. I pointed out to him the technical impossibility of such a reproduction.—L. P.

97.

Paris,* 23-2-'83.

Dear Pietsch,—My old ailment is worse than ever; I cannot even write myself. The operation, although painful, has nothing to do with it. It was not an abscess from the bowels, but a tumour from the abdomen, that they removed, and I am now adorned with a beautiful six-inch scar. But my old trouble, the convulsive spasms in my chest, is in full bloom, and the pain is continuous. I can neither walk, nor stand, nor drive, nor sleep, nor write. A lovely prospect! I am heartily sorry that you are also troubled with an infirmity (Frl. Arnholt declares that this word "Gebresten" does not exist in German). In old age one feels the thorns of the roses which one has plucked, or failed to pluck, in youth. I cry Patience! to you, as I cry it to myself—a bitter herb, that cures as little as other medicines. As for my poems in prose, a translation has been published at Dunker's, in Leipzig, under the title "Senilia". The translation is pretty correct and natural, but not without the inevitable blunders. On the very first page the horses "neigh" instead of snorting, etc.; but that sort of thing is unavoidable. You ought to have sent me a copy of your translation of "After Death", but never mind. I am sorry that Dohm is dead. That Wagner has cleared out at the first attack of an incurable ailment is only another proof to me of his unfailing good fortune. I know people who envy him. All the family here are well, thank God, and that is the principal thing.

Kind regards to your family and our friends. I hope you will be well soon. Hearty greetings.

Yours, Iw. TURGENJEW.

P.S.—Mr. Turgeneff compelled me to put in the parenthesis about "Gebreste," because I told him I didn't know the word.† Kind regards. L. ARNHOLT.

98.

Les Frênes,‡
8 September '83.

Ah, my friend, it is too much, too much sorrow for one heart to bear at the same time, and I do not understand how it is that mine is not yet broken. Our beloved friend completely lost consciousness about two days before the end. He did not suffer—his life ceased gradually, and with two short gasps all was over. He died like my dear Louis §, while still unconscious. He became beautiful again with the majestic calm of death. The first day the traces of pain had set a frown upon his face, which with its immobility gave it a strong and stern expression. On the second day his face became once again kind and gentle—at times one would have said that he was smiling. What a grief is ours! He was raised in bed and photographed. I will send you a proof of the portrait if it is successful. The religious ceremony took place yesterday in the Russian church. Many came from curiosity, but there were few of our friends there, as everyone is away from Paris now. The body will be taken to Russia in a few days. He expressed the desire to be buried in Russia beside his friend Bielinski.

The doctors thought that his life might have been prolonged for some time. It was the almost sudden cessation of the heart's action which brought the end in the space of a few minutes.

Grieve for me, my dear friend, and keep me all your friendship. I need all the support my friends' affection can give me now.

PAULINE VIARDOT.

It was I who sent you the telegram.

* Letter dictated to Frl. Arnholt.—L. P.
† The word is Gebresten, not Gebreste.—TRANSLATOR.
‡ This letter was written in French.—TRANSLATOR.
§ M. Viardot had died a few months earlier.

command of the army, Gordon Lord is second, and the next is Colonel Macdonald. The White Prophet is " a carpenter's son ", one Ishmael Ameer, who preaches a new compound of Christianity and Mohammedanism. He always attires himself in " spotless white ", and although he is destitute of private means, his laundry bill must amount to a pretty penny.

Far be it from us to attempt a summary of a yarn which Mr. Caine does not make very plausible in nearly eight hundred pages. Suffice it that " Gordon " is sent to capture the White Prophet, and gets converted to the prophet's views instead of doing so. Next he refuses to obey the general's orders, and forthwith has his sword broken and his medals torn from his breast and his fine uniform spoiled. Then he joins the prophet and complications innumerable follow, until one is thoroughly bewildered. In the long run, however, matters are somehow smoothed out, and the book comes to an end—not before time. " Gordon " Lord takes his father's place; the White Prophet disappears; and thereafter all goes well with Egypt. There are female characters in the book. Lady Nuneham is a feeble lady who lives till half-way through the second volume, when she dies pathetically in two chapters while a hymn is sung by the assembled company. Helena Graves, daughter of the general, is affianced to " Gordon ", and at first never makes her appearance without a motor car, which one might almost suppose her to take to bed with her as a child takes a doll. Later, wrongly fancying the White One to have killed her father, she gets herself up in Eastern garb and becomes his (the White One's) legal wife in order to betray him to Lord Nuneham. Much easier means of avenging her father's murder lie to her hand, but it is not in the nature of Mr. Caine's heroines (or heroes either) to choose the short way to attain an end if there is a long way. Their doings are perfectly unaccountable. If we might extravagantly suppose General Gordon, Mr. Stead, Mrs. Besant, Mr. Asquith, Lord Kitchener and Lord Morley to have been got together in Cairo, and half stupefied with hashisch, and given a few raps over the head with the butt-end of a rifle, we believe they might have behaved much as all the people behave in " The White Prophet ".

The pictures of social and official life in Government and military circles in Alexandria and Cairo may surprise those who have lived in either town; but not many of Mr. Caine's admirers know much of Egypt, and they will readily take his word for it that English commanding officers talk American slang and shriek or faint at the slightest hint of danger. Mr. Caine's admirers will also like the local colour and atmosphere got by the incessant employment of three or four Arabic phrases, and they will credit him with remarkable linguistic attainments. For ourselves, we humbly confess that none of all these things impresses us. " The White Prophet " is vulgar and pretentious; it never gets within a hundred leagues of literature; even in its badness it is undistinguished—it is bad as many hundreds of less advertised books are bad. Few writers, however, have the temerity—not to say the unparalleled effrontery—to rewrite the records of things achieved, for good or evil, by men who are still living or just recently dead. Good taste, manners, decency alike deter weaker spirits. Mr. Caine has no scruples, and as there are many ignorant people in this country, as in others, we suppose he will find plenty of readers who do not perceive that such stories as " The White Prophet " are not literature at all, are entirely untrue to life, and dull and tiresome.

A PHILOSOPHER-CRITIC OF POETRY.

"Oxford Lectures on Poetry." By A. C. Bradley. London: Macmillan. 1909. 10s. net.

THE writer of these admirable lectures may claim what is rare even in this age of criticism—a note of his own. In type he belongs to those critics of the best order, whose view of literature is part and parcel of their view of life. His lectures on poetry are therefore what they profess to be: not scraps of textual comment, nor studies in the craft of verse-making, but broad considerations of poetry as a mode of spiritual revelation. An accomplished style and signs of careful reading we may justly demand from any professor who sets out to lecture in literature. Mr. Bradley has them in full measure. But he has also not a little of that priceless quality so seldom found in the professional or professorial critic—the capacity of naïve vision and admiration. Here he is in a line with the really stimulating essayists, the artists in criticism. He has not, it is true, the Socratic felicity and sureness of a Matthew Arnold. His modesty of statement is serious, not ironic; he can hardly be said to buttonhole the plain reader with the objective, dogmatic effect which Arnold, beneath his air of sprightly open-mindedness, almost always achieved. Nor can we claim for Mr. Bradley the supreme gift of temperament which makes Pater's work unique—a gift which depends for its full fruition, let us add, on a spare and perfect choice of subject not always possible for the official lecturer. In these comparisons there is nothing odious. Their very suggestion is enough to show how excellent Mr. Bradley's work appears. And while he thus compels us to place him in the line of truly fine and impressive critics, he has, as we have hinted, a strain quite peculiar. The philosophic touch is very visible in all these papers. Nobody could doubt that at one time, if not now, abstract philosophy had charms for Mr. Bradley. Echoes of transcendental speculation, even some of its terms, recur often in his work. Not that his scope is narrowed thereby, or his judgment of poetry as a human product. His humanism has survived the abstruse discipline of the schools, and what we now perceive is nothing pedantic, but a certain austerity and insistence upon clear thinking which gives force to his conclusions about art and a pleasing pallor to his style. Allied, of course, to this philosophic note is the turn for scientific psychology which runs through many of these pages. Mr. Bradley is a keen analyst of " the poetic experience ", as he calls it; and the niceness of his discrimination, when he seeks to determine the precise effect upon the mind of this or that poetic utterance, imparts to much of his criticism a bloom of novelty which every reader must feel, though it is not easy to describe or illustrate. We feel this the more because he is withal so invariably sane, so free from mere idiosyncrasy. His analysis is always concerned, so to speak, with the normal experience, and never with fantasies of his own. The essay on " The Sublime " is a good example. It strikes us by its freshness, its intuition; yet at each step of the argument we confirm the writer from our own experience, and feel that he is drawing, with a sure hand, on the common consciousness of educated people.

The introductory lecture on " Poetry for Poetry's Sake " is an attempt, incisive and in many ways successful, to clear up the tangle of popular fallacy which obscures (even in the minds of most so-called critics) the relation of poetry to life, and of form to matter in poetry itself. Particularly good is the distinction so clearly made between the true " matter " of the poet and the mere " subject " of the poem, with which it is usually confused. Our age, Mr. Bradley thinks, " is already inclined to shrink from those higher realms where poetry touches religion and philosophy ", and in this paper—indeed by the consistent tone of all his lectures—he vindicates the value of poetry as something which is food and light for the spirit, while it can only express its meaning through itself. The lecture on " Hegel's Theory of Tragedy " is a discussion thoroughly congenial to the writer's mind. It suffers, however, from the compression incidental to its purpose, and presupposes much from the reader in the way of Hegelian understanding. Wider in appeal and interest is the Wordsworth lecture, which emphasises (as against the view of Wordsworth which critical authority has imposed) that strange and even mad side of his genius so indispensable in the total effect of his work. We think Mr. Bradley is a trifle misleading in his treatment of Pater's stray remark about Wordsworth and Surrey. No writer has felt more clearly than Pater the primæval grandeur, the weirdness of much in Wordsworth's vision of life. It is because Pater is so much preoccupied with the mystical substance of all Wordsworth's thought that he proposed for Wordsworth—a little rashly, perhaps—the Surrey test. We fancy, too, that Mr. Bradley is over bold in claiming so high a place for the Poems of National Independence. His quotations, however, throughout the lecture, are admirably made, and he really succeeds in exposing the weakness of Arnold's suggestion that Wordsworth "put by" the "cloud of human destiny". The popular conception of Wordsworth (based on a few hackneyed fragments of his work) as an amiable and rather complacent old pantheist has never, we suspect, deceived the true, as distinct from the "Social-Science-Congress", Wordsworthian. But there is room for Mr. Bradley's reassertion of the truth, none the less. We should like to hear Mr. Bradley on the relation of Wordsworth, spiritually, to Coleridge. This has not yet been adequately done. The poet of "Yew Trees", a poem to which Mr. Bradley very aptly calls attention, is nearer to the poet of the "Ancient Mariner" and "Kubla Khan" than most critics have suspected. We shall hope to find in Mr. Bradley's next volume one essay, at least, devoted to "Wordsworth as a Decadent"!

If space permitted we should like to argue several of Mr. Bradley's points. In his interesting though rather diffusive lecture on the Long Poem in Wordsworth's Age he shows scant consideration for the "comfortable" theory that the long poem is really a string of short ones. He thinks he states this theory fairly, but we are not sure we agree. Certainly a good deal of cant is talked about the "architectonic" unity of the world's long poems. Nobody thinks of the "Æneid" as incomplete, though we know it was only half of the projected scheme. In sober fact, the long narrative poem has never shown architecture, as the drama and the lyric have shown it. To admire the adjustment of parts to whole in a poem like the "Paradise Lost" is usually an effort of faith, not of sight. Long poems, in their historic origin, spring from the epic; and the epic sprang from the oral recital, in primitive ages, of fluent narrative more or less terminable at request. We envy and admire, as keenly as Mr. Bradley or any other lover of poetry, the sap and creative vitality of those ages which made it natural for men to attempt the big canvas, crowded by incident and action with which they really were familiar. We deny, however, that long poems, requiring as Mr. Bradley says "a substance which implicitly contains a whole interpretation of life", have ever been "unities" in any strict sense of the word. But the point is one that scarcely admits of brief discussion.

Perhaps the most enjoyable of the lectures is the wholly delightful one on "Antony and Cleopatra". Here Mr. Bradley, with all his restraint, becomes eloquent, and the result is a most moving and kindling piece of criticism. We cannot here deal in detail with the other Shakespearean lectures. All are good. In "Shakespeare the Man", particularly, we see once more that strong feature of Mr. Bradley's method to which we have already referred—his appeal to the normal, unsophisticated experience of the non-professional lover of poetry. Conducted on these lines, the higher literary education of the country is full of promise.

LUCAS MALET'S HALF SCORE.

"The Score." By Lucas Malet. London: Murray. 1909. 6s.

The two stories in Lucas Malet's new volume bear a certain resemblance to each other, though wrought in quite different styles. They are both confessions, one of a man on the point of death, the other of a woman on the point of matrimony. Nothing can save the man, who has a bullet in some important part of him; the woman saves herself by her good sense, and both obtain absolution from their confessors, though the woman's, being her lover, does not voice it so gracefully as the priest. There the resemblance ends.

"Miserere Nobis", as the first is called, is a brilliant piece of work, though just a little too determined to deserve that description. The whole scheme of its colour is determinedly vivid, attained sometimes with a sense of strain and by a too hard handling of contrasts, but producing at least the physical effect at which it aims, though it fails to make of its moral drama more than an almost incredible spectacle. The scene in which that spectacle is displayed to us is admirably used to frame the tragedy. It is a grim fourteenth-century building, half palace, half fortress, now used as a hospital. Above the whitewashed walls of the ward, the gods and goddesses of the Renaissance ceiling laugh and lust indifferently above the beds in which men groan and die, with white-robed nuns to wait on them, and pray as they hear behind the screens which surround the dying the confession of some terrifying sin. It is one of these confessions that we overhear, and an added contrast is supplied by the sinner's joyous voice, still in love with life, though he has taken his own life in sheer horror of it, telling to the grave Father beside him the flamboyant story of his crime, and hearing as he tells it, with vain regret, the sounds of life and love from which he is for ever exiled rise to the hospital fortress from the city below. The forced intensity of the style no doubt assists in the carrying through of the thing for English readers, for the story is such as could not be made acceptable if translated to these shores. We can observe with sympathy foreigners committing crimes, and even finding laudable excuse for them, of which in an English setting we could scarcely speak: and it needed an Italian of the ultra-sensitive type as hero to make alike conceivable his crime and his stupidity and the still gay detachment with which he can regard them both. The second story, "The Courage of Her Convictions", is far less successful, is, indeed, a very ordinary piece of work. Some part of its failure may be due to certain characters in it having already made an appearance in previous books of Lucas Malet. Such a use of material has the advantage of economy, when addressing readers already acquainted with it; but since it induces the author to trust to that acquaintance, and consequently only to present what may have affected the characters since they last appeared in print, it makes her work savour to the less instructed of an indifferent finish and fail of the effect which a completer knowledge might have insured. The little we are told in this short tale of Miss Poppy St. John and Mr. Antony Hammond leaves one quite indifferent to the outcome of their affairs, and makes the lady's long struggle with a proposal miss all the meaning it might conceivably have to old acquaintances.

SNAPSHOTS AT PAPAL HISTORY.

"The Last Days of Papal Rome." By R. de Cesare. London: Constable. 1909. 12s. 6d. net.

IN a work written by the historian of the last days of the Neapolitan kingdom certain qualities are guaranteed. Exactness, fulness of knowledge, a conscientious endeavour after impartiality, scholarly presentment—these are abundantly manifest in his new book. In fact the author possesses all the virtues of the modern historian. But, in a very marked degree, he also possesses their characteristic vice. If we have a quarrel it is not with Cesare in particular. He represents a class and stands for a tendency. Loosely speaking, history becomes every year more of a science. Must it necessarily become less of an art? Is it inevitable that, in the analytic fury of an inductive age, there should be a continuous production of historical matter that can only be regarded as so much raw material for an ultimate synthesis?

To come to the particular instance, why should the author of "The Last Days of Papal Rome" have produced a book interesting to the student of modern Italian history, of value to the specialist in international politics of last century; but abounding, quite unnecessarily, in difficult places for the amateur, who reads history because he has a general interest in human affairs? It is not a question of space. The author might have written a book of the same length, or a very little longer, containing the same quantity of new material, which should at the same time have been self-contained and able to stand upon its individual merits. It is a question of method. Instead of bringing a picture on to the canvas, grouping events and people about a central point of interest, and filling in a suitable background, the author has been content to take a series of instantaneous photographs. His men and women are every one a succession of attitudes. His portrayal of events is a succession of snapshots focussed from the Vatican. It follows that the reader must bring to the persual of this book a lively imagination and considerable knowledge, independently acquired, of the men and events of which the book itself will give him nothing beyond occasional glimpses and isolated views. With a subject eminently dramatic, abounding in interesting personalities and vivid paradox, the author might have given us a work as artistic in outline and effect as it is scientific in purpose and method. He has preferred to write a monograph, scientifically valuable but artistically of small consequence.

Specialisation, often more complete than intelligent, is almost entirely to blame for the catastrophe. The author has undertaken to write the history of the last twenty years of the existence of the Papacy as a temporal power. His history begins in 1850 with the entry of Pius IX. into Rome under French protection. It ends with the extinction of the temporal authority of the Papacy in 1870. From first to last one of the decisive factors in the situation was the occupation of the papal city by the French. For an understanding of the forces that between them led to the extinction of the temporal power it is, therefore, essential to stand for a while in Paris, and to be brought into lively contact with Napoleon III. But our author refuses to cross the Alps until he is actually compelled to do so. It follows that, when Napoleon acts, he appears to act suddenly and almost fortuitously. All at once we get a glimpse of him at Plombières. It is the famous meeting with Cavour in the summer of 1858, at which the fate of the Legations was determined. It is an instantaneous photograph, clear in itself down to the smallest detail; yet in a sense unintelligible, since it is not presented in synthetic relation to the events that preceded and gave rise to it. It is necessary to imagine that it just happened. Supposing that the reader has not read Ollivier, or something less pretentious, Napoleon remains incomprehensible from first to last. His actions seem like those of an arbitrary destiny asserting itself suddenly and capriciously at intervals from without.

Nor have we yet reached the limits of our author's specialism. He will go neither to Turin nor to Florence until he is compelled, and then at the shortest possible notice to the reader. For example, Cavour is photographed very finely in the act of achieving his coup de théâtre of September 1860. But the exact significance of his bold invasion of the Patrimony must be known independently, or taken upon the word of the author. For to the reader of this book Cavour is another of those unaccountable agencies that intervene for good or ill with disconcerting swiftness and caprice. Garibaldi is even more of an enigma. All at once he is sequestered by Ratazzi. In a short time he is at liberty and in action under the very nose of the Florentine Government. Soon he is marching upon Rome by way of Mentana. These snapshots are as effective as snapshots can be.

To some perhaps this may seem unfair criticism; it is certainly a little ungracious. In gratitude for what Cesare has done it is time to desist from pointing out what he never intended to do. He has, it is true, produced a work that can only be appreciated by collating it with other works written upon the same lines; but, at the same time, he has written a book that no student of Papal history can afford to neglect. One reflection cannot fail to strike the reader. The temporal power died as it had lived through the centuries. Its rule was as inefficient and unpopular in 1859 when Bologna revolted on the withdrawal of the Austrians as it had been when Innocent III. found that his papal rectors were as unpopular through the cities as were the German warriors they displaced. In Rome itself the two aristocracies, lay and clerical, faced each other in thinly veiled hostility, as in the ancient days of the house of Theophylact. The "commune", as ever, was negligible; except when, as occasion would have it with more or less regularity, it chanced to be galvanised into stormy self-assertion. Moreover, there was, as ever, the foreign occupation. There was even a crusade, a greater excommunication, and an œcumenical council. The people of Rome were those that had spent their days from time immemorial in alternately driving the pontiff from the city with sticks and stones and welcoming him back with rose leaves strewn in the way. Half of them, as from the times of the Gracchi, were of no occupation. They subsisted upon the Papacy, which had inherited the pauperising functions of the Empire. In things temporal the Papacy was blessed neither in what it gave nor in what it received. The phrase of Damiani, when he heard of the defeat of Leo IX. at Civitate in 1053, was truly prophetic. It contained within it the sum of all the praise and all the blame that an impartial posterity will affix to that period of papal history when the pontiff fought his enemies with the weapons of this world. "It was not for having denied His Master that Peter was the greatest of the apostles."

THE HABSBURG REALMS.

"Austria-Hungary." By Geoffrey Drage. London: Murray. 1909. 21s. net.

"THE data" for this comprehensive work of 841 pages "have been gathered", Mr. Drage says in his preface, "in many journeys, extending over more than twenty years, and were originally collated partly for use in my reports to the Royal Commission on Labour, partly as subsidiary to a book on Russian affairs, and partly as serviceable for debates in the House of Commons". It shows much research in many fields hitherto unexplored by those who have written on Austria and on Hungary. The statistical tables and other facts, collected as they have been at different times, are not always up-to-date; but the work is a valuable one, for it contains a great deal of information which has not up to this been given to English readers, at least in book form. It is also superior in some important respects to recent works, for it neither proceeds from a solitary visit to Austria-Hungary nor does it suffer from any particular party prejudice; indeed, Mr. Drage has done his best to keep the balance even between all parties throughout. He has perhaps avoided rather too ostentatiously, in his anxiety to preserve the judicial mind, some of those most controversial topics which are so essential to a proper understanding of the Dual Monarchy, and he devotes little attention to the details of those burning questions which divide the populations of such important provinces of Austria as Bohemia and Galicia. It is possible that he may regard minor party differences as proceeding from the wish of the younger to oust the older party leaders; still, there can be no doubt that Dr. Karel Kramar, the leader of the Young Czechs, is a greater personality than any of his rivals, and that there are vital differences which may have far-reaching consequences between Old, Young, Radical, Realist, Agrarian, Clerical, and Socialist Czechs, however much they may be united on purely national questions. It may be that universal suffrage will in time give greater prominence to social questions, but the Nationalists still carry on the fight between German and Slav in Bohemia. In Prague itself there is very little intercourse between the two, and Dr. Eppinger, the leader of the German Liberals, has proposed that, as in Moravia, where the races are far more mixed in the same electoral districts and vote for German and Czech candidates in separate Curias, so in Bohemia they should be split up also into separate Curias having their respective candidates and administering separate Budgets for education, theatres, and other national institutions; the German deputies looking after German and the Czech deputies after Czech interests separately. The political question in Galicia is almost entirely ignored, notwithstanding the very important bearing which it may eventually exercise upon the balance of power in Central Europe. It may be argued that the Poles themselves have sunk many of their differences and that most of their members have united in the Polish Club; but they are still divided into Conservatives, Liberals, Centre, and People's party. It is not quite fair to say that the peasants "are sunk in physical and moral degradation, a state of which they are conscious but which they attribute to their lords". This may be partially true of the Poles who have never left Galicia; but a great many peasants have been to the United States. Though the native Galician Pole has not much national feeling—a sentiment which has until lately been almost entirely monopolised by the nobility and the Clergy, he develops it when he reaches America. He realises that his best chance of securing work is to enrol himself in some local Polish Club or Confraternity, where he hears of the glorious past of his own country. He rarely stops long in America, but returns to Galicia when he has amassed enough money to buy the farm which his forefathers have tilled as peasants. The introduction of this new element is slowly effecting a revolution in some parts of Galicia, so much so that in many villages the local public-houses find it worth their while to subscribe to the "New York Herald". Much might also have been said of the many questions which in Eastern Galicia separate Ruthenians from Poles and Young from Old Ruthenians; for so great was the bitterness of racial antagonism at Lemberg that a wild fanatic was driven to assassinate Count Andreas Potocki, the enlightened Governor of Galicia, some fifteen months ago, though he had certainly shown more favour to the Young Ruthenians, it is true for political reasons, than any other Pole. The Old Ruthenians leant upon Russia, and had taught their fellow-countrymen that they were of the same race as their powerful neighbours across the frontier. It was, therefore, desirable to create a new party, and professors were instructed in the necessity of emphasising the distinction between the Ruthenian or Ukrainian who belongs to Little or Red Russia, and the Great Russian who has so much more Tartar blood in his veins. When, however, the Young Ruthenian began to depend upon Prussian support he became even more dangerous than those who looked to Russia for help, and he ceased to enjoy the favour of the Government at the Election for the Galician Diet, with the result that ten Old were returned as against eleven Young Ruthenians. The omission to give due weight to these and the Slovene and Croat questions in Southern Austria is all the more remarkable, as Mr. Drage has gone thoroughly into the question of the nationalities in Hungary, and exposed their grievances, as well as the difficulties of their Magyar rulers, with the greatest impartiality. Mr. Drage may argue, and with much fairness, that the compass of one volume would not have allowed him to deal at length with all these questions; but judging from the spirit in which he has approached the subject, no one could complain if he had published a more comprehensive work and dealt with Czech, Galician, and Slovene questions in Austria proper in the judicial spirit which he has shown in his whole work. On the other hand, he has published a most interesting map showing the comparative influence of socialism in Hungarian Communes; but has said little or nothing to explain this map in his text beyond dwelling upon the genuine grievances of the Hungarian labourer, and more especially since the passage by the Coalition Government of the Farm Servants Act of 1907, by which, if the servant fails to put in an appearance at the right time, he may be captured and haled back like a runaway. The farm servant is also forbidden to leave the farm, employ a substitute, or to receive visits from the outside without his master's permission, on pain of a fine of £2 1s. 8d., deduction from wages, or liability to damages. When he is under 18 years of age he may even be flogged by his master, whilst under Article 5 no passport of emigration shall be delivered to a farm servant until all relations between him and his master have been ended.

Mr. Drage supplies some extremely valuable information, which is not the less useful because some of it has already appeared in the Report issued by the Royal Commission on Labour, Vol. IX., on forms of land tenure and methods of cultivation, on industrial life, on the political rights of labourers, and on the social policy of the Government throughout all parts of the country. After dwelling upon Austria's connexion with the Balkans and the European outlook, he concludes with these words: "I will record my belief that whatever the result of the present crisis, in spite of racial and religious differences, in spite of external and internal dangers, the Dual Monarchy of Austria-Hungary will still remain a European necessity, and will in the future have an even greater part to play in the history of the world than in the past. In fact, the warlike races of the Habsburg realms may go far towards realising in Europe the proud device of the Emperor Frederick III.:—Austria erit in orbe ultima (A.E.I.O.U.)".

COLOSSAL!

"The Bride of the Misletoe." By James Lane Allen. London: Macmillan. 1909. 2s. 6d. net.

THE subject of Mr. Allen's new book is the crisis in the life of a married pair when the husband, but not the wife, begins to take things for granted and to glide towards middle age. It has, he tells us, neither the structure nor the purpose of a novel, and he draws attention to the fact that the time occupied is only about forty hours, and makes the assertion that no external event whatsoever is introduced. The method is pictorial, and the writer's effort has been to make a colossal pedestal and a colossal group. The effort is almost sublime, the result ridiculous. As in all inferior work, it is not only possible but necessary to separate the matter from the style. The matter, in fact, sinks entirely into insignificance compared with the style, which is laboured, self-conscious, unreal and ineffective to an extraordinary degree. Nobody will think twice about Mr. Allen's treatment of his subject, if indeed anybody succeeds in disinterring it from the words in which it is wrapped, drowned and overwhelmed. Probably Mr. Allen has taken as his model De Quincey at his very worst—the De Quincey who tells with so much circumstance and so little effect a story resembling that of "Lucy Gray". But De Quincey was always a musician, and when he fails it is always interesting to see how. Mr. Allen is not a musician, and he is only interesting because of the depth of the insincerity by which he has built up a style of which the one merit is its consistency. His method makes success impossible. His style is so unprecedented that we feel ourselves incapable of defining it. We shall attempt to suggest it by giving some examples.

When he wishes to say that Kentucky was made before man he says that it was made

"uncharted ages before man had emerged from deeps of ocean with eyes to wonder, thoughts to wander, heart to love, and spirit to pray".

Forms of sentence which he affects are seen in this:

"When morning came the sky was a turquoise and the wind a gale";

and this:

"What human traits you saw depended upon what human traits you saw with".

He is describing the preparation for celebrating Christmas Day, and he says:

"At intervals some servant with head and shoulders muffled in a bright-coloured shawl darted trippingly from the house to the cabins in the yard and from the cabins back to the house—the tropical African's polar dance between fire and fire ".

That last pendent clause is characteristic. Time after time we can see him either laying claim to a sensitiveness which he does not possess or making it an absurdity by his words, as here:

" The snow of Christmas Eve was falling softly on the old: whose eyes are always seeing vanished faces, whose ears hear voices gentler than any the earth now knows, whose hands forever try to reach other hands vainly held out to them. Sad, sad, to those who remember loved ones gone with their kindnesses the snow of Christmas Eve! "

We believe this to be a supreme example of the callous rhetorician's desecration of an emotion. Time after time we feel sure that he is writing of what he neither believes nor understands, as when he wishes to persuade us that his heroine regarded the clock as a " wooden God of Hours " and " had often feigned that it might be propitiated ", and " would pin inside the walls little clusters of blossoms as votive offerings ", and says:

" She was by nature not only alive to all life but alive to surrounding lifeless things. Much alone in the house, she had sent her happiness overflowing its dumb environs—humanising these—drawing them toward her by a gracious responsive symbolism—extending speech over realms which nature has not yet awakened to it or which she may have struck into speechlessness long æons past ".

These examples, a few out of a thousand possible ones, ought to be enough at least to convince any simple and honest reader that Mr. Allen is grossly untrue to life, if not that he—a man of undoubted ability—has scandalously misused words in a manner that might bring discredit or neglect upon better work by a superficial resemblance.

NOVELS.

"John Cave." By W. B. Trites. London: Treherne. 1909. 6s.

John Cave is an American journalist who is a slave to alcohol, and Prudence, whom he picks up in a restaurant, is an American cocotte addicted to opium, which she smokes both in private and in company very mixed in every sense of the word. Their continued intimacy does not tend to the reformation of either party, but Prudence, who of course has a heart of gold as well as " scarlet lips ", obtains from a friend of hers in the New York newspaper world a post for John on a Sunday magazine. Then John marries Diana, whose acquaintance he made by following her into the country and dropping a block of granite upon a dog which was attacking hers; but the couple simultaneously develop disloyalty to one another anent a Mr. and Mrs. Slocum —for no particular reason except the author's dislike to monogamic arrangements—and, Diana eloping with a third gentleman, John goes back to Prudence. By this time she is dying in a house of ill-fame, trying to remember something from the Bible appropriate to her case; and John bungles his suicide, though fortified for the occasion with a whole bottle of whisky. We do not propose to make any comment upon the poetic charm or the restrained art or the convincing vraisemblance of this pretty story.

"Sister K." By Mabel Hart. London: Methuen. 1909. 6s.

The pleasant love-story that runs through the pages of this book is spun out by misunderstandings of the usual type. If human beings were, as Homer called them, " articulate-speaking ", what would become of half our novels? However, this is one in which no serious harm is done by the lovers' distressing inability to grasp each other's meaning. The scene is laid chiefly in a great London hospital, and the novel is remarkable for the common-sense with which the writer discusses hospital nurses, good and indifferent. It is the literary and oratorical fashion of our nation to idealise nurses very much as Roman Catholic countries idealise nuns, and the most meagre amount of truth-telling about either is generally considered to prove that the speaker has no admiration for a fine calling or no reverence for religion. Whereas we all know—but are too great humbugs to say so—that neither every nurse nor every nun has a real vocation, and that a stupid or ill-tempered middle-class woman who has intruded into a way of life that requires exceptional qualities may do great harm and cause much suffering. Miss Hart writes as an observant gentlewoman, and her nurses are real.

"Harm's Way." By Lloyd Osbourne. London: Mills and Boon. 1909. 6s.

Mr. Lloyd Osbourne's new story is a study of a lively young American girl on her quest for the golden young man. Phyllis Ladd is the only daughter of a rich railroad president of Carthage, U.S.A., and in love with the idea of love she goes off for a season to Washington and thinks that she falls in love with, firstly, a frigid and wealthy young compatriot, and then with a sentimental German baron. In each case the rapid making of the engagement is followed by its rapid breaking, and Phyllis returns to her father believing that the race of golden young men has died out. Then she goes to a fourth-rate theatre, and, seeing a handsome young actor, the " star " of such establishments, soon makes an opportunity of knowing him. Mr. Osbourne does not make his hero a faultless person by any means; had he done so he would have made the story less real. As it is the romance has much in it of the conventional story of the wealthy heiress who elopes with a man who has difficulty in keeping his head above water, and things work on more or less conventional lines to a conventional end. Mr. Osbourne has a bright and easy way of writing, a facility in the rendering of dialogue and a knack of individualising his people, and these keep us entertained, though we should prefer to have them exercised over a less well-worn theme.

"A Family of Influence." By W. H. Williamson. London: Fisher Unwin. 1909. 6s.

Some lines of Tennyson's on the relative value of kind hearts and coronets and simple faith and Norman blood were, if we remember aright, prefixed to a certain mid-Victorian play; certainly there was in it an aristocratic dame whose teeth were set on edge by the mere sound of the name of Gerridge. Similarly the belated moral of this novel is that what a man himself is and does is of more moment than his ancestry, and though here the proud baronet can only go back to Charles the Second (as the author, with innuendoes, informs us), he, too, says " Shufflebottom! are there people with a name like that? " Also he struck his second son when the latter, declining the family living on the very proper ground that he felt no vocation for the Church, proposed to go into trade. Even Sir Anthony Absolute—but he, if irascible, was a gentleman. We have outgrown this sort of thing on the stage, but apparently not in fiction. Old-fashioned is a term of praise to many people, and therefore we do not use it; indeed we fear we may have been a little too complimentary to the book by our allusiveness. It is a réchauffé of a well-worn theme.

"The Bronze Bell." By Louis Joseph Vance. London: Grant Richards. 1909. 6s.

Mr. Vance has written a very engrossing, sensational romance of Hindu conspiracy. As a warning of Indian unrest, and of the danger of a second Mutiny, it lacks weight, it is too obviously constructed to excite and to mystify, and is not above the level of similar sensational fiction, though the style and manner of narration are by no means contemptible.

"Rose of the Wilderness." By S. R. Crockett. London: Hodder and Stoughton. 1909. 6s.

As a description of life in a wild moorland region of Galloway this book will serve very well. But what malign spirit impels Mr. Crockett, in season and out of season, to be arch? The sheer buffoonery of some episodes is comparatively tolerable. But the incessant archness! The story is by way of being the autobiography of a farmer's daughter. She marries a Church of Scotland minister not devoid of priggishness, and it is perhaps by way of compensation that she writes in the manner of one with whom Mr. Harry Lauder is collaborating.

SHORTER NOTICES.

"Giles and Phineas Fletcher: Poetical Works." Vol. II. Edited by F. S. Boas. Cambridge: At the University Press. 1909. 4s. 6d. net.

All the extant poetry of Giles Fletcher, together with that of Phineas published before 1633, was contained in the former volume of this book, which appeared last year. We now have the rest of Phineas' work, consisting of seven pleasant "Piscatory Eclogues", a number of miscellaneous pieces in English and Latin, and the best-known and most remarkable of all his poems, "The Purple Island". This last is a curiously elaborate allegory of Man. The first five cantos minutely describe the human body, the form and functions of every part both outward and inward; nothing, not even the vermiform appendix, which had not then acquired its present-day notoriety, is too insignificant for mention. The result, it need hardly be said, is often grotesque, and sometimes disgusting, yet it is all most skilfully done, and interspersed amongst the physiological details are many highly poetical lines. Passing from the physical to the emotional and intellectual qualities of mankind, Phineas finds his task more congenial, and the seven remaining cantos are in his best Spenserian manner; they flow easily on through a wealth of luxuriant imagery and phrasing, pervaded throughout with a strong religious atmosphere such as we should expect from this "excellent divine".

At the end of the volume is printed "Brittain's Ida", a poem formerly attributed to Spenser, whose name indeed appears on the first title-page dated 1628, but now almost universally admitted to be the work of another hand. Mr. Boas has satisfied himself that it was written by Phineas Fletcher, a view already urged by Grosart and others. He supports his contention by a considerable body of internal evidence, calling attention to many lines and turns of phrase, which occur almost identically in poems indisputably written by Phineas Fletcher. It is easy but dangerous to draw inferences from such similarities; however, in the present case the argument is strengthened greatly by the fact, which Mr. Boas points out clearly, that it was a habit of Phineas so to repeat himself. On the other hand, the poem as a whole, a sensuous, purposeless description of the loves of Venus and Anchises, is not quite such as we should expect from him, and, in the total absence of any corroboration by external evidence, we are still not altogether convinced by the ingenious theory here put forward. But if Phineas Fletcher did write it, the possibility of which we are far from denying, his reputation as a poet will certainly not suffer by its inclusion amongst his works.

"Texts Relating to Saint Mena of Egypt and Canons of Nicæa in a Nubian Dialect, with Facsimile." By E. A. Wallis Budge. London: British Museum. 1909. 12s.

Egypt is continually producing something new. Among the latest novelties are early Christian texts in the language spoken in Nubia in the ninth or tenth century. The most important of these is a manuscript found near Edfu, which has been acquired by the British Museum. It is exceedingly well preserved, and contains two works—one on the life of S. Menas and the other, apparently, on the Canons of Nicæa. To the first work a drawing has been attached of the saint on horseback, in the costume of a Roman soldier and with three crowns above him, the meaning of which is explained by Dr. Budge in his introduction to the present volume. The texts are written in the Coptic alphabet, to which three new characters have been added; the values of these have been determined by Drs. Schäfer and Schmidt. Dr. Budge contents himself with editing the texts, and does not attempt a translation, or even an analysis of them, but it is an open secret that Mr. Ll. Griffith, the Reader in Egyptology at Oxford, has succeeded in partially deciphering the language and fixing the signification of the grammatical forms. As was expected, the language proves to be an older form of the modern Nubian.

The reproduction of the manuscript leaves nothing to be desired, and is a beautiful specimen of photographic work. It is prefaced by a very full introduction by Dr. Budge, as well as by translations of two Ethiopic accounts of the martyrdom of S. Menas. Out of the abundant stores of his knowledge Dr. Budge gives all that the reader needs to know about the manuscript itself—the history of Christianity in Nubia and the story of S. Menas. Menas was one of the most popular of the Egyptian saints, and his church in the desert of Mareotis, near Alexandria, was one of the most splendid and frequented in Egypt before its destruction by the Mohammedans. Its ruins have recently been excavated by Dr. Kaufmann, and have yielded important remains of Coptic architecture. A spring of water over which it was built was famous for its miraculous cures, and the miniature oil-flasks which the pilgrims brought away from it as memorials of their visit are among the most interesting monuments of Christian Egypt. Illustrations of three of them are given in the present volume. S. Menas is usually represented upon them standing in the attitude of prayer with a camel-like creature on either side, concerning which there was more than one legend. A ship sometimes takes the place of the saint.

"Spain: a Study of her Life and Arts." By Royall Tyler. London: Grant Richards. 1909. 12s. 6d. net.

In his careful and elaborate study of the existing mediæval monuments in Spain the author discards all attempts at fine writing and that "picturesquemongery" which so long regarded Spain as first and foremost the land of romance, of hidalgos, brigands, Moorish maidens, and Inquisition mysteries. For he goes straight to the heart of his subject and bases his book on hard facts, which, if they make hard reading, are, as he points out, the result of still harder writing. To the student of mediæval Spanish architecture the book, with its detailed descriptions, careful ground plans, and well-chosen photographs, should prove of immense value. It is from this standpoint of stern fact, as opposed to romantic tradition, that, when dealing with the rivalry of north and south, the author devotes but one chapter to Andalusia, which, according to popular prejudice encouraged by Richard Ford, has always been considered the most interesting part of Spain. But, as a matter of fact, beyond the Mosque at Cordova, fragments of the Alcazar at Seville and the Alhambra atrociously restored, few monuments remain to testify to the former glory of what Spaniards call España Negra, and the one important Gothic church, the Cathedral of Seville, is great only by reason of its size. It is in the north that all the important monuments of Christian art that still exist are to be found—in the provinces of Castile and Arragon, provinces which, though the least visited, are the most interesting parts of the Peninsula. For the general reader, to whom the architectural details of cathedrals and monasteries form but poor pasture, there is yet much of interest in the descriptions of such typically Spanish pastimes as bull-fighting and pelota and the accounts of modern Spanish life in the great cities, notably in Madrid. The book is well got-up, and, although too heavy to be carried as a guide-book, should not be overlooked in view of a visit to any of the monuments it describes.

"The Real Francis Joseph." By Henri de Weindel. Translated by P. W. Sergeant. London: Long. 1909. 15s. net.

There are a large number of people of all classes who delight in the gossip of Courts, and the more ill-natured it is the better pleased they are. It is for this class of readers that this book has been written. No good qualities are allowed to the Emperor save industry and bravery. We may give one brief example of the author's capacity to criticise the policy of the sovereign he assails. On page 85 he tells us that "in 1866, much against the wishes of Francis Joseph, war was declared between Austria and Russia. It was Bismark's wishes (sic), not Francis Joseph's, which carried the day". On page 115 we learn that there was a grand battue "during the war with Russia in 1866, while the Austrian armies were being decimated *at the imperial whim*, and the country, *in consequence of this same infatuation of the Emperor*, was passing through a terrible domestic crisis". Clearly M. de Weindel is not a very consistent or trustworthy historian. He is evidently an adept at the baser tricks of the journalist's trade, retailing all the scandals he can rake together about the past of his victim and all the members of his house. Even for this inglorious business he is not over-well equipped, for he only tells us what everyone knows who has heard the gossip of Viennese cafés; he clearly has no real knowledge from within. The translator has on the whole done his work in decent style, and there are many excellent portraits.

"Croquis d'Orient: Patras et l'Achaie." Par le Baron Emile de Borchgrave. Bruxelles: Van Oest. 1908.

The Baron de Borchgrave, who has apparently travelled more than once in the South of Greece, has published the result of his studies in the mediæval annals of Achaia. They make pleasant reading enough, but have no pretensions at all to be regarded as the result of original research. It would, of course, be absurd to put this book in the same class as Mr. Miller's, or even Sir Rennell Rodd's, account of the Frankish princes and rulers of Greece in the Middle Ages. But M. de Borchgrave has read his authorities with care and has a real enthusiasm for his subject. There are a good many illustrations of the subject-matter of the text. The reproduction in most cases is not well done, but there are a few good photographs.

LAW BOOKS.

"The Law Relating to the Customs and Usages of Trade." By Robert William Aske. London: Stevens. 1909. 16s.

The peculiarity of custom and usage in English law has been its constant transformation from the local and particular into the general law of the land. It is in this way that what is known as the Common Law has grown up through being formulated by the Courts, all being brought under its operation. But new agricultural and trade customs are always growing; and sometimes the Courts will give their sanction to them and sometimes will not. We have a codified law of partnership and of bills of exchange, but a particular custom might grow up in a certain kind of partnership business not known as a general partnership rule, or the Stock Exchange might treat securities as negotiable of which the Courts had no previous experience. Lawyers must know the history of this kind of growth, whereby exceptions to the general law have been admitted into the body of the law, and the methods by which the Courts have regulated and controlled the process. Dr. Aske has dealt with this subject very satisfactorily. Not the least interesting part of his book is the collection of cases that have been decided as to particular customs, many of them amusing and quaint reminders of bygone times.

"Notes on the Companies (Consolidation) Act 1908." By L. Worthington Evans and F. Shewell Cooper. London: Knight. 1909.

The modesty of the title ought to be no prejudice to a book which is a very complete handling of the Act of 1908, and consolidates all the company law contained in the Companies Acts from 1862 to 1908. The Notes are a very thorough treatment of the decisions under the Acts now consolidated in this Act, and we may cite, as an indication of the editors' determination to make their work valuable, the two long notes by Mr. Stewart-Smith K.C. on the section relating to the "Liability of Directors" and on that relating to "Reconstruction." The co-operation of a solicitor (Mr. Evans), a member of the Bar, and a K.C. who is a well-known authority on company law, is prima facie a recommendation to the book, and the test of examination confirms it.

(Continued on page 236.)

"Local Government Law and Legislation for 1908." London: Hadden. 1909. 12s. 6d. net.

"The Law of Allotments and Small Holdings." London: Hadden. 1909. 5s.

Mr. W. H. Dumsday edits both these volumes with the knowledge and skill that come of familiar acquaintance with all branches of local government legislation. The first volume is the collection of Local Government Statutes, with Notes for 1908, issued as part of the well-known annual series of Messrs. Hadden, Best and Co. The experience of ten years has proved its value to all administering any department of local government.

The Small Holdings Act of last year, though it is printed with notes in the annual volume, is of special importance. Politically it was controversial, socially its future is in doubt. Mr. Dumsday has made a very complete edition of it, and in particular he has written a long and clear Introduction, which brings all the sections into logical order. Whoever may wish to explain or criticise the Act in rural constituencies will find it worth reading.

"The Law of Property in Land." By Stephen Martin Leake. 2nd Edition. By A. E. Randall. London: Stevens. 1909. 20s.

Leake's "Digest of the Law of Property in Land" still retains the place it has held for thirty-five years. Many have been, since it was first published, the books cast in more readable form for students. Its real office is as a secondary rather than a primary book, a medium between the class-book and the elaborate treatises on Real Property Law. The student and the practitioner alike may turn to it for condensed and accurate exposition. Mr. Randall has edited the book on its old lines, and has revised and added what the changes of thirty-five years have made necessary, so that a third of it now consists of his own original matter, and the work will continue to be as useful in the future as it has been in the past.

"Sanitary Law and Practice." By W. Robertson and Charles Porter. 2nd Edition. London: The Sanitary Publishing Company, Limited. 1909. 10s. 6d. net.

When the first edition of this book appeared we commended it to the notice of students preparing for the sanitary inspector's certificate and medical men preparing for degrees as medical officers of health. Since then there have been many additions to the law, such, e.g., as school medical inspection, as well as administrative changes. Many parts have been rewritten, and now even more than before Dr. Robertson and Dr. Porter present to students a thoroughly practical book. It was a wise choice not to include law reports. They are foreign to the general character of the book.

"The Law of Carriage by Railway." By Henry W. Disney. 2nd Edition. London: Stevens. 1909. 7s. 6d.

This is a book which should have a wider circle of readers than the legal. It was not intended, indeed, in the first instance for legal students, but for an audience at the London School of Economics, consisting mostly of men in the employment of the great railway companies. For these this book is an admirable text-book; but there is a more general public still to whom Mr. Disney's exposition of the law on this subject would appeal. Such chapters as those on the relations of the consignor of goods to the consignee, on delivery to the consignee, on the rights and liabilities after transit, on the carriage of animals, passengers' luggage, and those on the carriage of passengers, and the nature of their contract with the companies, would not be wrongly described as popular. We commend the book, therefore, to the large class of general readers. Others, such as lawyers and railway men, are not likely to overlook it.

"The Practical Statutes of the Session 1908." Edited by James Sutherland Cotton. London: Cox. 1909.

"Paterson's Practical Statutes," which have been issued for so many years, remains one of the most useful collections of annual Acts of Parliament published. The Introductions to each Statute are models of concise and lucid statement, and they are a source of diverse information which cannot easily be obtained elsewhere. It is curious to note the statutes which pass without public notice, and yet throw much light on social conditions. As examples we may notice the Act making married women with separate property liable to reimburse guardians for the cost of relief given to parents; the Act prohibiting the use of white phosphorus for making matches; and the Act making incest a crime, which was formerly only punishable in the Ecclesiastical Courts, though in Scotland and the Colonies it was, and is, punishable under the ordinary law.

For this Week's Books see page 238.

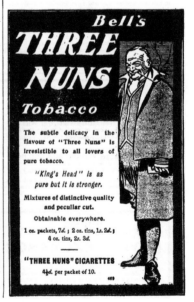

THIS WEEK'S BOOKS.

Fiction

The Severn Affair (Gertrude Warden); A Summer Wreath (Mrs. Campbell Praed); The Penalty (James Blyth); Doctor Dale's Dilemma (G. W. Appleton). Long. 6*s*. each.

Love, the Thief (Helen Mathers); Co-Heiresses (E. Everett-Green). Stanley Paul. 6*s*. each.

Splendid Brother (W. Pett Ridge). Methuen. 6*s*.

A Marriage in Jest (Mrs. Hugo Bartels). Ouseley. 2*s*. 6*d*.

Two Women (Baroness Albert d'Anethan). Fisher Unwin. 6*s*.

History

The Decay of the Church of Rome (Joseph McCabe). Methuen. 7*s*. 6*d*. net.

The Dawn of Christianity in Continental Europe (S. F. A. Caulfeild). Stock. 2*s*. 6*d*. net.

Gilbert White and Selborne (Henry C. Shelley). Werner Laurie. 6*s*. net.

Sport

The Record of the University Boat Race, 1829-1909 (Revised and Completed by C. M. Pitman). Fisher Unwin. 21*s*. net.

Le Lawn Tennis Moderne (P. A. Vaile). Paris: Hachette.

Verse

A Graftsman's Verse (George Earle). The Priory Press. 2*s*. net.

Miscellaneous

Britons Through Negro Spectacles (A. B. C. Merriman-Labor). Imperial and Foreign Co. 6*s*. net.

George Bernard Shaw (G. K. Chesterton). Lane. 5*s*. net.

Humours of the Country (Chosen by R. U. S.). Murray. 2*s*. 6*d*. net.

Invasion and Defence. Treherne. 2*s*. net.

Officers' Training Corps Examiner for Certificate "A", The (Captain R. F. Legge). Gale and Polden. 4*s*. net.

Poe Cult, The, and other Poe Papers (Eugene L. Didier). New York: Broadway Publishing Co. $1.50.

Shakespeare (Algernon Charles Swinburne). Frowde. 2*s*.

Studies in Lowland Scots (James Colville). Edinburgh: Green. 7*s*. 6*d*. net.

Reviews and Magazines for August.—The Architectural Review, 1*s*.; The Atlantic Monthly, 1*s*.; Revue des Deux Mondes, 3*f*.; Mercure de France, 1*f*. 25*c*.; The North American Review, 1*s*.

NOTICE.

The Terms of Subscription to the SATURDAY REVIEW are:—

	United Kingdom.	*Abroad.*
	£ s. d.	*£ s. d.*
One Year ...	1 8 2	1 10 4
Half Year ...	0 14 1	0 15 2
Quarter Year	0 7 1	0 7 7

Cheques and Money Orders should be crossed and made payable to the Manager, SATURDAY REVIEW Offices, 10 King Street, Covent Garden, London, W.C.

In the event of any difficulty being experienced in obtaining the SATURDAY REVIEW, the Publisher would be glad to be informed immediately.

Printed for the Proprietors by SPOTTISWOODE & Co. LTD., 5 New-street Square, E.C., and Published by REGINALD WEBSTER PAGE, at the Office, 10 King Stree Covent Garden, in the Parish of St. Paul, in the County of London.—*Saturday, 21 August, 1909.*

SATURDAY REVIEW

OF

POLITICS, LITERATURE, SCIENCE, AND ART.

No. 2,809 Vol. 108. 28 August 1909. [Registered as a Newspaper.] 6d.

CONTENTS.

NOTES OF THE WEEK.

Quite the most interesting Budget item for the week is the announcement that Lord Rosebery is to address a meeting against the Budget. True Lord Rosebery says that the announcement was "premature, at any rate". This is in effect a confirmation of the announcement. Public men find it so easy absolutely to deny embarrassing reports, part true part untrue, that when prematurity is the only waiver they can think of, the report is evidently true. Not that anyone can be surprised at Lord Rosebery being opposed to the Budget. He could be nothing else. The surprising thing is that he should have the courage to come out into the open and say so. It will be the definite breaking with his old party. He will then be the cross-bench man par excellence. So will he be most useful to the country. And what more happy or more dignified for him? Lofty, aloof from both parties, superior to either, Lord Rosebery from his solitary throne will from time to time Olympianly intervene in the affairs of men.

Other rumours are of course afloat. But the day for a Free Trade party, being the supposed moderate men from both the regular parties, is over. It might still be almost dazzlingly officered, but there would be nobody to officer. One notion at any rate may be scouted. Lord Rosebery is not answering signals of distress from the Unionist party. The Radical press goes on repeating day by day the story that the Opposition is disheartened and the Budget growing in popularity. Things do come to be believed by constant repetition, so there is nothing for it but constant denial. The Opposition simply could not be disheartened, seeing how extremely well they have done; and there is no evidence of the popularity of the Budget. There was no reason why it should be unpopular until understood; and it is difficult to understand. But, when the working classes realise how the Budget will stimulate unemployment, then will the truth about the Budget's popularity be out.

The Government is not going to alter the clauses in the Finance Bill which impose new licence duties on the public-houses. It will introduce them as first drawn. These clauses were objected to by the London Liberal members, who sent a deputation to the Chancellor of the Exchequer urging him to alter them and substitute a system of poundage either on sales or purchases, instead of fixing the licence duties in proportion to the assessed annual value of licensed premises. It was believed that his own friends had converted the Chancellor of the Exchequer, and that the clauses would be altered. Then Mr. Lloyd George wanted the brewers to discuss the matter with him after he had learned something he did not know before. But they remembered how he lectured and bullied them when they sent a previous deputation to him, and they will have nothing more to do with sending deputations to him. They are quite right to leave Mr. Lloyd George to flounder about in the mess he is in with the London Liberal members, and to fight their battle their own way.

Things seem to be coming to a crisis with Mr. Cox at Preston. He has recently issued a sort of manifesto to the Preston Liberals as to his attitude to the Budget, or rather to the land taxes. He has not changed in any way; he opposes those taxes now as he told them before the election he should oppose any taxes of the kind. He would not be in Parliament except as a free man. All this is true and is the strength of Mr. Cox' position. He has quite a good claim to be allowed to be a party to himself. Unfortunately such arrangements do not easily fit in with modern political conditions. What ought Conservatives to do with a Liberal who is most useful to them for the present, but might be a most painful thorn in their flesh in the future?

The Development Bill was introduced on Monday into the House of Commons. As described, it is to aid and develop forestry, agriculture, rural industries, and many other prima facie admirable objects calculated to promote the economic development of the United Kingdom. A Special Fund is provided to make grants and loans and, what is of special interest, for a Road Board to be formed to improve facilities for motor traffic. Already we know that the Budget provides for the net duties on motor spirit and motor licences going for this purpose. We have no quarrel with the objects, but the Government's methods of raising money make all their enterprises suspicious.

The main business of the House this week has, of course, been the Irish Land Bill. It must really have been quite a treat to Mr. Birrell after his luckless legislative past to be getting a large and extremely contentious Bill through so slickly. The truth is he has surrendered to the Nationalists on every point, and Unionists are naturally more or less exhausted by the constant Budget fight. All the same the Bill would have made small progress but for the help of the guillotine. The merits of the measure seem almost forgotten. The whole thing is a political move; and economics, justice, and everything else must go to the wall. Even the compulsion clause was let through almost without opposition. Yet it compels owners to part with their land at a price virtually fixed by the buyers to whom they are compelled to sell. Is this sheer exhaustion, or are the Lords counted on for redress?

The Bill for pretending that the sun is further on in the heavens than he really is has not obtained the approval of the Select Committee. It would not be surprising if the decision had been the other way. The idea caught on wonderfully in a very short time, and now, when the Committee have decided against recommending it, Mr. Willett is probably right when he says that a majority in the House of Commons would vote for it. Next year will show. There is a sort of moral fervour for the Bill which will survive many defeats; but farmers, the railways, the theatres and music-halls, and the Stock Exchange are against it. Its weakness is that counter-balancing pecuniary interests do not back it; and nobody gains by it except in a vague way either in hours or wages.

The Selection Board, now in effect the Army Council, have just arranged a nice little job. They have selected Sir Herbert Miles, whose appointment as Quartermaster-General recently caused much surprise, to be made a lieutenant-general over the heads of several of his seniors. Amongst these officers is Major-General Benson, who has performed most excellent service both in war and peace time, who was specially selected for promotion to major-general on account of his services, and who has since proved himself in every way qualified for the important positions he has held. Moreover, he now holds a major-general's post. Except that General Miles is a member of the Army Council, there can be no possible reason why General Benson should be passed over in his favour. The whole proceeding can only be described as a gross abuse of the privileges of the Army Council; and we hope that Mr. Haldane will be interrogated very closely on the subject.

Lord Kitchener, in the approved English fashion, has had his dinner of farewell at Simla. But though a customary function, it was an exceptional event, exceptional in the man. Lord Kitchener has been no ordinary Commander-in-Chief in India—even his harshest critics, his enemies, if we must speak plainly, will admit that. He has left a mark on the Indian Army, indeed on India, that must last. Some words of his given at this dinner explain why. His principle of action has been to do everything on a thought-out plan, and to do everything with an eye fixed on the future. In other words, he believes in science in administration. This is the right temper for peace preparation. It is the temper which will make the way clear for success in wartime, when other qualities and another temper are called for.

On Thursday Mr. Asquith explained to the House the general conclusions of the Imperial Defence Conference. It comes to this: the larger self-governing colonies, barring New Zealand, which takes a more Imperial view, will have and control their own defensive forces, naval and military, but these will be so assimilated as to be readily convertible for Imperial use. Their disposition and armament have been considered and arranged at the Conference. None of these conclusions will take effect until they have been approved by the respective Parliaments. The Conference has been useful as far as it could go; but the general result only reminds us how far we are from being an empire. The Prime Minister's phrase "Should these dominions desire to assist in the defence of the Empire, in a real emergency" has not a pleasant ring about it. But he could say nothing else.

The Australian State Premiers and the Federal Government have at last settled their differences as to the share of the Customs and Excise Revenue the States are to have. At any rate, they have agreed on a proposal to be laid before the various parliaments. Twenty-five shillings per head of population is to be paid out of this revenue to every State Government, with an extra grant to Western Australia. This means a large abatement of the payment hitherto made to the States, amounting in gross to some two and a half millions. The Federal Government, of course, gains by the exact difference. This is a happy conclusion of an old dispute, if it prove a conclusion and the parliaments assent. It will put the Commonwealth in a much stronger position to carry out its imperial policy. The States, too, will be wise to accept the settlement, for they are nearing the term of the "Braddon clause," and a little more delay would leave the Federal Government despot of the situation.

President Taft is taking a straightforward course with his income-tax proposals. Many authorities are of opinion that even as things are a scheme could be devised which would pass the Supreme Court, but the President prefers the more direct and more drastic method of adding an article to the Constitution. It will be a long and tedious business. The proposal must be sanctioned by thirty-five State Legislatures, and so far only one has given its consent. What is more important, the veto of twelve States will suffice to shelve the scheme. Georgia has already voted against it, and it seems not unlikely that eleven other Legislatures will be bribed, bullied, or cajoled into hostility. And even if the article were sanctioned, Congress would still have to pass an Income-tax Bill. On the whole, the Yankee capitalists seem safe for some time to come.

China has been warned in time and has settled all her differences with Japan. Both parties have got what they wanted. China receives full sovereignty and jurisdiction over Chien-tao, the border-zone between Corea and China proper and the cradle of the reigning dynasty. The only proviso is that death sentences shall be notified to the local Japanese Consuls. Japan, on the other hand, safeguards her South Manchurian line from competition, arranges for railway extensions into Northern Manchuria, and secures important mining rights. There has thus been an exchange of economic for territorial privileges. China, which is an Eastern Power, satisfies her sentiment, and Japan, which is (externally) a Western Power, gets the cash. Still if both sides are satisfied there is nothing more to be said.

The new Government in Teheran has discharged the little Shah's Russian tutor and is arranging for his education on modern lines, meaning thereby instruction in French revolutionary theories. Apart from this it does not seem to have done anything, least of all to have brought any money into the treasury. Indeed its only suggestion as yet is that heavy fines should be levied on the adherents of the ex-Shah, a scheme which shows no great advance on the financial policy of the old régime. For the rest the ex-Shah has leased a villa on the Black Sea, whence he can conduct intrigues at a convenient but not excessive distance. Has the Persian poison entered into the veins of the Ameer's subjects? There is reason for fear, for such news as has recently filtered through from Cabul suggests that the Ameer's position is none too happy.

Mulai Hafid has done something at last. He has captured the pretender Bu Hamara, otherwise known as El Roghi. After a defeat the Pretender took refuge in a mosque, but European civilisation has not touched Morocco for nothing, and his sanctuary was promptly invaded. The arrest was celebrated in fine style at Tangier, and the Diplomatic Corps no doubt paid pretty compliments to the authorities. But there is some uneasiness as to the captive's fate. Eastern monarchs have ingenious public methods of punishing their enemies, carefully calculated to make a strong impression on the spectators. No doubt Mulai Hafid is eager to give a demonstration of his power to his sceptical subjects; but, as Great Britain and France are preparing protests, he will do well to yield to their prejudices. After all, the Western Powers will be asked to lend money, and they can cause trouble if they turn nasty.

The Spanish advance from Melilla has begun. By now all the troops required have been brought up to strength and are being sent to the front. But disembarkation is a slow business through lack of a good harbour, and the equipment for a sub-tropical campaign is not yet all at hand. Pith helmets for the troops had to be ordered, and the camping-ground supplied with water and proper provisions. It is unwise to hurry the man on the spot, but a move was now fully due. There was serious danger of sickness if the troops were kept in their tents much longer. Spain must wipe that disastrous word "mañana" from her language. Happily her King does not lack energy, and we expect good things from the general of his choice.

Late in September the German Social Democratic party is to hold its annual conference at Leipsic, and already the little rifts within the lute are being carefully widened by the party press. As usual, the moderate South has provoked the anger of the uncompromising North. Last year it was Baden that went wrong, her Socialist deputies having attended the Grand Duke's funeral. This year Wuerttemberg has been guilty of respect to a living sovereign. It happened that when the Wuerttemberg deputies went over the Zeppelin works, the King invited them to lunch, and the Socialists actually accepted the invitation! They now defend themselves, first on the ground that the King of Wuerttemberg is really quite a nice fellow, and secondly by the argument that political differences need not be a bar to personal relations. But the intolerant Northerners bitterly retort that a man is known by the company he keeps, and demand an ex cathedra pronouncement at Leipsic.

The Reichstag has voted the £25,000,000 of new taxation, but the money is not coming in. Beer is sacrosanct on both sides of the North Sea, and the new German duty has provoked trouble. A beer strike is now raging in Thuringia. The blame is put on the brewers, who raised the price to such an extent as to make an extra mark profit per hectolitre, offering as an excuse their loss through diminished consumption. Hereupon the Social Democratic leaders urged their followers to resist this latest piece of capitalist spoliation, and drink nothing but syrups and mineral waters. The ingenious manœuvre would have failed but for the co-operation of the café proprietors, who were harassed by their waiters' demands for higher wages to compensate for loss of tips. Thus the distributors have ceased to order beer, while many consumers are ceasing to demand it, and the brewery companies are in distress. It is a very pretty little illustration of the play of economic forces only possible in a land whose people have a strong sense of discipline and no sense of humour.

The Swedish strike still continues, and has now entered on its fourth week; but public opinion, which has endured the infliction with exemplary patience, is at length becoming restive. That it has kept quiet for so long is due to the failure of the strike-leaders to destroy the mechanism of society. Suggestions for Government mediation are now being ventilated in the press and by petition to the Crown, the idea being that something should be done to settle the various small and isolated labour disputes which formed the basis of the movement. It is certain that the Government will take the first favourable chance of intervention. Not all the insistence on the self-control displayed by the workmen in maintaining the public order, which they lacked both the power and the courage to destroy, can alter the fact that the strike must have dealt a blow to the national finances, to the prosperity of the people and to the international credit of the country. Labour will one day have to answer for its lack of patriotism.

If flying meetings are to go pleasantly and smoothly, this week at Rheims shows that the weather must be good. Many people there were glad to get away; and yet by leaving they missed the two great events of the meeting—the flight on Thursday of Mr. Latham, whose success may almost have compensated him for his Channel misadventure; and that of M. Paulhan on Wednesday. Mr. Latham stayed in the air twenty-five minutes less than M. Paulhan did; but in the less time he made a flight of about ninety-six miles, the farthest ever made by man. This was the more remarkable as it was made during a storm; and gusts of wind had already wrecked M. Fournier's machine. Not to have been defeated by the wind was more significant than to have made a record distance.

Yet what hardly needed proof has been abundantly proved at Rheims—that the wind determines whether it is safe for an aeroplane to attempt any flying; though a dead calm is not necessary, as these two flights have shown. Up to a certain point a flier may depend on his machine; but he can never tell whether the next gust will not, by just going beyond that point, bring him down to earth. Probably for a considerable time to come flying meetings will be rather tame affairs, unless weather conditions are almost perfect. The events will be too irregular and uncertain. But even the young bird cannot be sure of getting exactly where he wants at first; and somebody's aeroplane is always doing better than the former best, as Mr. Latham's monoplane did better than M. Bleriot's biplane; and this seems very promising.

If games and dances and physical exercises oust a lot of the rubbishy subjects taught in elementary schools, we shall see something a little more like education. The Board of Education, to judge from the Physical Education Report, has a very reasonable notion of the sort of thing suitable for boys and girls up to fourteen. If we could only be sure that the teachers were competent to follow up the matter intelligently, there would really seem to be a prospect of considerable improvement amongst school children in physique, manners, discipline, cleanliness, and intelligence. But the teachers for so many years have had their noses kept over school books that they have not learned about the children themselves; and this is the knowledge they need most to lead the children's games.

There is a society for teaching morris dances and singing games that were known in olden days when children were not crammed, but educated, as the Greeks were, on music and dancing. But the teachers in schools generally not having been so trained themselves, they cannot so teach. They have to be taught first, and until they have learned the children will not get much good. The intention to instruct the teachers is what makes the importance of the new syllabus. Some of the instruction has to be in print, but the Board must see that the teachers go through the physical training under competent instructors, such as those of the Association that teaches games and morris dances, and not drill the children from the instructions in the syllabus alone. To get rid of books as much as possible is what is wanted in the schools.

Sir Joseph Thomson, Cavendish Professor of Experimental Physics at Cambridge, the newly elected President of the British Association, gave his address on Wednesday at Winnipeg, where the seventy-ninth annual meeting is being held this year. It is twenty-five years since the first meeting outside Great Britain was held at Montreal. Canada has changed a good deal since then, and the President's first point was that the change has been accomplished by applied science. Since the Montreal meeting a new body of science relating to the physical universe dates from the discovery of the Röntgen rays, and it was the history of discovery during this period that the President for the most part discussed. It was very wonderful, very fascinating, and an admirable occasion for the exercise of faith by the unscientific. Such subjects should beget enthusiasm in the student; but Sir Joseph Thomson thinks the excessive competition for scholarships deadens it.

"Blanco Posnet" has been acted in Dublin, and the world has not come to an end. Neither have we heard that Mr. Shaw has been consumed in flames or gone off in an evil odour. What has gone amiss? Surely after all the pother, all the letters, all the talk, something ought to have happened. Yet nothing did happen except that the play was acted and the audience pleased. Guesses why the play was forbidden here have been unceasing. Now we must all give it up. The play was the last chance; the play at any rate would solve the riddle. But the play has been given, and not a glimmer of light does it throw on the reason for its prohibition. It is easy, of course, to explain: we can all explain it, all who know our way about; but a rational explanation is what we were hunting for. That we shall never have now.

Of course, if drama is to have nothing to do with truth, is not to touch men and women as they are, is to treat them as soulless to please the conventions, plays like "Blanco Posnet" must not see the light. But it is difficult to keep patience, if we ought to keep it, when we think of the scores of prurient plays, whose whole standpoint is irreligious, accepted without a shriek, without a qualm, and a play of the high seriousness of this one of Mr. Shaw's hunted as "improper". Convention is very useful—you cannot carry on civilisation without it—and he is a fool that outrages convention. But convention was made for man and not man for convention. When a man comes along big enough to look behind convention at truth, he is not to be stoned because what he has seen is not quite what we expected or wanted.

Mr. W. G. Cavendish-Bentinck, who died suddenly on 22 August, was one of those cultivated and able men whose talents were little known outside an intimate circle of friends. As acting Portland Trustee of the British Museum for eighteen years he hardly ever missed a meeting, and brought an intelligent mind to bear on all the manifold and important subjects there discussed. He was of great assistance to the present Duke of Portland, when the latter began the difficult work, not yet finished, of examining and classifying the vast amount of important political and literary correspondence, covering over two centuries and a quarter, now at Welbeck. Mr. Cavendish-Bentinck in his early life intended to follow his father's example and a political career—and represented Falmouth in Parliament for eleven years—but after his defeat in 1895 he never stood again.

GOVERNMENT BY PHYSICAL FORCE.

IN a House of Commons where the division-bells can only muster 260 members, and where therefore it is safe to assume that in the chamber itself not more than 130 are present, a Bill has been passed this week confiscating the whole land of Ireland. The Estates Commissioners and the Congested Districts Board between them have been given power to acquire compulsorily any land they choose at a price to be fixed by themselves, the buyers, with a view to resale to the peasants. There is, of course, nothing objectionable in the principle of the compulsory acquisition of land for a public purpose, provided that the buyer does not fix the price. The moment that term is introduced the business becomes simple confiscation. Our object, however, is not to criticise Mr. Birrell's Land Bill, but to point out that a measure revolutionising the rural life of Ireland is carried, by the guillotine form of closure, in a House of Commons where less than forty per cent. of the members pass before the tellers, and probably less than twenty per cent. hear the debate. This Irish Land Bill is neither more nor less important than the Finance Bill, which is being forced through Committee by means as bad. When we add to the use of the closure the fact that members of Parliament are compelled to sit up all night, week after week and month after month, we have got down to Government by physical force pure and simple. It is as much a physical contest as if the Prime Minister were to take hold of one end of a rope and Mr. Balfour the other, and, supported by their respective followers, were to engage in a tug-of-war. Indeed, such a struggle would be healthier and less degrading than the present pitting of avoirdupois against argument. The Government can command some 500 supporters, and 150 obey Mr. Balfour's whip. It is confidently reckoned by the Ministry that the 500 will shortly reduce the 150 to such a pitch of exhaustion that the remaining clauses of the Budget, or, indeed, of any measure the Cabinet choose to table, will be quickly and silently passed. This seems likely enough to happen, for the Ministerialists can arrange a system of relays by which their friends can steal away to seaside or moor, whilst the devoted band of Unionists are growing weaker and paler. It must be maddening for the Opposition to watch the changing ranks of the enemy, and to see opponents reappearing, bronzed and rosy by their hasty holiday, while they, like horses blindfold, tread the weary mill-track. There is no fancy or exaggeration about this picture. It is sad, prosaic truth. To such depths has Parliamentary Government descended.

England is being governed by physical force, and apparently the people of England do not care—nay, rather, assisted by the picturesque reporter, regard the thing as a joke. Physical force in politics assumes many shapes. Oliver and his troopers, the Duc de Morny and his prefect of police, Mr. Pease and his battalions of obedient voters, all are incarnations of the same factor of brute force. And the man in the street is amused by the unspeakable vulgarity of the reporter's pen, chuckles over Mr. Churchill's pyjamas after lunch in his golf club, or patronisingly pities "those poor devils in Parliament". Has seriousness really departed from the British people? Will nothing rouse them to a sense of their danger? Lord Beaconsfield said that a nation could only be governed by one of two means, tradition or military force. France, which has broken with tradition, is governed by the army. Great Britain, which is fast breaking with tradition, is governed by the Cabinet and the Pease battalions, and, as we have said, it matters little what precise disguise may be assumed by force. We earnestly wish it were possible to induce the electors of this country to take a serious view of the situation and to reflect upon some of the most obvious consequences that must flow from a continuance of the present state of things. To put it in a commercial light, surely the average business man must see that the legislative output of all-night sittings must be inferior in quality. Let anyone try to imagine a large administrative concern conducting its business by the same methods as the House of Commons transacts the business of the nation! Imagine the London and North-Western Railway, or the thread-mills of Messrs. Coats, or Harrod's Stores, keeping their employees at work all night for months! Of course the "hands" in these gigantic establishments would not stand it for a week. But the liberty and rest allowed to a railway porter, a mill-girl or a shop-walker are denied to the representatives of the people, chosen by democratic suffrage as the flower of the nation. Putting aside the indignity and intolerable strain imposed upon some six hundred gentlemen, their work must be bad, just as it is admitted that the work of the overworked employee in office or factory is bad. Finally, we should like to ask the constituencies whether they are really indifferent to the intellectual calibre and moral character of their House of Commons. There will always be an adequate supply of candidates of a sort on both sides. Plutocrats eager to buy peerages, professional and commercial failures anxious to become guinea-pigs, briefless barristers on the hunt for county court judgeships, adventurers of every pattern, will always be found to stand for Parliament. But a few more sessions like the present must repel men of character, of brains, and of assured position from submitting themselves to a life of laborious trifling, of degrading servility and of brutal compulsion. There is only one kind of occasion that can justify the Executive in resorting to all-night sittings for the carriage of its Bills—namely, the safety and order of society. The Unionist Government resorted to all-night sittings to carry its Crimes Act in 1887. But that was a measure necessary to enable the Executive to carry out its primary and essential function, the protection of life and property, in the face of avowed obstruction by the Nationalist members. The Budget and the Irish Land Bill are not necessary for the preservation of life and property, and they have not been (admittedly) obstructed. They are Bills embodying the speculative socialism of the present Government, and they are being forced through the Legislature at the expense of the health and self-respect of the law-makers, and to the ultimate cost of those who have to obey the laws.

THE IRISH LAND BILL.

"WILL they get us compulsion?" That is the one question which has been asked of late in the Irish Congested Districts, and it marks the limit of agrarian knowledge regarding the Land Bill. The Congests want more land, for nothing if possible, and for the rest their mind is a blank. They do not even know about Mr. Dillon's famous confession that the League defies them to enter the prairies. The admission was made in Swinford last April, and the Leaguers have but strengthened their defiance since then. Yet the plea for compulsion was specially to get land for the relief of congestion. Mr. Dillon's quoted dictum of "No Mayo men in Roscommon" has been discussed in this Review before, and made widely known to the British public; but it remains unknown among his congested constituents in East Mayo, who, if they knew how he allows "the people's organisation" to be worked against them, might have a different opinion of his heroism. Mr. Birrell is as helpless as Mr. Dillon to prevent the League grabbing the land and perpetuating congestion, but both statesmen are agreed in acquiring by compulsion the land which they dare not put to the purpose for which the owner is compelled to sell it. The landlords must be harassed by the law to relieve congestion, but the League will not permit congestion to be relieved, and the Government dares not face the League, which, of course, remains equally free to terrorise the arbitrating authority through which the compulsion is to be administered. When Government itself is triumphantly defied, its minor servants can hardly hope to be more successful. In addition, the principle is initiated of forcing the owner to part with his property at a price which he may not arrange; and the Board to control the whole business will include nine political hooligans from the County Councils, all under the control of the League, elected to impose its terrors on local government. Stranger still, this amazing clause has been passed by a majority of 213 votes to 29, as if Unionism in the House had ceased to be interested in the rights of Irish property. Well, the day must come when the effects of Irish anarchy, encouraged by Government, will be felt in British life. These islands are too closely connected to have first principles applied in one and permanently inoperative in another.

In addition to all these facts, we have the example of the prairies already divided. In these the land has been acquired without compulsion, at prices as near the true value as the League would permit; but the settlers commonly confess their regret at having left congestion. They complain that they cannot meet the higher responsibilities, and it is certain that they are exhausting the reserve of fertility in the soil. To meet this compulsion is demanded, in the hope that Mr. Birrell's arbitrators may give them the land on still lower terms to accommodate their agricultural incapacity. There is not a word about raising their capacity to accommodate higher responsibilities. Incapacity is accepted as the governing fact, and all else must accommodate itself to this. Any improvement on this head would involve education; but Sir Horace Plunkett has been removed, and Mr. T. W. Russell has been put at the head of agricultural education, qualified as a stationer, an hotel keeper, and an agitator. Besides, the state of elementary education leaves agricultural instruction practically useless, however perfect in itself, and no statesman at present living dares to touch the question of primary education. The newly made holdings are largely sub-let. The new tenant right in the divided prairies is worth about twenty years' purchase, so that the man who gets fifteen acres in Roscommon has a free gift of something like £150 made to him. Thus the "landless men" around the prairies, the sons of tenants, and some who have nothing to do with land, get their neighbours' property for nothing, with the approval of Parliament, so that their reasons for joining the League are very strong. These are the men who combine in Roscommon to keep out the Congests of Mayo. We have it from Mr. Dillon, who also threatens to "let loose the dogs of war" unless Mr. Birrell secure him such compulsion as will meet the approval of the hooligans.

Mr. Birrell's next notable achievement this week has been in passing the clause that limits the size of farms, which, if made law, must certainly help to keep the land unproductive and to starve out the Irish race. The farms are to be such as may find occupation for a family of working people. The farmer himself must be a working man, industrially uneducated at that, and so unfit to become an employer. There is to be no room for either an employing or a wage-earning class. There is to be no room for the larger farm that could find scope for the larger mind, and accordingly industrial intelligence must be kept away from the soil. This must necessarily tend to keep the soil unproductive, the population ignorant, and the country poor. The economic interplay of the classes, their means and their motives, which act for the development of industrial production elsewhere, is to be suspended in Ireland and in the name of "remedial legislation"! However, it suits those who control Irish "public opinion". Its ignorance is their power. They prefer the kind of farm that keeps intelligence conveniently low. A man capable of being an employer might think for himself, and so the smallness of the farm is to make his presence impossible. We are to have a dead level of agrarian mediocrity, with no place for the man of culture whose character might help to raise that of his neighbours towards the outlook of a progressive community. Civilisation advances chiefly through the rare and gifted individual, but for him there is to be little or no room on the agrarian face of Ireland. Up to now we have seen the natural effect in the displacement of the peasants by the more economic ox, but now the owner of the ox is to be prevented by law from buying additional farms. The peasant is to be preserved, but on such a carefully low status that he may always remain ungovernable, unfit to see what is good for him, and willing to follow those who make a traffic in leading him. Mr. Birrell calls it "Democracy," and takes for the popular will the agencies that make volition impossible. The whole scheme goes to confirm the Irish character as a quantity incalculable in Imperial affairs, sacrificing industrial civilisation to political traffic. It suits the Irish leaders to have it so, and it suits the present Government to pretend that the Irish leaders represent "Democracy"!

THOSE DUKES.

"OH! these Dukes, how they harass us!" The Chancellor of the Exchequer's phrase (or at least the sentiment which inspired it) has caught on. It was sure to catch on with those it was intended to catch on with. The little bit of claptrap has been entirely successful, and there is not a Radical stalwart of them all who is not convinced that he is suffering some personal wrong (presumably is being kept out of the enjoyment of landed estate) by these personages, of whom, of their virtues and vices, morals and manners—to say nothing of their financial position—he knows no more than he does about the Dukes of Edom. With that sort of person, then, "Down with the Dukes!" is a capital cry, especially when the chorus is led by a Cabinet Minister, a species that is wont to be rather more mealy-mouthed. But will that cry make a single convert from the other sections of the sovereign people? It will not touch the hard-shell Conservative—of course. Will it affect that forty per cent. or thereabouts of the electorate which is not hard-and-fast Whig or Tory? We do not believe that it will, provided only that the man in the street can be adequately informed as to the true nature of the Lloyd-Georgian indictment of "the Dukes". But, before adequate information can be given it must be had, and there are few subjects upon which it is less easy to obtain full and accurate statistics than as to the possession of landed property in this country. That sounds strange—very strange—if the Lloyd-Georgian theory is correct, and if the soil of England is in the grip of a handful of idle rich—in a word, of Dukes. There are less than thirty of these parasitic patricians, and it ought, surely, to be an easy thing to ascertain the sum of their acres and rent-rolls. Easy enough it is, and mighty fine the figures look. There is he of Sutherland, for example, who, fortunately for his tenantry, owns well-nigh a million and a half of acres! It sounds prodigious until you remember Lord Tullibardine's little picnic the other day, when Scottish Radicals learnt for the first time the agricultural value of the Duke of Atholl's Scottish deer forest. Still, the ducal acreages are broad, and the rent-rolls not bad; but the question is—How far is it right to regard these twenty-seven Dukes as the sole, or at least the principal, freeholders in England?

It is not possible to answer that question with mathematical accuracy, but it is very easy to show that the suggestion that the land is in the grip of a few great landowners is a grotesque caricature of the truth. To get at any approximation to the facts we have to go back more than thirty years, to a return made by the Local Government Board in 1876. That return shows that there were then considerably more than a million freeholders in England, Scotland and Wales, of whom more than 800,000 owned less than a single acre apiece. At that time there was only one solitary owner of more than 100,000 acres in England; there were only twenty-four such landowners in Scotland; and there were no more than 382 owners of from 10,000 to 20,000 acres. Three-and-thirty years ago, therefore, the theory of the territorial omnipotence of the aristocracy was purely mythical; but it has even less—much less—basis of truth at the present day than it had in the 'seventies of the last century. Although there are no statistics available which will give us a complete account of the whole situation, there is a consensus of expert opinion that these figures must be revised in a sense which ought to bring tears of thankfulness into the eyes of our democratic Chancellor of the Exchequer. Thanks to the growth of the wealth of the community, the extension of building societies and the subdivision of estates, it is estimated that the present number of freeholders is three times as large as it was in 1876. That the Government are not unaware of the true position is shown by their exemption of registered societies from the operation of the new taxes.

The Dukes, however, are making their own position plain to the public with a candour which ought not to be wholly without effect. Thus, the Duke of Northumberland, replying to Sir Edward Grey's suggestion that Dukes should reduce their expenditure and cut their coat according to their cloth like meaner mortals, has said he is quite willing so to do; but, after enumerating the various items ear-marked for reduction, he has to add that he cannot help seeing that these economies mean loss of employment to all those who depend upon his maintenance of "these things"—things the absence of which will not appreciably affect the amenity of his personal existence. That sort of solicitude is not peculiar to this particular Duke. No holder of that rank in the peerage has been more roundly abused than the Duke of Westminster, who was specially subjected to the limelight of Limehouse. Nevertheless, we have a tenant on the Grosvenor estate in London bluntly proclaiming in a letter to the "Times" his conviction that "the ordinary man in the street would prefer to be a tenant of the Duke of Westminster rather than of the Crown". Similarly, there was dismay amongst the tenants on one of the Duke of Bedford's estates when that landlord announced his intention of selling the property. These benighted victims of the feudal tradition were, apparently, of opinion that they might go farther and fare considerably worse. In so far, indeed, as it is possible to discern the trend of public opinion in the letters addressed to the daily press, it seems rather more than likely that the Chancellor of the Exchequer will live to regret having gone out of his way to complain how "these Dukes harass us". He has set all sorts and conditions of men thinking a good deal more about the great landlords than most of us are in the habit of doing. Do "these Dukes" really "harass us"? And, even if they do, are we quite sure that there is any alternative in practical politics which brings us nearer the ideal of a quiet life? The Chancellor could hardly have done a greater disservice to the land clauses of his Budget than to challenge the public, of all classes, to ask themselves the simple question, What are we going to get by making it practically impossible for a great landlord to be as good a landlord as he ought to be, as good a landlord as most great landlords are?

GERMAN AFFAIRS.

IN the height of summer a great calm is wont to fall on German politics. The Emperor goes away, first on his northern cruise and then to his country home far from the capital; the Chancellor seeks health and rest in some distant villa; the deputies and publicists scatter abroad to study with characteristic German thoroughness the condition of foreign countries on the spot. Only towards the end of August do leading men return to the neighbourhood of Berlin, there to enter on the political confabulations preliminary to the opening of the new Session. This year the customary break has been lacking. The Emperor lingered near the capital longer than his custom; the Chancellor was busy moving into his new home and learning the routine of his new work; the deputies hurried away to explain their conduct to their constituents; and the publicists stayed in Germany to write leading articles on domestic politics. For, despite the great counter-attraction of Count Zeppelin's achievements and projects, the echoes of Prince Bülow's retirement still resound throughout the Empire, and the ex-Chancellor did not excite greater attention in the hour of his greatest triumph than now in the days of his defeat.

The general interest in the circumstances of Prince

Bülow's resignation are not due to any suspicion that he may again return to office. On the contrary, he is well known to be glad to be quit of it all. The prevailing political unrest is caused by the fact that the Prince's fall did not mark the end of a crisis, but rather the beginning of one, with the result that everyone is wondering what everyone else is going to do. Possibly the wonder is premature. The German is a slow-moving man, and Herr von Bethmann-Hollweg is an official of cautious temperament, certain to feel his way before he commits himself to any very definite policy. At the same time, important issues must be raised in the earliest days of the new session. The last session closed with the defeat of the Government on a first-class measure. The division was extremely close, and Prince Bülow found himself supported by all the groups that would normally compose the Opposition. The majority thus broke violently with its own traditions. Will it be able to hold together? Its main elements, the Conservatives and the Centre, are indeed used to co-operation, for they formed Prince Bülow's working majority during the first six years of his term of office. On the other hand, during the recent period of mutual antagonism the Conservatives aided the Government in a policy of coercion in Poland, to which the Centre, dependent as it is to no slight degree on the Polish vote, was bitterly opposed. In particular, the Conservatives are mainly responsible for the insertion in the new law as to public meetings of the paragraph which empowers the authorities to insist that the speakers shall use the German language. The authorities have not hesitated to apply this provision with the utmost rigour, and within the past few days have prohibited an English member of Parliament from delivering a speech in English. This incident is sufficient indication that the law is being strictly enforced in Poland, and the Centre Party can hardly remain deaf to the bitter complaints of their co-religionists.

The Polish question is likely to be the main obstacle to the harmonious co-operation of Clericals and Conservatives, because it tends to raise the invincible religious and racial antipathies, which are never very far below the surface of German political life. There is also, however, another matter on which the two sections of the new majority may be unable to see eye to eye. That is the reform of the Prussian franchise. The late Chancellor admitted some months back that the present three-class system could not be maintained in its entirety. Such reforms as the Prussian bureaucracy will sanction will be by no means thoroughgoing, but even the slightest change will scarcely be to the tastes of the feudal-minded Junkers from east of the Elbe. On the other hand, the Centre may be forced to demand a bold policy. It claims to be a democratic party; it appeals to great numbers of voters in industrial Rhenish Prussia; and its purely agrarian tactics in the recent financial struggle have met with strong criticism from a section of its supporters. In this matter the Centre, indeed, may be strong enough to force the Conservatives to give way, for they too have been unpleasantly reminded of the discontent of their humble electors. A cleavage has manifested itself in the ranks of the once all-powerful Agricultural League. At the initiative of small-holders farming in districts near Berlin, and therefore in touch with democratic thought, a new Peasants' League has been formed, which is reported to be making dangerous headway in the eastern provinces.

It is clear, then, that all is not well with the new majority. Neither of its elements is quite certain of its position in the country, and each cherishes some suspicion as to the aims of the other. The question of the moment is not whether the Clerical-Conservative bloc could stand any considerable strain, but whether the Left is capable first of uniting to overthrow it and then of establishing a stable majority in its place. Now the Left is composed of a Liberal and a Socialist wing, and co-operation between the two is a matter of some difficulty. The Socialists will have none of the individualism of which all sections of the German Liberal party are more or less enamoured. To the Socialists individualism is simply a philosophic term for the power of private capital, against which they are pledged to fight. Moreover, a recent incident has encouraged them to persevere in an uncompromising policy. Just after the new financial arrangements became law, there was a bye-election in a constituency which had been represented by a National Liberal since the establishment of the Empire. This time a Socialist was returned by a moderate majority. The surprising result led to a careful analysis of the votes cast. It appears that many of the Catholic voters, who were simply ordered to abstain from supporting the Liberal candidate, exceeded their instructions and voted for the Socialist; but that even this would not have secured his return had he not also been supported by a number of recalcitrant members of the Agricultural League. The election is thus very significant and may give the more militant Socialists cause to declare that their party alone represents the democracy and has nothing to gain by coalitions with Capitalist groups.

On the other hand, the Liberal party has some distance to travel before it will be in a position to think of negotiations with possible allies. It is at present split up into three main groups, which may be described as representing the Philosophic Radicals, the Capitalist Radicals, and the Democratic Radicals. These groups have in the past devoted much time to mutual criticism, which has only lost them votes and won them the outspoken ridicule of all sections of their opponents. In the present crisis, however, they show signs of rising to the occasion. Prince Bülow taught them the elements of co-operation in the course of his endeavour to bring them all into his bloc, and the triumph of the financial policy to which they are all opposed, though for slightly different reasons, has brought home to them the necessity for further combined action. If there should be a revival of the powerful and united Liberal party of Eugen Richter's time, what attitude would it adopt towards its Socialist neighbours in the Reichstag? Clearly if the Capitalist section predominates, any full union of the Left will be made impossible. If, on the other hand, the new party is led by the Democratic Radicals, who are enthusiastic advocates of a strong progressive social policy, the prospects of union will become far more hopeful. Proceedings at the initial meeting of the new Hansa Bund suggest that the Democratic Radicals will most probably control any combination that may ensue. At that meeting there assembled some six thousand men of business fairly representative of industrial Germany, although it may be admitted that the financiers and the merchants rather outnumbered the producers proper. This vast audience was addressed by Herr Kirdorf, who, as the managing director of a huge firm and the moving spirit of a great Cartel, is one of the leading capitalists in Europe. After citing some rather startling figures to prove the heavy burden imposed on industry by the social legislation of the last thirty years, he was about to argue that the new League must resolutely set its face against further developments on such lines, when the meeting howled him down. The episode is significant of the position which the Democratic Radicals would occupy in a rejuvenated party, and on the Socialist side men would not be wanting who would meet them half-way. Revolutionary Socialism is a decaying force in modern Germany, and the more moderate Revisionist movement, which does not fear the Greeks, even when they bring gifts, has made such strides, especially in the south, that it has threatened to split the party. Of an immediately United Left there is indeed only the faintest possibility, but union is in the air.

SCIENCE AT WINNIPEG.

THE President of the British Association opened his address at Winnipeg by saying the correct and inevitable things about science and what is called Imperialism. Until five-and-twenty years ago, the meetings of the Association had always been held in the British Isles; in 1884 the Society went to Montreal and since then has visited Toronto and South Africa. The number of scientific men who can attend meetings at these great distances is necessarily limited, but the arrangements of the Association provide that a representative selection is present, and it is good both for the visitors and the colonists that the word British should be given its extended meaning. Science itself is international, but the organisations engaged in advancing it must for long remain chiefly national. The President, remembering that he was a Cambridge professor as well as a physicist, seized the occasion of the great publicity of a Presidential Address to ventilate a problem specially acute at Cambridge, but not unknown elsewhere. In Sir Joseph Thomson's opinion the £35,000 a year given at Cambridge in scholarships does great harm to the competing schools and the successful scholars. The scholarships are awarded on the results of competition in practically a single subject in each case. The competing schools devote most of the time of their clever boys in the last year or two to the one subject in which they have most chance of being successful, and the selected scholars continue to specialise at Cambridge in that one subject. Thus they attain a very high standard of knowledge and a very low grade of education. The competitive taint reaches further than the regions discussed by the President. The Colleges compete for the clever specialised boys with the object of showing well in the University honours list. Perhaps on his return from Canada Sir Joseph will continue his attack in Cambridge itself; for, after all, it is a Cambridge problem, to be settled in Cambridge.

There was nothing local about the body of the President's address. He dealt with the problems of matter and force, of the texture of space and the forces that sway it, and pointed to the vast revolution that is taking place in the fundamental conceptions of physics. The direction of events has been apparent for a good many years, even to those who are not expert physicists. In 1895 a writer in this REVIEW, discussing the addresses delivered at the meeting of the British Association in that year, showed how, largely from mathematical data, the old crude conceptions of a universe of atoms and molecules of matter played on by forces was being displaced, how the distinction between the elements and even the distinction between matter and force was breaking down. Since then, and chiefly on the experimental side, the progress of knowledge has been so unexpected and so exciting that the word "renascence" is more than appropriate. The discoveries that quickened physical science with new life and that gave a new and coherent meaning to a great array of detached and unco-ordinated observations and deductions came from the discovery and investigation of the Röntgen rays. These rays were found to excite phosphorescence in certain substances, particularly the salts of uranium, and Becquerel tried to find out if phosphorescence would produce the rays. He found that uranium salts, made phosphorescent by exposure to sunlight, gave out rays with properties similar to those of the Röntgen rays. Later on, however, it was found that the rays were given out even if the salts had been kept in the dark, and that they were a property of the metal itself and not of the phosphorescent condition. Soon afterwards thorium was shown to have similar properties, and still later came the great discovery of M. and Mme. Curie of two new substances, radium and polonium, with enormously more powerful radiation. Still later, Rutherford, in Canada, found that an enormous number of substances were radio-active. Thus an experiment, in itself futile, but diligently pursued, led by a side issue to discoveries of enormous importance.

Further investigation of radio-active substances led to results still more unexpected and significant. Crookes showed that there could be separated from uranium something that was radio-active, leaving the uranium itself negative in this respect. Becquerel followed by showing that the separated radio-active material soon lost its powers, and that the neutral body re-acquired activity, and Rutherford and Soddy elaborated the theory, now fairly well established, that radio-active elements are not permanent but are gradually breaking up into elements of lower atomic weight. They are not immortal, but have a range of life varying from thousands of millions of years in the case of uranium to a few seconds in the case of the gaseous emanation from actinium. And they are vast reservoirs of energy, some of the energy being set free with each emanation. The quantity of energy stored in this fashion suggests some interesting side issues. A gramme of radium is capable of producing as much energy as would be set free in burning a ton of coal. These considerations have an important bearing on the age of the earth, a subject that has been discussed frequently at meetings of the Association. When biologists, in the early days of evolution, were speculating as to the formation of the existing plants and animals by the slow accumulation of small modifications, they were accused of making unlimited drafts on the bank of time, and the physicists calculating the age of the earth on the basis that it was slowly losing its primitive heat by radiation into space, were inclined to dishonour such drafts. It is plain that the presence of radium in the crust of the earth completely destroys the basis on which physicists formerly made their estimates. The question, however, is only of academic interest from the point of view of evolution; as the successive strata actually show the succession of life, say from lower to higher mammals, it is plain that there must have been time enough for the change to take place.

We must now look on matter with new eyes. The old phrases as to inert matter, and so forth, and the old ideas of permanent, indestructible elements have disappeared, to be replaced by conceptions of matter as undergoing ceaseless change and as being inseparable from the conception of energy. On the other hand, the new knowledge of electricity, set forth in plain language by Sir Joseph Thomson, further breaks down the distinction between matter and energy. For now the structure of electricity can be spoken of and described. Negative electricity is particulate, consisting of innumerable units all of the same kind and exceedingly small, compared with the smallest atom; and the evidence is at least pointing towards a conception of positive electricity as also particulate, although the particles must be different and probably much larger. Then, again, the ether, formerly regarded as not much more than a useful hypothesis, is now to be accepted as a definite, ponderable substance capable of acquiring and losing momentum. Molecules, atoms and corpuscles, the various forms of energy and the various forms of matter, are gradually appearing simply as different phases or conditions of a continuous whole.

Scientific men are themselves only beginning to grasp the bearing of the new conceptions of the cosmos towards which the advances in physical science are tending, and they themselves, as well as the general public, are much indebted to the President of the British Association for his luminous synthesis of the tendencies of modern science. But it is to be observed, notwithstanding the vapourings of those who invoke every wonderful discovery of radium or Röntgen rays or wireless telegraphy as in some strange fashion making science less materialistic, that every advance towards scientific monism, whilst it leaves untouched the ultimate conceptions of theology, leaves less real ground for the silliness of pseudo-scientific mysticism.

THE CITY.

WHATEVER the cause, the fact is indisputable that a great many people are investing their capital in the bonds of foreign Governments, especially in South America. Politicians, of the Conservative kidney, will tell you that the reason is that foreign bonds are mostly "bearer" securities, that is, bonds with coupons attached, passed by hand, and that in these Lloyd-Georgian days people think it safer. Undoubtedly inscribed or registered securities, such as are the bonds of all British and colonial and municipal authorities, take the income tax off at the source, and are traceable in a manner that cannot be denied to the authorities of Somerset House. Another explanation is however possible, and even probable, namely, that foreign bonds pay a higher rate of interest. When a man gets 5 per cent. from Russian, Chinese, Japanese, and Argentine bonds, why should he put up with 3½ per cent. from British, colonial, Indian, or municipal securities? It is not, perhaps, realised by those who write about gilt-edged securities how great is the pressure upon the ordinary man (and woman) to get a higher rate of interest than formerly. The cost of living is much higher than it was, not only by reason of the higher standard of luxury, but also because food and servants are dearer. Add to this the increased income tax and the ever-increasing local rates, and it will be seen that the man who was drawing £1500 a year from a capital of £50,000 is almost forced nowadays to invest it so as to bring him in £2500 a year, if he is to continue living in the same style as before. This is much to be regretted. We dislike this constant investment of British capital in foreign securities, not only on patriotic grounds but because we foresee the day when a great deal of this capital will be lost, and great misery caused thereby. A business man may, but the ordinary person cannot, get 5 per cent. on foreign bonds with safety. We have no belief in the capacity or even in the intention of all the South American Governments to meet their engagements punctually. Argentina, Brazil, Uruguay, are all flourishing to-day: they will not always flourish, and then there will be trouble. The same remark applies to Japanese securities, particularly municipal bonds. We have no great confidence in the good faith in money matters of the Japanese, and municipalities like Osaka, Kobe, Tokio, and Yokohama have all been borrowing freely. The interest on these loans must be paid out of rates, and there may come a day when rates cannot or will not be paid by the ordinary Japanese occupier. Many people have a touching faith in the honour of the Chinaman, justified, we agree, by the character of individual Celestials. But Chinese finances are drifting into chaos, and in high finance it is not the individual Chinaman that has to be dealt with, but mandarins and the Government. Russia, again, has never defaulted: but it is difficult to say what might not happen if there were to be a real Russian revolution.

We agree with some of our contemporaries that the gambling in Union and Southern Pacifics has been rather a disgusting affair. As the Union Pacific dividend just declared is at the usual rate, it is obvious that there is no real justification for the sensational rise, and all the rumours about Mr. Harriman's health have been nauseating; playing poker on the prospective coffin of a magnate, as somebody said. We have all along told our readers that we knew nothing about the antics of Wall Street, and that a man who gambles in Yankee rails, unless he is in a ring of three or four men, may just as well play pitch-and-toss. The misfortune is (and it is a calamity) that a large section of the clever and vigorous American nation spend all their time and brains in gambling in American railway shares and bonds. Union Pacifics have fallen from 225 to 210, and seem likely to remain there for the present, but we do not know. Steel Commons have fallen from 81 to 78.

In the Mining markets there has been absolute stagnation. Alaska Mexicans have paid a handsome dividend, and risen to 3⅞, their real value being nearer 7. Alaska Treadwells remain about 7, and are probably paid for. In the Kaffir market Gold Fields are the only shares with any life, and dodge about just under 7. Crown Mines have paid a dividend at the rate of 120 per cent. National Minerals remain unchanged at 12s. 6d., and as yet the rise to £1 predicted by the chairman has not materialised. We have heard nothing of the results of the process, for treating refractory ore, which is to knock spots out of Murex Magnetic.

INSURANCE: POLICIES AT LOW PREMIUMS.

IV.

We have already explained various forms of policies which can be obtained at low premiums. In doing so we have discussed the relative merits of policies that do and policies that do not share in the profits of a life office. We hope we made it clear that the selection of a participating or non-participating policy is largely a question of whether the largest possible provision in the event of early death is the important consideration, or whether a good return at some comparatively distant future for money invested is the more desirable.

All life assurance policies which require the payment of premiums throughout the whole of life may be considered to be policies at low premiums, but among participating policies there are very considerable differences in the cost. Thus a man of forty, for the assurance of £1000 at death, may pay as much as £39 10s. or as little as £28 5s. In both cases he shares in the profits of the life office. Clearly he cannot expect to receive such large bonuses for the small premium as he does for the large. Thus there is introduced not merely the question of the bonus systems adopted by different offices, but the relative merits of companies from a profit-sharing point of view. The low rate of premium just quoted, £28 5s. for an assurance of £1000, is that of the Scottish Provident Institution, which, since its foundation in 1837, has made a point of charging extremely low rates of premium and deferring participation in the profits until the premiums paid accumulated at four per cent. compound interest amount to the sum assured. This, of course, has the effect of assuring a much larger sum from the outset for a given premium than could be obtained if a higher rate of premium were paid. Thus, if the annual premium were £100 a year, the sum assured would be £3540 if the annual cost of assuring £1000 were £28 5s., and would be only £2532 if the premium for a £1000 policy were £39 10s. There is seen to be a guaranteed addition to the sum assured of £1008.

Very similar considerations to those which arise in connection with non-profit and with-profit policies occur in connection with low and high rates of premium for participating assurance. If the assured dies soon, his estate gains greatly by the low-premium policy having been selected. If, however, he lives a great many years, the high-premium policy yields a considerably larger sum at death. Here again it must be recognised that the value of insurance protection for the £1008 of difference between the sums assured under the two policies is a thing of definite commercial value, not the less valuable and worth paying for because the man happens to live a long time. We may repeat that this life assurance protection in the case of those who do not happen to die soon is just as well worth paying for as fire insurance protection is worth paying for, even though no fire happens.

Although the strongest life offices, which in the nature of things yield the most profitable results to policy-holders, have on the whole well maintained their rate of bonus in recent years, it is impossible to overlook the chance that the profits in the future may be less than in the past, partly because of a tendency to depreciation in capital value, and partly, it is to be feared, as a result of financial legislation. The life offices have protested against some of the Budget proposals, and though to a slight extent some of their objections have been met, it seems extremely probable that they will be adversely affected in the event of the present Finance Bill becoming law. Life assurance companies, particularly those doing life business only, are subject to very unfair treatment in the matter of income tax. They have to pay upon their interest earnings instead of only upon profits, and the inequity of this arrangement is increased when the income tax is raised. Hence for various reasons the attractiveness of what may be called the guaranteed bonus, which results from low rates of premium, becomes more pronounced than it used to be, because there is little chance of the bonuses of any life office being much larger than before, and a very considerable probability that future bonuses will be at a lower rate than they have been in the past.

LICENCES AND THE FINANCE BILL.

By George Cave K.C. M.P.

AT last Part I. of the Finance Bill (Duties on Land Values) has been partly rewritten and partly postponed, and the discussion on Part II. (Duties on Liquor Licences) is in sight. This discussion, according to the Prime Minister, is to be " short, sharp and decisive ", and it may be worth while to consider what it will decide.

Putting aside the duties on manufacturers and others, which are not the subject of this paper, and the duties on off-licences, which are, it is understood, to be reconsidered, the proposals affect (1) retailers of beer and spirits on the premises (including keepers of hotels and restaurants having on-licences) and (2) clubs in which intoxicating liquor is supplied. The annual duty on a full on-licence, which now varies according to the value of the premises from a minimum of £4 10s. to a maximum of £60, is to be raised to half the gross annual value, with a minimum based on population; but in the case of an hotel or restaurant in which the liquor trade is less than one-third of the whole a reduction is to be made. The annual duty on a beerhouse licence, which is now fixed at £3 10s., is to be raised to one-third of the annual value, with a like minimum. Clubs are to pay threepence in the pound on their receipts from the sale of intoxicants. Translating these abstractions into concrete examples, a full on-licence holder assessed at £100 who now pays £25 per annum will pay £50, one assessed at £200 will pay £100 instead of £30, one assessed at £500 will be raised from £45 to £250, and one assessed at between £700 and £1500 will find his annual charge increased from £60 to from £350 to £750 according to the rental value of his house. In the case of houses assessed at £700 or upwards an option is given to pay on " compensation value ", but the relief so offered is of very uncertain value. Hotel-keepers will, notwithstanding the contingent reduction allowed, suffer heavily, the duty imposed on the larger hotels amounting to thousands of pounds. The beerhouses, where profits are usually small, will have their duty multiplied many times over. It needs no great exercise of imagination to see that these heavy charges suddenly imposed must in many cases eat up the profits of these small tradesmen, and there are probably few members of Parliament whose letter-bag does not bring to their notice cogent instances (supported by names and figures) of the impending ruin. In the case of houses which are " tied " to brewers or distillers some part (not yet defined) of the extra duty can be thrown on the firms which supply the liquors, and certain large brewing firms have calculated the additional charge falling upon them (including the manufacturers' duty), one at £25,000 per annum, another at £33,000, another at £49,000, and two others (whose ordinary dividend amounted last year to £61,000) at £104,000. But holders of free houses, with no large firms behind them, will be the first to feel the pinch and to go under. In short, if the Bill stands, many thousands of traders must shut up shop, lose their capital and start afresh.

In contemplating these proposals the first question which occurs is, Why is it done? The liquor trade produced for the Chancellor of the Exchequer last year 38½ millions out of a total taxation of 130¼ millions. He desires to call upon this rapidly falling industry for a further £4,200,000, of which he proposes to raise £1,600,000 by an increase in the spirit duty. He might raise the balance of £2,600,000 by an increase of from 1s. 6d. to 2s. per barrel in the beer duty; and although there might be some grumbling, no great harm would be done. Or he might treat the licensed houses as he proposes to treat the clubs, and a poundage of 6d. on all retail sales would give him what he requires. Why, then, does he prefer a tangle of oppressive and ruinous charges on a limited number of individuals? The answer is to be found in a study of very recent history. On 27 November 1908, the House of Lords, by a majority of 272 to 96, rejected the Licensing Bill, mainly on the ground that the Bill proposed to close a number of houses on payment of a grossly insufficient compensation, and after a " period of grace " of twenty-one years to confiscate to the State the goodwill of the surviving houses. Thereupon the hearts of Ministers, according to Mr. McKenna, were " filled with rage ". They dared not advise an appeal to the country, for, by the admission of their spokesmen, the country was against them. But there was a better way. Mr. Lloyd George, speaking in September, said: " Even if the Bill be rejected, we are by no means at the end of our resources "; and after the fate of the Bill had been ascertained Mr. McKenna gave the interpretation of the Chancellor's declaration. " It is ", he said, " surprisingly simple. . . . If the House of Lords will not let you deal with a certain subject in the ordinary way by an ordinary Bill, then you will agree that the House of Commons are more than justified in dealing with the same subject in such a way that the House of Lords cannot refuse their assent. . . . It is open to us now, through the means of taxation, not only to raise a great deal of money, but indirectly by the very act of raising money from the taxation of licences to effect one of the main objects of the Bill—the reduction of superfluous licensed premises ". Mr. Ure, then Solicitor-General for Scotland, bluntly advocated a " swingeing duty " on all licences. Mr. Churchill gleefully prophesied that the licensed trade would find that they had " leaped from the frying-pan into the fire ". And Mr. J. A. Pease, the Liberal Chief Whip, gave the necessary socialistic tinge to these prophecies when he said " I imagine that people will expect that Mr. Lloyd George will cause the abolition of the redundant licences by placing taxation on them, so that the people may get back their own ". To put it shortly, the Government determined to reintroduce the Licensing Bill as part of their next Budget and so to close the weak houses and annex the profits of the remainder without compensation or time limit.

The Chancellor's speech at the Law Society (and those who are attracted by the interesting study of the effect produced on a speaker by his audience may profitably compare it with the speech delivered at Limehouse), disclaimed any desire to use the Budget for vindictive purposes; and doubtless he would say that he is not acting vindictively, but is merely " dealing with the licensing question by financial means ". In the course of the recent Swansea School case it was said by one of the judges that, " had the local education authority designed to degrade and disorganise the school, they could have taken no more likely means to that end than those dictated to them by their sense of public duty ". And similarly it may be said of the Chancellor of the Exchequer that, had he intended to revenge his defeat of last autumn by a merciless blow at the brewer and the publican, he would have adopted the course which has, in fact, been suggested to him by an unbiassed consideration of the needs of the Revenue. Whether, when the necessary results are pointed out to him, he will persist in this course, or will seek a juster way, is one of the questions which the coming debate will decide.

THE FUTURE OF THE ZOOLOGICAL SOCIETY.

By Dr. P. Chalmers Mitchell F.R.S.

II.

THE Council of the Zoological Society has obviously reverted to the opinion of its predecessor of 1847 that the distinctive and specific function of the Society must be care of the living collection of animals. There was much lost ground to recover, and old buildings, old methods and want of funds made the difficulties serious. But in the last five or six years the task had been grappled with zealously and with a great measure of success. Precisely as in 1847, the new policy has not only largely increased the income at the disposal of the Society but has brought new life and an extended scope to the scientific side. We need not dwell on such changes as a renewed attention on the part of the governing body must have suggested at once. The air of better discipline, more sedulous attention to cleanliness and upkeep of woodwork and ironwork, and the general improved smartness and efficiency imply care rather than knowledge, watchfulness than design. What is of greater interest is the evidence that new ideals as to the housing and display of animals are at work.

The new buildings and enclosures show a tendency to give their occupants more space, more fresh air and more liberty. The idea that animals must be sheltered from every wind that blows and kept at an evenly high temperature has been displaced by the conceptions that air and light are of fundamental value, and that inhabitants even of the tropics require the stimulation of changes of temperature, of rain and wind. The old view of ranging creatures in small dens, liked stuffed animals in a museum, so that their markings and points might be compared, has yielded to the desire to place them under such conditions that they may display at least some part of the characteristic business of their lives.

The parrots were formerly restricted to cages or chained to perches. A large flight cage has now been provided, in which macaws, cockatoos, and many parrakeets have abundant room to fly, and of which a few have shown their appreciation by breeding. Smaller outdoor compartments have been added to the south side of the parrot-house. Gulls, cormorants and herons, which formerly had their wings clipped and were confined to small enclosures, have now been given a huge aviary roofed with wire-netting, and containing trees, rockwork, and ponds. The penguins have been taken from their hutches and placed in the sea-lions' enclosure, where they have repeatedly bred. The new covered aviary for wading birds is one of the most successful innovations, and contains, almost at full liberty, redshanks and plovers, avocets and curlews, ruffs and reeves which dabble on the sandy margin of their pool or whistle and pipe amongst the reeds. Cranes and bustards, storks and secretary birds are now to be seen stalking in large enclosures. So far the birds of prey have not received adequate treatment. The owls, formerly imprisoned in dark and sunless cells, now take full advantage of their new opportunities of air and light, and some of the smaller hawks have been given better accommodation; but the eagles and vultures remain most inappropriately housed. No doubt their turn will come. The small perching birds and birds of paradise, of which the Society has been able recently to give an unrivalled display, have been given an extremely well-arranged house.

Amongst mammals, changes of the same order have been in progress. The new deer and cattle sheds have yards sufficiently large for the animals to be seen at a distance, and the paddocks recently added from the park are quite spacious. The elands and some of the larger antelopes have been provided with a spacious sandy enclosure with trees, rockwork and water. The kangaroos, or at least some of them, have been given paddocks; when a pair of the very rare and interesting tree-kangaroos recently arrived, instead of being placed in a box-like cage, they were put in the new squirrels' enclosure, on the trees of which they could display their apparently unnatural and clumsy agility, thus affording one of the most curious sights that has ever been witnessed in London. The seals and sea-lions have now an almost ideal habitation. The lions and tigers have been given permanent bridges placing their indoor quarters in communication with the outdoor yards. The dogs and wolves have had their house transformed to quarters that are at least tolerable. It has been announced publicly that new quarters are to be provided for the bears, lemurs and many of the smaller mammals.

The London Gardens, like many old institutions, have grown up without any general plan. New houses and enclosures have been set up in situations apparently selected only from temporary convenience, with the result that similar creatures are scattered over the whole of the area available, and a visitor who wishes to see, say, the complete collection of antelopes or deer, must traverse the greater part of the Gardens. It is proposed to amend this want of arrangement as quickly as possible and to bring together kindred animals. At the same time a rearrangement of the Garden staff is in progress. Formerly the superintendent was in immediate charge of the whole collection; under him the assistant-superintendent, and under him again the head-keeper, were responsible for everything connected with the menagerie. In future the mammals are to be in charge of a chief officer, the curator of mammals, and the animals under his control are to be grouped in divisions, such as large carnivora, deer, cattle, antelopes, monkeys and so forth, each division having its own head-keeper and a staff of keepers and helpers. A similar arrangement has been made for birds, under a curator of birds; whilst a curator of reptiles is to be provided later. Thus the responsibility for the well-being of the living animals will be more definitely assigned with a consequent closer care and attention.

A serious and unexpected difficulty in construction lies in the way of attaining the best results at the London Gardens. Plans for buildings have to conform with the provisions of the London Building Acts. These provisions, designed to protect a great human population crowded on a limited area, and with special reference to the wiles of the jerry builder, have none of the flexibility necessary if new materials, modes of construction and design are to be tried, whilst their chief objective is incongruous with the ideal arrangement for animals. Buildings for human beings are intended to last for many years; buildings for animals should be of such a design and such materials that they can be scrapped without regard to initial cost. However carefully sanitation may be attended to, the soil on which the buildings are placed and the materials themselves become contaminated, and new houses on new parts of the enclosure should be provided at intervals. Moreover, under ideal circumstances, there should be, so to say, a rotation of animals, a part of the Gardens occupied by one kind of animals being given up, after a few years, to another kind, with the consequent complete change of buildings. Finally, the application of scientific knowledge to the proper housing of animals is so new that it ought to be experimental, and money ought not to be wasted on such expensive permanent buildings as are contemplated by the London Building Acts.

Regent's Park, on a clay soil, in the smoky atmosphere of a great city, can never be an ideal place for animals, and there have been rumours and suggestions as to the transplantation of the Zoological Gardens to a locality with fewer disadvantages. Such rumours, for the present at least, may be dismissed. So long as the Society derives its income from Fellows and the public, the Gardens must be as near Central London as possible; and even if the large sum required for laying out new ground and erecting new buildings could be obtained, and if permission were granted, there would be no great advantage in moving to another of the London parks, whilst transference to Richmond Park, the Crystal Palace, or somewhere near Hampstead or Highgate would be a dangerous experiment financially, and no great gain from the point of view of soil and climate. But there is an alternative that the Society no doubt will bear in mind. There is still cheap and good land to be obtained within twenty or thirty miles of London. The Society ought to acquire several hundred acres of such land and gradually develop it, not as a zoological exhibition for visitors, but as a farm for growing suitable food and a breeding and recuperating ground for animals. The abundant space, freedom from disturbance, and seclusion required by breeding animals are conditions almost impossible to combine with arrangements for exhibiting animals to the public. The shelters and enclosures on such a farm would be more simple and less costly than those required on grounds open to the public and intended to attract visitors. The country quarters would serve admirably for experimental work in cross-breeding and acclimatisation, and would form a reservoir from which the exhibition grounds in Regent's Park could be kept supplied.

A NOTE ON "BLANCO POSNET".

By Lord Dunsany.

A LARGE crowd assembled last Wednesday night outside the Abbey Street Theatre, like Jonah outside the walls of Nineveh, to see what would happen to it.

It appeared that Mr. Shaw had called a spade an agricultural implement, instead of using vaguer and more devious language, though he had since agreed to leave out the word "agricultural" to oblige the Lord Lieutenant. There was even worse than this, though nobody knew what.

Before their horrified eyes we went in to fill every seat and to hear the profanity of Mr. Shaw; to hear "The Showing-up of Blanco Posnet," forbidden in England for blasphemy and indecency, and not by any supersensitive puritan, but by the Censor who had already passed so many musical comedies.

Besides those who were attracted by the horror of what they would hear, many came to judge between the views of Mr. Shaw and the Censor on the subject of decorum, and there came, too, old audiences loyal to their national theatre, among them a man who boasted a scar from former wars in the shape of a gap where two teeth should have been, lost when they tried to wreck the theatre as a protest against Synge's "Playboy". "Ah, Synge was a great man", he said regretfully; "and we were very drunk". Everyone knows what happened. The company acted splendidly, especially Mr. O'Donovan; the play was welcomed tumultuously as a huge success, the patent of the theatre was no longer in danger, the years of Mr. Gates' patriotic work and Lady Gregory's would not be wasted; but those hardened sinners who had endured in the street the banners of the Puritans, and had walked on boldly to hear blasphemy, were disappointed men. They had heard blasphemy better done in any public-house, and they had paid four shillings for every seat in the pit; not only this, but they had listened to a sermon, hopelessly moral and elevating.

I think that the reason for the terrible reputation that this truly religious play has brought from England is that a great number of Englishmen attach an intrinsic value to words while Irishmen more often look to the idea that those words represent. And so sometimes a man sees a "bad word" in a play, and he says, "This must be an immoral play": he probably prefers his immorality in the form of suggestion, finding it thus more easily digestible when he turns it over and chews it in his imagination; it is the form in which the modern English stage is accustomed to give it to him.

Such few words as have been left out of this play for fear of "shocking the nation" (a phrase of Mr. Shaw's) leave the play where it was before, the thought that those words represent remains unaltered; it is like tearing off a very small piece from a £5 note; it is like leaving out the last three letters of the word "damn", whereby many writers hope to attain to Heaven when they die. When England's taste for song found vent in the last lines of "Limericks" a joke about a sea-gull seeing the sea would have pleased millions, but that conveys nothing to us over here; the idea is judged on its merits. One might write an abominably pernicious play using only words that one had heard in a sermon.

The idea of Mr. Shaw's play is a good one and has been appreciated here as it deserves.

And now as I write that tide of human thought that waits for no man is setting eastwards—I mean the Irish mail which is due to leave Westland Row at 7.45. It waits for no man, but an additional halfpenny stamp may sometimes overtake it.

LETTERS FROM SOLITUDE.

By Filson Young.

I.

. . . . Connemara.

Like many of my generation, I have lost the art of writing letters, and with it, I am sure, a certain fulness of life that accompanies the communication of one's thoughts to friends at a distance. There are certain things, often trivial but nearly always interesting, that can only be written in letters; one cannot make articles or poems or books out of them—at least I cannot; and at present I find that they are the only things I want to say. And as the first quality of a letter is that it is addressed to someone in particular, and not to everyone in general; that one is sure of a sympathetic interest and understanding at the receiving end; so I am going to write these letters to four people; sometimes I shall be speaking to one, and sometimes to another; but the one who is addressed will always know. They are all women, of course—at my age one does not write long letters to a man; two of them are old and two are fairly young; but as their ages in the aggregate amount to more than two hundred years, I shall not be accused of frivolity. But why publish them in the Saturday Review? you say. Alas, it is my desolate habit not to be able to write otherwise than for publication. I could not write an article or a book on the chance of its being published—I have to know first that what I write will be published and read; and if I were to write to my four friends privately my letters would be scrappy notes, and tell them nothing. It is not a pretty trait, that; I do not excuse it; perhaps it is because I have always made my living by writing, and associate all writing with labour. Another explanation, and certainly a more agreeable one, is that I am saddled with the artist's need for expression. I have always had it and, as one of you well knows who watched me through that time, for years expressed myself in music; but as my music was seldom published or played, I forsook music for a means of expression in which I have had more success. Some people are like human gramophone-disks, always ready to experience something, and then anxious to tell the world about it. If they are pleased or annoyed, made happy or hurt, their first instinct is to give expression to their sensations. It is an instinct which one learns with years to hold in check; things ripen of themselves within one, and, sweet or bitter, come to fruit in their own good time. I will exercise my machinery of expression with these letters, which will at any rate interest the four friends to whom I write them, and may afford some innocent pastime for those who like reading other people's letters.

And first let me tell you why I am here, at the western extremity of Ireland, miles and miles from anything in the shape of a village, where, unless I fish for trout, there is nothing for me to do and no one for me to speak to. A certain amount of solitude is necessary to the soul's health, but one too easily loses the art of being alone; I lose it very quickly. The life of London or of any metropolis soon engenders in me a kind of panic terror of being bored, which means that in this state of disease one is bored if one is alone. So every minute is filled up, wisely or unwisely; nightly as one unfolds one's dinner napkin, one screws oneself up to the concert pitch, and takes a part in the busy orchestra; and having played till one is tired, has no inclination for a solitary performance. This is a thoroughly unhealthy state of affairs—a fact which was made painfully apparent to me by the horror and boredom with which at first I viewed my noble and desolate surroundings. I felt like a street-arab set to play in an empty field. So I mean to stay here until I have learned once more to be alone. I have to do it constantly, and have tried it in many places; and as some people go to a spring every year to take a cure for some bodily ailment, so I find that every year now I must take this cure of solitude until I have learned not to shun my own thoughts, and not to find every kind of life but the set scenes of society fatiguing. I feel them fatiguing enough, God knows, and pretend to despise them; but they are the easiest kind of life. It is harder to think one's own thoughts than to play with the thoughts of others.

It is not so easy to find a solitude where life is tolerable. I know Ireland very well, but not from the hotel point of view, and there are many Irish hotels, alas! where even one's narrow bed may not be solitude. I wanted air that would brace and not enervate, a freedom from tennis-players and golf-talkers, simple food and clean lodging, a room to work in and the life of men and women around me to observe, if not to take part in. Well, I went to one hotel on the north-east coast, and was told it was just the thing. It took half a day to get there; I arrived late in the afternoon and fled the next morning; and the hours I spent there seemed like years of my life. The place was not a real place, but the fond dream and invention of a railway company. It lay at the end of a great spit of arable land, and consisted of a railway station, a wharf constructed to contain one passenger steamer, two streets of cottages built by the company for their employees, an electric generating station (for the hotel), a laundry (for the hotel and steamers), and a golf links. The hotel lawn was fenced with sleepers, like a station approach, and there were only two ways of getting out of the hotel. One led directly to an opening in the quay wall, so that if the steamer was not there to catch you you fell into the water, and the other led into the railway station. The road from the station led to the golf-links. I hate golf; I could not go and look at the steamer without taking a ticket for England, for it was jealously screened from view by the hotel wall; the laundry was not working, there was a notice saying "No Admittance" to the electric-light works, so I went back to the hotel and dined in extreme misery, ashamed of my silence amid the loud talk of what was perhaps the most abandoned company of golfers I have ever seen. Bright and early next morning I went out by the railway door and returned to Dublin, and took fresh counsel; and as a result here I am at the opposite extremity of Ireland, far from railways and hotels, and farther still from golf.

None of you knows Connemara, so I must try and give you some pictures of my surroundings, though I will not attempt to describe the grandeur and desolation of this great barren glacial country, with its magnificent mountain range in the centre, and interminable vistas of rocky bog-land broken by a thousand in-reaching arms of the sea. But this sea is not like any sea that you know; no traffic comes or goes upon it; hardly a fisherman fishes in its teeming waters; it is far from the open Atlantic, shallow, and strewn with half-tide rocks covered with golden seaweed. The cabins along its shores are so tiny and so scattered that only an accustomed eye would discover their existence; life everywhere is sad and silent, and the attempts at cultivating some little patch among the rocks, and raising a crop of oats or potatoes, are miserable and heartbreaking. All the hills, all the plains that you can see are a sad green dotted with grey; there is as much grey as green; the grey is rock, and the green is the bitter useless grass that grows on the bog. Here and there are little chocolate mounds where the turf has been cut and stacked for fuel. One winding white road leads to the railway fourteen miles away. The railway will take you to Galway in two hours; from Galway to Dublin is three or four more hours; from Dublin to Holyhead is eighty miles, and from Holyhead to the nearest of you is a long way.

You see already the first effect of solitude—to send one's thoughts out, as Noah's dove went out, to find some sign of a place where they may rest. I will tell you in another letter something of how life goes here; but now the mountains are taking on their evening colour—the mauve behind the black, the grey behind the mauve, and the farthest of all, behind the grey, a mere shadow wavering in the sky. The sun is setting, and the bell from the little convent is ringing for Compline. I will not go to Compline, but I will alter a word of the salutation with which it is begun, and say to each of you, "Pray, madam, a blessing".

THE SPLENDID CRANK.

"DO well unto thyself and all men will speak well of thee" said the Psalmist. One might rather have expected this from the Preacher; yet it is too well observed, too true, to be the gibe of a cynic. The crank does not do well unto himself; hence men are not inclined to do well unto him. He is not as other men; therefore he must be mad. He does not think first of himself; therefore he must be madder. He aims at something the world cannot understand; therefore let the world persecute him. The ordinary motives of men will not explain his actions; he is uncanny. In an eternally true sense he is not all here; therefore the vulgar say he is not all here in their sense. He is out of the common; and should for that be shut out of the community. Either he is deficient—the ill, the maimed animal to be hunted by all the pack of well ones; or he is something too great and good for human nature's daily food—he must be laughed down. He is a constant protest; who can stand him? He is an Ugly Duckling; let us make his life a misery while we can. He may turn out a swan, as Julius Cæsar did, and then we shall not be able to worry him. It will be for him to worry us; but, being a crank, he will not worry us. He will forget what we did and give us a chance to murder him, which we will be careful to take.

The crank is a fool; he is always a fool; but no one calls him stupid. We all know he is not stupid. Were he stupid, he would not be a crank. We should understand him if he were stupid; we could sympathise with him; could like him, and like him the more for being a little less than one of us. But it is not that he has less than we; it is rather that he has something we have not; something that comes between him and us. We cannot belittle him; we dare not sneer at him. What we can do is try to laugh him out of his difference from us, or laugh his difference from us out of him. Crank is not an ill-natured term; it is good-humoured rather. It is at first a note of unintelligibleness; a shrug of the shoulder; it is giving him up as impossible. We must leave him to his ways: he to go one way, the world another. And if he does go one way and the world another, it is better perhaps for the peace of both; better for the comfort of either. But we are seldom able to part with him in that easy fashion; and he too can seldom leave the world alone. The unwelcome insistent feeling that he is something greater than we begins to irk us. Why can he not leave us alone? We can no longer good-humouredly tolerate him; we cannot treat him as a thing not responsible, a thing to be pitied. He will not be pitied; he rather pities us; which is maddening. This crank, who lives in the clouds, who hunts shadows forgetting the substance, pities us common-sense men who know so well how to look after ourselves! It is too much. And a new attitude to the splendid crank is gradually assumed. The consciousness that there is a splendour about him ferments within us. We jeer at S. Simeon on his pillar: but we know that we could not have done it. We would not if we could; perhaps: but it is very much more certain that we could not if we would. Simeon was ridiculous, but he was a greater man than we. The crank is generally a failure, apparently; and his very failure, while it provokes our contempt, provokes even more our respect. Who is not stirred more by the bones of Mr. Cunninghame Graham's Spanish captain* dead for a forlorn hope, a lost cause, than by a thousand prosperous careers? Ultimately the splendid crank either invincibly attracts or repels utterly. Laughter and contempt become love or hatred. Either we surrender or we rebel; become the disciple or the assassin. When a man is called a crank, we may be quite sure there is something great about him. "He was a crank." There is the contemporary epitaph on the world's greatest men, and it was precisely the average cultivated Roman's on Jesus Christ.

* In "Success" (Duckworth).

A WEST AFRICAN RIVER.

By E. A. Brackenbury.

FROM the borders of the German colony of Kamerun to the junction with the Niger at Lokoja the river Benue runs for some five hundred miles through British territory and forms the chief highway and trade route of the lower portion of Northern Nigeria. The rainy season usually begins in May, and the Benue steadily increases in volume during the next six months, attaining its greatest size in October. This is the time to choose if you wish to travel quickly on the river, for the fussy little stern-wheel steamers can then ascend the river, and have occasionally been able to traverse Kamerun and even reach the borders of French Congo near Lere.

But the deck of a stern-wheeler, travelling when the river is in flood, is not the best place from which to see and enjoy the Benue; for the surrounding country is flooded, the grass and reeds are at their tallest, and consequently much that is of interest is hidden. When the rains have finished and the river has dropped to its lowest level during the months of February, March, or April it is possible to see a good deal of the people, birds and animals living on its banks. The most comfortable conveyance at this time of year is a barge, which is not unlike a small houseboat, and is propelled by six or eight natives with long poles made of palm fronds. The barge is provided with a roof, and there is usually enough accommodation for one's native cook and "boys" in the stern; at each end is a raised deck on which the polers stand, two or more men who steer at the stern, and the remainder of the crew work on the forward deck, the captain of the barge sitting on the top of the roof to direct operations. The poles are like those used in punts on the Thames, but are a good deal lighter and are not shod with an iron tip, although they are sometimes bound at the ends with fibre to prevent their splitting; they are used exactly as a punt-pole, and as the bed of the river in most places consists of good firm gravel a fair rate of speed, particularly when going downstream, can be kept up.

At the end of the dry season the Benue is only about one-fourth of the size it attains in the rainy months, when in many places it is nearly a mile in width; the high banks are now separated from the stream by broad stretches of sand and gravel which form the happy hunting-grounds of birds and places of encampment for the Fulani cowherds, who bring their cattle at this time of year to feed on the grassy pastures near the great river. These cattle camps are quite a feature of the Upper Benue; lower down the river the tsetse flies swarm and make the keeping of cattle impossible: but similar encampments are made on the lower river by the fish-curers, who catch quantities of large fish, which are smoked and dried on the sandbanks. Of the cattle camps the most interesting are those of the Bororo Fulani, who represent the purest type of that curious race whose origin is so shrouded in mystery.

These Bororo live an entirely nomadic life, their stay in any place being limited by the quantity and quality of the grass and water suitable for their cattle. Their houses are the rudest kind of grass huts, fresh shelters being made at each encampment. They do not intermarry with the Fulani settled in the towns, who have a considerable strain of negro blood in their veins, but keep very much to themselves; nominally Mohammedans, their religion is, however, largely tinged with paganism, due possibly to the wild tribes among whom they wander. Their food consists almost entirely of milk and butter provided by their cattle; if grain or clothes are required, the women take their dairy produce to the neighbouring villages and barter it for native cloth, guinea-corn, or salt. They are engaged wholly in tending cattle and have no other arts or crafts. In appearance they are tall and slim, complexion yellowish-red, with straight black hair and aquiline features; presenting a great contrast to their negro neighbours.

On the banks of the Benue are numerous villages of the pagan tribes who make their living by fishing or hunting. Most of these peoples are of a low type, and are probably the aboriginal races of the country. They live in closely packed villages with houses of the well-known beehive type, and owing to their insanitary habits and improvident way of living they fall easy victims to epidemics and famine: for although tropical Africa is a most bounteous mother, yet famines are not unknown. A sudden plague of caterpillars or a shortage of rain is quite sufficient to reduce some of these river tribes to starvation; many of them rely entirely on one kind of crop, and if that fails they die.

Two other interesting races to be met with on the Benue are the Nupes and the Kakandas. These people are closely related, the Nupes claiming that the Kakandas were conquered by them; they intermarry and are the chief traders on the river. Their canoes are in evidence everywhere. The Nupes have flat-bottomed, square-ended punts, while the Kakanda canoes have sharp prows and slight keels, with numerous cross-pieces of wood joining the two sides of the canoe. In the centre of the Kakanda canoe is a mast flying a white flag shaped like a church banner, and there is a raised frame to which the cargo is lashed. Both Nupes and Kakandas live on their canoes; their wives and families accompany them on their trading trips with a varied assortment of live stock. Shelters of grass mats or pith screens are erected in the canoes, and are pitched on the sandbanks at night. Their chief cargo is salt, which they bring up from the Niger towns and sell on the Upper Benue for sheep, horses, grain, cloth or natron; the latter article is brought down in great slabs by Beriberi traders from near Lake Chad.

The birds of the Benue are a never-ending delight in the dry season. I am not an ornithologist, and can only give them their local names. Black spur-winged geese, knob-billed ducks and whistling teal are all common, but are wary and hard to approach. There are also many kinds of cranes, storks and waders, besides pelicans, ibises, egrets and a variety of plovers. Of the cranes the most beautiful are the "crown birds", with their yellow crests and wings of chocolate, black and white. One of the commonest little birds is the "Niger bird"; his plumage is a delightful symphony of French grey, black, white and buff. He is a most cheeky and officious person, and the way in which two of them will hustle and drive away a black-and-white crow, at least four times as large as themselves, is amusing to see. There are also flocks of bee-eaters, called by some of the natives "Saiihaiiaiki", probably in reference to their note, which live in holes in the banks of the river, much as sand-martins do in England. With their blue heads, magenta bodies, and forked tails they make a fine show in the bright sunshine; especially a flock of them at rest on a sandbank. Round the villages will be found pigeons and doves of different kinds, particularly the green fruit pigeon, with his beautiful pale yellow breast; he is a very swift flier, and by no means an easy mark; but if you can shoot him, he makes an excellent dish. Vultures and hawks abound, conspicuous among them a fine black-and-white fish hawk with a melodious cry; there are also many kingfishers of various sizes and colours.

From time to time antelopes, troops of baboons, and a few hippos may be seen. The hippos are often met with in family parties of three; father, mother and child, the little one showing off his powers of diving in a clumsy way to his delighted parents. Crocodiles are very numerous in some parts of the river, many of them of large size; and it is possible with luck to come across that strange beast the manatee, which looks like a fresh-water seal.

On the Upper Benue the country is for the most part open and park-like, with ranges of wooded hills running parallel to the stream; lower down the bush becomes denser and in places impenetrable. Travelling alone in a barge is apt to become slightly monotonous in spite of the varied life to be seen on the banks, and one eagerly welcomes the sight of another barge, which is perhaps bearing another white man in the opposite direction; a halt is called, books and papers exchanged, and if the newcomer has a gramophone so much the better. Some superior persons affect to despise the gramophone, and no doubt where better music is to be obtained the machine can be dispensed with; but in the wilds of Africa the gramophone is a perfect godsend: it cheers the homesick exile as nothing else can.

HOMELESS.

By W. H. Hudson.

At a remote spot in the West of England I got into an omnibus at the station to travel to a small town six or seven miles away. Just before we started a party of eight or ten queer-looking people came hurriedly up and climbed to the top seats. They were men and women, with two or three children, the women carelessly dressed, the men pale and long-haired, in ulsters of light colours and large patterns. When we had travelled two or three miles one of the outside passengers climbed down and came in to escape from the cold, and edged into a place opposite to mine. He was a little boy about seven years old, and he had a small, quaint face with a tired expression on it, and wore a soiled scarlet Turkish cap on his head, and a big pepper-and-salt overcoat heavily trimmed with old, ragged imitation astrachan. He was keenly alive to the sensation his entrance created among us when the loud buzz of conversation ceased very suddenly and all eyes were fixed on him; but he bore it very bravely, sitting back in his seat, rubbing his cold hands together, then burying them deep in his pockets and fixing his eyes on the roof. Soon the talk recommenced, and the little fellow, wishing to feel more free, took his hands out and tried to unbutton his coat. The top button—a big horn button—resisted the efforts he made with his stiff little fingers, so I undid it for him and threw the coat open, disclosing a blue jersey striped with red, green velvet knickerbockers, and black stockings, all soiled like the old scarlet flower-pot shaped cap. In his get-up he reminded me of a famous music-master and composer of my acquaintance, whose sense of harmony is very perfect with regard to sounds but in colours he takes pleasure in screaming discords. Imagine a big, long-haired man arrayed in a bottle-green coat, scarlet waistcoat, pink necktie, blue trousers, white hat, purple gloves, and yellow boots! If it were not for the fact that he wears his clothes a very long time and never has them brushed or the grease-spots taken out, the effect would be almost painful. But he selects his colours, whereas the poor little boy probably has no choice in the matter.

By and by the humorous gentlemen who sat on either side of him began to play him little tricks, one snatching off his scarlet cap and the other blowing on his neck. He laughed a little, just to show that he didn't object to a bit of fun at his expense, but when the annoyance was continued he put on a serious face, and folding up his cap thrust it into his overcoat pocket. He was not going to be made a butt of!

"Where is your home?" I asked him.

"I haven't got a home", he returned.

"What, no home! Where was your home when you had one?"

"I never had a home", he said. "I've always been travelling; but sometimes we stay a month in a place." Then, after an interval, he added: "I belong to a dramatic company".

"And do you ever go on the stage to act?" I asked.

"Yes", he returned, with a weary little sigh.

Then our journey came to an end, and we saw the doors and windows of the Working Men's Institute aflame with yellow placards announcing a series of sensational plays to be performed there.

The people on top came down and straggled off to the Institute, paying no attention to the small boy. "Let me advise you", I said, standing over him on the pavement, "to treat yourself to a stiff tumbler of hot grog after your cold ride", and at the same time I put my hand in my pocket.

He didn't smile, but at once held out his open hand. I put some pence in it, and clutching them he murmured "Thank you", and went after the others.

CORRESPONDENCE.

"A HEAVY TOLL."

To the Editor of the Saturday Review.

Sir,—I read Sir George Arthur's protest against your reviewer's remarks on the "heavy toll" on our Household Cavalry in Egypt in 1882 with some amusement, a feeling which I am sure will be shared by all soldiers who have any practical experience of the "wastage" of cavalry on active service. The two "affairs" near Ismailia on 24 August and at Mahsama on 25 August were part of the everyday work of mounted troops in war, for which one man killed and eleven wounded (eight of these only slightly) was surely nothing very terrible. So also with that other "heavy toll" at Kassassin on 28 August, when out of a regiment near 460 strong three men were killed and eight wounded.

The fact is that Sir George Arthur, true to the old, but now happily exploded, traditions of our cavalry, seems to imagine that the very important duties which fall to the mounted arm when not actually taking part in a "pitched battle" are "mere wastage" and "desultory skirmishing". It would no doubt be highly convenient if all the wastage in men and horses incurred by a cavalry which carries out properly its work could be avoided, so that all ranks could be preserved in undiminished strength until the traditional "pitched battle" was fought. The famous German cavalry general, Von Bernhardi, drily remarked of those who wish to obtain successes in war without wastage: "Advantages in war must be fought for, they cannot be filched". Sir Garnet Wolseley's spirited and decisive advance on Tel-el-Kebir and Cairo naturally enough entailed some casualties among the troops honoured with the task of clearing the way. Among these was our Household Cavalry, which had not been in action since Waterloo, and whose officers and men, owing to the nature of their service, certainly had no exceptional advantages as regards war training. That they did so well and suffered so little are alike greatly to their credit. But to talk of "a heavy toll" in their case is sheer nonsense.

Your obedient servant,
Grey Scout.

A SPLENDID OPPOSITION.

To the Editor of the Saturday Review.

Coton Grange, Shrewsbury, 24 August 1909.

Sir,—In summarising in your article on the Budget the concessions wrung from the Government by the Opposition, you have omitted the very important one of the practical exemption of agricultural land from the increment tax. It was on this point alone that the Administration was seriously threatened with a revolt of its own supporters; but the credit of exposing thoroughly the injustice of the tax belongs to Captain Pretyman.

Never did an Opposition do its work better than the present one in exposing the crudity and iniquity of some of the financial proposals of Mr. Lloyd George and his colleagues.

Yours truly,
J. Blevin.

"THE MISCHIEF-MAKER AT OXFORD."

To the Editor of the Saturday Review.

12 Boulter Street, Oxford, 21 August 1909.

Sir,—I have read your interesting article on the above subject, and think that there is a great deal to be said for that side of the question. Dr. Evans is evidently a supporter of Mr. Strauss, the present Liberal member for North Berks and a well-known Free Trader. Dr. Evans is said to have spoken against "those new-fangled doctrines of Protection laid before the country in the proposals of Mr. Chamberlain, with the complicity of Mr. Balfour". This really calls for some explanation, or I fear he cannot be regarded seriously.

It is also quite true that the persecution which Lord Hugh would be likely to receive from Unionist Tariff

Reformers is not a thing to be admired. So long as he is true to his party he ought to be allowed to be a Free Trader. I quite agree with the sentiment "Let him square his convictions for once and stand as a Tariff Reformer, and where would Dr. Evans be?" That is really all we want. As an opponent of the present fiscal system of long standing I consider your leading article in excellent form.

Yours truly, HENRY PASH.

To the Editor of the SATURDAY REVIEW.

26 August 1909.

SIR,—Your article in last Saturday's number anent the election candidates for Oxford University seems to me to be wide of the actual case. No one denies that Lord Hugh Cecil is a very talented man and a great loss to the House of Commons—his brother, Lord Robert, would be a great loss also. But what we have to look at is the fact that both these gentlemen are opponents of the first plank of the Unionist policy, and we are asked because they are clever men to allow them to be elected. Should a Unionist Government be elected it is, and must be, a fact that they could not command a majority as large as the present Government when they start with Ireland, Wales, and Scotland greatly against them, as they always have been. The two former countries will always follow the Liberals and the hope of Home Rule; the latter, being the most Conservative people in the Kingdom, vote Liberal the same as their forefathers did fifty years ago, though the policy of the Unionist party now is the policy nearly of the Liberal party of that day. Very well, we have the first constructive policy. The first thing that must—both from imperial, financial, and social points of view—be taken in hand is Tariff Reform, and we should have these two gentlemen and Messrs. Abel Smith and Norman Bowles against us, because if the two Cecils are to be elected why not the others? This would inevitably end in weakening the Government and in another General Election. Then probably back would come this present Socialist Government, so that the aforesaid gentlemen, instead of safeguarding the Union with Ireland and the Church etc., would have handed this country over bound to the Socialists, and the colonies would make arrangements for their increasing commerce with other countries. There is no doubt that Lords Robert and Hugh Cecil are clever men, but on this matter are they not trying to run the country on economics instead of on commercial lines? The former they understand, the latter they have never had a chance of learning. Are the Unionist party to be directed by Mr. Balfour, Messrs. Bonar Law, Wyndham, Long, Lords Curzon, Milner, etc., or are ninety-nine per cent. and these leaders to be handed over, gagged and bound with the Empire to the economics of the aforesaid very clever men, who are wholly out of touch with the majority?

Yours truly, J. W. BIGGS.

THE ROYAL COMMISSION ON SPIRIT.

To the Editor of the SATURDAY REVIEW.

20 Queen's Road, Wimbledon S.W.

15 August 1909.

SIR,—The report and finding of the Spirit Commission are startling in the extreme to those conversant with the subject. "Bonding and landing" of British and foreign spirit respectively appear to be futile and in direct opposition to the investigations on the maturation of potable spirit by the Society of Chemical Industry. That Society found ". . . that if spirit could be matured by artificial means there would be no need of compulsory bonding to bring about maturation, and six millions of capital would therefore be at once set free".

The Commissioners appear desirous of admitting into the market for the consumption of human beings—not pigs—palatable poison for filling the asylums! Is it possible the Commissioners have read the report of the Lunacy Commission just issued, and which can be obtained from Eyre and Spottiswoode, King's printers, East Harding Street, E.C. (2s. 11d.)?

The "blending" and vending of potato (plain) spirit coloured and flavoured to resemble brandy, whiskey (Scotch and Irish), rum and gin may be very interesting to some people, but why the nation should be compelled to pay "the piper", pecuniarily and morally, is what, as Lord Dundreary would say, "No fellah can understand".

The Commissioners tell us, soberly and seriously apparently, that whiskey ten days old is as wholesome as that ten years old! Well, it may be that the years given to the subject of the maturation of potable spirit are all wasted: we have all been reasoning from wrong premises. Speaking as an individual with some knowledge of the subject, the finding (sic) of the Commission will not influence my choice of potable spirit of any kind; I shall still use for my consumption spirit as old by years (not sophistication) as I can obtain it. The Government by their iniquitous spirit taxes are forcing the majority of publicans to vend poison from which to satisfy their unholy demands, filling the asylums and ruining the health of the whole nation.

Yours sincerely, H. R. GAWEN GOGAY.

A. E. I. O. U.

To the Editor of the SATURDAY REVIEW.

12 Nelson Street, Edinburgh,

21 August 1909.

SIR,—To-day's issue of your excellent weekly, which notices with well-deserved appreciation Mr. G. Drage's opportune work on Austria-Hungary, translates the Austrian A. E. I. O. U. into "Austria erit in orbe ultima." This differs from the reading given me, and, nisi fallor, commonly accepted in the Dual Monarchy. Turning to Hallam's "Europe during the Middle Ages", where I remembered having met the famous device, I found that it was first used by Frederic III., who adopted it on his plate, books and buildings, and that the initials, conformable to the information I had received de viva voce, stood for "Austriae est imperare orbi universo", or, in German, "Alles Erdreich ist Oesterreich Unterthan", a bold assumption for a man who was not safe in an inch of his dominions.

It seems only necessary to mention the discrepancy in the SATURDAY REVIEW to obtain the most correct interpretation of the five quasi cabalistic characters, whose significance has so much increased by recent events, and I remain, with thanks for your courtesy,

Yours truly, J. F. SCHELTEMA.

FRANCIA'S MASTERPIECE.

To the Editor of the SATURDAY REVIEW.

Livorno, 23 August 1909.

SIR,—I fear I do not quite understand Mr. Bell's letter. What can he mean exactly by saying "it seems to me that the suggestion of Catholic doctrines in a special degree is beyond the province of art"? If a painter receives a commission to paint a piece for an altar dedicated to one of the mysteries of the Catholic faith, what else can he do but represent that mystery as fully as may be? Would Mr. Bell have the painter of an Annunciation altar-piece leave out the Holy Ghost in order not to emphasise the doctrine of the Incarnation in "a special degree"? Then again, "Surely", says Mr. Bell, "the indication of the Immaculate Conception in a picture . . . is to confound art with theology". But surely, one might just as well say, to indicate in a picture the Annunciation, the Nativity, the Assumption, is "to confound art with theology". What other objective has religious art save the mysteries of religion?

Francia's picture of the Immaculate Conception at Lucca is in no way obscure: rather is it very luminous. It is no fault of his if writers without proper equipment of knowledge have judged wrongly of its meaning. Mr. Bell cites an altar-piece of Francia now numbered 81 in the Bologna Gallery as a "religious picture which needs no explanation". I invite him to tell you without opening a book what mystery, if any, of the Christian faith it represents, and why certain saints are introduced into it rather than others. I submit that

TURGENEFF'S GERMAN LETTERS.

TO JULIAN SCHMIDT.

* 1875—1881.

99.

König von England, Carlsbad
Friday, 9 July 1875.

My dear Schmidt,—This note will be handed to you by Mr. Paul Pissemski, the son of the well-known author, who wrote "Tausend Seelen". Probably he will bring his father with him, but the latter unfortunately can speak neither French nor German; however, you will certainly be interested to catch a glimpse of him—he is a very interesting and original personality. You will be able to see the signs of authorship in him at once!

Mr. Paul Pissemski will stay some time in Berlin. He is a jurist—a very capable one—and will be ultimately a professor at the University of Moscow, at whose expense he is now passing his second year of study abroad. Besides, he is a very pleasant and agreeable young man, and if you can be of any assistance to him I shall be extremely grateful.

I have received your feuilleton on Daudet's novel, and have sent it to Paris at once. It is like everything that you write—entirely correct and just.

You have never yet told me whether you know Flaubert's "Education Sentimentale", and whether you would like to have a copy.

I shall stay at Carlsbad till Wednesday the 14th, and then go back to Paris.

A few lines in answer would be very agreeable.

Best wishes and hearty greetings to your wife and yourself. Yours, Iw. TURGENJEW.

100.

50 Rue de Douai, Paris
Thursday, 27 January '76.

Dear Friend,—I am utilising the departure of a worthy acquaintance of mine to send you Flaubert's "Education Sentimentale" (two thick volumes). You will probably receive it at the same time as this letter. The book is not exactly enthralling reading, but it is extremely striking, and its almost entire failure in France is characteristic. The French utterly refuse to swallow such bitter pills as that.

I have received a few very courteous lines from Toret. He is staying at present in the South of France, and that is all I know about him. I am surprised that he has not written to you.

My story is not appearing in the "Gegenwart", I am ashamed to say, but in the "Deutsche Rundschau". It is a very slight little thing, and I commend it to your attention.

I am not a man of my word, and have not kept my promise to the "Gegenwart". Heaven knows how it came about. The editor has written me a reproachful letter, and I have made my excuses as well, or as badly, as possible, and proposed another story to them by way of compensation; but they preserve a gloomy silence.

You do not know Paul Lindau, do you? Otherwise, you might have acted as mediator. . . . I have just remembered that you are not on the best of terms with him; so consider all that unsaid and work per Pietschium, to whom I owe a letter, and to whom I want you to give my kind regards.

I have had an attack of gout. It was not very severe, but I still cannot put on a boot.

I am most eagerly awaiting what you promised to send me.

Have you got Taine's new book, "L'ancien régime"? You ought to read it.

Very probably I shall come to Berlin at the end of April, and of course I shall see you then.

Kindest regards to your dear wife and cordial good wishes to yourself, from

Yours most sincerely, Iw. TURGENJEW.

* Continued from page iv Supplement SATURDAY REVIEW, 27 February, 1909.

101.

Rue de Douai, Paris
14 February 1876.

My dear Friend,—Yesterday I sent you A. Daudet's new novel, "Jack", at his request.

Yesterday too my Russian friend, to whom I entrusted the two volumes of the "Education Sentimentale", returned here from S. Petersburg. He assured me that he gave them to a commissionaire at the station with instructions to take them to 14 Schillerstrasse. Did you receive them all right? Please let me have a few lines in reply. The commissionaire's number was 9.

What do you think of the last elections? The Republic is the Republic and Gambetta is its prophet. In Germany (and here too) people thought there would be a Bonapartist Restoration. But it is a long way away now.

Kindest regards to your wife and my other friends. Au revoir in May.

Yours, I. TURGENJEW.

102.

50 Rue de Douai, Paris
Saturday, 25 March, '76.

My dear Friend,—Rougon is Rouher, but much more broadly and strongly conceived: the resemblance is only superficial. As to Marci and Bougon you have guessed rightly. Clorinde is *not* Mme. de Montauban, but Countess Castiglione—but there the likeness is really frappant. The chief error in this otherwise striking book is Rougon's petty, provincial entourage. It is all too tiny for a fellow like that, but unfortunately Zola does not know the great world sufficiently well and is far too retiring ever to study it thoroughly.

The Emperor and the Empress are speaking likenesses.

To-day I am sending you "La Faute de l'Abbé Mouret". The beginning and end of this book are perhaps the best things that Zola has written. In the middle of it, where he tries to reproduce the wilderness of "Paradou" and starts off in an ultra-poetical direction (remarkable enough for a realist), lies the Achilles' heel of the work.

Pietsch has arrived. We have already lunched with him and also with Korn, the publisher of the "Schlesische Zeitung", and have had a deal of talk.

Kindest regards to your wife and best wishes to yourself. Yours, I. TURGENJEW.

103.

Les Frênes, Bougival
Saturday, 6 October 1876.

Mercy! Mer-er-er-cy I sing, like Alice in "Robert the Devil". I am a criminal; yes, for the first time in my life I passed through without stopping. (As an extenuating circumstance I am able to allege that I arrived in Berlin at 11 P.M. and left very early the following morning.) Still I repeat "Mercy!" and I count on your kindness and magnanimity.

I have been very busy this year. In Russia I wrote a monster of a novel (that is to say a monstrously long one), and I have just finished the copying of it. The MS. leaves for S. Petersburg in a week, and appears in a monthly in January. As to the translation, that is still in obscurity. At any rate you and your wife (to whom I send my kindest regards) shall *most certainly* have the *first* copy of any translation (whether in the form of a feuilleton or otherwise).

Was the poet called Leconte de Liste? If he was, tell me so, and I will send you one of his books at once.

And so I really didn't send the photograph? I could have sworn that I had . . . .

Apparently I am an undutiful dog! But you shall certainly have it the first time I go to Paris (at present I am sitting here without ever stirring. Now I have got rid of the accursed copying and shall be able to keep my promise.

My heartiest greetings once again. Do not write to me till the photograph is in your hands.

Your old friend,
IW. TURGENJEW.

104.

50 Rue de Douai, Paris
Sunday, 13 February '77.

My dear Friend,—Here is Zola's photograph at last! It is like him, but the expression is not strong enough and the colouring is too light. He has quite black hair, whereas in the picture it is almost blond. His general appearance is that of a clever, rather crude and unpolished Parisian ouvrier. His "Curée" (which you have already received) has created an extraordinary furore here—thirteen editions in three weeks. I wonder what *you* think of it.

Improbable as it may sound, I am coming to Berlin, but it will be in April. I hope I shall be certain to find you there.

Kindest regards to your dear wife and heartiest good wishes to yourself.

Yours, IW. TURGENJEW.

105.

50 Rue de Douai, Paris
Friday, 30 March 1877.

My dear Friend,—I am sending you to-day my new novel in the French translation, which is excellent. The German translation (in the "Petersburger Zeitung"), although authorised, is swarming with mistakes. Much of it is turned quite upside-down and all of it is commonplace. The descriptions have been entirely bungled, and present no picture at all. Compare, for instance, the beginning of chapter 21, where Markilov and Nezhdanov leave the town at night. The German text is simply *disgusting muck*, and presents no sort of consistent picture.

Before a month is over I shall see you in Berlin, and shall be able to chatter to my heart's content. Meanwhile my kind regards to your dear wife and cordial good wishes to yourself.

Yours, IW. TURGENJEW.

106.

50 Rue de Douai, Paris
Wednesday, 25 April '77.

My dear Friend,—Before 10 (say ten) days are over I shall be sitting in your room and chattering away. To-day I will merely tell you that I have received the Vienna paper and "Im neuen Reich", and that I at once translated the article on himself to Zola. He felt your criticisms, but you speak also of your admiration for his "great talent", so that is all right. Your estimate of "Virgin Soil"* is both kindly and *just*. We will speak of it later; at present I only want to make one observation. When I was writing the book, I was not entirely free. It was to appear in Russia, and so I had to take certain considerations into account, which somewhat crippled me—quite a new experience. Even in its present form the novel only just escaped being put on the fire. The majority of the Committee of Censors condemned it, and it was only saved by the president (the Minister of the Interior), thanks to my publisher's diplomacy. With fine foresight, and in spite of my protest, he divided the thing into two parts. The real venom was in the second part, and so he managed to slip the whole work through. They wanted to avoid any sort of scandal, and the Minister declared that if he had read the whole book he would have forbidden it unconditionally; but as it was, etc. But all this is "de l'histoire ancienne", and seems trivial and insignificant at the present moment, when we are standing on the threshold of a vast event, and—but I will talk about all that when we meet.

Well, au revoir in the near future. My kindest regards to your wife and all my other friends.

Yours, IW. TURGENJEW.

* In "Im neuen Reich", Part I.—FRAU SCHMIDT.

107.

50 Rue de Douai, Paris
Saturday, 23 February '78.

My dear Friend,—My slackness is shockingly incorrigible, and I must beg for your forgiveness. Perhaps these notes will arrive too late, but I send them nevertheless. Gustave Flaubert was born on 12 Dec. 1821 at Rouen, Emile Zola on 2 April 1840 in Paris, Alphonse Daudet on 13 May 1840 at Nîmes, Edmond de Goncourt on 26 May 1822 at Nancy. They gave me the information themselves.

There is only one copy of Flaubert's only photograph. He made me a present of it and I cannot give it to you. He must have been very handsome when he was a young man. Now he is fat, and quite bald, with a red face, rather like Frederick Lemaître, the celebrated actor. Do you possess the latter's photograph?

Have I given you the "Nabob"?* I will send you a copy in any case. If you have it already, you can give this one away.

I am certainly coming to Berlin, but when—"that is the question". At any rate this one will be solved more quickly than the Eastern question. Kindest regards to your wife and best good wishes to yourself.

Yours, I. T.

108.

Les Frênes, Bougival
13 October 1878.

My dear Friend,—You have probably abused me vigorously in your own mind, when you heard that I did not stop at Berlin on my way back, and you are quite right. But I tell myself that I was compelled to do so. As evidence of my repentance I send you by to-day's post

(*a*) The "Nabab"—at last.
(*b*) "La Chanson des Gueux" by Jean Richepin.

The last-named is quite a marvellous poet—such a poet! A good deal of it you will scarcely understand, as it is written in Parisian argot (many Frenchmen do not understand it either), but some of it, e.g. p. 30, is of really classical beauty. As especially audacious and whimsical I recommend "Fleurs de boisson", p. 173. Every page shows a strangely ardent temperament, which has a cheering effect amid the pale cast of thought of these times. . . .

I hope this little present has softened your heart a little and I cry Pardon, pardon! With kindest regards to your wife and best wishes to yourself,

IW. TURGENJEW.

109.

Moscow, 24/12† June '81.

Dear Friend,—Yesterday I forwarded you two copies of the last volume of my collected works, one for yourself, the other for our friend Pietsch. The whole book is "cram full of love" and its appurtenances.

At the end of August I shall be in Berlin again and shall see you. Did you receive the 80 marks (for yourself and Pietsch) which you lent me, and which I sent you from S. Petersburg? My permanent address in Russia is c/o the "European Courier", 20 Gaternaïa, S. Petersburg.

Kind regards to your dear wife and the heartiest good wishes to yourself from

Yours, IW. TURGENJEW.

* Daudet's "Le Nabab".—TRANSLATOR.
† 24/26 in text.—TRANSLATOR.

it would be impossible to explain this picture with certainty without knowing the dedication of the altar for which it was painted. The dedication alone can give us the name by which an altar-piece should be called, for the altar alone brought the picture into existence. All such titles as "The Madonna in Ecstasy", "The Madonna in Glory", "The Madonna in Adoration" merely serve to obscure meaning, for ecstasy, glory and adoration, even though physically visible, have nothing to do with the dedication of the altar, and hence nothing to do with the essential meaning of the picture. But it is perhaps unfair to criticise Mr. Bell's letter, for, as you point out in your editorial note, he has neither seen the picture nor read my book.

It cannot but be gratifying to me to learn that a critic of the standing of Professor Placido Campetti, the chief local authority on art matters, should take so favourable a view of my book, and it is good of Mr. Mercer to translate his remarks. May I, however, point out a misconception into which Professor Campetti has fallen—likely enough owing to a want of clearness of exposition on my part? He writes that Francia's Immaculate Conception "was removed from the Stiatta Chapel to that of the Guinigi, where it may now be seen". No; it was removed from the Stiatta Chapel to the nave, and back again from the nave to the Stiatta Chapel, where it now hangs. The double arched chapel, so long called of the Micheli, and of their heirs the Guinigi, is really two chapels, the western half Stiatta (Immaculate Conception), the eastern half Guinigi Magrini (Assumption). This fact I have proved by evidence that cannot be gainsaid, and the guide-books will have to add another chapel to their accounts of the Basilica of San Frediano.

I am, Sir, your obedient servant,

MONTGOMERY CARMICHAEL.

BETTER DEAD.

To the Editor of the SATURDAY REVIEW.

46 Blythe Vale, Catford S.E.

SIR,—Only the SATURDAY REVIEW would voice a truth in such plain words as in your paragraph beginning "Day after day Hyde Park is strewn with repellent bodies, the more objectionable because not dead". You only are not afraid to say that our verminous human wreckage should not be allowed in the West End of London—in the drawing-room of the Empire. Yet the vast mass of decent people are being "stunk out" of pleasant places in London, which they, and they only, planned and made and paid for.

On many occasions I have acted as guide to colonial ladies (mostly Australasian), and have included a walk upon the Embankment, at some time after 11.30 or 12 P.M., as one offering a fine impression of our mysterious river. But gaunt shadows rise from the niches begging, often with veiled threats; nameless horrors of filthy naked skin and tattered duds are stretched about the steps; loathsome remarks are aimed from the benches, until, tingling with shame and irritation, the owners, citizens and visitors of London's finest boulevard, must leave it to the sewer rats who have proved their ability to slime-out all life else. And we have a Government that dare not for its life remove those benches or give positive orders to its police for the prohibition of tramps within a certain area. Are there not parks and places unlimited in the East End? By sheer pressure there will come a time when the law will be forced to say to its citizens: Refuse honest work, drink, bet, steal, disgust father, family and friends, borrow repeatedly from all and sundry, remain incorrigible under various reformatory treatments, steal again, lead a life of tramping and begging your way from prison to workhouse, and workhouse to prison, fall so low that your life's variety of beastliness is written in every break of your sodden hulls—do this, and the drawing-room of the Empire shall be shut to you. It will come, but cannot we help it along? The movement must be initiated by the press, and I believe that every decent Englishman, whether workman or duke, will be in favour of barring out the sewer rat from the whole of the West End. The City Traffic Bill is a beginning—small but significant.

JOHN BLAND.

REVIEWS.

THE ELUSIVE SPIRIT OF PARIS.

"A Wanderer in Paris." By E. V. Lucas. London: Methuen. 1909. 6s.

THIS Wanderer in Paris, like his stalwart forerunner Der Wanderer in "Siegfried", may fatigue some people by dwelling a little too long on a ten-times-told tale. But whereas Wotan is tedious by reason of his detailed expositions of his state and domestic and strictly private affairs, Mr. Lucas loses his grip on our attention and interest by giving us not enough of himself. Everyone knows something of Paris nowadays. So long as the railway companies organise cheap excursions, so long will young men cross the Channel for a few days and come back to write newspaper sketches which tell us that there are trees on the boulevards and that some cafés are open all night. And, alas! so long also will other men feel imperatively moved to write books about Paris, essaying to interpret for us the ways and the thoughts of a strange people. The list of such books in the British Museum catalogue is appalling. No one would wish to read many of them, but if half a dozen are chosen at random amongst them they will be found to be much alike. Every adventurer begins by warning us that the "sights" of Paris are not Paris; everyone insists that Paris is not France. Then they all describe the sights, and inform us that Paris contains in epitome the history of France. Mr. Lucas has tried to do something different, without quite succeeding.

The cause of the book's shortcomings may be perceived at a glance. To modern people there is nothing so strange in modern Paris that a mere description should entrance us. The direct method that might result in an interesting volume on Tibet results in a dull book when Paris is the subject. Nothing presented to the reader has the quality of strangeness, nor even of novelty in the draper's sense. Paris has been over-described, every stone of it. Paris Mr. Lucas has never ceased to look at as an outsider looks; he has not got to the secret of its charm, fascination and enchantment; all that is rare and wonder-creating in its soul eludes him. He doubtless is aware of a magical presence, but he has never grasped it; he interprets nothing, but gives accounts of things we can all see for ourselves in a short time and at a small cost. As we have said, he repeats an old tale, and does not communicate the thrill he alone has experienced, or has felt more strongly than others.

After all, it is one of the hardest things in the world to reproduce in a book of description the colour, feeling and atmosphere of any city. There are not a dozen such books in existence. The writer must be familiar with his theme, and must have a great love for it, else the familiarity will pass into indifference. If Mr. Lucas loved Paris well enough to translate its magic into words, he would live in Paris: its air, colour, odours and movement would be necessary to his life. Novelists, we fancy, will always do better than mere descriptive writers. When they use busy towns as a background to human dramas, the towns are thrown into an intelligible relation with beings like ourselves, and the spirit that dwells behind mere bricks and mortar may speak to us. A story of Dickens or Thackeray gives us a more vivid notion of London in early Victorian or late Georgian times than a hundredweight of books on "London as it was": these, with all their illustrations and exact details, evoke no image that seems solid and real to the mental vision. For the life of older Paris and a true picture of its streets and buildings we must go to Balzac; and perhaps someone is now doing as much for the Paris of the present day—though we have doubts. Certainly Mr. Lucas has not done it.

Still, we are grateful to him for the rendering into light and rippling English of one's sensations on entering Paris in the evening—the cries of "La Patr-e-e", the merry chanting of the cabdriver, and the absurd "Vivent les femmes" which he once saw written on a wall. He might have given us much more—how in walking or driving through the humbler quarters one sees the crowds of hatless workgirls on the arms of their sweethearts or husbands, making haste to little cafés and cheap restaurants; how one hears the babble and joyous laughter from the groups seated at round-topped tables on the open terraces; how one watches the mobs struggling for places on the omnibuses as though the day's work being over, there were no morrow of toil to think about. And an arrival at Paris in the early morning of summer is delightful. Of course, the wretched chiffoniers do not exhilarate us; but the roads are sweet and clean; and there are plenty of cafés where business has already commenced, so that one need not set about one's own affairs breakfastless or trust to the uncomfortable refreshment-bar of a railway station. Sunday, or any other day, Paris seems to open its arms to receive you: you can at any rate fill your stomach before considering what to do next.

But the crowds and cafés of Paris are only a small part of its existence. For domestic life one must go to the provinces; though it is not so near to extinction in Paris as the late Mr. Hammerton tried to convince us. There are still some middle-class houses in the capital; and many middle-class families do not take all their meals, or hold their birthday-parties, in restaurants. Sundays are nearly the only days on which "wanderers" in Paris may witness genuine family life going on outside. Then, indeed, the restaurants are filled with women and children; and in the Casino de Paris, the home of seductive wickedness the night before, the squalling of babies sometimes mars the performance. All improprieties are taken out of the songs and dances, and a good deal is introduced of an element which we hardly have seen in England since the "good old" harlequinade grew too old-fashioned for the up-to-date English child.

This domestic life—narrow though it is—and still more the artistic, musical, and theatrical life which help to make the real modern Paris what it is, await an interpreter. Mr. Lucas pays too much attention to what are simply the ' sights ". That may be right enough in a guide-book; but we complain of finding too much of that sort of thing in a book which pretends to be other than a guide. And we should be justified in grumbling even at the guide-books when they point out the Eiffel Tower as a " sight ". It is a " sight ", of course—an abominable one: a monstrosity, a disgrace to a civilised people. There it stands, rusting away in its uselessness, dwarfing the Chamber of Deputies and ruining one of the finest Places in the world—la Concorde. As for the other sights, they are rather for the student than the sightseer on a char-à-banc. Most English visitors, however, go to Paris less to see sights than to see a sparkling life of amusement and gaiety. The right kind of sightseer, taking a Baedeker and dodging the harpies of the chars-à-banc, will come away with a truer idea of the town if he wanders about the Cité for a few hours than he will ever gain by staring at pictures and statues in the Louvre. And it must not be forgotten that in endeavouring to get into touch with the spirit of Paris the suburbs must not be neglected—and some of them are a considerable distance away. Thus, Versailles and Fontainebleau are most emphatically suburban Paris, while many places nearer at hand are pure " province ". But the real, living Paris, though not difficult to get a vague, faint sense of, cannot easily be made fully to disclose itself: one must gradually learn to love it, and, to do that, must live in it.

FERRERO'S ROMAN HISTORY.

"The Greatness and Decline of Rome." By G. Ferrero. Vols. III., IV. and V. Translated into English by the Rev. H. J. Chaytor. London: Heinemann. 1908-9. 6s. per vol. net.

IT is undoubtedly a great misfortune that Mommsen never wrote the history of Augustus. It is true that the commentary on the Monumentum Ancyranum and the half-volume on the principate in the " Staatsrecht " amount, when taken together, to a larger contribution to the subject than is left for Gardthausen or Seeck to make. Yet there is all the difference between the provision of this material and the embodiment of it in a continuous narrative which has an air of finality. It is impossible to say whether Schiller, in the history of the Empire which he undertook avowedly as a temporary measure pending the appearance of the fourth volume of the great History by Mommsen which never appeared, represented his master's views on Augustus or not; but Schiller would be the first to admit that his work was an imperfect substitute. Not everyone feels obliged to follow Mommsen implicitly. Yet it is extraordinary to what an extent the History, a comparatively early work of Mommsen, and in some ways a comparatively unimportant one, still dominates the field. No one who writes an account of the Roman Republic can neglect Mommsen any more than if he is dealing with the provinces of the Empire. He may differ from Mommsen or criticise him, but he can hardly avoid starting from him.

This consideration was not without its effect on the first two volumes of Signor Ferrero's history. They were full of interest, but they often left the impression of a continuous and hostile commentary on Mommsen. The author could not help this. His third, fourth, and fifth volumes, which carry us from the death of Julius to the death of Augustus, enable us to judge better what Ferrero can do when he is not hampered by his embarrassing predecessor. The world's loss is certainly the modern historian's opportunity.

Modern writers are in much the same position as the public were at the death of Augustus. They do not know what to make of him, and the facts appear to justify them in making out of him anything that they choose. Accordingly, in approaching a new historian of this period, we are obliged to judge him mainly by reference to his general historical capacity. The characteristics of Ferrero as an historian are already well known from his earlier volumes. He is always readable and never uninteresting; he is continually engaged in finding connexion between contemporary movements of all kinds, even where that connexion may be hard to see. Ferrero would not be a modern historian if he were not confident in his opinions. He attaches importance to the evidence of Horace's writings as throwing light on contemporary feeling, and a reader might search these volumes without finding any indication that the dates and order of those writings have been matters of dispute. He seldom has a doubt as to the meaning of an obscure word in one of his authorities or as to the occasion on which a monument was erected. He is not afraid to express his views in vigorous language. If he implies doubts as to the safety of his inferences (this seems to occur more frequently in the fifth than in the preceding volumes), there remain the vast majority of cases in which no alternative is suggested and the historian's tone suggests that there is scarcely room for argument. It is hardly necessary to add that Ferrero is a good scholar, that his volumes show abundant evidence of research, and that, apart from the slips or misprints which are inevitable in so long a piece of work, the book is accurate. It is clear that Ferrero has established a claim to be heard on those great questions about Augustus which can be solved, if at all, on general historical grounds, and not by an examination of the ancient evidence.

What are we to make of the personal character of Augustus? Hardly anyone has been found to maintain that he possessed an attractive or a sympathetic nature. It has been customary to argue that he sacrificed the deepest individual feelings to political objects, sometimes, as in the case of Tiberius and Julia, with disastrous results. Few modern critics have been willing to believe that the responsibility for the horrors of the proscriptions belongs entirely to the other triumvirs. Those who take the most favourable view of the object and effect of Augustus' moral reforms have admitted that they come with a bad grace from their author. But Ferrero is not content with admissions of this kind. At one period he gives his hero this testimonial: " A monster incarnate, with all the hideous vices of a tyrant, cruelty, pride, luxury and treachery, Octavian was the abomination of Italy ". Surely not even the depreciators of Augustus into whose company we are introduced by Tacitus can have equalled this. It may be true that we are apt to forget, as did some of the contemporaries of Augustus, the early failures in the subsequent success and the many barbarities in the reign of order and peace to which they were the prelude. But Ferrero is not free from one very common characteristic of modern writers—the unconscious bias against those who have been generally praised and in favour of those who have commonly been blamed. It is hardly surprising that Ferrero's characters of Antony, Julia and Tiberius should appear to be more favourable than his character of Augustus: this is just what would be expected from a modern critic. Let it be admitted that the personal character of Augustus is a very difficult question, that he was at the best " inter bona malaque mixtus ", that he has no right and probably made no claim to be considered as a model for universal imitation. Yet there is absurdity in believing that a combination of vice and feebleness, an astuteness shown mainly in shirking awkward decisions and in appropriating the results of others' work, could have produced the change which Augustus effected.

Was the dyarchy a sham or a reality? Did Augustus intend to establish a monarchy and to disguise that monarchy under respectable forms? Or was he seriously of opinion that the government of the world required the co-operation of many minds and that the unity of control which was needful to organise an effective army and to secure uniformity in provincial administration must not be allowed to become one-man rule? It is surprising to find that Ferrero is a strong supporter of the latter alternative. Yet there is no direct evidence of the presumed intention; and there is more probability in the opinions of Augustus' contemporaries than in the remote inferences of Ferrero.

Does the Empire represent an improvement on the Republic? Consciousness of the defects with which the Roman Republic justly stands charged is too often regarded as equivalent to a conviction that the Empire escaped them all. The evidence of Tacitus is quite enough by itself to convince us both that the provincial administration of the Empire was generally better than what had gone before, and also that some of the worst abuses occasionally survived under it. But it would be well in any case if modern critics could escape the temptation to import their party predilections into a purely historical question. Ferrero begins his fifth volume with a strong denial of the disinterested nature of Roman rule as a whole, but he ends the volume with a sufficient testimony to the improvement of administration by the end of the reign of Augustus. It might not be unfair to claim him as among those who hold the improvement to have been effected partly as the result of the less satisfactory features of the imperial rule. Provincial government became a career when political interest had ceased, from whatever reason, to have its centre at Rome, when a prominent Roman would be happier elsewhere than in the capital and when military reputation had its uncomfortable side. The change of machinery which we call in loose language the substitution of the Empire for the Republic introduced better results in the administration of the Roman world, but it would be hard to deduce from this any safe conclusion as to the merits of various forms of government in ruling dependencies. Augustus devoted special attention to the development of the western provinces, and Ferrero rightly claims this as among his chief merits.

The admirers of the Roman Empire state in very various language the exact nature of its contribution to the history of the world. Ferrero dwells especially on the indivisibility of the State, which he connects as a doctrine with the republican conception of the Roman system, and alleges to be the basis of modern monarchies. It would be easy to dwell on the paradoxical nature of this view, to remind ourselves that modern monarchy (as students of Gierke know only too well) has a very complicated history, and to hint a doubt whether an Italian is the best judge, any more than an Englishman, of the real spirit of modern European monarchies as a whole. But it certainly does appear as though the feat of linking personal rule on to the traditional system which had supported Rome through so many crises—a feat which, though not wholly successfully accomplished, was not without its effect, as Ferrero truly says, on the monarchy of the Flavians and the Antonines—bore a great part in effecting that connexion between monarchy and law which forms one of the sources of modern constitutionalism.

ROMANTIC, NATURALIST, AND SYMBOLIST.

" A Century of French Poets." By Francis Yvon Eccles. London: Constable. 1909. 10s. 6d. net.

THE virtue that is in literary formulæ lies, not so much in what they achieve, as in what they fail to achieve. They are mainly of use in suggesting their own inadequacy. They illuminate by affording to the mind a sudden and comprehensive view of the hundred and one diversities and incongruities which they are unable to include or reconcile. They are of sovereign efficacy only so long as they are not the objects of a too implicit trust. They are of value till they are applied; and in the act of application they lose their value.

Those who have a taste for formulæ will always enjoy themselves among the French poets of the nineteenth century. The labels are ready, and so legibly written. All that the neophyte has to do is to stroll casually through, affixing them to the right people. The whole century can be put into a nutshell. There was the Romantic outburst. Then, as was only to be expected, came the Naturalist reaction. Finally, as again was only to be expected, came the return to a subtler individualism with the Symbolists. Surely it is a very simple matter.

It is undoubtedly a simple matter for those who place implicit trust in formulæ; and, so, miss their value. In their favour it must be admitted that a generalisation is a statement of truth, and that it is an advantage to get truth stated even at the risk of a little compression of its material. But it should not be forgotten that a generalisation of the nutshell variety states truth by suppressing it, a fact that may cause nutshells to be regarded with suspicion. In fact, it may be realised that the above formulæ—Romanticism, Symbolism, and the rest—when applied to individual cases may lead to more misconception than understanding; and that their value, as already said, lies in the diversities and incongruities which they force into the light when they come to be applied.

The author of " A Century of French Poets " has rendered a real service to literature by putting within the limits of a single volume enough of the material for which these formulæ have been constructed to discredit their unintelligent application. His book affords a survey through the century of every manner and tendency in French poetry which was to be of permanent value. It affords this survey by means of the poetry itself, selected with fine discrimination and generous catholicity of feeling. In a period so rich in every kind of literature that it is hardly yet possible to see the wood for the trees, such a volume will prove of value to more than the casual reader.

Let us begin with the formula of Romanticism. No one would deny to Alphonse de Lamartine his title as the first of the great Romantic poets. He is this by virtue of his fervid lyricism. He is emotional, personal, confidential. So far the Romantic formula fits. And then it breaks down. Lamartine's handling of the Alexandrine was " more timid than Racine's "; his vocabulary was as old as Rousseau. This is an unfortunate beginning. Worse follows with the advent of Alfred de Vigny. De Vigny harks back to the Classics in the systematic trend of his thought; he belongs to the Romantics in his choice of themes; he is claimed by certain of the Symbolists as one of their earliest ancestors. Hugo comes next, hardly welcome to the formularist; since he included, or rather transcended, all the formulæ of his time. A little later there emerges the figure of Théophile Gautier. Where is the label for him?

Leaving this as a challenge, we pass on to Charles Baudelaire, Romantic, Naturalist, and Symbolist rolled into one with a superadded flavour which was all his own. Finally there was Paul Verlaine, full of transitions, who began as a disciple of Vicomte de Lisle; and, in his later years, blended the subtlety of the Symbolist with the candour of the Romantic.

Formulæ, it seems, do not sit well upon these men. And the reason is not far to seek. Every stage in the history of a literature contains what has gone before. Reaction is not contradiction: it is fulfilment. The literary outburst of the nineteenth century in France was not the result of a new formula that was an abrogation of one that was old. It was the sign of a new life. After a dreary interlude poets once more began to be born. The new wine had come, and there was a cry for new bottles. But there was no breach with the past. The old creative days had come again; and the form taken by the art of the Racines and the Corneilles of the new age was called Romanticism. The Romantic was the old Classic striving to express more, and with more resources at his command for that expression. The Naturalist inherited his labours, secured his rear, and indicated the path of future conquests. The Symbolist added a delicate something which has yet to be absorbed and put into relation with the rest. Every advance hailed itself as a new tendency, as a reaction, or as a revolution; for the present does not behold itself in true perspective. There has been neither reaction nor revolution. There has been continuous development.

AN AMIABLE AMERICAN.

"England and the English from an American Point of View." By Price Collier. London: Duckworth. 1909. 7s. 6d. net.

MR. COLLIER'S view of England will appear to the greater number of his fellow-countrymen to be an Englishman's rather than an American's. Mr. Collier admits that Americans do not like Englishmen; but, on the whole, his book is a eulogy on the English people, the English aristocracy and the governing classes especially, English character and English social life. He has lived in this country thirty years; and it seems we have made him an intelligent Conservative who believes that British institutions, taking them all round, are the best, and the governing classes the finest in the world. English people would be very greedy of flattery indeed if they were not satisfied with what Mr. Collier says of them. What he says disparagingly is often only the commonplaces that have been charged against us by foreigners from time immemorial. Socially we are stiff, unprepossessing, insular, with a conceit of ourselves and our own ways which is irritating. This we expect in any book about Englishmen. Mr. Collier adopts this conventional vein, but modifies it by the rider that in the country, where their true occupations and affections are, these gauche, morose beings become the easiest, most charming and amiable people on the face of the earth. Only on very few points need any fairly self-satisfied Englishman take the trouble to quarrel with Mr. Collier. For some reason, however, that we find hard to understand, English women do not please him so much as the men. According to him they are not good-looking, and they dress atrociously. Their white-and-red complexions, for example, are refreshing only at a distance. When you approach them you find the apparent rosy tint becomes beefy. Still, after thirty years, Mr. Collier experiences the unpleasant shock of it. As regards dress, we might have explained Mr. Collier's uncomplimentary opinion by supposing it to be a matter on which as a man he was ignorant, and that he had copied his descriptions probably from some French source. But Mr. Collier himself cuts us off from this explanation. He explains his own delusion. English women dress badly, he finds, because their dress allowances are so small. England is a man's country, and the men's own demands have to be first gratified, so that their women have to take what is left over, and they cannot afford anything but the cheapest and coarsest materials. We suspect that Mr. Collier, who is generally so fair to Englishmen, has, in this matter of complexion and clothes, been got at by envious American women. There is evidence that he does not see these things for himself. How else could he assert that London shop windows by their contents show that it is the men and not the women on whom the money is spent? To talk of gun-shops and men's dressing-bag shops! This is not an advertisement column, or how many gorgeous establishments might we cite to confute him! We only ask: in all these thirty years has he never walked along Oxford Street, or down Regent Street, or visited S. Paul's Churchyard? Has he never met his countrymen in Selfridge's?

Passing from Mr. Collier's misguided treatment of this delicate subject, we only find one chapter in his book where he appears to set himself to write a description of English ways such as will give Americans who "dislike Englishmen" the sort of pleasure they will expect. That is the chapter entitled "The Land of Compromise". And yet even here Mr. Collier writes more like an Englishman who holds strong views against all the things that are now lumped together as socialism than like an American who is on the prowl for anything disagreeable to say about English characteristics. Such an American would hardly say "The people is a free people in the sense that nowhere else in the world is the individual so little ruled, hampered, or oppressed; but politically they are bound fast by the chains of a House of Lords which, entirely independent of them, rejects their measures when it so pleases"; and then add "I believe that the House of Lords is, as a rule, a surer interpreter of the sober wishes of the English people as a whole than the House of Commons". Mr. Collier, indeed, is all for aristocratic government, and the compromises which he most dislikes in British politics arise from political power passing, as in America, down to social strata of the people who ought not to have political power. The real disposition of English people, he holds, is to leave government to competent governing classes, and that they have done so till recent years explains the unexampled success of England, both in national and imperial government. If, as he contends, we are losing this power which made us the admiration of the world, the cause, he believes, is the extension of democratic government. Often in reading his strictures on the political side of English life we feel that he intends to hit his own country as hard as he hits England. Moreover, he always finds mitigation for political degeneracy in the personal character of the dominant self-sufficient Englishman of his admiration, and this he does not find in America. Thus, though he draws a very depressing picture of the low physical and mental condition of our poorer classes, and compares them unfavourably with similar classes in America, he declares that, comparing a thousand Englishmen of the better classes with corresponding Americans, the Englishmen are very much superior. With all his severities on the incongruities he finds amongst us, he generally ends on a note of admiration which is as inconsistent as anything we find in his criticisms, if we are to take them literally. His account of our affairs would make us wonder that we survive. He appears to wonder too, and he does not explain how it is at all. "There must needs be colossal strength and pluck, marvellous financial elasticity, unbounded confidence, tremendous earning power, and a vast reservoir of national virtue somewhere to explain these huge incongruities. One begins to understand the reasons for the nonchalant self-satisfaction of the English, which Germans, Americans, and others are fain to call conceit, or obstinacy, or stupidity, as the occasion demands." One can only suppose that he means we are better than our institutions. He has made a really interesting book on that theme.

THE RELIGION OF THE SCRIBES.

"Some Aspects of Rabbinic Theology." By S. Schechter. London: Black. 1909. 7s. 6d. net.

OUTSIDE the pale of Jewry the adjective "Rabbinic" does not directly suggest a high form of religion. It is commonly associated with such phrases as "subtleties of exegesis" or "tithing of anise and cummin". A certain portion of the extant sayings credited to the ancient Rabbis are concerned with particular details of the kind, and many illustrate the methods by which they proved that what was good in equity was also good in their law. But the comprehensiveness of the sacred law, which they administered for the well-being of their several communities, does not necessarily prove that Rabbinic religion was a thing apart from the needs or beyond the capacity of common humanity. And neither isolated apophthegms nor judicial pronouncements can give a complete picture of the Scribe who uttered them, unless, indeed, they be read in the light of his presuppositions, which include a belief in the supreme authority of the law. Now the law—the Torah—includes the five books of Moses, the Prophets and the Writings, making in all three-fourths or more of the Christian Bible. However much the Rabbis perverted it in their decisions, this Torah was read in synagogue on Sabbath, and was translated into the vulgar tongue concurrently with the reading. So the subjects of the Rabbis had sufficient familiarity with the supreme authority of their faith to enable them to challenge any particular innovation which was repugnant to the tenour of the whole. That the Rabbis perverted the Torah is an assumption of unscrupulous enemies who never examine the evidence relevant to their quarrel. That the Torah is good, most sections of the Christian Church are still pledged to believe. A Christian cannot afford to approach the Rabbinic religion, which rests upon it and lives thereby, with a self-confident contempt. And approach it he must, if he would understand the remaining part of his Bible or construct for himself a valid apologetic. Dr. Schechter should therefore find a large audience for his "presentation of Rabbinic opinion on a number of theological topics". Repentance, forgiveness, and reconciliation with God, imputed righteousness, the joy of the law, the Kingdom of God—all these are household words in the Christian vocabulary; for the Church inherited from the synagogue. In this book the ideas and doctrines for which these words stand are expounded with a simplicity and a directness which come from a complete mastery of the Rabbinic literature. Himself Rabbinically trained, Dr. Schechter has added (one might almost say) a new chapter to the Talmud, and a chapter unlike all the rest in this, that it is immediately intelligible to any modern man who can read English, and so far as his selected topics are concerned it explains the rest. Few beside Dr. Schechter himself could say if there is other Rabbinic material to quote that would be more than merely parallel and illustration to what he has written.

The topics selected (some of which are named above) are described as large and important principles in which Rabbinic thought and Israel's faith are most clearly represented and which are most in need of elucidation, because so often misunderstood and misinterpreted. In quoting his authorities Dr. Schechter does not give their dates: he assumes "that so long as there is no evidence that they are in contradiction to some older or even contemporary opinion they may be regarded as expressive of the general opinion of the synagogue". He even appeals to living testimony in addition to the written evidence of Talmud and Midrash and their legitimate successors.

Apart from this living testimony, the authorities quoted are rigidly limited to Hebrew books. The Pseudepigrapha are ruled out as a product of the various sects hovering on the borderland of Judaism. The Psalms of Solomon, in particular, with other apocryphal and apocalyptic works, are disqualified. Consequently Dr. Schechter has "no real contemporary evidence from the most important period in the history of Rabbinic theology". The Mishnah is a compilation made in the second century C.E. Its sources must necessarily be earlier: "there must have been some Rabbinic work or works composed long before our Mishnah, and perhaps as early as 30 C.E.". But this work is not extant, and so the Rabbinism, here elucidated, is formally post-Christian. This result leaves the way open for the suggestion that (so far as there is any good in it) this Rabbinism is debtor to Christianity, as it was evolved out of the tenets of the Nazarene heresy. The suggestion does not admit of demonstration, and it is commonly entertained as a convenient prejudice. Nevertheless it exists, and the only possible disproof of it lies in the tracing of a vital connexion between Rabbinism and pre-Christian Judaism, as it is to be found in Philo, Josephus, and all the Apocrypha. Speaking in the name of "Catholic Israel" Dr. Schechter ignores the very possibility of such indebtedness to a sect which in its development was largely non-Jewish. His uncompromising attitude towards the older literature is all too faithful a reproduction of the procedure of the Rabbis, who led Israel to their tents and to their God after the destruction of Jerusalem and the discomfiture of Messiah bar Cochba. Like the Hebrew of Ecclesiasticus these Apocryphal books have emerged from the various lumber-rooms, to which they were literally or figuratively consigned; and it is not impossible that the sects, of which Dr. Schechter says they are a product, were sects which contributed themselves to the compilation of Catholic Israel as we find it in the Mishnah.

But Dr. Schechter promises other aspects of Rabbinic Theology, and we can only hope that this instalment will be read so widely that he will be impelled—and enabled—to fulfil the promise speedily and to interpret for us these books also which now he relegates to the borderland of Judaism.

NOVELS.

"The Heart of a Gypsy." By Rosamond Napier. London: Duckworth. 1909. 6s.

It is hard to do justice to this fascinating story without relying on the catch-phrases habitually applied by insincere critics to the work of bad, pretentious writers. Atmosphere, nature, open air and so forth spring to the pen. And the scene is laid chiefly in the West Country, which its most staunch lovers can admit to have been over-written. Here we have Exmoor, but with no suggestion of Blackmore or veiled challenge to Mr. Eden Phillpotts. The theme of the story is such as William Black enjoyed, but it is treated with an art unknown to the scene-painter of the Highlands. A gypsy waif, adopted by a poor Devonshire parson, filled in every fibre with a hedonist pantheism, a love of trees and sunshine and heather, gives her heart to a great London surgeon, and tries loyally to adapt herself to the air of Harley Street. Meridiana Pharaoh is a creature of pure charm, but Mrs. Napier has also a very pretty talent for analysing less agreeable women. The note of tragedy is not forced, and there is no breach of the Ten Commandments. Further, the first effect of London on a wild nature is described with perfect truth. Again, the book is written naturally, with no literary grimacings. For these and other reasons the average cockney critic will write himself down an ass by pretending that the book is wanting in originality, or power, or courage, or whatever the latest Grub Street shibboleth may be. We hope that it will find readers intelligent enough to recognise that gypsies need not conform exactly to the Watts-Dunton pattern (excellent as that is) nor Devonshire to the Phillpotts formula.

"The Adventures of Captain Jack." By Max Pemberton. London: Mills and Boon. 1909. 6s.

Mr. Pemberton is terribly heavy-handed when he wishes to sparkle (the metaphor is as good as his style), and the only touch of humour in this latest production is the fact that the publishers include it in a "Thrilling Adventure Library". Captain Jack (a stage Irishman who speaks a dialect never heard outside an English music-hall) and his friends (three dull dogs) sail round the Mediterranean enjoying Thrilling Adventures, and playing schoolboy jokes, and digging each other in the ribs. Mr. Pemberton makes the dialogue at times bristle with French phrases, the quality of which may be judged from his ingenuous notion that "faire la cour" is literally translated by the phrase "to make the heart"!

"Beyond." By Frank T. Bullen. London: Chapman and Hall. 1909. 6s.

This story suggests Sandford and Merton gone to sea, and some of their experiences take us into the province of Marryat. Denys Devereux, a young squire, and Willy Demzy, his peasant protégé, sail in a Whitby whaler to the West Indies and the South Atlantic in the days of Nelson. Mr. Bullen has none of the Marryat touch, and some of the incidents are grotesque. But when he takes his heroes to harpoon whales and fight gigantic cuttle-fish and explore the fringe of the Antarctic, he writes chapters that every healthy boy will read with delight.

"The Bishop and the Lady." By Martin Lutrell Swayne. London: Methuen. 1909. 6s.

This story of the flirtations of a very silly and unscrupulous widow might have been made tolerable had the author been able to write light dialogue. As it is, every chapter is rather like a heavy mince-pie. The elements of piquancy are there, but the result is indigestible. The Bishop (a waxwork bishop) and his brother-in-law, the cynical Sir Cyprian (widower), and Sir Cyprian's romantic son, and a supermannish man of science are all attracted by the aforesaid very silly woman, and the tale of their doings is nearly as tedious as a certain play about a widow which has been running in London for some years. But Mr. Swayne, to do him justice, manages an effective and unexpected fall of the curtain.

"The Third Circle." By Frank Norris. London: Lane. 1909. 6s.

This is a collection of short stories by the late Frank Norris, rescued from newspaper files by an admiring friend. The stories do not show Mr. Norris at his best, but they were well worth collecting. The author had the seeing eye and the gift of conveying vividly what he saw. It is strange to note with what persistency his mind turned to tragedy. Was it some foreboding of the tragic brevity of his career?

"The Actress." By Louise Closser Hale. London: Constable. 1909. 6s.

For people who are interested in stage life and all its details, here is an authentic account of an American company's doings in London. It is fairly bright and interestingly told, but for a young lady who prides herself on being amusing, and who despises the British sense of humour, the heroine is decidedly disappointing as a specimen of American brightness. However, as during most of her stay in London she is under a cloud of depression, owing to her persistent and unnecessary misunderstanding of her lover's intentions, she is not at her best in private life, although as an actress she has quite a sensational success. But we do not quite believe in the eccentric comedy character-actress, who is in real life a pretty girl. It is, at any rate, an unusual combination of gifts.

"Cecilia Kirkham's Son." By Mrs. Kenneth Combe. London: Blackwood. 1909. 6s.

A brightly written tale of filial devotion, the scene of which is laid partly in India. Mystery and a topical interest are supplied by the seditious plottings of wicked natives; but everything comes right in the end.

"The Forbidden Theatre." By Keighley Snowden. London: Laurie. 1909. 6s.

The Puritanical town of Kingley, in the West Riding of Yorkshire, was much perplexed by the offer of a local magnate to endow a municipal theatre. It did not want a theatre. But the donor was like the man who said to a neighbour in a restaurant: "Confound it, sir, you *shall* eat mustard". The engagement of the artistic magnate's son to the Nonconformist mayor's daughter brought a Montagu and Capulet atmosphere into the place. Mr. Snowden expends much talent, descriptive and analytical, in making us realise with melancholy conviction what a dull place of residence a West Riding town can be. The future historian of our provincial society will, we hope, be more grateful for his efforts than the average novel-reader is likely to be.

SHORTER NOTICES.

"Lady Lettice, Viscountess Falkland." Edited by M. F. Howard. London: Murray. 1908. 6s.

The editor has made a real contribution to the devotional literature of the Anglican Church in giving us this choice edition of John Duncon's picture of the spiritual life of "Lady Lettice, Viscountess Falkland". The old-fashioned view that saw only saints in Puritans and sinners in Cavaliers finds an absolute refutation in this picture of the soul of a devout Anglican woman. The annals of Puritanism may be ransacked in vain for a similar example of saintliness. Indeed, Lady Falkland, in her sacramental devotions, is near to the holy women of the Church of Rome, and in her later years she truly trod the via dolorosa. John Duncon, to whom we owe this picture of a devout soul, was an Essex cleric driven from his living by Puritan tyranny, who found in Great Tew a refuge and a field of spiritual labour. As his editor observes, he was a narrow theologian and had little literary power. He was however well acquainted with the Fathers, and, like many Laudian Churchmen, had studied François de Sales and apparently the Spanish mystics. He displays, his editor tells us, some of the austerity of the Puritan. The ascetic note is manifest; but is it Puritanical? It may be traceable to the influence of François de Sales, for, as the life of Mère Angélique shows, the aloofness from the world on which the Puritan prided himself was more truly apparent in the devout souls of the contemporary Gallican Church. Lady Falkland had a deep sympathy with the monastic ideal. It was her passionate desire to repair the loss her sex had suffered through the dissolution of the monasteries, and she had formed a "contrivement" that there might be places for the education of young gentlewomen and for retirement of widows (as colleges and the Inns of Court and Chancery are for men) in several parts of the kingdom. But the Civil War wrecked the scheme.

"The Romance of Fra Filippo Lippi: a New Version of the Love Story of the Friar-Artist and the Nun Lucrezia." By A. J. Anderson. London: Stanley Paul. 1909. 10s. 6d. net.

"I am poor brother Lippo, by your leave. You need not clap your torches to my face." This clapping of torches to the face of the great Carmelite painter is just what a certain type of English writer on Italy loves to do. We have dealt before with the pretentious and worthless monograph of Mr. Edward Strutt. Mr. Anderson, with the remarkable feeling for literary English that characterises him throughout, observes "I don't want my critics to jump on me, as I am jumping on Mr. Strutt". Nevertheless, he treats Mr. Strutt's book as a monument of critical erudition, its chief defect apparently being his not "inquiring about the moral theology of a Catholic marriage". Only five writers, Mr. Anderson assures us, need be considered on the subject of the Friar's life and work; the rest, including, we suppose, Crowe and Cavalcaselle, as well as Herr Ulmann, "are mostly mere journalists who have skimmed through a few books in order to make attractive and remunerative copy". His own contribution is this sentimental and amateurish romance, dealing with the loves of Filippo and Lucrezia, with no particular psychological insight and a merely superficial knowledge of the fifteenth century, the atmosphere of which he is quite incapable of suggesting. The chief merit of the book is that Mr. Anderson deals very reverently with the religious aspect of the story (as, notably, in the matter of Lucrezia's repentance), and shows a sympathetic appreciation of the normal life of a Roman Catholic convent at the present day. But we are bound to add that the edifying experiences of his "little friend" Cecily, whom he "sometimes took out to a theatre or to lunch at the Cecil before she left for her convent", are ludicrously out of place in a work of this kind.

"Greek Architecture." By Allan Marquand Ph.D., L.H.D. New York: Macmillan. 1909. 10s. net.

Professor Marquand's handbook on Greek architecture is an important addition to the well-known series edited by

(*Continued on page 266.*)

Professors Gardner and Kelsey. But it is far from easy reading. In some four hundred pages, liberally interspersed with diagrams and illustrations, the writer has tried to cover the whole field of materials, forms, proportions, decoration, and composition, with all their technicalities of nomenclature, not only of the buildings but also of the monuments known to ancient Greece. The result is inevitable. One looks in vain for anything but the severest succession of well-authenticated facts set down like carefully arranged paving-stones of equal size and equal importance. The effect is depressing. Were it not for the reproductions of detail, such as those of the grand column base from the Temple of Apollo near Miletus, or of the superb antefix from the Parthenon, it would be difficult to realise that the materials dealt with were among the most glorious works of art known to civilisation. At times, however, he touches upon questions of great interest, such as the entasis or swelling given to so many Greek columns in the middle part of the shaft. Penrose's elaborate investigations, published by the Dilettanti Society, go far to prove that the effect was to correct as far as might be the unpleasant optical illusion which makes columns with straight sides appear attenuated, and their outlines concave instead of straight. So delicate was this entasis, and so slight the convex curve added by the Greek architect, that in the Parthenon and Erechtheum it is only in modern times that it has been recognised at all.

"The Works of James Buchanan." Vols. VII. and VIII. Collected and Edited by J. B. Moore. J. B. Lippincott Co. 1909. 21s. each.

Volume after volume of this sumptuous edition appears, each with hundreds of letters, State papers, and speeches. As we have said before, there is no account prefixed of the course of events covered by each volume. The search for anything of real and permanent interest among this welter of trivial documents is almost hopeless. The period covered is from June 1846 to June 1853; during the first half of that time Buchanan was Secretary of State and dealt with foreign affairs. But why are letters published such as the following: "To Mr. McLane.—Allow for funeral expenses of Secretary of Legation in London"; "To the Speaker of the House.—Submit annual immigration statistics," and so forth? The remaining volumes should contain matter of wider interest, at all events at intervals, for at the close of this period Buchanan was appointed Minister to Great Britain by President Pierce.

"These Little Ones." By E. Nesbit. London: Allen.

Short stories for children about children, but starting problems too deep for their parents, and challenging adult judgment in child language that has a literary charm. Some of the "great" writers ought to realise how very much more can be said in child words than has ever been thought by the greybeards. The book makes us live back again through our childhood, in the trifles that made our tragedy and in the tragedy that made our amusement when the informed mind was working out its sense of proportion. Two of the tales are particularly good; one of the poor lad who tried to find his romance in a rubbish heap while his parents swore and drank; the other of the little girl who found her way to the great auction at the big house, bought back daddy's writing-desk after his death with her own pocket-money, and presented it to mother. The big farmer, who lifted her up to bid and stopped the competition against her, remains in our pleasant recollections of books.

"Revue des Deux Mondes." 15 Aout.

This number is somewhat dull. The two best articles are an account of the youth of Mme. de Genlis by Mlle. Bourgain and a criticism of Lord Tennyson by M. Firmin Roz. This writer takes a wide and sympathetic view of the great poet in this anniversary study; in fact, he grasps many aspects of his genius which might be supposed to appeal to his countrymen only. His renderings of some of Tennyson's finest lyrics into French prose are often both close and happy, but of course miss entirely the rhythm and charm which give most of their haunting effect to the originals. The elegance and ease of Tennyson's turns of phrase make a natural appeal to a Frenchman when he has once mastered the difficulties of the language, but it is no easy matter to convey the impression to other Frenchmen. M. Roz has to a great extent succeeded in doing this. "For his country and the world in general it is well that Tennyson has lived."

For this Week's Books see page 268.

THIS WEEK'S BOOKS.

BIOGRAPHY

Saint Teresa of Spain (Helen Hester Colvill). Methuen. 7s. 6d. net.

FICTION

The Bride (Grace Rhys); The Search Party (George A. Birmingham). Methuen. 6s. each.
Poppea of the Post Office (Mabel Osgood Wright); A Certain Rich Man (William Allen White). Macmillan. 6s. each.
The Eagle's Nest (Allan McAulay). Lane. 6s.
The Prodigal Father (J. Storer Clouston). Mills and Boon. 6s.
True Tilda (A. T. Quiller-Couch). Bristol: Arrowsmith. 6s.
The Mount (C. F. Keary). Constable. 6s.

REPRINTS

The Sowers (Henry Seton Merriman); The Slave of the Lamp (Henry Seton Merriman). Constable. 2s. net each.
Secrets of the Past (Allen Upward). Alston Rivers. 3s. 6d. net.

SCHOOL BOOKS

A General Text-Book of Elementary Algebra (A. E. Layng). Blackie. 4s. 6d.
Asia (Ellis W. Heaton). Ralph Holland. 1s. 6d. net.
Cicero—Select Letters (Rev. T. Nicklin). Blackwood. 2s. 6d.

SCIENCE

The Geology of Ore Deposits (H. H. Thomas and D. A. MacAlister). Arnold. 7s. 6d. net.

THEOLOGY.

The Gospels in the Light of Modern Research (Rev. J. R. Cohu). Oxford: Parker. 6s. net.

TRAVEL

The Motor Routes of England (Gordon Home. Southern Section). Black. 5s. net.

MISCELLANEOUS

British Motor Tourists' A B C, The. Upcott Gill. 1s. net.
Englishwoman's Home, An. Sampson Low. 1s. net.
Highway of the Air, The: An illustrated Record of Aviation. Funk and Wagnalls. 7s.
Liberty and Progress (C. Y. C. Dawbarn). Longmans. 9s. net.
Linguistic Survey of India (Edited by G. A. Grierson. Vol. III.). Calcutta: Superintendent of Government Printing.
Town Planning in Practice (Raymond Unwin). Fisher Unwin. 21s. net.

REVIEWS AND MAGAZINES FOR SEPTEMBER.—The Cornhill Magazine, 1s.; The State, 6d.; Blackwood's Magazine, 2s. 6d.; Fry's Magazine, 6d.; Harper's Monthly Magazine, 1s.

NOTICE.

The Terms of Subscription to the SATURDAY REVIEW are:—

	United Kingdom. £ s. d.	Abroad. £ s. d.
One Year	1 8 2	1 10 4
Half Year	0 14 1	0 15 2
Quarter Year ...	0 7 1	0 7 7

Cheques and Money Orders should be crossed and made payable to the Manager, SATURDAY REVIEW Offices, 10 *King Street, Covent Garden, London, W.C.*

In the event of any difficulty being experienced in obtaining the SATURDAY REVIEW, the Publisher would be glad to be informed immediately.

Printed for the Proprietors by SPOTTISWOODE & Co. LTD., 5 New-street Square, E.C., and Published by REGINALD WEBSTER PAGE, at the Office, 10 King Street, Covent Garden, in the Parish of St. Paul, in the County of London.—*Saturday*, 28 *August*, 1909.

THE

SATURDAY REVIEW

OF

POLITICS, LITERATURE, SCIENCE, AND ART.

No. 2,810 Vol. 108. 4 September 1909. [Registered as a Newspaper.] 6d.

CONTENTS.

NOTES OF THE WEEK.

The Prime Minister has relieved the Chancellor of the Exchequer of the conduct through Committee of the licensing part of the Finance Bill. Was this a greater relief to the House or to Mr. Lloyd George? Hard to say. But the effect on the debate is very obvious and happy. Mr. Asquith, right or wrong, is master of his matter. He can always explain his proposals if he cannot justify them. If so complicated and portentous a Budget had to be, it is a great pity it did not come during Mr. Asquith's Chancellorship. It should not have come hereafter.

After property-owners the brewers, and the fight on the licensing clauses began with the proposal to clap an additional tax on the manufacturing licences of brewers and distillers. Mr. Asquith's arguments were in the main that the brewers had no reason to grumble because first the sugar duties had been taken off, and next that they had acquired an "accomplished habit" of passing on liquor taxes to the consumer. Mr. Austen Chamberlain reminded Mr. Asquith that the sugar duties were taken off at the Dundee election "for electoral reasons". What the Government thus gave away they are intending to make up by the increased taxes on the liquor trade.

Mr. Asquith met Mr. Chamberlain in the style of a man who could not positively deny the accusation. "What do you mean, sir? I scorn to reply to such language." So what remains after Mr. Chamberlain's point is that Mr. Asquith has not denied it. Mr. Asquith's other argument about transferring the tax to the consumer brought up the notorious argument of Mr. Churchill about "blackmailing". Was this the view of the Government, Mr. Balfour wanted to know. Mr. Asquith admitted that the "picturesque language" of his young colleagues—particularly cutting, this—was nonsense. But apart from this: Suppose the brewers can pass the tax on to the consumer, they and all employed in the liquor trade, including in it even farmers, suffer. The consumer's demand is reduced. This is what the soap or the cocoa and tea trades would say against special taxation. The ultimate argument to which the Government is driven is that the liquor trade deserves to be harried, and the more it suffers the better it is for the prosperity of the country. Now by the division on Friday afternoon the licence duty is to be according to compensation value. This compensation under the Kennedy judgment has always been denounced by Liberals as unfair, yet it is to be the basis of taxation!

Hotels under the licensing clauses will have to pay about twenty times more than they pay at present. The cases of hotels and clubs are somewhat similar, and the Chancellor will probably for them adopt the principle of poundage, which would be an addition to the present excise duties for liquors consumed in them. But there are various differences between clubs and hotels which, as hotel proprietors urge, make the poundage system without allowances unfair to them. Thus they say the distribution of a thousand pounds' worth of liquor in hotels costs thrice as much as in clubs, and that the net profits on their liquor are very small indeed. As the net return on capital invested in hotels only averages four per cent., the hotels will suffer severely if the extra taxation turns their small profit on liquor into a loss. In Germany the total taxation of an hotel does not exceed the ordinary taxation borne by a private house. Visitors are considered at home. Under the Budget the licence duty alone will be greater than the whole taxation on a similar place in Germany.

On Thursday Mr. Asquith found himself defending the taxation of manufacture—home manufacture, of course. "These moderate duties on the manufacture of beer", he said, and then he edged off on some pedantic difference between manufacture and "monopoly". The subtlety is to disguise the fiscal spectacle of taxing home production while letting foreign products come in free. Mr. Lloyd George ties himself in a similar tangle by concessions to "small breweries" in Ireland. If it be right to make fiscal arrangements to encourage the starting of a small brewery in Ireland, can it be wrong to afford similar encouragement for starting a big factory in England? Such is the confusion that comes of levying necessary revenue off the productive energies of our own people in order to maintain a free market for the products of the competing foreigner.

The two motives which can most deeply move the Irish party are faith and whisky, but of late the whisky has been getting far ahead of the other inspiration. They can support the Budget and even keep quiet about the faith until the bottle is touched; then they stand up for the cause of Ireland like one man; and the Government teetotalers give way to them in various important concessions, including a reduction in favour of " small breweries ". In return for the Welsh teetotalers' generosity to the Irish bottle, the Irishmen help them to harass the owners of property in Great Britain. No doubt, the poorer a community the smaller ought to be the initial quantity that can be sold under a licence; but what appeals to the professional patriots in Parliament is that they cannot hold their seats and neglect the bottle. Let them differ from the publican and the priest, and there is an end of the Irish Parliamentary party.

The United Irish League is already making winter preparations for the great increase in crime which will be necessary to make Mr. Birrell's Land Bill a popular success. It is felt in Ireland that the provisions for compulsory sale, hampered by any sort of honesty, might move too slowly at prices fatally just; and so the criminal compulsion of the League must reinforce Mr. Birrell's legislation. If a landlord does not take kindly to the statutory compulsion, his rent can be refused, and the tails can be cut off his cows, all in the interests of " the cause ". On the other hand, should the Bill be thrown out, the increase in crime is likely to be still greater. The better course for the Lords is to pass the Bill, but with its criminal clauses amended; and the Commons can hardly complain of a desire in the Upper House to make an Act of Parliament less encouraging to crime. Mr. Birrell's Bill puts a premium on theft and bloodshed without a provision to make the compulsory clauses inoperative where crime is cultivated to make them workable.

The advertisements for a teaching staff for Mr. Birrell's " National University " in Ireland have been out, with a strong injunction against " canvassing "; but the difficulty appears to be met by making appointments before the advertisements are issued. For instance, it was believed many months ago in Dublin that the Chair in Economics had been reserved for Mr. T. M. Kettle M.P. (without his knowing it, of course), and now the belief is confirmed. Economists are not aware of anything ever done by Mr. Kettle in economics, unless a few week-ends spent cow-hunting; and his friends declare that his claim to the professorship is on the ground that he wants to get married, a reasonable ground for securing a good appointment, if not exactly academic. It is only fair to the rest of the Irish party that they should know what is going on.

In a letter published this week, arising out of correspondence as to the Oxford seat, Lord Hugh Cecil makes his loyalty to the Unionist party clear. He states categorically that as between a tariff-reform Unionist and a free-trade Radical he should vote for the Unionist. This is what we have always required of a Unionist. He must in every case, whatever his fiscal view, prefer a Unionist, be he free trader or tariff reformer, to a Radical. If he does not make this his rule he should be excommunicate of the party. One reservation Lord Hugh does make. He is not sure he would vote for a tariff reformer in East Herts, Norwood, or East Marylebone, where they are trying to oust a Unionist free trader. He is, of course, supposing there should ultimately be no free-trade Unionist in the field. His reservation is only human; but even between a Unionist " malignant " and a Radical the Unionist should have his vote.

When the Town-Planning Bill goes to the Lords the clauses as to the compulsory acquisition of land ought to be revised, and they no doubt will be. One clause, as Lord Robert Cecil and Mr. Lyttelton showed, will lead to preposterous results. A railway company acquires lands under parliamentary powers for purposes approved by Parliament. Then there comes in a municipal authority who can take the land for other purposes. An appeal to the Local Government Board would be to an authority naturally supporting the locality. The Board of Trade would be the more natural department; but the railway companies ought not to be interfered with in such matters.

Another clause takes away the right to the extra ten per cent. allowed to owners for land acquired compulsorily for public purposes. There is no reason why owners when their land is taken for one purpose should lose what they get when it is taken for other purposes; though something may be said for a less allowance when the land is taken for town improvements. To take away the whole allowance by Acts for special purposes will be carried further with deliberate intention by Liberal Governments. Then by the present Bill owners are not to be allowed to have their interests represented by counsel. The plea is saving of costs; yet the solicitor is left in! Thus an Act which is admirable in principle is made one more occasion for high-handed indifference to the rights of people who own land.

Lord Lansdowne made the customary protest on Tuesday against House of Commons bullying. The Commons chop and change their plans and expect the Lords to fit in with their convenience. If only the Peers would have the courage to stand up to the Commons and tell them that they were going to do their work in their own way and in their own time! They should refuse to be hustled by the Commons into dealing in a day with a Bill that has occupied the Commons for a month. Are they afraid of the mischief the Commons might be at in the meantime? They would have finished their programme, and would have nothing to do, while the Lords were quietly going through theirs. They would not, like the Lords, have the sense to do nothing, but would fill up their time with new Bills, which would reach the Lords just when they had finished their regular programme; and so on ad infinitum. Parliament would be sitting for ever.

The mistake is in allowing the Commons to get a start of them. The Lords should insist on having work —a first-class Government measure—given them early in the session. This would then go down to the Commons when they were sending up the Bills they had finished with, and would occupy them while the Lords were engaged upon the other items of the session's programme. The two Houses would be keeping step, and work would go on more smoothly and be better done. It is nothing but the leisure forced on the Lords by the Commons during the earlier months that compels them to hurry over a mass of work at the end. If the Irish Land Bill and the Town-Planning Bill had been taken in the Lords first, they would now have a free run with the Finance Bill without any inconvenience to the other House.

The Trade Boards Bill was read a second time in the House of Lords on Monday. It is one of those measures which may be said to have been forced by circumstances on both political parties. But the most sanguine forecasts of its effects cannot ignore the speculative character of the measure. It is in no pedantic opposition to State action, but in doubt as to whether the State can do what it sets out to do, that the Bill is criticised. The most hopeful view of it is that taken by Lord Lansdowne. It may tend to introduce trade-union organisation into the disorganised trades to which it applies, and if it does will in the end do much good. But the fact stands that in either case a certain number of people who now do get at least some wages will find themselves without work; it may be through foreign competition. Lord Crewe's remark that other nations would also pass humanitarian legislation only shows how real the danger is.

We can find no trace in the records of the Paris Congress of the question—just the one which international trade unionism might discuss with profit—whether trade union conditions which increase the cost of production can be adopted in one country without encouraging unfair competition in imports from other countries where the same conditions are not adopted. In the absence of any means to make such changes and conditions international, British trade unionists stand in the curious position of protecting themselves against one another and exposing themselves to the competing foreigner, who stands to gain what they lose in attempting to improve themselves. Would it not be better if our trade union leaders tried to understand their own country before going to enlighten Paris?

There are good reasons for the Swedish Government refusing to interfere at the present stage of the strike between the employers and the men. Surely and steadily the men are being defeated, and the end of it will be their collapse. Employers would not thank the Government for an interference which would make their anticipated victory less complete. The higher and middle classes, who have organised the remarkable "Public Security Brigade" which has done so much to render the so-called general strike almost innocuous, are in sympathy with them. The real criticism on the Government is that it ought to have prevented the strike at the first. A strong Government could have done it; but the most purely parliamentary Government in Europe was weak, as the French Government was weak when it allowed the labour troubles in France to come to a head. They were both afraid of a seemingly popular movement.

Greece has had her crisis this week. The Military League demanded reforms, mainly in the direction of removing the Royal princes and favourites from the control of the army. When M. Ralli refused its leaders audience, a considerable number of officers and men took up a position on Goudi Hill. M. Ralli resigned, M. Mavromichalis accepted office, the princes asked to be relieved of their commands, the new Prime Minister fell into line with the reformers, and the crisis was at an end. M. Mavromichalis says that the movement was at no time directed against the dynasty, and that the sole object of the army was to bring about changes in its administration, good alike for the Crown and the army. The truth seems to be that the army, holding the politicians responsible for recent events in Crete and elsewhere, decided to take matters into its own hands. The result is that for the moment Greece is governed by the military acting through M. Mavromichalis.

Mulai Hafid is not devoting all his time to the torture, moral if not physical, of El Roghi. At the moment when the Spanish advance was beginning he sent orders to the Moorish leaders in the Riff to abandon their hostility to Spain. That was the last thing they were prepared to do. Even though they were not spoiling for a fight, they did not intend to further Mulai Hafid's ulterior views by surrender to a European Power. On the contrary, some of them see an opportunity to prejudice a position already none too secure. Hence they snapped their fingers at his commands and proceeded to attack the Spanish post at Souk-el-Arba, apparently with disastrous consequences to themselves. Both sides are busy concentrating forces, and the sending of the Moorish women and children to the interior may be taken as a sign that the serious business of the campaign is at hand.

The French fleet has been engaged in two remarkable actions during this week, and has greatly distinguished itself. The first thrilling deed was the bombardment of an old war vessel on which were a number of cats and dogs. The enemy suffered severely. We hope international complications may not follow through the intervention of the Anti-Vivisection Societies. In the next engagement the cruiser "Gloire", in its enthusiasm to test the actualities of fire practice, sent two shots into the cruiser "Marseillaise", on board of which was Rear-Admiral Aubert. These two events appear rather to show that recent reports of the decadence of the French Navy may be exaggerated.

The "Frankfurter Zeitung" has been lecturing some of its sprightlier contemporaries for publishing naughty pictures of the King. The admonition is in the terms of homiletic patronage so characteristic of Liberalism all the world over. Certain of the more obvious absurdities of the English, we are grandiloquently informed, may be exposed, but the King should be respected. The article has brought this Frankfort newspaper much unmerited approval from the English Press. It is a flagrant case of the pot calling the kettle black. How does this journal, which prates of respect to foreign potentates, itself treat the King? In the very issue of the weekly edition which prints the warning to caricaturists, it is regarded as an open question whether the King actually sent a congratulatory birthday letter to the Emperor at Ischl or only allowed the English papers to say that he did. And when the Tsar was at Cowes, the "Frankfurter Zeitung", after quoting the King's words as to the pacific purpose of the British fleet, added that it was not necessary to believe them! Caricature may be less offensive than innuendo.

Lord Charles Beresford and Sir William White have both been urging upon the Canadians the importance of an Imperial Navy controlled as one unit. The Imperial Conference, a great event in its way, has not convinced the colonists that their best interests as well as the Empire's would be served by allowing their contributions to the Navy to be merged in the forces directed by the Imperial Government. Colonel Foxton, the Australian delegate, and Mr. Cook, the Australian Defence Minister, in their comments on the Conference still adopt too local an attitude. Mr. Cook thinks that the colonies may defend the Pacific whilst Great Britain looks after home waters, and Colonel Foxton says that the Admiralty would be in control only in war time. "In peace time the Australian fleet unit will be under the exclusive control and administration of the Commonwealth Government." He talks of the Admiralty "lending" the Australian fleet part of its personnel. The phrase has not the Imperial ring.

The journey between New York and London has been shortened by about half a day by the Cunard Company, with the co-operation of the Great Western Railway, whose enterprise deserves every advantage that may be got from the achievement. The mails will be transferred at Queenstown as usual, and the time is saved in the remainder of the route, by Fishguard and across Wales, instead of by Liverpool. It is good to know that the Liverpool people do not fear any disadvantage from the change, and yet it is hard to see how traffic can be diverted from one route to another and the left route not suffer. These things, however, have their own mysteries, and the people of Liverpool ought to be the best judges of their own business.

The week at Rheims ended as it began, and records continued to be broken. The touch of fitness came at the finish with the victory of Mr. Curtiss, the countryman of the Wright brothers. Mr. Latham's prize will also give pleasure to sportsmen of all nations, and it is to be feared that he has for ever lost that pity guaranteed to him by the "Figaro" of some weeks back on behalf of all the ladies of France. If the end were a chapter of records, it was also a chapter of accidents. M. Blériot deserves sympathy; but it must be admitted that his machine behaved well. True it set him alight; but then it also extinguished him. M. Blériot is paying for his experience. It will be remembered how he was made to hobble to his machine for the Channel flight.

It used to be thought that only an acrobat could fly; but the fact that mere pupils, driving machines that they have had no part in inventing, have met with fair success seems to show that it is simply a case for a cool head and a little practice. If this is so, there will soon be many in the field; for there is no doubt about it paying. Even the losers are to be induced to lose by the offer of substantial sums. Meanwhile on this side the Channel we are apparently beginning to mean something; and if Colonel Cody makes the first shot at Manchester, we wish him well. Nevertheless, although any attempt to enliven British enterprise in this direction is to be commended, it is odd that an Australian level-headed man of business should tempt Providence by inviting people to fly over London.

If the telegrams received at Brussels and Copenhagen are to be believed, the world will add this week to its list of successful heroes; but, until these telegrams receive very strict confirmation, the world will do well to restrain its enthusiasm. One thing is certain: whether Dr. Cook has discovered the North Pole or whether he has not, he will have an interesting story to tell. His last dash for the Pole in the company of Esquimaux, and his subsequent disappearance and reputed death, are thrilling enough. Meanwhile, one would like to know how Dr. Cook will prove his case. Can he do so by celestial photography, or by the production of a machine that is too honest to allow itself to be tampered with?

Fortunately Dr. Cook's reputation is above suspicion. He is a quiet man; and while people followed Peary and Shackleton with attention, Dr. Cook went out almost unnoticed. But his work in Alaska, in the Antarctic, and in the scaling of Mount McKinley is well known to explorers. He is the kind of man it would be a pleasure to congratulate, if he has indeed arrived. But he will have to make out a plain case. We have become so used to failure that we are beginning to disbelieve in the possibilities of success. Even those who think of airships remember André and shake their heads.

The Portrait Gallery and the nation are unfortunate in losing the services of Mr. Lionel Cust, while yet in the prime of life, and for a cause—the danger of prolonged strain on the eyesight—which everyone will regret. Mr. Cust's combination of wide and exact knowledge of painting in general, and of English portraiture in particular, with administrative ability, made the choice of a successor difficult. Mr. C. F. Bell, of the Ashmolean Museum, has claims of special knowledge and official experience which, if he had been a candidate, could hardly have been overlooked. In appointing another Oxford man, however, Mr. C. J. Holmes, the Slade Professor, the Government have undoubtedly chosen the best available successor to Mr. Cust. If not at present known by studies on the particular subject of portraits, in knowledge of English painting, of which portraiture forms so large a part, Mr. Holmes is passed by few living men. He is a good critic, perhaps a better painter; he has had experience of business; and the admirable temper and good sense of his editorials in the "Burlington Magazine" are valuable qualifications for his new directorship. The candour with which certain negligences and mistakes of the Government in matters of art have been exposed in the "Burlington" make this appointment the more to its credit.

So Mr. Russell Wakefield, Rector of S. Mary's, Bryanston Square, and one time Mayor of Marylebone, is to be Dean of Norwich. All things—no, not quite all things, not a bishopric—to him who can wait. Mr. Russell Wakefield has been marked out for preferment, even dignity, ever since this Government came into power—marked out by the public and himself. Well, if a very energetically Liberal Churchman did not come by his own now, when should he? And no valid objection could be taken to Mr. Wakefield's appointment. He is a man of wide culture and still wider activities—so wide that the care of his parish becomes a detail in his daily round. He is an attractive personality, too, and will surely make his deanery a centre of much varied life. His decanal duties will not nearly satisfy his appetite for doing. He should be sympathetic with his Bishop—one of the Gladstone Churchmen. As theologian he would be, we suppose, a sort of blend or cross between High and Broad, or, putting it in terms of mensuration, 6 Broad × 3 High.

THE BUDGET AND THE COUNTRY.

MINISTERS, little and big, seem never tired of repeating that the Budget is immensely popular, is getting daily more popular, and that the House of Lords will not dare to throw it out. According to them it is now a settled thing that the House of Lords will pass the Budget as it leaves the Commons. Maybe Ministers are taking Robespierre's precedent to heart and putting their confidence in repetition. The force of repetition no doubt is considerable; still Robespierre did not come to the best of ends. Rather Ministers remind us of fearful persons who reassure themselves by saying over and over again that they are not afraid. They say it aloud too, partly for the comfort of hearing the brave tone of their own voices, partly to assure others of their courage. But this is not so easy to do. Some are not persuaded but only made suspicious by these repetitions, which strike them as vain. If it is so obvious that the country is in love with the Budget, what is the need of saying it so often? If it is so certain that the Lords will not reject the Budget, it must be within most men's capacity to make the inference for themselves. So far as we have observed, Unionist speakers, certainly those of the front rank, are not imitating the Ministerial example by eternally saying that the Budget is extremely unpopular, and that it is certain the Lords will reject it with ignominy. "They can't say that because they know it is popular." This explanation of their restraint is at least complimentary to Unionist veracity. But any way this unceasing talk about the popularity of the Budget is stupid. It is always very difficult to know whether a particular measure is popular or not; the guides to a judgment are most uncertain. As to the Budget, there is almost nothing to go by. There has been but one by-election, and that was neutral as evidence of popularity. If the reduction by half of the Government majority at High Peak went to show that the Budget was unpopular, its not being reduced by more went to show that it was popular. All the fuss and controversy there has been over supposed and actual adverse votes and disturbance at Budget protest meetings has been perfectly idle so far as the question of the Budget's popularity is concerned. No doubt as between Mr. Walter Long and the "South Wales Daily News" we should prefer Mr. Long's account of the proceedings at Swansea. We should always prefer the account of a responsible politician who was there to any newspaper's report, and we do not know that Welsh Radical newspapers and Welsh people are more truthful than others. But as evidence of public opinion the whole matter is irrelevant. Everybody knows that any party that has an effective organisation at all can by concentration of disciplined force break up any open meeting of opponents and negative the resolution. At any rate they can do it until the tactics are observed and noted by the other side and then countered. Nor are meetings generally a trustworthy guide to public opinion. They are meant to stimulate enthusiasm, to encourage helpers and supporters, and only secondarily to influence political opinion. Unionist meetings during the election campaign of 1906 were as enthusiastic and well attended as could be wished. Meetings are attended almost exclusively by the very keen, and there are always far more keen men on both sides than would fill any number of halls. The "Daily Mail" may be upset by an adverse vote or two at Budget protest meetings, but discerning minds are not affected. There is simply no evidence either way as to the general public view of the Budget. One has to judge a priori. It is illogical but true that there is usually a general feeling about questions of this sort, grounds for which are not and cannot be stated in black and white, but which none the less is often correct. The feeling of some of the most competent experts about the matter is that on the whole the Budget is not growing in popularity.

Certainly there would be nothing strange in the Budget being popular. On paper it could hardly be otherwise, and it is not easy for the man in the street to know even what the Government's proposals in fact are, still less what they mean and what they are likely to lead to. If the bulk of electors had time and intelligence to follow day by day the discussion of the Budget in Committee, we should be perfectly confident of the country rejecting the Budget and withdrawing support from the Government. A Cabinet of very able debaters is not beaten in argument time after time if it has a good cause to defend. A very able and strong Prime Minister at the head of a majority of over two hundred does not alter his proposal at most important points in deference to the arguments of a small minority, if that proposal is sound. And the argument against the Government is all the stronger if the Unionist minority is inferior to their opponents in ability. These points would tell with the public if the public could be let into the details of what goes on in the House. But into those details the public does not go. It does not want to go into them, and hardly could if it did. Yet that is the task set to the Unionist worker. The man in the street must not be left to judge the Budget on a mere general view; which is all in favour of the Government, who have carefully constructed their Budget on that calculation.

If a debt has to be paid by a community of, say, six people, and a proposal is made to charge it on two of them, the other four paying nothing, it is quite certain that the four will support the proposal and the two will oppose it. It is also certain that the four will be satisfied that it is just, and the two will be satisfied that it is iniquitous. Having in mind this elementary proposition of human nature, the Government proceeded to put the burden of new taxation on so small a portion numerically of the whole community that it was certain a great majority of the electors would, at any rate at first sight, be pleased with the Budget. Thus from the electioneering point of view the Budget was truly and carefully laid. We need not claim any moral superiority in those who are taxed over those who escape. The landowner may be attacking the Budget on the same ground as the clerk and the artisan may be supporting it—self-interest. But the Government have so contrived that the argument from self-interest—other things being equal—shall tell wholly in their favour. Preach self-interest, selfishness, naked, undisguised, unqualified, and their side must gain. The argument is useless to us. The Government have only to appeal to cupidity and self-interest; the less they trouble to prove the justice or patriotism of their plan, the better for them. We have to appeal to justice, fair play, and a sense of honour. Mr. Lloyd George and his friends, with their sublime faith in human goodness, have made their calculation which appeal is the easier and the more likely to go home. We are left with the better but certainly the harder part. We believe it can be shown that ultimately these new taxes will not be to the advantage of any class in the community; but the probable injurious results are necessarily indirect. The breaking-up of the landowning class, even if another some day grew up and took its place, would be most hurtful to the nation. The depreciation in the value of ground rents must in the end affect an immense number of men of very small means. But considerations such as these require thought to be appreciated. This is the position the Unionist party has to face. We have done wonders against great odds in the House. If we attack with the same persistency and the same intelligence in the country, we shall do wonders there too. But we shall not help ourselves by underrating the difficulty.

As to the Ministerial pronouncements on the House of Lords, it is impossible that they can know anything about the matter. No one knows, not Lord Lansdowne himself, what the Lords will do with the Bill. But Radical Ministers of all men probably know least. The decisions of the Lords do not lie in the lap of the Government; and the present Ministers are less likely than anyone else to be taken into the confidence of the powers that be in the Upper House. We suppose they are assuming that the Lords will pass the Finance Bill from fear of its general popularity. But what would the position be if they did this? The Government would be triumphant; they would have beaten the Lords and got an admission that the Budget was approved by the country. This would give them an opportunity of going to the country too good to miss. Suppose they dissolved, say, at the end of the year; what position should we be in? If we defended the Lords on the theory of bowing to the will of the country, we should be estopped from criticising the Budget and have to admit that in the Commons Mr. Balfour and the Opposition were opposing the popular will. If we still denied that the Budget represented the will of the people, we should stultify the Lords entirely. They would have sacrificed their principles to a miscalculation of public opinion. On the other hand, if they throw out the Budget, our position will be clear and strong. The Lords condemned the Budget on merits, and held that the country did not approve it and would support it less and less the more they understood its details. That is a fighting position to take up. We are not posing as "in the know", but as a sporting event we would very much rather bet on the Lords throwing out the Finance Bill than passing it. If anybody offered us odds against their throwing it out, we would take him cheerfully. We might even give odds of six to four on their doing it.

PARLIAMENTARY COLLAPSE IN GREECE.

GREEK constitutionalism has received its death-blow amid considerable popular apathy; everything has passed off as quietly as it should do at a well-conducted execution. All political parties are regarded with such contemptuous indifference by the Greek public that the capitulation of one or other of them to a military committee is only viewed with hopefulness. At any rate, the new régime can hardly be more corrupt or more inefficient than the old. What fails to disturb Greece need not worry the outside world. In some quarters the new movement is regarded as anti-dynastic, but we have the unanimous assurance of the Athens press—which is rather a better press than the country deserves—that the monarchy is safe enough, and that it is only intended to replace by responsible officers the Princes who nominally control the various departments of the Greek army. And even if the dynasty should fail to weather the storm, there will not be much of a scramble for the vacant throne. True, an English nobleman might find it more acceptable now than it appeared in days gone by, when death duties were as yet undevised and land taxes unthought of; but even in his case the change might be a transference from the frying-pan to the fire. No great foreign Power is likely to force one of its unoccupied princes upon the country. Greece lies too near the edge of the European powder magazine for such risks, and Turkey, which might be tempted to take advantage of her rival's weakness, is well aware that the Powers would tolerate no annexation of territory. If the Greeks have any common-sense, which is by no means certain, they will realise that it is wisest for them to wash their dirty linen as quietly as possible and to stick to a dynasty whose powerful connexions have won the country something of a place in the sun. But, whatever be the international upshot of the recent outbreak, it is at least certain that Greek Parliamentarianism has capitulated without a struggle to military rule.

This fact will be disputed by that section of British opinion which is the slave to forms and phrases. We shall be told that the Ralli Ministry duly resigned, that the King sent for a Premier whose military and naval policy was more likely to meet with the approval of the electorate, and that the rules of the parliamentary game have been most scrupulously observed. All this is very true, and is nevertheless pure bunkum. It is even less of a metaphor than usual to speak of the parliamentary game in Greece. Party politics are a game there, and a dirty game. Parliament is spoken of as the source of power, but in fact it is obviously the instrument of power wielded by an extra-parliamentary authority. Nor is it only in Greece that Parliament is used as a convenient political machine by an alien control anything rather than constitutional. The gutter press—we apply the term to those organs which pander to the dearest political prejudices of our democracy—assures us that the tyrant Abdul Hamid has been deposed, and that the constitutional sovereign, Mehemet V., reigns in his stead. This is much the same as saying that the tyrant Charles I. was replaced by the constitutional monarch Cromwell, a doctrine which even Radical Wales would have some difficulty in swallowing when put in this bald form. What really happened in both cases was that a better-trained military force wrested power from a worse-trained military force, and abundant parallels are to be found in the history of the Roman Empire, a régime which even democratic ignorance would hardly call constitutional.

Parliamentary government has been tried all over the world, and only British peoples have made it even seem to succeed. Look first at other countries where the institution is supposed to flourish. There is France, where the Parliament has accomplished nothing, or next to nothing, since the Republic was established, and where all the real work is done by the huge bureaucracy controlled by the Ministry of the Interior. The one truly parliamentary régime which France has ever had was the July monarchy, and it fell in a street brawl. Then there is Germany, a monarchy obviously thoroughly military, and very properly typified by an Emperor who is always in uniform. It is true that there is a Parliament, but the Government is cynically regardless of members' principles, though it finds itself obliged to tout for their votes. Or, again, there is Spain, nowadays a constitutional country after many vicissitudes. That country lacks both a stable bureaucracy and a stable army, but their place is taken by the Church, the whole weight of which has been decisively behind the Prime Minister in the recent crisis. These are all countries which might be instanced by the parliamentary fanatic. But there is no difficulty in discovering cases in which constitutionalism is obviously a farce. To say nothing of the Latin-American republics, and even of the non-Latin-American republic, there is Persia, where Parliament has been given a splendid opportunity. So badly did the two last Shahs govern that they could not even raise funds to pay their mercenaries. Yet the constitutional régime, to which all men looked for help, could do nothing except talk. Or, again, there is Portugal, where the political forms are normally suspended whenever there is a crisis. Finally there is the peculiarly interesting case of Sweden. That country is now suffering under a general strike. It is a phase of the struggle between Capital and Labour, the problem of the century; and what steps does Parliament, the representative of public opinion, the unchallenged source of political power and centre of political authority, take towards a solution? It takes none whatever, but with disingenuous hypocrisy assumes credit for its impartial inertness.

There is a section of English opinion which advocates parliamentary institutions as a universal political remedy, with all the facile rhetoric of the vendor of a quack nostrum. Is your trouble dishonest Tchinovniks? Then try a general election. Is there not a toman in your treasury? An assembly of paid deputies will give you prosperity. Have you to administer a country of diverse races and religions? All will be well if you shut up a few specimens of each in one room. Be the people black, white, or yellow, be the issue racial, religious, or economic, the one sovereign specific of parliamentary institutions is recommended with eternal iteration and myopic confidence. Was there ever such an appalling case of the fallacy of the undistributed middle? Because the parliamentary system pleases the peculiar genius of the English and the Scottish peoples, because by its aid those peoples dealt with a problem primarily religious, therefore it must be applicable to all the world!

Travelling in France at the time of the Revolution, Arthur Young recommended the adoption of the English system of government. We laugh at him nowadays, but he had more excuse than the enthusiasts of to-day. They have seen the system applied and he had not. It is one of the most tragic jokes in history that the statesmen of Europe should have seen in our House of Commons the explanation of our victory over Napoleon. An effective oligarchy armed with sea-power will normally conquer a single genius armed with land-power, as the Romans proved when they defeated Hannibal. But the parliamentary system still enjoys undeserved credit.

WORKERS AND WORKLESS.

THE Trade Boards Bill in the Lords makes us think of unemployment—the spectre is re-appearing. When future students of politics come to look into the history of our own time, will anything surprise them so much as the blind refusal of a great party to acknowledge that the fiscal policy of a country can seriously affect the conditions of employment of its people?

It will be recorded how capital was taxed in the vain effort to increase interest; how it was sought to make the unemployed the pensioners of the State, how people still fortunate enough to find work were compelled to contribute to the cost of others whom a worn-out economic system could no longer support, how an English Finance Minister preached confiscation as an alternative to industry.

Unemployment, say economists, is a natural concomitant of our existing industrial system. The Government accepts the theory, confesses impotence and offers, prompted presumably by prickings of conscience, non-contributory old-age pensions, labour exchanges and invalidity and sickness insurance. These are palliatives not remedies, and leave the disease untouched. Even Sir Robert Giffen has turned at last and now roundly takes the Government to task for a financial policy which is steadily driving capital abroad and so giving to foreign workers employment and wages which rightly belong to our own people. Many people do not seem yet to realise that the penal clauses of the Budget, for one rich man they hit, ricochet on to scores of the poor. When an individual has provided for the bare existence of himself and his dependants he spends the excess of his income on luxuries, which though perhaps, in the strict material sense, economically unnecessary to the spender, provide employment for those to whom the money goes. The certain and inevitable effect of heavy taxation is the limitation of expenditure on non-necessities, with the consequent throwing out of employment of those who have hitherto supplied such luxuries. What have these workers to turn to?

However the rigid economist may rejoice at the cessation of theoretically unproductive manufactures, his satisfaction is small comfort to those who have lost their living, and the conversion of a once independent worker into a State-assisted citizen can hardly be to the benefit of the community. While the change is in progress these workers go to swell the ranks of the unemployed, therein to lose heart and hope, to forget their skill and cunning, and in all probability to exchange for habits of industry the loafer's To-morrow will do.

But what will the Government palliations effect? The old-age pension scheme in the main transfers the burden of the aged poor from the local rates to the Treasury, though incidentally it may to a slight extent lessen competition by the withdrawal from the labour market of a few aged workers. Labour exchanges, even if successful, cannot increase the volume of work, their function is simply an efficient notification of existing requirements. Sickness and out-of-work insurance, excellent as it is if properly contributory, provides no extra work, but rather by its toll on the employers and the State tends to diminish the capital available for industrial enterprise. None of these so-called remedies in any way increases the wages fund of the country; that rises or falls with the volume of trade, which is mainly dependent in this country on foreign markets, now gradually but steadily being closed to our manufactures. The alternative of Tariff Reform has at least the merit of attempting to strike at the root of the difficulty; it offers no anæsthetic, but seeks a radical cure.

The Government have too quickly assumed that their social legislation will be at once successful. Just as with old-age pensions so with labour exchanges: drafting first and inquiry to follow. With the Bill practically through Parliament there comes a hurried visit of officials to Germany, that Mecca of Radical social reformers for all policies but those which have really made the country what it is to-day. The officials will have found in Germany that the success of a labour exchange depends almost entirely on the tact and discretion of the officials in charge. The conditions are even more difficult in England. With us the trades union system is highly developed, strong in some places and weak in others. Where employers and workers agree and officials are tactful the exchange will probably work well; friction and suspicion can only lead to an empty register. The labour world is not too calm to-day.

Following the usual custom of his colleagues, the President of the Board of Trade has chosen the medium of the press to advertise his insurance proposals. Employers, workmen and State are all to contribute, and when unemployment comes the worker will be supported for many weeks by a fund to which he has contributed but a third. This tax on industry is heavy, and like all taxes on capital will probably be cast in the long run on the wages fund. Why Mr. Churchill has chosen to start his scheme with the best-paid trades in the country is not altogether clear. The argument is that a trade like shipbuilding is subject to long periods of depression, and therefore especially needs an unemployment fund. Yet Mr. Churchill proposes to limit his payments to a period totally inadequate to cover a long period of depression; and the answer of worse-paid trades reasonably may be that abnormally high wages in a period of prosperity carry with them the obligation to put by money for days of slackness. The textile trade, among others, is at present excluded on the ground that slackness of trade never means total unemployment but mere shortness of time, but that is no ground for making men with reduced wages help to pay unemployed benefits to those whose total average wages year in and year out in all probability exceed their own. This is not all, for textile workers frequently lose their employment; firms stop and factories close, and workers thus cast on the market would find unemployed benefits of the greatest value to keep them going until they had time to search for new places. It may well be asked, too, whether the trades unions have been consulted, whether Mr. Churchill has inquired why unions are restricting their unemployed funds, and are seriously considering whether these have any real economic value. In regard to sickness insurance the great friendly societies must be closely consulted, otherwise there is serious danger of destroying habits of thrift which it has taken years to produce.

As to the Trade Boards Bill, which has now passed its second reading in the House of Lords, it is to be feared that the problem of unemployment will be complicated by it. One of the things to be expected from it is that the attempt to fix minimum wages will be followed by the non-employment of many who earn some wages, even though in any satisfactory sense they cannot be called living wages. For this class of person who are not competent to earn wages at a fair market rate, what use can the Exchanges be? No employment can be obtained by people who are not competent; and no system of insurance can apply to them. They fall out of employment, and the only way of paying them unemployed benefit is through the Poor Law. The President of the Board of Trade hands over to his colleague at the Local Government Board an additional number of paupers. The only mitigation of this reflection is that already these people are half their time on the poor rates because they do not earn normal wages.

The social reform work of this Government is done in a hurry—it has about it at least a suggestion of political advertisement. The duty of the Unionist party is clear. They should insist on a thoroughly representative Commission to inquire into the unemployed question at large, inviting friendly societies, trades unions, social workers, Government officials and employers to give evidence. Only in this way can a properly co-ordinated scheme be prepared; piecemeal legislation such as is now seeing the light is hardly more than a beating of the air.

TOWN-PLANNING OR TOWN-TRAINING?

TOWN-PLANNING, though now in Parliament and in everybody's mouth, is nearly as new and unfamiliar to us as is flying; yet soon, no doubt, we shall be carrying out our studies of the first at the altitude of the second, with bird's-eye views in reality, and perspectives no longer merely on paper. In the matter of airships and aeroplanes natural selection may be peculiarly trusted to give instant decision as to our efficiency and skill, landing us promptly either as Icarus or as Blériot; but of good and bad town-planning unfortunately there can be no such ready test. The badly planned town does not fall down—more's the pity—but creates and keeps up evils of many kinds. Our vast Victorian expansions have neither retained the advantages of the old towns nor of the new, but rather the disadvantages of both. For their main streets, though varied even to bewilderment, remain without beauty or real individuality, while private streets are too often monotonous in their wealth or dismal in their poverty. The former are too narrow for their ever-growing traffic, the latter often wastefully broad, with long acres of costly macadam or paving, even where the old green lanes, with but little amendment, might have been preserved.

Housing improvements have, it is true, long been in progress, and not without results, though mostly far less than they seemed to promise. For to destroy overcrowded and insanitary houses without supplying new ones, as was too long the fashion in every city, was often primarily efficacious in raising rents for the still more overcrowded remainder; while the philanthropic building of high tenements set up a new rate of over-population per acre, with the deleterious effect of high staircases upon the health of women and children. Thus local evils, become dramatically obvious, were relieved by the municipalities at the public expense; while new evils, more generally diffused, were being created.

What real improvement in house accommodation the mass of the people have been enjoying has been coming about in a more normal and desirable way—through the gradual exodus of the middle class to the suburbs, leaving their houses to the small shopkeepers, clerks and skilled workmen, whose homes in turn become accessible to the poorer. A commendable desire has been stirring among the lower middle class and the artisans to get for their children and themselves some of the physical advantages of suburban dwelling. Hence the vast "dormitories" which have grown up around London, expanding old villages into mushroom towns, and so largely defeating their own object. Landowners and large employers have in many places come in to help this spontaneous movement, giving it a better thought-out direction. Model villages and garden cities have appeared; good in intention if not always quite happy in result.

At this stage the Town-Planning Bill makes its appearance, and with it we come face to face with the more ambitious town-planning movements of the Continent and the civic transformations of the United States. Haussmann is becoming for most an example; thus Mr. Inigo Triggs, who has boldly, but too hastily and uncritically, attempted the first English Manual of Town-Planning,* holds him up once and again in preface and in text for admiration apparently unqualified by even a moment's reflection, much less a week of actual inquiry in Paris as to the historic city which he so ruthlessly destroyed, the new evils which he so unthinkingly created. Uncritical as any town councillor upon his Paris holiday, he sees only that narrow streets have been replaced by broad ones, but knows nothing of the spacious gardens which so often lay behind the old houses. He has not climbed the lofty stairs to their evil garrets, nor looked down into the

* "Town-Planning, Past, Present and Possible." By J. Inigo Triggs. London: Methuen. 1909. 15s. net.

narrow sunless courts, too often mere wells of air-sewage, vast tubes for wholesale tubercle-culture which Haussmann has hid behind his pompous frontages. He has never thought how the population was ploughed aside and piled up into these lofty tenements, each household, poor or prosperous, with fewer and smaller rooms than before; nor how rents and municipal taxation, and with this the price of food, were all necessarily thus raised, and the condition of the people correspondingly depressed. Yet all this, however unknown to the admiring tourist, lay deep behind the discontent and unrest which tempted on the Franco-German war, and which exploded in the Commune; and is to this day a great and notable factor among those elements of decadence which Frenchmen and foreigners alike deplore—from the limitation of population to their narrowed homes, to that deterioration which the exchange of even the smallest garden outlet for the boulevard of a great city everywhere involves, and this peculiarly upon a fundamentally (indeed for the most part recently) peasant stock. Nor is it much better when we step behind the boulevards of imperial Berlin, which have sprung up since the war; not even when we visit the masterpieces of Haussmann's greatest successor, Dr. Stübben, in Cologne or Düsseldorf. We find our housing endeavours difficult enough in this country with current site prices; but when we go to the vast empty areas which each great Rhenish city has pegged out for its expansion throughout this opening century, we find that the finger of its land speculator has grown thicker than our landowner's loins; and tenement life for the German people thus threatens to be stereotyped. In America too—where Olmsted and Mayor Quincy transfigured Boston and L'Enfant laid out Washington—we note the appearance in nearly every considerable city of a swarm of new architects, largely fresh from Paris, at any rate essentially of the school of Haussmann. These are all for attempting the greatest tasks first; alluring unsophisticated city fathers with their exercises at the Ecole des Beaux Arts, brushed up into gorgeous architectural fashion-plates, in its worst style, or absence of style, and hustling not a few cities into gigantic extravagances, from which a reaction, and one disastrous to real good, must soon appear. Plainly then it is time to ask How is this new Bill to protect us from similar civic and therefore national misfortune?

It is we, the public of every borough and city, who must educate our coming masters, municipal, professional, and Government, and we must, therefore, first educate ourselves. It is time to go forth, then, and survey our city, both out and in, and mark it well, alike in past and present, from bulwarks to palaces. We shall then become conscious of the city as a life and growth in its geography, its work, its people, from simplest and humblest beginnings to their complex modern resultants. We see its many analogies to other cities here and there in needs and wants; we see resemblances in functions, in qualities, in defects; but we must not act until we have learned to know our city as having an individuality of its own. As we respect this, as we value and love it, it will become safe to think here of extensions, there of alterations and improvements. These now readily suggest themselves; let these be sketched out, with alternatives, by various skilful hands, each and all chosen not for specialised fitness alone, nor yet for general knowledge, but, as far as may be, for both together. Selection will still be difficult, but it can no longer go wholly wrong.

But all this dream of making or re-making our modern cities offhand and wholesale, yesterday by a Haussmann, to-day by a Stübben, and to-morrow by their copyists or their rivals, is not only megalomania in thought, but also lèse-humanité in action. It is fraught with more disasters than were ever the paper constitution-makings, the passionate turmoils of past political revolutions. A city, a complex modern city above all, is not to be thus made wholesale from without, but must grow gradually, organically, from within. There is a too common type of architect, of borough engineer also, who would cheerfully undertake to construct a coral reef; and he is even now preparing for us his wholesale perspectives, now of what may be but stone coffins and brick vaults in place of streets of homes, and again of public buildings, each but a collective sarcophagus for our scribes. This is, and should be as yet for our inexperience of city-making, but the day of small things: though if we be faithful with these, the ten talents and the many cities will come soon enough, even before we are fully ready for them.

We must begin with repairs and cleansing, reaching the hygienist and the housewife's standard, not merely the town council's. Our old houses, our existing town thus set in order, our next needs will be seen far more plainly; and the direction of their possible growth will also become more clear. Our action upon our city's growth is thus more like the gardener's, not merely tending, and where need be pruning, but above all training his trees here for foliage, there for flower, for fruit, for use and for beauty, yet neither separate from the other. Town-planning thus becomes town-training—a the assistance of the collective life and growth.

THE CITY.

THE end of August account is seldom an exciting one on the Stock Exchange; and had it not been for the antics of Union Pacifics and the domestic jars of the Peking Syndicate there would have been absolutely nothing to write about. Wall Street seems to have made up its mind that Mr. Harriman is not going to die just yet; and so Union Pacifics have settled down soberly in the neighbourhood of 207, and Steel Commons do not appear to have any intention of descending below 77, a prodigiously high figure, measured by dividends. The shares of the Peking Syndicate, after soaring to 15⅝, dropped to 12 and then recovered to 13¼. It is evident that there is a great deal of friction between the French shareholders in the Peking Syndicate and the board, or rather Mr. Carl Meyer, the chairman. The French shareholders believe enthusiastically in the value, present and prospective, of their property, and certain estimates of profits to be derived from the sale of coal appeared in the French newspapers. These estimates may have been exaggerated, or they may have been correct; but as they did not emanate from the directors there was absolutely no obligation on the board to take any notice of them. Suddenly a letter was sent to the papers, signed by the secretary on behalf of the board, stating that the estimates of profit were grossly exaggerated, and "crabbing" Peking shares in the hearty fashion which is generally done by powerful "bears" in command of a newspaper. As our contemporary, the "Financial News", points out, if the French estimates of profits are "gross exaggerations" then the prospectus, on which the money of the public was obtained, must have been a gross exaggeration, for the French journalists do little more than revive the statements of the prospectus. To say that a profit of 10s. a ton on coal may be realised, that there is a large area for the sale of the coal, that iron-smelting works may be erected, and that there may be petroleum on the property is an almost verbatim extract from the prospectus, so that if there are any misrepresentations afloat it would seem as if Mr. Carl Meyer and his colleagues were their authors. How can any class of shareholders, French or British, thank the board for doing their utmost to prevent a rise in the price of the shares, especially as many investors bought them at £25? There is clearly some incompatibility of temper between the chairman and his shareholders, and why the matter cannot be settled by the foreign group obtaining control we have never been able to discover.

In the foreign railway market Leopoldina Ordinary have slipped back a point to 73, and now, we should say, is the time to buy, as they will slowly rise to 80, as their increases of traffic are steady and substantial. Whether the dividend on Buenos Ayres and Pacific Ordinary will be reduced to 6 or 5, or at all, continues to exercise a good many speculators and investors. In the meantime the shares are steady in the neighbourhood of 103.

There is absolutely nothing doing in mines. Alaska

Iexicans are steady at 3⅜, and Alaska Treadwells at 7. n the Kaffir Circus Consolidated Goldfields are the only hares which have moved upward to over 7, though they ave pulled after them South African Gold Trusts, a ompany under the same management, whose shares at ¾ are undervalued. Gold Trusts will probably pay a ig dividend at the end of the year, and they are cer-ainly worth 5. Spring Mines are cheap at 25s., a price o which they have fallen from 35s., owing to the pecial settlement taking place on Thursday. A cer-ain type of speculator always buys for special settle-nent, because there is nothing to pay at the moment, nd then sells when the settling day approaches. We elieve that Spring Mines is a good property, and well vorth buying after so heavy a drop; but perhaps it vould be as well to wait till the next settlement, which egins for mines on Tuesday, is over. The stream of ubber flotations still continues; volvitur et volvetur. t is not finished yet, and will not stop until the price f rubber falls, as some day it must, back to the neigh-ourhood of 5s. Most of these flotations are honest nough, but what subscribers will not realise is that n nearly all of these companies the shares cannot get ny dividend for four or five years. If people can fford to do without interest for three or four years, hey will be rewarded by getting 30 or 40 per cent. n seven or eight years. But life is short.

NSURANCE: POLICIES AT LOW PREMIUMS.

V.

IN writing about policies at low premiums it has to be recognised that the rates of premium referred to are or assurances of various kinds all effected at the same ge. The age at entry is, however, a most important actor in determining whether the premium for assuring given sum is high or low. At age fifty whole-life ssurance with profits, subject to the payment of pre-niums for the rest of life, costs about £45 a year for £1000. A similar policy subject to annual premiums easing at age sixty-five would cost £61 a year; and articipating endowment assurance payable at age sixty-ive, or death if previous, would involve an annual pre-nium of £74 10s. Policies of the same amount and of the ame kind effected at age twenty-five would cost £22 year for life, £23 a year until age sixty-five, and £26 year for endowment assurance payable at sixty-five or revious death. Thus a form of policy which involves a igh rate of premium if taken late in life calls for the ayment of a small premium if the assurance is effected vhen young. Moreover, variation in age at entry always ntroduces one distinction, and generally two differences, etween policies that are of the same kind. When pre-niums have to be paid for life or until age sixty-five, oung men will have many premiums to pay and old men omparatively few. The younger the age at entry the maller the premium, but in most circumstances the arger the number of premiums required.

The second difference referred to arises in connexion vith participating assurance and emphasises the im-ortance of taking policies early in life. Thus endowment ssurance maturing at age sixty-five and effected at fifty eceives bonuses for only fifteen years. A similar policy aken at age twenty-five receives bonuses for forty years. Hence the sums assured under participating policies on he lives of young men are very much larger than on the ives of old men when the bonuses are taken as rever-ionary additions.

The length of time during which participation in profits s likely to continue has an important bearing on the question whether with- or without-profit policies should e taken, or whether it is wise to pay high premiums in nticipation of large bonuses or low rates of premium in he expectation of only small bonuses. Clearly for an ld man the rate of premium is of greater importance han the question of bonuses. Normally, the premiums re adjusted to suit the bonus system, and even offices vhich charge high premiums and give large bonuses noderate the premium rates for the older ages at entry because large additions from bonuses are not to be expected by people taking policies at an advanced age. The fact remains, however, that the older a man is at the time he takes his policy the less important the question of bonuses becomes, and the more attractive are participating policies at low rates of premium, or even non-participating assurances at premiums that are lower still.

The methods of bonus distribution adopted by various life offices should also be considered in relation to the age at entry, and, under endowment assurance policies, to the length of the endowment period. A great many offices distribute surplus on the compound reversionary bonus plan, whereby a uniform addition is made to the sum assured calculated on the amount of the original policy, and on previous bonuses as well; this method produces steadily increasing bonuses if the rate of bonus remains uniform. Thus a compound bonus of 35s. per cent. per annum is £87 for the first five years on a policy for £1000, while the bonus for the sixth quinquennial period at the same rate is £133. A uniform simple reversionary bonus is given by other offices. This is reckoned on the original sum assured only; it may be at the rate of £2 per cent. per annum, in which case on a policy for £1000 it would increase the sum assured by £100 every five years, and this addition would be made in the first quinquennial period and in all subsequent ones without any alteration. Other things being equal, the simple-bonus system gives larger additions to the sum assured at first, and smaller increases later on, than are yielded by the compound-bonus plan. A policyholder effecting his assurance at an age which makes it probable that he will receive a great many bonuses is likely to do well by selecting an office which distributes its surplus on the compound system; while when policies are taken at an advanced age or for endowment periods of short length, such as fifteen or twenty years, it is likely that the simple-bonus system will prove the more profitable.

These considerations bring us back to the fact on which we have often insisted and upon which too much stress cannot be laid, that the most important thing in the choice of a policy is the selection of that form of assurance that is best suited to the circumstances of the policyholder.

THE FUTURE OF THE ZOOLOGICAL SOCIETY.

By Dr. P. Chalmers Mitchell F.R.S.

III.

THE most important change decided on by the Zoological Society is the removal of the central offices and library from Hanover Square to the Gardens. The immediate result of this step is to free a considerable sum of money, hitherto locked up in a needlessly expensive site, with the result that many needed improvements at the Gardens can be put in hand forthwith. The ground added to the Gardens two years ago is to be laid out, and a new house for lemurs, a large pond with rockwork for the polar bears and spacious dens with pools for the other bears, and new aviaries for eagles and vultures are amongst the improvements promised as soon as the designs can be settled and the work accomplished. The general effect of the removal, however, is more important than the temporary acceleration of improvements. The two sides of the Society will be brought together and integrated. The Council and committees will be forced into intimate connexion with the chief establishment they have to administer, so that problems of policy, of finance and practical efficiency will be discussed on the field of operations. Those who are attracted to the Society chiefly because of its work in abstract science will find it difficult to escape the allurements of living animals and may come to an awakened sense of responsibility as guardians of sentient creatures. In a badly administered zoological museum opportunities may be lost, specimens may deteriorate and scientific work may be slack. So also in a collection of living animals, but with the addition that living creatures sicken and die. On the other hand, those who may be called the lay Fellows will have the scientific objects of the Society forced on their notice; they will come to realise that the Society exists not only to keep curious pets in beautiful gardens, but to procure the advancement of scientific knowledge.

The presence of the library at the Gardens will be of direct service to those zoologists who wish to consult the literature about an animal immediately before or after seeing it, and may induce many Fellows who are not professional zoologists to pass beyond interest in animals to knowledge of them. It is intended, moreover, to revert to an old custom and to arrange for short lectures, less than an hour in duration, to be given weekly on Saturday afternoons. The new lecture hall will provide suitable accommodation for these, and the expositions are to be varied, sometimes dealing with new arrivals at the Gardens, sometimes on a group that happens to be well represented (at this moment, for instance, every living species and several varieties of equine animals are represented at the Gardens), sometimes an untechnical account of some anatomical or pathological subject. It is also announced that an effort is to be made to develop the educational possibilities of the Gardens. The closer fusion of the scientific and popular sides should lead to a greatly improved system of descriptive labels, a feature in much need of proper attention. At the present time elementary school children are admitted to the Gardens at the rate of a penny each, on week-day mornings. They are in charge of their teachers and such visits are permitted by the education code to be counted as school attendance. It is proposed to arrange courses of lectures and demonstrations for the teachers to provide them with material by which they may turn the visits of the children into something more than the gratification of curiosity. A similar arrangement has been carried out most successfully in the case of the American Museum of Natural History in New York.

An important function of the Society is the publication of memoirs containing the results of zoological research. In accordance with a venerable and respectable tradition such memoirs are issued in volumes entitled the "Scientific Proceedings" and "Transactions" of the Society, and supposed to be a record of what takes place at the evening scientific meetings. But the reading of such memoirs is for the most part an unreal convention. Many are taken only in title, and for others a brief abstract suffices. The subsequent discussion varies almost inversely as the permanent value of the memoirs presented, for those who are expert in a difficult matter will say little until they have had the opportunity of studying in detail the new contribution laid before the meeting. The unreality of the convention of reading is still greater because now it is an accepted principle that priority and the right of the author to his own work dates not from the reading of his memoir but from its publication. It is when specimens can be exhibited or when topics relating to living animals are raised that discussion is most possible and the meetings most valuable, and it is to be expected that the removal of the library and the meetings to the Gardens, whilst not affecting the publication of specialised technical work, will stimulate interest in the much neglected bionomic aspects of zoology.

The transference of the library to the Gardens has an important bearing on another side of the Society's scientific activity. Statistics of deaths in the menagerie show that a considerable proportion of the losses occur within a few weeks after arrival, and there can be little doubt that newcomers not infrequently introduce diseases. Early last year a new principle was introduced. Two large reception houses were built in such a fashion as to be suitable for all except very large animals, and in these, so far as possible, animals are placed on their arrival and retained in quarantine until the authorities are satisfied as to their health. This year another new building is being erected to serve as an infirmary. Hitherto there has been no special accommodation for animals that required medical or surgical treatment or seclusion and special attention. Under the new system arrivals will be filtered through the reception houses, whilst from these and from the general collection all those that are ailing will be removed to the infirmary. Apart from the direct advantage to health, it is hoped that the new arrangement will provide a valuable opportunity for the clinical study of the diseases of animals, a branch of investigation almost untouched except in the case of domesticated animals. The Zoological Society for many years has made use of the anatomical material at its disposal, but until recently there has been very little clinical or pathological investigation. A new post-mortem room with the requisite ancillary offices has been built, whilst large and well-equipped laboratories for anatomical and pathological work have been provided. There are now the material, the arrangements and the equipment for such work, and under the capable direction of the Society's prosector and pathologist, and with the advantage of immediate access to the magnificent library, the Gardens ought to become an active centre of research.

The indications are plain that the new developments of the Zoological Society are to make for increased activity on all sides of its work. The problem of convenient access, however, remains to be solved, and will become still more acute when the work is concentrated at the Gardens and the improvements tend to attract more visitors. The actual distance from such a central point as Oxford Circus is not great, and for those who drive there is no difficulty. For such special occasions as evening meetings it will be simple to provide a private service of motor-omnibuses, but the Society cannot have the prosperity adequate to the work it is doing and to its appetite for more work until there is a direct and easy route to the Gardens. A glance at the map shows how such a route should run. The Broad Walk of Regent's Park continues the line of Portland Place to the eastern boundary of the Gardens. It should be transformed into a stately avenue, like Unter den Linden in Berlin, the present avenue being retained as a central footpath, with on either side a roadway for wheeled traffic, and under it, starting from the Regent's Park Tube Station, a sub-way with electric cars. The new avenue should be driven south through the floral garden on the north of the Marylebone Road and the crescentic private garden at the foot of Portland Place, whilst the central walk with its line of trees might well be continued to the Langham Hotel along the middle of the broadest street in London. Northwards the avenue should be continued across the canal, skirting Primrose Hill to emerge at Chalk Farm. It would then serve as a much-needed exit northwards from central London, relieving the congested traffic of Albany Street and Park Road. Perhaps if the results of the new motor taxation are really applied to improve road communication the Zoological Society may profit incidentally.

THE BELLMAN.

THIRTY years ago or more, when "The Hunting of the Snark" was a new book, an ingenious friend was fond of declaring that it was a profound allegory. None knew better than he that the author had no such intention, had only written it to promote innocent mirth, to "giggle and make giggle". He professed, however, to find in it a hidden meaning, and could, had he wished to do so, have defended himself by the example of "the ingenious of our age, as well as those who lived when Rabelais wrote". They discovered that Gargantua was Francis I., and that the Bishop of Valence sat for Panurge: why should not a modern sage make a key to "The Snark"?

The Bellman therefore was a "Leader of Thought", one of the class that by repeating a remark often enough ("What I tell you three times is true") had collected a following of disciples, promising to show them Truth. Our friend would triumphantly point to the fact that the Bellman supported each man "on the top of the tide, by a finger entwined in his hair". What does this mean, he would say, except that no great discovery is ever made till the world is prepared for it? You must wait for "the top of the tide", and then personal influence will do the rest.

But the Bellman was an agnostic, which, according to

our Interpreter, caused the failures of his voyage. He had made a clean sweep of charts :

"' Other maps are such shapes, with their Islands and Capes.
But we have our good captain to thank,'
So the crew would protest, ' that he's bought us the best—
A perfect and absolute blank '."

This, he would say, is precisely the objection of the agnostic to creeds. They are " such shapes ". As the crew objected that Italy wasn't like a boot, when you got there, nor England like Mother Goose, so the agnostic finds one article of one creed impossible, another of another, and makes away with them. But

" Soon they found out
That the captain they trusted so well
Had only one notion of crossing the ocean,
And that was—to tinkle his bell ".

The bell is ringing loudly in our ears to-day. Almost everyone seems to have a hand on the rope, tolling the knell of the passing day of Prosperity. And, unfortunately, very few bellmen suggest a remedy. A few do. It is perfectly right and praiseworthy to show how calamity is to be avoided—for a Lord Charles Beresford to say " You must have so many Dreadnoughts and so many destroyers, or you'll go to the demnition bow-wows ". He is on his own ground, and he tells you what, in his opinion, you ought to do. But what service is rendered by a threat of impending calamity unless it be accompanied by suggestion? Jeremiah did not save the Jews, nor Cassandra the Trojans. They had to dree their weird. And is such " a clamor and a clangor of the bells " as " The City of Brass " likely to be of any help in saving England?

" They can only shriek, shriek,
Out of tune,
In a clamorous appealing to the mercy of the fire,
In a mad expostulation with the deaf and frantic fire."

Unfortunately we can all understand that Mr. Kipling should think we are in a bad way and sorrow as one who has no hope. A great many of us feel that way, but recognise that it is no use to say so, and that it may be hurtful. It was amusing the other day to see " The City of Brass " called " magnificently fearless ". What has a man to fear who expresses the common feeling of his auditors? If the expression of pessimism be a mark of magnificent courage, we need not at least be afraid that in that quality we have degenerated. For, from every street, from every country village, the recruiting sergeant could raise a battalion of die-hards who feared no foe in shining airship.

Mr. Kipling is not by any means our only bellman, and has only been selected here as a modern and conspicuous instance. The others also howl—in herds, like baying wolves—and, for the most part, are quite as bare of comfort or advice as he is. This is partly owing to the quaint belief which seems to possess most of our public men that it is not their business to make suggestions until they are in a position to carry them out. Almost daily, in the debates, we have a harried Minister asking " How would you do it then? " and the indignant answer, " That's our business. When we are in power we will tell you ". Even when they have a plan it is too often sketchy, approximating to the Bellman's best chart, " a perfect and absolute blank ". A friend who lives in the country says that the Tariff Reformers who come down converting the rustics (and say that they want it—badly) cannot or will not answer the simple question, " What will be the first cost of Tariff Reform? " He, who is himself a Tariff Reformer, asserts that by this they damage their cause. They admit that a certain sacrifice will have to be made, but when asked " What sacrifice? " ride off on side issues as to the immediate return the sacrifice will bring in, increased prosperity etc. etc., none of which he is at all inclined to deny. But for an answer he looks in vain on their chart. It is " a perfect and absolute blank ". Their method, in fact, is that of Dingdong, the " canting sheep-seller " of Rabelais, who, to Panurge's patient " How much? " answers only with reiterated praise of the virtues of his sheep.

Let us admit, soberly and sadly, that all is not well with us, and let us give ear to him who can suggest what we can do to be, in a mundane sense, saved. But for maniac shrieks the world has no use. If they have any effect on it they will make it give up in despair. Nor is there on earth a man who cannot evolve as much pessimism as is good for him out of his own inner consciousness.

ANTINOMIAN DRAMA.

By Max Beerbohm.

Again and again, in the course of the sittings of the Censorship Commission, " the young girl " has been trotted out and pondered on with the customary solicitude. Her twin brother, as usual, has been passed over. Yet, really, is he not just as important as she? If ignorance of the facts of life be a necessary basis for innocence in her, and if it be moreover the best means of preparing her for life, let us keep her blindfold, by all means. But we surely ought, at the same time, to keep an eye on the twin brother. " The boy—what will he become? " A great and good man, let us hope; bating that, a steady, harmless citizen. His character is not yet formed; it is still elastic, malleable. Let us not shirk our responsibility. Let us be careful that this boy be, so far as in us lies, exposed to none but wholesome influences. We need not, I think, withhold from him the knowledge that evil exists in the world. We may as well tell him quite frankly that he has the choice of being wicked or good when he grows up. But, since it is not in human nature to choose virtue for its own sake, we must guard him from the suspicion that wrong-doing is not always unattractive and unsuccessful and despised, and virtue not always triumphant and delicious and revered. " Dear young friend, what is it that weighs on your mind? Come, out with it! We have told you always to bring your little troubles to us. You are not sure whether you want to be a policeman or a burglar when you grow up? Well, you must choose for yourself. We don't want to bring any irksome pressure to bear on you. Only remember that whereas the policeman is the idol of the community, and spends his old age peacefully in receipt of a huge annual pension, and then goes to heaven, the burglar invariably comes to a bad and miserable end. Indeed, his whole life is a series of such ends: he is always being caught by the policeman, and cast into prison, amidst the hoots of an outraged populace eager to tear him limb from limb, poor fellow! We merely mention these facts in passing. Far be it from us to dictate to you in the choice of a career. What is that you say? Will we give you half-a-crown so that you may go to a theatre to-night? Certainly, dear child, certainly. What play do you want to see? ' Arsène Lupin '? H'm. From the French, we suppose. Still, there can be no harm in it; otherwise it would never have been licensed. Go, dear child, and have a pleasant evening."

If there were no licenser of plays, the public (it is argued) would straightway develop a sense of responsibility, and would vocally condemn as assaults on morality many plays of a kind which now they accept as harmless on the strength of Mr. Redford's imprimatur. " Arsène Lupin ", let us hope, would be banned promptly. Its power for mischief is incalculable. The hero (save the mark!) is a man who started life with all the advantages of health, strength, genius. To what use has he applied them? To burglary. For ten years he has been cracking cribs with the utmost neatness and despatch, and so cunningly that he has never come within the arm of the law. Nor, alas, is he in the least ashamed. On the contrary, he is very well pleased with himself. And one notes with distress that the authors, MM. Francis de Croisset and Maurice Leblanc, seem to be very well pleased with him. They present him not as a man whose character has been ruined by sin, but as an instance of the powerlessness of sin to make the sinner less admirable than he was at the outset of his black career. What a man does, apparently, matters not at all, and has no relation to what he is. Arsène Lupin is, so we are assured by one of the characters who know him most intimately, " a man with a heart of gold ". And all that he needs for redemption after ten years of iniquity is " a wife, a home, and [this in a voice husky with emotion] a child ". The most disquieting part of the matter is that the audience seems to endorse this theory without a moment's demur. You might imagine there would be some measure of sympathy for a humble detective who, in the exercise of his duty, is flung violently to the floor by Lupin, and then has his arm almost wrenched out of its socket, while one of Lupin's confederates robs him of some papers which he had secured in the interests of justice. As a matter of fact, the audience roars with laughter and delight. And when, at the very end of the play, Lupin makes good his escape (quite impenitent, but with every prospect of getting " a home, a wife, and a child " presently), and the principal detective, mistaken for him, is flung violently to the floor by one of the lesser detectives, the unanimous verdict seems to be that justice has been done; and the evening ends sweetly in tears and laughter.

If the audience were composed entirely of members of the criminal classes, its behaviour would seem natural enough. But I have no reason to suppose that the audiences at the Duke of York's are below the average level of respectability that one finds in other theatres. It is a strange thing, this lack of esprit de corps among the virtuous. There is honour among thieves, and a loyal spirit of comradeship. The enemies of society rejoice in one another's triumphs, are touched by one another's failures. But among the decent people on whom they prey there is no corresponding emotion. Every one of these decent people is angry if he happen to be singled out as victim; but he cannot count on the sympathy of any one of his peers. " Law and order " —one would think, off-hand, that this would be an inspiring and a sacred ideal, for which orderly and law-abiding people would be glad, at a pinch, to lay down their lives. But the fact is that the human biped, though physically gregarious, is incurably individualistic in spirit. In law and order he sees merely a trouble-saving device. He is delighted at any infraction of it which does not directly incommode himself. Such an infraction appeals to his romantic sense, and its perpetrator is thereby endeared to him. If it were possible to make him see the romance of the common good, there might, by the way, be some hope of a practical future for socialism. But, to make him see this romance, you would have to construct him all over again, on a quite different principle; which you might find rather difficult. Meanwhile, he will certainly continue to sympathise with every malefactor whose misdeeds are not of a timid or humdrum order, as against the officers of the general convenience, and will rejoice in every score off these officers, and will mourn whenever a sensational scamp is laid by the heels. All England's heart went out to " D. S. Windell "; and all Europe's to Köpenick; and I am very sure that our frank delight in these prototypes of Arsène Lupin—our sympathy with them, so well worked up by and so loudly echoed in the press—must have had an evil influence on the minds of the rising generation. We have no official censor of the press, or of human nature. But we have Mr. Redford, whose duty it was either to prohibit " Arsène Lupin " altogether, or to insist that the central figure should not be so gifted, so brave, so successful, and so good.

However, the mischief is done, and we may congratulate Mr. Gerald Du Maurier on a part in which there is excellent scope for his peculiar dexterity and grace of style, and for his inventive humour. The one other part which counts is that of Guerchard, a Gallicised version of Sherlock Holmes, made very real by Mr. Dennis Eadie, that Protean actor. Miss Filippi and Mr. Eric Lewis do next to nothing admirably.

LETTERS FROM SOLITUDE.

By Filson Young.

II.

. . . . Connemara.

The day I came here was a day of deluge and drifting mists and squalls, and my drive from the station was a two hours' submersion. There was nothing to be seen but the road and a bit of the bog on each side; indeed, it was at times impossible to hold up one's eyelids under the weight of wind and water that pressed against them. The inn stands bleakly at the head of a bay far away from the open sea; it looked very drear and isolated, but I was glad to get under the shelter of a roof. My solitude began at once; my fellow-guests, all fishermen, were out on their various stands, lake and river, and I had the dingy coffee-room to myself for lunch. After that, the deluge continuing, there was nothing for it but to unpack my belongings and settle down for an afternoon indoors. I had brought some books with me—Swinburne, Davidson's last poems, Morris's History of Ireland, " Henry Esmond " and a few others—among them George Moore's rewritten " Sister Teresa ", which he had given me in Dublin. I nibbled at several of them, and then finally settled down to " Sister Teresa ", which I finished before the day was done. I was disappointed in this new version—or rather new book on the same subject, for it is an entirely new book; and though I regard George Moore as a great writer and a great artist, this book only deepens my conviction that people should never rewrite their books or tell their stories a second time. I think it is not nearly so good as the old " Sister Teresa ", although it is written with a very masterly technique. It is almost entirely in dialogue, there is hardly a page of description, and that in itself is a very considerable achievement. But I had been talking to Moore about the later books of Henry James, and had been pleased with his remark that reading them was like eating cork—you chewed and chewed and chewed, but it was savourless; no nourishment came of it. Well, I did not exactly find " Sister Teresa " like cork, but I did find a flatness and monotony in the story. George Moore is a master of the art of telling a story, but this is a story without symmetry and relief, and the great wedge in the middle about Egypt and hawking in the desert seems to be dragged in so laboriously that it has little interest. It is merely a pause in the interminable chatter of the convent and the helpless struggles of Owen Asher to keep Evelyn. I dislike Asher as much as ever I did, and begin to lose interest in Evelyn; but I suppose Moore means her to become less interesting as the Church tightens its grip upon her; her little burst of life is over; she is beginning the long death of the convent. Of course, there are many good things in the book, and many things delightfully characteristic of George Moore and his style. Here is one:

" We use words, but words mean so little. What do we mean when we speak of Nature? Where does Nature begin? Where does she end? And God? We talk of God, and we do not know whether he eats or sleeps, whether he wears clothes or goes naked; Moses saw his hinder parts, and he used to be jealous and revengeful; but as man grows merciful, God grows merciful with him—we make him to our own likeness, and spend a great deal of money in the making.

" Yes, God is a great expense, but government would be impossible without him."

Perhaps I read the book a little too fast to do it justice, and gave myself mental indigestion. I shall read it again presently to make sure that I do not like it. There is no writer like George Moore, and one cannot afford to be wrong about him.

In the evening the anglers came back very wet, and sat round the dinner-table talking of the day's sport. I confess that I find the talk of fishermen less tedious than any other kind of sporting " shop ". For one thing it is a solitary occupation, and acquires a certain dignity from that circumstance, for a man who can be cheerfully silent and alone all day is never a fool, and is often capable of genuine thought. They were the usual types—a colonel or so, a doctor, a snug elderly gentleman who lived contented on what he had, and sought fishing in this place and that, and one or two nondescripts who seemed to have no conscious life away from their rods and flies. They sat there munching away and exaggerating the difficulties and surprises of their failures, and putting down their successes to an extraordinary and sudden access of skill on their part, in spite of something like perversion on the part of the fish, as is the manner of all sportsmen. Anyhow their talk passed the short, windy evening; and to-morrow, as Montaigne said, is always "a new day".

And this to-morrow was really a new day. The sun shone, the sky was cloudless, the air very hot and still. It was no weather for anglers, but it was good enough for me, and I walked out along the road that runs beside the shore. In this glacier land, you must remember, there is no variety of colour except what the light and distance give. On one side of the road the land slopes, a tumble of scrub and stones, upwards to the low, olive-green hills of the shore; beyond them rise greater hills, deeper in colour; beyond them the mountains, peak after peak of mauve and grey; beyond them again the empty blue sky. And on the other side of the road lie great rocks, with patches of short grass on them where perhaps a little black cow is feeding; and then the stones of the beach, the tawny gold of the seaweed, and the untroubled blue of the sea. In these sheltered bays, far away from the unrest of that Atlantic of which their waters are a part, the tides seem to creep in and out most stealthily. At low water the blue level is broken by hundreds and hundreds of island rocks and stones, all covered by the wet golden weed; as the tide rises the weed moves and lifts, becomes smaller in area, becomes merely a patch of purple under the blue, vanishes altogether, until a floor of unbroken water stretches from shore to shore, and washes gently against the grey rocks. It is the only sound—this still small voice of the deep-throated ocean far away, telling you that the tide is about to turn again.

Hour after hour, as you sit or lie there in the heather, this silence of an empty land sinks deeper and deeper into your spirit. Such sounds as there are only serve to reveal the silence—now the cry of a seagull, now the drone of a bee, now the splash of a rising fish, and rarely, very rarely, the soft thud of bare feet on the road as someone passes by. And if you turn from the world we call inanimate to look for life and movement in the world of men and women, the silence and stagnation will only seem the deeper. The few peasants you see, those who are not gathering seaweed on the rocks for kelp-burning, seem to be waiting for something that never comes. Yesterday there was some talk of a Government inspector coming in the afternoon—something to do with old-age pensions—and hour by hour, from early morning, the people came in from the mountains and islands and sat down by the roadside—not speaking, barely moving, not eating or drinking, but just waiting. Most of them were old and bent; many, young or old, were beautiful of face and feature, their deep melancholy grey eyes seeming to look out into another world; and, alas! it is to another world that most of them turn their thoughts and hopes. For these are people who really look for the resurrection of the dead and the life of the world to come, and who look for little else. Of what moment, then, a few hours by the roadside, a few years of bitter existence on these stony hills, a few burnings by the sun and drenchings by the rain, a few toils, a few tears, a little hunger and a little sorrow? It is all of very little account to them, and so they lose in the fight against wild nature which is the peasant's unending crusade; and the gorse and the heather and the bramble, that have neither heaven to lose nor soul to save, creep in upon the little fields and surprise the enemy in his spiritual sleep.

Towards evening I climbed a hill and looked abroad over the country of Connemara, as far as Joyce's Country and Iar Connaught to the east, and as far as the sea to the north and west and south. Water everywhere! Down at the sea level one could see only hills; up on the hills one can see little besides water. From the Killaries to Galway Bay the sea runs inland in every direction, its bays formed like trees, branching and branching into smaller bays and inlets. And among the hills, strung like turquoise necklaces about their throats, lay the lakes—not ten nor twenty, but hundreds. And over all the evening sun was shedding its soft light—especially on one little round hill, ruggedly crowned, the sides of it ablaze with the great-belled Connemara heather, that reminded me strongly of S. Michael's Mount, and of that other western land where also there are solitudes and wide seas; so that some verses in Davidson's last volume came into my head, and rang in it until I was home again among the discontented fishermen. I will put them down here, so that there may be at least one pleasant page in my letter:

St. Michael's Mount, the tidal isle,
    In May with daffodils and lilies
Is kirtled gorgeously awhile
    As ne'er another English hill is:
  About the precipices cling
  The rich renascence robes of Spring.

Her gold and silver, nature's gifts,
    The prodigal with both hands showers:
O not in patches, not in drifts
    But round and round, a mount of flowers—
  Of lilies and of daffodils,
  The envy of all other hills.

And on the lofty summit looms
    The castle: none could build or plan it.
The foursquare foliage springs and blooms,
    The piled elaborate flower of granite,
  That not the sun can wither; no,
  Nor any tempest overthrow.

And now I look over these pages, and wonder quite sincerely if they are in the least interesting? Certainly there is no art in them; there is merely a record of some commonplace doings of a lonely person who in his secret soul hates being alone. And yet if they are dull, it is because I have consciously made a selection from among my commonplace doings, and not put down everything. If I had told all—what I had to eat, the serious difficulties about the chairs, what I really felt when the post came and there was nothing for me, how the waiter was drunken and the waitress imbecile, how there is a little lawn in front of the hotel on which now a drove of young turkeys feed, now a squadron of ducks, now a mob of chickens, but never all three together—would that be interesting? If I could keep myself out of it I daresay it would; but you know I could not; and I will spare you my reflections on turkey-life. In my next letter you shall have a real piece of local human drama.

AN OLD-TIME PARSON'S TITHES BOOK.

THREE hundred years ago the Cornish parish of S. Austell had as its vicar one Ralph May or Maye—spelling was nothing accounted of in his day; he reigned there for nearly forty years. Of his ministrations we know nothing, though we may suspect from his reliques that, like another "parson of the good old stock", he held that

"true religion was to do
As you'd be done by; which could never mean
That he should preach three sermons in a week".

But if we are in the dark as to his care of the flock, it is quite otherwise as to the fleece, for a recent unexpected find has thrown a flood of light on his business dealings with his parishioners; his "journal intime", in the shape of his "Tythes-book", was discovered a few years ago among the musty records of the parish chest. It is a marvel that it should have survived the vicissitudes of three centuries—private account books mostly find their way to the flames—and indeed it may be doubted whether any similar document is still in existence; these archives, by the way, may owe their preservation to the fact that Parson May was succeeded by his son and his grandson;

moreover, the vicars of S. Austell have been long lived; Stephen Hugoe was incumbent for sixty-two years, and two others for over forty years each, so that there have been fewer " new brooms " than usual to sweep out the chest. Anyhow, they have survived, and this discoloured and dilapidated ledger, the contents of which recall the tables of sines and tangents or the calculations of Arab merchants, has awakened from its long sleep to speak to us about the sweets of office and the means of subsistence and the chaffering and bargaining of an " old-time parson " in " the spacious times of Great Elizabeth ". Litera scripta manet.

But let us examine it within and without. It is evidently of home manufacture; the leaves are crudely stitched together and the paper is coarse to a degree. On the side it is stated that " this book of Tythes was given by Mrs. Hugoe to Mr. Harte "—Harte was a friend and flatterer of Pope and tutor to the hopeful son of Lord Chesterfield—" on his coming to the living of St. Austell in 1757 ". The first page is headed " St. Austell Vicaridge. Receipts in ye yeares of our Lord god 1599, 1600, 1601. R. May, Vic.", but the entries actually extend from 1598 to 1606—some few are as late as 1620. They profess to be in Latin, and most of them are in that language, but with a curious admixture of English—the old order was then changing—an entry will sometimes begin with the one tongue and end with the other; some pages, however, are entirely in Latin and others as exclusively in English; the reader shall have an extract—only a few lines—from page 3:

Carvarth, inhabitantes.

[1599]

	5d.	2d. ob.	2d.	2d.		
+ John Vyvian senr.	vaccae.	vituli.	herbae.	poma.	recepi 12d.	
Año 1600.	rec. 12d. ut in precedente [anno].					
	6d.	4d. ob.	2d.	2d.		
Año 1601.	vaccae.	vituli.	herbae.	poma.	canabi.	rec.
	6d.	4d. ob.	2d.	2d.	2d.	1d.
Año 1603.	vacc.	vitul.	herb.	poma.	canab.	matrices.
					2d.	2d.
					pulli.	lina.

16d.
privata acquisita 6d.; pro vellere lanae debito anno precedente.

It may be well, however, as Ben Jonson was not the only gifted Englishman who knew " little Latin and less Greek ", if we give a like extract from another page (page 8) in a translation:

12d. 4d. 2½d. 4d. 2d.
[1599] John Treleavane owes a mortuary; cows, calves, ewes, fruit,
2d. 7d.
grass; private earnings, 12d. A funeral fee; received.

4d. 6d. 4d. 2d. 2d. 1d.
1600 cows, calves, ewes, fruit, grass, fowls; private earnings of Nicholas, 12d.; received: private earnings of John Treleaven, 12d.; received.

2d. 5d. 3d. 4d. '4d. 2d.
1601 cows, calves, ewes, fruit, grass; private earnings 12d., hemp: received.

Only a few lines, but how much do they reveal! He takes the parishioners, roughly, in their geographical order and sets down their precise dues, and each petty item had to be calculated afresh each year. But every animal in field or fold, almost every apple-tree or medlar in garth or orchard, is accounted for. Our good vicar, it must be remembered, lived on the " small tithes "—those from the cereals fell to the lay rector. But these small tithes afforded him some fine pickings; many pennies (and he does not discard halfpennies or farthings) make pounds. And how few things escaped his net! Not only did every tenth colt, calf or lamb (there is no mention of pigs) or its value fall to his share, but a tenth part of the value of each animal born; as soon as it was weanable it became titheable. Each fleece, too, was laid under contribution: " vellus lanae " is of not infrequent recurrence. And if sheep, cows or calves were sold or left the parish the claim, the lien, went with them; thus Agnes Scollier paid 22d. " pro agno vendito ", and we often hear of " vacce delocate or boves delocati ". And so sharp was his outlook that in one place he gives a list of the sheep pastured in Trewydel on 13 June 1604: " of old wethers 23; young wethers 81; old yewes 28; Rammes 3; yew hoggets 43 ", but this list may have reference to agistment; tithe was payable on the profits made by feeding cattle on commons or elsewhere. It was also paid on barren stock, like geldings or steers. Then there is frequent mention of hens (pulli) and geese (anser: the word is always singular, but the charge, 8d., shows that it was a flock of geese; moreover, no one would keep one goose). Eggs, too, paid their quotas, and hives; mel (honey) is occasionally mentioned. Milk did not apparently furnish him any perquisites, though in some parishes every tenth quart was left at the vicarage or in the church porch. Nor does Mr. May appear to have maintained, as some parsons were by custom bound to do, " a common Bull and a Boar . . . for the increase of calves and pigs ". The mention of flax or hemp reminds us that these were the days of the spinning-wheel, when every housewife made her own linen. The charges for hay seldom exceed 2d.—once it is 12d.—but three parishioners are charged viiid. apiece on hay that they had bought—probably on their profits. Not much rye was grown in this district, but rye-bread was not unknown; peas and beans were seemingly scarce.

But in this seaboard parish the Vicar's gains were much augmented by the tithe of fish, the " harvest of the sea "; such tithes, indeed, have been paid in Cornwall almost within living memory. The different boats mostly compounded for a fixed annual sum; the Trinity and the Perel [Pearl?] paid 12s. each; the Colt, which seems to have done a brisk trade in pilchards and "maccrell", "xxs. and 6d." But, alas! the good man did not always get his dues, for he complains of the arreragia piscium—and not of fish alone; John Honye, for example, paid vijs. in 1602, but " he oweth other vijs." For Thos. Allyn's debts R. Tredinam had stood surety. Stephen Dadow paid 8s. 2d. for de antique (sic) per patrem debita. Farmers and graziers often compounded, as well as mariners; Easter was the usual time for settlement. The compositions do not seem to have been reduced to writing—apart from this book; probably few of Mr. May's flock could read or write, but they were made in the presence of witnesses; the agreement for 15s. de anno in annum with J. Josephe was made " testibus Wo. Carlyan et Eduardo Hooper ". Most of the tithe-payers seem to have toed the line in person: sometimes they got a trifle back; of Johannes Scollier, who paid xs., the Vicar records that he gave him 6d.; of Phillip Dadow that " computavit pro omnibus et est dismissus quietus ". Sometimes the money was remitted by friend or neighbour—the parish then covered some 13,000 acres, so the distances were considerable. Scollier, who got the sixpence, on another occasion " solvit per manus Thome Congon "; " R. ffarrowe exoneratur per manus Johannis filii sui "—this looks as if no receipts were furnished. There were evidently fixed days for payment, and the Vicar probably sat in the church to receive his dues; he certainly did for his Easter Offerings; he tells us what these oblacions yielded in 1600: driblets arrived most days of Easter week, the first day only 12d., the second xijs. vjd., tercio in ecclesia ijs. ijd.; on the fourth vijs. xd.; on the fifth xxxviijs. 8d., and on the last iijli js. 4d.; altogether £6 3s. 6d. Of the tithes received on account of private earnings—only day labourers were exempt from this payment—of servants' wages, of mills and fords, as well as of Mr. May's payments, and notably those to his curate, Sir Martyn Parnell, something may be said hereafter.

OUR CHALK FLORA.

IN Nature's garden there is an intimate connexion between vegetation and the soil. Indeed, soil and situation are the two main factors in determining the flora of a neighbourhood. Given the latitude and the geographical formation, it should not be difficult to draw up a list of plants likely to be found in the district. The most conspicuous illustration of this close association between geology and botany is to be seen in our chalk flora. A large number of plants, including some of the most interesting of our indigenous species, grow only on the chalk. The presence of calcareous matter in the soil seems to be necessary to their existence. The wild clematis, or old man's beard, called by Gerarde the herbalist "Traveller's Joy", because of "its decking and adorning waies and hedges where people travel", is a member, although not a very strict one, of our chalk flora; yet it affords a striking example of the influence of soil. "A person might walk", says the author of the "Flora of Berkshire", "from Lechlade through the meadows to Oxford, or from Shrivenham through the vale to Abingdon, or from Hungerford down the Kennet valley to Reading, and remark that clematis was not to be seen in the county. Another traveller, journeying along the Faringdon road, or from Reading past Sonning and Wargrave to Henley, or from Henley to Marlow and Maidenhead, might say with equal truth, 'What a conspicuous feature in the vegetation of Berkshire is the clematis!'" Its distribution depends entirely on the nature of the soil.

But nowhere is our chalk flora to be seen to better advantage, or under more typical conditions, than on the wide open downs of the South of England, such as those which stretch across Hampshire and Sussex into Kent, or those which form the backbone of the Isle of Wight. After a botanical ramble along the sea-shore there is perhaps nothing more fascinating to "a searcher after simples" than one on the downs. The fresh air, the springy turf, the vast expanse of heaven, the sense of space and freedom, all combine to lend vigour and inspiration to the expedition. Thousands of tiny plants star the elastic sod with their delicate blossoms. The brilliant little lotus or bird's-foot trefoil is very conspicuous, and often gives a tinge of yellow to the wide sweep of downland. With the lotus mingle the purple blossoms of the aromatic thyme, the two species of bedstraw, both yellow and white, the milkwort of inconstant colour, with blue, pink, or white flowers, the delicate cathartic-flax dear to the old herbalists, and the exquisite little squinancy-wort, a famous remedy for quinsy. But rarer and more interesting plants may sometimes be met with on the chalk downs. The beautiful Anemone pulsatilla, with silky stems and large purple flowers, which "flowring for the most part about Easter hath mooved me", says Gerarde, "to name it Pasque-Floure or Easter-floure", is often plentiful where it occurs, but it is very sparingly distributed. It still grows, where John Ray found it in the year 1660, "on the left hand of the way over Gogmagog hills leading to Haverill, so soon as you come to the top of the hill". It is also to be seen in fair abundance on the lower slopes of a down which divides the counties of Bedford and Hertford. On this same down, but later on in the season, when the long feathery achenes of the Pasque-flower are conspicuous, the blossoms of the rare purple milk-vetch will be scattered here and there over the short turf. This scarce and dainty little plant, clothed with soft black and white hairs, and, for its size, large blue-purple flowers, was known to Ray as the purple mountain-milkwort. He found it, he tells us, on the Gogmagog hills and on Royston and Newmarket heaths.

In the month of June, when the mountain-milkwort is in flower, several choice species of wild orchids are blossoming on the downs. It is remarkable how many kinds of this attractive order of plants are only to be found on calcareous soil. Indeed it is this order that gives to the chalk flora its special distinction. On the chalk hills of Kent and Berkshire there might be found, at least in former days, the strange species known as the monkey and the military orchids. It is to be feared that these fine plants are now nearly, if not quite, extinct. Still, orchids have a curious habit of suddenly appearing in a new locality. Their ways are full of mystery, and it is never safe to say that such a species is extinct. Within the last few years a colony of the rare man-orchis, "resembling a little man having an helmet upon his head, with his hands and legs cut off", has established itself in the Isle of Wight, where previously it was unknown. Solitary specimens of the extremely scarce lizard-orchis, an evil-smelling, uncanny-looking species, have lately been met with on the chalk hills of Kent. Within five or six miles of Shakespeare's Cliff at Dover the rare spider-orchis is still not uncommon, while the bee-orchis, "resembling in shape the dead carkasse of a Bee", is plentiful. The beautiful little fly-orchis, "in shape like unto Flies", is another member of the chalk flora, and the very striking burnt or dwarf orchis, abundant in places on Salisbury Plain and also to be found on Tennyson's beacon at Freshwater, and the slender musk-orchis, which smells like bees-wax or sandal-wood.

Later on in the season, when the down orchids are over, except indeed the frog-orchis, which is often to be found in flower in September, other choice plants appear upon the chalk hills. The delicate harebell will be abundant, and the deep blue clustered-bell-flower, and in some places on the Hampshire and Sussex downs the round-headed rampion. This local species, known to the early botanists as the "mountaine-horned rampions", is still growing, where Mr. John Goodyer found it early in the seventeenth century, "plentifully wilde in the enclosed chalky hilly grounds by Maple-Durham neere Petersfield". On the downs of the Isle of Wight, and also at Beachy Head, the very rare tufted-centaury—first recorded as a British plant in the year 1879—blossoms in August; while throughout October, and even in November, the dark purple flowers of the autumnal gentian or felwort will be in bloom.

But while the choicest and most delicate members of our chalk flora are to be found on the open downs, other localities often produce fine species. The steep slopes of some of our chalk hills in Hampshire are clothed with beech-trees, under the shadow of which several rare species love to dwell. Scattered over Selborne "hanger" the pale parasite known as yellow bird's-nest or monotropa will be found in plenty. In striking contrast with this sickly-looking plant, the tall spikes of the stately white helleborine, another member of the orchideæ which haunts chalky districts, gleam beneath the shadow of the beeches. In another wood not far distant its rare relative, with flowers of purest whiteness and elegant sword-shaped leaves, blossoms in company with the graceful butterfly-orchis.

Disused chalk-pits too, and rough broken ground where rabbits have burrowed, are favourite localities with many plants. Such showy species as foxglove, and yellow mullein, and viper's-bugloss with its exquisite azure flowers, will often be seen in lavish abundance, and sometimes Atropa belladonna, the deadly-nightshade. This "furious and deadly" plant, of weird and uncanny associations, is never indigenous except on the chalk, or among old ruins where calcareous deposits abound. In Hampshire it is a rare and local species, but it may be found among the ruins of Basing House and of Netley Abbey; while in an old chalk-pit not far from Selborne it is abundant. It also grows in profusion on a weird, elevated tract of desolate chalk warren, where the stone-curlews come to breed, in congenial company with rank masses of hemlock and henbane and black mullein. On the same chalky upland the very rare ground-pine, a curious hairy plant with crowded leaves and solitary yellow flowers spotted with red, flourishes in one or two places.

An old disused chalk-pit is also the favourite haunt of one of the rarest and most beautiful of British plants. When the wild tulip is found, it is usually in such a locality. It may seem a somewhat suspicious situation for a native plant, suggesting the possibility of introduction, but in certain parts of England it appears to be beyond question indigenous. One such haunt may be visited within a few miles of Selborne. The ancient quarry is close to the turnpike road, separated only by a belt of trees, but passers-by little imagine what a treasure it contains. In early spring, before the rank herbage has grown up, one side of the hollow is almost carpeted with the long linear leaves of this choice plant. For some reason, difficult to determine, it is a species that is shy of flowering, and in some years scarcely a blossom can be found. But last season, when a visit was made to the secret haunt, as many as a dozen fragrant flowers lit up with their bright yellow petals the deep recesses of the chalk-pit.

CORRESPONDENCE.

SIR WILLIAM EDEN'S FLOWERLESS GARDENS: A REJOINDER.

To the Editor of the SATURDAY REVIEW.

SIR,—Sir William Eden's article on "Gardens without Flowers" in the SATURDAY REVIEW of 24 August raised hopes doomed to disappointment. "Gardens without Flowers." What a delightfully original idea! How different will be the reading of it from the usual commonplace, well-worn gardening remarks. And the first lines (though I seem to have read something very like them often before) touch what I like to think the artistic chord in me, and all is yet well.

Then the Monte Carlo garden is instanced as an example of vulgarity; but as further on Sir William Eden talks of "the suitability of things is what is admirable" and "the relation of correct tones", possibly the beds of begonias, cinerarias and "the terrible crimson rambler", are exactly the setting fitted for the mob which yearly frequents the garden, and likes something to look at as "criard" as itself.

But now we are no doubt coming to the keynote of the whole article. We are told to go to Italy, and gardens at Tivoli, Rome and Florence are given as examples of flowerless ones. Sir William Eden, unfortunately for his argument, describes a part—and in one or two instances a small part only—of each garden which he writes down "flowerless".

The Villa d'Este is really his only safe standpoint. The "noble stone pines in the Borghese at Rome" can hardly be considered as part of the garden proper. True, the "Borghese Gardens" are always spoken of, but "Park" would more correctly describe the wild, uncultured ground where stand the pines. I was often in the Borghese last April, and in and near the "Giardino del Lago" a blaze of colour assailed the eye—in great part obtained by an indiscriminate use of cinerarias of every hue, planted or potted out. Again, in the Boboli Gardens at Florence, Sir William Eden remembers the cypress round the fountains; so do I. But I also remember on reaching the formal, box-bordered "Giardino del Cavaliere", the lamentable profusion of zinnias—most hideous of flowers—of all shades from mustard-yellow to magenta and vermilion.

Sir William Eden has, in fact, made an unfortunate choice in support of his article in recommending Italy to the notice of his readers. Take Mr. G. Elgood's book, "Italian Gardens". Although there are many illustrations of yew hedges, cypress, statues, in almost every case these are followed by other "bits" in the same gardens, where colour reigns supreme—either given by the many flowers planted in the formal beds, or by that device, loved of Italians, of massing pots of flowers closely together round a statue's pedestal or a fountain's basin. Then Sir William Eden instances Penshurst as a beautiful garden without flowers. I have never been at Penshurst, but in a volume of "Gardens Old and New" I was looking through only recently I came upon "A Border at Penshurst", which looks to be decidedly full of what are apparently flowers.

So again Sir William Eden seems to have chosen out one part of a garden and taken it as a whole. But when he tells us "never to have flowers against a balustrade", then I marvel still more at Italy having been quoted at all. Will anyone deny for a moment that one of the great characteristics of Italian gardens is the mass of roses spreading over balustrade, wall, even statues, in a wild tangle of unrestrained growth? Ask anyone who has been at the Italian lakes in May what most struck them there. The answer will in all probability be the blaze of colour in the gardens which no painting can exaggerate and the mass of roses, especially "Persian yellow", wreathing itself literally everywhere.

And as I am on the subject of roses, may I ask Sir William Eden where we are to be allowed to grow them? He tells us that, along with carnations and sweet peas, they are impossible grown in beds. If impossible there, unpermissible against a balustrade, unadvisable on walls behind herbaceous borders, where may we have them? Surely he does not advocate the expensive system of entirely growing under glass, with its necessary accompaniment of unsightly greenhouses?

In spite of Sir William Eden pleading for the flowerless garden, he is kind enough to give us a "réchauffé" of Robinson, Earle, Clarke, Cooke and others in his advice as to colour-schemes. He is entirely original once only—when he tells us to compare a yellow viola to a Titian. Unfortunately this brilliant suggestion for testing the effect of subdued colouring is followed immediately by the Robinson-cum-Earle etc. one of keeping orange and yellow together. Would a clump of Lilium croceum, grounded with the yellow viola "Klondyke", give exactly a "subdued effect"?

Before I dry my pen, may I be allowed to extend my sympathy to Sir William Eden on the lack of imagination his friends seem to suffer from? It must be dreadful to know that however often he dines out, so surely will sweet peas and gypsophila or smilax and malmaisons adorn the board. Perhaps even Shirley poppies and maidenhair fern would prove a welcome variation. Non-imaginative hostesses, please note.

He is also to be pitied for the behaviour of the ladies he "arms" in on these festive occasions. To disentangle the strange assortment of knick-knacks he describes from a jungle of smilax must be almost as trying to the temper as groping about under the table for them after dinner. And then only to see amusement on the face of the fair one! Dining-out women of England, I blush for you!

A last word. May I suggest to Sir William Eden to try a big patch of Nepeta Mussini, with Salvia "Blue-beard" behind it, near grey stone? I think he would like it.

Yours truly,
HORATIA D. MEYSEY-THOMPSON.

IRISH INDUSTRY.

To the Editor of the SATURDAY REVIEW.

House of Commons, 27 August 1909.

SIR,—The singular criticism which the SATURDAY REVIEW nowadays thinks it fit to publish about Ireland teems with such inaccuracies that one gave up as vain the idea of writing to correct them. But as I am reading a recent issue of the SATURDAY REVIEW which has been brought to my notice, there happens to be on my writing-table the refutation of one of these comments, and I may as well send it on. Sneering at the conference in Belfast convened by that most admirable body, the Belfast Industrial Development Association—a body of which the Lord Mayor of Belfast and leading manufacturers and business men of the North are active members—the writer of your Irish paragraph says: "While they increase their talk, year after year, industry declines". It is the last published Report of Irish Imports and Exports issued by the Irish Department of Agriculture and Technical Instruction which lies before me. In that return the total value of Irish trade for the last four years for which these figures are available is thus given:

	1904.	1905.	1906.	1907.
Imports...	£54,140,075	£55,480,926	£57,611,944	£61,617,225
Exports...	51,037,545	52,569,548	57,233,698	60,521,245
Total ...	£105,177,620	£108,050,474	£114,845,642	£122,138,470

These figures, by the way, are worthy of attention, apart from their bearing on your paragraph. The paragraph is a remarkable specimen of misrepresentation, and I cannot imagine how the SATURDAY REVIEW comes by such ideas about things which are fairly obvious even to the cursory newspaper reader. It speaks, for example, of the Industrial Development Association as "a body of Irishmen who talk industry to each other so industriously that they have no time to do anything industrial", and who call "anyone really understanding the matter" "a liar" and "boycott him" if he attempts to tell the causes of "the ruin". It makes out

TURGENEFF'S GERMAN LETTERS.

(CONCLUSION.)

TO JULIUS RODENBERG.

1874-1882.

110.

50 Rue de Douai, Paris
Wednesday, 23 November 1874.

Dear Herr Rodenberg,—I must apologise for not having answered your kind letter at once. I have been unwell ever since I received it, and have not yet quite recovered. I shall be delighted to collaborate in your "Rundschau", but I cannot yet say when I shall be able to do so. I have two works on my hands, one a very long novel and the other a very short story. The novel would not attract you in any case; the story does not yet exist outside my brain. As soon as it is in black and white you shall have it—probably* in the Russian text. I hope it will be by the end of January. Everything else can be easily arranged.

I have read the first number of the "Rundschau", and congratulate you on it. You are quite right in saying that you have the highest aims, and it is likely that you will attain them. Germany must have her "Revue des Deux Mondes" in the end.

Are you not coming to Paris this winter?

I shall not be in Berlin before the spring.

With very kindest regards,

Yours sincerely,
IWAN TURGENJEW.

111.

50 Rue de Douai, Paris
Wednesday, 17 February 1875.

My dear Herr Rodenberg,—A thousand apologies; it is really unpardonable of me not to have answered your kind letter at once. Now to the point! I will play "cartes sur table" with you. I have not written a line for nearly five months, and if things go on like this I shall probably have to give up my literary efforts entirely. Not to mention the long novel, the little story has stuck fast and refuses to progress. What is there to do in the circumstances? Only one thing—to promise you that if ever I complete anything at all, no other review than the "Rundschau" shall have it. That is little enough, but you may take it, such as it is, as a certainty. I cannot name any definite time. Perhaps it will be sooner than I expect at the moment. Now you can overwhelm me with reproaches, and I must just meekly bow my head and ask you still to keep a little friendship for me and to have a little patience.

With kind regards and feelings of deep repentance,

I remain yours sincerely,
IW. TURGENJEW.

112.

50 Rue de Douai, Paris
Wednesday, 24 November '75.

My dear Herr Rodenberg,—I should have blushed for shame when I read your kind letter, only received to-day, if I had not this time something a little less indefinite and "vague" to tell you. I was finally cornered by my Russian publisher, shut myself up in a little inn at S. Germain for a week, and completely finished a story, which I must now copy and send in a few days to S. Petersburg, so that it may appear on 13/1 January.

I make you the following proposition. You shall have the MS. on 15 December—the second copy will not be ready before that. Have the story translated by Kayssler or anyone else you like, and send me the translation for revision. The language of the story is difficult in places, particularly for a stranger. I will send the translation back immediately. Or, if you like, you can send me the proof instead of the MS. (that certainly would be better), and then you can fire away. It need not be divided, but can appear in a single number—it is not more than fifty pages. It is not very likely that anyone else will translate the thing (from the printed Russian text), but anyhow we shall have at least a month's start. Tell me what you think of all this, and remember that I am sincerely anxious to oblige you.

With kind regards, Yours,
IW. TURGENJEW.

113.

50 Rue de Douai, Paris
3 December '75.

My dear Herr Rodenberg,—Here is my answer to your letter of the 29th November. My MS. was sent to S. Petersburg the day before yesterday; will arrive there to-morrow, and will be printed at once, as the January number of the review in which it is to appear will begin with it. When I sent the MS. I wrote to the editor, giving him your address, and he will let you have a print of it. Thus you will get the story by 20 December at the latest. I could not have copied it quicker myself. The January issue does not appear till the 1st O.S., that is the 13th. So we are sure of our start. Dr. Kayssler will find it easier to translate the original from the print. I must have the proof of the German text, for the following reason: There is an old gentleman in my story who has had a stroke, and does not use the words which he means to use. That often happens, as you know, in cases of apoplexy. He finds himself in a dramatic situation, where he has to speak (his intellect is quite unimpaired), and yet he speaks in a confused way, as usual. But this effect must not be too much emphasised, or the reader will not understand. That is a great difficulty. I hope I have overcome it to a certain extent; but that doubles the difficulty of translation. You shall have the proof back very quickly.

I hope you will approve of my proposal. My kindest regards to Herr Kayssler and yourself.

IWAN TURGENJEW.

114.

50 Rue de Douai, Paris
Saturday, 17 March 1877.

My dear Herr Rodenberg,—I ought to have answered you long ago. If I did not, it was for a reason which I have only just made up my mind to disclose, since in your presence no subterfuges (the so-called "eau bénite de cour") are admissible. You shall have a dose of the pure truth. I cannot do anything for the "Rundschau" any more than I can for any other review, Russian or other. For various reasons, which it would be tedious to enumerate, I have renounced every kind of literary activity. I have laid down my pen, and shall never take it up again.

This resolution is unalterable, and I prefer to let you know it quite frankly.

That will not prevent me following your interesting publication with the greatest interest, and wishing you the greatest success and the best of everything.

With kindest regards, IW. TURGENJEW.

P.S.—I am writing to the same effect to Paul Lindau, to whom I had made a conditional promise of a contribution.

115.

50 Rue de Douai, Paris
Wednesday, 2 May 1877.

Dear Herr Rodenberg,—I have just received your letter and need not tell you how much pleasure it gave me. The fact that you like my book is to me a certain testimony of its value. But my determination is as much fixed as ever. The little story which has attracted your reviewer's attention was written at the very beginning of this year and has not appeared at all in Russia. The editor of the "République des Lettres", a little Paris review, to whom I promised something a

* Text "improbably", but this seems to be wrong.—TRANSLATOR.

long time ago, was contented to have a translation of this insignificant little thing. That is all. I am thinking of leaving for Russia in a few days, and hope to see you in Berlin, where I shall stop for a short time. We shall have many things to talk about, but I do not think literature will be the chief theme of our conversation. That is falling into the background everywhere, especially in Russia. Well, au revoir before long. With kindest regards, Yours sincerely,

IW. TURGENJEW.

116.

50 Rue de Douai, Paris
12 January 1882.

Dear Herr Rodenberg,—I have just received your postcard and hasten to answer it. I must ask you to be sure to send me a proof of my sketch by post. I will send it back by return. My publisher at Riga, E. Behre (who unfortunately has just died) sent me all the proofs of the eleven volumes to Paris; it caused no delay and I was able to make many improvements. I promised Herr Kayssler to give him some hints, but unfortunately I have not done so. I do not doubt his knowledge of Russian or his talent as a translator, but in this last sketch there are some very difficult passages, for instance in the gipsy scene Misha in his cups says something which seems quite senseless (literally it is "Paf! To the forehead! To the ceiling! Oh, you scamp, you Paul de Kock!") But this senseless stuff must be made sense of, something like this: "Whoop, halloa, over you go, heels over head," etc.

As to the title, perhaps "The Desperado" will be more correct; "The Desperate Man" would do quite well.

So please send me the proof. We have plenty of time before 1st February and I will not keep it more than a day. With kind regards,

IWAN TURGENJEW.

117.

50 Rue de Douai, Paris
17 January '82.

Dear Herr Rodenberg,—I received the proof yesterday evening and am sending it to-day with my improvements to Herr Vätel. The translation is good, but the real meaning of many Russian words is incomprehensible to Herr Kayssler, and so some strange things have occurred; for instance, "greshnik" means "sinner" and also "cocked hat" (such as navvies wear in Russia). Herr Kayssler has substituted one for the other etc.

I have carefully corrected it all. Please see that all my corrections are inserted. It is most important. With kind regards, Yours sincerely,

IWAN TURGENJEW.

TO BARTHOLD AUERBACH.

1868.

118.

7 Schillerstrasse, Baden-Baden
1 April 1868.

Dear Auerbach,—Your letter has given me much pleasure—it shows that you have not forgotten me—and the kind words contained in it have made me feel not a little flattered. I hope the book, which I have just sent you, may give you as favourable an impression as the earlier ones.

To come to the main point, it is extremely unfortunate that there is no convention as to literary copyright between Germany and Russia (as there is, for instance, between Russia and France). This I have often observed to you in former years. It means that anyone has the right to translate and even to mutilate an author, and what chance has the author of getting paid any fee? If he does, it is merely as a matter of domestic policy and not as a right of ownership. The fact that Stassülevitch has offered you such a high fee in spite of this is the best proof of your popularity among us. If his means do not permit him to pay for such a comprehensive work as yours on the same scale, I think he would be only too glad to have it, if the price was reduced a little. Have you asked him about it? I should feel it a great pleasure and honour to write an article about you, not by way of recommendation, for it is long since you needed any recommendation in Russia, but by way of preface, and in order to put an obstacle in the way of the pirates, since they would not have the right to reproduce my article. You can write to Stassülevitch to this effect, and as I shall soon (say in six weeks) be going to S. Petersburg, and stopping a few days in Berlin on the way, we can talk it all over. Unfortunately I have not the time to translate your novel myself, but I shall be glad to revise the translation. Tell me how long you will be staying in Berlin. I shall leave here on 1 June at the latest. With hearty good wishes, I remain, as ever, Yours sincerely,

I. TURGENEFF.

P.S.—Mme. Viardot sends her kindest regards in return for yours. We are now working at a third operetta. You have probably heard of the two earlier ones.

P.SS.—*When* is your new book going to appear? I could take the MS. with me to Russia, and we could then impose on the publisher, whether it be St. or some-one else, the condition that the work should appear in Germany and Russia at the same moment.

TO EUGEN ZABEL.

1882-1883.

119.

50 Rue de Douai, Paris
26 May '82.

Dear Sir,—Very many thanks for your kind letter. The Berlin public's expression of sympathy was somewhat unexpected, but that fact makes it still more agreeable and affecting. I could wish I had deserved it more than I have, but it has given me the greatest pleasure. I am much better, though recovery, at any rate complete recovery, is still far off. In a few days I hope to be well enough to be carried to the country—to Bougival.

I see our friend Pietsch almost every day, of course. With kindest regards, IW. TURGENJEW.

120.

50 Rue de Douai, Paris
6 January '83.

Dear Sir,—Many thanks for your very kind letter. Unfortunately I cannot comply with your wish. Plenty of essays on my life and works have appeared in different English, French and German newspapers and reviews, but I do not possess any of them, except those by Pietsch and J. Schmidt, which you probably do not want, and I cannot give you any idea where they are to be found. I am also unfamiliar with Wengeroff's composition. As to my biography, the principal dates, birth etc., are pretty well known, and the remaining details have no interest for the public—they consist of nothing but purely personal matters, and are quite unnecessary for an estimate of my literary activity, which is the principal aim of your work.

With kindest regards, IWAN TURGENJEW.

P.S.—I have accidentally found among my books a number of the "British Quarterly Review" for Oct. 1, 1869, which contains an essay on myself. If you like, I will send it you.

A new edition of my collected works is just being published by Glazunoff at S. Petersburg. I shall be pleased to send you a copy. The last volume will not appear till July.

that the conference is mostly attended by knaves and fools, "gombeen shopkeepers" and others. Let me illustrate. In the same newspaper from which your paragraphist learned that there was a conference at all, he should have learned (1) that the conference was presided over by the Lord Mayor of Belfast, Alderman Sir Robert Anderson J.P., the head of the dry-goods trade of the North and probably of all Ireland; (2) that the first resolution, which dealt with the extension of technical instruction in connexion with the woollen industry, was proposed by Mr. John Horner, a prominent Belfast business man, and was supported by Mr. McKnight, a large woollen manufacturer, and Mr. Dobbs, an Antrim county gentleman interested from the double point of view of a flockmaster and a public-spirited Irishman; (3) that the second resolution, which had to do with the relations between the leather industry and the boot and shoe trade, was moved by Mr. Christopher Dunn, of Cork, the largest leather manufacturer and owner of the largest tannery in Ireland, and supported by Mr. Long, of Limerick, another leather manufacturer, by Mr. Williams, of Belfast, head of the largest combined leather and boot and shoe manufactory in the North of Ireland, by Mr. Harper, of Belfast, another large boot and shoe manufacturer, and by Mr. Field M.P., President of the Cattle Traders' Association; (4) that the third resolution, which dealt with the improvement of industries connected with agriculture, was moved by Mr. Fletcher, of the Department of Agriculture and Technical Instruction, and seconded by Sir Alexander Shaw, head of the great Limerick bacon manufacturing firm and President of the Irish Bacon Curers' Association. And so on. I have only mentioned some names and some resolutions. There were others present. There were leaders of the linen manufacturers, including Mr. Thompson, President of their Association; and I can assure you that the conference and its discussions were quite different from the description in your editorial paragraph.

Many things in Ireland are so constantly misrepresented in the press, and in so many ways, that workers have to renounce the task of refutation, even though the misrepresentations mean an added difficulty in the way of their work. Those who work most have least time for newspaper exploitation. But I do think it a pity to see a paper like the SATURDAY REVIEW, from which one expects at least the temper of a scholar and a gentleman, lending itself consistently (I have dealt with only one case out of many) to this style of criticism.

Yours faithfully,

JOHN P. BOLAND,

Vice-President, Irish Industrial Development Association.

[The very causes which increase a country's imports and exports may be those which increase its poverty. From the national point of view the real test of industrial production and progress is the number and condition of the people living by industry, and under this test Irish industry is proved to be still steadily dying out, with the continued decay of a vast majority uncompensated by the progress of a small minority. All this may be seen in detail in Mr. Ernest Aston's admirable article in the "Westminster Review", recently reproduced as a pamphlet.—ED. S. R.]

VEGETARIANISM AND PHYSICAL DEGENERATION.

To the Editor of the SATURDAY REVIEW.

15 Grosvenor Road, Westminster S.W.
17 August 1909.

SIR,—Those who perceive signs of physical degeneration and decadence in the British race, and seek a cause for it, should extend their investigations to the region of gastronomy, where they will find food for reflection and possibly a solution of the problem. I refer to the radical change in the dietary of the individual and the increasing tendency to abandon flesh-food in favour of vegetables, fruit and farinaceous slops, under a system of dietetics commonly known as "vegetarianism". The foundations of the British Empire were laid and the splendid fabric built up by a carnivorous race; and the question now arises, Can that fabric be maintained in its integrity by a generation given over to the gastronomical views of Mr. Eustace Miles and his nucivorous disciples? How frequently nowadays do we encounter the individual loudly proclaiming the virtues of vegetarianism, glorying in his abstinence from animal flesh and expatiating on "food values", "proteids" and the hundred-and-one gastrological expressions with which the vocabulary of the vegetarian is so liberally besprinkled. The Japanese are pointed to as a fine example of vegetarianism carried to a successful conclusion, and other nations are advised to follow suit, irrespective of climatic conditions, environment and physical organisation, and oblivious of the fact that the Japanese, sensitive to their diminutive stature and puny appearance, recently appointed a Government Commission to investigate the physiological cause of this racial defect, with the result that the medical experts recommended a more liberal dietary, in which meat should have a prominent share. The Japanese, I submit with all respect, are a mushroom nation, and owe their present position more to a fortuitous combination of circumstances in the "Welt politik" than to anything else; and the student of ethnology, bearing in mind the slow and tortuous evolution of the Roman and British Empires, will apply the test of time before ascribing to this Oriental people the physical qualities necessary for the attainment of true national greatness.

Amongst the virtues claimed for vegetarianism is that by therapeutic action it subdues, if not actually eliminates, the "combative" passions in the human breast, resulting from an overheated condition of the blood due to animal food; and, further, that children nourished on fruit and vegetables exhibit a docility of nature and equanimity of temper conspicuously absent in those indulged on animal flesh. Perhaps so; but is it desirable that the virility of the British race should be emasculated by a system of dietetics which avowedly eliminates the physical traits, associated though they be with primordial man, that went to form an empire such as ours, owing its creation and grandeur to love of conquest, pugnacity and sheer physical prowess, qualities—or defects, as the peace-at-any-price party (mostly vegetarians) would have it—which may at no distant date be again called into play in defence of our existence as a nation? The food-reformers should recollect that during the momentous period in our history covered by the Napoleonic menace to England the destinies of the country were controlled by a brilliant and lofty-minded young statesman whose dietary régime is known to have included beef-steaks, three bottles of port wine daily and liberal potations of brandy! The parrot-cry of the flesh-abstainer is "Conform to Nature". So be it: *which* Nature—the fructivorous ape, the carnivorous lion or omnivorous man? In his anxiety to "conform to Nature" your vegetarian sees nothing derogatory in placing his gastric economy on a level with that of the undiscerning ape who, owing to the limitations of *his* nature, is constrained to seek sustenance from the kindly fruits of the earth within reach of his paw. It would be interesting to know whether the ascent of man in the mental scale synchronised with his adoption of a meat diet. Here is a hot-weather breakfast menu (by a London physician) culled from a daily paper of last week: "A couple of apples, toast, watercress, tea or coffee". This is not the fare of some modern holy eremite or sickly old valetudinarian, but, if you please, of a full-blooded Briton revelling in the joy of life, under the unwonted but normal temperature of eighty-three degrees in the shade!

The vegetarians further declare that their régime is conducive to longevity, and urge statistics in support of their claim. Let us grant it. I have before me a magazine article written by an authority on vital statistics, wherein is set forth the rule of life observed by certain aged public men verging on centenarians. In nearly every instance the subject is a vegetarian, a non-smoker, and a teetotaler; his food and drink are weighed with mathematical nicety, his hours regulated with Greenwich-time exactitude, his repose, exercise and relaxations mapped out with monastic severity. These venerable patriarchs are, of their own showing, obsessed by one stern tyrannic thought—to live! In the words of Hamlet, "There's the respect that makes calamity of so long life"—but the pitifulness of it all! To live at all costs.

In the course of my official duties I have had occasion to assist at the medical examination of about a thousand recruits for a well-known colonial military corps. The young men were drawn from the best procurable specimens of British manhood; but of those rejected fully two-thirds had carious teeth, caused, in the opinion of the examining medical officer, by lack of proper food—that is to say, the food of the kind requiring hard mastication, and therefore involving full use of the teeth. Dentists, Army and Navy recruiting officers, school inspectors all tell the same tale.

The catacombs of Hythe Church, in Kent, contain many thousands of skulls of ancient Britons or Saxons, in nearly every one of which the teeth are sound, albeit bearing evidence of hard wear and tear on bones and animal flesh. Therefore, since the state of the teeth is an index to the state of the general osseous structure of the body, we may safely deduce that our carnivorous forefathers were of stronger mould and hardier physique than the present generation, who are being urged to "conform to Nature" on a mess of herbage.

In tendering my apologies for trespassing at such great length on your valuable space I fear that my strictures border on the intemperate, but it is difficult to dilate with restraint on the ethics of the vegetarian creed which, in the opinion of the present writer, literally attacks the very vitals of the nation.

I am, Sir, your obedient servant,
HERMANN ERSKINE.

BETTER DEAD.

To the Editor of the SATURDAY REVIEW.

Chelsea S.W. 31 August 1909.

SIR,—It is somewhat surprising to see the SATURDAY REVIEW advocating such drastic treatment towards those unfortunate members of the community, the human derelicts who abound in the parks and open spaces of the metropolis. Are we so sure they have come by their present horrible condition through moral delinquencies that we can with justice mete out punishment or advocate their extinction? It is possible that unemployment may in some cases be the cause of their condition, and probable that the apathy of society may be responsible for the want of employment. I know personally the case of a young naval reservist with a wife and child to support who recently went on tramp to secure employment, being unable to obtain it in London. Having an innate horror of the casual ward, and being penniless, he preferred to sleep by the roadside, which does not conduce to cleanliness. Unfortunately the country had no more need of his services than London, and on his return I suggested calling on our large hotels and restaurants, as he was formerly employed in indoor service. The nationality of the managers, however, precluded the possibility of his employment in this direction, for, incongruous as it may seem, to be of British nationality, either in London or the provinces, is actually a bar to employment in this line of business. The community can compel this man to defend its hearths and homes and rewards him by assisting foreigners to deprive him of his own. The gulf between the employable and the unemployable is easily bridged over, and it is quite possible that this defender of British interests will eventually become one of the vanquished in the parks. I do not know what constitutes the privileges of British citizenship, but should imagine that the right to live was one of them, and until the means to do so decently are granted to the genuine unemployed, society should suspend judgment upon these outcasts.

I am, Sir, your obedient servant,
H. G. HILLS.

REVIEWS.

BERNARD SHAW: BY HIS APE.

"George Bernard Shaw." By Gilbert K. Chesterton. London: Lane. 1909. 5s.

IF Mr. Chesterton were a dull man he would probably have sub-titled his book on Mr. Shaw "An Appreciation". To sub-title it "A Lark" or "An Exercise in Chaffing" must have been tempting, as this is what the book is. But Mr. Chesterton is something more than a joker, and Mr. Shaw cannot be quite completely disposed of on the method of "Wisdom While You Wait". When you do not take a man's ideas altogether seriously, and at the same time you are kindly disposed to him personally, you chaff him. If you are smart, as Mr. Chesterton is, a bystander will be amused for a time; but there is a limit to the amusement of listening to one person chaffing another, however cleverly the banter is done. Besides, chaff is always intended to bring out the chaffer's cleverness, and this is evidently Mr. Chesterton's primary purpose, the revelation of Mr. Shaw being only secondary. It would be absurd to take the book seriously as being anything but this. Mr. Chesterton starts with remarking on the absurdity of writing a book about Mr. Bernard Shaw at all, and the indefensible foolishness of attempting to explain a man whose whole object through life has been to explain himself. If the reader reminds him, he says, that this is a book about Shaw, "I can only assure him that I will reasonably and at proper intervals remember the fact". Mr. Shaw might treat Mr. Chesterton in the same offhand casual way if they were talking together, or if Mr. Shaw took it into his head to write a book out of anything that it might occur to him to say about Mr. Chesterton. There would evidently be no real literary interest in either production. One could say at most that it was good-tempered, and perhaps prefer the new style of chaffing match to the vulgar insults and scurrility of the old. But these intimacies and personalities paraded in public are not good form at the best. In Mr. Chesterton's book there is a considerable amount of the fun-at-a-fair sort of amusement, Cheap Jack patter, mountebank contortions, and the strong fellow showing his muscles. The muscles are sometimes very weak, and at others contorted painfully without doing much work; and one is as unenlivened by the unnecessary stupidity of a statement such as that Mr. Shaw was born as other men are as irritated by sentences which are merely verbal puzzles, but which some of Mr. Chesterton's admirers may take for brilliant paradoxes, or epigrams, or wisdom, or whatever they may choose to call sentences that are only unnaturally twisted.

We do not profess to understand Mr. Chesterton's remarks about Mr. Shaw as a paradoxist. Mr. Chesterton for some reason refuses to admit that Mr. Shaw has any right to his reputation as a paradoxist. Most likely he denies it because to admit it would have prevented some pages of Mr. Chesterton's own efforts in that vein going into his book. Mr. Shaw, however, it is admitted, has made or perpetrated just one paradox. On this unique occasion Mr. Shaw said "I am a typical Irishman; my family came from Yorkshire". It takes a lot of explaining according to Mr. Chesterton. In the first place it is an Irish bull which is a paradox people are too stupid to understand. And an Irish bull is like a dogma, not dark and mysterious, but like a flash of lightning. If Mr. Shaw had deigned to analyse his particular flash of lightning it would have come out in this way: "That I am an Irishman is a fact of psychology which I can trace in many of the things that come out of me—my fastidiousness, my frigid fierceness, and my distrust of mere pleasure. But the thing must be tested by what comes from me; do not try on me the dodge of asking where I came from, how many batches of three hundred and sixty-five days my family was in Ireland. Do not play any games on me about whether I am a Kelt, a word that is dim to the anthropologist and utterly unmeaning to anybody else. Do not start any drivelling discussions about whether the word 'Shaw' is German or Scandinavian or Iberian or Basque. You know you are human: I know I am Irish. I know I belong to a certain type and temper of society; and I know that all sorts of people of all sorts of blood live in that society and are therefore Irish. You can take your books of anthropology to hell or to Oxford." And so Mr. Chesterton goes on kindly and cleverly explaining to us about paradoxes, and Irish bulls, and dogmas; and lots of other things such as Puritanism and purity, and prunes and prisms, but not politics, as the topics are suggested to him either by the fact of Mr. Shaw having been born or his having written and done certain other well-known things. But as to this one specimen of Mr. Shaw's paradoxy, is it not more likely that Mr. Shaw was thinking of Swift, whose family was of Yorkshire, than of all that medley Mr. Chesterton makes out to be running in his head? Whether this is so or not, the saying is typical, Mr. Chesterton remarks, of Mr. Shaw's way of thinking and speaking. Why, then, is Mr. Shaw not admitted amongst the paradoxists? This is Mr. Chesterton's secret, and we believe no one who has read his disquisition on the art of which he himself is so persistent a practitioner has discovered it. This seems to have puzzled readers more than any other criticism of Mr. Chesterton; from which we may conclude that most of the other criticisms of Mr. Shaw's character and writings embody the opinions generally held now as to both. But it is only fair to add that Mr. Chesterton alone of all possible writers of a Shaw book, biography or whatever we are to call it, could have set them out so cleverly, humorously, frankly, and yet so inoffensively. We wonder, however, why Mr. Chesterton, who tells us so much of Mr. Shaw's Irish ancestry and his Puritanism and purity, and asceticism and fastidiousness, in order to explain his writings, does not tell how Mr. Shaw became a critic of such technical subjects as art and music. Perhaps Mr. Chesterton does not know. He confesses that on his musical side Mr. Shaw baffles him. Otherwise he might say, with the French magazine, "Je sais tout". It would be embarrassing for Mr. Shaw to meet Mr. Chesterton if it were not for this mystery of music. Nobody likes anybody to know everything about him.

THE CLASSICAL PINT.

"Lucretius, Epicurean and Poet." Complementary Volume. By John Masson. London: Murray. 1909. 6s. net.

MR. MASSON has written this book as a sequel to his study of Lucretius published in 1907. Here he is more in his right; in the other book the meenister latent in every Scotsman pierced through, and the conception of Lucretius as an artist and a poet was wooden. An account of the coincidences between the ancient and the modern atomic theory is within Mr. Masson's powers, and of use as far as it goes. The polemic indeed with which he treats the question what formula of to-day was intended and anticipated by Lucretius, and what not, is idle. Lucretius anticipated nothing. The greatness of his system, and of the wonderful Greeks who originated it, consists in this, that without microscopes they conceived the existence of substance falling below the perception of the eye; and explained the specific properties of the visible universe by presuming a substance devoid of specific qualities and all qualities except motion and resistance. This is their service towards the growth of the human mind; beyond this it is useless to find titles for them. Mr. Masson's book is in a small way typical of the frequent actual attempt to extract more from the classics than they hold. The study of the past is, it is true, only useful as far as it yields sensations and ideas profitable to our culture; and it is equally true that the ideas and feelings which satisfied one generation have no bite on the next. Still it is stultifying the whole study of the past—at whatever period, for the past is past, as Lucretius would have said, if it is fifty or a thousand years gone—to pour water on the crushed grapes and offer the vinetto as good wine. This is what is being done now. Young people who take an interest in Greek are disciples of one of two distinguished preachers. The one, an airy and sinuous intellect, has played with antiquity from Homer to Statius, and made the authors between these two points say the contrary of what they meant. He has not done so much harm, for even the man in the street feels that it is spinning plates and forced cards that dazzle his eyes and paralyse his judgment. The other master is more subtle, and works not on our intellect but our senses. He catches us by what we think is good, and kind, and even tender, passionate, and craintif. He shivers himself, and we thrill and think the ancients were dolls who moved on the like wires. Neither of them is right; those who know admit it. The ancient world was in no particular as Mr. Verrall and Mr. Murray render it. Yet the experts say that the continued study of Greek in England is due to these two teachers. Must we then feed youth on wind? and does the vitality of a subject depend on its misrepresentation?

The study of the past is not like that of the present, that is of the material universe, nor that of the future, its destiny. It is in itself unessential, and only of value when we can assimilate it. We can never revive it, never see the great Achilles that we know. Some treatment it is certain must be given it before it takes a meaning. A third leading light in philology has said that unless we give the shades our blood to drink, as Ulysses gave his to Tiresias, they will not speak. Ulysses gave Tiresias sheep's blood, not his own piratical juice; but the metaphor is striking and embodies the truth that we find in literature what we bring to it. Transfusion of blood, however, is a process with its own dangers. Who does not remember the pale patient who was given a pint of kid's blood and butted the doctor? The current picture of the ancients is as violent. Mr. Verrall's Greeks are casuists, unwearied griphologists, who spent lifetimes in throwing dust in the eyes, drawing herrings across the paths, of men present and to come. The Hellene of Mr. Murray combines the devil-worshipper with the Nazarene, the erotic humanitarian with the steady promoter of the Glory of God. Such spectres our blood calls up from Endor.

The past is past. The men who lived then were not as we, and have no relation, except as being men, to us. We cannot realise them. They are both more like us and farther from us than we suppose. If we saw them as they were, what should we think of them? Distance and ignorance is the lot to which we must resign ourselves. All we can do is to ascertain the conditions of their period and to contemplate them therein. On this side lies what is still to be done in the field of the classical past. Excavations in Thessaly are, as we write, laying bare the basis of early Greek history, and dispelling the mist of scientific reconstruction; an organic explanation of the theory of ideas has for the first time been drawn by Professor Stewart from the physiology of ecstatic contemplation. The site of Sparta, dug down to the sand of the Eurotas, shows a pure Dorian polity from the beginning, and the art products of the bottom layer are no small argument for the self-denying ordinance which Lycurgus imposed upon his people. The Hittites are rising from their mounds to prove Mr. Sayce's daring guesses of the 'seventies. A power of central Asia Minor, they stretched down to Smyrna and Lemnos, and their ebb had a direct effect in permitting the Trojan War and the colonisation of Ionia. Some years ago it is true, but the rich drops of truth flow slowly, Signor Chiapelli gave a psychological account of Socrates, that electric man who, like a schoolman, was weaned from science by the call of Apollo and spent thirty years of mission work among Athenian gentlemen. Aristophanes made no mistake when he swung him in a basket and made him survey the sun. His familiar, the forbidding voice, shows he belongs to the Pauls and Catherines, who see and hear what other men miss. On these lines, namely the discovery of new monuments and the adducing of the permanent, that is the physical, elements of humanity, we may still dissipate learned error, give a meaning to convention, and interpret our old texts. When these resources stop, the dead must be buried.

ROMAN COUNT AND ENGLISH GENTLEMAN.

"Lord Arundell of Wardour." London: Longmans. 1909. 8s. 6d. net.

THESE papers were well worth collecting, for the late Lord Arundell of Wardour was something more than a country squire in politics or a very estimable, devout and conscientious man. He could keep his end up in a discussion of first principles, hold his own against Lowe in defence of abstract ideas, and import even into Primrose League chairmanship a certain literary and philosophic flavour. If a twelfth Baron, besides being a kind and considerate landlord, a true gentleman, a hard rider and a wholesome influence in the county, is also "a pamphleteer on guano and on grain", he has done as much, perhaps, as can be expected for his order. But Lord Arundell was something of a student and a thinker as well, and had a gift of pointed and easy expression, at any rate with the pen. Of Bright and Lowe, for example, he says happily that "although these rival luminaries are occasionally in conjunction, still it is well known that they belong to totally different constellations"; or he speaks of titles as the Corinthian capital of the social structure. "Depend upon it, that those who wish to see the capital destroyed do not see with pleasure the column itself erect."

The discussions in this volume of "social inequality and natural right" are not just crambe repetita, but contain a number of serviceable quotations from French, English and American thinkers, and some good reflections of the writer's own. The incompatibility of equality with liberty is pointed out, and also the circumstance that, while subordination is a fundamental law of the universe, the lines of social inequality are for ever interlacing and intersecting. A human being who is subordinate in one capacity has usually an acknowledged superiority in some other sphere. "In the ocean of life every wave, if it has sufficient persistency and retains its individuality, either through its own impetus or the momentum it receives from others, is pretty sure some time or other to come uppermost. Though whether it is worth while to have leaped above the rest unless at the same time we catch the sunshine of heaven, will be matter for our consideration after we have sunk back again into the abyss."

In home politics Lord Arundell broke away from the precarious dependence upon Liberalism traditional since Emancipation days with his co-religionists, partly because the old Liberal antagonism to historic Christianity was particularly in evidence in the foreign policy of the 'sixties, partly because he had himself all the instincts of a thoughtful Conservative. Disraeli wrote to thank him for expostulating with editors of party Conservative prints upon the silly and unprincipled adoption of the Orange and Whig platform. "If you place the Constitution of England upon the Revolution of 1688, as upon its foundation, you place it upon a revolutionary basis, and throw away every shred of Conservative principle." On the other hand he urged upon the "Tablet" that "there exists between the Catholic and Conservative an ensemble de doctrines admises, as Lord Derby has proclaimed", and that "the Tories, without having received any substantial support from the Catholic body, and hampered by the parasitical incubus of the Orange faction", had tried to deal equitably with Ireland. A Conservative Government may need to have Conservative principles forced on it, but this is working down stream instead of up. In the House of Lords Lord Arundell, though no orator, was regarded as an invariably candid, temperate and courageous champion of thought-out principles, and a formidable pricker of popular bladders. His knowledge of Italian politics was considerable, and the almost universal Garibaldi-worship was set by him in its true light. The spectacle of Evangelicals enthusiastically fêting a man who had at Naples persecuted everything connected with Christianity, or of fashionable English society going mad over a revolutionary red-shirt, was truly an amazing one. Lord Arundell defended the temporal power, and showed how much Italy and Rome owed to the Popes. On the other hand, he was not an ultramontane, and argued in the "Tablet" against the "directa potestas" of the See of Peter over kings and civil governments. Of course it was easy to show that Popes have often acknowledged the divine right of kings and rulers. But perhaps it was amateurish to forget how often, and how magnificently, they have denied it.

THE LAST YEARS OF GAMBETTA.

"Contemporary France." By Gabriel Hanotaux. Vol. IV. 1877-1882. Translated by E. Sparvel-Bayly. London: Constable. 1909. 15s. net.

IN this volume M. Hanotaux brings to a close his survey of French history since the War. With the death of Gambetta he rings down the curtain. For want of a better title, the period that then came to an end may be called the heroic age of the Third Republic. As the writer truly says, it was followed by an epoch of "party quarrels too trivial for much record". In the politics of later years he may feel himself too closely interested to write of them judicially, but his account would be the more interesting therefor. With the period under review he deals in an impartial and statesmanlike fashion. Many pages of this volume are devoted to the contemporary European situation, and we find in them more than one criticism which recalls the masterly historian of Richelieu. In fact, this fourth volume is much the best of the work, and is more worthy of the author's reputation than those which preceded it.

The men who established the Republic during these five years may not have been giants, but they were vastly superior to their successors. Gambetta was unquestionably a great man who had in him the touch of genius. Nothing is more remarkable than the development of Gambetta the orator into the clear-sighted and far-seeing statesman. The history of these five years falls into two parts. Up to the resignation of Marshal MacMahon in 1879 Gambetta was fighting on behalf of his party to defend the Republic against the attacks of the Monarchical parties and the Church. When the policy of the newly elected Leo XIII. came into play a détente with the Church followed, but Gambetta at the same time began to find his parliamentary position impaired by the jealousies of lesser men, headed by the new President, Jules Grévy. The contest thus lay between a self-contained lawyer, endowed with the cunning and avarice characteristic of the small French bourgeois, and the fiery and impulsive southerner, who had developed in these later years into a sagacious statesman. M. Hanotaux says, truly enough, that the election of Grévy was a mistake, for he had no sympathy with the best impulses of the French people. His one idea was to conduct the Presidential office like a business and to make as much out of it as he could. Under him financial scandals among politicians grew and flourished, and his régime undoubtedly gave to the politics of the Third Republic the mean and sordid impress which, far from disappearing, has been deepened by time and now made ineffaceable.

The triumph of Gambetta might have meant the establishment of a dictatorship, perhaps not in theory, but in effect. But even in France it was not possible to keep out of office for ever the man who had really been the victor in the struggle with the Conservatives. Had he been able to induce the strongest members of his party—the Ferrys, the De Freycinets, the Waddingtons—to serve under him we might have seen the inauguration in France of something like a stable system of Cabinet Government with the best men of the party in office together for some years. This would have led to a very different development of the national polity from that which France has had to endure, and many of the worst scandals in her public life might have been avoided. The petty jealousy of M. Grévy and other politicians of his kidney prevented the only man of real greatness and creative capacity which France possessed from organising the forces of the newly established régime, which he had done so much to create, into an harmonious system. Gambetta also was in touch with the statesmen of Europe, and had wise and consistent views as to the foreign policy of his country. Whether, after the collapse of his Ministry, he would ever have re-established himself at the head of affairs had he lived and retained his health may be doubted. The jealousy of lesser men is very effective under such a régime as that in force in France. It prevented him from securing as colleagues any of the other leaders of the Republican party. This gave his Ministry the appearance of an ill-disguised dictatorship, which was exactly the object aimed at by the sly jealousy of President Grévy. Had the Scrutin de Liste been voted by the Chamber, Gambetta would have triumphed. The retention of voting by small constituencies has made permanent the system of government by corruption and petty interests which has prevailed until to-day. Its disappearance would partially at least sweep away this corrupt system, but the Parliamentary Republic might disappear with it.

Had Gambetta retained power France would have gone hand in hand in Egypt with England. It is not very profitable to speculate on what that might have involved, but in any case the aspect of the Eastern Question would have been changed. The chapters in which M. Hanotaux treats of the circumstances preceding and attending the Berlin Treaty were published in the "Revue des Deux Mondes", and widely commented upon while the controversy over the policy of Austria in the Near East was acute. It is, therefore, unnecessary to repeat here what has already been said on the matter in the SATURDAY REVIEW. Nothing, however, can be clearer than that the occupation of Bosnia and Herzegovina was deliberately arranged between Russia and Austria before the outbreak of the Russo-Turkish War, and that it was the price paid by Russia for having a free hand. It is also perfectly evident that Bismarck's policy was to push Austria on to the East, and that the British plenipotentiaries deliberately thrust themselves forward to be the mouthpieces of that policy at the Congress. With all these facts well known to every student of foreign affairs the violently hostile attitude of our Foreign Office to Austria during the late dispute is the more astonishing. Not less astonishing is our apparent incitement of Russia to strong measures, knowing, as our statesmen must have, the strict limitations imposed on Russian action by previous engagements.

M. Hanotaux admits that France effaced herself at Berlin more than she need have done, but at least she secured some of the spoil. We have in this volume an account of the preliminaries to the occupation of Tunis. Perhaps at some later period the author may give us the history of the establishment of the Protectorate. This has proved the most successful of French colonial experiments, and he himself was the author of it. The incompetence of the Monarchical parties is made abundantly clear in M. Hanotaux' account of the last months of the MacMahon régime. At that time they had no lack of able men, but they quite failed to take advantage of Republican jealousies or to carry with them the sympathies of the people. Perhaps the true explanation is to be found in the lack of fibre in the class which might have carried out a change by concentrated effort. This was bitterly expressed by the Duc de Broglie when watching a well-dressed crowd in the Champs Elysées: "These people are better suited for a coup d'état than for the serious effort we mean to demand of them."

A MODERN NONCONFORMIST ON EARLY CHRISTIANITY.

"The Conflict of Religions in the Early Roman Empire." By T. R. Glover. London: Methuen. 1909. 7s. 6d. net.

IT was to be expected that in a volume like the present, which is an elaboration of certain lectures delivered at Mansfield College, the view of the first ages of Christianity should be adjusted to the focus of the dissidence of dissent. A lecturer at Mansfield would of course say that in his opinion the founder of Christianity was not responsible either for the name or for the idea of the Church, and add to this arrogant opinion "minds of the class to which his belongs have as a rule little or no interest in arrangements, and nothing can be more alien to the tone and spirit of his thinking than the ecclesiastical idea as represented by Cyprian or Ignatius". Yet everyone who has studied the records of primitive Christianity, anyone who has read the New Testament, is aware how good a case can be made out for the opposite point of view. In short, this volume is, so far as it touches on theological problems, an essentially partisan work. Regarded as a denominational treatise it is worthy of careful attention, if only for the light that it throws on the theological tendencies of modern Nonconformity. The interesting chapter on Tertullian which closes the book illustrates the strength of the old Puritanical feeling. To our author Tertullian embodies the noblest aspirations of the Church of the second century, and the adhesion of such a character to the Faith is, we are told, the measure of the power of the Gospel to transform the classic world. We appreciate much of what is here said of that stern Montanist, whom we freely admit to have been the "noblest Puritan of them all". Our author shows how disingenuously Gibbon garbled the awful picture which his hero drew of the Dies Iræ, and asks with justice whether even the most lurid lines in this awesome presentation are not a reasonable comment on the brutal persecution in which S. Perpetua perished. Naturally also the Apology is held up to our admiration. The fact remains that it is a work which some good Christians will always admire and other good Christians will always detest.

But if the old Puritan note is conspicuous in some portions of the book, other chapters, such as those entitled "Jesus of Nazareth" and "The Followers of Jesus", illustrate the growing cleavage between Nonconformity and traditional Christianity. We wish that those Churchmen who believe that there exists a wide residuum of dogmatic theology common to Anglicans and Dissenters, and seek to construct a system of religious education on this imaginary basis, would study these chapters. The Mansfield lecturer, they would note, encourages a view of the founder of Christianity absolutely opposed to the doctrine of Nicæa, though not far from that propounded in the City Temple. The Nonconformist minister of the future is apparently expected to teach that Christ was the eldest of the five sons of Joseph the Carpenter, and that "there is a growing consensus of opinion among independent scholars that Jesus instituted no sacraments".

Controversial matters apart, the book is interesting. Its author is a good classical scholar, and the chapters that discuss Lucretius, Vergil, and Plutarch make fascinating reading. And whatever we may think of his theological view, he has clearly explained the attitude of the Roman world of Marcus Aurelius and Celsus and Lucian to the new religion. What is most pleasing about these pages is the refreshing independence of judgment. On Marcus Aurelius, who was to Renan the hero of a dying world, and to F. W. H. Myers the "saint and exemplar of agnosticism", he passes a severe but just criticism. "He worked, he ruled, he endowed, he fought—he was pure, he was conscientious, he was unselfish—but he did not believe and he was ineffectual." Mr. Glover realises clearly that Christianity created a new civilisation, and he shows also that it was not the conversion of the Empire that destroyed the ancient civilisation.

NOVELS.

"The Lady of the Shroud." By Bram Stoker. London: Heinemann. 1909. 6s.

Vampires do not quite harmonise with the atmosphere of Ruritania, and in writing a political romance of the Balkans with a suggestion of the supernatural Mr. Stoker will probably disappoint the two sets of readers.

whom he hopes to amalgamate. The story is told in a series of letters and diaries, and is none the better for that. Rupert Sent Leger, whom we leave installed on the throne of the Land of the Blue Mountains, is a gallant enough hero, and it was very creditable on his part to love a young lady who appeared mysteriously in a shroud (sometimes dripping with sea-water) at odd moments, even though he was not quite sure that she was a normal human being. But the reasons for her odd proceedings are not quite convincing, and one cannot help comparing her with Iolanthe, sentenced to live at the bottom of a pond although her chest was delicate. Once more Mr. Stoker introduces a kind of Scots dialect only to be heard on the London stage.

"The Socialist." By Guy Thorne. London: Ward, Lock. 1909. 6s.

Does Mr. Bernard Shaw go about like Socrates διαφθείρων τοὺς νεανίας? Mr. Thorne gives us an undergraduate duke, kidnapped in a London slum, and rescued by a brilliant dramatist of Socialist views. Of course the duke turns Socialist, and marries a gifted actress who takes leading parts in Socialist plays, and has a very uncomfortable life. But then he escaped marriage with the beautiful and very patrician daughter of a pompous peer-bishop, and as the duke was a young cub (though Mr. Thorne does not know this) the lady was well out of it. The story is heavily splashed with highly altruistic idealism, and is rather amusing in ways that the author does not intend.

"Mr. Burnside's Responsibility." By Thomas Cobb. London: Mills and Boon. 1909. 6s.

When a flighty married woman throws herself at the head of a blameless member of Parliament, and her jealous husband accidentally overdoses himself with a powerful narcotic the night after a "scene" between the trio at the legislator's lodgings—the whole story becoming public property at the inquest—ought the blameless gentleman to marry the lady for the sake of her reputation and his own? Such is the rather artificial problem propounded by Mr. Cobb in this story, in which he deals with his usual skill with the manners and prejudices of a rather artificial stratum of society.

"The Silver Spoon." By G. H. Stevenson. London: Blackwood. 1909. 6s.

An imprudent marriage with a caddish medical student, the genteel poverty that followed, an elopement prevented by a carriage accident, and a reconciliation after the much-hoped-for death of a rich uncle—such are the materials of this tale, which is written with a singular lack of distinction. The landlady's cat as a subject for humorous reference might well be allowed to sleep, and the jests about seasickness and the hour at which honeymoon couples retire for the night are, to put it mildly, puerile.

"The Member for Easterby." By James Blyth. London: Long. 1909. 6s.

This story is tainted throughout with vulgarity. Mr. Blyth's realism is offensive, the disgusting details in his description of Augustus Bloomfield are quite intolerable, and beyond what is permissible in portraiture.

SHORTER NOTICES.

"Guiseppe Baretti and his Friends." By Lacy Collison Morley. London: Murray. 1909. 10s. 6d. net.

Mr. Morley has produced an interesting book, and what is better it is the result of real knowledge of the subject of which he treats. We confess that we feared it might be only another example of the unscrupulous book-making, only too common in these days, which is usually not founded on any serious study, but is the result of the most superficial knowledge picked up by skimming books already in print on the same subject. As Mr. Marion Crawford pointed out in the introductory chapter written by him, Mr. Morley is deeply versed in Italian literature and knows the Italian character. He is therefore well qualified to explain Baretti to English people. Those already well versed in Johnsonian literature will be glad to have a full account of Baretti's career in Italy. His adventures in search of a pension and the story of his persecution by various Italian Governments make clear to the uninitiated the obstacles to a literary career in eighteenth-century Italy. Mr. Morley makes a sufficiently attractive picture of his hero to explain why he became not only intimate with but respected by Johnson, Burke, Lord Charlemont, and the rest of that brilliant circle. He had clearly not only great social gifts, but was also a perfectly honest and independent nature, qualities the more remarkable in a man who always lived practically as a dependant. He showed his worst side in his quarrels with Mrs. Thrale, and from them he has been too often judged. Mr. Morley's useful and impartial monograph gives the proper perspective.

"Charles Le Brun." Par Pierre Marcel. (Les Maitres de l'Art.) Paris: Librairie Plon. 1909.

Charles Le Brun, the hero and protagonist of the bombastic art of Louis XIV., and Sir Joshua Reynolds may at least be compared in one respect. In 1648 Le Brun, by a long and brilliant series of intrigues and the exercise of immense social and political tact, succeeded in effecting the foundation of the French Academy. About 120 years later Reynolds, though perhaps personally holding aloof from the plots and cabals of the movement, was also upon the winning side in the favour of our "Grand Monarque", and as King George's first President took his place at the head of a movement whose influence became almost as powerful and in the end quite as self-destructive as the French one. M. Marcel writes with spirit and humour of the rise and ultimate fall of his hero. It would be absurd to expect anything but appreciation from a French writer on the founder of French academic art. For us the gigantic pompositics of Versailles and the Louvre are a source of boredom, almost of disgust, hysterical in conception and heavy in colour. But for all his faults as a draughtsman and executant, Le Brun, like David and Greuze after him, produced at times a portrait or group of real charm and something approaching sincerity. The illustrations are adequate and fairly representative, but they would have been more interesting if they had included some of the artist's numerous drawings. The pastel study of the head of his Royal patron is one of the finest things of its kind.

"A Romance of the Nursery." By L. Allen Harker. London: Murray. 1909. 6s.

Mrs. Harker has issued a revised and enlarged edition of her pleasant story of child-life entitled "A Romance of the Nursery", and the fact seems to indicate that many readers have learned to value her delightfully natural narrative, and have come to appreciate the whimsical little Paul, the slightly priggish Fiommetta, and the other children and grown-ups with whom the slight story has to do. The book is supposed to be written by one of the Staniland children, Fiammetta being a little visitor and centre of romantic interest because of her abduction and her recapture owing to a dream. The story, as has been said, is slight; it is in the author's light descriptive manner, in the succession of simple episodes in which the children are presented, in the lack of any straining after effect, that the charm of the whole lies. And charming it will be found, both by juvenile readers and by all of their elders who can find pleasure in a sweet and wholesome presentation of life.

"The Dictionary of National Biography." Vol. XVIII. London: Smith, Elder. 1909. 15s.

This volume of the D. N. B. reissue, which takes us from William Shearman or Sherman to Sir Frederick Stovin, contains perhaps rather a larger percentage than usual of attractive names: Sheridan and James Shirley, Mrs. Siddons, Sir Philip Sidney, Sir William Siemens, Adam Smith, Sydney Smith—the Smiths of more or less distinction claim 170 pages—Smollett, Lord Somers, Robert Southey, John Speke, several Spencers, Edmund Spenser, Richard Steele and Laurence Sterne, the Stanhopes, the Stanleys and the Stewarts, Robert Stephenson, and Robert Louis Stevenson. These by no means exhaust the list of leading names in the volume, but they suffice to show how well S holds its own in the national chronicle. The more we study the Dictionary the more we seem to realise how indispensable it has become to all properly organised reference libraries.

SCHOOL BOOKS.

"The Beginnings of the Teaching of Modern Subjects in England." By Foster Watson. London: Pitman. 1909. 7s. 6d. net.

The historian of the English grammar school to 1660 and the translator of the "Linguæ Latinæ Exercitatio" of Juan Luis Vives has written another book, which all those

(Continued on page 296.)

who are interested in education or who are members of the teaching profession will find abundantly interesting. It is a volume packed with information, giving as it does a separate historical account of the introduction and establishment of the modern subjects as one by one they became recognised portions of the school curriculum. Most of these "beginnings" only become distinctly visible, except to the eye of the miscroscopic historian, about the beginning of the sixteenth century. It was then that Juan Luis Vives was to be found urging upon teachers the advisability of being at any rate able to address their scholars correctly in the vernacular. Progress was gradual to begin with. English as a school subject found its first enthusiast among the masters in Richard Mulcaster, his "Elementarie" being the first shrewd blow for the cause of the mother tongue. In the course of the century text-books written in English began to appear; and, with the passing away of the Middle Ages, when the language of the Church was the medium of international converse and dealings, the days of Latin were numbered.

As for the other modern subjects whose "beginnings" are here traced, modern science could not very well begin before Bacon; modern languages waited upon the growth of the European nations and literatures; geography waited upon the discovery of the world; and arithmetic, which was an "extra" at Ashford Grammar School in 1623, soon took its place upon the syllabus. Finally it was again Richard Mulcaster who came to the front in a defence of mathematics. He held that, from the training they gave and the results they achieved, they did "work some good thing", and he gave them his support as a subject to be included in the schools.

A praiseworthy feature of the book is the absence of any invidious comparisons between the old and the new. The author has sought merely to present the essential facts and circumstances relating to the introduction of modern subjects into English education. A friend of the new order, he does not condemn the old; but contrives to have a sympathy with his subject which makes his pages pleasant reading. To those who wish to go accurately into these matters Mr. Watson's book will prove valuable. He wastes no space, and is ready with introductions to a number of delightful old masters and fogeys who are not to be met in the ordinary way. His knowledge of the bibliography of ancient text-books is also remarkable.

"Notes on British History." Parts I. and II. London: Rivington. 1909. 2s. net.

The compiler of these notes confesses, perhaps without knowing that he does so, that they are the product of a vicious system of education so far as history is concerned. Apparently it is never possible to give more than two hours a week to the subject; and since it is not advisable that this small time should go in the taking of notes by the student, here are the notes ready printed to his hand. Like most note-books this one may be of value as a summary of events; but where it proceeds to generalisation its tabulated remarks are either unnecessary or unintelligible. The book is intended for those who wish to obtain University scholarships, but we do not advise any such candidates to sit for an examination on the strength of having learned these notes by heart.

"Practical Organic Chemistry." By Sudborough and James. London: Blackie. 1908. 5s. net.

This is a companion book to Sudborough's edition of Bernthsen's "Organic Chemistry", and will be found of use to students who require a comprehensive guide to their practical work in the laboratory. The number of experiments recounted is larger than that usually given in a text-book of this character. The book will be found particularly useful to a lecturer who wishes each of his students to perform a different experiment at the same time, in order that he may give them a greater interest in what they are doing and a more distinct sense of independence than is felt when a whole class is set to work upon the same operation. A feature of the book is the inclusion of a discussion upon some of the more common physical methods used in the study of carbon compounds.

"Cicero: Select Letters." By the Rev. T. Nicklin. London: Blackwood. 1909. 2s. 6d.

This is a good selection, with accurate notes, in which regard is had for the work of Mendelssohn, Lehmann, and Schmidt in the correction of the less recent edition of Tyrrel and Purser. The recommendation that students should not translate without first appreciating the type of the particular letter that he is translating is admirable and quite necessary. Some of the letters are written in just the language of educated conversation; others are in the vein of Burke. Accordingly it behoves the translator to fix the type of his letter before rendering it into English.

"A Scientific Geography." VI. "Asia." VII. "The British Empire." By Ellis W. Heaton. London: Ralph, Holland. 1909. 2s. net.

These are more than usually interesting text-books. The Empire is treated under its geographical aspect, the units being climatic. A general treatment is given of trade routes, of the problems of imperial commerce, of the influence of geographical conditions upon the possibilities of defence and government, and of the course likely to be taken in the development of the native resources of the great geographical provinces. It is crammed with information, and with statistics that are too interesting to be difficult. The book on Asia discusses similar questions and problems after the same method.

"Geography of the World." By A. F. Evans. London: Blackie. 1909. 3s. 6d. net.

Here are some four hundred pages of harmless necessary facts likely to be of use to intending examinees. The kind of student into whose hands it will probably fall will feel grateful for the papers added at the end of each part, and for the assurance that all the questions these papers contain have been set in actual examinations. At first sight the absence of maps is a little remarkable in a geography book, but the defence almost disarms criticism. Since maps in geography books are generally bad maps, it is better to have none at all and to use an atlas.

"Practical Arithmetic for Schools." By W. G. Borchardt. London: Rivington. 1909. 4s. 6d.

This is an excellent text-book, which will prove of real value to the intelligent student or to the teacher. It is comprehensive in the best sense, discarding the ancient pedantic distinction between arithmetic and algebra, and making free use of the graph, the ready reckoner, the logarithm, and the vernier. The book cannot be too warmly recommended.

"French Idiomatic Expressions, with English Equivalents." By Frederick Rothwell. London: Sands. 1909. 2s. 6d.

This book is reminiscent of Henri Bué, but it is more comprehensive. The idioms are arranged alphabetically, the most important word in the sentence determining its place in the book. The author is a little liberal in his idea of what constitutes an idiom; but the book may be all the more safely recommended, since it leaves no loophole for stupidity on the part of the student.

For this Week's Books see page 298.

The busy man's greatest asset is the saving of time.
ARGYLLS
save time and save expense.
The ideal Cars for private or professional use — for town work or country pleasure.
12/14 H.p. Standard Side-Entrance Car, £285
12/14 H.p. Two-Seater Car £275
14/16 H.p. Standard Side-Entrance Car, £375
14/16 H.p. Two-Seater Car £355
Easy Buying – Easy Driving
Easy Running.
Head Office, ALEXANDRIA-by-GLASGOW
Glasgow Depot—92-94, Mitchell Street.
London—6, Great Marlborough St., W.

IN ADVANCING AGE.

The 'Allenburys' DIET

REAL HAMBURG GROUND
KROPP RAZOR
English Manufacture.
Always Ready for Use.
WARRANTED PERFECT

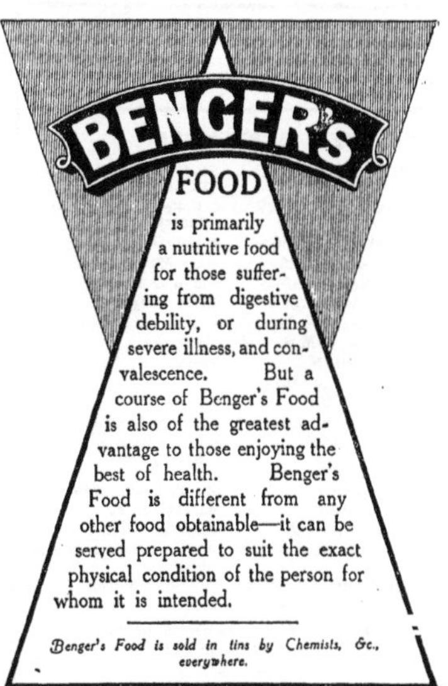
BENGER'S
FOOD
is primarily a nutritive food for those suffering from digestive debility, or during severe illness, and convalescence. But a course of Benger's Food is also of the greatest advantage to those enjoying the best of health. Benger's Food is different from any other food obtainable—it can be served prepared to suit the exact physical condition of the person for whom it is intended.
Benger's Food is sold in tins by Chemists, &c., everywhere.

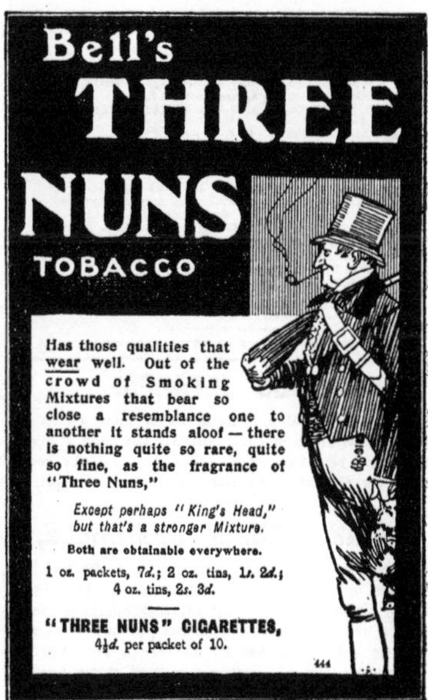
Bell's
THREE NUNS
TOBACCO
Has those qualities that wear well. Out of the crowd of Smoking Mixtures that bear so close a resemblance one to another it stands aloof — there is nothing quite so rare, quite so fine, as the fragrance of "Three Nuns,"
Except perhaps "King's Head," but that's a stronger Mixture.
Both are obtainable everywhere.
1 oz. packets, 7d.; 2 oz. tins, 1s. 2d.; 4 oz. tins, 2s. 3d.
"THREE NUNS" CIGARETTES,
4½d. per packet of 10.

THIS WEEK'S BOOKS.

BIOGRAPHY

Francis Atterbury (H. C. Beeching). Pitman. 3*s*. 6*d*. net.
The Life of William Huntington, S.S. (Thomas Wright). Farncombe. 5*s*. net.
The Last King of Poland (R. Nisbet Bain). Methuen. 10*s*. 6*d*. net.

FICTION

Anne Inescourt (Marcus Servian). Griffiths. 6*s*.
The Return of the Petticoat (Warwick Deeping); Troubled Waters (Headon Hill). Paul. 6*s*. each.
The Street of Adventure (Philip Gibbs). Heinemann. 3*s*. net.
The One Moment (Lucas Cleeve); The Punishment (Thomas McKenn); The Real Man (Henry Byatt). Long. 6*s*. each.

HISTORY

The Birth of Modern Italy (Edited by Duke Litta-Visconti-Arese). Fisher Unwin. 12*s*. 6*d*. net.
South Africa (Ian D. Colvin). Edinburgh. Jack. 6*s*.
Robespierre and the French Revolution (Charles F. Warwick). Fisher Unwin. 8*s*. 6*d*. net.
Henry Hudson in Holland (Hen. C. Murphy). The Hague: Nishoff. *fl*. 10.

REPRINTS AND TRANSLATIONS

Lord Arthur Savile's Crime (Oscar Wilde). Methuen. 5*s*. net.
An Introduction to the Articles of the Church of England (G. F. Maclear). Macmillan. 10*s*. 6*d*.
Master Flacksmann (Otto Ernst), 3*s*. 6*d*. net; The Evolution of the Sciences (L. Houllevigue), 6*s*. 6*d*. net. Fisher Unwin.

SCHOOL BOOKS

The Dawn of Mediæval Europe, 476-918 (J. Howard B. Masterman). Methuen. 2*s*. 6*d*.

THEOLOGY.

The Book of Job (Rev. David Davies). Simpkin. 5*s*. net.

VERSE

Mimma Bella (Eugene Lee-Hamilton). Heinemann. 5*s*. net.

MISCELLANEOUS

Economic Calculus and its Application to Tariff, The (Ewart S. Grogan). Simpkin. 1*s*. 6*d*. net.
Monologues and Duologues (Mary Plowman). Skeffington. 2*s*. net.
Revaluations, Historical and Ideal (Alfred W. Benn). Watts. 3*s*. 6*d*. net.
Works of James Buchanan, The (Edited by John Bassett Moore. Vol. IX.). Lippincott. 12*l*. 12*s*. for 12 vols.

REVIEWS AND MAGAZINES FOR SEPTEMBER.—The Empire Review, 1*s*.; The Financial Review of Reviews, 1*s*.; The Musical Times, 4*d*.; Travel and Exploration, 1*s*.; The English Review, 2*s*. 6*d*.; The Socialist Review, 6*d*.; The English woman, 1*s*.; The Treasury, 6*d*.; The Art Journal, 1*s*. 6*d*.; The Connoisseur, 1*s*.; The Contemporary Review, 2*s*. 6*d*.; Revue des Deux Mondes, 3*fr*.; Mercure de France, 1*fr*.50; United Service Magazine, 2*s*.; The Westminster Review, 2*s*. 6*d*.

MESSRS. METHUEN'S NEW BOOKS

Messrs. METHUEN will publish on September 9 Four New Novels.

(1) **THE SQUIRE'S DAUGHTER,** by ARCHIBALD MARSHALL; (2) **HAPPINESS,** by MAUD STEPNEY RAWSON; (3) **LOVE AND THE WISE MEN,** by PERCY WHITE; and (4) **GIANNELLA,** by Mrs. HUGH FRASER. Each, crown 8vo. **6s.**

They have just published a delightful story full of comedy by G. A. BIRMINGHAM, Author of "Spanish Gold." It is entitled **THE SEARCH PARTY.** Kindly order at your Library or Bookseller's. Ask also for the cheap edition of **SALTHAVEN,** by W. W. JACOBS. Crown 8vo. **3s. 6d.**

Messrs. Methuen have just commenced the publication of the new edition of the Works of Oscar Wilde in 12 volumes, fcap. 8vo. 5s. net each. The first volume is **LORD ARTHUR SAVILE'S CRIME, AND OTHER STORIES.** The second is **THE DUCHESS OF PADUA.**

Kindly note that Messrs. Methuen will publish on September 9 the following books:—(1) **MICHELANGELO,** by GERALD S. DAVIES. With 126 Plates, wide royal 8vo. 12s. 6d. net. This is the new volume of that fascinating series "Classics of Art." (2) **NAPOLEON'S BROTHERS,** by A. H. ATTERIDGE. With 24 Illustrations, demy 8vo. 18s. net; and (3) **THE AUSTRIAN COURT IN THE NINETEENTH CENTURY,** by the Right Hon. Sir HORACE RUMBOLD, Bart., G.C.B., G.C.M.G. With 16 Illustrations, demy 8vo. 18s. net.

They will shortly publish **IN THE CANARIES WITH A CAMERA,** by MARGARET D'ESTE, with 50 Illustrations, of which one is in Colour, from Photographs by Mrs. R. M. KING, and a Map. Crown 8vo. 7s. 6d. net.

A WANDERER IN PARIS, by E. V. LUCAS, crown 8vo. 6s., is now ready. This book contains 16 Coloured Illustrations by W. DEXTER, and 32 other Illustrations. It is uniform with Mr. LUCAS'S **A WANDERER IN HOLLAND** and **A WANDERER IN LONDON.**

Two volumes of the highest interest to the general reader who loves biographical history and Court chronicles are **THE ROSE OF SAVOY,** by H. NOEL WILLIAMS, with many Illustrations, demy 8vo. 15s. net; and **THE COURT OF LOUIS XIII.,** by Mrs. K. A. PATMORE, Illustrated, demy 8vo. 10s. 6d. net.

GENERAL LITERATURE

THE CONDITION OF ENGLAND. By C. F. G. MASTERMAN, M.P. Crown 8vo. 6s. [*Second Edition.*

A book of enthralling interest and indispensable to the student of the new social and industrial conditions.

"He has essayed a great task, and succeeded well."—*Daily Chronicle.*

"It is a brilliant, glowing work, the interest of which is unfailing."—*Daily News.*

RUBENS. By EDWARD DILLON. With 484 Plates. Wide royal 8vo. 25s. net. [*Classics of Art.*

This is a very fine book, and wonderfully cheap.

"Rubens the magnificent is here treated magnificently."—*Daily Chronicle.*

"Mr. Dillon's excellent narrative is as careful as it is spirited." *Yorkshire Post.*

TOWN PLANNING: Past, Present, and Possible. By H. INIGO TRIGGS, A.R.I.B.A. With 170 Illustrations. Wide royal 8vo. 15s. net.

"All who are interested in the question will find much that is bound to interest them."—*Scotsman.*

"This splendid volume is probably the most elaborate work of its kind that has yet appeared in this country."—*Daily News.*

THE DECAY OF THE CHURCH OF ROME. By JOSEPH McCABE. Demy 8vo. 7s. 6d. net.

"The book is well and agreeably written and the tone is always moderate and courteous."—*Spectator.*

"A singularly impressive and penetrating volume."—*Daily Telegraph.*

ELIZABETH: ELECTRESS PALATINE AND QUEEN OF BOHEMIA. By MARY-ANNE EVERETT GREEN. Revised by S. C. LOMAS. Demy 8vo. 10s. 6d. net.

AMONG THE DANES. By F. M. BUTLIN. With Coloured and other Illustrations. Demy 8vo. 7s. 6d. net.

"A welcome and valuable addition to the literature of travel." *Pall Mall Gazette.*

"A very chatty, pleasant volume."—*Daily Chronicle.*

THE LAST KING OF POLAND AND HIS CONTEMPORARIES. By R. NESBIT BAIN. With 16 Illustrations. Demy 8vo. 10s. 6d. net.

ST. TERESA OF SPAIN. By HELEN H. COLVILL. With 29 Illustrations, demy 8vo. 7s. 6d. net.

ENCHANTERS OF MEN. By ETHEL COLBURN MAYNE. With 24 Illustrations. Demy 8vo. 10s. 6d. net.

Contains vivid studies of twenty-three beautiful, witty, and fascinating women.

"The book succeeds in giving us living portraits."—*Standard.*

"Miss Mayne's writing is in the best meaning of the word 'racy,' and is full of fragrance and a quivering eagerness to win sympathy for women as women." *Pall Mall Gazette.*

ANNI DOMINI: a Gospel Study. By LADY MABEL LINDSAY. In 2 vols. super-royal 8vo. 10s. net.

In this book the author has taken the Gospel Text, and, making it the nucleus, has sketched round it the people, the scenery, and the historical conditions which formed the environment of our Lord's daily life.

MESMERISM AND CHRISTIAN SCIENCE: a Short History of Mental Healing. By FRANK PODMORE. Demy 8vo. 10s. 6d. net.

FICTION.

SPLENDID BROTHER. By W. PETT RIDGE, Author of "Erb," &c. Crown 8vo. 6s.

"It is a beautiful book."—*Liverpool Post.*

"There could not be a better proof of Mr. Pett Ridge's literary power than is given by this novel."—*Spectator.*

LORDS OF THE SEA. By EDWARD NOBLE, Author of "The Edge of Circumstance." Crown 8vo. 6s.

"A great, almost tremendous drama."—*Daily Chronicle.*

"A book that ought to be read."—*Daily News.*

THIS DAY'S MADNESS. By MAUDE ANNESLEY, Author of "The Wine of Life." Crown 8vo. 6s.

"Original both in story and treatment."—*Morning Post.*

"A vastly entertaining novel and one of unusual distinction." *Pall Mall Gazette.*

AVENGING CHILDREN. By MARY E. MANN, Author of "The Parish of Hilby." Crown 8vo. 6s.

"The book is strangely attractive."—*Standard.*

"It is a charming story, excellent in design and execution." *Pall Mall Gazette.*

THE CASTLE BY THE SEA. By H. B. MARRIOTT WATSON. Author of "The Flower of the Heart." Crown 8vo. 6s.

"A splendid mystery intermingled with a romantic love-story."—*World.*

"Genuinely entertaining."—*Standard.*

THE BRIDE. By GRACE RHYS, Author of "The Wooing of Sheila." Crown 8vo. 6s.

A ROYAL INDISCRETION. By RICHARD MARSH. Crown 8vo. 6s.

"Replete with a most delightful humour."—*Manchester Courier.*

"An ingenious idea, used freshly and amusingly."—*Morning Leader.*

WATCHERS BY THE SHORE. By J. E. PATTERSON, Author of "Fishers of the Sea." Crown 8vo. 6s.

"A strong, moving, and refreshing book."—*Scotsman.*

"An exceptionally fine and dramatic novel."—*Daily News.*

"The virtue of the book is its fidelity, its obviously true characterization, its intensely real descriptions."—*Morning Leader.*

DEEP SEA WARRIORS. By BASIL LUBBOCK. With 4 Illustrations. Crown 8vo. 6s. [*Second Edition.*

"A fascinating book, a real book of the sea."—*Daily Mail.*

"All those who love the sea should read this book of absorbing interest."—*World.*

"Written with masterly vigour and picturesqueness."—*Morning Leader.*

METHUEN & CO., 36 Essex Street, London, W.C.

Printed for the Proprietors by SPOTTISWOODE & CO. LTD., 5 New-street Square, E.C., and Published by REGINALD WEBSTER PAGE, at the Office, 10 King Street Covent Garden, in the Parish of St. Paul, in the County of London.—*Saturday*, 4 *September*, 1909.

THE
SATURDAY REVIEW
OF
POLITICS, LITERATURE, SCIENCE, AND ART.

No. 2,811 Vol. 108. 11 September 1909. [Registered as a Newspaper.] 6d.

CONTENTS.

NOTES OF THE WEEK.

By anticipation Lord Rosebery's Glasgow speech was almost as sensational as his Chesterfield speech. Nor did he disappoint expectation. It was a rousing speech, which will give Mr. Asquith and Mr. Lloyd George plenty of points to answer. The Budget, said Lord Rosebery, is not a Liberal measure; it is a measure to brand landlords as criminals, and to institute an inquisition unknown hitherto in Great Britain or to mankind. It is a menace to every form of property, to capital and to labour. Money is to be raised under a new form of bureaucracy, which is not Liberalism but Socialism, and to be squandered with spendthrift recklessness. The Budget attacks the rich, but is it a poor man's budget? The worker will soon feel the pinch, and the sequestration rather than taxation of capital proposed by the Government must ultimately aggravate the problem of unemployment. By their finance the Government have given away free trade. If the Prime Minister was right when he declared that Tariff Reform was the only alternative, then in Lord Rosebery's opinion free trade cannot survive the Budget.

The Radical press on Lord Rosebery to-day will be instructive reading. We looked into the "Nation" the other day, only to find that Lord Rosebery does not in the least matter. He is found out, done for, exposed, blown up completely. He is seen through and through. But, if so, why trouble to discuss him? If he is not a leader of anybody, why give him a "leader" all to himself, and flay and slay him with all this fury? And why do thousands flock to hear him, and why do the Radical papers report him word for word? Our own notion is that Lord Rosebery is still more or less alive. He is at Elba, not S. Helena yet; and candidly we hope he will break out of Elba. The "Westminster Gazette", a cool judge of men and political things, seems also to think Lord Rosebery is not yet the late Lord Rosebery. It has been suggesting that his right place is the place of Moderator. It will find him very much out of place after Glasgow.

Roughly, the classes affected by the Budget clauses debated this week are those whom Mr. Churchill styles "Swindlers"—those whom Mr. Lloyd George styles "Blackmailers" being, with the land clauses, finished with for the moment. But there is another class altogether that is going to be affected by these liquor clauses. When the working man comes to realise thoroughly that his beer is costing him more, he will surely resent the hardship. Bread, Beer and Bacca are looked on as the prime necessities of the farm labourer's life. Bread up, Bacca up, Beer up: and a Liberal Government in power! We advise all Unionist speakers and electioneers to rub in these Three B's.

It appears from the Budget debate on Tuesday there are several ways to "tie" a public-house within the meaning of the Finance Bill. One is to have the house owned by the brewer or distiller, and the tenant bound to go nowhere else for his supplies. Another way is to have the tenant permanently so much in debt that he is forced to buy from his creditor, which, in effect, differs little from the first way. In either case, the customer is the licence holder, and the Government means to shift the increase in the duty, or part of it, from the customer to his creditor. The method adopted is to "enable the licence holder to recover as a debt" from his tying creditor some portion of the duty, determined by agreement, and, failing that, to be determined by the Commissioners. The amount recoverable is to be a "fair" amount, but, as in the case of Irish rent, no two can agree as to what is "fair". The most interesting knot in the tangle is its detailed system of trade legislation by means of the Budget and without consulting the country.

The faith was not in danger, the Bottle stood adjourned, and the boys were told by Mr. Redmond that they could make holiday, which they did. Mr. Healy risked the disloyalty of remaining at his post. In the absence of the others the Bottle came up again. Did Mr. Healy get the Government to bring it up? He made a brilliant speech in defence of the Bottle, behind Mr. Redmond's back, and for this devotion to the cause he is to be removed from the Party—that is, until Mr.

Redmond gets orders from Cardinal Logue to the contrary. The men of the Bottle at home, including the men of the faith, wanted to know why the cause had been left to the care of Mr. Healy alone. The man is wrong who does less for the cause than Mr. Redmond; but he is still more wrong who does more. Mr. Redmond is the standard. To exceed his virtue is a vice. Mr. Healy's next great sin is his ability, which stands out to the disadvantage of the others; and an Irishman's way to the top is by getting others down under him. That is one reason why "the nation" dies out. The presence of one capable man demonstrates the incapacity of the others, and it is easier to level him down than to level themselves up. Tim will not go. When Mr. Redmond set out to oppose his election for North Louth he was ordered by the ecclesiastics to drop it, and the honourable "mimber" for Cardinal Logue is not less strong now.

There is only one really safe constituency for the free lance, and that is inside the Government. He is no sooner there than he ceases to harass the party and the party ceases to harass him. The proof of great ability in a free lance is, as a rule, getting a place in the Government of the day and becoming forthwith the most trustworthy henchman of that Government. If he does not get into the Government, sooner or later he will find himself at the bottom of the poll. We are very much afraid this is where Mr. Harold Cox, thanks to the Budget, will find himself ere long. The Preston caucus has sent him its ultimatum, and he has replied with a message of defiance and an interview of the same character. "A deputation", he declares, "came to me at the House of Commons, and to my surprise asked me to gracefully retire in favour of another candidate. . . . I intend to stand at the next election in support of the same causes for which I fought in 1906—Free Trade, fair play for all religious denominations, equity in taxation and economy in public expenditure . . . it is a question of the responsibility of members of Parliament not only to their consciences but to their constituencies. According to the views of the Preston Liberal Executive, any man who gets into Parliament with their assistance becomes their slave; his pledges to the constituency are to count for nothing; he is to cease to have either conscience or will."

Mr. Cox' views about the duty of a member are as conscientious as his views about a good deal of predatory radical legislation. But, alack, they won't wash in the brutal laundries of party politics to-day. His linen—like that of one or two on our own side—is over-fine for the work. Independence and individuality are splendid qualities in a man; it is doubtful whether a man is worth calling a man who has not practised them most of his life. Mr. Cox has practised them outside party politics with conspicuous success. But within party politics the rule of the thing now is that sooner or later a man must either fall into line or busy himself in some other employment. Caucuses think absolutely nothing of Burke and Bristol. Free lances and party caucuses—Liberal, Conservative, Labour—cannot live together: they would be mutually destructive like Carlyle's Squalid and Beautiful. Hence, whilst we greatly admire Mr. Cox' gifts of understanding, wit and character, we can't think that he is exceptionally unfortunate. He drank the port, and cannot hope like Pitt to congratulate himself on somebody else having the headache.

"Development" night brought lively discussion, though attendance was so poor that late in the evening a count had to be moved. The debate would have been still livelier had it not, in the biblical sense of the word, been prevented. "Hands off the Sinking Fund!" had been a cry too warmly raised for the comfort of Mr. Lloyd George, and he had removed them. Moreover the irresponsible Commission had disappeared. But an Executive was left, limited by advice only, with power to spend sums of money upon objects that were, in its opinion, calculated to work the good of a democratic people. It was upon this Executive that Sir Robert Cecil made his chief attack. But in any case, as regards the allocation of these hypothetic sums, it seems a choice between the devil and the deep sea; irresponsible Executive on one side, and on the other parliamentary control with attendant opportunity for local jobbery.

Mr. Lloyd George did not make much of a reply. He wasted more time than was necessary in defending the objects of the Bill, which on the whole are excellent. His expressions of surprise that no member for a rural constituency had spoken against the measure were a little pointless. No doubt it was banter that he intended, and banter is an excellent thing to pass the time when it is getting late. His large-minded appreciation of "development" machinery, as it was found working in France, the United States, Hungary, and other places, was also a little wide of the mark. Because an institution flourishes well in a certain soil, that hardly seems a strong argument for having it transplanted into a soil of totally different quality.

We are not deeply moved by the talk and print—common among Conservatives as well as Liberals—as to the way the farming industry is to be encouraged by development grants. Ordinarily what the farmer and the luckless landowner want just now is to be left alone for a time. And, despite the craze for small holdings, we need to grow, not currant-bushes and cocks and hens in miserly little plots, but large expanses of corn; for foreign countries are not flooding the markets with dirt-cheap grain as they were doing for five-and-twenty years and more. Just fancy, bread at over a shilling, and this benign free-trade Government in power! We don't know whether bread is "the sweeter because no longer leavened by the sense of injustice", as Peel put it—we do know it is precious dear.

While Mr. Redmond is trying to preserve his distinction by the removal of Mr. Healy and the suppression of his ability, the Molly Maguires are making for the removal of Mr. Redmond, and even followers of his own do not believe that he can be in the next House of Commons, unless as a follower. It is estimated that Mr. Redmond costs "the cause" over £1500 a year, and it is felt that five Devlins could be hired for the money, each Devlin being worth five Redmonds, making a difference of twenty-four to "the cause." The need to calculate the thing in this way now arises from the slump in the funds, with less than £4000 left against a general election, and Mr. Redmond taking a full sixth of this. Besides, the price of great men rises with the fall in supply. Fifteen hundred for one man, with only £3500 for seventy-nine others, is a lop-sided proportion, especially if one of the seventy-nine is worth five like the fifteen-hundred man. In spite of their "education," a minority of the peasants have in some way grasped the rule-of-three, and since they cannot see the use of further subscriptions at home, the patriots abroad tighten their purse in sympathy.

We have consulted Parliamentarians as to whether the Land Bill could admit of an amendment providing a test colony of the congested to prove whether they were capable of occupying the prairies at an honest price for the land; the uniform opinion is that such a matter must be in the discretion of the Lord-Lieutenant, and that such a provision in the Bill would be irrelevant—though it is the one thing that could be of value in regard to the only real land problem that exists for Ireland. The fact that men have not enough land to live is an imperative reality, but all the other land problems have been invented for party politics, and accordingly the Bill is all about the things that do not matter, without a word about the thing that does. The factor of Executive discretion makes it a matter of accident whether the Lord-Lieutenant for the time treats crime with "sympathy" or puts the law into force; but why not pass a separate Bill for the congested, providing for a test colony and placing the will of Parliament beyond the vagaries of the Viceroyalty? It would require increased expenditure on police to guard the congested migrant against the grabbers of the League; but it would be novel and instructive to have the police employed in a purpose so constructive.

The Irish genius for destruction, which helps to make Irishmen such fine soldiers, was illustrated on Wednesday in a resolution proposed to the Trades Union Congress by Mr. James O'Grady M.P. declaring the Territorial Army scheme injurious to trade unionism, and pledging the trade unionists to oppose Mr. Haldane's ideal. "It was their duty", added Mr. Hayday, "to render the movement unpopular", on the ground that the Territorials, instead of studying how to cripple their employers and frighten away capital, might "talk of nothing but the expansion of the Empire". The resolution was carried, "no one voting against it", and so we get British trade unionism, under the direction of an Irishman, definitely declared to be in conflict with British patriotism. The presence of a man who leads men so is a distinct damage to the community that includes him; but it helps to show that though Demos may be awake, his eyes are not yet opened.

Do the working classes fully appreciate all the labour leaders in and out of Parliament do for them? Each year now a labour leader's life becomes a greater grind than ever. One of his new duties is to take a trip round the world. Mr. Keir Hardie did this heroically a while ago and helped the English working man in some mysterious way by making great speeches to the natives of India. Now, with equal altruism, Mr. W. Crooks M.P. is preparing to make the same weary, weary trip round the earth, all on behalf of the working classes. And yet a "forced levy" is necessary. How wrong, how shameful! Almost as heroic and as useful to the cause of labour as these world trips is the hard work the leaders put in at the Trades Union Congress each year. They have worked this week in the talking line as hard as ever.

Mr. Ben Tillett was one of the chief heroes. He termed Mr. Haldane "a liar"; and, called to order by Mr. Shackleton, the chairman, cried out that all the members of the Cabinet were "liars". How is it that all working men do not recognise that it is worth having leaders who can say such brave things as these? The very valuable question too was discussed by Mr. Thorne and others—Has the working man a country to call his own? Mr. Thorne seemed to think he has, but another arguer said reproachfully, How could the working men have a country seeing that their great business in life is to combine against the capitalists of the world? We believe that a great number of people who are discontented with themselves and their lot in life spurn the notion of patriotism. Patriotism, they sneer, is all very well for people who are well off and comfortable—it won't do for those who are the reverse. But the argument of the labour leader goes still further. It almost comes to this: that no man can be said to have a country of his own who is intent on getting something substantial out of another man. If this be so, exit the patriot and exit the fatherland.

Dr. Jameson's decision to seek a seat in the first Parliament of United South Africa, instead of devoting his time to Rhodesia, his original intention, piques curiosity. Does it mean that he has been approached with a view to his becoming first Premier? Or does it mean that he has discovered something in the situation which makes it necessary for every friend of the British in South Africa to assert himself? His statement that a coalition arrangement, making for the total disappearance of racial difficulties, is now out of the question may open the eyes of some people to the realities of the situation. Perhaps the intention to adhere to old party lines may even have opened Dr. Jameson's eyes. Whatever the inwardness of his changed plans, they clearly point to one conclusion—party spirit in South Africa still stands in the way of that new-found union of hearts which made the passing without serious amendment of the Act of Union imperative in the future interests of the colonies. Racialism is not only not dead: it is not even dying.

Lord Kitchener's farewell order to the Indian Army strikes the note of the strong man confident that his seven years' work will endure. They have been seven years of trial, through which the Army has passed untouched by the insidious propaganda of the Nationalist "reformers". Lord Kitchener says that all efforts to corrupt the loyalty of the native soldier have been unavailing. To no small degree the credit for that fact belongs to himself. Like all truly strong men, he has shown himself considerate of everyone who has worked under him; he has encouraged the officers and men alike to assume responsibility and take personal initiative, and the reforms he has introduced have compassed at once the strategic position of the country and the welfare of the Army. At a time when the enemy without has in some measure given place to the enemy within, Lord Kitchener's influence on the domestic economy of the Indian Army has been not less important than his work on the frontier.

The Spaniards are setting about the serious business of the Riff campaign with a spirit and a thoroughness that are the best answer to their critics. On Saturday last the Moors used the white flag as cover for an attack, and on Monday the Spaniards sent out two columns to administer punishment, which they did in the smartest possible way. The Moors will think twice before they abuse the white flag again. Equally smart has been the police work at home by which the anarchist leader, Señor Ferrer, who is believed to have been responsible for the Barcelona rising, has been captured.

The fillip given to aviation by the week at Rheims continues to keep men in the air. Marseilles will have its fortnight; Brescia has its week; Tournai, Blackpool, and Brussels are preparing for theirs. Lest people should embark upon these projects too lightheartedly, aviation has claimed its victim in M. Lefebvre, whose death at Juvisy on Tuesday last was a sharp reminder to his fellows of the perils that wait upon the conquest (save the mark!) of the air. M. Lefebvre was one of the three Wright pupils who all succeeded in distinguishing themselves at the recent meeting. From the first he was noticed for his unusual daring in the turning of corners and in flying at a high altitude. Whether he fell the victim of his own peculiar daring, or of the danger that is, at this stage, inseparable from any attempt to fly, cannot definitely be known.

The record for cross-country flight achieved on Wednesday morning by Colonel Cody brings us definitely into the arena as a competitor. Forty miles in sixty-three minutes is not a record either for time in the air or distance covered, yet it is so far better than anything we have done that it may be regarded as a legitimate source of national gratification. If Colonel Cody came down rather suddenly, smothered in oil, this was only because he tried to keep up too long. Meanwhile prizes are being offered for the British aviator who can fly a British-made machine. There is the £4,000 of Baron de Forrest, and there is the medal of the North British Academy of Arts, Science, Literature, and Music. It remains to find some candidates.

The Pole has been discovered again, and, this time, there seems to be no doubt about it. The contrast between the ways in which the two announcements fell upon the world was complete. That of Commander Peary was loud. As for Dr. Cook, he has made a muddle of his case, if ever he had one. At first he almost seemed ashamed of his achievement, and the news went wandering about the world asking to be taken in. Then, when it had contrived to get itself printed, it proved inconclusive, matter for faith only, with the evidence making off in another direction.

No distance North, and not out of sight of land! —so Peary vows. Peary wishes to make short work of Dr. Cook's claim to have been there first. Certainly he has no doubt about his own title, witness his telegram to President Taft making him a present of the Pole and its appurtenances. President Taft is to be congratulated on not having allowed his head to be turned, and on replying in a fashion entirely non-committal. The personal tone that the controversy has assumed is a pity. "He took my dogs", says one. "Yes, but he took my victuals", says the other. It will be humanly interesting to see the two men publicly confronted. Meanwhile our own Geographical Society does well, perhaps, to reserve its recognition of the prior discovery.

As was to be expected, the Committee appointed to consider the question of holding London County Quarter Sessions at the Old Bailey has reported against the plan. There were two strong influences against it —that of the City Corporation and that of the Bars of the present Sessions. Taking the Sessions to the Old Bailey would abolish the sole control of the City over the Old Bailey and bring in the conjoint control of the County Council. It would also let in as competitors for the practice with the Sessions Bars that now have the monopoly of it other barristers who do not belong to them.

Thus the dreams of the lives of Sir Edward Clarke and Sir Harry Poland, according to their own statements, are not to be fulfilled. Both these distinguished Old Bailey advocates believed the plan was possible and best, in addition to convenience and dignity, for such interests of justice as the speedy trial of prisoners. They believed that the difficulties about accommodation and the staff at the Old Bailey, which the report lays so much stress on, could be managed. If the City were in love with the project no doubt it could. Now a new Sessions House will have to be built at considerable cost, either on the present Newington site or elsewhere. The Newington site would be more economical; an available site in Bloomsbury would be more convenient. In all probability it will be the latter that will be chosen; and it has long been spoken of.

Several ladies, and no man, have lately retired from the profession of literature on the ground of insufficient appreciation. That is the worst of making literature a profession, instead of simply writing. People who simply write have never need to retire, even for an advertisement. In fact, no one can retire who ought to be writing. The latest to retire is "Frank Danby", confessing to a circulation of forty thousand, and complaining that she cannot achieve fame. How could she expect fame on a circulation like that? She might have studied the fate of Miss Corelli and Mr. Hall Caine. Still, there may be something in it that we do not understand. Mark Twain's account of his own death increased his sales, and Mr. William O'Brien preserves his political popularity by retiring from public life at least once in five years. Every time he returns he finds public life still alive, and so it will be with literature, though it need not be so with many books.

Leaders of the two great parties, the "Times", judges of the High Court, and various other people of overrated authority may breathe again; for, as we understand, Mr. Harris is giving them and himself a holiday. "Vanity Fair" is turning over a new leaf. We wish it all good luck. It has been for some while past somewhat startling at times, even personal in its criticisms. But many of its notes have been good to warm oneself by: Mr. Harris, as man of letters and of journalism, touches nothing which he does not set on fire. He burns—and it must be said he often tries to make others fizzle too. He has another merit that has made "Vanity Fair" often so good to dip into—he writes with force and simplicity that uncommon language the English. We hope he will continue writing it, even at the possible cost of the statesmen, judges, bankers and Oxford and Cambridge.

AS THE POLES ASUNDER.

"WHY do they believe Shackleton and Peary if they won't believe me?" The question is to the point, and we shall answer it.

The week just passed has chronicled an achievement for which the world has waited nearly four hundred years. There has been a fascination about the search for the North Pole which has continued undimmed down the ages because of the apparently eternal inaccessibility of the goal. Now we are confronted by two claimants for the highest honour an explorer can obtain—the attainment of 90 deg. N. There are four alternatives in the competition for credibility: A and B may be both right or both wrong; A may be right and B wrong, or B may be right and A wrong. Each has made a categorical claim; how are these alternatives to be tested and settled?

When an explorer returns and says he has done a specific thing, he is entitled to be taken at his word; and in ninety-nine cases out of a hundred, before the polite exchange of compliments is over, he has spontaneously produced evidence of the truth of his statements. When Lieutenant Shackleton returned from the neighbourhood of the South Pole a few months ago, his first announcement was accepted as accurate; but while the man in the street in his thousands was reading the long telegram, there were half-a-dozen keen minds at work jotting down the positions on maps, calculating mileages and dividing them by days, setting one statement against another, so that if any discrepancy existed it would be brought to light. Some of these were friends of the explorer, never doubting the truth of what he said; some perhaps were critics who had predicted that the expedition would be a failure, anxious to vindicate their own prescience at the expense of the explorer's reputation; and some were mere scientific Gallios caring neither for the honour nor the discredit of the man, but simply desirous of testing the statements before accepting them. The public never heard of this; it probably does not yet know whether Shackleton has proved his assertions; or faces the world on the mere statement of what he has done. The public does not know, but the experts do, that no discrepancy was found in Shackleton's story; that all his original records have been examined and corroborated by independent authorities; and that, all the time it read of honours and fêtes, no honour worth having was offered without tests having been made, and no distinction bestowed until the word of a man no one dreamed of doubting was established out of the mouths of two or three witnesses. So the public does not know how much weighing of probabilities, how much "ringing up" of people specially fitted to form opinions, took place in the newspaper offices, before the headlines which appeared a few hours after the first telegrams came in were penned. It is worth while to glance at the sort of evidence which led the newspaper man—who is anxious not to mislead his readers—to hit upon the headlines: one day, "Reported Discovery of the North Pole by Dr. Cook"; and a few days later, "Peary reaches the Pole".

To begin with the reason for the more positive statement, Commander Robert E. Peary is an American who is able on occasion to speak great swelling words on the greatness of his nation and his own destinies; not the sort of speeches which a British explorer would make; in fact, when only his first writings were known, sixteen years ago, they did not attract much attention in this country, nor was the man looked upon as a very serious explorer. But Peary went on; year after year he went up into the Arctic; year after year his reports attracted more and more attention; at length in 1897 he came to London and gave a lecture to the Royal Geographical Society. The Arctic veterans of the Franklin Search saw him, questioned him about his experiences, and pronounced him good. His maps were fitted into the framework of earlier explorers of repute of many nations, and they were found to fit. Whenever Peary made a statement, important or trivial, that could be confronted with the statement of a known authority or another of his own, the two were compared; whenever he produced a photograph it was found to correspond with description. In a word, Peary conquered prejudice and proved that he was truthful; and the confidence of the Royal Geographical Society—a tribunal the adverse verdict of which means the non-bestowal of rewards—was expressed by giving him one of the coveted gold medals. Year after year Peary went on, forcing his way farther and farther into the shifting wastes of the frozen sea, and year after year he came back in the bitterness of disappointment, having done his best, but yet confessing failure. Had he been the sort of man who would tell a lie he could have done it. He knew so much of the Far North that it would probably never be detected; but the man who can do what Peary had done up to 1907 is the kind of man who cannot tell lies regarding what is nearest to his heart; and he is the kind of man who shows unasked to competent authorities the proofs which would reveal any deviation from truth in his narrative. Each year Peary had proved one fresh point in his reasoned scheme for reaching the Pole. He tamed the shy savagery of the Arctic Highlanders, and won the respect of these mistrustful people, so that they were ready to follow him over the sea-ice in the darkness of the Arctic night. He tested the powers of the Eskimo dogs, the amount of provisions requisite to accomplish a given number of miles; in fact he worked out like a mathematical problem the conditions precedent to reaching the Pole. Thus when he went North last year, an old man as polar explorers go, full of experience, with perfect equipment and a volcanic fervour of desire to reach the Pole this time, his friends knew that it was not the applause of success he was striving for, but the thing itself. The public were quick to see that the man who had left so little to do in the matter of miles to travel, who had many a time gone through hardships as great as he could ever be called upon to face, could be trusted not to depart from his own tradition of first telling the truth and then probability or inconsistency; and what they heard gave the London newspapers printed the headline "Peary reaches the Pole" they had questioned London geographers who know Peary as an intimate friend, and Arctic travellers, keen to detect the slightest improbability or inconsistency; and what they heard gave them full confidence in the man and in his word. We know that Peary will submit his records not to satisfy doubt, but to confirm belief; and if anyone can then prove them to be in error the fact will not be hidden. In the case of Peary we judge the man by the flawless record of his past; and, what will appeal even more strongly to some minds, by the fact that Captain Bartlett, the captain of his ship, who was with him, confirms the news.

Dr. Frederick A. Cook may, for all we know to the contrary, have reached the Pole a year before Peary. He says that he did so. He was subjected, so far as he would subject himself, to the same tests as Shackleton and Peary. In 1891-92 he had been a member of one of Peary's North Greenland expeditions, and there he became acquainted with the Eskimo. But Peary and he did not go out together again. In 1897 Cook joined the Belgian Antarctic expedition, and for a ghastly year he lived on board the "Belgica", drifting helplessly in the Antarctic floe. He wrote an eminently readable book on the expedition, full of rhetorical outbursts—not very much more extravagant than some of Peary's. His companions liked him, but they did not all take him too seriously. Later Dr. Cook made a notable expedition in Alaska, and started to scale the giant heights of Mount Mackinlay, the loftiest peak of North America. He made the last stages of the ascent alone, and wrote a book describing the achievement. Mountaineers are keen on the first climbing of virgin peaks, they keep careful records of such exploits, and a man is had in reputation when he establishes by definite rules his claim to such distinction. This Cook failed to do. He had no evidence to offer but his word. He had no observations to show, no companion to substantiate his statements. His experiences struck experienced mountaineers as almost more than improbable. We have, however, no proof that Dr. Cook did not climb Mount Mackinlay, and we do not say that he did not.

Now comes the statement that he has reached the Pole at the first attempt. Ploughing with the heifer of Commander Peary, he has solved his riddle; but unfortunately the answer is not convincing. We should find it easier to believe that Cook reached the North Pole than that several other statements in his narrative were correct. He had a year to write a telegram, and yet he states that the telegram as despatched from Lerwick and printed in the Paris edition of the "New York Herald" is full of telegraphic and typographic mistakes. He gave a temperature of 83 deg. below zero Centigrade, and when the absurdity of such a degree of cold was pointed out, he said he meant Fahrenheit, and that 83 deg. below zero Fahrenheit is quite common in the Arctic regions. Let it be granted that the Lerwick telegraph clerk or the Paris printer deliberately changed "Fahrenheit" to "Centigrade", the fact remains that no polar expedition ever found a temperature lower than 73 deg. below zero Fahrenheit, so far as we have been able to discover. Then the observations of latitude were given to the nearest second, and the telegram laid great stress on the seconds. A second of latitude is 100 feet; to be within two or three miles of the truth is exact enough for any polar traveller, and in later interviews Cook says that is all he claims. But the crowning marvel of the journey—greater even than going to the Pole with no white companions, but only two Eskimo boys—was that Dr. Cook solemnly says to newspaper reporters, to Princes, Kings, and even to Professors, that he left all his records, his diaries, his observations, his instruments—the charter of everlasting fame, the insurance policy against infamy—in Greenland, to be forwarded thence to America, while he came on by a Danish steamer to Europe.

WORRYING "THE TRADE".

THE House of Commons in Committee has been wading chin-deep in the technicalities of the licensing laws, and the gentlemen of the long robe have been thoroughly enjoying themselves. The subtleties of unearned increment and site value were bad enough, but they were child's play compared with the valuation of hotels and public-houses whose annual value exceeds £500 a year. The law of licensing is embedded in a series of statutes running back for over a century, and most barristers who are briefed in public-house cases are specialists. Is it not scandalously absurd that an attempt should be made to amend and consolidate this most difficult branch of municipal law by three or four sections in the Finance Bill, discussed by an exhausted and exasperated Committee in the month of September? We do not profess to understand—and we do not believe anybody else does—on what basis of valuation the new licences for hotels and public-houses assessed at over £500 a year are to be levied. The compensation value under the Act of 1904 is to be turned into annual value, and the new duties are to be half that amount. The capital sum to be awarded as compensation for the extinction of a licence under the Act of 1904 is arrived at by a multiplication of the annual difference between the value of a house with and without a licence, and that sum is added, we believe, to a multiplication of the profits or business done. How is that sum to be turned back again into annual value? Of course the Government originally intended to leave the whole matter to the officials of the Treasury and the Commissioners of Excise. My Lords of the Treasury were to make "regulations", and the clerks of Somerset House were to do sums in arithmetic, and between these bands of confederates the unhappy licensee was to be tossed about and comforted with an illusory right of appeal to the judges, who could only hand him back, after making an order for the payment of costs, to his tormentors. The "trap", however, was discovered in time, and once exposed had to be hastily abandoned by the Government. The appeal to the Courts, though costly it must be, will be on all points, and will at least protect the hotels and large public-houses against the arbitrary extortion of the myrmidons of Mr. Lloyd George.

The only part of these clauses which is comparatively clear is that relating to the public-houses under £500 a year assessed value and the beer-houses. The publican's licence duty is to be half the annual value of the premises, and the beer-house duty is to be a third of that value, with minimum duties which must in the case of a great many beer-houses exceed the annual value of the premises. A great deal of parliamentary time has been wasted by the folly of the Government in trying to settle by statute the peculiarly intimate relations of business between the manufacturer and the retailer of liquor. It is intended by the Bill to enable the publican to recover from the brewer the excess of duty now proposed to be levied, just as an ordinary tenant deducts from his rent the income tax under Schedule A which is collected from him. But this endeavour to protect the tied tenant from his landlord merely illustrates the absurdity of laws which try to regulate the private bargains of men. The difference between a free and a tied house is largely illusory. The number of so-called "free houses" whose occupiers have sufficient capital to buy their beer and spirits with ready money is infinitesimal. The licensee of a free house who is obliged to buy his liquors on credit is just as much tied to his brewer and distiller as the tenant of a tied house. Every man who owes another money is tied to his creditor, in which sense most people are tied to their bankers. The manufacturers and retailers of liquor are in fact partners, who, on the whole, get on very well together, and certainly do not require the intervention of a Government official or a judge to settle the terms of their partnership for them, or to enforce its obligations. It may be taken for granted that the brewers will pay the excess duties—if they can. But is it not obvious that in nine cases out of ten the brewer must do one of three things—raise the rent, or increase the price of his beer, or shut up the house? What is the use of giving the tenant a legal right to recover the excess of duty as a debt if the landlord cannot afford to repay him without raising his rent or his price? The Prime Minister indeed hinted broadly, with sardonic humour, that the beer might be watered. Higher prices for worse beer, or ruin, seems to be the alternative before a great many brewers and publicans. Another very objectionable feature is the new "register" that is to be compiled by the Somerset House officials from "returns" of the most intimate character extracted from the publicans. Details as to his methods and profits in business of a far more searching and confidential character than those now demanded for the purposes of income tax are to be tortured out of the publican by the inquisitor of excise. The only comfort is that the Chancellor of the Exchequer is here on the line of greatest resistance, as he may discover before he is many months older.

THE CULT OF THE COW-HUNTER.

THE increase in lawlessness required to make the Land Bill workable, especially the compulsory provisions, has now to be reckoned against the like results of throwing out the measure, and the decision is not more difficult for the Lords than the alternatives are tragic to Ireland. With more than £50,000,000 worth of land sold beyond the financial provision to pay for it, there was obviously no need for compulsion, unless to get the land for less than the honest price. For years lawlessness has been elaborately organised to lower the price of the land, with the increased land hunger raising it at the same time. On the whole, the price has risen, in spite of the lawlessness, and now the Government tries to accommodate the law-breakers, reinforcing the terrors of the League by the terrors of the law, to suit the cult of the parliamentary cow-hunters, to whom peace is public death. Men were shot to make them sell their property at the buyer's price, but they refused, and now the House of Commons comes to the assistance of the moonlighter, "in accordance with Irish ideas". The law-breaker having failed to depress the price of land, Parliament is asked to reinforce law-breaking, and the Commons have already consented. Up to now there has been at least a pretence of governing Ireland; this is the first time that "Government" has openly undertaken to realise the purpose of the criminal for him by legislation.

The compulsion by the law has not even the merit of superseding the compulsion by the League, which is but stimulated by it. While Mr. Birrell has been contriving his clauses, his Irish allies have been contriving their crimes to correspond; and already a League message is passed in confidence through the country to the effect that no rent must be paid to the landlord who does not welcome sale by force, with its necessary element of confiscation. Recent attempts to recover rent overdue have shown resistance to the law organised with a perfection worthy of the darkest days, and indicating evident inspiration from headquarters. Yet for twenty-seven years there has been a statutory tribunal at work to revise unfair rents, and in that period the total rental of Ireland has been reduced about forty per cent. With the institution of the "fair rent" tribunal which has worked so generously to the tenant, an end of rent agitation was promised; but all through last winter the region of Loughrea was virtually in a state of siege, with the police in the district increased more than tenfold, every man armed night and day. The police authorities expect the coming winter to be worse than the last. Compulsory sale implies statutory arbitration, but it is obviously easier to menace the arbitrator than the owner, the latter having so much more to lose, not to mention how the official system comes more and more under the sway of the agitator and the criminal every day. Official valuers are now found inspecting estates for purchase during the day, and during the night denouncing the owners as persons who ought to be cast out without a penny; and these Government officials are appointed practically at the dictation of the League and the priests, who can make the law unworkable should their nominees be refused. The whole plea for compulsion has been founded on the need to relieve congestion; but it is now openly confessed by Mr. John Dillon that the League will not permit the removal of the congested, so that the crime may not be compensated by the claim that necessitates it. "No Mayo men in Roscommon", shout the Roscommon Leaguers. The quotation is from Mr. Dillon, and though he lives between the two counties, with the congested behind him and the prairies before him, he dares not attempt the purpose for which the compulsory sale of the land is required with the confiscation incidental to it. The landlord must be forced to sell, by arbitration under terror; but the League grabs the land for its own favourites, and congestion remains as before, a problem to perpetuate crime for the convenience of those who base the security of their statesmanship on their capacity for lawlessness. The rapid progress of land purchase outside congestion has been increasing a class of peasant proprietor for whom agrarian war has no more attraction, and the parliamentary purse has run down in proportion; but congestion remains, an asset too rich to be easily given up. In the evidence before the Royal Commission on Congestion several years ago it was shown, even with documentary proof, how the priests prevented the removal of the congested from their parishes, and the facts were enough to check that; but since then the scheme to perpetuate congestion has been set to work from the other end, with the peasants round the prairies organised to keep out the unfortunate congests. There are no regions in Ireland so valuable as the congested districts to the interests that flourish on the ruin of the country.

Such is the outlook, assuming the Bill passed as it stands, and the outlook for its rejection is still worse. In that case Mr. Dillon is to "let loose the dogs of war", as if the strife of the past had not been dog-like enough; and he is eloquently supported by Father Henry, parish priest of Foxford, who advises the people of Mayo that "you must take the matter into your own hands, and no power and no effort will stop you from doing so"—after all that Mr. Birrell and Mr. Russell have done to conciliate the clergy in the interests of good government! It is hard to see how the Lords could reject the Bill, and it is harder to see how they could pass it as it stands; but they can amend it, especially its criminal clauses, and their conflict with the Commons then stands on the footing of an attempt to preserve Ireland from barbarism. One way to modify the criminal effect of the compulsory clause would be by declaring it inoperative on any estate where the compulsion of the League was exercised in sympathy with it; but that would necessarily be in the discretion of the Executive Government for the time, and probably the safest course is to put out compulsion wholly. For this course there is the farther ground that the whole nine counties to be scheduled as congested do not contain enough land to end congestion, even assuming the opposition of the priests and the League withdrawn. The most valuable provision of all would be a test colony of migrants, capitalised and directed for the utmost production from their new farms; but this, too, is regarded by the legislators as a matter of Executive discretion, while the Executive itself is controlled by those who keep congestion as their milk cow. The British side of the business is still more grave. It is the first statutory attempt in our time to transfer real property by force, unless in exceptional areas for the collective convenience, as in the building of a railway or the widening of a street; and a principle so far-reaching, once sanctioned by the State, as it is already by the House of Commons, could hardly have its location confined to one side of the Channel. Ireland is a bore, we know, but if the Lords cannot defend Irish individual liberty they must at least consider the logical effect on their right to own their own property in Great Britain. Coerced by Irish anarchy, compromised by British socialism, and dependent on the Parliamentary gag to put five-sixths of the scheme through the Commons without discussion, the Government have done this thing; and now it remains for the House of Lords to say for the nation whether the time has come to initiate a change in the law of property which would be even more revolutionary to the social basis than a transition to republicanism. If "priests and people" must go on destroying each other in Ireland, that is no reason for intruding the methods of their destruction elsewhere, and the Lords are faced by an issue that goes far farther than Ireland. The question is whether the national conscience has become so degraded as to tolerate the methods of those who call themselves the Government.

IN AETHERIAS AURAS.

ENGLAND has achieved a record, the first of its kind in this country. Colonel Cody has hitherto been measuring his period of flight in minutes. He can now measure it in hours; in fact, it works out at about one and one-twentieth hours. It is the first creditable performance of an aeroplane upon English soil. For airships there is, of course, a national record of longer memory. There was the achievement of last August, when the airship of Captain Lovelace succeeded in killing a spectator. There are the less remarkable performances of the "Nulli Secundus", which sailed all the way from Aldershot to London in October 1907. But it never got home, being wrecked on the point of return, when it lay at anchor at the Crystal Palace. Now we have a real record. In this connexion it must be remembered that there are few aviators who do not possess a record of some kind—for altitude, for distance, for time in the air, for speed, for flight with a passenger, for Channel-crossing, and so forth. It seems necessary, therefore, to be very particular in setting forth the nature of this new record. Briefly, it is a record for cross-country flight, as distinguished from other kinds. So far as this goes we are at the moment supreme in the air.

The phrase "conquest of the air", adopted and used by many of the writers upon this subject, is a little premature, not to say presumptuous. Man at present is at best barely tolerated above the surface of the earth. He is a slave to the idiosyncrasies of a new element. For instance, he endeavours to make himself as light as possible. This is humouring the caprices of the slave he has "conquered" with a vengeance. It is a case of that direct imitation which is flattery. The air possessing no weight as compared with itself, let us make ourselves as flimsy as possible, and the air will acknowledge the compliment by being kind. This is not "conquest", but subjection. If this is "conquest", then leaves and feathers have made some headway, for they can travel when the wind is good to them. We are, in truth, only just beginning to feel our way very feebly, and it will be a case of fair-weather flights for many long days. Even birds and insects, with their superb equipment, are mostly helpless in squalls and gales. Comparatively an aeroplane is a much flimsier construction than the smallest bird, and its adjustments are not instinctive.

One way to conquest, in the real meaning of the word, seems to lie, not in the direction of getting rid of our special attribute as creatures possessing weight, but in the direction of making use of that very attribute to bring into subjection a hostile element. At present weight, with the aviator, is a disadvantage, a clog; whereas with the best fliers of nature, the greater birds, weight is part and parcel of their power to fly. It balances the flier and gives momentum. It is part of the driving force. The aeroplane, if it is to be a "conqueror" of the air, and of high practical utility, must harness weight and bring it to its aid as nature does. If it fails to do this, then it must probably remain subject to the caprices of the air, and its only government will be that which rules by obeying. Aviation, that is to say, will remain more of a sport than a serious means of adding to man's control of natural agencies.

The experiments at Rheims should not be allowed to fill the horizon too exclusively. The monoplane and the biplane are part of an endeavour to adapt the principle of bird-wing flight to practical aviation; and it is premature to eliminate from consideration possibilities that lie elsewhere. It will be remembered that Mr. Edison, in September last year, gave it as his opinion that any attempt to develop the art of flying by imitation of the natural flight of a bird would break down owing to the fact that the wings of a bird act automatically, whereas the movements of the type of aeroplane with which we are now so familiar depend upon the reasoned adjustments of the aviator. A practicable aeroplane would have to be automatic in its action, the human element acting merely in the control of mechanism, as in the case of the steam-engine. But, while he doubted of the future of that type of machine which has just, in the forms of monoplane and biplane, come through the ordeal at Rheims with surprising success, he nevertheless predicted that in five years there would be a transatlantic service of flying machines carrying passengers! He pinned his faith upon the helicoptal aeroplane, a circular arrangement of planes making use of the principle of the spiral and steadied by a gyroscope. In face of a declaration from such a source the Rheims controversy concerning the relative merits of monoplane and biplane fade into very thin air, especially as the evidence is by no means conclusive. The honours were so evenly divided that dogmatism is as impossible after the event as it was before. Mr. Curtiss won the speed race in a biplane; but M. Blériot in a monoplane travelled with the greatest speed over ten kilometres. Mr. Henry Farman on a biplane flew farthest; but Mr. Latham on a monoplane was not very badly beaten. The controversy cannot really be regarded as of much importance at a stage when the ultimate form and principle of the flying machine is still matter of conjecture. The Rheims week will have done more harm than good if it has tended to stereotype the art of flying. If the bird-wing principle has brought itself into such prominence that endeavours in other directions are discouraged, the "conquest" of the air may be retarded rather than accelerated by this meeting of experts. It is true that M. Paulhan flew in a wind blowing at a rate of twenty-five miles an hour, and that Mr. Farman carried aloft two passengers at passengers' risk. These are episodes. Against them are to be set others which persuade in a contrary sense. Mr. Orville Wright's passenger was killed last year, and M. Lefebvre paid the penalty of the world's dawning confidence in the Wright machine last Tuesday.

THE CITY.

MR. HARRIMAN is dead, and so passes away one of the most remarkable figures in American railway finance. An autocrat, his schemes demanded autocratic methods, and were generally for the public good. Without him the Union Pacific and Southern Pacific roads might have been languishing in the hands of a Receiver. There is no need for panic. The railways he controlled are now well established on a financial basis, and can run by themselves. His illness was exploited in the characteristic Wall Street manner. The wonder is that any solid basis is ever found for making a market in securities when such slender threads as a man's temperature can pull down the whole fabric. Speculators in American securities have been provided with ample sensation this week, and the net result to real investors is a heavy depreciation in their holdings. Other markets have not been very satisfactory. Cheap money would seem to have lost its power of raising prices, and it is waste of energy for financial advisers to dwell upon its advantages when seeking to guide investment. The cynic will tell you that everything now goes by contrary in the Stock Exchange, and that the only thing that will bring about an improvement in gilt-edged securities is an international war, everything else having failed. Perhaps when the holiday season is really over and men's thoughts are once more directed to serious business we may find views change: certainly it is remarkable in presence of many favourable factors that so much pessimism prevails. Encouraging from the City point of view are the latest trade returns. Compared with the corresponding month of last year, imports in August show an increase of 13.2 per cent. and exports of 5.8 per cent. There is still much leeway to be made up before the decline of the first five months of the year is effaced, but all the indications are in favour of further improvement—apart from the prospect of new trouble in the Welsh coal trade.

The issuing house will no doubt claim a big success for the Cuban loan. If the City generally were consulted on the matter the very reverse would be stated. For the man in the street was given no opportunity of subscribing. The loan was considered too good to go outside a favoured few, and though it was advertised on Wednesday that the subscription list was open, only about thirty minutes was allowed for sending in applications. Meantime a premium of 3 per cent. had been established on the bonds. Thus once again the investor is shut out from participating in the good things that are supposed to be created from time to time for his special benefit. There is of course nothing dishonest or immoral in these proceedings, but it is not surprising that the public are disgusted, considering how they are solicited when loans of more doubtful character are offered them. We are promised many more loans in the next few weeks, and large numbers of industrial issues are pending. The creation of new rubber companies continues. Scarcely a day passes without an appeal for capital for the development of some estate. There seems no lack of funds for the purpose, despite the long wait before the majority can earn adequate dividends. Wild rubber propositions have the pull over newly planted estates, as the trees are ready for immediate tapping, and profits accrue from the commencement of operations. Prices obtained are considerably below the cultivated product, but where labour is plentiful and ordinarily cheap there is always a big margin of profit. As the supply of cultivated rubber increases—as it must do—and the price comes down to a more reasonable figure, the demand for the wild will correspondingly decrease. Manufacturers now accept wild rubber because there is not enough of plantation to go round, but they prefer the latter, even though they have to pay a little more. The time, however, is far distant when wild rubber will cease to find a market. Some of the attempts made to interest the public in obscure rubber properties are amusing. We wonder how many people recognise in the much "puffed" Nilambour the old Indian Glenrock—the seventh reconstruction of a mining company formed in 1880!

The recent departure of the Underground Electric Railways Company of London in publishing a monthly revenue statement has encouraged a hope in a few that our principal home railway companies will follow the example. We sincerely trust not, and those who remember the illusory monthly returns published some years ago by the South-Eastern Railway, and the speculation which they engendered, will deprecate any return to the practice. If any other objection need be urged we would mention the Grand Trunk Railway, the monthly statements of which afford about as much indication of the real financial position of the company as the expert forecasts furnished by the daily press do of the weather. The home railway market is now dead, but however much we should like to see a revival of speculative interest, we hope it may be brought about by other means than those suggested.

The settlement discloses a large "bull" account in Chartered and Gold Fields, and there is evidence of the existence of a big speculative account in Kaffirs generally. This position is not conducive to firm markets, and the weakness of the last few days is thus easily explained. It is possible that a good deal of the stock thrown upon the market in the last débâcle is still being "nursed", as the public have not bought with any freedom in the last two months. Complaint is made that the issuing houses do not give adequate support to the market, but these are not philanthropic institutions, and are "out to make money" as are the Stock Exchange and the public. Their business is to sell shares, not to buy, and only in emergencies do they come forward and take stock. It is not likely that they are going to relieve a lot of speculators of bankrupt holdings. There are many bargains in the Kaffir market, but the public must be prepared to put down the money if it wishes to obtain the full benefit; it is useless to buy to "carry over".

"MID-CHANNEL."

By Max Beerbohm.

NOBLESSE oblige; and Sir Arthur Wing Pinero ought to abandon his cult for low life above stairs. Time was when he gave us glimpses of beauteous Princesses and cynical Dukes. They were not altogether convincing. One seemed to have had something like them in the pages of Ouida and other far less gifted novelists. Perhaps they did not convince even Sir Arthur (then Mr.) Pinero. For in recent years he has concentrated himself more and more closely on a study of the least pleasing elements in the various strata of the middle-class. Uneducated young women aping the manners of their superiors, and educated young women with a lurid streak of commonness in them, have had a particular fascination for him; and very cleverly he has depicted them. But, as an artist, he ought not to allow any one phase of life to master him; and I was hoping that now that he had received the royal accolade, and passed into the pages of Debrett, he would treat himself to other and wider ranges of vision.

Accordingly, "Mid-Channel" is somewhat a disappointment to me. Zoe Blundell, the central person of the play, is yet another sample of that betwixt-and-between type in which Sir Arthur has specialised; and she is much nearer to the class beneath her than to the class above her. She is, indeed, crudely and monotonously vulgar in thought and in speech. I cannot divine in her circumstances any reason why she should be so. She is the daughter of a successful doctor. As such, presumably, she had the advantages of a good nurse and a good governess when she was a child, and of decent, though possibly dull, society when she "came out". In this society, however, moved a very vulgar young man, whose wife she became. She loved him entirely for himself and the good that was in him; for his vulgarity was not counterbalanced by wealth. They were very poor, he and she—so poor that they had to live in that dark and squalid alley, Fitzjohn's Avenue. But in after years, when, through the husband's industry on the Stock Exchange, they had been able to migrate to splendid and salubrious Lancaster Gate, they always looked back on those days of their pathetic early struggles as the happiest days of their lives. As it had been their specific aim to rise in the social scale, one would suppose that whenever the husband was at home it would have been his wife's aim to refine him. But Sir Arthur's belief in the inevitable vulgarity of stock-brokers is as firm as his belief in the benightedness of Fitzjohn's Avenue. So far from refining her husband, poor Zoe became vulgar herself. Indeed, by the time she is thirty-seven years old, she has outdone him in vulgarity; and he rebukes her for her "damned slang"; whereat she rounds on him with the explanation that it was by contact with the friends whom he used to bring to the house that she lost her natural delicacy of speech. Thus does Sir Arthur show us the irony of life, the canker that may be at the heart of even the fairest rose. A hovel where love is—what more idyllic? But peep within, and you may see there the flash gang of which we know the Stock Exchange to be composed, poisoning with their vile locutions the shell-like ears of Angelina, wife of Edwin. One of these brutes, just arrived, says to her "Let's have a squint at you". Another, being thirsty, asks her to give him "a drop of water". Another, being hungry, suggests "a snack". Others are loudly talking of money as "coin", of children as "kiddies", and so forth and so on. And all these horrid equivalents will, by the time the hostess is verging on middle age, have become ineradicable from her vocabulary. Her only consolation will be that but for them she might not be deemed by Sir Arthur Pinero worthy to be the central figure in one of his plays—nay! might not even be able to smuggle herself in as a subordinate. In "Mid-Channel" there is but one person who is not saliently vulgar; and this is an elderly woman who has little to do with the play, and whose daughter describes herself as "a straight, clean girl". Peter Mottram, the *raisonneur* of the play, is not vulgar only when he is *en train de raisonner*. At such times he becomes quite portentously refined, and evolves the simplest platitudes in terms of most laborious metaphor. He has discovered that not all husbands and wives are as happy together as they appear. But, important though it is that the world should receive this tremendous revelation with as little delay as may be, he involves himself in a long, long disquisition on two flawed vases of Chinese enamel. Another discovery of his is that people, as they grow older, are apt to lose the impulses and illusions of youth; and for him this matter is inextricably interwoven with the aspect of the pewter cups and other trophies of athleticism which he has seen ranged on the sideboards of his friends; and he develops the analogy with a patience that appals. But the greatest of all his discoveries is that on which Sir Arthur bases his play: to wit, that husbands and wives sometimes get on each other's nerves after the passions of youth are spent, and before the acquiescence of eld supervenes. In the bed of the sea, half-way between Folkestone and Boulogne, is a ridge, which has the effect of making the water choppy, and—if you want the analogy worked solemnly out in all its ramifications, you must go to the St. James's: I admire Peter Mottram's patience, but can't copy it.

On the aforesaid basis Sir Arthur might have written a good light comedy. The first act (granted the needless vulgarity of the characters) promises well. Zoe Blundell and her husband agree to bicker no more, and then, by easy gradations, they proceed to bicker worse than ever. No matter that Sheridan did this business perfectly: Sir Arthur does it very well indeed. The trouble is that he (a light-hearted man of the theatre) feels he owes it to his opinion of himself as a thinker, and to his reputation for merciless study of life, to build up a tragedy. Mr. Blundell leaves his wife in Lancaster Gate, and takes a flat, and starts a liaison with a woman who once occupied a good social position, but has been divorced and has since then been associated with various men. As presented by Sir Arthur, she shows no trace of her past advantages, and has all the manners of the least reputable type of chorus girl. In fact, there is no dramatic contrast whatsoever between her and Zoe. This difference she has: she is not Blundell's wife; and so, following a sacred tradition of the stage, Blundell takes to the bottle. That a middle-aged man of sober habit must suddenly become a drunkard when he separates from his wife and takes a mistress, is a proposition which one's experience of actual life does not support. However, Blundell takes the stage-traditional course. Zoe, meanwhile, visits Italy, and from Siena (a city on which we should like to hear her comments) she wires to a young man who has flirted with her, suggesting that he should come and cheer her up. She becomes his mistress, but, soon after their return to England, learning that he has played with the young affections of the "straight, clean girl", and learning moreover that her husband, for whom she cares far more than for him, is tired of his separation from her, she proceeds to give the young man what he calls "the boot", and goes straight to her husband's flat. Meanwhile, Sir Arthur has been reading "Tess"; and so, after Zoe has forgiven the penitent Blundell his infidelity, she proceeds to confess her own infidelity, under the impression that he will cry quits. Needless to say, Zoe, in real life, would have no such delusion; nor, being the shallow little vulgarian she is, would she feel any need to ease her soul by gratuitously telling the truth. Sir Arthur, however, is out for poignancy. Zoe, cast forth by Blundell, proceeds to the flat of the young man, to see whether he will eventually marry her. She finds that he is now engaged to the "straight, clean girl", and, rather than discommode him, she throws herself out of a window "off". Of course we are thrilled. But the thrill is not a legitimate artistic one. Zoe would no more kill herself than she would have confessed to her husband. Her suicide is a mere device for effect—an effect of physical horror. So why stick at trifles? Why not let the audience actually see Zoe climb on to the window-sill and disappear head over heels?

LETTERS FROM SOLITUDE.

By Filson Young.

III.

. . . . Connemara.

On a recent afternoon a little party straggled along a Connemara road, and then struck into the mountains. It consisted of, first, two constables, then a peasant woman, then another constable and the sergeant, then the local magistrate who is also the local hotel keeper, his son and clerk, the doctor and myself. The peasant woman was in custody for having that morning struck her mother-in-law, an old woman nearly eighty years of age, over the head with a pair of tongs; and as the old woman was thought to be dying the magistrate was going to take her depositions. So we climbed the mountains, no formality being observed, the prisoner walking a quarter of a mile away from her warders, and all of us intent upon our footing as we strode or leaped from stone to stone, or skirted a brown spongy patch of bog. Then we came to the "village"—four cabins hanging on the mountain side, each no bigger than the inside of a motor-omnibus, and each the centre of a tiny cultivated patch of land, where poor little fragments of crops feebly waved among the rocks. No road or path—just these four cabins and their little plots looking down over the lake-studded plain that lies between these southern hills and the great soaring inland mountains.

We stooped and went into the cabin in which the persons of the drama had their home. In a corner by the peat fire the poor old victim lay groaning on a heap of rags on the earth floor. Her son, a weak, complaining creature, sat beside her holding her hand. The prisoner, his wife—a patient, intelligent woman with a face of strength and suffering—sat on a box opposite to them. No greetings were exchanged. Her two children—beautiful little creatures with dark hair and great violet eyes—sat solemnly and speechlessly together on a tiny bench. The rest of us were crowded somehow into the bare, clean little hut, which was furnished only with a dresser, a table, two chairs, a box and a bench. A few chickens cheeped gently among our feet, and on a bed of heather at the far end of the room the family cow rustled and sighed. We kept both doors open for light and air, and while the doctor was making his examination I learned the facts.

It was the familiar situation of mother-in-law and daughter-in-law, contracted here into the space of a few square yards. Ten years ago this old woman's son, John let us call him, married this pretty Margaret from another country. She was an heiress, and brought him a dowry of fifty pounds. Old Mary, the mother, resented her coming into the house; old as she was, she still intended to be mistress; but until the fifty pounds was spent they all lived together; the man gave up all attempts at work, and loafed and drank and bullied the wife on whose money he was living. Then—after who knows what shame and suffering in body and mind?—she ran away alone to America, and there lived and worked for two years, regularly sending home money to husband and children—for she had left the two little ones behind her in her flight. She bore a third child soon after she left home; and I suppose the pull of the other children drew her back again, for she returned last winter. Since then there had been continual squabbles and fightings; she had twice to seek the protection of the police from her husband; and on the morning of the tragedy things came to a climax. She was baking a cake of bread for the children's breakfast; the old woman, who did not want bread herself and could not bear that anyone else should have it, threw the cake into the fire. The daughter-in-law turned on her and struck at her with the tongs; they came down on her head, cutting it badly; the son struck at his wife and caught his mother as she fell. The police were sent for, and the prisoner was marched off four miles to the barracks, whence she had now been marched back, presently to be marched to the barracks again—twelve miles' walking—driven five miles in a car to the station, and taken by train to Galway Jail—another two hours' journey: and all day without food. It was indeed a singular circumstance that none of the persons in the drama had eaten anything all that day. The old woman, who had lost a lot of blood and was now very low, was sinking from exhaustion; the son had not made any attempt to feed her or himself. I asked him if there was any milk in the house. "Ah, no, your honour; it's too poor I am to have any milk", he whined; but the prisoner said calmly, "There's some in that cup on the dresser, sir". "Have you an egg?" I asked him. "Ah, niver a one, sir, at all." I looked at the prisoner. "You'll find one under the basin, sir." We beat up the egg in some milk for the old woman, who took a little very reluctantly; and later, when I asked the son if she had finished it, he said she had. "Get up and let me see what you're hiding there." He rose and disclosed the mug, still half full. "Ah, and it's ill in meself I am, your honour, and after needing something to put strenth in me." It was only by reference to old-age pensions, wrapped up in an assumption of his love of his mother, that one was able to convince him of the importance of keeping her alive.

The doctor's report being unfavourable, the depositions were taken, much confusion being caused by the ill-put questions of the sergeant. It was something like this—the old woman answering in mournful, wailing, but beautiful broken tones:

Sergeant: "How were you feeling in yourself this morning, Mary?"

Mary: "Oh, it was wake, wake, I was."

Sergeant: "But were ye any waker than usual?" (Question repeated.)

Mary: "It's wake this long time I've been."

Clerk (reading): "I, Mary Manisty, got up early this morning, being in my usual health——"

Sergeant: "Now tell us what happened. Come, on, now; what happened next?"

Mary: "That woman shtruck at me with the tongs, and I'd a been kilt only for me son, and——"

Prisoner (rapidly): "Sure I went to put a cake on the fire for the children, and I niver wished the old woman any harrm, and me goin' in fear of me life of that man ever since I came home, and had to run out of the bed from him lasht night, an' I just gave her a tip with the tongs, an' I didn't mean to hurrt her at all."

Sergeant: "Whisht, woman. You'll be able to tell your story in court." (Producing the tongs) "Is this the tongs she shtruck ye with, Mary?"

Mary (whimpering): "Shure it is, your honour, and she'd a kilt me——"

Sergeant: "Where did she shtrike ye?"

Mary (undoing her bandages): "Here, your honour, and I niver wanted her in the house at all, and it's me own house me husband left me——"

Sergeant: "What part of the tongs did she shtrike ye with?"

Prisoner (pointing): "With that part, sir."

Sergeant: "Whisht, woman, now." (To Mary) "Did she shtrike you with the shoulder of the tongs?"

Mary (crying): "On me head."

Sergeant: "But was it with the shoulder of the tongs she hit ye?"

Mary: "It was, long life to your honour."

Clerk (reading): "Margaret Manisty, my daughter-in-law, whom I now see, then struck me on the shoulder with the head of the tongs (produced)——"

(Together)
Doctor: "No, on the head."
Sergeant: "On the head, with the shoulder of it."
Prisoner: "It was on the head I shtruck her."
Magistrate: "With the shoulder, on the head of her, wasn't it, Mary?"
Stranger: "The shoulder of the tongs, not——"
John: "Ay, and the wall all shpattered with blood."
Constable: "Sure it wasn't the head of the tongs at all."

Clerk (correcting): "On the head with the shoulder", etc.

And so on. The dreary little tragedy was reconstructed step by step, the rich quavering wail of the old woman with the great grey eyes and wrinkled face answering the briefer speech of the men and the sweet quiet tones of the younger woman. Through the open doorway, golden in the dying sunlight, lay all of the world that some of them had ever seen—the plain and the mountains and the far-away shining of the sea. Once the baby, who was in the adjoining room, began to whimper, its small voice rising louder in an appeal for attention. Its mother made an instinctive movement towards the sound, but the constable's detaining hand was on her arm and she sat back again, listening to the small voice that none responded to. When the end came, and it was time for the prisoner to start on her long journey to Galway (whence she might possibly never return), she kissed the two little ones tearlessly, and sent the five-year-old girl, a baby herself, in to mind the infant and take up the parent's burden. To her husband or the old woman she spoke no word and made no sign, and marched stoically out with the constable into the golden evening, to be dealt with as the Fates should decree.

It was obvious that the old woman would die from sheer exhaustion if she were not fed; though the doctor, hardened by long experience, merely told them to "mind and feed her up", and departed with the rest of us. A bottle of port, carefully disguised and marked "medicine; a tablespoonful after food", was made ready at the hotel when I got back; the son and several neighbours had promised that someone would come for it in the evening; but no one took the trouble to come, and I went to bed with sad misgivings as to the future of the daughter-in-law and her children if the worst should come to pass.

The third act of the drama took place the next day, which was Sunday. I got a large bottle filled with broth, and with that in one hand and the port in the other started on the four-mile walk to the cabin. It was very hot, and once off the road on the boggy mountains the horse-flies attacked me, and, as both my hands were occupied, bit busily on my unprotected flesh. Whenever I sat down to rest and do battle with them, I was fortified by a vision of the dying old woman, and the many lives that might depend on my errand, and so arrived, physically demoralised but mentally exalted, at the door of the hut. It was barricaded; and only after considerable parley was it opened, and I and my burden admitted. I expected to find that death had come before me; but, on the contrary, the old woman was sitting up in her corner looking very bright and brisk, the son sitting beside her in the same attitude as yesterday, and a neighbour, who opened the door to me, sitting at talk with them. Amazing vitality! The eighty-year-old victim who the morning before had lost half a pint of blood at least and whom we found in a sinking condition, was apparently on the mend, although she had taken nothing but some stewed tea in the meantime. I was made welcome and received with all honour; but not a drop of my broth or port would the patient touch. When it was put to her lips she sank back and shook her head. This was too much; I remembered the flies, and embarked on cajolery. Here was I, I said, after walking eight miles to bring her something to make her well; would she do something to please me?

"Ay, an' that I would, your honour!"

Then would she take some of the nice broth—just to please me?

"I would indeed, your honour; and" (loudly) "if it was poison itself I'd take it." And with perfect docility she drank down the broth.

But the tragedy was over. She was not going to die; in that case (the magistrate had promised) the prisoner would be released in a few days; and, for good or ill, they would all be together again. So the only thing left was to offer a few words of advice as to the desirability of living and letting live, and so forth. Had they missed her since she had gone? Yes, and indeed they had missed her; missed (although they had not known it) the calm practical strength of her presence, and consciously missed the order and energy she had brought into the feckless little household. Then, if they had missed her for a day, how would it be if she never came back for ten years? That was a fortunate shot, which went well home. They promised readily enough, if she came back, to welcome her and to be kind and not cross to her. The old woman followed me about the room with her great grey eyes, and when I was leaving, kissed my hand and blessed me very prettily; and her beautiful resonant salutation of "Long life to your honour!" followed me out into the hot sunshine.

I confess I was despondent enough about the effect of my advice, although I could not but be happy at their warm recognition of my friendly intention. More than the bottles and the advice, the eight-mile walk I had taken would do them good; and I had all the conventional sensations of bringing away from my mission much more than I had taken to it. Yet, to my great surprise, I heard later that the commonplace advice had produced a wonderful effect, simply because it came from a stranger who could not be suspected of "taking sides"; and that they had acted on it as they would not have acted on the advice of people well known to them and important in their lives. . . . So you see that even in these solitudes one's thread gets caught up and tangled with other threads; for it is often when one is most lonely that one is least alone.

THE OLD OLD STORY.

THE philosophy of Fiction has probably not been properly considered, and Empiricism reigns. Interesting questions cluster about the plot, and the most foolish romance takes us into the deep and sunless places of the human mind. For all the stories in the world are old and moth-eaten, ancient things that were told by our ancestor, Probably Arboreal. They were narrated by the primitive Cave-Woman to Pithecanthropus Erectus as the gentleman was innocently gnawing a bone; we steal from a low-browed, hairy man who hafted an axe on the ooze of malarious rivers, and Pterodactylus came through the forest.

Fiction works on dark, inherited instincts, on irrational impulses, just as the delight in running water and a dark wood is a relic of the time when man was a nomad on the road that leads to "the world's end", and when he who was a Wanderer had to follow the track of the drinkable streams.

A story must be old and follow paths in the brain that have been worn by the passing of ancient stories told by the Cave Woman in the twilight of the race, or the mind fails to grasp it. These primitive stories told in the nursery to Doris, who says she wants "another", are the Forms under which man comprehends all history. They correspond to the Ideas of Time and Space in the Kantian philosophy. Man cares not for historical truth; he is all for romance and Bruce's spider. He is mad for "bonnie Prince Charlie" and a "bleezing" piper: he is for Romance and Queen Mary. The story of Jeanne d'Arc, who was the least of all things in France, touches the heart because it follows the well-worn lines of Cinderella.

It is in this half-realised world that the novelist works and produces effects he knows not how. He makes us recall old things, just as, when the honest watch-dog sees the moon, there stirs in him a remembrance of the days when the packs were out and his ancestor, a gaunt wolf, stretched himself on a long trail in the snows of the Glacial period. In this connexion a curious evolution has been taking place in fiction, and the effect of it is to connect the novel still closer with Probably Arboreal and Pithecanthropus Erectus.

At first the novelist told his story in a bald and straightforward manner. Scott was hardly an artist, and when he uses a subsidiary theme it does not blend with the main current of the story. It is a matter of juxtaposition and propinquity in time, and the Waverley Novels consist of two threads ravelled together. Charlotte Brontë and Jane Austen all tell their tale in the simple and straightforward manner of Scott. But Dickens has advanced far beyond Scott, and in his hands a process to which we may give the name of "Echoing" is full grown. His characters all rise with shadows of Fate projected across them. In the course of the story incidents are related which dimly resemble the circumstances of the principal figures and the subsidiary theme is an "Echo" of the main plot.

Perhaps one of the most artistic uses of a process to which for the moment we may give the name of Echoing is to be found in Mrs. Johnston's "Old Dominion". A ship tacks up the estuary of the Chesapeake, a criminal sits in the straw of the hold. He stands in sharp contrast to Mistress Patricia in her pride, her Venice lace, her shoes "galooned with silver". It scarcely needs a child's discernment to know that before the end of the vexed tale, he who is down will be exalted. This is the main thread, but it is Echoed by countless episodes. Hints of the doom to which the story climbs are scattered along the course of the book; the footsteps of Fate are heard approaching. There is the tale of the man and the lone woman who live for love's sake in a forest rimmed about with wolves and the lean red Indian. "We shall die that way," the lone woman says quietly, "but what does it matter so that we die together?" . . . "You are happy?" Mistress Patricia asks as her pride melts. And then, with a light on her face, the lone woman answers, "Yes, I am happy!" So she and the lone man die in a burning house, and over the intervening space the mind takes a leap; we know the end to which the tale of Mistress Patricia and the broken man travels.

But, though this is a new development in the novel, the practice of later writers varies in the most interesting manner. Hardy scarcely uses this subtle method, or, if he uses it, it is in a simple and rudimentary form. The dominant idea in his novels is always that of a vast and unbroken succession in time, and when Knight goes over the cliff in "A Pair of Blue Eyes", he is to be with the geological ages in his death and to be reduced to the same state as the fossilised Trilobites, the zoophytes, the mollusca he sees embedded in the grit of the cliff over which he hangs suspended. Hardy, in the main, uses the Echo in a simple form, and in the "Woodlanders", which is a tragedy, the ancient pain of the world twists the trees into shapes that have the horror of Dante's forest. Melbury and his daughter "elbowed old elms and ashes with great forks in which stood pools of water that overflowed on rainy days and ran down their stems in green cascades", and "the Unfulfilled Intention . . . which makes life what it is, was as obvious here as it could be among the crowds of a city slum". It is an omen; the least observant reader cannot fail to note the subtle hint which it is the business of the artist to instil that the book creeps onward to a tragedy and to that scene where Marty tends a lone grave. But, though Hardy uses the Echo for the most part in this simple and rudimentary form, there is a fine instance in "A Pair of Blue Eyes", though, even in this, the idea is not complex.

Stephen and Elfride walk hand in hand to the village churchyard on a night of joy, and, as he sits down on a flat tombstone, he attempts to draw her towards him.

"No, not here", she says.

"Why not here?"

"A mere fancy", the girl answers, and in the tale she sits down beside him. It is spring in that world, and Stephen and Elfride, who feel the throb of the mounting blood, have much to say to one another, ancient things that were well worn when Noah was thoughtfully awaiting the return of the dove. He asks her if she had never loved another, and when Elfride vows that she has never before recognised another sweetheart, the youth blunders on.

"But", he asks, "did nobody ever love you?"

And Elfride hesitates. "Yes," she admits, "a man did once, 'very much' he said." "Where is he now?" Stephen asks. "Here," she answers. "Here," the man says, "what do you mean by that? . . . Where here?"

"Under us. He is under this tomb. He is dead, and we are sitting on his grave." It is an omen and the story climbs to a tragedy. But this use of the method of Echoing is simple and primitive and hardly has the subtlety of the process in its fully developed form, nor the delicacy which is shown by Dickens and other writers who have so often used this method to hint at the climax to which their stories move, the tragic pain with which they are infused.

But, if Mr. Hardy uses this method with hesitation and reserve, the thing is practically full-grown in the hands of Dickens. He is full of hints and foreshadowings; the characters are seen in a Romantic light. When David Copperfield arrives, lonely and weary, at his school, he sees one name carved high on the schoolroom door, and it is the name of "J. Steerforth". It is an omen and a premonition of the coming doom, the sad ending of the tender tale of Little Em'ly, when, on a night of joy, Mr. Peggotty sets a guttering candle in the window, and when dazed and bewildered he cries, "Em'ly fur away . . . Well!" Even Little Em'ly climbs about the knotty and gnarled knees of the "bacheldore" with hints of the far-off end. Ham stands looking long and earnestly at a streak of oily light that lies like a far-off flaw on the surface of the deep. He does not know why he stares at it, but we who read know that on a night of storm and stress, he and the false Steerforth will die together where the oily light shines on the surface of the hungry sea.

But these, though admirable instances of the management of a great theme, are hardly examples of what we have called the Use of the Echo. Indeed, Milton employs this simple form of suggestion with fine skill to emphasise the fact that, not Satan, but the Fall of Man is the central theme in his great epic. The innocent pair in the bowers of Eden do not, indeed, appear till far on in the story; but when, in the First Book, Satan on the burning marle speaks of his projected revenge on the new race, "whereof so rife there went a fame in Heaven", suddenly the murky air is lightened; a shout goes up; there flashes out "millions of flaming swords". The horrid cry on the burning marle, the lights, the brazen clash of shields "in the din of war" draw the attention of the reader to that unseen race in the trees of Eden.

But Dickens uses this method with finer art. In "David Copperfield" he manages to surround the child wife with a thousand charms, and yet, bit by bit, the conviction is slowly forced on the reader that the loves of Dora and David are fleeting. As the hero goes down the stairs of a gaunt London house where David had been praising Dora to the silent and suffering Agnes, a sightless beggar follows him in the night, tapping the pavement with his stick and crying with the melancholy cry of the mendicant, "Blind; blind; blind!" That wild and eerie cry in a London night is a stroke of genius, worthy even of the Romantic brain that conceived Admirable Guinea and the tattered figure of John Silver. And lastly, the theme of the passing loves of Dora and David is echoed no longer by fugitive hints but by a long narrative. The jealousy of Dr. Strong and his wife are worked in for a great artistic reason, and as the curtain goes down on the episode, we behold David meditating on the subject. "I was thinking" he writes, "of all that had been said. . . . 'There can be no disparity in marriage like unsuitability of mind and purpose. The first mistaken impulse of a mistaken heart.' . . . But we were at home, and the trodden leaves were lying under foot, and the autumn wind was blowing!"

Dickens is full of these hints and suggestions. So, when Mr. Peggotty goes out to search the world for Em'ly, Dickens says nothing of his own emotions; he flings the gnarled figure of the Yarmouth fisherman, black and dark against a sky of evening, and suggests moral grandeur simply by a rosy light. "He turned alone at the corner of our shady street, into a glow of light in which we lost him." And long afterwards, when Mr. Peggotty finds the girl who had danced at his knees, but changed and saddened, they sail away into the seas. The story closes on their future, but they go to happiness, for the light is rosy around them. Little Em'ly sails into the sunshine, but on the old country, the home land, the dear land, this England, the shadows gather, and on the Kentish hills the night has "fallen darkly".

The older writers know nothing of this use of suggestion. In the parting from England of Little Em'ly and Micawber, the Echo is little more than the Romantic use of scenery, though of scenery steeped in emotion. In other instances it takes the form of a long story running side by side with the main plot, twisted into its strands and anticipating the climax to which the story climbs.

This is the latest word in fiction. It is on the side of the art of writing a consequence of the Romantic Movement, but it goes beyond it, and in the words of Stevenson, 'those irrational acceptations and recognitions" of the artist "reclaim, out of a world which we have not yet realised, ever another and another corner."

A GOTHIC GRANGE.

By Laurence Binyon.

We had entered into an arresting stillness. Outside, in the great sunshine, there were the peaceful living sounds of the farm. Black and white oxen were grazing the short fresh herbage. Poplar-leaves made a cool trembling in the air. A boy who sat on some crumbling brickwork above a pond was angling in the still water. Beyond, in the vast fields, where the luminous stalks of wheat melted at a little distance into a sea of clear gold, thickened above with the browned spikes of the solid ears of corn, reapers were at work: sunburnt men and women in blue, bending over their sickles as the stalks fell crisply. Over all was the immense sky of Flanders, clear and hot; but the far distance showed impalpable sign of storm, and at intervals there was faint thunder.

The great unbroken slope of the roof, of ruddy tiles, a little mossed, made the long wall it covered seem low. But at once, on entering, the impression was one of space and grandeur. Also of a wonderful stillness. Perhaps the actual sounds within accentuated the stillness. Along one side of the interior, against the further wall, ran a wooden partition, with a low roof of boards. This low roof was heaped with fodder, and in one corner an old man and a boy were forking hay from a load on the floor to replenish the layers above. In the dimness and solitariness of the place the rustling, hushing sound of the tossed hay seemed the incarnation of silence. And then the eye began to take in the structure of this strange and magnificent interior. One seemed to be standing in a deserted cathedral. There was the central nave, and the aisles on either side, the great pillars and the buttresses; but all of wood, of naked oak, instead of stone. What forests must those have been which bore trees so formidable, out of which could be hewn these immense square columns, forty feet at least in height, even and straight from top to bottom! And above, what gigantic beams met to support the roof! Here was all the secret of Gothic building laid bare; no screen of stone disguised the bony framework of the architect's design, with its planned poise of thrust and counterthrust. The lesson was perfect. One marvelled at the perfection of the whole, hardly defaced or decayed in six centuries of time, and at the endurance of the ancient timber, seamed in places and worn a little at the bases of the pillars by rubbing and use, but in the upper parts preserving its fresh edges as axe and plane had left them.

Yet, try as one might to study the structural anatomy and understand its form and detail, the mind was irresistibly drawn away to be absorbed in the sentiment of the place. The spirit of the distant age which had built them seemed still to dwell within the walls; no modern molestations had dislodged it from its home; here, the age of commerce, appraising everything for instant and temporary use, seemed centuries away. An age of unhurried labour, executing large thoughts, choosing its time, seasoning its materials, disdaining alike parsimony and pretentiousness; that was an age which truly understood magnificence, the public virtue we know so little of. To some, the close modelling of a timbered barn upon the plan of a stone church may seem but the evidence of an ecclesiastical habit of mind, unable to free itself from rigid grooves. Certain stupidities of modern Gothic provoke indeed a natural disgust with ecclesiastical features misapplied. But we will justify the instinct of these old builders. For this great grange, which, season after season, and century after century—while Europe has been desolating itself with wars and alarms, bloodsheddings, exactions, fires and plunderings, dynasties falling and lands invaded—has with every harvest been stored full, and given out again of its abundance; has it not, with its benignant offices to man and beast, a just title to sanctity? Has it not a part in the immemorial religion of men? Are not this mystery and solemnity proper to the place? Profane thoughts, thoughts of the world, of gain, of fortune, of position and what not, are felt to be unseemly here, where the naked, delving Adam seems so eternally true an image of humanity, and the child of civilisation is brought to understand how all the efforts and accomplishments of ages have but disguised the nearness of man to the soil and his dependence on kindly earth.

Who could pass a half-hour among these shadowy pillars and not wish to be a painter? And yet how could pigment ever convey the aerial subtlety of this interior? Windowless, the grange admitted daylight only at one or two small doorways; but what a new thing it seemed to make of common light! Just as one lets water trickle between the fingers, to feel the pure coolness of it the better, so the light seemed to steal in shy floods into that spacious obscurity, to be treasured there. Through a chink between old boards the green light of the grass shone strangely vivid. And on the edge of the shadow, where a door stood open, a butterfly, winking its scarlet and black wings, glowed richly. But these only enhanced the quality of the pale interior light, which seemed spiritualised and unearthly as it hovered among the intricate order of the lofty beams and lost itself in the upper gloom.

Such subjects have proved a constant attraction to the painters of Europe. There is indeed a deep fund of latent poetry in the attachment of man to the earth, from which he gets his sustenance; a poetry more naturally expressed by pictorial means than any other. And if we consider the greater masterpieces of landscape art in Europe we shall find, I think, this vital relation between man and the earth implicit in nearly all of them. Seed-time and harvest; the ploughman, the reaper; the woodcutter, the fisherman; windmills and watermills, locks on rivers, and such old barns and granaries as I have been describing; all these refresh us with a savour of antique primeval life and associate us with the earliest hopes and victories of man. The world will not willingly lose its grasp of the continuity of the race; and such things bring us back, as poetry does, to what is elemental in life and enduring. There is another poetry of the mountains and the waters; and from that perhaps more inspiration will be drawn by painters of the future. But this homelier poetry of the soil, half-religious in sentiment, will never lose its fascination and freshness; and never have I felt its power and beauty more deeply than in this great sequestered grange—a kind of abbey of the harvests one might call it—lost in a corner of the rich Flemish plain.

SHAKESPEARE IN FRANCE.

(In three articles.)

I.

THE DRUNKEN SAVAGE.

THE first evidence that Shakespeare had crossed the Channel is to be found in a note written by one of Louis XIV.'s librarians in the royal catalogues. Among other things, it is affirmed of Shakespeare: "Ces belles qualités sont obscurcies par les ordures qu'il mêle dans ses comédies". Some years later Prévost, the first Frenchman of literary importance to sit in judgment upon the plays as a whole, wrote very much to the same effect, but with more amenity of phrase. Speaking of the tragedies, he says: "Quelques-unes sont un peu défigurées par un mélange de bouffonneries indignes." Subsequently there appeared the "Lettres sur les Anglais" of Voltaire, in which the "Cato" of Addison was hailed as the one reasonable tragedy written by an Englishman; in which the plays of Congreve were declared to be the summit of English comedy; in which English writers of tragedy might read of their productions that they were "presque toutes barbares, dépourvues de bienséance, d'ordre et de vraisemblance". Nor had Voltaire by any means done his worst. He began by objecting to cobblers and gravediggers; but in the hatred of his later years he delivered a riper and completer judgment upon Shakespeare in bulk. There was, for instance, his verdict upon "Hamlet": "Une pièce grossière et barbare, qui ne serait pas supporté par la plus vile populace de la France et de l'Italie". There was the classic judgment upon Shakespeare as the drunken savage. There was the mea culpa addressed to D'Argental, in which Voltaire repents at large for having introduced Shakespeare to his countrymen, and mourns over the national drama about to be eaten by Hottentots.

The case of Voltaire presents very forcibly one important aspect of the history of France's reception and treatment of the English dramatist. Voltaire is the first and best known of the critics who take a firm stand upon the national tragedy of Racine, and identify their struggle with Shakespeare as a struggle for the unities and decencies of the old theatre. As the battleground remained substantially the same throughout, it is worth while to survey it as it stood when Voltaire declared his war to the knife. It may be stated at the outset that it will be the purpose of these articles to show that the apparent vicissitudes in French opinion have been all upon the surface, that fundamentally the position has not altered for better or worse since the time when the precepts of Boileau and La Bruyère were fresh in the ears of Paris; and that neither the censure of one party nor the eulogy of others has very much pertinence as a criticism upon the Shakespeare that the English know for their own.

Time therefore will not be lost in dwelling upon the conditions that prevailed in the days of Voltaire, since it is proposed to show that these conditions have subsisted fundamentally from start to finish.

Shortly after his return to France, Voltaire began to produce those pearls which he had picked from the vast trough of the English barbarian. "Zaïre", "La Mort de César", "Sémiramis" would never have been written if Voltaire had not read "Othello", "Julius Cæsar" and "Hamlet". Shakespeare had hold of him, and he returned filled with the spirit of reform. Perhaps, after all, the tragedy of Racine admitted of development; perhaps all the old rules were not equally sacred; perhaps the unities of time and place were not eternally rigid; perhaps prose might, without sacrilege, be used for purposes of tragedy; perhaps a vocabulary of three thousand words was not sufficient for tragic expression; perhaps a little real action might be allowed within the limits of a play, to the relaxation of that stern system of monologues, explanations and news-bearing that had almost been stereotyped into sanctity; perhaps a little blood-shedding upon the stage might not come amiss, or a ghost, or a Frenchman, or a common person. There was a young man who had never read Shakespeare, but who was already suggesting these things. This was La Motte Houdard. Voltaire, of course, suppressed him heavily; but, none the less, Voltaire let it be known that he, too, was a reformer. He changed his scene within the same town; he killed Cæsar and Zaïre, not on the stage, it is true, but only just off, and you could almost hear it being done; in "Adélaïde du Guesclin" he even introduced a man with his arm in a sling, and a cannon; and, as a fitting climax to all this, although he sent Sémiramis decently away into a tomb to get killed, yet he had the temerity to bring this personage out again, actually bleeding.

But Voltaire was pulled up short in his splendid work as the emancipator of French tragedy. The first translations of La Place appeared in 1745, and Shakespeare was shown to the French people with little of his nakedness covered. Moreover, La Place had written a preface, in which he prophesied a new art of tragedy, and questioned the unities in their entirety. Tragedies in prose now began to appear, and comedies in which an appeal was made for tears. Hippolyte Lucas had even found a name for these monstrosities, calling them "drames". Diderot was laying down that all actions and all conditions of life were material for "drama"; and the tragédie bourgeoise was making progress upon the boards. Voltaire rubbed his eyes, and found that he had grown old. He took it into his head that Shakespeare was at the bottom of it, and that he himself was partly responsible. Furious and repentant, Voltaire came forward as a protagonist in the conflict that now opened; and thus it was that Shakespeare in France became forever involved in a conflict with the unities and decencies of French tragedy. This aspect of his struggle for recognition must not be overlooked, for it is a much more comprehensive one than at first sight appears. The unities stood for more than their surface value. They stood for the highly specialised and refined kind of emotion that the Frenchman looked for in Racine, and could indulge without æsthetic misgiving. The art-form which Racine had been compelled to use as a Frenchman writing for Frenchmen may cease to exist, but the æsthetic needs which that art-form in his day alone could satisfy will remain as long as France has a literature. At bottom the duel will always be a duel between Racine and Shakespeare.

The struggle waxed fiercer in 1776 with the translation of Le Tourneur. One of the warmest partisans that Shakespeare ever found in France was at that time in the field in the person of Mercier. Mercier cried aloud for prose in tragedy, for the mingling of the tragic and comic element within the limits of the same play, for the admission of all ranks of men and women to the high dramatic field; and, as a culminating piece of impiety, he denounced French tragedy as unreal. Voltaire foamed unpleasantly at the mouth, but in vain, for Le Tourneur sold, while Mercier and Madame Montague, already known as La Shakespearienne, replied unabashed.

What these apologies for Shakespeare meant exactly will be noticed hereafter. At present it is Shakespeare's struggle with the unities that is under discussion. This struggle brought against him a host of critics whose criticisms were, in the literal sense of the word, absurd. That is to say, they were the criticisms of men who were deaf. Their ears were attuned to the message of a peculiar genre, and they literally could not hear Shakespeare at all. Nor was this school confined to the men of Voltaire's day and generation. "Othello" did not obtain a hearing in Paris until "Hernani" had prepared the way by partially discrediting the amenities of the old theatre. The vein of criticism that dates from the librarian of Louis XIV. runs through the history to the end. Chateaubriand and Le Blanc follow Voltaire. Chateaubriand's earlier opinion brands the tragedies of Shakespeare as monstrous farces, and declines to consider them as artistic productions for the theatre. Le Blanc writes: "Pour avoir ignoré les règles, ou pour n'avoir pas voulu les suivre, Shakespeare n'a pas produit un seul ouvrage qui ne soit un monstre dans son espèce". Alphonse de Lamartine then writes: "Réunir dans la même pièce la comédie de Molière et la tragédie de Corneille, c'est faire grimacer toutes les deux". From first to last the unities, and that aggregate of sentiment and tradition that clustered about them, stood in the way of an impartial comprehension of the English Shakespeare that France has never succeeded in naturalising. By way of attraction or repulsion they influenced every opinion that was passed upon him, from the bitter scurrilities of Voltaire to the measured appreciation of Madame de Staël, or the unmeasured eulogy of Hugo.

CORRESPONDENCE.

MR. MILES' MEALS.

To the Editor of the SATURDAY REVIEW.

Chandos Street, Charing Cross, W.C.
September 1909.

SIR,—I have just read a letter in your paper signed by Hermann Erskine. I think that I should be justified in starting an action for libel against this writer when he accuses me of living on "a mess of herbage" and on "vegetables, fruit and farinaceous slops" and of being "nucivorous". Had this gentleman written to me I would gladly have told him what foods I prefer to take, and he would then have found that I eat fewer vegetables than most meat-eaters, certainly not more farinaceous food and decidedly less farinaceous slops, but that my favourite food bases instead of meat are—besides my own proteid food ("Emprote")—cheese, nuts, sometimes beans or lentils, and sometimes eggs. I never take porridge, and I do not often take pudding. I will gladly tell any reader of the SATURDAY REVIEW who is interested what meals I do prefer. I do not pretend that these meals suit everyone, but they are worth trying.

Now as to the extraordinary remarks of this writer. He begins by alluding with contempt to "food-values" and "proteids". It would be equally ridiculous for a critic of national defence to allude with contempt to ships, airships, guns and gunpowder. For the generally accepted statement that proteid is the most essential, the indispensable element in our food supply I need only refer the reader to such authorities (nearly all of them flesh-eaters) as Atwater, Bunge, Church, Michael Foster, Gamgee, Robert Hutchison, Landois and Sterling, Pavy, Pawlow and Virchow.

Then he speaks of the alleged docility of the people whom he calls by that most misleading name "vegetarians". Some of the Japanese and Indian troops, who rarely touch flesh foods, are splendid fighters. So were the Persians and Greeks and Romans at their best. So were the Scots. I shall give directly a few other instances of physical strength and endurance; but that the above fighters were living on "a system of dietetics which avowedly eliminates the physical traits" is a strange contention.

The implication that England owes her Empire to a meat-eating population is also based on ignorance. An examination into the diet of the small farmers and yeomen of old England—and we need not omit Scotland and Ireland, with their diet of buttermilk, oatmeal and potatoes—will show that over a great part of the country the prevailing diet was without flesh food, except, perhaps, once a week, and included such staples or bases as cheese, pease-pudding, cereals, etc.

Now with regard to what the writer says about long life, I agree with a great part of it. Sheer age, without open-mindedness, is of little use. Neither should I dream of disputing that "vegetarianism" has had abundant failures, through ignorance and through an unwise choice of the sloppy and pappy foods which the writer justly condemns, and for other reasons. I always have insisted on these failures as undeniable facts. But it is a shame to condemn principles because caricatures of these principles have existed. The fair plan is to examine results—actual results—of well-balanced non-flesh meals.

And as it is on the physical plane that the writer challenges us, we meet him there. And we cite a few examples of what are distinctly physical attributes—namely, endurance and strength. For these two bodily attributes imply little or no mental or spiritual attributes. Long-distance athletes and weight-lifters are not necessarily good specimens—though some are—intellectually. Well, Herodotus tells us that the builders of the pyramids of Egypt lived chiefly on lentils, onion and garlic. De Lesseps bore witness to the splendid physical work of the non-flesh-eating Arabs and Hindus on the Suez Canal.

Then there are the Chinese porters at Hong Kong, the carriers of Constantinople, of Smyrna, of Athens, of Rio Janeiro and of the Bakongo tribe (who can carry from sixty to a hundred pounds weight on their heads, and run for twenty miles a day for six days), the South American rubber-gum gatherers, and many others. Probably the Saxon Brothers (at present, I believe, in America) are the strongest men in the world.

As to endurance, the walking race between Dresden and Berlin, a distance of 125 miles, was won by Karl Mann in 26 hours 52 minutes: he arrived not at all exhausted. The other non-flesh-eaters also easily beat the meat-eaters. And similar records of endurance have been and are being given by cyclists like Olley, runners, swimmers and so forth.

The records are all the more remarkable when we remember how very few people there are, comparatively, who go in for athletic competitions on non-flesh diet in contrast to the tens of thousands of meat-eaters.

With respect to endurance, again, the experiments of Professor Irving Fisher, of America, who carried out his investigations without any prejudice, were decidedly in favour of the non-flesh diet in practically every case. Similar experiments in Brussels led to similar results.

As to teeth, the subject is a difficult one to deal with, since several factors combine to bring about dental decay. I do not think it is at all fair to put down the use of slops to the influence of food reform. The families that indulge in wet porridges and puddings are just as likely to be meat-eaters as not. But I know that in many cases (as in my wife's) the adoption of sensible food reform has absolutely stopped decay of the teeth.

The fact of it is that the effects of a well-balanced dietary without flesh foods have to be considered not from the point of view of what a theorist imagines, nor from the point of view of the failures of haphazard, unscientific and inartistic "vegetarianism", but from a careful study of actual instances.

I do not wish to be personal, but I must say that the writer's method of argument, which omits almost all that can be urged in favour of the other side, is not in the least suited for a practical and scientific discussion of a very important topic—a topic of more than national moment. The writer is obviously better suited for entering the arena of party politics. I think he would be a successful speaker in that field.

Yours truly,

Eustace Miles.

COSAS DE ESPANA.

To the Editor of the Saturday Review.

2 August 1909.

Sir,—Seven years ago you published a letter of mine in the Saturday Review in which I mentioned that, from information of an authoritative character which I had received, it appeared that a meeting of the Grand Masters of the so-called Freemasonic Lodges of Rome, Lisbon, and Madrid had been held at Barcelona, a meeting which was also attended by M. Combes. The purpose of this assembly was to inaugurate a virulent anti-clerical campaign in every Latin country, the object of which was the destruction of the Roman Catholic religion, which is equivalent to the de-Christianisation of those countries, a catastrophe which it is believed would lead to the overthrow of the monarchy in each and the creation of a federated Latin republic organised on the lines of the atheistical one that now governs or misgoverns France.

Before proceeding, allow me to say that, while I do not for a moment believe that either Mr. Nathan, M. Combes, or the Grand Master of the Italian Freemasons ever for an instant personally plotted or approved of the assassination of the King of Portugal and his son, it must be confessed that the refusal on the part of Mr. Nathan and his friends of the Municipal Council of Rome to address a letter of sympathy to the Queen-mother of Portugal after the murder of her husband and son (although she is an Italian Princess) does justify one in believing that at least they were not sorry for the deed after it was done. They may not even have hinted at the instigation of such a murder, but the campaign which they organised at Barcelona is at the bottom, not only of that dreadful occurrence, but of the mischief which has devastated Barcelona during the past few weeks.

Immediately after this meeting the intended campaign opened very vigorously at Lisbon, where a subventioned anti-religious Press, distributed among the working classes, soon inflamed their worst passions and presently led to the sacking of several convents, and finally to the expulsion from Portugal of the few remaining religious orders that had been spared by the Revolution of 1830. The campaign continued, religion was held up to ridicule, and the monarchy accused of every imaginable crime. The result of all this teaching was the assassination of the King and Crown Prince and the abortive attempt to proclaim a republic, which only failed thanks to the revulsion of public feeling in Portugal against the prime movers in the conspiracy. Meanwhile, Spain was deluged with filthy periodicals and horrible papers, mostly owned, edited, and published by disreputable Jews and self-styled Freemasons—a combination which the well-known Italian Deputy, Signor Santini, when writing lately in the Saturday Review of the same Association in Italy, described as "beyond words abominable and wicked". In Spain, again, as in Portugal, riots and disturbances ensued as a consequence of all this agitation; and I need not allude to the dastardly outrage which disturbed the happiness of the King and Queen of Spain on their wedding day, beyond saying that there can be no doubt that had the young Sovereigns been assassinated, a republic would have been immediately proclaimed, as has now been done in Catalonia. The fact is that ever since the date of the fatal meeting at Barcelona between the various heads of the subversive parties, the socialists and anarchists in that unfortunate city have been kept in a state of constant excitement by their skilfully concealed wire-pullers, so that scarcely a week has passed without an outrage in some part of the city. A friend in Malaga sent me recently a bundle of Spanish socialist and anarchist papers; and all I can say about them is that the "Asino", which is generally considered to be the most disgraceful publication of its sort in Europe, is mild compared with some of the obscene and blasphemous productions which have been published with impunity in Spain during the past five or six years. "So sure as we live", wrote my friend, now nearly six months ago, "if there is a disaster in Morocco we shall have rioting all over the South of Spain, and an attempt on a large scale on the part of the subversive agitators to get the government of the country into their hands and thus hoist themselves into prominent and remunerative positions. The political agitators are never quiet; their agents are everywhere disseminating abominable pamphlets and generally exciting the people, not only against the monks and nuns and the clergy in general, but also against every form of constituted authority. I have seen a man come into a café on the outskirts of Malaga, sit down quite quietly and ask for a glass of wine, so that at first his movements passed unobserved. Presently, however, he pulled out of his pocket a large and gaudily coloured caricature of the Pope, surrounded by a lot of semi-nude monks and nuns. What they were doing cannot be described; but in a corner of this picture appeared at a window the young King and Queen of Spain with broad grins on their faces, while out of their mouths proceeded scrolls on which were written what they were supposed to be saying, and which it is impossible for me to translate." In another Spanish socialist caricature the King and Queen are shown riding in a motor car over the prostrate bodies of a number of working men; and in yet another the Pope and the Queen are seen flogging a working girl. And so forth. What wonder then, that after some seven years of this sort of propaganda, the deluded people of Barcelona should, now that a favourable opportunity has occurred, rise and commit atrocities which have unfortunately compelled the troops to inflict reprisals of a horrible nature, in which hundreds of unfortunate working people have been shot down. But meanwhile, those who have excited and urged them to commit these acts of violence—I mean the Masonic wire-pullers, the editors of socialist newspapers, street agitators, etc.—are allowed to escape without so much as a reprimand. Indeed it seems to be the rule all over the world for the poor "man in the street" to receive the punishment of offences which he has only committed at the bidding, so to speak, of men who, by their education and superior position, are ten thousand times more guilty than their unfortunate tools. The civilised world is, or pretends to be, horrified at what has happened at Barcelona; but I have yet to see a single article advocating the punishment of the gang of concealed rascals who have brought about the horrible outrages of which Barcelona and other cities of Spain have been the scene. It is the social agitator, the man who suggests murder and rapine, who should be punished, and not the poor misguided working people who have been deceived by the fair promises of these professional politicians, perfectly well aware of what they are doing, and only agitating and flattering the mob in order to get its votes, and thus, when the revolution comes, obtain for themselves lucrative official positions. Only five years ago M. Aristide Briand shouted to an excited mob of strikers, "Take up your guns and shoot down your masters! Burn their factories and destroy their houses; you are justified in doing it!" Now, M. Briand becomes Prime Minister, and the world bows down before him.

Signor Santini, in the letter above alluded to, tells us joyously that the horrible "Asino", which he considers is unfit for decent people to discuss, is not likely to do much harm in Italy, because "the immense majority" of the Italian people are good Catholics. At the same time he is highly indignant that Mr. Ernest Nathan, whom he describes as a member of that abominable gang of "evildoers", the Freemasons, should have been elected Syndic of Rome; and no doubt he is equally indignant, though he does not say so, that Signor Podrecca, the proprietor and editor of the filthiest paper published in Europe, the "Asino", has been elected a member of the Italian Parliament. Signor Santini does not seem, however, to realise that had the Catholics, who are in "the immense majority", protested against the publication of such papers as this and the active propaganda of anti-religion and anti-everything carried on by the persons whom he stigmatises in far stronger language than I, as a foreigner, should like to use, Signors Nathan and Podrecca would not be in office. The same may be said of the good people of Barcelona, who are now lamenting the destruction of their shops, their churches, and their convents, or weeping over the innumerable victims of the agitations of the last few days. Had they manifested themselves in a manful manner against the propaganda of revolution, blasphemy, and indecency which has been going on with impunity for so many years in the beautiful capital and province of Catalonia, that part of Spain would not be in the forlorn condition it is to-day.

The people who allow the storm to be sown must reap the whirlwind. Another proverb tells us that "Prevention is better than cure". No government should allow anarchical unrest to get as far as the stage of street fighting; subversive agitators of all kinds, journalists, conspirators, and public speakers, whether anti-militarists, anti-religious, anti-monarchical, or whatever be their pet "theories", should be dealt with severely at the earliest stage, *before* the violent doctrines they preach have begun to soak into the public mind. Had this been done in Spain five years ago, and every paper of the "Asino" order suppressed, blood would not be running in the streets of Barcelona to-day. It was a "wicked agitation" of an anti-clerical sort that led to the murder of the inoffensive King Humbert of Italy in 1900; yet the men who pulled the wires and those who incited to the outrage (though they were well known) have never been punished, while the half-witted youth who perpetrated the crime still languishes, half blind and insane, in solitary confinement for life—a living death indeed!

What has happened in Spain within the past week will inevitably take place in France some day should any calamity occur which would offer an opportunity for the manifestation of anti-military and anti-religious insanity, if so I may call it. Italy, too, will have to undergo much the same dreadful experience unless she acts with foresight and energy against the combination of evildoers whom Signor Santini considers "so mischievous and, above all, so abominable". I am not too sure, either, that what I have said of the Latin countries is not applicable to our own, where a very active and dangerous propaganda is at present in full swing. It were well if, before seeing the mote in our brother's eye, we noticed the beam in our own.

I am, sir, yours truly,

A Traveller.

BETTER DEAD.

To the Editor of the Saturday Review.

2 Myrtle Road, Acton, 2 September 1909.

Sir,—In your issue of 28 August you accorded space for the insertion of the callous remarks of one signing himself John Bland, who desires, as his letter abundantly proves, to deprive the poor of their last right—the right to exist at all on the earth. May I be accorded a like courtesy in the interests of common humanity?

I wonder if it has never occurred to this fastidious (in externals) and perfumed (though not with the myrrh and aloes and cassia of spiritual sanctity) Mr. John Bland that at any moment some adverse stroke of circumstances entirely beyond his control may leave him penniless, friendless and homeless, even as those are whom he wishes to hound from the earth, which is the Lord's? Let him imagine (if he possesses sufficient of so human a quality) himself, weak and faint with hunger and deadly tired, creeping into some park or on to the Embankment to rest his bruised and weary body, and being cast out from that refuge by order of such inhuman legislation as he desires to bring into force against others.

Many of these persons are placed in the position of

physical degradation so offensive to Mr. John Bland through no fault of their own, and even he himself may be less assiduous with his toilet in the deplorable state I have pictured for him above; and even if it be admitted that the physical degradation of the poor sufferers from excessive poverty may cause a momentary shock and sensation of unpleasantness to persons not capable of higher thoughts, yet the spiritual leprosy which the letter of John Bland exhales is a far deeper danger and menace to society.

MARIE LANTROW.

THE SPLENDID CRANK.

To the Editor of the SATURDAY REVIEW.

Wick Court, near Bristol.

SIR,—In face of your having written " When a man is called a crank, we may be quite sure there is something great about him ", it may appear ungracious to suggest that you have not quite done justice to your subject. But is it not possible that this greatness, offensive as it may be to the crank's contemporaries, is of supreme benefit to future generations? I would suggest that if, to most of us, the crank who lives in the clouds is an altruistic fool and impossible as an ordinary companion, still, it is the very fact of his aloofness, of his living nearer to heaven than we ourselves, which gives him power to raise humanity at large. It is true cranks hunt shadows; but these are the shadows cast before of coming events; perhaps, too, they sometimes impress on earth shadows cast from heaven's facts, and so temper earthly material life with somewhat of the spiritual. Galileo, Copernicus, Martin Luther, S. Francis of Assisi, Robert Owen the founder of co-operation, John Brown the abolitionist, Lovelace and his six companions, Blake the poet, and, to some degree, Keats and Coleridge, were, to their contemporaries, all cranks, and so suffered the contumely originality or greatness of thought in action must always suffer in our foolish world—" Great is thy power, O Dullness ! " With their bones we inter the evil done to such men in life, and justify ourselves by crowning them, dead. But the good they did lives after them—good for their ignorant persecutors.

Long live the crank ! When sick of partridges and pheasants, motors and dinners, the dreary jog-trot of human converse on Budgets and babies, Dreadnoughts and school treats, socialism and the last society scandal, we can always—if the crank is to be found !—turn for relief to the clouds of heaven and chase their shadows. It is the crank, not the amorphous baby, who, trailing clouds of glory as he comes, tells us we are more than mere earthly gamblers at the devil's table of speculation for prizes of rank, wealth or power.

Yours faithfully,

F. C. CONSTABLE.

THE ZOOLOGICAL SOCIETY.

To the Editor of the SATURDAY REVIEW.

53 Chancery Lane, W.C.

SIR,—In the articles recently contributed to your columns by Dr. Chalmers Mitchell, stress was laid on the many improvements introduced in the Zoological Gardens as regards the housing of the animals. One point, however, on which Dr. Mitchell is silent, should I think in fairness be stated—that the changes referred to were to a large extent forced on the Society from without, as a result of Mr. Edmund Selous' series of articles on " The Old Zoo and the New," which first appeared in the SATURDAY REVIEW and were reprinted as a pamphlet by the Humanitarian League.

Yours faithfully,

HENRY S. SALT.

REVIEWS.

SOPHIA AND CAROLINE.

"The Hanoverian Queens of England: Sophia Dorothea of Celle; Caroline of Anspach." By Alice Drayton Greenwood. London: Bell. 1909. 10s. 6d. net.

SCIENTIFIC historians would condemn such books as this, as insisting too much on the influence of personalities on the course of history. " Les biographies ", writes M. Denis, in the " Fondation de l'Empire Allemand ", " exagèrent l'action des héros sur l'évolution du monde, elles réduisent la destinée de l'humanité à une série d'accidents. Je ne crois pas aux accidents et je ne crois guère aux héros." Of what importance, it might be asked, was the quarrel between the hard and unsympathetic George I. and his excitable, emotional and foolish wife, Sophia Dorothea? Are we really to believe, as Miss Greenwood suggests, that the evolution of our Cabinet system was due simply to the fact that our first Hanoverian king was ignorant of English, and that he accordingly left his Ministers much to themselves? Would Sir Robert Walpole never have controlled the government of the country if he had not gained the support of George I. by promises of an increased civil list, or continued to rule after his death if it had not been for the influence of Queen Caroline over her husband, George II.? Above all, would the main lines of English history have been much altered had her destinies been guided by an altogether different set of personalities?

Whatever may be the answers to such questions, there is without doubt another side to history. " History ", said Froude, " is nature's drama. To bring the past before us and make the actors live again, to teach us to sympathise with what is great and good and to hate what is base "—this, according to him, is the true function of the historian; and it is closely akin to that of the dramatist. There is a truth in all this, and in any case the virtues, the vices and the follies, the intrigues, the loves and the enmities of mankind, their triumphs and their tragedies, will always be attractive. Yet even so the question remains whether anyone who wishes really to understand the characters and realise the atmosphere of a bygone age had not better read the original authorities, even if many of them are not as truthful as one could wish.

This book makes no pretension to be a complete history of the period. The references to foreign affairs are scanty; and though home affairs are treated somewhat more fully, we must go elsewhere for an adequate account of the state of parties and the constitutional or economic problems of the day. The domestic life of the two heroines, the family quarrels, the Court intrigues and the Court pageants—these form the main part of the book. Nor, again, is Miss Greenwood the first in this peculiar field. Apart from foreign books, the period has been already treated in much the same way and with much the same conclusions as to the main characters on the stage by Mr. Wilkins in his " Love of an Uncrowned Queen " and his " Queen Caroline the Illustrious ". Miss Greenwood, however, has given us a very readable book, written in a clear and forcible style. She has taken every pains to make her work accurate and thorough; her judgment is sound and sober; she avoids the besetting temptation of the biographer to belaud her heroines, and in her preface she gives us a very useful criticism of her authorities.

The two women whose characters she has undertaken to portray present in every way a startling contrast. Sophia Dorothea of Celle, the unfortunate wife of George I., though intelligent and accomplished, was a mere lover of pleasure with no serious interests in life. Forced for family reasons to marry her cold and unsympathetic cousin, whom she never liked, she quickly consoled herself for his infidelity by intrigues of her own, more especially with the worthless libertine, Count Philip of Königsmarck. Even if we believe her own assertion that her relations with the Count were never criminal, she so completely compromised herself that she could never expect to be allowed to hold the position of Queen-Consort, or that it would be forgiven by her pitiless husband. The terrible suddenness of her fall, the unfathomable mystery as to the exact fate of Königsmarck, the tragedy of her long captivity, have attracted the attention of many biographers, and also of the dramatist.* Yet the whole story is discreditable to all concerned, and Sophia herself excites in us no sentiment but that of contemptuous pity.

Caroline of Anspach was of a far different mould. Descended from a younger branch of the masterful Hohenzollerns, she had been brought up at the Court of Berlin and had fallen under the influence of Sophie Charlotte, the wife of the Elector King, Frederick, and of Charlotte's mother, the ambitious and able Electress Sophia. From very early years she showed signs of character; she refused the brilliant offer of the hand of the Archduke Charles, the future Emperor. She associated with men of letters and took a lively interest in politics. According to some, it was her love of power which induced her to follow the wish of the Electress Sophia and become the bride of her grandson, the future George II.; and in this they believe is to be found the key to her conduct during life.

There is much truth in this view, no doubt. That she feigned to follow George II. while she really led, that she pretended an ignorance of high questions of policy, discussed in her presence, while she was guiding him to the decision already decided upon between Sir Robert Walpole and herself, and that she did this with such consummate skill that the suspicions of her vain husband were never aroused—all this is not incredible, and it enhances our admiration for her ability and her extraordinary self-restraint. It may, too, have been a love of power which led her not only to acquiesce in her husband's "amours", but even with amazing complaisance to be the confidante of his mistresses. But that the affection she so constantly displayed for him was also feigned is difficult to believe. Strange though it is, there was a stronger bond of union between these two very different characters. George II. had his mistresses, as was the custom then in Courts at least. Yet he never wavered in his admiration and affection for his wife. Caroline, who with all her virtues was not refined or sensitive, thoroughly appreciated the doctrine of the day—"Conjugal faithfulness is the honour of women, but the honour of a man consists only in that of his wife"†—and, for the rest, was really fond of her vain, garrulous husband, with all his coarseness and his limitations.

The society to which we are introduced in these pages was indeed an unloveable one. The private virtues of the two first Hanoverian kings were confined to a blunt honesty, to a certain sense of justice without mercy, and to personal courage. They were unlettered, parsimonious, and coarse men. They both quarrelled with their sons. In the case of George I. the fault lay chiefly with him, while in that of George II. it was his worthless son, Fritz, who was most to blame. Yet what can we think of a mother who, if we are to believe Lord Harvey, openly denounced her son as the greatest ass, the greatest liar, the greatest "canaille" and the greatest beast in the whole world, and heartily wished he were out of it? The statesmen were with few exceptions hopelessly corrupt; the clergy, worldly and time-serving; the worship of brutal common-sense, the deadness to all things spiritual, pronounced. Thackeray in his "Four Georges" declared that the only person of all the Court to whom he feels genuinely attracted is Mrs. Howard (Lady Suffolk), the patient, kindly, dignified maid of honour. He might perhaps have included the witty and vivacious Mary Bellenden, the gentle and loveable Molly Lepell, and the downright and simple Jenny Warburton. Indeed, the women are far more attractive than the men. They are brighter, better company, better tempered and many of them more moral; and if Queen Caroline shocks us with her want of refinement, she had at least the taste to appreciate it in the ladies of her bedchamber.

* "A Princess of Hanover," by Margaret L. Woods.
† The saying of the Duchess of Orleans.

THE CLEVER NOVEL.

"Open Country." By Maurice Hewlett. London: Macmillan. 1909. 6s.

WHENEVER Mr. Maurice Hewlett's characters open their mouths they seem to have an air of conscious cleverness and to be quoting from the narrative portions of Mr. Maurice Hewlett's works of fiction. At times the effect is startling—and baffling: one wonders whether the inverted commas have slipped in by accident or been lifted out in error. True, to get the smart manner, the spoken sentences are made very brief; but were we to take a scene where two people are engaged in a duel of wit, lightly chucking epigrams at one another, without any "he saids" and "she saids"; and were we to read it aloud to some ordinary wide-awake person, that person might easily mistake the whole passage for narration and think Mr. Hewlett was coruscating more brilliantly and galvanically than usual. A superficial listener might hear a few pages of Meredith and pass a similar remark; and it is true that Meredith's people are much given to talking Meredithian. But this fact simply reveals how wide a gulf lies between the art of the great novelist and the artfulness of the small one. Through the Meredithian phraseology we become conscious of the presence of real, separate characters, living beings of flesh and blood, ambitions and fears, passions and weaknesses; while in Mr. Hewlett's books we find only puppets, mostly empty, who rattle off Hewlettese. On the one hand we have creative art; on the other imitative trickery and smartness. Meredith may report in his own way what his characters said, and the report may be coloured by Meredithian turns of phrase; but we feel sure that, after all, in essence they said the thing reported; and we learn the shades of thought and feeling that impelled them to say it. Meredith wrote often, far too often, as a virtuoso; but at his best the force of his inspiration carried him far beyond any vain desire to show off: truth of expression, not display, was then his aim. Mr. Hewlett always lets us know how smart he is, forgetting that cleverness, especially self-conscious cleverness, is the last quality that should make itself felt in a work of art. There are many persons in "Open Country", and many of them possess extraordinary names, but fundamentally they are all Mr. Hewlett—their own mouths declare the fact. Even the rich merchant, Mr. Percival, speaks epigrammatically "when" Mr. Hewlett is "so disposed", and is the author of schoolboyish comic-verse. In some respects he is the best person in the story. He is a tradesman and, we dare say, an honest one, proud of his family, a trifle afraid of his wife, and astute enough to be still more afraid *for* his wife, with her fine talent for getting snubs and her insatiable appetite for swallowing them. His good-nature, affectionate disposition and broad stomach are homely and comforting to meet in a crowd of persons struggling to appear clever—indeed, those attributes to an extent compensate for some desperate endeavours of his own after smartness. We have met his wife and daughters before—in other writers' novels—with the exception of one daughter, Sanchia. This damsel, though not freshly (nor altogether faithfully) observed, does not recall so poignantly the fashions of the year before last; but in bending her to his iron will, and making her talk as he writes, Mr. Hewlett has broken her. The hero of the piece, Mr. John Maxwell Senhouse, has grown purely fantastic since the days when he figured in "Half-Way House". Intended to be a quaint child of Nature, he is simply impossible. Something—human nature—is wanted to reconcile his contradictions into a consistent whole, a solid human figure moving through the pages of the book. A secondary hero, Ingram, speaks as unvocally as the rest, yet leaves such an impression of yokel stupidity that one marvels how he should have led Sanchia Percival from the strict path of conventional virtue. The accomplishment of this feat and the behaviour of Senhouse and the family in the circumstances make up the whole story. Everything in it is possible—almost commonplace nowadays—yet nothing appears real. Even Mrs. Percival, pathetically struggling to get a footing in society—largely a society of baronet-ish nonentities—is not like life. As conventionally drawn by the trade-novelists her figure is familiar; but Mr. Hewlett has pushed her from the conventional, through the real, to a something on the farther side of reality. This may, indeed, be said of nearly all Mr. Hewlett's puppets. They impress us less as genuine, if blundering, attempts to create real personages than as the conventional types of trade-fiction in a grotesque disguise. They are no more human and alive than the persons of Mr. Guy Thorne; only their get-up is different and less usual. Mr. Hewlett seems to strain after something more real than realism and even reality. It is as though an engineer sought something rounder than a circle for the wheels of an express locomotive. What the locomotive would look like, and how it would run, we cannot guess; but we do know that while Mr. Hewlett's figures do not tax our credulity, because they are unlike anything conceived before, for the same reason they are incredible.

"Open Country" affords several opportunities for a writer capable of interpreting the silent moods of nature; and these opportunities are not seized. Senhouse, out gipsying, comes upon a scene that stirs him—woods in sunlight and shadow; and for a moment it seems likely that we shall get something new—especially new in Mr. Hewlett's work. But no: the moment passes: Senhouse is thrilled not by the vision that meets his eye, but by the possibility of turning it to account as such things have been turned to account by poets and painters in the past: he sees in nature only an artist making allusions to bygone master-works. He tries verse, and does not hit it off; then seeing before him a veritable Corot he tries to transfer that Corot to his canvas. Whether he would have succeeded, or what the picture would have been worth if he had, must remain for ever a puzzle; for in the very white heat of his reminiscent inspiration Sanchia interrupts him by taking off shoes and stockings and walking into a pond. With Mr. Hewlett "Place aux dames" was inevitable, and we are at once asked to transfer our attention and interest to the gambols of a man and a young girl alone in a wood together. Nothing very disastrous, however, occurs—as is the custom in Mr. Hewlett's stories. The atmosphere of nature is never captured: it is as false as the atmosphere of the middle-class drawing- and dining-rooms in "Open Country". Mr. Hewlett will not let nature speak and, like Walt Whitman, "nudge himself to listen", any more than he will let his characters speak; Mr. Hewlett must speak for nature as he speaks for his dolls. So nature is made, not to whisper sweet secrets as nature does, but to chat with Hewlettese airiness and flippancy of poets and painters. It is hard to say whether the backgrounds—interior as well as exterior—are thrown out of perspective by the queerness of the people who stand in front of them, or whether, after all, Mr. Hewlett's queer unhuman human beings are not made queerer by the backgrounds. Such society, middle-class or aristocratic, never met together on this earth; such fields and waters and woods never existed outside Mr. Hewlett's books. We do not demand photographic representations of drawing-rooms and hill and dale, nor phonographic reports of conversations; we only ask for trees which do not spout volubly of Corot and for a few people who will honestly utter what is in them without grimaces and shots at being smart. Not only the people in "Open Country" but the very buildings and fields never leave off going through Mr. Hewlett's literary antics.

We lay down the book rather glad to be done with it. The unceasing click of the epigrams, sham or real; the continual search after fine allusions, the strain to be if not original at any rate unusual, the lack of human, over-brimming humour and the pervading acid tone—all these help to damp our spirits; and the dullness is not lightened by the references to ladies' white skirts and even their white legs (lower extremities). Still the novel is clever; and, as a great many folk admire cleverness above all things, we presume that Mr. Hewlett has his great admirers. As we presume also that Mr. Hewlett wishes to be admired, and to be admired precisely for his cleverness, he may fairly be congratulated on being likely to mount to the summit of his ambition by means of "Open Country".

"RHYMES AND RHYMES."

"Sonnets." By Lord Alfred Douglas. London: The Academy Publishing Company. 1909. 2s. 6d. net.

"Fleet Street, and other Poems." By John Davidson. London: Grant Richards. 1909. 5s. net.

"A Vision of Life." By Darrel Figgis. With an Introduction by G. K. Chesterton. London: Lane. 1909. 3s. 6d. net.

"Poems at Home and Abroad." By the Rev. H. D. Rawnsley. Glasgow: MacLehose. 1909. 2s. 6d. net.

"Wind and Hill." By Geoffrey Winthrop Young. London: Smith, Elder. 1909. 3s. 6d. net.

"Mimma Bella." By Eugene Lee-Hamilton. London: Heinemann. 1909. 5s. net.

THE "Sonnets" of Lord Alfred Douglas need little by way of appreciation, and less by way of criticism. There is no man living able to produce a book of sonnets quite so flawless in their grace and music. If there is any criticism to be made, it is this: the writer is less happy as he becomes more personal. The personal note is difficult to strike with the unerring precision that is required to send it home to the ear and to the mind in the true fullness of its appeal. In a sonnet it is impossible to separate content and expression. If the content is crude; or if, even though it be sincere, it appears on the face of it to lack sincerity, the sonnet stands like some perfect vase hopelessly marred:

"I have enticed and merited distress,
By this, that I have never bowed the knee
Before the shrine of wise hypocrisy,
Nor worn self-righteous anger like a dress."

There is an artificiality in the mood of this quatrain that exacts its penalty in self-contradiction. To repudiate self-righteousness in poetic numbers is to invite the charge, if not of self-righteousness, then (as in this particular case) of something even less poetic, namely, self-pity. It is this strain that spoils some of the best of the sonnets, a strain of querulousness that perhaps may be forgiven in a man who has "fought with beasts and wrestled with despair"; but, none the less, to be deplored for his poetry's sake. Curiously enough, since this volume is plainly calculated to make an immediate appeal to the small public that reads poetry, the writer of the note appended at the end of the book seems to anticipate for these sonnets "homage given grudgingly from cautious mouths", or no homage at all. Such aggressiveness before the event is not easily explained; and we should like to record a firmer faith in the ability of Lord Alfred Douglas to please his generation than his literary sponsor seems to possess.

The poetico-scientifics of John Davidson are too familiar to need appraisement at this time of day.

"Fleet Street was once a silence in the ether.
The carbon, iron, copper, silicon,
Zinc, aluminium vapours, metalloids,
Constituents of the skeleton and shell
Of Fleet Street—of the woodwork, metalwork,
Brickwork, electric apparatus, drains
And printing presses, conduits, pavement, road—
Were at the first unelemented space,
Imponderable tension in the dark
Consummate matter of eternity.

. . . .

The warm humanities that day and night
Inhabit and employ it and inspire,
Were in the ether mingled with it, there
Distinguished nothing from the road, the shops,
The drainpipes, sewage, sweepings of the street."

Such speculations, like that as to whether the bricks of Fleet Street are happier in their lot than the rings of Saturn, are ingenious; but they are like the specu-lation of Hamlet concerning the dust of Alexander. When a poet asks us to consider of these matters, we reply with Horatio : "'Twere to consider too curiously to consider so". In "The Crystal Palace" we have another quality of work, a close realistic description of common things, very vital, and presented with a richness of vocabulary that is astonishing. In "Cain", John Davidson is at his best and worst. It is fine rhetoric occasionally touched with a real emotion that brings it almost to the level of good poetry. It is informed with a spirit of revolt, and an assertion of the dignity of man before God that classes so much of John Davidson's work as "religious" in that sense of the word he himself would have accepted.

Mr. Figgis is unfortunate in his literary godfather. Mr. Chesterton discovers him in an introduction. There Mr. Figgis finds himself in the company of Francis Thompson as one of a small band of latter-day Elizabethan poets. Mr. Chesterton's reasons for so acclaiming Mr. Figgis seem to be that the latter has an extensive vocabulary and a belief that "God's in His heaven". We can assure Mr. Figgis that there is nothing whatever Elizabethan about his poem "A Vision of Life", and that, until he gets rid of certain affectations of archaism and a certain laborious endeavour to liberalise the dictionary of modern poetic speech, he will never give his real gifts as a versifier any chance to appear for what they are. "Forgive my curious temper" is unfortunate in a twentieth-century volume as an attempt to say "Pardon my asking you so many questions". In the phrase "face to spiritous face" the word "spiritous" is susceptible of a most unkind interpretation which would be nearer to its actual grammatical meaning than the one intended by Mr. Figgis. Such other phrases as "disturbed uncertainty", "complicated elements", "proportions spacious" (this last being descriptive of a terrible majestic spirit), "problematical bliss" are excellent enough in prose, so far as they go; but "I stood on quaking limb" is not happy: it suggests a frightened stork. Finally, if anyone should imagine that Mr. Figgis is Elizabethan when he is erotic, let us, at any rate, assure him that he is not :

"Rare love, mellow, voluptuous love,
Shone from her wondrous eyes, fell from her tongue
Melodious, dwelt on the delicate bloom
Of her seductive limbs . . ."

and so on. An Elizabethan poet would have left all this out, and come to the point.

Canon Rawnsley is the poet of "daisied fields" and "milk-white sheep", of foxgloves and daffodils, of the rain and wind, and of the seasons that lay their hands in shifting benediction upon Helvellyn. His matter is the simple old-world matter which is always new; and his treatment of it has all the charm of that simplicity which is the result of a nice discrimination in the choice and placing of simple phrases :

"There is no day in all the year
To weary mortals given,
When God's sweet mercy seems so near
And earth so sure of heaven

As when, in middle March, we wake
To find spring's promise true,
And summer falls on lawn and lake,
Full-made from out the blue."

These are lines easily read; and if they are as easily forgotten, so much the worse for us, it may be.

Geoffrey Winthrop Young keeps his garden less neatly trimmed; but it is a garden that is best left to grow a little wildly. His inspiration is very genuine; and for the present it is very boyish. To employ a phrase of his own, the song he sings is "just a clean noise of youth"; and he finds the best of his "Real Pleasures" in "sun and rain and the smell of grass and trees":

"Only a hill: earth set a little higher
Above the face of earth: a larger view
Of little fields and roads: a little nigher
To clouds and silence: what is that to you?
Only a hill; but all of life to me,
Up there, between the sunset and the sea."

Of other things there is, as yet, an impatience; but it is already an impatience that is half out-grown. Already he has begun to ask questions of earth and ocean; and, though he asks them as a "boy fronting the dark," it is quite clear that when his exaggerated zest in the novel sensation of being alive has lost enough of its edge to permit of other things intruding into the poetic field, Geoffrey Winthrop Young will write even better poetry than he does now, if only he can contrive to deepen his inspiration without losing the glad note of his early manner.

Few poets have had an experience so rich in pain as had Eugene Lee-Hamilton. He is best known perhaps by his "Sonnets of the Wingless Hours", published in 1894; and "Mimma Bella" sounds a last melancholy chord that harmonises only too well with this earlier strain. Published posthumously, these sonnets form an elegy upon his little daughter, whose death it was that killed him :

"Two springs she saw—two radiant Tuscan springs.

. . . . . .

Now when the scented iris, straight and tall,
Shall hedge the garden gravel once again.
With pale blue flags, at May's exulting call,
And when the amber roses, wet with rain,
Shall tapestry the old grey villa wall,
We, left alone, shall seek one bud in vain."

If Lee-Hamilton is not a "master of the sonnet", this is because the sonnet has found but few masters, and because he himself had not the inevitable instinct for the perfect line without which no perfect sonnet may be written.

"With something like a superstitious dread"

would be an ugly line anywhere, and in a sonnet it may not be allowed. Nevertheless some of these sonnets take a high place, and all are marked by some felicity of phrase or fancy that gives distinction to the whole. They add something to that "sense of tears" which informs the best poetry of all ages :

"The little golden drop is in them all,
But bitterer is the cup than may be told."

SHANGHAI: THE MODEL SETTLEMENT.

"Historic Shanghai." By C. A. Montalto de Jesus. Shanghai Mercury Ltd. 1909.

SHANGHAI is an interesting and important place, but whether it has been so long enough to make it "an anomaly if not a reproach" that its history should still be unwritten is a question—well, perhaps, of terminology. For though it had its vicissitudes before the Treaty of Nanking opened it to foreign commerce these were scarcely of world-shaking importance, and the shorter term "story" might be more applicable to its subsequent growth. In setting himself to remedy the defect the author has, at any rate, found abundant though somewhat scattered material in the "Chinese Repository", the "Chinese Miscellany", the "North China Herald", and other local publications. Some may regret indeed that he has not quoted more freely from those earlier and less accessible records, instead of giving so much space to Gordon's exploits which have been fully related in Hake's "Story of Chinese Gordon", Wilson's "Ever-Victorious Army", and other works. Civil war in China has meant always massacre, plunder, and destruction. There was considerable cleavage of opinion among the foreign community at the time as to whether the Taipings or Imperialists should be supported, or let alone. Authority favoured the latter, and by so doing probably decided the fate of the rebellion. That is to say, it was decided to drive back the Taipings throughout a radius of thirty miles round Shanghai—which was, in effect, not only to set in motion against them forces superior to their own, but to secure to the Imperialists a base of operations for which both sides had eagerly striven and for which either would, it is believed, have bargained—even to the constitution of Shanghai as a free city with a radius of dependent territory as the price of our goodwill. It was at Shanghai, amid the fiscal chaos caused by the Civil War, that the Imperial Maritime Customs Service was born; and it was amid similar administrative chaos that the foundations were laid of the Municipal Government which has gained for the foreign quarter at Shanghai the title of "Model Settlement", in the teeth of obstruction and intrigue where gratitude and wisdom should have dictated cordiality and imitation.

It was with a perception, certainly, of the promise of Shanghai as a port near the mouth of the Yangtze that the right of trading there was exacted in the Treaty of Nanking; but the concentration of enterprise which has made it the chief port of Eastern Asia was fortuitous in so far that the project of making Chusan an entrepot for the trade of Mid-China, on the same footing as Hong-kong in the south, had at least presented itself to Sir Henry Pottinger and his colleagues. The site of the present settlement was then agricultural land, and plots were bought at from forty-five dollars to seventy-five dollars a mow (one-sixth of an acre), that are now worth as many thousands. Mr. de Jesus tells the story of its development and the growth of its trade, of its riots and vicissitudes, with somewhat meticulous detail, which invites equally meticulous criticism. The so-called Kiang-nan Arsenal, for instance, can hardly be called "a development of the small foundry established by Li Hung Chang during the Taiping War"; for that first little arsenal—it was more than a foundry—which was created by Dr. Macartney under Li's auspices was transferred to Soochow and eventually to Nanking, in the great Viceroy's wake. The "Kiang-nan" was a separate creation. Nor is it quite accurate to ascribe the sale of the Shanghai Steam Navigation Company to subsidised Chinese opposition. It was the China Merchants' Steam Navigation Company that purchased the steamers, but it was the appearance of a powerful British Company ("The China Navigation", which is still running) that precipitated the sale. We note also, by the by, that the author perpetuates an amusing mistake made by Mr. Hake in quoting from the "North China Herald" as genuine a letter purporting to emanate from a Taiping source which bears, one would have thought, sufficient evidence of being a squib.

We have been concerned so far with the modern features of the story; but the Shanghailander, to whom it is all so familiar, will turn back probably with greater zest to the introductory chapter which relates, from Chinese records, the emergence of Shanghai as a fishing village on the mud-flats that were gradually formed by the Yangtze and its affluents and its early experiences from floods, pirates, Japanese invasions and other disasters. It can boast among other distinctions that it was the birthplace of the Jesuits' distinguished disciple Siu Kwang-ki (better known as Paul Siu), who rose to be a chief Minister of State and whose name is associated by tradition with more than one familiar spot in the neighbourhood—notably with the great college at Sikawei, near which stood a tomb decorated by the last Ming Emperor with a double row of stone figures as an honorific tribute to his worth. This was practically the first incident in foreign associations which have found ulterior expression in a vast commerce that has by no means yet reached its limit. It is well, in the meantime, to have on record details of the earlier phases of a story that may have to be writ larger on a later day.

NOVELS.

"A Reaping." By E. F. Benson. London: Heinemann. 1909. 6s.

We hazard a guess that Mr. E. F. Benson does not see why his academic brother should have it all his own way in discussing life and death and things in general. So the novelist sets out to meet the essayist on his own ground, but scores a point by making his meditations centre round imaginary persons. This book is by way of being the diary of a year spent mainly in the country by a young married couple. They own a pleasant young cousin called Legs—at least Legs is a youth of a kind very likeable in flesh and blood but a little tiresome on paper. When the diarist is tired of discoursing on music and gardens he lets a friend be killed or a baby be born—and here we see how the essayist-brother, starting from scratch so to say, loses that particular hole. All this is agreeable enough to read, except that the important things touched upon—the bunkers in the course—are a little out of keeping with the small-talk.

"The Wanton." By Frances Harrod (Frances Forbes Robertson). London: Greening. 1909. 6s.

She was not really a wanton, but the public may be more desirous of hearing about the beautiful Beltis if they start with the belief that she was no better than she should be. Mrs. Harrod has evidently read up the times of the Emperor Frederick II., and the incongruous modernity of her dialogue will not be resented by those to whom her story will most appeal. Wardour Street English may be repellent—but Beltis is terribly far removed from Nicolette whom Aucassin loved. Apart from its setting, and from the author's evident desire to emulate Mr. Hewlett in giving the Philistine false alarms, the story is not undramatic. Cecilia, the correct and heartless woman, wedded a romantic knight whom her cousin and playmate, Beltis the passionate, had learned to love. There is incident in plenty—and the affectation of fine writing to satiety. What the author means by saying that "it took the Reformation to instil into woman the monstrous conviction that to be with child could ever be a dishonour" we cannot imagine. The Middle Ages attached a certain value to chastity.

"Fancy O'Brien." By Ella MacMahon. London: Chapman and Hall. 1909. 6s.

Although the main incident in this study of the small-shop-keeping class in a Dublin suburb is the seduction of Bridgie Doyle by Fancy O'Brien, it is saved from sordidness by the idealism of the author's standpoint. Her power to depict the humour and tenderness no less than the savagery of the Irish character is as evident as her pride in them; nor are we left without a hint that a trip to Blackpool and a friendship with a cynical Saxon with a cockney accent contributed to Fancy's lapse from the standard morality of the Isle of Saints. But if the shamrock stamped on the book's green cover occasionally obtrudes itself between the pages, these latter have something of the freshness and austerity of the plant itself.

"Katherine the Arrogant." By B. M. Croker. London: Methuen. 1909. 6s.

There is nothing remarkable in the subject matter or in the manner of the telling of this story. The plot depends in a strained way on the unlikely circumstance of two platonic lovers remaining in ignorance of each other's names. The minor characters are drawn with exaggeration, yet, with all their emphasis, leave an undecided impression.

"Dragon's Blood." By H. M. Rideout. London: Constable. 1909. 6s.

Mr. Rideout gives a very interesting description of life in a remote Chinese village, where there are only some half-dozen Europeans. The writing is so graphic that one can feel the nervous tension of the white people at signs of a rebellion among the natives, and over all is the sense of the aching loneliness of their lot.

SHORTER NOTICES.

"Flora of Cornwall." By F. Hamilton Davey. Penryn: F. Chegwidden. 1909. 21s. net.

The Duchy of Cornwall, with its extensive sea-board and wide stretches of heath and moorland, has long been a happy hunting-ground with "searchers after simples". From the far-off days of the seventeenth century, when John

Ray, in company with Sir Francis Willughby, found the now extinct cotton-weed "on the gravelly-shore between Pensans and S. Michael's Mount", and the wild asparagus "growing on cliffs at the Lezard Point in Cornwall", a number of able botanists have investigated the county flora. How rich that flora is we have been lately reminded by the publication of Mr. Hamilton Davey's work on the plants of Cornwall and the Scilly Isles. As many as 1180 species are claimed for the county. Several of the choicest plants have unfortunately disappeared, such as the magnificent sea-stock, the Roman nettle, and the sea-pea which formerly grew on the beach near Penzance. Of plants peculiar to the county in Great Britain Mr. Davey enumerates no less than twenty species. Among these we note a graceful brome-grass, confined to one locality near Par, two species of rushes, and three clovers or trefoils found by the late Rev. C. A. Johns, the author of "Flowers of the Field", between the Lizard Head and Kynance Cove. The Cornish heath is locally abundant in the western part of the county. The Scilly Isles can boast of a little slender bird's-foot, the Ornithopus pinnatus, not found elsewhere in Britain. The ciliated rupturewort, found by Ray near the Lizard Point, still blossoms in its old locality. In comparatively recent years the purple viper's bugloss, found at S. Just by Dr. Ralfs, has been added to the British Flora; and a new fumitory, F. occidentalis, was discovered by Mr. Pugsley in 1904.

Other interesting plants, not indeed confined to Cornwall, but having their main range within the limits of the county, are the Cornish bladder-seed and the Cornish moneywort. In many parts of the Duchy the hedgebanks and roadsides are adorned, to an extent unknown elsewhere, with the handsome flowers of the bastard-balm and of the exquisite evergreen-alkanet. The common-balm—the word "common", being the equivalent of the Latin "officinalis", indicates the supposed medical properties of the plant—is also frequently met with, and is still believed to possess incredible virtues. The splendid tree-mallow continues to flourish on the lofty Cornish cliffs, above which, on the short springy turf, the lovely vernal-squill puts forth every May its pale-blue, star-like flowers.

"The Dawn of Mediæval Europe: 476—918." By J. H. B. Masterman. London: Methuen. 1909. 2s. 6d. net.

This is a very readable little book, and certainly the best of possible introductions to the study of a difficult period. It is not merely a chronicle, but presents the history with some regard for style, and with an admirable sense of proportion. The generalisations are sound, and may be trusted so far as they go. They leave the reader with an impression that, if the author had an opportunity of expanding his volume, he could produce a book which would be of value to the well-read student in this period as well as to the beginner. The bibliography at the end is both discreet and comprehensive.

"Y. America's Peril." By P. A. Vaile. London: Griffiths. 1909.

It cannot be denied that Mr. Vaile has produced an amusing book, but his method is too vindictive. Everything that is base, grotesque, and unlovely in the United States has been noted and recorded by the author with glee and enthusiasm. We observe, however, that he admits that there is something to be said on the other side. Indeed, no nation at once so criminal and so grotesque as the America depicted in these pages could exist. It would soon fall a victim to its own corruption or to the combined forces of avenging civilisation. There is some excuse for Mr. Vaile, who has been nauseated by the fulsome adulation of the Americans by writers who have been lavishly entertained by them, and who appear to think that the sum of the United States is contained in Broadway and Pennsylvania Avenue. Mr. Vaile promises, or threatens, another volume, in which he will depict the other side of the shield. If he produces a book really intended to balance this, we fear the laudatory hyperbolism of his predecessors in that line will be eclipsed. It is true that the United States is only a nation in the making, and not yet civilised; but the unrestrained ferocity of the author conveys the impression of a castigation without discrimination.

Barr's Catalogue of Daffodils, 1909.

The horticulturists' catalogues are beginning to come in. One looks first and most keenly, perhaps, to Messrs. Barr's Daffodils. The daffodil is so delightful a flower that we cannot help welcoming anything that brings it before us, even though it reminds us that summer is past. The daffodil seems capable of really indefinite development, and on the whole, though some of the earlier varieties can never be beaten, one must admit that the newer, if we cannot say absolutely the newest, flowers are finer than their predecessors. This year Messrs. Barr have several new seedlings, notably Chieftain, a grand Incomparable, one of the most beautiful of all the daffodil groups, though our own choice for the loveliest of all would be Leedsi. Then we have Red Chief, a showy brilliant Barri, and another very striking Barri, Warley Scarlet. It is interesting to see how old famous varieties have to retire into the background. Emperor and Empress are now hardly in the front rank of Trumpets. But Madame de Graaf must always hold its own. Peter Barr, we note, has dropped to ten guineas.

THE SEPTEMBER REVIEWS.

Mr. R. B. Cunninghame Graham in the "English Review", Dr. Dillon in the "Contemporary", and Mr. Garvin in the "Fortnightly" are the only writers in the Reviews who discuss the question of Spain's action in the Riff. Mr. Cunninghame Graham and Dr. Dillon take one side; Mr. Garvin the other. To Mr. Cunninghame Graham the fighting in Morocco is naturally hateful, especially as he, like Dr. Dillon, is convinced that Spanish action is nothing more than an attempt to enforce respect for illicit mining concessions obtained from El Roghi. If Spain will only comprehend the full significance of the cry "Spain's future it is in Spain!", then, Mr. Cunninghame Graham thinks fifty years hence she may once again be a great Power. If not, if she persists in wasting slender resources in bolstering up the claims of the few capitalists whose "jobs have been so disastrous" to her in recent years, then her condition, which Dr. Dillon describes as one of "mental, moral, and physical inanition", will we suppose grow rapidly worse. Mr. Cunninghame Graham's sympathies and prejudices are easy to understand; they lead him to conclusions which would be less easy to justify. There is not much evidence of inanition in the way Spain tackled her Barcelona troubles, nor in the manner in which she has set about asserting her authority in the Riff. If the concessions which are responsible for the Moorish rising were illegal, how comes it that the Sultan has ordered the tribesmen to abandon their hostility to Spain? Mulai Hafid has endorsed the action of the man who is now his prisoner and was not his subject when he gave the concessions. Mr. Garvin takes the reasonable view of the case. Spain, without bringing upon herself troubles greater even than those she has now to face, could not withdraw from the position she had taken up around Melilla. If her King and Government had courted the fate which events in Morocco are supposed to hold in store for her, they could

(*Continued on page* 326.)

probably have adopted no means to that end more sure than retreat directly the tribes showed fight. Spain's honour is involved in this unfortunate affair, but not along the lines her critics suggest. She will, as Mr. Garvin says, not lose an opportunity of arriving at a settlement with the tribes if one presents itself, but if fanaticism elects to fight it out she will not flinch. "Even the chief Republican journal has declared for a resolute prosecution of the campaign, whatever acconnts should have to be settled with the Government afterwards."

The "Nineteenth Century" begins and ends with important articles on the unrest in India and the general effects of British rule. The Rev. J. A. Sharrock traces much of the recent trouble to certain misconceptions about India: education has been too literary, we have been diffident in regard to religion, even to the point of banishing it from the schools and apologising for it, and we have not taken sufficient trouble to encourage those who are loyal to us. In the new Legislative Councils, he says, Christians as well as Muslims and Hindus must have seats. Mr. Sharrock is convinced that India will ultimately become a Christian country. Disloyalty is not merely the work of certain English politicians who have taught the Bengali that if he gives sufficient trouble he will get all he cries for, but has been fostered by the deliberate policy of ignoring all religious instruction in colleges and schools. "Any religion with a belief in God", Mr. Sharrock says, "is better than none; and we have given them none, while boasting of our liberality." That is a point of view to which less attention has been given than it deserves. Mr. Elliot G. Colvin, for the benefit of those who have no special knowledge of India, meets and exposes the "distortions and exaggerations" of English and American writers who endorse the licence of the native Press; and Sir Edmund C. Cox devotes himself to answering the aspersions of a Hindu murderer and an English labour member of Parliament. It was hardly worth while to go into elementary history in the pages of the "Nineteenth Century" in refutation of Mr. Victor Grayson. Mr. F. H. Barrow in the "Empire Review", in an attempt to explain what Hinduism really is, takes up somewhat the same line as Mr. Sharrock. He thinks the Hindu is unconsciously approaching Christianity, and is trying to fit the political ideals of Christendom into his own ideals. "The fermentation brought about in Hinduism by the preaching of Christianity has rendered possible the new Indian nationalism." In the "Contemporary" also the Rev. N. Macnicol examines the spiritual forces at work in India; he shows what forces are still alive "in many a deep heart", and points to the pathetic spectacle of the educated young Indian who has lost the faith of his fathers without finding a new one. The "combination of Indian religious intensity with Western science and Western politics" is bound to be explosive. Sir Andrew Fraser in "Blackwood" concludes a short article on race hatred and the responsibility which rests upon the people as well as the Government of India, with the noteworthy suggestion that the time has come for providing in India itself the training in law, medicine, engineering, and the like, which will fit Indians to take their place beside the men from England. "It ought not to be necessary for Indians to leave India so as to acquire the status of barristers before the Indian Courts." We fail however to see how an Indian training would in any way save the Hindu from the unrest which is fostered by the native demagogues who take their cue from English Radicals.

Vox et Præterea Nihil in the "Fortnightly" gives an account of the relations of Baron Aehrenthal and M. Izvolsky in the negotiations as to South-Eastern Europe which puts the Austrian statesman in an unpleasant light and will not tend to encourage confidence in a peace dependent upon the mutual confidence of Austria and Russia. In the same review C. de Thierry throws out some useful hints as to openings for young Englishmen in South Africa, and Lord Monkswell congratulates Mr. Haldane on the position of the Territorial Force. In the "National" are articles on the Rôle of a National Army by Lord Alan Percy, who says that "some National Service party must appear to raise the cry for universal service"; on Party Government and the Empire by Mr. W. J. Courthope, who invites the Unionists to supplement constitutional machinery in imperial matters; and on Lord Kitchener in India by Sir George Arthur, who shows what Lord Kitchener has done not only for the Army as a whole but for the native regiments. "Lord Kitchener's command will long be associated in the minds of the native troops with bettered conditions of service." The "solid and tangible boons he has conferred will serve to butter the parsnips of the native soldier more effectively than any amount of exalted talk". Mr. Hobson, in the "English Review", on South Africa as an Imperial Asset is much more concerned with the future relations of the colonies to the Empire than with the position of South Africa; in characteristic Liberal vein he insists on those points that might make for trouble rather than those that make for union. If Mr. Hobson were capable of humour, we should be able to appreciate his suggestion that if there had been no war union might have been "achieved as early, though the Dutch supremacy which it embodies and assures would have been less conspicuous". The man who can seriously write such a sentence is not qualified to discuss South African affairs. Sir C. Kinloch-Cooke, in the "Empire Review", is agreed that South African union must have come, but he regrets that the Boers have been allowed to take the position of top dog, and shows his consciousness of facts by urging the necessity for increasing the white population of South Africa "from British sources". Lord Desborough, in the "Financial Review of Reviews", discovers the real yellow peril in the scarcity of gold, the fluctuating rate of exchange between gold and silver using countries, and the effect of the fall in the price of silver on the business of East and West. He enters a plea for the issue of ten-shilling notes to replace the half-sovereign, and thinks some arrangement will have to be made between the Great Powers, restoring the monetary function of silver and raising the exchange.

At this season the miscellaneous items in the magazines and reviews should be unusually numerous and attractive. The "English Review" gives a study of Mr. Lloyd George—not an article, but one of his inimitable caricatures—by Mr. Max Beerbohm, and Mr. Ford Madox Hueffer starts a serial entitled "The Call". In the "Nineteenth Century" Mr. P. D. Kenny has an article on the Irish priest entitled "His Parochial Majesty"; Miss A. E. Keeton writes on "Debussy: his Science and his Music"; Mr. Sidney Low on "Matrimony and the Man of Leters", in a way that suggests no real man of letters ought ever to marry. Mr. Low also appears in the "Fortnightly" with an article on Darwinism and Politics. Among the other contributions in the "Fortnightly" are an article on Admiral Saunders, Wolfe's colleague, which is apposite this month when the 150th anniversary of the fall of Quebec is to be celebrated; Some Neglected Aspects of Horace Walpole, indicated in an interesting essay by Mr. Norman Pearson; and The Master Hoaxer, James de la Cloche, whose claim to be a son of Charles II. is disposed of by Mr. Andrew Lang. The Story of Halley's Comet, which is to be expected again some time next spring, is told in the "Nineteenth Century" by Mr. E. Vincent Heward and in the "North American Review" by Mr. Ralph B. Larkin. In the "Contemporary" Mr. Jack London writes amusingly on the Bêche-de-Mer English of the South Sea Islands; in "Blackwood" there is a charming article on the Green Links of Peshawur by Mr. A. H. Grant; in "Cornhill" we have an account by Colonel Algernon Durand of his tiger-shooting experiences in Central India; and in "Travel and Exploration" Major P. W. Sykes' description of his pilgrimage to the tomb of Omar Khayyam.

For this Week's Books see page 328.

BEAUTIFUL FLOWERS for WINTER DECORATION from SUTTON'S BULBS.

Before ordering Bulbs for the coming Season, everyone should write for a copy of

SUTTON'S BULB CATALOGUE for 1909,
Containing particulars of the best varieties of NARCISSI, HYACINTHS, TULIPS, &c.
Price 6d. Gratis and post-free to Customers.

SUTTON & SONS, The King's Seedsmen, READING.

FIRST IN OFFICIAL TESTS
FIRST IN PUBLIC FAVOUR

DEVON FIRE

NONE BETTER THAN THE BEST

Sole Proprietors & Manufacturers
CANDY & Co Ltd
London Showroom: 87 Newman St.
Works: Heathfield Devon

GIVES UNIVERSAL & COMPLETE SATISFACTION

During the last half-century everyone travelling in hot climes has made a point of carrying some

DR. J. COLLIS BROWNE'S

CHLORODYNE

so as to stop immediately an attack of

DIARRHŒA, DYSENTERY, OR CHOLERA.

Hot weather in the British Isles strikes suddenly, and everyone should take a little precaution. Don't wait until you actually need the Chlorodyne; but always keep it by you. Avoid disappointment, and insist on having Dr. J. Collis Browne's Chlorodyne, it

ACTS LIKE A CHARM.

Of all Chemists.

1/1½. 2/9 & 4/6.

AUSTRALIA by ORIENT LINE,

UNDER CONTRACT TO CARRY HIS MAJESTY'S MAILS.

FROM LONDON EVERY ALTERNATE FRIDAY, calling at PLYMOUTH, GIBRALTAR, MARSEILLES, NAPLES, PORT SAID, and COLOMBO.

Managers—F. GREEN & CO.: ANDERSON, ANDERSON & CO.

Head Offices—Fenchurch Avenue, London.

For Passage apply to the latter firm at 5 Fenchurch Avenue, E.C., or to the Branch Office, 28 Cockspur Street, Charing Cross, S.W.

P. & O AUTUMN PASSENGER SAILINGS (1909)

(Carrying Mails under Contract with H.M. Government.)

EGYPT, INDIA, STRAITS, CHINA, JAPAN, AUSTRALASIA.

CALCUTTA AND INTERMEDIATE PORTS.

Steamer.	Tons.	From London.	From Marseilles.
SUNDA	5,000	Sept. 4	...
SIMLA	6,000	Sept. 18	...
MALTA	6,000	Oct. 2	Oct. 10
CALEDONIA	8,000	Oct. 14	Oct. 20
SARDINIA	7,000	Oct. 30	Nov. 7
NUBIA	6,000	Nov. 13	...
BORNEO	5,000	Nov. 27	...

Carrying First and Second Saloon Passengers at Intermediate Fares.

P. & O. Return Tickets, available for 2 years, at a Fare and a Half. For Passage and all information apply at the Company's Offices, 122 Leadenhall St., E.C., or Northumberland Ave., W.C., London.

UNION-CASTLE LINE.

ROYAL MAIL SERVICE.—To SOUTH and EAST AFRICA.—Via Madeira, Canaries, Ascension, St. Helena, and Lobito Bay.

Steamers	Service	London	Southampton
* KILDONAN CASTLE	Royal Mail	—	Sept. 11
§ DURHAM CASTLE	Intermediate	Sept. 10	Sept. 11
* BRITON	Royal Mail	—	Sept. 18
† GERMAN	Intermediate	Sept. 17	Sept. 18

* Via Madeira. § Via Teneriffe.
† Via Las Palmas, Ascension, and St. Helena.

Special Trains from Waterloo to Southampton every Saturday.

Donald Currie and Co., Managers, 3 and 4 Fenchurch Street, E.C. West End Agencies—Sleeping Car Co., 20 Cockspur Street S.W., and Thos. Cook and Son, 13 Cockspur Street, S.W.

R. ANDERSON & CO.,

BRITISH, INDIAN, AND COLONIAL ADVERTISEMENT CONTRACTORS,

14 KING WILLIAM STREET, STRAND, W.C.,

GIVE THE BEST TERMS for Company and General Advertising. Advice, Estimates, and all information free of charge. Replies received.

Awarded 25 Gold Medals and a Ten Guinea Challenge Cup.

BARR'S POPULAR 21/- COLLECTION OF DAFFODILS contains 6 Bulbs each of 26 Fine Distinct Varieties suitable for Pot-culture or for the Flower Border. (Half the Collection for **10/6.**)

BARR'S WOODLAND 21/- COLLECTION OF DAFFODILS contains 500 Strong Bulbs in 20 Fine Showy Varieties suitable for Naturalising.

Descriptive Catalogue of all the finest Daffodils in Cultivation, Free.

BARR & SONS,

11, 12, & 13 King Street, Covent Garden, London.

THIS WEEK'S BOOKS.

ART

Michelangelo (Gerald S. Davies). Methuen. 12*s*. 6*d*. net.
Art in Great Britain and Ireland (Sir Walter Armstrong). Heinemann. 6*s*.

BIOGRAPHY

The Life and World-Work of Thomas Lake Harris (Arthur A. Cuthbert). Glasgow: Pearce. 2*s*. 6*d*.
Carlyle's First Love (Raymond Clare Archibald). Lane. 10*s*. 6*d*. net.

FICTION

The Ghost Pirates (William Hope Hodgson); The Adventures of a Pretty Woman (Florence Warden). Stanley Paul. 6*s*. each.
Dorrien Carfax (Nowell Griffith). Smith, Elder. 6*s*.
The Key of the Unknown (Rosa Nouchette Carey); Open Country (Maurice Hewlett). Macmillan. 6*s*. each.
Love and the Wise Men (Percy White); The Squire's Daughter (Archibald Marshall); Giannella (Mrs. Hugh Fraser); Happiness (Maud Stepney). Methuen. 6*s*. each.
The Wood-Carver of Lympus (Mary E. Waller). Melrose. 6*s*.
Cut off the World (Frank T. Bullen). Fisher Unwin. 6*s*.
My Lady Wentworth (Allan Fea). Mills and Boon. 6*s*.
The Tragedy of the Pyramids (Douglas Sladen). Hurst and Blackett. 6*s*.
Black Mark (A. Whisper). Edinburgh: Blackwood. 6*s*.
Paths Perilous (Sidney Pickering); The Sheriff of Dyke Hole (Ridgwell Cullum). Chapman and Hall. 6*s*. each.
The Son of Mary Bethel (Elsa Barker); The Knight of the Golden Sword (Michael Barrington). Chatto and Windus. 6*s*. each.
To my King ever Faithful (George David Gilbert). Nash.
Aunt Jane of Kentucky (Eliza Calvert Hall). Cassell. 6*s*.
Margaret Hever (Elizabeth Martindale). Duckworth. 6*s*.

GIFT BOOK

The Romance of Modern Chemistry (James C. Philip). Seeley. 5*s*.

HISTORY

Napoleon's Brothers (A. Hilliard Atteridge). Methuen. 18*s*. net.
Johnsonian Gleanings (Aleyn Lyell Reade). Francis.
Inns, Ales, and Drinking Customs of Old England (Frederick W. Hackwood). Fisher Unwin. 10*s*. 6*d*. net.

LAW

Equity: also the Forms of Action at Common Law (F. W. Maitland). Cambridge: at the University Press. 12*s*. 6*d*.

REPRINTS AND TRANSLATIONS

The White Stone (Anatole France). Lane. 6*s*.
Everyman's Library (Edited by Ernest Rhys): The Conquest of Mexico (2 vols.); The Last Chronicle of Barset (2 vols.); Macaulay's Speeches on Politics and Literature; The Bayard of India. Dent. 1*s*. net each.

TRAVEL

An English Honeymoon (Anne Hollingsworth Wharton). Heinemann. 6*s*. net.
Travels in the Upper Egyptian Deserts (Arthur E. P. Weigall). Edinburgh: Blackwood. 7*s*. 6*d*. net.

MISCELLANEOUS

Aerial Navigation of To-day (Charles C. Turner). Seeley. 5*s*. net.
Beggars (W. H. Davies). Duckworth. 6*s*.
Dates of Genesis, The (Rev. F. A. Jones). Kingsgate Press. 5*s*. net.
In Memoriam: The Very Rev. William Lefroy (Rev. B. Baring-Gould). Jarrold. 2*s*. net.
In the Abstract (Norman Alliston). Sonnenschein. 2*s*. 6*d*.
Lighter Studies of a Country Rector (John Vaughan). Sir Isaac Pitman. 5*s*. net.
Psychical Science and Christianity (E. Katharine Bates). Laurie. 6*s*.
"Rosemary: that's for Remembrance" (Elenor Mordaunt). Scott Publishing Co. 3*s*. 6*d*.

In the event of any difficulty being experienced in obtaining the SATURDAY REVIEW, the Publisher would be glad to be informed immediately.

KING'S COLLEGE (University of London).

THE THEOLOGICAL DEPARTMENT.

Complete instruction is given for all theological degrees in the University of London, and students are prepared for Holy Orders in the Church of England.

KING'S COLLEGE (University of London).

This includes the FACULTY OF ARTS (including ARCHITECTURE), the FACULTY OF LAWS. The classes in Laws are arranged by an inter-collegiate scheme with University College and the London School of Economics. The FACULTY OF SCIENCE with (*a*) DIVISION OF NATURAL SCIENCE. Preparation for Science degrees and also for the Institution of Chemistry examinations. (*b*) DIVISION OF MEDICAL SCIENCE. Preparation for preliminary and intermediate medical examinations, for which the college is a University centre. FACULTY OF ENGINEERING. Systematic courses in civil, mechanical, and electrical engineering and metallurgy. EVENING CLASS DEPARTMENT. Full courses for University degrees in arts and science, and various special classes.

KING'S COLLEGE FOR WOMEN

(University of London).

The College is in Kensington Square. The faculties represented are ARTS AND SCIENCE. There are also two other departments—viz. HOME SCIENCE AND ECONOMICS and FINE ART. The more advanced students in science attend classes at King's College.

For information and prospectus apply to the Secretary, King's College, Strand, W.C.

ELTHAM COLLEGE, KENT.

(THE ROYAL NAVAL SCHOOL.)

PUBLIC SCHOOL LIFE AND EDUCATION, with Special Classes for all Naval and Military Examinations. Special Fees for Officers in the Navy and Army. Recognised by the Army Council. Large Playing-fields. Gymnasium, Swimming Bath; Chemical and Physical Laboratories; Cadet Corps, &c. Recent Honours: Open Scholarship, Balliol College; 1st, Open Scholarships, Hertford and Merton Colleges; 1st place Naval Clerkships; Admissions to Sandhurst, Osborne, &c. NEXT TERM BEGINS SEPTEMBER 15th.

Apply Headmaster, Rev. A. E. RUBIE, D.D.

ELY CATHEDRAL.

Visitors will find First Class Hotel Accommodation at the "LAMB" Family Hotel, which is situated close to the Cathedral. **MODERATE TERMS.** Omnibus meets all trains.

Proprietor, S. AIREY.

THE CONDUIT STREET AUCTION GALLERIES.

The attention of Executors, Trustees, Solicitors, and Owners, who may be desirous of selling Works of Art, Family Jewels, Old Silver, Furniture, Pictures, Prints, Miniatures, China, Coins, Books, Old Lace, Furs, Musical Instruments, Guns, and other Valuables, is drawn to Messrs.

KNIGHT, FRANK & RUTLEY'S

AUCTION GALLERIES, 9 CONDUIT STREET, AND 23A MADDOX STREET, W., which are Open Daily to receive goods intended for early sales.

VALUATIONS are prepared for Fire Insurance, Estate Duty, and all other purposes. As to Insurance, owners are reminded that, for security, Messrs. KNIGHT, FRANK & RUTLEY'S detailed inventory and valuation of the contents of a Town or Country Mansion is an important adjunct to their Fire Insurance Policies.

Sport Society Drama	THE **BYSTANDER** SIXPENCE. Every Tuesday.	Politics Literature Fiction

THE BEST OF THE LIGHT ILLUSTRATED WEEKLIES.
A PICTORIAL RECORD OF THE WEEK'S DOINGS.

TERSE AND TRUTHFUL CRITICISM.
"WORLDLY" SHORT STORIES.
SPORT: a Speciality. GOLF, HUNTING, LAWN TENNIS.

⁂ You do not only glance at "THE BYSTANDER," you READ it. It is Unique, Sparkling, Daring, Original.

Published by the Proprietors of the "GRAPHIC," Tallis House, Tallis Street, E.C.

IN COMMEMORATION OF THE 150th ANNIVERSARY OF THE

BATTLE OF QUEBEC,

THE WOLFE BANQUET

(F.-M. Sir GEORGE WHITE, V.C., in the Chair),

TO BE HELD AT

THE WHITE CITY, SHEPHERD'S BUSH,

SEPTEMBER 13, at 7.30.

Tickets (One Guinea, including Wines) may be had of

The HON. SECRETARY, WOLFE BANQUET, ROYAL COLONIAL INSTITUTE, W.C.

484 pp. letterpress. Size 9 by 7 ins. 25 Plates, 160 other Illustrations from Photographs and Pen and Ink Sketches and Folding Plan of Cliffs by the Author. Price **21s.** net.

MY LIFE AMONG THE WILD BIRDS IN SPAIN

BY

COLONEL WILLOUGHBY VERNER

(LATE RIFLE BRIGADE),

Author of
"Sketches in the Soudan,"
"The Military Life of H.R.H. George, Duke of Cambridge."

Although this account of Life in the Wilds of Southern Spain, and of the Wanderings and Adventures of a Naturalist amid the semi-tropical wilds of South-Western Andalusia, is primarily devoted to a description of the larger birds such as the Great Bustards and Eagles in their remote haunts, it also contains many descriptions of the scenery, mountains, woodlands, plains and marshes, as well as the inhabitants, the trees, the flowers, &c., of that fascinating and but little-known region. Neither are the great historical and antiquarian interests of the country, such as the battlefields and pre-historic graves, overlooked.

SOME PRESS OPINIONS.

SATURDAY REVIEW.—"One of those rare books which are virgin observation from end to end. Its width of experience makes the volume worthy to go down in that special list of international nature-history books which Mr. Roosevelt in his hours of leisure is perfecting. The author provokes an inevitable comparison with Mr. Millais, the first of our naturalists. Both men have the artist's hand to express what they see. . . . With the further help of the numerous photographs and tailpieces, the plains, the lagunas, the sierras of Spain, are very present to the eye while one reads these original rambles of a born naturalist in search of hidden homes."

TIMES.—". . . A story of glorified birdnesting, egging *in excelsis.* He talks rather as one may do in the smoking-room or from his armchair, telling unaffectedly of the incidents of what must be an almost unique birdsnesting career of over fifty years. On disputed points . . . he speaks with the authority of long and intimate experience. . . . Not the least interesting part of the volume is the illustrations, especially those from photographs of the author's taking, which are often surprisingly good considering the extraordinary disadvantages under which they were taken and that the conditions made it impossible to use any instrument but a hand kodak. On more than one occasion the taking of the photograph was more dangerous than the ascent or descent to or from the nest, thrilling though these often were."

ATHENÆUM.—"An inveterate birdsnester, unrepentant but not undiscriminating, Colonel Verner commands far more respect than many plausible humanitarians. . . . Long accustomed to supplement his journal with a sketch book, the author eventually calls in the aid of photography to complete his records. . . . All that Colonel Verner has to tell us of the birds of Spain is bound to carry great weight, owing to the continuity of his observations, for from the early seventies he has repeatedly visited the same scenes, and during the last few years has wintered in the country. . . . The culminating feat of Colonel Verner's long birdsnesting career was only accomplished in 1908 with a successful campaign against the famous Lämmergeyer or, as he prefers to call it, The Bearded Vulture. He has the evidence of his own eyes that the title of 'bone-breaker' is no misnomer. The excellent sketches of this and other grand birds upon the wing are a welcome feature. The scenes of the final act—the succession of bitter disappointments, dangerous predicaments, and eventual triumph—come with singularly dramatic effect. The indomitable veteran ends with a heartfelt 'Nunc dimittis.'"

LONDON: JOHN BALE, SONS & DANIELSSON, LTD., Oxford House, 83-91 Great Titchfield Street, Oxford Street.

THE EVERSLEY SERIES.

Globe 8vo. cloth, 4s. net per Volume.

Matthew Arnold's Works. 8 vols.
Poems. 3 vols.
Essays in Criticism. First Series.
Essays in Criticism. Second Series.
American Discourses.
Letters, 1848—1888. Collected and Arranged by G. W. E. Russell. 2 vols.

A Memoir of Jane Austen. By her Nephew, J. E. Austen Leigh. To which is added "Lady Susan," and Fragments of two other Unfinished Tales by Miss Austen.

The Eversley Bible. Arranged in paragraphs, with an Introduction by J. W. Mackail, M.A.
Vol. II. **Deuteronomy—2 Samuel.**
Vol. III. **1 Kings—Esther.** Vol. IV. **Job—Song of Solomon.**
Vol. V. **Isaiah—Lamentations.** Vol. VI. **Ezekiel—Malachi.**
Vol. VII. **Matthew—John.** Vol. VIII. **Acts—Revelation.**
*** The Text is that of the Authorised Version.

Essays by George Brimley. Third Edition.

Calderon. Eight Dramas of Calderon freely translated. By Edward FitzGerald.

Chaucer's Canterbury Tales. Edited by A. W. Pollard. 2 vols.

Dean Church's Miscellaneous Writings. Collected Edition. 9 vols.
Miscellaneous Essays. | **Dante,** and other Essays.
St. Anselm. | **Bacon.** | **Spenser.**
The Oxford Movement. Twelve Years, 1833—1845.
The Beginning of the Middle Ages. (Included in this series by permission of Messrs. Longmans and Co.)
Occasional Papers. Selected from *The Guardian*, *The Times*, and *The Saturday Review*, 1846–1890. 2 vols.

Life and Letters of Dean Church. Edited by his Daughter, Mary C. Church.

Lectures and Essays by the late W. K. Clifford, F.R.S. Edited by the late Sir Leslie Stephen and Sir Frederick Pollock. Third Edition. In 2 vols.

Emerson's Collected Works. 6 vols. With Introduction by John Morley, M.P.
Miscellanies. | **Essays.** | **Poems.**
English Traits and Representative Men.
The Conduct of Life, and Society and Solitude.
Letters and Social Aims.

Letters of Edward FitzGerald. Edited by W. Aldis Wright. 2 vols. New Edition.

Letters of Edward FitzGerald to Fanny Kemble, 1871-1883. Edited by W. A. Wright.

More Letters of Edward FitzGerald. Edited by W. Aldis Wright.

Pausanias and other Greek Sketches. By J. G. Frazer, D.C.L.

Goethe's Maxims and Reflections. Translated, with Introductions, by T. Bailey Saunders.
*** The Scientific and Artistic Maxims were Selected by Professor Huxley and Lord Leighton respectively.

Thomas Gray's Collected Works in Prose and Verse. Edited by Edmund Gosse. 4 vols.
Poems, Journals, and Essays.
Letters. 2 vols.
Notes on Aristophanes and Plato.

J. R. Green's Works. 16 vols.
History of the English People. 8 vols.
The Making of England. 2 vols.
The Conquest of England. 2 vols.
Stray Studies from England and Italy.
Oxford Studies.
Historical Studies.
Stray Studies. Second Series.

Guesses at Truth. By Two Brothers.

Earthwork Out of Tuscany. Being Impressions and Translations of Maurice Hewlett, Author of "The Forest Lovers." Third Edition, revised.

R. H. Hutton's Collected Essays. 7 vols.
Literary Essays.
Theological Essays.
Essays on Some of the Modern Guides of English Thought in Matters of Faith.
Criticisms on Contemporary Thought and Thinkers. 2 vols.
Aspects of Religious and Scientific Thought. Edited by his Niece, Elizabeth M. Roscoe.
Brief Literary Criticism. Edited by his Niece, Elizabeth M. Roscoe.

The Choice of Books, and other Literary Pieces. By Frederic Harrison.

The Meaning of History, and other Historical Pieces. By Frederic Harrison.

Poems of Thomas Hood. Edited, with Prefatory Memoir, by the late Canon Ainger. In 2 vols.
Vol. I. **Serious Poems.**
Vol. II. **Poems of Wit and Humour.**
With Vignettes and Portraits.

Thomas Henry Huxley's Collected Works. 12 vols.
Method and Results. | **Darwiniana.**
Science and Education.
Science and Hebrew Tradition.
Science and Christian Tradition.
Hume. With Helps to the Study of Berkeley.
Man's Place in Nature, and other Anthropological Essays.
Discourses: Biological and Geological.
Evolution and Ethics, and other Essays.
Life and Letters. 3 vols.

French Poets and Novelists. By Henry James.

Partial Portraits. By Henry James.

Modern Greece. Two Lectures delivered before the Philosophical Institution of Edinburgh, with Papers on "The Progress of Greece" and "Byron in Greece." By Sir Richard C. Jebb, Litt.D., D.C.L., LL.D. Second Edition.

Letters of John Keats to his Family and Friends. Edited by Sidney Colvin.

Epic and Romance. By Prof. W. P. Ker.

Charles Kingsley's Novels and Poems. 13 vols.
Westward Ho! 2 vols. | **Yeast.** 1 vol.
Alton Locke. 2 vols. | **Hypatia.** 2 vols.
Two Years Ago. 2 vols. | **Poems.** 2 vols.
Hereward the Wake. 2 vols.

Charles Lamb's Collected Works. Edited, with Introduction and Notes, by the late Rev. Canon Ainger, M.A. 6 vols.
The Essays of Elia.
Poems, Plays, and Miscellaneous Essays.
Mrs. Leicester's School, and other Writings.
Tales from Shakespeare. By Charles and Mary Lamb.
The Letters of Charles Lamb. Newly arranged, with additions, 1904. 2 vols.

Life of Charles Lamb. By the late Canon Ainger, M.A.

Historical Essays. By the late J. B. Lightfoot, D.D., D.C.L., LL.D.

The Poetical Works of John Milton. Edited, with Memoir, Introduction, and Notes, by David Masson, M.A., LL.D. 3 vols.

John Morley's Collected Works. 14 vols.
Voltaire. 1 vol. | **Rousseau.** 2 vols.
Diderot and the Encyclopædists. 2 vols.
On Compromise. 1 vol. | **Miscellanies.** 3 vols.
Burke. 1 vol. | **Studies in Literature.** 1 vol.
Oliver Cromwell. 1 vol.
The Life of Richard Cobden. 2 vols.

Science and a Future Life, and other Essays. By F. W. H. Myers, M.A.

Classical Essays. By F. W. H. Myers.

Modern Essays. By F. W. H. Myers.

Records of Tennyson, Ruskin, and Browning. By Anne Thackeray Ritchie.

Works by Sir John R. Seeley, Litt.D. 5 vols.
The Expansion of England. Two Courses of Lectures.
Lectures and Essays.
Ecce Homo. | **Natural Religion.**
Introduction to Political Science. Two Series of Lectures.

Shakespeare. By Walter Raleigh.

The Works of Shakespeare. With short Introduction and Footnotes by Professor C. H. Herford. In 10 vols.
*** The Plays may also be had in separate volumes, cloth, 1s. each; roan, gilt tops, 2s. each.

Works by James Smetham. 2 vols.
Letters. With an Introductory Memoir. Edited by Sarah Smetham and William Davies. With a Portrait.
Literary Works. Edited by William Davies.

The Works of Alfred, Lord Tennyson. Annotated by the Author. Edited by Hallam, Lord Tennyson. 9 vols.
Vol. I. **Poems.** | Vol. II. **Poems.**
Vol. III. **Enoch Arden: In Memoriam.**
Vol. IV. **The Princess: Maud.**
Vol. V. **Idylls of the King.**
Vol. VI. **Ballads and other Poems.**
Vol. VII. **Demeter and other Poems.**
Vol. VIII. **Queen Mary and Harold.**
Vol. IX. **Becket and other Plays.**

Selections from the Writings of Thoreau.

Essays in the History of Religious Thought in the West. By Brooke Foss Westcott, D.D., D.C.L., Lord Bishop of Durham.

The Works of Wordsworth. Edited by Professor Knight. In 10 vols. Each volume contains a Portrait and Vignette etched by H. Manesse.
Poetical Works. 8 vols.
Journals of Dorothy Wordsworth. 2 vols.

MACMILLAN & CO., LTD., LONDON.

MESSRS. CONSTABLE & CO.'S LIST

FOR IMMEDIATE PUBLICATION.

THE ROMANTIC MOVEMENT in ENGLISH POETRY. By ARTHUR SYMONS. Demy 8vo. 10s. 6d. net.

THE LIFE OF JOHN DEE. By CHARLOTTE FELL SMITH, Author of "Mary Rich, Countess of Warwick." With Portrait and Illustrations. Demy 8vo. 10s. 6d. net.

Apart from fugitive articles in magazines and dictionaries, this is the first attempt to set out in all its detail the life of a most remarkable character. Dee was more than a skilled astrologer and alchemist, as the author is able to show. He was a student of wide knowledge, and his influence on the mind of Elizabeth and on the intellect of his time form the subject matter of a really noteworthy book.

HISTORICAL ROMAN COINS: FROM EARLIEST TIMES TO THE REIGN OF AUGUSTUS. By G. F. HILL (of the British Museum), Author of "Historical Greek Coins." With 15 Plates. Demy 8vo. 10s. 6d. net.

CERE'S RUNAWAY, AND OTHER ESSAYS. By ALICE MEYNELL. Crown 8vo. 3s. 6d. net.

EXTINCT ANIMALS. By Sir E. RAY LANKESTER, F.R.S. With over 200 Illustrations. Crown 8vo. 3s. 6d. net. New Popular Edition.

"Readers of this fascinating book will find nothing that is not expressed with the utmost lucidity of text and illustrations."—*Times.*

MODERN ASTRONOMY. By H. H. TURNER, F.R.S. Crown 8vo. New Popular Edition. 2s. 6d. net.

"This highly interesting work."—*Athenæum.*

"Professor Turner's wholly admirable and concise little book."—*Spectator.*

THE ETERNAL VALUES. By HUGO MÜNSTERBERG, Author of "Psychology and Life," etc. Demy 8vo. 10s. 6d. net.

TIME AND CLOCKS. A Description of Ancient and Modern Methods of Measuring Time. By H. H. CUNYNGHAME. With Illustrations. Crown 8vo. 2s. 6d. net. New Popular Edition.

A volume of fascinating interest, describing for the general reader, Sundials, Water Clocks, Portable Sundials, Grandfather Clocks, Chronometers, the application of electricity as a means of impulse in clocks; in fact a history of the various methods employed by man to mark the passing of time.

THE ADVERTISEMENTS OF THE "SPECTATOR." Being a study of the Literature, History and Manners of Queen Anne's England as they are reflected therein, as well as an illustration of the Origins of the Art of Advertising. With Appendix of representative Advertisements now for the first time reprinted, and an Introductory Note by GEORGE LYMAN KITTREDGE. By LAWRENCE LEWIS. Price 6s. net.

Contents.—INTRODUCTION—I. HISTORY, LITERATURE, AND MANNERS—II. THE "SPECTATOR" CONSIDERED AS A PERIODICAL—III. THE VARIOUS FORMS OF ADVERTISEMENTS—IV. PUBLISHERS' ETHICS IN QUEEN ANNE'S DAY—APPENDIX.—SPECIMEN ADVERTISEMENTS OUT OF THE "SPECTATOR."

CHARLES W. ELIOT, President of Harvard University, 1869-1909. By Dr. EUGEN KUHNEMANN. With Frontispiece Portrait. Demy 8vo. 4s. 6d. net.

STUDIES IN CHRISTIANITY. By BORDEN PARKER BOWNE, Author of "The Immanence of God." Crown 8vo. 6s. net.

AUTOBIOGRAPHY OF NATHANIEL SOUTHGATE SHALER. Illustrated. Demy 8vo. 16s. net.

This most interesting life will take place among the more notable of modern memoirs. Professor Shaler was a man of extraordinary personal qualities, as well as a prominent figure in the scientific and educational world. His fascinating recollections form a remarkable book.

RECENTLY PUBLISHED.

CONTEMPORARY FRANCE. Vol. IV., **1877—1882.** THE COMPLETION OF MR. HANOTAUX'S HISTORY. Demy 8vo. With Portraits. 15s. net. Vols. I, II, III, previously issued, price 15s. net each.

THE LAST DAYS OF PAPAL ROME, 1850—1870. By R. DE CESARE. Translated by HELEN ZIMMERN, with an Introductory Chapter by G. M. TREVELYAN. Illustrated. Demy 8vo. 12s. 6d. net.

"An admirable version of a book well-known to Italian students. It appeals to enduring human sentiments. The author is a patriotic Italian scholar, with an imtimate knowledge of the epoch, which he describes with a light and picturesque touch."—*Standard.*

"Impartiality and intimate social and family khowledge are the special keynotes of his work."

Extract from Mr. G. M. Trevelyan's Introduction.

PORTUGAL: its Land and People. By W. H. KOEBEL. With 21 Beautiful Plates in Colour by Mrs. S. ROOPE DOCKERY, and 59 Illustrations in Half-Tone. Royal 8vo. 16s. net.

"Mr. Koebel has a genuine love of the country, and describes the varied aspects of the landscape and rural life, with the popular customs, in an easy style which is pleasant to read."—*Times.*

"Mr. Koebel will induce many people to follow in his footsteps, and his pleasant and chatty volume will be the best guide they can have."—*Globe.*

"The plenteous photographs are exceptionally good, and the illustrations in colour by Mrs. S. Roope Dockery are very pleasant additions to a volume which should enjoy, for many reasons, a wide popularity."—*Daily Telegraph.*

A CENTURY OF FRENCH POETS. By F. Y. ECCLES. Demy 8vo. 10s. 6d. net.

A selection illustrating the history of French Poetry during the last hundred years, with an Introduction, critical Notices of the Writers represented, a Summary of the Rules of French Versification, and a Commentary.

New Novels at all Libraries.

LOW SOCIETY.

By ROBERT HALIFAX.

"The life and the talk are convincing, and the humour true and unforced."—*Times.*

"The interest of the book lies in the series of vivid types presented to us, and the skill with which they are woven into their background to make an effective and convincing whole."—*Athenæum.*

WITH the WARDEN of the MARCHES.

By HOWARD PEASE.

"Mr. Pease evidently knows all about the old Border days, and his pages are full of the pleasant and interesting details of scholarship. If any one wishes to realise what life was in those times of feud and foray we cannot think of a more trustworthy and fascinating instructor."—*Pall Mall Gazette.*

"It is evident that Mr. Pease knows and loves every foot of these marches and dales."—*Athenæum.*

THE ACTRESS.

By LOUISE CLOSSER HALE.

"A perfectly healthy, thoroughly humorous story told with a more than ordinary degree of literary capacity."—*Athenæum.*

"Miss Hale has keen observation and as keen a sense of humour; she expresses herself both clearly and freshly, with many a quaint turn of phrase—in a word, her book is delightful."—*Sketch.*

DRAGON'S BLOOD.

By H. M. RIDEOUT.

"Mr. Rideout's style is vigorous, graphic, and entirely devoid of superfluities, and his book takes an unrelaxing grasp of the imagination."

Pall Mall Gazette.

"One of the best books which have appeared this year."—*Observer.*

"We shall be glad to see the next volume from this author's pen. He has the skill to set down that which he has seen in words which are sometimes almost magical in their pictorial power."—*Academy.*

THE SHADOW OF THE CATHEDRAL.

By VINCENT IBANEZ.

"Balzac might have written this romance and boasted of it."—*Bystander.*

"'La Catedral' is singularly true, and will have a certain attraction even for the merely curious reader by its pictures of a life unlike ours."—*Times.*

"A great book."—*Standard.*

THE MOUNT.

By C. F. KEARY, Author of "The Journalist."

"The work of a genuinely distinguished mind in a day when distinction among novelists is rare."

Spectator.

"The few readers who can appreciate good style and subtle observation have long appreciated Mr. Keary's work, but 'The Mount' should make him popular."

Standard.

ORDINARY PEOPLE.

By UNA L. SILBERRAD, Author of "The Good Comrade." [*Shortly.*

THE OATH OF ALLEGIANCE.

By ELIZABETH STUART PHELPS.

With 5 Illustrations. [*Shortly.*

These stories show Mrs. Ward in her most delightful and appealing vein.

London: CONSTABLE & CO. LTD. 10 Orange Street, W.C.

Printed for the Proprietors by SPOTTISWOODE & CO. LTD., 5 New-street Square, E.C., and Published by REGINALD WEBSTER PAGE, at the Office, 10 King Street, Covent Garden, in the Parish of St. Paul, in the County of London.—*Saturday*, 11 *September*, 1909.

THE

SATURDAY REVIEW

OF

POLITICS, LITERATURE, SCIENCE, AND ART.

No. 2,812 Vol. 108. 18 September 1909. [Registered as a Newspaper.] 6d.

CONTENTS.

NOTES OF THE WEEK.

The intellectual epicure loathes a surfeit, whether of blame or praise. We can quite see, then, why when death duties came up this week Mr. Balfour should be glad to change his tone. This is finance at last, he said: and he would only put Ministers on the hook as if he loved them. Yet we think he might have given the hook a little more barb. Death duties, of course, have been taken smilingly by Conservative Chancellors of the Exchequer and First Lords of the Treasury. Honest men, we suppose, are sometimes put to it to handle and apply—in party politics at any rate—the plunderings of their predecessors. But surely Mr. Balfour and his colleagues do not mean, if they come into office, to stereotype the stealings of this Government? That would be a little too cynical.

Yet not a voice has been raised this week in Parliament against some of the most brutal proposals of the Government. Take the case of a poor hard-working professional man or clerk, who cannot save anything to speak of, but just manages to insure his life for, say, a thousand pounds, so that his wife and two or three children may not be flung on the rates if he dies. There are thousands of cases of this kind. His widow can by safe investment get about £40 a year, or between fourteen and fifteen shillings a week, from this thousand. Fourteen-and-six a week is not an excessive income for a woman, a lady very likely, and two or three children to live on. Many a plump Labour leader makes five times that, and grumbles at it. But here the Government come along and find an easy victim. Mr. Lloyd George and Mr. Asquith propose to take from the widow a thick slice of her fortune. To Sir William Harcourt's £30 they add another £10 for legacy or succession. They take from her at least one whole year's income! This may be very good finance. But from the point of view of humanity it is devilish.

With tears in his voice the Chancellor of the Exchequer sorts out many of the smaller oysters to swallow as well as the bigger ones; and often indeed the smaller ones are delicious eating. We do not plead for humane finance. Let us leave that to the Government. But it is rather sickening when the Government do this sort of thing and their supporters pretend they are acting humanely. We open the "Daily Chronicle" on 15 September as an exceptional treat and find under an article called "Husbands, Wives, and Taxes" this passage: "The new tax is safeguarded from hardship by generous exemptions in the case of widows and small estates". What a candid and discerning writer!

It is arguable that small struggling professional men are fools to vote at all when such taxes are clapped on by one side and more or less winked at by the other. What is the use of their troubling to vote at all? it may be asked; they'll be taxed to death all the same. But it is quite sure they will be foolhardy among the foolhardiest if they do not vote against the party who devise such taxes at their expense. After all, the Conservatives at worst are only passive sometimes at their expense—the others are always active.

We must refer to two other monstrous proposals of the Government during the past week. One is to fine a man heavily who makes a present of money to anyone five years before his death. This was changed to three years, a change as ridiculous as the original proposal. It would be more logical to ordain that a fine should be imposed on every present of money a man makes whether five or fifty years before his death. But the whole thing is grotesque rubbish. We shall make ourselves the laughing-stock of history if we pass this Budget. The other proposal looks like irony. The payer of death duties can hand over his land instead of his money if he choose! The Government are going to take their tenth or half or whatever it is like the tithe-owner before commutation. The Duke of Sutherland will pay in deer forests, the Marquis of Bute in coal, Professor Stuart in mustard and Mr. Rowntree in chocolate.

Lord Robert Cecil's character sketch of the Chancellor of the Exchequer in Tuesday's debate had, we think, a slight flaw, historically. He declared that despite "many great qualities" Mr. Lloyd George loved tyranny for its own sake. Whereupon Mr. O'Connor suggested, "like Robespierre". "No," replied Lord Robert, "Mr. Lloyd George is more entertaining than Robespierre." This is the conventional view we know—that Robespierre was a mean figure intellectually, the dull, unentertaining mediocrist. Carlyle seems to have stereotyped this view for ever. But Lamartine's "History of the Girondists" gives one a very different picture of the man. Robespierre was a monster, no doubt, but not the less for that, one of the most "entertaining" figures of his century and country.

We are all in a way attracted by the theories of Mr. Ure, the extraordinary Solicitor-General for Scotland, Mr. Anacharsis Ure he should have been baptized. We cannot help liking him for his exceeding honesty, as Lord Rosebery says. He outs with everything. No bag, indeed, is big enough to hold the wild cat of Mr. Ure. But Mr. Chiozza-Money has theories on property only less signal than Mr. Ure's on land. He ventilated one of these in Tuesday's debate. It was this: Capital is not destroyed when absorbed by the State, but only removed from private to public ownership. Of course, if we take to arguing in this vein, capital and property appear almost indestructible. Suppose even the burglar break into Mr. Money's house and remove his plate and other effects, nothing need be lost or destroyed. The plate is only removed from one private person to another private person.

The appeal of the Primate to the Government on Wednesday as to the neglected reports of the Poor Law Commission cannot be ignored by the most engrossed of the Budget Ironsides. Lord Crewe expressed his gratitude at being reminded of the matter, but craved indulgence. He had not had time to study the report as it deserved. This is a pity, for months ago that report should have been obtained and studied by Liberal Ministers. The study of the report was, in fact, a logical preliminary to the framing of the Pensions scheme. But it is no use crying over milk already spilt, when the whole can is like to be upset. Meanwhile gratitude is due to the Primate from all who have the interests of the nation at heart. This vast problem will have to be grappled with, and it is no hasty drafting of inchoate Bills that will meet the case.

The contrivance "for the Development of the United Kingdom" came up in Committee on Wednesday. A "memorandum" came up, too, of advances from the Treasury under already existing powers, and as a model for farther extension; and this revealed the maximum proportion of £250,000 for England, and just twice as much for Ireland, where they can always find use for something that they think they get for nothing. There is money also "for various purposes", and everybody is to be "developed" at the expense of everybody else. On Thursday the thing was made less ridiculous by accepting Lord Robert Cecil's amendment to have the expenditure controlled by a permanent Commission instead of Mr. Lloyd George's "Advisory Committee." Yesterday the application of the closure resulted in a scene. Mr. George's autocratic methods are too much for Lord Robert Cecil's patience.

A scheme like this might be really useful but for the omissions that make it so foolish. The assumption is that potentially productive regions are now kept unproductive by want of transit; but where transit is already as perfect as possible we find production hindered most by uncertainties which cannot be touched by transit, and which arise from the very policy that starts the "development" theory. The industrial capitalist among us seems unable to count on settled conditions for six months at a time, and so it must remain as long as his normal sphere of activity is "free" to be upset by any accidental clearance at any accidental price throughout the world, alike in cauliflowers and in calico. To-day our producer finds himself able to make a profit; to-morrow he finds his profit stopped and his capital threatened by an industrial accident at Taganrog or Dakota. This State bolstering of transit is essentially in the nature of protection for home industry, and so we find ourselves protecting the carriage of what cannot be produced, and exposing to decay the production of what is producible.

There was another private meeting of the Imperial Home Rule Association in Dublin on Wednesday night, to consider their action in view of their treasurer having gone over to Mr. Redmond as his candidate for South Dublin, while remaining their treasurer. Since the Imperials alarmed "the boys" with their loyalty to the Empire, and the dread of this getting abroad in Ireland, there has been a scramble to annex the head men; and there has been a scramble among the head men to get themselves annexed. There is really no need to "consider". The course for the Imperials is clear. Let them get another set of head men, and let these also be taken over by "the boys", all protesting their loyalty to the Empire; and so on until all "the boys" shall have become loyal, and the Irish party is improved out of existence. Then we have Home Rule as a proposition in Imperialism. Meantime, for men of ambition it is worth knowing that the way to a place among "the boys" and to a "sait" in the House is to become a head man of the Imperials; that is, imperialism as a means to parochialism.

Lord Ashtown is expected to make a speech in the House of Lords on the Land Bill, and his experience as a boycotted farmer in Galway ought to make lively material for Mr. Birrell. With all the "peace", it takes about £1000 a year of the taxes to protect Lord Ashtown; and his offence against "the Cause" is that he makes his farms profitable, with a handsome margin left over after allowing for rent and taxes, and after paying £3000 a year in agricultural wages. The plea of "the Cause" is that the land cannot bear rent. This capable capitalist of Galway finds farming so profitable that he can buy up incapable peasant proprietors and replace them by capable bullocks, showing how the land can be turned back again into big farms at a profit should peace be permitted after the Treasury has staked nearly £200,000,000 in making small farms. It is a most upsetting affair, this Woodlawn enterprise, to statesmen as well as to agitators; and the Peers will do well to listen carefully. There is far-reaching instruction in the Galway balance-sheets, and they have all been professionally audited.

Our little note about that Industrial Conference in Belfast, where hopeful producers advertised their products to a decaying market, has caused widespread indignation in Ireland, with leading articles of the most red-hot kind, and full reproductions of Mr. Boland's letter to the SATURDAY REVIEW—but without the few lines that were added under it. This is the old rage that ever prevents the people of Ireland from seeing facts as they affect themselves. If facts are pleasant, all is well; if not, away with them, and down with "the nation". They do not yet see that Ireland's purchasing power, for either home products or imports, remains small until she learns to produce the means with which to purchase them; and they are equally ignorant of the fact that a country can increase her exports and imports while producing less and growing poorer. This has been Ireland's case for some time, and the proofs are beyond question; but Mr. Boland cannot see it, and the patriotic editors suppress the facts that correct him. If a people dare not face the truth even in their industry, how can they be expected to make progress in anything?

Has Mr. John Burns really been translated? Many rumours have been spread and have found their way into the papers, as to his silence on the Budget. He certainly has kept his enthusiasm for it under control. Whilst Mr. Burns seems never out of his Government Office, Mr. Churchill seems never in it; the one, it is complained, will attend to nothing but his own business, the other to nothing but the business of other Ministers. And yet, oddly enough, it is said they are both playing for their own hands! As to Mr. Burns and the Budget, we do not profess to know at all how he regards it. But let our people make no mistake about this: when the time comes for an election, Mr. Burns, like Mr. Churchill and Mr. Lloyd George and the rest of them, will go into the business with professions of out-and-out democracy. The statesman of to-day on the Government side will be the socialist of to-morrow—if to-morrow bring the General Election.

There is nothing surer in the world of party politics than this. It is all very reasonable for the "Spectator" and other Unionist journals to praise Mr. Burns and others who for the moment are playing the game of statesmanship, but it is dead sure that when the moment comes for Mr. Burns to touch the hearts anew of his friends in back streets of Battersea, he will have to take off his Court dress and "go in bald-headed". It will not do for him even to slip on a great-coat over the Court dress, as he does when he goes to see the unemployed waiting for their soup, for in this case a bit of the gold might show, which would be fatal. With one or two exceptions the moderates will go into the coming General Election as Jacobins, and some of the Jacobins will go in as Hébertists.

Party politics have lost a pathetic figure in Lord Tweedmouth. The last few years of his life were crushing with grief. "The cares of the world" laid hold of him with a vengeance, and we should say that few of his friends are sorry he is past all that. He was not a most attractive man to those who did not know him or did not know him well; and his somewhat assertive voice and manner in the lobbies and elsewhere scarcely gave the idea that he was refined or sensitive. But his intimates, we believe, can tell a very different story. And we all knew him as a brave man and a man who cared for and honoured his country. In the very cruel accumulation of his misfortunes is something suggestive of fate not blind but malign—the sort of fell malignity one is oppressed by in Hardy's stories.

At the Wolfe dinner on Monday night Colonel Seely announced a discovery that "we were a great people". The discovery had been made "a few years ago", not by the gallant politician, but by "a farm labourer". It concerned a dead hero of ours, and the labourer said of him "He died for a good cause, and they was brave men as killed 'im". Then the statesman saw that we were "great". There are several other instructive discoveries awaiting him, but farm labourers like this are not met every day. With others as well as the Colonel, the main theme was the proof of our greatness in "shaking hands with a brave foe when we have conquered him"; not one word from the standpoint of the other fellow, his readiness to shake hands with his conqueror when he is conquered. There is no greater cause for foreigners misunderstanding us than this national defect in our mental objectivity, which the Colonel illustrates so well.

The speech of the Kaiser at Karlsruhe on Saturday strikes a true note; and the ears which on such occasions are bent carefully down to detect a false ring will hardly be gratified unless they be of that peculiar quality which hears nothing but what it wants to hear. Once more the army is soberly declared to be the rock upon which peace is built. A feeling of national security is the best safeguard against unneighbourly suspicion and the chances of panic. Such propositions are self-evident, but they need to be stated. Until a nation can declare itself to be kriegsspielfreudig, it cannot be said to know the blessings of peace—a paradox which is a truism.

The Young Egypt Congress at Geneva has done its best to show how completely unfit its members are for independence and autonomy. Mr. Keir Hardie's presence alone would suffice to put them out of court. But, as though more were wanting, the delegates must needs welcome certain Irish Nationalists as frères d'infortune. How far the Egyptians enjoyed the rhetoric of Messrs. Hardie and Kettle we do not know—they probably found the subsequent excursion on the lake a refreshing contrast—but we are quite sure Messrs. Keir Hardie and Kettle were full of enthusiasm for the speeches in Arabic. Those in French they possibly did not follow. Ireland must be a little jealous of Egypt. She has been fighting for Home Rule for the best part of a century: Egypt has only lately awoke to her rights, and the Young Egyptian announces that he will get them soon. Nor will he suffer the indignity of asking them of Great Britain. He will get them from the Khedive direct. Such a snub England will feel keenly.

Lord Kitchener is the youngest Field-Marshal of modern times, not excepting Lord Wolseley. He is not yet sixty, so we may hope he will serve the Empire for at least another ten years. The mystery as to his new appointment does not clear. Mr. Haldane shelters himself behind the general statement that the time is not yet ripe for revelations. The truth seems this—the Government do not wish to have Lord Kitchener at their side. He is not a lover of shams. By placing him at Malta, and charging him with the inspection of all the troops in the African continent, they have given him plenty to do elsewhere than in Whitehall. If this be their object, they have got the wrong man.

Great Britain, thinks Lord Dudley, is still first in the world's markets, but is losing her lead year by year. Recognition of that accounts for the preponderance of opinion among the delegates of the Chambers of Commerce of the Empire and the striking confession of Sir Albert Spicer, the President of the Sydney Congress, that he would vote for the preference resolution though personally opposed to it. The free traders among the delegates made an appeal, hardly less significant, that the mother-country should be allowed to decide for herself what is best in her own interests. The desire throughout the Empire for commercial reciprocity is quickened with every meeting of the business men of the Empire. The next Imperial Conference should be solid for preference.

The report of the Tariff Commission issued on Thursday morning takes the work a long step further, and affords grave study for those who say that Protective countries cannot export with success. For example, from 1895 to 1907 Germany's exports of manufactures into our colonies increased 135 per cent., and those of the United States 315 per cent.; while our own increased only 95 per cent., though our colonies make substantial concessions in our favour. The report is rich in instructive things like this.

The demand for aviators seems to exceed the supply; at least they find it so at Boulogne. Captain Ferber is the only competitor this luckless enterprise has succeeded in attracting. There is a warning here for stage managers in a new line of business. The stars must be booked well in advance. At Brescia this was done; and the meeting has been strikingly successful, especially from the point of view of Mr. Curtiss, to whom it brought new laurels. Meanwhile neither M. Latham nor M. Blériot seems to like Wembley, and there is small prospect of a performance there. Our condolences this week are asked for Mr. Cody, who has damaged himself and his machine rather badly. Mr. Cody is all the more in need of public sympathy, as official sympathy does not seem to have been offered to him with a liberality at all in proportion to his importance.

Commander Peary and Dr. Cook will have to make haste or they may find that people have grown a little tired of them before they have cleared accounts. They deserve to go a little into the background as a penalty for having contrived to make themselves more interesting than was at all necessary. Since Dr. Cook challenged discussion by his deviousness, and Commander Peary deafened all ears by the vigour of his self-announcement, there has been no rest for anybody. Now, although we have both accounts substantially complete, the personal question remains exactly where it was. One thing alone is certain. Peary must "nail" Cook or beg pardon.

Meanwhile, it would be well if the people in this country, who have just shown such marked interest in Arctic exploration, were to turn from what has been done by America to what remains to be done by Great Britain. Next summer Captain Scott is to go to the Antarctic to continue the work of Lieutenant Shackleton. Though the immediate aim of the expedition is the establishment of a new base from which the Pole may be more easily approached, yet the Pole is always there to be discovered, and, if it is discovered this time, it will be by motor sledge. British enterprise has achieved such swift results in the South, that it is only fitting that it should proceed to a worthy conclusion. But £40,000 is required. Perhaps those journals which have made money out of the American discovery would like to head the subscription list.

On Wednesday at Lichfield was celebrated the bicentenary of Dr. Johnson. It does not seem two hundred years since Dr. Johnson was born. He is so very much nearer to us than scores of other people whose centenaries we are just clear of having celebrated. His proximity is easily explained. Dr. Johnson does not live by his books. Few read the "Lives of the Poets", fewer still consult the Dictionary; though both are works of classic excellence. He does not live by his deeds, or by his opinions. Deeds have a way of throwing doers into the shadow; and opinions grow speedily old. He lives by his conversation, in the widest sense of that word; by the play of his personality upon other personalities.

To say that he found a Boswell does not explain him. It was the fortunate accident that brought the born biographer into contact with the born subject for biography which has to be thanked for that "Life of Johnson". It so happened that at a certain period of English social history a man existed who reacted vigorously and articulately to all the ideas and prejudices of his age, and that at the same happy time another man was found to devote himself body and soul to the observation of these multifarious reactions; a man who, for posterity's sake, was content to be kicked, that he might record the manner of the kicking. The result was that perfect piece of life, which is as near to us to-day as it was to those who saw some of the actual living.

As for Lord Rosebery's address on Johnson, we wish it had not been quite so good. We sat up very late after a heavy day's work and read it in the pamphlet form which Mr. Humphreys has just published; and one pays for such indiscretions next morning. There is nobody who can touch Lord Rosebery in these literary exercises. In this Johnson address there was not a touch too much and not a touch too little. It is better than his "Pitt", which we have read half a dozen times despite Lord Acton's angry criticism of the book as spurious history.

A million and a quarter copies of Lord Rosebery's Glasgow speech were sold by Wednesday, and the thing is still selling. Yet the Radical critics insist that Lord Rosebery is followed by nobody; that he is wholly ineffectual and vapid"! But in truth the speech has been a great success. We hope, by the way, that no host or hostess was troubled in vain at Glasgow. At Chesterfield, at the time of the great speech there, a leading family understood it was to entertain Lord Rosebery, and made tremendous preparations to do the thing well. All the people were turned out of their rooms, the house was upside down. At the last moment it was announced that the great man was going back south by special train after the speech. It is bad enough entertaining angels, but to make in vain preparations to entertain them is quite too much.

LORD ROSEBERY'S MANIFESTO.

LORD ROSEBERY'S speech at Glasgow is a stimulating reminder that the art of political oratory is not yet extinct. It is at the same time a tantalising example to our hustled and scuffling statesmen of the necessity of leisure for the preparation of an effective manifesto. How our worn-out House of Commons leaders must envy Lord Rosebery the opportunity of thinking, not only what he shall say, but how he shall say it! Long ago Lord Chesterfield pointed out to his son that the subject-matter of politics is common property; the facts are equally known and almost equally accessible to all who "meddle with the government of men". As that acute philosopher observed, what makes the difference between a good and a bad speech is not superior information, but the style in which the facts are marshalled and the manner of the speaker. Lord Rosebery knows no more about the Budget than any member of Parliament or political journalist. He could not give us any new information; but he put familiar propositions in a new setting, and said what he had to say in a manner that no other living statesman can surpass. The Glasgow speech is full of mordant, portable phrases that will linger in the mind. The Radicals can find nothing to say against the speech except that Lord Rosebery was not a successful party leader and that he is a landowner. It is true that Lord Rosebery did fail as a leader of Jacobins, but that is partly because he has the judicial mind, like the last Lord Derby but one, and partly because he had the misfortune to stray into the wrong party when he was young. As for his landlordism, we must repeat his own query: When did the landowners become criminals and pariahs? Mr. Asquith may put in a good party answer to Lord Rosebery. But Mr. Lloyd George's simile of "the soft-nosed torpedo" only deepens the disgust with which grave and decent men regard the levity of the Chancellor of the Exchequer.

Lord Rosebery cruelly, but with perfect accuracy, characterised the Budget as "a long and haphazard catalogue of impositions" and as "a revolution without a mandate". These latter words seem to us to indicate, as clearly as language can, what the House of Lords ought, in Lord Rosebery's opinion, to do with the Budget. A revolution without a mandate is obviously a catastrophe which can only be prevented by a reference to the electors. Yet because Lord Rosebery stated what everybody knows, namely, that he is not the leader of the House of Lords, and that, as he has always been in a minority in that assembly, he cannot assume the responsibility of advising it as to its action, it has been triumphantly proclaimed by the Radicals that he is opposed to the rejection of the Bill. This is indeed the perversity of a frightened faction. When a statesman says that it is "not in the best interests of the nation that this financial measure should pass" he must mean that it should be rejected, or he means nothing. One of Lord Rosebery's most skilful hits, in the picturesque line, was his deputation of the present Cabinet with the Bill in their hands to a centenarian Mr. Gladstone—"they would soon find themselves on the stairs, if not in the street". Bitterly as we opposed Mr. Gladstone in his life, let us pay this tribute to his character: he would never have stooped to the use of finance as "a weapon to solve constitutional problems"; he would never have condescended to wield the Budget as a scourge for the backs of his political opponents.

Lord Rosebery went straight to the heart of the matter when he showed that the only sincere and logical justification of the otherwise absurd taxes on land is that private property in land is wrong. Mr. Lloyd George and his unofficial lieutenants, Mr. Keir Hardie and Mr. Snowden, are all avowed nationalisers of land. If this be not the basis of the Budget, then all the arguments for the confiscation of unearned increment apply irresistibly to all kinds of property, to Consols as well as to dirty acres. There are some Radicals who are in favour of "expanding" the doctrine of unearned increment so as to include money and shares. Not, we think, very many, because there are too many captains of industry in the Radical party, too many Brunners and Monds and

Pearsons and Furnesses—to say nothing of their latest acquisition, Baron de Forest—who would not relish this kind of logic when applied to their millions of share certificates and bonds to bearer. Mr. Henry, the bosom friend of the Chancellor of the Exchequer, might also resent his dealings in copper being treated as unearned increment. So that for the present, at all events, we think that money and shares, and all that is called in Bankruptcy Buildings " rash and hazardous speculation ", are safe from Mr. Lloyd George. But only for the present, because Mr. Chiozza-Money, in the debate on the death duties on Monday, explained with a candour that arrested Mr. Balfour's attention the collectivist idea that the State can spend an individual's income better than he can himself. As an antidote to such doctrines Lord Rosebery did well to expound to the business men of Glasgow the basic theory of all civilisation, namely, that the State guarantees the undisturbed enjoyment of their property to its citizens. Civilised men surrender to the State their natural right to defend their persons and their property with their own hands. But the consideration for taxes and obedience is the protection of property, and if the State not only fails to perform its part of the bargain, but practises robbery, society is dissolved into its original elements, and civil war supervenes. The latter is not quite so impossible an event as some people imagine. The Northern and Southern States went to war about a question of property, nominally about State rights, in reality about the ownership of slaves. It is not difficult to imagine a country like our own embarking on a civil war about the ownership of land.

We are glad that Lord Rosebery had the courage to attack " sans phrase " the death duties, which he described as " the gravest part of the Budget ". There is too much disposition on the part of Conservatives—we noticed it in Mr. Balfour's speech on Monday—to apologise for opposing these duties. Unionists as a rule are so anxious to show their willingness to pay that the death duties are handled in the most gingerly fashion. We agree with Lord Rosebery that this taking chunks of capital out of the national store and wasting it for the most part on such unremunerative objects as official salaries, is one of the most objectionable features of the Budget. But it is part of the Socialist programme to multiply salaried officials, who become, as in France and in the United States, election agents of the Government. To the financial theorist income tax appears to be as much a subtraction from capital as the death duties. In theory it is so; but in practice it is not. It is an interesting historical fact that Sir William Harcourt resorted to death duties because he thought a graduated income tax impossible. Lord Rosebery was Prime Minister at the time, and he now tells us that his Chancellor of the Exchequer saw no way of differentiating between earnings and inheritance but by a scale of death duties. But Mr. Lloyd George rushes in where Sir William Harcourt feared to tread; and we have both a graduated income tax and expanded death duties. To make the death duties an important part of the revenue is to live on the national capital, to spend it as income. Does it never occur to these Socialist financiers that in the event of war there may be no reserve to draw upon?

With the unerring hand of a master Lord Rosebery touched a chord in our national character when he dwelt upon the inquisitorial proceedings which this haphazard catalogue of impositions will necessitate. Chatham's saying was none the less impressive because of its familiarity. A really good quotation ought to be an old friend in a new light. The clause which proposed to make gifts " inter vivos " for a period of five years before death liable to duty was so preposterous that we could not believe it would stand. " For five years before death, according to the provisions of the Government, you are to live under death's icy hand. You may be walking about physically well, physically as other men, but financially you are a ghost." Alarmed by the revolt of two or three Liberals, the Government modified this clause. A man is only to be like Sir Aylmer Aylmer—dead for three years before his death. This striking and humorous passage in Lord Rosebery's speech led up to a fine peroration about the tyranny of Socialism and an impassioned plea for individual liberty, already we fear a lost cause, a forsaken belief. Only the coming election can show whether these fears are groundless. If the result of that election should set the seal of popular approval upon this tyrannous and inquisitorial taxation, then we can only say, with Lord Rosebery, that the character of the British nation is much changed.

"YOUR MONEY OR YOUR LAND."

If Ministers were still practising concealment of their animus against the country gentleman, the last rag of pretence was thrown away when Mr. Lloyd George suggested that land may be taken in satisfaction of the death duties. The idea has been embodied in one of the new clauses awaiting the attention of the House of Commons. A great effort, we think, should be made to defeat the proposal. It was not to make things easy for the new squire that the Chancellor of the Exchequer adopted this insidious afterthought. The object is to break up the inheritance. Nor is the trap unskilfully prepared. Rather than raise a lump sum of money which can only be repaid after several years of self-denial, the incomer may be tempted to " cut off a great chunk of his estate " and hand it over to the tax-collector—in the hope of enjoying the remainder without debt or incumbrance. There are, of course, many properties that comprise outlying or disconnected pieces which it may be more profitable to part with than to retain. But in such cases the owner, if he had no cash at his bank, would naturally sell them and thus discharge the Treasury claims. There would be no occasion for him to pay his taxes in kind. The debtor to whom Mr. Lloyd George wishes to apply the screw is the man who has come into a reasonably compact and self-sufficing estate. The value of the whole would be quite disproportionately impaired by the sale of a part. Here the tax-collector has the squire at his mercy, and may be trusted, with his highly developed sense of professional duty, to drive an unconscionable bargain. Practically he can dictate terms, for the State debtor knows that a tenth part, say, of his acreage would not fetch ten per cent. of the market value put upon the whole estate.

In considering this scheme we have confined ourselves to the case of agricultural land, since it has little or no application to urban property. The possessor of ordinary town sites and buildings, whether in large or small quantities, is a comparatively free agent. He can deal almost at pleasure with his possessions. Where, again, there are more or less continuous estates, like those belonging to the Duke of Westminster or Bedford, the question of impecuniosity should not arise. It would be a regular part of the chief agent's business to provide against such an emergency. Nor is he likely to be caught napping by the Treasury. Very different is the position of the country gentleman, whether on the grand or petty scale, who, even if he were a trained man of business, would not, as a rule, be able to negotiate on equal terms, since the other party, as creditor, could use a very cogent form of pressure. No wonder that in the debate on Monday afternoon in the House of Commons a vigorous protest was made by Mr. Evelyn Cecil. In his pleasant, smiling way Mr. Haldane tried to put the question by, and passed on to what he thought were less uncomfortable topics.

" Land nationalisation is bound to come ", so Mr. Lloyd George has declared, " but it must come by easy stages ", and one of those stages, it seems, is whittling away the country gentlemen's estates. What the State will do with these scattered plots and patches of land is a question that the Chancellor of the Exchequer has, perhaps, not asked himself. Probably they would be handed over, after several months of circumlocution between the Treasury and the Board of Agriculture, into Lord Carrington's keeping. He would be instructed, perhaps, to co-operate with the various county councils concerned and carve the annexed territories into small holdings. Or, again, these odds and ends of farms might be treated as objects for the Development Fund and generally advertised in majorem Ll. Georgii gloriam. The one thing certain about their destiny is that in no wise could these State lands be made to pay their way. But it was for no such humdrum banausic purpose that they would have been acquired. The object of the whole operation is to further the general policy of exasperating, impoverishing, and turning adrift the country gentleman.

So far as a single motive may be discerned in the course of the Campbell-Bannerman-Asquith Administration it has been found in the humiliation of the County and pampering the snobbish villadom of the towns. This was the meaning of the Act for reducing the qualifications of county magistrates, so that any little social climber who had made himself useful to the Liberal party could be admitted to rub shoulders with gentlemen. Altering the law was not enough: an organisation in the House of Commons (in membership largely identical with the reduction-of-armaments group) was formed and kept up for the express purpose of applying pressure to the Lord Chancellor. Happily, at the outset, it managed to stroke Lord Loreburn's fur the wrong way. That easily ruffled politician and excellent sportsman flatly and repeatedly declined to flood the bench with political nominees. Although, quite properly, he has taken care that the claims of presentable Liberals should not be overlooked (as in too many counties had been the case), he has fairly well maintained the standard of personal merit and dignity. For this "treason to Liberalism" he has been maliciously attacked, sometimes with open and clumsy upbraiding, but more often with sympathetic paragraphs to the effect that his obviously failing health would very soon necessitate his retirement. In spite of these delicately conveyed suggestions, the self-confident and straightforward gentleman whom all Oxford cricketers affectionately remember has gone on and intends to remain as wicket-keep for the team.

It was, undoubtedly, because the county councils in England and Scotland are largely manned and still more largely influenced by country gentlemen that the Government have aimed a series of blows at local government. One of the reasons why the Scottish Small Landholders Bill was rejected by the House of Lords, after it had been mercilessly shown up by Lord Rosebery, was that the county councils were to be placed under official tutelage. In the corresponding English measure the same feature has been successfully inserted, and was made the subject of vulgar boasting by Mr. Winston Churchill. All this was of a piece with the taking over of Mr. Agar Robartes' Land Tenure Bill, an elaborate scheme for setting up an incomprehensible tenants-right system in England which could be fruitful in nothing but litigation and quarrels between landlords and tenants. It happened, however, that the Ministers who had charge of it were somewhat conspicuously ignorant of country matters, and the Bill, before it reached Lord Carrington and was converted into an ordinary Agricultural Holdings Act Amendment Act, had been transformed into a fairly inoffensive example of superfluous legislation. Not such was the idea with which the Government started, for Sir Henry Campbell-Bannerman and his confidential advisers, Lord Pentland and Mr. Churchill, should not be cheated of such credit as is due to men taking service against the class to which they belong.

From the sweeping success which the Liberals made at the general election in the counties they seem to be strengthened in their inveterate belief that they can always win the labourers' vote if they rail at the squire and parson. We shall see. The results of recent contests in rural districts have not been encouraging to the fomenters of village strife. So far, there is no evidence that the peasantry are overcome with gratitude to the party which has set up a few of their number, not always of the highest local reputation, in rather dubious small holdings, and dribbled out pensions to some old folk. Not even when the sum of the Government's rural achievements has been swollen with the Development Grant Act will anything have been done to justify the grand and mendacious promises with which the Radicals bought their way into power.

GERMANY AND SEA-POWER.

EVERYONE deplores the costly race in armaments between Great Britain and Germany; everyone would welcome some agreement whereby a limit might be set to the ever-growing expenditure on warships. It is common knowledge that the British Government took the initiative in suggesting negotiations and that the German Government refused to entertain the suggestion; so many have jumped to the conclusion that the German is a quarrelsome fellow to whom we may one day have to teach a lesson at the sword's point. As a fact neither the German people nor the German Government are hopelessly Chauvinistic, but the most disquieting feature in the present situation is that the British authorities are only prepared to do a deal on terms which any patriotic German would think it positively dishonourable to accept. It may be regarded as certain that no British Government would conclude, and that no British Parliament would sanction, any agreement which did not ensure us an overwhelming naval superiority, represented by the two-Power standard or some equivalent formula. To invite the Germans to conclude a bargain under such conditions is, to German eyes, something of a humiliation. It is tantamount to the suggestion that Germany should accept a position of permanent and indisputable inferiority, and as such is emphatically repudiated by a great Empire always a little touchy as to its dignity.

There is thus revealed a fundamental difference between the British and the German attitudes towards the two-Power standard formula. To the Englishman it is something of a law of nature, as though the sea supremacy of Britain were established by the grace of God. To the German that same formula is a challenge to the world, which any Power determined to assert its independence must necessarily take up. It is a challenge which Germany in particular finds herself forced by her destiny to accept. Not only does she hold her over-sea possessions by the sufferance of Great Britain, in itself an irksome thing, but her position among the nations is permanently depressed by the silent and relentless influence of British sea-power. It is Germany's ambition—and it is not for us to condemn an ambition which we happen to find inconvenient—to become a world-power, and the most obvious sign of world-power is having a world trade. As things are now, Germany's inter-continental trade is largely dependent on British goodwill. If an outlet for German goods is found in the North Sea, Britain with her fleets lies clean across the main trade route. If an outlet be sought in the Mediterranean, Britain again possesses Gibraltar and controls the Suez Canal and is thus able to dominate the situation. And in case Germany should ever forget the precarious tenure under which she holds her place in the world's markets, she has the European history of the last two centuries to warn her that an extension of her seaboard westwards or an expansion to the Mediterranean would be regarded by Great Britain as casus belli. It is, indeed, the law of our national existence that we cannot allow the strongest land Power on the Continent to be master of the coast-line impinging on our sphere of influence. But it is not unnatural that the German should ask what right has Britain thus to enforce her will upon Europe in general and upon his own country in particular.

The mere assertion, then, of our naval superiority is not unnaturally regarded by many patriotic Germans as an act of defiance; but when that assertion takes the shape of the two-Power standard formula, defiance becomes changed into menace. To the English mind unassailable superiority is essential; to the German mind it is outrageous. For hundreds of miles the German frontier is coterminous with that of two great military Powers, but Germany has never presumed to establish a two-Power standard in army corps. A German army equal to the forces of France and Russia combined would be interpreted both by France and Russia as a threat, and Great Britain would scarcely dispute the interpretation. But if a German two-Power army is intolerable, wherein lies the justification of a British two-Power navy? Many a leading article in the German press has indignantly denounced the sheer hypocrisy of the British people in thus arrogating to themselves a preponderance which they would be the first to deny to an alien Power in another element. Again and again are German readers bidden to regard the British Navy as corresponding to the German Army, and the conclusion is pressed home that neither Britain at sea nor Germany on land may claim a position of absolute supremacy, but must be content to be first among equals.

The argument rests on the obvious fallacy that sea-power and land-power are in some way comparable, though, as every Englishman knows, a naval battle is far more decisive than any land fight can be. If Great Britain were to be defeated by an inferior sea Power, as she was defeated by an inferior land Power at the beginning of the South African war, she would be compelled to sue for peace. In the war with Japan Russia met with an unbroken series of defeats both ashore and afloat. But when the Treaty of Portsmouth was concluded her position on land was by no means hopeless, whereas her position at sea had been lost irretrievably. It would be easy to go through history multiplying instances of this elementary distinction between military and naval warfare. It is a distinction which the British people know well. Their experience has taught them that a land campaign may be successfully "muddled through", despite initial losses, but that the least mistake at sea means ruin. Unfortunately experience has taught the Germans no such lesson. They know that twice within half a century—first at Kunersdorf and afterwards at Jena—the power of Prussia was shattered as utterly as military power can be. They know that it was only a very few years before the defeated State was as strong as ever. But they do not know that there neither was nor could be any recuperation after the Nile or Trafalgar. Much irate and intolerant criticism would be avoided if it were remembered that many Germans have never seen the sea, that German history is practically empty of naval traditions, and that the average German is altogether destitute of that knowledge of the meaning of sea-power with which the average Englishman is endowed by instinct. Only when Germany has fought a naval war, only when she has realised that a single battle ends everything and that neither money nor patriotism is of the least avail, will she begin to understand that the two-Power standard represents no more than the minimum of British national and imperial safety, and carries with it not the least suggestion either of defiance or of menace.

No stronger illustration of the German ignorance of sea-power could be desired than the actual history of her naval development. Ten years ago she scarcely possessed a warship worth consideration. To-day she boasts a navy superior to any in Europe except our own. How did it come about that the German Empire, which for nearly a generation knew not the sea, attained so sudden a consciousness of its tremendous importance? Partly, no doubt, in virtue of the growth of German trade; partly through the acquisition of colonies; partly through an increased sense of imperial cohesion; but chiefly because of the action of Great Britain herself. In the early stages of the South African war certain German mail steamers were seized by British warships. The incident attracted little attention in this country and was thought to have been closed by the payment of compensation. But no one who was in Germany at the time can forget the storm of indignation which swept over the country. The seizure of the "Bundesrath" came indeed as a revelation to the German people, and, backed by the enthusiastic appeal of the Emperor, roused them from their false security. It must be remembered that Germany has no natural frontiers. Her only defences are the swords of her soldiers. When that safeguard has failed, and it has failed more than once, Germany has become the battle-ground of Europe. It is the first maxim of the new Germany, which came into being between 1806 and 1870, that German soil must be kept inviolate, and we, who have never seen the smoke of an enemy's camp-fire on English ground, can scarcely imagine how completely the German appreciates the fact that his army is the sole guarantee of national prosperity and even of national existence. The seizure of the German mail steamers ten years ago came like a thunderbolt. It suddenly brought home to the German people that they had yet another frontier to defend. It was as if Poland or Lorraine had been discovered to be denuded of troops. The danger was inevitably exaggerated by a people taught to think only in terms of land-power, but from the moment of its realisation the construction of a great German navy was inevitable. It is in vain to plead that the German people do not understand. The whole course of their history makes it impossible that they should understand, and they cannot now be reasoned into understanding. Only we must make allowances for the natural limitations of their point of view, that we may cease first to offer them terms which they must necessarily regard as degrading and then to misinterpret the grounds on which our proposals are rejected.

CITIZENS OF THE WORLD.

JOHNSON defined patriotism as the last refuge of a scoundrel. There are, it appears, Englishmen who are determined to give that refuge a wide berth. They are not sure that they relish being called Englishmen. Unlike George III., they do not glory in the name of Briton, or Britain—which is what the young monarch really wrote. They would have enjoyed finding themselves under the rule of the first George, who did not understand a word of English. We refer to certain speakers at the Trades Union Congress, who raised the question whether a trades unionist can call any country "my own, my native land". The awkward fact of some local nativity cannot be evaded. But the enlightened working man need not love it or acknowledge any duty towards it. He not only will not say, with the mere Conservative, "My country, right or wrong"; nor will he merely refuse to say, with the mere Liberal, "My country, and therefore always wrong"; for he ought not to say "My country" at all. The true proletarian has no patria, no propria tellus. For he belongs to a brotherhood of Internationals, banded in every clime and country to fight property and capital, and therefore he may call no land his own. When capital is driven out of one place it tries to take refuge elsewhere, as a coney ferreted out of one burrow dashes for safety to another. A Labour party, however, which knows its business will have stopped them all. Whithersoever on the face of the earth the investor betakes his accumulations, he must find the "workers" organised to relieve him of what he has saved and prevent him from saving any more.

There seems, at first sight, to be something monastic, ascetic in this idea of detachment from the ties and entanglements of country and of blood. The postulant desiring to be enrolled in the Company of Jesus had this duty of renunciation impressed upon him as his first lesson. The Franciscan went forth into the wide world, leaving home and kindred behind, that he might extend the universal kingdom of the Redeemer. There have been black and grey, as well as red, Internationals. And, without being Jesuit or friar, every Christian has been taught that he is a pilgrim in a land that is not his, compelled to "seek a country", and that, his citizenship being in heaven, he can here only exercise a lodger's franchise. In the early days of Christianity, it is true, this was brought home to ordinary men and women more strongly than it is nowadays. Was it not Tertullian who observed that the Christian is at home everywhere and an exile everywhere? And while the Church was still in the missionary stage, before the nations had brought their honour and glory into it, or the fowls of the air had come to lodge in its spreading branches, its universal, extra-territorial and international character was more plainly seen and emphasised. In the mystical Body there is neither Jew nor Greek, neither barbarian, Scythian, bond nor free. But even after the stooping of that which is Heavenly and from Above to mate with this, that and the other race or nationality, becoming bone of its bone and flesh of its flesh, growing into its life and taking up that life into itself, the difficulty of adjustment between the Catholic and the particular or national was, and still is, the pivot of history. At the Reformation the nationalist feeling and self-consciousness rose in revolt against the larger idea of a single Christendom. England especially succeeded in getting its religion off its own bat—for Scotland became an appendage of Geneva—and the Whig conception of an "established" or "national" Church has always been that of a parliamentary arrangement for reflecting the religious ideas and aspirations of the average ratepayer. Nevertheless, the Church of England has managed fairly successfully to assert her own origination from and part and lot in the universal Fellowship and its quod semper, quod ubique, quod ab omnibus.

Then, again, there are the Jews and the Gypsies and the Freemasons. And though, ever since the days of Byron, Liberalism has made a speciality of the independence of small nationalities—Greece, the Balkan States, Poland, Ireland, Finland, the Boers—yet, really and truly, Cosmopolitanism rather than Home Rule is the Liberal ideal. The lives and passions and interests of men are thought of as homogeneous, like water always finding its own level, and Humanity is regarded, not as a succession of land-locked seas and lakes, but as a great ocean laving every shore, one and indivisible. There is something grand in that notion, and it need not necessarily imply a formless monotony if we could think of the ocean merely as filling and glorifying and uniting an endless variety of diversified gulfs and bays and lochs and firths and inlets. As a matter of fact, the Cosmopolitanism of Liberal thought has been an ugly thing, effacing the beauty and interest of the multicoloured universe. It has meant a single world-market, a single type of hideous dress, a uniform dullness of thought, and it is trying to impose on mankind a common lingua franca gibberish. But the doctrine of the solidarity of the human race need not necessarily do this. Only we would remind Liberals that the Brotherhood of Man and the common bond of Humanity is a mystical and spiritual idea—quite as much a religious dogma as anything in the Athanasian Creed.

Our friends the trades unionists, however, do not trouble themselves with any such conceptions. The internationality which they aim at is based not on community of faith or community of blood, but on community of interest. Nor is their solemn league and covenant an alliance for self-protection of the poor and miserable. Trades unionists are well-paid working men who are trying to become bourgeois. They have not the least intention of lifting up the hands that hang down or strengthening the feeble knees. Their one aim is to smash Capital. And, as Capital knows nothing of the kindred points of heaven and home, Labour must equally be detached from those points. It is to turn its back on United Italy and Yankee Doodle and England, my England. "Love thou thy land", we used to be told, "with love far-brought from out the storied past"; love and revere the strong mother of a lion-line, lifting her rocky face to storm and sea and streaming torrent. And then we were bidden to pledge the loyal hearts who long to keep our English Empire whole, the strong New England of the South, the England under Indian skies and the dark millions of her realm, and so forth.

"Hands all round!
God the traitor's hope confound!
To this great name of England drink, my friends,
And all her glorious empire, round and round!"

No doubt that was all very mid-Victorian, but we seem to remember Shakespeare had something handsome to say about this sceptred isle, this other Eden, demi-paradise, this precious stone set in the silver sea, this blessed plot, this earth, this realm, this England, this nurse, this teeming womb of royal kings. Shakespeare lived, however, in an unenlightened epoch, and had he been a trades unionist he would probably have expressed himself very differently.

The first duty of Labour being to sit loosely to all ties of race and country, to expatriate and forisfamiliate itself, it leaves patriotism—England and so forth—to the dukes. Exiles returning from antipodean lands, men of Anglo-Saxon breed who have never before visited the Old Country, have spoken of the strained gaze, the beating heart, and the eyes filled with tears, with which the far-off cliffs of England have been first descried. It would seem, however, that to-day no one can have that feeling for his country upon less than two pounds a week. The duty of "doing for" Capital forbids it. The outcome of an age of altruism is class-war to the death, and "homo homini lupus" is the humanitarian's creed.

THE CITY.

THE course of prices has justified our statement last week that Mr. Harriman's death need cause no panic amongst holders of American securities. Anticipating the end, Mr. Harriman made every preparation, and no sooner was he dead than all the leaders of Wall Street finance came forward to combat any attempts that might be made to break up the market. Extraordinary results have followed, prices not only being sustained, but in many cases advancing above the level of a week ago. There have been sharp fluctuations, and at one time Union Pacific dropped about $10, but the net result is as stated. So far as the roads lately controlled by Mr. Harriman are concerned, there is reason to believe that Mr. Harriman's policy will in the main be steadily pursued by his successors. There may, and probably will, be less conservatism in the distribution of profits, but the internal management will be pursued on the old lines, and nothing is likely to be done to interrupt the progress of the last few years. Good internal management, however, cannot control Stock Exchange prices, and it yet remains to be seen whether the remaining powers will deem it politic or profitable to continue that support to the market which Mr. Harriman was able and willing to extend in times of crises. To gauge the future of the American market we must know what is to be the course of money in New York—and this it is impossible to ascertain or predict with any certainty. At the moment funds there are as plentiful as in London. Presently, however, money will be wanted to move the crops, and rates for accommodation will rise. Provided the rise is only normal, the stock market will not be materially affected. But if rates advance above the normal, then money which is now finding employment in Wall Street will be called in, and the chief support of the market will be withdrawn. In preparing for this contingency it is well to bear in mind that New York is now very largely indebted to Europe as a result of loans obtained on bonds and bills, that the creation of these is proceeding, and that Europe may not always be willing to continue the accommodation. London has indeed looked askance at American bills since the crisis in 1907, and as the year proceeds and money here begins to grow dearer, the difficulty of placing paper will increase. On the other hand, we have to remember that the crops in the United States have still to be gathered, that the harvest promises to be a very good one, and that the money which will have to be paid by Europe in purchase of grain and other food-stuffs will go a long way to set off this indebtedness.

The beginning of the gold drain to Egypt reminds us that the cotton crop of that country is far above the average, and that the higher prices obtainable may necessitate the withdrawal from the Bank of England of between three and four million sovereigns. Happily the Bank is in a very strong position and can spare all this amount without serious inconvenience. Unfortunately, however, the Bank is not adding to its supply of gold, except by obtaining sovereigns for which there is no immediate use in the country, and these will be called back as the year draws to a close. Of the monthly shipments of two millions or thereabouts from South Africa the Bank is getting no proportion. First Austria and now Russia is absorbing the supply, and so the Bank is accumulating nothing against the demands which will be made upon it from countries other than Egypt, South America probably being the most persistent. Russia may not long continue to take the metal, and the Bank may yet get a good deal of South African gold before the year is out; but, if not, we must prepare for higher money rates in Lombard Street. We should probably get them in a modified degree if the trade of the country improved, but while the indications now are favourable to an expansion in business it is difficult to foresee what the course will be if a General Election should come upon us in the next two months. A political crisis would interfere with trade, though when it was over the reaction would be proportionately great.

Surprise is expressed that the slight improvement reported in trade finds no reflection in the traffic returns of home railways. Week after week heavy decreases are recorded. The fact is that the improvement so far is largely on paper. Manufacturers have been buying more freely, but the country generally has not been spending more, and so there is no increased movement of goods traffic on the railways.

INSURANCE AT LOW PREMIUMS—VI.

IN the first of these articles on life-assurance policies at low premiums we described term insurance, which provides for the payment of the sum insured in the event of death only if it occurs within a specified term. There is a chance, but no certainty, of a claim arising under the policy, wherefore we call it "insurance", as distinct from "assurance", which may be used for forms of policies that are sure to result in a claim at some time or other, provided the payment of premiums is kept up.

There is another form of policy which involves a chance, but not a certainty, of resulting in a claim. It is appropriately called "contingent survivorship", and provides for the payment of the sum insured on the death of one person if he dies before another specified individual, and only in these circumstances. Since there is only a chance, but no certainty, of a claim resulting the rate of premium is very low, and policies of this kind may be taken with advantage when, for example, a man wants to make provision for his wife should he die first, but in the event of his survivance has no particular need for insurance. If a man and his wife are both aged thirty-five an annual premium of £18 7s. 6d., payable only so long as both of them are living, secures £1000 for the wife should the husband die first. A non-profit whole-life policy for £1000 effected at the same age would cost £22 10s. a year and would involve the payment of premiums throughout the whole of life if the full benefit of the policy was to be obtained. These policies are seldom to be recommended, however, when the ages of the two lives are approximately equal, and their chief value is for cases where reversionary interests are concerned. Thus if a man of thirty is sure to come into some money on the death of a man of sixty, provided the younger man survives the elder, but not otherwise, the contingent reversion can be made the equivalent of an absolute reversion by taking a policy of this kind. The annual premium for the insurance of £1000 in the event of a man of thirty dying before one of sixty is £12 6s. 8d., payable so long as they are both living. A policy of this kind makes possible the sale or mortgage of a contingent reversion. If the younger man survives to inherit the property the buyer or the lender is secure: if the elder man survives the younger, the latter never coming into the property and having no power to dispose of it by will or otherwise, the policy provides the equivalent of the money he would come into under the reversion if he lived.

Another form of life assurance that is useful in exceptional cases is concerned with two, or it may be more, lives in a different way. Take, for example, two brothers, who so long as either of them live can afford to support their sister, but if they both died she would be unprovided for. A last-survivor policy, assuming both brothers to be thirty-five years of age, would cost only £15 a year for the assurance of £1000, which would be paid after the second death. This again is not a policy which is frequently advisable, but there are cases which it suits admirably; the reason for the premium being so low is that the probable date of death is a good deal later than if only one life is concerned.

Another method of providing adequate insurance protection at a low rate of premium is applicable to policies of almost every kind. The lowness of the premium is apparent rather than real, but the system has some practical utility. Instead of assuring for £1000, a policy can be taken which assures the payment of £50 a year for twenty years. It is true the beneficiaries receive altogether £1000 in this way, but the value of this benefit is only equivalent to £750 in cash at death. In effect the policy is for £750 instead of for £1000, but £50 a year for twenty years is nearly as good as, and sometimes better than, £1000 in cash, especially when there is a chance of the money being invested foolishly.

A valuable adjunct to a policy payable by instalments in this way can be secured at a small additional premium. The contract with the assurance company can be that while £50 a year, or its equivalent value in cash, will be paid to the estate of the policyholder, yet if some named beneficiary survive the assured by more than twenty years the income of £50 a year will be continued to that beneficiary so long as he, or more frequently she, survives. The least that can be paid is twenty instalments, while there is a possibility of the instalments being much more numerous. If a man dies when his wife is thirty-five, and she lives till eighty, she will receive the £50 a year for forty-five years.

CRICKET.

THERE comes a day in the year when on the sporting page of the morning paper cricket and football intelligence—for so it is called—appear in juxtaposition. It is an evil day. That unholy alliance means, first, the end of summer; second, it means the beginning of those innumerable league matches with their enormous following, the size of which constitutes the pride of those who, without being sportsmen themselves, talk of England as a country of sportsmen, the despair of those who, being sportsmen, realise the place of sport in life and see that you will seek it in vain in the professional football enclosure. This year the transition was especially noteworthy owing to the football dispute, which made it doubtful whether the football season was really to be allowed to begin. The rights of that quarrel will be variously judged, but one thing is certain: a game has forfeited its right to be a game in the true sense of the word when the considerations of which the dispute was the outcome are allowed to find a place. Well, professional football has reached that unenviable goal, and it is a warning. Cricket must not be allowed to travel even a step down that steep road of perdition. It must continue to be founded in the first place on the amateur, and in the second place it must remain in the strictest sense immutably territorial. Directly a game becomes professional and nothing else, the number of players decreases, and in a word you may say that the ideal of professionalism becomes the provision of a spurious pleasure by the smallest number for the greatest. "We work in order to play" said the Greek Anacharsis, and he did well to emphasise the contradiction between the two terms in his saying, and to point to the ideal whereby all should play for love in order to work and none for money in order to live.

We have often said there is a danger lest the amateur disappear more and more from first-class cricket. He is being extinguished by the exacting claims of first-class cricket as now played. During this year, with the Australians in England, one has been able to see the apotheosis of the modern cricket programme. One has also heard of the monotony of Australian cricket, of the hasty stoppages for rain, their tea intervals, and general delays. The two do not stand isolated; but the one is the result of the other. Those who have never played cricket do not realise the extra effort required in order to strive for uncertain victory, and do not understand why it is that the Australians prefer, as undoubtedly they do, the tranquil alternative of a creditable draw. Long programmes generally mean dull and unenterprising cricket; the amateur does not care for such; we suffer from long programmes in England, and hence the amateur disappears. There are exceptions, it is true. Kent, and possibly Somerset and Hants, still remain strongholds, but the position of Middlesex is eloquent. The old University players are one by one disappearing, and there is nobody to take their place. To drop in and out of first-class cricket intermittently and with credit belongs to few. Thus it comes that the novice shuns so drastic a career, and besides, very often he has something else to do.

The season has not been of very great interest. Beyond the cricket of Kent there has been a singular lack of exhilaration, and the Test matches were, by all who saw them, confessed to be unparalleled for their joyless monotony. It is probably true to say that there is a lack of great players at the present moment, but at the same time it is also true that the general level of cricket is high. Ten or twenty years ago there were greater individuals, but now there are many more players of considerable capacity. It was then easy to pick an unquestioned English Eleven, but in 1909 it would have been easy to choose three, but hard to say a priori which was the strongest combination among them. Again we may seek for the cause in the same old grievance, and say that much cricket though it produces many cricketers, tends to stifle the very great, in the same way that much study makes Jack a dull boy. Indeed, the panacea for all cricket difficulties is the curtailment of the cricket programme, and the simplest way to that end is to diminish the number of first-class counties, or else to split the existing first-class counties into separate divisions. That will put an end to foot-weary cricket, and restore, if anything can, the amateur to the game.

There is no easier attitude than the attitude of pessimism, and especially in the realm of sport. Around a great game there always springs up a vast parasitic growth, obtruding itself unduly, exploited by the press, which catches at the irrelevant and leaves the core untouched. The chief hope for cricket lies in the jealous affection with which so many regard it; they know the dangers, and in defence of the game as a happy blend between amateur and professional they must be prepared to act.

THE BOYS AND THE BOTTLE.

By "Pat."

SEVERAL times of late I have been down among the boys where they are struggling for Ireland among the cosy couches in the House of Commons smoke-rooms, and I do not remember having seen greatness achieved in a more comfortable manner; but the purpose of my visits has been much more serious—to get the boys to take an interest in Ireland as well as struggling for her. I do not like struggling. It suggests conditions of activity in which the results are of uncertain quality, even when there are results; and so might the boys do something for Ireland if only they would take an intelligent interest in her instead of struggling for her among the taxpayers' cushions.

Jolly fellows, most of the boys, and I wish the British public were acquainted with them. They have no way to make themselves known but through their speeches, and since they can never say what they think in their speeches they remain unknown, especially the good that is in them, with all kinds of misunderstanding to cause all kinds of mischief between England and Ireland. Not content to rise above mere fact, they always choose the fiction that makes them most objectionable, and then the British public, always weak in fiction, ask "If these be the best they can send from Ireland, what sort of a —— crowd must they be at home?" If only the boys would say what they thought, they would be found much like other people, but then—well, the cushions are less comfortable in Connaught, and the distance of Westminster affords exactly the right perspective for the most comfortable kind of greatness. Familiarity breeds distrust of fiction.

I have been trying to touch the latest twists in the current motives of "the cause", but at the mention of "the cause" I find them cold. At the mention of the faith I find them colder. Is not this a great change, and why? I have even pictured myself to them with a pike on an Irish hillside trying to shed the last drop of my blood for something I could not understand; but they only stared at me, explaining that pike-and-hillside pictures had ceased to sell, had become a drug in the fiction market, unless in America, where a few dollars could still be raised in this way, assuming "the ambassador of the cause" unusually eloquent. No "cause", no "faith", no pike, no hillside, and what then? No dollars and no cushions, unless the bran-sack by the fireside of the bar parlour, where, after any length of time, familiarity grows dangerous to greatness. I notice an increased respect even for myself every time I return from London, the greatness of which is instinctively appreciated in Ireland. Suppose I were only a "mimber" of Parliament squatting on a bran-sack in the bar parlour night after night, casting the pearls of my oratory to corner-boys and exploiting my genius as a statesman to increase my turnover at the bar. No, London is the place to be a great man, and the only greater way to an Irishman's greatness at home is by pulling his neighbours down under him. Greatness is essentially comparative, and it is the province of statesmanship to decide which is easier—to get yourself above your neighbour or to get your neighbour below you. When everybody struggles to pull everybody else down the effect on the community is not at all the same as when everybody studies to get above everybody else; but the pulling-down plan is the popular one in Ireland, among "a nation of statesmen", where "you can kick an orator out of every bush", as Mr. Redmond once boasted in Australia. If only I could kick an orator into every bush, making sure that he could never come out again, I should spend the rest of my life planting bushes, and leave the Irish question finally settled.

When I had almost given up the hope of finding any current inspiration, divine or human, to move the boys, I thought of the Budget and mentioned the Bottle; their eyes lighted up, they gathered round me, and then I understood why they had supported everything else in the Budget, and fought as if at Fontenoy in defence of the Bottle. Since then I have never met them without mentioning the Bottle, and now they almost love me—except the honourable "mimber" for Archbishop Healy, who must have a Nonconformist strain in him. They can even forgive my cruel analysis of the League and the priests. They say I am to be one of the most popular men in Ireland. I have but to familiarise myself with the Bottle, and I become a "mimber" of Parliament, leaving a name to be enshrined under a special label by the Four Masters of the future. The cause of Ireland has become a cereal distillation; Kathleen Ni Houlihan, corked in "a quarter of a reputed quart", can be carried in the breast-pocket, and hilarity may provide the permanent antidote to its own reactions, a discovery of perpetual motion in the process of parliamentary happiness.

With all my watchfulness, the transition from the spiritual to the spirituous had come about without my knowing it, but I could see there was a new spirit in the air when the honourable "mimber" for Cardinal Logue, behind the backs of the boys, did battle for the Bottle, and set Mr. Redmond working to expel him for his devotion. Mr. Healy might do battle for the cause without danger to the popularity of the boys; but a man of such brilliant ability must not be allowed to get between Mr. Redmond and the Bottle. It was a great blunder, that holiday Mr. Redmond gave the boys, when the defence of the Bottle was left to the devoted "mimber" for Cardinal Logue.

Parliament is a pleasant place, in spite of the ventilation, but it means money, money means subscriptions, and nearly all sources are drying up, except the Bottle.

Mr. Healy could see this, and it was cruel of the Chancellor to renew the battle of the Bottle in the absence of the boys. The peasants refuse subscription as they become the owners of their holdings. What more can the peasants get for subscriptions? Forty years ago they were promised " the freedom of Ireland ", but it did not interest them. What they wanted was land. That was the reason the leaders mixed the freedom and the land together; but now again they are getting separated, and where the peasant has got the land he will not give a shilling a year for the freedom. Besides, after forty years' promises, he finds that he can get the land only by paying for it, and he has all the time given his subscriptions on the understanding that he must have it for nothing; so that even where he has not yet bought his holding he grows unwilling to give subscriptions. The promises to him have not been kept, and it has a cooling effect on further promises. A peasant paying twenty pounds a year in rent, and believing that he could save £19 19s. of it, might well join the League with the odd shilling; but now he finds himself buying instead of simply getting, and the difference puts odd shillings in a new relation for him. A man who has been " led " for forty years to sacrifice his peace in quest of the impossible must have learnt something. He gives no more subscriptions, and when there are no subscriptions there is no " Cause ". The priests are glad enough to control a party in Parliament, but the boys are worth the money to them only so long as the money is provided by somebody else. The " greater Ireland beyond the seas " makes it a rule to subscribe only in proportion to the subscriptions at home, which are now practically confined to the Bottle. Hence the great and sudden importance of the Bottle. The gombeen publican can always drill up those in his debt " for the good of the Cause ", and so every " mimber " surrounds himself with a local guard of gombeen publicans. It is the last stand of the noble eighty, in an entrenchment of alcohol, and glass is not good material for fortification.

There is a search now for men who can pay their own way, and it adds wonderfully to the variety of " the Cause ". The culture of Oxford is hired to grace the crudity of the professional cow-hunter, and the village publican lounges among the parliamentary cushions with the landlord son of the Irish Unionist leader, descended from the princes of Leinster. The newest recruit is my old friend " Colonel " Saul Lynch, on the way to his proper place among the prophets; the same hero who led his nomad traitors against the King in South Africa, and was pardoned by the King through the late Mr. Davitt and Sir Thomas Lipton. Why only " Colonel "? Did he not command a " brigade "? and is not that work for something more than a " Colonel "? Had President Kruger not been so bustled at the time, the valour might have been duly recognised, and we might now have Field-Marshal Saul Lynch taking the oath of allegiance to Edward VII. I notice, however, that even " Colonel " has been dropped since the oath of allegiance came to be contemplated, though our statesman was quite sensitive about his military dignities at the time I told the story in the SATURDAY REVIEW of how the King had let him out of gaol to his Christmas dinner. The dual allegiance to Kruger and to King Edward comes rather close in time, even for the versatility of the Irish mind; but the dropping of the " Colonel " may help to smooth the moral curvature of the performance.

I find the boys by no means enthusiastic about the " Colonel ", and the daily papers reported only " Hear, hear, from three or four of them " when the leader of the Irish brigade " put the New Testament to his lips " in the House of Commons. Were they shocked by the suddenness of the transition? I think not. Should the whole truth come out, the boys have reason enough to be uneasy over their connexion with the Boer War. Mr. Redmond ought to remember a cheque for £100 put into the purse of his parliamentary party from an Irish patriot of long standing; a cheque drawn on an Amsterdam bank, from a sum of £4000 placed there by Dr. Leyds to the credit of the Irish patriot, for services contracted to help the Boers against the British. If Mr. Redmond cannot remember this cheque, he may remember the later one, for a like sum, drawn by the same patriot on the same bank from the same deposit, and returned by the Parliamentary party—when they got to know that the secret of the first cheque had not been well kept. If Mr. Redmond cannot remember these transactions he might consult the most reverend bishop who acts as his treasurer to the Parliamentary Fund; and if they all deny it together, I still know that it is true. Besides, I could not accept the denial of the man who charged Sir Horace Plunkett with " infamous falsehood " when he had before him all the facts to show that the statements attributed by him to Sir Horace had never been made by him. The " Morning Post " has the whole story, early in August, and Mr. Redmond has not yet given a word of explanation. On the contrary, he has set up Mr. Stephen Gwynn and the " Irish Press Agency " to justify it. Thus the new prophet comes into the right school—except for the memory of the Amsterdam cheques, which may have been the cause for only " Hear, hear, from three or four of them ". How much of Kruger's money may still remain to " foight " the battle of the Bottle " on the flure o' the British House o' Commons " I do not know; probably not much, because the total was not large, the value of Irish professional patriotism having fallen low even before the Irish Brigade went to South Africa. It is right to add that the Amsterdam cheques were not drawn by the " Colonel ".

On the other hand, the boys are not rebels; it is only that they must have subscriptions. Rebellion does not flourish among cushions, and Ireland is now the last place to find an Irish rebel. Absence from Ireland is necessary to the ignorance that induces rebel subscriptions, and the Bottle yields the ordinary bond that brings home the Yankee debenture. The box-office depends on the bill of the play, and every great actor has his particular audience. The old stock répertoire is all but played out. It can no longer " draw ", even with " the flure o' the House " for a stage. Touring does not produce its cost, and there is not one in the cast who can be " starred ", not even Saul of Pretoria. Actor-managers never like to employ better actors than themselves, and the honourable " mimber " for Cardinal Logue must be " fired " from the company to accommodate the pre-eminence of mediocrity. It is not possible to level up the cast by levelling down the company; and Ireland, organised for decay, already reproduces it in her playboys, the organisers, who have organised their own ruin—unless they can be saved by the Bottle. At the death of a host its parasites desert it, but not sooner, even when the host is a nation.

WOLFE.

By Edward Salmon.

A CENTURY and a half is a long time to wait for the full meed of a nation's recognition. If genius does not always command instant homage, if too often the mere trickery of talent is accorded a place to which it has no title, posterity may generally be trusted to adjust matters. Posterity's judgment is final. One hundred and fifty years after his death, posterity is delivering itself of the verdict that must obtain for all time henceforth as to the place on the national roll of fame which belongs of right to James Wolfe. How does it happen that the man whose glorious death gave to Britain a new Empire has been so little honoured; that only now is the movement afoot to give him that larger national memorial which his great work merits? When Wolfe died, Pitt found it difficult to tell Parliament what he felt the nation had lost; Parliament, in the moment of emotion, voted him a monument in Westminster Abbey, where he should surely have been laid. The nation had been lifted by his daring and his genius from a state of despondency and doubt to the very empyrean of joy and exultation, and the Government, of which Pitt was a member, refused his mother the means to carry out the modest bequests of his will. The glory on the one hand, the parsimony on the other, were fit symbols of the fate in store for Wolfe's memory. The monument was not placed in the Abbey till fourteen years after the fall of Quebec, and within two years of its erection the American colonies, for whose sake Britain had bled and Wolfe had died, were in revolt. The French enemy had been driven out and the grateful American seized the first opportunity to strike at the hand which had relieved him of his century-long nightmare. Maybe it was felt at home that the conquest of Canada had paved the way to the loss of the thirteen colonies, and that Wolfe's and Amherst's work had gone for nothing. If only Wolfe had lived to deal with the situation his exploit had created!

Whatever the explanation, Wolfe's fame was meteoric. Others laid claim to the credit of his achievement, and the historian too readily accepted his enemies and rivals at their own valuation. Wright in the 'sixties—more than a century after his death—did something to show what manner of man Wolfe was and what his title-deeds to fame were. Mr. G. M. Bradley, most devoted of Canadian chroniclers, in a better position than Wright to judge of the imperial character of Wolfe's work, advanced matters a stage further some thirty years later, and then came the biographer of Townshend to prove after all that Wolfe died giving effect to the plan of others. Happily the archives have yielded up their treasures of fact, and even the biographer of Townshend to-day probably sees that Wolfe is entitled to every shred of credit for the masterly performance which made Canada British. I find nothing more piquant and gratifying in Mr. Beckles Willson's biography of Wolfe,* appropriately published on the 150th anniversary of Quebec, than a note from Brigadier-General C. V. F. Townshend, who says he now understands why Wolfe "did not hit it off with his brigadiers". Jealousy of his preferment "explains the friction and consequent misunderstandings". To say so much is to make Wolfe's victory appear greater than ever, for clearly in fighting Montcalm Wolfe had to bear up against not merely the sore trials of the campaign but the want of sympathy in those who should have been his staunchest supporters. The moral as well as physical strain, which made Wolfe ill, would have broken an ordinary man, and there would have been no victory on the heights of Abraham. Without that victory Amherst's chances of early triumph in Canada were slender.

No one who has studied Wolfe's life in its fullness—the fullness of its action together with the fullness of its thought as revealed in his correspondence—can have a moment's hesitation in saying that if ever hero-worship was justified it is justified in the case of the conqueror of Quebec. Sir George White says that he reads the story of Wolfe's campaign on the S. Lawrence with feelings akin to awe. And Sir George White wears the V.C. Wolfe's martial instinct, derived mainly from his father, was of that order which we look for in the creations of a Kingston or a Henty. He was a volunteer for the Cartagena expedition at thirteen, and was only spared the risks of that disastrous affair by an opportune illness. He was an acting adjutant in the war of the Austrian succession at sixteen, and by the time he was twenty-one he had been through the severities of the campaigns in Flanders and in Scotland. Dettingen, Falkirk, Culloden, Laffeldt made of him a seasoned veteran at an age when most lads are learning the A B C of their business. During eight years of troubled peace he made himself the most efficient of British soldiers, as the regiments with which he was connected were admittedly the most efficient in the British Army. Where everybody else failed at Rochefort, Wolfe stood forth as the one individual whose counsel was worthy of Pitt's designs. At Louisbourg Amherst was in command, but Wolfe's was the animating spirit. Even the sailors with Boscawen talked of Wolfe's batteries and the booming of Wolfe's guns, and the French themselves protested in effect that he did not play the game because they never knew where he would turn up next. When the engineer directing the approaches said his motto was "Slow and sure", Wolfe promptly rejoined "Mine is 'Quick and sure'—a much better maxim", and "Celer et audax" was the motto he gave the 60th Rifles. Had Wolfe been in command at Louisbourg, Quebec would conceivably have been taken, certainly would have been attacked, in 1758. Pitt knew what he was about the following year when he set Amherst to look after Ticonderoga and Crown Point whilst Wolfe was given the tough job of the campaign at Quebec.

For years past Wolfe had been denouncing the lack of efficiency and of enterprise in the British Army; he had educated himself beyond his fellows, had fought his way to preferment through every obstacle which nepotism, corruption and official stupidity placed in the path of men who had nothing more than their natural gifts to recommend them. He was only thirty-two when he was appointed to the Quebec command, and he confessed that he was called upon to play a greater part "in this business" than he wished or desired. "The backwardness of some of the older officers has in some measure forced the Government to come down so low", he told his uncle. Pitt sent Wolfe forth on an expedition which was to be a microcosm of British imperial power. Saunders, with his fleet linking up the divisions of Wolfe's army, was a perfect example of combined operations the secret of which Wolfe was the first to seize, as Mr. Julian Corbett has shown. Quebec was Wolfe's and the army's victory, but without Saunders and his fleet the campaign would have been impossible. Mr. Beckles Willson, with admirable but hardly discriminating devotion, strongly resents any attempt to place Saunders on a level with Wolfe. But this much must be said. In Saunders Wolfe had an ideal colleague, and it would have been well for the good name of certain other people if there had been more of his loyal disinterestedness on the military side. The story of Wolfe's stupendous task and accomplishment would then have been more pleasant reading and Wolfe's true claim on posterity would never have been called in question.

As a letter-writer Wolfe belonged to his century. Without literary pretensions, he managed to put much that was worth reading into English that seldom jars. Many of his reflections, which might be expected from a man twice his years, would be regarded as priggish to-day. One wishes there were more such prigs in the world. Wolfe could not enter into the distractions of the youth of his day, and his one lapse was long on his conscience. Devoted son, staunchest of friends, keen soldier, he found enjoyment in his studies, was partial to the society of ladies, was fond of his dogs, and so far as opportunity served, was a sportsman. Impatience of folly and incompetence was the keynote of his character. He was as anxious to avoid the company of fools as Dr. Johnson himself. His irritability was aggravated by a disease which was a sufficient handicap. The subacidity of many of his letters was not wanting even in the interchange of notes with his antagonist Montcalm. "Lettre d'une forme polie", says Montcalm in his journal, "et d'un style âcre de Wolfe." That admirably sums up the impression left on one by much of Wolfe's correspondence. Wolfe has been called the Nelson of the Army; Mr. Willson detects so many points of likeness in the two men that we should rather call Nelson, who came after him, the Wolfe of the Navy.

* "The Life and Letters of Wolfe." By Beckles Willson. London: Heinemann. 1909. 18s. net.

LETTERS FROM SOLITUDE.

By Filson Young.

IV.

. . . . Connemara.

This letter is all about an island—a little island, as islands must be if one is to love them and make them one's own. It is called Inishmuskerry, and lies about a mile beyond the mouth of one of these long Connemara bays; it faces south-west to the open Atlantic, and the sea horizon is only broken by the three swelling curves of the Aran Islands and the white finger of their lighthouse. Your first sight of it is only a low jagged line of rock, less than a quarter of a mile long, with the sea breaking white at one end;

but as you approach you see the green of grass above the rock, and a gleam of white where there is a sandy bay. You come nearer, and some of the black masses of rock detach themselves, and show you that the island is even smaller than you thought it; nearer still, and the little coast-line resolves itself into points and bays, until at last, rounding a steep rocky foreland where three or four cormorants are nearly always sitting, you sail up a calm little sound with the black detached wall of barrier rocks on one hand and a pearly white strand on the other. A few yards away, on the other side of those low rocks, the seas are breaking and bursting into snow and thunder; here are absolute calm and stillness, the shallow green waters sleeping in the sunshine and revealing the garden of sea-plants that hardly stirs beneath you.

You bring your boat alongside a flat rock, make her fast, and land. The island is uninhabited, or at least so they had told you; but you find that it is not so, for on your arrival clouds of black-headed terns get up from the rocks and begin to swoop and scream over your head; and as long as you remain there they will keep you under observation, and very indignantly talk about you, up there in their sunny world of wings. But you soon forget their voices, which, like the continuous roar of the surf about you, become as undisturbing as silence, and you are free to enjoy your possession of the island; for everything that we love and enjoy becomes our very own, and the extent of our possession is only the extent of our love.

And how shall I begin to tell you of the charms of Inishmuskerry? I will keep to the shore first, as I always do when I visit it. For those who like to walk into the sea on a sparkling white carpet and through clear emerald water, there is no place in the world for bathing equal to the white strand on Inishmuskerry. It is steep; you are in deep water in a moment; it is calm, but round by the rocks you can swim into all the surf you want. And then, when you have reluctantly left the water, and gone back to it again half a dozen times, you can lie naked on the hot sand and watch the terns and gulls swooping over you, and let the sun turn the salt on your body to stinging crystals, and be lulled by songs of Halcyone and Ceyx into a sleep that is half a dream, and a dream that is deeper than any sleep. And then when you have dreamed a little you may rise and eat, for food eaten in such a place has a savour of its own; and as landing on islands is one of the great joys of sailing on the sea, so eating when you land is one of the minor ways of enjoying an island.

And not until you have eaten and rested do you leave your little beach and strike across the grass that carpets the middle of the island. It is at the highest point only some twenty feet above sea-level, but it rolls about in little plains and valleys, and, small as it is (a walk of five minutes will take you from one extremity to the other), it contains almost every variety of pleasant feature. There is a spring, and a little pond of wild lilies; the pasture is deep and rich, and, in these barren parts, precious on that account; someone pays four-and-twenty pounds a year for Inishmuskerry, and his cattle come and grow sleek here. There is a little hut on it where the herd may spend a night. At the seaward end there is a great pile of stones that once supported a flagstaff, and two hundred years ago a man used to live here and watch other flagstaffs on other islands and points, so that when a foreign ship was sighted its coming might be signalled from one flagstaff to another, and the inhabitants ashore warned. For Inishmuskerry has not always been a mere habitation of seabirds and cattle. Tiny as it is, the drama of life has been enacted on its small stage, and love and strife, birth and death, played their parts here. If you look closely at the turf you will see the traces of furrows, parallel, and showing the hand of man; for in the old days the kelp burners had a few huts here, and tilled each of them a patch of earth to grow the potatoes on which they lived.

And there are other and smaller furrows, the graves of little children; the signalman had three children who, dying on the island, sleep here undisturbed through the centuries. They were, I am sure, the real island people, for Inishmuskerry is too small for men or women to live contented on it; they would always be looking across at the shore, and wondering what the people there were doing and saying. But to the children the shore must have been a mere world of fable; this was the real world for them, with slippery rocks and roaring surges for perils and all the wild flowers of spring and summer for joys; with grey misty days for melancholy, and bright sunshine and shouting winds for gladness. These few yards of grass and rock were all their world; long, long ago they lived and played and died here—little lives and deaths, suitable for a little island like this . . . I had visited Inishmuskerry several times before I knew of these graves or heard their history, but from the first I had been aware, in spite of the screaming gulls and the watchful cormorants and the ancient roaring sea, of a strange atmosphere of innocence and peace; and if matter has any memory, or spirit any persistence, it should not in this country of dreams and fables be hard to believe that those small innocent spirits, unheard and unseen, still inhabit the island and keep it sweet with the haunting presence of youth.

And now that the children are dead the real island people are the terns and the puffins and the dark, satanic cormorants that perch in rows on the rocks and watch the sea with unwinking eyes. The terns especially have an air of proprietorship, and deeply resent the intrusion of a stranger. Just now they have special reason to do so, for this is their breeding-place, and you have to walk warily over the grass lest you hurt one of the young birds that are lying there, still in the elementary stage of their education—soft, fluffy little birds, very tame and easily picked up, and not at all resentful of a caressing hand. The gulls are always talking, always in a fuss; the cormorants never. They sit and sit by the hour, silent and motionless on a range of rock, and then with a flap of black wings launch themselves out like projectiles over the sea and are gone from sight. There is a heron, too, a very shy heron; there is a little drove of kittiwakes, and a wild bee that came over in my boat one day, and was very much astonished at the aridity of planks and ropes, and finally sat down on a withered pansy that was in the buttonhole of a coat lying on the floor, and sulked there until we made the island. Now she is glad, for on Inishmuskerry there are many kinds of wild flowers flourishing among the grasses, as well as the sea-holly, thrift and sea-pansy that grow in the sand of the shore; and when I am walking there I often hear the swift drone of her wings as she flies about on her fragrant business.

Have I wearied you with my island? If I have, the fault is mine, and not Inishmuskerry's; you would never tire of it if you knew it; there are such flowers in its field, such shells on its shore as would enchant you through many a long summer's day. You may even have your choice of climates there; you may sit on the south-western rocks, with the fresh wind and roaring surf about you, or lie in the sandy hollows amid the shy and delicate perfumes of wild flowers. Do you remember a certain great sea-wind at night that filled the darkness with the brushing of sable wings; a wind of infinite weight and infinite softness, that wrapped all the world in black velvet? Well, I found it again on Inishmuskerry the other day, when the white clouds were charioting northwards over a deep sky, and sun and wind and sea were all jousting together. This wind was heavy and soft, but instead of being dressed in black velvet it wore the colour of deepest blue, and its wrapping had not the thickness of velvet but the softness of silk; it brought me again the message of the velvet wind. And although Inishmuskerry has its melancholy, misty moods, I will not go to it then, for I would see it always as I know it now—a place so redolent of happiness that even if you went there unhappy, you would find hope growing among its asphodels and heather.

I have told you so much about this island because I think such places are among the best and most beautiful things in one's life. You cannot lose them, they cannot fail or betray you, they are your very own always. From them you may often get a calm Pisgah-view, and see, beyond dim and foamy horizons, the sunshine touching the shores of some promised land. And although it is one thing to see the land, and quite another thing to reach it, it is always something to have seen it with your eyes, and to know that it is there; even if you go down off the very shores of your island, and see and are seen no more.

LEAR AT THE HAYMARKET.

By Max Beerbohm.

MR. TRENCH has shown excellent high courage in using "King Lear" to inaugurate his tenancy of the Haymarket. Tragedy is not popular; and the most horribly tragic of all Shakespeare's plays has been, in recent times, the least popular. In the lusty Tudor days, before "nerves" had been heard of, men were able to revel in the gloomiest exhibitions. They were not afraid of the dark. We are. They liked to have their blood curdled. We have no blood to spare for that process, thank you. Thunder and lightning, barren heaths cowering under starless skies, exile and despair, the breaking heart, the tottering reason, treachery most foul, death sudden or lingering, seemed to the Elizabethans very jolly indeed. With music of flutes and scent of roses, and plenty of sweetmeats and amber wine, and not a cloud in the sky, we can just support the cruel burden of existence. In a word, we are civilised. "We don't want to be harrowed" is our constant cry. It was impossible to harrow the Elizabethans. "King Lear" ran through three editions in the first year of publication, and was no doubt advertised as "endless fun for young and old". Shakespeare himself was in many respects a highly-civilised man; very far in advance of his time. He would never have been able to conceive the story of "King Lear" on his own account; and, had he been as superior as Mr. Trench to the lust for lucre, he would never have taken "The True Chronicle History of King Leir and His Three Daughters" as a basis for work. In their original forms the stories of Macbeth and Hamlet were as barbarous as that of Lear. But Shakespeare breathed into them much of the spirit of his own premature civilisation; so that twentieth-century audiences can just manage to put up with them. The story of Lear he left barbaric. Whereas Hamlet and Macbeth are both of them modern and "sympathetic" persons, in "King Lear" all the characters except Cordelia, the good and the bad alike, are savages; and their story is one of almost unrelieved horror. "That's but a trifle here" says Albany when the news of Edmund's death is brought; and, oppressed by the steady accumulation of agonies "here", we smile a sickly smile at the aptness of the remark. If Shakespeare had invented his own plots, his genius would not seem greater to us than it does to-day. But it is useless to deny that his work would have been more satisfactory. And "King Lear" is especially one of the plays that are cumbered by their origin. There is too much in it that is merely silly or merely brutal—too much that Shakespeare did not transmute in the crucible of his brain. Mr. Trench, in his admirably written note on the play, says: "What insight, what imagination, to build on that first scene—a mere display of pettish temper on the part of a wilful old man—the mighty structure of the tragedy! . . . His tragically profound sense of humour perceived that the scene supplied a scope for irony which great imaginations have always found in human affairs." This is a handsome and ingenious excuse. But I suspect the truth is not that Shakespeare "perceived" anything of the kind, but that he just went straight ahead without taking the trouble to make sense of nonsense. Suppose Mr. Trench wanted a house built for himself, and the builder said "I don't mean to bother about the foundations", would that builder be complimented on his "great imagination"? Would not his sense of humour strike his client as rather *too* "tragically profound"? However, it is right that one poet should stick up for another. And Shakespeare's great imagination certainly did begin to work at high pressure so soon as he got Lear out upon the storm-swept heath with the clown, and in the hovel where Poor Tom gibbered. Shakespeare never did anything more tremendous than the crescendo of those scenes, nor anything more exquisite than the diminuendo of the scenes in which Lear's life totters to its end.

If the theatrical presentment of such scenes is not to fall ludicrously short of one's vague mental conception of them, there must be an artist with high imagination, and with great power of design, to create the backgrounds for them. Mr. Charles Ricketts has risen to the level of his great opportunity. His scenery has a large and simple dignity of line and colour. It is a fit setting to tragic issues. It looms ominous in infinity. Darkling forests, sheer scarped cliffs, rude structures of stone—all are admirably right. I cannot praise his storm-swept heath, because I did not see it. Lear raved in inky darkness, which the streaks of lightning strove vainly to illumine. This was a pity. One needed to see Lear as well as to hear him. In real life, on so very stormy a night, one would not be able to see anyone, even at close quarters. But neither would one be able to hear him. The stage-manager at the Haymarket does not carry realism so far as to make Lear inaudible. That would be manifestly absurd. But hardly less absurd is it to make Lear invisible. Lear's face and figure are needed to illustrate his words. We should be surprised to see footlights and limelights on a stormy night out-of-doors. In the storm-scene of "King Lear", if they were used rightly, we should not notice them. Obscurantism, on the other hand, is noticeable, and a nuisance. Away with it!

I have never seen a better Lear than Mr. Norman McKinnel's; but then, I have never seen another one. Salvini's was before my time; and Irving's I missed. I imagine that the beauty and dignity of Irving's presence must to some extent have atoned for his lack of lung-power, and his inability to declaim blank verse. Mr. McKinnel's lungs are magnificent, and he has a true ear for the rhythm of verse. But his voice lacks variety, and is not in itself of a beautiful quality. And his presence, though impressive, is not regal. Lear was a barbarian, but he was a king. And much of the pathos of his tragedy is lost through our difficulty in believing that he, as presented by Mr. McKinnel, has ever been anything more than a solid and trustworthy liege. Still more of the pathos is lost through the impassiveness of Mr. McKinnel's face. It is a face that has only one expression: a sort of glum astonishment. Wrath, sorrow, fear, remorse, cannot be mirrored there. When he speaks of "these hot tears, which break from me perforce", the words ring strange, as coming from one whose lachrymal glands are under such perfect control. All that can be done by accomplishment and keen intelligence Mr. McKinnel does. What he leaves undone is the fault only of his physical and temperamental limitations. It is when Lear's spirit has burnt itself out, when his fury has spent itself and him, that Mr. McKinnel, who has given us all the forcefulness of Lear, but nothing of the fire, really rises to the level of the part. In that marvellously conceived speech which begins with the words "Pray do not mock me. I am a very foolish fond old man", Mr. McKinnel achieves a fine and memorable effect of pathos.

Miss Ellen O'Malley, looking curiously like the early portraits of Miss Ellen Terry, is charming and touching as Cordelia. As Goneril and Regan, Miss Ada Ferrar and Miss Marie Polini have an air of wishing to show how charming and touching they too could be if they hadn't been cast for such unpleasant parts. In pantomime the two Proud Sisters of Cinderella are always played by men. In the case of Goneril and Regan, who are uniform with them, this tradition might well be followed. Mr. Fisher White, as Cornwall, is as barbaric as one could wish. Mr. Hignett puts plenty of fantasy into his impersonation of the clown; but, for the right effect of the clown's juxtaposition to Lear, it is a pity that Mr. Hignett is not a smaller and more agile man. Mr. Quartermaine is excellently weird as Poor Tom. It is a pity that Mr. Hearn makes Gloucester so decrepit from the outset. There is hardly any contrast between Gloucester before his sufferings and Gloucester after them. It is also a pity that Edmund was not meant by Shakespeare to be a quiet, blameless, rising young Civil Servant of the twentieth century. For then Mr. Dawson Milward's rendering of the part would leave nothing at all to be desired.

A NEW IDEAL FOR GARDENERS.

By Sir Herbert Maxwell.

DESPITE the present exuberance of gardening literature there are no signs of slackening demand, so intense and widespread is the prevailing fervour for horticulture. Most of its disciples are inspired by the sentiment which Linnæus chose as his motto, " Tantus amor florum "—content if they can cause the long procession of flowering shrubs and herbs to brighten their borders, without much concern for the relation between garden and environment. It is not to such simple enthusiasts that Sir George Sitwell addresses his essay on " The Making of Gardens ".* They will search his pages in vain for precepts of cultivation, for advice about choice of species, preparation of soil, considerations of climate and aspect. In short, the author has nothing to say about the practical part of garden-making; he only philosophises about gardens when made, especially great ones made a long time ago.

Sir George Sitwell has made the gardens of Italy his special study, having visited nearly two hundred of them: a delightful occupation which has had the unhappy result of inspiring him with profound dissatisfaction with English garden design, which he finds " is seldom related as it should be to the surrounding scenery; it is often wanting in repose and nearly always in imagination ". Could he support this complaint on a June morning in the gardens of S. John's or New College, Oxford, or floating down the " backs " at Cambridge?

" These old Italian gardens, with their air of neglect, desolation and solitude, in spite of the melancholy of the weed-grown alleys, the weary dropping of the fern-fringed fountains, the fluteless Pans and headless nymphs and armless Apollos, have a beauty which is indescribable, producing upon the mind an impression which it is difficult to analyse, to which no words can do justice." Sir George then devotes many charming pages to describing what he proclaims as indescribable, and others, less charming, to analysing the impression which he pronounces so elusive.

In decrying our " wet, bird-haunted English lawns " he seems to have left out of account the part played by a Mediterranean sun and the lapse of centuries in the making of these Italian gardens. One may be as sensible as himself to their grave dignity, their fantasy and their atmosphere of romance; one may deplore with him the elaborate ugliness of many English pleasure-grounds, and yet ask what scenes can be found in Italy fairer than the sunlit alleys at Albury, the flower-girt fountains at Endsleigh, the duchess' garden at Belvoir, the hoary terraces at Balcaskie or the sea-girt pleasaunce at Culzean.

However, Sir George Sitwell has his ideal, and it is no common obstacle that will deter him from attaining it. Most of us regard gardens as accessory to our dwellings; certainly in a season such as afflicts us at present few will be found to share Sir George's regret for " the earlier days when everyone's parlour was under the sky ". The house he admits as a necessary excrescence in the landscape, but it must be adapted to its environment, not the environment to the house.

" This, then, leads up to what I believe to be the great secret of success in garden-making, the profound platitude that we should abandon the struggle to make nature beautiful round the house and should rather move the house to where nature is beautiful." This is as much as to say that no man of moderate means who has inherited a house in an unsatisfactory landscape need attempt to make a beautiful garden. A disappointing doctrine, this, to those of us who have sat at the feet of Mr. William Robinson and imbibed the faith that the true virtue of horticulture is that, rightly applied, it beautifies any human habitation, lofty or lowly. In another passage the author writes as follows:

" These great villas at Frascati, Tivoli, and Albano were never intended for winter residence. . . . A house or garden which is expected to look fairly well all the year round can never reach the ideal, and the advantage of knowing what months it will be occupied and of planning for those months alone is too obvious to be worth discussing."

If this indeed be Sir George Sitwell's ideal it is wholly at variance with another ideal cherished by Englishmen, namely, that of the home. That can never be fully attained in a house which is abandoned to a caretaker for half the year. Richest in association are those gardens that are most continuously occupied by their owners; and this Sir George appears to recognise, though he expresses himself in somewhat cryptic phrase:

" The centres which deal with sensation and emotion being the same, a faint stirring of past experiences involves also a more vivid renewal of the emotion common to such past experiences and of other feelings of pleasure which have been accidentally associated with them. . . . The reproduction in idea of past feelings tends to revive, not only others accidentally connected with them, but all others of the same class. So the masses of plexuses in the brain which deal with impressions intermixed with pleasurable emotion being intimately connected and the nervous discharge following the lines of least resistance, other feelings of beauty and happiness are partially aroused, there is a dim representation, vague, massive, multitudinous, of all kinds of pleasure, and an indefinable sense of well-being."

A plain man may ask what all this has to do with making a garden, and feel somewhat incredulous as to the measure in which the designers of Italian gardens bothered themselves about " the masses of plexuses in the brain " or " the nervous discharge ".

We are told that " Abel was a keeper of sheep, but Cain was a tiller of the ground "; nevertheless, most people will agree in considering horticulture conducive to orderly behaviour. But when Sir George Sitwell asks us to believe that " the garden, like beauty in a landscape, is inimical to all evil passions ", he surely forgets a good deal that went on in the gardens of the Italian renaissance. Perhaps it was owing to its faulty design that the sixteenth-century garden at Whittingehame became the scene of one of the most dastardly conspiracies in history; for it was there that Morton, Maitland, and Archibald Douglas, parson of Glasgow, planned the destruction of Henry Darnley. On the whole, it will probably lead to a better result if, in laying out a garden, one frankly makes pleasure and beauty the main objects and leaves the ethical influence to take care of itself.

It will be clear from these observations that I am unable to follow Sir George Sitwell to all his conclusions. Descending to plain matter of fact, may I submit to the author that, in preparing future editions, he will reconsider the allusion on page 6 to Anglo-Saxon keeps and Corinthian arches? If any Anglo-Saxon keep exists it must be unique; and, although the treasure-house of Atreus at Mycenæ has been cited as a proof that the arch was not unknown to Greek builders, they never made it an architectural feature.

* " An Essay on the Making of Gardens." By Sir George Sitwell Bart. London: Murray. 1909. 5s. net.

CORRESPONDENCE.

MR. MILES' MEALS.

To the Editor of the Saturday Review.

15 Grosvenor Road, Westminster S.W.
15 September 1909.

Sir,—I have adopted the above title to this communication, not because I desire to shift my ground, but because it appears to afford the keynote of Mr. Miles' reproach. After reading that gentleman's letter, I was forcibly reminded of Mark Twain's advice: " Punch, brothers! " says he, " punch by all means, but punch with care ". Mr. Miles is under the delusion that I have punched him—below the belt! And in his anguish he talks about invoking the law with a view to obtaining redress for the damage he has sustained in the contest. "Bardell v. Pickwick" is funny, but "Miles v. Erskine and the SATURDAY REVIEW" would be funnier. There can surely be no question of unfairness when combatants invite assault in the region of their gastric economy. Mr. Miles is a humourist, but he is also an English sportsman, and of all men should know how to receive with equanimity the volleys of his opponent.

Now to the battle once more. The fact that Mr. Miles has fully disclosed his dietary régime for my enlightenment in no way disposes of my assumption that he is prominent amongst those who advocate and practise abstention from flesh. Why is he so hurt that I should have indicated inter alia certain kinds of diet of which he acknowledges himself to be a partaker to the exclusion of animal meat?

Now I myself am a meat-eater, and glory in the fact; but I have no cause to feel offended because the vegetarians—I beg pardon, the food reformers—call me "carnivorous" in the general sense that I referred to Mr. Miles as being "nucivorous". Nobody denies that the Japanese and Indian troops are splendid fighters, but the net result of the Japanese capacity in that respect yet remains to be seen. They have had but one "round" in the contest, and their staying power is a matter of speculation, as I pointed out in my previous letter. Mr. Miles makes no comment on the fact that the Japanese are now importing European cattle in order to introduce a meat diet as part of the national food—another point I touched upon. The average native of India, vegetarian of vegetarians, can hardly be quoted as a model of manly physique. The Persian hordes were, with few exceptions, successively overcome by every well-organised enemy, and ultimately degenerated, mentally, morally, and physically. The Greeks have left for all time an indelible mark on the art, literature, and drama of the world, but their military and economic achievements in the ancient "Weltpolitik" were of a comparatively ephemeral character. Alexander the Great fell a victim to the pleasures of the table, both liquid and solid, but history does not record whether or not, meat formed an item in his gastronomic excesses.

Nobody denies that the Scotch were, and still are, "bonnie fechters". England and the world in general have had ample evidence of that—I am a Scotsman myself, as my name implies—but again, as a race, they can hardly be regarded as coming within the category of Empire-makers, until quite recently, since the Scot entered the firm of John Bull somewhat late in the day—alas! only after he had been well chastened by the aforesaid John Bull, and he remains for ever a valued but by no means dominant partner.

With regard to the Romans, Gibbon indicates that the proletariat fared well in dietary matters, and that the favourable agricultural and pastoral conditions of the country, afforded ample means for cattle rearing on an extensive scale. The Romans in their turn fell before the Goths, who subsisted entirely on flesh. Moreover those who study the minutiæ of the contemporary military historians will learn that the butcher and cook were important functionaries in the Roman legionary system, and that the "Army Service Corps" carried, among other impedimenta, all the paraphernalia for dressing and cooking meat.

I have no desire to alter my attitude or deviate from my line of argument, but Mr. Miles lays too much stress on the expression "physical degeneration", seeing that the tenor of my first communication clearly conveys the impression that the phrase was used in the abstract and not in the concrete sense, and as applying to the human organisation in its physiological entirety.

It would indeed be the reductio ad absurdum to maintain that a meat diet ipso facto makes for national greatness, but I hold that by an inexplicable process of nature, such diet conduces to the solidarity of a nation in relation to the idiosyncrasy for acquiring and retaining power and dominion in the affairs of this world, where the race is to the swift and the battle to the strong. Let the food reformers and flesh abstainers turn their thoughts to a nation across the North Sea. It is fairly well established that the absurd and useless excrescence known as the Great Pyramid, was reared about seven hundred years after the Deluge, and that the actual builders were hordes of slaves or forced labourers, working under the ancient equivalents of the "kourbash" and "corvée". These poor wretches may doubtless, under the peculiar climatic conditions, have subsisted on "lentils, onions and garlic", but our knowledge of human nature, even in those far-off days, leads us to the shrewd conclusion that their masters in consummating the colossal obelisk —the admiration of Messrs. Cook's clients—reserved for themselves the more grateful and comforting nourishment to be found in the "flesh-pots of Egypt"!

It may interest Mr. Miles to know that the "fellaheen" excavators of the Suez Canal worked under conditions practically identical with those of the pyramid-builders.

"The Chinese porters at Hong Kong" and the "water carriers of Constantinople" may be very sturdy fellows, and their diet admirably adapted for the particular form of physical exertion demanded by their humble calling, but neither the Chinese nor the Turks have exhibited any signs that their physical qualities are being utilised towards the attainment of national greatness, unless indeed we regard recent episodes in the near East as evidence of a desire to acquire the "righteousness that exalteth a nation".

As for the athlete, because a man specialises in a particular branch of athletics and eschews animal meat, since he finds it necessary to the maintenance of his condition and pre-eminence in the domain of sport, it by no means follows that the ordinary individual should go and do likewise: a sense of physical and mental well-being, accruing from a system of dietetics avowedly adopted for the attainment of a single object, is not per se an indication that one is equipped for the multifarious duties of life towards the community at large.

Many of the world's greatest men have achieved their successes under the most distressing conditions of health: Julius Cæsar an epileptic, Cardinal Richelieu a neuropath, and Huxley a dyspeptic. "Quite so", exclaim the food reformers; "had these men conformed to our views they would have been cured of their ills and done better work." I beg leave to doubt it; they would in all probability have degenerated into good, normal-minded, easy-going individuals. It would be like robbing the fakir of his bed of nails or the monk of his hair shirt. I enunciate no paradox when I say that the physiological disabilities of these great men were part of the price paid for their gifts. Nature is cruel in order to be kind, and attains her ends by pain and suffering, of which child-birth affords a concrete example. The martyr buys his crown. Nothing is given in this world, everything is paid for. Cecil Rhodes suffered intensely from cardiac trouble, but he gave us a continent! Scott wrote the Waverley Novels in a state of mental agony resulting from financial embarrassment. Keats (a consumptive), Byron and Shelley suffered terribly both in body and mind, but we have the expression of their pain, and the world is the gainer. Who knows the physical and mental conditions under which Shakespeare wrote his immortal works? We are told that he died of a "feaver" contracted at a drinking bout; had he subjected himself to the dietary régime of an Elizabethan Eustace Miles he might have "forsworn sack", lived to a good old age, and given us half-a-dozen more "Hamlets" and "Macbeths" into the bargain!

Mr. Miles and I seem to be at variance in regard to the authorities we have consulted as to the diet of England's mediæval population. I can find nothing in the works of contemporary writers to support his assertion that the "small farmers and yeomen of old England" subsisted mainly on "cheese, pease-pudding, cereals, etc." On the contrary, meat appears to have figured more prominently in the daily menu of the middle and lower classes than it does at the present time, for the simple reason that the woods and forests abounded in wild animals: stags, wild-boar, hares and rabbits might be had for the killing.

According to Doomsday Book everybody kept swine, from the lord of the manor down to the humble "villein". Shakespeare, whose plays faithfully reflect the manners and habits of life of the people, frequently alludes to the "venison pasties", "capons" and other meat dishes indulged in by his characters, drawn as they were from all classes of the community.

My soldier father, himself a grandson of the Chancellor Erskine, one of the "beef-steak-and-three-bottle" school, was a meat-eater. He excelled at racquets and all manly sports, and enjoyed splendid health, begat thirteen children, served his country all the world over, and died in his eighty-eighth year, maintaining his faculties to the end.

I must again, but for the last time of offending, ask your indulgence for trespassing on your space, for although "I could discourse upon this theme until my eyelids can no longer wag", that is no reason why I should inflict myself further upon your readers. The food reformers have raised a Frankenstein in our midst, and I shall indeed feel happy to think that I have had a hand in sounding that monster's death-knell.

I am, Sir, your obedient servant,

Hermann Erskine.

VEGETARIANISM AND PHYSICAL DEGENERATION.

To the Editor of the Saturday Review.

Holland House, Great Malvern,
5 September 1909.

Sir,—Although it may be quite true that the "dietary régime" of distinguished statesmen of the first quarter of the last century included a liberal allowance of beef-steaks, port wine and brandy, it may be questioned whether that of the rank and file who fought at Waterloo, or of the man-before-the-mast at Trafalgar, had been much else than bread, potatoes, cabbages and occasional bacon, varied, in the case of the Scots and Irish, by oatmeal in some shape or form. And yet, what grit behind those old bayonets! What untiring energy in the frame of the little powder-monkey! And, as for the "combative passions", they are strong enough in the Irish peasant, and it is little beef-steak that he gets year in and year out!

No, depend upon it, physical degeneration is less a question of diet than of a dozen other things, the chief of which may be described as the environment of childhood. Get the people back to the soil and to the seashore, and at least the foundation of physical regeneration will be laid. Happily the Empire possesses, in the temperate zones, a broad acreage and an extensive seaboard, both waiting to be occupied. Here at home —thanks to the infatuation of the hour—everything tends to make it impossible for men to live, much less bring up children, on the soil. The popular quack nostrum of the nationalisation of land not only expels capital and labour from the soil of the old country, but at the same time checks emigration by holding out the hope of a social millennium, which the knowing ones who remain at home will richly enjoy.

Alas, the solution is not so simple as to be found in a freer consumption of butchers' meat!

I am, Sir, yours obediently,

Watkin W. Williams.

THE GREAT NAIL—ONE PENNY.

To the Editor of the Saturday Review.

Sir,—It has been reserved for Messrs. Peary, Cook and Co. to discover and make the North Pole ridiculous. No man of any other nationality could have done one half they have done in the field of Arctic exploration. Hudson left us the legend, Franklin laid down his life. Nares, Rae, and Ross worked, dreamed, starved, sledged, trudged, wintered in the dark, and devoted their heroic lives to the great idea. None of them seem to have cared an atom about themselves. Not one of them thought about advertisement. Money never entered into their calculations. We do not hear that any one of them took a megaphone on any of his expeditions. They did not think of securing the exclusive right to any telegraphic system; above all, they were not jealous of each other's fame. Quietly and heroically they plodded on towards their goal, each man at his life's end content to have pushed the trail a little further to the north. The tale of their endeavour was more enthralling in our school days than any fairy story ever penned by man. The "Erebus" and "Terror" seemed to embody something romantic in their very names. When we were boys all of us wished to go and search for Franklin. An Arctic exploration carried something ennobling with it in the contempt of hardships and of death that the explorers showed. It never entered anybody's head to sneer or to cast doubts upon the motives of the self-sacrificing men who passed their lives in doing what everybody knew never brought in a penny to the whole band of them.

After the Englishmen came Nansen, Nordenskiöld, and others, and still the work went on, and still the glamour of perhaps the one adventure science has ever entered into in the world endured. Now, perhaps in order to pull down and bedaub with mud the last of our illusions, Messrs. Cook and Peary, with their bags of gum-drops for the Esquimaux, their cinematographs, advance agents, and "Old Glories", appear upon the scene, and straight the whole thing turns to comedy. Spread-eagle telegrams, and others of abuse, succeed each other. One great explorer stars it in the Dutch provinces. The other telegraphs to say that he will sue him for breach of copyright.

Good-bye romance, good faith, honour, and anything that we had hitherto connected with the cold, silent North. The Pole has now become a side show, and when the rival heroes have done vilifying one another they had better form a company and set up turnstiles at the North Pole and charge a penny to go in and see the "Mammoth Nail".

Yours faithfully,

R. B. Cunninghame Graham.

CAPTAIN HATTERAS AND THE NORTH POLE.

To the Editor of the Saturday Review.

2 Chesterfield Street, Mayfair,
9 September 1909.

Sir,—Jules Verne, whose romantic works have in so many cases proved prophetical, wrote some forty years since a book entitled "Les Anglais au Pôle Nord, ou Le Voyage du Captaine Hatteras". In this book he describes an imaginary discovery of the North Pole by an Englishman, Captain Hatteras, who, like Commander Peary, had devoted the best years of his life to attaining this object. When this explorer reaches his goal he finds he has been forestalled by an American, who arrived a few days before him and has already planted the U.S.A. flag on the Pole itself. In Jules Verne's account of the North Pole this is stated to be in an open icebound sea, with no land in sight.

I am faithfully yours,

Jessica Sykes.

BETTER DEAD.

To the Editor of the Saturday Review.

The Chicago Daily News—London Office,
Trafalgar Buildings, Trafalgar Square W.C.
13 September 1909.

Sir,—May I call the attention of Marie Lantrow to the errors into which her kindness of heart has led her in taking to task Mr. John Bland for his "callous remarks" on the subject of the habitual frequenters of the Thames Embankment?

Marie Lantrow states that Mr. Bland "desires, as his letter abundantly proves, to deprive the poor of their last right—the right to exist at all on the earth". The grounds for this flagellation are that Mr. Bland, in a temperate but vividly expressed letter to the Saturday Review of 28 August, asked why in the name of logic and progress the proper authorities—be whom they may—have deliberately chosen to allot to the most impressive by night, the freshest, the finest boulevard of the metropolis of the British Empire, the rôle of overflow tramps' casual ward, and allow there a nightly herding together of unspeakably filthy and verminous degenerates whom the none too æsthetic passers-by of the New Cut, the Mile End Road, the rough-and-tumble thoroughfare in which Chevalier "knocked 'em", and Saffron Hill would never tolerate for one hour.

If Marie Lantrow and readers of her letter will refer to their SATURDAY REVIEW of 28 August, they will search in vain for the hypothetical and cruel aims which having been put into the mouth of Mr. Bland are eloquently decried.

If Marie Lantrow knew her Embankment—not by any means the same spot as the romantically dowered Thames Embankment of popular twentieth century fiction—she would never fall into the error of drawing a harrowing picture of John Bland, overtaken by a righteous retribution, dragging his "faint, bruised, and weary body" on to the Embankment, there to receive the heartlessly repugnant glances, and subsequent strictures in the Press, of passing gentlemen of his kidney. The poor man does not, to quote Mr. Bland, "beg with veiled threats; stretch his filthy naked skin and tattered duds about the steps, and aim loathsome remarks from the benches". The typical Embankmenter does; and he is a distinct class of society. If a decent upbringing and a decent intercourse with the world has been working on you for twenty, thirty, or forty years, you cannot become a typical Embankmenter by the simple process of losing your money, your friends, and your home. You may lose, in addition, your sight, a leg, and the use of your hands, and, worst of all, your self-respect, and yet you won't pick up the little manners and aspects of an Embankmenter.

It is rarely indeed that a member of the tolerably respectable poor need sleep on the Embankment; cheap lodging-houses and casual wards in plenty are to be found in the heart of London. Moreover, the poor man may be very poor, and very shabby, and very miserable, and still not a revolting sight to witness.

But a discussion of the poor man, his rights and troubles, is altogether beside the point. Why is the noble sweep of the Thames Embankment ordained to be London's human garbage-heap?

Yours truly,
GEORGE BASSETT DIGBY.

"THE JEW AND HUMAN SACRIFICE."

To the Editor of the SATURDAY REVIEW.

Royal Societies Club, S. James' Street S.W.
14 August 1909.

SIR,—In his excellent notice of Professor Strack's work on the above subject your reviewer observes: "On the Continent the calumny [that the Jews are in the habit of sacrificing Christian children] is still sedulously circulated and widely believed". Of the truth of this observation I have just received a singularly interesting —I might almost say startling—illustration. It occurs in the course of a critique of my own book, "Israel in Europe", in a recent issue of the French Orientalist review "Mélanges". The writer, after blaming me severely for treating the "ritual murder" tradition as a myth, goes on to state: "Cette tache, qu'on a certainement grossie, on essaie vainement de la soustraire au verdict de l'histoire; les faits parlent encore: 'experto crede Roberto' devrais-je ajouter, si je pouvais trouver plaisir à rappeler une page de mon enfance, où je dus le salut à un vrai fils d'Israël".

As you will see, the writer, a French scholar of some standing, actually believes that he himself in his childhood had narrowly escaped being sacrificed by the Jews! After this, what is left for the half-civilised masses of Eastern Europe?

Yours truly, G. F. ABBOTT.

REVIEWS.

JANE AUSTEN.

"Jane Austen and her Country House Comedy." By W. H. Helm. London: Nash. 1909. 7s. 6d.

NO one can deny that Jane Austen has proved a good "stayer". After a period of comparative neglect in the middle of last century, her popularity, aided by the cheap reprint, came with a rush towards the end. She has easily outdistanced her early rivals. Few read Fanny Burney nowadays except out of curiosity, and it needs a very tough kind of curiosity to get one through either "Cecilia" or "Camilla". "Evelina" is the only one that will do at all, and that is certainly a splendid, witty story. Little, too, of Miss Edgeworth is read to-day, except perhaps her tales for children; still less of Miss Ferrier, though she is worth reading. Of Miss Mitford only "Our Village" survives. Indeed it is a question whether Jane Austen has not now surpassed in popularity Sir Walter Scott, despite his success at what he called the "big bow-wow strain". Besides the many reprints of her works, we have further proof of Miss Austen's popularity in the numerous books that are continually being written about various aspects of her life and novels. In the last few years we can call to mind such books as "Jane Austen, her Contemporaries and Herself", "Jane Austen, her Homes and her Friends", "Jane Austen and her Times", "Jane Austen's Sailor Brothers"; and now we have Mr. Helm with "Jane Austen and her Country House Comedy". And yet it is curious that there is not one satisfactory Life of Jane Austen in this country. Her nephew, the Rev. J. E. Austen Leigh, had seen but few of her letters when he wrote his sympathetic Memoir in 1870. Fourteen years later Lord Brabourne published nearly a hundred new letters, but his volumes were neither edited nor printed with any conspicuous care. "Lord "Overtley" for "Lord Orville", "Easton" for "Exeter" and "Lynn" for "Lyme" within a few pages hardly inspire confidence in the rest of the letterpress. Of the existing Lives, by far the best and most complete is that published in 1891 by an American admirer, Mr. Oscar Fay Adams. Yet not even Mr. Adams has studied the Letters with very strict attention. For instance, he repeats the usual statement that Jane Austen, together with her mother and sister, left Bath in 1805 after her father's death, and took up her residence that autumn in Castle Square, Southampton. But the Austens remained in Bath till the summer of 1806 (this is proved by Jane's letter dated 1 July 1808, where she says to Cassandra "It will be two years to-morrow since we left Bath for Clifton, with what happy feelings of escape!"); and any careful student of the letters written from Southampton can scarcely fail to infer that the earliest were written from lodgings, and that the move into Castle Square was not made till March 1807.

The chief events of Jane Austen's life are easily told. Born at the country parsonage of Steventon, she spent her first twenty-five years there: five years followed at Bath, two and a half at Southampton, and the last eight were spent at Chawton. But her quiet home life was varied by occasional visits to one brother's country seat in Kent or to another's house in town. All her six novels were written in the country, the first three at Steventon, the remainder at Chawton. Though she fortunately escaped ever being made a literary lion, as an author she met with considerable success. Her first book brought her in nearly £150, and not only did she receive a hint, which she took as a command, to dedicate her fourth novel to the Prince Regent, but she had the pleasure of seeing it made the subject of a review in the "Edinburgh".

Mr. Helm, however, is but little concerned with the events of Jane Austen's life except so far as they exerted any influence on her writings. In dealing with her various residences, however, he does make one admirable suggestion, namely, that the London County Council might well consider the idea of placing a plaque on 10 Henrietta Street, Covent Garden, for this is the only one of Henry Austen's London residences where his sister stayed which remains unaltered at the present day. 16 Michael's Place, Brompton, where Jane stayed in 1808, is gone, and even the name of the block is altered to Egerton Mansions. The house at 64 Sloane Street has been rebuilt, so too has 23 Hans Place, with its "love of a garden" from which Jane could talk across the intervening gardens to the Tilsons at No. 26. But the house at Henrietta Street, to which Henry removed for a short year between living in Sloane Street and Hans Place, must still, except for its plaster front, be much the same as when Jane stayed in the upper part in 1813 or witnessed the opening of an account in Henry's ill-fated bank on the ground floor.

Mr. Helm's volume, indeed, is more in the nature of an appreciation than a Life. The headings of his chapters—"Dominant Qualities", "Equipment and Method", "Contact with Life", "Ethics and Optimism" etc.—indicate its scope. Nor need the devoted admirer of Jane Austen quarrel much with his judgment. It is true Mr. Helm holds her to have been unemotional and, in the ordinary sense of the word, unsympathetic; he considers, rather unnecessarily, that in her the conjugal instinct was not strongly developed, and the maternal instinct still less, and he holds that no patience is possible with those who regard Jane Austen's work as equally excellent in every part. No doubt people are tiresome enough about Jane Austen; some see nothing in her works, while others consider her second only to Shakespeare, and see no exaggeration in Mr. Collins or Sir Walter Elliott. Mr. Helm's admiration is sane and well balanced. He points out clearly enough that one of the reasons why her novels have so abiding a freshness is that the material factors of manners and habits are little noted, and that "with a few slight changes such as making 'post-chaise' read 'motor' and 'coach' read 'train', or retarding the dinner from three or five to eight or half-past, cutting out the occasional 'elegants' and otherwise changing a word here and there in the dialogue, long scenes from any one of Jane Austen's novels could be acted without material alteration, in the costume of to-day, with no serious offence to the unities". This, like much of Mr. Helm's criticism, is true enough.

Besides using passages from her novels to illustrate Jane Austen's qualities, Mr. Helm makes frequent quotations from her published correspondence. The Letters were deemed trivial and disappointing at the time of their publication. There are but few allusions to her writings, and still fewer to public affairs. One casual mention of Bonaparte and one of Nelson, and a couple of references to Sir John Moore, almost complete the allusions to public affairs. But it must be remembered that nearly all her letters that have survived were written to her sister Cassandra. Even to-day devoted sisters probably do not waste much time when they write in commenting on the Budget or the Suffragette movement. In fact, Jane's letters are full of exactly what we might expect them to be—details of dress, balls, household affairs, and not always too kindly remarks about the people she met. For, as Mr. Helm reminds us, despite her brother's opinion, Jane Austen was not faultless, and, not being a fool either, she could not help remarking on her neighbours' little weaknesses.

Mr. Helm has something too to say of the various misprints in Jane Austen's novels. Jane was indeed no skilled proof-reader, and though she says in a letter to her publisher that she returns "Mansfield Park" as ready for a second edition as she could make it, it is a melancholy fact that the second edition, besides leaving two of the most glaring misprints unaltered, contains several others that were not in the first. Mr. Helm quotes two or three of Dr. Verrall's ingenious emendations, and rightly makes short work of his suggestion that Jane Austen really wrote "derelict" and not "direct holidays" in connexion with William Price's stay at Mansfield Park. Dr. Verrall also was quite correct when he emended the following passage in "Emma": "The want of proper families in the place, and the conviction that none beyond the place and its immediate environs could be attempted to attend, were mentioned" into "tempted to attend"—but then no good edition reads "attempted", which, if we remember rightly, was only one of a great number of misprints introduced into one of the earliest of the modern reprints. Finally, on the subject of misprints and faulty punctuation, what are we to say of Mr. Helm, who quotes on page 72 the famous remarks of Lady Catherine de Bourgh to Mr. Collins, as reported by the latter?

"Mr. Collins, you must marry. A clergyman like you must marry. Choose properly, choose a gentlewoman for *my* sake, and for your *own*; let her be an active, useful sort of person, not brought up high, but able to make a small income go a good way."

Here, half the characteristic insolence of Lady Catherine's speech is lost unless we punctuate according to the first three editions: "Choose properly, choose a gentlewoman for *my* sake; and for your *own*, let her be an active useful sort of person", etc. But nearly all the modern editions are full of misprints, and it is earnestly to be hoped that in the centenary edition which Mr. Helm foreshadows special attention may be paid to the text. Apart from this, Mr. Helm's volume seems singularly free from error, though we do not think Steventon was the birthplace of "Mansfield Park", as stated on page 237, and we fancy "Margiarna" must be a misprint on page 61. We think, too, that Mr. Helm might have mentioned somewhere that the very charming sketch that forms his frontispiece is only a work of the imagination. Finally, we see no reason why Mr. Helm's thoughtful and appreciative volume should not have the result he desires—namely, of bringing "new members into the large but comparatively restricted circle wherein she is regarded, not always as the first of English novelists, but at least as second to none in the quality of her work".

REVOLUTION IN THE FLESH.

"Robespierre and the French Revolution." By Charles Warwick. London: Fisher Unwin. 1909. 8s. 6d. net.

HE suffered from chronic indigestion, and was bilious in hue; his features were mean; his veins showed greenishly through the skin, and he wore green glasses; he rarely looked a man in the face; his limbs were feeble and angular; his step was irresolute; his attitudes were affected; his articulation lay between a squeak and a scream; his eyes were blue and vague, and his lips nastily thin; he was pock-marked; he was five feet two inches in height; he winked horribly and continually; he was very particular about his linen and his waistcoats; he was a highly nervous man; his reserve was impenetrable; he was moved by no wholesome human passions; he had nothing that could be called genius; he had no natural gift for oratory; he was possessed neither of resolution nor foresight; in all qualities of the mind and heart he was beneath mediocrity; in conversation he was a vulgar provincial trying to be mistaken for a Parisian. Such was Robespierre; or, perhaps it would be better to say, such was a piece of him. It remains to wonder at the use he made of himself. If there is one name in history more than another which will be for ever associated with scenes that attain to the sublimity created by sheer terror, it is the name of this absurdly self-appreciative, small-souled, and physically conspicuous deputy from Arras. He may not have shared in, or been ultimately responsible for, the Reign of Death; but the fact remains that with the execution of Robespierre the tide of blood swept suddenly out on the ebb; and that, rightly or wrongly, the history that lives in the hearts of men sees in him the incarnation of the Revolution and the great apostle of the guillotine. Is this common impression seriously discredited because the documents are against it? In the fifteen weeks before Robespierre's own execution there were over two thousand deaths, and Robespierre knew that he was held accountable. "Death—always death!—and the scoundrels throw it on me." But it has long been realised that during these months Robespierre had little influence in the Great Committee; that he did not attend the Convention; that actually he was not responsible. Is mankind wrong, then, to see in Robespierre an incarnation of the Revolution and of the logical sequence of its horrors?

Mankind is most certainly right. Robespierre may be washed as white as snow, yet the truth remains untouched. He stands at the heart of the Revolution. We are not considering Robespierre as a private individual, and it is a side issue that, in this respect, the more he is whitewashed the uglier he appears. We are considering Robespierre as an incarnation of the Revolution, and endeavouring to account on broad, general principles for his power. Under this aspect, the fact that explains Robespierre better than any other is the fact that from first to last his career was bound up with the rise and fall of the Jacobins. It was not in any of the various Assemblies of the Revolution that he came truly to his own. It was in the "Société des Jacobins" with its "Unité, Liberté, Egalité, Indivisibilité de la République, Fraternité ou la Mort" that Robespierre night after night protested his integrity, alluded to the classical philosophers, generalised on human destiny, and slowly began to loom large before the people of Paris as the eighteenth century in human flesh, the predestinate idol of the Triumph of Reason.

This Triumph of Reason was complete when, in June 1794, Robespierre lit the pyre at the Festival of the Supreme Being on behalf of the French nation. Tradition was shattered; the foolish religions of the past were down; the iniquitous social structure lay in ruins; the unaided reason of man, speaking through its great prophets, through Voltaire and through Rousseau, to the confusion of priests and kings, of theologies and polities, had triumphed. And indeed what a simple and beautiful rationalism was here, something worthy, as it had been found, of the easy couplets of Alexander Pope and of the even easier verses of his French imitator!

It is here that Robespierre stands in history. He was the best possible creature of all those that the Revolution brought forth to represent and lend a fitting glory to those few simple ideas upon which the Revolution was based. The narrow intensity of his provincial studies was just the kind of training to fit him for the part he played. Sounding passages from the great classical writers haunted his brain. For the Bible he substituted Rousseau. He came to the Jacobins fully equipped. He practised upon them till he could say what he wanted to say with something approaching eloquence, and he never bored them. He echoed their own ideas and aspirations, and they pushed him forth into the Revolution as the man of the Revolution, which he most certainly was. His faith was the faith of the Revolution—faith in a few simple ideas that must be logically followed. To pause and reflect that human destiny was too profound and too old a thing to be included in a few formulæ—this was treason. To hold that these ideas were socially and ethically barren, leading into blind alleys, products of an eighteenth century intelligence that looked upon life with a vision limited and thwarted by the blinkers of rationalism—this was impiety. These ideas sufficed, and they would suffice for ever.

Such was the meaning of Robespierre, approaching him from the purely historical point of view. From another, that of personality, he is if anything a vastly more interesting subject. Whatever else he was, he was not a dull person. Mr. Warwick has painted him afresh in all the ancient and lively colours that are so familiar to readers of Revolution history. The author has much to say on many points of interest, and the new volume brings to a fitting conclusion his earlier work upon Mirabeau and Danton. Mr. Warwick is conscientious; and if, in this respect, he has a fault, it is that he does not dogmatise sufficiently. His presentment of Robespierre almost fails to be a portrait, and only just misses being a collection of preliminary studies.

CHILDREN AND THE STATE.

"Children in Health and Disease." By David Forsyth. London: Murray. 1909. 10s. 6d. net.

GROWING interest in child-life and increasing intelligence expended upon the direction of it are noteworthy features of our times. It may be that the national consciousness has at last been aroused to the portents of our falling birth-rate, and that children, like other human possessions, become more appreciated as they become scarcer. At all events, it is a compensation that an epoch which has witnessed an unprecedented shrinkage in the prolificacy of the race should have been marked also by something like a systematised effort to secure greater civic efficiency in the rising generation. Without doubt a saner spirit pervades the educative field, and to-day we find common-sense, and some realisation of the physiology and psychology of childhood, moulding methods of education in a measure previously unattained.

Until the passing of the Education Act of 1870 the State evinced but a detached interest in its youthful citizens, but with the appearance of that Act the theoretical position, at least, was completely altered. We are not concerned to argue the academic wisdom or otherwise of this domestic revolution, nor to attempt a balance of the gains and losses which have followed and are following it. For good or for evil the State decreed book-learning for its children, and by doing so undertook a duty whose expansion is as logical as irresistible and whose end is not yet in sight. For with the imposition of elementary education upon the masses the State became a guardian of childhood in a novel and extremely comprehensive sense, though we may doubt whether at the time the true comprehensiveness of the new relation was properly appreciated. Indeed, we may be sure it was not, since there are, as we shall see, corollaries attached to the apparently simple proposition that a child shall be educated—corollaries which the State neglected for close upon a generation, yet which cannot be neglected without stultifying the main proposition.

It might have been supposed that the essential unity of the intellectual and bodily man was a postulate and needed no labouring. "It is not a mind, it is not a body that we erect", says Montaigne, "but it is a man, and we must not make two parts of him." The statement seems platitudinous enough; and it has not failed to encounter the disregard commonly meted to obvious truths. Thirty-nine years ago the edict went forth that all children were to be educated in reading, writing and arithmetic, and "educated" they were. That is to say, they went to school and were duly submitted to a daily dose of instruction; but as to whether they were capable of profiting from the instruction received the State evinced not the slightest interest. Deafness, blindness, bodily ill-health, mental dulness and other such disabilities only too common among the school community elicited no attention; and so for thirty years we saw, but did not observe, the wasteful and largely futile issue of the great scheme of national education. Gradually, however, it began to dawn upon the authorities that they had commenced, so to speak, at the wrong end; that the education to which they were committed, if it were to be of any notable service, inevitably implied far more than was originally contemplated. It was manifestly ridiculous to give the usual oral instruction to a deaf child, or to give blackboard demonstrations of desirable things to a child who could not see them. Moreover, advances in medical knowledge of childish ailments made it abundantly clear that large numbers of the physical faults which hampered educationalists were preventible by timely interference, and that much could be done to educate even the hopelessly handicapped by the use of specialised and appropriate means. Accordingly in 1893 statutory provision was made for the appointment of medical officers in connexion with the blind and deaf, and in 1899 others for the purposes of the mentally defective and epileptic. But here the advance rested until public interest was aroused, at about the time of the South African war, by a War Office Memorandum drawing attention to the progressive deterioration of the classes from which the Army was recruited. In 1903, consequently, an Interdepartmental Committee was appointed, which, after exhaustive inquiries, recommended the systematic medical inspection of school children. Two years later the Education Committee of the London County Council inaugurated a tentative scheme by appointing twenty "part-time" medical inspectors, to each of whom was assigned one of the metropolitan school areas. The duties of these officials comprised not only the examination of physically or mentally defective children (with a view to having remediable defects remedied in time and proper provision made for those whose condition could only be palliated), but included the giving of advice to teachers with regard to matters of general school hygiene. Finally, at the instance of both political parties, an obligatory clause was inserted in the Education Act of 1907, binding local education authorities to provide for the medical inspection of children at the time of their admission to a public elementary school, and empowering them to make arrangements for attending to the health and physical condition of the children in their schools.

It will be apparent from this brief sketch of the educational movement in recent years that we have long been grasping at the shadow of education and missing its substance. Book-learning may or may not be an essential factor in the vitality and efficiency of a modern race, but no such question can be entertained touching the matter of health; and this seems now to be fully appreciated. The mere appearance of such a book as the one before us is a sign of the times; for it is not a medical text-book, but a scientific consideration, in more or less popular terms, of the circumstances affecting the bodily and mental welfare of children, and is dedicated to educationalists and publicists as much as to physicians. In it Dr. Forsyth has collected a quantity of facts which will certainly be useful to students of school hygiene in general. But it is too long, and many pages are devoted to matter so obvious that it is hard to pardon the author for burdening his text with it; while elsewhere one encounters subjects which, in the detail accorded to them, can only appeal to physicians. Nevertheless we may welcome the book, for it is an earnest of newly awakened public interest in what can claim to be one of the most urgent problems of the time.

TEUFELSDROCKH'S BLUMINE.

"Carlyle's First Love: Margaret Gordon, Lady Bannerman." By Raymond Clare Archibald. London: Lane. 1909. 10s. 6d. net.

THIS volume would be a slender one if all the pages that do not deal directly with Margaret Gordon were cut out. Mr. Archibald, however, appears to have taken some pains to rake together everything ascertainable about her ancestry and her ancestors' connexions and friends; and it is all duly set forth and illustrated with portraits. To the general reader Margaret's main interest is that Carlyle was in love with her for a little while and utilised his experience for "Sartor Resartus"; and probably only those who find a deep joy in family records will devour this whole work with any great appetite. Margaret Gordon's father came of an undistinguished stock: he himself was an Army surgeon. Her mother's line, the Pattersons, made a couple of notable alliances. The sister of one Robert Patterson married Jerome Bonaparte in 1803; but when Jerome became a puppet-king he divorced her. She lived on to the age of ninety-five, and died as late as 1879. The widow of the same Robert married the Duke of Wellington's brother; but in view of the divorce we suppose it cannot be said that the Wellesley and Bonaparte families were in any way connected. Margaret Gordon, like these ladies, might never have attracted public notice, had not fate associated her name with a much greater name, that of Thomas Carlyle. Nowadays no one cares a jot for Jerome Bonaparte nor the Duke of Wellington's brother, nor thinks about whom they married or divorced; but the object of Carlyle's calf-love—if we dare call it so—and the original of Blumine will continue to make her appearance in literary biographies for some time.

Margaret Gordon was born in Canada in 1798. When she was twenty Carlyle, and Irving as well, met her. She seems to have fascinated them both a little; with Carlyle a few letters were exchanged; but a match with a poor schoolmaster seemed undesirable to her relatives, and in 1820 a "good-bye" was said in Kirkcaldy. She came to London and put on airs and the latest fashions; and in 1824 she married Alexander Bannerman, "banker, wine-merchant and manufacturer". To these avocations he added another later, that of Governor of Prince Edward Island, Nova Scotia—or somewhere that way, as Carlyle scornfully wrote. He was knighted; and he died at the age of seventy-six in 1864. So far as one can judge the marriage was a fair average one. Margaret did not expect, nor perhaps desire, the raptures of a "Tristan and Isolda" union; for she was a level-headed young woman with an eye for a solid position in life. She lived twelve years after Sir Alexander's death, and died in 1876.

The year after the "good-bye", out of which the tragic episode in "Sartor" is spun, Carlyle was introduced to Jane Welsh; he promptly fell in love again, vowed to love Jane far more deeply than he ever had Margaret; and five years afterwards married her. The time-dishonoured squabbles as to whether she was a suitable wife or he an unsuitable husband were always foolish, and are now grown a bore; and this book perhaps serves a useful purpose in showing that, however he fared with Jane Welsh, Carlyle could scarcely have hoped to get on much if any better with Margaret. The impression left indeed is that the former was in every way a superior woman to the other. Possibly Mr. Archibald did not mean to demonstrate this, but it is this he has succeeded in demonstrating. That Margaret Gordon and Carlyle's early passion for her were the starting-points for Blumine and the disastrous cataclysm in "Sartor Resartus" no one can doubt; but to affirm so much is not to accept Blumine as a portrait nor the incident of the parting as a photographic description of what actually happened. Carlyle was above all things a phrase-maker and a writer of books, and there is not the slightest reason to believe that everything he wrote was literally or even figuratively true. Many a young man after a love-disappointment feels as if the world has come to an end; and the shattering of his hopes may have appeared grave enough to Carlyle. But he recovered very swiftly. He did not see Margaret again until long years had passed, and perhaps the mournful glance she cast his way did not exist outside his own fancy. However, those who want to know the little there is to be known about the lady will find it in Mr. Archibald's volume. That the book is worth the labour it must have cost is more than we should care to vouch. The relatives of distinguished men are generally tedious, and still more so are the relatives of a lady whose only claim to distinction is that a famous man loved her for a brief hour in his youth.

CLIO EN DÉSHABILLE.

"An Introductory History of England." By C. R. L. Fletcher. Vols. III. and IV. London: Murray. 1909. 5s. each volume.

WANTED, a history of England as good as Green's, free from his Liberal prejudices, yet without any superior airs of frigid impartiality. This was the desideratum we lately discussed. And here comes Mr. Fletcher with his breezy, boyish volumes—but with nothing of schoolboy pomposity—bashing in many (not quite all) of the old left-centre conventions in which Englishmen are trained, our civil and religious liberties, our admirable party system, our excellent representative institutions, and the rest. Saint George for England is on the cover, but inside he is a champion rollicking about on a polo pony, in an Oxford blazer, and smoking a short pipe. Mr. Fletcher's pages are elegantly strewn with "isn'ts" and "couldn'ts", with "etc.'s" and "(?) 's", with immortal phrases from Mr. Kipling like "Pay, pay, pay", with jocularities like "The Age of W(h)igs"—a chapter heading—and with other literary artifices which we do not remember to have met with in Clarendon or Gibbon. Well, the conception of history has changed a good deal. In Herodotean days it was liturgic, and the historian claimed a religious inspiration. With Macaulay history became an immense party-pamphlet. For Mr. Fletcher it is a putting out the tongue at solemn frauds. He slaughters the Philistine with slang, drags the Whig Clio from her pedestal, and kicks about her false wig and padding. Yet somehow we seem to recall writers—like Fuller—who have made the Muse of history racy without making her vulgar. History as light literature is all very well. Mr. Fletcher begs his readers not to let him bore them. The day of prunes and prisms being over, we dare say his jolly volumes will be welcomed in the schoolroom. How funny that an Irish pig should be the gintleman that pays the rint, that the plural of Wolfe (James) should be Wolves, that Queens and Juntas should squeal to neighbouring Powers for help, that "empty ass" or "immeasurable ass" should be the description of a James II., Monmouth, Sacheverell, or George IV. When, however, Charles II.'s (allegorical) hooking of a salmon is illustrated by the monarch's fondness for swearing by "God's fish", it is possible that the meaning of that very profane oath may be known even in the schoolroom, and Mr. Fletcher's exquisite joke give a little shock.

It is a pity, because there is plenty of genuine humour and sound history in these volumes, and we have a real admiration for an historian who says he has forgotten what it was Arkwright invented, who tells "Headmasters in Conference" that they are going to make chewed pap the basis of education, and who asks God to bless the Highland boatmen who sank the first steamer that ever defiled Loch Katrine—at the bottom of which she still lies. William of Orange is described as a king who was a Whig against his will and never more than king of a faction; his War Office as displaying all the vices of senility in the infancy (why not the teething?) of our standing Army; the "effectual truth of things" as meaning brute force; and Frederick the Great (who relied on that truth) as, at his accession, a young man who was not a gentleman, devoted to flute-playing and cheap French philosophy. Chesterfield is said to have been universally dreaded because he was known to be writing memoirs of his own times; and, after mentioning that Fox, by an astonishing volte-face, spoke of the French, directly they became the friends of his own country, as our natural enemies, Mr. Fletcher adds "However, they soon went to war with us, so that he was again able to regard them as his friends". Nevertheless, "Fox, with all his iniquities, was a man of flesh and blood; Grey was the Spirit of Whiggery walking about in the clothes of a man". Diva Britannia in these pages is an Empress of the Sea intent on halfpence—"at one time a busy bumboat woman, but anger her and she is transformed into an armed mermaid". After a world-shaking struggle she hangs up her crown in the Abbey and dozes off again, or allows dirty political party squabbles to fritter away her might; for the old Sea-Queen is often sick of an acute attack of parliamentary inflammation. There is a good chapter on the American struggle, and one on Ireland—spiritually-minded, but "a country more unfit for self-government it is hard to imagine". Mr. Fletcher quotes Grattan's prophecy when the Irish legislature was abolished: "We will avenge ourselves by sending into the ranks of your Parliament, and into the very heart of your Constitution, one hundred of the greatest scoundrels in the Kingdom". On the other hand, the state of Scotland before the "sorrowfu' Union" was one in which parliaments and law courts played a very small part—for society was still based on patriarchal and kindly relations, not on the nexus of cash payment—but in which crime was rare and pauperism (which is a different thing from poverty) unknown. Intercourse with England changed all that, and the frugal Caledonian, with his simple and penurious virtues, has become the Scotch hotel-keeper or millionaire.

Mr. Fletcher's dislike of the Covenanters—persecuted with whips but persecuting with scorpions—makes him fairly gracious towards Scottish "Episcopalianism." But it is astonishing that he could write a History of England from 1660 to 1815 and hardly once mention the Church of England. When he does do so, it is usually to blunder. He thinks that James II. was Head of the Church of England, whereas the last sovereign to bear that title was Mary Tudor, who got it repealed in 1553. He says that the Church came back at the Restoration "entirely without the aggressive sacerdotal spirit of Laud's Church", and yet took up an "uncompromising attitude" towards dissent. He does not think that the sectaries suffered much oppression, after all, in Charles II.'s reign, but he writes like Green about the Bartholomew of 1662. Similarly he accepts the conventional view of the Huguenot expulsion. There are various girdings at "Puseyites", and we find the astonishing assertion that in the religious movement of the closing seventeenth century, when the S.P.C.K., the S.P.G. and the societies for "reformation of manners" were founded, "High Churchmen took little part". Nor has Mr. Fletcher ever heard that the Church of England claims to be a part of the Catholic Church—at any rate, he always uses "Catholic" in the sense in which it was used when Regent Street was in building. On the ecclesiastical side we fear Mr. Fletcher is whiggissimus. Whitefield, by the bye, went to Oxford in 1732, not in 1728.

Mr. Fletcher does justice to the Old Chevalier, so absurdly maligned in "Esmond". Though he speaks of the "fatal Act of Settlement" he disavows being a Jacobite in principle. But, "when the alternative came to be between an unspeakable German boor and a simple, pious, valiant young man of stainless honour", resolved in his Catholicism but respectful towards others' faith, "I for one", says Mr. Fletcher, "would have voted for my legitimate and native King". He calls him "the most gentle, tolerant, honourable soul who ever threw away a crown", the "rightful King". His last thought on Scottish soil was bitter regret that his troops had been obliged to burn some crops and cottages in their retreat, and his last act was to send some of his slender stock of money to relieve the sufferers. He was a finer, more religious character than Prince Charlie, of whose great adventure, however, Mr. Fletcher says that the reality vies in interest with any romance that could be written. He pithily divides English history into the age of heroics, the age of common-sense, and the age (our own) of hysterics. But the heroic age did not altogether die in 1660.

NOVELS.

"The Castle by the Sea." By H. B. Marriott Watson. London: Methuen. 1909. 6s.

It is evidently a mere coincidence that a somewhat disreputable baronet should be seeking hidden treasure in his abandoned estate by the sea, alike in this novel and in Mr. George Birmingham's "Spanish Gold", but the comparison that inevitably suggests itself somewhat handicaps Mr. Marriott Watson. There is much philandering in "The Castle by the Sea", and the essential motifs of the two novels differ widely. Taking the present one on its own merits, we may say that it is entertaining enough, with its medley of mistaken identities and smugglers' caves and duns besieging the innocent tenant of the castle. The aforesaid tenant, a man of letters, gives the impression of a certain deficiency in breeding—impalpable perhaps, and clearly unperceived

(*Continued on page 358.*)

by his inventor, but real enough to make us indifferent to his fortunes. Still, it is an amusing company that Mr. Marriott Watson has collected, and no one will drop the book halfway through.

"Midsummer Madness." By Morley Roberts. London: Nash. 1909. 6s.

Most of these nine stories are nightmares, and not bad of their kind. We like the experiences of an editor chased from the Temple to Greenwich by a lunatic contributor, and the adventures of a clergyman lost in Soho whose unfortunate nasal resemblance to an unknown person involved him in a good deal of homicide. But Mr. Roberts is less agreeable when depicting the unclean side of a sculptor's mind, or describing the working in London of a West African blood fetish (an Anstey theme treated after the Kipling manner, but not very effectively). There is power in the picture of London engulfed in so vast and lasting a fog that only a blind man is able to save the characters of the story. And a sketch of a French peasant of the Landes whose mind became obsessed by the great Sud express train has a certain pathos. But the stories suggest a series of attempts to startle magazine readers.

"Marcia." By Marguerite Curtis. London: Blackwood. 1909. 6s.

Marcia was afflicted with a dual personality. The one Marcia was truthful and even pious, but after periods of emotional stress the other Marcia would crop up, imagine pleasant fictions and substantiate them by lies and the forgery of letters. The good Marcia had only a hazy recollection of what the naughty one did, though for other things her memory was known to be excellent, and after situations painful both to herself and her friends she very properly put aside all thought of marriage with her lover. It is a sombre story, but as the author assures us there was a real Marcia it has a pathological interest; and the rather irritating iteration of similar phrases is perhaps inevitable in a novel cast in the form of reminiscences.

"The Invincible Amelia." By E. Maria Albanesi. London: Methuen. 1909. 3s. 6d.

We are sorry to see Madame Albanesi, who has done some good work, descending to such paltry stuff as this. The "Invincible Amelia" has nothing to recommend her. She is both second-rate and vulgar. Unfortunately, her creator does not seem to recognise this glaring fact, but rather holds her up to admiration as a sort of feminine "Admirable Crichton". We should be sorry to think such a detestable person as Amelia could exist, and, if we took the author's story as a serious character-study, we should be inclined to say that she had made an indecent exposure of the worthlessness of her sex.

"A Dog's Life in Burma." Told by the Dog. London: Drane. 1909. 3s. 6d.

Humour of a very elementary kind is obtained by putting this bald narrative of a pleasure trip in Burma —undertaken by the Colonel Sahib, the Mem Sahib and the Missy Sahib—into the dog's mouth; and it may be that the type of reader who finds the author's style really funny will also be grateful for the lavish and young-lady-like underlining with italicised words. To us it all seems rather amateurish.

SHORTER NOTICES.

Everyman's Library: "The Bayard of India," by Captain L. J. Trotter; "The Chronicles of Barset," and other volumes. London: Dent. 1909. 1s. net.

The People's Library: "The Crown of Wild Olive," by John Ruskin; "The Master of Ballantrae," by R. L. Stevenson, and other volumes. London: Cassell. 1909. 8d. net.

The rivalry of the reprint grows keener. Everyman's Library, in itself a marvel of cheapness, is challenged by the People's Library, which is cheaper still. Mr. Dent has now completed four hundred books in the first, and has another hundred to come; Messrs. Cassell are steadily adding to their People's Library—it now numbers over one hundred volumes —and the only limit to these reproductions is the limit of literature itself. Five millions of Everyman's Library have been sold, and over one million of the People's Library. Both libraries are nicely printed and bound, the paper is serviceable, and the brief introductions are all that is necessary. Except on the score of price, there seems little to choose between them. Not everybody, of course, who is looking for a cheap book wants it for a few pence. The People's Library may be had in leather for eighteenpence, and Everyman's for two shillings, a volume. In that form no one need hesitate to give any work in either Library a place on his shelves.

"America's Motherland." By T. W. D. Smith. London: Middleton. 1909. 1s. net.

America's Motherland seems, according to the editor of this "concise guide for American visitors", largely to consist of that portion of England which stretches from London to Stratford-on-Avon. Mr. Smith has called in Miss Marie Corelli and Mr. Clement Shorter to write parts of his brochure referring more particularly to Shakespeare's country—"the Mecca of many an American pilgrimage"—and to Cowper, Penn, Burke, Shelley, and Disraeli. Other sections deal with Byron's country, the ancestral home of the Washingtons, Sherwood Forest, &c. As the guide is intended for the visitor who wishes to tarry awhile in places of interest, it might appear to be more suited to the average foreigner than to the American, who rushes hither and thither in a motor-car and is content to know that he has put his name in a record number of visitors' books. It is, however, obviously prepared with a special eye to American predilections, and within its self-imposed limitations is full of useful hints. It will at least show the American that there are places in England with which it might be worth his while to make more than a ten seconds' acquaintance.

"Self-Government in Canada." By F. Bradshaw. London: King. 1909. 3s. 6d. net.

Mr. Bradshaw's book on Lord Durham's report to which Canada owed its self-government is now issued in a cheap edition. For all who are interested in colonial history and development in the second quarter of the nineteenth century the story is of immense interest. The book is also a useful supplement to the Life of Lord Durham which has appeared in the interval since the first edition was published. In this cheaper form we should have thought Mr. Bradshaw would have added Mr. Stuart Reid's work to his bibliography. He gives a list of certain small corrigenda, but the original volume otherwise is unchanged.

"Revue des Deux Mondes." 1 Septembre.

This number has several papers of real interest. Mme. Marcelle Tinayre has a third article on modern Turkey which contains some points on the inner life of Turkish homes. The usual European illusions on the matter vanish at the contact of reality. The Turk is usually the husband of one wife, because it is cheaper, and there is no luxury in her surroundings—at the most some hideous mid-Victorian furniture. There is also a delightful sketch of a visit to a Turkish girls' school. The system of teaching is curious. Passages of the Koran in the original Arabic are committed to memory without any explanation of their meaning being conveyed to the pupils, because "women have no need of instruction of the kind". Mme. Tinayre promises to give us an account shortly of a visit to the ladies in a Constantinople harem. It will be interesting to learn her views as to the "Désenchantées". Admirers of Matthew Arnold's "Obermann" will welcome M. Michaud's appreciation of Senancour.

For this Week's Books see pages 360 and 362.

NOTICE.

The Terms of Subscription to the SATURDAY REVIEW are:—

	United Kingdom. £ s. d.	Abroad. £ s. d.
One Year	1 8 2	1 10 4
Half Year	0 14 1	0 15 2
Quarter Year	0 7 1	0 7 7

Cheques and Money Orders should be crossed and made payable to the Manager, SATURDAY REVIEW Offices, 10 *King Street, Covent Garden, London, W.C.*

In the event of any difficulty being experienced in obtaining the SATURDAY REVIEW, the Publisher would be glad to be informed immediately.

POOLE & LORD

INDIAN AND GENERAL OUTFITTERS,

322 OXFORD STREET, LONDON, W.

(NEARLY OPPOSITE BOND STREET.)

INVENTORS OF THE

"Sans-Plis" SHIRT.

Prices from 7s. 6d.

The "SANS-PLIS" Shirt is superior to any other for Indian and Colonial wear. Being entirely free from gathers, it is cooler, much stronger, and will bear the Indian mode of washing better than any shirt in use.

A single shirt, or other article, made to *measure*, and accurate patterns preserved to ensure correctness in the execution of future orders.

Makers of Drawers with Flexible Hip Belt Bands.

"BREECHES CUT."

CONNOISSEURS OF COFFEE

DRINK THE

RED
WHITE
& BLUE

DELICIOUS FOR BREAKFAST & AFTER DINNER.

In making, use less quantity, it being much stronger than ordinary COFFEE.

BARR'S BEAUTIFUL HARDY DAFFODILS

GOLD MEDAL

THE MOST LOVELY OF ALL SPRING FLOWERS

Awarded 25 Gold Medals and a Ten Guinea Challenge Cup.

BARR'S POPULAR 21/- COLLECTION OF DAFFODILS contains **6 Bulbs each of 26 Fine Distinct Varieties** suitable for Pot-culture or for the Flower Border. (Half the Collection for **10/6.**)

BARR'S WOODLAND 21/- COLLECTION OF DAFFODILS contains **500 Strong Bulbs in 20 Fine Showy Varieties** suitable for Naturalising.

Descriptive Catalogue of all the finest Daffodils in Cultivation, Free.

BARR & SONS,

11, 12, & 13 King Street, Covent Garden, London.

AUSTRALIA by ORIENT LINE,

UNDER CONTRACT TO CARRY HIS MAJESTY'S MAILS.

FROM LONDON EVERY ALTERNATE FRIDAY, calling at PLYMOUTH, GIBRALTAR, MARSEILLES, NAPLES, PORT SAID, and COLOMBO.

Managers—F. GREEN & CO.: ANDERSON, ANDERSON & CO.

Head Offices—FENCHURCH AVENUE, LONDON.

For Passage apply to the latter firm at 5 Fenchurch Avenue, E.C., or to the Branch Office, 28 Cockspur Street, Charing Cross, S.W.

THE CONDUIT STREET AUCTION GALLERIES.

The attention of Executors, Trustees, Solicitors, and Owners, who may be desirous of selling Works of Art, Family Jewels, Old Silver, Furniture, Pictures, Prints, Miniatures, China, Coins, Books, Old Lace, Furs, Musical Instruments, Guns, and other Valuables, is drawn to Messrs.

KNIGHT, FRANK & RUTLEY'S

AUCTION GALLERIES, 9 CONDUIT STREET, AND 23A MADDOX STREET, W., which are Open Daily to receive goods intended for early sales.

VALUATIONS are prepared for Fire Insurance, Estate Duty, and all other purposes. As to Insurance, owners are reminded that, for security, Messrs. KNIGHT, FRANK & RUTLEY's detailed inventory and valuation of the contents of a Town or Country Mansion is an important adjunct to their Fire Insurance Policies.

SALE THURSDAY NEXT.

27 WHITEHEAD'S GROVE, CHELSEA.

By Order of the Executors of J. W. F. H. King, Esq., deceased.

ANDREWS & HITCH will SELL by AUCTION, on the premises as above, on Thursday next, the 23rd inst., at 12 (noon), the whole of the Contents of the Residence, comprising:

ANTIQUE FURNITURE,

PICTURES AND PRINTS,

A LARGE LIBRARY OF BOOKS,

Including Patristic Literature, Theological and Classical Works.

Catalogues of the Solicitors, Messrs. Dixon, Weld & Co., 1 Lancaster Place, Strand, W.C.; and of the Auctioneers, Andrews & Hitch, King's Road, Chelsea. Telephone No.: Ken 593.

BEAUTIFUL FLOWERS for WINTER DECORATION from SUTTON'S BULBS.

Before ordering Bulbs for the coming Season, everyone should write for a copy of

SUTTON'S BULB CATALOGUE for 1909,

Containing particulars of the best varieties of NARCISSI, HYACINTHS, TULIPS, &c.

Price 6d. Gratis and post-free to Customers.

SUTTON & SONS, The King's Seedsmen, READING.

Bell's THREE NUNS *Tobacco*

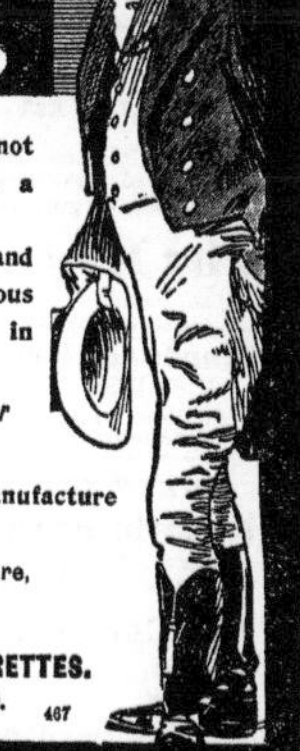

The man who does not like "Three Nuns" is a non-smoker.

The delicate flavour and peculiar charm of this famous mixture cannot be found in any other blend.

"King's Head" is similar but it is stronger.

Mixtures of unique manufacture and choicest quality.

Obtainable everywhere, 6½d. per oz.

"THREE NUNS" CIGARETTES.

4½d. per packet of 10. 467

THIS WEEK'S BOOKS.

Biography

A Beau Sabreur (W. R. H. Trowbridge). Fisher Unwin. 15s. net.
Memoir and Letters of Francis W. Newman (J. G. Sieveking), 10s. 6d. net; Sir Joseph Banks (J. H. Maiden), 6s. net. Kegan Paul.
Life of Dean Lefroy (Herbert Leeds). Jarrold. 2s. net.
The Life and Letters of James Wolfe (Beckles Willson). Heinemann, 18s. net.
My Recollections (Countess of Cardigan and Lancashire). Nash. 10s. 6d. net.

Fiction

The Scandalous Mr. Waldo (Ralph Straus). Heinemann. 3s.
Shadow-Shapes (Ella Erskine). Elkin Mathews. 3s. 6d. net.
The Screen (Vincent Brown). Chapman and Hall. 6s.
Arsène Lupin (Edgar Jepson and Maurice Leblanc); Tess of Ithaca (Grace Miller White). Mills and Boon. 6s. each.
Re-Birth (Rathmell Wilson); The Adventures of Susan (Cyrus Townsend Brady). Greening. 6s. each.
Johnny Lewison (A. E. Jacomb). Melrose. 6s.
In Ambush (Marie Van Vorst); Northern Lights (Gilbert Parker); The Severins (Mrs. Alfred Sidgwick). Methuen. 6s. each.
Mr. Justice Raffles (E. W. Hornung); The Paladin (Horace Annesley Vachell). Smith, Elder. 6s. each.
The Patience of John Morland (Mary Dillon). Nash. 6s.
Between Two Stools (Maynard Thorpe); Irish Drolleries (J. J. Moran); A Dual Personality (D. B. M.); Dr. Challoner's Chart, and other Stories (A. E. Winslade), 3s. 6d. each. Anthropoid Apes (Andrew Merry), 6s. Drane.
Stradella: an Old Italian Love Story (F. Marion Crawford). Macmillan. 6s.
The Rose of Dauphiny (Philip L. Stevenson); The Vortex (Fred Whishaw). Stanley Paul. 6s. each.
Le Vaisseau de Plomb (G. Leghartier). Paris: Plon-Nourrit.
Cricket Heron (Irving Bacheller). Fisher Unwin. 6s.
The Holy Mountain (Stephen Reynolds). Lane. 6s.

Gift Books

The Secrets of the Sargasso; Chillagoe Charlie (Robert M. Macdonald). Fisher Unwin. 5s. each.
Fairy Tales (Hans Christian Andersen). Heinemann. 6s. net.

History

French Vignettes (M. Betham-Edwards). Chapman and Hall. 10s. 6d. net.
History of Scotland (P. Hume Brown). Vol. III. Cambridge: At the University Press. 4s. 6d. net.

Law

Husband and Wife in the Law (Edward Jenks). Dent. 2s. 6d. net.
Foreign Judgments and Jurisdiction (Sir Francis Piggott). Butterworth. 35s. net.

Reprints and Translations

Poems (Oscar Wilde); The Duchess of Padua (Oscar Wilde). Methuen. 5s. net each.
The Cloister and the Hearth (Charles Reade). Chatto and Windus. 12s. 6d.
The People's Library.—The Black Tulip (Alexandre Dumas); Mansfield Park (Jane Austen); Lavengro (George Borrow); The Master of Ballantrae (R. L. Stevenson); The House of the Seven Gables (N. Hawthorne); Villette (Charlotte Brontë); The Sketch Book (Washington Irving); The Crown of Wild Olive and The Ethics of the Dust (John Ruskin); The Four Georges and The English Humourists of the Eighteenth Century (W. M. Thackeray); Reminiscences of Scottish Life and Character (Dean Ramsay). Cassell. 1s. 6d. net each.
The "Brother Luiz de Sousa" of Viscount de Almeida Garrett (Edgar Prestage). Elkin Mathews. 3s. net.

School Books

A Geography of the British Isles (A. Morley Davies), 3s.; Siepmann's Primary French Course, Part III. (Otto Siepmann), 2s. 6d.; Practical Exercises in Geography (B. C. Wallis), 2s. 6d.; Le Jeu de l'Amour et du Hasard (Edited by Eugène Pellissier), 2s. 6d.; Lettres de Mon Moulin (G. H. Clarke), 2s. 6d.; Thucydides, Book II. (Edited by E. C. Marchant), 3s. 6d.; Problem Papers in Mathematics (R. C. Fawdry), 4s. 6d. Macmillan.
First Latin Lessons (C. M. Dix). Rivington. 2s.

Science

The Periodic Law (A. E. Garrett). Kegan Paul. 5s.

Theology

The Study of Religion in the Italian Universities (Louis Henry Jordan). Frowde. 6s. net.
Passages of the Bible (J. G. Frazer). Black. 5s. net.

Travel

Things Seen in Holland (Charles E. Roche). Seeley. 2s. net.
The Holy Land (John Kelman). Black. 5s. net.
Through Persia: From the Gulf to the Caspian (F. B. Bradley-Birt). Smith, Elder. 12s. 6d. net.
Through the Yukon and Alaska (T. A. Richard). Mining and Scientific Press. 10s. 6d. net.

(*Continued on page 362.*)

THIS WEEK'S BOOKS—*Continued.*

VERSE

Sonnets and other Verses (W. M. MacKeracher). Toronto: Briggs. 50c. net.
The Exile, and other Poems (John Levo). Kegan Paul. 2*s.* 6*d.* net.
The Golden Treasury of Australian Verse (Edited by Bertram Stevens). Macmillan. 5*s.* net.
The Romance of the Twisted Spear (Herbert Sherring). Smith, Elder. 6*s.* net.
Ceres' Runaway, and other Essays (Alice Meynell). Constable. 3*s.* 6*d.* net.
The One and All Reciter (Marshall Steele), 2*s.* 6*d.* net; New Poems (Richard Le Gallienne), 5*s.* net. Lane.

MISCELLANEOUS

Critical Essays of the Seventeenth Century, Vol. III. (Edited by J. E. Spingarn). Oxford: At the Clarendon Press. 5*s.* net.
Dictionary of National Biography (Edited by Sidney Lee. Vol. XIX.). Smith, Elder. 15*s.* net.
Handbook of Marks on Pottery and Porcelain (W. Burton). Macmillan. 7*s.* 6*d.* net.
Introduction to the Architectures of European Religions, An (Ian B. Stoughton Holborn). Edinburgh: Clark. 6*s.* net.
Jane Austen and her Country House Comedy (W. H. Helm). Nash. 7*s.* 6*d.* net.
Life and Labour in Australia (E. Waltham). Drane. 3*s.* 6*d.*
Shakespeare Allusion-Book, The (Re-edited by John Munro. 2 vols.). Chatto and Windus. 21*s.* net.
Socialism and the Social Movement (Werner Sombart), 3*s.* 6*d.* net; Homer and the Iliad (F. Melian Stawell), 10*s.* 6*d.* net. Dent.

REVIEWS AND MAGAZINES FOR SEPTEMBER.—The Open Court, 10c.; The Forum, 25c.; The Architectural Review, 1*s.*; The International, 1*s.*; Revue des Deux Mondes, 3*f.*; The North American Review, 1*s.*

WOLFE MEMORIAL FUND.

FIRST LIST OF SUBSCRIPTIONS.

As was stated by Sir Frederick Young, the Honorary Treasurer, at the Wolfe Banquet on Monday evening, over £400 has been received for the purpose of erecting a National Memorial to Wolfe at his birth-place. Among the first list of subscribers are the following:—

	£	s.	d.
H.R.H. The Duke of Connaught	10	10	
The Marquess of Lansdowne	25	0	0
Earl of Ranfurly	5	0	0
Earl Stanhope	2	2	0
Viscount Galway	5	0	0
Viscount Milner	2	2	0
Lord Strathcona	50		
A. M. Grenfell	25		
F. Norton Garrard	5		
Sir Robert Finlay	5	0	0
Major-General Ralph Allen	1	0	0
C. M. Watney	5	5	0
Robert Mond	25	0	0
J. M. Synge	5	5	0
Sir W. Vaughan Morgan	5	0	0
F. J. Johnston	20	0	0
Dr. James Douglas	27		0
A. A. Dawson-Lambton	10	5	0
Hon. J. Howard	1	1	0
R. B. Polhill-Drabble	5	5	
A. O. Wolfe Aylward	5	5	
Mrs. Horace Pym	5	5	
Major-General Scrase Dickins	1	1	
J. E. Wolfe	5	5	
Colonel C. A. M. Warde	21	0	0
S. Vaughan Morgan	5	0	0
J. Richard	3	3	0
H. C. Billingsley	3	0	
H. G. Seamen	2	2	0
Sir George White	3	3	0
A. M. Cohen	2	2	0
Dr. H. Montagu Butler	1	1	0
W. H. Gadsdon	1	1	0
Captain W. G. S. Kenny	1	1	
Major-Gen. H. Hallam Parr	1	1	0
Col. W. A. St. Clair	1	1	0
George Wolfe	50	0	0
Sir Frederick Young	1	1	0
Master of Elibank	1	0	0
J. F. W. Deacon	1	0	0
John Laskin	0	5	0
Anonymous	0	1	0
Sydney le Mesurier	5	5	0
Rev. C. G. Acworth	2	2	0
A. Maude	1	1	0
Major E. P. Coates, M.P.	3	3	0
E. C. Horton	1	1	0
Second Form, Blundell's School, Tiverton	0	5	0
Major R. L. Stable	1	1	0
J. A. Hughes	1	1	0
Edwin Cait	1	1	0
George Stone	1	1	0
Sydney Pawling	1	1	0
Albert Lund	1	1	0
T. J. Macnamara, M.P.	1	1	0
J. G. Colmer	1	1	0
Rev. J. E. Campbell-Colquohoun	3	3	
Col. Bonham Carter	2	2	
Sir Archibald Douglas	1	1	0
C. Freeman Murray	1	1	0
Hooker Bros.	1	1	0
G. F. Robson	0	2	6
H. E. Botting	0	5	0
G. S. Streatfeild	1	1	0
Major G. Fowler Burton	5	0	0
G. Beckles Willson	5	5	0
Lieut.-Col. E. Montagu	1	1	0
Harold Streatfeild	1	1	0
John A. MacDonald	5	0	0
Col. Seely, M.P.	5	5	0
G. N. Watney	1	1	0
Sir Gilbert Parker, M.P.	2	2	0
Mrs. Lloyd	5	5	0
Lieut.-Col. Dudley Carleton Smith	1	1	0
Sir Lees Knowles	5	5	0
S. H. Hodgson	1	1	0

Subscriptions should be sent to SIR FREDERICK YOUNG, Royal Colonial Institute, Northumberland Avenue, W.C.

A Combination of Going Concerns owning and working Indigenous and Plantation Rubber and Balata Properties in British Guiana. These Properties produced in 1908 about 700,000 lbs. of Balata, and earned profits largely in excess of the amount required to pay the Dividend of 7 per cent. per annum on the Preference Shares of the Company. The estimated Balata production for the year 1909 is 1,100,000 lbs.

The SUBSCRIPTION LISTS will CLOSE to-day, SATURDAY, September 18, 1909.

THE

Consolidated Rubber and Balata Estates, Ltd.

Registered under the Companies (Consolidation) Act, 1908.

CAPITAL ... £250,000,

DIVIDED INTO

240,000 Cumulative 7 per cent. Participating Preference Shares of £1 each and 200,000 Ordinary Shares of One Shilling each.

NOTICE IS HEREBY GIVEN that a Prospectus is being issued by the Company offering for Subscription

176,500 CUMULATIVE 7% PARTICIPATING PREFERENCE SHARES AT PAR.

PAYABLE AS FOLLOWS:

2s. on Application.
3s. on Allotment.
5s. one month after Allotment.
5s. two months after Allotment.
5s. three months after Allotment.

£1

The Preference Shares are entitled to a Cumulative Preferential Dividend of 7 per cent. in each year, and after payment by way of Dividend on the Ordinary Shares of a sum equal to the amount so paid as Dividend on the Preference Shares, are entitled to one-half of any further profits which it may be determined to distribute by way of dividends. They also rank in priority to the Ordinary Shares for return of Capital.

THE SUBSCRIPTION OF 120,000 OF THESE SHARES IS GUARANTEED.

Directors.

Sir ROBERT HARVEY, Kt., D.L., 13 Arlington Street, London, W. (Chairman of the Nitrate Railways Company, Limited), Chairman.
J. BROWNE-MARTIN, 36 Victoria Street, London, S.W. (Director of the Westminster Electric Supply Corporation, Limited).
HENRY SHIELD, 3 Huskisson Street, Liverpool, M.Inst.C.E. (Director of the Liverpool Nitrate Company, Limited).
JAMES GREIG, 18 Belsize Park Gardens, London, N.W. (Director of the Delhi and London Bank, Limited).
GEOFFREY DE M. G. HOARE, London Commercial Sale Rooms, Mincing Lane, London, E.C. (Messrs. Edward Till and Co., Rubber and Balata Brokers).
PAUL L. OSTERRIETH (Messrs. Osterrieth and Cie., Rubber and Balata Brokers), Antwerp.

Local Agents.

Messrs. GARNETT & CO., George Town, Demerara.
S. DAVSON & CO., LIMITED, New Amsterdam, Berbice.
JOHN DOWNER (Messrs. Downer & Co.), New Amsterdam, Berbice.

Bankers.

NATIONAL PROVINCIAL BANK OF ENGLAND, LIMITED, Bishopsgate Street; and Branches.
ANGLO-SOUTH AMERICAN BANK, LIMITED, Old Broad Street, London, E.C.

Brokers.

London: MONTAGU OPPENHEIM & CO., 22 Austin Friars, and Stock Exchange.
London: JOHN GIBBS, SON & SMITH, 29 Cornhill, London, E.C., and Stock Exchange.
Liverpool: HORNBY & OCKLESTON, 3 Tithe Barn Street, and Stock Exchange.
Glasgow: T. R. LAMB, 121 West George Street, and Stock Exchange.

Solicitors.

For the Company: BRISTOWS COOKE & CARPMAEL, 1 Copthall Buildings, E.C.
For the Bartica and Balata Syndicates: TEMPLER DOWN & MILLER, 31 Lombard Street, E.C.

Auditors.

BLEASE & SONS, Chartered Accountants, 2, 3 and 4 Cheapside, E.C., and Liverpool.

Rubber and Balata Brokers.

EDWARD TILL & CO., London Commercial Sale Rooms, Mincing Lane, E.C.

Continental Agents.

OSTERRIETH & CIE., Antwerp.

Commercial Agents.

HARRISONS & CROSFIELD, LIMITED, 3 Great Tower Street, E.C.

Secretary and Registered Offices.

JAMES EDWARDS, 55 and 56 BISHOPSGATE STREET WITHIN, LONDON, E.C.

Prospectuses and Forms of Application can be obtained at the Offices of the Company, or from the Bankers, Brokers and Solicitors, as above.
London, 14th September, 1909.

STANLEY PAUL'S
NEW 6s. NOVELS
ENJOYING IMMENSE POPULARITY.

TROUBLED WATERS
"HEADON HILL'S new Story holds the reader's interest from first to last without a break. It has verve, vividness, and virility; and few who begin it will be at peace until they have read it all."—*SCOTSMAN* (First Review).
"Mr. HEADON HILL is at his best in 'Troubled Waters.'" *MORNING POST.*

THE ADVENTURES OF A PRETTY WOMAN
FLORENCE WARDEN'S latest Novel.
"One of her best stories."—*THE TIMES* (First Review).
*** This is indeed high praise, considering Miss Warden has written nearly One Hundred Novels.

THE GHOST PIRATES
"There's too many bloomin' shadders about this 'ere packet."
WILLIAM HOPE HODGSON "unfolds a tale so realistic as to freeze the young reader's blood and make his two eyes, like stars, start from their sockets . . . a tip-top thriller."—*BEDFORD GUARDIAN.*
"Weird and fascinating."—*LITERARY WORLD.*

THE ROSE OF DAUPHINY
PHILIP L. STEVENSON'S new Novel ready to-day. Many leading critics compared this author's last novel with the novels of Stanley Weyman and Alex. Dumas. The Publishers heartily recommend it to all in search of a good book brimful of intrigue and adventure.

THE VORTEX
FRED WHISHAW. (*Ready to-day.*)

CO-HEIRESSES
"EVERETT-GREEN gives us in this novel an opportunity of studying character in striking contrast. The girls who are the co-heiresses could not be more dissimilar; neither could the two men with whom they mate. The story, as do all Miss Everett-Green's novels, excels in its pictures of home life. No novelist of to-day can call up more realistically the atmosphere of an English fireside."—*SCOTSMAN* (First Review).

SHOES OF GOLD
HAMILTON DRUMMOND'S last Novel, already in a Second Edition, has been brilliantly noticed by twenty-eight leading critics and by many as the best novel of 1909.

LOVE, THE THIEF
HELEN MATHERS. (*Fourth Edition.*)
DAILY NEWS says: "We have read many tales of mysterious crime, but none has kept its secret more securely or furnished more excitement than this."
WESTMINSTER GAZETTE: "Miss Helen Mathers has chosen to make a voluntary exit from her career as novelist, and she does so with a particularly fine bow. 'Love, the Thief,' is in its way as remarkable a performance as her first success, 'Comin' thro' the Rye.' . . . The gift of making a story tell itself is not one possessed by every novelist, and we regret that one who has it in so marked a degree should be determined to exercise it no longer."

OTHER NEW 6s. NOVELS
STOLEN HONEY - Ada and Dudley James
(*Second Edition.*)
THE SECRET TERROR - - - "Brenda"
THE GAY PARADINES - Mrs. Stephen Batson
STRANGE FIRE - Christopher Maughan
A NOVEL EVERY CHURCHMAN SHOULD READ.

POPULAR 1s. NET BOOKS
BROTHER ROGUE AND BROTHER SAINT - - Tom Gallon
THE DEATH GAMBLE - - Geo. R. Sims

THE ROMANCE OF FRA FILIPPO LIPPI
By A. J. ANDERSON. Illustrated, 10s. 6d. net. (*Second Edition.*)
Early Opinions:—
BOOKMAN.—"A live and vivid romance."
WORLD.—"Mr. Anderson has made Fra Lippi's life a genuine romance."
DAILY CHRONICLE.—"There are few artists of the fifteenth century whose works are so unfailingly enjoyable, so delightful in colour, so winsomely appealing in expression, as those of the butcher's son of Florence, this most unclerical of Carmelite friars."
C. K. S., in the *SPHERE*, says:—"He has given us what is undoubtedly a fascinating romance. The book is admirably produced."

WOMAN IN MUSIC
By GEORGE P. UPTON, Author of "The Standard Operas," &c.
An ideal present for a lady.
Fascinating sketches of the love affairs of the world's greatest musicians and a general view of women's influence on music. 3s. 6d. net.

THE DAUPHINES OF FRANCE
FRANK HAMEL. In demy 8vo., fully illustrated. 16s. net. (*Ready shortly.*)

London: STANLEY PAUL & CO., Clifford's Inn.

THE LATEST FICTION
Quite a New Idea
THE HUMAN MOLE
SECOND EDITION NOW READY.
THE HUMAN MOLE
By COLIN COLLINS.
The *SPECTATOR* says: "An exciting melodrama, in which the reader will forget the incredibility of the means by which the 'Human Mole' attains his ends for the sake of the lively adventures that are described."

THE HUMAN MOLE
By COLIN COLLINS.
The *PALL MALL GAZETTE* says: "Quite a new idea. Distinctly engrossing and most skilfully designed to pin the reader's interest to it for hours at a time. We warn any seaside sojourner who picks up *this* book that he will not enjoy the sea or the scenery until he has finished it."

THE MASTER SCHEMER
By MRS. VERE CAMPBELL.
The *DAILY TELEGRAPH* says: "It is a story, cast in a turbulent mould, of love tumultuous and violent, but it is a story, all the same, through which rings a deep and unmistakable human note. . . . Admiration may be freely expressed for the resource and ingenuity displayed in the manipulation of a tale which deals frankly and unflinchingly with the more passionate feelings and problems of life. . . . The story swings along at headlong pace. There is neither pause or halt until the tragic end is reached, while the developments, although springing naturally from each other, are so skilfully contrived as to hold the attention firmly engaged. 'The Master Schemer' is a book that by virtue of its inherent strength and cleverly sustained interest ought to appeal to a wide circle of readers."

THE WANTON
By FRANCES FORBES-ROBERTSON.
The *GRAPHIC* says: "A romance well thought out, well worked out, and distinctly in advance of the best of her former stories."
SECOND EDITION NEARLY EXHAUSTED.
THIRD EDITION AT PRESS.

THE WANTON
By FRANCES FORBES-ROBERTSON.

THE MARQUIS CATILINI
By ROWLAND STRONG.
The *DAILY TELEGRAPH* says: "This is a very remarkable novel. Brilliantly written, intensely vivid, it is that extremely rare combination of a tale of action and a perfect picture of real life and real human beings."

READY IMMEDIATELY.
MR. GURNER GILLMAN'S NEW NOVEL.
HER SUBURBAN HIGHNESS
By GURNER GILLMAN, Author of "The Loafer," &c.

Messrs. Greening take pleasure in announcing that they are now publishing a New Work by **ENA FITZGERALD,** *whose first work,* **"PATCOLA,"** *caused much attention. Ask at your Library for*

THE WITCH QUEEN OF KHEM
A Story of Egypt.
By ENA FITZGERALD. Price 6s.

Other Recent Novels of Merit are
THE SPITFIRE — EDWARD PEPLE
MOON OF VALLEYS — DAVID WHITELAW
REBIRTH — RATHMELL WILSON
ADVENTURES OF SUSAN — CYRUS BRADY
HENRY OF NAVARRE — MAY WYNNE
SEALED ORDERS — A. E. CAREY
Price Six Shillings each. At all Libraries.

THE NEST OF THE SPARROWHAWK
The above is the title of the new romance by the **BARONESS ORCZY** *(Author of "The Scarlet Pimpernel") now appearing in "THE IMP," which should be ordered at once from your newsagent, or can be had direct for 2s. for a year, post free.*

GREENING & CO., LTD., 91 St. Martin's Lane, W.C.

Printed for the Proprietors by SPOTTISWOODE & Co. LTD., 5 New-street Square, E.C., and Published by REGINALD WEBSTER PAGE, at the Office, 10 King Street, Covent Garden, in the Parish of St. Paul, in the County of London.—*Saturday*, 18 *September*, 1909.

THE

SATURDAY REVIEW

OF

POLITICS, LITERATURE, SCIENCE, AND ART.

No. 2,813 Vol. 108. 25 September 1909. [Registered as a Newspaper.] 6d.

CONTENTS.

NOTES OF THE WEEK.

Mr. Balfour is least of all a man of sensations, yet judging by the hubbub in the press his Birmingham speech is more the sensation of the moment than was Lord Rosebery's or Mr. Asquith's—indeed Mr. Asquith in this Birmingham duel seems to have deliberately fired his pistol in the air. What is the general impression made by Mr. Balfour's speech and what is likely to be the effect? The two all-important points of course are the action of the House of Lords and Fiscal Reform. There are in the Unionist party, it must be said, those who would have wished Mr. Balfour to say outright (1) what he hopes the Lords will do with the Budget and (2) what kind of taxes he proposes to include in Fiscal Reform. This direct impulsive way is very much Mr. Chamberlain's way, as we are reminded anew by his call to the Lords "to force a dissolution". But it is not Mr. Balfour's. It never was. It never will be. And we must not forget that the astutest statesmen, parliamentary and other, have sometimes favoured the Balfour rather than the Chamberlain tactics. Who knew exactly what Mr. Gladstone meant to do until he chose that they should know it?

The tone of Mr. Balfour's speech should certainly relieve those who half fear that if the Lords touch the Budget in a vital spot the Flood may come again, or the world be shrivelled in flame. As he said in this speech, it is not the Lords who will decide about the Budget. If the Budget is to be slain, as we hope it will, its slayers will be the people, not the peers. The House of Lords can put the issues before the country; that is all.

Another batch of Budget concessions to the ballot-box! Mr. Lloyd George appears to have discovered that an inconveniently large number of voters owned the small houses in which they lived; and accordingly these are to be exempt from increment duty, at and under an annual valuation of £16 through the country, £26 in boroughs, and £42 in London. Still more far-reaching is the exemption of "agricultural land where, immediately before the occasion on which the duty is to be collected, the land was, and had been for twelve months previously, occupied and cultivated by the owner thereof"; but this is limited to fifty acres, inclusive of any other such land occupied by the same owner, and limited also to an annual valuation of £75. Other portions of the victim's property may have lost in value, but there is to be no relief on this, as allowed in Germany. Now our investor in building sites has but to turn market gardener, splitting a too large plot into small ones in the names of his family to cheat the Treasury as best he can until he is ready to build; but meantime he may not let the land to a market gardener, since the amendment specifies that he himself must be both owner and occupier. This legislative premium on subdividing must work against building schemes on an economically large scale, thereby increasing rent on the very class whose votes are wanted.

There is to be an "allowance" in motor duty for a car that has been used six days in the year on military work in connexion with the Motor Reserve, and there will be an exemption on land used for sport or recreation. In addition, there is the promised concession in the landlords' income tax, that they may not pay several times on the same incomes; and next comes a Scotch deputation, presumably Radical, demanding the relief of "unrestricted sale" in Scotland under the licence duties. The Scotch Radicals in the House have held a meeting of their own on this, and voted against the Budget in a majority of nine. Now, is there any other body of people strong at the ballot-box who would have "concessions"? The Chancellor is in the right mood, and the General Election is not far off. During the all-night sitting on Thursday the Government majority sank to the threatening figure 13.

It is unfortunate that the settlement estate duty was not more thoroughly discussed in the House. The doubling of this objectionable impost will act with cruel hardship on widows and spinsters of the middle classes. In the case of a widow left with children she may expect to be faced with an extra impost of 2 per cent. upon her few hundreds, just at the time when all her resources are needed for educational purposes. Though the return of the settlement estate duty is promised in cases where estate duty has already been paid, this is only if, after a lapse of years, the solicitor employed remembers to ask for it—too late, that is, to be of any real value. It almost seems as if the Government, by this ill-considered measure, desired to augment the suffragette ranks.

In its transformed shape, the Development Scheme ought to become known as the "Robert Cecil Bill". Lord Robert has practically reconstructed it, at least in its methods of working, and his tactics have been worthy of his insight. First he started amendments which the Government were forced to accept; then, on Wednesday, he discovered to them that further amendments were necessitated by his former ones. The Government were again forced to accept; and now it stands that compulsory powers may be acquired by any authority through which advances are made under the Bill, instead of being confined to two of the public departments. The Bill is much improved, but it still embodies the fundamental evil of expending the taxpayers' money on industrial purposes from which the individual capitalist could not hope for adequate return and security. There are necessities in which the State may so expend, but they have not up to now included industrial necessities as defined in the Development Bill. A Government that drives private capital out of the country had better provide public capital for private purposes, as long as it lasts—until the individual instinct is destroyed and the Socialistic squab is starved in its stolen nest.

That members and witnesses may eat without being out of order at Parliamentary committees or inquiries is well known. Few who attended the South Africa inquiry will forget the ample refreshers Mr. Pope allowed himself in sandwiches, and Mr. Rhodes' bottle of stout was quite as noticeable. It seems, however, from a ruling the other day, that members, though they may eat and drink, must not smoke, Captain Craig being stopped when he attempted to light his pipe. A pipe has not come so prominently into parliamentary notice since Sir John Rigby dropped his favourite briar on the floor of the House. Smoking in committee would be a little too much; but what are we to think of a Government that acts as if it wanted to rob its opponents of their smoke as well as their sleep? The Development Bill has been run in a way that seems to show the Prime Minister really wants to wear down the opposition thus. He has made it almost physically impossible to attend to the Development Bill and the Budget on the same day.

This is worse in a way than the guillotine: that after all only kills the debate, whereas this other device would kill the debaters. We prefer the old "patrician bullying of the Front Bench", as Bright called it, to this new and barbarous method. However, though the country never cares a rap about charges of closure and guillotine, we fancy a good many electors will, with the British love of a good fight and of a plucky little opponent, really be influenced by the way the Unionists have fought on through the summer and autumn with their backs to the wall. We hope they will put up "a great finish" just before the Bill passes to the Lords: that always appeals to a sport-loving public.

We believe the denial of Lord Crewe that Ministers encourage rowdy scenes at Budget Protest meetings was genuine in its passion. If there is one thing a Cabinet Minister loathes more than another just now it is rowdyism at public meetings: the suffragettes, if they have done nothing else, have put the fear of God into Cabinet Ministers in this matter. Ministers, then, being themselves in a state of shivering sensibility to interrupters, are no doubt guiltless. But Lord Malmesbury did well to raise the question in the House of Lords on Monday. Surely that very gentle perfect knight Sir Henry Norman ought to be able to check the beasts of the Budget.

The latest wild cat of Mr. Ure has turned out to be but a tame old tabby. He has been trying to claw the Duke of Buccleuch for refusing "ostentatiously" a guinea to a football club and for making £150,000 out of the citizens of London by selling them some vacant land. It has now come out that the Duke knew nothing about the football club, and that the story of the sale of London property is a pure mare's nest. And Mr. Ure—whom we unintentionally lowered to the Solicitorship-General for Scotland last week—is Lord Advocate! Was ever Government banned or blest with such a series of great law officers of the Crown as is this Government? We are reminded of William Pitt's withering scorn for these high personages.

We suppose that with this last short story by Mr. Ure the fiction about the Dukes and the Budget will end. The Liberals have, of course, scored by it. A large number of ignorant people, thanks to Mr. Lloyd George's stories about the Duke of this and Mr. Ure's about the Duke of that, and thanks to a thousand other stories of the same nature, believe that the class which the Budget really hits is the ducal class. They actually think that in taxing a Duke, a Marquess, or an Earl, the Government does not tax anybody else; that the Government can take a thousand or ten thousand extra in death duties or land taxes or income tax from, say, the Duke of Westminster or the Duke of Buccleuch without inconveniencing or impoverishing anyone but the Duke of Westminster or the Duke of Buccleuch. They seem to think the Duke keeps all his money hoarded in a stocking somewhere.

They are blind as moles to the fact that every shilling which the Duke has is, in some form or other, aiding someone or another. Even suppose it banked, the bank is largely putting it out to interest, thereby indirectly but surely employing labour. It is all filtering down to the working classes, through the commercial classes and through the professional classes. Tax a Duke by an extra sovereign, tax him by an extra shilling, and somebody who works directly or indirectly for this Duke must suffer in some degree. The thing is absolutely certain. It must be in the A B C of every system of political economy founded on truth and common-sense. But a million fuddled heads overlook it. It is the business of every lying demagogue to make the million overlook it.

Unhappily the fuddled heads have too often been encouraged in this ignorant, absurd notion that a Duke's wealth only benefits the Duke by emotional men of genius. Ruskin thought it wicked to have more than a certain number of thousands a year; and others take the view that it is a waste of good money. But, immoral or not, the money filters down to the worker, is distributed among the masses, as surely as water finds its level. When there arises a class of those "poor but honest men" the Dukes which says "We will keep our money all to ourselves; we won't let outsiders have any of it; we will put it in a stocking or in the roof or in a hole under the lake"—then it will be time for a Chancellor of the Exchequer to strike relentlessly. As it is, the Government, pretending to strike only their foes, are hitting plenty of their own friends, could the friends only see it.

Lord Dunraven will move the rejection of the Irish Land Bill, and Lord McDonnell is always behind Lord Dunraven; an irresponsible enterprise, assuming the intention to be in earnest. The rejection of the whole Bill would mean an immediate revival of organised crime, with the excuse that Parliament had failed or refused to finance land purchase. Parliament cannot evade the fact that there is over fifty millions' worth of land sold without money to pay for it, and it is not enough to plead that the Treasury has met the annual £5,000,000 cash provided in the last Land Act. The new Bill provides £5,000,000 a year more, but in paper; and though the effect is doubtful, the plan ought to have a trial on its merits. The paper is meant in the first instance to liquidate the purchase arrears, offering scrip instead of cash to the landlord who has sold, and on the current prices of land stock he stands to lose £6 to £7 per cent. on the cash bargain he has made with his tenants; but the alternative, assuming the Bill rejected, is to leave him where he is now, with his land sold, without money to finish the transaction, and with a fine winter's prospect opened for the outrage industry.

While the rejection of Parts I. and II. must increase crime to suit the agitator, the adoption of Part III. would be still more criminal. Here it is proposed to enforce sale for the relief of congestion, while Mr. John Dillon admits that the League will not permit congestion to be relieved. Much land bought for this purpose already has had to be turned to other purposes, the Government actually becoming farmer itself, through the Congested Districts Board, instead of putting the congests on their purchased prairies. The men round the prairies, who have no claim on the land, defy the congested migrants to come in; and the Government, while calling for compulsion, make allies of those who organise the defiance. The same menace is maintained even against the reinstatement of evicted tenants, and the Estates Commissioners officially admit that it is their chief hindrance in finding holdings for the evicted. Thus while experts are employed at one end to put the people on the land, the League is active at the other end to make it impossible; and the Government dares not oppose the League. Since compulsory sale is demanded solely to get land for the congested, and since the League, encouraged by the Government, will not let the congested have the land, why should the House of Lords sanction compulsion?

The Housing and Town Planning Bill has met with some significant amendment in the House of Lords. By venturing just now to discuss any measure at all, the Lords are, of course, filling up the cup (an excellent metaphor, but a trifle worn). How dare they! Here is another Liberal measure spoiled and wrecked from sheer party spite! Surely we may plead that, this time, the House of Peers simply could not help it. Bills must be discussed somewhere. Discussion, being driven out of one House, naturally flies to the other; and the Lords feel a certain responsibility in the matter. Somebody must think of the ratepayers. That is left to Lord Onslow. Somebody must have compassion upon the local authorities. That is left to Lord Belper.

What, exactly, are these amendments which have "wrecked" the Bill? The House of Lords, it appears, does not believe in bureaucracy; and does believe in certain fundamental privileges of the subject, which have been admitted, off and on, since Magna Carta. The measure, as unamended, permitted the Local Government Board to make a final order for the compulsory purchase of land. Lord Camperdown prefers that in disputed cases a loophole should be left for the authority of Parliament. In another matter, that of the compulsory execution of repairs, Lord Beauchamp prefers that an appeal should be allowed to the County Court. Moreover, the Peers feel bound to accept both these amendments. It is unfortunate for the Local Government Board that the rights of the subject should find support in such unexpected quarters; but there it is. The amendments were very properly resisted on the plea of cost. This is an economical Government.

The Lords have been set quaking again this week, for a small straw, borne down upon the wind of revolution, has floated finally to earth. The Duke of Norfolk, arraigned for breach of privilege by eminent Ministers and constitutionalists, has, it is true, escaped with his neck and members (the penalties for high treason are really awful); but surely his impeachment will be proof to his fellow-Peers that the Government means business in dealing with the like of him and his House! His accusers could not bring him to book, because, forsooth, the precedents were against them; but how long will the self-elected guardians of our Constitution allow such obstacles to stand in the path of true progress? It requires nerve to rejoice beneath a suspended sword, and it will probably be small comfort for the Lords to know that, while they are left alive, they will be allowed to write letters of sympathy to parliamentary candidates. Still, such at present is the law; and certain great Parliamentarians are looking a little foolish.

Great minds may think alike, but they rarely speak so much alike as Lord Curzon and Lord Kitchener seem to have done in their farewell speeches. Somebody has been comparing Lord Kitchener's speech on 20 August 1909 with Lord Curzon's of 16 November 1905, and the parallel passages certainly are wonderfully parallel. We suppose it a case of unconscious assimilation. Men of letters are sometimes very cautious, wisely cautious, of not reading matter in their own line. However much a man tries to keep himself quite fresh and original as a writer, he is apt to assimilate lines and phrases and ideas of others, and it is not good when these get into his work unacknowledged. Perhaps something of the kind has happened here.

It is a pity that this "amusing reappearance of certain remarks" of his own, as Lord Curzon puts it, should be made the occasion of a fresh effort to exploit his differences with Lord Kitchener. Lord Curzon has promptly shown the falseness of the statement that Lord Kitchener was despised and rejected by him as a military reformer. Lord Kitchener, he explains, went to India mainly at his earnest request, and in his measures of Army reorganisation received his hearty and consistent support. They differed on "a grave constitutional and administrative issue which had nothing to do with the Army reorganisation". Lord Curzon's letter will remove a good deal of misapprehension as to the precise relations of the two strong men of India during his Viceroyalty.

There was just a touch of very delicate satire in Sir Edward Grey's speech to the cosmopolitan pressmen who have been in conference during the week. Of all people a Foreign Secretary is in a position to gauge the harm done by the irresponsible journalist whose prejudices may be his chief guide in writing on international affairs. There is no need for him to suppress his own national sympathies to be fair to others. That was the point on which Sir Edward Grey insisted, and it is one which should be borne in mind not less in London than in Berlin and Paris and S. Petersburg. Happily Foreign Secretaries, in the days when the Press has seemed to consider that other countries were its proper sport, have known how to ignore "public opinion" manufactured in the newspaper offices. And now the very culprits have met and fallen on each other's necks with vows of eternal goodwill. Sir Edward Grey's little lecture must have struck home with not a few of the delegates.

The larger Imperial view seems to be taking hold of Australian statesmen the more closely they look into the question of Imperial defence. Mr. Cook, the Australian Minister of Defence, made a speech on the right lines in support of the Defence Bill, which is the outcome of the Imperial Conference. Australia is anxious to be a buttress rather than a burden, and will provide the nucleus of a navy, together with 2,300 officers and men. Training for both her local army and navy will be compulsory, and at a cost of £2,500,000 she hopes to have ready for Imperial service a total of 260,000 men. Part of her forces will be trained and equipped with a special eye to service overseas, and all will be interchangeable with other forces within the Empire. Mr. Deakin and his Government have dropped the Dreadnought, but they have substituted something more general and more practicable, which in no way falls short of their promises.

Spain scored smartly in her advance into the heart of the Beni Sicar country on Monday. Cavalry and infantry alike distinguished themselves in very difficult circumstances, and if the war were now to be brought to a sudden close Spain has at least given a fine answer to carping critics. Not less admirable than the dash and efficiency of General Marina's army is its humanity. With women and children rushing wildly from villages into the very zone of fire the Spaniards, "to their lasting honour", as the newspaper correspondent says, never allowed a shell to drop near them. The self-control was the more sterling because the Moors are not likely to adopt reciprocal methods. The Maghzen has formally protested against the Spanish advance, and invited European intervention. Europe may be trusted not to come between Spain and the Riffs, who have flouted the Sultan's authority and Spanish rights with equal assurance. Spain's good faith in the matter is as certain as her courage.

The death of Captain Ferber, following hard upon that of M. Lefebvre, makes it quite clear that for some time aviation will require much devoted enthusiasm in the aviator in order to induce him to face the chances of the air. The Rheims contest seemed to demonstrate that aeroplane races were less dangerous than motor races; but it must not be forgotten that, while it is only dangerous for a motor to travel at high speed, it is dangerous for an aeroplane to travel at all. It is true that the accident to Captain Ferber happened by the merest chance, just when he had alighted safely upon the ground; but, on the other hand, it will be remembered that within the last few days Colonel Cody has had a nasty fall, and that Mr. Latham has crippled his machine. It is only the more earnestly to be hoped that aviation spectacles will attract none of that type of onlooker that enjoys the peril of the tight-rope dancer or that instructive performance known as "looping the loop".

The curtain has been rung up again upon the proceedings of the Joint Committee on Stage Plays. It will be remembered that, when Mr. Barrie was asked whether he had said all he had to say, he replied that he had—for the time being. It is to be inferred that he recollected that he was billed for a subsequent performance. Probably he was reproved, behind the scenes, for giving away the stage-management in this fashion. Since then, however, the whole pretence has broken down, and evidence is set circulating in print before it is delivered in the committee-room. We were given the great advantage this week of reading the evidence of a witness in advance of the proceedings. He describes himself as "novelist and dramatist", and this witness is Mr. Hall Caine.

Commander Peary has retired. It is by far the most sensational thing he has done, so far. Perhaps he has despaired of any possible crescendo as a means of producing an additional stir among those who are still interested in the North Pole, and has consequently muted all the strings of his orchestra in order that our ears might be startled by a sudden stillness. Whether this be the explanation or not, he has definitely retired, and he has refused public honours. Moreover, he has now no intention of "nailing" Cook. He will wait, probably with the idea of allowing Cook to "nail" himself. Still, even Commander Peary must perceive that Dr. Cook's case does not wear at all badly as time goes on.

Rejected by the sea, the body of John Davidson was spared none of the indignities which must be suffered posthumously by those who die a violent and self-inflicted death. To be quite safe, men must begin and end within the pale. Even the sea could not save John Davidson from the profane rigour of a sacred law. The foreman of the jury had his say. A medical man assured the court that the corpse "had an intellectual skull, with a rather high forehead". The Home Office was consulted upon a legal technicality, and only then could John Davidson be decently returned to the sea, which had given him up in order that everything might be made plain, and that society might rest more comfortably with a sense of justice done.

THE DUEL AT BIRMINGHAM.

SOMEBODY, we think it was Swift, suggested that the quarrels of nations should be settled by a duel between the two sovereigns or their commanders-in-chief. What might have been the result of a personal encounter between Lewis and William, or Marlborough and Turenne, no one can say. But if the question between the Government and the Opposition could be settled by the speeches of Mr. Asquith and Mr. Balfour at Birmingham, with the nation as umpire, we should have no fear of the verdict. The Prime Minister was indeed singularly unconvincing, not to say perfunctory, in his performance of Friday week. The ponderous, mechanical periods were duly delivered beneath the sounding-board, and were duly applauded by the audience and the Ministerial press. But the argument was beaten out very thin, and Mr. Asquith, in his threats to the House of Lords and in his attempts to minimise the effect of the Budget, seemed to be the unwilling executor of other people's orders. Nor does it seem to have struck the usually logical mind of the Prime Minister that to dismiss Lord Rosebery's speech as "Much Ado About Nothing", and in the next breath to describe the intervention of the House of Lords as a revolution, was inconsistent. Lord Rosebery says the Budget is a revolution: Mr. Asquith says that its rejection by the House of Lords would be a revolution. In a sense both propositions are true. The Budget is a revolution in the sense that it is a violent departure from the methods of taxation hitherto adopted in this country, and a substitution of the financial devices invariably resorted to by revolutionary demagogues, whether in ancient Greece, in eighteenth-century France, or in modern South America. The canons of taxation universally admitted by all thinkers and writers, who are not of the Georgian school, are that taxes must be clear as to amount, certain in operation, and uniform in incidence. The vagueness and uncertainty of the new taxes, and the selection of two classes, the owners of land and the dealers in liquor, to bear their incidence, are in the true revolutionary style. Mr. Asquith's assertion, or rather repetition of the Chancellor of the Exchequer's favourite dictum, that the State can spend a man's income better than he can himself, is pure Socialism. On the other hand, the rejection of the Finance Bill by the House of Lords would be a revolution, or rather a counter-revolution, in the sense that the thing has not been done for more than two centuries. The question is whether the revolution of Mr. Lloyd George should be countered by a revolution on the part of the Lords.

On this point Mr. Balfour wisely said nothing, for which he has been taken to task and accused of a failure to lead by the very organs of opinion which formerly denounced him for dictating to the House of Lords. When it was a question of the Education or Licensing Bill we were told that Mr. Balfour insolently paraded his influence over the Second Chamber, and ordered Lord Lansdowne to do for him what he had failed to do for himself. Very dexterously, by a mere turn of the rhetorical wrist, Mr. Balfour managed to move the whole discussion out of the region of revolution and counter-revolution by saying that the issue would be decided neither by the House of Commons nor the House of Lords, that it would not be settled at Westminster, but in the constituencies. That was very clever, and made Mr. Asquith's solemn peroration about a revolution suddenly shrivel up and seem exaggerated. There was something really distinguished in the way Mr. Balfour lowered the controversial temperature and calmly indicated and discussed the alternative policies now presented to the British nation. Those alternatives are Socialism or Tariff Reform. The arguments for and against a socialistic reconstruction of society are the arguments for and against the Budget, which Mr. Balfour tactfully refrained from repeating. We are not sure that Mr. Balfour did not make a mistake in declining to discuss the details of tariff reform. After all, the General Election, whether it comes in November, or in January, or in February, is approaching quickly, and it will not be possible for candidates to avoid details. No one expects Mr. Balfour to name the articles which he contemplates placing in his tariff, but he might come a little closer to the heart of the matter, especially with regard to colonial preference. What new taxes on food is he thinking of, if any? This is a question which will certainly be put to Unionist candidates, and if each man is left to answer it according to his own views there will be a pretty confusion. It is hardly fair, as it is certainly dangerous, to turn each candidate loose to trade on his own stock of reason and knowledge. Is it proposed, for instance, to place duties on meat and dairy produce? Sooner or later these questions will have to be answered, and the sooner an authorised programme is issued the better. It is not easy, we know, to handle economic details before an audience of ten thousand. Gladstone discussed the figures of his Budget, we remember, from a waggon on Blackheath Common to an audience which was probably larger than and certainly not as quiet as that in Bingley Hall. But Gladstone had an altogether exceptional voice, which he much strained by speaking out of doors. Mr. Balfour could, of course, easily arrange a much smaller meeting if he is willing to explain the details of his fiscal policy. Mr. Balfour, however, may feel, as Gladstone felt about his Home Rule plan, that every time you explain a point you make an enemy. This is especially true about taxation; still, we repeat that Mr. Balfour might with advantage be a little less general. Barring this criticism, nothing could have been better than Mr. Balfour's survey of the originally slow, but latterly rapid, declension from "the pedantic individualism" of sixty years ago to the Socialism of to-day. It is remarkable how the Radical party has swung from the possibly exaggerated theories of Bentham and Mill to the collectivism of Marx and other anarchists. It is undoubtedly due to the failure of the system of free imports that we are face to face with Socialism. Had Cobden's prophecy come true, and free exchange been adopted as the international system, England's commercial supremacy would have been maintained, and we should not now be at our wits' end for revenue and a cure for unemployment. But France, Germany, and the United States, having borrowed our money to make railways and bought our machinery and copied our processes of manufacture, have proceeded to keep our goods out of their markets and to dump their goods in our markets. Statesmen like Mr. Asquith, "suckled in a creed outworn", have no remedy for unemployment and no cure for a declining revenue except laying the landlord and the publican under exceptional tribute. The money which they will get by these disreputable and perfectly foolish extortions will be much less than they think, while the blow which they deal at the security of property may be mortal. As Mr. Balfour pointed out, it is not enough to keep capital from leaving the country; you must provide security for it at home, not only when it is actively employed in industrial enterprise, but when the fruits of that activity are garnered in. Unfortunately the operations of capital on a large scale, as Bagehot long ago pointed out, are quite unintelligible to the ordinary man, even amongst the educated and comfortable class. Amongst those who labour with their hands the language of Lombard Street is about as well understood as Chinese. To make the rich and the titled jump and squeal is an exquisite pleasure to the majority of the lower class. What is the staple argument for the Budget amongst a crowd? Why, that the Dukes are against it. Somebody wrote to the "Westminster Gazette" on Thursday comparing the House of Lords to the Convention of Notables in the French Revolution, and quoting a passage from Carlyle about the exemption of the French nobility from taxes! How can the rapier of Mr. Balfour's ratiocination pierce such impenetrable ignorance as this? How indeed can any argument cope with the reckless mendacity of class hatred?

THE WILD MEN IN THE GOVERNMENT.

EVER since Mr. Asquith and Mr. Haldane in 1906 were led into the House of Commons and did penance for having withstood the Labour party over the Trade Disputes Bill they have been credited with nursing resentment against their persecutors. Being of like passions with ordinary politicians they were supposed to be on the look-out for a chance of "getting back" on the oppressor. In an unregenerate world this was counted to their honour, and they indulged in occasional platform flourishes that seemed to justify the compliment. Mr. Asquith, strong, staunch and steady, vowed he would never "go wool-gathering with the Socialists", and Mr. Haldane, clanking his War Office spurs, swore by Mars and Bellona he would not "toe the line". By these unsolicited protestations it was revealed that further pressure had been secretly applied to these independent statesmen. But the country could rely upon them. Sir Henry Campbell-Bannerman, perhaps, had been weak or temporising; allowance should be made for his feeble health. Things would be very different when Mr. Asquith had come by his own. With the help of Mr. Haldane and Sir Edward Grey, not to mention Sir Henry Fowler, the wild men inside and outside the Cabinet would be thoroughly domesticated—clothed, manicured and kept scrupulously clean.

Why is it that this pleasing expectation has been disappointed? Not for a moment do we suggest that the Prime Minister has forgiven Mr. Winston Churchill's promise of Home Rule or the pledge as to instant dissolution upon the Peers' rejection of the Finance Bill. That would be almost as improbable as that he believes in Mr. Lloyd George's finance. Nor can he shut his mind to the intrigues directed against his personal authority. He must very well see that these restless juniors mean to put him out, him and his friends. Their struggle against increasing the Navy seems to have been inspired neither by love of peace, trust in Germany, nor economy, but largely by the hope of driving the Foreign Secretary out of the Cabinet. Then why were they not stamped upon as soon as they had made themselves objectionable and before they became formidable? Their importance is magnified by office. Mr. Lloyd George turned adrift in Wales might soon have ceased to count greatly, and even Mr. Churchill, though his talents are substantial, might not be making much noise in the world if he had not been given a sounding-board. A year ago Mr. Asquith had him in the hollow of his hand. What party was there for the renegade to desert to? The Unionists did not want him back. The Socialists are not enamoured of patrician adventurers. His only career lay with official Liberalism. If at the first display of insubordination he had been sent packing he might have been compelled to make submission before being allowed to come back to favour and, on good behaviour, to official employment.

Mr. Asquith's masculine intelligence, however, is not combined with such great strength of will. Below his self-reliance is a well-founded self-distrust, and the Premiership which was to rally the Liberal party upon its Centre has been a series of running defeats inflicted by the Left. The truth is that Mr. Asquith knows well that his qualities do not touch the imagination of the masses. It would be vain for the party to "go to the country on Asquith". The King of the Cappadocians has plenty of loyal supporters at Westminster (mancipiis locuples, but eget æris, he lacks magnetism). The same may be said of his friends. Much sap went out of Liberal Imperialism when it was cut away from Lord Rosebery. He possesses just those qualities in which the Asquith set are notably deficient, and Sir Henry Campbell-Bannerman, not a genius but a shrewd judge of men, knew that he ran no risk in admitting these statesmen to his Cabinet. From the first they had to be his servants.

The position of these moderate, capable statesmen after Sir Henry's retirement was very much that of a steady-going business firm which has for years been doing a decent humdrum business and is suddenly pulled up short by the death of its experienced managing partner. As long as he was at the head of affairs the old routine answered fairly well. Sir Henry kept the Socialists in good humour because he was always in good humour himself. They allowed themselves to be led because they thought they were leading him. No sooner is the old firm broken up than the customers begin to ask questions—have they been getting value for their money, and might they not find better value elsewhere? It is clear that the business will soon drop away unless new blood is brought into the firm and up-to-date methods introduced. It was under some such idea that Mr. Lloyd George and Mr. Winston Churchill were promoted to high places. Though the one had made a success at the Board of Trade and the other a mark—of sorts—at the Colonial Office, it would be ridiculous to pretend that their abilities—in a party abounding with clever young men—had marked them out for instant and highest reward. Mr. Herbert Samuel and Mr. Masterman, for instance, would have been an impressive reinforcement of the Cabinet. But, with all their comparative originality and superior character, they did not possess just those powers of which the Ministry was believed to stand in need. They did not push or advertise themselves. For the street-corner oratory of which Mr. Balfour spoke at Birmingham, and which might be expected to bring in new business, it was necessary to go to the hustlers.

Mr. Asquith decided that the Government must make it worth the while of Mr. Lloyd George and Mr. Churchill to join him in the respectable old firm. He yielded them almost their own terms, and from that day forward how much of the power has been taken out of his hands! The energetic bummers who were to put life into the decaying business are now running it on the approved American lines. After a fashion the venture has been a success. The amount of turnover done has been considerably increased, if not in proportion to the extra noise and bustle. New customers have been attracted, and no account is taken of the old supporters driven away. These, however, have departed for good, and could never be recalled. It would therefore be useless for Messrs. Asquith and Company trading as the Liberal Party Limited to get rid now of their compromising new partners. Too late it is discovered that their connexions are undesirable and their methods unprofitable. They are doing what they were expected to do. They have made things "hum". It cannot be said that the inner politics of Liberalism have been dull since Mr. Lloyd George and Mr. Winston Churchill have taken charge of the Government. There is something diverting in the efforts of the "old gang" to keep up the air of dignity and pretend they are directing affairs. Also there is just a possibility that the aspiring juniors may land themselves in trouble. So far, they have been sensible enough not to quarrel with each other or, at least, to conceal their differences. But there are other rocks ahead. Are there not some able men who may not consent to be quietly shelved for the better advancement of Mr. Lloyd George and Mr. Churchill? There is Mr. Lewis Harcourt, for instance, who has a supple mind and a strong will—with something of the urbanity that distinguished his father's later style in Parliament. Who knows—he may yet give a fall to rivals counting prematurely on the succession to Mr. Asquith.

THE MEN AND THE LAND.

AN evidently sincere man like Lord Carrington can be unusually interesting when associated with a Government like the present, and Mr. Lloyd George ought to study his admission in an agricultural speech at Shrewsbury the other day in support of the Budget: "It is not until the men come back on the land that there will be found a fair share of comfort, happiness and contentment among the people of old England". This is a novel way of supporting a Budget that vastly advances the methods by which the men have been driven from the land. When these methods began, old England had still a healthy proportion of the people on the land, but now there are only about a fourth of them on it, with a corresponding decline in the chest measurements for the Army and Navy. The continuity of a nation is much more a question of thorax than of theory, but Lord Carrington's admissions show how the theory is at the expense of the thorax. His sincerity is as charming as it is instructive, and in the interests of the nation they ought to have a man like him in every Radical Government. There is no motive but conviction for such a man in such a position, and his honesty is like a mirror to reflect the methods of the other men.

He talked also of "development" and the instalments of State socialism by which they are to improve the farmer—and catch his vote. There is one way in which the State could develop agriculture enormously—by permitting it to develop itself. In spite of statesmanship, science and common-sense have really done something for the farmer, and if only the knowledge already established could be brought within his practice it would do more to increase agricultural production than any sort of tinkering to "develop" industries and to favour classes at the expense of one another. There can be no "developing" of industry without increased production, and the first essential to this is an increase in applied knowledge. Could not Lord Carrington do something towards this instead of inventing socialistic theories for the agriculture of the ballot-box?

The process indicated could be as much an education as a profit. For instance, it is now known that the proportion of organic fertility in the soil can be increased by the application of inorganic matter; but how many British farmers are aware of this vast transition in agricultural knowledge? Better still, there is a direct profit on the inorganic application, not to mention the organic bye-product; and the botanical effect is as fascinating as the chemical effect is instructive. This summer a paper was read by Mr. George Ryce before the Congress of Applied Chemistry in London, showing how the legumes in pasture and meadow were increased by potash. Commercial profit was not his business; but we know that the "albuminoid ratio" in the legumes is higher than in the grasses; that they tend to increase the nutrition even in the grasses growing among them; and that when they have finished their function they leave behind in the soil, deposited from the air, at no cost to the farmer, a net margin of nitrogenous plant food. In this way we have seen grey hillsides turned green through the winter, and in the summer richly perfumed with flowering clover, even without any outlay in either cultivation or seeding; and we have seen the food production of the area increased by fifty per cent., with three beasts thriving where two had found only what could keep them as they were. This indicates how agriculture could develop itself if only statesmanship would permit it, and education were directed to the great problem of food production.

In spite of all, the farmer has learnt something, and has applied some of his knowledge. With all its hindrances, political and educational, British farming has raised its profit margin in recent years, and there are instructive tendencies at work which cannot be expressed by the statistician. The latest official figures do not indicate any marked movement up or down as regards either the total area cropped or the total production from it; yet we know that large tracts have gone to grass, an equation evidently cancelled by a corresponding increase in production elsewhere. Where tillage stops, the methods are likely to have been the worst; but where it starts, they are likely to be the best, levelling up at the top what is lost at the bottom, with the additional advantages of demonstrating the fact that "farming can pay", and spreading the knowledge of the means to do it. In the southern counties this year and last we have seen many great fields ploughed for grain where the plough had not been seen for many years; and now we have the pioneers admitting a satisfactory profit, even in the production of grain. On farms that had been declared profitless we have seen penniless men rising to comfort, and even to comparative wealth, in the last fifteen years; men who began on borrowed money, who have reproduced it double and paid it back, leaving themselves industrial capitalists, employers of labour, leaders of the local mind, able to give handsome subscriptions to purposes of public good.

Last week came news from the United States which may add farther to the impetus in British agriculture—the meat kings of Chicago unable to continue export contracts, and even buying back some of their own products from London. In a double way the urban industrialism of America has made for a check on this export of agricultural produce, first by attracting the agricultural producer from the soil, and then by multiplying the millions of their own who consume his produce. In large regions at the back of the Eastern cities grain has ceased to be grown, and these cities have already developed a back-to-the-land problem of their own. Better still for the British farmer, the conditions and causes at work in this American transition are of a permanent nature, liable to passing variation, but on the whole making for a definite effect. It is simply the natural adjustment of industrial civilisation among the Americans, whose economic system steadily matures towards social symmetry, the classes and their industries supplying the increased demands of one another instead of depending on huge exports, narrowly specialised, to pay for imports which they could not produce. They have protected their manufactures to raise a vast demand for their own agricultural produce, and every farther stage in this development among them means an improved opportunity for the man who can put knowledge, capital and character into British agriculture.

After our primitive pretence to agricultural education in this country the chief hindrance to the farmer is the fiscal uncertainty that leaves him unable to calculate his prospects for any length of time ahead; not exactly Free Trade, but rather the industrial insecurity inseparable from its peculiar application among us. The farmer might still flourish under Free Trade if only it could secure him any steady outlook in the conditions of his productive activities; if only he could see his way to a steady profit over such a series of years as would justify him in venturing on an initial process. For instance, he knows that he can grow wheat at a profit to-day, but he also knows it was impossible a few years ago; and with his necessarily conservative ways of mind he will think over the matter for several seasons rather than turn his capital into plant and stock that may be idle or unprofitable a few years later, perhaps exhausting more than his whole gain in the need to convert his instruments of production back again into another form, less liable to uncertainty for the time. It is not exactly the lowness of the prices in his market, among which he could pick and choose to direct the incidence of his production for his highest gains, assuming some workable continuity in this; it is rather that he cannot calculate on continuity of any kind, his market being held "free" as a kind of international clearing-house for every accident of policy or of season throughout the world that can influence the price of what he is producing.

Not only is capital in farming less easily convertible from one form to another than in different industries, but the farmer himself is less fit to foresee the need and to direct the conversion. A loom can be adjusted to a new fabric in a few hours, and in a day the calico-printer can transform his cylinder surfaces to accommodate a new design; but it may take as many years successfully to convert ploughs and threshing machines into material for the production of cheese or butter; and thus we can see how Lord Carrington's ideals are fundamentally defeated by the fiscal methods with which he so strangely associates himself. True, when there is a slump in wheat, and we buy it for less than the home cost of production, the consumers of the nation have a clear gain in the difference; but then what is the total loss incidental to the nation as a whole? When the nation buys imported wheat for less than the cost of production the nation's farmer ceases to produce wheat; and since nothing can compensate diminished production, is it not obvious that the nation loses the whole in order to gain the fraction? This, however, opens a vast field of inquiry which cannot be fully explored in the last paragraph of one short article; and our immediate purpose is to set the philosophers of the Cabinet thinking again, and more carefully, on Lord Carrington's eloquent admission: "No fair share of comfort, happiness and contentment" until "old England" shall have grown wise enough to kick out of her councils the raw theorists who have driven the men from the land.

EDUCATION IN RUSSIA.

TWENTY-TWO volumes of special reports upon educational subjects have already been presented to both Houses of Parliament by command of his Majesty. "Education in Russia" makes the twenty-third. It contains a great deal of information that will surprise the British ratepayer in several ways. For one thing, it should cause him to modify his uninformed conception of the Russian Empire as a vast tract of land, somewhere in the East of Europe, given over to barbarism and sunk in neglect of all that is modern. Russia is very commonly supposed to be just emerging from the Middle Ages. There is no time to indicate the essential erroneousness of this common belief; but, at any rate, it can be pointed out at once that the supposed mediævalism of Russia is abruptly discredited in this matter of education. Her educational system may have serious defects; but it ranks as one of the completest of modern attempts at the organisation and administration of a comprehensive national system of mental training. The Russian experts number among them authorities of European reputation; witness the name of Professor Paul Vinogradoff, equally well known in Moscow and in Oxford. The system they have erected compares very favourably with that prevailing in Great Britain and in Germany; and it is infinitely superior to that which prevails in France.

The lessons here contained for British legislators are mostly brought home by way of contrast. In the matter of education England and Russia stand at opposite poles. The legislator in Russia had all the advantages of a clean slate; whereas it is the peculiar privilege of England that her slate is never clean. English public schools are ancient and private growths. Each has its peculiar traditions; each possesses a distinct character. The State cannot touch them without destroying them for what they are. In Russia, on the other hand, the entire secondary system of education is a recent thing, imposed from above, and practically uniform in character throughout the Empire down to the separate items on the curricula and the books recommended for the use of students. There is no idea in Russia of treating education as a private concern. The freedom of instruction characteristic of an English public school would amaze a Russian professor. The Englishman, on his side, is left with as great a misgiving and perplexity when he reviews the great secondary schools of Russia, with their centralised administration, their hierarchy of State teachers, their definite programmes, and their direct responsibility to the State. It is useless to expect an Englishman to place trust in a system that leaves no room for an Arnold or a Thring; where the master is a specialist in a subject, and not the form-master of his boys; where the school is simply a place of learning, and does not aim at being a microcosm of the world; where all boys are equally pupils, with none of the discipline that makes room for prefect and captain. It would be quite as useless to expect a Russian to place trust in a system that left the character of a place of education dependent upon tradition and personality; where no responsibility existed, except that which was due to public opinion; where there was no settled relation between school and university; where reform was left to private initiative. Again, to descend to the primary schools, although the Russian slate was not quite so clean in this respect, yet, as between the two nations, there is room for considerable surprise on both sides. That a citizen because he paid rates, or that a locality because it helped to provide a school, should claim to dictate in any way whatever concerning its curriculum would astonish any Russian who had had anything to do with the administration of education in his own country. An Englishman would be taken equally aback to find that most of our vexed questions, religious or administrative, do not exist there. Russia, in fact, had a vacuum to work in and certain definite ideas and principles upon which to proceed.

The vividness of the contrast between the two systems will best be illustrated by giving the briefest possible account of the Russian scheme as administered under the Ministry of Public Instruction. At the head of the Ministry stands the Minister, appointed by the Emperor. Under him work three important bodies with specialised functions. There is the Council of the Minister, in which all proposals involving change are discussed; in which all the more important financial estimates are examined; in which all questions relating to the internal administration, whether of schools or of universities, are settled. By the side of this body stands another, which for the performance of its duties subdivides into nine sections, dealing respectively with inspection, higher education, boys' schools, girls' schools and the training of teachers, primary schools, technical and professional schools, scientific institutions, private schools and Jewish schools, pensions and accounts. By the side of this stands the Scientific Committee, which considers educational matters simply, examines schemes of instruction, draws up curricula and advises upon books. The net seems to make a pretty wide sweep. It will be asked whether there is anything left for local administration, and, if so, how much of this is given over to local initiative and local control. The answer comes plainly enough. The Empire is divided into twelve districts; each district is administered by a curator appointed by the Ministry of Public Instruction as its local representative. This official does most of what remains to be done, after the central body have taken their share. He supervises work in the schools and universities. He makes all appointments not reserved for the higher authority. He has an army of inspectors, directors and other officials, by means of whom every school in the district is brought into line with the rest. It is a case of centralisation in excelsis, the application of a huge piece of administrative machinery to the needs of the human mind.

It is the secondary schools that fall most completely under this centralised system. Here again a contrast with England is noted. The higher education in England is more respected by the State than the lower. In Russia the reverse is true. It is the primary school that has most liberty. The liberty is, in the majority of cases, quite delusory; it consists in giving to the Zemstvos a minute share in their management. In Russia the primary schools are, many of them, spontaneous local growths; and represent the movement of the nation towards self-education, which preceded the assumption of the task of national education by the State. But even here the real control is wholly in the hands of the central government, which allows itself to be helped by local bodies on which the Zemstvos, or the towns which provide the schools, have only an insignificant minority representation. They provide and maintain, but they may not have any effective voice.

The whole system is a study in centralisation. Whether the schools be administered by the Ministry of Public Instruction, whose organisation we have briefly examined, or by the Holy Synod, or by the Department of Finance, of Agriculture, or of War, there is the same spectacle presented of a bureaucracy determined that nothing shall escape the control of a central hand. Primary school, secondary school, technical institute, or university—all are supervised, administered, organised, correlated, and controlled from the centre. Those outside Russia who are interested in education will draw countless profitable conclusions from a close study of the countless advantages that the system contains. Regarding the countless disadvantages and blemishes which are inseparable from the mechanical working of a vast machine, it is needless for a foreigner to indicate them. The Russians themselves are busy upon their own problems, and bringing to them an impartiality and sagacity that are wanting in many countries supposed to be more civilised. They are quite awake to the perils of their system; and in the case of the universities they are beginning to question the efficacy of State control. The Government, which began by forbidding the formation of societies among university students, even for literary and social purposes, is now aware of the suicidal nature of its own decree. Before long the autonomy taken from the universities in 1884 may be given back to them on terms which may permit of their taking their true place as independent centres of thought and feeling, where the thought and feeling of the Empire itself are broadened and unified.

THE CITY.

IT looks as though the period of cheap money had come to an end. No one need be surprised if we have an advance in the Bank rate in the next fortnight. The Bank of Germany has put up its rate, and the Bank of England must follow suit if it is to come into competition. There are local reasons for the action of the Reichsbank, but those reasons are sufficiently important to affect the International market. The Imperial Treasury has been drawing heavily upon the Reichsbank, Russia has demanded gold in payment of breadstuffs, and an inflated speculation on the Bourse has necessitated the use of considerable money. In order to make good the deficiency caused by these abnormal requirements London—the only free market for gold—has been drawn upon. For weeks past all the arrivals of the metal from South Africa have been bought for export to either Germany or Russia—it matters not which, as the one is directly connected with the other. Thus the Bank of England has had no opportunity of adding to its stock, while having to provide huge amounts of sovereigns for Egypt and South America. The moment would now seem to have arrived when the Bank of England must place itself in competition with Germany for the gold that weekly arrives from the Cape. It is practically impossible to ward off the drain of sovereigns to Egypt and South America, but not impossible to check the export of the raw metal. If the value of money is raised here there will be less inducement to take gold, and if it is raised sufficiently high the export will cease altogether. The first step towards this result will be an advance in the Bank rate, and the directors must perforce take it. As we pointed out last week, Egypt will be taking sovereigns for some time to come—probably four or five millions. These will go whatever is the ruling Bank rate. Shipments to South America will also be made irrespective of the value of money here. All the Bank directors can do therefore is to fill up the gap made by these withdrawals, and this it is in their power to do if they make it worth the while of Germany and Russia to stand aside from competition when gold is put up for sale in our market. It is an elementary principle that gold will always go where it can be most profitably employed, and if London can offer greater inducements than either Germany or Russia the metal will remain here. At the moment the Bank of England appears very strong, but the directors have to look ahead, and it is better to be a little premature than too late.

Dearer money will probably arrest the recovery in gilt-edged securities, and certainly as regards Consols it seems hopeless to look for any improvement. Apart from any consideration of home politics, Consols have lost their attraction for the investor, who now demands a higher rate of interest than they give. It has been suggested in Parliament that something might be done to restore their popularity by the issue of £50 certificates, but Consols are already transferable in amounts of a penny or multiples of a penny. We recall the fact that efforts have recently been made by Canada to attract the small investor by offering £10 bonds for sale, and that the response has been far from encouraging. Moreover, the offer was widely advertised. It is probably not within the knowledge of the small investor that English railway stock is transferable in amounts of £1 or multiples thereof, though few of the companies will open an account for less than £10. Still, it might be very useful for small investors to know that they can buy £10 of London and North-Western Railway stock. Perhaps the best method of popularising investment would be the issue of small bearer certificates, but as these offer facilities for evading taxation, the Chancellor of the Exchequer is not likely to approve their creation.

New York continues to give support to American securities, but whether it will do so if money gets much dearer in London is a moot point. The time is approaching when Wall Street will require all the financial assistance it can get, and if the value of money abroad rises, the "all" will be much restricted. At the moment ample money is available for bolstering up the market. A feature of the week has been a revival in South African mining shares, more particularly in Rhodesians. So far it partakes much of the nature of a gamble, and may by its recklessness defeat the end in view, but there are reasons for popularising the movement, and it may be supported by the financial houses to serve ends of their own. It is common knowledge in market circles that several big "deals" are in contemplation, and that these cannot be carried through successfully without public assistance. To obtain this assistance the market must be made to look more attractive, and this can only be done by advancing prices and sustaining them at the higher level while the operations are in progress. So long as there was any danger of the labour supply on the Rand running short it was deemed futile to engineer any upward movement, but now there is a chance that the public may take a hand. That the public are disposed to be more venturesome is shown by the great activity in rubber shares, many of which are advancing far ahead of prospects. It would be as well to ascertain, if possible, how many companies have sold their output for the next twelve months "forward". We hear of several having placed the larger portion, and at prices considerably under the ruling figures. This looked to be good business in the early part of the year, but is now proved to have been a mistake. It is interesting to note that the big American buyers of rubber were more farsighted than London manufacturers, and early in the year increased their stocks well in excess of requirements. They can now resell portions of their surplus stock at a considerable profit, and buy forward for future requirements at nearly two shillings per pound under the current price.

The Argentine Great Western Railway invite subscriptions for £1,000,000 5 per cent. debenture stock issued at £108.

INSURANCE: POLICIES AT LOW PREMIUMS.

VII.

It would be entirely inappropriate to conclude a series of articles dealing with policies at low premiums without describing deferred assurances for children, which provide the best kinds of policies at the lowest annual cost. The essential feature of these policies is that from the time they are taken out until age twenty-one money is being accumulated as it were in a savings bank; if the child dies before reaching the age of twenty-one all the premiums that have been paid are returned; on reaching that age the premiums remain at the same rate as before, and the sum assured under the policy will be paid at death whenever it happens, or on reaching a specified age. If on the attainment of age twenty-one the continuance of premium-paying is inconvenient, the policy has a substantial cash surrender value, or it can be exchanged for a policy payable at death upon which no further premiums have to be paid. The continuance of the policy after age twenty-one is, however, the strikingly attractive feature of this form of assurance.

If such a policy is effected in the first year of a child's life it costs £9 5s. a year for the assurance of £1000 at death at any time after age twenty-one, at which date the policy begins to share in the profits. By this time—the policy being effected at birth—twenty premiums of £9 5s. each, or £185 in all, have been paid, and this at 2½ per cent. compound interest would amount to about £240. If at age twenty-one a man went to a life office he could, in return for a single payment of £40, secure the assurance of £100 payable at death, with profits in addition; and for a single payment of £240 could obtain a similar policy for £600. He could also at age twenty-one take another policy, to be paid for by annual premiums of £2 1s. for each £100 assured; so that for an annual payment of £8 4s. for the rest of his life he would have whole-life policies assuring £1000 at death and sharing in the profits, which is exactly the same thing as deferred assurance gives him at an annual premium of £9 5s. a year from birth till death.

The deferred assurance policy, however, normally requires no medical examination, and has the great practical advantage that if started in childhood it is not likely to be discontinued, while it is moderately improbable that money will be regularly saved from birth till twenty-one for the purpose of buying life assurance by a single premium.

This description of the nature of the transaction helps to explain how the striking advantages it presents are accomplished. There are three causes for these advantages. In the first place when assurance is effected early in life there is normally a long period during which compound interest is at work accumulating the savings more and more rapidly as time goes on. In the second place, when the policy participates in profits, assurance commenced young is likely to yield bonuses for a much larger number of years than a policy effected late in life. By the time a man who begins to share in the profits at age twenty-one reaches sixty-five the sum assured under a policy for £1000 may have been increased by bonuses to more than £2000; but by the time a man commencing assurance at age forty reaches sixty-five the policy for £1000, assuming the same rate of bonus, amounts to only £1500. The young man and the middle-aged one are not buying the same thing; the policies are identical in character, the rate of bonus on each is equal, but assuming an approximately normal lifetime the young man is buying £2000 and the older man only £1500.

The third cause for the advantages of assurance commenced young is less obvious to people unfamiliar with the subject, though it has been explained frequently in these articles. When a policy is bought by a single premium, such as £40 for the assurance of £100 at death, the amount of protection is—speaking roughly—£60. The cost of protection, that is to say of a term policy such as we have been describing recently, is something like 11s. to secure the payment of £60 in the event of death within twelve months. The capital sum of £40 yields more than double this amount in interest, so that in one sense there is nothing to be provided for protection purposes, the single premium paid merely being accumulated at a lower rate of interest than if there were no protection involved. Even under an annual premium policy effected at a young age the cost of protection is very small; most of the premiums are available for accumulation at compound interest; there is a long period during which this accumulation can continue, and during which bonuses are received. When a policy is taken out later in life the cost of protection is much larger because the death rate is heavier. As compared with assurance effected young, the period for the accumulation of compound interest and for profit-sharing is short; so that in every way extremely great advantages attach to commencing assurance early in life.

DR. JOHNSON AND HIS EULOGISTS.

That Lord Rosebery is a good Johnsonian is certainly an addition to his claims upon our respect. But his Lichfield address contained a bêtise, for which it is not easy to forgive him—we mean, of course, the John Bull label. Johnson was as different from the typical Englishman of his day as Hume was from the typical Scot, and Voltaire from the typical Frenchman. There really is no single point of contact between the greatest and wittiest moralist of the eighteenth century and the grumbling, stupid farmer whom tradition has imposed upon us as the typical Englishman, except, perhaps, a common hatred of the American colonists. John Bull is credulous: Johnson was sceptical. John Bull grumbles at the weather, his food, his Government: Johnson, though melancholic, was not affected either by the weather, or by his food; and for politics, in the ordinary sense of the term, he did not care a rap. Mere grumbling, foolish repining at Providence, he detested, and rebuked wherever he found it. He was a good hater, certainly, but his prejudices were not insular. He knew more of European history and Continental literature, particularly French, than any of his contemporaries, except Burke and Gibbon. He was a cosmopolitan in the best sense of the word, for he compared his countrymen impartially with the citizens of other countries. He never took the conventional view, and he loved a paradox as dearly as the typical Briton loves a platitude. So far from being a boaster and thinking England could whip the world, Johnson was rather prone to depreciate the strength and wisdom of his countrymen. Decidedly, Lord Rosebery's attempt to paste the John Bull label on the Lichfield statue was not a success.

Johnson's Toryism was temperamental, and was not adopted from self-interest or based on a study of political theories or history. The Whig dogs were dissenters and canted about liberty. But except 'Mund Burke, "who, we know, acts from interest", Johnson did not know any of the politicians, and the absence from his talk of all allusions to the stirring politics of his time is really remarkable. It is astonishing, for instance, that there is only one mention in the Biography of Chatham (the glorious part of whose career opened before Johnson was fifty), and that is a criticism of the orator's blunder in saying "that had his colleagues not come to the bedside of a sick man, he would have taken up his bed and walked". There is only one mention of the younger Pitt: "I do not know Pitt; but Fox is my friend". There are only two other allusions to Fox in the book, one complaining of his influence over Reynolds, and the other defending his silence at The Club—"a man who plays nightly for the applause of the House of Commons will not throw for sixpences with us". This refusal to talk politics is the more extraordinary because, as we know, Johnson was frequently in the gallery, in days when it was difficult to get there, and composed the reports of the debates. Probably it was the drudgery of this means of livelihood that disgusted him with politics. It certainly was stupid of Lord Bute and Lord North not to use Johnson as Bolingbroke and Harley used Swift. Mr. Sidney Lee was not effective on Johnson. As a pure man of letters Mr. Lee isolated Johnson's edition of Shakespeare, and showed without difficulty that Johnson and Garrick between them had done more for Shakespeare than anyone else. But though it was impossible for Johnson to edit anything without making valuable contribution to the national stock of criticism, his Shakespeare is the least of his literary achievements. Quite a tradition of twaddle has been passed on from generation to generation about Johnson's prose style, its Latinisms, its mechanical antitheses, its pomposity. The truth is that though many of the Idlers and Ramblers were pot-boilers, Johnson's style is always noble and vigorous, and it is natural that an age which shuffles along without any style and mistakes slang for wit should be bored by the Johnsonian period. Under the influence of strong personal feeling Johnson has given us two of the finest pieces in the language—the Preface to the Dictionary and the letter to Lord Chesterfield. Personal resentment is the strongest spur, apparently, in the flanks of genius. The Letter to a Noble Lord was provoked by the Duke of Bedford's attack on Burke's pension.

No; it is not to the statesman or the man of letters that we must turn for the best panegyrics on Johnson; it is to the pulpit. The sermons of Canon Beeching and Canon Henson are the best things that have been said about the bicentenary. This is as it should be, for Johnson is greater on his moral than on his literary side. Dryden and Pope wrote as correctly, Gibbon as majestically as he; yet nearly all the brilliant satirists of the eighteenth century are disfigured by insincerity. Canon Beeching compares Johnson to the author of Ecclesiastes in his gloomy view of life, and discovers the likeness, which we pointed out many years ago in the SATURDAY REVIEW, between the Fleet Street philosopher and Jowett. "Perhaps no one except Jowett in our own generation", said Canon Beeching, "ever realised so keenly that his gift of wisdom implied a special mission to advise others to the best of his power." Canon Henson, preaching in the Abbey, where Johnson sleeps, asked: "Why was his name to-day the most widely reverenced and the most deeply loved of all the names which Englishmen cared to recall from his age? The answer was given in a word—character. . . . The days of Johnson had returned, but with every circumstance of spiritual peril intensified. The delusions which held the generation upon which the hurricane of the French Revolution broke with the dismaying shock of sudden and unwelcome surprise had reared their heads again, and were holding our generation also. Might the memory of the great moralist help to open our eyes and clear our minds of cant!" Thus perorates our Canon of Westminster, and inclines us to say: "A fine application. Pray, sir, had you ever thought of it? I had not, sir."

"THE MAKING OF A GENTLEMAN."

By Max Beerbohm.

MR. SUTRO is a highly successful dramatist. But against the ease with which he pleases the public must be set the difficulty he finds in pleasing the critics. When he writes dramas with strong scenes in them, the critics accuse him of sacrificing truth to effect, and manipulating his characters so as to secure those strong scenes; and I myself usually chime in. When he writes mere comedies, the critics complain bitterly of the absence of thrills. In that chorus I do not join. Mr. Bourchier, timorous man, does not invite me to the Garrick Theatre; but on leaving that temple a few nights ago I did not ask the keeper of the box-office to return me my money on the ground that I was not palpitating and haggard and forworn with emotion. Let us concede to Mr. Sutro the right to do what he sets out to do, and judge him according to the way in which he does it. "The Making of a Gentleman" is possibly not a classic. I daresay posterity will be able to get on quite well without it. But I take it to be, for us, in the autumn of 1909, a very good piece of work. The persons of the play are not essentially fresh. The homely but wealthy manufacturer with the heart of gold; the good-for-nothing son who lives on his bounty; the unscrupulous nobleman who also lives on his bounty; the daughter of his old clerk, who loves him for himself alone; the lady with a foreign title and an evil past, who yet has scruples and a capacity for disinterested devotion to the son—they don't sound startlingly new, as catalogued drily here. But Mr. Sutro has taken them and breathed plenty of life into them, and has given them freshness in detail. Though evidently his prime aim is to please the public, his play is far more convincing, gives us a far better illusion of reality, than Sir Arthur Pinero's laborious and wholly successful attempt to make us feel ill. Unflinching realism, merciless integrity, slices of life, the scalpel—such are the catch-words which doubtless were revolving in Sir Arthur's brain when he composed "Mid-Gutter". But never for a moment does that play impress us as true to human life. The photographer has grouped together, in the harshest light, certain specially ill-favoured persons, and before removing the cap from the lens of the camera, has said "Look unpleasant, ladies and gentlemen, please!—Now!" The result is a meaningless and unrelated ugliness. Fools are they who think ugly themes are to be eschewed by artists. But it is right to condemn ugliness to which the artist has given no moral or philosophic significance; and there is none in "Mid-Gutter". The fact that Zoe and her husband agreed when they married "to have no brats of children" has no bearing on what they have become. It is dragged in, for a moment, merely to give simple folk the idea that Sir Arthur is a profound critic of the age he lives in. To Zoe and her husband, children would have been but an added casus belli Billingsgatiani. And as if even they, when they were bride and bridegroom, would have made their compact in the words suggested by Sir Arthur! One of the several reasons why Sir Arthur fails as a photographer is that he seems to have so little notion of what people say, and of how they say it. One of Mr. Sutro's chief assets is the keenness of his ear for human speech. Of course, characters in a play must not talk exactly as we do in real life. If they did, the play would be interminable, and we should have but the vaguest idea of its drift. Human speech, for dramatic purposes, must be abridged and sharpened, all the time; and yet we must be kept unaware of the process. In the art of writing seemingly natural and actually telling dialogue Mr. Sutro is, with Mr. Henry Arthur Jones, foremost among our playwrights. Mr. Shaw has an ear for the rhythm of human speech; his characters never talk like books; but there is always something noticeably metallic about the concision of their utterance. Except when Mr. Shaw determines to show us that he can achieve beauty with the best of 'em—as in the long speech made by the mystic priest at the close of "John Bull's Other Island"—there is no charm of rhythm in his dialogue. Mr. Sutro never sets out to display beauty of word and cadence. But he is a constant purveyor of it. From first to last, his characters talk as charmingly as concisely. The charm is no more protruded on us than the concision. But it is there, an added grace, and subconsciously we enjoy it. It is a pity that Mr. Sutro, the most literary of our playwrights, does not publish his plays.

Apart from the quality of the dialogue, "The Making of a Gentleman" would not perhaps be deeply impressive in the study. I do not think we should lay the book down with a sense that our experience of life had been extended, and our insight quickened. Segregating ourselves from the magnetic public which Mr. Sutro set out to please, we might become more conscious than we are, in the theatre, of the inherent oldness of the story, and less conscious of the freshness with which Mr. Sutro has decked it out. The central figure of the play is Archibald Carey, the son of the successful but homely manufacturer aforesaid. The father's ambition has ever been that his son shall be a gentleman. Nowadays the habit of doing nothing is not deemed essential to gentility. Indeed, it is regarded as rather bad form. All the fashionable youths of to-day do definitely something—are in the army, or in business, or in politics. Loafing is outmoded. And one would suppose that even the homely Sam Carey would have known this, and would have wished his son to do something. However, let us accept Mr. Sutro's premises. Archibald Carey has plenty of intelligence, and any number of good impulses, but, unluckily, no character; and from his lack of character Mr. Sutro distils some admirable scenes of comedy. Sam Carey arrives at the flat in South Audley Street, and confesses to his son that he has been speculating with his capital and is ruined. He has just enough left to enable him to go back to Canada and re-inaugurate there—on a small scale—his business in pickles. Archibald does not reproach him. He is, on the contrary, deeply touched. Also, his manhood responds joyously to the notion of accompanying his father and leading a hard new life in a hard new world. The father becomes very husky, and the curtain falls. The next act takes place in the house of Archibald's sister, Rosie, who has married the son of Lord Parkhurst. Rosie has reason to believe that a certain Baroness von Ritzen would like to marry her brother. This lady has the disadvantage of not having been respectable, and the advantage of being a widow with twenty thousand pounds a year. Rosie and Lord Parkhurst take Archibald in hand. Rosie dilates on the charm and beauty of the Baroness, and Archibald cannot help feeling flattered by her predilection for him. Lord Parkhurst applauds his manly and filial determination to go to Canada. He describes the climate, the lack of civilised society, the long day's unremitting toil with no apparent reward, "but it's life, my boy—life!" And very soon Archibald is "off" Canada, and proceeds to the boudoir of the Baroness. She has heard of Sam Carey's losses, and instantly divines the object of the visit, and does her best to make the young man uncomfortable. He manages, however, to express his proposal, and in the agony of the effort he realises that he really is rather in love with the lady. The scene is extremely amusing and well-invented, graduated with great skill. But one cannot believe that the Baroness, being really anxious to marry him, and having had her pride salved by his belated sincerity, and being a spirited woman of the world, accustomed to take what she wants, would refuse to marry him without the consent of his papa (whom she has never seen). See him of course she presently does—rough old Sam, in his homespun clothes, much embarrassed by his intrusion into the luxurious boudoir, but with all the strength of his sound puritan stock opposed invincibly to his son's betrothal. It is an old situation; but here again Mr. Sutro's tact and insight save it from being tedious. The end of the play consists in old Sam's gradual yielding to the force of the argument that his son, having been brought up to do nothing, and encouraged to do nothing, is good for nothing, and had better attach himself to a Baroness with a past than to a country with a future.

Old Sam is played by Mr. Bourchier with that restraint which he has gradually acquired, and which was all that was needed to make a fine actor of him. Mr. Kenneth Douglas well presents the humour of Archibald. The Baroness is a rather difficult part, in that she is a complicated character, who remains mostly in the background. There is little time for an actress to make the audience understand her. Miss Ethel Irving succeeds where an actress of less well-developed method would certainly fail. Mr. Edmund Maurice is amusing as Lord Parkhurst; and Mr. A. E. Benedict, as Lord Parkhurst's son—a golf enthusiast, whose conversation is described by his father as "nauseous and asphyxiating"—plays with a keen sense of character and fun.

THE UNEXPECTED PERIL.

UNLIKE the youth that all men say
  They prize—youth of abounding blood,
In love with the sufficient day,
  And gay in growth, and strong in bud;

Unlike was mine! Then my first slumber
  Nightly rehearsed my last; each breath
Knew itself one of the unknown number.
  But Life was urgent with me as Death.

My shroud was in the flocks; the hill
  Within its quarry locked my stone;
My bier grew in the woods; and still
  Life spurred me where I paused alone.

"Begin!" Life called. Again her shout,
  "Make haste while it is called to-day!"
Her exhortations plucked me out,
  Hunted me, turned me, held me at bay.

But if my youth is thus hard pressed
  (I thought) what of a later year?
If the End so threats this tender breast,
  What of the days when it draws near?

Draws near, and little done? Yet lo,
  Dread has forborne, and Haste lies by.
I was beleaguered; now the foe
  Has raised the siege, I know not why.

I see them troop away; I ask
  Were they in sooth mine enemies—
Terror, the doubt, the lash, the task?
  What heart has my new housemate, Ease?

How am I left, at last, alive,
  To make a stranger of a tear?
What did I do one day to drive
  From me the vigilant angel, Fear?

The diligent angel, Labour? Ay,
  The inexorable angel, Pain?
Menace me, lest indeed I die,
  Sloth! Turn, crush, teach me fear again!

ALICE MEYNELL.

LETTERS FROM SOLITUDE.

By Filson Young.

V.

. . . . Connemara.

You will have noticed that I soon moved from my first headquarters in Connemara, and found others, no less solitary, but far more congenial. It was not until I had come some ten miles westward, nearer still to the salt wilderness of the Atlantic, that I realised that the melancholy of that first halting-place was not, as I had thought, due to some mood of my own, but was really inherent in the place. Human existence was a depressing business for everyone there; here, ten miles away, it is quite different. The land is as stony and barren as ever, and the landscape the same sonata of bog, mountain and sea; but here people's faces are brighter, happier, more hopeful; they smile here continually, and do not complain of poverty. Why? Because this part of Ireland is perhaps one of the best examples of what the reconstructive efforts of the various organisations for the betterment of the people have accomplished. If anyone should still think that reconstructive work in Ireland is a mere wasteful and cumbersome machinery of charity, let him come to Connemara, and stay, as I did, first in a place which has not been thoroughly worked over by the reconstructive agency, and then in a place like this which has. The difference can only be described as astounding. It is not merely the neat, clean weatherproof houses, and the better methods of working and living; it is the positive difference in the people—in their intelligence, their greater robustness of mind, their physical health—I would even say their happiness, if I felt that there was any possible way of judging what happiness in others is, or wherein it consists. One would think that they were a different race from the cowed, silent, hopeless people of the untouched districts; but they are exactly the same, with an interest in life added, and a temporal ambition put beside the eternal. "We will always like to be working", said a man who was doing some unnecessary jobs about the boat I was sailing; and he added, with a delightful mixture of persons and tenses used by the Irish who have only a little English, "A working man, he was better to be working always; we will always be better myself when we had something to do". How unlike the traditional Ireland; and yet it is already becoming a characteristic point of view with people in this place.

There is a great island here, close to the mainland, containing excellent land for pasture and tillage. This was bought and divided into holdings each of a size sufficient to support a family in decency and comfort. Then people who had holdings on the worst land in the neighbourhood—holdings that would hardly support a frog—were transported to the new land. Sound, plain little cottages were built for them instead of the huts of turf and stone in which they had lived before; a harbour was made for their boats and, in some cases, money advanced for boat-building. All the work was done locally and for fair wages; and the people who had formerly barely existed began to live, to make some margin of money over their needs, and to pay the instalments, in rent and purchase, which ultimately made them the sole possessors of these new lands and houses. Is not that a really satisfactory story? Of course it is not always quite plain sailing, and there are plenty of discouragements; but one positive piece of work, visible and accomplished, is more powerful than a hundred failures, and is the most eloquent of all arguments. My friend who "will always like to be working" is not himself a child of the Congested Districts Board, but a man whose own holding was, with fishing and kelp-burning, sufficient to support him and his family; but he has shared in the moral effect produced by the betterment of the others, and is an example of the way in which the benefits of positive action extend to many others besides those who receive direct help.

And after this re-establishment on the land comes the education that alone can make it a permanent benefit instead of a temporary relief. On the wildest part of the road that leads to this extremity I passed two little plots of land, each the size of a small cottage garden. All round them were desolate bog and rock, scraped and trenched here and there to grow a few potatoes; but on these little plots were flourishing a field of rich hay and a heavy crop of oats. The contrast was startling; but two placards explained this little lesson of the Department of Agriculture—placards stating the constituents, weight, and cost of the few pounds of chemical fertiliser with which the fields had been dressed. It was to me at once a most primitive and a most striking example of Horace Plunkett's work in Ireland—a work so humble in its beginnings, so obvious and so elementary and so patient, and yet so far-reaching in its results and possibilities. Very eloquent, very touching to the wayfarer on that lonely road are these two waving crops. Round them are the sodden bog and the glacial mountain, showing what Nature will do if left to herself; near them the pitiful crops of poor foodstuff, showing the best that the peasant of these parts, untaught and unhelped, has done for himself; and there stand the little fields, waving and ripening in wind and sun, to show what the same peasant, by due labour of draining and banking, and by a simple external aid easily within his means, can accomplish if he will. Better than any pamphlets, lectures, or tracts is the lesson of these two fields. "I cannot", says the hopeless peasant. "You can", shout the little fields; and the peasant, passing that way again, takes heart to say "I will".

I sailed one day to the Aran Islands; it took us two and a half hours to go to Kilronan and five to beat back, and it was wonderful to be feeling one's way after dark through these rock-strewn seas; but it was more wonderful still to be on the Islands, and to be aware of their utter difference from the rest of the world—their amazing detachment from any life but their own, their apparent prosperity, their unrealisable antiquity, the beauty of their children, the humour and character of their ancient men and women. They seemed to be inhabited entirely by artist's models. And of the view from the summit of Inishmore, from the cliffs of Moher in Clare right out to Kilkee, to the incomparable mountains of Connemara, from Galway to Slyne Head; who shall write? There are days that one remembers always, but cannot describe; and this day of sun and wind on Aran, of wide views, of ever-changing seas and skies, of nightfall at sea, of anxious progress homewards by ghostly reefs and headlands lit only by their foam—this day is of that unforgettable, uncommunicable company that goes to make memories at once mysterious and splendid.

I have told you nothing of that other side to one's life here—the world of bog and mountain, stream, and lough, of which the sea-trout is lord. Long days with a fishing-rod on a lough are absorbing enough while they last, but there is not much to tell about them; the drift down-wind, the intent rhythmical casting, the recurring procession of Blue-Jay, Claret-and-Grouse, and Butcher over the brown water; the rare—too rare!—curve of light and splash that means a sea-trout; the long row up the lake with lines trailing and eyes free to watch the silver furrows on the dark lough or the cloud shadows that darken the heather on the soaring mountain side, with no sound but the cry of the curlew or the occasional hopeful remark of the gillie—these are dream-like things, selfish joys which one cannot communicate and cannot share. For you see I have come to the end of my cure, and am beginning to fall in love with solitude; so I must move on into the world again, and let all these things that are realities now fall into their due place in my life, as backgrounds and memories. Memories are like sunsets; as the sunset to a summer's day, so is memory to a little piece of life like this; the active properties, sensation and experience, are gone, and only a soft and fading picture remains. Gradually the less essential things disappear; joys, pains, excitements, discomforts fade out, until at last the ultimate essence and result will alone remain.

In that day I shall see, a dark, low line against the sunset, my island of Inishmuskerry.

THE ROMANTIC MOVEMENT IN ENGLISH POETRY.*

By John F. Runciman.

Of all living writers, Mr. Arthur Symons would have seemed to me the best equipped to treat the subject immediately suggested by the title he has chosen for his new book; and though he employs the word "Romantic" in a much wider sense than is customary, and takes in a vast field of poetry which is not commonly regarded as Romantic, this very fact makes his thorough competency and mastery of the material the more striking. By the Romantic movement Mr. Symons means no less than the coming back to life of poetry at the end of the eighteenth century after its long and death-like sleep. He justifies his use of the phrase with skill, energy and resource. All poetry, he says, except that of the eighteenth century, has been Romantic; the poets of the Renaissance were Romantic poets; and if Keats was a Romantic poet, then Shakespeare was a Romantic poet also. The Renaissance was a Romantic movement, and what is commonly called, and what Mr. Symons himself calls, the Romantic movement was a Renaissance. This is an extension, with a vengeance, of Stendhal's dictum that all literature was Romantic when it was new. We will consider presently Mr. Symons' defence of his position—if we may apply the term "defence" to a very spirited assault upon an ordinary article of the literary creed of Englishmen—but it must be noted that in his introductory chapter he lays more stress on the word "movement" than on the word "Romantic"; and, far from dealing with all Romantic poetry—which, to follow his definition, means all genuine poetry—he is occupied solely by the revival of poetry. This narrows very considerably a formidable field; but as he deals with all the poets, great and small, so long as they can be called poets, who were born before 1800 and lived into the nineteenth century, the field, however narrowed, still cannot be said to be a narrow one. A large number of small and important "poets" get separate notices. All are discussed from Mr. Symons' point of view, a point of view to which he holds consistently, though by no means fanatically or absurdly; the whole book is clearly and logically arranged, and it is written throughout in that musical and crystalline English, easy without looseness, of which Mr. Symons is so fine a master.

In fact, I should be inclined to call this book the most brilliant that Mr. Symons has ever written. When he praises, he gives ample reason for the praise; when he gibes—as he does, very prettily, often—he gives no reasons, but quotes a line or two from the person gibed at. Happily, none of these persons are living, or Mr. Symons' own life would not be secure. Hannah More, for instance, is given what the ordinary literary agent would call a "favourable notice"; but amidst all the kindness comes the remark that this lady's works are not, after all, so bad to beguile a "dull afternoon". This is disagreeable criticism carried to the highest point of perfection. I thoroughly enjoy these little excursions. Henry James Pye, poet-laureate from 1790 to 1833, "meatless and savourless"; Mrs. Piozzi, "who wrote one verse in one century and lived nearly twenty years into the next"; "Samuel Rogers was not a poet"—such remarks fill the soul of a hardened critic, who has had to handle inferior persons, with a certain well-earned delight. But even better than the skilful damnation is the praise. It is much easier to damn and be interesting than to praise without making the reader drop the book; and Mr. Symons has achieved this hard task. His essays on Coleridge, Shelley, Keats and Wordsworth are amongst his finest. Thank goodness, one says in reading about Shelley, we have at last got away from the "beautiful, ineffectual angel"; in reading about Coleridge we are not worried by the great opium question; in the Keats Fanny Brawne makes a very brief appearance. Each poet is given his proper meed of approbation; and since we all like to know why we like poetry, and especially why we like the poetry of particular poets, these discussions will be gratefully read by lovers of Coleridge, Shelley, and Keats. I must not forget that Wordsworth, though he is a subject for fair discussion, is here discussed with a fairness that is much more fair than usual—which is, indeed, generous.

It would be ridiculous for me to find fault with Mr. Symons when he is dealing with the subject of poetry—the subject that he knows so much better than anyone. Yet I mean to quarrel slightly with him for his use of the word "Romantic". Of course, it is a word that has been abused with a great deal of thoroughness; since about 1830 it has been worked harder than any vocable in our language. It is applied to a poem—or more commonly a mere piece of versification—of which the subject is southern, or supernatural, or passionate in character; it is applied to young ladies who sigh for the days of Gretna Green; it is used to mean a thousand other things, so long as those things are not soiled by contact with the dull, workaday world. But in art it has been used to define one phase of the great revival of the spirit of art which took place at the beginning of the nineteenth century; and in extending its meaning so as to include other phases I cannot see that Mr. Symons has rendered literary or artistic men any good service. A word like "Romantic" had no meaning until a meaning was quite arbitrarily attached to it: we know what that meaning was, and though Stendhal came in to muddle matters, there seems to me no reason for qualifying all genuine art with the adjective "Romantic". This is what Mr. Symons does. All genuine poetry, he says, has been Romantic. Why, then, Romantic? Why not, simply, poetry?

This is a question of terminology. It will come as a slight shock to many of Mr. Symons' readers to find Landor and Keats classed as Romantics. As we ordinarily use the word, they were not; but, of course, as Mr. Symons uses the word, they were. No one can deny that they shared in the great revival of poetry; and if Romantic must be applied to that revival, well then, Romantic they were. But in that case we need new words to define the very great difference between the marble, sculptured verse of Landor and the sinuous, sensuous music of Keats. I will not attempt to argue the point, but simply go on to pass a few remarks on the most interesting book that has been put in my hands for a long time. I find the book chiefly interesting as the expression of the personality of one of the most interesting men it has been my good fortune to know, Mr. Arthur Symons. His joy in the beautiful thing—whether in poetry, music, painting, or sculpture—was always wonderful to witness; and here we find him positively revelling in beautiful things. He has tried to be critical, and he is critical in a much better sense of the word than he himself would admit. He says "Much fine literature has been written under the name of criticism. But for the critic to aim at making literature is to take off something from the value of his criticism as criticism. It may produce a work of higher value. But it will cease to be, properly speaking, what we distinguish as criticism". Of this statement Mr. Symons' own work is a flat contradiction: his criticism has its value as criticism because it is literature—because as a literary artist Mr. Symons can send home to us precisely what he feels and thinks about other literature. For example, no mere critic who was not a literary artist could tell us that "romance rose out of the grave of Chatterton". Could a writer who was not a literary artist say this?—"He remains alone in English literature, to which he brought, in verse and prose, qualities of order and vehemence, of impassioned thinking and passionless feeling, not to be found combined except in his own work". Mr. Symons is speaking of Landor: does he wish to be judged as a critic or as a maker of literature? I judge him as a critic who becomes a maker of literature by the mere exercise of his faculty of criticism. It is the literary man, not the critic, who speaks of Landor's "lofty homeliness of touch".

A hundred things might be quoted as illustrations

* "The Romantic Movement in English Poetry." By Arthur Symons. London: Constable. 1909. 10s. 6d. net.

of Mr. Symons' really marvellous way of combining criticism and literature. Apparently he contradicts himself at times, but the contradiction is never more than apparent: a few lines of explanation would make it all clear. Probably only those who have tried—as I have tried—to put into words the sensations and thoughts aroused by great works of art will realise what a feat is here achieved. The great and little poets of a hundred years are summed up in a free, clear and more or less just fashion: the point of view is kept, though not, as I have said, fanatically, and not self-consciously. In the future, when people have given up reading English poetry, a habit which is fast dying out, they will read Mr. Symons' book, and so learn all about the poetry of one of the most important periods in the literary history of England.

THE STRANGE DOCTRINE OF SIGNATURES.

THE curious doctrine of Signatures may be gleaned in part from the English herbalists, but more particularly from William Coles, who made it the keynote of a book, published in 1659, called "Adam in Eden; or, Nature's Paradise". In the seventeenth century men had begun to scoff at the belief of their forefathers that herbs, stones, and minerals were stamped in sympathetic characters to show their application in the cure of disease, and Coles through his book made a bid to recover the early doctrine from the limbo of outworn creeds. One Oswald Crol, a chemist of repute and a devout follower of Paracelsus, had lately published in Germany a discourse entitled "De Signaturis Rerum", and the subject had so captured the fancy of our herbalist that he began to reinterpret Nature by the light of far-off days, when the earth expressed in all her substance a language of signs and images amongst which empirics moved as in a kindergarten of medicine.

The doctrine had its origin in the East. It was naturally familiar to disciples of the Eastern philosophers; Roger Bacon wrote of Signatures, and the Rosicrucians talked of them in their revivals of forgotten things. It was, in short, an integral part of the mighty system of sympathy and antipathy, attraction and repulsion, by means of which the macrocosm was supposed to minister to the microcosm:

"Man is one world and hath
Another to attend him".

Our remote forefathers thought that things provided for the preservation of man were not left uncertain of application. They conceived on the contrary an attraction or sympathy between the intention of God and the understanding of man, such sympathy being established through the medium of the "Soul" or "Spirit" of the world. According to Talismanic lore, this spirit it was that received occult properties from the sun, moon, and stars to convey them into herbs, stones, minerals, and animals. "Everything", the adepts learnt, "was impressed with the peculiar virtues of its star to produce the like operations upon other things on which they are reflected." Often a seal or image was visibly stamped upon some substance to show its sympathetical use in the cure of disease.

To realise the apparent need for one of the most gracious dispensations of olden time, we may recall the first helplessness of the exiles from Paradise, as trembling they stood without the gates of joy; free indeed by the knowledge of good and evil, but wanting in experience to discern the nature of food or poison, blessing or curse. There existed no longer the bar against experimental enterprise: but there were penalties to reward a mistake. Whom could they question? God walked no more with them. The earth was dumb.

Then sprang to their eyes the warning language of signs and symbols, and a school of food and medicine was opened. As though God had said "Take man and nurse him for Me", the Mother of the Dust extended her ministrations, becoming thenceforth a natural medium in those communications of the Divine with human intelligence, whereby Love sought to mitigate the curse pronounced by Justice. She brought forth herbs fit for food and medicine with their purpose stamped upon them in legible characters: yellow flowers, as celandine, to exhibit a cure for the bilious disease; red herbs, as tormentil, to stand forth as blood-staunches; snake-like roots, as in viper's grass, to show a cure for envenomed wounds; eye-like blossoms, as of vervain, to cure ophthalmia; heart-shaped leaves, as of wood-sorrel, to use in cardiac disorders; palmate leaves, as of the fig-tree, for warts and pains of the hands; and many other signs for the instruction of man, her helpless child and nursling. Nor did the Great Mother forget to distinguish for the most part her noxious plants by giving them deterrent colours or unwholesome odours. Henbane, as Anne Pratt has remarked, is open to suspicion both in hue and odour, and the same author has pointed out that "dull yellow, dim purple, or green flowers often characterise noxious plants, though these distinctions are not invariable".

It is reasonable to assume that colours were the first Signatures known to primitive man, since their appeal is to the material rather than to the intellectual perceptions. Red and yellow juices were known, it has been said, even in the palæozoic forest, and surely red wounds and the "yellow disease" were likely to have made the first appeal to medicine in a youthful world. It is noteworthy that Signatures of colour have been the last to survive. So late, even, as 1812 there is in Sir John Hill's "Family Herbal" the praise of red herbs for the healing of red wounds or hæmorrhages, and the writer has found to-day, in a village in Buckinghamshire, some survival of belief in the yellow flowers of the dandelion to cure bilious affections; but although a cottage dame of her acquaintance applies in orthodox fashion yellow to yellow, like to like, she is yet unconscious of the doctrine of healing by Signature. It is, in fact, doubtful whether the doctrine ever obtained in this country among the unlearned. No mention of its theory is found in the "Saxon Leechdoms", though there is a hint of some practice in the recommendation of adder's tongue for snake-wounds, and in the description of "gromel" as a cure for stone.

William Coles, following his German contemporary, "the most renowned, . . . most learned, . . . most exquisite, . . . most profound Crollius", presented in his herbal three hundred and forty-three medicinal herbs, one hundred and forty of which show Signatures of healing. He leads with the wall-nut tree, than which no more interesting example could be quoted:

"Wall-nuts", wrote Coles, "have the perfect Signature of the Head: the outer husk or green Covering represent the Pericranium or outward skin of the skull, whereon the hair groweth, and therefore salt made of those husks and barks are exceeding good for wounds in the head. The inner wooddy shell hath the Signature of the Skull, and the little yellow skin, or Peel, that covereth the Kernell of the hard Meninga & Pia Mater, which are the thin Scarfes that envelope the brain. The kernel hath the very figure of the Brain, and therefore it is very profitable for the Brain, and resists poysons."

It was apparent, however, that no effort on the part of its "modern" advocates could make the old doctrine to live again. By the seventeenth century it had become outworn. If in its origin it had represented a dispensation to meet the earliest needs of humanity, it was now no longer needed as a primer of instruction. There is something almost humorous in the manner in which Crol and Coles worked at discovering Signatures. In their self-appointed task, which they "prosequited with extraordinary dilligence", they dragged forth images of an astonishing subtilty. Not content to read off "Nature's Book" as it was read by eyes of old, they must, as it were, wring fresh meanings from the grudging dame: say that "Misselto of the Oak" is in question as a cure for "falling sickness" or epilepsy:

"The viscosity", wrote Coles, quoting Crol, "and tenacious quality of the Bird-lime representing those melancholy and phlegmatick humours . . . by which it is caused, or else as Bird-lime doth detain whatsoever it fastens to, so this Disease ceasing (? seizing) upon the Body as the Remora doth upon a Ship, will suffer it to go no further but maketh it to fall down ". Yet two hundred and two herbs lack signature!

Our author makes nevertheless a delightful medium through which to view the ancient doctrine. He may be sympathised with in his abandonment to the fascination of his subject, for it shines in all the glamour of the faery past. In the larger view it is a story of the Great Mother when youth and joy were in her veins, a story that is worthy of remembrance, since every tradition of the earth is a part of our inheritance of herself.

BOOKS ON ITALIAN ART.

By Laurence Binyon.

WHAT is the secret of the special fascination of Italian art for English people? That this fascination exists no one can deny. The Germans and the French, of course, pay their large homage of admiration to the masterpieces of Italy; but, unless I am mistaken, there is not in those nations the same peculiar instinct of affection that springs up with us in each generation as it comes. We do not rave about the same masters that our grandfathers and great-grandfathers raved about; but the passion remains. There are some, no doubt, who will tell us that the cult is mostly habit and convention, a snobbery of the mind. Instead of studying with sentimental enthusiasm the productions of second-rate and third-rate Italians, we ought to be true to our Northern blood, and take the Dutch and the Flemish and the early Germans to our hearts; or else we ought to accept modernity in its fulness and give our minds to the modern art of France. Well, I am persuaded that the charm of Italy, and the Italian cult that charm has inspired in us, are very real things, and by no means affectations. I do not know how it is to be explained, but there seems certainly to be a sort of affinity, something inbred, which literature and history attest as existing between the genius of that race and of our own. No Italian artist is so remote from the sympathies of normal English taste as, say, Boucher, in one direction, or Goya, in another direction, or Grünewald, in yet another. No doubt there is a superficial, popular, sentimental side to this preference; but at bottom there is a real congeniality, and the English mind is at home in Italian air. Whether this is for our good or not, is another question with which I am not now concerned.

Endless are the books which have been issued by London publishers of late years, devoted to Italian painting; and it is permissible to be a little weary of them. There have been so many; and so very few have been real additions to our knowledge and enjoyment. But Italian sculpture has not, at least in England, been overdone by much writing. The Florentine Sculptors of the Renaissance make a subject which is not by any means hackneyed; and, adequately treated, it could not fail to be stimulating and delightful. A book with this title is one of the recent additions to Messrs. Methuen's handsome series, "Classics of Art". Though in an English version, it is from a German pen, that of the renowned Dr. Bode. And since Florentine sculpture has been one of Dr. Bode's special studies, and since his directorship has enriched the Berlin museums with a remarkable collection of the work of Italian sculptors, we take up the volume with high anticipations. It must be said at once that these anticipations are only very partially fulfilled. Though a few pages of introduction serve to sketch the development of sculpture in Florence, the rest of the book is not, as we should expect, a connected account of the sculptors and their works, but a variety of essays, largely on controversial points. If you have an appetite for the quarrels of the learned, there are many of Dr. Bode's pages which will satisfy your craving. Some of this argumentative matter is in the nature of a slaughter of the slain, a laborious trampling on theories already everywhere discredited. For nearly all these essays, in their original form, appeared several years ago; and controversies of specialists soon become stale reading. In any case they are quite out of place in a book intended for the general reader. As may be imagined, therefore, there is rather too much of Dr. Bode and his opponents in the book, and too little about certain of the Florentine sculptors; especially about the greatest of them all, Michelangelo. There is a disquisition on some of that master's youthful works, chiefly directed against the theories of Dr. Wölfflin, who has presumed to differ from Dr. Bode; but that is practically all. Again, of Agostino di Duccio, the artist of the charming reliefs at Perugia and Rimini, we are told almost nothing, and there is no illustration of his work. He is mentioned several times, as an imitator of Donatello's, but always with indifference or disparagement. It is a pity that Dr. Bode did not take the trouble to treat his subject in a comprehensive way, and give the world the results of his long researches and immense knowledge in a more considered form. These essays are very well for students already thoroughly familiar with the main works of the Renaissance in Florence; for those in need of guidance and illumination they are misleading, since emphasis is continually being laid on minor points and obscure questions of authenticity. It need hardly be said, of course, that, taken simply as a series of essays on various aspects of the subject, the book contains much that is extremely valuable. Some of Dr. Bode's opinions—such as, for instance, the ascription of the plaster relief in the Victoria and Albert Museum, called "Strife", and certain other works of the same kind, to Leonardo—are still very debateable, no doubt; but his opinions as to authorship are always suggestive. The most readable chapters are those which trace the treatment of certain subjects by different sculptors—Madonna groups, busts of boys, and the "putto". Yet we feel that when not arguing for an attribution or combating an adversary Dr. Bode finds writing less congenial. In the chapter on the Madonna groups he seems to get suddenly tired, and dismisses Michelangelo's Madonnas with a strangely superficial judgment. According to him, "scarcely one of these compositions recalls the Madonna and the Holy Infant, hardly even any mother and child, so impassively do they regard one another, so slight a connexion does there seem to be between them". At the same time Dr. Bode tells us that "purely artistic problems alone occupy Michelangelo". We conclude from this that Michelangelo's sole interest in creating that most noble and profoundly conceived Madonna of the Medici Chapel was the problem of sculpturing a given group in the round; a conclusion I believe to be entirely untrue.

The Germans are famed for their thoroughness in study; and rightly, though this virtue is in many cases—not of course in critics of Dr. Bode's rank—discounted by a total want of discrimination. For laborious accumulation of useless facts, and for wildly fantastic theories, no one can hope to rival a certain type of German mind. In England, though we also have our furious theorists, the tendency is rather to be slipshod than pedantic. Among the multitude of our "art books" there is a great deal of frothy rubbish. But now and again appears a work of real devotion, not less thorough than the German ideal, and sane as well as thorough. Such a book was Mr. Horn's "Botticelli"; and such another is Miss Ffoulkes' "Foppa" ("Vincenzo Foppa of Brescia, Founder of the Lombard School." By Constance Jocelyn Ffoulkes and Mgr. Ridolfo Maiocchi. Lane). It is true that Foppa is a master of infinitely less importance than Botticelli; and most people will think it a quite superfluous labour to have made so imposing a monument to a painter of his rank. Yet scholarship of this devoted kind is too rare and fine a quality to be lightly disparaged or disdained. It is a reproach to us in England that no similar piety of study has been given to the work of some of the earlier artists of our own country. What deserves especial praise is the admirable temper of Miss Ffoulkes' writing; it is quite free from the barren acrimonies of the partisan and from exaggerated laudation of its subject; it is also lucid and unpretentious in style. Like Mr. Horne, Miss Ffoulkes and her Italian collaborator believe that no sound study of the history of art can proceed without the control of documents; and those relating to Foppa are printed at the end of the book.

The results of all this research and labour are offered simply as a contribution to knowledge of the early Lombard school, a school of which not too much is known. Our interest in the school would perhaps have been greater if its normal growth had not been suddenly arrested and transformed by the invading genius of Leonardo. But before the time of that splendid irruption from Florence there can be no doubt that the Brescian Foppa, by the power of his grave and tranquil art, was predominant in moulding the type of Lombard painting.

CORRESPONDENCE.

THE SCENERY OF KING LEAR.

To the Editor of the SATURDAY REVIEW.

Arena Goldoni, Florence.

14 September 1909.

Sir,—My notice has been drawn to a false report which concerns my work and that of a fellow-artist, Mr. Charles Ricketts. It is so serious a report that I hasten to correct it, and to do so, if you will permit me, through your columns.

It is reported that in the production of "King Lear" at the Haymarket, Mr. Ricketts has been guilty of appropriating my method of employing stage-scenery. The accusation has already appeared in several London papers, and seems to me to be a very grave one to make against so talented an artist as Mr. Ricketts. This report has been on foot for several years, in fact it started soon after I had left England, when I was called to work in German and Russian theatres. It is a grave charge to make against an amateur in the theatrical world that he copies the idea of an artist who has just introduced that idea to the public—an idea, moreover, to which no copyright can be affixed.

If such an accusation were made against some poor fellow without an ounce of originality in his head, or a spark of conscience or pride in his heart, it could be overlooked, for these people must live, and this kind of theft is not actionable. But to accuse Mr. Charles Ricketts of so gross an offence is to conjure up an impossible kind of man to the imagination—a being so pitifully mean that I hasten to write these few words, stating at the same time that I know Mr. Ricketts personally, and he may or may not know my work, but that although I have never seen his stage-work, I am convinced that what the critics have mistaken for my method is Mr. Ricketts' own method, and that if Mr. Ricketts employs large blue sky-backgrounds, or towering trees in straight lines, or schemes instead of confusions of colour, or lights which lend a poetry to the scene, instead of lights blended by vulgarity, he is but following a "method" employed since time immemorial by all men of taste.

For the artificial manner in which he treats all this he cannot be responsible. He is working inside a theatre under artificial conditions, and therefore everything he does must become *theatrical*. Mysterious or open, gay or gloomy, it will all be tinged with the atmosphere of the theatre; he will give us theatrical mystery or theatrical gaiety, not the mystery and gaiety so long associated by us with his sensitive works of art. There is something sad about this. To me it has always seemed a pity that those born outside the theatre should be attracted into an atmosphere which even we who are well acclimatised to it desire to change to a fresher, purer air. It may be the heroic hope of Mr. Ricketts to let in this purer air for us from outside, and if this is so his attempt can only command our sympathy, for in doing so he runs the danger of losing some of his freshness; he must become tainted with that fearsome thing "the theatrical", whereas we who are born in that atmosphere are sometimes proof against its attacks.

This accusation against Mr. Ricketts of "cribbing another man's idea" is an accusation which is quite common to-day. Thus only yesterday the same artist was found fault with for printing books having some faint likeness to those of the Kelmscott Press, whereas the Vale Press, which was established shortly after Mr. William Morris' first book appeared, had very few characteristics in common with it. Again, only the other day a religious play, called "Eager Heart", was produced, and everyone said it owed its existence to the fact that "Bethlehem" had been produced a few years previously. Could anything be more without foundation? Why, someone will shortly be accusing Mr. William Poel of slavishly copying the methods of production employed by Shakespeare, or Richard Strauss will be told he is an imitator of Wagner. It will be said of Burne Jones that he founded his style upon that of Rossetti, or that the methods employed by the enterprising burglar of to-day are only stolen from Charles Peace.

And if you tell me that some of these statements are the truth, I can only remind you that, whenever one artist has stolen from another, the debt has been publicly acknowledged. Therefore Mr. Ricketts has not, cannot have, stolen from me, for he has made no such acknowledgment, and that ends the matter.

Yours faithfully,

GORDON CRAIG.

THE FOOD QUESTION.

To the Editor of the SATURDAY REVIEW.

Brenchley, 20 September 1909.

SIR,—A case overstated is a case weakened, and it is as dangerous to give instances as to give reasons. Mr. Hermann Erskine, in support of his thesis, that much good work has been done by men heavily handicapped, makes this astounding assertion: "Scott wrote the Waverley Novels in a state of mental agony resulting from financial embarrassments".

When Scott's "financial embarrassment" began, no one, I suppose, exactly knows. It is doubtful whether Constable and the Ballantynes knew: it is certain that, after they did know, they kept Scott in the dark. But surely Mr. Erskine will not say that Scott was in "mental agony" in 1821, in that idyllic summer which even "Gurlyle" admits was "very beautiful; like a picture of Boccaccio's: the ideal of a country life in our time". If, in 1821, Scott suspected himself of embarrassment, Scott was a dishonourable fool. It may have been foolish blindly to trust Jocund Johnnies and Napoleons of the Book-trade, but the southron booby who doubted Scott's honour would meet short shrift at the hands of an Erskine.

Now, in 1821, Scott was writing "The Pirate". On the splendid list of the novels "The Pirate" is the fourteenth—roughly speaking, the middle one. In most people's opinion, there is no comparison between the work that preceded it and that which followed. Though "Quentin Durward" and "Redgauntlet" belong to the later half, it is almost "Hyperion to a mummy".

Unfortunately for Mr. Erskine, Sir Walter's case, if anything, contradicts his theory. While happy, rich and strong Scott wrote splendidly; after sorrow and loss and sickness had fallen on him, less well. I do not myself believe that his troubles were the sole cause of his falling-off. There is such a thing as writing too much. But they were a cause. It is impossible to believe that Scott wrote the Waverleys "in a state of mental agony".

He did dictate one of them (I think "Woodstock", but am not sure) while in violent physical agony. All honour to him for his courage. Mr. Erskine would have done well to have confined himself to this instance.

Apologising for interfering in the battle of the foods, which is a very pretty quarrel as it stands,

I remain yours etc.,

CECIL S. KENT.

To the Editor of the SATURDAY REVIEW.

12 Charlotte Street, Bath,
13 September 1909.

SIR,—In view of Mr. Eustace Miles' convincing letter I have no wish unduly to frighten the meat-eaters. Mr. Hermann Erskine speaks of the docility of vegetarians, and almost foreshadows the downfall of the British Empire through the growth of the movement. May I mention an instance of British pluck and endurance which may help to reassure him?

It is not generally known that "Freddy" Welsh, the pugilist, is a strict vegetarian. Welsh is probably the fiercest and cleverest fighter at his weight in the world, besides being a man of exceptional intelligence. He has never been beaten and hardly ever "extended", and, in the words of an American descriptive writer, has made the men in his class in the United States "look like five cents". If Mr. Erskine has ever had the gloves on he will appreciate the force of the remark.

I can assure him that the only thing which could possibly beat Welsh at the present moment is a diet of good old British beef and beer.

Yours faithfully,
HUGH BLAKER.

To the Editor of the SATURDAY REVIEW.

Bad Ems, 20 September 1909.

SIR,—Among the various nations referred to by Mr. Hermann Erskine he does appear to admit at least that the Romans attained to greatness.

Unfortunately for his particular argument the Romans at the time of their fall before the Goths were flesh-eaters, whereas at the time of their greatness they were not. Mr. W. Warde Fowler, in his "Social Life in Rome in the Age of Cicero", says: "The Italians, like the Greeks, were then as now almost entirely vegetarian. . . . It was only when the consumption of meat and game came in with the growth of capital and its attendant luxury that a vegetarian diet came to be at all despised".

Mr. Erskine sees signs of degeneracy, and thinks to find the cause in vegetarianism. He makes no reference to the enormous consumption of tea and sugar, whereas it is these that are probably exercising more harmful influence than any other article of diet, except perhaps meat.

Yours faithfully,
F. R. CAVE.

To the Editor of the SATURDAY REVIEW.

98 Hampton Road, Bristol,
20 September 1909.

SIR,—Your correspondent the Rev. Watkin Williams seems to consider that physical degeneration is "less a question of diet" and more a consequence of early environment. To get "the people back to the soil and seashore", would that insure the "foundations of physical regeneration" without the supply of good substantial diet consisting of meat and proteid food? Our traditional diet, seconded by the exigencies of a bad climate, and furthered by indulgence in sport, has made John Bull what he is, has been, and will be. Is your modern Briton—in the aggregate—as physically degenerate as your correspondents seem to suggest? The late Mr. Cecil Rhodes (and he had seen much and travelled far) considered the existing British race—as a race—the finest ever yet evolved in history, and his territorial acquisitions were secured—as he stated—to give further expansion to that race.

The ubiquitous German Emperor, after spending a few weeks' holiday a few years ago on our southern coast, was more than ever impressed by the physical qualities of our race, enthusiastically commenting on the superb, unequalled material we possessed for our would-be nascent army; and surely this has not been the result of a practically vegetarian diet, on which your correspondent states the Guards of Waterloo were reared. After several years' sojourn in America, on returning to the motherland I was most struck by the general superior physique, sturdiness, and virility of the parent stock, from which the majority of Americans has sprung. This inferiority in the United States may be due in some measure to the greater infusion of foreign elements, but, I think, mainly to the differences of diet and of climate, exclusive of national indulgence in sport, the zest for which is equally prevalent in both countries. "Liberal allowances of beefsteaks, port wine and brandy", with meat-eating and solid food in general, form far less the diet of the American than the Englishman. With us the frequent indulgence in meat, as well as in general heavy feeding, is demanded by the rigours of a bad climate; while lighter and different food, as well as drinks, is instinctively required in America and in other countries where the climate is far drier, clearer, and sunnier, more buoyant and less exacting. Meat-eating, more universal in England than in any other civilised country, and solid feeding in general, combined with inclemency of climate and love of sport, have principally made the Englishman what he is; and if we wish to continue an imperial race, let the Roast Beef of Old England for ever prevail.

I am, Sir, yours etc.,
ROBERT HAUSER.

THE CEDARS OF SURREY.

To the Editor of the SATURDAY REVIEW.

Glendora, Hindhead, Surrey
20 September 1909.

Sir,—It is an interesting fact that the county of Surrey, which was the birthplace and residence of the famous publicist, John Evelyn (1620-1706), of Wotton, Dorking, author of the classic work on sylviculture, has still some of the finest trees of the kingdom—especially cedars.

At Kew, on the Thames, there are some splendid and vigorous specimens surrounding the Pagoda in the Royal Gardens. Farnham Castle, in the south, is noted for those planted by Bishop North about 1781. In Oatlands Park, Weybridge, there stands a famous cedar planted by Prince Henry, youngest son of Charles I. It is now some 14 ft. 6 in. in girth at a distance of 2 ft. 6 in. from the ground. In Addington Park, near Croydon, the former seat of the Archbishops of Canterbury, there is another beautiful tree, probably about the same age, since Mrs. Randall Davidson, wife of the present Archbishop, told the present owner of Addington Park that it is nearly three hundred years old. Addington, by the way, is a very ancient place, called in Domesday Book Edintone, and having a parish register dating back to 1559.

Even on its London borders Surrey could boast of its cedars, for up to about twenty years ago two fine specimens, I am told, stood on the lawn of Turret House, South Lambeth Road, the former residence of the Tradescants, father and son, who were gardeners, respectively, to James I. and Charles I.

It is fancied by some that the Crusaders first brought cedars here; others think that Evelyn did so, as he travelled abroad at an early age; but it seems established now that an expedition, sent into the Holy Land by the Bishop of London and two nobles, returned in 1640 with the first cedar cones, some of which are now growing and flourishing in the Earl of Pembroke's park at Wilton. Others may have gone to Weybridge, Addington, or Lambeth.

I am, Sir, your obedient servant,
J. LANDFEAR LUCAS.

BETTER DEAD.

To the Editor of the SATURDAY REVIEW.

2 Myrtle Road, Acton, 20 September 1909.

SIR,—Mr. George Bassett Digby, having accused me of putting "hypothetical and cruel aims" into the mouth of Mr. John Bland, will perhaps be prepared to deny that the tone of that gentleman's letter (which tone I resented and decried) was one of scorn and contempt for the miseries and degradation of a section of the destitute of his fellow-beings—that it breathed no note of pity or sympathy for them, no vaguest recognition of the Sublime Intelligence in whose image they were created, no trace of knowledge of the attitude of One who, when He saw the multitude (composed of just such as those whom Mr. John Bland, with lauded "temperance" of language, describes as "sewer rats, the unclean, the outcasts of society"), had compassion on them because they fainted, and were as sheep having no shepherd. The more fallen and ruined these poor frequenters of the Embankment, so much the more greatly does the tone of Mr. Bland deserve condemnation in comparison with that gracious Example.

It is surely more pardonable for these poor scorned creatures, who are grudged even the resting-place of the hard stones of the earth and the shelter of the open sky, to "beg with veiled threats" and "aim loathsome remarks from the benches" of parks and Embankment than it is for John Bland and his champion to pour vituperation on the unfortunate from the shelter of their exclusive "drawing-rooms" and the favour and protection of society.

Is not Mr. Digby wrong in his conclusion, and is not this the poignant point of wonder and amazement—that the sight of the pollution of the perishable "noble sweep of the Thames Embankment" should arouse compassion in his breast, while the sight of the pollution of the noble image of the Divine in these poor occupiers of its resting-places appears but to rouse in him bitterness and disdain?

I am, Sir, yours sincerely,

MARIE LANTROW.

KING LEAR.

To the Editor of the SATURDAY REVIEW.

Haymarket Theatre, S.W.

21 September 1909.

SIR,—I see that your admirable critic, Mr. Max Beerbohm, attributes the brief criticism of the play, "King Lear", contained in the programme of the performance at the Haymarket Theatre, to my pen. I regret that I cannot claim the credit of having written this criticism.

Yours faithfully,

HERBERT TRENCH.

A WOOD SONG FOR A CHILD.

NOW one and all you Roses,
Wake up, you lie too long!
This very morning closes
The Nightingale his song;

Each from its olive chamber
His babies every one
This very morning clamber
Into the shining sun.

You Slug-a-beds and Simples,
Why will you so delay?
Dears, doff your olive wimples
And listen while you may.

RALPH HODGSON.

REVIEWS.

"MITRED ROCHESTER."

"Francis Atterbury." By H. C. Beeching. London: Pitman. 1909. 3s. 6d. net.

THOSE who still think of the last Bishop imprisoned in the Tower—when will the Church of England again be fortunate enough to have prelates in prison?—as a mere "political parson" would do well to read this volume in the "Makers of National History" Series. Dean Stanley, who was pugnacity itself, abused his great predecessor at the Abbey as a "worldly theologian", and Macaulay labours to give the impression of one who fought for religion without it, suppressing such a trifling circumstance as Atterbury's refusal of Walpole's bribe (May 1722), by which he was to have the bishopric of Winchester at the next vacancy, and a pension of £5000 a year meanwhile. Dr. Beeching somewhat unnecessarily observes that faith unfaithful kept him falsely true, as though Atterbury owed a natural allegiance to the Hanoverian Elector; but the remark shows, at any rate, that his favourable estimate of Atterbury is not actuated by any Tory bias.

That Walpole, having the intercepted letters to the King over the water in his pocket, and the Bishop of Rochester in his power, should have gone in person to the Deanery to buy Atterbury off, demonstrates the precarious position of the new dynasty. Even then the blow did not fall for several months, during which Atterbury, "the most popular Churchman in England", made no attempt at escape. He was, Canon Beeching remarks, the only man in the country capable of organising a conspiracy. Lord Stanhope speaks of his "great and surpassing genius". He was the last Englishman proceeded against by a bill of pains and penalties—in other words, outside the law. Finally, after ten months in the Tower, the Bishop, stripped of all his dignities, went into perpetual exile. At Calais he heard that Bolingbroke also was there on his way to England. "Then", said Atterbury, "I am exchanged." He took over the direction of the Chevalier's affairs in Paris at a critical moment of European politics, but the favourable conjuncture, through no fault of his, came to nothing. Atterbury, though a hot-tempered and litigious man, was not a hot-head, and if any counsels could have retrieved the Jacobite hopes they were his.

What made this prelate a Jacobite and a conspirator? Dr. Beeching thinks that the picturesque story of his proposal, at Anne's demise, to go out in his lawn-sleeves and proclaim King James the Third rests on some earlier suggestion of his to that effect. He was a fearless man. Yet he was not by conviction a high legitimist. Though he had sworn no allegiance to George, in pudding time come o'er, Atterbury was not a nonjuror and had been chaplain to William and Mary. Stackhouse avers that he began life as a Whig, and there is a whiggish, social compact flavour about a 29 May sermon preached before the Commons in 1701, in which the Prince is said to be obeyed by his subjects "chearfully, because they know that in obeying him they obey those Laws only which they themselves had a share in contriving". For asserting that "the supreme ecclesiastical jurisdiction as annexed to the Imperial Crown of this realm can be exercised no otherwise than in Parliament", Atterbury was refused institution to the deanery of Carlisle by Bishop Nicolson; but then Nicolson was a latitudinarian, and the Liberal cue has always been to magnify the ecclesiastical supremacy of a Protestant monarchy. Atterbury certainly was a Tory, but hardly a divine-right one. If the Stuarts had been restored, he would, as Dr. Beeching says, have applauded on 1688 principles. And yet we find him, after Anne's death, an arch-Jacobite plotter. Dr. Beeching's explanation is certainly the right one. Atterbury's governing preoccupation was a passionate devotion to orthodox Christianity, and he foresaw that the triumph of Hanoverianism must give an immense impulse to Deism and Socinianism. The

Whigs, once they get a free hand, will abolish the hierarchical constitution of the Church, "appoint a small allowance to the Parsons and prescribe them what doctrines to preach from the pulpit, introduce a general comprehension and blend up an ecclesiastical Babel of all the sects and heresies upon the face of the earth". The first stroke, he saw clearly, would be the desynodising of the Church of England, and from 1717 for a hundred and thirty years Convocation was actually silenced. But the rights of Convocation were under Atterbury's especial championship, particularly—when the Episcopate became Whig—the rights of the Nether House. This Archdeacon Denison of an earlier day had fought a tremendous battle for the constitutional prerogatives of the clerical parliament, and for the independence of a presbyterate from which alone the safeguarding of the Faith could be looked for. Of course the anti-episcopalianism of the Highchurchman is a phenomenon as old as S. Jerome. What is more open to criticism in Atterbury's line of action is that by insisting on Convocation being—under the "premunientes" summons—an integral part of Parliament, and on the Lower House being related to the Upper as Commons to Lords, he went far to destroy the assemblies of the Church as Synods. The "Sacred Synod of this realm" is far older than the civil legislature, and, moreover, a bi-cameral Synod is unknown to Catholic theory. Convocation is indeed an utterly anomalous body.

Canon Beeching draws a scholarly and impartial picture of this remarkable divine, loved by his friends, sweet-natured, generous, sincerely religious, above jobbery, yet with a talent for getting into hot water, a born controversialist, and rather fond of a subterranean passage to a perfectly legitimate end. Atterbury was a scholar and man of letters, but before all things he was —in the old-fashioned sense of the word—a churchman. He ended his life as a confessor.

THE PYRENEES.

"The Pyrenees." By H. Belloc. With 46 Sketches by the Author and 22 Maps. London: Methuen. 1909. 7s. 6d.

MR. BELLOC'S knowledge of the intricacies of the mountain system of the Pyrenees is both thorough and extensive. Very few people—not excluding those who pride themselves on a good general knowledge of geography—appreciate the difference between the actual conformation of mountain ranges and the popularly accepted ideas as to their shape. The author points out truly enough how this is the direct outcome of the schoolroom, where curved lines of shading, indicating the general trend of the main watershed, are taken by most people to delineate the actual shape of a particular range. The result is that most travellers, when they find themselves approaching any mountain range for the first time, are sorely perplexed at what they see before them, since it is totally unlike what they expected. The Pyrenees afford an excellent example of this, and Mr. Belloc explains how, instead of being one simple single chain of hills running from the Bay of Biscay to the Mediterranean, they consist of two such main walls, starting from either sea and running parallel until they overlap near the centre. Nor is this all, for on the Spanish side numerous big spurs jut out, many of them T-headed, and some even with double T-heads. These T's extend laterally and their heads overlap in such a manner as to present a series of lofty parallel ridges, each one of which as it is approached from below seems to be the highest summit of the main chain, until other summits open to the view far beyond.

On the French side the big spurs run out truly and are not thus T-headed. This explanation may appear to be somewhat unscientific, but it is quite the best and most easily grasped that we have read. We cannot commend too highly this chapter dealing with the physical nature of the Pyrenees. That dealing with the political character of the region is also very instructive, and it is most interesting to see how the various almost insurmountable topographical barriers have led to the division of the inhabitants into well-marked and widely differing races.

With the chapter on Maps we are frankly disappointed. It is both involved and unnecessarily complicated, and in his repeated attempts to make clear his meaning the author has merely succeeded in bewildering his readers. It is obvious that he has a knowledge of maps and mapping superior to most people, but this knowledge lacks system and discipline. Some of his remarks are decidedly naïve. Thus, he commences by giving the somewhat obvious advice that, for a man wandering in an unknown country, a decent map and a small compass are necessary. But, as he calls a small compass a "toy", and later on advocates a "large cheap compass", it is difficult to know what he really means. A cheap compass is all very well, and much can be done with it; but all travellers and explorers know that the better a compass the more generally useful and reliable it is. It would be equally logical to recommend the traveller to wear cheap boots or carry a cheap watch. Both may serve well enough, but, on the other hand, they may not.

In his universal condemnation of Spanish maps he is apparently unaware that a considerable portion of the Peninsula has been admirably surveyed. How to obtain such maps is a totally different question. For one who is obviously fairly well acquainted with the topographical art, he uses at times somewhat curious expressions. Thus a map showing hill-shading by means of hachures he styles "hatched", whilst the art of delineating slopes he calls "hatching"! Such expressions are more suggestive of the occupation of a barn-door fowl than of a scientific cartographer.

The author, however, has apparently created for himself entirely new expressions to describe the topographical features of a country. Thus, instead of saying that double cols are often met with in the Pyrenees, he says that they are "damnably common". Most text-books on topography give a list of "Conventional terms in use in describing features of ground", but Mr. Belloc evidently prefers the unconventional. Where, however, he shows a genuine lack of method and of the art of imparting instruction to others is in his otherwise excellent hand-sketches illustrative of the difficulties which are presented to the traveller engaged in crossing a mountain pass. In one of these sketches he very reasonably elects to show the mountain summits by thick black marks filled in above the highest contour, whilst the portions of the valleys below the lowest contours are shaded diagonally or "hatched" as he calls it. Here the term is admissible. So far so good. But on page 190 he reverses the process and fills in the lowest parts with black "blobs". It may be fun for him, but it is death to the unfortunate student of his book who, having grasped the salient fact that the hill-tops are shown black, naturally views such quick changes with abhorrence.

The confusion thus wrought calls to mind the tale of the general of old Peninsular days who upon being shown one of the elaborate military sketches from High Wycombe (the Staff College of a hundred years ago) remarked: "A most excellent plan, sir! I see you colour all the artillery positions on the hill-tops blue". Report says that nobody dared explain that the blue patches were ponds in the depths of the wooded ravines below the hills.

In spite of these vagaries, Mr. Belloc's rough sketch-maps convey to the practised topographer a good idea of the ground. But we doubt whether one in a thousand of his readers will possess enough knowledge of the art to "read" them so as to appreciate the really good points he makes. Map-reading is a science which requires careful study, like everything else worth knowing. The skeleton maps of the various valleys described are excellent of their sort, but they all have the fatal drawback of being inserted in the wrong places in the book, and are further so designed as to make it impossible to refer to them when reading the very intricate letterpress.

On the other hand the landscape sketches, especially those where some serrated peak towers high above the wreaths of mist drifting across the precipitous wooded valleys far below, are simply admirable. None will appreciate these more than those few fortunate people who have had the happiness to explore remote mountainous regions similar to the Pyrenees.

We have pointed out some very obvious defects, but in spite of these we can say truly that anybody who sets himself to explore the Pyrenees without first providing himself with this book, a good map, and a compass, preferably not a cheap one, would deserve to come to grief when crossing one of the famous cols described by Mr. Belloc as being so "damnably common".

AN INCORRIGIBLE STORY-TELLER.

"True Tilda." By A. T. Quiller-Couch. Bristol: Arrowsmith. 1909. 6s.

"IF a man was to come an' tell me a story like that, I'd call 'im a liar." This was what Sam Bossom said, who was a coalheaver, a bargee, and, on the word of Tilda herself who had good reason to know, a white man in spite of his black face. The occasion was not in the least remarkable, as occasions go in the novels of Mr. Quiller-Couch. Tilda, a small circus girl, who had that morning lain helpless at the hospital of the Good Samaritan, had a few hours later rescued Arthur, a still smaller boy, from the clutches of Dr. Glasson (Squeers redivivus), who kept an orphanage. Tilda and Arthur had emerged through the manhole by which Sam Bossom was at that moment delivering eighteen tons best Newcastle to the aforesaid Doctor. Sam naturally saw everything at a glance; connived at the escape; and then, when he had done this as a matter of course, expressed his surprise afterwards. We suspect that many readers of "True Tilda" will behave much in the same way. If they question the truth of that wonderful world where the wizardry of coincidence plays its beautiful game with the facts of life, they will not do so till they have shut the book and put it well away. Then, if they break out like Sam Bossom, they are of course at liberty to do so, as their taste and inclination prompt; but, for our part, we have no sympathy with anything they may have to say. We consider that it reflects discredit upon anyone to be surprised at anything that this book contains, either at the time of reading or afterwards. "True Tilda" has, in fact, the essential characteristic of a good story, for a good story should contain nothing new under the sun. To admit surprise is simply to admit that you have not been there before. There is, of course, a current superstition that this is an age of novelty. Meantime the fact remains that our serious plays are variations on a single theme (and that theme as old as Adam); that our lighter plays are not variations at all; and that a novel which contains anything new is unworthy of the name.

"True Tilda" will satisfy the most critical person. There is no occasion to fear the smallest deviation from accredited models. Acquaintance may here be made with old friends, who act up to their old credentials, with the old results. The old illusions, that could be so finely created by the old story-tellers, are all here; and the old feelings, that are aroused in the old breast of the youthful reader (nothing is so old as youth), come bubbling up from their old sources in the old inevitable manner. It is no use questioning the reality of Dr. Glasson; and endeavouring to be indifferent to him, because he is a figment of Mr. Quiller-Couch's imagination. Nature is too strong for us; and, whether we like it or not, we have got to hate this ancient monster from the first moment that he appears. "He was elderly and bald, with small pig-eyes, grey side-whiskers, and for mouth a hard square slit much like that of the collecting-box by the gate. A long pendulous nose came down over it and almost met an upthrust lower jaw. He wore a clerical suit, with a dingy white necktie; the skin about his throat hung in deep folds, and the folds were filled with an unpleasing grey stubble." What more is necessary? It is impossible not to rejoice when the Doctor is hustled into the canal by a knowing dog, as of course he is; and it is impossible not to glory vindictively when he sits down upon something sharp, as of course he does. When we take leave of him, hurrying off upon a fiendish errand to Monte Carlo, which we know is to bring him into a woeful blind alley, then we are left beautifully satisfied.

Beautiful satisfaction is, in fact, the prevailing emotion to be indulged in the reading of "True Tilda". In the hands of Mr. Quiller-Couch the perfectly impossible becomes the perfectly credible. Tilda and Arthur set out to find a wonderful solution to dark problems, which, for the fun of the thing, we pretend to be as enigmatical to us as they are to them. How Arthur, beginning somewhere near Birmingham, ultimately arrives at an island which is the island of his destiny, discovering Prospero in a chemist's shop at Stratford on the way, is a story that must not be spoiled by indiscreet hints dropped to intending readers. We can only assure such as do intend that there is something of a treat in store, so long as they will only leave the thing they call their critical sense behind them. And, as already intimated, we can assure them of fresh introductions to many old and estimable acquaintances. There is, for instance, the dashing young Diana of the countryside, Miss Sally, who rescues the orphans in fifteen hansom cabs. There are Mr. and Mrs. Mortimer, Thespians of the highway, rolling stones, but, in more senses than one, comfortably moss-grown. There is, of course, the necessary baronet (necessary to account for Arthur) who marries in haste and repents even more hastily. These are but few.

As a sample of Mr. Quiller-Couch's latest quality we quote Tilda's instructions to Arthur, who is about to wash in a rustic pool:

"Be sure you don't fergit be'ind the ears. You may think you're on'y a small boy an' nobody's goin' to search yer corners; but back at the Good Samaritan there was a tex' nailed up—'Thou Gawd seest me'; and Sister said 'E was most partic'lar just in the little places you wouldn't think."

There is here neither profound humour nor wit of the most delicate; yet it pleases, being wrought of good

(*Continued on page 388.*)

homely material which is displayed to good advantage. Mr. Quiller-Couch's style has one virtue which distinguishes it from many another less readable—it is not marred by any affectation of good writing. This, perhaps, is only another way of saying that "Q." was born to be a good story-teller. And he is a good story-teller—an incorrigible one.

SHORTER NOTICES.

"The Record of the University Boat Race, 1829-1909." Revised and completed to date by C. M. Pitman, O.U.B.C. London: Fisher Unwin. 21s. net.

All rowing men will welcome this addition to the standard works on oarsmanship and its records. In the last few years we have had the complete story of Henley Regatta and the records of the O.U.B.C., compiled in each case by well-qualified hands; but since 1884 no new edition of Messrs. Goldie and Treherne's "University Boat Race" has been published, and in consequence there has been no authoritative account of the contests of the last twenty-five years. Mr. Pitman has done his work admirably. The history of the older races has been improved and enlarged, the story of those from 1884 to 1891 has been carefully compiled from the best contemporary records, and that of the last eighteen years has been provided by personal observation. No one could read the accounts of the best races—the victory of the Oxford seven-oar over the Cambridge Subscription Rooms, the race of 1859 when Cambridge sank, the wonderful victories of Cambridge in 1886 and of Oxford in 1896 and 1901—without a feeling of excitement and enthusiasm. The description of the races which Mr. Pitman himself either witnessed or rowed in is notably free from prejudice and remarkably accurate. In these later chapters Mr. Pitman indulges occasionally in critical remarks on the styles of the crews. To some these remarks will not prove altogether palatable, but the opinions expressed would certainly be endorsed by most oarsmen of experience. The book holds, besides, much statistical information. It should be of value to many not only as a work of reference, but also for the good reading which it contains.

"Sir Joseph Banks: the Father of Australia." By J. H. Madden. London: Kegan Paul. 1909. 6s. net.

Whilst we at home are getting together the funds for a memorial to Captain Cook, in Australia they are raising money for a statue to Banks, who was with Cook in the voyage of the "Endeavour" and the discovery of Botany Bay. Mr. Madden seems to have missed the chance for a good biography of Banks. He certainly has the material at command. He has given us a collection of notes divided into sections and subsections which are a little confusing at times, and for the general public there is rather too much botany in the book. Mr. Madden has shown the utmost devotion in recording whatever scrap of information he could gather about Banks, and the book, the proceeds of the sale of which are to go to the Banks Memorial Fund, is one to be kept for reference purposes. It usefully supplements Sir Joseph Hooker's "Journal of Sir Joseph Banks", which appeared a few years ago. Australia owes gratitude to Banks for his interest in her early days; the suggestion that Botany Bay should be utilised for colonisation purposes was his, and Linnæus even proposed that the country should be called Banksia.

"French Vignettes: a Series of Dramatic Episodes, 1787-1871." By M. Betham-Edwards. London: Chapman and Hall. 1909. 10s. 6d. net.

One lady novelist has set the example, if not the fashion, of retiring from business, perhaps other literary ladies may follow; but though we may hope we hardly anticipate that this will happen. However, not to digress before beginning, here is Miss Betham-Edwards with a book for which she claims to have done some original research. It seems to us rather a pity that she should have gone to such trouble. She thus opens an essay on the Second Empire:

"Louis Napoleon Bonaparte was born in 1808."

Heartily agreeing with the general sense of this line, we close the volume.

"The Small Holdings and Allotments Act 1908." By Aubrey John Spencer. London: Stevens and Sons. 1909. 7s. 6d.

This is a companion volume to Mr. Spencer's "Agricultural Holdings Act 1908". The Small Holdings and Allotments Act 1908 not only consolidates the previous Acts relating to small holdings and allotments and contains new provisions, but it refers to other Acts, such as the Agricultural Holdings Act 1908, on the subject of compensation for improvements, and to the Lands Clauses Acts and further enactments. Mr. Spencer discusses these subjects with knowledge and skill, and gives all the rules, regulations, and circulars which in any way apply to the subject; so that his book is at once compendious and self-contained and excellently adapted for the use of those who may consult it.

"The Cloister and the Hearth", by Charles Reade, illustrated by Byam Shaw (London: Chatto and Windus, 12s. 6d. net), has been added to the S. Martin's Library of Standard Authors. Sir Walter Besant said this was not only Charles Reade's greatest work, but, he believed, the greatest historical novel in the language. Mr. Byam Shaw's illustrations will hardly please every lover of the novel, but they may appeal to new readers who are attracted to it in its newest form. Some of them are striking. It is a handsome edition.

"Dictionary of National Biography." Vol. XIX. London: Smith, Elder. 1909. 15s. net.

The reissue of the "Dictionary of National Biography" is drawing rapidly to a close. Three more volumes, and the new issue, with its many important revisions, will be complete. The present volume, from Stow to Tytler, is of special interest from the literary point of view. We note Canon Ainger's account of Tennyson, Leslie Stephen's Swift and Thackeray, Thomas Seccombe's Suckling and Thomson, and others on Jeremy Taylor, John Taylor, Anthony Trollope, Trelawny, Tyndale, and Tyndall. Two of the best essays in this volume are Mr. Cosmo Monkhouse's Turner and Mr. Stanley Lane Poole's Palmerston.

"The Army Annual Year-Book and Almanack, 1909." Edited by Major B. F. S. Baden-Powell. London: The Army Press. 1909. 7s. 6d. net.

A useful publication, giving information on all kinds of subjects connected with the Army. Besides statistical matter, such as the strength of the Land Forces from 1792 to 1906, recruiting returns, &c., it contains short articles on the manœuvres of the year, the health of the Army, the military inventions of the year, and many other matters. All are presented in convenient form, for the benefit of those whose business or pleasure it is to study military affairs.

For this Week's Books see page 390.

THIS WEEK'S BOOKS.

ART

Benozzo Gozzoli (Urbain Mengin). Paris: Plon-Nourrit. 3/*r*. 50*c*.

BIOGRAPHY

John Dee, 1527-1608 (Charlotte Fell Smith). Constable. 10*s*. 6*d*. net.

FICTION

The Sinking Ship (Eva Lathbury); Lord Alistair's Rebellion (Allen Upward). Rivers. 6*s*. each.
The Gleaming Dawn (John Baker). Chapman and Hall. 6*s*.
Great Possessions (Mrs. Wilfrid Ward). Longmans, Green. 6*s*.
Toil of Men (I. Querido); The First Round (St. John Lucas), 6*s*. each. One Day and Another (E. V. Lucas); Tremendous Trifles (G. K. Chesterton), 5*s*. each. Methuen.
The Mysterious Light (Janet B. Orr). Stockwell. 2*s*.
A Perfect Genius (Bertram Smith). Harper. 6*s*.
The Path to Honour (Sydney C. Grier); The Man's Man (Ian Hay); The Background (W. J. Eccott). Edinburgh: Blackwood. 6*s*. each.
Strange Fire (Christopher Maughan). Paul. 6*s*.
The Silver Horde (Rex Beach). Harper. 6*s*.
Influences (Paul Methven). Chatto and Windus. 6*s*.
Jenny Peters (C. H. Dudley Ward). Fisher Unwin. 6*s*.
Diamond Cut Paste (Agnes and Egerton Castle). Murray. 6*s*.
The Palace of Danger (Mabel Wagnalls); The Phrases of Marcella (Captain Henry Curties). Long. 6*s*. each.

HISTORY

The Return of Louis XVIII. (Mrs. Rodolph Stawell). Heinemann. 10*s*. net.
Garibaldi and the Thousand (George Macaulay Trevelyan). Longmans, Green. 7*s*. 6*d*. net.
My Friends the French (Robert Harborough Sherard). Laurie. 12*s*. 6*d*. net.
Historical Roman Coins (G. F. Hill). Constable. 10*s*. 6*d*. net.
The French Procession (Madame Mary Duclaux). Fisher Unwin. 12*s*. 6*d*. net.

GIFT BOOKS

The Rose and the Ring (M. A. Titmarsh). Chatto and Windus. 3*s*. 6*d*. net.
Beasts of Business (Ascott R. Hope), 3*s*. 6*d*.; Adventurers in America (Ascott R. Hope), 6*s*. Black.
New Zealand (P. A. Vaile), 1*s*. 6*d*. net; The Children's Book of Art (Agnes Ethel Conway and Sir Martin Conway). Black. 6*s*. net.
The Fairies' Fountain, and other Stories (Countess Evelyn Martinengo Cesaresco), 3*s*. 6*d*.; Tanglewood Tales (Nathaniel Hawthorne), 6*s*. Fisher Unwin.

LAW

International Law (T. Baty). Murray. 10*s*. 6*d*. net.

REPRINTS AND TRANSLATIONS

Masters of Literature:—Scott (Edited by Arthur James Grant); Fielding (Edited by George Saintsbury). Bell. 3*s*. 6*d*. net each.
The Sayings of Confucius (Leonard A. Lyall). Longmans, Green. 3*s*. 6*d*. net.
Extinct Animals (E. Ray Lankester). Constable. 3*s*. 6*d*. net.

SCHOOL

A Class Book of Physics (R. A. Gregory). Macmillan. 4*s*. 6*d*.

THEOLOGY

The Psalter of the Church (James C. Carleton). Cambridge: At the University Press. 4*s*. net.
Introduction to the New Testament (Theodor Zahn. 3 vols.). Edinburgh: Clark. 36*s*. net.

TRAVEL

In the Canaries with a Camera (Margaret D'Este). Methuen. 7*s*. 6*d*. net.

MISCELLANEOUS

Advertisements of the "Spectator," The (Laurence Lewis). Constable.
Botany of To-day (G. F. Scott Elliott). Seeley. 5*s*. net.
Internal Values, The (Hugo Münsterberg), 10*s*. 6*d*. net; Abraham Lincoln and the London "Punch" (Edited by William S. Walsh). New York: Moffat. $1 net.
Organ, The (H. Heathcote Statham). Chapman and Hall. 7*s*. 6*d*. net.
Romantic Movement in English Poetry, The (Arthur Symons). Constable. 10*s*. 6*d*. net.
Savoy Operas (W. S. Gilbert). Bell. 15*s*. net.

REVIEWS AND MAGAZINES FOR SEPTEMBER.—The Economic Journal, 5*s*.; The State, 6*d*.; Mercure de France, 1/*r*. 50*c*.; The Anti-Vivisection Review, 6*d*.

ALL WHO LOVE GARDENS,

WATERWAYS, SPORT, AND

OLD-TIME TRAVEL

should secure a copy of

MEMORIES OF GARDENS.

By ALEXANDER INNES SHAND.

With a Special Memoir by

SIR ROWLAND BLENNERHASSETT, Bart.

10s. 6d. net.

THE WEST STRAND PUBLISHING CO. LTD.

10 King Street, Covent Garden, W.C.

7th and Revised Impression.

"SATURDAY" BRIDGE,

By W. DALTON,

Is the Best Book on the Best Game.

That the popularity of Bridge is as great as ever is proved by the continuous steady demand for the work.

"'SATURDAY' BRIDGE"

is admitted to be the Standard book on the Game. It is the leading Bridge Authority, and takes its name from the "SATURDAY REVIEW," in which its chapters appeared.

Of all Booksellers 5s. net, or post free 5s. 3d., direct from the Office.

THE WEST STRAND PUBLISHING CO., Ltd.,

10 King Street, Covent Garden, W.C.

THE CONDUIT STREET AUCTION GALLERIES.

The attention of Executors, Trustees, Solicitors, and Owners, who may be desirous of selling Works of Art, Family Jewels, Old Silver, Furniture, Pictures, Prints, Miniatures, China, Coins, Books, Old Lace, Furs, Musical Instruments, Guns, and other Valuables, is drawn to Messrs.

KNIGHT, FRANK & RUTLEY'S

AUCTION GALLERIES, 9 CONDUIT STREET, AND 23A MADDOX STREET, W., which are Open Daily to receive goods intended for early sales.

VALUATIONS are prepared for Fire Insurance, Estate Duty, and all other purposes. As to Insurance, owners are reminded that, for security, Messrs. KNIGHT, FRANK & RUTLEY'S detailed inventory and valuation of the contents of a Town or Country Mansion is an important adjunct to their Fire Insurance Policies.

484 pp. letterpress. Size 9 by 7 ins. 25 Plates, 160 other Illustrations from Photographs and Pen and Ink Sketches and Folding Plan of Cliffs by the Author. Price **21s.** net.

MY LIFE AMONG THE WILD BIRDS IN SPAIN

BY

COLONEL WILLOUGHBY VERNER

(LATE RIFLE BRIGADE),

Author of "Sketches in the Soudan," "The Military Life of H.R.H. George, Duke of Cambridge."

Although this account of Life in the Wilds of Southern Spain, and of the Wanderings and Adventures of a Naturalist amid the semi-tropical wilds of South-Western Andalusia, is primarily devoted to a description of the larger birds such as the Great Bustards and Eagles in their remote haunts, it also contains many descriptions of the scenery, mountains, woodlands, plains and marshes, as well as the inhabitants, the trees, the flowers, &c., of that fascinating and but little-known region. Neither are the great historical and antiquarian interests of the country, such as the battlefields and pre-historic graves, overlooked.

SOME PRESS OPINIONS.

SATURDAY REVIEW.—"One of those rare books which are virgin observation from end to end. Its width of experience makes the volume worthy to go down in that special list of international nature-history books which Mr. Roosevelt in his hours of leisure is perfecting. The author provokes an inevitable comparison with Mr. Millais, the first of our naturalists. Both men have the artist's hand to express what they see. . . . With the further help of the numerous photographs and tailpieces, the plains, the lagunas, the sierras of Spain, are very present to the eye while one reads these original rambles of a born naturalist in search of hidden homes."

TIMES.—". . . A story of glorified birdnesting, egging *in excelsis*. He talks rather as one may do in the smoking-room or from his armchair, telling unaffectedly of the incidents of what must be an almost unique birdsnesting career of over fifty years. On disputed points . . . he speaks with the authority of long and intimate experience. . . . Not the least interesting part of the volume is the illustrations, especially those from photographs of the author's taking, which are often surprisingly good considering the extraordinary disadvantages under which they were taken and that the conditions made it impossible to use any instrument but a hand kodak. On more than one occasion the taking of the photograph was more dangerous than the ascent or descent to or from the nest, thrilling though these often were."

ATHENÆUM.—"An inveterate birdsnester, unrepentant but not undiscriminating, Colonel Verner commands far more respect than many plausible humanitarians. . . . Long accustomed to supplement his journal with a sketch book, the author eventually calls in the aid of photography to complete his records. . . . All that Colonel Verner has to tell us of the birds of Spain is bound to carry great weight, owing to the continuity of his observations, for from the early seventies he has repeatedly visited the same scenes, and during the last few years has wintered in the country. . . . The culminating feat of Colonel Verner's long birdsnesting career was only accomplished in 1908 with a successful campaign against the famous Lämmergeyer or, as he prefers to call it, The Bearded Vulture. He has the evidence of his own eyes that the title of 'bone-breaker' is no misnomer. The excellent sketches of this and other grand birds upon the wing are a welcome feature. The scenes of the final act—the succession of bitter disappointments, dangerous predicaments, and eventual triumph—come with singularly dramatic effect. The indomitable veteran ends with a heartfelt 'Nunc dimittis.'"

LONDON: JOHN BALE, SONS & DANIELSSON, LTD., Oxford House, 83-91 Great Titchfield Street, Oxford Street.

This Prospectus has been filed with the Registrar of Joint Stock Companies.

The List Opened on Friday, the 24th September, 1909, and will close on or before Tuesday, the 28th September, 1909.

THE ARGENTINE GREAT WESTERN RAILWAY CO., LTD.

Incorporated under the Companies Acts, 1862 to 1886.

SHARE CAPITAL (Issued).	
5 per Cent. Preferred Stock...	£2,125,000
Ordinary Stock	2,125,000
	£4,250,000

DEBENTURE CAPITAL (Issued).	
4 per Cent. First Debenture Stock ...	£1,700,000
4 per Cent. Second Debenture Stock ...	1,700,000
5 per Cent. Debenture Stock	1,600,000
	£5,000,000

Issue of £1,000,000 Five Per Cent. Debenture Stock,

Secured by a Trust Deed reserving to the Company the right to create and issue further Debenture Stock for £400,000 (forming part of the present issue), and a further amount (of which this issue forms part) at the rate of £4,000 per mile of additional line acquired by the Company or of new line of the Company for the time being constructed or in course of construction or about to be constructed in excess of the mileage belonging to the Company in operation on February 6th, 1907. The present issue and any further stock which may be issued pursuant to the right reserved to the Company as above-mentioned will rank *pari passu* with the £1,600,000 Five per cent. Debenture Stock already issued.

At £108 per cent., payable as follows:—
£5 on Application.
5 on Allotment.
20 on November 15th, 1909.
30 on December 30th, 1909.
20 on February 15th, 1910.
28 on March 15th, 1910.

Total £108 per £100 Stock.

Bearer Scrip will be issued after allotment, and will be exchanged for registered Debenture Stock Certificates after April 1st, 1910, the registered Debenture Stock being transferable in amounts not involving a fraction of £1.

The interest is payable by warrant to the Registered Holders on April 1st and October 1st in each year. The first payment of Interest at the rate of 5 per cent. per annum, calculated upon the instalments as due, will be made on April 1st, 1910, on presentation of the Coupon attached to the Bearer Scrip.

Payment in full on Allotment, and on the due dates of the instalments, can be made under discount at the rate of 3 per cent. per annum.

The Directors of the Argentine Great Western Railway Company, Limited, have authorised the London Joint Stock Bank, Limited, and Parr's Bank, Limited, as Bankers of the Company, to receive applications for £1,000,000 5 per cent. Debenture Stock of the Company ranking *pari passu* with the existing issue of £1,600,000.

The whole or any part of the Stock is redeemable at the Company's option at any time after June 30th, 1930, at 110 per cent., on six calendar months' notice to the Stockholders. This Stock has a charge upon the undertaking of the Company (subject to the First and Second Debenture Stocks), under Trust Deeds, dated February 6th, 1907, January 19th, 1908, and August 9th, 1909, made between the Company and the Trustees.

The Buenos Ayres and Pacific Railway Company, Limited, works this Company's Railway and is entitled to the gross receipts of the undertaking and covenants to pay to this Company the sums necessary for the payment of the following interest and dividends, viz.:—

1. Interest on the First, Second and Five per cent. Debenture Stocks (including the £1,000,0000 Debenture Stock of the present issue) and on any issue of Debenture Stock or Debentures hereafter made by this Company with the previous consent of the Pacific Company. 2. Dividend on the Preferred Stock:—(*a*) At the same rate as may be paid on the 5 per cent. First Preference Stock of the Pacific Company; and in addition, (*b*) A dividend equal to the dividend or bonus in excess of 5 per cent., but not to exceed 6 per cent., as may be paid for the year on the Ordinary Stock of the Pacific Company; (*c*) A dividend of ½ per cent. per annum in respect of every year for which dividends or bonuses at a rate exceeding 7 per cent. per annum shall be paid on the Ordinary Stock of the Pacific Company; and (*d*) A dividend of ½ per cent. per annum in respect of every year for which dividends or bonuses at the rate of 10 per cent. per annum or in excess of that rate shall be paid on the Ordinary Stock of the Pacific Company. 3. Dividend on the Ordinary Stock:—(*a*) At the same rate as may be paid on the 5 per cent. Second Preference Stock of the Pacific Company; and, in addition, (*b*) A dividend equal to the dividend or bonus in excess of 5 per cent., but not to exceed 6 per cent., as may be paid for the year on the Ordinary Stock of the Pacific Company; (*c*) A dividend of ½ per cent. per annum in respect of every year for which dividends or bonuses at a rate exceeding 7 per cent. per annum shall be paid on the Ordinary Stock of the Pacific Company; and (*d*) A dividend of ½ per cent. per annum in respect of every year for which dividends or bonuses at a rate of 10 per cent. per annum or in excess of that rate shall be paid on the Ordinary Stock of the Pacific Company.

The margin of the income of the Buenos Ayres and Pacific Railway Company, Limited, on June 30th, 1908, after the payment of the interest on its Debenture Stocks and including amounts payable under the agreements for working this Company's Railway, the Bahia Blanca and North Western Railway, the Argentine Transandine Railway, and the Villa Maria and Rufino Railway, was £747,432. The Reserve Funds of the Buenos Ayres and Pacific Railway Company, Limited, at June 30th, 1908, stood at £840,674 6s. 11d. It has paid Seven per cent. per annum on its Ordinary Stock for the past five years.

The Reserve Funds of this Company at June 30, 1908 were as follows:—General Reserve Fund, £108,483 14s. 10d.; Insurance Fund, £29,361 8s. 11d., both invested on approved securities. The interest on the Reserve Funds is paid to the Pacific Company.

The present mileage of this Company's Railway open to traffic is 535 miles.

Various Branch Lines are in course of construction, which, when completed, will make the total length of the system 764 miles. The main line between Palmira and Mendoza is being doubled in order to deal more adequately with the increasing traffic on that section. The authority of the Argentine Government has been obtained for the construction of other Branch Lines, having a total length of about 144 miles.

The gross receipts of the system worked by the Buenos Ayres and Pacific Railway for the four years ending June 30th, 1908, compare as follows:—

Year ending June 30th, 1905	£1,913,760
Year ending June 30th, 1906	2,592,943
Year ending June 30th, 1907	3,063,547
Year ending June 30th, 1908	3,655,772

and the receipts of the Argentine Great Western Railway included in the above figures are as under:—

Year ending June 30th, 1905	£618,569
Year ending June 30th, 1906	741,723
Year ending June 30th, 1907	945,846
Year ending June 30th, 1908	1,158,092

For the year ending June 30th, 1909, the estimated gross receipts of the whole Pacific system are £4,134,487, against £3,655,772, an increase of £478,715; the figures relating to the Argentine Great Western Railway being £1,282,973, as against £1,158,092, or an increase of £124,881. Since July 1st last the estimated gross receipts of the whole Pacific system for the 12 weeks ended 18th instant are £776,481, against £787,563, a decrease of £11,082; the figures relating to the Argentine Great Western Railway being £190,917 as against £258,641, a decrease of £67,724. This decrease is due to the opening by the Buenos Ayres and Pacific Company of its line from Justo Daract to La Paz, the gradients of which are superior to those on this Company's line, but under the working agreement the consequent diversion of traffic does not affect the position of the Debenture and Shareholders of this Company.

The General Manager reports under date of the 18th instant as follows:—"Prospects Argentine Great Western Section excellent. 15 per cent. increase probable in vine production with corresponding development in passenger and general cargo traffic."

The proceeds of the present Issue will be appropriated towards repayment of the capital advances by the Buenos Ayres and Pacific Railway Company, and will be applied by that Company towards the cost and equipment of branch lines, and the purchase of Locomotives and Rolling Stock, and to the general requirements of this Company's Railway.

A preference in the allotment as regards 50 per cent. of this Issue will be given to applications received before the actual closing of the List from the holders of the Preferred and Ordinary Stocks of this Company, and the holders of Ordinary Stock and Ordinary (1911) Shares of the Buenos Ayres and Pacific Railway Company, Limited. Applicants should state the amount of their holdings on the Application forms.

Applications on the form accompanying this Prospectus, together with the deposit of £5 per cent., should be forwarded to the London Joint Stock Bank, Limited, 5 Princes Street, London, E.C., or to Parr's Bank, Limited, 4 Bartholomew Lane, London, E.C.

If no allotment is made the deposit will be returned without deduction. Should a smaller amount be allotted than applied for, the surplus paid on application will be appropriated towards the balance due on allotment. Non-payment of any instalment upon the due date will render the amounts previously paid liable to forfeiture. Interest at the rate of 6 per cent. per annum will be charged on instalments in arrear.

Application will in due course be made for a Stock Exchange quotation for this Issue.

Apart from Contracts made by the Company in the ordinary course of business, the following have been entered into within the two years immediately preceding the date hereof:—

Contracts dated November 9th 1908, and May 19th, 1909, and made between the Company and the Buenos Ayres and Pacific Railway Company, Limited.

Contract dated January 20th, 1909, and made between the Company and Messrs. Sheppards, Pelly, Price and Pott for underwriting £1,000,000 5 per cent. Debenture Stock, for a commission of £30,000, which commission has been paid.

Contract dated September 22nd, 1909, and made between the Company and Messrs. Sheppards, Pelly, Price and Pott for underwriting the present issue, for a commission at the rate of £3 per cent. on the amount of such issue.

The above Contracts may be inspected at the Offices of the Solicitors on any day while the List remains open, between the hours of 11 and 4.

The Preferred Stock carries equal rights with the Ordinary Stock of attending Meetings and voting, each £20 of Stock carrying one vote on a poll.

A Brokerage of 5s. per cent. will be paid by the Company on allotments made to the public in respect of applications bearing a Broker's stamp.

Prospectuses and Forms of Application may be obtained at the Offices of the Company, Dashwood House, 9 New Broad Street, London, E.C.: of the Bankers; and of Messrs. Sheppards, Pelly, Price and Pott, the Brokers of the Company.

Dashwood House,
9 New Broad Street,
London, E.C.
September 23rd, 1909.

Trustees for the Five per cent. Debenture Stock.
THE CONSOLIDATED TRUST, LIMITED.

Directors.
THE RT. HON. LORD ST. DAVIDS (Chairman).
HON. C. N. LAWRENCE.
C. M. ROSE.
HON. ARTHUR STANLEY, M.P.

Local Board at Buenos Ayres.
SAMUEL H. PEARSON (Chairman).
J. A. VILLALONGA.
J. A. GOUDGE.

Bankers.
THE LONDON JOINT STOCK BANK, LIMITED, 5 Princes Street, London, E.C.
PARR'S BANK, LIMITED, 4 Bartholomew Lane, London, E.C.

Solicitors.
ASHURST, MORRIS, CRISP & CO., 17 Throgmorton Avenue, London, E.C.

Brokers.
SHEPPARDS, PELLY, PRICE & POTT, 57 Old Broad Street, London, E.C.

Auditors.
DELOITTE, PLENDER, GRIFFITHS & CO., 5 London Wall Buildings, London, E.C.

Secretary.
J. T. DILLON.

Printed for the Proprietors by SPOTTISWOODE & CO. LTD., 5 New-street Square, E.C., and Published by REGINALD WEBSTER PAGE, at the Office, 10 King Street, Covent Garden, in the Parish of St. Paul, in the County of London.—*Saturday, 25 September, 1909.*

SUPPLEMENT TO THE

SATURDAY REVIEW

OF

POLITICS, LITERATURE, SCIENCE, AND ART.

No. 2,813 Vol. 108. 25 September 1909. GRATIS.

SUPPLEMENT.

LONDON: 25 SEPTEMBER, 1909.

THE ALES THAT ARE NO MORE.

"Inns, Ales and Drinking Customs of Old England." By Frederick W. Hackwood. London: Fisher Unwin. 1909. 10s. 6d. net.

"SOMEONE has said that an 'innless' England is inconceivable." With this sentence Mr. Hackwood begins a book into which he has collected much readable matter. Whoever "someone" was, he spoke truth. The associations, historical, literary and social, connected with English inns and taverns probably outnumber those of the English "Great Houses", and many a man has a pet inn of his own, a Bunch of Grapes where he has a delight to sit.

With the advent of every Licensing Bill we are threatened with the destruction of these pleasant resorts. The Trade, we are told, can bear no more. Mr. Hackwood comforts us a little. He devotes several chapters to the blundering legislation which has for centuries persecuted the trade (with occasional intervals of injudicious petting). The Trade, the victorious Trade, has survived it all, and may again. It is not the trade it was: not so profitable to the provider nor so pleasant to the consumer. Railways dealt it a nasty knock, and though Mr. Hackwood is of opinion that bicycle and motor have brought back custom, one fears that this is only true to a very slight extent. Too many hosts feel inclined, like Dickens' friend, to "take and drown themselves in a pail".

Inns at the present day tend towards one of two forms: the hotel and the "pub". The former, "replete with modern comforts", is, for those who like it, a pleasant residence; for those who don't, it is the dreariest habitation yet contrived of man. Arriving in the afternoon, you dress for a table d'hôte dinner, eat you know not what (your plain man hates to have to dine with a dictionary), spend your evening sitting about the passages with perfect strangers, too often to the sound of the "band as before", and go up to bed in a lift! The tramp who curls up out of the drizzle under a rick gets more of the homing feeling which ought to be associated with going to bed. In days of yore men loved the snugness of a tavern. Sheffield Duke of Buckingham, though at home he chose "instead of a little dozing closet (according to the unwholesome custom of most people) this spacious room for all my small affairs", from which "I am more sorry than my coachman himself if I am forced to go abroad any part of the morning", yet, after he had dined, drove away to Marybone to "bowl time away" certainly, but also to preside in the tavern attached to the gardens. Chatham is said to have been "at once impressed" by the noble proportions of the "Castle" at Marlborough. (The great Earl of Chatham, by the way, was not in 1767 what Mr. Hackwood calls him, "the Idol of the Nation". He lost three-fourths of his popularity on the day, in July '66, on which he was lowered to the peerage.) Chatham loved state, but to most men the attraction of the tavern lay in its snugness. Now the modern hotel is not snug. The pub—sometimes—is "pernicious snug". But alas! the pub has become a place for drinking only. Drinking is out of fashion, and the pub is hopelessly ungenteel. Whose fault is that? Of the gentle who forsook or of the vulgar who abide by it? The gentle did not play fair: they have their improved taverns, their clubs (the difference between distribution and sale is too fine for ordinary sight); for the present

"The poor must steer
For his pint of beer
Where the saint can't choose but spy him".

Mr. Hackwood, of course, deplores the "National Vice". He has unearthed what he takes to be "the earliest of teetotal poems known", by Joseph Rigbie, gentleman, at the Brazen Serpent, 1656:

> "Drink beastiates the heart, and spoils the brains,
> Exiles all reason, all good graces stains", etc.

"Beastiates" is good. Mr. Hackwood, we take it, would not go these lengths; he shows a rather malicious pleasure in the circumstance that ginger wine, to which "some teetotalers in their innocence do not object", is, compared to a light hock or claret, "highly alcoholic". But we are rather tired of hearing the aristocratic drinking of the eighteenth century ascribed to "a low moral standard". Will it be fair in a future historian to say "How low was the standard of morals in England when a motor car was considered a suitable present for a Bishop!"? But drinking and driving are fashions which go on all fours. Johnson, the "sullen moralist", admitted that a man was happy when he was drunk, and (with an after-reservation) when he was driven rapidly in a post-chaise. Driving and drink have the same object—exhilaration. Drink and driving are open to abuse. A modern minister would be disgraced if he were seen "in liquor". Brilliant Carteret would have blushed to be seen in a hurry.

Mr. Hackwood's portly octavo is crammed with pictures, a fact which necessitates a rather maddening separation of plate from context, but, to do the book justice, each plate bears in the corner a reference to its proper page. The frontispiece, Hogarth's second Election Plate, is attractive in colour. We have Beer Street and Gin Lane and one of Cruikshank's "Drunkard's Children" plates. Mr. Hackwood, writing of Jolly Good Ale and Old, could hardly avoid Beer Street; with the two others we could have dispensed. But they match the chapters on the "Gin Fever" of Hogarth's time and the "Gin Policy" of Cruikshank's, which are not pleasant reading. The most agreeable passage is that which gives one tradition of the origin of "Old Tom" gin. "An old Government spy set up an illicit establishment outside which was the sign of an old Tom cat projecting into the street. By depositing a penny through a slot in the figure a supply of gin to that value could be made to trickle from a pipe concealed in the cat's forepaw"—a "penny-in-the-slot" of 1755.

Some of the pictures are postcardy. Except where an inn betrays by its construction the purpose for which it was built, there is not much point in giving its picture. The "Bell" e.g. at Finedon, Northants, claims to have been an inn in 1042; but the present building looks more like a deanery than an inn. The plates of drinking apparatus appeal more to the connoisseur than to the ordinary man, though we own to coveting the three delightful "Tobies" on page 304. The signs are quaint but mostly familiar, as "The man loaded with mischief". Of the tavern-keepers, Elinour Rummin is only a rough woodcut, of conventional design, such as in her day and long after is found on every broadsheet and ballad. We are sure it is not like Elinour because it is not like a woman. Why then is Elinour "the famous alewife of Leatherhead" and Mother Louse "the alewife of tradition"? She was as real a person as Dr. Fell or Anthony à Wood, in whose time she flourished. Says Granger of the plate here reproduced (vol. iv. p. 217): "This print which is well executed and much like the person represented, gained the engraver (David Loggan) a considerable share of his reputation. It was drawn from the life at an alehouse near Oxford, which was kept by this matron. . . . She was probably the last woman in England who wore a ruff".

In one place Mr. Hackwood has blundered rather badly. One of the oldest inn bills which can be produced dates from 1274, in which year Richard de Insula, Bishop of Durham, and his Prior stopped at the "Angel" at Blyth, Notts. They ran up a bill—

	s.	d.
In pane	10	0
In cervisia et vino	33	5
In coquina	27	5½
In prebenda feno et littera	18	9

on which Mr. Hackwood remarks "the charges for bread, for the venison and wine, for the provender etc., would all appear to be reasonable, but the item set down for cooking would appear to be somewhat excessive". But cervisia is beer, not venison! The festive old prelate's little bill is divided between the bakery, the cellar, the kitchen, and the stable. If they gave him venison they charged him "in coquina".

All who hanker after the old tavern life will find much of interest in Mr. Hackwood's book. Perhaps, after all, that life was not as attractive as it seems. Perhaps finer things have been written about than were ever "done at" the Mermaid. As that old life is lost, it is better to believe so—if you can.

EUROPEAN MUNICIPALITIES.

"The Government of European Cities." By W. B. Munro. New York: Macmillans. 1909. 10s. 6d. net.

THERE appears to be quite a boom in American textbooks on European methods. Peripatetic professors shoot out from their universities, have a series of lightning interviews, and then produce a book. Mr. Munro has whirled through a number of Prussian, French, and English cities, and now we have what he terms in his own language a "viewpoint". It is frankly American; and evidently does not look kindly on Continental methods of checking the sovereign people by official interference. "Arbitrary interference from Paris", we read, "is, in view of republican traditions, somewhat surprising." The French wisely never mix traditions with government; they keep them for their speeches. The only country we can think of where republican traditions are properly followed out is the little State of Andorra, and there they have no politicians, everybody works. Though French cities boast mayors and councillors and all the paraphernalia of local self-government, everything that matters is overshadowed by the Ministry of the Interior, whose watch-dog, the Prefect, is the real power, and not always behind the scenes. In the circumstances, apathy at local elections is not unnatural, though perhaps surprising to one accustomed to the machine-made politics of the United States. Even so, it is interesting to learn that "French councillors compare very favourably with American councilmen". Merci, M. le Professeur. The position of those joint rulers of Paris, the Prefect of the Seine and the Prefect of Police, is clearly and interestingly sketched. The only traditions they follow are of promptness and force, unrepublican perhaps, but very effective in a place which has an awkward trick of boiling over at unexpected moments.

Crossing the German border one still finds the restraining hand of the central government on local effort, though to nothing like the same extent as in France. German cities have grown in population even more quickly than American, but that has never prevented their efficient administration. The presence or absence of central control probably to a large extent explains the cause of success in the one case and of failure in the other. The Prussian local electoral system, though wide numerically, is in practice much restricted by the three-class system of voting. The classes are constituted entirely on a tax-paying basis, and the result is that about 60 per cent. of the councillors are chosen by from one-tenth to one-fifth of the voters. Thus, those who pay really control expenditure. Mr. Munro, as an apostle of theoretical equality, does not appear to like the system. In America, if report be true, the large ratepayers prefer to wait until the elected of the people are installed in office; they are then more approachable and easily amenable to methods happily impossible in undemocratic Germany. The strength of the Prussian municipal system is the "Magistrat", an executive board of paid and unpaid members chosen by the Council and in close relation to it and to the central authorities. The paid members are all experts like the permanent officials of an English city, and their selection needs confirmation by the higher authorities. Mr. Munro's examination of the duties and function of this checking and revising body is quite the best part of his book, and well worth close attention.

English readers will naturally find a criticism of our own methods of local government more interesting than that of strangers. The present criticism is a little disappointing—too much ground is covered; too little space given to essential details. Mr. Munro fails to see that the great asset of English local government is the solidarity of local feeling. He harps too much on trivial points, such as the non-residence of a councillor in his ward. Evidently he has in mind the American idea of delegation; but this as yet has little footing in England. With us a councillor represents the town at large, and any attempt to gain a sectional advantage for a particular part of it would be very detrimental to his influence with the council as a whole.

The standing committee system is examined superficially and at times not altogether accurately. Nominally, of course, committees choose their own chairman; in practice, however, a suggestion comes from the dominant party, and it is the chairman who, with the permanent head of the department his committee controls, is really responsible for its good administration. Upon his personality depends the length of rope given to the permanent officials.

An English city has no difficulty in getting capable men; their tenure is certain and the pay good. So long as the Americans persist in the iniquitous spoils system there can be no comparison between the methods of the two countries. Mr. Munro has hardly kept himself up to date in regard to the position of the City Treasurer and the working of Finance Committees. The automatic growth of municipal expenditure, especially in those departments theoretically remunerative, has given rise to a strong movement in the direction of compelling a general previous submission of all suggested expenditure to the Treasurer and Finance Committee, much on the system that the Treasury controls the Budget. Other heads of departments are naturally strongly opposed to such control, seeing in it a threatened diminution of their own importance. Enough is not made of the radical difference in England between the audit of municipal accounts and that of other local authorities. The test is the power of review in order to disallow illegal expenditure. Generally speaking, this power does not exist in the case of provincial municipalities. No mention is made of the strong and growing feeling in favour of greater central control over expenditure. We are not able to agree with Mr. Munro's cursory summary of the relations between municipalities and their general employees. The pressure on the council is far greater than he imagines, and is none the less dangerous because applied to individual councillors at election times. Small compact bodies of electors pledged to vote only for those who will give them special consideration at all times exercise a very real pressure, and particularly so when parties are evenly divided. We suffer seriously from the same trouble in parliamentary elections in the case of postal, telegraph, and dockyard employees. Though the suggestion to disfranchise municipal employees has never been seriously pressed, there certainly is a growing belief in the advisability of erecting them into a separate constituency.

We have searched vainly throughout this book for any serious examination of the rating system of the four countries under review. The Americans, we believe, tax site values, and the Prussians, in many cases, increment values. In England for some years there has been a keen controversy on the suggested taxation of unimproved land in urban areas. Mr. Munro passes all this by; it is hardly unimportant detail. Even a comparison between English and American methods of rating would have been most valuable at a time when land taxation is so much to the fore, and we regret the omission.

In the United States literary men have steadily fought against the all too frequent mangling of our common language. Yet from a Harvard professor's writing we can compile the following: We "owe considerable to the helpful suggestions" of the "councilmen", and when the "dickerings" resulting from the "candidacy" are over, the council, "when it does convene", will settle its "conciliar procedure" at the next "quarterly sederunt".

NOVELS.

"The Tragedy of the Pyramids: a Romance of Army Life in Egypt." By Douglas Sladen. London: Hurst and Blackett. 1909. 6s.

There are, then, already two Richmonds in the field—but they are quite distinguishable. The noisier, Mr. Hall Caine, was also the first; but his domination has not long remained uncontested, for here comes a rival, Mr. Douglas Sladen, with another "romance of army life in Egypt". The first did not confine himself to the army, but let an eagle glance wander over all forms of English activity in the land of fleshpots. Nevertheless we must say—and emphatically—that by recognising his own limitations Mr. Sladen has succeeded in writing a much better story. Neither author, we suppose, is an Israelite: both have gone to Egypt for material and spoiled not the Egyptians but the English. Whether things past happened, or present things are happening, or things future will happen, according to one of these rivals, or to neither, is not the present question. Novelists must find their material somewhere and write about something or somebody; Messrs. Caine and Sladen have neither of them produced anything like literature, but the one has spun a dull yarn and the other an amusing and entertaining one. Intelligent readers will not regard them as serious authorities on Egyptian questions.

"The Mount." By C. F. Keary. London: Constable. 1909. 6s.

This, told simply, might have turned out an entertaining and even a beautiful story. Unluckily Mr. Keary refuses to be simple. Half-daring, half-afraid, with recollections of the big psychological novels of last century vivid in his mind, he is incessantly tempted to emulate many of the great novel-writers and some of the bad ones, and he as constantly wavers when the crucial test comes. Where he should be strong and decisive he is weak and fumbling, and he strives to cover up the feeble patches with "literary" phrases. One may perceive the thread of genuine narrative running through the book; but at times it is distorted into absurd melodrama, and at other times it is hidden under sentences which, to speak plainly, no mortal dare swear he understands. Some of the phrases are mere death-traps, in which we find all our sympathy and goodwill strangled. A good, straight-ahead story is what Mr. Keary can write, and we would wish him to forswear the "literary" and return to his true path. The market is at present overcrowded with thoroughly bad novelists, and it is a pity that a good one should perish through a foolish affectation.

"The Bill-Toppers." By André Castaigne. London: Mills and Boon. 1909. 6s.

Acrobats and other music-hall artistes of the kind have been treated with much success in sentimental drawing-room ballads, but are not often met in novels. Lily Clifton, the heroine of Mr. Castaigne's story, is an empty-headed little girl with no vice or nonsense about her, and we should imagine the record of her career as a trick bicycle rider, from appearance as an infant prodigy to triumph in a sensational performance in Paris, to be remarkably true to life. Mr. Castaigne takes us into a very odd world, the inhabitants of which are at home in every continent, and describes with apparent knowledge the freemasonry which links together places of entertainment all over the globe. Lily is exploited first by her parents and later by a disreputable husband, but runs straight according to her lights amid many troubles. Her biographer is conscious of the darker side of such an existence, but does not emphasise the ugly features. The story is quite entertaining, and, in a sense, instructive.

"This Day's Madness." By Maud Annesley. London: Methuen. 1909. 6s.

Many a comparatively successful playwright would be grateful to Miss Annesley if she would explain how her inexperienced, youthful, and by no means brilliant heroine contrived to write and produce four successful plays in eighteen months. Judging from Pamela's own conversation, and from the "good things" in other people's, which we are told she wrote down for subsequent dramatic use, we should say that a still lower level of general theatrical taste must be reached before her plays could be accepted by even the least intellectual of managers.

SOME AUTUMN LITERARY NOTES.

The publishers promise an autumn season of considerable activity. Whether it is to be a notable season, or commonplace, only the books on the stocks can determine. Publishers' catalogues of forthcoming works are always inviting, even though the performance may not be equal to the promise. We may get a good deal of pleasure out of the mere anticipation which literary announcements encourage, and the publisher's own account of the contents of his new books serves as hors d'œuvres to the substantial fare to come. What are the principal items to be found in the autumn lists of some of the chief houses?

Messrs. Macmillan have a big thing at the head of their announcements in Dr. Sven Hedin's book "Trans-Himalaya: Discoveries and Adventures in Tibet", which should be as good reading to the adventure lover as to the scientific explorer and student. Sir William Meyer has translated M. Joseph Chailley's "Administrative Problems of British India". Colonel Sir Thomas H. Holdich will give the results of twenty years of official wanderings on the ancient highways and among the cities of the trans-frontier regions under the title "The Gates of India". Colonel Patterson will follow up his "Man Eaters of Tsavo" with further adventures in East Africa: "In the Grip of the Nyika". Mr. John W. Fortescue will advance his "History of the British Army," seven years in volumes v. and vi., from the Peace of Amiens in 1802 to the death of Sir John Moore at Coruña and the evacuation of Spain by the British in the early days of 1809. "The English Church in the Nineteenth Century", by Mr. Warre Cornish, will form volumes viii. and ix. of "A History of the English Church". Professor H. M. Gwatkin's "Early Church History (to A.D. 313)" will appear next week. Professor Shield Nicholson has been studying the theories of Adam Smith from the Imperial point of view, and publishes his views opportunely in "A Project of Empire". Mr. Walter Jerrold's "Middlesex" will be added shortly to the "Highways and Byways" series. A new volume of stories and poems by Mr. Rudyard Kipling, "Actions and Reactions", is nearly ready.

Messrs. Smith, Elder have on their list three books concerned with the future of the British race from different points of view. They are Sir W. Earnshaw Cooper's "Britain for the Briton", showing the necessity of co-operation in agriculture and other industries, and the grave economical blunder England has made in her treatment of agricultural interests; Mr. Ellis Barker's "Great and Greater Britain", a series of essays on Imperial problems; and Professor James Long's "The Coming Englishman", which will deal with various movements intended to benefit the people. Mr. G. W. E. Russell has written a memoir of Sir Wilfrid Lawson, Mr. J. E. Vincent tells "The Story of the Thames", and Mr. Laurence Harris in "With Mulai Hafid at Fez" gives an account of his extraordinary experiences at the Court of the present Sultan of Morocco. In "George I. and the Northern War" Mr. James Frederick Chance makes a study of British Hanoverian policy in the North of Europe in the years 1709 to 1721, and "Fifty Years of New Japan" has been compiled by Count Shigenobu Okuma, late Prime Minister of Japan and Minister for Foreign Affairs, and others, under the editorship of Marcus B. Huish, of the Japan Society.

Messrs. Smith, Elder's new fiction includes "Her Mother's Daughter", by Katharine Tynan; "Corporal Sam, and Other Stories", by A. T. Quiller-Couch; and "The Caravaners", by the author of "Elizabeth and her German Garden".

Messrs. Longmans have ready or nearly ready Mr. C. Y. C. Dawbarn's book on the question of the unemployed, "Liberty and Progress", Professor W. James' "Meaning of Truth", Mr. G. M. Trevelyan's "Garibaldi and the Thousand", Professor C. H. Firth's "The Last Years of the Protectorate", which is a continuation of Gardiner's "History of the Commonwealth and Protectorate", and Mrs. Lecky's memoir of her husband. The pièce de résistance of Messrs. Longmans' list would however seem to be Mr. J. G. Millais' eight-guinea work, "The Natural History of British Game Birds". Mill's "Political Economy" is apparently still in steady demand, and a new edition edited by Professor W. J. Ashley is in preparation.

Mr. Heinemann will publish Lieutenant Shackleton's "Story of the British Antarctic Expedition, 1907-1909" in two volumes, with maps and about 300 illustrations, some in colours; "Lombardic Architecture: its Origins, Development, and Derivatives", by G. T. Rivoira; "A History of Japanese Colour-Prints", by W. von Seidlitz; "The Memoirs of the Duchesse de Dino" (afterwards de Talleyrand and de Sagan), edited, with notes and a biographical index, by Princess Radziwill (née Castellane); and "The Great French Revolution", by P. Kropotkin. On 28 September Mr. Heinemann will issue the first volume of a new series of Health Books, called "Why Worry?" It is intended to appeal alike to the man of business and the man distracted by his social engagements.

In Mr. John Lane's autumn list appear "William Makepeace Thackeray", a biography by Lewis Melville, who has for some years past devoted himself to the collection of material relating to Thackeray; "The Life of Joan of Arc", by Anatole France, translated by Winifred Stephens; "The Last Journals of Horace Walpole" (1771 to 1783), containing Dr. Doran's notes and edited, with an introduction, by A. Francis Stewart; and, most opportunely, "Dr. Johnson and Mrs. Thrale", by A. M. Broadley, with an introductory chapter by Thomas Seccombe.

Messrs. Chapman & Hall are issuing "Memorials of St. Paul's Cathedral", by Archdeacon Sinclair; "A History of St. Paul's School", by Michael F. J. McDonnell; "The Smugglers", being picturesque chapters in the history of an ancient industry, and "The Tower of London: Fortress, Prison, Palace", both by Charles G. Harper; "The Gateway to the Sahara", observations and experiences in Tripoli, by C. W. Furlong; and "Yet Again"—more "works" doubtless—by Max Beerbohm.

Messrs. J. M. Dent & Co. are publishing an English translation of the sixth edition of Professor Sombart's "Socialism and the Social Movement", which was first published in 1896. The sixth edition is four times the size of the first, and brings the history of Socialism in the great countries of Europe and in America down to the present time. The book has been translated into no fewer than seventeen languages, including all the principal European tongues and Japanese. The work of translation has been done by Dr. M. Epstein, who had the advantage of working with Professor Sombart for two years.

Messrs. Chatto & Windus announce in their Art and Letters Library "Stories of the French Artists from Clouet to Ingres", drawn from contemporary records, collected and arranged by P. M. Turner and C. H. Collins Baker; and "Stories of the Spanish Artists until Goya", drawn from contemporary records, collected and arranged by Luis Carreño. The firm will also issue shortly the authorised English translation of "Venice in the Eighteenth Century", by Philippe Monnier; and "Lives of the Medicis: from their Letters", by Janet Ross. "Astronomical Curiosities", by J. Ellard Gore, will appear in October.

Messrs. Ginn and Company will publish shortly a "History of English Literature" by William J. Long, giving an account of the great English writers, their works, and the literary periods in which they lived. The quotations, outlines, summaries, historical introductions, complete indexes, and a good working bibliography will, it is hoped, be found of real value to students. The book will be illustrated and will contain as frontispiece "The Canterbury Pilgrims", lithographed in nine colours from a direct copy taken from a manuscript in the British Museum.

Messrs. Cassell & Co. during this week will publish "Charles Dickens and His Friends", by W. Teignmouth Shore, who seeks to introduce his readers into the very midst of Charles Dickens' large circle of friends, and to give an idea of their views in so far as they throw light on the lesser-known traits of the novelist's character. "Cassell's Little Classics" is a new series which will add another rival to the many cheap editions of the world's masterpieces. Introductions are contributed by G. K. Chesterton, Austin Dobson, Stuart J. Reid, A. T. Quiller-Couch, and others. Among the first twenty-five volumes are Ascham's "The Schoolmaster", Maundeville's "Voyages and Travels", Lamb's "Essays of Elia", More's "Utopia", Ruskin's "Unto this Last", and Shelley's 'Prometheus Unbound".

Messrs. LONGMANS & CO.'S List

NEW BOOK BY MR. G. MACAULAY TREVELYAN.

GARIBALDI AND THE THOUSAND

By GEORGE MACAULAY TREVELYAN,
Late Fellow of Trinity College, Cambridge.
With 6 Maps and numerous Illustrations. 8vo. 7s. 6d. net. *(Inland postage 4d.)*

BY THE SAME AUTHOR.

GARIBALDI'S DEFENCE OF THE ROMAN REPUBLIC. With 7 Maps and 35 Illustrations. 8vo. 6s. 6d. net. NINTH THOUSAND. *(Inland postage 4d.)*

ENGLAND IN THE AGE OF WYCLIFFE. NEW AND CHEAPER EDITION. 8vo. 6s. net. *(Inland postage 4d.)*

NEW NOVEL BY MRS. WILFRID WARD.

GREAT POSSESSIONS.

By MRS. WILFRID WARD,
Author of "One Poor Scruple," "Out of Due Time," &c.
Crown 8vo. 6s. *(Inland postage 4d.)*

LIBERTY AND PROGRESS. By C. Y. C. DAWBARN, M.A. Part I. THE EMPLOYED. Part II. THE PRINCIPLES OF EMPLOYMENT. Part III. OUR UNDERPAID AND UNEMPLOYED. 8vo. 9s. net. *(Inland postage 5d.)*

THE BASIS OF ASCENDANCY: A Discussion of Certain Principles of Public Policy involved in the Development of the Southern States of America. By EDGAR GARDNER MURPHY, Author of "Problems of the Present South." Crown 8vo. 6s. net. *(Inland postage 4d.)*

"For the effective union of high thinking and telling common sense this book has not been equalled in the vast mass of discussion of the complex question with which it deals."—*New York Times.*

CHRISTIAN IDEAS AND IDEALS: An Outline of Christian Ethical Theory. By ROBERT LAWRENCE OTTLEY, M.A., Canon of Christ Church and Regius Professor of Pastoral Theology and Hon. Fellow of Pembroke College, Oxford. 8vo. 7s. 6d. net. *(Inland postage 4d.)*

THE SAYINGS OF CONFUCIUS. Translated by LEONARD A. LYALL. 8vo. 3s. 6d. net. *(Inland postage 4d.)*

This is an attempt to produce the style, as well as the literal meaning, of the "Lun-yü."

THE SILVER LIBRARY—New Volume.

THE ENGLISH IN THE WEST INDIES. By JAMES A. FROUDE. New Impression. With 9 Illustrations. Crown 8vo. 3s. 6d. *(Inland postage 4d.)*

LONGMANS' POCKET LIBRARY—Two New Volumes.

THE LIGHT OF THE WORLD: Or, the Great Consummation. A Poem. By Sir EDWIN ARNOLD, K.C.I.E., C.S.I. With Photogravure Frontispiece of W. HOLMAN HUNT'S "LIGHT OF THE WORLD." NEW EDITION. Fcap. 8vo. gilt top, cloth, 2s. net; leather, 3s. net. *(Inland postage 3d. each.)*

DEUTSCHE LIEBE (GERMAN LOVE): Fragments from the Papers of an Alien. Collected by F. MAX MÜLLER. Translated from the German by G. A. M. With Photogravure Portrait. NEW EDITION. Fcap. 8vo. gilt top, cloth, 2s. net; leather, 3s. net. *(Inland postage 3d. each.)*

HANDBOOKS FOR THE CLERGY.
Edited by the Rev. ARTHUR W. ROBINSON, D.D.

PREACHING. By the Very Rev. F. E. CARTER, M.A., Dean of Grahamstown. Crown 8vo. 2s. 6d. net. *(Inland postage 3d.)*

LONGMANS, GREEN & CO., 39 Paternoster Row, London, E.C.

RE-APPEARANCE OF

"THE THRUSH"

A MONTHLY PERIODICAL FOR THE PUBLICATION OF ORIGINAL VERSE,

DECEMBER 1st, 1909.

New Feature—Literary Articles on All Subjects.

CONTRIBUTIONS (which will be paid for) should be addressed to

THE EDITOR, "THE THRUSH" OFFICE,
12 & 13 Henrietta Street, Covent Garden, W.C.

Smith, Elder, & Co.'s List

NEW 6s. NOVELS.

BY THE AUTHOR OF "THE WATERS OF JORDAN."

THE PALADIN:
As Beheld by a Woman of Temperament.
HORACE ANNESLEY VACHELL.

DAILY NEWS.—"The best story Mr. Vachell has written for a long time, skilfully put together, and, for a comedy of respectable society, very human."

MR. JUSTICE RAFFLES
E. W. HORNUNG.

SCOTSMAN.—"A great deal of enjoyment can be got from a tale so ingeniously constructed, so vividly written, and so full of uncommon, puzzling, and dramatic situations."

NEW AND CHEAPER EDITION.
With Illustrations by ARTHUR TWIDLE. Crown 8vo. 3s. 6d.

SIR NIGEL

By **A. CONAN DOYLE**, Author of "The White Company," "Micah Clarke," "Rodney Stone," &c.

SHEFFIELD DAILY TELEGRAPH.—"As a picture of the period, the novel is beyond all praise . . . a wonderfully interesting, exciting story of chivalrous adventure, which cannot fail to excite comparisons with Scott's 'Ivanhoe.'"

NEW AND CHEAPER EDITION.
4 vols. With Illustrations. Crown 8vo. 3s. 6d. each.

HOW ENGLAND SAVED EUROPE

By **W. H. FITCHETT, B.A., LL.D.**, Author of "Deeds that Won the Empire," "Fights for the Flag," &c.

DAILY CHRONICLE.—"His pages are full of panoramic movement and picturesqueness, while his portraiture of the leading actors in the great amphibious drama are ever lifelike and vivid."

The Waterloo Library.

Crown 8vo. 3s. 6d. per Volume.

PALL MALL GAZETTE.—"The best 3s. 6d. Series on the market. . . . The paper is quite excellent, and the print is fine and clear."

THE BRASS BOTTLE. F. ANSTEY. With a Frontispiece.

NOTES AND JOTTINGS FROM ANIMAL LIFE. FRANK BUCKLAND.

THE CRUISE OF THE "CACHALOT." FRANK T. BULLEN. With 8 Full-page Illustrations and a Chart.

THE LOG OF A SEA WAIF. FRANK T. BULLEN, F.R.G.S. With 8 Full-page Illustrations by ARTHUR TWIDLE.

PETER'S MOTHER. Mrs. HENRY DE LA PASTURE.

TIMES.—"A delightful book. . . . There is a fragrance about it very like the fragrance of a Devon meadow."

ADAM GRIGSON. Mrs. HENRY DE LA PASTURE.

DEBORAH OF TOD'S. Mrs. HENRY DE LA PASTURE.

JESS. H. RIDER HAGGARD. With 12 Full-page Illustrations.

THE GAMEKEEPER AT HOME. RICHARD JEFFERIES. With Illustrations.

NEW VOLUME READY SHORTLY.

THE AMATEUR POACHER. RICHARD JEFFERIES.

GRAPHIC.—"We have rarely met with a book in which so much that is entertaining is combined with matter of real practical worth."

*** *OTHER VOLUMES TO FOLLOW.*

London: SMITH, ELDER, & CO., 15 Waterloo Place, S.W.

THE LATEST FICTION

Quite a New Idea

THE HUMAN MOLE

SECOND EDITION NOW READY.

THE HUMAN MOLE

By COLIN COLLINS.

The *SPECTATOR* says: "An exciting melodrama, in which the reader will forget the incredibility of the means by which the 'Human Mole' attains his ends for the sake of the lively adventures that are described."

THE HUMAN MOLE

By COLIN COLLINS.

The *PALL MALL GAZETTE* says: "Quite a new idea. Distinctly engrossing and most skilfully designed to pin the reader's interest to it for hours at a time. We warn any seaside sojourner who picks up *this* book that he will not enjoy the sea or the scenery until he has finished it."

THE MASTER SCHEMER

By MRS. VERE CAMPBELL.

The *DAILY TELEGRAPH* says: "It is a story, cast in a turbulent mould, of love tumultuous and violent, but it is a story, all the same, through which rings a deep and unmistakable human note. . . . Admiration may be freely expressed for the resource and ingenuity displayed in the manipulation of a tale which deals frankly and unflinchingly with the more passionate feelings and problems of life. . . . The story swings along at headlong pace. There is neither pause or halt until the tragic end is reached, while the developments, although springing naturally from each other, are so skilfully contrived as to hold the attention firmly engaged. 'The Master Schemer' is a book that by virtue of its inherent strength and cleverly sustained interest ought to appeal to a wide circle of readers."

THE WANTON

By FRANCES FORBES-ROBERTSON.

The *GRAPHIC* says: "A romance well thought out, well worked out, and distinctly in advance of the best of her former stories."

SECOND EDITION NEARLY EXHAUSTED.
THIRD EDITION AT PRESS.

THE WANTON

By FRANCES FORBES-ROBERTSON.

THE MARQUIS CATILINI

By ROWLAND STRONG.

The *DAILY TELEGRAPH* says: "This is a very remarkable novel. Brilliantly written, intensely vivid, it is that extremely rare combination of a tale of action and a perfect picture of real life and real human beings."

READY IMMEDIATELY.

MR. GURNER GILLMAN'S NEW NOVEL.

HER SUBURBAN HIGHNESS

By **GURNER GILLMAN,** Author of "The Loafer," &c.

Messrs. Greening take pleasure in announcing that they are now publishing a New Work by* ENA FITZGERALD, *whose first work,* "PATCOLA," *caused much attention. Ask at your Library for

THE WITCH QUEEN OF KHEM

A Story of Egypt.

B; **ENA FITZGERALD.** Price 6s.

Other Recent Novels of Merit are

THE SPITFIRE	EDWARD PEPLE
MOON OF VALLEYS	DAVID WHITELAW
REBIRTH	RATHMELL WILSON
ADVENTURES OF SUSAN	CYRUS BRADY
HENRY OF NAVARRE	MAY WYNNE
SEALED ORDERS	A. E. CAREY

Price Six Shillings each. At all Libraries.

THE NEST OF THE SPARROWHAWK

The above is the title of the new romance by the* BARONESS ORCZY *(Author of "The Scarlet Pimpernel") now appearing in "THE IMP," which should be ordered at once from your newsagent, or can be had direct for 2s. for a year, post free.

GREENING & CO., LTD., 91 St. Martin's Lane, W.C.

Messrs. Methuen have just published
A NEW BOOK BY

Sir GILBERT PARKER

ENTITLED

NORTHERN LIGHTS

The demand for it was so great that a Second Edition was called for before publication.

PRESS OPINIONS

"They are admirable sketches, quite absorbing to read."—*Observer.*
"It will cast its spell over all who read this delicately wrought volume." *Manchester Courier.*
"The stories are all good."—*Standard.*
"Each affords a finished picture of the truest kind."—*Morning Post.*

Sir GILBERT PARKER'S well-known Novels

Crown 8vo. **6s.** each

Published by Messrs. METHUEN

PIERRE AND HIS PEOPLE...	*6th Edition.*
MRS. FALCHION	*5th* ,,
THE TRANSLATION OF A SAVAGE ...	*3rd* ,,
THE TRAIL OF THE SWORD	*10th* ,,
WHEN VALMOND CAME TO PONTIAC	*6th* ,,
AN ADVENTURER OF THE NORTH ...	*4th* ,,
THE SEATS OF THE MIGHTY	*16th* ,,
THE BATTLE OF THE STRONG ...	*6th* ,,
THE POMP OF THE LAVILETTES, 3/6	*3rd* ,,

Published by Mr. HEINEMANN

THE LANE THAT HAD NO TURNING.
THE RIGHT OF WAY. *5th Edition.*
DONOVAN PASHA. A LADDER OF SWORDS.
THE WEAVERS. *7th Edition.*

METHUEN & CO., 36 Essex Street, W.C.

Werner Laurie's New Books.

MY FRIENDS THE FRENCH. By Robert Harborough Sherard, Author of "The Life of Oscar Wilde." Illustrated. 12s. 6d. net.

PSYCHICAL SCIENCE AND CHRISTIANITY. By E. Katharine Bates, Author of "Seen and Unseen," "Do the Dead Depart." 6s.

WHERE THE FISHERS GO. The Story of Labrador. By P. W. Browne. 200 Illustrations. 6s. net.

CHATS ON ELECTRICITY. Told in plain Language for the non-technical. By Frank Broadbent, M.I.E.E. Illustrated. 3s. 6d. net.

THE GRIZZLY BEAR. The Narrative of a Hunter—Historical, Scientific, and Adventurous. By William H. Wright. Illustrated. 7s. 6d. net.

THE MARRIAGE OF HILARY CARDEN. By Stanley Portal Hyatt, Author of "The Little Brown Brother." 6s.

GILBERT WHITE AND SELBORNE. By Henry C. Shelley. Illustrated. 6s. net.

WERNER LAURIE, CLIFFORD'S INN, LONDON.

Printe for the Proprietors by SPOTTISWOODE & Co. LTD., 5 New-street Square, E.C., and Published by REGINALD WEBSTER PAGE, at the Office, 10 King Street, Covent Garden, in the Parish of St. Paul, in the County of London.—*Saturday, 25 September*, 1909.

THE

SATURDAY REVIEW

OF

POLITICS, LITERATURE, SCIENCE, AND ART.

No. 2,814 Vol. 108. 2 October 1909. [REGISTERED AS A NEWSPAPER.] 6*d*.

CONTENTS.

NOTES OF THE WEEK.

Outside the House of Commons the Budget debates have now very little interest. The one question is, Will the Lords somehow give the Bill a mortal wound or not? We think there is no doubt that Unionist opinion on the whole strongly favours such a stroke. There is certainly another section of opinion in the party: nimium tutus, timidusque procellarum. They would not "put it to the touch to win or lose it all" because they think the Budget is popular with a large class who persist in considering it a poor man's as against a rich man's Bill. They fear to lose the election, but still more they fear the maiming of the House of Lords which might result if the Government swept in with triumph. We quite understand this point of view, which has been put before us within the last few days by a politician of high intelligence, a member of the last Government.

But we cannot agree with it. If the House of Lords does not strike, it will surely dispirit its own public—which, as the Unionist figures at even the last election prove, is a public of many millions after all—and it will come beyond doubt into the contempt of its opponents. Moreover, suppose the Liberals were to get back by a small majority after a stroke at the Bill by the Peers—would it be fatal to the Peers? We think it would be by no means so. The House of Lords is not in danger of being swept away after an election at which millions of electors declare in its favour. At worst, it might have to lie up or hibernate for a while. It would take a rest cure.

Of course, if the Unionists were to be swept clean into the sea and the Radicals and Socialists and Nationalists came in by a huge majority, then it might be all up with the Peers—and in such a case it might be all up ere long with every decent Liberal, indeed with all that is solid and substantial in our social system. But who really fears such a smash-up of everything? It is much more likely that the Unionists will come back to power. We do not believe in the theory that the Budget is extremely popular. It is certainly well liked by a crowd of people who have a shrewd notion that it is a step in the right direction for getting hold of other people's property. But it obviously and admittedly does not confer any direct benefit on the vast bulk of the working men; on the contrary, it puts up the price of their drink and their smoke. Will working men twenty-five years old, thirty-five, forty-five, fifty-five years old, really love a Budget that does this? We cannot think it.

A disgusting feature of the political situation is the loud vain brag of sections on both sides. The press is chiefly answerable for this. Unless, it seems, a General Election can be run on low music-hall lines, it is not worth running at all for circulation purposes. Accordingly every idling inkster on the Unionist side swears the Radicals are blue with terror, whilst every one on the Radical side swears the Unionists are in that state. Of course, the side which his paper graces or disgraces is bursting with confidence, full of great heart, longing for the others to come on. How hateful this all is, how false! Serious politicians take a very different view, and impudent brag is the last thing they care about on the eve of a profoundly important election. Why should general elections, football matches and crimes be made such very low comedy of? The first and the last have surely a serious enough side.

It is shocking to notice the way in which the General Election date and the latest popular crime are whipt on and off the posters of certain newspapers according to the supposed appetite of the public at the time. Is the election "off" at the moment? Then on with the crime. Is the palate of the crime-taster sated for an evening or so? Then on with the latest speech of Mr. Asquith or Lord Rosebery. The posters of some papers are a standing disgrace to London. They constantly shock, disgust, alienate decent people; and we strongly think the time has come to deal with them sternly by law. We want a Censor of Posters far more than we want a Censor of Plays.

One of Mr. Lloyd George's Budget concessions is a nice commentary on Radical criticism of mere landowners and capitalists. When the Chancellor proposed to tax clay as a mineral he forgot Mr. Greville Montgomery M.P. and the clay-workers whose interests he represents. But Mr. George was not prepared to listen, even though Mr. Montgomery is a supporter of the Government—and the Budget. Then Mr. Montgomery set to work in a manner very much after Mr. George's own heart in other days, and, if need be, he was ready with an amendment. He showed how clay has been held by the Courts not to be a mineral, how the tax would prejudice the building trade, and how it would inevitably hurt the worker. Mr. George, thus met within his own ranks by the very arguments urged by his opponents, gave way. Clay is exempt. Abundant supplies of untaxed clay, the sweeter because unleavened by the sense of injustice, are to be available to Mr. Lloyd George's supporters after all! It is a very pretty little object-lesson in Radical finance, and not without a certain grim humour.

What a Cabinet Minister or any other member of the Government has in the bank has nothing to do with the merits or demerits of his programme; nor does his salary affect the issues—unless it happen he is giving away a fifth of it to the public as a patriotic British Ministry once did when the country needed more ships and men. So we dislike personal references to this liberal because he is rich, or that radical because, despite his programme, he dines with a duke when he can. But there are exceptions, and we must say that Mr. Pretyman was justified the other day in admiring the wise investments of Mr. Ure. Down with the land interest, down with unearned increment, exclaims Mr. Ure—and buys a great lump of Clydesdale Bank shares which go up enormously in value; a splendid case of increment 'unearned'" and yet untaxed!

One always does so much admire the wise and happy politician whose broad and generous public faith is perfectly united with a wise employment and enjoyment of the good things which, as Mr. Snowden has declared, "make life worth living". He reminds one of the adroit man who is able at once to run the spiritual and the carnal side of things, a sort of clever circus performance, one foot on the pure white horse of the soul, the other on the dappled beast of the world.

The Radical and Unionist Commission has drawn up its report on the Atholl Deer Forest. This forest is owned by one of the dukes who so cruelly monopolise land for sport, and prevent the making of happy, smiling small-holders etc. And what does this unanimous report show? Why, that the land is utterly unfit for small holdings and utterly unfit for afforestation, and that, as a fact, the Duke employs more men by keeping it a deer forest than if he turned it into sheep farms. What a blow for the "Daily News" and "Daily Chronicle" enthusiasts—and a blow hit by people of their own political faith too!

Lord Curzon at least has a clear mind on the Land Bill. In his speech on Wednesday he described the Government's congestion scheme and its compulsory contrivances as "an almost inevitable instrument of bribery". That is how the money has gone in the congestion traffic so far, and the Bill would vastly extend the facilities. His next point was that for their millions of purchase-money the British taxpayers had no security but "the economic soundness of the experiment" in Irish land purchase; no security but the "economic soundness" and the economic soundness on a background of bribery. Strong language, but evidently chosen for accuracy. In milder terms, Lord Curzon's view is that of Sir Horace Plunkett, who foresees bankruptcy and repudiation unless the peasant's industrial character can be raised to the level of his increased responsibility. To this education is essential, but all are curiously silent as to education, and so the distressful circle goes round and round.

Lord MacDonnell "replied" to Lord Curzon, and succeeded in confirming him. He did not mention the "bribery", but his method betrays his consciousness of it, and he ought to know. He makes "three suggestions", and every one indicates his distrust of his fellow-countrymen: (1) He would take all land purchase and all the cash connected with it out of the hands of the Congested Districts Board. (2) He would deprive that Board of "all functions in regard to agriculture, fisheries and industries". (3) He would confine what remained of its "functions" to the Board's "present area". Having thus reduced the Board's statutory facilities for bribery to the narrowest limits, he would pass the work on to the Estates Commissioners and the Department of Agriculture—both bodies that are more free from clerical and Nationalist control than the Congested Districts Board could be. Though one of them "replied" to the other, the only difference between our two noblemen is that Lord MacDonnell proposes plans to meet the evils defined by Lord Curzon, but without mentioning them. We deal in a leading article with the attitude of the Lords towards that part of the Bill which they mean to amend radically by improvements that have the approval of the Irish peers in the House.

We should like to know how many new institutions, workable and otherwise, will be added for the tired attention of the citizen when this Government have done inventing theories. The latest is our "Road Board", which was to "carry any of the new roads over or under highways by means of bridges"; but on Wednesday this "over-or-under" scheme was dropped, "the Solicitor-General intimating that the changes made in the Bill had rendered it unnecessary". Lord Robert Cecil again? The withdrawal of Mr. Adkins' amendment leaves the new authority to project its roads without the consent of the existing authorities; and the sub-section proposing "no speed-limit" on the new roads is "unanimously struck out". No matter what this Bill "develops", its own development is rapidly negative.

If Mr. John Redmond had accepted the resolution of the Longford Leaguers, and got his Welsh friends to lift him into the House of Lords, "the boys" would not now be at such a disadvantage regarding the amendments to the Land Bill, which are going to spoil the most pleasantly criminal of the clauses in a place where "the boys" may not challenge the Prime Minister to a boxing match. It is another injustice to "the cause" that the Irish party, unlike the Tories and Liberals, have no representatives in the Upper House; and to an experienced conscience the oath is no greater strain than the oath for the Lower House, though it is understood that the top brand of patriot may enter the Commons only. To meet the financial slump in "the cause" the management is just now "starring" a special "draw" in the person of a seasoned martyr, Mr. O'Meagher Condon, of the American Molly Maguires; and when the touring season is over, something will have to be done for him in the way of a "benefit" performance. While Mr. Birrell and Cardinal Logue are still in charge, why not meet the double difficulty by getting Mr. O'Meagher Condon a seat in the Lords, with a special privilege to carry a revolver during debates? It would enable "the boys" to have themselves represented in "another place", and without directly compromising their integrity as patriots.

A certain amount of pained outcry against the "forcible" feeding of the suffragette prisoners at Birmingham was, of course, only to be expected. The interested partisan is making as much capital out of the situation as possible, and doing all he can to work upon the finer feelings of the amiable spectator. No one can deny to the individual the luxury of sentiment; but a Government, whatever else it may be, may not be sentimental. The responsibility of having created the situation does not rest with the Home Secretary, and it is absurd to expect him to compound a felony. Moreover, sympathy, this week, is out of place. The Suffragette goes to prison as a protest against an iniquitous law. She desires martyrdom, because it is part of her campaign to be a martyr. She has succeeded now beyond her wildest hopes. If the amiable spectator would think a little before indulging his finer feelings, he might perhaps end by hardening his heart.

The sly picketing of post-offices, with a view to buttonholing the aged pensioners who come to apply for their allowance, and informing them confidentially that the rejection of the Budget means the stoppage of supplies, is a kind of electioneering which we do not look for in this country. Rather, we expect the shouted lie such as that about Chinese slaves. If, as seems only too probable, certain Radicals have been going in for this sort of thing, it is to be hoped that the men in authority will take steps to wipe away a very dirty stain from the Liberal shield. That shield, Heaven knows, is already enough disfigured by a blot that no amount of cleaning can efface. Mr. Balfour has not forgotten about Chinese labour. He did well to mention the fact in a letter the other day.

"It is remarkable that there does not seem to be any demand for small freeholds in England and Wales", says Mr. Edwin S. Montagu in the "Times" in connexion with Mr. Balfour's speech and small holdings. It would be far more remarkable if there were any such demand, since the Government promises confiscation for such investments. Besides, the small holder is concerned with the production of the soil rather than with the possession of it, which is to him a smaller matter; and he will not put his capital into the smaller gain to leave himself short in settling the greater. No matter what the small holder may gain by buying fee simple to cancel his rent, he expects very much more from using the same capital reproductively in the soil; and then, should he have to remove, as he often must, the greater mobility of his assets makes his investment more convertible and his migration less destructive. However, Mr. Montagu has to defend the Government; and the need makes difficulty, even in the plainest facts.

Mr. Buxton may be congratulated upon an excellent deal. Wireless telegraphy is young, and its possibilities lie all in the future. In a few years it would probably have been necessary to multiply many times the £15,000 for which the Post Office has secured the transfer of the Marconi coast stations and the rights enjoyed in respect of these under the agreement of 1904. There is little doubt that wireless telegraphy will kill the cable. The installation of a cable, even now, costs eight times as much as the installation of a Marconi system over the same distance. The establishment of a private monopoly in the control of a system that has so much history in front of it would have been little short of disastrous. Meanwhile the purchase has a deep national significance. The Admiralty has throughout been kept informed of the proceedings. Wireless telegraphy is one of the great strategic factors in future operations.

There was a general waking-up to a national shortcoming in the House of Lords last Monday, when the report of the Treasury Committee upon the organisation of Oriental studies was considered. Great Britain, more in contact with the East than any other country, and weighted with a high responsibility in her intercourse with its peoples, has made next to no provision towards enabling her officers, civil servants, and traders to speak to the East in the tongues of the East, and, by sympathetic study of Eastern history and literature, to bridge the gulf that separates two antithetic civilisations. Material advantage alone would make it worth while to do something. The German trader sends out his invoices into Mesopotamia, and round the Persian Gulf, in Arabic or Hindustanee. British firms use English or French. But moral necessity transcends material advantage; and moral necessity there is for a nation that has taken up the task of bringing East and West together throughout the vast tract of the Indian Empire to look carefully to this matter. Lord Morley and Lord Curzon could not fail to be at one here with every Britisher, however little the England for which he stands. The sum required, an odd £12,000, must be had at once. We are behindhand enough as it is.

The first effects of preference on British goods in Australia have been precisely what they were in Canada. British trade with the Commonwealth compared with foreign was unprogressive; it was declining relatively if not actually. For four years the percentage record was steadily against the mother-country. In 1908 preference came into force and affected imports to the value of £26,000,000. The decline was at once arrested, and the result of one year's experience has not merely been a substantial gain to the British trader but given him a new opportunity of which he has not yet taken full advantage. The Australian Minister for Trade and Customs disclaims any desire to suggest a fiscal policy to Great Britain, but the figures he has just published clearly convey to him the moral which they will convey to all on this side who are not slaves to theory.

The super-Dreadnought "Helgoland" was launched at Kiel last Saturday, and the second vessel of this type followed her into the water on Thursday. "Super-Dreadnought" is an alarmist term employed in certain newspapers. There is really no occasion for concern. A ship of the improved German type is of about the same displacement as an English Dreadnought, and it carries the twelve-inch gun. It is noticeable that the launching of the "Helgoland" was made the occasion for a protest against navy expansion by the "Berliner Tageblatt". Well, Herr von Holstein has prophesied a reaction against navy fever, and has pointed to the time when a German who preaches economy will not be regarded as wanting in patriotism.

At the meeting of the Hungarian Chambers on 27 September Dr. Wekerle announced the resignation of his Cabinet. This has been pending for some time, as he only consented to retain office after tendering his resignation last July on condition that he should be replaced when the Chambers reassembled. The difficulties in the way of finding a successor are considerable. It appears to be certain that M. Kossuth, the leader of the Independent party, will be sent for, though his appointment as Prime Minister would be bitterly resented by the strict Catholics. As the Independent party has an actual majority, it seems only consistent with parliamentary usage that their leader should succeed to power and settle outstanding questions in accordance with their views. The Andrassy group, however, wish to settle these questions and to form a new majority constructed on the basis of the compromise of 1867.

It would appear, however, as if M. Kossuth were to have his chance, and he will certainly deserve the thanks of both halves of the Monarchy if he finally succeeds in settling the language question in the Hungarian Army. If this be not arranged in accordance with Hungarian ideas it appears very probable that the large credits demanded for military purposes will not be voted. The suffrage question has yet to be put on a satisfactory basis, and it is said that the retiring Cabinet desired to drop the provisions for plural voting and to insure that illiterates not hitherto entitled should have votes in future. It will be curious to see M. Kossuth's attitude on this matter. But the situation in both Austria and Hungary is for the moment dominated by finance, and it is possible that the large programme of naval expansion determined on will have to be curtailed. The settlement of the bill for a spirited foreign policy must react on internal politics.

Spanish successes in Morocco—and General Marina by very smart work is already in possession of Mount Gurugu—have had their effect not merely in Spain but with the croaking quidnuncs who prophesied nothing but evil from the campaign. The Spanish Government have decided on the restoration of the constitutional guarantees everywhere except in Barcelona and Gerona. That is their answer alike to the charges of tyranny and lurid accounts of seditionary unrest. Even in Barcelona the reign of terror is and has been merely imaginative. The gaols are not full of prisoners, and executions in the fortress moat of the Montjuich are not of frequent occurrence. The "Times" correspondent says public confidence is quite restored and business goes on as usual. Tourists flocked to the city during August, and an Esperanto Congress, attended by 1200 foreigners, was held in September. The Spanish Government and the Spanish Army have both given the lie most effectually to their detractors.

Aeroplanes are so much more interesting than dirigibles that they tend to thrust them into the background. The disaster to the "République", however, brings the dirigible into horrible prominence this week. It is a vessel of the flexible and unicellular type, and the tearing of the envelope meant immediate disaster. "Zeppelin III.", whose tedious performances and petty accidents have been sporadically recorded in the daily papers for the last month, seems at last to have justified the principles upon which it is constructed. The rigidity of the envelope prevents it from an easy tear, and the division of its gas-chambers makes such a tear when it occurs comparatively harmless. But the future is with the aeroplane. On the face of it, it looks safer and easier to ride in a balloon than to drive a machine heavier than air. But, remembering that the balloon is many years older than the aeroplane, it is only necessary to contrast Mr. Wilbur Wright's performance at the Hudson-Fulton celebration this week with the ignominious displays of Mr. Baldwin and Mr. Tomlinson to realise that the aeroplane is the safer horse.

Coincidence could hardly be more fortunate than in the Hudson-Fulton celebration this week. Henry Hudson gave his name to the river on which Fulton made his first successful experiment in steam navigation, and Fulton may fitly be regarded as the connecting-link between the voyageurs of the early seventeenth century and those of the early twentieth. Fulton's "Clermont" was as big a step in advance of Hudson's "Half Moon" as the "Lusitania" is in advance of the "Clermont". The spectacle of the replicas of these two pioneer craft on the Hudson to-day making a bravely picturesque but hopelessly ineffectual show in the midst of the modern leviathans has been among the most curiously realistic things in pageants. And as though to illustrate the difficulties the ancient mariner had to encounter, even with the aid of Fulton's invention, the ungainly little steamer of 1809 very nearly succeeded in sending the "Half Moon" to the bottom in the efforts of both to move along the river.

It was with a kind of dreary consternation that we contemplated every likelihood of an indefinite extension of the Peary-Cook squabble. Mr. Whitney's arrival with Dr. Cook's evidence was to have settled everything. Mr. Whitney has arrived, but the evidence has not. It seems that Commander Peary with very proper spirit refused to carry coals for Dr. Cook. He was not going to have that person's property brought along in the Roosevelt. Accordingly, the evidence is still derelict in a cache at Etah. Of course, Commander Peary did not imagine for a moment that it was evidence he was having left behind. He took it for luggage merely. Commander Peary is an honourable man: so are they all. But it is very unfortunate. We are tired of it all. We almost wish that we were back in the Middle Ages, and that we might have the matter settled by wager of battle. Let them prove something or other upon one another's bodies, and have done with it.

THE POLITICAL SITUATION.

It is now generally agreed that the General Election cannot take place before January. The excitable editors and impatient candidates who predicted a dissolution in November overlooked the prosaic facts of the situation, which are that a good many Bills of first-rate importance still remain in a far from finished state. There is the Irish Land Bill, which though it has passed second reading will be subjected to a vigorous alteration in the Committee of the House of Lords. There are the Town Planning Bill and the Development Bill, both of which will be drastically amended. The Government have no intention of dropping these Bills, and before the final stage, when the House of Commons is called upon to agree or disagree with the Lords' amendments, many weeks must elapse. The Finance Bill cannot very well come on for second reading in the House of Lords before the third week in October. So that the necessary business of Parliament cannot possibly be wound up before the middle of November. The mere issue of the writs takes some days; and we gather from the newspapers that a good many Liberal members are not going to seek re-election, and that consequently candidates are still to seek. A dissolution this year would come perilously near Christmas, and for various reasons a General Election in December would not be popular. It is also probable that as the moment for the plunge approaches the members of the Government in a very human way desire to put it off. Last, but by no means least, every Prime Minister requires a certain interval before a General Election in which to look round and provide for some of his friends. There are always a great many supporters of a party hungry for reward. The rich want peerages, or at least baronetcies. The poor want billets, in the shape of permanent appointments, county court judgeships, commissionerships, and so forth. Mr. Asquith will have an unusual number of commissionerships to dispose of, for his Development, Town Planning, and Finance Acts all call for the appointment of an army of Government officials, and in his majority of three hundred and fifty there must be many gaping mouths. Mr. Balfour always showed himself unsympathetic towards these "claims upon the party", and we fear that he did not by his Olympian indifference to the struggle-for-lifers contribute to the solidarity of his party. The hounds must be fed as well as halloed on by their whips.

But will there be an election in January? And does this depend on the rejection of the Budget by the House of Lords? And will the House of Lords reject the Budget? These are the questions which politicians feverishly discuss in their clubs, without arriving at any solution. It has to be admitted that the Conservatives are divided in their opinions. The majority are in favour of the rejection of the Finance Bill by the Lords on second reading, but some are against taking the admitted risk of such a step. These doubters and waverers shake their heads and ask, Is it worth while to risk the existence of the House of Lords upon a Budget which is bound to be popular with those who have no property? They argue that the evil results of the Budget, its inquisitorial character, its unfruitfulness, its injury to property and consequently to employment, will not be believed until they are felt by the masses. The issue will be put by the Socialists to the country thus: Will you have the Budget or the Lords? And, plead the waverers, there can be but one answer to that question. The stalwarts reply that the Unionists will put the issue thus: Will you have the Budget and no Second Chamber, or will you have Tariff Reform and a Second Chamber? And to that alternative, urge the stalwarts, there can be but one answer.

The key of the situation is in the hands of Lord Lansdowne, and his responsibility is very great. Now, Lord Lansdowne sometimes does quite unexpected things. On Tuesday, for instance, he declined to support Lord Dunraven's amendment for the rejection of the second reading of the Irish Land Bill, saying that he would amend it in Committee, and only if the Government refused to be reasonable in the matter of amendments would he consider the question of rejection on third reading. Suppose he takes some similar course on the Finance Bill? Suppose, that is, he advised the Lords, instead of rejecting the Finance Bill on second reading, to draw up a reasoned statement of objections to "tacking", and to invite the Government to listen to reason in a conference of the two Houses. What then? If the Government refused a conference they would certainly be in a worse position than before. There are a certain number of peers who proclaim their intention to vote against the second reading of the Budget, give what advice Lord Lansdowne pleases. These peers contend—and they are warmly supported in their contention by their friends in the House of Commons—that if they pass this Budget they will be false to the trust reposed in them by the Constitution, and that they will then have no reason for existing.

It remains to consider the probable course of the Government. There are some who maintain that the Government will not dissolve even if the Budget is rejected, and some who aver that they will dissolve even if the Budget is passed. It is worth remembering that the Prime Minister has said many times that the House of Lords must not and will not be allowed to dictate the time of a dissolution. Obviously the money must be obtained, but as the land taxes will bring in less than nothing they could be dropped without causing any financial derangement. The House of Lords is not likely to reject the Finance Bill "sans phrase"; there will probably be a demand for a conference, or a statement of objections; a golden bridge will be built for the Government to retreat, if they wish to do so. All depends on whether the Government desire to go on or to dissolve. If the Government wish to go on, some means or other will be found of patching up the business. But does the Government wish to go on? Some people say that the Government are so anxious to get a new mandate that even if the Lords pass the Budget they will go to the country in January. On this subject the Cabinet is likely to be divided. We can well understand that Mr. Lloyd George, the most powerful member of the Government, wants a dissolution. The Chancellor of the Exchequer is at the top of his wave; he can only sink into the trough of waters from this date, and as it is more than likely that he will be seriously out of his reckoning at the end of the financial year, he may sink rapidly. Besides, Mr. Asquith and he have pledged next session to the Welsh Disestablishment Bill, which excites no enthusiasm and will be thrown out by the Lords. All these promises and disappointments will be buried under a General Election. On the other hand, Mr. Winston Churchill, the next most powerful member of the Government, must be feverishly anxious for another session of official life, because next session will be his crowning opportunity. The Bill to provide insurance against sickness and unemployment will be in charge of the President of the Board of Trade, and may be even more popular than the Budget. With Mr. Churchill will be all the members of the Cabinet who wish to remain where they are. This party will be very strong, must always be so in every Cabinet. As we said above, if the Government are determined to have another year's existence, they can and will manage it somehow, even if the Budget be thrown out. If, however, as gossip says, Mr. Lloyd George is master of the situation, there will be an election in January or February.

THE LORDS AND THE IRISH LAND BILL.

WE venture to think that the second reading debate in the House of Lords upon the Irish Land Bill will occupy a high place in the annals of the British Parliament. We do not mean that the debate was adorned with oratory that will live or with argument that was strikingly new either in its essence or in its presentation. It was notable rather for the calm, businesslike and reasoned criticism of what was the chief measure of the session after the Budget, and for the courageous declaration that the Bill would be radically amended in the public interest. In the public interest we say advisedly. Reading the debate as a whole, what stands out is the prominence given to that part of the Bill which least concerns those whose interests are commonly supposed to dominate the Upper Chamber in its dealings with property in land. The Bill emerges from the first real discussion of its principle with an entirely new perspective. What was the background is now the foreground. What was regarded as a three-cornered fight between the British taxpayer, the Irish tenants, and the Irish landlords is now to be discussed in its bearings upon economic development and social progress in Ireland. And the British interest in the Irish Bill is not confined to the financial risks it imposes upon the general taxpayer. The issues upon which the Lords have fastened go to the root of problems just now affecting other parts of the United Kingdom. Parliament has an Irish question every year; but the Irish question of the present session, putting aside the husbanding of eighty-five precious Irish votes, is essentially the same as its English analogue—how to make small holdings pay.

In order to make our position clear, it will be necessary to state certain facts which are known to all who are familiar with the land situation in Ireland and with recent legislation affecting it. We believe that, as the result of the Lords' debate, many people, including members of Parliament who have never taken any interest in the Irish land question, will now be moved to do so; and therefore we must ask those of our readers to whom what we must now say will be stale to pardon the repetition.

The Government had no option but to introduce a Bill to meet an urgent case. The policy of land purchase in Ireland was no party policy; it was a matter of common agreement. The Wyndham scheme agreed to by all parties in 1903 had come to a standstill. The amount of property to be dealt with, and consequently the amount of money required to finance the operation, appear to have been seriously under-estimated; nor was it contemplated that landlord and tenant would almost rush into each other's arms in order to avail themselves of the new opportunity which Parliament had afforded. The plan for financing the transfer of the land consisted roughly of raising money by means of a new stock. The landlord was to be paid in cash, and whatever loss in flotation might occur from the stock not realising its face value was to be made good out of certain funds which had previously been earmarked for various other Irish purposes. The taxpayer was not to be called upon to make good any part of the deficiency, for already under this scheme he had contributed twelve millions which was to be given as a bonus to bridge over the gap between what the landlord could afford to take and the tenant to pay for the land. The basis of settlement was liberal, and was generally so regarded. But it fell upon evil days. Owing to its success in composing the difference between the two parties to an agrarian conflict centuries old, money was needed at an earlier date than was anticipated. Then it was discovered that the transaction was much larger than had been contemplated in 1903, and owing to changes in the money market the larger amount required could not be obtained at an early date without a much greater loss than was provided for in the Wyndham scheme. Therefore the Government had to readjust the Wyndham financial arrangements, and no objection could be taken to any reasonable proposal under which the general taxpayer and each of the two parties directly concerned should share proportionately in the sacrifice which must be made in order to meet the untoward circumstances above indicated.

The proposals of the Government for overcoming this difficulty could not have been expected to satisfy the three parties to whom they relate—the taxpayers, the landlords and the tenants—and we do not intend to discuss them here in detail. The controversy that has arisen over them has centred mainly round four points: (1) the proposed payment in a depreciated stock instead of in cash; (2) the substitution of compulsory for voluntary purchase; (3) the readjustment of the bonus; and (4) the proposed abolition of the zones, the maximum and minimum limits of price between which no question of value could be raised if the parties agreed to buy and sell. Although the Lords may not think it proper to take any action with regard to the finance of the Bill, it is probable that the last word has not been said upon it. It is whispered that the Government have up their sleeves an offer which will be tempting at least to the embarrassed landlords, and which will be conditional upon the acceptance of certain portions of the Bill to which the Irish Parliamentary party attach special importance. Nor is it unlikely that the Government would be glad of a compromise by which compulsion would be restricted to the acquisition of land needed for the relief of congestion. The abolition of the zones is justified on the ground that the system led to certain abuses; and it is thought that by amendment abuse can be prevented in the somewhat rare cases in which it appears to have existed. As regards the bonus, there are such obvious objections to the Government's proposal to vary it in inverse proportion to the price agreed to between landlord and tenant that it is not improbable the uniform rate may be restored.

So far then as the Government are genuinely desirous of expediting land purchase in Ireland, we too must recognise that they are confronted with difficulties not of their own making. If they on their part realise that the situation is one for compromise, we are sure the House of Lords will meet them in a conciliatory spirit. But unhappily the Bill contains (in Part III.) provisions which go far beyond the necessities of the case. Land purchase on a huge scale at the expense and risk of the taxpayer is a costly means to a great end. It is only justified if accompanied by such Government action as is required to foster the industry of the class to which the chief source of the nation's wealth is entrusted. This point of view was put by Sir Horace Plunkett in an essay* which we have before us as we write, and which we commend to our readers. "There can", he writes, "be no turning back. In a not remote future some two hundred millions sterling of imperial funds will have been invested in the latest final settlement of the Irish land question. Is that investment secure? My belief is that the investment is secure, and the moderate prosperity of the Irish peasantry assured, if, and only if, the peasants are induced to put more capital, more skilled work and better business methods into the industry of farming. . . . The statesman who is to solve the Irish land question must recognise that the most skilful handling of the financial complications, the most complete satisfaction of the two interests immediately concerned, will be no solution of the real problem; that whether we are to be blessed with a settlement or cursed by the continuance of agrarian strife depends upon the economic soundness and the moral effect of the agrarian revolution to which history has given the impulse and Parliament is giving the direction."

The direction given by Parliament up to the present time may be briefly summarised. During the last twenty years there has been added to the machinery of government in Ireland a Department of Agriculture and Technical Instruction, for giving to the Irish farmer 'those forms of assistance which every progressive Government considers necessary for the welfare of the farming community, especially where the holdings are small. Furthermore, a voluntary movement has developed a system of agricultural co-operation far in advance of any similar efforts in Great Britain. The Government have ignored these facts. Under influences quite well understood by all who have any knowledge of recent events in Ireland, influences stoutly resisted by Mr. Bryce, but allowed by his successor to predominate, they have tacked on to Irish land purchase an administrative machinery for which there is no precedent in the history of civilised countries. In the House of Commons no time was allowed for the discussion of the extraordinary and far-reaching proposals of Part III. Lords Lansdowne, Curzon and Dunraven simply riddled them, while Lord MacDonnell, who had already in his remarkable "Minute of Dissent" from the Dudley Commission's recommendations blown them to atoms, foreshadowed radical amendments. But the spokesmen of the Government, especially the Lord Chancellor, treated them as mere matters of detail for discussion only in Committee.

* "The Unsettlement of the Irish Land Question." By Sir Horace Plunkett. Dublin (E. Ponsonby) and London (Simpkin, Marshall), 1909. Price 6d. The pamphlet is reproduced with additions from "The Nineteenth Century" for June.

The precise method of the Government for satisfying their Irish dictators is plausible, but will not stand for a moment under the close examination to which it is to be subjected in the Lords. Before the new system of agricultural development (based upon organised self-help on its non-official side and upon local contribution and administration as a condition of assistance from public funds on its Governmental side) was under way, the Congested Districts Board was founded by Mr. Arthur Balfour in 1891. For eighteen years it has exercised paternal sway over the economy of poor western districts, its most important work being in the purchase and sale with improvements of estates and the development of fisheries. The Board was a temporary expedient and should gradually be restricted in function and area. The Government say it has done such good work and is so popular that it must be preserved. Then they proceed to abolish it utterly, retaining nothing but its name. This entirely new creation is given twice the area, three times the funds its predecessor controlled. It is to buy compulsorily what land it wants and to distribute it as it likes—the whole operation to be independent of the Government, which had hitherto recognised some responsibility where such powers were exercised and the general taxpayer was footing the bill. The constitution of this body is, however, altogether popular. Seven out of its nineteen members are to be appointed by the Government, presumably under the influences which dictated the measure itself, and nine are to be elected by the western County Councils. The justification for this extraordinary proposal is that in the coming redistribution of "grazing ranches" the poor "congests" will not get their share. The sons of farmers in the neighbourhood—"the landless men"—will get the preference. A body thus constituted can be trusted to save the manless land from being grabbed by the landless man.

It cannot be too clearly understood that in saving the country from these preposterous proposals which have been rushed through the House of Commons, the Second Chamber is fulfilling its highest purpose. Not only will its members be disinterested in the action they are called upon to take, but it is common knowledge that they can get valuable concessions on those parts of the Bill in which they are financially concerned if they will not "mangle" the part which concerns not them but only their country. And they have to make their decision at a time when every demagogue in the country is seeking to bring them into conflict with the representative Chamber. The coming week will provide one test of the Constitution as it stands. Problems of vast importance to the rural population in all parts of the United Kingdom are pressing for solution. The principles underlying the working out of the agrarian revolution in Ireland are applicable elsewhere. We look to the House of Lords, who know the conditions, to show that they also possess the true statesmanship which is needed for their treatment.

HENS, GOATS AND SMALL HOLDINGS.

IT is unfortunate that we have no inclusive and accurate information as to the progress and profit of the small-holdings movement in this country. The thing is of the livest interest and importance just now, as Mr. Balfour's remarks at Birmingham suggest. It seems we are to go into the General Election, at which small holdings are sure to be an issue in many constituencies—and yet the country is in the dark about small holdings! What we know definitely is that there are small holdings, that they have increased in number, that they are often a mere hobby, that they are not often the sole source of a family income on a fair standard of living, that their success depends in an essential way on postulates not easily assured, such as co-operation, with special facilities in banking; and that they afford an attractive subject for popular oratory by knowing politicians who have never done any farming, small or large. Judging by the oratory, small farming appears to be highly commendable to everybody but the man who commends it.

At first the small holding is a sweet Arcadia, a pocket edition of the pioneers' epic, combining the beauties of both solitude and civilisation, not too near a slum and not too far from London; and this, assuming faith and courage, is kept up for a few years, after which the oviduct of the hen that ought to be laying is found to have its executive capacity in some mysterious way discouraged by " a clay soil ", with a doubt that it may be something else, as in the instance of Mr. F. A. Morton, who, after " winning a living on four acres ", discovered that " My profits have decreased as the number of the hens increased ". In other words, the process of diminishing return has set in. We must investigate the relations of the " clay soil " to the refractory oviduct, and the first economic fly is in the Arcadian cream. It is well now if the four acres be a hobby, with an income from elsewhere to take up the tale where the family hen has dropped it; but in Mr. Morton's case there is no such irrelevant source of continuity, and so the " living " which he wins becomes a little trying, " exasperated by the problem of getting mature birds to lay ". It is an ancient problem, this of making birds lay more eggs, and reveals its economic limits on four acres, on which a living demands more intensive production than that of a laying hen who refuses to lay.

Then regarding the style and manner of the " living " : " To rise on a winter morning, to light the fire and heat the food for the fowls, to read one's newspapers and letters, feed the fowls and goats . . . . ; then to eat one's breakfast, after preparing it; afterwards to dig a little, and again feed the fowls and goats; to scramble over the preparations of dinner; more digging or similar work, and then finally to house the fowls and goats for the night, and retire to eat one's dinner, which not improbably has got a little bit burnt ". All the time it is a " living " only for one on the four acres, and there is no woman. Add woman, and we want four acres more, eight acres for two. The addition of woman suggests the addition of more, one, two, three, perhaps nine, each wanting its four acres, forty-four acres in all, at which point the small holding ideal is obviously shattered, and the small holder has his dimensions automatically multiplied into ordinary farming. The disaster arises even less from the " clay soil " than from the addition of woman, and yet it is not easy to see how a progressive community can proceed without woman, either back to the land or in any other direction. Without her, civilisation is really stopped, and the dinner is " not improbably burnt "; but with her, the potential increase in the number of necessary dinners expands elevenfold beyond the economic boundaries of the small holding.

The behaviour of Mr. Morton's goats is not less gravely instructive than that of his hens. Having dropped goats, he changed his mind and started again, with a reputed matron possibly of Anglo-Toggenburg lineage, " due to kid in about a week's time ", and with satisfactory conviction supporting her reputation by her appearance; but after " digital examination " and a length of time, all this marketable motherhood turned out to be merely the inflation of excessive age, and the mountain could not produce even a mouse. Our small holder bought another goat, chancing that her character might be more worthy of her reputation, and he complained of the first to " the vendor ", who now sent a third; so that he had three wrong goats to feed in place of one right goat. While some of them declined to kid, others kidded beyond all sane calculations, so that before the goat farmer knew where he was he found himself with about a dozen, big and small, male and female, with milk and mainly without it. Indeed, there was among them all only one goat that could conceivably approximate to his agricultural anticipations, and she had " a difficulty in satisfying the demands of her surviving kid ". The gravity of the enterprise lies in its contribution to our national salvation. All this important information, with much more, is found in Mr. Morton's excellent book " Winning a Living on Four Acres ", a true and faithful history of the enterprise, which, however, leaves some questions unanswered as to how a progressive community can be raised on the economic basis of small holdings.

That is not the only expert book on the subject which suggests essential questions as yet unanswered. In his " Small Holders " Mr. Edwin A. Pratt makes a similarly constructive confession of failure, exactly as if he, too, had passed personally through the various stages of practical experience, in hens, oviducts, " clay soils ", goats, kids and old-age inflations. His " Prefatory Note " starts: " The main purposes of the present volume are to urge the need of co-operation on the part of small holders, if their production of commodities for sale . . . . is to be a commercial success "; and in this essential need he appears to include co-operative finance. Very well, but British individualism is very slow to co-operate at agriculture, either in method or in finance, and the farming experience of the great Co-operative Wholesale Society itself does not seem to reveal any very tempting outlook for capital. There may be some examples of real success in small farming, on a basis affording the presence of woman and the progress of man; but there is no evidence of it yet, and, on the other hand, we have Mr. Boyd of Dumbarton, un-co-operated, growing potatoes by the thousand acres at profits that enable him to drive in a motor-car. Since the productiveness of the soil is the real question, which is the better outlook, the vagaries of Mr. Morton's goats or the profits of Mr. Boyd's potatoes?

Nature herself is prodigal in her empiricism, and these experimental shots among eggless hens and superannuated goats may yet get a bull's-eye somewhere. An extremely interesting scheme, founded on a thought-out system, has just been started in Kent, at " May's Farm ", by " The Residential Small Holdings Company, Limited ", with a capital of £2000 and forty acres. Here the main idea is permanence in tenure and elasticity in the farm area to accommodate the needs of man as varied by woman. Should man insist on agrarian monasticism and inflated goats, he may have his four acres, but the normal man may have something like four acres for each of his family. The tenant may never be disturbed so long as he pays the rent, which can never be raised, so that all agricultural increment values belong to the tenant, who may also sublet, but on the same terms as he gets himself from the head man. Thus in addition to his yearly produce the tenant is rewarded by owning all increment values from direct enterprise on the farm, and the head man has such increment as arises in the selling value of his fee simple. The transfer is already complete, and the company is about to begin building. The whole scheme arises out of a book, " The Redemption of Labour "; an attempt among the readers and students of the plan to put it into practice, with means to finance its extension as fast as the newly created tenancies succeed and induce others to be created. From the outline before us, it appears that the underlying principle is the increased application of productive capital and industrial energy to the soil, combining the utmost industrial motive with the utmost elasticity in accommodation, so that the man with a mind large enough for fifty acres may not be shut out by regulations for the man of four. In many ways the plan is like the dual ownership that has proved so disastrous in Ireland, but then it may be hardly safe to compare a people so completely devoted to fitting themselves for success in another world only. The men of Kent still keep a healthy grip on this world in spite of the static wisdom which works to clear them from the land and to starve them in the slums.

THE PASSING OF THE AUSTRIAN DREADNOUGHTS.

THERE is one fact in the relations of Germany and Great Britain which cannot be over-emphasised— the existence throughout the German middle class of an alarm about the navy equal to our own. True, the German well knows that we could not injure him by land; but his commerce has so far increased in value that he fears for his entire mercantile marine. The existence of a powerful fleet, he is sure, is essential to the life of the German nation. So far, so good. Great Britain does not grudge the Kaiser his ships. But Germany, whilst she has declared her intention of taking such steps as shall free her from being "at the mercy of England" (this phrase has been used by German publicists again and again), has never pretended to be able to build or maintain an effective fleet of anything like the size of that which Great Britain must possess. She has, on the other hand, aimed at building so strong a fleet that with any sort of ally in Europe she could make the two-Power standard impossible for us to maintain; and thus she looked forward to bringing about a condition of equilibrium in sea-power—a situation from which neither side dare stir.

This was the policy dictated by those circumstances in which she found herself placed during and immediately after the Boer War. And a brief survey of recent history will make this plain. She learnt, as we have pointed out lately, that her mercantile marine lacked protection. Damage done to her commerce, during a war in which she herself was not engaged, enabled her to form some estimate of Great Britain's power as a belligerent—a power against which her huge land forces could not hope to prevail. Her relations with other States were far from satisfactory. Few statesmen believed in the permanence of the Austro-Hungarian Empire, and Italy seemed to be drifting from her Teuton allies. Germany's first effort, therefore, was to improve her position in Europe. She was met by a rapprochement between England and France. Spain became of the party, and Russia was soon to go the same way. It therefore became a matter of extreme urgency for her to bring about, with the few materials at her disposal, that balance of power in Europe to which all Continental statesmen have looked as the only guarantee of peace. But since England, by her recent alliances, had somewhat thrust herself into European affairs, these calculations were forced to concern themselves with the production of such weapons as were best fitted to cope with the distinctive armament of England. It was therefore plain that no ally could be of permanent service to Germany who could not be induced to adopt the rôle of a Mediterranean sea Power equal, at the least, to the task of destroying the ordinary British fleet in those waters. The Dual Monarchy had aspirations of which the aims of Germany permitted her to approve. The determination mutually to support one another, irrespective of the attitude of Italy, constituted a pact which is now some years old. The Dual Monarchy was at first obliged to devote her energies to strengthening and improving her army. But it is not impossible that the arrival in England some five years ago of Austrian naval officers on an errand connected with the examination of the turbine form of marine engine may be referable to a realisation of the necessity of taking early steps towards naval efficiency. We happen to know that at the time such comment as was evoked in circles cognisant of the mission took the form of surprise that the British Admiralty should be so slow to use what quite a small Power thought worth considering.

The weakening of Russia consequent upon the war with Japan made the task of realising Austrian aspirations apparently easy. But the history of the Bosnian coup has yet to be written. That the Turkish revolution precipitated events we know; but how far the method adopted by Austria was a departure from the preconceived arrangement we can only guess.

Up to this time the consolidation of the Austro-German understanding (an understanding evidently quite independent of the terms of the Triple Alliance) had proceeded without a hitch. Germany had already embarked upon an ambitious naval programme; she had contrived to make her power felt at Constantinople and at Algeciras, always with the support of Austria; and although the Bosnian coup d'état was destined from the first to prove a most expensive move in the game, one which could not fail to check the immediate development of her plans, Germany stood loyally to her ally. Apparently all Europe could not prevail against this combination. And the fact that Germany, directly a settlement had been reached between Austria and Turkey, went on with her naval programme with unabated vigour plainly indicated a strong desire to obtain as much headway as possible before the inevitable disclosures of financial incompetence should have to be made. In spite of figures which have since come to light, the Austrian press was actually permitted to talk of building sixteen Dreadnoughts! It is possible that Germany did not know the extent to which Austria was financially involved through the Balkan imbroglio. For herself, she hoped up to the last to be able to impose new and important taxes. But it was precisely over this question that Prince Bülow fell; and, with the appointment of Dr. von Bethmann-Hollwegg, a new phase in the diplomatic struggle between Briton and Teuton began.

The incoming Chancellor is forced to approach the situation from a very different standpoint from that which it appeared prudent for Prince Bülow to adopt. First, it is plain that no material increase in the German naval programme can be attempted, nor the acceleration of the present one be long maintained, without taxation which it appears improbable that the German people will tolerate. Secondly, the patriotism manifested by the British Colonies in offering one or two Dreadnoughts has taken definite shape in the adoption of a comprehensive scheme for imperial defence by sea and land.

Dr. von Bethmann-Hollwegg has not been slow to assume a more friendly bearing towards England than his predecessor had adopted. Indeed, that particular newspaper which is said to derive its information from the present Chancellor, so far from declining to discuss the limitation of armaments—which earlier in the year had been the official attitude of the Wilhelmstrasse—expressed itself sympathetically as to the project, though, to be sure, it maintained, as all good Germans should, that the necessary overtures must come from England. During the whole of the past month the press of Germany was charged with numerous articles devoted to this question. More than one writer of distinction accused the Government of embarking upon a scheme in which the nation will shortly be unable to persist. Meanwhile the Chancellor went to Vienna. He arrived in time to get first-hand evidence of the disgust of Austrians and Hungarians alike when they awoke to the terrible financial burdens with which their Balkan policy had saddled them. After deducting from revenue the Turkish indemnity and the cost of mobilisation, the two countries were asked to find a sum approaching thirty-two millions sterling. The army was to enjoy an increase of four millions, and provision was to be made for the building of Dreadnoughts, fast cruisers and all the necessary supports of a big fleet. The Vienna correspondent of the "Times" was of opinion that the building of two Dreadnoughts, two fast cruisers and six torpedo-boats was "likely to be dropped, if indeed it were found possible to find a place in next year's estimates for any Dreadnought at all". It is not surprising that a Cabinet crisis was precipitated in Buda-Pesth by the announcement of the programme and estimates for 1910. The kingdom of Hungary and the empire of Austria, so wonderfully united in the spoliation of Turkey, are now quarrelling over paying the bill; whilst the latest news is to the effect that "in order to facilitate a settlement, the military and naval authorities may postpone their demands for extraordinary credits". In any event the plan for providing an Austrian fleet capable of destroying or even materially harassing the English and French fleets in the Mediterranean is for the time being hopelessly wrecked. Without that support in the Mediterranean which an Austrian fleet is alone capable of yielding, Germany could hardly hope to attain to equality with Great Britain at sea.

Events have proved too strong for the Teuton alliance, and the present Chancellor, a man whose political life has been devoted chiefly to the consideration of domestic problems, will, it is hoped, be ready to see in the failure of his predecessor's scheme an opportunity for the peaceful development of his country's resources, an undertaking which need never prejudice a cordial understanding between that country and Great Britain.

THE CITY.

THERE has been no improvement in the money position during the week, and each day brings us nearer to a rise in the Bank rate. Two million sovereigns have been taken for Egypt and South America, and all the gold in the open market—also nearly a million sterling—has been bought for export to Russia. In Paris the market rate of discount has risen to 2½ per cent., in Berlin the rate keeps firm at 3½ per cent., while in Vienna it is as high as 3⅞ per cent. Here the market quotation is only 2⅛ per cent., and while "short" money is so abundant the rate cannot improve, and no advance in the official minimum could bring about a permanent rise. But continued withdrawals of gold from the Bank must deplete floating supplies, and if there is any doubt on this score the Bank directors could take some of the money off the market before advancing their rate. It is certainly advisable that something should be done to check the drain of gold to the Continent, or the position of the Bank will be very weak by the end of the year. As we explained last week, an advance in the official rate would not stop sovereigns going to Egypt and South America, but it would place the Bank in a position to compete for the weekly arrivals of gold from South Africa, and the acquisition of these would go a long way towards filling up the gap caused by the withdrawals. In the Stock Exchange the prospect of dearer money has not so far adversely affected investment securities. On the contrary, there has been a broadening of the investment demand which may or may not be due to the prospect of a change of Government. A noticeable feature has been an inquiry for Consols, which can now be bought to yield a full 3 per cent. They are still over two points above the lowest figure touched since the drop in interest to 2½ per cent., but there were causes other than political for the special weakness of 1907. A yield of 3 per cent. from the premier security of the world must always attract the careful investor, whatever views he may hold of the party in power.

American securities have continued to soar, the most remarkable movement being in Steel Commons, which are now well over 90. This is more than double the price earlier in the year, and compares with 21 in 1907. In 1904 the shares were dealt in at 8. The rise is based on the assumption that the shares are to be put upon a 5 per cent. basis. This, of course, means a permanent basis, but he would be a bold man who placed any reliance upon the dividends of the United States Steel Corporation. Wall Street speculators are working to get the shares to par, and may succeed, but it is just as well that they be left to labour by themselves. A good deal of money continues to find its way into foreign railway securities, and the new issue of Argentine Great Western debenture stock was readily subscribed. There has been a pause in investment in foreign Government securities, and this is probably due to the large number of new issues that are pending. At least half a dozen Brazilian loans are contemplated—mainly provincial. Argentina may indirectly appeal to the market, Turkey still awaits financing, and if the matrimonial schemes of Portugal are successful we may be called upon to assist in the rehabilitation of Portuguese finances. So many of the American railways are handicapped by heavy bond obligations that the issue of 400,000 $5 (£1) shares in the Pacific-Oregon Railway and Navigation Company is noted as an interesting departure. The territory to be served by the line now in course of construction is rich in minerals, timber and agricultural possibilities. All the profits from development will go to the shareholders, and it is estimated the carrying of timber alone will furnish dividends for forty years to come. The latest rubber issue is the East African Rubber Plantation Company Limited, which on Monday will invite subscriptions for £60,000 of its capital. The company has been formed as the result of a Foreign Office Report drawing attention to the development of rubber cultivation in German East Africa. There are, it is said, 600,000 trees in the estate to be tapped next year.

Rhodesian mining shares have remained active, but the buying is still largely professional. Attempts to make a market in a new share—Bucks Reef—have not been very successful, and after rising from 2 to 2⅞ the price has dropped back to 2¼. Little is known regarding the property, except what is supplied by "the shop", and the market resents the introduction and the tactics indulged in to tempt the public to become buyers. Several very doubtful "deals" are in progress in the mining market just now. Thus from a nominal £10 the shares of the Wallis Syndicate have been advanced to £25. Except that the company has an option over properties in West Africa, little is known concerning it. Equally uncertain are the prospects of the West African Development Syndicate, whose £1 shares stand at over £8. The recently issued Brazilian Golden Hill is a very dubious proposition, and those who may be tempted to buy the shares of the Russian Mines and Estate Company would do well to inquire into the antecedents of the promoters. It is incomprehensible why the shares of the recently reconstructed Ashanti and Gold Coast United stand at a premium of 60 per cent., or why the 4s. shares of the Asgard Gold Company should be quoted at 18s. 6d. In all these shares there is a very limited market, but the premiums are maintained because it is thought the public will be led to believe that high prices reflect intrinsic merits.

INSURANCE: POLICIES AT LOW PREMIUMS.

VIII.

WE explained last week that perhaps the best policies at low premiums are deferred assurances for children. The plan is for premiums to be paid until age twenty-one, which are returned if the child dies before coming of age; the full sum assured is paid at death after twenty-one, at which time the policy begins to share in the profits. The advantages of these policies are numerous. For instance, policies can be obtained at a low premium which if effected at older ages would involve a prohibitive cost. If the assurance is effected at birth, subject to the payment of premiums only until age fifty or previous death, the annual premium is £9 15s. a year for with-profit assurance of £1000. A similar policy effected at age thirty would cost £33 14s. 2d. a year, and would receive bonuses that would amount to much less than assurance which began to share in the profits at age twenty-one. If effected at birth a policy for £1000 subject to premiums ceasing at age fifty costs only 10s. a year more than a policy which involves the payment of premiums throughout the whole of life. The difference between the annual premium on policies of the two kinds taken out at age thirty is £9 5s. 10d. The better policy involves a very small increase in the premium when commenced young, but a very great increase if it is not effected until later in life.

Similar considerations apply to endowment assurances. To secure £1000, with profits in addition, at age fifty or at previous death after twenty-one costs £13 14s. 2d. a year. With-profit endowment assurance maturing at age fifty would cost £43 16s. 8d. if commenced at age thirty, or £41 9s. 2d. if started at age twenty-one. Thus policies of a vastly attractive character cost but little if commenced in childhood, but cost inconveniently or prohibitively much if they are not taken out until after manhood is reached.

Life assurance in one form or another is essential for nearly every man and advantageous for a great many women; parents would do well to recognise this fact and to commence policies for their children at the earliest possible moment. There are many circumstances in which it would be more to the advantage of sons and daughters for parents to pay premiums on policies for children than for policies on their own lives. These deferred assurances are frequently of the utmost value for girls, especially if there is a prospect of their having to keep themselves. An annual payment of £18 12s. 6d. from birth until age forty will secure the payment of £1412 in cash when that age is reached; of this amount £412 is derived from bonuses. The sum of £1000, with whatever profits may have accrued, is paid at death at any time after age twenty-one. If a policy of this character were taken out for a girl she would probably be able to pay the premiums out of her income when she commenced working; but if no assurance were started until she began work the amount she could provide for herself would be most inadequate.

These deferred endowment assurance policies can be made payable at any selected age from about thirty-five to sixty-five; the longer the endowment period the smaller is the annual premium and the larger the amount paid at the end of the endowment period. For policies of £1000 effected at birth and maturing at age forty-five the annual premium is £15 15s., to mature at age fifty the premium is £13 14s. 2d., at age fifty-five £12 3s. 4d., and at age sixty £10 19s. 2d.

As the endowment age increases the premiums decrease, and the sum assured, payable at maturity, becomes larger on account of the greater number of bonuses received. By age forty the amount payable would be £1412, by age forty-five £1547, by age fifty £1694, by age fifty-five £1854, and by age sixty £2031. The smaller the annual premium the better are the results for those who survive to the end of the endowment period. It is difficult to emphasise too strongly the attractions and advantages of policies of this kind.

MR. H. B. IRVING IN "THE BELLS".

By Max Beerbohm.

A WAVE of filial piety is passing over the land. It is pleasant to have a wave restoring old landmarks to us, instead of washing them away. On all sides we find that the surviving sons of men who were eminent in their day are determined to perpetuate the fame of their fathers by doing as exactly as possible what their fathers did before them. Mr. Herbert Gladstone (so I learn from one of the permanent officials at the Home Office) spends the greater part of the day in transcribing his father's pamphlets on the Armenian atrocities of 1876, and will proceed to Midlothian, so soon as Parliament is dissolved, in order to stir the electors to a full sense of the iniquity of Lord Beaconsfield's foreign policy. No one who was in the House of Commons during the recent debate on the land-taxes will ever forget the profound impression made when Mr. Winston Churchill rose from the Treasury bench and declaimed his father's speech on the question whether Mr. Bradlaugh should be allowed to sit in the House. Mr. Lewis Harcourt is reading hard for the Parliamentary Bar, where he will presently recite a selection of his father's most trenchant orations. Lord Hugh Cecil has very kindly offered to contribute to this Review a series of the articles which his father wrote for it in the distant past. At the Queen's Theatre, Mr. H. B. Irving is playing Matthias in "The Bells"; and it will be remembered that he appeared recently in "The Lyons Mail" and in "Charles the First". On the outer door of Sir Philip Burne-Jones' studio is a card bearing the legend "No models required". This is because Sir Philip is making a copy of "Love among the Ruins", and will presently make copies of "King Cophetua and the Beggar Maid", "The Legend of the Briar Rose", and other favourite works of his father. M. Schutzheimer, the universally-respected millionaire, whose splendid hospitality in Park Lane was one of the most notable features of the past London season, has decided to return to Hamburg and do business there in a small way for the rest of his life. "Dat vot vos goot enough for my fahder, dat is goot enough for me" he replied to an illustrious personage who was trying quietly to dissuade him from his intention. Thoroughly popular throughout the length and breadth of the Empire is the announcement that King Edward has decided to re-open the great exhibition of 1853 in Hyde Park, wearing a costume modelled precisely on that of the Prince Consort. There is indeed something very human, very touching, in all these manifestations of filial piety. The world is the sweeter for them. But, much as I hate to strike a jarring note, I cannot help asking whether the world is also the stronger for them. French writers have often accused the English people of a comparative lack of reverence for parents. It is well that we have not ignored the rebuke. But let us not, in our anxiety to deserve it no longer, rush to an extreme. Reverence is one thing, slavish reproduction another. A thing that is admirable at the moment of its doing is not necessarily admirable ever after. Times change, and it is our duty to change with them. Let us try to keep ourselves elastic, malleable, fresh. Human progress may be all a delusion; but, for sake of our self-respect, let's keep the delusion up as long as we can. My heart goes out to all these men who are so active in the filial-piety crusade. But I am convinced that they might be employing their time to better purpose. Not by imitating their grandfathers did their fathers achieve greatness, but by striking out lines for themselves—lines appropriate to themselves and to the age in which they lived. All the pietists whom I have instanced are men of high ability; and some of them have genius. I think the greatest service and honour they could do to their fathers' memory would be to use their own powers in their own fashion, freely.

Take, for example, the case of Mr. H. B. Irving. Here is an actor with truly fine gifts, with truly great potentialities. His face, his voice, his hands, are admirably expressive, and have the advantage of not resembling those of anyone else—except, in some measure, those of the late Sir Henry Irving. A personality as distinct as it is powerful is his. By years of hard work he has acquired the means of expressing artistically the force that was in him from the first. Gone are all the crudities that once marred his work. He has entered his prime. Nor is he an actor who depends merely on personal force and on beauty of method: he is a thinker. What his performances lack in emotional warmth is counterbalanced always by their strong intellectual quality—whenever, at least, the part he is playing is one which is strong enough to bear intellectual pressure. Decidedly, here is an actor whom the drama needs. I hope the drama may get him. Filial piety is all very well, up to a point. "The Bells" was all very well in the year of grace 1871. Crude stuff though it must have seemed even then, it gave Mr. Irving's father his first chance of frightening an audience by the imagination and uncanny magnetism that were his. Mr. Irving's father was right to believe in the play, and to fight Colonel Bateman into producing it for him. We respect him for the daring and the initiative that he showed. Would that his son, entering into possession of the Queen's Theatre, had imitated those fine qualities! The line of least resistance was for his son to imitate his performance of Matthias, for the benefit of sentimentally-minded old playgoers and archæologically-minded young ones. In point of finance, the immediate result is very good, I have no doubt. But how about prestige? Is Mr. Irving content merely to show that he can rival Miss Cissie Loftus? Not that he shows even that. The filial-piety crusade has not yet spread among daughters, and Miss Cissie Loftus does not merely give imitations of Miss Marie Loftus, the mother whom she prettily resembles. Mr. Irving's natural resemblance to his father is strong enough to rob him of any great credit for cleverness in "The Bells". I commend to him the impiety of being henceforward himself. Not even Hamlet, sadly lacking though he was in initiative, spent *all* the time in following his father's ghost.

CONDUCTORS AND THEIR METHODS.

I.—MR. HENRY J. WOOD.

By Filson Young.

IF Mr. Wood had no other claim to consideration he would be famous as the man who had made good orchestral music on a large scale popular and possible in London. There were pioneers before him, of course; there were societies and orchestras subsidised by associations of rich amateurs; there were a few enthusiastic musicians who gave orchestral concerts willingly, not hoping that they would pay, but content if the concert-giver could get out without serious loss. The association of Mr. Wood and Mr. Newman which changed all that is an old story now; but it is a story that has brought great and deserved credit to Mr. Wood and great convenience to the London public. Among other things, it has raised Mr. Wood from the position of a city organist to that of the chief of English conductors; I do not think that anyone could seriously and justly deny his right to that title. For a long time, indeed, he was the only English conductor equipped with a modern technique and modern methods; for brief as the history of the art of conducting is, it has already passed through at least two phases—the school of Wagner and Bülow and Richter, who were its authors and beginners, and whom most of the great German conductors have followed, and the school of Nikisch who, although originally one of Wagner's young men, has carried the art of conducting a stage further than that to which his masters brought it, and whose influence on the modern French and English schools is strong. Mr. Wood was the first conductor in England to realise that a very perfect manual technique is as important for a conductor as for a pianist; he was also the first to acquire it. For a great many years his prestige was unchallenged, his position unthreatened; no one else had a chance. But like all great pioneers he sowed more than he could reap himself, and other men have come up to share the harvest with him. It is inevitable, and he will be the last to regret it; for time and the seasons cannot be bound to the ploughshare of one man, nor are those his only harvests which he gathers with his own hand. In a way Mr. Wood has had a great part in preparing the success of some of the younger men who are now becoming his rivals. For a long time their rivalry was not serious; but last year a wave of new life went over orchestral music in London, and instead of one conductor and one orchestra there were half a dozen. Mr. Wood's position was no longer unchallenged; one felt that the time had come for him either to make good his own position by further energy and advance, or to prepare for that slow process of retiring into the background which is the ultimate fate of every successful man, however brilliant he may have been.

This season, however, Mr. Wood has already shown that he is going to hold his own. The season of Promenade Concerts which is now drawing to a close has roused quite a new degree of enthusiasm among its frequenters; they have had excellent value for their money, and have heard an unusual number of new works as well as all their old favourites; and to carry through a season like this, with a long concert every night conducted in a stifling atmosphere, as well as going through all the work incidental to other orchestral engagements, is a feat in which no living conductor has achieved so much success as Mr. Wood. It is true that of the new works produced by Mr. Wood there are more foreign than English compositions; he has always shown a preference for foreign music, notably for that of the Russian and Slav schools; in fact, we owe a great deal of our knowledge of such music here to him. I am delighted that he should continue on this line; there are going to be plenty of other people looking after English music—in fact, we are in for something like an orgy of it, and that also is an excellent thing and a sign of native artistic life. But modern English music has many grave disadvantages from the conductor's point of view, and Mr. Wood is a conductor who has always above all things played for his own hand. He has not the rehearsal time to spare for a complex work unless it is likely to take a permanent place in his répertoire and to add to his own glory as a conductor—a perfectly comprehensible point of view. In pursuing this policy he has no doubt sometimes missed good things—for example, Mr. William Wallace's "François Villon" was one of last season's successes which, as I had something to do with bringing it to a hearing, and am extremely proud of the result, I have assiduously boomed whenever I have had an opportunity. But this singularly fascinating work, which should be ideal from Mr. Wood's point of view in conducting, and in which he would particularly shine, was left to Mr. Landon Ronald to produce. There are other examples of a similar kind, and I cannot help thinking that Mr. Wood might profitably keep a closer watch on the work of our own composers lest haply he should let other chances like this go by.

I have said that the production of new works by English composers has grave disadvantages from a conductor's point of view. Such works are almost always difficult and require serious rehearsing to make anything of them; they are generally scored for a large and therefore expensive orchestra, and the box-office receipts show quite clearly that the economic response to them is not commensurate with the artistic enthusiasm which produces them. Often works like these, which have cost time and money to produce, become practically obsolete after their first performance; in other words, every penny spent in producing them has to be written off; whereas the same money could often be invested in the preparation of other new works which would almost certainly prove popular. I think this state of things will gradually change, but in the meantime the guarantors of concerts, and often the members of the orchestra themselves, have to bear the losses incidental to musical patriotism.

But from Mr. Wood's point of view there is another reason why he leans so much to music of quite a different school—because it particularly suits his genius as a conductor, and music of the English school, with rare exceptions, does not. And what is the nature of this genius? I am told that Mr. Wood is nicknamed by members of his orchestra the "Band-sergeant", and that name indicates the direction in which a great part of his successes and a certain part of his defects lie. He is a great organiser, a great disciplinarian, a great business man, a great showman; he undertakes to produce a certain effect on the public, and he produces it. His rehearsals are more like barrack-yard parades than like the easy-going, pipe-smoking, just-run-it-through-gentlemen-please conversaziones of the old days; programmes are mapped out like the time-tables of a great railway system; it is pure business from first to last. That is a great strength; let no one think that any kind of excellence, artistic or otherwise, is achieved by loose and slipshod methods. Yet there remains in the art of interpreting music an entirely intangible, ethereal quality that cannot be bound or scheduled or reduced to a departmental system; and sometimes from amid all Mr. Wood's perfect organisation and perfect discipline that wayward spirit escapes and flies away, and the result is hard and mechanical and soulless. That it should be so is not wonderful; that it should so seldom be so is to me very wonderful indeed.

I have spoken of Mr. Wood's technique and of his sympathy with Slavonic music. It has indeed moulded him, moulded his mind, his artistic sense, and affected even his appearance, so that now he looks more like a foreigner than an Englishman—an effect to which the flowing tie and peg-top trousers contribute. Mr. Wood is a great master of savage rhythms and of extreme nuances, but not of those subtler dynamic variations which make their balance and contrast within a much smaller range; he is great at the thunder and the whisper, but not at that steadier and more human diapason that is the body of life and art in this world; he can always produce an effect, but he is not so good at interpreting a condition or a mood. Perhaps this is little more than saying he is, like most of us, imperfect; that the upper part of his face, with its fine brow and magnetic eyes, is not matched by the lower part; that he is a god with feet of clay—or say Orpheus in peg-trop trousers.

He has certain mannerisms with which the world is familiar—a fixed routine of gesture which personally I think vulgar and tiresome and unworthy. I would not like to say that my opinion is shared by the majority of his public, or that the circus-like performance which he goes through when conducting a great work is not carefully calculated to assist his personality. But it is a pitiable thing, after listening to a really fine interpretation of a noble work, full of fire and rhythm, passion and tenderness and understanding, to see the interpreter behaving like a mountebank before the audience, with gestures comparable only to those of a trapeze performer who has just alighted on the canvas, bending on this side and that and describing, between bearded lips and the utmost reach of his arm, arcs in the air which Ruskin might have described as "curves of beauty", but which for my part I find exceedingly deplorable and disagreeable. Yet it would be easy to exaggerate the importance of these defects of manner. They are the defects of Mr. Wood's qualities, the qualities which have raised him where he is, high above most of us who criticise him. Forget his antics and gestures in the moment of applause; watch his right wrist when he is at work—that most wonderful wrist in the world of conducting; watch the left hand, which talks to the horns and wood-wind and 'cellos like a familiar spirit; watch that glance which is always ready to look up from the score a second or two before some unimportant entry to reassure the player that the master's eye is on him and the master's mind controlling his work—look at these and you will be studying the elements of a technique which is in many ways unrivalled in the world, and marks in England the greatest height to which we have so far attained in this art.

BY ONY AND TEME AND CLUN.

By Lord Dunsany.

MR. GRANT RICHARDS has brought out a new edition of the well-known "Shropshire Lad", by A. E. Housman. On the cover there is designed a branch of a chestnut tree, with its bunches of blossom and large leaves, beneath which a sunset blazes over Shropshire. Besides this design there is a paper cover with one of Mr. William Hyde's illustrations reproduced on it. It represents woodlands all in the autumn, and a small road winding into darkness under vague distant hills. These pictures of autumn and sunset prepare one's mood for the poems of Mr. A. E. Housman, with their frequent graveward trend and their mournings for the friends of the Shropshire Lad when evil things befell them. As one opens the cover one sees Shropshire fields with little valleys among them sheltering hamlets, and between the cover again and the last page appear the chimneys of London, uneasy with troubled winds, and the strange untravelled land of London roofs, ugly enough perhaps, and yet romantic with the mystery of lands where no man goes, a region haunted only by those wildest and stealthiest of the animals that dwell with man. And from cover to cover we follow the fortunes of the Shropshire Lad from

"valleys of springs of rivers
By Ony and Teme and Clun"

to London, whither he goes leaving Severn shore to others, the same thoughts and the same troubled dreams.

The book begins with the year '87, when the beacons rose up along the Shropshire hills. In a poem called "Réveillé" we hear the cry of the open, empty highways in the dawn and see wide prospects of remote towns and forelands a-glimmer with the morning, all luring a man to rise up early and to see behind the hills before the long sleep comes on and the ending of journeys. Here are three lines of his poem:

"Hear the drums of morning play;
Hark! the empty highways crying
'Who'll beyond the hills away?'"

How well they call up the glamour of still, white roads, untrodden, waiting for footsteps, when the centre of some way from city to city is as safe for the little creatures of field and wood as their own secluded haunts.

We read how quiet it is in the grave, how still and apathetic:

"In the nation that is not
Nothing stands that stood before".

There is a poem, too, called Bredon Hill, in which the first and third line in every verse end with disyllables, and the second rhymes with the fourth, then comes a fifth line rhyming with second and fourth, like the echo of bells, as it seems to me, over water. It tells how the Shropshire Lad and his love heard from a hill-slope the bells in valleys calling:

"Come all to church, good people".

But they did not heed, for these were not yet the wedding peals, until one day, when the snows were over Bredon,

"My love rose up so early
And stole out unbeknown
And went to church alone".

So that they tolled one bell only, and the mourners followed after. Now him alone the bells call noisily.

And the Shropshire Lad tells how the lads come in to market: the mill-lads, the shepherds, the lads from barn and forge, from town and field and till, and there among them the lads that will never be old. He wishes that there was some token whereby you might tell them from the rest; but they are indiscernible, unguessed-at, so that you cannot talk friendly with them and say farewell

"And watch them depart on the way that they will not return".

He hears an aspen prophesying to itself and boding evil things; and a dead man comes up to question him; on idle hills the sound reaches him, like a noise in dreams, of drums and bugles of that great army of soldiers that lie dead on forgotten fields.

Then the day comes when through the hills of Wyre he goes away from his home and out of sight of Clee, the day when he speaks to his hand and tells it that because it has held true fellows' hands it must keep from shame the name of Shropshire in London. And after that stray breaths of winds that come eastward, or memories of lost and happy highways, or a knowledge that at a certain time the golden broom and hawthorn are out near Wenlock, are all that the Shropshire Lad has to do any more with Ony and Teme and Clun; only his soul still lingers, startling wayfarers, by starlit fences and about glimmering weirs "far in a western brookland".

These haunts of the Shropshire Lad and hills and rivers of his retrospection are well depicted by Mr. William Hyde. One of his pictures shows Clee rising up out of drifts of may. Another shows a sky all full of tranquil flame, with a new moon shining from it on the Teme, a moon just entering into her borrowed kingdom, for the sun is a long while set. It is an evening such as those that bode the change of seasons. Another shows a prospect of wide Shropshire, indistinct, vague and misty with the approach of night, limited by black hills. Distinct and bright in the foreground a little hamlet stands, for a while holding out against the night; all round it seems to be silent and is dusk. And not unlike this picture seem the brief abiding-places of the lads and girls of whom the poet writes, quiet sunny places round which eternity seems to be drawn quite close and quite dark; it is round Hughley steeple, Portland is black with it, Shropshire lads enter it in Asia and Shrewsbury, they drift down to it on Severn and Nile, they are thrust into it by knives of brothers, by the noose of the hangman, and others seek it suddenly for themselves, and all the while by Hughley steeple, either to north or south—the suicides lie to the north, and the south is holy ground—the Shropshire Lad wots of a grave that waits for him, and whether he choose the north or whether the south, it is but a choice of friends. And already his bones have spoken to him, and strangely and wonderfully have asked for how many more nights and days his flesh and thoughts will live, to irk them and hustle them about and to fill the round white skull with "its humming hive of dreams", proud in their little hour that for a brief while "the immortal bones" obey them, the immortal bones

"That shall last as long as earth".

Such are some of the fancies with which Mr. A. E. Housman has decked those rural places, of which it is so musically written:

> " Clunton and Clunbury,
> Clungunford and Clun,
> Are the quietest places
> Under the sun ".

SHAKESPEARE IN FRANCE.

II.

APOTHEOSIS.

BESIDES the famous preface to "Cromwell", in which Shakespeare is acclaimed as the leader of humanity in the last phase of its art, Hugo published a volume which, from its title, purported to deal with Shakespeare and the plays of Shakespeare. A certain proportion of the book does actually concern itself with the poet; and, after looking through these portions with care, the reader is left to ask what it is that Hugo has said. Unhappily Hugo has not been sufficiently collected to make himself altogether intelligible. Something has taken his breath away. Hugo's "Shakespeare" is one of the most wonderful pieces of jabber extant; it is torrential. When the faint shadow of a thesis emerges it is this: "Shakespeare is a genius: a genius must be accepted whole: therefore let no dog bark". Nay, the barking itself becomes a tribute when it is directed against Shakespeare:

" Sauvage ivre? Soit. Il est sauvage comme la forêt vierge; il est ivre comme la haute mer. Shakespeare, c'est la fertilité, la force, l'exubérance, la mamelle gonflée, la coupe écumante, la cuve à plein bord, la sève par excès, la lave en torrent, les germes en tourbillons, la vaste pluie de la vie, nulle réticence, nulle ligature, nulle économie, la prodigalité insensée et tranquille du créateur."

So Shakespeare finds his apotheosis; and, in order that full justice may be done to this side of French criticism, it is necessary to recall other verdicts, couched in less extravagant terms, but fully as sincere as this of Hugo. The eulogists are, for the most part, either men who are working for emancipation from the too rigid application of old formulæ, who use Shakespeare for their own purposes with noisy admiration and occasional misgiving; or they are the men of slender inspiration who, while they appreciate the art of Racine and place it higher than that of their dear barbarian, yet must perforce wonder at the irresistible fertility and the unscaled heights and depths of Shakespearian tragedy. Before attempting to show that the French can never, in the strict sense of the word, appreciate our countryman, it is only fair to notice that many Frenchmen have praised him.

Prévost was the first of Shakespeare's eulogists, as he was the first to deplore his irregularities. "Shakespeare n'observe pas les unités, mais en récompense si l'on passe aux mœurs, aux caractères, aux passions, et à l'expression des sentiments, on ne trouvera presque rien dans toutes ses œuvres qui ne puisse être justifié." Prévost meant what he said, although the effect of his words is apt to be discounted by the fact that he learned to appreciate Shakespeare because he found it impossible not to appreciate Madame Oldfield. Chateaubriand may be cited next; for Chateaubriand, in his maturity, throwing aside his earlier prejudices, acclaimed Shakespeare as one of the five or six dominating geniuses of all time, placing him with Homer, Dante and Rabelais. "On renie souvent ces êtres suprêmes; on se revolte contre eux; on compte leurs défauts; on les accuse d'ennui, de bizarrerie, de mauvais goût, en les volant et en se parant de leurs dépouilles; mais on se débat en vain sous leur joug." Diderot writes much to the same effect: "C'est l'informe et grossier colosse de Notre-Dame: colosse gothique, mais entre les jambes duquel nous passerions tous". By way of Guizot, who showed how Shakespeare preserved the unity of interest though he disregarded the unities, we come to Lamartine: "Tout est à lui; le clavier entier de la nature de l'homme est sous ses doigts". Then there were Dumas, Berlioz, and Flaubert. The last named wrote to George Sand: "Je ne lis plus rien de tout sauf Shakespeare; tout paraît médiocre à côté de ce prodigieux bonhomme". These quotations might be indefinitely continued.

Concerning the French eulogists of Shakespeare, two facts at once emerge. In the first place his work is regarded as a triumph of nature. He is not accepted as a great artist. He is spoken of in terms that suggest a natural phenomenon. He succeeded only where he rose above rules, not because he could make use of them. There were very few critics who, like Guizot, sought to appreciate him as an artificer. Lamartine put the general view of his countrymen very well when he wrote: "Où trouvez-vous le plus d'art, dans Racine ou dans Shakespeare? A coup sûr je vous répondrai: dans Racine. Racine a su choisir. Shakespeare ne le sait pas. Mais où trouvez-vous le plus de nature? Je réponds sans hésiter: dans Shakespeare".

In the second place a reserve is made by the majority of French critics. Shakespeare is allowed to be a tragic genius in order that his instinct for comedy may be denied. This point will have to be discussed at length, since it contains within it one of the explanations of the French attitude towards Shakespeare. For, if one reason why the French have failed to appreciate Shakespeare is to be sought in the fact that their tragedy has come down from Racine, the one other reason of equal importance is this: the French have no word to correspond to the English word "humour".

Leaving this point for further elucidation, it may be recorded, in conclusion of this note upon Shakespeare's apotheosis, that it coincided with the victory of the Romantics. The strain of eulogy was always ready to be raised, but it did not attain full volume till a new impulse had come into French literature. The fate of Shakespeare was, as already maintained, bound up with the battle of the unities. The victory of the Romantics, when they burst the strong fetters forged in the ancient days of Boileau, was a victory for Shakespeare, so far as it went. The French were no nearer to an appreciation of Shakespeare; but they could praise him a great deal more heartily, and he made a glorious battle-cry. It was right and fitting that it should have been De Vigny who translated "Othello", and that the production of this play should have followed that of "Hernani". Historically it was right and fitting. Whether it were so right and fitting æsthetically, and whether the Romantics were right in claiming Shakespeare as one of themselves, is another matter. That they did so claim him is clear enough. The Romantics undertook to be a law unto themselves. Moreover, they looked into themselves, and wrote. Hugo, therefore, is distinctly claiming Shakespeare as his peer and ally when he says: "L'œuvre capitale de Shakespeare, n'est pas Hamlet. L'œuvre capitale de Shakespeare, c'est tout Shakespeare". According to Hugo, Shakespeare's drama is nothing but a revelation of its author. "Il est dans sa peau; il est lui. De là ses originalités absolument personnelles: de là ses idosyncrasies qui existent sans faire loi."

NIGHTFALL.

AFTER a day of black showers, which had drenched for the twentieth time the uncleared remnant of the harvest, the evening came still and clear, and the sun dropped to a cloudless setting. The last trace of the storm hung in the east, a mountain-range of dull red vapour, half sunk in brown drifts of haze. The drip from the trees slackened and ceased; in the motionless air every leaf held the last drop dazzling against the level light. It was an hour which might give to a landscape of the nobler order that magic illumination beheld but once or twice in the year; for anyone who had the chance of seeing the western light kindle on the mists as they lifted off the hills, or strike across a wooded plain in shafts of smouldering haze, or burn upon some expanse of still-moving water, it was a sunset to be watched expectantly. Even for those whose paths lay among far less inspiring scenes, it had a promise not to be neglected. While it burned far away on mountain-sides and wide floods and ridges of dun woodland, watched, it is to be hoped, by duly attentive observers, it lit with a certain distinctive effect a piece of plain country, a little valley between low hillsides, slopes rising to the tall, broken hedges or thin copse which made the horizon three fields away. Along the valley a narrow lane wound between lines of half-grown oak and elm, which still showed on the verge of autumn the fresh green of the "midsummer shoot" among the darker foliage. As the sun sank and the sky above his setting turned to a liquid clearness of colourless light, a man who lived in that shallow hedgerow-quartered vale, and employed a good deal of a somewhat solitary leisure in country walks, came down the lane and stopped at an opening between the trees to watch the sight before him. In younger days he had seen abundance of those more obvious splendours in a finer country; as he turned to the glow between the hedge-oaks he had in mind the recollection of a sea-sunset—the blue shadows thrown across the foam by a breaker that lifted itself, dark and slow, out of a sea of orange fire. But he had learned long since that the commoner manifestations, as most would call them, have sometimes in their fineness and subtlety an appeal at least equal to that of the more exalted visions. To-night the pearl-white glow in the west, the low light which touched the stubble-fields with a brownish glory, put the thought of the Atlantic surge out of mind. There is a schooling of perception in these matters, which may show its effect in later life, the solitary man had sometimes thought, by a finer discerning of light as distinct from colour, and in another direction, by a sensitiveness to lesser details, foreground touches and secondary lights of the picture, beside the central focus of the scene. Here there was more to see than the sun's edge over the knoll of trees, and the immense clearness of the sky. A blackbird suddenly swerved across the lane, poised for a second on the hedge with drooped wings and spread tail, full in the level ray, and dropped into the meadow-grass; the stroke of its wings made a foxglove in the hedgeside sway a little; the withered spike, all brown with the rusted seed-pods, bore one last bell at the top, which shone in the sun against the dark of the elm-boughs. The beauty in the instant's vision of the bird, the bright black eye turned upon the intruder, the faint bars on the dark breast-feathers, the translucent gold-brown of the half-spread wings would be remembered hereafter as part of the whole impression of the hour, together with the deep serenity of the light, the smell of the wet road-side, the sway of the foxglove flower as it caught the light and showed the paler speckle through the purple of its bell. The picture, distance and foreground and detail, a momentary notice with a permanent power, stamped on the memory through the senses in a way which the solitary knew very well, raised once more an old question of the meaning in beauty such as this and the emotion which rarely failed to answer it, of the actual relation of this instant, caught and fixed in its passing, set up before him like a signal, learned like a lesson, to the whole scheme of life. How did such hours as these come by their association, intense but seemingly irrational, of pleasure, or, as to-night, of strong melancholy? It was not that the bird's song was over, with all the chances of winter to come before it could be heard again; or that the foxglove spires which shone along the hedge in July were rotting towards the ground; or that the fast-fading light was bringing on the dark and the cold. The melancholy in the scene went far beyond the reach of such simple reasons as these. Did the unaccountable pathos of the landscape and the light come from an assurance of the signs of an inward sense, undecipherable and unguessed?

When the sun was down, the watcher turned and took his customary evening walk to the end of the lane where it joined the high-road. Before he had reached his own gate again, the country had grown dark under the rapid changes of an autumnal twilight. The stubbles glimmered in spaces of shadowless grey; the rough pastures scarcely showed their thickets of ragwort and silvery clots of thistledown; but there was still a sheen from the afterglow on the brows and ridges of the fields, and the tufted shapes of bush and hedge were outlined with a greenish bloom. The melancholy of the dusk was no less than it had been at the sunset hour; but it was perhaps more easily to be accounted for. As the solitary stood with his hand on the latch of his gate, the end of another unmarked day was very clearly before him. The question rose in his mind, as it had risen somewhat too often of late, whether these exercises of his in perception and reflection were a fair purchase of time, and not a playing-away of still-shortening daylight. As far as his own experience went, he was almost alone in his practice of this kind of diversion; the singularity, which was in general a good argument for the rightness of his choice, began to raise uneasy doubts. There had been great poets, it was true, who seemed to be of his way of thinking; but he was no poet, even of the smallest species. The extreme insignificance of these concerns of his to the great world, to the stirring minds of the time, was a thought which began to trouble his prepossessions a little, in spite of their entrenchment in the roughnesses of an odd humour. For the moment it seemed almost probable that the things which certain of his friends were busy about—a clause in a Bill, a part in a play, a fall in prices, a microscopic discovery—might be justly thought of more serious interest to intelligent people than his own fancies about birds' wings and foxglove-bells and the last pale ray of sunset across the lane. He stood for some time at the gate, before the half-wild garden and the low, dark house, guessing with a sort of experimental dismay whether the deliberate choice of forty years might have been wrong after all. The reasonable certainty came back at length; he found his courage to think his amusements of as solid worth as those more popular diversions of his friends, perhaps in their immediate pleasure, assuredly in the harmlessness of their result. He lifted the latch of the gate and entered his inner fastness, answering in his own sense the question, "Dieu mettra-t-il les belles pensées au rang des belles actions?" Of the beauty of the thoughts, derived from such sources of inspiration as he frequented, it was allowable to be fairly well assured.

A CALL AT MIKINDANI.

By Frederick Hale.

When I came on deck after sunrise I remembered a remark that the Old Coaster had made the previous evening: "Mikindani, gentlemen, to-morrow morning, and you'll see one of the finest bays in the world". His pronunciation of the name, with a heavy accent on the penultimate, had reminded me that he was a German speaking of a port in German East Africa, and I had somewhat discounted his praise of it for that reason; but as I leant over the deck-rail scrutinising the low line of densely wooded coast that stretched away to the western horizon, I felt my curiosity already stimulated by the appearance of its dark forest. There was an atmosphere of seclusion, of elusive mystery, about its shores that seemed to challenge adventure, and the morning mist, blurring and softening their outline beneath a delicate blue haze, set the imagination peopling them with creatures of mythology and romance. The sky was dotted with patches of light-grey cloud that stood in clear-cut relief against a vivid steel-blue background; the breeze of the night before had fallen to a dead calm, and the sea was still and treacherous-looking. Alongside the track of the ship a couple of sharks on the look-out for offal had tailed on, and they followed us restlessly as if impatient with our speed of eleven knots an hour, their sleek forms glistening in the dark water as they turned and flashed about each other. Far away in the offing some whales were spouting; they were the first we had seen on this voyage, and their presence caused much excitement among those passengers who found the days monotonous.

The reduction of speed was the first intimation of our approaching port; it was quickly followed by a change of direction and the appearance of a second officer on the bridge. Shortly afterwards we went below.

When we returned to deck, the ship, to our surprise, was steaming slowly up a wide bay, evidently making for land, though not a sign of habitation was to be seen. We brought our glasses to bear, and the Old Coaster pointed out the bar ahead of us. We were in an outer bay, and the harbour lay beyond, through a narrow channel that called for careful piloting. After a little scrutiny we distinguished the features of the strait, and gradually the inner bay unfolded itself, line by line, in a scene of exquisite beauty.

On either side there was the same stretch of dark forest, nearer now and less forbidding. Little sandy creeks appeared at intervals, with green glades above them where occasionally a cluster of white huts might be seen half hidden behind a widespread baobab tree, or nestling among tall cocoanut palms. The little brown huts, with their low-hanging eaves, gave an air of intimate homeliness and security to the strange coast, seeming to welcome us or to invite us further inland. Soon we had a glimpse of the port itself, lying at the foot of dark and gloomy slopes at the far end of the bay. A low, white-walled, red-roofed house with towers and wings appeared, surrounded by smaller buildings of the same effective colouring, with numerous huts grouped and scattered about their outskirts. The principal building, standing out among its dependents against a magnificent background of forest-clad hills, suggested the home of some hero of German legend.

We glided in softly. The throbbing pulsation of the engines had ceased, and the silence around us was almost unbroken. The heat had grown intense; the sea, with not a breath on its surface, was burning with subtle flames of colour. Here and there a solitary native was fishing from his little dug-out canoe, his erect, motionless figure silhouetted in clear, sharp outline. The whole place had an atmosphere of strange, exotic charm, so potent that one almost feared its influence, finding the richness of its untempered tones too full for endurance. Everything spoke of peace and luxury—the peace of simple minds and the luxury of natural wealth. Everything spoke of the beauty of unimpeded life and the perfection of primitive attainment, as in the paradise of one's dreams. Yet the earth hung, as it were, in suspense, like a drooping stem bowed with the burden of its own luscious fruit, and awaiting the hour of its fall.

As the ship crept up the bay, moving always more slowly, we seemed to float without effort through the quivering air; the most restless of us became subdued, and we relapsed, by a sort of tacit consent, into a world of unreality; the senses yielded to a delicious languor, enchanted by the play of soft rich colour and the rhythm and flow of ever-changing outline. Nature, as a prelude to further wizardry, had drugged us with opiates, and only her spells could rouse us.

The ship made fast about a mile from land. We had hoped to go ashore, and we watched for the coming of the doctor who would "pass" the vessel and give us the necessary permission. He arrived with ceremony, dressed in the customary white suit and helmet, and seated in the stern of an eight-oared boat manned by natives in uniform. Almost at the same time we were surrounded by a swarm of canoe-men, great wide-eyed fellows, black and perspiring, paddling their little out-rigged craft in a press alongside. They scrambled on board and commenced a brisk bidding for the sale of curious wares, offering us musical instruments, bows and arrows of native make, fruit of various kinds, coral and shells. A strange barbaric medley of humanity they presented! Here and there was an Indian amongst them, and one distinguished, with a mixture of dislike and amusement, the sly sleek face of an Arabian Jew contrasted with the full lips and distended nostrils of the gaping negroes. The features of the pure East-coast native are convincing proof of the moulding influence of natural conditions on character. His expression of generous expansiveness is typical of his country; so, too, is the faint inscrutable smile that he assumes on occasions of diplomacy, and the suggestion of treachery that lurks beneath it. Traders have taught him the art of bargaining; accordingly he exaggerates the value of his goods like an auctioneering cheapjack, and will ask two pounds for an article that he sells you half-an-hour later for five shillings.

Travellers have a weakness for collecting rubbish, and my friends proved no exceptions. They were still haggling when a quartermaster drove the vendors back to their canoes, and they lined along the side of the vessel, keeping their attention to the upturned faces of the men below. It was then that I discovered the impossibility of going ashore. The boat was leaving almost immediately! With no cargo to load, and no passengers to embark, there was no need for delay. "Who, besides", said the captain, "would take the trouble to land at such a place?" I shook my head at him, and turning to the Old Coaster invited his sympathy. He made no answer. He too, then, was a Philistine after all! But what of his praise of this glorious bay? He was gazing after the vanishing figure of the doctor, and his face had a look of quiet admiration. After a while he spoke; his admiration developed into a mixture of eulogy and abuse, and I learnt many things. It was pointed out to me, amongst other matters, that the official value of the gentleman who had just left us was complex and peculiar; that he was sole representative of his race in the local government of Mikindani, and that all the offices of administration were combined in his person. "How delightful", the cynic would say, "to be governor of an East African port, and to be practically the only European who lives there!" And the serious would reply: "How precarious! How nerve-trying to an imaginative man!" Once upon a time Germany gave him a little garrison for company, and the members of that little garrison died or were invalided home. Now he rules alone, and there are no more deaths; the passing world respects him, not as the governor of Mikindani, but as the one white man who can live there. Such is the power of malaria.

The fruit of the drooping bough, so fair and tempting to the eye, is poisonous to him who would stay to pluck it. The bay is a mockery of men's hopes, alluring them to destruction. We, for other reasons, were forbidden to brave its dangers, yet it was perhaps well for us that we came and went so quickly. It was of the nature of such an impression that it should be brief and fugitive. Had we been allowed to land, the touch of earth might have robbed it of its glamour. The spell of the place would have been broken; the instinct of the tourist would have impelled us to rush hither and thither, analysing its beauties, criticising its wonders, till we had destroyed the delicate fabric of illusion. As it was we glided softly out again, leaving the fishermen still erect and immobile in their canoes, and the iridescent sea as motionless as they. The little huts drew back and disappeared; the white towers receded into the distance; the dark forests melted away and were lost on the horizon. Before the sun was overhead we had gone far from Mikindani, and were steaming northward on the way to Zanzibar.

CORRESPONDENCE.

THE PRETENSIONS OF THE COMMONS.

To the Editor of the SATURDAY REVIEW.

London, 24 September 1909.

SIR,—It is surely time that the soi-disant Liberal party was clearly taught and definitely informed, in view of its obvious ignorance on this constitutional question as on most other matters—political, economic, and so forth—that the mere ipse dixit of the House of Commons, however sententiously conceived and solemnly announced to a sceptical and contemptuous nation, is of itself absolutely valueless politically, and carries no constitutional weight or executive authority whatever. The "Liberal" party are, and always have been, great sticklers for precedent and custom, which ideas are usually associated only with Conservatism, when it happens to suit their temporary convenience and is thought to serve some immediate party or personal political advantage, and to carry weight with the uninformed, the jealous, and the bitter, semi-revolutionary mob that this conglomerate political party so fitly represents and is recruited from.

The present mis-government has made itself even more foolish than before over this futile and spiteful attempt to impeach the Duke of Norfolk of a high political crime and misdemeanour against the State—that is, against the Government and the party, of course. The solemn assertions of privilege, which for the past three centuries successive transitory Houses of Commons have seen fit to publish and have wasted time in formulating, have no constitutional value or legal force whatever, and are as impotent as the breath that was expended in their utterance. They are in no sense binding on the House of Lords or on any individual peer, save and except, and only so far, as they may, in any particular instance, have been formally accepted and ratified by the House of Lords *and* the Sovereign in due and solemn constitutional form.

Neither on questions of Supply, nor any other Parliamentary matter, has the mere ipse dixit of the House of Commons in these or any other times the slightest constitutional force. Similarly, any formal concurrence by the House of Lords with any such enactment of the Commons never has had, and never can have, any constitutional authority or executive effect whatever unless it has also received the formal and constitutional assent of the Sovereign. It is perfectly useless for the "Liberal" party to cite precedents or ipse dixits of the House of Commons or of constitutional practice where these have not received the necessary and indispensable constitutional assent and formal enactment of the three Estates of the Realm. The doings of the several Parliaments that overthrew the monarchy in the seventeenth century, committed an ever infamous act of regicide, and usurped the royal and the whole Parliamentary and Governmental authority, constitute no legal precedent whatever. The various declarations of the rights of the Commons in those and subsequent times by the House of Commons of the moment—illegally constituted and frankly self-instituted as it was during the entire period of the Commonwealth—have never been binding on the remaining two Estates of the Realm. Of course, if a measure has received the assent of the other parties in the Constitution, it is another matter. King, Lords, and Commons—all must concur in the passing of any measure, if that measure is to possess constitutional validity. A resolution of the House of Commons is not law; but if the House of Lords has at any time tacitly or deliberately assented to the Money Bills of any particular House of Commons, and the same have afterwards received the Royal Assent, those Bills have been duly passed and have become law and binding on the State in due legal and constitutional form.

The House of Commons is not omnipotent in the State. The Lords have the absolute and indisputable right now, and the Sovereign eventually, to amend, assent to, or to reject the present and any other Finance Bill coming up from the Commons (where it is customary, but not legally or constitutionally necessary, to initiate such or any other Bill) if they choose, and failing agreement with the House of Commons. The Liberal party cannot get round this, and they must know it.

Members of the Government are insistent that they have received no complaint against the present Finance Bill from the working classes. I do not suppose that they or anyone else ever expected they would, seeing that, even on their own admission, it is not the so-called working classes that are called upon to find the money for the revolutionary, socialistic schemes which the Budget projects.

Only the Lords and the Sovereign remain to save the country and the Empire from irreparable disaster.

If the lower classes of this country, at the wanton instigation of the present Government, want a revolution, they can surely have it now and welcome, and the sooner the better. It is wanted, indeed, to decide once for all whether the irresponsible parasitic mob majority of the nation is to prevail, or the unhappy thinking and truly working and cultivated minority which, ever since the advent to political power of "triumphant democracy", has had to suffer and to pay the whole national and imperial bill of costs.

Your obedient servant,

O. W.

COMPULSORY EVENING SCHOOLS.

To the Editor of the Saturday Review.

21 Harcourt Road, Sheffield,
20 September 1909.

Sir,—A Welsh stipendiary has recently condemned three colliery boys guilty of theft to regular attendance at evening schools. Although those of us who are engaged in evening work recognise the compliment thus paid to the value of the evening schools, we are by no means sure of the effect of such a proceeding, or of the line of thought which led to it, upon the schools themselves.

Evening teaching is at present to many of us the most hopeful work we undertake, because our evening pupils are still volunteers. If evening schools become compulsory there is a grave danger that the spirit which now animates the work in them and which is of the essence of true education would be destroyed. If, of course, parents are sufficiently interested to insist upon their children's attendance, as the chairman of the Lancashire Education Committee, Sir H. Hibbert, suggested recently that they should, or if boys' brigades, lads' clubs and similar organisations insist upon evening-school attendance as a condition of membership, no objection to these forms of compulsion can be raised; but there is a possibility that legal compulsion may result in the substitution of a mechanical putting-in of hours for the present pursuit of knowledge in evening schools—and all but the most statistically minded will realise that this change would be a sacrifice of the substance to the shadow.

Yet, since compulsion in some form or other is likely to come before long, it may be as well to consider whether we cannot gain from it the good which it contains while at the same time we avoid its drawbacks. Probably the period of compulsion would include the three years from fourteen to seventeen. If therefore the compulsory evening schools of the future were to be divided into two classes, one providing a three-year course, while the other offered a more extended course, we should still have a means of differentiating the willing from the unwilling students among ex-elementary school-children; for the former would volunteer to enter upon a course which would carry them well towards their twentieth birthday, whereas the latter would be compelled to enter the schools where the legal minimum of attendance could be enforced.

In both classes of school the teaching would be largely vocational, i.e. based upon the principles of the various callings in which the students were engaged; but the more extended courses would be necessarily more liberal and varied and therefore more attractive than the three-year courses. Vocational education in the elementary schools is open to several objections: school authorities might easily overstock some trades and starve others by an unwise distribution of boys among the various trades taught in school; neither is it easy to be certain of the special aptitude of a boy who has not yet reached his fourteenth birthday; nor is the primary-school period by any means too long for securing the unspecialised training and knowledge which everybody needs. But where, as in the evening schools, vocational teaching is possible because the students have already chosen their trades, it is perhaps the most valuable means of education; for the student has before him throughout his daily work the matter of his evening studies, which therefore become intensely real and practically valuable to him and in consequence very stimulating. The syllabus for barbers' classes in Germany affords an amusing instance of the value of a lack of humour in securing thoroughness. An English class conducted on similar lines would be hampered by constant fits of merriment. For the girls, the vast majority of whom remain at home doing nothing in particular after they have left day school, a thorough evening course in domestic subjects would be most valuable; and these courses might well be taken by the married women teachers whom a few authorities are, with unaccountable shortsightedness, at present dismissing from the day schools.

I remain yours faithfully,

Frank J. Adkins.

KING LEAR.

To the Editor of the Saturday Review.

London, 29 September 1909.

Sir,—In a recent article printed in the Saturday Review Mr. Max Beerbohm remembered that the parts of Goneril and Regan would, upon the Elizabethan stage, have been taken by male actors. He seemed to regret that these horrid creatures must now be impersonated by women. This does not, therefore, seem a very good place to assert that, of all Shakespeare's creations, Goneril and Regan are perhaps the most unmistakably feminine; and that there is sex in almost everything they say or do. Yet I intend to assert it.

Take the farewell to Cordelia. "Prescribe not us our duties"—so Regan; and after her Goneril: "Let your study be to content your lord, who hath received you at fortune's alms." Are these feminine touches, or are they not?

Again, take the great scene with Lear. What is all this talk of fifty knights; or twenty-five knights; or ten? Could a catastrophe have been built upon such trifles without the help of a woman? Surely it is the woman's particular glory to build tragedy upon a domestic difference.

Take the blinding scene. "Out, vile jelly!" Cornwall, being a man, must express himself, even at such a moment as this, with a certain conscious picturesqueness of phrase. "The other, too!" This is the feminine cry. There is a womanly directness and simplicity about it.

It is needless to proceed in detail. What could be more feminine than those exquisite sisterly passages where Goneril and Regan arrange how their father is to be managed; or the yet more sisterly passages where they strive with such natural emulation for the possession of the bastard Edmund? There is the eternal feminine here, as it showed among the caves, a little full-blooded perhaps, and reduced to its simplest terms; but quite unmistakable. There is, in fact, no natural feminine emotion that Goneril and Regan can be shown to lack. Goneril would have made a savagely devoted mother. Mark how she shrinks from her father's curse, which was to "create her child of spleen".

If the truth must be forced home by comparison, just compare Edmund, the light-hearted villain, with his "fa, sol, la, mi". There stands the man villain, taking pleasure in the evil exercise of his wits. Beside him stand the two women in the full light of their passionate wickedness, which ebbs and flows with the love (I call it love because I am afraid of them) and hate that lives in the blood.

Yours faithfully,

John Leslie.

To the Editor of the Saturday Review.

Queen Anne's Mansions S.W.

23 September 1909.

Sir,—Having recently witnessed the performance of "King Lear" at the Haymarket, I would ask you to allow me to state in your columns the impression it left upon me. The great fault I found—and it is one that may be noticed in most of the representations of Shakespeare's tragedies—was the poor elocution of most of the actors. To a lover of the noble poetry of the tragedies it is distressing to listen to such an unsatisfactory delivery of it on the stage. Why do so many of our actors seem to try to make poetry sound as much as possible like prose?

There was much in Mr. McKinnel's acting that was unsatisfactory. The great fault of his presentation of the part seemed to me to be that it was pitched throughout in too subdued a key. One of the critiques I have read praises Mr. McKinnel for his restraint! What is wanted here is surely not restraint but fire, and in this latter quality his impersonation was woefully deficient. His delivery quite failed to convey the impression that he felt the passion which the situation and the words of the dramatist called for. His voice seldom rose to the requisite pitch and at times sank to indistinct mutterings.

As regards the setting of the play, the attempt at archaic realism seemed overdone. The castle of Gloucester was represented by a sort of artificial cave (so to speak) built up of huge blocks. Cornwall's advice—"Shut up your doors, my lord" (Act II. sc. 2)—was impossible of adoption for the simple reason that, so far as one could see, there were no doors to shut! And this in an age in which letter-writing seems to have been freely practised.

It might be thought that in a play of such length, where some curtailment for stage purposes is inevitable, the harrowing scene of the blinding of Gloucester might have been omitted. It may with reason be replied that unless this is represented on the stage the audience is left in ignorance as to why Gloucester appears in the later scenes as a blind man. The blinding is certainly carried out in a manner to spare as much as possible the sensibilities of the audience, so perhaps on the whole the retention of this horrible scene is justified.

I missed several of those familiar lines which linger in the memory of all lovers of this great play, e.g.:

"Howe'er thou art a fiend
A woman's form doth shield thee." (Act IV. sc. 2.)

"Men must endure
Their going hence even as their coming hither;
Ripeness is all." (Act V. sc. 2.)

Why omit these fine and familiar lines?

I am, Sir, yours truly,

F. Venning.

MR. BALFOUR AND THE UNIONIST PROGRAMME.

To the Editor of the Saturday Review.

London, 30 September 1909.

Sir,—In your leader on Mr. Balfour's speech at Birmingham you express a certain disappointment, a disappointment which seems to be shared in some Unionist quarters, that Mr. Balfour did not give us an authorised programme. It is perhaps a pity that Mr. Chamberlain is not able to undertake the preparation of "The Unionist Programme" of 1909 as he did "The Radical Programme" of 1885. A book issued on similar lines written with equal authority would be a boon just now.

But how Mr. Balfour could outline such a programme at Birmingham I fail to see. He was there to combat and destroy the position taken up by the Prime Minister a few days earlier, and I think it will be agreed he did his work pretty thoroughly. The constructive period must come later in a different set of circumstances.

I am yours truly,

Unionist.

REVIEWS.

PROFESSOR ANTI-EVERYTHING.

"Memoir and Letters of Francis W. Newman." By J. Giberne Sieveking. London: Kegan Paul. 1909. 10s. 6d.

FRANCIS WILLIAM NEWMAN was born at 17 Southampton Street, Bloomsbury, on 27 June 1805. He was four years younger than his more celebrated brother, John Henry, the future Cardinal, but, according to many who knew them in their early years, the younger gave promise of a career fully as distinguished as that expected from the abilities of the elder. It would perhaps be difficult to find two brothers whose views and lives were destined to be so divergent, if we leave out of consideration the third brother, Charles Robert, who appears to have been a very undesirable relation, as he is described by Francis as one "of whom we do not speak, because he is as unfit for society as if he were insane". His moral ruin, he adds, "was from Robert Owen's Socialism and atheistic Philosophy".

Francis Newman was sent with his brother John Henry to school at Ealing, and, later, followed him to Oxford. Their religious paths soon showed that divergence which was to increase with age. It is said that in preparing a bedroom for his brother, John Henry hung on the wall a picture of the Virgin, which on his arrival Francis promptly removed as savouring too much of popery. Before two years had been passed at the University "a most painful breach", which was "unhealable", according to the statement of Francis, took place between the brothers, and this in spite of the many benefits which in his "rising manhood he had received" from his elder brother. The divergence of view, which made Francis say that "we seemed never to have an interest or wish in common", and John Henry with more fraternal feeling to declare that "much as we love each other, neither would like to be mistaken for the other", was painfully evidenced by the publication by Francis shortly after his brother's death of "The Early Life of Cardinal Newman". There was no sort of need that he should have published this sketch, the object of which was, if possible, to diminish the reverence and admiration expressed for the Cardinal at his death. At the time of publication it was thought a mistake, if not an outrage, and most people, after many years have passed, will not be inclined to disagree with the author of this present memoir "that it is impossible to justify Francis Newman's thus of his brother".

In 1826 Francis took first-class honours in Classics and Mathematics, gaining also a Fellowship at Balliol. His success was described as one of the best "Double Firsts" ever known in the schools; but as he felt himself unable in conscience to subscribe to the Thirty-nine Articles, he was obliged to resign his Fellowship and could not even take his M.A. By this dictate of his conscience and his consequent determination not to take Orders in the Established Church, Newman apparently sacrificed his prospects of a brilliant worldly career.

On leaving Oxford Francis Newman fell in with two men, who for a time exercised great influences over him: these were Lord Congleton (then Mr. Parnell) and a Mr. A. N. Groves. He agreed to join them in an expedition which is called "the Syrian Missionary journey", the story of which is told in that interesting "Personal Narrative" which Newman published in 1856. Judging from this account, however, it is somewhat difficult to understand wherein consisted the missionary character of the journey.

In 1834 Francis Newman had settled down as classical tutor at Bristol College, and in 1836 he went through the ceremony of baptism in one of the chapels in Bristol. This possibly may have been done at the instance of a lady, Miss Maria Kennaway, whom at this time he married, and who was a zealous Plymouth Sister. It was as a teacher of classics and mathematics that Francis Newman passed the best years of his life. From Bristol in 1840 he passed to Manchester New College, where he was professor of classical literature. Afterwards he came to London, and taught Latin from 1846 to 1869, when he retired with the well-deserved title of "Emeritus Professor". Many who studied under him have described him as an ideal professor. He seems to have had a peculiar genius for imparting knowledge, and if at any time he became conscious that some of his class had not fully understood what he had been explaining he would go over the ground again in such a fresh and new way that even those who had previously grasped his meaning were not made to lose time, but always obtained valuable information from the second explanation. His views as to the proper method of teaching and learning languages might be studied to-day with profit. It is only within a very few years that it has dawned upon some teachers that it is best to teach all languages as living tongues, and that the beginnings of Latin and Greek should not be made so burdensome and distasteful by overmuch learning of "matter quite unworthy of being retained in the mind". Newman desired to find someone capable of writing a good "Latin novel" for the use of students—a Latin comedy which would stimulate the imagination of youthful scholars, "and would convey numerous Latin words which do not easily find a place in poetry, history or philosophy".

A considerable interest attaches to the history of Francis Newman's religious opinions. The author of the "Phases of Faith" has usually been regarded as an agnostic of the aggressive type. But he was not so. That he was for a time, and possibly for a considerable part of his early youth, alienated from the Christian faith can hardly be doubted; but even as early as 1836 the fact that he submitted to re-baptism at Bristol marks a change in his religious or anti-religious principles. It was not, however, till towards the close of his life that he gave any sure indication of a return to Christianity—and there are, we believe, well-informed people who gravely question this. The influence of Dr. Martineau, for many years an intimate and esteemed friend, and of Miss Anna Swanwick brought him before his death to confess, although perhaps somewhat vaguely, his belief in the truth of Christianity. A letter written to Miss Swanwick when Newman was ninety-two years old states that he wished "once again definitely to take the name of Christian". Another friend records the following: "Not more than three or four years before Dr. Martineau's death I was sitting in an omnibus at Oxford Circus, when Dr. Martineau, accompanied by his daughter, got in and took seats by my side. After I had expressed my pleasure at seeing them, he said, 'I think you ought to know that the other day I had a letter from Frank Newman saying that when he died he wished it to be known that he died in the Christian faith'." There is, too, a certain pathetic sentence of Newman's in which he seems to refer to his earlier views in matters of religion. "It is a sad thing", he writes, "to have printed erroneous fact. I have three or four times contradicted and renounced the passage . . . . but I cannot reach those whom I have misled."

Besides his professorial work Francis Newman was from very early years of his life in the forefront of social reform. He was known to many friends and opponents as the Professor "Anti-Everything", and he was pleased to accept this description of his general attitude to social questions. Many, he once wrote, "might wish to know in how many 'antis' I have been and am engaged. Certainly more than you will care to make known will go into two pages of your magazine". To begin with, he was a convinced and strict vegetarian, being for many years president of the society. Then most of the causes which he supported by his name and pen are still with us, so that the "Memoir" as it recalls them appears to be dealing in actualities. The food question and the drink question always interested him, and he blamed the Governments of his day severely for not dealing with them in a way which might remove the standing disgrace to our civilisation. Parliament, he said at one time, will not act because "it sits on the beer barrel". Newman was also a strong advocate of female suffrage, declaring that the exclusion of women from the rights of citizenship on equal terms with men could not be made to square with the most elementary notions of justice. He held also strong views as to the holding of land by large landowners, and he looked back with regret to the times of the mediæval guilds when there was much more co-operation and much less centralisation than has since prevailed. "Back to the land" was his cry half a century ago, and to try in every way to develop rural industry was in his opinion the only hope for England's future prosperity. "It is essential to the public welfare", he writes, "to multiply to the utmost the proportion of actual cultivators or farmers who have a firm tenure of the soil by paying a quit-rent to the State." In the great political questions of the day Newman took the deepest possible interest, and he suffered apparently real mental distress when in his opinion the leaders of the country were directing its destinies wrongly.

This volume will certainly revive the memory of Francis W. Newman, and make many people think more kindly of the Cardinal's brother than they may have been wont to do. Mrs. J. Giberne Sieveking has done her work well, though perhaps some may be inclined to think that there is overmuch of the biographer and too little of the subject.

CHARLES READE, THE NOVELIST.

"The Cloister and the Hearth." By Charles Reade. London: Chatto and Windus. 1909. 12s. 6d. net.

CHARLES READE spent five hours a day in a room that he called "the workshop". The most conspicuous piece of furniture in this room was a large table, battered and worn, underneath which there stood an odd score of tall folios, the nature of their contents being indicated by labels upon the backs. At this table Charles Reade would sit, selecting, cutting, and pasting into its proper place every scrap of fact or experience, written or printed, that he judged to contain anything of interest—anything, that is, which might conceivably be of use to him as literary material. Everything was indexed. Anything could be found at a moment's notice. The culmination of the system was to be found in the Index ad Indices. From the Index ad Indices he could find his way to the correct index. From the correct index he could find his way to the particular slip or cutting that he wanted. His workshop was a triumph of method. His art was a triumph of empiricism.

It was the peculiarity of Charles Reade that he must begin with dry bones in order to arrive at something very like flesh and blood. He had the power to imagine and to inform his creatures with the breath of life, but his imagination was of the kind that abhorred a vacuum. Taking certain facts which he had seen correlated in his actual experience, he would pass them through his intelligence, plunge them into the great reservoirs of his emotion, and bring them forth again more real than reality itself. The greater artists dare more highly than this. They get their fundamental truths from life; and, having these touchstones, they build up their masterpieces by rearranging and not necessarily by accepting what they see. Charles Reade had not enough imagination for this. He was safe only in his workshop. There he could not go wrong. He had all his facts to hand. He had imagination enough to explain them, to quicken them into something more real; but his imagination faltered when he was asked to shape the bricks as well as to build the house.

It was this quality of Charles Reade's mind that marked him out as the man to write the best historical novel in our language. Facts are facts, whether they be three hundred years old or as many minutes. Facts about hermits, after being transmuted in the brain and heart of Charles Reade, issued again to the light with as real and true a life of their own as facts about the contemporary prison-house. By the intensity of his imagination, and by its characteristic limitations, Charles Reade was born for the express purpose of breathing into the dry bones of a vanished period a life so convincing and so eternally true that criticism becomes almost impossible. This process of transmutation was not an easy one. Reading the letters he wrote from Oxford to Mrs. Seymour at the time he was writing "The Cloister and the Hearth", we catch him in the act and watch the mental agony it cost him. It will perhaps be well to make a selection from sentences that occur in the course of this correspondence:

"Alas, indeed, stuck! That is to say, I have found such a wealth of material about hermits in Magdalen College that I have filled three more of those gigantic cards. . . . I must now try to use only the very cream, and that dramatically and not preachingly. . . . I think this story will wear my mind out. However, I see that if I had not read all about hermits and worked out these cards, this part of my story must have been all false. . . . Good Heavens, how often have I been stuck! . . . I cannot tell whether it will succeed or not as a whole . . . . but there shall be great and tremendous and tender things in it."

In these vigorous sentences we see the whole process—the accumulation and intelligent rejection of material; and, finally, that giving out of himself by which he breathed upon it and gave to so much concrete matter its own peculiar life.

Charles Reade, like many another, did not realise the nature of his genius or recognise the necessity under which he lay to work as he did. In the course of those very letters to Mrs. Seymour already quoted he writes: "God knows whether I am in the right path or not. Sometimes I think it must be dangerous to overload fiction with fact. At others I think fiction has succeeded better in proportion to the amount of fact in it". Now, with Charles Reade, fiction was fact touched with emotion. In his case the attempt to distinguish the two was useless. He was incapable, to any great extent, of the fiction which is a rearrangement of fact. He must have the fact itself, out of a record, a blue-book, or a newspaper. In "It is Never too Late to Mend" he describes scenes from Australian life. He had never been to Australia. Here then, it seems, was fiction with a vengeance. It was nothing of the sort. Had he actually been there, comprehended the life and its setting as a whole, quintessentialised it in his own mind, and then allowed his fancy to play when it came to the grouping of detail, and to the depicting of the interplay of emotions whose truth he had himself conceived from general study of the fundamental processes of human nature—then he would have produced a work which was fiction, as we intend the word. He was unable to do this and to do it well. He must have "fact", and "fact" he had when writing "It is Never too Late to Mend". He had never been to Australia. But there were books on flora and fauna. He had never seen the conditions of life in Australia. But there were reports and statistics.

Charles Reade has been taken at his word by one well-known critic. It has been asserted that his fact did kill his fiction, and that his fiction was better when written outside the workshop. That is to say, "Griffith Gaunt" is better than "It is Never too Late to Mend", "Christie Johnstone" is better than "The Cloister and the Hearth". It would require a great deal of space to do justice to this view and to examine the exact amount of truth which it contains. The view here expressed is in direct contravention. In spite of the melodramatic character of the types in novels like "It is Never too Late to Mend", "Hard Cash", or "Foul Play"; in spite of the resourceful hero, the terrible villain and his tool, the sweet young girl and the potential courtesan—in spite of all these things we believe that these novels are truer than those of the type of "Griffith Gaunt", where Charles Reade was trying to write with unfettered fancy and from first principles.

All these realistic novels are left behind in their turn by "The Cloister and the Hearth". His modern realistic work is marred by obvious faults of manner. Founded on facts, their intention is true; but this intention finds a violent and theatrical expression which revolts all the finer literary sensibilities. Moreover, the preaching habit grew upon Charles Reade with years. It brought him at last to the point of writing a whole novel in denunciation of tight-lacing, and to the point of meditating another upon the advantages of being ambidextrous. Now, in "The Cloister and the Hearth" there are no didactics; and the crudity of his intenser manner loses its power to wound by being thrown back into the past. It comes through to the reader like a vivid light that has passed through an ancient window of stained glass. It comes through subdued and touched with old-world tints; and it floods a noble building in which it is a delight to walk, a delight made sacred by a feeling that is almost all of it gratitude and something akin to awe. "There shall be great and tremendous and tender things in it."

ETON OF SORTS.

"Eton Memories." By an Old Etonian. London: Long. 1909. 10s. 6d. net.

ETON is the only school that seems to evoke and furnish a continuous demand and supply of self-regarding literature. This may be accounted for partly by the numbers and the purchasing power of the Etonian circle—and thus possibly Eton literature may be one of the evanescent luxuries doomed to extinction by the new type of Budget—but it still more depends upon the almost romantic quality of affection with which Etonians regard their old school.

The book before us—"Eton Memories"—is almost an extreme instance of the cult in question. Its form is somewhat unaccountable, but it appears to be a record, more or less fanciful, of a boy's life at Eton between 1820 and 1830. Its principal interest is that it reflects a type of schoolboy existence that is barely credible nowadays. The boys who appear in these pages have not the faintest resemblance to the modern public-school boy. They are precocious, insubordinate, rather offensive young men, whose main interest in life appears to be to obtain amusement by putting other people in painful and humiliating positions. Three-quarters of the book seems devoted to practical jokes of this kind. Work is seldom mentioned, and then only as a sort of penal routine; games are the hobby of a limited few; the chief zest of school life seemingly consists in defying the authorities, dames and tutors, not so much by way of open insubordination, but by inflicting on them as far as possible small annoyances and petty aggravations, varied by the destruction of the property of inoffensive persons, such as hearse-drivers, itinerant vendors, and cattle-drovers. Somehow or other the reminiscences do not leave a very pleasant taste in the mouth. They show, it is true, a certain robust and spirited quality, and a reckless daring which would be more attractive if it were not quite so self-conscious. But the book has the wrong kind of good-humour, because the point of too many of the anecdotes is the discomfiture of people who cannot retaliate; while the sportsmanlike element is often lacking, for the simple reason that the perpetrators of these jests take too much care to escape detection. Yet there is no doubt that the book is interesting as reflecting, however one-sidedly, a condition of things which has long since disappeared, and which the writer does not succeed for an instant in making even superficially attractive or desirable. Moreover, there are many incidental touches of a picturesque and entertaining kind. But the semi-farcical character of the whole treatment detracts from the verisimilitude of the book, and thus lowers its value as a faithful representation of contemporary manners. The aim of the writer appears to have been to treat the whole thing from the point of view of an Early Victorian sporting novel. Even Dr. Keate himself, who plays the part of Ursa Major throughout the book, has evidently been touched up for the sake of picturesqueness. Many of his phrases are obviously characteristic enough, such as the repeated prophecy made to offenders of every kind that if they "pursued such vicious courses, they would live unrespected and die unregretted"; and there is a harangue delivered to the school at absence, when Keate had been confronted by a copy of his own bust, which has the stamp of actuality about it:

"Such conduct, and by many old enough to know better, deserves severe punishment; it is opposed to all decency and order, and unless the principals forthwith give themselves up, the whole school must suffer. It might be called a masquerade, but it is great tomfoolery, whilst it shows on the part of some upper boys the worst example—contempt for authority. As to the nonsensical exhibition which has just been cast in my way, it is too vulgar a joke to pass by, and yet it is extremely childish."

There is a delicious inconsequence about this oration, and a sense of the unveiling of a battery of threadbare phrases, only vaguely applicable to the particular offence, which makes the scene a very real one; but a few pages away there is an account of an inquisition held by Keate into the case of a boy whom he had detected riding a pony in the troupe of a passing circus.

"'Hear me, sir', said Fluke. 'When the clown, on his beautiful Lilliputian steed, attracted the crowd around him, he invited the boys to ride, and with the word dismounted, and although I resisted all I could, I was forced on the animal's back. You know, sir, what celerity and force clowns possess. . . . I, for the honour of the school, held on to his neck, feeling at the same time considerable uneasiness lest I should fall backwards, pony and all.'"

This is, of course, pure farce, and not very good farce. Not such were the excuses made in the presence of the redoubtable cocked-hat and the shaggy twitching eyebrows! And this element vitiates the book throughout. What might have been extremely interesting, if its substantial accuracy could have been depended upon, becomes worse than dull when it is a mere piece of crude immature imagination. And thus it leaves on the mind a sense of unpleasant bravado and exaggeration, without any of the attractiveness of romance; it is rather a sordid chronicle; and the only comfort is to reflect that there were probably plenty of boys of the date who lived a more sensible and kindlier life, even if the type so pretentiously displayed seemed a heroic one to the youthful subjects of George IV.

There are a good many mistakes scattered through the volume, such as Provost Lodge, Western's Yard, Eton Wish (for Eton Wick), and so forth. Gray is credited with the line "and drowsy ticklings lull the distant folds"; but the least desirable feature of the book is the illustrations. These profess to be by the hand of an Etonian, but give the impression of having been copied from photographs or drawings by someone with no knowledge of the place. Not to travel far for instances, the illustration called "My Dame's" is not the house described in the text; in the picture of the chapel from Keate's Lane, the bell-turret is represented on the wrong side of the ante-chapel; while in the illustration called "Masters' Houses, Eton", not only are the principal buildings of a date long subsequent to the events of the book, but the entrance to Keate's Lane, which is the most familiar Eton thoroughfare, has been extruded altogether from the scene. These are blemishes which any Old Etonian could detect, and which would have been removed by the most cursory revision.

AMENDED SOUTH AFRICAN HISTORY.

"South Africa." By Ian D. Colvin. (Romance of Empire Series.) London: Jack. 1909. 6s. net.

THE romance of history is inherent; it hardly needs extraction even for him who regards history as interesting only in its adventures, its coincidences, its anecdotes, its dramatic developments. To set out with the deliberate purpose of telling merely of stirring deeds, of the conflicts of races for supremacy, of the heroism of some, of the wickedness of others, is largely to ignore the permanent and essential forces at work in a country's life-story. Soldiers may fight and change the course of history, but it is the psychology of peoples and the policies of statesmen which direct affairs before the crisis, often govern the crisis itself, and take up the running when the crisis is over. Obviously history cannot be written with an eye to romantic incident only, any more than a man's life can be summed up in his quarrels. It is the weakness of a series such as that to which Mr. Colvin's book belongs that every chapter must have its exciting adventure, its "curtain" in fact. Mr. Colvin appears to have made a gallant but ineffectual struggle to escape from the series' environment, the environment which finds new expression in the coloured pictures that are meant to illustrate his text. He aims at writing serious history, and in more than one chapter has contributed to the elucidation of questions which have long been the subject of bitter recrimination. But he seems to be handicapped by the consciousness that this is a book primarily for boys, that he is expected to write to a certain order of intelligence, with the result that his manner is not always equal to his matter. Yet the book is the outcome of a research which is unusual in works of this sort, and there is an element of imagination about it which lifts it outside its class. Mr. Colvin tells the story of the early days with many graphic touches, in the main steering clear of dates—fortunately perhaps, if there were to be many misprints such as 1846 for 1486 on page 7. He is clearly qualifying to be the historian of South Africa, and even Dr. Theal will find some passages of this book worthy of his attention.

Thoroughly British as he is, Mr. Colvin is British without unfairness to the Dutch; he has the gift of seeing something of the other side, which is not always the historian's characteristic. He invites South Africans to study their common history in the assurance that the heroes are not all on one side and the blacklegs all on the other. But whilst noting the shortcomings of the British and the good in the Dutch, he shows how authorities like Dr. Theal have done a wrong to the British name, and by so doing have served to keep alive enmities which were better dead and forgotten. The story of Slachter's Nek is one which Britons have always regarded as reflecting on British humanity, if not on British honour. The story as told hitherto is that of a brave Boer, "wanted" for trying to foment a native rising, being shot by a Hottentot at the instance of the British, whilst those associated with him were publicly hanged. "The official papers which gave the true story", says Mr. Colvin, "have all been published by Mr. Liebbrandt, but very few people like to read a thousand pages of old letters and legal evidence, and unfortunately the writer who should have made the truth clear, Dr. Theal, has only been one more raven croaking on the tree." The rebel Boer had sought to accomplish what is the most dastardly thing in the eyes of British and Dutch alike—to set the blacks on to massacre the whites. "As a matter of fact, the Dutch were as much concerned in hanging the rebels as the English. Dutchmen were in command of the forces that attacked them; Dutch burghers helped to capture them; a Dutch official prosecuted them; a Dutch judge sentenced them; a Dutch magistrate hanged them; and all the English Governor did was to pardon one of them." If the facts are as Mr. Colvin sees them after his study of Liebbrandt's papers, Slachter's Nek was not the result of Governor Somerset's brutal tyranny but of the savagery of a pack of border ruffians determined, in their own words, "to extirpate the villains of Englishmen out of our country". Slachter's Nek, handed down in the Taal—the official survival of which Mr. Colvin regrets as tending to keep the country bilingual and divided, has done an infinite amount of mischief. The truth could not appear at a more auspicious moment than the present. If the Boers are in earnest in their latest manifestation of friendship they will welcome it not less cordially than the British, and the younger generation which begins to read history with Mr. Colvin will at least not be fed upon all the horrors and libels on which its fathers supped.

THE KING OF GAMES.

"Court Tennis, Racquets and Squash." By Frederick Charles Tompkins. Lippincott. 1909. 3s. 6d. net.

THE tennis player is no spoiled child of author and publisher. Cricketers, golfers, lawn-tennis players are urged to their doing and undoing by every kind of writer, from the author who would extol the "complete" player to the scribe of the weekly and daily press. So we welcome the above treatise with more than common interest. It is a shapely, even distinguished-looking, little book, as pleasant to the eye as it is fitted, in the author's phrase, for "one's pocket". If to criticise is to find fault, our criticism is soon ended; but it begins at once. Why "Court Tennis"? Surely a vile phrase: and to come from a nephew of the great Edmund—it is enough to make him turn in his grave! Says our author, "in the minds of the majority of people 'tennis' is associated with an outdoor game, and they are therefore at a loss to understand", etc. Well, this is carrying tenderness to the weak brother to an extreme indeed. Besides, does not the lawn-tennis player speak of his "court"? No, Mr. Tompkins, let us stick to "Tennis" and "Lawn Tennis" and leave the "minds of the majority of people" to take care of themselves.

Our author rightly begins his treatise with a plan of a tennis court and two excellent reproductions of photographs showing the two sides of a court. True, he calls them "courts", though the usual names are "service-side" and "hazard-side", and we venture to think that even to the minds of the majority of people "service-side" and "hazard-side" would present no difficulty. The plan should have indicated the "service pent-house"—the part of the side pent-house a ball must touch in service, and we should be puzzled by what appears to be a circular cutting in the pent-house for the marker's box, did not the photographs of the court show that it is an eccentricity of the draughtsman, and we are still in the dark as regards the little indentations in the dedans. Apart from these trifles we have nothing but praise. Mr. Tompkins' descriptions and hints are as good as they can be, and we are pleased to note that he states plainly one of the small things about tennis which will puzzle an onlooker (who is not a tennis player), let him be a very Solon for wisdom—it is that the score of the winner of the last stroke is called first. The chapter on service is good, but we do not like his lax use of the word "drop". The "drop" is one of the three main varieties of service, and though, of course, in a giraffe service the ball "drops" on to the pent-house, the two services have nothing whatever to do with each other. The giraffe service is an underhand wrist service made to rise high in the air, to touch the edge of the pent-house in falling, and to fly thence to the utmost limits of the service-court. The "drop" is served from near the main wall, rises high in the air, drops on the pent-house, and falls as near as may be in the angle of the battery walls. The author should read his sentence on page 68 referring to overhead railroad service—as printed it is misleading to a novice; and on page 88, among the hints, we think he must mean "defending" and not "playing for". These hints are excellent, and we particularly commend those on the barring of certain services and strokes by players who constantly play together and grow to rely too much on these parts of their game. It is an admirable suggestion which we do not remember to have seen given before.

To the best of our belief Mr. Tompkins' book is only the fifth to deal with "Tennis" in nearly ninety years. In 1822 came "A Treatise on Tennis", by "A Member of the Tennis Club"—now a rather rare book—full of excellent hints and out-of-the-way tennis lore. Not the least amusing of these is a table of "the odds as usually betted". Thus, "upon the first stroke being won between even players, that is, 15 love, the odds upon a single game are 7 to 4, but 6 to 4 is more usually betted. Thirty love 4 to 1, but 3 to 1 more usually betted", and so on, all through the set. But the author concludes: "The odds are very precarious; to say nothing of the difficulty of making a match so near as to leave neither party the favourite". After this work, tennis lovers had to wait fifty-six years before Mr. Julian Marshall's full and admirable "Annals of Tennis" appeared in 1878. After that there was a small book of the "All England" Series, to which Mr. Marshall contributed, in 1890; and six years later appeared the Badminton volume, containing Mr. J. M. Heathcote's fascinating records and descriptions and an admirable paper by Mr. Alfred Lyttelton. And now there is the present little book. We remember also Mr. Marshall's article in the "Encyclopædia Britannica";

and another, a model in its learning and lucidity, by Mr. G. E. Ross, in the "Encyclopædia of Sports", and that is all; all that there is in prose—a modest list for the "king of games". J. K. S.'s immortal "Parker's Piece, May 19, 1891", stands by itself as the single poem of the game.

Good as Mr. Tompkins' work is within its limits, we wish that he could have seen his way, or that another could see his way, to give some worthy portraits of the great players of the last twenty years. In Mr. Heathcote's pages the giants of his early days live again and, short as these pages are, we read with keen interest of Barre and Biboche, Edmund Tompkins and George Lambert. But we should like companion pictures of Mr. Heathcote himself (amateur champion for twenty-three years, if you please, and only the merest shade behind the professional champions of his time), of Mr. Lyttelton, of Saunders and Latham, of "Punch" Fairs and Ferdinand, of Mr. Miles, and Mr. Jay Gould. Where is the historian of these? If Mr. Ross had the leisure we would urge the task on him. No man has followed the game with more devotion or written of it with greater insight than he—has he not materials he could fashion to a book? Such work is a labour of love and the material reward is not great, but he would earn the eternal gratitude of all who care for tennis. So we take our leave of Mr. Tompkins (of whom we have pleasant memories in his London days), and congratulate the Philadelphia Club on an "instructor" accomplished and excellent as well in the pocket as in the court.

NOVELS.

"In Ambush." By Marie van Vorst. London: Methuen. 1909. 6s.

The reformatory influence of the Right Woman is little short of miraculous. Sydney Adair, alias Bill Flanders, had been a highwayman, bank-robber, and general outlaw out West before he stole the money and the wife of his partner, Tom Moody, and vamoosed up Klondyke way; and neither Mrs. Moody, with whom he lived there, nor the Princess Trebesco, to whom he became affianced in Cairo, nor any of the ladies of the harem he was reported to keep at Wady Halfa, nor the gay Parisiennes, whom he took down to Auteuil, improved him a bit. But the beautiful young Kentuckian, Helena Desprey, crossed his erratic path on her "finishing" tour, and lo! that Denver bank received back the sum (plus interest) stolen from it fifteen years before; the States of Colorado and California, which Flanders had upset a good deal, got two million dollars between them for local charities, and Tom Moody's Irish relatives came into a little fortune. He was a splendid fellow, despite the warrants out against him, and twice saved Moody's life, besides rallying the Lancers in that charge at Omdurman; and the more Helena learnt about his past the more she forgave him, and when she found he had wiped quite a lot of it out she ran away with him. The book is capital melodrama, ingeniously devised, as we have seen, to win the vote of that large section of novel-readers every unit in which believes herself to be the Right Woman for somebody or other.

"Concerning Himself: the Story of an Ordinary Man." By Victor L. Whitechurch. London: Unwin. 1909.

Every curate should be made to read this book. We are not going to discuss the author's views on dogma, but he talks very soundly about the way in which religion is presented to the average English boy. Gerald Sutton, who herein writes his life-story, had reached the age of ten (and heard much about spiritual matters) before a friendly curate of the right sort put into his mind the quite novel and startling idea "that religion had anything manly about it". How he gradually developed a working faith, passed through a theological college (after a period of close contact with agreeable Roman Catholics who hoped to convert him), and settled down into a sensible country parson, are matters told effectively. The inevitable love interest is commonplace enough, but Mr. Whitechurch has some humour and observes very closely. He gives a faithful picture of life in a small cathedral town, and the odd vicissitudes through which young Sutton passes (going for a time from a good private school to a Board School) enable him to bring out one or two points which most of us pretend to ignore. Mr. Whitechurch is the only man we have come across with the courage to say (what is certainly true) that Board-school boys in England are absolutely devoid of that instinct against "sneaking" which forms the basis of such morals as the middle- or upper-class boy possesses. That is a thing of some importance in an age of democracy—but we are all afraid of being called snobs if we tell the truth about our political masters.

"Love, the Thief." By Helen Mathers. London: Stanley Paul. 1909. 6s.

Miss Mathers has for some years assiduously turned out novels. If there was nothing strikingly brilliant in them, neither was anything harmful; if they were unoriginal and devoid of literary qualities, they never lapsed into sensationalism or vulgarity; above all, Miss Mathers has been regular, punctual, always up to time. Yet she cannot make fiction-writing pay. Well, well! We wonder how long it was before Balzac made fiction-writing pay? Did Keats or Shelley make a profit out of their poetry? However, these questions are hardly pertinent, for Miss Mathers does not pose as an artist, but as a woman of business. That being so, it would savour of ill-natured irony to deplore a loss to literature: she is giving up story-spinning and going into some other business, just as, we daresay, at this moment other ladies are giving up, say, millinery and going into some other business. As for "Love, the Thief", it resembles many stories by Miss Mathers in being eminently fit for "the home". The tailors' and dressmakers' dummies do and say the right and respectable thing, with slips, and in the end there is nothing to wail or knock the breast about. In "the home" itself no one will wail or knock the breast either because the tale is finished or because the tale marks the finish of a confessedly unsuccessful business career. There are as good fish in the sea as ever came out: in "the home" there will not as yet be any lack of harmless novels that kill time if they do not enliven the understanding.

"Margaret Hever." By Elizabeth Martindale. London: Duckworth. 1909. 6s.

This story is concerned with the wobbling of Margaret's heart between the elderly bore to whom she is engaged and the insufferable cub who makes love to her under the other's nose. If the respective representatives of enduring affection and youthful passion had been drawn—as there is no reason why they should not have been—the one something less of a numskull, and the other just a little of a gentleman, the situation might have been interesting; as it is, the behaviour of Margaret's heart is unaccountable. Nothing in the literary reputation of the two lovers will explain it; for whilst on the one hand the younger man's art was "consummate", the romances of the elder were "perfect in style", and "apparently"—the author means clearly—"the outcome of an enlightened psychology". We regret our inability to apply any of these phrases without considerable modification to this "outcome".

SHORTER NOTICES.

"Masters of Literature":—"Scott", by Professor H. J. Grant; "Fielding", by Professor Saintsbury. London: Bell. 1909. 3s. 6d. net.

These two volumes are the first of a series which are to present the Masters of Literature to the British public by way of passages selected and explained with reference to context by the "critic in charge". The enterprise is either a bravely cynical one; or it is immoral. If it issue from a frank recognition of the fact that a classic writer is a writer

(*Continued on page* 418.)

THE

Scottish Provident Institution.

The Distinctive System of this Institution offers the substantial advantage of With-Profit Assurances at rates differing little from those usually charged for Non-Profit Policies.

Accumulated Funds, £14,000,000.

Head Office: 6 St. Andrew Square, Edinburgh.
London: 3 Lombard Street, E.C. 17 Pall Mall, S.W.

Head  *Office.*

Governor—
Sir Nevile Lubbock, K.C.M.G.

Incorporated A.D. 1720.

ROYAL EXCHANGE

ASSURANCE CORPORATION.

Fire, Life, Sea, Accidents, Motor Car, Glass, Burglary, Annuities, Employers' Liability, Fidelity Guarantees.

The Corporation is prepared to act as TRUSTEE and EXECUTOR.

Apply for full particulars of all classes of Insurance to the Secretary, ROYAL EXCHANGE ASSURANCE, ROYAL EXCHANGE, LONDON, E.C.

ATLAS ASSURANCE CO. LTD.

Head Office ... 92 CHEAPSIDE, LONDON, E.C.

FIRE — LIFE
ACCIDENT — BURGLARY

Including Uncalled Capital, the Resources of the Company

EXCEED FIVE MILLIONS STERLING.

LIFE BONUS YEAR, 1909.

All With-Profit Assurances effected in 1909, and in force at Dec. 31, will be entitled to participate.

Active and Influential Agents Wanted.

SAML. J. PIPKIN, General Manager.

LONDON, EDINBURGH & GLASGOW ASSURANCE COMPANY, LIMITED.

Incorporated 1881.

For the Year 1908.

Premium Income - - - - - - £598,024.
£98,473 added to the Assurance Funds.
The Assurance Funds are now over £1,000,000 Sterling.

SUMMARY OF TWENTY YEARS' RESULTS.

Year.	Premium Income less Annuities.	Income from Interest, Dividends and Rents.	Assurance Funds at the end of the Year.
	£	£	£
1888	120,907	2,159	54,617
1898	333,241	5,663	219,969
1906	598,024	36,073	1,012,144

ADDITIONAL REPRESENTATIVES WANTED.

Head Office:
Euston Square, London.

Apply **THOS. NEILL,**
General Manager.

THE EQUITABLE Life Assurance Society.

Founded 1762. FUNDS, 5 MILLIONS.

MANSION HOUSE STREET (Opposite the Mansion House), LONDON, E.C.

Ask for Particulars of

SPECIALLY LOW RATES FOR DEATH DUTY POLICIES.

No Commission Paid. Expenses, Half the Average.

Clergy Mutual Assurance Society, 1829.

OPEN TO THE

CLERGY AND THEIR RELATIVES.

LOW PREMIUMS—LARGE BONUSES—ABSOLUTE SECURITY.

Funds, £4,351,197. Income, £471,097.
Bonuses Distributed, £4,256,464.

Office:—2 & 3 The Sanctuary, Westminster, S.W.

NO AGENTS EMPLOYED. NO COMMISSION PAID.

GENERAL LIFE ASSURANCE COMPANY

Mortgages.] ESTABLISHED 1837. **[Annuities.**

CAPITAL—£1,000,000. FUNDS IN HAND—£2,000,000.

Chief Office: 103 CANNON STREET, LONDON, E.C.

Board of Directors.

Alfred James Shepheard, Esq., Chairman.
Lord Arthur Cecil, Deputy Chairman.

H. J. Bracey, Esq.
H. E. Duke, Esq., K.C.
Hon. R. C. Grosvenor.
Sir John Jardine, K.C.I.E., M.P.
William Muller, Esq.
Robert Henry Scott, Esq., F.R.S., D.Sc.
Rt. Hon. Viscount Valentia, C.B., M.V.O., M.P.

Double advantage policies issued ecuring two payments of the amount assured—one payment on the attainment of a specific age, and a second payment at death thereafter.

Advances made on Reversions, vested or contingent, and Life Interests, and on Personal Security in connection with a Life Policy.

JOHN ROBERT FREEMAN, *Manager and Secretary.*

LONDON AND LANCASHIRE LIFE OFFICE.

New Special Features:

GUARANTEED SPECIAL ENDOWMENT SCHEME

with GUARANTEED BONUSES on Maturity.

VALUABLE OPTIONS AND EXCEPTIONAL PRIVILEGES.

ASSURANCES FOR CHILDREN WITHOUT MEDICAL EXAMINATION.

Write to General Manager, 66 & 67 CORNHILL, LONDON.

PRUDENTIAL ASSURANCE COMPANY

(LIMITED)

HOLBORN BARS, LONDON, E.C.

INVESTED FUNDS - - £70,000,000.

ALLIANCE

ASSURANCE COMPANY, LIMITED.

Head Office: BARTHOLOMEW LANE, LONDON, E.C.

ACCUMULATED FUNDS EXCEED £16,500,000.

Chairman:
Right Hon. LORD ROTHSCHILD, G.C.V.O.

THE OPERATIONS OF THE COMPANY EMBRACE ALL BRANCHES OF INSURANCE.

DEATH DUTIES.—Special forms of Policies have been prepared by the Company providing for the payment of Death Duties, thus avoiding the necessity of disturbing investments at a time when it may be difficult to realise without loss.

INCOME TAX.—Under the provisions of the Act, Income Tax is not payable on that portion of the Assured's income which is devoted to the payment of premiums on an assurance on his life. Having regard to the amount of the Tax, this abatement (which is limited to one-sixth of the Assured's income) is an important advantage to Life Policyholders.

Full particulars of all classes of Insurance, together with Proposal Forms and Statement of Accounts, may be had on application to any of the Company's Offices or Agents.

ROBERT LEWIS, General Manager.

who is praised, discussed, and left unread; then it is a cynical enterprise, with courage in it. For the purposes of literary small-talk upon Fielding, a little volume of three hundred odd pages, taking you through his novels and giving you samples by the way, is a most convenient thing to have. It may, however, defeat its purpose; for, if the shallowness of the interest in classic literature be so unblushingly displayed, there will cease to be occasion for a pretence grown so transparent.

But we suspect that the enterprise is not so much bravely cynical as frankly immoral. Thus we read in the "prospectus": "It is needless to enlarge upon the value of a series of this kind for a student who is getting up a given author. The present series is, in fact, in a large measure constructed to suit his special needs". In other words these are literary cram-books, very excellent cram-books, on particular authors. To all students who require that literary smattering properly necessary for the attainment of a degree in letters at some of our Universities these books may be recommended. For the slipshod reviewer they will be mines of pure ore. For the literary small-talker they will come as a boon and a blessing. But for the few who care to read their Fielding without the direction of a "critic in charge"; who can eat a Waverley novel whole, despising tit-bits; who want their Thackeray without Chesterton, their Dickens without Seccombe, their Hazlitt without Lucas—why, let these old-fashioned people fare further, without much fear of faring worse.

"The Law of Compensation for Industrial Diseases." By Edward Thornton Hill Lawes. London: Stevens and Sons. 1909. 7s. 6d.

"Accidental Injuries to Workmen." By H. Norman Barnett and Cecil E. Shaw. London: Rebman. 1909. 7s. 6d. net.

These two books are of the very highest type in the class to which they belong. In treating of the Workmen's Compensation Act 1906 it is difficult to say whether the legal or the medical aspect is most striking. Lawyer and doctor each must understand the other's special department of knowledge. Mr. Lawes' book contains information about diseases which make it look almost like a medical treatise; Messrs. Barnett and Shaw's book opens with an admirable legal Introduction by Mr. Thomas J. Campbell. But a distinction must be made. Mr. Lawes primarily writes for lawyers; Messrs. Barnett and Shaw are medical men, and they write primarily for doctors, who have so many important duties under the Act. Their book, we believe, is the only one which treats all the accidents and diseases which may form claims for compensation from the standpoint of the medical profession. Mr. Lawes' book is to be distinguished from the many books on workmen's compensation in that it is not a treatise on the whole subject. It is limited to the legal and medical aspects of the subject of compensation for industrial diseases. We may say that we believe the reader who is a layman either in medicine or law would find both books well worthy of a place in his library. The Act of 1906 is a great chapter in the history of civilisation and society, and these books would repay reading for the light they throw on the industrial and social environment of the working classes.

"Shall we Ever Reach the Pole?" By F.R.A.S. New and Revised Edition. London: Morgan. 1909. 6d.

Thirty years ago this remarkable pamphlet attracted some attention. F.R.A.S. clearly does not believe the Pole has been reached or ever will be reached, because, in his opinion, there is no Pole to reach. Basing his ideas on the experiments of M. Plateau, the Belgian physicist, he came to the conclusion that the earth must be hollow round the axis. Hence in a note to the reader of this new edition he asks us to consider whether either of "the Arctic veterans" who are "hurling epitaphs" at each other has "got there". His pamphlet will quicken public curiosity as to the evidence to be produced.

"The Tactics of To-day." By Colonel C. E. Callwell. London: Blackwood. 2s. 6d. net.

That a sixth impression of this admirable little handbook should have been issued is sufficient evidence of its excellence, to which we called attention at the time it was published. Its reappearance, however, reminds us, with a feeling of regret, that its gifted author is no longer on the active list of the Army. In these days of "push" and advertisement, it is greatly to be deplored that no place should have been found for Colonel Callwell on the General Officers' list.

The Adventures of a Civil Engineer: Fifty Years on Five Continents." By C. O. Burge. London: Rivers. 1909. 7s. 6d. net.

Mr. Burge's book is very readable, though as a story of adventure it does not amount to much. A more appropriate name might have been found for what is just the autobiography of a man who in many parts of the world has worked at a profession which more than most others affords material for a diversified narrative. Being evidently a man of observation and humour, the writer has a good deal to tell that is amusing. If some of his stories are rather venerable they may, from their very age, have an element of novelty for a new generation. A man who has heard Dan O'Connell addressing a Dublin crowd can draw on the past with some impunity. Unchanging India has supplied little worth recording. The early experiences of Ireland and the strange contrast they present with the present day are distinctly diverting.

"Henry Hudson in Holland." By H. C. Murphy. The Hague: Martinus Nijhoff. 1909.

This "inquiry into the origin and objects of the voyage which led to the discovery of the Hudson river" was originally published by Murphy, the United States Minister at the Hague, in 1859. It is opportunely reprinted by Mr. Nijhoff in this the tercentenary year of the great discovery. The book was the result of much painstaking research, and, as it is not now easily available, should be welcomed in its new form by students of the seventeenth-century voyages. Mr. Nijhoff thinks that possibly further documents may in time be unearthed. We know all too little of Hudson, and what we know we owe in no small measure to Murphy.

For this Week's Books see page 420.

THIS WEEK'S BOOKS.

ART

The National Gallery (General Editor, T. Leman Hare).. Jack. 10s. 6d. net.
The International Art Series:—William Hogarth (Edward Hutton). Fisher Unwin. 5s. net.

BIOGRAPHY

The Reminiscences of Carl Schuz (Frederic Bancroft and William Dunning. 3 vols.). Murray. 36s. net.
The Last Journals of Horace Walpole during the Reign of George III. from 1771-1783 (A. Francis Steuart. 2 vols.), 25s. net; Madame de Maintenon (C. C. Dyson), 12s. 6d. net. Lane.
Francesco Petrarca, Poet and Humanist (Maud F. Jerrold). 12s. 6d. net. Dent.

FICTION

The Tireless Rider (J. Wesley Hart); A Bridge of Fancies (James Cassidy). Culley. 6s. each.
The Upper Hand (Mrs. Frederick Dawson). Grant Richards. 6s.
The Odd Man (Arnold Holcombe); Trial by Marriage (Wilfrid Scarborough Jackson). Lane. 6s. each.
The Burnt Offering (Mrs. Everard Cotes); The Column of Dust (Evelyn Underhill). Methuen. 6s. each.
Hedwig in England (By the Author of "Marcia in Germany"). Heinemann. 3s. 6d. net.
Actions and Reactions (Rudyard Kipling). Macmillan. 6s.
The Unlucky Mark (F. E. Penny). Chatto and Windus. 6s.
Ann Veronica (H. G. Wells). Fisher Unwin. 6s.
The Witch Queen of Khem (Ena Fitzgerald); Her Suburban Highness (Gurner Gillman); The Serpent and the Cross (Stephen Andrew). Greening. 6s. each.

GIFT BOOKS

Rubaiyat of Omar Khayyam (Edward FitzGerald). Black. 7s. 6d. net.
The Red Book of Heroes (Mrs. Lang). Longmans, Green. 6s.

HISTORY

The Reformation Period (Henry Gee); The Mediæval Church and the Papacy (Arthur C. Jennings). Methuen. 2s. 6d. net each.
A Literary History of the English People (J. J. Jusserand). Fisher Unwin. 12s. 6d. net.
Epistolæ Obscurorum Virorum (Francis Griffin Stokes). Chatto and Windus. 25s. net.
Memorials of S. Paul's Cathedral (William Macdonald Sinclair). Chapman and Hall. 16s. net.
The Merry Past (Ralph Nevill). Duckworth. 10s. 6d. net.

REPRINTS AND TRANSLATIONS

Lady Windermere's Fan (Oscar Wilde); A Woman of No Importance (Oscar Wilde). Methuen. 5s. net each.
Penguin Island (Anatole France). Lane. 6s.
How to Study the Stars (L. Rudaux); Greece in Evolution (Edited by G. F. Abbott). Fisher Unwin. 5s. net each.
The Prologue to the Canterbury Tales of Geoffrey Chaucer, 2s. 6d. net; The Confessions of Saint Augustine (Bouverie Pusey), 7s. 6d. net; Dramatis Personæ and Dramatic Romances and Lyrics (Robert Browning). 6s. Chatto and Windus.
David Hill (Rev. W. T. A. Barber). Culley. 2s. 6d.

SCHOOL BOOKS

Plane Trigonometry (H. S. Carslaw). Macmillan. 4s. 6d.
Words and Places (Rev. Isaac Taylor). Routledge. 6s.
A Text-book of Botany for Students (A. F. M. Johnson). Allman. 7s. 6d.

TRAVEL

Southern Rhodesia (Percy F. Hone). Bell. 10s. 6d. net.
China (Mortimer Mempes), 5s. net; Kashmir (Sir Francis Younghusband), 20s. net. Black.
The Soul of a Turk (Victoria De Bunsen). Lane. 10s. 6d. net.
The Face of China (E. G. Kemp). Chatto and Windus. 20s. net.
Our Entry into Hunan (C. Wilfrid Allan). Culley. 2s. 6d.

MISCELLANEOUS

Chats on Old Silver (E. L. Lowes). Fisher Unwin. 5s. net.
Darwinism and Modern Socialism (F. W. Headley). Methuen. 5s. net.
Fruit Ranching in British Columbia (J. T. Bealby), 3s. 6d. net; Montaigne and Shakespeare (John M. Robertson), 7s. 6d. net. Black.
Stephen's Book of the Farm (Revised by James Macdonald). Edinburgh: Blackwood. 21s. net.

REVIEWS AND MAGAZINES FOR OCTOBER.—The Cornhill Magazine, 1s.; The Century, 1s. 4d.; The Treasury, 6d.; Harper's, 1s.; Scribner's, 1s.; The Fortnightly Review, 2s. 6d.; The Socialist Review, 6d.; The Nineteenth Century and After, 2s. 6d.; The Empire Review, 1s.; The World's Work, 1s.; The Connoisseur, 1s.; Blackwood's, 2s. 6d.; The English Review, 2s. 6d.; The Contemporary Review, 2s. 6d.

NEW NOVEL BY

H. G. WELLS

ANN VERONICA.

Ready October 4. – – – Price 6s.

Town Planning in Practice. An Introduction to the Art of Designing Cities and Suburbs. By RAYMOND UNWIN. With 300 Illustrations, Maps and Plans. Crown 4to. cloth.	21/- net.
The Record of the University Boat Race, 1829-1909, and Register of those who have taken part in it. Revised and completed to date by C. M. PITMAN, O.U.B.C. With a Frontispiece. Medium 8vo. cloth. (Edition limited to 550 Copies, of which 500 are for sale.)	21/- net.
A Beau Sabreur. Maurice de Saxe, Marshal of France, His Loves, His Laurels, and his Times (1696-1750). By W. R. H. TROWBRIDGE, Author of "Seven Splendid Sinners," &c. With a Photogravure Frontispiece and 38 other Illustrations. Demy 8vo. cloth.	15/- net.
The French Procession. A Pageant of Great Writers. By Madame DUCLAUX (Mary Robinson). With 6 Photogravure Plates. Demy 8vo. cloth.	12/6 net.
A Literary History of the English People. Vol. III. From the Renaissance to the Civil War. II. By J. J. JUSSERAND. With a Photogravure Frontispiece. Demy 8vo. cloth.	12/6 net.
The Birth of Modern Italy. The Posthumous Papers of Jessie White Mario. Edited, with Introduction, Notes, and Epilogue, by the Duke LITTA-VISCONTI-ARESE. With a Photogravure Frontispiece and 40 other Illustrations. Demy 8vo. cloth.	12/6 net.
Inns, Ales and Drinking Customs of Old England. By F. W. HACKWOOD, Author of "Old English Sports." With a Coloured Frontispiece and 53 other Illustrations. Demy 8vo. cloth.	10/6 net.
Notes by the Way. With Memoirs of Joseph Knight and Woodfall Ebbsworth. By JOHN COLLINS FRANCIS, Publisher of the *Athenæum*. With 8 Illustrations. Buckram. "The charm of the book is in its discursive reference to all sorts and conditions of men and books. I shall always value very highly this attractive volume."—Mr. CLEMENT SHORTER in the *Sphere*.	10/6 net.
Greece in Evolution. Studies Prepared under the auspices of the French League for the Defence of the Rights of Hellenism. By TH. HOMOLLE, HENRY ROUSSAYE, TH. REINACH, ED. THERY, G. DESCHAMPS, CH. DIEHL, G. FOUGERES, J. PSICHARI, A. BELL, M. PAILLARES. With a Preface by the Right. Hon. Sir CHARLES W. DILKE, M.P. Translated from the French under the editorship of G. F. ABBOTT. Large crown 8vo. cloth.	5/- net.
Chats on Old Silver. By E. L. LOWES, Author of "Chats on Old Lace." With a Coloured Frontispiece and 64 other Full-page Plates. Large crown 8vo. cloth. [*Unwin's "Chats" Series.*	5/- net.
How to Study the Stars. Astronomy with Small Telescopes and the Naked Eye, and Notes on Celestial Photography. By L. RUDAUX. Translated by A. H. KEANE, LL.D., F.R.G.S. With 79 Illustrations. Large crown 8vo. cloth.	5/- net.
The Sovranty of Society. By HUGH E. M. STUTFIELD. The *Standard* says: "There is no lack of robust common sense in this straight talk, and the book ought to open a good many eyes to modern tendencies which are disquieting." The *Daily Chronicle* says: "Mr. Stutfield gives us a constant flow of literary champagne. His chapters are well written, true, and clever."	5/- net.

Full particulars of the above-mentioned books will be found in Mr. FISHER UNWIN'S AUTUMN ANNOUNCEMENT LIST, a copy of which will be sent post free to any address on application.

T. FISHER UNWIN, 1 Adelphi Terrace, London.

CHATTO AND WINDUS'S EARLY AUTUMN ANNOUNCEMENTS.

THE SON OF MARY BETHEL. By ELSA BARKER. "The book has power and reality behind it, and cannot fail of a true influence and appeal."—*Manchester Guardian.*	6/-
THE KNIGHT OF THE GOLDEN SWORD. By MICHAEL BARRINGTON. "A vigorous story."—*Times.* "A splendid story."—*Pall Mall.*	6/-
Mrs. PENNY'S *NEW ANGLO-INDIAN STORY,* **THE UNLUCKY MARK.** *Just Issued.*	6/-
KING HAL—OF HERONSEA. By W. WILLMOTT DIXON, Author of "The Rogue of Rye."	6/- Oct. 7.
A brilliant Story by a New Writer. **INFLUENCES.** By PAUL METHVEN. First review: "Mr. Paul Methven is a skilful deviser of plots and has a vivacious way of writing. . . . The story is sure to interest, for it has the qualities which go to make popularity." *Daily Telegraph.*	6/-
A New Story by COSMO HAMILTON. **PLAIN BROWN.**	6/- Oct. 15.
MELBA. AN AUTHORIZED BIOGRAPHY. By AGNES M. MURPHY. With Chapters by MADAME MELBA on **"THE ART OF SINGING"** AND ON **"THE SELECTION OF MUSIC AS A PROFESSION."** Also an Introductory Note by J. A. FULLER MAITLAND. Photogravure Frontispiece and 37 Portraits, Views, and Facsimiles.	16/- net. Oct. 15
THE CONFESSIONS OF ST. AUGUSTINE. Translated by Dr. E. B. PUSEY. Edited by TEMPLE SCOTT. Introduction by Mrs. MEYNELL. 12 Coloured Illustrations by MAXWELL ARMFIELD.	7/6 net.
THE CLOISTER AND THE HEARTH. By CHARLES READE. With 30 Plates in Colour and 10 in Line by BYAM SHAW, R.I. Title, End Papers, and Cover Designed by the Artist.	12/6
THE RAINBOW BOOK. By Mrs. H. M. SPIELMANN. Coloured Frontispiece and 15 Illustrations by ARTHUR RACKHAM, A.R.W.S., And 21 in Black and White by other well-known Artists.	5/- net.
THE FACE OF CHINA. By E. G. KEMP, F.R.S.G.S. Travels in East, North, Central, and Western China. With some Account of the New Schools, Universities, and Missions, and the old Religious Sacred Places of Confucianism, Buddhism, and Taoism, and a Map of China. With 64 Illustrations after Water Colours and Sepia Drawings by the Author.	20/- net.
THE COLOUR OF ROME. By OLAVE M. POTTER. 60 Illustrations in Water Colour and Sepia by YOSHIO MARKINO, who also contributes an introductory chapter.	20/- net. Oct. 7.
THE ROSE AND THE RING. By WM. THACKERAY. With Coloured Frontispiece and 44 Illustrations (12 in two tints) and decorated end-papers by GORDON BROWNE.	3/6 net.
DRAMATIS PERSONÆ: AND DRAMATIC ROMANCES AND LYRICS. By ROBERT BROWNING. With Ten Full-page Coloured Plates by ELEANOR FORTESCUE BRICKDALE.	6/- net.
THE PAINTERS OF VICENZA. By TANCRED BORENIUS. With 15 Full-page Plates.	7/6 net.
TRAVELS WITH A DONKEY IN THE CEVENNES. By ROBERT LOUIS STEVENSON. 12 Coloured Plates and 12 Facsimile Drawings by NOEL ROOKE.	7/6 net.
ASTRONOMICAL CURIOSITIES. By J. ELLARD GORE. (Two Illustrations.)	6/- net. Oct. 7

CHATTO & WINDUS, ST. MARTIN'S LANE, LONDON.

SALES BY AUCTION.

SEASON 1909-10.

MESSRS. HODGSON & CO. beg to announce the OPENING of their AUTUMN SEASON for the

SALE OF LITERARY PROPERTY.

The following Sales are arranged or in course of preparation, and Catalogues may be had on application :—

On TUESDAY, OCTOBER 12, and Three Following Days, at 1 o'clock, VALUABLE MISCELLANEOUS BOOKS, including a Selection of Standard Works from the Library of a Gentleman, removed from Emperor's Gate, S.W., and other properties, comprising the Historical Writings of Freeman, Froude, Gardiner, Brewer, Lecky, Thiers, Guizot, Hallam, Motley, Gibbon, Grote, Rawlinson, Mommsen, Duruy, and many others—a Set of Valpy's Delphin Classics, 141 vols., large paper—the Works of Shakespeare, Bacon, Locke, Johnson, Fielding, Burns, Thackeray (Library Edition, 22 vols.), Dickens, Matthew Arnold, &c. ; First Editions—a few Books in Sixteenth and Seventeenth Century Literature—Camden Society's Publications, 122 vols.—a Set of the Henry Bradshaw Society, 36 vols.—Ormerod's History of Cheshire, large paper, 3 vols. ; and other Topographical Books—Rare Seventeenth Century Tracts on Currency, by Briscoe, Houghton, Lowndes, Vicaris, Malynes, and others—Eden's State of the Poor and other Books on Political Economy—Works on Natural History by Wm. Yarrell, F. O. Morris, Darwin, Lydekker and others—Books on Sport, including a Set of the Bengal Monthly Sporting Magazine—Books of Travel, some relating to America—Theological Literature, &c.

To be viewed and Catalogues had.

On WEDNESDAY, OCTOBER 20, and Two Following Days, the VALUABLE LIBRARY OF A GENTLEMAN (deceased), collected during the early part of the Nineteenth Century, and now removed from Devonshire, comprising the First Editions of Keats's Poems, 1817, and Endymion, 1818, both in remarkable condition, and in the original boards, uncut—First and other Early Editions of Madame D'Arblay, Sir W. Scott, Leigh Hunt, Dickens, Lever, Blackmore, and others—Books illustrated by Rowlandson, Cruikshank, Phiz, &c. ; Ackermann's Oxford, 2 vols., and Winchester College, Papworth's Views of London, and other Rare Books with coloured plates—a Collection of Books relating to Shakespeare and the Drama—Works on English Topography and Genealogy, including an extensive Collection of Books relating to the County of Devon—Standard Historical Works, &c., the whole in clean condition and mostly in the original boards or cloth bindings.

Also THE LIBRARY OF THE LATE E. J. NANKIVELL, ESQ., removed from Camden Park, Tunbridge Wells, comprising the New Library Edition of Ruskin, 37 vols., half-morocco—the Cambridge Modern History, 9 vols.—the Historian's History of the World, 25 vols.—Hunter's Imperial Gazetteer of India, New Edition, 26 vols.—Modern Books in History, Science, and General Literature.

Catalogues on application.

EARLY in NOVEMBER, the VALUABLE LIBRARY collected by the late ADMIRAL LEMPRIERE, removed from Alton, Hants, comprising Froissart's Chronicles, 3 vols., Paris, 1514, Le Miroir des Princes, 1517, and other examples of the Early Parisian Presses—Books in Eighteenth Century Literature, including a fine copy of Goldsmith's "Vicar of Wakefield," First Edition, 2 vols., original calf—Books of Travel, several relating to America—the Writings of French Classical Authors, Foreign Historical Works, and Court Memoirs, the whole in good condition and mostly bound in handsome Eighteenth Century calf gilt bindings. Catalogues are preparing.

DURING NOVEMBER, VALUABLE LAW BOOKS, HANDSOME GLAZED MAHOGANY BOOK-CASES, SECRETAIRES, &c.

Auction Rooms, 115 Chancery Lane, W.C.

Telephone : 7291 Central. Established 1807.

THE CONDUIT STREET AUCTION GALLERIES.

The attention of Executors, Trustees, Solicitors, and Owners, who may be desirous of selling Works of Art, Family Jewels, Old Silver, Furniture, Pictures, Prints, Miniatures, China, Coins, Books, Old Lace, Furs, Musical Instruments, Guns, and other Valuables, is drawn to Messrs.

KNIGHT, FRANK & RUTLEY'S

AUCTION GALLERIES, 9 CONDUIT STREET, AND 23A MADDOX STREET, W., which are Open Daily to receive goods intended for early sales.

VALUATIONS are prepared for Fire Insurance, Estate Duty, and all other purposes. As to Insurance, owners are reminded that, for security, Messrs. KNIGHT, FRANK & RUTLEY'S detailed inventory and valuation of the contents of a Town or Country Mansion is an important adjunct to their Fire Insurance Policies.

H. SOTHERAN & CO., BOOKSELLERS.

GENERAL AGENTS FOR PRIVATE BOOKBUYERS AND PUBLIC INSTITUTIONS IN INDIA, THE COLONIES, AMERICA, AND ABROAD.

A Monthly Catalogue of fresh Purchases. Specimen number post-free.

LIBRARIES PURCHASED OR VALUED AND CATALOGUED AND ARRANGED.

Telegraphic Address: BOOKMEN, LONDON. *Codes* : UNICODE and A B C.

140 STRAND, W.C., and 37 PICCADILLY, W., LONDON.

Telephone : CENTRAL 1515. Telephone : MAYFAIR 3601.

R. ANDERSON & CO.,

BRITISH, INDIAN, AND COLONIAL ADVERTISEMENT CONTRACTORS,

14 KING WILLIAM STREET, STRAND, W.C.,

GIVE THE BEST TERMS for Company and General Advertising. Advice, Estimates, and all information free of charge. Replies received.

AUSTRALIA by ORIENT LINE,

UNDER CONTRACT TO CARRY HIS MAJESTY'S MAILS.

FROM LONDON EVERY ALTERNATE FRIDAY, calling at PLYMOUTH, GIBRALTAR, MARSEILLES, NAPLES, PORT SAID, and COLOMBO.

Managers—F. GREEN & CO.: ANDERSON, ANDERSON & CO.

Head Offices—FENCHURCH AVENUE, LONDON.

For Passage apply to the latter firm at 5 Fenchurch Avenue, E.C., or to the Branch Office, 28 Cockspur Street, Charing Cross, S.W.

"The Lost Sheep."

By ALF. U. SOORD.

From the Picture exhibited at the Royal Academy.

Published in five different sizes and sold with or without a frame.

A DELIGHTFUL XMAS or WEDDING PRESENT.

Prices on application to

THE AUTOTYPE FINE ART COMPANY, Limited,

74 NEW OXFORD STREET, LONDON.

Publishers of Reproductions of the Celebrated Pictures in all the important Galleries of the World. Lists sent free.

Illustrated Catalogue, post free, price One Shilling.

THE ENGLISH REVIEW.

MONTHLY. OCTOBER. 2s. 6d.

Four Cartoons by MAX BEERBOHM.

1. MODERN POETRY ... ... ARNOLD BENNETT. RACHEL ANNAND TAYLOR. ALFRED E. RANDALL. EZRA POUND.
2. EDWARD HUTTON ... ... THE CHURCH IN LUCINA'S HOUSE.
3. ANNE DOUGLAS SEDGWICK ... THE NEST.
4. ELIZABETH MARTINDALE ... TWO ESSAYS.
5. S. PEREZ TRIANA .. .. DON MARCELINO.
6. MAX BEERBOHM ... ... FOUR STUDIES.
7. C. F. KEARY ... ... THE ANTIQUARY.
8. FORD MADOX HÜEFFER ... ... A CALL—3.
9. THE MONTH : EDITORIAL... ... ... THE CRITICAL ATTITUDE—ENGLISH LITERATURE OF TO-DAY.
10. SIR CHARLES W. DILKE, BT., M.P. FOREIGN AFFAIRS.
11. SIDNEY WEBB ... ... THE ECONOMIC ASPECTS OF POOR LAW REFORM.
12. M.P. ... ... THE POLICY OF THE GOVERNMENT.
13. W. T. GOODE ... ... THE PRESENT MOMENT IN SPAIN.
14. J. A. HOBSON ... ... THE TASK OF REALISM.
15. W.G. ... ... REVIEW—THE PLACE OF HISTORY IN EDUCATION.

Subscription : One Year, 30s. ; Three Months, 7s. 6d.

CHAPMAN & HALL, Ltd., 11 Henrietta Street, London.

FIRST NUMBER OF NEW VOLUME.

The Expository Times

Edited by Dr. JAMES HASTINGS.

Contents of October Number.

Notes of Recent Exposition. In the Study.
The Faith of Jesus ... ... Principal P. T. FORSYTH.
The Vital Energies of the Gospel ... ... Prof. W. P. PATERSON.
Great Text Commentary. Literature.
Clauda or Cauda ... ... Dr. J. RENDEL HARRIS.
Studies in Pauline Vocabulary ... ... Rev. R. MARTIN POPE.
The Ideals of the Prophets ... ... Canon S. R. DRIVER.
The Law of Purification ... ... Principal BUECHLER.

Other Contributions by Prof. Denney, Prof. Law, Dr. J. Moffatt, Dr. Keane, Prof. Nestle, Mrs. Gibson, and Prof. Sayce.

Price 6d. Monthly. Annual Subscription, 6s.

Edinburgh : T. & T. CLARK, 38 GEORGE STREET.

SECOND EDITION. Price **2s. 6d.** net.

CATHOLICISM ON A PHILOSOPHICAL BASIS.

By B. C. NIXON, M. E. UNDERDOWN, and H. CUNLIFFE.

SWAN SONNENSCHEIN, LONDON.

And of all Booksellers.

Pp. x+492. Price 7s. 6d. net.

THE MORPHIA HABIT AND ITS VOLUNTARY RENUNCIATION.

By OSCAR JENNINGS, M.D. (Paris).

London : BAILLIÈRE, TINDALL & COX, 8 Henrietta St., Covent Garden.

New and Revised Edition. 6d. post free.

SHALL WE EVER REACH THE POLE?

Those interested in the POLAR WARFARE should read this brochure, which furnishes, from the work of M. PLATEAU, the Belgian physicist, and others, good scientific ground for believing that it is not possible to reach the Pole.

LONDON: R. MORGAN, NORWOOD, S.E.

JOHANNESBURG CONSOLIDATED INVESTMENT COMPANY, LIMITED.

(Registered in the Transvaal.)

REPORT OF DIRECTORS

To be submitted to the Shareholders at a Meeting to be held in the Board Room, Johannesburg Consolidated Investment Company, Limited, Consolidated Building, Fox Street, Johannesburg, on Tuesday, the 2nd day of November, 1909, at 11 a.m.

The Directors of the Johannesburg Consolidated Investment Company, Limited, beg to submit herewith the Balance Sheet and Profit and Loss Account of the Company for the year ended 30th June, 1909.

The operations of the Company during the year have resulted in a profit of £478,313 14s. 9d. The balance brought forward from last year's Accounts was £79,295 11s. 8d., making a total available profit balance of £557,609 6s. 5d.

An interim dividend of 10 per cent. in respect of the current year was declared on the 21st June, which absorbs the sum of £395,000, leaving £162,609 6s. 5d. to be carried forward to the next account.

Under the provisions of the Articles of Association, the declaration of dividends by the Board of Directors is limited to interim dividends. This limitation has been found to be exceedingly inconvenient in practice, and certain alterations of the Articles in this and other respects will be proposed at a Special Meeting of Shareholders convened for that purpose, of which due notice has been given.

The Directors have made no departure from their usual practice of taking Stock and Shareholdings and Mining and Real Estate assets into the Accounts at book figures. The current value of these assets exceeds the amount at which they stand in the Balance Sheet by an enormous sum, which constitutes a very large inner reserve in the Company's favour, in addition to the Reserve Fund of £250,000 which appears in the Accounts.

The financial position of the Company is the strongest ever presented to the Shareholders, the liquid cash assets alone exceeding the liabilities by the sum of £933,184 3s. 7d.

During the year covered by the Accounts now presented the adjustment of the loan owing to the Company by the Langlaagte Royal Gold Mining Company, Limited, has been arranged. The property of the latter Company has been sold on terms which, after providing for its Shareholders, have enabled it to repay this Company a substantial sum in settlement of its debt. This transaction had not been completed on the 30th June, and the figures will therefore only be reflected in next year's Accounts.

The year under review has been one of great activity in the Witwatersrand, and your Directors have been able to dispose of a considerable amount of its undeveloped claim holdings on very satisfactory terms, principally in exchange for shares in adjoining Gold Mining Companies. As a result of these arrangements, the Company has acquired important holdings in such companies as the Crown Mines, Consolidated Main Reef, Main Reef West, and a large additional interest in the Consolidated Langlaagte Mines.

Since the closing of the Accounts further satisfactory business of this character has been negotiated which will considerably extend the Company's mining interests on the Witwatersrand and materially enlarge the scope of its operations.

The group of Gold Mines with which the Company is associated have, during the year, produced in the aggregate gold to the value of £2,274,601, and have distributed dividends amounting to a total of £680,146. It is satisfactory to record a further substantial reduction in working costs; and speaking generally, the Mines are working on a solid and satisfactory basis.

In addition to the Mines actually producing gold, two important properties in which the Company is largely interested have been taken in hand, and their finances placed upon a sound footing—viz., the Van Ryn Deep and Randfontein Deep. Both these Mines cover a large area of valuable reef-bearing ground, and on both of them shafts are being sunk with all possible speed. In each case arrangements have been made for the provision of the funds estimated to be required in order to bring the respective Mines to the producing stage. The sole technical control of both these Mines has passed to the Engineering Department of this Company in Johannesburg.

The Directors are pleased to report that the returns from the Carlton Hotel, Johannesburg, have, during the past few months, shown improvement. Every effort is being made by those responsible for the management to make the Hotel a commercial success, and it is hoped that their action in keeping it open through a long and trying period of depression will prove to have been fully justified.

It is with deep regret that the Directors record the loss they have sustained by the death of their late colleague, Mr. Henry Barnato, which took place last November. Mr. H. Barnato was one of the Permanent Directors, and had been associated with the Company from its inception.

The surviving Permanent Directors have appointed Mr. A. R. Stephenson to be a Permanent Director in the place of Mr. H. Barnato.

The Directors further regret having to record the death of their colleague, Mr. E. B. Gardiner, M.A., which followed very shortly after he had resigned his seat on the Board owing to ill-health. Mr. Gardiner joined the Directorate in 1902, and rendered the Company very valuable services.

In terms of the Articles of Association, four of the Directors, viz., Mr. J. Emrys Evans, C.M.G., Mr. J. Friedlander, Mr. Isaac Lewis and Sir John Purcell, K.C.B., retire by rotation, and offer themselves for re-election.

Messrs. J. P. O'Reilly and Henry Hains, the Auditors of the Company in Johannesburg, and Messrs Chatteris, Nichols & Co., the Auditors in London, retire from office and offer themselves for re-election.

By order of the Board,
THOMAS HONEY,
London Secretary.

LONDON:
30th September, 1909.

PROFIT AND LOSS ACCOUNT, for the Year ended 30th June, 1909.

Dr.	£	s.	d.
To Directors' Fees, Salaries, Office and other Expenses, Johannesburg, London, and Paris, *less* Amounts received from other Companies ...	32,749	9	5
Balance, being realised profit for the year, carried to Appropriation Account ...	478,313	14	9
	£511,063	4	2

Cr.	£	s.	d.
By Profits realised on Stocks and Shares, Dividends, Commissions and Sundry Receipts, *less* Amounts written off ...	511,063	4	2
	£511,063	4	2

PROFITS APPROPRIATION ACCOUNT.

	£	s.	d.
To Dividend No. 11 of 5 per cent. to Shareholders registered at 30th June, 1908 ...	197,500	0	0
Interim Dividend of 10 per cent. declared 21st June, 1909 ...	395,000	0	0
Balance carried to Balance Sheet ...	162,609	6	5
	£755,109	6	5

	£	s.	d.
By Balance of Profit and Loss Account at 30th June, 1908 ...	276,795	11	8
Do., at 30th June, 1909 ...	478,313	14	9
	£755,109	6	5

BALANCE SHEET, 30th JUNE, 1909.

CAPITAL AND LIABILITIES.

	£	s.	d.	£	s.	d.
Authorised Capital (under Resolution of 23rd November, 1905 ...	4,500,000	0	0			
of which £4,345,000 is Registered Capital.						
Capital Issued ...				3,950,000	0	0
Reserve Fund ...				250,000	0	0
Sundry Creditors ...				706,505	9	2
Interim Dividend of 10 per cent. declared 21st June				395,000	0	0
Profit Appropriation Account— Balance ...				162,609	6	-
Contingent Liabilities— Uncalled Capital on Investments, &c. ...	£261,256	14	8			
				£5,464,114	15	7

ASSETS.

	£	s.	d.	£	s.	d.
Investments in Stocks and Shares ...				2,576,391	12	10
Mining Loans and Mining Investments ...				387,436	18	8
Real Estate and Buildings ...				774,556	13	1
Cash Advances and Mortgages ...				78,840	1	6
Loans at Short Call on Market Securities ...	1,158,766	2	9			
Sundry Debtors and Dividends Accrued ...	263,621	7	7			
Deposits with Bankers ...	200,000	0	0			
Cash at Bankers and in hand ...	17,302	2	5			
				1,639,689	12	9
Office Furniture...				7,199	16	9
				£5,464,114	15	7

S. B. JOEL, Chairman, A. R. STEPHENSON, } Directors.

THOMAS HONEY, Secretary.

We have examined the accounts of the Johannesburg Office of the Johannesburg Consolidated Investment Company, Limited, and have found them correct. We have also verified the Securities in South Africa.

J. P. O'REILLY, HENRY HAINS, } Auditors,
Incorporated Accountants.

Johannesburg, 9th July, 1909.

We have audited the accounts of the London Office of the Company, and find them correct, and they and the audited accounts of the Johannesburg Office are properly incorporated in the above Balance Sheet and Profit and Loss Account. We have also verified the Securities in London.

CHATTERIS, NICHOLS & CO.,
Chartered Accountants,
Auditors.

London, E.C., 25th August, 1909.

A Prospectus has been filed with the Registrar of Joint Stock Companies, which states among other things the following:—

The Subscription list will open on Monday, 4th October, 1909, and close on or before Wednesday, 6th October, 1909, for Town, and on or before Thursday, 7th October, for Country.

The East African Rubber Plantation Company, Limited.

Incorporated under the Companies (Consolidation) Act, 1908.

CAPITAL - - - £90,000.

Divided into 90,000 Shares of £1 each.

PRESENT ISSUE 75,000 SHARES.

60,000 Shares of the above are now offered for subscription at par, out of the proceeds of which £10,000 will be appropriated for Working Capital and the general purposes of the Company. 15,000 Shares will remain unissued for provision of further Working Capital if required.

PAYABLE:

2s. 6d. per Share on Application.
7s. 6d. „ „ „ Allotment.
5s. 0d. „ „ „ the 1st November, 1909.
5s. 0d. „ „ „ the 1st January, 1910.

Directors.

J. BARR ROBERTSON (Director Oceanic Railway Co. of Mexico, Limited), 10 Walbrook, London, E.C.

CECIL DE WINTON (Director of Cicely Rubber Estates Co., Limited), Hole Park, Rolvendon, Kent.

EDWARD HOWARD HALE (late Manager of the Trinidad Land and Finance Co., Limited), Dunster House, Mincing Lane, London, E.C.

THOMAS RITCHIE, J.P., Overstrand Lodge, Cromer (Director of the Pataling Rubber Estates Syndicate, Limited).

Solicitors.

GOLDBERG, BARRETT & NEWALL, 2 & 3 West Street, Finsbury Circus, London, E.C.

Bankers.

THE COMMERCIAL BANK OF SCOTLAND, LIMITED, 62 Lombard Street, London, E.C.; Head Office, Edinburgh; and Branches in Scotland.

Brokers.

BROWNING, TODD, & CO., 18 Old Broad Street, London, E.C.

Produce Brokers.

HALE & SON, 10 Fenchurch Avenue, E.C.

Auditors.

SMITH & LONGCROFT, Chartered Accountants, 41 Bishopsgate Street Within, E.C.

Secretary.

B. S. KIRKMAN, Dunster House, Mincing Lane, E.C.

PROSPECTUS.

The Company has been formed to acquire as a going concern the three Rubber Plantations, known as Goltzhof, Kwata and Mahezangulu, and also about 1,250 acres of uncultivated land of the Lewa Plantation, all situated in the North-East of German East Africa, and comprising together an area of about 3,100 acres.

These properties are freehold, and are planted with Ceara Rubber (*Manihot Glaziovii*). The first of them, Goltzhof, is about 10 miles from the railway station Muhesa, and the other two are in the valley of the Luengera River and about 25 miles from the railway station Korogwe. The stations Muhesa and Korogwe are on the Usambara Railway, which runs direct to the seaport Tanga, and thus gives communication by railway in a few hours between the Plantations and the seaboard. The 1,250 acres of uncultivated land of the Lewa Plantation are situate ear to the Goltzhof Plantation.

The Government dues on all the properties do not exceed £100 per annum, and there is no export duty on Rubber.

On the Kwata and Mahezangulu Estates about 250,000 trees are planted, about 200,000 of which are ready for tapping this year, and the remaining 50,000 next year.

On the Goltzhof (Kwanhanja) Estate about 330,000 to 350,000 trees are planted, about 50,000 of which are ready for tapping this year and the remainder next year, making a total of 580,000 trees at the producing stage in 1910. About 100 acres are at present planted with Cotton Trees and Kapok, and 25 acres with Ironwood and Lemon Trees. This property adjoins the well-known Lewa Plantation, which it is reported is already producing 100/120 tons of Rubber per year. There are approximately a further 1,909 acres of land available for planting.

The above statements with regard to number of planted trees, area, and development, are based on a declaration made by Messrs. C. J. Lange and R. Rady.

CEARA RUBBER.—The following testimony in regard to this variety of Rubber is taken from British Official Reports made to the British Foreign Office.

Extract from Report on German East Africa, by Vice-Consul Douglas Young, for the year 1907-8. [Parliamentary Paper, Cd. 4,446-45, p. 64, issued in May, 1909.]

"A development little less remarkable than that of sisal cultivation is shown by plantations of Ceara Rubber (Manihot Glaziovii). It is estimated that in the next two or three years the total number of trees in the colony will have increased to some 6,000,000. The chief districts in which this Rubber is grown are Wilhelmstal, which alone is expected to possess 4,000,000 trees by the end of 1912, Lindi, Kilwa and the lowlands of Moschi, while plantations are springing up at many points along the two railways.

"No separate statistics are available of the exports of Ceara Rubber as compared with the native varieties, but as the trees are not tapped as a rule until they have acquired the age of three years, the amount can scarcely be very large at present, and in any case would give little indication of the great future which is believed to await the cultivation of Manihot Glaziovii in German East Africa.

"The sudden preference shown by Rubber planters for Manihot Glaziovii has led to the great neglect of other valuable varieties, such as Castilloa, Kicksia, Hevea and Ficus."

Extract from Report on the Trade of Zanzibar for 1908, by Vice-Consul R. M. Kohan. [Parliamentary Paper, Cd. 4,446-136, p. 11, issued in July, 1909.]

RUBBER.—"The planting of young Ceara Rubber Trees in Government plantations, and the distribution of seeds to native cultivators undertaken by the Agricultural Department, represent a total of some 300,000 to 400,000 young trees now growing in both islands, and some of these trees should be ready to tap towards the end of 1910. The tree is extremely popular, especially in Pemba, owing to its easy propagation and rapid growth, and has been extensively planted in the gardens of the natives.

The following Extracts are taken from translations of reports of well-known and reliable planters in German East Africa, copies of which accompany this Prospectus.

"It should be regarded as of special importance for the yield of the trees that these trees, as far as it was possible, have been raised from the seed of trees which on the Lewa Plantation have produced up to 20 lbs. of Rubber."

"About the development of the trees the best only can be said. All three Plantations should be ready for tapping towards the end of this year."

"As regards the ground, I consider it on all three Plantations as specially suitable for Rubber growing."

"The meteorological conditions I consider favourable, as I have not experienced any unfavourable influence on the development of the trees for about thirteen years."

"There are plenty of labourers to be had at low wages."

The soil on these properties is of sandy clay, the ingredients of which have been found to be highly favourable for the rapid growth of the Ceara tree. The average rainfall in the district during the last ten years has been from 45 to 55 inches per annum, and this is regarded by experts as ample for the purpose of obtaining the best results from the Ceara tree.

Although the present market price of well-cured Ceara Plantation Rubber is little, if any, below Para (Ceara realised over 9s. per lb. at the Rubber Public Sales in London 21st September, 1909), the Directors prefer to base the following estimate of profits on an average selling price of 4s. per lb. The cost of production, including all expenditure up to time of sale in Europe, is estimated at 1s. 7d. per lb., leaving a net profit of 2s. 5d. per lb.

The following Estimates are considered conservative:—

580,000 trees in 1910, yielding $\frac{1}{4}$ lb. per tree = 145,000 lbs. at 2s. 5d. per lb. = net profit £17,520.

580,000 trees in 1911, yielding $\frac{1}{2}$ lb. per tree = 290,000 lbs. at 2s. 5d. per lb. = net profit £35,040.

580,000 trees in 1912, yielding $\frac{3}{4}$ lb. per tree = 435,000 lbs. at 2s. 5d. per lb. = net profit £52,560.

580,000 trees in 1913, yielding 1 lb. per tree = 580,000 lbs. at 2s. 5d. per lb. = net profit £70,080.

The above estimates do not take into consideration the profits which will accrue from the further cultivation of the Estates and the increased production as the trees grow older.

The Plantations have reached an advanced stage and are reported to be in the very best condition, and it is considered that the working capital will be amply sufficient to develop the Estates in the most efficient manner, and to produce increased returns. On each Plantation there is a house for the European Manager, and the labour conditions are also reported to be very favourable.

The following information is given in pursuance of Section 81 of the Companies (Consolidation) Act, 1908:—

The Memorandum of Association of the Company, with the names, addresses and descriptions of the signatories and the number of shares subscribed for by them respectively is printed in the fold of this Prospectus, and is to be deemed part of it.

The minimum subscription upon which the Directors may proceed to allotment is fixed by the Articles of Association at 20,000 Shares, but the Directors will not allot unless and until 48,000 Shares of the present issue have been applied for.

The Vendor to the Company is the G.E.A. Syndicate, Limited, whose registered office is at Dunster House, Mincing Lane, London, E.C. The purchase price payable to the Vendor has been fixed at £61,500, payable as to £25,500 in cash and £14,000 in fully paid shares and as to the balance at the option of the Directors of the Company in cash or partly in cash and partly in fully paid shares. Nothing is payable for goodwill.

The G.E.A. Syndicate, Limited, is the promoter of this Company, and it is proposed that the properties shall, in the first instance, be transferred to a Trustee for this Company. The Vendors to the said G.E.A. Syndicate, Limited, are Carl August Robert Hachfeld and George Otto Fischer (trading as "Gustav Schaar"), of 22 and 24, Grosse Backerstrasse, Hamburg, and the purchase price payable by the said Syndicate to the said Carl August Robert Hachfeld and George Otto Fischer has been fixed at £40,000, payable as to £20,000 in cash and £11,000 in fully paid shares and as to the balance at the option of the Directors of the Syndicate in cash, or partly in cash and partly in fully paid shares.

Of the Shares now offered for subscription 48,000 have been underwritten by the G.E.A. Syndicate, Limited, for a commission of £2,500 in cash and £1,000 in Shares. Part of these Shares has been sub-underwritten by various parties and the commission in respect of such sub-underwriting is payable by the Syndicate.

Prospectuses and Forms of Application for Shares can be obtained from the Company's Bankers, Brokers and Solicitors, and at the Offices of the Company.

30th September, 1909.

FIFTY-NINTH REPORT OF

THE YOKOHAMA SPECIE BANK, LIMITED

(YOKOHAMA SHOKIN GINKO).

Presented to the Shareholders at the HALF-YEARLY ORDINARY GENERAL MEETING, held at the Head Office, Yokohama, on Friday, 10th September, 1909.

CAPITAL PAID UP....Yen 24,000,000 | RESERVE FUNDS....Yen 15,900,000

PRESIDENT.—BARON KOREKIYO TAKAHASHI.

DIRECTORS.—NAGATANE SOMA, Esq. ROKURO HARA, Esq. IPPEI WAKAO, Esq. MASNOSKE ODAGIRI, Esq. TCHUNOSUKE KAWASHIMA, Esq. RIYEMON KIMURA, Esq. KOKICHI SONODA, Esq. YUKI YAMAKAWA, Esq. VISCOUNT YATARO MISHIMA. HYOKICHI BEKKEY, Esq.

AUDITORS.—NOBUO TAJIMA, Esq. FUKUSABURO WATANABE, Esq.

BRANCHES.—Antung-Hsien, Bombay, Chefoo, Changchun, Dairen (Dalny), Hankow, Hong Kong, Honolulu, Kobe, Liao Yang, London, Lyons, Fengtien (Mukden), Nagasaki, Newchwang, New York, Osaka, Peking, Ryojun (Port Arthur), San Francisco, Shanghai, Tieling, Tientsin, Tokio.

HEAD OFFICE.—YOKOHAMA.

TO THE SHAREHOLDERS.

GENTLEMEN,—The Directors submit to you the annexed Statement of the Liabilities and Assets of the Bank, and of the Profit and Loss Account for the half-year ended 30th June, 1909.

The gross profits of the Bank for the past half-year, including Yen 1,141,676.80 brought forward from last account, amount to Yen 11,989,849.89, of which Yen 8,994,008.01 have been deducted for interests, taxes, current expenses, rebate on bills current, bad and doubtful debts, bonus for officers and clerks, &c., &c., leaving a balance of Yen 2,995,841.88 for appropriation.

The Directors now propose that Yen 400,000.00 be added to the reserve fund, and recommend a dividend at the rate of twelve per cent. per annum, which will absorb Yen 1,440,000.00.

The balance, Yen 1,155,841.88, will be carried forward to the credit of next account.

Head Office, Yokohama, 10th September, 1909. BARON KOREKIYO TAKAHASHI, Chairman.

BALANCE SHEET.

30th June, 1909.

LIABILITIES.	Y.	ASSETS.	Y.	Y.
Capital (paid up)	24,000,000.00	Cash Account—		
Reserve Funds	15,500,000.00	In Hand	15,056,283.83	
Reserve for Doubtful Debts	468,795.79	At Bankers'	17,784,561.95	32,840,845.78
Notes in Circulation	4,744,993.28	Investments in Public Securities		20,555,994.84
Deposits (Current, Fixed, &c.)	119,409,870.68	Bills Discounted, Loans, Advances, &c.		64,874,187.60
Bills Payable, Bills Rediscounted, Acceptances, and other Sums due by the Bank	75,401,779.49	Bills Receivable and other Sums due to the Bank		118,715,009.41
Dividends Unclaimed	4,998.02	Bullion and Foreign Money		2,991,204.11
Amount brought forward from last Account	1,141,676.80	Bank's Premises, Properties, Furniture, &c.		2,549,037.38
Net Profit for the past Half-year	1,854,164.38			
Yen	242,526,279.02	Yen		242,526,279.02

PROFIT AND LOSS ACCOUNT.

	Y.		Y.
To Interests, Taxes, Current Expenses, Rebate on Bills Current, Bad and Doubtful Debts, Bonus for Officers and Clerks, &c.	8,994,008.01	By Balance brought forward 31st December, 1908	1,141,676.80
To Reserve Fund	400,000.00	By Amount of Gross Profits for the Half-year ending 30th June, 1909	10,848,172.89
To Dividend— Yen (6.00 per Share for 240,000 Shares)	1,440,000.00		
To Balance carried forward to next Account	1,155,841.88		
Yen	11,989,849.89	Yen	11,989,849.89

We have examined the above Accounts in detail, comparing them with the Books and Vouchers of the Bank and the Returns from the Branches and Agencies, and have found them to be correct. We have further inspected the Securities, &c., of the Bank, and also those held on account of Loans, Advances, &c., and have found them all to be in accordance with the Books and Accounts of the Bank.

NOBUO TAJIMA, FUKUSABURO WATANABE, } AUDITORS.

The requirements of Section 274 of the Companies (Consolidation) Act, 1908, complied with in Great Britain, September 3rd, 1909.)

THE

PACIFIC-OREGON RAILWAY & NAVIGATION COMPANY

(Chartered in the State of Washington, U.S.A., March 23rd, 1909).

CAPITAL - 10,725,000 Dollars (£2,145,000)

Divided into 2,145,000 Shares of the nominal value of Five Dollars (£1) each.

PROSPECTUS IS BEING ISSUED INVITING SUBSCRIPTIONS FOR

400,000 Fully Paid up Shares of the Nominal Value of Five Dollars (£1) each—Equivalent to £400,000.

(Payable 5s. per Share on Application, 15s. per Share on Acceptance.)

The Company has an assured freight revenue from two sources, sufficient to produce substantial dividends the first year the line is in operation. The first dividend will be paid on October 1st, 1910.

No period of waiting for the development of trade is involved. The markets are established, and are able to absorb at once all the produce that the railway can bring them.

The first section of the line that is to be built, from Prospect to Medford (on the Southern Pacific Railway), opens up vast timber belts estimated by the United States Forestry Reports to contain eight billions of feet of the finest timber in regular commercial use. Saw-mills are already erected, and enough business is guaranteed to keep the railway working to its full capacity from the start.

In addition, there are adjacent to the line coalfields in actual working, conservatively estimated to yield over seven hundred million tons of the best coal mined on the Pacific Coast.

There are other mineral and agricultural resources that present extraordinary potentialities, which, however, are not taken into consideration for the present.

The shares are all of one class and there are no bonds or debentures. The subscribers to this issue thus participate in the whole of the profits earned.

A brokerage of 6d. per share will be paid in respect of shares sold on applications bearing brokers' stamps.

Applications for shares must be made on the form accompanying the full Prospectus, which can be obtained from the Issuing House:—

Messrs. Leopold Mayer & Company, Ltd., 23 St. Swithin's Lane, London, E.C.;

or from the Solicitors

Messrs. COX & LAFONE, Tower Royal, Cannon Street, E.C.,

and from the Brokers

Mr. E. P. House, 13 Sherborne Lane, London, E.C., and London Stock Exchange.

Messrs. F. FERGUSON PAGE & CO., 32A Brown Street, Manchester, and Manchester Stock Exchange.

A New Company now offering Shares for Public Subscription.

EGGS LIMITED

propose to establish Poultry Farms near the large towns of England.

20% DIVIDEND

Send for Prospectus (on the basis of and with reference to which alone Shares will be allotted) to Dept. "X," EGGS LIMITED, 79 Queen Street, E.C.

ELY CATHEDRAL.

Visitors will find First Class Hotel Accommodation at the "LAMB" Family Hotel, which is situated close to the Cathedral. **MODERATE TERMS.** Omnibus meets all trains.

Proprietor, S. AIREY.

POOLE & LORD

INDIAN AND GENERAL OUTFITTERS,

322 OXFORD STREET, LONDON, W.

(NEARLY OPPOSITE BOND STREET.)

INVENTORS OF THE

"Sans-Plis" SHIRT.

Prices from 7s. 6d.

The "SANS-PLIS" Shirt is superior to any other for Indian and Colonial wear Being entirely free from gathers, it is cooler, much stronger, and will bear the Indian mode of washing better than any shirt in use.

A single shirt, or other article, made to *measure*, and accurate patterns preserved to ensure correctness in the execution of future orders.

Makers of Drawers with Flexible Hip Belt Bands.

"BREECHES CUT."

THE RICCARDI PRESS BOOKS

The Medici Society has pleasure in announcing that the first books printed in the **new Riccardi Fount** are now at press. In this Fount Mr. H. P. Horne has undoubtedly surpassed both his previous attempts in the same direction. Based upon the design of the larger Fount used in the famous first Florentine editions of Horace, printed by Antonio Miscomino in 1492, the Riccardi Types may confidently be said to surpass, **both in brilliance and in legibility,** all modern efforts to reproduce the ancient glories of the Printing Press. Encouraged by the public appreciation of the Medici Prints, of which the *Burlington Magazine* has said that "Nothing of the kind **so good or so cheap** has ever before been offered to the public," the Society hopes shortly to render available the noblest typography of modern times at prices within reach of the general purse.

Of the Riccardi Press Books, now at press, a list will shortly be ready to forward post free to all applicants.

NEW MEDICI PRINTS,

SUBJECTS MARKED * ARE JUST PUBLISHED: THE REMAINDER WILL BE READY SHORTLY.

		s.	d.	
*GIORGIONE	...**Figures in a Landscape**	21	0	net.
BOTTICELLI	...**The Birth of Venus**	25	0	"
*M. DA FORLI	...**The Archangel Gabriel**	17	6	"
PISANELLO	...**The Vision of St. Eustace**	17	6	"
*BRAMANTINO	...**Putto with Grapes**	12	6	"
*AMBROGIO DI PREDIS	**Beatrice d'Este** (Milan)	12	6	"
*AMBROGIO DI PREDIS	**Beatrice d'Este** (London)	31	6	net.
P. DE HOOCH	...**Interior with Soldiers**	15	0	"
GAINSBOROUGH	...**The Painter's Daughters**	15	0	"
ZUCCHERO	...**Queen Elizabeth**	17	6	"
CLOUET...	...**Elizabeth of Austria**	15	0	"
HOLBEIN	...**The Duchess of Milan**	17	6	"
* "	... " " (Monochrome)	5	0	"

Packing and Postage of all Prints is extra at 6d. each; additional Copies (up to 6) in same parcel 1d. each beyond the first.

The Society's New Prospectus with over 100 Illustrations, and full particulars of over 200 Reproductions after the Old Masters (in Colour), Frames, Annual Subscriptions, &c., post free 6d. stamps. Summary Lists post free.

IMPORTANT NEW SERIES—POPULAR MEDICI PRINTS.

THE POPULAR MEDICI PRINTS will reproduce only Paintings of the first order in their several "Schools." They will be mounted to a uniform size of about 17 by 14 inches, and will be sold at the uniform rates:—In tinted overmount, with real gold line, each **6s.** net; in best bronze-gilt mount, each **7s. 6d.** net. Postage 4d. each; per additional print in same parcel (limit in parcel 12) 1d. each.

READY DURING FIRST FORTNIGHT OF OCTOBER. (Illustrated List Free.)

Bellini, Giov	**Doge Leonardo Loredano**	**National Gallery**
Bronzino	**Venus and Cupid**	**do.**
Francia	**The Entombment**	**do.**
Moroni	**The Tailor**	**do.**
Fragonard	**The Fair-Haired Boy**	**Wallace Collection**
Greuze	**A Girl With a Dove**	**do.**
Gainsborough	**The Parish Clerk**	**National Gallery**
Morland, Henry	**The Laundry Maid**	**do.**

DÜRER DRAWINGS. The Society will shortly issue a series of 64 reproductions (many after water-colours) after the drawings of Albrecht Dürer. A completely illustrated catalogue is in preparation and will be forwarded upon receipt of 6d. stamps.

PHOTO-RELIEFS. Among the various recent advances in Photography, few, if any, are more striking than that, whereby—as perfected by the well-known Italian firm of Giacomo Brogi—a flat surface offers to the beholder the illusion of a modelling in relief. 18 Subjects, after the Della Robbias, now ready. Price 25s. net each. Illustrated List free.

PRIMITIVES. **The Medici Society will be pleased to send post free on receipt of 3d. stamps an Illustrated List of nearly 100 Facsimile Reproductions (in colour) after the Primitives of the Flemish, Italian, and German Schools.**

THE NATIONAL PORTRAIT SERIES.

I. Janssen, C. **John Milton** (age 10) **12s. 6d.**
II. Unknown **William Shakespeare** (Stratford) **15s. 0d.**
IV. Zucchero. **Queen Elizabeth** (*Shortly*) **17s. 6d.**
From the Collection of the Marquis of Salisbury at Hatfield House.

The National Portrait Series is issued with a special view to use in Schools and Public Libraries.
Illustrated Leaflet post free.

THE DIVINE MINSTRELS.

A Narrative of the Life of S. Francis of Assisi, with his Companions. By AUGUSTE BAILLY. Translated by Major ERNEST BARNES. Crown 8vo. cloth, Coloured Top, with Photogravure Frontispiece after the Picture of "S. Francis," by Gerard David, 5s. net. Whole limp vellum, silk ties, gilt tops, 12s. 6d. net. [*October* 15.

In this simple but exquisitely sympathetic narrative of the life of the Saint of Assisi, free of all expository or other disturbing element, and written with the consummate literary art which is the secret of his nation, M. Bailly has given us a book which will not fail of appeal as well to the most confirmed "Franciscan" as to the unregenerate few who find, in these pages, their first introduction to one of the most perfect histories in the world.

PHILIP LEE WARNER, Publisher to the Medici Society, Ltd.,
38 ALBEMARLE STREET, PICCADILLY, LONDON, W.

Printed for the Proprietors by SPOTTISWOODE & Co. LTD., 5 New-street Square, E.C., and Published by REGINALD WEBSTER PAGE, at the Office, 10 King Street, Covent Garden, in the Parish of St. Paul, in the County of London.—*Saturday*, 2 *October*, 1909.

THE

SATURDAY REVIEW

OF

POLITICS, LITERATURE, SCIENCE, AND ART.

No. 2,815 Vol. 108. 9 October 1909. [Registered as a Newspaper.] 6d.

CONTENTS.

NOTES OF THE WEEK.

Balmoral might be the gathering-place of a band of conspirators just now, to judge by the rumours and gasping comment of some people. Of course gossip will wag its tongue if the Prime Minister visits the King at a time when political affairs are deeply interesting; but the pretence of knowing what such a visit exactly means is too obvious altogether. A number of authorities have announced that Lord Lansdowne is to join Mr. Asquith and Lord Rosebery at Balmoral directly—a round-table conference, in fact, with the King in the chair. We suppose the name of no man and no house have been so often taken in vain during the last year or two as Lord Lansdowne and Lansdowne House.

Civilised men tend to politeness when the moment draws near for a stark trial of strength between them. Nothing could exceed the punctilious courtesy of the most vindictive duellists of old when the time came to pace out the ground. So, as the real critical moment of the Budget duel draws near, the chief combatants tend to lower rather than raise their tones. The Chancellor of the Exchequer's statement on Wednesday on the course of public business was quite humane. It is hard to realise that war to the knife is close when one hears or reads such statements as this, but we may usefully recall the reply of M'Intre when Lesley tried to avert the duel—"In my opinion persons that have carried this matter so far as we have done, and who should part without carrying it any further, might go to supper at the Graemes Arms very joyously, but would rise the next morning with ragged reputations."

Party politics in this country are written of chiefly by people who have had no sort of political training, who have never mixed with politicians, and know nothing whatever of the House of Commons. Hence most of the written and printed stuff on politics is quite wrong-headed. Take the stuff that has been written on the Budget concessions, to which one more was added on Wednesday. These concessions would form an exceedingly interesting and curious study. Mixed motives have prompted them all through. Uninformed hacks cannot perceive this, and as a result the comment on these concessions in the Unionist press has been undiscriminating usually. People who chance to know anything of Mr. Lloyd George know quite well that several of these concessions have been prompted mainly by a wish to be fair. He is a most dangerous politician, and his Budget would be disastrous, but one or two concessions to the agricultural interest have been genuine enough.

But who can really believe that the latest concession to Irish Nationalist demands is one of "fairness" only? Mr. Samuel hardly expected anyone with a sense of humour to take his words in this quite gravely. The truth here is plain enough—the Government had crossed the Nationalists once or twice already, and the time comes when it is politic to cave in to them. So the publicans of Ireland are to have a preference over the publicans of England. They support with hard coin the Irish cause. Mr. Dillon actually admitted it. The "swindler", as Mr. Churchill styles him in England, is a saint at the same game in Ireland. And this is a Government that wants to put down the drink evil!

It has been felt by many people lately that what is wanted at this moment is not so much a general as a good bye-election—and now we are to have it in Bermondsey! The truth is neither side—excepting the brainless braggers—really can feel at all sure as to the way the masses of the electorate regard the Budget. It is more than possible the masses themselves don't quite know how they regard it. This bye-election should give us some clue. It is suggested, we see, that Dr. Cooper was killed by the brute overstrain of the Government's all-night sitting!

Lord Rosebery is giving his farewell performances. But his good-bye to politics, like the singer's good-bye to the public or the actor's to the stage, can be sustained for a good long time. The farewell note has its value in attraction, and Lord Rosebery has never neglected the showman's finesse. He will not speak at Birmingham. In "present circumstances" he is unalterably resolved not to make another speech on the Budget. This will certainly add to the interest of the next speech he does make. We do not see why he should be lectured for not regularly campaigning against the Budget. It is just because he is out of the hurly-burly that everybody listens when he speaks: descend into the scrimmage and he loses his vantage. Does anybody suppose Lord Rosebery does not know this? Another farewell is his resignation of the Presidency of the Liberal League. To most of us, we should say, this would seem to be nothing but his taking farewell of himself. We had not realised there was a Liberal League apart from Lord Rosebery. One never heard of it except when it gave Lord Rosebery occasion for a big speech.

Mr. F. E. Smith's speech at Limehouse was miserably reported in the "Times" and most of the other papers. The "Standard" did report it in full, but on the whole we must say the Unionist press was very stingy in the matter. Mr. Smith is one of the few men on the Unionist side who can equal Mr. Churchill and at least stand up to Mr. Lloyd George on a platform of the Limehouse sort. And his speech had some most effective points. The point about the Government taking trouble not to find the working man food, but to prevent him drinking anything, was particularly good. The Unionist press should really report speeches of this kind more generously just now. Ordinarily, no doubt, the fewer reports of electioneering speeches the better.

Moderate Liberal members like Mr. Ridsdale of Brighton have just enough backbone to kick against the Budget. But, alas, there is the end of their backbone. With the sad exception of Mr. Cox, they one and all, having applied the tip of their toe delicately to the Budget, proceed to bolt. They find that they have not time or health to stand at the next election. Why are beautiful angels always so ineffective in politics?

We hope that the working classes have been following the Lords' debates on the Housing and Town Planning Bill. This "wrecked" measure was reported to the House last Monday; and we looked in vain for any echo of the shrill outcry against certain amendments which lent a hectic picturesqueness to radical head-lines when first they were made. But Liberals seem to be feeling curiously chastened; and the proceedings were almost genial. It was instructive to find Lord Onslow showing a much nearer appreciation of working-class circumstances than Mr. John Burns, whose breach with the working classes is comparatively recent. It were surely as well that houses built for the working classes were enjoyed by those classes. Bournville stands as an object-lesson here. Not one-third of the houses in Bournville are inhabited by Mr. Cadbury's workpeople.

So far, the action of the Lords on the Land Bill has been on the whole admirable. They have thrown out the proposal to refuse the purchase-money for large farms unless a proportion of them were tilled. The idea in the proposal was in itself excellent—to encourage increased production and increased employment of labour; but, on the other hand, should the farmer fail to agree with the League, he may have the produce of his tillage and his wages stolen. So long as the League has its way increased production remains practically impossible, whatever Parliament does; and so the tillage clause could only harass the large farmer without a compensating advantage to anybody. The only serious mistake of the Lords so far has been in refusing Lord MacDonnell's amendment enabling the Estates Commissioners to reallot congested areas without the consent of the occupants. Some such increased liberty is quite essential to the relief of congestion in places where the "farms" are mixed in plots among each other, each holder trying to make out that what he gives is better than what he gets. Lord MacDonnell's proposal was a really valuable one.

Every vote cast in favour of the Budget is a vote for separation between England and Ireland. Mr. Healy may write articles in the "Daily Mail" in defence of the House of Lords, but Mr. Redmond does a far finer service to the Opposition. He has cabled to Mr. J. Ryan, United Irish League, that "with the veto of the House of Lords will disappear the last obstacle to Home Rule". It is put with a strength and truth we must all praise.

There is no reason why the Americans should be either prompt or generous at the present moment—not one useful citizen has been shot for "the cause" in Ireland during the past six months. This appeal from "the cause" ought really to have been addressed to the Radicals, the Socialists and the clergy, for whom alone the "strugglers" have done anything in the present Parliament. They have helped the Socialists to attack property in Great Britain, but what have they done for Home Rule? Nothing, and after thirty years of the political confidence trick Irish-American credulity is rather less than it was. Mr. Redmond's appeal winds up, as we say, with the Lords as "the last obstacle to Home Rule"; but he says nothing of the first obstacle, namely, the Home Rulers. The hat goes round this time with the Galway pathos of Mr. T. P. O'Connor. Why do the Irish Unionists contest the seats, empty "the war chest" and burst "the cause"?

M. Delcassé's speech at the banquet of the Franco-Scottish Society at Bordeaux was laudatory of the Anglo-French entente. Naturally he is not less pleased with it now than he was before M. Clemenceau made his blunder about Algeciras and gave M. Delcassé his revenge. His obiter dicta were more topical than the ancient history of the entente. Other foreigners also think the English quite the most sentimental of people. It is Mr. Shaw's theory too. But what M. Delcassé said about the King is quite apt for a week filled with rumours of conferences at Balmoral. The King, said M. Delcassé, by his very rare talent for never doing anything but what is necessary, when it is necessary, and in the degree in which it is necessary, has won the admiration and respect of the world.

Spanish losses in the sharp fighting on Thursday week have been magnified into a reverse. As only thirty-eight Spaniards were killed and less than two hundred and fifty wounded, the affair cannot be considered very serious, however unpleasant. General Marina's request for another brigade no doubt lent colour to the accounts of the check he had sustained. As a fact, he would have wanted the additional men in any case. He finds his numbers unequal to the work of guarding communications, holding positions gained, and attacking Beni Bu Ifror, which is declared to be the limit of Spanish operations. But if Mulai Hafid should join in, where the end would be neither Spain nor any other could say.

The French are terribly nervous lest Spain should become ambitious. They protest their confidence in Spanish moderation and good faith, and their protesting betrays their nerves. General d'Amade, feeling much the same way, takes a different line. He openly suspects Spain of large ideas of conquest and sees ruin to French hopes in Morocco. "If France does not bestir herself, the one natural route of penetration, from Ujda to Rabat by Taza and Fez, may be lost to her and Taza become a Moorish Fashoda". Certainly we can understand French touchiness as to Morocco. They have made such a bungle of the Moorish business themselves, they may easily imagine themselves outwitted by some, perhaps any, one else.

Political crime in Bengal during 1908 was more serious than appeared even from the newspaper accounts. The Inspector-General of Police has drawn up an informing report. Officers of the Government and everyone who was suspected of sympathy with them were subject to dacoity organised by the seditionists. The Inspector-General says he has little doubt that the increase in serious offences against person and property was "the indirect result of the organised and partially successful efforts of the agitators to weaken the authority of the Government and bring its officers into contempt". Sympathy, passive if not active, was given by wealthy and educated natives to a movement which aimed at ousting British rule. And these "partially successful efforts" were rewarded with the new Councils which the Government have hopes of starting in January next.

Chang Chi-tung was one of the few names in Chinese politics familiar to English readers. A typical literate of the old school, he commanded all the respect with which his countrymen regard high literary attainment. He commanded, besides, the respect which they give to that much rarer quality in the mandarinate—integrity: he had great opportunities, but he died a poor man. These characteristics gained for him great influence; but he had, almost necessarily, the defects of his qualities. With the attainments he had also the limitations of a Chinese scholar. His intelligence enabled him to perceive the value of Western scientific knowledge and appliances; but the limitation showed itself in opposing Li Hung-chang's railway schemes on the ground that they were too near the coast and that foreigners could too easily get at them from the sea! He advocated, instead, a central trunk line, so he was moved from the viceroyalty of Canton to Hankow and told to build it! He was an advocate, too, of China doing for herself. That was the origin of his ironworks and his cotton factories. But his capacity for management was less than his capacity for appreciation, and he earned the epithet of bungler.

He joined Liu Kun-yi, then Viceroy of Nanking, in preserving peace in the Yangtze valley during the Boxer crisis in 1900, and he sent guards to receive into safety across the border of his viceroyalty the foreigners whom Tuan Fang protected and sent south from Shansi while Yu Hsien was massacring all he could reach in Shansi. Patriotically and arrogantly Chinese, he tried to minimise foreign influence and enterprise by drafting mining regulations which make impossible the participation of foreigners in mining enterprise for which the Mackay treaty provides. The other day he grossly evaded the spirit of his agreement to give preference to British interests in the construction of the Hankow-Canton railway, in consideration of the Hong Kong loan which enabled him to buy out other inconvenient claims. But he understood that foreigners had come to stay. He was a clever man in some ways, and as a literate perhaps superior to his great rival and contemporary Li Hung-chang. But he was less great a statesman.

The trade of the West Indies has notoriously been passing steadily from British into American hands. Yet the West Indians have shown again and again that they would rather do business with the Empire to which they belong. Great Britain does nothing to encourage this spirit, but Canada realised long ago that a great chance was being lost. A Commission representing the West Indian traders has met in Montreal this week, and the evidence shows the extent to which America has captured the market. Unless something is done, when an imperial preference scheme comes it may be found that the West Indies are irretrievably committed to the United States.

Any sign of trade improvement is naturally pleasing, but we cannot extract more than hope from the Board of Trade Returns for September. They show that both imports and exports improved on the month; but if we take the nine months of the year we find that against an increase of fourteen millions in imports and nine and a half millions in re-exports, has to be put a decrease of over eight millions in exports. What other moral can this bear than that we are rapidly improving our business as the carriers and half-way-house men of other people's goods whilst falling behind as manufacturers and producers? Perhaps the census of production, of which the first return is now published as a Blue Book, will ultimately throw some light on the subject. It is a pity we have no similar return for 1907. The figures, assuming they were approximately correct, would enable us to form some estimate of the extent to which, as a nation, we are holding our own or losing ground industrially.

It was soon after the Government came in that the Census of Production Act was passed, and this Blue Book is the first fruits of it. There are carefully prepared tables as to the nature and extent of the home trade in five great industries. The Act set up a kind of inquiry which had not before been made; and its origin is to be found in the desire of the Free Traders about that time to make a point as to the extent of the home trade as against Tariff Reformers, who were laying much stress on the quantity and quality of our export trade. Elaborate statistics are useful to a certain extent; but they generally arouse more controversy than they settle; as for example the Board of Trade returns. Still, it is desirable to have this book as a pendant to them.

Many people and more especially soldiers on the staff have been asking why it was that, whilst Sir Horace Smith-Dorrien, the Commander-in-Chief at Aldershot, commanded one side, the Commander-in-Chief of our second force, the Salisbury troops, Sir Charles Douglas, was not given command of the other side, but was passed over in favour of Sir A. Paget. Rumour has it that General Douglas was offered and declined the honour. Many a reputation has been damaged by a command in peace manœuvres, and those who profess to know say that General Douglas, true to his traditional policy, which earned him the name of "Cautious Charley" in South Africa, preferred to stand aside and let others take the risk.

This year the Church Congress is justified of its existence. An assembling of Churchmen at a moment when an attack on the Church in Wales has been sounded is opportune enough. That the place of assembly should have happened to be Welsh too is more than opportune. If the reply to the threatened attack is sustained in the tone of these Swansea speeches, the disestablishers will have their work cut out. It is easy to resist disestablishment on wrong—untenable—grounds, and the rank and file of Churchmen could do with some education on this point. The Bishop of S. Davids, presiding at the Congress, and the Archbishop of Canterbury have set a good example. There was no confusion of Church with State, nor any denial of the power or constitutional right of Parliament to disestablish and disendow, if it will. The answer to the demand for disestablishment is that the Church fulfils her trust to the State, and could not fulfil it so well if disestablished.

Indeed, it is this very progress of the Church in Wales, the growing recognition of her record, that is dulling the ordinary Welshman to disestablishment, but whetting to exasperation the political dissenter. He sees his case going, and fears it will be gone long before trial. Who does not remember Mr. Dillwyn's warning to the House that the Church was improving so fast in Wales that if disestablishment were not done quickly, there would be no reason for doing it at all? And there is a peculiar, though by no means technical, difficulty in the disestablishers' way in Wales. They are trying to cut off an integral part of the Church. Even if they were otherwise weaker, Churchmen would have strong enough ground of resistance in their objection to the Church being broken up. As Lord Hugh Cecil put it, seeing that there is neither a Welsh Church nor a Welsh State, you can hardly divorce them. It is very much to the credit of the Congress that it could take the threatened Bill so gravely, for it will not see the light during this Parliament, and, if it does at any time, will be exposed by its father. Mr. Asquith knows that the English people take no interest in disestablishing the Church anywhere, and would lie low for a Government that wasted a whole session on any such business.

If the Suffragettes show that the forced feeding of prisoners who starve themselves is illegal, they will be able to do pretty well what they like. After three or four days without food they will have to be discharged. The Birmingham magistrate has refused the summons applied for on behalf of Miss Ainsworth. The prison authorities have always assumed the right of compulsory feeding. If it is not legal, the law would have to give it them. Not to mention other instances, hanging would be abolished if a murderer chose to starve instead of to hang. Perhaps they would discharge him as if he were a Suffragette. Lunatics of another type may raise the same question yet. The Suffragettes have now the best cry they ever had. It would be the queerest thing in politics if they got the vote because people did not like their taking their meals with a stomach pump.

It is not a bad idea that Harvard University should own a house in Stratford-on-Avon. We do not so easily catch Miss Corelli's enthusiasm that Shakespeare may have been at the wedding of the founder of Harvard's mother; and known his father in Southwark. Shakespeare is one of the most difficult of persons to catch anywhere. We suppose there is no doubt that Katherine Rogers did marry Robert Harvard of Southwark from the house now belonging to the University which takes its name from their son John. If it is not, it does not greatly matter. We have gazed with equal enthusiasm on two old houses, in each of which the same great writer was born—according to contradictory legends.

The great Shakespearian discovery of Dr. Wallace is only great comparatively. The fact that little is known of Shakespeare's personal history makes it difficult to retain perspective in the light of any new revelation. At the expense of appearing ungracious to Dr. Wallace, it is necessary to insist that this perspective be kept. It is not of supreme importance, either to letters or to mankind at large, to know whether Shakespeare had one-tenth, one-twelfth, or one-fourteenth share in this, that, or the other theatre; although it is comforting to know, as we have long known, that Shakespeare was a man of property. It is all the easier to insist upon this point, as Dr. Wallace has been a little superlative in his announcement. Mr. Sidney Lee has already put in a plea for former students and discoverers; and this plea was not at all unnecessary.

Discovery seems anxious to associate itself with comedy just now. There was the Pole, which we are glad to be rid of for a time; and now a touch of liveliness has come to lend colour to the very serious announcements of Dr. Wallace. Sir Herbert Tree has been badgered with letters about a memorial bronze to be erected upon the alleged site of the old Globe. What if the topography be all wrong? Well, Sir Herbert and his friends are going to risk it, and no harm will be done worth talking about. There will not even be any danger of honouring Bacon unawares in this case.

The little red flag on the horse-cab is only one of the signs that the cab-horse is becoming a played-out animal. It is but a question of time, and the time is getting very near, at least in London and the larger towns. Sales of London cabs and cab-horses are announced which show that the horse-cab is tottering to its fall; nobody any longer wants the stock. No wonder the poor cabman is doleful and has no hope even in the red flag. What is the use of "improved business methods" in a business already doomed speedily to disappear altogether from the earth?

THE LATEST MOVE.

SOMETIMES in politics the explanation given by a Minister is true, though of course it is described by his opponents as "a blind" or "a bluff". The House of Commons will adjourn from Monday or Tuesday next for a week, until, that is, the 18th inst., when the London Elections Bill will be taken, and the report stage of the Finance Bill will follow. The Chancellor of the Exchequer, in explaining the course of business to the House, stated that a clear week was necessary in order that the very numerous amendments and new clauses promised by the Government to be brought up on the report might be carefully considered by the counsel who draughts the Government Bills, by the Attorney-General, and by himself. The Attorney-General has been telling everybody that he requires a week to get up the amendments. Why should it not be true? It is at least "vraisemblable", and there is nearly always an interval, more or less prolonged, between the committee and the report stages of a Bill. Why, then, should everybody see in this adjournment for a week some deep stroke of Machiavellian policy? Simply because the political world is in a feverishly excited condition, and everything is distorted, and nothing is seen in its natural light. In normal times nobody would have thought of questioning the sincerity of Mr. Lloyd George's explanation or of trying to find some hidden motive.

It is now affirmed, on by no means despicable authority, that the Government have decided to dissolve Parliament as soon as the Finance Bill has passed its third reading in the Commons, without sending it up to the Lords. The reasons given for this unconstitutional course are that the Prime Minister and the Lord Chancellor and Mr. Haldane wish to keep the House of Lords out of the scrimmage; and that they believe the Budget declines in popularity the longer it is before the country. They, the Government, are also said to wish to take the election on the old register (contrary to their usual practice), because they have been told by their agents that a large number of "silent voters" (i.e. moderate men) have been frightened into putting themselves on the register who will not be able to vote until after 1 January. Such is the story current in the lobbies and in the Pall Mall clubs. It may of course be true; anything may be true in these days. But the course suggested is certainly quite contrary to constitutional practice. It has been the constitutional custom for more than a century that a Prime Minister does not dissolve a Parliament elected under his auspices until he has lost the confidence of the Legislature, as indicated by a vote of the House of Commons, or until the approach of the seventh year of its life. The last Parliament, it will be remembered, was dissolved by Sir Henry Campbell-Bannerman in the sixth year of its life, the Liberal Government being in a minority. This Parliament was elected, not exactly under the auspices of the present Prime Minister, but of his party chief. On what grounds can the Prime Minister ask the Sovereign to dissolve a Parliament in the fourth year of its existence in which he has a majority of over three hundred? But, waiving the custom of the Constitution, which does not command much respect from the present Ministry, why should Mr. Asquith ask the King for a dissolution before sending the Finance Bill up to the House of Lords in the regular way? We have given the reasons with which the Government are credited, and which deserve examination. The first is that Mr. Asquith, Lord Loreburn, Mr. Haldane, and presumably Lords Morley and Wolverhampton, do not wish to throw the House of Lords into the melting-pot, but, on the contrary, wish, if possible, to keep them out of the struggle. We can well understand that the Sovereign would do everything in his power to assist in this laudable object; but is it not directly contrary to the policy and the speeches of Liberal statesmen since 1893, when Gladstone first seriously threatened the House of Lords upon the rejection of his second Home Rule Bill? Would not Mr. Asquith wreck his party if he were to throw away voluntarily the best chance he is ever likely to get of beating the Peers and the classes supporting them? The speeches of Liberal leaders for the last fifteen years have been insincere babble if they shrink at the eleventh hour from the battle with the hereditary Legislature. And their hypocrisy and cowardice would be so plain to the meanest mind that it would spell political ruin. Hypocrisy and cowardice are, we know, qualities of official Liberalism. But, however willing the older members of the Cabinet might be to swallow their speeches for the sake of avoiding a row, we cannot believe that the Prime Minister, still less of course Messrs. George and Churchill, would agree to so suicidal a step. Why should the Government be afraid of sending the Budget up to the House of Lords? Are they afraid of the Lords passing or rejecting it? If the House of Lords should pass the Budget the party would be deprived of a battle-cry, it is true; but then the party's leaders could remain in office for another year or two. If the House of Lords reject the Budget, then the Socialists will be able to ask the electors: Will you have the Budget or the Lords? It is inconceivable that this Government should sacrifice their trump card to a secret tenderness for the Peers or to squeamishness about opening a revolution. And think what an advantage to the Tariff Reform party it would be to eliminate the question of the Second Chamber from the controversy! We could then get a plain and pure issue between Tariff Reform and the Free Trade Budget. The other reason given for an immediate dissolution, without waiting for the verdict of the Lords, is that the Socialists are so little in love with their own Budget that they want to hurry the electors into voting for it with the least possibly delay. The country is hot for the Budget at present; it will soon grow cold, and the more the Budget is examined and discussed the sooner will the process of refrigeration begin. Such is the supposed argument, but it does not convince us. It may be quite true that the more the Finance Bill is analysed the less lovely it appears, but that view is not likely to occur to its parent or his enthusiastic followers. That the Radical party have so little belief in the Budget, which is proclaimed from the housetops as the greatest of all time, that they dare not expose it to criticism for another three months after it has been exhaustively debated for six months, is a proposition which seems to us nonsense. Still, in politics there is such a thing as the psychological moment; and if the Government think that it has arrived, absurd as it may appear when logically argued, a dissolution in November will take place.

DISESTABLISHMENT ON THE SHELF.

WHEN the meeting of this year's Church Congress was fixed for Swansea, the intention was that the gathering should be a muster of the forces of Anglicanism, English and Welsh, in the war that the Government was threatening to wage against the Church in Wales. The demonstration has been magnificent; but happily it stirs a feeling of unreality. The Government's campaign against the Church in Wales was abandoned ere it was begun, and whatever be the result of the General Election, Welsh disestablishment will be outside practical politics for many a long day. It was, however, a pleasant task for the Congress to hail the true hero of the hour, and to give to the Bishop of S. David's his deserved ovation. It is not too much to say that Bishop Owen and his brother of S. Asaph have materially altered the religious history of Wales. Twenty years ago Welsh disestablishment seemed inevitable. Not only was the Liberal party unanimous in its favour; it could claim strong friends, notably Mr. Chamberlain, in the Unionist ranks. The "Young Wales" M.P.s, T. E. Ellis, Mr. Lloyd George, and Mr. Samuel Evans, who were then at the commencement of their parliamentary careers, were urging it in season and out of season, and some ugly tithe riots in the Principality had startled the London press. Certain Churchmen even had come to the conclusion that resistance was hopeless, and would have welcomed a Disestablishment Bill on moderate lines from a Conservative Government. It was at this crisis that the Bishop of S. Asaph and Dr. Owen came forward as the champions of the doomed Church, and brought home to the English people the knowledge that the Church was a living and progressive body in Wales, that it was numerically greater than any one of the rival Nonconformist denominations, and that it was doing a great work for Christianity and civilisation. English Church opinion was at once aroused, and when in 1895 Mr. Asquith endeavoured to carry a monstrous measure of sacrilege and spoliation, English and Welsh Churchmen united in a solid opposition. It was then that the present Prime Minister learned to his cost the danger of basing arguments on the statistical romances of the Welsh vernacular press. The Bishop of S. Asaph and Dr. Owen supplied the opponents of the Bill with correct figures, and in the opinion of impartial members of the House Mr. Asquith's case ignominiously broke down. The fiasco hastened the general election of 1895, and inquiries of Radical wirepullers after the event revealed the fact that the Church had lost the party more votes than even Irish Home Rule.

The Liberal leaders learned from the fiasco the lesson that for political purposes Welsh disestablishment was a bad egg. Consequently when the party councils assembled to prepare for the dissolution of 1906, it was quietly determined that Welsh disestablishment should be shelved. Sir Henry Campbell-Bannerman was implored by certain Welsh M.P.s to give it a place in his election manifesto. He refused, and in his great oration at the Albert Hall, when he discussed almost every topic under the sun, on the Welsh Church he said never a word. All the consolation that the Welsh Nonconformists could get was the announcement that the chairman of the Welsh party, Sir Alfred Thomas, was satisfied that something would be done. However, when the victory was won and the Welsh dissenter began to press for a share of the spoils, the Government was in a nasty dilemma. The English social-reform Radicals were disinclined for a repetition of the fiasco of 1895, and, if rumour may be trusted, Mr. Asquith showed no enthusiasm to fight another Liberationist battle on unverified statistics. Then there occurred to Mr. Lloyd George and his colleagues the happy idea of a Royal Commission. They reasoned, one may guess, in this manner. Arrange a friendly Board with a sympathetic chairman. Let all the stale gossip about Church abuses be raked up, and let the Nonconformist minister be patted on the back. Welsh dissent will for a time be kept quiet under the eulogies of Royal Commissioners, and perhaps some figures may be collected, which in the dim and distant future will support a new Liberationist Bill.

And the Commission might really have worked out in this way, only Mr. Lloyd George appointed the wrong sort of chairman. Lord Justice Vaughan Williams, who in an evil hour for Welsh Radicalism was invited to fill this post, has emphatically a legal conscience. And he managed the Commission in a way that drove the Welsh agitators to frenzy. He required statistics to be strictly proved. He had the hardihood to examine in ordinary legal style Nonconformist ministers and Nonconformist deacons, and he closured in the sternest manner all attempts to introduce under the name of historical evidence the scandals of a bygone day. The Commission has not yet reported; but there is hardly a Welsh Nonconformist Radical who does not bitterly regret that it was ever called into being. For it is absolutely clear from the figures that have been given in evidence that the Church is the largest denomination in the Principality. If before the Commission sat the chances of carrying a Welsh Disestablishment Bill were gloomy, the prospect is now hopeless. English Liberal M.P.s have read the account of the proceedings with disgust, and have come to the conclusion that a Welsh Disestablishment Bill would be not only a nuisance, but also a danger. Talk to Radical members for industrial districts and they will tell you that on the statistics substantiated before the Commission it would be impossible to put a case for Welsh Disestablishment before an English working-class audience in a way that would elicit the faintest sympathy. Such M.P.s know that if a parliamentary session were to be wasted on so ridiculous a subject the chance of their return to S. Stephen's would be nil. So that while the Welsh Nonconformist ministers have been urging the Government to redeem its pledge, influential English politicians have been using every influence to defeat them, a fact that the unhappy preacher on the Kymric hillside has little suspected. Practically the Englishmen have won. Mr. Lloyd George is perfectly well aware that a Welsh Disestablishment Bill will be unpopular with most of his supporters, and also suspects that it will make havoc with his cause at the polls. But to put off the Welsh preachers with lame excuses another session would, he knows, be a dangerous step, especially in view of the gigantic strides that socialism is making in the Welsh coalfield. Let the Welsh Church Bill be again shelved, and let Parliament sit on. Mr. Keir Hardie, who, as visitors to the Swansea Congress know, is the hero of many of the Welsh working men, will at the next election fix the parliamentary representatives of industrial Wales. There is one escape from the dilemma, and that is dissolution. The Welsh preacher can in that case be told that only the wickedness of the House of Lords stands in the way of the spoliation of the Church; he will be urged to help the Government against the Peers, and he will be offered in return another idle promise to the effect that very soon his wish shall be realised. As he is a simple fellow, he will probably fall into line, though not with quite his old enthusiasm; and as a result of his slackness the Liberal wirepullers expect to lose three Welsh seats to the Tories. It is well for official Liberalism that Welsh Nonconformists have not realised that the political result of the Government's policy has been to drive Welsh disestablishment out of practical politics for an indefinite period. If they knew the truth few Welsh Liberal M.P.s would see Westminster again.

LORDS AND THE LAND BILL.

IT is a coincidence, and a very instructive one, that the House of Lords should be proving the necessity of the bi-cameral system at the very moment when the Radicals seem most set upon making an end of it. Ireland and Liberal policies for Ireland have more than once given the Upper Chamber a clear and easy opportunity to justify its existence. They are doing so again to-day, and if the people of this country could only be induced to read an Irish debate and to interest themselves in Ireland, even when she is comparatively at peace, they would need nothing more than the discussion in the Lords of the Irish Land Bill to convince them that a Second Chamber has still its uses. It is for this reason that we again this week go over ground traversed in our article of last Saturday. Here was a Bill involving British credit to the tune of something like two hundred millions sterling, upsetting or at least radically changing the solution unanimously applied six years ago by all parties and interests to the most contentious of all Irish problems, and yet rushed through a yawning House of Commons with six out of every seven clauses wholly undebated. Probably not one Englishman in a hundred thousand realised that the closure was being utilised to effect a secret and pernicious revolution, and that the House of Commons had set its ignorant seal upon a measure that threatened to bring the policy of land purchase in Ireland, and with it the progress of the country towards contentment, to a sudden stop. It was left for the House of Lords to examine with thoroughness the work that the Lower Chamber had scamped, to raise an effective protest against legislation in the dark, and to restore to the business of law-making its lost basis of open and informed discussion. To do that as the House of Lords has done it during the past week, with knowledge, discretion and freedom, is to fulfil the highest function of a revisory chamber.

There are at least three points that are common ground in this matter of Irish land among Unionists and Nationalists, landlords and tenants, alike. The first is that the process of transferring the title-deeds in the soil from landlord to tenant must go on, that there is no other way of bringing the agrarian struggle of seven centuries to an end, that Ireland, to be at rest at all, must become a country of peasant proprietors. That is the ultimate settlement of the land tenure question to which everyone subscribes. It will probably disappoint many hopes and raise many anxious problems of its own; if it robs the agrarian question of most of its old social and political bitterness, it will certainly invest it with a new economic acuteness; and the novel problem of how to make as much as possible out of the land will present difficulties as formidable as the old problem of who was to own it and how little he was to pay for it. Nevertheless there is no one in Ireland or in Great Britain who would now dream of reversing the policy of land purchase. A second and equally accepted point is that the Wyndham Act has broken down and needs amendment. It has broken down partly because of its overwhelming success in inducing landlords to sell and tenants to buy, and partly because the state of the money market has made it impossible to finance the resultant transactions without serious loss either to the Treasury or to the Irish ratepayers. In this dilemma it is a further point of agreement that landlords, tenants, and the State should all sacrifice something to promote an object in which all have a common interest. The financial clauses of Mr. Birrell's Bill have therefore to be considered from the standpoint of their fairness to the three parties chiefly interested and of their efficacy in furthering the progress of land purchase. Now it is clear at once that they depart widely from the principles that underlay the Wyndham Act. For voluntary negotiations between landlord and tenant Mr. Birrell substitutes compulsion; for a low tenants' annuity he substitutes a higher one; for a uniform rate of bonus he substitutes a graduated scale; instead of payments in cash he offers a mixed system of cash and stock; and instead of allowing agreements within the zones to be automatically effective he proposes to invest the Estates Commissioners with powers to sanction or refuse them at will.

It is at least arguable that these changes go a long way towards destroying the inducements held out by the Wyndham Act. One of them at any rate, the one that introduces the principle of general compulsion, is clearly inadmissible. With over £50,000,000 worth of agreements still to be financed, there is no necessity for compulsion, while its presence in the background is bound to affect and must ultimately supplant the speedier and more harmonious system of voluntary sales. The Lords will carry all sensible men with them in striking out a provision that in its present form is at once needless and harmful. They have done good work, again, in protecting the zones against the attempt to undermine them, in safeguarding the grazing industry, which, if it is the bane, is also the mainstay of Irish agriculture, and in championing the claims of the "congests" against those of the landless men. Their amendments to the purely financial clauses they forbore to press to a division, but their objections are bound to tell when the two Houses meet in conference. What indeed the Nationalists look forward to is buying the support of the Lords to Part III. of the Bill by meeting them half-way in the matter of the bonus and the price at which the stock which they are invited to take instead of cash is to be issued. We hope and believe that the Lords will assent to no such bargain. From the standpoint of Irish well-being Part III. is perhaps the most mischievous portion of the Bill. Lord MacDonnell, the greatest administrator, and Sir Horace Plunkett, the greatest constructive thinker on agrarian problems that Ireland has produced in the past half-century, have joined in condemning it; and we have yet to come across a rational defence either of its principles or its details. What Part III. does is to enlarge the area of the Congested Districts Board till it embraces a third of the whole of Ireland, to endow it with £250,000 a year, to give it the first call on all land within its area and compulsory powers for its acquisition, and to introduce on to a body hitherto non-elective and therefore non-partisan nine elected members—that is to say, nine United Irish Leaguers—who will quickly control both the policy of the Board and its finance. And this it does for the ostensible purpose of relieving congestion.

The objections to these proposals seem to us unanswerable, though we by no means oppose a strictly limited and ad hoc system of compulsion for the specific purpose of promoting the migration of the "congests". They practically place the West of Ireland under a separate government of its own, and thus create a new line of division in a country whose fundamental curse is its lack of unity and common interests. They set up a board for dealing in semi-paternal fashion with the economic conditions of the people; they expose the board to the full current of local faction and intrigue; and they give it a free hand to spend imperial funds as it pleases. Paternalism may or may not be a necessary policy in some of the more backward and depressed districts of the west. But two things may at least be asserted about it. The first is that of all bodies an elected one is the most unfitted to act with the impartiality that is the essential and redeeming feature of paternalism. The second is that the need for State-aiding the West of Ireland, thanks to old-age pensions, to the gospel of self-help preached by the co-operators, and to the activities of the Department of Agriculture, is year by year diminishing. There is nothing, moreover, as Lord MacDonnell has clearly pointed out, in the functions and duties of the new Congested Districts Board that could not be undertaken with less expense and greater efficiency by the Estates Commissioners and the Department of Agriculture. For the sake of endowing the United Irish League with £250,000 a year Mr. Birrell duplicates the machinery of administration and sets the West to experiment on its own wild lines with problems that throughout all the rest of Ireland are being treated on uniform lines and on sound character-forming principles. It only rounds off the absurdity of his proposals to add that they seem expressly designed to thwart the main object they have in view, and that so long as local opinion is enthroned as the decisive factor in the purchase and allotment of the grazing ranches, the "congests" will remain as they are and where they are, and the local men will carry off the spoils of the cattle-driving war.

AUSTRIA AND THE PAN-GERMANS.

THE lapse of forty-three years softens many memories. Forty-three years ago Prince Ludwig of Bavaria was fighting for a United Germany of which Austria should be the head. That dream was shattered in a six weeks' campaign, and now it is close on forty years since Prince Ludwig and the country over which he will one day rule became part of a United Germany of which Berlin and not Vienna is the capital. The Prince had no need to fear any charge of disloyalty to the new German Empire when he consented to unveil a monument commemorating the wound he received in fighting for an idea long since dead. How dead it is his own speech showed. It was addressed to the Austrian Germans, and bade them remain loyal to their country—that country which they now tend to regard as de-teutonised, but which the Prince once hoped to make the main prop of Teutonism in Europe. And in truth it is a little hard for these ardent patriots to believe that in these days of universal suffrage, when the Reichsrat cannot meet for fear of Czech obstruction, Austria is still a German State. Prince Ludwig endeavoured to calm their fears and to assure them that their position was made secure by the powerful backing of the German alliance. This enabled him to give a very politic turn to his speech and to praise both his earlier and his later overlord. But is it quite honest intellectually? Is it fair to say to the Austrian Germans, You must continue to be loyal to your Hapsburg Emperor because the Hohenzollern Emperor will see that you come to no harm? Assuredly it would be possible for some Pan-German journalist in Vienna to show that Prince Ludwig's apparent rebuke is really a justification of the Pan-German propaganda.

We may concede to our imaginary Pan-German that Prince Ludwig's speech does not say the last word on a very important matter, and that the position of the Austrian German is not as easy as the Prince would make out. We live in an age when Teutonism is determined to assert itself. Once it seemed as if Vienna would lead the forward movement and would establish German culture in the plains of Lombardy, thence to move forward in due course to Rome itself. That great historical ambition, which linked up the middle of the nineteenth century with the most inspiring traditions of the mediæval Empire, is beyond all hope of realisation to-day. Austria-Hungary is still a progressive State with a forward policy; but her glance has shifted from the Apennines to the Balkans. Moreover, Austria-Hungary has become a dual monarchy. The German must share his triumphs with the Magyar, possibly with the Slav as well, and the centre of pure Teuton activity has shifted to Berlin. The Pan-German may not unreasonably ask why he should be cut off from the expansionist movement in its modern aspect, or if not cut off at least only allowed to shine with the reflected glory of a victorious ally. That is the Pan-German's case. Because Berlin leads the way he would fain go with Berlin.

It is a strong case, strong in its simplicity and the obvious truth of the facts on which it is based. And yet there is much to be said for Prince Ludwig's point of view. Suppose the Austrian Germans put themselves under Prussian leadership, would they be happy? Prince Ludwig should know, for he speaks with the experience of the best part of a lifetime, and he advises his friends across the frontier to stay as they are. In fact the Prussian ideals are somewhat strange to the South German. He has no knowledge of sea-power, does not grasp the need for oversea expansion, and is a little perplexed that Great Britain should suddenly bulk so largely on the German horizon. He finds himself in a whirl of new ideas which he tends to distrust because of their novelty, and he likes them no better when they are propagated with all the harsh efficiency of Prussian methods. This matter of the navy is really a test case. Comparisons have often been made between the membership of the British and the German Navy Leagues. They are in some ways misleading. The German Navy League is an educational institution, but no one has to teach Englishmen the elements of the theory of sea-power. If a Tariff Reform League were established in Germany to-morrow it would only be joined by the enthusiasts who wished to make the scientific tariff more perfect still. But the comparatively small number of its adherents would not prove that the average German had no grasp of the theory of modern protection. It would prove just the opposite. And so with the Navy. The League has been very active in Bavaria of late, and has received the patronage of members of the Royal House, commendably anxious that their country should share the wonderful material successes of the new Empire. But Prince Ludwig knows that the movement has brought mental disquietude, and he tells the Austrian Pan-Germans that the success of their work would mean that they would be invited to consider the situation in the North Sea, which would not interest them at all.

The Prince is quite right. The Prussian and the Austrian do not see things in the same way. The Prussian looks forward to the future, but the Austrian looks back upon the past. The Prussian fixes his thoughts on sea-power, but the Austrian laments the loss of Italy. A veteran of 1866 can speak of the war without bitterness, but a veteran of 1859 cannot think of that year of disaster without passion. Prince Ludwig can bid the German of Vienna to be loyal to Francis Joseph, but he could not bid the German of Milan to be loyal to Victor Emmanuel. The traveller in Austria is at once struck by the poignancy of the regret felt for the loss of the Italian provinces. It is forced upon him when he makes the short journey from Munich to Innsbruck and finds himself in a town where the very match-boxes bear a motto telling the oppressed German brethren to be of good cheer. To the Austrian mind the goal of the Teuton is the south, not commerce nor colonies nor material wealth, but the sunshine and the beauty and the traditions of Italy. It is not for nothing that the Austrian Sovereign bears the title of Cæsar and wears the crown of Charlemagne. The Cæsar of the North stands for none of these things.

The Austrian may be well aware that the hope he cherishes is vain, but it is not the less precious for that. Not to-day nor to-morrow will he set forth on the reconquest of Italy, and yet some day, somehow, he tells you in his dreamy way, his chance may come again. But it will never come without the German alliance. Suppose that the policy of the Pan-Germans bore fruit, and that despite the forces of tradition and religion and despite the serious obstacle imposed by Bohemia, Austria proper passed over to the Hohenzollerns, leaving the Hapsburg monarch to bear rule over Magyars and Slavs. How such a State would flourish no man can say; but it may be assumed with certainty that its temper would be anti-German. It is the Pan-Germans' hope that by joining the German Empire they would deflect its energies towards the south. They are wrong. The dominant spirit in the Empire would still be Prussian, and the Prussian does not understand these southern impulses. Besides, he has other business on hand, the business of protecting his long coast-line on the Baltic and the North Sea. Till that work is done, and its doing may mean that Great Britain will be forced to abandon the two-Power standard, Prussia, and with Prussia the Empire, has no time to think of expansion elsewhere. A wise people will not scatter its energies over two fronts at once, least of all so sane and practical a people as the Prussians. And so it is that if the Austrian Germans should ever break with their Sovereign, they will at the same time have to break with their traditions and bid good-bye to their visions of Mediterranean sovereignty.

Far different are the prospects if the alliance rests firm. Its influence will ensure the predominance of Teutonic ideas in Vienna, but the two kindred peoples will work out the same ideas in different ways. Germany is building a fleet for Prussian purposes in the North Sea. The Austrians have seen the value of the new weapon, and are determined to build another fleet for Austrian purposes in the Mediterranean. As the greatest naval Power, Great Britain cannot be indifferent to the shipbuilding programme of any State, but it is not against Great Britain that the Austrian Dreadnoughts are primarily and immediately aimed. All Italy knows that, and for this reason is steadily gravitating towards the Anglo-French entente. There is in existence an agreement between England, France, and Spain which establishes a sort of Monroe doctrine in the Western Mediterranean. The scope of that treaty may yet be extended so as to include Italy. It is true that for the moment the future Austrian fleet seems unlikely to materialise for lack of funds. But when a people's heart is set on a thing the money is always forthcoming. In days gone by, when Austria was poorer than she is now, enthusiasm found the gold, whether the foe was Napoleon or Piedmont, both rivals, be it observed, in the fight for the possession of Italy. The Austrian Dreadnoughts will be built, because they represent an old hope in a new form; it may quite possibly be necessary to build them as a means to inducing the Empire to pay for them. Only one thing can stop their building, and that is the rupture of the German alliance. As things are, the German parallel will provide the Austrians with the driving-force to carry through their schemes. But they will carry them through as Austrians, not as Prussians. Prince Ludwig is right; the Germans across the frontier will do best as they are.

HOW SHALL WE SAVE OUR PICTURES?

THE National Loan Exhibition at the Grafton Galleries is a cry of distress and an appeal to the nation. The show is not the main thing. The Trustees of the National Gallery invite the public to inspect the treasures they have collected as though they said "Come and look your last; before long these precious possessions will in the inevitable course of things have vanished from your shores; we are helpless and cannot do anything to save them". The very plan of holding the exhibition appears to increase the danger and to expose the owners of the treasures to stronger temptations to part with them. Even this risk must be run, so urgent is the pressure. And yet the hope of raising sufficient funds by this means, to enable the National Gallery to compete with the wealthy foreign buyers, who are so much better able than we are ourselves to buy the coveted masterpieces as they come into the market, is a pathetic fallacy. One American millionaire could at a moment's notice find more money than the trustees could raise by their exhibition. The really important thing the Trustees have done is to get from Mr. Lewis Harcourt and Mr. Balfour speeches demonstrating that the State must be prepared to purchase with State funds if the tendency of our works of art to emigrate to other countries is to be checked. At present England is the greatest centre of masterpieces in the world. It has become so because the ancestors of those who now own them were an aristocratic class which a century or two ago was the wealthiest in Europe. The ancestors were buyers, the descendants are more and more likely in the immediate future to become sellers. Pictures under English law and custom have gone with the land. Land and pictures have accumulated together; and now when everything points to the breaking-up of accumulated land, the associated pictures are in danger of going with it. The State is attacking land, and even a Liberal Government in mid career recognises the injury it may do to art, and through Mr. Lewis Harcourt admits that it is rather alarmed at what it is doing. All works of art are in future, Mr. Harcourt informed his audience, to be exempt from the payment of death duties. This is an extension of the privilege which, in fear of what is now happening, has been given to pictures entailed with land.

Mr. Balfour believes this will have some effect, but far from enough. Just as to avoid raising capital to pay land taxes owners may, under the Budget, hand over the land instead, so to raise capital for the same or other purposes the owners of pictures will be tempted to sell. It is a far greater temptation to sell an unproductive picture than a productive or possibly productive part of an estate; and so the peril of the picture is greater than the peril of the land. But the State has as yet not devised any plan by which it may become the possessor of the pictures which its own action may force into the market. This handing over of pictures to it may or may not in the end play its part in keeping pictures in England. In any case the State ought to be prepared at any moment, when some great picture may be on the point of leaving its owner's hands, to be the most formidable competitor for it. Only the most paltry sums can be provided by any Government as the law stands. Ten thousand pounds was the limit of the Government offer when the Duke of Norfolk recently sold his Holbein. The balance of forty thousand pounds was raised by public subscription; but this showed ominously enough that we have no private persons in England who are willing to spend fifty thousand pounds on a picture as a permanent possession. Instead we have "dealers in old masters" who buy as speculators. They intend to sell again; it may be to some European gallery where the Government has more resources; but more probably to some American multi-millionaire who has such wealth as no Englishman can ever hope to possess. Unless the State's funds are made adequate to meet the purchasing power of the American multi-millionaire, the destiny of our pictures is to go to America: Hic exitus illas sorte tulit. The desire to have a picture gallery of renowned works as an appendage of social position is dying out in old countries. American multi-millionaires are a little old-fashioned. They copy tradition as nouveaux riches always copy an aristocratic fashion. Our feeling about great pictures now is that they ought to be in national rather than in private galleries. It is an aggravation of misfortune if English pictures are to go not even into other English private collections but into those of Americans.

Everything, therefore, shows that the State ought now to become the patron of art in a much wider sense than it has ever yet been. Mr. Harcourt and Mr. Balfour both urge that the State should make larger grants of money. We need something more definitely formulated than this. Mr. MacColl once described a scheme in the SATURDAY REVIEW which would be sufficient for the purpose. If the Government obtained power by Act of Parliament to raise and set aside for the purpose a fund of a million pounds, this would be quite enough to secure all the works that are of such national value that they cannot be allowed to pass into foreign hands. The owners of such pictures would prefer to sell to the Government, if it were, as it is not now, an effective competitor against the foreign clients of dealers. The dealers and not the sellers of the pictures get the huge sums which the foreign principal ultimately gives. The owner would probably get as much as he gets now if the State were the purchaser.

It would be to the good if the direct buying of pictures by the State were to lessen the influence of the dealers in matters of art. They encourage the pernicious superstition that the collecting of "old masters" is the be-all and end-all of the connoisseur of pictures. It is a very profitable superstition for the dealers, as it is through their hands that the traffic is conducted, and they have a monopoly of it. A new picture may be bought directly from the artist, but the dealer alone gets to know when the "old master" that hangs in the house of some needy owner is "ripe" for sale. A private buyer cannot ask a man whether his domestic gods are for sale. Everything tends to inflate the pecuniary prices for "old masters". It is their rarity even more than their special qualities which stimulate the lust of possession in the American multi-millionaire; and often he buys them to say that he has them more than to admire them. The dealer reaps the advantage of this mania and the collector puts his head into the mouth of the dealer; he is bled of money which he might more usefully spend if he exercised his independent taste and judgment. Is the purchase of "old masters" the only way in which collectors can be patrons of art? Too exclusive devotion to this form of art patronage rather suggests that collectors have not knowledge and taste enough to discriminate in contemporary art. The excessively dear "old masters" of to-day were perhaps excessively cheap when they were new. Collectors now might take the hint and emulate the shrewdness of their predecessors who made collections. This course is still open to them, though they cannot compete for antiquities with American millionaires. Let them buy good modern pictures which will become in due course "old masters". This is what their fathers did. The Reynoldses and Gainsboroughs came to be on the walls of our great houses because they were the great painters of their day. They were not added later as great deceased masters. Our landowners and nobles think that they cannot afford to buy pictures; they must rather sell them. They cannot, it is true, afford to buy "old masters" at the dealers' rates, but they could afford to buy modern pictures which will one day prove a good investment. How many owners of great country houses have been buying Johns and Steers and Rothensteins for the hundreds that could not secure a single fine "old master"? If they had been, they would now have good pictures to fill the place of those they have had to sell and interest accumulating upon them.

THE CITY.

THE directors of the Bank of England on Thursday raised their rate of discount from 2½ to 3 per cent. It is a good move, and thoroughly justified. It will not check the outflow of sovereigns to Egypt and South America, but it should turn the Continental exchanges more in our favour, and may stop Russia from competing for the weekly arrivals of gold from South Africa. The movement should also check the volume of American finance paper, which is a menace to our market and an encouragement to reckless speculation in Wall Street. Money and political uncertainties have alike contributed to depress the stock markets this week. The Stock Exchange hates to be kept in suspense, and the worst piece of news causes less disquietude than the anticipation. Consols have been comparatively steady, and the fact is noteworthy, because there is a tendency to decry the security at every political move. It is perfectly true that the investment demand has fallen off, and probably correct that the demand has been checked by the socialistic tendencies of the Government; but it is not true to assert that the market is a narrow one, and the statement that "jobbers" will not quote a price without knowing whether the broker is a buyer or a seller is open to quite a different interpretation from that which it is desired to place upon it. "Jobbers" try to ascertain the wants of brokers because they are out of stock, and to make a price and then find that the broker is a buyer renders them liable to be "caught short". It is significant that when on Monday there was a scare at Paris in connexion with Spanish designs on Morocco, Consols were the only important security unshaken. All speculative stocks were immediately offered and depreciated.

Wall Street has this week had a money spasm. It was bound to come, and will probably be followed by others. To maintain prices it is absolutely essential that money remain cheap and abundant, and this cannot be arranged for all time. It is beginning to be recognised that Europe will not go on finding the wherewithal to finance New York. There has been too much borrowing this year on bonds and bills. It is even asserted that the indebtedness to Europe on American paper is nearly as large as it was two years ago, when the whole fabric of United States finance was brought to the ground. This is probably an exaggeration, and in any case the United States is better able now than then to carry its indebtedness; but the edict has gone forth that financial assistance will not be given so readily in the future, and if this line of policy is pursued Wall Street may find itself in a very awkward position. The New York banks are not unmindful of the dangers of the situation, and in calling in loans on Wednesday they sounded a note of warning that Wall Street cannot well ignore. Messrs. Morgan and the National Bank came to the rescue subsequently, but it is not likely that these will continue to take upon themselves the whole burden of financing Wall Street.

The continued decrease in home railway traffic is a cause for much disquietude. It is as well to point out, however, that much of the loss is in passenger receipts, and that the comparison is with a period when the White City was attracting hundreds of thousands of excursionists from all over the country. The decrease in the Great Northern return is also partly explained by the Licensing demonstration in London on 27 September 1908. This added several thousand pounds to the company's receipts last year. If we examine the goods receipts of the principal lines we find increases are much more common than decreases. True, the expansion is small, but it is in evidence, and is of much more importance than the temporary loss in passenger earnings. It is difficult, we know, to convince investors that any improvement is taking place in the outlook for home railways. But to ignore facts is foolish. Trade is improving, and the cost of working our railways is steadily declining. Moreover, prices are low and dividend yields high. And when we realise the prices paid for American railway securities, and the great risks run by the fluctuations which take place in American trade, the existing prices of home railway stocks are not easily accounted for. There was a big jump in Hull and Barnsley on Thursday, accompanied by amalgamation rumours, but the fact seems to be that a trust company was buying and that there was no stock in the market.

An unexpected drop in the price of the raw material early in the week disclosed the sensitiveness of the rubber share market. The drop proved to be quite temporary, but it should remind speculators in the shares that the market is as liable to fluctuation as any other. The prominence given to the movement has induced a pause in the flotation of new ventures, the number of which was increasing at too rapid a pace to allow of digestion. Many dozens, however, are in preparation and awaiting a favourable opportunity of issue, and the moment is opportune to direct the attention of would-be investors to the all-important question of management. The tendency is to take too much upon trust. "So many trees—so much rubber. So much rubber—so much profit." This is the argument, and on paper it produces some very fine results, but if the trees are handled badly the supply of rubber will fall off, and profits will be reduced to a minimum or disappear altogether. The necessity for good management is thus of prime importance, and in estimating future dividends it might be as well to make allowance for possible losses arising out of careless administration.

INSURANCE: POLICIES AT HIGH PREMIUMS.

I.

When a life policy is effected at a low rate of premium the sum assured is large, and in the event of early death the life office has to pay to the estate of the assured a very much greater sum than it has received in premiums; this means that there is a large amount of insurance protection. When a high rate of premium is paid the sum assured for a given premium is comparatively small, and there is but little insurance protection. If a man of thirty pays £100 a year for a non-profit whole-life policy which requires premiums to be paid throughout the whole of life, the sum assured being payable at death, the amount of the policy exceeds £5000. If instead of paying £100 a year for life he pays £100 a year for only fifteen years, the sum assured at death is about £3000 instead of £5000; and if he pays £100 for one year only, the policy secures but little over £200. Whereas under the first of these policies he has insurance protection for about £5000, under the last of them he has protection for only £100. Thus for policyholders of the same age the essential difference between assurance at high premiums and low premiums is the amount of insurance protection obtained. When provision for others in the event of premature death is the essential thing, a policy at a low premium should be selected; when this is not required and capital for a man's own future is what is necessary, a policy at a comparatively high rate of premium is the better.

Assurance at high premiums is found in its extreme form when paid for by a single premium. A man of forty can make a single payment of £1000, in return for which he is definitely guaranteed the sum of £1412 at the end of twenty years, or at his previous death. This policy shares in the profits and is likely to amount to £2020 at the end of twenty years. The amount of the insurance protection is small in this case, and the annual cost of it is more than paid by the interest that is earned upon the single premium of £1000. Hence the whole of the single premium is available for accumulation at compound interest. In the instance just given the policyholder would receive back his £1000 at the end of twenty years, with compound interest at £3 12s. per cent. To obtain a net return of £3 12s. from shares or other investments the dividend, subject to income tax, would have to be at the rate of £3 16s. 6d. per cent. It is thus apparent that single-premium policies constitute an investment of a lucrative kind when the security afforded is taken into account.

It is sometimes urged that money paid for life assurance is locked up, and that a heavy loss is incurred if for any reason the policy has to be surrendered; this is not true even of assurance at annual premiums in some companies, and is certainly not the case when policies are paid for by a single premium. From the very outset 90 to 95 per cent. of the single premium can be borrowed immediately on the sole security of the policy, and after the assurance has been in force for a few years a larger sum than was originally paid can be obtained either as a surrender value or as a loan. This feature of single-premium policies is well known to many members of the Stock Exchange, who, as opportunity offers, buy policies of this kind, which enable them to obtain at a moment's notice a loan equivalent to the amount invested. They can walk into the life office with the policy, and walk out with the money.

In many ways endowment assurance at a single premium is a great deal better than a sinking-fund policy effected by a single payment. A man can go to an insurance company and pay £1077 in return for a guarantee of £2000 at the end of twenty years. We have just seen that a man can pay £1000 for an endowment assurance policy securing £1412 with bonuses in addition at his death within twenty years, and probably yielding £2020 at the end of that time. The sinking-fund policy is a guaranteed contract which does not share in the profits, and the endowment assurance gives more advantages and better results.

Policies under which the sum assured is paid only at death whenever it occurs can also be effected by single premiums. For age forty at entry one payment of £420 secures £1000 without profits at death, and a similar with-profit policy for £1000 can be secured for a single payment of £526.

In subsequent articles we shall describe other policies at high rates of premium, such as whole-life assurances subject to premiums for ten years, and endowment assurances for short periods. For those with sufficient capital to leave dependents well provided for, policies at high premiums have many attractions.

SHAKESPEARE IN FRANCE

III.

SHAKESPEARE AND THE GALLIC MIND.

The question still remains: Though the French consented to sit through De Vigny's "Othello", and though the incipient merriment of a Parisian audience at sight of Hamlet sitting upon the ground was drowned in the applause of Dumas' faithful battalions, were they, as a matter of fact, any nearer to an appreciation? Was Shakespeare anything more to his admirers than the great Romantic who transcended the formulæ which the Romantics themselves had overthrown?

Before an answer to this question can be given a word is necessary upon the relation in which Teutonic humour stands to Gallic comedy. The French have no word for humour, because they have no use for such a word. The Gallic laugh has nothing whatever to do with humour. It is the cruel, critical laugh that passes judgment upon the follies of life as they present themselves when held up to view by the Molière of the passing generation. It is laughter of the brain. The deeper laughter that comes not so much from a perception as from a feeling of the fundamental incongruities of nature; the laughter of the man who stands aloof from what he sees and sympathises with it at the same time; the broad, silent laughter that claims kinship with the whole of life, springing from the deeps of its tragedy and eliciting a sudden smile from the midst of tears; this kind of laughter is not Gallic, and the French have no word for it. The French feel their tragedy and think their comedy. Consequently, the two remain distinct. The humour of the English is not a product of the intelligence. To define it as an outlook upon life is not sufficient. Rather, it is a way of feeling life and of reacting to it. It lies, therefore, in the same plane as tragedy. Villemain did well to declare that the grave-scene in "Hamlet" was for the English alone, though little praise is due to him for the interpretation he desired to have placed upon that remark. The grave-scene in "Hamlet" is one of the finest examples of humour in Shakespeare; and, once again let it be stated, the French have no word for it.

Many Frenchmen are aware of what, as a race, they lack. The spectacle of Paul Stapfer, the best of the modern critics upon Shakespeare, endeavouring to give his countrymen some idea of the extraordinary psychologic compound called "humour" by the English is a fine example of the thing he is trying to explain. An even better example is afforded by De Stendhal, who went solemnly round the theatres with a notebook to find out what it was that made the people laugh. De Tréveret is another who knows that something is missing but does not quite know what it is: "Ce mélange de badinage, de philosophie, de caprice, et d'imagination que les Anglais appellent *humour*".

Shakespeare did not write comedies in the French sense. The only play that approaches the comedy in the French sense is "The Merry Wives of Windsor", which accordingly is the one invariably selected for favourable comment by their critics. Moreover, if the French proceed to enumerate Shakespeare's comic personages as they understand the word, these turn out to be, not Dogberry, not Gobbo, not Sir Toby Belch, but Biron, Benedick, Jaques, and Timon.

The French, being blind on one side to Shakespeare as a man of humour, and blind, from their centuries of training in the school of Racine, to Shakespeare as a tragic writer, an appreciation seems a long way off. For the Romantic outburst must not be regarded as a revolution. It was a development from Racine, and not an abrogation. Hugo, in writing "Cromwell", thought that he was imitating Shakespeare. There is perhaps nothing in literature that is less like anything that Shakespeare wrote, or possibly could have written. "Athalie" is nearer to "Hamlet" than is "Cromwell".

The straightest way to measure the real dimensions of the fundamental misunderstanding of Shakespeare by the French is to take some of the more prominent and typical of their critics, and watch them in the act of reading the plays. There is not one of them all that feels quite comfortable. There are bursts of admiration or censure, but they seem unaccountable. The acquired instincts that they have so unceasingly trained to an appreciation of their own literature fail them here, and the result is incredibly fantastic.

Let us, for instance, return yet again to Chateaubriand. It was Chateaubriand that began the legend of a Shakespeare who wrote in a spirit of universal mockery and doubt. "Shakespeare, cet esprit si tragiqué, tua son sérieux de sa moquerie, de son dédain de lui-même et de l'espèce humaine; il doutait de tout: *perhaps* est un mot qui lui revient sans cesse." Philarète Chasles, who made a profound study of Shakespeare's works, came to the same conclusion; and, to the satisfaction of his countrymen, proved that Shakespeare would never have written his tragedies or risen above the frivolity of his earlier manner had he not read the essays of Michael de Montaigne.

Next, it is worth while to watch Lamartine as he reads "Romeo and Juliet". How distressed he becomes when confronted with "les ignobles obscénités dont la nourrice de Juliette salit l'oreille virginale de l'amante de Roméo"! How sure he is that the inclusion of a clown in the play is "une concession du poète à l'habitude ricaneuse du peuple qui fréquentait son théâtre"! How bored he becomes when "une scène triviale entre les valets et les servantes autour des buffets amuse le peuple"! And how charmed he is with the nightingale that was a lark after all! And then he turns the pages and comes to "Othello", which he reads painfully through to the end. "Voici la dernière scène de cette abominable boucherie plutôt que tragédie; il y a horreur, mais peu de talent; l'horreur seul a attaché le peuple à cette abomination."

Then there is the Shakespeare of Taine; the Shakespeare who has imagination and passion, without morality or reason; the man whose fecundity was appalling, and untouched with conscience, like the fecundity of nature; the man who was indifferent to ideas and religions and philosophies, and utterly unselective in his material.

Then there is the Shakespeare of Mezières, a most moral man with solicitous regard for the virtues and standards of society. He will have no intriguing valets in his plays, because servants should be kept in their place. He will never neglect to force home his moral lesson with pitiless rigour. For example, do but notice how Lear and Desdemona reap the consequences of their injudicious conduct. And what better moral lesson could one have than the punishment of Falstaff at the very moment when his wickedness seemed about to triumph? According to Mezières, Falstaff is an instructive figure in more ways than one. For instance, why do the Germans like him better than the French? Because the Germans have had no Voltaire, no Molière, and no Regnard. The French know better. "Falstaff ne s'élève pas à nos yeux au-dessus de la bouffonnerie. C'est un bouffon très divertissant, mais ce n'est que bouffon. Il reste dans la région secondaire où nous rencontrons chez-nous Scapin, Sosie, et Mascarille."

An Englishman feels quite helpless here. What is the use of setting Mezières to read Dame Quickly's account of Falstaff's end? Like others of his countrymen he would discover in it evidences of a death-bed repentance. What is the use of telling him that we would not exchange those words of Dame Quickly for all the comedies of Molière and Aristophanes put together? The French have no word for humour.

In 1870 De Tréveret read a paper to the Sorbonne. It was a paper upon Falstaff. Falstaff, it appears, from among that class of Shakespearian personages "plus singuliers que risibles" shone forth as Shakespeare's one good piece of comedy. De Tréveret's paper tries to be an appreciation, and at the outset he seems to be getting very near to Falstaff indeed. Then suddenly occurs a most wonderful sentence: "Issu d'une noble famille, Falstaff n'a pas conservé le sentiment de l'honneur véritable". So Falstaff is judged, and passes in true French fashion to remorse and death. Moreover, "le progrès des lumières, la vigilance des gendarmes, la sévérité de l'opinion publique" will not permit his like to come upon the earth again.

A striking indication of French taste and opinion is afforded by the adaptations that were freely made for the purposes of the French stage. Though these changed in character as time went on, they got no nearer to being like their originals than they had been in the days when Ducis reduced "Hamlet," "Othello," and "Macbeth" to the unities, or when the revolutionary Mercier pieced together a "Romeo and Juliet" in which the Capulets and Montagues embraced one another in the last act. In the "Hamlet" of Dumas, a Romantic triumph, Ophelia is the daughter of Claudius and the price of her father's forgiveness. In the "As You Like It" of George Sand, Celia is the heroine, Jaques the most fully elaborated character, and the moral of the piece is its making. The moral, of course, is admirable. Man in close contact with nature loses all his baseness.

In conclusion, it would be difficult to do anything better than quote Jusserand, who holds substantially the same views that have been maintained in these articles. Shakespeare aided the emancipation of French drama, but the old foundation remained unaffected. "Ce conquérant, ce nouvel Attila n'a asservi personne. . . . Croire qu'il se soit acclimaté parmi nous, que son génie ait pénétré le nôtre et l'ait transformé, c'est une erreur." The French onlooker may applaud a scene, a striking word, an episode. He does not applaud Shakespeare. "Il admire par moments, mais sans s'abandonner tout à fait; il est en présence d'un génie trop différent; les différences l'inquiètent autant que les beautés le frappent." Perhaps Jusserand, who makes this statement, was the one Frenchman of note who really knew what it was that his countrymen missed.

AN ELIZABETHAN PARSON AND HIS CURATE: WAYS AND MEANS.

PARSON RALPH MAYE, whose multifarious and sometimes microscopic sources of income appear in his recently recovered "Tythes Book",* in several of his pages throws a curious light on the status and emoluments of his coadjutor, Sir Martin Parnall, curate of the adjoining parish of S. Blazey. There were, needless to say, no "assistant curates", such as we know now, in the land in A.D. 1600, but there were pluralities, and at that date and for long afterwards the benefice of S. Blasius, five miles away, was tacked on to the "Vicaridge" of S. Austell, and "Ser Martyn"—we can please ourselves as to the spelling—was the humble Levite to whom Mr. Maye had committed that portion of his charge. And as our Vicar recorded his payments almost as punctiliously as his receipts or his debita or arreragia, we get an instructive glimpse into the resources and almost into the ménage of this most impecunious cleric. It is to be hoped that he did his duty manfully by the flock, for certainly he had little enough to do with the fleece.

But before we occupy ourselves with this gentleman's exiguous stipend, something more must be said, if only to heighten the contrast, as to the Vicar's incomings.

* SATURDAY REVIEW, 4 September 1909.

For in addition to the fish, flesh and fowl, the hay, hemp and honey, which yielded him their annual tributes, he levied, he was entitled to levy, a charge on practically everything connected, however indirectly, with the produce of the soil or the sea : the miller, for example, and the miller's man paid toll as well as the farmer or the hind, and the women who salted the pilchards as well as the owners of the boats or seines which captured them. This accounts for the mention of mills—no doubt corn mills : John Hodge paid 3s. 4d. annually for his at Boscoppa, apart from his private earnings : the mill at Spit paid 2s. ; it looks indeed as if the water that drove the mill contributed to the ecclesiastical exchequer, as " privy fford " is of fairly frequent mention : Morishe the " tynner " paid for his " privy ff." xijd. And it explains the inclusion of " men " and " women " among titheable objects ; after a great haul of fish the Vicar " recd. of Otis Hayne for the *same men* "—the same as had paid before—" and right, xiijs."—quite a windfall it was (the date is 14 September) ; and he also had " from Rouse' sayne *and the women* xvs. iijd.", and for " a sharing of profits on Sep. 7, xliijs."—over £3 in one month. The mills must hide their minished heads before such draughts of fishes ; they were clearly not like those at Doncaster :

" The Doncaster mayor, he sits in his chair,
  And his mills they merrily go,
And his nose it doth shine with the drinking of wine,
  And the gout is in his great toe " !

These " personal tithes " (personales decimae are mentioned in one account), having been paid in the unreformed Church, were secured to later incumbents by 2 and 3 Edw. VI. cap. 15—butcher, baker and candlestick-maker must each pay " the tenth part of his clear gains " to the parish priest. This is the meaning of " privata acquisita ", which charge appears almost as regularly as that for " vaccae " or " vituli " : it averages about xijd. per annum. Stephen Clemens, however, paid 2s. 6d. yearly, but then John Carlyane was let off (in 1602) with 3½d.—his year's gains must surely have exceeded 3s. 11d., perhaps he was one of the unemployed. Wm. Renold " paid xviijd. pro se et suis filiis ; another paid a like amount pro se et genero suo ; John Hamblye paid 6d. and 12d. in alternate years. All these apparently farmed or traded on their own account. But Parson Maye by no means overlooked " wagesmen's tithes ", as he calls them ; fancy having to go round and collect them ! " Servus Davies " paid 12d. ; Thomas Congen's wages were 5li, but what he paid does not appear—perhaps he evaded payment altogether ; Ambrosse Skewes' wage reached £6—almost as much as Sir Martin had for his year's ministry. John Hambly at Tregongeeves gave his man 40s. wage and his maids Agnes and Alison 13s. 4d. each, but doubtless they were boarded in his house ; for one or all of these he paid 2s. 4d. in 1600 ; for one servant 2s. in 1602 ; in 1604, only 8d.—these marked fluctuations must have been most embarrassing. In one place the Vicar has set down a list, a few lines of which may be cited, of

Austle Servants in Anno Domini 1599 that Paid.

Nicholas Dalamyne serves R. Tonking, wages 13s. 8d.	viijd.
Thomas Nicoll, serves Coisgarne	xiiijd.
Margery Allen, serva ejusdem Domini	8d.
Robert Nicholas servit sua manu	12d.
Wm. Payne, servant	xvjd, rec.
Epsigh Carlyane, serves Richard Body	xd.
John Briban serves Mr. Kendall	xvjd:
John Cowlyn, servus ejusdem	xxd.
Marget Robyn, serva ejusdem	viijd.

We have also lists for 1600, 1601 and 1604, and it is to be remarked that these three have few names in common—the inference from which is either that servants paid most irregularly or that they did not retain their places much longer than they do nowadays ; possibly they were engaged at the annual " Statutes " or hiring-day and remained their year ; of one, a servant of Mr. Kendall (he had five), Elizth. Paulye by name, Mr. Maye remarks, " Dudum venit et non stetit mensem " (" she came but lately and did not stop a month ")—the servant problem is evidently a perennial ; of Elizth. Robin, who only paid 6d., that she " serves p. d." ; probably she was an old-time charwoman. This is the smallest sum paid ; Pasco Dadow and " John the Tynner " each paid iijs.—presumably this was for skilled labour. John Dadow junr. would seem to have paid xxd. twice in 1599. But it is more reasonable to ascribe this to a clerical blunder on the parson's part than to young John's inexperience.

We must pass by the mortuaries or " corse-presents " payable on the death of every householder and the funeral fees (funerale or sepultura), which averaged about 6d. But we may remark that Mr. Maye had no idea of working for nothing ; he charged Rose Trewenyk, for example, iijs. iiijd. for " writing her invent "—he had " laid out " for her xiiijs. " for her commission and the proctor's fees ". And this brings us back to the S. Blazey curate.

" Passing rich on forty pounds a year " ! Such a sum far exceeded Sir Martin's wildest dreams ; his fixed stipend was apparently £8 per annum, for the Vicar mentions 40s. as the summa of one quarter. No doubt this represents a much larger sum according to the present value of money, but when compared with Mr. Maye's charges and imposts it seems pitifully small. It was paid, too, in pitiful driblets and the account was always overdrawn. On 26 March 1600 we come across this " Memorandum—that I reconed with Sir Martyn and he dothe owe me, above all things due unto him at the 14th of May next, the full some of xxs. more ". Then follows the reckoning ; here are a few items : " I payd him at Whitson Day fayre at Bodmin, 10s."—the poor curate had clearly found himself at the fair, where astonishing bargains were going, with nothing in his pocket ! " More : White paid him iiijs." " Item : more at severall tymes in money xxs." " So I owe "—thus he concludes—" Ser Martyn no wages . . . and he must allow me in the next accompt the hole Receipts of the Regester booke." One wonders whether the old gentleman ever got them, in spite of Sir Martin's signature at the end allowing the figures. It is possible, however, that Mr. Maye's bark was worse than his bite, for on one occasion the curate received xls. all at once, but this was " against his daughter's wedding "—we may imagine the trousseau and the breakfast which this exceptional largess would supply ! Moreover, the following half-year's account would suggest that the curate's " wages " had been considerably advanced :

Item. Paid Sir Martyn at S. Blasy, Sep. 4, 1602—monye	xs.
Item. For a subsidy	vijs.
and to Eles Bennett	xijd.
more the 8th of November	xxijs.
more the 6th of December at Bodmyn	xs.
more the last of January	xxs.
more by Trenaur in February	xs.
more to your wiffe in Fowey, the 5th of March	vs.
paid yourself the 1st of Aprill, 1603	xs.
for the Regester booke ended at the 25th of March last	vs.
more to make up his quarter his payment which will be full at the 14th of May next	xxs.
[Signed] Marten Parnall.	

There is, we believe, a society among us for maintaining the rights of curates. They may recognise in these accounts the hole of the pit whence their grievances were first digged.

A REPERTORY THEATRE.

By R. B. Cunninghame Graham.

THE red-haired Spaniard from Ceuta, who had been hired to keep the mules from eating up our horses' corn—for in a fondak an Arab never ties his mule—was a sententious man. After having thrown a stone which narrowly escaped knocking out a horse's eye, he said in answer to a question, " No, Tetuan is not a bad place on the whole. . . . I am a mason, and just now am working on a mosque—a nice job for a Christian, eh? " No one compassionating him, he continued : " The worst thing is that there are no amusements in the place. A man without amusement soon grows vicious ". This he enunciated with so grave an air some might have thought he had evolved and not inherited the phrase. " The infidel, of course " (he meant the Moors), " do not require amusement as we Christians do. Give them a cup of weak green tea, flavoured with mint, and they will sit for hours and talk about the price of barley or on the attributes of God, for all is one to them, and be as happy as a strolling player upon the evening of a holiday." He stopped and tried to light a cigarette with a flint and steel, and, failing, put the cigarette behind his ear, saying, "I'll leave it for the next bull-fight, as we say in Spain; not that they ever have a bull-fight in this benighted land. Why do we come here? I sometimes ask myself. True, here there are no taxes, and bread is cheaper than in Spain, but after all it is a purgatory for us who come as pioneers of progress to this accursed land".

He did not look precisely like a pioneer of progress as he stood in the muddy fondak yard, his naked feet shoved into alpargatas which he wore down at heel like Moorish slippers, his jacket dangling from one shoulder like a cloak, and with a grey felt hat from Cordoba, battered and napless, kept on his head by a black ribbon tied underneath his chin. Still, we must take men as we find them, as we take banknotes at their face value, and generally their estimate of themselves and of their worth is nearer to the truth than any we can form. So it may well have been he was a pioneer designed by fate to show the Moors all that is worst in European progress, and bound himself to suffer in the showing, debarred from bull-fights, gambling and politics in what he styled "a cursed land of unwashed burnooses and of lice".

No one could say he was not civil in his manners, or fluent in his speech to a degree that would have made the future of a public speaker in the north. Then he was tall and strong and not bad-looking in a sort of villainous and cut-throat style, and certainly a good shot with a stone. For his abilities in his craft I cannot speak, not having had the curiosity to go and see the mosque where he was working, but he possessed a flow of ready and most idiomatic Arabic, an unusual thing for a Spaniard born in "Las Plazas Fuertes", that is Ceuta, Las Alhucemas and all the rest of Spain's possessions on the coast.

He took his cigarette from behind his ear, just as a clerk resumes his pen, and looked at it regretfully, and, when I handed him a match, lighted it, perhaps as a concession to the progress he was introducing, and then began to smoke with that peculiar relish, drinking the smoke and then expelling it a minute after in the middle of a flood of words, which only Spaniards of his class can ever perfectly attain. His action somehow called to mind a certain Irishman who drove me to a meeting at a place, the name of which I have forgotten, somewhere near Lurgan. All that I can recall is that the meeting was in a gaunt, dilapidated hall, stuck in the middle of the fields, and had been built by an old clergyman who had lived a blameless life till sixty and then "renagered", as the people said, and turned an atheist. Such things happen infrequently except amongst the Kelto-Saxon race. Having "renagered", he had to testify . . . . just as the Moors will call in a loud voice to any European who has put on their clothes, saying, "Testify, O wearer of the haik!"; so it seemed necessary to him to justify his creed.

Accordingly the quondam clergyman, now turned atheist, to show his faith in the nonentity of God, erected in the fields, a mile or two outside the village where he lived, a temple made with hands, and, having frescoed it inside with pictures of the pagan deities, called it the "Hall of Apollo", making, as it were, a sort of testimony of the bricks to his own idiocy.

The country people, more astute or more imaginative, called it the "Hall of Vanus", and to it I was bound.

Of course it rained, and as we passed by public-house or licensed premises the driver jerked his whip towards them, remarking, as a man talks in a dream, "Finucane keeps good spirits" or "Little Bob Coleary has nate whisky". Still I was obdurate, till he, drawing a green and freckled apple from his pocket, tendered it to me.

I asked him "What is that for?" and he replied "Sure it will keep down the drouth"; so we stopped at the first shebeen, and he drank whisky whilst I shivered in the rain.

Perhaps the remembrance of the episode softened my heart towards the red-haired dweller in "Las Plazas Fuertes", and so I tendered him the match.

It did not break the ice between us, for none existed; but it somehow drew us together, just as that acid-looking apple drew me towards the man upon the road in the Black North whilst shivering on his car.

My friend talked on, throwing a stone or two occasionally at a marauding mule, and telling me about the lives and habits of the Europeans in the town, by which I learned that Sodom and Gomorrah had been cleanly living places compared to Tetuan. As by an afterthought, he said, "Seeing that you speak Christian you might care to see 'Don Juan Tenorio', which is being played to-night at the dramatic circle in the consulate".

I did, and said that I would like to go, and he, calling loudly to a boy "Oh Mojamito", after the fashion of his countrymen, who tack a Spanish termination on to an Arab name, perhaps for euphony, there and then constituted him his "caliph", as he explained to me, to keep away the mules. He added "Now I am free to take you to the theatre, which in fact I had wished to see, but could not for want of necessary funds". Having hypothecated, as it were, some of his salary, which I advanced him on the spot, he dipped his hands into a drinking-trough for mules, sleeked down his hair with water, and having picked a marigold growing upon a wall, stuck it behind his ear, and so was ready to escort us to the play.

By devious ways he led us, through meandering lanes, talking quite at his ease to a young lady of the party, although she did not understand a word he said—which perhaps was well, considering the frankness of his speech. At last he led us to the place, having explained that in the dearth of all amusements the Spanish colony had organised theatricals to pass away the time, their idea being to give stock pieces, such as "Don Juan Tenorio" and the like, which everybody knew. "I see", I said, "a repertory theatre"; to which he answered "Repertory—I rather like the name". We took the most expensive places at a peseta each, and entered through a door at which just such another as our guide stood taking tickets, smoking a cigarette.

The hall, a long, low building off a narrow Moorish street, was lit by tin petroleum lamps, some hanging from the roof and others stuck against the wall. Most of them flared and smoked, and all of them gave out a rank, metallic smell. At one end of the room was a small stage, only a little larger than in a theatre of marionettes, but high above the floor. The walls were painted a pale yellow, something between the colour of a light montbretia and a canary bird. Upon them elongated vases, reminding one somehow of stained-glass figures by Jean Goujon, were drawn in a dull red. They held bouquets of what one might call superflowers, so violent were their colours and so difficult to tell the species to which they might belong. The audience was composed of almost all the Spanish colony in Tetuan and a few Moors and Riffs. In the front row the wives and daughters of the diplomatists and of the officers attached to the obsolescent military mission, and of the beef contractor, the doctor and the interpreter, were seated in a row. Most of them had a little run to fat, and nearly all wore white silk blouses over black silk skirts. Their fans were in their hands, and a light whir as of a locust's wings filled all the hall as they perpetually opened and shut them with the peculiar grace that only Spanish women ever attain to in the manipulation of this most potent instrument of war. Their faces were all white with powder, which in the case of those of lesser category (for all had brought their servants to the show) was carried up into the hair by natural instinct, so as to avoid a hard effect where the powder ended and the black hair began. Needless to say, their hair was done with taste, either piled high upon the head or, with the younger women, brought low about the ears and parted in the middle, looking a little like two waves upon the sides.

Though few of them were handsome seen alone, their great black eyes, long eyelashes, and the intense and jetty blackness of their hair, setting their dead-white faces, as it were, in a frame, gave to them in the mass a beauty which threw the looks of women in more ambitious theatres into the shade by its look of wildness and intensity.

The men were, on the whole, inferior to them, as often happens in the South, where Nature seems to have put out her best effort in the women of the race. Still, they had most of them that air of nervous hardness which many Spaniards have, and, from the superannuated colonel who filled an elusive post on the unnecessary and futile military mission, to the stout beef contractor, they looked like men no one could venture to insult.

At one end of the room a group of Moors, looking like figures made out of snow wrapped in their fleecy haiks, and silent and impassive, sat on their chairs uneasily, just as a European sits uneasily when squatted on the ground. Now and then one of them furtively drew up a leg and tucked it under him upon his chair, and nearly all of them let the beads of their Mecca rosaries slip through the fingers of one hand, leaving the other free to make a movement now and then either of deprecation or assent. The play, "Don Juan Tenorio", as was set forth upon the green and flimsy handbill, is one of the stock pieces of the Spanish stage, and all the actors and actresses were amateurs, drawn from the Spanish residents in Tetuan.

Nothing could possibly have been more democratic than the composition of the company. The receiver of the Customs was Don Juan; the corporal attached to the consulate, the comendador; his wife, the heroine; a tall, thin Spanish girl, the duenna; and yet they all looked, walked and spoke as if they had been born upon the stage.

The poverty of the mounting of the piece, the common dresses made of cotton velvet, and the smallness of the stage, so far from spoiling gave an air of such intense reality to the whole thing, it would have been difficult to match in any theatre. Nothing could have been more intensely natural than the first scene, in which Don Juan Tenorio comes home from Italy. The naked stage, with a deal table in the middle of it round which were set two or three Austrian chairs, took one, incredible as it may seem, back to the Middle Ages, at the first words the actors spoke. Nothing apparently upon the stage seems harder to set forth than poverty. Here all was poverty; but for all that nothing was sordid, and it seemed natural to see a man dressed in trunk hose, with a long rapier by his side and an imperfect recollection of his part, swagger across the stage, because you did not think it was a stage, so strongly did the actors dominate the accessories and focus interest upon themselves. They came and went, spoke (when they could recollect their parts), exactly as they must have gone about and spoken at the epoch of the play. They quarrelled fiercely, so fiercely that sometimes the phlegmatic Moors moved on their chairs uneasily, although their movements may well have been caused by the novelty of their position and the cramp in their legs. Occasionally upon the stage swords flashed, and swarthy men attired in cotton tights which bagged a little at the knee, and yet did not in the least make them ridiculous, set on each other with such good will it was a marvel no one was maimed for life. The prompter was a man of genius, voluble, as one could plainly hear, but yet discreet, as his remarks, "Now, Don Luis, 'tis time to draw your sword", or "Brigida, don't let him press your hand till you have got the purse", most amply testified. At times I fancied by the sudden change of voice that when an actor had forgotten all he had to say the prompter boldly read it from the book in a loud key, although the actor still stamped about the stage like a demoniac. These were the blemishes upon the surface, but underneath the heterogeneous company of Spanish amateurs, ill dressed and acting on a stage scarce large enough for marionettes, defective in their parts, and playing to an audience a good half of which knew little of the language that the actors spoke, in some strange way brought mediæval Spain before one's eyes as I have never seen it done in the most ambitious theatre in Spain. It may have been because Spain always has been poor, for three parts of the gold from Potosi filtered to Antwerp and to Genoa; it may have been because things always have been done in Spain in a haphazard way, that the haphazard method of the actors really set forth her mediæval life as in a looking-glass. At any rate, an English lady sitting by my side, who knew but little Spanish, watched the whole play in rapt attention, her colour going and coming at each episode, and when the piece was over said she had never seen such acting in her life in any theatre.

When it was finished and everybody duly slain before our eyes, over the Spanish Consul's sweet champagne the actors wandered in and out, and a fat Moorish Custom House official involuntarily gave the measure of their unconscious art, for, seeing Don Luis Mejia still in his mediæval clothes, but smoking an anachronistic cigarette, he looked amazed and said in halting Spanish, "By Allah, I thought that you were dead!" and wished to feel the place where he was sure the sword had run into his side.

HAVEN.

THE village seen from across "the harbour", as the wide estuary is called, seems to have come from the dim woodland massed over the rise to the north and crowded, leaving here and there a cottage by the way, down the narrow spit of land nosing a pathway out into the water. There it has stood, for centuries, among the trees round the little square grey wooden-towered church.

It shows at high tide a gleaming border along the farther margin of the waters lapping and washing along the low sea wall.

It calls the eye across the waste as you make your way down the harbour along the scrub-grown shore amongst the rank sea-spinach and lavender. On a day when the buffeting wind, driving the low clouds helplessly across the sky, would possess you altogether, and the plaintive sea-mews whirl in broken circles above the troubled water, you will scarcely pass the angle of the high sand bank where the causeway turns towards the distant sea without a last glance.

Seen thus from afar the Old House falls back into the picture, offering no saliency for the seeking eye, appearing only as a greyish surface to the left of the derelict tidal-mill. You would grant it the wide outlook across the flats available to all the dwellings owning rearward eyes on that side of the village, and it might occur to you to wonder whether it would claim free range beyond the little low headland marking the bend. It would not further engage your thought, it would make no mark, preserving unplumbed its peculiar quality. You would not even discover, though you observed its pallid featureless front across the narrowest reach of the estuary, that it has won by some score of yards the race towards the low shore.

But this vision of it as a part, indistinguishable from its fellows, is, when once you know the Old House, an endearing contact—a comfortable everyday "set-off" to the riches of first experience.

What better way to inherit the quality of the place than to have come away from some long-sustained pressure, by chance and not greatly expecting, to arrive at nightfall and drive the undeviating mile along the neatly hedged road from the station through the fading light, to recognise your destination by the sudden turf under the horse's feet and the low archway of light flashing upon the darkness? Then a magic—shut away deep and secure from the stirring world which held you but an hour ago—in the musty lamplit front room, old things, old thoughts, old ways crowding round you, casting a spell potent enough to keep you a while with them alone—sinking deeper and deeper, going moment by moment further from your late distress—postponing for their sake the drawing back of curtain and blind and the pouring in—impinging and enfolding—of the soft dense south-coast air.

All night long the spirit of the Old House possesses you, penetrating more and more completely as you lie content beneath the passage of the long hours—blessed by the intermittent breathing of the wind in the wide chimney, by the gracious stirring, as if ghostly fingers touched them in the darkness, of the flowered window draperies, till forgetfulness and sweet memory touch all the garnerings of your being and the hour is rich with the promise of healing. The faint call of a sea-bird sounds friendly and intimate, a last sense before the sudden dropping of unsummoned sleep. . . .

Robbed of its burden, unfurling already anticipatory wings, weariness holds you, ensconcing you with gently retaining hand in face of the morning window. And then there dawns the welcome truth about your kindly tent. For the Old House stands alone on the edge of the world. The village you came through last night has vanished. There is no dwelling, no creature, no challenge of movement in all the scene framed by your wide-flung sash.

On either hand unhampered miles of muddy sand, jewelled with shallow pools, softly shining grey, silver and saffron, weed-grown, here and there a gleaming emerald, and across the way at comfortable range for the hungering eye a little bare strand backed by soft dun distances, and to the west access away and away and away until the sea lies a dim line along the far horizon.

And all over the scene, making the living emerald soft and deep and powerless to claim a disturbing value, lowers the grey sky, a slowly shifting shroud.

And the afternoon brings the procession of the returning sea. Hour by hour its voice draws nearer, until at last it comes in a heavy foamless swell on and on, filling the channel, flowing and beating round the little promontory, washing up almost to your feet. And as you listen to its lapping and watch its breathing under the soft lambency of the moving light, the early autumn gloaming falls, blotting out the little strand in a soft mist, moving towards you across the water, growing and deepening until the night is round you once more. The days pass. . . . No sign reaches you, if you have been wise, no greeting claims you.

For daily adventure you may go out into your picture and meet the rain driving over the sea on the wind, the ceaseless south-west wind. Out across the ford you may go from ridge to ridge at ebbing tide and round the bend to the wilderness of distant waters. On and on, thoughtless, drinking the unimpeded air. And one day when the measure is full, when the wind and the rain and the thick salt air have done their work and your heart is strong within you, the sun comes.

From the glinting water your contented eyes turn to the kindling distance, and there away beyond the little naked strand the unsuspected hills shine out crowned with gold and bronze, mass beyond mass.

CORRESPONDENCE.

WORKING MEN AND THE BUDGET.

To the Editor of the SATURDAY REVIEW.

London N.W. 4 October 1909.

SIR,—You ask in your notes of 2 October whether "working men twenty-five years old, thirty-five, forty-five, fifty-five years old" will "really love a Budget" that "puts up the price of their drink and their smoke". I am waiting patiently for the time when "working man" as a term of invidious distinction shall have been abolished; but pending that blissful day I write as a working man who for the past twelve years has been sufficiently liberal to read the SATURDAY, and I reply to your question that if the Budget made tobacco prohibitive and beer a penal offence the working classes would still be silly unto insanity if they failed to do all they could (when they are asked) to push this Budget through, and then, after that, "more also".

In spite of the wail of the Dukes on behalf of their poorer brethren, in spite of the great concern of the Conservative press for the luxuries of the lowly, you know, Sir, as well as I do, that the Budget would have gone through without a word if the beer and tobacco taxes were all that was in it. I have a certain amount of respect (not much) for a ground landlord who comes out openly and says that he will oppose the Budget because the Budget hits him. The animal may be wicked to defend himself when attacked, but at any rate he is a natural animal and a plausible; what is so sickening to sensible working men of any age you name is the pernicious assumption of sympathy displayed by ducal folk for those who have to pay as much on a fourpenny ounce of tobacco as they have to pay on a pound's worth of undeveloped land. The working classes will be wise to take this sympathy with a very large pinch of (untaxed) salt, and meanwhile hammer away at those "capital values". The pivot of the Budget is the land taxes. On that all turns, and if the Government in a moment of weakness or fright were to delete this part of their Bill the agitation against the Budget would drop the moment after, and for all the landed classes cared the workers could pay two shillings a pot and sixpence a pipe to make up the deficit. As regards the first, it would probably turn out to be a very good thing for many hundreds of thousands of my countrymen. They simply wouldn't drink, the Chancellor wouldn't get his money, and in order to meet his expenses (which, with respect to armaments, might, with a sober country, be somewhat less) would have to turn again to the one final and inevitable source of revenue—the pockets of those who live fatly on other people's labour.

One last word, if you will permit me. You deprecate, in a succeeding paragraph, the "music-hall" method of running the politics of the country. The only politics which the music-hall ever knew is the politics of beer. You can hear it every night in those places of amusement, which are only enlarged public-houses. There it is natural, but I do not expect to hear it in the SATURDAY. Better the Lord Hugh Cecil aspect of things than this (and I, an agnostic, say it). It was a bad day for the workers of England when Lord Northcliffe began to edit a paper. It will be a worse day if they allow him and his party to edit the country and to go back to power by the mandate of their own insobriety. If they are willing to pay more for their glass or to sacrifice it altogether for the time, they may one day own England, and have real beer into the bargain. I enclose my name and address.

Yours truly,
A LIBERAL READER.

CHRISTIANITY IN ITALY.

To the Editor of the SATURDAY REVIEW.

27 September 1909.

SIR,—In my letter concerning the present condition of Christianity in Italy which you recently published I mentioned the encouragement which the Spanish Freemasons had received from Signor Podrecca and his paper, the "Asino". Since then the Grand Master of Italian Freemasonry, Ettore Ferrari, has issued a circular, dated 20 September, in which he very openly endorses the action of the rioters at Barcelona and alludes in no concealed terms to "those two suffering countries, Spain and Russia, where the voice of liberty is being crushed". M. Aristide Briand's organ, "L'Action", has been particularly violent of late with respect to the arrest of Ferrer and the closing of certain schools in various parts of Spain in which the teaching was distinctly revolutionary; and I notice, not without a little amusement, that the "Daily News" publishes an interview with M. Leroux, a gentleman who was as steeped in all that has taken place in Spain lately as was ever Ferrer, and whose known approval of the attempt on the King and Queen of Spain was one of the causes of his expulsion from that kingdom.

The Paris "Temps", a paper which cannot be accused of clericalism, commenting on all these extraordinary manifestations of sympathy, gives in its issue of 18 September a specimen of the sort of teaching which has caused the schools in question to be closed. In these schools the children have been told that "soldiers and officers are murderers, whose mission is to kill and to sack". The national flag is "a filthy rag put on a pole to deceive the people". It is "a symbol of tyranny and misery". Every year "the Governments of Europe kill more men and women for their simple pleasure than there are stars in the firmament". "Property has been created by spoliation. Religion is an appalling falsehood—there is no God, no Christ and no future state. Science has proved these facts. Christ was an adventurer, the son of a prostitute and a carpenter, who had the audacity to impose himself upon the world as the Son of God. All Kings are monsters, who ought to be uncrowned and punished for their iniquities as the Kings of France and of England were punished centuries ago. In the great revolution which is coming we must destroy the middle classes and the wealthy; we must destroy everything, so as to have a clear table on which to build up a new civilisation. If amongst the political men of the day there are one or two who pretend to sympathise with us, do not believe in their sympathy, but kill them when the opportunity occurs. We must abolish every existing law; expel and exterminate all monks and nuns and priests; we must expel and slay all magistrates and lawyers; we must demolish every church; we must confiscate all the money in the banks and all the money belonging to every class of citizen, military and civil. No one must be allowed to go out of Spain or to take any money or jewels out of the country. The railways must be confiscated to the good of the State, of the Commune. All the existing Ministers, courtiers and persons at the head of the Government must be massacred and a new set of men elected in their places, who must be of our way of thinking. Long live this revolution which shall avenge all injustice!" This abominable document, of which I give you a synopsis, was actually printed in large capitals and nailed up in every school under the control of the revolutionary party; and it is for closing these schools that the lives of the King and Queen of Spain and of the Ministers of that country are in danger!—it is to the scoundrels who invent and publish such an infamous thing as this that M. Aristide Briand and the Italian Freemasons extend their sympathy! In the meantime the Italian Government allows Signor Podrecca not only to continue the publication of the "Asino" (than which in the whole history of journalism nothing more abominable has ever been published), but also to go the round of Italy holding anti-Christian meetings before excited audiences of the lowest classes. In almost every one of his speeches he takes great care to insinuate that it is quite justifiable to put an end to the Italian Monarchy, even by the most violent means, should the Government make any attempt to silence him. On 20 September in various parts of Italy the Socialist and Republican speakers openly advocated assassination, regicide and universal pillage. Signor Giolitti nevertheless remains perfectly impassive, and does nothing to put a stop to these outrages, which, if they are not checked in time, may lead Italy to her destruction.

I had the pleasure of meeting recently a very distinguished Italian who was the most intimate friend of Garibaldi, whose eyes he closed in death. He too lamented the terrible mistake his countrymen were making in "monkeying"—to use his own expression, "scimietare"—the French in all that is worst in that decadent nation; above all, in its wild anti-theism.

Yours truly,
A Traveller.

DRUNKENNESS IN SCOTLAND.

To the Editor of the Saturday Review.

Sir,—It is extremely doubtful if it is generally known in England, or at any rate the southern part of England, the extent to which drunkenness exists in Scotland.

For the first time in my life I have been staying for a few weeks in localities not far removed from Dundee or Edinburgh, and have done a certain amount of travelling about in this direction. The drunkenness I have seen has been so frequent that it has excited my interest and curiosity, and I have tried to get opinions on the subject from others living here.

I am told that the curse of Scotland is the grocer's licence, and this applies especially to women. I am also told that I have seen no real drunkenness unless I have seen the crowd after a football match, and that the state of any railway station in the vicinity defies description, both police and railway officials being equally powerless.

My own experience makes this latter appear quite possible. Coming up here, I had to change at a small station and wait there for half an hour. In that half-hour I saw a dozen men more or less drunk, some of them lying about and having to be literally carried into the compartments of the train. It certainly was Saturday evening. From my personal observation the streets of the big towns compare most unfavourably with those of southern England.

This very afternoon two drunken men have been lying on the road, vomiting, within thirty yards of houses; the farmer who employs them, quite a good fellow, appears not to think much of it. Yet my wife, my children, my servants, have to pass this disgusting spectacle or else stay at home.

Whether the habit of spitting has anything to do with drunkenness I do not know, but very little effort, judging by results, seems to have been made up here to put down this horrible habit, and third class on the railway becomes almost impossible.

Disgusted Englishman.

FRANCIS NEWMAN'S RELIGIOUS CREED.

To the Editor of the Saturday Review.

4 October 1909.

Sir,—In the recently published "Memoirs and Letters of Francis W. Newman", by J. Giberne Sieveking—in many respects a highly interesting and a very instructive biography—it is asserted that the distinguished subject of it reverted in his last days to the creed of his earlier life.

This assertion, two or three times repeated, rests upon vague statements, found in, I believe, two letters written in his last illness in 1897, when he was in his ninety-second year, and upon the reports of two correspondents of the biographer. In not one of the cited statements is there the slightest proof that Francis Newman wished it to go forth to the world that he had renounced the convictions first published in his "Phases of Faith" some fifty years before his decease, and reiterated in numerous books and periodicals during all that long period—so far, at least, as supernatural and dogmatic Christianity is concerned. The passing remark in one of his latest letters—or in a verbal observation to an orthodox friend—e.g. that "Paul was less and less to him and Christ more and more" (the remark was suggested by his reference to his recent book "Paul of Tarsus"), obviously can be made to mean nothing more than that the theological critic had modified his earlier estimate of the relative value of the teaching of Jesus of Nazareth (as presented in the Synoptics) and of Paul of Tarsus (as presented in the letters attributed to that second founder of the Christian creed, as it was in the early stage). There is not the least intimation, either in this relative preference or in the other (alleged) last utterances of Francis Newman, that he had adopted dogmatic Christianity.

I venture, in the interests alike of abstract and of biographical truth, to object to this too common exaltation of expediency (or what is thought to be so) above fact.

Criticus.

KING LEAR.

To the Editor of the Saturday Review.

Eddlethorpe, Malton, 5 October 1909.

Sir,—I notice that some of your correspondents take exception to the representation of the blinding of Gloster in the version of "King Lear" now being acted at the Haymarket. I do not enter into the question of the propriety of exhibiting this scene upon the stage, but I venture to draw attention to a point which may be of interest.

It has been my fortune at certain times to live among peoples who are in exactly the same state of civilisation as the characters described in "King Lear"; though, it is true, I have never witnessed an incident of such violence as that of the blinding of Gloster, I have actually seen some that went near to it, and as a consequence during that brief scene "King Lear" ceased to be a play for me—it became an actual event.

The ruthlessness of Regan, the grim determination of Cornwall, the helpless, frantic terror of Gloster, the sudden protest of the servant, and, above all, the deadly hurry of the whole scene were portrayed with an exactness which was amazing to one who has seen similar actions in real life and similar scenes untruthfully represented on the stage. The whistling whips in "The Sign of the Cross", the hoarse "Ha ha's" of "Uncle Tom's Cabin", the howls of Thyreus in "Antony and Cleopatra" and such like have never imposed on me any more than does the clown's red-hot poker at Drury Lane, but in "King Lear" it was otherwise.

If any one of your readers desires to see how elementary people behave when they are annoyed or thwarted I commend them to pay particular attention to the conduct of this scene; it is neither beautiful nor pleasing, but nevertheless it is instructive.

I am, Sir, your obedient servant,

Mark Sykes.

To the Editor of the Saturday Review.

Temple, 4 October 1909.

Sir,—May I add my impressions of the performance of "King Lear" to those which you have already received? Let me say at once that it appears to me to be the most satisfying presentation of an "Elizabethan" drama which I remember. In particular, Mr. McKinnel, after the first scene, of which an angel from heaven could not make anything, seemed to me to be an ideal Lear. He exhibited none of that excessive restraint of which the critics accused him, and for this one who, like myself, believes firmly that plays of that period were originally, and always ought to be, performed with a full-mouthed violence devoid of any subtlety or finesse, is duly grateful. It is to be wished that some of the other members of the company would follow his example, but the tradition of inaudibility, set by Sir Henry Irving and followed at a respectful distance by Sir Herbert Tree, has not been entirely neglected even in this admirable presentation. The "slanging matches" however, if the expression may be permitted, were given in a healthy, unexpurgated fashion which must have caused some qualms to the worthy dames in charge of the girls' schools in the upper circle. It is to be regretted that the young ladies should, in addition, be misled by the dissertation affixed to the programme—a specimen of the type of criticism with which one is only too familiar—into supposing that the worst faults of the play are its greatest merits.

One or two points of detail may be noticed. The company should make up its mind, now and for ever, whether it is going to say "revénue" or "révenue" and stick to it. The excæcation of Gloster, the stage management of which appears to be taken from "La Petite Maison d'Auteuil" at the Grand Guignol, should extend to both his orbs. In the next act I fully expected to see a one-eyed Gloster searching anxiously for a non-existent samphire-gatherer. The confusion is made worse by the fact that a messenger subsequently describes the scene as Shakespeare wrote it and not as Mr. Trench produces it, and the young ladies upstairs must have been considerably puzzled. When Lear finally leaves his daughters there is a "confused noise without", which sounds for all the world like the rapid departure of the King's motor car. Possibly, however, it was meant for thunder. Finally, by a curious contretemps, at the moment when Lear was referring to "the vines of France and milk of Burgundy" someone in the refreshment-bar illustrated his point by loudly dropping a tray laden with both species of liquid. Altogether a most interesting entertainment.

Yours faithfully,

G. S. Robertson.

REVIEWS.

STUART IRELAND.

"Ireland under the Stuarts and during the Interregnum." By Richard Bagwell. Vol. I. 1603–1642. Vol. II. 1642–1660. London: Longmans. 1909. 32s. net.

THE history of Ireland under the Tudors has already been written by Mr. Bagwell, while the eighteenth century has been treated in great detail by Lecky. But of the period between the death of Elizabeth and the battle of the Boyne, which laid the foundations of modern Ireland, there has hitherto been no critical history. Mr. Bagwell observes that in Ireland "no party will be pleased with the present work", since its aim is to bring out the facts. Well, a writer who brings out the facts of the most controversial and the most important chapters in the troubled records of his country need not pay attention to the partisans. Our author is diligent and judicious, tells his story clearly, and has produced a work which ought to be (though it will not be) carefully studied by everyone who intends to allude to the events of the seventeenth century in Ireland. He is, perhaps, a little too contemptuous of certain legends which have obtained wide currency. Thus he writes curtly and, we believe, justly: "There is no reason whatever to suppose that Owen Roe O'Neill was poisoned". But many good people cherish the belief that Owen Roe was poisoned, and that Cromwell's triumph over the Irish was facilitated not by fate but by treachery. In Tudor times there was no a priori improbability in the removal by poison of a formidable enemy of England. The Puritans did not use poison—but Mr. Bagwell might have done a much-needed service towards the creation in Ireland of a sound view of history by going into this particular episode, and showing to the unlearned how and when the allegation arose, and why no credence should be given. He gives references, of course, but Irishmen with "popular sympathies", for all their genuine interest in the past of their country, do not look up seventeenth-century authorities. They prefer to take their views from Mrs. J. R. Green and other "patriotic" writers.

In the seventeenth century we find the most notable and tragic instances of the manner in which Ireland suffered from events beyond the seas. That has been the perpetual misfortune of the country. The accession to the throne of England of the King of Scots seemed to promise a reversal of the more oppressive features of Tudor rule. James had very little Gaelic blood, but he represented a line of Gaelic kings: he had little sympathy with Roman Catholicism, but the son of Mary Queen of Scots was more welcome to Catholic Ireland than any English sovereign. Then Gunpowder Plot checked the tendency to religious toleration, and the untiring campaign of the counter-reformation changed the spirit of Irish rebellion from clan-turbulence into a religious war. Later on the massacre of the Waldenses sharpened the swords of Cromwell's troopers. But Ireland herself bore the seed of plentiful troubles. The flight of the Earls, Tyrone and Tyrconnel, pardoned rebels who felt that their lives were not safe, in spite of Acts of Oblivion, while the men who had been fighting them for years remained in authority, gave the opportunity for the colonisation of Ulster. Given the forfeiture of tribal lands and the irruption of unsympathetic Protestant colonists, an agrarian rebellion was bound to come. When it came, in 1641, the actual slaughters and outrages were so multiplied by rumour that every Englishman honestly believed that scores of thousands of his countrymen had been murdered in cold blood. The view of the native Irish taken in England was exactly like the view of the natives of India which prevailed in England in 1857, but it had less justification in fact. Long before the Irish war could be decided England and Scotland were plunged into the Great Rebellion. The resultant chaos in Ireland cannot be explained in less space than that given to it by Mr. Bagwell. There was a Scots army in Ulster, looking to Edinburgh for its politics, fighting the Ulster rebels consistently and the

Royal and Parliamentarian forces according as Presbyterian Scotland adhered to the Solemn League and Covenant or upheld the Stuart cause. There were the Roman Catholic Kelts, with little cohesion, intent upon extirpating the new landowners, never actually declaring against the King, yet never obeying his officers even when, after the tragedy of Whitehall, all the Irish professed to rally to the cause of Charles II. There were the Roman Catholic gentry of the Pale, for the most part Norman or old English in blood, always attached to the Crown, yet unwillingly allied with the Keltic rebels when the King (before his final rupture with the English Parliament) denounced them. For a time Rinuccini, the papal nuncio, was established at Kilkenny, excommunicating good Catholics wholesale for purely political reasons, intent altogether on promoting the ends of Rome, yet nominally supporting the heretic King whose officials he opposed; defied at last by the Lords of the Pale, and driven to rely on Owen Roe—whom he detested. The Protestants in Munster, fighting for life against the rebels, distrusting the King, were bewildered and divided when the Civil War broke out in England. Meanwhile two men, Ormonde (an Anglican) and Clanricarde (a Roman Catholic), knew no principle but loyalty. Clanricarde, denounced in his day by the bishops of his Church, remains something of a popular hero. But Ormonde has never been forgiven because in 1647, finding Dublin untenable, he surrendered it to the Parliament and not to the Confederate Irish. Seldom has a Governor been in a position of such difficulty. Parliament and the Confederates at the moment alike professed some sort of allegiance to the King. Ormonde felt that he could not hand over a town full of Protestants to the Romanists against whom for six years he had campaigned. But the result of giving Dublin up to the Parliament was that, when the Roundheads threw off all pretence of loyalty, the key to Ireland was permanently lost to the Royal cause. The surrender of Dublin was the necessary preliminary to Cromwell's victories in Ireland. Mr. Bagwell, more than any previous historian of modern times, does justice to the Irish Cavaliers. Orangemen dislike their memory because they were united with Romanists against the Puritans, and Nationalists traduce them because they were loyal to the King.

Through these tortuous times moves the enigmatic figure of Owen Roe O'Neill, a fine commander (trained in the Spanish service), a reticent man, a brave and clement soldier, a dubious politician. Mr. Bagwell considers him more of a Royalist than a Nationalist, yet he preferred co-operation with the Parliamentary forces in Dublin to junction with Ormonde at the critical moment after the death of Charles I.

We have no space to follow Mr. Bagwell into his examination of the Irish career of Strafford and Cromwell. Strafford in Ireland represented efficiency divorced from justice, and yet he might, given time, have made the country peaceful and prosperous. It is one of those ironies which recur in this century that Strafford's harshness to the poor Irish was pressed—to his destruction—by the English Puritans, who were soon to forbid quarter to all Irish serving in England (and their women), and to rejoice in the bloody tidings of Drogheda—where probably not a single victim of the slaughter had been concerned in the massacres of English settlers. Of Cromwell's doings Mr. Bagwell gives a faithful and impartial description, but we do not learn from him such incidents—small but significant—as the complacent report of the victor at Drogheda to Bradshaw that one of the garrison in the church, when Cromwell had ordered the steeple to be fired, "was heard to say, 'God damn me—God confound me. I burn! I burn!'"

One point that any careful reader of the book will notice—perhaps with surprise, in view of Andrew Marvell's well-known summary of the Irish campaign—is that these confused and ill-ordered wars contained much really admirable fighting. The defence of Limerick against Ireton was a fine feat of arms (eclipsed by the Jacobite defence against William some forty years later), and several actions in the open field, though of little tactical importance, were very well contested. Almost all English writers pretend that the Irish fought badly in these wars. But bravery in the field could not avail against confusion in the Council Chamber. And yet it is not surprising that in such a welter of political and religious and agrarian feuds no man was ready to trust his neighbour.

We hope that Mr. Bagwell will give us the final volume of the book, in which he promises a review of social conditions. During these troubled times Trinity College was beginning its work, Ussher was amazing the world by his erudition, and the old Gaelic literature was a living force. Geoffrey Keating, no critical historian, was yet a fine writer, and in his work we find the promise of a literary renascence which the Cromwellian Settlement drove beneath the surface, to linger in the mouths of peasant bards.

We cannot end this notice without a reference to the Irish historian—sympathetically mentioned by Mr. Bagwell in his preface—who had for years studied this period most carefully, but was fated to produce little published work on Stuart Ireland except an admirable edition of the Ormonde Papers. The untimely death of Cæsar Litton Falkiner removed the only one of our contemporaries who possessed that really intimate knowledge of the times requisite to an adequate critical study of Mr. Bagwell's able and conscientious work.

THE SHOP-GIRL.

"Ann Veronica." By H. G. Wells. London: Unwin. 1909. 6s. net.

THE heroine of Mr. Wells' latest novel is a difficult young woman. To keep our heads at all it will be necessary to divide her into three compartments. There is the Prehistoric Compartment, which is a very big one. There is the Early Victorian Compartment, which is a very small one. There is the Modern Compartment, which stands in a peculiar relation to both of these.

We will take the compartments in order of date, beginning with the Prehistoric. Ann Veronica, having broken off an engagement with one man because she loved another, approached the other without loss of time. After she had broken the ice a little, a conversation ensued: "What do you want?" asked the man bluntly. "You!" replied the Prehistoric Compartment. And then, of course, as the Prehistoric Compartment pointed out, "Once you begin with love, you have to see it through". Accordingly we are not surprised when these archaically simple souls go a little further. The man, whose name was Capes, said:

"We're going to do work; we're going to unfold about each other; we're going to have children."

"Girls!" cried Ann Veronica.

"Boys", said Capes.

"Both!" said Ann Veronica: "lots of 'em."

Capes chuckled: "You delicate female!"

"Who cares," said Ann Veronica, "seeing it's you?"

So much for the Prehistoric Compartment. It is a further proof of the direct and unadorned simplicity of the relations of these two lovers that they were unable to contemplate marriage, since Capes was already a husband. His wife lived apart from him because he had been a co-respondent, and she objected to a certain strain of coarseness in his character. The man was, in fact, very human; and his private life had been unromantically beastly, as he admitted to Ann Veronica. Ann Veronica did not mind this. In fact, Ann Veronica loved him the more tenderly as, in this very strain of coarseness, she found a guarantee that he needed her the more.

We arrive at compartment number two—the Early Victorian. At present the compartments must, for the sake of clearness, be kept absolutely watertight. For purposes of the story Ann Veronica must on occasion be simple, ignorant and trustful, with no knowledge of men and their infirmities. So please forget all about compartments one and three for the moment.

The Early Victorian Compartment, finding itself alone in London (it was compartment number three that got her there, but that is coming), bethought itself of a dear, friendly, middle-aged and moneyed gentleman who had sympathised with it on a previous occasion. It went to his offices, and borrowed £40, in spite of the fact that this gentleman had prominent eyes. Such a friend was worth having, and the Early Victorian Compartment dined with him frequently. Then they went to "Tristan"; and, at the end of the first act, Ann Veronica discovered that the middle-aged gentleman had his hand upon her waist. His explanation followed: "It is no good. I want you". The situation was a little complicated. In fact, it required discussing. Accordingly, the Early Victorian Compartment agreed then and there to come and discuss it "somewhere where we can talk without interruption". So they had dinner in a cabinet particulier; and, when the door was locked, innocent discussion resolved itself into a personal encounter wherein the Early Victorian Compartment changed suddenly into compartment number three, which had learned jiu-jitsu. The result was that the middle-aged gentleman, instead of meeting with a proper reward for his kindness, was nearly throttled and very much upset.

Now for the third compartment. We have had a peep into it already in this matter of the jiu-jitsu; but that was a trifle. It was the Modern Compartment that left its home because it was not allowed to go to a fancy-dress ball as a corsair's bride. Ann Veronica's father actually used force, and held the door when persuasion failed, so that her universe fell all about her. It was the Modern Compartment that listened to discussions, when those who were "altogether in the van" talked familiarly of Christ, Buddha, Nietzsche and Tolstoy. It was the Modern Compartment that got itself locked up for raiding the House of Commons in a pantechnicon, which enterprise seems to have been entered upon as a reaction against the late ascendancy of the Early Victorian. It was the Modern Compartment that knew what a co-respondent was; that swore at a policeman; that "chucked" Manning (gentleman engaged to it); that, remembering its debt to the middle-aged man in the course of Ann Veronica's so-called honeymoon, said "My God!" and "Oh, cuss it!" with a vigour that surprised her lover into remarking "You do use vile language".

So much for the three compartments. Enough has been said to show that Mr. Wells has produced a very difficult young woman. Put the three compartments together, and you get Ann Veronica. No one will attempt to deny that here you have an exceedingly interesting study in human nature.

But Mr. Wells' book is more than a study in human nature. There are profound moral and psychological discoveries in it. For instance, Mr. Wells seems to have discovered a child-expelling instinct latent in all fathers and mothers. Moreover, if you have little moral sense, and if you are sufficiently reckless and egoistic to defy society with the requisite confidence, you are bound to fall on your feet. It is apparently a matter of faith. Ann Veronica fail? It is unimaginable. Accordingly, Capes at the right moment gets a play accepted, and Capes' wife disappears from the story. They are now at liberty to have children, and live happy ever after.

It is time to be serious. What has happened to Mr. Wells? What we have here seems to be realism run mad and into unpleasant places. The love-story of Capes and Ann Veronica is not a piece of art. For instance, it is conceivable that two creatures of the opposite sex placed in these circumstances might talk as these two creatures talk. But, by setting down the words as spoken, Mr. Wells says more, and therefore less, than is artistically contained in the situation. Listen to Ann Veronica: "I wish I could roll my little body up small, and squeeze it into your hand, and grip your fingers upon it. Tight". This hits the reader with a forcefulness that is almost ugly, and certainly grotesque. To get the spirit of such a mood, all the letters must be transmuted. Without some such transmutation the thing reads like a piece of stupid eroticism. Such are the perils that wait upon the realist.

Moreover, the unpleasant impression left by this book cannot be entirely explained away by ascribing it to overdone realism. There is throughout a vicious insistence upon the material aspect of life, more especially upon the physical aspect of sex. Certain admirers will be found to see here a healthy corrective of the tendency to ignore necessary elements in human nature and in social science; but in this book the insistence on things physical is beyond all proportion. Mr. Wells is looking at the world through the spectacles of a hectic materialism. His usually clear perception of values has deserted him. We hope that this is not the beginning of some insidious disease in his view of things.

SKELETON EPICS.

"Northern Lights." By Sir Gilbert Parker. London: Methuen. 1909. 6s.

SEVENTEEN good stories of North American life, mainly interesting in the primitiveness of their passion and the realism of their rough environment, in circumstances that strip hearts and souls of their conventions, exposing their realities in the play of primary impulse. There is no lack of action to suggest the life, but there is more character than is usually revealed in stories of action. A few of the personalities are types of uncommon strength and truth. Take Mitiahwe, the Indian girl, and the grandeur of her loyalty to "her white man". She has married him in her own way, which is not his way, and he longs for civilisation again, where he may not take her. The woman in her sees this in spite of him, and everything makes for separation, except one—she is a woman, he is a man, and their blood is young. Against all odds Mitiahwe wields her sole power with the pathos of primitive desperation. Can she keep her man? There has been no child, and she prays to her god: "O, Sun, great Father, have pity on me, for I love him and would keep him. And give me bone of his bone and one to nurse at my breast that is of him. O, Sun, pity me this night, and be near me when I speak to him, and hear what I say". Then she told him there was a child, when there was not; but there was one later, and so "she kept her man, but truly she was altogether a woman". She had conquered colour, creed, race, civilisation itself, and because she was "altogether a woman", which, though only sketched, goes very deep, and might be considered by some who are women and a little too much more. The theme is more extensive than the latitudes, and the simple force of the treatment is finely appropriate.

Our next heroine is a white girl, but lacking the single-mindedness of the savage; she is uncertain whether to "go north with Abe Hawley, or south with Nick Pringle, or east with someone else"; and in due course she goes one way with one man, only to turn and go another way with another on finding that the first has already a wife, deserted. No suggestion of anything seriously wrong in Nance all the time, and what is suggested is rather the moral elasticity of the civilised mind in the uncivilised environment, where derivative convention does not seem to hold its own against the primitive virtues. Mitiahwe's fidelity is but fortified in its intensity by the same environment that makes Nance such a moral uncertainty; and red motherhood levels up character to a plane far above the white spinster. We know how much lower than the savage can be the ethics of the civilised in savage conditions, and though Sir Gilbert Parker does not appear to have consciously intended the criticism in his contrast of the two girls, it is implicit in his impressions of Canadian life and character along the shifting border-line between the white man and the red.

Abe Hawley alone deserves a whole biography, and makes us long for the details to fill the dramatic outline in which he passes now and then through the stirring perspective; a fascinating ruffian of the first order, who lives between love and smuggling, ready to cut a throat or to woo a maiden; a terror to the fiercest, but like a big lamb when he meets Nance. Abe is a personification of animal ethics, modified by such traces of humanity as survive the necessities of the life that he has led; and accordingly he "goes north" with Nance, whose wonderful powers of resistance make the union tolerable to one's sense of proportion.

The most interesting feature of these stories, from a literary point of view, is the easy sureness and truth of their outlines. There is not a finished picture among them, but there is not a sketch that does not afford a finely finished picture; and the wonder is that the painter has been content to draw the line at the higher manifestation of his evident power. At every point, however good, he makes one feel that he could be so much better if he tried; and he seems to find it so easy to write well that he does not feel the need to write his best, which has probably to come. Then, he has written a full score of books, which, for a young man, however gifted, are far too numerous to contain his best. A man may write his best in one book, but never in twenty; and his best book may be worth much more than all the others put together. The sketches of too many others have no such interest for us, but these compel the wish that their author would some day sit down away from irrelevant strain, fill in one of his fine outlines, and let us see the finished picture.

THE GREAT EARTH-CALDRONS.

"The Natural History of Igneous Rocks." By A. Harker. London: Methuen. 1909. 12s. 6d. net.

THERE have been many treatises on volcanoes, but few specially devoted to the processes that underlie volcanic action. The igneous rocks known to all of us, the ejected dust and scoriæ of a great eruption, the lavas that remain hot for months, grey and grim and rugged, across the devastated fields, these are only the superficial representatives of matter that plays an enormous part within the crust. During the stress and storm of volcanic activity we can only guess at what is going on beneath us in the unseen caldrons of the earth. After long ages of rest, after even the mineral springs have ceased to flow, the gradual action of rain and frost and rivers may reveal to us, as a huge cast of crystalline rock, the source of all this surface turmoil. In the study of igneous rocks, as Mr. Harker observes, we must reverse the maxim of the school of Hutton and of Lyell, and "must seek rather to use the history of the past to explain the phenomena of the present. Geology may thus repay part of the debt which she owes to Physical Geography".

Mr. Harker's treatise is for the scholar, and almost for the specialist. It may not appeal even to all who regard themselves as trained geologists; but, on the other hand, there is much in it that will attract both the chemist and the physicist. The results of a large number of experiments on melting-points, the order of crystallisation of minerals, variations of volume with temperature, and so forth, are brought together in the form of diagrams. The chemical compositions of igneous rocks are compared by "variation-diagrams" which show, with a simplicity that may truly be called artistic, how the ordinary bases—lime, magnesia, alumina and the rest—vary relatively with the percentage of silica present. There are two fine plates illustrating types of volcanic activity, from photographs by that untiring traveller, Dr. Tempest Anderson; but no further concession is made to those who may think first of igneous rocks as providing natural features in a landscape. The appropriateness of the title chosen for the book may well be questioned by workers in other fields of "natural history". Natural history, as Mr. Harker no doubt feels, should be based on a study of the laws of growth and evolution. In discussing these laws, as they affect the constitution and distribution of the masses that were at one time molten in the crust, he stops short of any description of igneous rocks as they present themselves to observers in the field. His own very memorable studies among the wilds of Skye were recorded some years ago with the same clearness of purpose and the same reserve. Perhaps the microscope, with its fascinating revelations of the histology of igneous rocks, has led us on the same road as that travelled by many zoologists and botanists. The study and comparison of internal details go far towards a natural grouping of the types examined and towards the establishment of that delightful thing, a sequence. But this, even among igneous rocks, is not the whole of natural history. We want, as it were, in our common walks across the country to feel the power and pulsation of these unseen masses in the earth. We want to trace their influence on the form of a hillside, or, it may be, on the barriers of a continent. We want to picture the insidious growth of a great caldron, or the flooding of a land with lava; and ultimately to trace out, in granite or in basalt, the picturesque course of old age and decay. If we look in vain for these things in Mr. Harker's treatise, it is only because we have misread the intention of his title. If we are already familiar with igneous rocks in the broad sense, we shall welcome the book as enabling us to realise their mineral characters and their relationships far more adequately and philosophically than before. Its whole tendency is wisely opposed to the minutiæ of artificial classification. The work is so good, thorough and consistent that it will escape the fate of many text-books; it will not be recommended to those average students who regard geology as an easy subject in which to score marks at examinations.

One of the great problems of the igneous masses that are so prominent in the structure of the earth's crust is how they came into their present position in regard to the surrounding rocks. Have they eaten their way upwards, absorbing or "stoping" off the material above them, and thus enlarging their own caldrons; or have they been forced into place by earth-pressures, which raised the rocks into an arch and thus provided them with a field for thermal operations? On the former hypothesis, modification in composition must have occurred through the enormous quantity of material absorbed; on the latter, the variations that are so noticeable in the mass when it has cooled down and lies exposed must be mainly attributed to "differentiation", accompanying the crystallisation of the mineral material. Mr. Harker points out that there is everything to be said, as all geologists must admit, for the localisation of molten masses in the domes provided by earth-movements. This, indeed, is one of the first conclusions forced upon observers who have mapped large areas in the field. But it may be felt that so whole-hearted a champion of differentiation has not done justice to the evidence of intermingling, on what may be called a continental scale, that is revealed in Canada, Finland, Saxony, not to mention smaller areas nearer home. When we sit on the bare glaciated isles of Spikarna, we forget the wash of Baltic waters round us, and feel that we are immersed in one of the old granite caldrons, with the processes of absorption in full progress. But Mr. Harker in this book introduces us to so large a field of research that we must not ask him to come out and explain to us the phenomena of the gnarled and ever-varying older gneisses, which are, after all, the most continuous igneous masses that we possess. His brilliant work on gneisses of Tertiary age in Rum make us hope, however, for further help from him in this broad and fascinating field.

ARCHÆOLOGY IN THE CARNATIC.

"Mysore and Coorg from the Inscriptions." By B. Lewis Rice. London: Constable. 1909. 12s. 6d.

MR. RICE'S book is a practical illustration of the excellent scientific work that is now being done in India under Government auspices. It sums up the results obtained from the numerous inscriptions which have been collected, facsimilied, and published by the Mysore Archæological Department, and which are contained in twelve sumptuous volumes. Between eight and nine thousand inscriptions have thus been edited, with transliterations and translations into English, the earliest of which go back to the reign of the famous A'soka, the Constantine of Indian Buddhism.

Mr. Rice has directed the archæological work and superintended the publication of the inscriptions, and he now looks back upon what he has done with justifiable pride. The past history of a large portion of India has not only been placed on a trustworthy basis, but to a large extent rescued from oblivion. The very names of the princes who ruled for centuries over Mysore had been forgotten, and dynastic movements have come to light all memory of which had been lost. The archæological recovery of the past history of Mysore has been a reproduction on a small scale of that of Assyria.

The earliest contemporaneous inscriptions are those containing the edicts of A'soka. But there are others of later date, which refer to a Jain migration from the north, when the emigrants were accompanied by Chandra Gupta, the Sandracottus of Greek writers, who reigned from B.C. 321 to 297, and was the grandfather of A'soka. Chandra Gupta would thus have been a Jain by religion, which might, perhaps, help to explain his grandson's conversion to Buddhism; indeed, if the Mysore tradition is to be trusted, he would have come southward as the companion and chief disciple of a great Jain teacher, whom he is said to have survived only twelve years. The twelve years, it may be added, were spent in the characteristically Hindu occupation of performing penance.

The edicts of A'soka are written in Mâgadhi, and are chiefly devoted to impressing upon his subjects the duties of religion. They are bidden to follow the example of their king, who had entered the sacred Order and so discovered that the men who had been esteemed "true" were really "false", along with the gods they worshipped. Heavenly bliss was not the privilege of a few; it could be attained by all, by the humblest as well as by the mightiest. There can be little doubt that the "false" ones whose real character was thus unmasked were the Brahmins. The creed of Buddhism was a protest against the teaching of Brahminism, which declared that the people "that knoweth not the law is accursed".

One of the dynasties brought to light by epigraphic research is that of the Pahlavas, or Parthians, who reigned in the east of the Dekhan. It is interesting to find Parthian influence extending so far to the south. Their opponents here were the Chalukas, whose name Mr. Rice would connect with that of the Seleucian Greeks. But it is not princes and dynasties alone with which the discovery and study of the inscriptions have made us acquainted. The final chapters of Mr. Rice's volume pass in review the facts derived from them as regards administration, manners and customs, art, literature, and religion. Some of these facts are sufficiently curious. Perhaps to the Western mind the most curious of all are those relating to voluntary suicide for religious or political reasons. On one occasion a whole battalion of a thousand men slaughtered themselves along with their prince Lakshma. On another the chiefs were joined in their work of self-immolation by their wives and servants, male and female. A favourite mode of leaving the world was by fastening a hook at the end of a bent bamboo to the topknot of hair and then striking off the head, which bounded up into the air like "Garuda", the divine kite. At times we hear of literary and mnemonic prodigies. One celebrity whose name is recorded could write letters with both hands at once, and go through a hundred feats of memory at the same time. Another was a poet, Soma by name, who wrote poetry successfully in no less than eight languages.

The inscriptions are, for the most part, on stone or metal. The metal employed was generally copper, the inscribed plates of which were strung together on a ring, and so could be carried about. The inscriptions on stone were sometimes on rocks, sometimes on the walls of temples or other buildings, though the most favourite monument was a pillar or stela. "Their primary object", says Mr. Rice, "is, in general, to record the erection of temples or other public structures, the endowment of gods and Brahmins with lands and gifts, or to commemorate acts of heroism or self-sacrifice." But, naturally, other matters are referred to in them, and past history is frequently recapitulated or alluded to. It goes without saying that for genealogical purposes they are especially valuable.

THE DÉCLASSÉE'S REVENGE.

"My Recollections." By the Countess of Cardigan and Lancastre. London: Nash. 1909. 10s. 6d. net.

LADY CARDIGAN has revenged herself upon a society which refused to receive her by inventing a series of scandalous libels upon some of its members who are dead. The great ladies whose characters she takes away would no more have spoken to Lady Cardigan than to one of

"Those pedestrian Paphians who abound
In London when the daylight's o'er".

With one exception, the stately homes whose interiors Lady Cardigan pretends to depict resolutely closed their doors upon a woman who, with every advantage of birth and fortune, chose to defy not only morality but decency. The stories told by this doting déclassée have not even the excuse of wit; they are gross and brutal, but not in the least amusing. Of course, the fiction that Disraeli ever thought of marrying for her money a woman whom everybody cut is ludicrous. We understand that the book has had a great sale, at which we are not prudish enough to affect surprise. Most people like scandal about Queen Elizabeth, even when they know it to be untrue. The harm done by such a book is great. Not only are the relatives of the libelled dead annoyed, but the picture of Victorian society is accepted as true by those who do not know it. The most revolting passages are pounced upon by the halfpenny newspapers, and greedily read and repeated by the enemies of aristocracy. We cannot exonerate from blame the publishers who have published such a book for the sake of gain.

NOVELS.

"Watchers by the Shore." By J. E. Patterson. London: Methuen. 1909. 6s.

Throughout this book we seem always to be keeping an eye upon the weather and are seldom out of earshot of the rhythm of rowlocks. Nor, in Mr. Patterson's company, do we wish it otherwise. The chapters describing the wild race of two rival luggers for the narrow haven of Shingle Street when neither would give way, and the stranding of a disabled brig on the outer spit in a gale, present a masterly combination of picturesqueness with exact nautical lore. Moreover they are not like mere boards hung up in a theatre inscribed "This is the sea"; they are of the essence of the story, necessary recitals of events acting upon the lives and affected in turn by the characters of the men and women taking part in them. For first of all this tender yet virile tale is one of human interest. And although the web of character no less than of circumstance is of a mingled yarn, good and ill together, how rarely the characters in contemporary story-writing show us the defects of their qualities or any thread of the gold that is shot through darker stuff. We welcome Mr. Patterson's beach salvagers and fishermen of the Suffolk foreshore because they do. Not all Knut Sloggett's indubitable wisdom and humour and goodness of heart prevented his getting very drunk the night after he had finished breaking up his beloved old boat. It was the large and stubborn uprightness of Gideon Sheldrick—we accept the author's description of him as a Rodinesque figure—that itself led him to harbour dark thoughts of murder against the seducer of his adopted daughter Joan. Even the pitiful plottings of Huldah's crazy jealousy, by which she largely contributed to the girl's downfall, had their springs in her wifely pride in Gideon. If Joan herself and her betrayer Caleb are a little less impressive, they too are human and touching because of clashing qualities. Basil's "dictionary words" seem to us overdone; but he was only the publican's son, and perhaps Mr. Patterson meant to make him ridiculous. He certainly had no idea how to handle a boat.

"The Return of the Petticoat." By Warwick Deeping. London: Harper. 1909. 6s.

She rebelled "against Nature's classification", and with the amused connivance of an eminent physician and a highly respectable solicitor she got herself up as a man, purchased Red Ghyll Farm and went to live there. She was becoming warmly interested in Tom Swaine, her "man about" and general factotum (of superior education), when the usual accident causing a fainting-fit occurred, and Tom very nearly unbuttoned his master's shirt-front. This alarmed her so much that, leaving Tom in charge, she straightway went off to Australia in order that she might die there and return as that twin sister whom with admirable foresight she had invented. Re-established at Red Ghyll as its mistress, the sentimental relation with Tom was helped on by the loss of his arm whilst about the shooting of a fox at her instigation, and led at last to a most happy mésalliance. It seems a pity that a well-written story in which several of the minor characters are moving and life-like sketches should have so far-fetched a framework; but if the author means to recommend to ladies, rebellious like his heroine against the disabilities of sex, the figurative resumption of petticoats and the ardent pursuit of Tom Swaines, we cannot but applaud his intention.

"The Street of Adventure." By Philip Gibbs. London: Heinemann. 1909. 3s.

The only Liberal penny morning paper in London dramatically closes its existence with a notice that its current issue is the last. We seem to have heard of this in real life, and it would perhaps be indiscreet to ask whether or not the portraits of the staff in this novel are drawn from persons connected with the defunct Liberal organ. Run on these lines not even a Liberal paper could have thriven long. The description of the inner working of a newspaper office is interesting, but the story leads to nothing. We cannot feel any enthusiasm for the hero, Frank Luttrell, who starts as a reporter on the "Liberal" and ends in the same capacity elsewhere, and does nothing to show that he has any marked qualification for his work—except perhaps "an Oxford manner"!

SHORTER NOTICES.

"A Study of Mathematical Education." By Benchara Branford. Oxford: At the Clarendon Press.

We are glad to learn that Mr. Branford's book is to be translated into the German. It is not only of value as a practical guide to the intelligent teaching of mathematics, but it is also of interest to all who feel attracted to the study of the organic development of the human mind. It is a well-established truth that the growth of a child's intellect shows in miniature the intellectual history of the race. Mr. Branford has in this book some attractive chapters in which this growth is carefully followed from its first beginnings to maturity, with special reference, of course, to the conception and handling of number and the algebraic symbol. These chapters, of intrinsic interest in themselves, have a direct bearing upon his subject; for the peculiar secret of Mr. Branford's method lies in his insistence upon the necessity to follow the mental processes of a pupil, and not to force them forward prematurely. On its practical side the book is of immense value, and bears evidence of the greatest care. It is not the work of a theorist, but of a man whose experience is wide enough to enable him to proceed empirically without fear of generalising upon a practice too limited to warrant his inferences. There is at the present moment every need of such a book. The teaching of mathematics has swung violently away from the old formal paths, and tends to lay too much stress upon the practical aspects of the subject. Mr. Branford's book is nicely calculated to restore the balance.

"The French Procession." By Mary Duclaux. London: Unwin. 1909. 12s. 6d. net.

Madame Duclaux' title, and especially her sub-title, "A Pageant of Great Writers", indicate quite plainly for what kind of readers she has prepared these sketches of French writers. They are the readers to whom publishers are issuing all sorts of books on French subjects, on French history, biography, or literature, with the object of making them as amusing and as easily read as French fiction. To serious students of these subjects the purpose is contemptible and a proof of the mental levity of the modern reader. These sketches of French writers, ancient and modern, are a form of light entertainment which Madame Duclaux composes very cleverly. They are not important in any critical or historical sense, but they are fresh and brightly written. She seizes the points where a Frenchman becomes emotionally interesting to an English reader, especially to an English-woman or girl, and the result is a series of rapid little essays which, however slight they may be, are not commonplace or dull. Madame Duclaux has made her selections from the old writers and the new. In a sense she covers the field of French literature from Ronsard to Anatole France. The superficial reader, who is satisfied if supplied with interesting information, hardly deserves the good writing which Madame Duclaux (who in English is A. Mary F. Robinson) has devoted to his service.

"The Short Story in English." By Henry Canby. New York: Holt. London: Bell. 1909. 6s. net.

Mr. Canby says of his own book that it "invites criticism and risks dulness". This sounds as if the writer himself were tired of his subject. Enthusiasm for the subject should be sufficiently glowing in the writer not to permit of any doubt of enthusiasm in the reader. Besides, there is no real need for such doubt. Those who are sufficiently interested in literature to be willing to follow the growth of a particular type of literary expression through the centuries will read this book without boredom. It is written by a man who knows his subject, has read widely, and has reached conclusions. As a study in evolution it is disappointing. The affiliation of the ordinary modern short story to anything older than the needs and purposes of the present moment is a difficult, if not an impossible, task. As for the short story of James or Kipling, this is the natural expression of an analytic and self-conscious temper peculiar to an advanced cvilisation. The slender threads that bind it to the past are shown as thickly and distinctly as possible by Mr. Canby, but the organic continuity still appears as slight as ever. It is not necessary to go back before Chaucer to understand Henry James. But it is interesting, as a historical and literary exercise, to do so; and Mr. Canby is a trustworthy guide.

"Masques and Phases." By Robert Ross. London: Humphries. 1909. 5s. net.

We have here a collection of literary knick-knacks: "essays" is hardly the word. There is some delicate trifling with a number of subjects, artistic and so forth, which pleases at its best, and irritates at its worst. At its best it is good-humoured trifling, with taste and knowledge behind it. At its worst it is a little precious, and leads nowhere. The author does not seem to have been under any pressing obligation to himself to write these articles; but, being written, they are perhaps worth a pen, some ink, and a little paper—perhaps not quite so much ink and paper as has been given to them.

Messrs. Methuen are now bringing out a very comely and convenient edition of the works, in poetry and prose, of Oscar Wilde. Each volume is 5s. net, beautifully printed and bound in plain neat green cloth. We must say we far prefer this way of book production to the "fetching" devices of end-papers and "pretty" bindings which are a feature to-day of so many reprints. The "pretty" book which is voted "artistic" is nearly always bad to the eye of anybody who can really discriminate between the good and the spurious in these matters. And how tawdry these rubbishy and pretentious bindings become after a few years! The opening volumes in this admirable edition of Wilde are "Lady Windermere's Fan", "A Woman of No Importance", and "Lord Arthur Savile's Crime" and "Poems". As to this last, one must confess to a slight sense of disillusionment in glancing through the sonnets and other early verses which once seemed of such rare merit. For the most part this early work consists of graceful and delicate verse. It lacks the real fire and force of true poetry.

"Revue des Deux Mondes." 1 Octobre.

Among several excellent articles in this number we would call particular attention to M. Gabriel Faure's on "Cities and Landscapes of Upper Italy". The cities he deals with in particular are Vicenza, Brescia, and Bergamo, none of them among those universally visited. Yet what a wealth of art and associations they all contain! It is in Vicenza alone that the architecture of Palladio can be properly studied, for with the exception of Venice no other city contains any important work of this great artist. The writer particularly signalises the Guisti garden at Verona as worthy of attention, but it is often passed over by hasty visitors to Verona. Madame Marcelle Tinayre continues her series of papers on her recent visit to Constantinople.

(*Continued on page* 450.)

This one contains an interesting story of her life told by the wife of a Turkish Pacha. We wonder how much it owes to the adroit manipulation of the accomplished novelist! There is a good but not very conclusive article on the future relations between Japan and America by M. Felix Klein.

THE OCTOBER REVIEWS.

If the monthly reviews in any way reflect public opinion, Ministers need only turn to them to find the writing on the wall. There is a negligible quantity in their favour, and practically everything against them. "Blackwood" has its usual vigorous political essay, taking as its text "the three speeches"—those of Lord Rosebery, Mr. Asquith, and Mr. Balfour. Between the upper and the nether millstones, in the persons of the Liberal Imperialist and Unionist leaders, the Prime Minister has a bad time of it in Maga's pages. The "National" considers that "the constitutionalist crisis" opened with Lord Rosebery's speech on 10 September; and finds that the efforts of the past month have hardened opinion among the Unionists as a fighting unit. Verax in the same Review says that the real and sufficient reason for the rejection of the Budget is that the Government are prepared to surrender for ever the naval supremacy of Great Britain; by that Verax means that Mr. Lloyd George and Mr. Winston Churchill have not the slightest intention of devoting to the Navy the enormous sum—some £24,000,000—necessary to bring it up to the proper standard. "A Member of the House of Lords" makes it pretty clear that the peers have no option but to throw out the Finance Bill. If the Bill passes, the Government will at once proceed to fortify the position they have gained without running the risks of an appeal to the country. "A Member of the House of Lords" is confident that the Radical Government, if it still existed after the election, would be less powerful for mischief than it must be if allowed to continue unchecked. In the "Nineteenth Century" Mr. Ellis Barker, out of his knowledge of what has been done in Germany and France for the small-holder, advises the Unionists as to the programme they should adopt when Tariff Reform and Land Reform have brought the victory which he anticipates. Sir John Dickson-Poynder, writing on the valuation proposals of the Government, says that whereas the Government estimate that valuation can be made for £2,000,000, experts estimate that such a valuation by owners would cost £13,000,000. If that is so, clearly the work cannot be done by the State for less than a sixth of the amount. Then he pictures the confusion which must follow the valuation as proposed of areas that are not conterminous with existing local government areas. In the "Fortnightly" Mr. J. L. Garvin aptly defines the new Socialism, not as embodying a theory of the millennium, but as a mode of direct taxation. The question of the British Budget has become one of European interest. To foreign Socialists it seems to point to the earthly paradise: to the more moderate of Continental observers England seems in peril of becoming a lost nation. "Unless there be some startling change in the existing tendency", he says, "either our sea-power must go"—as Verax suggests—"which is not to be thought of, or we shall soon be in sight of a £200,000,000 Budget." Any politician, he says, who regards this "prospect of appalling gravity" lightly must be mad. Is there any evidence that the Government realise where they are plunging? Mr. F. W. Hurst in the "Contemporary" denies that the new death duties and taxation of capital mean ruin. He endeavours to explain when wealth is not capital. If he saves £20 and then spends it on something which would help his business or his profession, it becomes capital. If he spends it on motoring or smoking it is not capital expenditure. Could anything be more absurd? Then Mr. Hurst tells us that if the foreigner pays Customs duties there can be no protection in the home market, as though the relief from taxation would not in itself be an enormous boon to all concerned in home trade. M.P. in the "English Review" discovers in the social measures of 1909 beginnings of various reforms which may have consequences almost incalculable. He blesses the Development Bill, but as he puts off to a period fifty or a hundred years hence the full benefits which it may confer, it hardly strikes one as a matter for immediate enthusiasm.

Sir Charles Dilke, writing on foreign affairs in the "English Review", is gently critical of Sir Edward Grey's policy in dealing with recent events in South-Eastern Europe, and concludes that the result has "strengthened a proposal long popular among non-official Liberals for some measure of control in foreign affairs by a committee as recommended by the example of the French Parliament and the Senate of the United States". Lord Courtney is discursively historical and a little platitudinous in his "Contemporary" reflections on peace or war, ending in the assurance that there should be no ground of serious quarrel between the United States and Canada. The future will be happy, he seems to think, in proportion as we admit that "Canada must be recognised as absolute master of her fate". The suggestion may induce some readers of the "Contemporary" to turn to the "Nineteenth Century", in whose pages Professor Wrong, of the University of Toronto, explains the attitude of Canada as he sees it. He says that in the end Canada has always had her way; she will steadily become more independent, more ambitious to rank among the nations of the earth, but her own way will not lead to separation from Great Britain, consequently not to union with the States. As for the future of the Empire, Mr. Wrong finds the problem "intellectually insoluble". Incidentally he regrets that the Canadians get little information about Europe. They have given up their full but biassed cable service through the United States, for a service of their own, "and it is proving a doubtful blessing". Instead of the copious flow of Americanised news from Europe they now have only a few paragraphs, and are growing more ignorant of England in consequence. The conclusion is quaint: Mr. Wrong appears to prefer that the Canadians should have a surfeit of biassed and misleading news rather than a smaller quantity which is to be depended on. Mr. F. A. Acland's essay on "A Canadian Experiment" in the "National" is an explanation of the generally satisfactory working of the "Act to Aid in the Prevention and Settlement of Strikes and Lock-Outs in Mines and Industries connected with Public Utilities" passed in 1907. Mr. Archibald Hurd in the "Fortnightly" criticises the arrangement with the colonies for the creation of "Baby Navies". He examines the question in some detail and is convinced that the creation of a series of small colonial navies is not good economically or strategically. The Imperial Conference missed the opportunity for an object-lesson to the world. "It might have reached an agreement for the maintenance of one combined fleet, a challenge by an imperial democracy against the present competition in fleets." As it is "the colonial policy is one of pride and prejudice—of pride in nationality and prejudice against a community of interest—rather than a policy of imperial sense and sensibility". Two other articles of imperial interest in the "Fortnightly" are by Mr. Morris Colles and Mr. P. A. Vaile. Mr. Colles enters a plea for an English-speaking copyright league which shall save the Empire at least from drifting into a series of water-tight compartments, hurtful to all concerned, and Mr. P. A. Vaile outlines a new scheme for imperial scholarships which reverses the Rhodes scheme. He would send young men to the far corners of the Empire, rather than "bleed the intellect" of the colonies by bringing it to England, never to return.

Mr. Arthur Baumann's article in the "Fortnightly" on "Money and Brains in Politics", though a little hard on the rich who secure party preferment, is a timely warning against the danger of looking for Unionist candidates among the well-to-do only. There is a serious disproportion between Unionist talent in Parliament and Unionist talent in the country, and a very small levy on the incomes of rich Conservatives would, as Mr. Baumann says, provide a fund that would enable several hundred desirable candidates to come forward who are now prevented by lack of means. The parliamentary candidate as he was and as he is to-day is the subject of an anecdotic paper in the "Cornhill" by Mr. Ian Malcolm. Mr. Stephen Gwynn in the "Nineteenth Century" controverts the views of Mr. Ian Malcolm and Mr. P. D. Kenny as to Ireland. His case against the Union is that "lawless agitation, which invariably at some point or other degenerates into crime, is the necessary prelude to any serious legislative reform"—surely a very neat if unwitting, way of showing the folly of surrender to lawless agitation. Mr. Gwynn is, of course, quite unable to recognise the picture which Mr. Kenny draws of Ireland, though he admits that there is "a small substratum of reality" in it. Mr. Roosevelt contributes a first instalment of his impressions and doings in East Africa to "Scribner"; Mr. Sydney Brooks elects, in half a dozen pages of the "Century", to describe the successes and failures of British rule in India; A Conservative Indian in the "Asiatic Quarterly" has a good word to say for Lord Morley's reforms as marking an epoch in the political progress of India. One wonders how those reforms would have been regarded by some of the famous writers of old John Company, whose literary energy Mr. Beckles Willson reviews in the "Fortnightly". Mr. Max Beerbohm has four characteristically inimitable if rather cruel caricatures in the "English Review". They are studies of Miss Mona Limerick, Earl Beauchamp, Captain Hugh Warrender, and Mr. Augustus John.

For this Week's Books see page 452 and 454.

WHAT Celebrities Say about SANATOGEN

Ten thousand doctors have written in praise of Sanatogen.

Thirty thousand doctors throughout the world are known to prescribe it.

Hundreds of thousands of people have been restored from conditions of grave illness to complete health by its use. Among them are many well-known men and women who have voluntarily testified to the debt they owe Sanatogen in restoring their health.

A selection from their letters is published below.

The Right Rev. the Bishop of Norwich

"Mrs. Sheepsbanks is taking Sanatogen regularly, and deriving great benefit from it."

Mr. Marshall Hall, K.C.

"I think it only right to say that I have tried Sanatogen, and I believe it to be a most excellent food."

Sir Gilbert Parker, M.P.

"I have used Sanatogen with extraordinary benefit. It is to my mind a true food tonic, feeding the nerves, increasing the energy, and giving fresh vigour to the overworked body and mind."

Madame Sarah Grand

The gifted Authoress: "Sanatogen has done everything for me which it is said to be able to do for cases of nervous debility and exhaustion. I began to take it after nearly four years' enforced idleness from extreme debility, and felt the benefit almost immediately."

Lord Ronald Sutherland Gower

The Sculptor and Historian: "I feel it only due to the benefit conferred on my general health by Sanatogen to write and inform those interested in that wonderful medicine that in a couple of months' time it has cured me of all gouty trouble."

Mr. E. F. Benson

The well-known Author: "I have tried Sanatogen, and believe it to be an excellent tonic."

The Rev. Father Bernard Vaughan

"Sanatogen promises when you are run down to pick you up. It does so."

Mr. Hall Caine

The celebrated Author: "My experience of Sanatogen has been that, as a tonic nerve food, it has on more than one occasion done me good."

Mr. Henry Arthur Jones

The famous Dramatist: "Sanatogen seems to me a very valuable food and nerve tonic. I have several times taken a course of it when I've been run down, and always with excellent results."

Mr. Eden Phillpotts

The well-known Writer: "Sanatogen appears to be of real value to the brain worker, a useful food and tonic combined. I can give it high praise from personal experience."

Maxwell Gray

The Writer: "I have found Sanatogen helpful in digestive troubles and nervous weakness. I have taken it from time to time under medical advice."

Dr. C. W. Saleeby

The well-known Medical Author: "Sanatogen is a specially adapted food that has solved the problem of giving phosphorus in such a way that the nervous system can take hold of it."

Mr. Armiger Barclay

—the distinguished Author: "Your valuable preparation possesses remarkable recuperative properties."

Sanatogen can be obtained from all chemists, in tins from 1*s.* 9*d.* to 9*s.* 6*d.* A beautifully illustrated pamphlet containing much valuable information will be sent, post free, to those mentioning this paper, on receipt of a post card addressed to The Sanatogen Company, 12 Chenies St., London, W.C.

AUSTRALIA by ORIENT LINE,

UNDER CONTRACT TO CARRY HIS MAJESTY'S MAILS.

FROM LONDON EVERY ALTERNATE FRIDAY, calling at PLYMOUTH, GIBRALTAR, MARSEILLES, NAPLES, PORT SAID, and COLOMBO.

Managers—F. GREEN & CO.: ANDERSON, ANDERSON & CO.

Head Offices—Fenchurch Avenue, London.

For Passage apply to the latter firm at 5 Fenchurch Avenue, E.C., or to the Branch Office, 28 Cockspur Street, Charing Cross, S.W.

P. & O. AUTUMN PASSENGER SAILINGS (1909)

(Carrying Mails under Contract with H.M. Government.)

EGYPT, INDIA, STRAITS, CHINA, JAPAN, AUSTRALASIA.

AUSTRALIA, CHINA & JAPAN; also BOMBAY via ADEN.

Steamer.	Tons.	From London.	From Marseilles.
MONGOLIA	10,000	Oct. 8	Oct. 15
MARMORA	10,500	Oct. 22	Oct. 29
MOREA	11,000	Nov. 5	Nov. 12
MOOLTAN	10,000	Nov. 19	Nov. 26
MANTUA	11,000	Dec. 3	Dec. 10

P. & O. Return Tickets, available for 2 years, at a Fare and a Half. For Passage and all information apply at the Company's Offices, 122 Leadenhall St., E.C., or Northumberland Ave., W.C., London.

UNION-CASTLE LINE.

ROYAL MAIL SERVICE.—To SOUTH and EAST AFRICA.—Via Madeira, Canaries, Ascension, St. Helena, and Lobito Bay.

Steamers	Service	London	Southampton
* ARMADALE CASTLE	Royal Mail	—	Oct. 9
§ DUNLUCE CASTLE	Intermediate	Oct. 8	Oct. 9
* NORMAN	Royal Mail	—	Oct. 16
† GASCON	Intermediate	Oct. 15	Oct. 16

* Via Madeira. § Via Teneriffe. † Via Las Palmas, Ascension, and St. Helena.

Special Trains from Waterloo to Southampton every Saturday.

Donald Currie and Co., Managers, 3 and 4 Fenchurch Street, E.C. West End Agencies—Sleeping Car Co., 20 Cockspur Street, S.W., and Thos. Cook and Son, 13 Cockspur Street, S.W.

Awarded 25 Gold Medals and a Ten Guinea Challenge Cup.

BARR'S POPULAR 21/- COLLECTION OF DAFFODILS contains 6 Bulbs each of 26 Fine Distinct Varieties suitable for Pot-culture or for the Flower Border. (Half the Collection for **10/6.**)

BARR'S WOODLAND 21/- COLLECTION OF DAFFODILS contains 500 Strong Bulbs in 20 Fine Showy Varieties suitable for Naturalising.

Descriptive Catalogue of all the finest Daffodils in Cultivation, Free.

BARR & SONS,

11, 12, & 13 King Street, Covent Garden, London.

SPEEDILY CURE ACIDITY, FLATULENCE, HEARTBURN, IMPURE BREATH, INDIGESTION, DIARRHŒA, &c.

PREVENT MANY AN ILLNESS. Highly recommended by the Medical Profession. Sold by all Chemists and Stores. Biscuits, 1s., 2s. and 4s. per tin; Powder, 2s. and 4s. per bottle; Lozenges, 1s. 1½d. tin.

CHARCOAL CHOCOLATES. Highly nutritious and digestible. Sold in tins, 1/- each.

J. L. BRAGG, Ltd., 14 Wigmore Street, London, W.

A large sample sent for three penny stamps for postage.

Will be found most excellent as a sustaining and nourishing food when a light and easily digested meal is required. Whilst exceedingly helpful to the invalid and dyspeptic, it is admirably adapted for general use, especially as a light supper repast. In tins, 1/6 and 3/-, of Chemists.

The "Allenburys" DIET is a food for Adults, and is quite distinct from the well-known "Allenburys" Foods for Infants.

Allen & Hanburys Ltd., Lombard St., London.

THIS WEEK'S BOOKS.

Art

The Painters of Vicenza, 1480-1550 (Tancred Borenius). Chatto and Windus. 7*s.* 6*d.* net.

Biography

Charles Dickens and his Friends (W. Teignmouth Shore). Cassell. 6*s.*
Purcell (John F. Runciman). Bell. 1*s.* net.
A Memoir of the Right Hon. William Edward Hartpole Lecky (By his Wife). Longmans, Green. 12*s.* 6*d.* net.
Chateaubriand and his Court of Women (Francis Gribble). Chapman and Hall. 15*s.* net.
Handel (R. A. Streatfield). Methuen. 7*s.* 6*d.* net.
The Reminiscences of Charlotte Lady Wake (Edited by Lucy Wake). Edinburgh: Blackwood. 12*s.* 6*d.* net.
The Life of Sir Sydney H. Waterlow, Bart. (George Smalley). Arnold. 10*s.* 6*d.* net.
Byron: the Last Phase (Richard Edgcumbe). Murray. 10*s.* 6*d.* net.

Fiction

The Glimpse (Arnold Bennett). Chapman and Hall. 6*s.*
Chetwynd's Career (Horace Wyndham). Nash. 6*s.*
The Empress of the Andes (Florence Warden). Laurie. 2*s.* net.
The Price of Lis Doris (Maarten Maartens). Methuen. 6*s.*
Some Everyday Folk and Dawn (Miles Franklin). Edinburgh: Blackwood. 6*s.*
The Haven (Eden Phillpotts). Murray. 6*s.*
Germaine (Henry C. Rowland). Lane. 6*s.*
The Beggar in the Heart (Edith Rockett). Arnold. 6*s.*

Gift Books

Mokey: the Autobiography of Donkey (Kathleen Clare Watson). Jarrold. 3*s.* 6*d.*
Betty Vivian (L. T. Meade), 5*s.*; The Attic Boarders (Raymond Jacberns), 3*s.* 6*d.*; Muriel and her Aunt Lu (May Baldwin), 5*s.*; His First Term (John Finnemore), 5*s.*; The February Boys (Mrs. Molesworth), 3*s.* 6*d.*; Jack in the Rockies (George Bird Grinnell), 2*s.* 6*d.*; A Trip to Mars (Fenton Ash), 3*s.* 6*d.*; Son Riley Rabbit and Little Girl (Grace Macgowan Cooke), 2*s.* 6*d.* Edinburgh: Chambers.

History

History and Ethnography of Africa South of the Zambesi (George McCall Theal. Vol. II.). Swan Sonnenschein. 7*s.* 6*d.*
The Short Story in English (Henry Seidel Canby). Bell. 6*s.* net.
Early Church History to A.D. 313 (Henry Melvill Gwatkin. 2 vols.). Macmillan. 17*s.* net.
Historical Record of the 76th "Hindoostan" Regiment (Compiled and Edited by Lieut.-Colonel F. A. Hayden). Lichfield: Lomax.
In the Days of the Georges (William B. Boulton). Nash. 15*s.* net.
Memoirs of Scottish Catholics (William Forbes Leigh. 2 vols.). Longmans, Green. 24*s.* net.
Sir Walter Scott's Friends (Florence MacCunn). Edinburgh: Blackwood. 10*s.* net.
Maria Edgeworth (Constance Hill). Lane. 21*s.* net.

Law

The Legislation of the Empire (C. E. A. Bedwell. 4 vols.). Butterworth. 50*s.* net.

Reprints and Translations

Persuasion (Jane Austen); Emma (Jane Austen). Dent. 5*s.* net each.
Better Food for Boys (Eustace Miles). Bell. 1*s.* net.
The Old-Spelling Shakespeare:—The Second Part of Henrie the Fourth. Parts I. and II. (Edited by F. J. Furnivall). Chatto and Windus. 2*s.* 6*d.* net each.
The History of her Foundations (Sister Agnes Mason). Cambridge: At the University Press. 4*s.* 6*d.* net.
The Merrie Tales of Jacques Tournebroche (Anatole France). Lane. 6*s.*

School Books

An English Course for Evening Students (Frank J. Adkins). Swan Sonnenschein. 3*s.* 6*d.*
The Ruskin Nature Reader (Edited by G. R. Bennett). Dent. 1*s.* 6*d.* net.
Black's Literary Readers (Edited by John Finnemore). Black. 1*s.* 6*d.*

Theology

The Holy Spirit in the New Testament (Henry Barclay Swete). Macmillan. 8*s.* 6*d.* net.
The Soul of St. Paul (A. L. Lilly). Griffiths. 3*s.* 6*d.* net.
The Apocalypse (Rev. J. J. Scott). Murray. 3*s.* 6*d.* net.
Our Bible Text (Rev. W. O. E. Oesterley). Skeffington. 2*s.* net.
The Gospel of Reconciliation or At-one-ment (Rev. W. L. Walker). Edinburgh: Clark. 5*s.*

Travel

Travels with a Donkey in the Cevennes (Robert Louis Stevenson). 7*s.* 6*d.* *net*; The Colour of Rome (Olave Muriel Potter), 20*s.* net. Chatto and Windus.
Rome (Edward Hutton). Methuen. 6*s.*
Home Life in Ireland (Robert Lynd). Mills and Boon. 8*s.* net.
A Scamper through the Far East (Major Herbert H. Austin). Arnold. 15*s.* net.
A Military Consul in Turkey (Captain A. F. Townshend). Seeley. 16*s.* net.
Bosnia and Herzegovina (Maude M. Holbach). Lane. 5*s.* net.
Cathedral Cities of Spain (W. W. Collins). Heinemann. 16*s.* net.

(*Continued on page* 454.)

Rudyard Kipling's New Book
Actions & Reactions

IN THREE EDITIONS.

1. Uniform Edition: Scarlet cloth, extra crown 8vo. 6s.
2. Pocket Edition: India paper, limp leather, fcap. 8vo. 5s. net.
3. Edition de Luxe (limited to 775 copies): Hand-made paper, sateen cloth, 8vo. 10s. 6d. net.

Highways and Byways in Middlesex. By WALTER JERROLD. With Illustrations by HUGH THOMSON, and a Map. Extra crown 8vo. gilt top, 6s. [*Tuesday.*

TWO BEAUTIFUL COLOUR BOOKS.

The Water Babies. By CHARLES KINGSLEY. With 32 Illustrations in Colour by WARWICK GOBLE. Crown 4to. 15s. net. Also an Edition de Luxe, printed on Hand-made Paper and limited to 250 copies. Demy 4to. 42s. net. [*Next week.*

The Forest Lovers. By MAURICE HEWLETT. With 16 Illustrations in Colour by A. S. HARTRICK. 8vo. 5s. net. [*Tuesday.*

The New New York. A Commentary on the Place and the People. By JOHN C. VAN DYKE. Illustrated by JOSEPH PENNELL. 8vo. 17s. net.

BISHOP WESTCOTT.

The Two Empires: the Church and the World. Being Lectures on Early Church History. By BROOKE FOSS WESTCOTT, D.D., late Bishop of Durham. Crown 8vo. 6s.

Early Church History to A.D. 313. By Professor HENRY MELVILL GWATKIN, Author of "Selections from Early Writers Illustrative of Church History to the Time of Constantine." 2 vols. 8vo. 17s. net.

NEW 6s. NOVELS.

Open Country. **Maurice Hewlett.**
Stradella. **F. M. Crawford.**
An Old Italian love tale.
The Key of the Unknown. **Rosa N. Carey.**

A Latin Anthology. With Photogravure Frontispiece. Pott 8vo. 2s. 6d. net. Limp leather, full gilt back and gilt edge. 3s. 6d. net. [GOLDEN TREASURY SERIES.

MACMILLAN & CO., LTD., LONDON.

THE ENGLISH REVIEW.

MONTHLY. **OCTOBER.** **2s. 6d.**

Four Cartoons by MAX BEERBOHM.

1. MODERN POETRY ... ... ARNOLD BENNETT. RACHEL ANNAND TAYLOR. ALFRED E. RANDALL. EZRA POUND.
2. EDWARD HUTTON ... ... THE CHURCH IN LUCINA'S HOUSE.
3. ANNE DOUGLAS SEDGWICK ... THE NEST.
4. ELIZABETH MARTINDALE ... TWO ESSAYS.
5. S. PEREZ TRIANA .. .. DON MARCELINO.
6. MAX BEERBOHM ... ... FOUR STUDIES.
7. C. F. KEARY ... ... THE ANTIQUARY.
8. FORD MADOX HÜEFFER ... ... A CALL.—3.
9. THE MONTH: EDITORIAL... ... ... THE CRITICAL ATTITUDE—ENGLISH LITERATURE OF TO-DAY.
10. SIR CHARLES W. DILKE, BT., M.P. FOREIGN AFFAIRS.
11. SIDNEY WEBB ... ... THE ECONOMIC ASPECTS OF POOR LAW REFORM.
12. M.P. ... ... THE POLICY OF THE GOVERNMENT.
13. W. T. GOODE ... ... THE PRESENT MOMENT IN SPAIN.
14. J. A. HOBSON ... ... THE TASK OF REALISM.
15. W.G. ... ... REVIEW—THE PLACE OF HISTORY IN EDUCATION.

Subscription: One Year, 30s.; Three Months, 7s. 6d.

CHAPMAN & HALL, Ltd., 11 Henrietta Street, London.

MR. MURRAY'S NEW BOOKS.

BYRON: THE LAST PHASE. By RICHARD EDGCUMBE. Demy 8vo. 10s. 6d. net.

THE LIFE OF SIR WILLIAM BROADBENT, Bart., F.R.S., K.C.V.O. A Short Record of His Life, told mainly in his own Letters, showing the early struggles which led up to a successful professional career, and giving an example of determined and high-minded perseverance in the face of difficulties. Edited by his Daughter, Miss BROADBENT. With Portraits. Demy 8vo. 10s. 6d. net.

LETTERS FROM THE PENINSULA (1808-1812). By Lieut.-General Sir WILLIAM WARRE, C.B., K.T.S. Edited by his Nephew, the Rev. EDMOND WARRE, D.D., C.B., M.V.O. With a Portrait and Map. Demy 8vo. 10s. 6d. net. [*Ready next week.*

INTERNATIONAL LAW. By T. BATY, D.C.L. (Oxon.), LL.D. (Camb.), of the Inner Temple, Barrister-at-Law. Demy 8vo. 10s. 6d. net.

A New Novel by AGNES and EGERTON CASTLE.
DIAMOND CUT PASTE.
6s.

A New Novel by EDEN PHILLPOTTS.
THE HAVEN.
6s.

A New Novel by MAUDE GOLDRING.
THE TENANTS OF PIXY FARM.
6s.

JOHN MURRAY, Albemarle Street, W.

RE-APPEARANCE OF

"THE THRUSH"

A MONTHLY PERIODICAL FOR THE PUBLICATION OF ORIGINAL POETRY,

DECEMBER 1st, 1909.

New Feature—Literary Articles on All Subjects.

CONTRIBUTIONS (which will be paid for) should be addressed to

THE EDITOR, "THE THRUSH" OFFICE, 12 & 13 Henrietta Street, Covent Garden, W.C.

WHO WAS SWEDENBORG?

A Lecture on **EMANUEL SWEDENBORG: HIS LIFE AND CHARACTER,** will be sent **free and post free** to all applicants on their sending their names and addresses to the SECRETARY OF THE SWEDENBORG SOCIETY, 1 BLOOMSBURY STREET, LONDON, W.C.

Pp. x+492. Price 7s. 6d. net.
THE MORPHIA HABIT AND ITS VOLUNTARY RENUNCIATION.
By OSCAR JENNINGS, M.D. (Paris).
London: BAILLIÈRE, TINDALL & COX, 8 Henrietta St., Covent Garden.

The Sorrows of Ireland.

By "PAT." 1s. net.

THE WEST STRAND PUBLISHING COMPANY, LTD., 10 King Street, Covent Garden, W.C.

THIS WEEK'S BOOKS—*Continued.*

VERSE

Poems for Travellers (Mary R. Dubar); The Poetic Old World (Lucy H. Humphrey). Bell. 5*s.* net each.
The Tragedy of Nan and other Plays (John Masefield). Grant Richards. 3*s.* 6*d.* net.
The Poetry of Nature (Selected by Henry Van Dyke). Heinemann. 6*s.* net.
The World's Triumph (Louis James Block). Philadelphia: Lippincott. 5*s.* net.
The Scarlet Gown (R. F. Murray). Glasgow: MacLehose. 2*s.* 6*d.* net.

MISCELLANEOUS

Annual of the British School at Athens, The. No. XIV. Macmillan. 2*s.* net.
Book-Prices Current. Stock. 25*s.* 6*d.*
British Year-Book of Agriculture, 1909-10, The. Vinton. 5*s.* net.
British Mountain Climbs (George D. Abraham), 7*s.* 6*d.* net; Auction Bridge (Archibald Dunn), 5*s.* net. Mills and Boon.
Family Names and their Story (S. Baring-Gould). Seeley. 7*s.* 6*d.* net.
Fascinated Child, The (Edited by Basil Mathews). Jarrold. 2*s.* 6*d.* net.
History Sheet or Case-Paper System, The (Henry F. Aveling). King. 2*s.* net.
Masques and Phases (Robert Ross). Humphreys. 5*s.* net.
Morphia Habit, The, and its Voluntary Renunciation (Oscar Jennings). Baillière, Tindall and Cox. 7*s.* 6*d.* net.
Religion of H. G. Wells, The, and other Essays (Rev. Alexander H. Crauford). Fisher Unwin. 3*s.* 6*d.* net.
Romance of Symbolism, The (Sidney Heath). Griffiths. 7*s.* 6*d.* net.
Schoolboys and School Work (Rev. the Hon. E. Lyttelton). Longmans, Green. 3*s.* 6*d.*
Short Masonic History, A (Frederick Armitage). Weare. 4*s.* 6*d.* net.
Story of the Electric Organ (J. W. Hinton). Simpkin, Marshall. 5*s.* net.
Ten Great and Good Men (Henry Montagu Butler), 6*s.*; Ten Years of Game-keeping (Owen Jones), 10*s.* 6*d.* net. Arnold.
Yet Again (Max Beerbohm). Chapman and Hall. 5*s.* net.

REVIEWS AND MAGAZINES FOR OCTOBER.—Revue des Deux Mondes, 3*fr.*; The Englishwoman, 1*s.*; The Financial Review of Reviews, 1*s.*; The Antiquary, 6*d.*; The Asiatic Quarterly Review. 5*s.*; The Musical Times, 4*d.*; The Geographical Journal, 2*s.*; The Hibbert Journal, 2*s.* 6*d.*; The Country Home, 6*d.*; The East and the West, 1*s.*; The Humane Review, 1*s.*; The Church Quarterly Review, 3*s.*

NOTICE.

The Terms of Subscription to the SATURDAY REVIEW are:—

	United Kingdom. £ s. d.	Abroad. £ s. d.
One Year	1 8 2 ...	... 1 10 4
Half Year	0 14 1 ...	... 0 15 2
Quarter Year ...	0 7 1 ...	... 0 7 7

Cheques and Money Orders should be crossed and made payable to the Manager, SATURDAY REVIEW Offices, 10 *King Street, Covent Garden, London, W.C.*

NOW READY. PRICE, SIXPENCE NET. — **THE FIRST NUMBER OF** — **NOW READY. PRICE, SIXPENCE NET.**

THE RE-UNION MAGAZINE.

"Comprehension, not Compromise."

Conducted from a sound Anglican standpoint, this Magazine aims at advancing the cause of the re-union of Christendom by the propagation of ideas, the formation of public opinion, and the free discussion of various divergent points of view. A very strong list of contributors and supporters has been obtained, including representative men in the Anglican, Roman and Greek Communions, and the Church of Scotland, as well as prominent Nonconformists.

Among the contributors to and supporters of the magazine are the Archbishop of Melbourne, the Bishops of London, Gloucester, Aberdeen and Orkney, Thetford, Northern and Central Europe, Madagascar, and Harrisburg, Archdeacon Cunningham, Canon Randolph, Canon Erskine Hill, the Duke of Newcastle, Earl Nelson, Viscount Halifax, Professor Dr. Cooper, Professor White, and many others.

Among the Special Articles are:—

Re-Union: An Anglican's Point of View. By Rev. R. F. BOROUGH.

The Ecclesiastical Position in Scotland.—I. By F. C. EELES.

Comprehension, not Compromise: A Congregationalist's Interpretation. By ARTHUR C. TURBERVILLE.

Russia: A Christianising Power. By The Lord Bishop of Northern and Central Europe.

A Monastery of Intellect. By RAYMOND BLATHWAYT.

Mixed Marriages. By STEPHEN GASELEE.

A French Point of View. By MAURICE LEGENDRE.

At What Shall We Aim? By BISHOP VERNON HERFORD.

The Outlook for Re-Union in the United States. By Dr. CALBRAITH BOURN PERRY.

The Invisible Church of Christ. By HAROLD BAYLEY.

Wanted: An Anglican Order of Jesuits. By Rev. FORBES PHILLIPS.

The Central Board of Missions. By the Archdeacon of Chester.

THE RE-UNION MAGAZINE.

THE RE-UNION MAGAZINE can be supplied by all newsagents and booksellers, price **6d.** net. In case of any difficulty the Publishers (address below) will send post free to any part of the world for **7½d.** per copy. The annual subscription (12 numbers) is **8s. 6d.** post free to any part of the world. Address the Publishers: THE RE-UNION MAGAZINE, 16 CLIFFORD'S INN, LONDON, E.C.

If you want to know all about the AUTUMN NEW BOOKS just get ***THE BOOK MONTHLY*** for October, which only costs 6d., and is beautifully illustrated.

Publishers:
SIMPKIN, MARSHALL & CO.,
Stationers' Hall Court, London, E.C.

THINGS JAPANESE,

Political, Commercial, and Social, are of great interest to many business men in Great Britain. The latest Political News, the best Commercial Information, and the most interesting General News and Special Articles appear in the

JAPAN WEEKLY CHRONICLE,

Published in Kobe every Thursday, and delivered in England by post, viâ Siberia, in 17 days. The *Japan Weekly Chronicle* consists of 42 pages, slightly larger than those of the *Saturday Review*, and is published at 25 sen per copy (6d.). Post free for 12 months, Yen 13 (26s). Subscriptions and advertisements received at the London Office, 131 Fleet Street, E.C.

Sport Society Drama — **THE BYSTANDER** — Politics Literature Fiction

SIXPENCE. Every Tuesday.

THE BEST OF THE LIGHT ILLUSTRATED WEEKLIES.
A PICTORIAL RECORD OF THE WEEK'S DOINGS.

TERSE AND TRUTHFUL CRITICISM.
"WORLDLY" SHORT STORIES.
SPORT: a Speciality. GOLF, HUNTING, LAWN TENNIS.

⁂ You do not only glance at "THE BYSTANDER," you READ it. It is Unique, Sparkling, Daring, Original.

Published by the Proprietors of the "GRAPHIC," Tallis House, Tallis Street, E.C.

Price 1/- net.

Inferences at Bridge

By W. DALTON,
Author of "'SATURDAY' BRIDGE."

"Card players will find in its chapters an admirable whetstone for sharpening their wits."—*Nottingham Guardian.*

"As good a Bridge Manual as we have seen."—*Glasgow Herald.*

"Sure to be a favourite with readers who wish to perfect themselves in the refinements of this fashionable game."—*Scotsman.*

"A study of this little treatise will improve the play of a good many people who think they are competent."—*Athenæum.*

"Inferences at Bridge" appeared in the SATURDAY REVIEW. The articles have been revised, with additions by the author, and are issued in handy form by
THE WEST STRAND PUBLISHING CO., LTD.,
10 King Street, Covent Garden, W.C.

Printed for the Proprietors by SPOTTISWOODE & Co. LTD., 5 New-street Square, E.C., and Published by REGINALD WEBSTER PAGE, at the Office, 10 King Street, Covent Garden, in the Parish of St. Paul, in the County of London.—*Saturday*, 9 *October*, 1909.

THE

SATURDAY REVIEW

OF

POLITICS, LITERATURE, SCIENCE, AND ART.

No. 2,816 Vol. 108. 16 October 1909. [REGISTERED AS A NEWSPAPER.] 6*d*.

CONTENTS.

NOTES OF THE WEEK.

Lord Lansdowne and Mr. Balfour have been to see the King after all, Mr. Asquith following immediately. Of course the newspapers know all about what was said and why the meeting took place; but nobody marks them. It is hard to tell whether the "Times" article is meant to be a lecture to the King, whom it alternately patronises and beslavers, for interfering with politics, or a censure on Mr. Asquith for dragging him in. The "Times" had better leave alone what it evidently knows nothing about. Mr. Asquith would know what to do in a matter of this kind. Some sort of settlement would naturally suit Mr. Asquith better than fighting out the Budget in a general election. If the Liberals should lose, Mr. Asquith will be out of power; if they should win on the Budget, Mr. Lloyd George will be cock of the walk and Mr. Asquith's position be made impossible. Hence Mr. George's violence at Newcastle.

He is reported by one of his admirers to have said that he intended at Newcastle to out-Limehouse his Limehouse speech. As this was his standard, it is explained how the Newcastle speech was just what it was. But in the interval he had learned partial discretion. He took care at Newcastle to avoid slandering particular persons by name, and you may slander a class, as he is quite well aware, with impunity. This was the line he took at Newcastle. Both he and the Lord Advocate have discovered that lies and exaggerations, when coupled with names, are too easily identified and disproved, and the calumniator shown to be mean and malicious. When Mr. Lloyd George shows on the face of his speech that he has made up his mind to practise this sort of pettifogging cunning, he cannot wonder that his profession of Welsh lawyer has rather struck the public imagination.

After his speech, how are the Government going to say that the Budget is not a socialistic Budget? They cannot deny at any rate that their Chancellor talks socialism. What was all that nonsense about the landowners not having made the land, nor the mineowners the minerals, but Lloyd George playing at Henry George? True it is the primitive socialism of the uneducated; instructed socialists do not talk such crude stuff. Still, it is socialism, for it means abolishing individual property under pretence of a divine law. Naturally a paper like the socialist "Vorwärts" derides our Chancellor as claiming the whole in principle but only daring to take twenty per cent. in practice. But this sort of predaceous piety makes good electioneering. Gladstone knew it, and if Lloyd George has not Gladstone's art he has all, and more than all, his demagogy.

This speech has made it impossible for any wavering Unionist Free-trader to doubt as to his duty. Lord Hugh Cecil, in his speech at Manchester on Wednesday, defined the position even more precisely than in his recent letter. As between the dangers inherent in the socialistic Budget and the risks involved in Tariff Reform there can be no choice. The slippery slope of Protection, said Lord Hugh, is not such a steep and slippery slope as the alterations proposed in the very foundations of property. Unionist Free-traders are not prepared to be further exploited for the benefit of Lloyd-Georgism. Of course Lord Hugh does not agree with Lord Rosebery, Mr. Balfour and Mr. Asquith that Tariff Reform is the only alternative to the Budget. Of one thing, however, he may be sure. Whatever be the case to-day, if the Finance Bill became law the capital interest of the country will be hit so hard that Tariff Reform alone could save the business of the country.

Sir Edward Carson at Liverpool spoke of Mr. Lloyd George and his speech with the same freedom of personal invective that Mr. Lloyd George allows himself against the "Dukes." But after all, the Chancellor began it. If the "Welsh attorney" sees all the wickedness of Toryism embodied in Dukes, Lloyd George is a convenient symbol for everything that is outrageous in Liberalism. It is a plain fact in the present situation, as Sir Edward said, that when the baser work of stirring up passion is to be done, Mr. Asquith keeps in the background and Mr. Lloyd George comes to the front.

Mr. Snowden is not feeling happy about the House of Lords. He has apparently been reading a little history, and has no faith left in Liberal agitation. The present Radical outcry is so ancient a thing, and Demos has never come a bit the nearer to his own. It is surely a pretty state of affairs when a Minister goes upon a long journey without his dinner, when there are secret conclaves and mysterious calls, with Demos left in the cold, fobbed off with rumour. This does not look as if the Lords were as negligible as they should be, and these Liberals seem to be tacitly according them a place in the Constitution. Liberals had better be careful, is the inference. There is an old saying about the upper and nether millstones. Is the Liberal party of any real use to anybody?

The Bermondsey Conservatives, or rather the local Conservative association, have pinned their faith on a local man, in fact a local of the locals. It is true that in such parts local familiarity is a real force. We hope Mr. Dumphries will prove equal to his undertaking. If he wins the seat, he need not speak much in the House, after all. There could hardly be a more important election. One thing is quite certain. The Liberal will not get in. Mr. Lloyd George and Mr. Churchill have been playing with the social democrats, and now they have got their return for it. The socialists are making sure that in any case a Liberal shall not win.

The House of Lords had a good many objections to make to the Development Bill, but they gave it its second reading on Thursday. Nor does it seem likely that in Committee anything will happen to affect seriously the passing of the Bill. But to found on the good will shown to the principle of the Government's measure any speculation as to the intentions of the Lords on the Budget, as the Liberals are doing, is one of the silliest of all the rumours. The Bill, it is true, depends on the provisions for grants made in the Budget, but there is too great a disparity between such a small bribe and such a big object. Lord Carrington did point out that the grants for the benefit of agriculture were to do work now done by the great landlords. This is worth noting, as a commentary on Mr. Lloyd George's speeches, as well as the confession that the grant will redress the "somewhat heavy death duties". But altogether the bait is too small to make the Lords take the Budget.

The latest tame bear in the Irish National Show has quite failed to draw, and "Captain" O'Meagher Condon, the professional "martyr", is withdrawn after a very short run, notwithstanding the "profound impression" which Mr. Dillon was going to make with him on "British statesmen and the British public". Mr. Dillon never did realise a situation, and honest men will wish his showmanship to continue. The success of Mr. Parnell was due largely to his keeping Mr. Dillon quiet and preventing him from saying the wrong thing, but there is no such restraint now. In various parts of Ireland leading Nationalists have resented the attempt to squeeze more money out of them by the martyrdom trick. At Limerick a strong patriot said: "I am not here except to do honour to Captain Condon. I did not come here to get a lecture on the benefits obtained through the Irish Parliamentary party, for I know what they do for the country—a gang of robbers". At Claremorris a strong patriot said: "I protest against this council presenting an address to men who have come over from America like a Buffalo Bill circus, and are being shown round by Mr. J. Redmond and Mr. Joe Devlin". Things began to look bad for the show. The advance agents read the signs, and the "martyr" was taken off the bill.

All this is very sad, and the ghost walking so lame. What can "the Cause" do now? Time has lessened the number of first-class "martyrs", even if they were not objectionable, and there is not another sensation in view that has any money in it. We have followed Mr. Redmond's oratorical flutter on the Radical platforms, and can find his traditional "no far-distant date" nowhere in it. For more than a generation the "no far-distant date", eloquently mounted, could always catch American dollars; but after thirty years of it, and the "date" more distant than ever, even the Connaught emigrants in the American kitchen grow weary if not suspicious.

How will Mr. T. P. O'Connor be able to face the American rebels with Mr. Redmond on the party platforms of the "brutal Saxon" and the Leaguers of Longford recommending him for the House of Lords? The purse is very low, and that is always the measure of "the Cause". Here is an idea! Take a life-sized figure of "Molly Maguire", in a green sash and Emmett breeches. Let Mr. Joe Devlin keep the door, at a dollar a fool, and let Mr. Redmond hold forth on Molly, showing how, in her day, she cultivated "Irish public opinion" by putting those who could not agree with her to ride naked on a saddle set with "thorns or the bristles of a hedgehog". It might not make the "date" less "distant", but it would fill the purse, a matter so much more important than Home Rule.

Señor Ferrer has paid the extreme penalty for his mischief-making, mischief that meant, as he very well knew it must, loss of life. He who attempts to upset the existing order by violent revolution must expect to forfeit his life if he fails. He appears to have been fairly and fully tried. The demonstrations of sympathy and indignation on the Continent are misplaced. It is significant that these demonstrations in Paris took the form of violent attacks, with bloodshed, on the police. Evidently it is thought that the most fitting tribute to Señor Ferrer's memory is an outbreak against common order. The French Government have been commendably prompt in putting down the rioters. In Spain itself public opinion evidently regards the execution as necessary. This should satisfy foreigners, whom the matter concerns far less than the Spanish.

M. Briand has been to Périgueux, but no one is any the wiser. His speech was a splendidly articulated speech. His utterance was as clear as his message was indistinct. M. Briand has in fact passed along the road trodden by many of his predecessors. In youth his ideas were simple and few, as befitted a son of the Revolution. Since then he has been gradually educated into the vagueness that assails a certain type of mind when confronted with more than one side of a question. Fortunately he retains his beautiful voice, and that gift of generalisation which has never deserted a French statesman in his hour of need. Modern French politics may be resolved into a convenient formula: they are a battle of the young who generalise clearly from one idea with the mature who generalise vaguely from a sense of confusion.

Who can take the idea of a Chinese parliament seriously? The old Empress decreed that China should have constitutional government, and several edicts followed. Apparently they have been really holding elections for provincial councils, which are shortly to meet. Either way they are to have no power: they are to deliberate, to talk, but they are to do nothing. Would it not be better if, instead of playing at parliament, the Imperial Government straightened out its finances, and saw about paying officials a decent salary so that they need not have to squeeze to live?

Indiscretion seems to be the better part of official reticence. So think General d'Amade and Mr. Crane, the American Minister at Peking. Patriotism has its claims, and, though it may lead the patriot into hasty speech entirely to the detriment of his country's dignity or welfare, it is none the less patriotism, and not at all disgraceful. France has managed her little affair quite creditably. Spain will be pleased, because General d'Amade has been rusticated; General d'Amade will enjoy his holiday with a feeling that at any rate he has relieved himself and earned the esteem of all true-hearted Frenchmen. America is more severe upon her no less deserving son. Mr. Crane's diplomatic rustication is likely to last some time.

Did Mr. Harriman, who, it appears, has left the wonderful fortune of about fifty-three million pounds, ever—shall we say?—feel like it? The papers speak of his accumulations; but really that conjures up wrongly the picture of the old-fashioned miser who really did accumulate, and found in so doing what is now recognised as the pleasure attending a certain kind of insanity. His heaping-up was the heaping-up of power in the sort of enterprises that make such men the real masters of their country. It is unfortunate for them that their ambitions cannot be more varied; but this is the fault of their country, which turns its best organising brains into magnified company promoters, and its inferior men into politicians. We wonder whether some day an American will say to himself: "Why, I guess with £50,000,000 I can found a dynasty".

Again for another year the Law Courts have begun their sittings, and for many months the judges will be busy demonstrating the already well-proved fact that they are too few to do the work laid out for them. Lord Loreburn must sigh as he thinks how impossible it will be in the future as it has been in the past to get justice done as speedily as he has said it ought to be done. It would be otherwise if the Government to which he belongs had chosen to reform the Courts instead of planning to destroy them by a revolution. Consistently with their usual policy of offering people what they do not want, instead of making more High Court judges they proposed to let the High Court and the Bar go to decay and apply artificial culture to the County Courts. The House of Lords fortunately stopped that, and so we shall have to wait for a Conservative Government to give the High Court the judges it needs.

In the short time the Courts have been sitting, several interesting cases have been heard. The feeding of famished suffragettes is still on the legal merits sub judice, except as to the Home Secretary. No summons is to be issued against him, and this takes all the savour out of the case for the suffragettes. They will not care a hatpin about the governor and the doctor. The real point at issue—the legal power to feed prisoners starving themselves—will be settled just as well without Mr. Gladstone as with him. But the dear ladies wanted to show that his was the hand that fed them in order that they might bite it.

Mr. Gladstone has struck at the very root of the Suffrage movement by his decision that no more information shall be given to the press as to what takes place in the prison cell. If the women who are sent to gaol for disturbing the peace choose to starve themselves, or to resist forcible feeding, they will at least no longer enjoy the compensation of a free advertisement. The whole spirit will be taken out of their self-imposed sufferings when notoriety is not the instant reward. Very naïve is the protest made by Lady Constance Lytton and others whom the Home Secretary has released against their will. Why should they throw stones at motor cars and the windows of houses and not enjoy the pains and indignities that other women have to endure? Liberty is really harder to bear in such circumstances than prison fare itself.

A bit of Government sharp practice wants exposing. It is very well to provide Mr. Churchill with a chance to make up for time lost this session, but not at the expense of serious busines interests. The Assurance Companies Bill, having passed the Lords, was sent to the Commons; but it was never intended that so important a Bill should be run through the Commons at the fag-end of this wearying session. Suddenly the Government announce that they are going to do this, just to fill up the interval while the Finance Bill is in the Lords. The consequence is that many of the insurance companies are taken by surprise. They are not to have the time and opportunity they expected to examine a measure, substantially altered in the Lords, which affects their interests widely, and in some respects injuriously.

Take one instance. The Bill favours foreign re-insurance companies at the expense of British. Some of the biggest insurance companies do their re-insurance business (the sharing of their own risks) with foreign offices. Indeed, they pay two million pounds per annum to foreign re-insurance companies in respect of property insured in the United Kingdom. They do this in the ordinary spirit of trade jealousy. They grudge sharing their business with their English rivals lest they should take their custom away. This class of business is encouraged by the Bill. Under the present law only life offices have to deposit £20,000. By this Bill the deposit will have to be made by every insurance society —life, fire, accident, or employers' liability. It will put an end to many of the offices registered in the United Kingdom who have been doing re-insurance business in other branches than life assurance. Their business will all be taken by the foreign offices, and so the foreign insurance business will be encouraged to the detriment of British.

These foreign offices have no restrictions placed on them by the Bill. They are free from all obligation to make deposits with the Board of Trade as security for the business they transact in the United Kingdom, though their assets are in foreign countries. Compare this with the conditions imposed by the British Colonies and the United States of America, Japan, and other countries, all of which require that the largest of British offices should make very large deposits with their Government before they can underwrite a single risk in any of these foreign countries. British offices ought not to be allowed to place their re-insurance business abroad unless the foreign offices are put on the same footing as the British.

The police have beaten the Automobile Association in the fight about motor traps. Three Judges have decided that the police were obstructed in their duty by a "scout" of the Association who signalled to motorists that they were near a "control" tract set and watched by the police. The scout said he was really assisting the police in preventing the law being broken. No doubt he smiled at his joke, as the Judges did and other people will. There was evidence in the case that before the trap was reached the cars were going above the limit; but the police were bound to corroborate this evidence. By signalling the scout prevented them, and this was the obstruction. But a motorist who just tells a friend of a trap need not fear he is obstructing. The decision goes far enough and not too far.

Events among the flying men have not been going smoothly during the week. It would be unfair to the Aero Club to refer to its dispute with the promoters of the Doncaster meeting as a squabble, for the Aero Club is not squabbling with anybody. The Aero Club is the representative in Great Britain of the International Aeronautical Federation. What authority it has it derives from that fact, and it is not over-stepping that authority. Rightly enough, it says to Doncaster: Fly if you like; but if you persist in flying despite our recommendation not to do so, then we do not recognise you, and your competitors will find themselves disqualified for future competition under our rules. That is straightforward enough, and in the best interests of the flying men themselves. The new art is highly technical, and requires strict organisation under men with special knowledge. There is only one existing body that can give it this necessary direction, and that is an international body. The representative of that body in Great Britain is the Aero Club.

The fact is that Doncaster is just a financial speculation, and it is in danger of landing the speculators into an unpleasant place. Flying machines are a popular form of excitement just now, and there is a great hurry to make a good thing out of them before the slump sets in. Few of the meetings hitherto have been well planned or thoughtfully executed. Boulogne was a failure; Doncaster is laying bare the speculative skeleton beneath the flesh of high endeavour; Juvisy has revealed a lack of imaginative forethought unparalleled even in the annals of a French railway. It is to be hoped that this phase in the history of the art will soon be completed; that crowds will cease to assemble for a spectacle; that the excited amateur will in the interests of science be eliminated. As things are, we can only wish the International Aeronautical Federation well in its endeavour to bring some sort of discipline into things.

The Polar comedy improves. Commander Peary has proved Dr. Cook to be an impostor out of the mouths of Dr. Cook's Esquimos. But Dr. Cook, it seems, instructed these Esquimos to be discreet in their revelations. They were not to tell Commander Peary about that trip to the Pole. Their discretion must have exceeded the wildest anticipations of Dr. Cook. Surely the calm smile, of which the Press seems to be a little tired, was quite warrantable in the circumstances. The Esquimos came out of it well. Dr. Cook is profoundly touched by their loyal obedience to his instructions. Commander Peary believes all they say. Between them they will turn the heads of these poor boys. We are not informed, by the way, whether the public appearance of Mr. Barrille was received by Dr. Cook with or without the smile. The moral of the whole comedy seems to be this: when one goes exploring with the intention of getting there at all costs, it is advisable either to pay one's guides well, or to make away with them.

A society that calls itself by the portentous name of League of Progressive Thought and Social Service has been holding some meetings this week. Mr. Shaw was amusing in his way. Mr. Caine was equally amusing in his. These two writers and thinkers have much in common. Both take themselves very seriously (we prefer Mr. Shaw's way of doing it). Both are keen social reformers. Neither believes in Mr. Redford. We are glad that they have recognised their affinity. Now that we have a book by Caine with an introduction by Shaw, we may live in hopes of a book by Shaw with an introduction by Caine.

The issue between the "Westminster Gazette" and Mr. George Edwardes is much more than a private matter between the two parties. One's first impression on reading the correspondence published is wonder that the "Westminster" should adopt something of a deprecatory or even apologetic tone in answer to Mr. Edwardes. So far from having anything to apologise for, the "Westminster" had the strongest ground for extreme resentment. Because it did not give unqualified praise to a play he brought out, Mr. Edwardes immediately threatened the "Westminster" with the withdrawal of his advertisements. This is an attempt to influence a newspaper's criticism, or rather notices, by absolutely illegitimate means. It might be described by an uglier name. Such action should be met with determination by the whole press. It is a deliberate suggestion that newspapers should put in a favourable notice in order to get an advertisement.

THE LLOYD GEORGE STYLE.

MR. LLOYD GEORGE is a lawyer, and so is aware of the various defences to an action for slander. In his platform speeches he is careful not to preclude himself from pleading one in particular—"vulgar abuse". Should any of his friends the landlords bring an action for slander against Mr. George in respect of any of the pretty things he is so fond of saying of them, he would doubtless plead that he never said it, and "if he did, it was mere vulgar abuse". In that he would say truly. And this defence would be all the happier that while it would save him from paying damages to the landlord, mere vulgar abuse being a thing not to be taken seriously, not a charge that can be assessed in damages, his unsophisticated hearers, working laymen, would take it entirely seriously, and fully believe that a grave and damaging charge had been made, and in much the same language they would use amongst themselves. Mr. Lloyd George is not a lawyer for nothing. How different this platform flinger of mud from the sucking dove in the House! Abuse is not needed as a reserve defence for things said in Parliament, which are privileged, and would not tell with members who are not quite ignorant enough to believe them.

Really one cannot help feeling that it might be well worth while for the country to petition the King—this would hardly be dragging his Majesty into political controversy—to make Mr. Lloyd George a peer, Parliament voting him two or three good landed estates with a palace apiece and a tidy rent-roll. Somehow or another, too, the entrée to his neighbours' houses both in London and the country would have to be secured. How much of this ranting against dukes and landlords should we hear then? One of the most unpleasant characters of the extremely—disastrously—unpleasant style of political advocacy Mr. George is adopting is its obviously personal animus. There is a reserve, we will not say, of venom but certainly of malice about Mr. George's references to aristocrats and landowners that is plainly not political. It is the tone of a man who would destroy the thing he cannot attain. No doubt the itch in those who have not to ruin those who have, though they gain nothing by it themselves, is natural; but it is a nature that a Chancellor of the Exchequer should have schooled into submission. At any rate he ought not to parade it before the uneducated and inflame a most unlovely feeling. Mr. George is setting the worst possible example in political advocacy—we cannot say argument, for he never argues on the platform, though he tries to in the House. It is relapse into a mode that one hoped had rather died out. Mr. George looks about for a popular prejudice. "Who is unpopular?" he thinks. Is there any set of men whom people think badly of without knowing anything about them. "I have it", he says. "Dukes and landlords." So he proceeds to paint dukes and landlords blacker even than the Radical workman imagined them. In order that so black a figure can be seen at all he has to paint the poorer people who live round the duke—servants, tenants, and dissenting ministers—a dazzling white. The income of the rich is set side by side with the income of the poor without comment. Thoroughly successful and thoroughly dishonest advocacy! The trick is very easy—it has no subtlety—but happily few on either side in politics care to practise it. The play is easily trumped by a dishonest opponent—he need not be at all clever. As a matter of mere party tactics the Unionist leaders would doubtless have been wise to accept the land taxes without demur, and concentrate attack on the increase of the beer, spirit and tobacco duties. Mr. Ben Tillett has pointed out how this would have dished Mr. Lloyd George and put the working classes against him. He is quite right. The ground would have been cut from beneath Mr. George. He would have lost his outcry against landlords, the device which was to divert popular attention from the tobacco and beer duties. And it could have been done without hurting the average Unionist; for, after all, it is but a small minority of Conservatives that are owners of land. Unfortunately there is some honesty in politics, and Unionists have their modicum. Common honesty forbad their accepting taxes that were unjust to a particular class, unprofitable to the State, and socially and economically injurious. It was a choice between tactics and merits; and, foolish as it may appear, they preferred merits. At least they will come into court with clean hands. They have not swallowed principle for the sake of advantage. We need not claim for those whom these taxes would affect directly and adversely that they are opposing them on altruistic grounds; but the bulk of the party are. At any rate they are opposing them on public not on private grounds, to the disadvantage of the party in an election.

Mr. Lloyd George was very careful at Newcastle, as everywhere, not to go into the merits of his taxes. He wanted his audience to go away with one idea only, that the duke and the landlord were going to be made to smart. He did not show his working-class hearers how they would benefit if the landlords lost. By the present Budget working men pay a great deal more than they paid before. If the land taxes ultimately produce much, what relief from taxation working men would get would not appreciably affect their lives. If Mr. Lloyd George had taken pains to show them what they would gain, instead of what landlords would lose, there would have been disillusion indeed. It is the old story. The crowd are urged to pull something down on the vague promise that they will get their pickings out of the ruins. The thing is pulled down, and their pickings prove extremely meagre. It is not they who get the pickings, they discover; and after a time they become more wary. Old Liberalism was absorbed all the time in pulling down amid the applause of the multitude. But the day came when the working man discovered that he had got extraordinarily little out of the spoil of churches and landlords; and he turned to the Conservatives and social reform. There has not been much pulling down for now a good many years, and the multitude are beginning to forget their lesson. What is any relief from taxation the working man might get by heaping burdens on the land compared with a month's employment? How will spoiling landlords help an unemployed man to get work? These land taxes, with the death duties, will in the end break up the landed class; some, the dukes probably amongst them, will go on, though with difficulty; but the country gentleman as a class will gradually disappear. How will the closing of a country house and the migration of its owner and occupant from the country to London benefit the working classes? Mr. Lloyd George knows well enough that it will not; but he knows that these taxes can bring about the great social and political change he is aiming at.

It is strange that the collectivist does not see that Mr. Lloyd George is creating a most dangerous type of individualism. From the point of view of the employee, from the point of view of the State socialist, he is going for entirely the wrong men. One may admit—we at any rate frankly hold—that individuals may be too rich for the advantage of the community. We do not want Harrimans here. But the man who has his wealth mainly in land necessarily is the least dangerous of all rich men. He is largely immobile; his property is visible and tangible; if he does anything hurtful to the State, or fails to carry out his responsibilities, there is his property to come down upon. Through his land he can always be got at. The land is a constant hostage for his good behaviour. But on the landless rich man the State has no hold. He can go where he likes and live where he likes. He can enjoy his income without any regard to his neighbours or his country. If things look serious for him, he can invest in foreign securities and quit the jurisdiction. The sort of man Mr. Lloyd George seems to be so familiar with, the extremely rich commercial man, who, he says, abounds more in the Liberal than the Unionist party, is a potential danger to any community. His son is often more mischievous still, not being brought up to work and having no responsibilities. The aggregate wealth of such a man is more than that of the landed aristocrat and his command of cash infinitely greater. Yet the Radical Government would heap all the burden on the men with land. What vulgar ignorance is in Mr. Lloyd George's talk of men with two or three palaces and so many thousands of acres! Does he really suppose these palaces make it easier for their owners to pay heavy taxes? Does he not know that many of them, if they closed their palaces, could live an easier and a more luxurious life in London? We have in mind a family, the hereditary owners of one of the noblest houses in England architecturally and historically, whose income hardly exceeds the cost of repairs, and who live in a few rooms, a corner of the house, as it were, rather than sell it. No doubt to Mr. Lloyd George such people are blank fools; their fine sentiment would not be in his way. These with their palace and their park he would select for special taxation, while struggling Sir Christopher Furness he would let go free.

The socialists and the working classes generally will make a great mistake if they unlearn the lesson they learnt from the results of the old Liberal régime. They learnt that it was not the "swell" they had to fear, not the duke nor the bishop; but the commercial rich man who lived solely by the maxims of political economy and to whom every other man, and woman, was but a machine to make him money. He was a creation of Liberal economics, of Free Trade; hence Mr. George's tenderness for him in contrast to his spite against the Tory land-owning aristocrat.

THE BERMONDSEY ELECTION.

BERMONDSEY, like Byron, has suddenly awoke to find itself famous. In the same way Peckham two years ago, a South London constituency, whose very whereabouts was unknown to Fleet Street and Pall Mall, accidentally became the centre of the world's desire. The explorer who crosses London Bridge and walks due south will find himself in the heart of "the Borough", which is bounded on the east by Rotherhithe with its docks and wharves, and on the west by Blackfriars and the Stamford Street district. There is a dignity about decay; and Bermondsey is a victim of Free Trade, if ever there was one. It was once the centre of a flourishing leather-tanning industry, but most of its mills are now closed, having been ruined by the importation of American and Austrian leather. Yet, if Bermondsey tries to send its leather to the United States or the Continent, it is met by crushing duties of 60 and 70 per cent. The poor-rates have sometimes been as high as 11s. in the pound, nearly double that of the West End. You will find in Bermondsey a great many respectable poor, the most pathetic and in some ways the most admirable of all classes, whose struggle to keep in the path of honesty and decency is heroic. Of late years the manufacture of jam has to some extent taken the place of the tanning industry, and the celebrated Hop Exchange stands at the London Bridge end of the constituency. The Borough used to be a notorious resort of criminals, and, though modern improvements have cleared out some of these rookeries, there is still too large a proportion of the hereditary victims of crime and disease in the population to make Bermondsey the place one would choose for an evening's promenade.

Such is the arena of one of the most important political battles of modern times. The Unionist candidate, Mr. John Dumphreys, is emphatically a local champion. He is Bermondsey from the crown of his head to the sole of his feet. Until the last few years he was an actual working tanner, engaged for weekly wage in one of the leather mills of the district, with hands imbrued with the chemical process. But for thirty years he has been a public speaker, and he is now an old servant of the people. He has represented his beloved Borough on the London School Board, he has been twice Mayor of Bermondsey, and is still a Councillor. Like Cleon, of the same trade, his lungs are tough; and he is as much at home with a Bermondsey mob as the ordinary man is with his wife and children. It would be affectation to pretend that Mr. Dumphreys will add to the debating strength of the Conservative party in the House of Commons. But he is the best specimen of a Conservative working man that can be found, and if he does not win Bermondsey no one else can. For Mr. Dumphreys is not regarded by his fellow working men with that jealousy which is sometimes excited by elevation above their class—his character has protected him from that. He is fortunate, too, in his opponents. The Socialist candidate is too much of a doctrinaire, and deficient in brutality for the *rôle* he has chosen. The polished jokes and elaborate epigrams of the genial journalist who has been chosen to represent the almost defunct Liberal party are likely to miss their mark in the shops and yards and schoolrooms of Bermondsey. The betting is two to one on Mr. Dumphreys.

It is as certain as anything can be that we shall win Bermondsey—so certain that we almost wish there were not two opponents in the field, as the victory will thereby be deprived of some of its moral effect. Mr. Dumphreys will talk of nothing but tariff reform; indeed, he can talk of nothing else, for he knows no other subject. He has been preaching tariff reform for thirty years, and his return to the House of Commons will be a fitting reward of his life-long adherence to his creed through good and evil report. Twenty years ago "Jack Dumphreys" was regarded as the crack-brained advocate of a hopeless fallacy. In a fortnight's time he will be the member for Bermondsey on the tariff reform ticket. For what can his Socialist and Radical opponents say in answer to his "Si monumentum quæris, circumspice"? They have made a solitude of Bermondsey, and they call it Free Trade. What are these ridiculous land taxes, which cannot begin to be collected for three or four years, and which can never reach the Bermondsey ratepayer, to the man who pays to the rates an amount equal to half his rent, and who lives in daily expectation of his trade being ruined by dumping competitors? Then there is the question of closing a large number of public-houses in consequence of the new licence duties. In a poor district like Bermondsey the "pub" is very often the only place resembling a club to which the working man can resort. Unearned increment and undeveloped land duty must be empty, if not absolutely unmeaning, sounds to the ear of a dock labourer or a tanner. Except in their appeal to class-hatred, and to a vague cupidity, we cannot understand how the land taxes can be popular with the urban voters. They are, of course, told that the ground landlords are responsible for the rents which the middleman receives. But it ought not to be difficult to explain that land and houses, so long as they are subjects of ownership, must command their market value; and that laying taxes on land, which is the raw material of houses, is not likely to reduce rents. One other lie is certain to be thrust down their throats, namely, that if the Budget is rejected, old-age pensions will stop. It would be well, therefore, for Mr. Dumphreys and his friends to remember that nothing can stop old-age pensions but the repeal, by Parliament, of the Act which was passed last year. We regard this election as more critical for the party of tariff reform than any that has yet occurred.

BACK TO HOME RULE.

THE tameness of the Irish party in the present House of Commons has disappointed Nationalists in Ireland and checked the flow of subscriptions from the United States. But there can be no doubt that the Government would greatly prefer a series of scenes in the House to a single speech of the kind that Mr. Redmond delivered this week to the Liberals of Ashton-under-Lyne. It must be peculiarly annoying, when they are contending that the powers of the House of Lords can be destroyed without danger to the country, and should be swept away in the interests of the English poor, to be reminded that the Budget is by no means the only question that will be decided by the next General Election. Yet Mr. Redmond is so inconsiderate as to go on tour round Liberal as well as Labour meetings proclaiming that Home Rule is a live issue, that no Irish votes will be given to the Liberals except in return for a definite pledge of an immediate Home Rule Bill, and that the veto of the House of Lords must be destroyed because that House, and that House alone, stands in the way of Home Rule.

It is all perfectly true, of course, but that only makes the position worse for the Government, and increases the inconvenience of Mr. Redmond's frankness. So long as the Irish Nationalists confine themselves to fiction about events in Ireland no English Liberal resents their behaviour. When it comes to telling the truth about the political position in the British Isles at large, it must be hard to forgive. The one thing that had to be concealed was the fact that the Peers alone prevent the adoption of fundamental changes in the Constitution on which the genuine opinion of the electorate has not been taken. The argument as to the position of the Lords that appeals most to the average Englishman, of all the instances that can be adduced from our recent history, is the undeniable fact that the Upper House defeated Home Rule in 1893 and that the country, as soon as it was given the chance, enthusiastically endorsed the action of that House. In 1892 the electorate that returned Mr. Gladstone to power was influenced by many factors, of which the desire to break up the United Kingdom was by no means the strongest. But when the Commons had passed the Home Rule Bill the Lords insisted that, before it could be sanctioned, the electorate must be asked to say definitely whether they wished for it. As we all remember, the Liberals were afraid to appeal to the country on that particular issue. Their fears were justified when, in 1895, the constituencies crushed the Ministers who were identified with the Home Rule cause.

Since 1895 the primary object of Liberal tacticians has been to prevent England from paying attention to Home Rule, while assuring Ireland that the Union of Hearts was none the less sincere for having lost the exuberance of its first fine careless rapture. They were, in truth, as unable to be careless as they were—and are—unwilling to be rapturous. In 1906 we were assured that Home Rule was a bogey. For the South African War had shown Englishmen what are the real sentiments towards the British Empire of the Nationalists who purr contentedly about the supremacy of the Imperial Parliament over a mere Irish legislature when they speak on English platforms. Mr. Redmond might with fair safety have unveiled many memorials to the Irish rebels of 1798, claiming proudly that he stood for exactly the same cause as the United Irishmen of that year. The public in Great Britain does not read speeches delivered in Ireland, and, if it did, would not understand that the men whom Mr. Redmond has not only eulogised but claimed as his political ancestors, were those who a century ago sowed mutiny in our Navy and brought about civil war in the British Isles at the moment of England's greatest peril. But living Englishmen know and remember how the Nationalists, only nine years ago, gloried in Boer successes and vilified those Irishmen who were fighting under the Union Jack. Mr. Arthur Lynch is a member of Mr. Redmond's party, who dare not repudiate him because they dare not set themselves against the sentiment of sedition.

Though Home Rule was smothered in pigtails at the 1906 election, and though the Liberal majority was too huge to be dethroned by the Irish vote, the Government has not ventured to repudiate it. It is difficult to repudiate a cause which for twenty years one has been trying to invest with a quasi-religious mantle. Moreover, a great many earnest Radicals in the country have been taught by their leaders to believe in Home Rule, and the leaders cannot afford to shock the stalwarts who vote straight at every election, however conscious they may be that their prospect of victory depends on voters who are not hard-and-fast party men. Then again the Irish vote in Great Britain must not be alienated, and it has already availed to commit Mr. Churchill to a declaration which Mr. Asquith does not venture to cancel. That Mr. Churchill, of all Ministers, should have committed himself is very significant, since it is generally known that he, and not Mr. Birrell, would have been Chief Secretary for Ireland had not the Nationalists flatly refused to accept a man who had denounced them during the Boer War.

Mr. Churchill has no difficulty in swallowing principles; but it must have cost him an effort to suppress personal pique. The Liberals can hardly hope for a bare majority without Irish support in the constituencies, or for a working majority without an Irish alliance in the House.

It is true that the present Government, while giving academic approval to Home Rule (and incidentally proving themselves incapable of ruling Ireland), have not revived either of Mr. Gladstone's Home Rule Bills. But, if once more in power, they cannot enjoy immunity from the embodiment of their theories. Hitherto they could plead that a new Home Rule Bill would be immediately rejected by the Lords, and that to introduce one would be either to court a serious rebuff or to be driven to appeal to the country on an unpopular issue. Even so, Mr. Birrell's absurd Irish Councils Bill must inevitably—as we showed at the time—have laid the foundation of a Parliament in Dublin, and was secretly accepted by the Nationalist leaders because this was understood. The Nationalist rank and file rejected it contemptuously, because the politicians had promised to secure a sweeping measure; they refused to honour their leaders' secret agreement with the Government to accept a shilling in the pound on account. Consequently there can be no more half-measures: the dogs of war will tear Mr. Dillon to pieces—in spite of his affection for them—if there is any more humbug about halfway houses.

But the more important point is that, if the Liberals win the next general election by persuading the country to crush the House of Lords, there will be nothing to prevent the Government from proceeding with any degree of disruptive legislation to which they may be forced by the Irish vote. The question before the country is not whether landowners shall be taxed and employment diminished, but whether the power of the Lords to suspend revolutionary legislation shall be destroyed. We fancy that many voters who might see no great objection to compelling the Lords to pass the present Budget will be most reluctant to put it out of their power to preserve the integrity and safety of the United Kingdom against a temporary majority in the Commons. Yet that is the plain issue before the country. Our Constitution does not admit of the mechanism by which, in many countries, constitutional changes are treated by a special procedure. In England a measure to destroy one of the elements in the State is treated in exactly the same way as a Bill to alter the status of hares and rabbits. An appeal to the country on the Budget at the present juncture means an appeal on the position of the Second Chamber. A small Liberal majority must be at the beck and call of the Nationalists. A large Liberal majority would be able to override the House of Lords not only on the Budget but on all current questions. Many Liberals would be as glad to remove Irish members from Westminster as some Nationalist members would be aghast at having to live in Dublin. The Liberal party, irrevocably pledged to Home Rule, would be for the first time able to fulfil the pledge. It would, if triumphant, force the Lords to yield on all the important questions which were in issue at the election. It cannot contradict Mr. Redmond's statement made from a Liberal platform that the gravest of these questions will be Home Rule.

A NAVAL WAR STAFF?

The Admiralty have issued an official statement of a character we have been familiar with in recent years. Against precedent, it is unsigned, and, purporting to take the public into its confidence about a new "Navy War Council", in reality it tells us very little, while words are introduced which mean nothing that can help us to the facts, such as "further development of the policy which has actuated the Board of Admiralty". As a rule these "further developments" have been nothing of the sort, but useless re-shuffles based on no far-seeing plan and reminding one of nothing so much as Lowell's lines:

> "Change just for change is like those big hotels
> Where they shift plates and let you live on smells".

The War Office when they formed the General Staff and carried out similar changes were content to issue the actual orders, leaving the public free to judge and criticise, and no doubt profiting as wise men should by the discussion excited. This method is evidently repugnant to the Admiralty, and we must endeavour as best we can from the Board's own advertisement of its plans to sift the value of the changes. The first object is stated to be "to place on an established footing the arrangements made in previous years for the study of strategy and the consideration and working out of war plans". To do this the Admiralty take strategy and war plans out of the hands of the thinking branch or Naval Intelligence Department and hand them over to the Naval Mobilisation Department, which has hitherto, as its name clearly indicates, been concerned with the mechanical business of providing for the rapid manning and readiness for sea of our fleets. How this shift round of duties can be called a "further development" and placing on an established footing arrangements made in previous years passes our comprehension. There is a family resemblance to one of those redistributions of the fleets by which the Admiralty finally came back to the point from which they started—a Home Fleet with reserves, an Atlantic Fleet and a Mediterranean Fleet. Each change produced chaos for the time, invisible to the public eye, but palpable to the sailor, who knows too well the long process of rubbing shoulders before things are in ship-shape order. This time there appears to be a new invasion of the work of a colleague, the Second Sea Lord, who is responsible for the personnel, and who should therefore deal with all the methodical details of mobilising the personnel. This will now come under the First Sea Lord, just as the Third Sea Lord's responsibility for the material was invaded by the First Sea Lord being made Chairman of the Designs Committee and of the Dockyards Committee. Incidentally the First Sea Lord was also made Chairman of the Estimates Committee, with the revision every year of the whole of the Estimates; and yet with all this absorption in petty detail and the duties of Chief Naval Aide-de-Camp to his Majesty, the Cabinet Committee were surprised at the Admiralty failing to produce plans for war that carry any weight with the senior officers of the Navy. Apart from the invasion of the Second Sea Lord's work the immediate net result from the naval point of view of the redistribution of duties at the Admiralty is to get rid of officers who had given offence to the Board by giving evidence on the absence of proper war plans before Mr. Asquith's Committee. There can be no question that these highly talented officers have been got rid of, since others of equal rank are substituted for them. The least the Admiralty can do, having removed them from Whitehall, is to find them ships and remove from them the stigma of unemployment. This will in some measure alleviate the shock to the service at so flagrant a breach of the pledge of the Prime Minister that no officer giving evidence before his Committee would be in any way prejudiced in his career.

As the Naval Intelligence Department will continue to exist alongside the Naval Mobilisation Department, its duties will now be restricted to the collection of information in conjunction with our naval attachés at foreign capitals. "Under the presidency of the First Sea Lord, the officers directing the Naval Intelligence Department and the Naval Mobilisation Department, and the Assistant-Secretary of the Admiralty (a civilian), will join the Standing War Council." Then it is added that the Assistant-Secretary will also act as Secretary of the Council. The business of the Secretary is to obey orders, and it is merely farcical to put him in as a member of a committee and call it a War Council. The First Sea Lord, in addition, can call in whom he pleases, including the Rear-Admiral in command of the Naval War College. It is at the Naval War College that the galaxy of intellect belonging to the flag list and captains of the Navy is assembled, working out war problems untrammelled by details of routine duties of any sort. Formerly the War College was at Greenwich and the Rear-Admiral in command was close at hand. Now the War College is scattered at the dockyards, a change for the worse made in 1906. It came about through the undue importance which the Board attributed to the matériel, oblivious of the fact that the one aim and object of the War College is to enlarge the minds of officers, by history and study away from the dockyards, to conceptions such as Moltke used to teach in his lecture-rooms. It results that present arrangements are such that the sentence in the Admiralty communication, to the effect that "the Rear-Admiral in command of the Naval War College will be associated with the Navy War Council and will attend and act as a member of the Council, when the business is such as requires his presence", may be regarded as a dead letter and will only be used when it is thought desirable to stifle the free flow of thought at the Naval War College, which has by no means flowed invariably in the direction which the Admiralty desired. The real truth is that the description "Navy War Council" is a misnomer. A council implies some sort of equality of membership, whereas there is none in this council of two and sometimes three rear-admirals presided over by an admiral of the fleet. It is simply the beginnings of a Naval War Staff, and there is apparently no other reason for the new title having been chosen except the apparently incurable love of the Board for mere appearances and also pique at the censure of the Cabinet Committee which used the words "Naval War Staff" in indicating what was desirable. "The Committee have been impressed", wrote Mr. Asquith and his colleagues, "with the differences of opinion amongst officers of high rank and professional attainments regarding important principles of naval strategy and tactics, and they look forward with much confidence to the further development of a Naval War Staff, from which the naval members of the Board and flag officers and their staffs at sea may be expected to derive common benefit." Here the Cabinet Committee clearly indicated the bringing of the entire Naval War College into a Naval War Staff, so that all exercising important commands afloat should pass through this War Staff and become imbued with the methods and principles of the great officer whom, like a Moltke, we should naturally choose to stamp his personality on those who will carry through the campaigns which have been thought out as far as possible in advance.

We do not for one moment dissent from the absolute supremacy of the First Sea Lord, who is responsible to the First Lord of the Admiralty for strategy and plans of war, over the Naval War Staff. To accentuate the fact of that leadership we consider that the new body ought to be given its proper title instead of being called the Navy War Council. The whole efficiency of the machine will depend on its chief, even as Moltke was able to impress his character and methods on the German Army through the workings of the General Staff. Not only should his staff be the channel of all communications from the First Sea Lord affecting war plans or the distribution of the fleets for war, but the members of it, who have by understudy to understand his methods, should themselves be constantly changing from the Staff to sea service where they will be responsible for acting on those ideas. Strictly speaking, as they pass to the sea service they would still be members of the Naval War Staff, just as in armies we have the General Staff at headquarters and the General Staff in the outlying commands. Mr. Haldane very truly observed of the General Staff which he formed for the Army that "if they proved themselves to be pedantic theorists, if they got out of touch with the Army, or if they exercised their authority by interfering in the details of administrative business for which others are responsible, the failure of the present attempt to form a General Staff is certain". Every word of this reads like an indictment of the designated President of the new Navy War Council. His pedantic theories have been disproved in every single case except the revolutionary scheme for a single class of executive officer to take the places of the three distinct classes of executive, engineer and marine officers, and in this case he can only be proved wrong when these young cadets have honeycombed the service and are responsible for the safety of our ships. He is utterly out of touch with the Navy, for it is eight years since he commanded at sea, and Mr. Haldane's salutary and inflexible rule is that an officer is to go back to regimental duty if he has been four years at the War Office. As for the interference with the administrative business for which others are responsible, it has been on an unexampled scale. Hence, unless these methods are completely altered by the passing of Sir John Fisher, we can never hope to realise for the Navy what we have the right to do from a real Naval War Staff, the ideal Mr. Haldane had before him for the General Staff, that "if, on the other hand, they show themselves capable of mastering the science of war, of fully understanding war organisation in all its branches, and of imparting their own knowledge to the Army at large, the influence of the General Staff in this country will become as far-reaching as in Germany or Japan". It may be taken as certain, with the Kaiser as the supreme War Lord, that the methods of the General Staff have been applied to the German Navy, and that we have to face a rivalry more stern and more worthy of our steel than was ever in the past, for there is a brain animating the whole body of this new German Navy, and it would be a vain search to endeavour to find any indication of a guiding brain in the past in the navy of France or Russia.

SPANISH POLICY AND FOREIGN VIEWS.

It is sincerely to be hoped that there will be no attempt to make scenes in this country over the anarchist. If such attempts are made, it is no less to be hoped that there is enough common-sense in the country to resist them. The lesson of the "Affaire" should not yet have been entirely lost. If any warning were required, it might easily be found in the nature of the outbreaks in Italy and France. They are purely partisan demonstrations masquerading under the convenient disguise of a general zeal for liberty.

No doubt it is unfortunate that events during the last ten days have not been propitious for the good relations of Spain and France. It is no less unfortunate that both the patriots and the anti-militarist politicians have been stirred up in Paris. This will make the situation doubly difficult for the French Government when the Chamber reassembles. M. Pichon has shown so much discretion that he may safely be trusted to steer a safe course, but injudicious interpellations both on the subject of Morocco and Señor Ferrer are almost certain to be presented.

Nothing can be more entertaining to the detached observer than the exaggerated nervousness of French opinion with regard to Spanish action in Morocco. Even the best-informed Frenchmen, including M. Hanotaux, do not know the terms of the agreements between the two countries regarding Morocco, and, as the French Government expresses itself as perfectly satisfied with Spanish assurances, and sees nothing to object to in the Spanish operations, it might reasonably be supposed that public opinion would be satisfied also. But General d'Amade's tirade is clearly not the mere indiscretion of an individual. It is true he may feel that had he been better supported by his Government, he might have done more. But French opinion in general is irritable because it feels that French policy in Morocco has been throughout a failure, after much preliminary flourishing. The French must be fully conscious that though the Spaniards have had a harder task at Melilla than they had at Casablanca, yet the Spanish operations have been better conducted and more successful.

But France cannot afford at the present juncture to quarrel with Spain. Indeed, she has no ground save jealousy. Spain has no intention of undertaking a great campaign or conquering vast tracts of territory. Had she any such designs she has neither the money nor the forces to prosecute them. Her rights in Morocco are defined and secured by treaties with France and with other Powers, and we have the word of the French Foreign Minister to the effect that she has not transgressed them.

It need hardly be pointed out that the relations between the French and Spanish Governments are absolutely correct and that no countenance is given on either side to Chauvinist sentiments. It is however unfortunate for both that the trial and execution of Señor Ferrer should have occurred at this particular moment. It may help to inflame irritation already existing, and has brought into the field elements which would certainly not have objected to the eclipse of French influence in Morocco. The position of the French Government will be made more embarrassing from the fact that the many sections of the anti-clerical party will all be equally furious at Señor Ferrer's execution. These people are not by any means all anti-militarist, and some will therefore be inflamed against Spain on more grounds than one. But one ground is no better than another. It is alleged indeed that French sense of justice is revolted by the nature of the trial under which Ferrer was condemned. But ordinary English opinion would be and has been scandalised by the manner in which French trials, both military and civil, have been conducted. The procedure is entirely different from ours, but it may suit the French, and it is not any business of ours so long as the French people like to maintain it. In the same way Spanish methods of conducting trials may not tally altogether with the French. It is quite comprehensible that French anti-clericals, anarchists, Republicans, and anti-militarists should join hands to protest all in their own fashion against the summary trial and execution of a Spanish anti-clerical Republican. The same thing may be said of Italian anti-clerical sentiment, but there can be no excuse for any movement of the kind among moderate men in our own country. Spanish opinion will be well able to gauge the nature of the politicians with whom the French Government has to deal, but it would rightly resent any ill-informed agitation in Great Britain. So far as French protests are concerned, there is not the slightest reason for believing that Señor Ferrer would have had a fairer trial or more lenient treatment in France. In a state of siege accused persons are tried and dealt with by military methods. If Señor Ferrer was guilty, it cannot be contended that his sentence was otherwise than deserved. If he was guilty, he has been stirring up the people of Barcelona to change their government by violent means which actually resulted in death and disorder. People who embark on propaganda of this nature are well aware that they take their life in their hands; if they fail they must expect to pay the penalty. It is argued that the crime was political, and that therefore rigorous imprisonment for a time would have been enough punishment. But a Government's first duty is to protect itself, and the height of folly would be to let loose a dangerous propagandist who had already shown the capacity he possessed for mischief. They would have received no gratitude from Republicans in Spain, nor would the anarchist danger have been in the least diminished. They would have been laughed at for weakness, and would have lost all the credit they have already gained with conservative and moderate opinion in their own country and abroad for the resolute attitude they have adopted towards the revolution. In fact, if the Ministry intended to protect public order effectually there was no course but the one adopted.

It is alleged, of course, that the trial was unfair, but that is not a matter on which outsiders, certainly not foreigners, have any means of judging. There is no reason at all for supposing that the evidence against Ferrer was otherwise than convincing. He was clearly very well defended, and the case was carefully reviewed by the military governor, and finally by the Cabinet, who must have weighed in the balance all the possibilities of prejudice being created in foreign and friendly countries if the sentence were enforced. Yet all these authorities concurred without hesitation in the infliction of the death penalty. It must not be forgotten how easy it would have been for either the King or his counsellors to earn a spurious popularity by remitting it. They are responsible for law and order in Spain, and they determined to carry out the sentence. There is no reason to suppose that the country as a whole will be less satisfied with their action now than with the prompt suppression of disorder in Barcelona.

This view is borne out by the manner in which the Spanish press comments upon the event. The only charge made by Moderate Republican journals is that the Government have been stupid in allowing the charges of criminal agitation against Ferrer to be mixed up with questions of secular education and liberty of instruction. Of Ferrer himself they speak as a "criminal and an agitator". If this is the only accusation that can be brought with any truth against the authorities, then they stand absolutely justified in taking stringent measures against a most dangerous enemy. It must not be forgotten that among the people employed by Señor Ferrer in the school he conducted at Barcelona was Morral, the infamous ruffian who attempted to assassinate the King and Queen of Spain on their coronation day.

In any case, we sincerely hope that opinion in Great Britain will be allowed to restrain itself, and in any event will receive no encouragement to indulge in ignorant outbursts. The facts are very imperfectly known here, and Spanish opinion (even Liberal opinion) finds no fault with the conclusion at which the Government felt obliged to arrive. Therefore foreign remonstrance would be unfair and ridiculous.

THE CITY.

THE directors of the Bank of England have followed up their action of a week ago by further advancing the rate of discount to 4 per cent. No one is surprised, and Lombard Street and the Stock Exchange are actually relieved by the movement. The circumstances called for action, and when action is necessary the City likes it to be prompt. There were some who advocated a rise of only ½ per cent., but the majority recognised that half-measures would mean more suspense, whereas now the view is that the directors have removed any possibility of a further advance this year. The position as regards American finance has not improved, and it has become imperative to take drastic steps to check the discounting in this market of American finance bills. This consideration has probably weighed more with the Bank authorities than the actual state of the Reserve, though, of course, it is hoped at the same time to get some gold to fill up the gap caused by the withdrawals of sovereigns for Egypt and South America. Germany, however, is as keen as we are to attract gold, and was before us in advancing its discount rate, which is now 5 per cent.

Stock markets, which previously had been very depressed, have shown an improving tendency since the change in the Bank rate. With great assurance New York sent buying orders for its securities, and Paris also. The feature of the week has been the fall in Consols to 82¼. It resulted from no pressure to sell, and when a few buyers, attracted by the low figure, came forward there was a sharp recovery to 82¾. At anything under 83 Consols yield a full 3 per cent., and this is a return that tempts many of the insurance companies with funds awaiting investment; they have certainly been buying this week. Home railways remain a disappointing market, but this is largely because the traffic returns are misread. We have the Great Western reporting a decrease of £8000 for last week. On analysis we find that the whole of this is due to passenger receipts, goods actually showing an increase of £1000. Similarly with other lines, though perhaps not to the same extent. But the point to emphasise is that whatever improvement there is in trade is reflected in railway earnings, and that the loss in passenger receipts is due to special causes which will not operate after the end of the month.

The resignation of Sir Charles Rivers Wilson from the Grand Trunk Railway marks a new era in the history of the company, because it means that more power will be given to Mr. Hayes, and that American methods are penetrating the office. It is asserted that the control will still remain in London, and that the appointment of Mr. Hayes as president is merely a change in the name of his office; but it will give Mr. Hayes a much greater prestige in America, and as he is known to favour the transfer of control to Montreal any efforts he may make in this direction will probably receive a good deal of support. The objection to the passing of control—and it is a reasonable one—is that the line was built with English money, and that the majority of the shareholders are English. On the other hand, it must be acknowledged that the history of the company is not a recommendation for the maintenance of the present system, though it would be difficult to say that any better results would have accrued under a Canadian régime. There is nothing interesting in the directors' report beyond the announcement of this change. Of more importance is the report of the Mexican Railway Company, which shows that the anticipations of the chairman of a large saving in working expenses have been fully realised. From 61.37 per cent. the ratio to gross receipts has been brought down to 51.30 per cent. The saving is largely due to the substitution of oil for the patent fuel previously used by the company. As a result a decrease of $220,000 in gross earnings has been converted into an increase of $215,000 in net receipts.

Unconfirmed rumours of trouble at the settlement caused Kaffirs to be very depressed in the early part of the week, but, like others, the market has "bucked up", and once more the hope is entertained that we are on the eve of "big things". It is quite apparent, however, that there is a large "bull" position open, and that while everybody is waiting to sell on a rise any pronounced upward movement is out of the question.

MASTERPIECES AT THE GRAFTON GALLERIES.

By Laurence Binyon.

THE opening of the exhibition of Old Masters at the Grafton Galleries last week was indeed a memorable occasion. At last we are beginning as a nation to wake up to the fact that something must be done; that there are a certain number of pictures of the very highest order in the private collections of England which are in danger of being captured by foreign buyers, and which ought not to leave the country if any means can be found of retaining them for the nation. At last we have evidence that the necessity of taking action is recognised by the State. Individual effort and generosity may be counted on for much; but the co-operation of Government is indispensable; for it is not only large funds that are needed, but the whole system and machinery of public purchase want to be reorganised. The situation was discussed in this Review last week, and I am not proposing at the moment to discuss it further. The exhibition of these treasures from private collections will no doubt stimulate yet further prodigious offers from millionaires in America and elsewhere; and there are some who think that on this account the policy of the committee responsible for the exhibition was mistaken. But, after all, we cannot rouse the public to an active sense of the dangers of the situation by a policy of silence and suppression; owners cannot be compelled to hide their treasures away; and the same argument would hold good against the winter exhibitions at Burlington House and against any exhibition of Old Masters—except bad ones—whatsoever. All London is flocking to the Grafton Galleries, and as the pictures will be there till the end of the year, let us hope that not only will the National Gallery profit handsomely by the receipts, which are to go to it, but—what is more important—that the nation will be stimulated to a frame of mind which will make effective action possible.

And what of the exhibition itself? Perhaps some of the early winter exhibitions at Burlington House may have surpassed it in interest and importance, but certainly for many years London has seen nothing comparable to it. Though it is not very large, the choiceness and splendour of the show tell all the more. Indeed, it is so choice that one can hardly understand the admission of the few inferior paintings included. But we can have little to complain of where masters like Raphael, Correggio, Titian, Tintoret, Van Eyck, Rubens, Velasquez, Rembrandt, Hals, Van Dyck, Reynolds, Gainsborough and Watteau are represented, and most of them nobly represented. Yet some of the most delightful pictures on the walls are by men of lesser rank. And the roomful of drawings, chiefly from Mr. Heseltine's magnificent collection, is a feast in itself. Certain predilections seem to have limited the committee's choice. There are but few Primitives. There is a complete absence of landscape. Dutch genre is unrepresented save by the brilliant little Vermeer belonging to Mrs. Joseph. Portraiture, on the other hand, is predominant. The arrangement by schools which prevails at the National Gallery, though undoubtedly the best arrangement, forbids us one pleasure, that of seeing the supreme painters of the different schools side by side; and here the eye can pass from portraits by Titian, Rubens, and Van Dyck to portraits by Rembrandt and by Reynolds. Some of these pictures are famous and familiar. But a few have never been shown before; and among these is pre-eminent the superb portrait from Temple Newsam (No. 84), formerly called Titian but recatalogued, on the authority of Mr. Herbert Cook, as Giorgione. This alone would make the exhibition memorable. It is surely one of the finest portraits in the world. We are arrested at once as by a living presence. It is the portrait of a young man, who might well be an Englishman of to-day, so far as appearance goes, his pale features thrown into relief against the darkened background, gazing out with calm intensity of resolution. One cannot fail to be interested in the man, to wonder who he was and what he achieved in life. The air of quiet power and nervous force in the sitter harmonises well with the supreme distinction of the actual painting, which is masterly without being facile. There is in this portrait a certain material strength and objectiveness which, together with the painting of the features, the white linen at the throat, the red sleeve and gloved hand, seem to proclaim, not Giorgione, but Titian as its author. Giorgione was famous in his day for half-length portraits. Vasari says that he had seen numbers of these, "bellissimi"; and if already the name had begun to attract to itself the work of other hands, that only proves Giorgione's great prestige in portraiture. This fact makes it doubtless tempting to try to make Giorgione accountable for a good deal more than it was recently the fashion to allow him. Nevertheless, I fail to appreciate the reason for ascribing this particular portrait to his hand; still less the vastly inferior portrait of Giovanni Onigo (No. 60) in the adjoining room. Another "Giorgione", the little "Holy Family" (No. 81), is surely by Catena; the types of face, the homely charm of sentiment, the light gay blues and reds—everything—point to the painter of the adorable "Sta. Cristina" at Venice. Lastly, there is the much-discussed "Woman Taken in Adultery" from Glasgow. The gorgeous colour of this picture may blind us at first to an inherent weakness of conception and to the violent means taken to give a show of drama to the design, with insufficient motive. I suppose each of us conceives a Giorgione of his own, according as we imagine him to have developed. To some perhaps the weaknesses of this picture will be no ground for doubting his authorship of it: but to me at least it is very difficult to believe that the painter of the Castelfranco and Madrid pictures could have developed into the painter of the Glasgow picture, in spite of the landscape and other passages of great beauty in this canvas.

Giorgione, however few pictures he might have painted, would still be eminently a productive genius, in Goethe's sense of the word. Few painters have been so potent and fruitful an inspiration to other men. Near by hangs a picture which shows it: the wonderful "Circe" of Dosso Dossi (No. 87), one of the most delightful works in the collection, and one which certainly would enhance the glories of the National Gallery were it ever to come there. A modern painter would doubtless scorn Dosso's animals, especially the absurd though happily modest and unobtrusive lions, and would make them infinitely more true to life; but perhaps on this very account he would almost certainly lose the atmosphere of enchantment which steeps this painting. The trees which lift their diaphanous foliage against the low flush of the sky are Circe's trees, if not the trees of Nature, and, like the blue depths of wood beyond them, belong to the world of mystery in which she reigns. This poetic seizure of an imaginative atmosphere is seen at a yet greater pitch of mastery in a painting which hangs opposite, the "Christ Taking Leave of His Mother before the Passion", by Correggio, now thought to have caught in his youth from Dosso some stimulus of magic and romance. But how supremely original does the young Correggio show himself in his conception of the scene, with its passion of tenderness and pathos, to which the marvellous beauty of the sad light in the sky and of the glooming landscape contribute so much! With all the exultation of his mature powers Correggio never again entrances us with the peculiar deep and solemnly lyrical mood of this and one or two other early masterpieces.

To return to the Venetians; there hangs as pendant to the Temple Newsam picture another portrait of a young man, in this case ascribed to Titian (No. 86). By no means so fine in essential qualities as the other portrait, this is painted with a splendid if rather more obvious mastery. Indeed the emphasis of texture in the fur and dress makes the head, with its somewhat sentimental pose, look comparatively weak, though in itself beautifully painted. One feels a certain want of the powerful harmony we expect from Titian, though I could not suggest any other name than his. A noble piece of the master's senatorial portraiture is the Giacomo Doria (No. 59) in the large room, where it hangs with Van Dyck and with Reynolds. Another fine example of portraiture by a Venetian is the group of Cardinal Ferry Carondelet and his Secretary (No. 65), by Sebastian del Piombo, a picture painted at Rome under the influence of Raphael, under whose name it is catalogued, though Sebastian's authorship is palpable and generally, I believe, accepted. Two authentic Madonnas by Raphael, from the Panshanger collection, add another high distinction to the exhibition. Raphael, like Michelangelo, has been so much judged by his imitators that it is always good to study him in his genuine work, where even those out of sympathy with its atmosphere must recognise the unassailable qualities of his art, the sheer genius in it, the spontaneous masculine rhythm, the natural greatness of style; and "that element of sculpture which exists in all good painting", so strong in him, is excellently bracing and refreshing after the unsubstantial stuff we are too prone to accept in modern art because of the emotional appeal which disguises it. With Raphael, perhaps more than with any other master, we feel that art has arrived at a moment of perfect ripeness; the next step will be decay, but the very consciousness of what must follow gives unique value to that peculiar balanced perfection.

Florentine art is meagrely represented in comparison with that of Venice; but Filippo Lippi's tondo, delicate, luminous and lively in colour, is an admirable masterpiece of its time; and in the portrait of Sassetti and a Boy, damaged though it is, Ghirlandaio shows the fine humanity that was in him, which broke at times through the professional stateliness of an art unperturbed by gusts of inspiration.

The rest of the exhibition claims another article.

"DON."

By Max Beerbohm.

MR. BESIER'S new play, produced by Mr. Trench at the Haymarket, has distinct quality. It is quite apart from the ruck of clever comedies that might have been written by any clever man with a knack for play-writing. It conforms with no current pattern of manner or method. Here and there, in the discussions between the characters, are traces of Mr. Shaw's influence. But it would be impossible for a young dramatist to escape this influence altogether. The important thing is that Mr. Besier is evidently a man who can see and think for himself, and that he can construct as setting for the result of that activity a form of his own. The construction of "Don" is as daring as it is original. The play begins almost in the key of farce; and only when it has progressed some way do we realise that the effect of farce comes not from the treatment, but from the nature of the theme; and only in the middle of the last act are we aware that the play has drifted out of comedy into strong drama, narrowly evading tragedy, and coming to a happy ending which, though one could hardly have foreseen it, is justified by the nature of the situation. It is always, in play-writing, dangerous to have more than one manner—dangerous to demand of the audience more than one mood. To change your manner without incoherence, and to make your audience change its mood without confusion, is a very delicate job. Mr. Besier is to be congratulated on having done it.

Conceive a young man bringing to the house of his parents, and into the presence of the girl to whom he is engaged to be married, a woman whom he has taken away from her husband, and with whom he has spent the night; and conceive him offering at first no explanation, and being merely impatient at their unreadiness to receive the woman with open arms. Assuredly this is a situation of farce? But, if we attach due weight to the character of the young man as depicted for us, his behaviour presently resolves itself into comedy. His parents, Canon and Mrs. Bonington, are quite ordinary people, uninspired, practical, discreet. But he, Stephen, is a thinker and a poet, whose writings have already got for him a European reputation, and —though, as Mrs. Bonington tells us, "he takes a great interest in strikes, and reads 'The Daily News' every day"—he has not had time to learn the knack of behaving like other people, or even to notice how they behave. He is a dreamer, and accustomed to put his dreams into practice as well as into words. He is always going gloriously off at tangents, sped by a sublime logic of his own, and going, in the opinion of his friends, rather too far. It was all very well for him to befriend a waitress in distress, named Fanny; but when she, seeing that he did not reciprocate, and was indeed quite unconscious of, the passion he had inspired in her, became the wife of a Plymouth Brother of the lower orders, there the matter should have ended, with a good riddance. Having become engaged to General Sinclair's charming daughter Ann, and being wildly in love with her, Stephen ought to have taken no notice of the letter in which Fanny told him that her husband was a brute and a bully. He might have known that his conduct would be misconstrued; yet off he went to Fanny's home, and, finding her in a state of collapse, insisted on taking her away with him, and spent the night with her in an hotel, nursing her, and in the morning took her forth on the way to his father's house, with the best intentions, and quite as a matter of course. Meanwhile the Canon and Mrs. Bonington, and General, Mrs. and Miss Sinclair, had been apprised of the elopement by a letter from the infuriated Plymouth Brother, Albert Thompsett. In the middle of the first act, Stephen breathlessly appears in their midst, with Fanny drooping on his arm, and with no idea that there will be any doubt as to the propriety of his action. Where should he bring the poor girl, if not to the house of his mother? General Sinclair, as a plain soldier, is indignant. The Canon, as a plain clergyman, is appalled. His wife is also appalled, but fluttering and eager to forgive. Mrs. Sinclair's fury is tempered only by her sense of the ludicrous. It never occurs to anyone, except to Miss Ann Sinclair, that Stephen may but have been acting according to his own rather too dazzling lights. She alone suspends judgment. The others fume in their several manners; and when Stephen, having insisted that Fanny shall be accommodated with a bed and a meal of eggs beaten up in beef-tea, has leisure to explain to them just what he has done, and why he has done it, still they are incredulous: his unworldliness is too much for them, and he appears in their eyes a heartless and tasteless libertine. To Ann, whom alone he convinces, he confides his intention of appearing as co-respondent, so as to free poor Fanny. "Then", says Ann, "you will have to marry her". He says he would assuredly not commit the crime of marrying a woman whom he does not love; and he cannot for the life of him see why Ann, knowing him to be innocent, should care whether he is co-respondent or not. The war between idealism and convention, between what matters to Stephen and what matters to everyone else, is waged briskly. The great thing is to prevent a meeting between Stephen and Thompsett. This Thompsett—a man of great physical strength, and of great ferocity and determination—is travelling from his robbed home to the Boningtons' house, having received from Stephen news of his wife's presence there. Throughout the second act the audience is held in suspense for his arrival. And it is when we at last see him that the play slips into drama. Thompsett is an admirably drawn figure—the brutish, slow-witted man who has "got religion", and who "got" Fanny with the same dull fanaticism. The Canon, frightfully embarrassed by fibbing, tries to assure him that Mrs. Thompsett had come straight from her home to the rectory; but he is interrupted by the entry of Stephen, who promptly tells the truth, adding to it a lie as to his relations with Fanny. There is a long, tense, very effective scene between the two men; and finally the knot is cut by Fanny's confession, through which Thompsett "gets" the belief that Stephen has done no wrong, and promises to be a kinder husband henceforth. Usually, these conversions are a mere device to secure a happy ending. Thompsett's conversion, however, is quite in character, and brings a very clever play to a worthy conclusion.

Mr. McKinnel plays Thompsett magnificently. In parts which demand an effect of uncouth strength and emotion, held stolidly in reserve, Mr. McKinnel has no rival; and Thompsett is his reward for having had to play King Lear. Mr. Quartermaine, as Stephen, is rather too neat and acute in manner, too dapper, to suggest the poetry of Stephen's innocent and tumultuous soul. Miss O'Malley, as Ann, shows great sensibility and prettiness of method. And the other parts are well and amusingly played.

"Don" is preceded by "Gentlemen of the Road", a little play by Mr. Charles McEvoy—a very early little play by Mr. Charles McEvoy, I suspect.

SAN PELLEGRINO AND ITS NEIGHBOURHOOD.

By Richard Davey.

IT has been said, though it may seem paradoxical, that the comparatively few English men and women who visited Italy in the eighteenth century saw far more of the country than do the majority of their degenerate descendants in our day, who rush by train from capital to capital and thereby miss many interesting places in a land whose most insignificant village can boast of the possession of at least one fine work of art. The leisurely way of travelling a hundred years ago, either by very slow lumbering coach or by horse or mule, enabled our ancestors to saunter at their leisure through out-of-the-way cities full of historical or artistic interest. Montaigne, le Brosse and Young, who have described so many quaint but now obsolete scenes of Italian life common in every town and village in their day, could not, however, have told us much about the Valley of the Brembana, for until thirty years ago this region, one of the loveliest in Europe, was virtually unknown to the majority of Italians, let alone to English people. No post roads existed then, and even to reach San Pellegrino from Bergamo one had to go a weary journey on muleback by tortuous and dangerous roads, occasionally infested by brigands as late as the first half of the nineteenth century. Now a commodious electric railway takes you in less than an hour from Bergamo to San Pellegrino, and from San Pellegrino on to San Giovanni Bianco, whence conveyances can be obtained to drive into the heart of a region even more beautiful than the renowned Dolomites, for here the loftiest mountains are entirely covered with verdure and there is an interesting and lovely flora.

Lady Mary Wortley Montagu was possibly the first Englishwoman of any note who ever visited Bergamo, unless indeed we claim Miss Angelica Kauffmann as a countrywoman because "she spoke English so very well and was so influential with Sir Joshua Reynolds", whose style she certainly copied in the very effective "Holy Family", painted here for the Colleoni family, which still hangs in the sumptuous tomb-house of their ancestor the great Condottiere Bartolomeo. "Miss Angel" lived some years at Bergamo after her unfortunate adventure with the pseudo-Ambassador of Sweden in London, and her house and studio are still in existence. As to Lady Mary, she found Bergamo "much to her liking" and the neighbouring scenery very beautiful, though even she never visited the Brembana Valley that opens at the city's gates, but has only recently been brought into prominence by the increasing popularity of San Pellegrino, the "Contrexéville of Italy". In the time of Lady Mary and "Miss Angel" there were no roads between Bergamo and San Pellegrino and no accommodation for such strangers as came to drink of the waters (known even to the Romans for their efficacy in cases of gout and uric trouble), except a wretched old wayside inn. The Grand Hôtel, the most sumptuous in Italy, would surely have surprised and even overwhelmed "Miss Angel" and her lively patroness, Lady Wentworth, who would, however, have felt quite at home in the Casino, where they could have had a flutter at a game of chance, in much the same way that they were accustomed to do in that famous Ridotto at Venice which I discovered recently behind San Moisè, still in possession of its exquisite eighteenth-century decorations, but fallen from its high estate of one hundred and fifty years ago as the Monte Carlo of its time to become a cheap kinematograph exhibition!

The famous waters of San Pellegrino that four hundred years since cured Pope Pius IV. (de' Medici), when Cardinal, of his gouty ailments, flow no longer, as they did in his time, from a common pump in the middle of the street, but rush out of a pretty fountain in the grounds of the modern Kursaal. He was a native of the place, and the old house near the parish church, with a fifteenth-century fresco over its arched doorway, is said to have formed part of the Medici palace in which this famous Pope first saw light. In his Holiness' day the only sound that might have disturbed his ears of a night was that of the Brembo, which still dashes impetuously through the richly wooded valley, through Ambria with its "Orrido"—thus the Italians appropriately call a darksome gorge—through picturesque Zogno with its magnificent church, through Sedrina with its three ancient bridges, through old towns and villages and varied and verdant scenery to Bergamo itself, a city so beautiful and fortunately still so flourishing as to deserve something more than a flying visit.

There are two distinct towns at Bergamo, an upper and a lower. In the lower you will find a picture gallery worthy of any capital and a "modern hotel" and some well-managed "institutions", not the least of which is the Istituto Italiano d'Arti Grafiche, one of the most important art printing establishments in Europe, employing fifteen hundred men and women.

The picture gallery at Bergamo owes its origin to the generosity of three citizens who collected pictures at a time when it was safer and easier to do so than now. Count Giacomo Carrara, for instance, made his collection in the eighteenth century, when the Bond Street dealer and the American millionaire were unknown, and pictures which are now worth their many thousands could be bought for a few hundred lire. He was a man of great taste and judgment, and was happy in being able to pick up in some instances, and to inherit in others, some of Moroni's finest works, in which this gallery is singularly rich. To Carrara's magnificent collection have been added those of Counts Morelli and Lochis, formed at a somewhat later date, when Napoleon dispersed the monastic treasures of the country. The three collections have hitherto been kept apart, which, as they are under one roof, has resulted in considerable confusion of dates and "schools"; but it is now proposed to set aside certain unwise testamentary conditions and rearrange the gallery, both as regards its various "schools" and its lighting. When this is done the visitor will be better able to appreciate a collection of no less than twenty portraits by Moroni, of which the full-length portraits of Bernardo Spini and his wife, Pace, are perhaps the finest works of this master, whose "Tailor" and "Venetian Nobleman" in our National Gallery are universally admired, though he is otherwise little known in England. Lorenzo Lotto, also a native of Bergamo, is better represented here than anywhere else in Italy; and there are at least half a dozen admirable specimens of Moretto, another Bergamasc painter. Fra Ghislandi, an eighteenth-century master of the highest merit, described by some critics as the Velasquez of Italy, has several portraits of supreme beauty in this gallery, among them a lovely picture of "A Young Artist" which suggests, not indeed Velasquez, but Reynolds at his best. Ghislandi seems to have been particularly happy in the delineation of youth, but as he was a monk he never painted women. It would be a pleasant task to describe even a few of the more celebrated pictures in the gallery—the fine Velasquez, for instance, the three undoubted Botticelli, the "San Sebastian" of Raphael, an early and rather weak work, and the excellent examples of Carpaccio, Paris Bordone, Santa Croce, Titian, Palma Vecchio, Lorenzo Lotto, Gentile and Giovanni Bellini, Beltraffio, Paul Veronese, Carlo Crivelli, Guardi, Luini, Gaudenzio Ferrari, etc.; but my present object is to generalise, and thereby attract the attention of tourists to a little-known part of that lovely country, and not to describe exhaustively either its manifold beauties or its artistic treasures.

The gallery does not exhaust the sights of Bergamo, and the upper town, reached by a funicular, is even more attractive than the lower. Here, as on a sort of acropolis, stand the two great cathedrals, Santa Maria Maggiore and Sant' Alessandro; the mausoleum of the Colleoni, with Amadeo's superb monument to the famous Condottiere and his far more exquisite tomb of that hero's young daughter Medea, one of the simplest and most elegant works of the best period of the Rennaissance. Near the cathedrals stand the Town Hall and the ancient Piazza, through the arches of which you catch glimpses of the far-away hills rising above a long stretch of gardens and vineyards. Turning up a narrow street—unchanged since the Middle Ages—and just beyond a palace with an exquisite wrought-iron balcony, you reach the house where Colleoni died. After many vicissitudes, after being an inn for nearly two hundred years, the fine old mansion has fallen in its old age upon gentler times and, well restored and cared for, it is now an excellent example of a domestic dwelling of the "quattrocento". It contains one beautiful room, full of curious fifteenth-century frescoes, having at the upper end an equestrian portrait of the Condottiere which evidently suggested the famous statue at Venice. There is also an excellent portrait of Colleoni by Moroni, taken from an earlier and probably contemporary picture.

You might wander for days and yet not exhaust all the picturesque charm of this ancient city, which may be made the starting-point for many excursions not mentioned by Baedeker and Murray; but San Pellegrino offers greater advantages for this purpose, since there you are half way to a hundred places of unexplored interest—sheltered valleys as fresh and green as those of Ireland, and little lakes that mirror on their placid waters villages, convents and ruined castles, and even the peaks of snow-covered Alps. People who, like Hamlet, are "scant of breath" will be perhaps relieved to learn that San Pellegrino boasts of a funicular to carry you in about twenty minutes to the top of one of the highest mountains in the neighbourhood, whence a number of easy mule-paths enable one to take countless walks into the valleys beyond, even as far as Clusone, a fair sized town, where there is a remarkable "Dance of Death" in the parish church.

There still remain in some of the village churches hereabouts many fine pictures—at Bordogna a superb Paul Veronese; at Serina a wonderful Palma Vecchio—this celebrated artist was a native of the village. One day recently I went on an excursion to Villa d'Almé to visit the Sanctuary of Almenno, which is not mentioned in any guide-book that I have ever seen. Part of the church dates from the fourth century, and was formerly attached to the castle in which Arduin, the last of the Lombard kings, died. The more modern church of the fourteenth century contains a very remarkable tempietto, or altar in the shape of a small temple, designed by Bramante and painted with excellent and well-preserved frescoes by Palma Vecchio, which were only recently released, at the expense of the present rector, from a coating of whitewash that had covered them up since the plague of 1550. He also discovered in the crypt below a most remarkable fresco of the "Pietà" by Mantegna.

As I write, the moon is shining brightly, the Brembo rushes along cheerily, the band at the Casino opposite my window is playing the "Merry Widow Waltz" for the benefit of the throng of fashionable balneanti, whilst the pious are pouring out of the brightly lighted parish church into the crowded street, in which the youths who have run a Marathon race this afternoon from Bergamo, some twenty-five miles away, to the Hippodrome in the hotel grounds are being fêted by their enthusiastic admirers at a score or so of little tables arranged under the lime trees. It is a very gay and peaceful scene, full of delightful contrasts, in which civilisations old and new seem to blend. The peasants, a fine-looking race of men and women, are but little changed in mind, manners and customs from what they were five hundred years ago—a very straightforward, pious, gracious folk, who mingle, with that unconscious stateliness peculiar to Italians, with the throng of great ladies and gentlemen who bear names as old as European history itself and wear the slightly exaggerated garments that Milan and Turin produce after French models—the ladies in tight-fitting Directoire gowns and enormous hats like cartwheels, whereas the men pay us the compliment of trying to dress like Englishmen, only more so!

May the Lord preserve Italy from going too far on the downward path of Progress (spelt with a big P)! Will the nations never learn how to move on their own lines without borrowing all that is worst in the civilisation of their neighbours? Your Italian who remains an Italian is as delightful as his surroundings, but once he tries to be a Frenchman or a German, an American or even an Englishman, he becomes a thing of horror and the reverse of a joy for ever. D'Annunzio, Italy's most prominent modern writer, frankly admits that he would prefer an invasion of German soldiers to the present invasion of German art and "architecture"—consisting of ponderous masonry, hideous carvings and wrought-iron decorations—which, together with French decadentism, is becoming only too general in modernised Italy. Abbasso l'arte moderna e viva l'Italia!

HENRY PURCELL.

By Filson Young.

THE spread of what we call civilisation, and the decay of national feeling, produce some unfortunate results; among others the neglect of the work of great men in the past whose genius does not happen to be in tune with the cosmopolitan spirit of our own time. One often, for the sake of convenience, has to speak of the Modern English school of music. But there is really no such school. There is a modern school of music and there are English composers who belong to it; but they do not make an English school. The last great English musician who was essentially English in the sense that his work was stamped with the quality and characteristics of the England of his day, and who could only be produced by that England, was Henry Purcell. His work is extremely neglected in these days; partly because he was a great man and yet one who worked in a narrow compass, partly bcause we are very busy in England at present taking our part in the development of modern music as a whole, and do not care to go back for inspiration to what is both great and English in our own traditions; the modern taste prefers a small man working in a wide field to a great man working in a narrow one.

We are not so rich in great musicians in our English past that we can at all afford to neglect the greatest of them. There is need, therefore, that people should be continually reminded of the greatness of Henry Purcell; of the extreme beauty and pleasantness of his music, and of the desirability that it should be more often heard and more widely known. No writer has done more to call attention to these facts than Mr. John F.

Runciman, both in this REVIEW and in other places; and he has crowned his work in this direction by the monograph* which he has just published in Bell's Miniature Series of Musicians. The little book is modest in price and form; there is no attempt to make it a formal biography, because no one knows anything about Purcell's life; but within its small compass it contains the result of a profound knowledge, a devoted study, a wide scholarship, and probably years of intimate research among the works of Purcell. It is so seldom that a little book comes out which is really all that it should be that one is under special obligation to record and advertise the appearance of such a book; to inform people who are interested in the subject that they will find here accurate and scholarly information and illuminating criticism presented in a perfectly finished literary form; and to urge upon them, in this particular case, the importance of reading the book, reviving their interest in its subject, and doing what they can to further the author's intention of restoring Purcell's music to its proper place in the hearts of his countrymen.

Mr. Runciman is perfectly certain of his ground in assigning to Purcell the pre-eminent place which he holds among English composers, and he takes a very firm stand upon that ground. It is possible that he under-estimates the work of some of Purcell's predecessors and followers; what is vital is, that he does not and cannot over-estimate the importance of Purcell's own work. He shows, more clearly than one ever remembers having seen such an explanation made before, the technical reasons why Purcell's music was at once quite different from, and much greater than, that of his predecessors. It is almost impossible to explain musical technicalities to the lay mind; one is in danger of writing like a mere contrapuntist; for although the structure of music is very intimately concerned with such matters as thirds and sixths, diminished sevenths and augmented elevenths, subjects by augmentation and inversion, fugal treatment *per recte et retro*, they have indeed nothing to do with making it great music or little music. Purcell was a fine contrapuntist, but he was not finer than dozens of men who went before and came after him. What he did was to perceive, almost among the first who perceived it, that the technical and mathematical science of music was a means and not an end in itself; that the real expression of music was the expression of a poetic feeling and the extension of human experience into a sublime dimension. Therefore, woven into all his counterpoint there is the golden thread of poetry, which remains untarnished and unalterable, though the fabric that surrounds it may get rusty and obsolete. What is so very interesting and astonishing in Mr. Runciman's book is that he explains this, which one would have thought inexplicable; and explains it in a way that any intelligent amateur of music, not technically learned, can plainly understand.

I have one quarrel with Mr. Runciman, and it is a quarrel of merely personal opinion and criticism. I share his contempt for most of the music which the Church of England has produced since the Reformation; share it most heartily; but I must protest against his definite statement that "the Church of England has had no religious musicians worth mentioning". It is true that there were whole generations of Church composers, honestly pious and damnably inartistic, who merely "grubbed through life in dusty organ-lofts". But they were not all like that. Because my space is limited, and because one exception will prove my point as well as three, I cite the instance of Samuel Sebastian Wesley. It is true that he inherited some of the defects that sprang from his brilliant but unhappy father's cracked head; that he had fads and restrictions; that he clung to the mean-tone temperament in tuning and to the G and F keyboard compass when these were obsolete; but I cannot agree that his music is "not worth mentioning". I claim that it is both worth mentioning and remembering and hearing; that there is in much of it that human poetry which is so great a stranger to the organ-loft; tinged with melancholy and decadence and a sense of the passing of things perhaps, but eloquent and abiding none the less, and informed with a modern feeling for harmony which was most beautifully combined with a Bach-like suavity in the movement of parts. Has Mr. Runciman ever seen, I wonder, that little-known book "The European Psalmist"—a collection of hymn-tunes, most of them written and all of them harmonised by Wesley—which for importance in its way can only be compared with Breitkopf's collection of Bach's "vierstimmige Choralgesänge"? It is not practically important as music now, but it is infinitely important as showing what manner of musician Wesley was. A thing that has to be remembered, moreover, in criticising the work of Church composers is that their work was almost all written for performance in Gothic cathedrals. As Mr. Runciman himself certainly knows, the setting in motion of great sound waves in a cathedral is an art in itself; you are not dealing with notes and chords so much as with large sound waves; and many a composition which would sound sublime in a cathedral would sound feeble enough if tried over on a piano or performed in a small parish church—and vice versa. Music of this school does not always stand the test of severe analysis at the music-desk; it is music written for a certain instrument, and that instrument a cathedral, for the cathedral performs the music as well as the organ and voices, joins with them, a very orchestra of stone and space and proportion, the secret of which we have lost.

I have said so much in extenuation of some of the music which Mr. Runciman condemns; but Purcell's music, of course, needs no such extenuation. It is great in itself, and independent of any definite machinery of expression; it sums up a certain fresh spirit which is precious to us as that of the youth and glory of England; and I cannot do better than end this article in some beautiful and melancholy words of Mr. Runciman's own:

"We once had a glorious school of composers. It departed, with no sunset splendour on it, nor even the comfortable ripe tints of autumn. The sun of the young morning shone on its close; the dews of dawn gleam for ever on the last music; the freshness and purity of the air of early morning linger about it. It closed with Purcell, and it is no hyperbole to say the note that distinguishes Purcell's music from all other music in the world is the note of spring freshness. The dewy sweetness of the morning air is in it, and the fragrance of spring flowers. The brown sheets on which the notes are printed have lain amongst the dust for a couple of centuries; they are musty and mildewed. Set the sheets on a piano and play: the music starts to life in full youthful vigour, as music from the soul of a young god should. It cannot and never will grow old; the everlasting life is in it that makes the green buds shoot."

BEHIND THE HARVEST MOON.*

By LORD DUNSANY.

OVER the cover is a latticework and behind it a branch of the cherry tree all in blossom; from behind this there looks at you a huge round harvest moon. Whoever turns the pages behind the harvest moon will know how fared the spirit of O Ko San; and why there is a ghost in the Violet Well and weeping in the valley of Shimizutani whenever the nights are wet; and who the lady was that Heitaro met beneath the great willow in Kyoto, and what befell her when at dead of night they cut the willow down. They will know why at Kumedamura, eight miles south-east of Sakai, in Idsumo, stands Fuezuka, the Tomb of the Flute; where people worship, bringing incense and flowers, not in one season rather than another, but the whole year round. For the wronged husband, once blind and now dead, came with his flute by night to the house of Ichibei, his friend, and told him all his wrongs. And

* "Purcell." By John F. Runciman. London: Bell. 1909 1s. net.

* "Ancient Tales and Folk-Lore of Japan." By A. Gordon Smith. London: Black. 1909. 20s. net.

Ichibei arose and went to the house that had been Yoichi's, the blind flute-player, his friend. And he spoke to her that had been Yoichi's wife as she sat in the house with her lover, and asked her many questions. Thus the hour of ten went by and thus eleven. Still Ichibei sat talking and listening to lies. Now for the seventh time Asayo, who had been Yoichi's wife, "was assuring Ichibei that everything that was possible had been done for her blind husband", and the hour of midnight came upon them as she spoke, and a storm of wind arose, and they heard the sound of Yoichi playing his flute. And Ichibei slipped away at once, and escaped alone from the doom that comprehended the whole of that guilty house.

There too is to be found what vengeance Akechi takes on all the fishermen of Biwa because one of them once betrayed him to his death, and what the rustling was that Jogen heard by night about the haunted temple in Inaba, just before his marrow froze and he became paralysed.

And there is the beautiful story of O Kinu who dived for the haliotis shell in Oiso Bay, and Takadai the Samurai that loved her. And O Kinu would not marry so far above her station, and Takadai sickened for love. And one night Takadai went out to sea and drowned himself, so that his spirit lingering where he died might sometimes see O Kinu as she came diving down to look for the haliotis shell. But the spirit of Takadai passed into many gulls and they came wheeling into Oiso Bay, though so little known in that part of the sea, and hovered, to the wonder of the fishermen, over the place where Takadai had gone down. Far away they took his body to Kamakura, but his spirit had not ease, even though O Kinu prayed for it in the temple and built to his memory a tomb, and still in stormy weather, year in year out, hung over Oiso Bay the unwonted gulls. And only O Kinu knew that dead Takadai was watching there in fear lest she should ever marry a living man.

And O Kinu married no one, but the typhoon came down nine years later and drowned O Kinu in the sea, and then the spirit of Takadai rested and the sea-gulls went away.

One of the most beautiful pictures in this book, nearly all beautiful, is the one that shows O Kinu putting out into the bay to see the place where Takadai had died. And the white gulls are all about that place, and ever there come in to it more and more. Perhaps it is evening; but I think more likely it is about the dawn, for the sea-mist is rising and passing softly away. The tide is high, for it is very close up to O Kinu's village, the pleasant village of Oiso in Sagami, and it is still rising, for there is no trace along the shore of the pebbles that the ebb leaves wet. And Oiso with its old-world thatches of straw and its fantastic fir tree, Oiso with its little bay and the far gray guardian mountains half shutting it from the sea, seems such a place as an elf-king might well choose to be the capital of faëry.

I think that the chief delight of this book is its pictures. One shows a bitter, frosty morning, the lake frozen, rushes white and stiff, and the shore heaped up with snow; two crows are abroad searching; and the trees with their great gnarled fingers grip the world, against the winds of the winter.

Another shows twelve gusts of wind coming down by night out of the mountains and arousing the evil passions of the lake. Not unlike it is the picture of high and sudden winds, underneath which arise the clamorous multitudes of the clutching fingers of the insatiate sea whose salted heart is athirst for the blood of men.

Pleasant is the picture of the black rocks where written prayers are tied because of what Denbei and O Tagahana did, long ago in the Firefly Valley.

And there is an interior of a temple with saintly carven figures and the bloom of the lotus before them, the lotus bloom that Egyptian sculptors loved four thousand years ago, the same that waylaid Odysseus and his men. And Oba Kogi-Chika is looking for Yoritomo who is hidden in the great tree, and all the other trees of the forest seem to be in the secret.

Another lovely picture is the restful idol of Kwannon, and the islands and the sleepy inland sea, and one behind the other, white and small, three venturous sailing ships of the Japanese. Yogodazu, too, is shown just after sunset, as two cranes are flying home, by the side of a melodious ravine, saving the life of a bee who is in the toils of a spider. And it was well for Yogodazu that he did, for he was in trouble, but that night the bee appeared to him in a vision and promised him victory. And Yogodazu began to raise objections, so hopeless seemed his case. But the bee smiled. And Yogodazu in the end took the bee's advice and defeated his relation-in-law and built a temple to the bees, and prayed there once a year for the rest of his life.

A storm by night over Sagami Bay, and the fishing boats are all drawn up in rows, in comfort on the beach, and the houses of the fisher folk are glowing and warm. It is the night that O Cho San drowns herself because all the men of the isle are quarrelling over her beauty, and there had been no trouble in Hatsushima till she was born—not for three hundred years. And still when men pray at her shrine on the 10th of June, the Shrine of O Cho San of Hatsushima, her spirit drifts over the isle in rain.

Read how an emperor came along the shore of lonesome Naoshima, playing upon a four-stringed instrument of music a very beautiful but crafty tune; and how famous Saigo took farewell of the resolute Watanabe, calling for all not to forget so admirable a man, and bowing low to him, and fixing for the place of his beheading the three pine trees, and for the time dawn.

And here I take my leave of the fireflies and the plum trees and the shadowy moonlit temples, and forests full of chrysanthemums, and the snow, and spirits of peonies and lotus lilies and swords, and holy Fuji-Yama; all of which lie behind the lattice and the cherry and the huge round harvest moon. And I take leave of them with these words running in my head, written by Robert Bridges to the nightingales:

"Beautiful must be the mountains whence ye come".

CORRESPONDENCE.

WOLFE AND POSTERITY.

To the Editor of the SATURDAY REVIEW.

Syra, 26 September 1909.

SIR,—Is not too much fuss being made about General Wolfe? Not, indeed, of his exploits: we cannot easily over-estimate the splendour of his services or admire too much the nobility of his character. But this fashionable attempt to set him up as a martyr, thwarted by his fellows, unvalued by the nation he served: is it fair to his colleagues, is it just to his countrymen? Is it really true, as Mr. Edward Salmon claims in your columns, that he has had to wait a century and a half for the full meed of the nation's recognition? Has Mr. George Wolfe good cause for saying, as he did the other day at the commemoration dinner, that "this was the first time any genuine effort had been made to mark what General Wolfe had done for the country"?

An important point must not be lost sight of. It is that the deeds of prominent men of action are judged by two separate and distinct tribunals. On the one hand there is the general public, on the other the small body of critical opinion. Of the general public it is enough to say that it cares nothing for the details; it judges wholly by results, and gives all the credit of a campaign to the victorious commander-in-chief, sometimes wrongly, sometimes with justice. (I have myself heard men of breeding and education seriously maintain that Wellington was a greater soldier than Napoleon simply because he defeated him at Waterloo.) The much smaller body, on the other hand, examines minutiæ, weighs the plans and the methods of execution; in fact, forms a reasoned critical judgment.

But which of these bodies constitutes "the nation", "posterity"? Obviously the first. And is it too much to say that the great mass of living Englishmen have been brought up to regard the conquest of Canada as begun and ended by Wolfe's glorious victory and heroic death on the Plains of Abraham?—that for a hundred such there are, say, ten who even remember by name the gallant Saunders and the patient Amherst, and perhaps one who has even heard that a brigadier-general present claimed to have discovered the way that led to such memorable success?

The fact that such a claim was made is of itself nothing very new or startling or disgraceful; it certainly cannot convict "the nation" of ingratitude or forgetfulness. There have been many occasions, before and since, where the merit of the supreme decision or the critical movement has been claimed for a subordinate. Undoubtedly it was Colonel Hardinge who called up the division that turned the tide of battle at Albuerra: probably it was to Sir Charles Douglas that came the inspiration to break through the French line at the Battle of the Saints: perhaps we owe the taking of Gibraltar to the decision of Sir John Leake or Prince George of Hesse-Darmstadt: and certainly we may reject the pretensions of General Townshend to the first place among the conquerors at Quebec. But the general public cares for none of these things; for posterity these were the exploits of Beresford (or very likely Wellington), Rodney, Rooke, and Wolfe.

But if critical opinion bears out this last judgment it does not find it necessary to do so at the expense of others, to pass over the brilliant seamanship and loyal co-operation of Admiral Saunders, or to forget that in Amherst's Montreal campaign which finished the war "we seem" (to quote an historian, Mr. Julian Corbett, with no particular axe to grind) "to have before us one of the most perfect and astonishing bits of work which the annals of British warfare can show".

But the modern popular biographer is never content to depict his hero of his natural size among his fellows. The note must be forced, staccato, the colours heightened, the shadows deepened: the star actor must monopolise the limelight, whether it be an English hero who little needs such a treatment or a French mistress who as little merits it. So that even Mr. Salmon, who can be just to Saunders, has to tell us that "Wolfe had to bear up against not merely the sore trials of the campaign, but the want of sympathy in those who should have been his staunchest supporters"; that is, presumably, his brigadiers, whose most "unsympathetic" act was to reject his three tentative plans for a last desperate attempt below the city made at a moment of sickness and dejection, and to propose instead an attempt above which was not, but certainly led him to his own masterly and successful plan of attack at Anse du Foulon.

The truth is that no great man needs this appeal ad misericordiam less than Wolfe does. To call him in many ways singularly fortunate is not really to decry his singular merit. Yet these points deserve attention: (1) He was chosen at an early age for a great command by a Government that selected for contemporary expeditions such incompetent leaders as Mordaunt, Abercromby and Albemarle. (2) Of his superior in America, Amherst, it can be said "he behaved with conspicuous loyalty. All the high talent for administration which he possessed he devoted heart and soul to the preparation of Wolfe's force, and no expedition had ever been better equipped than that which Wolfe eventually found at his disposal" (Corbett's "England in the Seven Years War"). How great a contrast to the case of his noble adversary, Montcalm, ever harassed and thwarted by the vain and jealous governor, Vaudreuil! (3) His relations with his naval colleague made their amphibious warfare a model for all time: how different from those he had himself seen of Hawke and Mordaunt in the luckless Rochefort campaign! (4) Hard things have been said of his subordinates; but two of his brigadiers were men of his own choice and devoted to him, while the third, if intractable and opinionated, was at least an able and seasoned soldier. (5) And in his death? In this same war while Wolfe was earning fame and success in the lines before Louisbourg another young soldier marched at the head of a British force through American forests. In Lord Howe Wolfe recognised a kindred soul. "The noblest Englishman that has appeared in my time, and the best soldier in the British Army" he calls him; "a complete model of military virtue" is Pitt's verdict. No one who served with him questioned his exceptional promise, but the first blind shots of the first petty skirmish with the foe cut short his career, and to measure his loss and his greatness there was nothing but the swift ruin that came upon the force of which he had been the life and fire. Wolfe's fragile, pain-racked body gave up his glorious spirit at the supreme and perfect moment: well might he declare that he died in peace.

Commemoration dinners, statues and monuments, a host of biographers—these may mark, they do not create, the memory of his deeds. The New England chaplain, himself a soldier of the war, knew better when he preached to his flock: "Is he dead? I recall myself. Such heroes are immortal; he lives on every loyal tongue; he lives in every grateful heart".

Yours faithfully,
ROBERT WEATHERHEAD.

THE 60TH AND ITS MOTTO.

To the Editor of the SATURDAY REVIEW.

10 October 1909.

SIR,—In the interesting account of Wolfe which recently appeared in your REVIEW there is a small mis-statement of fact which would hardly deserve correction were it not that it was given some publicity at the time of the Wolfe celebrations, and has since been repeated in the papers. It is to the effect that the 60th Rifles, for their intrepid conduct at the taking of Quebec, were granted the motto "Celer et audax". All will agree that no more suitable motto could possibly be granted to a corps of riflemen, whose especial attributes are rapidity of movement and boldness. Unfortunately for the historical accuracy of the tale there was no regiment of Rifles at the taking of Quebec or anywhere else in the British Army until over 40 years later.

The regiment which distinguished itself by its celerity and daring at Quebec was the 60th Royal American Regiment of Foot, which had been raised some few years previously for service in America only—it being composed largely of foreigners. This regiment was clothed in red, and equipped and armed, as were all other line regiments, with "Brown Bess" muskets. In 1816 it was clothed in green, and in 1824 it was reconstituted as a "British corps" and brought to England, as described by the regimental historian, Captain Wallace. It was now that its name was changed from 60th (Royal American) Regiment to 60th (Duke of York's Rifle Corps and Light Infantry), a title, in 1830, changed to 60th (King's Royal Rifle Corps).

It was about 1824 that the regiment was permitted to resume the motto "Celer et audax", which, according to regimental tradition, had been conferred on it at the taking of Quebec. The exact circumstances of the granting of this motto, who gave it (for Wolfe was mortally wounded early in the day), who authorised it, and why such a proud distinction was discontinued, will no doubt be fully set forth in the history of the King's Royal Rifles, now in preparation.

The whole question has been curiously complicated by the addition in 1798 of a 5th Battalion of German riflemen to the 60th, which wore the green jacket and gained for the regiment its many Peninsular "Honours". But, so far as is known, this battalion of Rifles seems never to have borne the famous regimental motto "Celer et audax", for it was disbanded in 1818, and it was not until 1824, six years later, that the motto was "revived". Hence the plain fact remains that however well-merited the splendid motto of the present King's Royal Rifle Corps may be, or however suitable it may be considered for such a corps, it has nothing whatever to do with their prowess as riflemen as has been so recklessly stated and so universally repeated.

Your obedient servant,
VERITAS.

IS FRANCE DECADENT?

To the Editor of the SATURDAY REVIEW.

10 October 1909.

SIR,—As a Frenchman I am perhaps hardly able coolly to discuss the question "Are the French a decadent nation?"; but I regretted to see such a rash statement as that made in the last letter of "A Traveller" and printed in your REVIEW.

The SATURDAY REVIEW has always endeavoured to present without malignance or injustice the home policy of France; and this is all the more reason why I think it important that misstatement should not be permitted here.

"A Traveller" regards anti-theism as an evident sign of decadence. But on his next journey to or from Italy let him remain for some days in the French "province"; let him on Sunday visit the churches in towns or small villages; let him ask here and there the opinion of parents on the religious teaching of their children; let him visit the hospitals and cemeteries, and realise how infinitesimal is the number of families in which religion is treated as of no account, and marriages or funerals regarded as purely civil ceremonies.

No doubt he will understand then that wild anti-theism, which is an acute form of the political disease "anti-clericalism", is still very scarce, and he will reassure himself.

I am yours truly,
FRENCHMAN.

DR. JOHNSON AS JOHN BULL.

To the Editor of the SATURDAY REVIEW.

The Mill, Whitstable, Kent,
1 October 1909.

SIR,—In the article in the SATURDAY of 25 September entitled "Dr. Johnson and his Eulogists" the writer condemns what he calls Lord Rosebery's "bêtise . . . the John Bull label". I know too little about the great Johnson to take up the cudgels for Lord Rosebery, but may I make one suggestion—that Lord Rosebery is not alone in his thus labelling the subject of his recent address? Boswell, in the "Journal of a Tour to the Hebrides", says: "He was indeed, if I may be allowed the phrase, at bottom much of a John Bull, much of a blunt, true-born Englishman". In view of this, perhaps the writer of the able article in the last SATURDAY may be said himself to have committed a mild bêtise in his sentence, "Decidedly, Lord Rosebery's attempt to paste the John Bull label on the Lichfield statue was not a success". Bozzy's being the original labelling, to Bozzy surely the blame—or the praise.

Yours truly,
BETTINA VON HUTTEN.

"AMERICA'S PERIL."

To the Editor of the SATURDAY REVIEW.

4 Whitehall Court, London S.W.
7 October 1909.

SIR,—In your review of my book "America's Peril" you say "It cannot be denied that Mr. Vaile has produced an amusing book, but his method is too vindictive", and "It is true that the United States is only a nation in the making and not yet civilised; but the unrestrained ferocity of the author conveys the impression of a castigation without discrimination". "Not yet civilised"! I am afraid the American who sees this will say "Save me from champions like this!"

I never object to any reviewer's opinions. I express mine very freely, and always concede to others the same right. I must confess, however, that I do not quite like the words "vindictive" and "unrestrained ferocity", although the latter amuses me.

The fact is that I could not be vindictive about America or the Americans. I like it and admire them too much for that. I am scathing at times, I know. I intended to be. The book is one-sided. I admit it in my preface, but, as I there state, it is unfortunately the side that America presents most prominently to the world. I was well aware that the admission would be forgotten—as it has been—by nearly all reviewers. My object has, however, been served, and the ugliness of American life caused by the all-absorbing and scorching dollar-grapple has been made very apparent. I was restrained enough to withhold this book from publication for quite two years after it was written, until, in fact, I had revisited America and a very good friend of mine, an American gentleman, had read it for me and said that it was not "too strong".

I am etc.
P. A. VAILE.

FRANCIS NEWMAN'S LATER VIEWS.

To the Editor of the SATURDAY REVIEW.

12 October 1909.

SIR,—Will you kindly allow me space in which to reply to the letter by "Criticus" in your last issue?

He states that my assertion (in "Memoirs and Letters of Francis W. Newman") that Newman reverted in his last days to the creed of his earlier life "rests upon vague statements". Now, Sir, I cannot let these words pass without remark. There is certainly no vagueness about the fact that Francis Newman returned in some measure to his former faith during his latter years. It is impossible to read his letters, or those of others who knew him latterly, and then doubt it. It is equally impossible in a short memoir to give these letters in full, but they show that there was no doubt in Martineau's mind, nor in that of Temperley Gray, and others.

There is a spirit breathed forth in Francis Newman's later points of view that is more than convincing to those who weigh one letter with another, and it assures the reader that, though much dogma seemed always a difficulty in his religion, yet none the less the ship of his personal religion was steering straight for Christianity at the end of its long voyage across a sea of doubts.

I do not think in this connexion that we should forget that famous sentence of Vogüé's: "L'écrivain est surtout puissant par ce qu'il ne dit pas".

I am, Sir, yours faithfully,
J. GIBERNE SIEVEKING.

"KING LEAR."

To the Editor of the SATURDAY REVIEW.

London, 8 October 1909.

SIR,—Mr. Leslie's letter in yours of 2 October is useful in its insistence on the uncompromising sex-portrayal of Regan and Goneril.

Goneril is fearless, direct, brutal; unscrupulous rather than cruel. The "moral fool, . . . milk-liver'd" Albany—Mr. Dawson Millward might have made a hit in this part—is not Goneril's fitting lord, and this splendidly elemental female is capable of any crime to possess her natural mate, Edmund.

But if Goneril is tigress, Regan is quintessential cat, domesticated, never civilised. She fawns and is fair spoken, but those brief touches—"Put in his feet", when Kent is condemned to the stocks; "What need of one?" when Lear's retinue is to be curtailed; "The other, too!" of Gloster's eyes, and the instruction for him to be bound "hard, hard"—show the feline delight of torturing a captured prey. Deceit and insinuation are Regan's methods. She is capable of intercepting letters, of corrupting serving-men; yet risks nothing, never gives herself away. Hark how she puts a gloss on parricide

"Edmund, I think, is gone,
In pity of his misery, to despatch
His nighted life; moreover, to descry
The strength o' the enemy".

And listen to the hollow mockery of her arrival at Gloster's castle. She finds the poor father distracted at the supposed treachery of Edgar:

"Our good old friend,
Lay comforts to your bosom: and bestow
Your needful counsel to our business
Which craves the instant use".

True to her characteristics of vanity, deceit and virulent spite, it may be gathered that Regan plights herself to Edmund mainly to snatch him from Goneril. And there is Gloster's comment, "Your cruel nails". Does Mr. Max Beerbohm maintain that Regan is a sexless monster? The fact is, she is as womanly as Cordelia.

Your other correspondent notes that an archaic setting is out of keeping with the text of the tragedy. Surely Mr. William Poel's method stands justified by the Haymarket production! A play so bound up with legal procedure and the complexities of civilised conditions, full of allusions to customs and fashion of the day, is ludicrous except in Elizabethan setting.

I am, Sir, yours truly, M. J. LANDSEER.

"HOW SHALL WE SAVE OUR PICTURES?"

To the Editor of the SATURDAY REVIEW.

Constitutional Club, Weston-super-Mare,
10 October 1909.

SIR,—In view of your interesting article, "How shall we Save our Pictures?" with the conclusion that "unless the State funds are made adequate to meet the purchasing power of the American multi-millionaire, the destiny of our pictures is to go to America", I venture to think that a capital sum suggested by Mr. MacColl of one million pounds voted and set aside by the Government for that purpose would be soon consumed by the successive competition and caprice of multi-millionaires. Three of the latter who died recently—within the last four years—viz. E. H. Harriman, Russell Sage, and Marshall Field, left an average fortune of not less than twenty-five million pounds (and there are, and have been, Americans worth double and treble that amount). Consequently an expenditure of a quarter of a million pounds by any one of them for a work of art—and more than that price has been given by a single individual—would be like an ordinary English millionaire, in comparison, signing a cheque for ten thousand pounds for the purchase of a picture. Accordingly, in order to check the expatriation of works of art, in addition to the allotment of capital, an inventory would have to be made of private art treasures, and an excessive tax levied on their exportation, as is being done in Italy, where alarm about the deportation of "old masters" is rife. This might have the desired effect.

One favourable indication, however, is that a large proportion of the works of art purchased by wealthy Americans are given to their public museums and galleries, or find their way there after the owner's death. The art treasures bought by Mr. Pierpont Morgan, Mr. Gould, Mr. Frick, and other millionaires, are to a large extent given to public institutions; that can seldom be said of the art purchases of our men of wealth. The desire of founding a family with all its accessories is not the ambition of the average wealthy American. Rich men, as well as well-to-do, give and bequeath with far more frequency, and with far more liberality, in proportion to their wealth, than is the case in England. Yet why should we so loudly declaim against our pictures going to America, where they mainly do go? We do not clamour when they find their way to the colonies. The late Professor Freeman, in his "English People and its Three Homes", constantly emphasises the fact that an American is an Englishman, and vice versa. The exported works of British art to a large extent find their new—yet still the same—home in the public galleries of America; there to be gazed upon and admired by countless Englishmen born in a vaster England. They are not lost to the race, as if they found their final resting-place in French, Russian, or German galleries. And since, within recent times, America has become the wealthiest and one of the most powerful nations, it has been the policy, and the best policy, of the British Government, as well as the older English people, to court her and to endeavour to draw tighter the family bonds of friendship, and consequently all means of furthering that object are worthy of encouragement. The taste for British art and literature, as well as things English in general, should flatter us—please rather than displease. When I was staying and travelling in America, on entering a museum or gallery, I remember with what pleasure and satisfaction I descried an English landscape or portrait painted by a well-known British artist, and surely the sons and grandsons of the Englishmen in America must, in similar circumstances, feel the same thrill of pride for the accomplishments of the race. I am, Sir, yours etc.,

VIATOR.

[If our correspondent can see no difference between a British picture going to a British colony and its going to a foreign country, we have no common ground for discussion. To speak of the United States and its people as English in these days is merely absurd. For good or for bad the American people is a blend of every race under the sun. The purely English element gets steadily less.—ED. S. R.]

REVIEWS.

THE BOOK OF JOB.

"The Book of Job." By David Davies. Vol. I. London: Simpkin, Marshall; and Cardiff. 1909. 5s. net.

IN consequence of the same law of contrasts which causes a cockney age to marvel, as no previous age has done, at cataract and canyon and the eternal snows, the snippet-fed mind of to-day is fascinated by the majestic glooms and glories of the Book of Job. It must be studied with the Revised Version open, and yet it required the strong, rich music of the Jacobean English to make us feel its amazing beauty and power. What a gulf separates the dignity and imaginativeness of the human spirit, or at least the oriental spirit, in its primitive and patriarchal stage, from the same spirit at the end of four thousand years of the sophistication which we call Progress! But we are still puzzling ourselves over that old problem of providence and pain, though with a less naïve and childlike eagerness, for it is the way of childhood to be intense and curious about what is most profound and metaphysical.

A scissors-and-paste theory of inspiration wishes to break up the sublime unity of the Book of Job. It would be far easier to believe "King Lear" to be the work of a syndicate. "Job" is one of the very highest peaks of dramatic literature. On the other hand, personal drama was never, in early ages, pure fiction. The story of the afflicted prince and patriarch, "greatest of all the children of the East", and of God's dealings with him, was doubtless an Arabian tradition about a character understood to be historic, the dialogue portion of which was afterwards thrown into poetic form by inspired genius, probably in the era of Solomon. The book was then given a place, either as an original document or as a translation, in the Sapiential literature. Ezekiel speaks of Job as an individual who had really existed, and this was the usually accepted rabbinic view. The atmosphere of the tale, moreover, is entirely non-Hebraic, containing as it does no references to the Law of Moses nor yet to the glories and deliverances of Israel's history. It is not then the composition of exiles hanging their harps by waters of Babylon. The allusions to the non-Jewish astronomic mythology of the Orient, to the long-forgotten wars of the giants, the imprisoned Orion, the sweet influences of the Pleiades, the day-devouring leviathan or the land-devouring dragon of the deep, point also to an extra-Israelitish origin, primitive but not rude and barbarous. Job, like Melchisedech, was a saint outside the Covenant. What Dr. Liddon used to call the inspiration of selection placed his agonised questionings with God in the Sacred Canon, where more and more—but supremely in the New Testament—they found the answer which had seemed so dark, so wrapt in whirlwind and cloud. There is nothing narrow, particularist or local about this book, which Hugo was inclined to call the anonymous masterpiece of the human spirit. Its God is the Father of all men, and its "Vindicator" is the Saviour of all, in every age or clime, that believe.

Job has often been compared with Prometheus Vinctus, but his daring expostulation with Heaven is never defiant nor his uplifted outcry impious or insolent. He is at one with his interlocutors in upholding the absolute righteousness and goodness of the Most High, even while his bewildered spirit beats its wings against the inexorable bars of the Divine decree. Nor are the pious platitudes of the reproachful Comforters in the least like those of a Greek chorus, as the white of an egg tasteless, for they are always amazingly forcible and vigorous. Eliphaz, Bildad, Zophar and Elihu keep their end up with anything but feebleness. Only their arguments are an immense and most exasperating ignoratio elenchi, yet not so irritating, perhaps, to a chafed and wounded spirit as that unctuous optimism of a good digestion and pachydermatous cheerfulness which so often consoles the modern sufferer with breezy Browningisms and self-complacent assurances that all is well with the world. Pestered by the new theology which denies the reality of sin and the new science which denies the reality of pain, the thrall to both sin and pain may feel a desire, with the unhappy king, to sit upon the ground and talk of worms, of graves and epitaphs, or to cry out with the Apostle, "Infelix ego homo! Quis me liberabit de corpore mortis hujus?" He would fain lie down in the dust with that sad bedfellow under the "Miserrimus" tombstone in the Worcester cloisters, or "inch by inch to darkness crawl", deeming perhaps that he alone is blest who ne'er was born. Johnson in his melancholy was enraged by Soame Jenyns' "Enquiry into the Origin of Evil", wherein evil was satisfactorily demonstrated to be only another kind of good. Yet, like Job, Johnson was an energetic believer. The Byronic pose and the novel of fictitious misery were not then invented, or he would have made short work of them. He believed that sorrow predominates in life over joy, yet that life is "worth living", for God has willed it, only we cannot understand His purpose, seeing that men are led by a way they know not. Johnson feared to die, for he trembled to meet his Judge. Job dug for death as for hid treasures, for in the grave the wicked cease from troubling and the weary are at rest. But neither was he driven by despair into wretchedness of unclean living, or tempted to suicide. "All the days of my appointed time will I wait", said Job, "until my release come." There is no contention of two voices in his breast, no Hamlet-like soliloquising, but the issue is between him and his Maker. He is the pleader challenging the Almighty to show cause, and again he will stand forth as the defendant, and calls for the indictment to be produced. Until that last cry, "Now mine eye seeth thee; wherefore I abhor myself and repent in dust and ashes", he insisted on his integrity before God and man.

Certainly Job's "patience" is endurance rather than meekness. God has made man in His own image, and so has given him, in a sense, a right and locus standi to test the Divine righteousness by the standard in his own conscience. Nevertheless, man must recognise his own ignorance and limitation, and the distortion of his moral perceptions through sin. Man is not the measure of all things. There must be trust and resignation. The Augustinian teaching of the absolute Divine Sovereignty is extraordinarily humbling, and yet nerving and steadying. So far from crushing initiative, it has inspired frail creatures of the dust to high endurance and determined deeds. It has been the backbone of character. It is the strength even of Calvinism and of Islam. But substitute for a personal Wisdom and an overruling Providence the materialist's doctrine of hard and relentless Law, an invisible impersonal Chess-player who makes no mistakes, who exacts every forfeit and allows no false move to be retraced, at once conduct is paralysed by helpless terror. Huxley bade us combat the cosmic process; but without belief in grace and redemption it does not appear how this is to be done. Job believed that the cosmic process is, behind the veil, profoundly righteous. He was not a pagan, nor yet an Omar Khayyám. How to explain his own undeserved affliction he knew not, but a Divine justice he knew there must be. He was not tempted to take refuge in a Manichean dualism, as though God were not almighty, but were hemmed in by barriers of circumstance, through which His goodness can only partially pierce. Somewhere or other Job knew that his Vindicator lived, and would stand at the latter day over his dust, and he would see God for himself, and not another.

The Book of Job has certain resemblances to antique tragedy. There is the peripeteia, the headlong fall of a man of high place and eminent virtue—yet not flawless—from the summit of prosperity to the depth of misery. And there is the Greek "irony", for the reader knows, what Job does not know, the explanation of his tragic ruin in that other scene which takes place in heaven, where the probation of his disinterestedness is arranged. This is well brought out in the latest Commentary on Job, by Mr. Davies, of Penarth, where a protest is made against the modern whitewashing of "the Satan" by representing him as a faithful but churlish retainer, only anxious that his Master shall not be imposed upon, whereas in the text he is certainly a malignant enemy of goodness. For Christians, again, the double action of this drama has a far higher significance than it could have for those who knew not the coming mystery of the Cross, or only knew it dimly in such a spectacle as that of the just man suffering under God's hand.

A CHIAROSCURIST.

"The Annals of Tacitus." Books XI.—XVI. An English Translation, with Introduction, Notes and Maps. By George Gilbert Ramsay. London: Murray. 1909. 15s.

THE phrase "a scholar and a gentleman" has always had acceptance amongst us, and marks a real quality in English study of antiquity. We read to assimilate, and we reproduce our reading more or less directly in our action, especially in our public action. Gladstone and Homer, Cecil Rhodes and Plutarch, Lord Cromer and the Anthology, are instances of the conception that the field of the classics is the character, and that the character formed by them finds its pastime in them. It is an honourable view of study, and on the whole true. We cannot all be professors. The professor is necessary, to ascertain and verify the past, and to express it in terms suitable to each generation; but the recipients must not be professional, or learning returns upon itself and its blood is poisoned. For this audience, the scholar and the gentleman, Mr. George Ramsay, himself a shining example of both categories, has translated Tacitus' history of the Julian Cæsars. The characters of these princes are first-class historical matter, and the effect of Augustus, Tiberius and Claudius upon the world is of course amply worthy of any proconsul's study. The translation is in firm, clear English; interesting notes and admirable maps supply what extra information is necessary. All this is true; but in translation as translation there is a great gulf fixed between utility and success. The question must be put: Has Mr. Ramsay given us Tacitus? He thinks he has, and dwells on the point in his preface. He says "it is vain . . . to condemn a translation by saying of it that it may be excellent but that it is not Tacitus". Vain or not, it is exactly the truth about his version. The English is in some respects better than Tacitus' Latin; it is a well-bred, clean style, with plenty of motive power, unhampered by the original. It reads something like Lord Cromer's despatches; it has touches of Lord Rosebery; it is not in the least like Tacitus. Something is wanting; we will not say what.

Tacitus himself was not much of a proconsul. He did govern a province, as a late-found stone tells us, but he was below Cabinet rank, a good orator and magistrate; an observer. His book has not the first-hand value of an off-print of events which makes Cæsar's Commentaries unapproached; it is a study, by a man conversant with government, of the Emperors. Under a democracy, Tacitus says, the historian must understand the people, under an oligarchy the nobles; and now that Roman authority was practically single it was needful, however melancholy it were, to record and analyse the Princeps. The frame of mind in which Tacitus did this is clear. Born at Terni, near the Falls which no one now goes to see, where the Velino drops into the Nera and causes secular litigation between Rieti and Umbria, of an ordinary family (though two hundred years later an Emperor was eager to claim him for an ancestor), he belonged by temperament as by connexion to the Stoics who formed what Boissier called the Imperial Opposition. Excellent, high-toned people, we follow them from Claudius to Trajan. They included such different characters as the gallant Cæcina; poor little Persius with his weak chest, writing satire eight miles out in the Campagna between his mother and his sisters, his African professor and his aunts; Thrasea, Persius' hero; various philosophers and the widows of these, whom people visited in after-times as relicts of martyrs. Impracticable people, somewhat sour in aspect, Quakerish, and, if the word will out, accomplished prigs. Of this spiritual line Tacitus came; he was old enough to remember Thrasea's death; he must have been there when stout old Vespasian found himself obliged to execute Helvidius the elder: "non ante succensuit quam altercationibus insolentissimis paene in ordinem redactus ". He served in Domitian's governments and bowed the knee. At last, when the golden age dawned and men could " think what they pleased and say what they thought ", they all with one accord began to write. Juvenal chose scenes, Tacitus embarked on a consecutive chronicle. He did so as a kind of survivor, one who had overlived his time; he was ashamed with an almost hysterical regret to find himself alive: " nostrae duxere Helvidium in carcerem manus; nos Maurici Rusticique visus, nos innocenti sanguine Senecio perfudit ".

To refresh his reader, accustomed to Livy and the great wars of the Metelli and the Æmilii, he inserts at intervals military narratives, laid in Germany or Africa. They are the weak part of his book: Roman military history was always vague, but Tacitus' rhetoric is of the most écœurant, and it may be disputed whether Germanicus, Tacfarinas or Sacrovir has inflicted most suffering on the reader. Tacitus was not indifferent to the Empire, and gives valuable details about it; he looked back with some pity to its beginnings under Augustus; Trajan had made it really great. He does not disguise the advantage, efficiency and justice of the Imperial government, but he regarded it mostly as routine. The Empire, in its present educational expression having ceased to yield constitutional edification, is equated by us with "Military Frontier Policy", but to Tacitus the centre seemed, as it still was, at Rome. Here, at the caput rerum, policy was made; hence princes were despatched to the East and the North; here foreign chiefs were interned, hither came the Asiatic king to show cause, the provincial to accuse his collector, the Jew of Tarsus on his appeal from Cæsarea, and by the same Appia the mage Apollonius. Therefore Tacitus devoted most of his work to chronicling the actions and analysing the motives of the Princeps. A gloomy task! how different from republican annals, and even the struggles of consuls and tribunes! The necessity of Empire he admitted, but he was jealous of the Emperor. He did not put the most favourable construction on his acts. He thought, and with truth, that the position of Princeps entailed perpetual wakefulness, a trial of wit, to forestall the everlasting conspiracy, detect the points in the thicket; so he devoted himself to laying bare Imperial statecraft, and it is as a student of mind, a picturer of mental working, that he is strong. Whether he was always right we cannot tell; his events are confirmed and even the colour he put upon them in many cases is supported by Juvenal and that prince of mémoiristes Suetonius. But motive is always speculation. With the vast amount of evidence we have the world is not agreed about Napoleon. The reading of character is art, not science. There may be too much shade in the picture, there may be too little. In the last resort the reader settles it for himself. But with this proviso there is no doubt of the value of these portraits from Tacitus' hand. Fate has robbed us of the mad Caius, and left us little of Domitian; but we have an outline, in cold grey, of Augustus, and full pictures of Tiberius, Claudius and Nero. Their minds were not simple, and their likenesses are not done with a few strokes. To read the despot's heart, alike in the Greek period and the Cinquecento, taxed the greatest minds. No wonder that Tacitus' Latin is dark, intricate, and takes back what it has just said. Like his Tiberius, he is " compositus et velut eluctantium verborum ". To send or recall the centurion, to play the victim with talk about the weather, to try the limits of the præfect's power, the loyalty of the guard, and to foresee after all the mushroom, the knife or the pillow—no fluent Tullian Latin, no majestic Livian period, could render that; the translator, if he is to be more than useful, must give us Tacitus' casuistry, his smell of blood and his lampblack gloom.

BOHEMIAN PATRIOTISM.

"The Life and Times of Master John Hus." By Count Lützow. London: Dent. 1909.

THE little kingdom of Bohemia has had a tragic history. The westernmost of the surviving Slavonic nations, it is an island almost surrounded by people of German speech, and, like Ireland, it has received a large immigration of a race which accounts itself superior to the natives. The proportions in the two cases are the same; a quarter of the population of Bohemia is German, and, just as in Ireland, is mainly either aristocratic or industrial. The difference of language forms a barrier as strong as that of creed could be. The Hapsburgs have taken care that there shall be no difference in religion—Count Lützow cites an execution for the possession of a Bible as late as 1755; but the cleavage of speech has been quite as effectual. To-day there are two Universities in Prague, entirely independent and teaching in different languages. Less than a century ago it must have seemed that German influence would prevail and Czechish speech and sentiment die out; but in Bohemia there has been a patriotic revival, marked by the growth of a vernacular literature and by an interest in the nation's heroic age and its one citizen of European fame.

John Hus, of course, is a memorable figure, though there is no feature of his character and fortunes which does not appear elsewhere in the same age. At the end of the fourteenth century Western Christianity was everywhere at its worst, and the public discontent which was to lead to the Councils and ultimately to the Reformation was expressing itself loudly. In Bohemia, not only did the Church suffer, as in England, from absentee Italian holders of preferment; but also from the predominance of German clergy in high places, and especially in the University of Prague, where the natives, though a majority among the students and teachers, were almost excluded from posts of governance. The Slavonic rulers had made it their policy to favour Germans, as Peter the Great did in Russia at a later day, and to encourage German immigration. In fact, through marriage with German families, these princes were more or less alien in blood from their people; the house, soon to become extinct, which ruled in the days of Hus was in the male line that of Luxemburg. Thus Germans held a position to which their numbers in no wise entitled them, and, like most of the prosperous clergy of the age, they were corrupted by wealth. The inevitable discontent took both a religious and a national form. No encouragement for Czechish devotion could be found in richly endowed parish churches or monasteries, and without any thought of secession chapels were built in which Czechish sermons were preached to crowded congregations. There was clearly a strong spiritual revival which might have been guided if the ruling clergy had risen to their duty. But the beneficed clergy and the University made themselves mere champions of a vested interest, and were, of course, supported by the worldly popes of the period of the Great Schism. The patriots could only reckon upon the support, for what it was worth, of the kindly but drunken King Wenceslas, whose whole career was one of failure, and whose inevitable successor, as everyone knew, was pledged to destroy his work. Yet in spite of opposition, rendered the more formidable by the charge of complicity with the teaching of Wyclif, the movement gained ground, and soon had a triumph in obtaining the control of the University, though at the cost of its German members, who seceded to Leipzig and first made Germany a home of learning. The bitterness bred by this defeat has never ceased, Count Lützow tells us, to be cherished; and German historians have persistently misrepresented Bohemian history. He valiantly attempts to whitewash King Wenceslas and to minimise the influence of Wyclif; but his best apology, and it is a strong one, is the unvarnished account of the evils against which Hus and his party contended. Nor can we deny our sympathy to their patriotic spirit. While Germans regarded, and still regard, them as mere barriers to the spread of a uniform Teutonic civilisation, their purpose was to preserve their nationality, and it is significant that when an endowment was founded in 1388 for poor students to seek knowledge abroad, the Universities specified were Oxford and Paris.

Thus there was a clear issue: vested interests, German and ecclesiastical, on the one side; the spirit of reform and nationalism on the other. It is no wonder that the religious leaders, and still more their followers,

(Continued on page 480.)

exaggerated after the true mediæval fashion, and talked of Antichrist and the approaching end of the world, while the existing state of the Church grew steadily more hopeless in their eyes. Nor can we be surprised that the marriage connexion between the royal houses of Bohemia and England rendered the English movement of reform and protest familiar and attractive. Count Lützow is disposed to minimise English influence upon Bohemia; similar causes, he says, would in any case have produced similar effects in the two countries, and Hus, though he would not condemn Wyclif, was never his follower. In many ways he was the more conservative; he always, for instance, said his daily Mass and insisted upon the celibacy of the clergy. It is true that, like Wyclif, he proposed to subject the Church to the State in the interests of reform, holding with considerable reason that it was hopeless to expect the Church under John XXIII. to reform itself. But Hus was far more deeply interested in spiritual than in administrative matters, nor was he the beginner of the strife with the papacy. The burning of sham papal bulls in 1412, a protest against the sale of indulgences which had recently begun, was not his work; nor was this curiously exact anticipation of Luther's action approved by Hus after it had been accomplished.

Yet by that time the die was cast. His opponents had already been assailing him for four years, and as his religious influence over the people of Prague increased, so did the hostility of the beneficed clergy to whom his life and teaching were a reproach. In 1412 they obtained his condemnation as a heretic at Rome, and in 1414 he started, amid the fears of his friends, to appeal to the Council of Constance. He went under the safe conduct of Sigismund, King of the Romans though not yet Emperor, and the breach of that promise was to save Luther at Worms, when Charles V. refused to incur the disgrace of his predecessor. It is needless to say that his trial was a mockery and his death predetermined. His execution, at the age of forty, was the beginning, not the end, of trouble. At once there was a national revolt, marked by the adoption of communion in both kinds, a practice which Hus had not introduced though his doctrine of the responsibility and corresponding privileges of lay people had made this claim of equality with the priesthood seem natural to his avengers. Sigismund was the heir of Wenceslas, but he was never able to enter into possession of his inheritance. In a marvellous succession of victories the little Bohemian nation baffled the powers of Germany, engaged in what was a crusade as well as a war of conquest. Then followed internal dissension, the fierce Taborites, ancestors of the gentle Moravian Christians of later times, being suppressed by the dominant Utraquists, whose practice of communion in the two species was the law of Bohemia from 1433 to 1567. They failed, though they desired it, to obtain the episcopate, but maintained a well-ordered Church and their national freedom till the Thirty Years War. Though the Hapsburgs in the long run gained the crown, they had to submit to constitutional guarantees, and even the restoration of a hierarchy in communion with Rome did little to restore the people to that Church. After the German reformation the Utraquists became practically merged in the Lutherans, and Bohemian patriotism henceforth allied itself with North Germany. At length, in 1618, in anticipation of an expected attack on their liberties, the Bohemians revolted, and chose the Calvinistic Count Palatine, the son-in-law of James I., for their king. He was but the "winter king". The long war which was to end in the final check of Roman aggression began with the suppression of Bohemian liberty and with a systematic persecution which lasted from 1620 to 1781. The nobility were exterminated or expelled, and a new race of landlords introduced, as in the Ireland of the sixteenth and seventeenth centuries. Utraquism has utterly disappeared, and Moravians are hardly to be found on their original soil. But with the recent revival of Bohemian patriotism there has arisen a new pride in John Hus, and Count Lützow says many loyal adherents of the Pope desire that his reputation may be restored, like that of Joan of Arc. He has himself done his best for the cause. A learned historian, whose competence has been shown by earlier English works, he writes our language with ease and accuracy, though we could have wished that a more careful reading of the proofs had removed some slight blemishes and some errors in the printing of Bohemian names; nor can we think that his patriotism needed to be emphasised by giving such well-known places as Pilsen and Brünn their Czechish names of Plzen and Brno. His narrative brings him more than once into interesting contact with England: he introduces, among others, a Flemish diplomatist in the service of Henry IV., whom even the Dictionary of National Biography has failed to notice, Sir Hartung van Clux, K.G.

For this Week's Books see pages 482 and 484.

THIS WEEK'S BOOKS.

Art

The International Art Series: E. M. Degas (George Grappe). Fisher Unwin. 5*s*. net.
The National Gallery: Lewis Bequest (Maurice W. Brockwell). Allen. 5*s*. net.

Biography

John Milton (W. Grinton Berry). Jarrold. 2*s*. net.
Life of Sir William Broadbent (Edited by M. E. Broadbent). Murray. 10*s*. 6*d*. net.
Edmund Garrett: A Memoir (E. T. Cook). Arnold. 10*s*. 6*d*. net.
Marie Antoinette (H. Belloc), 15*s*. net; the Nine Days Queen (Richard Davey), 10*s*. 6*d*. net; Shelley, the Man and the Poet (A. Clutton-Brock), 7*s*. 6*d*. net. Methuen.

Fiction

Bella Donna (Robert Hichens. 2 vols.). Heinemann. 4*s*. net.
The Deeper Stain (Frank Hird). Bell. 6*s*.
King Hal of Heronsea (W. Wilmot Dixon); Plain Brown (Cosmo Hamilton). Chatto and Windus. 6*s*. each.
Old Friends and New (Mrs. George De Horne Vaizey). Hodder and Stoughton. 6*s*.
The Tyrant (Mrs. Henry De la Pasture); Jack Carstairs of the Power House (Sydney Sandys). Methuen. 6*s*. each.
A Woman of Mystery (Anna Katharine Green). Collier. 6*s*.
Special Messenger (Robert W. Chambers). Laurie. 6*s*.
The Tenants of Pixey Farm (Maude Goldring). Murray. 6*s*.
The Mystery of the Yellow Room (Gaston Leroux); The Pasque-Flower (Jane Wardle). Arnold. 6*s*. each.
Woodhays (Ernest F. Pierce). Bristol: Arrowsmith. 6*s*.
The Diverting Adventures of Maurin (Alfred Allison). Lane. 6*s*.

Gift Books

The Forest Lovers: A Romance (Maurice Hewlett). Macmillan. 5*s*.
Tales from Shakespeare (Charles and Mary Lamb); Gulliver's Travels (Jonathan Swift). Dent. 7*s*. 6*d*. net each.
A Lady of King Arthur's Court (Sara Hawks Sterling). Chatto and Windus. 6*s*. net.
Meg's Fortune (Emily Pearson Finnemore), 2*s*.; In Smuggler's Grip (Ernest Protheroe), 2*s*. 6*d*.; Lady Fabian (Edith E. Cowper), 2*s*. S.P.C.K.

History

San Celestino: an Essay in Reconstruction (John Ayscough). Smith, Elder. 6*s*. net.
A Cotswold Family (Mrs. William Hicks Beach). Heinemann. 12*s*. 6*d*. net.
Letters from the Peninsula, 1808-1812 (Edited by Rev. Edmond Warre). Murray. 10*s*. 6*d*. net.
The Roman Fort at Manchester (Edited by F. A. Bruton). Manchester: At the University Press. 6*s*. net.
The Days of the Directoire (Alfred Allison). Lane. 16*s*. net.

Law

The Law of Rentcharges (J. M. Easton). Stevens and Haynes. 7*s*. 6*d*. net.

Natural History

Leisure Hours with Nature (E. P. Larken). Unwin. 5*s*.

Reprints

The Electress Sophia and the Hanoverian Succession (Adolphus William Ward). Longmans. 10*s*. 6*d*. net.
The Importance of Being Earnest (Oscar Wilde); An Ideal Husband (Oscar Wilde). Methuen. 5*s*. net each.
Shakespeare's Plutarch (Edited by C. F. Tucker Brooke. 2 vols.). Chatto and Windus. 5*s*. net.

Theology

Texts and Studies (Edited by J. Armitage Robinson), 6*s*.; The Gospels as Historical Documents (Vincent Henry Stanton), 10*s*. net; Cambridge: At the University Press.
Laws of the Inner Kingdom (Henry W. Clark). Scott. 3*s*. 6*d*. net.
An Exegetical Commentary on the Gospel according to S. Matthew (Rev. Alfred Plummer). Stock. 12*s*.
Essays on Some Biblical Questions of the Day (Edited by Henry Barclay Swete). Macmillan. 12*s*. net.

Travel

An Overland Trek from India (Edith Fraser Benn). Longmans. 15*s*. net.
The Picturesque Hudson (Clifton Johnson), 5*s*. net; Highways and Byways in Middlesex (Walter Jerrold), 6*s*.; The New New York (John C. Van Dyke), 17*s*. net. Macmillan.
Houseboat Days in China (J. O. P. Bland). Arnold. 15*s*. net.

Miscellaneous

Astronomical Curiosities, Facts and Fallacies (J. Ellard Gore). Chatto and Windus. 6*s*.
Celestial Keys, The (Ireleda Sibbrena). Kegan Paul. 5*s*. net.
Equinox, The, Vol. I. No. 11. Simpkin, Marshall. 5*s*.
George Meredith: Some Early Appreciations (Selected by Maurice Buxton Forman); Moretum Alterum (James B. Winterbotham). Chapman and Hall. 5*s*. net each.
Good Company: a Rally of Men (E. V. Lucas). Methuen. 5*s*. net.

(*Continued on page* 484.)

THIS WEEK'S BOOKS—*Continued.*

In a Yorkshire Garden (Reginald Farrer), 10*s.* 6*d.* net; The Cottage Homes of England (Stewart Dick), 21*s.* net. Arnold.

Man's Survival After Death (Charles L. Tweedale). Grant Richards. 6*s.* net.

Meaning of Truth, The: A Sequel to Pragmatism (William James), 4*s.* 6*d.* net; Letters to "The Times" upon War and Neutrality (1881-1909) (Thomas Erskine Holland), 6*s.* net; The Family and the Nation (William Cecil Dampier Whetham). 7*s.* 6*d.* net. Longmans.

My Summer in London (James Milne). Laurie. 6*s.*

Psychotherapy (Hugo Münsterberg). Fisher Unwin. 8*s.* 6*d.* net.

Rambles of an Idler, The (Charles Conrad Abbott). Paul. 5*s.* net.

Small Garden Useful, The (A. C. Curtis), 3*s.* 6*d.* net; Great Britain and the Congo (E. D. Morel), 6*s.* net; Great and Greater Britain (J. Ellis Barker), 10*s.* 6*d.* net; London at Prayer (Charles Morley), 7*s.* 6*d.* net; Dictionary of National Biography (Edited by Sidney Lee. Vol. XX.), 15*s.* net. Smith, Elder.

Story of the Comets, The (George F. Chambers). Oxford: At the Clarendon Press. 6*s.* net.

Two Empires, The: The Church and the World (By the late Brooke Foss Westcott). Macmillan. 6*s.*

Why Worry? (George Lincoln Walton). Heinemann. 2*s.* 6*d.* net.

REVIEWS AND MAGAZINES FOR OCTOBER.—The Forum, 25c.; Cassier's Magazine, 1*s.*; The Quarterly Review, 6*s.*; The Dublin Review, 5*s.* 6*d.*

NOTICE.

The Terms of Subscription to the SATURDAY REVIEW are:—

	United Kingdom.	Abroad.
	£ s. d.	£ s. d.
One Year ...	1 8 2	1 10 4
Half Year ...	0 14 1	0 15 2
Quarter Year	0 7 1	0 7 7

Cheques and Money Orders should be crossed and made payable to the Manager, SATURDAY REVIEW Offices, 10 King Street, Covent Garden, London, W.C.

THE DIVINE MINSTRELS.

By AUGUSTE BAILLY. Authorised translation by Ernest Barnes, with photogravure frontispiece after Geraard David's painting "S. Francis," and a cover design adapted from Giotto's fresco "S. Francis preaching to the Birds." Crown 8vo. coloured tops. Cloth, 5s. net. Whole limp vellum, silk ties, 12s. 6d. net.

"Without in any way detracting from the peculiar charm of the original legend," Mr. Bailly, with the constructive genius of his nation, has retold the story of the Life of the Saint of Assisi with his Companions in the form of a consecutive narrative.

[*Published October* 19.

ITALIAN PAINTERS OF THE QUATTROCENTO AND CINQUECENTO.

By WILHELM BODE, General Director of the Royal Museums, Berlin; together with seventy-five reproductions in coloured collotype after the original paintings selected by the Author. The English translation by . . .

To be issued in Fifteen Parts in Card Portfolios (each plate separately mounted in grey and gold—dimensions of mounts about 25 by 19 inches). Price £5 5s. net per Part. The text (a volume in quarto, finely printed and convenient to handle) will accompany Part XV.

*** Part V. now ready: the remainder at intervals of four to six months.

Of the English Edition of 100 Copies, 50 are Reserved to America. A Few English Copies Remain for Subscription.

*** DRAWINGS BY ALBRECHT DÜRER.

On Monday, October 18, an Exhibition of 64 selected Drawings, from the collection by this Master in the Albertina Library, Vienna, reproduced in facsimile collotype, will be opened at the Medici Galleries, 38 Albemarle Street, Piccadilly. Entrance free on presentation of visiting card.

The complete catalogue, post free 2d. stamps, or with miniature illustrations of *all* subjects, 1s. stamps.

*** The subjects include many water-colours reproduced in the exact colours of the originals, and embrace Figure, Religious, Costume, Architectural, and Decorative Studies, *also* Birds, Flowers and Animals.

NEW MEDICI PRINTS NOW READY.

Speaking of "Special Plate 1909" the *Burlington Magazine* for October says: "The subtlety of Giorgione's colouring is conveyed with a fidelity as marvellous as that which reproduces every tiny crack in the aged canvas, and the traces of old varnish which survive here and there in the interstices. For those who cannot study at first hand such a superb facsimile ought to be invaluable. PRINTS LIKE THIS, WHICH ARE AT ONCE TRUE IN GENERAL EFFECT AND WILL STAND THE TEST OF THE MICROSCOPE IN THEIR DETAILS, CAN NEVER BE SUPERSEDED."

The Society's completely illustrated Prospectus, containing details of suitable frames, the annual subscription, &c., post free 6d. stamps. A special list, illustrated, of some 100 Colour-collotype Facsimiles after the Early Flemish, German, and Italian Schools, post free 6d. stamps.

C.S. = Colour Surface. Postage 6d. each extra; additional copies in same parcel 1d. each.

No. VIII.	BOTTICELLI	The Birth of Venus	C.S. 35 × 22	25s. 0d. net.
	The price will be raised to 30s. on November 1st.			
No. XVIII.	M. DA FORLI	The Archangel Gabriel	C.S. 22½ × 11½	17s. 6d. net.
Occasl. II.	BRAMANTINO	Boy Under a Vine	C.S. 17 × 13	12s. 6d. net.
„ III.	A. DI PRÉDIS (?)	Beatrice d'Este (?) [Milan]	C.S. 20¼ × 13½	12s. 6d. net.
* „ IIIa.	A. DI PRÉDIS (?)	Beatrice d'Este (?) [London]	C.S. 17¾ × 12¾	31s. 6d. net.
	* The Edition limited to 300 copies of the never before photographed or described version on canvas of the above famous portrait, which is now in a Private Collection in London, is rapidly subscribing.			
Spec. Plate '09.	GIORGIONE	Landscape with Figures	C.S. 20¼ × 18½	21s. 0d. net.
English V.	GAINSBOROUGH	The Painter's Daughters	C.S. 20⅝ × 13½	15s. 0d. net.
Flemish IV.	P. DE HOOCH	Interior with Soldiers	C.S. 17½ × 15	15s. 0d. net.

PHILIP LEE WARNER, Publisher to the MEDICI SOCIETY (Ltd.),
38 Albemarle Street, London, W.

Printed for the Proprietors by Spottiswoode & Co. Ltd., 5 New-street Square, E.C., and Published by Reginald Webster Page, at the Office, 10 King Street Covent Garden, in the Parish of St. Paul, in the County of London.—*Saturday*, 16 *October*, 1909.

SUPPLEMENT TO THE

SATURDAY REVIEW

OF

POLITICS, LITERATURE, SCIENCE, AND ART.

No. 2,816 Vol. 108. 16 October 1909. GRATIS.

Messrs. Constable & Co.'s Announcements

THE DESERTED VILLAGE BY OLIVER GOLDSMITH.

With 40 Full-page Plates in Colour and numerous Drawings in the Text,

By W. LEE HANKEY.

4to. cloth, **15s.** net. Edition de Luxe, limited to 250 copies, **42s.** net.

MR. RACKHAM'S MASTERPIECE.

THE FAIRY TALES OF THE BROTHERS GRIMM

With 40 Full-page Plates in Colour and 70 Drawings in the Text,

By ARTHUR RACKHAM.

4to. cloth, **15s.** net. Edition de Luxe, limited to 750 copies, **42s.** net.

READY IMMEDIATELY. MR. WALTER SICHEL'S NEW BOOK.

The Life of Richard Brinsley Sheridan.

By WALTER SICHEL, Author of "Emma, Lady Hamilton." In two volumes. Fully illustrated. Demy 8vo. 31s. 6d. net.

Drawn largely from manuscript sources to which the author was the first to have access, this brilliant work is at once the definitive life of Sheridan, and a new picture of eighteenth-century society. Much entirely new matter, including a manuscript diary by Georgiana, Duchess of Devonshire, and new letters from Sheridan to her and to Lady Bessborough appear in the volumes.

The Romantic Movement in English Poetry.

By ARTHUR SYMONS. Demy 8vo. 10s. 6d. net.

"It is written throughout in that musical and crystalline English, easy without looseness, of which Mr. Symons is so fine a master. . . . In fact, I should be inclined to call this book the most brilliant that Mr. Symons has ever written."—*Saturday Review.*

Hogarth's London.

By H. B. WHEATLEY, F.S.A. Profusely illustrated. Demy 8vo. 21s. net.

Mr. H. B. Wheatley has attempted in his new book, entitled "Hogarth's London," to gather much scattered information respecting the manners of the eighteenth century as painted by Hogarth, particularly in London. Hogarth was a thorough Londoner as well as a striking representative of the Englishman of his time, and hitherto, although much has been written about him, the special study of the wealth of detail he offers has not been definitely undertaken.

The Life of John Dee: An Elizabethan Crystal Gazer.

By CHARLOTTE FELL SMITH, Author of "Mary Rich, Countess of Warwick." With Portrait and Illustrations. Demy 8vo. 10s. 6d. net.

"An interesting addition to our knowledge of Queen Elizabeth is provided by this biography of her astrologer-in-chief. . . . A pleasant picture is drawn of her informal visits to his house, when she would ride across Richmond Park, pass through the East Sheen Gates, and, turning down the hill, stop at the old house between Mortlake Church and the Thames. . . . We are grateful to our author for these pleasant sidelights on the character of Queen Bess."

Evening Standard.

London Life of Yesterday.

By ARTHUR COMPTON-RICKETT, M.A., LL.D. (Cantab.), Author of "The Vagabond in Literature," &c. Demy 8vo. 7s. 6d. net. [*Ready next week.*

Wanderings in the Roman Campagna.

By RODOLFO LANCIANI, Author of "The Golden Days of the Renaissance in Rome," &c. Richly illustrated. 4to. 21s. net.

The Girlhood of Queen Elizabeth: A Narrative in Contemporary Letters.

By F. A. MUMBY, Editor of "The Letters of Literary Men." With an Introduction by R. S. RAIT, M.A., Fellow of New College, Oxford. With numerous Portraits, Views, and Facsimiles. Demy 8vo. 10s. 6d. net.

NEW VOLUMES BY GEORGE MEREDITH.

Poems Written in Early Youth (including Poems, 1851). Poems omitted from the later editions of "Modern Love" and "Scattered Poems." Crown 8vo. 6s. net.

Last Poems. Those hitherto unpublished in book form. Crown 8vo. 4s. 6d. net.

A Reading of Life, with other Poems. New Edition. 6s. net.

IN THE LIMITED EDITION DE LUXE.

A new volume (XXXIII.), being "Poems," Vol. IV. (Sold only to Subscribers to the previous volumes). 10s. 6d. net.

WITH AN INTRODUCTION BY HENRY NEWBOLT.

The Book of Cupid: being an Anthology from the English Poets. With an Introduction by HENRY NEWBOLT,

And 25 Illustrations by THE LADY HYLTON. Crown 8vo. 4s. 6d. net.

MRS. MEYNELL'S NEW VOLUME.

Ceres' Runaway and other Essays.

By ALICE MEYNELL, Author of "The Rhythm of Life," "The Children," &c. Crown 8vo. 3s. 6d. net.

Peaks and Glaciers of Nun Kun.

A Record of Pioneer Exploration and Mountaineering in the Punjab Himalaya. By FANNY BULLOCK WORKMAN and WILLIAM HUNTER WORKMAN. With Map and 92 Illustrations. 4to. 18s. net.

Historical Roman Coins: from the Earliest Times to the Reign of Augustus.

By G. F. HILL, M.A. (of the British Museum). With 15 Plates. Demy 8vo. 10s. 6d. net.

A NEW BOOK BY THE CHICHELE PROFESSOR OF MILITARY HISTORY AT OXFORD.

BRITAIN AT BAY.

Demy 8vo. By SPENSER WILKINSON. **6s.** net.

London: CONSTABLE & CO. LTD. 10 Orange Street Leicester Square

SUPPLEMENT.

LONDON: 16 OCTOBER, 1909.

VIGOUR OR RANT?

"Actions and Reactions." By Rudyard Kipling. London: Macmillan. 1909. 6s.

MR. KIPLING is as successful as usual in his new book. It contains eight stories which will not surprise his readers. "An Habitation Enforced" tells of an American millionaire's settlement in the dear beautiful old English home of his wife's forefathers. "Garm" is about a soldier and his dog and their perfect affection. "The Puzzler" describes the visit of a Colonial Minister to a Law Lord at his country retreat which began with a chase after an organ-grinder's monkey and ended, nevertheless (or therefore), in the accomplishment of a matter of immense importance. "The Gihon Hunt" shows how two Englishmen established a pack of foxhounds in Ethiopia and governed a province while seeming only to hunt. "A Deal in Cotton" is the story of the marvellous beginning of a cotton plantation in Africa. "The House Surgeon" is of a house that was for some time desolated by the discontented spirit of one who had fallen from a window in it—accidentally, but according to rumour intentionally—and died. And so on. At the end of each is a poem, to draw the moral or enforce it.

It is the combination of strength and tenderness that makes Mr. Kipling's work remarkable. Or would these virtues of his be more accurately named brutality and sentimentality? It depends on the point of view; and the point of view depends on whether the style of these three hundred pages appears to you vigorous, manly speech, or the ranting and whining of an unpleasantly accented unpleasant voice. Both views are possible, and we propose to give a few examples from this book which may simplify the choice between the two.

The two virtues which we will call strength and tenderness are nearly always found here in combination, as, for example, where the woodman, Billy Beartup, "lays his broad axe at the feet of" the American millionaire's wife—an act which few other authors can have witnessed. That story has, however, more of the tenderness than the strength. The millionaire succumbs to the beauty of the Kentish countryside where he goes at first only to restore his nerves: his wife curtsies to the old house, saying "Cha-armed to meet you, I'm sure. George, this is history I can understand. *We* began here". She discovers her maiden name on the floor of her pew at church. She kisses both door-posts of the old house which they have bought, when she finds that she is to be a mother in England. "Be good to me", she addresses the posts. "*You* know! You've never failed in your duty yet." And then the poem at the end implies that English soil actually calls American millionaires to come and settle on it:

> "I am the land of their fathers,
> In me the virtue stays;
> I will bring back my children
> After certain days". . . .

The verses ought to be invaluable to estate agents in Kent, Sussex, and Surrey, especially on gravel soils.

In the other tales what we have called strength and tenderness are more mixed. The dog "Garm" is named so after one "Garm of the Bloody Breast" who was a great person in his time. This animal breaks the backs of cowardly pariah dogs to prove that he "knew and was worth more than a man". There follows a moonlight scene of his old master in white uniform bending over the dog and saying:

"Good-bye, old man. For 'Eving's sake, don't get bit and go mad by any measley pi-dog. But you can look after yourself, old man. *You* don't get drunk an' run about 'ittin' your friends. You takes your bones an' you eats your biscuit, an' you kills your enemy like a gentleman. I'm goin' away—don't 'owl—I'm goin' off to Kasauli, where I won't see you no more. You'll stay here an' be'ave, an'—an' I'll go away an' try to be'ave, an' I don't know 'ow to leave you . . ."

We despair of being able to give a complete idea of the strength from which this tenderness springs, exemplified now in the mere phrase about dogs that are " not worth a cut of the whip ", and then in perfect combination with the tenderness in a poem on " the power of the dog " in this strain " :

" Brothers and sisters, I bid you beware
Of giving your heart to a dog to tear ".

But " A Deal in Cotton ", the best story, also gives the purest examples of these leading virtues of Mr. Kipling, so beautiful in themselves, so exceeding beautiful in company. His object is to upset the vulgar notion that the English are undemonstrative. He introduces at once a fat baronet, called the Infant, who is " devoted, in a fat man's placid way, to at least eight designing women ", but above all to Agnes Strickland, who nursed him through a bad bout of fever. It is her son, the young Assistant Commissioner invalided home from Africa, who tells the tale. She is there—" I think ", says Mr. Kipling, " I think his mother held his hand beneath the table ". But when he talks of cannibals she departs to play hymns. Then the son mentions how a native offered him " four pounds of woman's breast, tattoo marks and all, skewered up in a plantain leaf before breakfast ". The contrast is everything. The son tells his tale with the help of nourishing Burgundy, while the mother plays—

" The organ that had been crooning as happily as a woman over her babe restored, steadied to a tune ".

She will not let him finish his tale, but tells him to take his medicine, and then she will come and tuck him up in bed :

" Agnes leaned forward, her rounded elbows on his shoulders, hands joined across her dark hair, and—' Isn't he a darling ? ' she said to us, with just the same heartrending lift of the left eyebrow and the same break of her voice as sent Strickland mad among the horses in the year '84 ".

An Oriental servant finishes the tale, and Agnes passes " on her way to the music-room humming the ' Magnificat ' ".

The virtues are only latent in " The Puzzler ", as when the magnificent Law Lord with the nineteen-inch collar " lobs off at a trot which would not have disgraced a boy of seventeen ". The story shows that high imperial business is best accomplished in flannels—it is a kind of moral version of the story of Nero fiddling while Rome was burning.

Even in " The Mother Hive " the bees talk, not like Moth and Mustardseed, but like cockney soldiers after a wet night in their rough island strength. In the tale of " The Gihon Hunt " a certain Sheikh illustrates the two virtues by weeping over a dead foxhound as if it had been his son. Later on, the caricature of a humane reformer is introduced with consuming mirth in order that we may be prepared for the moral verses at the end, where Gallio, the too-long-abused Gallio, sings a triumphant song, disdaining the " crazed provincials like St. Paul " :

" One thing only I see most clear,
As I pray you also see.
Claudius Cæsar hath set me here
Rome's Deputy to be.
It is Her peace that ye go to break—
Not mine, nor any king's,
But, touching your clamour of ' conscience sake ',
I care for none of these things ! "

The strong man knows when to be only strong and can shed his tenderness with ease. That is the consummation to which the stories lead us. Is it really strength and tenderness? Claudius Cæsar might think so.

THE PERFECT DIARIST.

"Samuel Pepys." By Percy Lubbock. London: Hodder and Stoughton. 1909. 3s. 6d. net.

TWO kinds, very different kinds, of books can be written about Pepys : the historical monograph based on original research and carrying further in every direction the fine work accomplished by Mr. Wheatley ; the œuvre de vulgarisation, a chatty book summarising for the general public what Mr. Wheatley has garnered, placing it in a nice framework and adding the requisite touches of general comment and literary criticism—the book that a reader who has dipped into the immortal Diary or wishes to dip into it likes to have at his elbow to save himself the trouble of rummaging in books of reference for facts, and the trouble of thinking after he has rummaged. The first would be a labour of years, would be bought by first-class libraries and a handful of scholars, and might make a reputation for its author. The second, the œuvre de vulgarisation, will be very useful to everyone who has a taste for literature and does not bother about original research. Mr. Lubbock has kindly provided all who want the second with an excellent little vade-mecum. As librarian of the Pepysian Library he had the advantage of living in Pepys' own college, guarding the Pepysian treasures and learning all that the scholars have discovered about the diarist. He disarms criticism by telling us at once that his " sketch " is " based entirely on published materials " (which means practically Mr. Wheatley and his works) ; he gives us a succinct biography, summarises all the requisite information about the cipher, the books and the material available, and includes some nice pictures (with one of the Pepysian Library) of Pepys himself and two or three of his contemporaries, and adds the right quantity of analytical and literary criticism. The task is performed with pleasantness and good taste ; Mr. Lubbock's hand is light, he is interested in the man, has a very distinct impression of his own, and he uses his quotations and illustrations with skill. His pages are easy to read. They were probably not easy to write. We conclude therefore that Mr. Lubbock is fit to do something better. Meanwhile let us hope that he will send a good few readers to plunge into the Diary for themselves.

Those imperishable nine volumes which Mr. Wheatley first gave to the world, unmutilated by editorial prudery, have, we are all agreed, a unique place in our literature. Not merely the scholar or the seventeenth-century specialist, but everyone who has ever read a page of the Diary, would like to have them extended to thirty or forty volumes. But whereas the abrupt end on 31 May 1669 deprived the scholar of an original authority which would have been invaluable for the rest of Charles II.'s reign, the continuance of the diary was quite unnecessary for the literary critic or the lover of literature. It could not tell him anything that he did not know before ; it might have added to the quantity, but not to the quality, of his pleasure. Nor if our interest is purely psychological, the interest of the dissector in the laboratory of human souls, would additional volumes have given us any new light. The new evidence would have been superfluous, just because it would have been purely confirmatory. The man is completely revealed in the volumes we have. And much more than the man. His wife, his servants, his relatives and his friends are etched in often a few strokes. To anyone with the requisite touch of imagination Mrs. Pepys is a more living woman than Norah Helmer or Hedda Gabler, whom a well-known novelist once said he frequently took in to dinner. What is the reason of this? If we have a little quarrel with Mr. Lubbock it is that he does not plumply put and answer the question which every reader of Pepys asks himself : Why, when I don't care a rap about the tiresome politics and administrative business of 1675, do I find this Diary so enthralling? Is it because it is such an amazingly frank confession of a man's thoughts and feelings—but not frank as, say, Rousseau's is frank—the literary artist writing confessions with one eye on the public and another on his own feelings? Are we all potential Pepyses if we chose to do what Pepys did, and put on paper every night without flinching everything that we had thought or done that day? Imagine, for example, a well-educated civil servant of to-day, living in a flat in Kensington, with a young wife—a young man who went often to the theatre, enjoyed bridge at his club, loved the game and hated losing money, played the piano or the violin, subscribed to performances of the "Ring" and also liked to see what was going on at the Gaiety, took an interest both in the International and the Academy, bought books at second-hand book stalls and liked to know what the Royal Society savants were working at, attended church regularly and also went to Covent Garden fancy-dress balls, invested in trustee securities and dabbled in speculations in mines, preferred a pretty to a plain parlourmaid in his home, made copious good resolutions yet three or four times a year broke the Seventh Commandment—if such a young man kept a diary in which he recorded faithfully how he swore because he had foozled a shot at golf, cut himself shaving or lost his collar-stud, as well as every thought or act, foolish, nice, nasty, important, in the three hundred and sixty-five days of the year, would it be worth the paper on which it was written? Would anyone except the researcher anxious for documentary proof of trifling points in the history of 1909 want to read such a record two hundred years after it was written? If anyone thinks so let him make such a record for a week, concealing nothing, inventing nothing, and he will find it as interesting to read as the weekly washing-book of the laundry or the counterfoils of last year's cheque-book. And if the man who wrote it cannot make it interesting to himself, no one else except the diseased in mind will find it worth ten minutes' perusal. We are not all potential Pepyses. Nor does Pepys' Diary attract only the diseased in mind. Quite the contrary, it attracts all but the diseased in mind. And the reason quite plainly is that while Pepys apparently tells everything he is really selecting all the time. The selection is absolutely unconscious; but a diarist who unconsciously selects will also have the gift of describing what he selects. The two gifts of selection and description, in fact, go hand in hand. And if Pepys lived to-day his language would be just as simple, vivid and felicitous as it was in 1662. His secret was concealed from himself, because it was himself, and it was only fully revealed to the world when we had the unexpurgated Diary deciphered for us. There are no potential Pepyses. When they exist they write diaries. The difficulty for the world is first to produce the man and then to secure his diary. And the difficulty is so great that since the reign of Charles II. we have had many delightful letter-writers, many authors of memoirs, many so-called gossiping diarists. But there is only one Pepys as there is only one Boswell.

MOON-GAZING.

"New Poems." By Richard Le Gallienne. London: Lane. 1909. 5s. net.

IT is both easy and difficult to be severe with Mr. Le Gallienne. It is easy, because he can be so very irritating. It is difficult for much the same reason that it is difficult to be severe with a pretty child who is tiresome. His preciosity is often quite unendurable, yet his best effects lie so near to preciosity that it seems unreasonable to ask him to be less precious. Wrath comes steadily to a head, until the soft line turneth it away; and we are left wondering whether it is not beside the point to ask our poet to come closer to reality. It is asking him to be less himself, which is rarely a good thing.

Mr. Le Gallienne lives within the precincts of a tendency which in France already shows signs of having exhausted itself. He is something of a symbolist. Happily and naturally enough, symbolism is proving itself to be, not so much a serious movement, as a transitory cloud that will leave a very small wreck behind. The attempt to see through the meaning of a word to some enhanced and mysterious connotation subconsciously induced leads in the last resort to a species of emotional algebra where most of the quantities are unknown. Fundamentally, of course, the symbolists are right. The suggestive beauty of words, lines, and rhythms is at the back of all poetry; and it is in its peculiar arrangement of words, lines, and rhythms that poetry is enabled to say what prose may not. But, though a word poetically placed may have its meaning deepened and revealed as it was never revealed before, yet this is something very different from what the symbolists attempt when they get away from fundamental truth to their own perverse deductions from it. They do not so much seek to deepen the inherent meaning that lies in words as to look through the words themselves to certain nebulous conceptions which they arbitrarily associate with them. More often than not the point is reached at which nebulous conception becomes no conception at all, and the lines are so many arrows pointing to a pearly and shifting mist where the reader's own fancy may outline things for itself as it pleases. This way lies, not the apprehension of things deeper than speech, but the negation of all that speech was intended to convey:

> "O climb with me, this April night,
> The silver ladder of the moon."

It is not flippancy to insist that, before accepting the invitation, we should like to know where we are going. A fancy may be pretty enough; but fancies are of two kinds—the fancy that is sublimated thought, and the fancy that is thought's negation.

Talk about the symbolists passes a little over the head of Mr. Le Gallienne. His algebra is very elementary; and his "fancies" are obviously pretty, rather than vaguely significant. Pure symbolism will never come into English poetry. In France it was helped to its own by the fact that French words in the minds of the French tend to become more quickly charged with irrelevant association and with literary tradition than English words in the minds of the English. Mr. Le Gallienne would be reduced to very plain English indeed, if he were deprived of a certain small and cherished casket of gew-gaws. Take away his moon, and his pearls; forbid him to repeat, or invert, or toy with a mellifluous phrase; take from him his "dew and danger and delight", his "mouth where many meanings meet", and so forth—then he would find his cupboard a little bare. It would be cruel so to deprive him, cruel to him and to his readers. These readers would probably fare further and fare worse; and Mr. Le Gallienne himself would be left disconsolate like a child deprived of bricks with which he can build such dear little golden palaces.

In confirmation of all that we have said we might pass from chamber to chamber, from palace to palace, until we were tired of the journey. One door we open upon a little golden palace all complete:

> "What is the meaning of your hair—
> That little fairy palace wrought
> With many a grave fantastic thought?
> I send a kiss to wander there,
>
> To climb from golden stair to stair,
> Wind in and out your cunning bowers,
> O garden gold with golden flowers,
> O little palace built of hair!"

We pass to another:

> "The moon is up at half-past five,
> She frightens me among the pines;
> The moon, and only half-past five!
> With half the ruddy day alive—
> So soon, so high, so cold, she shines,
> This daylight moon among the pines."

The moon, and only half-past five! Fancy that!

MERE PASTE.

"Diamond Cut Paste." By Agnes and Egerton Castle. London: Murray. 1909. 6s.

THEIR latest novel may be considered for the authors in a measure as a new departure, since, if they have ever before attempted to deal with modernity, they have not done so for a good many years. Their "line", if one may so call it, has been the romance of half-historical adventure, laid in the seventeenth or eighteenth century, and dealing with life, not on the exacting terms of reality nor even with any great effort after probability, but according to the purely conventional acceptation of the period they selected, and obtaining what had to be added to represent the colour of life, not from any original study of the period, but from the phrases which have been consecrated to it by the usage of previous writers, and which have thus become the common stock-in-trade of the romancer who asks no more of the past than effective costumes, heroic simplicity, and the easy substitution of sentiment for character. Such requirements, coupled with ingenuity and invention, may quite easily succeed in making a readable book for idle people who ask no more than the beguilement of an hour, and for whom the only digestion with which literature is connected is that which it is expected to assist. In catering for such wants the authors have been quite successful. There has been no disturbing humanity in their creations, the morals and manners which history, drama and private chronicle lead us to imagine in the past have been carefully adapted to suit modern middle-class conventions, and there has never been a disturbing suggestion that hero or heroine would fail in the concluding pages to arrive for the reward of their subservience to the authors' plan. Moreover, the English in which these stories were written was of quite good quality, improved by its very failure to imitate the reality of the centuries with which it dealt. It was, in short, good romance English, unlike anything that ever was, but adhering carefully and effectively to what it was expected to be. Their latest venture may be considered to prove not only the wisdom in their selection of bygone periods but also how easily, when dressed in costume, the most moderate of talents may pass for something more considerable. To deal successfully with modernity a novelist must have either a forcible view of life or some skill in dealing with its presentation. Our authors are not only quite without these qualities, but have sacrificed in dealing with to-day the qualities which they seemed to have. In "Diamond Cut Paste", whatever the title may mean, we have an example of the trivial treatment of a trivial theme which one imagined as confined almost exclusively to the journals which picture "high society" for the benefit of the servants' hall. The treatment is perhaps not sufficiently lurid to appeal to that profitable circle, but its feebleness will probably commend it to the larger class of readers who in literature prefer even their milk watered. The effect of this diluted melodrama is to produce an appearance of emotions curiously out of proportion to their causes. Lady Gertrude, after finding her governess' hypochondriacal pulse "exceedingly quick and low, withdrew with a hopeless sensation that the world was out of joint beyond the power of her setting it right". "The room seemed to go round" with the same lady when her daughter explained a childish practical joke. The pulses of Coralie, a very modern American who has married into "the best society", "throbbed with a not unpleasurable excitement" when the motor-car in which she was being driven prepared to exceed the legal speed limit. One could much more easily understand her excitement if it had remained within it. The car, with "a rending and crashing of brakes, and a fierce convulsion beneath them", turns a somersault at a corner, flinging its four occupants unhurt into the neighbouring ditches, but reserves for itself the most amusing absurdity, the chauffeur announcing, while it is still upside down, that the machinery is in working order. However, as the accident is arranged solely to put into the hands of his wife an emerald necklace which Sir Reginald, a very stagey soldier, has bought for the lady with whom he has had the mildest of flirtations, one could not expect any harm to come from it, even to the car. Everything is, indeed, so mild, except the price of the necklace, that there is not a thrill to be extracted from the final scene in a darkened library at a dance, in the best stage style, when everyone, eavesdroppingly, overhears everybody else, though Sir Reginald's "countenance is stamped with emotion" on parting with the flirtatious lady who has begun to bore him, whose "breath is drawn hissingly within" on his telling her so, while "alternate waves of heat and chill passed over" his listening wife. The quotations, better perhaps than any depreciation, will explain the level which the book attains.

A GOOD VIEW OF RUBENS.

"Rubens." By Edward Dillon. London: Methuen. 1909. 25s. net.

IT required no little courage on Mr. Dillon's part to attempt the almost impossible task of combining readably in a single volume a life-history of Rubens with a critical and chronological survey of his painting. But he has succeeded admirably for all that, and his publishers have added to the value of the book by a series of nearly five hundred illustrations arranged as nearly as may be in the order of the painter's œuvre. The teeming events of the master's crowded life, for reasons which the author sets forth with cogency, are first dealt with. Rubens' life, even if he had never painted a picture, would have been busier than that of most of his contemporaries, and thanks to the patient enthusiasm of his countrymen the materials for dealing with it have been collected and worked out not only in the stupendous "Codex Diplomaticus Rubenianus", which still remains unfinished, but in the enormous mass of bibliography connected with the names of Rooses, Michel and others. Of even greater value is the critical appreciation which follows of the chief masterpieces of his brush, though the task of selection from some thousand works, the product of fifty years of uninterrupted labour, must have been no slight one. The criticism is fresh and spirited, sincere and sympathetic, yet entirely removed from that maudlin and ecstatic attitude which often disgusts and wearies even where its subject is admittedly one of the giants of the earth.

So vigorous and virile a personality as that of Rubens must always challenge either admiration or distaste. But to those who, like Byron, are out of temper with his "eternal wives and infernal glare of colour" or to those who, like Ingres, counsel "Look, but do not linger", the author's Apologia may be humbly commended. Mr. Dillon does well to remind us that the lives of Guido and Domenichino run parallel with that of Rubens, that Caravaggio, the arch-heretic of his day, was then a stalwart and dominating personality, and that Rubens' style followed upon that of the Seicento. The tendency to compare him to his disadvantage with the Flemish artists of the fifteenth century is indeed almost universal, and some excuse may be found for so doing in the curious abruptness with which, in the North at least, painting seems suddenly to abandon all remains of archaism and formality for the greatest freedom and flow of movement and life. Much at least of the modernism which showed itself even in Rubens' earliest work was due to his visit to Italy and the innate love of style traceable in all his art. An attempt has been made to link Rubens to his Flemish predecessors through his masters Verhaeght, Van Noort and Van Veen. Verhaeght indeed played little part in his education, though it has been suggested that Rubens' later fondness for landscape may be due to the older man's example. And even Mr. Dillon seems inclined to endorse the old belief that from Van Noort he derived or inherited the home-bred Flemish tradition in art as opposed to the influences of the South. The truth is, however, that practically no works of Rubens exist which can be attributed with absolute certainty to his pre-Italian days, while we are almost as much in the dark as to Van Noort's own painting, at least of the time when Rubens occupied his studio. There can therefore be no real basis for comparison. Even of Van Veen, the cultured eclectic, we know but little of the earlier work on which his reputation in the minds of Rubens and his fellow-pupils must have rested. But if it was Italy which opened Rubens' eyes and sent him back to Antwerp after eight brief years a master of the brush; it was no mere Italianising Fleming who now took his place among his brother artists. He already possessed an individuality that was all his own, and that fine sense of style—which above all his qualities appealed so strongly to his ardent admirer, our own Sir Joshua Reynolds—had set its seal upon all that he undertook. The combination is as irresistible as it is rare, and secures for Rubens his place of honour.

MEREDITH AND WATER.

"The Paladin." By Horace Annesley Vachell. London: Smith, Elder. 1909. 6s.

IF George Meredith had never written "The Egoist" Mr. Vachell in "The Paladin" would have produced a notable work. As it is, his book suffers inevitably by comparison, not only because he has chosen the theme of Meredith's masterpiece, but because he has adopted—not always very happily—some of his mannerisms and tricks of style. It is not possible to say of many pages of the book "These might have been written by George Meredith". But it is impossible to avoid detecting the resemblance in many turns of phrases, sentences and ideas. Mr. Vachell's prose has therefore something of the nature of patchwork. He is good—in patches; and he is bad, occasionally very bad—in patches. With a high aim, an unfailing seriousness and indomitable purpose, he set out, we feel, to write a great book. Somehow he just misses it. He might, perhaps, have done better if he had aimed less high, if he had been content to acknowledge to himself his own limitations, if, in short, he had allowed himself to be quite natural. The main defect of Mr. Vachell's work is that it is without charm. There is nothing winning in his manner. He cannot convey the loveable qualities even of those characters who he assures us are quite charming. He cannot win our unmitigated sympathy for his heroine Esther Yorke. We are sorry, of course, for her sufferings, but it is not the heartbreaking sorrow we feel for wronged and lovely women suffering undeservedly. It is an artificial sort of emotion—tempered by irritation at some of the absurdities of her conduct. And so with the Paladin himself. He must have been a finer fellow than the author allows us to see. He is presented throughout with satire, but somehow the satire does not bite. We never feel very pleased with him. We never feel very angry with him. He irritates at times, but more often he is merely tedious. He fails utterly to touch our emotions. He leaves us unmoved, unconvinced. Mr. Vachell has woven into his book an atmosphere of unrelieved gloom. From the first page to the last there is no note of joyousness. There is no warm glow of emotion, no touch of poetry, no lofty aspiration. Life is represented as a harsh, desperate thing—a drab battle in a drab world. Even the "comic relief" of the story (if we may introduce so melodramatic a description into a notice of so serious a work) is a lady who is smarting under a perpetual grievance, and who subsists on stout and steak. In the Paladin himself, Mr. Vachell has added nothing new to Meredith's creation. Harry Rye is an inferior "Egoist". He is a clean-bred, typical English gentleman, a sportsman, and one anxious always "to do the right thing". He has been brought up on pleasant platitudes by a worldly minded "little mater" who discourages the dear boy from doing anything rash. In his dalliance with the faithful lady whom he honours with his affection he follows in the footsteps of Sir Willoughby Patterne. That he makes a grievous mess of his life goes without saying. But that he should behave in the manner he is made to do towards the woman he finally marries and that he should be exposed in the consulting-room of a Harley Street physician are incidents for which the previous history of the Paladin as narrated by the author have not in the least prepared us. It is impossible to believe that a man with the Paladin's upbringing and consistent correctness of attitude would make love to another woman before his invalid wife's eyes in her own bedroom. Nor is this the only occasion on which the author makes great demands on his reader's credulity. Mr. Vachell must learn that while all things are possible for the novelist, it lies with him to make his readers feel not merely the possibility but the certainty of all that happens. Inconsistency of characterisation has spoilt better novels than "The Paladin". On the whole, then, we cannot consider Mr. Vachell's new book a success. It has its qualities—its seriousness of aim and purpose, its fluent, grammatical English and its evidence of real labour. But we prefer Mr. Vachell in his earlier work, in which he is more himself.

NOVELS.

"The Holy Mountain." By Stephen Reynolds. London: Lane. 1909. 6s.

At the first glance this novel appears to be a study in landslides—as good a title would be "The Perambulating Mountain". Considered more profoundly—though not much more profoundly—it turns out to be a satire on various fads, delusions and quackeries of to-day, Christian Science seeming to come in for a fair share of those zephyr-like lashings that may not do any good but at any rate work no harm. Such satire always impresses the untutored intelligence as clever and highly moral, and that is the best and worst that can be said of it (and really, when one remembers that the original of Pecksniff did not recognise his own portrait, the efficacy of the more biting sort may be questioned). The central idea of the story is that a young man in the present age by faith moves a mountain from its place, and then, disappointed by the results of his feat, more by accident than anything else, almost inadvertently, moves it back. Such a fantastic parable demands consummate mastery in the treatment. It must be a genuine parable, must show forth some truth difficult to grasp without it, else the mocker will say that those whose faith is mighty enough to move mountains would find something better to do with it than rendering useless existing maps and discomfiting local boards and borough surveyors. Without desiring to mock, that is our comment on the doings in "The Holy Mountain". It embodies nothing essential; there is no fervour behind it. Mr. Reynolds' imagination works too feebly and intermittently for such a theme, which the inventor of Gulliver, if he lived at the present time, might use to some fine purpose. The art of making the impossible seem not only possible but inevitable, and the incredible a thing that our understanding compels us to believe, is not an easy one. Mr. Reynolds wields a facile pen, and in this sort of fantasy or allegory it is his ruin. The voyages of Gulliver did not come easily out of a full inkpot through a smooth-running quill to sheets of pure white paper: they were first achieved by a white-hot, vivid, all-seeing imagination; Swift knew every nook and cranny of his topsy-turvy world, knew, so to speak, the natural laws that governed it, and wrought his picture all of a piece. It was an absurd world and was meant to be an absurd world, and its absurdity was consistent and therefore comprehensible. Mr. Reynolds, if he has the capacity, has not taken the pains to do the "fundamental brain-work". His fancy is everlastingly breaking down; highly serious passages and passages which are the very small beer of cheap satire are stuck together anyhow; after moments of attempted ecstatic elevation of mood there are longueurs of sheer farce and burlesque quite in the vein of Mr. Robert Hichens. Mr. Reynolds must seek to capture and master his runaway pen. It is quite possible that he may some day write a good book—"The Holy Mountain" is only a clever one. And there are so many clever writers and clever stories nowadays that readers must be growing rather tired of them.

"The Bride." By Grace Rhys. London: Methuen. 1909. 6s.

When the young barrister to whom Esther had been engaged to be married before she and her mother came down in the world took her to a fancy-dress ball at Covent Garden she mysteriously divined that his intentions were no longer honourable. And sure enough, when in spite of this discovery she motored down to a country inn with him, he lied about the car having broken down and about there being no train back, though in fact there was the 6.5; and Esther had to run alone to the station to catch it, and a horrid tramp spoke to her on the way. After four "formative" years of life in

London in reduced circumstances she was rendered "pale with horror" by another tramp as she took shelter under a tree in a thunderstorm; and now John came to the rescue. "The Miracle Happens" is the title of the next chapter, which means that John and she were therein properly introduced. John was a sculptor, but for some unexplained reason she never dared go to his studio until one morning it occurred to her to pay a surprise visit to her lover; and then (she was only twenty-five) she mistook a nude model for a statue, and fainted with fright when the girl looked at her. This unusually deceptive model was annoyed by Esther's behaviour and refused to sit any more to John; and John said he could never finish his statue "The Bride" without her, and pettishly began to hit "The Bride" on the head with a hammer. It is difficult to take any interest in such silly people, or in a story which in spite of its elaboration is on some points so curiously naïve and uninformed.

"The Prodigal Father." By J. Storer Clouston. London: Mills and Boon. 1909. 6s.

In returning to the vein of his early success "The Lunatic at Large", Mr. Clouston makes a considerable draft upon the charity of the reading public. There are times and seasons for everything, even for humour, and "The Prodigal Father"—after the manner of champagne at breakfast—strikes us as decidedly outside the fitness of things. We enjoyed "The Lunatic at Large" because it was brimful of innocent fun, and in the story of a precise Scottish lawyer subjected to a rejuvenating process on the lines of "Vice Versa", with a moral purpose such as Dickens gave us in the transformation of Scrooge, we looked forward to an even greater feast. But Mr. Walkingshaw was apparently too old to play the good fairy to his younger son and daughter without making havoc of the happiness of the rest of his family circle. It may be justifiable for the elderly philanthropist to rectify his testamentary dispositions so as to enable his daughter to marry a penniless artist—at the expense of his too grasping elder son; but there seems no excuse for carrying philanthropy to the length of depriving that unfortunate of his fiancée just because his younger brother has had the bad taste to make love to the girl. Nor does Mr. Walkingshaw grow in our esteem because in a state of skittishness he proposes to the unoffending Mrs. Dunbar—the feeblest scheming widow we ever met—only to repudiate her the next morning and "go on the spree" in London. Mr. Clouston forgets that humour has its limitations—George Graves would not shine in the title-rôle of "Othello".

"Deep-Sea Warriors." By Basil Lubbock. London: Methuen. 1909. 6s.

This story of a voyage from Calcutta to England in a sailing-ship ought doubtless to provoke from the conscientious reviewer (though he cannot tell a cutter from a schooner) a study of the difference in method between Mr. Lubbock and Mr. Joseph Conrad. Taking that as read (for it would be hard to write), let us say that our author has none of Mr. Conrad's detachment. The former writes as an army officer who for a bet ships before the mast, lives as one of the crew, fights and works and goes hungry and is soaked to the skin, and in the comradeship of the forecastle—and a scratch crew the "Benares" carried—learns more of human nature in the rough than often comes the way of an educated man. Mr. Conrad is more like an albatross viewing a ship objectively, taking higher flights—but we are slipping into the way which we have just abjured. This book is of absorbing interest: the men, their chanties, the weather, the seamanship, are wrought into a story which the veriest landsman must enjoy.

"Peter-Peter." By Maude Radford Warren. London: Harper. 1909. 6s.

This quaintly transatlantic story belongs to what one of its characters elegantly describes as "kid literature". Its very title is the beginning of a piece of infantile doggerel, and Peter loses all his money just when his wife is expecting Peterkin and he is hoping for Madgie. And when they retire to a farm to live the simple life on the hundred odd dollars that are left Margery lavishly presents him with both Peterkin and Madgie at once. By-and-by Margery has to go out teaching, and Peter left at home to mind the babes is inspired by them to write poems that sell like wildfire—a thing his pictures, painted before he started a nursery, had never done. The rest of the couple's time is filled in by strenuous matchmaking amongst their boarders. The book is dedicated to the writer's husband. We rather expected to find it dedicated to Mr. Roosevelt.

"Cackling Geese." By Brenda Girvin. London: Long. 1909. 6s.

It turned out that the reason Hélène did not live with her husband was because he was shut up in a lunatic asylum in France, and that the man who visited her was only her brother Henry; but not before the cackling had prevented her figuring as pianist at the sale of work in aid of S. Mary's Parish Hall. Meritorious as it is to point out the dire consequences of malicious gossip, a story chiefly about the silly tittle-tattle of a small neighbourhood is in danger of becoming, like its subject, a little wearisome. The author knows her suburbs; possibly she is a little anxious to make it clear that she is not of them. She also knows a good many French words, which she scatters liberally through her book. But who would have thought that a lady whose Gallic proclivities compel her to call the man who whistles for a cab outside a London restaurant a "concierge" would have omitted to correct a slip like "chef d'œuvres"?

"Avenging Children." By Mary E. Mann. London: Methuen. 1909. 6s.

Even in the days of pork-pie hats and chignons, we cannot believe that the blatant, tyrannical Mr. Blore, and his characterless daughter, all tremors and apparent obedience, were typical specimens of a middle-class parent and child. Grace is a foolish, dull girl, whose eventual happiness is more than she deserves. The other "avenging child" is, we presume, the handsome, artistic Alfred Clough, whose reckless courses punish his father for an early fault. But why because a man has an illegitimate son—a very excellent young man, by the way—his legitimate well brought-up offspring should indulge vicious propensities and commit suicide is what Miss Mann fails to make clear to us.

SHORTER NOTICES.

"Auction Bridge." By Archibald Dunn. London: Mills and Boon. 1909. 5s.

The lot of the novice at auction bridge is—like that of Gilbert's policeman—not a happy one, if he attempts to assimilate the methods recommended in the different books on the subject. The latest book flies in the face of everything which has been previously written. The author begins by saying that it is never right to overcall one's hand. This in itself is misleading, as there are times when it is absolutely necessary to do so—but we will let that pass. Having said so much, he proceeds to explain what he considers proper declarations. We read that the dealer should declare "One heart" on four hearts with any two honours, and nothing else in his hand—say knave, 10, 5, 2. This is one of the very worst and most fatal declarations at auction bridge. Again, we are told that the dealer, holding five winning clubs and two tricks in spades, should declare "Two No trumps", not "One No trump", without a possible trick in either red suit. He can do so, of course, if he does not mind losing 400 or 500 points above the line; but that is, apparently, a common occurrence with the author and his friends, as he tells us of a player who declared "Six clubs" over "Two No trumps", and lost 800 points on the transaction. What was it that we read about never overcalling one's hand?

Then as regards doubling. We are told that a one-trick bid should seldom be doubled, but that "a two-trick bid should generally be doubled". Now, if there is any meaning in the word "generally", it means in the majority of cases, and just fancy the terrible grief that a player would come to who made a general practice of doubling any two-trick bid made against him. His unfortunate partner would have our

(*Continued on page* x.)

A SELECTION FROM

MACMILLAN'S NEW AND FORTHCOMING BOOKS

RUDYARD KIPLING'S New Book
Actions and Reactions.

UNIFORM EDITION, scarlet cloth, extra crown 8vo. 6s.
POCKET EDITION, on India Paper, limp leather, fcap. 8vo. 5s. net.
EDITION DE LUXE (limited to 775 copies), Hand-made Paper, sateen cloth, 8vo. 10s. 6d. net.

TWO BEAUTIFUL COLOUR BOOKS.

The Water Babies. By CHARLES KINGSLEY. With 32 Illustrations in Colour by WARWICK GOBLE. Crown 4to. 15s. net.
Also an *Edition de Luxe*. Printed on hand-made paper and limited to 250 copies. Demy 4to. 42s. net. [*Oct.* 22.

The Forest Lovers. By MAURICE HEWLETT. With 16 Illustrations in Colour by A. S. HARTRICK. 8vo. 5s. net. [*Ready.*

*** *Illustrated Prospectus post free on application.*

BISHOP WESTCOTT.

The Two Empires: the Church and the World. Being Lectures on Early Church History. By BROOKE FOSS WESTCOTT, D.D., late Bishop of Durham. Crown 8vo. 6s. [*Ready.*

Early Church History to A.D. 313. By HENRY MELVILL GWATKIN, Dixie Professor of Ecclesiastical History in the University of Cambridge, Author of "Selections from Early Writers Illustrative of Church History to the Time of Constantine." 2 vols. 8vo. 17s. net. [*Ready.*

DR. H. B. SWETE.

The Holy Spirit in the New Testament. A Study of Primitive Christian Teaching. By HENRY BARCLAY SWETE, D.D., Regius Professor of Divinity in the University of Cambridge. 8vo. 8s. 6d. net. [*Ready.*

Essays on Some Biblical Questions of the Day. By Members of the University of Cambridge, Edited by HENRY BARCLAY SWETE, D.D., Regius Professor of Divinity. 8vo. 12s. net. [*Ready.*

Confirmation in the Apostolic Age. By the Right. Rev. FREDERIC HENRY CHASE, D.D., Bishop of Ely. Globe 8vo. 2s. 6d. net. [*Ready.*

Æsthetic as Science of Expression and General Linguistic. Translated from the Italian of BENEDETTO CROCE, by DOUGLAS AINSLIE, B.A. (Oxon.) 8vo. 10s. net. [*Ready.*

Handbook of Marks on Pottery and Porcelain. By W. BURTON, M.A., and R. L. HOBSON, B.A. Illustrated, crown 8vo. 7s. 6d. net. [*Ready.*

*** *Prospectus post free on application.*

THOMAS HARDY.

Time's Laughing-Stocks and other Poems. By THOMAS HARDY. Crown 8vo. 4s. 6d. net.

GOLDEN TREASURY SERIES.

A Latin Anthology. With Photogravure Frontispiece. Pott 8vo. 2s. 6d. net. Limp leather, full gilt back and gilt edge. 3s. 6d. net. [*Ready.*

The New New York. A Commentary on the Place and the People. By JOHN C. VAN DYKE. Illustrated by JOSEPH PENNELL. 8vo. 17s. net. [*Ready.*

The Picturesque Hudson. Written and Illustrated by CLIFTON JOHNSON. Globe 8vo. 5s. net. [*Ready.*

DR. SVEN HEDIN.

Trans-Himalaya: Discoveries and Adventures in Tibet. By Dr. SVEN HEDIN. With a Map, 8 Coloured Plates and about 400 other Illustrations. 2 vols. 8vo. 30s. net.

COLONEL PATTERSON.

In the Grip of the Nyika. Further Adventures in British East Africa. By Lieut.-Colonel J. H. PATTERSON, D.S.O., Author of "The Man-Eaters of Tsavo." With Illustrations. 8vo. 7s. 6d. net.

LORD ACTON.

Lectures on the French Revolution. By the late Right Hon. JOHN EMERICH EDWARD DALBERG, FIRST BARON ACTON, D.C.L., LL.D., &c. Edited with an Introduction by JOHN NEVILLE FIGGIS, M.A., and REGINALD VERE LAURENCE, M.A. 8vo. 10s. net.

RALPH NEVILL.

Light Come, Light Go. Gaming—Gamesters—Wagers—The Turf. By RALPH NEVILL. With 8 Coloured Plates and other Illustrations. 8vo. 15s. net.

HIGHWAYS AND BYWAYS SERIES.

Highways and Byways in Middlesex. By WALTER JERROLD. With Illustrations by HUGH THOMSON, and a Map. Extra crown 8vo. gilt top, 6s. [*Ready.*

NEW 6s. NOVELS.

Open Country. By MAURICE HEWLETT. [*Ready.*

Stradella. An Old Italian Love Tale. By F. MARION CRAWFORD. [*Ready.*

The Key of the Unknown. By ROSA N. CAREY. [*Ready.*

The Story of the Little Merman. A Story for Children. By ETHEL READER. With 8 Illustrations by FRANK C. PAPÉ. Crown 8vo. 3s. 6d. [*Oct.* 22.

THE GEM SERIES.

Miniature Volumes bound in peltine leather, gilt, with decorated titles. Fcap. 16mo. 1s. net each. [*Tuesday.*

Christmas, Christmas Eve, and Christmas Day. By WASHINGTON IRVING. With Illustrations by RANDOLPH CALDECOTT.

Country Pictures. By MARY RUSSELL MITFORD. With Illustrations by HUGH THOMSON.

Faithless Sally Brown and other Poems. By THOMAS HOOD. With Illustrations by CHARLES E. BROCK.

Goblin Market. By CHRISTINA G. ROSSETTI. With Illustrations by LAURENCE HOUSMAN.

In Memoriam. By LORD TENNYSON.

Rubáiyát of Omar Khayyám. Fourth Edition. Translated by EDWARD FITZGERALD.

MACMILLAN & CO., LTD., LONDON.

most sincere sympathy. The best part of the book is the last few chapters, under the heading of "General Hints". This part is distinctly good. It deals with the play of the cards, quite apart from the declaration, and a beginner will be able to glean some valuable information from these hints.

It is evident that Mr. Dunn has studied the game carefully, and formed his own theories about it, but it is equally evident that he can never have put his theories into practice, by playing the game seriously for money, or he would have been speedily disillusioned. The book is yet another instance of a little knowledge being a dangerous thing—dangerous to anyone who attempts to put its precepts into practice.

"The Works of James Buchanan." Vol. IX. Philadelphia and London: Lippincott. 1909.

This volume consists almost entirely of letters and despatches written by Buchanan while United States Minister in London. It is less disfigured by the inclusion of trivialities than its predecessors. A good many of the documents published here are of permanent interest in diplomatic history. Many of them deal with such matters as the right of seizure of an enemy's goods in neutral ships, a question frequently discussed by the British and American Governments during the Crimean War. The period covered is from June 1853 to the end of 1855. At times during this period controversy regarding the British protectorate over the Mosquito Indians was acute, and the possibility of war between the United States and ourselves by no means out of the question. Fortunately both Buchanan and Lord Clarendon were conciliatory in tone and temper. Buchanan, indeed, may be contrasted favourably with some of his predecessors at the London Legation. It is interesting to note that our Foreign Minister distinctly repudiates the American claim for European recognition of the Monroe doctrine, therein anticipating Lord Salisbury. This volume also contains the famous "Ostend Declaration" regarding Cuba made by three American Ministers in Europe, of whom Buchanan was one, probably the most grotesque violation of international comity known to history.

"Fifty Years of It." By J. H. H. Macdonald. London: Blackwood. 1909. 10s. 6d. net.

The reminiscences of an officer so distinguished as Colonel Macdonald, who has served in the volunteer force since 1859, ought to be of value. But the book is disappointing. Too much space is occupied with frivolous detail, and too many dull stories become wearisome. Nearly all these stories are hopelessly out of date. But Colonel Macdonald appears to think that drill has still the prominence it once had, and he claims that he has all through been in advance of the times, and has exercised a predominant influence on modern military training. In one place he says, "If I have ruined or helped to ruin the drill of the British Army", etc. He need really have no such qualms of conscience. Lord Airey, Lord Wolseley, Sir Redvers Buller, Sir Evelyn Wood, and other Adjutants-General were men who had ideas of their own, and acted on them without relying too much on the authority of even so distinguished a volunteer as the author. It is true that he talked a great deal on the subject with many leading Generals, from Commanders-in-Chief downwards—many of his conversations he relates in extenso; that he has written much in the "United Service Magazine" and other periodicals; and that he gives us numerous extracts from letters praising his work. But all this is far from convincing us that the author's influence on the training of the Army was more far-reaching than that of all the War Secretaries, Commanders-in-Chief, and Adjutants-General who held office during the period under notice.

"The Reunion Magazine." No. 1, October. London: Cope and Fenwick. 1909. 6d. net.

We welcome this magazine, which should be of real use in preparing the way for the reunion in Christendom. Undoubtedly ignorance stands in the way quite as much as any dogmatic difficulty. There is no valid reason why the American and Orthodox Churches should not be in communion with one another. But it would be fatal to try to rush things. The best service that can be done for reunion at present is the spread of knowledge.

"The Advertisements of 'The Spectator'." By Laurence Lewis. London: Constable. 6s. net.

At a time when most material for the reconstruction of vanishing periods has been made conveniently accessible, it is something to be grateful for when someone suggests an additional source of information that might well have been overlooked. To go to the advertisement for a sidelight upon manners would not occur to everyone; but it has occurred to Mr. Lewis. The result is by no means to be despised. The eighteenth-century gentleman may, in his chase after lost property, be followed through the culminating stages of last night's entertainment. The eighteenth-century lady may be indiscreetly followed into her very chamber, where she may be seen drinking strange quackeries, to make her fair, or applying the cosmetic, the presence of which may not be detected by the nearest friend. The books to be read, the garments to be worn, the theatres and shows to be visited—all are to be found here, puffed and praised a little archaically perhaps, but with a true modern appreciation of the superlative degree. No student of eighteenth-century society should neglect these advertisements.

"The Jena Campaign." By Colonel F. N. Maude. London: Swan Sonnenschein. 1909. 5s. net.

Each volume of the "special campaign series" has been interesting, and this last one is especially so. Colonel Maude has written a very clear and interesting account of one of the most momentous phases of modern European history. Jena may in truth be called the birthplace of the modern military system, since it was the dire straits to which Prussia was reduced in 1806 that induced her to set her house in order, and laid the seeds of the future greatness of modern Germany. Moreover, it was Napoleon's restrictions on her maintenance of an army that caused her to adopt the short-service system by which a whole nation can be trained to arms. Needless to say, this system has now been adopted by every great European nation except ourselves. We cordially recommend all those interested in the subject to read Colonel Maude's book.

"Dictionary of National Biography." Vol. XX. Ubaldini—Whewell. London: Smith, Elder. 1909. 15s. net.

Colonel E. M. Lloyd's sixty-eight columns on the Duke of Wellington are the principal contribution to the new volume. Nearly sixty columns are devoted to Mr. I. S. Leadam's Sir Robert Walpole, while some ten columns suffice for Mr. Austin Dobson's Horace Walpole—a proportion which strikes us as a good example of the relative importance allotted in the Dictionary to individuals. Sir Leslie Stephen's account of Bishop Warburton and of William Whewell, Sir Frederick Bramwell's of James Watt, Sir Alexander Arbuthnot's Viscount Wellesley, S. R. Gardiner's First Earl of Strafford, and the Rev. Alexander Gordon's Wesley combine to lend distinction to the latest volume in the reissue of the Dictionary.

"In the Days of the Georges." By W. B. Boulton. London: Nash. 1909. 15s. net.

No man who writes a book upon Court life can expect any very serious critical attention just now. Court life has, during the last year, proved to be the chosen field of the book-maker, and the number of these volumes has been as great as their contents have been negligible. "In the Days of the Georges" is good of its kind, not at all badly written, and resting upon a sound basis of contemporary evidence. But Georgian naughtiness is always a little tedious and the liveliness of the domestic annals of these kings fails to communicate itself to the onlooker. The incomparable Brummell, too, is all very well in his way; but we have soon had enough of him.

"The Religion of H. G. Wells, and other Essays." By the Rev. Alexander H. Craufurd. London: Fisher Unwin. 1909. 3s. 6d. net.

Mr. Wells must certainly feel flattered to find here so scrupulous a réchauffé of his opinions. To each of these opinions is attached a credo, or a non-credo, with or without reservations, which is instructive in so far as it reflects the mind of the author. Otherwise the instruction is not great in its amount, nor of a disproportionately high quality. The essays are quite readable, perhaps for these very reasons. The sententious mind will find them particularly pleasing; and there is much comfort here for those who have a sneaking affection for advanced views, without the courage or the logic to follow them through to the end.

LITERARY NOTES.

The autumn publishing season is prolific, though so far there have been no works calculated to lend it distinction. The only book that has apparently really "caught on" is one that had been better unpublished. To many of the principal volumes on the lists we drew attention three weeks ago. Dr. Sven Hedin's "Trans-Himalaya", which Messrs. Macmillan will issue, will be in two volumes, containing eight coloured plates and four hundred other illustrations. Then we are to have Lieutenant Shackleton's story of his Antarctic achievement from Mr. Heinemann.

Another big book, to be issued by Messrs. Longmans, is Mr. Millais' "Natural History of British Game Birds". Priced

(*Continued on page* xii.)

MESSRS. BELL'S BOOKS.

Write for Messrs. Bell's Full Autumn List.

NOW READY. Crown 4to. 15s. net.

Savoy Operas.

By W. S. GILBERT.
With a New Introduction by the Author.
32 Illustrations in Colour by W. RUSSELL FLINT, and Title-page and binding designed by the same Artist.

This volume contains four of the most popular of Sir W. S. Gilbert's Operas—"The Pirates of Penzance," "Patience," "Princess Ida," and "The Yeomen of the Guard," which have been revised by the author for the purpose.

NOW READY. Demy 8vo. Illustrated, 10s. 6d. net.

Southern Rhodesia.

By PERCY F. HONE, B.A.Cantab.

"It will prove of the greatest practical interest and value to those who have invested money in Southern Rhodesia, to all who study Imperial questions—and, most of all, to the young men . . . whose thoughts have lately been turning towards that most attractive and romantic territory."—*Standard.*

The aim of this book, which is the first history of Southern Rhodesia, is to give an accurate account of the country, its inhabitants, and its resources. The author possesses a thorough knowledge of the country, having been for some years engaged in farming, mining, and Government work out there.

VOL. I. NOW READY.
Demy 8vo. with Two Photogravure Portraits, 10s. 6d. net.

The Hanoverian Queens of England.

By ALICE GREENWOOD.

"Miss Greenwood is sincerely to be commended for having made an effort to fill a gap in English biography, and heartily to be congratulated upon the first results of her labours. An authoritative account of the Hanoverian Queens of England has long been needed, and it is surprising that we have been left so long without it."—*Daily Chronicle.*

READY WEDNESDAY NEXT. Fcap. 8vo. 6s.

A Handbook to Dante.

By F. J. SNELL, M.A., late Scholar of Balliol College, Oxford, Author of "The Age of Chaucer," &c.

This volume will be uniform with Mrs. Sutherland Orr's well-known "Handbook to Browning," and Mr. Morton Luce's "Handbook to Tennyson" and "Handbook to Shakespeare."

BOHN'S CLASSICAL LIBRARY.—NEW VOLUME.
READY WEDNESDAY NEXT. 3s. 6d.

THE TRAGEDIES OF ÆSCHYLUS.

A New Prose Translation from a Revised Text by WALTER HEADLAM, Litt.D., and C. E. S. HEADLAM, M.A.

A complete List of Bohn's Libraries, which now include upwards of 800 volumes, will be sent on application.

NEW AND REVISED EDITION (1909). 10s. 6d.

HOBLYN'S DICTIONARY OF TERMS USED IN MEDICINE, and the Collateral Sciences. Fourteenth Edition, revised throughout, with numerous Additions by JOHN A. P. PRICE, B.A., M.D.Oxon., Late Physician to the Royal Hospital for Children and Women.

THE QUEEN'S TREASURES SERIES.

Small crown 8vo. With 8 Coloured Plates and Decorated Title-Page, Covers, and End-Papers. 2s. 6d. net each.

NEW VOLUMES.

LOB-LIE-BY-THE-FIRE; or, the Luck of Lingborough, and other Stories. By Mrs. EWING. Illustrated by ALICE B. WOODWARD. [*Ready Wednesday next.*

LITTLE WOMEN. By LOUISA M. ALCOTT. Illustrated by M. V. WHEELHOUSE. [*Ready.*

NEW SIX-SHILLING NOVELS.

Crown 8vo. cloth, 6s.

The Deeper Stain.

By FRANK HIRD, Author of "King Fitz's A.D.C."

Mr. Hird's New Novel concerns itself with questions of modern social life, and will fascinate readers as much by the brilliance of the character studies as by the restraint and dignity with which the author has described the terrible problem which confronts his heroine.

"Mr. Hird's new novel will maintain and increase his reputation, because its characterisation is strong and faithful, and its description vivid and true. Beatrice Stratton, the very type of noble womanhood, and her husband, John Haughton, the representative of so much that is admirable in British manhood, will remain among the great figures of fiction."—*Manchester Guardian.*

Starbrace.

By SHEILA KAYE-SMITH, Author of "The Tramping Methodist."

"'Starbrace' must be included amongst the five or six novels that this year has so far given us that are worthy of remembrance. . . . The descriptions of Nature are quite remarkable; there is no set 'purple' patch, but Sussex is rendered in a way that is as unusual as it is beautiful."—*Standard.*

London: GEORGE BELL & SONS, York House, Portugal St., W.C.

DUCKWORTH & CO.'S ANNOUNCEMENTS.

A SELECTION.

Life, Sport, and Pleasure.

THE MERRY PAST.

By RALPH NEVILL,
Part Author of "Piccadilly to Pall Mall."
With a Frontispiece. Demy 8vo. 12s. 6d. net.

A racy volume of anecdotes, abounding in quips and stories of town and country life.

London.

A Portfolio of 20 Photogravures. By ALVIN LANGDON COBURN. With an Introduction by HILAIRE BELLOC, M.P. 25s. net.

A History of Aquatint Engraving.

By S. T. PRIDEAUX. Illustrated with Reproductions by the Collotype process and numerous Half-Tone Plates. Royal 8vo. 15s. net.

The Hills and the Vale. Collected Essays.

By RICHARD JEFFERIES. With an Introduction by EDWARD THOMAS, Author of "The Life of Richard Jefferies." Crown 8vo. 6s.

THE LIBRARY OF ART. New Volumes.

"The excellent Red Series."—Times.

Six Greek Sculptors.

(Myron, Pheidias, Polykleitos, Skopas, Praxiteles, and Lysippos.) By ERNEST GARDNER. With 80 Half-Tone Illustrations. Pott 4to. 7s. 6d. net.

The Lives of the British Architects.

By E. BERESFORD CHANCELLOR. With 45 Illustrations. Pott 4to, 7s. 6d. net.

Auguste Rodin.

By CAMILLE MAUCLAIR. With very many Illustrations and Photogravure Frontispiece. A new and cheaper edition. Small 4to. 7s. 6d. net.

Science and Religion in Contemporary Philosophy.

By PROF. E. BOUTROUX. Translated by JONATHAN NIELD. Demy 8vo. 8s. net.

Villa Rubein and Four Stories.

By JOHN GALSWORTHY. Crown 8vo. 6s. [*Shortly.*

W. H. DAVIES' REMINISCENCES.

Beggars.

By W. H. DAVIES, Author of "The Autobiography of a Super Tramp." Crown 8vo. 6s.

"A book about Beggars and their characteristics West and East. I contains a great many personal experiences, and is worth reading."—*Times.*

The Trader.

By CECIL ROSS JOHNSON. 6s.

"The Heart of a Woman."

Margaret Hever.

A Novel. By ELIZABETH MARTINDALE. Crown 8vo. 6s.

"The subject of Margaret Hever is the struggle in a girl's nature when invaded and hypnotised by the passion of a man whom she fears and strives to repulse."—*The Nation.*

DUCKWORTH & CO., Covent Garden, London, W.C.

at £8 8s. net, it will be ready on 28 October. Messrs. Longmans will also issue a facsimile of the original MSS. of "The Dream of Gerontius" by John Henry Newman. On Monday next will appear "The Relation of Medicine to Philosophy", by Dr. R. O. Moon. The work is an attempt to trace the influence exercised upon medicine by current thought and philosophy.

Mr. Murray is adding to his "Wisdom of the East" series the famous Buddhist parallel of the "Imitatio Christi", written in the eighth century by Santi Deva, who is called the Thomas à Kempis of India. No English translation of this work, which will be "The Path of Light", has previously appeared. The translation has been done by Dr. L. D. Barnett, the Keeper of Oriental Records at the British Museum. Another work which Mr. Murray is about to publish is equally fresh to English—or for that matter Italian—readers. It is a history of the Medici family as a whole. Colonel G. F. Young is the author.

The first item in Messrs. Bell's list is "The Savoy Operas", by Sir W. S. Gilbert, with coloured illustrations by Mr. Russell Flint: it appears this week. Next Wednesday Messrs. Bell will publish "A Handbook to Dante", by F. J. Snell; in November "The Works of John Hoppner", by William McKay and W. Roberts, of which there will be only 500 copies, price £5 5s. each; "A Lady of the Old Régime", by Ernest F. Henderson; and "The Builders of Spain", by Clara C. Perkins; in December "The Imperial Russian Dinner Service", by G. C. Williamson; and they have in the press Volume II. of "The Hanoverian Queens of England", by Alice Drayton Greenwood, containing Charlotte (Queen of George III.), Caroline of Brunswick (Queen of George IV.), and Adelaide (Queen of William IV.); and Volume V. of "The Itinerary of John Leland", newly edited from the MSS. by Lucy Toulmin Smith. "The Home Counties Magazine", edited by W. Paley Baildon, will in future be published by Messrs. Bell. The September number contains much matter of interest to the men and women of Kent and Essex and Hertfordshire.

Messrs. Blackwood will make the Blackie Centenary the occasion for the publication of "The Letters of John Stuart Blackie to his Wife, with a Few Earlier Ones to his Parents", selected and edited by his nephew, Mr. A. Stodart Walker. The letters contain reminiscences of seventy years of literary, artistic, and scientific association. Huxley, Spencer, Carlyle, Ruskin, Irving, Gladstone, and many more were among Blackie's friends. "The Work and Play of a Government Inspector", by Mr. Herbert Preston-Thomas, has a Preface by Mr. John Burns. "The Passing of the Shereefian Empire", by Mr. E. Ashmead-Bartlett; and "A History of Mediæval Political Theory in the West", by Mr. R. W. Carlyle, of Balliol College, Oxford, and Mr. A. J. Carlyle, of University College, Oxford, are also on Messrs. Blackwood's list.

The Oxford University Press have in preparation a new series of Oxford Studies in Social and Legal History, under the editorship of Mr. Paul Vinogradoff. The first volume is "English Monasteries on the Eve of the Dissolution", by Mr. Alexander Savine, and "Patronage in the Later Empire", by Mr. F. de Zulueta. A book on "Armour and Weapons", written by Mr. Charles ffoulkes, will have a preface by Viscount Dillon.

Messrs. Smith, Elder announce that Mr. A. T. Quiller-Couch's volume, "Corporal Sam, and other Stories", will be postponed to the New Year. During the next fortnight they will publish Mr. G. W. E. Russell's Memoir of Sir Wilfrid Lawson, and Professor James Leng's "The Coming Englishman". "The Caravaners" is the title of the new book by the author of "Elizabeth and her German Garden" which Messrs. Smith, Elder will publish early next month.

Mr. Heinemann has nearly ready a new book by M. Lenotre, entitled "The Tribunal of the Terror", a study of Paris in 1793-95. M. Lenotre's researches have added much to our knowledge of the French Revolution.

Mr. Edward Arnold has ready for publication "The Salmon Rivers and Lochs of Scotland", by Mr. W. L. Calderwood, the Inspector of Salmon Fisheries for Scotland. The book, while something in the nature of a work of reference, will, it is hoped, be found literary in character as well. "Unspeakable" is the word that sums up the condition of Turkey. Mr. G. F. Abbott attempts to show Turkey as she actually is, in his forthcoming book, "Turkey in Transition". Lady St. Helier's "Memories of Fifty Years" is to be published by Mr. Arnold on Thursday next.

Mr. John Lane next week will publish "Giovanni Boccaccio", a biographical study by Mr. Edward Hutton; "Later

(*Continued on page xiv.*)

Messrs. LONGMANS & CO.'s List.

William Edward Hartpole Lecky (A Memoir of). By his Wife. With Portraits. 8vo. 12s. 6d. net. (*Inland postage* 5d.)
"A singularly attractive picture of a fascinating character."—*The Times.*

"It is a fine story, finely told."—Daily Telegraph.

Garibaldi and the Thousand. By GEORGE MACAULAY TREVELYAN. With 5 Maps and numerous Illustrations. 8vo. 7s. 6d. net. (*Inland postage* 4d.)

The Electress Sophia and the Hanoverian Succession. By ADOLPHUS WILLIAM WARD, Master of Peterhouse. NEW EDITION. Crown 8vo. 10s. 6d. net. (*Inland postage* 4d.)
*** This is reprinted from GOUPIL'S EDITION DE LUXE, and Revised and Enlarged.

War and Neutrality: Letters to *The Times* (1881–1909). With Some Commentary. By THOMAS ERSKINE HOLLAND, K.C., D.C.L., F.B.A., Chichele Professor of International Law. 8vo. 6s. net. (*Inland postage* 4d.)

A History of Malta During the Period of the French and British Occupation, 1798-1815. By the late WILLIAM HARDMAN, of Valetta. Edited, with Introduction and Notes, by J. HOLLAND ROSE, Litt.D.Cantab. 8vo. 21s. net. (*Inland postage*, 6d.)

The Story of W. J. E. Bennett (1804–1886). Founder of St. Barnabas', Pimlico, and Vicar of Frome, and of his part in the Oxford Church Movement. By F. BENNETT, M.A. With Photogravure Portrait. 8vo. 7s. 6d. net. (*Inland postage* 4d.)

The Relation of Medicine to Philosophy
By R. O. MOON, M.A., M.D.Oxon., F.R.C.P. Crown 8vo. 4s. 6d. net. (*Inland Postage* 4d.)

THE EDINBURGH REVIEW.

Articles. OCTOBER 1909. Price 6s. [*On Wednesday next.*

I. THE REVISION OF THE UNITED STATES TARIFF.
II. THE WANDERER: GEORGE BORROW.
III. WHAT IS MORALITY?
IV. THE LAND FORCES OF THE CROWN: PAST, PRESENT, AND FUTURE.
V. SOME RECENT VERSE.
VI. THE LIMITATIONS OF EGYPTIAN ART.
VII. THINKERS AND IRONISTS.
VIII. ANGLO-GERMAN RELATIONS.
IX. RECENT POLAR EXPLORATION.
X. CARRYING ON THE KING'S GOVERNMENT.

OCTOBER 1909. Price 5s. [*On Wednesday next.*

THE ENGLISH HISTORICAL REVIEW.

Edited by REGINALD L. POOLE, M.A., LL.D.

Articles.

THE GERMANS OF CAESAR. By Sir HENRY H. HOWORTH, K.C.I.E. Part III.
KING JOHN AND ARTHUR OF BRITTANY. By Prof. POWICKE.
EARLY PRIZE JURISDICTION AND PRIZE LAW IN ENGLAND. By R. G. MARSDEN.
WOMEN PETITIONERS AND THE LONG PARLIAMENT. By Miss ELLEN A. MCARTHUR, Litt.D.
THE ENGLISH SILK INDUSTRY IN THE EIGHTEENTH CENTURY. By G. B. HERTZ.

Notes and Documents.

THE BATTLE OF TINCHEBRAI. By H. W. C. DAVIS.
THE OLDEST ACCOUNT BOOK OF THE UNIVERSITY OF OXFORD. By S. GIBSON.
PITT AND THE CAMPAIGN IN FLANDERS. By J. HOLLAND ROSE, Litt.D.
AND OTHERS.

Reviews of Books. *Short Notices.*

LONGMANS, GREEN, & CO., 39 Paternoster Row, London, E.C.

MEMORIES OF GARDENS.

By ALEXANDER INNES SHAND.

With a Special Memoir by

SIR ROWLAND BLENNERHASSETT, Bart.

10s. 6d. net.

THE WEST STRAND PUBLISHING COMPANY, LTD., 10 King Street, Covent Garden, W.C.

Invaluable to the Bibliophile

BOOK PRICES CURRENT

VOLUME XXIII. for 1908-9

Edited by **J. H. SLATER.**

Demy 8vo, Buckram gilt, **£1 7s. 6d.** net.

¶ The New Volume of BOOK PRICES CURRENT commences with the sale of Messrs. HODGSON'S on October 6 last year, and is carried down to the miscellaneous sale held at SOTHEBY'S, July 28–9, 1909.

FOLK-LORE AND FOLK STORIES OF WALES.
By MARIE TREVELYAN. Preface by E. SIDNEY HARTLAND, F.S.A., Fcap. 4to. cloth gilt, **10s. 6d.** net (by post, 11s.).
"The book contains much that is new; much too, that, although not quite new, has not been gathered up in a book before; but the whole budget forms a valuable and racy contribution, especially of South County Lore." *Manchester Guardian.*

THE HISTORY OF PEMBROKESHIRE.
By Rev. JAMES PHILLIPS. Demy 8vo. cloth gilt, **12s. 6d.** net (by post, 12s. 11d.).
Pembrokeshire, compared with some of the counties of Wales, has been fortunate in having a very considerable published literature, but as yet no history in moderate compass at a popular price has been issued. The present work will supply a long-felt need.
"Full of interesting details, ecclesiastical as well as secular."—*Spectator.*

THE CAT IN HISTORY, LEGEND, AND ART.
Written and Illustrated by ANNE MARKS. Crown 4to. cloth gilt, **6s.** net (by post, 6s. 4d.).
The cult of the cat must prove of interest even to those who are not professed lovers of the animal.

Milton on the Continent

A Key to *L'Allegro* and *Il Penseroso*.

By Mrs. FANNY BYSE.

Crown 8vo. cloth gilt, **4s. 6d.** net (by post, 4s. 9d.).

Second Edition, enriched by further observations concerning Milton's sojourn in the Rhone Valley and on the Simplon Pass, in the light of *Vaudois* legends and poems.

THE LIFE OF ROGER LANGDON.
Told by Himself. With Additions by his daughter ELLEN. Crown 4to. cloth gilt, **2s. 6d.** net (by post, 2s. 9d.).
"The story of a really remarkable life and career."—*Evening Standard.*

THE WAY OUT.
Or, From the Comparative to the Positive in Religious Thought.
By LAMPADEPHOROS. Crown 8vo. cloth gilt, **6s.** net (by post, 6s. 4d.).
In this volume, which might be called "The Old Truths from a New Point of View," the Author throws a fresh light and has an original restatement to make concerning Christ's Christianity.

THE HARP AND THE ROSE.
By "CARITAS." Cloth gilt, **3s.** net (by post, 3s. 3d.).
A collection of Poems which, like harp songs and wild roses, may help and cheer weary travellers on the dusty paths of this everyday world.

VERSES IN TWILIGHT.
By the Rev. PHILLIP WINTER DE QUETTEVILLE. Crown 8vo. cloth gilt, **2s. 6d.** net (by post, 2s. 9d.).
A volume of secular and religious verse, the sweet melody of which will charm the reader.

WHAT IS A PICTURE?

By G. G. MILLAR.

Fcap. 4to. cloth gilt, **2s. 6d.** net (by post, 2s. 9d.).
"A useful and well-written dissertation on the nature of art." *Sheffield Daily Telegraph.*

Write for Catalogue (No. 102) of Antiquarian and General Literature, free by post.

London: ELLIOT STOCK, 62 Paternoster Row, E.C.

Poems", by Mr. William Watson, the first volume of verse from Mr. Watson since 1903; and "The Song of Sixpence Picture Book", by Mr. Walter Crane.

Mr. Lee Warner, the publisher to the Medici Society, announces a new series of Riccardi Press books, the type for which has been specially designed by Mr. Herbert P. Horne. "The Story of Griselda", from Riggs' "Decameron", and "The Song of Songs which is Solomon's" will be among the first volumes issued in the course of a week or two.

Messrs. Duckworth have ready "London, a Portfolio of Twenty Photogravures", by Mr. Alvin Langdon Coburn, with an introduction by Mr. Hilaire Belloc. Mr. Coburn has been engaged on this work for some years, and the photogravure plates from which the pictures have been printed have been made by his own hands, not turned out of a factory. "The Grocery Trade: Its History and Romance", by Mr. Aubrey Rees, should prove a useful contribution to the history of trade and commerce from the fourteenth century to the present time—interesting alike to the trade, the home, and the student of civic history. Mr. Edward Thomas contributes an introduction to "The Hills and the Vale", the collected essays of Richard Jefferies, some of which appear for the first time in this volume. In Messrs. Duckworth's new series of Studies in Theology will appear "A Critical Introduction to the New Testament", by Dr. Arthur Samuel Peake; "Faith and its Psychology", by the Rev. William R. Inge; and "Philosophy and Religion", by the Rev. Hastings Rashdall.

Lieut.-General Sir R. S. S. Baden-Powell contributes an Introduction for Boy Scouts and Mr. Rudyard Kipling "A Patrol Song" to Mr. W. Percival Westell's new book, which is illustrated by Mr. Sedgwick, "Nature Stalking for Boys through Field Glass, Stereoscope, and Camera". Messrs. Dent, the publishers, will also start shortly an entirely new series of some of the greater and some of the lesser-known works of the Renaissance under the title of "The Renaissance Library", which is to be under the editorship of Mr. Edward Hutton.

Messrs. Black have several new colour books in hand, including Mr. Charles Whymper's "Birds of Egypt", intended to assist travellers and others to identify the birds which they see in the Nile Valley. "Eton", by Mr. Christopher Stone, will appear in their smaller series of colour books; and Mr. and Mrs. Adrian Stokes, who spent the greater part of four years in Hungary, have written and illustrated a book on that country. The Misses Du Cane are following up their book on "The Flowers and Gardens of Japan" with "The Flowers and Gardens of Madeira," and Mr. Sutton Palmer and Mr. A. G. Bradley co-operate in "The Rivers and Streams of England".

Messrs. Rebman's October list includes "Progressive Redemption", by the Rev. Holden E. Sampson, dealing with the Catholic Church in the light of the ancient mysteries and modern science; "The Prince of Destiny: the New Krishna", a romance by Sarath Kumar Ghosh; a new work on Naval Hygiene by Dr. James Duncan Gatewood, of the United States Naval Medical School; and a little book by Dr. Robert Park, entitled "The Case for Alcohol", based largely upon the researches and discoveries of the late M. Emile Duclaux, Pasteur's successor.

From Mr. Andrew Melrose we are to have "The Drama of Saint Helena" (Saint Hélène: Les Derniers Jours de l'Empereur), by Paul Freméaux; 'The Northward Trek: the Story of the Making of Rhodesia", by Stanley Portal Hyatt; and "Rosemary's Letter Book", by W. L. Courtney.

Messrs. George Allen have taken over the County Memorial Series and will publish the volumes on "Old Sussex", "Old Staffordshire", and "Old Yorkshire."

Mr. Frank Harris has at last apparently completed his book on "The Man Shakespeare and His Tragic Life and Story", which Mr. Frank Palmer is to publish.

The Priory Press will issue a new life of FitzGerald under the title "Omar's Interpreter".

A new monthly, "The Local Government Review", will appear shortly.

Printed for the Proprietors by SPOTTISWOODE & CO. LTD., 5 New-street Square, E.C. and Published by REGINALD WEBSTER PAGE, at the Office, 10 King Street, Covent Garden, in the Parish of St. Paul, in the County of London.—*Saturday*, 16 October, 1909.

THE

SATURDAY REVIEW

OF

POLITICS, LITERATURE, SCIENCE, AND ART.

No. 2,817 Vol. 108. 23 October 1909. [Registered as a Newspaper.] 6d.

CONTENTS.

NOTES OF THE WEEK.

The brotherhood of man, whose reign Dr. Salter announced he would begin, is making strides in Bermondsey. It seems to have set in with the blackening of one of Mr. Hughes' billposter's eyes by one of Dr. Salter's salvationists. But it is the habit of those who are in favour of sharing other people's property—they usually come to hard knocks. Honest men occasionally—though not so often as the tag supposes—come by their own in cases of this kind; and there is not the faintest doubt that Mr. Dumphreys is hot favourite. Two and three to one has been offered that he wins. It is a singular race, the three jockeys appearing to be a Christian Scientist, a pantaloon, and the tanner. "How they bellowed, stalked and flourished about; counterfeiting Jove's thunder to an amazing degree. Terrific Drawcansir figures, of enormous whiskerage . . . not without sufficient ferocity and a certain heroism, stage heroism, in them."

Whatever else the contest brings us—may it bring us better boot leather. Good leather can only be got by the hides being tanned in English oak bark. This process is a long one, and of late years most of the leather has been prepared abroad or at home with nasty foreign or—we are bound to add—nasty colonial chemicals. The oak trees are hardly worth stripping, so wretched is the price of bark, and soon there will be no place in the world for Martys. Happily Mr. Hardy has drawn the woodland scene in a picture quite imperishable.

We hate looking a gift Liberal in the mouth, but we must say this: The brave Liberals who mutiny against the Budget would be braver and vastly more useful if they would stick to their own guns—instead of running over to the Conservative side to help fire our guns for us. As it is, with one or two possible exceptions, no sooner does a Liberal declare his abhorrence of Liberal policy to-day than, instead of trying to reform it, he gets out of the Liberal party as fast as he can. We mentioned this lately, but it is worth mentioning again, for the Conservative papers seem quite full of these too discreet secessions and retirements. Nothing of course suits the Liberal party better than that its white sheep should get out of the flock at once. Thus will the strain of Lloyd George, Winston Churchill and Ure be kept pure.

Lord Joicey is one of the latest protesters against the Budget. If we remember aright, he could not, when in the House of Commons, quite gulp down the Compensation Bill. Mr. Chamberlain filled his cup to the brim—Mr. Lloyd George has fairly made it overflow. Lord Joicey is precluded from fighting the Budget in the way we should like to see protesting Liberals fight it, namely by sticking to their seats, so one has no complaint to make against him. But, for the others, how much more should we relish them if they would only remain our friendly foes the Liberals!

The Duke of Montrose on Wednesday gave a startling sketch of the life of Mr. Winston Churchill as, judging by his speeches, the public suppose it must be, and of the life as it really is. The imaginary Mr. Churchill is having his modest "chop and glass of ale" at a democratic inn with "Mr. Keir Hardie and Mr. Victor Grayson". The real Mr. Churchill, according to the Duke of Montrose, is "dining at a rich hotel, attending every fashionable party", and actually going to—Lansdowne House! It has long been a moot question whether the holder of extreme opinions is bound or not to abstain from Vanity Fair. Certainly Mirabeau did not abstain; even Danton had his weaknesses. On the whole we think the Duke of Montrose too severe: They took from Egalité in the end his head, but so long as he lived they did allow him his palace.

We recall the hasty complaint of a horsedealer when he was caught telling a fib. "It *is* unlucky, sir", he declared to a customer; "I never can make a mistake without being caught out!" Mr. Ure, Great Law Officer, seems in as bad a vein of luck as the horsedealer. Having made a trifling slip of £145,000 and the rest of his case against the Duke of Buccleuch, and been caught out there, he drops the Dukes for the

"Aged Poor". He makes another mistake, and is caught out again. The mistake this time is in suggesting to his innocent audience at Tring and at Newbury that if the wicked Unionists were in, the "poor old people" will lose their ten bob a week. Even the "Westminster Gazette" is getting tired of Mr. Ure.

The House of Commons reminds us at this moment of Browning's Grammarian. Dead from the waist down, it yet goes on properly basing the οὖν's and giving us the doctrine of the enclitic δε's of the Budget. As Browning meant to show, there is a kind of pedantry which, persisted in till death, can be even heroic; and we suppose the grammarians of the Budget might come into this singular category. The main feature this week has been the change of attitude by the Government as to agriculture and the increment. They were pressed some months ago to exempt agriculture. Swearing they would consent they have not consented after all. At least, agricultural land near urban centres is now to be taxed if the land acquires any building value. One is amused to notice that this stirs the ashes in the somewhat extinct volcanoes of Sir F. Channing even.

On Friday afternoon the House had something tangible, almost exciting, to think about. Mr. Lloyd George gave his promised revised estimate of his Budget receipts and losses. He expects a total loss of £2,100,000. Of this £800,000 is due to concessions. On whisky he expects to lose another £800,000; and the valuation will cost him £200,000 more than he calculated. But other taxes have done well. On death duties he will gain £1,300,000, the total gain reaching £1,850,000, which leaves the Chancellor of the Exchequer £250,000 to the bad. So the Sinking Fund has to give up another half million.

All the talk about the Lords thwarting the great will of the people is to Lord Milner merely wild claptrap. Nor is the suggestion that the rejection of the Budget would involve irremediable chaos anything more than "language of extraordinary extravagance". Rejection could only bring chaos if Ministers chose for a party advantage to make chaos the corollary. And if the Government appeal to the country failed? Tariff Reform would provide new sources of revenue and put new vigour into national industries. The worst feature of all about the Budget, in Lord Milner's view, is that it is intended to side-track Tariff Reform.

One of the most valuable proposals yet made for the Land Bill was refused on Wednesday by the Lords, but, in view of the facts, they could not well accept it. This was Lord Monteagle's amendment providing a colony of "probationary" allotments where congests could be shown how to farm before risking larger expenditure on their migration. The Government opposed it, no doubt realising their own incapacity to protect the colony against the League's grabbers and Mr. Dillon's "dogs of war", who defy the migrants to come in, and shout "No Mayo man in Roscommon". At Oatfield, Co. Galway, the Board have had thirteen new houses and farms of this kind on their hands for five years, and no congest dares to come near them.

Apart from the League and the "dogs of war", the congests are obviously incapable, alike in knowledge and capital, to undertake the more expensive holdings that would be large enough to assure their comfort. These men farm with the spade and depend on the British harvest to bring home the rent. Ignorant of implements, breeding, feeding, seeding and fertilising, how could they reproductively control the larger expenditure even if they had the capital? It is obvious that congestion cannot be much relieved by migration without some such proposal as Lord Monteagle's; but in opposing it the Government would naturally consider the Irish party, who do not see how they could survive the settlement of the land question.

Sir Edward Grey at the Sheffield Cutlers' feast on Thursday laid down a canon of conduct for Foreign Secretaries which tries his own record very severely. A Foreign Minister must first uphold the interests of his country abroad and then he must adjust any conflict of interest between his country and others without breach of international peace. And he had just been discussing Persia and the Balkans! There has been a settlement indeed without breach of the peace; but not without diminution, and serious diminution, of British interest. We have kept on terms with Russia in Persia by giving up nearly everything. Meantime the country is in a worse state than ever. In the Balkans we have to acquiesce in the very thing we swore we would never tolerate. Where is Sir Edward Grey's Balkan Conference?

Probably some of the people who just now prophesy "Revolution" are—like Dr. Cumming at another scare—taking ninety-nine-year leases of their houses. Yet with so much talk of home politics it is hard to concentrate on such a theme as India. Even the "Times" could not spare two columns for what it called the "brilliant and exhaustive address" of Lord Curzon on Tuesday. As a result there has not been a single full report of the speech in any London paper. Yet it was full of interest. Lord Curzon spoke of the tendency to disregard India imperially. India was unrepresented at the Colonial Conferences in 1902 and 1907; imperial defence has often been discussed without thought of India—in a sense its pivot; Cecil Rhodes overlooked her in his great will. The era of disregard, as Lord Curzon calls it, has hardly yet begun to pass away. Yet India is the supreme commercial asset of the Empire!

All this is true and deplorable. But there is this to be said: whilst we have officially disregarded India in the scheme of Empire, there has been, deep down in the heart of the nation, a conviction that to lose India would be to lose all. One has often heard people who always have a ready scoff for the colonies, and even declare them a "selfish lot", very little good to us, say that India is really essential: there is some slight consolation in this. We won India blindly, and —so far as the public goes—have held her blindly; and Lord Curzon declines to prophesy one word as to her future. But it is something that our people, even the least imaginative, so believe in her.

The China Association was fortunate in being able to announce a few days ago two great achievements. In March 1901 a School of Practical Chinese was organised, in order to give young men who contemplated an Eastern career an opportunity of acquiring a measure of colloquial and written Chinese before they started. The need of such a school was great; but the Association wisely awaited practical results before asking its members to turn their subscriptions into endowment. These conditions have since been fulfilled, and the school placed on a permanent financial footing. Moreover Sir Frederick Lugard has just brought to a successful issue the somewhat ambitious scheme for a local university at Hong Kong. A Parsee gentleman offered to provide the buildings, if the Colonial Government would provide the site, and if the public would subscribe the income. It is less than twelve months ago that Sir Frederick Lugard made his first announcement, and the project has already attained practical completion. It will give prestige to the colony, and the Chinese who subscribed liberally will be able to give their sons a Western education without sending them to the West.

In effect there was nothing more remarkable in the opening of the doors of the Montreal Tuberculosis Institute by the King in Chichester than in the automatic working of a lift. The King pressed the button and, in the words of the snapshot advertiser, the machine did the rest. But only a very dull or very scientific person would not be moved by the thought that a Sovereign whose dominions are scattered over the world can by a touch throw open portals three thousand miles away as surely as though he were on the spot. The shrinkage of the world before the advance of science could not be more happily illustrated. Mere distance is now no barrier to the effective unity of the Empire.

Onze Jan, as Mr. Hofmeyr was affectionately called, was a South African of South Africans, Dutch to the core, yet strenuously loyal to the British connection. As an organiser he called into being latent forces which went beyond his control. The Bond which he ran in the interests of the Dutch farmer was an instrument of sedition. With his resignation of the presidency in 1895 its unfortunate propaganda led straight to war. If Kruger had listened to his counsels, there would have been no effort on the part of the Boers to stagger humanity. From the imperial point of view the most interesting thing about Hofmeyr was his proposal, long before Mr. Chamberlain's Colonial Secretaryship, that a tax should be levied on foreign imports throughout the Empire to provide a fund for the growing demands of the Navy. For all his Dutch extraction, he knew that the integrity of the Empire meant everything to the future of South Africa.

Mexico was for so long regarded as a plum which would some day fall into the eager mouth of the United States that the meeting of Presidents Taft and Diaz on Mexican soil is, to say the least, suggestive. If Mexico occupies a position of independence to-day, the credit belongs wholly to General Diaz. For a quarter of a century he has been the elected despot. Mexico, strangely enough, has recognised his value to the full. What is to happen when this fine old man disappears? The United States have preponderant influence and interests in Mexico, as many a Briton has found to his cost, and if the country should again fall back into her bad old ways, they would not be slow to improve the occasion. Mexicans who love their country and realise the temptation which her resources provide cannot anticipate the future with whole-hearted confidence.

There has been a change of government at Madrid. A new shuffle of the cards brings Señor Moret and his Liberal group to the top. But Señor Maura retires with his following intact and well disciplined, still by far the strongest party in the House. Government in Spain, as in other of the Latin-speaking countries, is by arrangement between parties. No Cabinet can live without the support, at any rate the toleration, of the Opposition; so that when the Opposition leader thinks the time has come for him to have a turn of office, he refuses his support to the Government, which goes out. As in this instance, an accident may precipitate matters. Should the Opposition leaders be offended, they may withdraw their toleration of the Ministry before time. This is not quite cricket, but it is done. A change of Ministry need not in any sense mean a change of policy. It is not a question of policy. Señor Moret upset the Government not because he disapproved of Ferrer's execution but because one of the Ministers seemed to suggest that Liberals were responsible for the marriage bomb thrown at King Alfonso.

Mr. Cunninghame Graham showed a fine contempt for his audience, at the Ferrer demonstration at the Memorial Hall on Thursday, when he picturesquely described to them the people of Spain rising in their wrath and hurling Señor Maura from power. Every villager from Castilia to farthest Andalucia was throwing his cap into the air and shouting "Maura is fallen". It is extremely likely that not more than two or three in that audience would guess that this was not the severest history. It would be interesting to know how many Andalucian villagers knew that anything at all had happened to their Government at the moment when, according to Mr. Cunninghame Graham, they were throwing up their caps. However, Mr. Graham made his oratorical effect with great charm. What more was wanted? How he must enjoy himself in that galley! Side by side with the Nonconformist conscience, with Mr. Hall Caine, and that respectable Liberal, Mr. Wilson of Holmfirth.

It is rarely that a discoverer sees his discovery in right perspective. Lombroso's analysis of the criminal type is not the last word on the criminal. Crimes have been committed by men who were not born to crime, and they will continue to be committed by such men while society exists with its "shalt not" for the individual. But if Lombroso's was not the last word, it was an important and a striking word. It checked the tendency to regard the criminal as in all cases the well-meaning man gone wrong owing to unfortunate circumstances. Lombroso hunted down the crime which was the outcome of a crooked physique and a warped brain, the crime that results from a disturbing of that delicate balance of human qualities that makes man to be a social animal. The psychology of the criminal had been bared before this. Shakespeare knew all that Lombroso found. But Lombroso did a great work, and it was something to have measured the skull of Caliban. Regret for his death will be a regret that is personal only. His work was done, and his school was founded.

Whether Dr. Cook turn out to be a genuine person, or whether he be convicted of an eagerness to forestall Commander Peary great enough to blind him to the value of evidence, the sequel of the Polar controversy will be equally astonishing. The best reason for believing Dr. Cook is the difficulty of supposing that he may not be believed. The mind boggles at a man claiming a tall mountain and one of the Poles of the earth without having a vestige of a claim upon either. Could a man be so impudent? Could a man do either of these things and not be able to prove it? We are upon the horns of a veritable dilemma. However, whether Dr. Cook has discovered the Pole or not, he must be very sorry that he ever claimed to have done so, for he has thereby placed his mountain in jeopardy. We commend his spirit unreservedly. He will not let go his hold upon the Pole, and he intends to recover his mountain. If he prove unfortunate in both these enterprises, we shall feel a little sorry for him, and for ourselves. We shall have to congratulate Commander Peary.

Great Britain has been busy this week naturalising the art of flight. The inhabitants of this country are seeing with their own eyes that flying machines can fly in the sober British air as well as anywhere else. They will realise, as they have not realised before, that there really is something in this endeavour to come to terms with a new element. It is all very well to hear of an aeroplane sailing above the houses of Paris. It will be quite time to wake up when a similar sight is witnessed from Trafalgar Square. This has been the attitude of the majority of people up to the present. Doncaster and Blackpool will quicken the national interest; and perhaps Colonel Cody will before long get the official recognition he deserves. Meantime the prestige of this country may safely be left in his hands and in those of Mr. Farman.

Mr. Cody was turned into a British subject on Thursday. His achievements have been British achievements, but this was not enough. He must sign his papers to the strain of the National Anthem. The scene was a little demoralising, of the kind expressly calculated to kill decent patriotism in this country. There must have been many people present who will go away and be ashamed to be patriotic ever after.

It was a happy chance that brought Mr. Balfour and Mr. Lloyd George together at a meeting of the Cymmrodorion Society. That political leaders should have an opportunity to treat one another with humanity in the midst of a fervent controversy is as fortunate as the use made of it on this occasion was commendable. The humanity of Mr. Lloyd George was so great that Mr. Balfour confessed to some embarrassment; but when embarrassment expresses itself as Mr. Balfour expressed it there is nothing to deplore. The burden of the speech that followed was exactly in tune. To dwell upon the importance of nationality at a Welsh gathering was as timely as was the warning against local particularism. Culture must be national, and it must be cosmopolitan.

If it is not national, it will be neither hot nor cold. If it is not cosmopolitan, it will be of little value to mankind.

The unveiling of the statue of Tennyson at Trinity College, Cambridge, occurring in the same week as Trafalgar Day and the publication of a certain poem suggests some reflections. Tennyson was perhaps the one Poet Laureate who was, as a Laureate, successful. The reason of this is not far to seek. Tennyson was born to interpret his age and generation. He was no prophet reaching forward into the future. He was not concerned with mourning for the past. He voiced the thrill of his own epoch; he spoke the thoughts of his living countrymen; he made contemporary thought beautiful and contemporary feeling articulate. Much of the depreciatory criticism that lauds the form while it decries the content of Tennyson's poetry may be traced home to this fact. The sons of the generation to whom a poet spoke its own thoughts and emotions will respect the message of the poet according as they respect his generation. At present that generation is just old enough to be out of date, and not quite old enough to be appreciated.

The crude fallacies of the realist fell with a befitting dogmatism from the lips of Mr. Bernard Shaw in his lecture to the Photographic Salon last Monday. From Mr. Shaw we look for something a little fresher, or at least for something stated a little more freshly. The popular notion that a photograph has more truth in it than a painted picture, or that it is a jot nearer to reality, is as stupid a misconception as the one which supposes that you must necessarily get a tree on to canvas by painting every individual leaf and counting the branches. It is the same fallacy that supposes a drama in blank verse to be further removed from truth than a drama in prose. Even Mr. Shaw must perceive that the camera sees things a little differently from the eye, and that the eye of the mind is something different from the retina. Then, of course, there is the eye of the artist mind; but we do not hope to carry Mr. Shaw so far as this. But does he not know that there is nothing in art or out of it so grotesquely untrue as the photograph of a thing in motion, and that, if a photograph ever does happen to be true, its truth is purely a matter of accident?

Lord Curzon entertained the Glasgow students on Wednesday with some very sound sentiments. We like his idea of a football match with seven spectators and forty thousand players. Looking at games is not much in our way, but we should like to be amongst those seven spectators. He is quite right, though; it would be a splendid thing if the number of players and onlookers could be reversed. And we were very glad that he told the lads so plainly that he was in favour of compulsory military service. There was no hesitation to commit himself. It only wants a few more statesmen of Lord Curzon's standing to say the same and the thing will be done.

We note with great satisfaction the proposal to found a society for the promotion of Roman Studies: in other words, an Hellenic Society for Latin things. The Romans and their history are more worth studying than any other people—certainly for Englishmen. Every aspirant to political distinction should be made to give credentials in knowledge of Roman history. We should then be saved a good deal of nonsense now periodically served up in the House of Commons. We hope supporters of the scheme will write in large numbers to Professor Percy Gardner or Mr. G. A. Macmillan.

The Navy League must look to its laurels, literally—would it need not metaphorically!—or it will be accused of preferring the foreigner. Why could no English evergreen be found for Nelson's column on Thursday? There was bay and laurel. Consecrate, no doubt, but not British. There was oak; but scarlet oak, not English. We looked in vain for some ivy, which, if all else failed, should be abundant now.

BERMONDSEY AND FREE IMPORTS.

THE Bermondsey leather trade is, it happens luckily, as good an object-lesson in Free Trade as could be desired. Whatever the Free Traders may say, it is a simple fact that Bermondsey was once the centre of a flourishing tanning industry, which has partly disappeared and partly been shifted to other districts in the provinces, where it can be carried on more cheaply. Another industry has to some extent sprung up and taken the place of tanning. Jam factories are now working on the sites of former leather mills. As with Coventry, so with Bermondsey. The silk and ribbon industry of Coventry was ruined by French imports: there was a long period of misery, of idleness and destitution; finally the cycle and motor industry grew up, and Coventry smiled again. This is what economists pleasantly describe as the mobility of labour and capital. If one trade is ruined, say they, after the inevitable interval of starvation another trade will take its place. But how if the other trade is in its turn ruined, say, by the importation of cheap American cycles and motors? Are we to go on ruining one industry after another in order to demonstrate the mobility of labour and capital? And is the inevitable interval of starvation really unavoidable? Ought it not to be prevented? We gather that certain districts in the Midlands, where land is naturally cheaper than in London, have benefited by the ruin of Bermondsey tanners, and are exulting in the fact. There must be something rotten in the state of Denmark when one set of Britons can congratulate themselves on the ruin of another set of Britons. Then we have the makers of boots and shoes, and the manufacturers of leather goods, informing us of the astounding, undreamed-of fact that leather is their raw material, and that if duties are imposed on imported leather their raw material must be dearer! Again we have the same callous confession by one set of Britons that they care nothing for the fate of another set of Britons, but only for their own branch of the trade. The shoemakers and the manufacturers of leather might, however, have reflected that if duties are put on imported leather, duties will also be put on imported boots and leather goods. We are also warned, by the advocates of prunella, that if we put duties on leather we shall so increase the cost of production as to destroy our export trade in boots. The United States put a 20 per cent. duty on imported leather, and their exports of boots and shoes rose in value from £155,000 in 1894 to £1,829,000 in 1906, of which £445,000 worth came to this country, and most of the rest went to our colonies.

The Americans are not content with imposing a duty of 20 per cent. on English tanned leather. In sending cattle to this country for slaughter they stipulate in the contract that the hides of the animals shall be returned to the United States to be tanned. The men of Deptford, instead of passing on the skins to their neighbours in Bermondsey, actually pack them off to America, whence they return after their treble journey across the sea as chemically tanned leather. What an economic waste! Something of the same sort happens to india-rubber. The gum of the rubber tree, after having been coagulated, rolled, and dried in Ceylon or the Malay States or Brazil, is sent to Manchester, where it is again washed and rolled and cut into very fine strips or threads of rubber. These rubber threads are then sent from Manchester to France, Belgium, and Germany, to be made into belts, braces, and elastic webbing, in which form they are sent back to England. We would revive the manufacture of elastic webbing in this country by means of a tariff, and we repeat that this sending of material backwards and forwards from one country to another in search of cheapness is sheer economic waste. Nothing excites the Free Trader so powerfully as the assertion—whose fault is its obviousness—that in most cases the foreign producer will bear at all events a portion of the import duty. Mr. Churchill's eye rolls in a fine frenzy as he dismisses this "creed of quacks and gulls". Two things these gentlemen forget—one, that the foreign merchant must sell his goods somewhere at some price; two, that all the countries in the world owe England money, which they can only pay by means of trade-bills drawn on London against goods shipped to some British port. Take the case of tea. The producers of tea (who, although our own colonists, may for the purpose of the argument be regarded as foreigners) enjoy a monopoly, in the sense that they have no competition to fear from the home producer. They might therefore be supposed to command the market—that is, to be in a position simply to add any increase of duty to their price. But it is not the fact. When the duty on tea is raised, the consumption falls, which means that so many million pounds of tea are lying in the bonded warehouses and cannot be sold. As the agents of the tea estates in Ceylon cannot, like the rebellious Yankees, throw the tea into the water, they must sell it at a reduced price. In order to dispose of their produce, as they are bound to do, the tea companies take a slightly smaller profit—in other words, they share with the consumer the increased duty. The same thing happens in the case of tobacco. The planters in Virginia, in Cuba, and in Turkey must sell their produce. If an increased duty lowers demand, as it invariably does, the planter must lower his price, or lose his produce. This is what is meant by making the foreigner pay; and it is so familiar an operation to those engaged in the tea and tobacco trades that they can only laugh at the almost incredible ignorance of Free Trade politicians.

Lecky points out incidentally in one of his volumes that the whole history of political imposture does not contain a more successful instance of class selfishness beating down common-sense than the repeal of the Corn Law. It was purely a manufacturers' agitation, and it enabled them to lower the wages of their artisans at the expense of the landowners. A similar movement is afoot to-day, when the landowners are being made to pay the cost of social reform. Peel and Gladstone, it should not be forgotten, sprang from the same commercial class—were both sons of Lancashire merchants. On to the neck of the agricultural world they fastened their yoke, and there it has remained ever since, for a good reason. There are more people living on the interest of accumulated capital in Great Britain than in any other country. These rentiers form our leisured class, which supplies the men who are distinguished in every line except industrial production—lawyers, scientists, artists, authors, engineers. England's intellectual supremacy, which is no longer challenged even by France, is due to this class, which has generously paid for its keep by the industrial producers. So long as the industrial toe of our competitors—Germany and the United States—did not come so near our heel that it galled our kibe, all was well; we could afford to maintain our intellectuals at the cost of our industrials. But that day is past; we can no longer afford to sacrifice our industrial producers to our rentiers. Cheapness is the god of the rentier, naturally; but cheapness in the midst of unemployment and starvation is worse than useless. We agree with Lord Milner that Tariff Reform will increase the cost of living, though not much. There is very little difference between the margin of luxury left over to the American and English artisan, though there is this important difference—that the American artisan is master of his home market. Everything depends on the balance maintained between wages and cost of living. If you increase a man's wages by 50 per cent. and increase his cost of living by 30 per cent. he is 20 per cent. to the good, and if you add permanence of employment to that his advantage is enormous. Only fools make positive assertions about tariffs, which are and must be experimental. But there are times when experiments must be made on the economic body, just as there are times when the risk of an operation on the physical body must be taken. What has become of our national courage, or even of our power of observation, when we shiver at the idea of following the successful examples of Germany and the United States? With the single exception of Great Britain, the cheapest countries are the poorest—Spain, Italy, Turkey, Argentina, Japan. The dearest countries—the United States, Holland, Belgium—are the richest.

TOO MODERATE LIBERALS.

THE Apostolic precept "Let your moderation be known unto all men" would seem to have sunk deep into the minds of the Liberal centre. Centre we must call it, for that which lies or is supposed to lie between the extremes can hardly be anything else; but we are far from meaning, as the phrase might suggest, the most numerous contingent in the Liberal host. The assumption, no doubt, has always been that the bulk of Liberal members sympathised neither with whigs nor socialists, and might be trusted to keep the party at a steady jog-trot along the old road of easy progress. They were the ballast of the ship; and no matter what extravagance of sail some wild members of the crew—officers perhaps—might attempt to carry, they would keep her on a fairly even keel. Extreme men are suspect of the average, and the average must prevail. The sensible man, the man of the world, knows this; so the weight of influence would always be on the moderate side. After all, we need not worry ourselves too much about the hugeness of the Liberal majority or the wild cries of Mr. Churchill and Mr. Lloyd George. Thus the sober citizen, especially the moderate Liberal, comforted himself and was able to go to sleep again, even after the election of 1906. But the moderate Liberal did not realise his own moderation. He did not know how great was his self-restraint. Unlike most of us, the moderate Liberal has found it easier to keep himself under than anyone else; and apparently he has enjoyed the process. He has restrained himself to such purpose that no one knows for a certainty what he thinks about anything, and if anyone does know, he does not care. These gentlemen's moderation is indeed known, and it is almost the only thing about them that is. Where is it and what has happened to it, this band of sober, reasonable, conciliatory Liberals in the House? Are they all satisfied that the Budget is a most temperate, well-balanced, and equitable measure? Are they pleased with Mr. Lloyd George's moderation? Do they approve of his platform style? One could hardly help concluding that they do, from their silence in the House, their self-effacement in the country. One would not expect them to be aggressive on any side, for or against anything; but they are not even passively resistent to Mr. Lloyd George's performances. They attend; they say nothing; they vote. A sorrier, feebler, more miserable show than these moderate Liberals are making and have made all through could hardly be. That is, of course, if they do not approve and are not happy about recent developments and Liberal policy generally.

They are mum in public; but we can know something about their real feelings, for they talk in private. That is their one enjoyment. They can tell their friends what they feel; they can describe Mr. George or Mr. Churchill in choice language; they can grumble at the breaking strain on their party loyalty. It is no secret that there are quite a large number of Ministerial members who have no love for the Budget, and loathe Mr. Lloyd George's Limehouse and Newcastle exhibitions. They are unhappy: dissatisfied with themselves, with their party, with everything. They would check their own men but, naturally, would not help the Opposition. They do not know what to do: so they drift on and ultimately drift out. Sick of the whole thing, by a great effort they manage to screw themselves to the point of announcing that they will not seek re-election. Wounded, they slink off the field; do not, as certain high-spirited animals infuriate, become then really dangerous.

We must say that these discontented Liberals seem to us to play the very poorest of parts. We admit the difficulties of their position; we allow for natural reluctance to accentuate differences in their party; we can understand their desire to keep things smooth, outwardly at any rate, as long as possible. But are they not Englishmen as well as Liberals? Like it or not, they have to face the question: Is this policy for the good of the country? If they do not face it, but run away, leaving it unanswered, they are—no other word will do—cowards. If they do face it, and have to conclude that the policy, or a great deal about the policy, is not for the good of the country, they cannot, as patriots, either acquiesce or stand aside. They are bound to make their protest. They do not desire to leave their party: they are Liberals: they are not Tories. Who wants them to leave their party? Who wants them to come over? We certainly do not. They are probably much more useful to the country on the Radical side. But by lying low, by doing nothing, they are making it more and more difficult for moderate men to remain in the Liberal party. The sober citizen, who notes Mr. Lloyd George's antics and that no group in the party renounces him, is likely to conclude there is no place in the Liberal party for the moderate man. To resign and withdraw from public life is no protest worth having. That is merely to play the extremists' game. The extremists wish to make the party too uncomfortable to hold the moderate man; and if the moderate man allows himself to be pushed out—worse still, if he goes out without being pushed—he is obviously doing precisely what the extremist wants. As a party matter, too, he is helping the Opposition; for the more extravagant the Radical party becomes, the better the chances of the Conservatives. From every point of view there is strong reason why the moderate Liberal should make the voice of his discontent heard, when he would have a very fair chance of making his influence felt.

It is difficult to understand how a man of the calibre of Mr. Asquith could allow himself to be pushed off the track by a man of the calibre of Mr. Lloyd George. Merely outwitted by a party manœuvre, a domestic intrigue, the bigger man might easily be by the more cunning. But this is a long process and a deliberate plan. Mr. Asquith must have foreseen what has happened. Why did he acquiesce? The position of this very strong man in his own party has become tant soit peu ridicule—jockeyed by an openly disloyal colleague. Can he not make himself master in his own house? Recalcitrance—difference of attitude—rebellious groups—these are common characters of all political parties. Certainly they are no new phenomena in a Liberal party. One remembers 1885—Mr. Chamberlain and his programme competing with Mr. Gladstone. But no one at that time doubted Mr. Gladstone's authority. Everyone felt that he was very much the real as well as titular leader of the party. But Mr. Asquith himself must be aware that the public is beginning honestly to doubt whether he does lead his party any longer. It was surely fair to his loyal supporters—the imperialist Liberals, who are also the reasonable men in home politics—to let them see and feel that he was going to stand by them, and not allow the iconoclastic and non-imperialist wing to get the upper hand. Conversely, the imperialist Liberals ought, in fairness to Mr. Asquith, to have made it abundantly plain that they would not put up with any disloyalty to him on the part of Mr. Lloyd George and Mr. Churchill. But there has been weakness all round on the moderate side. On Mr. Lloyd George's side, we are bound to say, there has been no weakness; as little weakness as scruple or loyalty.

CHÂTEAUX EN CHINE.

AMERICAN rhetoric is apt to be hyperbolical, and the estimates which one sees expressed even in responsible quarters of the potential value to America of Eastern trade may be exaggerated; but the American Government is clearly in earnest in its purpose to uphold American interests in the East. The able articles of the "Times" special correspondent in the Far East have called attention to a number of questions that demand serious attention if the policy of our own Government is to deserve similar commendation and, especially, to a case where American and British interests were mutually concerned. An agreement—never, we believe, made public, but the existence of which seems unchallenged—between Prince Ching and Sir Ernest Satow, in 1903, stipulated that when China contemplated making a railway from Hankow to Szechuen she should have recourse to British-American finance. An agreement made in 1899 between two groups of British and German financiers under the auspices of their respective Governments reserved the Yangtze valley for British, and the valley of the Yellow River for German, enterprise. Yet the curtain rises on a Franco-British combination, into which Germany has been allowed to enter, for the construction of this very Hankow-Szechuen line, while no communication had seemingly been made to America in pursuance of the understanding of 1903. How it all came about is not clear; but one would have thought that it behoved our Government and our financiers to approach America, in pursuance of that agreement, directly negotiations for a Hankow-Szechuen railway loan were opened; and what happened seems to have been a reminder from Washington to that effect when it became known that other influences were at work. "Fling away your own interests if you like, but not ours!" and the terms of the loan were actually revised at the last moment, and the amount raised from £4,500,000 to £6,000,000 to permit the inclusion of America as a fourth partner in the group. It is all as curious as a Chinese ivory puzzle. There was the 1903 agreement! How and why was it ignored?

There seems a fatality about agreements connected with China. Scarcely a clause of the Shanghai treaty of 1902 has been fulfilled; and the SATURDAY remarked, at the time, that that treaty was itself a recapitulation of former agreements which had fallen flat. It was said two years ago, by one who knew China well, that our mistake lay in the fact that we thought when we had signed a convention with China it was all over, whereas in fact it was only beginning; and successive Governments seem unable to escape from the delusion. A people who are accustomed to see things begin and end with an edict may naturally fail to expect consequences from the signature of a treaty. Chang Chi-tung had a great deal to do with the negotiation of the Shanghai treaty which contains a clause, among others, providing for the participation of British and Chinese in mining enterprise. Yet one of Chang Chi-tung's first acts was to draw up a set of Mining Regulations which even his own countrymen condemned as impracticable, but which had, at least, the decisive effect of making British participation in mining enterprise in China impossible. It is a game in which practice has made Chinese statesmen adepts. Having been led to sign an agreement, how to escape fulfilling it? We saw them making the attempt the other day at Antung. The Portsmouth treaty permitted Japan to relay a light mountain line which had been hurriedly put down during the war, so as to make it serviceable for commercial use. The intention was obvious to a child; but the Chinese insisted that only similar light rails must be laid, at the same gauge, up and down hill over the same track. Japan lost patience and announced that, as China refused to listen to reason, she should proceed "on her own"; whereupon China promptly listened to reason. It is desirable sometimes to have a will of one's own, and to express it. Otherwise one is liable, in dealing with certain people, to be shouldered out of any interests soever.

"Quel pays de paperasses!" one was heard to exclaim who had experience of the forms and certificates required to compass marriage, twenty years ago, in France; but the papers are at least intended, there, to promote a conclusion. The epidemic takes another form in China. The recent outpouring of edicts in Peking announcing one reform after another has made a great impression in this country, and his Majesty's Minister is expected, doubtless, to maintain a sympathetic attitude towards a Government filled with such virtuous impulses. But one for whom the editor vouches as "having had exceptional opportunities for many years of studying the Chinese at close range" declares, in a recent number of the "North-China Herald", that it is largely empty talk, which delights the Peking mandarins "because it means new boards, new appointments, more opportunities for squeeze, and more openings for sinecurists. Hence we have one reform after another announced, but not a single one taken up seriously and carried through. The army, the navy, the currency, education, finances, police, etc., all are to be overhauled in the most wonderful way. Where the money is to come from no one asks and no one cares ". Costly educational establishments are being created without a supply of competent teachers. New warships are to be built, at a cost of millions, in disregard of the fact that each previous essay in that direction has resulted in the destruction or capture of the casual ships by the first enemy who comes along. Lekin is to be abolished, opium to be suppressed, and bribery to be eradicated; and yet, to quote the French proverb, the more it changes the more it remains the same thing. We may be referred to the institution of Provincial Assemblies as evidence that things do happen, and that this satire is unjust. " To-day " (Dr. Morrison telegraphed from Peking, last week) " marks an era in the establishment of constitutional government in China. In obedience to Imperial decrees . . . elections have been in progress for some time past, and the assemblies meet to-day. . . . The event may be one of great historical importance." Yes, but the question is in what direction and towards what end the portent may tend. The writer whom we have quoted says " the idea of a constitutional government in China, where each man's ambition is to serve his own ends, is a huge joke. The Government in Peking know this quite well, but they are anxious about revolution, and the talk of a Constitution is a piece of opportunism adopted to keep the discontented quiet ". This will sound, no doubt, unsympathetic to people at home who regard the British Constitution as sacrosanct (even if they seem uncertain just now as to its nature) and representative institutions as a panacea for all ills, and who regard the Chinese as a great people who are on the high road to Progress along representative lines. The curious thing is that it never seems to occur to such that peoples may be great without being alike; that a nation—especially a self-contained nation like the Chinese—evolves a religion, social customs and methods of government which suit it and become part of its being, yet may differ materially from those which suit another nation, and that drastic change is an experiment fraught with dynamic danger. China has had representative institutions of sorts in her guilds and in her gentry who act on, no doubt, and are acted on by the officials—but who form all together a rough synopsis of opinion which Peking rarely tries to ignore or override. The problem in the way of representative institutions and of reforms generally in China is that nowhere is the maxim of self and self-interest carried to so high a pitch. No man will work harder than a Chinaman when he is working for himself, but no man is more prone to scamp a job which he is doing for another. No man is shrewder at a commercial transaction in which he is interested; but his views of collective transactions are coloured largely by the prospects of " squeeze ". Will the modest invitation to unselfish collective action implied in the Provincial Assemblies change this peculiar morale or affect the tone of society or of thought, or the Government, in any way? The problem is an interesting one, and the solution may be unexpected—seeing that the problem itself is Chinese.

DUTCH COLONIAL ETHICS.

IN December the Dutch East Indies will celebrate once more the feast of the going and the coming man. Mr. A. W. F. Idenburg, Minister for the Colonies, has been designated to replace Mr. J. B. van Heutsz as Governor-General of the Colonies and Possessions of the Netherlands in Asia. The inner history of many selections for that high charge would make interesting reading. It is e.g. considerably less than a century ago that a " debt of honour ", contracted at écarté according to common report, got converted into an irresistible claim to the Buitenzorg throne. The favoured one had been a heavy loser at a quiet game with the Minister for the Colonies then in office, who entertained such grave doubts about the possibility of ever cashing the resulting I.O.U.s if his patient was not helped to something very good, that with discerning eye and on the spot he discovered in the guignard all requisite qualifications for the best-paid public function, the plum of plums in the service of the State. Preferment nowadays goes on different principles, of course, and the growing strategic importance of the Malay Archipelago in the coming struggle for the mastery of the Pacific may have had something to do with a soldier gaining the ascendant over civilians for a third time following.

An officer in the colonial army, Mr. Idenburg entered the political arena as a protégé of the denominational condottiere who rescued the Dutch press from the dullness of this year's slack season by letting it detect and expand upon alleged irregularities he committed in the collection of funds for electioneering purposes—not the first statesman of local fame, by the way, accused of trafficking in honours and dignities. A member of Dr. Abraham Kuyper's Cabinet, Mr. Idenburg retired from the scene, when another faction obtained temporary sway in Holland, as Governor of the Dutch West Indies, to reappear as soon as Dr. Kuyper's party again came to the front. Though General van Heutsz' term was to expire this month, Mr. Idenburg postponed his departure to the East Indies to coach his successor, Mr. de Waal Malefijt, in colonial tactics.

Besides Mr. Idenburg, two other serious candidates were in the field, anxious to fill the expected vacancy, and their chances rose by his accepting the leadership of colonial affairs in patria. It has always been considered a breach of official etiquette in a Minister for the Colonies to use that position as a stepping-stone to viceregal splendour. The last recorded abuse of power in that respect—a councillor of the Crown pocketing the coveted prize—caused a storm of indignation, and the hue and cry raised by Mr. P. Mijer's presumption in 1866, prevented repetition until Mr. Idenburg ventured to help himself. Fortunately for him, the most likely candidate next on the list at this juncture was put hors de combat, openly implicated in the Abraham Kuyper controversy, where he had shown more caution and discretion while following in the footsteps of his whilom chief. Colonial ambition was represented by the third candidate, typical of the Dutch official " se mirant dans son encrier ", whose zeal takes the shape of reports and statistics by the hundredweight to suit prevailing taste. His hopes, stimulated by the latest revelations anent bribery and corruption at home, were however blighted by the Minister for the Colonies Idenburg setting aside all conventional scruples of conscience preparatory to his metamorphosis from the chrysalid departmental phase into the Governor-General Idenburg.

Each of the preceding Governors-General, since the so-called ethical policy, much insisted upon in the Dutch Parliament, received a nebulous form but no substance, failed principally in the very thing that recommended his appointment. Mr. van der Wijck, bred in the Civil Service and on the authority of whose word this corps d'élite was said to lack backbone, sanctioned a reorganisation, conducted by Mr. Mullemeister, a member of his Council, which rather disorganised (the fault of most recent reorganisations!) and sadly impaired the foundation of Dutch rule—government of the natives by the native aristocracy. General Rooseboom, sent out ostensibly on the strength of a military reputation acquired in the peaceful command of Amsterdam, can scarcely boast of having bequeathed to the Dutch East Indies, as Lord Kitchener did to British India, an efficient army, not to mention the navy, or, despite an attempt at fort-building with ridiculously inadequate means and without the necessary artillery, even the material nucleus of an efficient plan of defence. Under General van Heutsz, the pacificator of Atjeh, that troublesome territory proved to be not pacified at all, far indeed from conquered after thirty-six years of warfare; and, worse still, the direction of the war, the attitude of the troops, their cruel ferocity in exterminating the enemy, exasperating instead of pacifying, gave rise to new scandal which led to the resignation of Colonel van Daalen—the scapegoat of collective sin.

Meanwhile there was, and is, the financial question. The most imperative among the instructions to all Governors-General refers to strict economy. In the official nomenclature strict economy does not mean, though, and never meant, the avoidance of prodigal expense; it means, when especially insisted upon, an extra squeezing of the almost squeezed-out colonial lemon. Characteristic in this respect, with regularly increased taxation of the natives, are the frequent circulars which inform the officials, who know how to read between the lines, that their advancement depends on the measure of their solicitude for the swelling of the revenue.

Will the new Governor-General of the Dutch East Indies prove more than a manager attached to a telegraph-wire, who hides his responsibility behind the orders he receives from Plein and Binnenhof at The Hague? Departing on a well-defined mission, will he prove the right man to give a practical turn to the theory of colonial ethics so loudly talked about? "Dal miracolo se conosce il santo", and if, as Minister for the Colonies, Mr. Idenburg has shown himself a handy debater, securing the passage of his colonial budgets with great capacity for accommodation to the currents and undercurrents of party politics, Governor-General Idenburg will find a much harder task awaiting him. Atjeh is not the only instance of the way things are mismanaged; and Holland, to keep pace with the times as a colonial Power, has urgent need of an able, energetic hand to control the inheritance of Jan Pietersz Coen. Above all, of clean hands in the colonies and at home: no vice-presidents or members of the Governor-General's Council who, by dabbling in mining stock, invite reminders of article 9 jct. article 3 of the Regeeringsreglement; no successors of Mr. Idenburg as Minister of the Colonies who, like one of his predecessors, incur suspicion of subordinating the public weal to private gain by too close relations with the market of colonial produce. May the economy which inevitably will be part of the new Governor-General's programme benefit in the first place the natives who pray for deliverance from Dutch "ethical" policy, forcing them to provide not for their own neglected wants but for ruinous extravagance, calculated to fill the pockets of shareholders in all sorts of ventures that spring up like mushrooms in the rank soil of Dutch colonial methods. Holland's colonial future is far from safe with such colonial ethics.

THE CITY.

THE rise in the Bank rate to 5 per cent. is the third reminder to New York that the spectacular display in Wall Street cannot be continued indefinitely —indeed, is becoming boresome. The first intimation was given three weeks ago when the rate was raised from 2½ to 3 per cent. It failed of effect, and last week the rate was advanced to 4 per cent. Still New York expressed indifference, and so the screw has once more been turned. Courage was required to take such a drastic step, but the directors of the Bank of England seldom fail of this when circumstances demand heroic measures. New York will now be compelled to take in sail, or it will quickly find itself on the rocks. It cannot continue the "bull" campaign without European assistance, and the high rates of interest now demanded by London should preclude the possibility of any further substantial support being afforded. Checked now, no great harm need result from the speculation. Conditions in the United States justify much of the rise in securities, and the over-discounting of the future is explicable, though unwarranted. The time has arrived to call a halt and take stock of the position. It is always a disagreeable proceeding on the part of the "bull" speculator to reduce commitments, but it must be done some time, and now is the most favourable moment. Accounts must be liquidated, and promptly. London banks will probably see to it that no large amounts of American securities are "carried" on this side; rates will be made so onerous at the forthcoming settlement that profitable speculation will be practically impossible. If New York banks follow the same course we may hope that the rise in the Bank rate will prove the salvation of the American market. Nothing we have said, however, applies to the speculation in United States Steel shares; this is out of the bounds of all prudence—a gamble in itself and unparalleled for its recklessness.

Stock markets, as a whole, have not been seriously affected by the rise in the Bank rate. Consols have kept steady at their previous fall, and the only sign of depression has been in stocks where recently speculation has developed. "Kaffirs" have scarcely moved because for some time past the market has been practically dead. Many land shares, however, which have been carried on borrowed money have been pressed for sale, and there are indications of the rubber share market feeling the pinch of dearer money. Banks are looking askance at these latter as security, and are especially disposed to curtail assistance to Mincing Lane sharebrokers. Malacca shares have been especially depressed, it being difficult to understand the financial methods of this company. The proposal to raise further money by £10 debentures is decidedly bad, and the option proposed to be given of converting the same into £1 shares would seem to be specially designed to foster speculation. For the inference is that the £1 shares will go well over £10. They may do, but we doubt very much whether they will ever be worth anything like the figure.

An effort is to be made to reawaken interest in Russian gold mining. The country is undoubtedly very rich in mineral wealth, and properly exploited should return handsome dividends. Perhaps the best example of a payable mine is that owned by the Lena Goldfields, Limited, the output from which has already exceeded ten millions sterling. In the financial year just ended the yield is estimated to produce £1,300,000. The company's shares have not so far attained much popularity, but they have recently been introduced in Paris, and more may be heard of them in the near future. A market deal is being arranged in Siberian Proprietary Shares, over which many people burnt their fingers a couple of years ago. The company's properties, however, have been systematically developed since then, and would seem to offer possibilities which are not discounted in the present price. In anticipation of a revival in the market Russian Estates and Mine shares continue to be "pushed", and it is necessary to repeat the warning of a few weeks ago, that the antecedents of the company will not bear investigation. As regards other mining shares, a surprise is promised by Lake View. It is rumoured that the accounts will reveal a large profit hitherto undisclosed.

A surprising announcement was made by the Chairman of the Mexican Railway Company at the meeting on Thursday. Owing to a shortage, the oil contractors have had to notify a restriction of the supply, and the company will be compelled to use coal on many of its locomotives. As oil was largely responsible for the saving in working expenses last year, nothing more unfortunate could have happened, unless it is the resignation from the board of the representative of the Mexican Government. No explanation of this step is given except that it is taken on personal grounds, but the shareholders should demand something more explicit. Among the issues of the week are the Brazil Railway Company's 4½ per cent. first mortgage 60-year gold bonds at £92.

INSURANCE: POLICIES AT HIGH PREMIUMS.

II.

FOR a given age at entry the highest rate of premium that can be paid is a single premium for endowment assurance, which secures the payment of the amount of the policy at the end of a fixed number of years or at death if previous. The shorter the endowment period the higher is the rate of premium. People can of course pay their premiums in any way they choose. A man can buy a twenty-year endowment assurance policy, or a policy under which the sum assured is paid only at death, by one, or five, or ten premiums, or by any other number of payments that suits his convenience. Generally the premiums for endowment assurances are payable throughout the whole of the endowment period, which is seldom less than ten years. The rate of premium varies somewhat, but not very greatly, with age, and is approximately a little less than £10 a year for non-profit ten-year endowment policies of £100, and a little more than £10 a year for with-profit policies. This form of assurance supplies a comparatively small amount of insurance protection and a large proportion of the savings-bank element. In a contract of this kind the rebate of income tax allowed on life-assurance premiums plays a very important part and helps to make such policies exceedingly profitable investments. It has been shown elsewhere that a man can pay £103 18s. a year for ten years, and if he can claim rebate of income tax at 9d. in the pound, reduce his net outlay to £100 a year. For this he can receive at the end of ten years the whole of his savings accumulated at practically 4 per cent. compound interest. Out of his total outlay of £1000 the sum of £51 is paid for protection, and £949 is saved. The policy yields him £1165 in cash if he survives to the end of the ten years, which is equivalent to the return of his £949 with the addition of £216 for interest. If this £1165 which he receives were regarded as a return on the £103 18s. a year which he pays to the life office, less the cost of the insurance protection, he would receive back his savings accumulated at 3 per cent. compound interest; but because he obtains rebate of income tax at 9d. in the pound, the 3 per cent. investment is converted into a 4 per cent. investment.

To obtain an equally good result from other investments it would be necessary that they should yield about £4 5s. per cent., which would be reduced by income tax to 4 per cent. Clearly, therefore, policies of this kind offer great attractions as investments for the wealthy. If the money paid for life assurance were entirely derived from unearned income, subject to rebate of income tax at a higher rate than 9d. in the pound, the results at the end of the endowment period would be still better.

When the endowment period is extended from ten years to fifteen years the rate of premium is lower, being at age forty about £68 a year for the assurance of £1000 with profits at the end of fifteen years or at death if before; the bonuses on a policy of this kind for £1000 may amount to £280. If the policyholder lives to the end of fifteen years, and if we ignore the value of insurance protection and the advantages derived from the rebate of income tax, he receives back all the premiums he has paid to the life office with compound interest at the rate of £2 15s. per cent. per annum. If entitled to rebate of income tax at the rate of 9d. in the pound, the investment yields £3 5s. per cent.; if rebate is allowed at 1s. 2d. in the pound the return is equivalent to £3 10s. per cent. per annum. If we make allowance, as we should, for the cost of insurance protection, the policyholder receives back at the end of fifteen years all the premiums he has paid, with 4 per cent. interest if he is entitled to rebate of tax at 9d., and at 4½ per cent. if he can claim rebate of income tax at 1s. 3d. in the pound.

These are results of a character with which comparatively few people are familiar. The insurance protection element is small and the savings-bank element is large. There is also the fact that the effect of income-tax rebate on the total outlay is much greater over a short period than over a long period, when the result of the investment is dealt with in terms of the rate of interest yielded. These things combine to produce results which are surprisingly lucrative when the security afforded is considered, and when it is remembered how high a rate of dividend subject to tax would have to be obtained in order to give equivalent results.

THE LABOURS OF LOMBROSO.

THROUGHOUT all nature, the abnormal individuals have ever been subjected to aggression and ill-treatment. Among the lower animals, and to a certain extent among men, it would seem probable that any deviation from the appearance or the habits of the herd is instinctively associated in the minds of the majority with something that is strange and external, and therefore with what is hostile and to be attacked. Hence the repugnance to foreigners and strangers evinced everywhere, and the contempt and hatred of, say, white and yellow people for one another, when they are forced to live in close proximity. The submerged criminal minorities are defective and troublesome; they are not proper, placid, or pleasant; they cumber the ground like the autumn leaves, and are always being swept away and thrown into dark places to corrupt out of sight. In the Middle Ages their existence was attributed to their own wicked perversity in listening to the seductions of the Devil; and this was most clearly stated upon all indictments up to a few short years ago. Cesare Lombroso was one of a band of scientific enquirers (including his compatriot Ferri, Westphal, Krafft-Ebing, and a whole vanguard of Germans) who began to seek material causes for physical actions. Nothing he imagined, and rightly, occurred by chance or through the promptings of unmeaning malevolence. He started to examine the whole structure of the convicted, and then found so many defects and peculiarities that he contended there were born criminals.

Having begun to weigh and measure Caliban and his tribe, and having found them mostly simious and misshapen, he was sometimes led to apply his formulæ indiscriminately; he would deduce too much from insufficient data, and frequently detected potential Hydes in distinguished Jekylls. In short, having made some discoveries, he was apt to exaggerate from them. Therefore, while we must be grateful for his many contributions to the incipient and much-needed science of criminology, we cannot accept all his conclusions and wide generalisations without occasional reservations and sometimes a grain of salt. Still he did good in laying so much stress upon the bad physique of the unfortunate, and in thus emphasising the undoubted truth that health is a great factor in conduct. "The moral demonstration", said Dr. Claye Shaw, giving evidence before Mr. Herbert Gladstone's Committee, "depends on the perfection of physical structure." Impair the mental machinery for an hour, by poison, by alcohol, by injury or disease, and where might not any one of us be landed; who could rely upon direction or self-control?

There are really no born criminals, and there is no criminal class; but there are innumerable born degenerates, and what they drift into depends upon circumstances. "Given a certain environment", said Dr. Bevan Lewis before the Committee alluded to, "and you will have crime; given a more favourable environment and you will have simply insanity". Even that strong exponent of the hardest officialism, Sir Edmund Du Cane, admitted that "a large number of prisoners are persons who are absolutely unable, or find it extremely difficult, through mental or physical incapacity to earn their livelihood even under favourable circumstances". A former governor of Pentonville declared, of a certain class of his habitual prisoners, that he had "those half-witted creatures coming again and again to prison". "Deficiencies in memory, imagination, reason", said the Rev. Dr. Morrison, who knew prisoners well, "are three undoubted characteristics of the ordinary criminal intellect." These unhappy beings in all the various stages of psychopathy and distortion are the material from which prisoners are made. When we consider how often ordinary people are overcome by temptation, and that many a lost boat's crew of decent Europeans have, from the mere force of conditions, been driven to cannibalism, we cannot expect the defective and the unbalanced to hold their own in a competitive community. So, doubtless, as Dr. Maudsley pointed out, we do manufacture our criminals like any other artificial product, only the process is a complex and unconscious one.

We must hope that the work of Professor Lombroso and of the many other modern writers upon the problems of criminology, may help forward and hasten the most urgent of all prison reforms, which is classification. There is infinite difference between those various groups of offenders who now fill the same dock, and receive—in different doses—the same sort of treatment, or rather punishment. What a man did on a particular day is only one symptom, and not always the most important, of the kind of man he is. It is only too certain, and it is sad indeed to reflect upon, that there are many persons hard and fast in prison at this hour, on account of abnormalities or defects which they could no more keep away by their own efforts than they could stave off mania or the spotted fever. For though the grotesquely mad are now taken care of and well treated, even if they have murdered people, and are sent to Broadmoor, the half-mad and obscurely afflicted are held to be swayed by merely normal desires and to possess full measure of self-control. All specialists know that it is otherwise, and that things will be altogether changed in the long run. It is not opposition that must be faced, but the dead weight of indifference. We want more men like Lombroso to set down facts, to ask of the afflicted, to weigh, and learn, so that in all our dealings with degenerates we may be able to look forward to the future, and not dwell morbidly upon what cannot be undone.

STAGE CROWDS.

By Max Beerbohm.

MR. CHESTERTON once chid me, in a brilliant essay, for not cherishing in my heart the ideal of democracy. It is quite true that I don't believe at all firmly in (what has always been to Mr. Chesterton a dark and mystical reality) the wisdom of the people. I would not stake sixpence on the people's capacity for governing itself, and not a penny on its capacity for governing me. Democracy, wherever it has been tried, has failed as a means of increasing the sum of human happiness. Autocracy, aristocracy, bureaucracy, and all the other modes of government, have similarly failed. In theory they are all of them admirable, but they won't work out in practice. They would, doubtless, if man were a rational and an unselfish animal. But man is not built that way, and cannot be trusted either to wield power wisely or to obey wise ordinances. He means well; but original sin and muddle-headedness, between them, make havoc of his good intentions. Political history is the term by which we dignify the record of his ludicrous flounderings. And the political history of the future will be just as amusing or depressing, you may be sure. And let us smile rather than be indignant, since we cannot hope to remedy the nature of things, and since, after all, there will be, as there has ever been, a general impression that life is worth living. The vitality of man will always rise superior to the circumstances of existence. In sounding this note of optimism I hope to conciliate Mr. Chesterton. Let him observe also that there is nothing invidious in my mistrust of his darling democracy, since the various other forms of tyranny seem to me not one whit more worshipful.

Furthermore, for his benefit I admit that in estimating the political capacity of the people, he has, and I have not, intimate first-hand knowledge as a basis. He has gone plentifully among them, making speeches to them, delivering lectures to them, canvassing them, and so forth. His impression of their magnificent sanity and sagacity has come through direct contact. He has been forced by the evidence of his eyes and ears to the conclusion that the historians whom he read at school—most of them, indeed, persons with a bias towards oligarchy—had been doing their little best to mislead him. I, all this while, have been deriving my knowledge of the people solely from the theatre. Neither by the popular demonstrations in the gallery nor by the dramatists' occasional presentments of popular demonstrations on the stage am I helped to reject the verdict of history. Wafted down to me from the gallery are shouts of laughter at the wrong moment; uproarious cheers for the cheapest and falsest sentiments; howls and groans, sometimes, for an author who has done fine work; salvoes for the charlatan. Speaking with the authority of an intelligent person somewhat expert in the art of the theatre, I say that the gallery is almost always wrong. Of course, the political and the aesthetic instincts are two different things. Misjudgment in the theatre does not preclude wisdom in the agora. But alas, the dramatists, one and all, when they deal with politics, present the people in the most despicable light. Innumerable are the mobs that I have seen on the stage; and I can recall not one that seemed to possess collectively one ounce of sense. The mode of presentment varies but little. You hear a confused and horrific hubbub before the curtain rises, and presently you behold the sovereign people—tanners, cobblers, blacksmiths, in the costume of the period, all with wild eyes and unshawn lantern jaws—hanging on the lips of some popular hero who is orating to them. At the close of his every sentence they roar themselves hoarse with rapture, those who are in the foreground turning to one another and repeating, with hideous grimaces and hideous gestures of approval, the last three or four words that have fallen from the orator's lips. We fear there is no doubt that they will tear limb from limb anyone who might dare to oppose the policy of their idol. And when, in due course, such a person bobs up in their midst, pale but determined, his life seems not worth a moment's purchase. There is a noise as of apes and tigers, with the most appalling convulsions all round—cudgels brandished, fists shaken, curses hurtling, eyes starting out of heads, lantern jaws strained to their utmost capacity. Somehow, above the din, the voice of the new orator is heard. His first sentence is punctuated by an ugly rush. But he bears a charmed life; he stands his ground, and proceeds to the next sentence. In a moment or two the din subsides, the lantern jaws slacken, the cudgels are given a rest, and the sovereign people are gazing into one another's eyes with every manifestation of dubiety. This condition of theirs passes not less rapidly into evident approval of the orator's point of view, thence into enthusiasm, thence into an ecstasy of rapture; and, so soon as the peroration of the brief and (as it seems to us) not very remarkable speech has been uttered, the sovereign people, with one accord, seize torches and rush off roaring, with the express purpose of slaying orator number one. The chances are, however, that they will promptly fall under his spell and return to make an end of orator number two.

I think that even Mr. Chesterton, if he were a seasoned dramatic critic, would find his faith in democracy somewhat shaken. In me, certainly, the theatre has destroyed utterly such belief as I may once have had in the political wisdom of the people. But I do vaguely suspect that the people are not quite such asses as our dramatists would teach us to suppose. The method of presenting them on the stage is traditional from Shakespeare, who very frankly hated and despised them and doubtless revelled in the opportunity of gibbeting them in the forum scene of "Julius Caesar". He, however, did have the grace to make Mark Antony's speech a subtle and an eloquent appeal. Whereas the average dramatist thinks that any perfunctory bit of fustian is good enough to make the people change its mind instantly. Without pretending to authority, I doubt whether—in England, at any rate, and in modern times—an orator ever has any practical effect. People who agree with him (so far as they think at all) go to hear and cheer their own opinions expressed by him. A few people who disagree with him go to interrupt. It is quite good fun all round, but I should be surprised to hear of any practical effects. I presume that most of the people in Trafalgar Square last Sunday were there because they were indignant against the Spanish Government, and wanted to hear Mr. Cunninghame Graham express their indignation. If there were present any people who approved the execution of Ferrer, could even Mr. Cunninghame Graham have moved them to join in the subsequent procession to the embassy? Suppose the whole multitude had been composed of men rejoicing in Ferrer's death—would a few words from the plinth of Nelson's column have turned their joy to horror, and have sent them headlong in the direction of Grosvenor Gardens? Suppose that on their way they had encountered, and wished to slay, the ambassador—would a few words from *him* have inclined them to tear Mr. Cunninghame Graham limb from limb? On the stage, yes, certainly.

MR. STRANG AND OTHERS.

By Laurence Binyon.

SOME time ago I dwelt upon the adverse and retarding conditions which face every man who nourishes a serious ambition in painting; one whose instinct for design is not satisfied with the problems involved in portrait and landscape, and who has no stomach for the sugared concoctions which pass for classic or romantic compositions in the eyes of the picture-going crowd. There is no great public for such men. A public may be there, ready to be interested and to enjoy, if only it could be reached; but there are so few opportunities for reaching it and impressing it. The men who have in them the most capability for creative design get no scope for exercising their talents congenially; every step has to be fought for, every advance in knowledge and mastery bought at the price of many experiments. It is a great waste. So we find artists of this type almost always driven to working out their ideas in small, on copper, stone, or wood, before they can get a chance of attempting to realise their ambition in painting. They come late, or comparatively late, to the more complex and difficult medium. All the more should be welcomed any evidence of appreciation and any promptings of encouragement from the public. The rumour that Mr. John is to be given a chance of showing his powers of design on a larger scale than has hitherto been afforded him is of good augury, if, as I hope, it is true. And London may note that Manchester has followed the example of Paris and of Venice in buying an example of Mr. Charles Shannon's romantic art, the picture known as "The Millpond".

The dear public which loves to recognise its favourites, with comfortable self-congratulation, by something obvious and tangible—a Wouvermans by its white horse, a MacWhirter by its silver birch—is apt to resent an artist who ventures into new fields and does things he has not done before. Mr. Shannon, I am sure, must have been often told that his lithographs were delightful, but that it was a pity he took to painting his subjects in oils. So too there will be many, doubtless, who profess to admire Mr. Strang's etchings very cordially, but regret that he should want to paint pictures. Since his election as an Associate-Engraver of the Royal Academy, Mr. Strang has taken to painting with more assiduity than he did. And now at the Leicester Galleries there is an exhibition of his work, in which there are a few drawings and a number of new etchings, but in which the pictures predominate. Not content with his activity in various processes, Mr. Strang is also surprisingly various in his painting. He has never before shown anything like the landscape studies here, in which he sets out to rival Mr. Steer and others in painting the brightness of bright sunshine. Without the signature few would guess the authorship of "From Cæsar's Camp", for instance. It is good to see an artist still keeping the alertness and flexibility of youth, and to Mr. Strang oil-painting seems always to be something of a joyous game. He sees the possibilities of a theme not yet attempted, a problem not yet tackled; and gaily picks up the challenge. The subject dictates the treatment. There is of course a danger in this experimenting. Mr. Strang is too easily enticed by the fun of trying something fresh; seized with an idea, he sets to work impetuously and gets it off his mind. But I think he would do better to brood over his ideas a little longer, to see if what pleased and possessed him yesterday still pleases and possesses him a month hence, or it may be a year hence. His powers are so great that one would like to see them taxed and engaged to the utmost in a work that concentrated and fused them all, a work absorbing his whole heart as well as his brain. These landscape studies will go to the enriching of his art; but the real Strang is to be found rather, I think, in the vein which produced pictures like the "Blind Musicians" (No. 11) and "The Horse Pond" (No. 14), where not the mere appearances of things but the animating forces within them are seized upon and expressed. These show a natural affinity with Daumier. The painter seems more at home in such scenes than in the Venetian idylls for which he has always shown a certain fondness. Glowing as the colour of them is, these designs do not seem to have been conceived and thought out in colour from the first, whereas the colour of the Venetian prototypes seems something "born, not made". Of late, Mr. Strang has been wont to add more and more colour to those portrait-drawings by which he has won much fame. In some cases one thinks that the native austerity of his style would suit better with monochrome; in many of these drawings that have been exhibited the colour has seemed to be either too much or not enough. But sparingly used, as in the beautiful "Portrait of a Girl" (No. 46), or used fully and frankly, as in the "Lord Wolseley", it becomes a felicitous enhancement. An oil-painting of George Meredith, a dry-point of Mr. Chamberlain and another of Mr. Bernard Shaw, are included in the exhibition. The last of these will rank with the many fine successes in portraiture of Mr. Strang's needle.

The adjoining room provides a contrast. It contains the water-colours of Mr. Dulac, painted in illustration of Omar Khayyám, and illustrations to "The Deserted Village", also in water-colour, by Mr. Lee-Hankey. Both of these sets, which have been made for reproduction in colours and publication in book form, are sure to be popular. As in his designs to the Arabian Nights, exhibited at the same galleries last year, Mr. Dulac again displays a fertile and pleasing invention. His designs would be more satisfying indeed if they were less given to prettiness of effect. There are stanzas in Omar, or at least in FitzGerald, which might as naturally suggest designs of Florentine "terribleness" and grandeur. Technically, Mr. Dulac's water-colours, enforced with line, are a compromise between the methods of East and West. Remembering certain exquisite pages of Persian painting, I am inclined to wish that he had not even remotely prompted a comparison with the native art; for no European can really catch that atmosphere. It would have been better, I think, to do as our forefathers would have done, and grappled with the universal elements in the subject, using the chiaroscuro and relief of European tradition, and leaving the local colour to take care of itself. But the local colour will doubtless prove an attraction, and Mr. Dulac employs it with great adroitness.

FONTAINEBLEAU OF THE VALOIS.*

"IT is situated among rocks and woods that give you a fine variety of savage prospects." So writes Addison of the Palace of Fontainebleau, in "Teacup Time of Gown and Hoop". Half a century earlier Evelyn has wandered to this "Hampton Court of France" (as he calls it) through "a forest so prodigiously encompassed with hideous rocks of whitish hard stone, heaped one on another in mountainous heights that I think the like is nowhere to be found more horrid and solitary. It abounds with stags, wolves, and boars. . . . In these solitudes rogues frequently lurk and do mischief". And even after the Crown of S. Louis has fallen before the red cap of the sans-culotte, the wolf still roams free in its forest brakes, and startles the melancholy Obermann from his reveries of death and immortality.

With the Renaissance commences the romance of Fontainebleau, or Fons Bleaudi, as it is called in the days when Thomas of Canterbury comes thither to bless the newly-built chapel of S. Saturnin. But from the times of the second Capet the Kings of France had chased the stag and the boar in its woodland glades, and from a gloomy donjon on the site of the present palace had the royal standard of France waved for nigh four hundred years, when one day, by chance, the "wizard" prince François the First rides by the mouldering tower and sees that the place is a "delicious desert". It shall be, he vows, the home of the new France, and Leonardo da Vinci, and Andrea del Sarto, and Benvenuto Cellini speed hither at his behest to mould the faery palace of the Renaissance. Stately courts and terraces of pleasaunce arise around the old donjon, and beyond appear "green lawns" and "luxuriant gardens" and lengthy avenues

* "Fair Women at Fontainebleau." By Frank Hamel. London: Nash. 1909. 15s.

and branching alleys where now grow strange and foreign plants and flowers which are tended by gardeners from many strange lands. And within the palace are stored pictures and statues and jewels and books which have come from every land in Europe. And for a moment in Fontainebleau the vision of the Renaissance is manifested to the world in Marguerite of Navarre, the authoress of the "Heptameron". Marguerite, though she is no Zwinglian, feels the thrill of the new awakening, and would an she could lead the brother, whom she loves not wisely but too well, into the path of tolerance and of a Catholic and humanist Reformation. And there wander in these days among these leafy glades women who are even fairer, if frailer, than Marguerite. First there comes from her Breton home, "to share the guilty splendours of a King", Françoise de Foix, Comtesse de Châteaubriand, who will glitter before the world for a moment as the Queen of Beauty of the "Field of the Cloth of Gold" and then, when her stormy reign is over, and the fair and flowerlike Anne de Pisseleu (hereafter to be Duchesse d'Etampes) has robbed her of her royal lover, will wend her way back to the rocks of Brittany, to meet a fate as hard as, perchance even more tragic than, that which in a later age will befall another erring beauty of Fontainebleau, La Vallière. In her place, the Duchesse d'Etampes, the belle et bonne, is Queen of the Fêtes, and everything that her heart desires is granted to her. Marot sings of her pink-and-white complexion and her "sens rassis", and the Emperor places on her finger a diamond ring. And she teaches to great men strange lessons. Rosso learns that it is a dangerous thing to paint Diane de Poitiers rather than herself as the Nymph of Fontainebleau, and Benvenuto, though he may design artistic gates and model a fair figure of Jupiter in silver, has to realise at last that inasmuch as his folly has made Madame his enemy, the palace of Fontainebleau is no lasting resting-place for him. But though the D'Etampes may destroy Diane's portrait, Diane herself remains. She is older by nine years than the D'Etampes, but she has the love of the heir to the throne. And as François slowly sinks into an unhonoured grave, the strife waxes fiercer, "la plus savante des belles et la plus belle des savantes"; but the last word is with Diane. This Diane de Poitiers, Nymph of Fontainebleau, is in a sense a child of the Renaissance, for though the years of her life are three score and four (some say three score and ten) the hand of Time never touches her, and her unfading beauty (as has been said) knows neither autumn nor winter. Yet in another sense she is not of the Renaissance. "See her at Fontainebleau", cries Michelet, "under a double aspect, there celestial, luminous queen of night, here Diane surrounded by sombre flames, a sombre Hecate". Diane the sombre Hecate is truly the first child of the counter-Reformation, for it is to her orders that Henri has lighted the fires of persecution in Paris. The children of the Renaissance are still at Fontainebleau; but their fine garments are covered with the dust of the theological turmoil, and their minds are distraught with the clamours of those who care little for the humanities and much for dogmas. And so, when Henri II., the last true king of the Valois, has fallen beneath Montgomery's spear in the lists of S. Antoine, wearing his Diane's colours to the last, and Diane herself is in the château of Anet "making her soul", the theological roar waxes louder in the palace halls. For if Diane has been Catholic, the Italian woman who reigns in her place is for the moment tempted to use the Huguenots and trusts to find in them her salvation from the house of Guise. It is in the Queen Regent's apartments that the assembly meets which is to herald the S. Bartholomew. The young king François II. sits in the chair of state, and by his side, enlivening with her beauty the gloomy scene, sits Mary Stuart, wondering and silent, as for the first time she meets Calvinism face to face. With them, watchful as a leopard, sits Catherine de Medici, the most sinister apparition that the gay palace will ever know. And there before the royalties are ranged the men whose names will be battle-cries of rival hosts o'er all the land of France. There stands François de Guise, the one hero that the princely house of Lorraine can claim, and near him is the Admiral Coligny, martyr to Calvinism and traitor to France, who will to-day for the first time declare himself before the world a Protestant. And there is present, too, the one just judge of an evil time, though at the same time a poor theologian, the Chancellor l'Hôpital, and likewise the old scarred veteran of François premier's wars, the Constable de Montmorency. And the Church militant is represented by four princely Cardinals, while the Reformation likewise finds its voice in the Bishop who has adopted the faith of Calvin, Monluc of Valence. It is this Bishop who, as he turns to the Queen, proclaims the end of the Renaissance. "Pardon me if I presume to entreat that you will order the ladies of the Court to sing the Psalms of David instead of foolish songs, and such spiritual melodies as can have the praise of God". Catherine de Medici smiles. Her smile some years later is turned to a frown when Guise and the Catholics burst into the palace and carry away her son Charles IX. lest he should become a Huguenot. She realises at last the folly of playing with the fires of religious discord.

This is Fontainebleau of the Valois. Those who would follow the pageant under the less romantic Bourbons will find it in "Fair Women at Fontainebleau"—the frowns of Christina of Sweden over the doomed Monaldeschi, the tears of Madame de Montespan, the rage of Napoleon when he cannot bend Pope Pius to his will; and, the prettiest picture of all, the child Marie Antoinette riding her donkey through the forest paths.

As a royal palace Fontainebleau has for many a year lain desolate, for in a republican France it has no place. But it is still the faery castle of romance; and in its galleries and courts, in its walks of chestnuts and its woods of pine the old France of chivalry and romance still dwells.

ON THE BURY DITCHES.

THE path up the hill lies deep buried in the woods: there is nothing, among the endless colonnades of the fir-stems, to show the traveller how far he is upon his way; only the steady drag of the ascent tells him that he has not missed the track and turned towards the valley-bottoms again. A clearing of the wood, a steep slope rough with oak-scrub and beds of withered foxglove and half-acre patches of seeded willow-herb, gives an outlook over the neighbouring hill-tops to far-off landmarks of Hopton or Wenlock Edge; higher still, a belt of deep bracken encircles the shoulder of the hill, and out of it rises the dark fir wood which crowns the summit. The outmost boughs feather low down to the fern, and beneath them the gloom is deeper than that half-daylight which broods beneath most English groves. In the dusk within the great ring the stems rise like grey pillars, clear of branches up to forty feet from the ground, save here and there for black mouldering sprays and contorted dragon-like limbs, gnarled and splintered by storms and age; across the brown floor of pine needles lie fallen columns with the base of matted roots upheaved. There is no path here; the traveller steers his course by guess through the glimmering aisles, silent-footed up the slant of the dry smooth glades without a leaf of green. In the heart of the wood a steep bank of shattery sandstone suddenly bars the way; and when this is climbed it is found to be the vallum to a clean-cut fosse five or six yards deep, stretching away to right and left till it is lost among the trees. Beyond this barrier is a second, and higher yet a third tier of ditch and wall; the vast triple work, buried in the twilight of the fir wood, encircles the whole hill-top. A little way beyond the inmost trench the explorer sees the sky again, and comes out upon the summit, a clear space of level turf some two hundred yards across, closed round by the circle of the firs.

This inmost keep is a hiding-place secure in a way which the old diggers of the trenches never knew. To-day there is nothing to be seen from the height but the tree-tops and the sky; only in one corner, where the woodmen have opened a road for the timber-wagons, is there a glimpse of the lower land. From their bare-edged ramparts the garrison once looked across scrub-strewn folds of the hill and the wide vale beneath to the horizon of dark heather-ridge or smooth grassy swell or stepped outline of high camps like their own; they watched, perhaps, the invaders' smoke-drift far away among the hills or the straggling cattle driven up the slope towards the stronghold from the coming foray. The old war-work, built with such vast toil, inexpugnable by time itself, has become a stronghold of inmost peace.

Anyone who takes the trouble to explore the whole circuit of the fort and measure with his eye the depth and width of the ramparts and the ditches will hardly escape an actually oppressive sense of the vastness of the labour spent upon the design. Savages, we should call them, the half-naked tribes who sapped the rock into scarps still thrice the height of a man, even after the wearing-down of centuries: what tools had they but sharpened stakes, and baskets for carrying the soil, and the little flint mattocks and hammers which we find among their graves? It discomforts us, who have made a religion of "labour-saying", to guess at the sum of toil which went to the digging of the camp, all the pain of bent back and cramped forearm and sore hand, of the sweat and the chill, the weariness of the endless attack on the scarcely yielding ground. We, who have come in the course of time perfectly to understand what part of life should be holiday, think with a sentiment between pity and anger of the men who once swarmed and burrowed here like ants about their mound. How lately we have learned those due proportions of work and ease we scarcely seem to understand. There is a figure which haunts the hill, sometimes to be met creeping along the wood path with an armful of dead sticks, sometimes resting on the grassy level within the ring, a survivor of a past age, whose theory of work is altogether in the following of the tradition of the men who trenched the rock. Old Meredith, a worn-out farm hand, with thin white hair falling on the bent shoulders of what was once a frame of heroic strength, with great bony hands palsied so that they can hardly keep the bundle of sticks together, and feeble knees resting perforce at every twenty paces of the path, is to the passing hour as thin a ghost as any one of the old Silurians who lie beneath the barrows on the down. To him, as he rests at the edge of the wood and looks over the landscape beneath, before he begins the enormous toil of getting down to the village with his load of fuel, it may well seem that the world, as his refrain goes, is turned upside down. The valleys between the wooded ranges, the little village-clusters and solitary farms still mock him with the image of the country that he once knew: the old names stand, but the race which owns them is strange. The deserted land, the half-score of stubble-fields where a hundred used to be, the idle ploughs standing in the half-finished furrows, the boys sauntering home from school, instead of being broken in to the ancestral toil, fill him with solemn scorn. Not for a moment is he tempted to envy these shirkers their ease: the tasks of his own prime are a standard which he maintains with a cheerful pride. He is ready to recount his labours to anyone who cares to listen, not as feats of his own strength, but as instances of the general worth of the old breeding. He had, the prooemium always goes, but one day's schooling in his life; he started to work in the fields when he was five. At eight he would go with the carter who took a wagon-load of corn the twenty-seven miles into Shrewsbury, starting before daylight, when the toll-gate was first opened, and bringing back a load of coal the same day. He was still a boy when, the wagoner drinking late at Ludlow, he drove the team—"four great horses"—all the way to the farm beyond Clunton, stabled and fettled them, and only left the gear on the ground because he could not reach to hang it on the racks. He became a man of note in almost every branch of country science: in haying and harvest, at wood cutting and barking, as wagoner, thatcher, thresher, he was the first hand in that country. At twenty-five he was getting three shillings a week and his meat at the Leasowes, carrying amongst other labours double bags of wheat from the bay to the granary—thirty score to a bag—more than a donkey's load. With such education as this went recreation on a like heroic scale—ring-fights at Clunton wake, nd less formal battles, not provoked but cheerfully joined, "whenever they put it on him", or a match to run two miles after the pony-races at Marsh Brook, that too ultimately decided by fists. On seven shillings a week he married, and on eight and nine brought up a large family. From the time that he was nineteen till he was turned sixty-five he worked in every harvest at pitching the sheaves on to the wagon, which is perhaps the hardest work in the world. He was a champion pitcher; he boasts that he could have three wagons loaded and roped in an hour. "I'd always use a shortish pikel", he says, "and I'd always have my own, 'cause I liked a handy tool. If any of the farmers wanted a piece of corn lugged, and there wasn't much time, it was 'Send for Meredith!' and I'd say 'You let me have plenty of good drink and I'll do it for you'. Once I cleared twelve acres after dinner-time. The dinner was brought to us in the field, and we didn't stay very long to eat it. We used to start work at harvest at six in the morning, and often we'd be going till ten at night. Sometimes I'd not get home till the cocks were crowing. Once, when it was a bad season, we kept on lugging two days and nights without we'd any sleep: we'd as much as we could eat and drink, but we never laid down: the horses, they slept as they stood. We got all the corn in, too, before the weather broke. Once, when I'd gone mowing grass at the Bryn with my two brothers, they never sent up the bread for us, and we couldn't stop for to fetch it, you see; and we were there three days with nothing but a little bit of bacon and some tea; we kept on mowing all day, just the same, and one night, as I was going back to the house, I see someone coming running, and 'twas my missus, with enough meat for seven; but I couldna touch a bit of it. I went home and to bed, and slept all night; but next morning I eat and eat, and thought I'd never stop. I'd always lead, mowing and harvest, but I liked the pitching best of all. But that's all over now."

Over and done the fifty years' labour of the untiring arm and well-stored head, spent in absolute peaceful profit to the world; gone the old busy thrift of the farms; gone also, it seems, in the space of a generation, the very temper for enormous toil possessed by earlier men, the spirit which looks down upon the neglected fields from the trenched circles of the hill.

THE LAIRD'S BELL.

By George A. B. Dewar.

Towards strangers of his own class the laird was wrapt about with a severe reserve: a reserve, I think, more shy than unkind. His servants, men and women kind, liked him well. The estate workmen all had good words to say of him. He treated them with a natural and perfect courtesy, save on the rare occasions when he flamed out against some fault of deliberate negligence or disobedience. He held it for proven that a gentleman must be considerate to all who serve him. To strangers in a class beneath his own who wished to cultivate him, he was quite impossible. He froze instantly, and however well their advances were meant, he could not thaw to them. He tried quite hard once or twice, wishing not to wound a well-meaning if pushing neighbour, to meet such social advances easily, but he failed at that. The laird was head of an old family, which through one thing and another—chiefly perhaps through not holding with the Earl of Lindsey that "nobility is consistent with merchandise"—had dwindled in estate and power. He was that rare thing in these times, the aristocrat; there could not for a moment be a doubt of it among those who understand the true tradition of aristocracy. He never boasted in his life—an aristocrat need not. He troubled little or not at all about other folks' ways; he held aloof—an aristocrat has this aloofness; it stamps the caste. The laird rarely took the name of anyone in vain—it is bad form in an aristocrat to do so. He had the grand reticence. At most he might now and then allow himself a cold sneer if, say, some upstart or rich pretender were discussed before him. Now, be it from loving-kindness, or be it from pride, this restraint is strength in a man. "They say? Who says? Let them say!" is fit for the coat of arms of a great family;

"They do? Who does? Let them do!" is fitter still. We who cannot weigh ourselves, who set us up to weigh the others?

Father, mother, brother, sister, cousins in near degree, he outlived all. For many years he had lived alone on the estate, and the sameness of his life was only interrupted at intervals when one of his family came to stay awhile with him. These visits grew fewer as time passed; his circle became very small. Self-centred as he seemed to strangers and the few neighbours in that land of barren heath and dusky wood, the laird had the family sense strong in him. He helped his own if they were in hardship. But it was as though some blight had fallen on that family. It could not thrive. Its race was run. One member of it after another died in the space of a decade or so. The laird spent most of his time roaming about the place in these lonely years, roaming in the wilds around his home. If some important call were made upon him whilst he was thus wandering, he could only be fetched back by the ringing of the bell in the old turret. This bell rang him home if ill news of some member of his family should reach the house when he was on a solitary round. Finally it came about that the bell was rung only at the grave summons "Come at once". A toll was in the note of that strange bell.

. . . . . .

The ringing of the bell through those wild heathy ways—the ringing of it through those gleaming holts! Come home, Come home, Come home—always the same warning, hasting words in the voice of the turret bell. But what tricks the uncertain air and the broken ground between them would play with the voice—sometimes sharply echoing with a mock; reverberating; tossed from knoll to knoll across the dells and dingles; or fitful in the fitful gusts of wind, but firm again and loud between them—Come home, Come home, Come home.

. . . . . .

So it rang from time to time through the lonely years, fetching the laird back from his long roamings, or from the hermitage, a little building at the highest point on the estate where he would often sit and read, for the sake of its quiet and absolute seclusion. But rarer as time went on grew the note, till at last what further need could there be for ringing? Had it not tolled out the lives of all the folk he cared for? Yet there was to be one more ringing after years of silence. It startled him, and then it angered him, for he judged that the bell must be ringing him back over some paltry matter that might wait. But, loud and imperious, it sounded sure enough the old note—Come home, Come home, Come home—not ceasing till he came down the avenue and entered the hall door. And now this strange thing happened. There were no tidings for the laird. No messenger had come. No servant knew anything about the bell. Much as he hated a scene—an aristocrat always hates a scene—the laird had the servants called into his study and demanded sternly who had rung him home and why. One and all they denied they had rung the bell—added they had not heard it ring. Were they drunk or drugged, were they a band of mutineers? He looked at them and blackened, as an aristocrat can blacken.

Then as if to solve the mystery of who rang the bell, he turned in wrath to the flagstaff turret. The bell was at the top of the turret, and to reach the rope a ringer must enter the little old damp cupboard in a room long disused, climb a wooden ladder fixed flat to the wall, and push up a glass trap-door. The little tower at its battlemented top being open to the sky, the builder had contrived this door as a guard against weather. The laird climbed the ladder and raised his hand to thrust up the glass trap-door. Doing so he raised his face and looked through the glass, and this gave him pause—over the trap-door were cobwebs and dead leaves. He stopped, as he well might, for a few seconds to think on what this implied. Then he thrust forth his hand again and shook up, after one or two attempts, the trap-door, which had stuck. A shower of dead leaves and grit came tumbling down thereupon into the cupboard, half blinding the laird for the moment. It must have come in on him then that the glass had certainly not been raised for a long time—probably years. Presently the laird came down the ladder, shutting the trap-door, and nothing more was said of the bell-ringing. What further could be said? The matter dropped. Perhaps the laird himself thought no more of it. At any rate that evening he sat in his study alone just as he had sat hundreds of winter nights, wild ones and quiet, for years past, over his book and his pipe at first, and later looking into the wood fire slipping to ashes. So he sat as of old, thinking . . . thinking.

. . . . . .

How came the bell to ring? Can it be that unseen hands sometimes touch cords in our life? May such things be, after all, as spirits moving about us, sometimes intervening, interceding in our affairs? May there be another world, a world spiritual, just without our gross ken? Now and then such ideas do flit about the brains of some of us, and we like to sport with them. There are hours and scenes that make honest thinkers half hope, even half hold it. One has known the feeling on a rapt night when the blue height is lamped by burning stars. One has known it in the God-lit belt of Orion, and in the vast streamers of the Milky Way.

There comes too soon again the damping day to quench those lights. There comes too soon again the earth earthy to preach another doctrine—that devil doctrine of a little heap of dust.

What did the laird think of such things? It was the same with him, I ween, as with the others. If he half hoped under the burning stars, he must doubt with the denying day. The earth has us with a tremendous hold. High moods or low, in the end we gravitate to her perforce. Yet whatever the laird thought of these vague things, and whatever you or I think of them, this fact remains, that the bell rang home the laird, and the laird died that night.

CORRESPONDENCE.

THE FERRER DISTURBANCES IN ITALY.

To the Editor of the SATURDAY REVIEW.

Venice, 18 October 1909.

SIR,—You may have noticed that nearly every one of the pro-Ferrer proclamations that have been made in Italy bears this endorsement "The Republican, Socialist, and Anarchistic Committees"—in other words, the subversive societies. In the last few days they have already endeavoured to destroy by fire several famous churches in Rome and Pisa; in Pisa they plucked out of the Church of San Stefano a splendid picture attributed to Andrea del Sarto and tore it into fragments. At Forli they hauled down the famous Column of the Virgin, a masterpiece of fifteenth-century art surmounted by a glorious figure of the Virgin by Sansovino. They broke nearly all the shop-windows on the Corso, Via XX Settembre, Piazza di Spagna, etc., in Rome. In Florence many soldiers and civilians were severely wounded and one or two killed. At Milan the same thing. In every city these demonstrators have gone down the principal thoroughfares shouting "Long live the Republic! Death to the monarchy! Death to religion! Death to the priests!" and "Death to the middle class—the 'borghesia'!" These disorderly demonstrations are of a purely artificial character; not one man in a hundred who is now shouting (three days after his execution!) "Long live Ferrer!" could tell you who he was, where he came from, or anything about him. It is remarkable, too, how the press has worked up the sentimental side of the picture by introducing on the scene the grossly neglected daughters of the unfortunate man. I am in a position to tell you that Ferrer was a man of most immoral life, who abandoned his wife and family to live with loose women, including the over-credulous dame who left him a fortune wherewith to continue his anti-religious propaganda, whilst at the same time leaving about 30,000 francs for Masses to be said for the repose of her soul.

Mr. Ernest Nathan, Mayor of Rome, has taken upon himself to proclaim to the Roman people that the Eternal City joins with the rest of Europe in denouncing "the foul murder of Francisco Ferrer, the great thinker and the apostle of education". Surely since this world began there was never anything quite so burlesque as this—the mayor of the capital of a monarchical country pushing himself forward, for the sake of popularity, with a proclamation in favour of a well-known Anarchist, a man who, by his inflammatory speeches and literature, was at any rate instrumental in bringing about the deaths of some hundred men, women and children, and the burning of property valued at sixteen millions of francs.

Podrecca and Barzilai are, of course, merely poor imitations of Ferrer; but Italy may one day regret that she did not assume the same firm attitude towards them that Spain has done towards Ferrer. The Conservative and non-anarchical press of Italy has remarked with surprise that the concluding lines of Mr. Nathan's proclamation to the people of Rome contain these significant words: "We approve and endorse with all our hearts the high purposes and ideals for which Francisco Ferrer sacrificed his noble life"—that is to say, the anti-religious and anti-monarchical; a distinct threat by the Mayor of Rome against the King of Italy.

The sensible and respectable people of Rome are as indignant as anybody at this ridiculous agitation, which has done the cause of Ferrer no good, and, if anything, has done it harm, and will probably result in strengthening the reactionary movement from one end of the country to the other. An Italian gentleman, not a clerical, said to me the other day he almost hoped that something worse might happen to awaken his countrymen from the apathy into which they have fallen, thanks mostly to the general well-being of the upper and middle classes; whereas the condition of the lower order remains, for all this agitation and all these committees, worse than it has ever been in the centuries, thanks to the increase in the price of food and rent and the very little practical good that has been done by listening to "tall-talkers", agitators and selfish politicians. I think we have a few of them in England.

I am very truly yours,

A Traveller.

THE "GLORIOUS" SCOT.

To the Editor of the Saturday Review.

Edinburgh, 10 October 1909.

Sir,—In yesterday's Saturday Review a "Disgusted Englishman" took exception to the "Drunkenness in Scotland". His austerity shows little community of feeling with the idiosyncrasies of the good people among whom fate has thrown him, and who regard the besotted by drink in the light of privileged beings to be humoured to the utmost extent, almost to be honoured in private and in public, in the street and in vehicles for common conveyance—even the first-class railway carriages offering an insecure refuge from ladies and gentlemen in a condition not less repugnant to the sober and staid than he reports of the third-class travellers. If this points hardly to a high grade of refinement, it speaks at least in favour of the forbearing temper of the local authorities, kindly disposed after the manner of the North African chiefs who condone almost any offence committed by their santons, crazy through fanaticism and excessive fasting as the Scots wha ha'e through the promptings of a constitutionally parched throat and excessive indulgence in usquebaugh, the fewest draughts they content themselves with being three, according to the classic rule preserved in James Howell's "Epistolæ Ho-Elianæ": the first to quench their thirst past, the second to relieve their thirst present, the third to tickle their thirst future.

In fact, this wondrous capacity of the Northerner for boozing and his consequential final total incapacity the disgusted Southerner complains of, is his most characteristic trait, and gives this city, his capital, its most distinguishing mark in the eyes of discriminating foreign visitors. Not Edina's beautiful situation and natural amenities, spoiled by unsightly railway tracks and the modern architect; not her imitation Greek temples (in this climate!) and poor imitation at that; not her plethora of statues whose pseudo-artistic forms are charitably covered with a thick crust of dirt by a sooty atmosphere; not her showy, shoppy Princes Street, which aspires to the appellation "noblest in Europe", notwithstanding the claims of heaven knows how many nobler boulevards, prados, corsos, Rings, etc.; not her squalid, unwashed, hooligan "historic mile"; not her castle or Holyrood—but Edina's hard drinking makes her conspicuous, her multitude of male and female topers in different stages of alcoholic bliss, her prominence among Christian and Paynim communities in the audacity of her tipsy beggars, undisguised tramps and ruffians or disguised as musicians. Musicians! Such discordant noises, such howling and yelling, nay yelping, never were tolerated anywhere else in the world.

Every copper begged goes to the pothouse, and every pretext to pass the flowing bowl will do—not only among the strolling pipers, the Caruso's and Tetrazzini's of the pavement. Yesterday the suffragettes came out brilliant with a didactic pageant and shrieking demonstration. Their hysterics carried the town, undesignedly combined with the permanent attraction of bars and cafés so-called. The demonstration's aftermath must have been far from gratifying to the friends of the cause: young girls, viragoes in their teens, decorated with the badge of woman's freedom, inflamed by the allusions to Scotch heroines—stool-throwing Jennie Geddes, amorous Flora MacDonald, etc.—shouting and pulling at the boys, parading up and down in the excitement of one or two drops too much, lolling on doorsteps, tumbling into the gutter, thoroughly franchised of modesty ad majorem Pankhurstæ gloriam!

That famous lady not responsible for the ribaldry of her army's accidental camp-followers, who wear the badge, one penny each, as they will wear anything, just for fun? Well, then, let us put the fault, if fault there be, on Scotch proclivity to the cup that cheers. And here we are back at our starting-point—the fault-finding, disgusted Englishman who grieves because that cup also inebriates.

I invite him to postpone his judgment until he has witnessed the bacchanalia connected with the ringing-out of an old year and the ringing-in of a new: a rare treat, especially when hogmanay is graced with frosty weather and slippery sidewalks. The spectacle at midnight of numberless tottering figures, losing their physical balance since they have lost their mental ditto, flopping down and crawling up, reinstating a haphazard equilibrium in earnest endeavour toward the next libation, trying to make headway from one hospitable roof to another, awakening a vision of jolly ghosts who went for a dram and unsteadily hurry back to their graves one second before the fatal stroke of the church-bell—that annual show repays a trip north with greater human interest than the hackneyed Trossachs, than Fingal's Cave or ancient Iona—at least to the student of Scotch character, and most positively so if he observe the same figures afterward repairing to kirk, men and women marching at measured Sabbath gait, starched and buckram. Whoever finds no delight, looking on that picture and on this, is not susceptible to the rich colour of life's low comedy as Jan Steen, Teniers, Van Ostade understood it best; I do not mention smaller fry like native Wilkie, though with the brush low comedian enough. And if the disgusted Sasunnach stays sufficiently long on this side of the border to catch the Albannach weekday joie de vivre against its background of Sunday gloom, he will perhaps distil wisdom from the advice of the poet:

> "To take what passes in good part
> And keep the hiccups from the heart".

I am, Sir, yours truly,

A Coimheach.

"HOW SHALL WE SAVE OUR PICTURES?"

To the Editor of the Saturday Review.

Lustleigh, Devon, 16 October 1909.

Sir,—Your correspondent "Viator" is labouring under a complete delusion if he imagines that the people of the United States to-day are English, the fact being that, owing chiefly to alien immigration, the vast majority of her people are thoroughly anti-English and have little in common with English ideas. The anti-English element, moreover, though Americans of British descent do not fully realise it, is rapidly increasing, and will more likely than not cause a collision between our two countries in the not-distant future. The real sentiment of the majority of Americans for England showed itself plainly at the time of the Boer War. That there is a minority friendly to England gives cause for congratulation to reasonable people in both our countries, and it is right to foster this friendly feeling. When, however, "Viator" says that the best policy of the older English people is to court America, I am tempted to reply—as regards the large anti-English majority in that country—"I do pray that we be better strangers".

This letter must not be taken to imply antipathy to Americans in general, for the writer has good friends in the United States, and first-class fellows they are. In view of "Viator's" letter I only wish to state the facts, and I do not see how it can be denied that a nation which tolerates the scurrilous abuse of Englishmen and English institutions that is poured forth in a constant stream by the so-called Irish-American and German-American press can have little friendly feeling for us, nor can it fully realise that the American Constitution is founded on the British.

Friendly rivalry between our two countries is good. Constant and "nagging" repetition of statements and misstatements of past events which are not fully understood, and which therefore had far better be forgotten, does nothing but harm.

It is to the interest of both Americans and Britishers to get together and keep together; if this is not possible we can at all events try to understand each other. If we achieve this desirable end we ought to be able to criticise each other without abusing one another. This would do nothing but good.

With regard to the question "How shall we save our pictures?" the answer seems to be: By means of an export tax.

Yours faithfully,
T. Edwards.

EDUCATION AND UNEMPLOYMENT.

To the Editor of the Saturday Review.

19 October.

Sir,—The more one sees of our present system of primary education the more one feels that it is turning out unemployed by hundreds every year, and that the remarks in the Report of the Poor Law Commission on this subject want underlining and repeating again and again. The simple facts are these:

1. The age at which boys and girls, but especially boys, can be withdrawn from school is fixed far too low. It is between fourteen and sixteen (and not much before) that some idea of the responsibilities of life and its problems can be impressed on the young.

2. The mistaken idea that, by getting the children "out in the world" and making them wage-earners, they are being done good to is one that must be fought against tooth and nail. No doubt for a few years they can add to the family exchequer; but at what a cost! So soon as they cease to be satisfied with a boy's wage they must throw up their work, and are out on the world—with no trade, no settled habits, and with most of what they have learnt at school forgotten—to swell the ranks of casual labour.

Our efforts, then, must be directed:

Firstly, to the raising of the school age, the extra years thus gained to be devoted in part to the rudiments of some definite trade, in part to the acquirement of extra knowledge, and in part (and this is most important) to physical training.

Secondly, to a general overhauling of the curriculum in our primary schools; much time at present is wasted on subjects of no importance. And

Thirdly, to the organisation of all juvenile labour—under eighteen—if possible through a Central Labour Department, or, failing this, through municipal and county authorities. I trust you will find space for the letter of one who has been a schoolmaster for several years and a manager of elementary schools, and has this matter deeply at heart.

Charles J. Magrath.

FRANCIS NEWMAN'S LATER VIEWS.

To the Editor of the Saturday Review.

17 October 1909.

Sir,—In her reply to my protest Mrs. Giberne Sieveking disallows the validity of my assertion of the vagueness of her alleged proofs of the reversion of Francis Newman to his early religious, or theological, creed. "There is certainly", she affirms, "no vagueness about the [assumed?] fact that Francis Newman returned *in some measure* [italics mine] to his former faith during his latter years." I hope that the esteemed biographer will not deem me to be hypercritical when I venture to submit that in this qualification "in some measure" there certainly may be detected "vagueness" in a high degree. It leaves a widely opened door to our interpretation of the nature, the extent, and the degree of the alleged reversion. As I already have remarked, Francis Newman very possibly may have revised some of his views as to Christianity—whether as to the comparative value of the teaching of the Founder of the first Christian society, or as to certain features of its later history. But that is far from proving—I must repeat my protest—that the conscientious and searching critic (whose investigations and most emphatic repudiations of the orthodox interpretations of the creeds of Christendom extended over some sixty years of his career) of the Gospel narratives accepted, in his last days, a supernatural origin for them.

But there is one fact—admitted and stated by the biographer herself (upon the same page on which she refers to a letter written by Newman, very shortly before his decease, to his friend Miss Swanwick, cited by the biographer as demonstrating the reversion)—which must be deemed, in itself, inevitably and logically conclusive and decisive of the question in debate. She records, with regret, that Francis Newman, at the very time of the correspondence between himself and his friend Anna Swanwick, had no belief (or, at best, a very slender belief) in continued existence.

Mrs. Sieveking refers to letters which (as she avers) make it impossible (or difficult) to doubt her contention. It will seem to every candid reader that in that case the production in full of the correspondence relating to so highly interesting, so important, a matter is called for and justly to be expected.

Mrs. Sieveking concludes her vindication of her presentation of the matter in question with the apophthegm of Eugène Voguë: "L'écrivain est surtout puissant par ce qu'il ne dit pas". No citation could be more à propos.

Criticus.

BOSWELL AND ECKERMANN.

To the Editor of the Saturday Review.

Springbank, Hamilton N.B. 16 October 1909.

Sir,—Lord Rosebery's praise of Boswell, in his Johnson speech, set me thinking of Sainte-Beuve's estimate of Eckermann, Goethe's Boswell:

"Eckermann, homme d'un talent personnel qui, seul et de lui-même, ne pouvait atteindre bien haut, s'est choisi la bonne part. Il ne peut désormais mourir, il s'est lié d'un lien indissoluble avec un immortel. Elisée nous a conservé le manteau et l'esprit d'Elie et il a gardé au front un rayon de sa flamme".

Yours faithfully,
James Bell.

REVIEWS.

GOVERNMENT BY THE KING.

"The Last Journals of Horace Walpole during the Reign of George III., from 1771 to 1783." With Notes by Dr. Doran. Edited, with an Introduction, by A. Francis Steuart. London: Lane. 1909. 25s. net.

HORACE WALPOLE was a good hater—what the French call "une mauvais langue"—and abused every one of his contemporaries except General Conway, his personal friend, and Charles Fox, whom he regarded as the torch-bearer of Whiggism. It must be admitted that "Horry" had good reason for his abuse, for the twelve years covered by these Last Journals were the most calamitous and disgraceful in British history. Anyone who takes the view that there is no such thing as a necessary man, and that institutions are more important than individuals, should be converted by reading these volumes. The five years of the elder Pitt's Administration (1757-61) were the most glorious in our annals. The twelve years of Lord North's Government were, as we have said, the blackest in our story. Yet Lord North actually succeeded Lord Chatham as Prime Minister. We admit that Lord Chatham's second Ministry was a tragic farce, owing to the ill health or madness of the great statesman. But ten years had not elapsed between Pitt's retirement before the Peace of Paris, in full possession of his faculties, and Lord North's accession to power. What produced the change from glory to disgrace, from victories in both hemispheres to defeat by a handful of provincials? The character of the nation assuredly had not changed, nor had its institutions. What had changed was its ruler: Lord Chatham had been succeeded by George III., governing by Lord North ostensibly, but in reality by Lord Mansfield, Jenkinson, Rigby and a bribed majority of the House of Commons, called Courtiers or King's Friends. The story of this system of corruption, with its consequent incompetence at home and abroad, has often been told. All historians and book-makers found their work on these journals of Horace Walpole, which are reproduced by Mr. John Lane in good type and with excellent notes for the benefit of those who prefer original to derivative authority.

How George III. not only reigned, but governed, by means of "the double Cabinet" has been exposed by the hand of a master in the "Thoughts on Present Discontents". Lord North was the Prime Minister; Lord Apsley (afterwards Lord Bathurst) was Lord Chancellor; Thurlow and Wedderburn were Attorney- and Solicitor-General; Lord Sandwich was First Lord of the Admiralty; Lord George Germaine was Secretary of State. The real Premier was the King, acting in secret conclave with Lord Mansfield (Lord Chief Justice), Rigby (Paymaster) and Jenkinson (holding some nominal and subordinate post). It was Rigby (an insolent and cynical buffoon who supplied Lord Beaconsfield with his pseudonym for Croker) and Jenkinson who issued the secret orders of the Court to the members of Parliament who took the King's money. How hard George III. slaved at his business of governing the British Empire; how he bribed and bullied; how with a civil list of nearly £1,000,000 he was always in debt, though he dined on boiled mutton and turnips; how he scanned the division lists, and wrangled over the smallest appointment—all these things are familiar to students of the period. But it is due to George III. to remember, what even Burke admitted, that the English people were behind him in the war with the American colonists, and that he was very unlucky with his generals and, perhaps it should be added, with his Ministers. Chatham was no doubt lucky in that the careers of Clive and Wolfe coincided with his own. George III. was unfortunate in being served by such a string of duffers as Gage, Burgoyne, the two Howes, Cornwallis and Dunmore (who were always turning up in London with "claims" for honours and rewards), and it would be difficult to pick out from history three such incompetent Ministers as North, Sandwich and Germaine. Somehow or other, fortune always seems to co-operate with genius; and if the King had not been a stupid man he would have managed to find better servants. It is absurd to suppose that in ten years all political, naval and military ability had disappeared from the nation. Chatham, we agree, had become impossible, but Conway was a good soldier and an honest man; the Duke of Richmond was clever and industrious, while Burke and Fox only wanted the salaries of office to turn them into brilliant public servants. But the King was afraid of Conway, because he was independent; he hated Fox, because he opposed the Royal Marriages Act and because he was a rake; and Burke was chained to Lord Rockingham, who was peevish and impracticable—"a nervous, incapable puppet", as Walpole calls him. And so his Most Gracious Majesty governed England himself, and did it worse than anybody else, except James II. Horace Walpole, in comparing the two Sovereign-rulers, says epigrammatically that while James lost his crown, George only lost his colonies. He did indeed lose as much as Chatham had gained for the Empire.

Horace Walpole's Journals are valuable not only for their historical chronicle but for the portraits of the chief actors. The son of Sir Robert Walpole was not likely to feel benevolently towards the Tories; but, barring a pardonable party bias, there is no excuse for his ill nature and unfairness towards men who had nothing to do with his father's downfall. But "Horry's" judgments are feminine; that is, they are purely personal. The picture of George III. is an odious one. The King's faults, his parsimony, his obstinacy, his attention to trifles and his political corruption are emphasised; while no mention is made of his bravery, of his fixed resolve to maintain his Empire at whatever personal cost, of his severe domestic trials. All this is due to the fact that the Duke of Gloucester married Maria Countess of Waldegrave, whom the King and Queen refused to receive at Court. We must say that George's brothers tried him pretty high in the matter of matrimony. The Duchess of Gloucester was the illegitimate daughter of Sir Edward Walpole, the brother of Horace, and her mother was a milliner's assistant. The Duke of Cumberland married one of the Luttrells, a family notorious for impecuniosity, insolence and immorality. Was it not natural that the King and Queen should be angry and refuse to recognise the Duchesses as royalties? Walpole's portrait of Lord North is very hostile. The Prime Minister was indolent and vacillating and servile at a time when he should have been the reverse of all these things. But in his private dealings with men North has generally passed for a good-natured man. Walpole declares that he was cruel and insolent—he certainly did not answer letters, which, no doubt, is the worst fault any man, public or private, can be guilty of. Lord Mansfield figures in these pages as a coward, a liar, and a conspirator against the Constitution. The celebrated Lord Chief Justice has inspired two such different men as Horace Walpole and Jeremy Bentham with intense hatred and contempt; so we suppose there must have been something bad about his nature. Against Burke's integrity Walpole makes the gravest charges. He declares that Burke and his cousin and brother, "his Irish tail", had bought for a mere trifle a huge estate in one of the West Indian islands from its native owners. In order to get the grant or purchase confirmed by the Government the Burkes took into partnership Charles Fox, who was at that time a Junior Lord of the Treasury under Lord North. The grant was disallowed as a swindle, for North permitted no one to plunder except himself and Rigby and Jenkinson and Sandwich. The story about the Clerkship of the Pells is still more extraordinary. The Clerkship of the Pells was the fattest sinecure of those days, being £7000 a year for life, with no duties. It was held by Sir Edward Walpole. On the death of Lord Rockingham, during the few days that his Government continued until the formation of Lord Shelburne's Ministry, Burke, still the Paymaster-General, came to Horace Walpole and proposed that his brother should resign the Clerkship of the Pells in order that Lord John Cavendish, Chancellor of the Exchequer, might appoint Burke in his place. Sir Edward Walpole was to be paid the full amount of his salary during his life, and Burke offered to give his personal security for the payment! Horace Walpole was civil, but he thought Burke was mad, and we think so too. Burke was always in difficulties, for he tried to get money by speculation, in which, like many another clever man, he always failed. Had it not been for Lord Rockingham, who lent or gave him large sums, Burke would have gone down. By his will Lord Rockingham cancelled a bond of Burke's for £30,000, and this was believed to be only one of many loans. Everybody who is interested in the eighteenth century ought to read these Journals, remembering that their author was a prejudiced and antipathetic observer of his contemporaries.

NAPOLEON'S BROTHERS.

"Napoleon and his Brothers." By A. Hilliard Atteridge. London: Methuen. 8s. 6d.

THE relations between Napoleon and his brothers have been the theme of much dispute. Some, like M. Marson,* attribute the failure of the Emperor in a large measure to their want of loyal support and their incapacity. Others not only hold that he treated them heartlessly, ungratefully and tyrannically, but that by his constant interference with the policy of the three whom he made kings he at once ruined their popularity and prepared his own fall.

Apart from this question, the history of the men of this Corsican family is interesting as furnishing studies of character under the influences of changes of fortune which for their greatness and their suddenness have few parallels.

The story of Napoleon's brothers, though treated by foreign writers, is, as Mr. Atteridge remarks, "but little known to English readers. . . . They are overshadowed by the greatness of the Emperor. We catch glimpses of them here and there as his mere satellites". Yet "their story is worth telling from a point of view that does not so utterly dwarf them". This is the aim of the book, and, although no new evidence has been dug out for us, Mr. Atteridge has succeeded in giving a very readable and well-arranged account.

Of the brothers, Lucien, who was younger than both Joseph and Napoleon, was the man of most character and independence. Napoleon, indeed, for a long time considered him a visionary with an ill-balanced mind. But though his earlier career, with his love for cheap oratory, his enthusiasm for Jacobin ideas, his absurd assumption of the name of Brutus and his desire to call the village of S. Maximin, where he was then a storekeeper in the commissariat, Marathon, would seem to justify this estimate, we must remember that he was then only a raw youth of eighteen; and Napoleon himself was soon to learn that he was much more than a mere club orator or a dilettante lover of literature and of art. In the two great crises of Napoleon's life Lucien played a leading part. It was his conduct as President of the Five Hundred that aided, if it did not secure, the success of the coup d'état of Brumaire; and after the fatal day of Waterloo it was he who vainly urged Napoleon to declare himself dictator, a bold measure which at least offered the best chance of saving the Imperial throne. Of his independence the best proof is shown in his refusal to abandon his second wife, Mme. Jouberthon, at Napoleon's dictation, a refusal which cost him his claim to the succession to the Empire in the future and all hopes of a kingdom in the present.

Joseph, the eldest of the family, never rises above respectable mediocrity. Napoleon, who had looked up to him in early days, began to push him as soon as he was in a position so to do. But neither in diplomacy, which he first tried, nor as a member of the Five Hundred under the Directory, nor as King of Naples had he made any mark. Then in an unfortunate moment for himself he changed the crown of Naples for that of Spain, which had just been stolen from the Bourbon, Ferdinand.

Joseph's apologists would tell us that had he been allowed to follow his policy of conciliation, and been given a freer hand, he might have gained the goodwill of the Spaniards, while his military failure they would attribute to the jealousies and the insubordination of Napoleon's marshals, an insubordination which the Emperor did not suppress. However that may be, Joseph at least displayed no great gifts as a soldier nor any of that personal magnetism and power which commands obedience. Napoleon's denunciation of his conduct as Lieutenant-General in Paris at the crisis of 1814 is no doubt exaggerated. "This", he said, "is what comes of employing people who have neither energy nor common-sense." Joseph is not to be held responsible for the failure to fortify Paris in time to check the advance of the Allies. It is doubtful whether the Emperor if he had reached Paris would have been able to hold it; yet a more resolute man would have resisted longer.

In the final crash after Waterloo Joseph behaved according to his wont. While Lucien was resolute and sanguine, he was depressed; and when Napoleon hesitated between abdication or a coup d'état, he shrank from advising the bolder course. But if he was not a great man, his last act showed that he was capable of self-sacrifice. He proposed that Napoleon, adopting his disguise, should avail himself of the means which he had prepared for his own escape. Joseph would have risked much, but if the Emperor had succeeded in escaping to America the conqueror of Europe would have at least avoided the humiliation of having to surrender to an English ship and his captivity at S. Helena. Joseph was, in fact, better fitted for the life of a quiet country gentleman, or at least for the post of a dignified ambassador at a friendly Court, and it was an evil day for him and his rich and respectable "bourgeoise" wife, Julie Clary, when he was tempted by the crown of Sicily and then of Spain to leave his comfortable estate at Mortefontaine.

The attachment of Napoleon for Louis, the fourth brother, is difficult to explain. Although a bright and interesting boy, he soon under the influence of prosperity proved himself a suspicious man, an idle and fantastic valetudinarian, a would-be poet with a love of dissipation. Yet this was the person who, in the opinion of the Emperor, "had none of the defects and all the good qualities of his other brothers". He always persisted in believing that Louis would become a great general. He selected him as the husband of his favourite stepdaughter, Hortense Beauharnais. He at one time designated him as his successor, and meanwhile made him King of Holland. In that position Louis certainly deserves our sympathy. The French rule was not indeed so unpopular there as in Spain, and his task was therefore not so difficult as that of Joseph. Nevertheless, Louis really attempted to identify himself with his new subjects, and his objection to seeing Dutch commercial interests sacrificed to the political exigencies of the Continental system, and part of the Dutch territories incorporated in the French Empire, was laudable enough.

With his departure from Holland he ceased to play an important part in European affairs. Refusing to comply with Napoleon's command that he should return to France and abandon his royal title, he retired to Gratz, in Austria, without his wife, from whom he had long been estranged. After the disastrous retreat from Moscow, he offered his services to the Emperor once more, but only on condition that he should be restored to Holland on conclusion of a general peace. On this being refused he retired to Switzerland, till the advance of Schwartzenberg in 1814. Then at last he returned to Paris against the wish of Napoleon, who however was at that moment too much occupied to trouble himself with the affairs of Louis, only to leave again on the approach of the Allies. Illness prevented him from taking part in the struggle of the Hundred Days, and so he passed away into exile. It is strange that Napoleon III., who established the Second Empire, should be son of one who had so deeply quarrelled with the first Napoleon.

As for Jerome, the best that can be said of him was that he was personally brave. His vigorous though probably mistaken persistence in attacking the château of Hougoumont at Waterloo extorted from the Emperor the remark, "Mon frère, je vous ai connu trop tard".

* M. F. Marson, "Napoléon et sa famille".

Apart from personal courage and a certain rollicking bonhomie, his career was contemptible. The youngest of all the brothers, he had never known the days of adversity. From the first he was something of a spoilt child. First as a sailor, then as a soldier, he imagined that he could become an admiral or a general without any diligence or trouble. When he went to war he behaved as if he were paying a visit of state. His personal wardrobe in the Russian campaign contained sixty pairs of boots, two hundred shirts, three hundred and eighteen pocket-handkerchiefs, and required in all seven heavy wagons, "while his whole campaigning kit stretched over half a mile".

His first wife, Elizabeth Patterson, he abandoned at the command of his imperious brother; he had even the indelicacy to suggest that she should remain as his mistress; to his second, Catherine of Wurtemberg, he was unfaithful. Recklessly extravagant and fond of display, he was always borrowing and always in financial difficulties. As King of Westphalia he thought chiefly of his pleasures, and, as Mr. Atteridge tells us, "when after the retreat from Moscow the houses of Westphalia were mourning for their sons dead under Russian snows, when Germany was quivering with eagerness for revolt, when Joseph's bankrupt throne at Cassel was tottering, there was feasting at the Palace of Napoleonshöhe".

If this estimate of the Emperor's brothers is a just one it would be idle to argue that any of them, with the possible exception of Lucien, assisted him in his rise; and if they were none of them traitors, like Napoleon's brother-in-law Joachim Murat and his wife Caroline, the sister of the Emperor, they were at least no real support in the days of his trouble.

The question as to Napoleon's ingratitude and tyranny is also not difficult to answer. From the days when in 1793 the Bonaparte family found themselves exiles from Corsica in France and in straitened circumstances we find Napoleon continually pushing the interests of his brothers, with the exception of the independent Lucien. Joseph he marked out as the diplomat and statesman, Louis and Jerome as the soldier and the sailor. But these favours were conditional on their being useful and obedient to the supreme will of their imperious benefactor. When in 1806 Napoleon, now Emperor, was looking for new kings to surround his imperial throne, it was but natural that he should select his brothers. He thereby avoided exciting the jealousy which would have been aroused if he had chosen outside his family, and hoped that family interests would keep them his obedient satellites.

Napoleon was not the first to attempt this family policy nor the first to experience how faulty it was. It had been tried in France in the days of the nobles of the fleur-de-lys, by Edward III. of England, and even by the nepotist Popes of the fifteenth century. In every case it had ended in raising a too-powerful nobility beneath the throne. With Napoleon's brothers the results were identical, only that they were kings—kings by the right of Napoleon in his eyes, kings by Divine right in theirs. Every attempt on their part to act as independent Sovereigns was therefore considered an act of treachery by Napoleon, and every attempt on his to guide their policy was denounced as an act of tyranny by them. As long as he was powerful enough to maintain them on their thrones the absurdity of their claim was not so flagrantly apparent. It stood revealed in 1814. They then still cherished the preposterous belief that when the Allies had at last extorted peace from the Emperor they would have a claim to be restored to kingdoms which they had only been able to hold by his armies and his victories.

THE TURKISH WOMAN'S STANDPOINT.

"Some Pages from the Lives of Turkish Women." By Demetra Vaka (Mrs. Kenneth Brown). London: Constable. 1909. 5s. net.

MRS. KENNETH BROWN'S name before she married was Mlle. Demetra Vaka. She was born and brought up in Constantinople, where her family had dwelt for centuries, and, herself a Turkish subject though a Greek, she lived as child and girl on terms of perfect familiarity and confidential friendship with the children of various Turkish harems.

This, for us her readers, is the important epoch of her career, when she laid in the instructive and unconscious knowledge of Oriental character and philosophy which is the informing element of her book. There followed a period no less essential. While still, as we gather, in her teens Mlle. Vaka was taken by her father to America, where she lived for six years, becoming in that period in all respects apparently Westernised. At the end of the six years she returned for a visit to Constantinople. The early friends of her childhood were by this time most of them married, but they had by no means forgotten her, and the old terms of intimacy and affection were soon re-established. During the time of her stay Mlle. Vaka lived in the best harem society of the place. But now she saw things not with the uncritical eyes of a child but with the discriminating gaze of a woman whose Western training had accustomed her to submit the whole contents of life to the test of rational analysis. With very keen and with very comprehending eyes Mlle. Vaka studied the usages of woman's life in Constantinople, and what she saw determined her on writing a book. The West, complacently satisfied with its own estimate, was, she very easily perceived, in a condition of gross and utter ignorance in regard to the whole Oriental point of view. Could she enlighten it?

This book is her attempt, and it answers the question as nearly in the affirmative, perhaps, as any book could. We have had so far for our knowledge of harem life to rely either on the voluptuously sentimental school which flourished on the secrets of that life or on the rationalist school which dealt indeed with facts, but with facts to which it applied only its own cocksure practical tests, and in which therefore it could find no intelligible meaning whatever. Here in this little book we have the almost unique combination of feelings in touch with Oriental views with a mind and reason capable of measuring those feelings and considering their influences and their claims. Here are the makings of an interpreter indeed! The author is one who can both receive and transmit. She understands the Eastern tongue, but speaks the Western. To her Oriental friends she is Demetra Vaka; to us she is Mrs. Brown.

What, then, has she to tell us? The reader must go to the book for an answer. Among much that is new, interesting and suggestive he will find one thing that stands out: it is that the Turkish system is supported and, in the eyes of its adherents, is justified by a profound philosophic theory of its own. Of course, everyone who gave the subject serious and disinterested thought had an inkling that this was so. No rule of life of general application subsists for centuries which is not, in some sort, a true response to human nature's needs and attributes. Even of the harem this must hold good. It must embody some idea of value to have lived so long.

Let us give in a sentence or two the thought suggested by many of the intimate talks between Mlle. Vaka and her friends. The idea these women have is that woman's sphere of development lies in the cultivation of the emotional and spiritual gifts and of the insight inseparable from such gifts; for it is in these, so they say, that the feminine nature is particularly rich. To man belongs intellect and practical energy, the faculties which deal immediately with the circumstances and appearances of our outward life. No woman in this sphere of action can hope to compete successfully; the utmost here open to her is that she should develop into an inferior, a second-class man. But in the other sphere her influence is supreme, and all the light and the colour which the spiritual and emotional faculties can bestow on life it is the woman's part to treasure and transmit. This is the thought which runs through the present book, and whatever the precise value may be which the reader allows to it, he will scarcely after reading these conversations dismiss it as altogether insignificant.

A GREAT FAMILY OF THE NEAR EAST.

"Les Mavroyeni: histoire d'Orient." By Theodore Blancard. 2 vols. Paris: Ernest Leroux. 1909. 7fr. 50c. per vol.

GENEALOGY has been denounced as the most inaccurate of all exact sciences, and this criticism is true with regard to many of the genealogies which have done duty in the past; but we are becoming much harder to please, and no genealogy will now be accepted by those who understand their work which is not proved up to the hilt. In these conditions some knowledge of family history is becoming more and more essential, for the story of great political changes can never be complete unless we have some means of gauging how they have affected the inner lives of the people. This story of a family is all the more interesting if its members have played their part in moulding the destinies of the country. The Mavroyenis have certainly done their share in Greece, in Turkey, in Roumania, in Crete, and in Samos, and it is not easy to master the history of the Near East without knowing something of the private history of men who have occupied such high and exalted positions as Hospodar of Walachia, Logothetes or chief lay officer of the Greek Church, or Prince of Samos. It may, perhaps, be unfortunate that M. Blancard has laid so much stress upon their alleged descent from the great Venetian house of Morosini, as he gives no more conclusive evidence of the truth of the pedigree than popular tradition and the conviction of such genealogists as F. Sales, C. M. Corrona, M. Persiani, and Thomas Hope, the author of "Anastasius". Much stress is also laid upon the presence of several Morosinis in Paros and in the Ottoman Empire during the wars of the seventeenth century, notwithstanding the existence of Machariote Mavroyeni, a Greek nobleman, who was Bailiff of Corfu on behalf of Venice as far back as 1441. It is furthermore stated that the Hospodar of Walachia frequently advanced this claim, but there is no evidence that he ever published the documents which it is alleged were subsequently destroyed. He was certainly one of the most remarkable men of his time. The son of Peter Mavroyeni, who had with his father and brothers fled from the Peloponnesus to Paros in 1715, he had certainly held the appointment of dragoman to the Turkish fleet for some time by 1770. Hadji-Djaafar Pasha was then Lord High Admiral, but in 1771 he was succeeded by Hassan Pasha, who remained Mavroyeni's friend and protector during his whole life. He enabled him at first to give the position of dragoman, hitherto monopolised by mere interpreters, an importance which it had never had before, by seeking his advice on many an occasion, and making him his intermediary with his Greek co-religionists, whom the dragoman saved on many an occasion from the vengeance of the Turkish Admiral. It was also Hassan who in 1786 succeeded, with the help of the Grand Vizier Youssouf Pasha, in securing for Mavroyeni the magnificent position of Hospodar or Prince of Walachia, notwithstanding the intrigues of Petraki, the Greek banker, in favour of Michael Drago Soutzo—intrigues which eventually cost the banker his life. The new Prince made himself extremely unpopular with the boyars or nobles by his impartiality between rich and poor. Much light is thrown upon the gallant struggle which he carried on for over two years against the united forces of Austria and Russia, and the manner in which he created a Roumanian army out of absolutely untrained peasants. It was a fruitless effort, and culminated with the loss of his life, sacrificed to his enemies by the Sultan Selim, who only appreciated subsequently what he had lost by the death of the most loyal Greek in his dominions. The story of the other members of the Mavroyeni family is that of the Ottoman Empire down to our days. Thus Stephen, who succeeded his uncle as dragoman of the fleet, was appointed on two separate occasions Logothetes, Archchancellor, or chief lay officer of the Greek Orthodox Church, and lost his life at the same time as the Patriarch Gregory V., when they were both beheaded in 1821. John, his brother, was Turkish Chargé d'Affaires in Vienna down to 1841. Peter, a third brother, married Princess Roxana Stourza, the divorced wife of George Balsch, and the grandmother of Nathalie, widow of Milan Obrenowitch, King of Servia. His son Peter helped to place Charles of Hohenzollern-Sigmaringen on the throne of Roumania and to put Roumanian finances on a sound footing. Madon, the daughter of Nicholas Mavroyeni, Spathar of Walachia, was one of the finest figures of the Greek War of Independence, to which cause she sacrificed all she could of the family fortunes, only to be treated with the basest ingratitude by her fellow-countrymen when once they had achieved their ends. Spiridion-Mavroyeni Pasha, who did so much for medical science in Turkey, saved the life of the ex-Sultan Abdul Hamid, and often preserved his co-religionists from Moslem bigotry. His domestic troubles were, however, destined to embroil him with his Royal master, and very nearly endangered his own life and property. The view of Apostolos Mavroyeni, who died at the age of 108, and was the last survival of the Greek War of Independence, is worth quoting: ". . . si notre armée était régulière? . . . "Assurément nous aurions vaincu. Mais le malheur a voulu que nous le soyons à cause de nous-mêmes. Depuis la libération du pays personne n'a sérieusement pensé à constituer une armée ni à chercher les moyens pour que, en temps de guerre la nation pût disposer d'une armée nombreuse et bien organisée. Nous attendions tout du bon Dieu". . . . "Rester les bras croisés et attendre l'aide de Dieu, cette façon de raisonner me parut étonnante". And yet M. Blancard is a great admirer of the results of Greek independence. He is not perhaps so hopeful of the capacity of the Young Turks to solve the many problems presented by the Ottoman Empire. They conformed their ideals of liberty, equality, and fraternity with the ambition to extend Mussulman domination over what he is pleased to call the "toiling nationalities" whose civilisation is superior to theirs. He fails to grasp the difficulty of applying constitutional principles without the experience of generations.

THE SACRIFICE OF LIS DORIS.

"The Price of Lis Doris." By Maarten Maartens. London: Methuen. 1909. 6s.

GRATITUDE to Mr. Maartens for his fine portrait of Lis Doris is mingled in us with extreme irritation at the astounding self-sacrifice to which he commits his hero. It is beyond belief, or at any rate our belief, that a genius—and Mr. Maartens cleverly contrives, without tiresome studio phrases, to make us feel that Doris is a genius—should at the very threshold of the temple of Fame allow another man to thrust him aside, and enter in his place, by stealing the credit of his pictures. The portfolio containing Doris' unsigned landscape studies is stolen from his room by his host, Odo Pareys, a wealthy amateur, who displays them as his own to his visitors, two artists of distinction, who acclaim them as masterpieces. Lis Doris stands by and, from a sense of gratitude to Pareys' wife, Yetta, makes no protest against this amazingly impudent imposture. It seems to us as unlikely that Pareys would have run the risk of exposure as that an artist—usually of all beings the most justifiably egoistic in his anxiety for recognition, the most insistent on his individuality and gifts of expression—should refrain from claiming the creatures of his imagination. We dare not say that such magnanimity is impossible, and if Mr. Maartens were to assure us that he knew of an actual similar case we should only say that we might safely hope it was unique. Extreme altruism is so frequently dangerous that it is fortunate it is also rare. Yetta's devotion to Lis Doris, in anonymously providing him with the means of study, lays a heavy burden of gratitude on the young man when his obligation is revealed to him by her husband. His lips are closed when he should have cried out and claimed his pictures. In future, to preserve Pareys' stolen fame, he must paint only portraits, which he is fortunately able to do, though with less enthusiasm and skill than he showed in his studies of "plein air". As a consequence the world was the

(*Continued on page* 508.)

poorer for the pictures in which he would have shown supreme excellence. His death is tragic; Mr. Maartens ruthlessly sacrifices him to the very end. Odo Pareys' son steals his betrothed, Odo Pareys' servant, a truculent melodramatic villain, takes his life. We wonder that Mr. Maartens allowed him to make so much money at portrait-painting. And, after all, since portrait-painting is usually more profitable than any other kind, Odo Pareys did Lis a service by forcing him into saleable work. But we suspect that Mr. Maartens conceives portrait-painting to be on a lower level than landscape. He is in his own way an artist when he draws for us his usual rigid Dutch Calvinistic characters, which depress us more than they amuse; indeed, the sense of humour displayed is always of the very grimmest. Mr. Maartens works with nervous, abrupt strokes, and describes his people from without, as they might appear to an observer, less than as a creator disclosing the workings of his creatures' minds, the honesty or dishonesty of their intentions. Strong and picturesque as his studies are, they arouse the suspicion that it is not merely because they are Dutch that they seem unfamiliar to us. There is something disproportionate in their semblance of life, they are in some instances distorted from their true outline, whether wilfully to suit the purpose of the plot, or unconsciously through the limitations of Mr. Maartens' powers of expression. With all his alertness and variety of phraseology, his stringent, forcible precision in the choice of words, we feel that he is frequently in difficulties: constraint hampers fluency, queer abrupt twists of dialogue, ideas striking off at tangents, mar the effect and give the impression of a mind more intricate than powerful.

NOVELS.

"The Sinking Ship." By Eva Lathbury. London: Rivers. 1909. 6s.

Vanda Fane is a middle-aged actress with a frivolous old mother, Mrs. Winchester, still upon the stage, and a serious young daughter Sybil, who up to the opening of the story has not emerged from domesticity. Vanda is becoming uncomfortably aware, in spite of another apparent triumph overnight, that she and her well-preserved husband, Mr. Conquest, are getting a little past the idyllic rôles upon which they have successfully rung the changes for years, when in walks Mr. Renshaw, scorning the butler's sevenfold denial. This young gentleman, after taking a science degree at Oxford, had written a real play round Vanda, and he proceeds at once to tell Mr. Conquest that the public are sick of sugar-and-water. Vanda is sick of it too, and notwithstanding the protests of old Mrs. Winchester, who has just made a hit in the expensive new sugar-and-water production, Mr. Renshaw's play "The Sinking Ship" is immediately put into rehearsal. This is all so likely to have really happened that we need not remark upon the curiosities of the play itself, of which we have a full description, or upon the fact that Sybil, who makes her début in it, declines to make-up her face. Presumably this is intended to be in some way allegorical—we have Sybil later in the book telling the dying old woman that the theatre is a "place of false reflection" where some day "the false gods will be turned out and the true God will come in"—whatever that may mean. But the book is so wordy that its intention is nebulous; and Miss Lathbury makes very little of what seemed a promising contrast between the three women. To say of a person that he is incoherent is not necessarily to assail his intelligence; but from the artist we are entitled to look for a definite format and some accuracy of detail. Even so great a master of cloud-effects as Turner sometimes condescended to make minute studies of rigging.

"Poppea of the Post Office." By Mabel Osgood Wright. The Macmillan Company. 1909. 5s.

It is refreshing to find an American writer who expects of her countrymen more than splendid extravagance and uncompromising vulgarity; even though in the search for ideals she must go back to the days of the Civil War—to the days before New York grew to greatness and—though she would not admit it—when the influence of the Old Country hung heavy on the land. On a night in winter a baby girl is left at the door of the post-office at Harky's Mills; the lonely old man adopts and educates the child, and the mystery of her origin is left unravelled—no one has claimed the girl, and he need never shatter her belief in the only "daddy" that she has ever known. The child grows to womanhood and suddenly comes upon the truth; she has no love for her lawful father, and refuses to desert her humble protector. Poppea is a truly sympathetic study, and Gilbert the postmaster in his simple faith is a type of manhood that we can ill afford to lose. The style recalls Winston Churchill at his best—we do not refer to that other Winston—but we do not like this: ". . . This was discounted on the East Coast by the terrifying career of the 'Merrimac,' beforetimes a United States cruiser, but now in Confederate hands, that, by closely sheathing the wooden vessel with metal plates, had converted her into a deadly ram which no wooden ship could withstand, and already having run amuck through the waters of Hampton Roads, showed the possibility of putting every Union port in peril." Even Bart Kennedy is more kind to the commas than that!

"Dorrien Carfax." By Nowell Griffith. London: Smith, Elder. 1909. 6s.

"As telegraphic to the numskulled fish flashes over the line the strike and jab of the angler's rod, so tumultuary, yet skilless of their trend, wrestled he with the import of her declaration". Without pretending to say to whom or what the trend belonged we understand just enough of this sentence to feel sympathetic towards the gentleman of whom it is written, after wrestling for over four hundred pages with Mr. Griffith's style. For the import of this story, which possesses a machine-made plot and some shadowy character-drawing, is well-nigh drowned in a torrent of needless and very ill-used words—words frequently inverted and entangled as in the sample above, or employed with what Falstaff calls damnable iteration. Not everyone is young enough to appreciate the humour of calling a person's right eye his "dexter optic", of explaining that a minute "embraces, as is world-widely known, some sixty seconds", or of nomenclature like "Captain Scuppers" and "Messrs. Spider and Web"; but no doubt readers may be found capable of revelling in these and similar exhibitions of high spirits.

"Sealed Orders." By Alfred Edward Carey. London: Greening. 1909. 6s.

This book is a curious piece of patchwork. Ostensibly a murder-mystery story, its criminology is tempered by folk-songs (with musical notation) and the author's gossipy remarks, by the way, on White of Selborne, over-population, British prestige, the women of Shakespeare, epitaphs in the Abbey, and many other subjects, including an amusingly incorrect description of the Trinity House flag. This little slip does not matter very much, but surely members of touring companies in Scotland should be told that a lady and gentleman who address one another as man and wife in the course of theatricals in that country, and are not at pains afterwards to allay the impression, have constituted a valid bond; whilst every prospective landed proprietor in love should be warned that a letter written to his inamorata, laying at her feet all his future interest in the estate, may be stolen by his rival (with claims on the lady created as aforesaid) and stamped as a legal document. It is hard to say which is most pleasing, the geniality of the author or the artlessness of his story.

SHORTER NOTICES.

"Tremendous Trifles." By G. K. Chesterton. London: Methuen. 1909. 5s. net.

Many things, as Carlyle said time and again, are wonderful enough for those who have eyes to see them. This ancient truth is the beginning and the end of Mr. Chesterton's new volume. The difference between Carlyle's and Mr.

(*Continued on page 510.*)

Chesterton's apprehension of this truth is, however, a somewhat large difference. It led Carlyle into deep waters; for it prompted him to peel away from his mental vision the scales of habit, and to see through words to the root conceptions that lay behind. It led with him to a bold undressing of Truth. Needless to say, Mr. Chesterton goes off in quite another direction. So far is he from wishing to deprive Truth of her garments that his whole art consists in tricking her out in fantastic apparel, in order that she may strike into the beholder, not so much a conviction of her own right to exist upon her ancient merits, as of Mr. Chesterton's own peculiar skill in the art of dressmaking. Mr. Chesterton, in fact, claims to be seeing a bed-post for the first time in his life, just because he happens to be writing an essay about it at the time, and to be writhing about it in strange verbal contortions. If Mr. Chesterton would only get rid of the idea that he is discovering new truth whenever he states an old one over again in perverted language, he might write a book of essays that would be of some real value as well as being pleasant and tiresome and wonderful and commonplace and silly all at once. But we shrewdly suspect that for Mr. Chesterton it is too late for repentance, even if his chosen public would allow him to repent.

"The Recent Development of Physical Science." By W. C. D. Whetham. London: Murray. 1909. 5s. net.

The fact that this book has run through four editions since June 1904 shows that there is a large body of readers who are interested in scientific developments without being technical experts in this or that particular branch of science. Mr. Whetham's book certainly deserves its four editions. Presupposing a little knowledge, but not too much, it allows the reader to follow the great physicists through to their discoveries, and to perceive the bearing of these discoveries upon kindred sciences and upon practical life. The general impression left by the book is an impression of the remarkable unity of the sciences. Arbitrarily divided and each possessing a language of its own, a discovery made in one will necessitate fresh speculation in another. Thus the discovery of radio-activity made it necessary to recast the age of the habitable earth. This would cause something of a revolution in the ideas of geologists and anthropologists. Moreover, the same discovery reached beyond science to philosophy, bringing again into prominence the old Greek idea of the fundamental unity of the universe. Knowledge is like a vast pool, and whoever casts into it a single stone sends ripples to the farthest shore.

"Sixpenny Dickens."

The new "Sixpenny Dickens", published by Messrs. Edward Lloyd, in paper covers, is a reprint of the Household Edition, distinguished from others by its double columns and illustrations by F. Barnard, an artist of decided talent, whose work is not so well known as it should be. "Phiz" (Hablot K. Browne) is the artist who did most for the original issues of Dickens' novels. "A Tale of Two Cities", when first published in book-form, was illustrated by him. Consequently, the expression used in this sixpenny reprint, "the original illustrations", is open to misconstruction. Barnard's work, as the Household Edition has been somewhile out of print, may be regarded as almost a novelty to the present generation. The plates are a little worn, and indistinct in dark passages, but the whole book is cheap at sixpence, and might be worth issuing bound at a regular price.

"One Day and Another." By E. V. Lucas. London: Methuen. 1909. 5s. net.

It is difficult to say very much about this little book; and the fact of this difficulty is perhaps its completest criticism. Censure would be beside the point, as there is nothing to censure. Serious appreciation would be equally out of place, as it would spoil the effect of these essays to take them too seriously. We must be content to say that these are pleasant essays, but the word "pleasant" should be underlined. We have here pleasantness quintessentialised. It is a book to keep upon the table. It would be fatal to put it up on the shelf. If it were put up on the shelf, it would probably never get taken down, which would be the greatest of pities.

"Some Memories of my Spare Time." By General Sir Henry Brackenbury. London: Blackwood. 1909. 5s. net.

It is disappointing that Sir Henry Brackenbury's reminiscences do not touch on that very interesting period of his career when, just before the South African War, he took over the duties of Director-General of Ordnance at headquarters. His work there was of immense national importance, and he was entirely successful. The labour was stupendous. When the war broke out it was found that the supplies of warlike stores were hopelessly inadequate. At one time it was necessary almost to denude the country of ammunition, and the strain imposed upon him was correspondingly great. But no doubt he is wise not to relate his experiences at this period of his career. Perhaps in a subsequent volume, and when it has become historical, he may do so. Nevertheless he has many interesting stories of his long and distinguished career, and we can cordially recommend his book not only to soldiers but to the general public.

"Astronomical Curiosities." By J. Elland Gore. London: Chatto and Windus. 1909. 6s.

We have here a model of sound packing. In a little book of 300 or more pages there is a sufficient number of small pieces of information to provoke as many notes of exclamation. They take the form, for the most part, of out-of-the-way facts and fallacies, not recorded in the popular text-book, but of interest to the student or to the dabbler in astronomy. It is an excellent book to pick up at odd moments. We challenge anyone to read it through at a sitting.

"Revue des Deux Mondes." 15 Octobre.

This number is somewhat dull. There is an article documenté but uninspiring on the Union of South Africa. The writer, M. Biard d'Aunet, strives to be impartial, and succeeds, but he writes without exciting interest. M. Bertrand has a good deal to say that is instructive about the general scramble of various religions in the Near East. He believes that European countries nearly concerned with the future of those regions may have a rude awakening so soon as any serious trouble may arise between any of the Great Powers. We think, however, that he expects a great deal too much from a "regenerated" Turkey. There is, in fact, no such thing, and it is mere absurdity to say that everything may be hoped by Turkey under its new régime "exalted by patriotic zeal and religious faith." The new Turkey is merely the old one with a military junta substituted for Abdul Hamid dictating to a Parliament.

For this Week's Books see page 512.

THIS WEEK'S BOOKS.

Art

The International Art Series: The Great English Masters (Fritz Stahl); Eugene Delacroix (Camille Mauclair). Fisher Unwin. 5s. net.

Biography

Melba (Agnes G. Murphy). Chatto and Windus. 16s. net.
Memoirs of the Duchess de Dino (Edited by the Princess Radziwill). Heinemann. 10s. net.
The Incomparable Siddons (Mrs. Clement Parsons). Methuen. 12s. 6d. net.
The Story of W. J. E. Bennett (F. Bennett), 7s. 6d. net; The Life and Times of Bishop Challoner (Edwin H. Burton. 2 vols.), 25s. net; Life of James Green (A. Theodore Wirgman. 2 vols.), 18s. net. Longmans.
Memoirs of Fifty Years (Lady St. Helier). Arnold. 15s. net.
William Makepeace Thackeray (Lewis Melville. 2 vols.). Lane. 25s. net.

Fiction

A Human Cypher (E. L. Haverfield). Hodder and Stoughton. 6s.
Sailors' Knots (W. W. Jacobs). Methuen. 3s. 6d. net.
Her Mother's Daughter (Katharine Tynan). Smith, Elder. 6s.
Gates of Brass (Mrs. Aubrey Richardson); The Silver Glen (Bessie Dill); False Gold (Lilias Campbell Davidson); The Old Bureaucrat (Sinclair Ayden). Digby, Long. 6s. each.
Lord Kentwell's Love Affair (F. C. Price). Heinemann. 3s. net.
The Prince of Destiny (Sarah Kumar Ghosh). Rebman. 6s.
John Thorndyke's Cases (R. Austin Freeman). Chatto and Windus. 6s.
With the Merry Austrians (Amy McLaren). Murray. 6s.
The Redemption of Kenneth Galt (Will N. Harben); The Involuntary Chaperon (Margaret Cameron). Harper. 6s.
The Pond and other Stories (Carl Ewald). Everett. 6s.

Gift Books

The Deserted Village (Oliver Goldsmith). Constable. 15s. net.
The Great Raid (Lloyd Williams). "Black and White." 2s. net.
The Faery Queen and her Knights (Rev. Alfred J. Church). Seeley. 5s. net.
The Irish Fairy Book (Alfred Perceval Graves). Fisher Unwin. 6s.

History

A History of Malta (By the late William Hardman). Longmans Green. 21s. net.
Social England (A. Abram). Routledge. 3s. 6d. net.
The Austrian Court in the Nineteenth Century (The Right Hon. Sir Horace Rumbold), 18s. net; The Court of a Saint (Winifred F. Knox), 10s. 6d. Methuen.
The Girlhood of Queen Elizabeth (Frank A. Mumby), 10s. 6d. net; The London Life of Yesterday (Arthur Compton-Rickett), 7s. 6d. net. Constable.
Men and Manners of Old Florence (Guido Biagi). Fisher Unwin. 15s. net.
A Century of Empire, 1801-1900 (The Right Hon. Sir Herbert Maxwell, Bart.). Arnold. 14s. net.
A History of St. Paul's School (Michael F. J. McDonnell). Chapman and Hall. 15s. net.
Italy To-day (Bolton King and Thomas Okey). Nisbet. 6s. net.

Science and Philosophy

Æsthetic (Douglas Ainslie). Macmillan. 10s. net.
Age Incidence, Sex, and Comparative Frequency in Disease (James Grant Andrew). Baillière, Tindall and Cox. 10s. 6d. net.
The Individual and Reality (Edward Douglas Fawcett). Longmans. 12s. 6d. net.
Air and Health (Ronald Campbell Macfie). Methuen. 7s. 6d. net.

Travel

The Salmon Rivers and Lochs of Scotland (W. L. Calderwood). Arnold. 21s. net.

Verse

Last Poems (George Meredith). Constable. 4s. 6d. net.
A Midnight Fantasy (Arthur Bennett). 2s. 6d. net.
Three Plays (Mrs. W. K. Clifford). Duckworth. 6s.
Love's Empire, and other Poems (A. M. Champneys). Bell. 3s. 6d. net.
New Poems (William Watson). Lane. 5s. net.

Miscellaneous

Armour and Weapons (Charles Ffoulkes). Oxford: At the Clarendon Press. 6s. 6d. net.
Art of Theatrical Make-up, The (Cavendish Morton). Black. 5s. net.
Britain at Bay (Spenser Wilkinson). Constable. 6s. net.
Editor's Chair, An (Ernest Foster). Everett. 2s. 6d. net.
Handbook to the Works of Dante (F. J. Snell). Bell. 6s.
Irish Ways (Jane Barlow). Allen, 15s. net.
Navy League Annual, The (Edited by Alan H. Burgoyne). Murray. 2s. 6d. net.
Orpheus with his Lute (W. M. L. Hutchinson). Arnold. 5s.
Self Help for Nervous Women (John K. Mitchell). Heinemann. 2s. 6d. net.

Reviews and Magazines for October.—Revue des Deux Mondes, 3fr.; The University Magazine; The Scottish Historical Review, 2s. 6d.; The Law Quarterly Review, 5s.; Mercure de France, 1fr. 50c.; The Eugenics Review, 1s.; The Sociological Review, 2s. 6d.; The North American Review, 1s.; The Edinburgh Review, 6s.; The English Historical Review, 5s.

SALES BY AUCTION.

BOOKS AND MANUSCRIPTS.

MESSRS. SOTHEBY, WILKINSON & HODGE will SELL by AUCTION at their House, No. 13, Wellington Street, Strand, W.C., on THURSDAY, October 28, and Following Day, at One o'clock precisely, BOOKS and MANUSCRIPTS, including the Property of a GENTLEMAN, comprising Standard Works in all Branches of Literature—Illuminated Manuscripts on Vellum—Books illustrated by Celebrated Artists—Works on Biography, History, Sport, and Travel—Engravings, &c.

May be viewed two days prior. Catalogues may be had.

Books, including the Library of B. M. JALLAND, Esq., J.P., D.L. (deceased), of Holderness House, East Yorkshire.

MESSRS. SOTHEBY, WILKINSON & HODGE will SELL by AUCTION at their House, No. 13, Wellington Street, Strand, W.C., on MONDAY, November 1, at 1 o'clock precisely, BOOKS including the Property of B. M. JALLAND, Esq., J.P., D.L. (deceased), of Holderness House, East Yorkshire, and other Properties, comprising Works relating to Mary Queen of Scots—Biography—History and Poetry—Americana—Illustrated French Works, including La Fontaine, Contes et Nouvelles, 2 vols. 1762—the Writings of Swinburne, Oscar Wilde, Stephen Phillips, and Zola, chiefly First Editions—Sporting and Natural History—Extra-Illustrated Books—Engravings—Architectural and Archæological Works—the Houghton Gallery—Ackermann's Microcosm of London—Walton and Cotton's Compleat Angler, with Venables' Experienc'd Angler, 1676—Boydell's River Thames—Books Illustrated by Rowlandson, Cruikshank, Bewick, Beardsley, Thackeray, &c.

May be viewed two days prior. Catalogues may be had.

H. SOTHERAN & CO., BOOKSELLERS.

GENERAL AGENTS FOR PRIVATE BOOKBUYERS AND PUBLIC INSTITUTIONS IN INDIA, THE COLONIES, AMERICA, AND ABROAD.

A Monthly Catalogue of fresh Purchases. Specimen number post-free.

LIBRARIES PURCHASED OR VALUED AND CATALOGUED AND ARRANGED.

Telegraphic Address: BOOKMEN, LONDON. *Codes*: UNICODE and A B C.

140 STRAND, W.C., and 37 PICCADILLY, W., LONDON.

Telephone: CENTRAL 1515. Telephone: MAYFAIR 3601.

7th and Revised Impression.

"SATURDAY" BRIDGE,

By W. DALTON,

Is the Best Book on the Best Game.

That the popularity of Bridge is as great as ever is proved by the continuous steady demand for the work.

"'SATURDAY' BRIDGE"

is admitted to be the Standard book on the Game. It is the leading Bridge Authority, and takes its name from the "SATURDAY REVIEW," in which its chapters appeared.

Of all Booksellers 5s. net, or post free 5s. 3d., direct from the Office.

THE WEST STRAND PUBLISHING CO., Ltd., 10 King Street, Covent Garden, W.C.

Pp. x+492. Price 7s. 6d. net.

THE MORPHIA HABIT AND ITS VOLUNTARY RENUNCIATION.

By OSCAR JENNINGS, M.D. (Paris).

London: BAILLIÈRE, TINDALL & COX, 8 Henrietta St., Covent Garden.

ELY CATHEDRAL.

Visitors will find First Class Hotel Accommodation at the "LAMB" Family Hotel, which is situated close to the Cathedral. **MODERATE TERMS.** Omnibus meets all trains.

Proprietor, S. AIREY.

RE-APPEARANCE OF

"THE THRUSH"

A MONTHLY PERIODICAL FOR THE PUBLICATION OF ORIGINAL POETRY,

DECEMBER 1st, 1909.

New Feature—Literary Articles on All Subjects.

CONTRIBUTIONS (which will be paid for) should be addressed to

THE EDITOR, "THE THRUSH" OFFICE, 12 & 13 Henrietta Street, Covent Garden, W.C.

Publishers: CHAPMAN & HALL, Limited.

THINGS JAPANESE,

Political, Commercial, and Social, are of great interest to many business men in Great Britain. The latest Political News, the best Commercial Information, and the most interesting General News and Special Articles appear in the

JAPAN WEEKLY CHRONICLE,

Published in Kobe every Thursday, and delivered in England by post, viâ Siberia, in 17 days. The *Japan Weekly Chronicle* consists of 42 pages, slightly larger than those of the *Saturday Review*, and is published at 25 sen per copy (6d.). Post free for 12 months, Yen 13 (26s.). Subscriptions and advertisements received at the London Office, 131 Fleet Street, E.C.

Sport Society Drama

THE

BYSTANDER

SIXPENCE. Every Tuesday.

Politics Literature Fiction

THE BEST OF THE LIGHT ILLUSTRATED WEEKLIES.
A PICTORIAL RECORD OF THE WEEK'S DOINGS.

TERSE AND TRUTHFUL CRITICISM.
"WORLDLY" SHORT STORIES.
SPORT: a Speciality. GOLF, HUNTING, LAWN TENNIS.

*** You do not only glance at "THE BYSTANDER," you READ it. It is Unique, Sparkling, Daring, Original.

Published by the Proprietors of the "GRAPHIC," Tallis House, Tallis Street, E.C.

Cloth, 2s. net. Paper, 1s. net.

THE SORROWS OF IRELAND.

By "PAT," Author of "Economics for Irishmen."

EVERYONE INTERESTED IN THE IRISH PROBLEM SHOULD READ THIS BOOK.

THE WEST STRAND PUBLISHING CO., Ltd., 33 Southampton Street, Strand, W.C.

Messrs. METHUEN have much pleasure in announcing that they have just published a new and delightful volume of Stories by W. W. JACOBS. It is entitled **SAILORS' KNOTS.** Crown 8vo. 3s. 6d.

They have also just published **THE TYRANT,** by Mrs. HENRY DE LA PASTURE, Author of "The Lonely Lady of Grosvenor Square." Crown 8vo. 6s.

The third Edition is now ready of **NORTHERN LIGHTS,** by Sir GILBERT PARKER, crown 8vo. 6s.; **THE SEARCH PARTY,** by G. A. BIRMINGHAM, Author of "Spanish Gold," a mine of honest fun, is in its Third Edition. Crown 8vo. 6s.

Messrs. METHUEN have just published twelve interesting books:—

1. **THE AUSTRIAN COURT IN THE NINETEENTH CENTURY.** By Sir HORACE RUMBOLD, late Ambassador at Vienna. Demy 8vo. 18s. net.
2. **MARIE ANTIONETTE.** By HILAIRE BELLOC, M.P. Demy 8vo. 15s. net.
3. **GOOD COMPANY: a Rally of Men.** By E. V. LUCAS. Fcap. 8vo. 5s. This is uniform with "The Open Road."
4. **SHELLEY: the Man and the Poet.** By A. CLUTTON BROCK. Demy 8vo. 7s. 6d. net.
5. **THE NINE DAYS' QUEEN: being the Life of the Lady Jane Grey.** By RICHARD DAVEY. Edited by MARTIN HUME, M.A. Demy 8vo. 10s. 6d. net. [*Romantic History.*
6. **THOUGHTS OF A TERTIARY.** By ELIZABETH WATERHOUSE, Editor of "A Little Book of Life and Death." Pott 8vo. 1s. net.
7. **ONE HUNDRED MASTERPIECES OF SCULPTURE.** With an Introduction and Descriptive Notes by G. F. HILL. Demy 8vo. 10s. 6d. net. A splendid book.
8. **THE DECLINE AND FALL OF THE ROMAN EMPIRE.** By EDWARD GIBBON. Edited by J. B. BURY, Litt.D. In 7 vols. Vol. I., 10s. 6d. net. This is a completely new Edition, reset, with many Illustrations and new Maps, and is a most desirable Library Edition.
9. **THE INCOMPARABLE SIDDONS.** By Mrs. CLEMENT PARSONS, Author of "Garrick and his Circle." Demy 8vo. 12s. 6d. net.
10. **THE COURT OF A SAINT.** By WINIFRED F. KNOX. Demy 8vo. 7s. 6d. net. This is a Life of St. Louis of France.
11. **AIR AND HEALTH.** By RONALD C. MACFIE. Demy 8vo. 7s. 6d. net. *New Library of Medicine.*
12. **MY PETS.** By ALEXANDRE DUMAS. Translated by A. R. ALLINSON. With 16 Illustrations by V. LECOMTE. Crown 8vo. 6s.

GENERAL LITERATURE.

THE WORKS OF OSCAR WILDE. A New Edition, reset in 12 vols. Fcap. 8vo. 5s. net each.

1. LORD ARTHUR SAVILE'S CRIME. 2. THE DUCHESS OF PADUA. 3. POEMS (including "The Ballad of Reading Gaol" and "The Sphinx"). 4. LADY WINDERMERE'S FAN. 5. A WOMAN OF NO IMPORTANCE. 6. AN IDEAL HUSBAND. 7. THE IMPORTANCE OF BEING EARNEST.

TREMENDOUS TRIFLES. By G. K. Chesterton. Fcap. 8vo. 5s. [*Second Edition.*
"Delightful to read."—*Daily News.*
"What pleases in this lively and amusing volume is its agile wit." *Morning Leader.*

ONE DAY AND ANOTHER. By E. V. Lucas. Fcap. 8vo. 5s. [*Second Edition.*
"The essays are inimitably refreshing."—*Morning Leader.*

A WANDERER IN PARIS. By E. V. Lucas. With 16 Illustrations in Colour by WALTER DEXTER, and 32 from Photographs after Old Masters. Crown 8vo. 6s. [*Second Edition.*
"Dainty and vivacious, humorous and pleasantly reflective."—*Daily Chronicle.*
"We do not hesitate to pronounce this fascinating volume a perfect model of its class."—*Daily Telegraph.*

DARWINISM AND MODERN SOCIALISM. By F. W. HEADLEY. Crown 8vo. 5s. net.

ROME. By Edward Hutton, Author of "The Cities of Umbria." With 16 Illustrations in Colour by MAXWELL ARMFIELD, and 12 other Illustrations. Crown 8vo. 6s.
This is the third volume in the series of books, that will eventually include all Italy, which Mr. Hutton is writing.

OLD ETRURIA AND MODERN TUSCANY. By Mary LOVETT CAMERON. With 32 Illustrations. Crown 8vo. 6s. net.

THE LAST KING OF POLAND AND HIS CONTEMPORARIES. By R. NISBET BAIN. With 16 Illustrations. Demy 8vo. 10s. 6d. net.
"The ground is covered with really exhaustive scholarship."—*Morning Post.*

HANDEL. By R. A. Streatfeild, Author of "Modern Music and Musicians." With 12 Illustrations. Demy 8vo. 7s. 6d. net. [*New Library of Music.*

NAPOLEON'S BROTHERS. By A. H. Atteridge. With 24 Illustrations. Demy 8vo. 18s. net.
"A complete book and unfailingly well written."—*Daily News.*
"Deeply interesting and instructive."—*Manchester Courier.*

A ROSE OF SAVOY: Marie Adélaide of Savoy, DUCHESSE DE BOURGOGNE, MOTHER OF LOUIS XV. By H. NOEL WILLIAMS, Author of "Five Fair Sisters." With a Frontispiece in Photogravure and 16 other Illustrations. Demy 8vo. 15s. net.

THE COURT OF LOUIS XIII. By K. A. Patmore. With 16 Illustrations. Demy 8vo. 10s. 6d. net. [*Second Edition.*

ST. TERESA OF SPAIN. By Helen H. Colvill. With 20 Illustrations. Demy 8vo. 7s. 6d. net.
"A fascinating book."—*Illustrated London News.*
"A most sympathetic study of Teresa."—*Daily Chronicle.*

FICTION.

NORTHERN LIGHTS. By Sir Gilbert Parker, M.P., Author of "The Weavers." Crown 8vo. 6s. [*Third Edition.*
"These stories will be read by future generations."—*Morning Post.*
"The stories are very readable and attractive, full of movement and colour." *Globe.*

THE SEARCH PARTY. By G. A. Birmingham, Author of "Spanish Gold." Crown 8vo. 6s. [*Third Edition.*
"Full of humour, humanity, and real interest."—*Westminster Gazette.*
"As hilarious a book as you could desire; witty and rich in the genius of mirth."—*Daily News.*

THE SEVERINS. By Mrs. Alfred Sidgwick, Author of "The Kinsman." Crown 8vo. 6s. [*Second Edition.*
"The charm, ease, and freshness of the book are altogether delightful." *Morning Leader.*
"A clever book; the situations are always well conceived."—*Times.*

SPLENDID BROTHER. By W. Pett Ridge, Author of "Erb," &c. Crown 8vo. 6s. [*Third Edition.*
"There could not be a better proof of Mr. Pett Ridge's literary power than is given by this novel."—*Spectator.*
"It is a beautiful book."—*Liverpool Post.*
"He is surpassed by none of his contemporaries."—*Standard.*

THE PRICE OF LIS DORIS. By Maarten Maartens, Author of "Brothers All," &c. Crown 8vo. 6s.
"The pictures of character are wonderfully firm and clear; their intimacy and vitality is surprising. This is a strong and valuable novel."—*Morning Leader.*

JACK CARSTAIRS OF THE POWER HOUSE. By SYDNEY SANDYS. Illustrated by STANLEY L. WOOD. Crown 8vo. 6s.
This is a thrilling story of engineering and adventure.

THE BRIDE. By Grace Rhys, Author of "The Wooing of Sheila." Crown 8vo. 6s.
"An extraordinarily interesting book."—*Guardian.*
"This fine, delicate, moving novel is a real book."—*Daily News.*
"Altogether a fascinating work."—*Manchester Courier.*

A ROYAL INDISCRETION. By Richard Marsh. Crown 8vo. 6s.
"Replete with a most delightful humour."—*Manchester Courier.*
"An ingenious idea, used freshly and amusingly."—*Morning Leader.*

IN AMBUSH. By Marie Van Vorst, Author of "The Sentimental Adventures of Jimmy Bulstrode." Crown 8vo. 6s.
"A story which will assuredly hold the reader."—*Edinburgh Evening News.*

DEEP SEA WARRIORS. By Basil Lubbock. With 4 Illustrations. Crown 8vo. 6s. [*Second Edition.*
"A fascinating book, a real book of the sea."—*Daily Mail.*
"All those who love the sea should read this book."—*World.*

TOIL OF MEN. By Israel Querido. Crown 8vo. 6s.
"A vivid, powerful, and terrible description of a year in the lives of certain Dutch peasants."—*Times.*

THE FIRST ROUND. By St. John Lucas. Crown 8vo. 6s.
"The book is exceedingly rich in observation, interest, and intellectual reactions."—*Pall Mall Gazette.*
"A novel written with genuine literary art."—*Standard.*
"It is a very good book indeed; the characterisation is excellent."—*Athenæum.*

THE COLUMN OF DUST. By Evelyn Underhill. Author of "The Grey World," &c. Crown 8vo, 6s.
"It is a book to set one dreaming; the style is terse, yet touched with beauty and feeling."—*Evening Standard.*

THE BURNT OFFERING. By Sara Jeannette Duncan (Mrs. Cotes), Author of "Those Delightful Americans." Crown 8vo. 6s.

THE SQUIRE'S DAUGHTER. By Archibald Marshall, Author of "Exton Manor." Crown 8vo. 6s. [*Second Edition.*
"It is an admirable picture of a pleasant land: every one in it is alive, every one is English. A graceful, gentle, entirely charming story."—*Morning Leader.*

LORDS OF THE SEA. By Edward Noble, Author of "The Edge of Circumstance." Crown 8vo. 6s.
"A great, almost tremendous drama."—*Daily Chronicle.*
"Mr. Noble has once more proved himself a master of craft." *Westminster Gazette.*

AVENGING CHILDREN. By Mary E. Mann, Author of "The Parish of Hilby." Crown 8vo. 6s. [*Second Edition.*
"The story is an achievement in the art of character drawing."—*Liverpool Post.*
"It is a charming story, excellent in design and execution." *Pall Mall Gazette.*

THIS DAY'S MADNESS. By Maude Annesley, Author of "The Wine of Life." Crown 8vo. 6s. [*Second Edition.*
"A vastly entertaining novel."—*Pall Mall Gazette.*
"Miss Annesley writes with a great freshness, buoyancy, and vigour. From the first she grips the reader."—*Liverpool Courier.*

HAPPINESS. By Maud Stepney Rawson, Author of "The Enchanted Garden." Crown 8vo. 6s. [*Second Edition.*
"Full of the comedy and the tragedy that makes so much of life."—*Scotsman.*
"A really fine book, largely conceived and admirably written."—*Times.*

LOVE AND THE WISE MEN. By Percy White, Author of "The West End." Crown 8vo. 6s. [*Second Edition.*
"The whole thing is done with great address, and the characterisation is crisp. A clever and enjoyable piece of work."—*Daily Chronicle.*

GIANNELLA. By Mrs. Hugh Fraser, Author of "The Slaking of the Sword." Crown 8vo. 6s. [*Second Edition.*
"The descriptions of life in Rome and the handling of situations are all carried through with sympathetic insight and knowledge."—*Liverpool Post.*
"The story is a very charming one, and told with an easy grace of style." *Sheffield Telegraph.*

THE CASTLE BY THE SEA. By H. B. Marriott WATSON. Crown 8vo. 6s. [*Third Edition.*
"Exhales the very breath of modern adventure. The most jaded lover of romance can hardly fail to fall a victim to its fascinations."—*Daily Telegraph.*

METHUEN & CO., 36 Essex Street, London, W.C.

The Subscription List will open on Monday, the 25th day of October, 1909, and will close on or before Wednesday, the 27th day of October, 1909.

BRAZIL RAILWAY COMPANY

(Incorporated under the Laws of the State of Maine, U.S.A.)

Share Capital authorised, $40,000,000, divided into 100,000 6 per Cent. Non-Cumulative Preferred Shares and 300,000 Ordinary Shares of $100 each. All the Ordinary Shares and 50,000 Preferred Shares are issued and fully paid.

BOND ISSUES:

4½ PER CENT. FIRST MORTGAGE 60-YEAR GOLD BONDS,
Authorised, £6,000,000—subject to increase as mentioned below.

5 PER CENT. 50-YEAR GOLD DEBENTURES,
Authorised, $5,000,000—Issued, $2,101,500.

ISSUE OF

£3,500,000 4½ per Cent. First Mortgage 60-Year Gold Bonds

(Part of the authorised issue above mentioned),

Of which £1,800,000 are reserved for issue in London and £1,700,000 for European issue.

THE BANK OF SCOTLAND

is authorised to receive subscriptions on behalf of the Company for

£1,800,000 4½ per Cent. First Mortgage 60-Year Gold Bonds

(Part of the above issue)

At 92 per cent., payable as follows:

£5 0s. on Application.
£30 0s. „ Allotment.
£28 10s. „ 5th January, 1910.
£28 10s. „ 15th February, 1910.
£92

or the whole may be paid up on allotment or on any day prior to the 5th day of January, 1910, under discount at the rate of 4½ per cent. per annum.

Interest at the rate of 6 per cent. per annum will be charged on overdue instalments.

The first full half-year's Interest Coupon in respect of the Bonds now offered for subscription will be paid on 1st July, 1910.

The Issue of £6,000,000 4½ per Cent. First Mortgage 60-Year Gold Bonds is created under the authority of the Bylaws of the Company and is secured by a Deed of Trust in favour of the Empire Trust Company of New York, U.S.A., as Trustee, dated June 1, 1909. Under the terms of the Deed of Trust the Bonds are constituted a specific first charge on all immovable property, both real and personal, and on all Bonds, Debentures, Debenture Stock and other Securities and Shares of other Companies which the Company owns or may hereafter acquire with Bonds or the proceeds thereof forming part of the said Issue as specified in the said Deed of Trust, and also a general floating charge upon all other assets and property of the Company other than the lands which the Company owns or is otherwise entitled to in the Republic of Brazil, under and by virtue of the concessions granted by the Federal Government of Brazil for the construction and operation of the Sao Paulo-Rio Grande Railway. The Bond Issue may, subject to and under the provisions of the Deed of Trust, be increased as therein mentioned, it being provided that all securities and assets acquired by such additional Bonds or the proceeds thereof shall form additional security for the entire Bond Issue.

The said Bonds will be dated July 1, 1909, and are redeemable at par on July 1, 1969, by means of annual payments by the Company to the Trustee, commencing July 1, 1914, to be applied in annual drawings at par or by purchase of the bonds on the market or by tender if they are at or below that price, or the whole or any part of the Bonds may be redeemed at 105 per cent. at any time on six months' notice, or on the Company going into voluntary liquidation, or amalgamating with any other Company or Companies. If part of the Bonds are to be redeemed, the particular Bonds will be determined by a drawing.

The Bonds are to Bearer, but can be registered as to principal at the holder's option in London at the Company's Office.

The Interest on the Bonds will be payable half-yearly on July 1 and January 1 by means of Coupons attached to the Bonds at the Offices of The Bank of Scotland, London, and at such other places as the Company may from time to time appoint.

Holders of the 5 per Cent. 50-Year Gold Debentures will be given later the option of exchanging their Bonds for 4½ per Cent. First Mortgage 60-Year Gold Bonds at the parity of exchange.

The following information is supplied by the President of the Brazil Railway Company, Mr. Percival Farquhar, by the authority of the Board of Directors:—

The Brazil Railway Company (hereinafter referred to as "the Company") was formed with the object of connecting and consolidating the railways in Southern Brazil into a comprehensive system, joining at the international boundaries with the railways of Uruguay, Argentine and Paraguay.

The enclosed map shows the great advantages which will result from the creation of this system.

Hitherto the States of Southern Brazil have had no direct communication with each other except through the ports on the Atlantic. When the Sorocabana Railway, the Sao Paulo-Rio Grande Railway, and the railways operated by the Compagnie Auxiliaire de Chemin de fer au Brésil are connected in about 15 months' time, a grand trunk system will be constituted in Southern Brazil, placing Rio de Janeiro and Sao Paulo in the north, Rio Grande do Sul, Montevideo and Buenos Ayres in the south in direct communication, and providing direct means of transportation to the eastern and southern ports. The States in Southern Brazil will then be in a position to compete with the Argentine in supplying food products for Sao Paulo and Rio de Janeiro, and there should also be a large passenger traffic between Rio de Janeiro, Southern Brazil, Uruguay, and Argentine, in addition to the export traffic.

The Company has leased and now operates the undertaking of the Sorocabana Railway Company for the period of the lease granted by the State of Sao Paula, which runs until June 30th, 1967. In addition to such lease the Company owns the whole of the issued share and debenture capital of the Sorocabana Railway Company with the exception of a few common shares and £175,000 Debentures. The length of the Sorocabana Railway line, operated under such lease, is 710 miles. The State of San Paulo has contracted to construct and hand over to the Company for operation approximately a further 100 miles of railway.

The Company has also leased and now operates the undertaking of the Sao Paulo-Rio Grande Railway Company for the period of the Concession (viz., ninety years) granted by the Federal Government of Brazil. In addition to such lease the Company owns 85 per cent. of the issued share capital of the Sao Paulo-Rio Grande Railway Company, which has 385 miles completed and recently put into operation, 523 miles under construction and survey, and 777 miles to be subsequently surveyed.

The Company also owns a very large interest in the capital of the Compagnie Auxiliaire de Chemins de fer au Brésil (hereinafter referred to as "the Compagnie Auxiliaire"), which operates under lease from the Federal Government of Brazil an extensive and practically the whole railway system in the State of Rio Grande do Sul, having 1,063 miles in operation, and a further 335 miles under construction.

The comparative gross and net earnings, before deduction of fixed charges and rentals, of the Sorocabana Railway and the Compagnie Auxiliaire are as follows:—

—	Sorocabana Railway		Compagnie Auxiliaire	
	Gross	Net	Gross	Net
1907	£793,537	£316,705	£423,688	£157,847
1908	769,997	336,866	494,750	209,322
1909 (estimated on basis of first nine months)	856,250	450,000	582,500	287,500

* On the basis of the earnings for the first nine months of 1909 the present annual income of the Company from the lines operated by it (after providing for the annual payments reserved by the lease) and from its holding in Companies operating connecting lines is	£252,000*
The interest on the present issue of £3,500,000 4½ per Cent. First Mortgage Bonds amounts to	157,500
A surplus remains of	£94,500

The consolidation and connection of the various railways will result in largely increased earnings, through interchange of traffic, economies in management, concentration of workshops and a better utilisation of rolling stock according to crop necessities. When the Company has developed its timber lands and realised its programme by the further improvements and developments contemplated by means of the proceeds of the authorised issue of First Mortgage Bonds, the gross and net earnings of the Company should largely increase; after providing for the interest on and amortisation of the Bonds, the surplus available for dividends in the near future should not be less than £550,000

The Railways referred to traverse the States of Sao Paulo, Paraná, Santa Catharina and Rio Grande do Sul, in Southern Brazil, which enjoy a temperate, healthy climate, have an area of about 320,000 square miles, with a population which has grown from 2,800,000 in 1890 to about 5,000,000 in 1908, and which, owing to the favourable climatic and agricultural conditions, must rapidly increase year by year as the means of communication are developed; the Federal Government are also encouraging, by active measures, immigration and colonisation. The four States constitute a vast undulating plateau of exceptional fertility, where wheat, maize, rice and cotton are cultivated to advantage, and the breeding of cattle is carried on under the most favourable circumstances. The State of Sao Paulo alone produces over 70 per cent. of the world's supply of coffee, and its rice production has increased to such an extent as to supply practically the entire demand of Brazil, which imported, as late as 1898, over 200,000 tons of rice.

At the present time the Sao Paulo-Rio Grande Railway has 6,000 men employed on the construction of its extension which will connect with the extension under construction by the Compagnie Auxiliaire, on which 1,500 men are engaged. The Sao Paulo-Rio Grande Railway has provided the money for the construction of its extension referred to by the sale of its bonds, the interest on which is guaranteed by the Federal Government of Brazil for a period of thirty years. The Federal Government also pays half the cost of construction of the extension now being built by the Compagnie Auxiliaire, the other half being borne by the Compagnie Auxiliaire, which has made arrangements for the provision of the funds.

The Brazil Railway Company is entitled, by virtue of the Concessions granted by the Federal Government of Brazil for the construction and operation of the Sao Paulo-Rio Grande Railway, to large areas of land which are situated along the line of that railway, and the greater part of which is covered with pine and hardwood forests. The measuring and taking possession of the lands, which should comprise about 6,000,000 acres, is now being proceeded with. These land grants should become of great and increasing value to the Company. In the Argentine, land has increased more than ten times in value since the railroads in that country were constructed, and the great value to the Canadian Pacific Railway Company and other Railway Companies of their land grants is well known.

The Company has also acquired extensive tracts of pine lands. Mr. Hiram C. Smith and Mr. John McComb, two of the best timber experts of the United States of America, have examined a portion of these lands, and have reported most favourably thereon, and copies of their reports may be seen on application at the Company's London Office. The markets for this timber in the River Plate countries (Argentine contains no construction timber) and in Brazil are practically without limit. Timber for building purposes is decreasing throughout the World, and the forests mentioned constitute an asset of enormous value which must increase from year to year. The profits to be derived from the development of these timber lands justify, apart from the other general traffic obtainable, the construction of a large section of the Sao Paulo-Rio Grande Railway system. After the timber has been cut the lands will be very valuable for agricultural purposes, and the Company has under consideration an immigration programme for the colonisation of such lands, the sale of which must necessarily be a source of large profit as the lines of communication are constructed and colonisation advances.

The Company owns approximately 50 per cent. of the capital of the Madeira-Mamoré Railway Company, which is constructing, for account of the Federal Government of Brazil, two hundred miles of railway around the series of falls and cataracts of the Madeira River, one of the most important affluents of the Amazon. The line will connect the navigation of the Amazon and Madeira rivers below the Madeira Falls with the 2,500 miles of navigation in Bolivia above these falls, thereby providing a quicker and cheaper route, *via* Manaos and Pará, for the transport to Europe of the valuable export products of Bolivia. This Railway, when completed, will be operated by the Madeira-Mamoré Railway Company under a lease from the Federal Government for sixty years on favourable terms.

The regions to be served by the Madeira-Mamoré Railway are particularly rich, especially in rubber. There is already a considerable traffic over the falls and cataracts of the Madeira River, in spite of heavy losses in transit, and high cost of transportation. When the construction of the Railway is completed and the line is in operation the losses in transit should be entirely avoided, and the high cost of transportation reduced, while, on the other hand, very profitable freight rates should be secured. Fifty-four miles of the Railway should be completed during November, and the entire line placed in operation in about 2½ years. The accompanying map shows the situation of the Madeira-Mamoré Railway and its relation to the valley of the Amazon.

The proceeds of the present issue of Bonds will be applied to payments in connection with the acquisition of the Company's various properties, and for the general purposes of the Company.

The Form of the Bond and the Trust Deed, in favour of the Empire Trust Company, of New York, securing the Bonds, can be inspected by intending applicants at the London Office of the Company, 31 Bishopsgate Street Within, London, E.C., during usual business hours while the list remains open.

Allottees will be entitled, on payment of all the instalments due on the Bonds allotted to them, to receive from the Bank, in exchange for their Allotment Letter and the Receipts for the Instalments, Provisional Scrip Certificates to Bearer, which will be subsequently exchanged for the Bonds.

If an allotment is not made to an applicant, the deposit will be returned in full through the post by cheque at the applicant's risk, and if an allotment is made of less than the amount applied for, the balance of the application money will be appropriated towards the sum due on allotment, and the balance, if any, returned to the allottee in manner before mentioned.

Failure to pay any instalment when due will render the previous payments liable to forfeiture and the allotment to cancellation.

An official quotation on the London Stock Exchange will be applied for in due course.

Application should be made on the accompanying form and forwarded with the necessary remittance to the Bankers.

Prospectuses and Forms of Application can be obtained of the Bank of Scotland, Edinburgh, London and Branches, and at the London Office of the Company, 31 Bishopsgate Street Within, London, E.C., and of Messrs. Kitcat and Aitken, 120 Bishopsgate Street Within, the Brokers to the Issue.

October 23, 1909.

*Note.—If the present interests of the Brazil Railway Company in these lines and holdings had been the same in 1907 and 1908 the Company's annual income therefrom would have been in 1907 £183,000, and in 1908 £170,000.

Board of Directors of the Brazil Railway Company.

PERCIVAL FARQUHAR, New York, President; Vice-President of the Sorocobana Railway Company; Vice-President of the Compagnie Française du Port de Rio Grande do Sul; President of the Port of Pará.

ALEXANDER MACKENZIE, Rio de Janeiro; Director of the Sao Paulo-Rio Grande Railway Company.

ALFREDO MAIA, Sao Paulo; former Minister of Public Works and Railways in Brazil; Vice-President of the Sorocabana Railway Company.

CARLOS SAMPAIO, Rio de Janeiro; Director of the Sorocabana Railway Company; Director of the Sao Paulo-Rio Grande Railway Company.

GASTON DE CERJAT, Sao Paulo; formerly General Manager of the Compagnie de Chemins de fer Brésiliens.

DR. F. S. PEARSON, New York; President of the Rio de Janeiro Tramway, Light & Power Company, Ltd.; President of the Mexico Tramways Company.

SIR WILLIAM C. VAN HORNE, K.C.M.G., Montreal; Chairman of the Board of Directors of the Canadian Pacific Railway Company; President of the Cuba Railroad Company.

JORGE TIBIRICA, Sao Paulo; former President of the State of Sao Paulo; Senator of the State of Sao Paulo.

H. MALCOLM HUBBARD, London; Director of the Port of Pará; Director of the Mexico Tramways Company.

B. H. BINDER, London; Chartered Accountant.

The number of Directors has lately been increased to fifteen, and five additional Directors will be elected shortly.

Trustees for the 4½ per Cent. First Mortgage 60-year Gold Bonds.

EMPIRE TRUST COMPANY, New York.

Auditors.

McAULIFFE, DAVIS & HOPE, Chartered Accountants. Threadneedle House, Bishopsgate Street Within, London, E.C., and Rio de Janeiro, Brazil.

Brokers.

KITCAT & AITKEN, 120 Bishopsgate Street Within, London, E.C.

Solicitors.

STOREY, THORNDIKE, PALMER & THAYER, Boston and New York, U.S.A.

H. MALCOLM HUBBARD, London.

Bankers.

BANK OF SCOTLAND, 19 Bishopsgate Street Within, London, E.C.

No. 14.

APPLICATIONS FOR THE BONDS MAY BE MADE ON THE FORM PRINTED BELOW.

BRAZIL RAILWAY COMPANY.

(Incorporated under the Laws of the State of Maine, U.S.A.)

Issue of £3,500,000 4½ per Cent. First Mortgage 60-Year Gold Bonds.

(Part of the authorised issue above mentioned)

OF WHICH

£1,800,000 are reserved for issue in London and £1,700,000 for European Issue.

LONDON ISSUE AT 92 PER CENT.

OF

£1,800,000 4½ PER CENT. FIRST MORTGAGE 60-YEAR GOLD BONDS

(Part of the above issue).

FORM OF APPLICATION FOR BONDS.

To the Board of Directors of the
BRAZIL RAILWAY COMPANY,
31 Bishopsgate Street Within, E.C.

Gentlemen,—I hereby apply for and request that you will allot to me £......... of the above issue of 4½ per Cent. First Mortgage 60-Year Gold Bonds, and I hereby agree to take and accept the same or any less amount thereof that you may allot to me upon the terms of the Prospectus dated the 23rd October, 1909.

I enclose a remittance for £................., being the deposit which is payable on application at the rate of £5 for every £100 of the said Bonds applied for, and I agree to pay the further instalments payable in respect of the Bonds allotted to me in accordance with the terms of the said Prospectus.

Ordinary Signature ....

Name (in full) ....
(State whether Mrs. or Miss)

Address.. ....

Occupation..

Date..............................1909.

Please write distinctly.

Printed for the Proprietors by SPOTTISWOODE & Co. LTD., 5 New-street Square, E.C., and Published by REGINALD WEBSTER PAGE, at the Office, 10 King Street, Covent Garden, in the Parish of St. Paul in the County of London.—*Saturday,* 23 *October,* 1909.

THE

SATURDAY REVIEW

OF

POLITICS, LITERATURE, SCIENCE, AND ART.

No. 2,818 Vol. 108. 30 October 1909. [Registered as a Newspaper.] 6d.

CONTENTS.

This week we publish the first of a series of four articles by M. Emanuel Lasker describing the chess match he is playing against M. Janowski, the French champion.

NOTES OF THE WEEK.

The gods which the radical and socialist parties have been setting up for "the People" have got broken in Bermondsey almost as badly as those in "La Foi". The brazen images named Increment, Reversion, and Super-tax have got badly battered, and the Isis of Free Trade has suffered desecration with the rest. And we suppose that from the radical point of view the worst of it is this—"the People", as M. Brieux rightly insists, must have their gods, and are going in now for those of the Conservative party. And what a wonderful knack Bermondsey has of knowing which gods are on top at the moment! In 1885 it went Liberal with the Liberals; 1886 Conservative with the Conservatives; 1892 Liberal with the Liberals; 1895 Conservative with the Conservatives; 1905 Liberal with the Liberals; and now Conservative again with a Conservative reaction.

Since an Irish mob of anti-Parnellites flung mud mixed with lime into Parnell's eyes, there has been no outrage so brutal, committed in the name of a constitutional movement, as that which occurred in Bermondsey on Thursday. There is a difference between the two cases. The Irishmen probably knew what they were doing; whereas these suffragettes have blundered into the glory that they covet. Their enterprise was too childish to be termed criminal. But, when badly brought-up children play with fire, they become a real peril, on the top of being a nuisance. A good whipping is the old-fashioned remedy; but we have grown too sentimental to return to Elizabethan methods. We are left with bread and water, and the locked door.

We are growing rather tired of the word "lie" as used in party politics just now: it tends to lose its exactitude. But Mr. Balfour gave it a freshness in his speech on Mr. Ure on Tuesday. Mr. Ure himself would hardly object to the word "calculated" as applied to his series of speeches at Newbury, Tring, Doncaster, and elsewhere. The idea of this lovely pilgrimage has been to suggest very plainly indeed to poor people all over the country that if the Conservatives come in, the old age pensions will no longer be paid. It is this that Mr. Balfour calls the frigid and calculated lie, adding that the Lord Advocate has dishonoured his profession and his country.

We doubt whether a party leader has, in the whole history of party politics in this country, ever spoken such a severe word about an opponent. It was not uttered with passion or in haste, but with cool deliberation, and we suppose that Mr. Ure will take steps to clear himself. So far he has not done so; otherwise, of course, we should not comment on the matter. All he has done has been to hurl a defiance and a tu quoque at Mr. Balfour, and to complain that he has been badly reported. But Mr. Ure must know quite well that this is no reply at all. He is head of the Bar in Scotland. It is a position of the highest trust and responsibility. In the natural order of things he becomes a judge. Hence, of course, he cannot rest under this charge made against him by Mr. Balfour. It is unthinkable that such charges should be made by the highest men in the State against one another and merely be angrily brushed aside.

Meanwhile many people are very doubtful as to what exactly Mr. Ure has been saying in this amazing series of speeches on the old age pensions; and it may be useful to quote what the "Standard" reports him as saying at Acton last week: "Many of the recipients of old age pensions are apprehensive of losing their pensions if the Budget is thrown out. I, for my part, share their apprehension, and I think their terror has been well founded. They will never get old age pensions out of Tariff Reform. . . . Why do the Conservatives refuse to renew the promise of a pension to the old folks? Their own Chancellor of the Exchequer has said: 'The proposal would involve so enormous a charge on the Exchequer that I always feel as Chancellor of the Exchequer that I never could advise my colleagues to accept the scheme.' They refused to give them because they were too dear, and they could not find the money. Are they in a better position to-day than they were then? . . . Assuming that the alternative for finding the money is Tariff Reform, and they pass Tariff Reform, it will be 1916 before they get any money from it, and where will the old people's five shillings a week come from?" And this is only one of many passages of the same kind in other speeches of Mr. Ure.

Party papers and party politicians—openly at any rate—must of course side with their own leaders in a quarrel. Otherwise there could be no party politics or organisation. Especially papers that are effective in elections, popular papers with large circulations, must back up their own people. But the line should surely be drawn somewhere. Suppose a Conservative leader, after the passing of the Allotments Acts or the Compensation for Injuries Act, had made a series of speeches throughout the country just before an election telling the people that the Liberals, if they came into power, would annul these Acts—could any decent paper or politician on the Conservative side have backed him up? We hardly think so. Yet this would be an exactly analogous case to Mr. Ure's; and the "Daily News" and, to judge by its poster on Thursday, the "Daily Chronicle" seem charmed with Mr. Ure's speeches on the old age pensions.

Death-bed conversions in party politics are not quite dignified. Seventy-four is too old surely for a man either to marry or to change his politics. Yet it seems Sir John Gorst is now a full-fledged Liberal, and that he is to stand as a Liberal at Preston. Sir John Gorst was badly treated by the Conservative party; and he has been known to treat Conservative leaders badly. He never could tolerate his inferiors in ability when these inferiors were set above himself. Who can forget his clever, wicked, daring and foolish reflections in the Manipur speech? We recall some very bitter scoffing remarks which Mr. Louis Jennings made to us about that "disloyal" speech. This was amusing, for it was just the sort of speech Jennings would have loved to make himself. These brilliant men—how little they appreciate each other!

Lord Robert Cecil and Mr. Bowles have been adopted as Unionist candidates at Blackburn. Norwood and Marylebone are happy and Blackburn is happy, and at last there really seems an end to this ridiculous dispute. It has been from first to last a tempest in a teaspoon, quite a small teaspoon, but such a raging, tearing tempest; and we have all ended up just as we were when we began. We congratulate the braves who have fought such a great fight, we congratulate them all. But, most of all, we congratulate the clever men who have brought about this capital arrangement.

The House of Commons is the only theatre in the world where the play is kept on though it has utterly ceased to draw its public. It is odd that the House of the people on the whole cares so little as to whether or not the people is attending to it. The debates, for example, on the Finance Bill during the past week have been full of close and conscientious work, and that on the licensing clauses was most informing. Especially it produced a speech from Mr. Sherwell, the expert, which was so terribly informing it informed nobody. The House, Mr. Asquith announced, is to adjourn on 5 November till 23 November. The House of Lords will reassemble on 8 November. It will thus have a whole fortnight to spend on the Budget; which will be ample.

On Monday, before taking holiday, the Lords left the Land Bill in a comparatively harmless condition, with its virtues increased and its vices diminished in a most depressing manner. The effective finance for land purchase is increased by reducing the temptation to irrelevant expenditure by the Congested Districts Board, whose million a year cannot now be spent in rewards for cattle-driving; and there has been no weakening of Mr. Birrell's admirable scheme for making the peasants pay £14,000,000 in increased annuities, which may induce them to study how organised crime depresses the value of Land Stock. The main changes are in limiting compulsion to proved necessity, in narrowing the vagaries of the Congested Districts Board, and in relieving its administration from the direction of elective cattle-drivers.

Lord Crewe "regretted" the improvements; but he is too much of a statesman to feel them very intensely, and probably they will be a relief to some of his colleagues in the House below. It is convenient to catch the Irish vote in support of social revolution in a British Budget; but it does not follow that there is any real desire to execute the wild promises which turned the Home Rulers into a socialist wing of the Liberal party, and the latest twist in Mr. Redmond's oratory suggests that he is far from satisfied with the results of the bargain. Unnatural alliances seldom produce anything permanently good. The gem of the debate was Lord Lansdowne's accurate estimate of the measure as it had left the Commons: "An attempt to include any proposal, however wild, which was thrown at his Majesty's Government by the Nationalist party".

The publication of the correspondence between Lord Charles Beresford and Mr. Asquith has revealed a state of affairs which has rudely shocked the country. The accusations of espionage, favouritism and intimidation which had hitherto been in the shadowy twilight of rumour, club gossip, or regarded as the accusations of clique, suddenly became a damning accusation which had been made and not disproved. Take the case of Rear-Admiral Sturdee, an officer of brilliant reputation, who became Chief of the Staff to Admiral Lord Charles Beresford when that officer was appointed by the Government, in the words of the First Lord of the Admiralty, for the purpose of commanding all the combined fleets in home waters in the event of war. The post was the most responsible post a captain could hold in this country. Yet this officer was not only forced away from his post by being informed that it would not count for time towards promotion, but no less than five captains refused this blue ribbon of the profession on the ground that it would prejudice their careers.

In the case of two such able officers specially selected to be heads of divisions of the Intelligence Department as Captains Campbell and Hulbert, we find both officers forced out of their posts into unemployment after they had given evidence concerning the want of proper preparedness for war of our Navy. This would be bad enough in any circumstances, but it becomes intolerable to the conscience of the nation after the Prime Minister had stated to the House of Commons, to Lord Charles Beresford in writing and to each of the officers on coming forward that their careers would not be prejudiced in the slightest degree by their evidence. The appointment of Captain Hulbert to a routine gunnery training course is no compensation for the injury which has been done by depriving him of a highly responsible post after he had only held it for six months.

The murder of Prince Ito at Kharbin on Tuesday was not wanting in the tragic irony which the Greeks loved. The Prince went to Korea at the close of 1905; his mission came to an end in July 1909. The result of his work during those three and a half years was the partial reconciliation of that province to the leadership of Japan. That reconciliation was the work of a statesman who could always sympathise with the opposition that he must overcome, who knew that to give to a race material prosperity alone was not to give them content. If any people had cause to respect and love Prince Ito, that people was the Korean. It was a Korean that murdered him.

The career of the Prince has coincided with the rebirth of Japan. The emergence of Japan into the circle of the modern nations has come about so swiftly and, to the eyes that have watched it from Europe, with such apparent ease that the strangeness of this sequence of events is not realised. That sequence was not so sure, nor so easy, as distance has made it appear. That Japan has been reconstructed is no argument that any other Eastern nation will reach a like result. It so happened that Japan had the man to act at the right time and in the right way. There was nothing foregone about the conclusion that has been reached. To watch Prince Ito bringing his constitution through the troubled waters of its novitiate is to realise that without him Japan would probably have had to be taken no more seriously than Turkey in her desire to be ruled by a Cabinet. Japan got her Cabinet, because Prince Ito knew when to assert and when to efface himself. Practically he was never effaced. In war, diplomacy, finance, administrative reform, his was the brain that informed the hand of the Executive. That Japan and China are contrasted to-day is owing to the fact that China has just lost Chang-Chih-tung and that Japan has just lost Prince Ito.

The meeting of the Tsar and the King of Italy is not a world-shaking event, but it is nevertheless an interesting episode. Austria has always been unpopular in Italy, and is at the present time extremely so in Russian official circles, therefore any proceeding which seems likely to give her pain will be welcome in those countries. On the face of it, nothing can be more correct than that the Tsar should return the King's visit, but it is impossible to forget that one of King Victor Emmanuel's allies is unable owing to his close relations with the Vatican to visit the Italian monarch in his capital. The route chosen by the Tsar was evidently intended to give point to the whole business. He carefully avoided Austrian soil both going and returning. The whole business is a distinct score for M. Isvolski, though in no adequate sense a Roland for Count Aerenthal's Oliver. The reception of M. Pichon on French soil was correct but had no special significance.

In Germany the Federal Council has renewed its sittings and is busy getting ready the estimates to be presented to the Reichstag on its assembly in a month's time. A deficit for 1909 and new taxes for 1910 are regarded as certain. The position of the new Chancellor is becoming very difficult. The Coburg bye-election, the third since Prince Buelow's resignation, has resulted, like its two predecessors, in the return of a socialist. The elections in the local Parliaments of Saxony and Baden show a marked increase in the socialist vote. This does not imply that the German people are becoming converts of Marx. It simply means that the prevailing disgust with the Government is finding expression in support of the one party which has been absolutely consistent in its opposition.

Time will show whether a union of the entire left wing is possible. A year ago no one dreamed of it; to-day the prospect deserves consideration. In the first place, a union of the sections of the Liberal party is practically assured. In the second place, the revisionist movement among the Social Democrats is rapidly gaining ground, to the unconcealed horror of those who loathe the idea of co-operation with the bourgeoisie. In the third place, the new Hanseatic League is making a great effort to attract workpeople as well as employers. The recently issued programme of the organisation proclaims neutrality in the case of a strike, a point of considerable significance. It is worth noting in this connexion that the Emperor took advantage of his daughter's confirmation to show marked attention to Prince Buelow. His conduct is regarded as a plain hint to the Conservatives that the monarchy may yet undertake to support a Government to which they are hostile.

M. Briand has as clever a tongue as any living politician. His speech in the Chamber on Thursday was an even better performance than the one at Périgueux. Apparently he has persuaded everyone that proportional representation is for certain reasons an excellent reform to be shelved, until the practical considerations which move practical men are good enough to point in the right direction. His appeal to practical men took the Chamber by storm; and his speech is to be posted up throughout the French communes. The first thing to do, says M. Briand, is to give the electors the notion of electoral justice. Then perhaps something can be done. Till then—well, there is a vexed question out of the way for the time being. But it will hardly encourage M. Briand to note how very successfully the practical details of a proportional representation scheme have been worked out in Johannesburg and Pretoria this week.

Sir Edmund Monson spent his life in the Diplomatic Service, reaching the top rung of the ladder at the Embassy in Paris. Those who knew him liked him; but very few did know him, and he knew very few. He was not an ideal Ambassador to France. In Paris he lived the life almost of a recluse, out of touch with society and most things characteristically French.

The greater minds of France continue to discuss the canons of art by killing each other; but one of the exceptions is M. Bernstein, who, in his duel with the "Figaro" critic last Wednesday, "held his pistol behind his back", while the critic "took a careful aim", apparently at some place where M. Bernstein was not. When only one fights, it is not more than half a duel, and so the exact value of "La Griffe", the play attacked, remains unsettled. There is really no future for the French duel unless it can be kept entertaining, and for this the Dublin model might be studied. Curran, a little man, was fighting a very big man, and the very big man complained, "See how little I have to fire at and how much he has", to which Curran replied, "Mark out a piece of him my own size for me with chalk, and the shots outside the line don't count".

The speech in which the Belgian Minister for the Colonies on Thursday outlined the scheme of reforms for the Congo may be taken as M. Renkin's answer to Sir Edward Grey. M. Renkin says that, beginning with large tracts in July 1910, by July 1912 the natives will be given the right to the produce of the soil and that taxes will be levied in money. He appears to ignore the question of freedom of trade, but promises an investigation with a view to revising the agreements with concessionaires. As for the stories of continued cruelty and oppression, after personal investigation on the spot he declares them to be false.

Señor Moret is not going to the Cortes with the war-credits. This looks as if the breach between the two parties were complete, and as if the old era of mutual arrangement were at an end. The Cortes is closed, and a general election will follow. The closing of the Cortes shows that the Liberal Prime Minister is convinced that feeling will only grow more bitter with every speech that is made. It also seems to show that Señor Moret himself deplores the breach that he cannot mend. Moreover, while Señor Moret will not actually condemn the execution of Ferrer, Señor Maura, his colleagues and his party are firmer than ever in insisting upon the just necessity of what they have done. On the surface the Ferrer execution has driven the Conservative party from power. As a matter of fact, it has made it stronger than it was before.

Señor Don Perez Triana, we are glad to see, has been appointed representative of Colombia in London and Madrid. Colombia, with the disappearance of President Reyes, is turning over a new leaf; and by way of initial letter happily entrusts its interests in England and Spain to one of the most distinguished South Americans in Europe. No wonder a number of shady gentlemen are agog with alarm. Señor Triana has for many years been engaged in showing up and bursting Central American finance bubbles. This does not earn the gratitude of the bubble blowers. Señor Triana is a man of quite wondrous versatility; brilliant linguist, littérateur, statesman, business man, diplomatist. We remember his speeches at the Hague Conference, where he represented quite a bevy of republics.

According to the "Daily Telegraph," Mr. Herbert Gladstone is to go to South Africa as the first Governor-General of the united colonies! Angels and ministers of grace defend us! What has South Africa done that she should have him? Mr. Gladstone is par excellence and by common consent the failure of the Cabinet; and by his own fault. He has shown some common-sense in dealing with the suffragettes, and that is the sole good point that can be put to his credit as Home Secretary. We can well understand that Mr. Asquith should welcome an opportunity of relief from Mr. Gladstone without hurting Mr. Gladstone's feelings. He was not so squeamish about Lord Elgin and Lord Portsmouth. But we had thought the day for sending our failures and mauvais sujets to govern the colonies was past. Perhaps this rumour is only a bad dream or a bad joke. But most people seem inclined to believe it.

Sir Wilfrid Laurier's logic strikes us as sadly wanting. In an address in Montreal he showed how superior the British Constitution is to the American—it is "more democratic, more elastic and more responsive to public needs"—and proceeded to recommend that Great Britain should copy the American Federal example. He would split up the United Kingdom into a series of watertight compartments, and wonders that Mr. Gladstone did not hit upon the federation principle in his attempt to carry Home Rule. Sir Wilfrid Laurier is clearly incapable of appreciating the difference between the uprooting of the old and the linking-up of the new.

The country owes a great deal to Lord Loreburn for the way in which he has resisted the demand that he shall pack the bench with political creatures. We know that he has put some very good Liberals on the bench —Liberals who ought to have been there long ago. But that is a very different thing from the unclean job some irresponsible radicals have been striving to make him do. The Government has now appointed an excellent Royal Commission to consider the whole matter of political appointments to the bench, with Lord James as Chairman.

The split among the flying men now seems to be past mending. It only needed a little oil upon the waters to make it smooth sailing to some sort of agreement; but the Doncaster meeting is an episode that the Aero Club finds it hard to forgive. Anyhow, there is to be some hot warfare, and that not of the prettiest kind. The Aero Club has boycotted the great national conference summoned by the Aeroplane Club to the Mansion House. This puts the Aeroplane Club in a ludicrous position. It has invited its enemies to the feast, and these have refused to appear, questioning the right of their self-constituted hosts to invite them. We cannot feel very sorry for the Aeroplane Club. It has been a little premature and officious. If there is to be a national body, it can only be formed with the Aero Club at the centre. Moreover, the constitution of this body has already been foreshadowed by the formation of the Aerial League. The Aeroplane Club does not seem to have a chance.

We are still left wondering about that bust by Leonardo Da Vinci; and we are inclined to think that Dr. Bode has been taken in. If Dr. Bode has been taken in, he will find himself in a tight place. But what credit to our own sculptor R. C. Lucas! Lucas or Da Vinci? No one seems to be able to declare offhand. Perhaps some of the credit or discredit may be ascribed to that exposure in the garden, or to that five hundred years or so of passing from hand to hand. Either of these alternatives leaves plenty of scope for the chances that have obliterated the means of giving judgment between the two men.

Mr. Edward Peacock will be sorely missed in the journalistic quarters of London which pass to-day for Bohemia. The Bohemia of the twentieth century is a vastly different thing from the Bohemia even of the mid-Victorian era. It is respectable, a trifle humdrum perhaps, essentially honest, and maintains tradition only in so far as the tweed jacket is preferred to the conventional evening dress. Mr. Peacock was for many years honorary secretary of the Savage Club, and that proclaims the man. In this position he was as happily placed as in the management of the "Morning Post". He was not the conventional manager: the aggressive self-consciously great little person. He was the courteous business chief of the Court daily.

BERMONDSEY.

IT is well that we have won Bermondsey. It may even be well that we have not won outright. This is suggestive perhaps of sour grapes; none the less it is possible for too much success and too complete a victory to lull the winning side into an unsafe sense of security. Not that we would not have had Mr. Dumphreys win absolutely if we could. It would have been much pleasanter to Unionists if he had. There is no gainsaying that; and this tantalising shortcoming of complete success can be turned into gain only by exceptional watchfulness and energy on our side resulting from it. The figures in this election show that Unionism has made great progress in Bermondsey, and probably in all South London. The total Unionist poll shows an increase on the poll of 1906 of over twelve hundred, and this is at the direct cost of the Liberal vote, which fell off by over fourteen hundred. As against Liberalism, therefore, Unionists have much ground in the result of this election for encouragement and hope. At least as certainly it gives us no excuse for resting on our oars or for taking things easily in any way. We have done much better than the Liberals, but we have only just succeeded in getting our man in. We cannot trust to a split opposition to see us through at the next general election. Circumstances this time were plainly in our favour. Mr. Dumphreys is very well known to Bermondsey people of all classes. He had been before the Bermondsey public for over twenty years, and he was personally connected with the main trade of the place. Mr. Hughes, on the other hand, was an importation. Then times are bad and it was evident that Bermondsey business had been adversely affected by Free Trade, if ever any local industry had. On the whole, things were much in our favour, and if Mr. Dumphreys had not got in, to pretend that we had not received a very nasty set-back would have been merely silly. As it is, the result is encouraging, though by no means entirely satisfactory.

As between the Liberal and the Unionist it was a question of Budget or Tariff Reform, and Tariff Reform won. This is the constructive answer to excessive direct taxation, and will no doubt, and naturally, tell in working-class constituencies much more than the most brilliant exposure of the unfairness of Mr. Lloyd George's land taxes, death duties, and burdens on brewers. Most of us can bear with some philosophy burdens put on other people, and it is no use to expect working people to cry over the financial sorrows of men who seem to them fabulously rich. It is, of course, unfortunate, it is depressing and squalid, that votes which go to determine the destinies of an empire and in theory are given on the highest public grounds should in fact be given on no other ground but personal interest. But if you object to this, you must not have democracy; if you will have democracy, you must not expect public motives to dominate elections. The man is a fool who expects a democratic vote to be given on very high lines. It is no serious charge against the poor that this is so. None of us who was not quite sure of his living from day to day would think of much else, and if an election gave us the chance, or we thought it did, of getting a bit more, we should certainly take it. But it does show the folly of democracy as a system of imperial government. Under it elections can but turn on personal interests, and policy will be framed accordingly. The budget as an electioneering draw is very effective on the negative side. It offers the pleasure of taking from those who have to those who have not—a pleasure to which human nature finds it difficult to rise superior. But when you are not yourself to have what is taken from the other man, and you are hard up, the fun of damaging the rich is not wholly satisfying. There the budget broke down. It could not even profess to help the Bermondsey out-of-works to get work and wages. Tariff Reform did, and Bermondsey workmen believed it. It was a choice between a negative pleasure and a positive gain, and they had the sense to prefer the positive.

We have no doubt that this is a correct diagnosis of the position as between Liberals and Tariff Reformers at this election. The incalculable quantity was Dr. Salter and his following. That this was a pro-budget element can hardly be disputed. Those who voted for Dr. Salter voted for a supporter of the budget, only rather more so. But whether all who voted socialist would have voted for Dr. Salter if the budget had been the only or main attraction in his window is quite open to question. We certainly should not admit for one moment that had Dr. Salter been out of the way, all who voted for him would have voted for the Liberal. Liberals naturally state the election in terms of pro-budget and anti-budget only, and as both Dr. Salter and Mr. Hughes were for the budget, they lump their total of votes together and infer that if there had been only one pro-budget candidate in the field, he must have won. But this is to beg the whole question of what determined Dr. Salter's supporters to vote for him. Those of them that were socialists unqualified voted for his socialism and, had there been no socialist to support, might not have voted at all, or might have voted for Mr. Dumphreys. However little one might infer it from the speeches of socialist leaders, every one who goes about amongst their rank and file knows that not a few of them will vote for a Conservative where there is no socialist candidate. Conversely, some who will always prefer a Conservative to a Liberal will not infrequently prefer a socialist to either. One cannot say what would have happened if Dr. Salter had not come forward. We must regard his following as a doubtful quantity that might be the undoing of either regular party.

But the budget produced its effect. We must not blink that fact. Probably the budget and the budget only prevented Bermondsey from being a second Peckham. But for it we have no doubt Mr. Hughes' vote would have sunk to a point that would have left Mr. Dumphreys an easy absolute majority of the whole electorate. Unionists must reckon with the budget as a seriously disturbing electioneering element. In front it must be met on merits point by point unwearyingly, but its flank must everywhere be turned by Tariff Reform. The double attack will avail. We have to meet the budget, not avoid it. We have no patience with those who would bid us shrink from opposing the injurious proposals of the budget because they are popular. No doubt these strategists, whose "strategic retreats" we all know by another name, will see in the Bermondsey election additional reason for accepting the budget. They will be pouring their cautions into the ears of Peers, bidding them save their lives by a timely retreat. But the British aristocrat, whatever his shortcomings, has never shown a penchant for the white feather, be it in war or in politics, at home or abroad. If the House of Lords, or its Unionist members, were all aristocrats we should have no fear of their passing the budget. We have not very much fear as it is. There will be some weak-kneed Peers on the Unionist side, no doubt; but they will be too few, we believe, to prevent the budget's happy dispatch. We do not need to be told that it is not to be rejected lightly or that for the House of Lords to disable a finance bill is a serious matter. Heaven knows we have been told this often enough by friends and foes during the last five months. Whatever the Lords do will not be done in a hurry. The budget is a serious matter, and will be met by serious action. We are told that if the Lords are allowed to meddle with a money bill they will be able to destroy any Government at pleasure, and so be masters of the nation. This is mere special pleading, for the House of Lords cannot upset in this way a single Ministry without promptly appearing at the bar of public opinion —an election must follow. If they acted either irresponsibly or in the mere interests of their own order, the nation would condemn them; and the outcome would be their own undoing. Public sanction is ample protection against encroachment by the Peers. Against encroachment by the Government we have no protection but the Peers. If the Government of the day is to be free to pass any finance bill unquestioned, there is no limit to its power. There is not a policy that cannot be put in the shape of a finance bill; and this would pass without any appeal to the country. We will ask the "Westminster Gazette", which is very strong on the danger of the Lords touching a money bill, if a Tory Government introduced a budget of an extreme protective nature, so violently protective as to amount to a serious provocation to foreign countries, would the House of Lords be doing their duty to the nation if they passed it without demur and without question? We hold that they would be betraying their trust. The Lords' power to give pause to executive aggression is too grave a matter for temporising. They must assert it now, or they may lose it for ever—by default.

ITALY AND RUSSIA'S ADDRESSES.

If the other two members of the Triple Alliance show no great objection to Italy enjoying a "tour de valse" with Russia, nobody else need. Of course it is very easy to explain the incident superficially. The Tsar owed the King a visit, and found the present a convenient season. But it is useless to pretend that there was nothing unusual or remarkable about the event. The route chosen was quite conspicuously circuitous. A much shorter way might have been found through the dominions of Francis Joseph, who after all is one of Italy's allies. But the intention is obvious. M. Isvolski has not yet by any means forgiven Count Aerenthal the nasty fall he gave him and Russian prestige in the Balkans last spring. In short, the world is not wrong for once in the significance it attaches to the meeting and the speeches of two Sovereigns. The general view is only emphasised by the half-timorous, half-swaggering attitude of the official Italian press. They long to defy altogether the feelings of their allies, but dare not, while they glory in the effort made by their ruler's independent action. "See what brave fellows we are", they seem to say to Germany and Austria. "After all, we mean to live our own lives, but at the same time we will do nothing to hurt your feelings."

The position of Italy indeed is not only illogical, it is almost contemptible. It was clear long ago that neither were her allies her friends nor her friends her allies. It is also clear now, especially since the Balkan crisis, that her friends' policy is entirely at one with that she wishes to pursue herself, while that of her allies is in every way repugnant to her. In short, she regretted and resented the triumph of the Triple Alliance, of which she is a member, over the Triple Entente, of which she is not. Yet, in spite of the double absurdity of her present position, no one doubts that Italy intends to renew the Triplice when the time comes, and no one believes that she will break off her official connexion with Austria and Germany. Her allies, therefore, are treating her faiblesse for other Powers with indulgent contempt. But it may reasonably be asked how far any State can be a trustworthy ally which believes that all her interests are bound up with the success of her nominal opponents.

We cannot remember an occasion when a member of an Alliance made such open parade of sympathy with the avowed objects of its rivals. Nobody who has studied the subject is ignorant of the far-reaching aims of Pan-Germanism in Turkey and the Balkan Peninsula. It is equally certain that Austria is regarded as the vanguard of the advance. The Drang nach Osten is equally to the advantage of Austria and Germany and contrary to the views of Russia. The great danger both for Austria and Germany is the development of the Slav element in the Austro-Hungarian Empire. At present the German and the Magyar dominate the situation, but that is by no means certain to last as the permanent distribution of forces. There are already 23,000,000 Slavs to 20,400,000 Germans and Magyars, and it is by no means certain that the Magyars will always remain on the German side. Slavs, too, multiply much more quickly than Germans, and seem to absorb rather than to become absorbed. It is remarkable that Vienna, formerly pure German, is now one-third Slav. Therefore in a few years' time Austria may be seriously threatened with a Slavonic question which might paralyse her efficiency as an ally to Germany.

The danger may be remote, but it has to be reckoned with, and might be a valuable asset for Russia in a Balkan struggle.

The interests of Italy lie quite as evidently on the side of the Slavs as those of Russia. All her ambitions are thwarted by the overwhelming power of Germanism in Central Europe. Italia Irredenta is not a forgotten dream, and, absurd as it may be, Italy still looks towards some expansion on the Albanian shores of the Adriatic. In any case it is against her interest that the strength of Austria on the eastern shores of the Adriatic or in the Mediterranean regions should be increased. Therefore, not only sentimental ties but the promptings of self-interest oblige her to espouse with warmth the cause of Montenegro. It is true she could do little for Prince Nicholas during the late dispute, but that does not make her resent the Austrian success the less. Therefore in the Balkans the cause of Russia and the Slav is in fact her own, and the success of Austria and Germany in every way disagreeable to her. No wonder, then, the Tsar should speak of the "constant and trustful co-operation" with which Russia and Italy will endeavour to compass their ends, which consist for the present in the laudable object of maintaining the status quo in the Balkans and peace in Europe. Russia is prepared for anything rather than war, and Italy could not face the peril involved in a rupture with her allies.

After all, the reasons which not only induce but compel Italy to remain a member of the Triple Alliance are very practical indeed, while those which separate her from them are mainly sentimental, though in a country like Italy sentimental reasons may be very powerful. First, Italy in a real breach with her allies would find herself in a very awkward military predicament. The forces of Germany and Austria combined are at present overwhelmingly strong, even over other European Powers. Italy could not for a moment withstand either Power singly. Her north-eastern frontier is very inadequately fortified, and her fleet is nothing to boast of. The Triple Alliance, therefore, has for her an additional drawback. It almost precludes her undertaking great schemes of defence on the Austrian frontier, while the absence of such defences prevents her breaking off the alliance. But there is, in the second place, a much stronger reason for maintaining the alliance than the military one. While the connexion with Austria may be a cause of embarrassment rather than of strength, that with Germany is undoubtedly an enormous potential benefit to the House of Savoy. Almost every month demonstrates that in every province and town of Italy there exist vast elements of unrest. Some of these concentrate in the milder shape of republicanism, while others are frankly anarchical. If Italian policy were to take any step which gave a definite advantage to a republican Power, that would undoubtedly encourage the simmering republicanism of Italy. It is the merest instinct of self-preservation which induces King Victor Emmanuel II. to cling to the German alliance at all costs. In spite of the correct attitude of the French Government towards foreign potentates, the tendency of the French people towards more and more violent forms of republicanism, anti-militarism and anti-patriotism only becomes more evident every day. No King, therefore, in the peculiar position of Victor Emmanuel will lend himself to promote the fraternising of two peoples which might easily prove fatal to himself. In fact, were Italy to abandon Germany for France the result in the event either of failure or success might prove equally fatal to the House of Savoy.

For these reasons, if for no others, any disturbance of existing arrangements is certainly not to be expected from the meeting at Racconigi. Its only serious import is to be found in the indication it offers that Russia deeply feels her failure in the Balkans, and is looking for an opportunity of revenge. The Austro-Russian entente in that region was at an end before, but we cannot believe that a Russo-Italian arrangement will necessarily keep the peace. One thing is certain. Unless the members of the Triple Entente are really ready to back their views with effective force, they will only march from one humiliation to another. If they are prepared to concert a policy which they are also ready to promote in unison, and if necessary to fight for, they may give pause to their opponents, and in such a contingency the influence of Italy might prove a decisive factor. But those who expect a rupture of the Triplice will be disappointed. An ill-assorted marriage by no means always leads to a divorce. The reasons for maintaining such unions are usually much stronger than those for a rupture, and it is so with the Triple Alliance.

LIBERAL WOMAN-FOLK AND THEIR MEN.

FAR be it from us to discuss at the present time so stale a question as woman suffrage or to advertise suffragette misdemeanours by their condemnation. There is, however, a lady concerned in this matter of the suffrage agitation whom the public as yet has hardly been able to see, thanks to the thick flight of suffragette missiles, but who, unlike the suffragette, has a real grievance against Mr. Asquith and his merry men, and whose influence will be felt one way or another when the General Election comes on. We refer to the Liberal Woman, for it is of her grievance that we have a word to say. Now let us in commencing make it clear to our readers what we mean by a Liberal woman. A Liberal woman in our sense is not any female who chances to call herself a Liberal. Nor is she necessarily the wife or daughter of a Liberal M.P. We mean by a Liberal woman a woman who is an active worker on a Women's Liberal Association united to the Women's Liberal Federation. That Federation is, if we only look at its leading spirits, a distinctly interesting body. Its president, Lady Carlisle, is, as everyone knows, a temperance fanatic, but she is recognised at the same time as a woman of ability, and in these days (for Liberal women) of stress and storm she has proved herself an astute wirepuller. The women who sit on the platform on the gala days of the Federation, and who are well known in political circles, are serious politicians and able speakers. Mrs. Eva Maclaren, Lady Slack, and Miss Balgarnie (to take three names at random) could all hold their own as orators with a good many Liberal M.P.s. However, it is not these leaders of the Federation that we want to consider to-day, but the rank and file of the body.

The ruling spirits in the local Women's Liberal Associations in the suburbs and country towns are the products in part of the Dissidence of Dissent, but also of higher education of women (being as yet new and crude) and of the cranks, fads, and enthusiasms that make up the so-called movement for social reform. The active Liberal woman here is often better educated than the men of her own political faith, and she has more time and taste for political intrigue, a fact well known to certain Liberal gentlemen, who, in spite of the recommendations of headquarters, local Liberal Associations have sent about their business. She is, needless to say, narrow and often intolerant. She fusses herself overmuch concerning the sins of priests and the crimes of publicans, and though she often is a useful member of an Education Committee, her colleagues are painfully aware that she may at any moment disturb local tranquillity by threatening a popular if ritualistic cleric with the Kenyon Slaney clause. But, be her errors what they may, she was a godsend to the Liberal party in the years that preceded the last General Election. In many a suburban and southern constituency the bazaars, the concerts, and the canvassing classes that she arranged gave the male Liberals funds and courage and useful volunteers, and many of the striking victories which the party won at the General Election were won by the enthusiasm which she aroused. Poor lady! she was out not only to put Sir Henry Campbell-Bannerman in power, but also to secure that her own name should be inscribed on the Parliamentary electoral roll. We have often said, and repeat, that the vast majority of Englishwomen are hostile or totally indifferent to the woman suffrage agitation. We have however no doubt that the Liberal woman desires the franchise far more passionately than does even the suffragette, for, like the male Liberal, she believes the suffrage to be a fundamental right, and she feels it to be an indignity that the public-house loafer should enjoy a privilege denied to her. It was in 1902, when the Women's Liberal Federation passed a resolution refusing its official countenance to any candidate who did not give a suffrage pledge, that woman's franchise became a serious question. The result of the resolution was apparent in the fact that at the last General Election four hundred and twenty members were returned pledged to some form of woman suffrage. The Liberal women were jubilant. They had gained for the cause which they had most at heart a great majority both in the Cabinet and in the House, and they felt that before the dissolution they would get their votes. The ordinary Liberal politician says nowadays that the cause was wrecked by the fantastic rowdyism of the suffragettes. This will not do, though it is probable enough that their antics have converted many a Liberal M.P. from an academic sympathy to an academic loathing for the whole cause. Nor is it the fact that any sense of responsibility prevented the Liberal M.P.s from precipitating a revolution for which they had no mandate from the country. The truth is this, that when the politicians and party wirepullers looked seriously into the question, they discovered that to enfranchise the women on the Municipal Register, which was what the Liberal ladies in their hearts desired, would be to lose seats to the Tories. If any doubt existed, the London County Council election demonstrated which side a female vote would go if party passion was aroused. The Liberal M.P.s, realising that to enfranchise the women on the Municipal Register would be to commit the happy dispatch, and knowing that the country would look askance at adult suffrage, made up their minds to do nothing for the voteless. We do not blame their decision; but we say that they should have honestly explained their difficulties to the women to whom they had pledged their support. So doing they would not have lost these women's respect. A more disingenuous policy was adopted, and an attempt was made to throw dust into the eyes alike of the militants and the Liberal ladies. A majority voted for Mr. Stanger's Suffrage Bill, knowing that it had been arranged that it should not go beyond the second-reading stage, and later, when the Liberal women were about to hold their annual conference, Mr. Asquith himself announced to a deputation of M.P.s that a great Reform Bill would be introduced to which the Government would permit a woman's suffrage amendment to be moved on certain conditions, one, and that the most important, being that it should be on democratic lines. This was astute. Not a Tory in the House would have voted for it, and if by a miracle it escaped through the Commons, its destruction by the Peers was certain. But the Liberal women took the pledge seriously, and so charmed were they with Mr. Asquith's "surrender" that they even offered to wager pairs of gloves (until they remembered their connexion with the Anti-Gambling League) that Mr. Lloyd George would move their amendment and that Mr. Asquith would vote for it. For a time the farce was well kept up. Mr. Lloyd George went down to the Albert Hall and brought to the women assembled in that building a message from the Cabinet of which the effect was that as they had a majority of 420 in the House they could count on their amendment becoming law, if only the suffragettes would cease their brawls. A message from the Cabinet! Some time later, when Liberal ladies heckled Mr. Birrell at Manchester, the interesting fact came out that the Cabinet had never yet considered the details of this precious suffrage amendment. How then in the name of common-sense could Mr. Lloyd George, or for that matter the Cabinet, tell serious people that an amendment would be passed, when they had not the vaguest idea what the amendment would be except that it would be one that every suffragist Tory would oppose? But what practical politician ever imagined that a Reform Bill would be introduced at all? Any way, the mask is now off, and Mr. Winston Churchill and Mr. Runciman have both proclaimed that woman suffrage is not to figure on the party programme at the next election. Mr. Churchill seeks to throw the blame on the militant suffragettes; but neither statesman has a word of sympathy for the Liberal women who have been so heartlessly bamboozled. Nor is this the worst. Injury has been added to insult, and the Liberal women are writhing under the Budget. That Budget with its *1s. 2d.* income tax and swingeing death duties is a cruel Budget for the spinster and widow with slender incomes, and they make up no small proportion of the members of the Women's Liberal Federation. No wonder that the women are angry. No wonder that the Women's Liberal Associations through the country are breaking up. No wonder that some Liberal men, with a sense of fair play, are deserting their party. London Liberal organs like the "Westminster Gazette" ignore these unpleasant facts, but readers of the "Manchester Guardian" know them well.

Yet as the General Election draws nearer a sense of fear seems to be creeping over some Liberals whether after all the anger of their women may not wreck them at the polls. The Liberal candidate for East Berks has been writing to more than one newspaper urging the Women's Liberal Federation to drop their 1902 resolution and, suffrage or no suffrage, stand with the male Liberals in the fight against monopoly of trade. So far he has got no response from those whose chief grievance is the monopoly of sex. When however the hour of battle draws nearer more powerful voices will doubtless re-echo the appeal. The Liberal women must stand firm to their convictions. Their conduct hitherto in a trying crisis has been quiet and dignified. But if after the way the Liberal politicians have treated them they still work on their behalf, they will get in return and deserve only these politicians' contempt. Common-sense suggests that they should leave their party to its fate. If the Liberals meet their deserts, it will be time for Cordelia to return to Lear.

MR. URE AS A PSYCHOLOGICAL STUDY.

MR. URE, his Majesty's Lord Advocate for Scotland, has conferred two boons upon the public. He has exhibited for our consideration a psychological study of a most unusual Scotsman, and he has procured the exhibition of a phase of Mr. Balfour's character very little suspected by any but his most intimate friends. The second is perhaps the greater boon. Vulgar abuse is common and easy, but an example of polished invective such as that with which Mr. Balfour has favoured the jaded politician is rare. Coming from such a source, with deliberation, with a carefully prepared stage, and with every item of the grave denunciation carefully set out with appropriate adjectives qualifying the necessary epithet, the incident is a veritable bolt from the blue, and we owe it all to Mr. Ure. This is the more extraordinary because Mr. Ure is a dull man. If he had not been dull, with a total absence of all that far-reaching perception usually associated with the canny Scot, he would never have said the things he has. The Buccleuch incident was bad enough. It took him a long time to discover he was in the wrong, and his dullness has prevented him even yet from discovering that members of an honourable profession usually apologise when they find they have made a mistake. But the old-age pension incident is a far more wonderful instance of his incapacity. His own journalistic monitors warned him very early in the day that he was not speaking the truth. They had even specifically endorsed the shocking word used by Mr. Balfour in a note denouncing the inaccuracy, but still he continued blundering along repeating his formula in quite a variety of ways. First came the assertion that the fears of the old-age pensioners that they would lose their dole were "not without foundation"; then that their alarm was "well founded"; then the "alarm" became "a terror" also "well founded"; and finally that he shared the apprehension of the aged poor that Mr. Balfour's party would take away their pensions. Truly it is a marvellous case of persistence in error, repeated day after day, and all over the country precisely as if his statement had been recognised as an accurate representation of a generally accepted fact.

The psychological interest in this incident centres in the point that there has never before been so extraordinary an example of lack of perception on the part of a Minister of the Crown. All the figures of speech that were ever coined to illustrate dullness and stupidity fall short of adequately describing this astounding example offered for our interpretation by this member of the Government. This was at once Mr. Balfour's difficulty and his triumph. He had nailed the lie to the counter in so many words. With lofty indifference or with the egotism of ignorance Mr. Ure passed this by. Perhaps he never reads the papers, and knows nothing of current events unless his "attention is called" to some daily record by an officious reporter. This seems to have happened, for the representative of a news agency lay in wait for him with Mr. Balfour's speech. At this point the extravagance of the psychology of the incident increases. Mr. Ure was surprised. It was clear he had never seen the obvious interpretation of his formula of condemnation. He had evidently framed it with much care. He had laid all the blame of the initial doubts on the old-age pensioners. He had merely added his confirmation of their alleged fears. The casuistry was perfect; and here was Mr. Balfour making remarks of quite a novel sort on a purely forensic declaration. No doubt Mr. Ure was genuinely surprised. He had seen and could see nothing else but the perfection of his method; and of course he never for a moment suspected his own dullness; but when Mr. Balfour spoke of the "frigid and calculated lie", of "lies carefully thought out, deliberately coined and then put into illegitimate circulation", Mr. Ure was shocked. He was literally and unmistakably concerned; and for the first time. Up to that hour he was clearly proud of his casuistry, and then for the first time he saw it stripped of its metaphysical aspect and set out for condemnation in all its grotesque simplicity as a piece of commonplace duplicity and a vulgar attempt at deception. Here we have the justification of Mr. Balfour's method. Ordinary rebuke had no effect upon Mr. Ure. It needed the cold chisel and the sledgehammer to get it into his dull brain that he had committed a political enormity, had injured his party, had despised the admonition of his journalistic mentors, had put his leader in a difficulty, more irritating because of its stupidity than the more grave offences of one or two of his colleagues. Perhaps he had aimed at emulating these reckless demagogues and had failed only because he had lacked their skill. This seems to be the more probable, because his defence was equally curious with all that had gone before. It was framed on the common formula "You're another"; and every phrase of condemnation and regret expressed by Mr. Balfour was spurted back with ludicrous repetition and in unconscious flattery of his denouncer.

It is probable that the evil consequences to the old-age pensioners likely to result from Mr. Ure's endorsement of fears they never entertained will be prevented by the exposure and denunciation of his casuistry. The pensioners have now complete assurance that they are in their country's keeping to the extent of their pensions. Unfortunately, however, one or two considerations remain concerning which the ordinary citizen may be excused if he feels a genuine concern. The office of Lord Advocate of Scotland is not merely a distinguished position involving temporary obligations during the retention of the office. It is associated in the legal mind with far-reaching possibilities. By common consent the holder of the office may, and usually does, aspire to assume by custom the highest seat on the judicial bench of Scotland, a position hitherto associated with the most distinguished Scottish lawyers of past times. It is disquieting to reflect that this curiously defective mind which Mr. Ure has exposed to us is in the way of becoming not only the chief exponent of the law of Scotland, but that it may, by virtue of precedent, be endowed with a seat in the highest Court of Appeal within the realm and determine causes of the first magnitude. We have had an instance within recent times of the impetuosity of a Lord Advocate in seizing a vacant seat upon the Scottish bench regardless of the interests of clients or the common decencies of public life. There was no restraining hand in that case, and we must expect a similar pusillanimity in the case of any future rush for preferment. Still, setting aside this serious public danger, we must acknowledge our indebtedness to Mr. Ure for having by sheer force of an obtuse persistence galvanised Mr. Balfour into a state of unwonted vigour. The country may now be assured that while a moderate amount of impropriety may fail to excite Mr. Balfour to action, we have here evidence of his capacity in a case of necessity of achieving perfection in invective.

THE CITY.

SOME improvement is discernible in the monetary position. High rates of interest and discount prevail, but only by maintaining quotations can we hope to check undue speculation in Wall Street and Germany, and it is to the existence of the higher charges that we owe the improvement which has taken place. To all outward appearance the gamble in Wall Street has not been interrupted, but undoubtedly the banks in New York are restricting accommodation, and the high rates demanded here for discount are putting a curb upon the indiscriminate creation of American finance paper. It has not been found practicable to refuse borrowers on American securities the money necessary for carrying over stock, but by exacting onerous rates of interest the banks placed difficulties in the way of continuing speculation, and if this policy is pursued the "bull" account should be gradually reduced. It would be foolish, however, to imagine that because the settlement has passed off so smoothly all danger of an upheaval in Wall Street has passed. The market there is so wrapped up in the speculation in Steel shares that any serious break in these would probably produce something approaching a panic. At the same time the market in these shares seems remarkably well held, an evidence of its stability being furnished by the firmness with which it was maintained after the announcement of the quarter's earnings. These make a very fine showing, but they fall below estimates, and certainly do not justify the big rise which has taken place in the shares in the last twelve months. A popular saying is that steel is either a prince or a pauper, and experience proves that a transformation from one to the other is easily accomplished. This is a "banner" year for the Corporation, and it is a prince in the industrial world. But two years hence it may be a pauper.

The goods traffic on our Home Railways continues to expand. It is always a long time before any marked improvement in trade is reflected in earnings, in the same way that earnings continue to show enlargement long after trade is on the wane; but the expected expansion is now in steady progress, and should become more pronounced in the next few months if confidence is restored by changes in the political world. Many brokers, who for months past have been advising clients to leave Home Railway stocks severely alone, are now advocating purchases, and there would seem to be ample justification for accepting their recommendation. The Argentine railway market has received a nasty shock. It appears that the payment of the 5 per cent. dividend on Buenos Ayres and Pacific stock is only possible by drawing upon the reserve. Without recourse to this the directors could not have paid more than 3 per cent. By reason of heavy borrowings for expansions the company's responsibilities have grown enormously in the last three years, and it is now announced that these are to be added to by a guarantee for another million capital for the Bahia Blanca. In course of time all the money spent will become productive, but the provision of interest in the meantime is a severe tax upon the company, and shows that the market considerably overrated its earning powers when last year it put the stock to 124. From this figure it has steadily declined until now it is no more than 92, which is its full value at the moment.

Another banking amalgamation is announced—Parr's with Stuckey's. It will form a powerful combination, and will probably lead to others. We regret the disappearance of our old country banks, but sentiment has no place in the business world, and London banks with few branches recognise that if they are to progress they must extend their ramifications. No better method presents itself than the absorption of already well-established country institutions. It is open to question, however, whether the disappearance of the private banker is a good thing for the country generally. To say nothing of the danger of the creation of huge banking combines or trusts, the removal of the private banker makes it increasingly difficult for the country trader and agriculturist to get the financial assistance necessary for carrying on their work. Country branches of big London joint stock banks are generally bound down by hard and fast rules. The managers have not the power to grant accommodation without consultation with the "head office", and this means vexatious delays and sometimes serious inconvenience. Moreover, the branch manager of a joint stock bank has not often the sympathy of the private banker, nor the personal knowledge of the applicant which a long acquaintance with his neighbours gives the resident private banker.

The Anglo-American Cold Storage Company, Ltd., is making an issue of share capital. A more appropriate title for the undertaking would have been "Count Ward's Relief Fund". The idea seems to be to shift from Count Ward to the public the responsibility of running a cold storage business in Tooley Street. For the privilege the public are asked to pay Count Ward £100,000 in shares for a goodwill that practically has no existence, and £42,500 in preference shares or cash for buildings and machinery which carry a mortgage of £25,000. To ensure the company going to allotment, Count Ward has himself underwritten (for a commission of 10 per cent.) the number of shares required to be applied for by the articles of association before allotment can take place. Count Ward thus appears as vendor, promoter and underwriter—an intolerable position in sound joint stock finance.

INSURANCE: POLICIES AT HIGH PREMIUMS. III.

In our second article we explained the lucrative character of endowment-assurance policies for short periods, such as ten or fifteen years; and in the first article dealing with policies at high premiums we described the good results obtainable from effecting life assurance at a single premium. It is often convenient to combine the two things. A man may save money every year for fifteen years, at the end of which time (if he is living) he receives from the life office a large sum in cash. Then the problem arises what to do with this capital. In many circumstances the best use to put it to is to employ it as a single premium, for a policy under which the sum assured is paid at death whenever it happens. The sum assured in this way will be much larger than the single premium paid; precisely how much larger depends mainly upon the age of the policy-holder at the time of paying the single premium. In cases of this kind it is usually best to take with-profit assurance. The bonuses can either increase the sum assured or be drawn in cash; if drawn in cash, whether bonuses are declared annually or quinquennially, they can be used to yield an income upon the capital outlay involved by the payment of the single premium. This income is relatively small at first, being perhaps 2 per cent. per annum upon the single premium, but it rapidly increases in amount as the policyholder gets older, until it may yield as much as or more than 4 per cent. per annum, in spite of the fact that the sum payable under the policy at death is greatly in excess of the amount paid as a single premium to obtain these benefits. A point that is worth notice is that the cash bonuses paid under a life policy are not, we believe, subject to income tax.

There is another valuable use to which short-period endowment-assurance policies may be put, and that is the provision of education for children. There are many excellent policies especially devised for this purpose, but for the most part they are non-profit contracts and are not on the whole quite so good for the purpose as endowment-assurance policies which participate in profits. Almost any life office will pay the sum assured by instalments spread over a number of years, instead of meeting the claim by a single payment in cash. The companies allow interest on the capital remaining in their hands, and this is a convenient method of obtaining an annual income for, say, five years, during which the expenses of education are the greatest.

Endowment-assurance policies have the further characteristic that in the event of the death of the assured within the endowment period no further premiums have to be paid and the sum assured is due forthwith. Educational annuities can be obtained which have this same provision, that in the event of the death of the parent before the annuities become due no further premiums have to be paid, but the child receives the full benefits of the policy. The value of this provision cannot be over-rated.

The death of a man may make it extremely important for a sum in cash to be available at once; this happens under endowment assurance, but is not the case under the majority of educational annuity policies. Should it be found feasible to devote the sum assured by the endowment policy to the original purpose of education, the fact that the money is available on the death of the parent, and before the greatest expense in connexion with education occurs, the money can be left with the life office or otherwise invested, thus accumulating to a larger sum and making more liberal provision for education.

We have frequently expressed the opinion that many people who take endowment-assurance policies would do better to take whole-life assurance subject to the payment of premiums so long as they live, or for a limited number of years; the reason for this opinion is that often the greatest necessity is for the largest amount of insurance protection in the event of premature death, and this is afforded by whole-life or limited-payment life policies, which, because the rates of premium are lower, assure a greater sum for a given annual outlay. When, however, it is evident that some special expenditure will be incurred at a known date in the future, as for instance for education or at the termination of a lease, then endowment assurance, which provides the necessary money at the necessary time, is the wisest kind of policy to take, and the returns yielded by it are of an exceptionally attractive character.

CONDUCTORS AND THEIR METHODS.

II.—DR. HANS RICHTER.

By Filson Young.

Modern conducting, that is to say the orchestral interpretation of music as a fine art, is a thing not more than fifty years old. It was revolutionised by Wagner and by the school of disciples which he sent out into the world to demonstrate his methods. The chief of these, von Bülow, did not live long enough to realise how far the new influence was destined to spread; but his colleague, Hans Richter, has lived to see the second generation of conductors spring up, and the art of which he is the living head develop possibilities which even von Bülow and Wagner probably never realised. Richter is so great that he can never become obsolete; but it is probably true that his method in any other hands than his own would already be regarded as old-fashioned, and those who should imitate his technique would find themselves taking up a wand that in their hands was lifeless.

A great many adjectives have been used in the attempt to fix and define the peculiar quality of Richter's genius as a conductor. The statement that he is a past master at his own business is not sufficient; for although his immense experience, and the numberless resources for meeting an emergency which are always at the command of the "old hand" would in themselves be enough to give him a unique position of authority among orchestral players, they would not account for his power over audiences often ignorant of the technicalities in which he works. It is his personality which accounts for that. There is a massive plebeian impassiveness in the very round of his back that suggests the peace and security, not only of the individual, but of a whole race of men. One might find grander terms for it, and yet do him less justice than by describing his principal attribute as an immense stolidity; stolidity allied to a prodigious slow momentum or power of going unsensitively on to the goal he has in view. Thus he not only arrives himself, but he sees that those under his command arrive with him.

His technical methods in conducting are wonderfully different from those of the ultra-modern school, although to many of them he has been the chief inspiration. The large wadded pole which he wields is not more different from the slender wand of Nikisch than is the ponderous stability of the one man from the volatile energy of the other. It is a saying attributed to Richter that he never makes two beats where one will do, never beats four in a bar where he can hold his rhythm together by beating two; and this is characteristic of the man and of his interpretations. This method means often the sacrifice of some very fine detail, or rather it means the necessity of trusting for it entirely to the player. For where a detailed phrase occurs on the fourth beat of a bar in which the conductor is only beating two or even one, it is impossible that he should control the player's phrasing. But it also makes for a large simplicity and coherence in the outline of the whole piece; and it is in the achievement of that outline that Richter is always supreme and never fails. He often seems to miss fine points, phrases the value of which has been discovered and exhibited by conductors whose mind is bent more on detail; but you never, in any performance conducted by Richter, fail to obtain a definite impression of a composition as a whole. Your impression may be right or wrong, or, let us say, more right or less right according as the music is of the kind that Richter himself understands and sympathises with; but it will never fail of a meaning of some kind, consequently it will never bore you or seem dreary as the same work might if presented by another conductor in a long series of brilliant episodes, each interesting in itself, but all remaining detached and incoherent at the end.

Undoubtedly the best place to study Richter's methods, and the place in which his qualities are most splendidly exhibited, is the Opera. He is the "old hand" there with a vengeance; of all the disconcerting accidents that can occur in the performance of an elaborate Wagnerian opera there is not one that has not happened to him already, there is not one that can disconcert him or for a moment disturb his phlegmatic security. The most nervous player can hardly fail to be reassured by that heavy motionless figure and grave incurious countenance; in the most tempestuous moments of musical storm and dramatic commotion he sits at his desk controlling it all, like an old scholar reading in a lamplit room. Nothing moves but the arm, except that occasionally the grave countenance and beard slowly revolve in a half circle to left or right; but behind the spectacles are eyes, weary-looking at all other times, that can be trained upon defaulting players with gimlet sharpness. He is utterly indifferent to applause; at the end of a great performance of "The Ring" he will step down from his desk, and look up at a house shouting with enthusiasm for him alone, with a countenance no more expressive of emotion than that of a cow looking over a fence. It is at once comic and grotesque and sublime, but it is much more sublime than anything else.

And if the Opera is his kingdom, "Meistersinger" is his throne in that kingdom. He is a part of "Meistersinger" as much as Pogner or Eva or Sachs; when he takes up the stick the whole of that great music seems to flow out spontaneously, inevitably, like a banner unrolled at his bidding. There is the place to study his method and his power of achieving an outline; there is the place to observe his peculiar methods of obtaining a climax, his manner of treating a long crescendo or diminuendo so that there is always a sense of something kept in reserve at the end of it; there, in a word, is the place to make a study of human achievement and mastery, of what can be done by work and enthusiasm and simplicity of purpose in this world of dissipated forces. The great conductor of the future ment and mastery, of what can be done by work and emotional magnetism of his age the dignity, the simplicity, and the humbleness of this man Hans Richter; it will be a task worth attempting.

AT THE GAIETY.

By Max Beerbohm.

I AM elderly enough to have seen two or three of the old Gaiety burlesques, though I am young enough not to weep bitterly over the reminiscence—young enough not to feel that the Gaiety, as it is to-day, insults my heart. To me, indeed, the place's main charm seems to be in its abiding likeness to what it was in the dear dim past. What though "the Sacred Lamp" has been snuffed out, and the arc-lamp of musical comedy installed? What though the old walls have fallen, and others have arisen on their site? The spell has not been broken. The old traditions still linger. The spirit, the "note", is as it always was. The temple stands true to its name, and true to that special and peculiar sort of gaiety with which we have always associated it. What though the masterpieces of literature and drama be guyed no more there? Gone are the rhymed couplets, and the puns, and other things that are sweet in retrospect: what matter? These were but the trappings and gauds that the Muse was decked in. Soul and body, she is her same old self.

It is easy to recognise, hard to define, the "note" of the Gaiety. One reason why the place is irresistible is that nowhere else do we feel that we are so far away, and so harmlessly and elegantly far away, from the realities of life. We are translated into a sphere where the dwellers have nothing whatever to think about, and would be incapable of thought if there were need for it. Nothing jars there. All the people (except the ladies of the chorus, whose languor is part of the fun) are in the highest spirits, with no chance of a re-action, yet never in the extravagance of their joy do they become loud, or infringe the bye-laws of deportment: they are all graceful and tuneful. They are all of them refined, though not in the least like "ladies" and "gentlemen" in actual life. They have a school, a higher school, of their own. Some of them are supposed to impersonate the aristocracy, others the proletariat; but in point of refinement there is nothing to choose between them: never a crude word or gesture. And all classes mingle on the easiest of terms. Every one wants every one else to have a good time, and tries to make everything easy and simple all round. This good time, as I need hardly say, is of a wholly sexual order. And yet every one, from the highest to the lowest, is thoroughly "good". The most attractive of the men do no harm to the ladies who love them at first sight. Not less instantaneous than theirs are the conquests made by the most unattractive men. A homuncule, made up to look as absurd as possible, has only to come by and wink at the bevy of lovely ladies to whom he is a perfect stranger, when behold! their arms are about his neck, their eyes devour him, they languish and coo over him, and will follow him to the world's end in deference to his wish for a good time. But be sure he will take no vile advantage. Absurd though he looks, he has his code of honour, like the rest, and never outsteps the bounds of that innocent libertinism which is the rule of Gaiety-land. Evil here is as remote as what we call propriety; and goodness and a good time go hand in hand. Gaiety-land is the Mohammedan paradise, reorganised on a perfectly respectable basis. Emotion is not more alien from its inhabitants than thought. True, there is always a thread of humdrum human love-story woven into the fabric of these plays. In "Our Miss Gibbs" there appears now and again a young man, with a Guards' riband round his straw hat, saying, in reference to Miss Gibbs, "I love her, and want to make her mine", quite soulfully. But who heeds him, or cares twopence whether the marriage will take place? In so far as we notice him at all, we do but deplore that any one so cloddish should have strayed into this ethereal domain.

The fact that in these plays (being what they are, an appeal to our eyes and to our sense of fun) there is no hint of love except "pour le bon motif", is what most of all bewilders Frenchmen when they visit the Gaiety. They cannot understand how an entertainment of this kind can be kept going without more or less explicit ribaldry; and, when they return to their own shores, it is always the Gaiety that abides in their memory as the most amazing of all our amazing institutions. Also, they never can get over their surprise at the lightness, the vivacity, the exquisite technical accomplishment, of the chief performers. These qualities they had deemed to be inalienably Parisian. And certainly nowhere in London are they to be found in such high degree as at the Gaiety. They are in the air there—have been so since the time of Nellie Farren and Fred Leslie and Kate Vaughan. They are a tradition, handed down through James Lonnen and Lettie Lind. They admirably survive in Miss Gertie Millar, Mr. Edmund Payne, and Mr. George Grossmith. Miss Millar, though her charm is so distinctly original, is not, certainly, a born comedian; but she has achieved an exquisite style in comedy, of a kind precisely fitted to the tasks laid on it; and this, with her charm, is all-sufficient. One cannot imagine her at any theatre but the Gaiety, nor imagine the Gaiety without her. Mr. George Grossmith has brought his innate comedianship to a fine point now; and his singing and dancing are perfect of their kind. I am told that the song "Yip-i-yiddy-i-yay" was imported from America; it may have been; but as rendered by Mr. Grossmith it becomes a pure symbol of the very spirit of the Gaiety; monumental, in its airy way; banality raised to the sublime. Mr. Edmund Payne, by temperament and physique, belongs rather to the music-halls (where he would certainly have outshone all but Dan Leno). But he, too, has schooled himself in the traditions of the Gaiety, and is a worthy *sociétaire*. All the minor parts in "Our Miss Gibbs" are played by people who have been carefully trained to produce the traditional effects. But, as always, the surpassing delight is the chorus. The look of cold surprise that overspreads the lovely faces of these ladies whenever they saunter on to the stage and, as it would seem, behold us for the first time, making us feel that we have taken rather a liberty in being there; the faintly cordial look that appears for the fraction of an instant in the eyes of one of them who happens to see a friend among us—a mere glance, but enough to make us all turn with servile gaze in the direction of the recipient; the splendid nonchalance of these queens, all so proud, so fatigued, all seeming to wonder why they were born, and born so beautiful. . . . I remember that when "The Belle of New York" was first produced in London every one prophesied that the example of that bright, hard-working, athletic American chorus would revolutionise the method of the chorus at the Gaiety. For a while, I think, there was a slight change—a slight semblance of modest effort. But the old local tradition soon resumed its sway, and will never be overthrown; and all the Tory in me rejoices.

A VIGIA.

By R. B. Cunninghame Graham.

WHEN the old Spanish navigators, sailing in virgin seas, uncharted, undeflowered by keels, passed by some islet about which they were doubtful, seeing it dimly as the mist lifted for a moment, or in the uncertain light of the false dawn, they called it a Vigia, a place to be looked out for, and their old charts are dotted here and there with the Vigia of the Holy Spirit, the Trinity, the Immaculate Conception, or the Exaltation of the Cross.

Their followers, sailing with ampler knowledge but less faith, kept a look-out for the mysterious shoals or islets, not often finding them, unless they chanced to run upon them in the dark and perish with all hands. These were Vigias of the seas, but there exist Vigias of the mind, as shadowy and as illusive, to the full, as any that Magellan, Juan de la Cosa, or Sebastian Cabot marked upon their charts. We all know of such islands, low lying, almost awash, as it were, in the currents of the mind. On them we make our land-fall when we choose, without a pilot, except memory, to guide us in the darkest night. We land and roam about alone, always alone, for those who once inhabited them and welcomed us whenever we sailed in, are now all harboured. Commonly we stay but little there, for though the men we knew are dead, their ghosts so jostle us that we are glad once more to re-embark and sail again into a world of noise, that modern anæsthetic of the mind, still knowing that one day we must return and swell the shadowy procession that walks along the shores of their dead, saltless seas. There is an island, whose whereabouts I do not care precisely to reveal, although only a little strait divides it from a land of mist, of money-making, a land of faiths harder by far than facts, and yet, there it rides swaying on the sea like some great, prehistoric ship, looking out westward in the flesh, and with the interior vision straining its eyes to keep its recollection of the past fresh and undimmed. Green grass, white sands, limpid blue seas, with windows here and there of palest green in them, through which you look into the depths and count the stones, watch sea anemones unfold like flowers, and follow the minutest fish at play fathoms below your boat; these keep it fresh, old and uncontaminated. One likes to think of virgin souls, and so I like to think of this oasis in the desert of the sea as virgin, in spite of tourists, steamboats and the stream of those who go to worship and defile. They have the power to trample down the grass, to leave their sandwich papers and their broken bottles in the ling, but the fresh wind coming across a thousand leagues of sea eludes them. That they can never trample down. So may a woman in a brothel be the mattress of the vilest of mankind and keep some corner of the soul still pure; for it is dull, befitting only to the spirit of the so-called wise, to say the age of miracles is dead. Those who have kept their minds unclogged with knowledge know that they never cease.

So old my island is that it seems young—that is, it still preserves an air as of an older world, in which men laboured naturally just as a bee makes honey; a world where the chief occupation of mankind was to look round them as the Creator did in Eden and to find all things good. So they pass all the morning, meeting their fellows and saluting them, and in the afternoon re-pass and re-salute, then work a little in the fields, lifting up hay upon a fork with as much effort as an athlete in a circus raises a cannon in his teeth, till it is time to sit down on a stone and watch the fishing-boats return upon the tides, the steersman sitting on the gunwale with his knee jammed against the tiller, and the sheet firmly knotted round a thwart. Just as of Avila, it might be said of my Vigia, that it is all made up of saints and stones, for not a stone is without its corresponding saint or saint without his stone. Thus in both places does the past so dwarf the present, that things which happened when the world was young seem just as probable as the incredible events we see before our eyes.

Upon a mound that looks out on a sandlocked bay the heathen crucified some of the new faith a thousand years ago, bringing as we might think their crosses with them ready made or rigging up a jury cross, fashioned from spars and oars, for not a tree grows, or has ever grown, upon the island where now the sheep feed peacefully on the short, wiry grass broken with clumps of flags. A little further on fairies appeared the other day, not to a man herding his sheep and dazed with solitude, but to a company of men who all declare they saw the Little People seated upon a mound. Fairies and martyrs both seem as natural as does the steamer landing its daily batch of tourists to hurry through the street where the kings sleep under their sculptured stones, gaze at the Keltic crosses and the grey, time-swept church which lies a little listed, as it were, to starboard, upon the grassy slope where once there stood the wattled temple of the

Apostle of the Isles. The mud-built church, where the Apostle chanted his last Mass, is nearer to us than the cathedral, now being killed with care. We see the saint lie dying, and his white, faithful horse approach and make its moan and, bowing down its head, ask for his blessing, as is recorded by the chronicler, with that old, cheerful faith in the impossible that kept his world so young.

So standing on the Capitol, the Church, Popes, Cardinals and Saints, the glory of the Middle Ages, the empire, the republic and the kings, melt into mist and leave us, still holding, as our one sure possession, to the two children suckled by the wolf. Some men, like Ponce de Leon, have sailed to find the fountain of eternal youth, landed upon some flowery land, left it, and died still searching, all unaware the object of their quest, had it been found, would have left paradise a waste. There in my island, whose longitude and latitude, for reasons of my own, I keep a secret, there is, I think, some fountain in which those who bathe recover, not their youth, but the world's youth, and ever afterwards have their ears opened to the voices of the dead.

So, seated on the ground amongst the flowers that grow in miniature amongst the grass, bedstraw and tormentil, upon the cairn-topped hill from which the saint of Gartan saw his vision, they see the history of the isle acted before them, as in an optic mirror of the mind. The setting still remains just as it was when the Summer Sailors from the north fell on the peaceful monks one day in June, twelve hundred years ago, and sacrificed them and their prior to their offended gods. The thin, white road which cuts the level machar into two, has probably replaced an earlier sheep track or a footpath of the monks. The dazzling white houses, with their thatched roofs secured against the wind by stones slung in a rope, only require a little more neglect to fall again into the low, black Pictish huts. The swarthy people, courteous and suave, in whom you see a vein of subcutaneous sarcasm, as they lean up against a house, sizing the passing stranger up to the last tittle at a glance, would all look natural enough with glibs of matted hair, long saffron Keltic shirts and the Isles kilt, made out of a long web of cloth, leaving the right arm bare.

Still in the Isle of Dreams remains the primitive familiarity between the animals and man, which only lingers on in islands or in the regions where no breath of modern life has set a bar between two branches of the same creation with talk about the soul. The still, soft rain yet blots the island from the world, just as it did of yore, and through its pall the mysterious voices of the sea sound just as menacing and hostile to mankind, as they did when the saint preached to the seals upon the reef. Perhaps—who knows?—he preaches yet to those who have the gift of a right hearing of the soft, grating noise the pebbles make in a receding wave upon the beach. The wind continues its perpetual monsoon, blowing across the unpolluted ocean for a thousand leagues. In the white coves the black sea-purses which the tide throws up like necklaces of an antique and prehistoric pattern are spread upon the sands, waiting the evening when the mermaids issue from the waves and clasp them round their necks. Soft wind and purple sea, red cliffs and greenest grass, the echoing caves and mouldering ruins, with the air of peace, all make the islet dreamlike, sweet and satisfying.

To have seen it once, is to have seen it to the last day of one's life. The horses waiting at the rough pierhead to swim a mile of channel with its fierce, sweeping tide, the little street in which the houses spring from the living rock which crops up here and there and forms a reef right in the middle of the road, are not a memory, but a possession, as real as if you held the title-deeds duly engrossed and sealed. When all is said and done, the one secure and lasting property a man can own is an enchanted city such as one sees loom in the sky, above the desert sands. That, when you once have seen it, is yours forever, and next comes a Vigia, which but appears for a brief moment, in the mind, as you sail past on some imaginary sea.

VATES SACER.

(After Polonsky.)

DRAG thou thy cross athwart the market-place,
Poet, that hast this title at the price
Of carrying such a cross as few men carry.
Keep silence; of barbarians beg no grace;
Suffer not them to approach the sanctuary;
Be no partaker in their sacrifice.

Such hearts as thirst for truth shall hear thy Muse,
Unbidden echoing all their inmost passion,
Sigh back the sigh no ear hath overheard.
She shall not dignify debauch, nor use
The sovereign glamours of her dazzling word
To sell for gold the tinsel foils of Fashion.

And if the mobs be blind, they and their betters,
(The Question and the Thirst, how should they know it?)
And the world be a world that never recked
What's good or bad, but, whilst they flaunt their fetters,
Fancy themselves in ruffling braveries decked . . .
Then be assured that there they have no Poet.

J. S. PHILLIMORE.

BRITISH GAME-BIRDS.

By COLONEL WILLOUGHBY VERNER.

PROBABLY every man who shoots imagines that he knows all about our common game-birds such as pheasants and partridges, although some may be more diffident where a knowledge of capercaillie, grouse, or ptarmigan is concerned. But as a broad rule the ordinary shooting man's acquaintance with our game-birds and their habits is limited to those days in the year, few or many, according to circumstances, when he finds himself posted for a drive or walking a turnip field; whilst only a comparatively small minority know anything whatever about rearing game or the life history of the birds whose death bulks so largely in the existence of the shooter. Even those select few who personally supervise the rearing of their game, and who in this and in other ways are in touch with their birds throughout the various seasons of the year, will find in this book of Mr. Millais a mass of information about our game-birds, from the splendid capercaillie down to the diminutive quail, which cannot fail to be as valuable as it is attractive. Never before has the whole life-history of our game-birds been told with such completeness of knowledge as is shown throughout this book.

Owing to the marvellous advances in recent years in the art of colour reproduction, the beautiful plates of these our most beautiful game-birds are presented with marvellous fidelity. The manner in which Mr. Thorburn has in every instance laid the scene of his picture in some wild spot which it is quite easy to see must be the home of the birds he depicts is simply delightful. For the birds form part of the magnificent scenery, and the scenery is the setting to the birds. Nor are Mr. Millais' fine black-and-white pictures of the birds in their favourite haunts one whit behind the others, and in every case, as is his wont, he grasps their life and action in a manner which is beyond criticism.

The book begins with the capercaillie, an aboriginal of our islands, which, becoming extinct towards the end of the eighteenth century, was happily reintroduced from the Continent forty years later, and is now more than holding its own. Mr. Millais gives a peculiarly good picture of one of these grand birds skimming over the tree-tops in a pine forest, and he graphically describes how, when thus flying, they are constantly missed by those unaccustomed to shoot them, their great bulk and easy flight causing a totally incorrect estimate of their pace, which far exceeds what it appears to be. I have seen exactly the same mistake made

* "The Natural History of British Game-Birds." By J. G. Millais. London: Longmans. 1909. £8 8s. net.

when driving great bustard, and it is simply astonishing how frequently these enormous birds are missed by those who have not seen them on the wing before, and for the identical reasons given by Mr. Millais in the case of the capercaillie. Another point of similarity between these two great game-birds is, according to Mr. Millais, that in spite of their brave " display " and pugnacious demeanour capercaillies never seem to fight seriously. This is precisely what I have noted with regard to the great bustard. Why capercaillies should avoid fighting, when their relatives, both the black and the red grouse, indulge in such furious combats, is a puzzle.

Prince Fürstenburg contributes an admirable description of the male capercaillie indulging in his " love-song " on the summit of a pine-tree, giving with considerable skill the phonetic rendering of the various notes. This account recalls to my memory most vividly how poor Crown Prince Rudolf of Austria, after a cheery dinner, surrounded by his ornithological friends, used to impersonate the love-sick capercaillie, including the final " cork-drawing " and " knife-sharpening " notes, so well described by Prince Fürstenburg. It is when emitting these last notes that the great bird is in such a state of frenzy as to become utterly deaf and oblivious to all the world, including his most dangerous enemy, the shooter. It is by taking advantage of these brief, yet repeatedly recurring, intervals that the sportsman in Austria and the Tyrol, by means of a succession of advances of three rapid steps, and no more, gets within gunshot of this wary bird. Many Englishmen affect to despise the man who thus approaches his game and kills it by a " pot-shot ". Yet to do so demands an amount of woodcraft and observation of wild birds which is most assuredly lacking in all but a very few of our shooters. Mr. Millais remarks incidentally that the Austrians view the slaying of a female capercaillie as most unsportsmanlike. He also calls attention to the curious mistake made by the late Mr. Howard Saunders when describing the song of the capercaillie, a mistake industriously copied by other writers. In advocating the shooting of blackcock with a small .22 rifle he shows some courage, for it is a method which the average shooting man will deride, but one which requires both " great skill and the employment of the hunter's instinct, the two great essentials of true sport ". In this I am most heartily with him, and without doubt it is these same essentials which prompt some of our keenest sportsmen to view snipe- and wildfowl shooting in a wild country as the very highest form of bird-slaying.

The chapters on grouse are fascinating, and abound with useful information. I wonder, by the way, how many people know that the " heather ", so-called, on the Yorkshire grouse-moors is neither heath nor ling, but crowberry! Mr. Millais, in spite of his great knowledge of birds, no doubt intentionally repeats the ornithological crime which so exercised Professor Alfred Newton, Lord Lilford, Colonel Irby, and other famous bird-men. For on page 55 he talks about a " Mallard drake ". I am ready to admit that every Mallard is a Wild Duck, but most certainly every Wild Duck is not a Mallard nor ever will be! It is perfectly true that many minor naturalists have elected to use the false quantity. Mr. Henry Seebohm did so. In the Fourth Edition of Yarrell Mr. Howard Saunders followed suit, much to the wrath of the distinguished naturalists mentioned above. But it was not till he brought out his " Manual of British Birds " (an abridgment of Yarrell) that he justified his departure from the path of orthodoxy by announcing that he followed American naturalists. It is hard to imagine a more unconvincing argument for doing what is obviously incorrect and in defiance of all the rules of etymology and derivation. Small wonder that Colonel Irby satirically dubbed this book—excellent as it is in many ways—" The Boy's Yarrell ". The undisputed fact remains that the word Mallard comes from " the French malart, the name of the male of the Common Wild Duck ", and to employ it as the name of the species and to talk of a Mallard drake and a Mallard duck is no less incorrect and absurd than to call the male of the Black Grouse a Blackcock cock, and the female a Blackcock hen! Curiously enough, there is a comical justification of my plaint later on in his book, for on page 98, when discussing the deeply interesting problem of the selection of mates among wildfowl, Mr. Millais says he " put ten Mallards into a pen ", to watch them selecting their mates. I read on, naturally expecting to hear about an adjacent pen with ten Wild Ducks, until it suddenly dawned upon me that half the " Mallards " were ladies!

The story of the Pheasants is a most fascinating one and well told, although bewildering to a degree where the question of determining the various species is concerned. The very latest authorities state that there are over twenty different species and sub-species. But whether we accept the maximum of twenty-three or the minimum of six is immaterial, for surely they must be all originally referable to the same species. Mr. Millais makes a gallant attempt to solve the vexed question by saying that when two distinct types of pheasants, occupying different districts normally, overlap and do not interbreed, they are entitled to specific rank. It sounds well enough, and may possibly apply in certain cases, but one's thoughts at once go back to the famous case of our black Carrion Crows and Grey Hooded Crows, which, normally inhabiting different portions of the earth's surface in the Old World, and accepted as well-defined species in each of these, in the regions where they overlap most assuredly do interbreed and with success.

With regard to our British race of pheasants, there can be little doubt that before long it will be composed, in the main, of the old dark-necked variety, which is believed to have been indigenous, and is known to have been here since the days of the Romans, crossed with the white-ringed or Chinese Pheasant, which was only introduced about a hundred years ago, and which has practically overmastered the ancient race. These are already much blended with the beautiful green Japanese Pheasant and the Mongolian race, all four species crossing readily and producing fertile hybrids. In certain localities there will undoubtedly be an admixture of several of the other species so beautifully figured in this book. Anyway, the upshot will be the production of a magnificently coloured and powerfully flying pheasant—that " sacred bird " which Sir William Butler has humorously described as having been more prejudicial to the efficiency of the training of the British Army for war than all the blunders of the War Office combined with all the ravages of cholera, typhoid fever, dysentery and other complaints.

Beautiful as are the plates and complete as is this history of our Game Birds, I would ask Mr. Millais to undertake the Life History of yet one more species, one that for centuries was more thoroughly British than some of those he describes and which only became extinct during the last century owing to the enclosing of our wild and open spaces. I mean the Great Bustard. No more magnificent game-bird flies, nor does any lend itself by its extraordinary " display " in the courting season to portrayal in more marvellous attitudes.

So also with the even more beautiful Lesser Bustard. The habits and habitats of both species on the brilliantly coloured flower-strewn vegas of Southern Spain, and amid its glorious sunshine, lend themselves with peculiar effect to such masters in the art of depicting game-birds in their haunts as Mr. Thorburn and Mr. Millais have proved themselves in this volume to be.

THE LASKER-JANOWSKI CHESS MATCH.

By Emanuel Lasker.

No name is more widely known among chess-players than that of Philidor, the French composer of light opera, who lived during the middle and nearly to the end of the eighteenth century. His book, " L'Analyse ", the first systematic treatise on the game, is famous. The principles that he there maintained are acknowledged. A pretty checkmate that frequently occurs with amateurs, and in masters' games is often an influence as a threat, is known in Anglo-Saxon countries by the name of the celebrated Frenchman. This is an honour such as belongs to no other master. The leading player after Philidor, Labourdonnais, was also of French nationality. His series of games with MacDonnell belongs to the classics of chess. France held among all the nations the undisputed sway of the chess-board until the middle of the nineteenth century. Then Staunton beat St. Amant in a match and gave the chess championship to England. In 1851 the German Anderssen took the honour away from Staunton; but he was defeated, seven years afterwards, by Paul Morphy, a French American from New Orleans, in a celebrated match that aroused the attention of "tout Paris." These were days when chess flourished in France. A chess-board was then in every good French family. Morphy was for a time a hero in Paris society. Napoleon and his son were fond of the game, and they set a fashion.

After this period of splendour several causes brought about the decline of French chess. The outcome of the war of 1870, in forcing the attention of the French upon practical needs, dwarfed their instinct for playing. Women had never understood the game. The powerful stimulus of their attention favoured the athletic sports. No great French master arose during the latter part of the nineteenth century. The love of country would have extended to the representative of the French chess-board, and have made the young enthusiastic, but there was no Frenchman to achieve victories over the champions of other nations. The vacant throne of French chess was then taken up by foreigners resident in Paris. Baron of Kolisch, Neumann, Rosenthal, and Janowski succeeded each other in that capacity. They did not stop the decay of French chess. It is true that Rosenthal was the teacher of Prince Louis Napoleon, that he was professionally attached to the wealthy "Grand Cercle des Echecs", latterly called "Grand Cercle", and that, in the year of the Exposition (1900) he arranged an international tournament at this club; but Frenchmen had little part in all this. The foreigner resident in France brought, perchance, his love of chess with him and founded a few chess circles in Paris. Baron of Kolisch, Neumann, Rosenthal, and young generation ignored the game entirely.

Latterly, however, a new movement has set in, destined to make the game popular among all nations that favour the spirit of progress. Numerous chess clubs have arisen in England, Germany, all the Slavish nations, Hungary, Italy, Egypt, South Africa, Australia, New Zealand, the United States, the Argentine; the membership of the old chess clubs has grown. Simultaneously with this movement—probably instigated by it—another has set in; a new type of chess master has come to the fore. The modern chess master, young in years, self-confident, sceptical of old authority, imaginative, energetic, shrinking before no obstacle, is pushing his investigations so far as to have already entirely altered, and certainly much improved, the manner of conducting the play. The public, that formerly admired the chess master as a genius whose laws were incomprehensible, begins to understand his work; and there is a vivid counteraction between it and him. The literature of chess, though more than a thousand years old, has in the last two decades doubled in size, and it has a large circulation. The cause of this new interest is, I believe, an influence that will last. The people in many parts of the world desire an active share in the management of their politics, commerce, education. The struggle for life and for progress has become more animated. Chess is the game of strategy "in abstracto". It is an outlet for the growing combative instincts and a teacher of strategy as well.

The effect of this movement is just beginning to show itself in France. A French chess club, the "Cercle Philidor", has a large membership. Billecard, a French chess master, has shown decided talent. In the art of composing artistic end games the Frenchman, H. Rinck, belongs to the set, Troitzky, Behting, the brothers Pawlow, whose work is known and enjoyed by tens of thousands. The Comte de Villeneuve is gifted in the same way. Larare worthily represents the art of problem composition. And the average strength of play of the French amateur has made considerable progress.

It is under these conditions and amid these surroundings that a match has been arranged between myself and the French champion, M. Janowski. The rules are as follows: The time limit is fifteen moves an hour. M. Nardus is umpire, M. Goetz director of play. Play takes place at the "Grand Cercle". Winner is he who makes the best score of ten games. The prize is two thousand francs. The honorarium for either contestant is three thousand francs. Play days are six in each week; Sundays are free. The hours for playing are from 2.30 to 7 P.M. each day. Each player has two off days that he can choose whenever he desires. The match commenced on 18 October. Here follow the two games played during the first four days of the match:

White Lasker	Black Janowski	White Lasker	Black Janowski
1. P–K4	P–K4	5. Castles	B–K2
2. Kt–KB3	Kt–QB3	6. R–K	P–Q3
3. B–Kt5	P–QR3	7. B×Kt ch	P×B
4. B–R4	Kt–B3	8. P–Q4	Kt–Q2

The move blocks the QB but frees the KB and the KBP; hence its advantages supervene. If P×P(9), Kt×P, B–Q2, B–Kt5 takes up a strong position.

9. P×P	P×P	11. Kt–B4	P–QR4
10. QKt–Q2	P–KB3		

Obligatory, because Kt–R5 would shut black into a narrow space.

12. B–Q2	P–R5	14. Q–K2	Kt–Q2
13. Kt–R5	R–R3	15. KR–Q	B–K3

Well done. The discovered attack on the queen is only an apparent danger.

16. P–QKt4	RP×P e.p.	18. B–B3	K–B2
17. RP×P	Q–R		

Of course not castles, because P–QKt4, Kt–Q2, Kt×P (menacing Kt×B ch), Q×Kt, Q×R, Q×B, Q×B ch. Now the bishop on K3 is defended.

19. Kt–R4 P–Kt3

If R–Q?, R×R, B×R, Q–R5 ch wins.

20. R–KB	K–Kt2	22. Kt–B5ch	. . . .
21. P–KB4	P×P		

If R×P, Kt–Kt2, and the combination cannot be done because of B–B4 ch. Black has a sufficient defence in either case.

22. . . . . B×Kt

Of course not P×Kt, P×P.

23. P×B	B–Q3	25. R×R	R–K
24. Kt–B4	R×R	26. Q–B3	Q–Q

The attack of white now breaks down, because Kt–K5, threatening both B–B4 ch and Kt×B, takes up a commanding position.

27. Q×P	Kt–K5!	28. Kt×B	Q×Kt

If now Q×R, Q–B4 ch forces Philidor's mate.

29. Q×Q	P×Q	35. P–QKt4	K–K4
30. B–Q4	P×P	36. K–K2	K–B5
31. R–R2	K–B2	37. R–R6	R–KKt
32. P–B3	K–K3	38. K–B3	R–Kt5
33. K–B	R–QB	39. R–R5	Kt–Q7 ch
34. K–K	R–QKt	40. K–B2	Kt–K5 ch

Drawn by repetition of moves.

THE SECOND GAME.

White Janowski	Black Lasker	White Janowski	Black Lasker
1. P–K4	P–K4	6. P–Q3	P–Q3
2. Kt–KB3	Kt–QB3	7. B–Kt5	B×Kt
3. Kt–B3	Kt–B3	8. P×B	Kt–K2
4. B–Kt5	B–Kt5	9. B–QB4	Kt–Kt3
5. Castles	Castles	10. Kt–R4	Kt–B5

In this difficult position the only move that repels white. Black now gets a doubled pawn—if Q–B3, P–KR3, B×Kt, B–Kt5!, Q–K3, P×B followed by P–KKt4—but the Kt on R4 is now misplaced and P–KB4 is prevented, two essential advantages largely counterbalancing the weakness of the pawn.

11. B×Kt (B4)	P×B	12. Kt–B3	. . .

Black threatened Kt×KP.

12. . . .	B–Kt5	13. P–KR3	. . .

In advancing his pawns on the side where he is inferior in strength he facilitates the task of black to make there an inroad.

13. . . .	B–R4	19. R–Kt5	Q–R3
14. Q–Q2	B×Kt	20. R (Kt5)–KKt5	QR–K
15. P×B	Kt–R4	21. P–Q4	P–KB3
16. K–R2	Q–B3	22. R–Kt4	P–Kt3
17. QR–Kt	P–QKt3	23. B–Q3	R–K2
18. R–KKt	K–R	24. P–QB4	. . .

White cannot stir. If R on K14 or Q moves, Kt–Kt2–K3–Kt4 will follow; if the bishop moves, P–KB4 is strong; but the move actually made has also drawbacks, since it leaves for the moment the QP unguarded.

24. . . . Kt–Kt2

This move is decisive. If Q×P, Q×Q, R×Q, Kt–K3 regains the pawn with an excellent position.

25. P–B3 Kt–K3

Menacing the deadly Kt–Kt4.

26. B–B P–KB4 27. QR–Kt2 .

If P×P, R×P black will continue R–KR4 and Kt–Kt4 whenever he pleases. In that case the RP cannot be defended.

27. . . . R–B3

This was a difficult move to discover. P–Kt4, threatening P–Kt5, was apparently much stronger, but would have been repulsed by P×P, R×P, B–Q3, R–B3, P–Q5 and R×KtP. Now, on the contrary, white has no sufficient defence.

28. B–Q3 P Kt4

Threatening mate in two by Q×P ch; if (29) P×P, the same sacrifice would make a mate in three.

29. R–KR P–Kt5

Closing up all hope for white to prevent Kt–Kt4.

30. B–K2 Kt–Kt4 31. KtP×P . . .

If KP×P, R×B; if Q×P, Kt×P ch, K–Kt3, Q–R5 mates.

31. . . . P–B5 32. R–Kt3 P×B

Resigns.

CORRESPONDENCE.

WANTED—A POLITICAL PROGRAMME.

To the Editor of the SATURDAY REVIEW.

74 Grosvenor Road, Highbury, London N.
18 October 1909.

SIR,—If private businesses were conducted as the affairs of the nation are conducted—that is, mismanaged by a House of Commons which, though containing a large number of able men, has been reduced to legislative inefficiency by the violence and animosity of the conflicting interests represented by the several groups into which the two once-great parties in the State have been subdivided—the richest institutions in the country would be ruined in no time. That such a state of things should be allowed to continue without emphatic protest by the people, independently of party ties, is evidence only too convincing of the intellectual apathy and the weakening of the sense of citizenship which are the two great dangers that threaten England at the present time, greater by far than the menace of a German invasion or the yellow peril.

The Unionist party has now a great opportunity before it of regaining the confidence of the country. Will it take advantage of this opportunity? That is the question which those who are more concerned with the general interests of the nation than with the particular interests of groups and sections are asking themselves, not without a certain amount of anxious doubt.

It is not necessary to agree with the political views and opinions of Mr. Winston Churchill in order to recognise the truth of his statement, made in the course of his speech on Saturday last at Abernethy, to the effect that the Unionist party has no policy. It is true that the great bulk of the party is committed to Fiscal Reform, meaning Tariff Reform, and that Mr. Balfour, as leader of the party, has fought a stubborn and courageous battle in the House of Commons against the Budget; but those two items, however important in themselves, do not constitute a sufficient programme on which to go to the country at the next General Election with any hope of success. Rightly or wrongly, the opposition to the Budget has not assumed the proportions of a national movement, and there are signs that a reaction in its favour is taking place, due no doubt less to decreasing dislike of its most objectionable features than to the progressive diminution of fear which always follows growing familiarity with unrealised dangers, imaginary or real.

The clear duty of the Unionist party lies in the construction of a political programme upon which to fight the next General Election. Mr. Balfour, with all his ability and intellectual distinction and alertness, is not an ideal leader. His qualities are largely neutralised by an apparently incurable fondness for very delicate and sensitive intellectual antilibration, delightful in itself because never sinking into casuistry or quibbling, but dangerous to stability and safety, and not understanded of the people, who, with less subtlety and coarser perception, like large, clear issues clearly stated in a form which appeals to their saving virtues of fundamental honesty and common-sense. But whether universally acceptable or not, he is universally accepted as the only possible leader of the party in the House of Commons and in the country, and to him all Unionists should unite in an immediate appeal for the construction of a political programme.

No one not engaged in political life or having otherwise a locus standi can hope to say or suggest anything at all likely to influence those who have a voice in the counsels of the party; and yet there are questions on which the plainest of plain men, the man in the street, as he is now more commonly called, can form an opinion for himself without guidance from above. Such a question is the danger of abolishing the veto of an Upper Chamber, however constituted and by whatever name it may be called, and leaving absolute power in the hands of the House of Commons, which, at best, only partly represents the nation's will and sometimes, in practice, does not represent it at all, to say nothing of the occasions on which it misrepresents it altogether. This is inevitable in a system of government by a bare majority, and the danger is increased a thousandfold when that majority, by reason of its size, is entirely mechanical and largely tyrannical. The case against government by majorities was put unanswerably once and for all by the late Archbishop Magee. He said: "I am unable to trust implicitly in the purifying and elevating influenee of the multiplication table, or to believe in the infallibility of the odd man". It may not be possible to get rid altogether, in practice, of the absurdity of assuming the infallibility of a majority, but that absurdity can be greatly reduced by the system of proportional representation, which gives greater weight to the opinions of minorities, fuller representation of the varied interests of the nation, and, by rendering enormous majorities impossible, removes the temptation to use power despotically.

Another question which the plain man can judge for himself is the present inequitable distribution of parliamentary representation. The redistribution of seats would follow, as a corollary, the introduction of the system of proportional representation, and if the further question of reducing the size of the House of Commons—not the Chamber itself but the number of its members—were added to the policy of the Unionist party—a policy which at present, as far as even sympathisers can see, is confined to (1) opposition to the Budget and (2) Tariff Reform, the first most ably presented, the second still, as far as the public are concerned, shrouded in mystery—the party would at least have a programme to which its leaders could appeal with confidence as being constructive, conceived in the interests of good government and therefore in the best interests of the nation at large.

I am, Sir, your obedient servant,
D. N. SAMSON.

IS FRANCE DECADENT?

To the Editor of the SATURDAY REVIEW.

SIR,—My attention has been called to a letter signed "Frenchman" which appeared in your issue of 16 October. This gentleman has, I think, quite mistaken the real meaning of my observations as to "decadentism" in France. I am quite of his opinion that at least two-thirds of the French people (if not more) are still Christians. I was made to realise fully this fact during a recent visit to France, when I saw the churches crowded and noticed from the newspapers that nearly all the marriages and burials among the better classes were still performed with religious rites. In short, I saw sufficient evidences of the continuance of Catholicism in France to be persuaded that had the Catholics of that country chosen to unite in defying the Government which oppresses them and which has done its best to ruin their Church, they could easily have withstood its anti-religious schemes. But, owing mainly I think to the decadent condition into which the pervading influence of rapidly growing neo-paganism has plunged them, they seem to me to be strangely lacking in courage and in a realisation of their numerical force. They have also an unenviable faculty for missing opportunities and playing into the hands of their enemies. Numerically they are far the strongest party, and the richest, for they include nearly the whole of the upper middle class and the aristocracy; yet, from a want of unity and courage, they have allowed themselves to be trampled upon in a manner which (even "Frenchman" must, I think, agree) shows that there is something wrong, and that something I hold to be a growth of decadentism—indifference and pusillanimity. And until the Catholic fellow countrymen and women of your correspondent exhibit a more courageous and manly spirit, I am afraid we must still consider them to be decadents.

Yours truly,
A TRAVELLER.

THE CHEDDAR CLIFFS.

To the Editor of the SATURDAY REVIEW.

The National Trust for Places of Historic Interest or Natural Beauty,
6 October 1909.

SIR,—For the past six or seven years the National Trust has been watching with great anxiety the disfigurement of the Cheddar gorge by extensive quarrying operations. This anxiety has been shared by many; for there are few that know the defile and do not regret the discordant note introduced into the impressive landscape by the sight of the scarred cliff side and the galvanised iron sheds, and by the sound of the steam crusher at work.

In 1903 the Trust made representations to the Somerset Council and other local public bodies on the subject, and as a result the County Council passed a resolution expressing a hope that the natural beauty of the cliffs might be preserved. Similar resolutions were passed by other bodies, including the Cheddar Parish Council. More recently the Somerset County Council, in exercise of their powers under the Advertisements Regulation Act, have made bye-laws to regulate the disfigurement of the cliffs by unsightly advertisements. It is thus made clear that the County Council fully appreciate the value of the gorge as one of the most striking features of the area under its jurisdiction.

But the preservation of the beauty of the cliffs is in reality a matter of more than purely county interest, for the gorge is one of our national "natural monuments".

There is nothing of its kind to compare with it in the South or West of England, and no mountain ravine of the North or of the Continent exceeds it in beauty or is so striking in contrast to the surrounding scenery. In spite of protests, however, the quarry has been continually worked, and the displacement about three years ago of some 50,000 tons of stone is an indication of the extent to which the disfigurement may increase if the quarry continues to be worked on the present scale. As the only method by which the damage may be checked consistently with justice to the rights of all parties, the National Trust has negotiated for the purchase of the property on which the quarry is situated, and now invites subscriptions for this object.

About £600 are still needed and this sum must be raised before Christmas.

It is hoped that readers of the SATURDAY REVIEW will be able to support the Trust, as they have generously supported it in the past, and send their donations to me at 25 Victoria Street, S.W. Cheques should be made payable to the order of the "National Trust" and crossed "National Provincial Bank of England".

I am, Sir, yours faithfully,
NIGEL BOND, Secretary.

[We cordially endorse Mr. Nigel Bond's appeal. Six hundred pounds is a very small sum to save a national possession such as Cheddar gorge.—ED. S. R.]

FRANCIS NEWMAN.

To the Editor of the SATURDAY REVIEW.

28 October 1909.

SIR,—It would seem that "Criticus", in his reply to my letter, prefers to rely on his own unproved conviction that Francis Newman persevered to the end in his repudiation of revealed Christianity rather than give credence to the personal witness of Dr. Martineau, a man whose veracity and reliability of statement have never been questioned, and who was, besides, Newman's close, intimate friend. What can be stronger than this statement of his? He said that he had had a letter from Frank Newman which stated definitely that "when he died he wished it to be known that he died in the Christian faith". If "Criticus" cannot believe the direct asseveration of a man's intimate friend neither would he be convinced by volumes of letters.

I am, Sir, yours faithfully,
J. GIBERNE SIEVEKING.

[We believe that the view of "Criticus" is that of some members of Newman's own family in a position to judge.—ED. S. R.]

CARLYLE AND SHAMS.

To the Editor of the SATURDAY REVIEW.

Springbank, Hamilton, 26 October 1909.

SIR,—In the "Memories of Fifty Years", by Lady St. Helier, just published, she records how Carlyle once offended against conventionality at the Deanery of Westminster, where he was invited to meet Queen Victoria.

It recalls to my mind another story of Carlyle, which not only records an offence of his against conventionality, but shows the determination of the man always to get at the root of things and, in this case, to make of a formal lesson a fruitful study.

It is well known that on the occasions of visits to friends' houses he would rarely be persuaded to attend "family prayers"; but on one occasion his hostess persuaded him to do so, and in honour of a guest so distinguished asked him to read the Bible lesson, which happened to be in the Book of Job. Carlyle became absorbed in the subject, and, regardless of conventional chapter endings, went on and on for what at least seemed to be hours and hours. To the bourgeoise hostess, preoccupied, like Martha of Scripture, about much serving and the household work of the day, which had no connexion with the relations of the patriarch with the universe, this was to take Job's story too seriously, and when through physical exhaustion Carlyle stopped, the household circle, as is sometimes said of a public meeting, broke up in confusion.

Yours faithfully,
JAMES BELL.

[Carlyle's unconventionality reminds us of a peer, lately a member of the Government, who when he reads the lessons at his own church persists in choosing his own chapter and ending the lesson when the fancy takes him.—ED. S. R.]

REVIEWS.

LECKY.

"A Memoir of the Right Hon. W. E. H. Lecky M.P." By his Wife. London: Longmans. 1909. 12s. 6d. net.

WE can imagine no life more satisfying than that of one who, having studied and written the politics of the past, is enabled to assist in the politics of the present. Such a combination of thought and action was achieved by Macaulay and Lecky, and the lives of both were singularly prosperous and happy. Gibbon can hardly be included in the catalogue, for, occupying a sinecure under Lord North, he was for a few years a silent and inactive member of Parliament. Hume and Hallam took no part in politics. Macaulay was of course much greater than Lecky, both in thought and action. Macaulay was a Cabinet Minister, was legal member of the Governor-General's Council in India, and, so long as there are people who read books, his eloquence will stir the blood. Lecky was no rhetorician; he was not a genius; he was a man of untirable industry and of an assiduously developed literary talent. How he would have done as a politician, if like Macaulay he had been popped into a pocket borough at the age of thirty, it is impossible to say. Macaulay began with politics and ended with his history.. Lecky began with his history and ended with politics. A seat in the House of Commons was not found for Lecky until 1895, when he was worn out with his life's work. His success in that assembly was, as might have been predicted, not commensurate with his reputation. He came too late into the callous world of pushing politicians to catch the "Don Juan" tone of the House of Commons. Curiously enough, both Macaulay and Lecky had the same fault as public speakers, that of speaking too fast. But though Lecky was dépaysé in the House of Commons, it would be unjust, as well as mistaken, to underrate the great services which he rendered to the Unionist cause in the press and on the platform. As early as 1880 Lecky, who started life as an admirer of Gladstone, awoke to the dangerous and unscrupulous character of that statesman's Irish policy. The Land Act of 1881 made Lecky a Conservative; and throughout the strenuous years between 1885 and 1895 the authority of his name, his letters to the "Times", his articles in the magazines, and his occasional speeches at meetings were powerful auxiliaries to the defeat of Home Rule.

We have inverted the order of Lecky's life, and dealt first with his political action. As an author he won an unusually early success. Born in Ireland in 1838, he was educated at Cheltenham and Trinity College, Dublin. He was not a dreamer, and began reading voraciously and methodically as soon as he had taken his degree, living a good deal in the south of Europe with his stepmother, Lady Carnwath. In 1865, when Lecky was in his twenty-seventh year, he published his first work, the "History of Rationalism", and it had an instant success, which was repeated and increased by his "History of European Morals" four years later. It is seldom indeed that a young author establishes his reputation by his first and second books. But Lecky's vast information and impartiality were recognised at once. And his method was at that time new. The two books, Lecky tells us, belong to the school of Comte and Buckle. "They are an attempt to examine the merits of certain theological opinions according to the historical method", that is, the writers of this school "especially believe that intellectual belief has not been due merely to arguments or other intellectual causes, but has been very profoundly modified in many curious ways by social, political and industrial influences". These books may live, because they are a mine of curious facts; with their method we have long been familiar. Buckle's fame has almost vanished, because he absurdly underrated the influence of the individual. Lecky avoided this fault, without running into Carlyle's other extreme of hero-worship. At thirty Lecky was the fashionable young philosopher of the hour. Ten years later, having married the author of this memoir, he settled down in Onslow Gardens to the work of his life, the "History of England during the Eighteenth Century", to whose eight volumes he devoted nineteen years. It would be absurd within the limits of this article to attempt a criticism of that history. Lecky's style is devoid of rhetorical ornament; his accuracy has never been disputed; the impartiality of his judgments extracts admiration from his political opponents. Perhaps the Irish parts are the most valuable, because it is so difficult to find an impartial history of Ireland. Though it lacks condensation, such a work can never die, until at all events Britons cease to take any interest in their past, a result that may be produced by board schools and halfpenny newspapers. We much regret for the sake of his reputation that Lecky wrote his last two books. In "Democracy and Liberty" Lecky says in two volumes what Sir Henry Maine had perfectly said in one. Maine's "Popular Government" is really the last word against Democracy, just as Mill's book is the last word in favour of Liberty. It is not possible to add to or improve upon what those great philosophers have said upon those subjects. "Democracy and Liberty" discovers Lecky's worst literary fault, diffuseness. "The Map of Life" is still further below the high-water mark of the History. Lecky had not mixed enough with the world, he had not seen enough of the seamy side of life, his virtue was too much "a cloister'd and fugitive virtue", to equip him for the perilous task of advising his fellows as to the course they should hold "on life's vast ocean". The library and the dinner-tables of the intellectuals are not a good conning-tower. Consequently "The Map of Life" is streaked with the obvious and the conventional, and sometimes is quite away from the centre of the subject. Lecky did not know, or had forgotten, the best things that had been said about ethics.

Mrs. Lecky has done her task exceedingly well. We cannot pay her a higher compliment than to say that it is executed with masculine judgment and skill. There is no indiscreet eulogy, and her own opinions of men and matters show a rare knowledge of society and politics. Of Mrs. Lecky's fairness and common-sense we cannot give a better idea than by quoting a sentence from one of her husband's letters, which she has allowed to stand: "After the ladies had gone up, my two philosophers (Huxley and Spencer) got into a most animated dispute about the inferiority of women in every respect, both, indeed, asserting it, but Huxley attributed it chiefly to the struggle for ascendency in the first human stage; Spencer to the expenditure of forces in generation. Huxley is very strongly of opinion that men are greatly superior to women, not only intellectually, but also morally, and in point of beauty, which must be very consolatory to us".

SHAKESPEARE AND HIS ENVIRONMENT.

"Montaigne and Shakespeare, and other Essays on Cognate Questions." By John M. Robertson M.P. London: Black. 1909. 7s. 6d. net.

MR. J. M. ROBERTSON'S "Shakespeare and Montaigne" contains a revised and expanded version of the essay of the same name published as a volume in 1897, with the addition of two shorter essays, "The Originality of Shakespeare" and "The Learning of Shakespeare", now first appearing in book form. The title scarcely does justice to the book. It does, indeed, deal at great length with the question of Shakespeare's debt to Montaigne and with the arguments of Professor Churton Collins and others against Mr. Robertson's view that this debt was considerable; but it touches a great many other questions, and expresses much of the critic's view of Shakespeare as poet and man, and of the best method of studying him. It is vigorous, albeit perhaps inevitably forensic, writing. Mr. Robertson is a well-read, clever and viewy man; he is always worth listening to. As to the influence of Montaigne on Shakespeare, he certainly strengthens the opinion that the poet had read the essays, at least in Florio's translation, though it is quite possible that the few passages which give the clearest evidence of this might have been suggested by quotations heard in conversation with Ben Jonson or Florio himself. These passages occur in " The Tempest ", " Measure for Measure ", the second quarto of " Hamlet ", and " As You Like It " ; and for the earliest of them Mr. Robertson assumes that Shakespeare had seen, or heard read, the manuscript of the translation which was not published until 1603, the year of the first quarto of " Hamlet ". The cumulative effect of his argument is very strong, although in several points he is obviously dealing only with possibilities, as when he traces " discourse of reason " to Florio, though it had appeared in English books before 1600. But these apparent repetitions of thoughts and even actual phrases, such as " common foppery ", from Montaigne are discussed chiefly to prepare the way for the argument that the essayist exercised a profound general influence upon the maturing Shakespeare's mind. We do not think that this influence is proved. It is certainly possible. It is perhaps the only probable influence which has yet been suggested. But at present it can only be a subject for research and disputation that " the nervous and copious speech of Montaigne " awakened Shakespeare to " a new sense of power over rhythm and poignant phrase, at the same time that the stimulus of the thought gives him a new confidence in the validity of his own reflection ". We know of no other instance of a prose-writer thus improving a poet's command of rhythm, and the point might have been more reasonably made had that improved rhythm been put down to the profounder thought which Mr. Robertson attributes to the influence of Montaigne. The point is repeated much later in the book, but merely repeated. " The poet's nerves ", says the critic, " have felt a new impulsion." This " new impulsion " was possibly due to the reading of Florio's " Montaigne ".

Mr. Robertson lays particular stress upon the probable fact that Shakespeare read the essays in a translation, because he holds the supposition that Shakespeare read French and other languages to be among the erroneous ideas which have let in the Baconian heresy. In " The Learning of Shakespeare " he condescends to the Shakespeare-Bacon, the Shacon or Bakespeare, controversy, and deals some blows which are as clever as they are forcible.

But the main or the most useful purpose of the book is to plead for " the naturalistic conception of Shakespeare as an organism in an environment ". It is as a contribution to this that he offers the suggestion that Shakespeare's culture must have owed much at the central period of his life to some external influence such as the thought of Montaigne. He has, we think, too low an opinion of the earlier stages of Shakespeare's development, and he certainly underestimates the early poems, which he regards as " simply manufactured poems, consciously constructed for the market ", though this assumption does but make the more admirable the sumptuousness of the style, the music and skill of the versification, and the fresh spirit of the whole. He regards Shakespeare's as " a temperament or mentality not at all obviously original or masterly, not at all conspicuous at the outset for intellectual depth or seriousness ", and the deepening and illumination of this temperament is what he wishes to explain. There is still, however, much to be done in making clear what this development was, apart from its causes, and this Mr. Robertson has not taken upon him to attempt. He is content to indicate three or four probable causes—the practice of acting, the influence of a woman or of women, of North's " Plutarch " and of Montaigne. We should like to see these more fully used, and in particular to know on what grounds the critic thinks Plutarch of so much more importance than a mine of precious substance that he seems to attribute to him Shakespeare's " virile treatment of virile problems ". " To the poet ", he says, " has now been added the reader ; to the master of the pathos of passion, the student of the tragedy of universal life." Until this has been attempted the book is incomplete, just as Shakespeare, with his " unparalleled plasticity and receptivity and responsiveness, happily balanced by a fine sanity of judgment ", was incomplete without the contact of Plutarch and Montaigne, according to the view of Mr. Robertson.

A QUEEN OF EVOLUTION.

"Memories of Fifty Years." By Lady St. Helier. London: Arnold. 1909. 15s. net.

THE difference between evolution and revolution is merely the point of view. Widening the basis of society, which Lady St. Helier and Lady Dorothy Nevill welcomed as evolution, was scorned and defied by the old Duchess of Cleveland as revolution. The breaking-down of the barriers began in the reign of the late Lady Waldegrave, and, gathering strength as it advanced, had better be described by Lady St. Helier : " Then of a sudden, as it were, the conventional rules were swept away, and those who had the courage and appreciation to open their houses to everyone who was interesting and distinguished found an ideally delightful society waiting for its new entertainers. Some courage was required to embark on this new enterprise, for society (in the old sense) viewed the step with suspicion and caution. Before long, however, the world began to realise the enormous crowd of brilliant men and women who had hitherto lived unrecognised and unappreciated at their very gates ; and those into whose houses they were welcomed found their rooms filled with distinguished guests, and the beau monde flocking in numbers to make their acquaintance." This process of intellectualising London society is a repetition of what took place in Paris just before the great revolution of the eighteenth century (absit omen !), when philosophers became fashionable ; and Lady St. Helier's position as a leader of the movement is more like that of the great French dames of the period than of the Lady Jerseys and Lady Waldegraves. In other words, Lady St. Helier owes her influence to intellectual sympathy and personal charm rather than to rank and wealth. " Zenobia " might dazzle the outsider by her gilded saloons and splendid retinue ; but it was by other arts that Lady Jeune gathered round her her devoted band of friends. The budding author, the potential Prime Minister, the future Lord Chancellor, however shy or however conceited—they are often the same thing—was instantly put at his ease and made to feel that he was really welcome in Lady Jeune's drawing-room. He would be casually introduced to the great man he was dying to know, and he would be drawn into talking on the subject nearest his heart, his last article, his last speech, his new play, or the cause célèbre in which he had just been briefed. A young man never forgets kindness of this sort, and probably there is nothing, short of murder, which Lady St. Helier could not get done for her if she chose to exert her power. Of course, there are many little contretemps inseparable from the cosmopolitan house, some of them amusing enough, as when Mr. W. E. Forster, having seen Mr. Parnell admitted, was denied the door; and when deadly enemies had to be introduced to one another week after week. We have seen such incongruous persons as Mr. Arthur Roberts and Mr. Arnold-Forster cheek by jowl in the back drawing-room at Harley Street. But the tact, the good breeding, the real benevolence of the hostess were contagious, and there never was anything but good-fellowship and amusement in that house.

The best story is, as usual, about Lord Beaconsfield. Sitting next Disraeli at dinner, Mrs. Jeune said that Lord Sherbrooke must be allowed one virtue, namely, his patient and affectionate behaviour towards his wife. " Do you think ", said Disraeli in his deep tone, " that he has ever seen her ? " A lady who tells you at the beginning of her book that she remembers dining between Dickens and Bulwer Lytton, and, at the end of her book, that she was taken out by Cecil Rhodes, must have had a wonderfully developed judgment of men. We wish sometimes that Lady St. Helier would give us her real opinion of the great ones of the earth who passed through her hands. She cannot really have admired and liked them all. Cecil Rhodes for instance? Altogether, the personal note is too much suppressed in these memories ; we do not know why. The first four chapters, which give us a glimpse of life in the Highlands sixty years ago, when Seaforth was still a real chieftain, and when the author lived with her grandmother at Brahan Castle, are not the least interesting in her book. In these days when the young are taught, not manners, but amusement, we would fain have learned Lady St. Helier's secret of educating girls into charming women. We should have been glad to be told more about the early struggles and professional successes of the late President of the Divorce Court. Lord St. Helier was not only a distinguished judge, but that much rarer thing, a lovable man. From Lord St. Helier there flowed an exquisite courtesy, based on his genuine modesty and his consideration for others. As a conversationalist, whether talking or listening, he was inexhaustible. We should have liked to hear about his traps to catch solicitors in his salad days. But when a dainty feast is spread before one it is unreasonable, and certainly ill-bred, to call for something which is not on the menu. Apart from its being a fascinating record of the past, every woman with social ambition should read this book in order to learn her lesson. But we can tell our imaginary pupil one thing which she will not find set down in these memories. Lady St. Helier owes much of her social success to the faculty of concentrating her mind on the business of the moment. She practises, if she has never read, the golden advice of Chesterfield to his son: "When you are reading Puffendorf, do not think of Madame de St. Germain, nor of Puffendorf when you are talking to Madame de St. Germain."

THE VALOIS AND THE HUGUENOTS.

"The Wars of Religion in France. 1559-1576." By J. Westfall Thompson. Chicago: University Press. London: Unwin. 1909. 21s.

DR. THOMPSON, who is Associate-Professor of European History in the University of Chicago, has produced a work which is the fruit of much research, and will prove useful to English and American students. Though not a book of great originality and power, it condenses in a clear form and enforces the views of the best authorities upon the period. Dr. Thompson has apparently studied the original documents in France, England, and Spain, and supports all his conclusions by quotations and references as amply as could be desired. This is a practice which may be recommended to some other authors who claim to write serious history. But we must raise a protest against the inconvenient size and weight of the volume, which would irritate the most patient reader. Otherwise it is well produced, being adequately illustrated with a few interesting prints and some essential maps, plans, and genealogies.

The period chosen by the author is one of the most confused in European history. With the exception of the story of the Italian Republics, there is probably none that presents such a complicated series of personal feuds and political and military manœuvres. The religious issue was perhaps dominant for a time, but never for long, and in some of the more important episodes it was by no means the principal factor. The feuds of great houses, the struggles of the Crown against the nobles, popular and local sentiment, and the demands of foreign policy all played as great a part as religious fanaticism in the quarrel, and at times were more important. This was so with the best-known episode in the struggle, the massacre of S. Bartholomew. It has for years been an article of faith, at least in non-Roman Catholic countries, that the tragedy was the outcome of a deliberate plot carefully hatched and long maturing. Every student knows now that nothing could be further from the fact. The Guises had been terrified by the prospect of two marriages, of Anjou to Queen Elizabeth and of Henry of Navarre to Marguerite of Valois, which were being urged on by their deadly foe Coligny. France was intriguing against Spain, and in April Alva discovered a letter from Charles IX. to Louis of Nassau promising to employ French armies to liberate the Netherlands. Elizabeth at the same time renounced the French alliance, and Charles then abandoned the Flanders expedition. This made Coligny furious, and he threatened another Huguenot war. Thus the massacre becomes the result of panic on the part of Charles and his mother Catherine. Partly also it may have been done to appease Spain and partly to get rid of Coligny. It was in fact a sudden inspiration of terror, not the outcome of long and deliberate plotting. Indeed, Dr. Thompson thinks that if the attempt on Coligny's life on 22 August had been successful, no massacre would have taken place at all. The Queen and the Guises feared that the Huguenots would rise in order to avenge the attempt on the Admiral's life, and so planned their massacre in order to avert the danger. The idea of giving indubitable proof of her own orthodoxy may have played its part in Catherine's mind as a subsidiary motive. In fact, when politicians get themselves into so embarrassing a tangle as that in which Catherine di Medici found herself in August 1572 they are apt to have recourse to desperate expedients which only make their case worse.

It must not be forgotten that the Parisian populace only wanted leave given them in order to do their part in such a work. Paris was furiously anti-Protestant, and the resolution to "lâcher le grand lévrier" saved the Court a good deal of trouble. Paris wanted no stirring up to massacre Protestants, only permission; it was a genuine act of popular resentment. The Duke of Guise made no concealment of his joy at Coligny's death, but certainly saved some Huguenots himself, and openly expressed his opinion that the King had killed a number of people who might have been very useful to him. What little credit was to be won from the approval of the Pope and Spain, Charles and Catherine no doubt accepted, but the author rightly states that the massacre was a blunder as well as a crime. Catherine was a great intriguer, but not statesmanlike. Had she diverted her ambition to recovering the position of France in Italy instead of endeavouring to conquer Flanders, she might have put before the country a clear issue by which she would have obtained popularity without involving her policy in so many complications with England and the Protestants of the Netherlands. But it was almost impossible for an Italian potentate of the period to pursue a clear course unhampered by motives of personal revenge. To call her a religious fanatic would be to overstate the case ludicrously.

The result of the massacre was a fourth civil war in which the Court was reduced to giving the Huguenots better terms than they could ever have hoped for before it. But their success was due less to themselves than to the assistance the Huguenot cause received from that band of able noblemen known as "Les Politiques", of whom La Noue and Damville were the chiefs and whose importance was much increased by the accession to their ranks of the Duc d'Alençon, the heir to the throne. We should be inclined to say that Dr. Thompson takes an unduly favourable view of this Prince, but he was perhaps the best of the Valois. On the other hand, while he fully acknowledges the difficulties of his environment, he hardly makes allowance enough for their effect on Queen Elizabeth's policy. After all, it was of the utmost importance to this country that her life should be preserved, and if anybody had ventured to ask her why she had indulged in so many fantastic and unreal projects of marriage when her age alone made them almost humiliating, she might have replied with some pride like Sieyès "j'ai vécu". And this was the greatest service she could have rendered to England. Spain was the great danger to France as well as to England; the collapse of either would have left her supreme in Europe. This was indeed the dominating factor both in French and English policy. But fanaticism and policy go ill together, and Elizabeth's policy was never fanatical, while Catherine's sometimes had that appearance; but what of the Huguenots', whose leaders actually proposed in 1575 to make an alliance with the Porte and introduce a Turkish fleet into the harbour of Aigues-Mortes, the port, we may note, whence S. Louis sailed on his crusade?

ALCHEMIST AND SAVANT.

"John Dee." By Charlotte Fell Smith. London: Constable. 1909. 10s. 6d. net.

MOST people have probably thought of Dr. Dee as a picturesque impostor in an age which, having got rid of religion, had taken up with superstition, and, having ceased to believe in the communion of saints, dabbled in necromancy, art-magic and dealings with the Devil. Miss Smith now writes a surprisingly detailed life of the famous alchemist, which depicts him as a quixotically disinterested and high-minded visionary of science. Dee was certainly a marvellously erudite man, whose private collection of books, manuscripts and curios, till it was plundered by a wizard-hunting mob, was of unique interest and value, and who did his utmost to procure the foundation of a State National Library just when it was possible to save the priceless literary riches of the dissolved monasteries from ignorant dispersal and destruction. He addressed to Mary a "supplication for the recovery and preservation of antient writers and monuments", urging the irreparable calamity of the loss of "the treasure of all antiquity and the everlasting seeds of continual excellency within this your Grace's realm". He also offered to set to work at his own charges in procuring copies of famous manuscripts in the royal and ecclesiastical collections of Europe. His own books were always not for himself, but for his friends. Under Elizabeth he endeavoured to bring about the introduction of the reformed Kalendar of Pope Gregory. What is of more immediate interest to the reader of to-day is Dee's advocacy of Admiralty reform and of the establishment, in addition to the Royal Harrys and Dreadnoughts of the day, of a "Petty Navy Royall", to consist of at least three score tall ships, thoroughly equipped and manned, as a "comfort and safeguard to the Realme". The supremacy of England's sea-power is an "incredible political mystery", and her Sovereigns must be "lords of the Seas" not with any aggressive object but for the protection of our commerce, the safeguarding of the world's peace, and in order that our "wits and travayles may be employed at home for the enriching of the Kingdom". All this sounds very modern. Trinity House was foreshadowed in the demand for a "Grand Pilot generall of England".

Potentates and their counsellors, however, were far more eager to get tin turned into gold or horoscopes drawn by the most eminent "mathematician" and astrologer of the age than to take advice about libraries and fleets. The "Polandish lord" Albert à Lasco, palatine of Siradia, carried off Dee and his skryer, the amazing Edward Kelley, from Mortlake to Cracow, and they were afterwards at Prague in the service of the Emperor Rudolph II., searching for the elixir of life and the philosopher's stone. The Tsar Feodor of Muscovy then invited Dee to come and advise about discoveries in the north-east, but Elizabeth in 1589 sent for him to come home. Kelley had been "wanted by the police" and kept out of the way, though Burleigh wrote this kind of letter: "Good Sir Edward Kelley, be assured of worldly reward. You can make yr Queen so happie as no subject she hath can do the like. Good knight, let me conjure you in God's holy name not to keep God's gift from yr natural countrie, but rather help make her Majestie a glorious and victorious power against the mallyce of hers and God's enemies". However, nothing was done for Dee, who for all his alchemy never had gold for his experiments and his books, and begged of friends "to keep us from hunger starving". When the author of "Demonologie" became King, Dee, the reputed "arch-conjurer of the kingdom", was in worse case than ever, and besought James to put him on his trial, being ready "eyther to be stoned to death or to be buried quicke or to be burned unmercifully, if the name of conjurer or caller or invocator of Divels or damned Sprites can be proved to have been duely reported" of him. The laws against sorcery had been sharpened before Elizabeth's death. Dee protested that, so far from being a companion of hell-hounds, he had striven to glorify the Most High in the investigation of the wonderful virtues and properties of His creatures, ever seeking the illimitable heights of knowledge through the spiritual and symbolic element in material things, and helped thereto by God's blessed angels. He held the ancient hermetic doctrine that physical science was the key to the treasure-house of the higher philosophy. Certainly, whatever admixture of craft that pre-Baconian passion for knowledge of the universe was alloyed with, its mysticism was of an exalted and idealising kind.

Miss Smith writes in a practised way, but her Latin is a good deal to seek. Costard's words, which head chapter xiv., should be printed as prose, not as verse; and there is nothing that needs explanation in Dee writing of his wife by her maiden name, though the custom is only now retained in Scotland. Nor does his reference to Kelley as having been "slayne" imply that Kelley came by a more sinister end than the fatal fall from a turret, for "slain" is still used in Lincolnshire for death by accident. We fancy "divelish hate" on page 296 should be "haine", rhyming assonantly with "name".

NOVELS.

"The Lordship of Love." By Baroness Von Hutten. London: Hutchinson. 1909. 6s.

The histrionic temperament is not nearly so uncommon as some people—particularly those who have it—imagine, but its development in the character of the half-Italian girl who is the heroine of this story is sketched in with unusual understanding, sometimes entirely sympathetic, sometimes playfully ironical. Beatrice Cavalsone, called for short Bice—a diminutive which the Baroness von Hutten begs the British public in a preface to pronounce like "Beechy"—was thrown at an early age upon her own resources and obtained an engagement in a chorus of small boys at the Teatro Leopardi by dressing up and pretending to be one. Apart from this mimetic proceeding, she found herself instantly in a congenial atmosphere. The universal smell of theatres—especially minor ones—which is neither wholly that of escaped gas nor size nor orange-peel, but a delicious blend of all three with romantic associations, was as ozone to her little nostrils. In the face of the open country she felt oppressed and out of place; obviously if one of the pleasures of your life is being stared at by people the open countryside leaves much to be desired. And when some trinkets that had belonged to her long-dead English mother fell into Beechy's hands the tearful reverie to which these relics led ended inevitably in a vision of her six-months-old self and the thought "Poor little baby! how I must have missed her". With deft touches like these the unfolding of Beechy's temperament is indicated, as she grew up, still supposed in the theatre to be a boy, amongst the odd, childish, kind-hearted operatic folk at the Leopardi. But by-and-by there was a tragedy amongst them, and with her instinctive avoidance of the unpleasant (which is also part of the temperament) she flew to Father Antonio, the old confessor, who had previously reproved her for continuing so long without petticoats. Then she lived in the convent, somewhat of a thorn in the flesh to the good priest and the quiet nuns, for eighteen months before she slipped out one night into the beautiful light and gaiety of the crowded streets, and of course made straight for the theatre. She had not forgotten her old friends, she said, though she had never thought of them—it was like one's summer hat which one does not think of during the winter, but which when summer comes one is delighted to wear again. But we must not multiply instances of the skill with which in the earlier chapters the engaging egotism of Beechy's character is displayed and which is quite the best thing in the book. For later, when Beechy looks up her mother's chapel-going relatives in Hartismere Road, Fulham, we encounter a good deal that is merely conventional, and rather out of date at that. Even the English Nonconformist conscience would hardly be equal to turning a travel-stained and hungry niece instanter into the street, though she combined in her own attractive person the dreadful qualities of foreigner, Catholic, and opera-singer. Yet this is the fate that Beechy is made to escape but narrowly. Nor does the wonderful self-effacement of the wife of the elderly butterfly Lord Charles, who captured Beechy's heart, nor the very unwonted restraint of his lordship's behaviour towards a child of the theatre, whose Catholicism was after all a little perfunctory, strike us as particularly convincing. We are almost tempted to regret that the author did not confine herself to her charming study of the child-artist, leaving the more commonplace presentment of the triumphs of the prima donna and the love of a promiscuous nobleman for another canvas.

"Johnny Lewison." By A. E. Jacomb. London: Melrose. 1909. 6s.

An artist must work in his own way, and perhaps his ideas ought not to be fettered by the conventional bounds of time and space, but there is no justification for the four hundred pages which Mr. Jacomb has devoted to a theme for which forty would have been a far too generous allowance. From the first it is obvious that Marjorie Wakeham will not marry Johnny Lewison, the son of the Jewish millionaire, and as Dick Chard, the Vicar's naval son, is the only other eligible male in Hothwell, the sequel of the romance can be guessed at once. But these summary proceedings are not after Mr. Jacomb's taste—he must hammer on at his task until every one of his characters has been made contemptible. The heroine, who repeatedly avows that she will never marry for money, surrenders unconditionally at the first glitter of the Lewison millions. Johnny Lewison, who is introduced as a dreamer and idealist, after his first passionate declaration of love degenerates into the most materialistic tyrant—the girl, for whom once nothing was too good, must now at a moment's notice become his chattel and the instrument of his desire. If Dick Chard is allowed to preserve some shred of decency and amiability, it is only because the author is too busily occupied elsewhere—and the minor players have all to be dipped in the blacking-bottle. Mr. Jacomb would doubtless pose as a cynic; but cynicism to be tolerable must possess originality.

"Aunt Jane of Kentucky." By Eliza Calvert Hall. London: Cassell. 1909. 6s.

Throughout the nine chapters of this little book the author, in the guise of a visitor, leads on Aunt Jane to give reminiscences of her earlier days, which she does in the quaint vernacular of her native State. The old lady does not require much encouragement, since every bit

(*Continued on page 540.*)

of "caliker" in her patchwork quilts and almost every flower in her garden remind her of some dead-and-gone episode or other; and although once she has the grace to say, "La, child, don't you ever git tired o' my yarns?" she does not (for obvious reasons) wait for an answer. The yarns are simple annals of the neighbourhood of Goshen, Kentucky, where people "got religion" and were unhappily not at one on the subject of infant baptism; but whilst these recitals present an amusing sketch of that evangelical community, their main purpose is to serve as pegs for Aunt Jane's moral reflections, which are cheerful rather than profound. There is a pretty picture of Aunt Jane in the tea-tray manner on the cover of the book, and yet another as its frontispiece; and pretty, too, is its sentiment—sometimes, indeed, getting rather near to the quality denoted by a duplication of that adjective.

SHORTER NOTICES.

"Secrets of the Past." By Allen Upward. London: Rivers. 1909. 3s. 6d. net.

"The Mystery of the Yellow Room." By Gaston Leroux. London: Arnold. 1909. 6s.

It is a searching test to put a detective story into comparison with a book such as Mr. Upward's. Historically true stories of crimes such as "Secrets of the Past", read soon before or soon after a story like the Yellow Room mystery, make the artificially constructed complications appear thin and bloodless. Yet M. Leroux' story is one of the cleverest of this kind that we have read. A mystery devised by an author, who keeps the secret of it until it pleases him to spring a surprise on his reader, loses all its interest from the moment of its solution. This barren ingenuity of the detective story is utterly outdone by the mysteries of real historic tragedies, which still remain uncleared after all the researches of historians. Another point that occurs in reading the two books is that M. Leroux ought to have compressed his drama as Mr. Upward has done. The crime story, if it is to keep its place in fiction, must get rid of much of the detective nonsense which makes M. Leroux' book repeat the stalest devices of the Sherlock Holmes stories in their decadence. Every one of Mr. Upward's narratives is an artistic short story; and it is this and not the historical subject-matter that makes Mr. Upward better worth reading than M. Leroux. In our time, whether Cesar Borgia killed his brother Francis does not matter more than who was the assassin of the Yellow Room. This is a new edition of Mr. Upward's book. Its success is deserved. If Mr. Upward did not too frequently drop commonplace phrasings into the midst of very good writing we should say his stories were done as well as they could be done.

"A Beau Sabreur: Maurice de Saxe, Marshal of France; his Loves, his Laurels, and his Times. 1696-1750." By W. R. H. Trowbridge. London: Fisher Unwin. 1909. 15s. net.

As may readily be imagined, this is no record of the science of war, nor does it pretend to hold up the hero of the tale as a grand soldier. Rather is it a chronique scandaleuse of the lives of the reigning sovereigns in mid-Europe during the first half of the eighteenth century, intermingled with those of their illegitimate children, such as Maurice de Saxe and of the hordes of great ladies who, with sublime effrontery, played the concubine to the various rulers, princes, warriors and statesmen of the period. In order to add more savour to the unsavoury tale the author has elected to give the life of his hero in the form of an autobiography. Whether in doing so he has chanced to write as the hero himself would have written must ever be a matter of opinion for each individual reader. It is, to say the least, rather startling to find the quasi-writer of such a book calmly describing the lapses from virtue of his mother, whence it came about that she, "the fair Aurora, brought me into the world nine months later". It would be hard to gather from this book that Marshal Saxe was a famous soldier, who, by his daring, took Prague by one of the most reckless "surprises" in history, and who by his coolness at Fontenoy turned the English success into a defeat. Rather is he set forth as a paladin of intrigue who died at the age of 55 utterly worn out by his debaucheries.

"Darwinism and Modern Socialism." By F. W. Headley. London: Methuen. 1909. 5s. net.

If Mr. Headley's thesis were quite new, it would provoke a general outcry. But he need not fear to find himself in the position of Malthus and others whose clear-headed brutality has shocked the gentle instincts of their time. The pitiless application of the doctrine of natural selection to human society has already been made, and accepted or rejected by most thinkers upon social subjects. Mr. Headley says some interesting things in the course of his argument, but the value of the argument is not strikingly great. Socialism, he maintains in the old style, must check natural selection. It must therefore check progress. But supposing the socialist state substituted for natural selection a selection that was premeditated and intelligent? In any case the propagation and preservation of the unfit proceeds merrily enough to-day, and could hardly be more thoroughgoing. Were we socialists, it would require more than this thesis of Mr. Headley to turn us aside.

"The Life of Joan of Arc." By Anatole France. A Translation by Winifred Stephens. London: Lane. 1909. 25s. net.

There is less to be said against this translation than against most. It is faithful, without continually jarring on account of its faithfulness. The same cannot be said of former translations of some of the works of M. France. We remember "The Red Lily". Here the task is easier. The matter of these volumes is more important than the manner; and conscientiousness has driven the translator into something like an achievement. For an historical work in English these volumes are very readable. How much of this readableness is due to M. France will be decided without much hesitation by all those who know how very readable M. France himself can be. Unfortunately, those who know this will not be likely to read the translation; so that the translator is likely to get a little more credit for her performance than she really deserves. Yet we do not grudge it her in the least. She must have worked very hard.

"Italy To-day." By Bolton King and Thomas Okey. London: Nisbet. 1909. 6s. net.

This book deserves its new edition. It is compact, pleasant to read, and trustworthy. One of the authors, Mr. Bolton King, has, it will be remembered, written one of the best histories of modern Italy extant. It is impossible to dive very deeply into the politics of a country in twenty-six pages; but the authors of this book contrive to give a tolerably complete outline of them in such a way that further details are unmistakeably suggested, and can be supplied from the imagination of the reader. There are not many handbooks of this quality to be had. The good handbook must contain a great deal of precise information in a digestible form. Unfortunately, precise information is not too common; and when it is obtainable it frequently gives mental indigestion to the feeder. But this is undoubtedly a good handbook.

"The Pickwick Papers." The Topical Edition. 2 vols. London: Chapman and Hall. 21s. net.

Editions of Dickens are infinite in their variety, and it is at least interesting to see that his old publishers find it worth their while to continue in rivalry with others who have availed themselves of the lapse of copyright. Mr. Charles van Noorden, who edits the present edition of "Pickwick", explains that the object is to produce an edition that shall form a complete topical commentary on the life of the time. To record traditions and preserve fading landmarks gives an entirely new turn to the work of reproduction. Hence illustrations and notes play an essential part in this Topical Edition, which will be welcomed by all true Dickens lovers. Among the notes are those given in the Victoria Edition by Mr. C. Plumptre Johnson, and in addition to the forty-three original illustrations there are 223 pictures of people, places and things which have some bearing on the text.

"George Meredith: Some Early Appreciations." London: Chapman and Hall. 1909. 5s. net.

A compilation of early notices of Meredith's poems and novels by Charles Kingsley, George Eliot, W. M. Rossetti, Swinburne, James Thomson, and others. Three articles are from the SATURDAY REVIEW. "Only he who begins honestly ends greatly", said Kingsley in noticing the poems in 1851. These appreciations serve to show not only how honestly Meredith began, but that, for all the years he had to wait for wider recognition, there were discerning critics of his greatness from the first. To many the most interesting item in the book will be Swinburne's emphatic protest against a certain narrow criticism of "Modern Love". Of some of the sonnets, Swinburne said "a more perfect piece of writing no man alive has ever turned out".

"The Poetic Old World." By Lucy H. Humphrey. London: Bell. 1909. 5s. net.

This is a little book for tourists. It provides the traveller with suitable lines for quotation in London or Assisi, in a churchyard or upon Dover beach. The idea is, we suspect, American. At any rate, the aim is to provide the best of

(Continued on page 542.)

GENTLEMAN seeks position as SECRETARY or similar post. Typewriting and Shorthand. Also French, German, and Italian.—Apply, "S," c/o *Saturday Review*, 10 King Street, Covent Garden, W.C.

everything. We must go to Oxford with Wordsworth and Matthew Arnold, to Coventry with Tennyson, up the Rhine with Byron, to Hamelin with Robert Browning. We hope that no one who carries this book in his coat pocket will ever mistake it for a Baedeker when pressed for time. The kind of person that loves to murmur lines by Thomas Moore at the meeting of the waters would be the kind of person to be particularly annoyed if he found himself in an uncomfortable hotel.

"The Poetry of Nature." By Henry Van Dyke. London: Heinemann. 1909. 6s. net.

A harmless anthology containing some of the best poetry inspired by the passing of the seasons and the gentle performances of Nature in earth and sky. The volume is appropriately bound in green, and the pictures are likewise appropriate.

THE QUARTERLY REVIEWS.

The quarterlies in their leisured and stately way provide so much that is attractive and important that it is never easy to select certain articles for mention without appearing to do injustice to others. Such essays as those in the "Edinburgh" on George Borrow the Wanderer, Some Recent Verse and Thinkers and Ironists, and in the "Quarterly" on the Soldier-President of Mexico, the Upper Anio, and Sport and Decadence are all inviting both in subject-matter and treatment. Then there are weighty articles on England, France and Russia, the Nationalisation of British Railways, and the United States as seen through foreign spectacles in the "Quarterly", and on the Revision of the United States Tariff and Anglo-German Relations in the "Edinburgh". But there are just four articles which demand instant attention. They are the surveys of the political situation, the needs of the Navy in the "Quarterly", and the Land Forces of the Crown, Past, Present, and Future in the "Edinburgh".

Dealing with the new Radicalism as distinct from the old Liberalism, the "Quarterly" says that "peace, retrenchment and reform" as a cry has given place to a desperate resolve to try class war, bloated expenditure and revolution. Disraeli said that "confiscation is contagious, and when once a community has been seduced into plunder, its predatory acts have seldom been single". What the "Quarterly" sees is that not merely property is at stake but liberty itself; "democratic tyranny" is coming "like a thief in the night with muffled footsteps. It begins with a system of bureaucracy no larger than a man's hand, and it develops into an all-embracing and all-crushing machine, from which there is no escape for the individual from the cradle to the grave". That is said in true "Quarterly" style. The "Edinburgh" likes the Government programme as little, but finds itself on the horns of a dilemma. It is almost as much concerned at the prospect and possible consequences of the Lords throwing out the Budget as at the passing of the Budget; the question is argued on constitutional lines, but the real trouble of the "Edinburgh", we suspect, is that anything the Lords might do to defeat the Finance Bill would bring about, if not a revolution in the relations of the two Houses, a revolution in tariffs. The idea of having to choose between Socialism and Tariff Reform is disconcerting to one who has declared anathema on both. Multitudes of good citizens, we are told, "would greatly prefer to tread the level plain of common-sense in the company of wiser men than those partisans who can see in political opposition and criticism nothing but 'Socialism' or 'revolution'".

The "Quarterly" has apparently had the opportunity of a peep behind the scenes in Downing Street. In March last, it says, the Cabinet was face to face with the possibility of disruption over the question of four or six Dreadnoughts. "It was due to the determination of Sir Edward Grey and Mr. McKenna, supported by the Board of Admiralty, that at last the Cabinet discovered that either an adequate programme must be put forward or the party would have to face the resignation of several of its most important members and of the whole Board of Admiralty." Hence the speeches of Mr. Asquith and Mr. McKenna which laid the truth before the country. The Navy's most urgent need is, says the "Quarterly", a new standard, and after a lengthy examination of the situation it sums up its views in "the simple formula of two to one in ships, officers and men as against the next strongest power". The cost would be "a relatively small insurance premium on the interests to be protected". Whilst the "Quarterly" takes this emphatic line with regard to the Navy, the "Edinburgh" is hardly less emphatic as to the Army. It demands that in peace we should command the means for war, that we should have not only naval supremacy but "an Army equal in organisation and efficiency and to the fullest extent possible in numbers to the best armies in Europe". The whole available strength of the Empire must be incorporated. "Any military system that neglects these cardinal principles is a mere waste of the people's patriotism, energies and substance." The Territorial Army, even when raised to its full establishment of 300,000 and reinforced by 100,000 Regulars, will not be strong enough to assume the entire charge of home defence in the absence of the Regular forces. The situation on the military side is, therefore, no more satisfactory than on the naval. How the ideals aimed at by the "Quarterly" and the "Edinburgh" are to be compassed by a voluntary system is hard to see.

The "Church Quarterly" must guard against becoming merely the organ of modernism, or it will lose influence. Professor Newsom's sketch of Tyrrell is well done, but it is a modernist manifesto. Tyrrell was a big man, not too well used, but he had his faults and shortcomings. More valuable than this article is that on "Gnosticism and Early Christianity in Egypt". Mr. Scott-Moncrief shows us an amazing picture of christianised paganism, mysticised grotesquely at one extreme and grossly materialised at the other. The question arises, Was there a similar transition stage in most other places, if we could get at the historic truth? French morals occupy some pessimistic pages in this number, pessimistic in spite of the writer's valorous attempt to be optimistic. But truth will out. France is sending morals after religion, and some of her better men are getting alarmed at the result, but so far have no remedy or palliative.

In the "Dublin Review" there is a thoughtful article by Mr. Belloc on the Taxation of Rent, and a pleasant one by Mr. Rowland Grey on Maria Edgeworth. The thoughtfulness of Mr. Belloc's article goes to show that rent ought not to be taxed, and the pleasantness of Mr. Grey's is in letters written by Maria Edgeworth. Father Thurston makes as good a case as possible for the removal of "Catholic Disabilities", and there are nine other articles. The ecclesiastical point of view predominates, but with an appropriate predominance.

For this Week's Books see page 544.

HELEN MATHERS

whose name as a novelist is a "household word," having decided to relinquish her literary work and to devote her attention to decorative schemes,

HAS JOINED

GILL & REIGATE

with a view to putting into practical effect the ideas of colour and harmony which have charmed so many of the readers of "Comin' thro' the Rye." In this capacity,

AS DECORATIVE ADVISER,

the resources of GILL & REIGATE'S workshops and studios have been placed at her disposal, and those who desire that distinctive note of comfort and refinement so closely associated with Helen Mathers and her work can arrange for

CONSULTATIONS DAILY,
from 10 to 4,

AT

GILL & REIGATE'S
GALLERIES,
73-85 OXFORD STREET, LONDON, W.

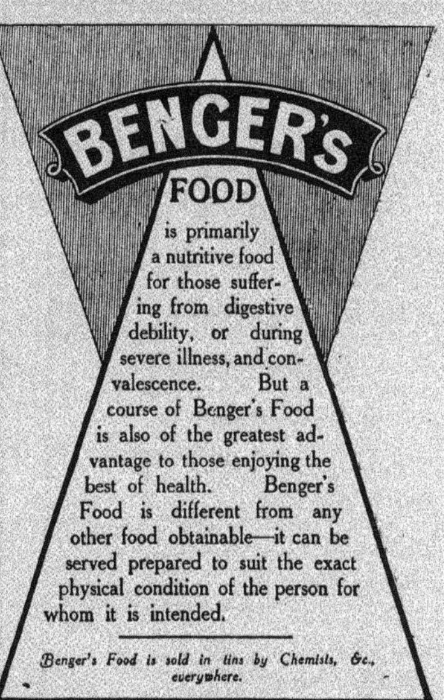

RAND MINES, LIMITED.

ABRIDGED TABULATED SUMMARY.

—	Glen Deep, Limited.	Rose Deep, Limited.	Geldenhuis Deep, Limited.	Jumpers Deep, Limited.	Nourse Mines, Limited.	Ferreira Deep, Limited.	Crown Mines, Limited.	Durban Roodepoort Deep, Ltd.
Financial Quarter ending	31st July, '09	30th Sept., '09	30th Sept., '09	30th Sept., '09	31st July, '09	30th Sept., '09	30th Sept., '09	30th Sept., '09
Mine.								
Development Work—								
No. of feet driven, sunk and risen, exclusive of Stopes	2,880	3,042	3,020	3,600	4,500	2,577	8,379·5	2,784
Estimated Tonnage of Ore exposed by drives, &c.	241,622	192,643	183,759	§ 213,808	§ 215,148	§ 157,812	§ 268,743	§ 102,280
Stoping—								
Tonnage Stoped, including Ore from development faces	71,829	132,545	108,480	77,886	130,588	119,014	405,624	78,364
Milling.								
No. of Stamps in operation	100	200	200	100	180	160	675	100
Ore milled (tons)	64,990	115,250	94,250	64,030	113,079	105,450	377,624	60,390
Duty per Stamp per 24 hours (tons)	7·810	7·140	5·653	7·405	7·323	7·800	7·397	7·733
Cyaniding.								
Total Tons treated	64,239	114,739	101,510	63,940	119,112	106,085	382,093	60,851
Gold Production.								
Milling (fine oz.)	14,125	24,358	16,672	15,345	29,938	39,065	100,172	14,652
Cyaniding (current milling) (fine oz.)	7,480	11,845	9,055	6,074	10,817	16,380	48,795	6,674
Cyaniding (Accumulations of Slimes) (fine oz.)	—	—	680	—	1,120	—	—	—
Total (fine oz.)	21,605	36,203	26,407	21,419	41,875	55,445	148,967	21,326
Total Yield per Ton Milled (fine dwt.)	6·648	6·282	† 5·459	6·690	† 7·208	10·515	7·889	7·062
Total Working Expenses.								
Cost	£63,827 19 11	£86,372 18 3	£93,130 18 11	£73,018 15 2	£117,710 13 2	£85,848 0 9	£307,376 15 5	£68,314 4 7
Cost per Ton Milled	£0 19 7·708	£0 14 11·865	£0 19 9·150	£1 2 9·692	£1 0 9·830	£0 16 3·386	£0 16 3·354	£1 2 7·492
Revenue.								
Value of Gold produced	£90,791 6 8	£151,873 5 7	£108,050 16 3	£89,848 1 1	£171,203 17 0	£232,846 13 3	£625,153 18 9	£89,367 13 6
Value per Ton Milled	£1 7 11·281	£1 6 4·265	£1 2 11·142	£1 8 0·772	£1 10 3·364	£2 4 1·949	£1 13 1·318	£1 9 7·162
Working Profit.								
Amount	£26,963 6 9	£65,500 7 4	£16,579 9 4	£16,829 5 11	£57,126 16 8	£146,998 12 6	£318,088 16 4	£21,053 8 11
Per Ton Milled	£0 8 3·572	£0 11 4·399	£0 3 1·992	£0 5 3·080	£0 9 5·534	£1 7 10·563	£0 16 10·162	£0 6 11·669
Interest.								
Debit	—	—	—	—	—	—	—	—
Credit	£373 15 7	£2,330 12 9	£2,094 19 6	*£2,299 16 10	*£1,081 12 9	*£2,467 16 5	*£12,099 14 1	£571 9 7
Net Profit	£27,337 2 4	£67,831 0 1	£18,674 8 10	£19,129 2 9	£58,208 9 5	£149,466 8 11	£330,188 10 5	£21,624 18 6
Estimated Amount of 10 % Tax on Profits	£1,548 0 0	£5,401 0 0	£1,677 0 0	£728 0 0	£3,617 0 0	£13,350 0 0	£27,505 0 0	£1,813 0 0
Reserve Gold (fine oz.)	1,676	6,745	1,098	5,283	611	1,430	11,293	208
Capital Expenditure	£934 13 5	£1,353 12 2	£4,578 16 9	£11,732 8 9	£21,670 2 3	£8,140 5 9	£59,082 7 6	£5,965 19 3
Interim Dividends Declared.								
Payable to Shareholders registered on books as at	31st July, '09	—	—	30th Sept., '09	31st July, '09	30th Sept., '09	—	—
Rate per cent.	10%	—	—	6%	12½%	27½%	—	—
Total amount of distribution	£60,000 0 0	—	—	£26,194 15 0	£84,375 0 0	£250,250 0 0	—	—

* Including Freehold Revenue. † Not including yield from accumulations of Slimes.

§ Exclusive of development work done during the quarter charged to Capital Account.

THIS WEEK'S BOOKS.

ART

The International Art Series: Fritz Boehle (Rudolf Klein), 5s. net; The Higher Life in Art (John La Farge), 8s. 6d. net. Fisher Unwin.
Peter Vischer (Louis Reau). Paris: Plon-Nourrit.

BIOGRAPHY

The Life of Joan of Arc (Anatole France. 2 vols), 25s. net; Giovanni Boccaccio (Edward Hutton). 15s. net. Lane.
Antonio Stradivari: His Life and Work (1644-1737) (W. Henry Hill). Macmillan. 7s. 6d. net.
The Divine Minstrels (Auguste Bailly). Lee Warner. 5s. net.
The Man Shakespeare and his Tragic Life-Story (Frank Harris). Palmer. 7s. 6d. net.
The Letters of John Stuart Blackie to his Wife (Selected and Edited by his Nephew, Archibald Stodart Walker). Edinburgh: Blackwood. 12s. 6d. net.
Sir Philip Sidney (Percy Addleshaw). Methuen. 10s. 6d. net.
The Autobiography of Sir Henry Morton Stanley, G.C.B. (Edited by his Wife, Dorothy Stanley). Sampson Low. 21s. net.
A Great Bishop of One Hundred Years Ago (Heneage Horsley Jebb). Arnold. 5s. net.
The Life of Mrs. Norton (Miss Jane Gray Perkins). Murray. 12s. net.

FICTION

Boom! (William Caine); The Secret of the Raft (Houghton Townley). Greening. 6s. each.
The Great Appeal (Joseph Keating). Everett. 6s.
Beyond Man's Strength (M. Hartley). Heinemann. 3s. net.
The Bluffshire Courier (Pentland Peile). Edinburgh: Blackwood. 6s.
Granite (John Trevena); The Lonely Lovers (Horace W. C. Newte); King Charles (Gerard Bendall). Rivers. 6s.
Robert Emmet (Stephen Gwynn). Macmillan. 6s.
The Battle (Cleveland Moffett). Milne. 6s.
The Wine in the Cup (Eleanor Wyndham). Laurie. 6s.
The Florentine Frame (Elizabeth Robins). Murray. 6s.
The Man who Stole the Earth (W. Holt White). Fisher Unwin. 6s.

GIFT BOOKS

The Children's Story of Westminster Abbey (G. E. Troutbeck); The Children's Story of the Bee (S. L. Bensusan). Mills and Boon. 5s. net.
The Story of the Little Merman (Ethel Reader), 3s. 6d.; The Water-Babies (Charles Kingsley), 15s. net. Macmillan.
Christabel in France (Mrs. Albert G. Latham), 3s. 6d.; The Islanders (Theodore Wilson Wilson), 2s. 6d.; Kinsman and Namesake (R. Stead), 2s. 6d.; The Cruise of the "Thetis" (Harry Collingwood), 5s.; The Rival Treasure Hunters (Robert M. Macdonald), 6s.; A Hero of Sedan (Captain F. S. Brereton), 6s.; The Hidden Nugget (Alexander Macdonald), 3s. 6d.; Children's Annual, 3s. 6d. Blackie.
The Silver Lattice (Edited by Richard Wilson). Nelson. 6s. net.

HISTORY AND ARCHÆOLOGY

Turkey in Transition (G. F. Abbott), 12s. 6d. net; South African Memories (Lady Sarah Wilson), 15s. net. Arnold.
The Last Phase of the League in Provence, 1588 to 1598 (Maurice Wilkinson). Longmans. 4s. 6d. net.
The Tribunal of the Terror (G. Lenôtre). Heinemann. 10s. net.
The Mediæval Hospitals of England (Rotha Mary Clay). Methuen. 7s. 6d. net.
Memorials of Old Sussex (Edited by Percy D. Mundy). Allen. 15s. net.
In Three Legations (Madame Charles De Bunsen). Fisher Unwin. 12s. 6d. net.

NATURAL HISTORY AND SPORT

Butterflies and Moths of the United Kingdom (W. Egmont Kirby). Routledge, 7s. 6d. net.
The Natural History of British Game Birds (J. C. Millais). Longmans. 8l. 8s. net.
The Master of Game (Edited by Wm. A. and F. Baillie-Grohman). Chatto and Windus. 7s. 6d. net.
Egyptian Birds (Charles Whymper). Black. 20s. net.

(*Continued on page 546.*)

CHAMBERS'S CYCLOPÆDIA OF ENGLISH LITERATURE.

Edited by DAVID PATRICK, LL.D.

3 vols., cloth, **£1 11s. 6d.** net; half-mor., **£2 5s.** net.

A History Critical and Biographical of Authors in the English Tongue from the Earliest Times till the Present Day, with Specimens of their Writing. Illustrated with nearly Three Hundred Portraits.

Mr. Clement K. Shorter, writing in the "Sphere," says: "I must offer my congratulations to Dr. David Patrick on the production of a book which seems to me to far exceed any previous effort in the way of a complete History of English literature.

CHAMBERS'S 20th CENTURY DICTIONARY.

1216 pages, 3s. 6d.

Pronouncing, Explanatory, Etymological, with Illustrations.

Contains over **100,000** references.

Journal of Education says:—

"A Miracle of Scholarship and Cheapness."

"IN USE EVERY DAY." ***A DICTIONARY OF UNIVERSAL KNOWLEDGE.***

Revised to 1908.

CHAMBERS'S ENCYCLOPÆDIA

It is safe to assert that no set of books will prove more generally useful in every household than the 1908 issue of this world-renowned work, which is a storehouse of information on every conceivable subject.

Glasgow News.

"For speedy reference, and satisfactory information on almost any topic, nothing can compare with Chambers's Encyclopædia."

COMPLETE in TEN VOLUMES.

Apply to your Bookseller for Cash Prices.

CHAMBERS'S CONCISE GAZETTEER OF THE WORLD.

Edited by DAVID PATRICK, LL.D.

768 pages, cloth, **6s.** net.

Pronouncing, Topographical, Statistical, Historical.

"Pall Mall Gazette" says:—"For all practical working purposes a thoroughly sufficient and admirable desk companion."

CHAMBERS'S BIOGRAPHICAL DICTIONARY.

Edited by DAVID PATRICK, LL.D.

1006 pages, cloth, **10s. 6d.**; half-mor., **15s.**

Dealing with many thousand Celebrities of all nations, from the Remotest Times to the Present Day; with copious Bibliographies and Pronunciations of the more difficult names.

CHAMBERS'S LARGE TYPE ENGLISH DICTIONARY.

Edited by Rev. T. DAVIDSON.

1264 pages, cloth, **12s. 6d.**; half-mor., **18s.**

A Library Dictionary of the English Language giving the Explanation, Pronunciation, and Etymology of Words; together with Compound Phrases, Technical Terms in use in the Arts and Sciences, &c.

STOKES' CYCLOPÆDIA OF FAMILIAR QUOTATIONS.

Compiled by E. E. TREFFRY.

773 pages, cloth, **3s. 6d.** net; half-mor., **7s. 6d.** net.

This volume will prove of immense value to Teachers, Public Speakers, Legal and Literary Men, and Readers generally.

"Nottingham Guardian" says:—"WE do not know any work of the kind in the market better adapted for everyday use."

Prospectuses on Application to W. & R. CHAMBERS, Ltd. **38 Soho Square, London, W. 339 High Street, Edinburgh.**

THE

NINETEENTH CENTURY & AFTER.

NOVEMBER.

UNIONIST OPPORTUNISM AND IMPERIAL DEMOCRACY. By FABIAN WARE.
THE FINANCE BILL. By the Right Hon. Lord AVEBURY.
PHANTOM MILLIONS. By W. H. MALLOCK.
THE CASE OF FRANCISCO FERRER: A CONFIDENTIAL FRIEND'S TESTIMONY. By ALFRED NAQUET (Ancien Sénateur de France).
RECENT EXPERIMENTS IN THE "PHYSICAL PHENOMENA OF SPIRITUALISM." By the Hon. EVERARD FEILDING (Hon. Secretary, Society for Psychical Research).
THE FALLACY OF THE ELDER BROTHER. By H. B. MAVOR (Assistant Master at Clifton College).
A TENTH-CENTURY DRAMATIST: ROSWITHA THE NUN. By Mrs. W. KEMP-WELCH.
THE QUESTION OF MEDICAL PRIESTCRAFT. By S. SQUIRE SPRIGGE, M.D.
DANTE'S SELF-PORTRAITURE. By the Right Rev. Bishop WELLDON.
THE VIRTUOSI. By NORMAN PEARSON.
CONTEMPORARY POLITICS IN FRANCE. By ANDRÉ BEAUNIER.
TWENTY-ONE YEARS WITH OUR INDIAN FELLOW-SUBJECTS. By Lady COX.
THE DEFENCE PROBLEM OF SCANDINAVIA. By AUGUST SCHVAN.
THE "NATIONAL GUARD": A HINT FROM THE UNITED STATES. By Lieut.-Colonel ALSAGER POLLOCK.

LONDON: SPOTTISWOODE & CO. LTD., 5 NEW-STREET SQUARE.

THE

FORTNIGHTLY REVIEW.

CONTENTS—NOVEMBER 1909.

IMPERIAL AND FOREIGN AFFAIRS: A REVIEW OF EVENTS.
M. IZVOLSKY AND COUNT VON AEHRENTHAL: A RECTIFICATION. By VOX ALTERAE PARTIS.
IN THE HOUSE OF COMMONS. By AUDITOR TANTUM.
HOW THE UNIONISTS MIGHT WIN THE GENERAL ELECTION. By J. ELLIS BARKER.
THE COMING BATTLE. By W. G. HOWARD GRITTEN.
HENRY FIELDING: SOME UNPUBLISHED LETTERS AND RECORDS. By G. M. GODDEN.
EYES AND NO EYES. By W. S. LILLY.
WHEN THE DOOR OPENED. By W. T. STEAD.
THE O.U.D.S. AFTER TWENTY-FIVE YEARS. By ALAN MACKINNON.
THE POLAR ESKIMOS AND THE POLAR EXPEDITION. By Dr. PHIL. H. P. STEENSBY.
EIGHT MONTHS OF PRESIDENT TAFT. By SYDNEY BROOKS.
WHAT ARE COMETS AND METEORS? By E. V. HEWARD.
TWO HISTORIANS OF THE EIGHTEENTH CENTURY. By H. D. ROOME.
THE END. By STIJN STREUVELS.

LONDON: CHAPMAN AND HALL, LIMITED.

For Your Library List

THE CAT IN HISTORY, LEGEND, AND ART

Written and Illustrated by ANNE MARKS. Crown 4to. cloth gilt, **6s.** net (by post, 6s. 4d.).

The cult of the cat must prove of interest even to those who are not professed lovers of the animal.

Milton on the Continent

A Key to *L'Allegro* and *Il Penseroso*.

By Mrs. FANNY BYSE.

Crown 8vo. cloth gilt, **4s. 6d.** net (by post, 4s. 9d.).

Second edition, enriched by further observations concerning Milton's sojourn in the Rhone Valley and on the Simplon pass in the light of *Vaudois* legends and poems.

LITERARY BYE-PATHS AND VAGARIES, AND OTHER PAPERS

By THOMAS NEWBIGGING. Crown 8vo. cloth gilt, **4s. 6d.** net (by post, 4s. 10d.).

A series of interesting essays on out-of-the-way subjects, with the true literary note that the book-lover enjoys.

THE WAY OUT Or, From the Comparative to the Positive in Religious Thought.

By LAMPADEPHOROS. Crown 8vo. cloth gilt, **6s.** net (by post, 6s. 4d.).

In this volume, which might be called "The Old Truths from a New Point of View," the Author throws a fresh light and has an original restatement to make concerning Christ's Christianity.

THE HARP AND THE ROSE

By "CARITAS." Cloth gilt, **3s.** (by post, 3s. 3d.).

A collection of Poems which, like harp songs and wild roses, may help and cheer weary travellers on the dusty paths of this everyday world.

VERSES IN TWILIGHT

By the Rev. PHILLIP WINTER DE QUETTEVILLE. Crown 8vo. cloth gilt, **2s. 6d.** net (by post 2s. 9d.).

A volume of secular and religious verse, the sweet melody of which will charm the reader.

Write for Catalogue (No. 102) of Antiquarian Literature, free by post.

LONDON: ELLIOT STOCK, 62 PATERNOSTER ROW, E.C.

THIS WEEK'S BOOKS—(*Continued*).

REPRINTS AND TRANSLATIONS

The Meaning and Value of Life (Rudolf Eucken). Black. 3*s*. 6*d*. net.
My Pets (Alexandre Dumas). Methuen, 6*s*.
Cape Colony To-day. Cape Town: Townshend, Taylor and Snashall.
The Plays of Æschylus (Walter Headlam). Bell. 3*s*. 6*d*. net.
Elections and How to Fight Them (J. Seymour Lloyd). Vacher. 3*s*. 6*d*. net.
The Pickwick Papers (Charles Dickens. 2 vols.). Chapman and Hall. 21*s*. net.
A Week in a French Country-House (Adelaide Sartoris). Smith, Elder. 5*s*. net.

SCHOOL BOOKS

Inorganic Chemistry (Part I.) (F. Stanley Kipping). Chambers. 3*s*. 6*d*.
English Literature (William J. Long). Ginn. 5*s*. net.

THEOLOGY

Confirmation in the Apostolic Age (Frederic Henry Chase). Macmillan. 2*s*. 6*d*. net.
The Ambrosian Liturgy (E. G. Cuthbert F. Atchley). Cope and Fenwick. 5*s*. net.
The Aristocracy of Grace (Rev. R. Ballantine). Stock, 3*s*. net.
Faith (William Ralph Inge); A Critical Introduction to the New Testament (Arthur S. Peake). Duckworth. 2*s*. 6*d*. net.
Sermons (Rev. Joseph Miller). Rivington. 6*s*. 6*d*.
Christianity at the Cross-Roads (George Tyrrell). Longmans. 5*s*. net.

TRAVEL

French Cathedrals (Elizabeth Robins Pennell), 20*s*. net; Romantic Corsica (George Renwick), 10*s*. 6*d*. net. Fisher Unwin.
The Heart of the Antarctic (E. H. Shackleton. 2 vols.), 36*s*. net; Italian Hours (Henry James), 25*s*. net. Heinemann.
High Albania (M. Edith Durham). Arnold. 14*s*. net.

VERSE

The Seductive Coast (J. M. Stuart-Young). Ouseley. 5*s*. net.
The Wheel of Life (Arthur Maquarie). Bickers. 5*s*. net.
Hero and Leander (Christopher Marlowe). Dent. 10*s*. 6*d*. net.
Poems and Baudelaire Flowers (Jack Collings Squire). New Age Press.
Songs in Wiltshire (Alfred Williams); Poems and Ballads (A. G. Hales). Erskine Macdonald. 5*s*. net each.
The Enchanted Island (Alfred Noyes). Edinburgh: Blackwood. 5*s*. net.
Rose and Vine (Rachel Annand Taylor), 5*s*. net; Goodchild's Garland (Henry Nemo), 1*s*. 6*d*. Elkin Mathews.
Songs of Memory and Hope (Henry Newbolt). Murray. 3*s*. 6*d*. net.

MISCELLANEOUS

American Newspaper, The (James Edward Rogers). Fisher Unwin. 5*s*. net.
Britain for the Briton (Sir William Earnshaw Cooper). Smith, Elder. 10*s*. 6*d*. net.
Commonweal, The (Alfred P. Hillier). Longmans. 4*s*. 6*d*. net.
George Meredith: a Primer to the Novels (James Moffatt). Hodder and Stoughton. 6*s*. net.
Journal of the Society of Comparative Legislation (Edited by Sir John Macdonell), 5*s*. net; Mosquito or Man? (Sir Rubert W. Boyce), 10*s*. 6*d*. net. Murray.
Maxims of Marmaduke, The (Charles Edward Jerningham). Methuen. 5*s*.
Memories of the Months (Sir Herbert Maxwell). Arnold. 7*s*. 6*d*.
Quintessence of Nietzsche, The (J. M. Kennedy). Laurie. 6*s*. net.
Rosemary's Letter Book (W. L. Courtney). Melrose. 7*s*. 6*d*. net.
Scientific Nutrition Simplified (Goodwin Brown). Heinemann. 2*s*. 6*d*. net.
Work and Play of a Government Inspector, The (Herbert Preston-Thomas). Edinburgh: Blackwood. 10*s*. 6*d*. net.

REVIEWS AND MAGAZINES FOR NOVEMBER.—Scribner's Magazine, 1*s*.; The State, 1*s*.; The Century, 1*s*. 4*d*.; The Treasury, 6*d*.; The English Review, 2*s*. 6*d*.; The Fortnightly Review, 2*s*. 6*d*.

CONSOLIDATED MINES SELECTION CO.

The thirteenth Ordinary General Meeting of the shareholders of the Consolidated Mines Selection Company, Limited, was held at Winchester House, London, E.C., yesterday, Mr. Francis Muir, Chairman of the Company, presiding.

The Secretary (Mr. C. W. Moore, F.C.I.S.) having read the notice convening the meeting and the Auditors' report,

The Chairman said he hoped the shareholders would agree with him that the report and accounts were so full and ample that there was not much left to be said from the chair. Their aim had been to cover, as fully as possible, the whole ground of their operations, so that every shareholder might have the fullest information at his command. He was sure they would endorse the note of satisfaction in the report touching the greatly improved position of the Company, as well as the confidence expressed that the wave of improvement they had enjoyed had not yet fully spent itself. Results had fully justified the optimism the Board dared to indulge in on the occasion of their last two or three meetings under conditions as depressing and disappointing as could well be imagined, and it was certainly pleasant to them to find that so many of their chief interests were at last justifying, and were likely still to justify, the faith with which they embarked in them. Put briefly, whereas last year at June 30 they showed depreciation amounting to £613,027 and a profit and loss debit balance of £26,675, or a total of £639,702 on the wrong side, they had this year a depreciation of only £71,734 and a profit and loss credit balance of £72,621; practically, therefore, the position of the Company had improved by £540,589 and the capital was again intact. In May, when the market was at its best, there was an appreciation in their assets of about £100,000, but to-day under present reaction, arising partly from dear money and the political uncertainty, the depreciation was somewhat greater than at June 30. The profit and loss account showed the satisfactory profit for the year of £99,296 17*s.* 1*d.*, and after deducting the debit balance brought into the account from last year, there remained at credit the sum of £72,621, which they proposed to carry to next account. It would be understood that with the depreciation in assets they could not consider the question of a division of this profit among shareholders. During the year they had purchased in the open market the Company's debentures amounting to £5,680, at a discount of £895, and since the closing of the accounts they had bought a further amount of £13,000, also at a discount, which would appear in next year's account. They had also arranged to take over from two of the largest debenture holders £104,000 of debentures against the issue of 100,000 reserve shares at par, they to have the option on a similar number of reserve shares at par, against a further £104,000 of debentures until April 1910. By this transaction the debenture debt was reduced to £263,580, and if the option mentioned was exercised it would stand at £159,580. By this repurchase a profit of £8,520 had been obtained, and if the further amount was repurchased the profit would be £12,520, which fully covered the underwriting commission and other costs connected with the debenture issue. There would also be a considerable lowering in the standing charges of the Company. Naturally, the financial position had greatly improved, their cash at bank and short calls amounting to £344,788, and the balance of cash and cash assets in excess of liabilities being £414,510.

The Chairman went on to deal with the information given in the report as to the progress of the Rand in general. From every point of view the progress had been remarkable. The tonnage treated, the values, savings, costs, capacity of plant, and dividends all told the same tale, and through all there ran the quiet confidence that while so much had been done there were still developments possible in the same direction which could in due time be accomplished. After reading the figures given on page 5 of the report, the Chairman alluded to the number of amalgamations which had taken place during the year and the good effects these had had in reduced capital expenditure and costs. Continuation of values in depth was also worthy of note, especially as measured by the condition disclosed on the Brakpan Mines at a distance from the outcrop of about 3½ miles. On the labour question their representatives expressed themselves with calmness, and there had been no shortage. Brakpan, in which they were interested, gave great promise for the future, and they had taken a prominent part in the flotation of the Springs Mines, embracing 1,160 claims. Outside the Transvaal they had not secured any fresh interests, although they had had a good many proposals before them for examination, chiefly in the United States and Mexico. The Chairman concluded by moving the adoption of the report and accounts.

Mr. Walter McDermott seconded this resolution, and it was carried unanimously.

Messrs. Carl Parcus and Maximilian Kempner were re-elected directors, and Messrs. Deloitte, Plender, Griffiths & Company having been re-elected auditors, the proceedings terminated with a vote of thanks to the Chairman.

Printed for the Proprietors by SPOTTISWOODE & Co. LTD., 5 New-street Square, E.C., and Published by REGINALD WEBSTER PAGE, at the Office, 10 King Street, Covent Garden, in the Parish of St. Paul in the County of London.—*Saturday*, 30 *October*, 1909.

THE

SATURDAY REVIEW

OF

POLITICS, LITERATURE, SCIENCE, AND ART.

No. 2,819 Vol. 108. 6 November 1909. [Registered as a Newspaper.] 6d.

CONTENTS.

NOTES OF THE WEEK.

There are people who think a debate in the House of Commons should never be anything more than a "businesslike discussion": that there should never be the least tinct of oratory—which they regard as "tall talk"—and that literary niceties and classic touches should be shunned. We dislike that point of view. It is as if a man were to insist that the Houses of Parliament ought to be plain, square businesslike buildings—none of your fine towers and traceries and Gothic decorations. Full-dress debates are not so good to listen to and read as they were in the days of the giants, but happily the House of Commons can still rise to occasions. The debate on the third reading of the Finance Bill began well with a speech by Mr. Austen Chamberlain, who has steadily enhanced his reputation. Then followed a part that was spoilt by a brutal personal incident, but there were notable speeches at the close.

Mr. Lloyd George made a good speech on the last evening of the debate. In some of his platform speeches during the last few months he has reminded one extremely of Mr. Chamberlain's platform speeches in the unauthorised programme days, when the Lords were likened to lilies. Some of our own people may be a little shocked when we say this (for people forget what they said in 1880 or 1885); but it is true; it is not so singular, for Mr. Lloyd George has always been a great admirer of Mr. Chamberlain. Later, Mr. Balfour presented the now familiar and accepted arguments against the measure with that rarity of expression which makes his speeches so good in the reading. The curiosa felicitas in words does not make a great leader of men, yet it is a precious gift. Mr. Balfour also showed a fervour in his speech on Thursday which is valuable. The talk about his being a cold detached philosopher and so forth is about half a truth, we imagine: it is just about as true as saying that Mr. Asquith is the mere advocate. The philosopher, the advocate and the "little Welsh attorney"—the public loves such nicknames.

In the old days, in Parliament and out of Parliament, the custom was this: when you were called a frigid and calculating liar and a dishonour to your country, you fought a duel—and were quite likely spitted as well as called harsh names. And what is the up-to-date custom? Is it to take a libel action or demand an inquiry? Certainly not: the right course and safe course is to furrage about among your accuser's past speeches, letters, telegrams, anything, and try to prove triumphantly that he himself is not above suspicion. Then all your friends cheer greatly, and the Prime Minister praises you and reproves your accuser.

When Brougham—we think it was Brougham—called Canning a liar in the House by simply saying a statement of his was untrue, Canning sat down; and everybody knew what that meant. What an absurd course! What he ought to have done of course was to get up and suggest that Brougham was something of a liar himself. The passages between Mr. Balfour and Mr. Ure, Lord Advocate, in the debate invite some reflections of the kind. For the rest, we suppose that everybody is now satisfied; and that "honour" is satisfied.

The Commons have refused all the vital amendments made by the Lords to the Housing and Town Planning Bill. Those amendments hang together and stand for a single principle. What the Lords have tried to do all along is to save for the individual or the local authority the right of appeal against the fiat of the Local Government Board. It is the appeal only which they have endeavoured to save. Thus in the matter of compulsory purchase the Board was to have its way unless its decision was appealed against. If an appeal were made, an arbitrator was to be called in. It was the appeal again—this time to the county court—that the Lords insisted upon in their amendment concerning the compulsory execution of repairs. Throughout it was the same, whether the appeal went to an arbitrator, to the county court, or to Parliament itself. This principle of the appeal has been refused by the Commons. The reasons given were childish. It costs time and money to maintain any system of national or personal protection. That is no argument for disbanding the Army or closing the courts. Mr. Burns' strongest weapon—the citation of the Small Holdings Act—broke in his hand. Mr. Lyttelton exposed his generalities with a concrete case.

While these disputes as to town planning are in hand, the Mansion House Council on Housing goes steadily on with its useful work. On Thursday its annual meeting was addressed by Councillor J. S. Nettlefold, of Birmingham, who told of the work similar to that of the Mansion House Council done by the Birmingham Corporation. The keynote of both has been the enforcement of existing laws on the owners of insanitary property. For many years the Council as a private body has shown what the London boroughs as public bodies ought to do more systematically on the model of the Birmingham Corporation. There is not the co-operation amongst them there ought to be, and it may be hoped that a conference such as Mr. Nettlefold suggested between municipal authorities, commercial and philanthropic companies, and other bodies will be arranged. It would stimulate a desire for common action and show the necessity for a common method in dealing with the housing problem in London.

Apparently everybody is not made quite happy by the dexterous settlement of the Marylebone squabble after all. At any rate, we are not. It appears that Mr. Jebb, who has caused all the trouble, insists on going on, though Lord Robert Cecil has retired to Blackburn. To say the least of it, this is grossly ill manners. The only courteous, in fact the only decent, thing to do was for him to make away with himself with the disappearance of Lord Robert. This was so obvious that everyone naturally supposed that with Lord Charles Beresford's acceptance of Lord Robert's reversion the whole matter would be smoothed out to every Unionist's satisfaction. Lord Charles as sole Unionist candidate would be perfectly safe to keep the seat. Mr. Jebb going on is mere fooling. He has not the ghost of a chance of getting in. The utmost he can do is to let in a Radical. The majority of Unionists in the division, Tariff Reformers as much as others, wish Lord Robert to represent them; and these certainly will not vote for Mr. Jebb because he happens to be a Tariff Reformer. It is time this mischievous person were suppressed.

Neither are things quite righted at Oxford. Dr. Evans persists with his idle candidature. He and his friends had a meeting this week. Dr. Evans' only argument in favour of himself is that the opposition to him is clerical. Well, the clericals are an extremely important and historic factor in Oxford. Why should they not be represented? But, in fact, Lord Hugh Cecil has a far wider support than that. He has the support of those who value high character, extreme ability, and the associations of a great name. Dr. Evans will find these far more numerous than his purely partisan following. Sir William Anson, we note, has agreed to stand along with Lord Hugh, which finally puts Dr. Evans out of court.

Not having become a member of the House of Lords, as the Nationalists of Longford advised him to do, Mr. Redmond is now going to pass a satisfactory Land Bill "on the hillsides of Ireland". Does it mean cow-hunting? The "University" is secured, and there is now no such reason to "give Birrell a chance"; but, on the other hand, the bishops are committed to the disturbing declaration that cow-hunting is "immoral". The new canon was imposed but quite recently, and cannot conveniently be put out of sight as earlier declarations can among a people who do not read history. However, there are numerous other offences that can be cultivated for "the undying character of the national spirit".

Since the "National President" of the Molly Maguires, supported by his "State chaplain", visited Ireland last summer they have been discussing in Dublin what "concessions" they would make to Germany for destroying the British Empire and "making Ireland free". Some suggest a new volunteer force to be maintained at Ireland's expense under German orders, but the most favoured proposal is a gift of Kinsale harbour as a naval station. It is just as well that Germany should know what is to be done in Dublin for her, and she will be the better for understanding also the fact that an Irishman, in Ireland, is never prepared to give anything for his country's freedom. His way is rather to get something for it. "Thank God, I've had a country to sell" is a famous Irish saying, and no one ever thinks of connecting it with any other people.

The municipal elections in London leave the Progressives still dejected. They are as they were at the famous election of 1906. Both Municipal Reformers and Progressives won or lost in this borough or that; but none of the Progressive gains can be compared with that of the Municipal Reformers in Battersea. Twenty-seven seats won by them there leave Battersea with only two Progressive representatives. In due course the Municipal Reformers will choose their own Mayor for the first time in Battersea history. Labour and Socialist candidates in London generally gained seven seats; but the avowed Socialists did not improve their position. In the country the Labour and Socialist gains together were seventeen, but Unionist and Liberal gains and losses balanced one another almost exactly.

Sir John Cockburn has been busy noting "signs of Imperial solidarity", and he duly set them forth in his Colonial Institute lecture this week. South African Federation, the Press and Defence Conferences, Empire Day, and the like are among the events which Sir John Cockburn regards as making for unity. But as what he calls Imperial democracy appears to depend for its success on the gradual disappearance of central authority, it is questionable whether the signs are all that he suggests. Nor are we reassured by such comments on his paper as were made by Lord Charles Beresford and Sir Frederick Young. Lord Charles welcomes the idea of colonial navies, and even proposes that they should carry their own flag, so that in the interchangeability of Imperial forces they should never lose their distinctive character. Sir Frederick Young urges that the colonies should be called colonies no longer, but nations. Imperial unity is the thing to work for in both our own and colonial interests, but the signs seem a little contrary at times.

Señor Moret has endorsed the statement that the attitude of the Riff tribesmen is now favourable to peace. The change is not due to anything done by the new Spanish Government, but to the excellent account General Marina's army has given of itself, to the desire of the tribesmen to prepare for the next harvesting season, and perhaps to orders from Fez. Mulai Hafid is confronted with many difficulties besides those incidental to the Spanish campaign. France and Germany are pressing for a settlement of outstanding claims, and new complications are ahead unless he can come to some arrangement. There is talk of a French loan, but France will hardly be eager, after wasting so much blood and treasure in Morocco, to find the money necessary to relieve Mulai Hafid. With a bankrupt exchequer at Fez and the Spaniards masters of the Riff the Moorish outlook is sufficiently dark.

The Greek Prime Minister must be at the end of his wits. He stands for constitutional government by the army—a difficult position. It was a position that Lieutenant Typaldos could not understand, with the result that he took away the Greek arsenal for a few hours. He did not see why the Ministry should draw the line at a Bill relating to persons. Since such Bills are the only Bills that are of any real interest to the Greek politician, it was like drawing the line at any Bill at all. And so a hasty demonstration was made with torpedoes in order to persuade the Prime Minister and his colleagues that a personal Bill was right and proper in the circumstances. This was all very natural. The strange thing about it was that it did not succeed. It will be a still stranger thing if the brave Typaldos is punished. Some words of Lear may be adapted: "Thou shalt not die. Die for high treason! No."

While the Greeks were busy demonstrating the futility of Greek politics the Germans were doing honour to Mommsen. The coincidence is an arresting one. Greek politics to-day are what they were a century before the Roman Empire, an object-lesson in the tragi-comedy of the small State that pretends to be great on the score of its memories. The immortal ridicule poured by Mommsen upon the Greek patriots, who withstood the Roman advance and could neither wisely submit nor forcefully resist, is a ridicule that every effete little nation must encounter when Empire is battering at the gate. The stern justice of history pronounces always in the same way. Greece to-day is ridiculous, as it was two thousand years ago. Mommsen is honoured in Berlin.

M. Briand pleases nobody except when he is speaking. This is the penalty of moderation. Audiences go home and find that what they have heard, though it was beautiful, was not satisfactory. At a meeting of the Ligue de l'Enseignement last Saturday M. Briand explained that his policy of conciliation was not a policy of surrender. More particularly he was going to remain faithful to secular education. But tenacity did not imply ferocity. Certainly the particular kind of tenacity which enables a French Prime Minister to keep his place does not. His advice to good republicans was excellent. Stand firm, but tread upon nobody. This advice ignores an important circumstance. It is rarely possible to find comfortable standing-room in politics without treading upon somebody. If you contradict nobody, you will seldom make a definite statement. But M. Briand does not believe in definite statements. He seems to be reaping his reward. The Bishop of Nancy, we note, is meeting him half-way.

If the so-called defeat of Tammany gave New York the minimum amount of honest municipal administration we might welcome it as a novelty. But these defeats of Tammany mean very little. They have happened before, and Tammany pulls itself together and wins again. In this election a Republican gang with a number of discontented Democrats who have been left out in the cold by Tammany have taken the place of the old Democratic gang. That is all. In other American cities the Grafters have won victories. In San Francisco the old gang is in again.

In New York the new Mayor, Judge Gaynor, is the Tammany man. He is famous as an anti-corruptionist —when the offender is a Republican. New York will probably be worse off than ever for the change. As the "Times" correspondent says, it marks the beginning of a four years' divided administration and endless political intriguing. The Tammany Mayor and the new Board of Estimates and Control will each be fighting for different apportionment of the graft. Tammany in full power at least knew its own mind and gave the city a strong government, though a corrupt one. The new men will surely be weaker, and what guarantee is there that they will be less corrupt? Apparently Tammany had nothing to teach them in the way of rascally practices during the election. After the next four years' experience New Yorkers will probably think it is not worth while worrying, and Tammany will come into its own again.

Cadiz, Ohio! Who would not live in Cadiz, Ohio? A city in its hundred-and-sixth year that has never had a murder. The foreman of the "Cadiz Republican" says so (in a letter to us this week), so it must be so. Cadiz, Ohio, the hub of civilisation, spends $2500 a year on lecturers and entertainers for a two weeks' Chautauqua; it has a Shakespeare Club, Choral Society, and a Cadiz Women's Club which studies English literature. And in the public library there are four volumes for every man, woman, and child in the town. And it has four banks and four loan associations. This is a delightful conception of civilisation. There must indeed be the real thing in Cadiz, Ohio. Yet a city that has not had a murder in a hundred years can hardly be civilised: can it?

Mr. Chirol's speech at the dinner of the China Association should, as he himself remarked, have been given elsewhere. His message was most valuable, but he was preaching to the converted—in fact, to the one audience in all England that realises the significance of China. From a British point of view things are not all they might be in China. Neither Mr. Chirol nor the Chairman attempted to make out that they were. The Chinese, no doubt, are taking in new ideas; but this seems rather to stimulate anti-foreign feelings. Unless the Government does much more to help the Englishman in China he will not be able to hold his own with the German or the American. Mr. Chirol has just come back from a survey of the Far East, and seems to have been struck with almost painful force with the advantage the German especially enjoys in the thought taken for him by his Government. Meantime there is little evidence of real internal reform in China. The finances are going from bad to worse. A paper reform, the beginnings of constitutional government, is in effect simply a blind to cover the apathy in everything that matters.

A great deal of trouble is going on behind the scenes in the Welsh Church Commission, and the trouble is aggravated by the action of the Home Office. Mr. R. M. Thomas, the secretary, who recently resigned—he is, by the way, a Churchman, and we think a Conservative—was during the sittings of the Commission appointed agent to Sir Watkin Wynn. It was arranged, however, that he should continue to perform his secretarial duties, and he worked exceedingly hard at them. Why then did he resign? This week he has told us that private business had nothing to do with the matter. It is of general knowledge that he has had differences with the chairman. Mr. Herbert Gladstone, however, professes complete ignorance of the reason, and admits that Lord Justice Vaughan Williams is quite within his rights in appointing a fresh secretary without consulting his colleagues. Those colleagues, or such of them as are Nonconformists, are naturally furious; but the Government seems indifferent to their temper. Why throughout all the long controversies about this Commission, we ask, have Mr. Lloyd George or the Home Office done nothing to assist their Nonconformist friends against the chairman? Is it that they honestly think their friends in the wrong, or do they wish to delay the appearance of the report for years? If they really wished to end the business, they could easily do it by cutting off supplies. This was the way in which a Conservative Government once brought a Welsh Commission to an end.

The Commission on Poor Law reform has issued its third and last report, which relates to the poor-law system in Scotland. Both as to England and Scotland the majority and minority differ mainly as to what is to be done when the Boards of Guardians are abolished, as both agree they ought to be. The majority propose to give the administration of the poor laws to County Councils and boroughs with the assistance of organised voluntary bodies. This, in the opinion of the minority, is only the Boards of Guardians over again. They would put each class of person receiving aid under the management of some already existing public body: the feeble-minded under the lunacy authority, destitute children under the education authority, the sick under the health authority, and so on.

To choose between these conflicting systems will be for some Parliament in a future more or less remote which depends on the political situation. Both political parties are pledged to deal with poor-law reform, and both the majority and minority of the Commission insist on its urgency. The idealism of the minority scheme will attract those with a penchant for immediate perfection. It is a fine conception to have special agencies with a mission in the highways and hedges to all who ought to be helped for distress of mind, body, or estate, whether they themselves do or do not feel that they fall below a scientific standard. In the case of infectious diseases and many sanitary matters the State takes the first step, but it is premature to administer the poor law in this spirit. Yet it is probable that poor-law reform will be in the direction of breaking up the workhouses, now crowded indiscriminately with every type of distressed humanity, and submitting their habitants to special treatment.

It is more than fifty years since the "Derby Day" made Mr. Frith famous. Few pictures have given so much entertainment to so many people, and it is safe to suppose that to the end of time it will continue interesting. Its author had a real painter's gift and a gift for staging incident, though the radius of his painter's vision was small and his stage gift in the same way ran to the multiplication of small incidents of equal importance. The dainty quality within his reach was best seen, perhaps, in the "Ramsgate Sands" belonging to the King. The "Railway Station", reproduced on lodging-house walls, must have cheered many a rainy day. In his sketches as compared with the finished pictures it was sometimes possible to catch the authentic observer and painter, before the cosmetic element of cosiness and rosiness had been rubbed over everything—the element that belongs to the slack part of Dickens' art. Mr. Frith's reminiscences, and perhaps still more those of his daughter in "Leaves from a Life", tell how jolly life was in the middle-Victorian, middle-class, middle-art homes like theirs; mild Bohemias with an easy charade-imagination that did not tax the nerves or the conscience. It is churlish of Death to have stopped the day's routine of a man who enjoyed it at ninety.

The halfpenny sensation of the week is the re-appearance of Julia and her revelations concerning the G.O.M. Julia's "discarnate" proceedings are almost as much talked about at this present moment as was the discovery of that other embalmed Julia whose beauty was the nine-days' wonder of the priests and nobles of mediæval Rome. It is impossible to be amused at Mr. Stead's latest performance. It is too puzzling. No joke can be intended because the joke would be too impossibly pointless and ill-mannered. We are confronted, then, with the necessity of taking Julia seriously, and bewilderment sets in. That these revelations could have been conceived in a human brain is a more amazing phenomenon than if the printing-press that printed them had protested against them and walked out of the room. The pathologic abyss so suddenly laid open to our view frightens away the tendency to smile.

By the side of Julia Dr. Bodie pales his ineffectual fire. His methods of deceiving the public are more in the ordinary line; and his showman tricks have been appropriately punished by a commonplace verdict to refund his gains. But we do not necesarily condemn him outright. We have read about Sludge, and would like to catch Dr. Bodie in a mood of similar candour. Does Dr. Bodie believe in himself? That is the point. The mind is capable of strange twists, and when it is possible for a man to get fame and living by the simple process of convincing himself that he is an extraordinary person, the path to such a conviction is surely not difficult to find.

A delightful event of its kind was the luncheon given at the House of Commons on Thursday to Sir Benjamin Stone; and nothing could have been happier than the Postmaster-General's little speech. The address to Sir Benjamin, one of "the seven stalwarts" of Unionist Birmingham, was signed by Mr. Asquith, Mr. Lloyd George, Mr. Churchill, Mr. Burns, as well as by the Unionist leaders. The House of Commons has indeed long had an affection for this pleasant gentleman, who has about him something that reminds one of the most benign characters in Charles Dickens.

THE BUDGET SEND-OFF.

MOST people will heave a sigh of relief at the news that the Budget has at last left the House of Commons. Whatever may be its treatment in another place, it is time that it was discussed by other tongues and from another point of view. The debate on the third reading was marred by one of those unpleasant personal quarrels which spring up suddenly in political controversy, and, like some foul tributary, soil, though they cannot interrupt, the current of events. Of the merits of the dispute between Mr. Balfour and Mr. Ure no educated and honest man can feel a doubt. Between saying that the fiscal policy of your opponents is not in your opinion adequate to meet the needs of the State and saying that they will repudiate the statutory obligations of the State there is a chasm wide as the Channel. Mr. Ure said both. He said that he did not believe it would be possible to meet the deficit of £16,000,000 by tariff reform, which was a perfectly legitimate remark. He then added that he understood the old-age pensioners were apprehensive as to the payment of their pensions, and that he, the Lord Advocate, shared their apprehensions, an observation which he repeated night after night at public meetings. Mr. Balfour described this performance as the coining and uttering of a frigid, calculated lie; and we do not think that all the wild and whirling words of recrimination and explanation uttered in the House of Commons on Wednesday and Thursday altered the situation in the least. Mr. Balfour cannot be accused of dealing in personalities as a habit. Indeed the only criticism that might be passed on his polemical methods is that, as a rule, he is too mild and polite. Mr. Balfour has not forgotten the Chinese slavery lie at the last election, and he perceived that it was intended to use the stoppage-of-pensions lie in the coming election. It is of course a very telling lie, and Mr. Balfour was perfectly right to arrest its circulation at the earliest moment and in the most striking manner. But what Sir Francis Clavering's footman called "the holtercation" quite upset the House of Commons and diverted attention from an historically interesting debate.

We must here repeat our astonishment that the Lord Advocate of Scotland can discharge the duties of his office and at the same time wander over England and Scotland making platform speeches every night. The Lord Advocate is paid by the taxpayers £5000 a year to do the legal business of Scotland. To make a speech in the provinces means the loss of the day, as far as office work is concerned. Is there really no legal work for the Lord Advocate to do? If so, why not abolish the office? It is quite true what somebody said in the debate, that the really alarming feature of our finances is the rapid growth of expenditure upon the Civil Service and officials of all kinds. Let us make a beginning of economy by cutting down the office of Lord Advocate, who apparently has no more to do than the King's Remembrancer or the Clerk of the Board of Green Cloth. The great sinecurist of the eighteenth century was the Clerk of the Pells, who was paid £7000 a year for doing literally nothing. If the Government want a peripatetic orator, surely he can be got for less than £5000 a year, especially in these days when a fearful fluency possesses all men, and is mistaken for eloquence. How many sheriff-substitutes must there be in the Parliament House who would gladly do the Lord Advocate's job for, say, £1500 a year? But, putting aside these disturbing personalities, the debate was in other respects worthy of the occasion, and philosophically entertaining. The House of Commons set itself down to discuss the question What is Socialism? As might be expected from a deliberative body composed of lawyers, business men, landowners, and journalists, much confusion of thought was discovered. Socialism is, in its proper sense, a theory of government which asserts that the State, or society, has wider duties towards its citizens than those of police and national defence. Socialism (in this sense) believes that the State or society is bound to see that its members are not only safe from robbers and invaders, but sound in mind, body, and estate. The unconscious practice of this theory of government was begun in this country by the Tory party in 1847, when they brought in and passed the first Act for the regulation of juvenile and female labour. For the next fifty years the Tory party talked prose (or Socialism) as volubly and unconsciously as the Bourgeois Gentilhomme. In Germany this doctrine of politics was for long confined to the professors of Universities until suddenly Bismarck, about thirty years ago, took it up vigorously, and applied it in all directions. This kind of Socialism is merely State regulation or protection of industry; and it is about the degree or amount of it that the opinions of sensible men differ. The Socialism of the Radical Party, which is the ground note of the Budget, is concerned, not with the regulation of industry, but with the distribution of property. Its aim is to transfer property, not from the rich to the poor, but from the individual to the State, by which it is to be administered in such a manner that "distribution should undo excess, and each man have enough." This is the object of the death duties and the super-tax, and the land taxes, and the licence duties. The justification for this transference of property is two-fold: first, because profit is earned by the State; and second, because the State can spend the wealth of individuals better than the individuals themselves. This deadly, paralysing nonsense is by no means new; it is as old as the Greeks, and one would have thought had received its coup de grâce from the French Revolutions in 1789 and 1848. Yet Mr. Lloyd George trots it out with all the pride of a man who says he has discovered the North Pole. It is against this pernicious and impossible system of transferring property from individuals to the State by taxation that the Conservative party is exerting all its resources. Let it be remembered that although the feudal tenures of land were abolished in France and Germany a hundred years ago, the change was not to State ownership, but to peasant proprietorship. Let it not be forgotten that the incentive to industry in nine men out of ten is the desire to make provision for their offspring. Dryden writes scornfully of Shaftesbury that he wore himself to fiddlestrings,

"And all to leave what by his toil he won
To that unfeather'd, two-legg'd thing, a son".

Precisely: that is the object of most men's toil, and all the Lloyd and Henry Georges in the world will not change it. The opposition to the Budget has human nature on its side, and therefore, be the fight never so prolonged, victory must be achieved by the Conservatives. We hope that in fighting the Budget in the country Unionist candidates will be careful to explain what they mean when they cry Socialism! Otherwise they may be met by Mr. Harold Cox's dictum that Tariff Reform is Socialism, which, in the sense explained above, is true.

"A FEW PATERNAL ACRES."

EVERYBODY should read Landor: a man is hardly well educated in literature until he has absorbed at least the poems to Ianthe. Landor had a noble independence in literature which would be still nobler in the case of many men if applied to the whole business of life. Even politicians might study Landor with advantage sometimes. Mr. Ure himself might find it not too late to reform if he would read and absorb and enjoy Landor. He would find the "Conversations" for example much more stimulating and much safer than his own imaginations. But though a course of Landor—of Landor, that is, in his books, not in his quarrels and lawsuits—would do many folk a deal of good, we would not plead that the Conservative party at the present time should adopt his severe rule of originality. "I have expunged many thoughts for their close resemblance to what others had written whose works I never saw till after. . . . I have resigned and abandoned many things because I reasonably doubted my legitimate claim to them and . . . because the retention might raise a clamour in my courtyard." This rigid rule of originality would never work in party politics. The Liberal party to-day thoroughly understands this. When Mr. Chamberlain started—in practical politics—the idea of old-age pensions the chief lights of the Liberal party opposed it. We remember Sir William Harcourt at the zenith of his influence declaring dead against it: the friendly societies, he considered, would be spoiled by it. But a few years later, never troubling itself for a moment as to whether it has "legitimate claim", that party seizes on Mr. Chamberlain's idea and works it for all it is worth. The Liberal party of late has also been working, for all it is worth, the back to the land idea. Which party has the "legitimate claim" here may be a moot point historically. In the 'eighties, in the form of three acres and a cow, it was the property of radicals, though eighty years earlier it seems to have been started by a Lord Winchelsea, who was not a radical. However, we may admit that though Conservatives carried out the allotments scheme—one of the best things done by Parliament in the last century—and also passed a far less efficient Small Holdings Act, the Liberals have run the thing for electioneering purposes of late a thousand times harder than ever any Conservatives ran it. The Conservative party has no time to lose: it has, somehow, lost far too much time already. The General Election is almost on us; and against this event we must have a very clear and strong small holdings or peasant ownership scheme to put before the electors in rural constituencies. Let us risk the clamour which indignant Liberals may raise in our courtyard—the louder the clamour indeed the better will it be for our prospects. We do not need by any means to steal the old clothes of the Liberals: there is plenty of new cloth, and it can be cut to a much better fit. Sir Gilbert Parker's pamphlet on the land question and Mr. Balfour's letter to him the other day are capital signs of activity in this direction. We hope that the Conservative candidates throughout England—Wales is past praying for—will go to the villages with a scheme that will greatly improve on the Liberal scheme. It ought to be easy in a way, for by an extraordinary piece of good luck the Liberal scheme has utterly ruled out the most attractive, as well as the soundest, feature of any reform of the kind. It has ruled out Ownership. It proposes to trust the villager, peasant, "small man in land", up to a point only—it will trust him to farm the land, but never to own it. Elaborate machinery is set up by which Irish peasants—the most thriftless people on earth probably—are to become owners: elaborate machinery is to be set up by which English peasants are not to become owners. The great "territorialist", as Lord Morley has styled him, is to be greater than ever. Instead of owning a mere county he is to own a whole country; and this "despot", this "tyrant", this feudal giant, is in his almighty condescension to suffer the small people to hire small holdings from him. On no account are they to own small holdings. And this is the great Liberal party which has thundered against the great landowners! This is the party that has talked about the necessity of peasant proprietorship! And it now insists that no small man—in England—shall be proprietor. He is to be a tenant under a huge landlord, the State. We do not profess to know who was behind this extraordinary arrangement, whether it was the Whig element in the Government or the Socialist element in the Government; but we should say that when the villagers come to grasp it they will not be at all delighted. Landowners, they may some of them say, are quite big enough as it is: we don't all want to be at the mercy of one who is trying to get the whole of the land into his own hands. Conservative speakers and canvassers cannot rub this point in too much in all the county constituencies. As it is, a small farmer can at least have human relations with his landlord in most cases: how can he have human relations with a Government Department in Whitehall?

No; if the small holdings scheme is to succeed in England it must be a scheme of peasant or small owners, not of peasant or small tenants. Mr. Balfour in his letter to Sir Gilbert Parker uses the expression "Magic of property". It may not be a very fresh expression, but it holds a truth which is world-old. There are some people, huge monopolists, who would hire out everything—houses, lands, horses, furniture. One can conceive a state of society where even wives might be hired out. But we are absolutely convinced, from long and close acquaintance with him, that the typical English villager who wants to go into the farming business "on his own" would prefer to except the land at any rate from this category. For thirty years in a corn, sheep and turnip country—it may be different in the jam districts—we have taken special note of the "small men in land" who have done well. Their great idea has been to own a bit of England some day for themselves and to keep it in their family, hand it down to their hardworking children. There is not the faintest shadow of a doubt about this. True, when this Liberal small holdings scheme was first started we said that we would on the whole rather have the tenant plan than the ownership plan; and certainly, if the country is to be flooded with small men in land who know nothing of land save what they have learnt from the newspapers, it is better to have a tenant system than an owner system. The first at any rate could be shot out more easily than the second. But if we are to get men of the earth earthy rather than of newspaper newspapery on the land let us make them independent and self-reliant owners rather than dependent and State-reliant tenants.

"Happy the man whose wish and care
A few paternal acres bound."

This, as we understand it, is Mr. Balfour's view and the view of the Conservative leaders at the present time. Who doubts for a moment that, when driven home, it must appeal to the villagers a thousand times more than the Whig plan of trusting nothing to the common poor man and the Snowden and Keir Hardie plan of trusting it all to the State? Which will the villager choose: a Government Department or his own little home and holding?

The paternal acres, then, are the thing. The only question is, How are they to be acquired by the villager who is fit to till them? We have known cases of just the right men to run small farms who have had the greatest difficulty even in finding enough money to go in as tenants. A man must have some stock and machinery, and after the villager has paid for these there will very rarely be anything over to pay for the freehold of his farm. This is the crux of the whole matter. The right man clearly must be helped if he is to become owner. He has made his own way so far by his own industry and character, but he never can hope to become capitalist enough to buy the land outright unless he can borrow the money. Now it is just here that the State can come in with real effect. The hidebound socialist—the ignorant socialist—may be dead against any scheme of ownership, the hidebound individualist—the ignorant individualist—may be equally dead against any State aid. Wise people, "moderate" people in the sense in which Gardiner the historian used the word, need attend to neither. It will be perfectly safe and sound for the State to help the right kind of Englishman to ownership. We have known in a single village at least a dozen active, ambitious and intelligent men to whom the State might lend with advantage. There are thousands of cases of the kind. It must be the work of the next Conservative Government to frame a good scheme to this effect, and we have no doubt it can and will be done. The prospects for a small owner are far better to-day than they have been for thirty years past. Corn can once more be grown at a fair profit, and, as we have shown in previous articles, land generally is "looking up". We do not want to see the whole country carved up into small holdings of a few acres apiece. This country is entirely unfit for such a peasant proprietary as that. The success of the French peasant and the success of Stein's policy in Prussia are beside the mark. As to the French, they were small peasant proprietors before the Revolution, as that great writer Alexis de Tocqueville shows. The thing is in the blood and bone of the French peasant. With us it is wholly different. Only a certain proportion of our country folk is fit for or desirous of small farming. We can add these men to the larger tenant farmers and the larger landowners, and strengthen the whole fabric. But they must be added as owners. This great and steadying reform rests wholly with the Conservative party. "Ownership" should be on the address of every Unionist candidate in the coming election.

THE REAL NAVAL MENACE.

WE confess to a feeling of nausea about the naval controversies which have so worried the Royal Navy, of which Kinglake wrote that its renown is "a treasure unspeakably precious. By our whole people, and, above all, by a British admiral, it deserves to be guarded with jealous care; for, if it be certain that the very life of England depends upon the strength of her Navy, it is also true that the strength of her Navy is in some sort dependent upon its sense of power, and again, that that sense of power must always depend in part upon the sacred tradition which hands down a vague estimate of the things our Navy has done and the things it has failed to do". There is no question that the provocation which has caused all these controversies has come about through weak and more or less incapable First Lords of the Admiralty. Associated with them there has been an autocratic First Sea Lord who remains in office at the age of sixty-nine, and, after eight years on shore, is utterly out of touch with the sea service, which frankly detests him. From the point of view of the man in the street there is opposed to this autocrat a popular Irish admiral whose service career is at an end, but in whom political life and mob applause have produced a tendency to minister to the public's view of this matter by making events revolve round himself. In neither case do we find the spirit of self-sacrifice, the bushido of the Japanese; but since Lord Charles Beresford has already been deprived of his command the full fury of the public will rightly fall on the man who has provoked all the deplorable strife in the Navy and on Mr. Asquith, who is responsible for his retention long beyond the usual term of office. For that retention of Sir John Fisher is surrounded by sinister signs, in that he above all other men has aided and abetted the Government in those mad reductions of the Navy in ships, men, and stores which have done so much to encourage Germany and America in the race of armaments and to lead the world to conjecture whether Great Britain was among the dying nations. There seems to be pervading all these naval intrigues an unholy compact which allows the renown of the Navy to go down before favouritism and intimidation, so long as the Admiralty does the will of the Treasury to save all expenditure except that which will promote retention of office. It is because the Navy for the first time for many years has been exploited for the sake of party that we witness all the deplorable controversies which are the product of the last four years. It is the strongest argument which should be put before the electors that as to the Navy the Liberal party cannot be trusted, and only a short interval is available to put things right before the period of severest stress is upon us when the German Navy will be ready. That interval of Mr. Balfour's government is necessary for us before all other things for a similar reason to that given a century ago by Napoleon that "peace is necessary to restore a navy—peace to fill our arsenals empty of matériel, and peace because then only the one drill-ground for fleets, the sea, is open". If that interval of sane government during peace is not given to us, then war may come upon us like a thief in the night. It will then be too late, and all the costly social reforms which are now on the statute book will be swept down the great maw of a gigantic indemnity.

It is not very creditable to Mr. Asquith that, his

correspondence with Lord Charles Beresford having been published, he should have first sheltered himself in Parliament behind the plea that the correspondence was not completed, and then behind a blocking motion put down by one of his silent supporters so that no discussion of a question in which his personal honour was involved could be entertained. Mr. Asquith chose to make himself chairman of a committee appointed to inquire into his own arrangements for war, and in these circumstances there was a reasonable disinclination on the part of officers to give evidence. Two of the heads of divisions of the Intelligence Department, whose reputation stood so high that they could afford to be more courageous than others, offered to give evidence if they received a safe conduct. Otherwise they said their careers might be "absolutely ruined". On 21 April Mr. Asquith wrote that "no prejudice of any kind to their future careers would result from their evidence, whatever it may be". The intimidation of members of committees, the punishment of officers who even attempted to send in reports to the Admiralty that any arrangements for which the autocrats were responsible had been found by the officers to be working unsatisfactorily—these things were too notorious to be ignored. Mr. Asquith's written guarantee, his preliminary assurance to each witness who had to give his evidence *confronted by Mr. McKenna and Sir John Fisher*, and finally the further solemn pledge on the floor of the House, seemed to argue some safety to men profoundly anxious to save their country. The cruel lie was soon exposed. Captain Hulbert later on complained to the committee that he had been subjected to pressure as to his evidence. Mr. Asquith brushed it aside as a "misunderstanding", as if there could be room for such in a deliberate threat to place an officer on half-pay. The tree, however, is judged by its fruits, and in this case the threat was amply fulfilled. Turned out of their departments by being ordered on leave, both officers were then placed on half-pay, while the work of genuine administration was prostituted in the service of this nefarious plot by a so-called reorganisation which involved getting rid entirely of all work connected with the defence of the Empire's shipping and trade or all that is involved in the food and wages of the working classes. The Admiralty state that "the experience of some years had shown that its work was not worth its cost". It would be interesting to hear of the comments of any single ex-Admiralty official who is free to express his opinion or of any chamber of commerce or shipping on this extraordinary pronouncement. In the midst of all this unpleasant notoriety to which the Navy is being subjected by the Government there comes the publication of the following message of Prince Henry of Prussia on relinquishing the command of the fleet which is being steadily increased in strength so quietly and resolutely, with an entire absence of ostentation: "Fearlessness, calm and purposeful work with the hour of trial alone in view, reticence, strict discipline, coupled with a kindly feeling on the part of superiors towards subordinates, true comradeship—these qualities must continue in the future in ever-increasing measure to distinguish the officers and men of the High Sea Fleet".

What a contrast this spirit affords to our own unhappy state! In contemplating its serious aspects let us always remember that there is nothing behind the Navy, nothing else between the poor and starvation in war. Have not the electors the right, after nearly four years of constant turmoil as to the Navy on which their whole existence is staked, to demand that it shall no longer be a pawn in a discreditable party intrigue? Is it not the duty of Parliament, which has run the four years' course that Lord Morley thinks long enough, to enable the electors by a General Election to relieve Mr. Asquith of the helm and confide it to one who will enable the Navy to prepare exclusively and whole-heartedly to confront the dangers which are fraught with such appalling misery to the working classes of this country?

PARLIAMENTS IN AUSTRIA-HUNGARY.

CHAMPIONS of parliamentary institutions must be filled with melancholy when they contemplate the bewildering chaos of Austro-Hungarian politics. Almost daily the situation increases in perplexity, and there seems no immediate prospect of a removal of the deadlock. It is true that the Dual Monarchy manages to get along pretty well although its Parliaments are not meeting, but this only shows that the brand-new parliamentary system is simply a political excrescence. This is scarcely a comforting state of affairs. For the whole civilised world is now engaged in a gigantic political experiment. During the latter part of the nineteenth century every country which claimed to be modern in thought adopted a system of representative institutions framed more or less closely on the English model. Quite lately we have witnessed the extension of the principle to the Orient. Never has democracy had such a world-wide opportunity, and for the first time since the Roman Empire a single people, and that our own, can claim to have given a pattern of government to the whole world. How is the great experiment going to answer? That is the problem of the century.

It is claimed for representative institutions that they form the one and only solvent of political discords. The discords of Austria-Hungary are racial. It must be confessed with sorrow that the Austro-Hungarian Parliaments afford an opportunity rather for the accentuation of these discords than for their resolution. For consider the sequence of recent events. The first step towards the present crisis in Austria was the passage by a provincial Diet of what in the constitutional jargon of that Empire was known as the Lex Axmann. This measure established German as the language of the province. It was drawn in the widest terms, and was vetoed by the Imperial Government on the ground that it encroached on the sphere of the Imperial Chamber. But out of this unconstitutional Bill two constitutional measures have been framed. The first makes German the language of the public offices, including the law courts. The second makes German the language of the schools. These Bills have been passed by the Diets of Salzburg, Vorarlberg, Upper Austria and Lower Austria. Of these provinces the last includes Vienna, the Czech population of which runs into six figures. The Austrian Cabinet has not felt itself able to advise the Crown to veto the Bills, and its two Czech members have at once resigned.

But the Czechs have other and far more drastic means of expressing their disapproval. In Bohemia there is a safe Czech majority, which has been making things most uncomfortable for the Germans. The German members of the Diet have explained that they will resort to obstruction unless their grievances are redressed. To this the Czechs have retaliated by saying that unless the Bohemian Diet can get through its work quietly they will obstruct in the Imperial Parliament and make the passage of the Budget impossible. It may be added that obstruction in Austria is a generic term including such refinements as desk-banging, ink-throwing and fisticuffs.

This then is the situation. Unless the Lower Austrian language law is modified, at least as far as the capital is concerned, the Czechs will harden their hearts. If the Czechs harden their hearts the Germans will obstruct in the Bohemian Diet. If the Germans obstruct in the Bohemian Diet the Czechs will make the Imperial Parliament unworkable. Altogether it is a pretty muddle, but, of course, there is a way out. It lies in recourse to paragraph 14 of the Austrian Constitution, that indispensable paragraph which is of more use than all the other paragraphs put together, because it provides for extra-parliamentary government. But there is one thing which paragraph 14 expressly forbids, and that is the levy of new taxes without the consent of Parliament. This year, as Dr. Bilinski, the Austrian Finance Minister, told the House last week, there is a considerable deficit, and unless the Budget is got through this deficit must remain uncovered. This fact is the last straw, and makes the Austrian deadlock complete.

Hungary too has a domestic difficulty. The Hungarian Bohemia is Croatia. It is now nearly two years since the Croatian Diet assembled at Agram. It promptly revolted against the methods of Budapest, was at once dissolved, and is not at all likely to be called together again while present conditions continue. The Croatian situation alone is enough to make the Hungarian Government profoundly suspicious of democratic experiments. But it is also deeply interested in the trend of events in Austria.

Some years ago the party which we have now learned to call the Coalition was formed in order to press upon the Crown the question of the use of Magyar in Hungarian regiments. It found itself able to take up a very strong position. It pointed out to the King that its leaders represented a political party elected by the Hungarian people. It claimed to voice the feelings of a nation in opposition to the ideas of bureaucrats in Vienna, and it obtained a good deal of sympathy in Western Europe. The Crown at first met its demands with a brusque negative, an attitude which provoked considerable hostile criticism. But Francis Joseph's sole object was to gain time. He used his opportunity to establish universal suffrage in Austria. And then the tables were turned. He told the Coalition leaders that there was now assembled in Vienna a Parliament thoroughly representative of all the nationalities of the Austrian Empire. This Parliament was prepared to endorse the use of the German language in the joint Army. On the other hand, the Hungarian House was elected on an antiquated system which gave a wholly artificial majority to the purely Magyar elements in the country. Let the Coalition leaders introduce universal suffrage into Hungary, let a representative Parliament in Vienna be confronted with a representative Parliament in Budapest, and the Emperor-King would see what he could do. The Coalition had appealed to the democracy; to the democracy let it go.

The Coalition accepted the Crown's terms. It took office on the understanding that it would pass a Suffrage Bill and then dissolve. It has spent more than three years in trying to devise a system of voting which should be universal and yet safeguard the Magyar majority. All it managed to produce was a scheme which would have given the non-Magyars one vote apiece and the Magyars about half a dozen. This naturally proved abortive. Meanwhile the hotheads have grown impatient. They have shifted their ground and, while dropping the military question for the time being, demand the establishment of a separate State Bank. One of their leading members is President of the House, and thus in a position to make things impossible for any Cabinet which will not accept their programme. But the Crown is adamant. It bargained for a Suffrage Bill to be followed by a dissolution. The terms were accepted, and it insists that they shall be carried out.

But even the moderate members of the Coalition are no longer enamoured of the notion of universal franchise. They have seen the system at work in Austria and the utter confusion it has produced. They know perfectly well that the Croats would fight the Magyars to the death if they had the chance. They know, too, the numerical weakness of the Magyar population. The Magyar claim of superiority over the other races of Hungary may or may not be well founded, but at least the Magyar leaders may assert that they stand for an old parliamentary tradition which has worked well in the past, and that they do not intend to throw the institutions of the kingdom into the melting-pot in order to imitate the chaos which now rules in the neighbouring Empire.

Such then is the situation in the two halves of the monarchy, and none can deny its gloom. Parliamentary institutions have not proved a political panacea; they seem rather to have intensified the existing evil. Still there is something to be said on the other side. Somehow or other the inevitable racial friction must be given vent. In the pre-parliamentary days it found vent in civil war, and even the worst parliamentary squabbles are better than that. It may be argued that the parliamentary arena enables the leaders of the racial parties to appreciate one another's strength. They can realise that there is a serious problem to be dealt with, and can exhaust their feelings in mutual invective which does no lasting harm. And when all the squabbling is over, the Crown, having carefully weighed the relative strength of the opposing forces, can intervene with all the prestige attaching to its extra-parliamentary position, and can suggest a compromise which may very well commend itself to public opinion as fair and reasonable, and at worst is likely to be accepted out of sheer exhaustion.

It is a somewhat paradoxical conclusion. What was advocated as an end turns out to be of some value as a means, and, not for the first time in history, it appears that an appeal to the democracy results in a strengthening of the monarchical principle. Viewed in this light, the position of affairs in Austria-Hungary may be of use to British statesmen. A small but noisy section of British opinion is demanding the grant of parliamentary institutions to India, and is supporting its demand by an appeal to the political experience of the British people. It is surely not superfluous to point out that the appeal no longer lies to the British people alone. Let us not overlook the Austro-Hungarian parallel. The course of events on the Danube proves two things. The first is that the mere grant of a Constitution will certainly fail to weld a congeries of races into a single nation. The second is that if parliamentary institutions are to succeed at all under such conditions the final verdict must lie with some authority above and beyond them, in Austria-Hungary the Crown, in India the English. Slowly and painfully we are finding out what democracy really means and how it can be made to work; and though such principles as can now be asserted may be disheartening to the enthusiast, they must neither be rejected nor ignored by British statesmen whose task is to govern every variety of race in every variety of time. We who have been pioneers in so much need not hesitate to take a lesson in our turn.

THE CITY.

THE improvement noted in the monetary position a week ago has not been maintained. The Bank finds great difficulty in attracting gold, and unless it is more successful in the next few days it may be necessary further to advance the official rate to 6 per cent. The fear of this, added to the political crisis, has a restraining effect upon the stock markets, which are furthermore depressed by recurring sales to close speculative accounts which can no longer be financed. No importance need be attached to the failures recently announced, though in one case some unpleasant disclosures are being made. Apparently the machinery of the Stock Exchange still admits of many irregularities, and these may easily bring distress upon innocent clients. Thus a client who sends a cheque in payment for stock may lose both money and stock if his broker fail before delivery, the procedure being to put all available funds into the common pot and set the whole against the broker's liabilities. The moral is that no stock should be paid for except against delivery or against a certified transfer, and this can easily be arranged through one's bankers. Certain brokers might object on the ground that the procedure is a reflection on their financial status, but if the practice became common any irritation would quickly disappear.

Home railway stocks rallied a little early in the week, but have lost most of their improvement. Confidence in the market is slow of return, but the small investor is coming forward, and if next week traffic figures bear out expectations there may be a decided change for the better. It should be remembered that most of the stocks now carry a full four months' dividend, that they are remarkably low in price, and that all the indications point to growing revenue. Dear money is against speculative purchases, and these we do not advocate; but the real investor should get a good return, first from dividends, and ultimately from the inevitable appreciation in capital value. The proposed arrangement between the North Eastern and Hull and Barnsley seems a good one, but there are difficulties in the way of its being carried through, and it would not be wise to build up too much hope upon its being carried through. Originally formed to combat the North Eastern, the Hull and Barnsley cannot well join hands with that company; and the Hull Corporation, who have the power of veto, will need to be very circumspect in dealing with the proposals.

There has been no great rush for the Turkish Loan on London account. Financiers here are not eager to provide the money necessary for the early maintenance of the new Constitution. The loan, however, does not lack sponsors, and what London refuses will be readily supplied by Paris. New capital issues have been quite numerous this week, dearer money notwithstanding. Presumably the rush is due to the approach of the end of the year, when many of the underwriting contracts expire. It is now or never with many of the issues. The Canadian Car and Foundry Company, Ltd., has been formed to amalgamate three companies already established. The Omnium Insurance issue was well heralded, but the prospectus suggests many pertinent questions as to the character of the business which is taken over. The "Bipsine" issue is remarkable for the addendum to the prospectus wherein it is stated that the directors have made a "conditional" contract to take over the "V.V." Bread Company. Apparently the "V.V." shareholders have not been consulted at all in the matter; and, as their consent is necessary, the contract may prove valueless. We certainly fail to see what benefit the "V.V." shareholders will obtain by throwing in their lot with "Bipsine". The proposed Anglo-Russian Trust is a daring project, but the Board inspires confidence, and there may be a good field for enterprise in Russia in the next few years.

It is regrettable that a portion of the responsible Press is so willing to place its advertising columns at the service of any "bucket shop" that can pay for the space. Some of the advertisements now appearing are so obviously designed to catch "flats" that there is not the least excuse for professing ignorance of their real purport. It would be absurd to suppose that proprietors of newspapers can inquire into the bona fides of every advertiser, but they are expected to use a little discretion in admitting to their columns appeals for money for gambling purposes. The mischief the advertisements do is proved by their continued repetition, for if they failed to secure business they would cease to be published. Instances are constantly cropping up of people being shorn of all they possess through dealings with "bucket shops", and the police courts frequently reveal cases of clerks robbing their employers in order to meet the claims of these swindlers, with whom they have played and lost, and played again and owed.

THE GRAFTON GALLERIES.

SECOND NOTICE.

BY LAURENCE BINYON.

MY first notice of the Grafton Galleries exhibition was mainly concerned with the splendid examples of the Venetian school. One Venetian picture I did not mention; and though not of the first importance, it is a picture that one would like to see in the National Gallery, for it is, I imagine, the only genuine Carpaccio in England. The large picture at Trafalgar Square which used to bear Carpaccio's name has for some years been restored to its rightful author, Lazzaro Bastiani. This "Holy Family in a Landscape" (No. 83) is in bad condition; but it has a great many of the typical qualities of the painter, whose childlike imagination captivates us in moods when far greater artists leave us cold. Who could resist the romantic zest of his invention, which has conceived so wonderful a setting to the sacred scene? Beside the broadening waters of a river rise strange rocks and Eastern trees, and along the shore in scattered procession come riding the Three Kings of the East, while in the foreground, among the wild things of the wood, the Mother adores her Child, and the Venetian pair who offered the picture kneel near by in their rich habits. It is all earthly, for Carpaccio was never far from earth and the pleasant delights of earth; but what a wild fresh charm in the ingenuous conception!

In an opposite corner hangs a little picture which carries us at once into a far different atmosphere. This is the small panel, said to be a work of the early Portuguese school (No. 77). One would have thought it to be French: but few people know much about early painting in Portugal. In any case it is an exquisite painting; and the religious spirit of the Middle Ages expresses itself not more purely in the mystical emotion of the subject than in the delicate colouring. The blackness and heavy shadows of the religious paintings of the seventeenth century in Italy and Spain were quite as fatal to their effect as the sentimental insincerity which pervaded nearly all of them. This little picture has not the lucid radiance of Angelico; the colour in it has a kind of cloistered temper suffusing it, congenial to the theme; but how tender are the tones of silvery gray in the still sky, the grays of the angels' robes, flushed with mauves and lilacs, and the solemn blue of the Virgin's dress! So much of what passes for religious art in Europe has so little inner spirituality that we recognise something rare and precious in a work like this. The angels in the trellised court where the mystic marriage of S. Catherine is being celebrated seem really beings of celestial nature as they sing or play on instruments of music or reach up to gather flowers from the boughs above their heads. It is only in some of the finest miniatures of the missal painters that we find a like spirituality of temper and delicate beauty of execution. If this is really Portuguese, it gives one a different and finer notion of early painting in that country than the examples generally known to students would support.

Spanish art is interestingly represented, if not magnificently. The famous "Water-carrier of Seville" from Apsley House (No. 31), "the earliest picture by Velazquez of which we have any authentic record", is now terribly dark; but, as was shrewdly observed by Watts, neither in the case of Velazquez' nor of Rembrandt's early pictures has time produced that magical improvement in quality which some modern painters profess to believe is an unfair advantage enjoyed by all old masters. Next to this hangs Sir Frederick Cook's "Old Woman Frying Eggs", another "bodegone" of Velazquez' youth. Hard and literal as this is in general effect, we can recognise in such passages as the painting of the melon and the earthen pan the sense of the born painter. It would be interesting to see beside this canvas some similar subject by one of the Dutchmen, who seem always to belong thoroughly to the world they paint, while in Velazquez the detachment strikes us, and the abstinence from comment, emphasis, or sentiment seems already to partake of an intellectual character—that most rare justness and veracity which were to be the mark of his mature portraiture. Some jovial piece by Jordaens would have been an apt contrast. In the "Fish-seller", by Velazquez' pupil Pareja (No. 40), which has not been shown before, we find the lesser man importing a kind of romantic atmosphere into the everyday subject. It seems strange that this should ever have been thought to be by the great master himself. The other side of Spanish art is represented by a gloomily imposing but rather empty Ribalta, and El Greco's astonishing "Supper in the House of Simon". This latter picture will probably provoke both dislike and enthusiasm. The personal element in the art of the painter is here developed to excess, and the intensity and abandon of the emotion, expressed with the courage of a nature determined to be absolutely itself and reckless of all academic canons and conventions, are attractive for their own sake to many modern minds. The majority of the public will dismiss the picture as grotesque, and vastly prefer the charming portrait of El Greco's daughter, with the brown eyes looking out from the fair, sensitive face and the bloom of life on her cheeks. The catalogue warns us that the "Lady in the Character of S. Elizabeth of Hungary" (No. 28) is not really by Zurbaran, but by some artist "of more delicate quality": it is certainly a very attractive picture. Lastly, there is a portrait of exceptional interest for Englishmen, Goya's half-length of Wellington. It was for this painting that the artist made the study in red chalk which is in the British Museum, and has been reproduced in Mr. Rothenstein's monograph and elsewhere. The study is much finer than the picture. The great duke was not fortunate in his English portraits; the painters of these saw too much of the Field-Marshal, too little of the genius. But in a moment of exaltation after battle Goya caught a glimpse of the inner spirit of the man, and drew the head with an unforgettable vividness, the lips a little parted and the eyes shining; it is not only the revelation of a man, but of a daring imagination and passionate purpose. Such is the drawing: it is a thousand pities that the painting falls so far short of the first intense conception. It seems to have been carried out in a colder mood, and to have been done in haste. None the less, it is deeply interesting.

Of the great portraits in the large gallery it is hardly necessary to write. Van Dyck and Titian, Rembrandt and Hals, Rubens and Reynolds are here to be seen, each with his own particular character of greatness. Special attention may be called to the Rubens (No. 29), which has never been shown before and is one of the master's finest portraits. Hals is at his firmest and most brilliant in the ruddy "Burgomaster" (No. 37), but neither in the famous "Man with a Hawk" nor the "Man with Close-cropped Hair" are Rembrandt's most subtle powers called out; the sitters were not sufficiently interesting personalities for that; and we feel his intimate genius more in the portrait of an old lady (No. 51), doubtless the same sitter as in the picture acquired for the National Gallery ten years ago. Reynolds holds his own by his male sense of character, colour and design, even in this exacting company, with the well-known "Sterne" and the two Dilettanti groups. And the Gainsboroughs are enchanting.

But one of the grandest portraits in the whole collection is to be found, not among the pictures, but the drawings. I mean the superb head of a Cardinal, in silverpoint, by Foucquet (No. 119). The two rooms of drawings demand, indeed, repeated visits. Mr. Heseltine's Watteaus form a collection unsurpassed for variety and brilliance. What singular completeness of beauty in the study of the lady (No. 48), whose face looks out at us from under the large veil and hat with almost disquieting reality of life, yet with what mobile delicacy! A largeness of style in the lines of the design lifts it above the world of prettiness. The Claudes show that fascinating draughtsman in less variety, but are all beautiful: and then what admirable examples of later Frenchmen, of Fragonard, of Boucher (if you like that artist, to me cold and tiresome), of Saint-Aubin, of Ingres! Note, too, the fresh, fragile sketch of a girl (No. 92) by that little-known artist, Trinquesse.

A MATTER OF SEX.

By Max Beerbohm.

LAST week, writing about the Gaiety, I permitted myself to laugh a little at the traditional languor of the ladies of the chorus. But for their air of ennui, I could have taken them quite seriously. There seems nothing at all absurd in the idea of pretty young women, dressed in the very latest fashion, singing and dancing in unison certain songs and dances in which they have been trained with a view to showing themselves off to the best advantage. What more natural, asks man, than that woman should wish to please? What more natural than that she should exercise fascination in public, at large, six or seven times a week? He would not care to do it himself. He would deem it beneath his dignity. He reserves his charms for private life. He doesn't mind showing off in a room; but in any public place he hates to draw attention—favourable or unfavourable—to himself. Observe any average man and woman entering a restaurant together. The difference in their costumes is a perfect symbol of the difference in their comportment. Whereas the woman has a garb of bright colours, and, belike, of some fantastic shape decreed by the mode of the moment, the man wears what is the nearest equivalent that our magic-bereft age can find for a cloak of invisibility. In the face and gait of the woman you can see that she is accustomed to be visible, and that she likes being looked at, while the poor man sulkily scowls and shuffles through the ordeal, or tries to carry it off with a high hand, failing utterly. I conceive that the average woman sees nothing ludicrous in the chorus at the Gaiety: the choristers are but doing for a salary, and in a trained manner, what she does casually for nothing. But "the chorus" is an arbitrary term. There are two choruses at the Gaiety. And I am certain that to the average man the male choristers seem to occupy a very absurd and lamentable position.

This difference of effect is the more interesting because, strictly, the one chorus is an exact pendant to the other. The men, like the women, have been selected for their good looks, and have been dressed in the latest fashion, and sing the same sort of songs in the same sort of way. They have been drilled to wave their walking-sticks at one moment, and at another to draw their handkerchiefs out of their cuffs and flick imaginary dust off their uniform boots, and perform simultaneously other bits of "business" equivalent to what the women have been drilled to perform. The only differences are that the men do not appear so frequently, and that they do not display that languor which seemed to me the one ridiculous thing about the performance of the women. They work with a will. I suppose it is the courage of despair that upholds them. They feel that since there is no escape they may as well put a brave face on the matter. But, heroes though they are, they excite only amusement and contempt among the audience. . . . Stay! I recall a conversation I had not long ago with a clever woman who writes books. We discussed, or rather I left her to expound, the question of what women most admire in a man—the qualities that especially attract them. I had said, perfunctorily, deeming it a truism, that beauty in the opposite sex meant much more to men than to women; whereupon, with the steadfast and minatory composure of a cross-examining counsel leading a witness on to dangerous ground, she asked me what, then, did I suppose woman most admired in man; and I, with a vague gesture, said "Oh, I'd always heard it was strength of character, and so on; a square chin, and all that". The swoop of her eagle glance made me wish I had a beard; but her mind is pre-eminently a generalising one, and swept me forthwith into the vast world-crowd of men who regard woman as a toy. I was but as an unit of the crowd she addressed. The reason, I heard, why men imagine strength of character to be a prime bait is that they imagine themselves the stronger sex. And stronger they are, doubtless, in point of muscle; and more concentrated in purpose; and in intellect more capacious. But (the lady continued) these advantages are accidental, not essential. They spring not from the nature of man, but from the defective training of woman. A very muscular, very purposeful, very intellectual woman—a woman trained in advance of the age we live in—is not very attractive to men, because men sub-consciously feel that she is a foe threatening their supremacy. And so she is. But when the battle shall have been won, and the principle of equality established, she will be just as attractive as any other kind of woman. Indeed (I gathered) there won't be any other kind of woman. They will all be what we, for the moment, call manly. And they will be attractive to the other sex in ratio to the amount of physical beauty that they possess. And it is exactly in that ratio that men, even now, are attractive to women. Strength of character: what does any woman, in her heart, care about that? She has been educated, on a man-made system, to think that she by nature needs a protector—some one to think for her and act for her; and the lesson has its superficial effect on her. She meekly repeats with her lips what she has been taught;

and often chooses a mate on the principles laid down for her. But her inward soul is true to itself. Centuries of oppression and misdirection have not availed to change it. First and last, it is physical beauty that women admire and desire in man. They are afraid to say so. They have been taught that it is immodest to say so. Some of them may not even be aware that it is so. But so it is (said my informant).

Perhaps, then, I have wasted my pity on the male choristers of the Gaiety. Perhaps to the women in the audience their aspect is giving just the same sort of pleasure that the men derive from the aspect of the female choristers. It may be that they are apt to receive bouquets and billet-doux from adoring ladies, and are all the while laughing in their sleeves at the men who sit despising their gambols. Maybe, it is not the courage of despair, but the consciousness of victory, that makes them seem so cheerful. Still, even so, their female counterparts on the stage, as not being despised by the women in the audience, and as being openly admired by the men, have the happier existence. In the future—I am not quite clear whether it is a remote or an imminent future—when woman's equality with man shall be established once and for all, here and there you will find a man rejoicing, and him you will know to be a chorister of the Gaiety, no longer overshadowed by his female rivals, no longer serving in a "man-made" theatre. Nightly the women in the audience will display frankly their delight in him. Week after week, the illustrated papers will reproduce full-page photographs of him, from this and that angle. He will be seen supping nightly in splendid restaurants, under chaperonage of his father or uncle, with splendid young Guardswomen. If he is careful, he may marry into the Peerage—who knows?

DR. HORNBY.

THE Provost of Eton was a man who possessed in an extraordinary degree the qualities and accessories of life that instinctively attract the admiration and respect of Englishmen. He had a stately and dignified presence, and a manner which was modest, genial and unaffected. His talk was graceful, lively and humorous, alike without pomposity or reserve. He had been a famous athlete in his youth, both as a cricketer and an oar, and he remained active and dexterous until a very advanced age. He was well-connected and came of a stock distinguished in the military and naval annals of the country. In mind he was alert and clear-sighted, but at the same time cautious and judicious. He could be depended upon to take a sympathetic and liberal view of a question up to a certain point, but beyond that he was tenacious of his opinions and courteously inflexible. It was in fact a typically English combination of qualities, and there was added to it a certain lightness of touch and an unfailing vivacity which made him the most charming of companions. His career was an eminently successful one, and the only wonder is that so richly equipped a personality did not set a deeper mark upon the age in which he lived.

His appointment to the Headmastership of Eton in 1868 was hailed as a triumph of enlightenment and progress. He was the first Headmaster for many generations who had not been an Eton Colleger and a Kingsman, and it was high time that the venerable tradition should be broken. Up to that date Eton had been in the hands of a close oligarchy consisting of the Provost and Fellows. The Provost was as a rule an ex-Headmaster, the Fellows were retired masters. The Fellows nominated boys to college, the Collegers succeeded to fellowships at King's, and returned to Eton as masters. On a vacancy in the Headmastership an assistant, generally the senior assistant, was nominated. Yet such a system worked better in practice than might have been expected. Hawtrey, for instance, was a man of cosmopolitan sympathies, liberal-minded and cultivated. But he was an exception to the rule. The traditions of the Headmastership were sound scholarship, unflinching Toryism, and strict discipline tempered by a due deference to the inherited liberties of the boys.

The Public School Commission disestablished the College as then constituted and suppressed the Fellowships. In 1868 the new governing body had to elect a successor to Dr. Balston, who had accepted office reluctantly and was conscientiously opposed to educational reform. Their choice fell upon Hornby, who was the precise opposite of the old-fashioned product. He was essentially a man of the world, and his educational experience had been wide and varied. He was an Etonian, it is true, but he was an Oppidan. He had resided at Oxford on a Brasenose Fellowship, he had been principal of a hall at Durham University, and he had for a short time held the second mastership at Winchester. He stood for Oxford and the humanities as against Cambridge and the verities. He was received at Eton with interest modified by suspicion, and was believed to be insufficiently equipped with practical scholastic experience. But the charm of his personality produced an immediate effect, and he was able to introduce without friction or opposition a large number of much-needed reforms. He introduced modern subjects into the curriculum and increased the hours of work. He was undoubtedly, in a sense, the creator of the modern, civilised, sensible Eton. His subordinates were capable and enthusiastic, and the place flourished greatly under his reasonable and gentlemanly rule. But he was in no sense, like Arnold or Thring, the exponent of new principles, nor the founder of a new type of commonwealth. He cannot be reckoned among the great Headmasters of the time. It was rather that new influences were in the air and that public attention was bearing heavily upon the patent demerits, the barbaric survivals, of the old type of public school. The new wine was already in the old bottles. Hornby by his closer touch with the world, by his greater width of experience, was enabled to give expression to these needs and to start the machine on the right lines, though he supplied but little of the impulsive power.

But it must also be frankly confessed that his personality hardly made itself felt in the great sphere in which he found himself. He formed no intimate relations with his masters, while to the boys he was a gracious and dignified monarch, rather than a commander to be dreaded and adored. He seemed to admit no one inside a certain fence of reserve. He was always courteous, considerate, and just, but he had none of the rough vigour and vehement earnestness that create difficulties and obstacles in their collision with human inertia, and then demolish them by sheer momentum. He was neither eager nor despondent; he had none of those acute reactions characteristic of exuberant natures which, by revealing the depths of personality, win devoted if almost compassionate adherence. Under Hornby things never came to a head. He valued tranquillity and he ensued peace by adroit prevention rather than by energetic dominance. He was firm enough in disciplinary matters and could be absolutely unbending if his mind was made up; but he preferred anything to a last resort. Thus his addresses to the boys on points of order were models of sensible argument and kindly consideration, but he did not aim at nor, indeed, desire any strong personal dominance. The system at Eton has always been that of divide et impera, and Hornby made no attempt to modify it. In the case of a man like Arnold, his personality penetrated the community he ruled from end to end; but at Eton Hornby ruled by delegation rather than concentration of authority, and gave his assistants a large degree of independence. In one celebrated case, where he dismissed a prominent colleague on a technical point, he made a grave mistake, but showed a tenacity of purpose worthy of a better cause. His urbanity, his policy of conciliation, had been sometimes mistaken for weakness; but just as he never courted applause, so he was in reality profoundly indifferent to adverse opinion and consistently self-contained.

As a teacher he was admirable. The subjects in which he was really at home were classics and theology, and he taught them soundly and lucidly, with refined appreciation and sincere enjoyment. But even here the impersonal element came out, and his sixth form regarded him with respect, admiration, and loyalty, but without just that quickened sense of personal responsibility and generous devotion which leaders of men instinctively evoke. He seemed so accessible, he proved so remote; yet his courtesy was unfeigned, his perception of character clear; what he shrank from was any show or expression of emotion.

The same qualities came out in his sermons from the school pulpit, which were models of lucidity, literary refinement, and reasonable piety. They convinced rather than inspired, and stirred reflection rather than emulation. If they lacked fire and directness, they edified and uplifted. They gave an impression of intellectual power, of wholesome ideals, of temperate strength; they never startled the careless or aroused the indifferent; but on thoughtful boys of equable temperament they produced a considerable effect, in harmonising intellectual and spiritual ideals.

The routine work of the Headmaster was in those days very severe, and Hornby bore his burden loyally and serenely. He hardly delegated any of his teaching, and took more than his share of examining. This gave him no time for personal inspection, and he was thus to the majority of boys an august but unfamiliar figure. The strain of work and responsibility was undoubtedly great and told severely upon his strength, so that the latter years of his Headmastership were years of quiet administration rather than vigorous organisation.

Strong and active as he always was, it was undoubtedly a relief to him when, in 1884, he was appointed to the Provostship, vacant by the death of Dr. Goodford. He was not yet sixty, but his life work was done. He had no ecclesiastical experience, and, as a churchman of the cautious and academical type, had little sympathy either with theological liberalism or with the advanced High Church party. He had no ambition to rule a diocese or direct the destinies of a cathedral. The dignified leisure of the Provostship was thoroughly congenial to him. He lived a quiet, almost secluded, life at Eton and at Keswick, where he had a house of his own. He read widely, and kept wonderfully in touch with literature and current thought. He preserved to the last a remarkable freshness and vivacity, both of mind and body, and never suffered from the disabilities of age. He entertained little, but was always the most genial and engaging of hosts. His memory was extraordinary, and he had a great fund of reminiscence and anecdote, animated by sympathetic comprehension and enlivened by apt and delicate humour. The Provost was never seen to greater advantage than at a public function of any kind. His natural dignity, his unaffected modesty, his ready geniality, his entire absence of pomposity and self-consciousness enabled him to preside with unexampled grace over a social gathering. His after-dinner speeches were the perfection of good taste and humour and appropriateness. It is remarkable that a task discharged with such entire ease and felicity was apparently so little congenial to him; for he had no taste for public appearances, and consistently withdrew from both social functions and official occasions.

He wielded considerable influence as Chairman of the Governing Body, and by his thorough knowledge of the conditions, his consistent definiteness of view, and his adroit handling of business, he kept the direction of the policy of the school to a large extent in his hands. Like many men who begin as reformers, his views had insensibly crystallised, and though his personal relations with his successor were uniformly cordial, he was not wholly in sympathy with Dr. Warre's vigorous and efficient measures of reform. But he never outstepped constitutional precedent, and though his educational theories might almost be called reactionary, yet no one ever doubted that he was actuated by the sincerest desire for the prosperity and welfare of Eton.

But in appreciating the worth and work of a man who has filled a high position, while it is legitimate and indeed desirable to use entire candour of criticism, we make a grave mistake if we imply or even seem to imply that a policy, positive or negative, is dictated either by a deliberate abstention or a lack of moral effort. The man's work is the expression of the man, his personality and character, and it is given to few to touch the whole gamut of human qualities. If there appeared to be in the work of Dr. Hornby a certain lack of initiative and emotional force, it was compensated for by many high and gracious qualities. He lived a serious, high-minded, unworldly life, of great simplicity and intellectual enjoyment. In all societies, he exerted a great personal charm. He had a singularly fortunate temperament, with that instinctive moderation, that fine balance of faculties which the Greeks accounted so high a virtue. He endured calamity manfully, he bore the burdens of life lightly. About his cheerful, tranquil nature there was nothing morbid or strained. He laboured abundantly and fruitfully, and he passes from the world in the fulness of days, with faculties unimpaired, after an old age of tranquillity and honour, and with a life behind him that can be called happy as few lives can claim to be called.

NATURE THE CONSERVATIVE.

In accordance with our modern trick of drawing far-sighted deductions of an ethical or social nature from so-called conclusions of science which are in themselves no more than first approximations to the truth, it has become the fashion of late for all sorts of writers, from professors of eugenics to popular playwrights, to warn us in no measured terms of the danger that civilisation is incurring through its habit of breeding only from its inferior stocks. Thus stated the thesis seems obvious enough; not only is the birth rate declining in the more advanced states, but the decline mainly affects the rich or perhaps more particularly the middle classes; it is the poor, and even the very poor, who nowadays possess large famllies.

The breeder of racehorses or milch cows proceeds along no such haphazard lines; not only are animals marked by any defect cast at once, but a further selection is made to pick out the very best for sires, and much thought is spent on the mating in order to secure the most desirable combination and intensification of qualities. Modern biology has returned to that study of the work of the breeder which Darwin made the foundation of his theories, and with the general appreciation of the value of Mendel's discoveries we are learning how plastic any race may become and with what quickness and certainty it may now be moulded by a guiding intelligence.

That the human race takes no heed of such possibilities or of the consequences of its heedlessness is obvious enough; no better example need be mentioned than the investigation which Dr. Eliot conducted into the birth rate of the families of Harvard graduates. Roughly speaking, he found that the average family of a Harvard graduate was no more than two, so that, allowing for wastage due to deaths before marriage and assuming that half the births were boys, any given Harvard class is not reproduced in the next generation. In this country, too, it is a matter of common observation that the men of the professional class marry late or not at all; it is not merely that they cannot afford to marry earlier, because standards of wealth are relative, but they are so much occupied in making their professional career, their lives are so rich in alien interests, that they pass through the critical marrying years without being drawn into the general stream of matrimony. Of women who take up a professional career the proportion who remain unmarried is even greater. They have stepped out of the ranks in virtue of their intellect, their training has intensified that side of their character and reduced their instinctive emotional appeal to the mere man, though they may have become not less willing to marry and certainly better fitted for the careers of wives and mothers. As the lady of immemorial tradition explained how she came to have acquired a third husband, "It isn't the money as does it, nor yet the good looks; it's the comither in my eye," and that gift often does not go with intellect.

But if we accept the fact that the race is in the main

being recruited from its lowest strata—from the improvident, the animal, even the criminal, members of society, in far greater numbers than from those whom the world usually delights to honour—is this process a new one, or can it even be described as breeding from the worst, without begging a good many questions? That the process has always been going on in all civilisations of which any record has been preserved may be surmised from the essential unchangeableness of human nature as revealed in history. Man in Periclean times, man even in the earliest of the Egyptian dynasties, was evidently very much what he is to-day; it is only by moving our datum back to the Stone Age that we can be very sure of anything to be called progress. We ought not to compare the course of human affairs to a spiral; a better simile would be the tide, where the waves surge unceasingly up and down but the general level of the water creeps only imperceptibly up the wall. In all ages the human race must have been bred from the broad common stock; the "best" have been the extreme variants in certain directions, the "sports", and like all sports they have been mostly sterile; had it been otherwise, the race would have changed in an accelerating fashion of which we have no evidence.

Moreover, have we any right to identify the "best" with the most intellectual or even with the most efficient from a common worldly point of view? Speaking biologically, the prime concern of the human race is not progress but life. "Give her the glory of going on and not to die"; the best for this purpose are those who do live and increase and multiply. Is Nature, indeed (understanding by Nature merely a convenient term for the dim instinctive trend of the race) so much in need of intellect as to be in any way striving to increase it or extend its sphere of action? The evidence would rather indicate that Nature has always been putting up a fight against intellect, and has been engaged in a constant endeavour to eliminate it both in the individual and the race. The keynote of Nature is stability; she is aiming above all at self-preservation, at life as it is, because such life has been tested by experience and found to work—everything else will be sacrificed to retain life and the possibility of further life. When we look at animals and plants we see how the whole external pressure of the environment seems directed towards the conservation of the existing type; we know that variation exists, but variations are always being smoothed out and eliminated. Darwin founded his theory of the creation of species on the accumulation of minute favourable variations, but it seems difficult to hold that view nowadays after an extended study of the facts of inheritance; hence the current school of thought considers that species arise by sudden and large steps quite different in kind from the normal variations round the type which Darwin had in view, the difference being that they are wholly handed on to the next generation. This theory presents its own logical difficulties, but it must be conceded that species and races are extraordinarily stable in the state of nature where they have to persist under the pressure of competition, that self-same competition upon which Darwin relied to bring the favourable variations to the front. The selective action of the breeder can only operate when his creations are protected from competition; his improved animals or plants when turned out into the world either revert to type or perish. There is a well-known experiment of Lawes in which he left a wheat field unharvested to sow itself and get on as best it could; in four years the wheat, for all its vigour and adaptability to all sorts of climates and soils, had disappeared—pushed off the land by the more aggressive weeds. We may fairly conclude that it is the stable conservative types of society that are most likely to persist, and that Nature is striving to eliminate intellect because a race dominated by intellect would become essentially unstable. Certain episodes in the French Revolution furnish examples of the strange fantasies into which the pursuit of reason may draw human beings, but the whole of history is full of instances of the extremes into which men can argue themselves—no madman has ever been half so dangerous as the logician. We have only to imagine the results of putting our own really clever and intellectual friends in control of any large section of public affairs—say, for example, in charge of the education of the young—to realise how jerky and erratic human life would become if intellect were made the guiding force in society. In the world as it is great rewards are often reserved for the intellect of the individual, but only on condition that he somehow makes his intellect work along ordinary lines. Thus the pressure of the circumambient stupidity makes the intellect of the individual effective for the purposes of the race by preventing it from developing in wasteful directions; to be valuable it must be repressed into the lead of a turbine and not allowed to break in foam over the waterfall. Such a conclusion, that Nature is in the main anti-intellectual, is confirmed by the further consideration that intellect, as Bernard Shaw says, is a masculine speciality. Of course nothing is more idle than to talk about masculine and feminine characteristics; only men and women exist, not man and woman. But little as any classification can apply to any individual, we are yet allowed to draw certain broad distinctions between the sexes, and in this general way it is true that woman must be regarded as the repository of the prime instinct of racial preservation. As mother she is self-regarding, though her unit is the family and not herself; from her position as mother again she derives her clear-sightedness, her practical instincts, and the distrust of adventure that marks the true Conservative valuing stability and persistence above all other qualities. Man has only indirectly the cares of the future generation on his hands—he has to be bribed by his senses to the service of the future race at all—and in him is developed the instinct of peacocking. For from the strictly practical point of view—that of handing on life to the next generation, of continuing to be—what else is intellect, art, altruism, the sense of beauty, even the sense of holiness, but vain display? They are illusions all, iridescences by which man strives to adorn the very ordinary part he has to play in the universe, and Nature is always fighting against these illusions in so far as they may tend to make man forget his essential rôle. Some of these illusions Nature has even turned to service as baits whereby man is drawn to woman; but against others, intellect in particular, an endless conflict is being maintained, and no better proof is wanted than the fact that woman, the true measure of permanent values, has always declined either to develop intellect herself or to make much of it in others.

FORBIDDEN THISTLES.

On someone asking whether it was not "wicked" to dabble in the Occult.

RAINY or sunny weather,
  Crop your thistle and grass:
Try the length of your tether,
  Beyond you cannot pass—
That is best on the whole—
  You are only an ass,
    Poor Soul.

But let no pedant priest
  Hobble you, fix your span;
You are the good God's beast,
  And not the slave of man—
That is best on the whole—
  Browse as far as you can,
    Poor Soul.

Sunny or rainy weather,
  Crop your thistle and grass;
God's will your only tether,
  And *that* you cannot pass.
So it is best on the whole—
  To be the good God's ass,
    Poor Soul!

M. B.

THE WIDOW'S MITE.

A FINANCIER lately left fifteen or twenty millions sterling to his widow, besides houses and lands. She may claim to be the richest woman in the universe. Two other widows identified by an enterprising journal run her close with sixteen millions each; but the lady to whom an ignorant public has granted that proud title hitherto may hide her head and her paltry eight millions for shame. They are all American of course; the note is pitched far too high for European rivalry. Indeed it is pitiful for anyone interested to look through a list of twelve widows, wives, and maiden ladies, the wealthiest extant, published by the same enterprising journal. Only one English name appears there, one German, and one Chilian. If Lady Burdett-Coutts, the typical heiress of legend, the embodiment of wealth beyond the dreams of avarice half a century ago, were living now, positively she would not be included in the dozen! Not rich enough! The antique pretensions of Miss Kilmansegg, Monte Cristo, Vathek and Lothair would be just ridiculous. Not only do the fortunes of these transatlantic dames pass record; they beggar imagination.

Doubtless the capital was invested profitably by the shrewd persons who collected it, and the return is even larger than would be computed normally. Without impertinence we may speculate how such gigantic incomes are used. A woman could not spend so much even though she gambled, for her opportunities are limited; but if past early youth she will not "chuck it away", as a man might. Relations and friends intercept a great deal, of course. We may venture to take it for granted that a vast sum is dispensed in charity—the woman who does not give when she has an unlimited amount of cash to spare must be a very rare monster. Also, we may take it for granted that a very large part falls into undeserving hands. It is understood that some widows carry on the business of the defunct, and those are the happiest probably, if competent. They have not altogether lost touch with the herd of workaday mortals. While conducting an operation on the Stock Exchange, and dividing the plunder, they may almost cease for the time to be conscious that everybody in the world is plotting against them.

But of the others few even spend their income probably. It suffices to meet any extravagance which a sane person could commit, and saving is an instinct of womanhood; it will be found even in the most reckless though under odd shapes. The hoard will pass, with accumulations, either to a second husband—not much to be envied—or, mostly, to an heir of the younger generation. Of such "golden calves" a score or two are already set up in the United States. Generally, it appears, they employ themselves in business, but they cannot be absorbed therein as their fathers were. Each generation differs from the last in tastes, fancies and ideas, but especially does the man who inherits a fortune differ from the man who made it, as a rule. As yet this jeunesse, so lavishly gilt, seems to content itself with the pursuit of "freaks" by way of amusement—unedifying but harmful only to those who share the sport, unless public decorum be worth consideration. But it is evident that if one of the lively crew turned his hand to mischief for a change he would have fine opportunities. Some thinkers in the United States have not failed to note this risk. The possession of wealth practically boundless by young men uncontrolled and irresponsible is a new portent, though something like it was seen in the last days of republican Rome—an evil omen, though the circumstances are so diverse.

In Europe hitherto the youth succeeding to a great fortune has found himself curbed and fettered by bonds, circumstantial and social, which indeed he could break through by main strength, yet so effective that instances of one disturbing public order without some grave object are very rare. A Duke of Buckingham might embarrass the Government "for fun", but in modern times only the last Duke of Wharton planned a serious disturbance of the public peace to amuse himself. But those restraining influences must be less powerful in the United States. A great English fortune is nearly always connected with land, which of itself has a steadying effect; but the infinitely larger hoards of the New World may be realised at short notice. It is "operations" of this sort, causing wanton panics and confusion, which people seem to fear. But one cannot help thinking that a man of evil nature, with a few millions of dollars at command, might raise trouble even more serious among the swarm of pauper aliens in New York, or among native desperadoes. But it is not necessary that he should be of evil nature. Quite a commonplace youth whose brains are affected by vicious living might conceive the idea of emulating Nero, the past-master of "freaks".

But Europe has an interest in the matter. One would like to be sure that any State is so firmly established, or any population so universally content, as to defy the agitator; but if such a one there be it is not Austria with a dozen hostile races, nor Spain with a Pretender waiting his opportunity and Republicans eager to try again, nor Russia, nor Italy, nor Great Britain with Ireland eternally irreconcilable. None of them could afford to smile if a foreigner, moved by enthusiasm to avenge some interesting nationality oppressed, or only seeking new and grander thrills, undertook to redress the wrong with a bottomless purse. He would not need to run any risks—his money would fly through the land like the Fiery Cross of old whilst he sat comfortable at home. There are countries in Europe where the Government or the Monarchy could be overthrown for a very reasonable sum. A few thousands would suffice to expel the Kings of Greece and Servia; the Bulgarian Tsar could be dismissed almost as cheaply. And there would be openings for personal adventure in these cases attractive to vivacious youth. The late "Empereur du Sahara" showed that a man with capital sufficient can still make himself a king, if he have the courage and energy which that gentleman did not display when the crisis came. Persia and Turkey offer great opportunities to a capitalist in search of excitement. He might buy up the clans of Albania bodily, and restore the throne of Scanderbeg. There is a prospect of the wildest and most various sensations in the idea. But he would not live long to enjoy them. This may sound fantastic; not so the marriage of one of these widows, or stupendous heiresses, to a princelet who lacked only money to raise a host of fanatics, adventurers and brigands. Patriots, too, with a grievance might well be tempted to mischief when they found themselves possessed of boundless wealth—in Bohemia, for instance, or Hungary, the Lithuanian Provinces of Russia or the Polish of Posen. The American wife would be more likely to encourage the enterprise perhaps than to dissuade them.

THE LASKER-JANOWSKI CHESS MATCH.—II.

By Emanuel Lasker.

THE "Grand Cercle" is a club that has a handsome suite of rooms upon the Boulevard Montmartre, not far distant from the Opera. Its members are wealthy men, few of them young. The predominating colour of hair is grey. The purpose of the club is to help men in quest of an easy and agreeable pastime to meet each other. One sees all games played there. Carpets covering every inch of the floor exclude noise. One dines well there, and the conversation at the dinner-table is animated. Latterly the club, finding its quarters too narrow, has added to them a suite of rooms of the neighbouring building, and connected the apartments. It is in one of these rooms that the match is taking place.

The paraphernalia are simple: a table covered with green cloth, in the centre of it the chessboard with its pieces, on the sides the scoring sheets, and a clock which measures the time consumed in thinking. On opposite sides, just before the chessboard, the two masters. Sitting on chairs, or standing, sometimes whispering, are M. Goetz, director of play, the seconds chosen for the day and a few spectators willing to look but to resign themselves to silence. In the adjoining two rooms men come and go, and a lively conversation takes place. The game is there being followed, explained, discussed. Everything is in good order, but unluckily the chess-board reflects the light strongly. The chess master needs his eyes often, and he has therefore an interest to use them economically. Brilliant surfaces excite and fatigue them. The manufacturers of chessboards do not realise this, or else they want to impress him who buys a present rather than to please the user.

The two masters are men of about the same age, approximately forty-one years. Their hair, originally black, is just beginning to be invaded by grey. Janowski is a very dark type; had he a moustache he would look a typical Spaniard, but he is beardless. He dresses with care and taste. He has the patience to study the position even when my clock is running. I am wandering about or sitting with closed eyes in a chair of another room whenever it is Janowski's turn to move. The strong artificial light of the room hurts my eyes. The lid of my right eye was operated upon four weeks ago, and is not yet in order; therefore my eyes are sensitive.

The Third Game.

Ruy Lopez.

White Lasker	Black Janowski	White Lasker	Black Janowski
1. P–K4	P–K4	4. B×Kt	QP×B
2. Kt–KB3	Kt–QB3	5. P–Q4	P×P
3. B–Kt5	P–QR3		

The character of the position is now declared. White has four pawns to three upon the king's wing, on the opposite wing black has the superiority, but is there hampered by having the QBP doubled and consequently less mobile than normally. On the other hand, black has two bishops upon a board showing few obstructions. The advantages of either party compensate and probably balance each other.

6. Q×P	B–KKt5	10. Kt(Q4)–K2	B×KKt
7. Kt–B3	Q×Q	11. K×B	B×Kt ch
8. Kt×Q	Castles	12. P×B	Kt–B3
9. B–K3	B–Kt5	13. P–B3	Kt–Q2

Black has succeeded in tearing the Q side pawns of white asunder; they would now fall an easy prey to any attack. The question is, whether the hostile pieces can find an approach to them. The road R–K–K4–QR4 is dangerously open. Again Kt–K4–B5 establishes the Kt in a strong yet unassailable position. The right side of white must therefore do some rapid fighting, in order to keep the opposing force occupied.

14. QR–Q Kt–K4 15. R–Q4 P–QKt3

preparatory to P–QB4, to drive the R away that blocks the road to the Kt.

16. P–KB4	Kt–Q2	18. R(Q4)–Q3	Kt–Kt
17. KR–Q	P–QB4		

The Kt has now found a way via B3, R4 to B5 that white cannot make unsafe. White must rapidly advance to force the pace of fighting on the other wing.

19. K–B3 QR–K

He desires to keep his rooks, and he rightly judges that the possession of the open file which he yields to the opponent is of no value; but the danger lies elsewhere.

20. P–B5	P–B3	23. R–K3	Kt–B3
21. B–B4	R–K2	24. P–Kt5	. . .
22. P–KKt4	KR–K		

forcing the exchange of pawns, thus making the backward KP free.

24. . . . Kt–R4

He abides by his original plan of campaign, not seeing that his left wing is already in imminent peril. P×P (25) B×P, R–B2 would have stayed the rush and, although the KP remained a dangerous assailant, with careful defence he would probably have drawn.

25. P–KR4	Kt–B5	28. P–R5	Kt–Q3
26. R–K2	R–B2	29. P–R6	. . .
27. R–KKt	K–Q2		

The KKtP which guards the P that blocks the way to white, the KBP, is thus destroyed. Its fall should have been foreseen six moves ago.

29. . . . BP×P

If P–KKt3 (30) P×KtP, RP×P (31) P×P, R×P (32) P–K5, R(B3)–B (33) P×Kt, R×R (34) K×R, R×B (35) R–KR, R–B (36) P–R7, R–KR (37) P×P, K×P (38) K–B3, marches to R6, then gains, after a rook check, the square Kt7 and wins the rook.

30. R×P	P–KKt3	35. R–Kt2	Kt–K
31. P×P	P×P	36. B–K5	K–K3
32. R×P	R(K)–KB	37. K–B4	K–B2
33. R–Kt7	R×R	38. K–B5	Resigns
34. P×R	R–KKt		

The KKtP can be won, but then the white king marches to K6 and queens the KP, also wins the defenceless black pawns.

The Fourth Game.

Four Knights.

White Janowski.	Black Lasker	White Janowski	Black Lasker
1. P–K4	P–K4	8. P×B	Kt–K2.
2. Kt–KB3	Kt–QB3	9. B–QB4	Kt–Kt3
3 Kt–B3	Kt–B3	10. Kt–R4	Kt–B5
4. B–Kt5	B–Kt5	11. B×Kt(B4)	P×B
5. Castles	Castles	12. Kt–B3	B–Kt5
6. P–Q3	P–Q3	13. Q–Q2	. . .
7. B–Kt5	B×Kt.		

Superior to P–KR3, as was played by him in the second game. The pawn on R3 was a mark for the attack, whereas on R2 it is beyond the reach of the knight and makes the position of the king safe against queen and rooks.

13. . . .	B×Kt	17. R–Kt5	P–KKt3
14. P×B	Kt–R4	18. QR–KKt	P–KB3
15. K–R	K–R	19. KR–Kt4	QR–K
16. R–KKt	Q–Q2	20. Q–B	. . .

White wants to bring all the heavy artillery of rooks and queen upon the knight's file. The manœuvre is hazardous, because it leaves the remainder of the board to the mercy of black, unless the partly open knight file, so strongly held, exerts sufficient pressure upon the black pieces to pin them to their posts.

20. . . .	P–KB4	23. P×QP	P×P
21. R–Kt5	P–B3	24. B–Kt5	Q–B3
22. Q–KB	P–Q4		

The QBP cannot be defended; if Q–QR, Kt–B3 and later R–QB.

25. Q–Kt2 Q–KB3

This wins the exchange by force. Kt–Kt6 ch is menaced. If (26) P–KR4, P–KR3 (27) R×KtP, Kt–Kt6 ch wins it likewise.

26. R×Kt P×R 27. B×P . . .

The best way out of his difficulties. He keeps open files for rook and bishop and can hope to make a good fight against the superior force of black by constantly threatening the imprisoned king.

27. . . . Q×P 28. Q–Kt5 R–K8

Until this point the game has been a faultless effort of the two masters to arrive at a decision, favourable to themselves, concerning their opinion of the merits of the chosen opening. It was like a well-conducted legal argument; but now the brain, excited by the partial success gained, and fatigued by the multitude of possibilities that it had to examine into, refuses to do service. It was easy to see that white menaced naught beyond the capture of the KBP, easy to defend it by Q–Q5 or Q–Q4, and it would have been wise to make preparations before trying to strike hard, since white could not threaten for a number of moves.

29. Q×P (B4) P–QKt3

P–QKt4 would have been preferable, to hamper the B and the QBP.

30. R×R	Q×R ch	32. B–Kt3	R–B3
31. K–Kt2	Q–K2		

The play of black is here far from being lucid. Better had he done Q–B3 and R–K. The open file is the natural post for the castle.

33. K–B	Q–Q3	36. Q–B3	P–QKt4
34. Q–QB4	K–Kt2	37. Q–K5	. . .
35. P–KB4	Q–Q		

Now white holds the all-important open file and black must make immense efforts to retake it.

37. . . .	Q–Q2	39. K–Q2	. . .
38. K–K2	K–Kt3		

If white advances the QP, R–Q3 follows, and it is difficult to see how white is to advance the pawn beyond the square Q5. This manœuvre would have sufficed for the draw; but white evidently plays to win.

39. . . .	R-B	40. B-K6	Q-B3

threatening Q-B6. If white now advances the QP, black executes the threat, captures the pawns on KB7 and KR7, and retires via R5 and B3 in time to stop the pawn. White had therefore naught better than the draw by B-Q5, Q-Q2, B-K6, etc.

41. Q-K3 . . .

Disappointed hope of a sure success makes him commit this unpardonable error.

41. . . .	R-K	45. B-Q	Q-K8 ch
42. Q-Kt3 ch	K-B3	46. K-B2	R-QB
43. B-Kt3	P-KR3	47. P-QB4	. . .
44. P-QB3	Q-KR8		

If P-Q4, P-Kt5.

47. . . .	P×P	50. Q×P	Q×Q ch
48. P-Q4	P-B6	51. K×Q	K-K5
49. Q-K3	R-K	Resigns.	

The score stood on Thursday night: Lasker five, Janowski one, drawn one.

CORRESPONDENCE.

LIBERAL WOMEN-FOLK; PRIMROSE-DAMES; POLITICAL FAITH.

To the Editor of the SATURDAY REVIEW.

Imperial Colonial Club, 84 Piccadilly W.
4 November 1909.

SIR,—I read with much interest and more dismay the article which appeared in the last SATURDAY REVIEW on "Liberal Woman-folk and their Men". I read it with interest because, in the course of several months of organising work for the Women's National Anti-Suffrage League, I came into contact with many Liberal women who viewed with concern the disintegration of their party associations by suffragist members. I read it with dismay because the writer of the article seems to me to justify political unfaith for personal expediency; and this applies as much to the Conservatives as to the Liberals. I also write of Conservative and Liberal women in the sense of your writer, and mean a woman who has attached herself to an organisation of either party, and who professes to uphold the principles of that party—whether imperial or domestic.

The woman who puts the vote above all other questions has a perfect right to her opinions. But, in common honesty, she has no right to allow her name to be borne on the books of a party association, and to use that association to forward her personal opinions to the detriment of that same party. The only course possible to a straightforward woman is that followed by the four women who have recently resigned their official connexion with the Birmingham Liberal Association; they regard "woman's enfranchisement as a claim superior to that of party", and they write: "Now that an election on other issues appears imminent we feel it would be unfair, both to you and ourselves, to remain till the moment for action in a position the duties of which we are unable conscientiously to discharge". This course has unfortunately not appealed to most women suffragists, and the Conservatives seem as likely to suffer as their opponents have done if we may judge by the recent correspondence between the Conservative and Unionist Women's Franchise Association and the Primrose League. This Suffrage Society works on the lines of the National Union of Women Suffrage Societies, and has the same policy except that it "does not work against a Conservative candidate should he not be in favour of the Enfranchisement of Women". The Grand Council of the Primrose League sanctions this attitude in that it regards the question as one "of opinion and not of principle"; it therefore is satisfied that members of the Primrose League have done all that is required of them in not working against an official candidate. Naturally, the Unionist Franchise Women now invite further support "as this statement makes it perfectly clear that by so doing they run no risk of injuring, even indirectly, principles in which they are so vitally concerned".

It is absurd for women of considerable social and political importance who have for years devoted themselves to the support of the Unionist party to pretend that they can suddenly abstain from taking an active part in the coming General Election without influencing "even indirectly" the fortunes of that party. Voters whom they have previously brought to the poll will naturally ask themselves what is the motive of this neutrality and will, in many cases, refrain from recording their vote—even if they do not allow themselves to be persuaded to vote adversely. At an earlier stage in the movement these women may have fondly thought that their votes would help to stem the tide of socialism and secularism. After months of discussion in the periodicals of all sorts of political and religious faith they can be under no such delusion and must be regarded as those who

"Knowing the end was foolish,
And guessing the goal was pain,
Stupid, and stubborn, and mulish—
Followed and follow again".

The Conservative party wants all the help and support it can get, and suffragists and anti-suffragists who believe in its principles should sink their differences in the face of the many more urgent problems now before the country. Unless they do so they must realise that they will have reason later to regret their inaction. And the leaders of the party will have, like the Liberals to-day, to say that "it is not an open enemy that hath done me this dishonour; . . . but mine own familiar friend".

I am, Sir, your obedient servant,
ANNIE J. LINDSAY.

LIBERAL WOMEN AND THE VOTE.

To the Editor of the SATURDAY REVIEW.

Reform Club, S.W., 4 November 1909.

SIR,—You say in your current issue: "As the General Election draws nearer a sense of fear seems to be creeping over some Liberals whether after all the anger of their women may not wreck them at the polls".

As the Liberal candidate for East Berks is described in the next sentence as writing to various newspapers, presumably under this sense of fear, I am bound to say that your contributor has entirely overlooked the main point of my efforts, to which he spares room to refer. The abstention of Liberal women from the coming election will result, so I expressed myself, not in the weakening of Liberalism but the collapse of the Women's Liberal Federation. I make this correction in order that readers of the SATURDAY REVIEW may not be beguiled by the alleged "sense of fear" which is coming over their opponents.

The prominence given in your article to the Women's Liberal Federation without any apparent knowledge of the existence of the Women's National Liberal Association (an older and more influential body) suggests that the inquiries made for you should be supervised by someone conversant with the facts.

Yours,
"THE LIBERAL CANDIDATE FOR EAST BERKS".

THE "GLORIOUS" SCOT.

To the Editor of the SATURDAY REVIEW.

25 October 1909.

SIR,—"A Coimheach's" delightful letter to your REVIEW of the 23rd does not go far enough in painting the picture of Edinburgh's Saturnalia.

After marching through the streets of Edinburgh and by the way picking up a huge mass of unwelcome and generally unsympathetic followers, Scotland's women, great and humble, rich and poor, came forth from the Waverley Market wildly excited; the Suffragettes dispersed, but the mob remained and quickly increased to immense proportions. Classes and masses became inextricably mixed, and seemed to enjoy it. Men and women, lads and lassies, felt all class prejudice broken down for the time. "A man's a man for a' that" seemed to be the motto of the women who embraced men, complete strangers up till that moment, and swept them into public-houses and hotel bars.

The afternoon wore on and the mob grew wilder; dusk showed gutters full of drunken men and women, and streets impassable for crowds of ladies not fou but with just a drappie in the e'e, waving their tartan plaids and showing their sex how to enjoy equal liberty with men in all things.

At first the aristocrats and great men of the north merely crowded to their club windows to gaze on the throng; but, irresistibly attracted by the wild excitement, they too joined in the madness, and soon with new-found friends were pressing into drinking-places and helping on the universal brotherhood of man. Gradually as the good drink mounted to the brain the serious political business of the day was forgotten, and famous Scottish songs rose with an awful skirl from ten thousand wetted throats. In side streets wild dances were started; ladies with dresses kilted to the knee footed it with ardent companions, amidst drunken hoochs and yells. Reels followed strathspeys in mad succession, only occasionally interrupted by playful charges of the Highland gentry, who with drawn skian dhus and the convenient but cool philabeg fluttering in the breeze showed that the ancient spirit of Killiecrankie was still alive.

The departure of the last train for Glasgow was a sight never to be forgotten. The station was packed with a seething mass of unsteady, lurching creatures. The railway officials with splendid determination flung passengers into the carriages regardless of class, and locked the doors. Everybody was drunk, so nobody could complain. This, no doubt, is the solution for "Disgusted Englishman".

Do I say that everybody in Edinburgh was drunk that night? Yes; and I go further and say that everyone in Scotland was in the same condition (except, of course, myself and possibly "A Coimheach"). But all, every man-jack of them, went to kirk the following day as stiff and buckram as could be (except myself and, I think, "A Coimheach", who stayed at home to write to you). The remedy for non-churchgoing has been found.

Far into the small hours of that wild night I parted from a learned member of the Franco-Scottish Society. Throwing back his head, he placed his bottle to his lips and took the last of the grateful spirit at a gulp; then, flinging the derelict from him, muttered "A splendid nicht of bonhomie and booze".

I am yours respectfully,
A Lover of Truth.

SMALL HOLDINGS.

To the Editor of the Saturday Review.

Croydon, 29 October 1909.

Sir,—The writer of the article "Hens, Goats and Small Holdings" in your issue of the 2nd inst. referred to the experiment to be made by the "Residential Small Holdings Company, Limited" to create small holdings on a rental basis, giving fixity of tenure and of rent to the tenants.

The company have only recently come to a fairly definite decision as to the lines they intend to follow, and therefore it seems only right to say now that the writer of the article ascribed a higher aim to the company than it actually has in view at the present moment. For where he writes of "a man with a mind large enough for fifty acres", evidently under the impression that in such a case a fairly large holding will be created, the company have determined to aim at giving only about five acres, while "for the man of four (acres)" the intention is to give one acre only, or less.

Although the chief object of those interested in the company is to put into practice the principles laid down by the late Major Shipson in "The Redemption of Labour", there is also the desire to benefit the greatest possible number of people.

The intention is therefore to build some houses to be let with about an acre of land to agricultural labourers and other wage-earners in the locality, and some to be let with from five to six acres each, to be farmed for a living. The company will retain and farm one holding for the present, and will help the tenants by ploughing, marketing produce, etc., for them, for which a reasonable charge will be made. It will also foster co-operation among the tenants. The latter are to have perpetual fixity of tenure and of rent, with the right to determine the tenancy at any time on giving six months' notice. The fact that this last is a necessary safeguard for them indicates the weakest point of the scheme. If Major Shipson's principles could be carried out in their entirety the tenants would increase steadily in prosperity, and although the company could never raise the rents it would also benefit, because the purchasing power of the money in which the rent was paid would also increase over all that was not food.

But agricultural rent contracts imply the surrender of a given amount of produce to the landlord, which for convenience is expressed in a fixed amount of money. The actual amount of produce, however, to be sold yearly to realise the sum of money required may vary enormously quite independently of harvests because of a rise or fall in the purchasing power of money over food. Any considerable fall is less probable than a rise, which would mean a fall in food prices. In such an event, if the tenants find themselves unable to pay the rents, they may be expected to abandon their holdings, and as in good times the company is going to refrain from increasing rents, it stands to lose on the balance.

It is, however, the main purpose of those interested in this movement to show that the risk for landowners is a real one if they let their agricultural land on the only terms which tenants can feel to be fair. If this is once appreciated it is hoped that the public and the landowners will study the remedies proposed by Major Shipson, as, after the legislation affecting landowners in recent years, first in Ireland and now throughout the whole country, it is obvious that if the private ownership of land is to continue some better form of tenure for tenants must be devised. For the people are slowly grasping the fact that if they are to have real economic freedom they must have free access to the land, if they are not to be doomed to semi-starvation because of the growing curse of unemployment.

When they are fully alive to this, if they are not given the access they need by fair means, will it be surprising if they get it by foul ones as soon as they fully appreciate the strength of an educated democracy armed with the vote? A study of Shipson's writings will show that access can be granted them by fair means to the benefit of the landowners and the entire country, and he wrote in his preface that "the dangers lie ahead not in the unwillingness of the rich to do justice or in a resolve of the poor to disregard it, but rather in the ignorance of both as to what justice is and how it may be obtained".

I do not doubt that with such study all fears as to the future of our country will be set at rest, for it will be seen that she still has a glorious part to play in advancing the civilisation of the world. But if they fail to do so, and allow these words to remain unheeded and continue to leave us "in ignorance as to what justice is and how it can be obtained", it is probable that the days of the civilisation of this Empire are numbered.

I am, Sir, your obedient servant,
Chela.

CADIZ, OHIO.

To the Editor of the Saturday Review.

Cadiz, Ohio, 16 October 1909.

Sir,—The "World's Work" for September quotes you as saying that the Americans are no more civilised than the Japanese. The reading of that paragraph recalled to my mind the following: About ten years ago a young Englishman arrived in this town to work for his uncle. He came directly to Cadiz from England. I met him after he had been here a few days, and he surprised me by inquiring when we would have a lynching or a murder. As this town was incorporated one hundred and five years ago, and has never had a murder or a lynching within its limits, I was somewhat surprised at such a question. In the conversation that followed I found that I knew much more about England than my friend from across the water knew about America. We had practically the same amount of schooling, but in our Cadiz schools we have a course in map study of England, with twenty pages of text on our mother country in our geographies, and we also include in our public-school course a 500-page text-book on English history and a work of equal size on English literature.

I also asked an English gentleman who filled a number of our annual lecture course in 1897 as to how this little city compared with one of equal size in England. One thing he said in answer was that the main thing to distinguish the two towns would be the amount of beer consumed abroad compared with what we drink here. I am forty years of age, and have never yet seen a woman intoxicated, and have travelled considerably. How many Englishmen can say as much? There are no saloons in Cadiz, and have been none in our county for the past fifteen years. We have a law in operation in Ohio that makes it possible forcibly to enter a place where liquor is supposed to be sold in prohibition territory and confiscate the "goods", if any are found. Such things have been done, and if it happens to be a rented building the owner can be made to pay $1000 liquor tax, and the "boot-legger" (one who sells or peddles liquor in prohibition territory) can be fined $200 and sent to the workhouse for sixty days. Such fines as the above have been assessed here in Cadiz. Sixty-eight out of eighty-eight Ohio counties are "dry".

I mentioned an annual winter lecture course. We spend annually $2500 to bring lecturers and entertainers here for a two weeks' Chautauqua in August, and through the winter months there are a number of clubs and organisations for culture and improvement, such as the Shakespeare Club, Choral Society, and the Cadiz Women's Club, which took English literature as the study for this winter. Our public library (not a Carnegie dollar in it) has four volumes for every man, woman and child in our town, and our four banks and four building and loan associations have about $3000 in deposits for each inhabitant of our city. We can show $5 postal receipts at our post office for each citizen, which entitles us to free city delivery.

Cadiz is an average American town, and about half of the population of the United States live very similarly to the manner of life in this place. Examine the pictures I enclose and note the bank statements, and point to an English town of equal size, 2150 inhabitants, not the suburbs of a city, that can be compared to this town in wealth, culture and learning.

Very truly yours,

HARRY B. MCCONNELL,

Foreman "Cadiz Republican".

A QUESTION OF GRAMMAR.

To the Editor of the SATURDAY REVIEW.

Halifax (N.S.), 12 October 1909.

SIR,—Mr. Asquith, in his introductory note to the edition of Bastiat's "Fallacies of Protection", recently published by the Cobden Club, says: "The 'Economic Sophisms' are no more out of date than 'The Wealth of Nations'". Is not the distinguished statesman's syntax a little faulty in the sentence quoted?

Yours etc.,

J. A. CHISHOLM.

REVIEWS.

MUDRAKING.

"Chateaubriand and his Court of Women." By Francis Gribble. London: Chapman and Hall. 1909. 15s. net.

"Byron: The Last Phase." By Richard Edgcumbe. London: Murray. 1909. 10s. 6d. net.

IF these books must needs come out, it is a happy chance that brings them out simultaneously. Chateaubriand and Byron were born to be mentioned in the same breath, born to be placed the one beside the other for the purpose of being compared and contrasted. Chateaubriand himself saw that he was destined to be bracketed with the Englishman. He cried out upon Byron for having committed the worst of plagiarisms, for having, in fact, borrowed from his personality without acknowledgment. Well, René was, at any rate, the first to be conceived; so perhaps he had a right to resent the conception of Childe Harold. But Childe Harold need not fear for his independent existence on that account. Childe Harold was no more a plagiarism upon René than René was a plagiarism upon Werther. René, Childe Harold, Werther, Obermann—these names are but symptoms of a common ailment. They were, to employ a homely metaphor, the measles of the young century. A new Renaissance was sweeping through Europe. There was young genius and young blood. There was an outworn society and decrepit ideals. Young genius grew melancholy, and wore the raiment of young cynicism. Young genius had its sorrows; it draped them beautifully, it allowed the lip to curl, the eye to cloud itself; it cultivated pilgrimage; it put vine-leaves in the hair, drinking the cup and apostrophising the dregs; it posed before the mirror of time with a coxcombry that was too transparent to be very hateful. Moreover, it had that perennial excuse for all sounding and beautiful folly, it was young. It needed the excuse badly enough. It had no respect. Byron respected neither Michael nor S. Peter. It had no regard for the truth, but lied in pure fulness of heart, almost as if it wanted to be found out. Did not Chateaubriand see flamingoes on the banks of the Mississippi? As for religion, it either loved it for æsthetic reasons, or openly blasphemed. It was faithless and cruel in its loves, unaccountable in its conduct, incorrigible in its weak sins, swift to apprehend evil and swifter still to run into it. It fed a curiosity that was insatiable and appetites that were boundless. It called its curiosity by the name of spiritual hunger, and the satisfaction of its appetites by the name of self-discovery.

If Chateaubriand and Byron make a very proper pair, so do these two books about them. From Mr. Gribble we know what to expect. Mr. Gribble is something of a scholar, and has read and written himself into a pleasing style. But it is difficult to fiddle upon one string. It requires an unbounded virtuosity, and even then the fiddling offends quite as much as it pleases. If man or woman were entirely made up of illicit sex relations, Mr. Gribble's knowledge of human nature would be great indeed. He has done this sort of thing so often. Madame de Staël could keep nothing from him. He followed Rousseau into dark, unsavoury places. George Sand could not undress herself completely enough for his liking; he must strip her of yet a little more. Mr. Gribble treated his subjects as delicately as was compatible with the operation he was performing upon them. The extent of his obligation to perform this operation he must be left to settle with himself.

Now it is the turn of Chateaubriand. The "Court of Women" is pleasantly diversified. There was one who loved him by letter until, on being met, she was found by the object of her epistolary affection to be too old to be loved in any other way. There was one who loved him truly, and devoted a life to his interests without the richest of returns. There was another, whom we like best, who was a frankly vicious young woman, and actually left Chateaubriand before he was willing to be left. One was an English girl from whom he ran away because he was a married man. This was an instructive case, showing that, even in this kind of contract, it takes two to make a bargain. It was characteristic of Chateaubriand that he loved this girl all his life, whenever he had time to think of it, till he met her again grown to middle age. As for the others, they are all there to be discovered by anyone foolish enough to read the book.

We are compelled to take Mr. Edgcumbe a little more seriously than Mr. Gribble; but we do so unwillingly enough. Mr. Edgcumbe makes certain claims; and, before refusing to allow them, it is necessary, not indeed to consider them very seriously, but at least to state what they are. He claims to have solved what is sometimes called "The Byron Mystery". It is unfortunately necessary, owing to Mr. Edgcumbe, to recall that the old Beecher-Stowe charge of incest was recently revived by Lord Lovelace in a volume entitled "Astarte". Mr. Edgcumbe sets out, with regret that is protested a little too much, to confute Lord Lovelace and to clear the memory of Mrs. Augusta Leigh. In course of doing so he is reluctantly—very reluctantly, as he tells us many times—compelled to besmirch the memory of Mrs. Musters, the Mary Chaworth of Byron's earlier years. He contends that Medora, the reputed child of Mrs. Leigh, was the natural daughter of Byron and Mrs. Musters, and that Mrs. Leigh consented to play the mother, and to accept the charge of incest, in order to shield Mrs. Musters. There is only one excuse for putting forward such a case. It must have proof, the clearest and most indubitable proof. It reflects very seriously upon Mr. Edgcumbe that such proof is not in the present volume forthcoming. Mr. Edgcumbe rests his case upon strained interpretations of certain poems that are in themselves utterly inconclusive, and upon the filling-in of blank spaces in certain correspondence with the name he would like to see in those spaces. At best his case is an artfully contrived piece of circumstantial evidence. There is nothing here in the nature of proof. His case would remain in doubt even if it were, on general principles, a credible case. It is the most humanly incredible case that ever came into court.

The absurdity of Mr. Edgcumbe's enterprise lies in the fact that if it had succeeded he would have defeated his own purpose. He sets out to clear Byron's memory of a stain. If he has succeeded in proving that Byron did not commit incest with his sister, he has also succeeded in proving that Byron allowed his sister to live under suspicion of that crime, when he could have set all right by a word. Byron, if the new theory be admitted, suffered his sister to bear the burden of a greater guilt in order to shield himself and his mistress from a lesser. This mistress, ex hypothesi accepting the sacrifice, was not worthy of it.

But Mr. Edgcumbe has not proved his case, and has put Byron in fresh peril with the public. He has set up against Lord Lovelace a theory of the most dubious kind. He has given his readers to understand that the truth lies between him and Lord Lovelace. His readers will certainly not accept Mr. Edgcumbe. Therefore they will tend to believe Lord Lovelace after all. We can only protest against this, and hope that Mr. Edgcumbe's book will not influence opinion one way or the other. The truth does not necessarily lie between these two writers at all.

But we have said too much about this already. Mr. Edgcumbe's book is best bracketed with Mr. Gribble's. It belongs to the same category, though it sets out more ambitiously. It is a useless and deplorable stirring of the mud. Both these books are impertinent studies in the seamy side of genius. The less wholesome aspects of Byron's life are best left unread, or read, as he himself intended, in his poetry. Chateaubriand, too, revealed himself quite sufficiently in his writings, and requires no one but himself to edit the transparent romances which he built upon his own varied experience. Mr. Gribble is too seasoned an offender to be whipped into any sort of repentance; and he offends with a grace that disguises the offence. As for Mr. Edgcumbe, we suggest that he republish his book with the second portion omitted. The first portion—that dealing with Byron's last days at Missolonghi—is at any rate quite harmless, if it is not quite necessary.

ALLUSIONS TO SHAKESPEARE.

"The Shakspere Allusion-Book: a Collection of Allusions to Shakspere from 1591 to 1700." Originally compiled by C. M. Ingleby, Miss L. Toulmin Smith, and by Dr. F. J. Furnivall, with the assistance of the New Shakspere Society; and now re-edited, revised, and re-arranged, with an Introduction by John Munro. London: Chatto and Windus. 2 vols. 21s. net.

MR. MUNRO'S introduction to these interesting volumes enhances their value, but the opening sentences are too stiff and magisterial. It is unfortunate that he should dwell so solemnly on "the necessity for absolute accuracy", for we have found several irritating misprints: e.g. "the Douce Collection at South Kensington" (i. 146) for the "Dyce Collection"; "1578" (i. 173) instead of "1598" as the date of Haughton's "A Woman will have her Will"; "Law's 'Day Tricks'" (i. 320) for "Day's 'Law Tricks'"; "Nathaniel Hooke" (ii. 27) for "Nicholas Hookes". On page 202 of vol. i. we are truly amazed to read that the song (from "Measure for Measure") "Take, oh, take those lips away" is "now generally given to 'Kit Marlowe' on Isaac Walton's authority". Walton has thousands of readers, learned and simple; and not a man or boy among them forgets that the "smooth song" attributed to Marlowe in the "Compleat Angler" is "Come, live with me and be my love".

The late Dr. C. M. Ingleby, whose "Centurie of Prayse" laid the foundation for the present work, was fond of girding at an abler scholar than himself, Alexander Dyce. It is a pity that his depreciatory references to Dyce, who rendered inestimable service to lovers of Elizabethan literature, have been allowed to stand; and we are sorry that Dr. Furnivall's somewhat acrimonious reflections on kind-hearted Halliwell-Phillipps were not unreservedly withdrawn. In a book dedicated to the praise of the "gentle" Shakespeare we do not want to be reminded of the "pigmy wars" of latter-day Shakespearean commentators.

Of all the panegyrics on Shakespeare the finest were Ben Jonson's before the First Folio and in the "Discoveries"; yet even to-day—so hard is it to stamp out a calumny that has once been bruited—may be found scholars (Mr. Munro is happily not among them) who persist in regarding Jonson's praise as hollow and insincere. A very weighty tribute was the poem of unknown authorship before the Second Folio, "A Mind reflecting ages past" etc., mysteriously subscribed "I. M. S." Among the most interesting of the early commendatory poems was Leonard Digges' eulogium prefixed to the 1640 "Poems". Digges testified most emphatically to the fact that plays of Shakespeare—"Julius Cæsar", "Othello", "Henry IV.", "Much Ado", "Twelfth Night"—never failed to draw crowded houses, while Ben Jonson's "tedious (but well-laboured) 'Catiline'" was refused a hearing, and even the "Fox" and "Alchemist"

> "scarce defrai'd the Seacoale fire
> And doore-keepers".

Yet among his contemporaries (particularly the younger men of letters) Ben Jonson had admirers who deliberately preferred his plays to Shakespeare's; and even in Dryden's time there were writers—Shadwell and others—who regarded Jonson as the greater master, though Dryden himself came at last to recognise clearly the supremacy of Shakespeare.

At the end of the second volume is a valuable appendix by Mr. Charles Crawford on John Bodenham's "Belvedere", 1600, a collection of snippets (single lines or double lines) from the poets and dramatists of the age. There are between three and four thousand quotations; and with immense industry Mr. Crawford has contrived " to trace to their sources about twelve hundred of these, or a third of the whole, including, I believe, all those from Shakespeare ". He writes:

" An examination of my results discloses the pleasing fact that, up to the present, Shakespeare holds the field against all contributors, as regards the number of passages quoted or misquoted from a single author, his figure, excluding ' Edward III.', being 213. Next follows Samuel Daniel, with 208, then Edmund Spenser, with 186. Drayton also contributes a great many single lines; but much of his work, in its original form, is not accessible to ordinary scholars."

" Venus and Adonis " was a far more popular poem than " Lucrece ", but in " Belvedere " Mr. Crawford has found ninety-two quotations from the sententious " Lucrece " and only thirty-five from " Venus and Adonis ". " Richard II." supplies forty-seven quotations, " Richard III." thirteen, " Romeo and Juliet " (text of 1597 quarto) twelve. " Belvedere " is a tiresome collection, and Mr. Crawford is the first scholar who has been at the pains to examine it carefully. Apart from its Shakespearean value, his paper has many points of interest.

In the middle of the seventeenth century there was an indifferent poet, Samuel Sheppard, who on several occasions refers to Shakespeare. The references in Sheppard's published writings are noted by Mr. Munro, but he has overlooked the unpublished " Faerie King ", circ. 1650. Twenty years ago an account of this tedious work was given in the SATURDAY REVIEW (10 August 1889), and we quoted the following poor stanza on Shakespeare:

" Shakespeare the next, who wrot so much so well,
That when I view his Bulke I stand amaz'd:
A Genius so inexhaustible
That hath such tall and numerous trophies rais'd;
Let him bee thought a Block, an Infidell,
Shall dare to skreene the lustre of his praise,
Whose works shall find (their due) a deathless date,
Scorning the teeth of Time or force of Fate ".

Sheppard was fond of paying high-flown, ridiculous compliments to the poets of his time: in an epigram on the " most excellent tragedy of ' Albovine ' " he assured Davenant

" Shakespeare's ' Othello ', Johnson's ' Cataline ',
Would lose their luster, were thy ' Albovine '
Placed betwixt them ".

Another unabashed, outrageous flatterer was Paul Aylward, who in 1645 commended Henry Burkhead's " Cola's Fury ":

" You I preferre. *Johnson* for all his wit
Could never paint out times as you have hit
The manners of our age: The fame declines
Of ne're enough prays'd *Shakespeare* if thy lines
Come to be publisht: *Beaumont* and *Fletcher's* skill
Submitts to yours, and your more learned quill ".

But Aylward may have been laughing in his sleeve; and we fear that " Philaster, St. John's College ", was quizzing Mrs. Jane Barker when he commended her " Poetical Recreations ", 1691:

" When in a Comick Sweetness you appear,
Ben Johnson's humour seems revived there.
When lofty Passions thunder from your Pen,
Methinks I hear Great *Shakspear* once again.
But what do's most your Poetry commend?
You ev'n begin where those great *Wits* did end? "

OUT-OF-WORK THEORIES.

" Unemployment." By W. H. Beveridge. London: Longmans. 1909. 7s. 6d. net.

SINCE Mr. Beveridge published his book he has been promoted to the control of the new Labour Exchanges. Here indeed is an opportunity seldom given for a practical conclusion to theoretical premises. It will be awaited with interest, and a curiosity not unkind. Able and careful controversialist as Mr. Beveridge is, we are inclined to think that his mind is unduly warped by horror of academic heresy. Developing the theory that in our modern industrial system cyclical fluctuations of trade are inevitable, his argument leads on to, and practically ends in, the organisation of the reserves of labour caused by such fluctuations; in other words, labour exchanges will provide men with the jobs they can do, and employers with the men they want. To stop here would leave but a lame conclusion, so we are given unemployment insurance to fill in the gap. Mr. Beveridge has his labour exchanges, and next year, or the year after perhaps, may get his unemployment insurance. Is the remedy sufficient? No one will deny that labour exchanges, if properly managed and freely accepted by employers and unions alike, will diminish unemployment to the extent of filling vacant places wanted by willing workers; but what of the willing workers for whom there are no vacant places? Insurance, a panacea, is the reply; but the power of any group of workers to insure themselves against unemployment depends on the average prosperity of their trade, and that in the end rests entirely on the market the trade can find at home and abroad. Then have fiscal changes nothing to do with international markets?—but we beg pardon, for tariffs are evidently among the " any such proposals " which " have to be attacked and defended on grounds alien to the present inquiry ". Even orthodox economists sometimes mix up cause and effect, and we rather agree with the practical heretic who thinks there would be less unemployment if there were only more jobs to go round.

Whatever views they may profess on fiscal matters, most of Mr. Beveridge's readers will agree with him that State and municipal employment cannot effectively provide a reservoir of labour for industrial fluctuations: he shows how this expedient tends to become relief work in which men get regularly more wages than ever they earn, and wages which have no relation to the competence or industry of the workers. Apparently " public business and public relief cannot be combined ".

One of our greatest modern social difficulties is the rapid increase in the numbers of casual workers. Mr. Beveridge would use his labour exchanges to convert the casual—docker, for instance—into a regular worker. Thus he cuts right across the Labour party's plan, " less hours for the few and more employment for all ", and gives a living wage to a certain fit minority, leaving the rest, who according to his theory are only occasional workers ordinarily living upon charity or the labour of their families, to the Poor Law as reformed. A drastic proposal, but certainly in the direction of sifting workers from shirkers, which after all is the main problem of casual unemployment.

Not the least interesting part of Mr. Beveridge's book is his examination of the difficulties which beset older workers in finding fresh employment. He seems to be against the popular view, and cites in support his distress-committee experience of the comparative absence of elderly applicants, but reasonably allows, on the other hand, that trades union returns are by no means comprehensive enough to settle the question. We prefer the experience of the workers themselves, and their general belief clearly is that even middle age tells strongly against them. No doubt the Compensation Act has done something to intensify the difficulty, but the main reason is probably the stress of modern competition—the young and vigorous elbowing out their seniors.

We cannot follow Mr. Beveridge in the easy view he takes of the mobility of labour: that changes in industry come so gradually that the few people displaced are usually absorbed in some other trade. No allowance is made for the long months of unemployment which occur in trades like shipbuilding and its allied industries. Labour exchanges cannot create work; even unemployment benefits come to an end, and no scheme has yet been proposed which will carry the workers over more than a short period of trade slackness. Once in the out-of-work morass a workman finds it very hard to get back to firm ground; most sink deeper, and even those who are able to grasp the chance reviving trade offers them have, in the bitter fight against want and misery, lost much of their old skill and efficiency.

Germany nowadays is held up as a model to all good social reformers, and our civil servants are always being hurried over there to look round. But are the conditions similar? and would the same results follow here? Germany's tariff protects her labour; what our workers produce is open to the competition of the world. Germany looks after her producers; in England we worship the consumer. Would not consideration for our own producers to some extent solve the problem of unemployment?

"OUR DEAR MISS EDGEWORTH."

"Maria Edgeworth and her Circle." By Constance Hill. London: Lane. 1909. 21s. net.

IF it is safe to judge from the continued reprints, the "appreciations" and the growth of ana, we may think that the restored fame of three or four literary ladies—"female writers" they would have called themselves—who flourished in England about the beginning of the last century rests for the present on a secure base. It would be a pleasing exercise among the curiosities of literature to compare the fervour of the first reception, the extent of the subsequent neglect, and the reality of the present return to favour in the several cases of Fanny Burney, Jane Austen and Maria Edgeworth: Susan Ferrier seems at the moment to await her turn. If we could wholly suppress a doubt whether handsomely illustrated biographies and cheap editions with "introductions" really mean that the text is read by any considerable number of people, the renewed vogue of the three novelists would be one of the most favourable symptoms in the present state of the fiction market.

This flourishing anew is perhaps most remarkable in the case of Miss Edgeworth. Through all the acclamation of her first success—no mere review applause, but a lionising by society sufficient to raise green envy in the most widely circulated of her modern sisters of the pen—in spite of the generous recognition of her powers by the chiefs of criticism, there are signs of a certain tinge of gentle ridicule in the appreciation of the authoress, a touch of affectionate quizzing, something of a "who'd-have-thought-it?" attitude such as might be shown to a petted infant prodigy. There are traces of this to be seen when Scott writes to Joanna Baillie in 1825: "I have not the pen of our friend Maria Edgeworth, who writes all the while she laughs, talks, eats and drinks, and I believe, though I do not pretend to be so far in the secret, all the time she sleeps too"; and the impression remains in Fitzgerald's letter from Edgeworthstown to Bernard Barton in 1841, when he reports "the great Maria" "as busy as a bee, making a catalogue of her books beside me, chattering away . . . really a very entertaining person". Besides this lack of the imposing, there was of course the presence of the didactic side of her character, the Harry-and-Lucy element which made Byron call Donna Inez "Miss Edgeworth's novels stepping from their covers", and Sainte-Beuve speak of Mlle. Scudéry as "une Miss Edgeworth . . . une excellente maîtresse de pension", and Ruskin in one of the footnote second thoughts in "The Stones of Venice" confess his earlier self "a little Edgeworthian gosling". Of course no one who is capable of enjoying "Castle Rackrent" or "The Absentee" will find the smallest check in such accidents as these; but there is matter for cheerful surprise in the fact that what we call the reading public has to all appearance got over an obstacle of some standing. The revival of taste seems to be on logical lines of selection; there is no sign at present of a restoration of Mrs. Radcliffe or Hannah More; it perhaps allows a hope of acts of justice yet to come, of rediscoveries of merit still largely self-obscured, a due recognition some day of Hood, perhaps even of Crabbe.

As a specimen of the present state of Edgeworthiana Miss Hill's book should encourage the faithful. It makes no pretence to criticism; it is a pleasantly discursive gathering-up of Maria's comings and goings, of scraps of her letters—in a few cases from unpublished manuscripts—of the doings of her relations and friends, sometimes to a rather distant remove, between the years 1801 and 1820. The width over which the net has been cast is a measure of the industry which has already searched the ground. Full praise is due to Miss Hill for the thoroughness with which she has chronicled the travels, the gaieties in high places, the acquaintance, the risks of a visit to Paris and a timely flight home, which have such a curious bearing—or want of bearing—on Miss Edgeworth's books. This is so capably done, and offers so many clues of reference which are consequent, if at times rather fine-spun, that the reader will probably regret the inclusion of several chapters whose connexion with the subject is thin to the point of invisibility. There is no sufficient excuse for giving us sections on the volunteer enthusiasm in Britain at the time of the threatened invasion, or on the restoration of the Bourbons, merely because Miss Edgeworth had been in France just before that time. Her sole connexion with the chapter called "After Waterloo" appears to lie in her description of a Lord Mayor's feast at Drogheda in honour of the victory and a joke about the disappearance of the Apollo Belvedere and the Venus de Medicis (sic) after the entry of the Allies into Paris. All this might well have been replaced by an expansion of the brief notes on the life at Edgeworthstown, which are confined to a couple of pages in the preface.

NOVELS.

"Great Possessions." By Mrs. Wilfrid Ward. London: Longmans. 1909. 6s.

One can imagine a conflict in the construction of "Great Possessions" between the author's personal inclinations and the concession she considered necessary to the public demand. The best work in the book is the part of it which is most detached from its project and least dependent on the working-out of a plot. The first two chapters, which do not even suggest a story, reach, in a vein of delicate reflection, a level from which the rest of the book declines. There is very little subtlety and not much penetration in their study of the widow suddenly faced with despairing suspicions regarding the husband she has just lost; but there is fine feeling, a wide quiet view, and a grave tenderness of handling. These are the qualities which give the book what distinction it possesses, but thereafter they have to struggle for expression through the tightening meshes of the plot. It is this plot which one imagines conceived as essential to a hold on the public's interest, but it does no service to the story as a work of art. It is the story of a lost will, and the very mention of so overworked a theme may well cause the reader to shudder. Lurid though some of its elements are, one realises that, apart from what she may have considered the public demand for sensation, the author only uses it as a means for producing a spiritual crisis. None the less, it hampers her particular gift of expression, which is evidently more happily employed with what one may call the sub-acute emotions, and a great deal of her space is wasted in the elaborate working-out of plot, done with a conscientiousness that does not conceal its perfunctory appeal to the constructor. It is wasted, moreover, in another sense, since, on the lines of its construction, a great deal more space should be devoted to the culmination of the drama, viewed even as a spiritual crisis, than Mrs. Ward allots to it. The curtain comes down so hurriedly in the last chapters as to produce a wrecked sense of proportion, and make one more than ever regret that so much labour has been spent on our preparation for a catastrophe of which we are to learn so little. The charm that Mrs. Ward can contribute to a romance must come not from a penetrative reading of character or from constructive capacity, nor from any imaginative suffusion of reality, but from a kindly and reflective view of life, coloured by a sincere and open-minded piety. Her descriptions of the London season as " a rest cure for aspirations and higher ambitions and anxieties and all the nobler discontents ", and of love as " God's anæsthetic ", give a measure of what may reasonably be expected of her—a wise understanding of much with which she is not in sympathy, and a sensitive presentation of all with which she is. She ought to do better work than her latest novel, and to do it by indulging entirely her own instincts for what is of spiritual interest, and paying no heed to what is supposed to be the market demand. There is a demand for serious fineness in the treatment of life which lies hidden to a bookseller's conceptions.

"The Key of the Unknown." By Rosa Nouchette Carey. London: Macmillan. 1909. 6s.

Even if Miss Carey had not permitted herself a gentle fling at " the twentieth-century young lady " through the mouths of two of the characters in this novel, it would have been fairly clear from its pages that she regards that heiress of all the ages with but a qualified approval. And perhaps her heroine, though she goes with a girl friend (and a chaperon, of course) to the Tate Gallery and the Walker Collection, and would therefore seem to have lived in comparatively modern times, is meant rather for a didactic fancy-portrait of what a really well-bred young lady ought to be than for a realistic study of anything young and feminine now existing in an imperfect and post-Victorian world. So regarded, it is impossible not to like the picture. It is tender and dignified, and drawn with all Miss Carey's practised art; and doubtless the twentieth-century young lady, studying it, will deduce therefrom her own detractions and put them to mending.

"A Summer Wreath." By Mrs. Campbell Praed. London: Long. 6s.

We should hardly call a row of apples a " wreath ", and there is no thread or connexion between the seven short love-stories that make up this volume except a great similarity of substance and colouring. Most of them exhibit cases of what is called in this class of literature " elective affinity "; and the title of one of them, " How Doris met her Fate; a suburban romance ", only needs the name changing to Janie or Gwen or Betty or Bridget to describe equally well the experience here recounted of each of those attractive young persons. The sub-title would still be quite accurate as an indication of the sentiment if not of the scene. They are wholesome and occasionally mildly picturesque stories, and they all end with the sound of wedding-bells—except the last; but then Aimée had already been married to Kenneth twice over.

SHORTER NOTICES.

"Modern Astronomy." By Hubert Hall Turner. London: Constable. 1909. 2s. 6d. net.

"How to Study the Stars." By L. Rudaux. Translated by A. H. Keane. London: Fisher Unwin. 1909. 5s. net.

There is no science that fires the imagination of the amateur like astronomy, and there is no science which so quickly frightens him away. It invites him to look into infinite depths and to discover new worlds; then it confronts him with a dull routine as a means to this wonderful end. From the beginnings of astronomy to the present day this outwardly most alluring of the sciences has progressed from discovery to discovery simply by dint of watching and recording and cataloguing small sidereal events. Keats was generalising upon a single instance when he wrote of that planet swimming into the ken of the patient watcher of the skies. Herschel was a lucky man. The other romances have been mathematical, as when Adams and Leverrier discovered Neptune. In Professor Turner's new book we have the plain unvarnished tale—a tale that concerns itself with the gradual perfection of instruments and the crystallisation of routine. There is romance, but it is not for the unimaginative multitude. It is romance of the camera, the spectroscope, the transit-circle, the altazimuth, and the almucantar. It is not dull for the general reader on that account. Professor Turner has no mercy on his ignorant readers; but, if they are not also lazy, they will like him for that very reason. Here is a welcome relief from the magic-lantern astronomy of most popular text-books.

" How to Study the Stars " will prove an excellent companion to Professor Turner's book. Being prepared by Professor Turner to take his subject seriously, the amateur will be ready to receive practical suggestion and instruction in the actual use of instruments. " How to Study the Stars " is exactly the book he will be looking for. It contains lucid advice and good diagrams. It will serve the purpose of a man who is well equipped with instruments as well as the man who has not even a telescope. In fact, the amateur will find here a veritable Baedeker of the skies, quite reliable and up to date.

"Criminal Types in Shakespeare." By August Goll. Translated by Mrs. Weekes. London: Methuen. 1909. 5s. net.

Mr. Goll is Chief Magistrate of Aarhus, Denmark, and is, as he ought to be in such a position, interested in the study of criminology. But he is at the opposite poles from Lombroso in his view of the criminal. He distrusts, as well he may, all attempts to range criminals in categories, as if they could be ranged as classes, sub-classes, species of the human race with the delicacy of the classifier of animals and plants. The exact opposite is Mr. Goll's view. " Lombroso's characteristics ", he says, " may perhaps be applied to a small group of strongly degenerated criminals closely approaching the feeble-minded and insane ", but generally speaking the criminal acts for the sake of ordinary human aims, out of ordinary human motives. He who understands, therefore, human nature best is best qualified to reveal to us what the criminal mind really is, and the origin and development of crimes. Shakespeare has a gallery of criminals' portraits. There are Brutus and Cassius, Macbeth and Lady Macbeth, Richard III. and Iago. We do not know why Mr. Goll treats Othello as a victim; he was surely as much a murderer as the others, and murder of wives for unfaithfulness real or supposed is quite a common motive. Mr. Goll appears to prove murder to be so normal that, except in cases of insanity where no doctor would hesitate to certify, we can go on treating murderers very much as we have been used to do. We cannot follow Mr. Goll in his appeals for the better understanding of criminals, because, granted we sympathise with Brutus and Cassius, Macbeth or Lady Macbeth or Othello in the strong temptations they were under to commit murder, does that suggest they ought not to be hanged? Practically Mr. Goll's book does not enlighten us much, but as a literary study of a set of Shakespearean characters it is worth reading.

(*Continued on page* 574.)

"Revue des Deux Mondes." 1 Novembre.

M. Charmes has some interesting remarks in this number on the Ferrer riots in Paris. He points out that the authors of the French manifestations when they looked on the other side of the Pyrenees found that their extravagances left their Spanish friends cold, and even embarrassed them. The insulting instructions given by French revolutionaries to the Spanish Government to pardon Ferrer, far from having the effect desired, served him ill. The threats uttered against them only hardened the Spanish Ministry against clemency. The Spanish people too are the last in the world to relish interference from outside in their national concerns. Madame Marcelle Tinayre gives her fifth and, we suppose, concluding article on her experiences in Turkey. M. Faguet has an appreciative paper on Michel de Bourges. Le Marquis de Ségur treats again the well-worn subject of Turgot's disgrace and dismissal from office. He quotes an interesting criticism of that great man by Malesherbes to the effect that he was a bad administrator, as he only knew men through books.

THEOLOGY.

"A Commentary of the Holy Bible." By Various Writers. Edited by J. R. Dummelow. Complete in one volume. London: Macmillan. 1909. 7s. 6d. net.

In the days of our childhood a Bible and commentary in one volume was the accompaniment of every respectable home; the particular volume most vividly present to our own memory was large and heavy, with illustrations which enthralled us, and a commentary which did not, because even then we could see that it skipped the difficult passages and gave wearisome sermons on those that were easy. Mr. Dummelow's Commentary is a more business-like piece of work; by the excision of the Bible text and by the use of thin paper he has brought it to a moderate size and a low price, and he has succeeded in producing one of the most useful books for a layman that we have ever seen. It is indeed more a companion to the Bible than a commentary on it; the introductions to the various books are comparatively full, but the comments on individual verses have been reduced to a minimum, so that we cannot rely on having every difficult text explained. The list of contributors shows a number of names high in the ranks of Biblical scholarship, and, what is more to the point, all the writers seem to have put their best into the work, and the result is a singularly even tone throughout the book. The critical position adopted is much the same as that in Dr. Hastings' Dictionary, perhaps a trifle more conservative; but a warm welcome is given to all the new light which science and criticism can throw upon Biblical problems, especially in the Old Testament. Altogether it is an admirable book to recommend to a busy man who is anxious not simply to read his Bible but to understand it. It is carefully printed on the whole, but we have noticed two mistakes: p. 625, col. 2, l. 7, "not desirable" is surely a slip for "most desirable"; and on p. 735, "Easter Eve" should be altered into "Easter Evening" or "the evening of Easter Day".

"The Faith and Works of Christian Science." By the Writer of "Confessio Medici." London: Macmillan. 1909. 3s. 6d. net.

The writer of "Confessio Medici" shows a good talent for controversy, and Christian Science has received a series of very damaging blows at his hands. He is not free from the besetting sin of controversialists, the sin of pressing his case too hard. His examination of the faith of Christian Science might well have been softened and compressed; there is too much repetition, explanation, and exposure of the nonsense which it propounds as philosophy; it would have been more effective if the quotations had been longer and the comments shorter; and, on the other hand, Mrs. Eddy's interesting excursion into etymology by deriving "Adam from the Latin demens, meaning madness, to undo, to spoil" (p. 58, n.) surely deserved a prominent place in the text instead of being banished to a footnote. He is more successful in his attack on the practical working of Christian Science; the long list of its successes and failures which he has tabulated forms a valuable series of data for judging the movement; successful at times in the treatment of functional disorder, it is powerless before organic disease. A philosophy of life which is blind to the existence of pain amongst the lower animals, and an ethical system which encourages the hideously cruel cases of neglect here enumerated, would seem to the ordinary reader self-condemned; but, alas, there seems no limit to the amount of nonsensical and mischievous teaching which will be swallowed by men and women who are in most respects shrewd enough.

"The Church of the Apostles: being an Outline of the History of the Church of the Apostolic Age." ("The Church Universal") By L. Ragg. London: Rivingtons. 1909. 4s. 6d. net.

This volume hardly reaches the level of the other volumes in the series. The author, indeed, knows his subject well, though not more than well; and he writes carefully, often gracefully. It is not his knowledge or his style that we feel bound to criticise; it is his point of view and the way in which he has approached his work. He has set himself to write a history of the Apostolic age from the orthodox High Church point of view—and far be it from us to quarrel with him for that; but he ought to have done more: he ought to have assimilated critical methods, or at least to have explained to his readers what problems and questions and difficulties have been raised by modern critics over incidents which he relates quite smoothly, without a word of comment. The consequence is that his book is not more than a handy companion to the New Testament; it will not teach the student much that he does not know already, nor is it likely to convince any reader whose views differ from the author's. He has written not so much to instruct as to edify; he has not produced a volume of history, rather a series of addresses suitable to an afternoon congregation in church—possibly the friends in Venice to whom the book is dedicated.

"The Wisdom of Solomon, in the Revised Version." With Introduction and Notes by J. A. F. Gregg. (The Cambridge Bible for Schools and Colleges.) Cambridge: At the University Press. 1909. 2s. 6d. net.

We are glad that the editors of this series are including the books of the Apocrypha in their commentaries; it is true indeed that they are rather slow about it. The first book of Maccabees appeared in 1897, and the book of Wisdom has only come to keep it company this year; we sincerely hope that other books will follow at somewhat shorter intervals. But few books are more interesting and valuable for the light they throw on the New Testament than Wisdom, and it is a real gain for the average student to have a handy edition of the book with a good introduction and short notes. We have nothing but praise for the excellent commentary which Mr. Gregg has compiled. It fully maintains the reputation of the Cambridge Bible for Schools.

For this Week's Books see pages 576 and 578.

THIS WEEK'S BOOKS.

Art

Beautiful Children (C. Haldane McFall). Jack. 21*s.* net.
The French Pastellists of the Eighteenth Century (Haldane Macfall). Macmillan. 42*s.* net.

Biography

Anna Van Schurman (Una Birch). Longmans, Green. 6*s.* 6*d.* net.
Sir Wilfrid Lawson (Edited by the Right Hon. George W. E. Russell). Smith, Elder. 7*s.* 6*d.* net.
M. K. Gandhi (Joseph J. Doke). London: "Indian Chronicle."

Fiction

Candles in the Wind (Maud Diver). Edinburgh: Blackwood. 6*s.*
The Trader (Cecil Ross-Johnson). Duckworth. 6*s.*
The Caravaners (By the author of "Elizabeth and her German Garden"). Smith, Elder. 6*s.*
The Street with Seven Houses (Sylvia Brett). Hodder and Stoughton. 6*s.*
Villa Rubein (John Galsworthy). Duckworth. 6*s.*
The Attic Guest (Robert E. Knowles). Melrose. 6*s.*
Dulall the Forest Guard (C. E. Gouldsbury). Gibbing. 3*s.* 6*d.*

Gift Books

Robinson Crusoe (Daniel Defoe). Bell. 5*s.* net.
Legends and Stories of Italy (Amy Steedman). Jack. 7*s.* 6*d.* net.
The Merchant of Venice (With illustrations by Sir James D. Linton). Hodder and Stoughton. 10*s.* 6*d.* net.
Father Tuck's Annual. Raphael Tuck. 3*s.* 6*d.*
The Story of Hereward (Douglas C. Stedman), 5*s.*; Cuchulain (Eleanor Hull), 5*s.* net; The Quest of the White Merle (Lilian Gask), 3*s.* 6*d.*; With Nature's Children (Lilian Gask), 1*s.* 6*d.* Harrop.
The Book of Friendship (Arranged by Arthur Ransome). Edinburgh: Jack. 6*s.*
The Animal Why Book (W. P. Pycraft). Wells Gardner. 5*s.* net.
Lob Lie-by-the-Fire (Juliana Horatia Ewing). Bell. 2*s.* 6*d.* net.
The Fairy Tales of the Brothers Grimm. Constable. 15*s.* net.
Not Out! (Kent Carr), 5*s.*; The Boy's Book of the Sea (W. H. Simmonds), 3*s.* 6*d.* Partridge.
Biffel: A Trek Ox (Stanley Portal Hyatt). Melrose. 6*s.* net.

History

Eton (Christopher Stone). Black. 7*s.* 6*d.* net.
South Africa (Frank R. Cana). Chapman and Hall. 10*s.* 6*d.* net.
Sikhim and Bhutan (J. Claude White). Arnold. 21*s.* net.
Christians at Mecca (Augustus Ralli). Heinemann. 5*s.* net.
Reminiscences of a K.C. (Thomas Edward Crispe). Methuen. 10*s.* 6*d.* net.

Law

Select Essays in Anglo-American Legal History (Various authors. 3 Vols.). Cambridge: At the University Press. 12*s.* net.
The Law of the Road (J. Wells Thatcher). Stevens and Sons, Ltd. 7*s.* 6*d.*

Reprints and Translations

The Little Flowers of S. Francis of Assisi. Chatto and Windus.
Modes and Manners of the Nineteenth Century. 3 Vols. Dent. 21*s.* net.
Gray's Poems: Peacock's Memoirs of Shelley (Edited by H. F. B. Brett-Smith); Keats' Poems. Frowde. 2*s.* 6*d.* net each.
Modern Astronomy (Herbert Hall Turner). Constable. 2*s.* 6*d.* net.
Saint Thomas à Becket (Monsignor Demimuid). Duckworth. 2*s.* 6*d.* net.
A Handbook for Travellers in India, Burma, and Ceylon. Murray. 20*s.* net.

(*Continued on page* 578.)

THIS WEEK'S BOOKS—(*Continued*).

SCHOOL BOOK

The British Isles (Lettice Jowitt). Black. 2*s.* 6*d.*

NATURAL HISTORY AND SPORT

British Sport Past and Present (E. D. Cumming). Hodder and Stoughton. 20*s.* net.
A Book of the Zoo (Eric Parker). Methuen. 6*s.*

THEOLOGY.

Religion and the Modern World (Sir Donald Macalister). Hodder and Stoughton. 5*s.*
The Shadows of the Valley (Rev. Alfred G. Mortimer). Skeffington. 5*s.* net.
The Unknown History of the Jews (E. E. Jessel). Watts. 3*s.* 6*d.* net.
The Unfinished Symphony (Hugh Falconer). Duckworth. 6*s.*
The Hibbert Journal Supplement, 1909. 5*s.* net.

TRAVEL

China: Its Marvel and Mystery (T. Hodgson Liddell). Allen. 21*s.* net.
Peaks and Glaciers of Nun Run (Fanny Bullock Workman). Constable. 18*s.* net.

VERSE

Later Poems from "Punch," 5*s.* net; The Poetry of Earth, 2*s.* 6*d.* net. Harrop.
The Wild Rose (Arthur Lyon Raile), 7*s.* 6*d.* net; Light among the Leaves (Hugh Moreton Frewen). Nutt. 3*s.* 6*d.*

MISCELLANEOUS

Cambridge University Calendar, 1909-1910. Cambridge: Deighton Bell. 7*s.* 6*d.* net.
Cookery Book of Lady Clark of Tillypronie, The (Edited by Catherine Frances Frere). Constable. 6*s.* net.
Education in the Far East (Charles F. Thwing). Boston: Houghton Mifflin. $1.50 net.
Far Eastern Question, The (Thomas F. Millard), 12*s.* 6*d.* net; Life in an English Village (M. F. Davies), 10*s.* 6*d.* net. Fisher Unwin.
Growth of Nations, The (W. Rose Smith). Sonnenschein. 3*s.* 6*d.*
Hills and the Vale, The (Richard Jefferies). Duckworth. 6*s.*
History of Story-telling, A (Arthur Ransome). Jack. 10*s.* 6*d.* net.
How to be Happy though Civil (Rev. E. J. Hardy). Fisher Unwin. 5*s.* net.
Imaginary Interviews with Great Composers (Gerald Cumberland). Reeves. 6*s.*
Kirk Life and Kirk Folk (James Wotherspoon). Foulis. 5*s.* net.
Land of Regrets, The (Isabel Fraser Hunter). Ouseley. 5*s.*
Modern Woman and How to Manage Her (Walter M. Gallichan). Laurie. 2*s.* net.
Myths and Legends of the Middle Ages (H. A. Guerber). Harrop. 7*s.* 6*d.* net.
Natural and Social Morals (Carveth Read). Black. 7*s.* 6*d.* net.
On Everything (H. Belloc). Methuen. 5*s.*
Twelve Masters of Prose and Verse (Wilfrid Whitter). Grierson.
Wayside Wisdom (E. M. Martin), 5*s.* net; Economic and Fiscal Facts and Fallacies (Sir Guildford Molesworth), 3*s.* 6*d.* Longmans.
Wedges (C. B. Wheeler). Gay and Hancock. 2*s.* 6*d.* net.

REVIEWS AND MAGAZINES FOR NOVEMBER.—Harper's, 1*s.*; Blackwood, 2*s.* 6*d.*; The Empire, 1*s.*; The Nineteenth Century and After, 2*s.* 6*d.*; The Englishwoman, 1*s.*; Mercure de France, 1*fr.* 50*c.*; Revue des Deux Mondes, 3*fr.*; The Contemporary Review, 2*s.* 6*d.*; The State, 1*s.*; The Financial Review of Reviews, 1*s.*; Current Literature, 25*c.*; United Service Magazine, 2*s.*; The Geographical Journal, 2*s.*; The Book Monthly, 6*d.*; The Re-Union Magazine, 6*d.*

NOTICE.

The Terms of Subscription to the SATURDAY REVIEW are:—

	United Kingdom. £ s. d.	Abroad. £ s. d.
One Year	1 8 2	1 10 4
Half Year	0 14 1	0 15 2
Quarter Year ...	0 7 1	0 7 7

Cheques and Money Orders should be crossed and made payable to the Manager, SATURDAY REVIEW Offices, 10 *King Street, Covent Garden, London, W.C.*

Ready Next Week. Price 2s. 6d. net.

THE "SATURDAY" HANDBOOK

FOR UNIONIST CANDIDATES, SPEAKERS, AND WORKERS.

EDITED BY

The Hon. GERVASE BECKETT, M.P., and GEOFFREY ELLIS.

This HANDBOOK is unique. It contains articles expressing the views of leading members of the Party in the House of Commons, and in addition notes and data on all the various subjects specially prepared for the information of all Unionists fighting the Party's battles in the coming election.

The HANDBOOK is consequently a guide at once to Unionist policy and to the facts which go to support that policy.

AMONG THE CONTRIBUTIONS ARE:—

Ireland - - - -	The Rt. Hon. Walter Long, M.P.
The Army - - -	The Rt. Hon. George Wyndham, [M.P.
Tariff Reform - -	A. Bonar Law, M P.
Urban Land - - -	E. G. Pretyman, M.P.
Navy - - - -	Arthur H. Lee, M.P.
House of Lords - -	Lord Robert Cecil, K.C., M.P.
Education - - -	Sir William Anson, K.C., M.P.
The Imperial Problem -	Sir Gilbert Parker, M.P.
Licensing - - -	George Cave, K.C., M.P.
The New Finance -	F. E. Smith, K.C., M.P.
Agricultural Land - -	Viscount Helmsley, M.P.
India - - - -	The Earl of Ronaldshay, M.P.
Social Legislation - -	Sir William Bull, M.P.
Unemployment - -	The Hon. Claude Hay, M.P.
The Budget - - -	Arthur Baumann
Foreign Affairs - -	Mark Sykes
Socialism - - - -	J. L. Garvin
The Position of the Church,	Harold Hodge

WITH A LETTER FROM

The Rt. Hon. A. J. BALFOUR, M.P.

ORDER FROM YOUR BOOKSELLER OR DIRECT FROM THE OFFICE. POST FREE, 2/9

THE WEST STRAND PUBLISHING CO., LTD.,
10 King Street, Covent Garden, W.C.

From CHATTO & WINDUS'S LIST. NEW **From CHATTO & WINDUS'S LIST.**

FLORENCE PRESS BOOKS.

Printed from a new fount of type specially designed by Mr. HERBERT P. HORNE after the finest examples of the Italian Masters.

THE FIORETTI, OR LITTLE FLOWERS OF S. FRANCIS.

A newly revised and in parts augmented Version of the Translation by Prof. T. W. ARNOLD. The Illustrations are reproduced in Collotype after the unique Drawings by an Unknown Hand, contained in the MS. of the "Fioretti" and "Life" preserved in the Laurentian Library. The edition is limited to 500 Copies on Hand-made Paper, size about 9 by 11 in., bound in paper boards, 30s. net; or in limp vellum, 42s. net. Also 10 Vellum Copies (sold), bound in limp vellum, Eight Guineas net each.

SONGS BEFORE SUNRISE. BY ALGERNON CHARLES SWINBURNE.

English Edition limited to 500 Copies on Hand-Made Paper, about 7¾ by 9¾ in., bound in paper boards, 26s. net; or in limp vellum, 36s. net. Also 10 Vellum Copies (all sold), bound in limp vellum, Ten Guineas net each.

MELBA

An Authorized Biography by AGNES G. MURPHY. With Chapters by MADAME MELBA on **The Art of Singing** and on **The Selection of Music as a Profession.** Also an Introductory Note by J. A. FULLER MAITLAND. With Photogravure Frontispiece, 37 Portraits, Views, and Facsimiles, **16s.** net.

THE FACE OF CHINA.

By E. G. KEMP, F.R.S.G.S. Travels in East, North, Central, and Western China. With some Account of the New Schools, Universities, and Missions, and the old Religious Sacred Places of Confucianism, Buddhism, and Taoism, and a Map of China. With 64 Illustrations after Water-Colours and Sepia Drawings by the Author. **20s.** net. Large paper, **42s.** net.

The *Scotsman* says: "Excellent use was made of her brush and pencil, as well as of her eyes and memory and the pages of her note-book."

The *Morning Post* says: "A particularly well-illustrated book."

THE COLOUR OF ROME.

By OLAVE M. POTTER. With 60 Illustrations in Colours and Sepia by the Japanese Artist, YOSHIO MARKINO, who also contributes an Introductory Chapter. Fcap. 4to. **20s.** net. Large paper parchment, **42s.** net.

"Mr. Markino's illustrations—we have seen none to equal them . . . each is presented with such force and freshness that it is felt by the spectator as an experience of the scene itself. The combination of such clear, unspoilt eyesight with such a gift of execution is rare."—*Nation.*

STORIES OF THE FRENCH ARTISTS FROM CLOUET TO INGRES.

Drawn from Contemporary Records. Collected and arranged by P. M. TURNER and C. H. COLLINS BAKER. With 8 Coloured Plates and 24 in Half-tone. Cloth, gilt top **7s. 6d.** net. Edition de Luxe, with 5 additional Coloured Plates, crown 4to. parchment, **15s.** net.

TRAVELS WITH A DONKEY.

By ROBERT LOUIS STEVENSON. Newly set in special large type, with 12 Coloured Plates and 12 Facsimile Drawings by NOEL ROOKE. **7s. 6d.** net. Parchment, **10s. 6d.** net; Vellum, **21s.** net.

THE CONFESSIONS OF ST. AUGUSTINE.

Translated by Dr. E. P. PUSEY. Edited by TEMPLE SCOTT. Introduction by Mrs. MEYNELL. 12 Coloured Illustrations by MAXWELL ARMFIELD. **7s. 6d.** net. Parchment, **15s.** net Pigskin, **25s.** net.

THE CLOISTER AND THE HEARTH.

By CHARLES READE. With 30 Plates in Colour and 10 in Line by BYAM SHAW, R.I. Title, End Papers, and Cover Designed by the Artist. **12s. 6d.** Parchment, **16s.** net.

DRAMATIS PERSONÆ AND DRAMATIC ROMANCES AND LYRICS.

By ROBERT BROWNING. With 10 full-page Coloured Plates by ELEANOR BRICKDALE. **6s.** net. Parchment, **12s. 6d.** net.

THE MASTER OF GAME. THE OLDEST ENGLISH BOOK ON HUNTING.

By EDWARD, Second DUKE OF YORK. Edited by W. A. and F. BAILLIE-GROHMAN. With Introduction by THEODORE ROOSEVELT. Photogravure Frontispiece and 23 Full-Page Illustrations after the Illuminations in the Original MS. in the Bibliothèque Nationale, Paris. Large crown 8vo. cloth, **7s. 6d.** net; parchment, **10s. 6d.** net.

EPISTOLÆ OBSCURORUM VIRORUM (1515-1517).

The Latin Text of the *Editiones Principes* with an English rendering, Copious Notes, and an Historical Introduction by FRANCIS GRIFFIN STOKES. English Edition limited to 500 Numbered Copies. With a Photogravure Frontispiece and Facsimile Title-Page. Royal 8vo. buckram, **25s.** net.

No English Translation, or Edition with English annotations, of this famous work has previously appeared, and it may safely be said that the light it throws upon the Religious, Social, and Political conditions of Western Europe during the early years of the Sixteenth Century cannot be neglected by serious students of the Renaissance.

NOTES ON THE SCIENCE OF PICTURE MAKING.

By C. J. HOLMES, M.A., Slade Professor of Fine Arts, University of Oxford. NEW EDITION REVISED. **7s. 6d.** net.

THE MIND OF THE ARTIST.

Thoughts and Sayings of Artists on their Art. Collected and Arranged by Mrs. LAURANCE BINYON. With 8 Illustrations. Crown 8vo. cloth, gilt top, **3s. 6d.** net.

THE PAINTERS OF VICENZA.

By TANCRED BORENIUS. With 15 Full-Page Plates. **7s. 6d.** net

New 6s. Novels.

PLAIN BROWN. By COSMO HAMILTON, Author of "The Blindness of Virtue," &c.

"Full of crisp and humorous vivacity."—*Times.*

"Brightly written novel. . . . All thanks to Mr. Cosmo Hamilton for keeping us on the laugh so long." *Pall Mall Gazette.*

"Youthful extravagance smiles broadly from its pages. . . . But the book is not the outcome of high spirits merely—there is feeling as well as fun in it."—*World.*

THE UNLUCKY MARK. By F. E. PENNY. Editor of "The Inevitable Law," &c.

"Through all . . . runs Mrs. Penny's fine sense of character and drama."—*Times.*

"Mrs. Penny excels . . . she handles her characters with skill and gets dramatic points without straining." *Daily Chronicle.*

INFLUENCES. By PAUL METHVEN. A brilliant story by a new writer. First Review: "Mr. Paul Methven is a skilful deviser of plots, and has a vivacious way of writing. The story is sure to interest, for it has most of the qualities which go to make popularity."—*Daily Telegraph.*

THE SON OF MARY BETHEL. By ELSA BARKER. The story of The Christ in a modern setting. "There is clearly sincerity and a great amount of power . . . many beautiful passages . . . for the author has been really stirred to the depths by the Gospel narrative."—*Morning Post.*

THE KNIGHT OF THE GOLDEN SWORD. By MICHAEL BARRINGTON.

"A vigorous story."—*Times.* "A splendid story."—*Pall Mall.*

"Mr. Barrington has an easy grace in the manner of his writing."—*Daily Chronicle.*

"Extremely good to read."—*Morning Leader.* "Extremely well written."—*Globe.*

KING HAL OF HERONSEA. By W. WILLMOTT DIXON.

"A fine novel, well constructed, full of incident and tense love interest."—*Sunday Times.*

BOOKS FOR THE YOUNG.

THE ROSE AND THE RING.

By W. M. THACKERAY. With Coloured Frontispiece and 44 Illustrations (12 in Two Tints) and Decorated End-Papers by GORDON BROWNE. **3s. 6d.** net.

THE RAINBOW BOOK.

By Mrs. H. M. SPIELMANN. Coloured Frontispiece and 15 Illustrations by ARTHUR RACKHAM, A.R.W.S., and 21 in Black and White by other well-known Artists. **5s.** net.

CAMPING IN THE FOREST.

With 12 Coloured Illustrations, many in Black and White, and Decorative End-Papers by MARGARET CLAYTON. Cloth, **3s. 6d.** net.

CHATTO & WINDUS, 111 St. Martin's Lane, London, W.C.

Printed for the Proprietors by Spottiswoode & Co. Ltd., 5 New-street Square, E.C., and Published by Reginald Webster Page, at the Office, 10 King Street, Covent Garden, in the Parish of St. Paul, in the County of London.—*Saturday*, 6 *November*, 1909.

THE
SATURDAY REVIEW
OF
POLITICS, LITERATURE, SCIENCE, AND ART.

No. 2,820 Vol. 108. 13 November 1909. [Registered as a Newspaper.] 6d.

CONTENTS.

We beg leave to state that we decline to return or to enter into correspondence as to rejected communications; and to this rule we can make no exception. Manuscripts not acknowledged within four weeks are rejected.

NOTES OF THE WEEK.

It is now taken for granted that the Lords will reject the Budget. Early in the week the "Times" stated that the decision to reject had been reached and gave the outline of an official Opposition amendment. No one seems to be much surprised, and there is no doubt that the great majority of Unionists would have it so. The party is in no mood for compromise. Neither is the Government. So lay on.

Being in for a pound over the Finance Bill, it would have been absurd if the House of Lords had hesitated for a moment to be in for a penny over the London Elections Bill. And the House of Lords did not hesitate a moment. They threw out the Bill almost as contemptuously as they threw out the Plural Voting Bill. The London Elections Bill was a Bill to castrate the London Conservatives, or at least a large number of them. The move was naked and unashamed. When a Liberal denies it—a Liberal, that is, who is not a perfect greenhorn—he may be described as winking the eye or pointing over the left shoulder. But do Liberals deny it? Of course they do so in Parliament; but that is strictly a parliamentary denial. We all hope we know what that means. There are denials, of course, which are demanded in common decency of a politician.

It was, for example, expected that the Prime Minister would make a strict parliamentary denial of the charge that his Lord Advocate had uttered at any time anything but the crystal clear truth. It would be indelicate, and, worse, it would be ridiculous, for a leader of one party to side with the leader of the other party against one of his own chief supporters on the eve of a general election. Try to imagine the effect not only on the House, but on the country—and the country is the main thing now—if Mr. Asquith had risen the other evening and reproached Mr. Ure severely and approved Mr. Balfour. One has only to imagine vaguely the effect to understand clearly that such an attitude in a party leader is simply impossible. A party leader cannot affect to be an angel guarding the gate of truth with a flaming sword against his own supporters.

In this matter a word may be said about Mr. Stanier's letter to the "Times" on Mr. Balfour's statement on old-age pensions. Mr. Stanier meant well, but his contribution to the subject was not valuable. His revised edition of the statement revises nothing. What are the facts? Mr. Balfour, before the pensions were granted, wrote an election letter saying: "Those who have hitherto doubted the value of our fiscal policy must now be converted to the wisdom of it, for though the radicals have promised old-age pensions only the Unionist policy can provide for their payment". Now here was the most ordinary partisan statement. It is as harmless and inoffensive as if Mr. Asquith were to say: "The Conservatives are promising the people the ownership of small farms and the aid of the State, but it is we with our policy of free trade and commercial prosperity who alone can give the people such benefits". However one looks at Mr. Balfour's statement, one can see nothing sinister or unusual about it. Its only crime is—if we may say so without offence—that it is somewhat common form: all party leaders who are compelled to write letters to candidates must adopt some common-form phrases and sayings—otherwise the electors would not attend to them.

But suppose the Conservatives had carried out an old-age pensions scheme, and then on the eve of a general election Mr. Balfour had crept about from rural constituency to rural constituency, addressing many meetings and at every meeting suggesting to the peasants that the Radicals, if they came in, would cease to pay these pensions? How then would straight men outside Parliament describe Mr. Balfour's conduct? How, indeed, might they not describe it!

The old-age pensioners may rest quietly in their beds, says Mr. Asquith, but it is likely that in many rural constituencies the Radicals will give them a sleepless night or two just before the election. A Conservative landowner—who is by no means a strong partisan, and as it happens is one of the minority in the party against the rejection of the Finance Bill—has written to us: "I find it difficult in the extreme to allay the anxiety of the aged people at L—— that their pensions will last. L—— and H—— (two villages) has each its agent, known to me well, in communication with Radical head-quarters. . . . I should not be surprised to have a very sudden mine sprung on us as we are waking up for the general election—possibly a sensational report about old-age pensions, or just before the election a cartoon of Mr. Balfour kicking old people downstairs." We have a shrewd notion this is the card which some of the Radicals are going to play—their trump. Ah-Sin was his name.

Sir Edward Carson made an interesting speech on Wednesday at Brixton. He told us he was once a Liberal, and amusingly explained the cause of his conversion—the National Liberal Club would not expel Mr. Gladstone! Sir Edward Carson is one of the most invigorating speakers in party politics to-day. He appeals to the fastidious and to the unfastidious man, which is a rare merit. He is a terrible hard hitter, but it is the hitting of manhood, never of malice. Why Sir Edward Carson should not come into the front rank of statesmen some people can never understand. He has the intellect and the distinction. The law is a great profession, and the law no doubt needs Sir Edward Carson. At the same time one may grudge the law having the first call on him at a time the Conservative party wants men of brilliant gift.

Sir Robert Perks has done with the Liberal party—one can read his message to his Louth supporters in no other sense. He is off because, so far as we can understand, the Government will not sack the Church enough and are sacking Capital too much. He has called to them to disendow the Church, and they answer by disendowing the commercial classes. He loves Nonconformity much, he dreads Socialism even more; and, though we do not attach deep importance to these defections of moderate and of rich Liberals, the loss of Sir Robert Perks to Liberalism is perhaps not quite a trifling loss. He has strong opinions, which is more or less common among politicians; he is fearless in pressing them home, which is extremely rare among men generally. It is possible he will take some Nonconformists with him out of the Liberal pen.

East Marylebone is still in turmoil, or the Unionists are. Nor can there be any peace until Mr. Jebb has retired. We will do him the justice to believe that he is a patriot, and wishes the seat to be kept for a Tariff Reform Unionist. If he goes on, not a Unionist, but a Free Trade Liberal, will represent East Marylebone. The utmost he can do will be to take away from Lord Charles Beresford enough votes to let in the Liberal. Both as a gentleman and as a Unionist he ought to follow the example of Mr. Mortimer, who retired from East Herts simultaneously with Mr. Abel Smith, and left the division free for a new start and a new man.

Lord Selby cannot be classed among the great Speakers of the House of Commons. At the time when he was discovered by Mr. Labouchere, he was one of the titular leaders of the Northern Circuit, where he was quite overshadowed by Charles Russell, and where his practice was not very large. Mr. Gully had arrived at that anxious period in a silk's career when he is asking for a puisne judgeship, and willing to accept a County Court judgeship. He had a good voice, dignified manners, and that clean-cut type of face that looks well in a full-bottomed wig. And then there was nothing against him, because nobody in the House of Commons knew him. In the Chair he was not to be compared to his predecessor, Lord Peel, who, with all his faults of temper, ruled the Commons with the hand of a master. Speaker Gully had comparatively easy times to deal with, for the violent phase of Irish obstruction had spent itself. When trouble arose unexpectedly, Mr. Gully showed himself a trifle timorous, and inclined to give way to the Nationalists.

In the morning one was relieved to find that the Birthday Honours list contained no new peers. Then, an hour or two later, one found there were two new peers after all. But irritation was soothed by the discovery that one of them was Sir Arthur Godley. For once, at any rate, honour to whom honour was due. No more loyal or more capable public servant has ever filled a great place under Government. If all new peerages were on this level, the House of Lords would by now be the world's model. The other peerage surprised nobody. Obviously Sir John Fisher could make himself a peer if he wished. In an enterprise of which he was the central beneficiary he was not likely to fail. Not that any formal objection can be taken to this honour. The First Sea Lord is necessarily a big figure, and none can deny that Sir John Fisher has made his mark conspicuous. Sir Ernest Shackleton stands out among the knights. What does so distinguished a man want with a knighthood? The vulgar herd was made up of Jesse Boot-s and suchlike successful tradesmen. In these days one cannot mind this. Indeed, one is only thankful they have not been made peers.

Lord Crewe spoke plainly and with common-sense enough to Lady Grove and the Women's Liberal Federation on Wednesday. He discovered himself—with the discretion of a Minister who wants to be nice and agreeable—as quite a supporter in theory of votes for women. The virtue of the thing seems to be in his mind that it might help Free Trade and help against liquor; on the other hand there is a vice—the women might on the whole tend to be too Churchy. In any case, whatever the virtues or vices of the women voters of Lord Crewe's imagination, the suffrage question is not to be one of the questions of the Election. Smashing glass in the Guildhall, flinging acid into officials' eyes, and behaving in the Savoy Restaurant as no midnight street-walker would care to behave outside it—it is all to no effect. They had better, like the real Revolutionists of France, sit at home in the chair and knit.

The rejection of the London Elections Bill was one thing—the Irish Land Bill is quite another. One may hope that the Irish Land Bill dispute between the two Houses may yet be settled. The attitude of the Government is harsh in the matter—mainly because Mr. Dillon (the real Irish leader, Mr. Redmond being his faithful serving man) insists on the whole Bill; still we think the House of Lords might with advantage at the present time make some concessions to the other side. One would not have the House of Lords get, among thoughtful electors outside the ring of partnership, a bad name for rejecting Bills in the mass.

What with the duties that are expected from an owner whilst he is alive and the duties that are exacted from him when he is dead, land, as we think Lady Bracknell said, is no longer much of a pleasure or profit. But if we can plant firmly and permanently on the land, say, a hundred thousand new men, small-farmer proprietors, the Radical party will find a fresh difficulty in undermining the land and agricultural interest in England; and it is well that Conservative opinion is really waking up to the very great importance of this reform. If Conservative candidates in South of England rural constituencies can see their way to declare for State aid toward ownership, there is no doubt that they will arouse enthusiasm in the villages. There is no reason why the State should not—with certain wise restrictions—be called to help those who help themselves. But what the Radical and Snowden element desire is vastly different—it is that the State should help those who help themselves to other folks' property.

The Prime Minister's speech at the Guildhall was a model of tact and graceful ease. South Africa, the Congo, and the Balkan question are safe topics, when everybody's head is full of the Budget and the House of Lords. An ordinarily-clever politician might have seen that this was the only course to take; but there is no other living statesman who could have treated these Imperial topics with the same breadth, and dignity, and polished rhetoric. Mr. Asquith is without a rival on these ceremonious occasions, which form a considerable part of public life. We are also grateful to the Prime Minister for not canting about the Congo. As for South Africa and Eastern Europe, all looks well for the moment, and we do not grudge Mr. Asquith his meed of self-gratulation. By the way, the reception of Ministers was decidedly cool, and by no means so cordial as it looked in the newspapers.

Mr. Haldane's speech hardly enlightened the defence problem. Of course, he praised his pet child, the Territorial soldier, and was optimistic about the future. This is the attitude which every War Minister is bound to adopt towards his own schemes. His ideals as to the unity of purpose which should guide the efforts of the naval and military authorities are certainly sound. But beyond developing the scope of the Defence Committee's work, we do not see that much can be done, naval and military men seeing things in so very different a light. However, all efforts which aim at a closer combination of the two services should be encouraged and fostered. In his speech Mr. Haldane did not forget that the Defence Committee was Mr. Balfour's idea.

Rear-Admiral Sir Percy Scott has delivered himself of a violent harangue proclaiming our Navy to be the best of all possible navies, and in every way better at this moment than ever it has been before. This flaring testimonial would count for more if one could forget certain past passages between Sir Percy Scott and Lord Charles Beresford. Lord Charles has expressed the view before now that the Navy is not in an ideal condition. Is it not strange that this admiral on the active list should come out and make this polemical pronouncement—for its whole object was polemics—in person to the world? Surely the orthodox and obviously right thing is for the Admiralty to make its views known through Ministers in the House of Commons.

Turkey has presented her Note, and has declared herself very anxious to have the Cretan question finally settled. So are many others. What does Turkey want? That is not so clear as what she does not want. She does not want, and she will not endure, that Greece should get hold of Crete. For the rest, Turkey is ready to make any amount of concession. Crete may be practically autonomous, so long as Greece is kept out. Why this hurry? Because the Greeks are making military preparations! The real reason is less diverting. The Young Turks who sigh for peace are compelled to throw a sop to their countrymen, who feel an historic hankering after that last island conquest of the Ottoman. Young Turkey has not to wait long for an answer. Russia has already declared herself. It simply cannot be done. To settle anything would be to unsettle everything.

The debate in the French Chamber on electoral reform nearly came to a resignation. The Chamber was found, on a division being taken, to be in favour of proportional representation and the scrutin de liste. But the Chamber is now too advanced for M. Briand, who, in his salad days, was too advanced for any Chamber in the world. There was a moment of suspense. M. Briand came to the tribune. He would resign if the Chamber did not declare itself to have erred. The Chamber recanted, and the Ministry was saved. The French people has now the kind of spectacle that it loves—a Ministry, with at least two ex-Radical leaders in it, saved at the expense of a standing Radical reform.

M. Briand's position is piquant. Here is a Prime Minister who virtually orders a national assembly to rescind an opinion that it has at that very moment recorded. The assembly does so, and it is an "incident". This is parliamentary government. On this occasion the proceedings were all the more astonishing, as the central figure was M. Briand. About a week ago M. Briand said that tenacity did not imply ferocity. Well, M. Briand has been ferocious. But his ferocity broke out not when he was holding on to reform, but at the moment he was dropping it.

Criticism by Frenchmen of French judicial procedure is their own privilege. From foreigners it may easily become an impertinence. Frenchmen are criticising the Steinheil trial severely enough; and it is not unlikely that Madame Steinheil will benefit by the judge's efforts to get a conviction. An Englishman with any humour will recall that a short time ago these Frenchmen, whose own ways seem to him so objectionable, were highly excited about the trials in Spain, and, as King Alfonso told them, interfered with what they did not understand. This is what Frenchmen would tell the too complacent Englishman who contrasted the Steinheil trial with English trials. It is just as well to remember that a nation has the judicial procedure as well as the government it deserves.

Really Sir Robert Hart is becoming rather trying. To him years seem to have brought not discretion, but recklessness. It would matter little were it not that everyone naturally thinks that a man who has lived in China for some half a century must know all about the Chinese that can be known. English "Chinamen" can go behind this fallacy. They understand and discount such pronouncements as Sir Robert's latest that in fifty years China will be wholly Westernised. It is doubtful if China can ever be Westernised at all, at any rate an inch below the surface. There is movement in China, certainly. But to talk in this wild way is merely deluding the plain man who is absolutely ignorant of China and the Chinese.

A coal-strike has broken out in New South Wales which may develop into a general strike. The Industrial Disputes Act has, at any rate up to the present, failed in exercising much influence on either the employers or the men. According to the account of the "Times" correspondent, the Northern coal proprietors "have fought with determination against the Industrial Disputes Act ever since it came into operation. The Southern and Western coalowners obeyed the Act, and consequently it is still doubtful whether their miners will join the strike". A later account shows that to some extent they have now done so.

For the time being the Industrial Disputes Act is given the go-by. Mr. Wade, the Premier, believes it can be put into useful operation yet if the parties are determined to make war upon the community. Who the suspected parties are he does not state. At present he thinks it would be unwise to set the criminal law in motion until all hopes of a conference are abandoned. Then the interesting question will be settled whether the Courts really are able to coerce the parties in trade-disputes as they do ordinary litigants. The precedent will be useful.

It is a very old custom for the Lord Chief Justice to receive the new Lord Mayor in his Court on the ninth of November. Almost, but not yet quite so old, is his practice of explaining to his civic lordship that legal business is in a bad way, and that there are too few judges to do the work. For years Lord Mayors have heard the same story. What we should like to see would be Mr. Asquith, Lord Loreburn, and the Attorney- and Solicitor-General, we were going to say in the dock—there is a dock now in the Chief Justice's Court—and hear Lord Alverstone ask in his most solemn tones,

Why don't you do it? It is really rather hard on the Lord Mayor to worry him with things he cannot help or alter.

Very likely these distinguished persons would stand mute or say to the Chief, You know quite well why. All lawyers do know that Mr. Asquith, Lord Loreburn, Sir William Robson, and Sir Samuel Evans are intending something else. They do not want to make more High Court judges, but to lessen the number; to take business from the London Courts and give it to County Courts. They may not consciously wish to dissolve the Bar, but their plan would come to that. As they cannot have their own way, they refuse to take the other; and Lord Alverstone, if he is not tired of asking for more judges, may go on until he is.

It is rather a surprise to find that professional football players are workmen under the Compensation Act and can recover from their clubs damages for injury. But they already have their trade-unions, so why not? We suppose it was a judicial joke to suggest that they may even be manual labourers. A Rugger player might be, but not the Soccer. Counsel put the case of a professional cricketer claiming compensation as a reductio ad absurdum of the footballers' claim, but it is not easy to see why; and after this decision there cannot be any distinction. Jockeys already come under the rule; and now all professional practitioners of sports, games, and pastimes may congratulate themselves on being raised to the rank of honest labourers. The honesty has been sometimes suspected.

At first sight the Report of the Censorship Commission seems to be a cowardly compromise—as lame a conclusion as even a Commission could come to. The Censorship is to remain, and even the office of Examiner of Plays. But it is to be legal to produce unlicensed plays. A left-handed privilege, for the general respectable public will naturally infer that an unlicensed play is wicked and shy at it; so its hapless author will be in his old bad case. Either he must submit to Mr. Redford or lose the largest public. If he elects to plunge and cut the Censor, it will be natural for him to plunge for something. The advanced play will become risky, and the risky riskier. And the distinction between music-hall and theatre is to go. We may be pretty certain this Report will please nobody.

The case for Leonardo Da Vinci as against Lucas does not improve in that matter of the bust. Mr. A. D. Lucas, Mr. Cooksey, and Mr. Whitburn have fitted in wonderfully together. The vicissitudes of the bust may now be followed through continuously up to its purchase by Dr. Bode. The Berlin authorities are reduced to mere hypothesis in their reply. They do not now deny that Mr. R. C. Lucas did execute a bust; but, they say, it was not the bust purchased by Dr. Bode. To which it may be replied: Produce the defaulting bust, and we will believe you. In evidence they point to what they believe to be an extant photograph of this mythical duplicate, which does not look quite like the reputed Leonardo bought by Dr. Bode.

"Notes and Queries" has just attained its jubilee; fifty years of disinterested usefulness. Fancy a paper going on for fifty years, and still in full vigour, which is, and always has been, written and edited all for love! It is read for love, too, and pilfered from freely and unacknowledged. How many books would never have seen the light but for "Notes and Queries"! This is the only charge against the paper. It is a free quarry for the whole tribe of book-makers. At least they might pay a royalty of thanks, but do not. What a resource is "Notes and Queries" to the literary browser who would tickle his intellect but not work it! Not many, we imagine, know that the word "folklore" was a coin of the first editor of "Notes and Queries", Mr. W. J. Thoms. He was plainly a benefactor. Joe Knight, too, will always be associated with this delightful child of the "Athenæum".

LORDS AND COUNTRY.

It is something to be able to make up your mind, no matter what that mind may be. The Unionist Peers have made up theirs, and three Unionists out of four are delighted with their choice. No doubt there are a certain number in the party, constitutionally unable to make a decision, who wish the Lords had decided otherwise, and would still have wished they had decided otherwise, had they decided to pass the Bill. There are some too who are convinced that rejection is bad tactics and are accordingly regretful. But these are very few. This does not in any way argue that they are wrong—indeed, the great preponderance of opinion in favour of rejection is the one thing that might make us sceptical of its wisdom. We do not deny that serious arguments can be brought against rejection; but so could serious arguments be brought against any plan. Broadly speaking, the Unionist Peers have resolved on the straight course. They have preferred straightforwardness to subtlety and we believe the public will do the same. "We believed these taxes to be bad, therefore we would not pass them unless the country expressly directed us to do so." That is a course of action the plain man, especially the non-politician, can understand and will rise to. It is easily commended to him; no enticing words of politicians' wisdom are needed to make it presentable. But to pass a Bill which they held to be bad, that would require a deal of explaining and excusing. Very fine theories have to be spun if the public are to see the honesty of that. It might be a quite honest action, we agree, but it would be exceedingly difficult to make the country believe it. It would savour too much of tactics, and too little of courage. The British aristocracy has always been plucky; its pluck has commended it a thousand times to the people, even its political haters. A course that at best was more politic than plucky would not be the course to commend a lord to a working man. The best that could be said for the alternative of compromise would be its intelligence, its wisdom; and intelligence is not a commendation to tell with the British public. "Tell the truth and shame the Devil" goes down much better than "Shame the Devil by superior subtlety". We believe the Unionist peers have decided rightly, and we are heartily glad that the period of calculation of party tactics is over.

It is mischievous, no doubt, that the issue before the country will be so much mixed that wrong inferences may be drawn from the result of the election. If the Radicals should get a working majority, it will be claimed that this is a condemnation of the House of Lords and of Tariff Reform and a vindication of the Budget; whereas it might, in fact, mean only one of these things. We believe that very many even of those who like the Budget would approve of the Lords' attitude. They would say, "We do not agree with the Lords about the Budget, but, thinking as they did, they were right to get it referred back to the country. They acted straightly". These would not wish to disable the Upper House, remembering that a time might come when the Lords could give check to a measure they disliked. Electors with such views would probably vote for the Liberals for the sake of the Budget, and would wrongly be held to have condemned the Lords' "veto" at the same time. To disagree with the majority of the Peers' opinion on a particular measure is a different thing from condemning the House of Lords as a factor in the constitution. Certainly it is unfortunate that issues so distinct should be inextricably mixed up as they are in a general election in this country. But whatever course the Lords took as to the Budget, this difficulty would arise. If they passed the Budget, a Radical victory would not the less be held to be a condemnation of the Lords for rejecting the Education Bill and the Licensing Bill. The Lords cannot be kept out of the next election.

We are not afraid of the "Down with the Lords" cry. We all know that lords are unpopular with stalwart Radicals, when they have not the pleasure of their acquaintance. But equally is the House of Lords popular with Conservatives. And the stalwarts on either side equate. The non-stalwart is the important man on this question, and we have never seen any evidence that the Lords are generally unpopular with the non-stalwarts. We believe, on the contrary, that they would strongly object to disestablishing the Lords, and would reject any proposal of the kind taken by itself. But we could well understand a good many of these rather taking to this Budget; the Lords cry may draw their attention off it, and from an electioneering point of view we should gain accordingly. We do not believe that the average non-politician will wish to get the Budget at the price of disestablishing the House of Lords. The Budget is undoubtedly the Government's best card, and we believe that it is in our favour, not in theirs, to make them play the anti-Lords card too.

There are two points, and we should say two points only, in the present position of the House of Lords which give serious pause to the sane elector who tries to think for himself: the so-called deadlock between the Radical party and the Upper House, and the advantage enjoyed by the Unionists from the Conservative character of the House of Lords. These do seem to interfere with the right working of the Constitution. But the deadlock between the Radical party and the Lords is no real deadlock, unless of a Radical Government's own making. The Radical Government that has a principal measure rejected by the Lords has only to go to the country, and if the country returns it again to power, the Lords will pass that measure. There is thus no deadlock. Whether it be right or wrong, there at any rate is the way out; and it is a certain way out, and always open. But the country may not return the Government again. No doubt: which explains the Radical talk of a deadlock, though this way out is always open to them. They want a way out which does not lead to a discovery of the popular view of their Bill. Conservatives, it is true, have such a way out; and we admit this gives them an advantage which is hardly cricket. We have never hesitated to say that the Lords are too compliant with Conservative Ministries. No doubt most of the Lords honestly approve of most Conservative measures: so they naturally pass them. But they have too often allowed themselves to be made a mere convenience of by Conservative Governments, and have suffered in the estimate of the country accordingly. But to make things equal something more than a stiffer attitude is no doubt needed. The Radical plan to equalise things is to make the Lords impotent to oppose either party. We would rather make them an equal check on both parties. We do not know that it would be at all a bad thing if the Lords regularly sent back first-class contentious Bills (excluding annual bills) until it became an understood thing that no Bill of that class could pass unless the country had had an opportunity in a general election of expressing its opinion upon it. It would mean delay, of course, and possibly in measures that were needed; but we should get better thought-out and more generally mature legislation, and the gain would be worth the delay. It would get rid of any unfair advantage Conservatives now enjoy, and the Lords would retain their necessary power of putting a check on legislation. To suppose that it would stultify the House of Commons and leave it with nothing to do during a Ministry's first Parliament would show very little knowledge of parliamentary work.

An objection very remarkable for its parentage has been taken to the House of Lords as a check. "The practical man", we learn, "may desire a check on legislation, but he cannot fail on reflection to see the uselessness of a check which always—according to those who exercise it—gives way before popular agitation". Then the sin of the House of Lords, according to the "Westminster Gazette", is that it is too sensitive to the popular will. This is significant as well as interesting, for it throws light on a familiar Liberal way of putting the issue. "Is the House of Commons or the House of Lords to be supreme?" they cry. The Unionist answer is, Neither, but the country. The Liberal would make the House of Commons supreme, and objects to the Lords because by compelling the reference of measures to the test of a general election, they make the country supreme over the Commons. Our Liberal friends would have the Lords give way to the House of Commons, which is to say the Government, but not to the country. We know the old story that the Commons is the mirror of the country; we also know that it is untrue. The country does not see itself in the House of Commons, and sometimes would be very sorry if it did. We know further that if the Commons did reflect the country, that would not make measures passed in that House necessarily welcome to the public, for the House of Commons is in the grip of the Government of the day. The House as a House, apart from the Executive, does nothing. Therefore it does not matter one straw whether the Lords are at issue with the Commons or not. The only important question is, Are the Lords in agreement with the country?

MINISTERS AT THE GUILDHALL.

IT requires no deep knowledge of politics or of human nature to picture the feelings of the City Corporation and its friends towards the present advisers of the King. Time was when the City of London was uproariously Whig, "the mansion-house of liberty", as Milton called it. But for the last thirty years the City has become more and more Tory, for obvious reasons. As the old party lines have been suddenly and rudely swept away in the last four years, and a bold attack made upon property by the guardian of the public purse, the feeling of antagonism against the Government has never been stronger than it is to-day in the City. That is no reason why the majority of his Majesty's Ministers should absent themselves from the Lord Mayor's banquet. It is an historic occasion, on which the bitterness of party feud is, by a polite fiction, drowned in the ancient loving-cup, which is passed round with so much ceremony. At the height of his unpopularity with "the classes", Mr. Gladstone and his Cabinet never omitted to accept the new Lord Mayor's hospitality. Mr. Asquith, Mr. Haldane, and Mr. Churchill were the only Cabinet Ministers who faced the music in the Guildhall on Tuesday. We really can excuse the absence of Mr. Lloyd George, both because he has undergone exceptional fatigue, and because he cannot but be aware that he is peculiarly odious to the monied class. But where were the Lord Chancellor and the First Lord of the Admiralty? It has been an almost invariable custom for the head of the Law and the head of the British Navy to appear at this representative gathering. Where were the Secretaries of State, Mr. Gladstone, Lord Morley, Sir Edward Grey, and Lord Crewe? We are compelled to condemn this wholesale abstention of Cabinet Ministers from the Guildhall as a breach of traditionary manners.

The lines of the Prime Minister's speech were chalked out for him by precedent and the environment. To such an audience it would have been impossible for Mr. Asquith to deliver a philippic against the House of Lords or to embark upon a vindication of the Budget. He was obliged to ignore what was filling the minds of the well-dressed guests about him and to lead their attention to the safe field of foreign and colonial politics. We are all so busy quarrelling over taxation that for the last two years we have tacitly agreed not to quarrel about South Africa and the Eastern question. We do not grudge the Prime Minister's compliments to his own Government on the establishment of autonomy in South Africa and the settlement of the Balkan difficulties, though we are far from sharing his complacency as to the future. For the moment everything seems to be for the best in this best of all possible (South African) worlds. It is flat blasphemy now to suggest a doubt of the loyalty of the Boers, or to hint a possibility of future separation from the Empire, when the Dutch have secured complete control of the Parliamentary machine. Confidence is a plant of slow growth; and we refuse to join in the chorus of gush about brotherly love and the fusion of races. The Dutch Boers are a much more stubborn and persistent race than the French Canadians, and after more than a century the French have not fused with the British in Canada. However, for the hour the fusionists have triumphed, and the Government are fairly entitled to crow over the supersession of the Lyttelton constitution by their own measure of complete autonomy.

With regard to the foreign policy of Sir Edward Grey we are even more dubious. Except for the reason given above, namely, preoccupation with internal finance, we do not know why there is a conspiracy of the Press to unite in praising the Foreign Secretary. Certainly his encounter with Count Aehrenthal was not so skilful or successful as to entitle him to be entrusted with a blank cheque by the nation. What were the facts? Bulgaria opened the game of grab by setting the Treaty of Berlin at defiance and proclaiming her independence. Austria immediately followed suit by converting the protectorate which she had been given by the Treaty of Berlin over Bosnia and Herzegovina into sovereignty—in other words, by annexing those provinces. It is our opinion that Count Aehrenthal by his promptitude saved Europe from war. It has subsequently become as certain as anything can be in the domain of secret diplomacy that Russia was, if not an agreeing party, perfectly informed beforehand of Austria's intention, and that her protest was purely political—i.e. made to satisfy the Panslavists in her own dominion. Sir Edward Grey should have known this, and should have backed Austria for all he was worth. But he did not know it; like the young man from the country he was not "at the centre of the situation". For he allowed himself to be drawn into a joint protest with France and Russia against Count Aehrenthal, and all to soothe the vanity of those regicide ruffians, the Servians. It is a golden rule of diplomacy that you should never protest, still less threaten, unless you mean to back up your words by force. Sir Edward Grey must have known that neither France, nor Russia, nor Great Britain had the faintest intention of going to war with Austria and Germany for the sake of Servia. He ought also to have seen, if his secret information did not tell him, that M. Isvolski was merely using him to play the Panslavist game. But Sir Edward Grey's diplomacy might have pushed us into a position—in fact very nearly did push us into an attitude—from which there would have been no retreat except by war or humiliation. As it was, Sir Edward Grey was fussy and feeble. He declared that certain things must not be done without the assent of the Powers of Europe in Conference; they were done, and nothing happened. We lost a golden opportunity of strengthening our old friendship with Austria, the next most powerful nation to Germany on the Continent, and we did not even secure the respect of Europe. Republican France and autocratic Russia are ineffective allies, and it is time the people of this country knew it. We wish we could share the Prime Minister's optimism with regard to the future of Eastern Europe. The situation in Greece, and the attempt of Turkey once more to place Crete beyond the reach of annexation by the Greeks, are combustible topics enough. On the subject of the misgovernment of the Congo the Prime Minister said what was fitting. It is inconceivable that a civilised country like Belgium, governed by highly educated men, can continue to tolerate barbarous methods in a country which she has now formally taken over.

THE THREE GOVERNORSHIPS.

THE approaching vacancies in the Indian Viceroyalty and the Governorships-General of South Africa and Canada will afford almost unequalled opportunities for the exercise of the highest patriotism or the meanest partisanship. We have no desire to attribute to the great majority of the Cabinet any but the most patriotic views before so grave a responsibility, but the temptation is always great to every party politician to view appointments from the standpoint of party advantage. Therefore, unless the emergency be overwhelming, it is impossible to eliminate this element from the calculations of party leaders; still it should not be difficult to reduce its influence to very small proportions. To do this, however, requires a strength of will in resisting social and party pressure which politicians on either side have not always possessed. Even if it be possible in the case of one appointment, it becomes more than trebly difficult when three are to become vacant almost at one time.

In any such conjuncture as this the Unionist party has some advantage over its rivals. It has certainly a much larger number of eligible candidates to draw upon, because in most appointments of this nature one essential condition is that the appointee should be of a high social position. This is obligatory in the case of Canada and Australia, but is perhaps less obviously so in the case of South Africa. Tact, industry, and a knowledge of affairs are also indispensable, and these qualities are generally present in the leading families which have for many years in this country devoted themselves to public work. When we come to the post of Viceroy of India—after that of British Prime Minister the greatest under the Crown—greater qualities than these are demanded: the capacity to assume the heaviest responsibilities and to decide on a policy, and sometimes to convince the Government at home against its will of the justice of that policy. These are the essential requirements for these appointments, and there are many minor qualifications almost equally desirable.

Now the Government is not too obviously supplied at the present time with a plethora of candidates fulfilling these indisputable conditions. They certainly have plenty to choose from if the eligible men would go; but then they clearly would not, for to do so would be to ruin their chances at home. The rôle of deputy constitutional monarch is not a good training for a return to the political arena; besides, five years' absence gives the pas inevitably to the rivals who remain here. A few years of the most successful Indian or colonial administration do not really compensate an ambitious man for the certain loss of the Premiership. Therefore those who are entitled to expect the highest honours at home will hardly risk their chances by accepting even the most dignified functions in a colony.

It has been suggested recently that partisan appointments to posts of this nature are to be deprecated, and that such posts, at least, as those we have named should not be given to leading party men. This seems to us a reductio ad absurdum of the very excellent maxim that they should not be bestowed upon men who have merely served their party and have no other qualifications. Obviously, too, they should not be used to weed out failures from the party hierarchy. But it is absurd to contend that when a man is otherwise qualified he should not receive such a post because he has taken an active part in home politics. If this rule is to be adopted, we shall strike out at once all our best-qualified candidates. Fortunately for this country, politics still attract many men of the soundest judgment, highest position, and keenest intellect, and if we are to forbid India and the colonies to have the benefit of their ripe experience of public affairs, we shall in the end injure irreparably both the Empire at large and politics at home. If the Liberals have the right to appoint to these high offices we do not grudge their bestowing them on Liberals, always supposing that their nominees are well equipped for the position.

Many rumours have been current of late regarding these three appointments shortly to be vacant. Most of them may be disregarded as invented in newspaper offices or as the tittle-tattle of clubs and drawing-rooms. But that which makes Mr. Herbert Gladstone the first Governor-General of united South Africa seems to have more foundation than the rest, and must therefore be weighed. The SATURDAY REVIEW has never professed to believe that the policy pursued by this present Government in South Africa was statesmanlike or likely in the end to prove beneficial to the Empire. But, things being as they are, every sane and patriotic man wishes the new régime to run as smoothly as it may. Now, if Mr.

Gladstone were well qualified in every other respect, his name alone would disqualify him. Nearly the whole British community there would feel that memories of a hated policy were being ruthlessly stirred up at a time when it is highly desirable that even the suggestion of former quarrels should be removed from any association with the Governor-General. This should especially be so in the case of the first man to occupy this post. Any such connexion must surely be fatal even to a good candidate. His wisest decisions would be subject to unfair criticism. But the case with regard to Mr. Gladstone is quite different. He is admittedly the most conspicuous failure in the present Ministry, which has been honourably distinguished by administrative success. The only vigorous legislation initiated and carried through by the Home Office was engineered and piloted by Mr. Samuel, at that time his able and industrious junior. The only conspicuous act of Mr. Gladstone himself that we can recall was the disgraceful reprieve of the Whiteley murderer, unless we include the weak blundering over the Roman Catholic procession in Westminster. In order to understand what the Home Office may become in capable hands, we have only to compare Mr. Asquith's two years and a half with Mr. Gladstone's four. Unfortunately his failure can only be attributed to a lack of industry little short of scandalous. There have been instances of important deputations, non-partisan, which have been disgusted by the failure of the Minister to reply coherently on matters with regard to which an hour's application under the coaching of a permanent official would have supplied him with all the points necessary.

We do not charge the Prime Minister with the wish to irritate wantonly the British element in South Africa; we can therefore only believe that if he sends Mr. Gladstone there, it will be because he wants to get rid of him. The same reason might justify the rumour that Mr. Winston Churchill is to go to India; but we do not believe for a moment that Lord Morley would assent to any such exasperating experiment. But a much stronger argument against its probability even is that for Mr. Churchill to accept the Viceroyalty would leave the field at home open to Mr. Lloyd George by neutralising for five years his most formidable rival. We have still enough confidence left in Mr. Asquith to believe that he would not make India a dumping-ground for his failures or a playground for his enfants terribles.

Canada is already so far advanced in the art of self-government that the choice of a Governor-General does not present quite such thorny problems as does India or South Africa. But any attempt to impose upon the Dominion one of our political failures will be deeply resented. Also a social position that counts is still demanded of the King's representative, and its absence will not be atoned for by amiable dilettantism or even by some literary reputation. We should imagine Mr. Asquith had already perceived that to have made some good remarks by the way is not proof of capacity to run a great country even as figure-head.

RELIGION AND THE FRENCH SCHOOLS.

THE French Republic is at the present time taxing French Catholics to support an educational system of which the chief object is the poisoning of their children's minds against the Christian faith. This tyranny is not a thing of yesterday. It commenced in the year 1882, when l'instruction morale et civique replaced "l'instruction morale et religieuse" in public education. But as long as the educational policy of M. Jules Ferry held the field, it was generally possible for Catholics, at the cost of personal sacrifice, to preserve their children from the pernicious influences of an anti-Christian training, as the law permitted, and politicians encouraged them, to maintain a private educational system on Christian lines side by side with the communal schools. To maintain these écoles libres, as they are called, has become for Catholics, since the expulsion of the religious orders and the passing of the separation law, an almost impossible task. French Christians are therefore face to face with the bitter fact that they must not only contribute to the support of anti-Christian education, but must perforce see their children subjected to its influence. If, however, anything could be added to their just indignation against this oppression, it is the hypocrisy which describes the most malign institution ever set up to injure the Faith as "l'école publique laïque et neutre". The description, however, unquestionably misleads Englishmen, who regard the French school as secular in the sense that Miall and the older Liberationists used the expression. A secular school in this, the English, sense means a school which absolutely ignores religion. In it the three R's and modern languages may be taught; but on the whole field that touches religion the teacher must be silent. Now whether this idea of a school that is honestly non-religious be practicable or not, it is certainly not the idea that underlies the French educational system, and the offensive primers or manuals which it employs. The idea of the French Republican educationist is (as is shown by those famous words of M. Viviani, which have startled even the "Times" newspaper) to put out in the Heavens the lights which shall never be lighted again. The French teacher, who is never seen at Mass, teaches the young Catholic child of a material and moral universe in which God has no place. Call this a neutral or a secular system! Since the days of Julian the Apostate history records no such insidious and dishonest an attempt to rob a nation of the Christian Faith. The tardy protest which the French episcopate is now raising against this tyranny is not primarily a claim for denominational privilege or even for denominational justice. It is only an appeal for common honesty and common fairness, a demand that schools which are in name neutral shall no longer be used as instruments for the repression of Christianity. If there was any sense of justice in English Nonconformity, its organs would at this crisis declare themselves on the side of the oppressed Church of France, for the French Bishops' case has for its justification the old Liberationist principle that the State should not employ its patronage or control to favour one form of belief (or unbelief) at the expense of another. But seldom has English Nonconformity or extreme Free Churchmanship been known to protest against injustice to the Catholic, and it shows to-day no intention to break its unworthy record. It will march in its thousands to the Albert Hall next week to raise its shout against the action of a Catholic Power in the Congo. When a freethinking State sets itself to poison the minds of Christian children against the Faith of Christ, it spins pretty apologetics for the unbeliever.

It is, however, something to the good that the stress of the facts has forced English supporters of French tyranny to admit that the Republic's action calls for apologies and excuses. In the days of the Separation struggle we were told that justice and religion were on the side of the persecutor. The British public, however, knows more of the attitude of French politicians to Christianity than it knew two years ago, and the apologists of the Viviani school of politics cannot deny that it is a trifle unjust to French Christians. They, however, have their excuse. The injustice, which in some small details might, they allow, be modified, is, they tell us, necessary for the preservation of the Republic, to which the Church is disloyal. Were Protestants and not Catholics the victims of this injustice, there is not a Protestant in Great Britain who would not deride the excuse as nonsensical. Because certain priests are believed, rightly or wrongly, to be in favour of replacing a republic by a monarchy, it is, according to our apologists, right and just that the State should use the money of Christian parents to proselytise their children into atheism or agnosticism. To state the proposition in simple words is to prove it ridiculous. But it is worse than nonsensical, it is dishonest. Assuming that the French priests are disloyal to the temporary constitution of their country, it is monstrous for the panegyrists of Cromwell, the stalwarts of passive resistance, the enemies of the House of Lords, to defend on such a ground the Republic's intolerance. Would it be right for a Conservative

Government to pass an Act for the compulsory education of Baptist children in the principles of the Church Catechism because Dr. Clifford is leading an agitation for the abolition of the Peers' prerogatives? It is no less unjust and dishonest to use the political views of French priests as an excuse for the perversion of French Catholic children from their parents' faith.

At the same time it is utterly false to say that the French clergy as a body are disloyal to the Republic. Individuals among them there doubtless are who hate it and all its works, and who would welcome an Orleanist or Bonapartist restoration. Practically, however, the bulk of the French priesthood accept the secular politics of the peasant class from which they spring, are just as loyal to the Constitution of their country as other citizens, and like them for the most part acquiesce in the bureaucratic tyranny of the powers that be. This fact of itself is far from being an unmixed blessing, either for France or for the Church. The passive submission with which from the days of Napoleon the French clergy have accepted every change of régime has convinced French politicians that anti-clericalism is a safe game for the bureaucracy. While, however, we may regret that thirty years ago the French clergy did not stand up to the State as the English parsons in their position would have done, the submissive manner in which bishops and priests alike bowed before the long régime of injustice and intolerance that followed MacMahon's fall is a complete answer to the idle charge of civic disloyalty.

If there is no justification for the plea that makes the disloyalty of the clergy the excuse for the persecution of the Church, there is less justification in the apology that all the French State desires is an education on German lines for its children. If this were its only wish, it could easily effect it by refusing State recognition to any Catholic school the pupils of which did not reach a certain standard in secular subjects. But the answer is more complete. The Republic has not adopted the German system of religious instruction. The talk of a business-like education for French children is as idle as the legend about clerical disloyalty. For a century, and more, ever since the day that the civil constitution of the clergy was introduced into the National Assembly, French Republicanism has laboured steadily and patiently to undermine and destroy Christianity or, in the words of its prophet, écraser l'infâme, and these State schools have been established to accomplish this and no other end. The war that the Republic has waged against Christianity has not been from first to last a war in the interests of democracy. As the civil constitution of the clergy wrecked all hope of a peaceful revolution and brought on France all the horrors of the Revolution and the Napoleonic wars, so it is to the frenzy of modern anti-clericalism that most of the misfortunes of modern France are due. It is this fact that makes it idle to talk of a reconciliation between the Church and the Republic. If the Republic ceased to persecute the Church it would cease to be the Republic of the Revolution, the child of the Encyclopædia and the contrat social. As Gambetta saw, an entente between the heirs of the Revolution and the Church would be an "ignoble comédie". There can be no chance of a real peace between the Church and Jacobinism. The hope for French Christianity lies in the movement for liberty and association as against bureaucracy that is now beginning to show itself in France. Meanwhile in its bitter struggle for the children's faith the French Church may claim the moral aid of Christendom.

THE PLOT AGAINST THE HIGH COURT.

LORD ALVERSTONE'S observations to the Lord Mayor on the state of business at the Law Courts were as painfully true as they were painfully not new. Ten years ago Lord Russell of Killowen anticipated him. Mr. Justice Jelf on Thursday followed to the same effect in his charge to the Grand Jury at Stafford Assizes. It is the fate of truisms to be ignored, and so both Conservative and Liberal Governments have given this question of the judges the go-by during all these years. It was a Liberal Attorney-General, Sir Lawson Walton, who, while the present Government was in office, declared that the breakdown of the Courts amounted to a scandal and a denial of justice. That nothing will be done by Liberals now is plain. The interval before a General Election will leave no room for anything but emergency business; and there is reason for believing that if the next Government were Liberal, it would pay no more attention to the Lord Chief Justice's complaint than to Lord Russell's. Two years ago, indeed, Lord Coleridge was appointed an additional judge in circumstances which showed that it was intended rather for the relief of Lord Coleridge than for the relief of the Courts. When the Criminal Appeal Court was set up it was well known that even with the additional judge the judicial bench would be proportionately worse under-manned than before. Lord Coleridge has been unfortunate beyond the usual lot of judges in the matter of health. But even if Lord Coleridge had done his work with the regularity of a machine, as it is absurdly assumed the judges are always able to do, the new Court would have nullified his best endeavours. Perhaps the most definite statement of the additional number of judges required is that of Lord Alverstone. He says there ought to be always in London ten or eleven judges, but that it is impossible to secure on an average more than six or seven. Four or five more judges then, at least, are absolutely necessary.

He also shows what results from the deficiency. If anyone should desire to have his cause tried there must be a delay of five or six months; and any appeal from a County Court judgment cannot be heard without a delay of four or five months. Why, then, are not more judges appointed? It is not on account of the expense. The sum of £25,000 a year would be a small price to pay for law proceedings so quick that, as the present Lord Chancellor has put it, every litigant would have his case heard, after it was ready for trial, within a few days. The reason the Liberals do not appoint more judges is that they have other views and other schemes. If they come back to office again, they will be as averse from appointing more judges as they have hitherto been. Their plan is not to strengthen the Courts in London but to weaken by decentralising and transferring most of their work to local Courts. They want especially to increase the jurisdiction of the County Courts. Their recent County Courts Bill made these Courts for most purposes the equals of the High Court. Even divorce cases, which County Courts have never had anything to do with, would be dealt with there if the Lord Chancellor and Lord Gorell had had their way. The Lord Chancellor greatly resented the collapse of his Bill in the Lords, and it may be prophesied with confidence that while Lord Loreburn advises the Government, there will be no additional judges appointed in the High Court. When a Conservative Government was in office the Liberals rushed to arms whenever the question of more judges was raised. They either said the judges could do more work if they tried, or that a revolution of the whole legal system was necessary from top to bottom. This was an argument that was rather popular. There is always a latent suspicion easily excited that lawyers themselves are responsible for the abuses of the law. A Conservative Government might have disregarded this prejudice if the case for additional judges had been as strong then as it is now, after the establishment of the Criminal Appeal Court. They might as it was, if an administrative act had been enough; but legislation was necessary and there was an Opposition ready to denounce and resist the appointment as a legal job. In the changed circumstances, and after the experience of all these years, another Conservative Government would find it much easier to appoint more judges, and would no doubt do so. But the Liberals would continue obdurate and harden their hearts. They sulk at the rejection of their County Court scheme. In revenge they would push on their scheme again and refuse to listen to the cry for more judges.

This question of more judges will be decisive of the

future of the legal profession. If County Courts take over a great part of the work of the High Court, more High Court judges will not be required, but fewer. It is only on the assumption that County Courts are to remain as they are that more judges are wanted in London. In a great measure it is by the growth of the County Courts that much business which would come to London or be done by the judges at Assizes is done by the County Court judges. The Bar alone has audience in London or at the Assizes, but in the County Courts solicitors too are advocates; as often in London as barristers, and in the country more often. Every extension of County Court jurisdiction therefore increases the scope of the solicitor's advocacy and restricts that of the barrister. If the County Courts Bill had passed, solicitors would have obtained almost all the rights of advocacy that barristers have. This naturally alarmed the Bar, and an attempt had to be made, if the Bill passed, to arrange between the two branches of the profession that barristers in cases over a certain amount should alone have the right of audience. It is quite certain that solicitors would not fall in with such a plan, and that it would not do. In any case barristers would have to migrate into the country for the chance of work, and instead of being too few judges in London there would be too many. The Courts in London would become almost wholly appeal courts. The distinction of barrister and solicitor would cease, and the legal system of ages be broken up. Whenever the legal profession has the question of fusion put to it directly, it is against this change. This is certainly so with the Bar, and probably with the solicitors, though at their recent annual meeting at Birmingham there was no formal resolution passed in favour of the appointment of additional judges, and they ascribed the defeat of the Government Bill to the opposition of the Bar. These controversies have been raised by the Liberal proposals, and if there are to be no more judges appointed till they are settled the Courts in London will remain in the confusion which has so long been their normal but unhealthy state. There are many reasons why it is better to keep the Bench and the Bar and the solicitor branch, generally speaking, in their present relations to each other. The Courts would work satisfactorily enough if the Bench were sufficiently strengthened; but it is the weakness of Liberals to suppose that nothing can be improved without destroying it. How soon or how late the demand for new judges will be met depends on the result of the next General Election.

THE CITY.

It looks as if a further rise in the Bank rate will be unnecessary. During the week quite a substantial amount of gold has been received from Austria and Paris, and a further influx is promised. The Paris remittances are not coming without assistance from the Bank of France, but there is no reason to cavil at the transactions and point to them as evidence of the straits to which the Bank of England is reduced. It is to the interest of the Bank of France that our Bank rate should not go any higher, and any assistance it may offer in strengthening our gold reserves is not altogether an act of philanthropy. It is not a case of the Bank of England borrowing gold as was the case in 1907, but of the Bank of France paying it out to protect itself. The Bank of England in the present instance has done absolutely nothing to solicit the metal except in the ordinary course of business. The important point is that the position of the Bank is improving. Stock markets have not been slow to recognise the change, and while there has been no pronounced advance in prices as a result, a distinctly better tendency has been observable. Disappointment continues to be expressed at the course of Kaffirs, but with nine-tenths of the market "bulls" of the shares no rise in prices can be sustained. The best thing that could happen to this market would be a good shake-out, eliminating the large number of small dealers and forcing brokers with clients of small means to close their commitments. It seems a drastic and rather a cruel proposal, but we are confident that no permanent rise can be engineered in existing circumstances, and therefore the prompt sacrifice of the small punter is really an act of kindness. The fall in Consols seems to be arrested, and our expectations in regard to home railway traffic are being borne out. This week's returns show quite a substantial gain in the aggregate, goods receipts continuing to expand steadily, while passenger earnings no longer show big decreases compared with abnormal figures a year ago. So far prices have not moved much, but the tendency is upwards, and at the settlement several small parcels of stock were lifted from the market as a result of the revival of investment. Meantime the position in Wall Street would seem to be improving, and for the time being at least all danger of a collapse appears to have passed. If, as is likely, a copper combination is arranged, yet another step will have been taken to prevent disaster to the market. The great restraining influence, so far as general markets are concerned, is the uncertainty of the home political situation.

Of the promotion of rubber plantation companies there is no end, and many disappointments are likely to be experienced by investors who swallow without inquiry all the statements contained in the prospectuses. The practice seems to be to sell all the estates on the basis of going concerns, whereas in the majority of cases several years must elapse before dividends commensurate with the risks are earned. It is generally assumed that there are no risks. To one, the management, we have previously referred; another is the danger of the white ant. This destructive insect is especially prevalent in Ceylon, and where jungle has been cleared for the plantation of rubber it is almost certain to appear when the roots of old trees are not completely removed. In the haste to plant the rubber these roots are very apt to be overlooked, and the work of destroying the insect adds considerably to the cost of production. No allowance, however, is made for emergencies in prospectus estimates of profit. As regards the immediate prospects of the raw material the market is beginning to waver, and there are not wanting indications of a sharp fall in price within the next few weeks. Supplies which have been kept back threaten to come forward, and if the quantity is as large as is reported a drop of a shilling a pound or more might easily result. We are inclined to think that the present is a good opportunity to sell rubber shares, as any material fall in the raw material would be immediately reflected in the share market. Repurchases could then be made on a lower basis, with the prospect of a return to the higher prices when the supply of the raw material once more became restricted.

The report of the Consolidated Gold Fields Company discloses a very strong financial position, and the directors are wise in setting aside half a million for the replacement of shares in mines which some day will be worked out. Meantime they can utilise the money in other channels, the sphere of their operations now extending to West Africa, the United States, and Russia. We notice that a recent purchase is an interest in the Lena Goldfields, Limited, a company owning an interest of about 74 per cent. in a Russian gold mine, which up to now has produced nearly thirteen millions sterling in gold. The full statement of the profits of the Russian company is not yet available, but it is estimated that the total for the year will be over £400,000. Pending the final result, the directors of the Lena Goldfields have declared an interim dividend of 10 per cent. per annum, and a promise is made of a further distribution on account of the profits for the year. Some weeks ago we referred to the manipulation of the shares of the West African Development Company. There was a sequel on Wednesday, when the price, which had been "made up" at 9¼, fell to below 5, with practically no market. It appears that one small dealer was heavily committed in the shares, and being unable to "carry over" he was "hammered". The closing of the account revealed the rotten state of the market, and will, it is to be hoped, warn off any of the public who may feel disposed to have a flutter in the shares.

We notice that the "Statist" endorses our warning

remarks concerning the Russian Estates and Mines, Limited. That journal has been very dilatory in the matter, and even now it has not traced the full history of the powers behind the promotion. In addition to assisting in the flotation of the Caucasus Minerals Syndicate and the Mount Elborous Mines—two companies around which much scandal arose—the promoter of the Russian Estates and Mines Limited was also responsible for the bringing into existence of the French Rhodesia and Transvaal Exploration Company, the shares of which were manipulated to 5 and fell to nothing, which is their value now. Indeed, the company has disappeared, leaving not a trace behind it. Which prompts us to ask: How is it that such a disappearance is possible?

INSURANCE: POLICIES AT HIGH PREMIUMS.

IV.

ENDOWMENT assurance policies effected at single premiums, or for short terms such as ten or fifteen years, are suitable in cases when a sum of money is sure to be needed at some definite date in the future; for instance, as a means of paying for education, or of replacing, when the lease comes to an end, the money sunk in leasehold property. Such policies are also a safe and lucrative method of investment for people who during a few years are earning a large income, out of which they want to accumulate capital for future use.

As the length of the endowment period increases the rate of premium that has to be paid diminishes. The reasons for this are obvious, since, except in the event of early death, the number of premiums to be received by the assurance company is larger, and the date at which the sum assured has to be paid is later. If the age at which the endowment matures for payment is made the limiting age of the mortality table—say, for example, ninety-seven—the endowment assurance policy becomes ordinary whole-life assurance. Thus as the endowment period is extended the character of the policy approximates more and more nearly to that of whole-life assurance, and the high premium gradually becomes a low premium.

A policy which assures £1000 with profits in addition at age sixty-five, or at death if previous, costs about £25 a year. If the policy is not taken out until age thirty-five, the annual premium becomes about £35; and if taken at age forty-five, the annual cost is £55. It has to be remembered that, although all these policies are with-profit endowment assurance maturing at age sixty-five, they do not secure equal benefits; the one effected at the youngest of the three ages receives bonuses for forty years, which may amount to £680, and yield a policyholder on reaching the age of sixty-five the sum of £1680 in return for a total outlay in premiums of £1000. The man of thirty-five will, on the same basis, receive £1510 at sixty-five, in return for a total expenditure of £1050; while the man of forty-five, who, in the course of twenty years, pays £1100 in premiums, cannot expect to receive more than £1340. The outlay is larger and the return is smaller, partly because the cost of protection is greater at the older ages, and partly because there is less time during which the premiums can accumulate at compound interest. Hence we reach once more the familiar conclusion that life assurance should be effected as early in life as possible.

When it is reasonably clear that a man who is at present earning an income will have to retire from work, or wish to do so, and has no means of providing an income for the future except by means of life assurance, an endowment assurance policy is the most suitable choice. Unfortunately, in many such cases, there is the further consideration that such a man also has to make provision for his family in the event of his premature death. If a man of thirty-five pays £100 a year for life assurance he can obtain a with-profit policy for about £3550, payable at his death whenever it happens, and subject to the payment of premiums throughout the whole of life. If he takes endowment assurance, payable at the end of thirty years or at previous death, the face value of the policy is only £2800, about one-fifth less provision for his family than he could make by taking a whole-life policy. At older ages the contrast is even greater: £100 a year for a whole-life policy would secure £2530 with profits, while the same premium paid for endowment assurance maturing at sixty-five would yield only £1760, or about two-thirds of the provision for his family that whole-life assurance would give. It thus becomes a case for each individual to decide whether a high premium policy providing the largest provision for his own future, or a low premium policy, securing the greatest amount of protection for those dependent upon him, is the more suitable.

There is always the possibility under a whole-life policy of surrendering it for its cash value at some future time, thus in a sense converting it into endowment assurance. A man of forty-five, who, at a cost of £100 a year, took a whole-life policy for £2530, could surrender it twenty years later for about £1110, with the cash value of the bonuses in addition. Comparing this with endowment assurance maturing at sixty-five, he would have, ignoring the amount of the bonuses in which both policies participate, £770 additional insurance protection during the twenty years and £650 less for himself at the end of that time. The surrender of a whole-life policy for the purpose of converting it into endowment assurance can in some ways be carried out more effectively if the policy is subject to the payment of premiums for a limited number of years only. In that case care should be taken that the company issuing the policy gives liberal surrender values.

ADVICE TO MR. CARTON.

By Max Beerbohm.

"SO", exclaims the young dramatist to the middle-aged one who is the central figure of Mr. Carton's new play at the St. James's—"so you think literary quality a negligible quantity in the art of playwriting?" I do wish Mr. Carton thought it so. His determination to write well is positively harrowing. If he placed himself in the hands of a teacher of the art of writing, he would be a centenarian before he had unlearned all the wrong principles that he has so industriously taught himself. Even then, there would be the fact—proved for the connoisseur by the sentence quoted above—that he was born without a sense for the value and the sound of words. That sense must be innate, cannot be implanted, can only be developed. But any man, by keeping his ears open, can acquire a good rough working notion of the manner in which his fellow-creatures converse. Any playwright can, if he will be so kind and unpretentious, write dialogue that is not unlike human speech. To get away as far as possible from human speech, and as near as possible to the crude pomposity that I have so often deplored in the writing of Sir Arthur Pinero, is evidently the ideal of poor misguided Mr. Carton. I wish he would be guided by me. Let him imagine for a moment that he himself is Lorrimer Sabiston, the middle-aged dramatist. Let him imagine that he has become a very rich man by writing the sort of plays that the public likes—plays at which he, however, laughs in his sleeve. Let him imagine himself wishing to write, just once, a true and fine play, but not wishing it to be produced under his own name, and persuading a needy young dramatist to take the responsibility for it. Would he, would he really, before dictating a letter which will save him from any attempt to fasten the play on to him hereafter, say to the young man "I hope you will find that pen to your liking"? Would he not say "I hope the pen is all right for you"—or something to that less would-be-lovely effect? And would he presently say "if you will allow me to encroach a little further on your leisure"? And does he ever really say "the former" and "the latter", as do his puppets? Those are locutions which a writer for print sometimes finds hard to avoid. Every good writer does manage to avoid them. Conceive a writer putting them deliberately into spoken dialogue! "You have been a pinchbeck Diogenes since first you began spoiling foolscap, with not a shilling nor a moral to your name"—is it thus that Mr. Carton would chaff a confrère? Surely, when he speaks of London, he says just "London", not "this little world that we call London". And surely, to a lady who has liked one of his plays, but not the others, he would not say "It left a passing footprint on the sands of even your approval". He would say "Even you liked it". In writing for print, a metaphor here and there is all very well; nay, it is delightful, if it be a fresh one and an exact one, and if it be worked out ingeniously. But how carefully would we avoid the company of people who could say nothing simply and directly—people who could not open their lips without emitting a metaphor (usually trite)! Such are the people whom Mr. Carton thrusts on us. The bedraggled shuttle-cock of oft-used imagery is bandied unceasingly between the resounding battledores of their respective intellects—as they would say. They simply can't stop. However agitated or depressed they may be, they must go on metaphorising. It is a sort of disease—of which *we*, not *they*, perish, hang it all! The younger dramatist in the play is embittered by unsuccess and by poverty, is at his wits' end. "The Thames Conservancy," says he, "has shown no sign of taking out a fire insurance policy against me." Lady Cheynley, whom Sabiston loves, is on the eve of eloping from a cruel husband with the younger dramatist (whom she loves because she believes him to be the author of Sabiston's masterpiece), and she remarks that "when one is going to take a plunge into unknown waters, Paris is the most appropriate spring-board". Sabiston wants her to live with him an untrammeled life in Italy; but, she tells him, "Romanticism is dead. The niggers have monopolised the moon. The banjo has ousted the guitar." Generally speaking, I cannot imagine a better way of cooling a lover's ardour than a smart-journalese utterance such as this. The ardour of Sabiston is, of course, only intensified by it. He would not wish the woman he loves to talk otherwise than he. But I put it to Mr. Carton that if he were in Sabiston's place, and were talked to in that style, he would get the lady off the premises as quickly as might be. I implore him to let his characters talk like human beings—even when, as in this play, he won't let them act as such.

The theme of the play is, in its quiddity, a good one. An eminent artist of middle-age, confronted by a radical change in the taste of the critics and (in some degree) of the public, is a theme on which Mr. Carton, if he had taken it seriously, might have based a fine comedy. Some years ago, somewhere, I read a short story in which the theme was treated well by a writer who had evidently steeped himself in the method of Mr. Henry James. The artist, in this instance, was a painter, a Royal Academician, fifty-five years or so in age, and full of vigour. For many years of his life he had been one of the idols of the critics and of the public. But in course of time, very gradually, the tone of the critics had changed; patrons had become less eager; old pictures of his that came into the market were sold for much-diminished prices. To him, as a very sensitive man, whom fame had always coddled graciously, these tokens were most bitter. He began to doubt—he who had never doubted yet—his own power. He had never truckled: his work had always been sincere; but, he was always asking himself, had he ever possessed the genius with which he had been credited? Also, had he been, all the time, on a false tack in his art? These new men, whom he was wont to regard as charlatans—what if, after all, they were as sincere as they were brilliant? What if his imperception was merely fogeydom? He could paint still as well as ever, in the way to which he had been trained. Aye, and he was sure he could beat these fellows on their own ground, if he chose to. One night, from the window of his studio, he "knocked off" a nocturne in the manner of the impressionists, and was immensely cheered to find how well he could do it. But next morning he began to have his doubts of it. No! the thing didn't pass muster. Overnight, he had thought what fun it would be to exhibit it in the enemy's camp, under an assumed name, and be hailed as a new-risen star. He saw now that there would be no such hailing for him. He must do his own work in his own way, less and less admired as the years went by. In the end, I remember, he committed suicide. This seemed to me a false conclusion. Elderly Academicians "don't do such things". But, for the rest, the tale was a fine study of what I take to be a typical case.

A far cry to Mr. Carton's treatment of the case! Lorrimer Sabiston, dramatist, is, as I have already indicated, a man who has no belief in the merit of his work, and has for years deliberately prostituted his natural and acquired gifts. In real life such a dramatist would not have enriched himself. He would not have been able to please the mass of playgoers. As Mr. Arnold Bennett in a recent comedy pointed out, the man from whom the public gets what it wants is always the man who wants what is wanted by the public. If we assume that a dramatist might manage to go on for years doing bad work for which he had no impulse, even then the story of Sabiston is not plausible. It is quite certain that such a man would not be able to sit down and produce a masterpiece, one fine day, for a lark. He would find his better self atrophied. He would find . . . but I am afraid Mr. Carton will think me awfully pedantic, and will wonder why I should prate about real life when his purpose was merely to turn out an exciting comedy of intrigue. So I will retire gracefully, admitting that the intrigue might be exciting enough, to the public at large, if it were not overlaid and bedevilled by Mr. Carton's disastrous dialogue. In that tropical forest of metaphors, Mr. Alexander, Miss Beryl Faber, Mr. James Carew, Mr. C. M. Lowne, and the rest of the company, vainly endeavour to hew with the hatchets of their histrionic skill a pathway through the exuberant vegetation of the author's fancy, to the sunlight of success; but the miasmal exhalations of . . . I desist for lack of skill in Cartonism.

CONDUCTORS AND THEIR METHODS.

By Filson Young.

III.—MR. LANDON RONALD.

Mr. Landon Ronald as a conductor is one with the musicians and composers of the young English school who, although themselves the reverse of academic, are really the true musical progeny of the more academic generation which preceded them, and which some of them affect to despise. One of the soundest characteristics of this young English school—the best of them, I mean—is their extreme technical accomplishment; a quality which they owe almost entirely to the despised contrapuntists. They are all aware that the contrapuntists were woefully lacking in inspiration; and they feel, no doubt, that the contempt they entertain for their methods can best be justified by a younger generation that shows itself not inferior to the old in technical ability.

Nothing could be less academic than Mr. Landon Ronald; nothing could be more accomplished or more modern. He does not affect the antique in any way, nor believe that in order to be great it is necessary to be old-fashioned. He is as up-to-date as his own new motor-car, and as commercially formidable as a Jersey City land agent or Dr. Richter. He is entirely typical of his own time, as any man who proposes to do great things must be. But he is a product of something much greater than his own time. He has the blood of a great race in his veins, which, mingling with his English blood, gives to his wide and solid ability that additional quality of imagination and emotionalism, of excess even, that has carried the Jews so very far on the two open roads of imagination of modern times—art and finance. Of course in this racial admixture lie also such snares and pitfalls as are likely to be encountered in Mr. Landon Ronald's career. The Englishman in him desires to be like other people; the Jew in him insists on an individuality of its own. The Englishman thinks of prosperity and a safe success; the Jew in him dreams of greater things, of a hazardous but splendid pre-eminence, and devises means for its attainment. The Englishman says, "Be like other people, but appear to be different"; the Jew says "Appear to be like other people, but be different". And in Mr. Landon Ronald the Jewish characteristics, seen in him at their very best, are winning everywhere because they are the greater. They represent the stronger, the more soaring side of his nature; and though their English partner works well in harmony with them, it is the negative part that he plays; it is they who lead and determine, they who are the dark, unknown, implacable Mr. Jorkins, and the Englishman who is the bland and deprecating Mr. Spenlow, of Dickens's famous partnership.

Mr. Landon Ronald is probably the most accomplished all-round musician at present (to use a delectable phrase) before the public. If he had not determined to be a great conductor he would certainly have been a great pianist; and if he had not been a great pianist he would probably have been a great violinist. The one thing in music that he probably would not have been is a great composer; instead, he is one of the most accomplished composers in his own line that one can imagine. Composition, oddly enough, represents the commercial side of him. The shop is filled with compositions—well written, always interesting, always acceptable to his public; and in the shop he serves for so many hours a day, handing you out songs, overtures, suites—what you will; all honest value for your money. But the dwelling-house behind the shop is full of dreams and poetry. It is there that what is great in him lives and matures; comes to itself a little more every day; and comes not by idle waiting for the hour, but by the closest study, the hardest work, the most unsparing effort. It is to that element in this double personality of Landon Ronald that I pin my faith; it is that element that inspires his orchestra; it is that element that is penetrating and will penetrate to a wider and more discerning world of taste than that rather inferior circle that buys, sings, and adores his sentimental compositions.

In the two seasons in which he has had an orchestra of his own he has advanced enormously in technique and in certainty of touch. No one can really judge him who does not hear him at his own symphony concerts. The New Symphony Orchestra, which he has made entirely his own, is certainly one of the best orchestras in London, and will in time be a great orchestra; but, like all young and more or less struggling organisations, it is often heard under disadvantages of place and rehearsal. You cannot, for example, judge any orchestra by hearing it in the Albert Hall, where it and Mr. Landon Ronald perform every Sunday afternoon. Yet his work there is quite admirable; whatever you hear there, whether it is a great or a trivial work, you may be sure that it will be done with care, with trouble taken to make its good points tell and to bring out what interest there may be in it; in a word, whatever Mr. Landon Ronald does, he takes trouble to do as well as he can. But to realise how thoroughly well he can do you must go to his symphony concerts in the Queen's Hall. There even an uninstructed amateur cannot fail to realise some of his most striking qualities—his splendid grip of the orchestra, his quite unusual concentration, and (what follows from it) that almost psychic quality of magnetic control without a little of which no one can be a good conductor at all, but of which Mr. Landon Ronald possesses more than any other living conductor except Nikisch.

His methods, where they are not entirely his own, are based on those of Nikisch. He is frankly an imitator, but of the right kind. He knows what he is trying to develop in himself, and whenever he sees something that will help in that development, a missing fragment of the pattern he is building within himself, he steals, begs, borrows, or imitates it. The result is not a patchwork of other men's methods; the result is Landon Ronald, because the thing towards which he is striving is not external, but within himself. The two most typically fine interpretations of his that I know owe practically nothing to any conductor that I have heard; they are the Elgar symphony and Weber's "Oberon" overture. I have heard the Elgar symphony conducted by Richter, by Wood, by Nikisch, and by Elgar himself; but I have no hesitation in saying that by far the broadest, finest, loftiest, and most sympathetic interpretation of that work is Mr. Landon Ronald's. And in the "Oberon" overture he displays a poetic sense quite startlingly unlike what only a casual appreciation might have led one to expect. The remote, dreamy entrance of the horns at the beginning, floating in as from another world, the light and rapid series of *crescendi* at the end, are wonderful for a true quality of fairy music such as I have not found so happily achieved in the rendering of any other conductor. His style is perfectly quiet, and free from antics or disagreeable affectations. Perhaps he is a little too much addicted to an undulating movement of the lower arm, wrist, and hand invented by Miss Maud Allan; but undoubtedly he means something, communicates something, when he uses it. The small, dapper figure expresses little; it is the striking head and powerful physiognomy, the burning, commanding, compelling eyes, the wide forehead, frowning or serene, and, above all, the changeless, unwinking attention to what is going on in the world round about him that brings his orchestra, and through them his audience, so completely under the power of his personality. There is brain dominating the sentiment, and intellect controlling the emotion; and as a result there are outline and proportion, those valuable qualities that are so rarely allied with a temperament so sensitive and volatile as his.

It will be a most interesting career to watch—so great already in its achievement, so full of promise, so beset with dangers. He will have to beware especially of the defects of his qualities, of temptation to deviate from the main certainty to follow the main chance; of letting his vitality stream off in other directions than from the end of his baton; of exercising, in his impatience with other people's incapacity, the commercial side of his faculties at the expense of the artistic; of caring too much for the applause of a crowd so long as it is large enough, without considering of what elements the crowd is composed. If he avoids these dangers he will go far and fare well, and stand at last in the company of those great ones to whose service his genius is devoted.

THE LASKER-JANOWSKI CHESS MATCH.—III.

By Emanuel Lasker.

SEVERAL spectators of the match expressed to me their wonder at the effort which the opposing masters appear to make. They drew the conclusion that chess is a hard game to play. This idea has a wide circulation, but is nevertheless erroneous. The rules of chess are simple enough for a child to understand. Knowing them, one may play chess at any rate of speed, according to one's desire and habit. Some play with so little mental labour that they contrive an average of twelve games an hour, and their fatigue afterwards is surely only of the muscular kind.

One may reply that it is difficult to play chess *well*. We may admit this fact, but all things well done, down to the boiling of water or listening to a story, are in their kind difficult. The physicist knows a great many points about the boiling of water of which the average man is ignorant. The listener who gets the maximum of pleasure out of what he hears is something of an artist. And thus every task, little or big, to be cleverly done requires uncommon knowledge and attention.

Chess is as easy as talking. The moment an idea flits through one's mind, one expresses it in words. A chess player does the same thing in moves.

Thinking in chess is mostly automatic. We observe a danger; say, the queen "en prise". Immediately the arm stretches forth to take hold of that queen. It shall fly whither? The eye runs over the board to seek a square likely to be a safe refuge, and, if possible, a point whence damage might be inflicted upon the opponent. The first act is instinctive; reflection comes afterwards. Again, we notice that the opposing king and queen are upon the same file. Can our rook pin the queen? What hindrances are there? The questions are pointed and simple to answer. A few moments of a sort of thinking that is little more than observation and the answer is arrived at, the move made.

Thus most problems that a chess-player while playing has to solve are elementary ones. It is different only when men of great skill meet. To the average mind their games need a commentary. But then these games have several qualities that make the essentials of a work of art. They inspire ideas, and they raise emotions of pleasure. The explanation that is needed is therefore a labour which has its recompense.

The Sixth Game.

Four Knights Game.

White Janowski	Black Lasker	White Janowski	Black Lasker
1. P–K4	P–K4	3. Kt–QB3	Kt–KB3
2. Kt–KB3	Kt–QB3	4. B–Kt3	P–Q3

The opening is thus converted into a Ruy Lopez.

5. P–Q4	B–Q2	8. Kt × P	Castles
6. Castles	B–K2	9. Kt(Q4)–K2	Kt–K4
7. R–K	P × P		

Until this point the masters have followed well-known lines; here is a departure. The idea is to exchange the bishop and to obtain thereby space for the development of queen and rooks. The weakness of the manœuvre is that it leaves white free to advance upon the king's side, where the square B5 is badly defended by black.

10. Kt–Kt3	B × B	12. P–QKt3	B–B
11. Kt × B	R–K	13. B–Kt2	P–KKt3

White menaced P-KB4. The best retreat of the Kt on K4 is QB3, where it cannot be disturbed; but this retreat is open only after the white knight upon Kt5 has been driven off by P-QR3, because otherwise, since the white Kt attacks QB7, if B×Kt (B6), the queen is prevented from recapturing, the KtP must retake, and the power of resistance of the black king side is greatly diminished.

This very real menace is entirely ignored by black, and he therefore immediately gets into difficulties.

14. P–KB4 Kt(K4)–Q2

Now the QKt blocks its companion, the KKt. That piece is thereby very badly placed. At any moment P-K5 might attack it, yet it cannot stir.

15. Q–B3 . . .

Not P-K5 at once, because P-QR3 follows, and the QKt must either block the bishop supporting the advanced pawn or go to R3, where, after P × P, it is in the line of the black bishop. White can, however, afford to wait, since it is only with difficulty that black can improve the weakness of his position.

15. . . .	P–QR3	17. QR–Q	. . .
16. Kt–Q4	B–Kt2		

The rook indirectly threatens the queen, the obstructions being removed by P-K5.

17. . . . Q–K2

No matter where the queen may move, white can make the sacrifice that follows. The move made prevents at least the worst consequences.

18. Kt(Q4)–B5 P × Kt 19. Kt × P Q–K3

If Q-B, P-K5 regains the piece. The weakness of the knight on KB3 is at last avenged.

20. Kt × B . . .

Much better than Q-Kt3, whereupon Kt-R4, Kt×B, Kt × Q, Kt×Q, R×Kt, P × Kt, QR-K with many chances to regain the pawn lost by the attack on the KP.

20. . . . K × Kt 21. P–K5 K–B

If (20) Kt-Kt (21) P×P ch wins the queen; if (20) P × P, (21) P × P, Kt×Kt, (22) R×Kt wins likewise.

22. P × Kt	Q × R ch	24. K–B2	QR–K
23. R × Q	R × R ch	25. Q × P	. . .

The straight way to win was to push the king side pawns, somewhat in this fashion: (25) Q-Kt4, R (K)-K3, (26) P-KR4, K-K, (27) P-KR5, Kt-B, (28) Q-B3, P-QB3, (29) P-B5, R-K5, (30) B-B3, R-K7 ch, (31) Q × R, etc. Black is occupied stopping the white pawns, and white wins by operations upon the defenceless queen's side.

25. . . .	R(K8)–K7 ch	28. Q–Kt5	Kt–B4
26. K–B3	R × BP	29. Q × P	Kt–Q6
27. B–Q4	P–QR4	30. B–K3	P–Q4

This threatens Kt-K8 ch, Q×Kt, P-Q5; but it is weak nevertheless. Black should have utilised the opportune moment for destroying the KBP by R-K3. Q-R8 ch would then have produced no change in the position, and therefore only drawn. By his premature attack black only succeeds in pressing white to better his position.

31. B–Q2 P–QB4 32. K–Kt3 . . .

He prepares to put himself into safety by P-KR3, then to pursue his attack at leisure. R-K3 now would fail on account of Q-Q8 ch, R-K, Q-Q6 ch, K-Kt, Q×P, threatening mate in two.

32. . . . Kt–B8 33. B × Kt Resigns

If R×B (34) Q-Q2 wins the last hope of black, the QP.

The Eighth Game.

Four Knights Game.

White Janowski	Black Lasker	White Janowski	Black Lasker
1. P–K4	P–K4	6. Castles	B–K2
2. Kt–KB3	Kt–QB3	7. R–K	P × P
3. Kt–B3	Kt–B3	8. Kt × P	Castles
4. B–Kt5	P–Q3	9. Kt(Q4)–K2	P–QR3
5. P–Q4	B–Q2		

Here black changes the policy that he had adopted in the sixth game. In combination with what follows the move appears to point in the right direction.

10. B–Q3 Kt–KKt5

The Kt, if driven off, will go to K4, where it attacks the bishop Q3 to good purpose.

11. Kt–Kt3 B–B3

Kt-Q5 would now be met by B-Q5.

12. P–KR3	B × Kt	14. P–KB4	Q–R5
13. P × B	KKt–K4		

Before capturing the bishop the knight K4 prevents the white queen from taking the important square B3; it also hinders K-R2.

15. Kt–B Kt × B 16. P × Kt P–KB4

He cannot preserve his powerful central pawns. P-K5 would be answered by P×P, P × P, P-B5, with the deadly menace of P-B6, tearing open the chain of pawns guarding the king.

17. Kt–R2	P × P	20. P–KB5	Kt–K4
18. P × P	QR–K	21. Kt × Kt	R × K
19. Kt–B3	Q–Kt6		

To recapture with queen would have been stronger; as, with the actual continuation, B-B3 would have threatened, and to hinder this white had no alternative but Q-Kt3, K-R, Q×P, B × P to the advantage of black.

22. R–K3	Q–R5	27. K–R2	Q–B7
23. Q–Kt3 ch	P–Q4	28. Q–K6 ch	K–R
24. Q × KtP	P × P	29. Q × P	Q–Kt8 ch
25. Q × BP	R(K4) × P	30. K–Kt3	Q–B7 ch
26. Q × B	R–B8 ch		

R (B8)-B3 would have been of no avail on account of R-K2. The game ended, therefore, drawn by perpetual check.

AN OLD-TIME MUSICAL DOCTOR.

DR. RICHARD BROWNE (or simple Brown) was not a doctor in music. In fact, until he attained his fiftieth year he was not a doctor at all, but plain "Richard Browne, Apothecary in *Oakham*, in the County of *Rutland*"; and he is so described on the title-pages of some of his not very numerous literary works. Nevertheless, he took a keen interest in music, and called it "this cælestial Science"; and he evidently devoted some study to the best methods of employing it as an adjunct and aid to medicine. The result of his thought and labour he had published by 1674. It is a tiny volume with a monstrously big name, from which the following selection may be made: "Medicina Musica: Or, a Mechanical Essay on the Effects of Singing, Musick, and Dancing on Human Bodies". His premisses are often surprisingly wrong, even for the seventeenth century; but his conclusions are generally just as surprisingly right. He argues with vigour, skill and a considerable degree of humour; and that he was a shrewd person is shown by his treating music as an aid to medicine and not as a substitute for it. He had been an apothecary before he became a doctor, and would do nothing to hurt his old trade; he took to prescribing medicines instead of making up other people's prescriptions; but his esprit de corps remained. Indeed he was not even an apothecary when the first edition of his little masterpiece came from the press. "When", he says, "I first publish'd the following Essay, I industriously endeavour'd to conceal my Name; not only upon account of the humble Opinion I had of the Work itself, but also lest my Age and Station in Life (it being wrote in the time of my Apprenticeship) might be a Bar to its Acceptance . . ." Later—but precisely in what year no one can do more than guess—"some particular Friends (whose Judgment and Sincerity I might rely upon)" persuaded him to risk a second impression; and "under their Authority" he hoped "to skreen" himself from censure. But he was as industrious to conceal their names as he had been at first to conceal his own; and, after all, this matters very little to us of a later generation, for probably "their Authority" would not impress us.

He had been an enterprising gentleman, this Richard Browne, although only a very few of his writings are known, and he gets little space in the "Dictionary of National Biography". He is said to have been educated at Queen's College, Oxford; but either his studies must have ended early or he was apprenticed very late. It may be that his connexion with medicine and medicines began late, for it was not until 1675, when he is reported to have been fifty years of age, that he took a medical degree at Leyden. This view is supported by the fact that he always wrote like an educated gentleman. "Medicina Musica" was intended largely for the use of "the fair Sex"; and when he seems in danger of uttering something perhaps a trifle indelicate for seventeenth-century feminine ears he dives discreetly beneath a few words of perfectly correct Latin. He avoids a coarser word by using "eructation"; and "deglutition" and "vellicate" also are pressed into the service of fastidiousness. But that he was well educated, and a pharmacist first and then a physician, is all we know of him. It is guessed that he was born about 1624 and lived to be seventy; he published, besides "Medicina Musica", an English grammar, a "Prosodia Pharmacopœorum; or, The Apothecary's Prosody", a "General History of Earthquakes" and one or two other works. An edition of the "Medicina" appeared as late as 1729. Brown, or even Browne, is not a rare name; and one can never feel sure that any medical gentleman referred to by that name in contemporary or slightly later documents is really *our* medical and musical gentleman.

To compare Richard Browne with his mighty namesake of the "Religio Medici" would be preposterous. But Richard had a fine vein of common-sense. In an age when bleeding was an almost universal remedy he had the hardihood to write: "To begin with Bleeding; it is but seldom indicated"; he was afraid of opium and said, "We ought to be very sparing in its Use, lest by too much endeavouring to alleviate the present Pain, we lay a Foundation for the future"; he always aimed at restoring "the Tone" of the system by "Cortex Peruvianus", steel, music and dancing. It was a fixed principle with him that cheerful people suffer less from illness than low-spirited people, and therefore a doctor's aim should always be to raise his patients' spirits. "Medicina" is largely filled with a formidable demonstration of the usefulness of music in doing this. "That Singing is an Enemy to melancholy Thoughts, and a pleasing Promoter of Mirth and Joy, is what we find by daily Experience", he wrote; but immediately afterwards a knotty point turned up: "All the difficulty is to conceive how any one can be pleased with his own Singing, when through a natural Deficiency of the Organs he is not in a capacity of modulating his Voice into a Tune. . . . One might reasonably imagine that the Sound would be offensive to him, were there not instances enough to prove the contrary. . . ." This problem greatly exercised Dr. Browne; but at length he hit on an explanation. A man may by an abominable voice drive his friends or neighbours to distraction, may clear the room of a large company, and yet be honestly enjoying himself. Mr. Browne thought the matter out, and spoke: "We cannot in reason imagine that any Pleasure can hence arise from immediate Sensation; but only from Reflection upon the pleasing Ideas of the Tune before form'd and treasur'd up in the Mind." He even recommends those with ugly voices not to be deterred by any modesty (or fear of inflicting suffering on others) from boldly singing up and thus doing good to their souls, their spirits and their bodies. The intimate connexion of these three, the soul, the spirits and the body, is proved in the terrific demonstration aforementioned. Proposition I. is: "There is a Sympathy betwixt the Soul and Animal Spirits"; and Prop. III.: "Digestion is perform'd chiefly by the Friction of the Stomach, as that is by the Influx of the Spirits into its Muscular Fibres", etc. Unluckily Mr. Browne had a pleasant way of omitting all proof, thus turning his Propositions into postulates, and referring the anxious reader to "Dr. Pitcairn's Opuscula". Who was Dr. Pitcairn? And who was Dr. Mead? and Dr. Friend? and Dr. Sydenham? These and others are cited as authorities; but it is to be feared they carry little weight for twentieth-century readers—whom, however, Mr. Browne had not in his mind when he penned his treatise. Still, in spite of formal propositions combined with absence of proofs, he establishes his main point—that music may be good for the human body, and he shows "in what cases it may be prejudicial". For instance, "In all Disorders in general where the Motion of the Solids and Fluids are rais'd above their natural Standard, Singing is not indicated"; and he points out quite seriously the dangers attending an attempt to sing when one is down with pleurisy or pneumonia. In cases of phthisis as well singing was likely to bring about "the sad catastrophe of blood-spitting". There is also a good deal about the value of quiet "Adagios" to soothe the fevered and over-excited, as well as the value of "lively" pieces for those who suffer from the "spleen and vapours". Those "lively" pieces seem not very lively nowadays; for when Browne served his apprenticeship Purcell had composed nothing—probably was not born, and the greater part of the music for "consorts" of viols came from the staider pens of composers who in their liveliest moments were somewhat solemn. Some of the lively pieces of John Jenkins would drive a modern low-spirited man to suicide; fashions in liveliness change, like other fashions.

Dr. Browne himself was obviously of a buoyant disposition. Only a doctor of his character could hope to cure patients by prescribing singing or dancing. Yet there is much wisdom in his little treatise; and it is curious that music should be more and more employed, both in lunatic asylums and hospitals, for maladies which are hardly to be recognised under their scientific denominations as the "spleen and vapours" of Browne. Browne himself did not enter into the question of "Melancholy and Madness": "that", he says, "was never my Design", so "I shall forbear to offer any thing on that Head, and here take leave to conclude".

CORRESPONDENCE.

UNIONIST WOMEN'S FRANCHISE ASSOCIATION.

To the Editor of the SATURDAY REVIEW.

11 November 1909.

SIR,—I read a letter in the SATURDAY REVIEW of 6 November by Miss Annie Lindsay, in which she has made statements concerning the Conservative and Unionist Women's Franchise Association, of which I am a vice-president. As Miss Lindsay appears to be in complete ignorance in regard to the working and organisation of our association, I think it only right to reply to her criticisms.

Our association was formed because it was felt that a great many Conservative and Unionist women, who were in favour of the franchise for duly qualified women, could only join an association which adhered to Unionist principles and placed imperial interests before everything. (The attitude of the Liberal ladies, according to Miss Lindsay, appears to be different.) Miss Lindsay proceeds to remark that "in order to remain straightforward" we should as suffragists resign forthwith any connexion with our party associations or leagues. I would venture to suggest to Miss Lindsay and other persons like her that in future, before they take the name of any society in vain, they should first of all endeavour to understand its objects. The Conservative and Unionist Women's Franchise Association works on lines which are strictly in accordance with party principles; the members do not "regard women's enfranchisement as a claim superior to that of party".

Among the printed objects of the society are the following:

"To work for women's enfranchisement by educational and constitutional methods, consistent with Unionist principles.

"To maintain the principles of the Conservative and Unionist party with regard to the basis on which the franchise should rest, and to oppose universal suffrage in any form.

"To convince members of the Conservative and Unionist party of the desirability of extending the franchise to duly qualified persons of both sexes, and as far as possible to give active support to official candidates at elections, when they are in favour of the enfranchisement of women."

The association also pledges itself not to oppose any official candidate who is against women's suffrage. Naturally as a body or organisation the association does not work for a candidate who is opposed to women's suffrage, nor would they be desired to do so; but individually, or as members of the Primrose League or other associations, they have done, and will do, work of which any Unionist might be proud. Miss Lindsay has evidently not studied the attitude of the great Conservative leaders towards the question of the enfranchisement of women.

Lord Beaconsfield, in a speech in the House of Commons on 27 April 1866 said: "I observe that in a recent debate in another place and country some ridicule was occasioned by a gentleman advocating the rights of the other sex to the suffrage. But as far as mere abstract reasoning is concerned, I should like to see anybody get up and oppose that claim. I may say that in a country governed by women, where you allow women to form part of the other estate of the realm—peeresses in their own right, for example—when you allow a woman, not only to hold land, but to be a lady of the manor and hold legal courts—where a woman by law may be a churchwarden and overseer of the poor—I do not see, where she has so much to do with the Church and State, on what reasons, if you come to right, she has not a right to vote."

And in a letter dated April 1873 he wrote: "I was much honoured by receiving from your hands the memorial signed by eleven thousand women of England, among them some illustrious names, thanking me for my services in attempting to abolish the anomaly that the parliamentary franchise attached to a household or property qualification when possessed by a woman should not be exercised. . . . As I believe this anomaly to be injurious to the best interests of the country, I trust to see it removed by the wisdom of Parliament."

The late Lord Salisbury, at a meeting convened by the Primrose League at Edinburgh, 12 November 1888, said: "I earnestly hope that the day is not far distant when women will also bear their share in voting for members of Parliament and in determining the policy of the country. I can conceive no argument by which they are excluded. It is obvious that they are abundantly as well fitted as many who now possess the suffrage by knowledge, by training, and by character, and that their influence is likely to weigh in a direction which in an age so material as ours is exceedingly valuable—namely, in the direction of morality and religion."

The Right Hon. Arthur J. Balfour, in the course of a speech in the House, 27 April 1892, in support of a Bill for the enfranchisement of women, said: "I think I may take it that every section of this House is only too glad to use the services of women when they think they can profit by them, and it does not lie in the mouths of any of us to say that taking part in framing the policy of the Empire is degrading to the sex. In any other department of human thought than politics such an argument would be described by no milder word than 'cant'. Cant it undoubtedly is. . . . You will give a vote to a man who contributes nothing to taxation but what he pays on his beer, while you refuse enfranchisement to a woman whatever her contribution to the State may be. . . . Depend upon it, this question will again arise—menacing, and ripe for solution—and it will not be possible for this House to set it aside as a mere speculative plan advocated by a body of faddists. Then you will have to deal with the problem of woman suffrage, and to deal with it in a complete fashion."

Therefore, to be told that in order to "remain straightforward" we must desert our party organisations, and by quoting our association as an example of "those who justify political unfaith for personal expediency", Miss Lindsay is not only inaccurate, but is ignorant of the real facts of the matter, and another time, before unjustly accusing her fellow-creatures, I would commend to Miss Lindsay's notice the sixth chapter of S. Luke, verses 41, 42.

I am, Sir, yours faithfully,

EDITH CASTLEREAGH.

WANTED—A POLITICAL PROGRAMME.

To the Editor of the SATURDAY REVIEW.

31 October 1909.

SIR,—Your correspondent, Mr. D. N. Samson, raises an interesting issue. His suggestions as to proportional representation and redistribution are very pertinent and will not, it is to be hoped, be disregarded. But there are also other necessities of the occasion to which he has not alluded. One, and that both urgent and widespread, will be the duty of repairing as speedily and fully as possible the mischief perpetrated by the present Government both in administration and legislation. Mr. McKenna's disreputable perversion, while at the Education Office, of his administrative trust to the furtherance of petty partisan purposes must be at once overruled on the advent of the Unionist leaders to power and responsibility. Indeed, Sir William Anson has in the House of Commons virtually committed his party to this elementarily just course. Then too, Sir, it is greatly to be desired that the Unionists, following the boldly wise example of their allies in the London County Council, will not scruple to repeal or at least radically amend any measures passed in this present Parliament which shall be proved generally inconvenient. A majority contrived as at the last General Election by any and every ingenuity of misstatement and proceeding to vote for legislative proposals ill prepared and worse debated cannot be said to represent much beyond its own want of principle, nor can its legislative productions claim anything of abiding authority.

More generally the Unionists have a great opportunity before them in restoring the dignity and freedom of the House of Commons and, outside its walls, in recalling the people to true notions of political life. In the one place there should be as complete as possible a restoration of the liberty of debate and a contentment with one or two first-class Bills fully and freely discussed in a session of reasonable length. In the other, i.e. the constituencies, no opportunity should be lost of impressing upon the electorate that sound and just administration is the first business of Governments, and that, the true province of law being the impartial protection of individual life, liberty and property, the less interference with private initiative and enterprise the better. I am, Sir, yours faithfully,

An Independent Elector.

A CHARGE OF PLAGIARISM.

To the Editor of the Saturday Review.

4 November 1909.

Sir,—In the October number of the "English Review" appears an article, under the signature of Edward Hutton, entitled "The Church in Lucina's House". Although the writer nowhere acknowledges his indebtedness, the whole source of his inspiration and many of his actual sentences are from Walter Pater's writings. The article follows closely the chapter "The Church in Cecilia's House" in Vol. II. of "Marius the Epicurean". A large number of passages are taken from this chapter, while Pater's phrases, expressions, and quotations are freely used throughout the article. It would be too mild to describe the article as a piece of patchwork.

Yours etc.,

A. M.

THE "QUICUNQUE VULT".

To the Editor of the Saturday Review.

53 Upper Brook Street W. 10 November 1909.

Sir,—The English language seems to provide an unfailing stumbling-block for modern scholars and ecclesiastics on the few occasions when they have to compose a collect or re-translate a passage in the simple and pure manner of the Prayer Book. The Archbishop of Canterbury's committee of seven distinguished scholars and divines has not escaped the common fate; but it would be a pity if the "Quicunque Vult", that entirely unique literary composition, the new translation of which was published in the "Times" last Wednesday, were as a result of their deliberations to be handed on to posterity containing the sentence "There is therefore one Father, not three Fathers".

The document itself expressly forbids us to confound the Persons; why, then, need we confound the numbers? I have the honour to be, Sir,

Your obedient servant,

Filson Young.

LATIN-SPEAKING PEOPLES.

To the Editor of the Saturday Review.

Hotel Great Central N.W. 28 October 1909.

Sir,—I read in the "Notes of the Week" published in No. 2817 of your Review: "Government in Spain, as in other of the Latin-speaking countries, is by arrangement between parties. No Cabinet can live without the support, at any rate the toleration, of the Opposition".

Would you kindly explain to a constant reader of your Review what is the meaning of the phrase "Latin-speaking countries"? M. Gaston Paris tried once to show that there was not a mother-tongue out of which other languages called French, Italian, Spanish, Portuguese were formed. No; he said that some countries went on speaking Latin according to their own ways, and so it came out that new languages were formed. His theory was that in Florence, in Paris, in Mexico and Bogota the people have gone on talking the language of Cicero in their own peculiar ways, which in some cases are certainly very peculiar. According to Gaston Paris the quoted expression is quite right. But if it is going to be universally accepted we have to include modern English in this qualification. The lines quoted furnish thirty-five per cent. of Latin element to have the expression of the thought complete. So that it would not be wholly unfair to call the English-speaking races half Latin-speaking countries.

Besides that, I ask leave to observe that by pushing only a bit farther the argument of Paris we could say, not the German-speaking nations, but the Sanskrit-speaking countries, as it is notorious that a language akin to the Sanskrit and unknown for the moment was the one that spreading, as Latin did, gave rise to the Indo-European group of languages.

Yours faithfully,

B. Sanin Cano.

[The countries we were referring to all speak a language based on Latin—in fact a Latin of their own. M. Gaston Paris' view was surely right. Thus it is accurate to speak of Latin-speaking nations, while it is inaccurate to speak of Latin races. If our correspondent likes to describe the Germans as speaking Sanskrit, we shall raise no objection.—Ed. S. R.]

LONDON'S NATIONAL MEMORIAL TO SHAKESPEARE.

Bankside, Southwark.

To the Editor of the Saturday Review.

9 November 1909.

Sir,—In the interests of this Memorial to the memory of Shakespeare, the following letters have reached me, and never at any time been associated with the National Shakespeare Theatre, nor is the "Theatre" scheme any part of the memorial which I inaugurated on 8 May 1903—viz., "to embrace the rebuilding of the old Globe Theatre [as far as this was possible] with a museum, and library, and picture gallery, with various offices for lectures and other purposes of the Memorial, which, from an educational point of view, is of paramount importance—sum required, £250,000. The Memorial is to be a corporate body consisting of Warden and Fellows. There would be something like thirty-six free lectures on dramatic art, music, poetry, law, and English literature to the young men of London, by the first professors of Oxford, Cambridge, and London, as the case may be, that the whole thing may be the better memorial to the memory of Shakespeare."

I am constrained to ask you to help to correct a wrong impression. I am, Sir, yours sincerely,

Richard C. Jackson.

"139 Canning Street, Liverpool,
6 November 1909.

"Re Shakespeare Memorial Scheme.

"Sir,—Your news astounds me! I was under the impression, as many still are, that the 'half-million' scheme was yours with enlarged scope, and that you were connected with it. It is entirely news to learn that someone has had the effrontery to copy your ideas. Perhaps some day there will be a statute to prevent this unfair cribbing of ideas.

"Yours very truly,
(Signed) W. Jaggard."

N.B.—It should be noted that the earliest mention of the other scheme, with which I have not the slightest sympathy whatever, since it would only benefit one section of the community, was printed in the "Daily Graphic" of 4 December 1904.

Another phase is demonstrated by the letter sent me from Mr. John Belcher A.R.A.

"20 Hanover Square W. 16 Sept. 1908.

"Sir,—When they decided to have a monument, I was put on the executive committee. Then the theatrical people wanted a National Theatre, and as I found the whole thing spoilt I retired in disgust.

"Yours very truly,
(Signed) John Belcher."

REVIEWS.

THE LAST OF THE TROUBADOURS.

"Francesco Petrarca: Poet and Humanist." By Maud F. Jerrold. London: Dent. 1909. 12s. 6d. net.

THE modern cult of Dante in England seems to have involved a comparative neglect of his chief successor. A pleasant book by two Americans dealt fairly adequately with one somewhat limited aspect of Petrarca's genius; but more recent works have completely ignored the researches of Italian and German scholars which during the last twelve years have put the literary and textual criticism of his vernacular poetry upon an entirely new basis. No such reproach can be brought against the present volume, which, from every point of view, is incomparably the best study of Petrarca that has yet been written in English.

Writing to Boccaccio, Petrarca claimed praise for himself chiefly "for having stimulated in many instances, not only in Italy, but perchance beyond its confines, the pursuit of studies such as ours, which have suffered neglect for so many centuries". This clearly states his position as the herald of the Renaissance. To the scholars of his own day Petrarca's Italian poetry probably seemed little more than an amiable weakness. It was his unfinished Latin epic, the "Africa", that gained him the laurel crown on the Capitol, and his Latin letters that enabled him to address the rulers of Church and State as an equal. With the exception of the "Secretum", which Mrs. Jerrold well calls "one of the world's great monuments of self-revelation", and possibly the Metrical Epistles and Eclogues, these Letters are the only Latin works of the poet that are now read for their own sake. Unquestionably Petrarca succeeded in his aim of making a more classical Latinity the literary language of the following age; but the vernacular literature of Italy in the fifteenth century paid dearly for his triumph.

Petrarca's Italian poems seemed to Shelley "as spells, which unseal the inmost enchanted fountains of the delight which is in the grief of love". It is particularly with regard to this collection of lyrics, the "Rime" or "Canzoniere" which the poet himself entitled "Rerum vulgarium fragmenta", that the researches of the last decade have been so fruitful. Since Giovanni Mestica first edited them from the famous Vatican manuscript, written in part by Petrarca's own hand and undoubtedly representing his own final recension throughout, we can read this wonderful spiritual romance, the poet's autopsychology, in the form in which he left it to the world. The splendid patriotic poems falling into their place, we read his inner life as a whole—its turning-point marked by the canzone that records his moral conversion. It is curious to find so distinguished an editor as Carducci pleading respect for "the almost religious custom" in retaining the apocryphal sub-titles referring to the life and death of Madonna Laura. "Tantum religio potuit suadere malorum."

The case is different with the "Trionfi", the allegorical poem in terza rima, upon which, begun more than twenty years before, Petrarca was still working at the time of his death. Here we have no authoritative text, although some of the poet's notes and corrections have been preserved. Herr Carl Appel has shown that Petrarca ultimately reduced the poem to ten cantos, discarding the two that are probably best known to English readers—the poet's meeting with Masinissa and Sophonisba, and the apparition of Laura to her lover in the night following her death. Mrs. Jerrold has, for the first time, given a complete interpretation of this singular poem, and proves conclusively, mainly from the evidence of his other writings, that it is simply an idealised picture, stage by stage, of the poet's own history. He is, as it were, rehandling the matter of his lyrics, and attempting to give it epical form. Read in this light, all the symbolical details become clear, and even the "Triumphus Pudicitiæ", with Laura's incongruous journey by Cumæ and Linterno to Rome in the company of Scipio, has a real significance. The poet's letters show that the journey was his own, the visit to Rome his own (probably that of the year of jubilee), and the "Triumph of Purity" is simply his own conversion.

Mrs. Jerrold translates admirably, even reproducing the stately movement and involved rhymes of the Italian canzone. She might, with advantage, have dealt at greater length with the metrical structure and history of the Petrarchan lyric, and we notice that the name of Antonio Minturno, the great Renaissance authority on this theme, does not appear in her bibliography. In his sonnets Petrarca departs little, if at all, from the practice of his predecessors, and it is noteworthy that the technical theory of what we now call the "Petrarchan" sonnet is already formulated in the "Summa Artis Rithmici" of Antonio da Tempo, who wrote in 1332, when the singer of Laura was only at the beginning of his career. In his canzoni, on the other hand, in spite of imitations from the Provençal, Petrarca shows himself more of an innovator, using this most stately of lyrical forms with a mastery and a freedom that no earlier Italian poet had attained.

The man himself, from his childhood in Provence to his death among the Euganean Hills, is portrayed with delicacy and insight in Mrs. Jerrold's pages. In spite of many failings, both public and private, his was a life devoted to noble ideals. His wish had been that death should find him "either reading or writing, or, better still, if God will, praying and weeping", and this wish was fulfilled. In a chapter entitled "In Petrarca's School", the author traces his influence upon English literature from Chaucer to Shelley. "Petrarch's invention is pure love itself", wrote Gabriel Harvey: "It is no dishonour for the daintiest or divinest Muse to be his scholar, whom the amiablest Invention and beautifullest Elocution acknowledge their master."

REAL TURKEY.

"Military Consul in Turkey." By Captain Townshend. London: Seeley. 1909. 16s. net.

"Turkey in Transition." By G. F. Abbott. London: Arnold. 1909. 12s. 6d. net.

TWO books on Turkey—both very necessary, both useful and welcome. Those who want to understand Turkey must get hold of both these books and read them without skipping. It is useless for the stay-at-home Englishman to read either alone, because each volume explains the things left unsaid by its fellow. Captain Townshend's experiences and Mr. Abbott's observations taken together form about as complete a picture of Turkey of to-day as can possibly be conceived. Captain Townshend gives us the people, the towns, the villages, roads, the mountains and rivers —the material in fact of which Turkey is made up. Mr. Abbott analyses the intellectual and spiritual forces which have acted, and still are acting and re-acting, on that material. The material lies in the provinces; the forces are, and always will be, pent up in the power station at Constantinople.

Captain Townshend's book should be read before Mr. Abbott's, not because it is of greater merit, but because it will form a solid foundation in the reader's mind, on which Mr. Abbott's work can conveniently rest. Captain Townshend is evidently fitted by nature to understand Turks and Turkey; he likes horses, enjoys a joke, can ride, shoot, tell a good story, and has served in the army. Now, strange as it may appear, these qualities of the ordinary English country gentleman help a man to describe and understand the Ottoman Empire and its inhabitants better than the most complete mastership of Turkish and Arabic grammar coupled with a profound knowledge of Oriental mysticism.

The English soldier-Consul, with his dogs, mounts, guns, and fishing tackle, appeals straight to the heart of the Moslem. "Wallah! But this is a man! Would that he were of the true faith!" must have been said of this author not once but a hundred times in the barracks and villages of Anatolia; probably he is too modest to know it. Captain Townshend gives the reader a plain, straightforward account of everything he saw and heard worth recording during the three years he was attached to the Levant Consular service. In the space of three hundred odd pages he sets down with extraordinary minuteness and accuracy every type, every class, every character, every detail of life and administration with which he came in contact; and that he should say so much in so short a space gives an idea of his discrimination, taste, and sense of proportion. Officials, peasants, merchants, pilgrims, soldiers, Levantines, cosmopolitans, Christians and missionaries, all the familiar actors of that drama which is eternally a-playing, on the high roads, in the inns and Government offices of the Ottoman Empire are set down to the very life. The subject is so broad that it would be unfair to quote or to particularise on the merit and excellence of any one of the admirable chapters in this book. Those who read it will learn how Captain Townshend dealt with a lady "of the tourists" who desired him to assist her to visit Tarsus, catch a steamer, get an interpreter, find a cold lunch, and change a five-pound note; how he acted as matrimonial agent to a gang of Perso-Hindi-Afghan-Gipsy horse-thieves; how he rode across the Taurus in winter; of Armenians and how he fared at their hands; of a Greek who offered him a "bakshish" of £200 for an English passport; of old Turks, young Turks, noble Turks, and villainous Turks; of intrigue, blood, disaster, comedy, and tragedy; of the preternaturally solemn children who bargain for turkeys with the dignity of bankers, and pass the time of day with the suave reserve of Ambassadors; of educated men governing provinces the size of Scotland who have the hearts of babes; of withered crones who veil their charms lest their beauty provoke a war like that of Troy; of missionaries who will nurse the Moslem who desires their blood through an attack of typhus, yet who preach against the "sins" of wearing low-necked dresses, singing hymns and keeping the pagan festival of Christmas Day; of Italian gangers, German surveyors, Mullahs, Hodjas, Hadjis, deserters, horse-thieves, and a whole collection of the most lovable blackguards in Christendom or Heathenesse. Of all these wonderful things will the readers of Captain Townshend's splendid book learn—Wallah! Billah! Tillah! Captain Townshend has given us the book we have been waiting for these many years. It will not appeal to the "prig", still less to the "righteous", but these are two products of our civilisation whose invincible ignorance precludes their ever getting nearer to the heart of the East than a statistical table of exports and imports or an occasional leading article in the "National" will permit; these people have a portable world of their own, and Captain Townshend's Turkey does not fit into any of its compartments.

Now we have said that those who have read Captain Townshend must then read Mr. Abbott. This second volume suddenly switches us away from the muddy roads, the bare hillsides, the biting winds of the Balkans and the Anatolian plateau, into the noisy streets of Pera and offices of Stambul; we leave the people and come to the forces that move them.

Mr. Abbott in his even more difficult task has succeeded as completely and as splendidly as Captain Townshend; he gives us what an enthusiast sometimes calls "the whole thing" when he is at a loss to describe a very complicated situation. There is no vital political factor in the government of Turkey of to-day that Mr. Abbott leaves untouched and undescribed. The educated new Turkish woman, the old Turkish gentleman, the young Turkish bounder, the Christian, the Liberal, the Committeeman, the general, the editor, Abdul Hamid and Mohammed V. are each laid bare, discussed, described and judged with a knowledge, impartiality and precision that should excite the envy of anyone who has vainly endeavoured to accomplish a similar task. Mr. Abbott's analysis of the situation into which these forces have worked themselves is really no less satisfactory than his descriptions of the forces themselves. He gives us a study of the ex-Sultan which should live as an historic document. This author alone, it may be confidently asserted, has given a truthful and graphic account of the character and personality of the man whose complexity, craft, simpleness, sagacity and folly have baffled pressmen and diplomatists for over thirty years.

But if it is difficult to do justice to so extraordinary an individual as the ex-Sultan, how much more hazardous an enterprise is it to sum up and weigh the faults and merits of so peculiar a body as the Committee of Union and Progress? Yet here again Mr. Abbott is at once as bold as he is successful; he sees through the academic superficiality, the pedagogic pomposity and the low blackguardism of some of its members, and still he is fully conscious of the immense patriotism, the devoted self-sacrifice, the high purpose and the great capacity which are the attributes of many of the others; and being able to detect and appreciate both these astounding opposites in one compound, he can give the untravelled English reader a view of a situation which many may examine but few can comprehend. With masterly directness he traces for the first time the whole sequence of events extending from the first revolution of July 1908 to the final crash of April 1909. The moves and counter-moves, the mutinies and counter-mutinies, starting with the fall of Kiamil and ending in the deposition of Abdul Hamid, are followed out and explained with perfect lucidity and fairness. A ready pen enables the author to clothe his recital with a useful and pleasing picturesqueness of scent, sound and colour: the smell of mastik, garlic and yeniji pervades the air; the grumbling of the narghilès, the wailing of the muezzins, the cheers of the multitude, the blaring strains of the bands of music, the crash of musketry and the yelping of the pariah dogs form a fitting accompaniment, while the background of curved domes, dark cypresses, graveyards and narrow streets make admirable painted scenery.

Mr. Abbott should refrain from referring to his ex-Majesty as "Abdul" and Captain Townshend should revise page 78. The little boy said "Hodja", not "Hadji", and a white turban doesn't—but there, as a Turk would say, "Zara Yok" ("It doesn't matter"); but Sir Richard Burton would have used some bitter words.

SCHOOLMASTERS ABROAD.

"Schoolboys and Schoolwork." By the Rev. the Hon. E. Lyttelton. London: Longmans. 1909. 3s. 6d.

A BOOK by the Headmaster of Eton, with a preface by the Headmaster of Winchester, the aim of which is "to set forth a rational curriculum of studies for boys in secondary schools", is, or ought to be, an event of unequalled importance in the educational world; but with every desire to make allowances for the difficulty of the task, and with every wish to do justice to the merits of the book, it must be frankly confessed that the Headmasters have missed a real opportunity, and that this tentative and desultory pronouncement is rather a confession that the difficulties of the situation are insuperable than a statesmanlike or practical solution. The book is not indeed without importance, because, inconclusive as it is, it contains some incidental judgments of a weighty kind; and it is not lacking in suggestiveness and interest. What might have been expected was a clear and judicious analysis of the difficulties of the situation and a concise and temperate statement of the lines on which reform might proceed. What the book actually is is a discursive treatise on secondary education, with a good deal of somewhat fanciful psychology and ingenious theorising.

The form of the book is in itself somewhat confusing. It seems that it was originally intended to be a joint production of the two Headmasters. As it is, the book is the work of the Headmaster of Eton, and the Headmaster of Winchester contributes a preface in which the difficulties of the situation are clearly and temperately stated. "Is it possible", Dr. Burge asks, "to construct a course of education by which a boy shall not be allowed to begin certain new subjects until his educators are convinced that he has the capacity for them?" That is, of course, the crux of the whole situation. It is very doubtful whether under present conditions anything of the kind is possible in a big school with only a limited number of masters. To discover a boy's aptitudes and to cater for his development is only possible under conditions which admit of much more individual attention than is possible at a large school; and, further, it must be confessed that the Headmaster of Eton does not succeed in establishing the case. Dr. Burge goes on to say that "the unhelpfulness of nearly all the criticism levelled at public-school education is due to the fact that there is little or no attempt to show exactly how improved subjects or co-ordination of subjects are to fill out the whole period of a boy's education". If the Headmaster of Eton had contrived to bring out this point, it would have been a solid contribution to the question. But this is precisely what the book fails to do; and when Dr. Burge goes on to say "these are the lines of education we hope at no distant date to lay down in our own schools" it is a disappointment to find that the lines laid down in the book are the vaguest outlines; no scheme is worked out, and we close the book without having any clear idea what is intended or how the programme is to take definite shape. What, then, are the practical measures that are proposed to meet the needs of the case? It must be honestly confessed that it is not easy to discover, because every possible reform suggested is so guarded with qualifications and exceptions that the existing confusion is hardly simplified at all. Mr. Lyttelton turns his attention to the preparatory schools, but he admits that no reform can be instituted unless the Headmasters of public schools are prepared to take concerted action, and this there seems to be no machinery for effecting. French is to have a secure place as well as Latin. Greek is to be postponed for the majority of boys until the public school—but even here there are to be exceptions. Handicraft and music are to be added, and in a singular little time-table that is appended all the strictly intellectual work (apart from handicraft and music) is to be compressed into four hours a day, in which time is allowed for preparation.

When we turn to the curriculum suggested for public schools we do not find ourselves on surer ground. The system which Mr. Lyttelton proposes is, briefly, this—that Greek should be dropped altogether for boys of inferior capacity, so as to secure adequate time for other subjects. For boys of greater capacity, but not necessarily of linguistic and literary ability, science is to be made an alternative for Greek. So far as it goes, this is sensible enough, as tending slightly to relieve the congestion of subjects, and as frankly recognising that Greek must be considered as a special subject; but the plan is one that is already in use at all schools which take up science seriously and have a modern side; it admittedly depends upon the Universities adopting a corresponding scheme of entrance examinations and making Greek an alternative with science. Then, too, the scheme is one which is obviously based on the desire to retain Greek as far as possible. It is obvious, therefore, that it is not a scheme which is framed to meet the real difficulty, namely, the congestion of subjects. Indeed, the result of the scheme would seem to be that the number of subjects will be increased rather than diminished, because English is to be thoroughly taught, while handicraft and music are to be added to the curriculum.

In his introductory chapters Mr. Lyttelton discusses the question of State control; he takes for granted that it means State aggression, and his chief argument for public-school reform is that if the public schools could produce a practical system of education, State interference would be indefinitely postponed. He brings out clearly the danger of State control, namely that at the present time the Headmasters, independent as they are, are yet to a certain extent amenable to public opinion, while to put the public schools under the direct and detailed control of a public Department would be to erect a bureaucratic tyranny of educational experts, which might prove disastrous to the best interests of higher education.

Of course the situation is a very complicated one. On the one side there is the parental public, vaguely claiming practical efficiency for the boys and discontented with present results; on the other side there are the schoolmasters pathetically desirous of preserving an ideal of intellectual culture, and nullifying the possibility by yielding to parental demands so far as to overload with subjects a crowded curriculum, and sacrificing thereby, in the case of many boys, both culture and efficiency. What is really needed is the interposition of a third authority which can balance and co-ordinate the rival interests and insist upon efficiency while safeguarding culture. Exoriare aliquis!

THE LAST DAYS OF THE VICARS APOSTOLIC.

"The Dawn of the Catholic Revival in England." By Bernard Ward. London: Longmans. 1909. 2 vols. 25s. net.

THE title of the Catholic Revival might mean either the Counter Reformation or the Oxford movement. How far it accurately describes the history of the Roman Catholics in England from the death of Bishop Challoner in 1781 to the restoration of the Hierarchy in 1850 must be judged by what Dr. Ward has to say in his later volumes. These first two only carry the history to 1803, and though the Relief Bill of 1791 removed the more galling of the Roman Catholic disabilities, it is still the day of small things. According to Joseph Berington, there were only sixty thousand of his fellow-churchmen in England in 1781, and of these three hundred and sixty were priests. The sermon that Cardinal Gibbons preached last year in Westminster Cathedral during the Eucharistic Congress told a very different tale. In 1782 two Roman Catholic labourers were fined for "not repairing to church". In 1908 the streets of London were filled with foreign Bishops and priests; seven Cardinals, one of them a Papal Legate, were present at High Mass in Westminster, a great procession passed unmolested through the streets of London, and nothing was wanting that could bear witness to the absolute freedom enjoyed by Roman Catholics in this country.

Between the one date and the other there is a long road to be passed. The history of the first stages of this journey is not altogether edifying. Active persecution had ceased, though outbursts like the Gordon riots still showed that Protestant fanaticism was only dormant. The night was over—a featureless twilight followed it. A transition period of this kind is never inspiring. These twenty years are no exception. Personal quarrels, academic controversies, petty rivalries loom large; there is little of the missionary fire of Campion and Parsons; there are none of the broad views and wide horizons of Wiseman, Newman and Manning. Neither the one nor the other was to be expected. Two centuries of civil ostracism had left their mark on priests and laymen alike. The priests, educated at Douai, or S. Omer, or Liège, still regarded themselves as sheep amongst wolves; the laity, debarred from public life, lived apart amongst themselves, suspicious and suspected of their neighbours.

Gradually their disabilities were removed, but the feeling that, though living in England, they were not real Englishmen could not be immediately eradicated. The character of their ecclesiastical administration tended to keep it alive. Since the Reformation England had been a missionary country under the direction of the Propaganda. Vicars Apostolic appointed by Rome, and not Diocesan Bishops, governed its four districts. The Catholic Committee and the Cisalpine Club, the two centres of liberal opinion, regarded this system as suggestive of Papal domination, and accordingly pressed for the restoration of a national hierarchy. From a purely administrative point of view also there was much to be urged against the government of the Vicars Apostolic. Their jurisdiction was never satisfactorily defined, and controversies about it were continually arising and never ending. Although in Bishop's orders, they had not the full authority of Diocesans, nor had they the support of a strong Papacy to take its place. The regulars regarded themselves as independent, whilst many of the seculars were more inclined to consult the wishes of the country gentlemen whose chaplains they were and upon whom they depended for their livelihood than to obey the "gentlemen of the mitre", as the Catholic Committee contemptuously described the nominees of the Propaganda. These internal difficulties and divisions could not but cripple the influence of a small and scattered flock. The parties were clearly defined: the ultramontanes, led by Dr. Walmesley, Vicar Apostolic of the western district, with their chief support in the north and their policy of no compromise; and the liberals, led by Lord Petre, supported by most of the country gentry and organised first in the Catholic Committee and afterwards in the Cisalpine Club. The former were bent on keeping their people separate and peculiar, the latter upon making them full and responsible citizens. Dr. Walmesley, for example, doubted the wisdom of repealing the Penal Laws: "I wish, therefore, it may be duly considered whether it would be expedient to ask for the Repeal of the old Penal Laws, or rather perhaps to let them remain unnoticed. . . . When so very few Catholics become mixed with such a multitude of Protestants, what religious duties can we suppose will they observe?" Ten years later he went even further in writing to the Archbishop of Canterbury, Dr. Moore, to urge him to oppose the very Relief Bill that the Catholic Committee had drafted:

"I therefore entreat your Grace to procure the suppression of the present Bill, which favour will remove my pressing anxiety, and will be at the same time a signal proof of your Grace's readiness to vindicate the rights of Episcopacy.
I am, with confidence in your Grace's protection,
Your Grace's very humble servant,
CHARLES WALMESLEY."

This is a remarkable letter for the "Senior of the Superiors of the English Roman Catholic clergy" to have written to a Protestant-minded Archbishop of Canterbury. Dr. Walmesley, good man and brilliant mathematician though he was, possessed neither tact nor the small arts of conciliation. Like his spokesman, Dr. Milner, "he undervalued the little etiquettes of society", and failed to see that the only way to get the position of his fellow-churchmen established was to show a united front and a conciliatory temper. It were indeed unjust to be too hard on him. There was a real danger of the Catholic Committee abandoning vital principles in the campaign for emancipation. In their celebrated "Protestation" of loyalty and abhorrence of certain doctrines imputed to them they went out of their way to declaim against Papal infallibility and Papal aggression. They were ready to distinguish themselves from the Papists by accepting the name of "Protesting Catholic Dissenters". The oath that they drafted went beyond the oath taken by their fellow-churchmen in Ireland. And throughout all the negotiations that preceded and followed the passing of the Bill they consulted their Bishops as little as possible, and did their utmost to prevent their intervention. If Dr. Walmesley's manners were blunt, and Milner's style offensive, it must be owned that the correspondence and the discussions of the Committee were very far from models of polite behaviour. At length, after various changes and chances, a Bill was passed, and the first step taken towards full and complete emancipation. But the internal disputes did not end with the passing of the Bill. Dr. Walmesley, with Milner as his mouthpiece, determined to bring his adversaries to their knees. Wilkes, a Benedictine monk and a member of the Committee, must be compelled to confess the errors of his ways and recant; the "Staffordshire clergy" to express their contrition for supporting Wilkes. A tiresome and interminable correspondence was the result. It is a relief to turn from it to a pleasanter picture. In the year that followed the passing of the Bill there arrived in England the first batch of refugee priests from France. Before many months had elapsed they numbered nearly five thousand. "It is impossible", wrote Sir Samuel Romilly, "to walk a hundred yards in any public street or thoroughfare without meeting two or three French priests". Such an invasion might easily have excited a Protestant outburst. As it was, it gave the English Government and the English people an opportunity that, be it said to their credit, they used to the full of giving a generous welcome to these victims of foreign persecution. The Government not only placed houses at their use, but made money grants towards their maintenance; nor could anything have exceeded the kindness and generosity of private individuals. For the English Romans the care of their unfortunate brothers was an opportunity to lay the controversies between the Committee and the Bishops. The immigration, therefore, did real good. In course of time many of the priests returned to the Continent, but, what is more important, the religious communities that had also arrived, with one exception, did not return. When it is remembered what most of these communities were, it will be realised how great an influence their stay has had upon Roman Catholicism in England. They were not foreign houses with French and Belgian monks and nuns like those that have been settling here during the last ten years, but English monastic houses and the English colleges founded for the conversion of England, with their English teachers and students. The ex-Jesuits of the Liège Academy, for instance, settled at Stonyhurst, the Benedictines of Douai first at Acton Burnell and afterwards at Downside. A Roman Catholic boy could henceforth be educated in his native land. The change from Douai to Downside or Liège to Stonyhurst marks a further step in the absorption of English Roman Catholics in the national life of the country. It is at this point that Dr. Ward ends his second volume. His fellow-churchmen are free to exercise the practices of their religion; they can be educated in England; they have yet to win their way into Parliament and the Universities, and have still to wait half a century for Diocesan Bishops and a whole century for emancipation from the Propaganda.

NOVELS.

"Influences." By Paul Methven. London: Chatto and Windus. 1909. 6s.

The influence of the country mouse Enid upon John Fane, the brilliant London playwright whom his friends called the Cynic, was to cause him to revise his views of the sex, to marry her, and to settle down in the country and grow roses. The influence of London upon Enid during that first season of hers when Fane met her was to give her an insatiable taste for theatres and bridge parties, and the kind of faintly Oscar-Wildeish dialogue with which he had originally dazzled her, but which, apparently, he found incompatible with gardening. The situation thus brought about is an interesting one, and the tendency of a blasé worldling fondly to deck out sweet-and-twenty with wholly imaginary qualities is a good theme for serious comedy. But afterwards the book drifts into sensational melodrama. We have again the seducer's lugger—now a steam yacht—in the offing, the well-worn rencontre of stony-broken lives upon the Embankment benches, and the conventional happy ending—even after Fane, in a fit of madness, had attempted to murder both Enid and her baby. Mr. Methven, however, writes so fluently and frequently contrives his thrills with so much ingenuity that the thinness of his story here and there may well escape notice.

"The Search Party." By George A. Birmingham. London: Methuen. 1909. 6s.

A book so laughter-compelling as "Spanish Gold" has not unnaturally claimed an encore, but Mr. Birmingham has passed from extravaganza into farce, from

(*Continued on page 604.*)

THE EMPIRE GUARANTEE AND INSURANCE CORPORATION, LTD.

The eighth annual general meeting of shareholders was held in the registered offices, 247 West George Street, Glasgow, on September 24. A. L. Bell, Esq., M.D., D.P.H., Chairman of the Corporation, presided.

The Chairman said: On behalf of the Board, I have again the honour to move approval of the directors' report and adoption of the accounts, and, notwithstanding an adverse balance, I do so with some degree of confidence in that, while you must join with us in deep regret that the result of the year's working has been a loss, you will, I am sure, readily appreciate the cause of that deficit, and support us in the stand we have taken against continuing to transact the class of business to which our loss is entirely attributable. In the first place, while a deficit of £13,000 is most regrettable to us, there seems to me no good reason for alarm on the part of the shareholders, especially as the loss is confined to one department of the business, and, what is of signal importance, can be so easily and fully explained, and can be surely avoided in the future. It will be within the recollection of those who attended the last shareholders' meeting that I stated that workmen's compensation was, for us, really experimental—that it was an unknown field which we had ventured to explore, and I indicated that our policy therein would be tentative, and would be determined by our experience. As a young Company, we were anxious not to miss a fair share of new business, which promised to be enormous, if we found it sound and profitable. As the year advanced, however, it was borne in on us with ever-increasing force that the liability attending workmen's compensation was being daily increased to such an extent that the most cautious forecast fell short, and the experience of the oldest offices was equally at a loss to estimate this increased liability. For not only did the Law Courts continue to interpret the new Act with unvarying and every-widening generosity towards claimants, but the Act itself has been a happy hunting-ground for the making and propagating of claims on every possible pretext. And so, gentlemen, looking at this class of business in the daily increasing light of our added experience, we had to decide whether it would be to the ultimate advantage or to the detriment of the Corporation to continue to accept workmen's compensation risks of the usual class. The Managing Director, on whom of necessity the heaviest responsibility fell, and myself, as well as our colleagues, recognised the fact that we had reached a point in our journey beyond which we might not go on the same lines and ever hope to retrace our steps. On the one hand, we could choose the broad, easy path of bounding increases, trusting that, whatever claims came to hand from day to day, the law of average would prevail, as it has been found to do in the more settled departments of insurance business, hoping that the evil days would pass, and profit and added prosperity emerge from the vaster amount of business done. On the other hand, there was the narrow difficult path, the course which I may characterise, without suspicion of self-praise, as the courageous and prudent course of looking squarely in the face facts drawn, not from theory, but from our own experience, and this course we have chosen in order to strengthen the Company. We had not hesitated in the lean years of the past to deny ourselves the pleasure of dividing profits; our policy and practice have always kept in view not present increase, but future strength; we have tried always to select only what seemed good in the light of our own experience. The issues were momentous, and the decision much more difficult than it may seem to-day. The Directors came to the conclusion that to accept workmen's compensation business would prove increasingly unprofitable in spite of a temporary surplus and dividend, and they believed to do so would be dangerous to the ultimate progress and wellbeing of the Company. We have decided to decline all hazardous risks such as iron and steel working, quarrying, mining, building, and suchlike. In the meantime, while we have thus discarded and refused a vast amount of new premiums, we have, of course, had to meet the exaggerated claims and the liability for which we had accepted previous payments. I trust your approval will follow the course your Directors have taken at an anxious and critical period of the history of the Company. With reference to the other departments of the Company's business, I need only say that without exception they show advance in the right direction; and, although that advance is much smaller than we expected it to be, I cannot shut my eyes to the fact that even here the malign shadow cast by workmen's compensation is abundantly in evidence. For partly because of the volume of this business pressing for attention, partly because of the greater ease with which it can be obtained, our agents have not applied themselves with the same assiduity to the other departments in which progress is slower and business more difficult to secure, with the result that our increases in the Life Department, in General Insurance, Personal Accident, Fire and Marine Insurance, have not been nearly so great as they would otherwise have been, and as they will be in the future now that our representatives are free to devote their time and energy to the work of the other departments.

The various questions raised by the shareholders having been satisfactorily answered, the Chairman moved the adoption of the Directors' Report and Statement of Accounts. This was seconded by Mr. W. K. Russell and was agreed to.

(Copies of the Report and Accounts for the past year can be obtained on application to the London Offices of the Corporation, 66 Finsbury Pavement, E.C., or 11 Regent Street, W.)

things that might quite well happen in Ireland to things that the untravelled Englishman might expect to be told about Ireland. A dispensary doctor (pale reflection of the imperturbable curate in "Spanish Gold") mysteriously disappears. The village assumes that he has escaped from his creditors to America, and when his determined fiancée comes from England to look for him, meets her with every form of kindly fiction. The lady's vigour and decision soon make the doctor's friends form a new theory, that he has preferred flight to marriage. A local ne'er-do-well's disappearance is accounted for by the obvious supposition that he has gone to America with the funds collected for the local athletic sports. But when two English members of Parliament vanish, and two policemen sent to search are no more seen, the young woman's reiterated assertion that there is something seriously wrong begins to find credence. It is all excellent fooling, and we shall not hint at the real secret.

"Two Women." By Baroness Albert d'Anethan. London: Unwin. 1909. 6s.

The author of this novel takes her characters to Japan, we should suppose, in order to describe some Japanese scenes and to introduce large quotations from her own poetry. The story in itself is not remarkable. A girl had eloped with a reputed widower whose first wife reappeared. She had then married a cynical baronet who agreed to assume the paternity of her infant daughter, but treated mother and child with cold brutality. (He is a servants'-hall sentimental-story kind of baronet.) So the daughter married a rich young bounder in order to escape from home, and when the bounder flirted with an adventuress there was obviously nothing to do except go to Japan, that the scenery and the poetry might bring the curtain down to soft music.

THE NOVEMBER REVIEWS.

On the eve of the annual meeting of Conservative and Unionist Associations at Manchester, and with a general election not far off, the political articles in the monthly reviews will claim special attention. What is to be the fate of the Finance Bill and of the peers should they throw it out? What is the policy which the Unionists will put before the country, and what are the claims on which the Government hope to secure a new lease of life? Mr. Keir Hardie, in the "Socialist Review", regards a General Election in January as certain, his "forecast" being based not on the assumption that the Lords will throw out or hang up the Finance Bill, "since I do not believe they will do either one or the other", but the general circumstances of the political situation. In the "Nineteenth Century" Lord Avebury, whom the "National" calls "the most fossilised of Cobdenite Mandarins", examines the Budget in detail and decides that it wages warfare not against poverty but against energy and industry, confidence and thrift—warfare from which the poor will in the long run suffer most. He is in favour of the Lords throwing out the clauses which contain Mr. George's "very novel and arbitrary proposals", and argues that if they can reject the whole they can surely reject a part. He quotes some remarks of Mr. Gladstone in 1861, in which the rights of the peers were clearly set forth; Mr. Gladstone said that in his opinion the House of Commons would be very much safer if the House of Lords did claim and exercise the power of amendment. In the same review Mr. Mallock institutes an inquiry into the actual amount of the annual increment of land values, and is satisfied that all the Government will get from their proposed tax will be £39,000. "As a matter of business the Government would behave far more wisely, and as a matter of principle they would not behave more unjustly, if they forced the landlords to pay them £1,000,000, as kings once extorted ship-money, and then invested this sum in the Canadian Pacific Railway, or acquired with it a preponderating interest in the Civil Service Stores, or in Harrod's." "Blackwood" discovers in Mr. Lloyd George himself an example of unearned increment. He receives £5000 a year: "What has he done to earn so large a sum? How can he compare his own services to the services of a zealous and intelligent landlord? It is not, in fact, to his own energy or self-sacrifice that he owes his income. The British democracy was none of his making. Why then should he profit by it? Had he stayed among his own Welsh hills he would have been precisely the same man. But he would not have had £5000 a year. Clearly it is a case of unearned increment, and as such it should be handed over to his constituents, or it should be heavily taxed for the profit of the community". Why, asks "Blackwood", are not brains valued by experts as land is to be valued? Then "Mr. Lloyd George might probably be given thirty shillings a week, while the rest of his salary, being unearned increment, should go to the comfort of the poor". With the exception of a short study in political depravity furnished by the case of Mr. Ure, the "National" confines its home politics to the Episodes of the Month, which, pointed as ever, emphasise in their own way the speeches of Lord Curzon and Lord Milner, and claim that among the assets of Unionism are Mr. George and Mr. Churchill, who are promoting the reunion and consolidation of the party.

Both the "National" and Mr. Fabian Ware in the "Nineteenth Century" are full of regrets that Unionism should have suffered a momentary set-back through the consideration extended to the Unionist Free Traders, and Mr. Ware warns Unionists that victory can only be achieved by loyalty to tariff reform. It strikes us as a little amusing to find Mr. Ellis Barker in the "Fortnightly" instructing the Unionists how they might—why might?—win the General Election. Land reform must go hand in hand with tariff reform, and the Unionist programme which "will appeal to the great majority of electors" is "British work for British workers; every man his own landlord; the British Empire for the British race". Mr. Howard Gritten follows with an article on "The Coming Battle"; he pins his faith to tariff reform and the House of Lords and asks "Who can doubt but that in the socialistic order of events the attack on the House of Lords would be merely the prelude to that on the monarchy?" Mr. Harold Spender has been looking up precedents with a view to what will happen if the Lords throw out the Finance Bill, and has found one in the legislative records of the Colony of Victoria for 1877. The chaos which Mr. Asquith predicts now, was the result then, until the Legislative Council gave way. A precedent drawn from a colony, which had not enjoyed complete autonomy during more than twenty years, is not perhaps very conclusive. In Mr. Spender's opinion it might be well to bear for a short season such troubles as befel Victoria thirty-one years ago, rather than submit to the claim of the House of Lords. But what if the chaos comes, and the country justifies the peers? Precedents more apposite because they belong to the Imperial Parliament itself are examined by Viscount Hill in the "Financial Review of Reviews" and Mr. Alexander Grant in the "Contemporary". Lord Hill comes to the conclusion that if the persons who criticise the Finance Bill because in parts it is something other than a Finance Bill make good their point, they have strong ground in ordinary legal theory for claiming the right to amend the Bill by striking out the extraneous matter as an alternative to absolute rejection. Mr. Grant thinks that because the Lords have passed the Budget year by year for the best part of a century without material challenge, therefore that right has become an "obsolete and abandoned privilege". In other words, the Lords have the right neither to reject nor amend a money Bill, which surely is the constitutional reductio ad absurdum. Nor will Mr. G. P. Gooch, in the "English Review", admit the claims of the Lords on any ground. He frankly admits that tacking would be contrary to the spirit of the resolutions on which the Commons take their stand, but he denies that any such charge can be established against the Budget. "Can any one seriously contend that the valuation of land is an object foreign to the taxation of land values, or that the increase of licence duties ceases to be a financial measure because the Licensing Bill was rejected a year ago?" Mr. Gooch has a conveniently short memory: the speeches of Mr. Lloyd George and Mr. Churchill provide ample evidence that the intention of the increased licensing duties is to accomplish the defeated object of the Licensing Bill.

Lord Courtney, in the "Contemporary", continues his reflections on Peace or War. He does not believe there are any questions open between Great Britain and Germany, or for that matter any other country, which "a frank, honest, good-natured diplomacy, based on a ready acceptance of inevitable facts", could not settle. Generally, his views are mere aspirations after disarmament, his idea being that we can only escape a dark future if we give up the effort to maintain "an overtopping superiority in physical resources which Time and Nature must deny us". On the other side, and much more in touch with facts, both as to human nature and nationality, is Baron von Stengel in the "National Review". Patriotism, in the German statesman's opinion, is greater than cosmopolitanism, and he does not hesitate to suggest that if the peace movement makes headway in Germany to a point which involves the neglect of warlike preparations, then the end of the German Empire is assured. Thus, while Lord Courtney thinks British salvation lies in one direction, Baron

(Continued on page 606.)

A Second Life

"If I only had another chance!"

How often are these despairing words uttered when a man feels his strength ebbing, his vital forces depressed, his health undermined—often as the result of his own errors or follies—and he realises the infinite possibilities which might lie in his grasp could he indeed receive, in Shakespeare's phrase, "a second life."

Happily for the world, this other chance, this "second life" is to be had for the asking by means of that

Tonic Food for the Brain and Nerves

which has been aptly described by a famous physician as "the last word science has spoken" on the subject of such remedial agents, and to which, by virtue of its health-giving properties, the name of Sanatogen—meaning "health-producer"—has been given.

So powerful is this health-producing property that the best physicians are not only constantly writing in the most eulogistic terms of its value, but they also prescribe Sanatogen every day to restore the health and vigour lost by debility and disease. Sanatogen, however, does more than this. It increases the vitality of those in perfect health, and gives them the power of putting forth the greatest physical and intellectual energy of which they are capable.

The constituents which give Sanatogen this power are known to every physician. What they are is described below in the plainest terms in the telling analysis of Sir Charles A. Cameron, the chief medical officer of health and public analyst for Dublin.

Medical testimony of its value can be read in the statement of Dr. C. W. Saleeby, the well-known medical author and one of the 12,000 physicians who have testified in writing to the supreme merits of Sanatogen as

A Revitalising Force

after wasting illness and as a restorer of health, not only in nervous diseases (with their innumerable symptoms of discomfort and distress, including loss of memory, insomnia, irresolution, weakness of the will, &c.), but also in anæmia, digestive disturbances, and consumption.

What Sanatogen has done is shown in the two typical letters of Sir Gilbert Parker, M.P., and Mr. Eden Phillpotts. They are selected from the scores of communications of famous men and women who have of their own free will put into writing the debt they owe to Sanatogen. Sanatogen may be obtained from all chemists in packets from 1s. 9d. to 9s. 6d. Free descriptive Booklet on application to the Sanatogen Co., 12 Chenies Street, London, W.C.

Medical Opinion

DR. C. W. SALEEBY, the well-known medical author:

"13 Greville Place, London, N.W.

"Sanatogen is a specially adapted food that has solved the problem of giving phosphorus in such a way that the nervous system can take hold of it. I would specially refer to its value in the feeding of invalids, whether during actual illness or during convalescence, and for nursing mothers."

A Telling Analysis

SIR CHARLES A. CAMERON, C.B., M.D., F.R.C.P., D.P.H., Medical Officer of Health and Public Analyst, Dublin, &c.

"On analysis it proved to be composed of 9·5% moisture, and 90·5% of dry matter, including 7·37% of ash. It contained 83·13% of Albuminoids (nearly wholly made up of casein, but including a little albumin), together with 2·2% of phosphoric acid, a small portion of which existed in the albuminoids, but by far the larger portion was in the form of sodium glycero-phosphate.

"I have arrived at the conclusion that Sanatogen is a substance of the highest nutritive value containing as it does a large amount, relatively speaking, of organic phosphorus—that is phosphorus which is offered to the tissues in exactly the form in which it can be easily absorbed. It is an excellent nerve food."

Typical Letters

SIR GILBERT PARKER, M.P., the popular novelist.

"20 Carlton House Terrace, S.W.

"I have used Sanatogen at intervals since last autumn with extraordinary benefit. It is to my mind a true food tonic, feeding the nerves, increasing the energy, and giving fresh vigour to the overworked body and mind."

MR. EDEN PHILLPOTTS, the well-known writer, says:

"Torquay.

"Sanatogen appears to be of real value to the brain-worker, a useful food and splendid tonic combined. I can give it high praise from personal experience."

·SANATOGEN·

von Stengel is sure that Germany's only hope is to be found in the other. And while both are speculating as to the future, events are afoot which certainly lend no support to theories of universal brotherhood. An anonymous writer in the "Fortnightly" corrects the view given a couple of months ago by Vox et Preterea Nihil concerning the relations of Russia and Austria in South-Eastern Europe. He tells us that the idea of Austria occupying the Sandjak was not Austrian, but Russian, which is a pretty commentary on Dr. Dillon's reference in the "Contemporary" to Austria-Hungary having "just banished from the Balkans the Russian spectre". Mr. T. Comyn-Platt, writing from Melilla on the Spanish army in Morocco, travels outside his immediate subject, and finds the state of Europe so electric that war may come at any moment. So far from the war in Morocco being a private quarrel between Spain and the Riffs, he says, there are all the elements of a long and fierce struggle, in which the nations of Europe may be embroiled. Dr. Dillon, in the "Contemporary", fills some twenty pages in discussing the many constitutional crises in Europe which in themselves may easily be a source of international anxiety.

Some of the literary articles in the reviews are specially attractive. Professor Dowden in the "Contemporary" answers in the affirmative with many qualifications the question, "Is Shakespeare self-revealed?" Dr. Welldon in the "Nineteenth Century" is more precise in showing Dante's self-portraiture. Mr. Henry D. Roome in the "Fortnightly" compares and contrasts the styles of Macaulay and Lecky as historians of the eighteenth century. Mr. Roome says it is a pity Macaulay never turned his hand to writing a play. Some of his history might have been at least as valuable in that form if not more entertaining. Mr. Charles Whibley in the "National" welcomes Mr. C. R. L. Fletcher's "Introductory History of England", because it is frankly anti-Whig. "The people", he says, "knows as much of its history as Macaulay and Green and other inveterate Whigs have chosen to tell it". At last their unchallenged reign is over. The article is a great compliment to Mr. Fletcher. Mr. Hannay writes in "Blackwood" in his usual informative way of the galleon, and Mr. Cunninghame Graham has one of his delightful South American sketches in the "English Review" under the title "The Captive".

For this Week's Books see pages 608 and 610.

PROVINCIAL MOTOR CAB.

The first ordinary general meeting of the Provincial Motor Cab Company, Limited, was held on Thursday, at Salisbury House, London Wall, E.C., Mr. Davison Dalziel (Chairman of the Company) presiding.

The Chairman said: You have all read the report, to which I do not think there is very much for me to add. You will see that at the date of the closing of the accounts we had succeeded in establishing a taxicab service in eighteen of the leading provincial towns—namely, Aldershot, Bath, Brighton, Birmingham, Bournemouth, Bradford, Bristol, Cambridge, Eastbourne, Edinburgh, Folkestone, Glasgow, Harrogate, Leeds, Liverpool, Manchester, Oxford, and Sheffield. Since that time services have also been started in Aberdeen, Ipswich, Birkenhead, and Newcastle; so that at the present time your business is in full working operation in twenty-two business centres in the United Kingdom. I need hardly dwell upon the many difficulties that have been encountered in establishing a business of this character in so many different centres. Local conditions vary considerably, and each town has proved practically the establishment of a new business, distinct in many of its characteristics from each of the other centres. At the same time these difficulties, as they have occurred, have gradually been overcome, until we consider that the general equipment of the business is in excellent condition, and everything points to a further important development of the Company's sphere of action, as well as a satisfactory return to the shareholders. It must be borne in mind that during a great portion of the period under review the business was in a purely experimental stage, and, in fact, for a time there were no cabs running at all, and that the results before you to-day were obtained by the small daily average running over the whole period of 148 cabs. It will perhaps interest you to know that during the first month of the new year—that is to say, in April of this year—this number had been increased to 270, and that during the last month this had risen to a daily average of 344, and that the average number of cabs in use for the six months ended September 30 was 302, as compared with 148 over the whole period of last year. Of the standard type of cars in use by the Company the principal ones are those made by the Charron Company and by the Wolseley Tool and Motor Car Company. Both these cars have given the board unqualified satisfaction, and it is the intention of the directors, as much as possible, to adhere in the future to these two particular makes of cars in the development of their business. As you are probably aware, we are utilising in the provinces cabs of a more powerful build than those in use in London. This has been necessitated by the heavy gradients existing in various parts of the country. I am of the opinion that there is still a large field for development in the provinces, and that in many towns where the Company's vehicles are now plying for hire there will shortly be an opportunity of considerably increasing the number of cabs in use. I think that is all I have to say to you to-day, in addition to the information contained in the report which was sent out by the board. However, I am at your disposal to answer any questions that you may be pleased to put to me. I beg to move: "That the accounts to March 31, 1909, and the reports of the directors and auditors be, and are hereby, passed and adopted."

Mr. Godfrey C. Isaacs seconded the motion, which, after some discussion, was carried unanimously.

The Chairman next proposed: "That the payment of an interim dividend at the rate of 7 per cent. per annum on the Preferred Ordinary shares on account of the profits for the current year, as recommended by the directors in their report, be, and is hereby, sanctioned, such dividend to be payable on December 20, 1909."

Sir Henry Seton-Karr, C.M.G., seconded the motion, which was unanimously agreed to.

THE CONSOLIDATED GOLD FIELDS OF SOUTH AFRICA, LIMITED.

SHARE CAPITAL:

Ordinary - - - - -	£2,000,000
Preference - - - - -	£1,250,000
First Mortgage Debentures	£275,000

Head Office ... ... 8 OLD JEWRY, LONDON, E.C.
Branch Offices PARIS, JOHANNESBURG, BULAWAYO.

CHAIRMAN: LORD HARRIS.

NOTICE IS HEREBY GIVEN that the Ordinary General Meeting of the Consolidated Gold Fields of South Africa, Limited, will be held at the City Terminus Hotel, Cannon Street, London, E.C., on Tuesday, November the 16th, 1909, at Noon.

The Report of the Directors for the year ending June 30th, 1909, states that the realised net profit on the year's operations, which is largely derived from dividends received on investments, after deducting Debenture Interest and all outgoings, shows a balance to credit of £1,283,891 11s. 2d., from which the dividend on the Preference Shares, an interim dividend of 2s. per share on the Ordinary Shares, and French Government Taxes, have been provided, leaving £1,002,823 3s. 6d., which, added to the sum of £68,260 15s. 4d. brought forward from last year, leaves £1,071,083 18s. 10d.

From this the Directors have made provision to the extent of £500,000 for the further writing down of the prices at which investments in the shares of crushing mines stand in the books of the Company, leaving £571,083 18s. 10d. available for dividend.

In addition to the foregoing realised profit, the Company's Share Investments (apart from any appreciation in value on properties and ventures) show on current market prices a further large unrealised profit.

Investments stand in the books at average cost or under, and all shares are taken into account at prices below those current at the date when the accounts were made up.

The changes that have taken place in the Company's holdings during the past year have not materially affected the general position or the nature of the investments.

The Directors recommend that a final cash dividend of 15 per cent. and a bonus of 10 per cent., both free of Income Tax, be paid on the 2,000,000 Ordinary Shares, amounting to £500,000, and making with the interim dividend 7s. per share for the year, leaving £71,083 18s. 10d. to be carried to the credit of the current year's Profit and Loss Account.

The Report and Accounts was posted to registered Shareholders on Saturday evening, the 6th November, and the Annual General Meeting of the Shareholders will be held on Tuesday, the 16th November, at the City Terminus Hotel, Cannon Street, London, E.C., at Noon.

Copies of the Report, containing full information as to the Company's position, Balance-sheet and Accounts, and Reports by the Joint Managers and Consulting Engineers, can be obtained on application at the Company's Offices in London and Paris, on and after Monday, November 8th, 1909.

By Order,

J. C. PRINSEP
H. L. SAPTE } *Joint Secretaries.*

Dated November 6th, 1909.

THIS WEEK'S BOOKS.

ART

Raphael (Adolf Paul Oppé). Methuen. 12*s.* 6*d.* net.
The International Art Series:—Auguste Rodin (Gustave Kahn). Fisher Unwin. 5*s.* net.
Some of the Moderns (Frederick Wedmore). Virtue. 15*s.* net.

BIOGRAPHY

A Lady of the Old Régime (Ernest F. Henderson). Bell. 10*s.* 6*d.* net.

FICTION

The Submarine Girl (Edgar Turner). Paul. 6*s.*
The House of Terror (Gerald Biss); For Charles the Rover (May Wynne). Greening. 6*s.* each.
The Oath of Allegiance (Elizabeth Stuart Phelps). Constable. 6*s.*
A Sense of Scarlet (Mrs. Henry Dudeney). Heinemann. 3*s.* net.
The Blindness of Dr. Gray; or, the Final Law (The Very Rev. Canon P. A. Sheehan). Longmans. 6*s.*
The Gateway (Harold Begbie); The Lady of Blossholme (H. Rider Haggard). Hodder and Stoughton. 6*s.* net.
The Valley of the Kings (Marmaduke Pickthall); On the Forgotten Road (Henry Baerlein); In the Shade (Valentina Hawtrey). Murray. 6*s.* each.

GIFT BOOKS

Dick's Angel (Mrs. Edwin Hohler); Peter and Christmas (Mrs. Edwin Hohler). Constable. 2*s.* net.
The Wonder Book of Light (Edwin J. Houston); The Wonder Book of Magnetism (Edwin J. Houston). Chambers. 3*s.* 6*d.* each.
The Poetical Works of Robert Burns (Edited by Charles Annandale. 4 vols.). Gresham Publishing Co. 30*s.*
Cranford (Mrs. Gaskell). Bell. 2*s.* 6*d.* net.
Afloat on the Dogger Bank (Henry Charles Moore), 2*s.* 6*d.*; Two Tapleby Boys (Mrs. Nevill Cubitt), 3*s.* Wells Gardner.
Mighty Hunter (Ashmore Kinson). Longmans. 6*s.*
Nature Stalking for Boys (W. Percival Westell). Dent. 3*s.* 6*d.* net.
By Right of Conquest (G. A. Henty), 3*s.* 6*d.*; John Bargreave's Gold (Capt. F. S. Brereton), 5*s.*; Three Fair Maids (Katharine Tynan), 3*s.* 6*d.*; The Log of a Privateersman (Henry Collingwood), 3*s.*; The Nicest Girl in the School (Angela Brazil), 2*s.* 6*d.*; A Final Reckoning (G. A. Henty), 3*s.* 6*d.*; The King's Liege (H. A. Hinkson), 2*s.*; The Starling (Norman Macleod), 1*s.*; Matthew and the Miller (Violet Bradey), 2*s.* 6*d.*; The Arabian Nights (Gladys Davidson), 5*s.* Blackie.

HISTORY

The Medici (Colonel G. F. Young. 2 vols.). Murray. 36*s.*
Roman Catholic Opposition to Papal Infallibility (Rev. N. J. Sparrow Simpson). Murray. 6*s.*
The Northward Trek (Stanley Portal Hyatt). Melrose. 10*s.* 6*d.* net.
The Union of South Africa (Hon. R. H. Brand). Oxford: At the Clarendon Press. 4*s.* 6*d.* net.
With Mulai Hafid at Fez (Laurence Harris). Smith, Elder. 7*s.* 6*d.* net.
Westminster Abbey (Francis Bond). Frowde. 10*s.* net.
The Lives of the British Architects (E. Beresford Chancellor). Duckworth. 7*s.* 6*d.* net.
The Great Revolution 1789-1793 (P. A. Kropotkin). Heinemann. 6*s.* net.
A Brief History of the Middle Temple (C. E. A. Bedwell). Butterworth.

TRAVEL

Rambles and Adventures in Australasia, Canada, India, &c. (St. Michael Podmore). Gill. 6*s.* net.
The Flowers and Gardens of Madeira (Florence Du Cane); Isle of Man (W. Ralph Hall Caine). Black. 7*s.* 6*d.* net each.
Netherlorn, Argyllshire, and its Neighbourhood (Patrick H. Gillies). Virtue. 12*s.* 6*d.* net.
The Great Wall of China (William Edgar Geil). Murray. 21*s.* net.
Sicily (Will S. Monroe). Bell. 7*s.* 6*d.* net.
By the Waters of Egypt (Norma Lorimer). Methuen. 16*s.* net.

(*Continued on page* 610.)

Greening's Latest Fiction.

Another DON Q. Story.

DON Q.'S LOVE STORY.

By K. & HESKETH PRICHARD.

By the Author of "THE FINANCIER."

THE DISC.

By HARRIS BURLAND.

First Edition exhausted. *Second Edition ready.*

By the Author of "THE DUPE."

THE HOUSE OF TERROR.

By GERALD BISS.

By the Author of "HENRY OF NAVARRE."

FOR CHARLES THE ROVER.

By MAY WYNNE.

By the Author of "THE BISHOP'S EMERALDS."

THE SECRET OF THE RAFT.

By HOUGHTON TOWNLEY.

The most Audacious and Humorous Book of the Season.

BOOM!

By WILLIAM CAINE.

Other Good Fiction in Demand.

THE HUMAN MOLE ... Colin Collins.
THE WANTON ... Frances Forbes-Robertson.
THE MARQUIS CATILINI ... Rowland Strong.
THE MASTER SCHEMER ... Vere Campbell.
THE SPITFIRE ... ... Edward Peple.
MOON OF VALLEYS ... David Whitelaw.
RE-BIRTH ... ... Rathmell Wilson.
ADVENTURES OF SUSAN ... Cyrus Brady.
SEALED ORDERS ... A. E. Carey.
THE WITCH QUEEN OF KHEM ... Ena Fitzgerald.
HER SUBURBAN HIGHNESS ... Gurner Gillman.
THE SERPENT AND THE CROSS ... Stephen Andrew.

Important Announcement.

A New Romance by the Author of

"THE SCARLET PIMPERNEL."

Messrs. Greening beg to announce that next week they will publish

THE NEST OF THE SPARROWHAWK.

By BARONESS ORCZY.

To prevent disappointment, order from your Bookseller or Library at once.

NOW READY.

SIR WALTER RALEGH

By STEPHEN LOVELL and WILLIAM DEVEREUX.

The Story of the Play by William Devereux now being successfully performed by Mr. Lewis Waller at the Lyric Theatre.

At all Libraries. *SIX SHILLINGS EACH.*

GREENING & CO., Ltd., 91 St. Martin's Lane, W.C.

THIS WEEK'S BOOKS—*Continued.*

Verse

An Ampler Sky (Lance Fallow). Macmillan. 3*s*. net.

Miscellaneous

Book of the Sweet-Pea, The (D. B. Crane). Lane. 2*s*. 6*d*. net.
Church and Nation; or, Wealth with Honour (Elliott E. Mills). Bath: National Unity Press. 10*s*. 6*d*. net.
Collected Works of Ambrose Brice, The. Vol. II. New York: Neale Publishing Co.
Coming Englishman, The (James Long), 5*s*. net; Dictionary of National Biography (Edited by Sidney Lee), 15*s*. net. Smith Elder.
Cupful of Kernels, A (J. M. Stuart-Young). Ouseley. 5*s*. net.
Epitaphia (Ernest R. Suffling). Gill. 7*s*. 6*d*. net.
Essays on Greek Literature (Robert Y. Tyrrell). Macmillan. 4*s*. net.
Essays Relating to Ireland (C. Litton Falkiner). Longmans. 9*s*. net.
Everyman's Book of the Dog (A. Croxton Smith). Hodder and Stoughton. 6*s*.
Famous Churches (Frederick Sherlock). Dent. 1*s*. net.
Industrial Diseases and Accidents (W. J. Green). Bristol: Arrowsmith. 7*s*. 6*d*. net.
King's Business, The (Frances Arnold-Forster). 3*s*. 6*d*. net.
New Zealand in Evolution (Guy H. Scholefield). Fisher Unwin. 10*s*. 6*d*. net.
Popular Science for Parochial Evenings (Rev. Charles T. Ovenden). Stock. 2*s*. 6*d*. net.
Shakespeare Folios and Quartos (Alfred W. Pollard). Methuen. 21*s*. net.

Reviews and Magazines for November:—The International, 1*s*.; The Westminster Review, 2*s*. 6*d*.; The Forum, 25*s*.

SALES BY AUCTION.

The COLLECTION OF COINS and MEDALS, the property of the late P. J. Prankerd, Esq..

MESSRS. SOTHEBY, WILKINSON & HODGE will SELL by AUCTION, at their House, No. 13 Wellington Street, Strand, W.C., on MONDAY, November 15, and Four Following Days, at 1 o'clock precisely, the COLLECTION of COINS and MEDALS, the Property of P. J. PRANKERD, Esq. (deceased), formerly of The Knoll, Sneyd Park, Bristol, comprising a few Greek Coins in Gold and Silver, a large Series of Roman Gold and others in Silver and Bronze, Ancient British and Anglo-Saxon Coins, English and Foreign Coins and Medals, Coin Cabinets, etc.

May be viewed. Catalogues may be had.

JAPANESE COLOUR PRINTS.

MESSRS. SOTHEBY, WILKINSON & HODGE will SELL by AUCTION, at their House, No. 13 Wellington Street, Strand, W.C., on MONDAY, November 22, at 1 o'clock precisely, JAPANESE COLOUR PRINTS, the Property of the late FRANK DILLON, Esq., and other Collectors, comprising Works by Utamaro, Hokusai, Hiroshige, and others, Drawings, Books, Kakemono, Makimono, etc.

May be viewed two days prior. Catalogues may be had.

The Collection of ENGRAVINGS and DRAWINGS, the property of the late FREDERICK HENDRIKS, Esq., F.S.S., F.I.A., Knight of Vasa.

MESSRS. SOTHEBY, WILKINSON & HODGE will SELL by AUCTION, at their House, No. 13 Wellington Street, Strand, W.C., on TUESDAY, November 23, and Following Day, at 1 o'clock precisely, ENGRAVINGS AND DRAWINGS, framed and in the portfolio, the Property of the late FREDERICK HENDRIKS, Esq., F.S.S., F.I.A., Knight of Vasa, of 7 Vicarage Gate, Kensington, W., comprising Mezzotint and other portraits, by J. Watson, J. Smith, J. Faber, E. Fisher, C. Wilkin, T. Watson, R. Houston, C. Turner, J. Dixon, J. MacArdell, R. White, W. Faithorne, R. Gaywood, F. Bartolozzi, and others. Etchings and Engravings by Old Masters, including: A. Dürer, Rembrandt, M. Schoengauer, G. Pencz, H. S. Beham, Lucas van Leyden, L. Cranach, The Hopfers, W. Hollar, Sir A. Vandyck, and others. Woodcuts by A. Dürer and others. Water-colour and other Drawings, and Drawings by Old Masters. Fancy subjects of the English school, Modern Etchings by J. M. Whistler, Seymour Haden, J. Jacquemart, and others, and a few Chiaroscuro prints, &c.

May be viewed two days prior. Catalogues may be had.

The Valuable LIBRARY of John Mitchell Marshall, Esq. (deceased), of Wallingford.

MESSRS. SOTHEBY, WILKINSON & HODGE will SELL by AUCTION at their House, No. 13, Wellington Street, Strand, W.C., on THURSDAY, November 25, at 1 o'clock precisely, the Valuable LIBRARY of JOHN MITCHELL MARSHALL, Esq. (deceased), of Wallingford, comprising an important and valuable Collection of Works, chiefly illustrated by Thomas and John Bewick; also original Water-colour and Pencil Drawings by Thomas Bewick, Engravings, a few Autograph Letters, Memoranda, etc., including first editions, in the finest condition, Catalogue of Works illustrated by T. and J. Bewick, extra illustrations inserted, some very scarce, Engravings of the Chillingham Wild Bull, on thin vellum and paper, the Kyloe Ox, on paper, the Cadger's Trot, a lithograph; original Water-colour and Pencil Drawings by Thomas Bewick, four Leaves of Thomas Bewick's Memorandum Book, Autograph Letters, etc.; Lord Lilford's Birds of the British Islands, Burton's Arabian Nights and Supplemental Nights, Pine's Horace, potest edition, Foreign Field Sports, Aiken's National Sports of Great Britain, and other sporting works; Gould's Birds of Great Britain, 5 vols., Claude's Liber Veritatis, 3 vols., 1777-1819, the Writings of Dickens, Smedley, and others, White's Natural History of Selborne, first edition, &c.

May be viewed two days prior. Catalogues may be had.

AUSTRALIA by ORIENT LINE,

UNDER CONTRACT TO CARRY HIS MAJESTY'S MAILS.

FROM LONDON EVERY ALTERNATE FRIDAY, calling at PLYMOUTH, GIBRALTAR MARSEILLES, NAPLES, PORT SAID, and COLOMBO.

Managers—F. GREEN & CO.: ANDERSON, ANDERSON & CO.

Head Offices—Fenchurch Avenue, London.

For Passage apply to the latter firm at 5 Fenchurch Avenue, E.C., or to the Branch Office, 28 Cockspur Street, Charing Cross S.W.

AXIM AND TARKWA GOLDFIELDS.

In view of the recent introduction on the Stock Exchange of the shares of the Axim and Tarkwa Goldfields, the following particulars may be found of interest.

The nominal capital of the Company, which has acquired the Aryiwassi Concession, Gold Coast Colony, from the Industrial Selections, Ltd., is £150,000, divided into 149,750 shares of £1 each and 5,000 shares of 1s. each. The purchase price is represented by 25,000 of the £1 shares, fully paid, and 5,000 of the same class of shares have been issued for cash, 5s. per share having been called up. The directors of the Company are Messrs. V. E. Pringle, H. A. Vincent, and C. H. Bennett. The Company, besides having obtained the Aryiwassi Concession, holds an option to purchase three other concessions from the Industrial Selections, Ltd., for £75,000, payable in cash or shares.

It is stated that the Aryiwassi Concession has lately been visited by Mr. J. J. Nicholl, M.I.M.E., who reports that the area of the concession is about four miles square, and is situated on the west bank of the Ankobra River, in the Lower Wassau district, and is about twenty miles from the nearest point of the Tarkwa-Kumasi Railway. Mr. Nicholl reports that he found four well-defined conglomerate reefs on the property, assaying from 1 to 4 oz. of gold to the ton. The reefs run east and west and dip to the north. He also discovered numerous alluvial deposits carrying from ¼ oz. to ½ oz. of gold to the cubic foot of dirt. He advises the erection of a preliminary 5-stamp mill near the southern boundary, where the principal reef is, and says the approximate cost would be less than £800, erected on the spot. He reports that there is an abundance of timber suitable for mining purposes, and that the property is well watered.

The Duebu-Heabah properties, comprising one of the concessions under option to the Axim and Tarkwa Goldfields, have also been reported on by Mr. Nicholl. He states that there are numerous reefs of auriferous quartz and quartzite on the properties, together with valuable alluvial deposits. The reefs run north-east and south-west, dipping to the west. He writes: "The lodes are of hematite and sandstone at the surface, or of quartzite at surface changing into lodes or reefs of quartz at an average depth of 30 ft. Several assays of outcrop and quartz taken from near the surface assayed from 1 oz. 6 dwt. to 3 oz. per ton, and the débris from the numerous old native workings on the quartzite reefs, of which there are many upon the properties, show from 10 to 12 dwt. to 2½ oz. of gold per ton." Mr. Nicholl has also gone into the petroleum-bearing possibilities of the Duebu-Heabah properties. He declares that he could find petroleum on the property, and that when he passed through a village to the south of Duebu-Heabah he observed a spring of yellow oil, which he is sure was naphtha.

Mr. Nicholl also visited the Mamponsa timber and gold-mining lands, another of the concessions under option to the Axim and Tarkwa Goldfields. This property is included in the so-called "Tarkwa Goldfields" district. Mr. Nicholl states that "the predominating strata is sandstone and quartzite, these rocks being both coarse and fine grained, and occasionally containing scattered pebbles, in some cases so rough as to become 'grit,' and becoming quartzite in depth." He says the property is honeycombed with old native workings, and that assays he has made from different samples went as high as 2 oz. to the ton, and would average 1 oz. to the ton. "There are three sandstone and quartzite reefs on this concession, running about north-east and south-west and dipping to the west. Assays I made from samples taken from these reefs went from ½ oz. to 3 oz. to the ton. There is also one known reef which is decidedly conglomerate, assaying from 1 oz. to 4 oz. to the ton." It is also said that "there are very valuable alluvial deposits on the property," which "gave as much as 6 dwt. to the cubic foot of earth."

In a report on the Abuyew lands and mines, the third concession held under option by the Axim and Tarkwa Goldfields, Mr. Nicholl says the area of the property is approximately 5¼ square miles. With regard to the geological and mineralogical features, he states that "the upper or overlying strata is of sandstone (of the lower tertiary epoch of disposition), laterite, quartzite, shales, and metamorphic schists. The secondary strata consists principally of sandstone-quartzite of an early epoch. The enclosing formations are mostly of basic igneous rocks, some of them forming well-defined diorite dykes, being slightly auriferous. A part of the sandstone formation forms a range of low-lying hills traversing the concession. The secondary (he goes on to remark) is the typical geological formation for auriferous conglomerate reefs in West Africa, differing in this respect from the geology of South Africa, where the auriferous conglomerate formations are found in granite. The general line of strike is N.E. and S.W., with a dip towards the N.W. of about 30 degrees. Along certain lines of strike in the metamorphic schists and sandstones frequent lenticular masses of quartz occur varying from 6 in. to 3 ft. in thickness; some of these are sufficiently large and continuous to be reckoned as workable lodes." Mr. Nicholl further states: "Assays I made from various samples of the quartz gave an average of over 10 dwt. to the ton. In addition to the reef formation the concession is rich in auriferous alluvial deposits, with a rich wash at an average depth of 15 ft., assaying over 8 dwt. to the ton." There is said to be a good supply of local labour.

THE . . . MEDICI PRINTS.

THE MEDICI SOCIETY exists for the purpose of bringing within reach of all the **finest obtainable replicas, in the colours of the Originals, of the finest works of the Great Masters of Painting.** Speaking of one of the latest issues, the *Burlington Magazine* has recently said:—"Among modern publishers of prints The Medici Society has already achieved notable distinction for the excellence of its colour facsimiles, but an even greater credit attaches to the taste with which the subjects have been chosen. . . . *Prints like this, which are at once true in general effect and will stand the test of the microscope in their details, can never be superseded.*"

The same authority has further said that, "nothing of the kind so good or so cheap has ever before been offered to the public." The *Daily Telegraph* speaks of "This young and vigorous Society, which has already rendered important services to art and art-lovers"; whilst the *Nation* critic, in an article examining the advance made in colour-reproduction, refers to the Medici Prints as "a class of work that, apart from its enormous educative value, has come to be something of first-hand æsthetic worth."

All lovers of Art are invited to pay an early visit to The Medici Galleries to inspect **The Medici Society's THIRD WINTER EXHIBITION,** comprising some 400 **"Old Masters." Among these, besides Medici Prints and similar colour-collotype facsimiles** after the Italian, Netherlands, German, and English Schools, are shown:

An Exhibition of the Complete Series of the reproductions of the old ARUNDEL SOCIETY (open until December 24).

An Exhibition of 64 facsimile Reproductions after selected Drawings by ALBRECHT DÜRER (many after Water-colours), chiefly from the Albertina Library, Vienna. The Illustrated Catalogue, post free 1*s.* stamps; unillustrated 2*d.* stamps. *** *The Dürer Exhibition closes on November* 20.

"The extraordinary fidelity to the originals [of these *Dürer* reproductions] can perhaps be fully appreciated only by those who know that wonderful series, or by someone who has been able to compare an original and a Medici facsimile side by side."—*The Morning Post.*

ITALIAN SCHOOLS.

Painter	Subject	Price	
BELLINI, GIAN ...	...**The Madonna of the Trees**...	15	0
BOTTICELLI ...	...**Madonna and Child** (*Milan*)	12	6
" ...	...**The Vision of St. Augustine**	10	6
" ...	...**The Birth of Venus**	30	0
BRAMANTINO ...	...**Putto with Grapes**	12	6
CARPACCIO, VITT.	...**Vision of St. Ursula**	30	0
CREDI, L. DI ...	...**The Annunciation**	17	6
FORLI, M. DA ...	...**The Archangel Gabriel** ...	17	6
FRANCESCA, P. DELLA	...**Portrait of a Lady** (*Milan*)...	15	0
GIORGIONE ...	...**Evander and Aeneas**... ...	30	0
" ...	...**Figures in a Landscape** ...	21	0
LEONARDO ...	...**The Last Supper**	25	0
" ...	...**Head of the Christ**	12	6
LIPPI, FILIPPO ...	...**Head of the Virgin** (*Uffizi*)...	10	6
LIPPI, FILIPPINO	...**The Virgin in Adoration** ...	17	6
LUINI, B. ...	...**Head of the Virgin** (*Brera*)	12	6
MANTEGNA, A.	...**The Madonna with Cherubim**	20	0
PISANELLO ...	...**Vision of St. Eustace** ...	17	6
PREDIS, A. DI ...	...**Beatrice d'Este** (*Milan*) ...	12	6
" " ...	... " " (*London*) ...	31	6
	*** *Edition limited to 300 Copies.*		
RAPHAEL ...	...**The Madonna in Green** ...	21	0
" ...	...**Madonna della Colonna** ...	17	6
TINTORETTO ...	...**Bacchus and Ariadne** (*Venice*)	17	6
TITIAN	... " " (*London*)	30	0
"	...**The Madonna of the Cherries**	25	0

ENGLISH SCHOOL.

Painter	Subject	Price	
GAINSBOROUGH	...**The Painter's Daughters** ...	15	0
HOPPNER ...	...**The Countess of Oxford** ...	15	0
REYNOLDS ...	...**The Holy Family**	15	0
ROMNEY ...	...**Lady Hamilton with a Goat**	25	0
ROSSETTI ...	...**Lady Lilith**	25	0

FLEMISH AND DUTCH SCHOOLS.

Painter	Subject	Price	
HALS, FRANZ ...	...**Family Group**	21	0
HOOCH, P. DE ...	...**Interior with Soldiers** ...	15	0
MATSYS, Q. ...	...**The Magdalen**	17	6
RUBENS	...**Fruitfulness**	12	6
TERBORCH, G. ...	...**The Concert**	17	6
VERMEER, JAN ...	...**The Pearl Necklace**	17	6
VOS, C. DE ...	...**Portrait of a Lady**	17	6

NATIONAL PORTRAIT SERIES.

Painter	Subject	Price	
JANSSEN, C. ...	...**John Milton (Æt. 10)** ...	12	6
UNKNOWN ...	...**William Shakespeare** ...	15	0
ZUCCHERO* ...	...**Queen Elizabeth with Rainbow**	15	0
	After publication	17	6

OTHER SCHOOLS.

Painter	Subject	Price	
CLOUET, FR. ...	...**Elizabeth of Austria** ...	15	0
HOLBEIN, HANS*	...**Christina, Duchess of Milan**	15	0
	After publication	17	6

(The same in monochrome (24" × 11"), *now ready*, 5s.)

* To be published shortly.

Packing and Postage of all Prints is extra, at 6*d.* each; additional copies (up to 6) in same parcel, 1*d.* each beyond the first. Flat packing extra.

FRAMES, suitable for all subjects, including replicas of fine originals contemporary with the Pictures reproduced, are a speciality of The Society. For particulars see prospectus. Those unable to visit the Galleries, are invited to write for:

The Medici Society's completely illustrated Prospectus, containing particulars of suitable Frames, the Annual Subscription, &c., post free 6d. stamps. Summary Lists post free.

Special List of PRIMITIVES illustrated—some 100 colour-collotype Facsimiles after the Early Flemish, German, and Italian Schools, post free 6d. stamps.

THE MEDICI SOCIETY, 38 ALBEMARLE STREET, LONDON, W.

Printed for the Proprietors by SPOTTISWOODE & CO. LTD., 5 New-street Square, E.C., and Published by REGINALD WEBSTER PAGE, at the Office, 10 King Street, Covent Garden, in the Parish of St. Paul, in the County of London.—*Saturday*, 13 *November*, 1909.

SUPPLEMENT TO THE

SATURDAY REVIEW

OF

POLITICS, LITERATURE, SCIENCE, AND ART.

No. 2,820 Vol. 108. 13 November 1909. GRATIS.

IMPORTANT NOTICE.—*Messrs. METHUEN have just published one of the most important books of the year, for which the demand everywhere is great:—*

THE SURVIVAL OF MAN: a Study of Unrecognised Human Faculty. By Sir OLIVER LODGE, F.R.S. Demy 8vo. 7s. 6d. net.

They have also just published the following Books:—

BY THE WATERS OF EGYPT. By NORMA LORIMER. Illustrated. Demy 8vo. 16s. net.
A CENTURY OF SPAIN AND PORTUGAL. By Lieut.-Col. G. F. WHITE. Demy 8vo. 12s. 6d. net.
MAN AND NATURE ON TIDAL WATERS. By A. H. PATTERSON. Illustrated. Crown 8vo. 6s.
FUNGI AND HOW TO KNOW THEM. By E. W. SWANTON. Illustrated. Crown 8vo. 6s. net.
THE SPIRITUAL COMBAT. By DOM LORENZO SCUPOLI. Newly Translated by THOMAS BARNS, M.A. Small pott 8vo. 2s.; leather, 2s. 6d. net. [*Library of Devotion.*

The last Three Volumes of the COLLECTED EDITION of the WORKS of OSCAR WILDE are also ready.

10. **DE PROFUNDIS AND PRISON LETTERS.** (This is the Fourteenth Edition, and contains new matter.)
11. **ESSAYS.** ("Historical Criticism," "English Renaissance," "London Models," "Poems in Prose.")
12. **SALOME.** (Containing a new Preface by the Editor, a Bibliographical Note and Two Plays: a Florentine Tragedy, "La Sainte Courtisane.") Fcap. 8vo. 5s. net each.

GENERAL LITERATURE

ON EVERYTHING. By HILAIRE BELLOC, M.P., Author of "On Nothing." Fcap. 8vo. 5s.

REMINISCENCES OF A K.C. By T. E. CRISPE, K.C. With 2 Portraits. Demy 8vo. 10s. 6d. net.

A BOOK OF THE ZOO. By ERIC PARKER. With 24 Illustrations from Photographs by HENRY IRVING. Crown 8vo. 6s.
The Author has tried in this book to make a round of the Zoological Gardens, and to show the animals to a visitor as they appear to one who has spent many hours watching their individual characters and habits in captivity.

RAPHAEL. By A. P. OPPÉ. With 200 Plates. Wide royal 8vo. gilt top, 12s. 6d. net. [*Classics of Art.*

THE AUSTRIAN COURT IN THE NINETEENTH CENTURY. By Sir HORACE RUMBOLD, late Ambassador at Vienna. With 16 Illustrations. Demy 8vo. 18s. net. [*Second Edition.*
"Its survey is wide; it abounds in personal touches and is never lacking in human interest."—*Daily Telegraph.*

MARIE ANTOINETTE. By HILAIRE BELLOC, M.P. With 35 Portraits and Illustrations. Demy 8vo. 15s. net.
"The story is told with a full appeal to contemporary evidence and with dramatic skill."—*Standard.*

GOOD COMPANY: a Rally of Men. By E. V. LUCAS. Fcap. 8vo. 5s. This is uniform with "The Open Road."
"The title is just; the characters are pleasant companions, the anthology very agreeable."—*Morning Leader.*

THE WORKS OF OSCAR WILDE. A New EDITION, reset in 12 vols. Fcap. 8vo. 5s. net each.
1. LORD ARTHUR SAVILE'S CRIME. 2. THE DUCHESS OF PADUA. 3. POEMS (including "The Ballad of Reading Gaol" and "The Sphinx"). 4. LADY WINDERMERE'S FAN. 5. A WOMAN OF NO IMPORTANCE. 6. AN IDEAL HUSBAND. 7. THE IMPORTANCE OF BEING EARNEST. 8. A HOUSE OF POMEGRANATES. 9. INTENTIONS.

TREMENDOUS TRIFLES. By G. K. CHESTERTON. Fcap. 8vo. 5s. [*Second Edition.*
"There is bubbling humour; there is ripe philosophy."—*Onlooker.*

ONE DAY AND ANOTHER. By E. V. LUCAS. Fcap. 8vo. 5s. [*Second Edition.*
"An elysium of humour and humanity."—*Pall Mall Gazette.*

A WANDERER IN PARIS. By E. V. LUCAS. With 16 Illustrations in Colour by WALTER DEXTER, and 32 from Photographs after Old Masters. Crown 8vo. 6s. [*Third Edition.*
"M. E. V. Lucas vient, en effet, en bon Samaritain, de se pencher sur la misère du voyageur mélancolique; il lui a donné un beau livre dont l'écriture est chatoyante et féline, un livre sur Paris tout plein d'images et de faits mais tout plein aussi d'humeur et de grâce familière."—M. CHARLES CHASSÉ, in *L'Opinion.*
"The soul of Paris is caught and reflected in these pages."—*Standard.*

SHELLEY: the Man and the Poet. By A. CLUTTON BROCK. With 12 Illustrations. Demy 8vo. 7s. 6d. net.
"A fine combination of penetration, accuracy, and charm."—*Morning Leader.*

THE NINE DAYS' QUEEN: being the Life of the Lady Jane Grey. By RICHARD DAVEY. Edited by MARTIN HUME, M.A. With 12 Illustrations. Demy 8vo. 10s. 6d. net. [*Romantic History.*
"This scholarly book is written with conspicuous charm."—*Standard.*

MATILDA OF TUSCANY. By NORA DUFF. With many Illustrations. Demy 8vo. 10s. 6d. net.

SIR PHILIP SIDNEY. By PERCY ADDLESHAW. With 12 Illustrations. Demy 8vo. 10s. 6d. net.

THE MAXIMS OF MARMADUKE. By C. E. JERNINGHAM. Fcap. 8vo. 5s.
"The vivacity of the author never flags."—*Daily Mail.*

THE PILGRIM FATHERS: their Church and Colony. By WINNIFRED COCKSHOTT, St. Hilda's Hall, Oxford. With 12 Illustrations. Demy 8vo. 7s. 6d. net.

THE MEDIÆVAL HOSPITALS OF ENGLAND. By ROTHA MARY CLAY. With many Illustrations. Demy 8vo. 7s. 6d. net. [*The Antiquary's Books.*

ONE HUNDRED MASTERPIECES OF SCULPTURE. With an Introduction and Descriptive Notes by G. F. HILL. With 101 Illustrations. Demy 8vo. 10s. 6d. net. A splendid book.
"An admirable study of the development of sculpture, well informed and well written."—*Scotsman.*

THE DECLINE AND FALL OF THE ROMAN EMPIRE. By EDWARD GIBBON. Edited by J. B. BURY, Litt.D. In 7 vols. Vols. I. and II. each 10s. 6d. net.
This is a completely New Edition, newly set in large type, with many Illustrations and new Maps.

THE INCOMPARABLE SIDDONS. By Mrs. CLEMENT PARSONS, Author of "Garrick and his Circle." With 20 Illustrations. Demy 8vo. 12s. 6d. net.
"A delightful book on a fascinating theme."—*Stage.*

THE COURT OF A SAINT. By WINIFRED F. KNOX. With 16 Illustrations. Demy 8vo. 10s. 6d. net.
This is a Life of St. Louis of France.

AIR AND HEALTH. By RONALD C. MACFIE. Demy 8vo. 7s. 6d. net. [*New Library of Medicine.*
A scientific and practical book on air in reference to health and disease, climate, dust, fog, and ventilation.

FOOD AND HEALTH. By A. E. POWELL, Lieutenant Royal Engineers. Crown 8vo. 3s. 6d. net.

MY PETS. By ALEXANDRE DUMAS. Translated by A. R. ALLINSON. With 16 Illustrations by V. LECOMTE. Crown 8vo. 6s.

ROME. By EDWARD HUTTON, Author of "The Cities of Umbria." With 16 Illustrations in Colour by MAXWELL ARMFIELD, and 12 other Illustrations. Crown 8vo. 6s.

A ROSE OF SAVOY: Marie Adélaide of Savoy, DUCHESSE DE BOURGOGNE, MOTHER OF LOUIS XV. By H. NOEL WILLIAMS. With a Frontispiece in Photogravure and 16 other Illustrations. Demy 8vo. 15s. net.

THE COURT OF LOUIS XIII. By K. A. PATMORE. With 16 Illustrations. Demy 8vo. 10s. 6d. net. [*Second Edition.*

ST. TERESA OF SPAIN. By HELEN H. COLVILL. With 20 Illustrations. Demy 8vo. 7s. 6d. net.

METHUEN'S POPULAR NOVELS

SIX SHILLINGS EACH

SAILORS' KNOTS (3s. 6d.)	W. W. JACOBS
THE TYRANT	MRS. HENRY DE LA PASTURE
NORTHERN LIGHTS	SIR GILBERT PARKER
THE SEVERINS	MRS. ALFRED SIDGWICK
THE PRICE OF LIS DORIS	MAARTEN MAARTENS
THE SEARCH PARTY	G. A. BIRMINGHAM
SPLENDID BROTHER	W. PETT RIDGE
TOIL OF MEN	ISRAEL QUERIDO
THE COLUMN OF DUST	EVELYN UNDERHILL
AVENGING CHILDREN	MARY E. MANN
THE BURNT OFFERING	SARA JEANNETTE DUNCAN
THE FIRST ROUND	ST. JOHN LUCAS
IN AMBUSH	MARIE VAN VORST
JACK CARSTAIRS OF THE POWER HOUSE	SYDNEY SANDYS
THE SQUIRE'S DAUGHTER	ARCHIBALD MARSHALL
HAPPINESS	MAUD STEPNEY RAWSON
LOVE AND THE WISE MEN	PERCY WHITE
GIANNELLA	MRS. HUGH FRASER
LORDS OF THE SEA	EDWARD NOBLE
THIS DAY'S MADNESS	MAUDE ANNESLEY
THE BRIDE	GRACE RHYS

METHUEN & CO., 36 Essex Street, London, W.C.

WILLIAM BLACKWOOD & SONS.

A NOTABLE LIST.

THE WORK AND PLAY OF A GOVERNMENT INSPECTOR.

By HERBERT PRESTON-THOMAS, C.B. With a Preface by the Right Hon. JOHN BURNS, M.P. 10s. 6d. net.

Mr. Preston-Thomas, late Government Board Inspector for the South Western District, has given us a book that will assist to the better understanding of a variety of Social Problems. He discourses of many subjects with wit and discernment, from "A Barmaid Show" to "The Privy Council," and from "The Royal Academy" to "The Shah of Persia."

THE LETTERS OF JOHN STUART BLACKIE TO HIS WIFE.

With a Few Earlier Ones to his Parents. Selected and Edited by his Nephew, A. STODART WALKER. 12s. 6d. net.

"Nothing that has been written upon the late Professor Blackie can be brought into even distant comparison with this volume as a revelation of a very remarkable personality. The marvellous variety and vivacity of these letters is scarcely to be even indicated in a brief review."—*Glasgow Herald.*

LADY WAKE'S REMINISCENCES.

Edited by LUCY WAKE. Illustrated with Portraits. 12s. 6d. net.

Like Archbishop Tait and her other brother, Sheriff Tait, Lady Wake possessed force of character and intellectual ability, and to the end of her long life she preserved her great interest in the world around her.

"Reminiscences told in so lively a vein, with so much literary charm, yet so sanely and unpretentiously written, acquire by the general suffrage of public opinion a permanent place in the biographical literature of the day."—*Pall Mall Gazette.*

"A real refreshment and delight to read."—*Northampton Mercury.*

SIR WALTER SCOTT'S FRIENDS.

By FLORENCE MACCUNN, Author of "Mary Stuart." With Portraits. 10s. net.

A book of the greatest interest to all lovers of the Great Magician. It contains chapters on Old Ladies of Sir Walter's Youth—Parliament House Friends—Makers of Minstrelsy—Buccleuch Group—Literary Ladies—Abbotsford Household—Scott's Relation to other Poets.

TRAVELS IN THE UPPER EGYPTIAN DESERTS.

By ARTHUR E. P. WEIGALL, Chief Inspector of the Department of Antiquities, Upper Egypt. With numerous Illustrations. 7s. 6d. net.

"Next to visiting the desert itself, we can imagine nothing so delightful as reading Mr. Weigall's fascinating story."—*Pall Mall Gazette.*

"Since the times of Eliot Warburton and Kinglake many writers have celebrated the delights of travel in the desert. None, I think, has realised the fascination of the desert more fully than Mr. Weigall."—*Westminster Gazette.*

THE ENCHANTED ISLAND, And other Poems.

By ALFRED NOYES, Author of "Drake: an English Epic," "Forty Singing Seamen," "The Forest of Wild Thyme," &c. 5s. net.

"A most notable achievement."—*Daily Telegraph.*

Messrs. BLACKWOOD have an interesting List of FICTION, and Novels that will be found well worth reading are the following, price 6s. each:—

TO-MORROW. A NEW BOOK.

By the Author of CAPTAIN DESMOND, V.C., and THE GREAT AMULET, both of which are now issued in the Popular Shilling form.

CANDLES IN THE WIND.

By MAUD DIVER. 6s.

Mrs. Diver's previous books have reached a circulation of 100,000 copies.

THE PATH OF HONOUR.

By SYDNEY C. GRIER, Author of "The Warden of the Marches," &c.

"The reader will find his interest increasing with every page."—*Scotsman.*

A MAN'S MAN.

By IAN HAY, Author of "The Right Stuff," &c.

"A bright, fresh book all through, with plenty of go and plenty of humour." *Times.*

BLACK MARK.

By "A WHISPER." A brilliant new author.

"The adventures of 'Black Mark,' a man of fashion in the days of George II., who turns highwayman to pay his gaming debts, and of Letty Beanders, are narrated with sprightly ease and dramatic skill."—*Athenæum.*

THE BACKGROUND.

By W. J. ECCOTT, Author of "His Indolence of Arrass," &c.

"An excellent book. . . . Written by one with a well-stored mind and an appreciation of the value of good style. The literary charm is all over it, and the author's *obiter dicta* are informed by good judgment and a sense of humour." *Aberdeen Free Press.*

SOME EVERYDAY FOLK AND DAWN.

By MILES FRANKLIN, Author of "My Brilliant Career."

"Noteworthy piece of fiction. . . . Exceedingly interesting. . . . We recommend this Australian story as one having genuine interest."—*Standard.*

THE BLUFFSHIRE COURIER.

By PENTLAND PEILE, Author of "Clanbrae."

The heroine's grandfather had been evicted from his crofting home on the Duke of Bluff's estate, and had migrated to America. By the turn of Fortune's wheel she comes back to the old place possessed of a great fortune. Her practical plans and a love idyll between her and the Duke's son go to the making of a charming love story.

WILLIAM BLACKWOOD & SONS, Edinburgh & London.

Select Gift Books

THE CAT IN HISTORY, LEGEND, AND ART

Written and Illustrated by ANNE MARKS. Crown 4to. cloth gilt, **6s.** net (by post, 6s. 4d.).

The cult of the cat must prove of interest even to those who are not professed lovers of the animal.

THOUGHTS FROM MANY CLIMES.

Quotations in English, French, and Italian, with the English translations of the Italian, with two Dialogues by E. CARSON. Demy 16mo. Japanese Vellum gilt, gilt top, **2s. 6d.** net (by post, 2s. 8d.); Velvet Leather, Gilt Edges, Silk Register, **5s.** net (by post, 5s. 3d.).

A book of meditative thoughts culled from French, Italian, and English authors, arranged for daily readings.

LITERARY BYE-PATHS AND VAGARIES, & OTHER PAPERS

By THOMAS NEWBIGGING. Crown 8vo. cloth gilt, **4s. 6d.** net (by post, 4s. 10d.).

A series of interesting essays on out-of-the-way subjects, with the true literary note that the book-lover enjoys.

Fiction.

PHILIP MENZE: A STORY OF COMMERCIAL LIFE.

By H. C. KNIGHT. Crown 8vo. cloth gilt, **6s.**

This story, of especial interest to "Gentlemen of the Road," will prove very attractive to all business men and women.

FOR THREE KINGDOMS.

By H. C. CROSFIELD. Frontispiece by Mr. NOYES LEWIS. Crown 8vo. cloth gilt, **6s.**

Recollections of Robert Warden, a servant of King James. Full of stirring incidents, a story that grips the reader from beginning to end.

A Striking New Work for Modern Thinkers.

THE WAY OUT. By LAMPADEPHOROS.

Crown 8vo. cloth gilt, **6s.** net (by post, 6s. 4d.).

Being a Mental Autobiography of Constructive Philosophy. By the Author of "From December to December."

Write for New Catalogue (No. R 102) of Antiquarian and General Literature.

LONDON: ELLIOT STOCK, 62 PATERNOSTER ROW, E.C.

EDWARD STANFORD'S LIST.

Murray's Handbooks for Travellers.

ROME AND THE CAMPAGNA.

17th Edition. Revised and Enlarged. Edited by NORWOOD YOUNG. 600 pages, 96 Maps and Plans. Crown 8vo. price **10s.**

EGYPT AND THE SUDAN.

Revised, Largely Rewritten, and Augmented. Edited by H. R. HALL, M.A., F.R.G.S. 800 pages, 58 Maps and Plans. Crown 8vo. price **14s.**

CENTRAL ITALY AND FLORENCE. 23 Maps and Plans. Twelfth Edition. **9s.**

SOUTH ITALY. Part I. 10 Maps and Plans. Ninth Edition. **6s.**

SOUTH ITALY. Part II. 9 Maps and Plans. Ninth Edition. **6s.**

GREECE. 38 Maps and Plans. Seventh Edition. **20s.**

Complete List on Application.

STANFORD'S GEOLOGICAL ATLAS OF GREAT BRITAIN AND IRELAND. With Plates of Characteristic Fossils. Second Edition. Revised and Enlarged. Preceded by a description of the Geological Structure of Great Britain and Ireland and their Counties, and of the features observable along the Principal Lines of Railway. By HORACE B. WOODWARD, F.R.S., F.G.S. Comprising 36 Coloured Maps and 16 Double-page Plates of Fossils, 200 pages of Text, illustrated by 20 Sections and Views. Crown 8vo. cloth, **12s. 6d.** net.

Detailed Prospectus gratis on application.

CORSICA: an Island of Rest. By JOHN MITCHEL CHAPMAN. With Coloured Map and 31 Illustrations, 392 pages, demy 8vo. cloth, price **7s. 6d.** net.

"This live, fascinating book. . . . We wish there were more like it." *Daily Telegraph.*

Prospectus on Application.

London: EDWARD STANFORD,

12, 13, and 14, Long Acre, W.C.

Geographer to His Majesty the King.

SUPPLEMENT.

LONDON: 13 *NOVEMBER,* 1909.

THROUGH MIDDLESEX.

"Highways and Byways in Middlesex." By Walter Jerrold. With Illustrations by Hugh Thomson. London: Macmillan. 1909. 6s.

LONDON has already been treated in the publishers' "Highways and Byways", but the Middlesex which is outside the metropolis offers an abundant field for the mixture of perambulation with historic and literary reminiscence which is the aim of this series. Mr. Jerrold has done his work with admirable industry and diligence. Novelty in such a subject is almost impossible—the expert, indeed, is wearied by the repetition of familiar matter—but the various points of interest for which we have looked are generally well taken up. In church architecture alone Mr. Jerrold disappoints us, omitting noteworthy details, though he is particularly strong on mortuary inscriptions.

However, within the compass of a single volume he has given us a great deal of sound information. He is some way above the ordinary writer of guide-books, and, had he kept to simplicity of language, would have been an excellent cicerone. As it is, he seems to strain after paraphrase and fine writing. He "bumps out" his text here and there, to use the effective idiom of the printer, and indulges in vain repetitions. He has not the lightness of the easy writer.

Mr. Thomson's charming sketches, which bring romance even into railway bridges, support throughout the enthusiasm of the text, which strikes us occasionally as overstrained. It is just the annoying part of Middlesex that scenes are not quite so "delightful" as Mr. Jerrold makes them. Dull bricks and mortar, ugly heaps of clay or refuse, hedges and flowers bravely growing, but dwarfed by dust, squalor due to growing suburbs and deserted villages, money and self-advertisement in the larger centres flaunting on Sundays—all these things are apt to reduce our pleasure. Acton now belies its name as a town of oaks; the trams have reached Uxbridge; the underground railway is at Hounslow, and we daresay that the less frequented road beyond has lost the country air it had when we last walked on it and spied the fieldmouse hurrying to his lair. There are patches of dullness and ugliness in the "beautiful valley of the Brent" belauded by the Metropolitan Railway. Horsenden Hill with two adjacent stations also figures on the hoardings as a place of resort for the Londoner. Here, Mr. Jerrold says, "within recent years . . . cowslips flourished in profusion". We could find no profusion of wild flowers last year when we chanced on this spot. Two or three wild hyacinths were in hiding. Perhaps they expected a crowd, for, in connexion with the inn which commands the hill, there was an open-air platform for dancing. The flatness of the Thames valley throws the hills into relief, but they are of inferior height to those of Surrey and Buckinghamshire, and we do not wonder that Mr. Jerrold strays occasionally across the border of his proper county.

The author himself lives at Hampton, and it causes us no particular exhilaration to learn that his house was once occupied "by one of those music-hall 'stars' which blaze brilliantly with fugacious light". We find a full and interesting chapter on Hampton Court. A pleasant poem by Mr. C. K. Burrow pictures the restful charm of the Dutch Garden, but one is more likely to encounter those "happy amateurs of noise" whom John Davidson discovered careering round the flower-beds. As critics we should have added some detail about the pictures to be seen inside Hampton Court and the available accommodation outside, and we may venture on an historic association which is up to date. That learned historian, S. R. Gardiner, informs us that Oliver Cromwell reduced the cares of Parliament by going down to Hampton Court for the "week-end", and the word startles us in his sober and dignified narrative.

Other chapters deal with Twickenham and Teddington; the Staines Corner; Harrow, Pinner, etc.; Edgware and Hendon; Edmonton and Enfield. Throughout we are pleased to see frequent notice of many bypaths which are apt to be swallowed up by the greed of private owners or imperilled by the operations of what Mr. Jerrold calls "the golfing fraternity". Sometimes his descriptions are clear enough to follow, but often research with a good map will be needed, a business to which walkers should not object. The unpretentious series of "Field-path Rambles" started by the late "Walker Miles" is of great use here.

In literary associations Mr. Jerrold revels, but we cannot regard all his views on criticism as fortunate. The Earl of Surrey is "the first smoothener of our versification"; Hood's feebly elaborate verses on the topiarian peacocks at Bedfont are not beautiful; nor do we think that "The Rape of the Lock" "stands alone in our poetry as a perfect example of narrative comedy". A letter of Pope quoted on page 40 includes a Latin epigram: in this the commas make nonsense, and a nymph has been misprinted into the masculine gender. We cannot pretend any interest in Letitia Matilda Hawkins as a dweller in Twickenham, but Traherne, a true poet, at Teddington is a new association, and the verses quoted from his "Wonder" are excellent. Abreast with the time, too, is the mention of this year's memorial at Brentford, which begins with Julius Cæsar and ends with Charles I. and the Battle of Brentford. Even Mr. Jerrold's optimism fails in this grimy district, and a word of caution is properly added concerning the "tram-congested High Street", a dangerous thoroughfare where we have been stopped many a time on tram, cycle and motor car.

The Thames is a highway, and one more appreciated in Middlesex than in London, so that a few pages might have been devoted to the river traffic. Thus the patriotic Evelyn says in his "Diary" (2 June 1662): "I saw the rich gondola sent to his Majesty from the State of Venice; but it was not comparable for swiftness to our common wherries, tho' managed by Venetians". Strawberry Hill, says Mr. Jerrold, "is said to have suggested Walpole's 'Castle of Otranto'—architectural stucco expressed in terms of romance—and the idea of the picture walking out of its frame in the opening chapter is believed to have been suggested by the author's portrait of Henry Carey, Lord Falkland, in white painted by Vansomer". The repetition of "suggested" is clumsy, also unnecessary. Belief can give way here to fact as stated by Walpole himself in his "Letters", 9 March 1765. Another instance of a clumsy sentence is the following: "It is in those associations which give to a locality that which may be defined—if so hard a word as 'definition" be applicable—as historical charm lies the interest of many places".

Laleham is "ever to be associated with the two most famous members of a family several members of which have won fame". On this village and the Arnolds Mr. Jerrold writes well. The ivy-covered tower of the church is pretty enough, but had the critic entered the porch he could hardly fail to have noticed its extraordinary decoration. On the river flats near Halliford we are introduced to "rich golden blooms of Caltha Palustris". This is pure pedantry. "Marsh marigold" is good English, and the flowers should have been so described. On the Lambs at Enfield and the two houses in which they successively lived, now duly marked with commemorative tablets, the author tells us just enough, adding a fanciful suggestion for further commemoration. "Tall elms no longer darken the door of the first house; their place has been taken by a couple of poplars. It is worth noting that the further one is covered by a very old growth of wistaria, the same climber which neighbours Bay Cottage at Edmonton; a coincidence that, if book-lovers needed an annual floral reminder of their hero, might make the beautiful Japanese flower the emblem for Elians' wear." This passage may serve as an example of the writer's style, which has a touch of affectation. The wistaria was, we may add, nothing like so old as Lamb himself; for it was not introduced into England until the nineteenth century was well advanced, and then, we believe, it came from China. Apart from the actual houses of the Lambs, there is little left as they saw it. Charles' favourite inn is a mere modern public-house: Edmonton, Enfield and Islington are not as they were. The chance of walking at noonday into the New River as George Dyer did is spoilt by the interposition of iron railings.

Stanmore Common is one of the few places that can be described as truly rural, and not overrun by trippers. It is a veritable birds' paradise, and reference is duly made to Mrs. Brightwen, who won so much wild nature thereabouts by kindness. We should not describe the cricket green as "grand". It is pretty enough, but small for a good hitter. Harmondsworth and Harlington are also, we think, fairly unspoilt, and here Mr. Jerrold and his illustrator combine to give us attractive details of churches and half-timbered houses.

MEREDITH'S LAST POEMS.

"Last Poems." By George Meredith. London: Constable. 1909. 4s. 6d. net.

IT was inevitable that these relics of Meredith's poetic work should be gathered up and presented in a volume no long while after his death. The thing is invariably done, and pardonable enough, human curiosity being what it is. Such gleanings from dead poets' harvests—for the most part occasional or fragmentary pieces—have always a more or less promiscuous air. The experienced reader is forearmed against disappointment. He knows how little he may expect, and thinks himself well rewarded by just a few gleams of the authentic fire. In this volume, to tell the truth, there is more of the real Meredith than we had anticipated. One or two of the poems are highly characteristic and beautiful examples. Among the mere "fragments" will be found several fine things; and even in those pieces which were evidently written to occasion there is often a freshness of imagery and condensed felicity of phrase that nearly, if not quite, touch our very exacting standard of Meredithian art. A man might be totally ignorant of Meredith, yet find enough in this small book to assure him that he was in contact with a writer of the first rank. We are, therefore, far from being sorry, as we fancied we should be, that the volume has been published.

"The Years had worn their Season's Belt" will stand with anything the poet ever wrote. We may call it Meredith's "Lucy Gray":

"She dwelt where twist low-beaten thorns;
Two mill-blades, like a snail,
Enormous, with inquiring horns,
Looked down on half the vale".

The little picture is in Meredith's best vein of happy audacity. As a whole, the poem is most unstudied in effect—Wordsworthian with all the difference of modernity. "On Como" is a typical landscape with cloud-effect and lightning—"thunderless lightning" which appeals so intimately to Meredith and may in some measure serve as a symbol of his mind. Sunset, storm, and the calm after storm are almost the only larger aspects of nature which can draw Meredith's eye away from the more abiding charm of soil-born things with their indigenous brightness and frail beauty. Several times that charm reasserts itself in these poems. None but he could have described "The Wild Rose":

"a plain princess of the weeds,
As an outcast witless of sin:
Much disregarded, save by the few
Who love her, that has not a spot of deceit,
No promise of sweet beyond sweet,
Often descending to sour".

And in the "dark hour" when "nought save uses held in the street" his remedy is found in "a wilding little stubble flower".

Not least delightful is the note of strength and hope. "Our Earth is young", cries the unsoured veteran. He believes in "scenes unsung,

Wherein shall walk a lusty Time".

Political and patriotic pieces are always a severe strain on poetic talent; poetic genius they seldom fit at all. One of the two Nelson poems, however—"October 21, 1905"—is Meredith at his best, with a restrained strength of rhythm not often found in him. Both in verse and prose Meredith was sometimes moved by contemporary occurrences to statements or ejaculations of impermanent value, and traces of this are naturally not wanting here. A patriot he always was, and we find the love of England and a profound sense of her history embedded deeply in that instinctive intellectual pride which veins—despite the personal modesty of the man—almost everything that Meredith wrote. We cannot refrain from giving, before we leave this volume, one splendid fragment:

"From labours through the night, outworn,
Above the hills the front of morn
We see, whose eyes to heights are raised,
And the world's wise may deem us crazed.
While yet her lord lies under seas,
She takes us as the wind the trees'
Delighted leafage; all in song
We mount to her, to her belong".

Nowhere has Meredith's philosophy of life expressed itself more aptly or nobly. He is among the very few essentially subtle writers from whom nevertheless the dim and dejected moods are alien. His mind is only at home in clear light. He belongs to the morning.

HISTORY'S BRIDE OF LAMMERMOOR.

"The Nine Days Queen." By Richard Davey. London: Methuen. 1909. 10s. 6d.

MR. DAVEY has given us an interesting book on the life and times of Jane Grey, and Major Martin Hume has added thereto a scholarly introduction explaining the tragedy of that nine days' queendom in the light of England's relations with foreign Powers. No pains have been spared in the way of research, and the author claims to have consulted "every available document as well in our national archives and in private libraries as in those of foreign countries concerning Lady Jane and her friends and foes". Yet when we have read his volume we feel that only indirectly has any fresh light been thrown on the life and character of that unhappy girl, the "Bride of Lammermoor" (to quote his own description) of history. Our real knowledge of Jane's character and life before her accession to her throne of sorrows is mainly drawn from Roger Ascham's well-known letter, which has immortalised alike the unhappy child's love of study and the brutality of her parents. The letters of other "Reformers" no doubt show that she was being unmercifully crammed to fit her to become the Queen of the "young Josiah". It must, however, be regarded as doubtful if she were an intellectual prodigy. She possessed no doubt the love of culture common to most of the princesses of the Renaissance, and, like Mary and Elizabeth, she was conversant with Greek and Latin. That she may have learned a little Hebrew is also possible; but to suppose that she was acquainted with the "tongue of Chaldea" and the "language of Arabia" is ridiculous. It is more certain that the Calvinistic divines who surrounded her were doing their best, and not without success, to make her a narrow minded bigot, and it is terrible to think to what atrocities she might have been urged, if Northumberland had triumphed over Mary and established Jane's throne on a sure foundation. On her personal character, we agree with our author that if at first she appears strained and artificial, she displays later, in the culmination of her misery, a "sweetness of nature and pious sincerity that render her worthy of her fame". But we agree with him also when he adds: "There was a strain of obstinacy and even of coarseness in (her) character, which leads one to think that had she remained Queen, she might have displayed in later life many of the less pleasing peculiarities of her Tudor ancestors". There is, however, in this estimate of Jane's character nothing original, and it has been generally accepted by all whose minds are not obsessed by Puritan prejudices. Mr. Davey, however, does bring out two facts of considerable interest—namely that there is no historical reason for thinking that much sympathy ever existed between Jane and Edward VI., and that Jane herself never felt the least affection for Guildford Dudley, whom she only agreed to marry under the constraint of blows.

Turning from his heroine to her age, we find Mr. Davey always an interesting, but sometimes an inaccurate historian. He repeats the old scandal that Edward VI. was, in the last stage of his malady, handed over to a female quack. The tale is first told by Hayward, an untrustworthy writer who gives no authority for it. Likewise he vainly struggles to palliate Somerset's execution of his brother Thomas Seymour. Thomas Seymour was no doubt a rascal, though he did not treat Catherine Parr so cruelly as scandal said; but if he was in truth a traitor, why did the Lord Protector proceed against him by a bill of attainder instead of giving him a trial? It is useless to say that Seymour's life would have been spared if the Council had not dissuaded the Protector from granting him an interview. On the actual question whether or not Seymour should be executed the Council was, in fact, divided, only one-half its members signing the warrant. The fact that he had only half the Council with him on the matter did not prevent Somerset from ordering the execution.

A more serious criticism on the book is the false perspective in which the author sees the religious struggle. With much that he says on the evils of the Reformation we agree; but he is quite mistaken in his view that the religious differences were as clearly stereotyped in the reign of Edward VI. as they afterwards became. The protagonists in the drama were by no means as certain of their own position as he would have us suppose. Take Somerset and Gardiner, for example. The one appears in these pages as a Calvinist, the other as a Catholic. Yet it is practically certain that if the former had lived the first Prayer Book of Edward VI. would never have been altered; and it is also a fact that the latter offered to accept the same book and to enforce its use in his diocese. The real doctrinal cleavage came when the Zwinglian Prayer Book of 1552 was sanctioned by statute; but Mr. Davey nowhere recognises this fact. But on the foreign politics of the period the book is admirable, and we should have liked to dwell on Major Martin Hume's view of the attitude of foreign Courts to the Northumberland conspiracy. It is amazing to read that the Catholic Court of France was prepared to back the enterprise and the Catholic Emperor to acquiesce in it. It is a grim reflection on the astuteness of diplomacy to read that the diplomatists were laying odds in favour of Jane Grey and against Mary Tudor. When Mary raised her banner at Kenninghall her cousin the Emperor actually branded the enterprise as "strange, difficult, and dangerous".

If nothing became poor Jane so well as her death, there is nothing in this her last biography to compare with the description of her appearance on the scaffold on Tower Green. It avoids all extravagance; but it gives us a powerful presentment of a pathetic tragedy. Mr. Davey is a Roman Catholic, but he may claim to have given us a more beautiful picture of the martyrdom of the saint of Protestantism than any Protestant pencil ever drew.

A STATIC POET.

" New Poems." By William Watson. London: Lane. 1909. 5s. net.

IT is rather a nice point how far we may justly expect a poet in every new volume to " enhance ", as journalists say, " his reputation ". In this book there is nothing to enlarge and little (so far as the several pieces are concerned) to detract from our fixed conception of Mr. Watson's poetic gift. The question arises: Is such a verdict actually unfavourable? Are we justified in a sense of disappointment? On the whole, we think we are. Naturally, from a poet already so mature and finished in style as Mr. Watson, it would have been idle to expect such technical developments as we look for in new works by quite young writers of raw power. Nor could we demand from him a larger fund of passion than we know him to possess. His limits here have long been evident, and we have been glad to find the natural compensation in that charm of lucid austerity which alone makes him rare among contemporary versifiers. But we feel, when all is said, that a good deal of water has flowed since Mr. Watson began to sing. Nobody asks a poet to become the mirror of ephemeral scenes, nor to play chorus to brief dramas of the day. None the less, we are aware of a real movement in life, a movement below the surface of mere events; and this stir of a conscious age (if we may so put it) inevitably affects the standpoint and appetite of his readers, even if the poet himself remain aloof. Growth and adaptation are necessary conditions of life in the organic kingdom, and we believe they are necessary conditions in the career of a poet. For ourselves, at any rate, we cannot read these present poems without some sense of their inadequacy. They are, in a word, innutritious. Any pleasure they afford is only the moonlike reflection of sensations we tasted long ago, and more freshly, in the work of the same writer. The poems in this book please, as well-turned Latin verses please the scholar; no more. Our time is singularly barren of creative achievement in verse. It is not by any means barren of poetic feeling. The new great poets are yet to come, but nobody with a vivid sense of his own age can fail to be conscious that there is a new and vital poetry, as it were, in the air. Faint stirrings of an enlarged romantic impulse are very discernible in the imaginative writings of the time, short as they may fall of powerful expression. In certain lyrics by John Davidson, for example, we have noted—with all the flaws and eccentricities—an indubitable aroma of distinctively modern poetry. We could mention a dozen writers (most of them in prose, it is true; but this does not affect our argument) who reflect, however weakly or obscurely, an imagination which belongs quite characteristically to the present epoch. Our preference, therefore, as readers of current poetry, is for the experimental, even the crude, if only it seem to help us towards the incarnation in verse of fresh and present emotion. Mr. Watson's lines, " written in my copy of Tennyson ", embody unmistakably that standard of form and " good taste " by which we are all too apt to close new avenues of artistic sensation. His indictment of the " phrase-tormenting fantastic chorus " is true enough up to a point, but the positive suggestion (if the verses have any real point), that style in the Tennysonian sense should afford the model for young poets, is merely absurd. In another verse Mr. Watson anticipates ironically the verdict of critics who demand his " message " and his " aim ", and, on receiving the answer

" Mere honest work my mission is,
My message and my aim ",

dismiss the poet as " a man of words ". Here, in fact, he unconsciously condemns himself. " Mere honest work " is precisely what we do not want in our poets. It is quite as tedious and as worthless as didacticism itself. Contempt of the charlatan we are all ready to share, but the mood is a trifle outworn. In the actual verse of the present moment what appals the critic is not the success of charlatanism, but the vast output of conscientious, iterative stuff.

Many of the poems in this book at least suggest the incongruity of classical form and ostensibly modern topic. The address to America, for example, where praise of trans-Atlantic energy and resources is tempered by warning against luxury, can only leave us cold. Such admiration as we feel is for typical Watsonian lines like

" Not unforetold by deep parturient pangs "

where the ear is gratified by a sonorous dignity. This dignity, be it said, nowhere forsakes Mr. Watson. Tennyson at his best, and Milton, have passed into the blood of his style. One or two poems in a lighter vein we cannot particularly praise. The " Tavern Song ", for instance, despite a good deal of " Sing hey! " and " Sing ho! " has nothing romantically rollicksome. It is a scholar's exercise in convivial mirth. At his weakest Mr. Watson's thought is thin, and tinged with a vague " liberalism " of outlook which we find all too familiar.

" When whelmed are altar, priest, and creed,
When all the faiths have passed;
Perhaps, from darkening incense freed,
God may emerge at last."

There is also more than a touch of the nobly sorrowing, self-confessed sceptic—again one of those trite assets of rhymed Victorian sentiment with which at this date we willingly dispense.

On the whole, we turn from this volume with a reluctant but very definite sense that fidelity to an ideal of formal perfection is not enough. Static poets are out of place in a dynamic age. Style is the salt of poetry, no doubt, but we are not content that the salt should merely keep its savour. We require a basis of meat.

LITERARY NOTES.

Mr. D. Morgan's new novel, "It Never can Happen Again", will be published by Mr. Heinemann on Tuesday next. It will be in two volumes, uniform with the author's previous works, at the price of ten shillings, which is surely a long price even for a long novel. Does this mean that Mr. Heinemann is going to abandon his Library of Modern Fiction, with its small format and moderate price?

Mr. Ernest T. Thornton, who was one of the Englishmen employed by the Amir to start and superintend various factories in Afghanistan, has, with Mrs. Thornton, written a book describing their experiences. It will be published by Mr. Murray.

The first volume of "Oxford Studies in Social and Legal History", edited by Paul Vinogradoff, covering "English Monasteries on the Eve of the Dissolution", by Alexander Savine, and "Patronage in the Later Empire", by F. de Zulueta, is nearly ready for publication by the Clarendon Press.

Messrs. Smith Elder, in the course of a few days, will have ready "The Book of Flowers", by Katharine Tynan and Frances Maitland, and "George I. and the Northern War", by Mr. J. F. Chance, who has been to the archives at home and abroad for his material.

The fourth volume of the Cambridge History of English Literature, to appear in a day or two, will be "Prose and Poetry: Sir Thomas North to Michael Drayton."

On November 17 Mr. John Lane will publish "Lake Victoria to Khartoum with Rifle and Camera", by Captain F. A. Dickinson, with an introduction by Mr. Winston Churchill, and on the 24th "Dr. Johnson and Mrs. Thrale", by A. M. Broadley, with an introductory chapter by Thomas Seccombe.

"Inns and Taverns of Old London", by Mr. H. C. Shelley, is on Messrs. Pitman's new list.

Mr. John Long has ready a new and cheaper edition of "Matilda, Countess of Tuscany", by Mrs. Mary E. Huddy, said to be the only life of the Countess in English.

On Monday the West Strand Publishing Company will publish "The 'Saturday' Handbook", edited by the Hon. Gervase Beckett M.P. and Mr. Geoffrey Ellis. It will contain a letter from Mr. Balfour and contributions by many leading Unionists. The Handbook should be of considerable public interest just now, as well as value to Unionist workers.

MESSRS. BELL'S BOOKS.

With 48 full-page Illustrations and a Map. 8vo. **7s. 6d.** net.

SICILY THE GARDEN OF THE MEDITERRANEAN.

By WILL S. MONROE.
Author of "Turkey and the Turks," "In Vikingland," &c.

Now Ready. Fcap. 8vo. **6s.**

A HANDBOOK TO DANTE.

By F. J. SNELL, M.A.,
Late Scholar of Balliol College, Oxford,
Author of "The Age of Chaucer," &c.

This volume is uniform with Mrs. Sutherland Orr's well-known "Handbook to Browning," and Mr. Morton Luce's "Handbook to Tennyson" and "Handbook to Shakespeare."

MASTERS OF LITERATURE.

A Series of Handy Single Volumes, containing the Finest passages from the Works of the Greatest Prose Writers, with full Biographical and Critical Introduction and Editorial connections.
Crown 8vo. Illustrated, **3s. 6d.** net each.

NEW VOLUMES.

DEFOE. By JOHN MASEFIELD.
CARLYLE. By A. W. EVANS.
THACKERAY. By G. K. CHESTERTON. [*Ready Shortly.*
EMERSON. By G. H. PERRIS. [*Ready Shortly.*

"This series has the admirable purpose of saving the time of those readers whose aspirations towards general culture are handicapped by want of leisure. . . . Professors Grant and Saintsbury could hardly have done their work better. None of the character-studies and incidents selected can be regarded as inferior to the highest achievements of Scott or Fielding. . . . They should be helpful to a wide class of readers."—*Outlook.*

Write for Prospectus and Full List.

THE QUEEN'S TREASURES SERIES.

With 8 Coloured Plates and Decorated Title-page, Covers and End-papers. Small crown 8vo. **2s. 6d.** net each.

JUST PUBLISHED.

CRANFORD.

By Mrs. GASKELL. Illustrated by M. V. WHEELHOUSE.

Full List and Colour Plate on application.

BOHN'S CLASSICAL LIBRARY.

NEW VOLUMES.

Now Ready. **3s. 6d.**

THE PLAYS OF AESCHYLUS.

A New Prose Translation from a Revised Text by
WALTER HEADLAM, Litt.D., and
C. E. S. HEADLAM, M.A.

READY WEDNESDAY NEXT. Vol. I

THE ILIAD OF HOMER.

Newly translated into English Prose by E. H. BLAKENEY, M.A., Head Master of the King's School, Ely.
In 2 vols., **3s. 6d.** each. Vol. I. containing Books I.–XII.

A Complete List of Bohn's Libraries, which now include upwards of 800 Volumes, will be sent on application.

MR. FRANK HIRD'S NEW NOVEL. Cloth **6s.**

THE DEEPER STAIN.

By FRANK HIRD, Author of "King Fritz's A.D.C."

"Mr. Hird's new novel will maintain and increase his reputation, because its characterisation is strong and faithful, and its description vivid and true. Beatrice Stratton, the very type of noble womanhood, and her husband, John Haughton, the representative of so much that is admirable in British manhood, will remain among the great figures of fiction"—*Manchester Courier.*

THE WORLD'S AUTHORITY.

WEBSTER'S INTERNATIONAL DICTIONARY.

TWENTIENTH CENTURY EDITION.

With an Appendix of 25,000 Words, Phrases, and Definitions.

2,348 Pages. 5,000 Illustrations.
Bound in Sheepskin, £2.

Write for Detailed Prospectus, with specimen pages, hundreds of opinions from eminent men, prices of various styles of binding, and *particulars of the system of payment by easy instalments.*

London: GEORGE BELL & SONS, York House, Portugal Street, W.C.

THE BOOKS OF THE SEASON.

MODES AND MANNERS OF THE NINETEENTH CENTURY

As represented in the Pictures and Engravings of the Time. By Dr. OSCAR FISCHEL and MAX VON BOEHM. Translated by MARIAN EDWARDES. Square demy 8vo. 3 vols., in slipboard case, **21s.** net; silk moirette, **25s.** net. 600 Coloured and Half-Tone Illustrations of Old World Fashion. Of the 83 Coloured Illustrations, 77 are coloured by hand.

VOL. III. OF THIS IMPORTANT WORK.

CROWE & CAVALCASELLE'S NEW HISTORY of PAINTING in ITALY.

A Reprint of the Original Text Verbatim. Edited and supplemented with Notes by EDWARD HUTTON. At least 300 Reproductions of Pictures. To be completed in 3 vols. Vols. I. and II. now ready. The Second Volume deals with the Sienese School, and the first part of the Florentine School, and will be followed by Vol. III., completing the work. Demy 8vo. **£3** net per set.

MILTON'S COMUS.

From the Original MS. at Bridgwater House. Fcap. 4to. **12s. 6d.** net.

By the courtesy of the Earl of Ellesmere, Messrs. J. M. DENT & SONS are now preparing an Edition of this unique MS., which will be beautifully printed and richly illustrated.

HERO AND LEANDER.

By CHRISTOPHER MARLOWE. From the Rare Edition of 1584, in the British Museum. 500 copies only on Hand-made Paper, small 4to. bound in half-white morocco with parchment side. **12s. 6d.** net.

This edition of "Hero and Leander" is the first volume of the RENAISSANCE LIBRARY.

Printed in a type which has been specially designed by Mr. Joseph M. Dent after the type of the great Venetian printer Jenson.

In the RENAISSANCE LIBRARY some of the finest pieces of literature inspired by the Renaissance in the English, Italian, French, and Spanish tongues will be printed in the most beautiful form the Publishers have been able to devise.

LES CLASSIQUES FRANCAIS.

A Series in the Original French. With Photogravure Frontispiece. Post 8vo. cloth, **1s. 6d.** net; limp lambskin, **2s. 6d.** net.

NEW VOLUME. *Full List of Volumes on application.*

LES FABLES DE LA FONTAINE.

Préface de JULES CLARETIE, de l'Académie Française.

WHIMSIES.

By GEOFFREY WHITWORTH and KEITH HENDERSON. With 12 Coloured Drawings by the latter. Fcap. 4to. **6s.** net.

The coloured drawings by Mr. Keith Henderson, whose illustrations to the "Romaunt of the Rose" are well known, will make this one of the most beautiful artistic books of the year.

TREES AND SHRUBS OF THE BRITISH ISLES.

By C. S. COOPER, F.R.H.S., and W. PERCIVAL WESTELL, F.L.S. Over 550 Species of Trees and Shrubs are described. 16 Full-page Coloured Plates and 70 Black-and-White. 2 vols. **21s.** net, or in 16 parts at **1s.** net per part. Detailed Prospectus on application.

Binding Cases for the two Volumes are now ready, and may be obtained through any Bookseller. Price 4s. net for the two Cases.

THE SOUTH COUNTRY.

By EDWARD THOMAS. Small crown 8vo. **3s. 6d.** net.

Mr. Thomas in this new book gives his impressions of a year's wanderings afoot as the seasons change through Kent, Sussex, Hampshire, Wiltshire, and Devon. It is a prose-poem of the most beautiful counties in England.

To be followed shortly by "THE HEART OF ENGLAND," by the same Author, and "THE HISTORIC THAMES," by HILAIRE BELLOC, M.P.

NATURE STALKING FOR BOYS.

Through Field Glass, Stereoscope & Camera.

By W. PERCIVAL WESTELL, F.L.S. **With an Introduction for Boy Scouts by General Sir R. S. S. BADEN-POWELL, and Verses from a Patrol Song, by special permission of Mr. Rudyard Kipling.** Four Coloured Plates and 100 Photographic Illustrations. Chapter on Nature Photography by Rev. S. N. SEDGWICK, M.A. Crown 8vo. **3s. 6d.** net.

A specially made Stereoscope suitable for viewing the stereoscopic pictures in this book may be obtained through any bookseller complete in case, and with instructions how to use same, **9d.** net, or post free **10d.** Ask for Dent's Stereoscope.

NATURE PHOTOGRAPHY FOR BEGINNERS.

By E. J. BEDFORD. With Coloured Frontispiece, and about 100 Reproductions of Stereoscopic Photographs taken by the Author. Square demy 8vo. **7s. 6d.** net.

There are special chapters on the choice of suitable apparatus; hints on developing and printing, lantern-slide making, stereoscopic photography, choice of subjects, &c. An important feature is the series of stereoscopic illustrations which, by means of a simple stereoscope supplied with the book, can be viewed by the reader.

PROSPECTUSES OF ABOVE BOOKS MAY BE HAD ON APPLICATION.

J. M. DENT & SONS, Ltd.,
24 Aldine House, Bedford Street, London, W.C.

Printed for the Proprietors by SPOTTISWOODE & Co. LTD., 5 New-street Square, E.C., and Published by REGINALD WEBSTER PAGE, at the Office, 10 King Street, Covent Garden, in the Parish of St. Paul, in the County of London.—*Saturday*, 13 *November*, 1909.

THE

SATURDAY REVIEW

OF

POLITICS, LITERATURE, SCIENCE, AND ART.

No. 2,821 Vol. 108. 20 November 1909. [REGISTERED AS A NEWSPAPER.] 6d.

CONTENTS.

NOTES OF THE WEEK.

King Manuel's popular reception in this country was straight from the heart. Every foreign king, or even a president, is cheered, as courtesy and decent feeling require. But it was not courtesy, it was not good manners, nor anything of convention that made the people of England welcome the young King of Portugal. They felt with him and for him; they were glad to see him because truly and spontaneously they wished him well. The appeal of King Manuel's position is compelling. Youth burdened with tremendous responsibility has always its own claim, a claim that is seldom resisted. Added to this was the thought of the bitterness in which King Manuel's reign was born and the sentiment that his country was our oldest ally. English goodwill towards Portugal and Spain has never stood so high, we should say, certainly has never been so real, as now.

"But this is a revolt", said the King. "Sire", was the reply, "it is a revolution." The Radical press announces that the Revolution has already begun: "The House of Lords declares Civil War" it proclaims on its posters. Yet, look where we may, we scarcely can find signs of a revolt, let alone a revolution. Lord Lansdowne's alleged declaration of war is at any rate worded much more like a message of peace. Except to the inflamed imagination, it reads suspiciously like an entente between the peers and the people—the people which is supposed to be in a state of "sacred rage".

But what man of honesty or common-sense really believes in this talk of revolution and civil war? Party politics are extremely interesting and even exciting, a general election of great importance is close at hand, and there is uncertainty whether either side will emerge with a strong working majority. This seems a reasonable view of the position, and what sign of revolution or civil war is there in all this? No doubt beyond this there is the feeling that things may be very unstable and unsteadying for some time to come unless the Conservatives do come in with a clear working majority. That is a very serious consideration, and no thoughtful man can possibly make light of it. But there is no earthly menace of revolution in it.

Even were the rage of the Radicals as sacred as their papers profess, and even were they to get something of a majority, the "sweeping away" business would be out of the question. There are far too many brooms on the other side for that. If Paris in 1789 had been as conservative as London is in 1909—or even as it was in 1906, our lowest water-mark—there would have been no great upheaval. Birnam Wood may march to Dunsinane, but the Keltic fringe is not going to march to London and blow up the peers. Like the undergraduates of Jesus College, Oxford, at the end of term it has not enough nails in its boots.

Nor do we imagine that Manchester and the cotton workers of Lancashire are going to march there. There is really good sign that Mr. Balfour's speech and presence at Manchester, and the enthusiasm of the National Union meeting there, are affecting that part of the country. The speech and the occasion surely find the Unionist party well knit together and in good trim for the fight. It has never been Mr. Balfour's way to make the clarion note so loud as some party leaders have made it. He, no doubt, is better at harmony than at noise. And there was very little noise in his speech on Wednesday. But the enthusiasm which he rouses tends to be more felt and lasting.

The Chief Whip did well at the Manchester gathering to warn Unionists to "watch" the pensions question well. In party politics lies that are described as nailed to the counter have a habit of escaping none the less, and doing a vast deal of damage. And we are much afraid the pension lie is likely to get clear of its nail again between now and the polling. If it does not venture to show its face on the platform, it may make a sly house-to-house visitation. We should like to learn that absolutely effective steps are being taken at headquarters and elsewhere to shadow it. Why not a special constabulary of Conservatives to shadow it? It should be borne in mind that there are other people to watch in this matter besides Lord Advocates. As Easterns say: "It is easy to see the King of Hades but not one of his imps."

Nearly everybody seems to have spoken during the last week or so. It is a solemn duty a politician owes to himself to clinch matters just now by a big speech. It is not necessary to read all the speeches; whilst as for listening to them—well, the ear is the most delicate, exquisite of human organs, so exquisite a great man utterly denied even Evolution could have built it. The ear should be respected. Besides, the clever men are probably holding back their good things, their pointed and witty sayings, for a season when they will not be drowned in the welter of words. Here and there, however, there is a phrase worth noting. Mr. Runciman has been likening the Liberals and their colleagues in the House to the "Ark of Liberty". When the flood subsides, the animals will come out, we imagine, in pairs. We suspect some of them will be glad to get out, unless an arrangement has been made for keeping such fellow-voyagers as Mr. Grayson, Mr. Keir Hardie, and Mr. Snowden on the one hand, and the "Liberal Imperialist" section on the other, in water-tight compartments.

Mr. Churchill is to tour Lancashire as the star speaker of his party. Frantic, indeed, was the appeal to him of the Lancashire and Cheshire Liberal Federation—a signal of distress. Mr. Churchill responds gallantly: he will raise the two counties with pleasure, and to keep up their courage till he comes, he sends them a sample of his oratory beforehand. "Why should this small cluster of titled persons be set up to rule all the rest of us?" This indignation at a title is delightful in the grandson of a duke. And how many Liberals have objected to a title when they could get one? Did Lancashire Liberals object when Lord Shuttleworth was set up by a Liberal Government as one of the titled cluster to rule over them? Mr. Churchill must get up some better gibes than this.

Lord Lindley late in life finds himself discussing a very different doctrine of "tacking" from that known to him in earlier days as a conveyancer. His letter to the "Times" is on tacking as a constitutional doctrine applicable to the Budget Bill. It is interesting as showing how Judges would treat the question if the Government attempted to levy taxes on the mere resolution of the House of Commons without a Finance Act passed exactly like any other legislation. Lord Lindley admits the general convenience and expediency of the Lords passing Budget Bills. But here the case of tacking comes in. Lord Lindley, however, does not find his illustration of tacking in the valuation clauses. To him the Bill appears an obvious attempt to destroy private property in land and to redistribute wealth. This is the feature which distinguishes it from an ordinary Finance Bill, and makes it unreasonable to expect the House of Lords to pass it.

There is some public interest in the correspondence published this morning between Mr. Carlyon Bellairs and Sir Edgar Speyer. Mr. Bellairs said somewhere that Sir Edgar Speyer was the only one he could remember of the numerous important men of finance attached to the Liberal party in 1906 who had come forward to support the Budget. This is significant, and Sir Edgar Speyer does not dispute it; but he denies Mr. Bellairs' aside that Sir Edgar Speyer's "wealth is largely in America". Mr. Bellairs should have used the word "business" instead of "wealth"; then there could be no misunderstanding. Sir Edgar Speyer's property apart from his business is in England, and so is liable to the Budget taxation. But it is a fair and significant point that the most prominent City man to support the Budget has a business which is mainly non-British.

The compromise accepted by Mr. Birrell leaves the Irish Land Bill still harmless. Compulsion is restricted in area. It is subject to a court of appeal specially constituted which checks "the lawless men", those who shout "No Mayo man in Roscommon", and who work the League to intimidate the Congests from taking the land provided for them. The statutory definition of a congested holding is brought down from £10 to £5, and the seller under compulsion may appeal against a price that cannot yield his present income. The £14,000,000 of additional annuities which the peasants stand to pay for the disorder which discredits land stock remains as Mr. Birrell left it. In short, the Irish party have got nothing but the clauses that help to put an end to their existence as a party.

Yet there still seems an element of doubt about it. The Government are obviously content with the Bill as it left the Lords this week; but will Mr. Dillon, the Irish leader, accept it in its present form? Some Conservatives now say that they will not be sorry if the Bill fails to go through after all. The tremendous figures of Irish land purchase alarm them. The figures are certainly somewhat alarming, but they are not new, and it is years too late to pull up or go back on land purchase. We greatly hope, then, that the Bill will go through. The Lords can afford for several reasons to be lenient here, as they have been with the Town Planning Bill, which they have passed.

On Wednesday night at Dublin Mr. Redmond was heard in defence of the Parliamentary party, and stated the extra taxation on Ireland at one-fourth of the estimate made by people who had studied the matter, such as Mr. Healy and Mr. Arthur Samuels. He added also that "they would listen to Tariff Reform" if the people of England "gave us Home Rule, with the power of protecting our own industries against English competition"—which shows that he does not understand Tariff Reform, whether he expects Home Rule or not. The pretty thing in Mr. Redmond's Irish estimate of the increased taxation is that it applies to "next year", and not to the full working effect. They can see through this kind of oratory, even in Ireland, and in proportion as Irish public opinion ceases to be strictly private Mr. Redmond's party goes out of existence.

A section of the Unionist party in East Marylebone, having driven away Lord Robert Cecil to Blackburn, has succeeded in driving away Lord Charles Beresford to Portsmouth. And this has been achieved by a gentleman who, whatever his title to journalistic distinction, is in the political world "to fortune and to fame unknown". To be sure Mr. Jebb is supported by the "Morning Post", whose editor has told us in the "Twentieth Century" (or is it the "Nineteenth"?) that Tariff Reformers will use any party to effect their end—the Unionist or another. Well, we hope Messrs. Ware and Jebb are satisfied with their handiwork in driving East Marylebone to distraction, possibly into the power of the Radicals. What we want to know is whether the friends of Lord Robert Cecil and Lord Charles Beresford will meekly accept a candidate who, after depriving them of the services of two really distinguished men, presents himself as the One Man Needful for East Marylebone? The intolerable presumption of the thing is not atoned for by canting about "folk-moots" and "straightforward politics".

However, Portsmouth is obviously the right place for Lord Charles Beresford. If ever round peg were in round hole, it should be Lord Charles Beresford as candidate for Portsmouth. This should have the double good effect of securing the seat for the Unionist party and putting the naval question in the forefront. There is some risk of more burning questions smothering the Navy in this election. At any rate, it will now have its proper place in the Portsmouth campaign. We can hardly doubt that Lord Charles will be able to carry with him the second Unionist candidate at the General Election.

Lord Milner, at any rate, does not see the Empire all couleur de rose. He knows perhaps more about the British nation throughout the world than any other Englishman, and he urges a new departure in imperial policy; "or you may have no Empire to consolidate". To carry Tariff Reform "in the end" will not do; it must be done before it is too late. We are glad that at Poole on Tuesday he disagreed with those who would have had the Lords pass the Budget that the country might get a sickener of Radical finance. This " savours too much of mere party politics ". Still more serious, the country cannot afford a year of this Budget merely to be made sick of it. It is too expensive an experiment.

Sir Wilfrid Laurier, in his reply on the address on Monday, put Mr. Monk, the anti-imperial Canadian Conservative, in his place with much vigour. The sentiments expressed by Sir Wilfrid towards the Empire and the British connexion were unexceptionable, and the Empire will be grateful to him for his testimonial to its good influence and greatness. These were all generalities. There was one little particular—concrete policy—which did not quite agree with these imperial sentiments. " Canada would have a navy, and that navy would not go to war unless the Parliament of Canada chose to send it." This is flat separatism. A navy on which the Imperial Government cannot count in a war with a foreign country is no part of an Imperial Navy; it is not imperial in any sense. It is a local force that has no more essential connexion with the Empire than a foreign navy. It is said that Australia too is thinking of a local navy unattached to the Empire. These are not pleasant signs.

The attempt to kill Lord Minto is a telling commentary upon the views of those who see in concession the great exorcist of revolution. Never through history has revolution been exorcised by concession. Moreover, the really clear-sighted revolutionary will always admit that, as revolution is only justified by success, so may it be legitimately quelled by the force which is greater than the force to which it appeals. That Lord Minto should have been attacked at the moment when the reforms towards which he has now been working for three years were on the point of promulgation is a frank invitation to the Executive on the part of the anarchist agitators to use what force it has to put them down. Should there be the least hesitation in accepting the challenge, the Executive knows what it may expect. Something different from concession, or from mild judicial process, is required. The anarchists have appealed to force. Let the appeal be allowed.

The reforms themselves, on the face of them, bear witness to the obstacles that lie in the way of their fulfilment. The framework of the scheme that determines in the new constitution the balance of Moslem and Hindu shows by its very artificiality that it has come from above, and that no practicable scheme could come from anywhere else. It is a workmanlike piece of occasional legislation. Suppose that an organic scheme, framed on general principles, were suddenly flung down to take its chance, and that the British Government were to retire to watch what ensued, the result would be not self-government but anarchy. The greatest responsibility that the British have to face in India is that of holding the balance between the two great sections of the Indian community, and of guiding them through that period of fusion which must precede any real self-government. If Great Britain had no other justification for her Indian Empire, it would be found in this—that, if to-day she abandoned her trust, either the Hindu or the Mohammedan would call her back to-morrow.

We are glad that Lord Ampthill had the courage to bring up once more the scandal of the treatment British Indians receive in the Transvaal. This is a sore in the imperial body politic from which the Government likes to avert its eyes; it is an unpleasant thing: therefore not to be talked about. It is enough merely to state the fact that the Transvaal refuses to British Indian subjects the elementary right of admission which it gives without restriction to Germans, Frenchmen, and foreigners generally. That the Imperial Government acquiesces in this proves that it is not an imperial government at all; if it cannot help acquiescing, it is a farce to talk of a British Empire. Nothing could be lamer than Lord Crewe's attempt at an apology. This thing has come to a head under a Liberal Government, whose stock-in-trade is humanitarianism. It is the old story—those who take humanity under their wing cannot find room for their own people.

The Shah, Sultan Ahmed, opened the Mejliss on Monday. The people, we are told, took the celebration with Oriental calm; but then, the people were not admitted. The Cabinet has resigned and will probably be re-nominated. In any case it does not matter. Nasr-ul-Mulk knows that the best place inside the Cabinet is not half so good as a place outside. So he will stay out in order that he may serve the Government. The Speech from the Throne was splendidly cheerful. Among other things it stated that " the relations of Persia with the foreign Powers were excellent, the only unsatisfactory feature in the situation being the presence of foreign troops in the country ".

Jamaica has again been visited by a natural calamity, this time a storm. Jamaica would really seem to be the sport of Nature. Yet the impression would be quite a wrong one. We here are apt to forget that these portents are placarded big before us, while the ordinary quiet time is unnoticed. We read of a terrific earthquake there, and then forget Jamaica until, may be years later, we read of a storm. This is very unfair and may be actually injurious to the island. The truth is that Jamaica is in most ways an island of the Blest, these disasters being no commoner than the hundred-and-one accidents one is liable to every day he steps out of his house in London. But these things in Jamaica are on so terrific a scale that one cannot forget them. Let a man be killed by a motor car in London and it is forgotten the next morning.

We were taken to task the other day for saying the Americans were no more civilised than the Japanese. The Japanese, we admit, might object; but, in the light of the following little incident, should the Americans? The other day in Knoxville, Mississippi, a negro, supposed to be an incendiary, was burned alive, and his daughter, rushing out to save her father, was shot. " The town ", we read, " is divided in opinion over the question whether Dunmore [the burnt nigger] should have been burned alive on the charge of arson without having had the opportunity of trial."

Purity is booming in the States. Now Mr. Hearst has purified New York, Mr. Taft is starting an inquiry into the frauds of the Sugar Trust, in which it is suspected that some of the highest officials in Mr. Roosevelt's Government and in the present took a hand. Even Congress, which resented Mr. Roosevelt's detectives inquiring too curiously into its members' proceedings, is going to help Mr. Taft; nominally at least. There is always the possibility that a Congress Committee may side-track instead of helping him. The Sugar Trust has defrauded the State of £400,000 by short weighing of its imports; and it has been made to refund that amount. The joint frauds of the Trust and the officials are now known as the Sugar Trust scandals, and the papers are making charges at large against officials. This is Mr. Taft's premier essai against the Trusts. Will he do better than Mr. Roosevelt did?

Inconvenience is already being felt in this country from the New South Wales coal strike. More than inconvenience will be felt if the strike continues. Mail steamers to Australia have to provide their own coal, and as this reduces the cargo room the Conference Lines are hinting that they will expect twenty-five per cent. more for freights. This is the first effect on merchants, and if they do not anticipate worse results, it is only because they believe that the strike is so disastrous to Australia itself that it must soon be ended.

It does not appear yet that the New South Wales Government has effected anything since last week. It still talks of the public interest demanding resumption of work before a conference. But neither persuasion nor threats seem to have had any effect. The criminal provisions of the Industrial Disputes Act have been applied neither to masters nor to men. There has been a resolution in the Legislative Assembly to nationalise a sufficient number of the mines to meet pressing requirements. It was defeated as an impossible project; and, as Mr. Wade, the Premier, said, the public would be no more secure against strikes, as the miners in the national mines would be as likely to strike as the others.

Really the life of a French deputy cannot be worth living. A week ago he had to vote against something he wanted; now he is asked to vote for something he does not want. What with M. Briand and his colleagues on the one hand and a crowd of irate constituents on the other, a French deputy cannot call his soul his own. Perhaps he does not want to do anything of the kind, for he seems to enjoy himself in his own way. Once again M. Briand is making a stand, and of course he will be successful. M. Cochery, his Minister of Finance, wants the taxes on alcohol and tobacco. M. Briand asserts that he will support M. Cochery, and that his Ministry shall stand or fall by the result. None of the deputies wants to face his constituents, which he must do presently, with any of these unpopular proposals. Why not issue Treasury bonds, and wait for the shelved income-tax? That must be as M. Briand will have it. Well, the French deputy is paid to suffer these discomforts.

An international map is not one of those things which come very close to men—international star maps perhaps still less; yet, almost unobserved by the mundane, these did come into existence some years ago. Now the geographers are resolved to be as completely equipped as the astronomers, and it may have been noticed that the delegates of numerous European Governments have been holding a conference in London this week to discuss this very esoteric subject. When it appears, it will be a luxury that most of us will cheerfully deny ourselves. There is nothing in the book-line more aggravating than a huge unwieldy atlas. Yet the conference is a good sign; we are living in a world so peaceful that the only international trouble is the lack of an international map. This conference too knows what it wants and can do it; an honourable distinction from peace conferences and social science and teachers' palavers.

It is something of a disgrace to Europe that the Hermes of Praxiteles should be housed in a building that may collapse upon it at any moment. The museum at Olympia has been twice repaired, and is again unsafe. The arguments against having the statue removed altogether are not very strong. Of course King George has pledged his word that Olympia shall not be robbed, and sentimental Hellenists will talk of vandalism if any sensible suggestion of the kind is put forward. But it is better that the Hermes should be safely lodged in Athens, or even in the British Museum, than that it should gloriously perish at Olympia. However, the museum at Olympia is to be patched up again, to which end the Greek Archæological Society is contributing £400; so that local feeling will not be outraged. The Hermes must be an undoubted "attraction".

Lady Gregory carries the comical criticism of Irish life a delightful step farther in "The Image", put on in Dublin last week at the Abbey Theatre. Two (Irish) whales, fighting, get stranded, and instead of annexing the treasure the people talk about it until the next tide runs away with one of the whales. The other leaves a sum of money, and the district council decides to put up a statue with it, but to whom? Great Irishmen are always so much greater than one another that no two of the people can agree. Some are for O'Connell, some for Parnell, and some for others, but everybody is afraid to mention his choice. Then comes the village fool pleading for "Hugh O'Laura". Who was he? Nobody knows, not even the fool; but the vote is by ballot, and O'Laura gets the statue, because every voter is afraid to vote as he thinks. Then it turns out that O'Laura is a character in a book, a book which nobody had read, not even the fool.

MR. BALFOUR AND LANCASHIRE.

"WHAT Lancashire thinks to-day, England will think to-morrow" used to be a saying when the cotton trade was a larger part of the industrial production of Great Britain than it is to-day. London and Lancashire still remain the most important electoral pivots, on which very many votes turn. Of London we are practically assured: the Unionists will sweep the Metropolitan board. Lancashire still remains something of an enigma, because, so it is said, employers and employees in its staple industry are dubious about Tariff Reform. We believe the truth to be that it is only the employers who are hesitating. The working classes, with a keener because a narrower perception, have, as to the majority, made up their minds to go for Tariff Reform. Be this true or not, Mr. Balfour, finding himself once more in the capital of Lancashire, was bound to address himself to the relation between Tariff Reform and the cotton trade. But before dealing with cotton Mr. Balfour turned aside to touch on the wider and more important question of the cost of living for all the working classes. It is one of the strongest points made by the free importers that you cannot have colonial preference without taxing food, and that you cannot tax food without increasing the cost of living to the working man. It is true that you cannot have colonial preference without taxing food; but it is not true that you cannot shift the taxes from one kind of food to another without increasing the daily budget of the labourer. Mr. Balfour repeated on Wednesday at Manchester what he said a year ago at Birmingham. "Certainly I should never have touched Tariff Reform: I should never have given my adhesion to any fiscal change of importance which was either calculated to or could increase the cost of living, the ordinary budget expenditure of the working classes of this country". We take this to mean that in dealing with the taxes on food neither an increase nor a decrease of taxation is sought. It is not by colonial preference that it is intended to widen the basis of taxation: what is aimed at is such a readjustment of taxes as shall enable us to give our colonies a preference for their corn and meat and dairy produce, while leaving the amount of revenue the same. New commodities will be laid under tribute; but the proportion of contribution will be undisturbed. We collect at the ports to-day £13,510,000 on tea, sugar, coffee, currants, cocoa, plums, prunes, raisins, figs, and chicory. Is there any reason, in principle or practice, why a portion of the duties on tea and sugar should not be transferred to the butter and eggs which we import in such enormous quantities from Denmark, Russia, and France? Russia taxes British goods on an average 130 per cent. of their value. In return we admit Russian eggs and butter duty free, while we tax the tea grown in India and Ceylon 50 per cent. of its value. Where is the sense in this? The policy is the more mad because in the case of tea the consumer pays the whole duty, as there is no competing supply. In the case of dairy produce Russia, Denmark, and France are all competing with one another and with the farmers of the United Kingdom, of Canada, of Australia, and of New Zealand. It is, therefore, as certain as anything can be in economics that duties on foreign dairy produce would, in part if not wholly, be paid by the foreign farmers. Meat, we admit, is a more difficult subject for taxation because in a northern climate it is more prized as an article of food than butter and eggs. Chicago competes with Smithfield; and the American Beef Trust is so rich that it would certainly pay a 5-per-cent. duty in order to keep its place in our market. If the Trust kept its place in Great Britain, this would not benefit Canada or Australia; but we should get the revenue to replace the reductions on tea and sugar and coffee and currants and cocoa, and the price of meat would not be raised. As for Argentine meat supplies, they are, we understand, practically in the hands of the American Beef Trust, or soon will be. If it is clearly understood that no increase of revenue is sought from food, but such a re-arrangement of duties as shall benefit the colonies, the cost-of-living argument presents no difficulty.

Having once more reassured the country on the question of cost of living, Mr. Balfour turned to the cotton trade in its relation to Tariff Reform, scoring a good point immediately. He was told and he had read, said the Unionist leader, that it was feared that Tariff Reform would increase the cost of production, a fear which is expressed in this fashion. We must on no account handicap ourselves by our tariff, exclaim the Free Trade Lancastrians, because we should then be beaten in the neutral and Eastern markets by our competitors. Who are these successful and dreaded rivals? They are the Germans, the French, and the Americans, who are all working under tariffs much higher than any contemplated by the Unionist party. If these competitors, who are ousting us from the colonial and Eastern markets, are not hampered, but apparently assisted by the tariff wall, what is Lancashire afraid of? Two other points Mr. Balfour made in connexion with the cotton trade which must have gone home to the business and the bosoms of his hearers. One was as to the future supply of the raw material; the other as to future competition in the Far East. It is dangerous for Lancashire to depend entirely for her supply of cotton on the United States, which will one day consume their own cotton. It is most necessary to develop new fields of supply in Africa and Egypt, as may easily be done. As to future competitors in the Far East, can Lancashire afford to neglect the case of Japan? Suppose Japan takes to manufacturing and exporting cotton goods, while keeping out our cotton goods by prohibitive duties, Lancashire would then find a retaliatory tariff necessary for self-defence.

Passing from Tariff Reform to the Budget, Mr. Balfour summed it up in the phrase "Bad finance and muddle-headed socialism". It is not easy to say anything new about the Finance Bill, but the land taxes gave Mr. Balfour an opportunity to open his policy of peasant-proprietorship. So far from agreeing that land should be transferred from its present owners to a department of the State, Mr. Balfour declares that if it is to be transferred at all it must be from the present to a large class of owners. It is true that if it had not been for the principle of private property in land, the North American continent would not have been cultivated, and become the richest country in the world. "Let Lancashire and let Britain beware of anything which shall render a man insecure in the possession of that which he has honourably acquired by honourable means and invested in legal investments" is a warning which, if not exactly novel, is still needed at this hour. We see that Mr. Balfour abandoned the position that the House of Lords has "co-equal authority" with the House of Commons. A second chamber exists for the purpose of seeing that on great issues the policy which is pursued is not the policy of a temporary majority elected for a different purpose, but represents the sovereign convictions of the people—such is Mr. Balfour's definition of the bicameral system. "If the action ends in disaster, the country, and the country alone, will have to bear the responsibility." We are not sure that Mr. Balfour and Lord Lansdowne are not pushing a little too far their principle that the whole weight of responsibility must be placed on the shoulders of the electors. The people are very ignorant, and have little or no time to study conundrums in taxation and socialism. Is not a portion of the responsibility on the statesmen who govern or advise them?

But Mr. Balfour was no doubt thinking less of moral responsibility than of ultimate power. In the long run the country and the country only can decide. Parliament is plenipotentiary, but not the House of Commons by itself. Parliament with the Crown makes a political trinity, and unless all its three constituents agree, the unity, in which alone is the power, collapses. The Liberal attempt to represent the House of Commons as the nation's lawful master is wrong both in law and fact. In fact we have gradually been getting away for many years from the representative theory. The electorate does not now periodically select political trustees to take over all their public interests and manage them on their behalf. Members of Parliament have become bare trustees: the country decides its own policy and keeps things in its own hands, watching its servants in Parliament very narrowly, and by no means standing aside from one election to another. The House of Lords is acting thoroughly in the spirit of the times in looking to the country more than to the House of Commons. Mr. Haldane evidently recognises this, and in his speech to the Eighty Club did not magnify the House of Commons as less astute Liberal advocates are wont to do. He came rather to the real point, and disputed the Lords' interpretation of the country's will. Well, the fact stands that Mr. Haldane and his leader and colleagues have not dared to take the view of the country on any of the Lords' proceedings during this Parliament; proceedings which he says cannot even be perverted into an expression of the electors' will. And they go to the country now simply because they cannot help themselves. Were any other than a Budget Bill in point, they would still avoid the electors. The Radical halfpenny papers placarded "Mr. Haldane's fighting speech"; but he is too much of a philosopher to make a fighting speech. Evidently, from this speech alone, he has great doubts about the whole business.

INDIA—THE PRELUDE TO REFORM.

THE Indian "Reform" scheme, published in its final form this week, was planned by Lord Minto three full years ago. On the very eve of its introduction an attempt has been made to murder its author. This sinister act is not a mere coincidence. It is the protest of the revolutionary party against any constitutional reform which leaves the British Government the de facto ruler of India. In this it confirms the history of the past three years. The first indication of the measure was followed by a demand on the part of the Congress through its President that the entire administration of the country—civil, financial and military—should be handed over to the natives of India. Emissaries were to be sent to every nook and corner of the country to preach this doctrine. The results prove the nature of the propaganda. The next three years, while the scheme was under discussion in India and in England, were marked by a series of riots and outrages directed against officials both Indian and European. Later on the sphere of operations was extended. A member of the Indian Council was assaulted in London by an Indian student, and the passing of the Councils Bill was followed by the murder of Sir Curzon Wyllie. Now the completion of Lord Minto's work is marked by an attempt to take his life. The lesson is clear and oft repeated. No concessions and no reforms will check a revolutionary conspiracy which has for its avowed object the overthrow of British rule. Force can only be met in one way—by greater force. Nor will it be suppressed by judicial proceedings. The trial of the Calcutta conspirators of May 1908 has not yet come to an end. The removal of the leaders, who are generally well known, and the break-up of their organisation is the only effective method. If "Reform" must be, the measures now published are good in their way. They may even produce great results if they are prudently and impartially worked, and if their privileges and obligations are not abused by those now called to administer them for the good of their countrymen. In any case the new regulations are now an accomplished fact, and it remains for all parties to join in securing them a fair and efficient trial. But they cannot take the place of executive action.

In the years of development, discussion and debate which have given it final shape the scheme has lost many of its original features. The Imperial Advisory Council and its analogues in the provinces have disappeared. They perished unwept. In their place has sprung up a scheme for Provincial Executive Councils—the most objectionable and dangerous feature of the measure as it now stands. Surely the history of recent events from Muzzaffarpur to Ahmadabad shows the danger of weakening the executive authority. The original constitution of the Legislative Councils, the number of their members, the methods of election and appointment, the procedure and the scope of authority—have all undergone material modification. In most respects the changes have been for the better. This cannot with any confidence be said of the step which deprives Provincial Councils of their official majority—an innovation which is opposed to expert advice. It is to be safeguarded by the power of veto and an official majority in the Viceroy's Council. The position is a false one. The frequent use of such safeguards would in itself become a cause of discontent and danger. It can be only irritating to appoint advisers and overrule their advice. These objections apply with even more force to the appointment of Indians to the various Executive Councils, notably that of the Viceroy himself, in which resides the supreme sovereign power in India.

Judging by what has recently happened, it seems safe to predict that immediate controversy will turn on the question of Mohammedan representation. So far back as October 1906 the Indian Mohammedans formulated two demands—first, that the number of their representatives must not be based merely on their numerical strength, but must take account also of their political importance and their services to the Empire. In the second place, every Mohammedan must be chosen by a purely Moslem electorate. Appointment by nomination would not satisfy their claims. These principles were fully admitted by Lord Minto, who gave a definite promise that they would be observed, and later by Lord Morley, who undertook that the promise would be met in full. This decision was received with dissatisfaction by the Hindu—or non-Moslem—leaders, who object to special favour being shown to the Mohammedan community. Thus a position of considerable bitterness and constraint has been created. Lord Minto has, however, firmly held to his undertaking, and successfully opposed even a very moderate and modified form of mixed electorate in a particular case. The result is that out of sixty-eight members of the Viceroy's Council eight are to be Mohammedans. Of these, six will eventually be chosen by Mohammedan provincial electorates and two by Mohammedan landowners of four different provinces in alternate Councils. To the eight so elected a ninth may be added by the Viceroy's nomination of a Moslem from the North-West Frontier province. In addition to this, the Mohammedans are eligible for and have their chance of election or nomination to all the other seats, official and non-official. On the population basis they would be entitled to only six of the elective seats. They have therefore reason to be very fully satisfied. Their leaders have recognised this, though not always with effusive gratitude. In the struggle for favour it is not always diplomatic to admit you have got all you wanted and more than you asked. Whether the arrangement will be accepted by the Hindu party without remonstrance is more than doubtful. Special favour to Moslems has been denounced in advance; those who wish to keep agitation alive will find in it a weapon ready to their hands. Moreover, there is a section among Mohammedans themselves who oppose the system. They do not wish to be treated as a class apart as though they were foreigners having no common interest with the rest of the population. They see a loss of dignity and status in being treated as though they were a special "interest" like a Chamber of Commerce or a small community such as Jews, Parsis or native Christians. They hold that a truer and nobler position would be that of independent citizens acting with their fellows as a powerful section of a great community. They further see in this class distinction the perpetuation of class hatred and dissension. It cannot be denied that there is force in these contentions. But the Mohammedans as a whole presumably know their own interests best, and they are resolutely opposed to leaving these in the hands of non-Moslem majorities whom they mistrust.

PORTUGAL AND THE ENGLISH EXAMPLE.

KING DOM MANUEL is a good enough linguist to read an English journal and an earnest enough thinker to ponder what he reads. One would gladly give more than the proverbial penny to have his thoughts upon the piece of news which has relegated even his own personality to a second place in the public mind. Only a night and a day after the young King's foot first touched English earth at Portsmouth it was known that Lord Lansdowne had disclosed his amendment to the Finance Bill and that one more hot and bitter struggle is to rage around the British Constitution. As an hereditary Chief of State the Portuguese King can hardly be indifferent to the fact that the hereditary principle is about to be challenged and assaulted in the very country where it has worked most fruitfully for the general weal. And, if he be well informed, he must know that the attack on non-elective authority in England is going to be pressed very far. It is true that, up to the present, there has been little open treason talked against the Throne, and that only one member of Parliament has publicly prophesied how, in a certain event, "the People" will "throw the crown after the coronets" into one common scrap-heap of discarded mediæval absurdities. But every keen-eyed, sharp-eared observer knows that the men who are pushing on the so-called Liberal leaders from behind cherish ultimate political ideals not widely different from those of the Portuguese Republicans whose ill-timed and unpatriotic agitation is the principal peril not only to the Bragança dynasty but to the very existence of independent Portugal.

A constitutional monarch cannot discuss the Constitution. But if King Manuel were free to tell us his mind he might have some timely and useful things to say about this British constitutional crisis which has synchronised with his visit. Although it was not till last Monday that he completed his twentieth year, Dom Manuel must no longer be thought of as a boy-king. For nearly two years he has ruled Portugal; and as four successive Portuguese Ministries have waxed and waned since he ascended the throne this serious young king has already stored up much knowledge of men and things. He has learned, above all, that the chief sorrows of his country flow from certain political conditions which, if we do not take care, may speedily reproduce themselves in Great Britain.

The curse of Portugal is the immense preoccupation of her people with the game of politics. Cities of less than seven thousand inhabitants often boast as many as half a dozen political newspapers whose main business is to excel one another in envy, hatred, malice and all uncharitableness. Even towns which we should call villages have their raucous Wednesday "Voice" and their scorching Saturday "Light". When the last lying word of these rags has been read, scores of the male townsmen assemble round the barbers' shops waiting for the ampler supplies of still more highly spiced vituperation provided by the closely printed halfpenny papers of Lisbon and Oporto. Worse follows. This game of politics, like our own game of football, has bred a plague of professionalism. A hungry horde of the least patriotic men in the country busily exploit the people's concern for their fatherland's prosperity and burden the community with a grossly over-manned body of non-producing political teachers and preachers. As a consequence parliamentary life is poisoned. Like certain school-teachers in England who are always discussing their pensions and promotions and privileges, with never a word about the interests of their pupils, so the majority of Portuguese deputies are incessantly bent towards their own private ends. Until the general election of last year some of them had never set foot in their constituencies. They abode snugly in Lisbon, battening upon the rural toilers more shamelessly than any of the old-régime aristocrats and courtiers whose tyranny was supposed to have withered for ever in the pure white ray of democratic institutions.

This obsession with partisan politics on all the three hundred and sixty-five days of the year is so imminent a danger for England that even little Portugal, despite many differences in the conditions, may fairly be held up as a warning. Nowadays our Imperial Parliament sits nearly all the year round. Editors have no longer to provide silly-seasonals for their readers while August dust thickens softly upon the deserted benches at S. Stephen's. And as a result of the demands now made by parliamentary life it may easily come to pass that there will be a stoppage in the supply of those fairly disinterested men who, whatever their faults, have framed the justest laws in the world during the few months of each year which they could spare, without fee or reward, from other occupations. In their places we shall have more and more of the professional politicians whose livelihood is won by going every day to work at the House of Commons as clerks go to work from nine till six in counting-houses. The trail of this political professionalism already lies unlovely over too many of the parliamentary paragraphs and lobby notes in certain Radical newspapers. With direct money stakes to be played for, our players must degenerate, like Portugal's. Indeed, in one respect we may be worse off than the Portuguese; for it is more essential to an English member of Parliament than to a Portuguese deputy that he should flatter his particular constituency by smartness and pushfulness.

With this shadow hanging over our House of Commons King Manuel would be rightly astounded if he saw his oldest friend and ally beginning to trifle away the safeguard which England, unlike Portugal, happily enjoys; namely, an effective House of Lords. The "Peers of the Kingdom" who form Portugal's upper legislative House are not necessarily peers in the sense of Burke and Debrett. They are less like our House of Lords than like life senators. Many of them, no doubt, are able and high-principled men; but, as a House, they lack the prestige and the traditions of wisdom which have often restrained England from following her demagogues into headlong deeds of iconoclasm such as she would regret but could never repair. This is the conviction of many a thoughtful Portuguese Liberal who, while scouting our hereditary House in theory, envies us its possession in practice. If such a Portuguese could speak to us at this moment, he would tell us that the great democratic superstition has been weighed in Portugal and found wanting; that a people can be cheated and oppressed as much by deputies and senators and presidents as by nobles and prelates and kings; and that, whatever theory may say, practice and experience prove the need for a twining and plaiting together of the elective and the non-elective powers.

It is to England that King Manuel and his people look for the perpetuation of their independence and for the inviolability of their colonial empire. It is with England, as the King significantly said at the Guildhall, that Portugal covets the best of all possible financial and commercial relations. Portuguese eyes are fixed at this moment with exceptional steadfastness upon the splendid equipoise of our institutions. With Portugal our example counts for much; and we shall do the little kingdom a poor service if we surrender one pin's-weight to those sham democrats who take the great name of liberty in vain.

ISVOLSKY v. AERENTHAL.

THE ill-tempered controversy between the Russian and Austro-Hungarian Foreign Ministers continues and shows no signs of coming to an end. The Press of all countries is summoned to give its aid. A leading English review opens its pages to the combatants, who are represented by writers disguised under phrases both obscure and inaccurate, and they are replied to by official scribes in S. Petersburg and Vienna. All this fuss both amuses and embarrasses Europe. The world cannot say to the leading statesmen of two Great Powers as Beatrice does to Benedick: "What! are you still talking? Nobody marks you". Unfortunately, heartily sick of the subject though we be, we have to mark them, for the Eastern Question is never settled and under present conditions may break out at any moment from several quarters. Greece is unsettled, Turkey suspicious, and Servia raging. The only thing which can firmly suppress the tendency to internecine war is a firm agreement between Russia and Austria; yet we find their Foreign Ministers still raining upon one another jeers and flouts, day after day, and endeavouring to convict one another of insincerity. As if anyone cared at this time, except the historian or the journalist, whether M. Isvolsky or Count Aerenthal first proposed to the other that they should make a bargain behind the back of Europe!

Something more than mere pique at a reverse in the political arena must be sought as the motive for this revival of controversy. If diplomatic rumour is to be credited, Count von Aerenthal has never forgiven M. Isvolsky for a defeat in other fields than those of diplomacy. He, however, might well rest content with the success of his Bosnian coup. M. Isvolsky recently got in a nasty return blow in the Tsar's ostentatious courtesies to Italy and avoidance of Austria. There surely the matter might well have been allowed to remain; but it has only proved the opening for a new wrangle which emphasises the estrangement of the two Powers.

No one will accept implicitly the statements of either side, which may well be affected by unconscious bias, and in such situations usually are. Whether Count von Aerenthal proved more slim than M. Isvolsky, or events worked for him more than for his rival, it is very difficult to determine. The story as told by both sides up to a certain point agrees. It is admitted that an agreement was made at Buchlau that in return for Austria's annexation of the provinces Russia should receive Austrian support in raising the question of the Dardanelles. Bulgaria was also to receive support in her declaration of independence, which was to be considered as her compensation for the action of the two Great Powers. The Russian version is that this agreement was hypothetical; the Austrian, that it was definite and positive. This is the kind of dispute which may easily arise between two perfectly honourable men when a question in discussion is not put into writing. The declaration of Bulgarian independence unfortunately precipitated matters and Austria acted at once. On 7 October the Heads of the European States received the official announcement of the Austrian Emperor's annexation manifesto. According to an Austrian account the Austro-Hungarian Foreign Minister had utilised the time since the Buchlau meeting in practical preparation for the coup already agreed upon while M. Isvolsky was comfortably touring round Europe interviewing various Foreign Ministers. Russia was therefore quite unprepared to deal her stroke and to attempt to solve the Dardanelles question in her own favour. A distinct contradiction takes place here. M. Isvolsky states that Count von Aerenthal promised him "considerable previous notice" of the date of annexation. Whether this was a misunderstanding or not, who can tell? In any case the Austrian reply is that the precipitate proclamation of Bulgarian independence forced their Foreign Office to act at once. The Russian retort is in effect that the action of Bulgaria was all engineered in Vienna and that the fact of the approaching Bulgarian declaration and its date were all communicated to if not arranged by the Austro-Hungarian Foreign Office itself. Whether this be so or not is really immaterial so far as Europe is concerned, for after all it does not matter much to the rest of the Powers whether Austria alone or Austria and Russia together were secretly preparing a surprise. It may well have been that Count von Aerenthal was convinced that certain of the Powers, ourselves assuredly, would never consent to the opening of the Dardanelles. It is impossible to believe that Austria's ally Germany could have viewed with equanimity any such disturbance of the existing balance of power in those regions. With her present views as to Eastern policy Germany could never consent to place Constantinople permanently at the mercy of Russia. It is not credible, therefore, that Austria could have believed that Europe would consent to a settlement such as M. Isvolsky desired. It is equally incredible that M. Isvolsky could have thought it possible that either England or Germany would assent to the proposal. If the Russian Foreign Minister ever seriously thought he could persuade Europe to consent to Russia receiving such "compensation", it shows a degree either of vanity or naïveté which easily explains his opponent's victory.

The only feature of the case we regret is that this country should have been dragged in as a protagonist in the matter. This was a development which, as the SATURDAY REVIEW has pointed out from the beginning, might have been avoided by the exercise of a little clear thinking and counting of forces. A statesman who is personally acquainted with the individuals he is dealing with, and is informed by personal observation as to the resources of his opponents, must always have an advantage over an adversary who may be equally able but has not the intimate knowledge enjoyed by his opponent. In foreign affairs, as in nearly all other matters, the professional will beat the amateur. Given equal conditions, the man who is prepared to win at all costs will beat the man who would like to win but considers other things as well.

We cannot see that the Russian Foreign Office has much to complain of, if, as it says, it was concerned in a manœuvre with Austria behind the back of Europe to force the hands of the other Powers. A Machiavelli, Machiavelli et demi. Russia herself thirty years ago not only invited Austria into the annexed provinces, but even suggested that she should take the Sanjak of Novi-Bazar also, from which she has now retired. This part has been brought out by the publication of the secret agreement made between Shuvaloff and Andrassy in 1878. By this arrangement Russia actually promised to raise no objection if Austria thought fit to eject the Turks and "definitively enter into occupation of that territory like the rest of Bosnia and Herzegovina". These quarrels, therefore, as to petty details continually renewed only tend to promote bad feeling and inflame wounds which ought to be allowed to heal. It is fortunate for Europe as a whole that the Conference was never summoned on which our statesmen were so bent at one time, but the absurdity of which, we take credit to ourselves, the SATURDAY REVIEW has always insisted on. It is bad enough that this wrangling should go on in newspapers and reviews, it would be a great deal worse to have it stereotyped at the Council Board of Europe with other Powers almost certainly taking sides.

It is not altogether out of place to note in this connexion that the plausible M. Milovanovitch is making another tour through the European Chancelleries. This enterprise has been modestly undertaken, but it is difficult to avoid the suspicion that Servia may be still in quest of some form of "compensation". According to his account given to the "Temps", his business was "to talk and to listen, to maintain or re-establish contact, nothing more". He has called the attention of Europe to the "moral sufferings" his country went through a few months ago. He also talks of a Balkan Triplice which is to include Servia, Bulgaria, and Montenegro. We shall be greatly surprised if the prudent Ferdinand will guarantee the status quo in the Balkans against Austria for the benefit of King Peter. We rejoice to learn from M. Milovanovitch that he finds the Powers determined on peace, and he may be well assured that civilised Europe has not forgotten her "moral sufferings" over the crimes of his own compatriots. It is because the Russo-Austrian bickerings may encourage the impudent ambitions of these barbarous little communities that they are especially to be deprecated.

THE CITY.

THE City welcomes the prospect of an early termination of the political deadlock, and is not at all perturbed by the statements of Lord Swaythling and Lord Welby as to the chaos which will prevail in the Money market when the Budget is rejected. It is recognised that some temporary financial accommodation will be required by the Government to meet the deficiency of the year; but the maximum amount should be ten millions, and this can be raised by two successive issues of Treasury Bills without in any way dislocating Lombard Street The monetary position this week has undergone a further improvement, and instead of anticipating a return of stringency the market is looking forward to an early reduction in the Bank rate. This may seem a sanguine view to take of the immediate future, but it is not unjustified when regard is had to the large addition which has been made to the Bank's reserve since the establishment of the 5 per cent. rate. Meantime the market is preparing for a reduction by lowering its quotations for discounts, and either it is showing an intelligent anticipation of forthcoming events or is indulging in speculations which may prove very costly. The Stock Exchange is not prepared to discount a reduction in the Bank rate because it can see no material increase in either investment or speculative business while a General Election is in prospect, and is rather disposed to reduce speculative commitments. Where possible, brokers are putting pressure upon clients with this object in view, and the last two days have seen heavy liquidations in Kaffirs. Real stock is also coming to market, it being impossible to see where the stimulus is to come from to arouse this particular section of the "House". It was hoped that Lord Harris would have said something inspiring at the meeting of the Gold Fields Company on Tuesday, but he very rightly adopted a cautious tone, and nothing in his remarks can be made an excuse for a "bull" campaign. At the same time Lord Harris had a very satisfactory tale to tell the shareholders, who may rest content that their interests are well safeguarded.

No further progress is reported in the arrangements which are being made in the United States for controlling the output of copper, but no effort is being spared to bring the scheme to fruition. And with the promise of success prices of American securities are kept up. There is the less difficulty in doing this now because money conditions in Wall Street have experienced the same relief as in London. The shifting of stocks from London to Wall Street has been accomplished without serious inconvenience, and with easier money in London there should be the less difficulty in renewing finance bills as they become due, and as they are now doing. This does not mean that existing prices of American securities are justified; on the contrary, we still think that there is gross inflation—in regard to industrials in particular. But the process of unloading by the manipulators is facilitated by the improved conditions, and thus a sudden collapse is averted, and the inevitable decline should be gradual and consequently less mischievous than was feared a few weeks back. A notable movement of the week has been a drop to 85½ in the price of Buenos Ayres and Pacific Railway stock. We were prepared for this when we commented upon the directors' report. At its present price the stock may be considered cheap for a lock-up.

Pekin Syndicate shares have had another of their sensational movements, rising over £2. A circular from the directors giving a report from the engineers has accompanied the rise, but is probably only partially responsible for the movement, which is, as customary now, being worked from Paris. The directors here must be very annoyed that their warning of a few months back as to the speculation in the shares is so persistently ignored, but they will probably know the reason why before many more months have passed. Paris interests are determined to remove all those members of the board who they consider have stood in the way of the development of the company's resources, and it will require a very strong man to circumvent their tactics. Meantime shareholders who have bought at lower figures might take some of their profits, coming in again on a lower level. Amazing though it may seem, we have yet another flotation by the Russian Estates and Mines, Limited! Particulars are advertised of the Mount Dzyshra (Caucasus) Exploration, Limited, which is to acquire certain petroleum and mineral rights from that company. No shares are offered for public subscription, but presumably the publication of particulars regarding the new venture is preparatory to making a market. The shares of Russian Estates and Mines, Limited, which a few weeks ago were dealt in at 15s., are down to 4s.; that is, just about 4s. more than their intrinsic value.

INSURANCE: POLICIES AT HIGH PREMIUMS.

V.

ENDOWMENT assurance policies, with which we have been dealing in recent articles, provide for the payment of the sum assured at the end of a fixed period or at death; consequently they involve a higher rate of premium than policies which become claims only at death. Assurance payable at death may be regarded as involving a high rate of premium when the payments to the life offices are limited in number, especially if the number of premiums be small, or if the policy be taken at an advanced age. These limited-payment policies have many attractions, and although they have become increasingly popular in recent years they are not yet appreciated quite as fully as they should be.

The smallest number of premiums is, of course, one. A single payment of about £345 at age thirty, of £420 at age forty, and of £516 at age fifty will secure £1000 without profits at death whenever it happens. Under policies of this kind the protection element is small and the investment element is large; in fact, the chance of the life office having to pay much more than the premium received, with accumulated interest, is more than balanced by the interest earned on the single payment which the company has received. Money invested in a single-payment policy is therefore not locked up, since the policy can at any time be surrendered for 90 or 95 per cent. of the amount of the single premium, and after a few years the surrender value exceeds the premium paid. A policy is about the best security that life offices can have for a loan, which they will grant to very nearly the extent of the surrender value. These features make single-premium policies a favourite investment with members of the Stock Exchange and others, since in a sudden emergency they can obtain a loan without delay. It is advisable to consider, when choosing the policy, the terms upon which a loan will be granted. Some life offices lend on such security at 4 per cent. interest, while others charge a higher rate. If the loan is to be repaid quite soon the rate of interest may not matter very much; but if the loan remains for a long time, and especially if the interest is not paid upon it periodically, it makes a great deal of difference whether the rate of interest is 4 or 4½ or 5 per cent.

People can take from any life office policies payable at death, subject to any number of premiums that suits their convenience. This may be five or ten or twenty, or the premiums may be payable until the attainment of a fixed age, such as sixty or sixty-five. Manifestly the fewer the number of premiums the larger is the amount of each premium for the assurance of a given sum. This means that the protection element is smallest and the savings element is largest when the number of premiums to be paid is smallest; if death occurs before the number of premiums originally agreed upon is paid no further payments have to be made to the life office. These policies, like nearly all others, can be taken either with or without participation in the profits of the assurance company. If the company is well chosen it is in almost every case the best plan to take a with-profit policy. In the majority of life offices the bonuses on limited-payment life policies are declared on the same basis as those on whole-life policies subject to the payment of premiums until death; but there are several peculiarities in the practice of life offices on this point which make companies in the first class for policies involving premiums until death somewhat second-rate for limited-payment life assurance. There are also exceptional conditions as to surrender values and other points which should be attended to in connexion with limited-payment assurance; the surrender values are always larger in proportion to the total amount paid in premiums than under whole-life policies subject to premiums until death; and the surrender values are largest in proportion to the premiums paid when the number of premiums payable is smallest. This is a direct consequence of the fact mentioned above that the saving element is greatest when the number of premiums payable is least. In good offices, under all policies, a considerable proportion of the accumulated savings is available as a cash surrender value. It is because under low-premium policies a large proportion of each premium has to be taken for the purpose of paying for insurance protection that the surrender values of such policies are so small as to be disappointing to the uninitiated. The relatively large surrender values attaching to limited-payment policies are among the circumstances which make assurance of this kind an attractive form of investment.

SMALL OWNERSHIP AND LAND BANKS.

By Sir Gilbert Parker M.P.

THE problem of the land might be deemed insoluble, the situation hopeless, were it not that other nations have had to face similar problems and situations as grave, and have found a solution and an issue from their difficulties. France has found in the very class whose wrongs convulsed her a bulwark against revolution and a source of national wealth. Her peasants, once the plague-spot and menace of her social system, are now the creditors and mainstay of the State. Stein, striving to infuse new life into Prussia as it lay gasping after long and disastrous wars, called into existence a race of country-folk who now, after a hundred years, form the surest guarantee of national stability, solve the problem of overcrowding, maintain the nation at a high physical standard, and enable industrial development to proceed unhampered. America has never allowed her feverish industrial activity to divert attention from agriculture; in no other country perhaps has the Government done more to develop agriculture than in the United States. Yet even there, with all the prosperity of town and country, a movement is on foot to create a more highly organised rural society. There is not a country in Europe where security and prosperity have not been sought and found in agricultural development; to a higher organisation of rural society our young colonists are turning for a solution of problems which beset them. And everywhere, except in the very youngest communities, where land is plentiful and labour scarce, the remedy for troubles such as ours has been found in the substitution, in greater or lesser degree, of small ownership for large tenancy.

Only in the multiplication of small farms owned by the cultivators can we, I am convinced, find a solution of our agricultural difficulties—an increased productivity, a relief of urban congestion, and an improvement of the national physique. The proposal is not a new one. Mr. Jesse Collings has done work in this cause which will yet secure for him the thanks of a whole people. But it has had to contend with two forms of opposition: the one, economic, which met it in earlier stages; the second, political, which is of more recent date.

The objection to small ownership is mainly political. Socialism sees in ownership a negation of its basic principle and a fatal obstacle to the realisation of its dreams. Without concerning itself, therefore, with the question whether ownership or tenancy would be the more congenial or profitable, it opposes itself resolutely to ownership and condemns the cultivators of the soil to a perpetual servitude to the State. There are others —not many—who prefer tenancy to ownership on other grounds, while admitting a close balance between the merits of the two systems. They think that, on the whole, the tenant who has practical fixity of tenure is better off than the freeholder, if only because, in the case of bad seasons and the like, he can get some indulgence from his landlord. To enter into that controversy is impossible here; but I would point to Ireland, where the tenant has fixity of tenure plus a periodical revision of rent, as a case where tenancy has not only failed to do what ownership is doing, but where, as is admitted on all hands, ownership is succeeding where it failed. It is urged also by critics that the demand for tenancies under the County Councils far exceeds the demand for the purchase of holdings, from which they argue that there is no great desire among the peasantry to become landowners. Against that should be set the fact that the terms on which land can be purchased now are not attractive. It is not many who can put down one-fifth of the purchase-money and pay off the balance at the rate of 4½ per cent., and still retain sufficient capital for current living expenses and working costs. And the statement that there is but a languid desire to own land is opposed to evidence given before Commissions, to statements made to myself and others who have taken up this question, and to the universal experience of other countries. I cannot believe that Englishmen are so differently constituted from other races that they alone of mankind prefer to work for a master and not for themselves.

The second objection rests on the argument that as the yeomen, statesmen and freeholders have failed, to try to re-establish the system would be to run counter to natural law. It needs but little reflection to see that such an argument has no real basis. To a large extent the disappearance of the small owners was due to artificial causes, to the operation of the Inclosure Acts, and to the desire of persons who had grown rich in commerce to obtain social prestige as "landed gentry"—an ambition which they gratified by offering prices for land beyond its intrinsic value. So far as the extinction of the freeholders was due to natural causes, they were of a kind which do not now exist in anything like the same degree. Markets are larger, more numerous and more accessible; there is a greater demand for those articles which are most suitable for small farms; agricultural education is more advanced; and, above all, there is a wider knowledge and experience of the effect of co-operation. In reinstating the small farmers on the land, therefore, we should not be merely putting back the hands of the clock, we should not be thrusting them again into the conditions under which they failed: we should be giving them a fresh start under a new order, with the accumulated experience of a century, gained under diverse conditions of race, soil and country, to encourage and guide them.

I recognise to the full the impolicy, if not the cruelty, of placing small owners on the land and then leaving them to sink or swim as fate may have it. Some, indeed, might succeed where conditions of soil and proximity to a market were exceptionally favourable, but very many would fail. Greater agricultural knowledge and larger facilities for transport would not avail, unassisted, to give them that fair prospect of success which we must offer to those whom we would attract back to the land. Great as is my faith in the "magic of ownership" as a stimulus to the ambitions and energies of those under its influence, it is not to be believed that it can work miracles. To enable it to effect its purpose the energies and ambitions which it calls up must be organised, must be given practical means of realisation. By combination alone can this be achieved. Co-operation is not only the handmaid of peasant ownership, it is a partner in the concern. So much has been written about co-operation as an adjunct to farming that it is not desirable, even did space permit, to elaborate the subject here. But one must point out that co-operation is the rudder which will enable peasant proprietors to steer clear of the three rocks on which they have hitherto been wrecked—want of working capital, inadequate means of production, difficulty of distribution.

Wherever the small farmer has been thrown upon his own resources he has, sooner or later, become the prey of the usurer or "gombeen" man. To enable him to succeed he must be given easy access to cheap money. The small owner, purchasing the means of production—seeds, manure, feeding-stuffs and the like—as an individual, always pays a high price and very often gets an inferior article. And he is, of course, always debarred from the use of modern machinery and high-priced implements. To avoid this, small owners must combine to purchase what they need in bulk and to use machinery in common. The small owner, working as an individual (unless he be in the near neighbourhood of a large market), can never distribute his produce to the best advantage, or even on terms which will enable him to meet competition. He cannot enter into contracts, he cannot get good terms from railway companies, he cannot take advantage of the turn of the markets, he is hampered by having to maintain farm buildings for the store of his produce and by having to lose time and money in the disposal of it. Small owners must, therefore, combine for the collection of the produce of the parish or district in common centres, whence it shall be distributed cheaply because sent in bulk, and, with the maximum of profit, because it has been properly graded and packed.

In all countries where small ownership is a national policy co-operation has been called to its aid in the form of land banks, purchasing societies and distributing societies. One need do no more than refer by name to Denmark and France, to Sir Horace Plunkett's work in Ireland, and to the co-operative credit devised in Germany by Raiffeisen and Schulze Delitzsche, which has spread across Europe and is invading the United States. But even in England, which has sadly lagged behind the movement, it is satisfactory to know that co-operative farming is making headway. As an instance one would mention the Eastern Counties Farmers' Co-operative Association, with its sub-committees of management, finance, estates, pigs, eggs, mills, roots and trading, the annual turnover of which has grown from £15,400 in 1904 to near £213,000 in 1908. In the nine years since the Agricultural Organisation Society was formed its turnover has increased from £9000 to nearly £1,000,000. These figures are encouraging, because they give an answer to those pessimists who say that English agriculturists will not combine; but they are very poor beside the £2,000,000 turnover of the kindred society in Ireland, and infinitely small compared with Continental operations.

To discuss the methods by which small ownerships may be called into existence might well fill another article as long as this. But it is essential to the success of the scheme that it should be possible for a man to become the owner of a holding without trenching on capital which might be devoted to its development. It is sometimes said that the Danish peasant owners are hard pressed. But the Dane has to find 10 per cent. of the purchase-money. Were he absolved from so doing he could use that money on development or to satisfy daily wants, and his position would be easier. Without insisting on the adoption of a precisely similar scheme, one would point to the land purchase system of Ireland as one which might be used as a model. By advancing the whole of the purchase-money through land banks the farmer's working capital is left intact, while by the use of State credit and the extension of purchase over a long period, the security of the State is increased and the energies of the owner are left unfettered.

PATRIARCHAL BASUTOLAND.

THE cosy doctrine that our national blunders somehow or other manage to get themselves retrieved is so firmly rooted in the average Englishman's mind that he would find it hard to point to the one or two actual instances in which the facts have squared with the theory. Lost ground, of course, is more easily recovered than lost credit. The Gladstone school avowedly saw nothing in "prestige". And yet Mr. Gladstone must have known that one schoolmaster can in a moment bring a noisy roomful of boys to order, when a colleague, known by all the boys to possess exactly the same official authority and punitive powers, finds himself helpless. Experience has shown that one has no firm grasp, but that the other (as a French master put it) "will stand no boozle-bam". And primitive races are very like boys.

Twenty-five years ago Egypt and South Africa were painful topics to any patriotic Englishman. Yesterday the effect of years of quiet work had made Egypt a satisfaction and South Africa a hope. To-morrow each will be an anxiety. Such a book * as that in which Sir Godfrey Lagden tells the story of Basutoland must be of intense interest to all who are moved by any sense of our Imperial obligations. After forty

* "The Basutos: the Mountaineers and their Country." By Sir Godfrey Lagden K.C.M.G. 1909.

years of vacillation we formed a policy and maintained it. For the last twenty-five years three Englishmen in succession—Sir Marshall Clarke, Sir Godfrey Lagden himself, and Mr. Sloley—have ruled Basutoland in peace without the presence of even a battalion of troops. Now the country is to pass from a direct Imperial protectorate to a special status under the High Commissioner of united South Africa. The Basutos, for reasons which their history explains, were so uneasy at the prospect of change that they sent to England a deputation, to whom Lord Crewe spoke comfortable words. Basutoland wishes to retain its present anomalous position as a British dependency in which Europeans may not own land, sell liquor, or prospect for metals. Their mountainous country contains fine cornland, tilled by themselves. Their young men go away to the Rand, make money, and return to settle down in family life. The Resident Commissioner with his small staff of magistrates maintains order, while the sectional chiefs, under the more or less nominal control of the Paramount Chief, look after the minor affairs of tribal life. It is an almost ideal state of things for the Basutos, who are not as militant as the Zulus, and are therefore not dissatisfied with the pax Britannica. But undoubtedly there will be growing pressure in the Parliament of South Africa to throw open this fine native reserve to trade, mining, and general European adventure. Sir Godfrey Lagden evidently has misgivings as to the future, and his book emphasises the necessity of keeping faith.

The peculiar interest of Basuto history is that the nation was formed not by conquest, but by the amalgamation of broken and fugitive clans under a petty chief. When the Zulu impis were sweeping over what is now Natal, in the early part of last century, their weaker neighbours fled over the Drakensberg. Moshesh, a Basuto chief of a small clan, gradually acquired ascendency far more by diplomacy than by arms. He bought off the hostility of Moselikatse, the founder of the Matabele kingdom, and by the time of the great Boer trek had become a powerful ruler. The advent of French Protestant missionaries, whom he welcomed, while never really accepting Christianity, profoundly influenced the development of his people. Moshesh prohibited liquor, witch-doctoring, and the alienation of tribal land—a very remarkable record for a Bantu chief. When the abortive policy was adopted of attempting to create a ring of protected native states between Cape Colony and the emigrant Boers, the British Government made with Moshesh the first of many treaties. But continuous fighting between Boers and Basutos led to the annexation of the Orange River Sovereignty, and Sir George Cathcart found it necessary to take the field against Moshesh, just as, a generation later, our annexation of the Transvaal involved campaigns against Cetewayo and Sekukuni. Our troops were repulsed by the Basutos in an official victory, and Moshesh was astute enough to pretend that he had been beaten and obtain excellent terms. But in 1854 we scuttled from the Orange River Sovereignty, leaving no settled boundary between Boer and Basuto. Constant fighting followed, in which we took no part (except that we allowed arms to pass into the Orange Free State, but not into Basutoland). At last, in 1867, just as the Free State was about to crush the Basutos, Sir Philip Wodehouse saved them by taking their country definitely under British protection. Naturally, the Free State Boers resented a policy which robbed them of their spoil. When Cape Colony was given responsible government in 1872, Basutoland came under the contagion of Cape politics. Colonial rule was unsuccessful, and after the colony had caused a troublesome war (in which the Basutos held their own) by attempting to enforce disarmament, the Imperial Government consented to resume a direct protectorate. Incidentally, it drove a hard financial bargain with the colony. To abandon the country would have been the signal for a general Bantu rising, but the Cape was quite unable to continue the war. So Imperialism on the cheap was the policy that commended itself to the Gladstone Cabinet. Sir Marshall Clarke was sent with a handful of police to control a turbulent Bantu people that had defied the Cape and was on unsatisfactory terms with the Free State, which would or could not police its own border. Moshesh was dead (having lost all control over his sons in his old age). By sheer force of character Sir Marshall Clarke succeeded, reduced to reason the stark old pagan Masupha, introduced order, kept out mean whites, persuaded the Basutos to live fairly quietly and to pay hut-tax. His successor, Sir Godfrey Lagden, carried on his work, and held the Basutos in leash during the Boer war. The country has always paid its way under the present system of administration, and is now well governed and prosperous. In Basuto affairs the High Commissioner of South Africa is responsible only to the Imperial Government. But when Basutoland is an enclave in a united self-governing South Africa, the High Commissioner must be influenced by his Ministers. It is easy to see why the Basutos are anxious.

THE CENSORSHIP REPORT.

By Max Beerbohm.

I CANNOT say I was disappointed by the Report of the Censorship Committee. Some knowledge of the English character, and of the official mind, had sufficed to save me from hoping for anything better. I should have liked the artists to wrench a victory. By temperament and habit, I am all on their side. If a man of genius wrote a play whose production might tend to lower the moral tone of the community, I should not wish that play suppressed. I make a present of that admission to the people who argue that a Court official is needed to stand between artists who are anxious to corrupt and a public eager to be corrupted. But the argument won't really be useful. Whether or not there is such a public, there are no such artists. And it is very natural that our artists should chafe under the control of an official appointed to keep his eye on them. The European Powers could afford to laugh when they heard that the eye of the Skibbereen Eagle was on them. But how if that obscure fowl had been appointed actual dictator of Europe? They would have rebelled then. Even so does dramatic genius and talent rebel against the licenser of plays. Not merely to depict life as it is, but to point therefrom some moral, is the aim of all the dramatic authors who count for anything at all to-day. Very often their moral fervour, their wish to do good, gets in the way of their artistic achievement. Their anxiety to be helpful to mankind does very often make their work clumsy. Propagandism in drama is a passing fashion, I daresay, and the playwrights of the near future will be as little anxious to do good as they will be to do harm. Meanwhile, being even more definitely moralists than artists, our playwrights have especial reason for resenting an official whose effect is so often to prevent them, not merely from depicting life, but from exerting a moral influence. I do not agree with Mr. Walkley that the outcry against the Censorship has been a fuss about next to nothing. His suggestion that the Committee should settle the whole matter by the toss of a coin was not less shocking than witty. Of course, it is well to preserve a sense of proportion. But that is an arbitrary term. Everything depends on the standard one selects. The fuss that is made about the British Empire would offend anyone who chose to take a wide enough survey. There have been many empires, and this particular one will doubtless come to grief in due time, and be forgotten. This planet will still go on revolving in its old orbit, at its old speed. And why—to carry our sense of proportion a step further—should we care if this planet itself came to grief? Our solar system would not be deranged. And, for the matter of that, why—in the face of infinity—bother about our solar system? Well, really, we don't—unless we happen to be astronomers. And even astronomers, I am told, are not wholly indifferent to the things that go on around them in their own homes. They like to see their puny domestic and local affairs being carried on for the best, and are worried when anything goes wrong. If I were a Briton, I should doubtless be very proud of the British Empire. As it is, I can quite enter into the feelings of men who are willing to devote their energies to the task of keeping it together. I should be sorry if no one raised a finger to help it. It may have done, and be going to do, more harm than good; but the world would be a dull place indeed if men did not love, and fight for, the things that most nearly concern them. It is right and natural that the welfare of the British drama should be a matter of passionate interest to British dramatists. It is right and natural that they should make a fuss about the Censor. Not merely through his refusal to license this and that strong and highly moral play, but by the fact that his office discourages from writing such plays many men who would write them if there were a fair chance of production, the Censor has been a strong impediment to the drama's progress, and, in some degree therefore, to the national good. Certainly, he should be sent packing. But, when a Parliamentary Committee was appointed to inquire into the matter, and some enthusiastic friends of mine seemed to think there was a possible chance that the Censor would be abolished, or that his power would be much modified, and way would be made for the dawn of a new era, I smiled.

Ten gentlemen in frock-coats, five lords and five commons, at a long green table—not by them ever are dawns of new eras ushered in. Their business is to find with dignity a common denominator in the opinions severally held by them. Two or three of the members of the Censorship Committee were, as one knows, appointed as disapprovers of the Censor, others as approvers, others because of their open minds. It was, as always, the duty of the first two kinds to examine witnesses from their respective points of view, and of the third kind to examine witnesses from no point of view. And I presume that in the secret conclave of the whole lot the two kinds talked from their respective points of view until, having no more to say, they held silence while the third kind shuffled together all the words that had been uttered, shuffling them long and vigorously till all the meaning was shuffled safely out of them, and then boiling them down to a scale on which they could conveniently be laid as an humble offering upon the altar of the god Compromise. How not to offend one another, how not to offend either of the opposing parties that had come before them—this, I take it, was the aim of the Censorship Committee, as of all such bodies. And very creditably the work has been done. In the whole kingdom there is only one person whom I can imagine being definitely perturbed by the Report, and that is Lord Althorp, who, while we have all been hurling hideous menaces in the face of Mr. Redford, has been elegantly aloof and immune. In future, the Report recommends, we ought to curse the Lord Chamberlain. Meanwhile, as a salve to him, he is recommended to go on with his idea of a small committee of appeal, "consisting of a distinguished lawyer, two gentlemen who are or have been actors and theatre proprietors, a playwright, and the Comptroller of the Lord Chamberlain's Department ex officio". Cannot one see them—especially the distinguished lawyer—at work? And can anybody for a moment suppose that this five-headed monster will be one whit less mischievous than a single Censor from whom there is no appeal? It will not, however, be more mischievous. Things will be in statu quo—a consummation which is, of course, the aim of the report in all its ramifications. To please the artists, there is talk of the duty of encouraging "writers of intellect who desire to present through the agency of the stage sincere and serious dramas, critical of existing conventions", and so forth; and it is recommended that a manager should be allowed to produce any play without applying for a license. But, suppose there be legislation to this effect, what difference will be made? Where is the manager who is going to risk those enormous penalties which will overtake him if the Public Prosecutor happen to hale him into court, there to be dealt with by a common jury? Nor do I see that the chance of being haled before a committee of the Privy Council, sitting in camera, is likely to lure our managers on. I repeat, however, that I am not disappointed.

THE LEWIS BEQUEST TO THE NATIONAL GALLERY.

By Laurence Binyon.

In 1849 the will of Thomas Denison Lewis was proved in London. By this will the sum of ten thousand pounds was left to the Trustees of the National Gallery in order that the interest on that sum might be "laid out for the use or objects of the said Gallery or otherwise in the improvement of the Fine Arts". The income amounts to about £246 per annum; an insignificant sum, one might think. Yet in the forty odd years during which this income has been available (the bequest did not take effect till the death of the testator's sister in 1863) the pictures acquired from the Lewis Fund would of themselves make a very choice collection, already worth several times the original amount of capital bequeathed. We have good reason to honour Lewis' memory. Rich men have made far more magnificent bequests; but there is something truly liberal and unpretentious in the spirit of this one, which makes no small or hampered conditions and seeks no vainglory. All honour, too, to the successive Trustees and Directors of our National Gallery, who have so well discharged the obligation laid upon them.

It was an excellent notion to publish, as Mr. Brockwell has done, the record of the purchases made out of the Lewis Fund.* The book consists of a descriptive catalogue of the pictures, with notes on their history where available, and a discussion of authorship where this is doubtful. The dates of purchase and the price given are added; and there are reproductions of most of the pictures. The essential information is repeated in tabular form at the end of the volume. An appendix, on which the author lays some stress, contains a list of authentic Italian pictures in the various public and private galleries of Europe and America. The authentic pictures are those accepted by Mr. Berenson. I do not quite see the particular relevance of these tables, or why they should be confined to the Italian schools, though they are of interest as showing how immensely rich this country still is in works of Italian art. But to return to the Lewis bequest. The present Director of the Gallery, who contributes a preface to the volume, frankly says that he does not believe it would have been possible to expend the sum available to better purpose. And really one is inclined to agree with him. At any rate, if in some cases the choice was not ideal, it is unlikely that any purchaser would have done better.

Few who go to Trafalgar Square take much notice of the labels denoting that certain paintings were acquired out of certain funds. Let us glance therefore at some of the more important works which compose this Lewis collection. To take the Italian schools first: the finest painting is certainly the superbly masculine head of a young man by Antonello da Messina. This was bought for just over a thousand pounds in 1883: its price to-day would of course be far higher. Rather more than this was given for the large Signorelli "Nativity"; but this was not so good a purchase. It is from the workshop of that great artist, rather than from his own hand, according to Mr. Berenson and other authorities; in any case, it is no true measure of Signorelli's genius. The Madonna and Child with S. John, by Fra Bartolommeo, bought in 1900, is an interesting rather than representative specimen of the painter; but it filled a gap. The exquisite little panel, "Amor and Castitas", now generally accepted as a work of Cosimo Rossolli, was bought for £500; and only £45 was given for the noble fragment of a fresco, "Four Heads of Nuns", by Ambrogio Lorenzetti. Later Italians are represented by two brilliant studies by Tiepolo. Among Flemish pictures the small portrait of a young lady as the Magdalene, by Mabuse, a desirable acquisition in itself, was also a memorable one, considering its price, £30. This we owe to the present Director's good judgment. Among several Dutch pictures the most notable is Hals' masterly half-length of a woman. The portrait of a man which hangs as a

* "The National Gallery: Lewis Bequest." By Maurice W. Brockwell. London: Allen. 1909. 3s. 6d. net.

pendant to it was given later. Sir Charles Holroyd's recent attempts to fill, in some measure, the sad gaps in the French school have mostly been made by the help of the Lewis Fund. In the case of the greater masters it would seem better policy to try to secure really representative works. The doubtful Ingres can hardly be called a fortunate purchase. But the Trustees must be congratulated on getting the admirable and authenticated example of Gabriel de Saint-Aubin for less than a hundred pounds; and the landscape by Georges Michel is of special interest to us in England.

The English pictures are more numerous than those of the other schools, and by no means the least important. It will suffice to name a few of them. The "Great Cornard Wood", by Gainsborough, and the "Windmill on Mousehold Heath", by Crome, are two masterpieces of English landscape. Only £231 was paid for the Crome. The group of portraits of Hogarth's servants is a piece of intimate character, well worth its place in a collection where the painters of our nation are to be studied. The two small paintings by Alfred Stevens, bought for a small sum, will be prized more and more as time goes on; and though opinions may differ as to the desirability of acquiring for the walls of a public gallery, instead of for a students' room, the many sketches and studies by Stevens, also bought from this fund, one is unwilling to criticise any action which serves to honour and enlarge the fame of our great sculptor. The brilliant picture by Hurlstone, which has revived a forgotten reputation, and Madox Brown's "Chaucer at the Court of Edward III." were wisely chosen. And the latest purchase of all, made this year, Mr. Arthur Hughes' "April Love", makes a fitting close to the list.

There is more than one reflection that this record suggests. When the agitation for the purchase of Holbein's "Duchess of Milan" was going on this spring there was considerable outcry among paint rs on the neglect of living art and the unjust devotion of collectors to the old masters; and the indignant letters written on that occasion all assumed that pictures by the artists of the past fetched inflated prices, quite out of proportion to their merit. The record of purchases from the Lewis Fund tells a different tale. Here we find excellent pictures, some of them of the finest quality, bought for prices which a popular modern painter would despise. Supreme masterpieces now fetch fabulous sums; but the collectors who can afford them are as rare as the masterpieces themselves. Generally speaking, I believe that living painters and the painters of the past are in much the same condition, as far as the market is concerned. Fashion and rarity are the main factors in sending up prices.

But there is another and more significant question raised by this timely publication. Who that cares for the art of our country can consider and digest this record of a trust well bestowed and help noting the obvious contrast with the administration of another and more famous bequest? The sum bequeathed by Chantrey produces an annual amount ten times that of the amount produced by the Lewis bequest. The annual sum from which the Lewis purchases have been made is actually less than the annual fee which the President of the Academy derives from Chantrey's fund in consideration of his duties as trustee! Does anyone pretend that the Chantrey purchases, year by year, are worth ten times the amount of the Lewis purchases? Can anyone doubt that the Trustees and Directors of the National Gallery would have made, on the principles observed in administering the Lewis fund, an infinitely worthier collection for the nation than the Royal Academy has done? The comparison provoked by Mr. Brockwell's book is disastrous for Chantrey's trustees.

THE LASKER-JANOWSKI CHESS MATCH.—IV.

By Emanuel Lasker.

THE match was ended on Tuesday, 9 November, with the score standing: Lasker, 7; Janowski, 1; drawn, 2. On the face of it an overwhelming defeat suffered by Janowski. But his is a nature of big contrasts; under stress it is capable as well of remaining indolent as of startling efforts. In a few international tournaments he has been nearly the last ranked, in several others he has been a brilliant leader. A characteristic story is told of him. When a boy he was beaten in two games at the odds of pawn and move by a chess friend whom he considered inferior to himself. Half furious, half despairing, Janowski stayed three days at home. Then he returned to the café and scorningly offered to concede the odds of the knight to his victor. The défi was accepted, and Janowski made his word good by winning five times in succession.

Janowski has the consciousness of his ability to make supreme efforts; hence no ill fortune can discourage him. He does not acquiesce in the result of the match, and asks for another in which draws do not count. I hardly believe, however, that the result of such an encounter would be far different from the one just concluded. The fact that the capacity of a man oscillates in showing a high maximum and a low minimum allows only one interpretation: the man is one-sided. A talent such as that is limited in adaptability. It is safe to assume that our faculties cause our will to seek the conditions that favour them and to avoid those unfavourable to them. The "all-round" man, as the phrase goes, has a larger variety of suitable opportunities to choose from, and his one-sided opponent is for that reason greatly handicapped.

Though the match has disappointed the lover of sport, it has satisfied the student. The games produced by it are of rare quality. Janowski has treated the openings in a novel manner and soundly; the positions which arose were interesting, and the course of the games was such as to permit a correct estimate of the value and quality of the new ideas tried out.

The Ninth Game.

Ruy Lopez.

	White Lasker	Black Janowski		White Lasker	Black Janowski
1.	P–K4	P–K4	5.	Castles	B–K2
2.	Kt–KB3	Kt–QB3	6.	R–K	P–Q3
3.	B–Kt5	P–QR3	7.	P–B3	B–KKt5
4.	B–R4	Kt–B3	8.	P–Q4	Kt–Q2

Of all the replies to the Lopez tried during the last fifteen years the line of play here adopted by black is on every score the most promising one. The black pieces are developed, the KP is well defended, considerable pressure is exerted upon the white QP, and black is ready to castle and to advance P–KB4. Room is left to the KB for B–B3. An attack by white would now be premature. The first player must try for small advantages only, or the "balance of position"—according to a general law discovered by Steinitz—must of necessity turn against him.

9. B–K3 P–B4 10. KP×P B×P

The tempting P–K5 would be met by P–KR3, B–R4 (B×P, P–Q5), P–KKt4.

11. QKt–Q2 Castles 12. B–B2 B–Kt5

If B×B, Q×B white holds what advantage there is in initiative. He would threaten Q–Kt3 ch, and be ready to establish his QR on Q, his Kt on K4.

13. Q–Kt . . .

The object is to force the KRP to advance so that the black king is weakened and the square Kt6 is added to the domain of the white forces.

13. . . . Kt–B3

He avoids weakening the king, but blocks both rook and bishop. To have given way to white would have been the lesser evil.

14. P–KR3 . . .

Forcing the exchange of the important bishop. If (14) B–R4, Kt–Kt5 menaces Kt×P and Kt–K6 as well. Against (14) B–K3 or B–Q2 the same attack wins, and the reply to B–B would have been (15) P×P,

Kt×P, (16) Kt×Kt, P×Kt, (17) Kt-B3, threatening Kt×P and Kt-Kt5.

14. . B-Q2

Trying to dodge the unavoidable. Now the catastrophe overtakes him.

15. Kt-Kt5	P-KR3	17. Kt-B7 ch	R×Kt
16. B-Kt3 ch	K-R	18. B×R	. . .

White having won the exchange, with correct play the issue is not doubtful. All that is left for white to do is to exchange the pieces and then to bring his king into action. The remainder of the game is a struggle for black to avoid exchanges, for white to compel them.

18. . . .	Q-KB	21. Kt-B3	R-Q
19. B-Kt3	Kt-KR4	22. B-B2	P-KKt4
20. Q-Q	Kt-B5		

A desperate attack.

23. P×P	P×P	24. B×Kt	KP×B

KtP×B would be met simply by Kt×KP, Kt×Kt, R×Kt, B×P, Q-R5.

25. Q-Q3	Q-Kt2	34. R-QB8	B-B3
26. Q-Kt6	Q×Q	35. K-B	P-QR4
27. B×Q	B-Q3	36. R-K4	R-Q8 ch
28. B-R5	K-Kt2	37. K-K2	R-Q2
29. R-K2	B-KB4	38. K-K	B-Kt2
30. R-K8	R-Q2	39. R-K2	B-B3
31. B-Kt4	B×B	40. R-Q2	R-K2 ch
32. P×B	B-K2	41. K-Q	B-K4
33. R-K	K-B2	42. R-K2	. . .

To exchange the bishop would allow the black Kt to assail the KtP, and, if P-B3, to establish itself via B5 on K6 in a fortified position.

42. . . .	R-Q2 ch	44. R-QR8	. . .
43. K-B2	B-Q3		

preparing the liberation of the hampered rook by P-QR3 and P-QKt4. Black now raises the useless siege of the castle.

44. . . .	K-B3	51. P-B3	B-B
45. R-KR8	K-Kt2	52. P-R4	K-R2
46. R(R8)-K8	R-B2	53. R-Q8	B-Kt2
47. R(K8)-K6	R-Q2	54. K-Kt3	B-B3
48. R-Q2	P-QKt3	55. R-Q5	B-Kt2
49. Kt-Q4	Kt×Kt ch	56. K-B4	B-B
50. R×Kt	R-B2		

The threat of white was K-Kt5-B6 and R-Q7.

57. R-KB5	R×R	59. R-Kt6	B-K2
58. P×R	P-R4		

Perhaps he was trying for P-Kt5, P×P, P-R5; but that would break down on account of P-Kt5.

60. K-Q5	B-Q	61. K-K6	Resigns

The Tenth Game.

Sicilian Defence.

White Janowski	Black Lasker	White Janowski	Black Lasker
1. P-K4	P-QB4	5. Kt×P	B-Kt2
2. Kt-QB3	Kt-QB3	6. B-K3	Kt-B3
3. Kt-B3	P-KKt3	7. B-K2	Castles
4. P-Q4	P×P	8. Q-Q2	. . .

The question is between this move and castling. If he wants to avoid the continuation that follows he must castle. The line of play adopted yields no advantage to white. It permits white to force the draw, but such a conclusion is, in theory, honourable for the defence, and, as a rule, to be avoided by the first player.

8. . . .	P-Q4	10. QKt×Kt	Q×Kt
9. P×P	Kt×P	11. B-B3	Q-B5

White is now prevented from castling. He has naught better than B-K2, Q-Q4, and a draw by repetition of moves.

12. P-QKt3 . . .

To avoid the draw he must continue Kt×Kt, P×Kt, P-B3, B-K3, B-K2, Q-KR4, castles K side, KR-Q or P-QR4. The position of black would then be slightly preferable.

12. . . .	Q-R3	17. Kt×Q	R×P
13. B-K2	Q-R6	18. Kt-Kt5	B-B4
14. P-QB3	R-Q	19. B-QB4	Kt-R4
15. R-Q	P-K4	20. B-Q5	B-B7
16. Kt-Kt5	R×Q	21. Castles	. . .

Intending to attack by Kt-Q6. He would have made a better fight with P-QKt4, Kt-Kt6, R-Q2, Kt×R, B×R, Kt-K5.

21. . . .	B×R	22. R×B	R-Q

All hope for black is now gone. If B×P ch, K×B, R×R, R-R8 ch. He cannot continue with Kt-Q6, and therefore his attack amounts to nothing.

23. P-Kt3	Kt-B3	27. B-Kt5	Kt-B6 ch
24. P-QB4	Kt-Q5	28. K-Kt2	Kt×B
25. Kt-B3	R-Kt7	29. Kt×Kt	R-Q2
26. Kt-K4	R×KtP	Resigns	

THE FIELD.

By Lord Dunsany.

WHEN one has seen Spring's blossom fall in London, and Summer appear and ripen and decay, as it does early in cities, and one is in London still; then at some moment or another the country places lift their flowery heads and call to one with an urgent, masterful clearness, upland behind upland in the twilight, like to some heavenly choir arising rank on rank to call a drunkard from his gambling-hell.

No volume of traffic can drown the sound of it, no lure of London can weaken its appeal. Having heard it, one's fancy is gone, and evermore departed, to some coloured pebble a-gleam in a rural brook, and all that London can offer is swept from one's mind like some suddenly smitten metropolitan Goliath.

The call is from afar both in leagues and years, for the hills that call one are the hills that were, and their voices are the voices of long ago when the elf-kings still had horns.

I see them now, those hills of my infancy (for it is they that call) with their faces upturned to the purple twilight, and the faint diaphanous figures of the fairies peering out from under the bracken to see if evening is come. I do not see upon their regal summits those desirable mansions and highly desirable residences which have lately been built for gentlemen who would exchange customers for tenants.

When the hills called I used to go to them by road, riding a bicycle. If you go by train you miss the gradual approach, you do not cast off London like an old forgiven sin, nor pass by little villages on the way that surely have some rumour of the hills; nor, wondering if they are still the same, come at last upon the edge of their far-spread robes, and so on to their feet, and see far off their holy, welcoming faces. In the train you see them suddenly round a curve, and there they all are, sitting in the sun.

I imagine that as one penetrated out from some enormous forest of the tropics the wild beasts would become fewer, the gloom would lighten and the horror of the place would slowly lift. Yet as one emerges nearer to the edge of London, and nearer to the beautiful influence of the hills, the houses become uglier, the streets viler, the gloom deepens, the errors of civilisation stand bare to the scorn of the fields.

Where ugliness reaches the height of its luxuriance, in the dense misery of the place, where one imagines the builder saying "Here I culminate. Let us give thanks to Satan", there is a bridge of yellow brick, and through it, as through some gate of filigree silver opening on fairyland, one passes into the country.

To left and right, as far as one can see, stretches that monstrous city; before one are the fields like an old, old song.

There is a field there that is full of king-cups. A stream runs through it, and along the stream is a little wood of osiers. There I used often to rest at the stream's edge before my long journey to the hills.

There I used to forget London, street by street. Sometimes I picked a bunch of king-cups to show them to the hills.

I often came there. At first I noticed nothing about the field except its beauty and its peacefulness.

But the second time that I came I thought there was something ominous about the field.

Down there among the king-cups by the little shallow stream I felt that something terrible might happen in just such a place.

I did not stay long then, because I thought that too much time spent in London had brought on these morbid fancies, and I went on to the hills as fast as I could.

I stayed for some days in the country air, and when I came back I went to the field again to enjoy that peaceful spot before entering London. But there was still something ominous among the osiers.

A year elapsed before I went there again. I emerged from the shadow of London into the gleaming sun; the bright green grass and the king-cups were flaming in the light, and the little stream was singing a happy song. But the moment I stepped into the field my old uneasiness returned, and worse than before. It was as though the shadow was brooding there of some dreadful future thing, and a year had brought it nearer.

I reasoned that the exertion of bicycling might be bad for one, and that the moment one rested this uneasiness might result.

A little later I came back past the field by night, and the song of the stream in the hush attracted me down to it. And there the fancy came to me that it would be a terribly cold place to be in in the starlight, if for some reason one was hurt and could not get away.

I knew a man who was minutely acquainted with the past history of that locality, and him I asked if anything historical had ever happened in that field. When he pressed me for my reason in asking him this I said that the field had seemed to me such a good place to hold a pageant in. But he said that nothing of any interest had ever occurred there, nothing at all.

So it was from the future that the field's trouble came.

For three years off and on I made visits to the field, and every time more clearly it boded evil things, and my uneasiness grew more acute every time that I was lured to go and rest among the cool green grass under the beautiful osiers. Once to distract my thoughts I tried to gauge how fast the stream was trickling, but I found myself wondering if it flowed faster than blood.

I felt that it would be a terrible place to go mad in; one would hear voices.

At last I went to a poet whom I knew, and woke him from huge dreams and put before him the whole case of the field. He had not been out of London all that year, and he promised to come with me and look at the field and tell me what was going to happen there. It was late in July when we went. The pavement, the air, the houses and the dirt had been all baked dry by the summer, the weary traffic dragged on and on and on, and Sleep spreading her wings soared up and floated from London and went to walk beautifully in rural places.

When the poet saw the field he was delighted; the flowers were out in masses all along the stream; he went down to the little wood rejoicing. But by the side of the stream he stood and seemed very sad. Once or twice he looked up and down it mournfully; then he bent and looked at the king-cups, first one and then another, very closely and shaking his head.

For a long while he stood in silence, and all my old uneasiness returned and my bodings for the future.

And then I said "What manner of field is it?"

And he shook his head sorrowfully.

"It is a battle-field", he said.

THREE SKETCHES BY TURGUENIEFF.

TRANSLATED FROM THE RUSSIAN BY H. STEWART.

[These sketches were first published in S. Petersburg in "The Messenger of Europe" of last September. They now appear for the first time in English.]

I.

THE MUSEUM.

I WAS ill and taking a cure of sea-bathing at Ventnor, a small town in the Isle of Wight.

That little place is not particularly well known; visitors are rare, and indeed there is nothing in it which could attract them thither.

The broad, sloping strip of yellow-brown sand which forms the beach stretches far beyond the limits of the town. It is nowhere built upon and is bare of vegetation. The bottle-coloured, green waves—cold, northern waves—rush up at the flow of the tide to a line of uniform houses. After the ebb you may see the erect figures of English people strolling over the moist, hard sand that is covered with threads of seaweed.

Later on I discovered that there was also at Ventnor a favourite place for excursion parties. That was the so-called "Museum".

From curiosity and boredom I went to look at it.

I was shown a tumble-down building, a small shed, in which the narrow openings of a few windows had been cut out at irregular intervals, manifestly long after its erection.

A man with a key in his hand, a respectable-looking Englishman, who wore a felt hat and a coat with mother-of-pearl buttons, sat awaiting visitors on a little bench at the entrance to the "Museum". He bowed gravely, opened the door, and invited me to enter.

After the bright daylight I could not at first discern my surroundings in the semi-darkness. The interior of the shed was like our Russian barns, only with a plain floor of boards.

Rare curiosities were hung on the walls and arranged on the floor and two shelves.

For the most part they were all objects cast out on the beach after shipwrecks. There were fragments of ancient ornaments, of different kinds of furniture, of broken crockery. Fossils, starfish and shells were set out symmetrically on the floor along the walls.

A great, clumsy object in a far corner involuntarily attracted my attention. I went up to it.

Before me lay the stern part of an old ship which seemed by various indications to have been Italian. With its shapely curves and swelling upper part the old galley stood out picturesquely in the soft evening-like light on the background of the white wall just behind it.

Scanning it more closely, I became convinced that this number at least of the Museum curiosities—they were all numbered—was undoubtedly of ancient origin.

The timber was so old that it seemed it might crumble away at the slightest touch. Mice and worms had gnawed and eaten it in all directions. A reddish-yellow, rust-coloured dross of hoary mould covered the rotten wood. In one place it was not so thick, and I fancied that I saw under it half-obliterated, scarcely visible letters.

I bent nearer and read: "La Giovane Speranza"—"The Fresh Hope".

II.

THE KISS.

I was walking on a summer noon down a winding path in a wood.

The wood was trim and young, a Russian wood with intermingled kinds of trees. White-boled spreading birches were mixed with low-growing aspens, grey-green like the skin of a snake. Young oaks grew here and there in the glades and at the outskirts; elms with drooping boughs stood out in dark blotches, melancholy trees in the summer-time.

The day was clear and warm, but the sun was not seen through the thick masses of foliage, and only below on the feathery grass bright and dark circles chased and played with and melted into each other.

As I followed their fantastic play, suddenly a substantial human shadow swept forward from somewhere or other, lay over them and occupied the space before me.

I started and turned round. I was not alone in the wood.

Two paces from me a woman's figure advanced gracefully and lightly without touching the grass.

I stopped. The woman drew near, and she also stood still before me. With one swift glance I managed to catch the features of a divine countenance and the contours of a marvellous body outlined through the light tissue of her waving garments. She was beautiful and young, but I did not know who she was.

Suddenly she made a movement, bent slightly over me and kissed me on the forehead.

I trembled. An indescribable emotion rose up within me, choking my breath, overpowering at once all there was of me. I stretched out my arms. I wished to prolong the feeling that coursed with a delicious tremor throughout my whole being. I lifted my head . . . . But there was no longer anyone by me.

She was going as gracefully and lightly as before, and as before she did not touch the earth. Behind her there seemed to be two wings, small and transparent. It was they which helped her to glide so lightly.

I rushed forward in her track, calling on her with a loud voice. I longed that she should kiss me on the mouth "with the kiss of her mouth". . . .

But in vain I called and ran after her. She withdrew ever further and further.

And while I pursued her vainly I spied another man not far from me in the wood. He was a young man, almost a boy. He was walking with careless step, and his curly, beautiful head was raised slightly in the air. Gaily and carelessly the inspired eyes looked ahead, and the rosy full lips, covered faintly with down, were smiling.

I saw how the woman stopped beside him, how with a swift movement the locks that fell in disorder by his cheeks quivered and tossed themselves backward, and how she kissed him straight on the purple, parted lips. . . .

And I understood suddenly who the woman was. I understood also who the young man.

Yes, it was she—the Muse, the inspirer of the poet. Her kiss I felt on my brow, a cold, incomplete kiss. . . .

Such a kiss, such an incomplete gift of inspiration she bestows on us, poets in prose, and treasures her kisses and caresses for him, for the careless, inspired singer of poetry.

III.

A PARTING.

It happened long ago, in those bygone days when Russian gentlefolk were wont to drive to one another's houses and stay there for long, for a week or for two, with horses, children and servants.

Once I chanced to spend some days in just such an old-fashioned hospitable home. All the society of the neighbourhood were gathered there, whiling time away. There were many young people, young beautiful women and girls. All of them gave themselves up with the enthusiasm of youth to careless merriment. Our amusements were simple and unsophisticated, walking through the woods, rowing in boats, and housegames in the evenings.

Among the women's faces I noticed involuntarily one face. It was that of a girl, also a guest in the house, a friend of our young hostess. She was not more attractive or more beautiful than the others, and perhaps I would not have marked her at all but for her glance, a pensive, melancholy glance, which more than once she fixed on me steadily and attentively.

I felt myself continually under the influence of that glance and did not know how to free myself from it.

I tried to talk with her. She answered always with a loud, seemingly unnatural, forced laugh, and what she said had neither meaning nor interest.

At length the time of my departure drew nigh. I was to drive off with my friend, our host's son. We had both come out on the balcony, and everyone assembled there to see us off. Everything was ready. We shook hands with the others and were already going down the stair, when suddenly someone's voice hailed me from above.

I turned round. Leaning with folded arms on the balcony rails, not more than two feet above my head she stood—the dark-eyed, laughing girl.

For the first minute I scarce recognised her—so changed was her face. It was covered with a deathlike pallor. Her eyes were opened wide and shone with a strange glitter, but the soft trembling lips were smiling as always. Quietly, without change of tone and without betraying emotion in her voice, she said:

"Take me with you! Take me!"

"But I—I'm going—— Where to?" I stammered. I was overwhelmed with surprise.

"Take me—from here. For ever!"

Suddenly she flung apart her folded arms and stretched them out in front of her.

"Old man! You're keeping us waiting!" my friend's voice cried gaily from below.

I ran down the stair and in a minute was seated in the carriage. The horses rounded the courtyard and set off down an avenue which ran exactly opposite the house. I lifted my head.

The young woman was still on the balcony. Her arms hung limply by her side. Once again for a moment her eyes rested their mysterious glance on me, and I felt a rebuke in it, in the closely-set, now pale lips. . . .

I could see how someone who was also on the balcony went up to her and spoke to her; she answered with her continual loud laughter.

Around also everything began to laugh loudly and noisily. And we too laughed as we glided on smoothly in the comfortable carriage along the soft, dusty road; but all the time a secret agitation, which I could not understand myself, did not leave me. I did not ask myself had I done well or ill. But the picture of the girl with outstretched arms lived in my imagination for many years afterwards.

CORRESPONDENCE.

MR. BALFOUR IN MANCHESTER.

To the Editor of the SATURDAY REVIEW.

Manchester, 18 November 1909.

SIR,—The newspaper reports of Mr. Balfour's reception in Manchester hardly convey an idea of the manner in which the Unionist leader came to grips with friends as well as opponents. At the White City reception eager men and women scrambled over each other to shake hands with him, until he pleaded, smilingly, "My friends, you want more hands than I've got to give you". At the Free Trade Hall, as later at the Ardwick Club, there was more than one almost dramatic moment. The singing of "Auld Lang Syne" by five thousand lusty men seemed to wipe out the memory of four bad years. Then there was the unexpected appearance of Lord Robert Cecil, whose earnestness in his assurance of loyalty to the chief figure, and in his appeal for union of empire, of country, of party, prepared us for his moving invocation, "May God defend the right!" By the way, there were 30,000 applications for 5000 seats, and it was freely stated that men offered £5 5s. for the privilege of standing.

Manchester clearly is not past hope.

Yours truly,

DELEGATE.

THE FORGOTTEN SIDE OF IMPERIAL EXPANSION.

To the Editor of the SATURDAY REVIEW.

Hingham, Norfolk, 6 November 1909.

SIR,—It is well as a rule to keep from religious appeals in secular journals, with however much goodwill they may be conducted. But the great difficulty of reaching that large body of well-disposed people beyond the small inner ring which upholds at least half of English Church work is a strong temptation to a wider appeal, and perhaps even a duty. In that spirit alone is it made here.

Anglican mission work in Rhodesia is in great straits. The most important English work is honourably maintained by the colonists themselves; but they can have little to spare for the native work. They are not hostile to it, it is a pleasure to say.

We at home therefore must carry on the pure mission work, and it is a hard fight. The res angusta foras is such that nearly half the missionaries of the diocese are at this moment working for their bare keep, and do it gladly. It is not to the credit of the English Church-people to have brought them to such a pass. Perhaps one such who reads this may care to help. It is a case where every one counts for more than one. For the natives themselves do know how to pay. The Knight Bruce Industrial College received £800 last year from its students in various ways, and from other stations over £200, etc. On few worldly investments is the return so large. And the crop is the Church of the ages to come—the great catholic company of our fellow-men.

M. UPCHER, Hon. General Secretary
(on behalf of the Committee of the Mashonaland Mission), to whom subscriptions may be sent.

THE FLOW OF GOLD.

To the Editor of the SATURDAY REVIEW.

19 Boscombe Road, Shepherd's Bush,
6 November 1909.

SIR,—We are again faced with a high Bank rate, and threatened with a further rise. The severity of the effects of this increase renders a discussion of the matter urgently necessary. The evil of an increased Bank rate falls upon a perfectly innocent section of the trading community. The discount of all bills of exchange becomes difficult in proportion to the increased rate; numerous business houses, which happen merely to have large debts to pay at such a period, stand in imminent danger of bankruptcy—the number of firms thus overthrown during the last American crisis reached many hundreds. There ensues a general stoppage of buying, followed by a closing down of factories and by unemployment. We have, even in normal times, an ever-present social question, which may be resolved into one of lack of demand for labour among employers. We perceive, however, that these periodical financial crises, by bankrupting numbers of competing firms, tighten the grasp of industrial monopolists. Further, even in normal times, our banks prepare for times of crisis by refusing credit advances upon ordinary industrial security such as stock and business plant. The entry of fresh competition into the employers' industrial arena is thus prevented. Is there no remedy for this evil?

Orthodox economists have declared that a scarcity of gold indicates over-trading, and that a cessation of home industry is therefore necessary. But a scarcity of gold may arise from many causes. Famine here will necessitate increased purchase abroad, and gold will flow out to balance the debt. An increase of prosperity in this country will call forth an additional volume of credit; and although the undertakings thereby floated may be perfectly sound, yet, when the volume of credit reaches a certain point in proportion to our gold reserves, the screw of an increased Bank rate must again be applied. Prosperity may show itself by an increased flow of capital abroad to finance foreign projects; gold may be withdrawn, as in the recent American crisis, to replenish the banks of a foreign country; yet again the Bank rate must be advanced and our entire home industry throttled. The question demands a discussion of root principles. Is it necessary that our exchange system be thus tied to a fluctuating quantity of a very scarce commodity—gold? A new school of finance is growing (vide the pages of the "Open Review") which denies this necessity. At present nine-tenths of the exchange of goods is carried on without the intervention of gold by means of a simple exchange of bankers' guarantees of the integrity of their clients; yet the whole of this vast superstructure of credit lies at the mercy of fluctuations in its gold basis. The new school asserts that this dangerous state of affairs is the result of governmental interference with the natural evolution of banking. But for governmental restrictions we had long since outgrown the necessity of using gold either as a credit medium or as a standard of value in banking operations. We demand freedom for the issue of an exchange medium which shall only be limited by the amount of commodities desiring exchange, not by the amount of gold in the vaults of the Bank of England. There is no room here to discuss the matter further. I shall be repaid if I am the means of drawing attention to this question.

I am, Sir, yours faithfully,
HENRY MEULEN.

REAL TURKEY.

To the Editor of the SATURDAY REVIEW.

Royal Societies Club, S. James' Street S.W.
13 November 1909.

SIR,—It is a common practice with authors to complain of the unfairness, real or imaginary, with which their works are treated by critics. I do not know if it is as usual for them to thank their critics for generous appreciation. Yet, even at the risk of departing from the precedent established by my splenetic brethren, I feel compelled to write and express to the reviewer of my "Turkey in Transition" my sense of profound gratitude for his unstinted praise. It is recognition like this, sincere and spontaneous, that recompenses the conscientious writer for his labour and encourages him to persevere in his path, despite the thorns with which it is strewn and the pit of obscurity to which it so often leads.

I am almost equally pleased with the high opinion expressed by your reviewer of the merits of Captain Townshend's book—merits which my work in the same field has enabled me fully to appreciate, and to which I have ventured to draw attention in the press. That writer seems to have taken for his guide the same principle as I did—candour; and he must be as gratified as I am to find that candour is not always rewarded with contumely.

I remain, Sir, yours gratefully,
G. F. ABBOTT.

LONDON GRADUATES' UNION FOR WOMEN'S SUFFRAGE.

To the Editor of the SATURDAY REVIEW.

114A Harley Street W., 18 November 1909.

SIR,—May I call the attention of your readers to the recently constituted "London Graduates' Union for Women's Suffrage"? This Union is open to all graduates of the University of London, is strictly non-party and is independent of other suffrage societies.

Among many anomalies produced by the exclusion of qualified women from the franchise on the ground of sex one of the most striking is the case of women graduates of those Universities which return a member to Parliament. It is instructive to consider the result of the present system of representation in connexion with a University constituency such as that of the University of London. This was the first University in the country to admit women as candidates for degrees. In 1878 the Senate and Convocation obtained a supplemental charter opening all degrees and honours to women students on the same terms as to men. In the University of London Act, 1898, this principle was again declared in the words "No disability shall be imposed on the ground of sex". In the University, step by step, women acquire their qualifications as men do, the degrees are open to both under the same conditions; they sit together in Convocation (which, besides being an advisory and elective body of the University, also forms its parliamentary constituency); they are equally eligible for the Senate and for the various offices of the University; they receive the same remuneration for the posts they occupy. Differentiation exists at but one point—over which the University has no control. The disability of women to take part in parliamentary elections rests on a general Act of Parliament, which requires that only male members of Convocation shall vote for the parliamentary representative of their University. In other words, a man is qualified to exercise this franchise because he is a member of Convocation, but a woman who is equally and similarly a member is debarred from any share in choosing the representative of the University in Parliament. The choice may greatly affect the welfare of the University; the qualification is an intellectual one which the woman has satisfied, and yet, because she is a woman, she is debarred from a privilege that her own students, if they are men, can acquire after a few years' probation. The recognition of these among other anomalies in our electoral system has brought into existence the London Graduates' Union. All London graduates who desire that the University tradition of equal treatment should be extended to the political enfranchisement of women are urged to join the Union without loss of time. Particulars and forms of membership can be obtained from the hon. secretary, Miss Jessie W. Scott, 114A Harley Street, London.

I am etc.,
L. Garrett Anderson M.D., B.S.
(Chairman of Committee).

NATIONAL THEATRES.

To the Editor of the Saturday Review.

De Crespigny Park, Denmark Hill S.E.
18 November 1909.

Sir,—According to the "Illustrated Handbook" of the National Theatre scheme, there appears to be a yearly deficit on each one of the so-called National Theatres which would mean to the men of London, in spite of the £500,000 they are asked to subscribe, a burthen upon the taxpayer of perhaps another £30,000 to be made up out of the rates each year, should this scheme (the most wild of ambitions) form another of England's useless foundations. We are told by this "Handbook":

1. The Théâtre Français, Paris, and the Théâtre de l'Odéon: in round figures, cost the State £10,600 a year.

2. The Royal Theatre, Copenhagen: its annual deficit about £10,000.

3. The Royal Playhouse, Berlin: costs about £10,000.

4. The New Theatre, New York: we are told what it purposes doing.

5. The Burg Theatre, Vienna: this costs the Emperor £24,000, and he has to support the Opera House. England would be expected to do as much as this—and, if all deficits are to be cast upon the taxpayer, one ought to ask where this poor creature is to get the money from. Figs do not grow upon thistles.

6. The Théâtre des Célestins, Lyons: this costs the town about £9600.

7. The Czech Theatre, Prague: this costs Bohemia £5400.

8. The Royal Playhouse, Dresden: this costs at least each year £8000.

N.B.—It should be noted in addition to the abovementioned figures, in some cases these items do not include heating, lighting, and, in another instance, paying the staff, nor for scenery, and never rent in these cases.

With every National Theatre it is a fact that the free tickets given to the press and its friends, the élite of persons associated with the drama (no matter if such may know one single aspect under which, or by which, dramatic art may be demonstrated, but simply because these creatures have daughters), these have to be provided with free tickets. The cost of these tickets is astounding, and for the amusement of this class of the community the taxpayer has to pay in order that a number of abject fools may have enjoyment without paying for it. The present writer has lived long enough in Paris and Berlin to know of what he writes from personal knowledge. Can any one of the promoters of the "National Shakespeare Memorial Theatre" remember the ignominious fate of our recently erected English Opera House?

Honest men have ever desired to pay the cost of their own pleasures—there is something to this effect in (shall we call it? the "dark ages" of) Homer; which, at the cost of not being properly understood by the crowd, we leave to be supplied by the imagination of those it alone concerns.

In another place Homer says, in so many words, "To desire pleasure at the cost of another is an abomination". To ask for, as to possess, a National Theatre which the "management" cannot make pay its own way is disgraceful, and never should be tolerated for a single moment. Such a "memorial" as this could in no way honour Shakespeare; it would only make his honoured name a curse to the taxpayer. There are thousands of honourable men of London who have no admiration for the stage or its associates, while they have no time left for the study of poetry; their eyes are burnt out of their defenceless heads toiling day and night to scrape together money for the due payment of those imposts which short-sighted, halfpenny politicians lay upon the shoulders of the people! The late Sir Theodore Martin reprobated the idea of a National Theatre, saying "such could benefit no person except ambitious managers unable to run a theatre by their own ability". "A State theatre", he said, "run at the cost of the rates would stifle every legitimate enterprise, placing a fictitious price on worthless people at the cost of the endowment."

Richard C. Jackson.

THE "QUICUNQUE VULT".

To the Editor of the Saturday Review.

15 November 1909.

Sir,—It is not easy to see wherein lies the impropriety which your correspondent finds in the slight change made in the re-translation of the words "Unus ergo Pater, non tres Patres" from "So there is one Father, not three Fathers" to "There is therefore one Father", etc.

What does appear open to question, both in the Prayer-book translation and in the new one, is the use of disconnected adjectives in the plural number. For instance: "Non tres æterni"—"They are not three Eternals" (same in both), "Tres immensi"—"Three Incomprehensibles" (Prayer-book), "Three Infinites" (new translation). Does the language admit of such employment of plural adjectives apart from their nouns, except in colloquial English?

Yours faithfully,
A. L. H.

[How about "sweets", "evils", "goods", "sharps", "flats"?—Ed. S. R.]

CARLYLE AND SHAMS.

To the Editor of the Saturday Review.

Scottish Conservative Club, Edinburgh,
10 November 1909.

Sir,—Your correspondent, James Bell, in your issue of 30 October, refers to a story of Carlyle on the occasion of a visit to a friend's house, stating that his hostess persuaded him to attend family prayers, and to read the Bible lesson. The true version of the story is as told by the late Provost Swan, Kirkcaldy, who was a pupil of Carlyle's. Carlyle often came and lived with the Provost; for he had a great regard for him. Provost Swan was a bachelor, consequently no hostess was in the house. He was a very devout and good man, and a respected Elder in the Free Church. He always had family worship in the morning and evening, which he generally himself conducted, unless some minister was his guest. The Provost asked the great philosopher if he would read a chapter to those at worship, which generally consisted of his servant and any guest that might be staying with him. After a little persuasion, Carlyle took hold of the big, old family Bible and proceeded to read the first chapter of Job, and got so interested he read on chapter after chapter, until he came to the sixth verse of the sixth chapter: "Or is there any taste in the white of an egg". He then stood up and shut the Bible, stating: "I never knew that was in the Bible before"; and walked out of the room to his sanctum to enjoy his pipe, leaving the good old Provost to finish the devotions, "which did not, like some public meeting, break up in confusion", as stated by your correspondent.

Yours truly,
William Williamson.

REVIEWS.

THE MAN SHAKESPEARE.

"The Man Shakespeare and his Tragic Life Story." By Frank Harris. London: Palmer. 1909. 7s. 6d. net.

THIS book, we are told, has "grown out of" a series of articles which appeared in the SATURDAY REVIEW some ten or twelve years ago. They were recognised at the time as brilliant work, and the forceful originality of the writer's standpoint was admitted even by many to whom his conclusions seemed no more than the fine flower of conjectural audacity. The same material has here been worked up and expanded to imposing proportions. A wealth of illustration has been added, astonishing in its variety, but more astonishing still by reason of the masterly skill which lends to every detail a cumulative and convergent force. If the fabric of the work be, after all, conjectural, we can at least say that no more confident, harmonious and creative piece of conjecture has appeared in modern literary criticism.

Briefly, the author's purpose is to disentangle the man Shakespeare from his writings—aided here and there, of course, by what is known otherwise. The method is simple but powerful. Accepting in the main the more or less scientifically determined chronology of the plays, he approaches them with the aim, at first, of discovering a type-character whose recurrent accents, under a score of thin disguises, suggest an authentic voice of Shakespeare himself. Having fixed this type-character by establishing a community of temperamental traits in figures which range from Romeo to Macbeth, he emphasises his conclusion by a negative but hardly less plausible mode of proof. He takes those characters (the Henry V. class) which by all laws of dramatic consistency should throughout show a polar divergence from the type-character and tries to convince us by a multitude of touches that even here—against the obvious design of their creator—the type-character persistently intrudes. More than that; he alleges a perpetual tendency of unconscious lapse into the type-character wherever Shakespeare is dealing with such minor figures as only claim from him a casual or sketchy handling. All this is enforced by really profuse and consecutive quotation; sometimes to the extent of a virtually continuous study, scene by scene, of a single character. From the sin of judicious omission, so gross and palpable in the ordinary Shakespearean theorist, these chapters are wholly exempt. Shakespeare's portrait is now projected, and our author—staking everything on its authenticity, as indeed he seems to admit—goes on to educe from the poems and plays, in order of their production, the outlines of Shakespeare's mental experience in ambitious youth, passionate maturity, and feverish decline. For Mr. Harris Shakespeare's "tragic" story is summed up in his insensate and prolonged love for Mary Fitton, the maid of honour who had originally betrayed him by yielding to his noble friend Herbert. To the torments of frustrate desire, exquisite in a nature at once acutely sensitive and sensual, are due the last reaches and terrible scope of the great tragedies. External evidence, necessarily scanty in bulk but chosen with nice judgment, is brought in from point to point to corroborate the tale.

For ourselves we have no stake in those standard conceptions of Shakespeare which for many professional critics have all the sanctity of vested interests. To our mind the mass of professional Shakespeare commentary is blasted at the outset by a patent want of imagination. The daring and independent layman, inspired by sheer love of life and poetry, is just the writer we most cordially welcome and most seldom see in the field of Shakespearean investigation. A writer like Mr. Harris, whose very iconoclasm is imbued with passionate appreciation—who disturbs old superstitions about Shakespeare only to vindicate his nervous and splendid humanity—is rare indeed. But while we admit the brilliance and cogency of Mr. Harris' d[illegible]nstration, we are conscious of some reserve. It is possible (outside mathematics) for a process of proof to be too complete, too perfect and rounded. This book, in fact, has the fascinating quality of a powerful novel, tinged everywhere with that realism of which its writer has elsewhere shown himself a master. It is essentially the work of an artist who will suffer no loose threads, and in whose hands the most diverse materials are meekly subservient to the unity of effect at which he aims. Moreover, the style is compelling. Aware that Mr. Harris is all the while building up his theory, we turn the pages with an eye everywhere alert for such windings and sophistries as are characteristic of writers resolved on proving a point at all hazards. Our vigilance is unnecessary, or else futile. From beginning to end he sustains with ease the demeanour of a plain man, plainly bent on enforcing obvious truths with a superfluity of evidence at his command. The originality of his views is the more striking, yet the more persuasive, by reason of this simple air and apparent freedom from paradox. Such work is more than interesting; it is exciting, and we willingly yield to the spell it exerts as we read. In calm afterthought, however, we hesitate to accept it as an infallible guide in the stubborn and tortuous region of objective fact. Mr. Harris himselves notes somewhere that the most subtle figure drawn by a dramatist becomes simple when we contrast it with an average man in real life. This is profoundly true, and we apply the principle to his own delineation of Shakespeare. Many of the lines in the portrait we accept, but the total proportions leave us somewhat sceptical. Particularly we feel this in the second part of the book. "Shakespeare's life story", we reflect, "cannot be reducible to factors so simple as those."

That Mr. Harris has realised Shakespeare more actually than any previous writer—a great achievement—is past doubt. Our wonder is whether this Shakespeare, whose lineaments pale or vivid are discerned in Romeo as in Orsino, Hamlet and Macbeth, Duke Vincentio and Posthumus, be necessarily the Shakespeare of flesh and blood. Admit that by every chemical test, negative as well as positive, we have elicited from the dramas an unmistakable type-character, embodying the distinctively Shakespearean temper and outlook. Have we really got so far, even then, as Mr. Harris would have us believe? To us it seems, or very largely seems, that we have simply got past the mask of the dramatist to the lyrical poet beneath. We are thus still confronted with that inscrutable complexity, the artist-mind. It is true we habitually speak of lyric as though it were peculiarly the vehicle of a poet himself, of his veritable passions, hope, or fear. But in plain English we are far from persuading ourselves that lyric utterance, however unstudied or spontaneous, is a faithful glass of the workaday life from which it springs. We think Mr. Harris has proved, admirably, that in Shakespeare the speech of thought (so to put it) carries more conviction than the speech of action; that Hamlet is more consistently "vécu" than Henry V. or Hotspur. Perhaps, in the broad, it is no illegitimate inference that the man Shakespeare was introspective and temperamentally irresolute. Take Marlowe, however. Everybody must agree that Marlowe is not a creator of individual men; that virtually, in all his plays, we are dealing with a lyrical, not an impersonating, Marlowe. Are we then justified in assuming that this poet, whose monstrous types are nothing if not energies incarnate, was a man audacious in design and swift to action? We fancy not. Concede again that the broad change in Shakespeare's dramatic outlook—that darkening sky and beckoning of sinister shapes which ushers in his great tragic period—implies some dreadful ripening in his personal experience, such as comes to most middle-aged men who can feel. Must we go on to furnish his inner life with erotic madness deduced from Troilus or speeches in Lear, with frantic jealousy from Othello, with misanthropic despair from Timon? Potentially, no doubt, and to some extent actually, Shakespeare had all these things. Most men of the Renaissance-artist type had a fair spice of them. Indeed, we have always thought too slight attention has been paid to those notes of decadence which obviously coexist throughout Elizabethan literature with the vernal vigour. But no Fitton theory, it seems to us, is enough to cover the ground of Shakespeare's most powerful development. The grand passions of artists are results, rather than conditions, of their imaginative susceptibility. And the most emotional utterances of a poet may be no index at all to the normal state of his mind, even within an hour of the poem's production. Poetry springs from experience of life, of course. But for a poet an old sorrow is as good material as a fresh one, probably better. We already have warned our readers that there is no crudeness in Mr. Harris' actual exposition of his theories. By the time he is ready to give these theories full play he has insidiously wound himself into us and fired us with the spirit of the game. Exempt from such fascination, we should smile (for example) at his dismissal of Shakespeare's later virginal figures as shadows of pure girlhood, pathetically chosen in reaction from the passionate and froward creature who had been his bane. No need to prove for us that Miranda, Perdita, and the rest are abstractions compared with Cleopatra. Of course they are. To be abstract is the fate of all virgins in drama. If we were asked to put our thumb on the one really striking psychological flaw, we should find it in the author's treatment of Shakespeare's humour. Having conjured up from a dozen impersonations the central mind of Shakespeare, and shown us its characteristics, he has the hardihood to bring in the humour by way of addition. This at least is how the process strikes us, and we feel that Shakespeare's humour is too fundamental to be so regarded. We cannot think of it as a specific quality, interspersed with and enlivening other qualities. It is unspeakably more than that. In essence the humour of Shakespeare is a tremendous and unapproachable capacity of detachment. Shakespeare the humourist, in other words, is a Shakespeare who will not give his heart away quite so vividly as the gentle reader, charmed or intimidated by Mr. Harris, may for the moment imagine.

With all these reservations, Mr. Harris has done much for the man Shakespeare. He has certainly demolished once for all the naïve effigy of a plump citizen, prosperously active or comfortably retired. He causes us to be strangely aware of the blood and sweat that must have gone to the making of those plays. We think he makes too much of Shakespeare's alleged "snobbery" and political hatred of the masses, of his failure to depict a middle-class puritan with sympathy, and of the fact that he nowhere paints a reformer. No artist, we believe, has ever triumphed in a sympathetic creation of demagogue, burgess, or visionary. (Mr. Harris' own tale "Sonia" comes as near as anything we know, but it is only a short story.) Some have succeeded in giving us the human traits beneath such characters; the types themselves have defied art, perhaps will always defy it. On all these points, none the less, Mr. Harris is full of suggestive insight. Those who have accepted as final the dogma that Shakespeare's personality eludes all detection will rub their eyes as they read this book and feel that at least they are on the track of something definite. For Shakespeareans the book is in the nature of a novum organum.

What equally concerns us is the remarkable freshness and fire of poetic appreciation with which the writer is endowed. We realise everywhere that he comes to Shakespeare's work with no academic predisposition, but as man of the world with a singular perception of poetry in its human and life-revealing aspect. His power of quotation (always in our opinion the last test of criticism) is equalled by his gift in discriminating gold from silver, and the bold but sure hand with which he rejects base metal. As critic of poetry Mr. Harris has none of those defects which usually attend, by a just nemesis, the prolonged pursuit of one idea. His sense of poetry has no blind spots. He weighs alike the exquisite phrase, the lyrical emotion, the strong clash or minute touch of character, and the broad philosophy of life. Most criticism of poetry is deciduous just because the critic's sensibility is unbalanced and leads him to set store by one or other of these factors at the expense of the rest. Mr. Harris' equipment, as judge of dramatic poetry, is wonderfully catholic. His fastidious observation of detail and setting occasionally almost reminds us of Wilde's unique essay on Shakespeare's use of costume. At the other end there is complete and intense recognition of Shakespeare the moral master; the austere breadth of Shakespeare's outlook on human destiny is nowhere missed. Nobody who cares for fine literature, however indifferent he may be to Mr. Harris' main thesis, should pass the book by. As a thesis, we call it a brilliant and fascinating tour de force. As a book concerned with the greatest poetry, we assign to it critical merit of the first order. In both aspects we predict for it a permanent importance.

THE QUEST OF THE SOUTH POLE.

"The Heart of the Antarctic: being the Story of the British Expedition, 1907–1909." By E. H. Shackleton C.V.O." London: Heinemann. 1909. 36s. net.

WHEN the two great scientific societies resolved to renew the work of Antarctic exploration, their object was not to reach the South Pole, but to explore in various directions from a base as far as possible within the unknown region, and to make scientific researches around the selected base. The distinguished commander of their expedition carried out their instructions with admirable completeness. Captain Scott with his companions made an exhaustive examination of the immediate vicinity of his base during two winters and three summers, and he sent out five or six extended sledge parties, the two most important being conducted by himself.

The general result was the discovery of a continuous range of mountains, running north and south, from Cape Adare to 83° S., where it turned to the N.N.E., with glaciers descending at intervals to the ice barrier, and of a vast inland ice cap averaging an elevation of 10,000 feet. Captain Scott is the first Antarctic land explorer, the creator of Antarctic sledge-travelling. There remained the exploration of King Edward VII. Land and the solution of the problem of the ice barrier. Captain Scott looked forward to a completion of his work when his naval duties would admit of his absence.

Mr. Ernest Shackleton was taken from the mercantile marine by Captain Scott, who appointed him to be one of the executive officers of the "Discovery". He was enthusiastic and zealous, proving a most useful member of the expedition, and he accompanied his chief on the memorable southern journey. But his health broke down and he was invalided after the first winter. From that time Mr. Shackleton was always anxious to return to the Antarctic work. When at length he obtained the needful funds, he announced his object to be the South Pole. The best-known route is from Captain Scott's base and along his southern line of march until the mountain range turns eastward, and then up one of the glaciers and over the ice cap discovered by Captain Scott. The distance is 750 miles, 250 of which Mr. Shackleton had already traversed with Captain Scott. A base having been selected, which had been worked out by the members of the "Discovery" expedition during two winters and three summers, any important additions to what had already been done could not be expected as regards scientific research.

Mr. Shackleton now gives us the story of his expedition. The vessel obtained for landing the party of fifteen in McMurdo Sound was the "Nimrod", of little over 200 tons, which had to take out the Manchurian ponies, a motor car, the winter hut in pieces, and the provisions. She was too small for the work. The command was given to Captain England, an excellent officer with previous experience of Antarctic navigation. He took the ship out from England to New Zealand, superintended the refitting and loading, navigated her, when overloaded and with encumbered decks, through the ice, landed the exploring party at Cape Royds, and navigated the ship, when nearly empty, back to New Zealand. He certainly did very important service to the expedition.

Mr. Shackleton wisely followed the system of his old leader, which he had learnt on board the "Discovery", in all matters respecting provisions, clothing, sledge and tent equipment, and diet while travelling; and he had with him two petty officers of the "Discovery", Joyce and Wild, who also had thorough practical acquaintance with Captain Scott's system. The winter hut was built at Cape Royds, on a spot where Captain Scott and Dr. Wilson had passed several days in the summer of 1904. There is an interesting chapter giving an account of the winter quarters, and another describing the ascent of Mount Erebus in the month of March by three of the party, who climbed the difficult slopes and on the 10th reached the edge of the crater, which is 900 feet deep and half a mile wide. A huge column of steam was rising from the abyss. The scene is admirably described by Professor David, of Sydney, the leader of the party.

But the centre of interest in this expedition was the attempt to reach the South Pole. The distance, combined with the difficulties of the way, was too great for men alone, although, if other means could be used for half the way, the remaining distance could be achieved. Mr. Shackleton's invention was the use of ponies. There were four available, and every one dragged a sledge. Provisions for ninety-one days were taken, weighing 773⅓ pounds, being 34 ounces per day per man. This would be considered insufficient in Arctic sledge-travelling; but it is practically the same as Scott's scale. The ponies took the sledges at a fairly good rate to the point where the mountains turn to the east, about seventy miles beyond Captain Scott's furthest point. Here the explorers had to ascend the glacier and begin their own sledge work. They were four in number—Shackleton and Wild with former experience, Lieutenant Evans R.N.R. and Dr. Marshall. The journey from the ship to the glacier, with ponies, took thirty-six days. With the provisions that remained it would not be possible to reach the pole; but a dash was made to attain the highest possible latitude. Mr. Shackleton's journal is very interesting, describing the scenery, the gradual ascent to a height of 10,000 feet, and the danger from crevasses. The ascent to the ice cap took them twenty-two days, from 5 December to the 27th, about the same time as Captain Scott took in ascending the Ferrar glacier; but he was confined to the tent by a gale during four days. Mr. Shackleton and his companions advanced over the ice cap, on half rations, for twelve days, being confined to their tent for two days. Captain Scott advanced westward over the ice cap for sixteen days, and the position of the magnetic pole was fixed by his observations. The Shackleton party endured great hardships and encountered dangers from hidden crevasses. It was a sporting and very plucky achievement, for which they deserve great credit. The return to the ship was necessarily rapid, owing to shortness of provisions, and was accomplished in fifty-three days.

By far the most important result of this journey was the discovery by Wild of six seams of what appears to have been coal, at 6000 feet above the sea. They were in the medial moraine in 85° S., and among them there was a fragment of fine-grained sandstone, with a black band running through it. The micro-slides of this specimen, examined at the Sydney University, prove that it is a coniferous wood. So that we at length have evidence of a warm climate near the South Pole in remote geological times, and of the existence of forest trees.

The sledge meters, during Mr. Shackleton's southward journey of a hundred and twenty-six days, recorded 1725 statute miles, but this includes relay work and back marches. Arctic and Antarctic work differs in several respects, and the sledge journeys are not comparable. But the great journeys of McClintock and Mecham, without the help of dogs, ponies, or anything but men at the drag ropes, will probably never be equalled. McClintock made 1408 statute miles at the rate of ten and a half miles a day, Mecham made 1336 statute miles at a rate of over twenty miles a day. The journey of Mr. Shackleton after leaving the ponies cannot be classed with these, but may be compared with Captain Scott's journey over the ice cap to the westward. They are about equal.

The second volume contains Professor David's narrative of a journey northwards to the position of the south magnetic pole, which was fixed by Captain Scott's observations 72° 51′ S.—156° 2′ S.E., calculated by Commander Chetwynd R.N. There was no particular object in going to the position itself; but the journey took the explorers over some new ground, and the narrative is interesting. There is also a good account of the work of Captain Evans, of the "Nimrod", in picking up the various travelling parties, before sailing for New Zealand.

Mr. Shackleton's own narratives are well told and will no doubt be popular with the general reader, and the work is admirably illustrated. It is noteworthy that this history of the Shackleton dash towards the South Pole has been published before the voluminous scientific results of the "Discovery" expedition have all seen the light. The Antarctic Joint Finance Committee still exists, and two volumes of the scientific results are still unpublished; nor are the accounts finally wound up and submitted to the councils of the two societies.

Meanwhile the South Pole remains to be reached. Mr. Shackleton's near approach, and events which have occurred since, can but whet the wish that the thing should be done, and by Englishmen. Fortunately, after much good service in the Navy since his return, Captain Scott is able to undertake the difficult task, at the same time doing all in his power to complete the geographical work within the Antarctic quadrant which is peculiarly his own. With this distinguished explorer success is, humanly speaking, assured.

KING MANUEL'S KINGDOM.

"Portugal: its Land and People." By W. H. Koebel. With Illustrations by Mrs. S. Roope Dockery. London: Constable. 1909. 16s. net.

ALTHOUGH a man with a ten-pound note in his pocket can transfer himself from London to Lisbon in forty-eight hours, Portugal, for most people, remains a kind of Ultima Thule. Travellers who have set eyes upon the tawny waters of the Tagus or the Douro generally return to the banks of grey Thames with the air of a Nansen or a Shackleton. Yet Portugal, in nearly all essential respects, is hardly less amenable than England. England, it is true, is netted over with a closer mesh of telegraph wires, and the Englishman boasts superior facilities for hurrying out of a place which bores him into another place which bores him still more. But, taking inn for inn, bed for bed, meal for meal, dish for dish, bottle for bottle, waiter for waiter, highway for highway, peasant for peasant, provincial Portugal is more comfortable to explore than provincial England.

Mr. W. H. Koebel, who, with the aid of Mrs. Roope Dockery, has made an engaging picture-book about King Manoel's country, cannot quite free himself from this traditional belief that whoso lands in Portugal is somewhat of a Columbus. With the exception of an unconventional jaunt around Estremoz, he does not appear to have gone out of hearing of the locomotive's whistle; yet he writes like a pioneer. His chapter called "The Far North", for example, merely records a visit to Vianna do Castello, one of the most civilised towns in the kingdom, which lies only two hours' railway journey from Oporto. Mr. Koebel apparently saw nothing of Algarve, the ancient southern kingdom, or of the highlands of Traz os Montes. He knows his Lisbon and his Porto, and his Regoa where the English buy port wine; but he has no word to say of Guimarães, the "Portuguese Sheffield", or of Covilhã, the "Portuguese Manchester"—those two dinless and smokeless towns sharpening tools and weaving fabrics under the enormous shadow of desolate mountains. He sojourned in the Swiss-managed hotel-palace at

Bussaco; but he records no pilgrimage to Vizeu, Portugal's Lincoln, where rests one of the grandest and most mysterious altar-pieces in the world; nor to Mafra, Portugal's Escorial; nor to Lamego, high among the hills of the Beira Alta; nor to the gaunt Estrella where the goatherds, without an inch of shelter, have learned to sleep in the midst of torrential rain merely leaning on the heads of their staves. What is still more unfortunate, Mr. Koebel would seem to have almost confined himself to the haunts of Englishmen. When he ventured further afield it was under the guidance of the Propaganda of Portugal, an otherwise excellent society whose cosmopolitan ideals are more helpful to the tourist than to the student. In such circumstances Mr. Koebel has naturally failed to make good the sub-title of his book. He saw too little of the Land, and is therefore unable to write very usefully about the People.

The People being mainly a rural People, an inquirer who is fain to study them in their habits as they live must needs break away from the tracks which link up the few urban centres. He must cut across the grain of the Land, with the mule instead of the iron horse to carry him. By rubbing the finer edges off his Latin and by committing to memory a few hundred Moorish words he must acquire a working knowledge of the lovable Portuguese tongue. He must dissemble a boundless curiosity under an unfailing tact. He must remember that every Portuguese bullock-driver or roadside potter or sardine-catcher or olive-gatherer believes himself to be a fine-spirited gentleman; and that, in nine cases out of ten, the bullock-driver or potter or sardine-catcher or olive-gatherer is quite right. He must early acquire the not very difficult art of probing local life without perpetrating religious or political indiscretions and without offending against the etiquette of a country where even the humblest tourist with a knapsack finds his inn-reckonings made out to the Most Excellent and Most Illustrious Senhor. If Mr. Koebel did these things he has not allowed them to come to fruit in his book; for, although he visited Portugal during a vastly interesting crisis in the little nation's life, he has contented himself with adding one more travel-book to the shelf, and has written hardly at all about the People's mind and the Land's need.

Taking his book, however, for what it is instead of for what one could wish it to be, Mr. Koebel has certainly improved upon most of his forerunners in the same field. From the days of Beckford onwards it has been the fashion with England's literary travellers to belittle the friendly and allied nation of Portugal. The late Oswald Crawfurd, who lived in the country for many years, could hardly speak too loudly in praise of its inhabitants; but the tourist with two portmanteaux and three words of Portuguese has nearly always chosen to print a long-drawn sneer at the Land and at all the people in it, with the exception of the English and Scots colonies in Lisbon and Oporto. Mr. Koebel, despite his limitations, deserves warm praise for having followed a more excellent way. He is not ashamed to write fairly and even handsomely about the people among whom he was happy; and it is a pleasant coincidence that his book should have come forth in the year of King Manuel's visit to Portugal's truest friend and oldest ally.

NOVELS.

"Bella Donna." By Robert Hichens. London: Heinemann. 1909. 2 vols. 4s. 6d. net.

This is one of the best novels we have ever read, and quite the best that Mr. Robert Hichens has written. It combines the two elements of which every good novel ought to be composed, subtle analysis of character and an exciting plot. The character of Dr. Meyer Isaacson, the fashionable physician, of German-Jewish origin, is perfectly free from prejudice and based on accurate knowledge of the type. "He looked intensely vital —almost unnaturally vital—when he was surrounded by English people, but he did not look fierce and hungry. One could imagine him doing something bizarre, but one could not conceive of him doing anything low." The intellectual, as distinguished from the commercial, Hebrew could not be summed up better. "Mrs. Chepstow (Bella Donna) was a great beauty in decline", and the viciousness of the déclassée of forty-five is perhaps a trifle exaggerated. The morbid passion of a female voluptuary of middle-age for a lusty young Egyptian financier in a fez is described with a realism which will shock some people. The infatuation of Nigel, "the damfool Britisher", of aristocratic belongings, for his Messalina is not, we think, overdone, though the strokes of the pen are somewhat heavy. We will not spoil the reading of this book by sketching the thrilling plot, which is enacted on the Nile and its banks. Needless to say, the Egyptian scenery and servants are described by Mr. Hichens with affectionate familiarity.

"Love and the Wise Men." By Percy White. London: Methuen. 1909. 6s.

This novel, according to the publishers' description on its wrapper, "is the study of a brilliant woman-hater and of his final conquest by a charming lady who has persuaded herself that it is her duty to despise man". But it is nothing of the kind. Really there ought to be a modicum of accuracy even in an advertisement. The story, like so many of Mr. White's, is told by a man standing outside the main current of the events—a man to whom things happen, a fly on the wheel, with something of the microscopic vision of a fly. David Kirke is educated by a philosopher uncle, who holds that the world is dominated by sex-obsession, and that children must by their early education be armed to withstand the unreal glamour of amorous emotions. So David and his friend Philip Kirke are sent to a peculiar school in France kept by a French philosopher who shares Mr. Kirke's views. The description of life at the French school is most amusing. Of course love—precocious romance quite unchilled by their physiological knowledge—comes to dominate both David and Philip. The plot is well worked out, and the book must be counted as one of Mr. White's happier efforts.

"Stradella: an Old Italian Love Tale." By F. Marion Crawford. London: Macmillan. 1909. 6s.

The last work of a veteran novelist must possess an interest of its own, but "Stradella" would not attract much attention from its intrinsic merits. The true story of the musician Stradella's elopement from Venice with a girl of good family supplies the framework for a graceful but somewhat mechanical story. Stradella and his bride remain shadowy figures, but two bravi who follow them—imaginary persons—have, paradoxically enough, the flesh and blood of real life as they move amongst the historical characters on the stage. The bravi are such cheerful and ingenious scoundrels that the failure of their designs becomes almost pathetic. We have a glimpse of Queen Christina of Sweden, and the Venice and the Rome of the late seventeenth century are skilfully depicted. But for all its fluency the story lacks distinction.

SHORTER NOTICES.

"Notes on Shooting in the British Isles." By Major Arthur Hood. London: "The Times" Publishing Co. 1909. 1s.

Books on shooting in the British Isles are many, but those which contain good first-hand information on the subject in all its branches are extremely rare. Major Hood is well known as a good game shot and as having had opportunities of shooting in some of the most famous localities; in fact, he writes as a man who has, in all probability, not only seen grouse and partridge driving, as well as covert shooting, at its very best, but has also shot woodcock, snipe, and duck at places where the best sport obtainable in these islands is to be found. Hence all that he has to say on the subject of home shooting is worthy of attention, and we have no doubt that all hosts of shooting parties will be especially grateful to Major Hood for his advice. Some of his suggestions, begot from wide experience, are admirable, notably those in connexion with partridge driving. No doubt some readers

will find fault with his style, but it should be remembered that he is a professor of the shot-gun and not of the pen; in fact, he especially excuses himself from discussing the joys of shooting over dogs and of driving, giving as a reason that since "abler pens" have done so, he has not ventured "to put his oar in"! The metaphor is understandable, if a little mixed. So also is his description of a famous grouse moor, situated on a mountain "rather steeper than the sides of most houses"! In the next edition of this book—for it will most assuredly be in demand, not only among those who shoot and understand shooting but among the immense majority of those who merely own guns and buy cartridges, yet are anxious to know something about the sport—it would do well if Major Hood asked some ornithological friend to revise his names of birds, both English and Latin. He might then possibly refrain from writing about Mallard drakes and Mallard ducks! He might also find a better name for the tarsus of a bird than "hock-joint"! These are, however, minor points. We note but one serious error in the whole book. He quotes Ireland and the Outer Hebrides as the best localities in our isles for snipe-shooting. Ireland, yes! since it lies along the line of migration from N.E. to S.W., as also do certain of the Inner Hebrides, well known to a few fortunate sportsmen. But Lewis, Uist and the other Outer Hebrides lie just outside the line taken by the migrating snipe. Those who have an extended experience of the Outer Islands know that when the small stock of native-bred snipe there have been shot, no more arrive to take their place during that season. On the other hand, in the Inner Islands, situated on the line of migration, good bags may be made repeatedly over the same ground at short intervals. The final chapter, styled "Random Remarks", is hardly in keeping with the rest of this really excellent little book, although some of the information given in it is both interesting and useful.

"Lectures on the Strategy of the Franco-German War, 1870, up to the Battle of Sedan." By Brevet-Major W. D. Bird. London: Rees. 1909. 6s. net.

For many years the only book available for those who wished seriously to study the Franco-German War of 1870 was the German official account. Many were the attempts made by English writers to present the campaign in a somewhat less biassed form, but one and all laboured under the difficulty that they were compelled to accept the German accounts as no others were available. The appearance of the French official account, which is an extraordinarily good book, enables the student to form a reasonably fair idea of the great events of the months July to September 1870. Considering the magnitude of the issues involved, the wide extent of the ground covered both in the preliminary strategical deployment and by the field of operations, and the great masses of men employed, it is no light work to attempt, as Major Bird has done, to present the whole circumstances in a small book of only 125 pages of open print. He has done so in a very fair manner, and this little book will be of great use to all who wish to get a good general idea of the campaign before entering into more extended and detailed studies of it. Of especial value are the small maps showing both the supposed positions of "the enemy" and the actual points they occupied on successive days. Nothing could demonstrate more clearly the extraordinary difficulties which beset every commander of an army in making his dispositions for the march or for a combat, owing to lack of correct information of his opponents' movements.

"Greece in Evolution." Edited by G. F. Abbot. London: Fisher Unwin. 1909. 5s. net.

This book is a kind of glorified pamphlet. It consists of a number of studies "prepared under the auspices of the French League for the Defence of the Rights of Hellenism", and written by members of the League. It seeks to interest the reader in the political objects of the League by pointing out what a beautiful country Greece is, and what fine fellows the Greeks have been. "Of all the ruins of Greece the Greek people is not the least interesting", wrote Edmund About in his "Memoir on the Island of Ægina". This, we are told, is no longer true. The land of Greece is a rational organism. Rationalism, as practised in Greece and as understood by France, Greece's modern sponsor, is a thing of doubtful value. Most of us would prefer the ruin to a rational Greece as she shows herself to-day. It is characteristic of the case for Greece pleaded in this volume by her eloquent advocates that, in discussing the economic factors that will govern her future, special prominence is given to the necessity for exploiting the very ruins upon which she professes to have turned her back. When Greece has been brought within sixty hours' distance of Paris, and has been covered with nice hotels, then, indeed, rationalism is going to have a real chance.

"Peacock's Memoirs of Shelley. With Shelley's Letters to Peacock." Edited by H. F. B. Brett-Smith. London: Frowde. 1909. 2s. 6d. net.

Peacock—save for Hogg—was perhaps the one man of Shelley's generation qualified to write of the poet without running into didactic absurdities. He had a queer blend of humour and sympathy that enabled him to understand his subject, and yet at the same time to stand between his subject and the world that ridiculed him. The memoirs are unpretentious, too, which is more than half their charm. They are, in fact, reviews written in correction of the heavier and less discerning biographies of the day. This neat, cheap, and handy little book should increase the number of Peacock's readers. If, as may be imagined, it impels some of them into an acquaintance with his novels, it will have served a good turn to Peacock as well as to Shelley; and, of course, to the readers.

"Dictionary of National Biography." Vol. XXI. Whichcord—Zuylestein. London: Smith, Elder. 1909. 15s. net.

There is a curious sort of interest in opening a volume of the Dictionary casually. Every name we know is of some significance in our national history. On whose story shall we come by merely taking a page at random? The first name which catches the eye in the present volume is that of Wordsworth, to whom Leslie Stephen has devoted nearly sixteen pages. We turn again and we come upon Charles Kent's Cardinal Wiseman, or Leslie Stephen's Wilberforce, or we dip deeper and find the Rev. Hastings Rashdall's long account of Wycliffe. Williams is the patronymic which occupies most space in this volume. The reissue of the Dictionary is now within one volume of completion. It is a marvel of both quality and quantity for the price charged, and the more the work is consulted the more conscious we are of the service it renders.

"A Scamper through the Far East." By Major H. H. Austin. London: Arnold. 1909. 15s. net.

For this book there is no room. If the author merely scampered through the Far East, he has no excuse for publishing his impressions, which can have no value. If he did more and remained there longer, he should not have called his book a scamper. However, he says himself his trip was a scamper and nothing more, so we cannot be doing him an injustice.

For this Week's Books see page 640.

THIS WEEK'S BOOKS.

Biography

Sheridan (Walter Sichel. 2 vols.). Constable. 31*s.* 6*d.* net.

Fiction

The Education of Uncle Paul (Algernon Blackwood). Macmillan, 6*s.*
The Senator Licinius (William Patrick Kelly). Routledge. 6*s.*
Miss Strangeways (Alice M. Diehl); A Legacy of the Granite Hill (Bertram Mitford). Long. 6*s.* each.
Fatal Thirteen (William Le Queux). Paul, 6*s.*
It Never Can Happen Again (William De Morgan. 2 vols.), 10*s.*; Leaves (Violet Clarke), 6*s.* Heinemann.
The Disc (J. B. Harris-Burland); Don Q.'s Love Story (K. and Hesketh Pritchard). Greening. 6*s.* each.
Ordinary People (Una L. Silberrad). Constable. 6*s.*
Suse O'Bushy (W. A. Allan). Bristol: Arrowsmith. 6*s.*

Gift Books

Miss Manners (Aileen Orr). Melrose. 3*s.* 6*d.* net.
A Book of Golden Deeds (Charlotte M. Yonge). Nelson. 6*s.*
Selected Tales of Mystery (Edgar Allan Poe). Sidgwick and Jackson. 12*s.* 6*d.* net.
Rubáiyat of Omar Khayyam (Edward FitzGerald). Hodder and Stoughton. 15*s.* net.

History

Hogarth's London (Henry B. Wheatley). Constable. 21*s.* net.
The Story of the Thames (J. E. Vincent), 7*s.* 6*d.*; Fifty Years of New Japan (Edited by Marcus B. Huish. 2 vols.). Smith, Elder. 21*s.* net.
The Last Years of the Protectorate, 1656-1658 (Charles Harding Firth. 2 vols.). Longmans. 24*s.* net.
A History of Mediæval Political Theory in the West (R. W. Carlyle). Edinburgh: Blackwood. 15*s.* net.
My Thirty Years in India (Sir Edmund C. Cox), 8*s.*; An Art Student's Reminiscences of Paris in the Eighties (Shirley Fox), 10*s.* 6*d.* net. Mills and Boon.
London in the Nineteenth Century (Sir Walter Besant). Black. 30*s.* net.
The Literary Profession in the Elizabethan Age (Phœbe Sheavon). Sherratt & Hughes. 5*s.* net.
The Cambridge History of English Literature (Edited by A. W. Ward. Vol. IV.). Cambridge: at the University Press. 9*s.* net.

Law

The Hague Peace Conferences (A. Pearce Higgins). Cambridge: At the University Press. 15*s.*
A Handbook of Public International Law (T. J. Lawrence). Macmillan. 3*s.*

Natural History and Sport.

Sporting Stories (Thormanby). Mills and Boon. 10*s.* 6*d.* net.
Natural History in Zoological Gardens (Frank E. Beddard). Constable. 3*s.* 6*d.* net.
Trees and Shrubs of the British Isles (C. S. Cooper. 2 vols.). Dent. 21*s.* net.

Reprints and Translations

The Angel of Forgiveness (Rosa Nouchette Carey). Macmillan. 3*s.* 6*d.*
The Japanese Spirit (George Meredith). Constable. 1*s.* net.
The Principles of Eloquence (Nikolaus Schleiniger). Kegan Paul. 7*s.* 6*d.* net.
The Powder-Puff (Frank Blei). Chatto and Windus. 3*s.* 6*d.*

Science and Philosophy

Consciousness (Henry Rutgers Marshall). Macmillan. 17*s.* net.
The Principles of Religious Development (George Galloway). Macmillan. 10*s.* net.
The Survival of Man (Sir Oliver Lodge). Methuen. 7*s.* 6*d.* net.
Great Issues (Robert F. Horton). Fisher Unwin. 7*s.* 6*d.* net.

Theology

Orpheus (Florence Simmonds). Heinemann. 8*s.* 6*d.* net.
Progressive Redemption (Rev. Holden E. Sampson). Rebman. 12*s.* 6*d.* net.
The Way Out (Lampadephoros). Stock. 6*s.* net.
The Divine Worker in Creation and Providence (J. Oswald Dykes). Edinburgh: Clark. 6*s.* net.
Authority in Religion (Rev. J. H. Leckie). Edinburgh: Jack. 5*s.*

Travel

Egypt (Pierre Loti). Laurie. 15*s.* net.
Hungary (Adrian Stokes), 20*s.* net; From Sketch-Book and Diary (Elizabeth Butler), 10*s.* net. Black.
In the Grip of the Nyika (Lieut.-Col. J. H. Patterson). Macmillan. 7*s.* 6*d.* net.

Verse

Sophocles (Arthur S. Way). Macmillan. 3*s.* 6*d.* net.
The Book of Cupid. Constable. 4*s.* 6*d.* net.

Miscellaneous

Broad Lines in Science Teaching (F. Hodson). Christophers. 5*s.* net.
From Cradle to School (Mrs. Ada S. Ballin). Constable. 1*s.* net.
Manufacture of Sugar Cane, The (Llewellyn Jones). Stanford. 13*s.* 6*d.* net.
Mind of the Artist. The (Mrs. Laurence Binyon). Chatto and Windus. 3*s.* 6*d.* net.
Stories from the Operas (Glaydys Davidson). Laurie. 3*s.* 6*d.* net.
Symposium of Plato, The (R. G. Bury). Heffer. 7*s.* net.

Select Gift Books

THOUGHTS FROM MANY CLIMES

Quotations in English, French, and Italian, with the English translations of the Italian, with two Dialogues by E. CARSON. Demy 16mo. Japanese vellum gilt, gilt top, **2s. 6d.** net (by post, 2s. 8d.); Velvet Leather, Gilt Edges, Silk Register, **5s.** net (by post, 5s. 3d.).

A book of meditative thoughts culled from French, Italian, and English authors, arranged for daily readings.

LITERARY BYE-PATHS AND VAGARIES

By THOMAS NEWBIGGING.

Crown 8vo. cloth gilt, **4s. 6d.** net (by post, 4s. 10d.).

A series of interesting essays on out-of-the-way subjects, with the true literary note that the book-lover enjoys.

Fiction.

PHILIP MENZE: A STORY OF COMMERCIAL LIFE.

By H. C. KNIGHT. Crown 8vo. cloth gilt, **6s.**

This story, of especial interest to "Gentlemen of the Road," will prove very attractive to all business men and women.

FOR THREE KINGDOMS

By H. C. CROSFIELD. Frontispiece by Mr. NOYES LEWIS. Crown 8vo. cloth gilt, **6s.**

Recollections of Robert Warden, a servant of King James. Full of stirring incidents, a story that grips the reader from beginning to end.

THE HUMAN GIRL

By GRAHAM MOORE. Crown 8vo. cloth gilt, **2s. 6d.** net.

A humorous and thrilling account of a girl's life at school. Just the book for a Christmas present for the girls.

A Striking New Work for Modern Thinkers.

THE WAY OUT

By LAMPADEPHOROS.

Crown 8vo. cloth gilt, **6s.** net (by post, 6s. 4d.).

Being a Mental Autobiography of Constructive Philosophy. By the Author of "From December to December."

Write for Catalogue (No. R 102) of Antiquarian and General Literature.

London: ELLIOT STOCK, 62 PATERNOSTER ROW, E.C.

VERNON HILL: A New Artist.

It is safe to assert that since the meteoric appearance of Aubrey Beardsley no new genius has appeared in the realm of black-and-white art whose work is so original, so daring, so decorative, so grotesque, and yet so poetic, as that of Vernon Hill. A youth only just past his teens, his inventions have the eternal quality of beauty; his imagination is so rich, so astonishing in its originality, and he is, besides, so gifted with rare humour, that his work defies comparison with anything known to us.

The

ARCADIAN CALENDAR for MCMX.

Quaintly and delicately done, too, are the prose poems that accompany the pictures. In their own way, they are hardly less fantastic. Lovers of art will, however, within a few days, be given the opportunity, on the publication of "The Arcadian Calendar," of judging for themselves of the justice of this announcement.*

* **3s. 6d.** net. 12 by 9 ins.

Published at THE BODLEY HEAD.

Inferences at Bridge

By W. DALTON,

Author of "'SATURDAY' BRIDGE."

"Inferences at Bridge" appeared in the SATURDAY REVIEW. The articles have been revised, with additions by the author, and are issued in handy form by

THE WEST STRAND PUBLISHING CO., LTD., 10 King Street, Covent Garden, W.C.

MACMILLAN'S NEW BOOKS.

Indian Speeches, 1907-1909,

BY

Viscount Morley.

Demy 8vo. 2s. 6d. net. [*Nov. 26.*

COLONEL PATTERSON'S NEW BOOK.

In the Grip of the Nyika.

Further Adventures in British East Africa. By Lieut.-Col. J. H. PATTERSON, D.S.O., Author of "The Man-Eaters of Tsavo." With Illustrations. 8vo. 7s. 6d. net. [*Tuesday.*

Lord Kelvin's Early Home.

Being the Recollections of his Sister, the late Mrs. Elizabeth King, together with some Family Letters and a Supplementary Chapter by the Editor, Elizabeth Thomson King. With Illustrations. 8vo. 8s. 6d. net.

The French Pastellists of the Eighteenth Century.

By HALDANE MACFALL. Edited by T. LEMAN HARE. With 40 Examples in Colour and 12 in Black. Demy 4to. 42s. net.

*** *Illustrated Prospectus post free on application.*

The Water Babies.

By CHARLES KINGSLEY. With 32 Illustrations in Colour by WARWICK GOBLE. Crown 4to. 15s. net.

Also an *Edition de Luxe.* Printed on hand-made paper and limited to 250 copies. Demy 4to. 42s. net.

Memorials of Edward Burne-Jones.

By G. B.-J. Cheaper Reissue. With 2 Photogravure Plates and other Illustrations. 2 vols. 8vo. 10s. 6d. net.

The Acharnians of Aristophanes.

With Introduction, English Prose Translation, Critical Notes, and Commentary. By W. J. M. STARKIE, M.A. 8vo. 10s. net. [*Classical Library.*

Sophocles in English Verse.

Part I. Oedipus the King Oedipus at Kolonus Antigone. By ARTHUR S. WAY, D.Lit. Crown 8vo. 3s. 6d. net.

NEW 6s. NOVELS.

The Education of Uncle Paul.

By ALGERNON BLACKWOOD, Author of "Jimbo," &c.

The story of the inner life of an imaginative and mystical man of mature years, who is led by a little child to "find" himself.

Robert Emmet: A Historical Romance.

By STEPHEN GWYNN.

Daily Telegraph: "Mr. Stephen Gwynn is to be congratulated on a fine piece of work: the writing is excellent, the emotion is never forced, and the situations are led up to and described with an ease and force which prove him a master of romance."

An Ampler Sky. A Volume of Poems.

By LANCE FALLAW. Crown 8vo. 3s. net.

The Principles of Religious Development:

A Psychological and Philosophical Study. By GEORGE GALLOWAY, M.A., B.D., D.Phil. 8vo. 10s. net.

SEVENTH EDITION. JUST PUBLISHED.

A Handbook of Public International Law.

By T. J. LAWRENCE, M.A., LL.D., Member of the Institute of International Law. Seventh Edition. Globe 8vo. 3s.

MACMILLAN'S ILLUSTRATED CATALOGUE POST FREE ON APPLICATION.

MACMILLAN & CO., LTD., LONDON.

SALES BY AUCTION.

JAPANESE COLOUR PRINTS.

MESSRS. SOTHEBY, WILKINSON & HODGE will SELL by AUCTION, at their House, No. 13 Wellington Street, Strand, W.C., on MONDAY, November 22, at 1 o'clock precisely, JAPANESE COLOUR PRINTS, the Property of the late FRANK DILLON, Esq., and other Collectors, comprising Works by Utamaro, Hokusai, Hiroshige, and others, Drawings, Books, Kakemono, Makimono, etc.

May be viewed. Catalogues may be had.

The Collection of ENGRAVINGS and DRAWINGS, the property of the late FREDERICK HENDRIKS, Esq., F.S.S., F.I.A., Knight of Vasa.

MESSRS. SOTHEBY, WILKINSON & HODGE will SELL by AUCTION, at their House, No. 13 Wellington Street, Strand, W.C., on TUESDAY, November 23, and Following Day, at 1 o'clock precisely, ENGRAVINGS AND DRAWINGS, framed and in the portfolio, the Property of the late FREDERICK HENDRIKS, Esq., F.S.S., F.I.A., Knight of Vasa, of 7 Vicarage Gate, Kensington, W., comprising Mezzotint and other portraits, by J. Watson, J. Smith, J. Faber, E. Fisher, C. Wilkin, T. Watson, R. Houston, C. Turner, J. Dixon, J. MacArdell, R. White, W. Faithorne, R. Gaywood, F. Bartolozzi, and others. Etchings and Engravings by Old Masters, including: A. Dürer, Rembrandt, M. Schoengauer, G. Pencz, H. S. Beham, Lucas van Leyden, L. Cranach, The Hopfers, W. Hollar, Sir A. Vandyck, and others. Woodcuts by A. Dürer and others. Water-colour and other Drawings, and Drawings by Old Masters. Fancy subjects of the English school, Modern Etchings by J. M. Whistler, Seymour Haden, J. Jacquemart, and others, and a few Chiaroscuro prints, &c.

May be viewed. Catalogues may be had.

The Valuable LIBRARY of JOHN MITCHELL MARSHALL, Esq. (deceased), of Wallingford.

MESSRS. SOTHEBY, WILKINSON & HODGE will SELL by AUCTION at their House, No. 13, Wellington Street, Strand, W.C., on THURSDAY, November 25, at 1 o'clock precisely, the Valuable LIBRARY of JOHN MITCHELL MARSHALL, Esq. (deceased), of Wallingford, comprising an important and valuable Collection of Works, chiefly illustrated by Thomas and John Bewick; also original Water-colour and Pencil Drawings by Thomas Bewick, Engravings, a few Autograph Letters, Memoranda, etc.; Lord Lilford's Birds of the British Islands, Burton's Arabian Nights and Supplemental Nights, Pine's Horace, potest edition, Foreign Field Sports. Alken's National Sports of Great Britain, and other sporting works; Gould's Birds of Great Britain, 5 vols., Claude's Liber Veritatis, 3 vols., 1777-1819, the Writings of Dickens, Smedley, and others, White's Natural History of Selborne, first edition, &c.

May be viewed two days prior. Catalogues may be had.

BOOKS.

MESSRS. SOTHEBY, WILKINSON & HODGE will SELL by AUCTION, at their House, No. 13 Wellington Street, Strand, W.C., on FRIDAY, November 26, 1909, at 1 o'clock precisely, BOOKS, including Works on Natural History, Biography, Poetry, Fine Art Publications, Illustrated French Works, Sporting Papers by Alken and others, Roxburghe Club, Costume, Essex House Press, American Newspapers, Portraits, Civil War Tracts, Voyages and Travels, etc. The writings of Charles Dickens, Leigh Hunt, G. Bernard Shaw, John Ruskin, Jane Austen, Sir Walter Scott, Stephen Phillips, W. M. Thackeray, Munich Gallery, Dictionary of National Biography, 66 vols., Portraits des Grands Hommes, The Original Letter-Book of Vice-Admiral George Darby, etc.

May be viewed Two Days prior. Catalogues may be had.

A PORTION of the valuable LIBRARY of a Baronet, deceased.

MESSRS. SOTHEBY, WILKINSON & HODGE will SELL by AUCTION at their House, No. 13, Wellington Street, Strand, W.C., on MONDAY, November 29, and following day, at 1 o'clock precisely, a PORTION of the valuable LIBRARY of a Baronet, deceased, comprising a collection of French books of the sixteenth and seventeenth centuries, mostly in fine bindings, many from the Firmin-Didot, Yemeniz, and Beckford collections; rare works on music, early herbals, &c., including the Basle Æsop of 1501, Albert Dürer's Apocalypsis, a remarkable series of works written or printed by Etienne Dolet, "Les Folles Entreprises," and other works by Pierre Gringoire, a complete series of the publications of the "Société des Anciens Textes Français," &c., the property of a gentleman, including Burton's Arabian Nights, original edition, 16 vols., and the property of the trustees of the late William Reid, jun., Esq., of Paisley, including works of the English dramatists and poets, fine art books, &c.

May be viewed two days prior. Catalogues may be had.

THE CONDUIT STREET AUCTION GALLERIES.

The attention of Executors, Trustees, Solicitors, and Owners, who may be desirous of selling Works of Art, Family Jewels, Old Silver, Furniture, Pictures, Prints, Miniatures, China, Coins, Books, Old Lace, Furs, Musical Instruments, Guns, and other Valuables, is drawn to Messrs.

KNIGHT, FRANK & RUTLEY'S

AUCTION GALLERIES, 9 CONDUIT STREET, AND 23A MADDOX STREET, W., which are Open Daily to receive goods intended for early sales.

VALUATIONS are prepared for Fire Insurance, Estate Duty, and all other purposes. As to Insurance, owners are reminded that, for security, Messrs. KNIGHT, FRANK & RUTLEY'S detailed inventory and valuation of the contents of a Town or Country Mansion is an important adjunct to their Fire Insurance Policies.

R. ANDERSON & CO.,

BRITISH, INDIAN, AND COLONIAL ADVERTISEMENT CONTRACTORS,

14 KING WILLIAM STREET, STRAND, W.C.,

GIVE THE BEST TERMS for Company and General Advertising. Advice, Estimates, and all information free of charge. Replies received.

H. SOTHERAN & CO., BOOKSELLERS.

GENERAL AGENTS FOR PRIVATE BOOKBUYERS AND PUBLIC INSTITUTIONS IN INDIA, THE COLONIES, AMERICA, AND ABROAD.

A Monthly Catalogue of fresh Purchases. Specimen number post-free.

BRARIES PURCHASED OR VALUED AND CATALOGUED AND ARRANGED.

Telegraphic Address: BOOKMEN, LONDON. *Codes*: UNICODE and A B C.

140 STRAND, W.C., and 37 PICCADILLY, W., LONDON.

Telephone: CENTRAL 1515. Telephone: MAYFAIR 3601.

SALES BY AUCTION.

THE VALUABLE AND EXTENSIVE LIBRARY of a Gentleman (recently deceased) sold by order of the executors.

MESSRS. HODGSON & CO. will SELL by AUCTION, at their Rooms, 115 Chancery Lane, W.C., on WEDNESDAY, November 24, and Following Day, at One o'clock, the above Valuable LIBRARY, comprising a Collection of Natural History and Scientific Works, including Cramer's Papillons Exotiques, with Supplements by Stoll, 8 vols. Donovan's Insects of New Holland, Leech's Butterflies of China and Japan, 3 vols., and other Entomological Books—Books on Botany, Conchology, Geology, &c.—Topography and Archæology—Books on Numismatics—Bibliographical Works, including a Copy of Hain, and Sotheby's Principia Typographica, 3 vols.—a remarkable Fifteenth Century Illuminated Horæ, with numerous Miniatures, executed for Charles VIII. of France; a few Early Printed Books—Chaucer's Works, 1602, and others in Black Letter—Books of Emblems—Goldsmith's Haunch of Venison, First Edition 1776—Best Editions of Beaumont and Fletcher, Ben Jonson, Shirley, Swift, and others—Gil Blas, by Smollett, 3 vols., 1819, Johnson's Chrysal, 3 vols., 1821, and other Books with Coloured Plates—Lord Byron's Copy of Hobhouse's Poems, 1809, &c.

To which is added a SMALL COLLECTION of OLD BOOKS, the Property of a Lady, including Marston's Plays, 1633—Milton's History of Muscovia, First Edition—Keats' Endymion, First Edition, &c.—also a Few Early Bindings—a complete Series of the First 1,000 numbers of the London Gazette—Scott's Tales of My Landlord, First Series, First Edition, 4 vols., original boards, &c.

To be viewed, and Catalogues had.

The LIBRARY of the late BRODIE McGHIE WILLCOX, Esq. (formerly M.P. for Southampton), removed from 28 Portman Square, W.

MESSRS. HODGSON & CO. will SELL by AUCTION, at their Rooms, 115 Chancery Lane, W.C., on FRIDAY, November 26, at One o'clock, the above Valuable LIBRARY (sold by order of the executors under the will of the late Miss M. E. WILLCOX for the benefit of various Charitable Institutions), comprising a Coloured Copy of Nash's Mansions of Old England, M'Ian's Highland Clans, 2 vols., Ackermann, and other Folio Books with Coloured Plates—a volume of Original Water-Colour Drawings of the Overland Route to India—Speculum Humanæ Salvationis (Spiegel des Menschen), Augsburg, A. Sorg, 1476—Oudry's La Fontaine, 4 vols., old mottled calf, 1755-9—First Editions of Dickens, Thackeray, Lever, and others; to which are added other Properties, including Library Editions of Hakluyt, Grote, Froude, Brewer, Scott, Lytton, Fitzgerald, &c.

To be viewed, and Catalogues had.

The VALUABLE LAW LIBRARY of the late S. G. LUSHINGTON, Esq., of the Inner Temple (by order of the Executor).

MESSRS. HODGSON & CO. will SELL by AUCTION at their Rooms, 115 Chancery Lane, W.C., on TUESDAY, November 30, at One o'clock, THE ABOVE VALUABLE LIBRARY, comprising the English Reports, complete to date, 98 vols.—a set of the Law Reports from 1875 to 1909, 255 vols., half calf—The Revised Reports, 107 vols.—Lord Halsbury's Laws of England, 10 vols.—Encyclopædia of Forms, 17 vols.—Daniell's Chancery Practice, 3 vols., and other Recent Text Books—Howell's State Trials, 34 vols.—Black Letter Year Books, &c.

Catalogues on application.

VALUABLE MISCELLANEOUS BOOKS.

MESSRS. HODGSON & CO. will SELL by AUCTION, at their Rooms, 115 Chancery Lane, W.C., on WEDNESDAY, December 1, and two following days, VALUABLE MISCELLANEOUS BOOKS, including the Library of the late J. B. PROUDFOOT, Esq., removed from Sydenham (by order of the Executor)—Valuable Architectural Books and Books on the Fine Arts—Books in Seventeenth Century Literature—First Editions, &c.

Catalogues are preparing.

ALL WHO LOVE GARDENS,

WATERWAYS, SPORT, AND

OLD-TIME TRAVEL

should secure a copy of

MEMORIES OF GARDENS.

By ALEXANDER INNES SHAND.

With a Special Memoir by

SIR ROWLAND BLENNERHASSETT, Bart.

"Memories of Gardens" should be in every library. It may be had through the booksellers, price 10s. 6d. net; or, if there is any difficulty in getting it, it will be sent post free for the published price.

THE WEST STRAND PUBLISHING CO. LTD.

10 King Street, Covent Garden, W.C.

SALVADOR RAILWAY.

The Ordinary General Meeting of the Salvador Railway Company, Limited, was held on Thursday, at Winchester House, E.C., Mr. Mark J. Kelly, chairman and managing director, presiding.

The Secretary (Mr. F. C. Tillbrook) having read the notice and the auditors' reports,

The Chairman said: The great expansion that has taken place in the local traffic affords a consoling and reassuring outlook for the future. The growth of what in technical language is called the local traffic affords pretty certain proof that your property is largely developing the country, and, as no currents of foreign immigration have as yet inclined towards Salvador, nor, indeed, towards any one of the five Central American States, it follows that what has been taking place in Salvador is that numbers of the more enterprising inhabitants are attracted each year from those parts where they enjoy no railway facilities to the central region which is served by your railway, where population grows apace, providing us with an appreciable yearly increase in the local traffics. The trade conditions during the year in the country have been unsatisfactory; nor could they be otherwise, having regard to the inflated rates of exchange which have prevailed. Bad trade has been at the bottom of the trouble, and the bad trade has been caused, primarily, if not solely, by the inflated exchanges, which, in our particular case, have caused the damage in a twofold way—directly, by reason of the loss on remittances to the head office, and, indirectly, because of the prejudicial influence upon trade. Personally, I have been at great pains to bring before the authorities and the people concerned the folly of these inflated exchanges, the injury they work to the general public of Salvador, and the damage they gratuitously inflict upon foreign capital invested in the country. The planters hold that the high exchanges constitute a clear and legitimate bonus upon the value of the coffee, the indigo, balsam, and other articles of export, while the importers clamour no less fervently, but undoubtedly with sounder reason, that the high exchanges, if, indeed, they really benefit the planters, are assuredly not less a tax, and a very heavy one, upon the goods consumed by the general public, and, still worse, a deterrent of active trade by reason of the enhanced prices at which goods must necessarily be sold to the consumer, with the corollary of a reduced consumption, while at the same time hitting the Government by reducing its revenue from Customs duties. This same fallacy of the so-called bonus on the country's exportable production has been a troublesome parasite in every one of the Latin-American Republics, and its death has been hard in many of them where it has yielded place to sounder economic practice, as is the case to-day in Mexico, Argentina, Brazil, Peru, Uruguay, Ecuador, and perhaps others, and where the establishment of a gold standard, or, at all events, the having in hand of more or less large sums of available gold, has had the inevitable effect of regulating the exchanges, whose fluctuations are now confined within narrow and well-defined limits. I hold that the gold standard must come. On the last occasion of our meeting you I went very fully into the subject of the proposed diversion of our traffic from Acajutla to Puerto Barrios by the concessionnaires of the railway to Guatemala, just referred to. A year has passed, and there are no signs that these concessionnaires are in a position to carry out their contract with the Government of Salvador, while the signs are not wanting that they are still unable to divert the bulk of the coffee in Guatemala itself, their own immediate field of action, from the port of San Jose, on the Pacific, to Puerto Barrios. And this reluctance of the Guatemala shippers (other than those advantageously placed by reason of proximity) to send their coffee across the Republic of Guatemala to Puerto Barrios would still more palpably be the case where Salvador is concerned. To accentuate the fact, to make it easier as well as cheaper for the Salvador shippers to make use of the Tehuantepec route, to dispel the idea of the long railway haul to Puerto Barrios, and, incidentally, to develop a direct interchange of commodities between Salvador and Mexico, your directors decided that we should establish a weekly steamship service of our own between Acajutla and Salina Cruz, the Pacific terminal of the Tehuantepec railway, for the benefit, preferentially, of shippers by your railway. With regard to traffic prospects for the current financial year, much, of course, will depend on the yield of our principal staple of export. We have opened a new source of revenue with the establishment of our sea carriage, and your directors are of the opinion that from this new undertaking we shall receive as substantial a return as was obtained from the acquisition, some years ago, of the warehousing and lighterage undertaking, which from the very first year of working it enabled us to commence the pleasing task of wiping out the debit balances accumulated in the first three years of the company's existence. I must not fail to mention here that our new undertaking has been favoured with the countenance of his Majesty's Government, the Governments of both Salvador and Mexico having been officially informed by the Foreign Office, through the respective Legations, of what we were doing, and encouraged to do whatever they may properly do to enable us to make this service a success. From the President of Salvador I have myself received warm assurances of support, and I have reason to believe that we shall be able to contract for the carriage of the mails. The steamship service will undoubtedly do much for us; but, even when we have two vessels, this undertaking must mark no final limitation to our efforts in the direction of earning more money. The failure of the concessionnaires I have already referred to to show any practical evidence of financial ability to carry out the works which they contracted for should be our opportunity to approach the Government of Salvador with the view of securing a concession to build and operate a desirable extension of your railway, which the board has long had in view. New works are peculiarly desirable, having regard to three capital facts which I must ask you to bear in mind—the first, that your railway may soon overtake the maximum development of which a line of only 100 miles is capable; the second, that your directors must be prepared to deal at any moment with the purchase of the 6,185 shares of the Acajutla Pier Company, upon which we are under an agreement to pay 12 per cent. per annum, if the occasion should arise to buy these shares outright at a price sufficiently attractive to allow of a considerable annual economy in our disbursement on this head; and the third fact, whose importance I am sure you will appreciate, is that, with reasonable anticipation, such measures in the way of extensions and acquisitions as I have outlined must be taken to increase the development of your business substantially before your present subsidy shall come to an end in 1916. A resolution will be put before you on the subject at the close of these remarks. As a matter of fact, they have extended already to a great length, and I have only to add that if, as I hope, this meeting accepts and shares the views of the directors, I propose to go out to Salvador almost immediately to enlist every possible support for your steamship business, both with shippers and with reference to subsidies, and to put forward my best efforts in the direction of the new works which we believe are necessary to a policy of active development of your business. The Chairman concluded by moving the adoption of the report and accounts and the declaration of a dividend of 2 per cent. on the preference shares.

Mr. M. Ulcoq seconded the motion, which was carried unanimously. It was then resolved: "That the directors' power to borrow conferred by Clause 45 of the articles of association as amended by special resolution passed November 18 and confirmed December 4, 1899, be extended so that the moneys at any one time owing shall not, without the sanction of a general meeting, exceed £1,250,000."

Printed for the Proprietors by SPOTTISWOODE & Co. LTD., 5 New-street Square, E.C., and Published by REGINALD WEBSTER PAGE, at the Office, 10 King Street, Covent Garden, in the Parish of St. Paul, in the County of London.—*Saturday 20 November 1909.*

THE

SATURDAY REVIEW

OF

POLITICS, LITERATURE, SCIENCE, AND ART.

No. 2,822 Vol. 108. 27 November 1909. [REGISTERED AS A NEWSPAPER.] 6*d*.

CONTENTS.

NOTES OF THE WEEK.

It has been on the whole a great debate in the House of Lords; though, recalling others during the last twenty years, we certainly miss one ruling figure. By how much less would the Home Rule Bill debate of 1893 live in the memory of those who heard it, had Lord Salisbury not been the chief and last speaker! The House of Lords now has no more a Salisbury than the Commons a Gladstone. It has no master personality. Yet, of its kind, nothing could be better than Lord Lansdowne's speech in opening the debate.

It was flawless in form, even-flowing, clear, correct. It had no flourish at the beginning or the end, and it was, intellectually, satisfying. In its touch of icy irony, its cold sneer here and there—as in the confession "I do not know what recreating the rural population means"—we have quite the ideal opposite to "naked democracy". The old ruling class may be doomed; but, as it happens, it can still support in the House of Lords a classic example of the aquiline style of speech.

The Lord Chancellor was warm. His speech was reminiscent of the democratic, humanitarian Bob Reid of the House of Commons. We have rather lost sight of that personality of late; it perhaps hardly comports with the full-bottomed wig and the woolsack. He made the important statement that the Liberals would not take office again without the power to deal effectively with the House of Lords question; and this was emphasised later by Lord Pentland.

Lord Cromer's speech was grave. One is interested by his argument that, if there be an exasperating struggle between parties, the vital matter of the defence of the Empire may suffer neglect. But it might suffer still more if the Peers were cowed at the last moment and the Radicals and extremists won all along the line, as they probably would after such a nerveless, miserable surrender. The Conservative party would come into the scorn of many of its friends as well as all its foes. A surrender has indeed been impossible for at least a matter of weeks past. The thing was still debateable—perhaps—in September or October, never after that. To be ready to debate it on November 23, as Lord Cromer and Lord Lytton seemed ready, this was as if Wellington had considered the question of withdrawing from Hougoumont at 10.45 A.M. on the eighteenth of June.

Lord Cromer must always command a respectful hearing, yet his speech on the whole was likely to leave many of his friends in a black fog of uncertainty. On and off he appeared to be speaking on both sides of either fence, and he ends up by refusing to vote on either. The Budget is bad; the Government is bad and extravagant; tariff reform is bad; socialism is worse; to take our thoughts off the vital question of national defence is fatal, and flinging out the Budget may lead to this ill; and it is bad to do anything to inconvenience Lord Lansdowne, a tariff reformer, who is going to do all he can to fling out this Budget and so invite the fatality in question. Was ever wisdom in such a welter? Most Englishmen, we think, will say: "In Heaven's name, give us, rather than this, a little foolhardiness, and the decision to speak and vote one way or another."

In some degree Lord Rosebery's attitude is like Lord Cromer's. To employ his own phrase, he stands first on one leg, then on the other, and then on neither. But we must say the feat is much more beautiful to follow than Lord Cromer's; Lord Cromer's movements are, alas, rather stiff and halting—Lord Rosebery still trips it on the light fantastic toe. What could be happier than his description of the dumping down of all the raw material of the Budget and the excruciating mess into which the Government plunged, and their two hundred and fifty amendments to try to fashion it into workable shape? Or, for lighter touches, what could be better than his quizzing Lord Camperdown as calling for a Balaclava charge?

We cannot help admiring that picture, too, of the great liners hurrying across the Atlantic with bonds and scrips for ballast, though unfortunately it rather guys his own argument and those in the notable speech by Lord Revelstoke—indeed, one of the chief arguments against the Budget—that it is sending investors abroad. From a purely literary point of view, perhaps, it is immoral to spare even our best arguments or friends when we have a good saying or image at their expense. The truly religious man of letters or the true artist is ready to sacrifice everything to beauty—it is his god. But in politics and the more solid pursuits of life the wise man will respect at least his own arguments.

Lord Rosebery went on to explain that the Lords would presently score by passing the Budget, and here surely he lost himself. If we follow his line of thought aright, when the Budget poison by and by begins to work in the veins of the masses, they, in their rage at unemployment and bad trade and increasing poverty, will greatly admire the House of Lords for—passing this "poison"! And there will be a great revulsion of feeling, and out will go the Liberals with a vengeance. To dish the Liberals, he would have the Lords craftily pass the one measure above all others on which the Liberals have set their hearts. It may be extremely subtle; we should say it is also extremely unsound.

Lord Milner discovered himself in a light almost new to some of us. He has been regarded as constructive rather than destructive in his policy—as an ardent lover of tariff reform rather than an ardent hater of the socialism of the Budget. But he declared that all the taxes were bad. It makes one's mouth water to hear from him that a matter of thirteen millions can be got by taxing the foreigner, and got without the least inconvenience to trade and employment at home! The most impressive part of his speech dealt with the death duties. He is a great expert here, and he warns us that if we again raise these duties from nineteen to over twenty-six millions, we shall begin to go down the slope. As it is "the accumulated wealth of the country seems to be on something like a dead level"—an alarming thing, considering how the wealth of the world is growing.

After Lord Cromer and Lord Rosebery came Lord Balfour of Burleigh; indeed every day of the debate seemed "to bring forth a noble knight" who came in all his arms into the lists and rode up and down and flung down his glove; and then, thinking better of the business, picked up his glove and pranced away without a tilt after all. We must say we hope we have got to the end of these noble knights who upbraid the foe and then betake themselves to the woods. A little of this sort of thing may spell discretion; but when indulged in by speaker after speaker it looks more like dastardy.

Some of the lighter—we will not say feather—weights spoke well. Lord Newton was bright and witty; the Marquis of Northampton spoke with force. Lord Ribblesdale always speaks well. Some very solemn folk may regard his jests on such a grave occasion almost as ribaldry. We do not. Ridentem dicere verum quid vetat? Besides, salted almonds are good things at a big feast. The Duke of Marlborough and Lord Beauchamp showed plenty of spirit. Perhaps the Duke did not quite come off in his jest about Lord Crewe being a self-constituted mute at the obsequies. Does he think mutes ought to make speeches? That would add a new terror to funerals. There were the usual time-dishonoured clichés. Even Lord Ribblesdale had out Pelion and Ossa once more, whilst Lord Pentland cast the Constitution into the melting-pot. Lord Milner used the goose and her golden eggs. Really it is time to put that very ancient bird out to grass with the Trojan horse.

Lord Loreburn and Lord Halsbury are ex officio on different sides over the Budget. Lord Loreburn would not be on the woolsack if he were not ready to back up the Government with all the circumstance of his office. Lord Halsbury is the last man in politics to leave his party without the prestige of his support as their ex-Lord Chancellor with an experience of the practical working of the Constitution which makes Lord Loreburn look juvenile. But the truth is there is no special value in their opinions as lawyers on the Budget question. In a certain class of case in the Courts—say about Trade Unions—it could be foretold they would decide in opposite ways, the reason being that they would be legislators and not judges. "I think it ought to be", "I think it ought not to be" is about what their arguments would come to. It is much the same with their quasi-legal opinions about the Budget.

Another pair of legal Siamese twins has appeared in the controversy, the "Times" being their arena. Professor Dicey and Sir Frederick Pollock are in the academic legal world what Lord Loreburn and Lord Halsbury are in the actual forum. If one did not know or could forget that Professor Dicey was a Liberal Unionist most likely to be against the Government, and had only read his book on the Constitution, one would say that he would be against the Lords, he is such a strong House of Commons man. Candidly we must say that we are not surprised at Sir Frederick Pollock's surprise that he takes the Lords' side now. But with these two it is exactly the same thing again as with Lord Loreburn and Lord Halsbury. In ability and learning Sir Frederick and the Professor are peers—though Sir Frederick is our only legal stylist. They would probably give the same sort of opinion on most strictly legal questions, just as Lord Loreburn and Lord Halsbury would. But when it comes to Constitutionalism one says—to use Lord Halsbury's illustration—"I say it is so"; the other says "I say it is not". They are not so crude in the Courts.

The Budget is exciting Ireland. The increase in Irish over-taxation becomes known in the village, and the board of guardians pass a resolution against the Irish party for supporting it; but then the League goes to work, by falsehood and intimidation, and the guardians rescind their resolution. This has been the way in Ireland since the Finance Bill passed its second reading in the House of Commons. Alike in passing the resolution and in rescinding it the guardians are unrepresentative of the people, because the people know little or nothing about the matter either way. They have been brought up to think what they are told, and, while it remains so, good government is practically impossible in Ireland. How can good government be provided for a people who are permanently incapable of thinking whether government is good or bad?

The sham fight made by the Irish party against the Land Bill compromise between the Government and the House of Lords may help to restore the prestige that has been damaged by the Budget; but on the other hand it is hard to disguise, even in Ireland, the fact that the Government have thrown the Irishmen over after having got their support on British questions all through the session. The Irish votes are there to swell the majorities against the House of Lords, but the Radical reward has been cut out of the Land Bill by a confidential arrangement between Mr. Birrell and the Peers. Yet there are people who credit the Irish members with political ability! Ireland's price for picking her statesmen from the village public-houses is very heavy, but she cannot yet see it, and even if she saw it she would be afraid to say so. Months ago we warned those credulous ones from Ireland in the House of Commons that it would suit the Government well to drop their most valued provisions of the Land Bill after their support had been got for the Budget.

Mr. Balfour will have to save the situation at East Marylebone; no one else can. The seat will be given to the Liberals unless the ground is cleared and a new Unionist candidate found, a man of distinction acceptable to the whole party in the division. We must say that things have only been made much worse by the committee of the Marylebone Constitutional Union fighting on a Mr. Boyton, of local celebrity, to succeed Lord Charles Beresford. Mr. Jebb, having got two first-rate men out of his way, is not likely to make room for an even less distinguished man than himself. He can hardly be expected to. Local politicians, at any rate in London, are taking themselves too seriously. It is absurd that every local man who has done some useful work canvassing or something else should think he has earned the reversion of the seat. Constituencies like East Marylebone are wanted for men who by position and ability can help their party in the House. At this moment there are men of first-rate capacity and of public experience—men who ought to be in Parliament—wanting a constituency. East Marylebone should be turned to account.

Apparently the bye-election at Uxbridge is not to come off; nor at Portsmouth. Yet all parties are working at Portsmouth as though they expected the election immediately. Well, Lord Charles Beresford need not have minded how soon it came. To wait for the General Election may be sensible, but Unionists can hardly be content. If only we had everywhere else the one man in all the world for the place as we have at Portsmouth! It is the man wins more than the cause. At Norwich, for instance, if Sir Samuel Hoare will stand, we shall win it back, in spite of the nearly four-thousand Radical majority. Sir Samuel has always been so much more than a party politician that even political opponents used to vote for him. He is a great patriot, and at this very grave crisis we feel sure he will not fail his country, but will yet fill the gap at Norwich.

In the negotiations between the Liberals and the Labour-Socialists as to three-cornered contests in Wales the Labour-Socialists have got a decided advantage. In five constituencies Liberal candidates are not to contest five seats now held by miner members, and in only one (East Carmarthen) is the compliment returned by the retirement of the miners' candidate. The Solicitor-General is to go from Mid-Glamorgan to Merthyr in order that the nominee of the Miners' Federation may have a clear field at Mid-Glamorgan. The result seems to warrant the Labour-Socialist party in insisting on what suits themselves and not caring to consult Liberal views in the matter. They are willing enough to agree when Liberals give way to their own men, but they are determined, they say, to fight every constituency where they believe they have any sort of chance. Whether it lets in a Conservative is a matter of indifference compared with keeping their own party acting independently.

Let us all note what Miss Pankhurst said a few days ago—it would be Mr. Balfour's turn next. The more intelligent suffragettes now understand quite clearly that the Conservative party has not the least idea of rewarding them because they have behaved in a disgraceful way towards members of the Government. The notion among the ignorant hitherto has been that a woman who binds herself to Mr. Asquith's railings or hits Mr. Churchill in the face will secretly please the Tories. As a fact, of course, such acts utterly disgust every decent member, indifferently, of the Conservative and of the Liberal parties.

Mr. Justice Grantham's ideas are often strikingly incoherent, but he surpassed himself in his remarks on sentencing the two women who spoiled the ballot-papers at Bermondsey, one of whom nearly blinded the presiding officer. He began by saying they had both been convicted of a serious crime, and he would treat them exactly as he would treat any other criminals. He finished by saying that as the defendants were people not of the same class as ordinary criminals the imprisonment would be in the second division. This is the division in which the offender is kept from the ordinary criminal. Since the suffragettes began to crowd into it we should think the ordinary criminal will give himself airs that he is not in it.

There are signs that both employers and men are becoming less dogged in the New South Wales coal strike. They are feeling their way towards a conference; and there is a suggestion that Lord Dudley, the Governor-General, should act as mediator. The men would accept an open conference; the employers are maintaining that the Wages Dispute Board should be resorted to. This is somewhat of a change, as it was the men's belief in the hostility of the employers to this Board that led to the strike. On the whole it seems that the men are in a more favourable position. The southern mineowners have never supported their northern fellows, and they are said to be privately negotiating with the men. The coalowners, too, are not supported by the Employers' Federation, as the coalowners do not belong to it. Above all, it is clear that the compulsory powers under the Industrial Disputes Act have broken down. It is quite understood that if the colliers' leaders were sent to prison there would be a general strike of all trades.

A year and a half after the trial began, the High Court of Appeal in Calcutta has given a judgment on the anarchist conspirators who were arrested after the murder of the Kennedy ladies in May 1908. The proceedings have been diversified by several attempts to blow up the trains in which the European Crown Prosecutor travelled, by the assassination of the Indian Public Prosecutor, of the informer inside the jail and of the detective-inspector of police in the public street. Seven of the thirty-three prisoners were convicted by the Indian assessors; this number was raised to nineteen by the judge. The Appellate Court has now acquitted one, and the judges have differed about four, whose case is relegated to a third judge. Through a technical informality the two chief criminals escaped the death sentence. They are to be transported for life. The judgment vindicates the employment of the summary method of deportation. It must be clear now that anarchy in India cannot be suppressed by judicial proceedings only.

Herr Kaempf, the Vice-President of the German Reichstag, was the principal speaker at the dinner given on Wednesday by the London Chamber of Commerce. He spoke of tariffs, and he pointed out two things. There are at present high tariffs, and they are going to be made higher and insurmountable; next that all nations were anxious to restore freedom of international trade. This reminds us of the talk about the desire of nations to disarm while they are straining to increase their armaments. Herr Kaempf is a Free Trader—there are Free Traders in Germany, in America, and in France. But we do not observe that he proposes Germany should imitate us and take off tariffs while other nations are building their walls higher. Tariffs are an "endless screw", as he says; and we are always getting an extra twist of it. We have no screw, and cannot twist. It is wanted—at least till the other parties take their screws off.

France has lost all patience with Mulai Hafid, and it is time that she did. M. Pichon has said the right thing at last, and the envoys of the Sultan who heard it will probably tell him to mind his P's and Q's. Mulai Hafid wants money very badly, and he also wants to get the French out of the Shawia and out of Casablanca. The fact that France has a footing in these places gives her the position of vantage, and she should have no difficulty in bringing the Sultan to terms. But there is no knowing what may not happen in Morocco, the chosen land of muddle and inconclusiveness. M. Pichon's speech reflects credit upon M. Pichon. That he should have had to make it at this time of day reflects discredit upon the way in which his country has conducted her business in Morocco, and upon the spirit in which opposition deputies in France approach questions of foreign policy.

It is real fun reading the accounts of the visit of the representatives of the British stage and dramatic criticism to the Comédie Française. In a sense the mission was elegiac and pathetic. It was to present a memorial to the Comédie Française of the admiration of British actors and critics for the genius of Coquelin. There is nothing amusing about this simple fact itself. It was an admirable idea, indeed, with which everyone must be sympathetic. But the French speeches! What amusement and amazement the Englishmen must have got from them!

Frenchmen do so delicately seize the nuances of the genius of our great living Englishmen; of those who were present especially. How subtly M. Claretie describes Mr. A. B. Walkley as "si honoré parmi les plus puissants publicistes de la noble presse Anglaise". Publicist indeed: Mr. Walkley must have shuddered a little at a name we generally give a man when we do not know what else to call him. As M. Claretie went on we suspect that each of the gentlemen he addressed hoped that only what he said of the others would get into the English papers. But here it is; and "we other Englishmen" congratulate them on the fame that is to be won by a trip to Paris. Only none of us will be safe from finding ourselves famous.

It is a long way from the political platform to the Sheldonian Theatre, and there are few who could so easily reach from one to the other as Mr. Balfour. Mr. Balfour appeared at Oxford with only a few notes in place of the carefully prepared lecture that the Romanes audience expects to receive. But there was no need for him to apologise for making a speech. From start to finish the speech was stimulating, provocative, and deeply interesting. He set out to speak of beauty, a subject in which, as he mournfully phrased it, he travelled as far as might be from his ordinary sphere of action. Yet, though Oxford is far enough from Manchester, Mr. Balfour seemed only grateful for the change of air. The rapidity of his removal had not in the least disconcerted him. For us, we are hard put to it to say which place has need of him more.

Dr. Bode still manages to look cheerful, but his case does not improve. At last the interior of the bust has actually been investigated. Waistcoat or no waistcoat, there was some sort of material inside. Whatever the antiquity of the bust, the stuffing of it is not very ancient. Moreover, the old photograph argument was, as we thought, of no great validity. It has been virtually confuted by comparing a negative of the supposed Da Vinci bust with that taken of his own by R. C. Lucas himself. One thing is certain, there will not be much glamour left about this work of art when they have done with it. How is one to admire a statue, however beautiful, that has suffered such indignities?

Windsor Castle threatened by the speculative builder is an alarming idea. Not the Castle itself literally, but a famous prospect from the river to the Curfew Tower. At present the eye travels over meadow land and rests upon a belt of trees which lie at the foot of the Castle walls, and above which rises the tower. This meadow is now being offered for sale as building land; and unless it is saved the eye will travel over such a prospect as the suburban builder loves to create. With the support of the King the National Trust is applying for funds to purchase the land. The Prince of Wales, we notice, has given £250, and we hope money will come in quickly to enable the Trust to put an end to the danger and save what is both an historic and a poetic national possession.

Any other choice for the Provostship of Eton than Dr. Warre is unthinkable. After a brief interval of absence Dr. Warre now returns to his old home, not again to leave it. One can hardly imagine a more ideal last Act of a busy and strenuous nor wholly peaceful life than the dignified leisure of the Provostship of Eton. The tie with Eton and all its associations—his life's work and its pleasure—is not severed; the only change is silk for cord. Dr. Warre has duties still—the Provost is chairman of the governing body—but they will hold him lightly, too lightly to be felt. It will be a pleasure to thousands in all parts of the British Empire to know that Dr. Warre is again at Eton.

ACT II.

WHO will not rejoice that another stage in the Budget play has been reached? One can at length begin to hope that this piece, whose endurance might become even the Japanese drama, will after all come to an end. How poignant the relief, too, that the second act consists of but one scene. Blessed contrast to the many scenes of the Commons' act—resolutions, second reading, committee, report, third reading. And for the new Act there is a new cast with many stars, and also quite a number of mutes whose names the political playgoer hardly recognises, if indeed he had ever heard them. All this gives a fillip to the Lords' performance, so that the speeches do not fall flat, jaded as the public is with the matter they discuss. It is a step nearer to the real fight. One would have done with these preliminary skirmishes and get to business. It says, indeed, very much for the Lords that after six months of the Budget in the Commons and on ten thousand platforms we can still read any of their speeches with interest. Who could say anything new about the Budget now? Could an old thought be even put in a new way? Yet the Lords' debate, so far from being followed languidly, is an amazing draw. At no time has the Budget in the Commons excited the outside public so much. It does not look at all as if the Lords were the obsolete survival, the antiquarian curiosity, the anachronism, the bore, that the champions of democracy would have us believe. It has always been a great annoyance to the demagogue orator that his audience finds a lord so interesting. He exhausts himself in demonstrating the childishness and absurdity of titles and coronets and robes, and then one of these tawdry gewgaws goes by and promptly the audience leaves him to go and admire. We do not know that the House of Lords' debate can actually add anything in the way of argument to the Budget controversy, but it will certainly serve the House of Lords as a House very well. It has shown the country, or brought home to it, if it did not realise, that the Peers are the reverse of effete, that they have men amongst them equal to any in the Commons, and amongst the speakers far fewer fools. The country will note, what it might very naturally not have imagined, that when the Lords have a chance they can get up a full-dress debate quite as well as the Commons, and carry it through with as much vigour and as much seriousness. There may be a scarcity of "incidents", which the halfpenny paper reader may think a sad fault in the Lords, and the performance may not be kept up so long; but the general effect, we are very sure, will be a conviction that the House of Commons is in no position to dictate to the Lords, and in any struggle between the two Houses cannot afford to give the Lords any points. This debate will be distinctly useful in making the truth about the Lords as a House of Parliament better known to vast numbers naturally ignorant of anything that is not given to self-advertisement.

If our Radical prophets, who have been very busy with the burden of the House of Lords, are right, the Peers should have filed in on Monday apostrophising the throne, "Morituri te salutamus". For the result of the approaching contest was in any event to be the dissolution of the House of Lords. Yet we could detect nothing of the swan-song in Lord Lansdowne's finished and flawless speech. If he was marching to his doom, he was doing it with a magnificent cheerfulness. Unfortunately for Radical oratory, the House of Lords is not a body easily frightened with noise, or easily impressed with it; which partly accounts for the pitiful show Liberals make in that House. Lord Lansdowne, speaking for all the Peers who were resolved not to treat with a policy they believed to be disastrous, but forthwith leave it to the only tribunal that could finally decide, spoke from the mens conscia recti. Whatever be the result, he would have done the straight thing. He could go to the country with clean hands. There was a freedom, a serenity about the speakers who supported Lord Lansdowne's amendment that did not mark either of the other groups. The Government spokesmen were all more or less oppressed—what were they among so many? And they had a text to preach from necessarily ungracious and naturally unpalatable to the congregation. Even if he is entirely right, it is not pleasant to hear a Peer in his own House arguing against the claims of his order and extolling the privileges of its rival. It savours of disloyalty. So that the Ministerialist Peers could get through only by half-apology or by brass. Earl Russell was more than brazen. In effect, he confessed himself a would-be assassin of the Lords' House.

Notwithstanding we easily allow the figures cut by Government speakers were not nearly so wondrous as the performances of the cross-bench Peers. True, the cross-bench mind is a wonderful thing. When Lord Cromer was speaking, one might have thought the "Spectator" had taken up its bed and walked into the House. It is pathetic when one who has so long been a leader of men is no longer able to lead himself. Certainly no one could follow Lord Cromer now, because he goes nowhither. Lord Lytton announced that he was going to follow Lord Cromer. He may stand still with Lord Cromer, but how is that following him? Lord Cromer on the whole objects to the Budget; he would wish it rejected, but he will not vote for Lord Lansdowne's amendment, which would result in the Budget's rejection. Why? Because he fears that the passing of the amendment would break up the Constitution, which would be a worse thing even than the Budget. Then why does he not vote against the amendment? He will not even commit himself to a choice of evils, though he has no doubt that one evil is worse than another. This is the grand result of cross-bench deliberations. In Lord Cromer such inconclusion is painful; the career of a great man of action should not lose itself in a no man's land of this sort. Over Lord Rosebery we cannot weep now. We have wept so often and so long over the inability of this most brilliant of men that we have no tears left. No one can have been surprised at his great speech in Glasgow and his speech on Wednesday leading to nothing. He gets there not quite by the same route as Lord Cromer. Lord Cromer got there in his wanderings in a maze; Lord Rosebery got there straight; thus: The Budget is as bad as can be: blue ruin to the country, the beginning of the end. The Lords are the only defence against such things as the Budget. Therefore the Lords must not defend us against the Budget for fear of incurring unpopularity and defeat in the country, and so ceasing to be effective as a defence. What is the good of a defence which must not take the risk of defending, Lord Rosebery did not explain. Put Lord Rosebery's position before any popular audience in the country and we would guarantee its contemptuous rejection, provided the meeting could be got to understand it; which is very doubtful. And how pleased the country would be if the Peers passed the Budget and told the people they had done so that they might have a taste of it and see how nasty it was and so spew it out with more vigour. Truly a bright idea to give a child poison—Lord Rosebery's description of the Budget—that it might be warned off taking poison again! And how painfully characteristic of Lord Rosebery that he should give this advice to the Unionist Peers not to reject the Budget only when it is too late! Had he made up his mind on the question a few weeks earlier, it might have sensibly modified the Lords' action. But his indecision saved us. Well, the cross-benchers must be left to their own counsels. We admire their detachment, we regard their honesty, but may we never have to depend on them in the hour of fight! For they say that in the General Election they are going to be on our side.

Very largely the debate has been a battle of experts —experts in land, in finance, in taxation, in law—and the wisdom of the pundits is, of course, very valuable. Lord Milner, for instance; ought not his experience as Chairman of the Board of Inland Revenue to outweigh a legion of mere politicians? But, unfortunately, there is Lord Welby on the other side. Experts and their superior knowledge can never count for what they ought, at least what on their face value they ought, for they always cancel out. It is the same in the Chamber as in the committee-room: if there is an expert for, there is an expert against. In balance of argument the expert element comes to nothing. But it adds much to the intrinsic value of the debate.

Naturally the constitutional question, Lords and Commons, has been much more to the front in this debate than it was in the Commons. The Lord Chancellor concerned himself little with anything else. He did not, as of course nobody can, dispute the legal power of the Lords to reject any and every Bill. But custom had deprived the Lords of the right to reject a money Bill dealing with the year's supplies. Lord Lansdowne had pointed out that the famous Commons resolution expressly reserved to the Lords the right to reject a Money Bill in its entirety; and there is no qualification as to what moneys the Bill deals with. The only plausible way of putting the Ministerial case is that the Lords had waived their right by leaving it so long unexercised. This is tantamount to saying that the Lords should periodically reject a harmless Budget to preserve their power to refuse right of way to a Budget through their House. What would Radicals say if they did? If the Lords have not rejected a Budget for a hundred years, it is because there has not in a hundred years been a Budget like this one.

THE FINANCIAL POSITION.

"OF course if you want chaos you can have chaos", said Lord Lansdowne, and the proposition looks indisputable, but is not really so. For with the worst will in the world, that is to say, crediting the Government with the utmost degree of malice and unscrupulousness, we really do not see how Messrs. Lloyd George and Churchill can educe chaos from the present financial position. The total loss of revenue produced by the rejection of the Budget is £56,700,000; that being the amount of the income tax and tea duty, grounded on financial resolutions, the amount of extra taxes or duties imposed by the clauses of the Finance Bill, and £3,500,000 from the Sinking Fund. This amount is made up as follows: Income tax, £37,100,000; tea duty (which begins on 1 July), £4,500,000; Customs (petrol, spirit and tobacco), £2,640,000; Excise (spirit, licences and motor cars), £2,760,000; estate duties, £4,150,000; stamps, £900,000; land-value duties, £600,000. As it is certain that the land-value duties cannot bring in a penny piece to the Exchequer this year, we may strike off the £600,000, thus getting a sum of £56,100,000 as the loss to the end of the year, i.e. 31 March 1910, involved in the rejection of the Finance Bill. But of this sum there was already received by the Exchequer on 13 November 1909, from income tax £5,894,000, from tea £2,500,000; and, taking two-thirds of the remaining extra taxes, Customs, Excise, and estate duties (the stamp duties are not leviable until the Budget is passed) at £6,366,000, making a total of £14,760,000 already paid in. Subtract £14,760,000 from £56,100,000 and you get £41,340,000 as the total shortage up to the last day of March 1910. But it will only be necessary to provide revenue for half that period, the two months up to the end of January, when the General Election will be over. The half of £41,340,000 is £20,670,000, which is the total amount the Government will be called upon to borrow in the event of their taking the reckless and unscrupulous course of refusing to bring in a Bill for the levying of income tax and tea duty. For that is the obvious thing to do, the thing that would be done by statesmen who had any sense of responsibility and who were not intoxicated with the fury of the baffled demagogue. The tea duty is unchanged, and about the increase of income tax there would be no haggling. Lord Lansdowne and Mr. Balfour have both pledged themselves to lend their assistance to pass any measure that may be necessary for carrying on the King's Government. The income tax and tea duty, from which there are, in round figures, about £34,000,000 still to come in, would be ample to provide for the requirements of Government up to the end of the year. And unless Ministers are really bent on making party capital out of the situation, a short Act for levying income tax and tea duty would settle the whole matter in a few days.

But we are afraid, from what Lord Pentland said, that the Government will not adopt this course—we say afraid, because of the demoralisation of public life which is thereby indicated. We are not afraid of the view which the country will take of such conduct. In his speech on Tuesday Lord Pentland said: "The noble Marquis" (Lord Lansdowne) "seemed to think that some Budget might be patched up, some temporary accommodation provided, and to indicate that there the trouble and difficulty would end. If the step proposed were taken it was an irrevocable step; things could never be again what they once were" (which is true of more things than the Budget). "They might have financial chaos, they would certainly have constitutional chaos. . . . If they took that step they brought matters to a deadlock, from which there was no escape but by some revolutionary change." The language is not quite clear, and Lord Pentland is not an important member of the Government, and it may well be that he was speaking, as the Americans say, "with his mouth". But the "Westminster Gazette" of the 24th inst., commenting on the above speech, writes: "The opening sentences here may be interpreted as a plain declaration that the Government will do nothing to relieve the situation created by the Peers. There will be no negotiations, no suggestion of compromise. The inevitable corollary is that not only will the whole of the new taxes drop absolutely, but that the collection of the income tax and the tea duties, which depends on resolutions of the House of Commons, will cease with the dissolution, and for the time there will be no power to enforce these imposts." The Government will do nothing to relieve the situation—it is almost inconceivable that a Cabinet Minister and a respectable newspaper should approve such a policy. And yet it is more than possible, it is probable, that such will be the policy of his Majesty's Government. The Cabinet is ruled by Mr. Lloyd George and Mr. Churchill, and we know what we may expect of them. The Prime Minister smiles with post-prandial benevolence upon his brace of demagogues. Mr. Haldane buckles on his armour, not without difficulty, and pants after the brace of demagogues. The Lord Chancellor, to whom the brace of demagogues cannot but be very distasteful, is cordially disliked by them and suspected of being a Whig. Lords Wolverhampton and Morley are ciphers, and Sir Edward Grey is one of those dangerous impostors who talk moderately and vote the party ticket. No; the supreme power in the State is in the hands of the brace of demagogues whom Mr. John Burns regards with "pale-eyed envy". What will Messrs. Lloyd George and Churchill say and do? They will strike a dramatic pose and say "We will not bring in a Bill, because that involves asking the consent of the Lords, and we will ask nothing from the Lords. Chaos? Exactly, but we want chaos! Chaos is the element in which we move and breathe and have our being. As the tree falls, so let it lie!" The Chancellor of the Exchequer and the President of the Board of Trade may be trusted to do all they know to produce chaos; but they will not succeed, because we are a nation of business men and do not lose our heads.

A sum of £20,670,000 may have to be provided for two months. The Government have power, by the Appropriation Act and other Acts, to borrow as much as £76,000,000 without coming to Parliament, and they may do so by issuing Treasury bills or Exchequer bills or by a loan from the Bank of England. As a matter of fact they need only borrow a small sum. There are in the Bank at the disposal of the Government some £6,000,000 of Exchequer balances, and there are £8,000,000 from the New Sinking Fund, being the surplus of last year's permanent charge for the Debt, less the interest and cost of management. These moneys (£14,000,000) could with perfect propriety be used by the Government for the temporary purpose of tiding over the General Election, leaving only the trifling sum of £6,670,000 to be obtained by Exchequer or Treasury bills. Such issues are constantly being made by the Chancellor of the Exchequer, and if the above plan were adopted there would not be a ripple in the money market or the Stock Exchange. In addition to the Exchequer balances and Sinking Fund, there are, we believe, some £10,000,000, called "appropriations in aid", in the hands of the departments which might be lent to the Chancellor of the Exchequer. So that if there is any heroic borrowing of any sum approaching £20,000,000, let the public know that the heroism is mere childish petulance and play-acting, for which there is no necessity whatever, and which is merely part of the design to abolish the House of Lords and destroy the Conservative party.

SAN SEBASTIAN, MONTE CARLO AND M. MARQUET.

It gives us no particular pleasure to recur to the subject of gambling in European countries; pharasaical comments on the failings of friendly neighbours being as much to our own distaste as to that of any other person who recalls uncomfortably the comments which follow references to the motes in his neighbour's eye. Yet it was not, we confess, without some private amusement that we heard of the wrath and amazement caused by our comments on Ostend last July, and of the indignant consultations in various circles as to whether the SATURDAY REVIEW could be prosecuted for its free criticism of the two worthy gentlemen who were "exploiting" the gambling there. Great, however, as must be our trepidation on hearing that M. Marquet and his friend and colleague, the King of the Belgians, disapproved of an article in this REVIEW, and actually consulted mighty international jurists as to what steps could be taken to annihilate us, we have overcome our alarm sufficiently to return to the subject. There are, in point of fact, two questions connected with gambling which seem to call immediately for a little outspoken criticism.

The first of these we approach with real regret, and a most whole-hearted hope that our information may be incorrect. The statement that a syndicate of financiers has obtained from the Spanish Government a concession to erect a large gambling establishment at San Sebastian is made definitely, however, by the "Pester Lloyd", which has a reputation for accuracy of which it is justly proud; moreover, the announcement merely intimates the conclusion of negotiations which have been going on to our knowledge for four years, and were very nearly brought to a successful conclusion (with certain discreditable English help) in the spring of 1906. The matter is now said to be settled; the syndicate is to pay a rent of £400,000 for its privileges; a considerable percentage of the profits will be paid to the Spanish exchequer; roulette and trente-et-quarante will be the principal games; and, in view of the opening of the casino in 1911, several hotel companies are paying large prices for the neighbouring land.

King Alfonso has shown himself to be so English in his social and political habits that this news will come with a most unpleasing shock to many English folk. Strictly speaking, the building of a large gambling-hell at San Sebastian, though it may vex English visitors to Biarritz and Pau, is no more concern of ours than the execution of Senhor Ferrer; and if the Spanish Treasury likes to recruit its finances by such methods that is entirely its affair. The scheme, however, shows a retrograde movement on the part of the Spanish Government and its head which we cannot help regretting. Nations and kings who are pushing their way to the front of civilisation, where voices count for something in the general morality and decency of the world, do not grant concessions like this San Sebastian affair. A hundred little blots of hypocrisy and gambling mar the philanthropy and morality of every country; this nation looks the other way elaborately while betting folk carry on their trade, the other carefully ignores lotteries or suchlike matters; but when you build a replica of Monte Carlo in your country your position in the comity of nations has sunk at once to the level of Belgium or of the Principality of Monaco.

This brings us to the second point we mentioned. The announcement has been widely made, as if it were a statement of some financial or social importance, that M. Marquet, of Ostend fame, has been appointed to a prominent position on the board of control of the casino at Monte Carlo. We are not at all inclined to decry the importance of the statement. Monte Carlo is not a place with which a profoundly moral person goes out of his way to profess sympathy. Of course if gambling is a necessity of human life, "on ne demande pas mieux"; Monte Carlo is a model of State-regulated vice, and that is the first and last word to be said about it. But its authorities have made a very great mistake if, in some momentary dissatisfaction with their dividends or in some slight irritation at the reproaches levelled at them by certain visitors, they have decided to offer a share in their finances and management to all the scum of Europe which proposes to ask for it. In the most friendly and kindly fashion we recommend them to advise M. Marquet to go back to Ostend and stay there; while, if they have already, as commonly reported, given him a prominent place on their board of control, we would venture to suggest to them that there is hardly any sum of money which it would not be worth their while to pay to induce him to resign it. It is merely a choice between his departure and the departure of numerous English visitors; with a further ultimate contingency which it is worth the while of the Principality to consider. The fits of hysteria which seize upon France are not always confined to the Paris police courts, nor are they always undesirable nor evanescent. If it occurred to the French nation one day that the Casino of Monte Carlo was a serious blot on French morals, and that the French Riviera would be "rounded off" in desirably symmetrical fashion by the annexation of the Principality of Monaco, the French nation would annex that Principality; and no nation in Europe would trouble itself to go beyond the mildest diplomatic remonstrance.

Such an accident might happen, we can assure the Prince of Monaco, even if he were on his best behaviour; and if his Government offer any share of their business to persons like M. Marquet the French Government will not only be allowed but urged to number Monte Carlo among the things of the past, not only during some future hysterical crisis, but immediately. We really take no credit for having prophesied what would happen at Ostend under M. Marquet's rule this summer. We suggested that a considerable number of the most reputable English visitors would stay away, and they did stay away. We hinted that the gambling would be found less honest than might be desirable, and numerous English visitors left the gambling-rooms after three or four nights' experience. We volunteered the news that a subsidiary gambling-room would be opened at the chief hotel of the place, hinting in addition our belief that two such very astute financiers as M. Marquet and the King of the Belgians would not allow these profits to be diverted from the public rooms without compensation; and the subsidiary room was, in fact, opened. We cannot state whether the compensation in question was paid, but, having a sincere belief in those financial powers of King Leopold and his friend which are known by the vulgar English word of "blackmail", we judge it to be probable. We volunteer now to the authorities of Monte Carlo prophecies similar in every detail to the above, and suggest that the consequences to them will be extremely tiresome. In Ostend M. Marquet soothes all susceptibilities by promising annually to go to prison and to close his gambling-rooms. In Monte Carlo his adventures will be a social and diplomatic nuisance to everybody concerned, and the authorities will, we think, be well advised if they invite him to transfer them elsewhere. Unless they get rid of M. Marquet they may find that in the end their own positions may be in peril.

THE DEFENCE CONFERENCE.

THE report of the Conference on Imperial Defence has just been issued. The idea of convening it arose out of a resolution of the Imperial Conference of 1907, but the proximate cause of its being summoned was the offer of naval aid to the Imperial Government by several of the self-governing colonies when the problem was being discussed last spring. Very properly the scope of the delegates' work was not confined to naval details. In the defence problem military and naval affairs go together; so that both the Admiralty and the War Office laid elaborate memoranda before the Conference. The two cases, however, are not quite parallel. The naval conditions must vary with geographical situation, while the military problem remains identical for all the great self-governing Dominions. There were separate meetings therefore. As to military affairs, a definite policy was agreed to by the delegates, and although "all resolutions come to and proposals approved by the Conference"—we quote from the Prime Minister's statement in the House of Commons on 26 August—must be considered as "ad referendum and of no binding force unless and until submitted to their various Parliaments", we can already form some opinion on the military issue. "Proposals for so organising the military forces of the Empire as to ensure their effective co-operation in the event of war" were discussed at a general meeting of the Conference. The subject, however, appeared to be one which could more suitably be considered by a sub-committee of experts. Accordingly, a sub-committee, under the chairmanship of Sir William Nicholson, the Chief of the General Staff, was assembled. Their report was afterwards approved by the Conference as a whole. We are, therefore, entitled to take it as authoritative.

The War Office memorandum laid down these principles for the consideration of the sub-committee: That, without superiority at sea, the Empire cannot be maintained; that it is the duty of self-governing colonies to provide, as far as possible, for their own territorial security, and that a definite scheme of mutual assistance should be prepared. It is interesting now to consider how far the mother country and the colonies have fulfilled their obligations. The War Office claims that these obligations have been met on our part by the maintenance of a navy which is designed to keep command of the sea, by the provision of a territorial force for home defence, and by the creation of an expeditionary force ready to proceed to any threatened part of the Empire. As regards the first contention it is enough to say that, whereas only a year ago the admitted need of the Empire was the maintenance of a two-Power standard, the plan now is just to keep ahead of the strength of one other Power. As to the Territorial Army, we need scarcely say that, in the opinion of almost every independent expert, that force is not, and as now organised and trained can never hope to be, competent to tackle the highly disciplined troops it would have to meet in the case of an invasion. Yet this is the one thing it claims to be able to do. Grave doubts also exist as to the real efficiency for war of Mr. Haldane's much-vaunted expeditionary force. Of course, we had an expeditionary force before Mr. Haldane, and a larger proportion of regular troops to endue it with life. Now we know that it is to be composed largely of special reservists or militia, its increased value under the change of name is very much open to question. The memorandum, however, assumes that this new force, some twenty thousand less than the old militia—at any rate in infantry and artillery—will be an enormous increase to our strength. Indeed, so inflated is the War Office with the supposed success of the change that it claims that this, with some other changes in the Volunteers, fulfils the well-known saying of the War Commission that "no military system will be satisfactory which does not contain powers of expansion outside the limits of the regular forces of the Crown, whatever that limit may be". This is mere nonsense. The War Commission had obviously in their minds something far more drastic than a mere change of name and alteration in terms of service of one or even two portions of the auxiliary forces. They probably contemplated what the Norfolk Commission a few months later actually recommended—a measure of compulsion. How, then, can we take Sir William Nicholson's memorandum seriously? Did the colonial delegates themselves take it seriously? And will the colonies be encouraged to fresh efforts thereby? Moreover, we know well that nothing so far has really been accomplished towards ensuring that on mobilisation we shall have an adequate supply of horses. Our peace establishment of horses is only a third of our war requirements, and even if this can be made good on mobilisation in a hurry—which is questionable—the wastage inseparable from six months' warfare would place us in an extremely difficult position. So much for the way the mother country has interpreted her duties.

The colonies as yet have certainly not done much. But they have come to some conclusions on the subject, though whether even these, when they become known, will be very welcome is open to question. The colonies are painfully jealous of any interference in their military as in their other affairs. Their representatives, however, have agreed that every part of the Empire is willing to "make its preparations on such lines as will enable it, should it so desire, to take its share in the general defence of the Empire". Moreover, they have recommended that, without impairing the complete control of the Government of each Dominion "over the military forces raised within it, their forces, the formation of their units, and their transport arrangements should be standardised; and that colonial patterns of arms, equipment, and stores should, as far as possible, follow the imperial pattern." They also make some recommendations towards a unification of the Imperial General Staff throughout the Empire, all of whom should, nevertheless, remain responsible to and "under the control of their own Governments". They also favour the creation of local staff colleges. These recommendations are, no doubt, good as far as they go. In view of the co-operation of the imperial and colonial forces in a big campaign it is most desirable that their organisation and departmental services should be standardised. So too is it desirable that there should be a free interchange of Staff officers. It will necessarily broaden the minds and the standpoints both of imperial and colonial Staff officers to gain experience otherwise denied to them. But there is no cause for enthusiasm. It will be long before Staff officers trained at local institutions will be of any real use, because the local staff colleges will not have at their service the means of instruction open to the home colleges or to the Indian. On this part of the programme, therefore, we are not enthusiastic.

A general examination of this report leads to wider considerations, not entirely military. It is to be noted that the colonial delegates are careful to make some reservations. Thus as to taking their share in the general defence of the Empire, we find such remarks as "should it so desire" and "under the control of their own Governments". The pertinent question arises, "Can a real imperial army be created under such conditions? Further, can the word 'Empire' be used intelligibly of such a loose collection of units as composes the British Empire"? It is true that other empires are composed of States which possess a certain autonomy, except as regards foreign affairs. But, unlike our case, there is always one supreme military control; and without that the word "empire" becomes unmeaning. Take Germany. Saxony has its King and its own system, and other German States also have their Sovereigns, though not all of regal rank, their Parliaments and their local institutions. But the German Emperor is Commander-in-Chief of all their armies, and they work, in military matters, as one whole. That, therefore, is an empire. But is there a British Empire? An empire based upon reservations regarding the disposition of its military forces is something of a contradiction in terms.

CRITICISM AND FAITH IN ÆSTHETICS.

THE ways of clear thinking lead straight into the valley of mysticism. The old conviction again reaches home as Mr. Balfour speaks to us from Oxford. The man who believes greatly in human reason is the man who has seldom followed any train of thought very far. The paths of reason are many and small; and they are all lost in the wide land where the Pillar of Cloud and the Pillar of Fire are the only guides. We can imagine that there are not a few critics to-day who will feel a little unsettled by what Mr. Balfour said at Oxford on Wednesday afternoon. Mr. Balfour has been down many of these ways that lose themselves where dogmatism ends and faith begins. Now it is the path of æsthetic criticism that he follows. For ages men have thrown a great deal of intellectual energy into the criticism of art and literature. Yet the total achievement has not been great. All the rules, from those of Aristotle onwards, have broken down. The men who framed the rules were often the men who disregarded them. The failure to get any satisfying æsthetic rule is revealed by the attempts that have been made to graft æsthetics on to morality, philosophy, or religion. Yet the fact remains that Milton never wrote worse than when he was justifying the ways of God to man, and that Ruskin, in spite of his ideas about art and morality, broke through his own principles repeatedly, because he was too good an æsthete to trust to the application of his own formula. Not only are there no discoverable laws by which beauty may be enmeshed; but the transitory rules framed from age to age are from age to age mutually hostile. In the same age they are hostile from man to man, and in the same man they are hostile from the man in his nonage to the man who has educated his sensibility. The Greeks derived æsthetic delight from barbarous music. Mr. Balfour derived æsthetic delight from bad story-books in his Eton days. What is here the lesson to be drawn? It is just this—that the laws of criticism have been mostly impertinent; and that, since good and bad art (as in our impertinence we term it) may each raise in men's minds the same pure æsthetic emotion, therefore there is "no philosophical or logical method of attaching æsthetic emotion to the moving wheels of the great system of which we form a part". In fact, high æsthetic emotion takes its place beside high moral feeling, and is not to be assayed by the coarse tests of human logic.

Such was the general trend of Mr. Balfour's thought. One of the first questions that it occurs to ask is this—What reference has a destructive argument of this kind to practical criticism? Must the critic throw away the standards by which he praises or dispraises, and lay down the pen in despair? Oh no, nothing of the sort. There is here an analogy to the position arrived at in the old controversy of necessity as against free will. Even if a man believe in necessity as a philosopher, yet, as a man, he must act as if his will were free. So here, even if the critic agree with Mr. Balfour that æsthetic standards have varied, that the same pure æsthetic delight may be produced in the human mind by the beating of the tom-tom as by a performance of Beethoven's Trio in B flat, yet he must believe in the culture of his generation and continue to hold the scales as before between Beethoven and the smaller musical fry. He must not pause to consider what happens in that region beyond thought where his standards will be found to waver like a rushlight. He stands in his place, the product of his age, to voice the æsthetic needs and opinions of his age. His judgment must be almost reflex, something involuntary. The good critic feels first, and justifies his feeling afterwards. He may justify it stupidly, as did Ruskin and Wordsworth and Aristotle. That hardly matters. The thing that does matter is that he should react spontaneously and truly, on behalf of his generation, to the developments in art and literature of his day. He will say to Mr. Balfour: You may be right in everything you say; it may be that the laws of beauty lie beyond us, and that all our varying standards are of no value at all; yet I stand here on behalf of the trained sensibility of my day and generation, and here I shall continue to stand in spite of you. Nor do we think that Mr. Balfour would reprove him.

Mr. Balfour's main contention that the laws of absolute beauty lie beyond us is profoundly true. But we do not reach that conclusion quite by the same ways. He seems to have been driven by his distrust of historical standards to flee to mysticism as a refuge. We would rather regard historical standards as pointing the way to the absolute beauty that lies behind the veil. Our own standards of beauty are as shadows cast by a sun that shines upon shapes of beauty in another world. Mr. Balfour's distrust, as he expressed it on Wednesday, seemed to us to be too deeply rooted. Take the example he himself gave. He confessed to having, as a boy, read worthless tales with lofty pleasure. Then, as discrimination grew, this pleasure was no longer his in so undiluted a form. Mr. Balfour infers from this that as his discrimination grew his sensibility waned; and the proposition emerges that as our so-called taste improves, the quality of our æsthetic emotion deteriorates. Surely this is truth upside down. Is the quality or quantity of æsthetic emotion higher when a mind reacts violently to a coarse stimulus than when it reacts less violently to the striking of a finer note in a manner that exalts and abides and ramifies? Apparently Mr. Balfour would answer yes. He was nearer to pure æsthetic emotion before discrimination had taken the edge from his young hunger for the beautiful. Apply this principle to the race. From the tom-tom to Beethoven is æsthetic degeneration! The great masters who handed on the sonata or the sonnet from age to age were obeying no high æsthetic law that prompted this new civilisation of ours to cultivate and refine upon its emotions in that process of getting nearer to nature in the Aristotelian sense which is self-discovery and self-fulfilment.

Yet the fundamental truth remains. The great evolutionary processes, by which æsthetic emotion and moral feeling are sifted and refined in process of time, lie outside the narrow formulæ that are applied by the critics of any one period. The real value of the work of a great critic lies, not so much in the touchstones he applies, as in the manifestation he makes in the course of his criticism of that Zeitgeist which he is there to embody. The best critic is not the man who invents a formula; but the man who, by exercising a trained judgment independently and honestly whenever that judgment is invoked, helps to pile up unconsciously a mass of opinion that is, as it were, the voice of a century passing judgment upon itself.

The lecture was not without its lighter passages. Mr. Balfour is never portentous, though portentousness is not unknown in the Sheldonian Theatre at Oxford. The hundred best books, the possible hundred best pictures, the possible dozen best philosophies were treated to some well-merited and well-phrased banter. Mr. Balfour had a congenial task in exposing the hypocrisy and æsthetic snobbery which account for so much of the apparent unanimity in matters of taste. Another portion of his lecture—that in which he contended that the æsthetic enjoyment of a trained critic has in it an alloy of sympathy with the artist in his struggle with his materials—was also admirably expressed. On that text alone it would be possible to raise many interesting questions. The delight in technique is something peculiarly satisfying and peculiarly apart from æsthetic emotion. In fact, æsthetic emotion presupposes that the other is for the moment in abeyance.

THE CITY.

THE City is waiting upon the decision of the Government in regard to the financing of the year's deficit when the Budget is rejected by the House of Lords. Apparently no one outside the Cabinet is aware of the action to be taken, and the various suggestions made are more bewildering than helpful. In the circumstances it is not surprising that the Bank of England directors on Thursday refused to lower their discount rate. The position as disclosed in the weekly return would have justified such a movement, but with the prospect of a definite course of action being outlined by the Government before the next meeting of the Bank Court the directors may be excused for taking advantage of the interregnum for further consideration of their action. In the interests of trade, however, they cannot postpone a reduction over Thursday next; and if there is to be borrowing by the Government, in whatever form, a lower rate than 5 per cent. would materially assist the operation. Meantime the Stock Markets remain in a very uncertain condition, the movements of one day being counteracted by those of another. Not for more than twenty-four hours is there any pronounced tendency, and always there is a feeling of nervousness amongst dealers lest they are doing wrong. Each recurring settlement arouses apprehension, and while the open defaults are few, it is well known that a good deal of financial weakness exists, and that monetary assistance has frequently to be given both to jobbers and brokers. In the case of brokers their troubles generally arise from defaulting clients, of which there have been more than the usual number during the past few months.

Home railway traffic continues to expand, but not with any corresponding effect upon prices. As Lord Revelstoke stated in the House of Lords on Monday, investors want "something foreign" nowadays, and whatever the reason for their choice it is undoubtedly a fact that Home Railway stocks have no attraction when set side by side with foreign railway securities. There is always a large business doing in the latter, with a freedom in dealings that probably no other market enjoys at the moment. Argentine issues have been especially firm this week, with Central Argentine up to par and Buenos Ayres and Pacific three points higher than when we last wrote. And while home and colonial Government securities have been languishing there has been a steady stream of investment in foreign Government bonds. A notable feature has been the demand for Russian bonds, which is not all on French account. Investors apparently recognise the improvement in the economic and social condition of Russia, and are probably drawing comparisons between that country and our own—very much to the detriment of England. The upheaval here is almost as great; but whereas the revolution that is now going on in Russia is all for the good of the country, here the reverse is the case. Russia will probably have millions of English money poured into it in the next few years, the Government there having abandoned its policy of laisser faire, and welcoming foreign capitalists who wish to assist in the industrial development of the country.

A good deal of apprehension has been aroused amongst shareholders of South African mines by a proposal made in Johannesburg that the monthly statements of output and labour be abandoned. Messrs. Wernher, Beit apparently agree with it; but there is an almost general consensus of opinion amongst the other groups that the existing practice should be continued. The suggestion that there would be a saving in expense if the proposal were adopted is probably true, but it is not a good and sufficient reason for putting it into practice. We all know that the monthly figures do not accurately represent the work done in the particular period to which they refer, but they are nevertheless extremely useful, and any attempt to suppress them would certainly be construed as an endeavour to place the ordinary shareholder at a disadvantage as compared with the controlling houses. The market is more reassured now, but we have probably not yet heard the last of the proposal. Kaffirs this week have moved very irregularly, but at the time of writing are showing a fair amount of strength. It would be unwise, however, to anticipate any pronounced revival just yet, as there is still a good deal of stock being carried for stale "bills", and every substantial rise in prices must bring in sellers.

The decision of the United States Courts against the legality of the Standard Oil Trust is a blow to the

Trust mania in that country; but it has not checked the negotiations for the proposed copper combination, and Wall Street is still hopeful of a successful issue. There will, of course, be an appeal against the Standard Oil judgment; and as this is likely to engage the attention of the Courts for another twelve months, ample time exists for speculation before the matter is definitely settled. Wall Street has been well sustained through a trying ordeal, and has probably forgotten by now that there is a Legislature seeking to wrest from unscrupulous millionaires the power to monopolise industries to the detriment of the public weal.

INSURANCE: POLICIES AT HIGH PREMIUMS.

VI.

LIMITED-PAYMENT life policies are the connecting link between endowment assurance on the one hand and whole-life assurance on the other. They resemble whole-life policies inasmuch as the sum assured is payable only at death whenever it occurs, and in common with endowment assurances the number of premiums to be paid is limited. The result is that they supply a larger amount of protection than endowment assurances and a larger proportion of the investment element than whole-life policies. Frequently they are the happy mean.

We have already mentioned that in proportion to the premiums paid the surrender values of limited-payment policies are larger than those of whole-life assurance: we have also said that even whole-life policies, when taken from a company that gives liberal surrender values, can be given up for a cash payment at the age of, say, sixty or sixty-five, thus converting them into endowment assurances. The result of doing this is less good at the time of surrender than if endowment assurance had been taken at the same cost, but this course is better than endowment assurance in that a larger amount of protection in the event of premature death has been provided at an equal outlay.

Limited-payment life policies can be converted into the equivalent of endowment assurance, by being surrendered for a cash payment, on better terms than whole-life policies can be given up; at the expense, however, of providing rather less insurance protection in the meantime. These features are simply illustrated in the case of a special without-profit policy issued by the Norwich Union Life Office. A man of forty can pay £42 2s. 10d. a year for twenty years at the most; if he dies before reaching the age of sixty the sum of £1000 will be paid to his estate. This is, for practical purposes, a twenty-payment life policy. On reaching the age of sixty he can, if he chooses, draw £913 in cash. Had he paid £42 2s. 10d. a year for endowment assurance, payable at the end of twenty years, the policy would have secured £921 at death before sixty, instead of £1000; and £921 at the end of the term, instead of £913. The limited-payment life policy gives £79 extra protection during twenty years, and £8 less as endowment at the end of the time. The proportions between protection and endowment vary according to age and term, and under with-profit policies bonuses introduce other differences. This particular Norwich Union policy gives a large number of options on reaching the age of sixty; for example, a man commencing at forty can at the age of sixty draw £315 in cash, in addition to a paid-up policy assuring the sum of £1000 at his death whenever it happens. If at that time he does not want to draw any cash, he can secure a paid-up policy for £1495 payable at death. To secure a policy for a larger sum than £1000 he must furnish evidence of good health; but as the cash amount of £315 which he could take is really used as a single payment to secure an additional £495 at death, the state of his health at age sixty need not, perhaps, be absolutely first class. If his health is really good, and insurance protection for his family is then found to be the essential thing for him to provide, he can continue paying premiums at the old rate of £42 2s. 10d. a year, and secure a policy for £2130 payable at his death whenever it happens. This policy illustrates in happy fashion the way in which limited-payment life assurance can be adjusted to meet a number of different circumstances. At the time of effecting the assurance a man may not be able to tell with certainty what his requirements will be twenty years later: he may want money for himself, or he may still require a large amount of protection for his family in the event of his death. There is a greater flexibility of adjustment about limited-payment life policies than attaches to either whole-life or endowment assurance; consequently it is by no means a bad rule, when a man is in doubt as to what kind of policy it is best to take, for him to decide upon life assurance subject to the payment of premiums for a limited number of years only.

THE VOICE OF MARINETTI.

By Max Beerbohm.

IF you hear a voice from afar, do not take the message seriously. Wisdom is a thing that can be expressed only in an under-tone. Life—even such part of it as our limited human brains can conceive—is a very weird, august, complex, and elusive affair. To have any positive theory of it, any single dogmatic point of view, any coherent "message", is an act of impertinence. To be an optimist or a pessimist, a realist or an idealist, a Thingumyite or a Somebodyan, to belong to any "school of thought" whatsoever, is to write oneself down an ass—for anyone who can read. The true sage, he who penetrates the furthest, and raises the most of the fringe that surrounds the darkness, dares but offer us guesses, to be taken or left; dares not enunciate any "truth" without a hundred-and-one reservations and qualifications. It is the awe-struck whisper, then, the tremulous murmur; not the cheery or angry megaphonic shout or screech that "carries" across frontiers. He may be heard by a few in his own land. He most assuredly will not have a European reputation. That sort of thing is reserved for inspired asses like Tolstoi or Nietsche—for men who have gone off at a tangent, men precipitated along one sharp narrow line which they mistake for the whole dim universe. It is natural that they, in their joy or their wrath, should shout or screech very resonantly; and let us not grudge them their lungs; and let us, by all means, listen to them: they are great fun. Take them seriously?—ah no! If they happen to be artists, expressing themselves through some art-form, through poems or plays or novels, let us delight in their concentration, the narrowness that enables them to express just what they can feel, just what they can understand, so much more forcibly than if they had a sense of proportion and a little of the modesty that comes of wisdom. Our Ibsens and D'Annunzios and Bernard Shaws and Gorkys—let us harken to them and revel in them. But let us mix up all their "messages" together, and strike an average, and not suppose even then that we are appreciably one whit nearer to the truth of things.

The very latest thing in "carrying" voices is the voice of Signor Marinetti. Up through the Italian peninsula, from peak to peak of the Swiss mountains, this voice has reverberated into Paris; and all the eminent Parisian poets and thinkers have been saying what they think of it; and many of them think quite highly of it. So much I judge from a copy of a magazine, "Poesia", that has been sent to me. Doubtless it has been sent to many other people. I feel that the voice of Marinetti is already well on its way to John o' Groat's House. Its message, that it may the quicklier fly, has been translated, by someone on the staff of "Poesia", into English. Marinetti is a poet, and has founded a thing called Futurism. He tells us that he is not yet thirty, and that none of the poets whom he has gathered round him is yet thirty; and it does not appear that he and they have done much in the poetic line so far; but all sorts of terrible things are just going to be done by them. The fat boy in "Pickwick" wished to make creep the flesh of one old lady. Marinetti, standing, as he tells us, "erect on the pinnacle of the world", with his disciples, wishes to make the flesh of all the human race creep. "We wish", he thunders, "to exalt the aggressive movement, the feverish insomnia, running, the perilous leap, the cuff and the blow". War, he declares, is "the only true hygiene of the world": he is going to "glorify militarism, patriotism, the destructive gesture of anarchist, the beautiful Ideas which kill, and the scorn of woman". Also, he and his friends are going to destroy museums and libraries. "A race-automobile adorned with great pipes like serpents with explosive breath—a race-automobile which seems to rush over exploding powder—is more beautiful than the *Victory of Samothrace.*" Do you not think so? You had better. "Time and Space died yesterday. We already live in the Absolute for we have already created the omnipresent eternal Speed." And one wouldn't like to be left behind. And oh, the Absolute is *such* a nice place to live in! "Therefore welcome the incendiarists with carbon fingers! Here they are! Here! Away and set fire to the book-shelves! Turn the canals and flood the vaults of the museums! Sap the foundations of the venerable towns!" The statues of Victor Emmanuel are better than anything Verrocchio could have turned out. Down with Dante! Up with Marinetti! His triumph, though, will be short-lived. Not that Dante will be re-instated in popular favour—oh no! But so soon as Marinetti and his troupe have reached the age of forty "other younger and more daring men will throw us into the waste-paper basket like useless manuscripts!" The scene will be rather an odd one; for the younger men will come "leaping on the cadence of their first poems", and will be "clawing the air with crooked fingers", and also "scenting at the academy gates the good smell of our decaying minds". Finally they will run Marinetti and his friends to earth "in the open country, in a sad iron shed pitter-pattered by the monotonous rain, huddled round our trepidating aeroplanes;" and "they will rush to kill us;" and "powerful and healthsome Injustice will burst radiantly in their eyes." I hope I shall be spared to see something of all this.

I should like, meanwhile, to see Marinetti. I should not be surprised to find in him a physical as well as a spiritual resemblance to the fat boy in "Pickwick". The people whose fancy delights in "Speed", and "the destructive gesture of anarchist", and all that sort of thing, are usually people of sedentary habit, loth to raise a little finger on their own account. To profess, as does Marinetti, admiration of "violence, cruelty, and injustice" is not characteristic of a violent, cruel, or unjust man. Such a man is apt to be rather ashamed of these things. It is only the very mild person to whom they are a lovely obsession. When I hear a man expressing "scorn of woman" I suspect he is a sentimentalist whom women don't happen to like. So, with the best will in the world, I fail to be frightened by Marinetti and his doctrines. When he glorifies "the beautiful Ideas that kill", I ask what are they?—knowing very well he couldn't tell me. When he says that "Art can only be violence, cruelty, and injustice," I murmur, with a smile, that those are three of the few things that art just *can't* be. When he asks why we "poison ourselves" by "a daily walk through the museums", I assure him that his metaphor has no relation to fact. There are a few pedants who walk daily in museums; but even they don't poison themselves; on the contrary, they find there the food that best agrees with them. There is the vast mass of humanity which never sets foot in a museum. There are the artists who go now and again, and profit by the inspiration. It must be a very feeble talent that dares not, for fear of being overwhelmed and atrophied, contemplate the achievements of the past. No talent, however strong, can dispense with that inspiration. But how on earth is anyone going to draw any inspiration from the Future? Let us spell it with a capital letter, by all means. But don't let us expect it to give us anything in return. It can't, poor thing; for the very good reason that it doesn't yet exist, save as a dry abstract term.

The past and the present—there are two useful and delightful things. I am sorry, Marinetti, but I am afraid there is no future for the Future. Perhaps you don't really mind. "We already live in the Absolute" because certain motor-cars can be driven at the rate of a hundred miles an hour. What more can one want? You yourself, Marinetti, have the added gratification that your voice has crossed Europe. And this feat you would not have achieved if you had been the sort of person who talks good sense.

BREAD AND TREACLE.

By George A. B. Dewar.

It has been said that the man in the most helpless position of all is he with ten children to feed, clothe and educate as ladies and gentlemen and a thousand a year to do it on. The husband of the Lady Susan answered to this description. He had not only the children—he had the park, gardens, glasshouses, stables and mansion house (whose roof wanted thousands spent on it) of Elvers Place to keep up into the bargain. How was it done? It might easily be shown on paper—Free Trader and Protectionist could both show it—that it could not be done; yet there is the fact that Lady Susan did it for years, her husband looking on helplessly. The Rev. Stiffbristle was an angry witness to the doing of it; a sarcastic witness to the looking on helplessly; angry and sarcastic because the Lady Susan not only ran the children, the stables, her husband, the garden, the park and the mansion house and its terrible roof, but never left off trying to run as well the village of Elvers Green, including its vicar. Camps and barrows dotted about the countryside show that at some time or other hundreds of now obscure English villages have been the scenes of fierce battle. But that long and passionate fight at Elvers Green no barrow or fosse commemorates. Greenworthy the local historian will overlook it, the Field Club will picnic on the battlefield and yet know nothing about it. Elvers Place is let to strangers, the eldest son is abroad, all the other sons and daughters—the daughters growing, alas! rather scraggy—are scattered far and wide, and the Lady Susan and her husband helpless on a thousand a year are no more. Stiffbristle's name is on the chancel wall. The brass gives the usual satisfactory dates as to when he entered and when departed this life, and how long he was vicar of this parish. It tells no more. He, like the vast majority of men and women, small and great souled, dull and entertaining, is one of the suppressed characters of history. Yet, could one but draw it all in fine detail, what an extremely interesting and moving story that would be of his struggle with the great lady of Elvers Green; the bitterness—sometimes the gnashing bitterness—of defeat, the glow of victory; the forced, polite words before strangers for appearance' sake, and just beneath them often the fires of righteous anger. "That Woman!" "That Man Stiffbristle!" "Impertinent!" "How dare she?" "Our Living, too!" "In *my* churchyard!"

For a few months after the Lady Susan had given him the living—£100 a year gross, the ten-acre glebe and the vicarage—Stiffbristle was high in favour. He was asked to dinner to meet the Dowager Lady de Vault and Lady Eastcheap. The Lady Susan, I should have explained, was a de Vault. Whilst she had married into land minus mortgages, her sister the Lady Ann had married into merchandise plus nobility. Lord Eastcheap was working partner in a very old-established firm which dealt in hides from Posen. It will be well remembered that their failure was quite a sensation in society. It was through no fault of their own; it was simply because of the utter stagnation in the Posen trade. Bitter tongues will often snarl that when this sort of people fails there always seems enough money for them to live in comfort. But not so in this sad case. The family travelled second for some years; and, of the two sons, one had to go straight from Eton to an Oxford scholarship, where his battels were so low they shamed the staircase scout.

In this company Stiffbristle basked—so far as a man may bask in vaults—but, alas! not for long. That which had befallen other vicars of Elvers Green befel Stiffbristle. There may be room in a village for a supreme lay ruler and a supreme spiritual ruler. Given fine tact, such a division of authority is conceivable. If the Lady Susan had been content to drill the bodies of her parishioners and Stiffbristle had confined himself to drilling their souls, the thing might have worked. But she wished to have a hand in both departments, and he had rather on the whole she had her interfering hand in neither. So they took to hating one another for the love of God, and there was war at Elvers Green, war all the week and again on Sunday. It was a war, so far as I understood, not of ritual but of management. There was war about the choir to start with—a musical war. Four of the daughters of the Lady Susan played the organ, but Stiffbristle wished to choose the chants. He protested against, I think it was, Gregorian chants for lesser Psalms. There was war in the school, in the parish room, in the cottage. The combatants had been known to join battle even at a mother's meeting. Stiffbristle was no longer asked to meet the Dowager de Vault at dinner at Elvers Place; that vault was closed for ever against him.

It went on for years, the two sides being on the whole evenly matched in spirit and resources. If the Lady Susan seemed to have got him by the short hairs during the week—as when for example she invited a neighbouring clergyman to do for Elvers Green what Stiffbristle himself ought to have been asked to do—the fortunes of war might shift on the seventh day; for then the Lady Susan must sit under her foe, and the text might be made to tell against her. Had not Pharaoh to bow before the high priest on occasion?

The thing reached a climax when the news went forth that the Lady Susan had announced that the children of Elvers Green must not have bread and treacle for their supper; it was absurd their having bread and treacle—they must have bread and butter. This had somewhat the effect on Stiffbristle that the Berlin Decrees of Napoleon had on England. He came out as a champion of the liberties of the people. England, he told the villagers, was a free nation. All parents had the right to decide on the supper of their own children. He had stood it for years, he would stand it no longer. Driven by bread and treacle past bearing, Stiffbristle went straight off to see the Bishop, and pour into his ears the long story of his martyrdom at Elvers Green.

The Bishop was commonly described as a courtier and a compromiser. A few who knew him intimately added that he was a Christian. He had a habit of going to bed at six o'clock in the evening when he wished to withdraw himself from the world. The Bishop was one of those rarest men who confer benefits simply by listening to people smarting under grief or injustice. There was a soothing, an exquisite sympathy in the way he lent his ear to sorrow. But how could even he help Stiffbristle? Not all the Bishops and Archbishops in their accumulated wisdom could have directed Stiffbristle how to prevent that woman from trampling on the liberties of Elvers Green. Convocation could not have prevented her. The Bishop could only advise as you or I could have advised Stiffbristle. Change with some other priest—this was all the Bishop could say. Alas, it was only easy to say!

So Stiffbristle went home with the good man's sympathy. He went home to discover this strange coincidence—that whilst he had gone to his Bishop she had gone to her God. People had said for years that the Lady Susan had no heart: and yet it was her heart that carried her off. At the very time Stiffbristle was pouring out his soul in the Bishop's ear, crying out against her pride, her tyranny over his people, she had a seizure. She was gone without a word—gone with one long mysterious sigh of death, no more.

"The hand of God"—was that the thought that flashed on Stiffbristle when he heard? Did he feel he had gotten the victory at last in a righteous cause? One cannot tell. To read the hearts of men is mostly left for the fools of this world; and to God in the next. But this is sure—Stiffbristle was a changed man thereafter. It was remarked at Elvers Green that he began to show a loss of spirit about this time. There were not wanting bitter tongues to say it must be because he felt the loss of the Lady Susan so deeply. Perhaps people who said this were wiser than they knew. At any rate the man wilted. The zest of his life, which is the zest of so many a life, the wrestling and boxing business, went out of him. Stiffbristle was no longer Stiffbristle. One might have produced some little Baptist or Methody Boythorne to bait Stiffbristle into good heart again, and even this might not have served. The truth seems to be that some natures are meant for peace and some for war. Some for suffering the little children to come unto them, and others for smiting the Amalekite. Stiffbristle must have been meant as a smiter. He must have been meant for opposition and competition. It was bread and treacle to him. Take away competition from a plant or a man that thrives on competition, and the thing relieved may degrade or perish. There were some snowdrops in my garden that spread from the flower border to the gravel path, and though I pounded down the gravel and rolled it till it became like cement, the snowdrops in their season would thrust up through this hard floor stronger, more resolute than ever. As with plants, so it is with men like Stiffbristle. He was even as the snowdrops.

THE MARRING OF A COUNTY.

THOSE most praiseworthy people whose industry sets before us from time to time something of the treasures which our ancestors have left us in every corner of our country unhappily remind us of the Sibyl who brought her books to market. Year by year the amount of our inheritance dwindles; but the price which we have to pay if we would preserve it is fixed. Our efforts of conservative taste are always about a generation behindhand. Forty years ago there were churches which had escaped the restorer, ancient houses which only needed a few touches to the tiling or the plaster to make them tight for another century, sites round which a wise man might have drawn a magic circle against the jerry-builders for a mere song. Twenty years on, and the church is gutted and scraped; the manor house is a tumbled ruin; the foreground of an unsurpassed landscape has been blocked up by a row of unwholesome cottages and an iron shed. Another twenty years, and one of the latest of the Sibylline gatherings from the past* tells us that we have still our lesson to learn; the phrases "destroyed", "allowed to perish", "modernised", "the ignorance, carelessness, and prejudice by which so much has been swept away in our own time" are in a too familiar strain. It would seem that there is some sort of compensatory connexion between the growth of a solicitous interest in antiquities and the practical energies which brush them out of our path. The very taste which has learned to demand a country cottage "with beams"—as a recent definition compendiously put it—proceeds to transmogrify the simple unity of a half-timbered Jacobean farmhouse into a commodious week-end residence, with a new front like a stage-scene, a built-out billiard-room, and electric light. And this curious double-headed taste—too well seconded by the efforts of the country builder, with a conception of the meaning of "old-world" dawning in his soul, and van-loads of ready-made "art" details bought from a "cutting-line" in a wholesale catalogue—affects not only architecture, but the landscape. All over the South of England, on almost every rise which looks over woods or heath to wide sweeps of horizon, there stand brand-new mansions, rarely in harmonious or even considered relation to the surroundings, "pricking a Cockney ear" in raw red brick or gleaming stone, perched high to catch the view whose obverse they necessarily destroy. No county has suffered so much from this one-eyed taste as has Sussex. Mr. H. Belloc, who has written a proem, "The Individuality of Sussex", to the book referred to above, expresses an

* "Memorials of Old Sussex." Edited by Percy D. Mundy. London: Allen. 1909. 15s. net.

optimist view of the future of the county, as regards the chances of crowding and vulgarisation. The hope is a pious one; but the arch inconsequence of the reasons adducéd might well exasperate anyone who has watched the course of things in the Weald for the last quarter of a century—even one who has been tamed by the influences of the soft air, the broad vaporous distances, the deep holding soil, working together to produce that steadying, lenitive quality which gives the county its distinctive virtue. To announce that the Wealden clay is a real obstacle to the invasion of modern settlers is mere trifling. The London clay, beside whose sour intractability, damp-holding, and foundation-settling qualities the Wealden staple is a docile and generous compost, has not perceptibly checked, it may be remembered, the suburban expansion in its area. Those who have made any notes of the quantity and the quality of the building in Sussex during late years—not only near the railway centres, but in the most out-of-the-way villages and upon the openest of forest ground; who know the sort of designs which the bye-laws habitually pass, and the utilitarian iron bridges which the county councils put up in place of condemned timber and stone, and the cruel cleverness of the experts who turn old cottages into modern antiques, and the public liking for corrugated iron and barbed wire, and the effects upon a once picturesque village of the possession of an "Improvement Association"—the people who consider these things will not have very much doubt as to how long "the isolation and the consequent individuality of Sussex" will remain. The mischief which we shall learnedly deplore in another score of years is now busy in every part of the county with scarcely a breath of disapproval to be heard against it. At the proper conjunction we shall begin to think it unthinkable (as we say) that any little speculator in bricks and mortar should have been allowed to deface with his æsthetics a county where nature and time, working on a curiously amenable architecture, had produced a kind of landscape beauty not to be found anywhere else in the world. It is not building, but building wrong, which blights the prospect. The finest and most characteristic views in Sussex generally owe something to farm-roofs or cottage timbering of the right kind coming into the picture. If we would but define for ourselves the points wherein the rightness lies, and see the reason why an old windmill or thatched gables or an oast-house are prettier than a new red-brick public-house with a glass "facia" and three gas-lamps, a girder bridge, or a zinc-roofed shed, we should be in the way of anticipating for once our customary posthumous wisdom in these concerns.

Sussex, of course, is not singular among the counties in the transformation which is going on; but for various reasons it is in the forefront of the battle, and in its peculiar mixture of gifts has perhaps more to lose than any other shire. There are other survivals, beside those of landscape and architecture, which there is still time for us to learn to respect and to conserve, dwindled relics and dear to buy though they may be. It is not only the brasses vanished from their matrices, the thirteenth-century paintings blackened by church stoves, the end of castles and monastic houses as road-metal, as set before us in Mr. Mundy's "Memorials", which we have to deplore. The learned compile glossaries of dialect, and the many write novels with rustic conversations, while for some forty years we have made our elementary education a machine for systematically stamping out the forms of the vernacular and replacing them by the tongue—of all within the four winds!—of lower middle-class London. It may be too late to save much of the vocal idiom—the north country will stick to its impregnable vowels for some time to come, but the southern wells are pretty deeply defiled. Yet of the dialect of thought, the mental syntax which perhaps even more than turns of the tongue used to distinguish the races of Britain, something may still be saved. If the rotund Sussex "a" must follow the "th" into oblivion, giving place to the soul-grating diphthong of Whitechapel, it is worth a struggle to keep even a remnant of the Sussex temperament, the way of looking at the world, the deep entrenchment of opinion, the elementary wit, which have not their like in the world outside the Downs, the Weald, and the Forest. The right South Saxon nature—a rare compound which unites a softness of fibre something like the Celtic impracticability, a gentlemanly yielding of the wall to the aggressive world, with an extreme tenacity of private concerns, and mingles a strain of real piety with a stoical humour—is too good a thing to be handed over to the polishing touch of the certified intellects of the Code.

It may be hoped that the solidity of reserve still maintained towards new things and new people may indicate a provision of nature for the permanence of the type. The efforts of our "educationalists" may after all have only overlaid the full relief of the race like a coat of churchwardens' whitewash on old carving, and in better days the old deep-cut light and shade may be seen again in unslurred sharpness. When the time comes for us to discover that the uniformity we have loved is a specific blight of the mind, a national danger to be met by commissions and talking leagues, the resisting powers of silly Sussex may prove invaluable as the groundwork of recovery.

Meanwhile, there is something to be done by those who are not content with always being in at the death of all kinds of desirable antiquity. They will lend a hand where practicable to the saving of landscape beauty from injury that is often quite gratuitous, in places whose fame is unlike that of Ullswater or Burnham Beeches, insufficient to raise the public in their defence. They will give no countenance to that impudent folly of "restoring" old craftsmanship by replacing it by a modern copy. They will encourage as far as they can a general temper of reverence for the past, a spirit which involves something both of filial piety and of gratitude, and is an excellent countervail against some exaggerated modern tendencies. The true conservative reveres, in that fine conclusion of Pliny's, the glory of the days of old, and that very age which, venerable in man, in cities is sacred.

THE NEW ZEALAND OWL.

By James Drummond.

NEW ZEALAND'S "morepork" owl is one of the few members of the great Strigidæ family that are not regarded with disfavour. There is hardly a race, barbarous or civilised, ancient or modern, which has not associated owls with misfortune and death. From remote ages poets have taken as much delight in decrying the owl as in praising the lark. It is always the "boding owl", the "moping owl", the "hooting owl", or the "screeching owl". The New Zealand owl, however, is loved by Europeans and revered by Maoris, and the Parliament of the country, following the people's wishes, has given it absolute protection.

It is a small bird as owls go, though its soft, fluffy feathers make it look larger than it is. It has a round, bullet-shaped head, large wings, strong, grasping claws, and a rather sombre, brown, rufous-spotted plumage. It loves the stately, almost songless forests of its native land, and usually shuns places where human beings gather. Sometimes it is seen out in the open, but when it is "at home" in the day-time it sits on the branch of a tree in the gloomiest depths of a dark forest, apparently lost in thought. I watched two of them sitting side by side in a forest in the Bird Sanctuary on the Little Barrier Island, near Auckland, a few years ago. They sat and stared and blinked until I went quite close to them, and then they seemed silently to fall from their perch, and, like beings from another world, they vanished amongst a network of hanging lianas and dense foliage.

When I spent ten days on the West Coast of the South Island in the early part of this year, trying to cement my friendship with several species of New Zealand's interesting native birds, owls were the first inhabitants of the forest to greet me. I was the guest of a miner, who is one of the most devoted bird-lovers

I have known. He lives on the banks of the lovely Mahinapua River, which flows eight miles from the Mahinapua Lake into the mouth of the Hokitika River, and so out into the Tasman Sea. He was waiting for me at Hokitika when I arrived there at dusk, and we paddled in a Maori canoe up the river until we reached a small grassy platform which runs out from the bank, and which is lapped by the waters of the river as they pass swiftly on to join the ocean. Behind the platform there is a natural shrubbery. In an opening in this shrubbery there is a path which crosses a swamp, and, turning at right angles, leads up to the portals of the forest through which it passes. For five chains or more, between avenues of towering trees, it has been formed by the dark trunks of hundreds of tree-ferns being thrown across it side by side and row upon row, while here and there a hollow has been bridged by a lordly pine which has fallen under the strokes of the axe, and which is now trampled under men's feet. The path ends at a clearing. In the centre of that clearing stands a wooden hut, small, modest, and comfortable, in which my friend lives alone, and which is the head-quarters of many wild birds. Parson-birds step through his doorway, robins hop upon his table to share his meals, fantails flit through his rooms in search of flies, and on several occasions during my visit he called down tom-tits from distant tree-tops to feed on insects in his outstretched hand.

As soon as I set foot in this clearing I heard the owls' loud hooting. The presence of these birds seemed to be in keeping with the sombre, moonlit forest and the gigantic spectral pines and rata trees. "Whoo-whoo", one of the owls cried, the first note longer and more emphatic than the second; and an answer came from the other side of the clearing in the same monotonous tone, utterly devoid of variation. Every night at almost all hours, from dusk until the first faint glimmerings of dawn chased away the shadowy forest ghosts, I heard the strange "whoo-whoo, whoo-whoo, whoo-whoo", now from one tree, now from another, never close, but always loud, and, I admit, always peculiarly boding. It is in the darkest hour, just before the dawn, that the "morepork's" cry is heard in its most effective setting. At that time there is usually not another sound in a New Zealand forest except the rustling of the leaves, the creaking of the boughs, and the sighing of the wind. Owls have the whole forest to themselves, and their hooting is made louder by the absence of all other evidence of animal life. They do not always wait for night to come and hide their actions. Before darkness has settled down, and while it is still quite light, they come out from their hiding places in hollow trees and set upon belated small birds which are hurrying to their nests. Sometimes, early in the evening, they come about the hut One of them has a favourite perching place close to the window, where he likes to sit and listen to my friend startle the silence with notes from his cornet.

In the old days in New Zealand, before civilisation, the "morepork" was treated as a supernatural being, and even now there is a strong belief amongst the Maoris that the family god, protector, or guardian angel assumes the form of an owl. There are some Maoris who still believe that when a chief takes his walks abroad he is accompanied by an owl, which hoots or screeches in the evening when he breaks his journey or reaches his destination. An incident that shows how the owl superstition is perpetuated occurred a short time ago. Some school-children finding an owl in a garden struck it down and apparently killed it. An old Maori woman took it from the children, that the cats might not get hold of it. She carried it to her hut and placed it under her bed. A few hours later she saw with terror the owl fly from under the bed into the room, through the door, and into the open. She was convinced that it was quite dead when she took it from the children. Nothing but a god, she said, could come back to life, and she saw in the incident the sign of a calamity which would follow an insult to a god. The Maoris generally, who are very fond of bird pets, refuse to keep owls in captivity, because, they say, the death of a captive owl is an omen of ill.

The members of some tribes believe that the owl has friendly feelings towards human beings. In the fastnesses of Tuhoe Land, in the great King Country, it is believed that the owl gives a warning of the approach of a hostile war party. It is alleged to have a peculiar cry: "Kou! Kou! Kou! Whero! Whero! Whero!" It is understood to say: "Arise! By fleeing you will escape the enemy, who assault an empty hamlet!" In one of the forests of Tuhoe Land two albino owls of supernatural powers, named Kahu and Kau, predict the success or failure of the bird-snaring seasons. If a person belonging to the district goes into the forest and takes some birds and bones them, and the two owls appear, the season will be good; but if the owls do not appear the season will be bad. When the chief Hone Heke, in one of the early Maori wars, attacked the Europeans at the Bay of Islands, the Maori warriors used the owl's cry as a means of communication. The parties, as they moved to their positions near the block-houses before daybreak, imitated the hooting. The British soldiers were so accustomed to hear the owls at night that they took no notice of the familiar sound, and the tactics of the Maoris were carried out without hindrance.

The Maori priests of olden times gave the owl a very honourable position in the "Battle of the Birds". A land-bird and a sea-bird quarrelled over a feeding-ground. A great battle took place, all the birds of the sea and of the land taking part in it. "An immense army of sea-birds came sweeping grandly from one side of the heavens to the other, making a terrible noise with their wings and throats. A mighty charge was made by the sea-birds. In the first rank, swooping down with mighty wings, came the albatross, the gannet, and the brown gull, all the other birds of the sea following closely. Then they charged at close quarters and fought, bird with bird. The river-birds came in close phalanx and dashed bravely right into their foes. They all stood to it for a long time, fighting desperately. At last the sea-birds gave way and fled in confusion. The big hawk sailed down upon them, pursuing and killing, and the fleet sparrow-hawk dashed in and out amongst the fugitives, while the owl, who could not fly by day, and who, therefore, could not take an active part in the affray, gave encouragement by hooting derisively: 'Thou art brave! Thou art victor!'"

The only charge made against the "morepork" is that it kills small native birds, which are now becoming rare; but it also destroys large numbers of vermin, and its few failings and foibles are readily forgiven. "I have listened to the music of our steadfast friend the 'morepork' for fifty years", writes a colonist in the North Island, "and the song of no other bird gives me half as much satisfaction. It is 'hooting, laughing in the forest', indeed, to the inestimable benefit of every settler. By the destruction of rats and mice, this bird has been of incalculable benefit to farmers, and I would make it a criminal offence either to destroy or injure it".

CORRESPONDENCE.

LIBERAL WOMAN-FOLK; PRIMROSE DAMES; POLITICAL FAITH.

To the Editor of the SATURDAY REVIEW.

Imperial Colonial Club, 84 Piccadilly,
19 November 1909.

SIR,—My letter of 4 November under the above heading was called forth by your article on "Liberal Woman-folk and their Men" and by the recent correspondence between the Conservative and Unionist Women's Franchise Association and the Primrose League, published in the "Morning Post" on 27 October. On 28 October a letter appeared, signed "Primrose Leaguer", regretting the decision of the Grand Council; this regret is shared by many Unionists—Primrose Leaguers and otherwise—who feel that an attitude of neutrality on the part of Unionist suffragists is bound to have an adverse effect, indirectly at least, at the General Election.

On 31 May this year the "Morning Post" published a correspondence between Mrs. Gilbert Samuel, Hon. Secretary of the Conservative and Unionist Women's Franchise Association, and Mr. Arnold Ward, at the Central Conservative Association, Watford. Mrs. Samuel asked Mr. Ward's opinion on the subject of pressing for legislation "when our party is returned to power". Mr. Ward expressed regret at an attempt to make the subject a party question "as likely to jeopardise principles far wider than the particular object you have in view". He says: "The fact that among your vice-presidents are to be found the names of a number of very influential ladies, closely connected with the leaders of the party, only increases the anxiety which has been aroused by your Association's programme". He asks if the Association proposes "to support or oppose Unionist candidates according to their views on women's franchise. If this is your intention, how do you reconcile it with party loyalty? If it is not your intention, what can be the object of the letter which you have circulated?" Mrs. Samuel then explained the objects of the Association, and stated its intention not to oppose any official candidate. To this Mr. Ward wrote that "in view of the strong opposition to your objects existing within the ranks of the party . . . your Association is not calculated to promote harmonious relations, but rather to divide the members of a great party whose first imperative duty it should be to ignore all points of difference and to work all together for the triumph of its accepted principles".

This correspondence caused some comment at the time, but not much uneasiness was felt until the Grand Council of the Primrose League announced that "members of the League are bound not to oppose official Unionist candidates whatever the candidates' views may be on the question of women's suffrage". It has been felt that an attitude of neutrality—however benevolent—is not enough for members of a League formed "to maintain the integrity of the Empire"; there are Unionist anti-suffragists who have expressed their intention of refraining from activity in the General Election if their official candidate is in favour of suffrage, and this feeling is as much to be regretted as in the case of Unionist suffragists.

My knowledge of the working and organisation of the Conservative and Unionist Women's Franchise Association is limited, like that of any other nonmember, to what can be gathered from a set of the leaflets published by it, a copy of the rules, and such notices of meetings and correspondence as have from time to time appeared in the "Morning Post".

I have read with interest the quotations from Conservative leaders, past and present, and have noted that all are dated before the question reached its present acute stage. Mr. Balfour has made no very recent pronouncement about the suffrage, and several other prominent Unionists are known to be opposed to it. I did not say that any suffragist "to remain straightforward must desert her party organisation". What I said was that the suffragist who puts the vote above all other questions should not "allow her name to be borne on the books of a party association, and to use that association to put forward her personal opinions to the detriment of that same party".

Many Unionists will welcome Lady Castlereagh's assurance that, while the Association as such will naturally not work for an official candidate should he oppose the suffrage, those members who are also "members of the Primrose League or other associations . . . will do work of which any Unionist may be proud". No reminder is needed of the work done by them in the past. I hope it may be my fate—and that of other anti-suffragist Unionists—to work under the leadership, in the coming election, of one of those ladies of the Conservative and Unionist Women's Franchise Association who "place imperial interests before everything".

I am, Sir, your obedient servant,

Annie J. Lindsay.

THE FLOW OF GOLD.

To the Editor of the Saturday Review.

23 November 1909.

Sir,—It is very encouraging to find a paper having the standing of the Saturday Review giving prominence to the subject which your correspondent, Mr. Henry Meulin, deals with under the title, "The Flow of Gold", in last week's issue. To one who has studied this subject it is not a little curious that our daily and weekly journals devote so little space to a subject which is certainly of greater importance than any proposed scheme of tariff reform or taxation of land values.

In an able address to the Bankers' Association of Liverpool last year Mr. (now Sir) E. H. Holden, the well-known general manager of the London City and Midland Banking Company, stated that "the business of the world is carried on by means of loans, that loans create credit, that the stand-by for the protection of these credits is gold, and that, therefore, gold controls the trade of the world".

The condition of the commercial man in England is very peculiar. In spite of all his diligence and enterprise he knows perfectly well that his success is largely due to influences and agencies over which he has no control, that not only is he liable to suffer for any indiscretions on the part of his own people, such as some foolish legislation or other circumstances arising in his own country, but he is also likely to suffer for the indiscretions or even for the successes of people in other countries. For instance, a short time ago the directors of the Pennsylvania Railway Company decided upon the construction of some extensive new works, and at the same time various speculators in Egypt decided upon similar undertakings in that country, the result of which was that there was an application to the Bank of England for large shipments of gold abroad, and the Governors of the Bank decided to raise the rate, the consequence being that thousands of our commercial people were compelled to pay an additional rate of interest on loans. And this is what is likely to happen at any time. In other words, owing to our financial arrangements, the Bank of England has the power to tax the whole of the commercial interests of Great Britain in order that foreigners may have free access to English gold!

The system is so extraordinary that it would be farcical were it not so terribly disastrous. We are the only country in the world where such a condition prevails.

Just now there is an enormous amount of agitation throughout the British Isles owing to the proposal on the part of the Government to put a tax on land values, and yet we cheerfully submit to a system where a dozen men in London may sit around a table at any time and impose a tax of from one per cent. upwards on bank loans, without exciting any comment. When one reflects that a large number of businesses are done on a margin of from one per cent. to two per cent., it is easy to see how disastrously the increase of the Bank rate affects them.

One of the chief arguments that has been used by tariff reformers against our free-trade system is that trade conditions have entirely changed during the free-trade period, and that our fiscal system needs reconsideration. If this is true of the tariff system, surely it is equally true of our financial system. We are still doing business on the basis which was created sixty-five years ago when trade was a mere bagatelle to what it is at the present time and before the gold standard had been adopted by other nations. The mere fact that our great industrial competitors have adopted the same monetary standard is in itself sufficient to demand a reconsideration of the Banking and Currency Acts.

It may sound strange to many, but I have no hesitation in asserting that the evils that have arisen and which have created this agitation in favour of tariff reform are directly traceable to our irrational and inadequate financial system, and if this subject were properly agitated both tariff reformers and free traders would find that they were what the Americans call "barking up the wrong tree". Free trade has failed in this country because it has been unaccompanied with free banking, and because of the absurd restrictions which have been placed upon the means of exchange. Similarly tariff reformers would find that with the adoption of a sane monetary and banking system English trade would have all the protection that it enjoyed from 1847 to 1874 when England was alone in the use of the gold standard. Since the latter date, international trade has become not so much an exchange of commodities as a scramble for gold.

The subject is, perhaps, too long for a letter. I merely make these few remarks hoping that your readers will see the importance of a complete study of this subject.

Yours faithfully,
A Reader of the S. R.

MR. URE'S LATEST.

To the Editor of the Saturday Review.

The "Old" Vicarage, Rye,
23 November 1909.

Sir,—When trying to answer Mr. Balfour's condemnation of his speech on the old-age pensions and the Unionist party Mr. Ure made the excuse that he meant that the Unionists, relying only on Tariff Reform for their revenue, would not be able to pay these pensions. I admit this was rather a clever "get-out"; whether a very truthful one or not I can't say; but I see he is now reported to have said at Weston-super-Mare: "Unionists were going to plunge the country into a great constitutional struggle, upset business and bring the financial affairs of the State to a deadlock upon a Budget which was the very Budget they would have brought in to-morrow had they been in office." Surely this takes all the wind out of Mr. Ure's reply to Mr. Balfour, for, providing the Unionists bring in a Budget the same as Mr. Lloyd George's, they will be in the same position to pay old-age pensions as the Radicals. Can Mr. Ure wriggle out of this? I would not ask you to insert this letter did I not know what a tremendous effect Mr. Ure's speeches have had on those in receipt of old-age pensions.

Yours faithfully,
T. G. Sharpe.

NATIONAL THEATRES.

To the Editor of the Saturday Review.

Reform Club, Pall Mall S.W.,
20 November 1909.

Sir,—Mr. Richard C. Jackson writes in to-day's Saturday Review strongly deprecating the establishment of the proposed National Theatre. He assumes that the object of a National Theatre is to rob taxpayers in order to provide casual amusement for nothing to certain playgoers. This is not so. The object of a National Theatre is to organise and build up a national drama on the level of its sister arts, to raise high standards of writing and acting all round, and to establish great traditions on our stage. With this idea in our minds the money actually spent upon the various National Theatres that Mr. Jackson mentions seems to be a wonderfully good and economical investment. The upkeep of a National Theatre costs about £10,000 a year. It costs us over £4000 a year to gaze at two pictures only in the National Gallery, the recently acquired Holbein and the Raphael Madonna. To gaze at all our collections, when the value of the sites is taken into account, costs us a fabulous sum. Beside it £10,000 a year is a mere fleabite, a mere nothing for a wealthy country to dole out to the art which has, or should have, incomparably the more vital and penetrating influence upon the tastes and conduct and lives of its citizens. The measure of a nation's advance in the arts is roughly the measure of its distance from the brutes. The arguments that Mr. Jackson uses against the establishment of a National Theatre may be equally used against the continued establishment and endowment of the National Galleries. The sites and pictures would sell for an enormous sum, which would be of great use to the Chancellor of the Exchequer just now. If on consideration Mr. Jackson finds that his arguments are sound, let him leave the drama alone, as it is not at present endowed, but let him organise a scheme for the sale of our national collections, and thus earn the gratitude of those fellow-taxpayers for whom he shows so much solicitude.

Your obedient servant,
Henry Arthur Jones.

THE SHORT STORY.

To the Editor of the Saturday Review.

24 November 1909.

Sir,—In the fine review of Mr. Harris' "Shakespeare" which appeared in the Saturday of last week, there occurs one of the most amazing sentences I have read for some time, a sentence that shows how very much we here in England are out of touch with the trend of literature in those benighted portions of the world outside of the sweet influence of the Brixton Pleiades.

The sentence is as follows, and as it is placed in parenthesis it is naturally the absolute opinion of the writer: "Mr. Harris' own tale 'Sonia' comes as near as anything we know, but it is only a short story."

Only a short story—one wonders if the writer of the review has read the three sketches by Turguenieff that appeared in your issue of last week.

It is precisely because "Sonia" is not a long-drawn-out novel that Mr. Harris has succeeded (as your reviewer allows) in placing before us a picture.

In spite of the fact that novels continue to pour out of the British press, it would seem that the novel as a means of artistic expression is an obsolete form. In France, Russia, Spain, Italy, and Germany the short story has either supplanted or is supplanting it.

With ourselves the drama is displacing it every day. Already even the press, which is usually a generation behind intellectual opinion, is beginning to give more attention to the dramatist than to the novelist. If English writers go on pouring out floods of enormous, formless novels, in which the subject is everything and the handling nothing, our literature will inevitably decline.

However, I observe with pleasure that our best writers—as Conrad, Hudson, Galsworthy, George Moore, Henry James, and Ezra Pound—are devoting themselves more and more to short pieces, and in them are doing some of their finest work.

I am yours faithfully,
R. B. Cunninghame Graham.

"NUMEROUS."

To the Editor of the Saturday Review.

Little Clarendon, Dinton, Salisbury,
20 November 1909.

Sir,—Will not the Saturday Review help by precept and example to reclaim this constantly misused word to its right use, and to reinstate its much-injured poor relation "many"? Et tu, S. R. To take one instance out of several from your last issue, why, in the name of the English tongue, not "many" but "numerous important men of finance" (p. 616)? The reminder is an impertinence that a hive and a family are numerous, the bees and the children not numerous but many. "Numerous", in its proper and almost extinct sense, is a most valuable word with no English equivalent.

And where is the ancient ear for English? Neither the Editor nor A. L. H. ("Quicunque Vult" correspondence) seems afflicted by the cacophony in the new rendering "There is therefore one Father".

I am etc.,
G. H. Engleheart.

[It is so rare in these days to find a man fastidious in the use of words that we gladly publish this letter; we think it seems to be at our own expense.—Ed. S. R.]

REVIEWS.

A MODERN BOOK ON SHELLEY.

"Shelley: the Man and the Poet." By A. Clutton-Brock. London: Methuen. 1910. 7s. 6d. net.

THE author of this volume tells us in his introductory chapter that he has written the book largely to please himself. At the end he ventures the hope that it may renew, in the breasts of "middle-aged" people, the youthful desire to read Shelley. All this is modest, and indeed the whole work is as unassuming as it is sane and enjoyable. Mr. Clutton-Brock is familiar with several modes of artistic expression, and particularly is able to illuminate his observation of literature by side-lights from what he knows of pictures. More important, his view of art itself is logically thought out and consistently applied. He possesses what is all too rare among writers of literary criticism—a clear, simple and central æsthetic theory which guides, without stilting, his judgment of particular works. For biographical purposes his style is excellent. He eschews theatrical effects, but he writes with a shrewd perception and a turn of dry humour which give real life to his narrative. Thus equipped, there was no reason why Mr. Clutton-Brock should hesitate about a new book on Shelley. There was more than room for a book of the right sort —a book addressed to the layman, dealing sensibly with the life and sympathetically with the poems, above all, presenting Shelley's astonishing unity, as man and artist, in a form entirely clarified from the sloppy sentiment which shifts and palliates no less than from the mechanical morality which condemns from outside. A book of this kind, essentially modern in tone and free from the professorial taint, would have been a genuine contribution to present-day criticism. Half-way through the present volume, we fancied that Mr. Clutton-Brock had actually filled the gap. Reviewing the book as a whole we can see that our expectations—very high ones, it is true—have not been realised. We can only say that the book will please, justly, many readers who have no inclination to "authoritative" biographies like Professor Dowden's, or who are deterred from that and other works by the qualities, or rather lack of quality, which Matthew Arnold so lightly but vividly indicated in his famous review. There is nothing ponderous in Mr. Clutton-Brock's exposition of the poems. He has the good sense to choose what is typical, however familiar, and never descends to wearisome detail. Unfortunately his chapters of literary criticism read as though they had first seen the light by instalments, and abound in repetition, useful enough in the journalist or lecturer who aims at a certain completeness in the serial part, but a bad flaw in the writer of a compacted work. His views of "romantic" poetry and the peculiar difficulties which the romantic poet had to face, sound views as they are, recur again and again. Shelley's attitude to Nature, especially his sense of a personality in her elemental forms, is emphasised with needless iteration. The author's ideas on marriage, and on the "polygamous" instinct he finds in Shelley, are always with us throughout the book, often in practically the same words. Certain idiosyncrasies of Shelley's temperament are so harped upon that their undoubted significance is blunted rather than enforced. We would undertake to improve the book enormously with no instrument but a knife. Excision, however, will not touch the book's main defect—its lack of unity. The first hundred pages or so are quite admirable; then the author's attempt to keep the man and the poet running in double harness seems to be too much for him. The portrait flickers. He tells us that what was best in Shelley "was always growing stronger", but this development (crucial test of a psychological study) is just what he fails to exhibit. He asserts it, but he does not bring it home to us in any cumulative way. We would not for a moment minimise the difficulty of such a task. Perhaps it is impossible after all. We only say that Mr. Clutton-Brock excites in us—perhaps unconsciously—a hope which he does not fulfil. Our disappointment is complimentary to the writer. We should not dwell upon it did we not recognise the sound and varied merits that make this book—taken page by page—so easy and instructive to read.

No doubt the general failure to understand Shelley has been due to an impossible discrimination between man and poet. Little poets may be considered well enough apart from their moral characters and political leanings. In the case of a great poet it is simply futile to swallow his poetry while we blink his mental and moral life in bulk. The attempt is cowardice. Shelley's opinions, and nearly everything that was questionable in his behaviour, were neither lapses from his real self nor mere trappings of his personality. It is not even enough to say of Shelley, as we might say if we were discussing the life of Burns, that the poetry and the conduct were fellow-fruit of one tree. Shelley's poetry and Shelley's conduct are more than mutually explanatory. They both belong integrally to that amazing idealism of which he will always remain the classical example. Alike in art and in life he carried the power of abstraction to a point which is not likely to be surpassed. Psychologically, he is the most verdant spirit in history. It is quite a mistake to suppose that the metaphysical faculty must imply unusual subtlety of character. Kant, we have no doubt, was privately a simple soul. Subtlety, in the sense of consciously mixed motives, was totally absent from Shelley's composition; and it was just this simplicity of consciousness which enabled him, in his poetry, to sustain such flights of insubstantial fancy as no other poet we know of could even have attempted without a sense of incongruity. His acts were symbols of his intellectual attitude. The youth who at nineteen designed to liberate Ireland, and who amused himself by attaching copies of his Declaration of Rights to fire balloons or setting them afloat on the sea, is one and the same with the author of "Alastor". Not only was he incapable of understanding the conventions of normal humanity; he did not even live, mentally, within the normal limits of evidence in matters of fact. The mysterious perils and episodes which he several times alleged in justification of flight from places where he had but recently resolved to stay "for ever"; his romantic fancy that he was suffering from elephantiasis; his self-persuasion (after his break with Harriet) that she had previously been untrue to him; his naked but unabashed appearance before a mixed company after bathing; these things and many like them, which occurring in an average man would suggest obvious doubts of his sanity, in Shelley are only remarkable as everything about him is remarkable. The essence of insanity is inconsistency. A more consistent figure than Shelley never walked. Mr. Clutton-Brock remarks acutely that if Shelley had loved Harriet, he would probably have made it a point of honour not to marry her. We hardly know which is the more pathetic, in the highest sense of pathos; the slowness of Harriet's gradual recognition that she had really been betrayed, or Shelley's own naïve wonder whether Wordsworth could have written his poetry if he had been worried (as was Shelley at the time) by money-lenders. Harriet's death did not fill Shelley with remorse. His subsequent attitude was in perfect keeping with all he had done before. There is reason to think that the tragedy made its mark on his spirit and in his poems, as Mr. Clutton-Brock shows, but we must quite reject any theory which would assume in Shelley the power of analysing his previous or present actions in a dry light. The dejection to which we owe not only the familiar "Stanzas", but a hundred fine passages, is an intuitive, rather than a reflective, sense that this world was not made for him. The conscious war of flesh and spirit no more existed for Shelley than for the purely Hellenic nature. Shelley, as one of John Oliver Hobbes' persons flippantly observes of women in general, thought his flesh was his spirit. Of course the war went on in him, as it does everywhere, but his perplexities arising from it were only apprehended like physical pain, and remind us of the perplexities of dumb animals caught in external devices which they cannot understand. This explains Shelley's habitual conception, in politics and poetry, of enormous artificial tyrannies preying upon the world; a conception which seems to us excessively crude, but which after all is very natural if we consider the sort of person he was. Mr. Clutton-Brock very truly points out that Shelley in his whole life knew very few normal people. His childlike nobility attracted cranks as a rock attracts mussels. The excellent earlier part of this book makes vivid, what we scarcely before realised, the prevalence a hundred years ago of "queer" people precisely similar to those of to-day, whom we often regard as purely modern excrescences. Stripped of the vast creative impulse which belonged to that time, Shelley would be thoroughly at home among vegetarian idealists in a "garden city" of 1909. We could say of modern "progressives" exactly what our author happily says of Shelley, that "the love of mankind in the abstract caused him to dislike most individual men because they did not love each other".

Much that is said of the poetry deserves comment, but special praise is due to Mr. Clutton-Brock's thoughtful, if somewhat diffuse, account of Shelley's romanticism. The romantic poets were "like architects who should set out to design a great building without a commission or a site". Shelley's higher animism, so to put it (the author does not give it this name), is also well expounded. Good, too, is the remark that "Shelley's earlier verse is empty where Keats' is clogged". We are delighted to find Mr. Clutton-Brock recognising, in the "Epipsychidion", notes alike of Donne and of Crashaw. Paradoxically, but not without shrewd truth, he also says that Shelley "at his best is rather a classical than a romantic poet". The point invites discussion too late.

"The loud deep calls me home even now to feed it
With azure calm out of the emerald urns
Which stand for ever full beside my throne."

These are not the lines of a "classical" poet in any eighteenth-century sense. They might occur in "Hyperion". Shelley, like Keats, had drunk deep of Helicon. In their finer moments both poets, under forms whose purity of outline at least rivals the ancients, express beauty with a restrained ecstasy of feeling that is entirely modern.

A RARE PERSONALITY.

"Sir Wilfrid Lawson: a Memoir." Edited by the Right Hon. G. W. E. Russell. London: Smith, Elder. 1909. 7s. 6d. net.

GIBBON says, with his solemn sneer, that it was not the business of the first Christians to make themselves agreeable in this world. And in truth an apostle is generally a tiresome and disagreeable person. Sir Wilfrid Lawson was a witty and charming man of the world, who devoted himself fanatically to a cause that was not worldly, resembling in this respect Laurence Oliphant. When the reminiscences of a wit are edited by a wit the result is expected to be an amusing volume, and Mr. George Russell's book will not disappoint those who get it. Sir Wilfrid Lawson stands out from the mob of politicians as a rare and sweet personality. The testimony of those who knew him in private and public life is unanimous and enthusiastic to the nobility of his character. A country gentleman of old lineage and ample estate, a public speaker whose vigour and purity of style were rather drowned in his inexhaustible humour, he might easily have become a Cabinet Minister had he consented to desert his life-work and bow the knee to the idols of party. How far removed he was from the servility of the partisan may be gathered from the following extract from his speech on the bombardment of Alexandria in 1882: "I say deliberately, and in doing so I challenge either Tory or Liberal to contradict me, that no Tory Government could have done what the Liberal Government did yesterday in bombarding these forts. If such a thing had been proposed, what would have happened? We should have had my right hon. and learned friend the Secretary of State for the Home Department (Harcourt) stumping the country and denouncing Government by ultimatum. We should have had the noble Marquis the Secretary of State for India (Hartington) coming down and moving a resolution condemning these proceedings being taken behind the back of Parliament. We should have had the President of the Board of Trade (Chamberlain) summoning the caucuses. We should have had the Chancellor of the Duchy of Lancaster (Bright) declaiming in the Town Hall of Birmingham against the wicked Tory Government; and, as for the Prime Minister (Gladstone), we all know there would not have been a railway train, passing a roadside station, at which he would not have pulled up to proclaim non-intervention as the duty of the Government." The way in which the foibles of his leaders are told off one by one is perfect parliamentary invective. Sir Wilfrid celebrated the same event in the following verses:

"The Grand Old Man to the war has gone,
In the Jingo ranks you'll find him;
He went too fast for Brother John,
But Chamberlain's still behind him.

'Land of Fools', said the Grand Old Man,
'Let nothing I do surprise thee;
And if any blame be cast on my plan,
The Grand Old Man defies thee.'

On Egypt's sands the Old Man fell,
But he would not own his blunder;
The Midlothian book, which we knew so well,
He took and he tore asunder."

How Gladstone must have writhed under this satire, as good of its kind as anything we know! Lawson has often been accused of cynicism. The truth is he despised the leaders of parties with the scorn natural to an honest man and a gentleman. The Dual Alliance of Mr. Balfour and Mr. Chamberlain moved him to "Hanky and Panky":

"Arthur and Joseph are two pretty men,
They declare their affection again and again.
When Arthur proclaims a thing to be 'so',
'That's just what I think', comes the answer from Joe.
'The name of Protection we stoutly abjure,
Free Traders at heart we both are to be sure.'
'Where thou goest, I go', exclaims Chamberlain Hanky;
'And I go where you go', replies Arthur Panky;
'For one thing is certainly clear beyond all,
That united we stand, and divided we fall.'"

Political verses of this kind are a national possession, and ought not to "pass in smother".

Sir Wilfrid Lawson's politics sat oddly on a baronet with a large rent-roll. He was a Little Englander and a peace-at-any-price man; he was against the Church and the House of Lords: of course in favour of universal suffrage, local veto, and secular education. The squabbles over primary education always excited the Pontius Pilate vein in his mind. "Forster's Education Bill" (this in 1870) "was perhaps more exciting than the Land Bill—the Bible being the great bone of contention—when it was to be read, where it was to be read, by whom it was to be read, to whom it was to be read, who was to pay for its being read—these points were discussed ad nauseam." And then he tells the following story: "One of the great points of discussion in 1870 was whether the Bible should be read in the schools 'without note or comment'. I have heard of an old woman who had clear views on this point. Her husband was blind, and someone said that it must be a great deprivation to him not to be able to read. To which she replied: 'Oh, no; I reads the Bible to him every night, and many's the bits I puts in for his good'!" Thirty-eight years later the same irrepressible humour bubbled up on the same subject, Mr. Birrell's Education Bill:

"It's a very good Bill in its way,
Though it alters its shape every day.
But everything's meant
With the best of intent,
Whatever the critics may say.

There's a bit for the Papist, a bit for the Jew,
A bit for the stern Nonconformist man too—
There's a bit for the Parson's assistance,
And a bit to help Passive Resistance;
But above all beside, whatever we've tried,
On Religion we place chief insistence.
We don't for ourselves demand it—not we—
But it's all for the good of the children, you see:
For them we debate and squabble and fight;
If the children are pious, then all will come right.

And so without ending,
We'll go on amending;
Through good and through ill,
We'll stick to the Bill,
Our faith in its future unending."

Who (but Gladstone) could be angry with such a man? Who would not love him? We think Lawson was happier in verse than in prose; though when he replied to a Tory Privy Councillor who had just made a speech on a liquor Bill, and who had a perpetual appearance of inebriety, "the right honourable gentleman was evidently full of his subject", the House of Commons roared. When the Tories said during an election "The flowing tide is with us", Lawson answered "The flowing bowl is with them". And, if we are not mistaken, Sir Wilfrid was the author of "Dam the tide", which Mr. Barrie so audaciously cribbed in "What Every Woman Knows". Only once did we hear Sir Wilfrid Lawson say a nasty thing, and then we think the provocation was sufficient. Referring to Mr. Harry Lawson in the short Parliament of 1885, Sir Wilfrid said, "I do not know the honourable gentleman; but he bears an honoured name".

But what of his life-work? Contemning place in Parliament, and praise in the market-place, Sir Wilfrid Lawson devoted his life to the making of men sober by Act of Parliament. He did not carry his Acts, and men have become sober—almost. From what has been written above it will be gathered that we do not undervalue the eloquence, the courage, and the wit of Sir Wilfrid Lawson. But though the drunkenness of Alexander the Great may have made drunkards—this is generally received—we doubt whether the speeches of Sir Wilfrid Lawson ever made a convert to total abstinence, and we are certain that none of his prohibitory laws would have done so. The climate, ignorance and the absence of rational amusements made men drink in the old days. Our climate is unchanged, but education, facilities of locomotion and multiplicity of indoor and outdoor amusements, perhaps also nerves and gout, have made men on the whole sober. Men's habits cannot be changed suddenly, any more than their minds, as Mr. Gladstone and Mr. Chamberlain both found out. But if we cannot allow Sir Wilfrid Lawson to have accomplished what is beyond the power of an individual, all honour to the apostle who braved abuse and gave up power to try to raise his fellows from the slough of a degrading vice.

MRS. SIDDONS.

"The Incomparable Siddons." By Mrs. Clement Parsons. London: Methuen. 1909. 12s. 6d. net.

SARAH KEMBLE was born at Brecon on 5 July 1755. Her father and mother were strolling, or perhaps we should say touring, players, and from her earliest youth the child was brought up in the atmosphere of the stage. In spite of this circumstance she received a tolerably good education, and her mother was at pains to teach Sarah the sounding elocution of the day. When eleven years old she played Ariel, her first Shakespearean part, and in her nineteenth year she married William Siddons, a bad actor in her father's company. At the end of the year 1775 she made her first and unsuccessful appearance in London at Drury Lane, but when she returned from the provinces seven years later she achieved an immediate and astonishing success. From then till her retirement in 1812 she held the boards, acknowledged queen of English drama. She died on 8 June 1831, in her seventy-sixth year.

These are the bare facts of a life that must always prove surprising to those who only know Mrs. Siddons as the greatest tragic actress of her time—perhaps the greatest tragic actress England has ever produced. Our stage-struck society expects actors and actresses to be no less interesting in their homes than on the boards of the theatre. Mrs. Siddons' failure in this can only be described as colossal. Her private life was one long tale of placid propriety. She was kind to her husband, an admirable mother to her children, and her recreations were needlework and modelling in clay; she went to church every Sunday morning; she was very fond of money, indeed her parsimony got her into trouble with her audience more than once; she was a prude, in a day when nearly all good women were prudes; and she was "lofty-minded" to the degree of having no sense of humour. She was very fond of food—we have the word of her butcher that she ate a surprising number of mutton chops, and she loved taking snuff. She was, it would seem, intelligent rather than clever, and a great solemnity brooded over her every word and deed.

It is a little difficult to discover the great tragic actress in all this, though it certainly prepares us for Mrs. Siddons' relative ill success in comedy; but if the unanimously enthusiastic evidence of her contemporaries may be trusted, it would seem that this solemn, homely creature became a consummate artist the moment she stepped on to the stage. The audiences of those days were oddly impressionable compared with the sophisticated audiences of to-day. They would cry like children when Mrs. Siddons wept on the stage; and in Edinburgh, roused to enthusiasm by her acting, they once encored the sleep-walking scene in "Macbeth". Audiences of this character would be more sympathetic with the players than with the dramatists, and doubtless their unrestrained emotionalism was of real assistance to Mrs. Siddons in the development of her art. She had all the physical attributes necessary for success: a wonderful voice, great physical strength, and especially that striking beauty which lives for us in the portraits by Romney, Reynolds, and Gainsborough. She had had years of hard work and good training in the provinces. Such a woman could hardly fail.

But her success was quite extraordinary, and it is clear that, in terms of her own day, Mrs. Siddons was a very great actress indeed. In spite of the mass of contemporary evidence, it is a little difficult to appreciate wherein the strength of her acting lay, for her critics praised her indiscriminately for her "naturalness" and the classic grandeur of her style. We know that her elocution was that of the ranting school of Quin rather than of the natural school of Garrick. But the truth probably is that when her mouthing manner of speech allowed it, she was a natural actress. Her tears were real tears, and her madness did not wear white satin. Her deaths on the stage were very realistic, and the tragic expressions of her features, and especially of her eyes, not only reduced her audience to a state of delicious terror, but frequently alarmed her fellow actors and actresses as well. The unnatural tones of her voice would tend to heighten the intense realism of her acting, and at the same time would help to conceal the extreme absurdity of the contemporary drama.

Her limitations are easier to fix, and are such as might be deduced from a study of her life. Her comedy was forced, though she was not readily persuaded of its inferiority; and sexual passion, if she did not ignore it, she at least regarded with marked mistrust. She would not play Cleopatra in "Antony and Cleopatra" because she said that she would hate herself if she played the part as it ought to be played; and her Rosalind in "As You Like It" disguised herself in "an ambiguous vestment that seemed neither male nor female". She was, we might venture to say, as careful of her reputation in acting as she was in life, and she conceived Lady Macbeth as a "fragile blonde".

Late in life Mrs. Siddons said emphatically "I was an honest actress, and at all times in all things endeavoured to do my best", and this assertion of her artistic sincerity was certainly justified. She studied her many parts as few actresses can have studied them, and her constant triumphs did not hinder her continual endeavour to improve her readings. Her limitations as an artist were largely due to the sentimentality of her age and the unchallenged rectitude of her private life, which prevented her from associating herself with emotions which her intellect condemned.

Mrs. Clement Parsons' biography is painstaking, and, as far as we have tested it, accurate, and may be commended to those who wish to know more of the woman who ruled the English stage for thirty years.

PICTURE-BOOKS ON CHINA.

"China: its Marvel and Mystery." By J. Hodgson Liddell. With 40 Illustrations in Colour. London: Allen. 1909. 21s. net.

"China." By Mortimer Menpes. Text by Sir Henry Arthur Blake. With 16 Illustrations and 64 Reproductions in Black and White. London: Black. 1909. 5s.

"The Face of China." Written and Illustrated by E. G. Kemp. London: Chatto and Windus. 1909. 20s. net.

"The Great Wall of China." With numerous Illustrations. By William Edgar Geil. London: Murray. 1909. 21s. net.

"Houseboat Days in China." By J. O. P. Bland. Illustrated by W. D. Straight. London: Arnold. 1909. 15s. net.

IT is not so very long since the public was accused of being absolutely indifferent about China, unless galvanised by a war or a Boxer outrage; but the appearance of five illustrated books within a few weeks seems to imply a belief that interest must be growing apace. Dr. Edkins declared—but that is more than thirty years ago—that the trouble originated with Sir John Mandeville, who (with Marco Polo) told such wonderful things about China that readers did not know whether they were dealing in fact or fiction, so agreed to look at it through coloured glass. Nor are we quite sure that the obsession has been dispelled even yet, for some of the illustrations before us are very highly coloured indeed. Bright colouring there is in China, without doubt, and the picturesque presentments of the buildings within the Palace precincts to which Mr. Liddell was fortunate in gaining access reproduce, no doubt, with a certain artistic licence the effects of the glazed material which is often employed about temples and official and ornamental buildings such as are here portrayed. But stones and bricks are generally grey, and mud and dust —elsewhere, at any rate, than in the loess region—are generally grey, and dust and dirt do widely prevail; so that the untravelled reader must not draw too strong an inference from the brilliant colouring, for instance, of the picture (page 60) of Bing-oo. It does not matter so much in the case of portraits, though the Chinese man in the street does not usually wear a red cap or have such pink arms and hands as one of Mr. Menpes' onlookers at a game of draughts (page 65); but everyone can discount for himself the colouring in his sketch, for instance, of "A Student" (page 17) or the admirably characteristic portrait labelled "Chopsticks" (page 33). Miss Kemp uses colours more sparingly, and her picture (page 6) of the familiar teahouse in the native city at Shanghai may serve as a corrective to Mr. Liddell's more brilliant presentment (page 44).

We recognise the difficulty—the practical impossibility, in fact—of reproducing the actual colouring under these conditions, and desire only, as we said before, to enter a caveat against a mistaken impression. This reservation apart, the reader who has not "been there" will be helped to form an impression of China and things Chinese by the generally characteristic and well-selected pictures of all sorts, down to thumb-nail sketches, which are placed before him.

The choice of topic in dealing with China offers a range as wide as that of scenery or type. Sir Henry Blake addresses himself chiefly to the people, their customs and characteristics, and compresses a great deal of information within his hundred and forty pages of letterpress. Mr. Liddell describes what he has observed, and as he confined his journeyings chiefly to the Treaty Ports and Peking he generally traverses trodden ground. Shanghai-landers will be amused by the romantic description quoted (page 33) from Chitty of the origin of their "Bubbling Well"; though they may doubt whether the lady whose tears produced it were really threatened with divorce: the Chinese remedy for childlessness is more usually a second wife!

It is scarcely necessary on the other hand to have "been there" to share the sentiments excited by his visit to the Temple of Heaven.—Miss Kemp takes a wider range. "The Face of China" is a record of travel in East, North, Central and Western China, and the illustrations recall varied incidents and features of her journeys; but the portrait of the author as a Chinese "female travelling scholar" (is such a thing known in Chinese sociology?) fails to lessen our objection to ladies travelling alone in China. She writes pleasantly, but a longer residence would have taught her that reform does not necessarily follow edicts deprecating malpractice; while more careful inquiry would have enabled her to assure herself that his Majesty's Government, while scrupulously fulfilling their promises in regard to opium, desire only (page 262) proof that China is doing her part. It is generally admitted that the Imperial Government is in earnest, and a measure of success has doubtless been attained. Still, not only were no statistics presented to the recent International Commission of Inquiry, but the Chinese representative admitted frankly that statements regarding the extent to which poppy cultivation and opium smoking had been reduced were "guesswork". It is significant that, whereas the gross amount of foreign opium imported into Shanghai fell from 33,219 cwt. in 1906 to 28,869 cwt. in 1908, that of native opium rose from 15,731 cwt. to 22,814 cwt. in the same period.

Mr. Geil's black-and-white views of the Great Wall and objects in its vicinity—albeit perhaps less attractive —are better suited than colour sketches to convey an impression of the scenery he describes. They are apparently reproduced from photographs, and testify to the clearness of atmosphere which permitted such sharpness of outline. He has been at pains to collect a great deal of information legendary, historical and archæological, and is impressed—we had almost written oppressed—by the potentialities of a race that could plan and execute such a stupendous work. But his style is sensational, from the Discours Préliminaire, as he calls his preface, to the demoniacal stories at the close; and the calculation (page 136) about the quantity of human blood that Genghis Khan shed during his career is distasteful.

Mr. Bland's should not, properly, be classified as a picture-book, though it contains not a few sketches, thumb-nail and others, pleasantly illustrating the reminiscences of houseboat excursions which it relates. The letterpress is, as it is intended to be, uneven —slight in some chapters, pregnant with suggestive reflections in others. The explanation offered, for instance, by a lay figure introduced under the guise of an American missionary, of the reasons "why the Caucasian is a failure at diplomacy in China", of the general contrariness in China of cause and effect, why European women are found to marry Chinese, etc., is delicious. It is all P'utzu! What P'utzu is, we leave our readers to discover for themselves.

ECCLESIASTICAL ORIGINS.

"Early History of the Christian Church." By Monsignor Louis Duchesne. Rendered into English from the Fourth Edition. London: Murray. 1909. 9s. net.

MONSIGNOR DUCHESNE worthily represents the great traditions of France in sacred learning. Like the Benedictines of S. Maur, he is an admirable antiquary, and, like some of them, he has had his troubles. His inquiry into the earliest history of certain of the French sees has led him to reject their traditional succession of bishops from an impossible antiquity, and he has brought a hornets' nest about his ears by this disturbance of local self-complacency. But his most solid work, and one which no living scholar has excelled, is the monumental edition of the "Liber Pontificalis", which now is unfortunately out of print. That famous document, which began to take shape early in the fourth century and gained its present form in the seventh, professes to give the chief facts in the life of every one of the first ninety Popes. To distinguish truth from tradition or deliberate invention, and to interpret its strange language and obscure antiquities, as Mgr. Duchesne has done, was a task of extraordinary difficulty and required a variety of knowledge to which few scholars have attained. But the author has also an expert acquaintance with the mysterious subject of liturgies, and has expounded it in the most interesting and instructive of his writings, the "Origines du Culte Chrétien". And now he has used the same literary skill to narrate the history of the Christian Church down to the close of the Arian controversy, in two volumes of which the former has just been translated into English. We trust that he will soon carry on the story through the great Christological controversies to Gregory the Great and the beginning of the Middle Ages. His previous researches have made him even more familiar with that period than with the earlier, and such a narrative would cover ground less adequately traversed than that to which his present volumes are devoted.

In dealing with the work of a thoroughly competent scholar it is less profitable to discuss details than to consider his point of view. And this is the more worthy of attention because Mgr. Duchesne is the head of a school and the representative of a tendency which we trust is gaining ground in his communion. In his judgment tradition unsupported by evidence has no weight, and he is remarkably free in his treatment of venerable assumptions. The most important of these is, of course, that in regard to the special rights claimed for the See of Rome. The belief in those rights, as making Rome the centre of unity, is maintained on other than purely historical grounds, but it is remarkable how candid inquiry has made the old confident assertions no longer credible. Pius IX. never doubted that S. Peter had been for twenty-five years Bishop of Rome, and took a special pleasure in thinking that he was the first to exceed the Apostle's term of office. Probably the mass of Roman Catholics have as little doubt to-day; yet the standard text-book of the Catholic Universities of Germany, that of F. X. Funk, merely says that S. Peter was at Rome at the beginning of the twenty-five years and suffered martyrdom there at the end of them. He does not profess to know where the Apostle passed the interval. Mgr. Duchesne goes a step further. While maintaining, with ample evidence, that S. Peter died at Rome, he says that there is no evidence of an earlier visit, and he bases the claims of the Roman See, not upon the bishopric of S. Peter, but upon the fact that Rome was his last scene of work and the place of his martyrdom. To the end of the present volume, which closes with the cessation of persecution, he is scrupulous not to overstate the Roman claims or the amount of recognition which the merits of the Roman Church received from Christendom at large; yet occasionally a turn of phrase shows that he is not quite emancipated from the current thought of his communion. It must, indeed, be difficult when a proposition is firmly held on one ground to prevent the intrusion of arguments, even though dubious, which are used by friends in maintenance of the same thesis. Quite as remarkable is Mgr. Duchesne's tolerance. The tradition of his Church has been the abhorrence not only of heresy but of all who came under suspicion of being heretics; and the reformed Churches, not to be outdone, have in the main been equally rigid. The old spirit has now disappeared. Origen is spoken of with constant sympathy, and his errors are made to appear as slight as possible in comparison with his services to Christendom. And so in other cases. Save where Gnostics and the like taught doctrines destructive of the faith, points of contact rather than of difference are emphasised, and Mgr. Duchesne is evidently glad when speculative error is compensated by confessorship or martyrdom. He recognises that the system of doctrine, like that of law, could only be worked out by the accumulation of decisions upon particular points, and that therefore the teachers who proved to be in the wrong were in a sense serving the cause of truth. Thus the old hostility, inevitable and often praiseworthy in the days of conflict, may now be laid aside, and those who would be the last to approve doctrinal eccentricity may recognise that the course of events had as much to do with its emergence as the wilfulness of men. And with this tolerant spirit our author joins a willingness to learn from scholars whose position is far from his own. Though he remarks that of the two evils, legend and theory, he prefers the former, his views on some important points are those of modern Germany. He is very cautious in his statements as to the Gospels, and seems inclined to give them a later date than many scholars would allow. He is also vague as to the origins of the Christian ministry, and much less confident than our own Bishop Gore, while he refuses to be wiser than Mommsen concerning the causes of persecution, and ignores recent speculations on that topic.

We could have wished that so wise and interesting a book had been worthily translated. The translation is of a class far higher than those hackwork renderings from the German which are too often a disgrace to English scholarship. The translator writes good English and has a competent knowledge of French; the lapses, due rather to haste than to ignorance of the language, are few, though sometimes provoking. But for the translation of a work which in parts deals with abstruse matters a third language is required—the technical language of the subject. Of classical antiquity and of Church history the present translator is quite ignorant, and though this is not manifest through many pages of flowing narrative it becomes discreditably conspicuous wherever a knowledge greater than that of the general reader is needed to interpret the author's sense.

THE GAY PROFESSOR.

"The Letters of John Stuart Blackie to his Wife." By Archibald Stodart Walker. London: Blackwood. 1909. 12s. 6d.

IS the memory of John Stuart Blackie still so living that this book may count on many readers? In his lifetime the Professor of Greek at Edinburgh was a notable figure in England and Scotland amongst the learned and literary, and in Scotland at least perhaps the best known by the populace in public meetings and festivities. But when the vigour and brightness and charm of his personality went with his death, and Edinburgh was bereaved of her most picturesque and characteristic resident, what remained of his work still able to attract attention? We believe very little either of prose or verse, though he wrote much of both. When those who knew Blackie personally have gone, his Greek Dialogues and his "Self-Culture" will probably be the only things of his read for their own sake. Until that time comes, say fifty years to allow all those to whom he taught Greek to die away, whatever he wrote will be read by them as a renewal of their knowledge of him, and of the admiration they felt for him in days when their susceptibilities were in their first keenness. So this book will have no lack of readers, though the formal biography of Blackie was published soon after his death fourteen years ago. Pupils who rose in class every morning to his Πάτερ ἡμῶν are in every English-speaking nation. They will recognise in these letters from their very beginning, and throughout the half-century, the authentic note of the thoughts and feelings so familiar to them on the lips of the man who taught them such Greek as they were capable of learning, and many things more valuable to them than Greek. It is remarkable indeed that Blackie's letters to his wife are so very like what he would have written to pupils with whom he was in regular correspondence; and there is nothing so intimate and personal that it causes uneasiness and embarrassment. Probably no man of more than ordinary mind and character had ever fewer thoughts that he could not and would not communicate fervidly to any intelligent listener. Such a clever and versatile man, of high ideals, a pure and transparent moral character, of poetic sentiment, will have far-reaching influence over young minds. Much more by direct contact than a profounder and more original thinker has whose personal qualities do not capture the imagination. It was said that Blackie taught anything but Greek. In the later years he taught less of his subject than any other professor did. He may have neglected his subject, but he did not neglect his pupils. One could see by cursory inspection of an ordinary junior Greek class that the majority of the uncouth youths had come from home where the humanities and the amenities had not been cultivated. Half of them were morose and recluse, over-valuing the book-learning and education of which they had not had a fair share. They were representative of the many warring sects and narrow fanaticisms of Scottish life of thirty years ago; the Homoousians and the Homoiousians of the Scottish theological and political and social worlds. Incalculable was the benefit to these youths, the coming-on ministers, journalists and schoolmasters, and to society about to be delivered into their hands, that Blackie should have thought of teaching them other things than Greek. He became a missionary of the gospel of sweetness and light to generations of the Gentiles who crowded his classes. He taught them by precept and personal example. In physical grace he so approached the Greek as to be non-Scottish or non-British. Intellectually and morally the Greek and the Christian culture were combined in him as completely as they are ever to be found. For such a man to impress just himself and his ideas consciously and purposely, with intent to make his pupils as like himself as possible, was to give them the benefit of the best education that could be given to the young Scotsmen under his charge. This Blackie did, and the Scottish people owe him gratitude for doing it to the extent to which he succeeded. They admitted it during his life, and they saw that this Edinburgh Socrates was not corrupting their youth, though with irony and sarcasm and humour, which it must be confessed sometimes ran into buffoonery, he scoffed at the idols of their temples and their families. These letters, as we have said, will give the greatest pleasure to those who knew Blackie personally or have the admiration and affection which all Scotsmen, perhaps without exception, felt for him. This alone is a fairly large circle into which the letters may go. But it would not be giving a quite correct notion of them if we did not recall that Blackie was also one of the most popular Scotsmen amongst Englishmen. He had a very wide acquaintance and friendship with Englishmen and Englishwomen of social, political and academic distinction. He was well known, too, amongst similar classes of foreigners. His letters from England, Germany, Russia and Turkey exhibit him with all his verve, humour, sagacity, naïveté, vanity and joy in life, in societies that are attractive to every class of reader.

NOVELS.

"The Haven." By Eden Phillpotts. London: Murray. 1909. 6s.

The methods which Mr. Phillpotts has adopted in his latest novel demand unqualified praise. He has tried to show us the life of a south-coast fishing town for a certain number of years with great simplicity and a delightful minimum of manipulation. The story brings into prominence the fortunes of a particular family, but only as the beam of a searchlight illuminates a special block of faces in a crowd. The Major family has not been selected for any peculiarity of adventure or of character; the father is a typical God-fearing Brixham fisherman, very circumscribed in his view of divinity, with an unshakeable faith in its operations on his behalf, and a serene capacity for misinterpreting the natural course of events and his own inclinations. Yet, for all his faithful obstinacy, never bigoted; and, for all his hardness, never wilfully unkind. His son and daughter seem scarcely to partake of his nature, and, the one sadly, the other determinedly, go their several ways to grieve him, and live the lives which most appeal to them. They are but boy and girl when first we meet them, but each presents grandchildren to their father, and one of these grows to a working age before the book concludes. It thus covers an entire generation, and in its quiet and unhurried, undirected presentation of progressive existence its hold on the reader will be found. That hold is unexacting, there is, most commendably, no effort made to heighten it, and it depends throughout on a sheer simplicity and directness which never attains the highest narrative quality, and even when it moves us most is plainly but a paraphrase, and often a somewhat distant one, of actuality. Mr. Phillpotts succeeds in producing a sense of character, and even of dialect, though obviously he reports nothing as it was spoken, and very little, probably, as it was thought. Dick Varwell, doubtless, was a philosopher, and a delightful one; but his symposiums—and he consumed an inordinate amount of liquor—have a cogency and a brilliance which one expects in vain from philosophers with much easier access to his modern arguments. Nor can we imagine such idyllic love-making from any country boy and girl as Ned and Deborah so charmingly offer us. "Every word that he faltered was beautiful to her: his humility, his fear, his promises; the name of her spoken at sea by night while she slept. . . . . To her it seemed that if he only looked and listened, everything round about would answer for her. The bees made mellow music and voiced her; the gulls cried out her happiness in their laughter; the grasshoppers chirruped it; the waves danced and flashed it. Heaven spread above her, and the great westering light aloft was not too large to tell of her delight." This admirable passage gives very nearly the distance which the author keeps from the real atmosphere of the life he pictures. He gives us a sense of things as they are, while always depicting them as they are not. He has not the master's power to deal with reality, naked and expressive; but he draws over it a veil of style, beneath which, with its crudities and incapacities, softened by a gentle iridescence, we are permitted to watch it working. The point to realise is that it is life indeed that lies beneath his veil, and not the puppets of romantic creation; and that he is diligent to present it to us, at that remove, faithfully, sympathetically, and as he knows it.

"The Pasque Flower." By Jane Wardle. London: Arnold. 1909. 6s.

The opening chapters of "The Pasque Flower" promise pleasant adventure, spiced with mystery and picturesquely set, but later it develops into a tame love-story. The hero's affections are divided between two cousins, neither of them very admirable specimens of the feminine sex, and it is impossible to care very much which of the two he eventually marries. Not that a novel need be uninteresting because the hero is lukewarm and diffident, and the heroine unsatisfactory, but such beings require an artistic treatment different from the pleasant superficial psychology of the ordinary novel of romantic interest. Miss Wardle writes carefully and intelligently, and her German business-man of good family is an excellent piece of portraiture and quite unhackneyed.

"Mr. Justice Raffles." By E. W. Hornung. London: Smith, Elder. 1909. 6s.

We confess that we are sick of the egregious Raffles. The only excuse for Mr. Hornung's idealisation of his cricketer-burglar would be a wish to undermine the notion, oddly prevalent in some educational circles, that good cricket implies superior morality. But what our schoolboys are toō much disposed to believe is that a good cricketer can do no wrong. Therefore Mr. Hornung will be taken to preach the doctrine that robbery is a legitimate and spirited pastime. We do not suppose that his books will have the same effect on public-school boys as is, according to police-court reports, produced on board-school boys by penny dreadfuls. All the same, this kind of writing is not cricket. In the present volume Raffles is outwitting a Jewish moneylender in a good cause. But Mr. Hornung's delivery is losing its power, and he ought to be taken off.

"F. E."

"Speeches delivered in the House of Commons and elsewhere, 1906-1909." By F. E. Smith K.C. M.P. Liverpool: Young. 1909.

Why should Mr. Smith apologise (see preface) for publishing his speeches? Demosthenes did it; Cicero did it; why not F. E. Smith? One must eternally regret that Cæsar did not do it (at least we have not got the book if he did). Mr. Smith has an eye on posterity, and is not going to make this mistake. He is quite right. After all, speeches of a politician, until he becomes a cabinet minister, are everything—his stock-in-trade, his record, his credentials, his claim on the future. Property so important to him he obviously ought not to trust to the changes and chances of newspaper reports for their preservation. It is safety for the speaker, and convenient for his critics, to have an authorised version to go to. At any rate, it removes one element of contention—what the speaker did or did not say; for in the nature of things he is estopped from going behind his own authorised version, even if he knows it to make him say what he did not. Therefore we trust Mr. Smith has been extremely careful that this should be a true version of what he said. He is much too important to the Unionist party to be able to take the accuracy of this volume lightly. We are glad in every way that Mr. Smith has published his speeches; partly, we admit, because, appalling as is the number of speeches an editor, poor devil, has to read, Mr. Smith has made speeches we are very willing to read again for pure pleasure. Epigram and the brilliancy of light play are, of course, better in the spoken than the read speech; nothing can quite make up for the countenance and the voice; but when one knows the man one can fill that in for one self. The first speech in the book—the first in Mr. Smith's parliamentary career and the foundation of all his greatness—makes the same impression that it did on first acquaintance. One feels now as then that the first question it raises

(*Continued on page* 670.)

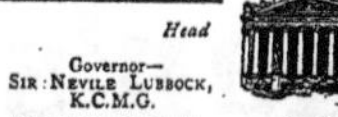

is: can he live up to it? It is dangerous to begin with your best. You may incur the fate of the man who went into the highest room and was told with shame to go lower. Accordingly most parliamentary debutants, following the advice of every old House of Commons mentor, begin studiedly piano. Not so Mr. Smith. He flings the old men's advice in their faces and opens with a flourish of trumpets. He pours forth a stream of glittering epigram. Well, he took a great risk with the most brilliant result. It might have offended; in fact it pleased. It is remarkable, because it would have been only political human nature that the veterans should, most of them, be annoyed that this raw recruit could do what they could not, and a few that he could do what they could. The proverb of the premier pas has never been so well vindicated. After that superas evadere ad auras has been simple work. One thing we are sure of: he who reads the first speech in this book will go on and read others. By the way, we observe thankfully that this collection contains none of the militant Protestant speeches. Mr. Smith can do without that crutch now.

SHORTER NOTICES.

"The Disappearance of the Small Landowner." By Arthur H. Johnson. Oxford: At the Clarendon Press. 1909. 5s.

This is a really useful little book on the land question which should serve to dissipate various obstinate errors both of Liberals and Conservatives. The old idea that the small owners in England, the peasantry, were wholly thrust out by barbarous Enclosure Acts is an ignorant idea. The Enclosure Acts certainly tended to that end, but one cannot help realising as one reads this book, or indeed any history of modern England, that the tendency was for the small owner or holder to go irrespective of Enclosure Acts. The rise of industry evidently diverted the peasant holders to the towns. Mr. Johnson also has a few very useful notes on the present position of the peasant proprietor in France. There is no doubt that in thousands of instances he lives a life of more labour and distress than the English peasant. We have little patience with the careless pens that are for ever dwelling on the prosperity and happiness of the peasants in France and Germany, and there is much utter poverty and wretchedness in the villages of both countries. The reforms of Stein and Hardenburg in Germany a hundred years ago have by no means made of the Prussian village a paradise to-day.

"Travels with a Donkey in the Cevennes." By Robert Louis Stevenson. London: Chatto and Windus. 1909. 7s. 6d. net.

These travels with a donkey bear any amount of reprinting. Stevenson rarely wrote in a better vein, and never, we think, revealed the secret places in himself so nearly as in this holiday diary of impressions. The small events that were to him adventures are made adventures for the reader, and every mood comes successfully through. Are the pictures a mistake? They are executed by Noel Roope; if we object, it is not because we object to him. The fact is that Stevenson's own word-colour is so delicately perfect, yet so surely given, that the interposition of another's art is apt to be resented.

"Poems by Gray." "Poems by Keats." London: Frowde. 1909. 2s. 6d. each.

The interest of these reprints lies in the exactness with which they reproduce original editions. The "Poems by Gray" are reprinted line for line from the original volume published in 1768; the "Poems by Keats" from the volume of 1820. It is a melancholy thing to read the publisher's apology for printing the unfinished "Hyperion". Over the date June 26, 1820, we read: "The poem was intended to have been of equal length with 'Endymion', but the reception given to that work discouraged the author from proceeding".

To their admirable edition of the **Works of Oscar Wilde (Methuen, 5s. net each)**, the publishers have lately added "The Importance of Being Earnest", "An Ideal Husband", "The Duchess of Padua". Will Wilde's plays survive for reading? It is certainly possible to read them now with some lively interest. We have lately read a part of "The Importance of Being Earnest", and its flippancy and wit are so good in their way that it might seem as if the plays must last. Yet we doubt it not the less. The point about these plays is their incessant cleverness. The play we mention above is a good example probably. Cleverness where persisted in without ceasing, without an occasional brilliant flash of the ordinary or mediocre, defeats its own ends. If all the world were full of clever men, women, and children never speaking save in paradox, not even asking for the bread and butter without being witty in the asking, what a bore it would all be. "The Importance of Being Earnest" overdoes cleverness. "I am sick of cleverness", says Ernest Worthing, "everybody is clever now. You cannot go anywhere without meeting clever people, and the thing has become an absolute public nuisance. I wish to goodness we had a few fools left." Algernon: "We have". Jack: "I should extremely like to meet them. What do they talk about?" Algernon: "The fools? Oh! about the clever people of course." It is undoubtedly true that the professional clever men of to-day, or of Wilde's day, depend largely for their success on the fools. The fool is their bread and cheese.

The "Saturday" Handbook (The West Strand Publishing Company. 2s. 6d. net), edited by the Hon. Gervase Beckett and Mr. Geoffrey Ellis, is something more than an ordinary handbook. Whilst providing powder and shot for the electoral campaign in the shape of hard facts and extracts from speeches and official publications, it contains special contributions by Mr. Walter Long, Lord Robert Cecil, Mr. Bonar Law, Mr. Wyndham, and others; these are a guide to Unionist policy. In a note Mr. Balfour expresses his approval of the general scheme of the Handbook.

"Revue des Deux Mondes." 15 Novembre.

In an extremely good paper, critical and appreciative of the work of Israel Zangwill, M. Augustin Filon remarks that in accepting the presidency of the "Ito," Mr. Zangwill becomes the first democratic leader the Jewish race has had in modern times. It must be remembered that he has been elected unanimously, without any limitation as to time or powers. There is an interesting study of the genesis and realisation of the schemes for tunnelling the Alps by the Gotthard and the Simplon, written by M. Bawnhes. He also describes the conferences held this year. The one was between Germany, Italy and Switzerland regarding the Gotthard, regulating traffic, rates, etc., and it certainly appears that Switzerland is to do all the work in keeping the line clear, etc., for the benefit of Germany. The Simplon Convention was signed on 18 June on behalf of France and Switzerland; this regulates the further shortening and facilitating of the means of approach to the tunnel on the Swiss side.

For this Week's Books see pages 672 and 674.

THIS WEEK'S BOOKS.

Art and Archæology

Les Sculptures de la Cathédrale de Chartres (Margaret and Ernest Marriage). Cambridge: At the University Press. 12s. net.

The Art Journal. 1909. Virtue. 21s. net.

The Evolution of Italian Sculpture (Lord Balcarres). Murray. 21s. net.

Biography

Pascal (Viscount St. Cyres). Smith, Elder. 10s. 6d. net.

The Correspondence of Priscilla Countess of Westmorland (Edited by her daughter, Lady Rose Weigall). Murray. 14s. net.

Lord Kelvin's Early Home. Macmillan. 8s. 6d. net.

Doctor Johnson and Mrs. Thrale (A. M. Broadley), 16s. net; César Franck (Rosa Newmarch), 7s. 6d. net. Lane.

Matilda, Countess of Tuscany (Mrs. Mary E. Huddy). Long. 7s. 6d. net.

Fiction

Golden Aphrodite (Winifred Crispe). Paul. 6s.

A Gentle Knight of Old Brandenburg (Charles Major). Macmillan. 6s.

The Hungry Heart (David Graham Phillips); Mary (Bjornstjerne Björnsen). Heinemann. 3s. net each.

The Settler (Ralph Connor). Hodder and Stoughton. 6s.

The Nest of the Sparrow Hawk (Baroness Orczy). Greening. 6s.

Nameless (Hon. Mrs. Walter R. D. Faber); Stories told by the Miller (Violet Jacob); Us Four (S. Macnaughton). Murray. 6s. each.

Gift Books

A Song of the English (Rudyard Kipling). Hodder and Stoughton. 15s. net.

A Book of Whimsies (Geoffrey Whitworth). Dent. 6s.

Stories from the "Faerie Queene" (Lawrence H. Dawson). Harrap. 5s. net.

A First Book of Wild Flowers (Margaret M. Ranklin). Melrose. 6s. net.

History

The Bourbon Restoration (Major John R. Hall), 21s. net; The Anne—Queen's Chronicle (Reginald Farrer). Rivers. 6s.

Ancient Ceylon (H. Parker). Luzac. 25s. net.

Japan in World Politics (Henry Dyer). Blackie. 12s. 6d. net.

A Short History of the Chief Campaigns in Europe since 1792 (General A. von Horsetzky), 18s. net; The Rise of Louis Napoleon (F. A. Simpson), 12s. net. Murray.

The Clerk of Oxford in Fiction (Samuel F. Hulton). Methuen. 10s. 6d. net.

A Colonial Autocracy (Marion Phillips). King. 10s. 6d.

George I. and the Northern War (James Frederick Chance). Smith, Elder. 14s. net.

Medallic Illustrations of the History of Great Britain and Ireland. Plates CI.-CX. Printed by Order of the Trustees. British Museum. 6s.

India under Ripon (Wilfrid Scawen Blunt). Fisher Unwin. 10s. net.

Natural History

Beasts and Men (Hugh S. R. Elliott). Longmans. 12s. 6d. net.

Reprints and Translations

The "Iliad" of Homer (E. H. Blakeney), Bell. 5s.

Principles of Political Economy (John Stuart Mill). Longmans. 5s.

Paradise Lost (John Milton). Harrap. 2s. 6d. net.

How to Write the History of a Parish (Rev. J. Charles Cox). Allen. 3s. 6d. net.

School Books

Elementary Arabic (Reynold A. Nicholson). Cambridge: At the University Press. 6s.

A Geography of India (George Patterson). Christian Literature Society. 1s. 4d.

A New Algebra (S. Barnard). Macmillan. 4s.

(Continued on page 674).

THIS WEEK'S BOOKS—(*Continued*).

SCIENCE AND PHILOSOPHY

The Idea of the Soul (A. E. Crawley). Black. 6*s*. net.
Blaise Pascal (Humfrey R. Jordan). Williams and Norgate. 4*s*. 6*d*.
Charles Darwin and the Origin of Species (Edward Bagnall Poulton), 7*s*. 6*d*. net; Old Criticism and New Pragmatism (J. M. O'Sullivan), 7*s*. 6*d*. net; Knowledge, Life and Reality (George Trumbull Ladd), 18*s*. net. Longmans.

THEOLOGY

Philosophy and Religion (Hastings Rashdall). Duckworth. 2*s*. 6*d*. net.
The Epistle of St. James (F. J. A. Hort). Macmillan. 5*s*. net.
The Birth and Growth of Toleration (Rev. J. O. Bevan). Allen. 5*s*. net.
History, Authority and Theology (Rev. Arthur C. Headlam). Murray. 6*s*. net.

TRAVEL

Vicenza (Mary Prichard-Agnetti). Hodder and Stoughton. 12*s*.
From Monte to Mosul. Bickers. 10*s*. 6*d*. net.
Sport and Travel in Both Tibets (Lady Jenkins). Blades, East and Blades. 10*s*. 6*d*. net.
The Great Pacific Coast (C. Reginald Enock). Grant Richards. 16*s*. net.
The Land of the Lion (W. S. Rainsford). Heinemann. 12*s*. 6*d*. net.
Lake Victoria to Khartoum (Capt. F. A. Dickinson), 12*s*. 6*d*. net; Seekers in Sicily (Elizabeth Bisland and Anne Hoyt). Lane. 5*s*. net.

VERSE

Life and the Great Forever (E. Charnes). Lane. 3*s*. 6*d*. net.
Napoleon: A Historical Tragedy (Algernon Byesen). Fisher Unwin. 5*s*. net.
A Hundred Verses from Old Japan (William N. Porter). Oxford: at the Clarendon Press. 2*s*. 6*d*. net.

MISCELLANEOUS

Acharnians of Aristophanes, The (W. J. M. Starkie), 10*s*. net; Indian Speeches (Viscount) Morley, 2*s*. 6*d*. net; Shakesperian Stage, The (Victor E. Albright). Macmillan.
Book of Flowers, The (Katharine Tynan). Smith, Elder. 6*s*. net.
Monthly Gleanings in a Scottish Garden (L. H. Soutar). Fisher Unwin. 6*s*. net.
Mother's Companion, The (Mrs. Cloudesley Brereton). Mills and Boon. 2*s*. 6*d*. net.
Music: Its Law and Evolution (Jules Combarrew). Kegan Paul. 5*s*.
Oxford Garland, The (Dona H. Ball). Sidgwick and Jackson. 2*s*. 6*d*. net.
Tales of Irish Life and Character (Mrs. S. C. Hall). Foulis. 5*s*. net.
Virginian Attitude Towards Slavery and Succession (Beverley B. Munford). Longmans. 9*s*. net.

MAGAZINES FOR DECEMBER.—Blackwood's, 2*s*. 6*d*.; The New Quarterly, 2*s*. 6*d*.

NOTICE.

The Terms of Subscription to the SATURDAY REVIEW are:—

	United Kingdom. £ s. d.	*Abroad.* £ s. d.
One Year	1 8 2	1 10 4
Half Year	0 14 1	0 15 2
Quarter Year ...	0 7 1	0 7 7

Cheques and Money Orders should be crossed and made payable to the Manager, SATURDAY REVIEW Offices, 10 *King Street, Covent Garden, London, W.C.*

In the event of any difficulty being experienced in obtaining the SATURDAY REVIEW, the Publisher would be glaa to be informed immediately.

Mr. HEINEMANN'S NEW BOOKS.

MR. DE MORGAN'S NEW NOVEL.

IT NEVER CAN HAPPEN AGAIN.

By WILLIAM DE MORGAN.

In 2 volumes, uniform with the author's "Joseph Vance," "Alice for Short," and "Somebow Good." Crown 8vo. 10s.

"It is indeed a worthy companion to 'Joseph Vance' and its two successors. . . . In Mr. de Morgan's new book we should estimate that there are about 300,000 words, and the most eloquent testimony to his charm is that we do not find it in any way too much. Whether depicting tragedy in slumdom, drama in a suburban middle-class home, or comedy in a country mansion, the author shows himself master of his materials."
DAILY TELEGRAPH.

Heinemann's Library of Modern Fiction.

BELLA DONNA.

By ROBERT HICHENS. 2 vols. 4s. net.

"One of the best novels we have ever read, and quite the best that Mr. Hichens has written."—*Saturday Review.*

THE HUNGRY HEART.
By D. G. PHILLIPS. 1 vol. 3s. net.

THE STREET OF ADVENTURE.
By PHILIP GIBBS. 1 vol. 3s. net.

HEDWIG IN ENGLAND.
By the Author of "Marcia in Germany." 1 vol. 3s. net.

BEYOND MAN'S STRENGTH.
By M. HARTLEY. 1 vol. 3s. net.

A SENSE OF SCARLET.
By Mrs. HENRY DUDENEY. 1 vol. 3s. net.

THE WHITE PROPHET.
By HALL CAINE. 2 vols. 4s. net.

THE MAGNETIC NORTH.
By ELIZABETH ROBINS. Popular Edition. Cloth, 2s. net.

THE HEART of THE ANTARCTIC.

By Sir ERNEST SHACKLETON, C.V.O.

2 vols. Fully Illustrated in Colour and from Photographs. Crown 4to. 36s. net.

AUTOGRAPH EDITION DE LUXE, limited to 300 Numbered Copies, each signed by Sir Ernest Shackleton and the members of the Shore Party, with additional Illustrations and text, printed on Dutch hand-made paper with special water-mark. Medium 4to. vellum, £10 10s. net.

ITALIAN HOURS.
By HENRY JAMES.
Illustrated in Colour by JOSEPH PENNELL. Demy 4to. 25s. net.

THE LAND OF THE LION.
By Dr. W. S. RAINSFORD. Fully Illustrated. Demy 8vo. 12s. 6d. net.

THE CONQUEST OF THE AIR.
By ALPHONSE BERGET. Profusely Illustrated. Demy 8vo. 12s. 6d. net.

ORPHEUS: A Universal History of Religions.
By Dr. SALOMON REINACH, Author of "Apollo."
Demy 8vo. 8s. 6d. net.

THE GREAT FRENCH REVOLUTION.

By P. A. KROPOTKIN. Demy 8vo. 6s. net.

THE TRIBUNAL OF THE TERROR:
A Study of Paris in 1793-95.
By G. LENÔTRE. Profusely Illustrated. Demy 8vo. 10s. net.

MEMOIRS of the DUCHESSE DE DINO.
Demy 8vo. 10s. net.

LEAVES. Essays and Sketches.
By VIOLET CLARKE. Crown 8vo. 5s.

Mr. RACKHAM'S NEW BOOK

UNDINE.

Adapted from the German by W. L. Courtney.
Illustrated in Colour by ARTHUR RACKHAM. Crown 4to. 7s. 6d. net.

N.B.—This is the only entirely new and original work by Mr. Rackham to be published this year.

ILLUSTRATED BY THE SAME ARTIST.

THE INGOLDSBY LEGENDS.
Crown 4to. 15s. net.

CATHEDRAL CITIES OF SPAIN.
By W. W. COLLINS, R.I.
With 60 Water-Colour Drawings by the Author. Demy 8vo. 16s. net.
Also an Edition de Luxe, 42s. net.

Mr. Heinemann's Illustrated List, Post Free.

London: WM. HEINEMANN, 21 Bedford Street, W.C.

Just published. La. cr. 8vo. 640 pp., cloth, 6s. net.

THE PRINCE OF DESTINY.

A Romance. By SARATH KUMAR GHOSH.
Author of "1,001 Indian Nights."

A presentment of **India by an Indian,** with its eternal patience, religious fervour, and **passionate love.** The book also reveals

BRITAIN'S PERIL IN INDIA.

In the circumstances depicted it would need the **extraordinary love** of an extraordinary man like the hero **to save Britain's cause.**

SOME PRESS OPINIONS.

THE DAILY TELEGRAPH:—"Enthralling . . . character splendidly conceived and drawn. . . . A treat provided only by the most skilful novelists."

OUTLOOK:—"Stirs the imagination and quickens the pulse."

THE BOOKMAN:—"We have read no book in which the atmosphere of India is so wonderfully reproduced."

Just published. Demy 8vo. **12s. 6d.** net.

PROGRESSIVE REDEMPTION:

The Catholic Church, its Functions and Offices in the World reviewed in the Light of the Ancient Mysteries and Modern Science.
By Rev. HOLDEN E. SAMPSON,
Author of "Progressive Creation" (*see below*).

This book is eminently indispensable to the practical labourer in the many fields of effort for the betterment of mankind and "reform" in human conditions, in which every individual soul who is not entirely selfish cannot help being employed. It gives in clear and forcible logic an exposure of the defects in modern efforts of humanity and reform, whether political, social, or religious, and breaks into pieces the delusions of sanguine thinkers and workers, who think that permanent and beneficial results will follow the methods of Christianization, philanthropy and social reform, which are carried out without reference to the Divine methods embodied in the Catholic Church.

Now ready. Two demy 8vo. vols. Cloth, **21s.** net.

PROGRESSIVE CREATION:

A Reconciliation of Religion with Science.
By Rev. HOLDEN E. SAMPSON.

A book that has confessedly baffled the reviewers, and of which Mr. Arthur E. Waite has said "it is of the quality of Revelation."

Just Issued. Crown 8vo. paper covers. Price **1s.** net: by post **1s. 1d.**

THE CASE FOR ALCOHOL,

Or The Actions of Alcohol on Body and Soul,
By Dr. ROBERT PARK.

Just Issued. Royal 8vo. with 105 Illustrations and 8 Coloured Plates. Cloth, price **25s.** net.

NAVAL HYGIENE.

By JAMES DUNCAN GATEWOOD, M.D.,
Instructor in Naval Hygiene, U.S. Naval Medical School.

The only book extant which attempts to deal with the subject of Naval Hygiene in all its bearings upon the *personnel,* construction and efficiency of Ships.

Descriptive Circulars on application.

London: REBMAN Ltd., 129 Shaftesbury Avenue, W.C.

SWIFTHAND.

A NEW, SIMPLE, & RAPID METHOD of WRITING.

Invented by the Right Hon.
Sir EDWARD CLARKE, K.C.

PRESS OPINIONS.

"Extremely ingenious and clever."—*The Road.*

"A modified shorthand with some advantages of its own, particularly in regard to legibility."—*Birmingham Daily Post.*

"Easily learnt by any person of ordinary ability."
Newcastle Weekly Journal.

"It is certainly a simple system that may be mastered in a very short time."—*Colonial Printer.*

One Shilling, of all Booksellers.

LETTERS FROM GEORGE ELIOT TO ELMA STUART.

Crown 8vo. cloth, **5s.** net.

"All admirers of George Eliot will surely join in a feeling of gratitude to Mr. Roland Stuart for publishing this little volume of letters addressed to his mother by the great novelist."—*Daily Telegraph.*

"Every admirer of the writings of George Eliot will be delighted with these charming letters."—*Publishers' Circular.*

LONDON:
SIMPKIN, MARSHALL, HAMILTON, KENT & CO., LTD

Printed for the Proprietors by SPOTTISWOODE & Co. LTD., 5 New-street Square, E.C., and Published by REGINALD WEBSTER PAGE, at the Office, 10 King Street, Covent Garden, in the Parish of St. Paul, in the County of London.—*Saturday, 27 November,* 1909.

THE

SATURDAY REVIEW

OF

POLITICS, LITERATURE, SCIENCE, AND ART.

No. 2,823 Vol. 108. 4 December 1909. [Registered as a Newspaper.] 6d.

CONTENTS.

NOTES OF THE WEEK.

Parliament was prorogued on Friday until 15 January. Curiosity was felt as to how the delicate fact of the collision between the two Houses would be put in the King's Speech. The "Gentlemen of the House of Commons" are thanked for their liberality, and regret is expressed that "that provision has proved unavailing". But the future will make everything right. The new Parliament is to assemble, as Mr. Asquith has told us, "at such a time as to make it possible to provide retrospectively and prospectively for the needs of the current financial year". There is to be no chaos after all.

The hundred-and-ten ton gun may be obsolete in the Navy. It is not so in party politics. The Prime Minister had it out on Thursday, and fired it off. The report was so loud that all the windows in Westminster ought to have been broken. The Prime Minister had loaded it to the muzzle, as his opening shot proved: "Mr. Speaker Sir we are met in circumstances unexampled in the history of the British Parliament. When the Finance Bill left this House it represented in a greater degree than can be said of any measure of our time the pure, well-sifted and deliberate work of an overwhelming majority of the representatives of the people on a matter which by the custom of generations and by the course of practically unbroken authority is the province of this House and of this House alone." Eighty-four words with a solitary full-stop for breathing space! If Mr. Stead could produce something of this sort, we really should begin to think there was a good deal in Julia's talks with Mr. Gladstone.

Mr. Balfour, in his reply to Mr. Asquith, put the Liberal passion for these abstract resolutions neatly—"they bind nobody, they help nobody, they hurt nobody; I doubt whether they encourage anybody; and I am sure they do not frighten anybody". Most of this is probably quite true, but one can quite understand why such abstractions are favourite Liberal weapons—they cannot be snatched out of their hands by the House of Lords. Moreover, perhaps it is not very discreet to bring these resolutions into too much ridicule. We have heard a Chairman of Committees say the less Bills that pass the better, and it is certainly true that the less Liberal legislation there is the better. Hence these abstract resolutions may be regarded not unkindly.

On Tuesday night the House of Lords flung out the Budget by 350 votes to 75, and next morning in the City Consols showed "a slight upward tendency". Indeed, look where we will, we cannot see any sign of that grim and stern revolution which Lord Denman, Captain of the Honourable Corps of Gentlemen-at-Arms, has promised us. Captain Hemphill, Chairman of the Political Committee of the National Liberal Club and Chevalier of the Legion of Honour, seems to have failed his admirers: after his call to the people, they must have looked for at least a head or two on a pike by now. Yet the people are so very peaceful and orderly that it is not even necessary for the police to ask anybody to move on!

The debate in the House of Lords has in truth cleared away the absurd delusion that anything in the remote nature of a Revolution is in the air. Is it good policy for the House of Lords to stake its influence on flinging out a money bill? That is a question much more for actual political tacticians than for Revolutionists. Last week three of the four chief speeches—Lord Rosebery's, Lord Cromer's, and Lord Balfour of Burleigh's—were almost wholly devoted to this question; and this week again it has been very much the same, Lord Morley, Lord James of Hereford, Lord Courtney, Lord Curzon, and Lord Cawdor each handling in his own style the same theme.

What could one imagine more decorous and constitutional than the way in which the whole matter has been dealt with so far? If the Constitution really is going to die this time, it is being given plenty of opportunity to do so in the way that Lowe pleaded for—wrapping its toga about it in the most approved style.

Lord Curzon's speech stands out as by far the strongest in the second half of the debate. It is doubtful whether it is not the best speech he has ever made, though perhaps his address on Empire at the Guildhall some years ago was rarer or more elaborate in thought. Lord Curzon has gifts of oratory, but his best gift, after all, is his manhood and spirit. That was his real addition to the debate. Before he spoke the peers had listened day after day to counsels of wily wisdom. Lord Rosebery, Lord Cromer, Lord Balfour of Burleigh, Lord James, Lord Courtney, Lord Morley, and Lord Crewe, counsel such as theirs well absorbed is enough to make of any young man—well, one is bound to say—a regular old woman. After many days with the Constitution-sticklers, it is a relief to find oneself in the company of an empire-builder.

Lord Curzon's confident and brilliant speech is the more valuable because everybody who knows anything whatever about him knows he is "a House of Commons man". Ignorant writers in Radical papers have an idea that Lord Curzon is a superior, splendid person who looks down from Viceregal heights on popular representation and so forth. Whereas in reality Lord Curzon has a passionate belief in this representation. We do not imagine this—we know it. We have heard him express it with all the impatience of sincerity. Mr. Balfour declares he is a House of Commons man; Lord St. Aldwyn is said to hold aloof from the Budget debate because he is at heart of the same persuasion; but Lord Curzon would go further than either of them in this matter. He would give the eldest son of a peer the power to stay in the House of Commons. Yet he does not hesitate a moment about speaking and voting for Lord Lansdowne's amendment; and one has not the faintest doubt that Pitt, Chatham and Canning would in a like case have done likewise.

Frankly, we are disappointed with the speech of the Archbishop of York. We got a good deal, but we expected more. Everyone knows that Dr. Lang has the voice and habit of an orator; so that goes without saying. But it is strange that this very remarkable man did not see that the opportunity for an ecclesiastic in the House of Lords is not to make an ordinary political speech. He might say, of course, if he pleased, that we were disappointed in his speech because he voted against our side. But we knew very well that Dr. Lang was a Liberal—or a cross between a Liberal and a Socialist—and would vote according to his sympathies. Quite right. Why not? But surely he should have told the House things that most peers were not in a way to know about, and not lecture them on "tacking" and resolutions. Any peer could do that as well as he. An archbishop is in the House as an archbishop, not as a peer. One digression, on the mind of the street-corner Socialist, was to the point; but he was soon back to his party politics. And really Dr. Lang's modesty was excessive.

Lord Denman made a terrific black list of the Dukes. The Duke of Rutland proposes the gagging of the whole Labour party. The Duke of Montrose would have Mr. Lloyd George and Mr. Churchill sit down to a chop and glass of ale with Mr. Keir Hardie and Mr. Snowden. The Duke of Beaufort would put Mr. Lloyd George and Mr. Churchill in the midst of twenty couple of dog hounds. The Duke of Montrose's plan sounds harsh. The Duke of Beaufort's plan seems terrible, but perhaps he, as a good hunting man, only wishes to see these two Ministers duly "blooded".

The debate ended with a quiet speech by Lord Crewe. He has grown into a distinctly good debater, though he is not biting or brilliant. When he says the House of Lords is resolving itself into a Committee of Public Safety, he strains analogy. That Committee was certainly a sinister body, and most of its members lost their heads; but at any rate it had the satisfaction of seeing most of the Constitutionists lose theirs first. And if we follow Lord Crewe aright, he and his friends are the Constitutionists in this drama.

Are the Lords, asked Lord Lovat, to be reduced to the ineffectiveness of a dog barking behind a carriage? The question was not put in the Budget debate, but when the Lords' amendments on the Development Bill came back from the House of Commons. The Commons are in an ungracious and churlish temper with the Lords, and they have spitefully claimed privilege over the money grants in the Development Bill. Lord Lansdowne showed that they have usually waived their privilege in similar instances in the past. By insisting on treating the Development Bill as technically a money Bill, the Commons refused to consider important amendments of the Lords on their merits.

Lord Crewe did not deny that this was what had happened. The whole purpose of the Bill is to grant money to certain persons for roads and economic development. If the Lords are to have no say on these grants nor the persons to whom they are to be made, they cannot do anything with the Bill at all except pass it. If this is not "Commons' arrogance", in Mr. Asquith's phrase, what would be? Privileges such as these cannot be kept out of future discussions about the relations of the two Houses. The Lords did not insist on their amendments, but they entered a protest against the Commons' action on their Journals, and recorded that the Bill involved questions of policy in which both Houses are concerned, and with which the Lords have in the past been accustomed to deal.

The essence of the controversy between Lord Carrington and Mr. Prothero over the sale of the Duke of Bedford's Thornley estate is in two brief sentences from Mr. Prothero's letter in Monday's papers: "Lord Carrington prophesies that the future income derived from the sale of the estate will be £30,000. If this proves correct, his Grace receives nothing for the land and under 2 per cent. on the capital expenditure"—which has been £1,815,353 since the year 1816. Mr. Prothero's estimate, on Lord Carrington's own calculations, stands uncontradicted, so that, taking the estate as a whole, anything derived from it by Mr. Lloyd George's proposed taxation would have to be in substance a tax on invested capital.

In his reply next day Lord Carrington rested his case on the statement that the estate had actually been sold "for over three-quarters of a million sterling"; but £30,000 on this is only 4 per cent., leaving us still to seek the taxable "increment". That is as to the selling value, assuming Lord Carrington's three-quarters of a million to be right; but then this selling value, as shown by Mr. Prothero, is a trifle of £1,065,353 less than the capital actually expended on the estate. In other words, at the price received the Duke loses much over half the capital investment, and gets 4 per cent. on the remainder. Trying to justify increased taxation for an estate like this is a poor kind of occupation.

Only one serious cattle-drive appears to have followed the removal of the more objectionable proposals from the Land Bill by the Lords, though Mr. William Redmond declared that he "would not be responsible for East Clare". The "Western News", published in Galway, says that "the cattle-driving period inaugurated for the first of November has passed off rather quietly", and denounces the national policy of "organised crime", quoting Mr. Birrell to ask "whether 'Hell in Ireland' comes within the Ten Commandments". The same paper openly charges the Irish party with having supported "the colossal robbery of Ireland" proposed by the Budget. Such print is new to Galway. The Nationalist members had better look out when these symptoms develop at the very nerve centres of agrarianism.

Everyone will be pleased that Admiral Sir Arthur Wilson has been appointed to be First Sea Lord in succession to Sir John Fisher. There is certainly reason for national self-congratulation on the merits of the appointment—Sir Arthur Wilson is the one man, we should say, whom the best men of all parties in the Navy—that we should have to speak of parties in the Navy!—would have hit on for the post. Also the nation may congratulate itself on the appointment, as much for what it supersedes as for what it brings. There is a chance now for the restoration of the old order and the good naval spirit.

Just when the members of our own Parliament are dispersing to the uttermost parts of the country, the German Reichstag meets to begin a new session. The German Emperor's Speech from the Throne to the assembling Reichstag precedes by only a few days the King's Speech to the dissolving Parliament. It coincided, indeed, with the decisive act of Tuesday, which was to set our members of Parliament scurrying. Last session in the Reichstag was occupied, as our Parliament was, with finance, and many domestic questions had to stand over. In the approaching session it would seem from the Speech that they are to be resumed as the principal business. The imperial insurance laws against sickness are to be extended, and life insurance introduced for the benefit of surviving relatives. The conditions of home work are to be regulated, and a Bill on Criminal Procedure to be re-introduced. In England the quarrels of the Montagus and Capulets will be too exciting for any useful work to be done.

King Manuel might or might not have enjoyed the sensation which King Pataud—to give this notorious vaurien his Paris nickname—arranged for him at the Opera. King Pataud, who once cut off all the electric supply in Paris, threatened to cut off the light at the Opera on the night King Manuel was there. The Bureau of the Opera were in the midst of a dispute with their electricians, and this was Pataud's method of bringing them to terms. It succeeded, and the light was not actually put out. Then King Pataud strolled along to a meeting where the other King, Jaurès, was discussing " Comment nous ferons la Révolution ", and happened to be deriding the Pataud attempt at revolution by practical jokes. Pataud arrived at this critical moment and bragged about his latest exploit, and also lied about it, as he said the lights had been put out. M. Jaurès, still disapproving, asked " Will the Proletariat see any clearer because the King of Portugal has been left for two minutes without a light? " But Pataud is not the sort of man to worry about that.

The tunnel through the Andes is finished, and Valparaiso will soon be within reach of Buenos Ayres. Chile and Peru thus come into contact with Brazil and Argentina. The building of this railway is symbolic of a change in South American politics. Chile and Argentina, once so ready to be truculent, have worked together in a scheme that brings them closer. South America is beginning to hear and obey a call to unite. Should South America once feel itself a peculiar unit among the continents, a new competitor will come into the circle of Great Powers. All the straws are blowing the same way. Brazil and Argentina have just helped Chile to get her dispute settled with the United States, and have won something like a diplomatic victory.

And who is to settle this dispute?—His Majesty King Edward VII. Notice, too, that the boring of the tunnel was a triumph for British engineers. The omens are good. South America will have to face a serious question. Is she to come among us with a character and voice of her own, or is South America to be lost in America? We hope and hope again that the small voice will not be shouted down. Nor is there any reason why it should be, if Europe wakes up in time to the importance of South America and refuses to be frightened away by the loudness (and it will probably be very loud) of the Pan-American rally. There is no need for anybody to be frightened. Even the President of a republic in the middle of revolution can hold his own by refusing to be deafened. The United States will probably let President Zelaya's Government die a natural death. True, by way of helping nature they have severed diplomatic relations. It was the least they could do after the tall talk, and it may or may not lead to war. But United States caution has been most marked.

Opportune object-lessons in the advantage of a tariff on the one hand, and of colonial preference on the other, have come this week from Canada and Australia. Canada has the power to retaliate, and is prepared to use it. Hence the Americans are officially advised to consider whether they should not postpone the imposition of the maximum tariff under the Payne Act till 1911 in order to escape border reprisals. The United States has to take into account the retaliatory powers of a colony, though she rides rough-shod over that colony's mother country. In tariff matters, as things British are now, the part is greater than the whole. Then Victoria, as the result of preference, is placing a large order for electrical appliances with England instead of Germany, notwithstanding Germany's lower tenders. The Canadian treaty with France has only been allowed to go through the Dominion Parliament without serious challenge because it can be cancelled at twelve months' notice, and so would not stand indefinitely in the way of reciprocal preference between Great Britain and the Dominion.

New South Wales, and Australia generally, is suffering so much from the coal strike that the public are ceasing to care who is to blame for it—the employers or the men. The one thing desired is that the parties should agree to a conference and to mediation. The Employers' Federation, the Government, and the public are agreed on forcing this mediation. The question is how and by what force it can be compelled; the Government threatens to use the Industrial Disputes Act, but 20,000 men cannot be forced to work or sent to prison. Anticipating failure, the suggestion is made that the Government should help the employers to obtain labour and force the opening of all mines and factories. The Government is just as helpless to do the one as the other; and the third proposal of the Labour party to nationalise the mines is as hopeless. It looks as if hunger alone will provide a solution.

In Mr. Dutt India has lost one of the best known of that group of visionary reformers who see her emancipated and governing herself under British protection. He gave a certain amount of respectability to a movement which he was not strong enough to keep under. His antagonism to foreign rule was softened by his twenty-five years in the Indian Civil Service, where he was the first Indian to reach the responsible post of Divisional Commissioner. After his retirement Mr. Dutt began to criticise the Administration to which he had belonged. Unluckily he selected for attack the Land Revenue System, of which, like most Bengalis under the Permanent Settlement, he knew little. His agitation, however, proved useful in evoking the vindication of British methods with which Lord Curzon's name is associated.

Messrs. Cadburys' action for libel against the " Standard " raises a most peculiar and interesting question. Messrs. Cadburys since 1901 have bought through brokers cocoa which came to the English market from the Portuguese island of San Thomé, but did not themselves own any plantations in San Thomé. It was unfortunate for Messrs. Cadburys, with their religious and philanthropic reputation, that this cocoa is produced by what is practically slave labour. Last year the " Standard " pointed this out in severe terms, and asserted that Messrs. Cadburys had been indifferent and had done nothing to put an end to this state of slavery. This was the libel complained of, and Mr. W. A. Cadbury has himself given evidence and has had Sir Edward Grey as witness to show that in the special circumstances the

" Standard's " allegations ought not to have been made. One of the remarkable characteristics of the trial is the cross-examination by Sir Edward Carson, which suggests and presses many of the bitterest political and social and religious controversies between Liberals and Conservatives and Churchmen and Nonconformists of late years.

After all Bath Street is not safe. Most municipal corporations are Philistines; but the Corporation of Bath are more. They seem to be an assembly of Goliaths. One had thought that these enterprising tradesmen had been shamed by national public opinion out of their little scheme to pull down one of the most interesting streets of old Bath to make room for a modern " handsome and commodious structure ". Messrs. Waring, who were to carry out the scheme, unlike their employers, had sensibility enough to draw back from the outrage. They wisely let the matter alone, and they have now no wish to put a defacing touch to a single pillar in Bath Street. But this does not suit the worthy Corporation at all. They see business for themselves in a new huge hotel. What is beauty to them? So they are forcing Messrs. Waring under legal threats to start demolition.

If Waring's should have the courage still to prove refractory, they would have public opinion everywhere and the sympathy of every really good citizen of Bath on their side. The Corporation is as wrong in its business judgment as in its taste. There are plenty of good hotels in Bath, and no one would choose the centre of the town, stifling, shut in, with no prospect, to stay at. But what Bath does want is the obvious eponymous thing—better baths and more. The Corporation's plan is to make a futile little addition to the baths, using up practically the whole space for a mammoth hotel. The right thing would be to use the whole space for baths. This would be doing something real to restore to this fine old city its lost fortunes.

The price of the modern novel is again to the fore. In the terrific battle which the " Times " waged against the publishers six shillings was declared to be exorbitant. It was said that eighty thousand words of fiction could be easily turned out at a profit for half that sum; the sale of four hundred odd copies at six shillings " covers "; and a novel that does not sell to that extent is not worth publishing at all. But here is Mr. De Morgan coming along with not eighty but two hundred thousand words, and Mr. Heinemann offering his work at the rate of five shillings per hundred thousand, which is substantially cheaper than the six shillings per eighty thousand rate. And yet the Libraries are not happy! Authors and publishers to-day seem to be the only class of people who have not the right to live.

The improper book, too, is getting a boom. Somebody is going to have a committee to taste the stuff beforehand, and decide whether it is too high for public consumption. Mrs. Grundy is to be up in arms, and she is to prod the authors of doubtful books with her gingham. But, alas! it is not only a question of some books to-day being too high—it is a question of books, high or low, to-day being far too many. A man who cannot write is yet often a prolific producer of printed matter in books and papers. If he has been somewhere, or knows something, or has thought of something, that is enough: the printing press is ready.

It is just as if an intelligent or well-informed man who admires a landscape or knows the features of a striking face were forthwith to get a box of colours and a camel's hair brush, and, without any idea of painting, proceed to make a daub and send it off to the public galleries and picture dealers, where it will be hung on the wall or in the window. Writing is not only an art, it is an extremely difficult art. Is it not a strange thing that to-day, when there is next to no chance for any writer in any province of print unless he can produce something uncommon, the multitude of undistinguished amateurs grows and grows?

BEFORE PHILIPPI.

" Why now, blow wind, swell billow, and swim bark!
The storm is up, and all is on the hazard."

AT last. Parliament has had its say, and the real action is about to begin. These preambles and preludes are rather trying. After a time they get on the nerves. Both sides know very well that the time for parleying is past; the issue must be fought out in the country, and can be settled nowhere else. So the sooner we get to business the better. We could say with young Octavius:

" Come, come, the cause of arguing makes us sweat,
The proof of it will turn to redder drops."

We do not mean by this that we are literally eager for our opponents' blood, neither are we predicting civil war; though there are issues involved in this controversy which in times past have been soluble only by force. In one sense it is so now; every general election is an appeal to force. Nobody believes because his side has lost that it was wrong, or was worsted in argument. Everybody whose side loses an election believes he was beaten by the brute force of ignorant numbers, and makes from it no sort of inference that success is anything else than what is meant by the success of a victorious army. True, the winning side does believe that righteousness has triumphed; so does every successful army. The real use of an election, as of war, is to find a way out of a seeming impasse. We all hope that way out found will be the best; but that an election is certain to do that, none of us, however enthusiastic a democrat, in the least believes. But it is something even to get to a settlement of any kind; to have done with these Homeric challenges before the battle.

Liberal leaders really seem to imagine that they will frighten, or at any rate greatly impress, us by their constant insistence on the extreme gravity of the occasion and the certainty that we are going out to our destruction. Pompous solemnity can go no further than the tragic warnings of Mr. Asquith and the awful denunciations of the Lord Chancellor. Evidently, as Lord Curzon wittily suggested, he thought he was sentencing the House of Lords and the whole Unionist party to death. All this concern of our opponents for our safety is rather absurd; it is in ill taste. We are not boys to be taught how to conduct ourselves. It is also very silly. Seeing that the thing they warn us against is the very thing they most want—our political ruin—are we likely to heed them? If they really believed we were choosing our battle ground so badly, and the time, they would be very silent indeed about it, for fear we might become aware of the position and change our plan. It is very clear to the Unionist leaders that the Government has been hoping by some means or another to put us off this fight. When the Archbishop of York suggests to us, with such kind thought for our interest, that it would be better tactics to pass the Budget, there is but one possible answer, " In vain is the net spread ". One would have thought Dr. Lang would perceive the futility of talking in that way. The forebodings of the cross-bench men were different. These were really afraid. Constitutional timidity visibly depressed them. The Cassandra mind is naturally always in favour of not taking action, for in all action it always foresees ruin to the actor. Lord Courtney of Penwith, whose wisdom we greatly revere, could not have been more solemn on the verge of a hundred years' war. It is not strange that these great minds have no followers. Mark Tapley himself would not have had the heart to follow them. Lord Curzon blew away all this heavy atmosphere almost with a single breath. *There* was a man men could follow.

It may be fantastic to speak of a good conscience in connexion with politics, but we are very sure that the great mass of Unionists will be sensibly heartened to the fight by the feeling that we have met a straight issue in a straight way. We have nothing to apologise for, nothing to explain. We have not finessed; we have played the game. If the Lords had passed the Budget, when the election came we should have to explain all over the country why they did. The only possible explanation would have been one of tactics, and we are confident that the non-party voter would have refused point blank to accept it. We should pay the penalty of excessive cleverness. That, if you will, would have been an unconstitutional course. The Lords may pass a Bill they do not approve because they believe the country demands it, but to pass a Bill they believe the country disapproves, that the country may feel the consequences, that is tactics you would never get any popular constituency to stand. To be accused of treating the Commons with bravado and insolence is nothing; we need not care a rap for talk of that sort; to be accused, and justly accused, of cowardice and double dealing would have been a charge we could not have repelled.

This issue of Government and Lords has, we all know, been gathering to a head these many years. That it has now come to a head is nothing to cry over. If we lose, defeat could not have been put off more than at most a few years; if we win, we shall have delivered the country from a standing menace. For this contest—we do not say this election—will settle things one way or another. Either we shall become in effect a single-Chamber country, or the right of the House of Lords to intervene between the House of Commons and the country will be vindicated finally. There will then be no more talk in our time of disestablishing the House of Lords.

In very rotund phrase Mr. Asquith's resolution makes the Lower House declare the Lords' rejection of the Budget a usurpation of the rights of the Commons. No doubt Liberals think this will be a capital catchword for electioneering purposes. They, or the more intelligent amongst them, are probably quite aware of its unreality. In constitutional form this is a contest between two estates of the realm. In fact it is nothing of the kind. It is a contest between Unionists and Liberals; nothing else. This very resolution a Conservative House of Commons would not pass: maybe after the election there will be a House of Commons that would straightway reverse this resolution. So far from this being a matter of Commons on one side and Lords on another, you could not form any idea, from the mere fact of a man being a commoner, whether he was against or in favour of the Lords' action on the Budget. In the old days of protest against Crown demands for supplies, it really was a matter of the Commons' resistance as Commons. But the House of Commons is as much divided on this question as on any other question; its view on it changes as quickly as on any other. It is unreal, too, to talk of the House of Commons now as a political entity, a political whole, at all. If it is, it is an extraordinarily feeble one; for it stultifies itself by flat self-contradiction almost periodically; it is always divided against itself; it takes no political action as a unit; it never acts independently of party leaders. In a certain social way, in a tradition of camaraderie, in a sense of the rules of the game, the House of Commons is a fact; the House has a mind and habit of its own; but politically the House of Commons is a fiction. The mere fact that it is always necessary to distinguish expressly between a Conservative and a Liberal House of Commons shows that: we see that the essential element is not the House of Commons but its Conservatism and its Liberalism. The House of Commons goes on: it is the continuing factor, but it has no effect in producing continuity of policy. In other words the House as a House is dead matter. It is important that the country should not be carried away by conventional phrases. We must see at this election that the electors realise what are the facts as distinct from the old forms which hide them. We can thus take the sting out of the Radical representation that the Lords are contending against the Commons.

If we thought the House of Lords' question would be an effectual red herring across the Budget, we should not be doubtful about this election. On the Lords we are perfectly satisfied that we can commend our case to the majority of the electors. Even if we were technically wrong from a constitutional point of view, we should not be very greatly afraid. We cannot at all agree with the Archbishop of York that the man in the street cares for constitutional points. It would be difficult, indeed, for him to do so, seeing that, as the Archbishop himself insisted, he knows nothing at all about them. We are persuaded that if he knew more, he would care less. There is something almost pathetic in a man being so far away from facts as Lord James of Hereford, who builds a solemn argument on the motions of Black Rod, or as Lord Courtney of Penwith, who is deeply concerned because the sentence of the next King's Speech, which thanks "Gentlemen of the House of Commons" will have to be turned otherwise. This Radical ritualism is quite an interesting phenomenon. We hope Lord James and Lord Courtney will argue on these lines against the Lords on many a popular platform.

THE LORDS AND SUPPLY BILLS.

It is now clear that the main issues before the country at the coming General Election will be three. First, has the House of Lords constitutionally discretion to reject a Budget? This is the question the House of Commons was occupied with on Thursday. Second, if the House of Lords has this discretion, has it used it rightly in rejecting this particular Budget? This becomes simply a discussion of the merits of the Budget. Those who like the Budget will judge that the Lords used their discretion wrongly in not passing it; those who dislike it will hold that they used it rightly. The point of pure tactics, whether the Lords—granted that the Budget is bad and that they have the constitutional right to throw it out—were wise in so doing can hardly come up for discussion on a platform. Third, if the Lords were right in rejecting the Government's plan for raising revenue, what is the alternative? The Liberal answer is, in effect, none; the Unionist answer is Tariff Reform. Thus the fiscal question becomes the third issue before the electorate. We believe these three questions contain the whole subject of immediate discussion. Others will be raised during the campaign—education, for instance, Home Rule, and Welsh Disestablishment—but they will not be dominant issues.

It is always wise to look first for points of agreement. We then have a starting-point of some kind, at any rate. This time we have it in the legal right of the Lords, which of course carries power, to amend or reject any and every bill sent up from the Commons. We have further agreement in the common admission that there is a difference between legal right and constitutional authority: that a House of Parliament, like the King, may have the legal right to do a thing, but constitutionally be not entitled to do it. It may be lawful but not convenient. And there is also agreement that in practice finance is mainly the business of the Commons. There is absolute agreement that at any rate the House of Lords cannot propose taxes and cannot impose them. These agreed points cleared out of the way, the issue is considerably narrowed. It would be simpler still, at any rate much more clearly grasped, had there been less loose thinking, or rather had there been any serious thinking, about the position of the two Houses as to finance amongst practical politicians of late years. We all knew that in fact the Lords did not concern themselves about Budgets, and we had come to expect the Government of the day to settle these matters in the Commons. Nothing occurred to make us examine the foundations of our belief. And we got into a loose way of speaking, which necessity is now checking. Mr. Balfour himself has used language allowing the House a control over finance which cannot be upheld on closer examination. Mr. Asquith on Thursday quoted words of Mr. Balfour which, we may be allowed to say, this Review took exception to at the time. In fact, we have more than once said that Mr. Balfour magnified the relative position of the House of Commons. On the other side Mr. Asquith has used words, quoted by Lord Cawdor on Tuesday, inconsistent with his present attitude. At first it was roundly claimed that constitutionally the Lords could not touch a money bill. Examination of the fundamental resolution of the House of Commons showed this view to be untenable, for the resolution implicitly left the Lords discretion to reject, though not to amend, a money bill. Then it was said that this did not apply to the bill providing the year's supplies, but only to separate money bills. There is nothing, in fact, in the terms of the resolution to bear out that construction. Authorities, great authorities, can be cited on either side.

It is this uncertain and disputed point on which the country will now have to give its opinion. It is the first of the three dominant issues of the election. The country is more likely in our judgment to decide on grounds of expediency than constitutional precedent. And perhaps very wisely, nor even technically incorrectly. The very idea, and the actual history, of constitutionalism is elasticity, a working adjustment, dictated by the moment, of rigid law to changing situations. If you allow constitutional usage to become as binding and rigid as law itself, you defeat its very purpose and bring it to an end. If constitutionalism is to be as inelastic as law, far better make it law and get rid of the dual conflict. Precisely what has happened with equity and law. If we value constitutional as against legal process, we must not make it a law of the Medes and Persians. And Englishmen have never done this. Lord Morley, as able a spokesman as the Government have at all, admitted expressly that he could conceive a case where it would be the duty of the House of Lords to throw out a Budget. Lord Morley would never say that it could be the duty of the House of Lords to violate the constitution. Therefore he admits that the Lords might be acting constitutionally in throwing out a Budget, and this is all we contend for. Of course Lord Morley does not admit that the present Budget is one of the possible cases he had in mind—cases which would justify the Lords in rejection. But that is irrelevant to the constitutional issue. To say that the Lords are not justified in this case is one thing; to say that by constitutional usage they never can be justified is quite another. Lord Morley does not hold that by not using it the Lords have lost the right to reject a Budget. He does not therefore support Mr. Asquith's main contention.

No wonder. Practical necessity makes such a ruling impossible. Who cannot conceive Budgets that no sane man would say the Lords ought to pass? If the next Ministry were Conservative and Protectionist and sent up a Budget imposing a tariff as high as the American, how many Liberals would insist on the constitutional duty on the Lords to pass it? We give their party the credit of containing very few such fools. Or if a Budget were sent up dangerously starving the Army and Navy, would Lord Cromer and Lord Balfour hold that the Lords must pass it or violate the Constitution? To say so would be reducing the Constitution itself to an absurdity. Practical necessity settles the claim that the Lords cannot constitutionally reject a Budget; even apart from the most serious argument of all, that such a claim would leave the House of Commons, that is the Government of the day, which really means two or three men at most, absolute masters of the country.

THE GERMAN PROBLEM.

ON Tuesday the Emperor showed his confidence in the new Chancellor by opening the Reichstag in state. The ceremony was a reminder that the German Empire is a military monarchy. Most of the deputies were in uniform, and the Socialists protested against the established state of affairs by wearing civilian dress. The Chancellor himself wore the uniform of the Dragoon Guards, a regiment in which he has recently been promoted to the rank of major. On his appointment he was merely a lieutenant, but it was felt incongruous that the chief Minister of the Empire should take precedence of a junior captain, and Herr von Bethmann-Hollweg has therefore attained a rank worthy of his civilian status. Possibly he may yet rise in time to the high dignity of a colonelcy, a position actually won by his predecessor. The day, however, is still far distant when a Civil servant of the Crown will be regarded as in any way the peer of the commander of an Army Corps.

The speech from the throne was a document of great caution. It contained a reference to the financial reforms of the past session which throws no light whatever on Herr von Bethmann-Hollweg's future intentions. It touched on foreign affairs no further than was necessary; and it did not allude to naval policy. For the rest its contents were forecast with some accuracy. The House is asked to sanction a new commercial agreement with Portugal and to renew the old arrangement with Great Britain. Railway development in the African colonies is to be continued; and there is a short programme of domestic legislation.

This part of the speech provided the one surprise of the day. Last session there was laid before the House a proposal for the reform of criminal procedure. The outlines of the new scheme met with general approval, but much criticism was anticipated on the points of detail with which the Bill naturally bristled. It was accordingly postponed, and it was generally expected that it would occupy much of the Reichstag's time during the session just opened. The Bill, however, has been dropped and its place taken by a proposal to extend the system of workmen's insurance and in particular to provide for the maintenance of widows and orphans. The plan is one with a past. It dates from the new tariff of 1905. When Prince Buelow proposed to increase the corn tax, the Catholic Centre only gave its assent on the understanding that the proceeds should be set aside to form the nucleus of a widows' and orphans' fund. It was then enacted that 1910 should be the date when the fund should first be distributed. The revenue from the tax has been so small that it was confidently anticipated that the scheme would be postponed. But it is the German way to go ahead, and the plan will be elaborated this session as promised. Critics of the Empire's financial policy do not conceal their surprise, and pointedly ask where the money is to come from.

There is indeed some ground for their inquiry. The estimates just presented show an anticipated deficit of some £7,000,000 to be covered by loan. Technically, of course, there can be no deficit on the Imperial Budget. All outstanding amounts must be covered within three years by the so-called matricular contributions of the federated States. But the States have lately refused to pay the enormous sums demanded of them, and the financial reforms of last year fixed their contribution at forty pfennigs a head till 1914. Nothing more, then, can be got from this source; the new taxes, which, it may be observed, have nothing to do with the protective tariff, but are without exception acceptable to orthodox economists, have broken down very badly and are enormously unpopular; the tariff itself, still a productive source of revenue, is fixed by treaty for some years to come; and there is a heavy deficit destined to become heavier still. That is the situation confronting the new Chancellor, and as yet he has given no hint, by deed or word, how he hopes to deal with it.

This silence, characteristic of the man, is emphatic of the difficulty of his position. Prince Buelow's original scheme was undoubtedly popular. It failed to please the reactionary majority of the Reichstag, and Prince Buelow accepted the defeat and did not dissolve. To the English observer his failure to insist on a dissolution last June is most bewildering. It admits of only one explanation. Prince Buelow did not dissolve because he could not get a dissolution. For that purpose he required the assent of the Federal Council, and it appears absolutely certain that its assent was refused. The Council meets in secret, so that its decision can only be inferred, but its composition makes the inference conclusive. For the Council is composed of delegates from the Governments of the various States. These Governments were certainly hostile to the proposed death duties, as being a tax which met with the approval of the Socialists. Bavaria is the citadel of the Centre; Saxony has actually abolished universal suffrage; and the majority of the Conservatives and Clericals in the Prussian Diet is overwhelming. Prince Buelow was thus faced with the opposition of the chief minor States and of his own colleagues in the Prussian Government. It was this opposition which drove him to resign, and it was this opposition which his successor was prepared to conciliate when he took office.

It must not be supposed that the German Empire is the theatre of a struggle between two Houses of Parliament. The Federal Council is not a House of Parliament in any real sense of the words. It is an assembly of delegates with no powers of their own who vote according to the instructions received from their respective Governments. Of these Governments Prussia is infinitely the most powerful. Her control of the votes of the smaller States assures her a majority; and, besides this, her sole veto is absolute. Prince Buelow's proposals were unacceptable to Prussia, and as long as the composition of the Prussian Diet remains unchanged there is no reasonable probability of their acceptance. Accordingly the actual question which is being put to the new Chancellor is not what he intends to propose in the matter of financial reform, but what he means to do in the matter of the Prussian franchise.

To a certain extent Herr von Bethmann-Hollweg's hand has been forced. In the speech from the throne with which the Prussian Diet was opened after the last elections the King declared his "firm determination" to reform the Prussian franchise. How much did the words mean? Were they simply put into the Sovereign's mouth by Prince Buelow or is the strong phrase intended to represent William II.'s own convictions? And what does the new Chancellor intend to do? Up to the present no scheme has been introduced, and reform to-day will be infinitely harder to carry than it was a year ago. For reform would mean the eventual success of the new finance. The death duties actually proposed are moderate enough, but they are dangerous for what they imply. As in this country, so in Germany, the masses are being encouraged to join battle with the interests, and the interests very naturally defend themselves. Where the right lies is not the business of this article to consider. All that is pointed out here is that the Prussian Chamber, elected as it is by an electorate graded according to its wealth, is rightly regarded as the stronghold of the interests, and forms the central point round which the constitutional battle must rage.

The struggle which entered on a new phase with the rejection of Prince Buelow's proposals last year is, in itself, no novelty. It is simply another aspect of that rivalry between the central Government and the federated States which has been the main issue of German politics since the establishment of the Empire. How it will be decided no man can say, and the new Chancellor is hardly the type of Minister to push matters to a crisis. His bureaucratic temperament is inclined to acquiesce in things as they are. He succeeded Count Posadowsky, whose liberalising instincts were displeasing to the Junker party, and he became Chancellor when Prince Buelow fell a victim to the hostility of the same group. These facts go far to indicate his line of policy, but since his accession to the supreme office he has scrupulously refrained from committing himself. His sphinx-like silence is, indeed, in the greatest contrast to the affability of his predecessor, than who no man knew better how to talk much and say nothing.

To the English mind it would seem that the Chancellor occupies an impossible position, and is silent because there is nothing which he is competent to say. Here is a political problem of extreme complexity which it will require the highest statesmanship to solve. Herr von Bethmann-Hollweg is a bureaucrat, familiar with papers and routine, but necessarily ignorant of men. Such a man, it would appear, is obviously incapable of dealing with such an issue. The argument involves a subjective fallacy; it forgets that the German and the Englishman are creatures of a very different type. It is not an accident that the highest Ministerial posts in the German State are filled by men appointed from the bureaucracy and not from the Reichstag—a glaring contrast with the English system, which throws a striking light on the differences of temperament between the two nations. It is quite possible that the new Chancellor may turn out to be just the type of man whom the German trusts. Moreover, it is easy to exaggerate the tensity of the present situation. In England a struggle for the reform and extension of the franchise would probably dwarf every other issue. But the Germans are not a political people, or at any rate not yet, and though the Socialists may blaspheme, the Prussian electorate may long continue unreformed. Saxony could even abolish universal suffrage. In England a similar proposal might have produced a revolution.

But when all the necessary qualifications have been made, it must be admitted that affairs are developing in Germany, though the development may be slow. Sooner or later the financial problem must again be faced, and it cannot be faced without raising the question whether ultimate sovereignty resides with the Empire or with the States. That question takes the form of an alteration in the Prussian franchise, and it is in the Prussian Chamber that the future course of German history must be determined. How a reform for which there is a great and growing demand can be carried in the face of a hostile and suspicious majority is a question only to be answered by a man of genius, and in speculating as to Germany's future it must be borne in mind that the one man of genius who now figures in German public life is the Emperor.

THE CITY.

So far there are no signs in the City of that financial chaos which was threatened if the Lords threw out the Budget. True the Bank rate has not been lowered as was hoped a week ago; but in the interval the position of that institution has unexpectedly weakened, and we need not go beyond the figures of the weekly return to find an explanation for the retention of the 5 per cent. quotation. The reserve is still high for a 5 per cent. rate, but it is materially below the total of a week ago, and if the directors then deemed it wise to postpone a reduction, it would have seemed very inconsistent to come down when the position was less strong. It is satisfactory to have Mr. Asquith's assurance that until fresh parliamentary provision can be made the necessities of State will be supported by resorting to borrowing powers conferred by the Appropriation Act. This apparently means that any deficiency will be met by the issue of Treasury bills—a course of procedure we have always urged as the only possible one in the circumstances. Lombard Street will readily provide money on this security, and we shall probably find the Continent anxious to buy the bills. The "bogey" of financial chaos may therefore be said to have been effectually laid, and while there promises to be a curtailment of business in the interval between the prorogation and the reassembling of Parliament, there is no reason to anticipate any further alarums on the score of finance. This is so much to the good of stock markets, which are already assuming a more cheerful aspect. Since the division in the House of Lords Consols have risen fully ⅝ per cent., thus recovering the whole of the dividend. This is scarcely a reflection of financial chaos; but we will not draw too fine an inference from the movement, as a recovery usually follows the deduction of the dividend. It cannot be denied, however, that the Stock Exchange supports the action of the House of Lords, and while it is not prepared yet awhile to engineer a rise in prices, it is already looking with more favour upon home securities, in the belief that the socialistic policy of the Government has been "scotched" once and for all time. A reduction in the Bank rate would probably do much to stimulate this feeling, and as it is the policy of the directors to assist the Government of the day, as far as possible, in making its financial arrangements, we may be sure that a movement will not be delayed longer than is absolutely necessary.

The special weakness of Kaffirs on Wednesday was attributed to many causes. One of the principal reasons was the selling of shares taken over at the last settlement from a defaulting broker. The holders tried to realise, and the market being unwilling to take the shares, prices were forced down quite out of proportion to the number offered. When the selling ceased there was a sharp recovery, but it is evident, as we have repeatedly pointed out, that the market is in a very weak state, and that any return of a "boom" is quite out of the question at the moment. Activity in Argentine railway stocks has continued, and Buenos Ayres and Pacific stock has this week "marked" 93, at which it may be left to rest for a while. Buying of foreign Government securities continues, but a nasty reminder of the uncertainties of investing too deeply in South and Central American Bonds is furnished by the slump in Colombian, concerning which there is talk of a possible default in the January coupon. A bad effect would be produced on the whole market if there was to be a lapse in Colombian honesty. It is the uncertainty and doubt as to the maintenance of credit that has always kept down South and Central American bonds well below the level of home and Colonial Government securities; and now when so much enthusiasm is being shown for such investments it may not be out of place to suggest a little more discrimination in purchasing.

The expected fall in the price of rubber has taken place, and rubber shares have had a sympathetic movement. We do not anticipate much further reduction, but there need be no hurry to repurchase shares sold in anticipation. Considerable attention has been given to the shares of the Associated Portland Cement Company during the week. On vague and undefined rumours the price of these has had quite a big rise, but the best figure has not been maintained, and careful inquiry in well-informed quarters fails to elicit any adequate reason for the appreciation. The proposed amalgamation of the Law Life and Phœnix Assurance Companies is only a sign of the times, and it is surprising that the moment should be chosen to float several new insurance companies. Capital provided for these new ventures is merely fostering a gamble in which the promoters stand to lose nothing and the public all.

INSURANCE: POLICIES AT HIGH PREMIUMS. VII.

ONE characteristic of policies effected at high rates of premium is that, other things being equal, a larger proportion of each premium paid is accumulated as savings, and a smaller proportion is applied for protection purposes, than under forms of assurance which call for low rates of premium. This consideration has a direct effect upon the surrender values of the policies. When much out of each premium is saved, large surrender values can be given; while when the bulk of each premium is required to pay for protection the surrender value is of necessity small.

It thus appears that the conditions of policies in regard to the terms upon which they can be surrendered are of even greater importance in connexion with policies at high rates of premium than under policies at low premiums. A difference of 20 per cent. between the cash surrender values of a good and a bad office may not amount to a large sum under whole-life policies; but it becomes very appreciable under limited-payment life policies and endowment assurances, which in any case call for substantial surrender values. Moreover, policies at high premiums are more apt to be regarded as investments than the less expensive forms, and, being looked at in this way, there is a greater chance of their being surrendered, or of being used as security for a temporary or permanent loan; hence from every point of view it becomes important to consider conditions of this kind. Taking, for example, policies effected in two different companies on the twenty-payment life plan at a premium of £100 a year we find that while one office guarantees a surrender value at the end of ten years of £635, another gives only £335; at the end of fifteen years the terms are £1058, as against £500; and at the end of twenty years £1530, as compared with £670. In both cases the cash value of bonuses not previously drawn is added to the surrender values, and the bonuses are larger and the terms for commutation more generous in the office which is the more liberal in the matter of surrender values. It is quite foolish if a man can take a better policy in a safer office, which would have a guaranteed cash value of more than £1000 at the end of fifteen years, for him to take a less good policy from an inferior company, which at the same cost, and at the same date, will be worth only £500.

All policies which have acquired a surrender value constitute good security for loans, which, if the policy is not assigned, can be obtained from the life office with the utmost promptitude; the amount of the loan obtainable depends upon the surrender value; but while some offices lend money in this way at 5 per cent. interest, other companies are satisfied with 4 per cent., and—especially if the loan remains unpaid for a long time and the interest upon it accumulates as a debt upon the policy—the difference between interest at 4 per cent. and 5 per cent. amounts to a considerable sum.

The surrender of a policy for cash is not the only way in which it can be dealt with. A policyholder can cease paying premiums and take a paid-up policy for a reduced amount, which becomes a claim in the same circumstances as the original assurance. When whole-life or limited-payment life policies are surrendered in this way the reduced sum assured is paid at death, and in the case of endowment assurances it is paid on reaching the endowment age or at death if previous. This is the usual, but not the necessary, practice, since if desired endowment assurance can be surrendered for a paid-up policy payable at death, and a whole-life policy can be exchanged for paid-up endowment assurance for a smaller amount.

If the paid-up policy acquired by surrender is of the same character as the original assurance, the general plan among life offices, when the surrendered policy was subject to a limited number of premiums, is to grant paid-up assurance for a sum that bears the same proportion to the sum assured under the original policy as the number of premiums actually paid bears to the maximum number of premiums payable. Thus if the original policy was twenty-year endowment assurance or a twenty-payment life policy, and ten premiums out of the twenty have been paid, the new policy, which calls for no further premiums, will be for ten-twentieths of the original sum assured. Almost invariably any bonuses declared on the original policy and not previously taken in cash or in reduction of premium, will be added in full to the paid-up policy. At this point the practice of life offices varies, some companies giving future profits to paid-up policies of this kind, and some offices allowing no further participation in surplus. How great a difference this variation in practice may make to the policyholder we must explain in a subsequent article.

BEETHOVEN—TREE.

By Filson Young.

IT is one of the minor tragedies of family life that the world will never know Mr. Max Beerbohm's true opinion of his illustrious relative. Does his mind maintain from Sir Herbert that remote and airy detachment which keeps his opinion of other men so fresh and independent; or is he moved by family pride to descend from his pinnacle and identify himself with the performer, rejoicing at his triumphs, weeping at his failures? I have given much secret thought to this problem; and at His Majesty's Theatre on Thursday week, in the watches of the entr'actes, I meditated long and deeply upon it, with no more fruitful result than the development of a suspicion that at the bottom of what takes the place of a heart in his anatomy, Mr. Max Beerbohm is a grovelling admirer of the great man; that with the rest of us he bows himself down in the house of Rimmon, submits to the spell of a personality, and reads over the portals of His Majesty's, "Abandon criticism, all ye who enter here". Is it really so? Would he, if his lips were unsealed, speak like others in derision, but privately admire and wonder? Does he sit in the stalls of His Majesty's, sucking the knob of his cane, round-eyed at the pageantry, his ears absorbing the luscious rhetoric, and secretly resolving that he too, in the privacy of his chamber, will practise to hold his limbs just so, and in just such tones of level melancholy will mutter

"Not all the watah in the wrough, wrude sea
Can wash the balm from my anointed head "?

Is it really so? I cannot tell; I am not (as he would say) privy to his thoughts; I can only wonder if even he escapes the common fate.

For Sir Herbert Tree is not so much an actor in the ordinary sense of the word as an arch-personality, a sensation, a spectacle, a great master of the art of importing his own individuality into various and splendid scenes and illustrating them by its light. His medium is less that of intellect than that of vision and illusion—or so at least has it always appeared to me. How often have I too not sat, expectant and wondering, at His Majesty's, watching the changing lights and colours and movements of some great spectacle, lost in the splendours of the Orient or the noble barbarities of the ancient world; and at length, when the sense of incompleteness has grown upon me sufficiently, whispered to my neighbour (fair or otherwise as the case may be), "When does Tree come on?" And how often have I not thrilled, with the rest of the house, at that pause in the action, that opening in the serried ranks of the crowded stage, that hush of expectation which heralds the witching moment; and finally heaved a sigh of relief when, with nicely calculated effect, the centre entrance of the great man has been achieved. The slightly dragging gait, the rolling eyes, the snap of the fingers, the rapid monotonous enunciation with its long vowels and consonant elisions, the air of doing everything casually and naturally but yet with the inimitable stamp of personality—they are all part of a kind of entertainment which cannot be identified with any of the classified forms of drama, but which Sir Herbert Tree has made greatly and successfully his own. Custom does not in the least wither it; his sound is gone out far beyond the circles from which his audiences are drawn; and in the remotest suburbs of the remotest provinces there are young men who have never set eyes on Sir Herbert, but whose claim to social accomplishment rests chiefly on their ability to say, rapidly and gloomily, in reply to an imaginary young lady proposing to begin her stage career by playing the part of Juliet: "Don't bang the doah after you when you go out".

I have said all this chiefly by way of confession, and to read myself and those who think like me a lesson in the injustice of believing that anything new is impossible in a familiar art. I went to hear Sir Herbert Tree's production of "Beethoven" with feelings of frank apprehension. I knew that there was nothing in the known facts of Beethoven's life to make a play about, and that the thing must therefore resolve itself into a mere exhibition of a more or less realistic Beethoven in unholy alliance with the powerful but extremely different personality of Sir Herbert Tree. And at the actual performance my sensations were of so various and acute kinds that I find it very hard to give an accurate record of them. Theoretically there is nothing to be said in justification of putting what amounts to an effigy of a dead great composer on the stage and using his personality and all the emotional aids which his immortal music can render in order to exhibit and glorify the art of an actor. It is likely that I am hypersensitive on the subject of Beethoven, and my view is certainly not representative of the public view; I should be sorry if it were, since the public is not trained to discriminate, and I am; but it is only fair to say that in actual fact the performance is much less an outrage on the feelings than anyone holding my views would probably expect. And this is almost entirely due to the extraordinary fineness of Sir Herbert Tree's impersonation. He deliberately laid aside his own personality in a way in which I certainly have never seen him do before. His "make-up" was, of course, magnificent, and far too much of his success has been attributed to it; his one or two trifling momentary lapses from the character showed to what a very great extent it was an intellectual make-up, which went much deeper than the paint and the powder and the clothes and the wig. In fact it was a completely successful feat of mental transference: Sir Herbert ceased to be Sir Herbert and became the Beethoven of his own imagination.

That it should have been the Beethoven of my imagination or anyone else's would have been too much to expect; but in no way did it shock me, nor did I ever find it an impossible thing to believe that Beethoven might have looked, behaved, spoken, and been like that. But I think that the great artistic absurdity (I use the word quite technically and respectfully) of a performance like this is that it emphasises and brings to light the dead part of a man who is fully and spiritually alive through his music. Of all the things in which men exist here after their physical death there is nothing more living than thought and music; and music being at once a more physical and apparent thing than thought, and a thing more capable of definite personal association with an individual, a musician is really always with us so long as his music is played. When I shut my eyes and hear Beethoven's music it never occurs to me that he is not a contemporary with me in life; but when I open my eyes and see an effigy of the man walking about the stage I have an odd sense of anachronism, and I suddenly realise that Beethoven has been dead a long while. It is an unpleasant, mortuary illusion; the incorruptible has put on corruption, and the immortal has put on mortality; one feels that one has been assisting at a resurrection of the earthly body—than which nothing could be more unpleasant, or, with the spirit soaring about you on its wings of sound, more unnecessary.

The entertainment as arranged by Messieurs René Fauchois and Louis N. Parker is quite effective, and only touches the absurd in the apparition and speeches of the embodied nine symphonies. The music, arranged by Mr. Landon Ronald and performed by an admirable orchestra and chorus, is provided for with a care and expensiveness which is as praiseworthy as it is unusual. I can imagine the whole thing being deeply, overwhelmingly impressive to a certain kind of temperament in which music induces deeply sentimental and emotional moods. And I think it is completely a triumph for Sir Herbert Beerbohm Tree. . . . But I do wonder what Max would have said.

AT DALMARY.

By R. B. Cunninghame Graham.

THE road led out upon an open moor, on which heather and wiry grass strove for the mastery. Here and there mossy patches, on which waved cotton grass, broke the grey surface of the stony waste, and here and there tufts of dwarf willow, showing the silvery backs of their grey leaves, rustled and bent before the wind.

The road, one of those ancient trails on which cattle and ponies were driven in old times down to the Lowland trysts, was now half covered up with grass. It struggled through the moor as if it chose to do so of its own accord, now twisting, for no apparent reason, and again going directly up a hill, just as the ponies and the kyloes must have straggled before the drovers' dogs. It crossed a shallow ford, in which the dark brown, moorland trout darted from stone to stone when the shadow of a passer-by startled them as they poised, their heads up stream, keeping themselves suspended, as it were, by an occasional wavering motion of their tails, just as a hawk hangs hovering in the air.

Beside the stream, a decaying wooden bridge, high pitched and shaky, reminded one that in the winter, the burn, now singing its metallic little song between the stones, brown and pellucid, with bubbles of white foam floating upon its tiny linns or racing down the stream, checking a little in an eddy, where a tuft of heavy ragweed dipped into the flood, was dangerous to cross.

The aromatic scent of the sweet gale came down the breeze, mixed with the acrid smoke of peats. Hair-bells danced in the gentle breeze, and bumble bees hummed noisily as they emerged, weighed down with honey, from the ling.

Across the moor, from farms and shielings, and from the grey and straggling village built on each side of the rough street, in which the living rock cropped up and ran in reefs across the road, came groups of men dressed in black clothes, creased and ill-fitting, with hats, grown brown with years of church-going and with following funerals in the rain; they walked along as if they missed the familiar spade or plough handle to keep them straight, just as a sailor walks uneasily ashore.

As they trudged on they looked professionally on the standing crops, or passed their criticisms on the cattle in the fields. Root crops, they thought, were back, taties not just exactly right, a thocht short in the shaws, and every cow, a wee bit heigh abune the tail, for praise was just as difficult a thing for them to give as blame was easy, for they were all aware their God was jealous, and it did not befit them to appear more generous than He. Hills towered and barred the north, and to the south the moors stretched till they met another range of hills, and all the space between them was filled with a great sea of moss, eyed here and there with dark, black pools on which a growth of water-lilies floated like fairies' boats. A wooded hill, which sloped down to a brawling river, was the fairies' court. Another to the south, steep, rising from the moss, the Hill of the Crown received its name, back in the times of Fingal and of Bran. Gaps in the hills showed where, in times gone by, marauders from the north had come to harry and to slay. The names of every hill, lake, wood, or stream were Gaelic, and the whole country exhaled an air of a romantic past.

In it, the dour, black-coated men, although they thought themselves as much a part and parcel of the land as the grey rocks upon the moor, were strangers; holding their property but on suffrance from the old owners who had named every stone, and left their impress even in the air.

It seemed the actual dwellers acted, as it were, a play, a sort of rough and clownish interlude, upon a stage set out for actors whom the surroundings would have graced.

Still, though they shared the land, just as we all do, by favour of the dead, they had set their mark upon it, running their rough stone walls across the moors, and to the topmost ridges of the hills, planting their four-square, slate-roofed houses in places where a thatched and whitewashed cottage, with red tropeolum growing on the corner of the byre, a plant of mullein springing from a crevice in the wall, and flauchtered feals pegged to the thatch with birchen crockets, or kept down with stones, would have looked just as fitting, as theirs looked out of place. A land in which the older dwellers had replaced the nymphs and hamadryads by the fairies, where, in the soft and ceaseless rain, the landscape wore a look of sadness, that the mist, creeping up on the shoulders of the hills, at times turned menacing, was now delivered over to a race of men who knew no shadows, either in life or in belief. If they believed, they held each letter of "The Book" inspired and would have burned the man who sought to change a comma to a semicolon, and if they had rejected faith as an incumbrance they could do without, denied the very possibility of any god or power but mathematics, holding the world a mere gigantic counting-house in which they sat enthroned. The moaning birches and dark murmuring pines, the shaggy thickets by the streams, and the green hummocks under which tradition held Pictish or Keltic chiefs reposed, the embosomed corries over which the shadows ran, as imperceptibly as lizards run upon a wall, turning the brown hillside to gold, which melted into green as it ran on, until it faded into a pale amethyst, faint and impalpable as is a colour in a dream, seemed to demand a race of men more fitted to its moods than those who walked along the road chatting about the crops. Still it may be that though the outward visible sign was so repellent, the unexpected and interior softness of the black-clothed and tall-hatted men was bred in them by their surroundings, for certainly their hard, material lives, and their black, narrow, anti-human faith could not have given it.

The road led on until on the south side of it a path, worn in the heather and the wiry grass, and winding in and out between the hillocks, crossed here and there by bands of rocks, outcropping, but smoothed down on the edge by the feet of centuries, broke off, not at right angles after the fashion of a modern road, but on the slant, just as a herd of driven animals slants off, stopping at intervals to graze.

The knots of black-clothed men, some followed by their dogs, slowly converged upon the path, and stood a minute talking, passing the time of day, exchanging bits of news and gossip in subdued voices, and mopping vigorously at their brows, oppressed with the unwonted weight of their tall hats.

"We've had a braw back end, McKerrachar", Borland remarked. The worthy he addressed, a gaunt, cadaverous man, so deeply wrinkled that you could fancy in wet weather the rain down the channels in his face, spat in contemplative fashion, rejoining in a non-committal way:

"No just sae bad . . . markets are back a wee." A nod of assent went round the group, and then another interjected:

"I dinna mind sae braw a back end for mony a year; aye, ou aye, I'll no deny markets are very conseederably back."

Having thus magnified his fellow, after the fashion of the stars, he looked a moment with apparent interest at his hat, which he held in his hand, and ventured the remark:

"A sair blow to the widow, Andra's death; he was a good man to her."

No one answering him, he qualified what he had said by adding:

"Aye, sort of middlin'", and glanced round warily, to see if he had overstepped the bounds by the too indiscriminating nature of his praise.

The house towards which the various knots of men were all converging stood at the foot of a green, grassy mound, which looked as if it might have been the tumulus of some prehistoric chief. On it grew several wind-bent ash trees, and within twenty yards or so of the front door of the grey cottage, with its low thatched eaves, there ran a little burn. Two or three mulleins, with flowers still clinging to their dying stalks, on which they stuck like vegetable warts, sprung from the crevices between the stones of the rough byre. A plant or two of ragweed grew on the midden on which a hen was scratching, and out of it a green and oozy rivulet of slush filtered down to the stream. On one side was a garden, without a flower and with a growth of straggling cabbage, gooseberry bushes, and some neglected-looking raspberry canes, as the sole ornaments. In the potato patch a broken spade was stuck into the ground. All round the house some straggling plum trees, with their sour fruit half ripened and their leaves already turning brown, looking as if they had fought hard for life against the blast in the poor, stony soil, gave a peculiar air of desolation, imparting to the place a look as of an oasis just as unfruitful as the waste which stretched on every side. On one side of the door, but drawn a little on the grass, not to obstruct the way, there stood a cart, with a tall, white-faced and white-pasterned horse between the shafts, held by a little boy. Peat smoke curled lazily out of the barrel stuck into the thatch that served as chimney, and cocks and hens scratched in the mud before the door, bees hummed amongst the heather, and once again the groups of men in black struck a discordant note.

Inside the house, upon four wooden chairs was set the coffin of the dead ploughman, cheap and made in haste, just as his life had been lived cheaply and in haste, from the first day that he had stood between the stilts, until the evening when he had loosed his horses from the plough for the last time, his furrow finished and his cheek no more to be exposed to the November rain. Now in the roughly put-together kist he lay, his toil-worn hands crossed on his breast, and with his wrinkled, weather-beaten face, turned waxen and ennobled, set in its frame of wiry whisker, and his scant hair decently brushed forward on his brow. The peats burned brightly in the grate and sent out a white ash which covered everything inside the house, whitening the clothes of the black-coated men who stood about, munching great hunks of cake and slowly swallowing down the "speerits" which the afflicted widow pressed upon them, proud through her tears to say "Tak' it up, Borland", or "It will no hurt ye, Knockinshanock; ye ken there's plenty more".

The white peat ash fell on the coffin lid just as the summer's dust had fallen upon the hair of him who lay inside, and lay upon the polished surface of the thin brass plate, on which were superscribed the dates of the birth and of the death of the deceased, his only titles to the recollection of the race with whom his life had passed. Now and again the widow, snatching a moment from her hospitable cares, brushed off the dust abstractedly with her pocket-handkerchief, just as a man might stop upon the way to execution, to put a chair straight or do any of the trifling actions of which life is composed. As she paused by the coffin the assembled men exchanged that furtive look of sympathy which in the North is the equivalent of the wild wailings, tears and self-abandonment of Southern folk, and perhaps stamps on the heart of the half-shamefaced sympathiser even a deeper line.

When all had drunk their "speerits" and drawn the backs of their rough hands across their mouths and shaken off the crumbs from their black clothes, the minister stood forth. Closing his eyes, he launched into his prayer with needless repetition, but with the feeling which the poor surroundings and the brave struggle against outward grief of the woman sitting by the fire in the old high-backed chair, in which her husband had sat so long, evoked, he dwelt upon man's passage through the world.

Life was a breath, only a little dust, a shadow on the hills. It had pleased the Lord, for reasons of His Own, inscrutable, but against which 'twere impious to rebel, for a brief space to breathe life into the nostrils of this our brother, and here he made a motion of his hand towards the "kist", then to remove him to a better sphere after a spell of toil and trouble here on earth. Still we must not repine, as do the heathen, who gash themselves with knives, having no hope, whereas we who enjoy the blessings of being born to a sure faith in everlasting bliss should look on death as but a preparation for a better life. No doubt this hope consoled the speaker for all the ills humanity endures, for he proceeded to invoke a blessing on the widow, and as he prayed the rain beat on the narrow, bull's-eye window panes. He called upon the Lord to bless her in her basket and her store, and to be with her in her outgoings and incomings, to strengthen her and send her resignation to His will. He finished with the defiance to humanity that must have wrung so many tears of blood from countless hearts, saying the Lord had given and that the Lord had taken, blessed be His Name.

All having thus been done that all our ingenuity can think of on such occasions, four stalwart neighbours, holding their hats in their left hands, hoisted the coffin on to their right shoulders and shuffled to the door. They stooped to let their burden pass beneath the eaves which overhung the entrance, and then emerging, dazed, into the light, their black clothes dusted over with the white ashes from the fire, set down the coffin on the cart. Once more the men gathered into a circle and listened to a prayer, some with their heads bare to the rain, and others with their hats held on the slant to fend it off as it came swirling down the blast. A workman in his ordinary clothes took the tall white-faced horse close by the bit, and, with a jolt which made the kist shift up against the backboard, the cart set out, swaying amongst the ruts, with now and then a wheel running up high upon one side and now and then a jerk upon the trace-hooks, when the horse, cold with his long wait, strained wildly on the chains. The rain had blotted out the hills, the distant village with its rival kirks had disappeared, and the grey sky appeared to touch the surface of the moor. A whitish dew hung on the grass and made the seeded plants appear gigantic in the gloom. Nothing was to be heard except the roaring of the burn and the sharp ringing of the high caulkins of the horse as he struck fire amongst the stones on the steep, rocky road.

Leaning against the doorpost, the widow stood and gazed after the vanishing procession till it had disappeared into the mist, her tears, which she had fought so bravely to keep back, now running down her face.

When the last sound of the cart-wheels and of the horse's feet amongst the stones had vanished into the thick air, she turned away and, sitting down before the fire, began mechanically to smoor the peats and tidy up the hearth.

THE "WASPS" AT CAMBRIDGE.

To the gallery and the stalls, to statesmen, critics, poets, Aristophanes makes separate appeal elsewhere. In the "Wasps" he asks applause from mankind in the bulk, from whole audiences of his own time and whole audiences of later days. And he has the applause he asks. Yet of necessity the pleasures of the "Wasps", spread as they are broadcast, come in less quantity to all than do those of the "Clouds" to a special few, and not many would pronounce the "Wasps" their favourite of the eleven plays. But no Athenian comedy that survives loses less by production on a foreign stage. Something less than Athenian brilliancy can grasp its humour in the bulk, and its fun is not too broad for the self-conscious propriety of these days. No such sudden lyric sweetness as startles the ludicrous Hades of the "Frogs" foredooms the chorus of the "Wasps" to failure; the plot all ages and places can understand, and of local and lost allusions there is a minimum. And all comedies of action gain when materialised upon the stage. There is a very great joy in seeing a solid Philocleon perform real absurdities among living folk. A probable, practical chimney pot with the old man's head coming out of the top is very much funnier than the imagined one that must serve the liveliest reader's turn, and the amateur donkey led out for sale with the guileful old dicast clinging beneath is vastly better than any beast that fancy unaided can construct. It is action too that fills the gaps and completes such splendidly ludicrous scenes as Philocleon's trial of his thieving dog. The household dog has embezzled a cheese, and the old judge, balked of a real prey, arraigns and would condemn the beast, but votes his acquittal by mistake. This is all delightful to read of course, but, if acted well, it is very much better to see on the stage. And the acting at Cambridge was very good. Bdelycleon, the old man's son, who cures him of "Lawcourtitis" and keeps him amused when he feels the loss, was a very delightful young Athenian, more Greek than any in the play, soft-voiced yet clear and vigorous, tall and pleasant and spirited, combining the comic abandonment with no small charm and dignity. But the dear old father was best of all. Whether querulous, tearful, furious, whether dignified, shameless, riotous, in every mood and moment he was Philocleon himself. And when son and father held the stage then the "Wasps" seemed in very deed the "Wasps". In some smaller parts too there was much good comedy. Clever and nearly vulgar enough was Sosias the slave, and the two halves of the delightful Ass became lively if not very lifelike dogs. The Baking Girl was a triumph of paint, and raged as to the manner born, while the Kitchen Utensils, if rather large, succeeded at least in looking their parts. So there was much material for five wild nights of the real Athenian Old Comedy. But much of each night was far from wild, and some went heavily as a funeral goes.

Dr. Vaughan Williams' music at some points comes as near as the limits of its aim permit to congruity with the spirit of the play. But often it falls far short of that. When the chorus has a light lyric piece to sing (there is one such in preface to the Parabasis), slow, gloomy thunders often overwhelm the grace and airiness and smiling pathos that are the beauty of the Greek. And it is a grave error to add anything to that great Parabasis, to break the heavy swinging strength of the long tetrameter lines with elaborate battle-music and a tasteless pantomimic drill. Between those very verses which tell of the fight at Marathon, how under the cloud of arrows the night-bird, the owl of Athens, could show itself as omen of the gods' good-will—Dr. Verrall's touch has made that picture clear—between the verses, disconnecting them, Dr. Williams inserts his posings and wheelings and parades till it seems that before each line is heard we must watch a weary chorus sombrely dance the Lancers through. And that last gorgeous riot in the final scene moves very, very lifelessly, with only half the gallop and swing that even in reading it seems to have. Philocleon gloriously drunk imparts to it all the vigour he can, but for all his efforts it is slow and dull. The chorus is too sedate and the music too uninspiriting. The chorus music throughout is too respectable. Mr. Pole, the leader, has dignity enough to grace the chorus of a tragedy. He wears always a face of gloom, moves through statuesque attitudes (not in themselves unbeautiful), and sings with a pained note in his powerful voice such as a proudly patient martyr might affect. Old men, feeble and fussy, pitiful figures on the whole, but old above all, the dicasts of the "Wasps" should be; at Cambridge some few of the chorus might be old, the leader knows no infirmity. He is upright, dignified, severe; and it must be admitted he is dull. He has trained his band with obvious care and skill, but it has surely been with a wrong end in view. Strange that the unequalled Lady Farringford of the A.D.C. should impart dullness and pomp into the most frankly comic of all comedies. Surely there is not dullness in Aristophanes. All manner of other faults he has, but from first to last he is madly gay. Did not Heine speak of that "Weltvernichtungsidee" for which no other language could find a word? And what is left of Aristophanes if that be hid? Mr. Butler and Mr. Robertson (son and father), the slave from Christ's and the animals from Trinity, these all worked hard and worked understandingly. Yet somehow through all the Cambridge play there seemed lacking the true spirit of the Old Comedy, that riotous, uproarious, divine incontinence of laughter which has shaken only Rabelais and the poet of the "Wasps".

THE CONSTANT Π.

LOOKING, the other day, through a row of school and college prize-books, the spolia opima of a friend, we saw, by the inscriptions, that most of them were for proficiency in mathematics. Not associating him with such studies, we displayed some little surprise.

"You did not think", he said, "that Master Silence was a man of this mettle? Very likely not. Yet I suppose he was—once. Of course a boy could pass with credit, even with honour, the tests of our boyhood and know very little of mathematics. But my tutors all praised me for having a mathematical head, an eye for an equation, and the like. They prophesied for me a Senior Wrangler's place and the career of a Newton. I got neither; why, I scarcely know, for certainly problems over which fellows with twice my brains despaired came easy to me. But the way of life which seemed the best for me to follow had no use for mathematics. Enough arithmetic to check my bankers' book (when I got one) and enough geometry to lay out a rose-garden is all I have ever needed. Experience has convinced me that the bankers' clerk may be safely trusted to do one, and a fairly intelligent gardener the other, of these things. I often wonder whether Peterborough formed Pope's Quincunx on correct principles. I wonder, more, that the many accusations of the public school and university 'curriculum', which I read, confine themselves to abusing the dead languages, especially 'compulsory Greek', and never mention mathematics as a waste of time. They may be more usefully taught now than they were in my day. As far as 'fruit', as Bacon called it, goes, I should have done better if I had devoted myself to Greek. Almost everything that is worth reading was written in Greek, and a great part of mathematics, as the word was understood forty years ago, bears no discernible relation to life. Two and two only make four in arithmetic, not in fact. You cannot find two oak leaves exactly similar, and if you did find two pairs exactly agreeing you would still have distinct leaves, not an homogeneous body of four, in the mathematical sense of that word. Two sides of a triangle are only mathematically greater than the third; it is a truism that often the longest way round is the shortest way home. And if in a barefoot hunt for the matches you tread on a tintack you will find that its point has considerable parts and an excruciating magnitude. These things are only axioms in vacuo, and Nature abhors a vacuum.

"Of mathematics as a study, pursued as its own end, I quite understand the fascination. There is a neatness about it, a compact certainty, which is very attractive. Young says 'An undevout astronomer is mad', and the Autocrat takes leave to question that dictum. But, though not perhaps quite in the sense that Young intended, it contains a certain truth. Of a surety a man is mad who espouses astronomy or any other science unless he thoroughly believes in it, is willing to devote himself to it, and, so, may be called 'devout'. I suppose I was not devout. I saw or thought I saw that many mathematical operations were only ingenious exercises of wit: that, given the premises, the result followed. The maker of a Jigsaw puzzle may be trusted to put it together. To spend a life doing so would, I thought, pall. The mathematicians, like Tom Thumb the great, 'made the giants first and then they killed 'em'. I think", he said, and smiled meditatively at the fire, "that the best thing I got out of mathematics was a firm conviction of the existence of π, the constant π."

Π is the ratio of circumference to diameter in a circle, the proportion one bears to the other. As circles differ from each other only in size, it is evident that π is always the same. A bishop, perhaps even an archbishop, could see that. Therefore is he "the constant π", "constant" not being a mere epithet, like the "judicious" Hooker or the "venerable" Bede, but the note of his existence. Π is immutable. Constat.

But π is also indefinable. No one can tell you what he is. He straddles quite over the whole way of the mathematician, as Apollyon did across the path of Christian, with straight legs and squared shoulders, and says "No! friend. Weigh the sun by all means, and much good may it do you. Calculate the orbits of comets, so that you can foretell their arrival to a minute. Me you shall not measure. There are limits. It is good for a man that there should be some things he doesn't know. I, Π, am one of those things. I will, with (or without) your leave, remain to you the unknown quantity, the Constant Π".

Of course, they have got very nearly to a knowledge of him. Order a wheel of a certain circumference, and the maker of it will use π in the making. But wheels are not mathematical circles, they are only rather round. Mathematicians have worked him out to an incredible number of decimals, but, perceiving that he would not "come out", have desisted, and are now, for the most part, resting in asylums squaring the circle. A miss of the million-millionth part of an inch is, to a mathematician, as bad as a mile. "'I've got within a single letter, brother Toby,' cried my father, 'of Erasmus his mystic meaning.' 'You are near enough, brother,' replied my uncle, 'in all conscience.' 'Pshaw!' cried my father, scratching on, 'I might as well be seven miles off.'"

Π is an Uitlander, not to say an undesirable alien, in the neatly kept country of geometric demonstrations and exact arithmetic. He belongs, in fact, to a wider realm than the mathematic, to pure metaphysic, and it was just like him to intrude among the figures and make himself objectionable by declining to submit to their laws. But, in his own place, π the constant, the incalculable factor, seems, as our friend said, to count. One who should know, for he has probably played more games of chess than any other man living, told us that there was a lot of luck in chess, and explained the seeming paradox quite easily and convincingly. On the other hand, a certain school rebukes the use of the words " luck " and " chance ". " You know ", they say, " that there can be no such thing." Well—there is, emphatically, something. And, while the formalist holds it profane to name that something " luck ", others feel it blasphemous to attribute the spoiling of a picnic to a special—and spiteful—providence.

" Peace, coxcombs, peace ! and both agree "

to call it π, the constant π.

Π, the intruder among the figures, seems to us a powerful weapon to use against the man who professes to believe in nothing that he cannot explain. He places great reliance on " exact science ". As " animal capax rationis " he cannot deny that, there, π exists—very much in his way. Nor can he assert that he knows what π is. Wrought out to eighty-seven places of decimals, π is still incomplete, not the real obvious π.

An ancient sage figured the Infinite as a circle whose centre was everywhere and circumference nowhere. To some this is nonsense : in others it excites " a vibration of the chords in the neighbourhood of the brain ". Π is the same in that tremendous circle as he is in the compass of a threepenny-bit. And, if we do not know him exactly, still we have him laboriously and, let us hope, correctly figured out to eighty-seven places of decimals, which ought to be near enough for anyone but a mathematician.

THE WIND.

THIS afternoon the sunlight paints upon the grimed brick wall the sharp black shadows of the bare hollyhock stems. Every leaf upon the pathway and the lawn shines brown and gold bronze or keenest yellow. The raw still air speaks of frost and the dropping of the few lingering leaves standing now for their moment of lonely individuality opaque and dry against the shimmering blue or showing, all sharp form and colour, on the background made by the white-washed walls of the little colony of studios across the way.

Once more the clumped trimmed bushes, the barberry and holly, the box and privet, the laurel and the yew, begin their monotonous supremacy, bearing—at this moment when the riches of autumn are told, and the memory of the past blossoming and the love of the blossoming that is to come are at their utmost gnawing intensity—but little immediate relief, giving, however, presently in return for a measure of patient acceptance a rewarding vision of the part they still may play. They remind you that they may beguile, draping their too perpetual faces in the soft shroudings of the urban winter, that they will wear the jewels of the morning, and perhaps, before they are again thrust aside, they will make the unwearied heart dance as they stand transformed beneath the burden of the snow. But, more than all these things, they tell how when they stand out there among their silent neighbours you will bless them for rendering up the voice of even the gentlest of the raindrops.

And on nights when the wind is still, when there is no rain to mitigate the sound of the ceaseless going to and fro, and sleep stands far off, the thought of them motionless beneath your window will be as a cup of quiet in your need, and sometimes, draining it, you may go away into memory, far and deep. The half-light which finds its relentless way through the window draperies to beat upon your closed eyelids will be forgotten, and you will be away—away in the rich depth of the long November night in the open country.

Darkness envelops you, obliterating the walls of your chamber, immense and formless. Your wide-flung, curtainless window throws not the faintest glimmer—for the sky hangs low over the sleeping fields. Nothing stirs. Your days have dropped and dropped since high summer to this serenest of all the sweetness of the year, this full moment between memory and promise. . . . You waken on such a night to find that you have been carried by dreamless slumber to the heart of tranquillity, surprising consciousness at its richest brimming. . . .

Suddenly in the stillness there sounds away across the marshes a little wailing voice. Five clear dropping notes it utters, and ceases. And then you know what has brought you from the depths. You wait, scarcely breathing. There is a long silence. Then again the little sound breaks, high and thin, and threadlike and very far away. So clear it is, out there, and intimate, that it might be speaking from your garden space or rising from the deep furrows of the stubble field beyond. But you know that it has come out of the sea and is wandering along the distant, desolate shore. And as you turn to give yourself the better to your listening, joy laughs at the thought of the clear countryside, nothing between you and the sound but the slope of naked fields and the wide marsh beyond. You lie listening. . . . There it is. . . . It has left the foreshore and is roaming along the margin of the marshes, creeping in and out among the sedges, complaining.

Presently you seem to see, as you hear it rise from whispering to a querulous shrillness, the rows of huddled willows, black and crouching, straggling along the dykes. You feel the conflict, the rattling of the scanty slender leaves, the straining of the maimed twig-like branches, the trouble of the scattered pools waiting since the falling of the autumn rains for the frost to bring them sleep.

Gathering strength like a wave, voices are sweeping up and up over the land now, borne on a wide undertone, shouting and moaning in long-drawn ululation, rising and falling, breaking and dying down to a low sobbing.

Surging onwards they have reached the flat dew-drenched fields. The dense hedgerows are answering with deep singing. Across the way the ever-green oak quivers under the threatening breath, harp-like in all its burdened branches. For a moment the stillness falls again, and then the tumult rushes forward in full strength, wild from the sea, gigantic, sweeping headlong until, with rapid blows and yells and mighty shaking, it seizes your dwelling and encircles it with a roaring, fierce, flamelike. In at your window, down your wide chimney it rushes. You are at the heart of the uproar. The wind has found its prey upon the bare hillside.

CORRESPONDENCE.

THE MAN SHAKESPEARE.

To the Editor of the SATURDAY REVIEW.

Hotel Cecil, London W.C.,

30 November 1909.

SIR,—My book " The Man Shakespeare and his Tragic Life-Story " has been uncommonly lucky : it has found amid the horde of journalistic scribes three or four critics, judges both honest and competent, among whom must be reckoned the writer of the review which appeared in the SATURDAY. It is because I recognise his competence and his interest in the subject that I would like to examine part of his criticism. He says :

" We already have warned our readers that there is no crudeness in Mr. Harris' actual exposition of his theories. By the time he is ready to give these theories full play he has insidiously wound himself into us and fired us with the spirit of the game. Exempt from such fascination, we should smile (for example) at his dismissal of Shakespeare's later virginal figures, as shadows of pure girlhood, pathetically chosen in reaction from the passionate and froward creature who had been his bane. No need to prove for us that Miranda, Perdita, and the rest are abstractions compared with Cleopatra. Of course they are. To be abstract is the fate of all virgins in drama."

Here the critic argues like a political gladiator whose

object is rhetorical triumph. The whole contention is mere word-fence. Is Tourgenief's Marianna an abstraction or at least as vital and as passionately differenced as any of his more experienced women? To go no further than Shakespeare: Is Juliet an abstraction in the sense that Miranda is an abstraction, or is it the fate of Portia to be abstract as Marina is abstract?

Again, when I attempt to outline and fix Shakespeare's limitations as an artist, your critic boldly sweeps away my lines:

"We think he makes too much of Shakespeare's alleged 'snobbery' and political hatred of the masses, of his failure to depict a middle-class puritan with sympathy, and of the fact that he nowhere paints a reformer. No artist, we believe, has ever triumphed in a sympathetic creation of demagogue, burgess, or visionary."

This last sentence is somewhat unfair: I have given twenty proofs of Shakespeare's "snobbery", stronger than his failure to depict a demagogue; a hundred proofs of his dislike of the middle classes, stronger than his failure to depict a burgess or a visionary; but, taking such special pleading as it stands, is it true to say that "these types themselves have defied art, perhaps will always defy it"? There are many sympathetic and masterly studies of the demagogue in literature, from Felix Holt to Bazarof; there are dozens of successful and sympathetic studies of burgesses: the SATURDAY critic must have heard of the immortal Birotteau and his assistant or of Mr. Arnold Bennett's shopkeeper in "The Old Wives' Tale", and as for visionaries they positively swarm in every literature, from Greatheart to Sylvestre Bonnard and the hero of "Resurrection".

Again your critic argues:

"Concede again that the broad change in Shakespeare's dramatic outlook—that darkening sky and beckoning of sinister shapes which ushers in his great tragic period—implies some dreadful ripening in his personal experience, such as comes to most middle-aged men who can feel. Must we go on to furnish his inner life with erotic madness deduced from Troilus or speeches in Lear, with frantic jealousy from Othello, with misanthropic despair from Timon?"

This criticism is specious special pleading. I do not deduce "erotic madness from Troilus or speeches in Lear" alone or even chiefly. I have proved that extraordinary sensuality is a characteristic of all those characters whom I regard as impersonations of Shakespeare himself. The Duke in "Twelfth Night" wants a surfeit of passion that the appetite may sicken and so die. Jaques, too, is one of Shakespeare's most characteristic figures; lewdness has nothing to do with his character, why is it attributed to him? He is, as I have shown, an alter ego of Shakespeare and another impersonation is the Duke in "Measure for Measure", who wishes to punish lewdness: why does Lucio accuse him of lewdness; why is Henry V. accused of lewdness by Poins; why does Ophelia talk lewdly and Juliet and Portia, and, above all, why after the unbounded sensuality of "Hamlet", "Othello", "Lear", "Antony and Cleopatra", and "Timon" is there no sensuality, no suggestive talk in his latest romances, in "The Winter's Tale", in "Cymbeline" or "The Tempest"? Moreover, his sonnets show extravagant sensuality, and all we know of his life bears out this obvious deduction from his works.

Your critic, Sir, has come some way with me and has shown himself very sympathetic and appreciative. He will not take it in bad part that I seek to defend my book from undeserved blame. Already the baser representatives of the nonconformist conscience in the press have not scrupled to impute to me the "erotic mania" which I lay to Shakespeare's charge at a certain definite crisis in his life. But from a critic of the SATURDAY I expect scrupulous fair play, with all the rigour of the game; so when he appears to fail, I protest; the protest is a token of my respect for him.

Yours faithfully,

FRANK HARRIS.

THE SHORT STORY.

To the Editor of the SATURDAY REVIEW.

SIR,—Mr. Cunninghame Graham cites with indignation the following sentence from a review: "Mr. Harris' own tale 'Sonia' comes as near as anything we know, but it is only a short story". The word "only" is understood by Mr. Graham to imply an insular indifference to the short story as a form of artistic expression. May I say that nothing was more remote from the intention of the writer?

The point out of which the sentence arose was this, that artists in general have not triumphed in the sympathetic delineation of demagogue, burgess, or visionary. The tale "Sonia" was allowed to be successful in such delineation; and the qualification—"but it is only a short story"—was added by way of suggesting that in a long story, which involves a more sustained and detailed psychology, the same success would be unlikely. Mr. Graham himself supplies just this explanation when he says "it is precisely because 'Sonia' is not a long-drawn-out novel that Mr. Harris has succeeded in placing before us a picture".

To the writer, personally, it happens that no form of art offers more pleasure than that of the short story. None would more readily admit the supreme quality of which that form is capable, or join more cordially in admiration of the instances to which Mr. Graham refers. Indeed, one might justly add Mr. Graham's own work to the list. Nevertheless, while it is true that the short story can achieve effects impossible in any other form, this fact cuts both ways. The great short-story writer has had to overcome many difficulties which do not exist for the novelist, but it is equally certain that he has escaped, by virtue of his form, some difficulties which the novelist is compelled to face. To have captured our sympathetic understanding for the revolutionary in the white heat of a condensed action is a feat less remarkable (from the standpoint of the passage questioned) than to sustain that sympathy in the elaborate structure and drier light of a long novel. Compare "Sonia" itself with "The Bomb", a novel by the same author on a similar theme. That the longer story has power in dealing with the anarchic type is unquestionable, but its force in this respect lies really in one or two scenes, virtually handled in the short-story manner, which seem to lose rather than gain by the length of the whole tale in which they are embedded.

That the short story is now supplanting the novel may be true. But this does not affect the point made, namely, that triumphantly complete portraiture of a visionary under the conditions of a long novel would be more surprising, and would more effectually help to dispel one's general feeling that the visionary type "defies art", than an equally triumphant sketch within the limits of the short-story form. This, and nothing else, was intended by the little word "only" which has so excited Mr. Graham's ire.

I imagine that the warmest admirers and even the best modern exponents of the short-story form will hardly carry enthusiasm to the point of disclaiming for it all limitations while they emphasise its peculiar merits. They cannot eat their cake and have it.

I am yours faithfully,

THE REVIEWER.

A VIGOROUS DENIAL.

To the Editor of the SATURDAY REVIEW.

37 York Place, Perth, 27 November 1909.

SIR,—Your notice of the Keats reprint in the Oxford Pocket Series contains these words: "It is a melancholy thing to read the publishers' apology for printing the unfinished 'Hyperion': 'The poem was intended to have been of equal length with "Endymion", but the reception given to that work discouraged the author from proceeding'". I wish that in justice to Keats you would also print this paragraph from Mr. H. Buxton Forman's much-annotated edition: "In a copy [of the poems published in 1820] which recently came into the hands of Canon Ainger, Keats has drawn his pen through and through this advertisement, writing at the head, 'I had no part in this; I was ill at the time'. The statement about 'Endymion' he has bracketed off from the rest; and beneath it he has written 'This is a lie'".

It dies hard, the foolish belief that Keats was a sentimental weakling chilled and killed by a rude blast of ridicule. He left "Hyperion" unfinished because he was dissatisfied with it.

I am yours faithfully,
A. Stevenson Nicol.

VEGETARIANISM IN INDIA.

To the Editor of the Saturday Review.

Civil Lines, Sitapur, India,
20 October 1909.

Sir,—It is indeed venturesome on my part to enter into a discussion which is going on among your English correspondents respecting the utility of animal food. Among other conflicting arguments there is one which is of supreme importance, and the truth of which can be known simply by observation without plunging into technical disputations about proteid and uric acid. It is the question of physical strength. As a tree can be known by its fruits so a cause can be determined by its effects. If from our experience we find the herbivorous or frugivorous nations physically superior to the carnivorous ones we should unhesitatingly pass judgment in favour of "food reform". Now I find that India is often pointed out as a country where the common diet is vegetables; and it is sometimes alleged by the food reformers that the strongest Indians are found to subsist on a pure vegetable diet. But this statement is altogether groundless, and is put forward only by those who have little knowledge of Indian dietary. The fact is that meat forms a part of the diet of all the Indian communities that can really boast of their physical strength. The gallant Rajputs, the sturdy Patháns, the valiant Sikhs—all of whom represent the warlike classes of India—are well-known flesh-eaters. The only abstainers are the Jains and a section of the Arya Samájists. But these communities have never been known to exhibit any sort of physical superiority over the flesh-eaters. They have never produced a warrior. Few of them ever aspire to be admitted into the ranks of the Indian Army, which is entirely composed of the flesh-eating classes named above.

As regards the effect of flesh diet on the brain, it is sufficient to remark that the most intellectual classes of India are, again, found to be flesh-eaters. The Pársis, the Bengalis, the Kashmiries, the Kaesths, all of them partake more or less of animal food. It remains to be added that the entire Mussulman community of India—forming a population of about sixty millions—the intellectual and physical activities of which are too well known to be repeated here, is, with only a few exceptions, a flesh-eating community.

This brief note will, I hope, remove the misconception of your English correspondents about the diet of Indians, and India will not be pointed out in future to show the favourable effects of vegetarianism on the physical constitution.

I am yours faithfully,
Abdul Majid.

REFORM IN CHINA.

To the Editor of The Saturday Review.

The University, Sheffield,
15 November 1909.

Sir,—After having read the interesting note in your journal of 6 November on Mr. Chirol's speech at the China Association, I could not resist writing to you a few lines, giving you my own opinion.

It was stated that "the Chinese are no doubt taking in new ideas, but this seems rather to stimulate anti-foreign feelings". I think that an impartial judge with a knowledge of the matter would discern that this resentment running through Chinese policy was a not unnatural result of the one-sided and anti-Chinese interventions which have been made. For instance, in the recent so-called "Chinese Railway Imbroglio", which has been stigmatised as anti-foreign, there was ample justification for the suspicions of the Chinese people that these railway concessions to foreigners would turn out to be detrimental to native interests. The Chinese have realised the advantages of railway development, but they fear to grant any more concessions. When reflection reveals to them the real nature of the aggrandising process devised by foreign Powers, they can only see that the obtaining of railway concessions is a new way of getting foothold in the country. The Chinese have been awakened to a sense of the dangers which threaten their national existence, and will stand firm against encroachment. "To ensure her own national existence", said the Rev. E. W. Thwing, "she must more strongly hold to the principle of 'China for the Chinese'." For this new movement China has been severely criticised, especially by European syndicates. But the so-called anti-foreign feeling in China can only be designated as a movement of resistance to foreign aggression. It would be juster to speak of the rise of national spirit or the awakening of national consciousness than to talk of anti-foreign feeling.

It was also stated in the note that "meantime there is very little evidence of real internal reform in China". Of course we could not compare China with this country; but her reform during the last few years has not been merely a paper one. Allow me to quote a few words from Sir Robert Hart on the present condition of China. He said: "China is changing in every quarter; education of the Western kind is welcome; railroads are increasing their mileage; the telegraph is at work everywhere; steamers on the coast and on the inner waters are increasing in numbers; newspapers are being established at all important points; post-offices are transmitting mail matter all over the country. . . . With such a country and such a people—a country rich in undeveloped resources and a people possessed of every good quality—the future before the Empire cannot be other than great. But the future will depend much on to-day, and it is to be hoped that her foreign relations will go on improving, and she will only have kindness to remember, and neither wrongs to right nor grudges to pay off".

But in this fighting world right must be supported by might. What can China do? Her position to-day in relation to other Powers is most difficult. Japan was allowed in the main to fight out her own battles for herself. There was no complicated network of foreign interests, no burden of foreign indebtedness to hamper her freedom of action. There were no foreign Powers watching for every opportunity to further their political or territorial ambition at her expense. But China, being very rich in natural resources, has naturally drawn the attention of the whole world. She is entirely by herself and single-handed. She has her vast Empire to look after, and so she needs every help possible, great tact and careful diplomacy to bring herself through this present critical period of her history. However, it is the hope of all well-wishers of China that the day is not far distant when she will be raised to the level of her neighbours and remain no longer a tempting bait to greedy Powers. China's advent to the position of a world Power will be a great benefit to the rest of the world in civilisation, in wealth, and above all in restoring the peace of the world and in maintaining it for the betterment of mankind.

I am, Sir, yours truly,
Cheng-chang Lu.

INDIANS IN THE TRANSVAAL.

To the Editor of the Saturday Review.

5 Pump Court, Temple E.C.,
30 November 1909.

Sir,—Will you, with your usual courtesy, permit me to express my appreciation of the reference in your issue of the 20th to the struggle for elementary civic rights of our Indian fellow-subjects in the Transvaal Colony?

The Transvaal British Indians are pursuing their campaign by adopting a course which is so thoroughly characterised by moderation, self-restraint and good sense that it alone, apart from considerations of justice, imperial policy or wider expediency, should justify their claim to treatment as civilised citizens of the Empire to all whose eyes are not blinded by racial or colour prejudice. The issue between the Transvaal Government and its small British Indian population of some thirteen thousand lawfully domiciled residents has been reduced to a simple question of, firstly, the removal of legislation in regard to those on the spot, which is resented because it imposes requirements implying that they are a body of criminals (the Registration Law is taken exception to on these grounds, and the pronouncements that preceded its enactment afford strong justification for this view); and secondly, an amendment of the Immigration Law, which, read together with the Registration Law, imposes for the first time in imperial legislation complete exclusion upon would-be Indian immigrants *because of their race and colour.*

Mr. Gandhi, the Indian leader, has shown General Smuts a method whereby the possibility of any further immigration into the Transvaal can be obviated by administrative means without the infliction of a statutory insult such as the existing law constitutes in respect of the whole three hundred millions of India; but, with an airy disregard of imperial considerations, General Smuts prefers his own parochial methods, careless of the far-reaching consequences his conduct cannot but have upon the peace and the integrity of the Empire. That the Colonial Secretariat might have avoided what has now become dangerously like an impasse is indisputable, but, having allowed the opportunity to slip, only heroic measures can now retrieve the lost ground. The outlook is anything but happy. I am assured that the Transvaal Indians will pursue their passive-resistance campaign to the very death. India is united in a feeling of deep resentment against the insult it feels has been inflicted with the tacit assent of the Imperial Government, and I doubt not that when the people of this country understand the cruel injustice and the breach of trust that have been perpetrated in their name they will insist upon a righting of the wrong.

Thanking you in anticipation,

I am etc.,

L. W. Ritch

(Hon. Sec., South Africa British Indian Committee).

THE BANKING QUESTION.

To the Editor of the Saturday Review.

London, 29 November 1909.

Sir,—I read with much interest Mr. Meulen's letter on the above subject in your issue of the 20th inst. In these days when the question of unemployment is so urgently before us it is important that no part of our present machinery should escape examination; and amongst other things we need to be assured that the banking system that now obtains enables the national resources to be used with as much efficiency as is consistent with practical safety and with the general social conditions that prevail.

Generally speaking, intelligently organised labour should always be capable of working at a profit, and it undoubtedly is a deplorable thing that we should not be able to provide employment for capable and willing labour. We have the labour and, it is to be presumed, the ability intelligently to organise it. What we seem to lack is adequate control of capital—of the means, that is to say, to support labour during the process of fresh production. The means is provided somehow—more or less. The unemployed contrive to live—pitiably it may be, but still to live—at the expense of the rates or of public and private charity. Whether, however, the necessary control of capital could be brought about, whether the capital which now is frittered away could be made efficient and effectual by the issue of bankers' credit, as Mr. Meulen suggests, is open to some doubt. But at least the subject deserves careful consideration.

One very important objection presents itself at once: there can be no reasonable doubt that the issue of credit must tend to raise prices. For the effect of such an issue would obviously be to increase the demand for commodities. This increased demand would probably stimulate and in part be met by increased production at home; but in part also it would be met by imports from abroad. Thus we might have a time of apparent prosperity, for which we should pay, in part at least, by an efflux of gold.

Credit is rendered possible only by surplus production in the past. It is limited not by future but by actual production, past and present. When we issue credit we give, in effect, to a number of people the means to subsist for a certain time, and, it may be, to produce, at the expense of the community. It is no use, for example, issuing credit notes entitling the bearer, say, to a quartern loaf if the quartern loaves in existence are fewer than the credit notes. And since credit is thus limited, it follows that it will command a price—which we term interest—a price which will fluctuate, of course, accordingly as free capital—that is, free access to the world's actual production—is plentiful or otherwise.

The available savings of the world tend to be represented by gold, because no doubt gold has such obvious advantages and is so universally acceptable. It is not only a token of work done; it is also a thing desired of man. And by the fusion of these two qualities it becomes a token of work done that men needed or desired done. It is conceivable that a paper note might be a satisfactory enough token of work done, but unless it were restricted so as to represent only such work done as men desired or needed done, it would certainly depreciate. And paper so restricted would be subject to the same shortages as gold.

The writer on this subject in your issue of the 27th complains that the flow of gold abroad, from whatever cause, restricts credit at home. It is undoubtedly unfortunate that a panic in America or development in Egypt should make credit more difficult to obtain in this country. But it is not the fault of gold or of our use of it. If I hold an instrument entitling me to support a man or a number of men for a given time, whether that instrument be a piece of coined gold or a paper certificate of credit, I cannot use that instrument both in America or Egypt and in this country. I cannot eat my cake and have it. The available savings of the world—the fluid savings, as it were—are limited, and can be used only once by the same holder. And if they go abroad, for any reason whatsoever, they are withdrawn for the time being from use in this country.

To me, therefore, the issue of bankers' credit seems an expedient of doubtful value. But the subject is one of considerable difficulty, and it is to be hoped that the courage of the Saturday Review in thus ventilating the question will induce our authorities in banking to justify the present system.

Yours faithfully,

W. P. Baines.

MR. CAMERON CORBETT'S POSITION.

To the Editor of the Saturday Review.

London, 30 November 1909.

Sir,—Mr. Cameron Corbett's latest performance is to intervene in the impending contest in the Tradeston Division by issuing postcards to the electors asking them to say whether or not he ought to come forward as the Liberal candidate at the General Election, and this, too, after the local Conservative and Unionist and Radical Association respectively had selected its own candidate. This extraordinary behaviour has aroused the indignation of the selected Radical candidate, who has addressed a letter of protest on the subject to the local daily paper. It is obvious, of course, that if he does stand the result will be to increase considerably the majority the Unionist candidate is certain to have. This is the greatest service Mr. Cameron Corbett has ever rendered to the electors, whom he has deceived and whose trust he has betrayed, and to the party which he has deserted.

I am yours faithfully,
PARTY LOYALTY.

A CAMBRIDGE FEAST.

To the Editor of the SATURDAY REVIEW.

London, 1 December 1909.

SIR,—One had supposed that the eating of small song-birds was a custom confined to plutocrats and the "smart set" which in older times would not have found its way into English society. The custom comes, as we all know, from the Continent; the poverty of the peasant is held to account for it, together with the soullessness of the uneducated Roman Catholic, but others say that it is favoured at the hotels for the benefit of the rich and Protestant English traveller.

Now we learn that the grave and reverend dons of Cambridge are anxious to be known as lark-eaters. At a feast at a certain Cambridge hall last week there appeared on the menu, in French as vile as the dish, "Mauviettes Farcées (sic) en Nids à la Financière". That is to say, larks presented in their little nests, to tickle the palates of the learned guests between turtle soup and turkey. A pretty idea, no doubt, the cook thought; as pretty as that of the gasping bird with open beak that looks "so natural" on a woman's hat.

There is no Professor of Poetry at Cambridge, otherwise one might bid these dining dons read of the skylark as sung by poets from Shakespeare to Alfred Austin. And while to Martin Luther the humble sparrow was his "doctor of divinity", and to S. Francis the small birds were his "little sisters", the modern doctor of divinity only cares for the "ethereal minstrel, pilgrim of the sky", as a tit-bit for a big dinner.

I am, Sir, your obedient servant,
E. G.

TOO MUCH CLEVERNESS.

To the Editor of the SATURDAY REVIEW.

65 University Road, Belfast,
29 November 1909.

SIR,—In speculating upon the chances that the plays of the late Oscar Wilde have of securing that immortality which is obviously to be the portion of some of his other works your critic complained that the plays were too brilliant—that is to say that the cleverness of the conversation became tedious. I am sorry he did that. For I am quite sure that the SATURDAY REVIEW critics are sufficiently clever themselves to be free from that most unpleasing jealousy which we expect from mediocrity; and for that very reason it seems quite a pity that one of their number should suggest that immortality will be impossible in the case of what seem to be the most brilliant prose plays in the English language.

There is nothing quite so severe as the test of immortality: we expect so much in a work that cannot die. And so, for Wilde's sake, it might be better if his plays continued to live for ever without bearing any critical trade-mark. The reason why there are so few epigrams in novels and plays is that the people who write novels and plays cannot invent epigrams. Clever conversation is only written by clever people; and it has become so unusual to expect it that critics either get so great a shock that they write no reviews at all or they fail to recognise the cleverness when they see it.

Yours etc.,
HERBERT PYM.

REVIEWS.

THACKERAY THE MAN.

"William Makepeace Thackeray." By Lewis Melville. London: Lane. 1909. 25s.

THACKERAY was late in being famous. He was not as a young man driven to letters by necessity; and, when necessity came, he was impelled, not directly into letters, but in another direction (witness the illustrations to "Vanity Fair"). Then finally, when he did decide to give to literature his best endeavour, he wrote sporadically under many pseudonyms. Michael Angelo Titmarsh, Yellowplush, Major Gahagan, FitzBoodle, Miss Tickletoby, were all more or less familiar to the reading public; but only a few were aware that these and other motley persons were all united in Mr. Thackeray. Moreover, there was a reason more fundamental than these why Thackeray's reputation hung fire. His greater work was the product of ripe observation. It is difficult to believe that Thackeray could have written "Vanity Fair" earlier than he did.

Against Thackeray and his work two charges have been made time and again. Both are equally untrue. Some say that he was a cynic; others that he was a sentimentalist. Thackeray was neither. He was a man of uncommonly fine sensibility. The woes and the humours of life were always very near to him and very real. With this sensibility went an extraordinary power of detachment, and the two things together made Thackeray a great humourist. Feeling did not obscure judgment. It invested judgment with a large humanity, that no mere adding-up of two and two can achieve. At the same moment he was sympathetic and critical. This looks very like a definition of the man of humour.

Look at Thackeray for a moment as editor of the "Cornhill"; not because it is necessary to say any more about these two charges, but because Thackeray as editor of the "Cornhill" makes a most delightful figure. It gave Thackeray a bad night to refuse a manuscript, and he had to refuse them by the gross. Sentimental! cries someone. Let that someone produce evidence that Thackeray ever printed one of those manuscripts that he ought not to have printed. Let that someone also read Thackeray's own account of the letters that made him hate the postman—the letters written by poor, good, hardworked, would-be contributors with sick mothers and dependent families. "Day and night that sad voice is crying out for help. Thrice it appealed to me yesterday. Twice this morning it cried to me, and I have no doubt when I go to get my hat I shall find it, with its piteous fate and its pale family about it, waiting for me in the hall." Thackeray could write this. Yet he was a good editor. Put the two things together; and then collate the following passage written when Thackeray was resigning, where the vein is a lighter one: "To say No has often cost me a morning's peace and a day's work. I tremble recenti metu. Oh, those hours of madness spent in searching for Louisa's lost lines to her dead Piping Bullfinch, for Nhoj Senoj's mislaid essay! I tell them for the last time the (late) Editor will not be responsible for rejected communications, and herewith send off the Chair and the great 'Cornhill' Magazine Tin-box with its load of care." Taking it that this disposes of even the ghost of one charge, let us have a last look at the other. Thackeray saw two tubs of oysters outside a shop. One lot was labelled a shilling, the other fifteenpence. "How these", he murmured, looking at the cheaper, "must hate the others!" Those who say that Thackeray was a cynic will see in this a forced sneer at human weakness. We do not see it like that. Thackeray was not sneering at humanity. He was voicing a deep sympathy with the less distinguished.

Thackeray, the man, has always been something of an enigma. The reason seems to be that he was a shy man. He appears to have been one of those who keep within themselves a corner secluded from the world. However intimate the friendship, however seeming frank the good fellowship, there is always one last ring-fence that few may break down. There is about Thackeray, through all his varying moods of surliness or loving-kindness, through all his flashes of grim humour or pitiless insight, a suggestion of a still sanctuary kept inviolate. He seems to have been as jealous for the seclusion he needed for his inner self as he was often boisterous in his expression of the superficial mood that possessed him. The real Thackeray will never be known; for the inquirer with eyes to see behind the veil will not be the one to tear it aside for a spectacle.

The Thackeray the world knew was himself a fascinating figure. A man who combined the humour of ripe judgment with a boyish zest in life was likely to charm and dominate and mystify his generation. Viewed from outside, he appeared, partly on account of that very shyness that hid the real man, as a bundle of contradictions. He was a man who could say a savage thing because of the very tenderness of his sensibility, who could wound a friend because of the very earnestness of his desire to please, who could appear self-conscious and awkward because of the very naturalness of his heart. Then in an access of health or spirits he could leap all barriers and appeal unerringly to friends and listeners. The way in which he regarded his own fame is typical of the Thackeray we have tried to know. No man ever enjoyed his fame more than he; but no man's head was ever less turned than his. The story is told that Charlotte Brontë, sitting opposite to him at dinner, regarded him for a long time as a hero. "And", said Thackeray, "I had the miserable humiliation of seeing her ideal of me disappear as everything went into my mouth and nothing came out of it, until at last, as I took my fifth potato, she leaned across with clasped hands and tearful eyes, and breathed imploringly: 'Oh, Mr. Thackeray! Don't!'" This is one of those stories which may not be true, but ought to be. It shows Thackeray in his typical attitude to life and to himself. He enjoyed the situation and criticised it implicitly as he enjoyed it. A hero perhaps—but there were the five potatoes. It takes a man of humour to see the two things together without laughing stupidly or unkindly or cynically or self-consciously, either at his admirer or at himself.

The injunction left behind him by Thackeray that no one should write his biography was as typical of the man as it is typical of the world to disregard it. The world has, in the person of Mr. Melville, twice offended. It was ten years ago that Mr. Melville wrote the first biography; and here we are faced with a second. Mr. Melville in ten years has had time to improve. He should have had time to improve himself out of any intention to repeat his offence. He has not succeeded in doing this; but he has improved a little in other respects. His first biography was a collection of scraps which did credit to the industry of the collector. In the second the scraps are better edited. But the Thackeray we have imagined behind the fence of reserve which the world will never succeed in breaking down is still as safe as he was or ever Mr. Melville began to drag out literary lumber for our instruction. Moreover, Mr. Melville will have frightened away competitors—all save Mr. Wright, the world's biography-monger. As a piece of book-making this biography is as complete as the author could make it with the information at his command or at the command of anyone hardened by the literary trade to rush in where others with more right to be there would not.

AUSTRIA INFELIX.

"The Austrian Court in the Nineteenth Century." By the Right Hon. Sir Horace Rumbold Bart., G.C.B., G.C.M.G. London: Methuen. 1909. 18s. net.

WE welcome a sympathetic, if somewhat superficial, history of Austria from so competent an authority as Sir Horace Rumbold, formerly Ambassador at Vienna. The feeble and fussy diplomacy of Sir Edward Grey during the Bosnia-Herzegovina crisis, supported as it was by the fatuous and provocative language of our press, has done something—we hope not much—to prevent that cordial understanding which ought to exist between two such old allies as England and Austria. Sir Horace Rumbold's book, if it is as widely read as it deserves to be, should convince educated Englishmen how unjustly we judged Count Aehrenthal, to whom we ought to be grateful for preventing a European war. On reading these pages it is impossible not to be struck by the ill luck which has dogged Austria for the last hundred years. Unfriendly critics might say it was incompetence, not ill luck, that led to the dismemberment of the Holy Roman Empire. Austria produced many very able statesmen in the last century; but it is a melancholy fact that in her three great wars, the first with Napoleon I., the second with Napoleon III. and Victor Emmanuel, and the third with Prussia and Italy, she did not produce a really great general. The Austrian troops, composed of Magyars, Czechs and Germans, were the finest in the world; but they were wretchedly generalled on each occasion, if we except the Archduke Albert's campaign in Italy in 1866. Indeed it is remarkable that both in 1859 and 1866 the Austrians beat the Italians, who would never have recovered Lombardy and Venetia had it not been for France and Prussia. Italy owes her unity less to the valour of her soldiers than to the cleverness of Cavour in sending troops to the Crimea, and thus securing the moral support of England and the material support of France. The war of 1866 was of course a deliberate design of Bismarck to wrest the German hegemony from the Emperor. It is easy to be wise after the event; and it appears to us, on reading Sir Horace Rumbold's chapters on this transaction, that Austria might have prevented the formation of the German Empire by a prompt cession of Venetia to Italy and by an appeal to Napoleon's hatred and fear of Prussia. Austria's prestige would have suffered by the surrender of Venetia without a blow; but she lost more by the war. If Austria's diplomacy at Paris had been bolder and more decided, there is little doubt that the two Emperors could have crushed Prussia for a generation. But Bismarck and Moltke were two men of genius, for whom the Emperor Francis and his Ministers and generals were no match. It is difficult to read the account of Sadowa without a feeling of indignation against the imbecility of General Benedek and his head of the staff Krismanic.

Meditating on the military misfortunes of Austria one cannot forget the enormous political difficulties with which an Emperor, who was his own Foreign Minister, had to cope. The dual system, which Gladstone tried to persuade us to adopt with regard to Ireland, has not been a success in the cases of Sweden and Norway and Austria and Hungary. The two Parliaments of Austria and Hungary and the annual meeting of the Delegations from the two Legislatures have been the most striking political failure of modern times. It may be that parliamentary institutions are unsuited to such races as the Magyars and the Slavs, as we are inclined to think. Certain it is that parliamentary government has to be suspended from time to time in the Austro-Hungarian Empire, and is now suspended. Nothing but the courage, the patience and the sweetness of temper of the Emperor Francis Joseph could manage this motley crew of races and quell the absurd pretensions of the so-called nationalities which compose his kingdom. Probably no other man could cope with the task. But Francis Joseph has behind him a reign of sixty years, during which no stain has rested, even for an instant, upon his character as a just, an honourable and a benevolent Sovereign. He has also behind him the memory of his domestic sorrows, which are tragic enough to silence the most malignant faction. Sir Horace Rumbold handles appreciatively and delicately the complex temperament of the unhappy Empress.

In the concluding pages of this history are one or two passages upon the British attitude during the last Eastern crisis which exactly represent our views. The secret treaty between Austria and Russia about Bosnia, which was made in 1878 before the Treaty of Berlin, was, it is said (and Sir Horace Rumbold evidently believes it), confirmed at a meeting in 1908 of Baron d'Aehrenthal, M. Isvolski, and Count Berchtold (Austrian Ambassador at S. Petersburg). The impudent claims of Servia were therefore doomed to neglect from the beginning, and nothing but the encouragement of the London press emboldened the Servians to arm, and thus gave Austria a welcome pretext for the military preparations which through last winter kept Europe on tenterhooks. " But the mischief ", writes Sir Horace Rumbold, " did not end here. The censure so freely passed on Austria in the Western countries and the almost hostile feeling evinced towards her had the result "—one which in our opinion cannot be too much deplored, but to which we in England largely contributed—" of drawing yet closer the irksome bond between Vienna and Berlin; of making Vienna more than ever dependent on Berlin; and of perpetuating what has been from the first an unequal compact, injurious to the best interests of the Dual Monarchy. It went, in fact, a long way towards the realisation of what had once been the dream of Schwarzenberg, namely the welding together of the whole of Central Europe, from the Baltic to the Adriatic, into one formidable union, with a population numbering some hundred and ten millions of souls and disposing of two million bayonets—to say nothing of present or prospective Dreadnoughts—and this time not under Habsburg ascendancy, but under the hard, unscrupulous lead of the most aspiring of Powers. Austria, it is to be feared, has now been driven for good into the arms of that Power." Exactly so. We should have thought that the European policy of Great Britain was pretty plainly chalked out, namely, the breaking-up of the Triple Alliance by detaching Italy and Austria from Germany. Italy, we have long known, is none too pleased with her position; and we now have it, on the weighty authority of Sir Horace Rumbold, that " the bond " is " irksome " to Austria. And yet Sir Edward Grey is hailed by our press, and the leaders of both parties, as a heaven-born Foreign Minister!

MR. GEORGE FREDERIC HANDEL.

"Handel." By R. S. Streatfeild. London: Methuen. 1909. 7s. 6d. net.

A LITTLE while since it might have been said that no good biography of Handel existed in English, or indeed in any language—for Chrysander's is incomplete. To-day no good one exists: if we change the tense of the verb the truth remains the same. Mr. Streatfeild's study is simply a little better than Rockstro's rubbish. Mr. Streatfeild's aim is not so new nor his daring so great as Mr. Streatfeild himself apparently supposes; for, although no fine and complete Life has come forth, much has been written about Handel and his opera-songs and oratorios, of which we must believe Mr. Streatfeild to be ignorant. His book is a kind of study in backward prevision; somewhat after the event he anticipates what was written—in, amongst other places, this REVIEW—ten to fourteen years ago. All the same, we admire his air, at once bold and bashful—modesty struggling with the heat begotten of the prophetic vision that peers with temerity into the dark backward and abysm of time. When he says that " what [a biographer] could claim, and I think with justice, would be that of all who have written music Handel was the greatest man ", we turn backward over our own pages to the year 1897, where we find " he [Handel] is not only amongst the very greatest musicians, but is certainly the very greatest man who ever followed music as a profession ". Turning further back to 1895 we see " The truth is that the man was greater, infinitely greater, than his music ", and Handel " is by far the most superb personage one meets in the history of music ", " the most astonishing lord of music the world has seen ". A sufficiently rash statement, made in our columns, that Handel was the greatest man who had lived, excited the wrath of the " Musical Courier " of New York, which pleaded hard for Nietzsche. In a word, Mr. Streatfeild need not fear condemnation on the score of over-novelty. And if his phrases do not come fresh from his own mint, his general purpose might even be called stale. Full fourteen years ago we noted that Handel was ceasing to be the Mr. Sankey of the grocers who love their little chapels; and here and elsewhere the claims of the true Handel have been steadily kept in view. For the rest, this " Handel " is not a bad book. It is journalism, but the tittle-tattle is less threadbare than such stuff usually is; and we are genuinely grateful for the attempt to set Handel in a picture of his friends and contemporaries. The wearisome anecdotage of Hawkins and Burney may now be reckoned as for ever discarded; and the refreshing quotations from Mrs. Delany and other letter-writers of an age of letter-writers are welcome as a substitute. Still, Mr. Streatfeild need scarcely assume a superior pose on the score of his literary as apart from musical learning. Musical learning he has not; and such a self-conscious touch as " the cultivated reader will not need to be reminded " of something in " She Stoops to Conquer " is a little comic. It reminds one of Mr. J. A. F. Maitland. Not many readers would plume themselves on being " cultivated " simply because they know there is such a play, though they might consider themselves crassly ignorant if they did not know it and its contents.

Handel the man must always remain something of a puzzle, because so little of his private life can be known, and where nothing can be known mankind is prone to suspect the worst. Or if, as in Handel's case, anything " worst ", or anything bad at all, seems preposterously out of the question, we still cannot deny ourselves the luxury of believing that at least something interesting went on behind the shutters when he had gone into his house and closed the door. Nature, at any rate human nature, abhors the vacuum that Handel and his biographers leave us instead of a room full of air perfumed and thickened with gossip and scandal. Hence, perhaps, the interminable tales of the guzzling and wine-bibbing which professional scandal-mongers have invented and handed on from almost the date of Handel's death. Yet there is a simple and quite reasonable explanation of the silence. Handel had no Boswell. He was a German and his servants were German; he had about him no one likely to set down in English any account of the hero's more obscure doings; and if these were not recorded in English, in what tongue would it have been of the slightest use to record them, seeing that by the end of his life Handel was a great name and nothing else outside of England? And, besides being a German, Handel was a musician: he went into English society a great deal, but always as a musician: he visited the houses of the great as an honoured (and probably well-paid) guest: we have no stories of him hobnobbing with the literary and artistic celebrities of his day—no such stories as those that form the very stuff and fibre of Boswell's " Johnson ". We hazard the conjecture that Handel's private indoor life must have been dull and without striking occurrences or brilliant conversations. Indeed, when we reflect on his stupendous activity in full view of the public, and recollect the immense quantity of music he wrote in his own home, we can fairly account for his private hours—at least until the period of his blindness. A colossal lonely figure, content with the society of his servants the two Smiths at home and with the friendship, reverence and affection of his " patrons " when he went abroad—no other picture can be conjured up of the composer in his darkened age. He is less pathetic in his grandeur than Beethoven, for his day's work was done before he was cut off from the busy world; also he had been a successful man of affairs, and does not remain, as Beethoven does, a type of the unappreciated man of genius dying in poverty and leaving works from which fortunes were to be made.

And in a sense Handel's good fortune has pursued him. His real greatness as a composer is more widely appreciated to-day than it ever was. Whilst the crowd still flocked at Christmastide to hear " The Messiah " both English and Germans were slowly learning to love the wondrous opera-songs; the gigantic creative and constructive power manifested in the oratorio choruses is felt more deeply now than it was in the days when only the superficial brilliance of "For unto us a Child is born" with its "Wonderful! Counsellor!" appealed to unmusicianly ears—nay, the marvellous scheme of that same chorus and the sheer inventiveness it shows are felt now as it was hardly possible for an eighteenth-century Burney to feel them. Gradually the popular preacher, the Mr. Campbell, of the little Bethel folk has lost his grip on Handel audiences; and as the preacher has receded the supreme artist has come forward. There was a time when the preacher hid the artist; but that time was before Mr. Streatfeild's. That Handel is fully and properly appreciated by all the world is much more than can be expected in the case of any artist of the first rank; until the millennium arrives there will always be an immense number of good people born incapable of understanding the things that are greatest in art. Whereas Mr. Streatfeild seems to be of opinion that Handel's only fame has been an unworthy one, it seems to us rather that even while his popularity overshadowed his fame, his fame was slowly growing, has never ceased to grow, and did not require a biographer to give it, so to speak, a start.

Yet, in the better time which we may hope is coming, we may hope to hear Handel's oratorios sung as they ought to be sung, and his opera-songs sung as they have not been sung since the old Italian opera passed away—which happened before Handel's own death. In that glorious day Purcell will also come to his own, and we shall see that these two composers, both English in their art, stand apart from all the German, Italian and Flemish composers, that while neither is a writer of religious music—in the sense that Byrde and Palestrina were religious musicians—both are masters of a kind of picturesque music with regard to which they stand alone. Handel wrote delicious love-songs, lovely songs inspired by every shade of sentiment; but it is in his glorious picturesque music that he is supreme—he is a landscape painter as great as Turner, but different from him. Yet he resembles Turner in his veritable passion for the sea. Nearly the whole of "Israel", as we quite recently pointed out, deals with the sea: the voice of the sea thunders or murmurs throughout. Whenever a chance offered in his other oratorios of painting a sea-picture he seized it and gave us such wonders as "When His loud voice", "Thus, when the sun", and, we venture to say, "The sound is gone out". Purcell needs no reflected glory; yet some of Handel's glory is reflected upon him, for the art in which Handel rose to be supreme was, if not invented, at least triumphantly employed by Purcell.

AN IRISH SKETCH-BOOK.

"Irish Ways." By Jane Barlow. With Illustrations by Warwick Goble. London: Allen. 1909. 15s. net.

WE cannot help wondering whether Miss Barlow is pleased with her illustrator. Mr. Goble has produced some spirited and faithful pictures of Donegal peasants, but his landscape sketches are sadly to seek. Of course, reproduction impairs, where it does not ruin, an artist's work, but it can hardly be the fault of a reproductive process that Mr. Goble's foregrounds are vague and dim hazes while the more distant vegetation is painted in some detail, and very distant clouds are sharply outlined. In one bogland scene an old man, in the traditional Irish costume so seldom seen off the stage, is sitting out of the picture in a most alarming way. The wonderful clear air of a fine day in Ireland is as absent from these pictures as it is from the conventional English idea of the Irish climate. The Irish rainfall may be heavy, but between whiles one can see vivid colouring and wide prospects that in all England probably only Cornwall can show. Miss Barlow, of course, knows this: "Everywhere, spread abroad in unstinted measure by the acre or even the mile, lie the pure and vivid hues that are prized when doled out thriftily in precious stones, and flower petals, and fragile wings". But Mr. Goble is very good indeed when painting a cottage interior, or a farmyard, or a village street.

We dwell on the pictures in this book because, to tell the truth, there is not very much to be said about the letterpress that could not have been said of half a dozen earlier volumes from the same pen. We all know by this time that Miss Barlow can write with charm, that she has a poignant sense of the pathos in humble lives which never degenerates into sentimentality. She does not make any of the mistakes of a tourist, and yet she remains a kindly visitor from the outer world to peasant cabins. She has not the remarkable flair for the niceties of dialect that marks the work of Miss Somerville and "Martin Ross", whose stories, if they were not so amusing, would be more generally recognised as possessing great merit in the sphere of realism. Miss Barlow is an artist, and Charles Kickham was profoundly innocent of art, yet every one of the characters who meander through the interminable pages of "Knocknagow" has a flesh-and-blood existence beside which the figures of the well-educated writer are misty and insubstantial. Miss Barlow can seize an episode well enough, but the Irish peasantry, for all their friendliness and good manners, take very good care not to reveal themselves to the visitor from a larger world. The only educated writers who can get the Irish peasant on to paper are those whose childhood has been spent in the country in Ireland. The best work of Miss Emily Lawless therefore possesses this certainty of characterisation, but, from internal evidence, we should suppose that Miss Barlow, like Maria Edgeworth, had not at her command the countless memories of the many friendships which a child—Protestant, landlord, and all the rest of it, if you will—enjoys with cottagers and dependants. For children the clan life of Ireland is still alive.

But the old delight in imaginative tales has fallen on hard times. Half-education has nearly killed folklore without introducing literature, and Miss Barlow is at her best in showing how the monotony of life in a western village can be stirred by the advent of a travelling library van. Her old schoolmaster, it is true, buys heavy volumes for a penny a stone at a country-house auction; a perfectly possible incident, which should be remembered when enthusiasts talk of a passion for learning in Ireland. But the young people crave for something more amusing.

These sketches and stories make very pleasant reading, and it is a pity that the price of the book will effectually prevent its reaching more than about one in ten thousand of the population of Ireland. There is here nothing controversial to excite the priestly or political boycott, and really some living Irish writer ought to try the experiment of a cheap publication of good fiction. Miss Barlow is not afraid to chronicle incidents of cheating, such as the swindling of an incompetent antiquary, and so we suppose her sketches, if dramatised, would be denounced by part of the Dublin press as a libel on Ireland. It is so odd that the writers who ably represent the worst features in Irish life should be peculiarly touchy about any imaginative work that hints that every Irish peasant is not a saint. Miss Barlow, to judge from her spelling of Gaelic words, is not a Gaelic League member, and so may be suspect to the idealists. She is quite wrong in thinking that O'Connell succeeded in putting down faction fights once for all, and we cannot imagine why she should suppose that a Roman Catholic may not marry his second cousin.

AROUND S. TERESA.

"St. Teresa of Spain." By Helen Hester Colvill. London: Methuen. 1909. 7s. 6d. net.

A VERY troublesome book to review—because it ought to be so much more interesting than it is and we ought to be so much more interested than we are. This cannot be S. Teresa's fault, and we do not think it is ours; so perhaps it is Miss Colvill's. Even though so many previous Lives of this great saint have been published, all the facts and details carefully put together here ought to prove very enjoyable reading. But somehow, although we sat down expectantly to a feast of good things, after solidly eating through course after course, we got up from the banquet with an unsatisfied craving, and with the doleful perception that the otherwise painstaking cook had persistently throughout forgotten to put in the salt. How the author fails it is sometimes difficult to define, but the whole impression left in the mind after reading the book is that S. Teresa herself has been left out, to give place to somewhat unnecessary discursions into contemporary history of her country or her friends. In a picture no background ought so to intervene and protrude itself as to be a detriment rather than a setting-off to the subject itself; but it is precisely that which does occur continuously in Miss Colvill's book. Often, as we are hoping to hear something interesting from S. Teresa's own accounts of her daily life, we are drawn up short and turned into the arid track of the author's reflections as to what S. Teresa might do if alive now in England; or our attention is unnecessarily distracted from the saint by a chapter being interpolated on that well-worn subject the Inquisition; again, a whole chapter on the lives of seven Spanish mystics is suddenly wedged in—contemporaries certainly and friends, more or less, of S. Teresa; but it would have been better merely to refer to them, than so completely to break the thread of the story and jumble the skein of our thoughts by this diversion from one mystic to another.

For, after all, what is wanted in a new account of S. Teresa such as this professes to be can only be a little more of S. Teresa's own sayings and daily life. Everything else has already been written and said about her that can be written or said, and by the most gifted writers and speakers. Miss Colvill's desire, as expressed in her preface, was to draw a sympathetic picture "of a great single woman" for "the advancing woman of to-day" to contemplate (and, par parenthèse, we do not applaud the choice of adjectives—so shudderingly suggestive of modern Pankhursts!). Miss Colvill would have succeeded better in her object if she had stuck connectedly throughout her sketch to S. Teresa herself, and given less of the history of other indifferent persons, or made it at any rate subservient to that of the great heroine of the piece, instead of often confusing the reader and throwing him off the track so completely as more than once to reduce him to the frame of mind in which poor Fray Julian of Avila must have been when on one of their many expeditions "the Great Reverend Mother is herself lost for over an hour"!

We wish some more of the amusing, witty letters, referred to, but, alas! not given, were inserted in this book. Her humour is so genuine, spontaneous, genial, as for instance when she writes to her good pious wealthy brother Lorenzo, recently returned from his money-making in Peru, who has been sending her a present of sweetmeats etc.: "I can't help laughing to think that you send me sardines, sweets and money, and I *send you a hair-shirt!*" Or, again, the delicious quaintness of her reply made "in converse with the Lord" when at Burgos, on her way to found a convent, the floods threaten to drown her and her sobbing nuns: "Teresa was not to be daunted, though her nuns were frightened. When they got to the Pontones and saw nothing but a world of waters and of sky, and knew that the least deviation of the rudder would plunge them in the flood, they made their confessions and sobbed the Credo. 'Eh, my daughters,' said Teresa, 'what better can you wish than to be martyred for the love of the Lord? See now, I will go first, and if I am drowned, then I will suffer you to go back!' But inwardly she sighed and said 'Oh, Lord! when wilt Thou cease to strew our path with obstacles?' And the Lord spake to her and answered 'Murmur not; for thus is it that I treat My friends'. At which Teresa sighed again, and said 'Ah, dear Lord! *and that is why Thou hast so few!*'"

It is quite perfect, this! Teresa, her courage, her strength of will, her faith, her perfect union of spirit with her Lord—and through it all her unquenchable humour! We have it all here condensed. Much more of this is what we would have liked the present book to give us, much less of meandering in by-paths. But, as Miss Colvill says, it is "most difficult knowledge", that of knowing "what to leave out"; and we should be ungrateful if to our expressions of disappointment as to what her book has not given us we were not to add our acknowledgment of what it has—a painstaking, minute account of the local colouring, gained by the author in her visits to the various convents of the Carmelites in Spain.

NOVELS.

"The Florentine Frame." By Elizabeth Robins. London: Murray. 1909. 6s.

There is a considerable lapse in Miss Robins' latest novel from the energy of "The Magnetic North" or the vivid drawing of "Come and Find Me!" Its theme is one very difficult to handle with effect—the affection of a mother and daughter for the same man. Such an accident can rarely be anything but unpleasant, and to treat it without facing all its tragic implications is to miss whatever advantage there might be in touching it at all. Miss Robins treats it with extreme discretion, avoiding almost entirely the tragic stress of it until one of the women has ceased to be. Just in one scene while the two are still alive she paints finely its poignancy for one of them, the other being too blindly convinced of the man's devotion to observe what has come to pass; but that one reticent moment is an indifferent climax for all the building-up of the story, and the moment of permitted drama, when the survivor makes discovery of what has happened, comes too late to compensate for the disappointments we have endured. Written of women by a woman it shows inevitably the woman's point of view, and the man, despite the virility credited to him, comes out as little more than a puppet, a peg on which their affections may be hung, a mere dumb instrument of tragedy. True, he almost declares his affection for the wrong woman, enough at least for her to understand him, but not explicitly enough to require an answer. As a man would have conceived him he would certainly not have stopped at that, neither would he, as he does here, have abandoned all hopes of the woman he loved on the strength of one elusive interview and without having definitely declared himself, or have married her daughter to obtain the luxury of keeping her within reach. True, to another type of man such pusillanimity might have appealed, but Chester Keith is anything but a pusillanimous person, and his intelligence should have been sufficient to have discerned Isabella Roscoe's more than liking for him. The scene is laid in New York, but we are given no clear account of its curious and interesting social entanglement. Mrs. Roscoe's surroundings are more suggestive of a New England coterie, save for the astounding incursion of Minna Butts, with her false hair, false eyelashes, false colour, toy dog and immature husband, who comes like a splash of vermilion into a low-toned landscape. Minna seems indeed to be a confession of failure. She is introduced, as unblushingly as comic lovers in a comedy, merely to produce amusing interludes. Where the other characters are drawn with subtlety and reticence she bursts upon the page like an overdressed caricature. Admitting that she has her exact prototype in life, and that caricature is her distinctive feature, she should have been put through the same process of toning by which the hard actuality of the other characters has been tempered. Her garish loudness kills the atmosphere of every scene into which she intrudes, and even the best desire to be amused by her cannot forgive the intrusion. Miss Robins has before shown a similar indifference to a tone relationship in drawing character, but she has carried it off by the sheer vitality of her tale. The vitality of her latest story is, however, not its distinguishing quality, and the contrast produces in consequence the more destructive effect.

"Robert Emmet." By Stephen Gwynn. London: Macmillan. 1909. 6s.

In Mr. Gwynn's "historical romance" of Robert Emmet there is more historical exactitude than is usual in such narratives. The names of the actors in the abortive rising of 1803, the sequence of events, the details of the conspiracy, are all matters of fact, and probably for that very reason the story is not throughout effective. The perpetual introduction of fresh characters, the constant rush of newcomers, which for us are mere names without personalities, is most bewildering. They may all be real enough to Mr. Gwynn, but he does not give them substance in his book. Robert Emmet, however, himself stands out clearly as a man of heroic mould in character, if not in appearance, enthusiastic, devoted, unselfish, single-minded, of keen intelligence, but too trusting to make a successful conspirator. Not even Mr. Gwynn can deny that he was confiding to the point of folly, nor prevent the impression that he was too much of a visionary, an idealist, to succeed, in spite of his active and practical ingenuity and readiness of resource. His devoted adherents were many of them as unwise as they were unlucky.

"The Severins." By Mrs. Alfred Sidgwick. London: Methuen. 1909. 6s.

This is one of the most amusing novels we have seen this year. The Severin family is a collection of the most happy-go-lucky, helpless, and foolishly unconventional women ever collected under one roof. The eldest son of the house, a shrewd and practical man, returns from India to find his shiftless widowed mother drifting into poverty, while his sisters, full of modernity, live their own lives, as the jargon goes, and collect round them an appalling crew of mercenary Bohemians. Michael Severin's own love story is full of charm. With strange fatuity the publishers, on the book's wrapper, observe that "Michael's own love affairs show him that although he criticises and deplores the family temperament, he shares in it himself". The only ground for this statement is the fact that Michael, who has a great respect for convention, discovers that life is more complex than he had supposed. But he never is in danger of developing what some people call an artistic temperament.

SHORTER NOTICES.

"British Year-Book of Agriculture, and Agricultural Who's Who, 1909-1910." London: Vinton. 1909. 5s. net.

In the week of the annual great Cattle Show it is appropriate to call attention to several books which are of particular value to agriculturists. The "British Year-Book of Agriculture" is in its second issue and is a very useful summary of all kinds of official information relating to agriculture. Here are lists of all the societies, institutions, farmers' clubs, chambers of agriculture, etc., within the kingdom. Here also will be found particulars of the breed societies, the agricultural shows, and again a directory of the agricultural colleges and schools, with a brief account of their courses of instruction and staff. An immense amount of detail is included which will often save a good deal of time to anyone with work to do in connexion with the industry; as far we have been able to test it the information has been accurately compiled. The final section of the book, modelled upon the well-known "Who's Who", is perhaps less needed, and the biographies are hardly so engaging as many of those contained in the prototype: probably the vanity is equally there, but an agricultural life is less favourable to its expression and may even still cultivate personal reticence as a virtue.

"Stephens' Book of the Farm." By James Macdonald. 5th Edition. Vol. III. Edinburgh: Blackwood.

Many generations of agricultural students, who in their turn have become teachers or lecturers, have been brought up on Stephens' "Book of the Farm", the original edition of which appeared more than half a century ago. From that time it has been the standard and almost the only generally comprehensive treatise on British Agriculture. Indeed it has too exclusively set the style of teaching, so that the majority of agricultural classes even to-day are given little more than a summary of Stephens' "Book of the Farm". This is harmful in many ways. One is that the "Book of the Farm" was and has continued to be a Scottish book, written by men familiar with Scottish practice and Scottish stock, ignorant of the agriculture of the South and the many variants that have been there evolved for special purposes. Then Stephens' point of view was essentially descriptive. It was never based on investigation or close examination of whatever accounts were available to show the profit and loss on different methods and operations of farming. In this unvital condition the teaching of agriculture has largely remained. It may be hoped that some of the younger race of instructors now growing up at our new agricultural colleges will investigate for themselves the actual practice of their own districts and make out their financial basis. Only the monetary return justifies this or that method of farming. The present edition has largely been rewritten, the editor has had the assistance of many men who are best qualified to give information about their own special lines of work. This third volume deals exclusively with live stock. It gives an account of breeds and management, and is illustrated by a number of photographs of typical prize-winning animals.

"Botany of To-day." By G. F. Scott-Elliot London: Seely. 1909. 5s. net.

Mr. Scott-Elliot is a well-known traveller and writer, who has studied plants under many different conditions and climates, and has contributed valuable observations to the advancement of his subject. This book is intended for popular reading, and forms one of a series of discourses for the layman on the movement of ideas in the scientific world. It is very unlike the ordinary botanical text-books, which have disgusted so many people who started on them with a real love of plants; he takes his subject from the standpoint which dictates most of the investigation of to-day, and considers the plant physiologically—as a living creature responsive to its environment and reflecting in various ways its position in the world. The book begins with the lowest forms of plant life, the green algæ and bacteria, and so by lichens, fungi, and ferns it passes on to the higher plants with their elaborate mechanisms for reproduction by flowers and seeds. The most valuable parts of the book, containing Mr. Scott-Elliot's own work and experience, deal with the great typical assemblages of plant life that we know as deserts, steppes, forests, salt marshes, &c., and the author discusses with vividness and authority the interplay of natural forces which has given rise to these characteristic associations of plant forms. The book is very much up-to-date, and, as it has a bibliography, might become a most useful guide to the student of the currents of scientific botanical opinion; there are references to such modern and even debatable topics as soil inoculation with the nodule bacteria, Mendelian breeding and Professor Biffen's new wheats, killing weeds by electricity, and such other matters. Indeed, Mr. Scott-Elliot is perhaps a little too anxious about the latest novelty. No man can be quite at home in all the ramifications of a science like botany, and in summaries and short views on matters about which one has only read, mistakes are bound to occur through not knowing the value of the witnesses and from lack of proportion. Thus the book here and there becomes a little journalistic, but this minor defect will not impair its value to the general reader, to whom, as a vivid and extremely well-informed account of the living science of botany work, it may be confidently recommended.

"History and Ethnography of South Africa before 1795." By George McCall Theal. Vol. II. London: Swan Sonnenschein. 1909. 7s. 6d.

The second volume of Dr. Theal's revised history describes the foundation of Cape Colony by the Dutch and covers about a century from the landing of Van Riebeck in 1652. It is practically a reprint of half the first and half the second volume of his original "History of South Africa". By the middle of the eighteenth century the African possessions of the Dutch East India Company had a white population of over five thousand, but Dutch rule did not extend very far beyond the Cape peninsula. Delagoa Bay had been occupied for ten years, and then abandoned, like Mauritius. The Dutch had more or less friendly relations with various Hottentot clans, but had little intercourse with the Bantu or Kafirs, except when ships were wrecked on the south-east coast. The Bantu as a rule treated shipwrecked sailors very kindly, and geographical knowledge was advanced more by these accidents than by deliberate exploration. The Bushmen, untamable hunters who preyed on their neighbours' flocks, were hunted like vermin alike by Dutch, Hottentots, and Bantu. The most important event was the introduction of French Protestant settlers at the end of the seventeenth century. The particularist tendencies of the French were vigorously repressed, and their language obliterated in the interests of Afrikander

(*Continued on page 702.*)

THE WESTMINSTER FIRE OFFICE

ESTD. A.D. 1717.
RECONSTITUTED 1906.

Head Office: 27 KING STREET, COVENT GARDEN, W.C.
City Office: 82 LOMBARD STREET, E.C.
APPLICATIONS FOR AGENCIES INVITED.

THE EQUITABLE
Life Assurance Society.

Founded 1762. FUNDS, 5 MILLIONS.

MANSION HOUSE STREET (Opposite the Mansion House), LONDON, E.C.

Ask for Particulars of

SPECIALLY LOW RATES FOR DEATH DUTY POLICIES.

No Commission Paid. Expenses, Half the Average.

LONDON, EDINBURGH & GLASGOW
ASSURANCE COMPANY, LIMITED.

Incorporated 1881.

For the Year 1908.

Premium Income - - - - - - £598,024.
£98,473 added to the Assurance Funds.
The Assurance Funds are now over £1,000,000 Sterling.

SUMMARY OF TWENTY YEARS' RESULTS.

Year.	Premium Income less Annuities.	Income from Interest, Dividends and Rents.	Assurance Funds at the end of the Year.
	£	£	£
1888	120,907	2,159	54,617
1898	333,241	5,663	219,369
1908	598,024	36,073	1,012,144

ADDITIONAL REPRESENTATIVES WANTED.

Head Office: EUSTON SQUARE, LONDON.
Apply THOS. NEILL, *General Manager.*

"There is scarcely any other Office, perhaps there is no other Office, which holds quite such strong reserves and has quite such good bonus prospects as the Scottish Amicable. It represents British Life Assurance at its very best." *Saturday Review.*

"There are few life Offices in the country possessing greater inherent attractions for new entrants than this flourishing mutual institution."—*The Statist.*

The large compound bonus of £1 15s. per cent. per annum was again declared at the last distribution of profits—31st December, 1905.

SCOTTISH AMICABLE
LIFE ASSURANCE SOCIETY.

LONDON - - 1 Threadneedle Street, E.C.
HEAD OFFICE—35 St. Vincent Place, Glasgow.

The IDEAL Policy

ISSUED BY
The CITY LIFE ASSURANCE COMPANY, Ltd.
(Formerly known as the British Homes Assurance Corporation, Ltd.),
PROVIDES
Life Assurance without Medical Examination.
For full particulars of this unique scheme send post-card to
M. GREGORY, Managing Director, 6 Paul Street, Finsbury, London, E.C.
AGENTS WANTED.—EXCELLENT PROSPECTS.

The Empire Guarantee

AND INSURANCE CORPORATION, LIMITED.

FIRE. LIFE. ACCIDENT.

PROSPECTUSES ON APPLICATION.

CHIEF OFFICE—247 WEST GEORGE STREET, GLASGOW.
LONDON OFFICE—66-68 FINSBURY PAVEMENT, E.C.

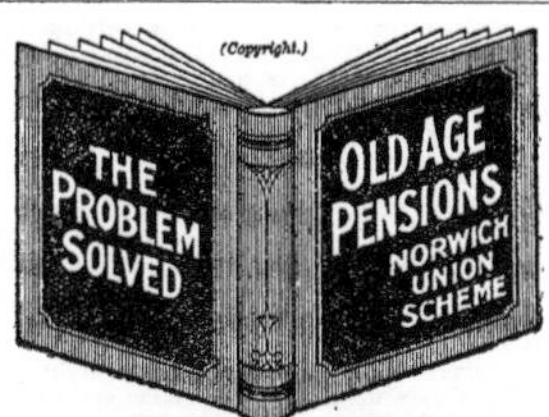

Write for particulars to Department 11,
NORWICH UNION LIFE OFFICE, NORWICH.

ATLAS ASSURANCE CO. LTD.

HEAD OFFICE ... 92 CHEAPSIDE, LONDON, E.C.

FIRE LIFE
ACCIDENT BURGLARY

INCLUDING UNCALLED CAPITAL, THE RESOURCES OF THE COMPANY
EXCEED FIVE MILLIONS STERLING.
LIFE BONUS YEAR, 1909.
All With-Profit Assurances effected in 1909, and in force at Dec. 31, will be entitled to participate.

Active and Influential Agents Wanted.
SAM J. PIPKIN, GENERAL MANAGER.

IMMEDIATE ANNUITIES
WITH
RETURN OF PURCHASE MONEY

For Particulars write . . .

GRESHAM LIFE ASSURANCE SOCIETY, Ltd.,

St. Mildred's House, London, E.C.

ASSETS EXCEED - £10,000,000

JAMES H. SCOTT, *General Manager and Secretary.*

EVERY MAN
who wishes for a sound investment
should read

"INVESTMENT POLICIES."

Sent post free on application to the

NATIONAL PROVIDENT INSTITUTION
for Mutual LIFE Assurance.

48 GRACECHURCH STREET, LONDON, E.C.

PRUDENTIAL ASSURANCE COMPANY
(LIMITED)

HOLBORN BARS, LONDON, E.C.

INVESTED FUNDS - - £70,000,000.

ACCIDENTS OF ALL KINDS,

SICKNESS, EMPLOYERS' LIABILITY,
BURGLARY AND FIDELITY GUARANTEE RISKS,
INSURED AGAINST BY THE

RAILWAY PASSENGERS' ASSURANCE CO.

Capital (fully subscribed), £1,000,000. Claims Paid, £5,700,000.
64 CORNHILL, LONDON. A. VIAN, *Secretary.*

solidarity. Religious toleration, as regards public worship, was denied not only to Roman Catholics, but to Lutherans and Moravians. All this was, of course, in harmony with the spirit of the times, but the facts lend a certain piquancy to Dr. Theal's commendation of the Dutch for their love of liberty.

"Ten Great and Good Men." By H. M. Butler. London: Arnold. 1909. 6s.

The ten "great and good men" are Burke, Canning, William Wilberforce, John Wesley, Lord Shaftesbury, John Bright, General Gordon, Dr. Arnold, Pitt the younger, and Erskine of Linlathen. As Dr. Butler says in his preface, these are "very unpretentious lectures"; but they have the charm of style which always distinguishes both the spoken and the written words of the Master of Trinity. They were delivered on different occasions to public-school boys or university students, and have without doubt led many who heard them to pursue further the studies they so ably suggest. Though Dr. Butler shows in many instances, especially when dealing with Burke and Canning, that he has a complete mastery of his subject, he is very rarely critical. He interests his hearers by copious quotation. We could have wished in several instances his comments had been less slight and fugitive, though there may be little new left to say on Burke, Canning, Wilberforce, or Wesley. These lectures give Dr. Butler little scope for his great gifts, and indeed they barely allow an opportunity for delivering an equitable judgment between his heroes and their rivals or opponents.

"Charles Dickens and his Friends." By W. Teignmouth Shore. London: Cassell. 1909. 6s. net.

There is something in the nature of wit that makes of it something which cannot be served up in the form of a réchauffé. A feast of wit is like a collection of diamonds, each facet catching the light at one particular moment. The light shifts, and every sparkle is lost to give place to another. To serve up a man's witty saying, divorced from its setting and isolated from those other sparks that set it off, should be made a piece of literary high treason. Mr. Teignmouth Shore would then have to be hung, drawn, and quartered many times over. The friends of Charles Dickens numbered among them most of the people worth knowing in his day. In this book we get glimpses of them all, with specimen examples of the wit in which many of them excelled. When the company includes Douglas Jerrold, Walter Savage Landor, Samuel Rogers, and others both greater and smaller than any of these, the result of this collocation of good things should be dazzling and delightful indeed. Yet the book is, if anything, dull. The reason has already been given. A witty saying introduced by a preface has lost all its salt; little remains, and the whole effect is something like a periodic letting-off of small crackers. Still, the book is worth looking at from its very strangeness. A collection of anecdotes and slight sketches of men and women, with nothing in common but their acquaintance with Charles Dickens, forms so irrelevant and motley a piece of book-making that it is worth investigation as a literary curiosity.

"The Return of Louis XVIII." By Gilbert Stenger. Translated by Mrs. Rudolf Stawell. London: Heinemann. 1909. 10s. net.

"How I do hate that man! I hate him worse than cold boiled bacon." Macaulay once said something to this effect, and then proceeded to write a history of his bugbear's doings, not a very impartial history. Partial history, however, does no harm when the personal equation is so easily read and applied as in the case of Macaulay. So here in the case of M. Stenger. Of the Bourbons and restored émigrés he writes in his preface: "They thought of nothing but themselves and of making the most of their happiness and dignity and royal position. . . . Their egoism was glaring and detestable: I have exposed it. Their appetite for power was immense: I have unmasked it". After that no friend of the Bourbons can complain of what follows, especially as this translation of M. Stenger's book is a very readable one. Partial history is generally good to read, and this piece of history forms no exception to the rule. Moreover, for the social side to the events that filled the months from the arrival of Napoleon in Paris in 1813 to the return of Louis XVIII. from Ghent in 1815, this translation will be found of real value to those who want information without having to look for it in a French book.

"Saint Thomas à Becket." By Monsignor Demimuid. Translated by C. W. W. London: Duckworth. 1909.

This is an interesting little book, not because it contains any very fresh or reliable history, but because it presents very forcibly the ultramontane view of Becket the saint. The saint is already there beneath the robe of the Chancellor; and, when the Chancellor has become Primate, no worldly, almost no human, thing may henceforth touch him. He first breaks with Henry over criminous clerks. We hear nothing of the sheriff's aid. Moreover, his canon law is not found wanting, though we have always understood that the "twice punished" argument was not to be found in Gratian. Then, of course, he never wavered at Clarendon. We are not allowed to have the human interest of that surrender and its retraction. No. Becket, noble and guileless, was circumvented by the cunning of false friends. Well, these views may be supported from the chronicles; but so can almost any other. We lean to a more human interpretation of S. Thomas for two reasons—because it is a more interesting interpretation, and because we believe that one who is altogether a man may also be something of a saint.

"Egypt." By Pierre Loti. Translated by G. A. F. Inman. London: Laurie. 1909. 15s.

Is it possible to translate an atmosphere? It is at any rate difficult, and, unless the translator is quite sure of himself, he would be well advised to leave Loti alone. This particular translation is good; but not quite good enough. It is pleasant to read, and catches some of that glamour which Loti's love of the East enabled him to throw into all his Eastern pictures. If the translation is not quite good enough, that is perhaps because in this enterprise it is not possible to be quite good enough. The translator deserves well of his readers, if only because he has felt the burden of his task. He has not imagined it unnecessary to do more than turn Loti into English. At the same time he has not done very much more. He has got sufficiently near to Loti to enable us to sympathise with the incompleteness of his achievement, instead of blaming him for his rashness in attempting it.

"Christians at Mecca." By Augustus Ralli. London: Heinemann. 1909. 5s.

This book gives an account of the various journeys to Mecca made from time to time by European pilgrims. The pilgrimages cover a period reaching from 1503 to 1894, so that there is some liberty of assortment in the information given (never very great) and in the pictures drawn. The stranger in the East is made at home in this book by some prefatory chapters on Moslem rites and the Great Mosque.

For this Week's Books see page 704.

THIS WEEK'S BOOKS.

Biography

Lady Hester Stanhope (Mrs. Charles Roundell). Murray. 6*s.* net.
Dr. Johnson (Mrs. Thrale). Edinburgh: Foulis. 6*s.* net.

Fiction

Tropical Tales and Others (Dolf Wyllarde). Paul. 6*s.*
Haunted Skoulton (Edward Hardingham). Haslam. 1*s.* net.
Theodora's Husband (Louise Mack). Rivers. 6*s.*
Big John Baldwin (Wilson Vance). Bristol: Arrowsmith. 6*s.*
Time and Chance (Francis Bancroft). Digby, Long. 6*s.*

Gift Books

Grimm's Fairy Tales (Githa Sowerby), The Doll's Diary (Rose Haig Thomas). Grant Richards. 5*s.* net each.
The Child's English Literature (H. E. Marshall). Jack. 7*s.* 6*d.* net.

History

The Roman Republic (W. E. Heitland. 3 vols.). Cambridge: At the University Press. 30*s.* net.
Relics and Memorials of London City (James S. Ogilvy). Routledge. 25*s.* net.
Trial of Captain Porteous (William Roughead). Glasgow: Hodge. 5*s.* net.
The Cradle of New France (Arthur G. Doughty). Longmans. 6*s.* net.
Moore's History of the States (Charles F. Moore). New York: Neale Publishing Co. $1.50 net.
The Art and Crafts of Ancient Egypt (W. M. Flinders Petrie), 5*s.* net; Master Musicians (J. Cuthbert Hadden), 3*s.* 6*d.* net. Edinburgh: Foulis.
Hope Street Church, Liverpool (H. D. Roberts). Liverpool: Liverpool Booksellers Co.
Memorials of Old Staffordshire (Edited by Rev. W. Beresford). Allen. 15*s.* net.
Stories of the French Artists (P. M. Turner). Chatto and Windus. 7*s.* 6*d.* net.

Science and Philosophy

Science and Religion (Emile Boutroux). Duckworth. 8*s.* net.

Theology

Modernity and the Churches (Percy Gardner). Williams and Norgate. 5*s.*
The Manual for the Sick of Lancelot Andrewes (F. E. Brightman). Rivington. 3*s.* 6*d.* net.
The Incarnation of the Son of God (Charles Gore). Murray. 2*s.* 6*d.* net.

Travel

A German Staff Officer in India (Count Hans von Koenigsmarck). Kegan Paul. 10*s.* 6*d.* net.
Trans-Himalaya (Sven Hedin. 2 vols.). Macmillan. 30*s.* net.
Oxford: Its Buildings and Gardens (Ralph Durand). Grant Richards. 21*s.* net.
Wild Life on the Rockies (Enos A. Mills). Constable. 6*s.* net.
The Rivers and Streams of England (A. G. Bradley). Black. 20*s.* net.

Verse

The Dublin Book of Irish Verse, 1728-1909 (John Cooke). Frowde. 7*s.* 6*d.* net.
Echoes of the Infinite (Marcus S. C. Rickards). Clifton: Baker. 4*s.* 6*d.* net.
Hamewith (Charles Murray). Constable. 5*s.* net.

Miscellaneous

Britannia's Calendar of Heroes (Kate Stanway). Allen. 5*s.* net.
Catalogue of the Tamil Books, A (L. D. Barnet). Printed by Order of the Trustees. British Museum. 45*s.*
Economics of Railway Transport, The (Sydney Charles Williams). Macmillan. 3*s.* 6*d.* net.
Handbook on British Colonies, 1909. 2*s.*
Heart of England, The (Edward Thomas). Dent. 3*s.* 6*d.* net.
How Old Age Pensions Began to Be (Francis Herbert Stead). Methuen. 2*s.* 6*d.* net.
Human Race, The (James Samuelson). Sonnenschein. 3*s.* 6*d.* net.
In the Evening (Charles Stewart). Murray. 6*s.* net.
Lighter Side of War, The (Morton Ballyfrench). Century Press. 6*s.*
Literary Bypaths and Vagaries (Thomas Newbigging). Stock. 4*s.* 6*d.* net.
People's Budget, The (D. Lloyd George). Hodder and Stoughton. 1*s.*
Sketches of English Life and Character (Mary R. Mitford). Edinburgh: Foulis. 5*s.* net.
Their Day in Court (Percival Pollard). New York: Neale Publishing Co. $3 net.
Warley Garden in Spring and Summer (Ellen Willmott). Quaritch. 21*s.* net.

Reviews and Magazines for December.—The Oxford and Cambridge, 2*s.* 6*d.*; Cornhill Magazine, 1*s.*; The English Review, 2*s.* 6*d.*; The Country Home, 6*d.*; The Socialist Review, 6*d.*; The Century, 1*s.* 4*d.*; The Nineteenth Century and After, 2*s.* 6*d.*; The Thrush, 1*s.*; The Contemporary Review, 2*s.* 6*d.*; The Westminster Review, 2*s.* 6*d.*; The Art Journal, 1*s.* 6*d.* net; Harper's Monthly, 1*s.*; The Financial Review of Reviews, 1*s.*; The Fortnightly Review, 2*s.* 6*d.*; The Connoisseur, 1*s.*; Revue des Deux Mondes, 3*fr.*; The Re-Union Magazine, 6*d.*; The Book Monthly, 6*s.*; Scotia, 7*d.*; The Antiquary, 6*s.*

From . .

Wells Gardner, Darton & Co.'s List

An Original book on a new plan. The Illustrations are all Mounted on Art Brown.

11 by 8½, fancy paper boards, cloth back, 5s. net.

The Animal Why Book.

By **W. P. PYCRAFT, F.Z.S., A.L.S.** Illustrated in Colours by EDWIN NOBLE, R.B.A.

A book of Natural History on novel and interesting lines. 32 Pictures painted in a bold and original style, beautifully produced in chromo lithography, besides others in black-and-white.

The New Volume in the Series of FINE ART GIFT-BOOKS.

8¼ by 5¾, printed on Superfine paper, cloth, gilt top, 6s.

A Wonder-Book of Beasts.

Edited by **F. J. HARVEY DARTON.** Full of Humorous Illustrations by MARGARET CLAYTON.

A volume of Romance and Adventure, where all the leading characters are animals. The Illustrations are full of humour, and the volume will delight "grown-ups" as well as children.

8 by 5½, printed on Superfine paper, cloth, 6s.

Bellerophon. "The Bravest of the Brave."

By **EDWARD FRASER.**

Mr. Fraser has written a stirring and romantic battle story of the hardest fighter of the Fleet of Nelson's time, and how Napoleon gave himself up a prisoner, with some account of the later "Bellerophons," including the present vessel of the "Dreadnought" type.

8 by 5½, cloth, 5s.

Seeing the World. The Adventures of a Young Mountaineer.

By **ASCOTT R. HOPE.** With Illustrations in Colour from Drawings by GORDON BROWNE, R.I.

An excellent tale for boys by a most popular and experienced writer.

Send a post card to Messrs. WELLS GARDNER, DARTON & CO., Ltd., 3 Paternoster Buildings, London, E.C., for a list of the latest new books for presents, beautifully printed in colours.

THE

NINETEENTH CENTURY & AFTER.

DECEMBER.

MR. GLADSTONE AND THE CRISIS OF 1909. By Sir FRANCIS A. CHANNING, Bart., M.P.
LORD BEACONSFIELD AS A TARIFF REFORMER. By Sir ROPER LETHBRIDGE, K.C.I.E.
IRISH POLICY AND THE CONSERVATIVES. By Colonel HENRY PILKINGTON, C.B. ("Patrick Perterras").
CAN RUSSIA ESCAPE THE FATE OF POLAND? By ADAM NOWICKI.
THE CENSORSHIP OF STAGE PLAYS. By BRAM STOKER.
OF THINGS THEATRICAL IN GERMANY AND ENGLAND: A COMPARISON. By GERTRUDE KINGSTON.
THE TRUTH ABOUT THE MANNING OF THE FLEET. By ARCHIBALD S. HURD.
THE OUT-CASTES OF INDIA. By the Right Rev. the BISHOP OF MADRAS.
SAUL AMONG THE PROPHETS: A PHILOSOPHER'S PLEA FOR RELIGIOUS EDUCATION. By Sir BAMPFYLDE FULLER, K.C.S.I.
LEONARDO DA VINCI AS SCULPTOR. By EDWARD McCURDY.
THEN AND NOW. By Mrs. FREDERIC HARRISON.
A TRANSATLANTIC INVASION OF 1816. By Mrs. STIRLING.
PSYCHO-PHYSICAL FORCES. By F. CARREL.
THE DEPRECIATION OF CONSOLS, AND A REMEDY. By MACKWORTH PRAED.
UNIONIST OR SOCIALIST LAND REFORM? By J. ELLIS BARKER.

LONDON: SPOTTISWOODE & CO. LTD., 5 NEW-STREET SQUARE.

THE ENGLISH REVIEW.

MONTHLY. CONTENTS OF DECEMBER NUMBER. 2s. 6d.

MODERN POETRY ...	ERNEST RHYS. JOHN FREEMAN. FREDERIC MANNING.
A PAGAN CREED ...	PROFESSOR GILBERT MURRAY.
THE STARVELING POET ...	EDWIN PUGH.
LETTERS FROM AMERICA ...	G. LOWES DICKINSON.
LUCY EVANS ...	GILBERT CANNAN.
THE WIFE OF ALTAMONT ...	VIOLET HUNT.
THE MONTH: EDITORIAL ...	THE PASSING OF THE GREAT FIGURE.
AFTER THE DESTRUCTION OF THE VETO	J. A. HOBSON.
THE CONTROL OF FOREIGN AFFAIRS ...	H. N. BRAILSFORD.
LES INTERETS DE LA RUSSIE ET LES DROITS DE LA FINLAND ...	L. MECHELIN.
THE RIGHTS OF FINLAND AT STAKE ...	PROFESSOR J. N. REUTER.
THE PLACE OF SATIRE IN EDUCATION	PROFESSOR FOSTER WATSON.

SPECIAL SUPPLEMENT:

"HISTOIRE DE LA PRINCESSE ZULKAIS ET DU PRINCE KALILAH," a hitherto Unpublished Manuscript by WILLIAM BECKFORD, the Author of "VATHEK."

CHAPMAN & HALL, LTD., 11 Henrietta Street, Strand, W.C.

The first year of the *ENGLISH REVIEW* (December 1908 to November 1909), handsomely bound in Three Volumes, can now be obtained from the Publishers, price 27/- per set. Single Volumes price 9/- each. The first volume includes, among many contributions, H. G. WELLS' Novel, "TONO-BUNGAY," while "THE HOLY MOUNTAIN," by STEPHEN REYNOLDS, appears as a Serial in Volume 2, and "A CALL," by FORD MADOX HUEFFER, in Volume 3.

—Illustrated Gift-Books—

THE FACE OF CHINA.

By F. G. KEMP, F.R.S.G.S. Travels in East, North, Central, and Western China. With some Account of the New Schools, Universities, and Missions, and the old Religious, Sacred Places of Confucianism, Buddhism, and Taoism, and a Map of China. With 64 Illustrations after Water-Colours and Sepia Drawings by the Author. **20s.** net; large paper parchment, **42s.** net.

THE COLOUR OF ROME.

By OLAVE M. POTTER. With 60 Illustrations in Colours and Sepia by the Japanese Artist, YOSHIO MARKINO, who also contributes an Introductory Chapter. Fcap. 4to. **20s.** net; large paper parchment, **42s.** net.

STORIES OF THE FRENCH ARTISTS FROM CLOUET TO DELACROIX.

Drawn from Contemporary Records. Collected and Arranged by P. M. TURNER and C. H. COLLINS BAKER. With 8 Coloured Plates and 24 in Half-Tone. Cloth, gilt top, **7s. 6d.** net; Edition de Luxe, with 5 additional Plates, crown 4to. parchment, **15s.** net.

THE MIND OF THE ARTIST:

Thoughts and Sayings of Artists on their Art.

Collected and Arranged by Mrs. LAURENCE BINYON. With 8 Full-page Plates. Fcap. 8vo. cloth, gilt top, **3s. 6d.** net.

THE CONFESSIONS OF SAINT AUGUSTINE.

Translated by Dr. E. B. PUSEY. Edited by TEMPLE SCOTT. With an Introduction by Mrs. MEYNELL. Large crown 8vo. cloth, with 12 Plates in 4 Colours by MAXWELL ARMFIELD. **7s. 6d.** net. Also an Edition de Luxe. Crown 4to. pure rag paper, with the plates mounted, parchment, **15s.** net; pigskin, with clasps, **25s.** net.

ANCIENT ENGLISH CHRISTMAS CAROLS, 1400–1700:

With some of later date, including poems by Algernon Charles Swinburne, J. Addington Symonds, Christina Rossetti, and Wm. Morris.

Collected, Arranged, and Illustrated from Medieval Books of Hours by EDITH RICKERT. With 8 Photogravure Plates. **7s. 6d.** net, boards; **10s. 6d.** net, in pigskin, with clasps.

THE CLOISTER AND THE HEARTH.

By CHARLES READE. With 20 Full-page Four-Colour Plates after Water Colours, and 10 after Drawings in Line, Title Page, Cover Design, and End Papers, by BYAM SHAW, R.I. Demy 8vo. cloth gilt, **12s. 6d.**; parchment, **16s.** net.

TRAVELS WITH A DONKEY.

By ROBERT LOUIS STEVENSON. Newly set in special large type. With 12 Full-page Reproductions from Water Colours, and 12 Facsimile Drawings by NOEL ROOKE. **7s. 6d.** net; parchment, **10s. 6d.** net.

THE RAINBOW BOOK.

By Mrs. M. H. SPIELMANN. With Coloured Frontispiece and 15 Illustrations by ARTHUR RACKHAM, A.R.W.S., and 21 in Black and White by many other well-known Artists. **5s.** net.

THE ROSE AND THE RING.

By W. M. THACKERAY. With Coloured Frontispiece, 44 Illustrations (12 in Two Tints), and Decorative End-Papers by GORDON BROWNE. **3s. 6d.** net.

THE MASTER OF GAME.

The oldest English Book on Hunting. By EDWARD, SECOND DUKE OF YORK. Edited by W. A. and F. BAILLIE-GROHMAN. With Introduction by THEODORE ROOSEVELT. Photogravure Frontispiece and 24 Full page Illustrations. Large crown 8vo. cloth, **7s. 6d.** net; parchment, **10s. 6d.** net.

A complete List of Autumn Announcements will be sent upon application.

CHATTO & WINDUS, 111 St. Martin's Lane, W.C.

Messrs. Longmans & Co.'s Standard Books

LORD MACAULAY.

Life and Letters of Lord Macaulay.
By the Right Hon. Sir G. O. TREVELYAN, Bart.

"ALBANY" EDITION. Large crown 8vo. 3s. 6d.
*** *An Enlarged and Complete Edition, with a New Preface and an Additional Chapter.*
POPULAR EDITION. Crown 8vo. 2s. 6d.
STUDENT'S EDITION. Crown 8vo. 6s.
CABINET EDITION. 2 vols. post 8vo. 12s.
"EDINBURGH" EDITION. 2 vols. 8vo. 6s. each.
LIBRARY EDITION. 2 vols. 8vo. 36s.

Complete Works.
"ALBANY" EDITION. With 12 Portraits. 12 vols. large crown 8vo. 3s. 6d. each, or £2 2s. the Set.

History of England, from the Accession of James II. POPULAR EDITION. 2 vols. crown 8vo. 5s.

Essays, with Lays of Ancient Rome, &c.
POPULAR EDITION. Crown 8vo. 2s. 6d.
"SILVER LIBRARY" EDITION. With Portrait and 4 Illustrations to the "Lays." Crown 8vo. 3s. 6d.

Miscellaneous Writings, Speeches, and Poems. POPULAR EDITION. Crown 8vo. 2s. 6d.

*** A Complete List of Lord Macaulay's Works sent on application.

JAMES ANTHONY FROUDE.

History of England, from the Fall of Wolsey to the Defeat of the Spanish Armada.
12 vols. crown 8vo. 3s. 6d. each.

Short Studies on Great Subjects.
CABINET EDITION. 4 vols. crown 8vo. 24s.
POPULAR EDITION. 4 vols. crown 8vo. 3s. 6d. each.
POCKET EDITION. 5 vols. fcap. 8vo. cloth, 2s. net each volume; leather, 3s. net each volume.

The English in Ireland in the Eighteenth Century. 3 vols. crown 8vo. 10s. 6d.

English Seamen in the Sixteenth Century. Crown 8vo. 3s. 6d.
ILLUSTRATED EDITION, suitable for Presentation, 6s. net.

The Divorce of Catherine of Aragon. Crown 8vo. 3s. 6d.

The Spanish Story of the Armada, and other Essays. Crown 8vo. 3s. 6d.

Cæsar; a Sketch. Crown 8vo. 3s. 6d.

Life and Letters of Erasmus. Crown 8vo. 3s. 6d.

The Council of Trent. Crown 8vo. 3s. 6d.

Oceana; or, England and her Colonies. With 9 Illustrations. Crown 8vo. 3s. 6d.

The English in the West Indies; or, The Bow of Ulysses. With 9 Illustrations. Cr. 8vo. 3s. 6d.

Thomas Carlyle: A History of his Life.
1795-1835, 2 vols. crown 8vo. 7s.
1834-1881, 2 vols. crown 8vo. 7s.

Selections from the Writings of James Anthony Froude. Edited by P. S. ALLEN, M.A. Crown 8vo. 3s. 6d.

SAMUEL RAWSON GARDINER.

History of England, from the Accession of James I. to the Outbreak of the Civil War, 1603-1642. 10 vols. crown 8vo. 5s. net each.

History of the Great Civil War, 1642-1649. 4 vols. crown 8vo. 5s. net each.

History of the Commonwealth and Protectorate, 1649-1656. 4 vols. crown 8vo. 5s. net each.
Professor Firth's continuation of this work, which was left unfinished by Dr. Gardiner, is just published under the title of "The Last Years of the Protectorate, 1656-58." 2 vols. 8vo. 24s. net.

The Student's History of England. With 378 Illustrations. Crown 8vo. 12s.

GEORGE G. CHISHOLM, M.A. B.Sc.

SEVENTH EDITION, REVISED (1908).

Handbook of Commercial Geography. With 38 Maps and 8 Diagrams. 8vo. 15s. net.

WILLIAM E. H. LECKY.

A Memoir of the Right Hon. William Edward Hartpole Lecky.
By his Wife. With Portraits. 8vo. 12s. 6d. net.

History of England in the Eighteenth Century.
LIBRARY EDITION. 8 vols. 8vo. Vols. I. and II. 1700-1760, 36s. Vols. III. and IV. 1760-1784, 36s. Vols. V. and VI. 1784-1793, 36s. Vols. VII. and VIII. 1793-1800, 36s.
CABINET EDITION. ENGLAND. 7 vols. crown 8vo. 5s. net each. IRELAND. 5 vols. crown 8vo. 5s. net each.

Democracy and Liberty.
LIBRARY EDITION. 2 vols. 8vo. 36s.
CABINET EDITION. 2 vols. crown 8vo. 10s. net.

Leaders of Public Opinion in Ireland: Flood, Grattan, O'Connell.
2 vols. 8vo. 25s. net.

History of European Morals, from Augustus to Charlemagne.
2 vols. crown 8vo. 10s. net.

History of the Rise and Influence of the Spirit of Rationalism in Europe.
2 vols. crown 8vo. 10s. net.

Historical and Political Essays.
8vo. 10s. 6d. net.

The Map of Life. Crown 8vo. 5s. net.

GEORGE MACAULAY TREVELYAN.

England in the Age of Wycliffe.
8vo. 6s. net.

NINTH THOUSAND.

Garibaldi's Defence of the Roman Republic. With 7 Maps and 35 Illustrations. 8vo. 6s. 6d. net.

FIFTH THOUSAND.

Garibaldi and the Thousand.
With 5 Maps and numerous Illustrations. 8vo. 7s. 6d. net.

The Rev. J. FRANCK BRIGHT, D.D.

A History of England. 5 vols. crown 8vo.
Period I. MEDIÆVAL MONARCHY. A.D. 449-1485. 4s. 6d.
Period II. PERSONAL MONARCHY. 1485-1688. 5s.
Period III. CONSTITUTIONAL MONARCHY. 1689-1837. 7s. 6d.
Period IV. THE GROWTH OF DEMOCRACY. 1837-1880. 6s.
Period V. IMPERIAL REACTION: VICTORIA. 1880-1901. 4s. 6d.

MANDELL CREIGHTON, D.D.

A History of the Papacy, from the Great Schism to the Sack of Rome, 1378-1527.
6 vols. crown 8vo. 5s. net each.

JOHN STUART MILL.

A System of Logic. Crown 8vo. 3s. 6d.

Political Economy.
NEW EDITION. Edited and with Introduction by Prof. W. J. ASHLEY. Crown 8vo. 5s. [*Just published.*
POPULAR EDITION. Crown 8vo. 3s. 6d.
LIBRARY EDITION. 2 vols. 8vo. 30s.

PETER M. ROGET.

Thesaurus of English Words & Phrases.
Classified and Arranged so as to Facilitate the Expression of Ideas and Assist in Literary Composition. By PETER MARK ROGET, M.D. F.R.S. Enlarged and Improved by the Author's Son, JOHN LEWIS ROGET. Crown 8vo. 9s. net.

FREDERIC W. H. MYERS.

Human Personality and its Survival of Bodily Death. 2 vols. 8vo. 42s. net.
ABRIDGED EDITION, in 1 vol. 8vo. 10s. 6d. net.

LONGMANS, GREEN & CO. 39 Paternoster Row, London, E.C.

NOTICE.

The Terms of Subscription to the SATURDAY REVIEW are :—

	United Kingdom. £ s. d.	Abroad. £ s. d.
One Year	1 8 2	1 10 4
Half Year	0 14 1	0 15 2
Quarter Year	0 7 1	0 7 7

Cheques and Money Orders should be crossed and made payable to the Manager, SATURDAY REVIEW Offices, 10 King Street, Covent Garden, London, W.C.

In the event of any difficulty being experienced in obtaining the SATURDAY REVIEW, the Publisher would be glad to be informed immediately.

GENERAL MOTOR CAB.

THE Third Annual General Meeting of the General Motor Cab Company, Ltd., was held on Wednesday at Salisbury House, E.C., Mr. Davison Dalziel (Chairman of the Company) presiding.

The Secretary (Mr. R. Gordon) having read the usual notices,

The Chairman said: You will all have received a copy of the balance sheet and profit and loss account, together with the directors' report for the period ended July 31, 1909. I think you will all agree with me that the result is satisfactory. The profit for the year, after deducting directors' fees, general expenses, interest, law charges, advertising, &c., amounts to £225,553 12s. 6d. Out of this there has been set aside £6,530 13s. to a special reserve against rolling-stock (bringing this reserve up to £110,426 4s. 1d.), £7,225 0s. 2d. has been written off for preliminary expenses, £57,160 16s. 8d. has been paid out in dividends (being the fixed dividend of 7 per cent. on the Preferred shares), £9,199 0s. 6d. has been added to general reserve, being 10 per cent. on the net profit after payment of the Preference dividend, and £3,646 17s. 6d. has been set aside for directors' commission, leaving, with the balance of £9,352 13s. 6d. brought forward last year, a total net balance of £92,143 18s. 2d. This we propose to carry forward. When the intentions of the directors in this respect were made known, I was unprepared for the announcement made in several newspapers that the General Motor Cab Company had passed their dividend, and one important journal described it as "a severe blow." It is quite needless for me to point out that we did not pass the dividend, that the Preference shares have received their fixed 7 per cent., and that we have received nothing but commendation from our shareholders for the conservative policy which is outlined in the proposal to carry forward the £92,143 18s. 2d. at our disposal. The year's business of your Company has been entirely satisfactory, and you will realise this more particularly when I tell you that the large profit of £225,553 12s. 6d. has been earned with only a portion of the Company's rolling-stock at work. We have already materially increased the number of cabs working, so that at present we have an average of about 1,850 running, and our receipts since the commencement of the present financial year show a substantial increase over the same period last year. It must be borne in mind that many difficulties present themselves in the establishment of an entirely new business such as this. We are gradually, but surely, approaching the desired end of having all our cabs employed. When this point is reached, we shall, without further capital expenditure, be earning no doubt largely increased revenue, so that we look forward to the future with satisfaction. It is quite possible that in the near future there may be some important developments in the motor-cab industry, not the least of which will be the introduction of the use of solid instead of pneumatic tyres. We are actually making exhaustive experiments with the Amans Pneumo Suspension, which promise well in this direction, and which, if they turn out as satisfactory as we have reason to hope they may, will have such a far-reaching effect upon your general expenditure in this respect that I almost hesitate to go into too much detail. It will be sufficient if I say that your expenditure in pneumatic tyres alone last year amounted to £100,982 17s. 9d., and for the current year, in consequence of the increased number of cabs, will probably reach nearly £200,000.

I should like now to dwell upon our decision to recommend the carrying forward of the balance to the credit of the accounts. We consider that, having regard to the increasing competition, it is a wise policy to strengthen the resources of the Company in every possible way. It was only natural that, having shown the way in motor cabs, we should have imitators. It would seem that a great many people are under the impression that they were especially put into the world to show other people exactly how motor-cab companies ought to be run; but I have already told you, and I am obliged to repeat it, that a motor-cab business can only be run successfully—and by "successfully" I mean as a dividend-earning concern—if it is run upon a large scale. It would be idle, of course, to ignore entirely the wild and totally unreliable stories which are constantly being circulated concerning the affairs of this Company. I would not say they all emanate from the Stock Exchange or the Paris Bourse, but I am bound to say a good many of them find a comfortable home within an area of a mile of these useful institutions. As I have already informed you, our cabs are maintained out of revenue. They are licensed only for one year at a time. At the end of each year they are overhauled and presented at Scotland Yard for re-licensing, and unless they are practically, both as to body and engine, in a condition of first efficiency, the licence is not granted. The statement that we are not running more cabs because the others are either in the repair shops or the scrap heap is a malicious slander. Certain Preference shareholders have raised a point that in the consolidation of the old £1 shares into £4 shares their voting power was reduced proportionately by one-fourth. They have asked us to see whether this cannot be remedied, and I may say that, providing there is nothing in the Trust Deed securing the Debentures to legally prevent this being carried out, we should support such a proposal, and that is being looked into by our solicitors. I have now a personal statement to make on behalf of the directors of the Company, which I feel sure will meet with your hearty approval. When this Company was originally formed, as you are no doubt aware, the Articles of Association provided that each director, in addition to his fixed fees, should receive a commission of 1 per cent. on the profits of the Company, after all standing charges had been made and after the Preference shares had received a dividend of 7 per cent. When the United Motor Cab Company was amalgamated with this Company one of the conditions of the agreement between the two Companies was that the directors of the United Motor Cab Company should also become directors of the General Motor Cab Company. It was also deemed advisable that a managing Committee should be appointed, of which the shareholders did me the honour of electing me chairman, and, so that no additional burden should be thrown upon the Company in consequence of the creation of this Committee, the directors themselves agreed that the 1 per cent. to which they were individually entitled should be cut down to ½ per cent., the remaining ½ per cent. to be specially set aside to remunerate the managing Committee for their special services. It was thus, at the creation of the managing Committee, that the cost of the managing Committee fell upon the directors themselves. I may say at once that when these arrangements were made the important financial consequences to the Company were not taken into sufficient consideration, and while the directors and the managing Committee have every right, legally and morally, to exact that which is properly their due, they have decided quite voluntarily to make a sweeping reduction in their fees. Under the new arrangement the 1 per cent. which the directors are entitled to by the Articles of Association is reduced permanently to ¼ per cent., the managing Committee being paid a fixed remuneration for their services. The principle of interesting directors in the result of the business which they conduct is not an unwise one so long as that interest is not carried beyond the bounds of reason. The percentage to which the directors are entitled in this case under the Articles is in their opinion too high. The reduction they have voluntarily made brings the total amount down to a reasonable and, I may say, a modest basis. This voluntary act on their part has reduced the expenses of the Company in the present balance sheet by about £10,000, and with the very possible increase in the Company's profits in the future the saving will automatically become larger. As some of your directors are not seeking re-election to-day, and as legally they would have been fully entitled to claim the full amount due to them, I think you will approve the course they have taken. Let me say in conclusion that my ambition—and it is shared by my colleagues on the Board—is to place this Company upon a financial basis which will earn the commendation of the most exacting advocates of careful administration and, at the same time, prove worthy of an enterprise of such great importance. You have a business in the future of which you may, in my opinion, have full confidence. The motor-cab business has come to stay.

Mr. Mamelsvors seconded the adoption of the report, and the motion was carried unanimously.

Printed for the Proprietors by SPOTTISWOODE & Co. LTD., 5 New-street Square, E.C., and Published by REGINALD WEBSTER PAGE, at the Office, 10 King Street, Covent Garden, in the Parish of St. Paul, in the County of London.—*Saturday*, 4 *December*, 1909.

THE

SATURDAY REVIEW

OF

POLITICS, LITERATURE, SCIENCE, AND ART.

No. 2,824 Vol. 108. 11 December 1909. [REGISTERED AS A NEWSPAPER.] 6d.

CONTENTS.

NOTES OF THE WEEK.

The political situation would be endurable but for its speeches. Election oratory is rarely for the fastidious, but surely there never has been such a chance as this for bad arguments and worse speakers. Does anyone really try to keep up with the platform doings of the week? And if nobody does, why do the papers cram themselves with such unusually bad copy? It is more entertaining just now to read the trade organ of the greengrocers or the ironmongers, advertisements and all, than to read the columns of newspapers out for electioneering. And the tortured British public has got another three weeks of this kind of thing. Decidedly we hope that the Peers will rarely exercise their right to fling out a Budget.

"The uncomplaining brow of Eliot" would have cause to look full of complaint could Eliot know the way in which his name is tossed about by Radicals to-day. Almost any Radical who drinks a whisky and soda in the smoking-room of the National Liberal Club is a potential Pym. Seldens are cropping up quite thick among the briefless barristers, and a Hampden may be hatched by the headquarters of the N.L.F. any moment. Is it not nauseous the way in which these great names, with Burke and Pitt flung in, are paraded by Radicals? Every Englishman with the instinct of history must feel that the name of Eliot or Selden should not be mixed up with a sharp wrangle among party politicians.

So far as we have noticed, Mr. Lloyd George and Mr. Churchill have left Eliot and Selden alone, and that is something to be thankful for. Perhaps they judge shrewdly enough that live personalities tickle an audience more than historical analogies. In Mr. Lloyd George's opening speech at the National Liberal, for instance, the most popular passages were those about the "Daily Mail", Lord Rothschild, and Mr. Garvin; whilst loud laughter and cheers rewarded Mr. Churchill's joke about Mr. Balfour: "Mr. Balfour is a leader, he does whatever his followers tell him, only when he knows his followers are wrong he does it half-heartedly."

Mr. Birrell, in a speech later in the week, declared himself an admirer of Mr. Balfour's strength of will in overcoming "physical infirmity". But in this hunt for obloquy Mr. Runciman was surely the leading hound. He could admire a gambler who damned the consequences, but the gambler who like Mr. Balfour hedged was "not fit for decent society". And people who lay themselves out for this sort of stuff would have one believe they are grandly defending Magna Carta or the Petition of Right!

But some of the speeches in the Peers campaign are really fresh and lively to read. Most outright Englishmen would rather have a few minutes with Lord Willoughby de Broke than hours with the high-falutin' Chancellor of the Exchequer or the ineffable President of the Board of Trade. Why does the "Times" report these pretentious orations not by the column but by the page? Lord Willoughby de Broke is a hard-riding, hard-bitten English sportsman. His speeches should be far better and fresher copy than the solemn, pretentious, high constitutional ones. He leads his field in a rattling good run of forty minutes; and he has a way not only of finding but of killing his fox.

Mr. Lloyd George at Carnarvon is as happy as usual in his attempts at history. How felicitous the exhortation to "the democracy" to march under Oliver Cromwell's banner in a campaign to set up the House of Commons supreme. The Dictator would hardly have been pleased at this glib-tongued talker, the champion of the "horridest arbitrament" he so much loathed, taking his name in vain. From history Mr. Lloyd George strayed into eschatology. The Liberal triumph is to herald a new earth; not a new heaven, we observe. Does not this spiritual fervour well become the man who lampoons the Burial Service in a political speech?

Whatever it was that drew the crowds to the Budget demonstration in Trafalgar Square, it was no doubt a huge assembly. It could not have been larger if held in the Square at all, as it overflowed into the streets and all the parapets were lined two or three deep. Curiosity accounted for the presence of the greater crowd which surrounded the nucleus of enthusiasts about the speakers. We do not think it is any use either Conservatives or Liberals trying to prove anything from it. If the Budgeteers did not pull down Nelson's Column to show their zeal, the anti-Budgeteers did not show theirs by any opposition.

What is taking place in the reciprocal withdrawal of Liberal and Labour candidates in constituencies where they would clash is a sign of tacit understanding. Mr. Henderson, the Chairman of the Parliamentary Labour Party, may protest that there has not been, and could not be, a formal arrangement because the constitution of the Labour Party does not permit it. Liberals have hitherto, to soothe their moderate division, affected to have quite different aims from the Labour Party. Now the Liberal and the Labour parties issue manifestoes on the House of Lords and Budget questions as like as Tweedledum and Tweedledee. Mr. Henderson says the Liberal Whip demanded that the new Labour candidates should be withdrawn. Mr. Henderson quotes refusal as a proof of independence of the Labour Party. On the contrary, it seems quite the thing to expect. They may quarrel, but they are accommodating, as Wales and Yorkshire show.

Thanks to the business common-sense of the tea and tobacco and spirit dealers, much of what was called the financial chaos which was to arise out of the rejected Budget will be avoided. Perhaps it would be too strong to call it patriotism, though we might when we remember the prophecies about disaster which seemed to give the Liberal prophets positive satisfaction. Tea particularly, it was said, would be got in in huge quantities without paying duty. The associations representing the tea, tobacco, and spirit traders have decided that it is better to make deposits to cover the higher taxes fixed by the Budget. When the new Parliament meets it is anticipated that for the current year to the end of next March these taxes will be legalised retrospectively.

They would have to pay then, but in the meantime difficulties would arise with their customers. If they had not paid the duties, it would be awkward to charge higher prices on the strength of taxes they had not actually paid. This action of the associations binds their reputable and recognised members not to get any advantage by taking their goods out of the Customs without paying the taxes. If unrecognised and doubtful speculators tried the game and would not make the deposits, the revenue officers would simply refuse them delivery. They could go to the Law Courts, but before their actions could come on the taxes would be legally and retrospectively imposed.

Cocoa, like beer and mustard, has long had a flavour of party politics in England (there is a cocoage as well as a beerage), but one hardly appreciated the strength of this flavour till a fortnight since. It is impossible to detach the case of Messrs. Cadbury from party politics; one might as well try to detach it from the "Daily News", the chief engine of the Liberal Party, the fount of Liberty, the champion of oppressed humanity the world over. The Cadbury case has given us all, what we have needed so much since the last general election, a terminological exactitude as to slavery.

It was admitted—after that election—that the term slavery was not quite exact as applied to indentured labour in South Africa. But now we have an example of the real thing. The blacks who grew the cocoa that filled the factories of Cadbury with grateful and comforting food for the masses were absolute slaves. The black babies born on the plantations of San Thomé were the goods and chattels of the planters who supplied Messrs. Cadbury, who in their turn supplied the British public. Now not the harshest critics ever said that the Transvaal mineowners could claim as their goods and chattels any yellow babies. The line was drawn there at any rate. We remember some fearsome pictures of the Chinese slaves with their cruel chains; but at least our Radical friends did spare us harrowing pictures of the fate of the children.

We know why the "Daily News" did not agitate the cause of the San Thomé slaves. That was made plain in the case. It lay low just for the sake of the slaves, and for nothing else in the world. We must all admire the "Daily News'" motives and its great restraint. It struck a master blow for freedom by saying nothing. May we take it that the attitude of the chief Liberal weekly, the "Nation", was identical? We think the "Nation", too, has refrained from agitating severely the case of the San Thomé slaves who produced the cocoa for Messrs. Cadbury and for Messrs. Rowntree. It is a very notable lesson in restraint!

The Irish National Directory, which is the League's House of Lords, will meet next Tuesday in Dublin to give the Irish Party absolution. They will also probably denounce Mr. Healy for not having sinned. Throughout the country there is a threatened outbreak of public opinion, and the party can trust to get a vote of confidence from its Upper Chamber, with the doors closed against critical discussion. There has not for twenty years been an occasion so great to call the National Convention; but the National Convention is the Commons of the League, with open doors, and more given to criticism, so that, in the circumstances, it is better not to run the risk. An open discussion printed through the country just now might put an end to the cause, not to mention the likelihood of the statesmen battering each other with chair legs.

Mr. Churchill, who is now "drumming" for free trade in Lancashire, has at any rate one client in Germany. Herr Gothein, the economist, hopes that free trade will win in England because the introduction of a tariff would be a serious blow to German industry. And then Herr Delbrück in the Reichstag dares say that Germany has managed to achieve an industrial conquest of the world by means of her tariff. Why modify a fiscal system under which so much has been accomplished? All he would do is negotiate a new treaty with Portugal because the Portuguese have dared to raise their tariffs against Germany. What Portugal can do with success it would, of course, be madness for Great Britain to attempt. At least, that is what Mr. Churchill asks his friends to believe.

The new session of the Reichstag has opened stormily, though scarcely more stormily than was expected. The difficulty about a suitable second Vice-President was soon overcome, but the Kiel dockyard scandal led to a great row. It is the rule in German politics that the Government must anticipate squalls whenever anything goes wrong with the bureaucracy. In his present stage of development the German knows that he is governed bureaucratically, grumbles at the system, loves to criticise it, but—is not yet ready to proffer an alternative. As to this Kiel business, Admiral von Tirpitz' replies smacked of all the dogmatism of German officialdom.

The disagreeable subject of official errors did not detain the gallant admiral for very long. Business-like administration was, he agreed, most desirable, but the idea of placing a mere man of business at the head of a naval base was, of course, absurd. Moreover, the yards were very economically managed on the whole. In a passage of great significance Admiral Tirpitz pointed out that in spite of a general advance in prices there had been a reduction of some fifty shillings a ton in battleship construction during recent years. This important statement is but another proof that, after some initial mistakes, Germany has learnt to build cheaply, quickly and well—a fact on which our Free Traders may ponder. Fortunately we in England do not now under-estimate either the power or the efficiency of the German battle fleet. But it is well to remember that Germany is still going ahead and beating her own records.

The Berlin Museum has at last spoken officially about the Leonardo-Lucas bust. The list of indignities is complete. First comes a chemist who analyses the wax. Then comes an entomologist who discovers larvæ of the anthrenus in the right hand. Then comes a botanist who discovers Italian fir inside. The Italian fir need disturb nobody; because in the time of Richard Lucas it was growing in England. Besides, against Italian fir we have to set those old-fashioned British quilts, also found inside. The examination has in fact proved nothing. We are thrown back again upon the evidence of witnesses.

All the witnesses speak against Dr. Bode, and now Dr. Bode has in a manner spoken against himself. He has thrown away all his old arguments; and, in the report, makes a final stand upon the evidence of a witness subpœnaed into court at the last moment. This new witness is Mr. Tolfree, a bookseller. Mr. Tolfree remembers setting aside this bust at the time of a sale held at the Tower of the Winds, Chilworth, because it did not belong to Mr. Richard Lucas at all, but to Lord Palmerston. Mr. Tolfree will have to prove something about that sale. Mr. A. D. Lucas himself denies that it took place; so does the firm accredited by Mr. Tolfree with carrying it out. The books of this firm are quite innocent of privity to anything of the kind. Is Mr. Tolfree a reed to run into Dr. Bode's hand?

The French Chamber has ratified the Convention of Berne. Some of the traffic which went through the S. Gothard tunnel will now go through the Simplon; and Paris is nearer to Lausanne. That is all the great event amounts to, and it is enough. Of course, it has a political history behind it. Gambetta wanted the Simplon tunnel in 1880. He thought that, as Italy and Germany had come together by way of S. Gothard, so Italy and France might meet in the Simplon. But France did not think much about the matter. It was Switzerland that pushed the business through. Switzerland wanted Paris tourists more dearly than France wanted to be independent of a route through German Switzerland. The effort to make political capital out of the achievement now comes too late in the day.

M. Briand has just had some talk with the Paris police. The police have been suggesting things to their Prefect—no, not Prefect; that is too harsh a word. He is the father of them all. Among other things the Paris policemen want to organise a professional union. M. Briand spoke kindly to them. He appealed to their patience. Let them remember that they were Civil servants, and at the same time soldiers. Really they must be moderate, if only for the sake of discipline. And was not their Prefect a "good and brave chief, who regarded them as the children of a large family"? If this is really the way to talk to policemen who are soldiers, we should perhaps begin to inquire a little anxiously into the discipline of the British policeman who has not submitted himself to a military yoke. Yet we can trust the truncheon.

The Mejliss, Persia's Parliament, has voted unanimously for borrowing abroad. Politics in Persia must be a sad business. Conceive the oppression of that unanimous vote. Persia is going to borrow foreign money and foreign men. She has decided to do the sensible thing, because it is the only thing she can do. Having done that, unanimity ends. The Nationalists will only borrow men from little countries. The Persians in general will not endure a Russian officer, yet it is exactly the Russian officer that Persia will have to endure. Russia is on the spot and inexorable exactly on that point. The Mejliss has little that it can look forward to with any sort of pleasure.

The Minto-Morley 'Charter'" for India, as it is now styled, covers four hundred and fifty-eight printed pages, and is introduced by an Explanatory Resolution itself almost as long as the original American Constitution signed by Washington. This enormous document is briefly and comprehensively set down by the "Bengali" newspaper as "a meaningless sham". This is ungrateful of Mr. Surendro Nath Banerjee, the proprietor, seeing that the Government has specially relieved him of the disqualification for membership incurred by his dismissal from the Indian Civil Service early in his career.

There is no great significance in the Message of the President of the United States to Congress apart from the paragraph on Central America. Put this with the admonition of the Secretary of State, delivered late last week to the Nicaraguan envoy, when his violence astonished even his own countrymen, and it is clear that interference in Nicaraguan affairs is contemplated. Several warships and a large force of marines are already in the neighbourhood. The world is likely to see shortly a startling development of Monroeism unless the revolutionary party receives so much encouragement and assistance that President Zelaya is overthrown from within. An unusual amount of space is devoted in the Message to foreign affairs, the Far East receiving considerable attention. The references to home affairs sound tame after the fulminations of Mr. Roosevelt, and are of little interest to foreigners.

The system of selection for the higher ranks in the British Army is becoming a scandal; it is one of the first things a Unionist War Secretary must take in hand. The supersession of Major-General Benson was unaccountable; and now he has retired from the Army. General Benson served with distinction in South Africa as Chief Staff Officer to the Sixth Division. He was the only officer who won the almost enthusiastic praise of the German General Staff in their official history of the war. After his return home he was specially selected for promotion to major-general, and he has since continuously held important appointments until last Saturday in that rank. He is now passed over for lieutenant-general by officers whose claims are certainly no greater than, if so great as, his. What makes the matter worse is that General Benson is a Canadian; and when we are hoping for a real Imperial Army it is particularly ill-timed to treat a distinguished colonial so unjustly.

At last we are to have two extra judges. Common sense has beaten the Treasury Screw. True the report of the Committee is a compromise and the new judges are extra to the establishment, to be absorbed as vacancies occur, unless Parliament orders otherwise. It is an open secret that the Committee began their work with a strong inclination against increase, but eventually were compelled by unanswerable evidence to the other conclusion. Commissioners, it was suggested, might easily get rid of existing arrears, and so leave the road clear again—until the next block we suppose. And what an opportunity for the unemployed "silks"!

But litigants pay their fees for a judge's time and experience, and ought not to be put off with substitutes, however much time and however little experience these may have. This was evidently the last straw for the Committee. The attempt to force Commissioners on the circuits has several times been tried by the authorities, but the Bar have always taken up the attitude that the appointment of a Commissioner is justifiable only towards the end of an Assize in which work has been unduly prolonged or exceptionally heavy. The Committee have also considered other matters, and practically agree to put the circuit system into the melting-pot. Possibly before many years are over we shall have local High Courts. What of the Bar then?

In November last year a curious libel action was brought against a Manchester paper, the "Sunday Chronicle", by Mr. Artemus Jones, a barrister, and he obtained a verdict for £1,750. Mr. Dawbarn wrote a sketch of Dieppe motor races and introduced into it the figure of an Englishman under the name of Artemus Jones, who lived the very respectable life of a churchwarden at Peckham, but was a very gay dog indeed at Dieppe. The real Mr. Artemus Jones was known as a barrister in the district, and, strange to say, he had already written for the paper under his own name. People there knew the name, but they did not know that he neither lived at Peckham nor was a churchwarden, and that there was nothing corresponding to him in the article but the unusual name.

Mr. Dawbarn did not even know of his existence. The "Sunday Chronicle" appealed, and the Appeal Court upheld the verdict; but Lord Justice Moulton in a very remarkable judgment dissented from the other two judges. The "Sunday Chronicle", backed up in this way, appealed to the House of Lords. Now the House of Lords has unanimously held that Mr. Artemus Jones is entitled to keep his verdict. It is therefore settled that a writer may libel a man without intending it, if his readers suppose that his remarks may be applied to some man they know. Lord Justice Moulton may not know the law better than the House of Lords; anyway he pointed out consequences which show the law would be better than it is if it were what he said it was.

The Municipal Reformers' sweep of the board at Battersea is bearing some fruit, at any rate. Too often on local bodies no result can be seen from any change of parties. The Highways Committee have had the good sense to recommend the removal of the Brown Dog. Their case is one of extreme common-sense. The figure is offensive to the medical profession, and costs the ratepayers over seven hundred a year to keep up. This is obviously not business. Seven hundred a year is too much to pay for flattering the sentiments of faddists who have been allowed to call the tune, but have not paid the piper. The Council has not accepted the Highways Committee's report entire; but referred it back with an instruction to remove the offensive inscription. This is not so good as taking away the whole thing; but it is certainly a gain. We hope the Council may even yet have the pluck to do the right thing.

If Dr. Cook be an innocent man, how the twigs have been limed to catch him! His Eskimos failed him. His guide up Mount McKinley gave him away. And now he is caught again. The appearance of Captain Loose and Mr. Dunkle—these are delightful names—will be the last straw. According to their story they found Dr. Cook without the observations wanted to make his claim to the Pole a good one. So they offered to manufacture some for him. The story goes on to say that the observations were made and given to Dr. Cook just before he sent his data to Copenhagen.

Cannot the week-end holiday be made to include Friday evening? Not that we have the smallest wish to take more hours from the week's work in this country, which is already severely restricted. It is rather our keenness for work that prompts the thought. If Friday evening counted as holiday, political leaders would not choose it for any of their great efforts. It would drop out as Saturday evening does now. The Friday evening speech cuts out the weekly Review. It cannot deal with it the next day, and therefore is immediately put out of date. Lord Rosebery made his Glasgow speech on Friday; Lord Lansdowne spoke at Plymouth on Friday; Mr. Asquith chooses Friday of this week for the Liberal send-off; and Mr. Balfour on the same Friday publishes his manifesto. For most speeches we are only too glad of the relief that Friday gives. But to have our mouths shut on these supreme efforts is irritating.

A RECONNAISSANCE.

THIS time Unionists take the field with the conditions in their favour; in 1906 everything was against them. Their party had been in office for eleven years without a break; a new and great departure in policy had just been made; the party had not had time to think this out and was seriously divided in opinion. This was fatal to the unity of plan and community of action necessary to success; it blighted enthusiasm, turning some former members of the party into active opponents, and leaving quite a large minority half-hearted, if not actually despondent. Doubts and divisions as to tariff reform had much the same effect on the party as a fighting force as the South African war had on the Liberals in 1900. On the top of this there was the depressing effect of a long term of office. Everyone knows that the odds are against the party in power, and these odds are greatly increased if the period of power has been long. So in 1906 every Unionist took the field knowing that everything was against his side and fully expecting to be beaten. More than this; most Unionists who took the trouble to think about the matter at all felt that it was better for the party that it should go for a time into Opposition and for the country that it should have a short period of Liberal Government. No party fighting in such a mood and in such conditions could win. On any reasonable computation nothing but overwhelming defeat was possible; and it came. This is not being wise after the event. Amongst themselves Unionists were saying freely before the election of 1906 that they could not possibly win. We should say comparatively few Unionists expected anything but defeat, though, of course, they did not look for the débâcle that came. So unusual a result is only explained by unusual conditions; and those in 1906 do explain it.

Now the situation is reversed. We are the attacking party. A Liberal Ministry are in office and have done less than they were expected to do, and painfully less than their supporters expected them to do. They have their explanation, of course; it is all the wicked Lords. But it is bad to have to explain at all; the fact is likely to be marked and remembered more than the explanation. The average elector, not of course the keen "politician," is apt to say to himself: All I know is that the Government promised to do this which I wanted done and have not done it. That man will not work keenly for his party this time. For Unionists on the other hand all is expectation. No shortcomings, avoidable or not, can be charged against them. As an Opposition they have done extraordinarily well for their numbers. No Opposition has ever made a better fight than Mr. Balfour and his little band against the Budget. Seldom has an Opposition made so great an impression on a Government Bill. Very seldom has a Government with a working majority made so many strategic retreats. As a Leader of Opposition in the House of Commons Mr. Balfour has been extremely brilliant. The behaviour of Ministerialists in the House is testimony enough to Mr. Balfour's quality as a debater. In the early days of this Parliament Liberal and Labour members alike were ready to laugh and to interrupt and to jeer whenever Mr. Balfour stood up, but Mr. Balfour's ability schooled them into better behaviour before many months were out. They have long since been educated or cowed into quite a respectful demeanour. "He never gets up but he draws blood" is the comment on Mr. Balfour of one of the very first of the Liberal Ministers. We will be quite honest and give his addition that for any other Unionist he did not care a rap or something less parliamentary. Unionists have for their leader obviously the first man in public life, and the leader is everything. Mr. Asquith, we all know, has first-rate ability; he is a big man; but he is not Mr. Balfour's equal. He has not more force than Mr. Balfour, and he is utterly without Mr. Balfour's flexibility and deftness. Neither has he the "magnetism" or the flair for a popular lead that Mr. Balfour also undoubtedly lacks. The general of neither host has all the qualities of a popular leader;

but, put one against the other, the Unionists have the advantage greatly. They go into the fight under the first public man of the day, feeling that they are on the winning side. For Unionists must be gainers in any case. There is not a Liberal member or a Liberal candidate that believes for a moment that his party will come back after the election as strong as it is now. The majority will on any computation be sensibly reduced. Success makes for success—only too much—and Unionists are certain of considerable success. Liberals cannot improve their position; they do not hope to keep what they have; they stand only to lose.

The constructive force on each side is Tariff Reform and the Budget respectively. Tariff Reform no longer divides the Unionist party: on the contrary, it is a most effective party tonic. The irreconcilable free traders have kindly purged the party of themselves, finding office and salvation on the other side. There are still Unionists who are free traders, but they are loyal to Mr. Balfour and are fighting as hard against the Government as any other members of the party. Tariff Reform has put more fighting enthusiasm into the Unionist rank and file than any Conservative policy in modern times; more, we believe, than did opposition to Home Rule. It is easier to be enthusiastic about something you are going to do than something you are going to prevent being done. Tariff Reform appeals to every side of Conservatism; to social reform as helping to provide employment, being the only policy before the country that even claims to increase the amount of work for the unemployed; to imperialism as recognising the closer relation to ourselves of a colony than a foreign country, and providing a plan, which the colonies earnestly desire, for drawing the Empire together. Negatively, too, Tariff Reform expresses the traditional Conservative dislike of Manchester doctrines, of laissez-faire and anti-imperialism. And the policy is now presented to the country in a better and more scientific form than it was in 1906. To Mr. Chamberlain we owe the impulse, for which he has won the gratitude of the larger part of the whole Empire, but Mr. Balfour has made this impulse a workable policy. Against this the Liberals set the Budget, the strength of which as an electioneering force is that it appears to lay a tremendous burden on the rich and to let off everybody else almost wholly. Naturally this is a popular policy with the majority, who think they will not pay. But it does nothing to increase the amount of work to go round amongst the unemployed; it does not claim to do this: Tariff Reform does. We have to put before the country the unfairness of the Budget, also, to make the people see that in the end part, at least, of the extra burden will fall on themselves. Mr. Lloyd George calculates that his appeal to envy of the rich will be more effective than our appeal to the popular sense of justice. He may be right, but we should not enjoy winning on his cry. Undoubtedly the Budget is the Government's best electioneering card—it is their only good one—we must trump it with Tariff Reform.

And the Lords? Liberals count on popular prejudice against a privileged class, a common, if unlovely, dislike of those who are more fortunate and more highly placed than ourselves. Against this there is to be put the British instinct of snobbery—not much lovelier—the love of a lord. Which of these two evil impulses is the stronger it would be hard to say. But Unionists will tap an immense reserve of force in the average man's fear of what may come after. He may have little love for the Lords and not particularly object to seeing them humbled; but will it end there? Unfortunately for the Liberals, enthusiastic Socialists leave him in no doubt that the humbling of the Lords will be the beginning, and not the end. There are not very many—though far too many—who have nothing to lose; and all who have anything at all will be thinking, It is the Lords' turn now; mine may come before long. These will vote for the Unionists and safety. Neither has the average elector any affection for the House of Commons. All Mr. Asquith's solemn talk about the constitutional position of the House as the people's representative falls on deaf ears. The country—rightly or wrongly—does not care a fig for constitutionalism, and will only ridicule the appeal of Radicals—the Socialists' allies—to the sacredness of constitutional precedent. The people will never wish to make the House of Commons their master. They see that the House of Lords cannot impose on them any legislation; cannot stop any without their being consulted. The House of Commons, cut loose from the Lords, can ride rough-shod over them, passing any laws it will. This "horridest arbitrament" is not to the stomach of the populace. Neither have the Government gone the right way to rouse the country against the Lords. According to them the Lords murdered their education policy, and they took it lying down; the Lords murdered their temperance policy, and they took that lying down. And why have they appealed against the Lords now? Simply because they cannot help it. They want money. The Liberal fanfarronade against the Peers rings hollow enough, when we remember they have not dared to ask the country to condemn the Lords until the Lords themselves made them. What is the use of Liberals talking of trusting the people when they are afraid to appeal to the people?

A BUSINESS MAN ON FISCAL POLICY.

It is refreshing to turn from the whoop of the politician and the shriek of the journalist to the calm and thoughtful utterance of a successful business man on fiscal policy. Sir Julius Wernher is in a peculiarly advantageous position from which to survey the fiscal condition of Great Britain. He is intimately and practically acquainted with the commercial systems of Germany, the United States, and the British Empire. He is the head of the great diamond-producing industry which has its seat in Kimberley. He is largely interested in the gold industry of the Transvaal, and he is the chairman of Fraser and Chalmers, the Anglo-American manufacturers of mining and other machinery, one of our most important exports. It was in the last capacity that Sir Julius Wernher made the speech on fiscal policy on which we are about to comment, and which attracted less notice than it deserved, probably because it ground no party axe. That is precisely what gives it a particular value in our eyes. Though naturally a supporter of the Unionist cause, Sir Julius Wernher does not speak as a partisan.

The point that struck us most is Sir Julius Wernher's emphasis of the fact that what tells in international competition is the capacity to produce on a large scale at a moment's notice. Large orders, which are practically open to tender, go to Germany or America, not because their workmen are better than ours, but because at short notice and within the time of the contract they can finish the work. This capacity of rapid production depends simply upon having a large plant running always at full pressure. This in its turn depends upon the certainty of the home market, which enables the manufacturer to produce largely and therefore economically, with "dumping" as a resource to fall back upon in the periods of depression caused by over-production or over-speculation. Sir Julius Wernher was slily incredulous of the heavy loss inflicted upon the dumping nation, which is one of the stock arguments of the Free Traders. Dumping is injurious, but to the country that is dumped on, not to the country that dumps. The rapidity with which Germany and the United States have recovered from their recent industrial crises was adduced by Sir Julius Wernher as a proof that their fiscal systems are not so erroneous as the Cobdenites would have us believe. England recovers much more slowly from the inevitable cycles of depression which visit trade. Sir Julius contradicted, mildly but explicitly, those who assert, like Lord St. Davids, that capital is always forthcoming for British industrial enterprises. Capital is always available for well-established going concerns, and it was no doubt of his highly prosperous Argentine railways that Lord St. Davids was thinking, though they are hardly home industries. But the old spirit of adventure, which gave Great Britain its former industrial supremacy, is gone, both in those who find the money and those who find the organising brains. Nothing is so difficult as to get capital for a new and speculative venture, either at home or in the colonies. Everybody is grown so cautious that nothing is done. This is not the mood by which a nation claims and keeps ascendancy in the world of trade.

The reason is obvious. People will not venture, because there is less prospect of the large gains which must be there to compensate for big risks. Anyone proposing to embark capital in a large industrial concern is open to the double danger of competition from abroad and socialistic legislation at home. This confluence of deterrent causes makes, as Sir Julius Wernher sees, for unemployment. He makes on this head the remarkable and informing statement that there is generally a shortage of unskilled labour in Germany. This is most important, as it is notoriously the unskilled and casual labourers whose condition gives most anxiety to the Government. Skilled artisans, the aristocracy of the working classes, are generally able to take care of themselves. They have their periods of depression like their employers, but they can wait, which they do with commendable patience and courage, for the turn of the wheel. It is the casual labourers who hang round the dock-gates for the day's job, the unskilled giants who do what may be called the dirty work, who are the trouble and the danger to society in bad times. Well, Sir Julius tells us that Germany, with her highly developed tariff system, is generally short of these men, whom she has to import from over her borders. It is just the reverse with Great Britain. The unemployment of our trade unionists and three-pound-a-weekers is negligible compared with the enforced idleness of our dock labourers and navvies. If by adopting the fiscal system of Germany and the United States we could produce a shortage of unskilled labour the problem of unemployment would be solved.

Sir Julius Wernher said another remarkable thing, though he wrapped it up in cautious language. Looking back at Great Britain's palmy days, at our former industrial hegemony, he said—we do not quote his exact words, but their effect—that a great effort, an extraordinary display of energy, of hard work, of thrift and enthusiasm, might still save us, and restore us to our old headship. But alas! the great effort, the extraordinary energy, where are they? Sir Julius Wernher is unable to descry them in the England of to-day. Quite the contrary, he says; the tendency is towards "the maximum of ease" and higher remuneration. Less work and more wages, to put it shortly, are the objects of our industrial classes of all grades, from the casual labourer to the clerk in the counting-house. They are determined, those who are "in fortune's Bridewell whipt to the laborious task of bread", to get more amusement, and the means of buying more amusement out of their employers. This may be a most laudable design, but unfortunately we cannot compete with the Germans on those terms, unless we defend ourselves by adopting their fiscal system. Nothing but the frugality and enthusiastic energy of our forefathers could enable Great Britain to recapture her industrial supremacy. And as that frugality and energy are not only not forthcoming, but are replaced by the opposite qualities, it is tariff reform or starvation. If the skilled artisans could control their trades-union officials, who have a kind of vested interest in the present commercial system, instead of being controlled by them, tariff reform would be a question of months.

Sir Julius Wernher touched on emigration as a symptom of industrial malaise. Bismarck had an idea, which looks paradoxical, that emigration was a sign, not of weakness, but of strength. The great State-Socialist maintained that emigration was the throwing off of superfluous strength by a body suffering from industrial plethora. There are emigrations and emigrations. Sometimes an exodus of inhabitants from their native soil is caused by religious persecution, as in the case of our Puritans to the United States, and as in the case of the French Protestants to England. Such immigrants, as a rule, form a valuable addition to the State which affords them asylum. Sometimes emigration is caused by the superfluous prosperity of the mother country, by the fact that there is no room for all to make a living. Some of the emigration from England and Scotland to Canada and Australia has been due to this cause. But more often emigration is due to unemployment and starvation at home. These were the causes that drove so many Irishmen to the United States, and these are the causes which now impel so many Englishmen to seek their fortunes in the Argentine Republic, in South Africa, and other parts of the globe. The conclusion of the whole matter is, according to Sir Julius Wernher, that we should cautiously try a gradual and moderate system of tariff reform.

THE LIBERAL CHURCHMAN'S DILEMMA.

As usual before an election, the Liberal Churchman, and especially the Liberal divine, is making broad his phylacteries. A pose of moral superiority and enthusiasm for righteousness has always something unctuously pharisaic about it, even when placed at the service of a semi-Sadducee party—what Stanley and Tait described as the irreligious party, Pusey as the sacrilegious party, and Liddon as the party of unbelief. If the Liberal Churchman is an ecclesiastic, he puts on a solemn mien of confessorship for conviction, whereas it is obvious that he has a far better chance of a deanery or bishopric if he attaches himself to the Liberal party than he would have if he remained undistinguished among the crowd of Conservatives. We are not imputing interested motives to any class or individual, but we are sickened by the pretence of renunciation of worldly prospects which the Liberal priest usually affects. He is a "marked man", no doubt, and that is why he becomes a dignitary when his friends are in office, and often when they are not. The way, notoriously, not to become a dean or bishop is to have uncompromising convictions of Churchmanship.

The Liberal Churchman is at the present moment casting about for excuses for voting with his party and against his Church. And when we speak of Liberal Churchmen we do not, of course, mean the large number of unintelligent electors who attend church, or at any rate would not repudiate membership of the Church, but who vote Liberal at an election. The bulk of the agricultural labourer class does this. And there are tens of thousands of other citizens who, with extremely vague ideas as to what Churchmanship means or Liberalism means, combine the two professions. The clergy, nervously afraid of the accusation of partisanship, have told them very little about either. We are thinking, however, of a much smaller and more educated class which, with its eyes open, essays to hold in combination the principles of Churchmanship and the principles of Liberalism. And we would put on one side the avowed Broad Churchmen. Though in the Church they are not of it; and, having once made up their minds that inconvenient statements in the Prayer-book may be glossed to mean what they like, there is nothing to prevent their voting Liberal except the dislike they usually cherish to separation of Church and State, the union of which ensures the latter being a little Christian and the former not too much so. However, the platform of the new Liberalism is not the libera Chiesa in libero Stato, but a "national" Establishment on "unsectarian" lines; so this scruple disappears. We are left then with the Liberal Churchman proper—attached by habit and conviction to the Church, but a member of the Liberal party. What is he going to do next month? We fear, in five cases out of six, he is going to vote with wilfully shut eyes for the Asquith-Clifford cause, "trusting in the Liberal Government's sense of justice towards the Church"—we believe that is the phrase—and afterwards he will say that he never thought the Church would be treated so unjustly. Like the two hundred "invited" men who left Jerusalem to join Absalom's camp, these people, after every disillusionment, say they went forth in their simplicity and knew not anything.

They never exercise the slightest influence on Liberal anti-ecclesiastical policy—what are Mr. Russell or Mr. Masterman doing in that way? They are the fly on the party wheel. Yet they embarrass the Church out of all proportion to their numbers, giving an appearance of division and enabling Liberalism to boast that the intellectual and spiritually (not to say unctuously) minded Churchmen are on its side.

It is this attitude of pseudo-spirituality—resembling the Gnostic superciliousness towards the mere "psychic" Catholic Christian—which makes the Liberal Churchman so superior a person when "Church defence" is spoken of. How nobly he despises endowments and "temporal privileges"! He will fling the ancient Cambrian Church to those who revile her as "the old alien Hag" rather than not be in sympathy with national aspiration. He forgets perhaps that from the day which sees Welsh Disestablishment enacted the final severance of Imperial Government and Christianity will inevitably date. "Justice to Wales" is promised faithfully for 1910. And 1911, if the present Government returns to power, is to see the universal overthrow of the denominational schools. This is the complementary policy of Liberalism. The Catholic religion is to be disestablished and despoiled in the State, and the new undenominational religion is to be established and endowed in the schools. The Liberal Churchman can give himself no airs of exalted virtue here, but must confess to a double deglutition of principles. He has to swallow both his Churchmanship and his Liberalism, for neither can approve the conferring of a legal monopoly, under State patronage and control, upon a residuum of emasculated religion, defined by the County Council and enforced by the police. Undenominationalism is simply Protestant Dissent upon the rates. Yet the Liberal Churchmen—some of them soi-disant High Churchmen—have one and all, except the Bishop of Birmingham, reconciled themselves to this peculiarly tyrannical and immoral kind of Erastianism. In fact the new Radicalism is every bit as Erastian as the old Whiggery. And Dissent is just as eager now as it was two and a half centuries ago to become the State religion, imposed by Parliament on the whole nation.

There are a good many other consequences of Liberal triumph which an attached Churchman, or indeed any Christian, might be expected to view with apprehension—for example, the proposed large extension of divorce facilities. And directly a Dissenting House of Commons finds time there will be more raging against "disorders in the Church"—that is to say, against observance of the Ornaments Rubric. The Army and Navy will be let down, and then farewell to any chance of influencing the Congo question. But all this will weigh little with the Liberal Churchman by comparison with having a hit at the brewers, or securing an additional five shillings a week to the trades unionist, or crippling the country gentry, or maintaining a free market for whatever is cheap and nasty. He cannot deny that, long before Liberalism left off Constitution-tinkering, the other party was at work on social reform. But such social reform had no pleasant predatory flavour. The twentieth-century Liberal, however, does not know whether he is an Individualist or a Socialist. At one moment he is using the old Manchester and Benthamite phrases about our civil and religious liberties, and the next he is back in a kind of de-Christianised Middle Ages, fixing prices and wages by statute, compelling people to be good against their will, and prescribing the natural religion of every true Protestant Briton. As a free trader he is against regulating the interchange of commodities, but as a collectivist he is in favour of regulating the interchange of labour—which determines the former. We do not deny that Toryism needs a good deal of educating and purging. We by no means say that an earnest Churchman is bound to be a mere party Conservative. But he will find in Tory principles, philosophically and even practically considered, all that is true in the socialistic theory. Combined with Liberalism, Socialism is not only painfully illogical, but it loses hold of religion and becomes purely materialistic. Humanitarianism by itself is the negation of God.

Yet it is simply the humanitarian idea which makes some religious minds think it right to profess Liberalism, since Liberalism rejects all ethical motive except humanitarianism. Thus it is that the Lords Spiritual, who have been so violently attacked for voting in past days on the wrong side, now try to justify their position in Parliament by never speaking except on what is considered to be the philanthropic side. The parochial clergy, too, have been the objects of so much insolent abuse for their want of sympathy with popular causes that they stand almost entirely aloof from politics; and while every tabernacle and meeting-house is ringing with electioneering harangues the English priesthood go on quietly preaching the Gospel and helping their parishioners. We must say we think this attitude is being overdone. Candidates who want to fight the Church's battle complain that the Church gives them no support. After all, Churchmanship must mean the influencing of the course of human affairs in accordance with certain sacred principles, not something which at election time can be either muffled or bartered.

CONSCIENCE AND COCOA.

MESSRS. CADBURY won a technical verdict in their libel action against the "Standard", but their legal victory was a moral defeat. The libel the "Standard" wrote of them was so direct and merciless, it attacked their character as religious professors and philanthropists so plainly, that we should not have been surprised if the jury had assessed the damages for the harm done them at twenty thousand pounds. Messrs. Cadbury brought the action for the sole purpose of vindicating their personal character and reputation. The attack was made upon them, it is true, in their character of cocoa manufacturers who had obtained their material for years from plantations cultivated by slave labour. But the trade quality of their cocoa was unimpeached and unimpeachable. Indeed, one of the chief merits of the slave cocoa of San Thomé was that it was peculiarly valuable commercially, and Messrs. Cadbury were unwilling to give it up for this reason. It would have been less difficult to deal with the troublesome question of slavery if the cocoa had not been of so fine a quality. It was as men therefore of peculiar standing in the world of philanthropy, especially of philanthropy in all questions between employer and employed, and not as cocoa manufacturers, that they brought their action against the "Standard". The contemptuous verdict of one farthing shows two things. One is that the "Standard" misconstrued Messrs. Cadbury's negotiations relating to the San Thomé slavery; the other that the jury, putting their own construction on these negotiations, thought that Messrs. Cadbury deserved no sympathy and were entitled to no real reparation. If they had been misunderstood, their prolonged dallying with the slavery question, the struggle between conscience and cocoa, had gone on so hesitatingly and timidly that they had contributed themselves to the making of a natural mistake. When a jury, in loyally following a judge's directions as to the legal point in issue, cannot avoid giving a plaintiff a verdict it marks its disapproval of the moral side of a plaintiff's conduct by giving him nominal damages. The humble farthing crumples up any high moral pretensions with which the plaintiff brings his action; and intimates to him that the less he appeals to them the less ridiculous he will be. Messrs. Cadbury's counsel told the jury that he believed when they had heard the record of the Messrs. Cadbury, and of the labour and expense they had incurred to improve the conditions of the native labourers, they would say it was an honour and a credit to them, and that they might well be proud of what they had done. The answer of the jury to this was to give Messrs. Cadbury a farthing, in spite of a Judge's summing up which was in effect a direction to give heavy damages.

Judging from the verdict, what do the jury believe Messrs. Cadbury ought to have done, if they were to be honoured and credited? Clearly that they ought long before 1908 to have ceased buying San Thomé cocoa. We are to assume from their verdict that Messrs. Cadbury did many things which showed they were uneasy about the slavery at San Thomé, and that they would like to put an end to it. All the credit this can give them, let them take. For honour there is not much room. There were too many obvious reasons why Messrs. Cadbury, as inheritors of the old Quaker tradition, and the more recent tradition of the "Daily News" and South African Chinese labour, should desire that the scandal should cease and as little as possible be known of the connexion they had had with it. This would save their credit without any special credit attaching to them for what they actually did. All this can be accounted for by mixed motives in which conscience, social, political, and religious respectability and commercial advantages can be discovered making their action ambiguous. There would have been no such ambiguity about ceasing to buy San Thomé cocoa. But this is the one thing they did not do. They left undone the one thing they ought to have done. If they had done this everybody would have exclaimed "What noble people these Cadburys are, and how worthy of their reputation for piety and philanthropy and indomitable resolution to make war against every form of slavery!" The farthing damages tells them that, instead of acting on their own moral and religious feelings, they were anxious to be assured by Sir Edward Grey, or the Aborigines Protection Society, or the Anti-Slavery Society, or Chambers of Commerce, that they might still go on buying San Thomé cocoa. Why may we suspect they preferred to leave the abolition of slavery to Sir Edward Grey rather than to "wash their hands" of it and take their own course? The answer is because it was easier and it involved no money loss. The American and German rivals would have no advantage over the British cocoa makers, all being put on the same footing. Messrs. Rowntree wrote to Messrs. Cadbury disagreeing with the method of attaining their ends by Government action upon Portugal. They thought cocoa manufacturers themselves ought to form a combination which would bring down prices and so force the planters to give in. But it would be necessary to win over the American manufacturers. This was found impossible. The Americans did not pretend to have a conscience. The result of individual action by a British cocoa manufacturer, as Messrs. Rowntree observed, would be great loss. This is the bed-rock of the whole stratum of delay which lies between 1901, when Messrs. Cadbury first knew of slavery in San Thomé, and 1908, when Messrs. Cadbury decided at last to cease buying San Thomé cocoa.

We are not forgetting Messrs. Cadbury's difficult position or suggesting that business men, barring the whole tribe of British cocoa manufacturers, would be expected to sacrifice business to scruples about slavery. But then it was precisely Messrs. Cadbury, as newspaper proprietors, who carried on that furious and reckless crusade—it was called a holy mission—against South African Chinese labour. There is not space nor necessity for describing what the horrors of San Thomé slavery were and are. We must refer to Sir Edward Carson's speech and cross-examination for that. Messrs. Cadbury did not even attempt to mitigate them. They never made this a matter on which solely their own conscience ought to decide, apart from policy international or otherwise. On the slavery question they were purists. They were of the straitest sect of the Pharisees; what a teetotaler is on liquor. Could a teetotaler cocoa manufacturer use liqueurs to make his goods more tasty? We suppose he might for chocolates and sweets. But what should we think of him as a conscientious teetotaler? He might conceivably not know of the use of liqueurs in his sweets, but when it was brought to his notice he must not go on using them seven or eight years longer, or teetotal societies will disown him and other people laugh at him. He simply must not even if he pleads that he expects the Government to bring in a Licensing Bill to prohibit the use of liqueurs in sweets in the course of a few years. Messrs. Cadburys may persuade themselves that what they did was for the best. The jury do not find that they were carrying on a pretence of negotiations with the real intention of stifling the whole thing; but the farthing damages means that they have nothing to plume themselves on, and that the only conduct which would have been straight was to refuse to buy San Thomé cocoa at the earliest stages without dwelling on consequences. The verdict of the jury must mean this, as everything else was done. This one thing thou lackest—and the young man went away sorrowing to find something else to do more convenient than what his conscience told him was right. The pious Messrs. Cadbury must take the consequences, one of which is a farthing damages. This misfortune has happened to them because they chose to stray into the paths of cunning worldly wisdom and diplomacy in a matter which was one simply for aye or no in a question of absolute wrong or right. Slavery to some men may be relatively right or wrong according to circumstances. Messrs. Cadbury have preached that in no circumstances can slavery be anything but absolutely wrong. Yet in San Thomé they went on year after year parleying with it and tolerating it. They did not shake themselves clear of it until a year came when they were obliged to. A conscience that works so slowly and laboriously may do for some, but not for British cocoa manufacturers. It ought to be worth more than a farthing.

PRESIDENT TAFT AND CENTRAL AMERICA.

PRESIDENT TAFT'S Message to Congress is in many respects a welcome change from similar pronouncements by his predecessor. He does not attempt to sermonise an inattentive universe nor does he bluster and futilely threaten the great moneyed interests of his own country. We shall see whether he may not recommend particular legislation in Special Messages, but the only matter calling for attention today is the very significant reference to the affairs of Southern and Central America. If Mr. Roosevelt's disciples find a lack of enthusiasm in Mr. Taft for their leader's home policy, they cannot reproach him for want of continuity in foreign policy. The President is inspired by the same ideas which led Mr. Roosevelt to collect foreign debts in S. Domingo and to set up a new State in Panama; matters have only moved a stage further.

We have been accustomed to fulminations by the ex-President, particularly in his Philadelphia speech as to the preservation of "civilisation and decency" by communities which were accustomed to appeal for protection to the Monroe Doctrine. But the utterance in the Message of Tuesday regarding Nicaragua goes further, and, when read along with Mr. Knox' admonition to the Nicaraguan envoy, seems to open up a serious prospect of actual armed intervention. If it should take place, it will only be another step forward in the establishment of a practical protectorate of the United States over Central America. This obviously became inevitable (supposing no other Great Power should intervene) directly the United States took over the Panama Canal, engineered the revolution in Colombia and induced this country to abandon its rights under the Clayton-Bulwer Treaty. The steps towards the consummation of the project have been rapidly taken during the last few years.

It is naturally a difficult task to awaken much interest in Europe over the politics of Nicaragua and her sister States. President Zelaya may be, and probably is, a sanguinary tyrant of the worst type. But he is President de facto and de jure. It is true that a revolution is in progress; such movements generally are in those parts; but President Zelaya is the recognised head of the State. Two filibusters from the United States have been taken in arms against his Government and executed. It is alleged that they have been tortured, but no evidence of this is adduced. The matter is not one on which a civilised Government can find any legal ground for interference, and is only imported for purposes of prejudice. The real reasons advanced last week by the Secretary of State for taking action are well worth consideration, for they set forth the methods by which the hegemony of the United States in those regions is being rapidly established.

In the first place, the Washington Agreement of 1907, by which the Central American States bound themselves to live at peace with one another and to abstain from intrigue, has given Costa Rica, Salvador and Guatemala an excuse for requesting the United States Government to interfere to check anarchy in Nicaragua. How this protest has been engineered it is not easy to prove, but it is easy to conjecture. Without doubt the same means of persuasion have been employed which are always available to bring about the election of presidents agreeable to Washington and the success of legislative proposals which may also secure approval in the same quarter. But the most ominous sentence in Mr. Knox' denunciation is that in which he intimates that some "constitutional" government in Nicaragua will have to bind itself by a Convention "for the benefit of all the Governments concerned as a guarantee for the future loyal support of the Washington Conventions and their peaceful and progressive aims". As the "Times" correspondent truly remarks, this seems to imply a determination to compel the Central American Republics to live harmoniously together, and, if so, marks a remarkable development of the Monroe Doctrine.

As we have pointed out before, the extreme assertion of Monroe principles was sure to lead in the end to this position: that the right of protection by the United States against foreign interference would involve the assertion of a right to maintain order in the States so protected. The time and method of its assertion would be determined solely by the convenience of the United States. We are likely to see this great advance made shortly. No remonstrance may be expected from the other Republics of Central America, and, once the right is admitted in one case, it will be advanced in all. It is obvious also that when a Great Power has secured an admission of its right to protect a lesser State against foreigners and also a peculiar right of its own to interfere in the internal affairs of the protected country to set them straight, we have at once all the essentials of a Protectorate such as exists already in Cuba and Porto Rico.

This result may not be attained immediately, but is hardly likely to be very long delayed. The steps by which the United States are obtaining complete mastery over Central America and the Caribbean Sea have been consistently thought out and rapidly taken. First Cuba and Porto Rico were annexed after a filibustering war. Then by the late President's direction, though for long against the wish of the Committee on Foreign Relations, United States warships have been collecting the revenues of S. Domingo and paying forty-five per cent. to foreign creditors, while the remainder goes towards purposes of internal administration. It is only fair to say that both debtors and creditors benefit by this, but the control of the United States Government is firmly riveted on the neck of the mulatto republic. By this prudent action the Americans have also secured for the purposes of their Navy Samana Bay, on the north-west of the island, one of the finest naval stations in the world. The refusal to allow the Danish Ministry to sell S. Thomas, S. Croix, and S. John to Germany also indicated a settled policy. When the Panama Canal is finished the United States will have a complete chain of stations establishing their grip upon the whole strategical system from Florida to Venezuela. Without the presence of an overwhelming British fleet our own West Indian possessions will be obviously at American mercy. In this connexion should be considered the Annual Report of the Secretary of the United States Navy published on Thursday in the English papers. This document deals generally with naval stations, but alludes especially to a matter which concerns this country above all others—the growth of trade in the Gulf of Mexico and the Caribbean region. Political and strategical advantages in those parts we cheerfully and cheaply abandoned by the abrogation of the Clayton-Bulwer Treaty, but our trade with Central and Southern America is surely a matter in which our Government may be reasonably expected to take some interest. It is well to remember that these Central American Republics are in a most backward condition, but every year, especially after the opening of the Canal, their trade capacities will grow greater. With the institution of an American Protectorate would come also the institution of preferential duties for the benefit of the United States. At present the South American greatly prefers to trade with Great Britain. It is a sore point at Washington that while Brazil exports more than double the amount to the United States that she does to this country she takes from us nearly three times as much as she does from them; and the trade of Chile with the United Kingdom is both in imports and exports treble that with the United States. This tendency is of course magnified in the case of Argentina.

In the future this healthy tendency will be checked unless we look to it. It might be a good move to acquire the debt of one of these Central American countries and satisfy the creditors, who have not received anything from the original debtors. Not long ago an attempt was made by Mr. Pierpont Morgan to buy up the debt of Honduras, and a similar effort in America might succeed in the future. One thing is clear—unless we show greater vigilance in protecting our pockets than we have in our policy, the enormous development of trade certain to come in those regions will be for the benefit of others less scrupulous but certainly farther-seeing.

THE CITY.

THE directors of the Bank of England are doing their best to assist the Government in making fresh issues of Treasury Bills. Without any material improvement in their own position, the directors on Thursday reduced the discount rate from 5 to 4½ per cent. This is the Bank's reply to the panic-mongers. And the continued improvement in prices which has taken place in the Stock Exchange is a further answer to these false prophets. The recovery in Home Railway stocks has excited most attention, though it is no more than was predicted here some weeks ago. We pointed out then that a very great improvement was taking place in Home Railway traffic, and that it could not be long before this was reflected in prices. The inevitable has happened, and, despite some relapse from the best points, prices are from 2 to 5 per cent. higher than they were a month ago. There is ample room for a further rise, and if in January a Conservative Government should be returned to power we may expect quite a "boom" in this class of security. Even if hopes in this direction are disappointed, there should be no permanent relapse, for investors must be impressed with the improved traffic prospects, and will look to intrinsic conditions of the companies to counteract the scare schemes of any Radical Government. It is a truism that Home Railway stocks will always find buyers when traffics are increasing, and the heavy fall which has taken place in values in the last two years is largely accounted for by the decline in revenue. A recent decision of the Railway and Canal Commission as to the rates for the carriage of house coal considerably improves the prospects of the various companies. Hitherto the companies have carried house coal on the basis of 20½ cwts. to the ton; now it has been decided that rates must be paid on the full quantity. This means that an additional charge of 2½ per cent. can be made, and, if one thinks of the enormous tonnage carried, it will be realised that the money gain to the companies will be very considerable. The most disappointing company at the moment is the Great Western, which is slower than others to recover traffic. The Fishguard experiment has yet to be proved successful from a business point of view. A certain amount of prestige is gained to the company by facilitating the delivery of mails, but it remains to be seen whether there will be any adequate compensation for the expenditure incurred.

The generally improved feeling in the Stock Exchange has brought in many buyers for Kaffirs, and an apparent scarcity of stock has induced a belief that we are on the eve of important developments in this market. We are still sceptical of any pronounced revival, believing that the finance houses are yet unprepared to offer the support necessary for the maintenance of prices. When the revival comes in earnest, it will be Rhodesian shares that will lead the way, as only these possess speculative possibilities. Practically all there is to be known about the Transvaal mines is public property, and there can be no speculation where there are no chances. West African mines will probably come forward at an early date, as here are all the elements of a gamble, and the progress made in developments suggests that there may be several pleasant surprises for shareholders. The further postponement of milling by the Prestea Block A is disappointing, but the reasons given for the action cannot be questioned.

There must be no "whitewashing" of the directors of the Law Guarantee Trust and Accident Society. The deplorable condition into which the affairs of the company have fallen is entirely due to them. Common sense should have convinced them of the risky nature of the business they were undertaking, and a little financial knowledge would have shown them that big reserves were imperative if they were to trust to the law of averages to bring them through a crisis. We can find no excuse for the chairman's sanguine remarks of some months ago, when he scouted the suggestion of a call on the shares. We agree that in the interest of shareholders voluntary liquidation is preferable to a compulsory winding-up by the court, but in the interests of the general public an official inquiry should be held.

A prospectus is issued of a "Rio de Janeiro 5 per cent. Benedictine Order Gold Loan". At first glance this would seem to be a loan of the Government or Province of Rio de Janeiro. It is nothing of the sort, and the description savours of sharp practice. The security offered is freehold property in Rio de Janeiro belonging to the Benedictine Order in Brazil, and while it may be worth all that is claimed for it, we consider that the risk of holding is too great for anyone outside the country. The issue lends point to last week's warning against too lavish an interest in South American securities.

FARMERS IN COUNCIL.

CATTLE SHOW week has come and gone, but the streets no longer show those rubicund waistcoats, broad-brimmed hats, and drab gaiters which provided annual jokes for the comic papers of the last generation. Partly this is owing to the growth of London—the countryman is more easily submerged in the crowds that hurry along the central thoroughfares—but it is more due to the farmer himself, who is nowadays sufficiently in touch with town to imitate its ways and adopt its garb. We met on Monday last in Regent Street the most magnificent representative of John Bull among our acquaintances—in a top hat and a frock-coat—and he was bound not to any of the sights but to a discussion on Mendelian breeding and the principles of heredity at the Farmers' Club. Cattle Show week still has its social side, but it is also a week of earnest enquiry and hard debate, because all the societies connected with agriculture, whether on its industrial, its political, its scientific or educational side, hold their meetings in London at this period.

But though the modern farmer is keenly interested in the organisation and the politics of his business, and has taken to discussing them with a readiness and a freedom from prejudice which did not exist in country affairs a generation ago, there seems little sign of an agrarian party in Great Britain. As yet, indeed, group politics have made no headway in our State, even Labour and Socialism have not as yet succeeded in convincing anyone but themselves that they are more than Liberalism writ new, and as far as agricultural life is concerned no such community of interest exists between the three classes living on the land as will supply driving power to an exclusive party. The landlords have always commanded both the votes and the real loyalty of their tenant farmers, to an extent which has always surprised the outside observer and not unfrequently disappointed the calculations of the politician. This has been due in part to snobbery—the farmer likes to class himself with the landlord and look down on the low lot who live by trade in the towns; in part again self-interest has been a factor—it has often been dangerous to be known to hold views in opposition to those of the squire; but in the main it has been a genuine spirit of following his natural leaders, men whom he knew at home and trusted. But no loyalty, no desire for unity, can disguise the fact that the interests of landlord and tenant are not always identical; they may, as in Ireland, become fiercely opposed, and there are not wanting signs of a coming divergence in this country. The labourers' interests again are not with any agrarian party; they may follow the landlords for their qualities of leadership, but they will be mostly against the farmers. Some labourers are old enough to remember the palmy days of tenant-farming in the third quarter of last century, enough to keep the tale alive on the countryside how that period of prosperity for the farmer was a time of bad wages and high prices for the labourers. During the last thirty years the labourer has gained a considerable cash rise in his wages, and with that an equal or greater increase in the purchasing power of each shilling, all gained directly in the teeth of times so bad as to bring about the downfall of many of his old masters. Small wonder that it is hard to convince the labourer that his interests are in any way bound up with the landlord and the farmer. The labourer, too, has old scores to pay off, and we have always thought that some of the bitterness of the Radical party against the landed interest is an inherited resentment at the old bad tyranny of the farmers in the past on the sons of those who were forced into the towns.

This threefold division of interests, with all the voting power at the silent inarticulate end, makes the united action of a country party very difficult of realisation in Great Britain, but so many efforts towards a common cause are being made that it may not be out of place to review the organisations which the agricultural interests now possess. Of these the Royal Agricultural Society, the Central Land Association, the Central Chamber of Agriculture, and the Farmers' Club are the most representative, and have all been meeting in London this week. With its ten thousand members, its seventy years' record, its exalted patrons, the Royal Agricultural Society takes precedence, but this venerable body has long forsworn all claims to leadership. It has declined all contact with politics or even with matters of legislation, and though it has recently gained a more elective constitution it is still a close oligarchy, which has settled down to think only of the success of its annual show. It has naturally become a landlords' society, though the great commercial interests connected with agriculture—the raisers of pedigree stock, the implement manufacturers, the seedsmen, etc.—have always been well represented in its management. The abstention of the Royal Agricultural Society from the field of politics has led recently to the foundation of a body definitely organised for action in legislative matters—the Central Land Association—which, though associated with no party and open to all classes of the agricultural community, is yet mainly recruited from the same class as are dominant in the Royal Agricultural Society—the landlords and their agents.

The Central Chamber of Agriculture exists to watch over all measures affecting agriculture; as it is in constant touch with more than a hundred county chambers and farmers' clubs, and has an organisation for collecting and focussing their opinions, it is perhaps the most effective political agency that farmers now possess. It will be found, however, that the landlord point of view is still very dominant in both the Central and its affiliated chambers up and down the country. Not only do certain landlords and agents take a good deal of natural interest in these societies, and as educated men soon acquire a leading part in their management, but also the traders connected with the business of farming—valuers, corn merchants, manure dealers, etc.—are always prominent at these meetings, and are always on the landlords' side—plus royaliste que le roi. Of course there are tenant farmers well to the fore in the county and in the Central chambers, but very often they are men with extensive business connexions, more dealers and valuers than farmers proper.

The Farmers' Club is one of the oldest societies connected with agriculture, and has perhaps a stronger tenant-farmer representation than any of the bodies mentioned before; it is in the main, however, a social meeting-place, and its discussions more often deal with actual farming and with scientific developments than with legislative proposals. The Farmers' Club is perhaps taking an increasing part in agricultural politics, but as a rule it acts in concert with the Central Chamber. Thus the various societies which have been meeting in London during the past week, which stand to the public for agriculture, to which again a member of Parliament would look for guidance as to the feeling of the farming interest, all in the main represent the landlord's opinions; in all of them his natural leadership and his point of view have been tacitly accepted. A new movement, however, and one which, though still in harmony with the older institutions, may eventually take a line of its own, is represented by the Lincolnshire Farmers' Union, an organisation which originated in that county but has since spread all over England. This is a farmers' society, which makes its members subscribe according to the acreage they hold; it deliberately excludes not only the landlords themselves but their agents and the traders and valuers who have so often been the landlords' supporters and spokesmen; the tenant farmer, who has not always been articulate in the past, means to have a society for himself. It is a society run by the younger generation of men who have been educated alongside the sons of professional men and traders, by farmers who look at farming as a business and not as a feudal inheritance; it is going to be an active class society, militant, narrow and even selfish, but effective. It has grown with remarkable rapidity, and is now formulating a series of test questions to be put to every Parliamentary candidate; and according to the answers, and not according to party, will the Farmers' Union throw its weight into the electoral scale. So far the Farmers' Union is in harmony with what we may call the landlords', we might even say with Conservative, policy; the coming of Tariff Reform will provide the crux. If the manufacturing party get their will and food is to be kept cheap by either no taxation at all or such a low taxation on colonial produce as will maintain prices at the level of the open market, these men will cross into the other anti-landlord and anti-manufacturers' camp, and they will easily take their labourers with them. But if on the other hand they get the protection for agriculture they look for, they can mitigate the worst effects to their labourers of any rise in food prices, particularly where as in Lincolnshire so much of the wages are paid in kind, and they thus can save the labourers' vote for a united country party. What we fear is that the agricultural community, whether landlords or farmers, have not got the leaders just now who can make their claims good against the powerful manufacturing interests; but if when Tariff Reform comes into its kingdom the views prevail of those who stand only for State and Empire, then the farmer will not be forgotten.

A CLASSIC FARCE.

By Max Beerbohm.

"The Importance of Being Earnest" has been revived by Mr. Alexander at the St. James's Theatre, and is as fresh and as irresistible as ever. It is vain to speculate what kind of work Oscar Wilde would have done had the impulse for play-writing survived in him. It is certain that a man of such variegated genius, and a man so inquisitive of art-forms, would not, as some critics seem to think he would, have continued to turn out plays in the manner of "The Importance of Being Earnest". This, his last play, is not the goal at which he would have rested. But, of the plays that he wrote specifically for production in London theatres, it is the finest, the most inalienably his own. In "Lady Windermere's Fan" and "A Woman of No Importance" and "An Ideal Husband", you are aware of the mechanism—aware of Sardou. In all of them there is, of course, plenty of humanity, and of intellectual force, as well as of wit and humour; and these qualities are the more apparent for the very reason that they are never fused with the dramatic scheme, which was a thing alien and ready-made. The Sardou manner is out-of-date; and so those three plays do, in a degree, date. It is certain that Oscar Wilde would later have found for serious comedy a form of his own, and would have written serious comedies as perdurable as his one great farce.

In "The Importance of Being Earnest" there is a perfect fusion of manner and form. It would be truer to say that the form is swallowed up in the manner. For you must note that not even in this play had Oscar Wilde invented a form of his own. On the contrary, the bare scenario is of the tritest fashion in the farce-writing of the period. Jack pretends to his niece, as an excuse for going to London, that he has a wicked brother whom he has to look after. Algernon, as an excuse for seeing the niece, impersonates the wicked brother. Jack, as he is going to marry and has no further need of a brother, arrives with the news of the brother's death; and so forth. Just this sort of thing had served as the staple for innumerable farces in the 'sixties and 'seventies and 'eighties—and would still be serving so if farce had not now been practically snuffed out by musical comedy. This very ordinary clod the magician picked up, turning it over in his hands—and presto! a dazzling prism for us.

How was the trick done? It is the tedious duty of the critic to ask such questions, and to mar what has been mere delight by trying to answer them. Part of the play's fun, doubtless, is in the unerring sense of beauty that informs the actual writing of it. The absurdity of the situations is made doubly absurd by the contrasted grace and dignity of everyone's utterance. The play abounds, too, in perfectly chiselled apothegms—witticisms unrelated to action or character, but so good in themselves as to have the quality of dramatic surprise. There are perhaps, in the course of the play, a dozen of those merely verbal inversions which Oscar Wilde invented, and which in his day the critics solemnly believed—or at any rate solemnly declared—to be his only claim to the title of wit. And of these inversions perhaps half-a-dozen have not much point. But, for the rest, the wit is of the finest order. "What between the duties expected of one during one's lifetime, and the duties exacted after one's death, land has ceased to be either a profit or a pleasure. It gives one a position, and prevents one from keeping it up. That's all that can be said about land." One cannot help wishing it were all that "the Dukes" had had to say recently. It is a perfect presentation of the case which they have presented so lengthily and so maladroitly. And it is only a random sample of the wit that is scattered throughout "The Importance of Being Earnest". But, of course, what keeps the play so amazingly fresh is not the inlaid wit, but the humour, the ever-fanciful and inventive humour, irradiating every scene. Out of a really funny situation Oscar Wilde would get dramatically the last drop of fun, and then would get as much fun again out of the correlative notions aroused in him by that situation. When he had to deal with a situation which, dealt with by any ordinary dramatist, would be merely diagrammatic, with no real fun at all in it, always his extraneous humour and power of fantastic improvisation came triumphantly to the rescue. Imagine the final scenes of this play treated by an ordinary dramatist! How tedious, what a signal for our departure from the theatre, would be the clearing-up of the mystery of Jack Worthing's parentage, of the baby in the hand-bag, the manuscript in the perambulator! But the humour of the writing saves the situation, makes it glorious. Lady Bracknell's recital of the facts to the trembling Miss Prism—" Through the elaborate investigations of the metropolitan police, the perambulator was discovered at midnight, standing by itself in a remote corner of Bayswater. It contained the manuscript of a three-volume novel of more than usual revolting sentimentality "—and Miss Prism's subsequent recognition of the hand-bag by " the injury it received through the upsetting of a Gower Street omnibus in younger and happier days " and by " the stain on the lining caused by the explosion of a temperance beverage, an incident that occurred at Leamington "—these and a score of other extraneous touches keep us laughing whole-heartedly until the actual fall of the curtain.

Or again, imagine an ordinary dramatist's treatment of the great scene in the second act—the scene when Jack Worthing, attired in deepest mourning, comes to announce the death of the imaginary brother who is at this moment being impersonated on the premises by Algernon. I call this a " great " scene, for, though it is (as I have hinted) essentially stale, it is so contrived as to be quite fresh. It is, indeed, and will always be cited as, a masterpiece of dramatic technique. If the audience knew at the beginning of the act that Jack was presently to arrive in deep mourning, the fun would be well enough. On the other hand, if, when he arrived, it had to be explained to them why he was in deep mourning, and what was his mission, there would be no fun at all. But the audience is in neither of these states. In the first act, Jack has casually mentioned, once or twice, that he means to " kill off " his imaginary brother. But he doesn't say when or how he is going to do it. As the second act opens and proceeds, the audience has forgotten all about his intention. They are preoccupied by Algernon. And so, when the sable figure of Jack at length appears, they are for a moment bewildered, and then they vaguely remember, and there is a ripple of laughter, and this ripple swells gradually to a storm of laughter, as the audience gradually realises the situation in its full richness. None but a man with innate instinct for the theatre could have contrived this effect. But the point is that only Oscar Wilde, having contrived the effect, could have made the subsequent scene a worthy pendant to it. Miss Prism's comment on hearing that the cause of the brother's death was a chill, " As a man sows, so shall he reap "; Dr. Chasuble's offer to conduct the funeral service, and Jack's hasty explanation that his brother seems " to have expressed a desire to be buried in Paris ", and Dr. Chasuble's " I fear that hardly points to any very serious state of mind at the last "—these are of the things that have kept the play young, and have won for it, in dramatic literature, a place apart.

It is a solemn thought that Mr. Alexander and Mr. Allan Aynesworth were playing their present parts fifteen years ago. They both, however, seem to have worn as well as the play itself. Miss Stella Patrick Campbell and Miss Rosalie Toller are charming in the parts of Gwendolen and Cecily.

OUR YOUNG PAINTERS, AND A CRITIC.

By Laurence Binyon.

THE last exhibition of the New English Art Club, held in the spring, was not only one of the most brilliant in the history of the club, but seemed to mark a certain change of temper, the infusion of a new current of life. I wonder if the late Mr. Frith, who so long outlived the fashions of his heyday, was aware that his work, after being the typical object of scorn for the superior person, had come to be regarded with a quite affectionate admiration—some of his work, at least—by a group of the rising painters of the end of last century? Probably not; but I seem to remember some controversy, I think in this Review, when the art of Frith had been compared advantageously with the art of Madox Brown. Such a comparison seems to me absurd. Yet it is easy to understand what repels in Madox Brown and what attracts in Frith's " Dolly Varden ", for instance. A frank joy in pretty things, in the sunshine and amenity of life, and in the pleasure of painting them; it is this which has been an abiding inspiration to the New English group of painters, and we have all enjoyed the gaiety and impulsiveness, the genuine spontaneous charm, of their pictures, year by year. But in shutting themselves out from other aspects of life, in shunning extravagant and heroic adventures, they have avoided, it is true, the laboriousness and grimness that inhere in the art of Madox Brown, but they have lost also his great ardour and his serious intensity. In the spring exhibition at Suffolk Street, dominated by the genius of Mr. John, it seemed as if the club were going out to conquer fresh fields and break its habitual limitations. No doubt this will be so. In the present show the club " marks time ", for the most part; but it is an admirable exhibition, with the usual high average of quality that we expect. Mr. Steer is as rich and broad and spacious as ever in his Severn landscape; Mr. Russell and Professor Brown are as successful in a kindred vein; and less prominent exhibitors, like Mrs. Cheston, have learnt in the same school to catch on canvas the light and breeze with notable skill and freshness. There is, of course, a Corfe Castle; the long siege of that ancient citadel by the New English painters will become one of the memorable events in its history; this time it is Mr. Arthur Streeton who has made it his own in a large canvas, full of sun and shadow, exceedingly vigorous and effective. Among landscapes the newer note, of which I wrote last spring, is present only in the paintings by Professor Holmes, who loves mountains and austere solitudes as much as his fellow-exhibitors delight in broad champaigns, breezy shores, and picnic-haunts. The " Harter Fell, from Mardale " has a beautiful solemnity of colour and design, which gives it a curious independence among its surroundings. Again, there are a number of pleasant interiors and domestic scenes, as usual; and particularly welcome is the " Baby's Bath " of Mr. Tonks, painted with a charm and naturalness that disguise the learning and mastery in the drawing of the grouped figures and the painting of reflected firelight on various surfaces and textures. I must also mention a picture by Mr. Charles Stabb, called " The Book of Poems " (No. 130). The reader, a girl in a blue dress, has laid aside her book, and her musing figure detaches itself against the white wall by which she sits. Subjects of this kind have been treated again and again by painters of the New English group; but Mr. Stabb by fine simplicity of design and colour, a simplicity anything but bare or jejune, has raised his picture above the level of mere genre, and given it an indefinable distinction. Another small and unobtrusive work is Miss Gwen John's " L'Etudiante " (No. 51), to me the most memorable thing in the whole exhibition. Here is that intensity, quiet and shy though it be, which counts for so much more than brilliancy, and which is so rare in contemporary art. It is a picture of singular delicacy and beauty. Mr. John sends an able portrait, but his little canvas, the strange " Girl on the Cliff ", and a large charcoal composition of a gipsy group belong more to the essence of his genius. Mr. Orpen is very well represented; and there are good examples of the portraiture of Mr. Connard, Mr. Von Glehn, Mr. Kelly, and Mr. Philpot; to say nothing of Mr. Sargent. Mr. Walter Sickert's " The New Bedford ", a vision of a music-hall interior, is one of the most original pictures in the gallery, one of the things by which this exhibition will be remembered. Among the drawings and water-colours, always an admirable section, Mr. Muirhead Bone's pastels and black-chalk studies form a splendid group, opposite a group of Mr. Beerbohm's caricatures. Mr. Dodd, in his chalk portraits and groups, Mr. Pearce, in his water-colours of French street-scenes, show each advancing mastery; and Mr. W. Tryon is a welcome addition to the little band of artists who are returning to the old methods of the water-colour drawing in no archaistic spirit.

The exhibition at Suffolk Street is only one manifestation of the productiveness of members of the New English Art Club. Mr. Orpen, for instance, has been even more brilliantly represented this season at the Goupil Gallery Salon, where also Mr. Connard's landscapes with figures were conspicuous. With these two exhibitions, and the choice collection at Messrs.

Knoedler's in Bond Street, where examples of Mr. Strang, Mr. Shannon, and Mr. Ricketts, as well as Mr. Nicholson, Mr. Orpen, Mr. John, Mr. Pryde, Mr. Glyn Philpot, and others of the younger school have been seen, there has been plenty of material this autumn for taking stock of the non-academic painters of the day. Mr. Wedmore's handsome volume, "Some of the Moderns" (Virtue, 15s.), comes therefore at an opportune moment. The book consists of brief essays on ten painters, with reproductions from representative pictures, eighty in all, grouped after each essay. Mr. Wedmore calls it "a study of certain interesting individualities in our contemporary art". The ten chosen are Nicholson, Roussel, Steer, Priestman, Walter Sickert, David Muirhead, Livens, Connard, Bone, and Orpen. The choice is not, I imagine, an exclusive one, though a sentence in the preface excites curiosity as to those Mr. Wedmore has purposely excluded. I have no wish to quarrel with the choice, but I think that the inclusion of certain other "interesting individualities" would have greatly enriched the scope and range of the volume. And, as this name or that occurs to the mind, how brilliant and vigorous, one reflects, is this school of painters now among us, none of whom is past his prime and most of whom are in their early maturity! Mr. Wedmore discourses sympathetically, in the style familiar to us, of the characteristics and the aims of each of his chosen group. It would be impossible, as it would be unfair, in the case of men who are still but midway (we hope) in their career, to attempt anything like a final summing-up. Mr. Wedmore does not attempt it, nor do his essays pretend to be in any sense biographical, though he communicates to us one or two interesting avowals on the part of the artists. Thus we learn something of Mr. Connard's views on flower-painting. He thinks that in the past flowers have been painted with too little regard to the fact that they reflect light so keenly and abundantly; and so he is fond of painting them in a vivid shower of sunshine. Here, it seems to me, is an apt point of departure for interesting discussion. Flower-painting is an enthusiasm of many of the younger generation, and preoccupation with light is characteristic, too, of the time. What gains or losses are involved in the modern approach to these themes? Mr. Wedmore hints that he is not entirely in agreement on this point with Mr. Connard, but in his tantalising way slips off to something else: he touches lightly and is away again, just when a question challenges. But, slight as these essays are, the main thing about them is that here is a critic who has the courage and good sense to realise that these painters (like others of their compeers and contemporaries) have earned the right to be treated with much more than the average patronising talk of promise, a note only changed when death lets loose a flood of belated praise; that they have accomplished definite things; that they have not only a future—or, as Mr. Wedmore would prefer to write, a Future—but a Past, and a very respectable past, too. Mr. Wedmore harps a little too much on his favourites' escape from popularity. His is the attitude of the collector, the "delicate observer"; his pleasure is enhanced by the feeling that it is not shared by vulgar eyes. But it is not well, at least for those who are producing, to cultivate this attitude exclusively; and to this tendency I would impute just that lack of certain qualities which I ventured to desiderate at the beginning of this article; the avoidance of those arduous complexities which endeavours in the epic or dramatic vein involve, and the absence of those profounder moods which we find in Millet, for instance, as in the finest works of our own Pre-Raphaelites. But I rather doubt if Mr. Wedmore would agree with me.

THE CONTEMPLATIVE HORSEMAN.

IT is a probable contention—the more so in a time when "mechanical means of progression" (how the phrase rattles like the machines!) are replacing the older ways—that no man can be said to have trained his soul properly who has not had a horse of his own. We may leave on one side all the labyrinthine rascality which his masters have heaped about the noblest of the brutes; when all the jockeyings and copings in the world have done their worst, they leave the creature a gentleman who knows how to treat with his own kind. The man who can saddle and ride his own beast, feed and groom him and talk to him, has to his hand a branch of learning which takes its place beside the experiences of men and of books. Even at our vaunted rate of progress we do not leave the past behind us quite so fast as we should like to believe: etymology is, after all, a tough link; and we may yet live to find that chivalry has really more to do with the stable than with the drawing-room—to say nothing of the motor-pit.

To own and use a horse is of course the only way to a full understanding of his ways: yet there are gifts, not to be despised, in a less close relation. There are some for whom the creak of saddle-leather has no irresistible allurement, who detest as much as Scott did "the mania of driving wheelbarrows up and down", even though they have not his alternative of "a handsome horse to ride", yet who are general lovers of the race, with a sympathy and respect—the word is advised—not the less active for its breadth. The owner, even if he escape the extreme curse of being horsey, lies open to prejudices, perhaps to silly pride. That material but somewhat neglected biographer Diogenes Laertius tells us that Plato, when once he had got upon horseback, dismounted, saying that he did not wish to become horse-proud. The Greek contains a pun, but the sense survives the bare translation. They who only sit behind hired cattle, or but watch the horse-world from the pedestrian level, have the chance of practising a humility which admirably clears the vision. To the dismounted horseman nil equinum alienum; all breeds and degrees are alike of concern, he looks with still fresh interest at the Shire horse in his pride, making nothing of his load, as at the poor vanner worked to the last ounce of his strength, at the old farm horse lumbering placidly home from the plough. No comparison, either envious or contemptuous, of any steed of his own affects this universal interest. He has an eye for a horse in another sense than that the phrase commonly bears: no friend, perhaps, has ever asked his advice at a sale: he has not the art of looking extremely knowing while he runs his hand over a doubtful hock. But he sees, it may be, more of a horse's soul than the wise are prepared to allow the creature; the arch of a restive neck and the crook of an aching pastern both move his care; he studies horse-faces as some people study human physiognomy, often with a real relief in the consistent good looks of the beasts. The true handsomeness of head and frame he looks for not so much in the fine-drawn breeds, the race-horse or the hack, as in the deep neck and massive shoulder of the heavier animals, forms nearest to the ideals of the Parthenon. The honesty, the grave patience, the dignity, the zeal of work expressed in the features of a fine cart-horse are, with the exception of certain unguessed meanings in a dog's eyes, the noblest trait that we know of animal character. Almost every species of the brute creation is parodied in human countenances: the likeness lies, it need hardly be said, not so much in mere exaggeration of anatomical proportions as in a suggestion of temper or spirit. The resemblance is in most cases entirely unpleasant; but the human features which seem to recall the ideal horse nature are nearly always good to see. But it is not the handsomer specimens of the race only that take the eye of the detached observer of horseflesh. For him the worn-out frame, the staring ribs and hollow flank which are still worth one or two journeys more, the overloaded cart-horse on the hill gallantly struggling in response to the whip and bridle-tugging of a blaspheming numskull, have a pathetic appeal which to some minds may seem to infringe the human prerogatives, a power of that kind which made Ruskin give "a kind of worship" to "yonder poor horse, calm slave in daily chains at the railroad siding".

For the observer of this fashion the horse is at once the crowning misery and the main solace of London streets. On one side are to be set the mishaps of the traffic, small and great, the sudden wrench of start or pull-up, the head jerked up out of the way of the jamming wheels, the slip and desperate struggle on the greasy wood-blocks, the smashing fall: on the other, the calm endurance, the generous strength, the steady order of the ceaseless stream, the well-taught squadrons that go to and fro by light or dark on journeys they know not whither till the last one brings them to the docks or the knacker's yard. The veriest screw whose head droops towards his broken knees as he tugs the luggage-piled four-wheeler has his part on the stage of town, and will leave a gap which we shall perhaps understand in the day—thrice blest for him and his mates!—when nothing moves in the streets but the crowds that dodge and scurry among the whizzing engines.

These, the nameless workers, we should salute as they go by, these and the countless troop that have perished inglorious within our own span. But while we honour these in the mass we shall have a special remembrance of the chance friends whose virtues served us so notably here and there: horses we sat behind, whose names we learned, whose build and character are fixed in the mind, together with this and that stretch of country or stage of road. There is that grey leader of the three who took the coach over Devonshire moors: who would forget—any more than he would forget the keen sweetness of the October nightfall, or the glimmering ranges of upland under the moonrise, or the little country town we rumbled through, all aflare like a stage scene with its market night—who would forget that magnificent use of muscle and valiant will, redoubled on the uphill at the mere challenge "Now, Jack!" without a flick of the whip in twenty miles? Who would forget the vision of the tireless tuck and drive of those fine-trained quarters, of the vague shape of rhythmic energy plunging through the dark, the fire that flew from the hoofs like an outbreak of elemental force within? We shall keep in mind the team, poor to look at but great in heart, who butted against a south-west gale over the folds of the barren country towards the Land's End, while the whole Atlantic seemed to pour itself against us in the weight of the wind and the sheeting rain. Unforgotten are others, of even less heroic make than these, but of as high a spirit; there was the weedy little bay in the hansom outside the station at Oxford whom we looked at doubtfully when the last train into the wilds had gone: it seemed as if a journey to Carfax would have been enough for his bent knees and too numerable ribs; but he covered the thirteen miles of oolite mud in a little over the hour, with every sign of enjoying himself. There are memories, too, of holiday as well as of toil: of the old grey hunter, long descended to the parson's chaise, who cantered restlessly up and down the meadow and did his best to break hedge when he heard the hounds running: of the Sabbath leisure of "Duke" and "Captain" at the farm spent in brotherly cropping of the grass, side by side in the ten-acre, as they went on work-days in the mowing machine or the reaper or the plough. So Xanthus and Balius must have fed together beneath the invisible yoke in green pastures through the long quiet after the end of Troy.

In some such ways as these may the horseless man pretend to a sort of general ownership, perhaps at bottom as real a title as that possessed by many a man with a long string, even of those who venture inside their own loose-boxes. For the passage money of his journeys, every one of which is a new adventure, from his hansom, his box-seat on the village 'bus, the board across the carrier's van, he commands the service of such a stud as no millionaire yet maintained. He may dream, nodding a little over some longish stage as the winter afternoon closes in frosty red and the horses shake themselves together at the last turning for home, of a realm where, escaped from some congenital awkwardness of practice and having the whole range of chivalry under his hand—heniochos, essedarius, écuyer, cavalier, Border rider, vaquero, as he will—he shall find again all his friends of the earthly roads, swift as Sleipnir, fine as Pegasus, and, by some turn of poetic justice, all his own to ride or drive.

CORRESPONDENCE.

VEGETARIANISM IN INDIA.

To the Editor of the SATURDAY REVIEW.

40, 41 and 42 Chandos Street, Charing Cross, W.C.

7 December 1909.

SIR,—The discussion in your columns as to the food of the best races of India is most interesting. I am glad to see so prominent a paper taking up the matter, since ardent advocates of a haphazard non-flesh diet do enormous harm in two ways, and they need to be publicly corrected.

First, some of the least scrupulous of them pretend that merely to abstain from flesh food means, ipso facto, health; whereas in India and elsewhere many of those who live without flesh food are miserably weak, and succumb readily to disease, partly because their diet is of such starchy and bulky foods as rice, and is poor in the body-building elements. On the other hand, these propagandists deny health to flesh-eaters, whereas many people, especially if they get plenty of air and exercise, seem to be able to neutralise or eliminate the waste products which flesh foods contain.

Secondly, the evidence is too often of a carefully selected type. Instances supporting a special plea are chosen and quoted; instances of the failure of that régime and of the success of the opposite régime are religiously ignored.

Eventually no cause is aided by untruths or suppressions of truths. I feel sure that the right policy of genuine reformers is to insist on bringing every truth to light and seeing all truths in fair perspective.

There have been thousands of failures on the haphazard, unscientific, inartistic "vegetarian" diet. I myself hear of such failures again and again. And I am convinced that the best and only honest way for a food reformer is to admit the failures, and then—if he can—to account for them and to suggest how they might have been avoided.

Yours truly,
EUSTACE MILES.

THE SHORT STORY.

To the Editor of the SATURDAY REVIEW.

4 December 1909.

SIR,—Your reviewer's rejoinder to my letter is made with great temper and point. I am glad to see from it that the influence of the Peckham Pleiades does not extend to him; but I am free to confess that I think he is right when he states "that triumphantly complete portraiture of a visionary under the conditions of a long novel would be more surprising . . . than an equally triumphant sketch within the limits of the short-story form".

Of course the short story has its limitations, as has the sonnet—and every other form of art.

I have never wished to eat my cake and have it, though occasionally I have lamented that there is so little cake about to eat.

Mr. Harris in his letter to this week's SATURDAY deals so well with the question of a visionary type in literature that I will say no more on that point, but to remark, in passing, that it seems to me a visionary type of the highest interest is dealt with and made interesting by no less than four writers in the New Testament.

Yours faithfully,
R. B. CUNNINGHAME GRAHAM.

LOTI'S "EGYPT".

To the Editor of the SATURDAY REVIEW.

1 Hillersdon Avenue, Barnes S.W.

5 December 1909.

SIR,—I notice that in a review of Pierre Loti's "Egypt" in your issue of 4 December the translation is ascribed to Mr. G. A. F. Inman. Will you permit me to point out that that is a mistake? The translation, whatever be its merit—and I do not flatter myself that it is great—or its shortcoming—and I am conscious that it is considerable—is the work of

Yours faithfully,
W. P. BAINES.

ALFRED GILBERT AND THE NATION.

To the Editor of the SATURDAY REVIEW.

Richmond, Surrey, 1 December 1909.

SIR,—An article on Alfred Gilbert in the current number of the "Studio" puts me in mind to ask a question I have long wished to ask. How is it that we have to look in vain in our national collections for a work by that greatly gifted artist?

You, Sir, I think I am not wrong in saying, interested yourself warmly in the acquisition for the nation of works by Rodin: is it well at the same time that we should neglect our own sculptor? Rodin and Gilbert are artists of two very different types, but each is supreme in his own sphere.

It might not perhaps be easy to get reproductions of some of Gilbert's delicately wrought decorative work; but replicas of such works as the "Icarus" or the beautiful figure which surmounts the Piccadilly fountain, or the study of a head, done long back in the 'eighties—these at least, I imagine, it would not be hard to procure, or others which might be mentioned.

Yours etc.,
A. G. ATKINSON.

DUTCH COLONIAL ETHICS.

To the Editor of the SATURDAY REVIEW.

Amsterdam, 2 November 1909.

SIR,—The English and the Dutch are the only nations who know how to colonise. If the former consider themselves superior to us, they might still judge us with goodwill. As a rule they do not to-day. Does this mean that they treat us as their equals, and consequently that they are obliged to judge us severely?

Maybe, but they do not only judge us, they condemn us without a hearing. Fifty years ago Wallace wrote a book, "How to Manage a Colony". He wrote of Java. Would the same scholar, so thoroughly acquainted with his subject, now agree with what the SATURDAY REVIEW of 23 October says about our colonial proceedings? I do not think he would; nay, I firmly believe he would find much to praise.

I cannot but admit that the SATURDAY REVIEW wishes to enlighten its English readers. So I say: Et audi alteram partem.

The position of a Governor-General in the Dutch Indies is far from being a sinecure. It implies the heaviest burden of responsibility that can ever be put upon the shoulders of anybody in our country. Does your critic think "£11,000 a year" is enormous for a man who has to represent royalty in the colonies like the Viceroy in British India?

After some blunders and insinuations about the last Governor-Generals he only says about Mr. Van Heutsz that the Atjeh war is now as hopeless as it was thirty-six years ago. He speaks of the cruelties committed by our troops—an allegation refuted long ago as pure slander—mentioning the General Van Daalen as the scapegoat.

Let us calmly reconsider the matter. We have not carried on war in Atjeh; we did carry on war in Groot Atjeh, a small part of the country, from 1873 to 1898—i.e. twenty-five years—and also here and there along the coast. Most of this time was passed in a watching attitude without any proper warfare. But after 1898 Groot Atjeh was entirely pacified, and only then we began earnestly to occupy ourselves with the numerous small states along the coast and in the interior. Now there are still occasional gangs of rebels—nothing strange in a country of secular anarchy—and these still disturb the settled population and our troops. But they are gradually disappearing, and in many parts of the country they never show themselves at all. The great work has been completely done, first under Van Heutsz's direct guidance, afterwards under his rule as a Governor-General.

The General Van Daalen did not succeed as a civil ruler, he was tactless with native chiefs, thinking he could make them obey by severity. His supersession was necessary, and no blame may be thrown on the Governor-General Van Heutsz for this proceeding.

The critic did not speak about the following achievements: 1. In the S. and E. division of Borneo, a country as large as Spain, resistance was definitely put down. 2. Jambi (E. Sumatra) was pacified; the small predatory states of Central Sumatra were subdued. 3. In Celebes there was a complete change, so that the slave-trade, head-hunting, petty feuds and the oppression of the natives by the chieftains are now things of the past. 4. Bali was entirely put under Dutch supremacy. 5. In many other regions—Nias, Halémahéra, Séram, the Timor Archipelago, etc.—considerable progress was made towards more civilised conditions.

All this we call ethical policy. But Van Heutsz did more to prove that he was a good ruler, one of the best we have ever had. For instance, he put the finances in order, and made an end of the absurdity that "Sumatra's West Coast", a peaceful and prosperous country, had to be subsidised with a couple of millions. Moreover, the burdens on the Java natives have been considerably diminished; the tax on native vehicles has been abolished; popular education has been taken in hand; good schools have been started teaching Dutch; a college for native judges has been erected; the "normal schools" for native teachers were improved; several Chinese Dutch schools and colleges were founded; a college for native military officers was opened at Batavia; the splendid harbour of Sabang Bay was built. No wonder that the President of the Java Bank congratulated the Queen on the choice of Van Heutsz. Taken as a whole, his work has yielded splendid results. After five years of extraordinary exertion, Van Heutsz wanted a rest, but, as the issue of the last elections had to be waited for, he consented to stay till the end of the year.

The Buitenzorg throne was offered to several suitable candidates, but they all declined. Mr. Idenburg, who had shown himself a good Minister in Surinam, was offered the post. Mr. Idenburg accepted.

In our opinion, Mr. Idenburg is now the man, just as Van Heutsz was in 1904. We look forward with confidence to the continuation of his predecessor's designs, for we are quite certain the charge of our colonies in East Asia, especially of their native population, has got into good hands. Ever since 1867 the Budgets for the Indies have been settled by law. It no longer depends on the Governor-General, but on Parliament, to decide what expenses have to be met. The old system has been altogether abandoned, and there is no room now for a precedent like that of 1842, which our critic thinks is still operative. Only enemies of capitalistic enterprise will assert that everything done to encourage the development of the country in trade, industry, and means of communication is detrimental to the natives, and for the sole advantage of the companies.

Of a man like Mr. Idenburg we may expect that he will promote the interests of anyone able to help him to make the Dutch Indies a colony of which we may be proud. The population, taken as a whole, are enjoying in an increasing measure welfare and protection. Why, then, should a British paper corroborate the impression, so often unjustly given, that Holland treats her colonies in a cruel and immoral fashion? I am a Colonial Dutchman. As one who loves the country of his birth, and Holland too, and as one who has devoted a lifetime to the study of colonial languages and ethnography, I cannot but feel indignant at this unworthy attack.

DR. A. A. FOKKER.

[We will deal with the subject raised in this letter next week.—ED. S. R.]

REVIEWS.

ERBA ITALICA.

"Italian Hours." By Henry James. Illustrated by Joseph Pennell. London: Heinemann. 1909. 25s. net.

THE writer of impressions of Italy can look back to a distinguished line of ancestors. It would, perhaps, be straining a point to include Vergil among the number, on the strength of the second Georgic, or Horace, in virtue of the ode to Septimius. But assuredly Claudius Rutilius showed the way, in the poem on his return to Gaul from Rome a few years after the first flood of barbarian invasion had swept through the gates of the city. At the end of the Middle Ages we have Petrarca, in certain of his letters and metrical epistles, and, in the early Renaissance, Æneas Sylvius Piccolomini, in the fascinating pages of his Commentaries. Coming down to our own time and language, Shelley, alike in prose and in poetry, interpreted some aspects of Italy with unsurpassable beauty and fidelity. Among contemporary writers no one, we think, can approach Mr. Arthur Symons in this field; his study of Rome, in his "Cities of Italy", is a masterpiece of its kind.

"I have not pretended", writes Mr. James, "to add the element of information or the weight of curious and critical insistence to a brief record of light inquiries and conclusions." The truth is that these inquiries are altogether too light to justify the drawing of any conclusions. It is somewhat late in the day to approach Italy with one's mind a tabula rasa. Indeed, does not such an attitude involve an unconscious assumption on the writer's part that his ignorance is better than the specialist's knowledge? Mr. James frankly asks to be regarded as "systematically superficial". We feel his subtle intellect just playing over the surface of things; but the true spirit of Italy, "the lady of lands", seems to have eluded him. Were an unsophisticated reader to light upon this volume, knowing nothing else of the writer, he would not easily gather that he was in fact one of the recognised masters of contemporary letters.

After all that has been written and sung of Italy, how should a man see her with his own eyes, how avoid the mere repetition of what has been said and thought many times before? And the pedant and the scientific critic of pictures have made her their happy hunting-ground. Mr. James protests, genially and not unreasonably, against the petulance of much of Ruskin's "Mornings in Florence" as particularly inappropriate "in this rich old Italy, where art, so long as it really lived at all, was spontaneous, joyous, irresponsible". This is surely of more general application. To "lie at our ease in the bosom of the past" is a phrase that Mr. James uses to represent his own sensations in Italy, and it is a happy one. His impressions are fresh and personal. If his criticism of works of art is not remarkably illuminating, it is sensible and to the point. Thus in Venice he writes of Canaletto that he "falsified without fancy", and in Florence of Ghirlandaio that his art is "the happy tact of a robust faith". The appreciation of S. Peter's is one of the best passages in the book. Mr. James notes that the supreme beauty of the great basilica is "the splendidly sustained simplicity of the whole", and he speaks of its "vast enclosed clearness" invoking the sense of ease. "There are no shadows to speak of, no marked effects of shade; only effects of light innumerable—points at which this element seems to mass itself in airy density and scatter itself in enchanting gradations and cadences. It performs the office of gloom or of mystery in Gothic churches; hangs like a rolling mist along the gilded vault of the nave, melts into bright interfusion the mosaic scintillations of the dome, clings and clusters and lingers, animates the whole huge and otherwise empty shell." And again: "To a visitor not formally enrolled"—he means one who is not a Roman Catholic —"S. Peter's speaks less of aspiration than of full and convenient assurance. The soul infinitely expands there, if one will, but all on its quite human level. It marvels at the reach of our dream and the immensity of our resources."

It is strange that the Roman Campagna has not yet found an adequate interpreter, much less an historian worthy of the theme. There is no district in Italy so rich in both classical and romantic association, or with scenery so haunting in its austere beauty. Its silence is like no other silences; its mystery seems to make the secret of other regions obvious by comparison. Here Paganism lingered on to witness the birth of Western monasticism at Subiaco and Montecassino. East and West still meet at the Basilian monastery of Grotta Ferrata. Tivoli and Palestrina invite the archæologist, while Fondi and Anagni make a special appeal to the student of mediæval Church history. It has been well said that "by whatever side human things and the history of the world interest you, on that side chiefly will you feel the attraction of the Campagna". If Mr. James' reminiscences of rides outside Rome and his sketches of the Castelli Romani lead us no further than the rest of the book, they are at least pleasant reading and communicative of delightful sensations. He is less successful in cities which he has only visited in the casual fashion of the tourist. Passages like this would become a cheap scribbler, not Henry James: "The great purple-robed monarch on the wall of Ravenna is at least a very potent and positive Christ, and the only objection I have to make to him is that, though in this character he must have had a full apportionment of divine fore-knowledge, he betrays no apprehension of Dr. Channing and M. Renan".

Mr. Pennell shows a predilection for dark tints, which disguise rather than suggest the colour and atmosphere of Italy. Two or three of his illustrations are hackneyed in subject and seem a little perfunctory; but the majority are decidedly unconventional in treatment, and some of the best are much above the average to which we have grown accustomed in works of this nature.

AN ANCIENT TALE OF WRONG.

"The Life of Mrs. Norton." By Miss Jane Gray Perkins. London: Murray. 1909. 12s. net.

THE memory of Mrs. Norton, like that of her predecessor in the Whig world, Mrs. Crewe, is fast fading into oblivion. We doubt whether the interest which once raged round the wrongs of the celebrated beauty will be revived by this book. Miss Perkins, we gather, is an American, and we are not sure that this old story of domestic scandal has not been dug up for the purpose of recording the ultimate triumph of suffering wives over brutal husbands. It is a favourite topic with American women, and our suspicion is aroused by the minute and tedious chronicle of every step in the sordid quarrel between George Norton and his wife, which cannot possibly interest the present generation. A woman with a grievance, who screams and scratches in public, is a bore, and it must have required all Mrs. Norton's beauty and wit to enable her to keep her place in society. But Mrs. Norton was very beautiful and very witty, and she was the granddaughter of Sheridan, and the sister of Lady Seymour, afterwards Duchess of Somerset, and of Lady Dufferin, and of Brinsley Sheridan, who eloped with an heiress and lived in Grosvenor Square; and she had been publicly accused of being the mistress of Lord Melbourne, who had been obliged to go into court and deny the charge, when he was Prime Minister. So that for years the town rang with the wrongs of Mrs. Norton; the custody of her children, the allowance which her husband would not pay, the copyright of her books and poems which he claimed, all being subjects of public controversy in the press, and naturally of gossip in society. George Norton was as bad a beast as ever breathed; but his drunkenness and meanness and cruelty to his wife are merely wearisome to us now. Perhaps the only feature of the case that may be excepted is the fact that Norton, having got his wife to use her interest with the Whig Government to appoint him (an ex-Tory M.P.) to a police magistracy, sued Lord Melbourne for damages as his wife's seducer. We doubt whether in the records of blackmail there is a more impudent stroke than this. Mrs. Norton had great conversational power, and, like many another clever woman, she thought that she must be able to write as well as she talked. But though it is true that the best prose is frequently colloquial, it does not follow that a good talker can write well. That Mrs. Norton was witty and that she had a hawk's eye for character is proved by her nicknaming Monckton Milnes (Lord Houghton) "the Bird of Paradox". But writing requires a long, expensive, and laborious education, and much practice. A writer who does not know the best things that have been said or written about life may be a genius, but cannot possibly succeed in producing good books. Mrs. Norton had a considerable dose of the Sheridan genius, but she was only half educated. Therefore she wrote bad poetry and bad novels. Who now could read "Lost and Saved" or "Old Sir Douglas"? The best things Mrs. Norton wrote were her songs, some of which are pretty enough. George Norton died, quite an old man, a few months before his brother Lord Grantley, and his wife, who did not make any pretence, said that, having lived so long, he might have lived a month or two more and made her Lady Grantley. After a long life of misery and strife Mrs. Norton married, in her sixty-ninth year, Sir William Stirling-Maxwell of Keir (ten years her junior), but died three months afterwards. If Miss Perkins had occupied herself less with Mrs. Norton's woes and had given us more of her sharp sayings and brilliant, saucy letters to friends, this book would have been more amusing.

THE SEARCH FOR EARLY MAN.

"The Stone Ages in North Britain and Ireland." By Rev. Frederick Smith. London: Blackie. 1909. 16s. net.

THERE are few men of science still living who remember the controversy that raged over the discovery by Schmerling, and almost simultaneously by Boucher de Perthes, of human remains in caves, associated with an extinct European fauna. Evidence that carried back the history of man into epochs appropriated by the geologists was naturally looked on with far more suspicion than would have been the case had it affected any other organism. The immense interest aroused by these and subsequent discoveries is shown by the issue of three editions of Lyell's "Geological Evidences of the Antiquity of Man" in a single year, 1863. By this time the early types of stone implements extracted from the gravels of the valley of the Somme had been paralleled by others from many parts of England. The suggestion that they were produced by accidental chipping in the deposit in which they lay had been abandoned in the face of cumulative evidence. The bones and skulls of man himself, including the first known example of the low-browed species now styled Homo neandertalensis, had already been accepted as contemporary with the palæolithic flints; and the makers of the polished neolithic types were now looked on as quite modern persons. At the same time, the doctrine that man's physical characters, at any rate, had descended from a simian ancestry was attracting

(*Continued on page 732.*)

renewed attention. This was largely due to the publication in 1859 of Darwin's "Origin of Species"; but the specialisation of the human skeleton made it seem probable that man, the genus Homo, had not arisen until recent geological times. Although his remains have now been successfully traced back into the glacial epoch, any assertion of a Pliocene or earlier appearance still meets with criticism that is just and natural. Flints alleged to be artificially chipped have been recorded from Lower Pliocene beds in Burma and from Lower Miocene beds in the plains of Blois. The latter case, put forward forty years ago by the Abbé Bourgeois, has been very carefully examined, and it is generally admitted that, if the chipping is really of artificial origin and not the result of forest fires, it was due to the ingenuity of some highly developed anthropoid, and not of Miocene man. It is, indeed, difficult to oppose the arguments of Boyd Dawkins and of Gaudry, who point out that mammalian forms of life have changed considerably since Lower Miocene times. Man, as man, can hardly have existed when the horse and the elephant, for example, had not yet settled down as definite types.

In the last eighteen years, however, abundant "eoliths" have been brought to light, that is, flints showing very primitive signs of chipping, or some slight artificial modification of the form which rendered them suitable as tools for early man. These were shown by Mr. Benjamin Harrison to occur freely in plateau-gravels in Kent, and to be presumably older than the present surface-features of the Chalk escarpment and the Weald. Mr. W. Lewis Abbott found, in 1897, similar forms in the pre-glacial forest bed of Cromer; and far older examples are claimed, even from Lower Eocene strata, by Belgian enthusiasts like M. Alphonse Cels. The difficulty of deciding on what is a true eolith is enormous; the earliest men, or even their precursors, must have selected stones of certain shapes, and such stones must of course occur in gravels of all geological ages. When the improvement of the implement by the chipping of its edge set in, eoliths were manufactured over wide areas, to be flung away, as is still done among the bushmen of South Africa, when they had served some temporary purpose. The search for eoliths must therefore be guided by an unusual amount of judgment, caution and discrimination.

Mr. Frederick Smith has brought together the results of many years' patient field-observation. He can remember the first somewhat grudging acceptance of Boucher de Perthes' work by English men of science; and he made experiments on the fracturing of flints while he was still a boy. His task in the present book is to prove that palæolithic man has left relics in Scotland and in Ireland as well as in England, and that even the glacial deposits contain numerous evidences of his presence. Dr. A. H. Keane, who supplies an introduction, believes that Mr. Smith has succeeded where others have often failed; and he wisely reminds critics of the flat denial which has too often met the announcement of such discoveries in prehistoric anthropology.

In all reason, man ought to have spread into Scotland as far back as late Pliocene times, and into Ireland also, which probably was then connected with Great Britain. Nothing in Mr. Smith's conclusions on this point seems immoderate. Two or three of his stones from these areas, as here figured, would no doubt be accepted by experts if they came from other places. On this point the author properly insists. But he has drawn into the argument an immense number of very dubious forms, often broken out of rocks extremely unsuitable for practical use, and often closely resembling stones bounded by natural planes of jointing or stratification. His illustrations seem singularly faithful, and are reproduced from really clever drawings. Again and again, in turning over the pages, one's eye is caught by forms that must surely be artificial; but again and again one finds that these are examples from other districts, brought forward as analogous with those on which the thesis hangs. The glaciated limestone specimens from Killiney, in the county of Dublin, must have been fashioned, if they were fashioned, in a region in which flint abounds, and where even the local quartzite would be more suitable. Earthy limestone seems actually to have been used in Ireland for shaped implements in neolithic times; but these may have been processional rather than serviceable forms. Mr. Smith's book is an interesting example of personal industry. His comparison between certain stone forms and the jaws and scapulæ of mammals, which would furnish rude weapons, is well reasoned. But no student of rock-fracture and of subsoils will be willing to accept a twentieth of his specimens as possibly of human origin.

ASTRAY IN AUSTRALIA.

"Australien." Von Dr. Robert Schachner. Jena: Gustav Fischer's Verlag. 1909. Mk. 10.

THERE is much about Australia that appeals to the German mind. The German student finds a variety of parallels with his own country. There is the conflict between the Central Government and the States, there is the spectacle of the Central Government compelled to rely upon indirect taxation for its revenue, there is the tendency to look to the State as the chief, and indeed practically the sole, organ of enterprise, and there is the statistical system, beautiful in its perfection, which even the German Empire cannot surpass. With all these familiar features it is to be expected that a German would write well of Australia, and Dr. Schachner has equipped himself for his task by prolonged and detailed study of Australian conditions. He has cross-examined men of every variety of opinion; he has even disguised himself as a workman in order to become acquainted with the spirit of the labour movement. Again, the book is systematically planned, as only a German would plan it. It falls into three sections. First, politics. An introduction gives a sketch of the history and character of the system of government. This is followed by an elaborate chapter of constitutional history. Documentary evidence is set forth at length. There are long quotations from the Constitution of the Commonwealth and from the programmes of the various parties. A third chapter deals with local administration and a fourth with finance. The second part of the book contains an elaborate and painstaking analysis of Australian fiscal politics; and Part Three discusses certain aspects of Australian civilisation, education, law, religion, literature and art. Lastly, the book is thoroughly up to date, even noting Mr. Deakin's return to office last June. Clearly the index of the book raises great expectations. Unhappily, its contents are disappointing. In the first place, the author is out of sympathy with the whole trend of Australian politics. He inclines, one may conjecture, to the school of Classical Liberalism, which is about as dead in Australia as it is in England. Consequently, Dr. Schachner both misunderstands and dislikes Mr. Deakin, whose policy he once goes so far as to describe as sophistical. There is, indeed, one passage in which the author perceives the truth. "It was no instinct towards State Socialism", he writes, "but sheer necessity, the insufficient capacity of private capital to cover an undeveloped country with a network of railways, that half a century back drove the State to construct lines." Had Dr. Schachner considered all that this statement implies in modern times, he might have taken a truer view of recent developments in Australian politics.

But it is not only domestic conditions that Dr. Schachner fails to grasp. He misinterprets, we believe, the attitude of Australia towards the Empire. It is no exaggeration to say that if the facts were as Dr. Schachner suggests, the independence of Australia might be proclaimed to-morrow. In this connexion he makes a number of statements which ninety-nine Australians out of every hundred would deny. First, in the matter of preference, he quotes with approval the statement of a person whom he calls Lord Churchill—

(*Continued on page 734.*)

THE

HOUSE OF COMMONS

AND

SANATOGEN.

Whenever your work involves long hours, severe nervous strain and a tax on the brain, you need a nerve tonic to help you through with ease. During the recent prolonged discussions on the Budget, with their late hours and incessant nervous wear and tear, many Members of the House of Commons, knowing the supremacy of Sanatogen above every other preparation, have made a habit of taking it daily to prevent them feeling the fatigue and strain and to keep their nervous energy and general health in their best and fittest condition.

You should follow their example.

The unanimous testimony of the Members of Parliament printed below offers as comprehensive and conclusive evidence of the supreme merits of Sanatogen as the most exigent could desire.

The Rt. Hon. Sir H. G. Aubrey-Fletcher, Bart., C.B., M.P.

"I have used Sanatogen for some time and appreciate its qualities."

Sir William Bull, M.P.

"I have much pleasure in stating that I consider your preparation, Sanatogen, is of decided value. It performs that which it promises to do, and I have recommended it to several friends."

Mr. R. S. Jackson, M.P.

"Some time ago my daughter, at the instance of her medical attendant, took Sanatogen, deriving considerable benefit therefrom. That being so, I recommended it to a lady relative of mine, who also tells me it has done her good."

Mr. George Nicholls, M.P.

"I think it right to say I have tried Sanatogen and believe it to be an exceedingly good nerve tonic, and does what you claim for it."

Mr. Arthur Fell, M.P.

"I must say I think Sanatogen has a wonderful effect in enabling one to withstand fatigue and want of sleep."

Mr. N. Joyce, M.P.

I have taken Sanatogen and I think very highly of it. My wife has also taken it. She thinks it has done her great service and will continue to use it regularly."

Mr. W. J. Burnyeat, M.P.

"My opinion is that Sanatogen is both a valuable food and tonic."

Sir Gilbert Parker, M.P.

"I have used Sanatogen with extraordinary benefit. It is to my mind a true food tonic, feeding the nerves, increasing the energy, and giving fresh vigour to the over-worked body and mind."

Sir Luke White, M.P.

"My experience of Sanatogen confirms the medical opinion; there is no longer that feeling of fatigue which one previously experienced, but there follows from its use a distinct restorative effect."

Mr. H. S. Staveley-Hill, M.P.

"I find Sanatogen a most excellent tonic and restorative after the hard work of the present session. It appears to me to contain all the qualities necessary for a tonic which secures the object in view, viz., the removal of lassitude, and gives increased vitality."

Mr. James F. Remnant, M.P.

"I have found Sanatogen a most excellent and invigorating tonic. I mean to take it again."

Mr. Alexander Cross, M.P.

"I have no doubt Sanatogen has bad a material effect in the vigour and physical fitness with which I have been enabled to go through my duties. It is only fair to say I have been rather surprised at the results. They have just been what you predicted."

Mr. Arthur Sherwell, M.P.

"I have derived much benefit from the use of Sanatogen. I have found it of great value during a period of high pressure of work."

Sanatogen can be obtained from all chemists, in tins from *1s. 9d.* to *9s. 6d.* A beautifully illustrated pamphlet, containing much valuable information, will be sent to you, post free, on receipt of a postcard addressed to The Sanatogen Company, 12 Chenies Street, London, W.C., mentioning SATURDAY REVIEW.

HELEN MATHERS

whose name as a novelist is a "household word," having decided to relinquish her literary work and to devote her attention to decorative schemes,

HAS JOINED

GILL & REIGATE

with a view to putting into practical effect the ideas of colour and harmony which have charmed so many of the readers of "Comin' thro' the Rye." In this capacity,

AS DECORATIVE ADVISER,

the resources of GILL & REIGATE's workshops and studios have been placed at her disposal, and those who desire that distinctive note of comfort and refinement so closely associated with Helen Mathers and her work can arrange for

CONSULTATIONS DAILY, from 10 to 4,

AT

GILL & REIGATE'S GALLERIES,

73-85 OXFORD STREET, LONDON, W.

CRAMER PIANOS.

PIANETTES - - - - - 25 gs.
UPRIGHT GRANDS - - 36 gs.
GRANDS - - - - - - 84 gs.
Players, Pianola, Cecilian, and others, 20 gs. each.
Interior Piano Players - - - - - 60 gs. upwards.
BECHSTEIN PIANOS, COLLARD, CRAMER, BROADWOOD,
AND OTHER GOOD MAKERS.

400 to select from at best discount prices for Cash, Hire, or Hire Purchase.

J. B. CRAMER & CO., Ltd.,
46 MOORGATE ST., E.C., and 126 OXFORD ST., W.,
LONDON.

Starving and Shivering on Christmas Day.

PRAY HELP

THE CHURCH ARMY

TO PROVIDE

CHRISTMAS CHEER

For thousands of Poor Households who would otherwise spend the day in **Hunger, Cold,** and **Misery,** and to bring Yuletide **Gladness** to thousands of poor men, women, and lads in our Labour Homes, Labour Relief Depots, etc.

Gifts of Groceries, materials for Dinners, Coals, Blankets, Toys, Clothing, etc., or Funds to buy the same, most gratefully received by Mr. COLIN F. CAMPBELL, Hon. Social Secretary, Church Army Headquarters, 55 Bryanston Street, Marble Arch, W. Telephone: Paddington, 3440.

Cheques crossed "Barclays', a/c Church Army," payable to Prebendary CARLILE, Hon. Chief Secretary, or Mr. W. F. HAMILTON, K.C., Hon. Treasurer.

it is one of his very rare slips—that commercial arrangements between Protectionist States are only productive of bitterness, and says that Australia suspects Great Britain of pure selfishness in advocating preference. Next, he states that the treaties with France and Japan are thoroughly offensive to Australian opinion. Thirdly, Australia is disgusted at the mother country's refusal to grant Home Rule to Ireland. Fourthly, the political activity of the King is viewed with grave suspicion. Fifthly, a New Zealand statesman once defended republican principles, and Dr. Schachner considers that this view is becoming more and more prominent. His final conclusion is that Imperialism is a dead and discredited movement. Comment is superfluous. It is not too much to say that whenever Dr. Schachner tries to interpret Australian opinion he makes a mistake, and as he is at once very German and very clever this is rather an instructive fact. But he rarely embarks on this dangerous task. For the most part he is content to give facts. Statistics of everything are cited without much comment, and as they are all to be found in the Australian year-books Dr. Schachner need never have left Jena. Even when it comes to politics he prefers to quote the official programmes of parties, apparently because he has not grasped the fact that British politicians are practical and therefore opportunist.

Part Three of the book is a sketch so slight as to be of no value at all. The charge that university education languishes would never have been made if the author had remembered that Australia is a part of the British Empire and that a fair number of her best students take an Oxford or Cambridge degree. And we really fail to see what value there is in a list of literary men and women of the Commonwealth with the titles of their chief works. Altogether, we can commend this book to those Englishmen who are anxious to recover their confidence in the superiority of their own people. Dr. Schachner's complete lack of political penetration will probably surprise them.

For this Week's Books see page 736.

THIS WEEK'S BOOKS.

ART

Gainsborough (Mortimer Menpes). Black. 63s. net.

BIOGRAPHY

Charlotte Grace O'Brien (Stephen Gwynn). Dublin: Maunsel. 3s. 6d. net.
George Edward Jelf (By his Wife). Skeffington. 3s. 6d.
Memories of Sir Walter Scott (James Skene). Murray. 7s. 6d. net.

FICTION

Love Besieged (Charles E. Pearce). Paul. 6s.
The Chase of the Golden Meteor (Jules Verne). Grant Richards. 5s. net.

GIFT BOOK

The Dream of Little Hazy Cream (Lady Arthur). Bickers.

HISTORY

India in Primitive Christianity (Arthur Lillie). Kegan Paul. 15s.
Musical Memories (William Spark). Reeves. 6s.
Light Come, Light Go (Ralph Nevill). Macmillan. 15s. net.

LAW

Cases and Opinions on International Law. (Part I. Peace. Pitt, Cobbett). Stevens and Haynes. 15s.

REFERENCE BOOKS

Whitaker, 1910. Whitaker. 2s. 6d.
Hazell's Annual, 1910. Hazell, Watson and Viney. 3s. 6d. net.
The Literary Year Book, 1910. Routledge. 6s. net.

REPRINTS AND TRANSLATIONS

With the Adepts (Franz Hartmann). Rider. 2s. 6d. net.
Shelley's Literary and Philosophical Criticism (John Shawcross). Frowde. 2s. 6d. net.
The Historic Thames (Hilaire Belloc). Dent. 3s. 6d. net.
The Case for Tariff Reform (J. Robertson Watson). Simpkin. 2s. 6d. net.
Memorials of His Time (Henry Cockburn), 6s. net; The Wild Flowers (J. H. Crawford), 5s. net. Edinburgh: Foulis.

SCIENCE AND PHILOSOPHY

Matter, Spirit, and the Cosmos (H. Stanley Redgrave), 2s. 6d. net; Mental Medicine (Oliver Huckel), 3s. 6d. Rider.

THEOLOGY

The Old Catholic Missal and Ritual, 6s.; The Office Peter and Paul (J. B. Wainwright), 5s. net. Cope and Fenwick.
Modern Substitutes for Christianity (Pearson M'Adam Muir). Hodder and Stoughton. 6s.
A History of the Use of Incense in Divine Worship (E. G. Cuthbert F. Atchby). Longmans. 60s. net.

TRAVEL

Wanderings in the Roman Campagna (Rodolfo Lanciani). Constable. 21s. net.

VERSE

England and Other Poems (Laurence Binyon). Elkin Mathews. 3s. 6d. net.
Historical Plays for Children (Amice Macdonell). Allen. 2s. 6d. net.
Songs before Sunrise (Algernon Charles Swinburne). Chatto and Windus. 26s. net.
Mingled Wine (Anna Bunston). Longmans. 3s. 6d. net.
Songs of Britain (Vivian Victor). Drane. 3s. 6d.
The Saviour of the World (Charlotte M. Mason). Kegan Paul. 2s. 6d. net.

MISCELLANEOUS

British Place-Names in their Historical Setting (Edmund McClure). S.P.C.K. 5s.
Decameron, The (A. C. Lee). Nutt. 12s. net.
Modern Journalism (London Editor). Sidgwick and Jackson. 2s. 6d. net.
Official Report of the Church Congress held at Swansea, The (Edited by the Rev. C. Dunkley). Allen. 10s. 6d. net.
Rhythm of Modern Music, The (C. F. Abdy Williams), 5s. net; Exposition and Illustration in Teaching (John Adams), 5s.; Iambica (J. Jackson), 7s. 6d. Macmillan.

REVIEWS AND MAGAZINES FOR DECEMBER.—Cassier's Magazine, 1s.; United Service Magazine, 2s.; Mercure de France, 1f. 25c.; The Geographical Journal, 2s.; The Englishwoman, 1s.; Busy Man's Magazine, 20c.; Current Literature, 25c.; The Open Review, 6d.

Printed for the Proprietors by SPOTTISWOODE & Co. LTD., 5 New-street Square, E.C., and Published by REGINALD WEBSTER PAGE, at the Office, 10 King Street, Covent Garden, in the Parish of St. Paul, in the County of London.—*Saturday, 11 December, 1909.*

SUPPLEMENT TO THE

SATURDAY REVIEW

OF

POLITICS, LITERATURE, SCIENCE, AND ART.

No. 2,824 Vol. 108. 11 December 1909. GRATIS.

BLACKIE'S XMAS GIFT BOOKS.

Two New Stirring Books by Capt. F. S. BRERETON

"Captain Brereton is an impetuous story teller. He seems to take one by the hand, and rush one headlong through a series of startling adventures."—*Saturday Review.*

"Captain Brereton has long since won his spurs as a skilful writer of boys' stories."—*Westminster Gazette.*

A HERO OF SEDAN:

A Tale of the Franco-Prussian War. Illustrated by STANLEY L. WOOD. Large Crown 8vo. cloth extra, olivine edges, 6s.

JOHN BARGREAVE'S GOLD:

A Tale of Adventure in the Caribbean. Illustrated by CHARLES M. SHELDON. Crown 8vo. cloth extra, olivine edges, 5s.

Reviewing "A Hero of Sedan," the *Spectator* says:

"The Franco-Prussian War does not belong to past history in the sense in which the Crimean War so belongs. It began an era of which we have not by any means seen the end. This is a statement which it does not concern us now to prove. We make it because it accounts for the special interest which a really good story of the campaign is bound to raise; such a story we have here. Captain Brereton knows his subject. We follow the adventures of his hero, who is not by any means one of the stock figures which serve this purpose, and at the same time get a clear idea of the campaign. . . . Altogether, it is an excellent story without a word about love in it—a feature very much to be commended.

By ALEXANDER MACDONALD

Through the Heart of Tibet: a Tale of a Secret Mission to Lhasa. Illustrated by W. RAINEY, R.I. 6s.

The Hidden Nugget: a Story of the Australian Goldfields. Illustrated by W. RAINEY, R.I. 3s. 6d.

By HARRY COLLINGWOOD

The Cruise of the Thetis: a Tale of the Cuban Insurrection. Illustrated by CYRUS CUNEO. 5s.

Harry Escombe: a Tale of Adventure in Peru. Illustrated by VICTOR PROUT. 3s. 6d.

By ROBERT M. MACDONALD.

The Rival Treasure Hunters: a Tale of the Debatable Frontier of British Guiana. Illustrated by CYRUS CUNEO. Crown 8vo. cloth extra, olivine edges, 6s.

By Staff-Surgeon T. T. JEANS, R.N.

Ford of H.M.S. "Vigilant": a Tale of the Chusan Archipelago. Illustrated by WM. RAINEY, R.I. Large crown 8vo. cloth extra, olivine edges, 5s.

NEW BOOKS FOR GIRLS.

By WINIFRED JAMES.

Saturday's Children: a Story of To-day. Illustrated by FRANCES EWAN. Large crown 8vo. cloth extra, 6s.

By ETHEL P. HEDDLE.

Clarinda's Quest: a Story of London. Illustrated by FRANCES EWAN. Large crown 8vo. gilt top, 5s.

By BESSIE MARCHANT.

Three Girls in Mexico: a Story of Life in the Interior. Illustrated by WM. RAINEY, R.I. Crown 8vo. cloth, olivine edges, 3s. 6d.

By Mrs. ALBERT G. LATHAM.

Christabel in France: or, The Further Adventures of Three Little Folk. Illustrated by PAUL HARDY. Crown 8vo. cloth extra, olivine edges, 3s. 6d.

By THEODORA WILSON WILSON.

The Islanders: The Story of a Family. Illustrated by GORDON BROWNE, R.I. Crown 8vo. cloth extra, 2s. 6d.

By ANGELA BRAZIL.

The Nicest Girl in the School: a Story of School Life. Illustrated by A. A. DIXON. Crown 8vo. cloth extra, 2s. 6d.

BEAUTIFUL NEW BOOKS FOR CHILDREN.

The Arabian Nights: Selected and Re-told for Children, by FRANCIS DAVIDSON. Illustrated by HELEN STRATTON. Large crown 8vo. cloth extra, olive edges, 5s.

Stories from Grimm. Fully Illustrated by HELEN STRATTON. Crown 4to. cloth extra, gilt top, 3s. 6d.; picture boards, 2s. 6d.

Little French People. Written and Illustrated with 24 full-page Pictures in Colour, by KATE J. FRICERO. Picture boards, cloth back, 3s. 6d.

Matthew and the Miller: a Tale for Children. By VIOLET BRADBY. With Coloured and Black-and-White Illustrations by H. R. MILLAR. Square crown 8vo. cloth extra, 2s. 6d.

Great Grandmother's Book: "The Daisy." An old-fashioned Picture Book for Children. With 16 full-pages in Colour, and numerous Black-and-White Drawings, by RUTH A. HOBSON. 3s. 6d.

How They Went to the Seaside. By S. R. PRAEGER. With 24 Full-page Pictures in Colour. Cloth extra, 3s. 6d., picture boards, 2s. 6d.

BLACKIE'S CHILDREN'S ANNUAL.

SIXTH YEAR OF ISSUE.

A handsome volume of 192 pages, with over 150 Illustrations, including Forty Full-page Pictures in full colour by the best artists. Picture boards, cloth back, 3s. 6d.; cloth, gilt edges, 5s.

A COLOURED BOOKLET, POST FREE.

Messrs. BLACKIE and SON have prepared a Booklet containing particulars of Gift Books for Grown-ups, Boys and Girls, and Picture Books for Young Children. This List, beautifully Illustrated in colours, on Art paper, will be posted free to any address.

BLACKIE & SON, LTD., 50 Old Bailey, E.C.

SEELEY & CO.'S NEW BOOKS

*** A miniature Illustrated Catalogue will be sent on application.

A MILITARY CONSUL IN TURKEY.

By Captain A. F. TOWNSHEND.
With 29 Illustrations and a Map. Demy 8vo. 16s. net.

"Captain Townshend's splendid book."—SATURDAY REVIEW.
"Vivid and entertaining."—YORKSHIRE OBSERVER.

FAMILY NAMES AND THEIR STORY.

By the Rev. S. BARING-GOULD, M.A.
Demy 8vo. 7s. 6d. net.

"Mr. Baring Gould has a most piquant theme. . . . This most entertaining of volumes."—EVENING STANDARD.
"Very instructive and entertaining."—SPECTATOR.

BOTANY OF TO-DAY.

By G. F. SCOTT ELLIOT, M.A., B.Sc.
Extra Crown 8vo. with 27 Illustrations, 5s. net.

"Teems with interesting matter. There is not a dull page."
DAILY TELEGRAPH.

SECOND EDITION.

AERIAL NAVIGATION OF TO-DAY.

By CHARLES C. TURNER.
Extra crown 8vo. with 70 Illustrations. 5s. net.

"Mr. Turner is well qualified to write with authority on the subject of aviation. . . . Sets forth the principles of flight in plain, non-technical language, for all to read and understand."
DAILY GRAPHIC.

THINGS SEEN.—New Volumes.

16mo. cloth, 2s. net; lambskin, 3s. net; buffed leather in box, 5s. net.

THINGS SEEN IN EGYPT.

By E. L. BUTCHER. With 50 Illustrations.

"Mrs. Butcher is thoroughly conversant with her subject . . . excellently written."—GLOBE.

THINGS SEEN IN HOLLAND.

By C. E. ROCHE. With 50 Illustrations.

"A charming addition to the series. Thoroughly well done and satisfactory."—MORNING POST.

ASPECTS OF MODERN OXFORD.

New Edition. By A. D. GODLEY, Fellow of Magdalen College, Oxford, M.A. Cloth, 2s. net; leather, 3s. net; buffed leather in box, 5s. net.

"The charm of Mr. Godley's little book remains with its passages of humour and quiet satire, and its excellent illustrations."—FIELD.

PROFESSOR CHURCH'S NEW BOOK.

THE FAERY QUEEN & HER KNIGHTS.

Retold from Edmund Spenser. By A. J. CHURCH, M.A. With Illustrations in colour. Extra crown 8vo. 5s.

"It would be difficult to present the stories in more charming guise . . . we reckon this among the season's gift-books."
GUARDIAN.

HEROES OF MODERN INDIA.

By E. GILLIAT, M.A. With many Illustrations. Extra crown 8vo, 5s.

"Every Englishman will be the better for a perusal of this virile and well-written book."—GUARDIAN.

ADVENTURES IN THE ARCTIC REGIONS.

By H. W. G. HYRST. With 16 Illustrations. Extra crown 8vo. 5s.

"Really thrilling reading—appears at a singularly appropriate moment."—LIVERPOOL COURIER.

THE LIBRARY OF ROMANCE.—NEW VOLUMES.

With many Illustrations. Extra crown 8vo. 5s. each.

THE ROMANCE OF MODERN CHEMISTRY.

By JAMES C. C. PHILIP, D.Sc., Ph.D.

"A fascinating exposition in popular language."
ILLUSTRATED LONDON NEWS.

THE ROMANCE OF MODERN MANUFACTURE.

By CHARLES R. GIBSON.

"We have seen no better gift book for an intelligent boy this autumn."—MANCHESTER GUARDIAN.

ALREADY PUBLISHED.

The Romance of—
Plant Life. G. F. Scott-Elliott, M.A.
Animal Arts and Crafts. H. Coupin, D.Sc., and John Lea, M.A.
Missionary Heroism. Rev. J. C. Lambert, D.D.
Early Exploration. Archibald Williams, B.A., F.R.G.S.
Modern Electricity. C. R. Gibson.
The Animal World. E. Selous.
Insect Life. Edmund Selous.
Modern Engineering. A. Williams.
Modern Locomotion. A. Williams.
Modern Mining. A. Williams.
Polar Exploration. G. Firth Scott.

The Romance of—
The Mighty Deep. Agnes Gilberne.
Modern Photography. C. R. Gibson.
Modern Sieges. Rev. E. Gilliat.
Modern Exploration. A. Williams.
Modern Mechanism. A. Williams.
Modern Invention. A. Williams.
The World's Fisheries. Sidney Wright.
Early British Life. G. F. Scott-Elliott, M.A.
Savage Life. G. F. Scott-Elliott.
Modern Geology. E. Grew, M.A.
Bird Life. John Lea, M.A.

SEELEY & CO., LTD., 38 Great Russell Street.

SUPPLEMENT.

LONDON: 11 DECEMBER, 1909.

AN IMMORTAL SPRITE.

"Sheridan." By Walter Sichel. London: Constable. 1909. 2 vols. 31s. 6d. net.

THIS is a great biography, and will remain the classical, authentic, unsurpassable Life of Sheridan. Only it would have been twice as good had it been half as long. These volumes are a mine of erudition: they are crammed with eighteenth-century lore. Mr. Sichel has had access to the Sheridan family papers at Frampton, to the diary of Georgiana Duchess of Devonshire (which he prints in an appendix), and various other first-hand sources of information. In short, there is not a book, a letter, a manuscript or a scrap of paper relating to Sheridan which Mr. Sichel has not read, and in his enthusiasm he has given us them all. We have to mark the same fault which marred his "Bolingbroke", an over-elaboration, a diffuseness, a lack of perspective. Mr. Sichel has proved himself a prodigy of industry: "mais il y a des longueurs". As an example of his discursive method we may give the following, on page 193, vol. i.: "But while Miss Linley warbles and her lover listens, a short ramble must be made through Bath past and present, though it is hard to be torn away from S. Cecilia and her minstrel". Accordingly Mr. Sichel is not torn away, but before starting off on his "ramble" through Bath he gives us verses from Sheridan to Miss Linley and return verses from Miss Linley to Sheridan, after which he trots us up and down Bath, a promenade which we have often enjoyed before. We know Mr. Sichel believes in atmosphere; but there are rather too many rambles of this kind into familiar bypaths. There is a chapter devoted to the pedigree of the Sheridans. It surely would have done to begin with the grandfather, Swift's friend; and when Mr. Sichel goes back to the Sheridans of the sixteenth century we feel inclined to say, with Racine's judge, "Avocat, passons au déluge". Then there is another chapter devoted to the family of the Linleys, which is rather too much, as who cares twopence about the ancestry of the Linleys? Indeed we do not get to "Sheridan's birth and childhood" before page 235, as Mr. Sichel adopts the original method of giving us a synopsis of the two volumes in an "overture" of one hundred and eighty pages, divided into Part I. The Man, and Part II. The Moment. This overture and the two final chapters are the best-written parts of the book, for in them Mr. Sichel moves easily and blithely and judicially, unhampered by the mass of details which he has shovelled in between, and with which he, and the reader, often struggle wearily. We suppose that the overture was written after the rest of the work, for in these opening pages Mr. Sichel seems to dance, like a man who has finished a gigantic task. We would willingly have danced from beginning to end if Mr. Sichel had only spared us some of his labour. But he insists that we too shall read all his hero's love-songs, sketches of plays, notes of undelivered speeches, aye, and large portions of his delivered speeches. There are very few speeches that are readable long after the event, and only those that are perfectly reported. The speeches of Sheridan's period were florid, artificial and very long, and shorthand had not been invented. As Selden says, "Rhetoric is either very good or stark nought". Rhetoric reported by a Johnson or a Cobbett from rough notes, aided by memory and malice, are indeed "stark nought", as anyone who tries to wade through these orations, which shook the world, will find. The only exceptions to the rule of unreadability are Burke's speeches, which he wrote out himself before or after delivery. Mr. Sichel should have suppressed a great deal of Sheridan's speeches (which must be abominably reported, they are so flat and commonplace) and a good many of his amatory and satirical verses, which are unworthy of his fame. There is another irritating practice. Quite a third of the matter is put into the footnotes. A fact is either worth relating or it is not. If it is, let it be put into the page. We hold strongly the opinion that footnotes should only be used for necessary explanation of obscurities, of persons or things, and that the authorities should be given together at the beginning or the end.

One of the inevitable consequences of Mr. Sichel's trying to tell us too much is that he makes mistakes which can only be due to an overtaxed memory. If a man resolves to drain his period to the dregs he is bound to slip. "Chatham's great Treaty of Paris" (page 19, vol. ii.) was neither Chatham's nor great. One of Macaulay's most dramatic passages describes how Pitt was carried down to the House of Commons to speak against the Treaty of Paris, which he did for two hours. The Duke of Bedford, who concluded the treaty, was accused of being bribed by France, and Henry Fox only obtained a majority in its favour by bribing members of Parliament. Samuel Whitbread was not "the inheritor of that brewery which had once been Thrale's". This was in the Borough, and was sold to Barclay and Perkins. Whitbread succeeded to his father's brewery, which was near Smithfield. Mr. Sichel actually speaks of Milton's line, "Drew iron tears down Pluto's cheek", as one of Burke's phrases! Mr. Sichel tells us on page 151, vol. i., that in the interval between the Rockingham and Shelburne Administrations Burke "pouched a sinecure for his son", to which there is a footnote referring us to Walpole's "Memoirs of George III.", and saying that "Lord Lansdowne declared the sinecure was for Burke himself". It is plain that Mr. Sichel has not read "The Last Journals of Horace Walpole", republished recently, where there is a minute account (vol. ii., page 454) of what happened. Burke came to Horace and had the effrontery to ask him to get his brother Sir Edward Walpole to resign the Clerkship of the Pells (£7000 a year) in Burke's favour, Burke offering his personal security that Sir Edward "should be no loser". Old "Horry" thought Burke was mad, naturally, but he was civil. A much less learned man than Mr. Sichel would not have made these mistakes, which are due to overcrowding. Mr. Sichel has a tendency to be voluminous rather than luminous.

But when all these faults have been noted, this biography is a noble delineation of one of the most extraordinary characters that ever crossed the stage of history. It is a solid and sympathetic record of a man who realised exactly the popular idea of genius. To make speeches from the front bench of the House of Commons while your play is being acted to a crowded Drury Lane—that, says the ordinary man, no one could do but a genius; and the ordinary man is right. For the same man to have made the Begum speech and to have written "The School for Scandal" is no common intellectual feat; and "The Rivals", "The School for Scandal" and "The Critic" were all written before the age of thirty. It is striking that two impecunious Irishmen should have sat side by side on the Front Opposition Bench, should have made the finest speeches of the day, and should have written works which still rank as classics. Sheridan and Burke had some points of resemblance. Both had the Irish ways of finance, the habit of treating other people's money as their own. "Thank God, that's settled!" Sheridan used to say as he signed an I O U and handed it to an importunate creditor. Both lived audaciously beyond their means, and both speculated disastrously—Sheridan in theatres, Burke in stocks and shares. But curiously enough, though Sheridan had ten times as much common-sense as Burke in dealing with other men or with politics, Burke managed his monetary affairs better than Sheridan, and died at Gregories in comfort. The fact was that Burke attached himself to Rockingham and Verney, from whom he had something like £50,000. Sheridan was foolish enough to devote himself to the Prince Regent, who dropped him when he grew old, and left him to die amidst squalor and duns. Burke also secured for himself two pensions by going over to Pitt—we do not, of course, mean that he joined the Tories to get a pension. But it would have been very easy for Sheridan to join Pitt after the murder of the French king, for he did not in the least share Fox's foolish and factious sympathy with the Jacobins, and a few years later he denounced Buonaparte and supported the war. Had Sheridan gone over to Pitt there can be no doubt that he too would have been well provided for, as he was much more useful in the House of Commons than Burke. But here again Sheridan's loyalty to persons stood in his way: he would not desert Fox, who repaid him by sneering at him behind his back, and by keeping him out of his Cabinet in 1806. It is no exaggeration to say that Sheridan's life was ruined by his loyalty to those two thorough-paced scoundrels, Charles Fox and the Prince of Wales. Mr. Sichel rightly dwells on Sheridan's sentimentality and his romantic devotion to "lost causes, and forsaken beliefs, and impossible loyalties". This sentimental perversity and his disgusting vice explain his ruin. No man of genius was ever ruined by mere monetary difficulty; there is always an auxiliary vice. "It was a moist age", as Mr. Sichel says. The finest ladies of Sheridan's time were coarser than the housemaids of to-day, or he would have been put out of their houses far sooner than he was, with his hiccoughs and his purple nose. Samuel Rogers has somehow come down to us as a cold-blooded, selfish, ill-natured man. Yet it was Rogers and Peter Moore, the promoter (the Hooley of those days), who were really kind to Sheridan when he lay dying without food, in stench, and with the bailiff threatening to carry him off to a spunging-house in his blanket. All honour to the poet and the promoter, and fie on the lords and relatives who crowded to his funeral, when he had "outsoared the shadow of our night"!

A BIRD-GUIDE FOR NILE TOURISTS.

"Egyptian Birds, for the most part Seen in the Nile Valley." By Charles Whymper. London: Black. 1909. 20s.

THIS is a decidedly pretty picture-book in which the birds most commonly to be met with in the Nile valley are figured with more or less fidelity. The colour process employed is not one which we greatly admire, but we have seldom seen it produce better results than in many of the fifty-one plates in this book. In some instances the general effect and atmosphere of reaches of the Nile are reproduced with marked success, as also are some of the birds—notably one of the delicately coloured Courser amid the sandy wastes of the desert, with which it harmonises perfectly. A picture of Kites on the wing is not so happy and is reminiscent of the "snapshot" photograph with the colours of the bird indifferently registered thereon. Again, that of the Buff-backed Herons gives but a poor idea of the snowy whiteness of these graceful birds. But this must be the fate of these attempts to produce coloured plates wholesale at small cost, and we must rest satisfied that most of them fulfil their main object—to enable the casual traveller in Egypt to identify many of the birds he may see on his journey.

Mr. Whymper's apologies for having figured the Sacred Ibis among the birds of Egypt are unnecessary. No reasonable naturalist endued with the historic sense ought to object to the introduction of this species here, connected as it has been for centuries untold with the whole legend of the Nile. Its presence here is doubly justified if only as a means of discounting the impudent lies of successive generations of dragomen who have so persistently assured credulous Englishmen that any herons or storks which chanced to come within view were the real "Sacred Ibis" they were clamouring to be shown. The other interloper in this book, Balæniceps, the Shoe-bill Stork, we also welcome, but for different reasons, and the picture of these quaint birds in the papyrus swamp is most pleasing and makes one long to go and see those kept in the Cairo

Zoological Gardens, said to be the only known living specimens in captivity in the world.

With regard to the best form of field-glass for identifying birds, Mr. Whymper, wisely, does not prescribe any particular pattern, but we think he would have done well to lay even more emphasis than he has upon the necessity of the would-be bird-watcher being provided with a glass, kept ready for instant use, whatever may be its make or the size of its "field". For where moving birds are concerned there is no time to be lost. Hence to use a field-glass with effect it should always be carried adjusted to the sight of the owner, and, if necessary, a case should be especially made for the glasses to fit in it when thus adjusted. It may, indeed, be taken as an axiom that a field-glass for bird-watching is as much for the instant private use of the owner as are spectacles.

Mr. Whymper, in his "Foreword", asserts that the scientific man will not find anything new in his book. Without claiming to be severely scientific, we must say that we have come across several decidedly new bits of ornithological information. Thus we had somehow always looked upon a Kestrel as a falcon and not as a hawk. Setting aside popular expressions, which may perhaps justify the employment of the word "Hawk" to include that of "Falcon", it is very certain that the "Drawing from a painting of a Hawk at Karnak" given on page 23 represents a bird with the unmistakeable primary feathers of the genus Falco, and not that of the genus Accipiter. Also, it never occurred to us to think of Vultures as in any way inimical to "defenceless little birds" as described on page 8. Again, the general description of the Griffon Vulture is rather misleading; one of the most marked characteristics of this species is the big ruff of snowy white down (not lance-shaped feathers) encircling the base of the neck. This ruff is, in the case of immature birds, replaced by a fringe of tawny lanceolate feathers. It is quite true that Griffons as well as Sociable Vultures and others of the same family identified on the wing can be readily distinguished by the extreme shortness and squareness of the tail; but so far is this from being a characteristic feature of the Egyptian Vultures or Neophrons that they are most easily identified by the great length of their cuneate-shaped tails; as also is the Bearded Vulture. Non-scientific readers of this book would reasonably suppose that the White Owl alone disgorged the indigestible portions of its food, whereas it is the universal habit of all the Raptores and of some other families as well. We do not understand why Mr. Whymper more than once alludes to game birds as "so-called game birds". We admit the looseness of the expression; but it is a very convenient one, and is well understood by every sportsman and naturalist, and hence needs no apology, especially in an eminently popular book like this.

We have made these few criticisms; still the book will serve admirably the purpose for which it is written, and will afford much pleasure and no little useful information to Nile tourists by steamer or dahabeah if they can spare some of their valuable time from mummies, monuments, and bridge-playing to a glance at the many beautiful birds which frequent the river.

NOVELS.

"Granite." By John Trevena. London: Rivers. 1909. 6s.

Mr. Trevena shows power, imagination and fervour in his writing to an unusual extent and intelligence in his views. He is as much preacher as novelist; he would probably say of himself that he hated humbug and pretentiousness, but above all does he evidently hate drunkenness. His loathing of intemperance and self-indulgence is an obsession. His story is set in "drunken Devonshire", his characters are for the most part poor and ignorant and incredibly superstitious, the hewers of granite, peasantry of Dartmoor, with whom, even when condemnatory, he is sympathetic. But the higher-placed among his dramatis personæ—the cynical squire, the self-indulgent vicar, the pampered rich woman—are all drawn with vitriolically bitter lines of hatred. Mr. Trevena's work would be more nearly first-rate if he imposed stronger restrictions on his exuberance of expression and imagination, if he were a severer critic of his own ideas as to what is worth saying and what is not. He takes himself and his mission too seriously, he is ponderous, incoherent, exaggerated, sometimes even absurd, and unfortunately his faults seem to be inherent in his way of thinking, and are not mere tricks of manner which could be dropped. Still there is much that is valuable in his work; the pictures of the Dartmoor peasantry are unforgettable: terrible and sordid in some instances, pathetically simple and attractive in others, but always strongly drawn, always as intensely realised, as they are ruthlessly, closely observed.

"Villa Rubein, and other Stories." By John Galsworthy. London: Duckworth. 1909. 6s.

Thanks to the sureness of Mr. Galsworthy's character-drawing and his knack of summing up physical traits in a few sentences, it is quite easy to visualise the members of the mixed household at the Villa Rubein at Botzen, and their neighbours. It is also a pleasant process. Even Herr Papa Paul, narrow and self-indulgent though he was and capable of setting the police on the track of his English stepdaughter's lover, could be magnificently expansive on a festive occasion, such as the thirteenth birthday of Greta, his own child. The nature of Christian Devorell, the daughter of Paul's deceased wife by a former marriage, was when the tale begins as yet unawakened on its emotional side; but between this girl of nineteen and her bachelor uncle Nicholas Treffry—a gruff, manly, old man, and a furious driver of horseflesh—there existed a beautiful mutual affection. And so when the inevitable lover arrived in the person of the masterful Tyrolese painter Harz, who had been mixed up with anarchists and was in other respects somewhat of a detrimental, there arose that clash of loves and duties which provides the dramatic interest of the story. It would be unfair to indicate the ending further than may appear by saying that its pathos is in part that of the proverb that the world belongs to the young; but we should be doing scant justice to the gallant Nicholas Treffry (and through him to Mr. Galsworthy) if we left it to be inferred that the sequel is no more than a mere illustration of that trite adage. There is in "Villa Rubein" little or nothing of the irony that colours some of the other stories included in this volume. We should indeed perhaps have called the story pretty had not such a word tended to leave out of account the strong quality of its portraiture. For even the minor characters stand out, distinct and typical—Miss Naylor, the prim, elderly governess; Dominique, the saturnine valet; Edmund Dawnay, the easy-going English doctor. But the daintiest portrait of all is that of the "little white moth" Greta, Christian's half-sister, who was always in difficulties with the English use of "shall" and "will", though she wrote none the less the most charming letters in that language. "Villa Rubein" occupies very nearly half of the book. The other stories, four in number, hardly come up to its level.

GIFT BOOKS.

"Oxford: its Buildings and Gardens." By Ralph Durand. With 32 Water-colour Drawings by William A. Wildman. London: Grant Richards. 1909. 21s. net.

We could make allowance for this book if we thought it marked the end of making picture books on Oxford. Unfortunately it is only one more in an interminable procession—output would be the better word. The pictures are, of course, the point, and they do not very greatly attract us. We know Oxford as well as anyone, and many of its buildings we could not identify in Mr. Wildman's illustrations. This is not necessarily a condemnation of the artist, we admit, for every building has unnumbered and changing aspects. Mr. Wildman may have seen what we have never seen, but we fancy some of his pictures are extravagant. Still they are better than many. The book is well printed and terribly heavy to hold. The collaborator, Mr. Ralph Durand, shows his kind by talking of "the long night of the Middle Ages". Here is the mere book-maker. Mr. Durand imagines he has beautified the work of the earthworms, as he calls Anthony Wood and other Oxford antiquaries. Beautify them is perhaps just what he has done. Their work looked well enough before he touched it. The earthworm has its use; this book has not.

"**Stories from the Faerie Queene**", **by Lawrence H. Dawson (Harrap, 5s. net).**—Perhaps we shall never have again stories retold simply as stories from great poets with the charm of Lamb's "Tales from Shakespeare". But it must be admitted that we have had tales from the "Iliad" and the "Odyssey", and from Dante and others, which have been told in good, pure English, free from vulgarity and affectation and tawdriness, and in which the adventure and romance have been rendered with freshness and spirit so as to give delight to the young imagination. Quite sincerely we can say that Mr. Dawson's book, which Miss Gertrude Demaine Hammond has illustrated very prettily in colours, has these merits. Mr. Dawson has told the stories as we have described, and there is no question of Spenser's philosophy, or allegory, or historical personages concealed under romantic names, which would be as unintelligible to five out of six men or women as they would be to children. But perhaps it is well to remark that the stories are by no means written in the spelling-book or words-of-one-syllable style; and that parents might be called on to explain such words as Paynim and Palmer or duenna and symbol and champaign, and their expository skill be put to some trial. They may even try finding the moral which Mr. Dawson has left unobtrusive if it is there. It is decidedly a good reading book for not too young children.

"**The Merchant of Venice**", **with Illustrations by Sir James Linton (Hodder and Stoughton, 10s. 6d. net).**

"How many things by season season'd are
To their right praise and true perfection."

Whether by the season season'd the colour book will ever reach true perfection—in other words, whether in due time we shall become conscious of merits we do not now detect—is a question as to which there can surely be but one answer. It will have to change its character a good deal before we can regard it as satisfactory. Some of the reproductions of Sir James Linton's pictures in this volume are charming and characteristic work, others are either not reproductions at all, or if they are then Sir James realised that he was in the toils of a process vastly different from the medium in which he has been so long accustomed to work. For whom this book—and it will no doubt be one of the gift-books of the year—is specially intended, we do not quite know. Mr. A. T. Quiller-Couch writes twenty-six pages of introduction, in twenty of which he tells the story of "The Merchant of Venice", as though the play were so difficult to follow that a variant of Lamb's Tales were indispensable to its proper understanding.

"**Savoy Operas**", **by W. S. Gilbert, with 32 Illustrations in Colour by Mr. W. R. Flint (Bell, 15s. net),** is no doubt intended as a companion volume to that in which last year Sir William Gilbert retold the story of "H.M.S. Pinafore". "The Pirates of Penzance", "Patience", "Princess Ida", and "The Yeomen of the Guard", are introduced with a brief account of their inception and history. Sir William got the idea of "The Yeomen of the Guard" from an advertisement at Uxbridge station which caught his eye during a long wait for the train. The text will of course make this an agreeable gift-book: the illustrations, though good of their kind, do not seem to catch the Gilbertian spirit. Sullivan did that in music; Mr. Flint must have found himself sorely taxed in attempting to bring it within the range of mechanical colour-printing.

"**The Rubáiyát of Omar Khayyám**" is in favour with the colour illustrator this year. There could perhaps hardly be a more difficult subject. To materialise the ideas of the poem must appear to many to rob it of its significance. FitzGerald's version is illustrated by Mr. Edmund Dulac (Hodder & Stoughton, 15s. net), without any sort of introduction or notes; by Mr. Gilbert James (Black, 7s. 6d. net), under the editorship of Mr. R. A. Nicholson, who is lecturer in Persian at Cambridge, and by Mr. Willy Pogány (Harrap, 10s. 6d. net), also without comment. Of the three there can be no question that the most costly is the best, though the treatment differs so widely and public taste in colour illustration is so inscrutable that it is quite possible the others may find favour.

Among the more notable of the books printed in colours from original and highly imaginative drawings is "**A Song of the English**", **by Rudyard Kipling (Hodder and Stoughton, 15s. net),** taken from "The Seven Seas". Mr. W. Heath Robinson's pictures are a happy blend of fact and fancy, and will no doubt be the more interesting to many Kiplingites because they must have had Mr. Kipling's own sanction as interpreting his verses. Less fanciful are the pictures with which Mr. W. Lee Hankey seeks to convey an idea in colours of "**The Deserted Village**" **(Constable, 15s. net).** Some of the illustrations are very pleasing, and Goldsmith's poem should find new friends in its latest presentment.

"**The Poetical Works of Robert Burns**" **(The Alton Edition, 4 vols.: The Gresham Publishing Company, 30s. net).** — Robert Burns' public continues to grow, and here we have an edition of his poems which by its effective "get-up", its conveniently arranged notes and marginal explanations of unfamiliar words, its pictures, which Mr. Claude Shepperson supplies, and its songs, which Mr. H. C. Millar has harmonised, should prove attractive. The work, prepared under the editorial direction of Mr. Charles Annandale, is substantial in form, yet light and easy to handle. In the first volume the editor gives a sketch of the poet's life, and the second opens with Burns' autobiographical letter to John Moore. The edition is therefore comprehensive, and should appeal to those with long purses who want to make a special present at this season.

"**The Book of Friendship**", **arranged by Arthur Ransome (Jack, 6s.).**—There is a sort of businesslike sentimentality in the idea that has led Mr. Ransome to make what he calls an anthology of friendship. We give Mr. Ransome credit for having collected the best things that have been said about friendship from the days of David and Jonathan to the present, but we should prefer to have them uncollected, and to come across them in the ordinary way of reading without being required to consider, say, Cicero's "De Amicitia" and Shelley's "Adonais" as equally something that has been said on the topic of friendship. There is something grotesque in two such things being bound together in the same volume, and in a jump from "Lycidas" to Walt Whitman's "On the Road"—which, by the by, does not belong to friendship, but to humanity at large—or to Borrow's "The Wind on the Heath", of which the same may be said. The best that can be said of Mr. Ransome's collection is that it is not made up of scraps, but of complete things, most of which are the best in literature. As a gift book it would make a very solid offering on the altar of friendship.

"**A Book of Golden Deeds**", **by Charlotte M. Yonge (Nelson, 6s.).** In Miss Yonge's idea a golden deed is not some display of mere daredevil courage or adventure for the sake of adventure or material reward. As a consequence of her high standpoint what her book loses in melodramatic interest it gains in worth. The instances she gives are "chiefly cases of self-devotion that stand out remarkably either from their hopelessness, their courage, or their patience, varying with the character of their age, but with that one essential distinction in all, that the dross of self was cast away." Her collection of golden deeds is derived from times ancient and modern, and from many races, beginning with the stories of Alcestis and Antigone, and ending with an account of child devotion in the Australian bush forty years ago. The full-page illustrations—of which it is curious that no list is given with the contents—are taken from well-known works in the great picture galleries.

"**The Red Book of Heroes**", **by Mrs. Lang, edited by Andrew Lang (Longmans, 6s.).** — Mr. Lang introduces Mrs. Lang's Christmas collection with a note of apology. "'Life is not all beer and skittles,' said a reflective sportsman, and all books are not fairy tales." Having exhausted the colours of the rainbow in finding titles for the fairy books of the past ten years, Mr. and Mrs. Lang turn to reality for their material and tell afresh the stories of men and women like Florence Nightingale, Gordon, Father Damien, Montrose, Hannibal and Havelock. If they are going through the rainbow again with a Heroes series they may find the colours fail them before they have exhausted the supply, and there should be more variety in their pages than in the fairy stories, so many of which seemed to have a common origin. There is nothing very distinctive in the literary treatment of these stories of heroes, but then they are issued with the Lang sign manual, and that will suffice. Even Mr. Lang's preface will pass perhaps for profound wisdom. "I think honour is the dearest and most natural of virtues; in their own ways none are more loyal than boys and girls"—a sentiment which must commend the volume more readily to the boys and girls for whom it is intended.

"**Legends and Stories of Italy for Children**", **by Amy Steedman (Jack, 7s. 6d. net).**—The cross and the lily figured on the inside covers of this book are a clue to the character of the stories themselves. Legends and stories of Italy when not very secular are very edifyingly moral and religious. The stories told here are mostly of apparitions of the Madonna and the miracles of holy men and women. Not that they are purposeless or told to induce a belief in their actuality as a

Roman Catholic might put them before his children. They are to teach piety, and all the virtues and kindness and humanity are their themes. These are the "pearls" which Miss Steedman in a somewhat gushing preface professes to believe children will seek eagerly for: "I will listen carefully", said the child, "but I love even the rough shells of your pearl stories". We do not wish to contradict Miss Steedman's criticism of her own stories, but we may hint that the "pearls" do lie just a little apparent near the surface. There are many pictures quite in keeping with the stories by Miss Katharine Cameron.

"The Story of Hereward the Champion of England", by Douglas C. Stedman (Harrap).—Mr. Stedman in his scholarly story of Hereward states that full justice has never been done to the champion. We are free to confess that in spite of the undoubted merits of his book we prefer Kingsley's treatment, and certainly the latter appears to bring us nearer to the heroic spirit of the times with their halo of the magical and marvellous. Mr. Stedman's is what we should call a Tennysonian version with its more obtrusive stress on the sentimental and moral side. But when we have said this, we have nought but praise for what is really a fine historical romance. Perhaps the closing scenes of the siege of Ely and the death of Hereward are the best in the book, though the adventures after the tournament at Poictiers and the wild homecoming at Bourne after the arrival of the Normans run them hard. A word must be said for the ballads and verses appropriately woven into the narrative. Miss G. R. Hammond's illustrations call for commendation.

HEROES AND HEROINES OF SORTS.

"Through the Heart of Thibet", by Alexander Macdonald F.R.C.S. (Blackie, 6s.).—Mr. Landor and Sven Hedin have revealed to us much of the romance of the forbidden land. "Through the Heart of Thibet" is a happy blend of information and adventure. The hero, George Gray, takes part in a secret expedition, which is intended to penetrate to the sacred city of Lhasa. Chinese secret agents appear early on the scene and attempt to thwart the expedition at every turn. None the less it passes on. It crosses the Brahmaputra, and in spite of obstacles reaches Lhasa, where the hero is kidnapped. The final scene, in which he poses as the new Dalai Lama, teems with dramatic excitement. The story ends with the discovery, in the guise of a Lama, of George's father, who was supposed to have died years ago on a surveying expedition along the border of Nepaul. "Through the Heart of Thibet" will add to Mr. Alexander Macdonald's established reputation as a story-teller.

"A Trip to Mars", by Fenton Ash (Chambers, 3s. 6d.).—Readers who delight in Jules Verne, Fenimore Cooper, and Rider Haggard will find in Mr. Ash a judicious combination of the three. "A Trip to Mars" is based on certain definite scientific theories, though in matters where the most modern research only offers possible premises and conflicting theses the author has necessarily had to choose one out of many, and has wisely stuck to it throughout. The story goes with a rare swing, and we fancy few boys will be able to lay down the book till they have reached the end. It begins with the arrival on the earth of a mysterious meteorite with the denizens of another world on board. They carry off with them to Mars two British boys, Gerald and Jack, and their guardian, who after manifold adventures on that planet return to earth. The chance is held out, however, that they may one day return to see their friends in Mars, or even go further afield. All boys who read the book will doubtless hope that Gerald and Jack will live to visit many other starry worlds as yet unconquered.

"The Red Caps of Lyons", by Herbert Hayens (Chambers, 3s. 6d.). As will be gathered from the title, episodes in the French Revolution form the theme of this story. A prominent merchant in Lyons is denounced by one of his discharged workmen as an aristocrat. The vicissitudes through which M. Legendre and his family pass during the reign of the sans-culottes bring out vividly how during the stress of those days men were led by fear to abandon their dearest friends. Imagination and historical facts have been blended by Mr. Hayens in "The Red Caps of Lyons" with distinct success, and the varying fortunes of M. Legendre will be followed with breathless interest.

"With Kit Carson in the Rockies", by Everett McNeil (Chambers, 5s.).—Mr. Everett McNeil portrays life in the wilderness of the Great West of America seventy-five years ago, in the days preceding the advent of the scientific and geographical explorer. The trappers and hunters who figure in his pages have to overcome such difficulties and dangers as must always face pioneers in opening up new and unexplored country. The author's delineation of the adventurous life led by these hardy men, whose trail "crossed and recrossed the Rocky Mountains" long before the days of the explorers, affords a good idea of their part in opening up the West. "With Kit Carson in the Rockies" is brimful of a healthy spirit of adventure.

"The Islanders", by Theodore Wilson Wilson (Blackie, 2s. 6d.). This story is concerned with the lives of three young children on an island in Morecambe Bay, under the guardianship of an elder sister, who contributes to their maintenance by her pen. Incidentally the author touches upon one of the insistent social problems of the day, but without giving undue prominence to it. The ménage causes much searching of heart to an old aunt, who objects to any member of her family writing penny story-books for money. The picture of the life passed on the island, with its peculiar charms and at times dangers, is well drawn.

"Kinsman and Namesake", by R. Stead (Blackie, 2s. 6d.).—In "Kinsman and Namesake" the author of "Will o' the Dales" again takes his readers to the North of England, introducing them to various historical personages at the opening of the fifteenth century. The story will be disappointing to Mr. Stead's devotees. A lack of definition in the outlines of his picture gives the reader a blurred impression of the times, and in the delineation of his characters there is a want of differentiation. The clashing of swords is that of the stage rather than of stern reality. We have failed to find anything in the tale to arrest attention.

"The Little Tin Soldier", by Graham Mar (Chambers, 2s. 6d.). In the pages of "The Little Tin Soldier" the reader is introduced to a child who has been kidnapped from home and carried off to the slums of the East End. His dominating love is for soldiers. This love is stimulated by the presence of an old soldier in the alley where the child passes most of his younger days, who protects him from the violence of his foster-mother. How "The Little Tin Soldier's" character keeps him unsullied by the coarser natures around him, and how he is transferred to more kindly and tender keeping and finally restored to his own, is told with a sympathetic pen.

"The King's Liege", by H. A. Hinkson (Blackie, 2s. net).—Maurice Hyde was a wonderful boy. He saved a countess from abduction, and upset a conspiracy to capture his Majesty Charles I. without being helped by anybody. How he did it by hiding in a cupboard, and being discovered, and being tied up, and getting loose, and carrying the news to Oxford, is told in language peculiarly suited to the story.

"Jack in the Rockies", by George Bird Grinnel (Chambers, 2s. 6d. net).—Instruction may be taken in great quantities if spiced with a semblance of narrative. We remember that we were often taken in like that in our day, and made to learn quite a lot of things when we thought we were just amusing ourselves. Well, every boy will be wiser for reading Mr. Grinnel's book. He will know a great deal about Indians, bears, bighorns, blacktails, geysers, and other transatlantic things, including a more than superficial acquaintance with the American tongue. This last will do him no particular harm, provided someone in authority warns him that American and English are different languages.

We detest all girls' books; out of a wretched mass we select these as the best. **"Saturday's Children", by Winifred James (Blackie, 6s.)**, is a pleasant story, full of humour, quite free from mawkishness, and natural in dialogue and details. One knows, when the two pretty girls set up housekeeping on little else than pluck and energy, that gods will soon spring from providentially sent machines to help them—and so they do, but without the extravagant improbabilities of most happenings of the sort. To tell the actual adventures, and their upshot, of the young girl without home or capital to back her, would be too depressing perhaps; but one sometimes fears the encouragement that books of this sort may give to the utterly inexperienced. There is no reason why it should not all end, as Miss Winifred James makes it, with marriage and success; only in life things do not always happen so. Meanwhile the story is considerably more wholesome, humorous and vivid than many of its kind. Miss Alcott would have liked it.

"Muriel and her Aunt Lu", by May Baldwin (Chambers, 5s.), gives a good account of Paris student life and how it affects English girls. It is just as well that the lurid and melodramatic notion of Paris (especially artistic Paris) should be corrected in schoolrooms by something nearer the facts. Normandy is brought in as a background when the girls go on a sketching tour, and is also well drawn, without picturesque exaggeration. The book is sensible and readable, without distinction.

"Barbara Bellamy", also by May Baldwin (Chambers, 3s. 6d.), is unconvincing. The most pedantic of present-day grandfathers could hardly keep a girl so utterly from modern ways of thought and speech as Barbara is kept. Her talk is just a shade too much accentuated and eccentric to be artistically amusing. Still, it makes a good situation when she comes in contact with ultra-modernity at a girls' public school; and Barbara is lovable, chiefly because, as her schoolmates remark, in spite of being "awfully learned, she was so awfully good".

"The Luck of Ledge Point", by Dorothea Moore (Blackie, 2s. 6d.), is a tale of the early nineteenth century, not badly written, and prettily illustrated by Mr. Charles Horrell. Napoleon and his dreaded invasion come in, and there is much excitement and adventure of a lively kind. Girls (or boys, for that matter) from twelve years old upwards should enjoy the story.

"Three Girls in Mexico", by Bessie Marchant (Blackie, 3s. 6d.), is the work of a favourite. It is a fresh, unusual story, with a fine young girl for its chief heroine; and as it places the three in the centre of Mexico, extracting perfume from yellow orchids, it breaks new ground with most readers. The style is simple and direct, and the whole book pleasing.

"Lady Fabia", by Edith Cowper (S.P.C.K., 2s.), is romantic without "sawniness", and told with very great vivacity and charm. Mrs. Cowper knows how to paint a real girl. The adventures of little Fabia, who is a girl in spite of having been a wife for a short time, make thoroughly interesting reading. They take place on the south coast in 1805, and smuggling, political intrigue, and lovers' plots are cleverly woven together. The character of Kitty Kirwan is well done. Altogether the little book is up to Mrs. Cowper's fastidious level.

SOME SCHOOL AND SEA STORIES.

"John Bargreave's Gold", by Capt. F. S. Brereton (Blackie, 5s.), is one of three books which turn on treasure-seeking. Every Christmas brings its treasure stories, reminiscent, in a more or less minor key, of Stevenson's masterpiece. Captain Brereton is not a Stevenson, but he is a good hand at piling up thrills. Here we have the attempt to recover the wealth aboard a Spanish galleon wrecked on the Mosquito Coast. The parchment which reveals the whereabouts of the sunken vessel is responsible for many of Duncan Hay's and Chris Hendry's startling adventures. We do not like the murder with which the book opens; but that apart, the story is one of Captain Brereton's best, varying its excitements with a certain amount of information, particularly as to the natives of the Caribbean Sea, and the work done by the Americans on the isthmus of Panama. The second treasure story deals with the "debatable frontier" of British Guiana. In **"The Rival Treasure Hunters", by Robert M. Macdonald (Blackie, 6s.),** there are two bands of explorers, one a set of heroes, the other of adventurers of the most unprincipled sort, who seek in the mountains a tribe supposed to know where a marvellous blue diamond is to be found. Mr. Macdonald's characters all have certain strongly marked lines of individuality, and belong to the picturesque order to be found in abundance on the confines of the British Empire. "The Rival Treasure Hunters" is capital. Its author's brother, Alexander Macdonald is hardly less happy in **"The Hidden Nugget" (Blackie, 3s. 6d.)** — a stirring tale of the new old sort beginning with a cryptogram in London and taking its heroes into the midst of bushrangers. The incidents are thickly sorted, and the narrative rarely hangs fire. The style is quite good, neither racy nor ponderous.

(1) "The Search of the 'Sargasso'", (2) "Chillagoe Charlie", by Robert M. Macdonald (Fisher Unwin, 5s. each).—Last Christmas Mr. Robert M. Macdonald published "The Great White Chief", which stood out as one of the boys' books of the season. This year he has produced a couple of books, written around two mysterious persons, one called the Chief and the other Chillagoe Charlie. The Chief is the captain of a cosmopolitan crew of scientists who, at the opening of the story, break away from their leader and sieze the "Sargasso", which possesses extraordinary steaming powers owing to certain scientific inventions. The rest of the book is taken up with the efforts of the Chief to run down and recapture the "Sargasso". He builds another still more remarkable ship, thanks to the inventive genius of his faithful first engineer Mac, and in spite of a magic powder that deprives him and Mac of half their memory he manages to get aboard of the "Sargasso" in disguise. The plot is at times somewhat intricate, the Chief proving himself such a quick-change artist as to make one doubtful of his identity. In "Chillagoe Charlie" the search for a mising relative may be regarded as the main plot. Tom Willoughby arrives in Queensland on the look-out for his uncle. Thanks to the long arm of coincidence or the finger of Providence he comes at the outset in contact with a mysterious stranger, who turns out later to be no other than the redoubtable Chillagoe Charlie, which is really only an alias of the missing uncle. The police are out after Chillagoe Charlie, and a good deal of the book is taken up in their amazing mistakes in arresting one wrong man after the other. Matters are complicated by certain evildoers adopting Charlie's sobriquet. The book is exciting and the local colour strikes us as particularly true to nature.

"The Cruise of the 'Thetis'", by Harry Collingwood (Blackie, 5s.). Last year Mr. Harry Collingwood gave his boyish admirers a thrilling story in connexion with the war between Chili and Peru. This year he has selected the last Cuban insurrection as the scene of another exciting tale. Jack Singleton, an Englishman, helps his old school friend, Carlos Montijo, in a gun-running expedition, which they successfully carry out on board the R.T.Y.C. steam yacht the "Thetis". This is followed by a series of strange adventures, including the disablement of the Spanish torpedo-boat by means of a submarine which enabled Jack and his men to descend and tie up the propeller. Later on the family Montijo are carried off and rescued by the hero, who also takes part in a full-dress defence of the Hacienda Montijo. The Hacienda is taken, but the Cubans, as they retreat, successfully ambuscade their enemies. The story ends with the blowing up of the "Maine" and the statement of the ultimate success of the insurrection, after which Jack decided to settle in the county next his friend Carlos, while the "Thetis" returned to the less exciting if safer career of a pleasure yacht.

"The Middy of the 'Blunderbore'", by Lieut. Charles Gleig, R.N. (Chambers, 3s. 6d.).—"If you want to get on in the Navy you've got to be a bit of a bounce and blow your own trumpet until you can make other people blow it for you", exclaims one of Lieut. Gleig's middies; but in this respect the Navy, we imagine, is not peculiar. The reader who looks for an exciting and animated description in these pages of life in the Navy will not be disappointed. That the principal middy who figures in them is cast in heroic mould and quits himself like a man is only to be expected; he is but maintaining the best traditions of the Service. Lieut. Gleig gives a clear insight into the work on board a modern man-of-war; he also has a sense of humour, and draws not only a realistic but an amusing picture of the middy ashore and afloat. He even provides a thrill for his young readers in the shape of that old favourite of sea fiction, the pirate.

"Ford of H.M.S. 'Vigilant'", by T. T. Jeans (Blackie, 5s. net). This sea-story is told by a man with first-hand knowledge of naval life as it is lived to-day. Staff-Surgeon Jeans, R.N., writes with authority. The narrative is direct and unvarnished. It would have to be a very dull boy who would not find here the real live thing. The ships described are actual ships, and the characters are drawn from life. The author has aimed at giving an accurate picture of warfaring in the Service, and he has succeeded.

"Not Out", by Kent Carr (Partridge, 5s.); "His First Term", by John Finnemore (Chambers, 5s.).—Mr. Kent Carr and Mr. John Finnemore will make the task of choosing a school story this year extremely difficult. Perhaps the decision may rest on style. Mr. Carr's work is full of dignity, often literary in a way somewhat unusual with boys' books to-day; Mr. Finnemore's is racy, almost slangy occasionally. But Mr. Finnemore strikes home with his first lines, whilst Mr. Carr prefers a more formal entrance. Both have a delightful gift of humour, though in that respect, too, Mr. Finnemore is the more spirited, and both are keenly alive to the public school code of honour. "Not Out" is a study of the new headmaster of Heronhurst who is early called the Goth, and a very admirable study it is. The story is so up to date that one of its best chapters deals with the Suffragettes, who invade the school. By the way we hardly know whether to be more shocked at young Cripps' fondness for bridge, or pleased that he slept with "Dalton" under his pillow. At least he had authority on his side. "His First Term" is an account of a Japanese boy's introduction to an English school, the familiar incident of the fight with the bully turning on jiu-jitsu—a novelty. The story of Lester and Ito's doings in the football field will make boy readers ardent supporters of the Anglo-Japanese alliance.

"Two Tapleby Boys", by Mrs. Neville Cubitt (Wells Gardner, 3s.).—This is an improving school story told with a dash of schoolboy slang and full of incident, some of it a little threadbare. Ralph is a nice, well-intentioned boy, led away into dreadful wickedness by naughty companions, who run a secret bridge club in cricket time. Prefects get upon the scent, and Ralph has a tussle with his best friend, who is himself a prefect and an excellent youth. However, Ralph gets through the fire in time, being nearly drowned in the next vacation, and confessing everything to his stern father, to

(*Continued on page* x.)

SMITH, ELDER & CO.'S PUBLICATIONS

Not for Christmas only

but for years to come

You will realise the usefulness, the value, and interest of your purchase of "The Dictionary of National Biography," edited by Leslie Stephen and Sidney Lee.

It comprises:—

22 volumes;

30,500 pages;

30,378 biographies of all men and women who have filled a noteworthy part in our national history from the earliest times down to the death of Queen Victoria. The whole written by a staff of nearly 700 specialists, including the editors—the late Sir Leslie Stephen, Mr. Sidney Lee, Lord Morley, Dr. Richard Garnett, Professor Jebb, Mr. Edmund Gosse, Professor Firth, Mr. Sidney Colvin, Sir Edward Fry, Lord Milner.

Reprinted on thinner paper, in the same type, and containing every word of the original issue, this work is now re-issued in **one-third the original size** (22 volumes instead of 66), **at one-third the original price.**

The Set in Cloth, gilt top, £16 10s. (instead of £49 10s.).

The Dictionary of National Biography.

EDITED BY

LESLIE STEPHEN and SIDNEY LEE.

In one volume—a guide to the vast and varied contents of the Dictionary and its Supplement, giving the leading facts and dates recorded in the substantive work.

Cloth, 25s. net; half-morocco, 32s. net.

The Dictionary of National Biography Index and Epitome.

Edited by **SIDNEY LEE.**

Ask your Bookseller to show you the volumes or write for Prospectus.

A NEW NOVEL.

By the Author of "ELIZABETH AND HER GERMAN GARDEN."

THE CARAVANERS.

2nd Impression. Large post 8vo. 6s.

World.—"One of the most amusing novels of the year. . . . It is also among the cleverest."

Observer.—"'Elizabeth' is always maliciously entertaining . . . we are grateful to the Baron for being so outrageous, and to 'Elizabeth' for meeting him and for letting us meet him, too."

Country Life.—"'The Caravaners' in wit, audacity, and a kind of elfish malice surpasses the most brilliant of its forerunners . . . no one could be blind to the wit and cleverness and literary skill with which one of the most amusing books we have ever read is worked out."

In 2 vols. Demy 8vo. 25s. net.

FIFTY YEARS OF NEW JAPAN.

Compiled by COUNT SHIGENOBU OKUMA, late Prime Minister of Japan, and Minister of Foreign Affairs, and others. Edited by MARCUS B. HUISH.

Observer.—"Quite the most valuable thing of its kind that we have on Japan, and really an extraordinarily interesting document to all and sundry."

With a Portrait. Small demy 8vo. 10s. 6d. net.

PASCAL.

By VISCOUNT ST. CYRES, Author of "François de Fénelon," &c.

Sphere.—"A Life of Pascal, which should have a multitude of readers."

Devon and Exeter Gazette.—"One of the greatest geniuses and best writers that France has produced. Viscount St. Cyres has brought together all such facts in Pascal's life as are likely to be of interest to an English reader."

Demy 8vo. 14s. net.

GEORGE I. and the NORTHERN WAR.

A Study of British Hanoverian Policy in the North of Europe in the Years 1709 to 1721.

By JAMES FREDERICK CHANCE, M.A., F.R.Hist.S., Author of "The Lighthouse Work of Sir James Chance, Bart."

Scotsman.—"Mr. Chance's valuable work is an erudite study, set forth with a fullness that materially enriches the available knowledge of the history of Europe."

Crown 8vo. 6s. net.

THE BOOK OF FLOWERS.

By KATHARINE TYNAN and FRANCES MAITLAND.

Globe.—"A charming production. Open it where you may, and you come across some pretty legend, some rescued folk-lore, which gives a new meaning to the common flowers and plants of this country of ours. No one who loves the blooms of England will fail to find the best kind of entertainment in this book."

Crown 8vo. 5s. net.

THE COMING ENGLISHMAN.

By Prof. JAMES LONG, Author of "British Dairy Farming," "The Small Farm and its Management," &c.

"*The Times.*—"Mr. Long, an agriculturist of high standing, discusses many of the problems of the day, and writes throughout in a spirit of a radical reformer for whom our present conditions in town and country fall far short of the ideal which he hopes the future will achieve."

LONDON: SMITH, ELDER & CO., 15 WATERLOO PLACE.

whom he had told a fib out of sheer funk. We warrant this story to keep the boy that reads it interested at the time, and good for at least a day after he has read it.

"The Attic Boarders", by Raymond Jacberns (Chambers, 3s. 6d.). "The Attic Boarders" will not disappoint readers of "A Discontented School". The motherless eldest daughter, who handles her many and troublesome housekeeping problems so valiantly and successfully, is a character which should prove a wholesome tonic to girl readers. The boarders of the rectory attics who help to cure her "bill-paying headaches" are not of the tame biped variety of paying guests, but four-footed creatures of the canine species, exception being made of a dog thief's child, whose short and tempestuous stay provides one of the most thrilling incidents in a delightful story. In addition to the dog-thief episodes there are adventures with tramps, with a spice of amateur detective work thrown in. The book should appeal not only to girls but boys, and should also interest all lovers of children and of children's pets. A special word of commendation is due to the illustrations, which are not of the aimless type that fasten on some perfectly irrelevant detail like "She went into the garden and cut a cabbage", but really add point and interest to the text.

FAIRY STORIES AND OTHERS.

"The Irish Fairy Book", by Percival Graves (Fisher Unwin, 6s.). Every year has its speciality in fairy tales; this year it is Irish folk-lore, very interesting from the point of view of the student, but too vague and curious to satisfy children. The eccentric procedure of the beings in these stories by various students of Irish legends is beyond the limits of fairy-tale probability. There are certain conventions and traditions in the behaviour of magicians, princes, fairies and giants which make it comprehensible and probable within its own limitations, but it is difficult to understand the bewildering adventures of these Irish heroes, possibly because they *are* Irish, and not easy to follow in their modes of reasoning and action. Though most of these stories have a poetic imaginative grace in the manner of their telling, some are written in a style too difficult for children, while the dialect stories will puzzle Saxon infants. The illustrations by George Denham in black and white are amateurish.

"Cuchulain, the Hound of Ulster", by Eleanor Hull (Harrap, 5s.). Miss Hull has arranged in a stirring narrative, told in a pleasant, simple manner, the cycle of legend of which Cuchulain is the central hero. Boys will probably enjoy the marvellous achievements of this Irish Hercules. The coloured illustrations, by Stephen Reid, are effective, if sometimes a little tremulous in drawing.

"The Fairies' Fountain", by the Countess Martinengo Cesaresco (Fisher Unwin, 3s. 6d.).—This is a reprint of the charming fairy tales published last year. They are daintily illustrated by Charles Robinson, and are well worthy of being revived.

"Prince Pimpernel", by Herbert Rix (Duckworth, 2s. 6d.), is a pleasant, rather old-fashioned little tale of a small hard-working maid-of-all-work's adventures in fairyland. The illustrations by Frank C. Papé are pretty and quaint.

"The Rainbow Book", by Mrs. Spielmann (Chatto & Windus, 5s.), contains many varieties of fairy-tale reminiscent of Mrs. Nesbit, Lewis Carroll, and Hans Andersen, but none of more than ordinary merit. They are pleasant and readable, however, and the illustrations by Arthur Rackham, Hugh Thomson, Bernard Partridge, and others are most attractive. We should recommend it as a gift-book for little girls rather than boys.

"Tales of Hans Andersen", translated by Braekstad (Heinemann, 6s.).—This is a cheaper reprint of the fine edition of the "Tales" originally published in 1900, with an admirable preface by Edmund Gosse. The essential qualities of Andersen's genius, above all the child-like nature of his appeal to the childish imagination, are described with very fine and precise appreciation. This edition of the most beautiful and poetical fairy-tales ever written is elaborately illustrated by drawings from Hans Tegner's pictures, which are of unusual excellence and characteristically Danish in every detail.

"The Water-Babies", by Charles Kingsley (Macmillan, 15s.).—A most sumptuous edition of Kingsley's popular and very priggish fairy-tale. The illustrations by Warwick Goble are richly coloured, and will probably be pronounced extremely pretty. They are of the popular kind, and many people will be found who will not think the price too high for them, or the Early Victorian tract which they illustrate.

"Grimm's Fairy Tales", illustrated by Arthur Rackham (Constable, 15s. net), will carry with them a meaning at once more real and more fantastic than they have had for the majority of youngsters in the past. Mr. Rackham does not illustrate Grimm for the first time, but his earlier work has been reconsidered, revised and added to in this volume. There are forty coloured pictures as well as many black-and-white. The size and weight of the book will make a miniature Pickford's van or a trolley indispensable in the nursery if small people are to move it from place to place without considerable physical exertion. Another and more manageable edition of Grimm is edited by Miss Githa Sowerby and illustrated by Miss Millicent Sowerby (Grant Richards, 5s.).

"The Gateway to Romance", by Emily Underhill (Nelson, 5s.). This book is nicely pictured, and the tales are nicely told. The tales are from "The Earthly Paradise" of William Morris, and very good tales they make. We do not at all resent having them retold in prose. In so much that Morris wrote the tale is the thing; the rest does not matter very much. This book has the double advantage of being readable by anybody, and suitable for children.

"The Dream of Little Hazy Cream, and other Rhymes", by Lady Arthur; pictures by Miss C. F. Frere (Bickers, 1s.), will amuse the uncritical small mind captivated by the adventures of Master Cream or Dolly Darling in the wilds of the nursery or among the elves who make mushrooms their hiding-places. The pictures, particularly those in colour, are very crude. Miss Frere has ideas, but in seeking to give effect to them she seems to have gone back to the days of Maria Edgeworth or Mrs. Barbauld.

"The Silver Lattice", edited by Richard Wilson (Nelson, 6s.), is a book of verse for boys and girls of over twelve. The collection includes well-known poems chiefly of narrative interest by Tennyson, the Brownings, Christina Rossetti, Longfellow, and many other distinguished poets, and a few old ballads, such as "Sir Patrick Spens", are added. The illustrations are excellent, being reproductions in colour of famous pictures by such artists as Millais, Landseer, and Watts. It is an admirable and handsome gift-book.

"The Little Merman", by Ethel Reader (Macmillan, 3s. 6d.), has really charming pictures, by Mr. Frank Papé. It is for people of nine or thereabouts, and should delight their hearts, being the tale of a mer-baby whom the land attracted. There is another story in the book, not quite so long, and concerning a queen of gnomes and a True Prince. Altogether a delightful little book.

"Lucy Mary; or, The Cobweb Cloak," by Agnes Grozier Herbertson (Blackie, 2s. 6d.), is for still smaller people, very simply written, and pretty, on lines that faintly suggest "Alice in Wonderland"; its pictures, by Margaret Tarrant, are coloured (which little ones always prefer), and happen to be very soft and pleasing, as well as cleverly drawn.

MISCELLANEOUS.

Every Christmas season brings with it now a large number of books of an elementary character which appeal to young people with hobbies and special tastes. There is nothing new about them, but they serve an informing purpose. **"The Boys' Book of the Sea", by W. H. Simmonds (Partridge, 3s. 6d.),** deals with some of the wonders within the sea as well as the adventures which have taken place on the sea from the days of the early voyagers down to Shackleton's Antarctic Expedition. Messrs. Seeley send out several volumes, such as the **"Romance of Modern Manufactures", by Charles R. Gibson,** and the **"Romance of Modern Chemistry", by James R. Philip (5s. each).** Messrs. Chambers add to their Wonder Books **"Magnetism"** and **"Light", by Professor E. J. Houston (3s. 6d. each).** **"The Children's Story of Westminster Abbey" (Mills and Boon, 5s. net)** is told, without pretension to literary effect, by Mr. G. E. Troutbeck, and **"Nature Stalking for Boys" (Dent, 3s. 6d.)** is described by Mr. Percival Westall with an introduction for boy scouts by Sir R. S. S. Baden-Powell. No better book could be given to the boy scout who has an eye for nature as well as his friend the enemy.

"The Child's English Literature", by H. E. Marshall (Jack, 7s. 6d. net), is a heavy book on a big subject for small people. It is not a bad book if such books must be. Mr. Marshall writes well, and has taken pains with his materials. But we think what he says of Shakespeare may be said of most of the others. Children "must remember that learning to know Shakespeare's stories through the words of other people is only half a joy. The full joy of Shakespeare can only come when we are able to read his plays in his very own words." Of course Mr. Marshall's hope is that he may rouse sufficient interest to send his readers to the originals. He certainly contrives to make his chapters entertaining from both the

(Continued on page xii.)

Handsome Gift Books.

MESSRS. J. M. DENT & SONS Beautiful Christmas Catalogue is Now Ready, and contains many choice literary items. A copy will be forwarded post free on application.

A FEW SUGGESTED SETS OF BOOKS ARE HERE GIVEN:

COMPLETE SET JANE AUSTEN'S NOVELS.
6 vols. in cloth case, 33s. net. 144 beautiful Illustrations by C. E. BROCK.

SCOTT'S WAVERLEY NOVELS
(EVERYMAN EDITION). Complete in 25 vols. Cloth, 25s.; leather, 50s.; Aldine morocco, 62s. 6d. net.

NOVELS OF CHARLES DICKENS
(TEMPLE EDITION). 32 vols. already issued, cloth, 1s. 6d. net; leather, 2s. net.

CAPTAIN MARRYAT'S NOVELS.
In 22 vols. Illustrated with Three Etchings in each book. £3 17s. net complete.

THACKERAY'S PROSE WORKS.
Illustrated with 300 Drawings by C. E. BROCK. Also Portraits, &c. Complete in 30 vols. £4 10s. net.

NOVELS OF MARIA EDGEWORTH.
Complete in 12 vols., in cloth box. £1 13s. 6d. net.

DICKENS' CHRISTMAS STORIES.
In 5 vols., with 40 Water-colour Drawings by C. E. BROCK. 12s. 6d. net the 5 volumes.

THE WORKS OF HENRY FIELDING.
Complete in 12 vols., with Photogravure Frontispieces, cloth, 18s. net; leather, 24s. net.

NOVELS OF THE SISTERS BRONTË.
With 60 Illustrations by EDMUND DULAC. Ten vols., cloth gilt, 25s. net.

NOVELS OF FRANCES BURNEY.
Portrait and 15 Photogravure Illustrations by W. C. COOKE. 5 vols., 12s. 6d. net.

THE WORKS OF LAURENCE STERNE.
Illustrated in Photogravure and Line by E. J. WHEELER. 6 vols. The set, in cloth box, 17s. 6d. net.

THE WORKS OF CHARLES AND MARY LAMB.
Very fully Illustrated. 12 vols., £2 2s. net.

EVERYMAN'S LIBRARY. Beautiful Sets of Books are included in this famous Library. A full list of the 400 volumes already published will be sent post free on application.

J. M. DENT & SONS, Ltd., 24 Aldine House, Bedford St., W.C.

Messrs. BELL'S BOOKS

CHRISTMAS GIFTS.

Write for Messrs. Bell's Illustrated Miniature Catalogue.

NOW READY. 500 Copies only for Sale. Price £5 5s. net.

THE WORKS of JOHN HOPPNER.

By WILLIAM McKAY and W. ROBERTS.

Imperial 4to. with 60 large Photogravure Plates, most of which are taken from Pictures never before Illustrated, and several of which will be reproduced in Colours.
(Published in conjunction with Messrs. P. & D. Colnaghi & Co., 13 & 14 Pall Mall East, W.)

This work has been in preparation for several years, and the wealth of material which it for the first time makes public will surprise those who only know of Hoppner's pictures through the Old Masters Exhibition at Burlington House and in other galleries. In addition to a preliminary chapter on Hoppner's life and friends, there is an exhaustive catalogue *raisonné* of his works, with short biographical particulars of his sitters; sections dealing with unidentified portraits and with pictures and portraits painted under fancy or classical titles; contemporary criticisms of both identified and unidentified pictures. The letterpress is printed at the Chiswick Press.

NOW READY.—Royal 4to. 25s. net. Also an Edition de Luxe of TEN COPIES ONLY on Japanese Vellum, £10 10s. net.

THE IMPERIAL RUSSIAN DINNER SERVICE.

By G. C. WILLIAMSON, Litt.D., Author of "The History of Portrait Miniatures."
With Coloured Frontispiece and upwards of 70 Collotype Plates.

In this Monograph Dr. Williamson traces the story of the famous and long-lost dinner service which Wedgwoods made for the Empress Catherine II. of Russia. The editions are strictly limited, and should appeal to all lovers of the ceramic art.

THE COLOUR BOOK OF THE YEAR.

Crown 4to. 15s. net.

SAVOY OPERAS.

By W. S. GILBERT.

With a New Introduction by the Author, 32 Illustrations in Colour by W. RUSSELL FLINT, and Title-page and Binding designed by the same Artist.

This volume contains the libretti of "The Pirates of Penzance," "Patience," "Princess Ida," and "The Yeomen of the Guard," which have been revised by the author for the purpose.

"This handsome volume will be a source of sheer delight to the many who rejoice in Savoy Opera. . . . Mr. Russell Flint's illustrations are throughout in striking harmony with the text. . . . We think that few persons have hitherto applied themselves to the study of the Gilbertian libretti, but there is no doubt that this delightful book will add greatly to their number."—*Athenæum.*

8vo. with numerous Illustrations, 10s. 6d. net.

A LADY OF THE OLD RÉGIME.

By ERNEST F. HENDERSON, M.A., Ph.D.

*** An account of Elizabeth Charlotte, daughter of the Elector Charles Louis and granddaughter of the Winter King. She married the Duke of Orleans, brother of Louis XIV.

"'Madame' is one of the most vivid and human figures that have come down to us from those glittering times."—*Observer.*

MR. FRANK HIRD'S NEW NOVEL. Cloth, 6s.

THE DEEPER STAIN.

By FRANK HIRD, Author of "King Fritz's A.D.C."

"Mr. Hird's new novel will maintain and increase his reputation, because its characterisation is strong and faithful, and its description vivid and true. Beatrice Stratton, the very type of noble womanhood, and her husband, John Houghton, the representative of so much that is admirable in British manhood, will remain among the great figures of fiction."—*Manchester Courier.*

Thirtieth Thousand. Crown 4to. 5s. net.

The PETER PAN PICTURE BOOK.

The Story of Peter Pan, retold by DANIEL O'CONNOR, from the play by J. M. BARRIE. With 28 Full-page Illustrations in Colour by ALICE B. WOODWARD, and specially designed Binding, Title-page and End-papers.

"It would be difficult to imagine anything more dainty. The pictures are exquisitely beautiful, and to follow the story in Mr. Daniel O'Connor's version is almost as fascinating as it was to see Mr. Barrie's quaint creation on the stage."—*Glasgow Herald.*

Crown 4to. 5s. net.

THE PINAFORE PICTURE BOOK.

The Story of H.M.S. Pinafore, told by W. S. GILBERT, with 16 Colour Plates, and numerous Black-and-White Illustrations by ALICE B. WOODWARD, and specially designed Binding, Title-page and End-papers.

Post 8vo. 5s. net.

THE ADVENTURES OF ROBINSON CRUSOE.

With many Illustrations in Colour and Black and White, and Title-page, Binding, and End-papers by GERTRUDE LEESE.

London: GEORGE BELL & SONS, York House, Portugal Street, W.C.

literary and the personal point of view, but we wonder how much a child would really know of English literature after wading through this bulky volume. We are afraid the child would be chiefly attracted by Mr. Skelton's highly coloured pictures, and they could hardly advance his knowledge of literature.

"The Children's Book of Art", by A. E. & W. Martin Conway (Black, 6s.).—It will be a very exceptional child who will be able to appreciate this "Book of Art", excellent as it is. It is impossible to give criticism of any real value, to distinguish between the methods and merits of painters, in such a way that a child may grasp what, after all, most grown-up persons are quite unable to perceive—the essential qualities and characteristics of good painting. Children can understand and remember anecdotes about painters, and they will appreciate a picture which contains a story; they may even in certain cases have a sense, vague and indefinable by themselves, of what is beautiful, but they are only bewildered by such a criticism as the following: "The higher art of composing into the unity of a group all its parts, and keeping their perfections within such limits as best co-operate in the transcendent perfection of the whole—this was the labour and the crown of both their lives". Such a sentence might well puzzle even an art critic. Throughout the book the phraseology is too difficult, as, for example, the remark about Rubens: "In his life, as in his art, he was exuberant"; or of Tintoretto: "Like Michelangelo he worked passionately rather than with the sober competence of Titian". Miss Conway's book would be a really useful guide for girls, say, of fifteen or sixteen, and the reproductions of the pictures of great masters of all countries and ages are really beautiful.

It is a not unhealthy sign of the times that among the new gift-books are a good many dealing with natural history. **Mr. Ascott R. Hope's "Beasts of Business" (Black, 3s. 6d.)** describes the horse, the dog, the elephant, the ox, the reindeer, the camel, and other animals employed by man in various countries as "friendly servants". The book has unobtrusive merits, chief among them being the writer's sympathy with dumb creatures. Incidentally Mr. Hope expresses wonder that the monkey, with his natural intelligence, has not been more often turned into a beast of business. Sailors used to say that monkeys could speak but were too artful to do so lest they should be made to work. **Mr. Eric Parker in "A Book of the Zoo" (Methuen, 6s.)** takes us through the Zoological Gardens, with an eye to humour and humanity rather than science, and tells us what he has observed of the animals in captivity by night as well as by day. No doubt we do not always see them to best advantage, and it is not every one's privilege to see them out of hours as Mr. Parker has done. The book will be an excellent companion for visitors young or old. It contains many illustrations from photographs by Mr. H. Irving. **"The World of Animal Life", by Fred Smith (Blackie, 5s.),** is less popular in tone, but is nevertheless in its second edition. Imaginary stories about animals are not without use when written with a due regard to the facts of life. A good deal may be learned of trek oxen and the conditions under which they work in South Africa from **"Biffel", by Mr. Stanley Portal Hyatt (Melrose, 6s. net).** The book is dedicated "to the memory of our Black Span, the best cattle transport-riders ever had, and of Peter, a goat with a white man's soul", and it winds up with men drinking to the success of the mines, "forgetful that but for the trek ox there would have been neither townships nor mines". The Basuto's love for Biffel—"my best of hind bullocks!"—is finely shown. Of a different order of stories about animals is the collection which Mr. F. J. Harvey Darton has edited under the title **"A Wonder Book of Beasts" (Wells Gardner, 6s.), illustrated by Miss Margaret Clayton.** These stories are, says Mr. Darton, concerned with animals, but except incidentally not with natural history. "Unnatural history, indeed, would be the proper scientific name for them if all that we are told about such creatures as the Fox and the Hen (to take the two who appear here most often) were the observed facts of their daily life." Mr. Darton's care, in a capital introduction, to warn his young readers that the wonders of these particular animal stories are not quite in accord with nature is in itself a little lesson happily given in the cause of truth. Whether children will like the stories more or less for the warning is another matter.

The Christmas book season without new editions of **"Robinson Crusoe", "Gulliver's Travel's", "The Arabian Nights", and "Lamb's Tales from Shakespeare"** would hardly be normal. Such books Messrs. Dent appropriately speak of as evergreen. This year we have Defoe's work illustrated in colour and black-and-white by Miss Gertrude Leese (Bell, 5s. net); "The Arabian Nights", selected and retold for children by Miss Gladys Davidson, and illustrated by Miss Helen Stratton (Blackie, 5s.); and "Gulliver" and "Lamb's Tales", both illustrated by Mr. Arthur Rackham (Dent, 7s. 6d. each). Here, as in "Grimm's Fairy Tales", Mr. Rackham has added to and worked up the drawings with which he illustrated Swift and Lamb nine or ten years ago.

THE DECEMBER REVIEWS.

Lord Lansdowne's motion referring the Finance Bill to the people came just in time to permit the monthly reviewer to take cognisance of what is called the crisis of 1909. In the "Nineteenth Century" Sir Francis A. Channing leads off with an article on what Mr. Gladstone would have done to abolish the revising power of the Lords over the House of Commons "in its most vital function". We agree that it is a fruitless speculation; but fruitless or not, Sir Francis is quite confident that Mr. Gladstone would have thrown himself "with almost a Berserker rage" into the fighting of this "constitutional revolution". Like Professor L. T. Hobhouse in the "Contemporary", Sir F. Channing is full of regret that the Liberals did not accept Mr. Gladstone's invitation in 1894 to go ahead with the issue of Lords versus Commons. That Mr. Gladstone himself, when he had the opportunity, did not embark on the campaign to which he urged the Liberal party in what proved to be his last speech is perhaps rather conveniently overlooked by the Radical to-day. Professor Hobhouse says the abolition of the absolute veto lies before Liberals as their next duty. But where is the absolute veto in this instance? If the Radicals can induce the country to accept the Finance Bill, the Lords will pass it, however little they may like it. It is not the will of the people that the Peers flout, but designs which it is hardly conceivable the people can endorse. After the destruction of the veto, to which Mr. J. A. Hobson confidently looks forward in the "English Review", what is to happen? Even Mr. Hobson is not prepared to accept the supremacy of the House of Commons unchecked as an ideal of democracy. Hence he insists that "a surgical operation upon the veto of the Lords must entail important after-treatment in the shape of constructive constitutional reform", such as adult suffrage, proportional representation, and the Referendum.

Mr. H. J. Darnton-Fraser in the "Westminster Review" enters on the somewhat heroic task of attempting to prove the hollowness of the cry that the Finance Bill is socialistic. "Any person of education and intelligence who takes the trouble to find out what socialism means, and what the Budget proposes, is driven to the conclusion that the alleged socialism of the Budget is an electioneering myth. To the unbiassed observer no other conclusion is possible." Mr. Darnton-Fraser is of course wholly unbiassed. A short study of the "Socialist Review" might be useful to him. In the "National" Mr. Charles A. W. Pownall, writing on "Bermondsey—And After", says there is not much in Socialism at present, but warns us that what Bermondsey has done the rest of England must do, for "with Ireland Nationalist, Wales Radical, and Scotland, despite Lord Rosebery's influence, but half convinced, the turnover of seats necessary to displace our present misrulers will have to be obtained in the English counties and boroughs and especially in the Metropolis." Observer in the same Review makes of Mr. Asquith as Prime Minister "a study in political deterioration", and Scotsman returns to "the Right Honourable Alexander Ure—to date (approximately)". "Blackwood" asserts that Liberalism is intellectually bankrupt, and pours contempt on the new Liberal who has no national principles, and is content to obey the people whom he professes to lead, but to whom he is disinclined to go for orders. "His life is one long speculation on the psychology of the masses, and his efforts are centred on anticipating what he imagines may be the demands of this intermittent *Vox Dei*. The wisest of men in such a paradoxical case would become muddled in their arguments."

The Reviews are taking up the land question seriously. In the "Fortnightly" Sir Gilbert Parker makes play with the phrase of Arthur Young. It is the "magic of ownership" which is to restore British agriculture to its rightful place, not the communal purchase and occupation of land offered by the present Government and its Socialist guides. With ownership must go co-operation. It was the lack of co-operation that ruined the old yeomen. The new peasants must work together as they are doing in Germany, Austria, France, and Belgium. Ireland shows us the way here with her 873 co-operative societies. English agriculture, concludes Sir Gilbert Parker, has a safe future, provided only that the individualism of the English freeholder can come to terms

(*Continued on page xiv.*)

The February Boys.

CHAMBERS'S XMAS BOOKS

"The name of Mrs. L. T. Meade is one over which every girl reader rejoices, and the books which Messrs. Chambers publish this season will not fail to make that talented writer more than ever a favourite." *Glasgow News.*

"Miss Baldwin's stories are the delight of young girl readers."—*Freeman's Journal.*

"Raymond Jacberns writes that happy mixture of incident and good sense which teaches children so much while keeping their interest engaged."—*Spectator.*

The February Boys. By Mrs. MOLESWORTH. **3/6**

"This charmingly told story is told as only Mrs. Molesworth can tell a simple and familiar story . . . if materfamilias wants a book to read aloud, she cannot do better . . . . We can assure her that the judgment of the audience will leave no doubt as to Mrs. Molesworth's skill."—*Spectator.*

Aylwyn's Friends. By L. T. MEADE. **6/-**

"A delightful story of girl-life, refreshing in its naturalness, and with an atmosphere as perfectly wholesome as it is charming."—*Glasgow News.*

Muriel and her Aunt Lu. By MAY BALDWIN. **5/-**

A Story of School and Art Life in Paris.

"One of her best productions, and, though combining instruction with entertainment, always fascinating and attractive."—*Queen.*

His First Term. By J. FINNEMORE. **5/-**

A Story of Slapton School.

"This is a rattling good book for boys; there is not a dull page in it, and the boys act and speak like schoolboys."—*School Guardian.*

Bravo, Bob! By ANDREW HOME. **3/6**

A School Story.

"Bob is a fine fellow alike in trial and triumph. . . . Written throughout in Mr. Home's manly, crisp style."—*Dundee Advertiser.*

Jack in the Rockies. **2/6**

By G. BIRD GRINNELL.

"Boys will be fascinated by the description of the wild life in the Yellowstone region. . . . Every boy who wants to scrape acquaintance with camp-life and the hunting-trail cannot do better than read 'Jack in the Rockies.'"—*Spectator.*

The Little Torment. **2/6**

By MARGARET KILROY.

"After becoming initiated into all her little ways, we can only hope that another year the fair author will let us see a little more fully into her life-story."—*Western Mail.*

Becky Compton, Ex-Dux. **5/-**

By RAYMOND JACBERNS.

"A comic element is supplied by the German pupil, Elise Schiffner who explains her position, her wants, and her opinions about English music with admirable frankness."—*Spectator.*

The Princess of the Revels. **3/6**

By L. T. MEADE.

"Presents some delightful pictures of life under adversity, and the character delineation, the charming style, and a moving narrative make an interesting story for girls."—*Freeman's Journal.*

The Red Caps of Lyons. **3/6**

By HERBERT HAYENS.

"An entrancing tale of the French Revolution, with a hero who performs wonders and has our sympathies throughout."—*Manchester Courier.*

A Trip to Mars. By FENTON ASH. **3/6**

"All boy and girl readers will receive from this book ideas which must widen the world of their experience."—*World.*

For a complete list of Messrs. Chambers's Xmas Books write for their Coloured and Descriptive List to 38 Soho Square, London; or 339 High Street, Edinburgh.

From . .

Wells Gardner, Darton & Co.'s List

An Original book on a new plan. The Illustrations are all Mounted on Art Brown.

11 by 8½, fancy paper boards, cloth back, 5s. net.

The Animal Why Book.

By W. P. PYCRAFT, F.Z.S., A.L.S. Illustrated in Colours by EDWIN NOBLE, R.B.A.

"A book of sterling merit."—NATION. "A capital book."—FIELD.

The New Volume in the Series of DARTON'S FINE ART GIFT-BOOKS.

8½ by 5¾, printed on Superfine paper, cloth, gilt top, 6s.

A Wonder-Book of Beasts.

Edited by F. J. HARVEY DARTON. Full of Humorous Illustrations by MARGARET CLAYTON.

A volume of Romance and Adventure, where all the leading characters are animals.

"A thorough book for children, well planned in every way and turned out without a fault."—PALL MALL GAZETTE.

8 by 5½, printed on Superfine paper, cloth, 6s.

Bellerophon. "The Bravest of the Brave."

By EDWARD FRASER.

Mr. Fraser has written a stirring and romantic battle story of the hardest fighter of the Fleet of Nelson's time.

"Better than half the stories of adventure."—YORKSHIRE POST.

8 by 5½, cloth, 5s.

Seeing the World. The Adventures of a Young Mountaineer.

By ASCOTT R. HOPE. With Illustrations in Colour from Drawings by GORDON BROWNE, R.I.

"Breezy and captivating. . . . An excellent book, well bound, well printed and illustrated."—SCHOOLMASTER.

THE NEW VOLUME in the TREASURE HOUSE SERIES

Crown 8vo, cloth boards, 2s. 6d. net.

HAMPTON COURT. By **Julia Cartwright (Mrs. Ady).** With 16 Illustrations on art paper. Uniform with

THE NATIONAL GALLERY. By **Alice Corkran.** With Illustrations from Photographs.

THE WALLACE AND TATE GALLERIES. By **Estelle Ross.** With Illustrations from Photographs.

Each of these volumes will prove a delightful companion for any boy or girl visiting these treasure houses of the nation.

Send to WELLS GARDNER, DARTON & CO., Ltd., 3 Paternoster Buildings, London, E.C., for their latest Catalogue (PRINTED IN COLOURS).

OXFORD UNIVERSITY PRESS

THE OXFORD ENGLISH TEXTS.

Library Editions, 8vo. uniformly bound in cloth with paper labels. The texts carefully collated with the original editions.

TWO NEW VOLUMES.

CAMPION'S WORKS.

Edited by PERCIVAL VIVIAN. 10s. 6d. net.

SPENSER'S POETICAL WORKS.

(The Faerie Queene, Vols. II and III) Edited by J. C. SMITH. 18s. net.

THE ENGLISHMAN IN ITALY.

Selected by G. H. WOLLASTON. Foolscap 8vo. 5s. net.

EIGHTEENTH CENTURY LITERATURE.

An Oxford Miscellany. Crown 8vo. 4s. net.

THE UNION OF SOUTH AFRICA.

By the Hon. R. H. BRAND, Secretary to the Transvaal Delegates at the South African National Convention. 8vo. 6s. net.

OXFORD LIBRARY OF PROSE AND POETRY.

Fcap. 8vo. cloth, 2s. 6d. net each; lambskin, gilt extra, 3s. 6d. net each.

NEW VOLUMES.

SELECT POEMS OF WINTHROP MACKWORTH PRAED.

Edited, with an Introduction, by A. D. GODLEY, with a Portrait.

SHELLEY'S LITERARY AND PHILOSOPHICAL CRITICISM.

Edited, with an Introduction, by J. SHAWCROSS.

PEACOCK'S MEMOIRS OF SHELLEY, with Shelley's Letters to Peacock.

Edited, with an Introduction, by H. F. B. BRETT-SMITH. With Portraits of Shelley and Peacock.

JAMES RUSSELL LOWELL'S FIRESIDE TRAVELS.

With an Introduction by E. V. LUCAS.

A HUNDRED VERSES OF OLD JAPAN.

Translated by W. N. PORTER. With 100 Illustrations from Japanese woodcuts.

POEMS OF GRAY.

A Facsimile Reprint of the Volume of 1768.

POEMS OF KEATS.

A Facsimile Reprint of the Volume of 1820.

THE OXFORD THACKERAY.

A new Illustrated Edition in 17 volumes. Arranged and edited by GEORGE SAINTSBURY. Including the copyright matter. With 1942 Illustrations. Price per volume: cloth, 2s. net; on Oxford India paper (to range with the Oxford India paper Dickens), 3s. 6d. net. The volumes may be obtained separately, and in a variety of leather bindings.

LONDON: HENRY FROWDE, OXFORD UNIVERSITY PRESS, AMEN CORNER, E.C.

with the principle of co-operation. Credit, the other necessary element, is implicit, given the will to work together. In the "National" Mr. Turnor approaches the subject from a slightly different point of view and reaches slightly different conclusions. Increased facilities for the purchase of land by tenants must be given; but small ownership must not be pushed too far. Tenancy is necessary as a probation for ownership. Mr. Turnor has not so absolute a faith in the "magic of property" as Sir Gilbert Parker. On the main points, however, there is agreement. For instance, Mr. Turnor insists strongly upon the part to be played in the future by credit and co-operation. Mr. J. Ellis Barker, in the "Nineteenth Century", views these questions more in their relation to the history and intentions of the two parties in their dealings with the land. He asks the question—Unionist or Socialist land reform? He then contrasts the Unionist policy of small holdings, affirmed in 1890 and 1906, with that of the Liberals as forecast in the present Finance Bill. That the present Government is making straight for land nationalisation Mr. Barker is assured. That way lies ruin for the land. Like Sir Gilbert Parker, Mr. Barker insists upon ownership as the basis of reform, flatly contradicting Mr. Asquith's statement that "the most hopeful tenure for a small holding is not that of a proprietor, but that of an occupying tenant". Lest these three articles should fail to force home the importance of the agricultural problem, M. Yves Guyot, in the "Financial Review of Reviews", sets out to prove that the increase of a nation's capital depends more upon its wheat harvest than upon its coal, iron, or precious metals.

Dr. Dillon and Mr. Garvin contribute their usual monthly survey of foreign affairs—the curious must sometimes find the comparison of their notes instructive—to the "Contemporary" and the "Fortnightly". In the "Fortnightly" there appears an article by Captain Battine on Austria-Hungary, appealing to the "intelligent interest" of people who would understand the problem of the Dual Monarchy. Captain Battine denies that Austria-Hungary is on the brink of dissolution, and describes as entirely farcical the forecast of a scramble plunging Europe into war on the death of the Emperor. Sir Edward Grey's action during the autumn is held to have cost Great Britain the advantage of Austria's moderating influence in the councils of the Triple Alliance. According to M. Adam Nowicki, in the "Nineteenth Century", Austria-Hungary has sustained a heavy blow by the understanding of Russia and Italy, which threatens the only sea route open to Austria. "The meeting at Racconigi is a further stage in the struggle between Austria-Hungary and Italy for predominance in the Adriatic—a struggle which it is daily becoming more difficult to conceal." But apparently M. Nowicki considers that Russia will be the ultimate loser. He asks the somewhat cryptic question "Can Russia escape the fate of Poland?"—says that history shows foreign policy rather than domestic to be the determining factor in the fate of States, and concludes that Austria has been thrown more than ever into the arms of Germany, thus adding enormously to the menace which Russia has to meet on her western frontier. Except for some characteristic opening notes, in which we are told that candour compels the admission that the Kaiser would no longer be a welcome guest in England, the "National" this month leaves European politics severely alone. But the "National" would not be itself without its anti-German page or two; and this month Mr. Maxse finds an ally in Mr. Blatchford. Strange bedfellows indeed! In the "English Review" are two articles on the rights of Finland; and a scheme for the control of foreign affairs by the democracy, outlined by Mr. H. N. Brailsford, following in the wake of Sir Charles Dilke. He wants a small Standing Committee of the House of Commons to be given the power in diplomatic matters, if not of veto at least of delay. His trouble is that diplomacy has now been taken outside party. "There is a governing class which in foreign affairs is always in power whatever label the administration wears. It is the class entrenched in society, in the clubs, in the City, in the Conservative press, and in the Diplomatic Service". The unhappy Radical gets no chance.

Mr. Lewis Melville has gathered into a most readable article for the "Fortnightly" some facts about William Beckford, of Fonthill Abbey, the author of "Vathek", and in the "English Review" appears an unpublished story of Beckford's in French, which Mr. Melville has unearthed, entitled "Histoire de la Princesse Zulkaïs et du Prince Kalilah". The "English Review" prints as usual various specimens of modern poetry, but Mr. Ford Madox Hueffer gives his views on the subject not in the pages of his own monthly, but of "The Thrush", which, by relying chiefly on verse, hopes to do something to rescue poetry from the neglect involved in "the stultifying conditions of modern life".

Select Books for Xmas Gifts.

THE CAT IN HISTORY, LEGEND AND ART

Written and Illustrated by ANNE MARKS. Crown 4to. cloth gilt, **6s.** net.

The cult of the cat must prove of interest even to those who are not professed lovers of the animal.

WHITE HEATHER

By ELLA MARY GORDON. Crown 8vo. cloth gilt, **2s. 6d.** net.

A dainty and elegant volume of verse which every poetry lover will enjoy.

THE HUMAN GIRL

By GRAHAM MOORE. Crown 8vo. cloth gilt, **2s. 6d.** net.

"A most readable tale. The dialogue is crisp, the situations conceived with skill. A story which should be popular amongst girls."—*Dundee Advertiser.*

FOR THREE KINGDOMS

By H. C. CROSFIELD. Frontispiece by Mr. NOYES LEWIS. Crown 8vo. **6s.**

Recollections of Robert Warden, a servant of King James. Full of stirring incidents, a story that grips the reader from beginning to end.

THOUGHTS FROM MANY CLIMES

Quotations in English, French, and Italian, with the English translations of the Italian, with two Dialogues by E. CARSON. Demy 16mo. Japanese vellum gilt, gilt top, **2s. 6d.** net; Velvet Leather, gilt edges, silk register, **5s.** net.

A book of meditative thoughts culled from French, Italian, and English authors, arranged for daily readings.

LITERARY BYE-PATHS, & VAGARIES

By THOMAS NEWBIGGING. Crown 8vo. **4s. 6d.** net.

A series of interesting essays on out-of-the-way subjects, with the true literary note that will appeal to all book-lovers.

PHILIP MENZE

A Story of Commercial Life. By H. C. KNIGHT. Crown 8vo. cloth gilt, **6s.**

This story, of especial interest to "Gentlemen of the Road," will prove very attractive to all business men and women.

THE FIRST DROP AND THE LAST

By PHŒBE ALLEN. Crown 8vo. cloth, **2s.** net.

An excellent story, founded on incidents in real country life. The book for parish libraries.

Write for Catalogue No. N102 of Antiquarian and General Literature.

LONDON: ELLIOT STOCK, 62 PATERNOSTER ROW, E.C.

NOW READY.—Small 4to. pp. x–270, 1s. net.

RELICTA.

Poems. By ARTHUR MUNBY.

"The book cannot fail to please a serious, quiet-minded lover of poetry."
Scotsman.

OTHER WORKS BY THE SAME AUTHOR.

POEMS, CHIEFLY LYRIC AND ELEGIAC. Small 4to. 5s.
VESTIGIA RETRORSUM. Crown 8vo. cloth, 2s. 6d.
ANN MORGAN'S LOVE. Crown 8vo. 1s.
SUSAN: a Poem of Degrees. Small 4to. 2s.

BERTRAM DOBELL, 77 Charing Cross Road, London.

NOW READY.
Royal 4to. Bound Cloth, pp. 274. Price £1 1s. net.

NATIONAL ANTARCTIC EXPEDITION, 1901-1904. MAGNETIC OBSERVATIONS.

With Map, Diagrams, and 43 Plates.
Preface by Sir ARCHIBALD GEIKIE, Pres.R.S.
PUBLISHED BY THE ROYAL SOCIETY.
Sold by HARRISON & SONS, 45 ST. MARTIN'S LANE, LONDON, W.C

WHO WAS SWEDENBORG?

A Lecture on **EMANUEL SWEDENBORG: HIS LIFE AND CHARACTER,** will be sent **free and post free** to all applicants on their sending their names and addresses to the

SECRETARY OF THE SWEDENBORG SOCIETY,
1 BLOOMSBURY STREET, LONDON, W.C.

A STRIKING NEW WORK FOR MODERN THINKERS.

THE WAY OUT

By LAMPADEPHOROS, *Author of "From December to December."*
Being a Mental Autobiography of Constructive Philosophy.
Crown 8vo. cloth gilt, **6s.** net (*by post*, 6s. 4d.). *Please write for Prospectus.*
LONDON: ELLIOT STOCK, 62 PATERNOSTER ROW, E.C.

SECOND EDITION. Price **2s. 6d.** net.

CATHOLICISM ON A PHILOSOPHICAL BASIS.

By B. C. NIXON, M. E. UNDERDOWN, and H. CUNLIFFE.

SWAN SONNENSCHEIN, LONDON.

FAVOURITE FICTION FOR XMAS.

By STANLEY WEYMAN.

The Long Night. 6/-
The House of the Wolf. 3/6
Pocket Edition: Cloth, 2/- net; Leather, 3/- net.
Sophia. 6/-
A Gentleman of France. 6/-
The Red Cockade. 6/-
Shrewsbury. 6/-
The Abbess of Vlaye. 6/-

By SIR A. CONAN DOYLE.
Price 3/6 each.

Micah Clarke. With 10 Illustrations.
The Refugees. With 25 Illustrations.
The Stark Munro Letters.
The Captain of the Pole-star.

By EDNA LYALL.
Price 3/6 each.

Doreen. The Story of a Singer.
Wayfaring Men. A Story of Theatrical Life.
Hope the Hermit. A Romance of Borrowdale.

By H. RIDER HAGGARD.

Price 3/6 each.

She. With 32 Illustrations.
Allan Quatermain. 32 Illustrations.
Colonel Quaritch, V.C.
Mr. Meeson's Will. With 16 Illustrations.
Stella Fregelius.
Black Heart & White Heart.
Swallow. A Story of the Great Trek. With 8 Illustrations.
Dawn. With 16 Illustrations.
The Witch's Head. With 16 Illustrations.
Pearl Maiden. A Tale of the Fall of Jerusalem. With 16 Illustrations.
Lysbeth. With 26 Illustrations.
Cleopatra. With 29 Illustrations.

Price 3/6 each.

Allan's Wife. With 34 Illustrations.
Beatrice.
Eric Brighteyes. 51 Illustrations.
Nada the Lily. 23 Illustrations.
Montezuma's Daughter. 24 Illustrations.
The People of the Mist. 16 Illustrations.
Joan Haste. 20 Illustrations.
Heart of the World. 15 Illustrations.
Dr. Therne.
The World's Desire. By H. RIDER HAGGARD and ANDREW LANG. 27 Illustrations.
Maiwa's Revenge. 1/6.

By E. Œ. SOMERVILLE and MARTIN ROSS.
"Capital fun."—*Daily Express.*

FURTHER EXPERIENCES OF AN IRISH R.M.

With 35 Illustrations by E. Œ. SOMERVILLE.

Some Experiences of an Irish R.M. 31 Illustrations. 6/-
Some Irish Yesterdays. 51 Illustrations. 3/6
All on the Irish Shore. 10 Illustrations. 6/-
An Irish Cousin. 6/-
The Real Charlotte. 3/6
The Silver Fox. 3/6

LONGMANS, GREEN & CO., 39 Paternoster Row, London, E.C.

THE ENGLISH REVIEW.

MONTHLY. CONTENTS OF DECEMBER NUMBER. 2s. 6d.

MODERN POETRY	ERNEST RHYS. JOHN FREEMAN. FREDERIC MANNING.
A PAGAN CREED	PROFESSOR GILBERT MURRAY.
THE STARVELING POET	EDWIN PUGH.
LETTERS FROM AMERICA	G. LOWES DICKINSON.
LUCY EVANS...	GILBERT CANNAN.
THE WIFE OF ALTAMONT	VIOLET HUNT.
THE MONTH: EDITORIAL	THE PASSING OF THE GREAT FIGURE.
AFTER THE DESTRUCTION OF THE VETO	J. A. HOBSON.
THE CONTROL OF FOREIGN AFFAIRS ...	H. N. BRAILSFORD.
LES INTERETS DE LA RUSSIE ET LES DROITS DE LA FINLAND	L. MECHELIN.
THE RIGHTS OF FINLAND AT STAKE ...	PROFESSOR J. N. REUTER.
THE PLACE OF SATIRE IN EDUCATION	PROFESSOR FOSTER WATSON.

SPECIAL SUPPLEMENT:
"HISTOIRE DE LA PRINCESSE ZULKAIS ET DU PRINCE KALILAH," a hitherto Unpublished Manuscript by WILLIAM BECKFORD, the Author of "VATHEK."

CHAPMAN & HALL, LTD., 11 Henrietta Street, Strand, W.C.

The first year of the *ENGLISH REVIEW* (December 1908 to November 1909), handsomely bound in Three Volumes, can now be obtained from the Publishers, price 27/- per set. Single Volumes price 9/- each. The first volume includes, among many contributions, H. G. WELLS' Novel, "TONO-BUNGAY," while "THE HOLY MOUNTAIN," by STEPHEN REYNOLDS, appears as a Serial in Volume 2, and "A CALL," by FORD MADOX HUEFFER, in Volume 3.

ART CHRISTMAS BOOKS TRAVEL

ART

A NEW BOOK FROM WALTER CRANE

THE SONG OF SIXPENCE PICTURE BOOK

By WALTER CRANE. **4s. 6d.**
Containing SING A SONG OF SIXPENCE, PRINCESS BELLE ETOILE, AN A B C OF OLD FRIENDS. Each, separately, **1s.** each, with New Cover and End Papers, uniform with the rest of Mr. Walter Crane's Toy Books.

"We are glad to welcome this reissue of three of Mr. Crane's unsurpassable picture-books for the young."—*Athenæum.*

THE ARCADIAN CALENDAR FOR 1910

Invented by VERNON HILL. A Series of 12 Designs descriptive of the Months, together with a Cover and Title-page. Folio, 8½ inches by 12 inches. **3s. 6d. net.**

A BOOK OF SATYRS

By AUSTIN OSMAN SPARE. Large folio. **21s. net.**

"These vigorous pen-and-ink designs are interesting. . . . He produces striking effects by sudden contrasts. . . . As a designer he is full of curious ideas.—*Athenæum.*

GEORGE BERNARD SHAW

By G. K. CHESTERTON. Crown 8vo. **5s. net.**

NEW POEMS

By WILLIAM WATSON. Crown 8vo. **5s. net.**
Also a Limited Edition of 75 Copies on Japanese Hand-Made Vellum. **£1 1s. net.**

"If a poet is to be judged by his power of interpreting the dreams and ideals of his fellows, then Mr. Watson must stand in a high place." *Athenæum.*

NEW POEMS

By RICHARD LE GALLIENNE. Crown 8vo. **5s. net.**

"His hand has lost nothing of its cunning."—*Daily Telegraph.*

TRAVEL

THE SOUL OF A TURK

Record of a Trip to Baghdad. By Mrs. DE BUNSEN. With 8 Full-page Illustrations. Demy 8vo. **10s. 6d. net.**

"The most delightful books are those which either depict the character of men and women or those which reveal the personality of the writer. Mrs. De Bunsen combines both these charms . . . her book must be read by those who would know Turkey. It must be read also by those who are trying to understand the elemental primitive feelings or instincts which form the background alike of religion and superstition."—*Morning Post.*

"This delightful book is full of shrewd observations . . . the whole book is full of charm and insight."—*Athenæum.*

SEEKERS IN SICILY

Being a Quest for Persephone by Jane and Peripatetica. Done into the Vernacular by ELIZABETH BISLAND and ANNE HOYTE. With 8 Full-page Illustrations and numerous decorations. Crown 8vo. **5s. net.**

LAKE VICTORIA TO KHARTOUM, With Rifle and Camera

By Captain F. A. DICKINSON, D.C.L.I. With an Introduction by the Right Hon. WINSTON SPENCER CHURCHILL, M.P. With numerous Illustrations taken by the Author. Uniform with "Big Game Shooting in the Equator." Demy 8vo. **12s. 6d. net.**

"An exceedingly vivacious account of excellent sport. . . . A really informing book, and of the photographs it can only be said that they are wholly beautiful."—*Pall Mall Gazette.*

BOSNIA AND HERZEGOVINA

By MAUDE M. HOLBACH. With 40 Illustrations by OTTO HOLBACH, and a Map. Crown 8vo. **5s. net.**

"An excellent, chatty, and picturesque travel companion." *Pall Mall Gazette.*

BIOGRAPHY

DR. JOHNSON AND MRS. THRALE

By A. M. BROADLEY. With an Essay Introductory by THOMAS SECCOMBE. With upwards of 50 Illustrations, 1 in Colour, 1 in Photogravure. Demy 8vo. **16s. net.**

"Mr. Thomas Seccombe is probably the most entertaining writer of introductions that we have to-day."—*Daily Mail.*

WILLIAM MAKEPEACE THACKERAY

A Biography. By LEWIS MELVILLE. With 2 Photogravures and numerous other Illustrations. 2 vols. demy 8vo. **25s. net.**

"Mr. Melville is certainly an enthusiast, and his zeal has made him seek Thackerayana in all possible places. . . . His record of the novelist's life will be found at once interesting and useful. The thoroughness with which the work has been done may be gathered from the fact that the 'Bibliography' gives particulars of close upon thirteen hundred items."—*Daily Telegraph.*

GIOVANNI BOCCACCIO: a Biographical Study

By EDWARD HUTTON. With a Photogravure Frontispiece and numerous other Illustrations. Demy 8vo. **16s. net.**

"Mr. Edward Hutton has written by far the best book in our language upon a theme as attractive in itself as any in literary history. It is a delightful volume. It is quick and it is balanced. It is learned and it is sympathetic. It throws a full light upon a changeable and paradoxical personality much misunderstood. . . . For English readers the biography is one of those reconstructions which are in themselves a revelation." *Observer.*

MARIA EDGEWORTH & HER CIRCLE in the Days of Bonaparte and Bourbon

By CONSTANCE HILL. With numerous Illustrations by ELLEN G. HILL, and Reproductions of Contemporary Portraits, &c. Demy 8vo. **21s. net.**

"A new book by Miss Constance Hill is a sheer delight; no one has a prettier touch in the re-creation of a forgotten period."—*Daily Telegraph.*

MADAME DE MAINTENON Her Life and Times, 1635-1719

By C. C. DYSON. With a Photogravure Frontispiece and 16 Black-and-White Illustrations. Demy 8vo. **12s. 6d. net.**

"In a lively and entertaining manner Mrs. Dyson relates the chapters of this wonderful story. . . . With graphic touch she depicts life at the Court of Le Grand Monarque. The illustrations to the volume are excellent."—*Daily Chronicle.*

FICTION

THE DIVERTING ADVENTURES OF MAURIN

By JEAN AICARD. [*Translated.*]

"Maurin is a great story-teller—'galégeades,' they call their yarns in Provence. . . . Sketches of prefects, and poachers, and peasants are cleverly drawn. There is not a dull page in the volume."—*Scotsman.*

"Those who imagine they know their France already will find a good deal to surprise and instruct them in this absorbing picture of provincialism.—*Globe.*

GERMAINE

By H. C. ROWLAND.

"From its first page this novel quickens the reader with its intense vitality and individuality.—*World.*

THE HOLY MOUNTAIN

By STEPHEN REYNOLDS.

"Deserves nothing but praise. . . . A clever story well told and an endlessly amusing caricature of the petty side of life."—*Punch.*

TRIAL BY MARRIAGE

By W. S. JACKSON, Author of "Nine Points of the Law."

"Sparkling and incisive. . . . Undeniably entertaining." *Evening Standard.*

THE EAGLE'S NEST

By ALLAN McAULAY.

"A brilliant *tour de force.*"—*Athenæum.*

THE ODD MAN

By ARNOLD HOLCOMBE.

"One of the most refreshing and amusing books that we have read for some months. . . . A book to put on one's shelves."—*Morning Post.*

ANATOLE FRANCE IN ENGLISH

NOW READY—A Translation by A. W. EVANS of
L'ILE DES PINGOUINS (Penguin Island).
By ANATOLE FRANCE.

Being the 10th Volume of the Uniform **6s.** Edition of the Works of Anatole France in English.

PUBLISHED. — "The White Stone," "Thais," "Balthasar," "The Well of St. Clare," "The Garden of Epicurus," "The Crime of Silvestre Bonnard," "Mother of Pearl," "The Red Lily," "Merrie Tales of Jacques Tournebroche."

JOHN LANE, THE BODLEY HEAD, LONDON & NEW YORK

Printed for the Proprietors by SPOTTISWOODE & Co. LTD., 5 New-street Square, E.C., and Published by REGINALD WEBSTER PAGE, at the Office, 10 King Street, Covent Garden, in the Parish of St. Paul, in the County of London.—*Saturday, 11 December, 1909.*

THE

SATURDAY REVIEW

OF

POLITICS, LITERATURE, SCIENCE, AND ART.

No. 2,825 Vol. 108. 18 December 1909. [REGISTERED AS A NEWSPAPER.] 6d.

CONTENTS.

NOTES OF THE WEEK.

Better than any speech any Unionist can make is the announcement of the malign bargain between Liberals and Irish. It is exact and explicit. Home Rule for years has not been quite definitely on or quite definitely off the Liberal platform. Now it is as much a plank as it was in '86 or '93. Every Liberal must walk it. If Mr. Asquith's statement in his Albert Hall speech does not bring every Unionist to the poll, nothing can. It is a direct and dreadful menace to the Empire.

Still three more weeks of election oratory—it is a horrible prospect for the country. During the past week everybody, on the Liberal side at any rate, seems to have made a series of speeches. The Prime Minister may be an honourable exception. He appears not to have spoken since the Albert Hall performance on Friday; but then such heavy pieces as he fires, charged with great round shot, need a vast deal of loading and priming. As for Mr. Churchill's speeches and Mr. Birrell's and Mr. Ure's and so forth, one has lost all count of them. The truth is, it is the same old speech dressed up again and again for different meetings.

A man is not going to exhaust himself out of his own constituency, unless the baits are large, by inventing a new speech at each meeting he addresses. Even the nobler Radical may value his own constitution above the British Constitution. We knew of a case lately where a north-country parson was staying in a south-country village when suddenly he found that there was a great call on his services as preacher. Three neighbouring parsons asked him to preach in their respective villages. Wishing to get the duty done within a single day, he preached morning, afternoon and evening. He took Balaam as his text and read the same sermon at each church. Hence he is known as Balaam in the district, and we imagine there are a good many Balaams engaged in electioneering just now.

When Lord North was shown a list of the generals who were to lead the British troops in the war with America he said "I know not what effect these names will have on the enemy—they fill me with alarm". A thought of the same kind may well come to people who observe Mr. McKenna and Dr. Macnamara standing forth just now as the leaders of the British Navy. Whatever effect these names may have on the enemy, they fill us with alarm. At Southend, where he has been electioneering, Mr. McKenna makes a list of the big ships he is building in a way that reminds one of a boy playing with his popguns; whilst Dr. Macnamara assures us that things are all nice and safe "under the White Ensign". What is so ludicrous as a lord-high-admiral manner in a party politician of the successful clerk type?

There have been two speeches this week of interest and freshness—those of Mr. Burns and Lord Curzon. Mr. Burns is not going to the Port of London, despite all the gossip. He certainly should be there. He has the weight and distinction which, to tell the truth, are a little to seek in the present holder of the office. But Sir Hudson Kearley does not see the fun of budging for Mr. Burns or anybody else. So Mr. Burns has come out once more as the bruiser of Battersea. But he is not the bruiser he was. He has been to school at the Local Government Board and has grown too responsible—and we rather suspect too Conservative at heart—to play the game well for Mr. Lloyd George and Mr. Churchill. He is a very cool admirer of the Budget—a short time ago he was, we think, not an admirer at all. He prides himself on his administrative record. He has worked far harder—in his office—than any other Minister. He has run the Local Government Board, whilst Mr. Churchill has succeeded in running himself and Mr. Ure has tried to run the party. All three have gone in for a big "screw"; Mr. Burns, however, has chosen not only to pocket but to earn his.

In short, Mr. Burns has been too openly virtuous for a long while past, and he is out of favour with his side. So he has gone into the fight without fervour, and we should not be surprised if he is really shaken severely in this contest. He has carried through the Town Planning Act, a measure of statesmanship, but what do the Hébertists of Battersea care for such a thing as that? What they want is swag. He might quote Mr. Lyttelton in his favour, and other Conservatives as well as the Conservative papers. But this would not withhold a single Unionist vote from Mr. Benn. When the election comes we must all forget our friends on the other side—it must be a dead cut.

For the rest there was a point or two in Mr. Burns' opening speech which may be recalled after the election. He said he did not think much of Back to the Land—the people who have left the quiet country for the live city are not likely to return. That is absolutely true. Of all hollow cries, Back to the Land is hollowest. It amuses us to find Mr. Burns and Lord Lansdowne in the same galley for once.

The Liberal press appears delighted with Lord Curzon's bold speech at Oldham—it is full of admissions which are to be used with much effect against the Unionists. We think they are welcome to the admissions. As if the election were going to be decided by fine analyses and weighings of argument! By putting the case for the House of Lords at its maximum Lord Curzon is doing a good service. He has proved himself so far the most valuable speaker on the Unionist side. He may by habit dwell on Olympus, but the gods have a way sometimes of coming down with effect among the common people.

The Radical papers are making a great mistake about the platform speeches of what they call the "Wild Peers". They seem to think they are scoring off them by reporting the original and racy parts of their speeches. The fact is these Peers of unconventional language are taking on, as we said they would, with popular audiences who know there may be a very good fellow behind a "bad word" and a very bad one behind a good. The affinity between the aristocrat and working men (proper) is notorious. When Lord Mansfield was at the Bar he was told by his clerk that a lady had called while he was out. "Who was she?" asked Mr. Murray. "I don't know", the clerk said, "she would not give me her name; but she did swear so she must be a lady of quality."

No lawyer ventures to say the Lords has not the legal right to reject a Budget Bill; not Mr. Asquith nor the Lord Chancellor nor Mr. Haldane who have admitted it. Lord Lindley, in his second letter to the "Times" of Tuesday, recalls that Mr. Gladstone and Lord Granville in 1861 made no distinction between legal rights and constitutional rights when they stated that the Lords could always reject even a Budget Bill. To those who say that the House of Lords cannot exercise the legal right, and refer to the analogy of the Crown's "veto", Lord Lindley points out that this power can still be exercised quite constitutionally on the advice of a Minister. His defence to impeachment would be that the country supported his advice, the King having dissolved Parliament for the purpose of submitting the question to it.

This is exactly the defence of the House of Lords as to the Budget. It cannot be impeached, as the Minister could be, if it mistakes the opinion of the country, but neither can the House of Commons, supposing the country is against the Budget. The Constitution has to assume that both Houses will do their best according to their lights, and in this instance they are like the King, they can do no legal wrong. It has been replied to Lord Lindley that no Minister under the present Cabinet system could conceivably give the advice supposed. Why not? An individual Minister may act and must refrain from acting in law just as if the Cabinet were not invented.

Mr. Markham M.P., it seems, did not say that "the Bentincks even robbed the Crown by seizing the Royal Forest of Sherwood". But he admits he said that the Duke of Portland is enjoying a large mineral income owing to the Enclosure Acts passed in the Mansfield district during the last century. There is a suggestio falsi here, perhaps due to the ignorance or recklessness which is so common amongst political speakers like Mr. Markham. The Duke of Portland's agent informs him of what he ought to have known—that the Enclosure Acts did not give the mineral rights to lords of manors. They already owned the minerals under the old English laws, and the Enclosure Acts gave them no rights over the minerals which they did not possess without them.

Mr. George had better stick to theory. He should never run his head against a concrete case—especially of his own making. Cardiff Castle is a concrete case. Mr. George said that the castle pays less in rates than "the small tailor's shop next door". The small tailor's shop turns out to be a large emporium, and next door proves to be 380 yards away in the heart of the city. Mr. George, therefore—very weak this—writes to explain. The small shop covers an area of 470 square yards, he says. But the explanation is itself a misstatement. The premises with their accessories to which he now refers, cover not 470 square yards, but 992. These points no doubt only relatively affect the merits of the question at issue, but they will certainly strengthen Mr. George's dislike of the dukes. Incidentally they afford a clue to the methods by which the Budget was compounded.

The Government and the Admiralty will have to meet Mr. H. H. Mulliner's challenge, or judgment must go by default against both. Mr. Mulliner apparently gave offence to the Admiralty, and was victimised accordingly, on account of his discovery nearly four years ago of the extraordinary arrangements Germany had made for building a navy that should surpass our own. He offers to give £100 to anyone who first obtains a categorical reply from a responsible Minister to the question "At what date were the Government first aware of the enormous acceleration for the production of armaments which commenced in Germany at the beginning of 1906, and which is admitted by Mr. McKenna to have been going on continuously ever since?" Under the present Government our naval supremacy has been imperilled, and the situation is now, says Mr. Mulliner, graver than ever. And the full facts on which action might have been taken were before the Admiralty in 1906. Were the Government informed?

It would be strange if Tariff Reformers were not confident; converts are made almost hourly. Sir John Turner, the Liberal alderman and leather manufacturer of Nottingham, has thrown over the associations and economic beliefs of a lifetime because he sees no chance of solving the problem of the unemployed except by tariff reform. He is one of many industrial leaders who at last look the facts fairly and squarely in the face. This is particularly the case in the motor trade. Mr. Harvey du Cros complains of the competitive advantage the foreigner enjoys in our markets. Tariff reform is the remedy. Mr. Scott Leefe says that if tariff reform comes, the French house of the De Dion-Bouton Company will pay the duty only till such time as they can transfer their factory to England. Mr. S. F. Edge foresees the dumping of American cars at an early date unless we have tariff reform. If the Americans are allowed to throw their surplus unchecked on the English market, Mr. Edge will transfer his business to the United States—and his firm pays £150,000 a year as wages. Tariff reform is insistent whichever way we turn.

The valour of the Labour party in boasting its independence of the Liberals seems to be oozing out of its fingers, judging by what is happening in Northumberland. Messrs. Burt and Fenwick ought to be opposed by a Labour party man, as they have refused to sign the Labour party Constitution. The miners indeed voted for a Labour man being put up to oppose them; but Messrs. Burt and Fenwick have talked the Council of the Miners' Association over. On the pretext that there is not time for any other candidature, they have sent the question back for another ballot. This is a weak submission to two Liberals most opposed to the Labour party, and if the miners have no more backbone than the Council there will be no three-cornered fight for the Morpeth and Wansbeck Divisions and Messrs. Burt and Fenwick will be returned, to the greater glorification of the Liberals and the nullification of the Labour party.

Sir Christopher Furness' co-partnership scheme, during the nine months it has been in operation, has given perfect satisfaction to the company. It comes up again just now through a letter from the secretary to the employé shareholders inquiring if they are equally satisfied, as the company wish to go on with it. The answer of the men, whatever it may be, ought to be valuable as indicating whether or not this kind of arrangement between employers and employed is likely to spread. During the nine months there have been no disputes at the Hartlepool yards. Orders have been executed without trouble or delay, in striking contrast to what has previously occurred; and it is because the company desire to have the like security for future orders that it now applies to the men. The fact that the employé shareholders receive a dividend of nine per cent. on their shares ought to be of weight in their reply.

French Socialists have been exhibiting a lack of competence to talk on social problems not confined to the fraternity in that country. M. Ruau, Minister of Agriculture, has had to instruct them on one or two matters. The small landholder is not dying out in France. Far from being crushed by the capitalist, he is doing better than anybody else in the breeding of stock and in market-gardening. Besides, why should the Socialist grumble, even if the peasant were being extinguished? It is just these small landholders that stand between the Republic and the Utopia of M. Jaurès. If a nation wishes to have an army at its disposal against the time when the Socialists sound the advance, let that nation foster the small holder and plant that army on the land.

The Paris papers did their talking in subdued tones about the German Chancellor's reference to Alsace-Lorraine. If the Alsace-Lorraine question no longer exists (as the Germans are glad to fancy), a troublesome chapter of history is closed. The question existed before France and Germany were nations, and France still sees in it a Western question to put beside those of the East. One thing is certain, France cannot in nature view Germany's "conciliatory" policy towards the Lorrainers as well meant for herself; and we do not expect her to meet Germany in these provinces with a very good grace. We only hope that she may keep some dignity, and induce hot-heads to think a little before they speak. It is poor exercise gnashing one's teeth at what cannot be helped.

The German Chancellor has undoubtedly strengthened his position by the speeches he has made since the Reichstag assembled. His tone was dignified and his matter conciliatory, and the German public are now convinced that, despite his previous lack of diplomatic experience, Herr von Bethmann-Hollweg is determined to exercise his influence in shaping the policy of the Empire. In a few days' time he is to start for Rome, and great importance is attached to a visit following so closely on the Racconigi meeting. It is now felt that the Chancellor will acquit himself with firmness and tact, and do all that is in his power to ensure the loyalty of the new Italian Ministry to the Triple Alliance.

Quite a pretty quarrel is now in progress between the States of the German Empire. The Constitution provides that inland navigation is free, but the Prussian Government has come forward with proposals for shipping tolls, the proceeds to be devoted to the improvement of the rivers and canals. This is all very well for Prussia, which is certain to profit by any expenditure, since all the rivers debouching into the North and Baltic Seas pass through Prussian territory. The other States, on the contrary, feel that Prussia is likely to reap all the profits while sharing the loss. Accordingly, the Governments of Saxony and Baden have taken the strong step of publishing a joint memorandum of protest. Their association is significant, for whereas Saxony is concerned only with the Elbe, Baden is interested in the Neckar, which is a tributary of the Rhine, and Prussia might have hoped to succeed in playing off one against the other. Her hope has been disappointed, and her whole policy has given rise to one of those scares of "Prussianisation" to which the federated Governments are always liable.

In Austria-Hungary the racial issue stands behind all political questions. The annexation of Bosnia last year turned many Serbs into Austrian subjects and brought Vienna into the closest touch with the Pan-Serb movement. The failure of Hungary to govern Croatia has embittered feeling still further, until to-day the mere fact that a man has a Servian name is regarded as presumptive proof of disloyalty. During the past few months the authorities have chosen to bring matters to a head. First they put fifty-three distinguished Serbo-Croatians on their trial for high treason. The proceedings dragged on for many weeks, and though a few convictions were secured the episode scarcely reflected credit on the Austrian Government.

To justify the proceedings at Agram, Dr. Friedjung, an historian of repute and a strong German, was commissioned, apparently by the chiefs of the Foreign Office, to write a series of articles in a Viennese paper. The politicians attacked have brought a libel action against him, and have certainly made out a strong case. Dr. Friedjung relied on what purported to be the minutes of a Pan-Serb organisation. The president of this body, Dr. Markovitch, who is a professor of Belgrade University, has voluntarily come forward to give evidence. His case is that the records of minutes are obvious forgeries, since he was attending a juristic conference in Berlin at the very time when the minutes represent him as presiding over a group of conspirators at Belgrade. Should his evidence be confirmed, and there seems no reason to doubt its truth, Dr. Friedjung, and the Government which inspired him, will be gravely discredited. The case, however, is not yet at an end, and other sensations may be in store for the public. As is usual in political trials, the attitude of the presiding judge has come in for much criticism.

Of King Leopold it can hardly be said that he should have died hereafter. A man of extreme energy and of ability, he played, of course, a prominent part. History will not be able to ignore him; it will be difficult to forget him. But the later years of his life were not the best. The Congo was not the only shade upon them. There are some domestic differences that cannot be the affair of the family alone. This is not the moment to attempt an historical estimate of the second King of the Belgians; but his epitaph can hardly be "We could better have spared a better man".

A Parliamentary "crisis" is soon settled when the Government has a Cromwell waiting at the door for it. This is what has happened in Turkey, though we are grandly told by some papers that the constitutional Government has emerged from the crisis with credit. The Cabinet made the question of a fusion of two steamship companies a matter of confidence; and lost by a large majority. But its resignation would not suit the convenience just now of the Committee that controls the army, and within a few hours the matter was brought up again and the first decision reversed by an equal majority. This is the farce of Parliamentary government, but so-called Parliamentary government must be this in Turkey; though English papers pretend to be serious about it.

Sir Alfred Jones is a loss to the Empire. He has died at a moment when affairs would have been profoundly interesting to him. None ever did more for those parts of the Empire with which he was more directly connected. He flung much of his energy and not a little of his wealth into the work, which Mr. Chamberlain as Colonial Secretary initiated, of developing our neglected estates beyond the seas, and both the West Indies and West Africa owe him more than is generally known. For the sake of the much-tried West Indies he sacrificed a great deal, and to him was chiefly due the successful inauguration of the British Cotton Growing Association. Big shipper as he was, he shared none of the fears as to the effect Tariff Reform would have on the British mercantile marine.

If Mr. Salting was a miser, he was not miserable in his three rooms over the Thatched House. It was certainly strange—a better word would be "unnatural"—for a man with a collection of works of art worth more than a million to live in three rooms. But he enjoyed life in his own way; and he built a truly magnificent gift to the nation. The nation at any rate must not criticise Mr. Salting's conception of a happy life and the enjoyment of wealth. He knew how to use his money better than most millionaires.

Mr. Frederick Greenwood was a journalist of dignity and public spirit. He searched for good copy as keenly as any journalist, but he had taste, discretion, a sense of responsibility; these are qualities not invariable among "the writing sort". Mr. Greenwood had not anything in the nature of genius: he dwelt in the safer regions of talent.

If Captain Loose and Mr. Dunkle—Arcades ambo—were speaking truth Doctor Cook is absolutely incompetent to discover the Pole. He is not able to make the necessary observations to prove his claim. In any case, Loose and Dunkle are a couple of rascals: Loose especially a clever one. The story they told to the "New York Herald" is that Loose made all the observations which would be made up to the Pole, Cook's own observations being mere rubbish. Loose even invented a set of chronometers with different rates according to Greenwich time. He is a humorous rascal too. When he handed over his observations he remarked that he guessed he was entitled to be considered the discoverer of the North Pole.

According to the story the two men were to have £800, and it is because Cook has not paid that they have given him away. If Cook does not go against them and the "New York Herald" for libel he will have to disappear permanently, as he has already disappeared temporarily. He is supposed to have sent the proofs to Copenhagen. Loose is so confident of his ability that he declares the Danish scientists could find no flaw in them. The whole question depends, then, not on the proofs as such, but on the relations of Cook, Loose, and Dunkle. Astronomers are not the best judges of this, though they might, perhaps, by viva voce examination of Cook find out whether he is or is not competent to make the observations he has sent in. If he is not, the observations must have been cooked by Loose. But the latest is that Loose has confessed that his story is a lie from beginning to end.

The time has really come to end the hansom-cab agony. The rickety old cabs that still linger on the streets, the rickety hacks that jolt them along, the forlorn drivers—London has little use for them, little save abuse. The taxicab is the one cab—with a few growlers—that is wanted to-day. But we are not quite so sure about the virtues of the taxi's drivers. They are beginning to growl already if one does not give them two shillings when their taximeter says one and eightpence.

EXORITUR CLAMOR.

In the din of speeches it will soon be impossible to distinguish the voice of any particular speaker, no matter how brilliant he may be. The great men, to indulge in a rather odd comparison, will be like the thrush or the nightingale singing undistinguished in the hubbub of chirps and cheeps around them. If only there were any resemblance between a politician's note and the worst of songbirds! To the concert of the parrot-house an election campaign may very well be compared, barring the beauty of the birds. He must be a great adept in parrots who could distinguish the scream of one macaw from another in the general noise. We seize the opportunity of doing this before the whole multitude of cockatoos, parrots, parakeets and lorikeets join in. At present Lord Curzon is able to make his voice heard far above the crowd, not drowned even by the call to arms of Mr. Balfour and Mr. Asquith or the piping plaint of Lord Rosebery. The fight and life this "effete oligarch" is putting into the attack is quite splendid. He has never been more effective. The Government election-advisers did not quite reckon with the extra energy the peers were going to throw into this fight. To hide their chagrin they are now pretending to make a huge joke of every peer's speech. Peers are not professional politicians, and because they have something to say and do not say it in the common form of the political hack, the Radical papers are puzzled. They know no language but that of the journalist, and a man who does not talk as the journalist does must necessarily talk ridiculously. It reminds us of certain Americans who think it "funny" when an Englishman talks English without a twang. The amateur is not as slick as the professional, but none the less in most things he is a great relief from the professional. In a few days the man who goes to meetings will know the stereotyped speech on both sides by heart and will give up listening after the regulation speaker's first words. But the "backwoods peer" he will still find quite refreshing. We hope every Unionist peer in the country will come out and speak. He is worth much more to us than the paid orator; and the Radicals have no similar force. They do not want it, of course; they thank their stars they have nothing of the kind. Nobody ever does want what he cannot get. All the same we observe that every one of their wretched remnant of peers is trotted out by the Radical electioneers whenever they get the chance. Yet not quite every one. Lord Courtney of Penwith would put out the fire of any meeting.

Very foolishly Liberals are making their whole campaign turn on the Lords, and very wisely Unionists are helping them to do this. There was a time when these purely political questions did interest people in this country very much; but the interest has died with the spirit that was behind it. That mid-Victorian prig, the intelligent Liberal youth, generally a mechanic or junior clerk, who read Mill and talked Bentham, or what he took for Mill and Bentham, is happily dead. Socialism has done much to kill him, and we thank socialism for it. Since his decease men have cared much more for social realities than for political forms. Lord Rosebery's Government owed its ignominious end largely to popular sickness of barren negation, such as the bill for the disestablishment of the Church in Wales. The working man is not such a fool now as to be content with injuring others: he wants to benefit himself. This Government is not so blind to facts as was Lord Rosebery's, and has given a good deal of time to substantial social work. But now it is foolish enough to undo the good effect of this by taking its stand on a purely political question of constitutional form. It would be difficult to imagine anything more sterile than the promise of Mr. Asquith's programme. Disestablishment of the House of Lords, a Home Rule Parliament for Ireland, Disestablishment of the Church in Wales, and a Franchise Bill, mainly as a sop to the women. Not a single vital matter that can touch the daily life of the people. Tariff Reform is, at any rate, a very living issue; it bears directly on the question of unemployment. Mr. Asquith's programme has nothing to compare with it in practical significance. It will not be very difficult to make working men see that if they give Mr. Asquith the power to go through with his programme, social reform must wait for many a year. Apart from merit, the Lords question alone will take him most of his time; and then Home Rule for Ireland; and then Welsh Disestablishment; and then a Franchise Bill. How will this strike the man who already has a vote but nothing else? Will the unemployed man enjoy seeing the time of Parliament given up to Irish politics or Welsh Nonconformity? Mr. Asquith's speech will do us a great service. It puts his party on the defensive; he even represents his designs on the Lords as defensive in essence; and he appeals to the people to quit themselves like men for—constitutional dogma. The effect of this is to shift the centre of gravity from the Budget to the Lords. It is no use saying that the overthrow of the Lords is the necessary prelude to the Budget. People may be mostly fools, and Liberals may be no better than others, but they are not fools enough, whether Liberals or Conservatives, to believe that they cannot get the Budget without destroying the Lords, when they know that the utmost the Lords could do, if the country wanted the Budget, was to hang it up till next February, when every tax it contained would be re-enacted and made retrospective. So far as the Budget goes, if the country wants it, the position next March will be in every respect the same as if the Lords had passed it. Is anyone such a fool as to get excited about a few weeks' delay as a violation of popular rights? Only the enthusiastic Radical. Others will think something quite different. They will be thinking that the real cause of the Government's fury against the Lords is not that they hung up a Budget which the country wanted, but that they made it impossible to pass a Budget which the country may not have wanted. That was their real offence. Evidently Mr. Asquith and Mr. Lloyd George are both very doubtful of the result of this election (as every sane man must be), and are proportionately sick that the Lords prevented the Budget going through without taking the risk of an appeal to the people. The little game was spoilt.

Lord Curzon's speech at Oldham showed how easy the Lords' case is to argue; though not to argue as well as he did. There is so much "merits" in it that a speaker can never be grounded for want of matter. Any comparison of personnel shrivels into nothing all Mr. Lloyd George's rhodomontade. Take almost any head of distinction you like, the House of Lords comes out much better than the House of Commons. Take law: Mr. Lloyd George, the provincial solicitor, is hardly the equal of Lord Collins, say. If this is unfair, take either Law Officers: neither Sir William Robson nor Sir S. T. Evans would claim to be the equal as lawyer to one or two of the Law Lords. Or finance: Mr. Lloyd George, in his other capacity, is hardly equal to Lord Welby or Lord Milner. At least, officials in the Treasury, who have to explain to him some of the elements of finance, hardly think so. Or take letters: even the brilliant Mr. Belloc or Mr. Mason is hardly equal to Lord Morley. There is something sublime in a Lloyd George putting down all these men "as effete".

And that stock piece for Liberal wit, the hereditary element, it is strange how well it comes out by comparison. How many of the peers that have got to the House otherwise than by heredity would be there but for their money? Had they been brilliant but poor, they might have been waiting at the gate of Paradise still, like the expectant Radicals Lord Curzon described. But the brilliant though poor hereditary peer has the House of Lords open wide to him; no other brilliant but poor man finds either House open to him. Heredity thus keeps a way open for brains without much money. The truth is, any given number of men will have an average number of brilliant sons, of able sons, and of stupid sons. The hereditary plan secures them all for the House of Lords. No brilliant hereditary peer can be lost to the country, and his environment and traditions give him every chance. The fools mostly leave public life alone. What other system does the sifting better?

We note a new version in superior Radical circles of the constitutional position of the Lords as to Finance Bills. The cry once was that in no circumstances could the Lords be justified in rejecting a Finance Bill. Lord Morley gave that away in the Lords' debate. Now we find the "Westminster Gazette" too admitting that situations might arise in which it would be the Lords' duty to reject a Finance Bill. It would still be unconstitutional; but the Lords would be justified in violating the constitution. This is surely the escape of a man hard pressed for a way out. But it does not help him very much. Whether you call it violating the constitution justly, or using a constitutional power, if you admit that there may be circumstances in which the House of Lords would be justified in rejecting a Finance Bill, the whole question becomes solely one of discretion. The constitutional argument goes. The only question is, Were the Lords right? If they were right, who will care to inquire whether they were constitutional? But it is just this constitutional point which makes Mr. Asquith's whole case.

TO UNIONIST FREE TRADERS.

WE have always been struck by the disparity between the individual ability of the Unionist Free Traders and the corporate stupidity of their actions. If ever a group of clever men played their cards badly, surely it is the members of the Unionist Free Trade Club. Lord Cromer, Lord Balfour of Burleigh, Lord James, Lord Robert and Lord Hugh Cecil, Mr. G. S. Bowles, and Mr. F. Lambton are all able and experienced politicians; they had an old-established cause to defend; and yet what a poor fight they have made! Compare their position with that of the Peelites, who revolted against Lord Derby and Disraeli, and who all became Cabinet Ministers! To be sure, the Peelites went over to Palmerston in the end, and the Unionist Free Traders cannot bring themselves to go over to Mr. Asquith, which is not to be wondered at. But one would have thought that they might have got together some sort of organisation, and put forward some candidates besides the gentlemen mentioned above, to whom, by the way, must be added Mr. Charles Seely, who persists in standing for Lincoln. Of course, it is not for us to complain of the weakness of the Unionist Free Traders. None the less, their failure to make any sort of position for themselves in the political world is one of the most astonishing facts in the period of transition through which we are passing.

We are not, however, concerned with the careers of three or four thoughtful and eloquent protestants—they are well able to take care of themselves. We are thinking of the men in the constituencies who share their views, inconsiderable indeed in numbers, but entitled to respect as educated, if somewhat perverse, adherents to an impossible attitude. For if one thing has finally demonstrated the impossibility of the Unionist Free Traders' existence as a political party, it is the advice addressed to them on the eve of the election by the Unionist Free Trade Club. That advice is to use their own discretion as to voting, but to do nothing which can imperil the Union or Free Trade! As the Prime Minister has authoritatively made Home Rule one of the planks in the platform, the Free Trade Unionist is in this cruel dilemma—that if he votes for the Radical candidate he is supporting Home Rule; while if he votes for the Unionist candidate he is voting against Free Trade. The pundits of the Free Trade Club might just as well have told the unhappy man to square the circle. It may be said that the Unionist Free Trader was in the same dilemma at the General Election of 1906. But that is not so, for not only was Home Rule not in the programme, but it was well understood that during this Parliament, at all events, it would not be brought forward. The patience of the Irish Nationalists is, however, exhausted. They say, naturally enough as men of business, "We have supported you British Socialists through one Parliament, in which you have had your chance of reforming the universe and clearing the way for Home Rule. That you have failed in everything you have undertaken, and are now laying the blame on the House of Lords, is none of our business. We will help you, certainly, to down the House of Lords, but only on condition that Home Rule is to be one of the first measures in the new Parliament". Some such language as this must have been held to Mr. Asquith by Mr. Redmond and Mr. Dillon, and was the "causa causans" of that passage in the Albert Hall speech. So that no Unionist Free Trader can lay the flattering unction to his soul now, as he did in 1906, that his abstinence from the poll will not really endanger the Union.

It is impossible not to sympathise with a conscientious man in such a plight. If he does not vote at all, he is guilty of what Pericles declared to be the greatest crime of a citizen, indifference. "Indifference", exclaimed that statesman, "is the only thing we do not tolerate in Athens". How then shall the Unionist Free Trader vote? We will not repeat Hume's advice, of two evils choose the less, because we will not talk of Tariff Reform as an evil for anyone. We will ask the Unionist Free Trader to ask himself seriously, What is my obvious duty as the citizen of an empire? We beseech him to consider (as Cromwell besought his Scotch theologians to consider) the possibility of his being mistaken on so complicated a question as the reform of the tariff. The wisest and most experienced men, professors of economics and practitioners of trade and finance, differ in this country and in all countries about fiscal systems. Further, we would remind our Free Trade Unionist that a fiscal system is a matter capable of annual adjustment and correction. If you make a mistake in 1910 you can put it right in 1911. About Home Rule there is no doubtfulness of issue: and there is no retracing your steps. To vote, therefore, for Home Rule in order to escape Tariff Reform is to vote for something you know to be wrong in order to avoid something as to which you cannot be certain whether you are right or wrong. Surely no serious, we had almost said no sane, man can hesitate when confronted by this alternative. We know, indeed, that there are some men who believe that a tariff on foreign imports would be a greater evil than Home Rule for Ireland. These are the bigots of a commercial theory, with whom it is as useless to reason as it is with fanatics of any creed. It has been well observed that when a man is inflamed against a doctrine, the more clearly you prove to him its merits or its innocence, the angrier he becomes. But the number of Free Importers of this complexion is happily small. The majority of those who are unconverted by Tariff Reform are much more afraid of Home Rule and Socialism. We are sorry to play upon their fears; we would rather rely upon their convictions. But as they cannot by any political gymnastic obey the orders of the Unionist Free Trade Club, let them for once sink the doctrinaire in the patriot.

LORDS AND LIBERAL BILLS: THE FACTS.

WHAT are the facts as to the Lords rejecting Bills sent up from a Liberal House of Commons during the present Parliament? In the first session (1906) it is noteworthy that, beyond a Water Provisional Order Bill, the House of Lords negatived only two measures in which the Liberals or the Labour party were interested. On second reading they threw out the Plural Voting Bill and an Aliens Bill. The former they did not denounce in principle, but argued that, when its provisions were made law, they should be part of a wide and general scheme of electoral reform. Briefly it aimed at compelling a man who lived in one place and worked in another to give up his double franchise and make his choice between the two. This would form quite a legitimate section in a genuine and comprehensive Reform Act, but, standing by itself, it seemed to the Peers to embody the spirit of class legislation. Its character was in their eyes rendered specially invidious because the University franchise, the one constitutional privilege enjoyed by persons of higher education, was treated as on the same basis as a faggot vote. But in rejecting Mr. Lewis Harcourt's measure the leaders of the majority made it plain that they would in the future be prepared to reconsider a scheme which at present was inadmissible because one-sided only, redressing anomalies favourable to one party, and ignoring those which told for the other. The Aliens Bill, also thrown out in 1906, was of Trade Unionist origin, and proposed to forbid the entry of foreign workmen during an industrial dispute. There was a good deal to be said for this Bill, but it was a great innovation on existing usage, and could only be justified if the Labour and Capital of the United Kingdom should agree together to build up a ring-wall against external competition.

If, however, the Lords killed no other Bills in 1906, they performed a series of drastic and dangerous operations upon Mr. Birrell's education measure. So severe was the surgery that the patient did not survive. But formally it owed its death to its author. Nor must we forget that it might have been saved if at the last moment, when a compromise over the Lords' amendments was all but reached, the Nonconformist leaders had not intervened. No Churchman can do other than rejoice at the loss of a Bill mischievous even in its improved shape; and that the changes introduced at the instance of Lord Lansdowne and the Archbishop of Canterbury were not altogether repugnant to Liberalism is proved by the fact that, whether for good or ill, they were revived in Mr. Runciman's ill-managed scheme for an "agreed Bill". Let us then sum up the legislative results of an exceptionally controversial session. The Bills passed by both Houses were one hundred and twenty-one; and only three of those approved by the Commons came to grief, or four if the Education Bill be included, in the Lords; while fifteen Bills from the Lords were rejected by the Commons. Moreover, in Private Bill legislation (where the Commons habitually waive their privilege) one hundred and fifty-two were passed by both Houses, and only one from the Commons was thrown out by the Peers.

The history of 1907 was less eventful. It was largely occupied, the curious may remember, with talk about Irish Devolution and with the Campbell-Bannerman resolution against the House of Lords. The two Chambers together, however, got through one hundred and sixteen Bills, and only two from the Commons were lost in the Upper House—the Land Values being rejected on second reading, and the Small Landholders Bill for Scotland being dropped on a motion to adjourn the debate. It may be remembered that Sir Henry Campbell-Bannerman graciously exonerated the Peers from blame as to the first of these measures—they had not been given time to study it. Seven Public Bills which had got through the Lords were thrown aside or otherwise maltreated by the Commons. The Private Bill record was one hundred and twenty-three passed by both Houses and one rejected by the Lords.

The work of 1908 was overshadowed by the impending doom of the Licensing Bill, of which we will say nothing more than that it does not lie with Radicals to taunt the Lords with having thrown it out on second reading. They had threatened to claim privilege against every amendment proposed in the Upper House. The other measure killed was the revived Small Landholders (Scotland) Bill. Its fate was due to the untiring exertions, inside and outside Parliament, of the same statesman who thinks that the Peers should have accepted the Land Clauses in this year's Budget. The total legislation of this year was one hundred and twenty-nine Public Bills passed by both Houses. The number might have been increased by one if the Commons had not declined to consider the Lords' amendments to the Land Values (Scotland) Bill. Nine other Bills from the Lords miscarried in the Commons, but one hundred and ten Private Bills were safely conducted through both Houses, one only being sacrificed by the Lords.

In the session just prorogued, of the measures promised in the King's Speech six received the Royal Assent, two were withdrawn, and one only was rejected by the Lords. The London Elections Bill was thrown out for substantially the same reasons as the Plural Voting Bill in 1906. The Welsh Disestablishment Bill was put aside by Ministers because they had no time to proceed with it. The same reason may be pleaded, though with less excuse, for the fate of Mr. John Burns' Dairy Bill. But the Irish Universities Bill, the Irish Land Purchase Bill, and the Housing Bill were all very important and, in detail, highly controversial measures. In all three cases the draft had been scamped in the Commons and improved in the Lords. Most of the amendments were, however, either rejected or watered away, and in the Development Bill a very innocent proposal from the Upper House was ignored because the Speaker felt bound to call attention to a supposed breach of alleged privilege. Beyond question the Lords submitted to very considerable sacrifice of their opinions because they were anxious not to provoke a constitutional crisis. To the list of sessional casualties must be added the County Courts Bill withdrawn at the end of August, and the Small Dwelling Houses (Scotland) Bill, which with certain useful reforms embodied a rather crude form of interfering paternalism. It finally died in the House of Commons because the Government would not agree to the Lords' amendments.

THE RESURRECTION OF SAN FRANCISCO.

LESS than four years ago San Francisco was an utter ruin—a waste of riven steel, shattered stone, desolate, appalling. To-day it is almost entirely rebuilt, nearly every trace of the earthquake and fire has disappeared, and the new city, according to American standards, is handsomer than the old. The celebration of this resurrection, begun in October, is not yet ended. This week there were elaborate festivities in connexion with the reopening of the Palace Hotel—that caravanserai described by so many travellers, centre and symbol of the wealth and luxury and pride of the most attractive city of the United States. Nevertheless San Francisco is now a city shamed, a byword among the cities of the world. Rescued for a short time from a gang of "grafters", who outdid even the Philadelphia "ring" in shamelessness, in hideous greed, in ruthlessness, in trafficking in human souls, San Francisco has now, deliberately, knowing well what it means, chosen to be ruled by men who come from the same class and hold the same political opinions as Eugene Schmitz and his crowd of Labour Union ruffians; men who have openly declared their sympathy with Schmitz, "Abe" Ruef, and the others whose crimes horrified the world. There will again be a Labour Union Mayor in San Francisco, a man whose campaign "slogan" was "San Francisco the Paris of America", who was a "political schoolmate" (as the Americans say) of Ruef and Schmitz. There will again be a Labour Union Board of Supervisors, Labour Union officials in every department. The city has made its choice, and already Los Angeles, Portland, and other cities of the Pacific coast are congratulating themselves on the opportunities they will have of profiting at the expense of "gang-ruled" San Francisco. For three years half a dozen courageous men have been fighting against the Ruef-Schmitz gang of "grafters". These men struggled against enormous odds. In the earlier days of the campaign they risked their lives every time they went into the streets. One of them was shot, another was kidnapped in daylight in the middle of San Francisco, was taken by force to a railway station, and was only saved by chance from being carried, in defiance of all law, to Los Angeles, where it had been arranged he was to be put into prison, or otherwise "got out of the way"—murdered. The home of one of the Reformers' witnesses was destroyed by a bomb. It has been an extraordinary fight, of interest to all, in America and elsewhere, who hate 'graft'", who care for public virtue and public service. The war had not been ended at the time of the municipal election last month; some few battles had been won, many had been lost. Now, by the decision of the voters, the three years' work is thrown away and the Reformers have been defeated by immense majorities. Mr. Francis Heney, Mr. Roosevelt's friend, who prosecuted Schmitz, Ruef, and other "grafters", was a candidate for the office of District Attorney. The votes given to him were 9000 fewer than those given to his opponent. The new Labour Union Mayor is Mr. P. H. McCarthy, who in his speeches made no secret of his sympathy with Schmitz, and promised the voters a "wide-open town"; everyone who has lived in the United States knows what that means. Only four members of the Reform Board of Supervisors were re-elected; the fourteen others are Labour Union men.

It is hardly necessary to tell again in detail the story of Mayor Schmitz, "Boss" Ruef, the corrupt police (many of them ex-convicts), the "boodling" Supervisors. English newspaper readers know what the "Municipal Crib" meant, know of the "Twinkling Star Development Company", the "Hotel Nymphia", and other (just printable) details of the record. They know how the City Hall gang bled all classes of the community, from the bootblack and pickpocket to the railway company and gas corporation, how it made million on million by the most elaborately organised systems of "big graft" and "small graft" ever evolved. The proprietor of a saloon, a gambling-house, a "French restaurant", any establishment which required "protection", was made to "give up" directly, but also in many indirect ways. He must buy his wines and spirits from a firm in which the boys were interested, paying high prices for bad goods. His cigars and cigarettes had to come from another concern owned by the grafters. Even his glassware must be purchased from the "right" people if he did not want his place raided. And "Abe" Ruef, the little, mean-looking, shabby, French-Jewish lawyer, who was the dominant figure in the gang, and of whom Schmitz was the willing slave—all have heard of him and his ingenious method of obtaining, under the guise of "counsel's fees", great sums of money from the persons who wanted favours from the city. They have read of his flight, his capture, the thousands of legal quibbles he and his lawyers employed to defeat the ends of justice; the weary trials, the ultimate conviction, the sentence passed twelve months ago of fourteen years in the gaol at San Quentin. Schmitz was convicted too, but soon got out of prison on legal technicalities, and was (and is) acclaimed in the streets by the admiring San Franciscans. It is a safe bet that Ruef will soon be out too.

Now, if Mr. McCarthy carries out his promises, the "French restaurants" will reappear—those unique establishments, the first floors respectable, quite decent citizens dining there with their wives and daughters; the upper floors—well, one cannot go into details. Also, it is to be supposed, the "pool-rooms" and faro banks will no longer have to take precautions against raids; in the dens of Chinatown will be conducted mysterious, unspeakable trades; the "Barbary Coast" will again be an Occidental Yoshiwara; "slot-machines" at every corner will tempt his last "nickel" or "quarter" from the ruined gambler, the errand boy, the out-of-work clerk. San Francisco will be "wide open"!

What is the meaning of this deliberate choice of evil? For that is what it is, though no imputation of "graft" has been made against Mr. McCarthy, who is head of the San Francisco Building Trades Council, and the other elected officials have clean records so far. It is a choice of evil because the election was fought on the question whether the citizens did or did not want reform, decency, honesty. They have declared against reform, and have put into office men of the same class as the Schmitz Supervisors. A queer lot these were, "very clusterfisted lubbers", as Tom Coryat would have called them—"Mike" Coffey, a cabman; "Jim" Kelley, a piano-polisher; "Tom" Lonergan, the driver of a baker's cart. The new Supervisors have just as little experience as that extraordinary "outfit"—again to use an Americanism. San Francisco wanted to be "wide open", and the Reform leaders were hated. In 1907 and 1908 the hatred of the "Prosecution "—as the Reform leaders were called—was indescribable. It showed itself among all classes, from the millionaires in the Pacific Union Club to the workmen travelling in the ferry-boats. Even the conservative and excellently edited "Argonaut" ended by joining the cry against Mr. Spreckels and his associates. It is not necessary to discuss the question of the good faith of the Reformers. They may have been over-bitter in certain cases, but their intentions have been honest throughout. The fact remains that San Francisco has voted for "graft", and the election is fatal to municipal reform in the United States. It is far more significant of corruption than a Tammany victory in New York. A large proportion of the voters in New York are ignorant foreigners, but a San Francisco election expresses the will of a population of normal American citizens.

" Drop down, O fleecy fog, and hide
Her sceptic sneer, and all her pride.
Hide me her faults, her sin and blame;
With thy grey mantle cloak her shame.
Then rise, O fleecy fog, and raise
The glory of her coming days."

When will they come, these days Bret Harte looked for?

THE THOMPSON APPEAL.

THE duty of an English law court is to interpret not criticise, still less to make the law. The fact that an Act of Parliament produces grotesque or evil results is a most excellent argument for its repeal. It is no argument whatever for treating it as a dead letter. Last Saturday the Court of Appeal, consisting of the Master of the Rolls, Lord Justice Fletcher Moulton, and Lord Justice Farwell, delivered judgment on the meaning of the first section of the Marriage with a Deceased Wife's Sister Act 1907. Their Lordships' judgments were lengthy, learned, laborious and verbose. They dealt with countless matters—parliamentary draughtsmanship, theology, rights of conscience, rights of laymen, rights of parishioners, "Fathers of the Church of England", excommunication, canon law, international law, and many more suchlike things. And at the end of all, their lordships declared that Parliament did not mean what it had said in the Act, but something quite different.

The Act says: " No marriage heretofore or hereafter contracted between a man and his deceased wife's sister, within the realm or without, shall be deemed to have been or shall be void or voidable, *as a civil contract*, by reason only of such affinity ". Dealing with the words " as a civil contract ", Lord Justice Fletcher Moulton declared that they were equivalent to the words " for all purposes ". To justify this construction he opined that " for all purposes known to the law marriage is a civil contract and nothing but a civil contract ". This until last week was not even the law of the Divorce Court. " Marriage ", said Lord Penzance, when the validity of a Mormon marriage came before him in the case of Hyde v. Hyde, " has been well said to be something more than a contract religious or civil—to be an institution. It creates mutual rights, as all contracts do, but beyond that it confers a status." If words mean anything, the Act of 1907 means that the Legislature refused to persons who contract a marriage under its provisions the status of married people and gave them only such rights as they may claim under a valid civil contract.

Extraordinary as was Lord Justice Moulton's explanation of the first clause of the Act, the construction put upon its first proviso by the Master of the Rolls was even stranger. The proviso which follows the sentence in the Act which we have already quoted runs thus: " Provided always that no clergyman in Holy Orders of the Church of England shall be liable to any suit, penalty or censure, whether civil or ecclesiastical, for anything done or omitted to be done by him in the performance of the duties of his office, to which suit, penalty or censure he would not have been liable if this Act had not been passed ". The explanation of the Master of the Rolls is expressed in the following portentous sentence: " To hold that the clergyman is at liberty to act in the performance of the duties of his office generally as if the Act had not been passed is, in my opinion, impossible ". In other words, the Master of the Rolls solemnly affirms that the Legislature declared that if a clergyman in the performance of the duties of his office acts generally as if the Act had not been passed he shall be liable to suits, penalties and censures, civil or ecclesiastical. It is not a coach and four that has been driven through the proviso. The Master of the Rolls takes upon himself to excise it from the Act because it does not agree with his views. The chief reason for this extraordinary conclusion was their Lordships' fears of producing grotesque consequences. It terribly shocked their sense of propriety that Parliament should positively order them to enforce even as civil contracts marriage relationships that were contrary to the law of God. Could Parliament, they asked themselves, have ever intended to place such grotesque folly on the Statute Book of a respectable and Philistine community? Impossible! And yet if their Lordships had only for a moment cast their eyes on the Table of Degrees as it stands in their judgment after the passing of the 1907 Act they would have realised in a moment that it is idle to say that Parliament did not deliberately introduce into our marriage law grotesque and blasphemous absurdities. As the law, expounded by the Court of Appeal, stands, the man who goes through a form of marriage with his deceased wife's sister is a sober, pious and conscientious son of the Church of England, whose marriage is agreeable to the law of God and the Church, and who has the amplest right to participate in every Christian privilege. A man who conscientiously believing it to be right goes through a form of marriage with the daughter of the sister of his deceased wife is not only the breaker of illogical civil statutes: he is an offender against the law of God and an open and notorious evil liver whom it is the duty of the parish priest to denounce from the pulpit and to repel from the Lord's Table. To think that any human being can regard a marriage with a deceased wife's sister as agreeable to the law of God and one with her daughter as contrary to it is insanity. On the other hand, it is quite easy to conceive that the Statute Book of an illogical nation may regard both marriages as religiously wrong, and yet may validate the one and not the other as a civil contract. But their Lordships gave a judgment which practically means that any clergyman may preach the blasphemous folly that the law of England, when it rides roughshod over logic, common sense and common decency by making a man's union with his dead wife's sister holy matrimony and with her niece incestuous concubinage, is the law of God.

The initial mistake, which has led the judges of the Court of Appeal into a morass more hideous than the one in which they believed that a strictly literal construction of the Act would have plunged them, arose from their usurpation of the functions of the Legislature in troubling their heads about the shock that British respectability would receive if they came to the opposite conclusion. It is fair to add that their difficulties were increased by the inconsistent provisions of the Act and the ridiculous legal fiction which forces the Courts to regard the Church of England as if it were literally the nation on its ecclesiastical side. The general idea that underlay the miserable statute is well known. It was an attempt to alter the law of the State without modifying the law of the Church. Unfortunately, instead of stating plainly that so far as the spiritual privileges of Churchmen, clerical and lay, were concerned the law remained unaltered, the protecting proviso was so framed as to deal only with the obligations of those clergymen who refuse to abandon their ordination vows at the bidding of Parliament, a secular assembly. Construed in its natural meaning, the proviso gives to these clergymen adequate protection. If its language be compared with the corresponding provision in the Matrimonial Causes Act of 1857, the theory of the judges that it applies only to matters connected with the solemnisation of these marriages cannot hold water. When Parliament wished to do nothing for a clergyman except to excuse him from solemnising the marriage of an adulterer or adulteress, it said so in plain language. If, as the judges imagined, Parliament had only in this instance wished to protect the priest from proclaiming the banns, solemnising, or allowing his church to be used for, such a marriage, it could and would have said so clearly. The fact that under the Deceased Wife's Sister's Marriage Act a clergyman is exempted from any penalty for any act done or omitted to be done by him in the performance of his duties would have suggested to any legal mind, save one occupied with considerations not of law but of policy, the idea that the Legislature desired to protect the clergyman not in one but in all the duties of his office. Still, the manner in which the proviso was framed was unfortunate. It threw upon the counsel for Canon Thompson the necessity of basing their case on the injustice to the individual conscience of the clergyman which would result if he was forced to administer the most sacred rite of the Church to persons openly defying the Church's law, rather than on the insult to the Church involved in the interference of a secular Legislature with the power of the Keys. An argument on this line made it possible for Lord Justice Farwell to shut his eyes to two centuries of history and to talk as if he were a churchwarden of Stuart days and as if Church and State were still identical. Churchmen, therefore, owe a deep debt of gratitude to the Bishop of Birmingham for the clear manner in which he has placed the real issues before the Church and the nation. The Church of England, as the Bishop reminds us, never has accepted the Deceased Wife's Sister's Marriage Act as a part of the ecclesiastical law. The Church stands where it stood before the Act was passed, on the old Table of Degrees. The Church cannot and will not allow a secular Legislature to interfere with its discipline in the matter of the Sacraments. The clergy are bound by their ordination vows to minister "the doctrine and Sacraments, and the discipline of Christ as the Lord commanded and as the Church and Realm hath received" (not as Lord Justice Moulton seems to have imagined "shall receive ") "according to the Commandments of God", and they cannot break their vows. The Ecclesiastical Courts under the coercion of the traditions and precedents of three centuries may be forced to sell the pass of ecclesiastical freedom to Cæsar. The secular judges may place consideration of worldly respectability and convenience above the Crown rights of Christ. An agnostic press may rail against priests who do their duty to their parishioners. It remains for the faithful sons and daughters of the Ecclesia Anglicana to meet them all with the same Christian firmness that French Catholics in recent days showed, when they flung back in the face of the French Republic its offer of gold and dishonour. Much strife there will be; probably imprisonment for some of the priests who do their duty; the whole position of the Establishment is unquestionably weakened by this judgment; but English public opinion never acquiesces for long in religious persecution, and in the end, if the Church stands firm, the freedom of the Church will be won back.

THE CITY.

STOCK markets have been quieter this week. Dealers have bought all the stock they consider necessary to meet immediate requirements, and the public is holding its hand until the result of the General Election is known. Considering the small volume of business, prices are well maintained—presumably because "bear" operators are loth to sell in view of the undoubted tendency of the investor to return to markets. Home railway stocks are being carefully watched, and the leading article in the "Times" of Tuesday on the revival of interest in this class of security has attracted a considerable amount of attention. The "Times" points out that much of the buying of foreign railway stocks in the last year or two has been due to the high return of interest, and that the prices to which they have been carried have so reduced the yield that their principal attraction has disappeared. Consequently it is now possible to make a comparison with the dividends to be obtained from home railway stocks, and their greater security as to tenure of property. Attention is called to the fact that foreign railways suffer disadvantages that are not felt by our home railways, that they are equally liable to labour troubles, and that they are worried and in some cases oppressed by the authorities of the countries where they are situated. The conclusion drawn is that home railway stocks are now at a level more in agreement with the present requirements of investors and that the future will justify any purchases that may be made at current prices. The moment is opportune to draw attention to the progress made by the District and allied "tubes". In the past five months the former has obtained £21,400 more net revenue than in the corresponding period of last year. This does not mean much to the company's ordinary stock, but it materially improves the position of the prior charges and makes the 4 per cent. perpetual debenture stock look cheap at 96. An advance in the price of ordinary stock should follow as a matter of course, despite its remote chance of a dividend. The progress made by the Bakerloo, the Great Northern and Piccadilly, and the Charing Cross and Euston lines is also sufficient to attract buyers of the prior charges of all these companies. The 4 per cent. perpetual debenture stocks can all be obtained under par, or an average of ten points below the ruling prices for similar rated stocks of the leading passenger railways. We are not saying that they are on an equality, but the disparity is not justified. The stigma the "tubes" were under at their inception is now removed, and the financial management is as good as that of any of the more important railway companies. If, as is contemplated, the whole of these "tubes" are amalgamated into one company, there should be a big saving in administrative charges.

The improvement in Indian railway traffic should not be overlooked. Last year, it may be remembered, there was great scarcity of food supplies in India, and the companies not only lost traffic, but had to compensate their staffs on account of the increase in the prices of foodstuffs. In some cases the increase in expenses as a result of this charge upon the companies was very considerable, and the result was that there was very little surplus to divide over and above the guaranteed interest. This year there is a great improvement. Crops have been good, especially cotton and seed, traffics are expanding, and working expenses are no more than normal. Consequently the dividend outlook is very much better. How striking is the change will be gathered by the experience of the Great Indian Peninsula Railway. At the meeting of this company early in the week the chairman said that there was every promise that the current half-year would terminate with a surplus of eight lakhs of rupees, instead of a deficit of between thirty-one and thirty-two lakhs.

A "tip" is going round the markets to buy Spies Petroleum shares, and, unlike most "tips", it seems to be disinterested. The company was formed in 1900 to acquire oil-producing land in Russia, the original capital being £700,000. Subsequently half of this was written off as lost by writing the shares down to 10s. In 1908 developments justified an increase in the capital to £500,000 in 1,000,000 shares of 10s., of which 930,000 are at present issued. Meantime large additions were made to the oil-bearing area of the company's property. In 1908 about 11½ million poods were produced, and the company returned a gross profit of £110,287, including the carry-forward and allowing for upkeep of machinery and plant. Of this about £57,000 was net profit, and a dividend of 12½ per cent. was distributed. The production has gone on increasing, and the board has declared an interim dividend at the rate of 15 per cent. per annum on account of the current year payable on December 21. The present price of the 10s. share is 19s.

Whilst substitutes for rubber are still being talked of, M. Albert Mans has patented an invention which is to provide a substitute for the pneumatic tyre, and a company has been formed, called the Amans Pneumo-Suspension and Solid Tyres, Limited. If the system does what it claims to do, it means a revolution in the automobile business. The tests are said to show that there is no sacrifice of comfort, and that the solid tyre has ten times the life of the ordinary pneumatic.

Two new issues this week are the Bembesi Goldfields of Rhodesia, Limited, with a capital of £100,000, and the Vienna Motor-Cab Company, Limited, with a capital of £200,000.

LAW GUARANTEE AND TRUST SOCIETY.

THE Law Guarantee and Trust Society, which has a subscribed capital of £2,500,000, and for nearly twenty-one years has been held in high esteem, has failed completely, and the greater part, if not the whole, of the £2,000,000 subscribed by the Ordinary shareholders will be lost. The causes are not far to seek. The business transacted by the society may be divided into two classes—the customary and the unusual. So far as the customary business is concerned, such as fidelity guarantee, personal accidents, burglary, and some classes of fire insurance, it has been successful, and these branches of the business have been sold to the Guardian Assurance Company, who have taken over the liabilities to holders of policies of this character, and have paid a sum of money for the goodwill and connexions attaching to them. This step affords most complete security to the insured, since the Guardian is one of the strongest and best insurance companies. The success of the customary business, and the fact that a first-class office could be found to undertake the liabilities and to pay for the goodwill in addition, is a significant fact. It shows that the business of insurance as usually conducted is sound, and that even when failure occurs the remedy of transfer or amalgamation is available to keep the policyholders secure.

It is the unusual business of insuring mortgages and debentures that has brought about the failure of the Law Guarantee. A frank statement of the position of the society has been made by the chairman, who is in no way responsible for the difficulties in which the society finds itself; he was invited a few months ago to take his present position in order, if possible, to avert impending disaster. One consequence of guaranteeing the capital and interest of mortgages and debentures has been that when the mortgages were called in, or the interest was not paid, the society had to take over or to realise the property mortgaged. The fall of value in properties now under the management of the society has been so great as to be almost incredible: property originally valued at £4,900,000 is estimated to produce only £1,700,000, showing a depreciation in value to the extent of nearly two-thirds of the original valuation. There are now under the management of the society ninety blocks of flats, fifty-six public-houses, seventeen hotels, six theatres, two breweries, and other properties. To lend sums running into millions on licensed and theatrical property has naturally proved an exceedingly unwise course, and it is difficult to imagine how any board of directors could have embarked on so hazardous an undertaking to so large an extent. It is a class of business that other insurance companies decline to touch, and again the significant fact is that the failure is due to business that is unusual among insurance companies.

It is necessary to emphasise the success of the customary and the failure of the unusual, since, unless this is recognised, it might be supposed that other insurance companies are unsound, which is the reverse of true. Apart from other distinctions, it has to be noted that claims under life, fire or accident policies occur, for the most part, against the wishes of the policyholders, and arise out of circumstances that are mostly beyond human control. With the insurance of mortgages and debentures it is different. Rights of foreclosure exist which are not likely to be exercised so long as people believe themselves to be fully secure. While confidence was felt in the Law Guarantee mortgages were allowed to remain, but when the security of the society was questioned policyholders began to call in their mortgages, thus increasing the difficulties of the society, causing more questions as to its financial stability and accentuating the demands for paying off the mortgages. It is perhaps within the bounds of possibility that the society might have surmounted its difficulties but for action of this kind on the part of the policyholders: however this may be, the fact remains that the unusual business conducted by the Law Guarantee readily lent itself to the piling-up of inconvenient claims in this way, while the usual classes of business undertaken by insurance companies cannot, in the very nature of things, bring about such results. This consideration is one of the reasons for the stability and soundness of the general run of insurance companies. At one time life offices were more ready to lend money on mortgages when guaranteed by the Law Guarantee than when no such policies were available. For some time past life offices have declined to accept these policies as affording any appreciable addition to the security.

A circular issued by a large number of influential shareholders insists upon the necessity of an inquiry into the past management of the society. This inquiry is certainly necessary in the interests of everybody concerned. At the meeting of shareholders many questions were asked about the emoluments of Mr. T. R. Ronald, the manager, and his directorships in other companies, of which the chairman gave a list numbering twenty. Much was also said at the meeting about the extensive employment by the society of Mr. Ronald's son as valuer. If the shareholders attribute a loss that may run into £200,000 largely to these two well-paid officials it is quite to the interests of these gentlemen that the whole of the facts should be known. Very little inclination to blame the directors was shown by the shareholders. At the bi-weekly board meetings the transactions to be considered were so numerous that the chairman said they could not be attended to properly. It is permissible to surmise that the directors were so occupied with details that they failed to recognise the general and unsatisfactory drift of the business as a whole.

There is an uncalled liability of £5 a share on 200,000 ordinary shares: it is to be feared that the whole of this amount will have to be called up, but it should be possible to allow the shareholders considerable time for paying the calls. It is probable that the policyholders are secure, and there may prove to be something for ultimate distribution among the holders of the 500,000 fully-paid preference shares of £1 each. This, however, is largely dependent upon the nature of the settlement with the Law Accident Insurance Society, with whom there is a dispute over certain reinsurance contracts. We gather that the Law Accident not only repudiates liability under these contracts, but that it makes a claim against the Law Guarantee for the return of some money already paid. The sums in question are large, and it will make much difference to the shareholders of the Law Guarantee whether the Law Accident have to pay or be paid.

However the matter is carried out, the liquidation of the Law Guarantee will be a matter of extraordinary complexity, and will take a long time to complete. The nature of the business is such that, especially with voluntary liquidation, it will probably be possible to allow the ordinary shareholders a considerable time—possibly some years—for paying up their liabilities in full, to this extent easing, if not minimising, the heavy loss that is bound to fall upon them.

'09.

AMONG the many minor idiocies of man, his undue respect for dates is not the least. He knows of course that the year is a purely arbitrary period, invented for the benefit of—the tax-gatherer, for instance, and that any other period, if selected by the wisdom of Antiquity, would serve the turn, and would have become by now quite as familiar to him and seem as if it were a real Heaven-appointed division of time. But many things—the importance placed on dates by his schoolmasters, as if the "when" of an action mattered half as much as the "how" and the "why", the convenience to the procrastinator of being able to fix a date for improvement, like that old Duke of Norfolk who used to say, "Next Monday, wind and weather permitting, I purpose to be drunk", and imitation—have combined to make the end of the year seem an event. No one really believes it. It would, at least, be an idiocy not "minor" at all if a man who had found the web of time homespun in 1909 should expect by unrolling it into 1910 to find it velvet.

The coming year is looked forward to with a little apprehension. Some people, a little while ago, were kind enough to hint at the possible advent of "chaos". Chaos sounded rather interesting. It is a grand mouthful of a word, with a ring of doom about it, and it was, some thought finally, abolished so many æons ago, that one rather hoped it would seem new. But—it was difficult to find how its prophets meant to bring it about: they reminded us of Carlyle's hen, who would not lay an egg for her dyspeptic master, sure that he would die, not foreseeing that he would wring her neck and purchase eggs at fourteen a shilling. Chaos couldn't get itself believed in. Now, however, it appears that we are not to have "chaos". But one change, the man who lives a fortnight longer will see, and rejoice in. If it were a change for the worse, we would leave to others the unpleasant task of pointing out its inevitability, but, as far as it goes, it is all to the good. True, it goes but a little way, but let us be thankful for small mercies.

It is this. In future, no man now alive will ever again, after 31 December next, be made angry by seeing his letters dated with that utterly asinine abbreviation of '09. Why—oh why!—the o? What earthly purpose did it serve? Yet, ten years ago, Post Office, business men, even some of the few private letter-writers who survive in an unepistolary age, adopted it. 00, 01, 02, etc., have ploughed deep furrows in our sense of the fitting. The powers of cyphering be praised, 09 is the last of the baleful brood. On 1 January next "as ever is", Post Office, business man, correspondent, must perforce return to a sensible notation and date 1/1/10. The o will leave us for ever.

True, it will come back—if men and numerals last so long, to agonise A.D. 2000. Poor posterity! Let us hope it will all be on the telephone and write and receive letters no more.

It would be interesting, had one access to a manuscript correspondence of the first ten years of the last century, to see whether our great-grandfathers used this strange unnecessary nought. Printed collections of letters do not show it. Byron's, e.g., are dated 1805, etc. In one, however, to his sister, dated "Jan. 7th 1805" a note is added to the date "in another hand —6", which may show that our ancestors were not such fools as to write 06.

"There was more leisure", it may be said, "in those days. Byron could spare the time to write 1805 in full—I'm too busy." It would be very interesting to know what is done with the time gained by these intangible savings. A business man writes, say, a hundred letters a day, saves the time it takes him to write 19 a hundred times over. How long is that? Long enough to light a cigarette? And is that how he spends the time saved, or what does he do with it? But why not save the time taken over the noughts and write 1, 2, 3 like a Christian? In two days he'd save time enough to light another cigarette.

It is a small matter—will remind many of the puff of smoke, and "These are my sorrows, Mr. Wesley". But, however we pique ourselves on stoicism, "many small articles make up a sum", and, with its daily, almost hourly recurrence, that idiot o has been, and will be for another three weeks, a bitter bore to all right-thinking mortals. To point out to the recipients a boon, even if it be not of one's own conferring, is a charity—sometimes. Feeling seasonably charitable, we say to all humanity, We believe next year won't be as bad as you fear (nothing ever is); we hope it will be as good as you can wish, and we know, and heartily congratulate ourselves and you on the fact, that in it you will have seen the last of "09".

"THE BLUE BIRD."

By Max Beerbohm.

A FEW weeks ago, writing here about silly Signor Marinetti, I developed a theory that the thinkers who acquire in their own day a European reputation are never, in the strict sense of the word, sages. A "carrying" voice implies shouting. Shouting implies cock-sureness—contentment with one definite point of view, one set of convictions. Wisdom, of which the essence is spiritual surrender and elasticity—wisdom, that immensely complicated thing, cannot be shouted. It can only be doled out in murmurs. Murmurs don't "carry". Therefore—but, just as I was completing my syllogism, I had the horrid experience which always does overtake the maker of any hard-and-fast generalisation: I remembered an exception which made nonsense of my rule. It was Maeterlinck that I remembered. And, as I was rather pleased with my generalisation, and, moreover, didn't want to have the trouble of writing my article all over again, I disingenuously suppressed that honoured name. It, however, must have occurred to many of my readers. Twenty years ago, Maeterlinck began whispering; and the whisper penetrated Europe, perfectly audible amidst the guffaws which it at first evoked. He has never, in the meantime, raised his voice; and always he has compelled the attention of us all—I mean, all of us who are not fools.

For proper appreciation of Maeterlinck, you must have, besides a sense of beauty, a taste for wisdom. Maeterlinck is not less a sage than a poet. Of all living thinkers whose names are known to me, he has the firmest and widest grasp of the truth. He more clearly than any other thinker is conscious of the absurdity of attempting to fashion out of the vast and impenetrable mysteries of life any adequate little explanation—any philosophy. He sees further than any other into the darkness, has a keener insight into his own ignorance, a deeper modesty, a higher wisdom. In his youth, the mystery of life obsessed him. He beheld our planet reeling in infinity, having on its surface certain infinitesimal creatures all astray at the mercy of unknown laws. And he shuddered. And he wrote certain plays which, as mere expressions of the pathos of man's lot, and the awfulness of the mystery of life, will not be surpassed. Little by little, the shudders in him abated. The more a man thinks about infinity, the better does he realise that what he can grasp of infinity is but a speck, signifying nothing; and, accordingly, the more important will become to him the visible and tangible creatures and things around him. Maeterlinck began to look around him, to "take notice" with babyish pleasure, with the fresh vision of a true seer. The world seemed to him a very-well-worth-while place. Who was he to say that we had no free-will? How could he possibly know that, or anything else? If we are but the puppets of destiny, and if destiny is, on the whole, rather unkind, still there seems to be quite enough of joy and beauty for us to go on with.

Such is the point to which Maeterlinck, in the course of years, has won; and such is the meaning he has put into "The Blue Bird", this masterpiece of his later years. An Optimist? No; he is too conscious of the sadness of things to be that. A Meliorist? He has too much sense of history, and too much sense of proportion, to imagine that the world, if seven specially selected maids with seven specially designed mops "swept it for half-a-year" or for a thousand years, would be appreciably tidier. So far as any one crude label can be affixed to him, he is just a Bonist. . . . Off go the two children, Tyltyl and Mytyl, in their dreams, to quest the blue bird, and they do find blue birds, and do catch them. True, these birds die when they are caught, or else lose their colour, or else flutter mockingly away. And, when the children awake in their beds next morning, the bird-cage contains only their own ordinary dove. But see! he *has* turned a *sort* of blue! And bright blue he becomes when the children send him as a present to the little girl who is ill. And she, at sight of him, is made well. True, again, he flies right away out of her hands, and is lost. "Never mind," Tyltil tells her. "Don't cry . . . I will catch him again." And again he will lose him. No matter. The quest, even if it were a vain one, were good enough. Sometimes in the wanderings of Mytyl and Tyltyl, as when the hour comes for them to set forth through the forest to the Palace of Night, there is the old Maeterlinckian note of terror. "Give me your hand, little brother", says Mytyl, "I feel so frightened and cold", and as the curtain falls, we experience that strange cold thrill of awe and pity which the dramatist so often, so cunningly, prepared for us in his earlier plays. But, for the most part, the thrills in "The Blue Bird" are of a quiet joy. Mytyl and Tyltyl are crouching in the grave-yard, to wait for the arising of the dead people at midnight. They talk together in whispers. The hour is at hand. The mounds quake, the graves open, a pale mist rises. Little by little, this mist gathers into masses of white, and the place is but a garden of tall white lilies. "Where are the dead?" asks Mytyl. And Tyltyl answers "There are no dead!" and the curtain falls. It always was in his contrivance of the ends of acts that Maeterlinck revealed the essentially dramatic quality of his genius. What of mystery and beauty these plays must necessarily lose by visual performance is always counteracted by what they gain—the special power that a true dramatist's work can never have for us except in the theatre.

Even if you happen to have an exceptionally keen theatrical imagination (which I haven't), you cannot, in reading a play, be thrilled by it so much as you may be in an actual theatre; for this reason: that there is not an audience of fellow-creatures around you, thrilled in company with you and unconsciously transmitting through you something of their own electricity. Only a theatrical performance of which you were the sole spectator, or else only a very bad performance indeed, could fail to be more impressive than a mere silent reading. (That is, if the play has, like "The Blue Bird", true dramatic quality.) The corporeal presentment of symbols and fancies is, as I have just suggested, a dangerous job. Such presentment, at best, cannot vie with the mind's images. And the perfect venue for a production of "The Blue Bird" would be some impossible combination of an actual theatre and one's own cranium.

In that actual theatre, the Haymarket, Mr. Herbert Trench has contrived a production which is, I imagine, as good as can be. The scenery is duly various according to the many moods of the play. Mr. Cayley Robinson and Mr. Sime (welcome!) and Mr. Harker have produced scenery that is always imaginative and beautiful—sometimes mystical, sometimes noble, sometimes frightening, sometimes funny, in just accord to the doings for which it is a background. And all the dresses have been designed in a not less eclectic and proper spirit. But the most remarkable thing in the production is certainly Miss Olive Walter as Tyltyl. Some time ago, when first I read the play, it seemed to me that Tyltyl would be an insuperable obstacle to anyone who might wish to put the play on the stage. For Tyltyl is hardly for a moment out of sight and hearing. On his shoulders rests the play's main burden. And it is essential that Tyltyl should be, or seem to be, a little boy, and not a day more than eight years of age. To seem on the stage like a little boy of eight is beyond the powers of any actual little boy of eight: he appears as an awful little automaton of eighty. And five minutes of him appear as an eternity. Imagine a whole evening of him! On the other hand, imagine somebody old enough to act, and to act throughout an evening, attempting to produce the illusion that he—or she—is only eight years old! That alternative "she" seemed to me, as I mused on the chances of "The Blue Bird," especially sure to be disastrous. And yet, here is Miss Olive Walter, Tyltyl to the life, and perfect from first to last. She may be no longer in her 'teens for aught I know; but, as she appears on the stage, she is not, in voice or gait or manner, a day more than eight; and is a boy, at that; as absolutely a boy as Mytyl is a girl. Who would have believed it?

CHILDREN'S CHRISTMAS AMUSEMENTS.

By Edward H. Cooper.

A CURIOUS feature of the theatrical world which one cannot notice without approval is the fashion in which so many actor-managers of repute surrender their theatres to the holiday world of children at Christmas. Pieces which are being played to paying houses are withdrawn or transferred elsewhere simply in order that the young folk may have a good time, although, in point of fact, the lessee or manager of the theatre is as often as not a considerable loser by the transaction. Plays for children were once upon a time a very paying business—long ago, in days before every man and woman with a typewriter and three or four fairly new nursery anecdotes thought they could write one and were willing to pay large sums for its production. Nowadays a considerable sum of money is lost every Christmas over these attempts to amuse the young folk. A play intended for their entertainment can be produced for about six hundred pounds, and can be run at a loss of about a hundred and eighty pounds a week. On the other hand you can spend twenty thousand pounds on its production. In one or two well-known cases the manager and author have produced their work simply and solely for the amusement of a circle of small friends, and repeated it next year for the benefit of the companions who have been told about it. The theatre world, as I say, seems to make up its mind to waste half its yearly earnings on amusing the children during their Christmas holidays.

And who can gainsay the fact that these plays and pantomimes are the ideal form of Christmas party? If you take it as a mere matter of numbers they must be the best; for, with a few rare exceptions, the small folk on the stage are enjoying themselves quite as much as their contemporaries in front. The tremendous gravity with which a Drury Lane fairy goes through its part might occasionally deceive a spectator into believing that the creature was doing work instead of enjoying itself thoroughly; but nobody who has taken a party of children to "Peter Pan" and watched their rapt, unsmiling absorption in the jokes of Smee and Starkey would make such a mistake again. His Majesty's, Drury Lane, and the Lyceum are, or shortly will be, between them employing considerably over two hundred children at their two daily performances; while the Haymarket and the Garrick have more than a hundred children engaged in the exquisite plays which they have already launched; so plenty of Christmas amusement would be guaranteed even if the auditorium of every theatre were empty. And the pantomimes of Mr. Robert Arthur—who would certainly be appointed Secretary of State for Christmas if any Government had the sense to create such an office—will shortly fill England with more delighted birds, and fairies, and cats, and demons, and flowers of whose numbers I have no idea.

Perhaps it is not till you have spent some Christmas holidays in places like Paris or Vienna that you realise the immense wealth of amusement provided for English children. I have tried to give children's Christmas parties in Paris at the theatres, and it is simply one of those things "qu'on ne fait pas"—at any rate not for a second time. The only possible proceeding is one which I have tried myself once with good effect—to see the whole piece or programme through one night, and then ask the manager, partly as an act of kindness to your guests and partly because the purchase of a considerable number of seats depends on his answer, to leave out certain portions of the aforesaid programme. When this promise is given it will be kept; but imagine the feelings of an ordinary London host who had not one single place of entertainment which he could suggest without premeditation and elaborate preparation to a party of Christmas friends! As a matter of fact, during the first three weeks of January in London I believe one might take a collection of ten- or twelve-year-old children to any theatre or music-hall in the city with absolute indifference. That is a statement which critics of English morals might feel inclined to offer as a retort to the new Association of Libraries or to the friends of the Dramatic Censorship.

Perhaps, however, even more remarkable than the endless annual round of decent novelty in this country is the affection displayed by generation after generation of young folk for the same story told almost in the same words, dressed in the same dress, and often acted by the same people. One wonders whether there is any revolution of youthful feeling which would cause the nursery world to "strike" for long against "Aladdin" or "Cinderella", or precisely how violent a degree of revolution would follow the removal of "Peter Pan" from Christmastide. In truth there are scores of grown-up people who simply would not tolerate any other entertainment at the Duke of York's theatre just now; who go there now and again even by themselves, knowing every word of the play, seeing ghosts in the boxes and stalls of the theatre, shrinking before the outbreaks of childish applause and laughter because it was at this point in the play that some ghost-figure in this box or that group of dress-circle seats used to lean forward breathless and thrilling, and demand afterwards on what terms she might be taken to "Peter Pan" every night for a fortnight. Failing to negotiate this bargain, the person in question would employ her time in writing out the whole play from end to end from memory, or go occasionally to some fancy-dress dance, or assortment of conjurers and ventriloquists, or skating party, and wonder why on earth her relatives knew no better than to bring her to such places when she might be sitting comfortably at "Peter Pan".

I dwell on theatre parties in this fashion because at the present day they are the simplest form of entertainment in existence. For some years past Christmas hostesses have been vieing with one another in the matter of elaborating child parties, very much as they do with June dances and receptions; till the children's fancy-dress ball at the Mansion House, which was once the wonder—and amongst schoolroom guardians by no means an admired wonder—of the year, is now merely one of a score of similar entertainments, from whose hosts you "head off" your children as from a perambulating tiger. If they must go, they must; but towards the end of the evening, in the room where the younger babes are playing games, there is mostly enacted a scene of which the following dialogue (ensuing on an attempt to get up a game of "Zoological Gardens") is a specimen:

"What animal will you be, Kitty?"

"The bear, please."

"And you, Geoffrey?"

"I don't know."

"Oh, think! Will you be a snake and crawl about?"

"No, thank you."

"Will you be a lion and roar?"

"N-n-no, thank you."

"Well, what do you want to be?"

"I want to be sick."

It is quite a delusion, I am assured by a very eminent nursery specialist in the medical world, to suppose that three or four weeks of this kind of thing do a child any serious, permanent harm. Three days after his return to school the average boy who has spent his holidays in this fashion is as well as if he had passed them taking constitutionals on Worthing Parade. But where on earth does the fun of it come in for anybody? The young gentleman himself does not enjoy being sick; his mother is equally little pleased during the two following days; and the average hostess, unless she is an idiot, cannot imagine that she has made herself very popular either among her senior or junior guests. There is no person on earth more easily amused than a child. Why spend time and money and pains on making it ill instead?

MINIATURES.

By Lord Dunsany.

THE ASSIGNATION.

Fame singing in the highways, and trifling as she sang, with sordid adventurers, passed the poet by.

And still the poet made for her little chaplets of song to deck her forehead in the courts of Time: and still she wore instead the worthless garlands, that boisterous citizens flung to her in the ways, made out of perishable things.

And after a while whenever these garlands died the poet came to her with his chaplets of song, and still she laughed at him and wore the worthless wreaths, though they always died at evening.

And one day in his bitterness the poet rebuked her and said to her: "Lovely Fame, even in the highways and the byways you have not forborne to laugh and shout and jest with trivial men; and I have toiled for you and dreamed of you, and you mock me and pass me by".

And Fame turned her back on him and walked away; but in departing she looked over her shoulder and smiled at him as she had not smiled before, and, almost speaking in a whisper, said:

"I will meet you in the graveyard at the back of the workhouse, in a hundred years".

THE RAFT-BUILDERS.

All we who write put me in mind of sailors hastily making rafts upon doomed ships.

When we break up under the heavy years and go down into eternity with all that is ours, our thoughts, like small lost rafts, float on awhile upon Oblivion's sea. They will not carry much over those tides—our names and a phrase or two and little else.

They that write as a trade to please the whim of the day, they are like sailors that work at the rafts only to warm their hands and to distract their thoughts from their certain doom; their rafts go all to pieces before the ship breaks up.

See now Oblivion shimmering all around us, its very tranquillity deadlier than tempest. How little all our keels have troubled it! Time in its deeps swims like a monstrous whale; and, like a whale, feeds on the littlest things—small tunes and little unskilled songs of the olden, golden evenings—and anon turneth whale-like to overthrow whole ships.

See now the wreckage of Babylon floating idly, and something there that once was Nineveh; already their kings and queens are in the deeps among the weedy masses of old centuries that hide the sodden hulk of sunken Tyre and make a darkness round Persepolis.

For the rest I dimly see the forms of foundered ships on a sea-floor strewn with crowns.

Our ships were all unseaworthy from the first.

There goes the raft that Homer made for Helen.

TIME AND THE TRADESMAN.

Once as Time prowled the world, his hair grey not with weakness but with dust of the ruin of cities, he came to a furniture shop and entered the Antique department. And he saw a man there darkening the wood of a chair with dye and beating it with chains and making imitation worm-holes in it.

And when Time saw another doing his work he stood beside him awhile and looked on critically.

And at last he said "That is not how I work". And he made the man's hair white and bent his back and put some furrows in his little cunning face; then turned and strode away, for a mighty city, that was weary and sick and too long had troubled the fields, was sore in need of him.

THE PRAYER OF THE FLOWERS.

It was the voice of the flowers on the West wind, the lovable, the old, the lazy West wind, blowing ceaselessly, blowing sleepily, going Greece-wards.

"The woods have gone away, they have fallen and left us; men love us no longer, we are lonely by moonlight. Great engines rush over the beautiful fields, their ways lie hard and terrible up and down the land.

"The cancerous cities spread over the grass, they clatter in their lairs continually, they glitter about us blemishing the night.

"The woods are gone, O Pan, the woods, the woods. And thou art far, O Pan, and far away."

I was standing by night between two railway embankments on the edge of a Midland city. On one of them I saw the trains go by, once in every two minutes, and on the other they went by twice in every five.

Quite close were the glaring factories, and the sky above them wore the fearful look that it wears in dreams of fever.

The flowers were right in the stride of that advancing city, and thence I heard them sending up their cry. And then I heard, beating musically up wind, the voice of Pan, reproving them from Arcady: "Be patient a little; these things are not for long".

WIND AND FOG.

"Way for us", said the North Wind as he came down the sea on an errand of old Winter.

And he saw before him the grey silent fog that lay along the tides.

"Way for us", said the North Wind, "O, ineffectual fog, for I am Winter's leader in his age-old war with the ships. I overwhelm them suddenly in my strength, or drive upon them the huge seafaring bergs. I cross an ocean while you move a mile. There is mourning in inland places when I have met the ships. I drive them upon the rocks and feed the sea. Wherever I appear they bow to our lord the Winter."

And to his arrogant boasting nothing said the fog. Only he rose up slowly and trailed away from the sea and, crawling up long valleys, took refuge among the hills; and night came down and everything was still, and the fog began to mumble in the stillness. And I heard him telling infamously to himself the tale of his horrible spoils.

"A hundred and fifteen galleons of old Spain, a certain argosy that went from Tyre, eight fisher-fleets and ninety ships of the line, twelve warships under sail, with their carronades, three hundred and eighty-seven river-craft, forty-two merchantmen that carried spice, four quinquiremes, ten triremes, thirty yachts, twenty-one battleships of the modern time, nine thousand admirals . . ." he mumbled and chuckled on, till I suddenly rose and fled from his fearful contamination.

THE HEN.

All along the farmyard gables the swallows sat a-row, twittering uneasily to one another, telling of many things but thinking only of Summer and the South, for Autumn was afoot and the North wind waiting.

And suddenly one day they were all quite gone. And everyone spoke of the swallows and the South.

"I think I shall go South myself next year", said a hen.

And the year wore on and the swallows came again, and the year wore on and they sat again on the gables, and all the poultry discussed the departure of the hen.

And very early one morning, the wind being from the North, the swallows all soared suddenly and felt the wind in their wings; and a strength came upon them and a strange old knowledge and a more than human faith, and flying high they left the smoke of our cities and small remembered eaves, and saw at last the huge and homeless sea, and steering by grey sea-currents went southward with the wind. And going South they went by glittering fog-banks and saw old islands lifting their heads above them; they saw the slow quests of the wandering ships, and divers seeking pearls, and lands at war, till there came in view the mountains that they sought and the sight of the peaks they knew; and they descended into an austral valley, and saw Summer sometimes sleeping and sometimes singing song.

"I think the wind is about right", said the hen, and she spread her wings and ran out of the poultry-yard. And she ran fluttering out on to the road and some way down it until she came to a garden.

At evening she came back breathless.

And in the poultry-yard she told the poultry how she had gone South as far as the high road, and saw the great world's traffic going by, and came to lands where the potato grew, and saw the stubble upon which men live, and at the end of the road had found a garden and there were roses in it—beautiful roses!—and the gardener himself was there with his braces on.

"How extremely interesting", the poultry said, "and what a really beautiful description!"

And the Winter wore away; and the bitter months went by and the Spring of the year appeared and the swallows came again.

"We have been to the South", they said, "and the valleys beyond the sea."

But the poultry would not agree that there was a sea in the South: "You should hear our hen", they said.

CORRESPONDENCE.

A NEW SPHERE FOR HEADMASTERS.

To the Editor of the SATURDAY REVIEW.

21 Harcourt Road, Sheffield,
4 December 1909.

SIR,—Recent Government statistics show that the increase in evening students under twenty-one years of age is less than one per cent., while the increase of those over twenty-one is 32.5. These figures suggest that evening schools are appealing to the adult rather than to the adolescent, and that therefore we should be careful lest we destroy the attractiveness of the school for the elder students when we undertake to compel the attendance of boys and girls in their teens.

This was, however, the subject of a former letter. May I now point out that if evening schools become compulsory there will be a good deal of additional teaching to be done, and that eventually the work in the evening schools will fall to the day-school teacher? Now the will-strain of day-school work is sufficiently exhausting in itself, and day-school teachers ought not to be tempted by the offer of relatively high pay to undertake additional work which fills time needed for recreation and self-development if the teacher is to remain efficient. But headmasters of schools are differently placed. Both in elementary and secondary schools they are unfortunately ceasing to be magistri in any real sense, for they no longer practise their chosen art, teaching. They are rapidly becoming administrators attending to the needs of the real magistri, the class masters, and filling in their spare time with clerical work. The loss resulting from this development is a double one. In the first place, the school loses the teaching power of the most experienced teacher on the staff, and, secondly, a headmaster, once having lost touch with the actual conditions of teaching, is apt to lose even the power of effective examination, if not that of effective organisation itself, the chief reason for his existence. Would it not therefore be a good thing if these well-equipped teachers were at the same time to renew their experience of actual teaching and to give the community the benefit of their skill and knowledge by taking as much as they could of the actual teaching—not organising—in the evening schools at relatively modest salaries? Veterans are required for teaching adults; and adolescence presents problems worthy the skill of the best teachers. Since, moreover, the present work of a headmaster is less exhausting than that of an assistant, and since, as a mature man, he needs less "off time" than the still-developing assistants—though by no means all assistants are juniors—the additional evening work is not so likely to injure him.

Even in the day schools he might with advantage teach more than he does. In elementary schools, faced with the problem of reorganisation under Circular 709, and in secondary schools, split into departments and sections under the influence of the specialists, the headmaster will see that there are many advantages in his again becoming a teacher; not indeed of a particular class or form—that is to chain oneself down—but of as many divisions as he can conveniently and regularly take in his own subject. By so doing not only will he be able to hold the school together, he will also gain a working knowledge of the actual value of the education given in his school, and, lastly and chiefly, he will gain a first-hand acquaintance with many more of his boys; matters surely more worth his time than form-filling and the chess game of time-table planning. If English headmasters are to retain the prestige they still enjoy, but which is really a relic of the days when schools were one-man concerns, and if they wish to avoid the ambiguity attaching to their position in Germany, they must take to teaching again.

I remain yours faithfully,

Frank J. Adkins.

THE COMBINE AGAINST THE TWO-VOLUME NOVEL.

To the Editor of the Saturday Review.

31 Farm Street W. 5 December 1909.

Sir,—May I, from the library subscriber's point of view, offer a word of protest against the extraordinary action of the circulating libraries in boycotting Mr. De Morgan's latest novel? The book is longer, I think, than your "Notes" of last week suggest, but the question here is not one of "quantities" or prices. The ordinary reader subscribes to a circulating library precisely in order that he may have access to certain more highly priced volumes which he could not afford to buy or which he would not care to buy without having first satisfied himself that they are worth keeping. One pays one's subscription—in advance—upon a tacit understanding that any book which may reasonably be asked for will sooner or later be procurable. Nobody, of course, expects to obtain expensive éditions de luxe or books of no general interest. But it cannot be pretended that Mr. De Morgan is not in demand or that ten shillings is in itself a prohibitive cost. If the novelist had written two volumes of sociological essays or a work on philosophy or history or geography, published at a guinea, the libraries would have taken it as a matter of course. Why should a brilliant thinker be penalised because, instead of embodying his views of life in a royal octavo of stodgy philosophy, he has turned out three hundred thousand words of entertaining fiction?

I understand the plea to be that it would ultimately be to the disadvantage of library subscribers if publishers reverted to the old form of fiction in two or three volumes. But even if this were true, the libraries have plenty of means of bringing pressure to bear on the publisher who offends. As it is, the whole inconvenience is being shifted on to their subscribers. To force these last—who believed that their library subscription insured them against any such necessity—to purchase a pig in a poke if they wish to read a much-talked-of novel seems to me a high-handed proceeding which would not be endorsed by any plébiscite of the persons it is supposed to benefit.

Your obedient servant,

Herbert Thurston S.J.

THE MAN SHAKESPEARE.

To the Editor of The Saturday Review.

Badminton Club, 100 Piccadilly W.
8 December 1909.

Sir,—It is rash for a mere student of Shakespeare to differ from so accomplished a doctor as Mr. Frank Harris; but I cannot believe that Henry V. is represented as a person of "extraordinary sensuality" simply because Poins says that he has been "lewd". "Licentious" is only a secondary meaning of that word; its primary meaning is "ignorant", and in the Bible it stands for "riotous"—"Certain lewd fellows of the baser sort." I have no doubt that it is in this sense that Poins uses it. The Prince asks him why he would think him a hypocrite if he professed sorrow for his father's sickness. It would be no answer to say "Because you are a person of extraordinary sensuality"—such men being commonly quite emotional persons. I think that, on the contrary, Shakespeare meant to represent the Prince as rather exceptionally chaste. Doll Tearsheet has no attractions for him; he calls her—ironically, of course—"this civil virtuous gentlewoman", and she treats him with the greatest respect. Let Mr. Harris read again—if he does not know the passage by heart—Henry's wooing of the French Princess, and I think he will admit that no man could make love with less appearance of sensuality; yet the lady is young and, presumably, beautiful, and her manners are of the prettiest. I think, too, that Mr. Harris is rather hard on Ophelia. When the poor dear is quite mad she sings a rather (but not shockingly) naughty song that she might have learned from her nurse and only half understood; but when does she talk "lewdly"? She snubs Hamlet icily when he tries to take liberties with her. Perhaps it is with prevision of Mr. Harris that Hamlet says "Be thou chaste as ice, pure as snow, thou shalt not escape calumny". When, as in the case of Jaques, Shakespeare really accused a person of licentiousness, he left no doubt whatever as to his meaning.

Yours faithfully,

H. Finlay Knight.

THE LAW GUARANTEE TRUST SOCIETY.

To the Editor of the Saturday Review.

28 Chepstow Villas, Bayswater, W.
16 December 1909.

Sir,—At the meeting of the Law Guarantee and Trust Society last Monday my remarks were apparently inaudible at the reporters' table, and were therefore not reported. As far as I could judge at the time, there were some people amongst those who could hear me who agreed with me. I said that I ventured to challenge the late chairman's view that the cause of the society's position to-day was the great depreciation in property. There are many people who think that a want of prudence and discretion in the management and direction of this unfortunate business is at least as much as any depreciation the cause of the present position. I quoted a case where debentures had been guaranteed and the company subsequently went into liquidation. The Official Receiver's report stated that out of the sum provided by the society's guarantee only two hundred pounds were available for working capital, and that this proved entirely insufficient. Surely this is a most damning commentary on the society's methods. To many shareholders the guaranteeing mortgages on public-houses when at boom prices and also on such a large number of flats is inexplicable, and indicates a policy in which the desire to build up a large premium income was apparently allowed to outweigh every other consideration. After the chairman's speech at the general meeting in March last one well-known company was asked what mortgages it had guaranteed on public-houses and flats, and the answer was "Two public-houses and no flats". This appears to me to be due to judgment, not to accident.

Mr. Harris in his admirable report states on page 36 "It is quite evident that the foundations of the society's business were never critically regarded". There are those who think that amongst the very eminent directors not one critical mind has been applied to the business as a whole since its inception. Speaking of the debenture-guarantee business at the general meeting last March Mr. Turner said "we regard it as a healthy and very important branch of our business". At that very time the society was acting as receiver for debenture-holders in many cases where outside opinion predicted a heavy loss. This opinion is amply confirmed by Mr. Harris' report.

At Monday's meeting I was asked to second the appointment of the committee of inspection, but declined, as I considered the proposed committee too legal in character, and that a commercial mind was wanted. I am glad to see that two creditors are to be added to that committee, and hope they will be commercial men. In conclusion, I would remind the directors that it was on the faith of their reputations they were entrusted with this enormous credit, and I venture to think that the onus is on them to show that the business has been conducted with prudence. Mr. Turner last Monday offered us the sympathy of himself and his fellow-directors. Speaking for myself, I have neither asked for it nor want it, but I submit with all respect that we are entitled to ask for evidence that ordinary common-sense has been applied to the transaction of the society's business in the past.

I am, Sir, your obedient servant,
MacIver Buchanan.

THE BANKING QUESTION.

To the Editor of the Saturday Review.

9 December 1909.

Sir,—Let me take Mr. Baines's points seriatim :

(1) That an increased issue of credit must raise prices. We must agree to this since an issue of credit means an issue of purchasing power. The essential and peculiar feature of a *credit* issue of purchasing power, however, is the condition of subsequent repayment, when precisely that amount of exchange medium is withdrawn from the market as was previously introduced. Prices would, therefore, again tend to the normal. Moreover, in these days of telegraphic communication, even the rumour of increased demand stimulates supply and further tends to keep prices level.

(2) That the prosperity resulting from a fall of interest here will result in a dangerous drain of gold abroad. This is the theory which has continually obstructed efforts to cheapen credit. The new school of finance admits that gold will probably flow abroad, but denies that such a drain of gold must be dangerous, or, indeed, that our internal exchange system need be based upon gold at all. Credit should be merely a system of mutual guarantee. Were we to permit the use of *circulating* substitutes for gold, i.e., banknotes, gold would flow abroad simply because it would no longer be needed here.

(3) That the issue of credit must be limited not by future, but by actual production, past and present, and that the price of such credit must necessarily fluctuate according as capital is plentiful or otherwise. Macleod's definition of credit as that which brings into commerce the present value of a future profit is more accurate, since the economic results when a borrower is enabled by the use of credit to produce value within a certain period, and when such credit merely enables him to exist until the sale of his own product, are similar. Moreover, we have even prevented the banker from regulating his advances according to the production of commodities : he must regulate his issues by the amount of his gold reserves, which reserves cannot be an index of the production of real capital in the country, since they fluctuate with circumstances entirely unconnected with production.

(4) That the flow of gold represents an export of the savings available for credit issue, and that the subsequent price of credit must therefore inevitably be raised at home. I reply that our credit system consists of a huge superstructure of paper credit, representing, however inadequately, the nation's production of commodities, the superstructure being based by our legal tender laws upon a slender gold reserve. Under a rational exchange system any export of capital abroad should be merely subtracted from the total volume of our surplus production, even though it should be exported in the form of gold. Yet, under our present system, the subtraction of each unit of gold from the basis of our credit structure obstructs the issue of fifty or more units of credit for internal commerce, the obstruction being increased snowball fashion in practice by consequent industrial bankruptcies.

Faithfully yours,
Henry Meulen.

REVIEWS.

THE VICTIM OF KAUNITZ.

"Marie Antoinette." By H. Belloc. London: Methuen. 1909. 15s. net.

THIS book is not in the strict sense a biography of Marie Antoinette. It omits, as we shall see, some important chapters in her career. It is a brilliant essay on the tragedy of the most pathetic of the victims of the Revolution, interspersed with pictorial narratives of those episodes in her life which specially interest the author. Needless to say, the subjective note is apparent throughout the volume. Mr. Belloc hates all Jews, Protestants, Freemasons, and British conventionalities, and never hesitates to show it. We cannot deny a certain sympathy with his judgment of Parliament and " British institutions ". But this distinguished Liberal member should avoid mere insolence, as when he calls his colleagues the " Dunderheads " of Westminster or when he says : " The English Home Office allows criminals of a certain standing to go free rather than endanger social influences whose secrecy is thought necessary for the State ; nor do we allow anyone to know what sums or how large are paid for public honours, nor always to what objects secret subscriptions of questionable origin in Egypt, for instance, are devoted ". Or again : " There are others to whom cheating, intrigue, and cunning are native ; such are at bottom, however high their station, the slaves, not the dictators or the helpers, of their fellow beings ; they have a keen nose for the herd, they will always follow it, and it is their ambition to fill posts where they can give favours and draw large salaries. Of this sort are our parliamentary politicians to-day ; from such we draw our Ministers. They have of poor human nature an expert knowledge such as usurers have and panders ".

Let us now come to Mr. Belloc's subject. He rightly considers that the fate of Marie Antoinette was the fruit of the diplomatic revolution that in 1755 altered the whole Bourbon tradition by making France the ally of Austria. It is, however, idle romance to imagine that when Kaunitz allied the Empress Queen with Versailles, he was in any way actuated by religious sentiment ; far less that the diplomatic revolution of the eighteenth century sprang from the religious revolution of the sixteenth. Maria Theresa may have fancied that the Seven Years War was in a sense a conflict between Protestant and Catholic Powers ; but Kaunitz was the last man to have dreamed of a renewal of the policy of counter-reformation days. Mr. Belloc's favourite Minister was in truth as strong an anti-clerical as his bête noire, Joseph II. When Pius VI. visited Vienna, he showed the fact in an impressive way by pressing instead of kissing his Holiness' hand. It is also an exaggeration to see in Frederick II.'s annexation of Silesia " the first mere conquest of European territory which had been achieved by any Christian Power since Europe had first been organised into a family of Christian communities ". Frederick's attack was, we allow, a piratical raid, but he could put forward for it the same sort of conventional excuses from ancient documents that had justified the wars of Catholic Powers on various portions of Italian soil from the days of Erasmus to the days of Alberoni. The truth is that in the eighteenth century the Chanceries of Europe, Catholic and Protestant alike, were guided by the principles of Macchiavelli. To turn to the victim of Kaunitz' diplomacy. When the line of coaches left the palace of Vienna on 21 April 1770, and the young Archduchess, now known as Marie Antoinette, took the western road for France, she had been taught nothing (she could hardly write her name properly) excepting the conventional manners of a Court. Had her good abilities been properly trained, her history might have been different. She would have understood France, and she would have known how to form a plan. That she never could form a plan is, in Mr. Belloc's view, the secret of her failure. She could neither organise nor intrigue. Of her early years as dauphine and queen he gives a sympathetic and interesting picture. The righteous if tactless protest of a pure girl against the wickedness of the Du Barry was the beginning of her sorrows. The failure of her ardent character to conciliate her elders increased them. Despised as a child, she was hated as an adult by the King's three sisters, and it was in their drawing-rooms that the fatal name of "Autrichienne" was given to her. But her fate, according to our author, was decided in the first three years of her reign. "Children had become", he says, "a craving to her, and when in these days no child came, she took refuge in every stimulant save wine—gaming, jewels, doubtful books, masked balls." "The fever now upon her caused her always to despise and sometimes to neglect the rules that were of the essence of her position". In one sense the evils need not be exaggerated. The debts that she incurred amounted in two years to less than £20,000, and never bore an appreciable proportion to the scale of the public embarrassment. But these follies nevertheless blighted the Bourbon lilies. French Royalty was public property, as no other Royalty is or has been, and Antoinette's follies were the "mark of a million eyes, all keen to observe whatever trifle was done between midday and dawn". Yet, in spite of these early failures, there seemed a chance in 1784 that she might see happy days. The American War had given back to the Bourbons something of their military glories. Children had been born to the Queen, and the inheritance in her family appeared secure. Under Calonne's management the finances seemed to be improving. Then like a bolt from the blue there fell on the Court the horror of the diamond necklace revelations, reviving the old scandals, and building, in Napoleon's picturesque phrase, the gate of the Queen's tomb. It adds to the tragedy that the honesty of the King and Queen was the chief cause of their undoing. Knowing that they had done nothing of which to be ashamed, they insisted on an open trial for the culprits. The politicians Vergennes and Mercy would have suppressed the whole matter, paid the La Motte woman something to be off, and would have done (as Mr. Belloc truly says) what modern statesmen do in similar circumstances. From a worldly point of view at least the trial was a blunder; popular prejudice exaggerated everything that told against the Queen, and it is only in our time that the calumnies against her have been disproved.

Our author, whose account of the "affair" is at the same time accurate history and thrilling romance, presents impressive pictures of the attitude of the Queen to the coming revolution—her foolish coquetting with the spirit of insurrection in Beaumarchais' play, her reckless subsidy to Austria, her breaking of Calonne, her choice of the atheist priest Loménie for Premier, and her other follies. One thing, however, he brings out clearly. Whatever were the faults of the King and Queen, they were (this is one of the most important points to realise) as much martyrs for the Faith as was Charles the First. They believed, and for this reason they could not acquiesce in the Civil Constitution of the clergy. But the world in which they lived could not comprehend their action. Mr. Belloc may exaggerate the influence of freethinking ideas in the National Assembly. He is an Ultramontane, and will not understand that Camus and the Jansenists, cranks and fools as they were, honestly believed themselves to be restoring Primitive Christianity. But he proves clearly that the French Church, which in Paris at least bowed before the Civil Constitution, had a far weaker grip on Christian truth than the French Church that yesterday threw the associations cultuelles into the face of M. Clemenceau. Mirabeau, Mr. Belloc thinks, might have saved the Crown had he lived. But he allows that neither could he understand the Queen nor the Queen understand him. The pictures of the ill-starred banquet to the Flanders regiment, when the song

"O Richard, O mon roi,
L'Univers t'abandonne"

heralded the doom of Versailles, and of the flight to Varennes are brilliant, but in the period that divides Varennes from 10 August Mr. Belloc flags. Of the Royal advisers and Ministers in the last year of the Monarchy he hardly troubles to write the names. Actually Narbonne is never mentioned, and Bertrand de Moleville's name only once occurs.

The attack of the Jacobin insurrection on the Tuileries seems to reawaken our author's interest in his subject, and the story of the last day of the French Monarchy is told from the soldier's standpoint as it has never before been told in English. We then pass to the Temple. Mr. Belloc observes that at first the royal family were kindly treated, and he surmises that if only the war had gone well for the Republic, the Queen would have been exchanged or perhaps unconditionally released. In his view she was a hostage, a hostage who when the allies closed round Maubeuge was sacrificed in revenge for a ravaged territory. It is picturesque to see the siege of Maubeuge and the trial of the Queen on the same stage; but if the connexion between the war and the murder has been minimised by other historians, we think that in this book it is exaggerated. One may also question whether Mr. Belloc does not go too far when he assumes that the Queen was in any real sense a traitor to the French nation. Certainly she never had any sympathy with the émigrés, nor did she desire the invasion of France by the allies until a Congress had first been held. She was, it must be remembered, a child of the eighteenth century, and it must have seemed to her as natural for the Powers with the consent of the French Monarchy to combine against the Jacobins as it had seemed to all Europe natural for them some years earlier to combine against the Jesuits.

But though we may differ from him in matters of detail and smile at his extravagances, let us say in conclusion that Mr. Belloc has given us a great book—a book which everyone who desires to see the Revolution as Frenchmen see it should study. It is a great thing that one who is so little of a royalist should have so brilliantly vindicated the fair fame of the murdered queen.

THE SIN OF ACHILLES.

"Homer and the Iliad." An Essay to Determine the Scope and Character of the Original Poem. By F. Melian Stawell. London: Dent. 1909. 10s. 6d.

AGALLIS (or Anagallis, for there is a varia lectio), a Corcyræan schoolmarm, wrote a book "on the Ball", in which she attributed the invention of that sphere to her compatriot Nausicaa; she further held that the Shield of Achilles contained engraved on its surface the ancient history of Athens. Hestiæa of Alexandria wrote about the Iliad, and wondered if the war took place round the actual Ilium. The triad (without prejudice to the rights, if any, of Dacieria) is completed by a Cambridge lady, Miss Stawell. The reviewer makes his best bow and sheathes his blade. Miss Stawell's book is a welcome and useful addition to the English literature on Homer. She does not carry Mr. Lang's magic pack of learning, and wants Mr. Murray's love of appropriating the lunes of every wild German. Her characteristic appears to be a feeling for literature; we find in her book many true and delicate remarks upon the art of poetry. Thus she has an easy task in rapping Wilamowitz over the knuckles and hauling Kirchhoff over the coals; easy, for anyone who can read Greek and is gifted with ordinary taste can make hay, and fun, of all the Germans, and some of our countrymen too. So true is it that learning dulls the eye of the soul, even where the soul possesses that organ.

Miss Stawell is not content with liking and interpreting. She sets up as a critic herself, and seeks to determine how much of the Iliad is original, or by Homer, and how much is later. This is a different thing. One may be able to appreciate the best situations of the Iliad and the debt that they owe to their setting, and see clearly how the reconstructions in vogue detract from their force, and yet fail to realise the real conditions of poetry in the heroic age. But such a realisation is necessary, else one's critical judgment comes practically to declaring what one likes to be original, and what offends one to be late. Mr. Murray ejects what pains him. Miss Stawell is not quite so feminine, in one case at least, for she puts Book IX., which naturally she likes, among the additions; but she betrays no general idea of what the Iliad was made out of. It is not an easy question. The data are the lays about the Trojan war, which we see in the Odyssey being sung in barons' halls at Ithaca and Sparta, and the Iliad and the Odyssey, great poems of 15,000 and 12,000 lines; these are the data, and the problem is to bridge the interval. Something existed, down to the eighth and seventh centuries, right to 600, out of which the Cypria, the Aethiopis, and the other Cyclic poems were formed. Whatever this something was, it was the same thing from which the Iliad and the Odyssey were created. Greek tradition saw a number of poets as Homer's predecessors, and gave them names which appear to us fantastic; the accounts in the Odyssey suggest a continuous and all-embracing national history in verse laid up in the heads and perhaps in the books of the Aoidoi, the professional bards. Out of which of these categories Homer made his two poems—continuous chronicle or already formed separate works—we cannot say. One lengthy specimen, however, of this kind of verse survives, the Catalogue of Ships, the oldest thing in Greek, the Domesday Book and Libro d'Oro of all later history. The state of Greece and Asia which it represents came to an end with the Dorian migration and the Ionic colonisation, and its accuracy is guaranteed in the minutest details by the latest discoveries in archæology. In the east an Amazon on stone at Boghazkeui proves Mr. Sayce's view that they were the armed Hittite priestesses whom Priam helped the Phrygians to fight on the banks of the Sangarius; the very name (Halizones) Homer gives these Hittites is found on the cuneiform inscriptions of Van. In the west we now hear there was a Mycenæan Sparta on the left bank of the Eurotas; Strabo, Bérard and Dörpfeld have assisted each other to recover Nestor's kingdom of Pylos, ninety ships strong, with its port on the sandy shore of Triphylia, claiming the whole course of the Alpheus, and containing the home of the Mycenæan Muse. On the north-west Dörpfeld has confirmed the Homeric Dulichium by his discoveries at Leucas, though this great excavator is blind to the evidence of his own spade; in the north-east Mr. Wace and Mr. Thompson find that an inspection of the Thessalian plains shows for the first time the meaning of the Homeric Baronies. When this survival from the prehomeric stratum of heroic poetry is found to be such a faithful record of fact and place, it is reasonable to suppose that the original version of the Tale of Troy, on which Homer and his successors worked, was a chronicle of real events, allowance being made for the notions of cause and effect and of the dependence of man upon God then prevalent. Events will have been recorded in their real order, and according to their relative importance. This, too, is the notion we gain from the Odyssey, where the Ithacan and Spartan bard is a kind of newsman. Our Iliad is very unlike this. It does not narrate the important events of the war at all, and those it does tell it distorts and expands to an unreal prominence. If we compare the story of the Iliad with the same episode as it must really have happened, we get at last a criterion by which to distinguish Homer's work from his predecessors'.

What Homer did in brief was to create an Achilleis. He chose the episode in the war where Achilles quarrelled with his overlord, and expanded it till he made it the national poem of Greece. The portions of the Iliad in which Achilles is glorified are Homeric, the rest is the old chronicle. This gives the good bits to Homer, as is just; the great genius naturally surpassed his ordinary predecessor; but—and Miss Stawell has seen this—not only the good bits, but the means, generally inferior, by which they are introduced. With us poetical quality and technique coincide. It was not so in those days, the technique of construction was weak. All the machinery that immediately follows the quarrel—Agamemnon's Dream, the Marshalling, the similes: the Epipolesis, Tichoscopia, probably the Duel—are either inventions of Homer or, like the Catalogue, brought from elsewhere. The palpable stopgaps of Book VIII. introduce the magnificent rhetoric of Book IX., wherein we see Homer absolutely at his best. His whole plan, in fact, of adaptation turns on this book. To heighten his hero's value and make his absence felt early, he emphasises the First Embassy rather than the Second; two there always were, for without the rejection of the first Achilles would have committed no sin, no Ate; to quarrel was within his right, but equally he was bound to accept terms, δῶρα, when offered. Like Meleager, he refused terms, set on humiliating Agamemnon to the dust; and, like Meleager, he paid the price. Though he failed in his civic duty, he allowed his heart to be touched to the extent of sending out his friend in his place. His friend fell; he then accepted terms in due form, but too late. This tragedy Homer made out of the chronicle. As Shakespeare dealt with Holinshed, Homer romanticised heroic history. So his poem lived. The conception was great; the fitting of it into the history does not escape the critical eye. But the effect justified the execution; when all else of the Tale of Troy withered, the Sin of Achilles, Homer's creation, lived.

SIR WILLIAM WARRE'S PENINSULAR LETTERS.

"Letters from the Peninsula, 1808-1812." By Lieut.-General Sir William Warre. Edited by his Nephew, the Rev. Edmond Warre. With Frontispiece and a Map. London: Murray. 1909. 10s. 6d.

IN view of the many interests of our operations in Portugal and Spain during the years 1808 to 1812, and Sir William Warre's presence, as a young officer of the staff, at most of the important battles and sieges of that period, it is disappointing that he has not more to tell us of his own personal experiences. For it is exactly in books of this description that the student of our wars at times comes across first-hand information, which throws fresh light on some contested or doubtful point and brings more vividly to the mind the actualities of our struggle in the Peninsula than the most exhaustive accounts, official or otherwise.

Yet young Warre had exceptional advantages. His father was a merchant at Oporto, and hence he had learnt Portuguese, knowledge invaluable to an officer at that time. Further, he had what was sadly lacking a hundred years ago, a fair military education. Joining the Army in 1803, he went in 1807 to the Royal Military College at High Wycombe to study for staff employment. Thanks to this, and also, no doubt, to his knowledge of Portuguese, he was taken by General Ferguson a year later on the expedition to Portugal, as A.D.C., and was at the battles of Roliça and Vimeiro. Later on he joined General Beresford's staff and was with him in the campaign of Coruña. In 1809, when Beresford was given command of the Portuguese forces, Warre, as one of his A.D.C.s, saw much of the raising and organisation of the various units and was given local brevet rank, as a British officer in the Portuguese service. Here, very probably, may lie some of the causes of the lack of anything very novel or illuminating in these letters, for Warre, as a junior staff officer to Marshal Beresford, not seldom found himself, to use his own words, in the position of "playing a second fiddle to a second fiddle". Be that as it may, the letters have the undoubted merit claimed for them by Dr. Warre of being written by the young officer to his parents "on the spot and without reserve". Yet, truth to tell, there is not much interest in his repeated references to home politics or his conjectures of the result of some action of Austria or Russia with Napoleon, for they are clearly based on the views of his uninformed military chiefs.

What is of genuine interest in these letters is his undoubted knowledge of Portuguese character and his freely expressed opinion, formed in 1809, early in the war, of the military value of Portuguese soldiers when rightly trained and well led by British officers. Never was a forecast more thoroughly justified by subsequent events. Warre left the Peninsula in 1812 to take up staff work at the Cape, and it was over a year later, after the desperate fighting in the Pyrenees, that Wellington wrote "the Portuguese have become the fighting-cocks of the British Army". Warre also recognised the fine fighting capacity of the Spanish private soldier, and there can be no doubt whatever that, had Spanish pride permitted of it, regiments formed on the same lines as the Portuguese "fighting-cocks" would have been an enormous addition to Wellington's strength. As it was, the general incapacity of the Spanish officers and the arrogant conduct of their generals, combined with the hopeless vagaries of the Spanish Government, made all reliance on them out of the question, a fact of which Wellington had more than one bitter experience.

Few things have caused more vexation and trouble to all who have studied and written on Peninsular operations than the chaotic spelling of names and places. Wellington himself cheerily led the way by misnaming the first battle he won on Spanish soil "Roleia", whereas, as is well known, the correct spelling at the time was "Roliça", or, as some maps give it, "Roriça". It may be taken as granted that Warre's orthography, with his intimate knowledge of Portuguese, was superior to that of most British officers; yet at places we are puzzled by it, and wonder whether we have been right in spelling "Alameda" as such, or whether Warre's rendering of "Alumeda" may not be right. He gives "Bussaço" as "Busaco", but this may be out of deference to his military superiors. It is the same with some Spanish names; thus he gives "Arroyo dos Molinos" as "Arroio del Molino".

His profound contempt for the Portuguese "titled and official classes" was no doubt well deserved, and his description how they habitually indulged in calculated misstatements of fact, frigid and the reverse, makes one realise that the residents of Lisbon were at least a century in advance of the present Lord Advocate. There is a good general map of Spain at the end of the book, which would have been all the better if it had not included the two degrees of longitude beyond its eastern limits and had included a similar portion on its western side, for it then would have opened clear of the text. Dr. Warre has shown a fine contempt for European geography in delineating an inland sea, some twenty-five miles in extent, in S.W. Spain, which in his map has supplanted the Isla Mayor below Seville.

THE SHAKESPEARE QUARTOS.

"Shakespeare Folios and Quartos: a Study in the Bibliography of Shakespeare's Plays, 1594-1685." By Alfred W. Pollard. With 37 Illustrations. London: Methuen. 1909. 21s. net.

IN his preface to this handsome volume Mr. A. W. Pollard tells us that one of the objects he has in view is to vindicate the editors of the First Folio of Shakespeare and the printers of the better Quartos from the disparagement of their modern detractors. His arguments are mainly directed against Mr. Sidney Lee, whose account of the provenance of the First Folio is submitted to rigorous and destructive criticism.

Since the text of Shakespeare began to be seriously studied, there have always been wrangles over the merits and demerits of the Folio and the Quartos. Steevens impishly delighted in vexing Malone by decrying the First Folio and extravagantly praising the Second. Horne Tooke, who knew little or nothing about the Quartos, maintained that "the First Folio is the only edition worth regarding"—a statement often quoted with approval by writers who shared his ignorance. Mr. Pollard distinguishes between the good and bad Quartos; but even some of the bad, mutilated Quartos preserve Shakespearean passages that are not to be found in the Folio. He is rightly severe on the tattered 1602 Quarto of "Merry Wives"; yet Theobald, the first and by far the most brilliant of the textual experts, retrieved from the Quarto's corruptions authentic Shakespearean fragments. In the scene (II. ii.) where he vainly importunes Falstaff for a loan, Pistol is made to exclaim in the Quarto, "I will retort the sum in equipage!"—a protestation that is in the true "swaggering vein of Ancient Pistol", and could never have been coined by a stenographer. Of "Richard III." Mr. Pollard observes that the text of the First Folio was founded on that of the Sixth Quarto (1622), "with additions and corrections from a transcript of the original". But there is one very notable correction that could not have been drawn "from a transcript of the original". In the scene (III. vii.) where Buckingham (as spokesman for the faint-hearted Mayor and citizens of London) presses Gloucester to assume the crown while Gloucester goes through the farce of refusing it, at last—after many rhetorical flourishes—Buckingham affects to take umbrage:

"Come, citizens; zounds, I'll entreat no more";

whereupon the demure hypocrite Gloucester reproves him with

"O do not swear, my Lord of Buckingham!"

So the passage stands in the Quartos, and nothing in the whole play is more Shakespearean. "O do not swear, my Lord of Buckingham!" In the Folio the gist and point are lost; an enactment had been passed in James' days against the use of profane language on the stage; "zounds" was adjudged to be profane; so "zounds, I'll entreat no more", was corrected by some reviser to the tame "we will entreat no more", and Gloucester's pious reproof had to be thrown out altogether. Yet some modern editors follow the Folio: O pectora cæca! It was always stimulating to hear Swinburne's scorn for these blind souls.

Mr. Pollard gossips pleasantly about Elizabethan and Jacobean printers and their methods of doing business. He has a theory of his own about the plan on which Heminges and Condell arranged the order of the plays in the First Folio—that certain plays of primary importance were to be given a prominent position, while others of secondary interest were to be relegated to comparative obscurity. His arguments on these heads we take to be mere moonshine. But on the subject of the misdated Quartos (the 1600 Roberts "Merchant of Venice", etc.), he effectively supports and strengthens the case that Mr. W. W. Greg set forth most ably in "The Library"; indeed, the evidence is now so clear and convincing that no scholar who values his reputation can continue to offer further resistance.

THE ROYAL RIVER.

"The Story of the Thames." By the late J. E. Vincent. With Illustrations and a Map. London: Smith, Elder. 1909. 7s. 6d. net.

TO write a good guide-book or itinerary is surely one of the most difficult tasks which can be set to a man of letters; to begin with, the author must be equipped with all that wealth of local and trivial detail which marks the true antiquary, yet he must possess such a sense of proportion and feeling for the broad stream of history as is generally antipathetic to the persistence of the antiquary over trifles and his preoccupation with the letter of the past. He must also be a man of science, or much of the scenery and many of the aspects of the country which might be made of the liveliest interest to the reader will be sealed books to him; for similar reasons he should be something of a sportsman. He must somehow know the topography of his district personally and lovingly; it will not suffice to get it up by a series of journeys made for the purpose; it ought to have been a hobby of long standing. With and above all this the writer must be an artist, appreciative of the associations and sensitive to the beauties of his playground, yet equally sensitive to the flatness born of an excess of adjectives and appreciative of the boredom brought about by a record of trivial impressions.

If such a combination of qualifications may well be deemed to be impossible, this book shows that the ideal is not wholly unrealisable when an English gentleman of education and culture at last gathers together the recollections of many years' traffickings in one of his beloved haunts. The author, the late editor of "Country Life", did not live to see the proofs of his book, a book which speaks in every chapter of thirty years' enjoyment of Thames-side by a man singularly equipped by his training and sympathies to blend with his delight in sport and the open air both a keen sense of natural beauty and an intellectual interest in the past and present history of the country. Of course, from the historical and antiquarian point of view the Thames has been well written up, and without any special research a man may put together from readily accessible books many vivid episodes which are local to the Thames valley, but which illuminate their period of English history. Oxford, Windsor and London belong, as it were, to the commonplace texture of history; but where else in England will the Civil War be brought more home to one than about the upper river?—the skirmishes at the bridges—Radcot, Newbridge, Cropredy; Burford, with its memories of Falkland and the Lenthalls; Ewelme again, from which it is no long walk to Chalgrove Field where Hampden fell. The lower reaches are instinct with the eighteenth century—Pope and Garrick, Walpole and Caroline of Anspach; from Windsor downwards the Thames traveller may remind himself and be reminded of pretty nearly everything and everyone of consequence in that most unspiritual but comfortably human of centuries. Nineteenth-century memories chiefly cluster round the lower reaches still—Putney, Hammersmith, Chelsea—though its two modern and, saving Spenser, its greatest poets belong to the upper waters of the Thames. All the exquisite winding stream from Godstow to Newbridge, still shy retreats and retired ground, are now ennobled and made for ever fair by Matthew Arnold's verse, and if Mr. Bridges has been less topographical, there are plunging weir pools and smooth sweeps of down in the Streatley country which will always owe an added grace to him. But if we allow ourselves to begin to enumerate the pearls which are strung together along Thames-side we shall forget Mr. Vincent's book, and it is much too charming a production to be passed over. The note of the book is set by the illustrations—they are neither photographs nor intensely chromatic colour-prints, but reproductions from various series of engravings, "Picturesque Views", published between 1791 and 1828. Alive as Mr. Vincent is to the delights of the river to-day, it is the flavour of the older world that he is always seeking to recapture, and he is never so happy as when he is showing, as in his extracts from Mrs. Powys' diary, that the Thames has always been a pleasure stream. Another feature of interest in the book is the discussion of the many Navigation Acts under which the river has been administered, and the accounts of how the locks and cuts have come to be, in the course of which the very unjustly abused body, the Thames Conservancy, gets its case very fairly presented. Mr. Vincent's book may claim to be a guide-book, probably the best one that has been written for the Thames, but it is also a book, and will form not only one of the pleasantest of companions on a river journey but an ever-ready friend for any dweller, temporary or permanent, by Thames-side.

NOVELS.

"The Caravaners." By the Author of "Elizabeth and her German Garden." London: Smith, Elder. 1909. 6s.

The title is in the plural, but the weakness and occasional weariness of the book results from its being concerned too exclusively with a single character, and being written with a mild ferocity to expose his infirmities. Major Otto von Ottringel, a German baron, is the unfortunate gentleman, and, by dubbing him the author of the book, he is made to appear as his own executioner, revealing on every page his futility, pompous ignorance, snobbishness, provincialism, and domestic absurdity. The rest of the party serve only to exhibit his arrogance and stupidity in the most unbecoming light, and consequently only incidentally acquire any kind of entity; we never see them in relation to each other save at a distance, and pending the Baron's effort to interpose with some fatuous misconception. He would be more amusing if he were not so ridiculous, and he would be much more amusing if there were much less of him. The humour of his absurdities is extracted so often that we lose all taste for it, and even begin, before the end, to resent so relentless an exploitation. The ignorant reader who learns to regard him as a typical German soldier will make as big a mistake about his nation as the Baron made about ours, and of that fact the author must have been perfectly aware however much she may have suffered from the type which she has drawn. The German officer with whom one has been professionally acquainted has never been the gross, ignorant, greedy, discourteous, uncompanionable creature which is here depicted. If in his views of the other sex he has seemed sometimes oriental, and been somewhat overpoweringly obsessed by military ideals, to reveal him, caravanning, as worse than a Turk and foretasting at every stage the savour of conquered England, is to detract both from the humour and the instruction which he might afford. Not that there is any lack of humour on almost every page of the book; but there is too pronounced a sameness in the note of it, and a sense, for all its cleverness and apparent suavity, of its having been extracted by exasperated nerves. The portrait fails likewise in consistency, for, the Baron being writer and commentator, the author has, despite his elemental stupidity, to entrust him with the delivery of her own good things as well as of his own banalities. Thus on the same page we find him remarking that "No woman (except, of course, my wife) shall ever be able to say I have not behaved to her as a gentleman should", and reflecting that "A socialist, as far as I can make out, is a person who may never sit down. If he does, the bleak object he calls the community immediately becomes vocal, because it considers that by sitting down he is cheating it of what he would be producing by his labour if he did not". Her heavy-handed slaughter of the Baron leaves the author with few opportunities for that light pleasantry in dealing with life by which she has been distinguished, and clever though the manner is with which in English she imitates a Teutonic diction, we would willingly sacrifice it for a few of those delicate felicities in recording her observations which she first gave us in the "German Garden".

"With the Merry Austrians." By Amy McLaren. London: Murray. 1909. 6s.

This novel is of interest rather on account of its pleasant picture of (hotel) life in the Austrian Tyrol than because there is anything remarkable about the story, which is in the main the old one of two men and a woman, prettily written. Such action as there is takes place in and about the Hôtel Pension Schloss Waldhof; and there is also an avalanche, an excursion to the Dolomites and Cortina, and a very amusing sketch of a boarding-house busybody.

"John Thorndyke's Cases." By R. Austin Freeman. London: Chatto and Windus. 1909. 3s. 6d.

Here are eight readable detective stories by the inevitable admiring medical friend and follower of the principal sleuth-hound. In the best of them an innocent person is invariably arrested by obtuse but well-meaning police officers, and the case for the prosecution demolished more or less dramatically by the superior science of John Thorndyke, lecturer on medical jurisprudence at S. Margaret's Hospital.

POINTS FOR CAMPAIGNERS.

"Campaign Points." Reprinted from the "Standard". London: The Standard Newspapers Ltd. 1909. 3d.

If a supplement to the "Saturday Handbook" be necessary—and where topics like Tariff Reform, covering so many points of doubt and difficulty, are concerned we cannot be too fully informed—then we do not hesitate to recommend this brochure, well entitled "Campaign Points." Tariff Reform has to stand or fall by hard facts. A sixty years' old fiscal system will only be abandoned if it can be proved up to the hilt that its usefulness is spent. That there is something wrong somewhere, that England with all her wealth should have the largest percentage of unemployed, that with all the skill and industry of her artisans she should lose her lead in the commercial race, makes explanation imperative. Why is it that when trade throughout the world begins to revive England responds last to the call? How is it that Germany and the United States have gone ahead so fast while Great Britain has relatively gone back, notwithstanding the overwhelming advantages which were hers at the outset? These are the questions which the man who does not choose to regard everything as for the best because he lives under one half of an ideal fiscal system, asks himself; and the answer will be found in this admirable series of points. The particular value of the pamphlet is that in most cases the facts it sets out are a categoric reply to free trade assertions and assumptions. Whether it be in regard to bread or chocolate, to iron or leather, the data in almost every case have been collected to expose a free trade fallacy or dispose of a fiscal reformer's doubts. In half a page we may learn the effect of an anti-dumping law; or how world tariffs, combined with competitive skill, have destroyed England's supremacy as a manufacturer; or, again, how tariffs have assisted protectionist rivals in exports in flat contradiction of the theory that tariffs kill exports. By the way, in section 24, page 23, the dates 1904-8, 1894-8, dealing with leather, have been trans-

(Continued on p. 760.)

posed by the printer; the text makes this quite clear, but the speaker who takes his facts and figures from the pamphlet must be on his guard against this purely mechanical slip. There is much besides tariff reform; the points against the Budget are numerous and equally well done. The Budget not only does nothing to bring the empire into closer relations; it keeps bolted and barred the door which the Government slammed; its alternative, tariff reform, would realise that Imperial commercial union which is the one great opportunity for the people of the British Isles in the twentieth century. The Colonies have saved us from absolute disaster, and the appeal of "Campaign Points" is to all who would seize an occasion that may not come again till the foreigner with his remorseless tariffs has done so much harm to British industry and got so firm a hold of Colonial markets that it cannot be utilised to the full. Tariff Reform, as shown in this pamphlet, means a big gun for battering down hostile walls; it means the material improvement of the Colonial market—our best, if judged by population; it means a minimum net yield of 16,000,000*l.* or 17,000,000*l.* to the revenue on a much more businesslike and reasonable computation than that made by Mr. Haldane and endorsed by the President of the Board of Trade. "Campaign Points" provides a goodly number of hard nuts on which the friends of the Government will break their teeth if they try to crack them.

SHORTER NOTICES.

"The Mother's Companion." By M. A. Cloudesley Brereton. London: Mills and Boon. 1909. 2s. 6d. net.

This book has been written for the series published by Messrs. Mills and Boon under the general title of the "Companion Series". Sir Lauder Brunton writes a preface, in which he very correctly speaks of the keynote of the volume as "a plea for the training of woman for the career of wifehood and motherhood". Mrs. Brereton has all the qualifications for writing on a subject which in unfit hands would fall into triviality, absurdity, or offensiveness, and, most likely of all, into the doing of harm. If the writer of a book of this kind does not do exactly the right thing, the book is not only a failure but an impertinence, so intimate and personal are the matters upon which she commits herself to advise and reprove her fellow women. The modern woman is not the kind of person for whom the "Mother's Companion" of half a century ago is now possible. Social, political, and economic questions about the various classes of women have become as important as those about the various classes of men. For physiology and psychology, both from the race and the individual standpoint, women have become more interesting than men, no doubt because the larger study of them is new. A well-qualified woman like Mrs. Brereton talking to women about themselves in this era is therefore a light on the obscurity to men as well. On some points the book is as suggestive to men as it is to women, and it will inform them of some things even about economics which women know better. We must not be thought to mean that the book is mainly sociological. Mrs. Brereton speaks simply and directly to women as wives and mothers on intimate matters, physical, mental, and domestic. Women who would welcome the opportunity of talking to a woman of trained intelligence and practical experience would be glad to read this book.

"Dictionary of National Biography." Vol. XXII. Supplement. London: Smith, Elder. 1909. 15s. net.

The great re-issue is at an end, and we hope has met with the support from the public and the libraries which so admirable an undertaking merited. It was a big thing to put the Dictionary in hand at all; it was certainly no small thing to face the risks involved in a new and cheaper edition. A work which in its cheapest form costs £16 10s. can hardly be regarded as a commercial proposition, as the Americans would say, but when it renders national service as the "Dictionary of National Biography" does, it should at least find a sufficient number of subscribers to prevent any loss to the enterprising firm which puts it on the market. If every library, public and private, which should have the Dictionary on its shelves has taken a copy, then perhaps merit has not been its own reward. We ought to welcome the work if only for the tribute it pays to the national genius. And the supplement shows that all the giants were not of the centuries preceding the nineteenth. Here we have biographies of men like Ruskin and Browning, of Froude and Sullivan, of Burne Jones and Jowett, of Max Müller and Huxley, of John Bright and Gladstone, and many others. The Supplement opens with Leslie Stephen's account of George Smith, to whose public spirit we owe the Dictionary, and almost closes with Mr. Sidney Lee's one hundred and ten pages on Queen Victoria—certainly not the least notable volume of this very notable work.

"Myths and Legends of the Middle Ages", by H. A. Guerber (Harrap, 7s. 6d. net).—Perhaps Mr. Guerber rather grandiloquently adds to his title "Their Origin and Influence on Literature and Art", but in his introductions to the stories and the "General Survey of Romance Literature" he certainly does give much information which helps the general reader to understand how the popular mediæval legends grew up and how they entered into the literature and history of all the modern European nations. The book contains a very copious selection from the Teutonic legends, such as the Niebelungenlied, those of Charlemagne and those connected with the Holy Grail, and from the Arthurian cycle. They are not only stirring stories of war and love and of the miraculous, but a kind of knowledge of mediæval life and thought with which everyone interested in history and literature ought to be in some measure acquainted. Mr. Guerber has had in view an intelligent class of readers who desire something beyond mere story-telling, and he has provided them with something not too learned and yet not superficially popular. The book is handsome, and has a large number of artistic photographs of pictures.

"Revue des Deux Mondes." 1 Decembre.

Among several articles of considerable power we think M. Leroy-Beaulieu's on the Fiscal Revolution in France and England will most repay attention by English readers at the present crisis. The writer is equally severe on Mr. Lloyd George and M. Cochery. As an economist of the straightest sect his conclusions will hardly be welcome to either party in this country. He demands a rigid orthodoxy in taxation which is not possible under present conditions considering the increasing demands on the public purse. Nevertheless his criticism of the proposed methods deserves close consideration. M. Bertrand's study of the political troubles in Barcelona and their probable outcome, though too friendly to the Catalans, deserves attention. He says Catalonia is the most progressive part of Spain, which is true, and that she believes she can impose her ideas on the rest of the country, which is doubtful.

CHURCH HISTORY.

"The Story of W. J. E. Bennett." By F. Bennett. London: Longmans. 1909. 7s. 6d. net.

Tractarianism was thought out by devout students, but translated into action by energetic parish priests like "Bennett of Frome". The Frome part of the story, however, is less absorbing than the earlier scenes in Knightsbridge and Pimlico. There was throwing of rotten eggs and oranges in the little Somerset town at first, and the "Times" declared that private patronage ought to be abolished when the Marchioness of Bath faced a Protestant mob side by side with her presentee. However, Frome-Selwood, though described a generation earlier as "a town unhappily proverbial for its mongrel Churchmen and liberalising religionists", soon learnt to love and rally round its uncompromising, but by no means unconciliatory, vicar. Bennett's real heartbreaking troubles had been in London. His own Oxford days had been pre-Tractarian—he went up from Westminster in 1823—and it was some time after his ordination before he came under the influence of "Puseyism". At his appointment to the new district of S. Paul's, Knightsbridge, the spiritual destitution of the latter was appalling, yet the district was immensely wealthy. Bennett, without any "Christian-Socialist" posing, threw all the fire of his eloquence into shaming the rich out of their self-satisfaction. When, a year or two later, he was turned out of this church, which became so famous as S. Barnabas, Pimlico—not by mob violence, of which he was utterly fearless, but by Bishop Blomfield, in whose hands he had placed himself—the parishioners told the Bishop of "the great and almost unparalleled personal sacrifices by which Mr. Bennett placed the whole of his private fortune on the altar at the head of subscriptions for the extension of the Gospel to the poor". The ceremonies which had excited so much fury seem to us now incredibly trifling. But in 1847 a Liberal reaction against Tractarianism was in flood, Lord John Russell was hounding public opinion against "the unworthy sons of the Church of England", and Blomfield was now in a state of abject alarm. So Bennett went out into the cold, and the "Times" said next morning that it might "fairly count the spolia opima of Mr. Bennett as among the first substantial triumphs of the Protestant cause". But the Westminster Play, after Bennett's death in 1886, called him "cedendo victor". He was never a man to run away from force or bullying, and the letters in which he dressed down Lord John Russell (a parishioner) are almost worthy to rank with Law's letters to Hoadly. There was no modern cant about Bennett.

(Continued on p. 762.)

He was a scholar and a gentleman, intensely beloved and respected, dignified in appearance and feeling, and his biographer pithily asks if he could possibly have had such influence had he been the new-style curate who dresses for a scrimmage like a harlequin and tells the lads of the parish to call him by his Christian name. "'Popular'", he adds, "is a word which, applied to a clergyman, makes one feel uncomfortable. It could not be applied to Mr. Bennett".

"The Mediæval Church and the Papacy." By Arthur C. Jennings. London: Methuen. 1909. 2s. 6d. net.

This is as skilful a summary as one could have of the events of three and a half crowded centuries. But we are more than ever convinced that compendious history is false history. The impression is here given of a barbarous era, marked by universal greed, ambition and selfishness. Who could suppose that it was also the era of the most exquisite idealism and beauty, of immense construction in institutions, in the science of worship, in architecture, art and philosophy? The world has never seen such passionate response to any spiritual call, such saintly lives, such an ardour of unearthliness. Mr. Jennings is too good a scholar to hash up some of the old conventions, such as that popular liberties were the aim of Magna Charta and constitutionalism of the Statute of Præmunire. He also points out that, gross as were the abuses of "provision", the Pope's nomination to high places in the Church was usually much better than the King's, and that the Præmunire and Provision Acts paved the way for the tyranny of Henry VIII. But Mr. Jennings is nevertheless rather a pronounced anti-clerical. His attack on Laud as a pompous, fussy little pedant sounds like the old Macaulay whiggery, as does what he says about Beket's stand against Henry II. having an aim which was "destructive to the Church's spiritual life" and having had a "remote connexion with religion in the modern sense". It is, of course, perfectly arguable that the ecclesiastical theory of Church and State was more wrong than right. But the issue at stake was such an immense one that even a short history of the Mediæval Church and Papacy which leaves it unstated and almost unglanced at is bound to present a puzzle picture rather than a related whole. This issue is the key to the whole struggle from the Conquest to the Reformation. No one till towards the end questioned the apostolic authority in spiritual things of the See of Peter. Its authority over temporal matters was sometimes submitted to—especially when it was convenient—but more often resisted. Nevertheless, there was a constant and ever-growing tendency to oppose to ultra-Papalism the conception of the inherent sacredness of all government, but especially of regal government. The modern world has resigned itself to the final break-up of life's unity, stepping down perforce to a permanently lower level of idea. Mr. Jennings points out that the first time the House of Commons was invited to determine doctrinal questions was by the Lollards in 1395. The Commons, we may remark, would not have defined transubstantiation as a change of the "accidents", as is done on page 70. Nor do we understand why "Let not a man contract with a relation of his former wife" was "one of the extraordinary prohibitions with which ecclesiasticism had environed liberty of marriage". It is the present law of the Church of which Mr. Jennings is a priest. On page vii "Our story finds its halting place in 1185" should read "in 1485".

"The Reformation Period." By Henry Gee. London: Methuen. 1909. 2s. 6d. net.

The English Reformation, if a necessary, was a very ugly, business. The framework of the old Church was distorted, as Dr. Gee observes, almost beyond recognition, and the elements of spirituality, or even of greatness, in the people who forced it through are almost indiscernible. As for results, Henry—Clodius accusans mœchos—told his people before his death: "Charity was never so faint among you, and virtuous living was never less used, and God Himself among Christians was never less reverenced, honoured and served". And, if possible, things were a good deal worse afterwards. What one of the Convocation prayers styles the "Sacrosancta Reformatio" was certainly not a second Pentecost. Yet it did put an end to an intolerable and immoral state of things, as well as to much that was lovely, gracious and of good report, and in spite of muddle and confusion the essentials of ecclesiastical and theological continuity were somehow preserved. Mary's first Repeal Act spoke of the things "which we and our forefathers found in this Church of England, to us left by the authority of the Catholic Church"—in ignorance of the theory of a new Church erected on the ruins of the old Ecclesia Anglicana. Henry's supremacy over the Church was not greater in theory, though more tyrannical, than that which the Conqueror and other Christian princes had claimed, and was much softened down under Elizabeth. As for the reformed body being merely a parliamentary Church, it is far from the case that synodical forms were not observed or that Parliament itself compiled rules of worship and formularies of faith. And the reaction was every bit as Erastian as the Reformation. It was not till Elizabeth and the Stuarts that parliamentary invasion of the liberties of the Church was sharply checked. Cecil had advised that "the care of all things belonging to the State ecclesiastical be remitted to the clergy". However, the Elizabethan Act of Uniformity made a bad beginning by interference with rubrical details. We confess we are totally unable to understand what so expert a writer as Dr. Gee means when he speaks, on page 217, of the Ornaments Rubrick of the 1559 Book as directly "opposed to the words of the Act", and as a "revolutionary order" the legal authority for which can only be guessed at. The Rubrick is taken straight out of the Act, though with an unauthorised modification, the words of the Act being reproduced more accurately in our present Book. Again, when Dr. Gee says that the "Romanist" view of matrimony as a sacrament is unscriptural, we should have expected him to remember that it is called a sacrament in the English Homilies. Nor does it seem right to say that with the restoration in any place of the Mass "Holy Communion ceased". Roman Catholics have always used the expression "receive Holy Communion". Once more, why should the being given "power to celebrate Mass as well for the living as the dead" imply a greater sacerdotal "control over a man's spiritual life" than the present English formula of conferring priesthood: "Whose sins thou dost forgive they are forgiven, and whose sins thou dost retain they are retained"? Dr. Gee, however, is not a partisan. He speaks highly of the mediæval monasteries, is sensible of the losses entailed by the Reformation, and observes of the Papacy: "There is, perhaps, nothing inherent in the idea of papal government which is wrong in itself, and no unprejudiced student of Church history can deny the vast benefits of control, organisation, and development directly due to it". This historical sketch of an unwieldy period is on the whole both lucid and fair. On p. 75 "put in use" is a misprint for "put in ure", and on p. 126 "oration" should be "oraison". In the phrase (p. 146) "matins, mass, evensong and procession", it might have been useful to explain that the last word means the Litany.

For this Week's Books see page 764.

By Appointment to H.M. the King.

"BLACK & WHITE" WHISKY

James Buchanan & Co. Ltd.,
Glasgow & London.

CONNOISSEURS OF COFFEE
DRINK THE

RED WHITE & BLUE

DELICIOUS FOR BREAKFAST & AFTER DINNER.

In making, use less quantity, it being much stronger than ordinary COFFEE.

BARR'S

CASH CLEARANCE SALE of SPRING FLOWERING

BULBS.

Daffodils, Hyacinths, Tulips, Crocuses, Irises, Polyanthus Narcissi, &c., all of best quality,

AND AT GREATLY REDUCED PRICES.

CLEARANCE LISTS ON APPLICATION.

BARR & SONS, 11, 12 & 13 King Street, Covent Garden.

Dr. J. Collis Browne's Chlorodyne

The ORIGINAL and ONLY GENUINE

Acts like a charm in DIARRHŒA and DYSENTERY.
Cuts short all attacks of SPASMS, HYSTERIA & PALPITATION.
The only Palliative in NEURALGIA, GOUT, RHEUMATISM, TOOTHACHE.

Convincing Medical Testimony with each bottle.
Of all chemists, 1/1½, 2/9, 4/6

The Best Remedy known for

COUGHS, COLDS, ASTHMA, BRONCHITIS.

ELY CATHEDRAL.

Visitors will find First Class Hotel Accommodation at the "LAMB" Family Hotel, which is situated close to the Cathedral. **MODERATE TERMS.** Omnibus meets all trains.

Proprietor, S. AIREY.

"The Lost Sheep."

By ALF. U. SOORD.

From the Picture exhibited at the Royal Academy.

Published in five different sizes and sold with or without a frame.

A Delightful Xmas, New Year, or Wedding Present.

"You cannot do better than present a few Autotype reproductions from their favourite Masters."—*Outlook.*

Prices on application to the

AUTOTYPE FINE ART CO., LTD.

74 NEW OXFORD STREET, LONDON.

Publishers of Reproductions of the Celebrated Pictures in all the important Galleries of the World. Lists sent free.

Illustrated Catalogue, post free, price One Shilling.

CRAMER PIANOS.

PIANETTES - - - -	25 gs.
UPRIGHT GRANDS - -	36 gs.
GRANDS - - - - -	84 gs.
Players, Pianola, Cecilian, and others,	20 gs. each.
Interior Piano Players - - - -	60 gs. upwards.

BECHSTEIN PIANOS, COLLARD, CRAMER, BROADWOOD, AND OTHER GOOD MAKERS.

400 to select from at best discount prices for Cash, Hire, or Hire Purchase.

J. B. CRAMER & CO., Ltd.,
46 MOORGATE ST., E.C., and 126 OXFORD ST., W.,
LONDON.

AUSTRALIA by ORIENT LINE,

UNDER CONTRACT TO CARRY HIS MAJESTY'S MAILS.

FROM LONDON EVERY ALTERNATE FRIDAY, calling at PLYMOUTH, GIBRALTAR MARSEILLES, NAPLES, PORT SAID, and COLOMBO.

Managers—F. GREEN & CO.: ANDERSON, ANDERSON & CO.

Head Offices—FENCHURCH AVENUE, LONDON.

For Passage apply to the latter firm at 5 Fenchurch Avenue, E.C., or to the Branch Office, 28 Cockspur Street, Charing Cross S.W.

EGYPT BY P. & O.

THREE SERVICES WEEKLY FROM LONDON.

Direct	(11 Days) ...	Friday	2 P.M.
Via Marseilles ...	(5 Days) ...	Thursday ...	11 A.M.
Via Brindisi	(100 hours) ...	Friday	9 P.M.

Handbook on application.

P. & O. S. N. CO. { 122 LEADENHALL STREET, E.C. / NORTHUMBERLAND AVENUE, W.C. } LONDON.

UNION-CASTLE LINE.

ROYAL MAIL SERVICE.—To SOUTH and EAST AFRICA.—Via Madeira, Canaries, Ascension, St. Helena, and Lobito Bay.

Steamers	Service	London	Southampton
* NORMAN	Royal Mail	—	Dec. 18
§ TINTAGEL CASTLE ...	Intermediate	Dec. 17	Dec. 18
* WALMER CASTLE	Royal Mail	—	Dec. 25
† GALICIAN	Intermediate	Dec. 24	Dec. 25

* Via Madeira. § Via Teneriffe. † Via Las Palmas and Lobito Bay.

MONTHLY DIRECT EAST AFRICAN SERVICE
To and from United Kingdom and Continent.

Donald Currie and Co., Managers, 3 and 4 Fenchurch Street, E.C. West End Agencies—Sleeping Car Co., 20 Cockspur Street, S.W., and Thos. Cook and Son, 13 Cockspur Street, S.W.

R. ANDERSON & CO.,

BRITISH, INDIAN, AND COLONIAL ADVERTISEMENT CONTRACTORS,

14 KING WILLIAM STREET, STRAND, W.C.,

GIVE THE BEST TERMS for Company and General Advertising. Advice, Estimates, and all information free of charge. Replies received.

THIS WEEK'S BOOKS.

ART AND ARCHÆOLOGY.

A Sienese Painter of the Franciscan Legend (Bernard Berenson). Dent. 6s. net.
The Collector's Handbook to Keramics (William Chaffers). Gibbings. 6s.

BIOGRAPHY.

Henry Fielding (G. M. Godden). Sampson Low. 10s. 6d. net.

HISTORY

The Regality of Kirriemuir (Alan Reid). Edinburgh: Grant. 6s. 6d. net.
The Dauphines of France (Frank Hamel). Paul. 16s.
The Revolution in Constantinople and Turkey (Sir W. M. Ramsay). Hodder and Stoughton. 10s. 6d. net.

LAW.

Foreign Judgments and Jurisdiction (Sir Francis Piggott. Part III.). Butterworth. 35s. net.

REFERENCE BOOKS

Debrett's Peerage, 1910. Dean. 31s. 6d. net.
Clergy Directory 1910. Phillips. 4s. 6d. net.

REPRINTS AND TRANSLATIONS

Ancient English Christmas Cards (Edith Rickerts). Chatto and Windus. 7s. 6d. net.
Crete the Forerunner of Greece (Charles Henry Hawes). Harper. 2s. 6d. net.

THEOLOGY

Orders and Unity (Charles Gore). Murray. 3s. 6d. net.
Church Life and Thought in North America, A.D. 200 (Stuart A. Donaldson). Cambridge: At the University Press. 3s. 6d. net.
The Nicene Creed (Rev. A. E. Burn). Rivington. 1s. net.

TRAVEL

Mexico (W. E. Carson). New York: Macmillan.

VERSE.

Poems Lyrical and Romantic (J. Barnard-James). Constable. 3s. 6d. net.
Sonnets and Elegiacs (Richard Chenevix Trench). Kegan Paul. 2s. net.
Time's Laughingstocks (Thomas Hardy). Macmillan. 4s. 6d. net.

MISCELLANEOUS

Addresses to Teachers (Dorothea Beale). Longmans. 1s. 6d. net.
Broad Lines in Science Teaching (F. Hodson). Christophers. 5s. net.
Catholic Encyclopædia, The. Vol. VI. Caxton Publishing Co. 27s. 6d. net.
Dictionary of National Biography (Sidney Lee). Vol. XXII. Smith, Elder. 15s. net.
Growth of Modern Philosophy, The (C. Delisle Burns). Sampson Low. 3s. 6d. net.
Principles and Methods of Taxation (G. Armitage Smith). Murray. 2s. 6d net.
Project of Empire, A (J. Shield Nicholson). Macmillan. 7s. 6d. net.

REVIEWS AND MAGAZINES FOR DECEMBER.—The Architectural Review, 1s.; Revue des Deux Mondes, 3 *fr.*; The North American Review, 1s.; The Economic Journal, 5s.
FOR JANUARY.—The Cornhill Magazine, 1s.

FROM MR. HEINEMANN'S XMAS LIST.

THE HEART OF THE ANTARCTIC.

By Sir ERNEST SHACKLETON, C.V.O.

2 vols., fully Illustrated in Colour and from Photographs. Crown 4to. 36s. net.

AUTOGRAPH EDITION DE LUXE.—Limited to 300 Numbered Copies, each signed by Sir Ernest Shackleton and the members of the Shore Party, with additional Illustrations and Text, printed on Dutch Hand-made Paper with special water-mark. Medium 4to. vellum, £10 10s. net.

ITALIAN HOURS.

By HENRY JAMES.

Illustrated in Colour by JOSEPH PENNELL. Demy 4to. 25s. net.

GREAT MASTERS, 1400–1800.

100 Photogravures of the Finest Works of the most Famous Painters, With Notes on each picture by Sir MARTIN CONWAY. In portfolio, £5 net.

MODERN ART.

A Comparative Study of the Formative Arts, being a Contribution to a New System of Æsthetics.

By JULIUS MEIER-GRAEFE.

With about 300 Illustrations. 2 vols. demy 4to. 42s. net.

AUTHORISED BY MR. WHISTLER.

THE LIFE OF

JAMES McNEILL WHISTLER.

By E. R. & J. PENNELL.

Profusely Illustrated in Photogravure and Half-tone. 2 vols. crown 4to. 36s. net. [*Fourth Edition.*

THE WORK OF JOHN SARGENT, R.A.

By ALICE MEYNELL.

With 58 Photogravures and 4 Lithographs. Imperial 4to. £6 6s. net. Also Editions de Luxe.

MR. RACKHAM'S NEW BOOK.

UNDINE.

Adapted from the German by W. L. COURTNEY.

Illustrated in Colour by ARTHUR RACKHAM. Crown 4to. 7s. 6d. net.

N.B.—This is the only entirely new and original work by Mr. RACKHAM to be published this year.

ILLUSTRATED BY THE SAME ARTIST.

THE INGOLDSBY LEGENDS.

Crown 4to. 15s. net.

A MIDSUMMER NIGHT'S DREAM.

Crown 4to. 15s. net.

RIP VAN WINKLE.

Crown 4to. 15s. net.

ALICE IN WONDERLAND

Pott 4to. 6s. net.

CATHEDRAL CITIES OF SPAIN.

By W. W. COLLINS, R.I.

With 60 Water-Colour Drawings by the Author. Demy 8vo. 16s. net. Also an Edition de Luxe, 42s. net.

UNIFORM WITH THIS VOLUME. 16s. net each.

CATHEDRAL CITIES OF ENGLAND.

By GEORGE GILBERT.

With 60 Water-Colour Drawings by W. W. COLLINS, R.I.

CATHEDRAL CITIES OF FRANCE.

By HERBERT MARSHALL, R.W.S., and HESTER MARSHALL. With 60 Water-Colour Drawings by HERBERT MARSHALL, R.W.S.

TUNIS, KAIROUAN, AND CARTHAGE.

Described and Illustrated with 48 Coloured Plates by GRAHAM PETRIE, R.I.

EGYPT: BELOW THE CATARACTS.

Described and Illustrated with 60 Coloured Plates by WALTER TYNDALE.

GREAT ARTISTS.

REMBRANDT.

By EMILE MICHEL. Profusely Illustrated. 2 vols. imp. 8vo. 42s. net; also a Cheaper Edition, 1 vol. 21s. net.

GAINSBOROUGH.

By Sir WALTER ARMSTRONG. Profusely Illustrated. 15s. net.

REYNOLDS.

By Sir WALTER ARMSTRONG. Profusely Illustrated. 15s. net.

RAEBURN.

By Sir WALTER ARMSTRONG. Profusely Illustrated. £5 5s. net.

SEVEN CENTURIES OF LACE.

By Mrs. T. H. POLLEN. Profusely Illustrated. Royal 4to. 30s. net. [*Second Impression.*

A GUIDE TO MODERN COOKERY.

By A. ESCOFFIER. New and Revised Edition. Demy 8vo. 12s. 6d. net.

Mr. Heinemann's Illustrated List post free.

London: WM. HEINEMANN, 21 Bedford Street, W.C.

MACMILLAN'S NEW BOOKS.

Trans-Himalaya: Discoveries and Adventures in Tibet. By Dr. SVEN HEDIN. With 388 Illustrations from Photographs, Water-colour Sketches, and Drawings by the Author, and 10 Maps. 2 vols. 8vo. 30s. net.

2ND IMPRESSION NOW READY.

In the Grip of the Nyika.

Further Adventures in British East Africa. By Lieut.-Col. J. H. PATTERSON, D.S.O., Author of "The Man-Eaters of Tsavo." With Illustrations. 8vo. 7s. 6d. net.

RALPH NEVILL.

Light Come, Light Go.

Gambling—Gamesters—Wagers—The Turf. By RALPH NEVILL. With 9 Colour Plates and other Illustrations. 8vo. 15s. net.

THOMAS HARDY.

Time's Laughingstocks and other Verses. Crown 8vo. 4s. 6d. net.

The Times.—"There have been a good many volumes of poetry published this year; but has there been one that surpasses or equals this in the indefinable quality of greatness by which human productions survive"?

The Rhythm of Modern Music.

By C. F. ABDY WILLIAMS. Extra crown 8vo. 5s. net.

A Project of Empire.

A Critical Study of the Economics of Imperialism, with special reference to the Ideas of ADAM SMITH. By J. SHIELD NICHOLSON, M.A., D.Sc., F.B.A. Professor of Political Economy in the University of Edinburgh. 8vo. 7s. 6d. net.

3RD EDITION COMPLETELY REVISED AND ENLARGED.

Introduction to Public Finance.

By Professor CARL C. PLEHN, Ph.D. Extra crown 8vo. 7s. 6d. net.

Macmillan's Guide to Egypt and the Sudan. Including a Description of the Route through Uganda to Mombasa. With 35 Maps and Plans. Sixth Edition, 5s. net.

Mexico. The Wonderland of the South. By W. E. CARSON. Illustrated. Crown 8vo. 10s. net.

NEW 6s. NOVELS.

The Education of Uncle Paul.

By ALGERNON BLACKWOOD, Author of "Jimbo," &c.

Robert Emmet: An Historical Romance. By STEPHEN GWYNN.

MACMILLAN & CO., LTD., LONDON.

NOW READY.

Royal 4to. Bound Cloth, pp. 274. Price £1 1s. net.

NATIONAL ANTARCTIC EXPEDITION,

1901-1904. MAGNETIC OBSERVATIONS.

With Map, Diagrams, and 43 Plates.

Preface by Sir ARCHIBALD GEIKIE, Pres.R.S.

PUBLISHED BY THE ROYAL SOCIETY.

Sold by HARRISON & SONS, 45 ST. MARTIN'S LANE, LONDON, W.C.

NOTICE.

The Terms of Subscription to the SATURDAY REVIEW are:—

	United Kingdom. £ s. d.	Abroad. £ s. d.
One Year	1 8 2	1 10 4
Half Year	0 14 1	0 15 2
Quarter Year ...	0 7 1	0 7 7

Cheques and Money Orders should be crossed and made payable to the Manager, SATURDAY REVIEW Offices, 10 *King Street, Covent Garden, London, W.C.*

In the event of any difficulty being experienced in obtaining the SATURDAY REVIEW, the Publisher would be glad to be informed immediately.

THIS IS PUBLISHED NOT TO INVITE SUBSCRIPTIONS BUT FOR PUBLIC INFORMATION.

Vienna Motor-Cab Co., Ltd.

Incorporated in England under the Companies (Consolidation) Act, 1908.

CAPITAL - - £200,000

Divided into 197,000 Participating Preferred Shares of £1 each, and 60,000 Deferred Shares of 1s. each.

Subject to the Directors' power before recommending any dividend to set aside out of profits such sums as they think proper as a reserve fund, the Preferred Shares will receive, in the first place, out of the divisible profits of each year, a dividend of 7 per cent. non-cumulative. 10 per cent. of the remaining profits will be put to a reserve fund, 5 per cent. of the then surplus will go to the Board of Directors as additional remuneration, and the balance will be divisible in two equal shares, one of which shares will be paid to the holders of the Preferred and one to the holders of the Deferred Shares.

67,000 Preferred Shares are reserved for Future Issue, leaving a Balance of 130,000 Participating Preferred Shares of £1 each for Subscription.

Directors.

Baron LEON DE STEENHAULT DE WAERBECK, Banker, Director of the Brussels Motor Cab Company (Limited), 83 Rue Royale, Brussels.
PAUL NAGELMACKERS, Banker, Director of the Brussels Motor Cab Company (Limited), 83 Rue Royale, Brussels.
Count ERNEST KINSKY, 10 Lenaugas·e VIII., Vienna.
HOFRATH ALPHONS VON GLASER, Director of the Compagnie Internationale des Wagons Lits, 2 Academie Strasse, Vienna.
JULES DE BORCHGRAVE, Chairman of the Company les Tramways d'Agram, 24 Rue d'Idalie, Brussels.

Bankers.

In LONDON—LONDON COUNTY AND WESTMINSTER BANK (Limited), 21 Lombard Street, E.C.
In BRUSSELS—MAGELMACKERS et FILS, 83 Rue Royale.

Solicitors.—BROAD & CO., 1 Great Winchester Street, London, E.C.

Brokers.—BIERER & CO., 8 Draper's Gardens, London, E.C.

Auditors.

DELOITTE, PLENDER, GRIFFITHS & CO., 5 London Wall Buildings, E.C.

Secretary and Registered Office.

GEO. H. JOHNSON, F.C.I.S., CAPEL HOUSE, OLD BROAD ST., E.C.

Office of the Company in Vienna.

V·I STROBACHGASSE 2.

This Company has been established for the purpose, amongst others, of carrying on the business of motor-cab proprietors, in Vienna, and of acquiring by lease, or in some other manner, license for the carrying on of such business.

The city of Vienna has at present about 2,000,000 inhabitants. It is visited yearly by nearly 500,000 people, and offers a field admirably prepared in all ways for the creation of an important motor-cab undertaking.

The takings of the motor-cabs at present in use in Vienna are, on an average, 60 kr. per day. A basis is taken on an average receipt per carriage per day of only 45 kr. Putting the net profit on each carriage at only 15 kr. per day, this for 300 carriages and 300 working days per annum gives the sum of Kr. 1,350,000. There should then remain an estimated net profit of Kr. 810,000, say, £32,400. A dividend of 7 per cent. on the 130,000 Preferred Shares now offered requires a sum of £9,100. The balance, after carrying 10 per cent. to Reserve Fund, and providing for directors' fees and further remuneration and general and administration charges, should permit of the distribution of a substantial further dividend to the holders of the Preferred Shares.

RAND MINES, LIMITED.

(INCORPORATED IN THE TRANSVAAL.)

Declaration of Dividend No. 18 and Bonus.

NOTICE IS HEREBY GIVEN that an INTERIM DIVIDEND of 100 per cent., and in addition a BONUS of 50 per cent., making in all 7s. 6d. per share, have been declared by the Board for the half-year ending 31st of December, 1909.

This Dividend and Bonus will be payable to all Shareholders registered in the books of the Company at the close of business on 31st December, 1909, and to holders of COUPON No. 13 attached to Share Warrants to Bearer.

The Transfer Books will be closed from 1st to 7th of January, 1910, both days nclusive.

The Dividend and Bonus will be payable to South African registered Shareholders from the Head Office, Johannesburg, and to European Shareholders from the London Office, No. 1 London Wall Buildings, E.C., on or about 11th of February, 1910.

HOLDERS OF SHARE WARRANTS TO BEARER are informed that they will receive payment of the Dividend and Bonus on presentation of COUPON No. 13 at the London Office of the Company, or at the Compagnie Française de Mines d'Or et de l'Afrique du Sud, 20 Rue Taitbout, Paris.

COUPONS must be left FOUR CLEAR DAYS for examination and will be payable at any time on or after 11th of February, 1910.

COUPONS and DIVIDEND WARRANTS paid by the London Office to Shareholders resident in the United Kingdom, will be subject to deduction of the English Income Tax.

COUPONS and DIVIDEND WARRANTS paid by the London Office to Shareholders resident in France, and COUPONS paid by the Compagnie Française de Mines d'Or et de l'Afrique du Sud, Paris, will be subject to a deduction on account of French Transfer Duty and French Income Tax.

Five Per Cent. Debentures.

NOTICE IS HEREBY GIVEN that the INTEREST due on the 1st JANUARY, 1910, will be paid against presentation of COUPON No. 26.

IN LONDON—At the Offices of the Company, No. 1 London Wall Buildings, E.C.

IN JOHANNESBURG—At the Offices of the Company, The Corner House.

COUPONS must be left FOUR CLEAR DAYS for examination, and may be presented at the London Office any day (SATURDAYS EXCEPTED) between the hours of Eleven and Two.

HOLDERS of the DEBENTURES are reminded that in terms of Notice given on 27th May, 1909, all Bonds outstanding are payable by the Company at £105 per centum at the London Office on 1st January, 1910, and that interest thereon will cease after 31st December, 1909.

The Debentures with Coupons Nos. 27 to 30 attached thereto should be lodged at the London Office of the Company, aud must be left FOUR CLEAR DAYS for examination.

Listing Forms may be obtained on application.

London Office, No. 1 London Wall Buildings, E.C.
14th December, 1909.

ELYSÉE PALACE HOTEL.

THE TWELFTH ANNUAL GENERAL MEETING of the Elysée Palace Hotel Company, Limited, was held on Thursday at Cannon Street Hotel, E.C., Mr. Charles Hodges, J.P. (chairman of the company), presiding.

The Secretary (Mr. Stephen Gorringe) having read the notice convening the meeting and the report of the auditors,

The Chairman said he regretted not being able to present a more satisfactory balance-sheet. They were feeling the effects of acute competition. "Another new hotel in our neighbourhood was opened, and, with those already in existence, this part of Paris seems, for the time, overdone; as a consequence, we have had less visitors both in the hotel and restaurant. Perhaps another reason is that a big wave of depression has spread over England and France, and America is only slowly recovering from her financial crisis of eighteen months ago. We find our visitors spend less per head, and seek to economise wherever possible in their daily expenditure." He trusted they had good grounds for hope that a change for the better was coming. "In the meantime we are doing our utmost to keep down expenses. Undoubtedly we shall effect a large saving in one item—namely, upkeep and maintenance. For the last five years we have been spending an average of £12,000, £4,000 of which has gone in alterations, additions, and reconstructions. This was necessary in order to keep ourselves in every way up to date. Especially has this been so in the matter of bathrooms, and I think I may now say we are thoroughly equipped, and have some 150 rooms with bath and lavatory en suite. As far as we can see, we have nothing more to do, and in the present year it is quite possible we may reduce this sum to £7,000; in other ways we hope to make savings without in any way lessening the high standard of our food and our cooking. We have also a new manager. With regard to the change of management, I may just explain that the agreement with Mr. Cesari expired at the end of last September, and on his part he did not seek a renewal, wishing for a time to take things more easily. We have been fortunate in securing the services of Mr. Ronacher as our manager. Mr. Ronacher has been for many years in charge of one of the best hotels in Europe, and comes to us with the highest credentials, and we have every confidence in his ability, feeling sure he will study the comfort of our visitors as well as the interest of our company. The trading profit, after charging £9,871 for maintenance and upkeep of the property, is £24,037, and the net profit, after deducting the fixed charges and administration expenses, and providing for the debenture stock redemption fund, is £1,001, and, with the £10,016 brought over from the previous year, shows a total credit to profit and loss account of £11,018, which the directors recommend shall be carried forward. With regard to the figures as to the profit for the year, I should like to point out that they are somewhat misleading, as we really show a profit on trading of £2,791. May I explain how I arrive at this? You will see a sum of £1,790 charged to debenture redemption account. These debentures are bought and cancelled; so that our debenture capital is reduced by that amount, and, as this process of redemption really amounts to a reserve, we are just this amount of £2,791 better off than last year. I now beg to move: 'That the report and accounts for the year ended September 30, 1909, be received and adopted and entered on the minutes.'"

Mr. Davison Dalziel, in seconding the resolution, said that the Elysée Palace Hotel had been a very successful enterprise. The company had paid in dividends during the nine years of its existence £134,146, which represented practically 47 per cent. of the capital. The directors themselves represented 80 per cent. of the entire share capital of the company.

The resolution was carried unanimously.

Army & Navy Gazette.

The leading Service Journal and Organ of the Territorial Force and Special Reserve.

PROMOTION AND THE SUPPLY OF OFFICERS.

AIRSHIPS AND AERIAL BOMBARDMENT.

(See issue of December 18.)

Published every FRIDAY in time for the Indian Mail. Price **6d.**

Offices: 22 ESSEX STREET, STRAND, W.C.

THE RE-UNION MAGAZINE.

Comprehension not Compromise.

CONTENTS FOR DECEMBER.

PRICE 6d. NET OF ALL BOOKSELLERS.

COPE & FENWICK, 16 CLIFFORD'S INN, E.C.

A copy of the full Prospectus has been filed with the Registrar of Joint Stock Companies.

The SUBSCRIPTION LIST OPENED on 17th day of December, 1909, and will CLOSE on or before 21st day of December, 1909, for both London and Country.

THE BEMBESI GOLDFIELDS OF RHODESIA

Limited.

(Incorporated under the Companies (Consolidation Act, 1908).

CAPITAL - - - - - - £100,000

Divided into 100,000 Shares of £1 each.

69,973 Shares of £1 each are now Offered for Subscription at Par,

Payable as to 1s. per Share on Application, 4s. per Share on Allotment, and the balance of 15s. per Share as and when required.

Of the 69,973 Shares now offered for subscription, 35,000 are set aside for working capital. 35,000 Shares have been underwritten.

DIRECTORS.

Colonel G. WENTWORTH FORBES, J.P., The Glebe House, Brackley, Northants, Director of the Colombian Central Railway, Chairman of London Board of the Century Insurance Company, Ltd.

J. F. A. RAWLINSON, 69 Piccadilly, W., Director of the Cartagena (Colombia) Railway, Director of Harrison, Ainslie & Co., Ltd.

Sir FREDERICK FRANKLAND, Bart., 3 Queen's Gardens, Windsor, Director of United African Explorations, Ltd.

SOLICITORS.

WELDON AND EDWARDS, Metropolitan Chambers, New Broad Street, E.C.

BANKERS.

THE STANDARD BANK OF SOUTH AFRICA, LTD., 10 Clement's Lane, Lombard Street, E.C.

LONDON AND SOUTH-WESTERN BANK, LTD., 170 Fenchurch Street, E.C., and Branches.

AUDITORS.

VINCENT AND GOODRICH, 34-6 Gresham Street, E.C.

BROKERS.

IRVING HARRISON AND CO., 3 Copthall Buildings, E.C., and Stock Exchange.

SECRETARY AND REGISTERED OFFICES (pro tem.)

A. NORMAN SMITH, A.C.A., 2 Tokenhouse Buildings, E.C.

ABRIDGED PROSPECTUS.

This Company has been formed for the purpose of acquiring, further developing, and working the properties known as the Grangebrook Mine, comprising the Basch Reef, Basch Reef Extension, Basch Reef Double Bank, and Brass Reef, all adjoining, as set out in the plan accompanying the prospectus.

The gold industry of Rhodesia has of late years made enormous strides, the last annual return being over £2,500,000 sterling, and it has produced about £10,000,000 since it was first opened up. Rhodesia bids fair to rank in the near future as one of the leading goldfields of the world, as is instanced by the attention now given by the public to Rhodesian concerns and by the enhancement in Stock Exchange values of several of the leading Rhodesian mines; among which are the Giant Mines of Rhodesia, Eldorado Banket, Enterprise, Globe and Phœnix, and others; the shares of all of which stand at very substantial premiums. This remarkable progress has largely been due to the great mineral richness of the gold-bearing strata and the gradual elimination of obstacles to development.

The Grangebrook Group of Mines occupy a central position in the Bembesi District of Southern Rhodesia, with excellent transport facilities, being situate only about eight miles north-east of the railway station of Bembesi on the north main line from Buluwayo to Salisbury, and about 35 miles north of Buluwayo.

Abundant native labour of a reliable kind is to be had in the district.

Fuel is also plentiful.

Water is to be obtained from the Bulmani River, 1¼ mile distant. It can also be obtained by sinking. A water right has already been acquired under the mining laws of Southern Rhodesia.

The area of the ground to be acquired consists of 40 reef claims, in four blocks of 10 claims, each claim measuring 150 ft. by 600 ft., with the right, under the law of the British South Africa Company, of extra lateral right of pursuit.

As may be seen from the reports and the returns issued by the Mines Office, Buluwayo, the quantity of ore worked in proving the mine during the period from June, 1906, to April, 1908, was 2,383 tons, which yielded from crushing £3,914 15s. 3d., and by the application of cyanide process £992 5s. 10d. (the cyanide process only being employed for a portion of the period, i.e., starting in January, 1908), making a total of £4,907 1s. 1d., or a yield of £2 1s. 2d. per ton. The figures are only given up to the date mentioned, as since that time a large quantity of rubble turned out during the development work has been milled, naturally decreasing the return per ton for a short period.

The smallness of the tonnage dealt with is accounted for by the fact that, during the period under review, the mining for gold was not so much an object as the development of the mine, the opening up of the reef, and the proving of the property. For the greater portion of such period there was only a 2-stamp mill employed.

The directors have obtained reports on the property from Mr. T. J. Britten, M.I.M.E., A.M.I.C.E., and Mr. J. A. Fraser, late Claims Inspector of the British South Africa Company, which can be seen at the offices of the solicitors of this Company. The information given in the prospectus relating to the properties is taken from these reports.

Mr. J. A. Fraser estimates that having regard to the amount already expended and work done in proving and developing the mine, 15 stamps can now be erected and the mine brought to a producing stage for an expenditure of £9,000.

The directors propose using the additional capital provided by this issue on further development work, and when this is far enough ahead of the mill to erect a larger number of stamps and so increase the output.

PROPERTY.—There are four blocks of claims, known respectively as the Basch Reef Block, Basch Reef Extension Block, Basch Reef Double Bank Block, and Brass Reef Block.

Each block consists of 10 claims, forming an area of 1,500 ft., along the strike of the reef, by 600 ft. deep.

The Basch Reef and Basch Reef Extension Blocks adjoin each other, which give a lateral strike to the property of 3,000 ft.

The Basch Reef Double Bank Block has been pegged on the east boundary line of the two former-mentioned blocks.

The Brass Reef Block has been pegged at an approximate angle of 45 deg. from the western boundary line of the Basch Reef Block, the south-eastern corner peg being situated near the centre of the west boundary line of the former.

The lode which is being worked and developed runs through the Basch Reef and Extension Block in a northerly direction, and dipping at an angle of 65 deg. to the east.

The formation in which this lode is encased can be traced through the entire length of the property, viz.:—3,000 ft., and outcrops of the lode itself can be found over the greater portion of the same length.

Over 1,300 ft. of driving and sinking has been done on this property to prove the width and value of the reef.

A cross-cut west to the footwall portion proves the lode to be quite 40 ft. thick. Drives on the footwall portion have been carried 64 ft. south and 41 ft. north, when prospecting cross-cuts were carried east to the hanging-wall to confirm width of lode and test its value.

The reef has some of the characteristics of a contact lode, as through the greater length of its strike it has a granitic rock for both hanging and footwall, the former giving place to schists before entering the extension block. The length of strike has a good augury for permanency in depth, and the possibility of being a contact lode improves the chances of the values continuing in depth.

Sufficient work has been done upon the property to prove the existence of a payable lode, which has a strike of fully 600 ft., with an average width of 4 ft.

The following assay returns have been received from Mr. T. J. Britten:—

No. on Plan.	Width of Lode. ft.	in.	Value dwts.	
1.	2	0	7.7	Taken in open working.
2.	2	6	4.5	" "
3.	3	0	4.0	" "
4.	4	0	15.7	Reef solid body.
5.	2	9	1.3	Reef split and broken.
6.	4	0	12.0	Reef compact body.
7.	7	0	4.5	Taken in stope drive.
8.	2	0	107.0	Taken in open working where foot lead branches off.
9.	4	0	3.2	End of south drive, 2nd level.
10.	4	0	39.5	Taken across 4 ft. of footwall of reef 40 ft. thick.
11.	4	0	6.5	Taken across 4 ft. of footwall of reef 40 ft. thick.

A sample of slimes dam assayed 3.5 dwts.

The above assays give an average of 18.8 dwts. per ton. Estimating value of same at 4s. per dwt., equal to £3 15s. 4d. per ton, and allowing working costs at 20s. per ton, this leaves a net profit of £2 15s. 4d. per ton, which on 90 tons per day for 330 days per annum, yields a net profit of £82,170 per annum.

The directors, however, base their calculations on an estimate of 11 dwts. per ton, and a 15-stamp battery being erected, with a capacity of 90 tons per day, which would give the following results:—

11 dwts. per ton, at, say, 4s. per dwt., equals £2 4s. per ton gross.

90 tons per day for 330 days per annum equals 29,700 tons per annum at £2 4s. per ton, equal to	£65,340
Less working expenses, including administration, royalties, &c., on 29,700 tons per annum, at, say, 20s. per ton	29,700
Leaving a net profit of	£35,640

sufficient to pay a dividend of 30 per cent. per annum, and carry forward over £5,000 to reserve.

Under agreement Claud Francis Hooton Brookes and Edgar Granger, both of Bembesi, in the district of Southern Rhodesia, South Africa, who are the Vendors, have agreed to sell the aforesaid group of mines to this Company for £50,000, payable as to £25,000 in cash, or partly in cash, partly in shares, and £25,000 in fully-paid shares of the Company. The agreement further provides that this Company shall pay all costs, fees, and expenses of its incorporation, the increase of its capital, the promotion of or flotation of the Company, and the transfer of the property to the Company. The agreement also provides that the Vendors have the right to nominate two directors of this Company.

For full list of contracts entered into and the information given in accordance with the Companies' (Consolidation) Act, 1908, see full prospectus.

Of the shares now offered for subscription, 35,000 have been underwritten by the Mexican and Rhodesian Finance Syndicate, Limited, for a commission, payable by the Company, of £3,500 in cash and £5,000 in fully-paid shares. Part of the shares have been sub-underwritten, but all commission in respect of such sub-underwriting is payable by the syndicate.

Copies of the memorandum and articles of association and originals or copies of the reports and agreements can be seen at the offices of Messrs. Weldon and Edwards, the solicitors to the Company, at any time during business hours on the days on which the subscription list is open.

Application for shares should be made upon the form accompanying the full prospectus, and forwarded, together with a deposit of 1s. per share, to the bankers of the Company. If no allotment is made the deposit will be returned without reduction; if the number of shares allotted be less than that applied for, the surplus paid on application will be credited to the amount due on allotment, and the excess (if any) returned.

The Company will pay a brokerage of 6d. per share on all shares allotted on application forms bearing brokers' and approved agents' stamps.

It is intended in due course to apply to the Committee of the London Stock Exchange for a settlement in the Company's shares.

Prospectuses and forms of application may be obtained of the Company's bankers, brokers, solicitors, and auditors, and at the offices of the Company.

To the Directors of THE BEMBESI GOLDFIELDS OF RHODESIA, Limited.

Please send me a copy of the prospectus issued by you, and dated 17th November, 1909, together with application form.

I enclose you cheque for £................., being 1s. per Share on .... Shares. Please reserve for me .... Shares, for which I will apply on receipt of form of Application.

Name in full..

Address ....

Description ....

THE RICCARDI PRESS BOOKS

The Riccardi Fount, designed for The Medici Society by Mr. Herbert P. Horne and here used for the first time, may successfully challenge comparison, for LEGIBILITY and BEAUTY of line alike, as well with the Designer's previous founts as with any other modern attempt to recreate the glories of the Early Printers.

"The Riccardi type, another of Mr. H. P. Horne's graceful designs, based on an Italian model of 1492, suffers at no point by comparison with the same artist's [earlier essay in the same direction]. . . . Full of character, equally free from any kind of affectation, . . . greater brilliance . . . certainly a pleasure to read. . . . [The first issue] demonstrates the beauty of the type and the perfection of the printing. . . . A very promising beginning."—*Birmingham Post.*

***** The detailed prospectus, printed in THE RICCARDI PRESS TYPES, will be sent post free on application.**

THE STORY OF GRISELDA. Being the Tenth story of the Tenth day from the "Decameron" of Boccaccio, translated by J. M. RIGG. 500 numbered copies on Batchelor hand-made paper ($9\frac{1}{2} \times 6\frac{1}{2}$), Michalet grey wrapper, 5s. net; limp vellum, with silk ties, 12s. 6d. net. Also 12 copies printed on vellum (10 for sale), bound in limp Kelmscott vellum, silk ties, 42s. net [*Ready.*

The Plates in the following are reproduced by THE MEDICI PROCESS:—

THE SONG OF SONGS WHICH IS SOLOMON'S, in the Authorised Version, with 10 Plates after the water-colour drawings by W. RUSSELL FLINT. 500 numbered copies on hand-made Riccardi paper ($10\frac{1}{2} \times 7\frac{3}{4}$), Michalet grey boards, canvas back and paper label, £2 2s. net; limp vellum, silk ties, £2 12s. 6d. net. Also 17 copies printed on vellum (15 for sale), bound in limp Kelmscott vellum, gold lettering, silk ties, with duplicate set of the Plates, mounted, in cloth portfolio, £12 12s. net. [*Ready.*

THE THOUGHTS OF THE EMPEROR MARCUS AURELIUS ANTONINUS. Translated by GEORGE LONG, with 12 Plates after the water-colour drawings by W. RUSSELL FLINT. 500 numbered copies, on hand-made Riccardi paper ($10\frac{1}{2} \times 7\frac{3}{4}$), boards, £2 12s. 6d. net; limp vellum, silk ties, £3 3s. net. Also 17 copies printed on vellum (15 for sale), bound in limp Kelmscott vellum, gold lettering, silk ties, with duplicate set of Plates, mounted, in cloth portfolio, £15 15s. net. [*Ready.*

Orders will be executed in strict rotation as received, preference being given only to Subscribers to the entire series of Riccardi Press Books. *Of the copies printed on vellum very few remain.*

***** The Original Water-colour Drawings by Mr. W. Russell Flint, mentioned above, are on Exhibition at The Medici Galleries until December 24. Admission Free on presentation of visiting card.**

THE MEDICI PRINTS

NATIONAL LOAN EXHIBITION AT THE GRAFTON GALLERIES.

The Medici Society has pleasure in announcing that by the generous permission of their owners, a small series of Medici Prints, *in the colours of the Originals*, will be issued in due course after selected pictures in this Exhibition. "*Prints like this,*" says the BURLINGTON MAGAZINE for October, 1909, "*which are at once true in general effect and will stand the test of the microscope in their details, can never be superseded.*" Subscribers to these prints may therefore be assured of possessing the most faithful replicas of these great pictures which can be obtained. They may also be assured that "*nothing of the kind so good or so cheap*" (the BURLINGTON MAGAZINE) will be obtainable otherwise than in these Medici Prints. Finally, since in consideration of the permission to reproduce these pictures, *The Society will make Special Contributions to the National Gallery Fund*, Subscribers will, incidentally, aid the prime object with which the above Exhibition has been organised.

Full particulars (illustrated) of these reproductions—*which will be executed in England by English Workers*—post free on application.

AMONG RECENT MEDICI PRINTS ARE:—

Holbein ... **The Duchess of Milan** ... **24 × 11** in. ... **17s. 6d.** net.

The same size in monochrome 5s. net. Special frame, exact replica of contemporary frame in N. G. 35s. net.

Carpaccio	... **The Vision of St. Ursula**	30s.	Botticelli	... **The Birth of Venus**	30s.
Giorgione	... **Storm Landscape**	21s.	Gainsborough	... **The Painter's Daughter** ...	15s.
Clouet	... **Elizabeth of Austria**	15s.	*Zucchero	... **Queen Elizabeth** ...	17s. 6d.
Pisanello	... **Vision of St. Eustace** ...	17s. 6d.	M. da Forli	... **The Archangel Gabriel**	17s. 6d.

(*Immediately.) Postage of all Prints 6d.; additional copies in same parcel 2d. each.

The above are a representative selection from nearly 50 Medici Prints now ready. Complete Lists post free. FRAMES suitable to each subject are a speciality of The Society. The Society's New Detailed Prospectus, with full particulars of Frames, Annual Subscription, &c., post free, 3d. stamps; or, fully illustrated, 1s. Special illustrated prospectus of some 100 "PRIMITIVES" of the Italian, German, and Flemish Schools, post free, 6d. stamps.

DRAWINGS OF ALBRECHT DÜRER. A Series of 64 Drawings, chiefly from the Albertina Library, Vienna, reproduced in facsimile collotype, including Architectural, Natural History, Botanical, Religious, Figure, and Portrait subjects. Every drawing, whether a full water-colour or otherwise, is reproduced in the *exact colour of the original.* Prices from 2s. to 15s. each; framed from 3s. 6d. each. Write for the completely Illustrated Catalogue, post free, 1s. stamps; or unillustrated, post free, 2d. stamps.

The *Times* says:—"The perfection with which this Medici process reproduces the forms, the colours, and the touch of the more precise painters, especially Dürer and Holbein, is little short of amazing." . . . "Almost disquieting in its accuracy and beauty," says the *Daily Telegraph* of the style of production. "The extraordinary fidelity to the originals," says the *Morning Post*, "can perhaps be fully appreciated only by someone who has been able to compare an original and a Medici facsimile side by side."

All lovers of Art are invited to visit the Medici Society's Galleries to inspect their EXHIBITION of "Old Masters," including Medici Prints and similar facsimile collotype reproductions in the colours of the Originals.

PHILIP LEE WARNER, Publisher to The Medici Society, Ltd., 38 Albemarle Street, W.

Printed for the Proprietors by SPOTTISWOODE & Co. LTD., 5 New-street Square, E.C., and Published by REGINALD WEBSTER PAGE, at the Office, 10 King Street, Covent Garden in the Parish of St. Paul, in the County of London.—*Saturday*, 18 *December*, 1909.

THE

SATURDAY REVIEW

OF

POLITICS, LITERATURE, SCIENCE, AND ART.

No. 2,826 Vol. 108. 25 December 1909. [REGISTERED AS A NEWSPAPER.] 6d.

CONTENTS.

We beg leave to state that we decline to return or to enter into correspondence as to rejected communications; and to this rule we can make no exception. Manuscripts not acknowledged within four weeks are rejected.

NOTES OF THE WEEK.

We suppose the oratory of General Elections always is bad, and always will be. Speakers who are at all fastidious, and cultivate niceties of phrase and thought, are unheard in the hubbub, or they hoard their good things against a quieter and favouring occasion. But has any election within the last twenty-five years been quite so crude and commonplace in the vast bulk of its talk as this election? We cannot recall one. Babel must have been better than this election; at Babel at least were many languages, whereas here we have not even that attraction. Who but an ignoramus, or a man professionally engaged in party politics, would sit down to read with zest more than two or three of the speeches made this week—say Lord Curzon's, Mr. Asquith's, or, for lighter stuff, Lord Willoughby de Broke's?

There is one good thing about all this bad oratory—it serves to show how hollow is the pretence that this is a mighty historic struggle. We must all know by now that it is just a very harsh and exasperating party quarrel. This is not to deny the importance of the struggle: indeed, it is by far the most important party fight of our time, and any Unionist or Imperialist who withholds his support from Mr. Balfour in January will be false to the country. That is clear and certain. But how egregious to affect, as many Liberals are affecting, that this is the beginning of another 1640 or 1688! There were great figures on those stages, great figures on both sides who were ready to give their lives to the causes they held just; that is not quite the same as lending one's carriage to bring up an old-age pensioner.

Lord St. Aldwyn has written to explain why he did not speak in the Lords' debate on the Budget. Nothing that he could have said would have altered the decision of his side, and he did not want to argue against his own friends. He dislikes the Budget, but he does not think it is Socialism. But if no speech or statement by Lord St. Aldwyn could have availed then, how in the world can any speech or statement by him avail now? If it has any effect whatever, it can only be an effect hurtful to his side—and Lord St. Aldwyn is anxious not to hurt his own side! Lord St. Aldwyn quite out-Cromers Lord Cromer. The fact is subtle lines of conduct at a time like this are fatal.

It must be either yes or no, and it is because they have thoroughly understood this that the Peers are on the whole doing so well in their adventures through the country. Their blunt, hard English is the sort of speech any man may understand. It is full of that strong sporting flavour which is relished by a great number of English people of the middle and working classes. Some of the Liberal papers have tried to make capital out of the fact that there are horse-racing Peers. We should have thought that a strong recommendation to the average English working man. He loves a horse-race. Everybody knows that when he buys the "Star" the first column he turns to is the racing column. Coe has done far more for the Radical press than ever cocoa did.

We would not say that all the peers who are speaking speak brilliantly. But even the least able of them could point to some ancestor of his who did good service for his country; and how many of the obscure talkers, hired talkers largely, who are speaking everywhere to-day, could make a like claim? After all there is something in family, though to-day we go in much more for money. A man may rightly get some credit through his forbears, though not so much as in the dignified and stable England of a hundred years, even fifty years, ago. There are things we do not want to borrow from Japan, but the veneration which the Japanese people have for their ancestors might be a very good thing for this country to-day.

Mr. Blatchford reminds one of Mr. Secretary Bashford. He scrambles out nightly, we suppose, on to the roof of the "Clarion" office and looks eagerly in the direction of the North Sea for a sign of fire. Mr. Blatchford is a pretty shrewd judge of naval matters, for, finding his own galley a bit leaky just now, he is for getting as quick as he can contrive into another. But perhaps the less other galleys—certainly Unionist and Imperial galleys—have to do with him the better. He is a useless deadweight as passenger, and as rower we may depend upon it he would soon demoralise the rest of the crew—that may be his game.

For exquisite literary form in electioneering the 'Daily News" excels just now. It is publishing a series of sketches describing the misadventures of a Duke. He is accursed by a tenant called Onions, who lives like "a pig in a pigsty", and is one of the "chattels" of the Duke. The word "chattels" is dangerous: surely it recalls a case which we fancy the "Daily News" is very, very anxious to forget. Were not the children of the slaves of San Thomé described as the chattels of the planters?

Why don't people take Mr. Asquith seriously on the question of Home Rule? Here is an issue that may be said to dwarf every other—one that has divided politicians into Unionists and the other sort from the moment it was raised. Yet a Liberal Whip denies his leader, and little astonishment is shown. Everybody, in fact, is taking the thing quite quietly. Liberals themselves seem to be trying to ignore it. The only people, apparently, who care are the Western Scots, who cannot forget their Ulster kinsmen, and the Nationalists themselves. Perhaps it is that all of it is so stale. It is the cry of the wolf that was never there. It is well to remember, however, that the animal did arrive at last, when nobody believed in him any longer.

Anyhow, the Nationalists are rallying to the old cry. Mr. Asquith has succeeded in buying his votes, paying liberally for them in paper. The transaction seems to indicate despair. Is it just a desperate bid for a working majority? Or is there here a light-hearted raining of golden promises which the giver knows he will not have the chance to redeem? Maybe; but Mr. Redmond is loud in anticipation. The Lords are to go, and the infamous Act of Union is to be torn and trampled underfoot at last. Unionists should really show more interest in the matter; though, of course, it is very difficult to be interested in so many things at once.

The Prime Minister is not happy in principles. Not long ago he defended the export of capital, and in his Birkenhead speech on Tuesday he repeated the old dogma that an import duty cannot produce revenue and at the same time assist the home producer: "If the imports come in to produce the revenue, it follows that the home producer is not protected", etc. The British exporter must cut his own prices, and often his wages, to hold the foreign market against increased duties, thereby paying foreign taxes out of British industry, necessarily putting the foreign producer at an advantage; but Mr. Asquith does not believe in the foreigner doing this. Party needs produce queer effects even on clear minds.

Then Mr. Asquith wanted to know how South Africa could gain under Preference. Solemnly he conjured up grave consequences from discrimination against South Africa, whose wool we could not protect in any way, being a raw material. But we have not all forgotten what Dr. Jameson told Mr. Asquith at the Imperial Conference. The answer to Mr. Asquith's question was ready enough: "Give us a preference on our wines". This did not even necessitate putting on a new import tax; all that was asked was to lower the existing duty in favour of South Africa as against France and Germany. But Mr. Asquith's free-trade rectitude would have none of it. The principle was the thing! But Dr. Jameson showed plainly enough what Tariff Reformers can do when they have the chance. Neither would the gain to South Africa be a small thing. Not, at least, if we are to believe the South African delegates, who ought to know nearly as well as Mr. Asquith.

Lord Curzon has again come off. His speech at Burnley has freshness. How sadly it has worn off nearly all the politicians' words already! No wonder, after nine months at S. Stephen's. Why, then, was not Lord Curzon's speech reported in full? If one picks out the "Times" as a defaulter, it is because it is the one paper to which one may generally look, safely, to find the actual words a man said. But the report of Lord Curzon was largely lacunæ filled with stars. We prefer Lord Curzon's own scintillations. Where on earth is the sense of filling the paper with snippets of every Tom, Dick and Harry among the speakers, and not giving what was said by the one man, or two, whose words one has the smallest desire to read?

Tariff Reform takes firmer hold of the people every day as its meaning becomes better known. And what Tariff Reform might have failed to do unaided, the Budget has assisted it to accomplish. Moderate men like Lord Durham join the Unionists in sheer despair of Radical policy. Employers of labour, life-long believers in Free Trade, are sorrowfully finding facts too much for them. Last week it was Sir John Turner of Nottingham; this week it is Sir Richard Garton of Battersea. Sir Richard started a factory in Mr. Burns' constituency to compete with American imports. He has succeeded so far that he now employs 400 or 500 men. Then America began to dump, and to save his men, with the hundreds of women and children dependent on them, Sir Richard Garton now sees there is only one way. He has become a Tariff Reformer.

There is no suspicion of politics in the decision of the House of Lords on the trade union case of Osborne v. the Amalgamated Society of Railway Servants. Lord Shaw, Radical of Radicals, agrees with Lord Halsbury, Lord Macnaghten, and Lord James that trade unions cannot levy contributions on their members to pay for representation in Parliament. To these may be added a unanimous Court of Appeal, in which sat Lord Justice Fletcher Moulton, very comparable with Lord Shaw. The decision is not so surprising as the one which played so important a part in the election of 1906; but it is not without importance in the election that is now pending. Most of the unions have money which they cannot now spend on elections, as an indefinite number of persons are entitled to demand back what they have paid. The Labour party will be hampered now and in future. Voluntary contributions may fail them, and they have not the ghost of a chance to make good by State payment of members.

Messrs. Burt and Fenwick have scored over the Labour party in the Northumberland Divisions of Morpeth and Wansbeck. They at almost one stroke also gain a victory over that party by the trade union decision. Mr. Richard Bell makes up the trio, and no man is more satisfied with the defeat of the union to which he is secretary than Mr. Bell himself. All three resisted the attempt to make them sign on with the Labour party; and Mr. Bell forfeited his seat for his contumacy. We can congratulate Mr. Bell on his revenge; but we are sorry that the Labour party in Northumberland, by caving in to the Liberals, after all their swagger, have lessened the chance of Unionists being returned for those Northumberland Divisions.

There is good reason for believing that the New South Wales coal strike is almost over. Christmas will very likely see the trams and railways at work as usual, and the risk of Sydney once more being in darkness gone by. What has happened has shown that the machinery of the Industrial Disputes Act was insufficient to make either employers or men submit their disputes to arbitration. The Government has had to strengthen the means at its disposal by passing a further Act against both; and this Act has, it is said, caused the strike congress to dissolve. The Western miners have resumed work, and the Southern miners have decided to follow suit. The result is that they submit to the Wages Board under the Industrial Disputes Act for a decision on their dispute. This Act has not altogether failed under a very excessive strain, and it allows the hope that in future it will prove equal to prevent as it has to arrest a strike.

"If this country is to remain a white man's country we must stand by the British flag." So says Mr. Maclean in the Dominion Parliament. The Premiers of British Canada have been saying the same; this is the reaction from Sir Wilfrid Laurier's French Canadianism, which would have a separatist fleet, probably some thousands of miles from where the freedom of Canada would have to be defended in the hour of need. There is to be a Canadian fleet, and the question is whether it will be a unit in the imperial power or a sign to attract an enemy without the capacity to repel him.

Mr. Herbert Gladstone is to go to South Africa. All doubt on that matter is now set at rest—or rather all hope of his not going is killed. His qualifications for service abroad seem to be that (1) he has not been a success at home, and has been a conspicuous failure at the Home Office; (2) he is the son of his father, and so his appointment will gratify Dutch sentiment, recalling Majuba; (3) he will be an irritant to the loyal English settler who does not love the new Boer régime. Fancy Mr. Asquith denouncing the principle of heredity after this! By any other name what sweetness or savour of any kind would Mr. Gladstone have?

The Indian elections under the reform scheme are turning out very much as might have been expected. The ill wind that has got into the heads of the Bengali leaders is blowing good to their Mohammedan rivals. In Bengal the regulations required that the representatives in Council of the various Local Boards should be members of the Boards they would represent. This reasonable condition excluded the Calcutta wire-pullers and carpet-baggers who have no stomach for the spade work of self-government. According to Mr. Banerjea it reduced the reforms to a "meaningless sham". Mr. Ramsay Macdonald then, following Mr. Hardie, described it as "an insult to the educated community". So the word went out to boycott the elections.

In the Deccan the extreme men have prevailed over the moderates—owing to sympathy with rabid, seditious journalists. This feeling has been further shown in the murder of Mr. Jackson, the Collector of Nasik, not for any act of his own but as the head of the district administration. Even more than the attempt on Lord Minto's life it shows the folly and futility of the policy which would reward sedition with political concessions, sweetly oblivious of criminal organisations. The high-placed heads of these conspiracies must be well known. But will the outrage convince Lord Morley that deportations are even more necessary in the Western Presidency than in Bengal and would be not less effective?

Everybody will watch the new King of the Belgians with interest. He is well gifted to do what lies before him, but his has been wary walking up to the present, and his opinion on several important matters is still to seek. Of one or two things we may be fairly sure. King Albert has not traversed the Congo in spite of dissuasion for nothing. Nor has he passed through the Military School and attended daily at the Foreign Office to no purpose. He has already shown interest in social questions, and Queen Elizabeth has humanised him. Altogether the only fear seems to be that his virtues are many enough to undo him. He seems to have trained himself as carefully as Richard Feverel was trained.

The Friedjung trial has ended unfortunately for the Austrian Government. Dr. Marcovitch having proved his alibi, Dr. Friedjung admitted that the minutes of the Slovenski Jug were forgeries, and the case collapsed. This result is due to the public spirit of some distinguished Serbs who volunteered to give evidence in the prejudiced atmosphere of a Viennese court. Sympathy will be felt for Dr. Friedjung, who is a writer of repute and who has been the victim of the stupidity of Foreign Office officials. But a trained historian ought to detect clumsy forgeries even when bureaucrats accept them, and the learned doctor must bear the ridicule he has brought upon himself. How far Count Aehrenthal and certain very exalted personages were deceived we do not know and are not likely to learn.

Englishmen who visit Rome must be careful when they write about it. There was one of our visitors there who did not know this, and he has raised the devil. Signor Nathan the Syndic has been crushing him ever since. The Englishman said very little—simply that he did not like modern Rome, which, he thought, was being spoilt in course of being improved. But this was enough for Signor Nathan, who has stormed and sneered heavily from that time. The artful fellow is making a national case of it. In good truth Signor Nathan's real bugbears are among his own countrymen—the artists and archæologists who are working to preserve the monuments of the city. He is only too glad of this occasion to work off a little of his old bile, and to inveigle some of the more misguided of the Italian newspapers into blind heroics.

Mr. Roosevelt has been made a member of the French Academy of Moral and Political Sciences, and will be received by the Institute on his return from East Africa. The honour, it appears, is merited by the "originality" of Mr. Roosevelt's "literary output". So runs the official bill. It is quaint, but is it a true one? The French journalists, unfortunately, rather give things away. The Mr. Roosevelt who is being honoured is not really a literary person at all. He is the "personification of Anglo-Saxon energy" and the "apostle of national idealism". Anyhow, we rather wonder at the French Institute. Can that body really afford to let itself down in this way?

At last Copenhagen has given its verdict, and Dr. Cook has gone out. There is no doubt as to what the University thinks of him. It does not merely say that the papers do not prove his claim. It says that these papers are lacking in clear information to an "inadmissible" degree. In other words it is useless for them to pretend to be those of a genuine scientific explorer. The judgment of the University is all the more conclusive because it so dearly wanted to believe in the man it had honoured and fêted in the days when Peary and Cook were both in the running. The judgment is, in fact, a frank admission of error on the part of a learned body. Perhaps that body will proceed along the bitter path of contrition still further, and apologise to Commander Peary. Anyhow, Commander Peary has come through it all with the delicious right to say "I told you so". Meantime, we wonder what has become of those calculations of Captain Loose that were going to prove so much.

Dr. Cook has had a wonderful career. There were some who doubted him from the very first; but he was always so modest for an American, and so plausible. Though his story and his photographs of the Mount McKinley expedition were questioned at the time of their publication, yet he would probably have been safe had he been satisfied with this one achievement. Grasping the Pole at a most sensational moment, he fell at once under a criticism that he has never for a moment been able to bear. At this date the pleasantest thing we can do is to pretend with Mr. Wack, his former attorney, that he is "an object of sympathy"—the victim of hallucination. It is a tall notion; but then we are dealing in things Transatlantic.

Mr. Justice Ridley has a reputation for doing most things in the wrong spirit and the wrong way. Probably no judge but he would try on his own account to limit counsel to speeches of the length he himself thinks right. Any of them would resent the attempt, as one of them did a few days ago. Closure in Parliament is bad enough, but closure of the Bar is positively dangerous. Mr. Justice Ridley may be right in saying that long speeches account largely for the courts being behind with their work; but if the closure is to be introduced, it must not be at Mr. Justice Ridley's caprice.

Copyright law is one of those things that never seem to get settled on a satisfactory basis. The Committee that has reviewed the subject has now reported its recommendations. The most important of these is the proposal to extend the protection of literary copyright from life and seven years or forty-two years, if that term is longer, to life and fifty years. Musical copyright is to be protected from the mechanical music-box makers of all sorts, and these are to be protected from each other. In future, we imagine, the street pianos will be limited to the performance of the classics.

Choreographic and other dumb-show entertainments, it is also suggested, should have more protection. There may be danger in the domestic charade, and imitation of popular actors and actresses will be at the risk of the amateur reciter: a welcome protection to the public. Perhaps the most curious recommendation is that architects shall be protected from any copying of the buildings they design. There will be trouble on many building estates unless, as they ought to be, the original architects, if there are any, should be too much ashamed of themselves to claim. Why does not the Committee recommend retaliation against the American law requiring the setting up in the States of every English book desiring copyright in America?

Who cared about politics in Battersea last Monday evening? Not Mr. Burns at any rate. The ferocious fire at Messrs. Arding & Hobbs' made a fireman of him for some hours; and, by way of addressing his meeting, he dismissed it as a mark of respect for those who had lost their lives. Mr. Burns is not at all popular just now with his old friends; but, if anything can wring a vote from an opponent, Mr. Burns should have made some headway that night. The old shirt-sleeve days were back again, and he toiled and grew black with the best of them. Mr. Burns is a man, take him for all in all. Though Mr. Burns was the centre figure of the occasion, he was not its hero. There was an assistant who lost his life by sending two women down the escape before him. Gratitude is due to a man who can dare so much, not simply because of the lives he saves, but because such an act smacks the cynic in the face. Man, after all, is more than a political animal.

The price of turkeys is up. In this Christian country the great fact about Christmas for the average good citizen will undoubtedly be the dearness of turkeys. Has Dickens vulgarised Christmas in England for all time? In the great Christian feast he taught a not unwilling people to keep their eyes fixed on their plates. The Christmas of Dickens might perfectly well be a pagan festival. Its kindly joviality, untempered by any spiritual touch, was after all hardly more than a decent Saturnalia—the Mid-Victorian version of Christianity. We are a little better now. Frank Christianity and frank paganism is better than respectable compromise.

THE PEERS' PROTAGONIST.

If the House of Lords is dead, or as good as dead, the Radical touch seems to have made their dry bones exceedingly alive. The traditional caricature—the languid gentleman with a drawl and a coronet—will have to be given up. Soon so many of "the people" will have seen a peer that it will be no good to represent him as anything but lively, plucky and full of "go". The anti-Lord party have made a mistake. They should not have drawn the peers. While they remained quietly in their places or spoke only in the House of Lords, it was pretty safe to talk of them as bloated and tyrants and fools and effeminate, as profligate boys or worn-out old men. But now that game is up. The people have seen for themselves and know that this sort of talk is, frankly, "rot". More irritating than any to the Liberal wirepullers is Lord Curzon. Lord Lansdowne they could at least explain. Only the plain fools amongst Liberals ever supposed that the Lords could not produce a statesman who could command polished language and play with perfect finish the part of grand seigneur. Lord Lansdowne may have been a difficulty, but he was a natural difficulty. But what was to be said of a peer who could speak on a platform as well as any man in the House of Commons; who could talk to the people as straight and true as any vulgar demagogue; who could throw as much life and blood into his words as any plebeian, whether the pantaloon type or the highwayman? It is easy to see how annoying our Liberal friends find Lord Curzon's speeches from the large attention they give them. No one ever says he is pleased with an opponent's speech unless he finds it very difficult to answer. When you cannot answer a man, the obvious thing to do is to say he has given you nothing to answer. Lord Curzon has given Mr. Asquith nothing to answer! Is there nothing to be said on the question, What are Liberals going to put in the place of the House of Lords? Do they want the Lords to be reformed or not? Do they want a one- or two-Chamber system? What have they to say to Lord Curzon's analysis of the personnel of the House of Lords? Is it true or untrue that the Lords contain a larger proportion of distinguished men than the House of Commons? Is it true or untrue that in nearly every department of public work—even in finance, which no Unionist has ever said was not primarily work for the Commons—the Lords contain experts and in most departments better experts than the Commons? Is it true or not true that the peers do their local work, especially in the country, on the whole in model fashion; that the peer is of solid value as a centre of social life in his rural neighbourhood? It would be easy, of course, for Mr. Asquith and his friends readily to answer to every one of these questions "untrue". But happily in most Liberal leaders' constitutions there is not enough uric acid to allow this. The facts about the peers under all these heads are too well known for it to be safe for their assailants to take on Lord Curzon. All they can do in answer is to harp on the exception. They might, for instance, put forward Lord Portsmouth, the ex-Liberal Minister, whom Mr. Asquith removed, as a failure in his social capacity locally, an unpopular peer whom his countryside did not regard with excessive respect. They might instance Lord Beauchamp, the disastrous failure as a Colonial Governor. And of course Lord Clanricarde and the late Lord Ailesbury and the late Lord Anglesea are always exhibited. It does not matter that they are "late". Liberals make the best, that is the worst, of the bad examples, and no doubt some of their hearers take these black sheep as fair specimens of the flock. But more do not. It is pretty obvious that these are the exceptions, and people are apt to infer—most illogically, no doubt—that exceptions prove the rule. One is not surprised that Mr. Asquith and Mr. Churchill say they are pleased with Lord Curzon's speeches.

Mr. Asquith touches but one of Lord Curzon's points, and his answer is not argument but laughter, forced. Lord Curzon had said the House of Lords, being unaccountable to popular election, better represents the continuing permanent feeling of the nation than the House of Commons. This Mr. Asquith thinks good enough for a romance. It is a great deal too good for nine romances out of ten; for a good romance should be truth well put. A little examination will show Lord Curzon's statement to be true. It is plain that the House of Commons after an election never represents the average feeling of the country. No one pretends that the country is usually, or often, so Radical as it was in 1906; nor so Conservative as it was in 1895. But the House of Commons remains during the whole time of the Parliament nearly at the point of party heat at which it came into being; so it soon ceases to be representative of public political feeling averaged over a number of years. And the House of Commons acts purely as a party machine: not a single Bill introduced by a Leader of Opposition would ever be passed. Naturally enough, he never introduces one. But the House of Lords, though its members are in party overwhelmingly Conservative, passes a great number of Liberal Bills. Of the Bills introduced by a Liberal Government it passes the vast majority. It probably passes quite as many proportionately as the relative predominance of Liberals in the country at the moment justifies. Suppose the coming election, as everyone expects, shows a considerable reduction in the Liberal majority, a rule-of-three sum will show that the Lords in their treatment of Liberal Bills have been more Liberal than was the general feeling of the country; yet not so Liberal as the House of Commons. It will have been nearer to the actual state of national feeling than the Commons. Worked out over a period, say, of fifty years, we believe Lord Curzon's case would be proved. Mr. Asquith's way of arguing is rough and ready, indeed; it certainly is not scientific. Because there is a Liberal majority in the House of Commons and a Tory majority in the House of Lords, therefore the Lords cannot represent the country. It would make a considerable sum in arithmetic to compute the number of fallacies such an argument contains. One assumption alone vitiates it: that a majority on one side or the other side in the Commons always signifies the general feeling of the public; also, the assumption that the country is always either wholly Liberal or wholly Conservative, as the Government is, but which the country in fact never is. Mr. Asquith wants the House of Lords always to mirror the House of Commons. This Lord Curzon never said it did, and would never wish it to do, we are very sure, for it would then be superfluous. In its party composition the House of Lords is of course more Conservative than the permanent feeling of the country, but in its acts and character as a House of Parliament, which is the important point, it agrees with that permanent feeling much better than the House of Commons.

It is strange that Mr. Asquith should again trot out—the hackneyed phrase meets the hackneyed point—the charge that the Lords had thrown out the Budget simply because it was an obstacle to Tariff Reform. If the country wants the Budget, what will Tariff Reform gain by a few weeks' delay? If the country does not want it, were the Lords opposing the electors in referring it to them? There is the true gravamen of the case against the Lords. They compelled the Budget to take the risk of popular appeal. This Mr. Asquith and his Government did not want. The bird they thought they had in the hand was being turned by the Lords into the bird in the bush.

Lord Curzon's unkindest cut was his challenge to the Liberals to say what they mean to put in the place of the Lords. Mr. Asquith says he is a two-chamber man; so he cannot mean indefinitely to leave his second chamber in a state of suspended animation—his present plan. Is he going to put in its place an elective chamber? And who is to elect it? He does not say; he would avoid the plight of the wretched man who told Lord Curzon the electors should be the same as the electors of the Commons A second chamber either a duplicate of the first and so merely redundant, or at variance with it and, as springing from the same popular source, equally authoritative: hence an eternal deadlock! Is this Liberal statesmanship? But Mr. Asquith has another difficulty before him. His extreme Left, the most powerful section of the party, is all for one chamber only. They see no fun in downing the Lords and then putting up in the Lords' place someone else who certainly will not be they. Mr. Asquith is asking the country to take a leap without knowing and without thinking where the leap will land it. It is the last thing any Liberal leader wants to think about. Out of the frying-pan, is their cry, and take your chance of the fire! Lord Curzon unkindly brings the elector too near to the fire for the jump to be pleasant. We hope Lord Curzon will have the strength to bring him nearer yet to it until a little scorching does the desired work of prevention. He will do it, if any man.

THE PAYMENT OF LABOUR MEMBERS.

THE decision of the House of Lords as to the payment of members of Parliament by the trade unions comes, as the decision in the Taff Vale Railway case did, when a General Election is near. In 1906 the decision that trade unions could be sued for damages and their funds made liable was one of the effective causes of the Liberal victory. It united the trade unions and many workmen without them in the demand for an Act which should reverse the decision. Such an Act was passed in the first session of the new Parliament. The case of the Amalgamated Society of Railway Servants and Osborne is in itself of far more political colour than the Taff Vale, but its influence on the elections will not be so important. The case itself arose out of a schism amongst trade unionists as to their compulsory contributions to the payment of members pledged to vote according to the directions of the Labour party, to whose constitution they had to submit. The party who objected to this compulsion has won the victory, and many Liberal trade unionists with representative men like Messrs. Burt, Fenwick, and Bell welcome it as much as the many trade unionist working men do who are also Conservatives. There can be no united demand for an Act to reverse this decision, and if a Bill were brought before Parliament to enable trade unionists to make compulsory levies on their members, the opposition would be as strong from trade unionist ranks as from any quarter. It is possible even that, apart from the future effect the judgment may have, its immediate result will be to hamper the candidature of Labour men at the approaching elections. Trade unionists in 1906 poured their contributions into the election chest without stint. Now it is probable that members who hold the opinions of Mr. Osborne, the trade union official who raised this question, will not only stop their contributions but demand back what they have already paid. It is assumed they will do this, and already Mr. Bell, the Secretary of the Amalgamated Society of Railway Servants, has sent circulars to the members stating that a sum of over £4000 belonging to the Parliamentary Fund will be distributed in consequence of the decision. The Executive is anxious to know what proportion of the subscribers may want their money back, and what proportion will be willing to allow it to be transferred to the Railwaymen's Parliamentary Association Fund.

The compulsory levies have hitherto masked the real feelings of the contributors. Many trade unionists may object not merely to their parliamentary representatives subscribing the constitution of the Labour party, but a considerable number may also object altogether to paying for any variety of member of Parliament. This uncertain question is raised just at the beginning of the election; and it cannot be known until after the event how much the uncertainty as to funds will affect the success of the Labour party candidates. The Labour party leaders sanguinely believe that the undeniable success they have had in bringing over the trade unions to their programme points to the sufficiency of voluntary subscriptions to see them through their difficulties during this election. They are certainly not so sure of the future as to rely solely on them, and they are talking of an alteration of the law. We have mentioned the difficulty of their getting the levies made compulsory. The other plan would be legislation for paying salaries to all members of Parliament. Trade unions are valuable organisations within their proper sphere of duties; but it cannot be believed that in order to enable them to return members of their own the general aversion from payment of members of Parliament will be sunk. The nation does not care for trade unions to that extent. Rather a curious point arises as to the reliance on voluntary subscriptions. Suppose the Labour party got all the money it wants to pay members, would it be legal for members so paid to sit in Parliament? What law could we say they were breaking by doing so, and what would be the procedure by which they could be restrained? All that the House of Lords decides is that members of trade unions are still members and cannot be deprived of their benefits merely because they refuse to pay levies for members of Parliament. If the unions attempt it, they will be restrained. What would be the similar process by which they could be restrained if they assumed the power of sending members pledged to their constitution under the system of voluntary contributions? Taking the judgments of Lord Shaw in the House of Lords, and Lords Justices Moulton and Farwell in the Appeal Court as guides, it would appear that this system too would be illegal. The constitutional reasons they give for holding this apply universally against returning members bound beforehand to act so and so, whether they are paid for by compulsory or voluntary levies. And this is not a law laid down for trade unions alone, but for any association whatever. This, however, is precisely the very important point which the House of Lords has not decided. It was sufficient to settle the case that had arisen to decide that the trade unions, as bodies acting under statutes, had no power to order levies for payment of parliamentary representatives. The question, therefore, still remains undecided whether, if the attempt is made to run the Labour party policy by voluntary subscriptions, the law can be invoked to prevent it. Who would be the parties aggrieved, and how they would proceed to stop it, is a question which neither the House of Lords judgment nor the separate opinions of Lord Shaw and the two Lords Justices enable us to answer. All we can say is that there seems still a probability that we have not heard the last of the great trade union cases which in recent years have added such well-known decisions to the law books.

Another important question of public policy is suggested by the judgment. According to it trade unions cannot expand their functions in a natural course of development. They are bound down by Acts of Parliament which leave them no room for growth. The presumption is that when they contemplate a new step it will be against the statute. Now this is not the way in which British institutions have been wont to establish themselves. Under the common law an organisation that has evolved a convenient custom has been presumed to be acting legally, and if the custom has been widely spread but found liable to abuse, the ordinary way has been to control it by Parliament. But in our day the process is reversed. We bring in Parliament in the first place and attempt by the minutest regulations to predestinate the embryo body to a future which we cannot foresee—a futile assumption of omnipotence without the possession of omniscience. More than this, we are threatened with an attempt to strangle the political constitution itself in the fetters of statute. Lord Shaw expressed very forcibly the objections to sterilising an organisation like the trade unions and prohibiting them from any growth by an inflexible statutory constitution. But the British Constitution is the very type of organisations which have arisen and grown under the freedom of the common law. Yet it is his party which proposes to do for this Constitution what he protests against as to trade unions. Liberals will doubtless back up the unions, while they clamour for the written constitution which is to stop all development in the future along the historic lines on which the Constitution has hitherto grown. We do not doubt that in this case the attempt will be defeated; but the prevailing tendency to turn every living institution into a lifeless automaton pulled by the strings of an Act of Parliament is unhealthy. This decision is objectionable on this account. It would have been unimpeachable if the ground for it had been that taken by Lord Shaw and the Lords Justices: the ground of the constitutional independent position of the member of Parliament; not the vicious one of the statutes.

THE LIBERALS AND THE NAVY.

MR. ASQUITH'S emphatic but ineffectual assurance at Liverpool that all is well with the Navy will not quiet national fears. On the contrary, it is calculated to raise even graver misgivings than his silence at the Albert Hall. The Government speak with so many voices that even their friends find it hard not to mistrust them. To-day Mr. Asquith asks the country to take his word for it that the Navy is in a position to maintain not only this year "but in the years that lie before us" British supremacy at sea, "the integrity of our shores, the protection of our commerce, the inviolability of our Empire". In March last, when Mr. McKenna startled the House of Commons and the nation by his revelations as to the progress of Germany, Mr. Asquith took a very different tone. He said we could no longer take to ourselves the comforting reflection that we have the advantage of speed in shipbuilding. What has happened in the interval to warrant his oracular confidence that the Navy now and henceforth will be able to discharge the duties he summarised so admirably? If the Government have been able to make good the ground lost, if they have regained the advantage as to which we could no longer comfort ourselves, they have indeed done wonders. But where is the evidence? We do not find it in the Estimates or in the number of new ships which are supposed to be in hand. In Mr. McKenna's opinion if in 1912 we have twenty Dreadnoughts to Germany's seventeen we shall have margin enough of security. Mr. Macnamara declares that all bogeys may be laid to rest because we shall have twenty Dreadnoughts to Germany's thirteen. What is happening in the German yards we do not and cannot know; it is quite clear the Government do not know, because the First Lord of the Admiralty suggests a possible seventeen German Dreadnoughts, whilst the Parliamentary Secretary says there will only be thirteen. On the eve of a General Election there is much talk of new ships being laid down, but with the four years' record of the Government to go upon we know pretty well what that amounts to. What guarantee, then, have we that the purblind policy exposed by Mr. H. H. Mulliner has been abandoned?

Neither the Admiralty nor the Government can be trusted for an instant if there is a word of truth in what Mr. Mulliner has said, and so far not one word has been called in question, though many irrelevant comments have been made. Here we have a plain, straightforward statement from an individual that he discovered for himself in 1906 what the authorities should have known, and that he placed the facts at their disposal two and a half years before they woke up to their significance. Or, in the interests of a cheeseparing policy misnamed economy, were those facts suppressed till they could no longer be withheld? According to Mr. Asquith, the Government were informed in November 1908. According to Mr. Mulliner, Mr. McKenna says that Ministers knew all about the extraordinary preparations which the Germans were making in 1906. Either way the case is alarming. If the Admiralty knew and did not inform the Government the assumption can only be that the permanent officials were fearful of the consequences of upsetting Ministerial equanimity, conduct which is assuredly not characteristic of permanent officials. If the Government knew, as Mr. McKenna suggests, they are traitors. Their assurances during 1906-7-8 have been shown to be worthless. Are their assurances in the last days of 1909 of more value? Mr. McKenna tells us to-day that we may sleep confidently in our beds. He echoes Sir John Fisher's "sleep quietly" speech in November 1907. When Sir John Fisher ridiculed all bad dreams as to Germany's preparations Mr. Mulliner's letter to the Admiralty explaining how the Krupp extensions had placed Germany in a position to beat "the whole capacity of Great Britain" was already eighteen months old.

If anything were calculated to give the country nightmare, surely it is the revelation that such high assurances are the merest claptrap, if not something worse. German energy in naval construction whilst Mr. Mulliner's invaluable information was secreted in someone's pigeon-hole in Whitehall is common knowledge. Are we to take it that in the last year the Germans have been idle whilst the British Government have been making heroic attempts to repair their self-confessed blunder? The crux of the Prime Minister's statement at Liverpool lies of course in the words "the years that lie before us". At the moment the Navy may not be wholly inadequate, but the effective life of ships, especially ships of war, is short. A year or two hence a considerable number of the vessels now in the fighting line will be obsolescent if not obsolete. Whatever else they may pretend, the Government can lay no claim to have maintained the two-Power standard. They abandoned the Cawdor programme, which provided a minimum of security, and we shall soon find ourselves, so far at any rate as the biggest and newest battleships are concerned, not with a two-Power but a one-Power standard. The least we should do now is to lay down two keels for every one laid down by Germany—if, that is, we can find out, and are prepared to use our knowledge when we have it, how many she puts in hand. That is the only formula of safety. A large naval loan may be necessary. Germany does not hesitate to raise loans in order to build a navy that may challenge the supremacy which Mr. Asquith says is now safe, and in finance as in naval matters Germany is showing us the way.

THE NEW KING OF THE BELGIANS.

THE new King of the Belgians is little known to statesmen or diplomatists, but well known to the great mass of the people, and he has their confidence. His reign opens brightly on that side at least. As heir-apparent it would have been less than useless for him to push himself to the fore in public. Instead of meddling with affairs he could not influence he chose the wise part of a student's life, surrounded himself with professors, and buried himself for years in books. He did this the more readily because he believed his knowledge in statescraft wanting. It was not until the death of his elder brother, Prince Baodoin, in 1891, when he was sixteen years of age, that the possibility of his succeeding to the Belgian throne occurred to him. Until then he had studied little. The moment he realised the responsibilities which lay before him he determined to fit himself for their discharge by study. As a matter of course he passed through the Belgian Military School, and received a commission in the Grenadier Regiment, in which he was rapidly promoted from sub-lieutenant to colonel; but he did not allow military duties to interfere with his studies. Up to the time of the death of Baron Lambermont he went daily to the Foreign Office to learn diplomacy. From diplomacy he turned to sociology, and at once the people's welfare became his greatest interest.

King Albert will not hinder Belgian expansion, but he has learned to keep his own counsels. No one knows what his opinion was on the Bill passed recently in the Belgian Parliament which introduced compulsory service into the army; and no one can speak with authority of his views on the Congo question; but there is good reason to believe he is of opinion that wide and sweeping reforms must be carried out without delay. His journey through the Congo from end to end, undertaken in spite of discouragement from all sides, was an assertion of independence which startled more than one high functionary and gave promise of vigorous action.

Labour laws are not wanting in Belgium. King Albert has pleaded in the Senate for their extension; but he is not a socialist dreamer. He has done much to aid those who are struggling to aid themselves. He takes special interest in Belgian sailors and fishermen, and dreams, as did Leopold II., of the creation of a Belgian marine. The greatest difficulty in his way is the lack of Belgian sailors. King Albert boasts of the brave race of Flemish sailors which flourished centuries ago. To revive the people's seagoing spirit he has established a training ship and promised to push the fortunes of its pupils.

The emphatic declarations of the new Belgian King with regard to the encouragement of art and literature will come as a surprise to many who thought all such things were banished for ever from the Belgian Court. In truth, King Albert cared little about art or literature until, as he put it himself, his wife brought art into the palace. Queen Elizabeth is a skilled musician, and has a sound knowledge of art and literature. She is the only member of the Belgian royal family, according to a great Belgian writer, who knows what books to read. The King admits she educated him, and, keen in all that he takes up, he is now a ready and appreciative patron of art, and a friend of every Belgian author. Leopold II. may not have violated the Belgian Constitution, but for many years past he bent the Ministry to his will and acted, in much, as a despot. Under King Albert's reign, it is promised, the Constitution will once more be respected in spirit as in letter. The rôle the King selects for himself is that of arbitrator. He hopes to find the means of uniting Capital and Labour, so that, "being united, they may fight side by side for a noble end, esteeming one another, and inspiring mutual confidence".

The military crisis being at an end, the Government remains unchanged. There are rumours that King Albert will clear out all the old Congo officials, and get rid of all those who served under King Leopold and are accustomed to his methods. As a matter of fact, all the Congo officials to whom reasonable objection could be made have already been replaced. It is not public servants that King Albert will have to get rid of, but the gang of capitalists, notaries, doctors, and Court officials who acted as King Leopold's men of straw in the formation of his numerous companies. It seems inevitable that actions will be taken to compel them to disgorge the millions of King Leopold's private fortune they are said to hold in secret trust. It is hinted that the latest and most extraordinary of King Leopold's companies, that for the preservation of Belgian sites, in which he vested the furniture, paintings, books, etc., now in the palace of Brussels, will be dissolved before it proceeds to allot its shares. In the meantime the Duke of Connaught and other royal guests have been lodged in the palace, which is virtually in a state of siege. One must sympathise with King Albert in the painful complications which King Leopold's action has caused. He has already found it possible to unite in Brussels the royal family disunited for so long. But he is assured the sympathy of Europe in his efforts to put the Belgian house in order.

COPYRIGHT REFORM.

INTERNATIONAL and municipal law have already been brought into almost complete accord on the subject of marine piracy and the slave trade so far as it affects African negroes. But there is a form of piracy by land well known to the author, the artist and the composer, viz. the appropriation, without payment or acknowledgment, of the product of his intellectual labour by his compatriots, or his cousins overseas, or by the enterprising foreigner. The municipal legislation of most civilised States now gives, under the name of copyright, an incomplete and imperfect protection to authors against literary and artistic piracy. The Berne Convention of 1886, with its supplementary Act and the declaration of 1896, was a first step towards the creation of a universal law of copyright. It has led to considerable improvement of the municipal law of the States which have joined in the International Copyright Union, and to qualified reciprocity in the recognition by each State adhering to the terms of the rights of authors belonging to other States of the Union.

The Convention has been in force long enough to justify a review of its working, and consideration of its defects, and examination into the numerous ways in which the up-to-date pirate has availed himself of the latest discoveries of modern science to enable him to take without payment the ideas of others in cases not provided against by the Convention or by the law of individual States. The Convention has accordingly been subjected to thorough revision, and the revised Convention signed in November 1908 is now before the nations for adoption or rejection.

Inasmuch as it is a cardinal principle of English law that these international agreements do not affect the rights of anyone within the realm until they are enforced by legislation, the Government in March last appointed a Committee to take stock both of the Convention and of our own law. That Committee has now presented a Report of great value and much interest. In the foreground of the Report one thing stands out pre-eminent: the need of harmonising and consolidating our own copyright laws. Even if not a single step be taken to adopt the new ideas of the Revised Convention, it is intolerable to have a matter of daily concern to authors and artists and publishers scattered over a series of ill-adjusted enactments spreading over nearly two centuries, on which scores of judicial decisions, not all consistent nor all illuminating, have been given. So far back as 1878 it was pointed out that the law was wholly destitute of any sort of arrangement, incomplete and often obscure, and thirty years have not appreciably mended matters. The Committee has further demonstrated the existing confusion by an epitome of the law as it stands to-day, and has clearly indicated the need of placing British law on a plain and uniform basis for the United Kingdom, and if possible also for the rest of the Empire.

But this alone will not suffice for the author or artist. The profits of much literary and artistic work, and in particular music and painting, depend on the public of foreign countries; and it is therefore necessary so to frame our laws as to entitle us, under the Convention or otherwise, to a protection in foreign States reciprocal to the recognition which we give to the copyright of foreign authors and artists. In some respects we are pretty fairly protected as matters at present stand; but in the Convention and Report are indicated a number of instances in which copyright needs further help from municipal or international law.

The Convention seeks to protect choreographic works and pantomimes (i.e. entertainments in dumb show), the acting form of which is fixed in writing or otherwise. It also seeks to protect architecture; and to protect authors of musical works against the adaptation of music to instruments which reproduce it mechanically; and to protect authors of literary, scientific, or artistic works against their public representation on the cinematograph. The Committee reports generally in favour of the extension of our law to cover these cases, but has for obvious reasons found great difficulty in the case of architecture. There is no trouble in protecting an architect's plans and models; but when his building is erected it is treated as fair game by copyists, and it will be very hard to get Parliament to prevent builders and others from taking ideas for new buildings. If complete enough protection is given, we shall have a horrid diversity of laboured originality in our buildings. In dealing with music and the gramophone, the Committee hesitate somewhat between the absolute right of the composer to control the reproduction of his works and the idea of compulsory licence (as in the case of patents) to prevent monopoly. Either method has its attractions and its defects.

From the mass of interesting matter in the Convention and Report space forbids selection of more than one other point, the idea of giving, as a general rule, for all copyrights a term of the author's life and fifty years, and to give to this term, so far as possible, an international recognition without the trouble and technicalities of registration in each country. This would be a very good general rule if equal rights or equal conditions are given by the law of each country to foreign works; but until by close bargaining we can ensure substantial equality, it is well to keep something in hand to bargain with.

Indeed—though the Report does not deal with it—it should not be forgotten that in certain countries copyright in favour of foreigners is conditional on the setting up or printing of the work within the protecting State, or on undertaking labours in connexion with it which will give to the workmen of the country recognising the copyright of a foreigner something in the way of wages in return for the monopoly thus accorded. This principle is recognised in the Patents Act of 1907 as regards the manufacture of new inventions, and is equally applicable to the publication of new ideas in the domains of literature and art.

The principle is this: that in giving to the foreign author the benefit of copyright in the United Kingdom we should not also give to the foreign trades which are engaged in the multiplying of books and artistic productions an advantage intended by the law only for the author of the work multiplied for circulation.

TARIFF AND IMPERIAL UNITY.

By Vates.

I.—AN IMPERIAL GOVERNMENT.

If it be accepted that a permanently fixed system, whether by theory or by arithmetic, cannot meet permanently unfixed needs, it follows that rigid finalities like Free Trade and the percentage formula of certain Tariff Reformers go out of court at once. Take a few examples of the foreign forces in economic variation which, operating beyond our control, disturb the productive process with us and can never be met by a permanently fixed system, however perfect at the time of its adjustment. To mention only one product and one country, the United States export wire nails at 20 to 30 per cent. less than the price in America; and, in varying forms, the same applies to numerous other products in several countries of Europe as well as in America, with the additional economic novelty of carrying German products for export at reduced rates. Farther, we find prices in Germany lowered as the distance from the seat of production increases, exactly the opposite of what we have been taught for several generations in our orthodox definition of "the market region". Again, in the latter half of the year 1900 the German combination in wire nails exported 19,000 tons, at a gross loss of £42,000, yet making a satisfactory profit on the total output, for home consumption and export taken together. Of course, the Free Trader will claim that the German example in wire nails means a present of £42,000 from the Germans to the peoples buying from them, and let it be admitted at once; but presents are not always worth accepting, and the cost of accepting this will be more clear if we see that the importation of a product at less than the cost of producing it must go to stop its production where it is imported, throwing the agents of production out of employment, which can never be compensated by the fractional gain of accepting such a gift. Besides, the gain is obviously to the commercialist, and the loss falls on the worker, whose only asset is his energy, now displaced and useless to him. Who will put his capital into the production of a commodity where he can buy it at 20 per cent. less than the price at which he can produce it, and then what happens to the man who depends on earning wages? The speculator takes the £42,000, and the workman goes to join a procession of the unemployed.

No one thinks that Tom, Dick and Harry can, with advantage to the country, carry their "democratic" intrusion into the conduct of the Foreign Office; but the work of fiscal adjustment is even more complex and, in many ways, not less esoteric; so that Parliaments themselves, in view of their party necessities, are intrinsically unfitted for the undertaking, even if we go the great length of assuming a parliamentary majority fit to understand it. What, then, shall we say of submitting the issue to the crowd and the ballot-box? It is in its nature a business which crowds cannot hope to understand; and, in their circumstances, the very best they can attempt is to select men who may understand it. Besides, the problem is essentially imperial, and our surviving fiction of an "imperial Parliament" makes it plain that we have no longer a Parliament that is imperial, though enough of imperial government survives to make raw material for imperial reconstruction. The self-governing colonies already describe themselves as "nations", and this political self-consciousness must grow with their maturity. Here, then, is a real basis of reunion: If a nation forms a national Government of men chosen from her parties, why cannot an Empire form an imperial Government of men chosen from her nations?

Let us begin with a cabinet of the Empire to study and control imperial fiscal interests, and not necessarily confined to these; the nucleus of a really imperial Government to recover and unify the half-lost mechanism of the imperial power, extending its authority as fast as its collective advantage is proved, if so it be, even to the issues of peace and war. In the outlook of international dynamics this means for England's future a choice between pre-eminence and subserviency. On the present footing her capacities and her responsibilities develop at different rates of progression, making the impossibility of her position a matter of time and accident. Her outlook is that of an organism unable to direct its own energies, and this is the stage next to disruption. In the coming years she must settle her destiny, making herself more than ever fit as the first power in the world, or receding to the grade of a secondary nation; a momentous decision, dependent on her imperial reconstruction, in which her colonies must be considered in the light of the liberties she has herself given them.

Then we must consider the peculiarities of the British instinct, its way of approaching problems, by intuition rather than by intellect, and often not the less effectively. A French scheme of ready-made definitions might have put an end to this Empire long ago, and no working definition has yet appeared of practical instinct. If the Empire is to be saved, this is the British way. Besides, restoration from the chaos that has grown requires stronger motives than argument. The natural and proper tendency of maturing communities is to grow in ways of their own; and if they remain imperially associated they must have an advantage from the association in accordance with that tendency.

Preferential import taxation is a preliminary necessity, and having adopted this in the United Kingdom, the Empire, in instituting its imperial Cabinet, agrees on a basis: (1) No product to be imported from any country outside the Empire into any country inside it on terms as favourable as are secured for the same product exchanged between two countries of the Empire; and the difference must always be enough to influence the location and direction of trade, provided that inefficiency in production is not subsidised or otherwise privileged at the expense of the consumer. (2) No product to be imported from any country either inside or outside the Empire into any country inside it at less than the normal cost of production in the country of origin; and normal cost of production implies the current rates of remuneration for the agents of production in that country.* (3) After guarding against the evils indicated in the two preceding clauses, the Cabinet proceeds to supplement taxation for the revenue required, devising for every country such incidence as suits it best. (4) A reserve fund, raised in proportion from the whole Empire, is controlled by the Cabinet for fiscal experiments or local emergencies, as in testing in an undeveloped region whether a subvention or other encouragement could start industry in economic proportion to the expenditure, to establish for local enterprise industrial data which it might not be able to establish for itself. (5) The Imperial Cabinet undertakes to provide for the naval defence of the Empire, controlled as a unity, and on the basis of contributions from the various countries in proportion to taxable capacity. (6) On the decision of the Imperial Cabinet every constituent country commits itself to the principle that the Empire as a whole must use force if necessary for its self-preservation against any disloyalty within it.

* Of course this need not apply to a product unproducible in the country importing it.

There remains a vital defect in the imperial organism if it has no provision by which its combined strength can come to the economic and industrial support of its weakest places, in the same way as its combined fighting power defends the less defensible points. For instance, a little help might have meant much in results when the Yankees were deliberately dumping to kill the beginnings of the great fruit industry in Canada, and a *temporary* bounty of 2d. a pound for a few years on exported butter enabled the colony of Victoria to establish her flourishing supply in other markets.* An Imperial Cabinet meets this defect also, and it would be selected by the constituent Parliaments of the Empire. It is not necessarily selected *from* the Parliaments, since the fittest man may have neither the time nor the taste for electioneering. A man charged to adjust the incidence of an Empire's import taxation requires to be as secure from "popular" interference in his work as a General on active service. Define his trust to him and criticise his conduct in the results; but, at work, let him have his faculties free from party fetters to judge for the nations what parties and even Parliaments are comparatively unfit to judge.

The aim is to enable the peoples of the Empire to select those fit to judge what they cannot well judge for themselves, and possibly, if not probably, the fittest man may not be found in public life at all. No country in the Empire may refuse the Imperial Cabinet's decrees, but no country is without a voice in declaring them. The Cabinet is supposed to be always sitting, because the interests it has to watch are always changing; its venue would be permanently in London, but committees of its members would travel over the Empire, that sound judgment may be reinforced by the indispensable knowledge of eye and ear, as well as by electric cables and blue papers, not to mention how the misunderstandings of distance are modified and tempered by human touch. The basis of representation ought to be on relative averages of population and foreign trade, varying automatically with the movements in the different countries, so as not to need imperial Redistribution Bills in the future. On such a footing, who knows whether the largest group in the Cabinet may not soon come from Canada, where less than half the corn-land still untilled could feed the whole of the British Empire, and where the production of grain can increase at the rate of doubling itself in about four years? It is a question whether, assuming all the food from the rest of the world shut out of the United Kingdom by prudent stages, the Canadians could not supply us wholly in a very short time and as cheaply as now, at prices brought down and kept down by the competition of Canadians among themselves—another of the changes that have come about since Free Trade established its dogmatic finalities, when the active sources of competitive food supply within the Empire were not extended and capable of immediate further development as they are now.

The Chairman or Prime Minister of this Imperial Cabinet would be appointed by the King from among its members on the advice of the majority. This new machinery of imperial government would be the outcome of an imperial conference called expressly, and would be embodied in an identical Bill passed by every Parliament (after consultation with the Indian Government) in the constituent countries of the Empire.

Another of the incidental functions vested in the imperial Cabinet is to set the Empire feeding itself, and without increasing the cost of food, surely a more "economic" proposition than the development of skilled industry on the basis of exporting half the product at less than cost and deriving a satisfactory

* Mainly the United Kingdom. The annual exports of butter from Victoria have gone up in sixteen years from £50,300 to £1,654,481. The subvention continued only for three or four years, and Victorian statesmen declare that the results were impossible without it.

profit on both halves from the increased price of the other half for home consumption. This is the economic impossibility which has become a constant fact through German and American "cartels"; and yet it is assumed by many that the whole British Empire, including so much of the best of the earth, could not maintain within itself the competition necessary to keep food below famine prices in one particular little island. If the rest of the world were sunk under the sea tomorrow, leaving the British Empire alone, it could hardly affect the food supply or its prices for much more than a couple of years in any particular country; and yet it is in our power, if we only see it, to bring about practically the same result in regard to food supply and prices without any hardship anywhere for one day, and without any such inconvenience to our neighbours outside the Empire. Should our imperial producers at any time make a "corner" in a particular commodity against any one constituent country, then would be the time for the imperial Cabinet to declare Free Trade in the country threatened.

There is no more need for Protection as a permanent policy than to remain fettered by the rival dogmatism of Free Trade. Both extremes are the expedients of emergency rather than the mechanism of the normal; and they ought to be reserved against crises when either may be applied, or even both at the same time, in different connexions. In short, we have an engine of tremendous power industrially and politically, now perfectly useless to us, because it has not occurred to us to empower qualified judgment in the control of it. The British working man could hardly do a greater good for himself than in handing over his engine to competent engineers, taking care that they are not interfered with and the machinery put out of order by the really irrelevant noise of party politics.

THE CITY.

THE City is wonderfully cheerful, all things considered. Investment brokers have been busy, the outstanding feature again being the demand for home securities, and more particularly home railway stocks. It is not an overwhelming demand, but it is sufficiently pronounced to show that the prestige of home investments is returning. A further batch of good traffics is published, not the least noteworthy being the gains shown by the District and the allied "tubes". Particulars are now available of the terms upon which it is proposed to amalgamate the "Bakerloo", the Great Northern and Piccadilly, and the Charing Cross and Hampstead Companies, and there is no doubt that if the scheme is sanctioned by Parliament, the prior charges of these companies will materially benefit by being consolidated—both as to security and by being rendered more marketable. The new company will have a total capitalisation of £16,800,000, of which £4,200,000 will be in the form of debenture stock for exchange of the existing debentures of the three companies. We also have particulars this week of the applications made by English railways for further capital powers. The total amount to be raised in the form of share capital is just under four and a quarter millions, and the borrowing powers sought involve a little more than one and a quarter million sterling. These are very modest demands, and show that the companies have benefited by the severe criticism to which they were subjected some two years ago. No one can say that the service has suffered through the curtailment of expenditure. On the contrary, we have had efficiency with economy. While the public interest has not been jeopardised, a considerable benefit has accrued to the shareholders, which they have yet to receive. Of the total of four and a quarter millions additional share capital which it is proposed to raise, one-fourth is for the Lancashire and Yorkshire Company, which is proposing to construct a railway at Chadderton and effect sundry widenings and improvements. Lest it be said that we are making too strong a case for the railways, we would remark that the amount of share capital raised this year is only £400,000. Contrasted with the proposed expenditure, a new era of extravagance would seem to have set in. But until lately this year has been a very bad one for the railways, and not an atom of excuse could be found for making fresh borrowings. In previous years, however, directors did not seek to find excuses; they raised capital when and how they chose. Now, with the promise of greater activity of trade and greatly increased traffics, the proposed expenditure sinks into insignificance. If we go back to 1908 we find that the amount of capital raised by British railway companies was twelve millions, and prospects then were exceedingly poor. Moreover, at the time the expenditure was sanctioned directors had not learnt the value of economy. Of course, if the railways are to have a return of prosperity, labour will want a share; but, under the prevailing system of conciliation boards and arbitration, there is the less danger of a serious strike for higher wages, and the companies can afford to accede to the men's additional demands if they are doing well. Nothing in all this must be taken as encouraging an immediate speculation in home railway stocks. The real investor can buy with safety, because he is assured of a remunerative rate of dividend and an ultimate appreciation in capital value; but the speculator should wait until the General Election is over before he enters the market, as a surprise at the polls might cause a sharp, if only temporary, break in prices.

The rise in the price of United Railways of Havana stock has aroused some criticism, the opinion being freely expressed that there is no justification for the movement. It would seem, however, that the Cubans themselves are buying, and they should be better able than the London market to judge of the prospects of the undertaking. We are informed that the price for the stock in Havana is 108, as against 91 here. This great disparity is partly due to the fact that the certificates in Cuba are "to bearer" and that there is a scarcity of the warrants; but it would also seem to indicate a keen investment inquiry, or buyers would wait until purchases were effected in London and the necessary formalities of exchange arranged. Last week's traffic shows an increase of £4251, bringing up the aggregate gain for the twenty-five weeks to £46,224. This does not mean much in the way of increased dividend for the current half-year, but the future is full of promise. An exceptionally good sugar crop is anticipated, raising hopes that the results obtained in 1906-7 will be repeated. A line mainly dependent upon a single crop is, of course, a precarious investment, as we were painfully reminded in 1907-8, when the sugar crop failed. But the directors are doing something to render the line more independent of the sugar traffic. Money has been spent on making through traffic arrangements, and the company is now getting business which it never had before. Hence there is good reason for the rise in the company's stock. At the same time it must not be forgotten that the railway employés are easily led, and that strikes, if they occur, are generally very serious.

INSURANCE: POLICIES AT HIGH PREMIUMS.

VIII.

IN previous articles it has been explained that policies effected at a high rate of premium involve a varying and relatively small proportion of each premium being used for protection purposes, and a comparatively large portion of each premium being accumulated at compound interest as in a savings bank. The money used for protection purposes is spent every year just as truly as the money paid for expenses of management or the premiums paid for fire insurance is spent. The surrender value of a life policy depends, for practical purposes, upon the total amount that has been saved out of the premiums paid, and consequently the conditions on surrender are much more favourable, in proportion to the total amount paid in premiums, under policies at a high rate of premium than under those at a low rate. It is nothing unusual for the cash-surrender value of a whole-life non-profit policy to be only 30 per cent. of the premiums paid after the policy has been in force for five years. On a whole-life policy with profits effected at a single premium the cash-surrender value would be considerably more than 100 per cent. of the premium. In view of these facts the conditions on which policies can be surrendered become more important under policies at high rates of premium than under those at low rates, though these conditions are always of moment and vary greatly in different offices.

A policy can be surrendered in various ways: it can be given up altogether for a cash payment or can be exchanged for a policy of a reduced amount upon which no further premiums have to be paid, and which matures at death, or—in the case of endowment assurances—at a specified date. Paid-up policies of this kind do not usually participate in future profits; but sometimes they do, and the difference between the results is very considerable. If a man of thirty takes a policy for £1000, subject to the payment of premiums for twenty years, the sum assured being paid at death whenever it happens, he can surrender this policy at the end of ten years for ten-twentieths of the original amount; the assurance being on the with-profit plan the reversionary bonuses for ten years on £1000 are added to the paid-up policy for £500. If the bonus is a simple addition to the sum assured at the rate of £2 per cent. per annum the bonus would amount to £200 and the paid-up policy to £700, which would be paid at the death of the assured without any further payments by the policyholder. In most offices this paid-up policy would not share in future profits; in some companies it would. If the bonuses were distributed on the basis of a uniform addition to the sum assured only, future bonuses would be calculated on the £500, not on the £700; and if the rate of bonus were 2 per cent. per annum, the addition to the sum assured would be £10 each year. In this example it is supposed that the policy is surrendered at the age of forty. The assured might well live to seventy-five, in which case the sum assured would be increased by £350, and at his death his heirs would receive £1050, instead of £700, simply as the result of having originally selected an office which gave future participation in surplus to paid-up policies. This increase of 50 per cent. in the amount payable is the result of a policy condition, and of nothing else. The variation in the rate of bonus or in the duration of life after the policy is surrendered would vary the percentage of gain, but in principle the benefit is derived from a liberal condition.

If the bonus system were on the compound reversionary plan, calculated on the sum assured and on previous reversionary additions as well, each bonus declared would earn future bonuses, and from the date of surrender the increase in the sum assured would be calculated upon the £700, not upon the £500. Other things being equal, a compound reversionary bonus is at a lower rate than a simple reversionary bonus, the latter plan yielding better results if the assured dies soon, the compound plan being the more advantageous if the assured lives long.

There is one company which declines, or at any rate used to decline, to give to paid-up policies the amount of reversionary bonuses on the original sum assured. Thus if bonuses to the extent of £200 had been earned on a policy of £1000, and ten premiums out of twenty had been paid, the new paid-up policy would have been for half the original sum of £1000 and half the declared bonuses of £200, making only £600 in all, and this policy would receive no share of future profits. When at the same outlay £1050 can be obtained instead of £700, or even instead of £600, it is manifestly foolish not to secure, when selecting the policy originally, conditions which may have so large an effect upon the results.

THE HORRID COMMONS.

THE masterly volumes in which Professor Firth appears as the continuator of Dr. Gardiner contain much that is of great interest at this moment.* As to-day, so just two and a half centuries ago, the horridest arbitrariness that ever was exercised in the world—Lord Lansdowne must have taken his apt Cromwellian quotation from these pages—was "so tender of the privilege of Parliament as to forget the liberties of Englishmen", and by "over-voting the lovers of freedom" was aiming by a law to "perfect their instrument of bondage and rivet it on the necks of the good people for ever, and thereby make them vassals and slaves perpetually". This, the Cromwellian statesmen considered, would never do. There must be an effective House of Lords which would "preserve the good interest against the uncertainty of the Commons' House", and be a sort of a citadel in which the party of progress could hold out, custos libertatis Angliæ. Cromwell told the Commons that he would not accept office—this sounds like Mr. Asquith reversed —"without there might be some other Body that might interpose between you and me on behalf of this commonwealth, to prevent a tumultuary and a popular spirit". "A Parliament consisting of a single assembly elected by the people and invested with the whole power of government" seemed to him "so strange a thing that neither ancient nor modern prudence can shew any example of the like"—unless it were the Thirty Tyrants of Athens or the Decemvirs at Rome. A "check or balancing power" was essential to civil liberty. Single-Chamber government had been tried from 1649 to 1653, with calamitous results. When he had secured his House of Lords, Oliver—once, according to Packer, "the greatest anti-lord in England"—declared that the ship of State had at last reached its desired haven, that those who had helped thereto would be blessed by future generations as the restorers of paths to dwell in, and that "if there be any higher work which mortals can attain unto in this world beyond this" he was ignorant of it. "What hinders this nation from being an Aceldama, if this do not?" Nathaniel Fiennes, on the same occasion, compared the two Houses to Ephraim and Manasseh and to Leah and Rachel, which did build the House of Israel.

There had been determined opposition in the Commons. Haselrig, like Mr. Asquith, invoked the shades of Pym, Strode and Hampden. "The other House", said another Republican orator, "was justly cast out, by their being clogs upon the passing of many good laws." To which it was answered that "the great reason was that bills passed too hastily here", and that that House "did pass more in a month than the best student in England can understand in a year. A check is necessary upon us". The Parliament of 1653 had done well to refuse to change its name to "the Representative of the People". Besides, it was held by some that "the spirit of those the Commons represent hath little affinity with, or respect to, the cause of God", and that the "future security of the honest interest seemeth (under God) to be laid up" in a House of Lords composed of "men of property and influence and of unshakable fidelity to the Cause". The interest of the godly might require the dissolution of that or of all Parliaments, which yet the Commons might object to. It is melancholy to find that it was considered essential by Cromwell and his friends that the Upper House should be a House of landlords and denominationalists. In fact, the republicans derided the new House as "having no interest, not the forty-thousandth part of England". It was endeavoured to reassure them by pointing out the strength of the military interest among the new "Lords". Whether they should be called a House of Lords or only "the Other House" was vehemently debated. The former name seemed safest. "We know not what this 'Other House' may do. It may claim to be the House of Commons, to open the people's purse at both ends."

* "The Last Years of the Protectorate." By Charles Harding Firth. London: Longmans. 1909. 2 vols. 24s. net.

As it was, thirty of the ablest Commoners were to be given seats in it. The objection is fatal to an idea which has doubtless occurred to enterprising minds in the present crisis, that the entire Liberal party in the Commons should be raised to the Peerage, or else that the Upper House should not be even the Other House, but the Same House, robed, coronetted, and seated on red morocco.

The misdeeds of the old House of Lords, however, were brought up against the institution. It had refused to concur in the trial and beheading of the King. Its negative had often grieved "the saintlike army", which was now practically, as in Plato's Republic, an estate by itself. The Protector told the Commons, however, that it was they, not the Lords, who were the overthrowers of the Constitution, and bringers-in of chaos. "And, if this be your carriage, I think it high time that an end be put to your sitting. And I do declare to you here that I do dissolve this Parliament. And let God be judge between you and me." "Amen", some voices answered—not, we must suppose, "after the old Cathedral manner." Oliver, though the "drudge" and "kickshaw" of the major-generals, resented the demagogy of "tribunes of the people". His Fifth Monarchy opponents retorted with various theological expressions, among which the Seed of the Dragon and the Babylonish Beast who had taken the crown from Christ's head to place it on his own figured prominently. Against such a monster the dagger of Ehud was the Scriptural remedy. Mr. Firth is evidently a little scandalised that "Killing no Murder" was read by staid Royalists like Clarendon with relish, not only for its wit, but for its reasoning. Private right of tyrannicide, however, was directly taught by Milton, and ordinary people might be excused for thinking that others besides regicides could play at that game.

It was decided that the choice of the new Lords—not to exceed seventy in number—should rest with the Protector. There was much self-denying competition in the Commons' House for a seat in Another Place, and many hopes expressed that the Lord would direct his Highness' selection. Lenthall, when chosen, rejoiced that all the elevated ones "shall themselves and their heirs be for ever peers of England". But, when the list was complete, the principal part, wrote Ludlow "were such as had procured their present possessions by their wits and were resolved to enlarge them by selling their consciences". The accident of birth was, alas! done homage to by the inclusion of seven of the Cromwell family; but, of seven members of the old Peerage summoned, all "disdained" to come except Cromwell's son-in-law, Fauconberg, and an indigent nobleman, "once well esteemed for honesty" —how history repeats itself!—the Lord Ure of Eure. Even Warwick "would not be persuaded to sit with Colonel Hewson and Colonel Pride, whereof the one had been a shoemaker and the other a drayman", while Say, of all people, used the most reactionary language about our old nobility, the insolency of the multitude, and the dishonour incurred by any peer of England who should make himself a felo de se, a stalking-horse and vizard for the supersession of the historic House of Lords by Cromwellian nominees.

The City was not as staunch for the good old cause as it had been. Finance was a more absorbing interest than politics, and Republicans asked sadly, "What is the City but a great tame beast that eats and carries and cares not who rides it?" But it felt the tax laid in 1657 on developed building land, and, said an M.P., "nothing is so like to blast your settlement as a land tax". The new excise was an impost "more burthensome than ship-money". The question of supply became a most anxious one towards the end of the Protectorate, and Henry Cromwell hoped that God of His mercy would save his father from the temptation to levy taxes by the sword alone. The Protector lamented the nation's ragged, unpaid and barefooted army, and his own pecuniary engagements to Charles X. were not fulfilled. Professor Firth eschews the rôle of commentator, but he might here perhaps have recalled the extent to which the Cromwellian family and most of the heroes of Puritan simplicity feathered their private nests. And the whole history leaves us once more in amazement at the tacit indulgence of historians towards acts of an upstart military despotism for one-twentieth part of which they would have damned the old monarchy with sternest reprobation. Cromwell himself was the supreme opportunist, and his alliance with the Scarlet Woman against not Spain only, but Holland, led to a certain toleration of Papists at home. The Sardinian Chapel just demolished in Kingsway was the place, if we remember right, where their attendance at Mass was first connived at. But the ferocious laws against Popery were strengthened, and for prelacy there was no mercy at all. Bishop Wren, for instance, spent the whole nineteen years between 1641 and 1660 in prison. Undenominational Protestantism was then, as now, the only State-endowed religion, and the "national Church" was confined to conforming "professors". The day before Cromwell took to his bed for the last time, Fox met him riding with his life guards in Hampton Court Park, and pleaded for mitigation of the Quakers' sufferings. "I saw and felt a waft of death go forth against him, and when I came to him he looked like a dead man."

CHRISTMAS.

By Arthur C. Headlam.

A LITTLE more than nineteen hundred years ago a little child was born. Whatever strange facts may have accompanied his birth, nothing of that was known to his neighbours. He grew up as a village boy in the country districts of Galilee. He was a carpenter, the son of a carpenter. He lived among the people and was held to be like the people, to live as they did, and to think as they did. The times were troubled ones. The old glories of Judaism seemed to have gone —the newer tinselled glory of the Herods was over. The strong might of the Roman legions was breaking the spirit of the people. Everywhere the tax-gatherer was collecting his tribute. Turbulent spirits were striving for revolt; religious dreamers were building up their apocalyptic visions of a kingdom which was to come. Then a voice was heard coming from the desert, with something of the sternness of the old prophetic utterance, saying that the "kingdom" was coming, telling men to give up their sins and to wash them away in the waters of baptism. The carpenter of Nazareth seemed to be seized with the contagious enthusiasm. He listened to the teaching; he was baptised as others; he withdrew into the desert. From the desert he came back and began to teach. Followers collected round him; he stirred up enthusiasm; he taught as no man had ever taught before. He healed the sick, he cleansed lepers, he cast out devils. Crowds flocked round him. Surely here was the Messiah! surely the kingdom had come! But the obvious notes of the Messiah were not there. Here was no commander to lead the turbulent spirits against the legions of Rome. Here was no supernatural figure that came down from heaven and appeared amidst the assembled worshippers in the courts of the Temple. They were disappointed. The Scribes and the Pharisees questioned him, and he would tell them nothing that they wanted to know. But a small body of true friends clustered round him. A short period of enthusiasm, a short period of disappointment—and he and his followers went to Jerusalem. He went as the Messiah. Some accepted him as the Messiah. There were hopes that there might now be a revolt. But the wise priests had no intention of embroiling the country with Rome—certainly not for one who seemed to think little of their authority or the authority of the doctors of the Law. The rigorous methods of Roman administration quenched the rising hopes. His disciples forsook him and fled.

A few years, and we find the little band of disciples who seemed to have so little courage—a group of ignorant Galilean peasants—preaching Jesus the Messiah. They are filled with a new and strange spirit. Crowds come to hear them—the message spreads through Palestine—the opposition that it arouses scatters the preachers far and wide. Damascus and Cyprus and Antioch become the centres of the new faith; and under the leadership of the pupil of a well-known Rabbi, who himself had been a persecutor, it makes marvellous steps onward, and in spite of opposition and persecution it spreads throughout the Empire. It rears its head in Rome; everywhere, like a silent leaven, it works through the world. Sometimes opposed, sometimes, perhaps, fostered, it seems to be ever growing. It creates a new life, a new hope, and a new enthusiasm. It withstands the cruellest persecutions and conquers the Empire.

And then we hear a knocking at the distant gates of Rome—the sound of new nations rising into being. Wild and fierce and strong barbarians, they sweep over the Alps; they overthrow the great cities; they ravage the provinces. The world seems to have come to an end. But that power seizes them. It captures the conquerors, and by them obtains a new dominion. It rears a great spiritual kingdom stronger than the old temporal kingdom of the Cæsars. It builds up a new and strange comity amongst new races. Revolt against the new power arises, as it arose against the old. New nations start into the world to gain a new life, and still inspired by the same faith. And even now, in many new lands, under tropical suns, in the great prairies of America, sometimes in new and strange guises, the old power lives on. In a very different way from his imagining thought, the stone which Daniel the prophet saw in his vision has grown and spread and filled the earth.

Whence came this power? whence came this force? Who was that child, born in that obscure province of the Roman Empire nineteen hundred years ago, whose birth portended such wonderful things to the world? The Christian Church takes us to Bethlehem; it shows us the little child lying in a manger; it bids us see the shepherds worshipping; it bids us see that strange caravan that had come from distant Eastern lands; it bids us gaze on that bright glory in the skies; it lets us hear the voice that said to Mary "He shall be great and shall be called the Son of the Highest; he shall reign over the house of Jacob for ever, and of his kingdom there shall be no end; that holy thing shall be called the Son of God". It bids us hear the voice which said to the shepherds "For unto you is born this day in the city of David a Saviour which is Christ the Lord", and to hear the angelic song, "Glory to God in the highest, and on earth peace to men of goodwill". What would it teach us by these stories which are woven into the very fabric of Western thought? It tells us that we must see in that peasant teacher the revelation of God in the world. And we, as we ponder over the pageant of Christian history, and think of the message which then came to men, and wonder what power would suffice to accomplish all that has happened, and as we feel in our hearts that peace which Christ alone can give amid the trials and temptations and disappointments of the world, may not we too say, as others have said before us, "Truly this is the Son of God"?

A CHRISTMAS LEGEND.

"I'LL mourn no more that Winter days are long;
I'll build a fire and sing a song.
Perchance some wayfarer unseen by me
Shall hear my song and go more heartily.

I'll open wide the door—a table spread
With herbs and honey, and with oaten bread.
Perchance some wanderer shall see the light
And find goodwill, and shelter for the night."

So said an exile in a hut of clay,
Snow-shrouded, on the Morn of Christmas Day.
Rich merchants passed, and laughed to see coarse bread,
Wild herbs, and honey, for a Feast Day spread.

And king and courtiers gave him alms unsought;
But all the day no wanderer asked him aught!
Yet, though no outcast came his Feast to share,
He entertained an Angel unaware!

ALTHEA GYLES.

CHILDREN'S BOOKS.

By EDWARD H. COOPER.

THERE is a famous writer on racing matters whose weekly articles in a contemporary are full of language which is constantly quoted, approvingly or otherwise, by his fellow-journalists, and which every man has longed to apply at one time or another to the events of the passing year and their actors. "An anserous and asinine crowd", "muddy-headed moon-calves", "the gullible herd"; who would not long to fling adjectives and substantives of this description at the head of some political or literary or social enemy? One ought not to use such language about children or Christmas, but the words recur to my mind with loving memory whenever I have read two or three score of modern books for children.

This year I have read fifty-three; last year I not only read about the same number, but had the honour of talking to half a dozen or so of their authors while the immortal works in question were being written; the year before that I read some incredible number (I believe over a hundred) of the same class of books; and the question which presents itself to me with yearly growing force is, What on earth is in the mind of the man or woman who deliberately sits down and writes three or four of them? It must be remembered that a large majority of authors of this description write their books, not in the fashion of even moderately intelligent novelists, at the rate of one per-annum, but at the rate of two and three, and sometimes five or six, in the year, all of which are published within a few weeks of one another, and seem for some obscure reason to bring their authors a mild but enviable and regular income.

The secret of the sale of these books is open to anybody who knows the nursery and school-room worlds. It is a matter of the bachelor uncle, the maiden aunt, and the well-meaning, but ignorant, friend. No human being who has ever spent an intimate week with a child, listening to the creature's opinions, and noting its actions, would ever dream of considering more than one per cent. of the child-books published every year nowadays for Christmas or birthday presents. In that week's conversation it is impossible that you could have failed to hear the young person's real private opinion of this literature. At first she suspects your bona fides. If you ask her opinion of a gift book, she puts you down mentally at first as a friend of the giver, a friend of the author, or possibly the author in person, who is in any case going to "tell" if she expresses her real opinion of the book. A day or two later comes the cautious admission that she "began to read" the work of art in question, but Miss X. (her governess) told her that she "might put it away". Later on, if in several ways you have shown yourself to be perfectly trustworthy, she will tell you her candid opinion of the book, occasionally in the most startling language. "I call So-and-so", a twelve-year-old lady wrote to me once, "sodden rot, only mother says I musn't use Guy's words without telling her beforehand." Then she criticised several other Christmas and New Year gift books with equal candour, the whole forming a letter which, if I published it, would cause a painful and somewhat considerable stir among authors, publishers, and critics whose work centres round the children's Christmas season.

But it must be remembered, among the more curious details of this matter, that not a hundredth part of the persons dealing with child literature know anything whatever about a child's personal tastes. They need to know nothing, because the child's taste, as I have said, is an infinitesimally unimportant part of the sale of the book; and in these busy times few people want to "get up" a subject which will bring them neither thanks nor profit. The publisher and critic "play up to" the bachelor uncle, whose 3s. 6d. is, naturally enough, the real matter. What is in his mind I do not pretend to guess. Naturally he is quite unaware that the modern child in its schoolroom reads "David Copperfield", "Cranford", and the stories of Charlotte Yonge; he never goes there, and if such a visit were anticipated the young person would be found buried in his own last gift book. It would be unreasonable to expect him to know any better, since his views are culled from the daily papers; and the dim suspicion which surely must occur to him now and then, that the omniscience of such critics stops at the bottom of the nursery stairs, rarely becomes a certainty to his mind. I remember it was not confirmed in my own mind till I had read numerous notices on the death of Charlotte Yonge, whose well-thumbed volumes stack the shelves of three-quarters of the children of my acquaintance. "A writer for the Parish Library", said a brief biography in a famous "yellow" journal. "Yet there is something in her books besides sanctified twaddle", a similar newspaper graciously admitted. "The kind of incident which she thought attractive makes her seem old-fashioned to those who have been trained in the work of George Egerton, 'Iota', and Sarah Grand", wrote another person, who, it is to be hoped, does not put his theories into practice by distributing cheap editions of "The Yellow Aster" and "The Heavenly Twins" or their successors as schoolroom presents at this season. In truth, when one reflects that it is stuffed up with such verdicts that the bachelor uncle goes to Hatchards in search of literary Christmas presents, one wonders why the result, as visible on schoolroom bookshelves, is no worse.

I have heard the theory advanced with much fervour that it would do the ordinary child less harm, intellectually and morally, to read the most scandalous of modern "grown-up" books than the dreary school stories, sentimental yarns about sick, widowed mothers, and fifth-rate adventure tales which litter the lists of modern publishers. There would be something to be said for the theory, but for one fact. The trashy plots of the stories which I have in my mind, coupled with the villainous slipshod English in which they are written, would debase youthful literary taste, and thereby do a considerable amount of damage—if the child ever chanced to read them. But the lady or gentleman in question does nothing of the sort. He or she has a private library kept for reading purposes, and another kept for the reception of gift books. Madame Albanesi summed up all the advantages of these literary gifts in a recent article, where she described how "the advent of a parcel still has its proper measure of mystery and excitement, and the dignity of twelve years melts into the eager haste of ten as the string is cut, the brown paper is unwrapped, and the neat arrangement of Christmas books is revealed". That "parcel" is the sum and substance of the whole matter, very much as leaving the house in a taxi or carriage is the "summum bonum" of many parties. "It's the going which matters to me, not the where", said a small, excited bundle of wraps to me once, when I was cross-examining her delicately as to her reasons for wishing to pay a third visit to a house where she had once frankly admitted that she was invariably and badly bored; and if that brown paper parcel described by Madame Albanesi had a dozen farthing Christmas cards in it, it would be just as popular.

The real difficulty is that books for children require an amount of work and knowledge altogether disproportionate to the money which you are going to make out of them. It strikes one at first as curious that writers like Mr. Barrie, Mrs. W. K. Clifford, Miss Cholmondeley, and Madame Albanesi herself, who know a child's mind as well, in schoolboy parlance, as if they had been down there with a candle, should not more often imitate the devotion of writers like Miss Yonge or Mr. Henty or Madame de Ségur, and give up a year or two to mere unadulterated child work. Then, on reflection, one perceives that one is asking these writers for a work of mere charity, which they may or may not feel inclined to give, but whose refusal cannot be met with reproaches. Mrs. Clifford's "Anyhow Stories" and "The Getting Well of Dorothy" show that their author can write nursery and schoolroom work which is very rapidly put apart by the child-reader from other gift books; while the work which the author of "Peter Pan" would do after this fashion makes one's mouth water to think of. It is rough luck on the small folk that their literature should not at least hit some happy medium between this and the actual publishers' lists of 1909.

A GREAT COLLECTOR.

By Laurence Binyon.

NOT every one who amasses rarities and costly things is a collector in the true sense of the title. One must be born of the race. And though a man be born with the instinct and the passion, how many impediments of nature or of fortune may prevent him from attaining a place in those chosen ranks! He may have the curiosity and the acquisitiveness, but lack that nice discrimination of the great collector, and amass with mere rapacity, casting his net in the deep waters of antiquity and fishing up coarse and fine alike; or he may find himself possessor of a superb gallery of forgeries. Of these last we need not speak; they are but copyists, and the root of the matter is not in them. But those who have the temperament generally learn; to collect is an education; and smatterers in the art, such as begin with toys like walking-sticks and postage-stamps, may find themselves—perhaps only on their death-beds—discovering a nobler appetite for porcelain or for sculpture. Fortune again is often unkind and contrary. Our great collector, Charles I., for instance, who gathered together what was, I suppose, the most splendid series of pictures ever collected by one man; how ill destiny served him, plaguing him with vexatious and unruly Parliaments when he should have been choosing Titians and giving gorgeous commissions to his architects and painters! Lack of means may hinder; but not at all in the degree that might be imagined. Even in these days when only masters of fabulous revenues, such as Oil Kings and potentates of that kind enjoy, are supposed to be able to acquire the greatest masterpieces, even now the born collector (witness Sir Hugh Lane) manages to secure fine examples of painting by the most renowned of names for comparatively little. Courage, patience, knowledge, a keen and fine taste; these may be backed against the deepest purse in the world, if the owner of that have not these gifts also. You may know the born collector by his manner; as he handles a choice piece, he is transfigured; he is all finger-tips and eye; nay, among the elect of this kind there are those who, becoming blind, can tell with some rarefied perception, between touch and smell, the period and the country, the make and the maker, of this or that specimen of pottery, of metal-work, of sculpture.

George Salting was of the great race. And fortune had amply endowed him with the means to gratify his instinct. For long years he spent all but a fraction of a great income on his manifold collections. He bought widely and bought well. It is true, he had his limitations. He was no pioneer. But to be in advance of the taste of the time, like Rossetti, to discover virgin fields, unexploited yet by dealers, this is the province of the genius with moderate means. Mr. Salting could afford to compete with a keen market; if he bought what it was the fashion to pay high for, no doubt the joys of contest brought his occupation richer zest. The days of anxiety he cost the dealers, those luxuries of hesitation, those dallyings of desire, were all indispensable; the pleasing torments of devotion. It may be said that his vast collections lacked character; that subtle impress of personality which certain collectors give to what they own, so that we feel it inconceivable that things of a particular type or quality should ever belong to them, while other things seem to be theirs by a sort of right. I have heard, I do not know how much truth is in the report, that rival collectors, wishing to divert Mr. Salting from their own special field, succeeded by telling him that they had acquired something (in a quite different line) of which he had no specimen; it was enough to start him on a fresh track. But whatever province he invaded, his captures were of the choicest. Collecting for him was the grand passion. Already, as we see from the newspapers, he is becoming a legend. His extravagant economies in the little comforts proverbially associated with wealthy bachelors touch the popular imagination. He had a part in life, and he played it, serenely unconscious of effect, to the full. We have too few of such characters in our day of smooth compromises. He had the simplicity and grandeur of a type. If Molière had created a collector in his comedies, he would have been such a man as this.

It seems to be fairly certain now that Mr. Salting's treasures are to become the nation's property. When we remember what beautiful things have been lost to this country by sheer short-sightedness; when we think of Lawrence's marvellous collection of drawings, the most magnificent ever made, offered to the nation for a moderate sum and rejected, to take only one striking instance, we are inclined to think that England has better luck than she deserves. Certainly other nations may well envy us so splendid a bequest; and if it is not shown that the will which has been found has been modified by a later one, it is a bequest unhampered by any of the irksome conditions so often attached to such legacies. In this will, I understand, the particular destination of the several collections is not specified; but it is to be presumed that the wonderful treasures in the Victoria and Albert Museum will remain in the galleries they have so long adorned. The Chinese porçelain lent to that museum by Mr. Salting is a collection unsurpassed in Europe, of its kind. It is not an historically representative series, like the Franks collection, but rather a dazzling array of the most prized and finished specimens of the ceramic art, of the three great periods, K'ang Hsi, Yung Chêng, and Ch'ien Lung. As Chinese art comes to be better known, taste will probably revert to the noble largeness of earlier design, as seen in the simpler wares of the Lung period. Of these Mr. Salting had but few authentic specimens. But matchless workmanship will always hold its place, and whatever vicissitudes of taste may come about, this collection is magnificently representative of the periods and styles it illustrates. Of the other choice things at South Kensington, the ivories, the metal-work, the Persian carpets, it would require the learning of many experts to write with due appreciation. These, like the pictures shown in the National Gallery, are more or less known to the public. It is of more interest to note some of the treasures which Mr. Salting kept in his own apartments. Among these is a collection, which has not, I think, been mentioned in the papers, of early Italian Medals: the finest private collection in the world, unless the Dreyfus collection be thought to rival it. It is practically confined to the fifteenth century, but remarkable not less for its admirably representative character than for the high quality of the specimens it contains. This, one may suppose, will go to the Medal Room of the British Museum; and if so, will make the section to which it would belong the richest in existence. A fine collection of jade must be mentioned; and among the pictures a Vermeer, together with good examples of most of the best Dutch masters (Steen, Ruysdael, Maes, etc.); and excellent Constables. Of drawings Mr. Salting had no large collection, but some incomparable things among them. He had one of the two or three genuine English portrait heads by Holbein outside the great series at Windsor; this was the beautiful drawing of a lady, bought a year or two ago, and exhibited this summer at the Burlington Club; and a splendid Dürer, the so-called portrait of Lucas van Leyden, dated 1525. Rembrandt, Van Dyck, and Gainsborough are also finely represented; and not the least is the collection of some forty portrait drawings of the school of Clouet, in quality perhaps superior to any of the similar collections in France. Lastly there is the marvellous series of miniatures, from Holbein—and what a matchless Holbein is the "Anne of Cleves", also seen at the Burlington Club this year!—through Hilliard, the Olivers, Coopers and Flatman, to Cosway and Engleheart. This collection alone would have made a lesser collector's renown.

Since the above was written, the definite announcement has been made that the Salting collection is bequeathed to the nation. The bulk of it is to go to the Victoria and Albert Museum, as was anticipated; but the condition is made that all the bequest to that Museum is to be kept together. A rather severe blow, this, to the newly adopted "classification by material", which has caused so much controversy.

A NOTE ON PADEREWSKI'S SYMPHONY.

By Filson Young.

ON Saturday afternoon last, at a concert of the London Symphony Orchestra conducted by Dr. Richter, M. Paderewski's Symphony was performed for the second time in England. It has had none of the advertisement with which such works are usually heralded, and by musical critics as a whole it has been received coldly. Unfortunately I myself heard it for the first time on Saturday, and as I do not pretend to be able to take in a work of this magnitude and complexity at one hearing, I do not propose to write a criticism on it. But I wish to lose no time in recording certain broad facts about it which are at once obvious, and which have not received due recognition either in this country or America.

The Americans found it dull and tedious; so also, one may remind them, did they find the Elgar Symphony at first, until their judgment had been influenced and their enthusiasm led by a body of critical opinion which they could not but respect. As to the Paderewski Symphony, therefore, I did not attach much importance to the American verdict; but when I heard it confirmed here I assumed that it was probably true. I was certainly not prejudiced in favour of the symphony before I heard it. Every criticism that I have read before or since has grudgingly admitted certain fine qualities in it, but has condemned it as a whole on account of its lack of proportion. This does not seem to me a just or true criticism, or one with which the verdict of the future will be in agreement. With all its faults of proportion, I feel that M. Paderewski's Symphony is among the finest and most beautiful pieces of music that have been written in our time. It is full of poetry, full of colour and rhythm, and informed also with an extraordinary spiritual depth, a limpid and serene element of which only the upper surfaces are moved, and which gives to their movement a profound and luminous significance. Great and thorough as one knows M. Paderewski to be as a musician, it was certainly a discovery to me that he could work with success on so great a scale. The orchestration is extremely beautiful and in many ways quite original; his treatment of string tone in the middle register, and of the low register of flutes and other wood-wind, struck me as unfamiliar and, what does not always follow, effective. The whole symphony, moreover, has a rhythmic freshness which is invaluable in a work of such length and complexity, and (to single out one more quality which distinguishes the symphony from most other music on the same scale) the tonality, that subtle affair of modulation and key relationship which is so hard to analyse or reduce to any system, gives the work a coherence and continuity that is very satisfying to the ear.

I repeat that I do not feel competent to give after one hearing any more detailed criticism of the work. I wish merely to pay a first tribute to it as a composition of the highest interest and importance, of which much more ought to be heard, and which will, I am certain, take a permanent place among the musical works of our time.

DECEMBER.

THE voices in the dawn chorus coming this morning from the fir-trees and the deep recesses of the evergreen oak swelled from thin cheeping, from single muffled notes, to some measure of an earlier richness.

Calling your hand to your curtain, the eager broken ripplings poured in at your bared window, poignant jewels of sound, in the brilliant twilight streaming from the waning wintry crescent hanging just above the garden space. The dark outlines of the blunt low hedgerows were broken here and there by the high poplars, motionless black plumes against the silver fields. Beyond, at the edge of the world the cold daylight answered the welcoming voices, widening above the little clouds clumped along its margin, until at last they glowed to saffron and promised rose and told of crimson bars to burn across the sky. And then the voices thinned and ceased and night had left the mild raw air.

And when full day was there, a blackbird broke, from the high beech hedge dotted with lingering leaves crowning the steep bank across the roadway, into sudden wild singing—and on through the sunlit hours, daunted by a passing midday shower, he has sung as though he could know no winter but must carol so through the lengthening days until the coming of April. And now his voice follows you as you go in the afternoon light away from the homestead and road, up the high bank, through the gate and along the field-path towards the little shaw nestling in the hollow at the foot of the slope.

The end of the year is at hand, and in this down-sheltered southern strip memory prompts a quest. The song sounds faint and far, a fringe of liquid shrillings, as you cross the stile between the last drenched meadow and the acre of ploughed land stretching to the margin of the shaw. Once well out on the little firm grass-fringed causeway you are free from its haunting.

The earth lies silent all round you. The chill sweet air and the pervading dampness carry you on. A moment's turn served for the picture from the stile—the gleaming enamel of the two broad fields through which you had come, the scanty irregular fencing, the high bank and hedge marking the horizon, obliterating the farm and the distant village, showing only the top of the old grey sailless windmill on the crest of the hill, cutting you off, giving you to the world of the fields, the expanse of teeming furrows, the little silent wood and the wide sandy flats, dotted with shining pools, stretching away and away, to the sea.

The pathway will take you along beside the wood to where the thicket breaks to a wide access at the foot of the slope. But there is a better way if you will leave your high security and plunge—when you reach the nut-bushes, a little forest of bare twigs forming the angle of the shaw—into the soft turned earth. You must drag your happy burdened feet step by step along the margin of the thicket, the strong sharp earth currents tingling to your finger-tips—bringing a sudden vision of the summer's fragrant bean-rows standing in the hot sunshine festooned with the songs of sipping bees—until just beyond the half-way a small gap shows, granting access to a little muddy alley. The straggling brambles spread long bare thorny tentacles across the slippery path, and the drenched bushes besprinkle you as you brush by.

The world is away. Your winding passage has brought you into the fellowship of the encircling trees. The little wood, which showed in the distance a dark colourless clump nestling compactly beyond the sloping fields, is growing and widening as it draws you in. The sounds of your passage are echoed back from an immense stillness. With a sharp turn the avenue opens, disclosing the heart of the woodland. On the floor of the clearing, lit by the misty afternoon gold, stand the great oaks. Shimmering downwards until it is lost in the velvet moss around their feet the silver lichen clothes them. Drip, drip, drip, the lingering raindrops fall from their sleeping branches. In the immeasurable stillness there is no sound but the sharp drip, drip. Sloping gently down to the thicket—a ruddy blur away beyond the gleaming boles—the clearing, sunswept, glistens from every jewelled blade, and on its breast redeemed in the sheltered solitude you find, a fitful arabesque, clumps of rich wrinkled leafage, bearing here and there, sharp and pale, the tender petals of a primrose.

CORRESPONDENCE.

UNEMPLOYMENT AND THE BANKING QUESTION.

To the Editor of the Saturday Review.

7 December 1909.

Sir,—The contribution of your correspondent, Mr. W. P. Baines, in your issue of the 4th raises a number of interesting and important points.

Mr. Baines says "What we seem to lack is adequate control of capital", by which I understand he means there is an insufficiency of liquid capital, which is undoubtedly true. There are two ways by which this may be provided. The one is that suggested by Mr. Meulen: the issue of credit notes against capital—not gold merely—which would provide an amount limited only by capital available and the demand for such notes. The other way is that provided by our present system—viz. increase the supply of gold. The latter is about the most irrational system one could well imagine, for it means that employment must depend upon the precariousness and accidental discoveries of gold, which is less sane than an Act limiting the hours of labour to correspond to the hours of sunshine.

"The available savings of the world tend to be represented by gold because no doubt gold has such obvious advantages and is so universally acceptable." So writes Mr. Baines, who seeks to make a virtue of necessity. Experience proves the contrary. Gold possesses no greater advantages for currency purposes than paper. Paper circulates to a much greater degree in those countries where gold and paper are equally available. And as regards its being "universally acceptable", this is due to law and law alone. All nations have enacted laws making gold legal tender, a condition that would make paper equally acceptable. Fifty years ago silver was more acceptable than gold, because silver was then the universal legal standard money. Gold was actually demonetised in Holland in 1847. My quarrel with the gold standard is that it greatly restricts the use of capital and is far too scarce an article for the needs of modern commerce. It is this that causes fluid capital to be scarce, so that if it is needed in Egypt and New York we have to stand idle and wait for its return. "You cannot eat your cake and have it", says Mr. Baines. No, but why confine yourself to a single cake when flour and butter and eggs and currants are so abundant? Why not have enough cakes to go round? Here is the very root of the problem of unemployment. All the prime factors of production, land, labour, and capital, are abundant. We haven't commenced fully to employ one half of the amount available. Wealth is produced so easily and quickly that the cry of this century is "over-production". The thing that worries the producer to-day is not how to produce wealth and capital, but how to get rid of it, how to exchange it. Millions are spent annually and wars are often waged trying to produce fresh markets. Where, then, is the difficulty? Surely in the mechanism of exchange. We produce more goods than our restricted mechanism allows us to exchange. It is—to use Mr. Baines' simile—our restricting ourselves to one cake—a golden cake—when we might have dozens far more digestible and palatable. After all, money and credit are mere inventions, and if the same freedom had been allowed by legislators in this field as in all other fields of invention, industry and production would not be in the insecure condition they now are.

This condition is aptly illustrated by the well-known pyramid standing upon its apex. The figure shows the same apex representing gold, supporting a huge volume of credit upon which the whole of our trade and commerce rests. With the idea of the inverted pyramid in mind, it is easy to see why the shipment of a comparatively small amount of gold affects our trade so disastrously. The shipment of, say, five millions in gold reduces credit ten or twenty times and cuts off a corresponding volume of trade.

One error Mr. Baines has made is that an increase of credit raises prices. This is not necessarily so. An increase in gold or credit might have that effect if all other conditions remained the same. But they do not. There are hundreds of new industries that would be started within a week if money could be obtained more easily and cheaper than at present. I do not mean merely "call" loans. New enterprises usually require time for development, and no one would start with borrowed money if it were likely to be called in, say, within three or four months. What is needed is cheap time loans for such industries. This would increase employment and production and the demand for credit would increase as fast as and faster than the supply.

A Reader of the S. R.

MR. CAMERON CORBETT AND TRADESTON DIVISION.

To the Editor of the Saturday Review.

Glasgow, 21 December 1909.

Sir,—"Politics have never been a scrupulous department of human affairs." Such is the opinion of a prominent writer on social problems; and the political manœuvring of Mr. Corbett at the time of his withdrawal from the Unionist party, and latterly during the past few weeks, gives a practical illustration of the truth of this dictum. At his committee meeting on the 17th inst. he complained that a reflection had been cast on the constituency because of his postcard inquiry. Why was the postcard inquiry adopted? And does it not come near to being an infringement of the Ballot Act? The constituency would have been spared this reflection had he, in a manly, straightforward, and constitutional manner resigned his seat at the time of his secession and contested it as a Liberal. After his act of tergiversation he chose to sit tight and record his vote for the measures of the Government—a fact of which he now boasts—though returned as a Unionist, and by the aid of the Conservative organisation. If that is what he regards as political honesty or political consistency, may the gift of smiling never depart from him! More than that, he has never, since his withdrawal from the Unionist party, addressed a public meeting of his constituents to explain his conduct and position. Yet he says there is nothing but sincerity and brotherliness existing between him and them. Surely this is the acme of cant and humbug! If, however, he has treated them with scant courtesy in the past, at this committee meeting he covertly insulted them by stating that if the link is broken between them as representative and represented, no charity will suffer and no donation be withdrawn. What has his future philanthropic or benevolent intentions to do with this political contest? The inference by the plain man is that should Mr. Corbett be again returned, perhaps the subscription will be in keeping with his majority. This is very near sailing to get round the Corrupt Practices Act, and is the plutocrat personified. He has been in Parliament for nearly a quarter of a century, and as a politician no other judgment is possible but that he has been a failure. Mr. Corbett is strong against the hereditary principle in the House of Lords. Perhaps it is not a perfect system. At the same time, he has much to be thankful for in being the eldest son of his father. Nothing is more certain than that he never would have been member for Tradeston had he been as poor a man as your correspondent, who takes leave to subscribe himself

Diogenes.

THE LIBERAL CHURCHMAN'S DILEMMA.

To the Editor of the Saturday Review.

1 Vernon Chambers, Southampton Row W.C.

20 December 1909.

Sir,—I cannot help thinking that in your article on "The Liberal Churchman's Dilemma" you have misunderstood the character and miscalculated the strength of Liberal Churchmanship. For I understand that by a Liberal Churchman you mean one who is by tradition or conviction a Liberal in politics.

The man of the type you describe, who puts politics before Churchmanship, exists no doubt, and is, as you say, a "marked man". But there are many of us who, convinced Free Traders as we are, consider that Protection would be a disaster to the material welfare of the country, but hold that spiritual and moral interests are of greater count, both in themselves and because prosperity ultimately depends on a nation's character. We find it impossible, therefore, to vote for our party as long as its leaders attack the Church and try to banish her teaching from the schools.

How many we may be it is impossible to say, but I am convinced that we are more in number than professional politicians suspect. We do not live in their world and seldom make our voices heard, but we vote, and every one of our votes that is alienated represents a dead loss to our party. I need not say with what sorrow we, who always prided ourselves on belonging to the party of progress that upheld the principle of religious equality, find ourselves so disillusioned when we contemplate the reactionary policy of religious persecution that the present Government has adopted. Yours etc.,

Clement F. Rogers.

To the Editor of the Saturday Review.

Capworth Lodge, Leyton, Essex,
15 December 1909.

Sir,—I do not call myself either a "Liberal" or a "Conservative" Churchman, because these names signify nothing definite to anyone not actively engaged in the rather dirty game of party politics. Nor am I strictly a "Socialist" Churchman, though my sympathies are with the Socialists, who are free at least from the vice of hypocrisy, who know what they want, and whom I am prepared to support in getting it, up to a certain point. As a Catholic layman and a member of the "English Church Union", I abhor the Liberal party and mistrust the Conservative. Of the two, however, I prefer the open enemy to the false friend, and I purpose doing all in my power next month to secure the return of the Liberal and Nonconformist candidate for the constituency in which I happen to reside, for the following reasons: I object to "Tariff Reform", and I want reform of the House of Lords. On these two issues the next General Election will turn. If, as I hope and confidently expect, Mr. Asquith will return to power, the Budget will go through, together with its land-valuation clauses, which are the cause of all the fuss, and Tariff Reform will be scotched if not killed. The next Parliament will probably be a short one. Welsh Disestablishment and another attempt at the establishment of the Nonconformist religion of Undenominationalism in the schools will be frustrated by the unreformed Second Chamber (or the Liberal party may even have learned wisdom by their past failures and succeed in settling the religious difficulty in the only equitable way—viz., by providing religious teaching of the kind desired by the parents for the three divisions—Church, Roman Catholic, and "simple Bible"), and the Government will bring forward some scheme for restricting the Peers' veto, which will, of course, not pass into law. Meanwhile, the responsible peers, who are quite as anxious for the reform, and consequent strengthening, of their Chamber as the Liberals are for reducing it to practical impotence, will, in all probability, be quite ready with proposals which will be submitted to the country at the next election but one, and if they recommend themselves to the good sense of the non-party electors (who, after all, are the overwhelming majority in the country), a way out of the present difficult and, in many respects, unsatisfactory situation will be found. For these reasons a Churchman may vote Liberal in January without impaling himself on either horn of the dilemma you present. There is no inconsistency in "thanking God there is a House of Lords" and at the same time desiring its reform. When thieves fall out honest men may come by their own.

Chas. G. Harrison.

[This letter is a delightful instance of the dishonesty

which men who think themselves peculiarly honest so often fall into. Very few "professional politicians" would confess that they were trusting to the Lords to thwart certain iniquitous legislation and at the same time were working and hoping for the return of the party pledged to destroy the House of Lords and pass the said iniquitous legislation. Such shamelessness is indecent.—Ed. S. R.]

THE DECEASED WIFE'S SISTER CASE.

To the Editor of the Saturday Review.

Lincoln's Inn, 20 December 1909.

Sir,—If I may venture to do so, will you let me thank you for your excellent article on the Thompson appeal? You stand practically alone in the lay press, but it is just those who have the courage to stand alone who win in the long run. Where stands the "Times" newspaper now? Nothing was more honourable and consistent in its former career than its outspoken line on this question—a line never departed from, even when it gave a general support to the Liberal party. Under its new management, it does not aspire to lead public opinion.

You have well expressed the logic of the matter. I would add the law, too, but for the respect I have for the very learned judges who have interpreted it in a contrary sense. On this point it is not unworthy of notice that the opinion of the learned Dean of the Arches was formed "not without some doubt and hesitation".

I read yesterday in a weekly paper, usually most well-informed, that the judgment would commend itself to all but "the extreme High Church party". This remark betrays absolute ignorance of the history of the controversy. Presbyterian Scotland appeals to the Westminster Confession, which lays down exactly the same rule as to the prohibited degrees as that of the Church of England. And in England the relaxation of the law had some of its strongest opponents in the Evangelical school. Are we to class the late Lord Shaftesbury and the late Lord Cairns as victims of "sacerdotal tyranny", wedded to "ecclesiastical rubbish"?

One word more. If the law as laid down in the Court of Appeal holds the field, it is to be hoped that the Church will follow the strong and clear lead of the Bishop of Birmingham. Any other course, dictated by dread of Disestablishment, would simply be

"Propter vitam, vivendi perdere causas".

Yours faithfully,

W. Digby Thurnam.

"BOERS WILL BE BOERS."

To the Editor of the Saturday Review.

Mamiaanshoek, P.O. Zwagershoek, Nylstroom, Transvaal, 3 November 1909.

Sir,—The Boers of the Orange River Free State province of United South Africa are loudly demanding that their children shall be educated in English and better taught the English language. A most laudable demand; and one would admire their good sense, and prophesy well of South Africa, were it not for a memory of recent history.

In 1903, the general medium of instruction being English, and the time devoted to the teaching of English and Dutch about the same, these same Boers would have none of it; the use of English was a device to root out their native tongue and to lure the children into undesirable doctrines. By their thousands they protested they would have none of it; rather would they undergo the martyrdom of a small money payment in the shape of school fees.

With much cry and little wool in the shape of grudging subscriptions, the private schools were started to preserve the "mother tongue" free and undefiled, amid much intellectual juggling with the question whether the said "mother-tongue" were the Dutch of Holland, the degraded patois of South Africa, or something between the two. The schools were confessedly only a bluff, to be financed somehow till the Crown Colony Government should surrender and amalgamate. This last fact, I might add, was blurted out to me in advance by one of the chief organisers of the "discontent" while unfortunately in his cups.

The bluff succeeded to admiration, and the Government surrendered on a compromise which logically paved the way for the coming of General Hertzog, with his system by which the medium of instruction is that of the majority in the school, with repetition for form's sake in the tongue of any minority. Surely this was what the malcontents originally clamoured for: "liberty for our children to be educated through the language they know", the "preservation of the mother tongue", etc., etc. Yet now we have these same Boers, headed by Mr. C. L. Botha M.L.A., Mayor of Bloemfontein, clamouring for the despised and rejected English as the medium.

Mr. Botha is amazing in his candour with regard to the various forms of the Dutch language, saying that "the parents won't allow" the giving of instruction through the "taal" because "the mother tongue of the Dutch children—my own mother tongue—does not provide the words to convey technical meanings of abstract ideas", while as to high Dutch "those terms of ideas would be as unintelligible to the child in high Dutch as they would be in English". Again, he refers to high Dutch as "practically a foreign language—which may be all very well in Amsterdam, but of no use in South Africa". Wherefore unless the Dutch medium—which last week, as it were, was the only means to salvation—be forthwith abandoned, Mr. Botha and the Boers are once more prepared to endure martyrdom.

Mr. Botha's arguments, almost his very phrases, are identically those used by the Crown officials in the original debate; but they were told that they merely exposed their ignorance, pardonable in newcomers, of the fluency with which the humblest bijwoner prattles high Dutch in the bosom of his family; that their quite erroneous statements of the poverty of the "taal" were a gratuitous and cowardly insult to the dearest feelings of a beaten foe.

This would all be very good farce, a distinct addition to the gaiety of nations, were it not for the disquieting thought that these people who have behaved so much like spoiled children are now to have as a plaything the native question, with which in all probability is bound up the destiny of the British Empire.

Yours faithfully,

C. R. Prance.

JAMAICA.

To the Editor of the Saturday Review.

148 Harbour Street, Kingston, Jamaica, 4 December 1909.

Sir,—Allow me to thank you for your note on Jamaica in your issue of 20 November. You are quite right when you say that the impression that Jamaica is always being visited by calamities is entirely wrong. As a matter of fact, there has been no storm here since 1903. We had five or six days of very heavy rain two or three weeks ago. Some of the rivers overflowed and several small bridges were swept away. A few peasants whose houses were built on the banks of the rivers were drowned; and for a short time communication was interrupted in several parts of the island. The losses altogether were insignificant. None of our great bridges has been destroyed; most of our planters agree that the benefit we have derived from the rains is greater by far than the loss we have sustained, and this is also the Governor's opinion.

The true situation in Jamaica is this. The island has never been better off. There is a larger area of land under cultivation to-day than there ever was before; revenue is coming in handsomely, and the Government has been reducing taxation. There exists a £100,000 fund to repair any damages that may be caused by such calamities as floods or hurricanes, and this fund is still intact. In addition to this, the Government has a floating balance of £50,000 to aid the revenue in case of any unforeseen falling-off. The Collector-General told me two weeks ago that he expected that the Customs duties alone would give a surplus of £40,000 this year, and surpluses are expected from other sources of revenue.

The Government and the legislators of the island are thinking seriously of improving the public service. It is proposed that the island, already healthy, should be made still further attractive to visitors, and so a determined effort is to be made to extirpate the germs of the very mild form of malarial fever which exists in some parts of Jamaica. Jamaica to-day is covered with luxuriant vegetation, and the capital, Kingston, is being steadily rebuilt. Altogether our prospects are excellent and our present position is a very happy one.

Yours faithfully,
H. G. de Lisser.

THE RAVENS OF FRESHWATER.

To the Editor of the Saturday Review.

Rochester, 15 December 1909.

Sir,—The Royal Society for the Protection of Birds has lately reported the wanton destruction, as it is believed, of the last pair of ravens in the Isle of Wight and Hampshire, after their eggs had been taken in spite of the vigilance of a watcher. Those responsible for this irreparable mischief deserve to be hounded out of the country. Unfortunately the evidence against them was not strong enough to justify a prosecution. It seems that the people of this country will not awake until too late to the fact that their rarest and finest birds are fast vanishing, through the greed and selfishness of a few people; but some day a bitter feeling of resentment will grow up against those who have caused the mischief. We want our birds, and it is our duty to keep them living objects of the greatest beauty, pleasure and interest; not lifeless specimens in private collections and museums, where they, with their eggs, can last at longest but a few years. Our birds belong to the nation as surely as the air and the sunshine do. The land for the people is now the cry: should this come about before the people are better educated, it is difficult to guess what would be the effect on our wild birds. It might be deplorable, but anyhow the people should have the opportunity of preserving the fauna of their country. The majority of landowners have betrayed their trust; some wilfully, others through apathy and want of care in not seeing their wishes and orders carried out. Let anyone who does not understand me read what Mr. W. H. Hudson wrote in your Review of 3 October 1908, under the heading "The Sacred Bird". How strange it is and how deplorable that our schools and universities, and education generally, have done so little in teaching the duty and the pleasure of preserving the Creator's priceless gift, the wild life of our country!

I am yours faithfully,
Frank C. H. Borrett.

[We need hardly say we sympathise heartily with our correspondent. Could not the Bird Protection Society keep a black book and enter in it the name of every fool who thinks the best way to preserve a rare species is to shoot its last survivor? If this black-list were published periodically in the "Times" most people passing as respectable would be shy of appearing in it; though of course some would be elated at seeing their names printed in any connexion. It would probably console such for being hanged that their names would appear next day in the report of the execution. Only the other day we heard of a Lesser Bustard being shot in Wiltshire; in the same county a White-tailed Eagle was shot on Marden Down this year. The "sportsman's" name can be got in this case, and we propose to advertise him, though he may come in the category we have just mentioned.—Ed. S. R.]

REVIEWS.

SHAKESPEARE AND HIS AGE.

"A Literary History of the English People: From the Renaissance to the Civil War." II. By J. J. Jusserand. London: Fisher Unwin. 1909. 12s. 6d. net.

No man was more creative than Shakespeare. A shameless commonplace, but we must begin with a truism in order to point the paradox that follows. Shakespeare was original: yet no man was more clearly the product and reflection of his age. Shakespeare was creative: yet no man subordinated creative impulse with such entire success to the needs of his contemporary hearers. The plays of Shakespeare are a final answer to those who cry out upon the harsh strictures of transitory art-forms, and are prone to believe that they will appeal to the future because they have failed to appeal to the present. Shakespeare cheerfully submitted to formulæ that were inartistic, or satisfied tastes that were degraded; and he contrived to do both without damaging his art or spoiling his theme. His genius broke through a medium that was coarse, only to be more completely triumphant. His appeal frequently tickled the ears of the groundlings, only to reverberate more loudly in the ears of mankind. It is, in fact, difficult to say whether Shakespeare triumphed because of his tools or in spite of them.

The crowd that turned in to Shakespeare's theatre would as soon have turned in to a bear-baiting in the neighbouring yard. This bear-baiting was, beyond all others, the alternative delight. Sometimes, by way of variation to the baiting by dogs, the bear was blinded and whipped to death by stablemen. The spectators were out to see bloodshed, and the manner of it did not signify. Some of them on the way to the theatre or yard might have passed some unfortunate vagabond naked to the middle and whipped through the streets in accordance with the precise instructions of the Elizabethan Poor Law. Here was an audience that required a great deal to arouse its horror; and, as it revelled indiscriminately in its young sensations, it was ever ready to buy the pennyworth of thrills. In most cases the pennyworth was a good one—especially at the theatre. The theatre soon came to be more popular than the bear-yard. There horror had no limit, except that set by imagination; and horror could be thrown into rude relief by grotesque interpolation of farce at a moment when nerves were on the stretch. Or, perhaps, there would be some outburst of poetic fervour, some bout of euphuistic wit, or some melting to a mood of pastoral, elegiac, and always ingenious love-making. There might, in fact, be anything, so long as it was unexpected and in violent contrast with what went before. The bill of fare was almost invariable—strong meat served in a rapid succession of courses ill-assorted for any but the strongest digestions. The people who came to Shakespeare's theatre were hungry for just this fare. They could depend on Kyd and Peele and Greene, on Lodge and Nash and Marlowe to give it them. In a popular play of the time, "Solyman and Persida", all the interesting personages are killed. "Moonshine and Lion are left to bury the dead." There is a list of properties belonging to the Lord Admiral's men. We read: "Item, j caulderm for the Jewe". This was for the boiling of Marlowe's Rich Jew of Malta. "Titus Andronicus" indeed! "Titus Andronicus" is quite a mild play, insipid by the side of some by Marston, Ford or Webster. Every variety of murder or rape is brought on to the stage, and dead bodies are adjured to swing or bleed or rot, as the case may be, under the eyes of the spectators, by this time a little jaded. Then, always at the right moment, out would come the clown, or there would be some wonderful word-play, or ingenious turn of the plot.

Shakespeare accepted all this, and the fact that he had to accept it never seemed to worry him. He took "Hamlet", a horrible old Elizabethan melodrama—the audience delighted in repetition—and gave it back to his generation with its horror and violence undiminished, with all the old twists of plot and rude alternations of crime and farce. But the horror and violence turned to supreme tragedy, and farcical interpolation gave us the grave-scene. Shakespeare denied his audience nothing they asked for. Euphuism? They should have it—transmuted to great human prose. Idyllics? They should have them—in the form of Comedies which will always be among the loveliest products of human fancy. Lofty patriotic flights? Shakespeare was ready with his Histories. Poetic rhapsody checking the flow of dramatic action? Shakespeare was ready to arrest counsels of state with line upon line about the virtues and wonders of the bee. Nice encounters of wit—mere verbal exercises? Shakespeare lifted even these from barren ingenuity to human significance. Old Gaunt punning on his name would bring down an Elizabethan house, and this, to us at any rate, appeals as intensely to-day. It is almost unnecessary to urge the point further. There was nothing that Shakespeare omitted to catch the attention of his own time. All the stock situations and devices—young women wandering as men, the plot within a plot, lost children, comedies of errors, ghosts and witches—all these things Shakespeare found to his hand and used over and over again. The fact that he borrowed his plots is only a small piece of the truth. He borrowed also his methods, and the form of his drama was moulded almost entirely in accordance with what his audience required of him. He even imported into his plays the necessary spice of obscenity. But here, too, the fundamental sanity and greatness of the man came through. Shakespeare's obscenity is never more than a frank and full-blooded recognition of the more elemental facts of the flesh. He was more refined than his age, but he was not fastidious; so that, although he was clean-minded, he could be Elizabethan in his coarseness.

M. Jusserand in this portion of his "Literary History" (it is the second part of the English translation: the French is differently arranged) is dealing almost entirely with Shakespeare and his contemporaries. To read the volume is to view Shakespeare as he is too seldom viewed, in his true historic setting. How far Shakespeare's work mirrors his personality Mr. Frank Harris has set us all thinking. There is no doubt that Shakespeare's work mirrors his age. His plays are a priceless commentary upon Elizabethan manners and feeling. Their value in this respect is evident as soon as they are placed by the side of the plays of his contemporaries, written for the same audiences. We can then perceive what it was that was due to Shakespeare's creative genius and what it was that he took from his age as the raw stuff of his art. Comparison lays bare the two things we most desire to know—the Elizabethan taste and spirit on the one hand, and the nature of Shakespeare's genius on the other. The man who has made this comparison most brilliantly and completely, and gained from that comparison a real insight into some of the manifestations of Shakespeare's genius, is a Frenchman—one of the very few Frenchmen who can approach Shakespeare with anything like a clear understanding. But M. Jusserand has a genius for criticism that transcends what we believe to be a racial disability. Certainly there is no living critic who could have made a study so vivid, and at the same time so scholarly, in the literature of a nation whose artistic spirit lies so far removed from that of his own.

A DIPLOMATIST'S WIFE.

"In Three Legations." By Madame Charles de Bunsen. London: Fisher Unwin. 1909. 12s. 6d. net.

THE life of few women can be pleasanter than that of a diplomatist's wife. The diplomatic couple are moved about from one foreign capital to another, and wherever they go are immediately received into the best society, a small and charming group, between whose members there exists a kind of family intimacy or freemasonry. Diplomacy is also a career in which a wife may be more useful to her husband than in any other, as the "chéfesses de mission" are sometimes quite as important as the chiefs. It is true that the telegraph and the telephone have robbed diplomacy of some of its power; but as long as men are men the spoken word and the hand-shake will do a great deal in business. Madame de Bunsen is the sister of Monsieur Waddington, who was Prime Minister of France and for ten years French Ambassador in London. Her mother's name was Chisholm, so that she may be described as three-parts English or Scotch. Her husband was the third son of the celebrated Baron Bunsen, and was Secretary, afterwards Councillor, to the Prussian Legations in Turin, Florence, and The Hague. The diplomatic experiences of the Bunsens were certainly exciting, for they were in Turin and Florence from 1858 to 1868, when Italian unity was making, and when Victor Emmanuel embarked in two wars against Austria—the first in alliance with France, and the second as the ally of Prussia. In 1870 the Bunsens were at The Hague when the war broke out between France and Germany—a very awkward position for husband and wife, of whom one was German and the other French. In one of her letters at this period Madame de Bunsen thanks her mother (née Chisholm) for her kindness to the German officers quartered in her château near Rouen! But Madame de Bunsen's interests and affinities were so mixed that she must have been a perfect Cosmopolitan.

Madame de Bunsen has humour and considerable power of description; her style of writing is easy and unaffected and accurate. She observed closely, reported conscientiously, and is never malicious or scandalous. Indeed, to judge from these pages, she seems to have been a perfect wife and mother, and a clever, well-bred woman of the world. Her description of the scene in the first Italian Parliament at Turin between Cavour and Garibaldi is vivid history. After the Treaty of Villafranca Cavour gave a dinner, at which the ice-cream was surmounted by a dove, to which he called the attention of his guests—"Voyez-vous la colombe de la paix?" When Victor Emmanuel moved his Court from Turin to Florence—which was described at the time as an ingratitude and an imprudence, but which was merely a step towards Rome—the Piedmontese were naturally furious with their idol, and riots broke out, which were suppressed with bloodshed. The mob surrounded the Palace and shouted: "Morte al Re! Abbasso Vittorio! Abbasso Casa di Savoia!" However, when the King returned, after a month, to pay a short visit to the Turinese, he was rapturously received, the very intelligent Piedmontese having perceived in the interval that United Italy was a different thing from the kingdom of Sardinia. "I am sending you a paper", writes Madame de Bunsen, "with a capital drawing of the meeting between Vittorio and Giandouja, who is the popular personification of the Piedmontese"—as if John Bull were dressed up. "The scene was really enacted in the Piazza san Carlo on Monday last. Quite an ordinary mask came up to the King's carriage in the Corso, and, after talking to him for some time, held out his hand, saying in broad Piedmontese, 'Toc la li' (Touch it then), and the King shook hands with him." Thus was the reconciliation between Victor Emmanuel and the Piedmontese effected. These touches give us an insight into the simple, excitable, Italian character. Talking of masks, Madame de Bunsen tells a very good story about the old Prussian King, first German Emperor, Frederick William. The King said he liked the freedom and unconventionality of masked balls, and so got himself up in a mask and domino. But when a passing mask patted him on the stomach and inquired, "Wie geht es, Alter?" (How goes it, old man?), the King drew himself up and replied "Alles sagen, aber nicht anrühren" (Say anything, but do not touch). The story is a lesson to kings not to play the fool. Madame de Bunsen writes shrewdly that, if any one wishes to know his precise social value, let him go to Berlin. After you have been told by Court chamberlains that you must not go into that room, and must not sit at that table, and been generally waved about for a few evenings, you begin to know your place. As someone said wittily, in France you are prayed to do this or that or the other; in Germany "alles ist verboten".

After Italy and Berlin the Bunsens naturally found The Hague dull until the news of the Franco-Prussian War arrived. Madame de Bunsen gives us an observant and humorous picture of the Netherlands Court, and of the meticulous luxury of the home life of the Dutch upper class. "The King also shook hands and graciously told me it was 'infernally hot' and he was going back to The Loo as soon as he could. H.M. speaks English remarkably well, but indulges sometimes in strong expressions", a comical error to which everyone is liable in speaking a foreign language. We once heard an Englishman answer a French lady who asked him how he liked the Exposition, "Ah, Madame, ça m'embête à crever"! The Frenchwoman's face was a study! After staying in a Dutch country house Madame de Bunsen writes: "We were certainly much impressed with the studied and excessive comfort of Dutch life. The great importance of meals, the amount of food, the particular excellence of the tea, of the coffee, of the chocolate, of the cream, of the fruit, of everything, in fact. But the whole time of our stay the words of Scripture, 'Man doth not live by bread alone', were running in my head, and I rather sympathised with Mlle. A., who bored herself horribly, and declared, 'qu'elle avait envie de leur jeter toute cette mangeaille à la tête'". This is from the first page to the last a most entertaining and instructive book, which is worth the fatigue of holding, for it is somewhat cumbrous in form. Why will publishers not produce two light volumes, instead of one that is so heavy as to require a Sandow or a reading-desk to hold it up?

A NEW HISTORIAN.

"The Medici." By Colonel G. F. Young. London: Murray. 1909. 36s. net.

WE bid a very cordial welcome to this important book on the great House of Medici. Colonel Young's name was unknown to us as a writer, known to us only as a gallant and distinguished Indian officer, and we will frankly confess that we entered on the reading of this voluminous work on so intricate, thorny and difficult a subject as the Medici with feelings of considerable trepidation. But the reading of a few chapters soon showed us that we were in the presence of a remarkable and a fine book, written by one with an infinite capacity for taking pains who had gradually become deeply versed in the subject. It is not the work of a literary craftsman, but so fascinatingly interesting has the author made it that one brushes aside altogether any questions of style. That is its chief and remarkable characteristic, the real secret of its success—interest, interesting; we read from beginning to end without our attention once flagging, and it is the story of flesh and blood Medici we read, not the fairy tale of impossible bogeys and transpontine tyrants. Sanity of judgment is another of the author's characteristics, and he has nearly, though not quite, emancipated himself from the thrall of legends which die hard. The book is well compacted, extraordinarily accurate, carefully dated; sufficiently full consideration is given to contemporary events; the observations on art are often quite noteworthy; and it is informed throughout with the natural directness, the love of essentials, the sense of fairplay, characteristic of the military mind. If this is really Colonel Young's first incursion into Italian history, we are frankly puzzled to know how the book ever came to be written, and it increases our admiration of a remarkable feat. In short we have here a really satisfactory history of the Medici which, with a few corrections and improvements and an occasional modification of judgment, is likely to remain the English standard work on the subject for many years to come.

The estimate of the Duke Alexander, for instance, needs considerable modification. Colonel Young will hear no good of him, and even adjudges him "stupid" and "incapable". It seems to us as if Colonel Young had failed to lay this one Medici bogey, and had allowed himself to be frighted from a proper study of the subject; else he could never have written as he has done: "Alexander is never known to have done or said a single thing worth being recorded". Does he know Ceccheregli's "Attioni et Sentenze"? Make all deductions for the eulogium of an enthusiastic admirer, and we still have here a fine substratum of wit and wisdom, and the record of happy judgments which would have done honour to just Solomon. No Prince that ever ruled in Italy had so fine a sense of justice, and none ever took so keen a relish in its even-handed administration. We are not for whitewashing the ill-fated "Moor"; we only ask for the same fair and sane treatment which Colonel Young has meted out to Catherine and Cosimo, to the Gottoso and Gian Gastone. (Colonel Young's account of Catherine—he devotes 168 pages to her—is perhaps the fairest and truest ever written of that remarkable woman.) Had Alexander but survived the tempestuous sowing of his wild oats—he was barely twenty-seven when foully murdered—he would certainly have fulfilled the rich promise of his nature, and proved the greatest ruler of them all.

The first and larger part of the book, dealing with the elder branch, is also the better. Colonel Young is obviously more in sympathy with Cosimo Pater Patriae and Lorenzo il Magnifico than with the Grand Dukes Cosimo and Ferdinand. Some of the Grand-ducal reigns suffer by compression. This was perhaps inevitable: as it is, the book runs to over 1100 pages. Still some vital points called for a fuller elucidation even at the expense of more interesting matter. For instance, the change in the constitution of the Florentine State from a Republic with Gonfalonier and Priors to an hereditary rulership seems to us inadequately dealt with. The compact between Clement VII. and Charles V. at Barcelona was that the Medici should be restored to their former position in Florence. That position was informal headship of the State. Charles V.'s Diploma, so as effectively to secure the position, makes Alexander and the issue male of his body, or failing such issue the nearest male agnate, not Duke of Florence, but hereditary head of the Republic of Florence ("Reipublicæ Florentinæ Gubernii Status atque Regiminis Caput"). It was the Florentines themselves who afterwards made him "Duke of Florence" and practically an absolute ruler. This was never ratified by the Emperor, who never once even addressed Alexander as Duke of Florence. (He, however, was already a Duke, Duke of Civita di Penna.)

The account of Cosimo's accession is not only inadequate but inaccurate. It is inaccurate to say that Cosimo was "given by the Emperor the rank of Duke of Florence". A fresh Imperial Diploma had become necessary so as to exclude Lorenzino, the nearest male agnate (his brother Giuliano was likewise excluded), and in this the Emperor only gives Cosimo, as in the case of Alexander, the status of head or chief of the Republic. Cosimo soon after the issue of this Diploma begins to sign himself no longer "Cosimo Medici" but "Duca di Fiorenza", and this he did because the Diploma, though it confers no title, does allow Cosimo "ex gratia nostra uti et frui ea omni auctoritate quod prædictus quondam Dux Alexander tempore sui obitus poterat et utebatur". To read Colonel Young one would suppose that Cosimo obtained the Republic of Siena "by conquest". How could he "conquer" an Imperial fief and at the same time be the ally of the Emperor? The truth is that Charles V. granted his son Philip II. the investiture of the lapsed fief of Siena, and that Cosimo obtained it from Philip by sub-investiture. These are not mere jurisprudential niceties, but fundamental laws which regulated the holding of important territories. It is also an error to say that Cosimo "was given" the "Island of Elba"; he only obtained the investiture of Portoferraio with some 12,000 feet of territory round the town; these and kindred subjects are fully dealt with in Spannaghel's monumental "Notizia della vera libertà di Firenze". A greater knowledge of feudal jurisprudence and practice would also have saved Colonel Young from two unfortunate pages in which he describes what he calls the "loss of Urbino" to Tuscany. Having in the first volume told us that Lorenzo di Pietro was wrongfully made Duke of Urbino by Leo X.—with which we are inclined to agree—he in the second volume enters a claim to the Duchy for the Grand Duke Ferdinand II. as descended through his grandmother, Catherine, from the wrongful Duke. And at the same time he claims the Duchy for Ferdinand's wife, Vittoria della Rovere, only child of the last lawful Duke, though the bull of investiture clearly limits the succession to heirs male only. Colonel Young considers that Urbino could by "no possible argument be declared a vacant fief", yet nothing could be clearer than that the Duchy reverted to the direct dominion of the States of the Church through failure of male issue. Colonel Young is of opinion that Urban VIII. intended to give the Duchy to a member of his own family. But it is a matter of history that he resisted the suggestion, because, like all the Popes since Pius V., he had bound himself on no consideration, not even for the good of the State, to alienate the cities or territories of the Church's Temporal Dominions by way of fiefs. (See Pius V.'s Constitution "Admonet Nos", of 20 March 1567.)

One other word by way of criticism. Authorities are cited frequently, but the page of the volume is seldom given. This hampers the careful student, and delays the conscientious critic. Too often, however, references are not given, and we have to be content with the expressions "we are told", "we read", "it has been said", "says an old chronicler", "says a scientist of our own day". These expressions are often serviceable, but who tells us and where we read should be accurately stated in an appendix. The bibliography of "Authorities consulted" is singularly incomplete and apparently based on no fixed principle. But few Italian works are mentioned, and far too many English. We miss most of all Galluzzi, Litta, and the thirty-three volumes of Cantini's "Legislazione Toscana"; there is no mention of individual lives such as Rastrelli's of Alexander or Cantini's of Cosimo, nor of special studies such as Borgognoni's of Lorenzino or Ferrai's on the first years of Cosimo's rule. Even the fountain head of so much information, Moreni's "Serie d'Autori risguardanti la celebre famiglia Medici", finds no place in the list. The genealogical tables at the end of each volume are without a single date, and that in the carefully dated book of a genealogically-minded writer is an unaccountable omission.

PERSIAN TRAVEL.

"Through Persia: from the Gulf to the Caspian." By F. B. Bradley Birt. London: Smith, Elder. 1909. 12s. 6d. net.

MR. BIRT sailed up the Persian Gulf from Muscat and landed at Bushire. From Bushire he rode over the kotals to Shiraz and visited the graves of Hafiz and Sadi. He then covered the distances between Shiraz and Ispahan, Ispahan and the capital, Teheran and the Caspian port of Enzeli, by "carriage dak", the system on which one drives throughout the livelong day in an old springless landau, changing one's driver and horses at every caravanserai. Thus he did not go in any direction off the beaten track between Bushire and Enzeli, nor did he adopt, like the authors of "Through Persia in a Motor Car", a sensational style of travel.

In a short introductory note he expresses the hope that the recent popularity of Persian travel among Europeans may add an interest to his book. Surely Persian travel is neither popular nor likely to become so. Possibly the existence of a very considerable literature on the subject misled Mr. Birt. But the number of trippers to Persia scarcely exceeds the number of books on Persia, as is well known. The thing has gone past being a joke, this writing of guide-books when there are none to guide. General Houtum Schindler of Teheran, who placed his intimate knowledge at Mr. Birt's disposal, might have told him this—the General Schindler who knows more about Persia than any foreigner alive, and to whose house all travellers go as though it were a bureau of information, a Cook's office. Visit Iran! There is no denying, however, that Mr. Birt has written a very superior guide-book indeed, one that ought to be in the hands of every Indian official who decides to return home via the Gulf and the Caspian. The expedition lies, so to speak, under the noses of Indian officials. The book will interest others too, although it will not compel them to set off to the Empire of Iran. The chapter on Teheran is disappointing, but the historical and literary information as to Ispahan, Shiraz and Persepolis is very readably given. The journey direct from Bushire to Enzeli is not necessarily an adventurous one, and Mr. Birt met no brigands. Even during the recent revolution it could be made safely enough, at least by foreigners. Means and methods are to hand. One is not by any means an explorer or even an unexpected visitor. It is possible indeed that the beaten track is the most amusing track to follow, because the means and methods that exist are extremely peculiar and not to be found anywhere else in the world. They have often been described before. Still Mr. Birt's account is the most detailed that we have seen of the nature of the "road" in Persia. He tells the traveller exactly what to expect.

The soul of Persia has baffled Mr. Birt. Travel literature about Persia has established a kind of convention for itself which he accepts in such passages as these: "The first feeling of bafflement and mystery still holds". And again: "These high dead walls baffle one at the outset . . . an overpowering sense of helplessness . . . a sense of disappointment. . . . One is forced reluctantly to acknowledge that the inner mind of the people is a closed book". It may be so. Yet Pierre Loti's cities, "de lumière et de mort", had a soul. Fortunately Mr. Birt's book is free on the whole from those triter reflections upon the vanity of human wishes etc., the stock-in-trade of many of his predecessors who would otherwise have been rendered speechless by the "glamours" of Ispahan and Shiraz.

Mr. Birt saw the first Mejliss at work in Teheran. Colonel Liakhoff's guns had not yet shattered the Parliament-house. It is a pity that he did not travel a few months later, when a unique revolution was in full blast. He had already taken the measure of both parties and had perceived the humours of the situation. "Western craze" is a useful expression of his. It must have been largely a snobbish affectation—Teheran has been snobbish ever since the Shahs began to visit Europe—but undoubtedly the middle and upper classes of the capital could discuss politics in the very phraseology of Mr. Swift MacNeill and the Irish party, and with as fine an appreciation of constitutional precedent.

THE CHARM OF RUNNING WATER.

"The Rivers and Streams of England." Painted by Sutton Palmer; described by A. G. Bradley. London: Black. 1909. 20s. net.

A RIVER nearly always forms the centre of attraction in any landscape that happens to include it, and if you try to make out the reason for its demand upon the attention you find this due to a very complex interaction of æsthetic and intellectual interests. In the first place, the river is generally the oldest thing in sight, older even than the everlasting hills themselves. This seems a paradox, but although there are ranges like the Malverns and Charnwood Forest in Leicester which have endured from the earliest geological times, which were islands in the remote Palæozoic seas, yet most of the hills of the Midlands and the South have taken shape long after the rivers began to follow their present courses. Nowhere can this be more clearly made out than in the gorges which the Weald rivers have cut through the Downs; Cuckmere and Arundel Gaps, the gorge of the Mole at Dorking and of the Wey at Guildford, where the rivers appear to leave the low country in order to carve a narrow way through the steep chalk scarp that faces them, are witnesses of a time before the Downs existed when the rivers ran northwards or southwards as to-day, but down either side of a great roll that stretched continuously from the Thames valley to the sea without any of the transverse furrows which make up its hill and valley system to-day. But, leaving these cold speculative ages for times when the river may be said to have at last begun to exist because man traversed its banks and was conscious of its course, there can be nothing which takes us further back into time; as highway or barrier it has always made history, and as surely as in any city you must go uphill if you want to find the cathedral so you must ascertain the river structure of a country if you desire insight either into its campaigns or its commerce. Where now the water is still slipping by one of the bridges, there man in the Stone Age first found the ford, there the Kelt in his migrations wore a trackway to and from the water's edge, there the Roman first passed dryshod, and there at last some mediæval guild of bridge-builders wrought out their meed of service to the world in the stone arch that endures to-day. Much water under the bridges—πάντα ῥεῖ—the world has always been seeing its philosophy in terms of running water. And what variety in the style and charm of the rivers themselves! Even in our own circumscribed borders we find many different types, from the broad streams diversified with stony shallows and sandbanks of the rocky North, to the deep-cut channels of the Severn sort that tell of sudden rises and eager-scouring floods, and to the placid meanderings of Thames and Avon where the water is level with the meadows and the bordering grasses quiver in the current. They have their own colours too: the chalk streams possess an intense, almost jewel-like, clearness and brilliancy; others like the Wye are warm brown, so that a bather's body below the surface takes an olive Mediterranean glow; the Thames and many of the Midland rivers are green—a pale, troubled opalescence when the stream is hurrying bankfull with the cold April thunderbursts, a still fainter and more fleeting hue, as though here and there a leaf had been dissolved, in the still summer reaches; while some of the Eastern fen rivers show curious black transparencies that are all their own.

But it is hard nowadays to know the rivers of England; except in one or two notable cases they do not exactly fit with popular pursuits. You need to be a fisherman, and a catholic one also, not a mere dry-fly enthusiast who knows only Test and Itchen, Mimram and Stour, but one who is not ashamed of bread-crust and float, or even of the ridicule that attaches to a bait-can and a punt. Best of all is it to explore the unfashionable rivers in canoe or boat, taking kit and tent with you. So shall you catch the old towns of England unawares, and find an out-at-elbows, free-and-easy access into their intimacy, as different from the ordered front-garden respectability of the high road as it is from the indecorous Peeping-Tom sort of entry among the chimney-pots which our railways seem to favour.

In the book before us Mr. A. G. Bradley tells us something of the immemorial charm that attaches to the rivers of England; he makes no attempt to characterise them one by one, but deals with them in groups, and picks out an example here and there for treatment in detail. The Thames is ruled out as possessing so many books of its own, but Wye and Severn have a

(*Continued on p.* 794.)

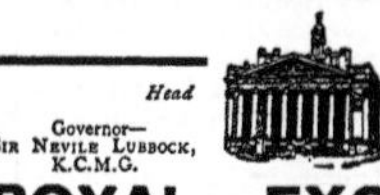

chapter apiece, as have the chalk streams, the Border rivers, and those belonging to Devon and the dales of Yorkshire. Mr. Bradley is so sound in his local history, so practised in the art of weaving the main stream of history into his topographical narration, and so passionate a fisherman that one could wish for no more informing and appreciative an introduction to the story of all these fair streams. Mr. Sutton Palmer's illustrations, to which perhaps we should have given the first place, are not only delightfully picturesque and faithful to the spirit of the scenes they represent, but possess a space and largeness of vision which is unexpected in work that has to be reproduced on so comparatively small a scale. Mr. Palmer is fond of great sweeps of gleaming valley and distant hill seen from a height, and the colour-printing process adopted has rendered very successfully the varying values of the distances. But we can never quite reconcile ourselves to these colour-prints; they lack the style of the interpretive artist, and we cannot imagine anyone treasuring them in the future as one treasures nowadays the engravings into which were translated Turner's visions of the rivers of France.

NOVELS.

"Hedwig in England." By the Author of "Marcia in Germany". London: Heinemann. 1909. 3s. net.

The shrewdness and pungency of this little book recall the criticisms of English life which Matthew Arnold put into a German mouth in "Friendship's Garland". But the Baroness Hedwig is a critic not of our public affairs but of our social life. She stays first with a family of very good position, and then with the most unattractive suburban household that ever was created on paper. In each case the defects existing in a particular class are concentrated in one family. The suburbans are snobbish, pretentious and bornés, but the father of the family is, besides, immoral and a hypocrite. In Mayfair Hedwig's hostess is an extreme devotee of pleasure and fashion, her daughter is uneducated and stupid, her son an insufferable young cub. Hedwig occasionally—not often—has to correct a false first impression, but as a rule she sums up very fairly from a German point of view a good many English traits. Her opinion on our national selfishness, as regards both family life and patriotic claims, is very largely sound. But London is not England, and Hedwig sees nothing of country life. Nor are the young men whom she meets at dances really typical of their class, though too many such are allowed to live. The story is slight, but the book should be read. Imagine a well-educated German girl of good family, compounded largely of sentiment and matter-of-fact, walking as a spectator first through a novel by Mr. F. E. Benson and then through a suburban study by Gissing. That is the England—or those the Englands—unfolded to the critical Hedwig.

"The Eagle's Nest." By Allan McAulay. London: Lane. 1909. 6s.

The nest is Corsica during the last quarter of the eighteenth century, and the eagle, as yet unfledged, is a young man of Ajaccio, by name Nabulione Buonaparte, a sous-lieutenant of artillery in the French army; but one Domé Tirolani is the real hero of the story, though the presence of a stronger and stranger personality in the cast somewhat militates against his taking his conventional place in the centre of Mr. McAulay's stage. However, a quotation printed on the title-page foreshadows the aim of the author as being rather to reconstruct the life of a place and a period than to write a conventional novel; and, looked at in this way, the book presents a strong and sombre picture of the Corsica of the day, its political intrigues and private vendettas, and a portrait of Napoleon as an eccentric, priggish, inhuman young man, which is by no means unconvincing even if it seems in part put together by the light of long subsequent events. The love affairs of the unfortunate Tirolani run their course amidst some admirably painted scenery; but they have little more than a subsidiary interest, and are brought to no such consummation as the conventional novel-reader usually looks for.

"A Perfect Genius." By Bertram Smith. London: Harper. 1909. 3s. 6d.

The escapades of Totty, facile princeps in mischief amongst his schoolfellows at Willisdean, make very entertaining reading. If "A Perfect Genius" smacks of pardonable exaggeration, Totty's institution of a school literary society wherein, despite an awe-inspiring syllabus, the only subject ever debated was "How to circumvent the authorities" comes near to justifying the title of these his further memoirs. He was at any rate a vastly resourceful scapegrace—if the word may be used of one so amply endowed with the saving grace of humour, and his extensive and peculiar knowledge of tight places and the paths that lead into them became of great use to him when later he attained to the dignity of a prefect and for a short time on one memorable occasion to that of head of the school. Mr. Smith has an admirable understanding of the peculiar standards of schoolboy honour, and his tersely written little book reproduces the patois of boys amongst themselves without that unreal and excessive slanginess sometimes supposed to create the right atmosphere for this sort of story.

SHORTER NOTICES.

"Eton." Painted by E. D. Brinton; described by Christopher Stone. London: Black. 1909. 7s. 6d. net.

Messrs. Black have included Eton in their series of Beautiful Books, though they published a portfolio of views of the school reproduced from Mr. Luxmoore's drawings only a year ago. Those to whom the three-colour process of reproduction appeals—and we are not among the number—will probably find much pleasure in Miss Brinton's illustrations, though the result seems unnecessarily crude in one or two instances. Mr. Stone, who is already known as the compiler of a very handy book called the "Eton Glossary", has wisely not attempted to give a detailed history of the school. When Sir Henry Maxwell Lyte has been over the ground there is but little left for subsequent writers. Mr. Stone, however, gives a very readable aperçu of the most salient points in Eton manners and customs during the last four hundred years, touching lightly on the contemporary accounts given by Cox, Malim, Thomas James, and the entertaining authors of the "Nugæ Etónenses". Nor has he neglected the very valuable correspondence concerning the two brothers Francis and Robert Boyle, who were at Eton from 1635 to 1638. With so short a space in which to deal with so large a subject it was perhaps unavoidable that the canvas should be rather overcrowded, and we wish that the style were a little less jaunty. In addition to his own share, Mr. Stone has had the good fortune to get his father, long known as an Eton master, to contribute two chapters on College in his day. Though the Rev. E. D. Stone missed the great days of College which, historically speaking, came to an end with Long Chamber, he gives a graphic description of much that has radically altered since his days. One is tempted to wonder whether the cause of education would not be better served by abolishing College altogether and spreading the scholars, like leaven, among the houses, as is done at most schools. We have noticed one or two small errors in the book. Lord Wellesley was not known as Lord Mornington at Eton, but as Lord Wellesley, and his more famous brother can hardly have been "Lord Wellington" when he made the familiar remark about the playing fields of Eton. We should imagine, too, that Tiger Clive is more likely to have been the nickname of Earl Powis than Bacchus Browning.

"A Survey and Record of Woolwich and West Kent." Woolwich: Labour Representation Printing Company. 1909. 9s.

This volume is produced by the South-Eastern Union of Scientific Societies. It is an admirably designed and well wrought, if as yet incomplete, collection of local surveys of the geology, the flora and fauna of the district, each by its own specialist. In the departments of archæology and history, the article on church architecture deserves praise which cannot be given to the too commonplace and merely descriptive treatment of the section on "Scientific Industries", military, mechanical, and electrical. Books like this improved as they may be, and synthetised and inter-

(Continued on p. 796.)

preted, are needed as the basis of the regional nature study which will become a more and more important feature in education. Starting from the geological and topographic facts, such surveys unite into geography, and they issue finally in a sociology founded on a sound basis of scientific philosophy and history. Towards this ideal such a volume is a real step, and it may be commended as an example for similar regional surveys and worthy of attention by other than professed naturalists and antiquaries.

"Selected Tales of Mystery", by Edgar Allan Poe (Sidgwick and Jackson, 12s. 6d. net).—In whatever form Poe's tales appear they are good to read, but we see very little to recommend them beyond their own merits in a book got up as this is. The size of it is unwieldy, and this is a serious fault in an edition of Poe, who ought to be read in any kind of volume, the shabbier the better, with the feet on the fender, and not in one which seems to aim at being a fancy book for the best parlour. The outside is ugly, and about as unpleasing as it can be, whilst inside the illustrations by Mr. Byam Shaw are either vapid or flaring. Take the frontispiece of the Masquerade at the Palace of the Duc di Broglio. It might just as well be a fancy-dress ball at Covent Garden. Or take the illustrations to the murders in the Rue Morgue, and the case of M. Valdemar—absolutely vacuous—and that of the Black Cat, which is only horrible. If this is illustration of Poe, we should prefer to have him left alone.

"With Mulai Hafid at Fez." By Lawrence Harris. London: Smith, Elder. 1909. 7s. 6d.

The first paragraph of the preface to this book contains two exclamation marks. The rest of the book maintains the level of heavily stimulated excitement. The author went to Fez with instructions to "interview" Mulai Hafid. We did not trouble to find out whether he ever succeeded in doing so. If he did succeed, then, having pleased his employer, he should have desisted from further offence.

"The Children's Story of the Bee", by S. L. Bensusan (Mills and Boon, 5s. net).—This book seems to be intended for children old enough to be trusted with a hive of their own. The "Story" is told picturesquely, and will doubtless be found absorbing by the young bee master who has a taste for natural history and a love of long words. The romances of the hive are very charming when romantically treated. The morals are so unexceptionable too. We advise parents who can trust their children to play with fire to buy this book. Be warned, however, that this is hardly the season to begin bee-keeping; also that parents who take our advice will be called upon to answer some awkward questions.

"The Prologue to the Canterbury Tales", designs by Ambrose Dudley (Chatto, 2s. 6d.).—It is difficult to understand to what kind of reader this production can appeal. The illustrations are too commonplace to add any value for grown-ups to the prologue, which it is preferable to read in companionship with the tales, while children, who might like the pictures, will be baffled by the archaic wording and spelling of the poem, which, if it had been slightly modernised, would be quite easily understood.

There is, perhaps, no one to-day who produces books with quite the taste and refinement of Mr. Foulis, who has just published a new edition of Mr. J. H. Crawford's pleasant and unconventional work, **"The Wild Flowers" (Edinburgh: Foulis, 5s. net).** We fail entirely to be impressed by most of the "beautiful" books of the day. Their showy get-up is meant to take the purchaser by storm. He gasps "How beautiful!" before he has time to consider the matter. Often the beauty is nought but gaud. Now the volumes which the Astolat Press produced a few years ago, mostly reprints of the English classics, really were beautiful books. The same can be said of Mr. Foulis' books. Time and thought and real taste are spent on their production, and the result is a volume which we may put on the bookshelf reserved for books that are good to handle and look at as well as read. Why is the art of book production so very rare to-day? The sense and understanding of good art is much more general than in the days when Moxon and the Pickerings were at work.

The student of the eighteenth-century voyages, discoveries and doings of European seamen in Eastern waters will find much that is curious and interesting in **"Unpublished Documents on the History of the Seychelles Islands Anterior to 1810" (Wyman, 7s. 6d.).** This volume, compiled by Mr. A. A. Fauvel from the papers of General Decaen, the last Captain-General of the French settlements east of the Cape of Good Hope, is accompanied by facsimile reproductions of numerous ancient maps and plans, dating from the year 1501, and a bibliography of manuscripts and books relating to the Seychelles. A useful introduction is supplied by Mr. W. E. Davidson, and the book is a distinct contribution to history down to the time when France surrendered Mauritius to Great Britain.

"The Century Magazine", May to October 1909 (Macmillan, 10s. 6d. net), well maintains the English side, American though the bulk of its contents necessarily are. For instance, there are articles on the London police from the New York point of view by Mr. William McAdoo; British Rule in India, by Mr. Sydney Brooks; and the Darwin Centenary, by Mr. Benjamin E. Smith. Then there are various articles such as those written by Mrs. Joseph Pennell and illustrated by Mr. Pennell on French Cathedrals, and by Mr. R. H. Schauffer on Romantic Germany. The pictures in the "Century" are always admirable, though we prefer the black-and-white to the occasional colour pages.

The **"Cornhill"** for December completes its fiftieth year. The number is full of reminiscences of editors and contributors, including an article by Mr. E. T. Cook, reviewing the history of the magazine. The King, we understand, has accepted a copy.

"Revue des Deux Mondes." 15 Decembre.

The article of most general interest in this number is by M. René Pinon, who deals with the Albanian question and its probable influence in the case of difficulties in the Near East. After a masterly review of the racial and religious elements always contending in that region, he proceeds to consider the manner in which Albania may be dealt with by Austria and Italy in the pursuit of their rival policies. He thinks it not impossible that an Albanian Confederation might arise under a native chief, but that would require a political renaissance in the country not yet in sight. The Power that wishes to dominate Salonica and the route thither must be in command of Albania. In the case of a break-up of the Ottoman Empire, Albania would become an autonomous State. The present Sultan is not popular in Albania, and in the spring trouble may again arise that might be Austria's opportunity. The whole paper is well worth study, though the writer wisely refrains from prophecy.

For this Week's Books see page 798.

THIS WEEK'S BOOKS.

ART AND ARCHÆOLOGY

Aquatint Engraving (S. T. Prideaux). Duckworth. 15*s*. net.
Early English Glass (Daisy Wilmer). Gill. 6*s*. 6*d*. net.

FICTION

Love and the Lodger (Priscilla Craven); The Wolf at the Door (Florence Warden). Digby, Long. 6*s*. each.
Major Owen and other Tales (Christopher N. Johnston). Edinburgh: Blackwood. 6*s*.

HISTORY

The Danes in Lancashire (S. W. Partington). Sherratt and Hughes. 5*s*. net.

REPRINTS AND TRANSLATIONS

The Tarot of the Bohemians (Papus). Rider. 6*s*. net.
The Campaign Guide. Edinburgh: Douglas. 5*s*. net.

SCIENCE

An Elementary Treatise on the Dynamics of a Particle and of Rigid Bodies (S. L. Lonley). Cambridge: At the University Press. 12*s*.

THEOLOGY

Encyclopædia of Religion and Ethics (Edited by James Hastings. Vol. II.). Edinburgh: Clark. 28*s*. net.

MISCELLANEOUS

Bulletin of the Keats-Shelley Memorial (Edited by Sir Rennell Rodd and H. Nelson Gray). New York: Macmillan.
Power of Speech, The (Edwin Gordon Lawrence). New York: Hinds, Noble and Eldredge.

MAGAZINE FOR JANUARY.—The Thrush. 1*s*.

THE THRUSH

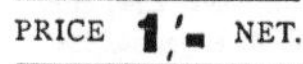
PRICE 1/- NET.

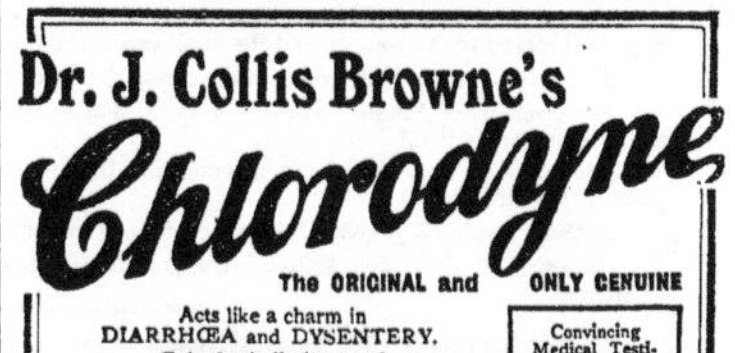
Dr. J. Collis Browne's
Chlorodyne

Printed for the Proprietors by SPOTTISWOODE & CO. LTD., 5 New-street Square, E.C., and Published by REGINALD WEBSTER PAGE, at the Office, 10 King Street, Covent Garden, in the Parish of St. Paul, in the County of London.—*Saturday, 25 December, 1909.*

Lightning Source UK Ltd.
Milton Keynes UK
UKHW020250051218
333419UK00007B/227/P